MW01069028

seliš nyoʔnuntn

Medicine for the Salish Language

English to Salish Translation Dictionary

Published by:
Salish Kootenai College Pres
Pablo, Montana

Distributed by:
University of Nebraska Pres
Lincoln, Nebraska

Gangers 360-805-8192
000965

Second Edition

Tachini Pete

All proceeds generated from this book will go to a fund to produce additional Salish language books for Nk̓ʷusm Salish Revitalization Institute. The Institute operates a private Salish language immersion school to educate children in all academic areas through the Salish language. This school operates on the generosity of donations from individuals, philanthropic organizations, corporations, and tribal, federal and state governments. Without the support of individuals the Salish language would not have a place to live and grow. For more information about Nk̓ʷusm visit their website at ***www.salishworld.com***.

Nk̓ʷusm

Nk̓ʷucn x̣ʷl̓ Qe Nuwéwlštn

For Tachini Jr., Kayenta, Sṫšalqʷ, and Staan.

Dedicated in memory of Sophie "supi" Mays.

lemlmtš pesyaʔ for putting up with my obsessive study of Salish.

Copyright © 2010 Tachini Pete. All rights reserved.
No part of this work may be reproduced or transmitted in any form or by any means, electronic or mechanical, including photocopying and recording, or by any information storage or retrieval system without the prior written permission of Tachini Pete unless such copying is expressly permitted by copyright law.
Address inquiries to, Nk̓ʷusm, P.O. Box 5, Arlee, Montana 59821.

Library of Congress Cataloging-in-Publication Data:
Pete, Tachini, 1971-
Seliš nyoʔnuntn = medicine for the Salish language : English to Salish translation dictionary / Tachini Pete [compiler and editor]. -- 2nd ed.
p. cm.
Includes bibliographical references.
ISBN 978-1-934594-06-3 (hardcover)
1. Salishan languages--Dictionaries—English. I. Title. II. Title: Medicine for the Salish language.
PM2263.P48 2010
497'.943—dc22
2010075050

Published by Salish Kootenai College Press, PO Box 70, Pablo, MT 59855.

Distributed by University of Nebraska Press, 1111 Lincoln Mall, Lincoln, NE 68588-0630, order 1-800-755-1105, www.nebraskapress.unl.edu.

Table of Contents

Salish Language

Welcome to the second draft edition of the English to Salish translation dictionary. This book was compiled and edited under the direction of Tachini Pete to encourage the use of the Salish Language. **This work is called a draft because it is seen as a work in progress; this second draft is not perfect; there will be changes in that appear in the third draft**. The information presented is derived mainly from the knowledge gained from the interaction with elders, learners, and academia. **This book is not intended to be a final official word on the Salish language.** Also it is not an academic presentation of the language. However, it is presented in a form that will enable people to use Salish words and language. It is hoped that this work will stimulate the ongoing conversation of creating a standardized Salish orthography.

This draft attempts to engage the reader, researcher, and learner by showing the structure and grammar of Salish. This will help people form the ever-difficult Salish sentence. This work also revives the usage of formal Salish. That is, the inclusion and use of suffixes that tend to be omitted. These "word endings" contain helpful information that provide students a more enriched understanding of the language. Anecdotal evidence of advanced learners of the language shows that when suffixes are used, retention of the Salish language is more meaningful. As well, the learner's comprehension is highly improved.

The Creator gave the Salish language to our ancestors. Parents and grandparents passed the language on to each successive generation. No one person or organization owns the language; nor should it be owned. Rather, it is held in common by the people that use it, just as the air and water.

This book will always be in the process of revision as new words are created and old words are revived and/or remembered. English translations will always be a point of debate as each individual brings a different perspective. The dictionary staff worked tirelessly to ensure that spellings and translations accurately reflect the language. The book is merely a resource for individuals learning and using the Salish language. Consultation of knowledgeable fluent speakers is recommended when creating any formal representation of the Salish language. The dictionary staff worked diligently to eliminate mistakes. If you find any errors, write them down and pass them on to the dictionary staff. We want all new editions to be as comprehensive as possible. All comments, additions, and/or corrections are greatly appreciated.

Tachini Pete started this project in 1993 at the beginning of his Salish learning. Tachini has spent over 15,000 hours during the past twelve years compiling and editing this document. Special thanks are given to the many teachers and the hundreds of hours spent with these patient and giving people. It is through their dedication and thoughtfulness that we have this book. Special recognition is also given to the late Sophie Mays for her many years of work teaching Salish. Sophie was Tachini's first Salish language teacher. Sophie contributed greatly to the work in this book.

The following contributors made this dictionary possible: Nk̓ʷusm, Salish Pend d'Oreille Culture Committee, Salish Kootenai College, Kalispel Tribe of Indians, and the United States National Park Service. The Kalispel Tribe funded publishing costs of this book. Their generous donation made the second edition available to the public quicker. Lemlmtš Qlispe

As a member of the Qlispe/Lower Pend d'Oreille people, it is with great honor and privilege that I acknowledge this very important dictionary of our people. The retention of words, stories and voices of long ago continues our legacy and livelihood into the future. What has been accomplished with this publication further connects us together with the elders of our past and the people of today, and if we are to retain our beautiful language this Dictionary will benefit all the generations yet to come.

We as a people now separated onto individual reservations and held together by relatives, history, traditions and cultural ties, need to retain and keep our language alive.

I want to give special thanks to our creator for all of those children and individuals who are working so hard at teaching and learning our languages.

Francis Cullooya

Editorial and Production Staff

Executive Editor
Tachini Pete

Entry Editors

	Tachini Pete
sčiyalmn	Malina Pete
	Tachini Pete, JR.

Consulting Salish Editors

čqʷoya	Louie Adams
čole	Johnny Arlee
supi	Sophie Mays
patlik	Patrick Pierre
stipn	Stephen Small Salmon
pleswe	Frances Vanderburg

Primary Salish Contributors

čqʷoya	Louie Adams
čole	Johnny Arlee
	Allen Beaverhead
	Eva Boyd
	Alice Camel
toloti	Dorothy Felsman
	Dolly Linsebigler
supi	Sophie Mays
pliciti	Felicite McDonald
patlik	Patrick Pierre
	Josephine Quequesah
stipn	Stephen Small Salmon
	Shirley Trahan
pleswe	Frances Vanderburg
	Lucy Vanderburg
	Anna Vanderburg

Proofreading

st̓lt̓la sċik̓ʷs	Arleen Adams
	Robert Bigart
scnpaqci	Diana Cote
	Trina Felsman
mlani	Melanie Sandoval

Text Design
Tachini Pete

Graphic Design
Tachini Pete

Covers
Matt Rogers Photography

Artwork
Antoine Sandoval

Cover Concept and Design
Tachini Pete
Robert Bigart

Pre-Press Development
Robert Bigart

Special thanks for the guidance and words of the following people: Patrick Pierre, Stephen Small Salmon, Dorothy Felsman, Frances Vanderburg, Mary Lucy Parker, Noel Pichette, Mike Durgelo, Sophie Haynes, Tony Incashola, Alik Quequesah, and Joseph Pablo.
The following contributors have passed on: Sophie Mays, Angie Matt, John Peter Paul, Agnes Paul, Joe Cullooyah, Margaret Finley, and Agnes Kenmille.

Front cover picture on Waterworks Hill, Montana, is of yarrow, a medicinal plant for healing wounds. Back cover and title page picture is of Rattlesnake Creek, Montana. Both pictures are courtesy of Matt Rogers Photography, Matt Rogers, 1809 S 14th W, Missoula, MT 59801.

Division page illustrations and page number icons by Antoine Sandoval, Arlee, MT.

Salish Language

Book Usage Guide and Abbreviations

There are many features in this book that are used to keep the page count down and to reduce repetition. Included are abbreviations and omitted English translation. On the lower right of each page is a table of abbreviations used through the book. Below is a diagram that shows how translation and conjugation of Salish words are organized.

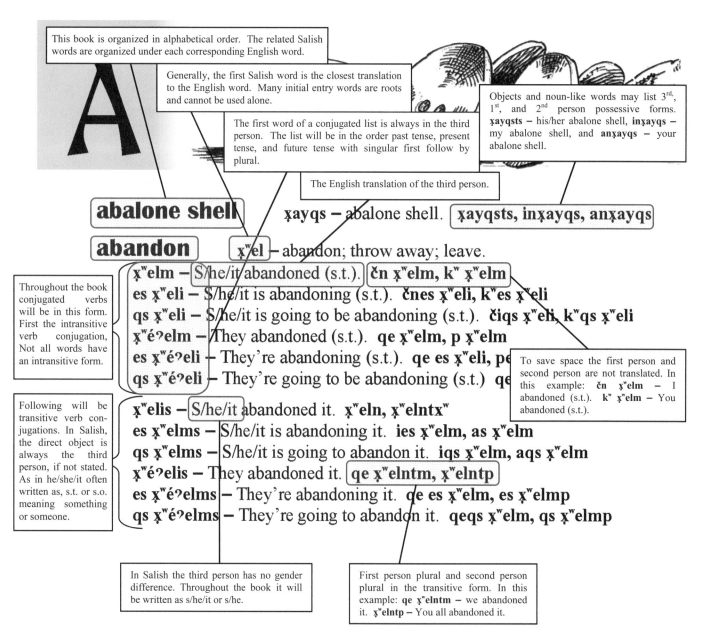

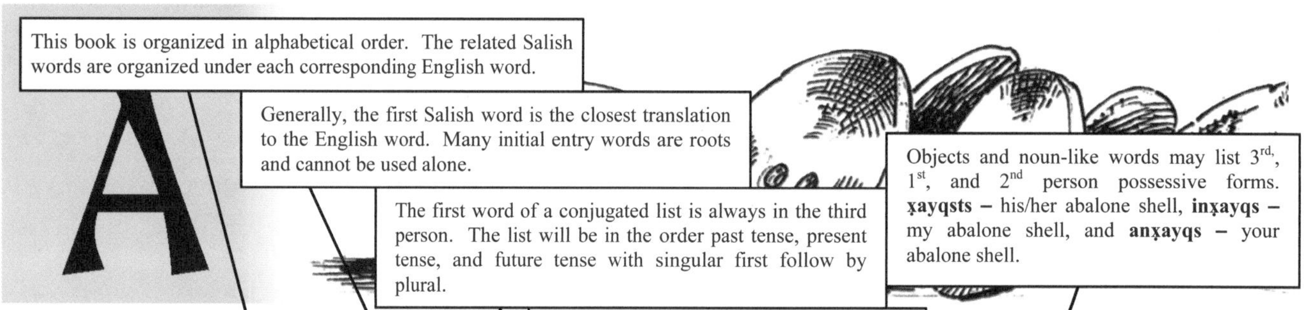

This book is organized in alphabetical order. The related Salish words are organized under each corresponding English word.

Generally, the first Salish word is the closest translation to the English word. Many initial entry words are roots and cannot be used alone.

The first word of a conjugated list is always in the third person. The list will be in the order past tense, present tense, and future tense with singular first follow by plural.

Objects and noun-like words may list 3rd, 1st, and 2nd person possessive forms. **x̣ayqsts** – his/her abalone shell, **inx̣ayqs** – my abalone shell, and **anx̣ayqs** – your abalone shell.

The English translation of the third person.

abalone shell **x̣ayqs** – abalone shell. **x̣ayqsts, inx̣ayqs, anx̣ayqs**

abandon **x̣ʷel** – abandon; throw away; leave.

x̣ʷelm – S/he/it abandoned (s.t.). **čn x̣ʷelm, kʷ x̣ʷelm**
es x̣ʷeli – S/he/it is abandoning (s.t.). **čnes x̣ʷeli, kʷes x̣ʷeli**
qs x̣ʷeli – S/he/it is going to be abandoning (s.t.). **čiqs x̣ʷeli, kʷqs x̣ʷeli**
x̣ʷéʔelm – They abandoned (s.t.). **qe x̣ʷelm, p x̣ʷelm**
es x̣ʷéʔeli – They're abandoning (s.t.). **qe es x̣ʷeli, pe**
qs x̣ʷéʔeli – They're going to be abandoning (s.t.) **qe**

Throughout the book conjugated verbs will be in this form. First the intransitive verb conjugation, Not all words have an intransitive form.

To save space the first person and second person are not translated. In this example: **čn x̣ʷelm** – I abandoned (s.t.). **kʷ x̣ʷelm** – You abandoned (s.t.).

x̣ʷelis – S/he/it abandoned it. **x̣ʷeln, x̣ʷelntxʷ**
es x̣ʷelms – S/he/it is abandoning it. **ies x̣ʷelm, as x̣ʷelm**
qs x̣ʷelms – S/he/it is going to abandon it. **iqs x̣ʷelm, aqs x̣ʷelm**
x̣ʷéʔelis – They abandoned it. **qe x̣ʷelntm, x̣ʷelntp**
es x̣ʷéʔelms – They're abandoning it. **qe es x̣ʷelm, es x̣ʷelmp**
qs x̣ʷéʔelms – They're going to abandon it. **qeqs x̣ʷelm, qs x̣ʷelmp**

Following will be transitive verb conjugations. In Salish, the direct object is always the third person, if not stated. As in he/she/it often written as, s.t. or s.o. meaning something or someone.

In Salish the third person has no gender difference. Throughout the book it will be written as s/he/it or s/he.

First person plural and second person plural in the transitive form. In this example: **qe x̣ʷelntm** – we abandoned it. **x̣ʷelntp** – You all abandoned it.

In general only one translation will be provided. Look at the main entry word translation to construct other English meanings. In this example the translation could also be, "S/he is repeatedly thowing away", or "S/he is repeatedly leaving (s.t.)."

It, s.o. or *s.t.*, is used to indicate the third person object. This object could be physical, emotional, mental, animate or inanimate. In Salish these are incomplete sentences without an understood or declared object.

Word forms will generally be listed in the following order when appropriate:

plural reduplication

es x̣ʷlx̣ʷeli – S/he is repeatedly abandoning. **čnes x̣ʷlx̣ʷeli, kʷes x̣ʷlx̣ʷeli**

es x̣ʷlx̣ʷelms – S/he is abandoning things. **ies x̣ʷlx̣ʷelm, as x̣**

As with *it*, *someone (s.o.)* is used to indicate the third person object. *Someone* is used when the English translation generally refers to human objects. Conceivably the object could be non-human.

diminutive derivations

łx̣ʷex̣ʷlm – S/he/it abandoned a little. **čn łx̣ʷex̣ʷlm, kʷ łx̣ʷex̣**

łx̣ʷex̣ʷlis – S/he/it abandoned a little of it. **łx̣ʷex̣ʷln, łx̣ʷex̣ʷl**

developmental derivations

x̣ʷell – S/he/it got abandoned.

x̣ʷelntm – S/he/it was abandoned by someone.

In many entries affixial information is provided. A full listing of affixes can be found in section 5 of this book.

successive derivations

x̣ʷlnuis – S/he finally abandoned it. **x̣ʷlnun, x̣ʷlnuntxʷ**

nominal derivations

sxʷx̣ʷelm – one tasked to abandon/throw away. *prefix:* ***sxʷ...*** *– one tasked to do.*

x̣ʷlemn – one inclined to abandon/throw away. **x̣ʷlx̣ʷlemn** *pl. suffix:* ***...emn*** *– one inclined to do.*

x̣ʷlx̣ʷlmuł – one that habitually abandons/throws away. *suffix:* ***...łmuł*** *– one that habitually does.*

scx̣ʷel – something that's been thrown away. *(i.e., people, child, spouse or item.) prefix:* ***sc...*** *– s.t. that's been done/made/prepared.*

snx̣ʷelmn – place you abandon things; dump; garbage receptacle. *prefix:* ***sn...*** *– a place of.*

sx̣ʷelmn – devil. **słx̣ʷex̣ʷlmn** – little devil. *suffix:...*

Examples and/or additional information will be provided in parenthesis. This information is included to help clarify meaning.

In order to keep the page count down diminutives will generally be listed on the same line. As in *devil* and *little devil.*

imperative derivations

x̣ʷeliš – Throw (it) away. *cmd.*

x̣ʷelskʷ – Abandon it. *cmd.*

x̣ʷelnt – Throw it away. *cmd.*

miscellaneous derivations

x̣ʷlscut – S/he abandoned something personal. **čn x̣ʷlscut, kʷ x̣ʷlscut**

es x̣ʷlscuti – S/he is abandoning something personal. **čnes x̣ʷlscuti, kʷes x̣ʷlscuti**

es łx̣ʷlmisti – S/he is getting rid of something that is self detrimental.

es łx̣ʷlscutisti – S/he is getting rid of something within one's self.

es x̣ʷlmnwexʷi – They're leaving each other.

Commands or imperatives will be denoted with the abbreviated and italicized *cmd.*

Something (s.t.) is used to indicate the third person object. It is use when the English translation generally refers to inanimate objects. Conceivably the object could be animate or human.

Guide to Salish Pronunciation and Orthography

ʔ is not written in English, but can be heard before **u** and **o** in **uh-oh**! This sound is produced by closing and then opening the vocal/glottal cords. It is called the *glottal stop*. The glottal stop naturally precedes all words that start with a vowel thus it is not necessary to write.

c is like the **ts** in ca**ts**.

c̓ is similar to **c** *(ts sound above)* but with pressure built up behind the tongue and suddenly released as a **c** *(ts sound above)*. It is called a *glottalized c* or *hard c*.

č is like the **ch** in **ch**ur**ch**, called a *wedged c*.

č̓ is like a **č**, *(ch sound above)* but with pressure built up behind the tongue and suddenly released as a **č** *(ch sound above)*. It is called a *glottalized wedged c* or *hard wedge c*.

h is like **h** in **h**ot.

l is like **l** in **l**ip.

l̓ is like **l** *(l sound above)* with glottal closure. It is called *glottalized l*.

ł There is no English sound equivalent similar to **ł**. It is produced while holding the tongue in the position of an **l** as is p**l**ay and then blowing air out the one or both sides of the tongue. It is called a *barred l*.

ƛ̓ There is no English sound equivalent similar to **ƛ̓**. It is produced by putting the tongue in the position to pronounce **l** as in p**l**ay. Build pressure behind the tongue, keeping tongue in the **l** position, then suddenly release from one or both sides of the tongue. A similar sound is produced when calling horses, only this sound is produced in reverse by sucking air in. It is called a *lambda*.

m is like the **m** in **m**ouse.

m̓ is like the **m** *(m sound above)* with a glottal closure. It is called a *glottalized m* or *hard m*.

n is like the **n** in o**n** or i**n**.

n̓ is like the **n** *(n sound above)* with a glottal closure. It is called a *glottalized n* or *hard n*.

p is like the **p** in spin.

p̓ is like the **p** *(p sound above)* but with sudden release of air. It is called a *glottalized p* or *hard p*.

s is like the **s** in **s**in.

š is like the **sh** in **sh**ip. It is called a *wedge s*.

k is like the **k** in s**k**in.

kʷ is like **qu** in **qu**een. The raised *w* indicates that the lips are rounded. It is called a *k w*.

k̓ʷ is like the **kʷ** with a glottal closure. The raised *w* indicates that the lips are rounded. It is called a *glottalized k w*.

q is like the **k**, but produced farther back in the throat.

q̓ is like the **q** but with simultaneous glottal closure. It is called a *glottalized q* or *hard q*.

qʷ is like the **q**, but pronounced with rounded lips. The raised *w* indicates that the lips are rounded. It is called a *q w*.

q̓ʷ is like the **qʷ**, but with simultaneous glottal closure. The raised *w* indicates that the lips are rounded. It is called a *glottalized q w* or a *hard q w*.

t is like the **t** in **t**op.

t̓ is like the **t** with a glottal closure. It is called a *glottalized t* or *hard t*.

w is like the **w** in **w**ell.

w̓ is like the **w** with a glottal closure. It is called a *glottalized w*.

x̣ is a fricative sound produced in the same position as **q**. It is called an *x-dot* or *dotted x*.

xʷ is a fricative sound like **h**, but produced in the same position as **k**. The raised *w* indicates that the lips are rounded. It is called x w.

x̣ʷ is like **xʷ**, but produced farther back in the throat in the position of **q**. The raised *w* indicates that the lips are rounded. It is called a *dotted x w* or *dot x w*.

y is like the **y** in **y**es.

y̓ is like the **y** with simultaneous glottal closure. It is called a *glottalized y*.

a is like the **a** in f**a**ther.

e is like the **e** in p**e**t.

i is like the **i** in mach**i**ne. When following a **q**, **q̓**, **qʷ**, **q̓ʷ**, **x̣** or **x̣ʷ** the **i** will have the sound of **ey** as in th**ey**. This is a good way to check pronunciation of the **q** letters. If you can hear the **i** as in mach**i**ne, following the **q**, **q̓**, **qʷ**, **q̓ʷ** letters then you know you are pronouncing the sound of a **k**.

u is like the **u** in r**u**de.

o is like the **o** in **o**rb or **o**ff.

´ The primary stress is written above the vowel which, in words of two or more vowels, receives the loudest stress. The stress mark is a grammatical mark rather than an alphabetic mark.

Vowels

Diagram 1. Vowel Chart

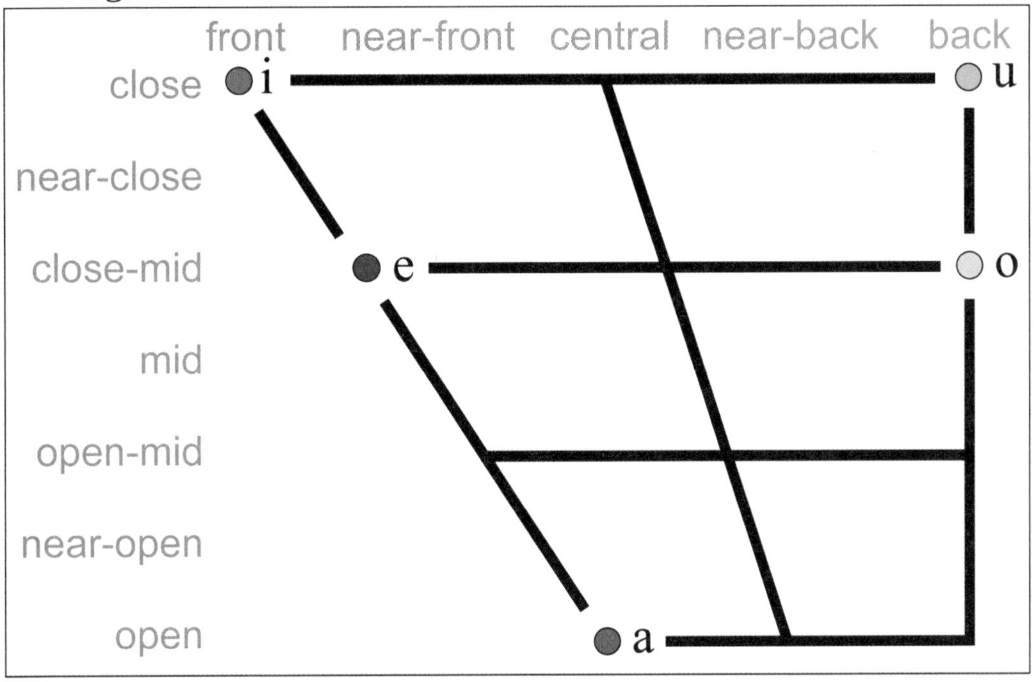

Diagram 2. Vowel Physical Position

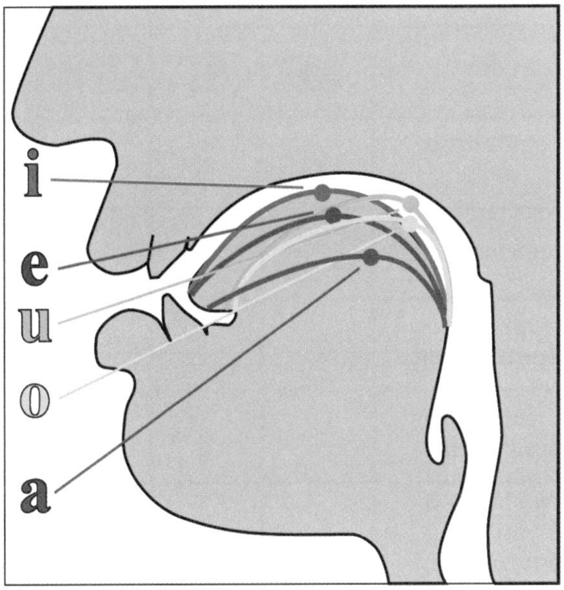

There are five written vowels in the Salish language. Diagram 1 is a vowel chart that shows the arrangement of vowel closeness and vowel openness. The vertical positions denotes vowel closeness. The horizontal position denotes vowel openness. "In phonetics and phonology, **vowel height** is the vertical position of the tongue relative to either the roof of the mouth or the aperture of the jaw. In high vowels, such as [i] and [u], the tongue is positioned high in the mouth, whereas in low vowels, such as [a], the tongue is positioned low in the mouth."[1] "Also, in phonetics, **vowel backness** is the position of the tongue relative to the back of the mouth in a vowel sound."[2] Diagram 2 illustrates graphically the position of the tongue in relation to the position in the mouth.

---

[1]Vowel height. (2008, March 26). In *Wikipedia, The Free Encyclopedia*. Retrieved 04:59, April 15, 2008, from http://en.wikipedia.org.

[2]Vowel backness. (2008, March 17). In *Wikipedia, The Free Encyclopedia*. Retrieved 05:16, April 15, 2008, from http://en.wikipedia.org.

Consonants

Table 1. Salish Consonants[1]

	bilabial	alveolar	palato-alveolar	palatal	velar	labial-velar	uvular	labial-uvular	glottal
plosive	p	t			k	k^w	q	q^w	ʔ
ejective stop	p̓	t̓				k̓^{w}	q̓	q̓^{w}	
affricate		c	č						
ejective affricate		c̓	č̓						
lateral ejective affricate		ƛ̓							
fricative		s	š			x^w	x̣	x̣^{w}	h
lateral fricative		ł							
nasal	m	n							
glottalized nasal	m̓	n̓							
approximant				y		w			
glottalized approximant				y̓		w̓			
lateral approximant		l							
glottalized lateral approximant		l̓							

The linguistic terms in Table 1 are explained in the following pages.

[1] *Note.* Modified table based on: Flemming, E., Ladefoged, P., & Thomason, S. (*c.* 1992). Phonetic Structures of Montana Salish (Manuscript: Department of Linguistics, MIT, Cambridge, MA. 1992).

Diagram 3. Consonant Place of Articulation

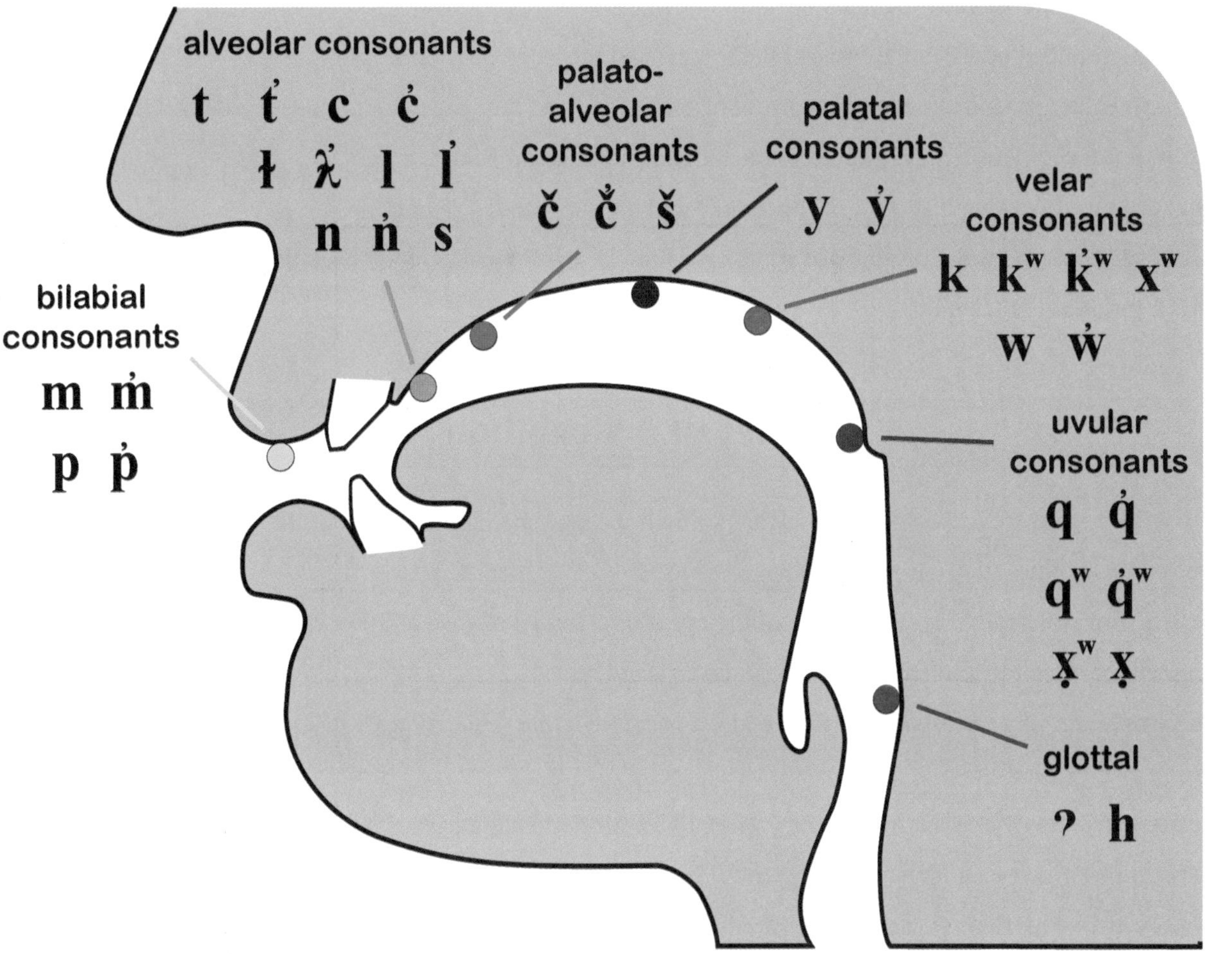

The Salish orthography includes 32 consonants and 5 vowels. A change in the alphabet in the 1980s and early 1990s eliminated four consonants and one vowel. These omitted letters are mentioned for people interested in further study of the language. The letters are the four pharyngeal consonants and the schwa vowel. The written forms of these letters would have looked like the following: ʕ ʕ̓ ʕʷ ʕ̓ʷ ə

"In articulatory phonetics, the **place of articulation** of a consonant is the point of contact, where an obstruction occurs in the vocal tract between an active (moving) articulator (typically some part of the tongue) and a passive (stationary) articulator (typically some part of the roof of the mouth). Along with the **manner of articulation** and **phonation**, this gives the consonant its distinctive sound."[2] Salish has seven places of articulation: bilabial, alveolar, palato-alveolar, palatal, velar, uvular, and glottal and thirteen manners of articulation. This is illustrated in Table 1, with the columns representing place of articulation and rows representing manner of articulation. Diagram 3 shows a representation of the physical location of point of articulation. Definitions of each point and manner of articulation follow.

[2] Place of articulation. (2008, January 12). In *Wikipedia, The Free Encyclopedia*. Retrieved April 14, 2008, from http://en.wikipedia.org/

Place of Articulation

Bilabial: produced between the lips.

Alveolar: produced between the front of the tongue and the ridge behind the gums.

Palato-alveolar: produced between the front of the tongue and the space behind the alveolar ridge.

Palatal: produced between the middle of the tongue and the hard palate.

Velar: produced between the back of the tongue and the soft palate (velum).

Uvular: produced between the back of the tongue and the uvula (hangs in the back of the mouth).

Glottal: produced at the glottis.

Manner of Articulation

Plosive is where there is a complete blockage of both the oral and nasal cavities of the vocal tract, and therefore no air flow.

Ejective stop is where there is blockage of the vocal tract with a release of air power by an upward movement of the glottis rather than by the lungs or diaphragm.

Affricates begin like a plosive, but release into a fricative rather than having a separate release of their own.

Ejective affricates are like affricates beginning like a plosive and releasing into a fricative all with an air stream powered by an upward movement of the glottis rather than by the lungs or diaphragm.

Lateral ejective affricate is an affricate produced on one or both sides of the tongue by blocking the vocal tract and releasing the pressure build up with an air stream powered by an upward movement of the glottis.

Fricative is where there is continuous frication (turbulent and noisy airflow) at the place of articulation.

Lateral fricatives are where frication occurs on one or both sides of the edge of the tongue.

Nasal is produced with an obstructed oral cavity allowing the air to pass through the nasal cavity.

Glottalized nasal is produced with an obstructed oral cavity allowing the air to pass through the nasal cavity simultaneously with a closure of the glottis.

Approximant is where there is very little obstruction.

Glottalized approximant is where there is very little obstruction simultaneously with a closure of the glottis.

Lateral approximant is produced on one or both sides of the tongue with very little obstruction.

Glottalized lateral approximant is produced on one or both sides of the tongue with very little obstruction with a simultaneous closure of the glottis.

A Brief History of Salish Orthography
and the controversial *i* or *ey* spelling

Language is a body of words and systems for communication and expression. People throughout the world created symbols to represent oral language which provided for widespread communication and the transfer of knowledge. Orthography is a system for writing these words and their proper letters. People of all cultures developed their own unique languages. The ability to write and record them is important for preservation. The Salish language is one that has been in oral form for thousands of years. When foreign cultures arrived they brought with them an orthographical system, the written word. The Salish orthography began as purely an academic pursuit and as an instrument of education for these foreigners who were working with Salish speaking people. Jesuit Fathers in the latter part of the 1800s created the first Salish orthography using the English alphabet. Since then, there have been numerous isolated orthographical systems used during the past 150 years. In 1879, Rev. J. Giorda published the first body of written Salish words in "A Dictionary of the Kalispel or Flathead Language." For nearly 100 years, the written language was primarily created and used by and for missionaries, anthropologists, and linguists. In 1974, Johnny Arlee and a group of other fluent speakers started the Salish Culture Committee. This group was concerned with the rapid decline of the language and culture. They set out to document and preserve the stories and wisdom that were still a part of the elders in that era. These efforts led to a need to create a standardized alphabet.

With the help of linguists, an alphabet based on the International Phonetic Alphabet (IPA) was devised. "British and French language teachers created the IPA in 1886. The general principal of IPA is to provide one symbol for one sound, a phonetic spelling."[1] It was based on an alphabet aimed at reforming English spelling to a phonetic system. IPA has had a few modifications; first in 1888, 1932, 1989, 1993, and most recently in 2005.

Similarly, Salish IPA has undergone minor alterations from its inception in 1976. In the early 1990s, use of the schwa and pharyngeal consonants were eliminated. Throughout this period there have been competing views about correct spelling. Some spellings have been ingrained and are now deemed correct. The development of our orthography is still in a formative stage; its evolution is not yet complete. It is early enough that changes can be made without much disruption. In the near future, the hope is that there will be many who speak and write the Salish language. It is for these people that this article is presented. Also, individuals interested in the future of the Salish language are encouraged to seriously consider the evidence presented in the following sections. Whereas it took several hundred years to standardize English spelling, Salish spelling has been rapidly becoming standardized in a mere 30 years. English spelling remains an over-burdensome system that requires countless hours of study and causes anguish for many young and old. However, it continues to evolve. Today, the Salish language is in such a precarious state that standardized spelling should be the least of our concerns. Let us not allow Salish to evolve into a complicated system of spelling such as English.

---

[1] International Phonetic Alphabet. (2008, March 30). In *Wikipedia, The Free Encyclopedia*. Retrieved, April 2, 2008, from http://en.wikipedia.org

<u>The inconsistency of *ey*</u>

This part of the article presents an argument and justification for the use of "i" in representing Salish pronunciation. The spelling of the "i" sound in certain circumstances with an "ey" originates from an indoctrinated familiarity of English spellings and sounds. When an "i" follows uvular consonants and the glottal stop, it sounds similar to the "*ey*" in English words like th*ey*, pr*ey*, and ob*ey*. In the English word, "th*ey*," one can hear the same sound an "i" makes when following Salish uvular consonants, "**q, q̓, qʷ, q̓ʷ, x̣, x̣ʷ**" and the glottal stop, "ʔ." <u>This irregular sound is a result of the distance between production points of uvular consonants and the vowel "i."</u> Uvular consonants are produced with the back of the tongue pressed near the uvula. The vowel "i" is produced furthest from the uvula compared to other Salish vowels. This distance creates a sound that blends the vowels as the tongue glides from the uvular consonant position to the "i" vowel position creating the familiar English "*ey*" sound. The glottal stop is even further away from the "i" vowel thus creating the same English "*ey*" sound. On the other hand, velar consonants are closer to the "i" vowel, consequently creating a distinct "i" or English long "ee" sound. *(See diagram 1. at the right.)*

This information, if taught properly, can help students produce correct pronunciations of the uvular consonants. English does not have these uvular consonants in the language so it takes Salish language students a lot of practice to master. Language learners can self correct and self monitor if the following rule is taught: <u>if you can hear a distinct English "ee" sound after attempting to say a uvular consonant then you know that, incorrectly, a velar consonant was produced.</u> This means that more practice is needed to accustom the mouth to produce uvular consonants. So then, if you hear the English "*ey*" sound after saying a uvular consonant, one should be assured that it was pronounced correctly.

This "*ey*" sound after uvular consonants is a single phoneme not two phonemes. A phoneme represents one sound. In Salish one phoneme or sound is represented by a single character. This means that this "*ey*" sound needs to be represented with one letter. The practice of using two letters has been perpetuated by comfort in the familiar, created by using the English "*ey*" over the span of many years. This use has been further instilled by uninformed unilateral assertions. In most instances the Salish spelling of "i" after "**q, q̓, qʷ, q̓ʷ, x̣, x̣ʷ**" and the "**ʔ**" has generally been with an "*ey*," or "*ey̓*."

As learners and teachers we want to represent Salish sounds in writing as close as possible. This English "ey" sound doesn't sound like a long "ee" sound so it continues to be represented with the English "ey" spelling. For fluent speakers the written language does not help pronunciation. For learners the written language can be vital to learning.

This article and the following sections show evidence to support the use of "i" to reflect the sound and grammar of Salish.

Diagram 1. Velar and Uvular Consonants

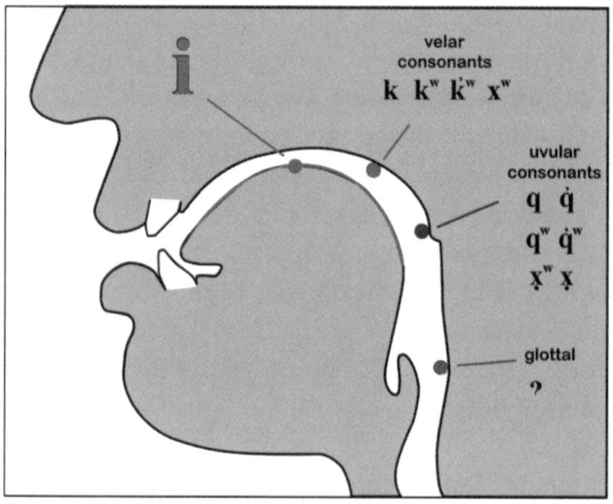

Diagram 2. Vowel Positions

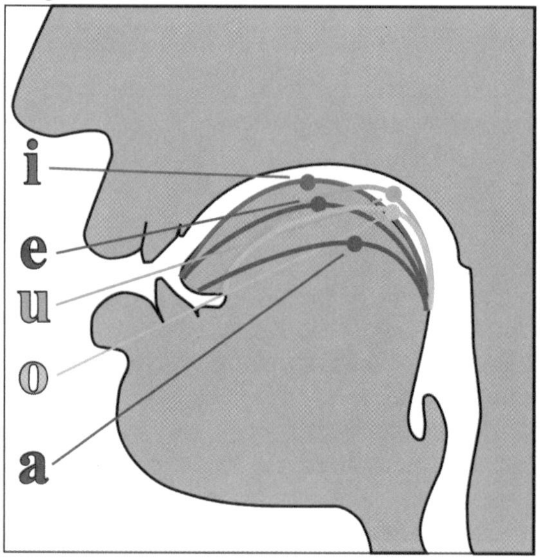

Supportive Grammatical Evidence

As stated above, in Salish, each letter is directly associated with one sound. Students of Salish are taught to associate each letter with one sound. This relationship of one-letter/one-sound has led most instructors to teach the alphabet before or in conjunction with language instruction. It is hoped that this will make students pronounce words correctly. Correct pronunciation is the goal of most instructors. At times this is an overzealous expectation detrimental to creating a safe and positive learning environment. In an effort to help students through this learning period, the "i" should be used to correctly represent the single phoneme produced. The instruction of using an "i" after uvular consonants will produce better pronunciation in students. This will be the result of providing students with a tool to check uvular consonant production, and ultimately correct pronunciation. This is a goal of all language teachers.

True "ey" Salish words

First, there are true "ey" sounds in Salish. In the examples below one can pronounce and hear each of the two letters. One way to test for a true "ey" sound is to stop on the "e." You should be able to hear a definite "e" sound followed by a true "y" sound as in the following examples. It is important to compare these sounds to those of the disputed ones.

Table 1 – Words with an *ey* sound:

This list of words contains true *ey* sounds. That is, each syllable of the *e* and the *y* can be heard distinctly. Refer to these words when comparing with words that appear to have an *ey* sound.

sxʷeyn – fisher	**weyt** – sick of animals
kʷleyn – cheese	**x̣ʷax̣ʷeẏm** – lazy person
smx̣eẏčṅ – grizzly	**es eycni** – S/he is talking back.
uheyiš – Bark! *(comm.)*	**snčmłq̇éyt,** *snčmłq̇é* – shoulder
ṅéyxʷe – trade	**xʷixʷeym** – S/he/it goes here and there.
xʷixʷeyuł – animals	**cpłéẏ** – eyebrow; brow

nweym – make prayerful offerings in sacrifice to the Creator
nweyls – lazy/tired; hate to do work; do something haphazardly
k̇ʷl̓l̓eysm – S/he changed (into s.t.).

Truncation Evidence

The examples in table 2 illustrate how one can check if the vowel should be an "i" or an "e." If the letter is a true "ey" then you should be able to stop at the "e" like in the two previous examples of **sčq̇ʷe** – Blackfeet and **snacłq̇e –** shirt.

Keeping with truncation at the "e," the word, **snyak̇ʷqin** – afternoon, should be spelled **snyak̇ʷqe** in truncated form. Rather it is often spelled **snyak̇ʷqey**. Similarly **ntox̣ʷqin** – noon, should be **sntox̣ʷqe** rather than the often spelled **sntox̣ʷqey**. In both of these examples spelling with an ending "e" would be incorrect because the familiar "ey" spelling represents one phoneme. This being the case, it should be spelled with an "i" to correctly represent the single phoneme sound. This will help students of Salish attempt a more accurate pronunciation of the single phoneme. If there is any doubt that the "i" isn't a single phoneme or one sound, compare it to any of the words in table 1. Listen carefully to the two phonemes of the "ey" in the words in table 1. Each letter is distinctly heard.

Table 2 – Truncation at the *e* of an *ey* sound:

These example words are truncated on the *e* of an *ey* sound. These words, when spoken, are generally "cut-off" at the *e*. A very distinct *e* is heard when *ey* words are truncated at the *e*.

sčq̇ʷeyšn, commonly said **sčq̇ʷe** – Blackfeet
snacłq̇eyt, commonly said **snacłq̇e** – shirt

<u>Morphological Evidence</u>

Morphology is the linguistic study of the internal structure of words and how it relates to word formation. This section shows some morphological evidence to support the use of "i" after uvular consonants. In Salish there are root words that have a strong "a" vowel. These root words pass this "a" to its suffixes. One of these words is, **tam –** not. When combined with a suffix the "a" is passed to the suffix. This is seen in the word, **tmalsm –** in doubt, from the word, **tam –** not, and the suffix, **els –** feelings. The "a" in **tam,** changes the "e" in **els,** to an "a." Another word, **psap –** nervous, has a strong "a." When a word takes on the continuative aspect (similar to "ing" in English) an "i" is added to the end of the word. With words that have a strong "a" the "i" is changed to an "a." For example **psap** – nervous, becomes **es pspma** – s/he is being nervous, just as **ƛ̓lip** – stop, becomes **es ƛ̓lpmi** – s/he is stopping.

The suffix **qin –** top**,** is often spell "qeyn." In the previous section the example **snyak̓ʷqin** – afternoon, was used. In truncated form it is often spelled **snyak̓ʷq*ey*.** Root words with a strong "**a**" transfer it to the suffix. One example is the descriptive root **ṗaṫ** describing something squishy/ moist. When the suffix **qin** is added it makes the word **ṗaṫqan,** an insult calling someone's head squishy. It transfers its strong "**a**" to overtake the "i" and morph it to an "a." It would be unthinkable to spell it as **ṗaṫq*ay*n.** Another example comes from the word **pmap –** go fast, in a word to describe the condition of dizziness. The **npṁpqan –** dizzy, is a combination of **pmap** and **qin**. The strong "a" in **pmap** changes the "i" in qin to an "a." This word would be incorrectly spelled as **npṁpq*ay*n**.

Table 3 – Strong "a" words:
To keep with the pattern of "ey" instead of "i" these strong "a" words would not be spelled with an "ay."
ṗaṫqan – has a soft sloppy head, would be spelled, **ṗaṫq*ay*n.**
npṁpqan – out of the head; dizzy; silly; buzzed, would be **npṁpq*ay*n.**

Table 4 – : Suffixal Consistency
In Salish suffixes are consistent unless influenced by a strong "a." One example is the suffix …**iċeʔ** – covered in. This suffix starts with an "i" making it a good example to show the sound an "i" makes after a uvular consonant.
es čq̓ʔiċeʔ – It has a pattern around it; tattoo (not spelled "**es čq̓ʔ*<u>ey</u>*ċeʔ**").
čax̣iċeʔ – wrapped with rope; it is covered with lines (not spelled "**čax̣*<u>ey</u>*ċeʔ**").

<u>Suffixal Evidence "…iċeʔ"</u>

The "**i**" sound can be shown in suffixes that have an "**i**." One example is the suffix "**iċeʔ**" which indicates "covered in." When this suffix follows a "**q, q̓, qʷ, q̓ʷ, x̣, x̣ʷ**" or the "**ʔ**" the word has been spelled with an "*ey*." Below are some examples of the "*ey*" spelling with a correlation to the same suffix.

One example is the word, **čq̓ċiċeʔ –** the cover is woven. Another word is, **čpƛ̓iċeʔ –** take a harness off. In both words, there is no dispute that the "**i**" is an "**i**" in the spellings. Now if the suffix …**iċeʔ** was in fact "eyċeʔ," the words **čax̣iċeʔ** and **čq̓ʔiċeʔ** would be spelled with and "*ey*." The words in table 4 have the same suffix, **iċeʔ**. When the "**i**" combines with the "**x̣**" and the "**ʔ**" it makes the "**i**" sound like the "*ey*" sound as in English th*ey*. Below are other examples with the **…iċeʔ** suffix that have a clear "i" sound:

čpƛ̓iċeʔ – to take a harness off.
es čq̓ċiċeʔ – It has a woven cover.
čsṗiċeʔ – to hit all over.
ṫmiċeʔ – damp all over.
čc̓miċeʔ – eggshell.

There is no question that these examples are spelled with an "i." There is no rule grammatically of morphologically that would change the "i" to an "ey."

Suffixal Evidence "…ičṅ"

Just as in the previous section the "i" sound can be clearly heard in words containing the suffix …**ičṅ** – the back. The following are used to illustrate how the "i" sounds like the "*ey*" in English when following one of the letters, "**q, q̓, qʷ, q̓ʷ, x̣, x̣ʷ**" or the "**ʔ**." Below are some examples:

snčmičṅ – the whole back
nqsičṅ – to scratch the back
čxʷstičṅ – to walk on a ridge
nc̓aličṅ – to have an achy back

Examples with uvular consonants:

mx̣ʷičṅ – snow on the ridge (not "**mx̣ʷ**_ey_**čṅ**").
nmq̓ʷmq̓ʷičṅ – bumps on the back; camel (not "**nmq̓ʷmq̓ʷ**_ey_**čṅ**").
nƛ̓aq̓ičṅ – to have a hot back (not "**nƛ̓aq̓**_ey_**čṅ**").

These examples show how the sound "i" after uvular consonants is similar to the *ey* sound in English th*ey*.

Intransitive Verb Evidence

There are grammatical rules in Salish that remain constant just as the previous suffixes do. Unlike English, Salish grammar rules apply without exception throughout the language. They are based on lexical and morphological rules. The following examples show how the "ey" spelling can create complications to the Salish grammar. Without adhering to these very specific rules there can be confusion, especially when you are a beginning student of the language.

In this grammar, there is the rule of adding "**i**" to create the continuative aspect. This rule is very familiar to most teachers and students. Since it is so commonly used, the spelling of "**i**," following one of the letters, "**q, q̓, qʷ, q̓ʷ, x̣, x̣ʷ**" or the "**ʔ**," is rarely spelled with an "ey." The following are some examples of this grammatical rule:

es susti – S/he/it is drinking.
es k̓ʷlsncuti – S/he is cooking.

es łoq̓ʷi – S/he is peeling/making bare.
es laq̓i – S/he is sweating.
es ac̓x̣i – S/he is looking.
es acqʷi – S/he is roasting (s.t.).

Now, compare the ending sound in **es laq̓i** – S/he is sweating, with the ending sound of **snyak̓ʷqi** – afternoon – and the "ey" sound in **kʷl**_ey_**n** – cheese. If said correctly, there is a distinct difference.

Third Person Plural Evidence

Another grammatical rule is when words change to the third person plural, "they" or "their." In this rule, the stressed vowel gets reduplicated and placed in front of the stressed vowel and separated with an "**ʔ**." For example, if the stressed vowel was an "**á**" the reduplication would look like "**áʔa**." This rule applies throughout the language without exception. Further, the reduplication happens only to one syllable or vowel. For instance, an "*ey*" cannot be reduplicated to "*eyʔey*." The following are examples of words without "**i**" after the "**q, q̓, qʷ, q̓ʷ, x̣, x̣ʷ**" or the "**ʔ**" and words that do.

snsuʔustis – their cup
sšeʔenšs – their rock
aʔaplsts – their apple

nmq̓ʷmq̓ʷiʔičis – their camel (not **nmq̓ʷmq̓ʷ**_eyʔey_**čis**)

The following examples show action words with the same rule above. That is, reduplication of the stressed vowel for third person plural, "they."

suʔúst – They drank, from the word, **sust** – to drink.
čłiʔíp – They hunted, from the word, **čłip** – to hunt.

čcoqiʔís – They beat someone (not **čcoq***eyʔey***s**), from the word, **čcoqín** – to beat someone.
qiʔíʔlm – They begged (not **q***eyʔeyʔ***lm**), from the word, **qiʔlm** – to beg.

čnmnmṗqiˀín – Each one of them went blind (not **čnmnmṗq**_eyˀey_**n**), from the word, **čnmṗqin –** to go blind.

qéˀeẏs – They had a nightmare (not **q**_eyˀeyˀ_**is**), from the word, **qéˀeẏs –** to have a nightmare.

Plural Reduplication Evidence

In the last example of the grammatical rule of reduplication, to create a plural, the syllables on each side of the stress vowel get reduplicated, and placed before the first letter of the three syllables. For example, the word, "**kʷil**" which means, "red," becomes, "**kʷlkʷil**," in the plural form "reds" or "two or more red objects." The following examples show words without the "**i**" after "**q, q̇, qʷ, q̇ʷ, x̣, x̣ʷ**" or the "**ʔ**" and then words that do.

x̣ʷlx̣ʷelm – to abandon things, from the word, **x̣ʷelm** – to abandon.
mq̇ʷmoq̇ʷ – mounds, from the word, **moq̇ʷ** – mound.
sqlqélixʷ – people, from the word, **sqelixʷ** – people.

sšṅšeṅš – rocks, from the word, **sšeṅš** – rock.

qʷnqʷin – two or more green objects from word, qʷin – green. If it were spelled "**qʷ**_ey_**n**" it would become "**qʷ**_y_**qʷ**_ey_**n**" which would be incorrect.
x̣tx̣itne – dagger. If it were spelled "**x̣**_ey_**tne**" it would become "**x̣**_y_**x̣**_ey_**tne**" which would be incorrect.
x̣px̣ipt – gnawed by bugs. If it were spelled "**x̣**_ey_**pt**" it would become "**x̣**_y_**x̣**_ey_**pt**" which would be incorrect.
q̇tq̇it – square. If it were spelled "**q̇**_ey_**t**" it would become "**q̇**_y_**q̇**_ey_**t**" which would be incorrect.

All the above evidence shows the need to spell words using the "**i**" after "**q, q̇, qʷ, q̇ʷ, x̣, x̣ʷ**" or the "**ʔ**." Without it, future Salish students will have confusion and anguish like those learning to spell the English language today. If we want to enable ease of use and consistency in Salish orthography we must not get complacent in our currently accepted Salish spelling of "i" with and "ey" after uvular consonants.

Writing and spelling are a means for communicating the spoken word in an abstract representation. Fluent speakers have an intimate knowledge of the language. Writing for them is merely an extension of their fluency. For people learning the language the written word is vital to their growing vocabulary. Correct pronunciation does not come from the written word. It comes from exposure to the spoken word in real-world contextual experiences. It also comes from practice, perseverance, and dedication. One of the most difficult world languages to learn is English. We are all fluent speakers of this language. If you have the capacity to learn English you have the capacity to learn enough Salish to become conversationally fluent; don't give up. Practice, practice, practice.

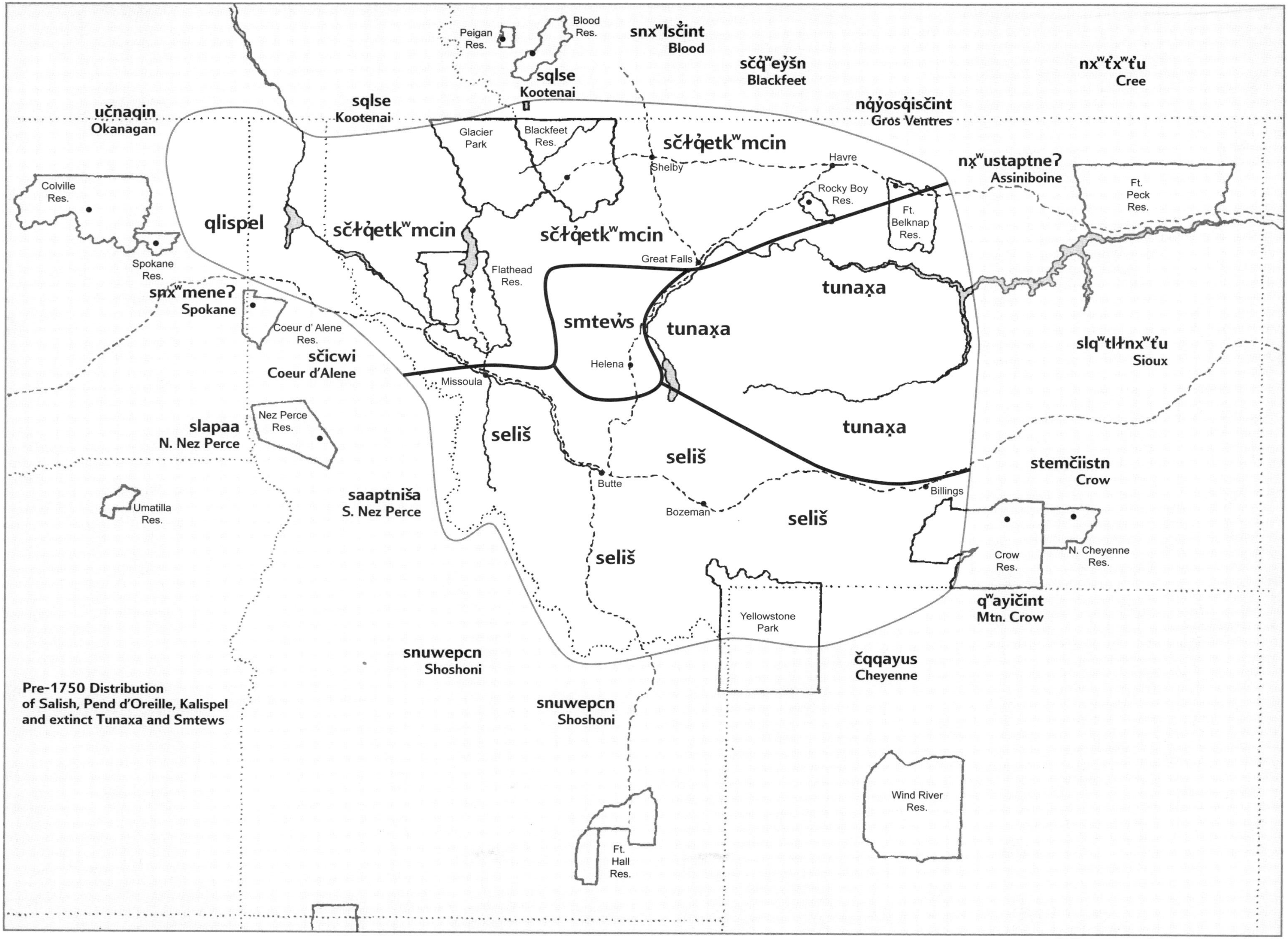

Pre-1750 Distribution of Salish, Pend d'Oreille, Kalispel and extinct Tunaxa and Smtews

A

abalone shell
x̣ayqs – abalone shell. **x̣ayqsts, inx̣ayqs, anx̣ayqs**

abandon
x̣ʷel – abandon; throw away; leave.

x̣ʷelm – S/he/it abandoned (s.t.). **čn x̣ʷelm, kʷ x̣ʷelm**
es x̣ʷeli – S/he/it is abandoning (s.t.). **čnes x̣ʷeli, kʷes x̣ʷeli**
qs x̣ʷeli – S/he/it is going to be abandoning (s.t.). **čiqs x̣ʷeli, kʷqs x̣ʷeli**
x̣ʷéʔelm – They abandoned (s.t.). **qeʔ x̣ʷelm, p x̣ʷelm**
es x̣ʷéʔeli – They're abandoning (s.t.). **qeʔes x̣ʷeli, pes x̣ʷeli**
qs x̣ʷéʔeli – They're going to be abandoning (s.t.) **qeʔqs x̣ʷeli, pqs x̣ʷeli**

x̣ʷelis – S/he/it abandoned it. **x̣ʷeln, x̣ʷelntxʷ**
es x̣ʷelms – S/he/it is abandoning it. **ies x̣ʷelm, as x̣ʷelm**
qs x̣ʷelms – S/he/it is going to abandon it. **iqs x̣ʷelm, aqs x̣ʷelm**
x̣ʷéʔelis – They abandoned it. **qeʔ x̣ʷelntm, x̣ʷelntp**
es x̣ʷéʔelms – They're abandoning it. **qeʔes x̣ʷelm, es x̣ʷelmp**
qs x̣ʷéʔelms – They're going to abandon it. **qeʔqs x̣ʷelm, qs x̣ʷelmp**

es x̣ʷlx̣ʷeli – S/he is repeatedly abandoning. **čnes x̣ʷlx̣ʷeli, kʷes x̣ʷlx̣ʷeli**
es x̣ʷlx̣ʷelms – S/he is abandoning things. **ies x̣ʷlx̣ʷelm, as x̣ʷlx̣ʷelm**

łx̣ʷex̣ʷlm – S/he/it abandoned a little. **čn łx̣ʷex̣ʷlm, kʷ łx̣ʷex̣ʷlm**
łx̣ʷex̣ʷlis – S/he/it abandoned a little of it. **łx̣ʷex̣ʷln, łx̣ʷex̣ʷlntxʷ**

x̣ʷell – S/he/it got abandoned.
x̣ʷelntm – S/he/it was abandoned by someone.

x̣ʷlnuis – S/he finally abandoned it. **x̣ʷlnun, x̣ʷlnuntxʷ**

sxʷx̣ʷelm – one tasked to abandon/throw away. *prefix:* ***sxʷ...*** *– one tasked to do.*
x̣ʷlemn – one inclined to abandon/throw away. **x̣ʷlx̣ʷlemn** *pl. suffix:* ***...emn*** *– one inclined to do.*
x̣ʷlx̣ʷlmuł – one that habitually abandons/throws away. *suffix:* ***...łmuł*** *– one that habitually does.*
scx̣ʷel – something that's been thrown away. *(i.e., people, child, spouse or item.) prefix:* ***sc...*** *– s.t. that's been done/made/prepared.*
snx̣ʷelmn – place you abandon things; dump; garbage receptacle. *prefix:* ***sn...*** *– a place of.*
sx̣ʷelmn – devil. **słx̣ʷex̣ʷlmn –** little devil. *suffix:* ***...min, ...mn*** *– instrument/tool.*

x̣ʷeliš – Throw (it) away. *cmd.*
x̣ʷelskʷ – Abandon it. *cmd.*
x̣ʷelnt – Throw it away. *cmd.*
x̣ʷlscut – S/he abandoned something personal. **čn x̣ʷlscut, kʷ x̣ʷlscut**
es x̣ʷlscuti – S/he is abandoning something personal. **čnes x̣ʷlscuti, kʷes x̣ʷlscuti**
es łx̣ʷlmisti – S/he is getting rid of something that is self detrimental.
es łx̣ʷlscutisti – S/he is getting rid of something within one's self.
es x̣ʷlmnwexʷi – They're leaving each other.

s.t. - something, the 3rd person
(s.t.) - something implied
s.o. - someone, the 3rd person
sl. - singular form
pl. - plural form
rt. - root word
cmd. - command
lit. - literally
fig. - figuratively
i.e., - for example
See: - Redirection to a related word.

x̣ʷllwisntm – S/he keeps getting left behind.
x̣ʷllwisis – S/he keeps leaving it behind. **x̣ʷllwisn, x̣ʷllwisntxʷ**
es nx̣ʷlmelsi – S/he is wanting to abandon (something). **čnes nx̣ʷlmelsi, kʷes nx̣ʷmelsi**
es x̣ʷlmutms – S/he can abandoned it. **ies x̣ʷlmutm, as x̣ʷlmutm**
es x̣ʷllutm – It can be abandoned; it is disposable.
x̣ʷllałq – S/he abandoned his/her spouse. **čn x̣ʷllałq, kʷ x̣ʷllałq**
es x̣ʷllłqotm – S/he is divorceable.

xʷuyš k̇ʷis x̣ʷeliš – Go throw (it) away. **x̣ʷllwisn łu stipn –** I keep leaving Stephen behind. **ies x̣ʷlx̣ʷelm łu inmomosqá –** I am getting rid of my broken down cars. **ṅem x̣ʷelntxʷ –** You will throw it away. **łiʔe scmlmálq̇ʷ eł es x̣ʷlx̣ʷélm pkʷéẇt –** There were clumps left lying all over.

abdomen **čłčmqni –** lower abdomen. *rt.: **čm** – extremity.*

olin – belly, stomach. *See: **belly**.*

…éẇs – suffix indicating middle, center. *See: **middle**.*

Abe **aplám –** Abe.

able **ax̣llwís,** *ax̣llwí* – hustle around for something; able and determined in doing something. *See: **busy**.*

above **čłqeẇs,** *čłqe* – on top of. *See: **top**.*

qaqlt – arrive at the top. *See: **top**.*

ššaĺús, *ššaĺú* – go uphill. *See: **uphill**.*

čqe – upstream. *See: **upstream**.*

čiwlš – climb. (also used to indicate going upstairs) *See: **climb**.*

nwist – up; above; up high. *See: **high**.*

x̣ʷcuʔsičṅ, *x̣ʷcuʔsi* – go over a mountain pass. *See: **pass**.*

čłqʷéẇs – drape up high; hang up high over an object; hang up. *See: **drape**.*

Abraham **iplahá –** Abraham.

absent **čuw –** gone; away; absent. *See: **gone**.*

absolute **i mi –** It is plainly evident; it is absolute; it is fact. *See: **know**.*
ha i mi – Is it for sure?
x̣ʷa i mi – probably; most likely.

x̣ʷa i mi u ta es mistexʷ – It is most likely you do not know it. **i mi lkʷut –** Of course it is far. **i mi u ta es mistexʷ –** Of course you do not know it. **i mi u ta –** For sure no. **i mi u unexʷ –** It is certainly true. **i mi u sḿa –** It is plain to see it is a cow. **i mi u čiqs xʷuyi –** I am going for sure. **i mi u šeẏ –** It is plain to see that's what it is.

accept **tkʷnem –** accept something. *rt.: **kʷen** – take.*
tkʷéis – S/he/it accepted s.t. **tkʷen, tkʷentxʷ**
es tkʷnems – S/he/it is accepting s.t. **ies tkʷnem, as tkʷnem**
qs tkʷnems – S/he/it is going to accept s.t. **iqs tkʷnem, aqs tkʷnem**
tkʷéʔeis – They accepted s.t. **qeʔ tkʷéntm, tkʷéntp**
es tkʷnéʔems – They are accepting s.t. **qeʔes tkʷnem, es tkʷnemp**

qs tkʷnéʔems – They are going to accept s.t. **qeʔqs tkʷnem, qs tkʷnemp**

tkʷent – Accept it. *cmd.*

t atwen u tkʷeis – Tony accepted it. **i tam łu tkʷen –** I accepted the wrong one. **qʷo tkʷent –** Accept me.

nšiẏelsm – in favor of s.t./s.o.; in acceptance of s.t.; show preference for s.t./s.o. *See: **agree**.*

tamm – not; deny; refuse. *See: **refuse**.*

accident

x̣ṅnumt – get injured; have a long lasting sickness. *See: **injure**.*

lxʷup – get hurt accidently. *See: **hurt**.*

accompany

čšin – go with; accompany.

čšnim – S/he/it accompanied. **čn čšnim, kʷ čšnim**
es čšnmi – S/he/it is accompanying. **čnes čšnmi, kʷes čšnmi**
qs čšnmi – S/he/it is going to accompany. **čiqs čšnmi, kʷqs čšnmi**
čšníʔim – They accompanied. **qeʔ čšnim, p čšnim**
es čšnmíʔi – They are accompanying. **qeʔes čšnmi, pes čšnmi**
qs čšnmíʔi – They are going to accompany. **qeʔqs čšnmi, pqs čšnmi**

čšntes – S/he/it accompanied s.o. **čšnten, čšntexʷ**
es čšnims – S/he/it is accompanying s.o. **ies čšnim, as čšnim**
qs čšnims – S/he/it is going to accompany s.o. **iqs čšnim, aqs čšnim**
čšntéʔes – They accompanied s.o. **qeʔ čšntem, čšntep**
es čšníʔims – They are accompanying s.o. **qeʔes čšnim, es čšnimp**
qs čšníʔims – They are going to accompany s.o. **qeʔqs čšnim, qs čšnimp**

čšnists – S/he/it accompanied s.o. **čšnin, čšnintxʷ**

čššin – S/he/it went along involuntarily *(i.e., a crowd pushing you along).* **čn čššin, kʷ čššin**
čšntem – S/he/it was accompanied by someone.

čšnint – Go with s.o. *cmd.*
čšnlwis – S/he/it goes around with *(i.e., a dog that follows someone everywhere). suffix: **...lwis** – indicate going around.*
es čšnwexʷi – They're accompanying each other. **qeʔes čšnwexʷi, pes čšnwexʷi**

ha es čšneľt – Did the child come with you? **ha es čščšneľt –** Did the children come with you? **qʷo čšnint –** Come with me. **kʷ iqs čšnim –** I am going to go with you. **ha kʷ iqs čšnim –** Do you want me to go with you? **ṅe tʔe swe qs ácṁi m še čšin –** If anyone is going to trap they should come along. **iqs čšníʔim łu isxʷsixʷlt qs k̓ʷis qq̇méʔe –** I am going along with my children, they're going to go fishing. **hoy nhéʔelsn u cun "xʷu ṅem čšncin" –** I felt sorry for him and told him, "Okay I will go with you."

nčšnmels – want to accompany. *circumfix: **n...els** – want.*
nčšnmels – S/he/it wanted to accompany. **čn nčšnmels, kʷ nčšnmels**
es nčšnmelsi – S/he/it is wanting to accompany. **čnes nčšnmelsi, kʷes nčšnmelsi**
qs nčšnmelsi – S/he/it is wanting to accompany. **čiqs nčšnmelsi, kʷqs nčšnmelsi**
nčšnméʔels – They wanted to accompany. **qeʔ nčšnmels, p nčšnmels**
es nčšnméʔelsi – They are wanting to accompany. **qeʔes nčšnmelsi, pes nčšnmelsi**
qs nčšnméʔelsi – They are going to want to accompany. **qeʔqs nčšnmelsi, pqs nčšnmelsi**

x̣eł – invite to go; invite to travel to someplace. *See: **invite**.*

The **i** following uvular consonants (UC) and the glottal stop **ʔ** sound like English "*ey*" as in the words th*ey*, h*ey*, wh*ey*, etc. Salish UC are: **q, q̇, qʷ, q̇ʷ, x̣, x̣ʷ**. For example, the suffix ...**qin** – head/top, is often spelled using English *ey* as "q*ey*n". So **qi, q̇i, qʷi, q̇ʷi, x̣i, x̣ʷi**, may be spelled with English *ey* as **q***ey*, **q̇***ey*, **qʷ***ey*, **q̇ʷ***ey*, **x̣***ey*, **x̣ʷ***ey* in other texts.

s.t. - something, the 3rd person
(s.t.) - something implied
s.o. - someone, the 3rd person
sl. - singular form
pl. - plural form
rt. - root word
cmd. - command
lit. - literally
fig. - figuratively
i.e., - for example
See: - Redirection to a related word.

accomplish

k̇ʷl̇nunm – succeed making something; accomplish something. *rt.: **k̇ʷul̇**– make/build/do; suffix: **...nu...** – transitive suffix indicating success.*
k̇ʷl̇nuis – S/he accomplished s.t. **k̇ʷl̇nun, k̇ʷl̇nuntxʷ**
es k̇ʷl̇nunms – S/he is accomplishing s.t. **ies k̇ʷl̇nunm, as k̇ʷl̇nunm**
qs k̇ʷl̇nunms – S/he is going to accomplish s.t. **iqs k̇ʷl̇nunm, aqs k̇ʷl̇nunm**
k̇ʷl̇núʔuis – They accomplished s.t. **qeʔ k̇ʷl̇nuntm, k̇ʷl̇nuntp**
es k̇ʷl̇núʔunms – They are accomplishing s.t. **qeʔes k̇ʷl̇nunm, qs k̇ʷl̇nunmp**
qs k̇ʷl̇núʔunms – They are going to accomplish s.t. **qeʔqs k̇ʷl̇nunm, qs k̇ʷl̇nunmp**

qʷoṁmałq, *qʷoṁma* – get close to doing/finishing something; getting near to some point; close to the end of a journey; winning. *See: **close**.*

accumulate

málq̇ʷ – rounded/spherical; balled object; accumulate. *See: **ball**.*

accustomed

qʷʔem – get accustomed/used to somebody or something.
qʷʔem – S/he/it got accustomed. **čn qʷʔem, kʷ qʷʔem**
es qʷeṁmi – S/he/it is getting accustomed. **čnes qʷeṁmi, kʷes qʷeṁmi**
qs qʷeṁmi – S/he/it is going to get accustomed. **čiqs qʷeṁmi, kʷqs qʷeṁmi**
qʷʔéʔem – They got accustomed. **qeʔ qʷʔem, p qʷʔem**

qʷemmstes – S/he/it made s.o. get accustomed. **qʷemmsten, qʷemmstexʷ**
es qʷemmims– S/he/it is making s.o. get accustomed. **ies qʷemmim, as qʷemmim**
qs qʷemmims – S/he/it is going to make s.o. get accustomed. **iqs qʷemmim, aqs qʷemmim**

qʷeṁmis – S/he/it got used to s.t./s.o. **qʷeṁmin, qʷeṁmintxʷ**
es qʷeṁminms – S/he/it is getting used to s.t./s.o. **ies qʷeṁminm, as qʷeṁminm**
qs qʷeṁminms – S/he/it is going to be used to s.t./s.o. **iqs qʷeṁminm, aqs qʷeṁminm**
qʷeṁmíʔis – They got used to s.t./s.o. **qeʔ qʷeṁmintm, qʷeṁmintp**
es qʷéʔeṁminms – They are getting used to s.t./s.o. **qeʔes qʷeṁminm, es qʷeṁminmp**

sqʷʔem – habit; practice.
sqʷʔems – his/her/its habit/practice. **isqʷéʔm, asqʷéʔm**

qʷeṁmint – Get used to it. *cmd.*
qʷaqʷemncut, *qʷaqʷemncu* – practice, drill, training. *See: **practice**.*
sčqʷamaqs – something one is used to; something liked. *(i.e., drugs)*
qʷeṁmnwexʷ – Get accustomed to each other.
es nqʷeṁmeẇsms – S/he got accustomed to be among them. **ies nqʷeṁmeẇsm, as nqʷeṁmeẇsm**
qʷeṁmulexʷ – S/he/it got used to the area/land/place. **čn qʷeṁmulexʷ, kʷ qʷeṁmulexʷ**
qʷeṁmuléʔexʷ – They got used to the area/land/place. **qeʔ qʷeṁmulexʷ, p qʷeṁmulexʷ**

ha qʷeṁmintxʷ – Are you used to it. **ha qʷeṁmintxʷ kʷqs xʷuy č nłʔay –** Are you getting used to going to Missoula. **qʷeṁmin łu snlaq̇i –** I got used to/accustomed to the sweat. **nqʷeṁmin łu sxʷṗq̇ʷʔleṁ –** I got used to/accustomed to being a ballplayer.

qʷamáqs – get accustomed to food. *suffix: **...aqs** – food, kind.*
qʷamáqsmis – S/he/it got used to the food. **qʷamáqsmn, qʷamáqsmntxʷ**
qʷamáʔaqsmis – They got used to the food. **qeʔ qʷamáqsmntm, qʷamáqsmntp**

sqʷamáqs – Food that you are accustomed to. **isqʷamáqs, asqʷamáqs, sqʷamáqsts**

čn qʷamaqs t kapi – I am just getting used to coffee. **isčqʷamaqs łu kapi –** I am used to coffee.

ache

ċaál, *ċa* – achy; sore; hurting; in pain.
i ċaál – It is painful; it aches.
sċaál – ache.

nċaléls – feel pain inside.
ċalċlt – painful *(physical or emotional).*

ċʔalax̣n – have a sore/achy arm. *See: **arm**.*
nċaléneʔ – aching ear. *See: **earache**.*
ċaléčst – have a sore/achy hand. *See: **hand**.*
ċʔalqín – headache. *See: **headache**.*
nċaličṅ – have an aching back; backache. *See: **backache**.*
čċaʔlelps – have a neck ache. *See: **neck ache**.*
čċaléls, *čċalé* – ill, sick. *See: **sick**.*
čċax̣ʷéls – sick to the stomach. *See: **sick**.*

ċa ye isčwax̣n – My arm hurts. **šeẏ łu pn ċa** – Now, that is painful. **čna ċʔál** – That one person got sick.

k̓ʷłċa – very painful.
k̓ʷłċa isčwax̣n – My arm hurts. **nłapa k̓ʷłċa tʔe u ƛ̓lil sqelixʷ** – Death can be very painful. **k̓ʷłċa tʔe u tnk̓ʷuʔ l snlaq̓i** – Sometimes it is painful in the sweat. **k̓ʷłċa tʔe u čłła l sxʷuymtkʷ** – It is painful to sit on the ice.

uxʷt – freezing; get frostbite. *See: **frostbite**.*

The **i** following uvular consonants (UC) and the glottal stop **ʔ** sound like English "*ey*" as in the words th*ey*, h*ey*, wh*ey*, etc. Salish UC are: **q**, **q̓**, **qʷ**, **q̓ʷ**, **x̣**, **x̣ʷ**. For example, the suffix ...**qin** – head/top, is often spelled using English *ey* as "q*ey*n". So **qi**, **q̓i**, **qʷi**, **q̓ʷi**, **x̣i**, **x̣ʷi**, may be spelled with English *ey* as **q***ey*, **q̓***ey*, **qʷ***ey*, **q̓ʷ***ey*, **x̣***ey*, **x̣ʷ***ey* in other texts.

acknowledge

tóls – point with the head or face; show acknowledgement. *rt.: **tol**– straight vertical; suffix: **...us**– face, fire.*
tólsm – S/he acknowledged. **čn tólsm, kʷ tólsm**
es tólsi – S/he is acknowledging. **čnes tólsi, kʷes tólsi**
qs tólsi – S/he is going to acknowledge. **čiqs tólsi, kʷqs tólsi**

tólsmis – S/he acknowledged s.o. **tólsmn, tólsmntxʷ**
es tólsms – S/he is acknowledging s.o. **ies tólsm, as tólsm**
qs tólsms – S/he is going to acknowledge s.o. **iqs tólsm, aqs tólsm**

tólsmiš – Acknowledge; point with your face. *cmd.*
tólsmnt – Acknowledge s.o.; point at it with your face. *cmd.*
tlsmnwexʷ – They acknowledged each other.

čtóls – point with the eyes; show acknowledgement by looking. *rt.: **tol**– straight vertical; circumfix: **č...us** – spherical object; eyes.*
čtólsm – S/he acknowledged. **čn čtólsm, kʷ čtólsm**
es čtólsi – S/he is acknowledging. **čnes čtólsi, kʷes čtólsi**
qs čtólsi – S/he is going to acknowledge. **čiqs čtólsi, kʷqs čtólsi**

čtólsmis – S/he acknowledged s.o. **čtólsmn, čtólsmntxʷ**
es čtólsms – S/he is acknowledging s.o. **ies čtólsm, as čtólsm**
qs čtólsms – S/he is going to acknowledge s.o. **iqs čtólsm, aqs čtólsm**

čtólsmiš – Acknowledge; point with your eyes. *cmd.*
čtólsmnt – Acknowledge s.o.; point at it with your eyes. *cmd.*
čtlsmnwexʷ – They acknowledged each other.

acne

sčečeʔus – pimples; acne. *rt.: **čeʔ**– lump; suffix: **...us**– face, fire. See: **pimple**.*

s.t. - something, the 3rd person
(s.t.) - something implied
s.o. - someone, the 3rd person
sl. - singular form
pl. - plural form
rt. - root word
cmd. - command
lit. - literally
fig. - figuratively
i.e., - for example
See: - Redirection to a related word.

acquainted

sxʷnwexʷist, *sxʷnwe* – get more acquainted with each other. *rt.: **suxʷ**– recognition; suffix: **...wexʷ**– action to each other.*
sxʷnwexʷist – S/he got acquainted. **či sxʷnwexʷist, kʷ sxʷnwexʷist**
es sxʷnwexʷisti – S/he is getting acquainted. **čnes sxʷnwexʷisti, kʷes sxʷnwexʷisti**

qs sxʷnwexʷisti – S/he is going to get acquainted. **čiqs sxʷnwexʷisti, kʷqs sxʷnwexʷisti**
sxʷnwéʔexʷist – They got acquainted. **qeʔ sxʷnwexʷist, p sxʷnwexʷist**
es sxʷnwéʔexʷisti – They are getting acquainted. **qeʔes sxʷnwexʷisti, pes sxʷnwexʷisti**
qs sxʷnwéʔexʷisti – They are going to get acquainted. **qeʔqs sxʷnwexʷisti, pqs sxʷnwexʷisti**

acquire

tixʷł – acquire something; get or receive something; gather.
tixʷł – S/he acquired. **čn tixʷł, kʷ tixʷł**
tíʔixʷł – They acquired. **qeʔ tixʷł, p tixʷł**

hayo qeʔ tixʷł čłkʷlkʷlé – Hey, we've got a calf. **hayo qs tixʷł nóx̣ʷnx̣ʷ –** Hey, he's going to get a wife! **x̣ʷa ṅem kʷ tixʷł scpupušénč –** Maybe you will get saddness. **ta kʷ qes čečečmscut x̣iṅe kʷ tixʷł łox̣te –** Do not be nasty, you might acquire a baby. **čn tixʷł ululim –** I got money. **čn tixʷł nqʷq̓ʷosṁi –** I acquired a dog. **nk̓ʷuʔ u eł čtxʷunt t nk̓ʷuʔ m kʷ tixʷł esel –** One and add one, you get two. **l čeṅ m ax̣í m kʷ tixʷł čłq̓iq̓á –** How do you get candy?

tixʷm – pick/get a plant object or clay. *See: **pick**.*

ẏaẏáat – rare; scarce; hard to acquire. *See: **rare**.*

across

čtl̓ihew̓s – across the land/valley. *suffix: **...éw̓s** – in between, middle.*

čtlihálqʷ, *čtlihá* – across anything that is a line; railroad track; or a border. *suffix: **...alqʷ** – wood; cylindical.*

ntl̓ihaqs – across the road; street; highway. *circumfix: **n...aqs** – nose, road, pointed.*

ntl̓ihew̓s, *ntl̓ihe* – across the canyon. *prefix: **n...** – inside; suffix: **...éw̓s** – in between, middle.*

čtl̓ihičṅ, *čtl̓ihi* – over the hill/mountain. *prefix: **č...** – upon; suffix: **...ičṅ** – back.*
čtl̓ihičis ci es moq̓ʷ – on the other side of that mountain/hill.

ntl̓ihełc̓eʔ – across the room. *prefix: **n...** – inside; suffix: **...ełc̓eʔ** – inside contents, body, meat.*

nisq̓ʷot, *nisq̓ʷo* – across the river.
steṁ łiciʔ č nisq̓ʷot – What is that on the other side of the river? **ha kʷ ṅe u qʷo xʷiyusnt č nisq̓ʷot –** Would you take me across the water? **stéṁ łišé č nisq̓ʷot –** What is that on the other side of the river?

niʔék̓ʷ – cross water. *See: **cross**.*

nx̣ʷcuʔsáqs – cross a road. *See: **cross**.*

nx̣ʷcuʔséw̓s – cross to the other side of something. *See: **cross**.*

čłx̣ʷcuʔséw̓s – cross to the other side of a plain or any flat land area. *See: **cross**.*

k̓ʷłnx̣ʷcuʔséw̓s – cross to the other side of a tunnel. *See: **cross**.*

čxʷstalqʷ – walk on a narrow object. *(i.e., log, railroad tracks, board, etc.) See: **walk**.*

act like

ax̣íl, *ax̣í* – do as someone/something; imitate; behave a certain way. *See: **imitate**.*

ncucuwečst – act in someone's place; substitute for somebody. *See: **substitute**.*

nql̓ql̓wečšnm – imitate a walk or dance. *See: **imitate**.*

ec̓x̣íl, *ec̓x̣í* – like; same. *See: **like**.*

cuut – way of doing something; one's mannerism; one's gift from Creator. *See: **way**.*

nčl̓pscut, *nčl̓pscu* – act as Coyote; be foolish; mimic others' actions just because they are doing it. *rt.: **snčlep** – coyote; suffix: **...cut** – action to the self. See: **foolish**.*

k̓ʷłpusncut, *k̓ʷłpusncu* – self-conscious; backward; shy; bashful; polite; considerate; does not impose. *See: **self-conscious**.*

add

čtxʷum – add.

čtxʷum – S/he added (s.t.). **čn čtxʷum, kʷ čtxʷum**
es čtxʷmi – S/he is adding (s.t.). **čnes čtxʷmi, kʷes čtxʷmi**
qs čtxʷmi – S/he is going to add (s.t.). **čiqs čtxʷmi, kʷqs čtxʷmi**
čtxʷúʔum – They added (s.t.). **qeʔ čtxʷum, p čtxʷum**
es čtxʷmíʔi – They are adding (s.t.). **qeʔes čtxʷmi, pes čtxʷmi**
qs čtxʷmíʔi – They are going to add (s.t.). **qeʔqs čtxʷmi, pqs čtxʷmi**

čtxʷntes – S/he added s.t. **čtxʷnten, čtxʷntexʷ**
es čtxʷums – S/he is adding s.t. **ies čtxʷum, as čtxʷum**
qs čtxʷums – S/he is going to add s.t. **iqs čtxʷum, aqs čtxʷum**
čtxʷntéʔes – They added s.t. **qeʔ čtxʷntem, čtxʷntep**
es čtxʷúʔums – They are adding s.t. **qeʔes čtxʷum, es čtxʷump**
qs čtxʷúʔums – They are going to add s.t. **qeʔqs čtxʷum, qs čtxʷump**

The **i** following uvular consonants (UC) and the glottal stop **ʔ** sound like English "*ey*" as in the words th*ey*, h*ey*, wh*ey*, etc. Salish UC are: **q, q̇, qʷ, q̇ʷ, x̣, x̣ʷ**. For example, the suffix ...**qin** – head/top, is often spelled using English *ey* as "q*ey*n". So **qi, q̇i, qʷi, q̇ʷi, x̣i, x̣ʷi**, may be spelled with English *ey* as **q***ey*, **q̇***ey*, **qʷ***ey*, **q̇ʷ***ey*, **x̣***ey*, **x̣ʷ***ey* in other texts.

es čtxʷtxʷmi – S/he is adding repeatedly. **čnes čtxʷtxʷmi, kʷes čtxʷtxʷmi**
es čtxʷtxʷums – S/he is adding things. **ies čtxʷtxʷum, as čtxʷtxʷum**

čtxʷntem – S/he/it was added to.

ntxʷetkʷm – add water. *prefix: **n...** – inside; suffix: **...etkʷ, ...tkʷ** – liquid*
čtxʷłuk̓ʷ – add wood.
čtxʷessň – add rocks. *suffix: **...essň, ...sň** – rock.*
čtxʷełxʷ – add on to a house. *suffix: **...ełxʷ, ...łxʷ** – house.*
čtxʷxʷsqáx̣eʔ – add a car; bought/borrowed a car. *suffix: **...sqax̣eʔ, ...sqa** – domestic animal; generally horse or car*
čtxʷxʷasq̇t – add days. *suffix: **...asq̇t** – sky, day.*
čtxʷcin – add something to food. *suffix: **...cin, ...cn** – action of the mouth*
nčtxʷsels – add feelings. *circumfix:: **n...els** – want, feel.*

qeʔqs čtxʷtxʷmisti yetłxʷa – We're going to be adding today. **nk̓ʷuʔ u eł čtxʷunt t nk̓ʷuʔ m kʷ tixʷł t esel** – One and add one, you get two. **k̓ʷinš m kʷ tixʷł še nk̓ʷuʔ u eł esel** – How much do you get when you add one plus two? **nk̓ʷuʔ čtxʷum t esel kʷemt eł čełe** – One plus two equals three.

nk̓ʷuʔ u eł nk̓ʷuʔ – one plus one.

Adele

atél – Adele.

Adeline

atlin – Adeline.

adhere

čċp̓aq̇ – stick/adhere something onto something; tape. *See: **sticky**.*

admire

čłyuxʷtm, *čłyu* – admire something; wish for something. *(Traditionally, to show admiration of someone's property made the owner obligated to give the object to the admirer. This word therefore means more than admiring. To make someone admire one's things is seen as negative. Abuse of admiration is also seen as negative.)*
čłyuxʷtm – S/he/it admired. **čn čłyuxʷtm, kʷ čłyuxʷtm**
es čłyuxʷti – S/he/it is admiring. **čnes čłyuxʷti, kʷes čłyuxʷti**
qs čłyuxʷti – S/he/it is going to admire. **čiqs čłyuxʷti, kʷqs čłyuxʷti**
čłyúʔuxʷtm – They admired. **qeʔ čłyuxʷtm, p čłyuxʷtm**
es čłyúʔuxʷti – They are admiring. **qeʔes čłyuxʷti, pes čłyuxʷti**

s.t. - something, the 3rd person
(s.t.) - something implied
s.o. - someone, the 3rd person
sl. - singular form
pl. - plural form
rt. - root word
cmd. - command
lit. - literally
fig. - figuratively
i.e., - for example
See: - Redirection to a related word.

čłyuxʷtmis – S/he/it admired s.o./s.t. **čłyuxʷtmn, čłyuxʷtmntxʷ**
es čłyuxʷtmms – S/he/it is admiring s.o./s.t. **ies čłyuxʷtmm, as čłyuxʷtmm**
qs čłyuxʷtmms – S/he/it is going to admire s.o./s.t. **iqs čłyuxʷtmm, aqs čłyuxʷtmm**
čłyúʔuxʷtmis – They admired s.o./s.t. **qeʔ čłyuxʷtmntm, čłyuxʷtmntp**
es čłyúʔuxʷtmms – They are admiring s.o./s.t. **qeʔes čłyuxʷtmm, es čłyuxʷtmmp**

es čłyuyuʔxʷti – Each one is admiring. **čnes čłyuyuxʷti, kʷes čłyuyuxʷti**
es čłyuyuxʷtmms – S/he/it is admiring things/people. **ies čłyuyuxʷtmm, as čłyuyuxʷtmm**

sxʷčłyuxʷt – one tasked to admire. *prefix:* ***sxʷ...*** *– one tasked to do.*
čłyuxʷtemn – one inclined to like or admire. *suffix:* ***...emn*** *– one inclined to do*
sččłyuxʷt – something that's been admired. *prefix:* ***sc...*** *– s.t. that's been done/made/prepared:* ***sc...*** *– s.t. that's been done/made/prepared*

čłyuxʷtmskʷ – Admire him/her/it. *cmd.*

čłyuxʷtmms ci t sqelixʷ – people who admire; fans. **imše čłyuxʷstmstxʷ –** You should admire it.

q̓exʷ – proud; admire. *See:* ***proud.***

Adolph
atól – Adolph.

affection
p̓ałkʷ – preferential affection.
p̓łkʷmstes – S/he had preferential affectionate love for s.o. **p̓łkʷmsten, p̓łkʷmstexʷ**
es p̓łkʷmims – S/he has preferential affectionate love for s.o. **ies p̓łkʷmim, as p̓łkʷmim**

p̓łp̓ałkʷt – affectionate.
scp̓ałkʷx̣menč – someone that has been preferentially loved.

es p̓łkʷmmncuti – S/he has preferential affectionate love for one's self. **es p̓łkʷmmncuti, es p̓łkʷmmncuti**

čx̣ssmels, *čx̣ssme* **–** physically affectionate with someone; make out with someone; lucky. *(In the short form this word is also used as an expression for having good luck.) rt.:* ***x̣es*** *– good; prefix:* ***č...*** *– upon; suffix:* ***...els, ...ls*** *– want, feel. See:* ***lucky.***
čx̣ssmels – S/he was physically affectionate with s.o. **čn čx̣ssmels, kʷ čx̣ssmels**
es čx̣ssmelsi – S/he is being physically affectionate with s.o. **čnes čx̣ssmelsi, kʷes čx̣ssmelsi**
qs čx̣ssmelsi – S/he is going to be physically affectionate with s.o. **čiqs čx̣ssmelsi, kʷqs čx̣ssmelsi**

es čx̣smnweʔ – They are being physically affectionate with each other.

čn čx̣ssmels łu čnes memscuti – I got lucky when I was playing. **ha kʷes čx̣ssmelsi t asx̣mnčew̓s –** Are you making out with your love?

q̓ix̣tm – cherish something or someone; fond of something possessed; treasure something or someone; show respect by cherishing a gift. *See:* ***cherish.***

affirm
k̓ʷ šey̓ – Oh, that's it!

k̓ʷ uc unexʷ, *k̓ʷ uc une* **–** Oh! That is right; Oh! Yes.

we – really; was; even though. evidential particle *expressing that the statement is unsupported by the apparent condition or situation. See:* ***true.***

afraid
čin – afraid of getting hurt; careful and cautious. *(i.e., falling, etc.)*
i čin – S/he/it is afraid. **i čn čin, i kʷ čin**

čint – afraid.
čint – S/he/it was afraid. **čn čint, kʷ čint**

es činti – S/he/it is afraid. **čnes činti, kʷes činti**
qs činti – S/he/it is going to be afraid. **čiqs činti, kʷqs činti**
číʔint – They were afraid. **qeʔ čint, p čint**
es číʔinti – They are afraid. **qeʔes činti, pes činti**
qs číʔinti – They are going to be afraid. **qeʔqs činti, pqs činti**

čintmis – S/he/it was afraid of s.t. **čintmn, čintmntxʷ**
es čintmms – S/he/it is afraid of s.t. **ies čintmm, as čintmm**
qs činti – S/he/it is going to be afraid of s.t. **iqs činti, aqs činti**
číʔintmis – They were afraid of s.t. **qeʔ čintmntm, čintmntp**
es číʔintmms – They are afraid of s.t. **qeʔes čintmm, es čintmmp**
qs číʔintmms – They are going to be afraid of s.t. **qeʔqs čintmm, qs čintmmp**

es čnčinti – S/he/it is repeatedly afraid. **čnes čnčinti, kʷes čnčinti**
es čnčintmms – S/he/it is repeatedly afraid of s.t. **ies čnčintmm, as čnčintmm**

es łčičnti – S/he/it is a little afraid. **čnes łčičnti, kʷes łčičnti**
es łčičntmms – S/he/it is a little afraid of s.t. **ies łčičntmm, as łčičntmm**

čnčsnuis – S/he finally got afraid of s.t. **čnčsnun, čnčsnuntxʷ**

čntemn – one inclined to be fearful; timid. *suffix:* ***...emn*** *– one inclined to do*
čnčntemn – one inclined to be constantly fearful. *suffix:* ***...emn*** *– one inclined to do*
čnčnłmuł – one that is habitually fearful. *suffix:* ***...łmuł*** *– one that habitually does.*

činčnt – dangerous.
es čintm – It is fear.
čnčnmscutlwis – go around being fearful. *suffix:* ***...lwis*** *– indicates going around.*

ta es čint x̣iṅe nlopetkʷ – S/he/it is not afraid he'll fall in the water. **ta es čint x̣iṅe lxʷup** – S/he/it is not afraid to get hurt. **imše kʷ čint** – You should be afraid.

k̓ʷłax̣lmist – afraid; give into; scared to offend; timid. *prefix:* ***k̓ʷł...*** *– under.*
es k̓ʷłax̣lmist – S/he/it is afraid/timid. **čnes k̓ʷłax̣lmist, kʷes k̓ʷłax̣lmist**

k̓ʷłax̣lmistmis – S/he/it was afraid of s.o./s.t. **k̓ʷłax̣lmistmn, k̓ʷłax̣lmistmntxʷ**
es k̓ʷłax̣lmistms – S/he/it is afraid of s.o./s.t. **ies k̓ʷłax̣lmistm, as k̓ʷłax̣lmistm**
qs k̓ʷłax̣lmistms – S/he/it is going to be afraid of s.o./s.t. **iqs k̓ʷłax̣lmistm, aqs k̓ʷłax̣lmistm**

ta qs k̓ʷłax̣lmistmntxʷ łu t̓eyeʔ – Do not give in to evil. **čn nte ṅem kʷ leči u čn k̓ʷłax̣lmi t anwi** – I was scared you would get mad.

nx̣él – afraid/scared of something. *See:* ***scared.***

kʷʔeł – jumpy; nervous; edgy; frantic. *See:* ***nervous.***

kʷssusm, *kʷssu* – startle. *See:* ***startle.***

African-American

q̓ʷyós – black person; African-American. *rt.:* ***q̓ʷáy*** *– black; suffix:* ***...us*** *– face, fire.*

p̓ič – glossy; shine something; *used to describe the shiny surface of rubber, dark sun tans and the skin of black people. See:* ***glossy.***

after

čł..., č... – prefix to indicate that *something is gone after.* *See:* ***fetch.***

afternoon

nyák̓ʷqin, *nyák̓ʷqi* – afternoon.
x̣est snyák̓ʷqi – Good afternoon.

The **i** following uvular consonants (UC) and the glottal stop **ʔ** sound like English "*ey*" as in the words *they, hey, whey*, etc. Salish UC are: **q, q̓, qʷ, q̓ʷ, x̣, x̣ʷ**. For example, the suffix ...**qin** – head/top, is often spelled using English *ey* as "*qeyn*". So **qi, q̓i, qʷi, q̓ʷi, x̣i, x̣ʷi**, may be spelled with English *ey* as **q***ey*, **q̓***ey*, **qʷ***ey*, **q̓ʷ***ey*, **x̣***ey*, **x̣ʷ***ey* in other texts.

s.t. - something, the 3rd person
(s.t.) - something implied
s.o. - someone, the 3rd person
sl. - singular form
pl. - plural form
rt. - root word
cmd. - command
lit. - literally
fig. - figuratively
i.e., - for example
See: - Redirection to a related word.

sntx̣ʷqin, *sntx̣ʷqi* – noon. *See: **noon.***

again

ułéˀ – again.

ha ułeˀ – Again? Are you going to (do it) again? **ułéˀ čiqs susti t nṫišk̓ʷ –** I am going to drink pop again. **kʷeṁt ułéˀ ye l sčx̣ʷéct –** Well, it is Monday again. **k̓ʷmiˀ ułéˀ čiqs susti –** I hope to drink again.

eł – back; again; once more. *See: **back.***

against

čłˀéˀ – against; pressed against something; leaned against something; eve of any day.

čłˀém – S/he/it was up against. **čn čłˀém, kʷ čłˀém**
es čłˀémi – S/he/it is up against. **čnes čłˀémi, kʷes čłˀémi**
qs čłˀémi – S/he/it is going to be up against. **čiqs čłˀémi, kʷqs čłˀémi**

čłˀéntes – S/he/it leaned s.t. against something. **čłˀénten, čłˀéntexʷ**
es čłˀéms – S/he/it is leaning s.t. against something. **ies čłˀém, as čłˀém**
qs čłˀéms – S/he/it is going to lean s.t. against something. **iqs čłˀém, aqs čłˀém**

čłˀémis – S/he/it leaned on s.t. **čłˀémin, čłˀémintxʷ**
es čłˀéminms – S/he/it is leaning on s.t. **ies čłˀéminm, as čłˀéminm**
qs čłˀéminms – S/he/it is going to lean on s.t. **iqs čłˀéminm, aqs čłˀéminm**

es čłˀé – It is against. *cmd.*

sčłˀéˀ – Saturday; end of the week.

čłˀént – Put s.t. against something. *cmd.*
čłˀémint – Lean against something. *cmd.*
čłeṁncut – get one's self close/next to/against something. *See: **close.***
łˀem – close in friendship or relationship. *See: **close.***

čłaqin – lean something so the top is against something. *(i.e., head, broom, gun, etc.)*

čłaqin – S/he/it leaned one's head on. **čn čłaqin, kʷ čłaqin**
es čłaqini – S/he/it is leaning one's head on. **čnes čłaqini, kʷes čłaqini**
qs čłaqini – S/he/it is going to lean one's head on. **čiqs čłaqini, kʷqs čłaqini**

čłaqis – S/he/it leaned the top against s.t. **čłaqin, čłaqintxʷ**
es čłaqinms – S/he/it is leaning the top against s.t. **ies čłaqinm, as čłaqinm**
qs čłaqinms – S/he/it is going to lean the top against s.t. **iqs čłaqinm, aqs čłaqinm**

es čłaqin – S/he/it is leaned against.

čłaqint – Lean its top against something. *cmd.*

Agatha

akát – Agatha.

łakat – little Agatha. *prefix: **ł...** – little.*

age

smx̣ʷóp – snows; age; year. *See: **snow.***

sk̓ʷṅšsmx̣ʷóp – how many snows; how old is s/he? *prefix: **sk̓ʷnš...** – how many?*

sk̓ʷṅšspéntč, *sk̓ʷṅšspé* – ask, how many years; how old is someone. *rt.: **spentč** – year; prefix: **sk̓ʷnš...** – how many?*

sk̓ʷṅšspéntč – How old is s/he/it? **či sk̓ʷṅšspéntč, kʷ sk̓ʷṅšspéntč**
sk̓ʷṅšspéˀentč – How old are they? **qeˀ sk̓ʷṅšspéntč, p sk̓ʷṅšspéntč**

q̓eẏnit łu ask̓ʷṅšspe – Write how old you are. **sk̓ʷṅšspe łu anṗiṗuyšn –** What year is your car? **kʷ sk̓ʷṅšspe u kʷ xʷist –** How old were you when you first walked? **čn nk̓ʷuˀspe u čn xʷist –** I was one year old when I first walked. **ṅe kʷ upn eɬ cil m lcíʔistmn kʷqs ntx̣ʷmsqá** – When you are fifteen I will let you drive. **sk̓ʷṅšspe u eɬ ƛ̓lil** – How old was s/he when s/he died? **k̓ʷṅšspe u kʷes k̓ʷuli l sqelixʷ nk̓ʷul̓mn** – How many years have you been working with the Culture Committee? **kʷ nte sk̓ʷnšpentč ɬu cniɬċ** – How old do you think s/he is?

spéntč – year. *See: **year**.*
čn clčspentč – I am five years old.

čéwlš – age; get old. *See: **old**.*

The **i** following uvular consonants (UC) and the glottal stop **ʔ** sound like English "*ey*" as in the words *they*, *hey*, *whey*, etc. Salish UC are: **q**, **q̇**, **qʷ**, **q̇ʷ**, **x̣**, **x̣ʷ**. For example, the suffix ...**qin** – head/top, is often spelled using English *ey* as "*qeyn*". So **qi**, **q̇i**, **qʷi**, **q̇ʷi**, **x̣i**, **x̣ʷi**, may be spelled with English *ey* as **q***ey*, **q̇***ey*, **qʷ***ey*, **q̇ʷ***ey*, **x̣***ey*, **x̣ʷ***ey* in other texts.

agree

nkʷɬmistmm – in agreement with something or someone. *prefix: **nkʷɬ...** – together with.*
nkʷɬmistmis – S/he/it agreed with s.o. **nkʷɬmistmn, nkʷɬmistmntxʷ**
es nkʷɬmistmms – S/he/it is in agreement with s.o. **ies nkʷɬmistmm, as nkʷɬmistmm**
qs nkʷɬmistmms – S/he/it is going to be in agreement with s.o. **iqs nkʷɬmistmm, aqs nkʷɬmistmm**
nkʷɬmíʔistmis – They agreed with s.o. **qeʔ nkʷɬmistmntm, nkʷɬmistmntp**
es nkʷɬmíʔistmms – They are in agreement with s.o. **qeʔes nkʷɬmistmm, es nkʷɬmistmmp**
qs nkʷɬmíʔistmms – They are going to be in agreement with s.o. **qeʔqs nkʷɬmistmm, qs nkʷɬmistmmp**

ɬnkʷɬmistmm – agree, a little, with someone.

nkʷɬmistmnt – Agree with s.o. *cmd.*

es kʷɬnmistmnwexʷi – They are in agreement with each other. **qe es kʷɬnmistmnwexʷi, pes kʷɬnmistmnwexʷi**

kʷ ies nkʷɬmistmm – I am in agreement with you. **nkʷɬmistmncn** – I agreed with you. **x̣iɬ x̣e nkʷɬmistmnt** – Be in good agreement with him/her. *cmd.* **ta qs tam nkʷɬmistmnt** – You have to agree with him/her.

nk̓ʷúʔumnwexʷ – become one with each other *(to be in agreement with each other). rt.: **nk̓ʷuʔ** – one; **...wexʷ** – action to each other.*
es nk̓ʷúʔumnwexʷi – They are becoming one with each other. **qeʔes nk̓ʷúʔumnwexʷi, pes nk̓ʷúʔumnwexʷi**

ɬnk̓ʷúʔumnwexʷ – in a little way, become one with each other.

nkʷɬnk̓ʷuʔm – become one with someone; to agree with someone. *rt.: **nk̓ʷuʔ** – one; prefix: **nkʷɬ...** – together with.*
nkʷɬnk̓ʷuʔmis – S/he become one with s.o. **nkʷɬnk̓ʷuʔmn, nkʷɬnk̓ʷuʔmntxʷ**

nkʷɬnk̓ʷúʔumncn – I became one with you; I agreed with you.

s.t. - something, the 3rd person
(s.t.) - something implied
s.o. - someone, the 3rd person
sl. - singular form
pl. - plural form
rt. - root word
cmd. - command
lit. - literally
fig. - figuratively
i.e., - for example
See: - Redirection to a related word.

nšiy̓elsm – in favor of s.t./s.o.; in acceptance of s.t.; show preference for s.t./s.o. *rt.: **šey̓** – there; circumfix: **n...els** – want, feel.*
šiy̓elsmis – S/he/it favored s.t./s.o. **šiy̓elsmn, kʷ šiy̓elsmntxʷ**
es nšiy̓elsmms – S/he/it is favoring s.t./s.o. **ies nšiy̓elsmm, as nšiy̓elsmm**
qs nšiy̓elsmms – S/he/it is going to favor s.t./s.o. **iqs nšiy̓elsmm, aqs nšiy̓elsmm**
šiy̓éʔelsmis – They were in favor of s.t./s.o. **qeʔ šiy̓éʔelsmntm, šiy̓elsmntp**
es nšiy̓éʔelsmms – They are in favor of s.t./s.o. **qeʔes nšiy̓éʔelsmm, es nšiy̓elsmmp**
qs nšiy̓éʔelsmms – They are going to be in favor of s.t./s.o. **qeʔqs nšiy̓éʔelsmm, qs nšiy̓elsmmp**

nšiy̓elsmnt – Favor it. *cmd.*

es šiẏilmcuti – S/he is favoring one's self. **čnes šiẏilmcuti, kʷes šiẏilmcuti**
es šiẏelsmnwexʷi – They are favoring each other. **qeʔes šiẏelsmnwexʷi, pes šiẏelsmnwexʷi**

ta kʷeṁt łu ƛ̓e qʷo šiẏélsmntm – No, s/he already favors me. **tam qʷo es nšiẏelsmms** – S/he/it is not in favor of me. **nšyelsmncn** – I am in favor of/with you.

nunxʷnmnwexʷ – believe each other (to agree with each other). *See:* ***believe.***

šeẏ – that in general; there, confirming/concurring; yes, concurring.
xʷu šeẏ – Okay, that.

ahead **es šʔit** – first, ahead. *See:* ***first.***

ƛ̓xʷupist, *ƛ̓xʷup* – win something; ahead *(i.e., a bet, card game, etc.).* *See:* ***win.***

aim **tx̣ʷmiṅč** – aim a weapon *(i.e., bow, gun, etc.).* *rt.:* ***tox̣ʷ*** *– straight; suffix:* ***...iṅč*** *– weapon.*
tx̣ʷmiṅč – S/he aimed. **čn tx̣ʷmiṅč, kʷ tx̣ʷmiṅč**
es tx̣ʷmiṅči – S/he is aiming. **čnes tx̣ʷminči, kʷes tx̣ʷmiṅči**
qs tx̣ʷmiṅči – S/he is going to aim. **čiqs tx̣ʷminči, kʷqs tx̣ʷmiṅči**

tx̣ʷmiṅčš – Aim. *cmd.*

air **sx̣x̣ap** – air.

airplane **ṫuxʷtn** – airplane. *rt.:* ***ṫuxʷt*** *– fly; suffix:* ***...tin, ...tn*** *– means of/device.*
łṫuṫxʷtn – little airplane. *prefix:* ***ł...*** *– little.*

airport **snṫuxʷtn** – airport. *rt.:* ***ṫuxʷt*** *– fly; prefix:* ***sn...*** *– a place of; suffix:* ***...tin, ...tn*** *– means of/device.*

alarm **liwmn** – bell.

alarm clock **liwmn spq̇niʔ** – alarm clock.

Alaska **ċaltulexʷ** – Alaska. *lit. cold world/land. rt.:* ***ċalt*** *– cold; suffix:* ***...ulexʷ*** *– land.*

alcohol **qʷéwutn** – alcohol. *rt.:* ***qʷéw*** *– crazy; suffix:* ***...tin, ...tn*** *– means of/device.*

nkʷilkʷ – wine. *rt.:* ***kʷil*** *– red.*

nx̣ʷóskʷ – beer. *rt.:* ***x̣ʷos*** *– foam.*

nx̣al – vodka. *rt.:* ***x̣al*** *– clear; prefix:* ***n...*** *– inside.*

alder tree **čičitṅéłp,** *čičitṅé* – alder tree; *Alnus incana.*
čṗnusntxʷ t čičtṅe – Put alders in the fire.

alert **xʷus** – wide awake, open-eyed. *See:* ***awake.***

čeʔl̓ – watching; alert.
links **ččeʔl̓ist,** *ččeʔl̓* – The dog is alert; it is barking continuously. *See:* ***bark.***

uak̇ʷq̇t – notice/see everything; not take surroundings for granted; alert *(acting in a wild way). rt.:* ***uʔiwa*** *– wild.*
es uak̇ʷq̇ti – S/he/it is acting a little wild; being alert. **čnes uak̇ʷq̇ti, kʷes uak̇ʷq̇ti**

Alex **alik** – Alex.

Alexander **aliksá** – Alexander.

algae **elis** – Alice.

Alice **elis** – Alice.

alike **eċx̣ax̣íl**, *eċx̣ax̣í* – alike; same. *See:* ***like.***
eċx̣ax̣í t anwi – S/he is like you.

i šey̓ – the same one.
nexʷ epł t šey̓ – S/he/it has the same.

alive **xʷlxʷilt** – alive; well.
es xʷlxʷilt – S/he/it is alive. **čnes xʷlxʷilt, kʷes xʷlxʷilt**
es xʷlxʷlíʔilt – They are alive. **qeʔes xʷlxʷlilt, pes xʷlxʷlilt**

xʷlxʷilsts – S/he/it saved s.o. **xʷlxʷilstn, xʷlxʷilstxʷ**
es xʷlxʷiltms – S/he/it is saving s.o. **ies xʷlxʷiltm, as xʷlxʷiltm**

xʷlxʷiltmis – S/he/it used s.t. for living. **xʷlxʷiltmn, xʷlxʷiltmntxʷ**
es xʷlxʷiltmms – S/he/it is using s.t. for living. **ies xʷlxʷiltmm, as xʷlxʷiltmm**

xʷl̓il̓ – S/he/it came alive.
eł xʷl̓il̓ – S/he/it came back to life.

scxʷlxʷilt – lifetime. *prefix:* ***sc...*** *– s.t. that's been done/made/prepared.*
nxʷlxʷiltn – life. *prefix:* ***n...*** *– inside; suffix:* ***...tin, ...tn*** *– means of/device.*
čxʷlxʷiltn – something that makes one alive. *suffix:* ***...tin, ...tn*** *– means of/device.*
xʷlxʷiltncutn – one that gives one life. *suffix:* ***...tin, ...tn*** *– means of/device.*

es xʷl̓l̓misti – S/he/it is coming alive *(born, hatched). suffix:* ***...ist*** *– action for/of the self.*
es xʷl̓l̓mscutisti – S/he/it is making one's self come alive.
xʷl̓l̓utm – S/he/it can get well/come back from sickness, depression, etc.
xʷlxʷltutm – S/he/it can be saved/brought back from sickness, depression, etc.
xʷlxʷltmutm – S/he/it is able to bring back from sickness, depression, etc.
xʷlxʷlstweʔexʷ – They saved each other. **xʷlxʷlstwexʷ, xʷlxʷlstwexʷ**
qeʔ xʷlxʷilt łu tl̓ t̓eyeʔ – Deliver us from evil. **ha puti es xʷlxʷilt** – Is s/he/it still alive? **wis iłn u xʷl̓il̓** – S/he finished eating and came alive.

nkʷƛ̓exʷncut – resurrect. *See:* ***resurrect.***

all **esyáʔ** – everything; everyone; all.
esyáʔaʔ – All of them. **qeʔesyáʔ, p esyáʔ**

pesyáʔ m p ċl̓ċl̓qinm – All of you put on headdresses. **siyent esyáʔ ci snčłemutn** – Count all the chairs. **x̣ʷaxʷʔéy esyáʔ sqélixʷ** – All the people laughed. **esyáʔ u es misten** – I know everthing.

milk̓ʷ – complete; whole; all over; all around. *See:* ***complete.***

all around **ml̓uk̓ʷ** – spread all around; propagate; grow, of non-living things.
ml̓uk̓ʷ – S/he/it spread all around. **čn ml̓uk̓ʷ, kʷ ml̓uk̓ʷ**
es mlk̓ʷmi – S/he/it is spreading all around. **čnes mlk̓ʷmi, kʷes mlk̓ʷmi**
qs mlk̓ʷmi – S/he/it is going to spread all around. **čiqs mlk̓ʷmi, kʷqs mlk̓ʷmi**

mlk̓ʷmstes – S/he made s.t. propagate. **mlk̓ʷmsten, mlk̓ʷmstexʷ**
es mlk̓ʷmims – S/he is making s.t. propagate. **ies mlk̓ʷmim, as mlk̓ʷmim**
qs mlk̓ʷmims – S/he is going to make s.t. propagate. **iqs mlk̓ʷmim, aqs mlk̓ʷmim**

The **i** following uvular consonants (UC) and the glottal stop **ʔ** sound like English "*ey*" as in the words th*ey*, h*ey*, wh*ey*, etc. Salish UC are: **q, q̇, qʷ, q̇ʷ, x̣, x̣ʷ**. For example, the suffix ...**qin** – head/top, is often spelled using English *ey* as "q*ey*n". So **qi, q̇i, qʷi, q̇ʷi, x̣i, x̣ʷi**, may be spelled with English *ey* as **q***ey*, **q̇***ey*, **qʷ***ey*, **q̇ʷ***ey*, **x̣***ey*, **x̣ʷ***ey* in other texts.

s.t. - something, the 3rd person
(s.t.) - something implied
s.o. - someone, the 3rd person
sl. - singular form
pl. - plural form
rt. - root word
cmd. - command
lit. - literally
fig. - figuratively
i.e., - for example
See: - Redirection to a related word.

nmlk̓ʷmeɫc̓ʔeis – S/he spread s.t. all over the inside. **nmlk̓ʷmeɫc̓ʔen, nmlk̓ʷmeɫc̓ʔentxʷ**
es nmlk̓ʷmeɫc̓ʔems – S/he is spreading s.t. all over the inside. **ies nmlk̓ʷmeɫc̓ʔem, as nmlk̓ʷmeɫc̓ʔem**

nmlk̓ʷmeɫc̓ʔemis – S/he/it got filled/spread with s.t. inside. **nmlk̓ʷmeɫc̓ʔemn, nmlk̓ʷmeɫc̓ʔemntxʷ**
es nmlk̓ʷmeɫc̓ʔemms – S/he/it is getting filled/spread with s.t. inside. **ies nmlk̓ʷmeɫc̓ʔemm, as nmlk̓ʷmeɫc̓ʔemm**

nmlk̓ʷmew̓sis – S/he spread s.t. amongst it. **nmlk̓ʷmew̓sn, nmlk̓ʷmew̓sntxʷ**
es nmlk̓ʷmew̓sms – S/he is spreading s.t. amongst it. **ies nmlk̓ʷmew̓sm, as nmlk̓ʷmew̓sm**

nmlk̓ʷméʔew̓smis – They got s.t. spread amongst them. **qeʔ nmlk̓ʷmew̓smntm, nmlk̓ʷmew̓smntp**
es nmlk̓ʷméʔew̓smms – They are getting s.t. spread amongst them. **qeʔes nmlk̓ʷmew̓smm, es nmlk̓ʷmew̓smmp**

mlluk̓ʷk̓ʷ – S/he/it got to be all over; it propagated. **čn mlluk̓ʷk̓ʷ, kʷ mlluk̓ʷk̓ʷ**
es mlk̓ʷk̓ʷmi – S/he/it is coming to be all over; it is propagating. **čnes mlk̓ʷk̓ʷmi, kʷes mlk̓ʷk̓ʷmi**

es mlk̓ʷmulexʷ – everywhere; all over the world; all over the land.
es nmlk̓ʷmew̓s – all amongst them.
es nmlk̓ʷmeɫc̓eʔ – the whole inside.

mlk̓ʷmiskʷ – Make it propagate; make it spread. *cmd.*

milk̓ʷ – complete; whole; all over; all around. *See:* ***complete.***

es mlk̓ʷmi ɫu sp̓aap – The fire is spreading all over. **es mlk̓ʷk̓ʷmi ɫu čsupulexʷ** – The weeds getting to be all over. **čn mlluk̓ʷk̓ʷ ɫu l es pk̓ʷlʔemi** – I was all over in the ball game. **qeʔ nmlk̓ʷmew̓smntm ɫu pipiit** – Happiness got spread amongst us. **es nmlk̓ʷmew̓s ɫu sm̓im̓iʔ** – the news is spread all amongst them.

alligator
skʷtiɫšl̓šl̓č̓é – alligator; big lizard. *rt.:* ***šl̓šl̓č̓e*** *– lizard; prefix:* ***skʷtiɫ...*** *– big.*

all kinds
nšƛ̓aqsm, *nšƛ̓a* – many things not the same; many things one after another. *circumfix:* ***n...aqsm*** *– kinds.*
nšƛ̓áqsm ɫu xʷixʷey̓uɫ – all kinds of wildlife. **nšƛ̓a ɫu p̓ip̓uyšn** – all kinds of cars. **nšƛ̓a ɫu sqelixʷ** – all kinds of people. **wičtn nšƛ̓a ɫu xʷixʷey̓uɫ** – I saw all kinds of animals.

nxʷʔaqsm – many kinds. *See:* ***kind.***

almost
x̣iɫ n̓e u – almost.
x̣iɫ n̓e u čn naq̓ʷ t ululim – I almost stole the money. **čn wičm t nɫámqeʔ l isčsáx̣x̣m x̣iɫ n̓e u qeʔ tamnqnwe** – I saw a bear so close we almost bumped heads.

čč̓ʔit – in motion to get close/near someone or something; drawing near. *See:* ***near.***
čč̓ʔit intoxʷqin – It is almost noon.

ƛ̓e – already. *See:* ***already.***
ha ƛ̓e kʷ qʷom̓ma – Are you almost ready?

qʷom̓maɫq, *qʷom̓ma* – get close to doing/finishing something; getting near to some point; close to the end of a journey; winning. *See:* ***close.***

alone
čɫn̓áqsm, *čɫn̓á* – alone.
i čɫn̓áqsm – I am alone. **i čn čɫn̓áqsm, i kʷ čɫn̓áqsm**

čnaqsm – S/he is one person. **čn čnaqsm, kʷ čnaqsm**

i ččnaqsm u ck̓ʷłči – All alone s/he arrived here. *(implies a hardship)*

i čmi u stipn u k̓ʷis swenš – Alone, Stephen went to dance.

nk̓ʷukʷk̓ʷwilš – solitary. *See: **solitary**.*

> The **i** following uvular consonants (UC) and the glottal stop **ʔ** sound like English "*ey*" as in the words *they, hey, whey*, etc. Salish UC are: **q, q̓, qʷ, q̓ʷ, x̣, x̣ʷ**. For example, the suffix ...**qin** – head/top, is often spelled using English *ey* as "q*ey*n". So **qi, q̓i, qʷi, q̓ʷi, x̣i, x̣ʷi**, may be spelled with English *ey* as **q***ey*, **q̓***ey*, **qʷ***ey*, **q̓ʷ***ey*, **x̣***ey*, **x̣ʷ***ey* in other texts.

alpine fir

maniṅłp – alpine/subalpine fir; *Abies lasiocarpa*.

already

ƛ̓e – already.

ta kʷeṁt łu ƛ̓e qʷo šiẏélsmntm – No, she has already accepted me. **ƛ̓e es x̣lpulexʷi –** It is already getting light. **ƛ̓e ep sqélixʷ ye lʔe u ciʔap łu ułselíš –** There were already people here when the Salish came in. **snwénštn qʷélm ƛ̓e esnkʷnéʔems –** They're already singing the war dance song. **ƛ̓e čn wisʔiłn –** I've already finished eating. **ƛ̓e ep sqélixʷ u cnpilš –** There were already people here when they came in. **hoy kʷeṁt ƛ̓e es łp̓mncuti –** They were already lining up. **čx̣ʷuyqntp néłi ƛ̓e čxʷʔéʔ t c̓ʔulixʷ –** You guys pile it up, because there are already a lot of deer. **ƛ̓e łu es wis suxʷumentm ye sqlixʷulexʷ –** They had already finished measuring out Indian land.

also

nexʷ – also, too.

u nexʷ ta es yoostép łu sčłip – Also, you guys do not know how to hunt. **nméƛ̓nt łu mulš t mlmlté u nexʷ ppo u nexʷ t apłsálqʷ łu ṅe kʷ wičm –** Mix cottonwood with aspen and willow and also applewood, if you can find it.

alumroot

ċpċup – alumroot; *Heuchera cylindrica*.

always

tmilq̓ʷ – always, repeatedly.

tmilq̓ʷ čʔemteẁs l es šiṫ łu łlqʷó – Little Prairie always sits in that tree. **tmilq̓ʷ m qeʔes nṫums –** We will always have a smile. **tmilq̓ʷ čn sust t kapi –** I always drink coffee. **tmilq̓ʷ čnes susti t kapi –** I am always drinking coffee. **tmilq̓ʷ u es k̓ʷuli –** S/he's always working.

iše – always; do.

iše čn sust t kapi – I drink coffee. **tma iše kʷ sust t sewłkʷ x̣ʷl̓ kʷes nx̣mpcin –** As you know, you drink water because you are thirsty. **iše iłn –** S/he/it eats. **ṅe kʷ p̓ʔum iše puxʷ łu asp̓uʔ –** When you fart it stinks. **ha iše nṫaṁcantxʷ łu annox̣ʷnx̣ʷ –** Do you kiss your wife? **ha iše kʷ ṫusm –** Do you eat marrow? **ha iše kʷ k̓ʷis čawm –** Do you go and pray?

ax̣l – every time. *See: **every time**.*

exʷ – gee; gee…always/again; oh. *See: **exclamation**.*

exʷ kʷes susti t kapi – Gee, you are always drinking coffee. **exʷ šeẏ kʷ emut –** Gee, you are sitting again! **exʷ iłṫṫétmstxʷ –** Oh, you made it easy.

> s.t. - something, the 3rd person
> (s.t.) - something implied
> s.o. - someone, the 3rd person
> *sl.* - singular form
> *pl.* - plural form
> *rt.* - root word
> *cmd.* - command
> *lit.* - literally
> *fig.* - figuratively
> *i.e.,* - for example
> *See:* - Redirection to a related word.

Ambrose

amló – Ambrose.

ambush

čx̣lem – ambush.

čx̣lem – S/he ambushed. **čn čx̣lem, kʷ čx̣lem**
es čx̣lem – S/he is ambushing. **čnes čx̣lem, kʷes čx̣lem**
qs čx̣lem – S/he is going to ambush. **čiqs čx̣lem, kʷqs čx̣lem**

čx̣lemis – S/he ambushed s.o. **čx̣lemn, kʷ čx̣lemntxʷ**
es čx̣lems – S/he is ambushing s.o. **ies čx̣lem, as čx̣lem**
qs čx̣lems – S/he is going to ambush s.o. **iqs čx̣lem, aqs čx̣lem**

snčx̣lmnwexʷtn – place of ambush.

amen **k̓ʷmiʔ ecx̣i –** amen. *lit. hope it is like that.*

American **suyápi –** white people. *(This term is used to describe Caucasian people; generally it refers to people who are not Native American. The term is also used to describe the English language.) See:* ***white people.***
snuyapcn – English. *See:* ***English.***
puʔsuyápi – spouse of somebody who is a white person. *See:* ***spouse.***
suypálqs – white people clothing, American clothing. *See:* ***clothes.***
suypsqáx̣e – American stock, horses, cattle, etc. *See:* ***horse.***

American bittern **x̣witx̣ʷu –** bittern, American bittern.

American coot **sṫláqšn –** American coot; mudhen; *Fulica americana.*

łẏé – rail; coot; *Rallus limicola.*

American crow **scáʔaʔ –** American crow.

American dipper **q̓ʷox̣ʷṁiṅeʔ –** American dipper; water osel; *Cinclus mexicanus.*

American kestrel **spiyálqn –** American kestrel.

Anaconda **momoo –** Anaconda, Montana.

Anastasia **anastá –** Anastasia.

ancestor **x̣ʷlčmusšn –** ancestor.

ancient **t sq̓sps –** ancient; long time ago.

Andrew **antli –** Andrew.

angel **ánš –** angel.

angle **es yutm –** angle.

piṅ – bend from one position to an curved/angular position. *See:* ***bend.***

qq̓ṁéyeʔ, *qq̓ṁé* **–** angling; fish.
qq̓ṁéyeʔ – S/he fished. **čn qq̓ṁéyeʔ, kʷ qq̓ṁéyeʔ**
es qq̓ṁéyeʔi – S/he is fishing. **čnes qq̓ṁéyeʔi, kʷes qq̓ṁéyeʔi**
qs qq̓ṁéyeʔi – S/he is going to fish. **čiqs qq̓ṁéyeʔi, kʷqs qq̓ṁéyeʔi**
qq̓ṁéʔeyeʔ – They fished. **qeʔ qq̓ṁé, p qq̓ṁéʔeyeʔ qq̓ṁéʔeyeʔ**
es qq̓ṁéʔeyeʔi – They are fishing. **qeʔes qq̓ṁéʔeyeʔi, pes qq̓ṁéʔeyeʔi**
qs qq̓ṁéʔeyeʔi – They are going to fish. **qeʔqs qq̓ṁéʔeyeʔi, pqs qq̓ṁéʔeyeʔi**

es łqq̓ṁéyeʔi – S/he is fishing a little.

sxʷqq̓ṁéyeʔ, *sxʷqq̓ṁé* **–** one tasked to fish; fisherman. *prefix:* ***sxʷ...*** *– one tasked to do.*
qq̓ṁiyeʔmuł – one that habitually fishes.
čqq̓ṁéyeʔtn, *čqq̓ṁé* **–** fishing pole.

q̓eyẇ – get/fetch fish from a trap/barrier. *See:* ***fetch.***

mul – fish/scoop something out of water. *(i.e., with a net, container, etc.) See:* ***fish.***

angleworm **yanáq̓ʷ –** angleworm, earthworm. *See:* ***worm.***

angry **áym –** angry, mad.

áymt – S/he/it was angry. **čn áymt, kʷ áymt**
es áymti – S/he/it is angry. **čnes áymti, kʷes áymti**
qs áymti – S/he/it is going to be angry. **čiqs áymti, kʷqs áymti**
áʔaymt – They were angry. **qeʔ áymt, p áymt**
es áʔaymti – They are angry. **qeʔes áymti, pes áymti**
qs áʔaymti – They are going to be angry. **qeʔqs áymti, pqs áymti**

áymtmis – S/he/it was angry at s.o. **áymtmn, áymtmntxʷ**
es áymtmms – S/he/it is angry at s.o. **ies áymtmm, as áymtmm**
qs áymtmms – S/he/it is going to be angry at s.o. **iqs áymtmm, aqs áymtmm**
áʔaymtmis – They were angry at s.o. **qeʔ áymtmntm, áymtmntp**
es áʔaymtmms – They are angry at s.o. **qeʔes áymtmm, es áymtmmp**
qs áʔaymtmms – They are going to be angry at s.o. **qeʔqs áymtmm, qs áymtmmp**

The **i** following uvular consonants (UC) and the glottal stop **ʔ** sound like English "*ey*" as in the words th*ey*, h*ey*, wh*ey*, etc. Salish UC are: **q**, **q̇**, **qʷ**, **q̇ʷ**, **x̣**, **x̣ʷ**. For example, the suffix …**qin** – head/top, is often spelled using English *ey* as "q*ey*n". So **qi**, **q̇i**, **qʷi**, **q̇ʷi**, **x̣i**, **x̣ʷi**, may be spelled with English *ey* as **q***ey*, **q̇***ey*, **qʷ***ey*, **q̇ʷ***ey*, **x̣***ey*, **x̣ʷ***ey* in other texts.

es łʔáymti – S/he/it is a little angry. **čnes łʔáymti, kʷes łʔáymti**
es łʔáymtmms – S/he/it is a little angry toward s.o. **ies łʔáymtmm, as łʔáymtmm**

čʔamtn – something that makes one mad.
amtemn – one inclined to get mad. *suffix:* ***…emn*** *– one inclined to do*
sʔamamsnuxʷ – something deserving/worthy of hate.

áymtš – Get angry. *cmd.*
áymtmnt – Get angry at s.o. *cmd.*
nʔaymls – have bad feelings; have inner anger. *See:* ***detest.***
aiṁeʔ – hate. *See:* ***hate.***
áymscut – S/he/it got angry at one's self. **čn áymscut, kʷ áymscut**
es áymscuti – S/he/it is getting angry at one's self. **čnes áymscuti, kʷes áymscuti**

es nʔaymlsi – S/he/it is working toward getting angry. **čnes nʔaymlsi, kʷes nʔaymlsi**
es nʔamtelsi – S/he/it is wanting to get angry. **čnes nʔamtelsi, kʷes nʔamtelsi**
es nʔamtelis – S/he/it is mutually/equally angry. **čnes nʔamtelis, kʷes nʔamtelis**
es nʔaymtelsi – S/he is feeling angry. **čnes nʔaymtelsi, kʷes nʔaymtelsi**
es amtmlwisi – S/he/it is going around being angry. **čnes amtmlwisi, kʷes amtmlwisi**
es nʔaymičṅi – S/he/it is turning one's back in anger. **čnes nʔaymičṅi, kʷes nʔaymičṅi**
es amtmnwexʷi – They are mad at each other. **qeʔes amtmnwexʷi, pes amtmnwexʷi**
es amtstwexʷi – They are getting each other mad. **qeʔes amtstwexʷi, pes amtstwexʷi**

nq̇aupáqs – have a broken nose. An expression indicating someone is angry. *rt.:* ***q̇au*** *– break bone; circumfix:* ***n…aqs*** *– nose, road, pointed.*

nq̇aupáqs – S/he/it got angry. **čn nq̇aupáqs, kʷ nq̇aupáqs**
es nq̇aupáqsi – S/he/it is angry. **čnes nq̇aupáqsi, kʷes nq̇aupáqsi**
qs nq̇aupáqsi – S/he/it is going to be angry. **čiqs nq̇aupáqsi, kʷqs nq̇aupáqsi**
nq̇aupáʔaqs – They got angry. **qeʔ nq̇aupáqs, p nq̇aupáqs**
es nq̇aupáʔaqsi – They are angry. **qeʔes nq̇aupáqsi, pes nq̇aupáqsi**
qs nq̇aupáʔaqsi – They are going to be angry. **qeʔqs nq̇aupáqsi, pqs nq̇aupáqsi**

nq̇auq̇aupáʔaqs – Each one of them got angry. **qeʔ nq̇auq̇aupáqs, p nq̇auq̇aupáqs**

ta kʷ qes nq̇aupaqs – Do not be angry/mad.

nšiwm – have angry/nasty/bad actions or words.

s.t. - something, the 3rd person
(s.t.) - something implied
s.o. - someone, the 3rd person
sl. - singular form
pl. - plural form
rt. - root word
cmd. - command
lit. - literally
fig. - figuratively
i.e., - for example
See: - Redirection to a related word.

nšiwis – S/he had angry actions toward s.o. **nšiwn, nšiwntxʷ**
es nšiwms – S/he is doing angry things toward s.o. **ies nšiwm, as nšiwm**
qs nšiwms – S/he is going to do angry things toward s.o. **iqs nšiwm, aqs nšiwm**
nšíʔiwis – They had angry actions toward s.o. **qeʔ nšiwntm, nšiwntp**
es nšíʔiwms – They are doing angry things toward s.o. **qeʔes nšiwm, es nšiwmp**
qs nšíʔiwms – They are going to do angry things toward s.o. **qeʔqs nšiwm, qs nšiwmp**

nšiwnt – Do angry things toward s.o. *cmd.*

qʷo es nšiwms – S/he is doing angry things toward me. **ta qes nšiwstxʷ –** Do not do angry things toward him/her.

léč – furious; really angry; mad; in a rage; violent. *See: **furious.***

čxʷttels, *čxʷtte* **–** enraged; angry; mad; vicious; the extreme of anger. *See: **enraged.***

nčesls – grouchy; angry feelings. *See: **grouchy.***

tmals – despise; disregard; spurn; pay no attention to; have no feelings for; have no care for; have no respect for. *See: **despise.***

hawawlš – tell off; yell at someone. *See: **tell off.***

čłkʷiccl̓š – hair stands up, as on a dog's/bear's back when angry. *See: **hair.***

animal

xʷixʷeyuł – animals.
łxʷixʷey̓uł, *łxʷixʷey̓u* **–** bird; small animal. *See: **birds.***

q̓ʷłq̓ʷłšulexʷ – little animals; rodents. *(**q̓ʷłq̓ʷł** – sound/action little animals make/do.) See: **rodent.***

tišulexʷ – insect; bug. *lit. earth crawler. rt.: **tiyeš** – crawl; suffix: **...ulexʷ** – land. See: **insect.***

ntišulexʷ – worm, insect, bug. *See: **worm.***

...sqáx̣eʔ, *...sqá* **–** suffix indicating horses, domestic animals, or vehicles.
es siyenusqáx̣eʔi – S/he is counting horses/domestic animals/cars. **čnes siyenusqáx̣eʔi, kʷes siyenusqáx̣eʔi**

mosqá – His/her car/horse broke down. **čn mosqá, kʷ mosqá**

ƛ̓lsqá – His/her horse/car is dead. **čn ƛ̓lsqá, kʷ ƛ̓lsqá**

ƛ̓asqáx̣eʔ – look for horses, domestic animals, or vehicles. *See: **look.***

nk̓ʷsqáx̣eʔ, *nk̓ʷsqá* **–** one horse, domestic animal, vehicle.
aslsqáx̣eʔ, *aslsqá* **–** two horses, domestic animals, vehicles.
čałlsqáx̣eʔ, *čałlsqá* **–** three horses, domestic animals, vehicles.
msqáx̣eʔ, *msqá* **–** four horses, domestic animals, vehicles.
clčsqáx̣eʔ, *clčsqá* **–** five horses, domestic animals, vehicles.
tq̓ńčsqáx̣eʔ, *tq̓ńčsqá* **–** six horses, domestic animals, vehicles.
sp̓l̓čsqáx̣eʔ, *sp̓l̓čsqá* **–** seven horses, domestic animals, vehicles.
hanmsqáx̣eʔ, *hanmsqá* **–** eight horses, domestic animals, vehicles.
x̣ńtsqáx̣eʔ, *x̣ńtsqá* **–** nine horses, domestic animals, vehicles.
upnčsqáx̣eʔ, *upnčsqá* **–** ten horses, domestic animals, vehicles.
upn eł nk̓ʷsqáx̣eʔ – eleven horses, domestic animals, vehicles.
xʷaʔsqáx̣eʔ, *xʷaʔsqá* **–** many horses, domestic animals, vehicles.

čn epł msqá t pus u aslsqá t snčłcaʔsqá u nexʷ nk̓ʷsqá t p̓ip̓uyšn – I have four cats, two horses, and one car.

ankle **sk̓ʷłčmcinšn** – ankle. *rt.: **čm** – extremity.*
smq̓ʷcinšn – tibia/fibula bone protrusion on the ankle.

annoy **mʔečstmm** – annoy. *suffix: **...ečst, ...čst** – of the hand.*
es mʔečstmms – S/he/it is bothering s.o. **ies mʔečstmm, as mʔečstmm**
qs mʔečstmms – S/he/it is going to bother s.o. **iqs mʔečstmm, aqs mʔečstmm**
es mʔéʔečstmms – They are bothering s.o. **qeʔes mʔečstmm, es mʔečstmmp**
qs mʔéʔečstmms – They are going to bother s.o. **qeʔqs mʔečstmm, qs mʔečstmmp**

mečstmłtumš – Bother (someone). *cmd.*

nċlos – An action showing disdain toward someone. *This is done with the arm out and the wrist slightly bent down; then by extending, spreading and curving the index and middle fingers in the direction of the recipient. This action is similar to flipping someone off by extending the middle finger.*
nċlosis – S/he showed disdain toward s.o. **nċlosn, nċlosntxʷ**
es nċlosms – S/he is showing disdain toward s.o. **ies nċlosm, as nċlosm**
qs nċlosms – S/he is going to show disdain toward s.o. **iqs nċlosm, aqs nċlosm**

es nċlsnwexʷi – They are showing disdain toward each other. **čnes nċlsnwexʷi, kʷes nċlsnwexʷi**

qʷo nċlosntm – I was shown disdain by someone.

The **i** following uvular consonants (UC) and the glottal stop **ʔ** sound like English "*ey*" as in the words *they, hey, whey*, etc. Salish UC are: **q, q̇, qʷ, q̇ʷ, x̣, x̣ʷ**. For example, the suffix **...qin** – head/top, is often spelled using English *ey* as "q*ey*n". So **qi, q̇i, qʷi, q̇ʷi, x̣i, x̣ʷi**, may be spelled with English *ey* as **q***ey*, **q̇***ey*, **qʷ***ey*, **q̇ʷ***ey*, **x̣***ey*, **x̣ʷ***ey* in other texts.

answer **k̇ʷłkʷenxʷcn** – answer someone. *suffix: **...cin, ...cn** – action of the mouth.*
k̇ʷłkʷenxʷcnm – S/he answered. **čn k̇ʷłkʷenxʷcnm, kʷ k̇ʷłkʷenxʷcnm**
es k̇ʷłkʷenxʷcni – S/he is answering. **čnes k̇ʷłkʷenxʷcni, kʷes k̇ʷłkʷenxʷcni**
qs k̇ʷłkʷenxʷcni – S/he is going to answer. **čiqs k̇ʷłkʷenxʷcni, kʷqs k̇ʷłkʷenxʷcni**
k̇ʷłkʷéʔenxʷcnm – They answered. **qeʔ k̇ʷłkʷenxʷcnm, p k̇ʷłkʷenxʷcnm**
es k̇ʷłkʷéʔenxʷcni – They are answering. **qeʔes k̇ʷłkʷenxʷcni, pes k̇ʷłkʷenxʷcni**
qs k̇ʷłkʷéʔenxʷcni – They are going to answer. **qeʔqs k̇ʷłkʷenxʷcni, pqs k̇ʷłkʷenxʷcni**

k̇ʷłkʷenxʷcis – S/he answered s.o. **k̇ʷłkʷenxʷcn, k̇ʷłkʷenxʷcntxʷ**
es k̇ʷłkʷenxʷcnms – S/he is answering s.o. **ies k̇ʷłkʷenxʷcnm, as k̇ʷłkʷenxʷcnm**
qs k̇ʷłkʷenxʷcnms – S/he is going to answer s.o. **iqs k̇ʷłkʷenxʷcnm, aqs k̇ʷłkʷenxʷcnm**
k̇ʷłkʷéʔenxʷcis – They answered s.o. **qeʔ k̇ʷłkʷenxʷcntm, k̇ʷłkʷenxʷcntp**
es k̇ʷłkʷéʔenxʷcnms – They are answering s.o. **qeʔes k̇ʷłkʷenxʷcnm, es k̇ʷłkʷenxʷcnmp**
qs k̇ʷłkʷéʔenxʷcnms – They are going to answer s.o. **qeʔqs k̇ʷłkʷenxʷcnm, qs k̇ʷłkʷenxʷcnmp**

k̇ʷłkʷenxʷcniš – Answer. *cmd.*
k̇ʷłkʷenxʷcnt – Answer him/her. *cmd.*
k̇ʷłkʷenxʷcnłnt – Answer for him/her. *cmd.*

qeʔ k̇ʷłkʷnkʷnxʷcnwexʷist – We answered each other.

ant **sxʷuxʷyeʔ** – ant.

anteater **sxʷiłnm l sxʷuxʷyeʔ** – anteater.

antelope **staánč**, *staán* – antelope; pronghorn.

anticipate **pspmals**, *pspma* – nervously anticipating. *rt.: **psap** – excited/nervous; suffix: **...els, ...ls** – want, feel.*
pspmals – S/he was nervously anticipating. **čn pspmals, kʷ pspmals**
es pspmalsi – S/he is nervously anticipating. **čnes pspmalsi, kʷes pspmalsi**
qs pspmalsi – S/he is going to be nervously anticipating. **čiqs pspmalsi, kʷqs pspmalsi**
pspmáʔals – They were nervously anticipating. **qeʔ pspmals, p pspmals**

s.t. - something, the 3rd person
(s.t.) - something implied
s.o. - someone, the 3rd person
sl. - singular form
pl. - plural form
rt. - root word
cmd. - command
lit. - literally
fig. - figuratively
i.e., - for example
See: - Redirection to a related word.

es pspmáʔalsi – They are nervously anticipating. **qeʔes pspmalsi, pes pspmalsi**
qs pspmáʔalsi – They are going to be nervously anticipating. **qeʔqs pspmalsi, pqs pspmalsi**

čpspmalsmis – S/he was excited over s.t/s.o. **čpspmalsmn, čpspmalsmntxʷ**
es čpspmalsmms – S/he is excited over s.t/s.o. **ies čpspmalsmm, as čpspmalsmm**
qs čpspmalsmms – S/he is going to be excited over s.t/s.o. **iqs čpspmalsmm, aqs čpspmalsmm**
čpspmáʔalsmis – They were excited over s.t/s.o. **qeʔ čpspmalsmntm, čpspmalsmntp**
es čpspmáʔalsmms – They are excited over s.t/s.o. **qeʔes čpspmalsmm, es čpspmalsmmp**
qs čpspmáʔalsmms – They are going to be excited over s.t/s.o. **qeʔqs čpspmalsmm, qs čpspmalsmmp**

čpspmlsmnwexʷ – They were anxious about each other. **qeʔ čpspmlsmnwexʷ, p čpspmlsmnwexʷ**
es čpspmlsmnwexʷi – They are anxious about each other. **qeʔes čpspmlsmnwexʷi, pes čpspmlsmnwexʷi**

psap – excited/nervous. *See:* ***excited.***

antifreeze

tmsnimaptn – antifreeze. *rt.:* ***nimap*** *– water froze; prefix :* ***tms...*** *– not.*

antler

qx̣min – antlers, horns.

łm̓q̓ʷmu – antler nubs. *rt.:* ***moq̓ʷ*** *– bump/hill/mtn.*

nk̓ʷnk̓ʷalqʷ – one spike. *rt.:* ***nk̓ʷuʔ*** *– one; suffix:* ***...alqʷ*** *– wood; cylindical.*

nłq̓iq̓e – two spiked/forked antler.

...elsčn – suffix indicating antler or horn. *See:* ***horn.***

sax̣mqn – rub one's antlers on something such as a tree. *See:* ***rub.***

Antoine

atwén – Antoine; Tony.

anxious

nx̣ʷeʔłels – anxious; want to hurry. *rt.:* ***x̣ʷełe*** *– hurry; circumfix:* ***n...els*** *– want, feel.*
nx̣ʷeʔłels – S/he was anxious. **čn nx̣ʷeʔłels, kʷ nx̣ʷeʔłels**
es nx̣ʷeʔłelsi – S/he is anxious. **čnes nx̣ʷeʔłelsi, kʷes nx̣ʷeʔłelsi**
qs nx̣ʷeʔłelsi – S/he is going to be anxious. **čiqs nx̣ʷeʔłelsi, kʷqs nx̣ʷeʔłelsi**
nx̣ʷeʔłéʔels – They were anxious. **qeʔ nx̣ʷeʔłels, p nx̣ʷeʔłels**
es nx̣ʷeʔłéʔelsi – They are anxious. **qeʔes nx̣ʷeʔłelsi, pes nx̣ʷeʔłelsi**
qs nx̣ʷeʔłéʔelsi – They are going to be anxious. **qeʔqs nx̣ʷeʔłelsi, pqs nx̣ʷeʔłelsi**

nx̣ʷeʔłelsmis – S/he was excited over s.t/s.o. **nx̣ʷeʔłelsmn, nx̣ʷeʔłelsmntxʷ**
es nx̣ʷeʔłelsmms – S/he is excited over s.t/s.o. **ies nx̣ʷeʔłelsmm, as nx̣ʷeʔłelsmm**
qs nx̣ʷeʔłelsmms – S/he is going to be excited over s.t/s.o. **iqs nx̣ʷeʔłelsmm, aqs nx̣ʷeʔłelsmm**

psap – excited/nervous. *See:* ***excited.***

čn psap u čn npc̓awsm – I was anxious and I soiled my pants.

pspmals, *pspma* – nervously anticipating. *See:* ***anticipate.***

nqaupups – *literally:* have an itchy butt; *figuratively:* anxious, restless and unable to sit still. *See:* ***itch.***
nqaupups – S/he/it was anxious. **čn nqaupups, kʷ nqaupups**
es nqaupupsi – S/he/it is anxious. **čnes nqaupupsi, kʷes nqaupupsi**
qs nqaupupsi – S/he/it is going to be anxious. **čiqs nqaupupsi, kʷqs nqaupupsi**

qʷim̓m – anxious; in a hurry; move quickly. *See:* ***hurry.***

any

šiʔmi – any; whatever.

šiʔmi sċacaál – any sickness.

kʷ y̓amim t sšéń̓š tam t šiʔmi tam tl̓ ntx̣ʷé u tl̓ č̓łq̓li – You gather rocks; not just any old rocks, and not from the river or from the lake.

miš – none; out of. *See: **none**.*
mišlexʷ – nobody around.

miš łu inʔululim – I do not have any money. **miš łu qesʔiłn –** We do not have any food.

> The **i** following uvular consonants (UC) and the glottal stop **ʔ** sound like English "*ey*" as in the words *they, hey, whey,* etc. Salish UC are: **q, q̓, qʷ, q̓ʷ, x̣, x̣ʷ**. For example, the suffix ...**qin** – head/top, is often spelled using English *ey* as "*qeyn*". So **qi, q̓i, qʷi, q̓ʷi, x̣i, x̣ʷi**, may be spelled with English *ey* as **q***ey*, **q̓***ey*, **qʷ***ey*, **q̓ʷ***ey*, **x̣***ey*, **x̣ʷ***ey* in other texts.

anyone

tʔe swe – anybody; anyone; somebody.
ha tʔe swe wičtm – Did anyone else see him/her? **ṅe tʔe swe qs áċṁ m še čšnin –** If anyone is going to trap, they should come along.

apart

es nitkʷe – It falls apart easily; it is tender. *(i.e., meat.) See: **tender**.*

apparent

i wnwi – it is plainly visible; evident; apparent; very clear; it is obvious. *See: **plain**.*

appear

łaaq̓ʷ – appear/show up; manifest; exposed to view.
łaaq̓ʷ – S/he/it appeared. **čn łaaq̓ʷ, kʷ łaaq̓ʷ**
es łaq̓ʷmi – S/he/it is appearing. **čnes łaq̓ʷmi, kʷes łaq̓ʷmi**
qs łaq̓ʷmi – S/he/it is going to appear. **čiqs łaq̓ʷmi, kʷqs łaq̓ʷmi**
łaʔaaq̓ʷ – S/he/it appeared here. **qeʔ łaaq̓ʷ, p łaaq̓ʷ**
es łáʔaq̓ʷmi – They are appearing. **qeʔes łaq̓ʷmi, pes łaq̓ʷmi**
qs łáʔaq̓ʷmi – They are going to appear. **qeʔqs łaq̓ʷmi, pqs łaq̓ʷmi**

cłaaq̓ʷ – S/he/it appeared here. **čn cłaaq̓ʷ, kʷ cłaaq̓ʷ**

łaq̓ʷmscut – S/he made one's self appear. **čn łaq̓ʷmscut, kʷ łaq̓ʷmscut**
es łaq̓ʷmscuti – S/he is making one's self appear. **čnes łaq̓ʷmscuti, kʷes łaq̓ʷmscuti**
qs łaq̓ʷmscuti – S/he is going to make one's self appear. **čiqs łaq̓ʷmscuti, kʷqs łaq̓ʷmscuti**
łaq̓ʷmscúʔut – They made themselves appear. **qeʔ łaq̓ʷmscut, p łaq̓ʷmscut**
es łaq̓ʷmscúʔuti – They are making themselves appear. **qeʔes łaq̓ʷmscuti, pes łaq̓ʷmscuti**
qs łaq̓ʷmscúʔuti – They are going to make themselves appear. **qeʔqs łaq̓ʷmscuti, pqs łaq̓ʷmscuti**

łaq̓ʷmstes – S/he made s.o./s.t. appear. **łaq̓ʷmsten, łaq̓ʷmstexʷ**
es łaq̓ʷmims – S/he is making s.o./s.t. appear. **ies łaq̓ʷmim, as łaq̓ʷmim**
qs łaq̓ʷmims – S/he is going to make s.o./s.t. appear. **iqs łaq̓ʷmim, aqs łaq̓ʷmim**
łaq̓ʷmstéʔes – They made s.o./s.t. appear. **qeʔ łaq̓ʷmstem, łaq̓ʷmstep**

łaq̓ʷmists – S/he made s.o./s.t. exposed to view. **łaq̓ʷmistn, łaq̓ʷmistxʷ**
łaq̓ʷmíʔists – They made s.o./s.t. exposed to view. **qeʔ łaq̓ʷmistm, łaq̓ʷmistp**

łaq̓ʷmusts – S/he made s.o. appear. **łaq̓ʷmusten, łaq̓ʷmustxʷ** *infix: **...us...** – face.*
łaq̓ʷmúʔusts – They made s.o. appear. **qeʔ łaq̓ʷmustem, łaq̓ʷmustp** *infix: **...us...** – face.*

łałʔáʔaq̓ʷ – Each one of them appeared. **qeʔ łałʔaq̓ʷ, p łałʔaq̓ʷ**

łłʔaq̓ʷ – S/he appeared a little. **čn łłʔaq̓ʷ, kʷ łłʔaq̓ʷ**

sxʷłaq̓ʷm – one tasked to show something. *prefix: **sxʷ...** – one tasked to do.*
sxʷłaq̓ʷmscut – one tasked to make themselves appear. *prefix: **sxʷ...** – one tasked to do.*
sxʷłaq̓ʷlwis – one tasked to keep showing up. *prefix: **sxʷ...** – one tasked to do.*
čłaq̓ʷtin – something that makes something known/evident.

> s.t. - something, the 3rd person
> (s.t.) - something implied
> s.o. - someone, the 3rd person
> *sl.* - singular form
> *pl.* - plural form
> *rt.* - root word
> *cmd.* - command
> *lit.* - literally
> *fig.* - figuratively
> *i.e.,* - for example
> *See:* - Redirection to a related word.

nłq̓ʷtin – place of appearance.

łaq̓ʷmscutistiš – Make yourself appear/show up. *cmd.*
łaq̓ʷlwis – go around showing up/to make appearances here and there.
es łaq̓ʷlwisi – S/he keeps showing up. **čnes łaq̓ʷlwisi, kʷes łaq̓ʷlwisi**
łałaq̓ʷcnwexʷ – They showed up with each other. **qeˀ łałaq̓ʷcnwexʷ, p łałaq̓ʷcnwexʷ**
łaq̓ʷcin – speak up once in a while. *suffix: **...cin, ...cn** – action of the mouth.*

ṅe eł cłˀaq̓ʷ m qeˀ xʷuy – When s/he/it appears again we'll go.

łaq̓ʷš – show something to someone by making it appear or exposing it to view; reveal something to someone.
łaq̓ʷšišm – S/he showed (s.t.). **čn łaq̓ʷšišm, kʷ łaq̓ʷšišm**
es łaq̓ʷšiši – S/he is showing (s.t.). **čnes łaq̓ʷšiši, kʷes łaq̓ʷšiši**
qs łaq̓ʷšiši – S/he is going to show (s.t.). **čiqs łaq̓ʷšiši, kʷqs łaq̓ʷšiši**

łaq̓ʷšits – S/he showed s.t. to s.o. **łaq̓ʷmšitn, łaq̓ʷmšitxʷ**
es łaq̓ʷšitms – S/he is showing s.t. to s.o. **ies łaq̓ʷšitm, as łaq̓ʷšitm**
qs łaq̓ʷšitms – S/he is going to show s.t. to s.o. **iqs łaq̓ʷšitm, aqs łaq̓ʷšitm**

łaq̓ʷšišmis – S/he showed s.t. for s.o. **łaq̓ʷšišmn, łaq̓ʷšišmntxʷ**
es łaq̓ʷšišms – S/he is showing s.t. for s.o. **ies łaq̓ʷšišm, as łaq̓ʷšišm**
qs łaq̓ʷšišms – S/he is going to show s.t. for s.o. **iqs łaq̓ʷšišm, aqs łaq̓ʷšišm**

łaq̓ʷšit – Show it. *cmd.*
es łaq̓ʷštwexʷi – They are showing each other. **qeˀes łaq̓ʷštwexʷi, pes łaq̓ʷštwexʷi**

čłaq̓ʷiċeˀ – exposed to view all over; completely exposed.
es čłaq̓ʷċeˀ – S/he/it is completely exposed to view. **čnes čłaq̓ʷċeˀ, kʷes čłaq̓ʷċeˀ**

čłaq̓ʷiċˀeis – S/he/it completely exposed s.t. **čłaq̓ʷiċˀen, čłaq̓ʷiċˀentxʷ**
es čłaq̓ʷiċˀems – S/he/it is completely exposing s.t. **ies čłaq̓ʷiċˀem, as čłaq̓ʷiċˀem**
qs čłaq̓ʷiċˀems – S/he/it is going to completely expose s.t. **iqs čłaq̓ʷiċˀem, aqs čłaq̓ʷiċˀem**

čłaq̓ʷisċˀencut – S/he/it completely revealed/exposed one's self. **čn čłaq̓ʷisċˀencut, kʷ čłaq̓ʷisċˀencut**

čłaq̓ʷiċˀent – Completely reveal it. *cmd.*

apple
ápls – apple.

apple juice
aplsetkʷ – apple juice; cider. *suffix: **...etkʷ, ...tkʷ** – liquid*
aplsck̓ʷłsˀeˀs – apple juice. *lit. the apple's juice.*

applesauce
snṫpus apls – applesauce. *lit. boiled apples.*

apple tree
aplsálqʷ – apple tree, applewood. *suffix: **...alqʷ** – wood; cylindical.*

applewood
aplsálqʷ – applewood, apple tree.

appoint
nk̓ʷnšmist – appoint; make a personal choice. *rt.: **nk̓ʷéṅ** – choose, pick, select, or try; suffix: **...ist** – action for/of the self.*
nk̓ʷnšmiststs – S/he appointed s.o. **nk̓ʷnšmiststn, nk̓ʷnšmiststxʷ**
nk̓ʷnšmíˀiststs – They appointed s.o. **qeˀ nk̓ʷnšmiststm, nk̓ʷnšmiststp**

nk̓ʷnšmiststm – S/he was appointed.

snk̓ʷnšmists – his/her appointment. **isnk̓ʷnšmist, asnk̓ʷnšmist**

qʷo nk̓ʷnšmiststm – I was appointed.

nk̓ʷéṅm – choose; pick; select; show the selection. *See:* ***try.***

t̓k̓ʷum – put something down/to place someone in charge/to appoint. *See:* ***put.***

April **sčiyál̓m̓n spq̇niʔ** – April *(month of the buttercup).*

apron **miɫʔil̓xʷé** – apron. *rt.:* ***xʷep*** *– cover; prefix:* ***miɫ...*** *– front.*

aquarium **snsẇewɫtn** – aquarium. *rt.:* ***sẇewɫ*** *– fish; prefix:* ***sn...*** *– a place of; suffix:* ***...tin, ...tn*** *– means of/device.*

arch **čɫpṅusm** – arched over. *rt.:* ***piṅ*** *– bend; prefix:* ***čɫ...*** *– surface; suffix;* ***...éẇs*** *– in between, middle.*

čɫpṅusis – S/he arched s.t. over. **čɫpṅusn, čɫpṅusntxʷ**
es čɫpṅusms – S/he is arching s.t. over. **ies čɫpṅusm, as čɫpṅusm**
qs čɫpṅusms – S/he is going to arch s.t. over. **iqs čɫpṅusm, aqs čɫpṅusm**

čɫpṅusnt – Arch it over. *cmd.*

piṅ – bend from one position to an curved/angular position. *See:* ***bend.***

area **...ulexʷ** – *suffix indicating land, place, or area.*
nk̓ʷuʔ čeɫlulexʷ – One of three or 1/3. *(in reference to area.)*
nk̓ʷuʔ msulexʷ – One of four or 1/4. *(in reference to area.)*
nk̓ʷuʔ clčstulexʷ – One of five or 1/5. *(in reference to area.)*
nk̓ʷuʔ t̓q̇nčstulexʷ – One of six or 1/6. *(in reference to area.)*
nk̓ʷuʔ sp̓l̓čstulexʷ – One of seven or 1/7. *(in reference to area.)*
nk̓ʷuʔ henmulexʷ – One of eight or 1/8 *(in reference to area.)*
nk̓ʷuʔ x̣ntulexʷ – One of nine or 1/9. *(in reference to area.)*
nk̓ʷuʔ upnčstulexʷ – One of ten or 1/10. *(in reference to area.)*

argue **x̣ʷċncut** – argue.
x̣ʷċncut – S/he argued. **čn x̣ʷċncut, kʷ x̣ʷċncut**
es x̣ʷċncuti – S/he is arguing. **čnes x̣ʷċncuti, kʷes x̣ʷċncuti**
qs x̣ʷċncuti – S/he is going to argue. **čiqs x̣ʷċncuti, kʷqs x̣ʷċncuti**
x̣ʷċncúʔut – They argued. **qeʔ x̣ʷċncut, p x̣ʷċncut**
es x̣ʷċncúʔuti – They are arguing. **qeʔes x̣ʷċncuti, pes x̣ʷċncuti**
qs x̣ʷċncúʔuti – They are going to argue. **qeʔqs x̣ʷċncuti, pqs x̣ʷċncuti**

x̣ʷċis – S/he argued with s.o. **x̣ʷċin, x̣ʷċintxʷ**
es x̣ʷċims – S/he is arguing with s.o. **ies x̣ʷċim, as x̣ʷċim**
qs x̣ʷċims – S/he is going to argue with s.o. **iqs x̣ʷċim, aqs x̣ʷċim**
x̣ʷċíʔis – They argued with s.o. **qeʔ x̣ʷċintm, x̣ʷċintp**
es x̣ʷċíʔims – They are arguing with s.o. **qeʔes x̣ʷċim, es x̣ʷċimp**
qs x̣ʷċíʔims – They are going to argue with s.o. **qeʔqs x̣ʷċim, qs x̣ʷċimp**

es ɫx̣ʷċncuti – S/he is arguing a little. **čnes ɫx̣ʷċncuti, kʷes ɫx̣ʷċncuti**
es ɫx̣ʷċims – S/he is arguing a little with s.o. **ies ɫx̣ʷċim, as ɫx̣ʷċim**

x̣ʷċšis – S/he argued for s.o. **x̣ʷċšin, x̣ʷċšit**

x̣ʷċncutn – arguer/lawyer. **x̣ʷċncutis, inx̣ʷċncutn, anx̣ʷċncutn**
x̣ʷċċnmuɫ – one that habitually argues. *suffix:* ***...ɫmuɫ*** *– one that habitually does.*
sx̣ʷċiċ – argument. **sx̣ʷċiċs, isx̣ʷċiċ, asx̣ʷċiċ**

The **i** following uvular consonants (UC) and the glottal stop **ʔ** sound like English "*ey*" as in the words th*ey*, h*ey*, wh*ey*, etc. Salish UC are: **q, q̇, qʷ, q̇ʷ, x̣, x̣ʷ**. For example, the suffix **...qin** – head/top, is often spelled using English *ey* as "q*ey*n". So **qi, q̇i, qʷi, q̇ʷi, x̣i, x̣ʷi,** may be spelled with English *ey* as **q***ey*, **q̇***ey*, **qʷ***ey*, **q̇ʷ***ey*, **x̣***ey*, **x̣ʷ***ey* in other texts.

s.t. - something, the 3rd person
(s.t.) - something implied
s.o. - someone, the 3rd person
sl. - singular form
pl. - plural form
rt. - root word
cmd. - command
lit. - literally
fig. - figuratively
i.e., - for example
See: - Redirection to a related word.

x̣ʷċiš – Argue. *cmd.*
ta kʷ qes x̣ʷċncut – Don't argue. *cmd.*

x̣ʷċint – Argue with someone. *cmd.*
x̣ʷex̣ʷċeʔ – little arguer, affectionately.
x̣ʷċnwéxʷ, *x̣ʷċnwé* – argue with each other.
es x̣ʷċnwéxʷisti – They are arguing with each other. **qeʔes x̣ʷċnwéxʷisti, pes x̣ʷċnwéxʷisti**
x̣ʷċċłtumš – argue with people; argue at large. *suffix: **...łtumš** – of people*

steṁ łu asx̣ʷċiċ – What is your argument? **qʷo x̣ʷċšit** – Argue for me.

Arlee
nłq̇alqʷ, *nłq̇a* – Arlee. *lit. thick trees. rt.: **łaq̇t** – wide; suffix: **...alqʷ** – wood; cylindical.*

arm
sčuwáx̣n – arm. **sčučuwax̣n** – arms. **sčuʔuwax̣n** – arms. *pl.*
snčmax̣n – armpit.
sčmelx̣n – upper arm.
sčq̇ʷmax̣n – bicep.
sčmusax̣n – inner elbow.
sčaw̓sax̣n – outer elbow.
sčx̣max̣n – forearm.
sk̓ʷłčmcnečst – wrist.

...ax̣n – suffix indicating arm.
schax̣n – right arm.
sċq̇ʷax̣n – left arm.
q̇aw̓pax̣n – broken arm.
usšnax̣n – long arm.
kʷtunax̣n – big arm.
q̇t̓q̇t̓ax̣ni – swinging arms. *See: **swing**.*

ċa ye isčwax̣n – my arm hurts.

sčchax̣n – right arm.
sčċiq̇ʷax̣n – left arm.

ċʔalax̣n – have a sore/achy arm. *rt.: **ċaál** – ache.*
ċʔalax̣n – S/he/it had a sore arm. **čn ċʔalax̣n, kʷ ċʔalax̣n**
es ċʔalax̣ni – S/he/it has a sore arm. **čnes ċʔalax̣ni, kʷes ċʔalax̣ni**
qs ċʔalax̣ni – S/he/it is going to have a sore arm. **čiqs ċʔalax̣ni, kʷqs ċʔalax̣ni**
ċʔaláʔax̣n – They had a sore arm. **qeʔ ċʔalax̣n, p ċʔalax̣n**

es čqqx̣nax̣n – His/her legs are stacked one on the other. **čnes čqqx̣nax̣n, kʷes čqqx̣nax̣n** *See: **stack**.*

armband
čiyallax̣n – armband. *rt.: **čyall** – wrap; suffix: **...ax̣n** – arm.*
es čiyallax̣n – S/he wears an armband. **čnes čiyallax̣n, kʷes čiyallax̣n**

čiyallax̣niš – Put on an armband. *cmd.*

armpit
snčmax̣n – armpit. **snčičmax̣n** – armpit. *rt.: **čm** – extremity; suffix: **...ax̣n** – arm.*

snupupax̣n – armpit hair.

arm wrestle
čmusax̣nm – arm wrestle.
čmusax̣nm – S/he arm wrestled. **čn čmusax̣nm, kʷ čmusax̣nm**
es čmusax̣ni – S/he is arm wrestling. **čnes čmusax̣ni, kʷes čmusax̣ni**
qs čmusax̣ni – S/he is going to arm wrestle. **čiqs čmusax̣ni, kʷqs čmusax̣ni**

nkʷłčmumusax̣is – S/he arm wrestled s.o. **nkʷłčmumusax̣n, nkʷłčmumusax̣ntxʷ**
es nkʷłčmumusax̣nms – S/he is arm wrestling s.o. **ies nkʷłčmumusax̣nm, as nkʷłčmumusax̣nm**
qs nkʷłčmumusax̣nms – S/he is going to arm wrestle s.o. **iqs nkʷłčmumusax̣nm, kʷqs nkʷłčmumusax̣nm**

es čmumusax̣nwexʷi – They are arm wrestling each other. **qeʔes čmumusax̣nwexʷi, pes čmumusax̣nwexʷi**

> The **i** following uvular consonants (UC) and the glottal stop **ʔ** sound like English "*ey*" as in the words th*ey*, h*ey*, wh*ey*, etc. Salish UC are: **q, q̇, qʷ, q̇ʷ, x̣, x̣ʷ**. For example, the suffix **...qin** – head/top, is often spelled using English *ey* as "qeyn". So **qi, q̇i, qʷi, q̇ʷi, x̣i, x̣ʷi**, may be spelled with English *ey* as **q***ey*, **q̇***ey*, **qʷ***ey*, **q̇ʷ***ey*, **x̣***ey*, **x̣ʷ***ey* in other texts.

x̣ʷlq̇ʷax̣nm – arm twist. *rt.: **x̣ʷollq̇ʷ**– roll; suffix: **...ax̣n** – arm.*
x̣ʷlq̇ʷax̣nm – S/he arm twisted. **čn x̣ʷlq̇ʷax̣nm, kʷ x̣ʷlq̇ʷax̣nm**
es x̣ʷlq̇ʷax̣ni – S/he is arm twisting. **čnes x̣ʷlq̇ʷax̣ni, kʷes x̣ʷlq̇ʷax̣ni**
qs x̣ʷlq̇ʷax̣ni – S/he is going to arm twist. **čiqs x̣ʷlq̇ʷax̣ni, kʷqs x̣ʷlq̇ʷax̣ni**

x̣ʷlq̇ʷax̣is – S/he twisted s.o.'s arm. **x̣ʷlq̇ʷax̣n, x̣ʷlq̇ʷax̣ntxʷ**
es x̣ʷlq̇ʷax̣nms – S/he is twisting s.o.'s arm. **ies x̣ʷlq̇ʷax̣nm, as x̣ʷlq̇ʷax̣nm**
qs x̣ʷlq̇ʷax̣nms – S/he is going to twist s.o.'s arm. **iqs x̣ʷlq̇ʷax̣nm, aqs x̣ʷlq̇ʷax̣nm**

x̣ʷlq̇ʷax̣nt – Twist his/her arm. *cmd.*

es x̣ʷlq̇ʷax̣nwexʷi – They are twisting each other's arms. **qeʔes x̣ʷlq̇ʷax̣nwexʷi, pes x̣ʷlq̇ʷax̣nwexʷi**

around

šlič – go round; turn on an axis; go in a circular course; rotate 360 degrees.
šlič – S/he/it went round. **čn šlič, kʷ šlič**
es šlčmi – S/he/it is going round. **čnes šlčmi, kʷes šlčmi**
qs šlčmi – S/he/it is going to go round. **čiqs šlčmi, kʷqs šlčmi**

šlčmstes – S/he/it turned s.t./s.o around. **šlčmsten, šlčmstexʷ**
es šlčmims – S/he/it is turning s.t./s.o. around. **ies šlčmim, as šlčmim**
qs šlčmims – S/he/it is going to turn s.t./s.o. around. **iqs šlčmim, aqs šlčmim**
šlčmstéʔes – They turned s.t./s.o. around. **qeʔ šlčmstem, šlčmstep**
es šlčmíʔims – They are turning s.t./s.o. around. **qeʔes šlčmim, es šlčmimp**
qs šlčmíʔims – They are going to turn s.t./s.o. around. **qeʔqs šlčmim, qs šlčmimp**

šlličč – S/he/it got turned around. **čn šlličč, kʷ šlličč**

šlčmiš – Go round. *cmd.*
šlčmiskʷ – Turn him/her/it around; revolve him/her/it. *cmd.*

ha kʷ šlič l snčłemutn – Did you go around the chair?

šlčmncut – make one's self turn around/on an axis. *See: **round dance**.*
šlčmncut – S/he/it turned around. **čn šlčmncut, kʷ šlčmncut**
es šlčmncuti – S/he is turning around. **čnes šlčmncuti, kʷes šlčmncuti**
qs šlčmncuti – S/he is going to turn around. **čiqs šlčmncuti, kʷqs šlčmncuti**
šlčmncúʔut – They turned around. **qeʔ šlčmncut, p šlčmncut**
es šlčmncúʔuti – They are turning around. **qeʔes šlčmncuti, pes šlčmncuti**
qs šlčmncúʔuti – They are going to turn around. **qeʔqs šlčmncuti, pqs šlčmncuti**

šlčmncutš – Turn all the way around. *cmd.*

> s.t. - something, the 3rd person
> (s.t.) - something implied
> s.o. - someone, the 3rd person
> *sl.* - singular form
> *pl.* - plural form
> *rt.* - root word
> *cmd.* - command
> *lit.* - literally
> *fig.* - figuratively
> *i.e.,* - for example
> *See:* - Redirection to a related word.

nšlič – go around the inside of something.
nšlič – S/he/it went around the inside. **čn nšlič, kʷ nšlič**
es nšlčmi – S/he/it is going around the inside. **čnes nšlčmi, kʷes nšlčmi**
qs nšlčmi – S/he/it is going to go around the inside. **čiqs nšlčmi, kʷqs nšlčmi**
nšlíʔič – They went around the inside. **qeʔ nšlič, p nšlič**
es nšlčmíʔi – They are going around the inside. **qeʔes nšlčmi, pes nšlčmi**

qs nšlčmí⁾i – They are going to go around the inside. **qe⁾qs nšlčmi, pqs nšlčmi**

nšlčmis – S/he/it went around the inside of s.t. **nšlčmin, nšlčmintxʷ**
es nšlčminms – S/he/it is going around the inside of s.t. **ies nšlčminm, as nšlčminm**
qs nšlčminms – S/he/it is going to go around the inside of s.t. **iqs nšlčminm, aqs nšlčminm**
nšlčmí⁾is – They went around the inside of s.t. **qe⁾ nšlčmintm, nšlčmintp**
es nšlčmí⁾inms – They are going around the inside of s.t. **qe⁾es nšlčminm, es nšlčminmp**
qs nšlčmí⁾inms – They are going to go around the inside of s.t. **qe⁾qs nšlčminm, qs nšlčminmp**

nšličš – Go around the inside. *cmd.*
nšlčmintxʷ – Go around the inside of it. *cmd.*

čnes nšlčmi l es q̇ey – I am going around the inside of the camp. **nšlí⁾ič l es q̇ey –** They went around the inside of the camp.

nšlčełxʷm – go round the inside of a structure or village. *(i.e., building, tipi, house, etc.)*
nšlčełxʷm – S/he/it went around the inside. **čn nšlčełxʷm, kʷ nšlčełxʷm**
es nšlčełxʷi – S/he/it is going around the inside. **čnes nšlčełxʷi, kʷes nšlčełxʷi**
qs nšlčełxʷi – S/he/it is going to go around the inside. **čiqs nšlčełxʷi, kʷqs nšlčełxʷi**
nšlčé⁾ełxʷm – They went around the inside. **qe⁾ nšlčełxʷm, p nšlčełxʷm**
es nšlčé⁾ełxʷi – They are going around the inside. **qe⁾es nšlčełxʷi, pes nšlčełxʷi**
qs nšlčé⁾ełxʷi – They are going to go around the inside. **qe⁾qs nšlčełxʷi, pqs nšlčełxʷi**

nšlčełxʷmis – S/he/it went around the inside of it. **nšlčełxʷmn, nšlčełxʷmntxʷ**
es nšlčełxʷms – S/he/it is going around the inside of it. **ies nšlčełxʷm, as nšlčełxʷm**
qs nšlčełxʷms – S/he/it is going to go around the inside of it. **iqs nšlčełxʷm, aqs nšlčełxʷm**
nšlčé⁾ełxʷm – They went around the inside of it. **qe⁾ nšlčełxʷmntm, nšlčełxʷmntp**

ṅem qe⁾ nšlčéłxʷ – We'll go around the inside of the camp.

nšlčusm – go around a fire.
nšlčusm – S/he/it went around a fire. **čn nšlčusm, kʷ nšlčusm**
es nšlčusi – S/he/it is going around a fire. **čnes nšlčusi, kʷes nšlčusi**
qs nšlčusi – S/he/it is going to go around a fire. **čiqs nšlčusi, kʷqs nšlčusi**

čšlič – go around something; make a circular path around something.
čšlič – S/he/it went around (s.t.). **čn čšlič, kʷ čšlič**
es čšlčmi – S/he/it is going around. **čnes čšlčmi, kʷes čšlčmi**
qs čšlčmi – S/he/it is going to go around. **čiqs čšlčmi, kʷqs čšlčmi**
čšlí⁾ič – They went around. **qe⁾ čšlič, p čšlič**
es čšlčmí⁾i – They are going around. **qe⁾es čšlčmi, pes čšlčmi**
qs čšlčmí⁾i – They are going to go around. **qe⁾qs čšlčmi, pqs čšlčmi**

čšlčmis – S/he/it went around s.t./s.o. **čšlčmin, čšlčmintxʷ**
es čšlčminms – S/he/it is going around s.t./s.o. **ies čšlčminm, as čšlčminm**
qs čšlčminms – S/he/it is going to go around s.t./s.o. **iqs čšlčminm, aqs čšlčminm**
čšlčmí⁾is – They went around s.t./s.o. **qe⁾ čšlčmintm, čšlčmintp**
es čšlčmí⁾ims – They are going around s.t./s.o. **qe⁾es čšlčminm, es čšlčminmp**
qs čšlčmí⁾ims – They are going to go around s.t./s.o. **qe⁾qs čšlčminm, qs čšlčminmp**

es čšlšlčmí⁾i – They are going around and around. **qe⁾es čšlšlčmi, pes čšlšlčmi**
es čšlšlčminms – S/he/it is going around and around s.t./s.o. **ies čšlšlčminm, as čšlšlčminm**

čšlšlčmis – S/he/it circled around s.o./s.t. **čšlšlčmin, čšlšlčmintxʷ**
es čšlšlčminms – S/he/it is circling around s.o./s.t. **ies čšlšlčminm, as čšlšlčminm**
qs čšlšlčminms – S/he/it is going to circle around s.o./s.t. **iqs čšlšlčminm, aqs čšlšlčminm**

čšlšlčmíʔis – They circled around s.o./s.t. **qeʔ čšlšlčmintm, čšlšlčmintp**
es čšlšlčmíʔinms – They are circling around s.o./s.t. **qeʔes čšlšlčminm, es čšlšlčminmp**

es čłšlčmíʔi – They are going around. **qeʔes čłšlčmi, pes čłšlčmi**
es čłšlčminms – S/he/it is going around s.t./s.o. **ies čłšlčminm, as čłšlčminm**
čłšlšlčmis – S/he/it went around and around s.t. a little. **čłšlšlčmin, čłšlšlčmintxʷ**

čšličš – Go around. *cmd.*
čšlčmint – Go around something. *cmd.*
es čšlčmnwexʷi – They are going around each other. **qeʔes čšlčmnwexʷi, pes čšlčmnwexʷi**
es čšličči – S/he/it is making it around. **čnes čšličči, kʷes čšličči**

qeʔes čšlšlčmiłlt – S/he/it is circling around us. **kʷ es čšlšlčminms** – S/he/it is circling around you.

čšlčmstes – S/he/it brought s.t./s.o. around. **čšlčmsten, čšlčmstexʷ**
es čšlčmims – S/he/it is bringing s.t./s.o. around. **ies čšlčmim, as čšlčmim**
qs čšlčmims – S/he/it is going to bring s.t./s.o. around. **iqs čšlčmim, aqs čšlčmim**
čšlčmstéʔes – They brought s.t./s.o. around. **qeʔ čšlčmstem, čšlčmstep**
es čšlčmíʔims – They are bringing s.t./s.o. around. **qeʔes čšlčmim, es čšlčmimp**
qs čšlčmíʔims – They are going to bring s.t./s.o. around. **qeʔqs čšlčmim, qs čšlčmimp**

qʷo šlšlčmiskʷłt – Go around it for me. *cmd.*

nčšličṅm – go around somebody's back. *suffix: **...ičṅ** – back.*
nčšličis – S/he/it went around s.o. **nčšličṅ, nčšličṅtxʷ**
es nčšličṅms – S/he/it is going around s.o. **ies nčšličṅm, as nčšličṅm**
qs nčšličṅms – S/he/it is going to go around s.o. **iqs nčšličṅm, aqs nčšličṅm**
nčšlíʔičis – They went around s.o. **qeʔ nčšličṅtm, nčšličṅtp**
es nčšlíʔičṅms – They are going around s.o. **qeʔes nčšličṅm, es nčšličṅmp**
qs nčšlíʔičṅms – They are going to go around s.o. **qeʔqs nčšličṅm, qs nčšličṅmp**

nčšličṅt – Go around his/her back. *cmd.*

čšlčełxʷm – go around the outside of a village/house/tipi. *suffix: **...ełxʷ, ...łxʷ** – house.*
čšlčełxʷm – S/he/it went around the outside. **čn čšlčełxʷm, kʷ čšlčełxʷm**
es čšlčełxʷi – S/he/it is going around the outside. **čnes čšlčełxʷi, kʷes čšlčełxʷi**
qs čšlčełxʷi – S/he/it is going to go around the outside. **čiqs čšlčełxʷi, kʷqs čšlčełxʷi**
čšlčéʔełxʷm – They went around the outside. **qeʔ čšlčełxʷm, p čšlčełxʷm**
es čšlčéʔełxʷi – They are going around the outside. **qeʔes čšlčełxʷi, pes čšlčełxʷi**
qs čšlčéʔełxʷi – They are going to go around the outside. **qeʔqs čšlčełxʷi, pqs čšlčełxʷi**

čšlčełxʷmis – S/he/it went around the outside of it. **čšlčełxʷmn, čšlčełxʷmntxʷ**
es čšlčełxʷms – S/he/it is going around the outside of it. **ies čšlčełxʷm, as čšlčełxʷm**
qs čšlčełxʷms – S/he/it is going to go around the outside of it. **iqs čšlčełxʷm, aqs čšlčełxʷm**
čšlčéʔełxʷm – They went around the outside of it. **qeʔ čšlčełxʷmntm, čšlčełxʷmntp**
es čšlčéʔełxʷms – They are going around the outside of it. **qeʔes čšlčełxʷm, es čšlčełxʷmp**
qs čšlčéʔełxʷms – They are going to go around the outside of it. **qeʔqs čšlčełxʷm, qs čšlčełxʷmp**

The **i** following uvular consonants (UC) and the glottal stop **ʔ** sound like English "*ey*" as in the words th*ey*, h*ey*, wh*ey*, etc. Salish UC are: **q, q̇, qʷ, q̇ʷ, x̣, x̣ʷ**. For example, the suffix ...**qin** – head/top, is often spelled using English *ey* as "q*ey*n". So **qi, q̇i, qʷi, q̇ʷi, x̣i, x̣ʷi**, may be spelled with English *ey* as **q***ey*, **q̇***ey*, **qʷ***ey*, **q̇ʷ***ey*, **x̣***ey*, **x̣ʷ***ey* in other texts.

s.t. - something, the 3rd person
(s.t.) - something implied
s.o. - someone, the 3rd person
sl. - singular form
pl. - plural form
rt. - root word
cmd. - command
lit. - literally
fig. - figuratively
i.e., - for example
See: - Redirection to a related word.

nčcnšncut – make a complete revolution; make a circle; meet one's own footprints/tracks. *This word is used to describe cycles such as birthdays, and the telling of time in hours. rt.:* ***čic*** *– happen upon; infix:* ***...šn...*** *– foot; suffix:* ***...cut*** *– action to the self. See:* ***meet.***

nčcnšncut – S/he/it went around; it is his/her birthday. **čn nčcnšncut, kʷ nčcnšncut**

ha kʷ nčcnšncut – Did you make it clear around; Is it your birthday?

nčcnšncut spq̓niʔ – one time around the clock.

ṗl̓čmncut – turn one's self over/back.
ṗl̓čmncut – S/he/it turned over/back. **čn ṗl̓čmncut, kʷ ṗl̓čmncut**
es ṗl̓čmncuti – S/he/it is turning over/back. **čnes ṗl̓čmncuti, kʷes ṗl̓čmncuti**
qs ṗl̓čmncuti – S/he/it is going to turn over/back. **čiqs ṗl̓čmncuti, kʷqs ṗl̓čmncuti**
ṗl̓čmncúʔut – They turned over/back. **qeʔ ṗl̓čmncut, p ṗl̓čmncut**

ṗl̓čmncutš – Turn over/back. *cmd.*
ṗl̓čṁim – turn something over. *See:* ***turn.***

ntax̣ʷlús – face toward some direction. *suffix:* ***...us*** *– face. See:* ***face.***

qéclš – run of an individual; run leisurely. *See:* ***run.***

ml̓uk̓ʷ – spread all around; propagate; grow, of non-living things. *See:* ***all around.***

arrest

kʷnem – take one thing; grab. *See:* ***take.***
kʷéis – S/he/it took s.t./s.o. **kʷén, kʷéntxʷ**
es kʷnems – S/he/it is taking s.t./s.o. **ies kʷnem, as kʷnem**
qs kʷnems – S/he/it is going to take s.t./s.o. **iqs kʷnem, aqs kʷnem**

kʷéntm – S/he was taken/arrested. *rt.:* ***kʷen*** *– take.*

sxʷkʷnem – one tasked to take/grab; police. *prefix:* ***sxʷ...*** *– one tasked to do.*

l̓čim – tie up something or things. *See:* ***tie.***
sxʷl̓čim – one tasked to tie something up; police. *prefix:* ***sxʷ...*** *– one tasked to do.*
snl̓čmin – jail; place where you are tied up.

k̓ʷłolocnečstn, *k̓ʷłolocne* – handcuff.
k̓ʷłolocnečstm – S/he was handcuffed. **čn k̓ʷłolocnečstm, kʷ k̓ʷłolocnečstm**
es k̓ʷłolocnečst – S/he is handcuffed. **čnes k̓ʷłolocnečst, kʷes k̓ʷłolocnečst**
qs k̓ʷłolocnečst – S/he is going to be handcuffed. **čiqs k̓ʷłolocnečst, kʷqs k̓ʷłolocnečst**

es k̓ʷłolocnečsti – S/he is getting handcuffed. **čnes k̓ʷłolocnečsti, kʷes k̓ʷłolocnečsti**

k̓ʷłolocnečsis – S/he handcuffed s.o. **k̓ʷłolocnečsn, k̓ʷłolocnečsntxʷ**
es k̓ʷłolocnečsms – S/he is handcuffing s.o. **ies k̓ʷłolocnečsm, as k̓ʷłolocnečsm**
qs k̓ʷłolocnečsms – S/he is going to handcuff s.o. **iqs k̓ʷłolocnečsm, aqs k̓ʷłolocnečsm**

k̓ʷłolocnečsnt – Handcuff him/her. *cmd.*

arrive

k̓ʷłčicš, *k̓ʷłči* – arrived there. *rt.:* ***čic*** *– happen upon.*
k̓ʷłčicš – S/he/it arrived there. **čn k̓ʷłčicš, kʷ k̓ʷłčicš**
es k̓ʷłčicši – S/he/it is arriving there. **čnes k̓ʷłčicši, kʷes k̓ʷłčicši**
qs k̓ʷłčicši – S/he/it is going to arrive there. **čiqs k̓ʷłčicši, kʷqs k̓ʷłčicši**

ck̓ʷłčicš – S/he/it arrived here. **čn ck̓ʷłčicš, kʷ ck̓ʷłčicš**
es ck̓ʷłčicši – S/he/it is arriving here. **čnes ck̓ʷłčicši, kʷes ck̓ʷłčicši**
qs ck̓ʷłčicši – S/he/it is going to arrive here. **čiqs ck̓ʷłčicši, kʷqs ck̓ʷłčicši**

k̓ʷłčicšis – S/he/it arrived at that place. **k̓ʷłčicšn, k̓ʷłčicšntxʷ**

es k̓ʷłčicšms – S/he/it is arriving at that place. **ies k̓ʷłčicšm, as k̓ʷłčicšm**
qs k̓ʷłčicšms – S/he/it is going to arrive at that place. **iqs k̓ʷłčicšm, aqs k̓ʷłčicšm**

t k̓ʷłčicš – arrive before.

čic – happen upon; meet someone; an accidental meeting. *See:* ***meet.***
nčcnšncut – make a complete revolution; make a circle; meet one's own footprints/tracks. *See:* ***around.***

áx̣lwis pasqá u k̓ʷłčicš – Through his persistence and determination Pascal arrived there. **put u tʔe swe epł ck̓ʷłčicš** – Somebody has just arrived. **t spisteṁ u kʷ eł ck̓ʷłčicš** – When did you get back?

nčcnus – arrive at the start of a time period, the beginning of an action, or the edge of a place. *rt.:* ***čic*** *– happen upon.*
nčcnus – S/he/it arrived at the start. **čn nčcnus, kʷ nčcnus**
es nčcnusi – S/he/it is arriving at the start. **čnes nčcnusi, kʷes nčcnusi**
qs nčcnusi – S/he/it is going to arrive at the start. **čiqs nčcnusi, kʷqs nčcnusi**

nčcnusis – S/he/it arrived at the beginning of s.t. **nčcnusn, nčcnusntxʷ**
es nčcnusms – S/he/it is arriving at the beginning of s.t. **ies nčcnusm, as nčcnusm**
qs nčcnusms – S/he/it is going to arrive at the beginning of s.t. **iqs nčcnusm, aqs nčcnusm**

npx̣̌mus – come to the end of a time period, an action, or a place; reach the full extent. *See:* ***end.***

iap – arrive/gather.
iáʔap – They arrived/gathered there. **qeʔ iap, p iap**
es iáʔapmi – They are gathering there. **qeʔes iapmi, pes iapmi**
qs iáʔapmi – They are going to gather there. **qeʔqs iapmi, pqs iapmi**

ciáʔap – They arrived/gathered here. **qeʔ ciap, p ciap**
es ciáʔapmi – They are gathering here. **qeʔes ciapmi, pes ciapmi**
qs ciáʔapmi – They are going to gather here. **qeʔqs ciapmi, pqs ciapmi**

niáʔap – They arrived/gathered in there. **qeʔ niap, p niap**
es niáʔapmi – They are gathering in there. **qeʔes niapmi, pes niapmi**
qs niáʔapmi – They are going to gather in there. **qeʔqs niapmi, pqs niapmi**

t pisteṁ u p eł ciap – When did you all get back?

qaqlt – arrive at the top. *See:* ***top.***

arrogant

q̓exʷmscut – show-off; snobby; arrogant; self admiring. *See:* ***show-off.***

nxʷtxʷtcin – arrogant talk; talk provoking anger.
es nxʷtxʷtcini – S/he speaks with arrogance. **čnes nxʷtxʷtcini, kʷes nxʷtxʷtcini**

arrow

ṫapmin – arrow. *rt.:* ***ṫap*** *– shoot; suffix:* ***...min, ...mn*** *– instrument/tool.*

arrowhead

snululmusl, *snululmu* – metal arrowhead.

snčlelstn – flint/stone arrowhead. *rt.:* ***čil*** *– upright protrusion.*

sncmalstn – bone arrowhead.

arrowleaf

sqáqʷocn – arrowleaf; wapato; water potato; *Sagittaria latifolia.*

arrowleaf basalmroot

táqʷu – sunflower root.

The **i** following uvular consonants (UC) and the glottal stop **ʔ** sound like English "*ey*" as in the words *they, hey, whey,* etc. Salish UC are: **q, q̓, qʷ, q̓ʷ, x̣, x̣ʷ**. For example, the suffix **...qin** – head/top, is often spelled using English *ey* as "q*ey*n". So **qi, q̓i, qʷi, q̓ʷi, x̣i, x̣ʷi,** may be spelled with English *ey* as **q***ey*, **q̓***ey*, **qʷ***ey*, **q̓ʷ***ey*, **x̣***ey*, **x̣ʷ***ey* in other texts.

---

s.t. - something, the 3rd person
(s.t.) - something implied
s.o. - someone, the 3rd person
sl. - singular form
pl. - plural form
rt. - root word
cmd. - command
lit. - literally
fig. - figuratively
i.e., - for example
See: - Redirection to a related word.

arthritic **sċaċalsċom –** aching bones, sore bones. *rt.: **ċaál –** ache.*

ashamed **ċˀeš –** ashamed.

ċˀeš – S/he/it was ashamed. **čn ċˀeš, kʷ ċˀeš**
es ċˀešmi – S/he/it is ashamed. **čnes ċˀešmi, kʷes ċˀešmi**
qs ċˀešmi – S/he/it is going to be ashamed. **čiqs ċˀešmi, kʷqs ċˀešmi**
ċˀéˀeš – They were ashamed. **qeˀ ċˀeš, p ċˀeš**
es ċˀešmíˀi – They are ashamed. **qeˀes ċˀešmi, pes ċˀešmi**

ċˀešmis – S/he/it got ashamed of s.t./s.o. **ċˀešmin, ċˀešmintxʷ**
es ċˀešminms – S/he/it is ashamed of s.t./s.o. **ies ċˀešminm, as ċˀešminm**
qs ċˀešminms – S/he/it is going to be ashamed of s.t./s.o. **iqs ċˀešminm, aqs ċˀešminm**
ċˀešmíˀis – They got ashamed of s.t./s.o. **qeˀ ċˀešmintm, ċˀešmintp**

ċˀešstes – S/he/it caused s.o. to be ashamed. **ċˀešsten, ċˀešstexʷ**
es ċˀešims – S/he/it is making s.o. be ashamed. **ies ċˀešim, as ċˀešim**
qs ċˀešims – S/he/it is going to make s.o. be ashamed. **iqs ċˀešim, aqs ċˀešim**

es ċeċˀešmíˀi – Each one is ashamed. **qeˀes ċeċˀešmi, pes ċeċˀešmi**

nċeštin – shame.
ċeˀšémn – one inclined to be ashamed. *suffix: **...emn –** one inclined to do.*
ċešċšt – shameful.
čċeˀšepleˀ – embarrassed. *See: **embarrassed.***

ṅem ċˀeš – S/he/it will get ashamed. **ṅem čn ċˀeš, ṅem kʷ ċˀeš**
ṅem ċˀéˀeš – They will get shamed. **ṅem qeˀ ċˀeš, ṅem p ċˀeš**

qʷo es ċˀešmiłtms incitxʷ – He's ashamed of my house. **ha kʷes ċˀešmi kʷqs wenš –** Are you ashamed to dance? **ha kʷes ċˀeš kʷqs ntx̣ʷmsqá –** Aren't you ashamed to drive? **ta kʷ qes ċˀešminm –** Do not be ashamed. **ta qes ċˀešmistxʷ łu annuwewlštn –** Do not be ashamed of your language. **ta kʷ qes ċˀeš m kʷ qʷlqʷe –** Do not be ashamed when you talk. **qʷo es ċˀešmiłtms inṗiṗuyšn –** He is ashamed of my car. **ta epł nċeštin –** S/he has no shame.

ashes **ċáx̣ʷċx̣ʷt,** *ċáx̣ʷ* **–** powdery ashes.

qʷli – turned to charcoal/ashes.
qʷlil – It got turned to charcoal.
qʷllmi – It is turning to charcoal.

qʷlmin – ash chunks; charcoal. *(used as a teething medicine)*

nqʷlil – It fell in the charcoal.
čqʷlilċeˀ – It got covered in charcoal.

ashtray **snx̣ʷelmn l ċax̣ʷċx̣ʷt –** ashtray.
čmenxʷtn snx̣ʷelmn – ashtray.

aside **k̓ʷlčlim –** separate from the main source/bulk/group and put aside. *See: **separate.***

ask **séw –** ask; seek information.

sewm – S/he/it asked. **čn sewm, kʷ sewm**
es sewi – S/he/it is asking. **čnes sewi, kʷes sewi**
qs sewi – S/he/it is going to ask. **čiqs sewi, kʷqs sewi**
séˀewm – They asked. **qeˀ sewm, p sewm**
es séˀewi – They are asking. **qeˀes sewi, pes sewi**

sewis – S/he/it asked s.o. **sewn, sewntxʷ**
es sewms – S/he/it is asking s.o. **ies sewm, as sewm**
qs sewms – S/he/it is going to ask s.o. **iqs sewm, aqs sewm**

čsewis – S/he/it asked about s.t. **čsewn, čsewntxʷ**
es čsewms – S/he/it is asking about s.t. **ies čsewm, as čsewm**
qs čsewms – S/he/it is going to ask about s.t. **iqs čsewm, aqs čsewm**

k̇ʷłsewis – S/he/it secretly asked about s.t./s.o. **k̇ʷłsewn, k̇ʷłsewntxʷ**
es k̇ʷłsewms – S/he/it is secretly asking about s.t./s.o. **ies k̇ʷłsewm, as k̇ʷłsewm**
qs k̇ʷłsewms – S/he/it is secretly going to ask about s.t./s.o. **iqs k̇ʷłsewm, aqs k̇ʷłsewm**

sewšts – S/he/it asked on behalf of s.o. **sewštn, sewštxʷ**
es sewštms – S/he/it is asking on behalf of s.o. **ies sewštm, as sewštm**
qs sewštms – S/he/it is going to ask on behalf of s.o. **iqs sewštm, aqs sewštm**

The **i** following uvular consonants (UC) and the glottal stop **ʔ** sound like English "*ey*" as in the words th*ey*, h*ey*, wh*ey*, etc. Salish UC are: **q, q̇, qʷ, q̇ʷ, x̣, x̣ʷ**. For example, the suffix …**qin** – head/top, is often spelled using English *ey* as "q*ey*n". So **qi, q̇i, qʷi, q̇ʷi, x̣i, x̣ʷi**, may be spelled with English *ey* as **q***ey*, **q̇***ey*, **qʷ***ey*, **q̇ʷ***ey*, **x̣***ey*, **x̣ʷ***ey* in other texts.

scsew – something that has been asked.
sxʷsewm – one tasked to inquire. *prefix:* ***sxʷ…** – one tasked to do.*
susułmuł – one that habitually asks questions. *suffix:* ***…łmuł** – one that habitually does.*
susucnemn – one inclined to ask questions. *suffix:* ***…emn** – one inclined to do.*

sewiš – Ask. *cmd.*
sewnt – Ask him/her/it. *cmd.*
seseẇeʔ – little questioner, affectionately.
sunwexʷ – ask each other questions.
k̇ʷłsew – ask about someone when not present. *prefix:* ***k̇ʷł…** – under.*
čsewpleʔ – ask permission; ask about someone. *See:* ***permission**.*
sułtumš – inquire; ask people; ask at large. *See:* ***inquire**.*
nsumels – want to question; want to ask. *See:* ***question**.*
sumlwism – ask around; interrogate. *See:* ***interrogate**.*
nsewpm – ask someone to repay their debt *(as a last resort the debtor has not paid and the lender has waited long enough). See:* ***debt**.*
nsucnmist – propose marriage to someone; ask permission to marry. *See:* ***propose**.*

ṅem qs sewms – S/he/it will be asking her/him/it. **ṅem iqs sewm, ṅem aqs sewm**
ṅem qs séʔewms – They are going to ask her/him/it. **ṅem qeʔ qs sewm, ṅem qs sewmp**
qʷo séwis – S/he asked me. **sewnt asłax̣t eċščéṅ –** Ask your friend how s/he/it is.

čutmist – ask for help/prayers. *rt.:* ***čaw** – pray.*
čutmist – S/he/it asked for help. **čn čutmist, kʷ čutmist**
es čutmisti – S/he/it is asking for help. **ies čutmisti, as čutmisti**
qs čutmisti – S/he/it is going to be asking for help. **iqs čutmisti, aqs čutmisti**

čutmistmis – S/he/it asked s.o. for help. **čutmistmn, čutmistmntxʷ**
es čutmistms – S/he/it is asking s.o. for help. **ies čutmistm, as čutmistm**
qs čutmistms – S/he/it is going to ask s.o. for help. **iqs čutmistm, aqs čutmistm**

s.t. - something, the 3rd person
(s.t.) - something implied
s.o. - someone, the 3rd person
sl. - singular form
pl. - plural form
rt. - root word
cmd. - command
lit. - literally
fig. - figuratively
i.e., - for example
See: - Redirection to a related word.

čomistm – ask for something/guidance. *rt.:* ***čaw** – pray.*
čomist – S/he asked s.o. for s.t. **čn čomist, kʷ čomist**
es čomistms – S/he is asking s.o. for s.t. **ies čomistms, as čomistms**
qs čomistms – S/he is going to ask s.o. for s.t. **iqs čomistms, aqs čomistms**

kʷ iqs čomistm – I am asking you for s.t.

nʔawqnm – call upon/ask for someone; challenge/encourage someone; beseech; exhort. *See:* ***call**.*

x̣lit – call for; holler for; beckon. *See:* ***call.***

asleep

itš – sleep. *See:* ***sleep.***

čsulšn – foot "fell asleep," went numb. *rt.:* ***sult*** *– freeze.*
čsulčst – hand "fell asleep," went numb. *rt.:* ***sult*** *– freeze; suffix:* ***...ečst, ...čst*** *– of the hand.*
čsolx̣n – arm "fell asleep," went numb. *rt.:* ***sult*** *– freeze.*

tmłʔenwen – have no feeling. *See:* ***feel.***

aspen

mĺmĺtéłp, *mĺmĺté* – quaking aspen; *Populus tremuloides.*

Assiniboine

nxʷustaptneʔ, *nx̣ʷusta* – Assiniboine.

ate

iłn – S/he/it ate. *See:* ***eat.***

atop

čłqeẇs, *čłqe* – on top of. *See:* ***top.***

qaqlt – arrive at the top. *See:* ***top.***

nwist – up; above; up high. *See:* ***high.***

attach

čołip – become attached to something to form one whole. *(i.e., someone affectionate to their significant other, etc.) rt.:* ***oył*** *– one piece, whole.*
čołip – S/he/it got attached. **čn čołip, kʷ čołip**
es čołpmi – S/he/it is attached. **čnes čołpmi, kʷes čołpmi**
qs čołpmi – S/he/it is going to be attached. **čiqs čołpmi, kʷqs čołpmi**

oył – one piece; whole; no holes/breaks/tears. *See:* ***one.***

attack

čxʷicut – more than one charges toward; attack; rush to; run toward. *See:* ***charge.***

attempt

k̓ʷn̓šmist – attempt; make a personal attempt.
k̓ʷn̓šmist – S/he attempted. **čn k̓ʷn̓šmist, kʷ k̓ʷn̓šmist**
es k̓ʷn̓šmisti – S/he is attempting. **čnes k̓ʷn̓šmisti, kʷes k̓ʷn̓šmisti**
qs k̓ʷn̓šmisti – S/he is going to attempt. **čiqs k̓ʷn̓šmisti, kʷqs k̓ʷn̓šmisti**

k̓ʷén̓ – try; sample; attempt; show out; make attention to. *See:* ***try.***

attention

tqĺsečst – gesture with the hand for somebody's attention; sign. *See:* ***gesture.***

attic

snwistełxʷ – basement. *rt.:* ***nwist*** *– up, up high; suffix:* ***...etxʷ, ...łxʷ*** *– house.*

attorney

sxʷqʷlqʷelt, *sxʷqʷlqʷe* – attorney; someone tasked to talk; speaker. *rt.:* ***qʷlqʷelt*** *– talk/speak; prefix:* ***sxʷ...*** *– one tasked to do.*

attract

es k̓ʷeʔnmmi – attracting; get somebody's attention. **sništełxʷ** – basement. *rt.:* ***išut*** *– down, low; suffix:* ***...etxʷ, ...łxʷ*** *– house.*

auction

čwewéʔm – auction. *rt.:* ***weʔm*** *– yell, holler.*
es čwewéʔm – S/he is calling out; auctioning.

auctioneer

sxʷčweweʔm – someone tasked to call out; auctioneer. *rt.:* ***weʔm*** *– yell, holler; prefix:* ***sxʷ...*** *– one tasked to do. See:* ***holler.***

August

sťšá spq̓niʔ – August *(month of the huckleberry).*

uyust – August *(a man's name).*

aunt **sk̓ʷúk̓ʷiʔ** – paternal aunt of a male *(father's sister)*; woman's nephew *(brother's son)*.
tetíkʷeʔ, *tikʷɬ* – paternal aunt of a female *(father's sister)*; woman's niece *(brother's daughter)*.
qáx̣eʔ – maternal aunt *(mother's sister)*; woman's nephew/niece *(sister's children)*.

ɬwéstn – aunt or uncle after death of connecting relative; stepparent.
sɬwélt – aunt or uncle after death of connecting relative.

automobile **p̓ip̓uyšn** – automobile; car. *lit. wrinkled feet. rt.: **p̓uy** – wrinkle; suffix: **...šn** – foot. See: **car**.*

avalanche **sṅillii** – avalanche.

avenge **éyčst** – revenge; got even; avenge wrongs done. *See: **revenge**.*

awake **xʷus** – wide awake, open-eyed.
xʷusmist – S/he/it stayed awake. **čn xʷusmist, čn xʷusmist**
es xʷusmisti – S/he/it is staying awake. **čnes xʷusmisti, kʷes xʷusmisti**
qs xʷusmisti – S/he/it is going to stay awake. **čiqs xʷusmisti, kʷqs xʷusmisti**

xʷustes – S/he/it kept s.o. wide awake. **xʷusten, xʷustexʷ**
es xʷusms – S/he/it is keeping s.o. wide awake. **ies xʷusm, as xʷusm**
qs xʷusms – S/he/it is going to keep s.o. wide awake. **iqs xʷusm, aqs xʷusm**

xʷusmis – S/he/it used s.t. to be wide awake. **xʷusmin, xʷusmintxʷ**
es xʷusminms – S/he/it is using s.t. to be wide awake. **ies xʷusminm, as xʷusminm**
qs xʷusminms – S/he/it is going to use s.t. to be wide awake. **iqs xʷusminm, aqs xʷusminm**

čxʷusmis – The thoughts of s.t. kept him/her wide awake. **čxʷusmin, čxʷusmintxʷ**
es čxʷusminms – The thoughts of s.t. are keeping him/her wide awake. **ies čxʷusminm, as xʷusminm**
qs čxʷusminms – The thoughts of s.t. are going to keep him/her wide awake. **iqs čxʷusminm, aqs čxʷusminm**

i xʷus – S/he is wide awake. **i čn xʷus, i kʷ xʷus**
xʷuus – S/he became wide awake. **čn xʷuus, kʷ xʷuus**

sxʷus – insomnia; being wide awake.
čxʷusmin – The thing thought about that keeps one awake.
xʷusxʷst – alert; energetic; wide awake.

xʷusiš – Be awake. *cmd.*
xʷusint – Make him/her be awake. *cmd.*

čɬxʷsneʔ – intentionally make someone sleeping wide awake; disturb someone's sleep.
čɬxʷsnʔeis – S/he made s.o. wide awake. **čɬxʷsnʔen, čɬxʷsnʔentxʷ**
es čɬxʷsnʔems – S/he is making s.o. wide awake. **ies čɬxʷsnʔem, as čɬxʷsnʔem**
qs čɬxʷsnʔems – S/he is going to make s.o. wide awake. **iqs čɬxʷsnʔem, aqs čɬxʷsnʔem**

qiɬt – wake up. *See: **wake**.*

čɬheʔenʔem – bother someone who is sleeping. *See: **wake**.*

peš – spry; lively; quick; alert; moves fast.
es pešpšcni – S/he/it is being lively. **čnes pešpšcni, kʷes pešpšcni**
qs pešpšcni – S/he/it is going to be lively. **čiqs pešpšcni, kʷqs pešpšcni**

The **i** following uvular consonants (UC) and the glottal stop **ʔ** sound like English "*ey*" as in the words *they, hey, whey*, etc. Salish UC are: **q, q̓, qʷ, q̓ʷ, x̣, x̣ʷ**. For example, the suffix **...qin** – head/top, is often spelled using English *ey* as "q*ey*n". So **qi, q̓i, qʷi, q̓ʷi, x̣i, x̣ʷi**, may be spelled with English *ey* as **q***ey*, **q̓***ey*, **qʷ***ey*, **q̓ʷ***ey*, **x̣***ey*, **x̣ʷ***ey* in other texts.

s.t. - something, the 3rd person
(s.t.) - something implied
s.o. - someone, the 3rd person
sl. - singular form
pl. - plural form
rt. - root word
cmd. - command
lit. - literally
fig. - figuratively
i.e., - for example
See: - Redirection to a related word.

i peš – S/he/it is alert/quick. **i čn peš, i kʷ peš**

pešpšcnemn – one inclined to be spry. *suffix: **...emn** – one inclined to do.*
pešpšt – active; nimble.

sčmċmaċs – have gummy eyes. *circumfix: **č...us** – spherical object; eyes.*
kʷ sčmċmaċs – You have gummed eyes; you are not really awake yet.

aware **miscut** – aware; conscious; know about one's self.
miscut – S/he was aware. **čn miscut, kʷ miscut**
es miscuti – S/he is aware. **čnes miscuti, kʷes miscuti**
qs miscuti – S/he is going to be aware. **čiqs miscuti, kʷqs miscuti**

miscutn – the knower of one's self.

enwenm – feel/sense. *See: **feel.***

away **čuw** – gone; away; absent. *See: **gone.***

lkʷut – S/he/it is far away. *See: **far.***

awe **čhomist,** *čho* – in awe of something or someone; overwhelmed; see something beautiful/good/wonderful.
čhomist – S/he was awed. **čn čhomist, kʷ čhomist**
es čhomisti – S/he is in awe. **čnes čhomisti, kʷes čhomisti**
qs čhomisti – S/he is going to be in awe. **čiqs čhomisti, kʷqs čhomisti**
es čhóˀomisti – They are in awe. **qeˀes čhomisti, pes čhomisti**

čhomistmis – S/he was awed by it. **čhomistmn, čhomistmtxʷ**
es čhomistms – S/he is in awe of it. **ies čhomistm, as čhomistm**
qs čhomisti – S/he is going to be in awe. **iqs čhomistm, aqs čhomistm**
čhóˀomistmis – They were awed by it. **qeˀ čhomistmntm, p čhomistmntp**

es čhohomisti – S/he is repeatedly in awe. **čnes čhohomisti, kʷes čhohomisti**

čhomistemn – one inclined to be in awe. *suffix: **...emn** – one inclined to do.*

héˀemist – restrain one's self; reserved; in awe of. *See: **reserved.***

awl **ƛ̓qʷomn** – awl.

axe **šlmin** – axe. *rt.: **šil** – chop; suffix: **...min, ...mn** – instrument/tool.*
łšl̓min – hatchet.

B

baby **łox̣ʷtél̓t,** *łox̣ʷté* – baby.
łox̣ʷtél̓ts – her/his baby.

scel̓t – newborn baby. *rt.:* ***sic*** *– new.*

snk̓ʷłˀox̣ʷelt – playpen; baby corral.

baby board **mx̣ʷol** – baby board; cradle board.

baby sack **sqq̇ttew̓s,** *sqq̇tte* – baby sack; baby wrap. *suffix:* ***...éw̓s*** *– in between, middle.*

snyew̓smn – baby sack.

mx̣ʷol – baby board, cradle board.

babysit **čšťel̓t** – watch over children; babysit. *rt.:* ***čšťim*** *– guard; suffix:* ***...el̓t, ...l̓t*** *– child, baby.*
čšťel̓t – S/he babysat. **čn čšťel̓t, kʷ čšťel̓t**
es čšťel̓ti – S/he is babysitting. **čnes čšťel̓ti, kʷes čšťel̓ti**
qs čšťel̓ti – S/he is going to babysit. **čiqs čšťel̓ti, kʷqs čšťel̓ti**
čšťéˀel̓t – They babysat. **qeˀ čšťel̓t, p čšťel̓t**
es čšťéˀel̓ti – They are babysitting. **qeˀes čšťel̓ti, pes čšťel̓ti**
qs čšťéˀel̓ti – They are going to babysit. **qeˀqs čšťel̓ti, pqs čšťel̓ti**

čšťel̓tis – S/he babysat s.o. **čšťel̓tn, čšťel̓tntxʷ**
es čšťel̓tms – S/he is babysitting s.o. **ies čšťel̓tm, as čšťel̓tm**
qs čšťel̓tms – S/he is going to babysit s.o. **iqs čšťel̓tm, aqs čšťel̓tm**
čšťéˀel̓tis – They babysat s.o. **qeˀ čšťel̓tntm, p čšťel̓tntp**
es čšťéˀel̓tms – They are babysitting s.o. **qeˀes čšťel̓tm, es čšťel̓tmp**
qs čšťéˀel̓tms – They are going to babysit s.o. **qeˀqs čšťel̓tm, qs čšťel̓tmp**

sxʷčšťel̓tm – one tasked to take care of children; babysitter. *prefix:* ***sxʷ...*** *– one tasked to do.*

ha kʷṅe u kʷ čšťel̓t – Would you babysit? **ha ṅem kʷ čšťel̓t** – Will you babysit?
ha kʷes čšťel̓ti – Are you babysitting? **ha kʷqs čšťel̓ti ṅe člux̣ʷ** – Are you going to babysit this evening?

babysitter **sxʷčšťel̓tm,** *sxʷčšťel̓t* – one tasked to take care of children; babysitter. *rt.:* ***čšťim*** *– guard; prefix:* ***sxʷ...*** *– one tasked to do.*

back **snčmičṅ** – back. *rt.:* ***čm*** *– extremity; suffix:* ***...ičṅ*** *– back.*
sčmṁelixʷ – whole back. *rt.:* ***čm*** *– extremity.*
snčmusičṅ – lower back; waist.
sčmew̓s – one side of an object; waist. *rt.:* ***čm*** *– extremity; suffix:* ***...éw̓s*** *– in between, middle.*
ásx̣ṁ – backbone.
snťx̣ʷičṅ – spine.

s.t. - something, the 3rd person
(s.t.) - something implied
s.o. - someone, the 3rd person
sl. - singular form
pl. - plural form
rt. - root word
cmd. - command
lit. - literally
fig. - figuratively
i.e., - for example
See: - Redirection to a related word.

sxʷƛ̓elnčst – shoulder blade.

swe łu l asnčmičn̓ – Who is behind you?

...ičn̓ – suffix indicating the back or ridge.
snt̓x̣ʷičn̓ – spine. *suffix: **...ičn̓** – back.*
es nkʷlkʷl̓čičn̓ – It has a hard back. *suffix: **...ičn̓** – back.*
nk̓ʷlk̓ʷl̓čičn̓, *nk̓ʷlk̓ʷl̓či* – beetle. *rt.: **k̓ʷelč** – cover w/ formed object; suffix: **...ičn̓** – back.*

nmlčičn̓ – turn one's back in anger to someone. *See: **turn**.*
nmnčim – turn one's back to someone or something. *See: **turn**.*
cqql̓ičn̓ – fall on your back.

eł – back; again; once more.
čn eł itš – I went back to sleep. **čn eł es itši** – I am going back to sleep. **i eł es kʷupm** – I am pushing s.o. again. **čn eł xʷuy č nłq̓a** – I went back to Arlee. **eł cʔukʷn** – I brought it back here. **n̓e eł cwis íʔim̓š tl̓ čłčéwm m qeʔ wenš** – When they finish moving back here from the plains, we'll war dance.

eł t – back to another; in succession to another.
eł t qʷoyʔe – It's my turn; back to me.
eł t anwi – It's your turn; back to you.

backache

nc̓aličn̓ – have an aching back; backache. *rt.: **c̓aál** – ache; suffix: **...ičn̓** – back.*
nc̓aličn̓ – S/he had a backache. **čn nc̓aličn̓, kʷ nc̓aličn̓**
es nc̓aličn̓i – S/he has a backache. **čnes nc̓aličn̓i, kʷes nc̓aličn̓i**
qs nc̓aličn̓i – S/he is going to have a backache. **čiqs nc̓aličn̓i, kʷqs nc̓aličn̓i**

backbone

ásx̣m̓ – backbone.
snt̓x̣ʷičn̓ – spine. *rt.: **tox̣ʷ** – straight; suffix: **...ičn̓** – back.*

skʷlqin – backbone marrow.

sqʷl̓a – inside backbone.

backpack

snq̓ʷéłtn – backpack. *See: **pack**.*

back up

nwéw̓pm – move backward in/on something. *(i.e., in a car, on a bike, etc.)*
nwew̓pm – S/he/it backed up. **čn nwew̓pm, kʷ nwew̓pm**
es nwéw̓pi – S/he/it is backing up. **ies nwéw̓pi, as nwéw̓pi**
qs nwéw̓pms – S/he/it is going to back up. **iqs nwéw̓pi, aqs nwéw̓pi**
nwéʔew̓pm – They backed up. **qeʔ nwew̓pm, p nwew̓pm**
es nwéʔew̓pi – They are backing up. **qeʔes nwéw̓pi, pes nwéw̓pi**
qs nwéʔew̓pi – They are going to back up. **qeʔqs nwéw̓pi, pqs nwéw̓pi**

nwew̓pis – S/he/it backed s.o./s.t. up. **nwew̓pn, nwew̓pntxʷ**
es nwéw̓pms – S/he/it is backing s.o./s.t. up. **ies nwéw̓pm, as nwéw̓pm**
qs nwéw̓pms – S/he/it is going to back s.o./s.t. up. **iqs nwéw̓pm, aqs nwéw̓pm**
nwéʔew̓pis – They backed s.o./s.t. up. **qeʔ nwew̓pntm, nwew̓pntp**
es nwéʔew̓pms – They are backing s.o./s.t. up. **qeʔes nwéw̓pm, es nwéw̓pmp**
qs nwéʔew̓pms – They are going to back s.o./s.t. up. **qeʔqs nwéw̓pm, qs nwéw̓pmp**

nwew̓psts – S/he/it caused s.o./s.t. to back up. **nwew̓pstn, nwew̓pstxʷ**
es nwew̓psts – S/he/it is causing s.o./s.t. to back up. **es nwew̓pstn, es nwew̓pstxʷ**

nwew̓pmis – S/he/it backed out from s.t. **nwew̓pmn, nwew̓pmntxʷ**
es nwéw̓pmms – S/he/it is backing out from s.t. **ies nwéw̓pmm, as nwéw̓pmm**

qs nwéẃpmms – S/he/it is going to back out from s.t. **iqs nwéẃpmm, aqs nwéẃpmm**

nwéẃpiš – Back up. *cmd.*
nwéẃpwi – All of you back up. *cmd.*
nweẃpnt – Back s.o./s.t. up. *cmd.*
nweẃpmnt – Back out from it. *cmd.*
nweẃpskʷ – Make s.o./s.t. back up. *cmd.*

eł nwéʔeẃpm – They backed up again.

nupmupsm, *nupmu* – back up; go backward. *circumfix: **n...ups** – butt, tail.*
nupmupsm – S/he/it went backward. **čn nupmupsm, kʷ nupmupsm**
es nupmupsi – S/he/it is going backward. **čnes nupmupsi, kʷes nupmupsi**
qs nupmúʔupsi – S/he/it is going to go backward. **čiqs nupmupsi, kʷqs nupmupsi**
nupmúʔupsm – They went backward. **qeʔ nupmupsm, p nupmupsm**
es nupmúʔupsi – They are going backward. **qeʔes nupmupsi, pes nupmupsi**
qs nupmúʔupsi – They are going to go backward. **qeʔqs nupmupsi, pqs nupmupsi**

nupmupsis – S/he/it backed s.o. up. **čn nupmupsn, kʷ nupmupsntxʷ**
es nupmupsms – S/he/it is backing s.o. up. **čnes nupmupsm, kʷes nupmupsm**
qs nupmúʔupsi – S/he/it is going to back s.o. up. **čiqs nupmupsm, kʷqs nupmupsm**
nupmúʔupsis – They backed s.o. up. **qeʔ nupmupsntm, nupmupsntp**
es nupmúʔupsms – They are backing s.o. up. **qeʔes nupmupsm, es nupmupsmp**
qs nupmúʔupsms – They're going to back s.o. up. **qeʔqs nupmupsm, qs nupmupsmp**

nupmupsiš – Back up. *cmd.*
nupmupswi – All of you back up. *cmd.*
nupmupsnt – Back s.o. up. *cmd.*

The **i** following uvular consonants (UC) and the glottal stop ʔ sound like English "*ey*" as in the words th*ey*, h*ey*, wh*ey*, etc. Salish UC are: **q**, **q̇**, **qʷ**, **q̇ʷ**, **x̣**, **x̣ʷ**. For example, the suffix ...**qin** – head/top, is often spelled using English *ey* as "q*ey*n". So **qi**, **q̇i**, **qʷi**, **q̇ʷi**, **x̣i**, **x̣ʷi**, may be spelled with English *ey* as **q***ey*, **q̇***ey*, **qʷ***ey*, **q̇ʷ***ey*, **x̣***ey*, **x̣ʷ***ey* in other texts.

backward

k̓ʷłpusncut, *k̓ʷłpusncu* – self-conscious; backward; shy; bashful; polite; considerate; does not impose. *See: **self-conscious.***

ta kʷ qes k̓ʷłpusncut – Do not be backward.

np̓l̓čsalqs – have a shirt/coat on backwards. *rt.: **p̓l̓ič** – turn over/around; suffix: **...lqs, ...alqs** – clothes.*
es np̓l̓čsalqs – His/her shirt is on backwards. **čnes np̓l̓čsalqs, kʷes np̓l̓čsalqs**

ta kʷ qes np̓l̓čsalqsm – Do not put your shirt on backwards.

čp̓l̓p̓l̓čšin – have shoes on backwards. *rt.: **p̓l̓ič** – turn over/around; suffix: **...šin, ...šn** – feet.*
es čp̓l̓p̓l̓čšin – His/her shoes are on backwards. **čnes čp̓l̓p̓l̓čšin, kʷes čp̓l̓p̓l̓čšin**

ta kʷ qes čp̓l̓p̓l̓čšin – Do not put your shoes on backwards.

np̓l̓čmups – have pants on backwards. *rt.: **p̓l̓ič** – turn over/around; circumfix: **n...ups** – butt, tail.*
es np̓l̓čmups – His/her pants are on backwards. **čnes np̓l̓čmups, kʷes np̓l̓čmups**

ta kʷ qes np̓l̓čmups – Do not put your pants on backwards.

s.t. - something, the 3rd person
(s.t.) - something implied
s.o. - someone, the 3rd person
sl. - singular form
pl. - plural form
rt. - root word
cmd. - command
lit. - literally
fig. - figuratively
i.e., - for example
See: - Redirection to a related word.

backwoods

nkʷéct, *nkʷé* – forest; backwoods; brush; thicket.

es t̓émp – bush.

bacon

lkʷošó – pig, bacon, pork, ham. *(approximation to French word)*

bad **t̓éyeʔ**, *t̓e* – bad; evil; mean. *See: **evil.***
  t̓e sx̣lx̣alt – bad day.

  čn t̓éyeʔ – I am mean, evil, bad. **ma še we cuncn epł t̓it̓éẏe sm̓t̓ṁa** – See, I told you there are a lot of mean cows.

č̇s... – *prefix indicating bad, ugly.*
  č̇sáłq – stink. *suffix: **...ałq** – smell, accompaniment.*
  č̇sus – ugly/bad face. *suffix: **...us** – face, fire.*
  č̇salqs – bad shirt. *suffix: **...lqs, ...alqs** – clothes.*
  č̇sasq̇t – bad day. *suffix: **...asq̇t** – sky, day.*
  tam kʷ ies č̇scinm – I am not saying anything bad about you. *See: **talk.***

nč̇seẇs – put bad in the middle; put bad amongst; put bad in between.
  nč̇seẇsis – S/he put bad in the middle s.t. **nč̇seẇsn, nč̇seẇsntxʷ**

čsč̇smscut – do something bad of one's self. *suffix: **...cut** – action to the self.*
  čsč̇smscut – S/he/it did s.t. bad. **čn čsč̇smscut, kʷ čsč̇smscut**
  es čsč̇smscuti – S/he/it is doing s.t. bad. **čnes čsč̇smscuti, kʷes čsč̇smscuti**
  qs čsč̇smscuti – S/he/it is going to do s.t. bad. **čiqs čsč̇smscuti, kʷqs čsč̇smscuti**
  čsč̇smscúʔut – They did s.t. bad. **qeʔ čsč̇smscut, p čsč̇smscut**
  es čsč̇smscúʔuti – They are doing s.t. bad. **qeʔes čsč̇smscuti, pes čsč̇smscuti**
  qs čsč̇smscúʔuti – They are going to do s.t. bad. **qeʔqs čsč̇smscuti, pqs čsč̇smscuti**

  čsč̇snuxʷ – worthy of being bad.

kʷuskʷst – ugly; scary looking. *See: **ugly.***

mtmitt, *mtmi* – no-good. *See: **no-good.***
  mtmi smx̣e – It is a no-good grizzly.

nʔaymls – have bad feelings; have inner anger. *See: **detest.***

badger **six̣ʷix̣ʷo** – badger; *Taxidea taxus.*

bag **čk̇ʷxʷépleʔ**, *čk̇ʷxʷé* – bag with a handle. *suffix: **...epleʔ** – permanence.*

q̇éċ – woven sack/bag. *See: **weave.***

čq̇ʔiċéʔ, *čq̇ʔi* – Indian suitcase, rawhide bag. *lit. it has a pattern around it. See: **pattern.***

ax̣éṅeʔ – beaded bag/handbag. *rt.: **i ax̣** – it has lines. See: **line.***
  łax̣éṅeʔ – small beaded bag/handbag.

čt̓k̇ʷłċełniut, *čt̓k̇ʷłċe* – something on the side to put stuff in; pouch on a belt. *See: **side.***

qq̇epeʔ – cornhusk bag.

bagel **suyápi snċax̣lexʷ** – bagel. *lit. Whiteman frybread.*

bait **čt̓kʷqnéyeʔ**, *čt̓kʷqné* – bait for fishing.

łqq̇méyeʔtn – bait for fishing. *rt.: **qq̇méyeʔ** – fish; prefix: **ł...** – little; suffix: **...tin, ...tn** – means of/device.*

ṁul̓e – bait.

bake **scnlóʔ** – something put in the oven. *rt.: **nlo** – put inside; prefix: **sc...** – s.t. that's been done/made/prepared.*

qʷl̓ep – bake underground; pit bake.

qʷl̓epm – S/he pit baked. **čn qʷl̓epm, kʷ qʷl̓epm**
es qʷl̓epi – S/he is pit baking. **čnes qʷl̓epi, kʷes qʷl̓epi**
qs qʷl̓epi – S/he is going to pit bake. **čiqs qʷl̓epi, kʷqs qʷl̓epi**
qʷl̓éʔepm – They pit baked. **qeʔ qʷl̓epm, p qʷl̓epm**
es qʷl̓éʔepi – They are pit baking. **qeʔes qʷl̓epi, pes qʷl̓epi**
qs qʷl̓éʔepi – They are going to pit bake. **qeʔqs qʷl̓epi, pqs qʷl̓epi**

> The **i** following uvular consonants (UC) and the glottal stop **ʔ** sound like English "*ey*" as in the words th*ey*, h*ey*, wh*ey*, etc. Salish UC are: **q, q̓, qʷ, q̓ʷ, x̣, x̣ʷ**. For example, the suffix ...**qin** – head/top, is often spelled using English *ey* as "q*ey*n". So **qi, q̓i, qʷi, q̓ʷi, x̣i, x̣ʷi**, may be spelled with English *ey* as **q***ey*, **q̓***ey*, **qʷ***ey*, **q̓ʷ***ey*, **x̣***ey*, **x̣ʷ***ey* in other texts.

qʷl̓epis – S/he pit baked s.t. **qʷl̓epn, qʷl̓epntxʷ**
es qʷl̓epms – S/he is pit baking s.t. **ies qʷl̓epm, as qʷl̓epm**
qs qʷl̓epms – S/he is going to pit bake s.t. **iqs qʷl̓epm, aqs qʷl̓epm**
qʷl̓éʔepis – They pit baked s.t. **qeʔ qʷl̓epntm, qʷl̓epntp**
es qʷl̓éʔepms – They are pit baking s.t. **qeʔes qʷl̓epm, es qʷl̓epmp**
qs qʷl̓éʔepms – They are going to pit bake s.t. **qeʔqs qʷl̓epm, qs qʷl̓epmp**

sxʷqʷl̓epm – one tasked to pit bake. *prefix:* ***sxʷ...*** *– one tasked to do.*
scqʷl̓epm – something that's been pit baked.

qʷl̓epiš – Pit bake. *cmd.*
qʷl̓epwi – All of you pit bake. *cmd.*
qʷl̓epnt – Pit bake s.t. *cmd.*

ncaqʷmn – something used to poke/stick into/through something, *(i.e., stick used in the camas bake, stick used to poke at the fire, etc.). See:* ***stick.***

ṅem kʷ nċiqm t aqł nqʷl̓éptn – You will dig your baking pit. **kʷéṁt qeʔqs qʷl̓épi** – Then we'll pit bake. **qeʔ qʷl̓epntm łu sx̣ʷéʔli** – We baked the camas.

acqʷ – roast something. *See:* ***roast.***

ṗiqém – make done; be ready. *See:* ***done.***
es ṗiyaq – It is done.

k̓ʷl̓sncut, *k̓ʷl̓sncu* – cook; prepare food. *See:* ***cook.***

baking pit

snqʷl̓éptn – baking pit. *prefix:* ***sn...*** *– a place of; suffix:* ***...tin, ...tn*** *– means of/device.*
ṅem kʷ nċiqm t aqł nqʷl̓éptn – You will dig your baking pit.

baking powder

nmex̣̌mn – something you mix; spices; baking powder. *rt.:* ***mex̣̌*** *– mix; prefix:* ***n...*** *– inside; suffix:* ***...min, ...mn*** *– instrument/tool.*

balance

nyeuʔusmist – balance. *(i.e., balance a stick vertically or horizontally, etc.)*
es nyeuʔusmisti – S/he is balancing. **čnes nyeuʔusmisti, kʷes nyeuʔusmisti**

q̓etm – make weighty as a means to counter balance; make weighty to make something sink down.
q̓etis – S/he added a counter balance. **q̓etn, q̓etntxʷ**
es q̓etms – S/he is adding a counter balance. **ies q̓etm, as q̓etm**
es q̓etms – S/he is going to add a counter balance. **ies q̓etm, as q̓etm**

q̓etmis – S/he used s.t. to counter balance. **q̓etmn, q̓etmntxʷ**

q̓eʔtemn – something used to weight something as to make it go down/sink/counter balance.

q̓etnt – Add a counter balance to it. *cmd.*
q̓etmnt – Use it to counter balance. *cmd.*

> s.t. - something, the 3rd person
> (s.t.) - something implied
> s.o. - someone, the 3rd person
> *sl.* - singular form
> *pl.* - plural form
> *rt.* - root word
> *cmd.* - command
> *lit.* - literally
> *fig.* - figuratively
> *i.e.,* - for example
> *See:* - Redirection to a related word.

es q̓etmnwexʷ – They are balanced in weight. **qeʔes q̓etmnwexʷ, p es q̓etmnwexʷ**

snq̇tq̇atáx̣, *snq̇tq̇atá* – teeter totter. *See:* ***teeter totter.***
q̇tq̇eteẇs – teeter totter; counter balance back and forth. *See:* ***teeter totter.***

q̇etnt ci i nk̓ʷu – Add weight to the other side *(to bring to balance).* **q̇etmnt ci luk̓ʷ** – Use that wood to make it go down *(to counter balance).*

bald **nłóq̇ʷosqn,** *nłóq̇ʷo* – bald on top of the head. *rt.:* ***łoq̇ʷ*** *– bare.*
nłóq̇ʷo – S/he is bald. **čn nłóq̇ʷo, kʷ nłóq̇ʷo**

čłóq̇ʷqn – bald head.

čłóq̇ʷp – become bald; loosing hair.

čttoqqin – loose hair; balding. *rt.:* ***tuwaq*** *– fall apart; suffix:* ***...qin, ...qn*** *– top.*
es čttoqqini – S/he is losing hair. **čnes čttoqqini, kʷes čttoqqini**

bald eagle **pqlqin,** *pqlqi* – bald eagle; *Haliaeetus leucocephalus.* *rt.:* ***piq*** *– white; suffix:* ***...qin, ...qn*** *– top.*
qełpqlqin – young bald eagle. *prefix:* ***qeł...*** *– offspring of.*

bale **lčéẇs** – tied up around the middle; bale of hay. *rt.:* ***lič*** *– tied up; suffix:* ***...éẇs*** *– in between, middle. See:* ***tie.***
es l̓čeẇs – It is bundled around the middle.

ball **sččxʷumeʔ** – ball, shinny ball.
snlolop sččxʷumeʔ – basketball.

sṗint sččxʷumeʔ – Hit the ball!

pk̓ʷlʔemi – playing ball. *(i.e., basketball, baseball, football, etc.)*

málq̇ʷ – rounded/spherical; balled object; accumulate.
mlq̇ʷmstes – S/he accumulated s.t. **mlq̇ʷmsten, mlq̇ʷmstexʷ**
es mlq̇ʷmims – S/he is accumulating s.t. **ies mlq̇ʷmim, as mlq̇ʷmim**
qs mlq̇ʷmims – S/he is accumulating s.t. **iqs mlq̇ʷmim, aqs mlq̇ʷmim**

scmlmálq̇ʷ – something that's been rounded. *(i.e., a ball or clumped together dirt or clay.)*
scmalq̇ʷ – one balled clump.
mlq̇ʷqan – spherical head.
mlq̇ʷéčst – fist. *suffix:* ***...ečst, ...čst*** *– of the hand.*

mlq̇ʷmstes łu skʷtnels – S/he accumulated respect.

mlq̇ʷmscutist – ball/curl yourself up. *(i.e., in a fetal position.)*
mlq̇ʷmscutist – S/he curled up. **čn mlq̇ʷmscutist, kʷ mlq̇ʷmscutist**
es mlq̇ʷmscutisti – S/he is curling up. **čnes mlq̇ʷmscutisti, kʷes mlq̇ʷmscutisti**
qs mlq̇ʷmscutisti – S/he is going to curl up. **čiqs mlq̇ʷmscutisti, kʷqs mlq̇ʷmscutisti**

mlmlq̇ʷmscutist – Each one is balled up. **qeʔ mlmlq̇ʷmscutist, p mlmlq̇ʷmscutist**

balloon **scnpew** – balloon; something that has been expanded by air. *lit. something that has been aired up. prefix:* ***sc...*** *– s.t. that's been done/made/prepared.*

scnpuxʷ – something that is blown through/into. *(i.e., an instrument.) prefix:* ***sc...*** *– s.t. that's been done/made/prepared.*

balsam fir **qʷelcn** – grand fir, balsam fir; *Abies grandis*; western red cedar; *Thuja plicata. (There is uncertainty with this word; some speakers identify it as western red cedar, Thuja plicata, while some identify it as grand fir, Abies grandis.)*

sṫikʷłp – grand fir; balsam fir; *Abies grandis.*

balsamroot

mtčẇé – arrowleaf balsamroot; sunflower; *Balsamorhiza sagittata.*

táqʷu – root of the arrowleaf balsamroot; *Balsamorhiza sagittata.*

banana

q̇ʷátx̣ʷ – banana. *lit. something bent.*

q̇ʷtq̇ʷátx̣ʷ – bananas; cucumbers.

band

čmṗqinčst, *čmṗqi* – band; finger ring. *rt.:* ***čm*** *– extremity; suffix:* ***...qinčst*** *– finger.*

es łoqʷ – It has a band.

łqʷéẇstn – hat band. *suffix:* ***...tin, ...tn*** *– means of/device.*

sqʷlápqn – hat band. *suffix:* ***...qin, ...qn*** *– top.*

čiyallax̣n – armband. *rt.:* ***čyall*** *– wrap; suffix:* ***...ax̣n*** *– arm.*

čiyallaqstšn – legband. *rt.:* ***čyall*** *– wrap; suffix:* ***...aqstšn*** *– leg.*

nk̓ʷaʔqsus, *nk̓ʷaʔqsu* – another group; one of a larger group. *(i.e., band of a tribe, a family group.)*

qeʔ nk̓ʷaʔqsus – We are part of one group.

i qeʔ nk̓ʷaʔqsus – We're one group.

The **i** following uvular consonants (UC) and the glottal stop **ʔ** sound like English "*ey*" as in the words th*ey*, h*ey*, wh*ey*, etc. Salish UC are: **q**, **q̇**, **qʷ**, **q̇ʷ**, **x̣**, **x̣ʷ**. For example, the suffix ...**qin** – head/top, is often spelled using English *ey* as "q*ey*n". So **qi**, **q̇i**, **qʷi**, **q̇ʷi**, **x̣i**, **x̣ʷi**, may be spelled with English *ey* as **q***ey*, **q̇***ey*, **qʷ***ey*, **q̇ʷ***ey*, **x̣***ey*, **x̣ʷ***ey* in other texts.

bangs

sčmuʔsus – bangs; forelock.

bank

npapaánč, *npapaá* – dirt riverbank; dirt cliff.

es npapaánč – It is a dirt bank.

snululimtn – money bank. *rt.:* ***ululim*** *– money; prefix:* ***sn...*** *– a place of; suffix:* ***...tin, ...tn*** *– means of/device.*

Bannock

ax̣ʷiċeʔ – Bannock people.

bannock bread

nṗéč̓lexʷm – make bannock bread. *rt.:* ***ṗeč̓*** *– radiant heat; prefix:* ***sc...*** *– s.t. that's been done/made/prepared; suffix:* ***...éẇs*** *– in between, middle.*

nṗéč̓lexʷm – S/he made bannock bread. **čn nṗéč̓lexʷm, kʷ nṗéč̓lexʷm**

es nṗéč̓lexʷi – S/he is making bannock bread. **čnes nṗéč̓lexʷi, kʷes nṗéč̓lexʷi**

qs nṗéč̓lexʷi – S/he is going to make bannock bread. **čiqs nṗéč̓lexʷi, kʷqs nṗéč̓lexʷi**

nṗéʔeč̓lexʷm – They made bannock bread. **qeʔ nṗéč̓lexʷm, p nṗéč̓lexʷm**

es nṗéʔeč̓lexʷi – They are making bannock bread. **qeʔes nṗéč̓lexʷi, p nṗéč̓lexʷi**

qs nṗéʔeč̓lexʷi – They are going to make bannock bread. **qeʔqs nṗéč̓lexʷi, pqs nṗéč̓lexʷi**

scnṗéč̓lexʷ, *scnṗé* – bannock bread.

ṅem čn nṗeč̓lexʷm – I will make bannock bread.

s.t. - something, the 3rd person
(s.t.) - something implied
s.o. - someone, the 3rd person
sl. - singular form
pl. - plural form
rt. - root word
cmd. - command
lit. - literally
fig. - figuratively
i.e., - for example
See: - Redirection to a related word.

Baptist

pati – Baptist.

baptize

lpatém – baptize. *(approximation to French word)*

lpatémis – S/he baptized s.o. **lpatémn, lpatémntxʷ**

es lpatémms – S/he is baptizing s.o. **ies lpatémm, as lpatémm**

qs lpatémms – S/he is going to baptize s.o. **iqs lpatémm, aqs lpatémm**

es lpatém – S/he is baptized, Catholic. **čnes lpatém, kʷes lpatém**

bar

snssustn, *snssu* – place to drink; bar; tavern. *rt.:* ***sust*** *– drink; prefix:* ***sn...*** *– a place of; suffix:* ***...tin, ...tn*** *– means of/device.*

snqʷeẁtn – place to get drunk. *rt.: **qʷew** – crazy; prefix: **sn...** – a place of; suffix: **...tin, ...tn** – means of/device.*

snx̣ʷoskʷtn – place of beer; brewery; bar. *rt.: **nx̣ʷoskʷ** – beer; prefix: **sn...** – a place of; suffix: **...tin, ...tn** – means of/device.*

es mlqtalqʷ – It is a cylindrical object; log; metal bar. *suffix: **...alqʷ** – wood; cylindical.*

čḿtḿmqʷalqʷtn – wrecking bar; pry bar.

barber

snčaʔilqntn – place to cut hair; barber shop. *rt.: **čaʔilqn** – cut hair; prefix: **sn...** – a place of; suffix: **...tin, ...tn** – means of/device.*

sxʷčaʔilqnm – one tasked to cut hair; barber. *rt.: **čaʔilqn** – cut hair; prefix: **sxʷ...** – one tasked to do; suffix: **...qin, ...qn** – top.*

čaʔilqn – cut hair. *See: **cut**.*

bare

łoq̇ʷ – make bare; peel *(i.e., peeling bitterroot, peeling camas, plucking the fuzz off a bird). See: **peel**.*

i łoq̇ʷ – S/he/it is bare/bald. *(devoid of filamental formations or coverings where naturally is should be)*

nłóq̇ʷosqn, *nłóq̇ʷo* – bald on top of the head. *See: **bald**.*

łóq̇ʷlexʷ – bare land.

łóq̇ʷolexʷ – becoming bare land.

čtmélxʷ, *čtmé* – naked; without clothes. *See: **naked**.*

čċslexʷ – get naked; get cleared of clothing. *See: **naked**.*

čpƛ̓ʔencut – undress one's self. *See: **undress**.*

npƛ̓alqs, *npƛ̓a* – remove/take off clothes. *See: **undress**.*

čpƛ̓iċéʔ – remove coverings/clothes. *See: **undress**.*

pƛ̓int – Take it off. *See: **remove**.*

pƛ̓qin – remove head cover/hat; bare head. *See: **hat**.*

pƛ̓pƛ̓šnim – remove footwear. *See: **shoe**.*

barefoot

pƛ̓pƛ̓šnim – remove footwear. *rt.: **pƛ̓im** – release from. See: **shoe**.*

es pƛ̓pƛ̓šin – S/he is barefoot. **čnes pƛ̓pƛ̓šin, kʷes pƛ̓pƛ̓šin**

es čpƛ̓šin – S/he has one shoe off; one foot is bare. **čnes čpƛ̓šin, kʷes čpƛ̓šin**

bare head

pƛ̓qin – remove head cover/hat; bare head. *rt.: **pƛ̓im** – release from. See: **hat**.*

nłóq̇ʷosqn, *nłóq̇ʷo* – bald on top of the head. *See: **bald**.*

bark

čiilélxʷ – tree bark. *suffix: **...elxʷ, ...lxʷ** – skin/hide*

sčmx̣ʷcin, *sčmx̣ʷci* – inside the bark.

nmx̣ʷcin, *nmx̣ʷci* – inside of cottonwood bark.

snmx̣ʷcinm – scar on tree from the removal of bark.

čqʷłn̓alqʷ, *čqʷłn̓a* – white birch; *Betula papyifera.*

sicqn̓ełp – red birch; *Betula occidentalis.*

ql̓elxʷ – green/fresh bark.

čťuplxʷ – bark fiber from the outside. *rt.: **ťup** – twist; prefix: **č...** – upon; suffix: **...elxʷ, ...lxʷ** – skin/hide*

nťuplxʷ – bark fiber from the inside. *rt.: **ťup** – twist; prefix: **n...** – inside; suffix: **...elxʷ, ...lxʷ** – skin/hide*

es čxʷƛ̓alqʷi – S/he is removing bark. *See:* ***whittle.***

čawálqʷm – peel bark; peel flower stems; peel cylindrical objects. *See:* ***peel.***

čawełpm – peel fibers off of bark. *See:* ***peel.***

čxʷk̓ʷełpm – clean bark/branches. *See:* ***clean.***

uhem – dog bark.
es uhemi – It is barking.
qs uhemi – It is going to bark.

es uhems – It is barking at him/her/it.
es uhéʔems – It is barking at them.

sxʷʔuhem – one tasked to bark. *prefix:* ***sxʷ...*** *– one tasked to do.*

uheyiš – Bark. *cmd.*

qeʔ hewšiłt – We were barked at.

čn sewneʔ t nqʷq̓ʷosṁi es uhemi – I heard the dog bark.

ččeʔl̓ist, *ččeʔl̓* – The dog is alert; it is barking continuously. *rt.:* ***čeʔl̓*** *– alert.*
es ččeʔl̓isti – The dog is barking continuously.
es ččéʔelisti – They are barking *(many dogs).*

we – The sound a dog makes when barking.

The **i** following uvular consonants (UC) and the glottal stop **ʔ** sound like English "*ey*" as in the words th*ey*, h*ey*, wh*ey*, etc. Salish UC are: **q, q̓, qʷ, q̓ʷ, x̣, x̣ʷ**. For example, the suffix ...**qin** – head/top, is often spelled using English *ey* as "q*ey*n". So **qi, q̓i, qʷi, q̓ʷi, x̣i, x̣ʷi**, may be spelled with English *ey* as **q***ey*, **q̓***ey*, **qʷ***ey*, **q̓ʷ***ey*, **x̣***ey*, **x̣ʷ***ey* in other texts.

barn

snt̓pyuʔtsqá – barn, stable. *lit. place for animals to stand. rt.:* ***t̓pyeẃt*** *– stand pl.; suffix:* ***...sqax̣eʔ, ...sqa*** *– domestic animal; generally horse or car.*

barn spider

tupn – black widow spider.

barrette

sk̓ʷl̓snapqn – barrette for holding or ornamenting hair. *suffix:* ***...qin, ...qn*** *– top.*

barroom

snssustn, *snssu* – place to drink; bar, tavern. *rt.:* ***sust*** *– drink; prefix:* ***sn...*** *– a place of; suffix:* ***...tin, ...tn*** *– means of/device.*

snqʷeẃtn – place to get drunk. *rt.:* ***qʷew*** *– crazy; prefix:* ***sn...*** *– a place of; suffix:* ***...tin, ...tn*** *– means of/device.*

snx̣ʷoskʷtn – place of beer; brewery; bar. *rt.:* ***nx̣ʷoskʷ*** *– beer; prefix:* ***sn...*** *– a place of; suffix:* ***...tin, ...tn*** *– means of/device.*

bar soap

c̓eẃstn – soap, bar soap. *lit. something to wash with. rt.:* ***c̓eẃ*** *– wash; suffix:* ***...us*** *– face, fire; suffix:* ***...tin, ...tn*** *– means of/device.*

basement

sništełxʷ – basement. *rt.:* ***išut*** *– down, low; suffix:* ***...ełxʷ, ...łxʷ*** *– house.*

bashful

ẏaasqelixʷ – shy/bashful of people. *See:* ***shy.***

c̓ʔeš – ashamed. *See:* ***ashamed.***

k̓ʷłpusncut, *k̓ʷłpusncu* – self-conscious; backward; shy; bashful; polite; considerate; does not impose. *See:* ***self-conscious.***

basket

snq̓c̓éstn, *snq̓c̓é* – woven basket. *rt.:* ***q̓ec̓*** *– weave; prefix:* ***sn...*** *– a place of; suffix:* ***...tin, ...tn*** *– means of/device. See:* ***weave.***

sčłq̓ʷastn, *sčłq̓ʷa* – basket made of bark; rawhide bucket. *suffix:* ***...tin, ...tn*** *– means of/device.*

s.t. - something, the 3rd person
(s.t.) - something implied
s.o. - someone, the 3rd person
sl. - singular form
pl. - plural form
rt. - root word
cmd. - command
lit. - literally
fig. - figuratively
i.e., - for example
See: - Redirection to a related word.

kʷqs k̓ʷuli t sčłq̓ʷastn – You are going to make a bark basket. **ƛ̓éʔentwi péce̓ʔmp u sčłq̓ʷastnmp –** All of you look for your diggers and your bark bags. **łu as k̓ʷul̓m sčłq̓ʷastn m še pn̓elxʷntxʷ ančiilelxʷ –** While you are making a bark basket you have to bend your bark.

čłqʷełtn – binder on the outside of a bark basket. *(made of a bough stem or bark strip) suffix: **...tin, ...tn** – means of/device.*

nłqʷełtn – binder on the inside of a bark basket. *(made of a bough stem)*

čaċmin – loop/holder. *(found on bark baskets) suffix: **...min, ...mn** – instrument/tool.*

basketball

nlolop sččxʷumeʔ – basketball. *rt.: **nlo** – put inside.*

nlopstes – S/he made a basket. **nlopsten, nlopstexʷ**

sxʷsnlolop sččxʷumeʔ – one tasked to put balls in the hoop; basketball player. *prefix: **sxʷ...** – one tasked to do.*

snlolop sččxʷumeʔ – the basket.

nlopiskʷ – Make a basket. *cmd.*

pk̓ʷlʔem – playing ball. *(i.e., basketball, baseball, football, etc.)*

es pk̓ʷlʔemi – S/he is playing ball. **čnes pk̓ʷlʔemi, kʷes pk̓ʷlʔemi**

sxʷpk̓ʷlʔem – one tasked to play ball; ballplayer. *prefix: **sxʷ...** – one tasked to do.*

či sxʷpk̓ʷlʔem – I am a ballplayer.

cq̓minm – throw an object. *See: **throw**.*

kʷnnunm – catch someone or something. *See: **catch**.*

čłtʔem – bounce something. *See: **bounce**.*

šičt – miss something targeted. *See: **miss**.*

bat

čsp̓sqé – bat/hit a ball. *rt.: **sp̓im** – strike w/ object; suffix: **...sqe, ...sqelixʷ** – people.*

t̓lt̓el̓w̓é, *t̓lt̓el̓w̓éliyeʔ* **–** bat.

iše t̓uxʷt łu t̓lt̓el̓w̓é – Bats fly.

sp̓áas – nighthawk, night bat, mosquito hawk; *Chordeiles minor.*

bathe

ċaw̓lš – bathe; sit in the tub. *rt.: **ċew̓** – wash.*

ċaw̓lš – S/he bathed. **čn ċaw̓lš, kʷ ċaw̓lš**
es ċaw̓lši – S/he is bathing. **čnes ċaw̓lši, kʷes ċaw̓lši**
qs ċaw̓lši – S/he is going to bathe. **čiqs ċaw̓lši, kʷqs ċaw̓lši**
ċáʔawlš – They bathed. **qeʔ ċaw̓lš, p ċaw̓lš**
es ċáʔawlši – They are bathing. **qeʔes ċaw̓lši, pes ċaw̓lši**
qs ċáʔawlši – They are going to bathe. **qeʔqs ċaw̓lši, pqs ċaw̓lši**

ċaw̓lšis – S/he bathed s.o. **ċaw̓lšn, ċaw̓lšntxʷ**
es ċaw̓lšms – S/he is bathing s.o. **čnes ċaw̓lšm, kʷes ċaw̓lšm**
qs ċaw̓lšms – S/he is going to bathe s.o. **čiqs ċaw̓lšm, kʷqs ċaw̓lšm**

ċuʔċaw̓lš, *ċuʔċa* **–** bathe; swim/play in the tub; moving around in the water.
ċuʔċaw̓lš – S/he bathed/swam. **čn ċuʔċaw̓lš, kʷ ċuʔċaw̓lš**
es ċuʔċaw̓lši – S/he is bathing/swimming. **čnes ċuʔċaw̓lši, kʷes ċuʔċaw̓lši**
qs ċuʔċaw̓lši – S/he is going to bathe/swim. **čiqs ċuʔċaw̓lši, kʷqs ċuʔċaw̓lši**
ċuʔċaʔawlš – They bathed/swam. **qeʔ ċuʔċaw̓lš, p ċuʔċaw̓lš**
es ċuʔċaʔawlši – They are bathing/swimming. **qeʔes ċuʔċaw̓lši, pes ċuʔċaw̓lši**

qs ċuˀċaˀawlši – They are going to bathe/swim. **qeˀqs ċuˀċaẇlši, pqs ċuˀċaẇlši**

snċuˀċaẇlštn – bathtub; tub. *prefix:* ***sn...*** *– a place of; suffix:* ***...tin, ...tn*** *– means of/device.*

ċaẇlš – Bathe. *cmd.*
ċuˀċaẇlš – Swim and bathe. *cmd.*
ċaẇlšnt – Bathed s.o. *cmd.*
ċeẇ – wash. *See:* ***wash.***

čiqs k̇ʷis ċuˀċaẇlš – I am going to go bathing. **čmlk̇ʷmásq̇t u čnes ċuˀċaẇlši**
yetɬx̣ʷá – I was bathing all day today.

The **i** following uvular consonants (UC) and the glottal stop **ˀ** sound like English "*ey*" as in the words *they, hey, whey,* etc. Salish UC are: **q, q̇, qʷ, q̇ʷ, x̣, x̣ʷ**. For example, the suffix ...**qin** – head/top, is often spelled using English *ey* as "q*ey*n". So **qi, q̇i, qʷi, q̇ʷi, x̣i, x̣ʷi**, may be spelled with English *ey* as **q***ey*, **q̇***ey*, **qʷ***ey*, **q̇ʷ***ey*, **x̣***ey*, **x̣ʷ***ey* in other texts.

bathroom

snɬˀó – toilet; outhouse. *prefix:* ***sn...*** *– a place of.*
čiqs xʷuyi č snɬˀo – I am going to the bathroom.

snċuˀċa – bathroom; place to bathe.

bathtub

snċuˀċaẇlštn – bathtub; tub. *prefix:* ***sn...*** *– a place of; suffix:* ***...tin, ...tn*** *– means of/device.*

battery

suwečm – lightning; electricity.

suwečm x̣ʷl̇ anpaqmn – batteries for your flashlight.

battle

plstwéxʷ, *plstwé* – kill each other; battle; war. *rt.:* ***puls*** *– kill; suffix:* ***...wexʷ*** *– action to each other*
es plstwéˀexʷi – They are killing each other. **qeˀes plstwéxʷi, pes plstwéxʷi**

plsqélixʷ, *plsqé* – killed a person. *See:* ***kill.***
puls – kill. *See:* ***kill.***

ilnwéxʷ – striking each other with arrows; battle; war. *rt.:* ***ilim*** *– penetrate w/ pointed object; suffix:* ***...wexʷ*** *– action to each other.*

ilpstwéxʷ – wounding each other; battle; war. *rt.:* ***ilip*** *– wound; suffix:* ***...wexʷ*** *– action to each other.*

beading

čk̇ʷul̇m – bead. *rt.:* ***k̇ʷul̇*** *– make/build/do; prefix:* ***č...*** *– upon.*
čk̇ʷul̇m – S/he beaded. **čn čk̇ʷul̇m, kʷ čk̇ʷul̇m**
es čk̇ʷul̇i – S/he is beading. **čnes čk̇ʷul̇i, kʷes čk̇ʷul̇i**
qs čk̇ʷul̇i – S/he is going to bead. **čiqs čk̇ʷul̇i, kʷqs čk̇ʷul̇i**
čk̇ʷúˀul̇m – They beaded. **qeˀ čk̇ʷul̇m, p čk̇ʷul̇m**
es čk̇ʷúˀul̇i – They are beading. **qeˀes čk̇ʷul̇i, pes čk̇ʷul̇i**
qs čk̇ʷúˀul̇i – They are going to bead. **qeˀqs čk̇ʷul̇i, pqs čk̇ʷul̇i**

čk̇ʷul̇is – S/he beaded s.t. **čk̇ʷul̇n, čk̇ʷul̇ntxʷ**
es čk̇ʷul̇ms – S/he is beading s.t. **ies čk̇ʷul̇m, as čk̇ʷul̇m**
qs čk̇ʷul̇ms – S/he is going to bead s.t. **iqs čk̇ʷul̇m, aqs čk̇ʷul̇m**
čk̇ʷúˀul̇is – They beaded s.t. **qeˀ čk̇ʷul̇ntm, čk̇ʷul̇ntp**
es čk̇ʷúˀul̇ms – They are beading s.t. **qeˀes čk̇ʷul̇m, es čk̇ʷul̇mp**
qs čk̇ʷúˀul̇ms – They are going to bead s.t. **qeˀqs čk̇ʷul̇m, qs čk̇ʷul̇mp**

s.t. - something, the 3rd person
(s.t.) - something implied
s.o. - someone, the 3rd person
sl. - singular form
pl. - plural form
rt. - root word
cmd. - command
lit. - literally
fig. - figuratively
i.e., - for example
See: - Redirection to a related word.

sxʷčk̇ʷul̇m – one tasked to bead. *prefix:* ***sxʷ...*** *– one tasked to do.*
čk̇ʷl̇emn – one inclined to bead. *suffix:* ***...emn*** *– one inclined to do.*
scčk̇ʷul̇ – something that's been beaded. *suffix:* ***sc...*** *– s.t. that's been done/made/prepared.*
sčk̇ʷul̇ – beadwork.

čk̇ʷul̇iš – Bead. *cmd.*
čk̇ʷul̇wi – All of you bead. *cmd.*
čk̇ʷul̇nt – Bead something. *cmd.*

ṅem čiqs čḱʷuli̓ yetłx̣ʷa – I am going to bead today.

łixʷm – picking up beads with a needle.
es łixʷqʷi – S/he is picking up the beads. **čnes łixʷqʷi, kʷes łixʷqʷi**

tixʷm – pick/get a plant object or clay. *See:* ***pick.***

čłḱʷum – pick something up using an instrument or tool. *(i.e., a needle for beads, a pitchfork for hay/rocks, etc.) See:* ***pick.***

beads **čłccṁus,** *čłccṁu* – beads.

beadwork **sčḱʷul̓ –** beadwork.
sčḱʷul̓s – His/her beadwork. **isčḱʷul̓, asčḱʷul̓**

scčḱʷul̓ – something that's been beaded.

i yal sčḱʷul̓ – It is round beadwork.

beak **snṗsáqs,** *snṗsá* – nose; bird beak; pencil tip.

beans **łṁt̓ṁtós,** *łṁt̓ṁtó* – beans. *rt.:* ***ṁtos*** *– kidney.*

bear **nłámqeʔ –** black bear; *Ursus americanus.* **nłmłámqeʔ –** black bears. *pl.*
nłałṁqeʔ – little black bear.
nłṁłáłṁqeʔ – little black bears.

nłamqcn – black bear growl. *suffix:* ***...cin, ...cn*** *– action of the mouth.*
es nłamqcni – A black bear is growling.

es nłamqalqsi – S/he is wearing black bear skin. **čnes nłamqalqsi, kʷes nłamqalqsi**

wičtn łu nłámqeʔ – I saw a black bear. **čn sewneʔ es nłamqcni –** I hear a black bear growling.

smx̣éy̓čṅ, *smx̣é* – grizzly bear; *Ursus arctos horribilis.* **smx̣mx̣éy̓čṅ** *pl. suffix:* ***...ičṅ*** *– back.*
słmx̣x̣éy̓čṅ, *słmx̣x̣é* – little grizzly bear.

wičtn łu smx̣éy̓čṅ – I saw a grizzly bear.

bearberry honeysuckle **nłámqeʔ sʔiłis –** bearberry honeysuckle; black twin-berry; *Lonicera involucrata.*

beard **supcín,** *supcí* – beard; hairy mouth. *rt.:* ***up*** *– hair; suffix:* ***...cin, ...cn*** *– action of the mouth.*
es upcín – S/he has a beard. **čnes upcín, kʷes upcín**
es upupcíʔin – They have beards. **qeʔes upupcín, pes upupcín**

supus – beard; hairy face. *rt.:* ***up*** *– hair; suffix:* ***...us*** *– face, fire.*
es upus – S/he has a beard. **čnes upus, kʷes upus**

beargrass **słčést̓iyeʔ –** beargrass; *Xerophyllum tenax. suffix:* ***...st̓iyeʔ*** *– grass.*

Bear Paw Mountains **čelšs smx̣éy̓čṅ –** Bear Paw Mountains, Montana; *lit. hand of the grizzly bear.*

bear rib grease **scocoó –** something that hangs in a line; describing the way bear rib grease is prepared.

scq̓ʷoʔct̓ – grease. *prefix:* ***sc...*** *– s.t. that's been done/made/prepared.*

beat **čcoqin –** beat on. *prefix:* ***č...*** *– upon.*

čcoqis – S/he beat s.o. **čcoqin, čcoqintxʷ**
čcoqíˀis – S/he beat s.o. **qeˀ čcoqintm, čcoqintp**

es čcoqnax̣ni – S/he is beating. **čnes čcoqnax̣ni, kʷes čcoqnax̣ni**
qs čcoqnax̣ni – S/he is going be beating. **čiqs čcoqnax̣ni, kʷqs čcoqnax̣ni**

es čcoqnaqsnms – S/he is beating up on s.o. **ies čcoqnaqsnm, as čcoqnaqsnm**
qs čcoqnaqsnms – S/he is going to beat up on s.o. **iqs čcoqnaqsnm, aqs čcoqnaqsnm**

es čcoqnwexʷi – They are beating each other up. **qeˀes čcoqnwexʷi, pes čcoqnwexʷi**
qs čcoqnwexʷi – They are going to beat each other up. **qeˀqs čcoqnwexʷi, pqs čcoqnwexʷi**

čcoqis isqʷsé – S/he beat my son. **xʷu qeˀqs occqeˀi qeˀqs čcoqnwexʷi –** Okay, let's go outside. We're going to fight.

The **i** following uvular consonants (UC) and the glottal stop **ˀ** sound like English "*ey*" as in the words th*ey*, h*ey*, wh*ey*, etc. Salish UC are: **q**, **q̇**, **qʷ**, **q̇ʷ**, **x̣**, **x̣ʷ**. For example, the suffix ...**qin** – head/top, is often spelled using English *ey* as "q*ey*n". So **qi**, **q̇i**, **qʷi**, **q̇ʷi**, **x̣i**, **x̣ʷi**, may be spelled with English *ey* as **q***ey*, **q̇***ey*, **qʷ***ey*, **q̇ʷ***ey*, **x̣***ey*, **x̣ʷ***ey* in other texts.

ƛ̓áq̇ʷ – verbally or physically fight one's spouse. *See:* ***fight.***

šƛ̓páqs, *šƛ̓pá* **–** win/defeat/beat at some contest or event. *See:* ***win.***

čsṗiċéˀ – whip, spank. *rt.:* ***sṗim*** *– strike w/ object. See:* ***whip.***

beautiful

swinumt – beautiful. *lit.* ***es wiˀ*** *– it is finished; meaning Creator's work is finished.*
swinumt – S/he/it is beautiful. **či swinumt, kʷ swinumt**
swiwinumt – S/he/it is beautiful. **qeˀ swiwinumt, p swiwinumt**

uł swinúˀumt – All of them are beautiful. **qeˀ uł swinumt, p uł swinumt**

winmtstilš – S/he/it became beautiful. **čnes winmtstilš, kʷes winmtstilš** *suffix:* ***...ilš*** *– autonomous.*
es winmtstilši – S/he/it is becoming beautiful. **čnes winmtstilši, kʷes winmtstilši**
qs winmtstilši – S/he/it is going to become beautiful. **čiqs winmtstilši, kʷqs winmtstilši**

winumtšts – S/he/it made it beautiful. **winumtštn, winumtštxʷ**
es winumtštms – S/he/it is making it beautiful. **ies winumtštm, as winumtštm**
qs winumtštms – S/he/it is going to make it beautiful. **iqs winumtštm, aqs winumtštm**

winmtscut – S/he/it made one's self beautiful. **čn winmtscut, kʷ winmtscut**
es winmtscuti – S/he/it is making one's self beautiful. **čnes winmtscuti, kʷes winmtscuti**
qs winmtscuti – S/he/it is going to make one's self beautiful. **čiqs winmtscuti, kʷqs winmtscuti**

winumtn – something that beautifies.
winmtscutn – something/someone that makes one beautiful.

x̣est – good. *See:* ***good.***

qʷamqʷmt – excellent; beautiful; pleasing. *See:* ***excellent.***

čhomist, *čho* **–** in awe of something or someone; overwhelmed; see something beautiful/good/wonderful. *See:* ***awe.***

s.t. - something, the 3rd person
(s.t.) - something implied
s.o. - someone, the 3rd person
sl. - singular form
pl. - plural form
rt. - root word
cmd. - command
lit. - literally
fig. - figuratively
i.e., - for example
See: - Redirection to a related word.

beaver

sqléẁ – beaver; *Castor canadensis.*
kʷtisqléẁ – big beaver.
sqqléẁ – little beaver.
scṅpu – baby beaver.
qmepeˀ – beaver testicles *(used for scent/fragrance).*
sċpselxʷ – beaver hide.

beaver tail **sqléẇ sups –** beaver tail.

because **x̣ʷl̓ –** for; because.

x̣ʷl̓ steṁ u tám t selíš u kʷes uwéwlši – Why are you not speaking Salish?
x̣ʷl̓ tá čnes nsuxʷneʔ – Because I do not understand.
čnes iłni x̣ʷl̓ čnes čšq̓me – I am eating because I am hungry.

néłi – naturally because; matter of fact.
néłi ṅem ẏapqiṅ qeʔqs cq̓ʷełt – because there will be lots for us to pack out.
čx̣ʷoyqntp néłi ƛ̓e čxʷʔéʔ t sẇewł – You guys pile it up, because there are already a lot of fish.

tma – as you know.
tma iše kʷ sust t sewłkʷ x̣ʷl̓ kʷes nx̣mpcini – As you know you drink water, because you are thirsty.
tma x̣ʷl̓ šeẏ kʷ šlim – that's why you chop wood (to make a sweat).

become **…wilš –** *suffix indcating developmental progression; getting to; in the process of.* See: ***getting***.

…ilš – *suffix indcating autonomous progression; getting to; in the process of.* See: ***getting***.

…ṁnuxʷ – *suffix indicating going through the time of; getting to be/becoming.* See: ***getting***.

…ip – *suffix indicating something became/happened due to natural process.*
ƛ̓lip – stop. See: ***stop***.
til̓ – shatter/break into pieces of stone, glass, iron or teeth. See: ***break***.

…t – *suffix indicating something is in a particular state due to natural processes.*
x̣est, *x̣e* **–** good; fine; beautiful. See: ***good***.
yopiyewt – strength; fortitude; financially sound. See: ***strength***.
yoyoót – strong. See: ***strong***.

bed **snčłʔitštn –** bed. *rt.:* ***itš*** *– sleep; prefix:* ***sn…*** *– a place of; suffix:* ***…tin, …tn*** *– means of/device.*

snʔitštn – place to sleep; bedroom. *rt.:* ***itš*** *– sleep; prefix:* ***sn…*** *– a place of; suffix:* ***…tin, …tn*** *– means of/device.*

t̓kʷéłp – bedding; mattress. *suffix:* ***…ełp, …łp*** *– tree; in the past boughs were used for bedding.*

nx̣cméneʔ – make a bed ready with covers; fix a bed.
nx̣cménʔem – S/he fixed the bed. **čn nx̣cménʔem, kʷ nx̣cménʔem**
es nx̣cménʔei – S/he is fixing the bed. **čnes nx̣cménʔei, kʷes nx̣cménʔei**
qs nx̣cménʔei – S/he is going to fix the bed. **čiqs nx̣cménʔem, kʷqs nx̣cménʔei**
nx̣cméʔenʔem – They fixed the bed. **qeʔ nx̣cménʔem, p nx̣cménʔem**
es nx̣cméʔenʔei – They are fixing the bed. **qeʔes nx̣cménʔem, pes nx̣cménʔei**
qs nx̣cméʔenʔei – They are going to fix the bed. **qeʔqs nx̣cménʔem, pqs nx̣cménʔei**

nx̣cméneʔiš – Fix the bed. *cmd.*

ṅe kʷ wis nx̣cménʔem m kʷ itš – When you finish fixing your bed you will sleep.

płqełpm – cover/fix a bed. *rt.:* ***płqem*** *– spread/unpack; suffix:* ***…ełp, …łp*** *– tree; floor, bed; in the past boughs were used for bedding.*
płqełpm – S/he fixed the bed. **čn płqełpm, kʷ płqełpm**
es płqełpi – S/he is fixing the bed. **čnes płqełpi, kʷes płqełpi**
qs płqełpi – S/he is going to fix the bed. **čiqs płqełpi, kʷqs płqełpi**
płqéʔełpm – They fixed the bed. **qeʔ płqełpm, p płqełpm**
es płqéʔełpi – They are fixing the bed. **qeʔes płqełpi, pes płqełpi**

qs płqéʔełpi – They are going to fix the bed. **qeʔqs płqełpi, pqs płqełpi**

płqełpis – S/he fixed the bed. **płqełpn, płqełpntxʷ**
es płqełpms – S/he is fixing the bed. **ies płqełpm, as płqełpm**
qs płqełpms – S/he is going to fix the bed. **čiqs płqełpi, kʷqs płqełpi**
płqéʔełpis – They fixed the bed. **qeʔ płqełpntm, płqełpntp**
es płqéʔełpms – They are fixing the bed. **qeʔes płqełpm, es płqełpmp**
qs płqéʔełpms – They are going to fix the bed. **qeʔqs płqełpm, qs płqełpmp**

płqełpiš – Fix the bed. *cmd.*
płqełpnt – Fix that bed. *cmd.*

k̓ʷl̓lexʷełp, *k̓ʷl̓lexʷe* – fix a bed. *suffix:* ***...ełp, ...łp*** *– tree; floor, bed; in the past boughs were used for bedding.*
k̓ʷl̓lexʷełpm – S/he fixed the bed. **čn k̓ʷl̓lexʷełpm, kʷ k̓ʷl̓lexʷełpm**
es k̓ʷl̓lexʷełpi – S/he is fixing the bed. **čnes k̓ʷl̓lexʷełpi, kʷes k̓ʷl̓lexʷełpi**
qs k̓ʷl̓lexʷełpi – S/he is going to fix the bed. **čiqs k̓ʷl̓lexʷełpi, kʷqs k̓ʷl̓lexʷełpi**

bedbug

łq̇łáq̇t, *łq̇łá* – bedbug.

k̓ʷeʔk̓ʷʔé – bedbug.

bedding

t̓k̓ʷéłp – bedding; mattress. *suffix:* ***...ełp, ...łp*** *– tree; in the past boughs were used for bedding.*

bedroom

snʔitštn – place to sleep; bedroom. *rt.:* ***itš*** *– sleep; prefix:* ***sn...*** *– a place of; suffix:* ***...tin, ...tn*** *– means of/device.*

bee

sqʷuʔł – wasp; bee; hornet.

mac̓pł – bumble bee.

beef

st̓m̓a – cow.

beehive

sqʷuʔłétxʷ – beehive. *rt.:* ***sqʷuʔł*** *– bee; suffix:* ***...etxʷ, ...txʷ*** *– house.*

beer

nx̣ʷoskʷ – beer. *rt.:* ***x̣ʷos*** *– foam; circumfix:* ***n...etkʷ*** *– liquid.*

nx̣šuskʷ – beer.

beetle

nk̓ʷlk̓ʷl̓č̓ičṅ, *nk̓ʷlk̓ʷl̓č̓i* – beetle. *rt.:* ***k̓ʷel̓č̓*** *– cover w/ formed object; suffix:* ***...ičṅ*** *– back.*
es nk̓ʷlk̓ʷl̓č̓ičṅ – It has a hard back. *suffix:* ***...ičṅ*** *– back.*

čk̓ʷlk̓ʷl̓č̓iċeʔ – beetle. *rt.:* ***k̓ʷel̓č̓*** *– cover w/ formed object; suffix:* ***...iċéʔ*** *– covered in.*

čč̓nč̓np̓iċéʔ – beetle. *suffix:* ***...iċéʔ*** *– covered in.*

before

t – *particle indicating before; ahead; in advance.*
čn t xʷuy – I went ahead.
es t misten – I already knew.
t skʷekʷst – this morning; the morning already past.

beg

qiʔl – beg; insist; persuade; coaxed into.
qil̓l̓ – S/he/it got persuaded. **čn qil̓l̓, kʷ qil̓l̓**
es qil̓l̓i – S/he/it is getting persuaded. **čnes qil̓l̓i, kʷes qil̓l̓i**
qs qil̓l̓i – S/he/it is going to get persuaded. **čiqs qil̓l̓i, kʷqs qil̓l̓i**

qiʔlm – S/he/it begged. **čn qiʔlm, kʷ qiʔlm**
es qiʔli – S/he/it is begging. **čnes qiʔli, kʷes qiʔli**

The **i** following uvular consonants (UC) and the glottal stop **ʔ** sound like English "*ey*" as in the words th*ey*, h*ey*, wh*ey*, etc. Salish UC are: **q, q̇, qʷ, q̇ʷ, x̣, x̣ʷ**. For example, the suffix ...**qin** – head/top, is often spelled using English *ey* as "q*ey*n". So **qi, q̇i, qʷi, q̇ʷi, x̣i, x̣ʷi**, may be spelled with English *ey* as **q***ey*, **q̇***ey*, **qʷ***ey*, **q̇ʷ***ey*, **x̣***ey*, **x̣ʷ***ey* in other texts.

s.t. - something, the 3rd person
(s.t.) - something implied
s.o. - someone, the 3rd person
sl. - singular form
pl. - plural form
rt. - root word
cmd. - command
lit. - literally
fig. - figuratively
i.e., - for example
See: - Redirection to a related word.

qs qiʔli – S/he/it is going to beg. **čiqs qiʔli, kʷqs qiʔli**

qiʔlis – S/he/it begged s.o. **qiʔln, qiʔlntxʷ**
es qiʔlms – S/he/it is begging s.o. **ies qiʔlm, as qiʔlm**
qs qiʔlms – S/he/it is going to beg s.o. **iqs qiʔlm, aqs qiʔlm**

ql̓l̓ncutn – persuader of one.

es ql̓ɫtúʔumši – They are begging.

aẏċn – have the voice of insisting, begging and pleading. *See: **insist**.*

áẏċ – urge; insist and plead; stubborn. *See: **insist**.*

behave **toẋʷ –** straight/right; straight/true; undistorted; not curved; not wrong. *See: **straight**.*
toẋʷš – Behave; be straight. *cmd. rt.: **toẋʷ**– straight.*
toẋʷwi – All of you behave; all of you be straight. *cmd. rt.: **toẋʷ**– straight.*

séwneʔ – hear; listen. *See: **hear**.*

k̓ʷɫpusncut, *k̓ʷɫpusncu* – self-conscious; backward; shy; bashful; polite; considerate; does not impose. *See: **self-conscious**.*
čn k̓ʷɫpusncut – I was self-conscious; I was backwards.

ẋiɫ exʷ ye ta es k̓ʷɫpusncut – S/he was really acting like a jerk.

ẋeʔe – keep someone in line; correct behavior; forbid bad behavior; prevent misdeeds; make someone behave. *See: **discipline**.*

behead **nič̓sm –** cut the face/head off.
nič̓sis – S/he cut the face/head off. **nič̓sn, nič̓sntxʷ**
es nič̓sms – S/he is cutting the face/head off. **ies nič̓sm, as nič̓sm**
qs nič̓sms – S/he is going to cut the face/head off. **iqs nič̓sm, aqs nič̓sm**

nẋʷtusm – cut off the face/head.
nẋʷtusis – S/he cut off the face/head. **nẋʷtusn, nẋʷtusntxʷ**
es nẋʷtusms – S/he is cutting off the face/head. **ies nẋʷtusm, as nẋʷtusm**
qs nẋʷtusms – S/he is going to cut off the face/head. **iqs nẋʷtusm, aqs nẋʷtusm**

behind **aw̓tpáqs,** *aw̓tpá* – follow; walk behind someone. *See: **follow**.*

ecċéwt – late, lagging behind. *See: **last**.*

k̓ʷɫʔaċẋmist – look behind/under. *rt.: **aċẋ**– look; prefix: **k̓ʷɫ...** – under; suffix: **...ist**– action for/of the self.*
k̓ʷɫʔaċẋmist – S/he looked under. **čn k̓ʷɫʔaċẋmist, kʷ k̓ʷɫʔaċẋmist**
es k̓ʷɫʔaċẋmisti – S/he is looking under. **čnes k̓ʷɫʔaċẋmisti, kʷes k̓ʷɫʔaċẋmisti**
qs k̓ʷɫʔaċẋmisti – S/he is going to look under. **čiqs k̓ʷɫʔaċẋmisti, kʷqs k̓ʷɫʔaċẋmisti**
k̓ʷɫʔaċẋmíʔist – They looked under. **qeʔ k̓ʷɫʔaċẋmist, p k̓ʷɫʔaċẋmist**
es k̓ʷɫʔaċẋmíʔisti – They are looking under. **qeʔes k̓ʷɫʔaċẋmisti, pes k̓ʷɫʔaċẋmisti**
qs k̓ʷɫʔaċẋmíʔisti – They are going to look under. **qeʔqs k̓ʷɫʔaċẋmisti, pqs k̓ʷɫʔaċẋmisti**

k̓ʷɫʔaċẋis – S/he looked under s.t. **k̓ʷɫʔaċẋn, k̓ʷɫʔaċẋntxʷ**
es k̓ʷɫʔaċẋms – S/he is looking under s.t. **ies k̓ʷɫʔaċẋm, as k̓ʷɫʔaċẋm**
qs k̓ʷɫʔaċẋms – S/he is going to look under s.t. **iqs k̓ʷɫʔaċẋm, aqs k̓ʷɫʔaċẋm**
k̓ʷɫʔáʔaċẋmis – They looked under s.t. **qeʔ k̓ʷɫʔaċẋntm, k̓ʷɫʔaċẋntp**
es k̓ʷɫʔáʔaċẋms – They are looking under s.t. **qeʔes k̓ʷɫʔaċẋm, es k̓ʷɫʔaċẋmp**
qs k̓ʷɫʔáʔaċẋmms – They are going to look under s.t. **qeʔqs k̓ʷɫʔaċẋm, qs k̓ʷɫʔaċẋmp**

k̓ʷłčlxʷmncut, *k̓ʷłčlxʷmncu* – make one's self go out of sight. *rt.: **člux**ʷ – go out of sight; prefix: **k̓ʷł...** – under; suffix: **...cut** – action to the self.*

k̓ʷłčlxʷmncut – S/he/it went out of sight. **čn k̓ʷłčlxʷmncut, kʷ k̓ʷłčlxʷmncut**
es k̓ʷłčlxʷmncuti – S/he/it is going out of sight. **čnes k̓ʷłčlxʷmncuti, kʷes k̓ʷłčlxʷmncuti**
qs k̓ʷłčlxʷmncuti – S/he/it is going to go out of sight. **čiqs k̓ʷłčlxʷmncuti, kʷqs k̓ʷłčlxʷmncuti**
k̓ʷłčlxʷmncúʔut – They went out of sight. **qeʔ k̓ʷłčlxʷmncut, p k̓ʷłčlxʷmncut**
es k̓ʷłčlxʷmncúʔuti – They are going out of sight. **qeʔes k̓ʷłčlxʷmncuti, pes k̓ʷłčlxʷmncuti**
qs k̓ʷłčlxʷmncúʔuti – They are going to go out of sight. **qeʔqs k̓ʷłčlxʷmncuti, pqs k̓ʷłčlxʷmncuti**

k̓ʷłčlxʷmncutš – Get behind something. *cmd.*

es k̓ʷłčilxʷ – It is out of sight.

k̓ʷłčlxʷmncut l es šiṫ – S/he/it went behind the tree.

The **i** following uvular consonants (UC) and the glottal stop ʔ sound like English "*ey*" as in the words *they, hey, whey*, etc. Salish UC are: **q, q̓, qʷ, q̓ʷ, x̌, x̌ʷ**. For example, the suffix **...qin** – head/top, is often spelled using English *ey* as "q*ey*n". So **qi, q̓i, qʷi, q̓ʷi, x̌i, x̌ʷi**, may be spelled with English *ey* as **q***ey*, **q̓***ey*, **qʷ***ey*, **q̓ʷ***ey*, **x̌***ey*, **x̌ʷ***ey* in other texts.

nččnčnaqs, *nččnčna* – catch up. *See: **catch**.*

ntuṅičṅm – fail to catch up to someone; unable to catch up to someone; behind. *See: **catch**.*

snčmičṅ – back. *rt.: **čm** – extremity.*
čmčṅełxʷ – behind the house. *rt.: **čm** – extremity.*
č asnčmičṅ – to your back; behind you.
swe łu l asnčmičṅ – Who is behind you?

belch

kʷakʷimt – belch.
es kʷakʷimti – S/he is belching. **čnes kʷakʷimti, kʷes kʷakʷimti**

believe

nunxʷéneʔ, *nunxʷé* – believe.
nunxʷénʔem – S/he/it believed. **čn nunxʷénʔem, kʷ nunxʷénʔem**
es nunxʷénʔei – S/he/it is believing. **ies nunxʷénʔei, as nunxʷénʔei**
qs nunxʷénʔei – S/he/it is going to believe. **iqs nunxʷénʔei, aqs nunxʷénʔei**
nunxʷéʔenʔem – They believed. **qeʔ nunxʷénʔem, p nunxʷénʔem**
es nunxʷéʔenʔei – They are believing. **qeʔes nunxʷénʔei, pes nunxʷénʔei**
qs nunxʷéʔenʔei – They are going to believe. **qeʔqs nunxʷénʔei, pqs nunxʷénʔei**

nunxʷénʔemis – S/he/it believed s.o. **nunxʷénʔemn, nunxʷénʔemntxʷ**
es nunxʷénʔems – S/he/it is believing s.o. **ies nunxʷénʔem, as nunxʷénʔem**
qs nunxʷénʔems – S/he/it is going to believe s.o. **iqs nunxʷénʔem, aqs nunxʷénʔem**
nunxʷéʔenʔemis – They believed s.o. **qeʔ nunxʷénʔemntm, nunxʷénʔemntp**
es nunxʷéʔenʔems – They are believing s.o. **qeʔes nunxʷénʔem, es nunxʷénʔemp**
qs nunxʷéʔenʔems – They are going to believe s.o. **qeʔqs nunxʷénʔem, qs nunxʷénʔemp**

es nunxʷénʔemsts – S/he/it is always believing s.t./s.o. **es nunxʷénʔemstn, es nunxʷénʔemsts**
es nunxʷéʔenʔemsts – They are always believing s.t./s.o. **qeʔes nunxʷénʔemstm, es nunxʷénʔemstp**

nunxʷénʔemtn – something that is believed.

nunxʷénʔemnt – Believe it. *cmd.*
es nunxʷénmwexʷi – They are believing each other.

s.t. - something, the 3rd person
(s.t.) - something implied
s.o. - someone, the 3rd person
sl. - singular form
pl. - plural form
rt. - root word
cmd. - command
lit. - literally
fig. - figuratively
i.e., - for example
See: - Redirection to a related word.

ta qes nunxʷéʔenʔemstxʷ – Do not believe s.o. **hoy nunxʷé –** S/he believed (s.o.). **kʷ iqs ewtusm, ta kʷ ies nunxʷénʔem łu ascʔuwewlš –** I am going to oppose you, I do not believe what you said. **nunxʷemncn –** I believe you. **imše nunxʷénʔemnt anpx̣px̣ot –** You should believe your elders.

bell **luliwlštn,** *luli* – bell.
liwmsts – S/he rang the bell. **liwmstn, liwmstxʷ**
es liwms – S/he is ringing the bell. **ies liwm, as liwm**
qs liwms – S/he is going to ring the bell. **iqs liwm, aqs liwm**

liwmstm – The bell was rung.

liwmskʷ – Ring the bell. *cmd.*

belly **olin –** belly, stomach.
es k̓ʷłncucw̓e inolin – My stomach's knocking.

...éw̓s – suffix indicating middle, center. *See:* ***middle.***

belly button **témusimu –** navel, belly button.

belly flop **ntʔetkʷmist –** make yourself hit the water. *(i.e., canonball, belly flop, etc.) suffix:* ***...etkʷ, ...tkʷ*** *– liquid*
ntʔetkʷmist – S/he hit the water. **čn ntʔetkʷmis, kʷ ntʔetkʷmist**
es ntʔetkʷmisti – S/he is hitting the water. **čnes ntʔetkʷmist, kʷes ntʔetkʷmisti**
qs ntʔetkʷmisti – S/he is going to hit the water. **čiqs ntʔetkʷmist, kʷqs ntʔetkʷmisti**

ntʔetkʷ t anʔolin – Hit the water with your belly.

below **k̓ʷłišut –** underneath; down below; under; beneath. *See:* ***under.***

nišut – down inside; deep inside. *See:* ***inside.***

belt **snlčew̓stn,** *snlče* – belt. *rt.:* ***lič̓*** *– tie up; suffix:* ***...éw̓s*** *– in between, middle; suffix:* ***...tin, ...tn*** *– means of/device.*

npul̓čaw̓stn, *npul̓ča* – yarn belt. *suffix:* ***...éw̓s*** *– in between, middle; suffix:* ***......tin, ...tn*** *– means of/device.*

sčk̓ʷl̓snlčew̓s – beaded belt. *suffix:* ***...éw̓s*** *– in between, middle.*

čt̓k̓ʷłcełniut, *čt̓k̓ʷłce* – something on the side to put stuff in; pouch on a belt. *See:* ***side.***

łq̓ep – wide rope; belt. *rt.:* ***łaq̓*** *– wide.*

belted kingfisher **ċalis –** kingfisher; belted kingfisher; *Ceryle alcyon.*

bench **łaq̓t̓ snčłemutn –** bench; wide chair.

bend **piṅ –** bend from one position to an curved/angular position.
es piṅ – It is bent.

pṅip – It got bent.
es pṅpmi – It is getting bent.

pṅntes – S/he bent it. **pṅnten, pṅtexʷ**
es pṅim – S/he is bending it. **ies pṅim, as pṅim**
qs pṅim – S/he is going to bend it. **iqs pṅim, aqs pṅim**
pṅntéʔes – They bent it. **qeʔ pṅtem, pṅtep**

pṅntéʔexʷ – You bent them.

pṅpṅnté ʔexʷ – You bent each one of them.

pṅint – Bend it. *cmd.*
pṅmiskʷ – Bend it. *cmd.*

pṅmscut – bend one's self. *(i.e., at the waist, elbow, knee, etc.)*
es pṅmscuti – S/he is bending one's self. **čnes pṅmscuti, kʷes pṅmscuti**

pṅinč – liver.
čłpṅusm – arched over. *rt.: **piṅ** – bend See: **arch**.*

pṅmiskʷ asčmqinšn – Bend your knee.

pṅelxʷm – bend bark/rawhide.
pṅelxʷis – S/he bent bark/rawhide. **pṅelxʷn, pṅelxʷntxʷ**
es pṅelxʷms – S/he is bending bark/rawhide. **ies pṅelxʷm, as pṅelxʷm**
qs pṅelxʷms – S/he is going to bend bark/rawhide. **iqs pṅelxʷm, aqs pṅelxʷm**

pṅelxʷnt – Bend bark/rawhide. *cmd.*

The **i** following uvular consonants (UC) and the glottal stop **ʔ** sound like English "*ey*" as in the words th*ey*, h*ey*, wh*ey*, etc. Salish UC are: **q**, **q̇**, **qʷ**, **q̇ʷ**, **x̣**, **x̣ʷ**. For example, the suffix …**qin** – head/top, is often spelled using English *ey* as "q*ey*n". So **qi**, **q̇i**, **qʷi**, **q̇ʷi**, **x̣i**, **x̣ʷi**, may be spelled with English *ey* as **q***ey*, **q̇***ey*, **qʷ***ey*, **q̇ʷ***ey*, **x̣***ey*, **x̣ʷ***ey* in other texts.

pṅalqʷm – bend a cylindrical object such as wood.
pṅalqʷis – S/he bent wood. **pṅalqʷn, pṅalqʷntxʷ**
es pṅalqʷms – S/he is bending wood. **ies pṅalqʷm, as pṅalqʷm**
qs pṅalqʷms – S/he is going to bend wood. **iqs pṅalqʷm, aqs pṅalqʷm**

pṅalqʷnt – Bend bark/rawhide. *cmd.*

łu as k̓ʷul̓m snlaqi m še pṅpṅalqʷntxʷ – While making a sweat house you have to bend poles.

pṅew̓sm – fold/bend something; bend something from the middle. *See: **fold**.*
es pṅew̓s – It is folded; it is bent.

pṅew̓is – S/he bent s.t. **pṅew̓n, pṅew̓ntxʷ**
es pṅew̓ms – S/he is bending s.t. **ies pṅew̓m, as pṅew̓m**
qs pṅew̓ms – S/he is going to bend s.t. **iqs pṅew̓m, aqs pṅew̓m**

pṅew̓snt – Bow it. *cmd.*

čpṅew̓sm – fold onto; bend onto. *(i.e., folding the top portion of a paper onto itself.) suffix: **…éw̓s** – in between, middle.*
čpṅew̓is – S/he bent s.t. onto it. **čpṅew̓n, čpṅew̓ntxʷ**
es čpṅew̓ms – S/he is bending s.t. onto it. **ies čpṅew̓m, as čpṅew̓m**
qs čpṅew̓ms – S/he is going to bend s.t. onto it. **iqs čpṅew̓m, aqs čpṅew̓m**

čpṅew̓snt – Bend it onto it. *cmd.*

npṅew̓sis – fold in. *(i.e., folding paper to make a paper airplane.)*
npṅew̓sis – S/he folded s.t. in. **npṅew̓sn, npṅew̓sntxʷ**
es npṅew̓sms – S/he is folding s.t. in. **ies npṅew̓sm, as npṅew̓sm**
qs npṅew̓sms – S/he is going to fold s.t. in. **iqs npṅew̓sm, aqs npṅew̓sm**

npṅew̓snt – Fold it in. *cmd.*

npṅusncut – bend one's self in the middle.
npṅusncut – S/he bent one's self. **čn npṅusncut, kʷ npṅusncut**
es npṅusncuti – S/he is bending one's self. **čnes npṅusncuti, kʷes npṅusncuti**
qs npṅusncuti – S/he is going to bend one's self. **čiqs npṅusncuti, kʷqs npṅusncuti**

s.t. - something, the 3rd person
(s.t.) - something implied
s.o. - someone, the 3rd person
sl. - singular form
pl. - plural form
rt. - root word
cmd. - command
lit. - literally
fig. - figuratively
i.e., - for example
See: - Redirection to a related word.

čłpṅew̓sm – bend over something; arch over. *rt.: **piṅ** – bend; suffix: **…éw̓s** – in between, middle.*

čłpṅeẁis – S/he bowed s.t. over. **čłpṅeẁn, čłpṅeẁntxʷ**
es čłpṅeẁms – S/he is arching s.t. over. **ies čłpṅeẁm, as čłpṅeẁm**
qs čłpṅeẁms – S/he is going to arch s.t. over. **iqs čłpṅeẁm, aqs čłpṅeẁm**

čłpṅeẁnt – Arch it over something. *cmd.*

t̓uẏ – bend down; bend toward; inclined/shaped/formed to.
t̓uẏis – S/he bent s.o./s.t. down. **t̓uyn, t̓uyntxʷ**
es t̓uẏms – S/he is bending s.o./s.t. down. **ies t̓uym, as t̓uym**
qs t̓uẏms – S/he is going to bend s.o./s.t. down. **iqs t̓uym, aqs t̓uym**

t̓uẏmsts – S/he caused it to bend down. **t̓uymstn, t̓uymstxʷ**

es t̓uẏm – It is bent down.
es t̓it̓uẏ – Each one is bent down.

sct̓uẏ – something that's been bent down.
sct̓it̓uẏ – things that have been bent down.

t̓uẏmskʷ – Bend it down. *cmd.*
čt̓oyqn – bow the head down; put the head down. *See:* ***bow.***

čt̓uẏ – bend toward; inclined.
čt̓uẏmis – S/he bent toward s.t. **čt̓uymn, čt̓uymntxʷ**
es čt̓uẏms – S/he is bending toward s.t. **ies čt̓uym, as čt̓uym**
qs čt̓uẏms – S/he is going to bend toward s.t. **iqs čt̓uym, aqs čt̓uym**

sal̓kʷ – bend out of position; inflect; turn form the course.
sal̓kʷis – S/he bent s.t. **sal̓kʷn, sal̓kʷntxʷ**
es sal̓kʷms – S/he is bending s.t. **ies sal̓kʷm, as sal̓kʷm**
qs sal̓kʷms – S/he is going to bend s.t. **iqs sal̓kʷm, aqs sal̓kʷm**

es sal̓kʷ – It is winding.

es sal̓kʷmncuti – S/he/it is bending/turning one's self. *(as a colt/calf would do when playing)*

łopqn – top bent over; top pulled down. *suffix:* ***...qin, ...qn –*** *top.*
es łopqn – tree top is leaning over, heavy with fruit.

łopqis – S/he/it bent the tree top down. **łopqn, łopqntxʷ**
es łopqnms – S/he/it is bending the tree top down. **ies łopqnm, as łopqnm**
qs łopqnms – S/he/it is going to bend the tree top down. **iqs łopqnm, aqs łopqnm**

es nłpqnops – tail is bent down *(between legs). circumfix:* ***n...ups –*** *butt, tail.*
es nłpqnopsi – It is bending its tail down *(between legs).*

pel̓q – bent upward; flare up/out; warped.
pl̓qstes – S/he bent s.t. upward; flared s.t. out. **pl̓qsten, pl̓qstexʷ**
es pl̓qems – S/he is bending s.t. upward; is flaring s.t. out. **ies pl̓qem, as pl̓qem**

pl̓qalqʷ – warped wood; bent/warped upward wood.

yalk̓ʷ – bend/make into a circular shape. *See:* ***circle.***

q̓ʷatx̣ʷ – curved object; naturally curved object. *See:* ***curve.***

tkʷmim – bent crooked. *See:* ***crooked.***

nwalqn – tip the head. *(Also, a saying to be drinking alcohol.) suffix:* ***...qin, ...qn –*** *top. See:* ***tip.***

beneath

k̓ʷłišut – underneath; down below; under; beneath. *See:* ***under.***

nišut – down inside; deep inside. *See: **inside**.*

Benjamin

pnwé – Benjamin.

pisamá – Benjamin.

bent

piṅ – bend from one position to an curved/angular position. *See: **bend**.*

łopqn – top bent over; top pulled down. *See: **bend**.*

q̇ʷaṫx̣ʷ – curved object; naturally curved object. *See: **curve**.*

tkʷmim – bent crooked. *See: **crooked**.*

berry

sṗiqáłq – berry; fruit; raisin. *rt.: **ṗiẏáq** – ready, ripe; suffix: **...ałq** – smell, accompaniment.*

kʷel – change outward perception; change color; ripening/dying. *See: **change**.*

besseya

čečłu – red besseya; kitten tails; *Besseya rubra.*

best

čmaqs – perform at the peak of one's ability; best at something; pinnacle. *rt.: **čm** – extremity;*

čmaqsm – S/he/it performed at the top. **čn čmaqsm, kʷ čmaqsm**
es čmaqsi – S/he/it is performing at the top. **čnes čmaqsi, kʷes čmaqsi**
qs čmaqsi – S/he/it is going to be performing at the top. **čiqs čmaqsi, kʷqs čmaqsi**

čmaqsm – S/he/it performed at the top. **čn čmaqsm, kʷ čmaqsm**
es čmaqsi – S/he/it is performing at the top. **čnes čmaqsi, kʷes čmaqsi**
qs čmaqsi – S/he/it is going to be performing at the top. **čiqs čmaqsi, kʷqs čmaqsi**

čmaqs – S/he/it is the best. **čn čmaqs, kʷ čmaqs**

sšimł x̣e – best; most good.

q̇ʷił – energy; motivation; internal drive. *See: **capable**.*
q̇ʷiłmist, *q̇ʷíłmi* – do one's best; try hard from energy. *See: **capable**.*
q̇ʷiłmistš – Do your best; try your hardest. *cmd.*

musčst – do one's best with hope of succeeding; do something with confidence. *See: **confident**.*

bet

ṫk̇ʷseẇs, *ṫk̇ʷse* – bet. *rt.: **ṫuk̇ʷ** – put/place something down;suffix: **...éẇs** – in between, middle.*

ṫk̇ʷseẇs – S/he bet. **čn ṫk̇ʷseẇs, kʷ ṫk̇ʷseẇs**
es ṫk̇ʷseẇsi – S/he is betting. **čnes ṫk̇ʷseẇsi, kʷes ṫk̇ʷseẇsi**
qs ṫk̇ʷseẇsi – S/he is going to bet. **čiqs ṫk̇ʷseẇsi, kʷqs ṫk̇ʷseẇsi**
ṫk̇ʷséʔeẇs – They bet. **qeʔ ṫk̇ʷseẇs, p ṫk̇ʷseẇs**
es ṫk̇ʷséʔeẇsi – They are betting. **qeʔes ṫk̇ʷseẇsi, pes ṫk̇ʷseẇsi**
qs ṫk̇ʷséʔeẇsi – They are going to bet. **qeʔqs ṫk̇ʷseẇsi, pqs ṫk̇ʷseẇsi**

ṫk̇ʷseẇsiš – Bet. *cmd.*

nṫk̇ʷeẇs – put down between; in betting: place/match a bet between them. *rt.: **ṫuk̇ʷ** – put/place something down; prefix: **n...** – inside; suffix: **...éẇs** – in between, middle.*

nṫk̇ʷusis – S/he put it down in the middle. **nṫk̇ʷusn, nṫk̇ʷusntxʷ**
es nṫk̇ʷeẇsms – S/he is placing it down in the middle. **ies nṫk̇ʷeẇsm, as nṫk̇ʷeẇsm**
qs nṫk̇ʷeẇsms – S/he is going to place it down in the middle. **iqs nṫk̇ʷeẇsm, aqs nṫk̇ʷeẇsm**

nṫk̇ʷułlt – It was placed down in the middle; the bet was matched.

The **i** following uvular consonants (UC) and the glottal stop **ʔ** sound like English "*ey*" as in the words th*ey*, h*ey*, wh*ey*, etc. Salish UC are: **q, q̇, qʷ, q̇ʷ, x̣, x̣ʷ**. For example, the suffix **...qin** – head/top, is often spelled using English *ey* as "q*ey*n". So **qi, q̇i, qʷi, q̇ʷi, x̣i, x̣ʷi**, may be spelled with English *ey* as **q***ey*, **q̇***ey*, **qʷ***ey*, **q̇ʷ***ey*, **x̣***ey*, **x̣ʷ***ey* in other texts.

s.t. - something, the 3rd person
(s.t.) - something implied
s.o. - someone, the 3rd person
sl. - singular form
pl. - plural form
rt. - root word
cmd. - command
lit. - literally
fig. - figuratively
i.e., - for example
See: - Redirection to a related word.

ṫuk̇ʷ – put something down; lay *something down; place something down. See:* ***put.***

toẍʷseẇs – even; straight between; match up in betting. *rt.:* ***toẍʷ***– *straight; suffix:* ***...éẇs***– *in between, middle.*
toẍʷseẇs – S/he matched the bet. **čn toẍʷseẇs, kʷ toẍʷseẇs**
es toẍʷseẇsi – S/he is matching the bet. **čnes toẍʷseẇsi, kʷes toẍʷseẇsi**
qs toẍʷseẇsi – S/he is going to match the bet. **čiqs toẍʷseẇsi, kʷqs toẍʷseẇsi**
toẍʷséʔeẇs – They matched the bet. **qeʔ toẍʷseẇs, p toẍʷseẇs**
es toẍʷséʔeẇsi – They are matching the bet. **qeʔes toẍʷseẇsi, pes toẍʷseẇsi**
qs toẍʷséʔeẇsi – They are going to match the bet. **qeʔqs toẍʷseẇsi, pqs toẍʷseẇsi**

toẍʷseẇsiš – Match the bet. *cmd.*

k̇ʷłtuṅeẇs – not matched up in betting; belt doesn't fit. *rt.:* ***tuiṅ***– *fail/deficient; suffix:* ***...éẇs***– *in between, middle.*
k̇ʷłtuṅeẇs – S/he did not match the bet. **čn k̇ʷłtuṅeẇs, kʷ k̇ʷłtuṅeẇs**
es k̇ʷłtuṅeẇsi – S/he is not matching the bet. **čnes k̇ʷłtuṅeẇsi, kʷes k̇ʷłtuṅeẇsi**
qs k̇ʷłtuṅeẇsi – S/he is not going to match the bet. **čiqs k̇ʷłtuṅeẇsi, kʷqs k̇ʷłtuṅeẇsi**
k̇ʷłtuṅéʔeẇs – They did not match the bet. **qeʔ k̇ʷłtuṅeẇs, p k̇ʷłtuṅeẇs**
es k̇ʷłtuṅéʔeẇsi – They aren't matching the bet. **qeʔes k̇ʷłtuṅeẇsi, pes k̇ʷłtuṅeẇsi**
qs k̇ʷłtuṅéʔeẇsi – They aren't going to match the bet. **qeʔqs k̇ʷłtuṅeẇsi, pqs k̇ʷłtuṅeẇsi**

k̇ʷłtwiṅtm – fall short of something; deficient in something; unable to attain something. *See:* ***deficient.***

nṫmčim – flick with the finger; place a bet down as in flicking down a card or money. *See:* ***flick.***
nṫmčim – S/he placed down a bet. **čn nṫmčim, kʷ nṫmčim**
es nṫmčmi – S/he is placing down a bet. **čnes nṫmčmi, kʷes nṫmčmi**
qs nṫmčmi – S/he is going to place down a bet. **čiqs nṫmčmi, kʷqs nṫmčmi**
nṫmčim – They place down a bet. **qeʔ nṫmčim, p nṫmčim**
es nṫmčmíʔi – They are placing down a bet. **qeʔes nṫmčmi, pes nṫmčmi**
qs nṫmčmíʔi – They are going to place down a bet. **qeʔqs nṫmčmi, pqs nṫmčmi**

imi – absolutely; for sure; of course; It is obvious.
ẍʷa i mi – probably; I bet.

ẍʷa i mi u ta es mistexʷ – I bet you do not know it. **i mi lkʷut** – Of course it is far. **i mi u ta es mistexʷ** – Of course you do not know it.

better

ẍstwilš – get better. *suffix:* ***...wilš***– *developmental.*
es ẍstwilši – S/he/it is getting better. **čnes ẍstwilši, kʷes ẍstwilši**

ṫuul̓m – something got better.
ṫuul̓m – S/he/it got better. **čn ṫuul̓m, kʷ ṫuul̓m**
es ṫuul̓mi – S/he/it is getting better. **čnes ṫuul̓mi, kʷes ṫuul̓mi**
qs ṫuul̓mi – S/he/it is going to get better. **čiqs ṫuul̓mi, kʷqs ṫuul̓mi**

ṫuul̓mist – S/he/it got one's self better. **čn ṫuul̓mist, kʷ ṫuul̓mist**
es ṫuul̓misti – S/he/it is getting one's self better. **čnes ṫuul̓misti, kʷes ṫuul̓misti**
qs ṫuul̓misti – S/he/it is going to get one's self better. **čiqs ṫuul̓misti, kʷqs ṫuul̓misti**

i ṫuul̓ – S/he/it is better.

nṫul̓etkʷ – the liquid got better.

es nṫul̓setkʷi – the water is getting better after being dirty.

siscut – act better; smarty. *See:* ***smart.***

q̇xʷq̇exʷt, *q̇xʷq̇e* – proud; vain; think much of; stuck-up. *See:* ***stuck-up.***

between **q̇eʔ –** put/placed inside something; inserted between. *See:* ***insert.***

nq̇ʔeẇs – between two objects. *rt.:* ***q̇eʔ*** *– put inside; suffix:* ***...éẇs*** *– in between, middle.*
nq̇ʔeẇs – S/he/it was in between. **čn nq̇ʔeẇs, kʷ nq̇ʔeẇs**
es nq̇ʔeẇsi – S/he/it is in between. **čnes nq̇ʔeẇsi, kʷes nq̇ʔeẇsi**
qs nq̇ʔeẇsi – S/he/it is going to be in between. **čiqs nq̇ʔeẇsi, kʷqs nq̇ʔeẇsi**
nq̇ʔéʔeẇs – They were in between. **qeʔ nq̇ʔeẇs, p nq̇ʔeẇs**
es nq̇ʔéʔeẇsi – They are in between. **qeʔes nq̇ʔeẇsi, pes nq̇ʔeẇsi**
qs nq̇ʔéʔeẇsi – They are going to be in between. **qeʔqs nq̇ʔeẇsi, pqs nq̇ʔeẇsi**

scnq̇ʔeẇs – something that's been put in between; sandwich.

The **i** following uvular consonants (UC) and the glottal stop **ʔ** sound like English "*ey*" as in the words th*ey*, h*ey*, wh*ey*, etc. Salish UC are: **q**, **q̇**, **qʷ**, **q̇ʷ**, **x̣**, **x̣ʷ**. For example, the suffix ...**qin** – head/top, is often spelled using English *ey* as "q*ey*n". So **qi**, **q̇i**, **qʷi**, **q̇ʷi**, **x̣i**, **x̣ʷi**, may be spelled with English *ey* as **q***ey*, **q̇***ey*, **qʷ***ey*, **q̇ʷ***ey*, **x̣***ey*, **x̣ʷ***ey* in other texts.

nq̇emuscut, *nq̇emuscú* – put one's self between things. *rt.:* ***q̇eʔ*** *– put inside; suffix:* ***...cut*** *– action to the self.*
nq̇emuscut – S/he/it got one's self between (s.t.). **čn nq̇emuscut, kʷ nq̇emuscut**
es nq̇emuscuti – S/he/it is getting one's self between (s.t.). **čnes nq̇emuscuti, kʷes nq̇emuscuti**
qs nq̇emuscuti – S/he/it is going to get one's self between (s.t.). **čiqs nq̇emuscuti, kʷqs nq̇emuscuti**
nq̇emuscúʔut – They got themselves between (s.t.). **qeʔ nq̇emuscut, p nq̇emuscut**
es nq̇emuscúʔuti – They're getting themselves between (s.t.). **qeʔes nq̇emuscuti, pes nq̇emuscuti**
qs nq̇emuscúʔuti – They are going to get themselves between (s.t.). **qeʔqs nq̇emuscuti, pqs nq̇emuscuti**

nq̇eq̇emuscut – put one's self between things. *(i.e., a crowd of people.)*

čn nq̇eq̇emuscut u čn čx̣ʷéct – I went into a crowd and passed through. **čn nʔułxʷ u čn nq̇emuscut –** I went inside the place and put myself in between.

snihews, *snihe* – middle; between. *suffix:* ***...éẇs*** *– in between, middle.*

beverage **scsust,** *scsu* – something that is drunk. *prefix:* ***sc...*** *– s.t. that's been done/made/prepared.*

beyond **x̣ił ci č ciʔ –** beyond; way over there.

bible **sx̣x̣épeʔ –** bible.

big **kʷtunt –** It is big.
kʷtunsts – S/he/it made s.t. big. **kʷtunstn, kʷtunstxʷ**
es kʷtunms – S/he/it is making s.t. big. **ies kʷtunm, as kʷtunm**
qs kʷtunms – S/he/it is going to make s.t. big. **iqs kʷtunm, aqs kʷtunm**

skʷtunt – bigness; something big.
kʷtnálqʷ – tall person.
čłkʷkʷtṅéẇs – It has a little big belly.

kʷtunskʷ – Make it big. *cmd.*
kʷtntwilš – get big; grow big. *See:* ***grow.***
kʷtnels – proud; think highly; have confidence. *See:* ***proud.***
kʷtncinm – praise; talk highly of someone; speak big of someone. *See:* ***praise.***
kʷtnlsmist – think highly of one's self; think big of one's self; self-conceited. *See:* ***proud.***

s.t. - something, the 3rd person
(s.t.) - something implied
s.o. - someone, the 3rd person
sl. - singular form
pl. - plural form
rt. - root word
cmd. - command
lit. - literally
fig. - figuratively
i.e., - for example
See: - Redirection to a related word.

l čeṅ u ecx̣lskʷtunt – How big is it? **čn ecx̣lskʷtunt t anwi –** I am as big as you. **čeṅ łu šymł kʷtunt –** Which is the biggest? **kʷtnéłxʷ łu kʷtisi –** Big Blanket has a big house.

kʷtił... – *prefix indicating something is great or big.*
kʷtiłqpełc̓e? – big plate.
kʷtiłx̣est – really good.
kʷtiłpx̣pax̣t – very wise.
kʷtisic̓m – big blanket.

kʷtiłq̓sip – really long time.
kʷtiscut – make one's self important, great; brag. *See:* ***brag.***

tečéṅ – great; really big.
tečnmcut – S/he/it did (s.t.) really big/great. **čn tečnmcut, kʷ tečnmcut**
es tečnmcuti – S/he/it is doing (s.t.) really big/great. **čnes tečnmcuti, kʷes tečnmcuti**
qs tečnmcuti – S/he/it is going to do (s.t.) really big/great. **čiqs tečnmcuti, kʷqs tečnmcuti**
tečnmcú?ut – They did (s.t.) really big/great. **qe? tečnmcut, p tečnmcut**
es tečnmcú?uti – They are doing (s.t.) really big/great. **qe?es tečnmcuti, pes tečnmcuti**
qs tečnmcú?uti – They are going to do (s.t.) really big/great. **qe?qs tečnmcuti, pqs tečnmcuti**

tečéṅ skʷtunt – It is really big. **ci sk̓ʷl̓sn?iłntm u tečéṅ suswisšn** – The eating rate was made to be really long.

ƛ̓e tečen t sq̓sip – really long time ago.

yult – large in girth. *(of cylindrical objects.) See:* ***girth.***
t čeṅ ec̓x̣lsyult – How big is the girth/diameter?

Big Arm **łqʷqʷ?e?** – Big Arm, Flathead Nation. *lit. little corner.*

Big Blanket **kʷtisic̓m,** *kʷtisi* – Big blanket; *(a person's name).*

Big Draw **ll?ot** – Big Draw, Flathead Nation.

big-eared bat **t̓ltel̓ẇéliye?,** *t̓ltel̓ẇé* – bat.

Bigfoot **sc̓wene** – Bigfoot, giant, Sasquatch.

Big Hole River **skʷumcné sewłkʷs** – Big Hole River.

bighorn sheep **ł?umnélsčn,** *ł?umné* – bighorn sheep, mountain sheep; *Ovis canadensis.*
nłmqélsčn, *nłmqé* – bighorn sheep ewe, mountain sheep ewe; *Ovis canadensis.*

big sagebrush **p̓up̓unéłp** – sagebrush; big sagebrush; *Artemisia tridentata.*

bike **snčmtéẇstn,** *snčmté* – something that is stradled, *(i.e., bike, horse, motorcycle, etc). rt.:* ***emut*** *– sit; prefix:* ***sn...*** *– a place of; suffix:* ***...éẇs*** *– in between, middle; suffix:* ***...tin, ...tn*** *– means of/device.*
snčmteẇsts – his/her bike. **isnčmteẇs, asnčmteẇs**

nšllčupstn, nšllču – bike. *lit. it spins on the back end.*

nłx̣ʷlq̓ʷupstn – bike. *lit. it rolls on the back end.*

billiards **čłx̣ʷlx̣ʷlq̓ʷi** – play pool/billiards.
es čłx̣ʷlx̣ʷlq̓ʷi – S/he is playing pool. **čnes čłx̣ʷlx̣ʷlq̓ʷi, kʷes čłx̣ʷlx̣ʷlq̓ʷi**

ha kʷqs k̓ʷis čłx̣ʷlx̣ʷlq̓ʷi – Are you going to go play pool?

billiard table **snčłx̣ʷlx̣ʷlq̓ʷi** – pool/billiard table.

bingo **čłqmqmnełqʷi,** *čłqmqmne* – play bingo. *prefix:* ***cł...*** *– surface; rt.:* ***qmin*** *– place things down.*

čłqmin – place things on the surface. *See:* ***lay***.
es čłqmini – S/he is placing things on the surface.

bipod
es ċalx̣ʷ – poles lashed together; bipod.
čełlċalx̣ʷ – tripod; three poles lashed together. *rt.:* ***ċalx̣ʷ*** *– poles lashed together.*

birch
čqʷłṅalqʷ, *čqʷłṅa* – white birch; *Betula papyifera*.

sicqṅełp – red birch; *Betula occidentalis*.

bird
sxʷexʷʔe – birds.
es xʷexʷʔe – birds take flight.
es xʷexʷʔemi – birds are taking flight.

łxʷixʷey̓uł, *łxʷixʷey̓u* – bird; small animal.

laʔli – unidentified bird.

łšál̓šl̓ – unidentified bird.

qáƛ̓aƛ̓lasulexʷ – unidentified bird.

łkʷakʷláqʷ – unidentified bird.

birth
k̓ʷul̓ – born; birth; made.
es k̓ʷul̓lel̓ti – She is having a baby.

es k̓ʷul̓li – S/he/it is being born.
čn k̓ʷul̓ ci č ciʔ – I was born over there.

es nċalew̓si – She is having pains inside the belly. *See:* ***ache***.

nċaléls – feel pain inside. *See:* ***ache***.

es enwncuti – She is feeling/sensing; starting labor. *See:* ***feel***.

birthday
čk̓ʷul̓ltn – time of birth.

nčcnšncut, *nčcnšncu* – make one revolution; meet your tracks. *rt.:* ***čicn*** *– meet; infix:* ***…šn*** *– foot, tracks.*

biscuit root
pčl̓u – biscuit root, white camas; *Lomatium piperi*.

Bismarck
pisamá – Bismarck, North Dakota.

bison
q̓ʷiq̓ʷáy – buffalo; bison; *Bison bison. lit. many blacks. See:* ***buffalo***.

nłox̣ʷénč – National Bison Range, Flathead Nation.

bite
k̓ʷʔem – bite.
k̓ʷʔem – S/he/it bit. **čn k̓ʷʔem, kʷ k̓ʷʔem**
es k̓ʷʔemi – S/he/it is biting. **čnes k̓ʷʔemi, kʷes k̓ʷʔemi**
qs k̓ʷʔemi – S/he/it is going to bite. **čiqs k̓ʷʔemi, kʷqs k̓ʷʔemi**
k̓ʷʔéʔem – They bit. **qeʔ k̓ʷʔem, p k̓ʷʔem**
es k̓ʷʔéʔemi – They are biting. **qeʔes k̓ʷʔemi, pes k̓ʷʔemi**
qs k̓ʷʔéʔemi – They are going to bite. **qeʔqs k̓ʷʔemi, pqs k̓ʷʔemi**

k̓ʷʔentés – S/he/it bit s.t./s.o. **k̓ʷʔentén, k̓ʷʔentéxʷ**
es k̓ʷʔems – S/he/it is biting s.t./s.o. **ies k̓ʷʔem, as k̓ʷʔem**
qs k̓ʷʔems – S/he/it is going to bite s.t./s.o. **iqs k̓ʷʔem, aqs k̓ʷʔem**

The **i** following uvular consonants (UC) and the glottal stop **ʔ** sound like English "*ey*" as in the words *they, hey, whey*, etc. Salish UC are: **q, q̓, qʷ, q̓ʷ, x̣, x̣ʷ**. For example, the suffix **…qin** – head/top, is often spelled using English *ey* as "q*ey*n". So **qi, q̓i, qʷi, q̓ʷi, x̣i, x̣ʷi**, may be spelled with English *ey* as **q***ey*, **q̓***ey*, **qʷ***ey*, **q̓ʷ***ey*, **x̣***ey*, **x̣ʷ***ey* in other texts.

s.t. - something, the 3rd person
(s.t.) - something implied
s.o. - someone, the 3rd person
sl. - singular form
pl. - plural form
rt. - root word
cmd. - command
lit. - literally
fig. - figuratively
i.e., - for example
See: - Redirection to a related word.

k̓ʷʔentéʔes – They bit s.t./s.o. **qeʔ k̓ʷʔentém, k̓ʷʔentép**
es k̓ʷʔéʔems – They are biting s.t./s.o. **qeʔes k̓ʷʔem, es k̓ʷʔemp**
qs k̓ʷʔéʔems – They are going to bite s.t./s.o. **qeʔqs k̓ʷʔem, qs k̓ʷʔemp**

k̓ʷek̓ʷʔém – chew; bite repeatedly. *See:* ***chew.***

k̓ʷʔent – Bite it. *cmd.*
k̓ʷʔencut – S/he/it bit one's self. **čn k̓ʷʔencut, kʷ k̓ʷʔencut**

es k̓ʷéʔemi – Biting something accidently; when flies are biting horses and deer.
čnes k̓ʷʔemi t scom – I accidently bit the bone. **qʷo es k̓ʷʔems t slaqs –** Mosquitoes are biting me.
kʷ iqs čk̓ʷʔelpsm – I am going to bite your neck.

k̓ʷʔaqs – hold (bite) something in the mouth.
k̓ʷʔaqsis – S/he/it held s.t. in the mouth. **k̓ʷʔaqsn, k̓ʷʔaqsntxʷ**
es k̓ʷʔaqsms – S/he/it is holding s.t. in the mouth. **ies k̓ʷʔaqsm, as k̓ʷʔaqsm**
qs k̓ʷʔaqsms – S/he/it is going to hold s.t. in the mouth. **iqs k̓ʷʔaqsm, aqs k̓ʷʔaqsm**

k̓ʷʔaqsnt – Hold it in your mouth. *cmd.*

es k̓ʷʔaqsm t sqel̓tč ci mla – That raven has meat in its mouth.

k̓ʷłk̓ʷʔem – bite something off.
k̓ʷłk̓ʷʔem – S/he/it was biting s.t. off. **čn k̓ʷłk̓ʷʔem, kʷ k̓ʷłk̓ʷʔem**
es k̓ʷłk̓ʷʔemi – S/he/it is biting s.t. off. **čnes k̓ʷłk̓ʷʔemi, kʷes k̓ʷłk̓ʷʔemi**
qs k̓ʷłk̓ʷʔemi – S/he/it is going to be biting s.t. off. **čiqs k̓ʷłk̓ʷʔemi, kʷqs k̓ʷłk̓ʷʔemi**

k̓ʷłk̓ʷʔentés – S/he/it bit s.t. off. **k̓ʷłk̓ʷʔentén, k̓ʷłk̓ʷʔentéxʷ**
es k̓ʷłk̓ʷʔems – S/he/it is biting s.t. off. **ies k̓ʷłk̓ʷʔem, as k̓ʷłk̓ʷʔem**
qs k̓ʷłk̓ʷʔems – S/he/it is going to bite s.t. off. **iqs k̓ʷłk̓ʷʔem, aqs k̓ʷłk̓ʷʔem**

k̓ʷłk̓ʷʔentén – It got bitten off.

k̓ʷłk̓ʷʔent – Bite it off. *cmd.*
čk̓ʷʔečstm – Bite a finger off.
k̓ʷłnk̓ʷʔaqsm – Bite a nose off.
k̓ʷłk̓ʷʔenʔem – Bite an ear off.

x̣ƛ̓im – chew away at something; gnaw. *See:* ***chew.***
x̣ƛ̓cin – graze/eat. *See:* ***graze.***
x̣ƛ̓cin – horse. *(word for horse because of the way it eats)*

x̣ƛ̓ulexʷ – graze on the land. *See:* ***graze.***

bitter

tax̣ – bitter; spicy.
i tax̣ – It is bitter.
i łttax̣ – It is a little bitter.
i ntax̣kʷ – It is bitter (liquid).

ntax̣elsm – have bitterness toward someone.
es ntax̣elsm – S/he had bitterness. **čn ntax̣elsm, kʷ ntax̣elsm**
es ntax̣elsi – S/he has bitterness. **čnes ntax̣elsi, kʷes ntax̣elsi**
qs ntax̣elsi – S/he is going to have bitterness. **čiqs ntax̣elsi, kʷqs ntax̣elsi**
es ntax̣éʔelsm – They had bitterness. **qeʔ ntax̣elsm, p ntax̣elsm**
es ntax̣éʔelsi – They have bitterness. **qeʔes ntax̣elsi, pes ntax̣elsi**
qs ntax̣éʔelsi – They are going to have bitterness. **qeʔqs ntax̣elsi, pqs ntax̣elsi**

čntax̣elsmis – S/he had bitterness toward s.o. **čntax̣elsmn, kʷ čntax̣elsmntxʷ**

es ntax̣elsmms – S/he has bitterness toward s.o. **ies ntax̣elsmm, as ntax̣elsmm**
qs ntax̣elsmms – S/he is going to have bitterness toward s.o. **iqs ntax̣elsmm, aqs ntax̣elsmm**
čntax̣éʔelsmis – They had bitterness toward s.o. **qeʔ čntax̣elsmntm, čntax̣elsmntp**
es ntax̣éʔelsmms – They have bitterness toward s.o. **qeʔes ntax̣elsmm, es ntax̣elsmmp**
qs ntax̣éʔelsmms – They are going to have bitterness toward s.o. **qeʔqs ntax̣elsmm, qs ntax̣elsmmp**

ntax̣elsmis – S/he had bitterness toward s.t. **ntax̣elsmn, kʷ ntax̣elsmntxʷ**
ntax̣éʔelsmis – They had bitterness toward s.t. **qeʔ ntax̣elsmntm, ntax̣elsmntp**

The **i** following uvular consonants (UC) and the glottal stop ʔ sound like English "*ey*" as in the words *they*, *hey*, *whey*, etc. Salish UC are: **q**, **q̇**, **qʷ**, **q̇ʷ**, **x̣**, **x̣ʷ**. For example, the suffix ...**qin** – head/top, is often spelled using English *ey* as "q*ey*n". So **qi**, **q̇i**, **qʷi**, **q̇ʷi**, **x̣i**, **x̣ʷi**, may be spelled with English *ey* as **q***ey*, **q̇***ey*, **qʷ***ey*, **q̇ʷ***ey*, **x̣***ey*, **x̣ʷ***ey* in other texts.

bitter cherry

pčłṅełp, *pčłṅe* – bitter cherry; *Prunus emarginata.*

bittern

x̣witx̣ʷu – American bittern.

bitterroot

sṗéƛ̓m – bitterroot; *Lewisia rediviva.*
sṗéƛ̓m spq̇niʔ – May *(month of the bitterroot). See:* ***May.***

nṫqétkʷnt asṗéƛ̓m l séwłkʷ – Put your bitterroot in water. **x̣ił kʷ speƛ̓m** – You are bitterroot; you are pouting.

Bitterroot Mountains

čkʷlkʷlqin, *čkʷlkʷlqi* – Bitterroot Mountains, Montana/Idaho; *lit. red top mountains.*

Bitterroot River

nstetcčxʷtetkʷ – Bitterroot River, Montana; *lit. waters of the Red Osier Dogwood. suffix:* ***...etkʷ, ...tkʷ*** *– liquid*

snʔaṁša – trail up the West Fork of the Bitterroot River. *rt.:* ***iṁš*** *– move camp.*

black

q̇ʷáy – black; dark. **q̇ʷiq̇ʷáy** – blacks; darks; buffalo. *pl.*
q̇ʷáyis – S/he made it black. **q̇ʷáyn, q̇ʷáyntxʷ**
es q̇ʷáyms – S/he is making it black. **ies q̇ʷáym, as q̇ʷáym**
qs q̇ʷáyms – S/he is going to make it black. **iqs q̇ʷáym, aqs q̇ʷáym**

i q̇ʷáy – It is black.
i łq̇ʷq̇ʷáy – It is a little black; blackish.

q̇ʷáynt – Make it black. *cmd.*
q̇ʷaynumt – S/he/it finally became black. **čn q̇ʷaynumt, kʷ q̇ʷaynumt**
q̇ʷaq̇ʷáyeʔ – blackie.
q̇ʷiq̇ʷáy – buffalo. *lit. – many blacks.*
sčq̇ʷeẏšn, *sčq̇ʷe* – Blackfeet.
q̇ʷáylqs – priest. *suffix:* ***...lqs, ...alqs*** *– clothes. lit. black robe/clothes*
q̇ʷyós – African-American.
čq̇ʷiq̇ʷá – prunes.
i ṅqʷáys – black eye. *rt.:* ***qʷáy*** *– blue.*
i q̇ʷáy ye ṗiṗuyšn – This car is black.

q̇ʷays – black face.
q̇ʷisis – S/he made s.o.'s face black. **q̇ʷisn, q̇ʷisntxʷ**
q̇ʷiʔisis – They made s.o.'s face black. **qeʔ q̇ʷisntm, q̇ʷisntp**

q̇ʷisntm – His/her/its face was made black.

ṗič – glossy; used to describe the shiny surface of rubber and the skin of black people. *See:* ***glossy.***

s.t. - something, the 3rd person
(s.t.) - something implied
s.o. - someone, the 3rd person
sl. - singular form
pl. - plural form
rt. - root word
cmd. - command
lit. - literally
fig. - figuratively
i.e., - for example
See: - Redirection to a related word.

black bear **nłámqeʔ** – black bear; *Ursus americanus.* **nłmłámqeʔ** – black bears. *pl.*
nłałṁqeʔ – little black bear.
nłṁłáṁqeʔ – little black bears.

wičtn łu nłámqeʔ – I saw a black bear.

black berry **nłámqeʔ sʔiłis** – bearberry honeysuckle; black twin-berry; *Lonicera involucrata.*

black-billed magpie **áṅṅ** – magpie; black-billed magpie; *Pica hudsonia.*

blackbird **ƛ̓čƛ̓áčqn,** *ƛ̓čƛ̓á* – blackbird; Brewer's blackbird; *Euphagus cyanocephalus.*

čłq̇ẏe ƛ̓čƛ̓á – red-winged blackbird; *Agelaius phoeniceus.*

čkʷaliyoqn ƛ̓čƛ̓á – yellow-headed blackbird; *Xanthocephalus xanthocephalus.*

ƛ̓čƛ̓á esq̇ẏe – lark bunting; *Calamospiza melanocorys.*

black bullhead **upupci** – channel catfish; *Ictalurus punctatus*; black bullhead; *Ameiurus melas.*

blackcap **mcukʷ** – black raspberry; blackberry; blackcap; *Rubus occidentalis.*

black-capped chickadee **ċípana** – black-capped chickadee; *Poecile atricapillus.*

black-chinned hummingbird **łx̣ʷx̣ʷṅi** – hummingbird; rufous, black-chinned, calliope; *Archilochus alexandri.*

black crowned night heron **smat̓q̓ʷul** – black crowned night heron; *Nycticorax nycticorax.*

black elderberry **ċkʷikʷ** – elderberry; black elderberry; blue elderberry; *Sambucus racemosa.*

black eye **i ṅqʷáys** – black eye. **i ṅq̇ʷiq̇ʷays** – black eyes. *pl.*

i čq̇ʷaẏs – black of the eyes.
i čq̇ʷiq̇ʷays – person's color of eyes (black).

Blackfeet **sčq̇ʷeẏšn,** *sčq̇ʷe* – Blackfeet.
qeʔ nčcničiłlt t sčq̇ʷeẏq̇ʷe – The Blackfeet caught up with us.

snxʷlsčint, *snxʷlsči* – Blood.
sxʷiyesčint – Ant People, a band of the Blackfeet.
łcċmiċeʔ – Small Robes, a band of the Blackfeet.

black hawthorn **sxʷexʷʔénčełp,** *sxʷexʷʔenč* – thorn bush, thorn tree, hawthorn; *Crataegus douglasii.*
sxʷeʔne – thorn berry.

snčl̓palqʷ, *snčl̓pa* – thorn wood, coyote wood; *grows east of the continental divide, has large thorns.*

black-headed grosbeak **nkʷtnáqs** – grosbeak; *Pheucticus elanocephalus.*

black lichen **sqʷl̓ápqn,** *sqʷl̓á* – cooked black tree moss, black lichen.
kʷ čsqʷl̓á – You gather black tree moss.

šawtmqn – black tree moss, black lichen; *Bryoria fremontii.*

black raspberry **mcukʷ** – black raspberry; blackberry; blackcap; *Rubus occidentalis.*

black-tail deer **puwélsčn,** *puwé* – black-tail buck; male mule deer; *Odocoileus hemionus.*
pupuwélsčn – black-tail bucks; male mule deers.
puwélsčnelxʷ – black-tail buck hide.

sṫulċeʔ – black-tail doe; female mule deer; mule; *Odocoileus hemionus.* **sṫl̓ṫulċeʔ** *pl.*
sṫulċeʔlxʷ – black-tail doe hide.

black-tailed prairie dog **heẁheẁmuł** – black-tailed prairie dog; *Cynomys ludovicianus. lit. one that habitually barks.*

słkʷu – white-tailed prairie dog; *Cynomys leucurus.*

black tree moss **sqʷl̓ápqn,** *sqʷl̓á* – cooked black tree moss; black lichen.
kʷ čsqʷl̓á – You gather black tree moss.

šawtmqn – black tree moss, black lichen; *Bryoria fremontii.*

black widow **tupn** – black widow spider; *Latrodectus hesperus.*

bladder **sntčeẏtn** – urinary bladder. *prefix:* ***sn...*** *– a place of; suffix:* ***...tin, ...tn*** *– means of/device.*

blame **čtem** – blame.
čtemis – S/he blamed s.o. **čtemn, čtemntxʷ**
es čtems – S/he is blaming s.o. **ies čtem, as čtem**
qs čtems – S/he is going to blame s.o. **iqs čtem, aqs čtem**
čtéʔemis – They blamed s.o. **qeʔ čtemntm, čtemntp**
es čtéʔems – They are blaming s.o. **qeʔes čtem, es čtemmp**
qs čtéʔems – They are going to blame s.o. **qeʔqs čtemm, qs čtemmp**

čtmtmłmuł – one that habitually blames. *suffix:* ***...łmuł*** *– one that habitually does.*

kʷ ies čtemm – I am blaming you. **qʷo čtemmntm** – I was blamed. **x̣ił kʷ čtmtmłmuł** – Gee, you are one who always blames.

blank **čmi u kʷes čx̣lx̣al u hoy** – Your eyes are open but you have a blank face. *derogatory statement.*

blanket **siċm** – blanket.
kʷtisiċm – big blanket.
łssiċm – little blanket.

es siċm – S/he is wearing a blanket. **čnes siċm, kʷes siċm**

snq̓ʷomi – comforter; quilt (stuffed blanket; thick blanket).

sṫqʷṫaqʷi – quilt (pieces sewn together).

blank tape **čloʔmintn** – something to put onto; recording tape. *See:* ***record.***

tmsewneʔ čloʔmintn – blank recording tape; has nothing to hear.

bleed **ƛ̓um̓st** – bleed.
es ƛ̓um̓sti – S/he is bleeding. **čnes ƛ̓um̓sti, kʷes ƛ̓um̓sti**

smll̓áqs, *smll̓á* – nosebleed. *rt.:* ***mlip*** *– overflow.*
es mll̓áqsi – S/he/it has a nosebleed. **čnes mll̓áqsi, kʷes mll̓áqsi**

bless **ččáwpleʔ** – pray for/over something; bless. *rt.:* ***ċáw*** *– pray. See:* ***pray.***

The **i** following uvular consonants (UC) and the glottal stop **ʔ** sound like English "*ey*" as in the words *they, hey, whey,* etc. Salish UC are: **q, q̓, qʷ, q̓ʷ, x̣, x̣ʷ**. For example, the suffix ...**qin** – head/top, is often spelled using English *ey* as "*qeyn*". So **qi, q̓i, qʷi, q̓ʷi, x̣i, x̣ʷi**, may be spelled with English *ey* as **q***ey*, **q̓***ey*, **qʷ***ey*, **q̓ʷ***ey*, **x̣***ey*, **x̣ʷ***ey* in other texts.

s.t. - something, the 3rd person
(s.t.) - something implied
s.o. - someone, the 3rd person
sl. - singular form
pl. - plural form
rt. - root word
cmd. - command
lit. - literally
fig. - figuratively
i.e., - for example
See: - Redirection to a related word.

ččáwpleʔ – S/he blessed. **čn ččáwpleʔ, kʷ ččáwpleʔ**
es ččáwpleʔi – S/he is blessing. **čnes ččáwpleʔi, kʷes ččáwpleʔi**
qs ččáwpleʔi – S/he is going to bless. **čiqs ččáwpleʔi, kʷqs ččáwpleʔi**
ččáʔawpleʔ – They blessed. **qeʔ ččáwpleʔ, p ččáwpleʔ**
es ččáʔawpleʔi – They are blessing. **qeʔes ččáwpleʔi, pes ččáwpleʔi**
qs ččáʔawpleʔi – They are going to bless. **qeʔqs ččáwpleʔi, pqs ččáwpleʔi**

ččáwpleʔis – S/he blessed s.t./s.o. **ččáwpleʔn, ččáwpleʔntxʷ**
es ččáwpleʔms – S/he is blessing s.t./s.o. **ies ččáwpleʔm, as ččáwpleʔm**
qs ččáwpleʔms – S/he is going to bless s.t./s.o. **iqs ččáwpleʔm, aqs ččáwpleʔm**
ččáʔawpleʔis – They blessed s.t./s.o. **qeʔ ččáwpleʔntm, ččáwpleʔntp**
es ččáʔawpleʔms – They are blessing s.t./s.o. **qeʔes ččáwpleʔm, es ččáwpleʔmp**
qs ččáʔawpleʔms – They are going to bless s.t./s.o. **qeʔqs ččáwpleʔm, qs ččáwpleʔmp**

ččáwpleʔnt – Bless it. *cmd.*

qeʔ ččáwpleʔnłlt – We were blessed.

blind

čnmqín, *čnmqí* **–** blind.
es čnmqín – S/he/it is blind. **čnes čnmqín, kʷes čnmqín**

čnmṗqín, *čnmṗqí* **–** go blind.
čnmṗqín – S/he went blind. **čn čnmṗqín, kʷ čnmṗqín**
čnmnmṗqíʔin – Each one of them went blind. **qeʔ čnmnmṗqín, p čnmnmṗqín**

čṗaq̇aq̇us – S/he/it blinded by lights. **čn čṗaṗaq̇us, kʷ čṗaṗaq̇us**
nṗaq̇aq̇us – S/he/it is blinded by lights. **čn nṗaṗaq̇us, kʷ nṗaṗaq̇us**

nċk̇ʷlus – snow-blind. *See:* ***snow-blind.***

blink

čcaps – blink.
čcpcapsm – S/he blinked. **čn čcpcapsm, kʷ čcpcapsm**
es čcpcapsi – S/he/it is blinking. **čnes čcpcapsi, kʷes čcpcapsi**
qs čcpcapsi – S/he/it is going to blink. **čiqs čcpcapsi, kʷqs čcpcapsi**
čcáʔapsm – They blinked. **qeʔ čcapsm, p čcapsm**
es čcpcáʔapsi – They are blinking. **qeʔes čcpcapsi, pes čcpcapsi**
qs čcpcáʔapsi – They are going to blink. **qeʔqs čcpcapsi, pqs čcpcapsi**

čcpcpsmuł – one that habitually blinks. *suffix:* ***...łmuł*** *– one that habitually does.*

čmi u es ncpcipsi – S/he only blinks.

nċipsm – wink; close eye. *See:* ***wink.***

čx̣aʔx̣apsus, *čx̣aʔx̣apsu* **–** stare. *See:* ***stare.***

čƛ̓lƛ̓lpus – not blinking; eyes are still.

blister

haqʷqʷ – It blistered.
sx̣qʷqʷé – blister.
haqʷqʷečst – blistered hand. **haqʷaqʷqʷečst** *pl.* *suffix:* ***...ečst, ...čst*** *– of the hand.*
haqʷqʷšin – blistered foot. **haqʷaqʷqʷšin** *pl.*
nhaqʷqʷeneʔ – blistered ear.
nhaqʷqʷups – blistered butt.

ptáq – sore spot, almost blistered.
ƛ̓e ptaq – It is already sore.
es ptqmi – It is getting sore.

nptkʷups, *nptqu* – sore butt. *(after riding a horse.)*
ptptqečst – sore hands. *suffix:* ***...ečst, ...čst*** *– of the hand.*
nptqełċeʔ – sore inside.
es nptqełċeʔi – S/he/it is sore inside. **čnes nptqełċeʔi, kʷes nptqełċeʔi**

nqlewiyecn – thrush; white blisters. *suffix:* ***...cin, ...cn*** *– action of the mouth.*

> The **i** following uvular consonants (UC) and the glottal stop ʔ sound like English "*ey*" as in the words th*ey*, h*ey*, wh*ey*, etc. Salish UC are: **q, q̓, qʷ, q̓ʷ, x̣, x̣ʷ**. For example, the suffix ...**qin** – head/top, is often spelled using English *ey* as "q*ey*n". So **qi, q̓i, qʷi, q̓ʷi, x̣i, x̣ʷi**, may be spelled with English *ey* as **q***ey*, **q̓***ey*, **qʷ***ey*, **q̓ʷ***ey*, **x̣***ey*, **x̣ʷ***ey* in other texts.

blizzard

qʷułmncut, *qʷułmncu* – dust, blizzard storm.
es qʷułmncuti – There is low visibility from a dust storm or blizzard; *(fig., this can be said of someone really "dancing up a storm," making dust).*

es p̓ič̓łqi – strong/big wind; blizzard, but does not refer to snow.

bloat

peʔxʷénč – bloat. *suffix:* ***...enč*** *– within.*
peʔxʷénč – S/he got bloated. **čn peʔxʷénč, kʷ peʔxʷénč**

q̓xʷpénč – bloat, constipated. *suffix:* ***...enč*** *– within.*

block

łusussšnalqʷ – wooden blocks. *lit. little long wood.*

yém̓mist, *yém̓m* – despaired; frustrated; troubled; worried; have a block; have a dilemma. *See:* ***despair.***

tqep – dam; restrict; choke off. *See:* ***dam.***

blood

snxʷul – blood.

ƛ̓um̓st – bleed. *See:* ***bleed.***

Blood tribe

snxʷlsči – Blood *(a band of the Blackfeet Nation).*

bloom

sčċek̓ʷełp – flower in a tree; blossom, bloom.
sčċek̓ʷełpm – The tree blossoms came out.
es čċek̓ʷełpi – The tree blossoms are coming out.

sċek̓ʷulexʷ – flower on the ground. *See:* ***flower.***

sċéʔek̓ʷ – flower. *See:* ***flower.***

čmkʷkʷełp – bud.

t̓lqʷqin – when buds first open up. *rt.:* ***t̓lip*** *– it came open.*

blooming sally

qʷqʷółnłp, qʷqʷołqnéłp – fireweed; blooming sally; *Chamerion angustifolium.*

blow

puxʷm – blow.
puxʷm – S/he blew. **čn puxʷm, kʷ puxʷm**
es puxʷi – S/he is blowing. **čnes puxʷi, kʷes puxʷi**
qs puxʷi – S/he is going to blow. **čiqs puxʷi, čiqs puxʷi**
púʔuxʷm – They blew. **qeʔ puxʷm, p puxʷm**
es púʔuxʷi – They are blowing. **qeʔes puxʷi, pes puxʷi**
qs púʔuxʷi – They are going to blow. **qeʔqs puxʷi, pqs puxʷi**

puxʷist – S/he blew on one's self. **čn puxʷist, kʷ puxʷist**
es puxʷisti – S/he is blowing on one's self. **čnes puxʷisti, kʷes puxʷisti**
qs puxʷisti – S/he is going to blow on one's self. **čiqs puxʷisti, čiqs puxʷisti**

puxʷis – S/he blew s.t. **puxʷn, puxʷntxʷ**
es puxʷms – S/he is blowing s.t. **ies puxʷm, as puxʷm**
qs puxʷms – S/he is going to blow s.t. **iqs puxʷm, aqs puxʷm**

> s.t. - something, the 3rd person
> (s.t.) - something implied
> s.o. - someone, the 3rd person
> *sl.* - singular form
> *pl.* - plural form
> *rt.* - root word
> *cmd.* - command
> *lit.* - literally
> *fig.* - figuratively
> *i.e.,* - for example
> *See:* - Redirection to a related word.

púʔuxʷis – They blew it. **qeʔ puxʷntm, puxʷntp**
es púʔuxʷms – They are blowing it. **qeʔes puxʷm, es puxʷmp**
qs púʔuxʷms – They are going to blow it. **qeʔqs puxʷm, qs puxʷmp**

puxʷš – Blow. *cmd.*
puxʷnt – Blow it. *cmd.*
k̓ʷłpuxʷm – blow from underneath.
npuxʷm – blow into/up.
puxʷs – blow a fire.
npuxʷs – blow into the eye.
npuxʷeneʔ – blow into ears.
npuxʷcneʔ – blow air out of ears.

ṅem puxʷm – S/he will blow. **ṅem čn puxʷm, ṅem kʷ puxʷm**
ṅem púʔuxʷm – They will blow. **ṅem qeʔ puxʷm, ṅem p puxʷm**
ṅem qes puxʷms – S/he will be blowing it. **ṅem iqes puxʷm, ṅem aqes puxʷm**
ṅem qes púʔuxʷms – They will be blowing it. **ṅem qeʔqes puxʷm, ṅem qes puxʷmp**

es puxʷi t ċeẇstn – S/he is blowing bubbles. **puxʷis łu ċeẇstn t sneẇt –** The wind blew the bubbles.

néẇt – wind blows.
qʷo newntm – I was blown over (by wind/air).
snéẇt – wind.
čłneẇtkʷ – waves on water.

plim – drift/float away by water or wind; carried away. *See: **drift**.*
łu t snéẇt plntem – It was carried away by the wind.

nosiš – Blow your nose. *See: **snot**.*

blue

qʷáy – blue. **qʷiqʷáy –** blues. *pl. (On the spectrum of color this word describes the lighter tones of blue while the darker tones of blue would be described with the word for black. The word used to describe green also includes some of the blue spectrum. This is the reason why the word for blue sky uses the descriptor green and the word for watermelon uses the descriptor blue.)*

qʷáyis – S/he made it blue. **qʷáyn, qʷáyntxʷ**
es qʷáyms – S/he is making it blue. **ies qʷáym, as qʷáym**
qs qʷáyms – S/he is going to make it blue. **iqs qʷáym, aqs qʷáym**

i qʷáy – It is blue.
i łqʷqʷáy – It is a little blue; bluish.

qʷáynt – Make it blue. *cmd.*
łqʷqʷáy – light blue.
i ṅqʷáys – black eye.

qʷaqʷayeʔ – little blue one.
qʷásqʷiʔ – blue jay.
ččqʷáyiċéʔ – watermelon. *suffix: **...iċéʔ** – covered in. lit. it is all blue.*

Blue Bay

čłq̇áqes, ***čłq̇á*** **–** Blue Bay, Flathead Nation. *lit. wide mountaintop.*

čkʷlkʷl̓áqs – place near Blue Bay. *lit. red barked trees on mountaintop.*

bluebird

nłqʷiqʷayáċeʔ, ***nłqʷiqʷayá*** **–** mountain bluebird; *Sialia currucoides.*

nłqʷiqʷayačṅ – western bluebird; *Sialia mexicana.*

blue elderberry **ċkʷikʷ –** elderberry; black elderberry; blue elderberry; *Sambucus racemosa.*

blue grouse **skʷiskʷs –** spruce grouse; Franklin's grouse; fools hen; *Falcipennis canadensis*; domestic chicken. *See:* ***chicken.***

sq̇óxʷlu, *sq̇ó –* sharp-tailed grouse; prairie chicken; *Tympanuchus phasianellus jamesi.*

qáłqłċeʔ, *qá –* ruffed grouse; *Bonasa umbellus.*

The **i** following uvular consonants (UC) and the glottal stop **ʔ** sound like English "*ey*" as in the words th*ey*, h*ey*, wh*ey*, etc. Salish UC are: **q**, **q̇**, **qʷ**, **q̇ʷ**, **x̣**, **x̣ʷ**. For example, the suffix ...**qin** – head/ top, is often spelled using English *ey* as "q*ey*n". So **qi**, **q̇i**, **qʷi**, **q̇ʷi**, **x̣i**, **x̣ʷi**, may be spelled with English *ey* as **q***ey*, **q̇***ey*, **qʷ***ey*, **q̇ʷ***ey*, **x̣***ey*, **x̣ʷ***ey* in other texts.

blue heron **smóq̇ʷeʔ –** great blue heron; *Ardea herodias.*

blue jay **qʷásqʷiʔ –** blue jay; *Cyanocitta cristata*; Stellar's jay.

blue racer **npƛ̓áċeʔ –** eastern racer, green racer; *Coluber constrictor.*

blue sky **čqʷinsq̇t –** blue sky. *suffix:* ***...asq̇t –*** *sky, day.*

ikʷkʷlil̓ – It is sunny *(blue sky).*

i čpaasq̇t – blue sky.

board **łq̇álqʷ –** board; dimensional wood.

boat **ƛ̓iyéʔ –** bark canoe; boat.

čn k̓ʷul̓m t ƛ̓iyéʔ – I made a boat. **cnkʷƛ̓etkʷn łu ƛ̓iyéʔ –** I pulled the boat out of the water.

sṫiłm – wooden canoe; dugout canoe.

bobcat **snqcups,** *snqcu –* bobcat; *Lynx rufus.*

body **sqel̓tč –** meat, body.

sčtełċeʔ – half of the body.

ƛ̓ll̓ełċeʔ – dead body.

boil **nṫpus,** *nṫpu –* cook something by boiling.

nṫpusm – S/he boiled (s.t.). **čn nṫpusm, kʷ nṫpusm**
es nṫpusi – S/he is boiling (s.t.). **čnes nṫpusi, kʷes nṫpusi**
qs nṫpusi – S/he is going to boil (s.t.). **čiqs nṫpusi, kʷqs nṫpusi**
nṫpúʔusm – They boiled (s.t.). **qeʔ nṫpusm, p nṫpusm**
es nṫpúʔusi – They are boiling (s.t.). **qeʔes nṫpusi, pes nṫpusi**
qs nṫpúʔusi – They are going to boil (s.t.). **qeʔqs nṫpusi, pqs nṫpusi**

nṫpusis – S/he boiled s.t. **nṫpusn, kʷ nṫpusntxʷ**
es nṫpusms – S/he is boiling s.t. **ies nṫpusm, as nṫpusm**
qs nṫpusms – S/he is going to boil s.t. **iqs nṫpusm, aqs nṫpusm**
nṫpúʔusis – They boiled s.t. **qeʔ nṫpusntm, nṫpusntp**
es nṫpúʔusms – They are boiling s.t. **qeʔes nṫpusm, es nṫpusmp**
qs nṫpúʔusms – They are going to boil s.t. **qeʔqs nṫpusm, qs nṫpusmp**

s.t. - something, the 3rd person
(s.t.) - something implied
s.o. - someone, the 3rd person
sl. - singular form
pl. - plural form
rt. - root word
cmd. - command
lit. - literally
fig. - figuratively
i.e., - for example
See: - Redirection to a related word.

čnes nṫpusi t sqel̓tč – I am boiling meat. **t qʷoyʔe u nṫpusn łu pataq –** I boiled the potatoes.

ptam – boil something.

ptáp – It boiled.
es ptpma – It is boiling.

ptpstas – S/he made it boil. **ptpstan, ptpstaxʷ**

es ptpams – S/he is making it boil. **ies ptpam, asptpam**

nptatkʷ – boil something liquid.
nptatkʷis – S/he boiled the liquid. **nptatkʷn, nptatkʷntxʷ**
es nptatkʷms – S/he is boiling the liquid. **ies nptatkʷm, as nptatkʷm**

nitkʷétkʷ, *nitkʷé* – over boil something.
nitkʷétkʷis – S/he over boiled it. **nitkʷétkʷn, nitkʷétkʷntxʷ**
es nitkʷétkʷms – S/he is over boiling it. **ies nitkʷétkʷm, as nitkʷétkʷm**
qs nitkʷétkʷms – S/he is going to over boil it. **iqs nitkʷétkʷm, aqs nitkʷétkʷm**

es nitkʷétkʷ – It is over boiled.

scnitkʷétkʷ – something that has been over boiled.

ta kʷ qes nitkʷétkʷm t uʔuseʔ – Do not over boil the eggs.

sċaṁċm – boil (inflamed swelling with pus).

ptáq – sore spot, almost blistered. *See:* ***blister***.

boiling pot

snt̓pustn, *snt̓pu* – cooking pan, boiling pot. *prefix:* ***sn...*** *– a place of; suffix:* ***...tin, ...tn*** *– means of/device.*

bolt

ptkʷmin – bolt; something put through a hole.

bone

sċoṁ – bone. **sċmċoṁ** – bones.

spasċó – skeleton.

ásx̣m – backbone.

k̓ʷnk̓ʷi – stickgame bones.

Bonner

nʔaycčstm – Bonner, Montana; place of large bull trout.

bonnet

ċlqin, *ċlqi* – war bonnet, head dress.

book

ččnp̓iċeʔ – hardcover book; book. *suffix:* ***...iċéʔ*** *– covered in.*
čk̓ʷl̓čiċeʔ – soft cover book. *rt.:* ***k̓ʷelč*** *– upturned formed object; suffix:* ***...iċéʔ*** *– covered in.*
snʔawʔawtn – books. *rt.:* ***aw*** *– speak; prefix:* ***sn...*** *– a place of; suffix:* ***...tin, ...tn*** *– means of/device.*

sk̓ʷłq̇yq̇eẏi ččnp̓iċeʔ – picture book.

čłqtčus – front cover. *suffix:* ***...us*** *– face, fire.*
čk̓ʷl̓čičṅ – back cover. *rt.:* ***k̓ʷelč*** *– upturned formed object; suffix:* ***...ičṅ*** *– back.*
čcneẇstn – book spine. *rt.:* ***čicn*** *– meet; suffix:* ***...éẇs*** *– in between, middle; suffix:* ***...tin, ...tn*** *– means of/device.*

ček̓ʷseẇs – separate something; open a book. *See:* ***separate***.
šṅéẇs – close a book. *rt.:* ***šin*** *– cover; suffix:* ***...éẇs*** *– in between, middle. See:* ***close***.
p̓lčmist – turn something over; turn a page.

skʷests – title; its name.
sxʷq̇eẏim – author; one tasked to write. *rt.:* ***q̇eẏm*** *– write; prefix:* ***sxʷ...*** *– one tasked to do.*
sxʷk̓ʷłq̇eẏim – illustrator; one tasked to draw. *rt.:* ***k̓ʷłq̇eẏim*** *– draw; prefix:* ***sxʷ...*** *– one tasked to do.*
snmimeyetn – table of contents.
snłmimeyetn – index.
sntx̣ʷcin – glossary. *rt.:* ***tox̣ʷ*** *– straight; prefix:* ***sn...*** *– a place of; suffix:* ***...cin, ...cn*** *– action of the mouth.*
łx̣ʷq̇ʷeẇs l q̇eẏmin – chapter.

sq̇y̓q̇ey̓i – illustration.
sk̓ʷłq̇y̓q̇ʔey̓ – picture.

q̇ey̓min – paper; suffix indicating paper or book.
nk̓ʷelxʷq̇ey̓min – page. *rt.: **nk̓ʷuʔ** – one; suffix: **...elxʷ** – skin/hide; suffix: **...q̇ey̓min** – paper; book.*
nk̓ʷelxʷ scsiyen – page number.

xʷuk̓ʷlxʷq̇ey̓min – blank paper. *rt.: **xuk̓ʷ** – clean; suffix: **...elxʷ** – skin/hide; suffix: **...q̇ey̓min** – paper; book.*
łp̓łip̓lxʷ – lined paper. *rt.: **łip̓** – line; suffix: **...elxʷ** – skin/hide.*
snq̇iq̇iim̓ – notebook. *rt.: **q̇iim** – write; prefix: **sn...** – a place of.*
snłq̇q̇iim – notepad. *rt.: **q̇iim** – write; prefix: **sn...** – a place of; infix: **ł...** – little.*
sčyallew̓s – spiral bound. *rt.: **čyall** – wrap; suffix: **...éw̓s** – in between, middle.*
čnp̓ew̓stn – binder. *suffix: **...éw̓s** – in between, middle.*
snččnpic̓eʔtn – folder.

> The **i** following uvular consonants (UC) and the glottal stop **ʔ** sound like English "*ey*" as in the words th*ey*, h*ey*, wh*ey*, etc. Salish UC are: **q**, **q̇**, **qʷ**, **q̇ʷ**, **x̣**, **x̣ʷ**. For example, the suffix ...**qin** – head/top, is often spelled using English *ey* as "q*ey*n". So **qi**, **q̇i**, **qʷi**, **q̇ʷi**, **x̣i**, **x̣ʷi**, may be spelled with English *ey* as **q***ey*, **q̇***ey*, **qʷ***ey*, **q̇ʷ***ey*, **x̣***ey*, **x̣ʷ***ey* in other texts.

sm̓im̓iłq̇ey̓min – newspaper.
słm̓im̓iłq̇ey̓min – newsletter.
snłm̓ey̓etn – brochure.
sm̓eyłq̇ey̓min – journal.
čk̓ʷl̓čq̇ey̓min – magazine.

scmeye – prediction.
syoiqʷeʔ sm̓im̓iʔ – fiction story.
stx̣ʷsm̓im̓iʔ – non-fiction story.

bookshelf

snq̇íimintn – bookshelf. *prefix: **sn...** – a place of; suffix: **...tin, ...tn** – means of/device.*

boot

sp̓čp̓ičšn – rubber boots; over boots. *rt.: **p̓ič̓** – glossy.*

słc̓m̓c̓m̓épšn – cowboy boots. *rt.: **c̓im** – constricted.*

sxʷlepsm q̇ešin – work boots; fire fighter's footwear.

sxʷpičm q̇ešin – sawmill boots; sawmill worker's footwear.

border

łp̓ulexʷtn – border; boundary.

čtlihálqʷ – across railroad track; border.

bore

nłx̣ʷéłc̓eʔ – bore out the inside; hollow out the inside. *(i.e., a pipe stem, a hollowed log, etc.)*
nłx̣ʷéłc̓ʔem – S/he bore out the inside. **čn nłx̣ʷéłc̓ʔem, kʷ nłx̣ʷéłc̓ʔem**
es nłx̣ʷéłc̓eʔi – S/he is boring out the inside. **čnes nłx̣ʷéłc̓eʔi, kʷes nłx̣ʷéłc̓eʔi**
qs nłx̣ʷéłc̓eʔi – S/he is going to bore out the inside. **čiqs nłx̣ʷéłc̓eʔi, kʷqs nłx̣ʷéłc̓eʔi**

nłx̣ʷéłc̓ʔeis – S/he bore out the inside of it. **nłx̣ʷéłc̓ʔen, nłx̣ʷéłc̓ʔentxʷ**
es nłx̣ʷéłc̓ʔems – S/he is boring out the inside of it. **ies nłx̣ʷéłc̓ʔem, as nłx̣ʷéłc̓ʔem**
qs nłx̣ʷéłc̓ʔems – S/he is going to bore out the inside of it. **iqs nłx̣ʷéłc̓ʔem, aqs nłx̣ʷéłc̓ʔem**

es nłx̣ʷéłc̓eʔ – It is hollowed out.

łóx̣ʷ – make a hole in something; puncture something; bore through. *See: **hole**.*

> s.t. - something, the 3rd person
> (s.t.) - something implied
> s.o. - someone, the 3rd person
> *sl.* - singular form
> *pl.* - plural form
> *rt.* - root word
> *cmd.* - command
> *lit.* - literally
> *fig.* - figuratively
> *i.e.,* - for example
> *See:* - Redirection to a related word.

bored

šáll – bored; tiresome; weary from dullness.
šáll – S/he got bored. **čn šáll, kʷ šáll**

es šálli – S/he is being bored. **čnes šálli, kʷes šálli**
qs šálli – S/he is going to be bored. **čiqs šálli, kʷqs šálli**

šallmis – S/he was bored by s.t./s.o. **šallmn, šallmntxʷ**
es šallms – S/he is bored by s.t./s.o. **ies šallm, as šallm**
qs šallms – S/he is going to be bored by s.t./s.o. **iqs šallm, aqs šallm**

šallmistmis – S/he was bored with s.t./s.o. **šallmistmn, šallmistmntxʷ**
es šallmistms – They are bored with s.t./s.o. **qeʔes šallmistm, es šallmistm**
qs šallmistms – They are going to be bored with s.t./s.o. **qeʔqs šallmistm, qs šallmistm**

šllamn – one inclined to get bored. *suffix:* ***...emn*** *– one inclined to do.*
šálšlt – dull; uninteresting; causing boredom.
łšalšlt – a little dull.
šállsnuxʷ – something deserving boredom.
čšlšals – bored eyes.
es šállmisti – S/he is bored with one's self. **čnes šállmisti, kʷes šállmisti**

hoy ṅem čn šáll ṅe eł cxʷuy – I will be (get) tired when s/he comes back.

q̇etyus, *q̇etyu* – nod off; have heavy eyes; cannot hold up head; *literally: weighted face. See:* ***nap***.

boring

picpcuxʷt – boring; tiresome; laborious.
npicpcuxʷcn – boring words. *suffix:* ***...cin, ...cn*** *– action of the mouth.*

piclexʷ – boring land.

born

k̓ʷuĺl – born, birth.
es k̓ʷuĺli – S/he/it is being born.
qs k̓ʷuĺli – S/he/it is going to be born.

es nk̓ʷuĺlċeʔi – S/he/it is being conceived/made inside her.

nk̓ʷuĺlċʔeis – S/he/it was conceived/made inside her. **nk̓ʷuĺlċʔen, nk̓ʷuĺlċʔentxʷ**
nk̓ʷuĺlċʔemis – S/he/it conceived/made s.o. inside her. **nk̓ʷuĺlċʔemn, nk̓ʷuĺlċʔemntxʷ**
nk̓ʷuĺlċʔemncn – I conceived/made you inside me.

snčk̓ʷuĺĺtn – birth place.

čn k̓ʷuĺl ci č ciʔ – I was born over there. **čeṅ asnčk̓ʷuĺĺtn** – Where were you born.

nƛ̓ĺlelt – stillborn.

es enwncuti – She is feeling/sensing; starting labor. *See:* ***feel.***

borrow

kʷułn – borrow; lend.
kʷułn – S/he borrowed. **čn kʷułn, kʷ kʷułn**
es kʷułni – S/he is borrowing. **čnes kʷułni, kʷes kʷułni**
qs kʷułni – S/he is going to borrow. **čiqs kʷułni, kʷqs kʷułni**

kʷułis – S/he borrowed/lent from/to s.o. **kʷułn, kʷułntxʷ**
es kʷułnms – S/he is borrowing/lending from/to s.o. **ies kʷułnm, as kʷułnm**
qs kʷułnms – S/he is going to borrow/lend from/to s.o. **iqs kʷułnm, aqs kʷułnm**

kʷułnš – S/he gave a loan. **čn kʷułnš, kʷ kʷułnš**
es kʷułnši – S/he is giving a loan. **čnes kʷułnši, kʷes kʷułnši**
qs kʷułnši – S/he is going to give a loan. **čiqs kʷułnši, kʷqs kʷułnši**

sckʷułn – something that was borrowed, lent. *prefix:* ***sc...*** *– s.t. that's been done/made/prepared.*

čkʷułntn – something that's borrowed on. *prefix:* ***č...*** *– upon; suffix:* ***...tin, ...tn*** *– means of/device.*

kłlisqáx̣eʔ, *kłlisqá* – borrow horses and domestic animals.
kłlisqáx̣eʔ – S/he borrowed a horse. **čn kłlisqáx̣eʔ, kʷ kłlisqáx̣eʔ**
es kłlisqáx̣eʔi – S/he is borrowing a horse. **čnes kłlisqáx̣eʔi, kʷes kłlisqáx̣eʔi**
qs kłlisqáx̣eʔi – S/he is going to borrow a horse. **čiqs kłlisqáx̣eʔi, kʷqs kłlisqáx̣eʔi**
kłlisqáʔax̣eʔ – They borrowed a horse. **qeʔ kłlisqáx̣eʔ, p kłlisqáx̣eʔ**
es kłlisqáʔax̣eʔi – They are borrowing a horse. **qeʔes kłlisqáx̣eʔi, pes kłlisqáx̣eʔi**
qs kłlisqáʔax̣eʔi – They are going to borrow a horse. **qeʔqs kłlisqáx̣eʔi, pqs kłlisqáx̣eʔi**

The **i** following uvular consonants (UC) and the glottal stop **ʔ** sound like English *"ey"* as in the words *they, hey, whey,* etc. Salish UC are: **q, q̓, qʷ, q̓ʷ, x̣, x̣ʷ**. For example, the suffix **...qin** – head/top, is often spelled using English *ey* as "q*ey*n". So **qi, q̓i, qʷi, q̓ʷi, x̣i, x̣ʷi**, may be spelled with English *ey* as **q***ey*, **q̓***ey*, **qʷ***ey*, **q̓ʷ***ey*, **x̣***ey*, **x̣ʷ***ey* in other texts.

boss

ilmixʷm – chief; boss. *See:* ***chief.***

ililmxʷscut – bossy; make one's self the boss.
ililmxʷscut – S/he acted bossy. **čn ililmxʷscut, kʷ ililmxʷscut**
es ililmxʷscuti – S/he is acting bossy. **čnes ililmxʷscuti, kʷes ililmxʷscuti**
qs ililmxʷscuti – S/he is going to act bossy. **čiqs ililmxʷscuti, kʷqs ililmxʷscuti**

both

es seʔsélm – both things.
čsélm – both people.

bother

mʔečstm – bother with behavior or actions. *suffix:* ***...ečst, ...čst*** *– of the hand.*
mʔečstm – S/he/it bothered. **čn mʔečstm, kʷ mʔečstm**
es mʔečsti – S/he/it is bothering. **čnes mʔečsti, kʷes mʔečsti**
qs mʔečsti – S/he/it is going to bother. **čiqs mʔečsti, kʷqs mʔečsti**
mʔéʔečstm – They bothered. **qeʔ mʔečstm, p mʔečstm**
es mʔéʔečsti – They are bothering. **qeʔes mʔečsti, pes mʔečsti**
qs mʔéʔečsti – They are going to bother. **qeʔqs mʔečsti, pqs mʔečsti**

mʔečstmis – S/he/it bothered s.o./s.t. **mʔečstmn, mʔečstmntxʷ**
es mʔečstmms – S/he/it is bothering s.o./s.t. **ies mʔečstmm, as mʔečstmm**
qs mʔečstmms – S/he/it is going to bother s.o./s.t. **iqs mʔečstmm, aqs mʔečstmm**
mʔéʔečstmis – They bothered s.o./s.t. **qeʔ mʔečstmntm, mʔečstmntp**
es mʔéʔečstmms – They are bothering s.o./s.t. **qeʔes mʔečstmm, es mʔečstmmp**
qs mʔéʔečstmms – They are going to bother s.o./s.t. **qeʔqs mʔečstmm, qs mʔečstmmp**

meméʔt – bothersome; pesty.

mʔečstmnt – Bother it. *cmd.*

ta qʷo qes mʔečstmstxʷ – Do not bother me.

el – tease; bother.
elsts – S/he bothered s.o. **elstn, elstxʷ**
es elms – S/he is bothering s.o. **ies elm, as elm**
qs elms – S/he is going to bother s.o. **iqs elm, aqs elm**

ta qʷo qes élstxʷ – Do not bug me, do not push me!

hetim̓ – tease *(more a playful tease than a bothersome tease). See:* ***tease.***

néhels – sick and tired; perturbed; disturbed; fed up. *See:* ***disturbed.***

s.t. - something, the 3rd person
(s.t.) - something implied
s.o. - someone, the 3rd person
sl. - singular form
pl. - plural form
rt. - root word
cmd. - command
lit. - literally
fig. - figuratively
i.e., - for example
See: - Redirection to a related word.

bottle

leputé – bottle. *(approximation to French word)*

bottom **k̓ʷłišut –** underneath; down below; under; beneath. *See:* ***under.***

nišut – down inside; deep inside. *See:* ***inside.***

bough **nťqełptn –** boughs.

nťqełpm – put boughs down.
nťqełpm – S/he put boughs down. **čn nťqełpm, kʷ nťqełpm**
es nťqełpi – S/he is putting boughs down. **čnes nťqełpi, kʷes nťqełpi**
qs nťqełpi – S/he is going to put boughs down. **čiqs nťqełpi, kʷqs nťqełpi**
nťqéˀełpm – They put boughs down. **qeˀ nťqełpm, p nťqełpm**
es nťqéˀełpi – They are putting boughs down. **qeˀes nťqełpi, pes nťqełpi**
qs nťqéˀełpi – They are going to put boughs down. **qeˀqs nťqełpi, pqs nťqełpi**

nťqełpis – S/he put down boughs. **nťqełpn, nťqełpntxʷ**
es nťqełpms – S/he is putting down boughs. **ies nťqełpi, as nťqełpi**
qs nťqełpms – S/he is going to put down boughs. **iqs nťqełpi, aqs nťqełpi**
nťqéˀełpis – They put down boughs. **qeˀ nťqełpntm, p nťqełpntp**
es nťqéˀełpms – They are putting down boughs. **qeˀes nťqełpi, es nťqełpmp**
qs nťqéˀełpms – They are going to put down boughs. **qeˀqs nťqełpi, qs nťqełpmp**

nťqełpntxʷ aslaqi – You put boughs down at your sweat lodge.

mšéłp – western red cedar boughs.

bounce **čłtˀem –** bounce something. *prefix:* ***čł...*** *– on the surface; rt.:* ***teˀ*** *– hit/bump into.*
čłtˀentes – S/he bounced s.t. **čłtˀenten, čłtˀentexʷ**
es čłtˀems – S/he is bouncing s.t. **ies čłtˀem, as čłtˀem**
qs čłtˀems – S/he is going to bounce s.t. **iqs čłtˀem, aqs čłtˀem**
čłtˀentéˀes – They bounced s.t. **qeˀ čłtˀentem, čłtˀentep**
es čłtˀéˀems – They are bouncing s.t. **qeˀes čłtˀem, es čłtˀemp**
qs čłtˀéˀems – They are going to bounce s.t. **qeˀqs čłtˀem, qs čłtˀemp**

čłtetˀem – dribble; bounce the ball on the ground. *See:* ***dribble.***

čłtˀent – Bounce it. *cmd.*
čłtˀełt – Bounce it to somebody. *cmd.*
yoyosčłtˀent – Bounce it hard. *cmd.*

t swe u čłtˀentes – Who bounced it? **qʷo cčłtˀełt –** Bounce it to me.

boundary **łp̓ulexʷtn –** border; boundary. *rt.:* ***łip̓*** *– line; suffix:* ***...ulexʷ*** *– land.*

bow **ckʷiṅč –** hunting bow.
ckʷṅčálqʷ, *ckʷṅčá* – western yew. *(Used to make bows –* ***ckʷiṅč.****)*

čaciṅčtn – bow string.

čťoyqn – bow the head down; put the head down. *rt.:* ***ťuy̓*** *– bend down; suffix:* ***...qin, ...qn*** *– top.*
čťoyqn – S/he/it bowed one's head down. **čn čťoyqn, kʷ čťoyqn**
es čťoyqni – S/he/it is bowing one's head down. **čnes čťoyqni, kʷes čťoyqni**
qs čťoyqni – S/he/it is going to bow one's head down. **čiqs čťoyqni, kʷqs čťoyqni**

čťoyqis – S/he/it bowed s.o.'s head down. **čťoyqn, čťoyqntxʷ**
es čťoyqnms – S/he/it is bowing s.o.'s head down. **ies čťoyqnm, as čťoyqnm**
qs čťoyqnms – S/he/it is going to bow s.o.'s head down. **iqs čťoyqnm, aqs čťoyqnm**

čťoyqniš – Bow your head. *cmd.*
čťiťoyqnwi – Each one of you bow your head. *cmd.*
čťoyqnt – Bow s.o.'s head down. *cmd.*

čskʷic – stoop over. *See:* ***stoop.***

q̇ʷaťx̣ʷ – curved object; naturally curved object. *See:* ***curve.***

yalk̇ʷ – bend/make into a circular shape. *See:* ***circle.***

pṅeẇsm – fold/bend something; bend something from the middle. *See:* ***fold.***

čpṅeẇsm – fold onto; bend onto. *(i.e., folding the top portion of a paper onto itself.) See:* ***bend.***

čłpṅeẇsm – bend over something; arch over. *See:* ***bend.***

npṅusncut – bend one's self in the middle. *See:* ***bend.***

piṅ – bend from one position to an curved/angular position. *See:* ***bend.***

q̇etyus, *q̇etyu* **–** nod off; have heavy eyes; cannot hold up head; *literally: weighted face. See:* ***nap.***

The **i** following uvular consonants (UC) and the glottal stop ʔ sound like English "*ey*" as in the words th*ey*, h*ey*, wh*ey*, etc. Salish UC are: **q**, **q̇**, **qʷ**, **q̇ʷ**, **x̣**, **x̣ʷ**. For example, the suffix ...**qin** – head/top, is often spelled using English *ey* as "q*ey*n". So **qi**, **q̇i**, **qʷi**, **q̇ʷi**, **x̣i**, **x̣ʷi**, may be spelled with English *ey* as **q***ey*, **q̇***ey*, **qʷ***ey*, **q̇ʷ***ey*, **x̣***ey*, **x̣ʷ***ey* in other texts.

bowl

snsx̣sestn – bowl. *prefix:* ***sn...*** *– a place of; suffix:* ***...tin, ...tn*** *– means of/device.*

es nčuxʷlexʷ – bowl in the land.

bow legged

sasalqʷáqstšn, *sasalqʷá* **–** bow legged.

bowling

čłx̣ʷlx̣ʷollq̇ʷi – bowl.
es čłx̣ʷlx̣ʷollq̇ʷi – S/he is bowling. **čnes čłx̣ʷlx̣ʷollq̇ʷi, kʷes čłx̣ʷlx̣ʷollq̇ʷi**

snčłx̣ʷlx̣ʷollq̇ʷi – place to bowl.

ha kʷqs k̇ʷis čłx̣ʷlx̣ʷollq̇ʷi – Are you going to go bowl?

box

čluk̇ʷc̓éʔ – box.

boy

słqʷqʷsʔel̓t – small boy.
ttẇit – boy, boy up to the age of puberty.
titwit – boys; to the age of puberty.
es łx̣ʷómʔeẏ – boy at the age of puberty.
kʷtiłttẇit – boy after age of puberty.
sqltmi – male; man; boy; to tell the sex of boy.
tʔéw – youngest; young (boy).

Bozeman

epsłxʷexʷʔenče – Bozeman, Montana; *lit. has small hawthorn bushes.*

bra

łqʷłqʷemxʷ – put on/wear a bra. *rt.:* ***łoqʷ*** *– put on/across; suffix:* ***...emxʷ*** *– breasts.*
es łqʷłqʷemxʷ – She is wearing a bra. **čnes łqʷłqʷemxʷ, kʷes łqʷłqʷemxʷ**

łqʷłqʷemxʷ – She is putting on a bra. **čn łqʷłqʷemxʷ, kʷ łqʷłqʷemxʷ**
es łqʷłqʷemxʷi – She is putting on a bra. **čnes łqʷłqʷemxʷi, kʷes łqʷłqʷemxʷi**
qs łqʷłqʷemxʷi – She is going to put on a bra. **čiqs łqʷłqʷemxʷi, kʷqs łqʷłqʷemxʷi**

łqʷłqʷemxʷis – S/he is putting a bra on her. **łqʷłqʷemxʷn, łqʷłqʷemxʷntxʷ**
es łqʷłqʷemxʷms – She is putting a bra on her. **ies łqʷłqʷemxʷi, as łqʷłqʷemxʷm**
qs łqʷłqʷemxʷms – She is going to put a bra on her. **iqs łqʷłqʷemxʷm, aqs łqʷłqʷemxʷm**

s.t. - something, the 3rd person
(s.t.) - something implied
s.o. - someone, the 3rd person
sl. - singular form
pl. - plural form
rt. - root word
cmd. - command
lit. - literally
fig. - figuratively
i.e., - for example
See: - Redirection to a related word.

łqʷłqʷemxʷtn – bra.

łqʷłqʷemxʷiš – Put on a bra. *cmd.*
łqʷłqʷemxʷnt – Put a bra on her. *cmd.*

pƛ̓pƛ̓emxʷ – remove a bra. *rt.: **pƛ̓im** – release from; suffix: **...emxʷ** – breasts.*
pƛ̓pƛ̓emxʷ – S/he removed a bra. **čn pƛ̓pƛ̓emxʷ, kʷ pƛ̓pƛ̓emxʷ**
es pƛ̓pƛ̓emxʷi – S/he is removing a bra. **čnes pƛ̓pƛ̓emxʷi, kʷes pƛ̓pƛ̓emxʷi**
qs pƛ̓pƛ̓emxʷi – S/he is going to remove a bra. **čiqs pƛ̓pƛ̓emxʷi, kʷqs pƛ̓pƛ̓emxʷi**

pƛ̓pƛ̓emxʷis – S/he removed her bra. **pƛ̓pƛ̓emxʷn, pƛ̓pƛ̓emxʷntxʷ**
es pƛ̓pƛ̓emxʷms – S/he is removing her bra. **ies pƛ̓pƛ̓emxʷm, as pƛ̓pƛ̓emxʷm**
qs pƛ̓pƛ̓emxʷms – S/he is going to remove her bra. **iqs pƛ̓pƛ̓emxʷm, aqs pƛ̓pƛ̓emxʷm**

es pƛ̓pƛ̓emxʷ – She is braless. **čnes pƛ̓pƛ̓emxʷ, kʷes pƛ̓pƛ̓emxʷ**

pƛ̓pƛ̓emxʷiš – Remove your bra. *cmd.*
pƛ̓pƛ̓emxʷnt – Remove her bra. *cmd.*

brace

nyawlsm – brace feelings; make feelings strong; tough something out. *(i.e., in preparation for bad news, etc.)*
nyawlsm – S/he/it braced one's feelings. **čn nyawlsm, kʷ nyawlsm**
es nyawlsi – S/he/it is bracing one's feelings. **čnes nyawlsi, kʷes nyawlsi**
qs nyawlsi – S/he/it is going to brace one's feelings. **čiqs nyawlsi, kʷqs nyawlsi**

nyawiyawt – unyielding; patient; tenacious.
nyawlsiš – Brace yourself. *cmd.*

ƛ̓e kʷ nyawlsm – You were already braced. **čnes nyawlsi x̣ʷl̓ čnes ċalqini** – I am toughing out a headache.

yomim – hold something steady. *See: **hold**.*

yomncut, *yomncu* – make one's self become rigid/tense. *See: **tense**.*

bracelet

sk̓ʷłčcnéčst, *sk̓ʷłčcné* – bracelet. *suffix: **...ečst, ...čst** – of the hand.*

brag

kʷtiscut – make one's self important, great; brag.
kʷtiscut – S/he bragged. **čn kʷtiscut, kʷ kʷtiscut**
es kʷtiscuti – S/he is bragging. **čnes kʷtiscuti, kʷes kʷtiscuti**
qs kʷtiscuti – S/he is going to brag. **čiqs kʷtiscuti, kʷqs kʷtiscuti**
kʷtiscúʔut – They bragged. **qeʔ kʷtiscut, p kʷtiscut**
es kʷtiscúʔuti – They are bragging. **qeʔes kʷtiscuti, pes kʷtiscuti**
qs kʷtiscúʔuti – They are going to brag. **qeʔqs kʷtiscuti, pqs kʷtiscuti**

kʷtiscutš – Make yourself important. *cmd.*

kʷtnmscin – talk big; to brag. *suffix: **...cin, ...cn** – action of the mouth.*
kʷtnmscin – S/he talked big. **čn kʷtnmscin, kʷ kʷtnmscin**
es kʷtnmscini – S/he is talking big. **čnes kʷtnmscini, kʷes kʷtnmscini**
qs kʷtnmscini – S/he is going to talk big. **čiqs kʷtnmscini, kʷqs kʷtnmscini**

es kʷtcnmisti – S/he is talking big about one's self. **čnes kʷtcnmisti, kʷes kʷtcnmisti**

braid

sitč – braid something.
sitč – S/he braided. **čn sitč, kʷ sitč**
es sitči – S/he is braiding. **čnes sitči, kʷes sitči**
qs sitči – S/he is going to braid. **čiqs sitči, kʷqs sitči**

sitčis – S/he braided s.t. **sitčn, sitčntxʷ**
es **sitčms** – S/he is braiding s.t. **ies sitčm, as sitčm**
qs **sitčms** – S/he is going to braid s.t. **iqs sitčm, aqs sitčm**

sitčš – Braid. *cmd.*
sitčnt – Braid it. *cmd.*

čstčpéneʔ – braid hair over ears. *rt.: **sitč** – braid.*
čstčtčpenʔem – S/he braided hair. **čn čstčtčpenʔem, kʷ čstčtčpenʔem**
es **čstčtčpenʔei** – S/he is braiding hair. **čnes čstčtčpenʔei, kʷes čstčtčpenʔei**

čstčtčpenʔeis – S/he braided s.o.'s hair. **čstčtčpenʔen, čstčtčpenʔentxʷ**
es **čstčtčpenʔems** – S/he is braiding s.o.'s hair. **ies čstčtčpenʔem, as čstčtčpenʔem**
qs **čstčtčpenʔems** – S/he is going to braid s.o.'s hair. **iqs čstčtčpenʔem, aqs čstčtčpenʔem**

sčstčpéneʔ, *sčstčpé* – braided hair; braid. **sčstčtčpéneʔ**, *sčstčtčpé* – braids.

kʷ iqs čststčpenʔem – I am going to braid your hair.

k̓ʷłstčapqn – braid hair in a pony tail. *rt.: **sitč** – braid.*
kʷłstčapqis – S/he braided s.o.'s hair. **kʷłstčapqn, kʷłstčapqntxʷ**
es **kʷłstčapqnms** – S/he is braiding s.o.'s hair. **ies kʷłstčapqnm, as kʷłstčapqnm**
qs **kʷłstčapqnms** – S/he is going to braid s.o.'s hair. **iqs kʷłstčapqnm, aqs kʷłstčapqnm**

sčchepeneʔ – right braid.
sčc̓q̓ʷepeneʔ – left braid.

snxʷi – braid/lock on top or to the side.

The **i** following uvular consonants (UC) and the glottal stop ʔ sound like English "*ey*" as in the words *they, hey, whey*, etc. Salish UC are: **q, q̓, qʷ, q̓ʷ, x̣, x̣ʷ**. For example, the suffix ...**qin** – head/top, is often spelled using English *ey* as "q*ey*n". So **qi, q̓i, qʷi, q̓ʷi, x̣i, x̣ʷi**, may be spelled with English *ey* as **q***ey*, **q̓***ey*, **qʷ***ey*, **q̓ʷ***ey*, **x̣***ey*, **x̣ʷ***ey* in other texts.

braid wraps

čl̓čl̓čpe – braid wraps.

łłtkʷhe – otter braid wraps.

brain

sc̓mqin – brain.

brake

čƛ̓lpšisqáx̣eʔtn, *čƛ̓lpšisqá* – brake pedal.

branch

sčšṫełp, *sčšṫe* – one branch. *rt.: **šiṫ** – stand upright; suffix: **...ełp, ...łp** – tree; floor, bed.*
sčšṫšṫełp, *sčšṫe* – branches.

sčc̓lc̓lšmełp, *sčclclšmé* – branches. *rt.: **c̓il** – protrusions; suffix: **...ełp, ...łp** – tree; floor, bed.*

sčillmnéłp – branches. *rt.: **čilil** – branch off; suffix: **...ełp, ...łp** – tree; floor, bed.*

mšełp – cedar boughs; western red cedar boughs.

čq̓aw̓ečst – break branches. *See: **break**.*

brand

p̓ix̣ – brand with a hot iron.
p̓ix̣m – S/he branded. **čn p̓ix̣m, kʷ p̓ix̣m**
es **p̓ix̣i** – S/he is branding. **čnes p̓ix̣i, kʷes p̓ix̣i**
qs **p̓ix̣i** – S/he is going to brand. **čiqs p̓ix̣i, kʷqs p̓ix̣i**

p̓ix̣is – S/he branded s.t. **p̓ix̣n, p̓ix̣ntxʷ**
es **p̓ix̣ms** – S/he is branding s.t. **ies p̓ix̣m, as p̓ix̣m**
qs **p̓ix̣ms** – S/he is going to brand s.t. **iqs p̓ix̣m, aqs p̓ix̣m**

p̓ix̣nt – Brand it. *cmd.*

s.t. - something, the 3rd person
(s.t.) - something implied
s.o. - someone, the 3rd person
sl. - singular form
pl. - plural form
rt. - root word
cmd. - command
lit. - literally
fig. - figuratively
i.e., - for example
See: - Redirection to a related word.

cxʷuyš qeʔqs p̓ix̣m łu šušweł – Come on, we'll chart out a course.

p̓ix̣sqáx̣eʔ – brand a horse/domestic animal with a hot iron.
p̓ix̣sqáx̣eʔ – S/he branded a horse. **čn p̓ix̣sqáx̣eʔ, kʷ p̓ix̣sqáx̣eʔ**
es p̓ix̣sqáx̣eʔi – S/he is branding a horse. **čnes p̓ix̣sqáx̣eʔi, kʷes p̓ix̣sqáx̣eʔi**
qs p̓ix̣sqáx̣eʔi – S/he is going to brand a horse. **čiqs p̓ix̣sqáx̣eʔi, kʷqs p̓ix̣sqáx̣eʔi**

čt̓čim – mark/brand with the hand.
čt̓čim – S/he marked. **čn čt̓čim, kʷ čt̓čim**
es čt̓čmi – S/he is marking. **čnes čt̓čmi, kʷes čt̓čnmi**
qs čt̓čmi – S/he is going to mark. **čiqs čt̓čmi, kʷqs čt̓čnmi**
čt̓číʔim – They marked. **qeʔ čt̓čim, p čt̓čim**
es čt̓čmíʔi – They are marking. **qeʔes čt̓čmi, pes čt̓čnmi**
qs čt̓čmíʔi – They are going to mark. **qeʔqs čt̓čmi, pqs čt̓čnmi**

čtečsqáx̣eʔ – mark a horse/domestic animal with the hand.
čtečsqáx̣eʔ – S/he marked a horse out. **čn čtečsqáx̣eʔ, kʷ čtečsqáx̣eʔ**
es čtečsqáx̣eʔi – S/he is marking a horse out. **čnes čtečsqáx̣eʔi, kʷes čtečsqáx̣eʔi**
qs čtečsqáx̣eʔi – S/he is going to mark a horse out. **čiqs čtečsqáx̣eʔi, kʷqs čtečsqáx̣eʔi**

brave
kʷtispúʔu – brave. *lit. big heart.*

bread
scnqʷl̓púl̓exʷ, *scnqʷl̓pú* – bread.

nqʷl̓púlexʷm – make bread.
nqʷl̓púlexʷm – S/he made bread. **čn nqʷl̓púlexʷm, kʷ nqʷl̓púlexʷm**
es nqʷl̓púlexʷi – S/he is making bread. **čnes nqʷl̓púlexʷi, kʷes nqʷl̓púlexʷi**
qs nqʷl̓púlexʷi – S/he is going to make bread. **čiqs nqʷl̓púlexʷi, kʷqs nqʷl̓púlexʷi**

ṅem čn nqʷl̓púlexʷm – I will make bread.

čłsnqʷl̓pú – go after bread.
čłsnqʷl̓pú – S/he went after bread. **čn čłsnqʷl̓pú, kʷ čłsnqʷl̓pú**
es čłsnqʷl̓pú – S/he is going after bread. **čnes čłsnqʷl̓pú, kʷes čłsnqʷl̓pú**
qs čłsnqʷl̓pú – S/he is going to go after bread. **čiqs čłsnqʷl̓pú, kʷqs čłsnqʷl̓pú**
čłsnqʷl̓púʔu – They went after bread. **qeʔ čłsnqʷl̓pú, p čłsnqʷl̓pú**
es čłsnqʷl̓púʔu – They are going after bread. **qeʔes čłsnqʷl̓pú, pes čłsnqʷl̓pú**
qs čłsnqʷl̓púʔu – They are going to go after bread. **qeʔqs čłsnqʷl̓pú, pqs čłsnqʷl̓pú**

nc̓áx̣lexʷ – make frybread. *See: **frybread.***

np̓éčlexʷm – make bannock bread. *See: **bannock bread.***

nłkʷlkʷaliʔúlexʷm – make corn bread.

break
máw̓t – break.
maw̓is – S/he/it broke s.t. **maw̓n, maw̓ntxʷ**
máʔaw̓is – They broke s.t. **qeʔ maw̓ntm, maw̓ntp**

mumaw̓is – S/he broke it repeatedly. **mumaw̓n, mumaw̓ntxʷ**

es maw̓ – It is broke.
maw̓ntm – It got broken.

maw̓nt – Break it. *cmd.*
maw̓łxʷm – wrecked/break a house, tipi, or lodge.

qʷo mawłxʷis t cišps – wolverine wrecked (broke) my tipi. **t spisċé u wičis t mali ci smx̣é qʷo es mumáwłtm innšnse** – Yesterday Mary saw that grizzly bear breaking my window. **es maw łu spq̇niˀs** – His/her clock is broken. **mawt łu inpumin** – My drum is broken (frame is broken).

moˀsqáx̣eˀ, *moˀsqá* – vehicle/horse broke; vehicle/horse does not work. *suffix:* ***...sqax̣eˀ, ...sqa*** *– domestic animal; generally horse or car.*

moˀsqá – His/her vehicle/horse broke down. **čn moˀsqá, kʷ moˀsqá**

The **i** following uvular consonants (UC) and the glottal stop **ˀ** sound like English "*ey*" as in the words th*ey*, h*ey*, wh*ey*, etc. Salish UC are: **q, q̇, qʷ, q̇ʷ, x̣, x̣ʷ**. For example, the suffix **...qin** – head/top, is often spelled using English *ey* as "q*ey*n". So **qi, q̇i, qʷi, q̇ʷi, x̣i, x̣ʷi**, may be spelled with English *ey* as **q***ey*, **q̇***ey*, **qʷ***ey*, **q̇ʷ***ey*, **x̣***ey*, **x̣ʷ***ey* in other texts.

q̇awm – break wood/bones.

q̇wup – It broke.

es q̇awpmi – It is breaking.

q̇awntes – S/he/it broke it. **q̇awnten, q̇awntexʷ**

es q̇awms – S/he/it is breaking it. **ies q̇awm, as q̇awm**

qs q̇awms – S/he/it is going to break it. **iqs q̇awm, aqs q̇awm**

q̇áˀawntes – They broke it. **qeˀ q̇awntem, q̇awntep**

es q̇áˀawms – They are breaking it. **qeˀes q̇awm, es q̇awmp**

q̇uq̇awis – S/he/it broke things. **q̇uq̇awn, q̇uq̇awntxʷ**

es q̇aw – It is broken.

q̇awntem – It got broken.

q̇wup – It broke.

q̇awnt – Break it. *cmd.*

q̇awpax̣n – broken arm.

nq̇awpmusax̣n – broken elbow.

q̇awpčst – broken finger/hand. *suffix:* ***...ečst, ...čst*** *– of the hand.*

nq̇awpłq̇eyt – broken shoulder.

nq̇awpłniut – broken rib.

nq̇awpews – broken lower back. *suffix:* ***...éws*** *– in between, middle.*

nq̇awpičn – broken upper back. *suffix:* ***...ičn*** *– back.*

k̇ʷłq̇awpus – broken cheek.

čq̇awpups – broken tailbone.

nq̇awpušn – broken hip.

q̇awpaqstšn – broken leg.

q̇awpšin – broken foot.

nq̇awpaqs – broken nose; *expression: to be angry.*

nq̇awpqin – The tree top broke.

q̇awx̣e – yellow bell.

es q̇aw łu inłṗmintn – My pencil is broken. **q̇awup łu inłṗmintn** – My pencil broke. **q̇awnt ci stmtmniˀá** – Break those snowberry sticks!

s.t. - something, the 3rd person
(s.t.) - something implied
s.o. - someone, the 3rd person
sl. - singular form
pl. - plural form
rt. - root word
cmd. - command
lit. - literally
fig. - figuratively
i.e., - for example
See: - Redirection to a related word.

čq̇awečst – break branches.

čq̇awečsis – S/he broke branches. **čq̇awečsn, čq̇awečsntxʷ**

es čq̇awečsms – S/he is breaking branches. **ies čq̇awečsm, as čq̇awečsm**

čq̇awečsnt – Break the branch. *cmd.*

tiľ – shatter/break into pieces of stone, glass, iron or teeth.

tľip – S/he/it broke (s.t.). **čn tľip, kʷ tľip**

es tľpmi – S/he/it is breaking (s.t.). **čnes tľpmi, kʷes tľpmi**

qs tľpmi – S/he/it is going to break (s.t.). **čiqs tľpmi, kʷqs tľpmi**

tľíˀip – They broke (s.t.). **qeˀ tľip, p tľip**

es tľpmíˀi – They are breaking (s.t.). **qeˀes tľpmi, pes tľpmi**

qs tl̓pmíʔi – They are going to break (s.t.). **qeʔqs tl̓pmi, pqs tl̓pmi**

tl̓ntés – S/he/it broke s.t. **tl̓ntén, tl̓ntexʷ**
tl̓ntéʔes – They broke s.t. **qeʔ tl̓ntém, tl̓ntép**

ntl̓pus – S/he/it has a broken neck. **čn ntl̓pus, kʷ ntl̓pus**
ntl̓peys – S/he/it has a broken tooth. **čn ntl̓peys, kʷ ntl̓peys**
ntl̓tl̓peys – S/he/it has broken teeth. **čn ntl̓tl̓peys, kʷ ntl̓tl̓peys**
ntl̓eysis – S/he/it broke s.o.'s tooth. **ntl̓eysn, ntl̓eysntxʷ**

qʷo ntl̓eysntxʷ – You broke my tooth. **ha tl̓ntexʷ qeʔac̓x̣snc̓u –** Did you break our mirror? **tl̓ip łu qpé –** plate broke. **t swe u tl̓ntés łu qpe –** Who broke the plate? **tl̓ntén łu qpé –** I broke the plate. **es til nšn̓se –** The window broke. **tl̓ip łu innšn̓se –** My window broke. **tl̓tl̓ip łu innšn̓se –** My window broke into pieces.

t̓uwáq – break rope/cord.
t̓uqntes – S/he broke the rope. **t̓uqnten, t̓uqntexʷ**
es t̓uqms – S/he is breaking the rope. **ies t̓qm, as t̓uwqm**
qs t̓uqms – S/he is going to break the rope. **iqs t̓uqm, aqs t̓uqm**

t̓uqent – Break the rope. *cmd.*
t̓uqew̓s – two pieces of a broken rope. *suffix:* ***...éw̓s*** *– in between, middle.*

xʷeƛ̓mist – relax *(loosen one's self)*; do what you want; pass time; recreate.
es xʷeƛ̓mi – S/he/it is relaxing. **čnes xʷeƛ̓mi, kʷes xʷeƛ̓mi**

snxʷeƛ̓mistn – place to relax/recreate; recreation area. *prefix:* ***sn...*** *– a place of; suffix:* ***...tin, ...tn*** *– means of/device.*
nxʷxʷeƛ̓mistn – certain place to relax, recreate, do what you want *(i.e., fishing hole, some place in the mountains, your shop, etc.).*

łexʷls – take a break, a rest.
łexʷls – S/he/it rested. **čn łexʷls, kʷ łexʷls**
es łexʷlsi – S/he/it is resting. **čnes łexʷlsi, kʷes łexʷlsi**
qs łexʷlsi – S/he/it is going to rest. **čiqs łexʷlsi, kʷqs łexʷlsi**
łéʔexʷls – They rested. **qeʔ łexʷls, p łexʷls**
es łéʔexʷlsi – They are resting. **qeʔes łexʷlsi, pes łexʷlsi**
qs łéʔexʷlsi – They are going to rest. **qeʔqs łexʷlsi, pqs łexʷlsi**

acacsqáx̣eʔ, *acacsqá* – break horses; restrain/catch horses. *rt.:* ***ac*** *– bind, tie, trap; suffix:* ***...sqax̣eʔ, ...sqa*** *– domestic animal; generally horse or car*
acacsqáx̣eʔ – S/he broke a horse. **čn̓ acacsqáx̣eʔ, kʷ acacsqáx̣eʔ**
es acacsqáx̣eʔi – S/he is breaking a horse. **čnes acacsqáx̣eʔi, kʷes acacsqáx̣eʔi**
qs acacsqáx̣eʔi – S/he is going to break a horse. **čiqs acacsqáx̣eʔi, kʷqs acacsqáx̣eʔi**
acacsqáʔax̣eʔ – They broke a horse. **qeʔ acacsqáx̣eʔ, p acacsqáx̣eʔ**
es acacsqáʔax̣eʔi – They are breaking a horse. **qeʔes acacsqáx̣eʔi, pes acacsqáx̣eʔi**
qs acacsqáʔax̣eʔi – They are going to break a horse. **qeʔqs acacsqáx̣eʔi, pqs acacsqáx̣eʔi**

sxʷacacsqáx̣eʔ – one tasked to break horses. *prefix:* ***sxʷ...*** *– one tasked to do.*

acacím̓ – repeatedly catching/restraining; break horses. *rt.:* ***ac*** *– bind, tie, trap.*
acacím̓ – S/he broke horses. **čn acacím̓, kʷ acacím̓**
es acacm̓í – S/he is breaking horses. **čnes acacm̓í, kʷes acacm̓í**
qs acacm̓í – S/he is going to break horses. **čiqs acacm̓í, kʷqs acacm̓í**

acacnúnm – succeed in breaking a horse; succeed in catching/restraining a horse. *rt.:* ***ac*** *– bind, tie, trap.*
acacnúis – S/he broke the horse. **acacnún, acacnúntxʷ**

es acacnúnms – S/he is finishing breaking the horse. **ies acacnúnm, as acacnúnm**
es acacnúnms – S/he is going to finish breaking the horse. **iqs acacnúnm, aqs acacnúnm**
acacnúˀuis – They broke the horse. **qeˀ acacnún, acacnúntp**
es acacnúˀunms – They are finishing breaking the horse. **qeˀes acacnúnm, es acacnúnmp**
es acacnúˀunms – They are going to finish breaking the horse. **qeˀqs acacnúnm, qs acacnúnmp**

breakable

iłt̓é – fragile; easily broken; breakable.

breakfast

kʷekʷstm – eat breakfast.

kʷekʷstm – S/he/it ate breakfast. **čn kʷekʷstm, kʷ kʷekʷstm**
es kʷekʷsti – S/he/it is eating breakfast. **čnes kʷekʷsti, kʷes kʷekʷsti**
qs kʷekʷsti – S/he/it is going to eat breakfast. **čiqs kʷekʷsti, kʷqs kʷekʷsti**
kʷéˀekʷstm – They ate breakfast. **qeˀ kʷekʷstm, kʷ kʷekʷstm**
es kʷéˀekʷsti – They are eating breakfast. **qeˀes kʷekʷsti, pes kʷekʷsti**
qs kʷéˀekʷsti – They are going to eat breakfast. **qeˀqs kʷekʷsti, pqs kʷekʷsti**

t steṁ u kʷ kʷekʷstm – What did you eat for breakfast?

break pedal

čƛ̓lpšisqáx̣eˀtn, *čƛ̓lpšisqá* – vehicle break pedal.

breast

sqaqˀém – breasts.

...emxʷ – suffix indicating breasts. *See:* ***section 2.***
schemxʷ – right breast.
sc̓q̓ʷemxʷ – left breast.
c̓alemxʷ – sore breast.
ušušsnemxʷ – long breasts. *rt.:* ***wisšn*** *– long.*
kʷtkʷtnemxʷ – big breasts. *rt.:* ***kʷtunt*** *– big.*
łkʷk̓ʷnemxʷ – small breasts. *rt.:* ***łkʷk̓ʷnumeˀ*** *– small.*
uxʷuxʷemxʷ – bare breasts. *rt.:* ***uxʷ*** *– droop.*
tqemxʷ – touch the breast.

breastfeed

qˀeméľt – breastfeed; nurse.

qˀemeľt – She nursed. **čn qˀemeľt, kʷ qˀemeľt**
es qˀemeľti – She is nursing. **čnes qˀemeľti, kʷes qˀemeľti**
qs qˀemeľti – She is going to nurse. **čiqs qˀemeľti, kʷqs qˀemeľti**

qˀemstes – She nursed him/her. **qˀemsten, qˀemstexʷ**
es qˀemims – She is nursing him/her. **ies qˀemim, as qˀemim**
qs qˀemims – She is going to nurse him/her. **iqs qˀemim, aqs qˀemim**

tatameˀ – suck on the nipple. *See:* ***suck.***

breast plate

sq̓ľaxʷcč, *sq̓ľa* – breast plate. *rt.:* ***q̓ľ*** *– hooked on to; suffix:* ***...axʷcč*** *– chest.*

breathe

pew – breathe.

es pupéwlši – S/he/it is breathing. **čnes pupéwlši, kʷes pupéwlši**

pupéwlš – Breathe. *cmd.*
péwlš – Take one breath. *cmd.*

npéw – pump up.
npéwmn – air pump.

The **i** following uvular consonants (UC) and the glottal stop **ˀ** sound like English "*ey*" as in the words th*ey*, h*ey*, wh*ey*, etc. Salish UC are: **q, q̓, qʷ, q̓ʷ, x̣, x̣ʷ**. For example, the suffix **...qin** – head/top, is often spelled using English *ey* as "q*ey*n". So **qi, q̓i, qʷi, q̓ʷi, x̣i, x̣ʷi,** may be spelled with English *ey* as **q***ey*, **q̓***ey*, **qʷ***ey*, **q̓ʷ***ey*, **x̣***ey*, **x̣ʷ***ey* in other texts.

s.t. - something, the 3rd person
(s.t.) - something implied
s.o. - someone, the 3rd person
sl. - singular form
pl. - plural form
rt. - root word
cmd. - command
lit. - literally
fig. - figuratively
i.e., - for example
See: - Redirection to a related word.

čn séwneʔ steṁ łu es pupéwlši – I hear something breathing.

yomspewlš – hold breath inside the body. *rt.: **yomim** – hold steady.*
yomspewlš – S/he held his/her breath. **čn yomspewlš, kʷ yomspewlš**
es yomspewlši – S/he is holding his/her breath. **čnes yomspewlši, kʷes yomspewlši**
qs yomspewlši – S/he is going to hold his/her breath. **čiqs yomspewlši, kʷqs yomspewlši**

yomscin – hold breath by closing the mouth. *rt.: **yomim** – hold steady; suffix: **...cin, ...cn** – action of the mouth.*
yomscin – S/he held his/her breath. **čn yomscin, kʷ yomscin**
es yomscini – S/he is holding his/her breath. **čnes yomscini, kʷes yomscini**
qs yomscini – S/he is going to hold his/her breath. **čiqs yomscini, kʷqs yomscini**

tqup – suffocate (not dead); restrict air flow; lacking air; winded/out of breath. *See: **suffocate**.*

breechcloth

nłqʷépustšn, *nłqʷé* – diaper; breechcloth; loincloth.

Brewer's blackbird

ƛ̓č̓ƛ̓áčqn, *ƛ̓č̓ƛ̓á* – blackbird; Brewer's blackbird; *Euphagus cyanocephalus. rt.: **ƛ̓éʔeč** – peek.*

bribe

qil – invite; attract; bribe.
qil – S/he/it bribed. **čn qil, kʷ qil**
es qili – S/he/it is bribing. **čnes qili, kʷes qili**
qs qili – S/he/it is going to bribe. **čiqs qili, kʷqs qili**

brick

kʷlepsšṅ – brick. *suffix: **...sšṅ** – rock.*

bridge

nx̣léẁs – bridge.
scnx̣léẁs – something that's been bridged.

bridle

kʷłʔaceptn, *kʷłʔace* – bridle. *rt.: **ac** – bind, tie, trap.*

k̓ʷłʔacpasqáx̣eʔ – bridle a horse; put a bridle on a horse. *rt.: **ac** – bind, tie, trap.*
k̓ʷłʔacpasqáx̣eʔ – S/he bridled a horse. **čn k̓ʷłʔacpasqáx̣eʔ, kʷ k̓ʷłʔacpasqáx̣eʔ**
es k̓ʷłʔacpasqáx̣eʔi – S/he is bridling a horse. **čnes k̓ʷłʔacpasqáx̣eʔi, kʷes k̓ʷłʔacpasqáx̣eʔi**

k̓ʷłʔacpasqáx̣eʔtn, *k̓ʷłʔacpasqá* – bridle.

k̓ʷłplpasqáx̣eʔ – unbridle a horse.

łax̣usm – put a bridle/hackamore/halter on. *rt.: **aax̣** – has lines; suffix: **...us** – face, fire.*
łax̣usis – S/he put a bridle on it. **łax̣usn, łax̣usntxʷ**
łax̣úʔusis – They put a bridle on it. **qeʔ łax̣usntm, łax̣usntp**

łax̣usnt – Put the hackamore/bridle on it.
łax̣usntm – Its face has been lined; a bridle has been put on it.

pƛ̓usm – take a bridle/hackamore/halter off. *rt.: **pƛ̓im** – release from; suffix: **...us** – face, fire.*
pƛ̓usm – S/he removed a bridle. **čn pƛ̓usm, kʷ pƛ̓usm**
es pƛ̓usi – S/he is removing a bridle. **čnes pƛ̓usi, kʷes pƛ̓usi**
qs pƛ̓usi – S/he is going to remove a bridle. **čiqs pƛ̓usi, kʷqs pƛ̓usi**
pƛ̓úʔusm – They removed a bridle. **qeʔ pƛ̓usm, p pƛ̓usm**
es pƛ̓úʔusi – They are removing a bridle. **qeʔes pƛ̓usi, pes pƛ̓usi**
qs pƛ̓úʔusi – They are going to remove a bridle. **qeʔqs pƛ̓usi, pqs pƛ̓usi**

pƛ̓usnt – Take the bridle off. *cmd.*

čax̣ċasqáx̣eʔtn, *čax̣ċasqá* – harness. *See: **harness**.*

łax̣ústn, *łax̣ú* – halter. *See:* ***halter.***

łxʷpusáx̣eʔ, *łxʷpusá* – halter. *See:* ***halter.***

bright

ṗáq̇ – shine; bright. *See:* ***shine.***

ṗéxʷ – bright; the red-hot glow of something heated. *See:* ***hot.***

bring

ukʷm – bring/carry something over somewhere.
ukʷis – S/he/it brought s.t. there. **ukʷn, ukʷntxʷ**
es ukʷms – S/he/it is bringing s.t. there. **ies ukʷm, as ukʷm**
qs ukʷms – S/he/it is going to bring s.t. there. **iqs ukʷm, aqs ukʷm**
úʔukʷis – They brought s.t. there. **qeʔ ukʷntm, ukʷntp**
es úʔukʷms – They are bringing it. **qeʔes ukʷm, es ukʷmp**
qs úʔukʷms – They are going to bring s.t. there. **qeʔqs ukʷm, qs ukʷmp**

ukʷnt – Bring it there. *cmd.*

ukʷn pumin č̓ snčłeliłtn – I brought the drum to the table. **č̓ čeṅ łu ukʷntxʷ** – Where did you bring it?

cʔukʷm – bring/carry something here. *rt.:* ***ukʷm*** *– bring; prefix:* ***c...*** *– indicating toward the speaker.*
cʔukʷis – S/he/it carried s.t. here. **cʔukʷn, cʔukʷntxʷ**
es cʔukʷms – S/he/it is bringing s.t. here. **ies cʔukʷm, as cʔukʷm**
qs cʔukʷms – S/he/it is going to bring s.t. here. **iqs cʔukʷm, aqs cʔukʷm**
cʔúʔukʷis – They brought it here. **qeʔ cʔukʷntm, cʔukʷntp**
es cʔúʔukʷms – They are bringing it. **qeʔes cʔukʷm, es cʔukʷmp**
qs cʔúʔukʷms – They are going to bring s.t. there. **qeʔqs cʔukʷm, qs cʔukʷmp**

cʔukʷnt – Bring it here. *cmd.*

cʔukʷštn snsustn x̣ʷl̓ cniłc – I brought the cup for him/her. **cʔukʷnt łu snčłemutn** – Bring the chair here.

ukʷmsqáx̣eʔ, *ukʷmsqá* – bring domestic animals/horses somewhere.
ukʷmsqáx̣eʔ – S/he brought horses. **čn ukʷmsqáx̣eʔ, kʷ ukʷmsqáx̣eʔ**
es ukʷmsqáx̣eʔi – S/he is bringing horses. **čnes ukʷmsqáx̣eʔi, kʷes ukʷmsqáx̣eʔi**
qs ukʷmsqáx̣eʔi – S/he is going to bring horses. **čiqs ukʷmsqáx̣eʔi, kʷqs ukʷmsqáx̣eʔi**
ukʷmsqáʔax̣eʔ – They brought horses. **qeʔ ukʷmsqáx̣eʔ, p ukʷmsqáx̣eʔ**

xʷiusm – take/bring along a person or animal. *rt.:* ***xʷuy*** *– go; infix:* ***...us*** *– face.*
xʷiusis – S/he/it took s.o. along. **xʷiusn, xʷiusntxʷ**
es xʷiusms – S/he/it is taking s.o. along. **ies xʷiusm, as xʷiusm**
qs xʷiusms – S/he/it is going to take s.o. along. **iqs xʷiusm, aqs xʷiusm**
xʷiusis – They took s.o. along. **qeʔ xʷiusntm, xʷiusntp**
es xʷiúʔums – They are taking s.o. along. **qeʔes xʷiusm, es xʷiusmp**
qs xʷiúʔums – They are going to take s.o. along. **qeʔ qs xʷiusm, qs xʷiusmp**

xʷiusnt – Take s.o. along. *cmd.*

xʷimsqáx̣eʔ, *xʷimsqá* – take/bring along domestic animals/horses.
xʷimsqáx̣eʔ – S/he brought along a horse. **čn xʷimsqáx̣eʔ, kʷ xʷimsqáx̣eʔ**
es xʷimsqáx̣eʔi – S/he is bringing along a horse. **čnes xʷimsqáx̣eʔi, kʷes xʷimsqáx̣eʔi**
qs xʷimsqáx̣eʔi – S/he is going to bring along a horse. **čiqs xʷimsqáx̣eʔi, kʷqs xʷimsqáx̣eʔi**
xʷimsqáʔax̣eʔ – They brought along a horse. **qeʔ xʷimsqáx̣eʔ, p xʷimsqáx̣eʔ**

The **i** following uvular consonants (UC) and the glottal stop **ʔ** sound like English "*ey*" as in the words th*ey*, h*ey*, wh*ey*, etc. Salish UC are: **q, q̇, qʷ, q̇ʷ, x̣, x̣ʷ**. For example, the suffix **...qin** – head/top, is often spelled using English *ey* as "q*ey*n". So **qi, q̇i, qʷi, q̇ʷi, x̣i, x̣ʷi**, may be spelled with English *ey* as **q***ey*, **q̇***ey*, **qʷ***ey*, **q̇ʷ***ey*, **x̣***ey*, **x̣ʷ***ey* in other texts.

s.t. - something, the 3rd person
(s.t.) - something implied
s.o. - someone, the 3rd person
sl. - singular form
pl. - plural form
rt. - root word
cmd. - command
lit. - literally
fig. - figuratively
i.e., - for example
See: - Redirection to a related word.

es xʷimsqáʔax̣eʔi – They are bringing along a horse. **qeʔes xʷimsqáx̣eʔi, pes xʷimsqáx̣eʔi**
qs xʷimsqáʔax̣eʔi – They are going to bring along a horse. **qeʔqs xʷimsqáx̣eʔi, pqs xʷimsqáx̣eʔi**

iqs xʷiusm łu isxʷsixʷlt qeʔqs k̓ʷis qqméʔe – I am going to bring the children along fishing.

nʔułxʷm – bring an individual person or thing inside.
nʔułxʷsts – S/he brought s.o. in there. **nʔułxʷstn, nʔułxʷstxʷ**
es nʔułxʷms – S/he is bringing s.o. in there. **ies nʔułxʷm, as nʔułxʷm**
qs nʔułxʷms – S/he is going to bring s.o. in there. **iqs nʔułxʷm, aqs nʔułxʷm**
nʔúʔułxʷsts – They brought s.o. in there. **qeʔ nʔułxʷstm, nʔułxʷstp**
es nʔúʔułxʷms – They are bringing s.o. in there. **qeʔes nʔułxʷm, es nʔułxʷmp**
qs nʔúʔułxʷms – They are going to bring s.o. in there. **qeʔqs nʔułxʷm, qs nʔułxʷmp**

cnʔułxʷsts – S/he brought s.o. in here. **cnʔułxʷstn, cnʔułxʷstxʷ**
cnʔúʔułxʷsts – They brought s.o. in here. **qeʔ cnʔułxʷstm, cnʔułxʷstp**

cnʔułxʷstm – S/he/it was brought inside.

nʔułxʷmsqáx̣eʔ, *nʔułxʷmsqá* **–** bring one domestic animal, horse inside.
nʔułxʷmsqáx̣eʔ – S/he brought it in. **čn nʔułxʷmsqáx̣eʔ, kʷ nʔułxʷmsqáx̣eʔ**
es nʔułxʷmsqáx̣eʔi – S/he is bringing it in. **čnes nʔułxʷmsqáx̣eʔi, kʷes nʔułxʷmsqáx̣eʔi**
qs nʔułxʷmsqáx̣eʔi – S/he is going to bring it in. **čiqs nʔułxʷmsqáx̣eʔi, kʷqs nʔułxʷmsqáx̣eʔi**

npilšm – bring things inside there. *suffix:* ***...ilš*** *– autonomous.*
npilšis – S/he brought s.t. in. **npilšn, npilšntxʷ**
es npilšms – S/he is bringing s.t. in. **ies npilšm, as npilšm**
qs npilšms – S/he is bringing s.t. in. **iqs npilšm, aqs npilšm**
npíʔilšis – They brought s.t. in. **qeʔ npilšntm, npilšntp**
es npíʔilšms – They are bringing s.t. in. **qeʔes npilšm, es npilšmp**
qs npíʔilšms – They are going to bring s.t. in. **qeʔqs npilšm, qs npilšmp**

cnpilškʷ – Bring them in here. *cmd.*
npilškʷ – Bring them in there. *cmd.*
npilšnt – Bring s.t. in. *cmd.*

nplšsqáx̣eʔ, *nplšsqá* **–** bring domestic animals, horses inside.
nplšsqáx̣eʔ – S/he brought it in. **čn nplšsqáx̣eʔ, kʷ nplšsqáx̣eʔ**
es nplšsqáx̣eʔi – S/he is bringing it in. **čnes nplšsqáx̣eʔi, kʷes nplšsqáx̣eʔi**
qs nplšsqáx̣eʔi – S/he is going to bring it in. **čiqs nplšsqáx̣eʔi, kʷqs nplšsqáx̣eʔi**

nplšeslqʷm – bring wood in there. *rt.:* ***npilš*** *– go in pl.; suffix:* ***...alqʷ*** *– wood; cylindical.*
nplšeslqʷm – S/he brought wood in. **čn nplšeslqʷm, kʷ nplšeslqʷm**
es nplšeslqʷi – S/he is bringing wood in. **ies nplšeslqʷi, as nplšeslqʷi**
qs nplšeslqʷi – S/he is going to bring wood in. **iqs nplšeslqʷi, aqs nplšeslqʷi**
nplšéʔeslqʷm – They brought wood in. **qeʔ nplšeslqʷm, p nplšeslqʷm**
es nplšéʔeslqʷi – They are bringing wood in. **qeʔes nplšeslqʷi, es nplšeslqʷi**
qs nplšéʔeslqʷi – They are going to bring wood in. **qeʔqs nplšeslqʷi, qs nplšeslqʷi**

nplšeslqʷis – S/he brought the wood in. **nplšeslqʷn, nplšeslqʷntxʷ**
es nplšeslqʷms – S/he is bringing the wood in. **ies nplšeslqʷm, as nplšeslqʷm**
qs nplšeslqʷms – S/he is bringing the wood in. **iqs nplšeslqʷm, aqs nplšeslqʷm**
nplšéʔeslqʷis – They brought the wood in. **qeʔ nplšeslqʷntm, nplšeslqʷntp**
es nplšéʔeslqʷms – They are bringing the wood in. **qeʔes nplšeslqʷm, es nplšeslqʷmp**
qs nplšéʔeslqʷms – They are going to bring the wood in. **qeʔqs nplšeslqʷm, qs nplšeslqʷmp**

es nplplšeslqʷi – S/he is bringing wood in repeatedly. **čnes nplplšeslqʷi, kʷes nplplšeslqʷi**

es nplplšeslqʷms – S/he is bringing the wood in repeatedly. **ies nplplšeslqʷm, as nplplšeslqʷm**

es łnplšeslqʷi – S/he is bringing a little bit of wood in. **čnes łnplšeslqʷi, kʷes łnplšeslqʷi**

sxʷnplšeslqʷm – one tasked to bring wood in. *prefix:* ***sxʷ...*** *– one tasked to do.*
nplšeslqʷnemn – one inclined to bring wood in. *suffix:* ***...emn*** *– one inclined to do.*

nplšeslqʷiš – Bring in wood. *cmd.*
nplšeslqʷnt – Bring the wood in. *cmd.*

nplšesšn̓m – bring rocks in there. *rt.:* ***npilš*** *– go in pl.; suffix:* ***...sšn̓*** *– rock.*
nplšesšn̓m – S/he brought rocks in. **nplšesšn̓m, nplšesšn̓m**
es nplšesšn̓i – S/he is bringing rocks in. **čnes nplšesšn̓i, kʷes nplšesšn̓i**
qs nplšesšn̓i – S/he is bringing rocks in. **čiqs nplšesšn̓i, kʷqs nplšesšn̓i**
nplšéˀesšm – They brought rocks in. **qeˀ nplšesšn̓m, nplšesšn̓m**
es nplšéˀesšn̓i – They are bringing rocks in. **qeˀes nplšesšn̓i, es nplšesšn̓i**
qs nplšéˀesšn̓i – They are going to bring rocks in. **qeˀqs nplšesšn̓i, qs nplšesšn̓i**

nplšesšn̓is – S/he brought the rocks in. **nplšesšn̓, nplšesšn̓ntxʷ**
es nplšesšn̓ms – S/he is bringing the rocks in. **ies nplšesšn̓m, as nplšesšn̓m**
qs nplšesšn̓ms – S/he is bringing the rocks in. **iqs nplšesšn̓m, aqs nplšesšn̓m**
nplšéˀesšn̓is – They brought the rocks in. **qeˀ nplšesšn̓ntm, nplšesšn̓ntp**
es nplšéˀesšn̓ms – They are bringing the rocks in. **qeˀes nplšesšn̓m, es nplšesšn̓mp**
qs nplšéˀesšn̓ms – They are going to bring the rocks in. **qeˀqs nplšesšn̓m, qs nplšesšn̓mp**

sxʷnplšesšn̓m – one tasked to bring rocks in. *prefix:* ***sxʷ...*** *– one tasked to do.*
nplšesšn̓emn – one inclined to bring rocks in. *suffix:* ***...emn*** *– one inclined to do.*

nplšesšn̓iš – Bring in rocks. *cmd.*
nplšesšn̓nt – Bring the rocks in. *cmd.*

ocqˀém – bring something out there.
ocqˀéis – S/he brought s.t. out. **ocqˀén, ocqˀéntxʷ**
es ocqˀéms – S/he is bringing s.t. out. **ies ocqˀem, as ocqˀém**
qs ocqˀéms – S/he is going to bring s.t. out. **iqs ocqˀem, aqs ocqˀém**
occqˀéˀeis – They brought s.t. out. **qeˀ occqˀéntm, occqˀéntp**
es occqˀéˀems – They are bringing s.t. out. **qeˀes occqˀém, es occqˀémp**
qs occqˀéˀems – They are going to bring s.t. out. **qeˀqs occqˀém, qs occqˀémp**

ocqeˀskʷ – Bring it out there. *cmd.*

ocqˀusm – bring someone out there. *rt.:* ***ocqeˀ*** *– go out; suffix:* ***...us*** *– face, fire.*
ocqˀusis – S/he brought s.o. out. **ocqˀusn, ocqˀusntxʷ**
es ocqˀusms – S/he is bringing s.o. out. **ies ocqˀusm, as ocqˀusm**
qs ocqˀusms – S/he is going to bring s.o. out. **iqs ocqˀusm, aqs ocqˀusm**
occqˀúˀusis – They brought s.o. out. **occqˀusntm, occqˀusntp**
es occqˀúˀusms – They are bringing s.o. out. **qeˀes occqˀusm, es occqˀusmp**
qs occqˀúˀusms – They are going to bring s.o. out. **qeˀqs occqˀusm, qs occqˀusmp**

ocqˀusnt – Bring him/her out there. *cmd.*

ocsqáx̣eˀ – take/bring a horse/domestic animal out of some place. *(i.e., a barn, corral, etc.)*
ocsqáx̣eˀ – S/he took a horse out. **čn ocsqáx̣eˀ, kʷ ocsqáx̣eˀ**
es ocsqáx̣eˀi – S/he is taking a horse out. **čnes ocsqáx̣eˀi, kʷes ocsqáx̣eˀi**
qs ocsqáx̣eˀi – S/he is going to take a horse out. **čiqs ocsqáx̣eˀi, kʷqs ocsqáx̣eˀi**

The **i** following uvular consonants (UC) and the glottal stop **ˀ** sound like English "*ey*" as in the words th*ey*, h*ey*, wh*ey*, etc. Salish UC are: **q**, **q̇**, **qʷ**, **q̇ʷ**, **x̣**, **x̣ʷ**. For example, the suffix **...qin** – head/top, is often spelled using English *ey* as "q*ey*n". So **qi**, **q̇i**, **qʷi**, **q̇ʷi**, **x̣i**, **x̣ʷi**, may be spelled with English *ey* as **q***ey*, **q̇***ey*, **qʷ***ey*, **q̇ʷ***ey*, **x̣***ey*, **x̣ʷ***ey* in other texts.

s.t. - something, the 3rd person
(s.t.) - something implied
s.o. - someone, the 3rd person
sl. - singular form
pl. - plural form
rt. - root word
cmd. - command
lit. - literally
fig. - figuratively
i.e., - for example
See: - Redirection to a related word.

cʔocqʔém – bring something out here. *rt.: **ocqeʔ** – go out; prefix: **c...** – indicating toward the speaker.*
cʔocqʔéis – S/he brought s.t. out here. **cʔocqʔén, cʔocqʔéntxʷ**
es cʔocqʔéms – S/he is bringing s.t. out here. **ies cʔocqʔem, as cʔocqʔém**
qs cʔocqʔéms – S/he is going to bring s.t. out here. **iqs cʔocqʔem, aqs cʔocqʔém**
cʔoccqʔéʔeis – They brought s.t. out here. **qeʔ cʔoccqʔéntm, cʔoccqʔéntp**
es cʔoccqʔéʔems – They are bringing s.t. out here. **qeʔes cʔoccqʔém, es cʔoccqʔémp**
qs cʔoccqʔéʔems – They are going to bring s.t. out here. **qeʔqs cʔoccqʔém, qs cʔoccqʔémp**

cʔocqʔém – S/he/it brought it out here.
cʔocqeʔskʷ – Bring it out here. *cmd.*

cʔocqʔusm – bring someone out here. *rt.: **ocqeʔ** – go out; prefix: **c...** – indicating toward the speaker; suffix: **...us** – face, fire.*
cʔocqʔusis – S/he brought s.o. out here. **cʔocqʔusn, cʔocqʔusntxʷ**
es cʔocqʔusms – S/he is bringing s.o. out here. **ies cʔocqʔusm, as cʔocqʔusm**
qs cʔocqʔusms – S/he is going to bring s.o. out here. **iqs cʔocqʔusm, aqs cʔocqʔusm**
cʔoccqʔúʔusis – They brought s.o. out here. **cʔoccqʔusntm, cʔoccqʔusntp**
es cʔoccqʔúʔusms – They are bringing s.o. out here. **qeʔes cʔoccqʔusm, es cʔoccqʔusmp**

cʔocqʔusnt – Bring him/her out here. *cmd.*

tmsqáx̣eʔ, tmsqá – bring a horse to water.
tmsqáx̣eʔ – S/he brought a horse to water. **čn tmsqáx̣eʔ, kʷ tmsqáx̣eʔ**
es tmsqáx̣eʔi – S/he is bringing a horse to water. **čnes tmsqáx̣eʔi, kʷes tmsqáx̣eʔi**
qs tmsqáx̣eʔi – S/he is going to bring a horse to water. **čiqs tmsqáx̣eʔi, kʷqs tmsqáx̣eʔi**

ckʷnem – fetch something that is within the immediate area; *lit. to go take something and bring it back here. See: **fetch**.*

cq̓ʷom – gather and bring things here. *(the plural form of **ckʷnem**) See: **gather**.*

brodiaea

sil̓us – brodiaea; wild hyacinth; *Brodiaea douglasii.*

broil

yexʷ – broil; put at a distance from a fire.
yexʷis – S/he broiled s.t. **yexʷn, yexʷntxʷ**
es yexʷms – S/he is broiling s.t. **ies yexʷm, as yexʷm**
qs yexʷms – S/he is going to broil s.t. **iqs yexʷm, aqs yexʷm**

broken

máw̓t – break. *See: **break**.*

broom

ċslexʷéłpmn, *ċslexʷe* – broom. *rt.: **ċslexʷ** – make bare/clean; suffix: **...ełp, ...łp** – tree; from floor covering which were boughs in the past.*

čłʔáx̣ʷłpmn – broom. *rt.: **ax̣ʷ** – scrape; prefix: **čł...** – surface; suffix: **...ełp, ...łp** – tree; from floor covering which were boughs in the past. lit. instrument to scrape.*

broth

sx̣sétkʷ, *sx̣sé* – soup; broth. *suffix: **...etkʷ, ...tkʷ** – liquid*

brother

qecč – older brother of a male. **qcqecč** *pl. See: **section 3: Kinship terms**.*
qecčs – his older brother. **inqecč, anqecč**

łqáqceʔ – older brother of a female.
łqáqceʔs – her older brother. **inłqáqceʔ, anłqáqceʔ**

sínceʔ – younger brother of a male. **snsínceʔ** *pl.*
sínceʔs – his younger brother. **isínceʔ, asínceʔ**

sísnceʔ – younger brother of a female.

sísnceʔs – her younger brother. **isísnceʔ, asísnceʔ**

qéws – older brother.

snkʷsixʷ – brother/sister/cousin. **snkʷsxʷsixʷ** *pl. rt.:* ***sxʷsixʷlt*** *– offspring; prefix:* ***snkʷ...*** *– fellow; member of.*
snkʷsixʷs – his/her brother/sister/cousin. **isnkʷsixʷ, asnkʷsixʷ,**
snkʷsíʔixʷs – their brother/sister/cousin. **qesnkʷsixʷ, snkʷsixʷmp**

sck̓ʷl̓snkʷsixʷ – foster brother. *prefix:* ***sck̓ʷl̓...*** *– s.t. that's been made.*
sck̓ʷl̓sínceʔ – foster younger brother. *prefix:* ***sck̓ʷl̓...*** *– s.t. that's been made.*
sck̓ʷl̓łqáceʔ – foster older brother of a female. *prefix:* ***sck̓ʷl̓...*** *– s.t. that's been made.*
sck̓ʷl̓qecč – foster older bother of a male. *prefix:* ***sck̓ʷl̓...*** *– s.t. that's been made.*

The **i** following uvular consonants (UC) and the glottal stop ʔ sound like English "*ey*" as in the words *they, hey, whey*, etc. Salish UC are: **q, q̓, qʷ, q̓ʷ, x̣, x̣ʷ**. For example, the suffix …**qin** – head/ top, is often spelled using English *ey* as "qeyn". So **qi, q̓i, qʷi, q̓ʷi, x̣i, x̣ʷi**, may be spelled with English *ey* as **q***ey*, **q̓***ey*, **qʷ***ey*, **q̓ʷ***ey*, **x̣***ey*, **x̣ʷ***ey* in other texts.

brother-in-law

sc̓éšt – brother-in-law of male. *See:* ***section 3: Kinship terms.***

seʔstem – brother-in-law of a female.

nq̓ʷic̓tn – brother/sister-in-law after death/separation/divorce of spouse.

brow

cpłéẏ – eyebrow; brow.

brown

čłkʷi – brown.

i pá – It is faded; tan; grey.

čłčé – brown horse.

čłpá – buckskin colored horse.

p̓um – orange; brown.

ṅem i kʷéṁt m p̓um – then it will be done orange/brown (the hide).

brown bat

t̓ɫ̓t̓el̓ẁé, *t̓lt̓el̓ẁéliyeʔ* **–** bat.

brown trout

sttṁáẏl̓qs, *sttṁá* **–** bullhead trout; brown trout; *Salmo trutta.*
čtl̓ic̓éʔetxʷ sttṁa – Rip the blankets off the bullhead.

bruise

iyus – bruise.

i ṅqʷáys – black eye.

emuk̓ʷ – bruised all the way through coming to the skin.

brush

nkʷéct, *nkʷé* **–** forest; backwoods; brush; thicket.

i nc̓án – It is a tight space inside. *(i.e., brush, thicket.)*

est̓émp – bush.

nxʷk̓ʷxʷk̓ʷeysm – brush/clean teeth.
nxʷk̓ʷxʷk̓ʷeysm – S/he brushed his/her teeth. **čn nxʷk̓ʷxʷk̓ʷeysm, kʷ nxʷk̓ʷxʷk̓ʷeysm**
es nxʷk̓ʷxʷk̓ʷeysi – S/he is brushing his/her teeth. **čnes nxʷk̓ʷxʷk̓ʷeysi, kʷes nxʷk̓ʷxʷk̓ʷeysi**
qs nxʷk̓ʷxʷk̓ʷeysi – S/he is going to brush his/her teeth. **čiqs nxʷk̓ʷxʷk̓ʷeysi, kʷqs nxʷk̓ʷxʷk̓ʷeysi**

nxʷk̓ʷxʷk̓ʷeysiš – Brush your teeth. *cmd.*

nc̓uʔc̓éẁistn – toothpaste.

s.t. - something, the 3rd person
(s.t.) - something implied
s.o. - someone, the 3rd person
sl. - singular form
pl. - plural form
rt. - root word
cmd. - command
lit. - literally
fig. - figuratively
i.e., - for example
See: - Redirection to a related word.

nxʷk̓ʷxʷk̓ʷeysiš ṅe kʷ wisˀiłnm – Brush your teeth after meals.

bubble **čx̣x̣als** – bubble. *rt.: **x̣al** – clear; circumfix: **č...us** – spherical object; eyes.*

buck **sx̣ʷl̓éščn**, *sx̣ʷl̓é* – white-tail buck; *Odocoileus virginianus. suffix: **...elsčn** – horn.*

puwélsčn, *puwé* – black-tail buck; male mule deer; *Odocoileus hemionus.*

nmcmccq̓ʷlépleˀ, *nmcmccq̓ʷlé* – buck. *(i.e., horse, bull, etc.) suffix: **...épleˀ** – permanence.*

buck brush **k̓ʷl̓itčyełp**, *k̓ʷl̓itčye* – buck brush, ceanothus.

bucket **łčépeˀ**, *łčép* – bucket.

sčłq̓ʷastn, *sčłq̓ʷa* – bark basket; rawhide bucket.
ƛ̓éˀentwi péċemp u sčłq̓ʷastnmp – All of you look for your diggers and your bark basket/rawhide bucket.

buckle **x̣ṗeẃstn** – buckle together. *rt.: **x̣ṗ** – line, coat; suffix: **...éẃs** – in between, middle.*
x̣ṗeẃsiš – Buckle. *cmd.*
x̣ṗeẃsnt – Buckle s.o./s.t. *cmd.*

snlče x̣ṗeẃstn – belt buckle.
ṗiṗuyšn x̣ṗeẃstn – seat buckle.

buckskin **siṗiˀ** – buckskin; buckskin rope; buckskin lacing.

ċulixʷélxʷ, *ċulixʷé* – buckskin, white-tail doe hide.

čłpa – buckskin in color.

spéčst – buckskin glove. *suffix: **...ečst, ...čst** – of the hand.*

sčpqłċaˀálqs, *sčpqłċaˀá* – buckskin shirt.

buckskin dress **sṗiẏálqs** – buckskin dress. *rt.: **siṗiˀ** – buckskin; suffix: **...lqs, ...alqs** – clothes.*

sx̣ʷpxʷálqs, *sx̣ʷpxʷá* – woman's traditional cloth dress. *suffix: **...lqs, ...alqs** – clothes.*

bud **sčmkʷkʷełp** – leaf/blossom bud.
es čmkʷkʷełpi – The trees are budding.

čtt̓ekʷełp – leaf bud opened. *See: **leaf**.*

t̓lqʷqin – when buds first open up. *See: **flower**.*

čkʷal̓ečst – bud; produce; makes something grow upon. *See: **grow**.*

buffalo **q̓ʷiq̓ʷáy** – buffalo; bison; *Bison bison. lit. many blacks.*
stṁáltms – buffalo cow.
sċułm – buffalo bull.
słwiqʷq̓ʷ – buffalo yearling.
čłkʷlkʷlélxʷ, *čłkʷlkʷlé* – buffalo calf; cow calf. *lit. red hide. (Buffalo calves have a reddish coat. This word has been adopted for use with cattle calves.) rt.: **kʷil** – red; prefix: **čł...** – surface; suffix: **...elxʷ, ...lxʷ** – skin/hide*
smčłq̓ʷiq̓ʷáy – female buffalo.
i piq q̓ʷiq̓ʷáy – white buffalo.

buffalo berry **sx̣ʷósm** – foamberry; buffalo berry; soapberry; *shepherdia canadensis.*

bug **tišulexʷ** – insect; bug. *lit. earth crawler. rt.: **tiyeš**– crawl; suffix: **...ulexʷ**– land. See: **insect**.*

ntišulexʷ – worm, insect, bug. *See: **worm**.*

bugle **npuxʷ** – bugle; blow inside. *(i.e., bull elk) rt.: **puxʷ**– blow.*
es npuxʷi – It is bugling.

sikʷ – whistle. *See: **whistle**.*

build **k̓ʷul̓łxʷ** – work on a house; build a house; carpentry work. *rt.: **kʷul̓**– do; suffix: **...etxʷ, ...łxʷ**– house.*
k̓ʷul̓łxʷ – S/he worked on a house. **čn k̓ʷul̓łxʷ, kʷ k̓ʷul̓łxʷ**
es k̓ʷul̓łxʷi – S/he is working on a house. **čnes k̓ʷul̓łxʷi, kʷes k̓ʷul̓łxʷi**
qs k̓ʷul̓łxʷi – S/he is going to work on a house. **čiqs k̓ʷul̓łxʷi, kʷqs k̓ʷul̓łxʷi**
k̓ʷúʔul̓łxʷ – They worked on a house. **qeʔ k̓ʷul̓łxʷ, p k̓ʷul̓łxʷ**
es k̓ʷúʔul̓łxʷi – They are working on a house. **qeʔes k̓ʷul̓łxʷi, pes k̓ʷul̓łxʷi**

ṅe qeʔ wis k̓ʷul̓łxʷ m šeẏ l qeʔ lciʔ – When we finish building the house, we'll live in it. **čn k̓ʷul̓m t ƛ̓iyéʔ** – I made a canoe.

k̓ʷul̓ – do; make; fix; work. *See: **work**.*

> The **i** following uvular consonants (UC) and the glottal stop **ʔ** sound like English "*ey*" as in the words *they, hey, whey,* etc. Salish UC are: **q, q̇, qʷ, q̇ʷ, x̣, x̣ʷ**. For example, the suffix **...qin** – head/top, is often spelled using English *ey* as "q*ey*n". So **qi, q̇i, qʷi, q̇ʷi, x̣i, x̣ʷi**, may be spelled with English *ey* as **q***ey*, **q̇***ey*, **qʷ***ey*, **q̇ʷ***ey*, **x̣***ey*, **x̣ʷ***ey* in other texts.

bulb **snčṗaq̇ustn** – light bulb. *rt.: **ṗaq̇**– bright; circumfix; **č...us**– spherical shape; prefix: **...tin, ...tn**– means of/device.*

bulge **mqʷeẇt** – bulge out. **mqʷmqʷeẇt** *pl.*
es mqʷeẇt – It is bulged.

ƛ̓čiṁ – protrude out; bulge out. *See: **protrude**.*

bull **nmlmlk̓ʷépls,** *nmlmlk̓ʷé* – male animal; bull; stallion. *suffix: **...epls**– testicle.*

sċułm – bull; steer.

bull elk **tšeċ** – bull elk; *Cervus canadensis*. *See: **elk**.*
šċelxʷ – bull elk hide.

snq̇axʷmi – elk teeth.

bullet **snčʔiṅč,** *snčʔi* – bullet; the loading of a gun. *rt.: **čeʔ**– lump; suffix: **...iṅč**– weapon*
nčʔiṅč – S/he loaded bullets. **čn nčʔiṅč, kʷ nčʔiṅč**
es nčʔiṅči – S/he is loading bullets. **čnes nčʔiṅči, kʷes nčʔiṅči**
es nčʔiṅči – S/he is going to load bullets. **čiqs nčʔiṅči, kʷqs nčʔiṅči**

nčʔiṅčis – S/he loaded s.o.'s gun. **nčʔiṅčn, nčʔiṅčntxʷ**
es nčʔiṅčms – S/he is loading s.o.'s gun. **ies nčʔiṅčm, as nčʔiṅčm**
es nčʔiṅčms – S/he is going to load s.o.'s gun. **iqs nčʔiṅčm, aqs nčʔiṅčm**

nčʔiṅčmis – S/he loaded a gun with s.t. **nčʔiṅčmn, nčʔiṅčmntxʷ**
es nčʔiṅčmms – S/he is loading gun with s.t. **ies nčʔiṅčmm, as nčʔiṅčmm**

nčʔiṅčš – Load the bullets. *cmd.*
nčʔiṅčnt – Load his/her gun. *cmd.*

łmlmilk̓ʷ, *łmlmi* – lead of a bullet.

łcċmeł – small projectile; bb.

> s.t. - something, the 3rd person
> (s.t.) - something implied
> s.o. - someone, the 3rd person
> *sl.* - singular form
> *pl.* - plural form
> *rt.* - root word
> *cmd.* - command
> *lit.* - literally
> *fig.* - figuratively
> *i.e.,* - for example
> *See:* - Redirection to a related word.

bullhead **sttṁáẏl̓qs,** *sttṁá* – bullhead trout; brown trout; *Salmo trutta*. *See: **brown trout**.*

Bullock's oriole **xʷiwxʷu** – Bullock's oriole; northern oriole; *Icterus bullockii.*

bull pine **sʔátqʷɫp** – Ponderosa pine; bull pine; *Pinus ponderosa.*

bull snake **sx̣ʷnu** – bull snake; gopher snake; *Pituophis catenifer.*

bull trout **aáyccst,** *aáy* – bull trout; Dolly Varden trout; *Salvelinus confluentus.*
ɫʔáyccst, *ɫʔáy* – little bull trout; immature bull trout.

nɫʔaycčstm, *nɫʔay* – Missoula, Montana; place of little bull trout.
nʔaycčstm – Bonner, Montana; place of large bull trout.

bulrush **tkʷtiṅ** – bulrush; *Scirpus subterminalis.*

bumble bee **maċpɫ** – bumble bee; *Bombus terricola.*

bump **čtéʔemistm,** *čtéʔe* – bump against something *(i.e., wall, person, etc.). rt.:* ***teʔ*** *– hit/bump into.*
čtéʔemist – S/he/it bumped (s.t.). **čn čtéʔemist, kʷ čtéʔemist**
es čtéʔemisti – S/he/it is bumping (s.t.). **čnes čtéʔemisti, kʷes čtéʔemisti**

es čteteʔmi – S/he/it is repeatedly hitting; hammering. **čnes čteteʔmi, kʷes čteteʔmi**

čteʔmistmis – S/he/it bumped into s.t./s.o. **čteʔmistmn, čteʔmistmntxʷ**
čteʔmíʔistmis – They bumped into s.t./s.o. **čteʔmistmntm, čteʔmistmntp**

čteʔmistmnwexʷ – They bumped/ran into each other.
tʔamnqnwexʷ, *tʔamnqnwe* – They bump each other's heads together.
čɫtʔem – bounce something. *See:* ***bounce.***
čtáʔalqʷ, *čtáʔa* – bump into wood or a tree.

čteʔmistmntm x̣ʷax̣ʷaa t ṗiṗuyšn – The fox was hit by a car. **čn wičm t nɫámqeʔ l isčsáx̣x̣m x̣iṅe u qeʔes tʔamnqnwexʷi** – I saw a bear so close we almost bumped heads. **tʔamnqnwe m sƛ̓pnun** – I will bump heads with it until I overcome it/win.

ta kʷ qes npmpqan – Do not bump your head.

bumper **snčtéʔemistn** – bumper.

bumpy **ɫṁq̓ʷeẇt** – small bump; bumpy. *rt.:* ***moq̓ʷ*** *– bump/hill/mtn.*
ɫṁq̓ʷmu – antler nubs.
ɫṁmoq̓ʷ – small bump/hill.
čmq̓ʷmq̓ʷalqʷ – bumpy wood. *rt.:* ***moq̓ʷ*** *– bump/hill/mtn; suffix:* ***...alqʷ*** *– wood; cylindical.*

moƛ̓ – rough/bumpy texture. *See:* ***rough.***

bundle **čɫčeẇs** – items in the bundle. *suffix:* ***...éẇs*** *– in between, middle.*

bunting **ɫṁṁék̓ʷt** – snow bunting; *Plectrophenax nivalis.*

ƛ̓čƛ̓á esq̓ẏe – lark bunting; *Calamospiza melanocorys.*

burn **ɫmaq̓** – get a superficial burn/scorch.
ɫmq̓ncut – S/he/it burned one's self. **čn ɫmq̓ncut, kʷ ɫmq̓ncut**
es ɫmq̓ncuti – S/he/it is burning one's self. **čnes ɫmq̓ncuti, kʷes ɫmq̓ncuti**
qs ɫmq̓ncuti – S/he/it is going to burn one's self. **čiqs ɫmq̓ncuti, kʷqs ɫmq̓ncuti**

ɫmaq̓ – S/he/it got burned. **čn ɫmaq̓, kʷ ɫmaq̓**

es łmq̇mi – S/he/it is getting burned. **čnes łmq̇mi, kʷes łmq̇mi**
qs łmq̇mi – S/he/it is going to get burned. **čiqs łmq̇mi, kʷqs łmq̇mi**

łmq̇ntes – S/he/it burned s.o. **łmq̇nten, łmq̇ntexʷ**
es łmq̇ems – S/he/it is burning s.o. **ies łmq̇em, as łmq̇em**
qs łmq̇ems – S/he/it is going to burn s.o. **iqs łmq̇em, aqs łmq̇em**

słmaq̇ – burn.

łmq̇ncutš – Burn yourself. *cmd.*
łmq̇ent – Burn him/her/it. *cmd.*

łmq̇ečst – S/he/it burned one's hand. **čn łmq̇ečst, kʷ łmq̇ečst**
nłmq̇ołqlt – S/he/it burned one's throat. **čn łmq̇ołqlt, kʷ łmq̇ołqlt**
nłmq̇cin – S/he burned one's tongue/mouth. **čn nłmq̇cin, kʷ nłmq̇cin**
łmq̇šin – S/he/it burned one's foot. **čn łmq̇šin, kʷ łmq̇šin**
čłmq̇us – S/he/it burned one's face. **čn čłmq̇us, kʷ čłmq̇us**
nłmpołqʷlt – burned mouth.
nłmpsq̇amel̓tn – burned throat.

ha kʷ łmaq̇ – Did you get burned? **čn łmq̇em t inpus** – I burned my cat.

p̓ix̣ – brand with a hot iron. *See: **brand**.*

ulip – burn up; catch fire. *See: **fire**.*

p̓aap – grass/timber caught fire. *See: **fire**.*

c̓áx̣ʷc̓x̣ʷt, *c̓áx̣ʷ* – powdery ashes. *See: **ash**.*

The **i** following uvular consonants (UC) and the glottal stop ʔ sound like English "*ey*" as in the words th*ey*, h*ey*, wh*ey*, etc. Salish UC are: **q**, **q̇**, **qʷ**, **q̇ʷ**, **x̣**, **x̣ʷ**. For example, the suffix **...qin** – head/top, is often spelled using English *ey* as "q*ey*n". So **qi**, **q̇i**, **qʷi**, **q̇ʷi**, **x̣i**, **x̣ʷi**, may be spelled with English *ey* as **q***ey*, **q̇***ey*, **qʷ***ey*, **q̇ʷ***ey*, **x̣***ey*, **x̣ʷ***ey* in other texts.

burrito

scp̓lk̓ʷew̓s – burrito. *rt.: **p̓lk̓ʷ** – roll, wrap; suffix: **...éw̓s** – in between, middle.*

čp̓lp̓lk̓ʷsʔiłn – burrito. *rt.: **p̓lk̓ʷ** – roll, wrap.*

burrowing owl

nčcw̓éʔ – burrowing owl; *Athene cunicularia.*

bury

laq̇ – bury.
láq̇m – S/he/it buried. **čn láq̇m, kʷ láq̇m**
es laq̇i – S/he/it is burying. **čnes laq̇i, kʷes laq̇i**
qs laq̇i – S/he/it is going to bury. **čiqs laq̇i, kʷqs laq̇i**
láʔaq̇m – They buried. **qeʔ láq̇m, p láq̇m**
es láʔaq̇i – They are burying. **qeʔes laq̇i, pes laq̇i**

laq̇is – S/he/it buried s.t. **laq̇n, as laq̇ntxʷ**
es laq̇ms – S/he/it is burying s.t. **ies laq̇m, as laq̇m**
qs laq̇ms – S/he/it is going to bury s.t. **iqs laq̇m, aqs laq̇m**
lq̇áʔaq̇is – They buried s.t. **qeʔ laq̇ntm, laq̇ntp**
es láʔaq̇ms – They are burying s.t. **qeʔes laq̇m, es laq̇mp**

lq̇łtmtmnéy – funeral; bury the dead.

čłlaq̇éneʔ – bury/cover with dirt. *(This term implies something will be buried permanently.)*
čłlaq̇énʔeis – S/he buried it. **čłlaq̇énʔen, čłlaq̇énʔentxʷ**
es čłlaq̇énʔems – S/he is burying it. **ies čłlaq̇énʔem, as čłlaq̇énʔem**
qs čłlaq̇énʔems – S/he is going to bury it. **iqs čłlaq̇énʔem, aqs čłlaq̇énʔem**

čłlaq̇enʔént – Bury it. *cmd.*

ha čłlaq̇enʔéntxʷ łu asc̓om̓ – Did you bury your bone?

s.t. - something, the 3rd person
(s.t.) - something implied
s.o. - someone, the 3rd person
sl. - singular form
pl. - plural form
rt. - root word
cmd. - command
lit. - literally
fig. - figuratively
i.e., - for example
See: - Redirection to a related word.

čłpq̓ʷenʔem – bury/cover something with a granular substance. *(i.e., sand, dirt, etc.)*
čłpq̓ʷenʔeis – S/he buried s.t. **čłpq̓ʷenʔen, čłpq̓ʷenʔentxʷ**
es čłpq̓ʷenʔems – S/he is burying s.t. **ies čłpq̓ʷenʔem, as čłpq̓ʷenʔem**
qs čłpq̓ʷenʔems – S/he is going to bury s.t. **iqs čłpq̓ʷenʔem, aqs čłpq̓ʷenʔem**

ha čłpq̓ʷenʔentxʷ łu asx̣ʷéʔli – Did you bury/cover your camas?

čłpkʷenʔem – bury/cover something with a large granular objects. *(i.e., rocks, wood, etc.)*
čłpkʷenʔeis – S/he buried s.t. **čłpkʷenʔen, čłpkʷenʔentxʷ**
es čłpkʷenʔems – S/he is burying s.t. **ies čłpkʷenʔem, as čłpkʷenʔem**
qs čłpkʷenʔems – S/he is going to bury s.t. **iqs čłpkʷenʔem, aqs čłpkʷenʔem**

bus

snukʷuṅwé – school bus; bus.
snukʷukʷuṅwé – bus that takes passengers; bus that travels around the country picking up and dropping off passengers here and there.

bush

esťéṁp – bush; *describing bunched at the bottom and bushed on top.*
čn sewneʔ tʔe t steṁ ẏe tl̓ esťeṁp – I heard something in the bush.

iliil – bush; *describing branched out branches. rt.: **ili** – pass into/through.*

nkʷéct, *nkʷé* – forest; backwoods; brush; thicket.

bushy-tailed wood rat

héẃt – pack rat, bushy-tailed wood rat; *Neotoma cinerea.*

sqʷʔópłxʷ – hole; den (as of a mouse or rat). *rt.: **qʷʔóp** – make soft; suffix: **...etxʷ, ...łxʷ** – house.*

business

nq̓ʔels – busy with something; pay attention to something; involved with something. *rt.: **q̓eʔ** – put inside; circumfix: **n...els** – want, feel.*
nq̓ʔelsmis – S/he took care of it. **nq̓ʔelsmn, nq̓ʔelsmntxʷ**
es nq̓ʔelsms – S/he is busy with s.t./s.o. **ies nq̓ʔelsm, as nq̓ʔelsm**
qs nq̓ʔelsms – S/he is going to be busy with s.t./s.o. **iqs nq̓ʔelsm, aqs nq̓ʔelsm**
nq̓ʔéʔelsmis – They took care of it. **qeʔ nq̓ʔelsmtm, nq̓ʔelsmntp**

čq̓ʔelsmis – S/he made s.t./s.o. one's business. **čq̓ʔelsmn, čq̓ʔelsmntxʷ**
es čq̓ʔelsms – S/he is making s.t./s.o. one's business. **ies čq̓ʔelsm, as čq̓ʔelsm**
qs čq̓ʔelsms – S/he is going to make s.t./s.o. one's business. **iqs čq̓ʔelsm, aqs čq̓ʔelsm**

nq̓aq̓ʔels – always busy; snoopy; nosy; prying.

scnq̓éʔels – business. *rt.: **q̓eʔ** – put inside; prefix: **sc...** – s.t. that's been done/made/prepared; circumfix: **n...els** – want, feel.*
scnq̓éʔelsts – his/her/its business. **iscnq̓éʔels, ascnq̓éʔels**
scnq̓éʔeʔélsts – their business. **qescnq̓éʔels, scnq̓éʔelsmp**

tam ascnq̓éʔels – It is none of your business. **ciqs xʷuy č x̣ʷiʔilqsá čn ep scnq̓éʔels** – I am going to Pablo on business. I have business there.

sntumistn, *sntumi* – store.

bustle

sčłċlčnups, *sčłċlčnu* – bustle. *rt.: **ċil** – standing upright.*
čłċlčnupsm – S/he put a bustle on. **čn čłċlčnupsm, kʷ čłċlčnupsm**
es čłċlčnupsi – S/he is putting a bustle on. **čnes čłċlčnupsi, kʷes čłċlčnupsi**
qs čłċlčnupsi – S/he is going to put a bustle on. **čiqs čłċlčnupsi, kʷqs čłċlčnupsi**

es čłċlčnups – S/he is wearing a bustle on. **čnes čłċlčnups, kʷes čłċlčnups**

čiqs k̓ʷuli t iqs sčłċlčnu – I am going to make a bustle.

sčt̓x̣čnups – bustle. *rt.: t̓ix̣ – protrude.*
čt̓x̣čnupsm – S/he put a bustle on. **čn čt̓x̣čnupsm, kʷ čt̓x̣čnupsm**
es čt̓x̣čnupsi – S/he is putting a bustle on. **čnes čt̓x̣čnupsi, kʷes čt̓x̣čnupsi**
qs čt̓x̣čnupsi – S/he is going to put a bustle on. **čiqs čt̓x̣čnupsi, kʷqs čt̓x̣čnupsi**

es čt̓x̣čnups – S/he is wearing a bustle. **čnes čt̓x̣čnups, kʷes čt̓x̣čnups**

busy

ax̣tčim – busy with something.
ax̣tčim – S/he was being busy. **čn ax̣tčim, kʷ ax̣tčim**
es ax̣tčmi – S/he is being busy. **čnes ax̣tčmi, kʷes ax̣tčmi**
qs ax̣tčmi – S/he is going to be busy. **čiqs ax̣tčmi, kʷqs ax̣tčmi**
es ax̣tčmíʔi – They are being busy. **qeʔes ax̣tčmi, pes ax̣tčmi**

ax̣tčmstes – S/he was busy with s.t. **ax̣tčmsten, ax̣tčmstexʷ**
es ax̣tčims – S/he is being busy with s.t. **ies ax̣tčim, as ax̣tčim**
qs ax̣tčims – S/he is going to be busy with s.t. **iqs ax̣tčim, aqs ax̣tčim**
es ax̣tčíʔims – They are being busy with s.t. **qeʔes ax̣tčim, es ax̣tčimp**

ax̣ax̣tčim – Each one of them is busy. **qeʔ ax̣ax̣tčim, p ax̣ax̣tčim**

ax̣tčemn – one inclined to be busy. *suffix: ...emn – one inclined to do.*
ax̣ax̣tčmuł – one that is habitually busy. *suffix: ...łmuł – one that habitually does.*

ax̣tčiš – Be busy. *cmd.*
ax̣tčmiskʷ – Be busy with s.t. *cmd.*
ax̣tčint – Be busy with s.t. *cmd.*
es ax̣tčmwexʷisti – They are busy with each other. **qeʔes ax̣tčmwexʷisti, pes ax̣tčmwexʷisti**
es nax̣tčmelsi – S/he is wanting to be busy. **čnes nax̣tčmelsi, kʷes nax̣tčmelsi**
es ax̣tčmscuti – S/he is busy with one's self. **čnes ax̣tčmscuti, kʷes ax̣tčmscuti**

ax̣tčmists – S/he is working at it. **ax̣tčmistn, ax̣tčmistxʷ**

es čax̣eplʔems – S/he is busy with s.t. **ies čax̣eplʔem, as čax̣eplʔem**
qs čax̣eplʔems – S/he is going to be busy with s.t. **iqs čax̣eplʔem, aqs čax̣eplʔem**
es čax̣éʔeplʔems – They are busy with s.t. **qeʔes čax̣eplʔem, es čax̣eplʔemp**

ax̣tčim es čk̓ʷul̓i – S/he is busy beading.

ax̣í – busy with; mess around with; perform.
ax̣í u čn uẏéčst – I finally finished.

ax̣ísts – S/he did it like s.t./s.o. **ax̣ístn, ax̣ístxʷ**
es ax̣ílms – S/he is doing it like s.t./s.o. **ies ax̣ílm, as ax̣ílm**
qs ax̣ílms – S/he is going to do it like s.t./s.o. **iqs ax̣ílm, aqs ax̣ílm**
ax̣íʔists – They did it like s.t./s.o. **qeʔ ax̣ístm, ax̣ístp**

ax̣ískʷ – Do it like this. *cmd.*

l čeṅ m ax̣ístn – How should I do it?
l čeṅ u ax̣ístxʷ – How did you do it?

lʔe u ax̣ístxʷ – This is how you did it. **ye lʔe m ax̣ístxʷ –** You will do it like this.
ax̣ístn t seẇłkʷ – I did it like water.

ax̣llwís, *ax̣llwí* **–** hustle around for something; able and determined in doing something. *suffix: ...lwis – indicate going around.*
ax̣llwís – S/he/it hustled around. **čn ax̣llwís, kʷ ax̣llwís**
es ax̣llwísi – S/he/it is hustling around. **čnes ax̣llwísi, kʷes ax̣llwísi**

The **i** following uvular consonants (UC) and the glottal stop ʔ sound like English "*ey*" as in the words th*ey*, h*ey*, wh*ey*, etc. Salish UC are: **q, q̇, qʷ, q̇ʷ, x̣, x̣ʷ**. For example, the suffix **...qin** – head/top, is often spelled using English *ey* as "qeyn". So **qi, q̇i, qʷi, q̇ʷi, x̣i, x̣ʷi**, may be spelled with English *ey* as **q***ey*, **q̇***ey*, **qʷ***ey*, **q̇ʷ***ey*, **x̣***ey*, **x̣ʷ***ey* in other texts.

s.t. - something, the 3rd person
(s.t.) - something implied
s.o. - someone, the 3rd person
sl. - singular form
pl. - plural form
rt. - root word
cmd. - command
lit. - literally
fig. - figuratively
i.e., - for example
See: - Redirection to a related word.

qs ax̣llwísi – S/he/it is going to hustle around. **čiqs ax̣llwísi, kʷqs ax̣llwísi**
es ax̣llwíʔisi – They are hustling around. **qeʔes ax̣llwísi, pes ax̣llwísi**

ax̣llwísts – S/he/it did s.t. by hustling around. **ax̣llwístn, ax̣llwístxʷ**
es ax̣llwísms – S/he/it is doing s.t. by hustling around. **ies ax̣llwísm, as ax̣llwísm**
qs ax̣llwísms – S/he/it is going to do s.t. by hustling around. **iqs ax̣llwísm, qs ax̣llwísm**

ax̣llwisemn – one inclined to hustle around for something. *suffix:* ***...emn –*** *one inclined to do.*

ax̣llwisiš – Hustle around. *cmd.*
ax̣llwiskʷ – Hustle around for it. *cmd.*
čn ax̣llmutm – I will be able to *(future; something that is coming up).*

čnes ax̣llwísi t ululim – I am hustling around for money. **čiqs ax̣llwísi t sʔiłn –** I am going to hustle around for food. **čn ax̣llwís u k̓ʷul̓n łu k̓ʷłnčmé –** I was persistent, determined, able in fixing the door. **ax̣llwís u wičts sxʷmalyé –** S/he hustled around and found a doctor. **ax̣llwís pasqá u k̓ʷłči –** Through his persistence, and in determination Pascal arrived here or there. **ax̣llwís łu qʷléwyeʔ u uẏé –** Valeria kept at it and got done. **kʷes ax̣llwísi x̣ʷl̓ ululim –** You are hustling around for money. **čiqs ax̣llwisi t ululim –** I will be hustling around for money.

ax̣l – every time. *See:* ***every time.***

ax̣íl, *ax̣í* **–** do as someone/something; imitate; behave a certain way. *See:* ***imitate.***

nq̓aq̓ʔels – always busy; snoopy; nosy; prying. *See:* ***business.***

but

pṅ – but *(contradictory)*, well *(as a rebuke)*, yet *(in spite of)*. *See:* ***response.***

butcher

xʷxʷicm – cut-up something up; butcher.
xʷxʷcntés – S/he cut-up s.t. **xʷxʷcntén , xʷxʷcntéxʷ**
es xʷxʷcims – S/he is cutting-up s.t. **ies xʷxʷcim, as xʷxʷcim**
qs xʷxʷcims – S/he is going to cut-up s.t. **iqs xʷxʷcim, aqs xʷxʷcim**
es xʷxʷcims – They are cutting-up s.t. **qeʔes xʷxʷcim, es xʷxʷcimp**

čt̓l̓qʷéẇsts u xʷxʷcntés u ƛ̓e q̓ʷáłq̓ʷłt – S/he gutted it and cut it up and packed it back to camp.

plsqax̣eʔ, *plsqa* **–** kill domestic animals.
plsqax̣eʔm – S/he killed a domestic animal. **čn plsqax̣eʔm, kʷ plsqax̣eʔm**
es plsqax̣eʔi – S/he is killing a domestic animal. **čnes plsqax̣eʔi, kʷes plsqax̣eʔi**
qs plsqax̣eʔi – S/he is going to kill a domestic animal. **čiqs plsqax̣eʔi, kʷqs plsqax̣eʔi**

snplsqax̣eʔtn, *snplsqa* **–** slaughter house.

plsqax̣eʔiš – Kill a domestic animal. *cmd.*

plsqax̣eʔm u xʷxʷcntés – S/he killed a domestic animal and butchered it.

butt

nt̓ʔóps – blow or thrust with the head.

snt̓apqi – butt with the head.

tʔamnqnwexʷ, *tʔamnqnwe* **–** Bump each other's heads together.
tʔamnqnweʔexʷ – They bumped heads together. **qeʔ tʔamnqnwexʷ, p tʔamnqnwexʷ**
es tʔamnqnweʔexʷi – They are bumping heads together. **qeʔes tʔamnqnwexʷi, pes tʔamnqnwexʷi**

Butte

snt̓apqin, *snt̓apqi* **–** Butte, Montana; *lit. loud sound coming from the mountain.*

butter

čmiƛ̓mn – butter.

buttercup **sčyal̓mn** – sage buttercup; *Ranunculus glaberrimus.*

butterfly **k̓ʷeʔlúlexʷ**, *k̓ʷeʔlú* – butterfly.

buttocks **soq̓mépł**, *soq̓mé* – buttocks.

schepł – right buttock.
sc̓q̓ʷepł – left buttock.
nc̓alepł – hurt anus.

n...ups, ps – circumfix indicating buttocks, tail, pants. *See: **section 2**.*
nkʷtnups – big butt.
nkʷkʷimeps – small butt.
nt̓łups – dirty rear. *rt.: **t̓ił** – dirty; circumfix: **n...ups** – butt, tail.*
nt̓uy̓mps – clenched buttocks.
nqʷyutups – bare butt.
ntqups – touch the buttock.

The **i** following uvular consonants (UC) and the glottal stop ʔ sound like English "*ey*" as in the words *they, hey, whey*, etc. Salish UC are: **q, q̓, qʷ, q̓ʷ, x̣, x̣ʷ**. For example, the suffix ...**qin** – head/top, is often spelled using English *ey* as "q*ey*n". So **qi, q̓i, qʷi, q̓ʷi, x̣i, x̣ʷi**, may be spelled with English *ey* as **q***ey*, **q̓***ey*, **qʷ***ey*, **q̓ʷ***ey*, **x̣***ey*, **x̣ʷ***ey* in other texts.

čʔemtupsm – keep someone from doing something; hold someone back. *See: **hold back**.*
es čʔemtupsms kʷtisi t nox̣ʷnx̣ʷs – Big Blanket's wife is keeping him home. *lit. Big Blanket's wife is sitting on his tail.*

button **čx̣p̓im** – button. *rt.: **x̣p̓** – line, coat.*

čx̣p̓uscut – S/he buttoned one's self. **čn čx̣p̓uscut, kʷ čx̣p̓uscut**
es čx̣p̓uscuti – S/he is buttoning one's self. **čnes čx̣p̓uscuti, kʷes čx̣p̓uscuti**
qs čx̣p̓uscuti – S/he is going to button one's self. **čiqs čx̣p̓uscuti, kʷqs čx̣p̓uscuti**

čx̣p̓ntes – S/he buttoned it. **čx̣p̓nten, čx̣p̓ntexʷ**
es čx̣p̓ims – S/he is buttoning it. **ies čx̣p̓im, as čx̣p̓im**
qs čx̣p̓ims – S/he is going to button it. **iqs čx̣p̓im, aqs čx̣p̓im**

x̣p̓mintn – button.

čx̣p̓uscutš – Button yourself. *cmd.*
x̣p̓int – Button it up. *cmd.*

k̓ʷłx̣p̓cnečst – button a cuff.
x̣p̓ołq̓ʷlt – button a collar.

łiliyá – button *(describes material wrapped around the button).*

buy **tumíst**, *tumí* – buy.

tumíst – S/he bought. **čn tumíst, kʷ tumíst**
es tumísti – S/he is buying. **čnes tumísti, kʷes tumísti**
tumíʔist – They bought. **qeʔ tumíst, p tumíst**
es tumíʔisti – They are buying. **qeʔes tumísti, pes tumísti**

tumistmis – S/he sold s.t. **tumistmn, tumistmntxʷ**
es tumistmms – S/he is selling s.t. **ies tumistmm, as tumistmm**
tumíʔistmis – They sold s.t. **qeʔ tumistmntm, tumistmntp**

es tutumísti – S/he is repeatedly buying. **čnes tutumísti, kʷes tutumísti**
es tutumístms – S/he is repeatedly selling things. **ies tutumístm, as tutumístm**

tumistmnwexʷ – buy from each other; exchange.

s.t. - something, the 3rd person
(s.t.) - something implied
s.o. - someone, the 3rd person
sl. - singular form
pl. - plural form
rt. - root word
cmd. - command
lit. - literally
fig. - figuratively
i.e., - for example
See: - Redirection to a related word.

t k̓ʷinš u kʷ tumist t čłq̓iq̓á – How many candies did you buy? **t esel čłq̓iq̓á u čn tumíst**– I bought two candies. **čn tumíst t i sic p̓ip̓uy̓šn** – I bought a new car.

teucn – buy food.
  teucnm – S/he bought food. **čn teucnm, kʷ teucnm**
  es teucni – S/he is buying food. **čnes teucni, kʷes teucni**
  qs teucni – S/he is going to buy food. **čiqs teucni, kʷqs teucni**

  teucis – S/he bought s.o.'s food. **teucn, teucntxʷ**
  es teucnms – S/he is buying s.o.'s food. **ies teucnm, as teucnm**

  teucnmis – S/he bought that food. **teucnmn, teucnmntx̣ʷ**
  es teucnmms – S/he is buying that food. **ies teucnmm, as teucnmm**

  teucišts – S/he bought food for s.o. **teucištn, teucištxʷ**
  es teucištms – S/he is buying food for s.o. **ies teucištm, as teucištm**

  teucnwexʷ – trade food with one another.

teulqs – buy clothes.
  teulqsm – S/he bought clothes. **čn teulqsm, kʷ teulqsm**
  es teulqsi – S/he is buying clothes. **čnes teulqsi, kʷes teulqsi**
  qs teulqsi – S/he is going to buy clothes. **čiqs teulqsi, kʷqs teulqsi**

  teulqsis – S/he bought s.o.'s clothes. **teulqsn, teulqsntxʷ**
  es teulqsms – S/he is buying s.o.'s clothes. **ies teulqsm, as teulqsm**

  teulqsmis – S/he bought that clothing item. **teulqsmn, teulqsmntxʷ**
  es teulqsmms – S/he is buying that clothing item. **ies teulqsmm, as teulqsmm**

teułxʷ – buy a house.
  teułxʷm – S/he bought a house. **čn teułxʷm, kʷ teułxʷm**
  es teułxʷi – S/he is buying a house. **čnes teułxʷi, kʷes teułxʷi**

  teułxʷis – S/he bought s.o.'s house. **teułxʷn, teułxʷntxʷ**
  es teułxʷms – S/he is buying s.o.'s house. **ies teułxʷm, as teułxʷm**

  teułxʷmis – S/he bought that house. **teułxʷmn, teułxʷmntxʷ**
  es teułxʷmms – S/he is buying that house. **ies teułxʷmm, as teułxʷmm**

tusqáx̣eˀ, *tusqá* – buy horses; domestic animals; car.
  tusqáx̣eˀ – S/he bought a horse. **čn tusqáx̣eˀ, kʷ tusqáx̣eˀ**
  es tusqáx̣eˀi – S/he is buying a horse. **čnes tusqáx̣eˀi, kʷes tusqáx̣eˀi**
  es tusqáˀax̣eˀi – They are buying a horse. **qeˀes tusqáx̣eˀi, pes tusqáx̣eˀi**

ṅeyxʷéẇs, *ṅeyxʷé* – trade; swap. *See: **trade**.*

buzzard

caqʷuyéˀ – buzzard, vulture; *Cathartes aura.*

buzz off

xʷuyš – Go. *cmd. See: **go**.*

ƛ̓ékʷš – Leave, get out of here, get out of the way. *cmd. See: **leave**.*

č ciˀš – Buzz off. *cmd.*

xʷistš – Walk. *cmd. See: **walk**.*

C

cabbage **picčł –** leaf; cabbage; lettuce.

cactus **sxʷyéneʔ –** prickly pear cactus; *Opuntia polyacantha*.

caddisworm **čc̓n̓čn̓p̓ic̓eʔ,** *čc̓n̓čn̓p̓i* – caddisworm; straw worm; *Trichoptera*.

cafe **snel̓iłntn,** *snel̓i* – café; cafeteria; restaurant. *prefix:* ***sn...*** *– a place of; suffix:* ***...tin, ...tn*** *– means of/device.*

cafeteria **snel̓iłntn,** *snel̓i* – café; cafeteria; restaurant. *prefix:* ***sn...*** *– a place of; suffix:* ***...tin, ...tn*** *– means of/device.*

cake **nt̓št̓išlexʷ –** cake. *rt.:* ***t̓iš*** *– sweet.*

calculator **sisyénmn –** calculator. *rt.:* ***siyenm*** *– count;*

calendar **snsinásq̓t,** *snsiná* – calendar. *rt.:* ***siyenm*** *– count; suffix:* ***...asq̓t*** *– sky, day.*

sinásq̓t – count days.
sinásq̓t – S/he counted days. **čn sinásq̓t, kʷ sinásq̓t**
es sinásq̓ti – S/he is counting days. **čnes sinásq̓ti, kʷes sinásq̓ti**
qs sinásq̓ti – S/he is going to count days. **čiqs sinásq̓ti, kʷqs sinásq̓ti**
sináʔasq̓t – They counted days. **qeʔ sinásq̓t, p sinásq̓t**
es sináʔasq̓ti – They are counting days. **qeʔes sinásq̓ti, pes sinásq̓ti**
qs sináʔasq̓ti – They are going to count days. **qeʔqs sinásq̓ti, pqs sinásq̓ti**

sinásq̓tiš – Count days. *cmd.*

es t sinásq̓ti – S/he is counting the days *(before some date)*. **čnes t sinásq̓ti, kʷes t sinásq̓ti**

čnes t sinásq̓ti – I am counting the days *(before some date)*. **ha kʷes t sinásq̓ti –** Are you counting the days *(before some date)*?

calf **čłkʷlkʷléxʷ,** *čłkʷlkʷlé* – buffalo calf; cow calf. *lit. red hide. (Buffalo calves have a reddish coat. This word has been adopted for use with cattle calves.) rt.:* ***kʷil*** *– red; prefix:* ***čł...*** *– surface; suffix:* ***...elxʷ, ...lxʷ*** *– skin/hide*

snq̓ʷmšin – calm; back of the lower leg.

calf elk **q̓y̓itš –** calf elk; *Cervus canadensis*. *See:* ***elk***.

call **x̣lit –** call for; holler for; beckon.
x̣litis – S/he/it called for s.o. **x̣litn, x̣litntxʷ**
es x̣litms – S/he/it is calling for s.o. **ies x̣litm, as x̣litm**
qs x̣litms – S/he/it is going to call for s.o. **iqs x̣litm, aqs x̣litm**
x̣líʔitis – They called for s.o. **qeʔ x̣litntm, x̣litntp**
es x̣líʔitms – They are calling for s.o. **qeʔes x̣litm, es x̣litmp**

s.t. - something, the 3rd person
(s.t.) - something implied
s.o. - someone, the 3rd person
sl. - singular form
pl. - plural form
rt. - root word
cmd. - command
lit. - literally
fig. - figuratively
i.e., - for example
See: - Redirection to a related word.

qs x̣líʔitms – They are going to call for s.o. **qeʔ qs x̣litm, qs x̣litmp**

x̣litntm – S/he/it was called on.

x̣litnt – Call for him/her/it. *cmd.*
x̣lx̣llitntm – Each one was called on.
x̣lH̓tumš – call on the people; call for s.o. from a group of people.

čnes x̣lH̓tumši – I am calling for a helper. **kʷémt es cololqʷé ɫu ep scx̣lit** – Then the ones who sent for these things came and got their orders.

nʔawqnm – call upon/ask for someone; challenge/encourage someone; beseech; exhort. *rt.:* **áwm** – *say; suffix:* **...qin, ...qn** – *top.*
nʔawqis – S/he/it called upon s.o. **nʔawqn, nʔawqntxʷ**
es nʔawqnms – S/he/it is calling upon s.o. **ies nʔawqnm, as nʔawqnm**
qs nʔawqnms – S/he/it is going to call upon s.o. **iqs nʔawqnm, aqs nʔawqnm**
nʔáʔawqnis – They called upon s.o. **qeʔ nʔawqntm, nʔawqntp**

nʔawqntm – S/he was called upon. **qʷo nʔawqntm, kʷ nʔawqntm**

nʔawqnt – Call on s.o. to talk. *cmd.*
nʔawqnmɫtumš – call on s.o. from a group of people to talk.
es nʔawqncuti – S/he is calling upon one's self. **čnes nʔawqncuti, kʷes nʔawqncuti**
es nʔawqnweʔexʷi – They are exhorting each other. **qeʔes nʔawqnwexʷi, pes nʔawqnwexʷi**
nʔawqnelm – S/he called on s.o. to volunteer. **čn nʔawqnelm, kʷ nʔawqnelm**
es nʔawqnelisti – S/he is calling on s.o. to volunteer. **čnes nʔawqnelisti, kʷes nʔawqnelisti**

kʷ ies nʔawqnm – I am calling on you to talk. **nʔawqncis** – S/he called on you. **nʔawqncn** – I called on you. **nʔáʔawqncis** – They called on you.

čsp̓alqʷm – make a telephone call. *rt.:* **sp̓im** – *strike w/ object; suffix:* **...alqʷ** – *wood; cylindical.*
čsp̓alqʷm – S/he called. **čn čsp̓alqʷm, kʷ čsp̓alqʷm**
es čsp̓alqʷi – S/he is calling. **čnes čsp̓alqʷi, kʷes čsp̓alqʷi**
qs čsp̓alqʷi – S/he is going to call. **čiqs čsp̓alqʷi, kʷqs čsp̓alqʷi**
čsp̓áʔalqʷm – They called. **qeʔ čsp̓alqʷm, p čsp̓alqʷm**

čsp̓alqʷis – S/he called s.o. **čsp̓alqʷn, čsp̓alqʷntxʷ**
es čsp̓alqʷms – S/he is calling s.o. **ies čsp̓alqʷm, as čsp̓alqʷm**
qs čsp̓alqʷms – S/he is going to call s.o. **iqs čsp̓alqʷm, aqs čsp̓alqʷm**
čsp̓áʔalqʷm – They called s.o. **qeʔ čsp̓alqʷntm, čsp̓alqʷntp**

čsp̓alqʷntm – S/he was called. **qʷo čsp̓alqʷntm, kʷ čsp̓alqʷntm**

čiqs kʷis čsp̓alqʷi č inʔilmixʷm – I am going to go call my boss. **ha kʷ ṅe u qʷo čsp̓alqʷntxʷ ẏetɫx̣ʷa** – Would you call me today? **l čeṅ m čsp̓alqʷštmncn** – Where would I call you?

skʷést – name; title. *See:* **name.**

call out

čošim – yell out; shout out. *(i.e., a war cry) See:* **yell.**

wéʔm – yell; holler out; talk while shouting. *See:* **holler.**

áwm – say/speak; pronounce; annunciate. *See:* **say.**
nʔawqnm – call upon/ask for someone; challenge/encourage someone; beseech; exhort. *See:* **call.**
kʷɬʔawʔáw, *kʷɬʔawʔá* – guess. *See:* **guess.**
awʔawm – say words out loud; read aloud. *See:* **read.**
scʔawʔáw, *scʔawʔá* – something that's been said; spoken words. *See:* **say.**
čáw – pray. *See:* **pray.**

calm **qim –** calm; undisturbed.

nqimlš – S/he was calm. **čn nqimlš, kʷ nqimlš**
es nqimlši – S/he is being calm. **čnes nqimlši, kʷes nqimlši**
qs nqimlši – S/he is going to be calm. **čiqs nqimlši, kʷqs nqimlši**

qmstes – S/he/it calmed s.o./s.t. **qmsten, qmstexʷ**
es qmims – S/he/it is calming s.o./s.t. **ies qmim, as qmim**
qs qmims – S/he/it is going to calm s.o./s.t. **iqs qmim, aqs qmim**

i qim – S/he/it is calm. **i čn qim, i kʷ qim**

qmqemt – S/he is at peace/content. **čn qmqemt, kʷ qmqemt**

qmstekʷ – Calm s.o./s.t. *cmd.*
qmqmncut – be calm with one's self; tarry.
nqmqmcin – talk calmly.
nqmqmetkʷ – calm water; undisturbed water.

qmip – calm from an agitated state. *suffix: **...ip** – action of natural cause.*
qmip – S/he/it got calm. **čn qmip, kʷ qmip**
es qmpmi – S/he/it is calming. **čnes qmpmi, kʷes qmpmi**
qs qmpmi – S/he/it is going to calm. **čiqs qmpmi, kʷqs qmpmi**

nqmpus – face became calm.
nqmpetkʷ – water calmed.

nqimls – feel calm; feel content; relaxed; patient.
i nqimls – S/he is a calm person. **i čn nqimls, i kʷ nqimls**

es nqimlsi – S/he is calming down/relaxing. **čnes nqimlsi, kʷes nqimlsi**
es nqiʔimlsi – They are calming down/relaxing. **qeʔes nqimlsi, pes nqimlsi**

nqmels – have calmness inside.

q̓ʷoy̓ – calm; serene. *(i.e., place with no wind, etc.)*
es q̓ʷoy̓i – The wind is calming/dying down.
qs q̓ʷoy̓i – The wind is going to calm/die down.

k̓ʷłq̓ʷoy̓m – S/he got out of the wind. **čn k̓ʷłq̓ʷoy̓m, kʷ k̓ʷłq̓ʷoy̓m**
es k̓ʷłq̓ʷoy̓mi – S/he is getting out of the wind. **čnes k̓ʷłq̓ʷoy̓mi, kʷes k̓ʷłq̓ʷoy̓mi**
qs k̓ʷłq̓ʷoy̓mi – S/he is going to get out of the wind. **čiqs k̓ʷłq̓ʷoy̓mi, kʷqs k̓ʷłq̓ʷoy̓mi**

q̓ʷoy̓is – S/he sheltered s.t. from the wind. **q̓ʷoy̓n, kʷ q̓ʷoy̓ntxʷ**
es q̓ʷoy̓ms – S/he is sheltering s.t. from the wind. **ies q̓ʷoy̓m, as q̓ʷoy̓m**
qs q̓ʷoy̓ms – S/he is going to shelter s.t. from the wind. **iqs q̓ʷoy̓m, aqs q̓ʷoy̓m**

i q̓ʷoy̓ – It is calm *(wind is calm).*

nq̓ʷoy̓mistn – wind shelter.
k̓ʷłq̓ʷoy̓ncutn – someone that shelters one.

q̓ʷoy̓nt – Shelter it from the wind. *cmd.*
q̓ʷoy̓lexʷ – area sheltered from the wind.
nq̓ʷoy̓kʷ – calm water; unmoving water.

nmeʔl̓els, *nmeʔl̓e* **–** cool off after being angry. *rt.: **meʔl̓** – be agreeable.*
nmeʔl̓els – S/he cooled off. **čn nmeʔl̓els, kʷ nmeʔl̓els**
es nmeʔl̓elsi – S/he is cooling off. **čnes nmeʔl̓elsi, kʷes nmeʔl̓elsi**
qs nmeʔl̓elsi – S/he is going to cool off. **čiqs nmeʔl̓elsi, kʷqs nmeʔl̓elsi**

The **i** following uvular consonants (UC) and the glottal stop **ʔ** sound like English "*ey*" as in the words *they, hey, whey,* etc. Salish UC are: **q, q̓, qʷ, q̓ʷ, x̣, x̣ʷ**. For example, the suffix **...qin** – head/top, is often spelled using English *ey* as "q*ey*n". So **qi, q̓i, qʷi, q̓ʷi, x̣i, x̣ʷi,** may be spelled with English *ey* as **q***ey,* **q̓***ey,* **qʷ***ey,* **q̓ʷ***ey,* **x̣***ey,* **x̣ʷ***ey* in other texts.

s.t. - something, the 3rd person
(s.t.) - something implied
s.o. - someone, the 3rd person
sl. - singular form
pl. - plural form
rt. - root word
cmd. - command
lit. - literally
fig. - figuratively
i.e., - for example
See: - Redirection to a related word.

nme?l̓elsis – S/he cooled off toward s.o. **nme?l̓elsn, nme?l̓elsntxʷ**
es nme?l̓elsms – S/he is cooling off toward s.o. **ies nme?l̓elsm, as nme?l̓elsm**
qs nme?l̓elsms – S/he is going to cool off toward s.o. **iqs nme?l̓elsm, aqs nme?l̓elsm**

nml̓ap – The liquid cooled down. *See: **cool**.*

nml̓mel̓čst – act calmly as a child playing with toys. *rt.: **me?l̓–** be agreeable; suffix: **...ečst, ...čst–** of the hand.*
nml̓mel̓čstm – S/he was calm. **čn nml̓el̓čstm, kʷ nml̓mel̓čstm**
es nml̓mel̓čsti – S/he is being calm. **čnes nml̓mel̓čsti, kʷes nml̓mel̓čsti**
qs nml̓mel̓čsti – S/he is going to be calm. **čiqs nml̓mel̓čsti, kʷqs nml̓mel̓čsti**

ml̓mél̓čstn, *ml̓mé* **–** toy; toys.

łexʷésčt, *łexʷé* **–** rest; relax; take a break. *See: **rest**.*

xʷxʷuṁ – relaxed/safe/secure; have no worries; have no cares; out of danger. *See: **secure**.*

i čłšiƛ̓kʷ – flat water; calm water. *See: **flat**.*

saṅ – tranquil; quiet and calm; tame; settled. *See: **quiet**.*

camas

sx̣ʷé?li – camas; *Camassia quamash*.
sx̣ʷé?li spq̓ni? – June *(month of the camas). See: **June**.*

kʷes x̣écti t sx̣ʷé?li – You are digging camas. **čłxʷépnéntxʷ łu asx̣ʷé?li –** Cover your camas with dirt.

itx̣ʷe? – baked camas.

pčl̓u – biscuit root, white camas; *Lomatium piperi*.

iẇéstn – death camas; *Zigadenus elegans*.

Camas Prairie

qln?ítx̣ʷe?, *qln?í* **–** Camas Prairie, Flathead Nation. *lit. raw camas. (North end of valley near stream)*

čmk̓ʷtáqs – place in Camas Prairie. *lit. long lasting snow.*

čłsčut – place in Camas Prairie. *lit. little half; describing either side of the prairie dividing stream.*

sx̣ʷll̓ésčn – place in Camas Prairie. *lit. little buck on the hillside; small hill on north end.*

camel

nmq̓ʷmq̓ʷičṅ, *nmq̓ʷmq̓ʷi* **–** camel. *rt.: **moq̓ʷ–** bump; suffix: **...ičṅ–** back.*

camera

sk̓ʷłq̓eẏmintn – camera.

Camille

kamél – Camille.

camouflage

wekʷmn – camouflage. *rt.: **wekʷ–** hide.*

camp

ccil̓š – spend the night away; overnight camp; overnight stay.
ccil̓š – S/he went camping. **čn ccil̓š, kʷ ccil̓š**
es ccil̓ši – S/he is going camping. **čnes ccil̓ši, kʷes ccil̓ši**
qs ccil̓ši – S/he is going to go camping. **čiqs ccil̓ši, kʷqs ccil̓ši**
ccí?il̓š – They went camping. **qe? ccil̓š, p ccil̓š**
es ccí?il̓ši – They are camping. **qe?es ccil̓ši, pes ccil̓ši**
qs ccí?il̓ši – They are going to go camping. **qe?qs ccil̓ši, pqs ccil̓ši**

snccil̓štn – overnight camping place; hotel, motel. *prefix: **sn...** – a place of; suffix: **...tin, ...tn** – means of/device.*

l še u ccil̓š x̣ʷl̓ k̓ʷnšasq̇t – S/he went camping for so many days. **qeʔqs k̓ʷis ccil̓ši –** We are going to go and camp.

q̇ey – camp; long stay camp; village.
es q̇ey – S/he is camped. **čnes q̇ey, kʷes q̇ey**
es q̇eʔéy – They are camped. **qeʔes q̇ey, pes q̇ey**

es łq̇q̇ey – small camp.

es q̇iʔq̇ey – camps.

čq̇eysšn̓is – S/he built camp on a large rock. **čq̇eysšn̓n, čq̇eysšn̓ntxʷ**
es čq̇eysšn̓ms – S/he is building camp on a large rock. **ies čq̇eysšn̓m, as čq̇eysšn̓m**

snq̇eytn – camp site.

sq̇imułxʷ, *sq̇imu,* **–** tipi. *See:* ***tipi.***
q̇ey̓łxʷm – put up a tipi. *See:* ***tipi.***
sq̇ey̓mn – pole, tipi pole. *See:* ***tipi poles.***

nšlíʔič l es q̇ey̓ – They went around the camp.

The **i** following uvular consonants (UC) and the glottal stop **ʔ** sound like English "*ey*" as in the words th*ey*, h*ey*, wh*ey*, etc. Salish UC are: **q, q̇, qʷ, q̇ʷ, x̣, x̣ʷ**. For example, the suffix ...**qin** – head/top, is often spelled using English *ey* as "q*ey*n". So **qi, q̇i, qʷi, q̇ʷi, x̣i, x̣ʷi**, may be spelled with English *ey* as **q***ey*, **q̇***ey*, **qʷ***ey*, **q̇ʷ***ey*, **x̣***ey*, **x̣ʷ***ey* in other texts.

camp robber

lk̓ʷłk̓ʷqi – gray jay; Canada jay; camp robber; whiskey jack; *Perisoreus canadensis.*

can

stpčé – can; tin.

łkʷl̓kʷal̓čqn, *łkʷl̓kʷa* **–** canned goods; tins.

l̓q̇ʷom – can do; prevail; succeed. *See:* ***do.***

Canada goose

tptpósqn, *tptppó* **–** Canada goose; *Branta canadensis.*

sƭaqt – geese.
ƭaqt – geese in formation while flying.

ƭaqt k̓ʷsixʷ – The geese gathered.

k̓ʷsixʷ – goose.

Canada jay

lk̓ʷłk̓ʷqi – gray jay; Canada jay; camp robber; whiskey jack; *Perisoreus canadensis.*

Canadian

kʷlkʷltalqs, *kʷlkʷlta* **–** Canadian. *rt.:* ***kʷil*** *– red; suffix:* ***...lqs, ...alqs*** *– clothes.*

čtlihálqʷ, *čtlihá* **–** across anything that is a line; railroad track; or a border.

Canadian lynx

snqcuł, *snqcu* **–** lynx; Canadian lynx; *Lynx canadensis.*

canal

sƭletkʷ – canal; ditch. *rt.:* ***ƭil*** *– tear; suffix:* ***...etkʷ, ...tkʷ*** *– liquid*
ƭletkʷm – S/he made a canal. **čn ƭletkʷm, kʷ ƭletkʷm**
es ƭletkʷi – S/he is making a canal. **čnes ƭletkʷi, kʷes ƭletkʷi**

ƭletkʷis – S/he made the canal. **ƭletkʷn, ƭletkʷntxʷ**
es ƭletkʷms – S/he is making the canal. **ies ƭletkʷm, as ƭletkʷm**

cancer

es x̣ƛ̓ełc̓ʔem – It is chewing away at his/her body. *(i.e., cancer)*

candle

smlk̓ʷtálqʷ, *smlk̓ʷtá* **–** candle. **smlmlk̓ʷtálqʷ** *pl.*
esłml̓k̓ʷtá – little candle.

s.t. - something, the 3rd person
(s.t.) - something implied
s.o. - someone, the 3rd person
sl. - singular form
pl. - plural form
rt. - root word
cmd. - command
lit. - literally
fig. - figuratively
i.e., - for example
See: - Redirection to a related word.

noẋʷmeɫċe – candle wick.

candy **čɫq̇iq̇áyalqʷ,** *čɫq̇iq̇á* – candy.

i čq̇áyalqʷ – The cylindrical object is marked. *This is indicating the twisted strip that was common on candy sticks in the past.*

cane **cḱʷéčstn,** *cḱʷé* – cane. *suffix:* ***...ečst, ...čst*** *– of the hand.*

canoe **sṫiɫm –** wooden canoe; dugout canoe.

ƛ̓iyéʔ – bark canoe; boat.

cantaloupe **čɫaẋáʔa –** cantaloupe; has lines all over it. *rt.:* ***aaẋ*** *– it has lines.*

canvas **sṗéċn –** rope; canvas.
spċnéɫxʷ, *spċne* – canvas lodge.
čɫpiɫmskʷ l asṗeċn – Spread it out on your canvas.

canvas dance **nqaqaá –** canvas dance.

canyon **čuxʷqne –** vertical walled canyon.

nččxʷenč – steep walled canyon.

nɫaqnetkʷ – arrive at the top of a dead end canyon going down stream. *rt.:* ***ɫe*** *– end.*
snɫaqnetkʷ, *snɫaqne* – top of a dead end canyon or impassable water looking down. *(i.e., lake inlet, etc.) rt.:* ***ɫe*** *– end.*

snɫeʔpcin – mouth of a dead end canyon. *rt.:* ***ɫe*** *– end.*

nppƛ̓mqne – enter a canyon.

es tóqʷ – ravine, draw; slope walled canyon. *See:* ***ravine.***

cap **snqqápqn –** baseball cap.

nšṅusu – baseball cap.

qʷacqn – hat.

ḱʷáľčqn – lid; cap; cover of a container. *rt.:* ***ḱʷeľč*** *– upturned formed object; suffix:* ***...qin, ...qn*** *– top.*

capable **q̇ʷiɫ –** energy; motivation; internal drive.
i q̇ʷiɫ – S/he/it is full of energy. **i čn q̇ʷiɫ, i kʷ q̇ʷiɫ**

q̇ʷiɫčst – S/he/it did with all energy. **čn q̇ʷiɫčst, kʷ q̇ʷiɫčst**
es q̇ʷiɫčsti – S/he/it is doing with all energy. **čnes q̇ʷiɫčsti, kʷes q̇ʷiɫčsti**

nq̇ʷiɫq̇ʷɫtn – something that makes one capable; energy.

q̇ʷiɫq̇ʷɫt – S/he is apt; able; capable; strong. **čn q̇ʷiɫq̇ʷɫt, kʷ q̇ʷiɫq̇ʷɫt**
q̇ʷaq̇ʷiɫeʔ – little energetic one, affectionately.

kʷ xʷist u kʷ ẋʷcuʔsičṅ t esmq̇ʷmoq̇ʷ hayo kʷ q̇ʷiɫq̇ʷɫt – You walked over the mountain; gee you are strong/able. **q̇ʷiɫq̇ʷɫt isnčɫcaʔsqá ta qs ayẋʷt –** My horse is strong/capable; it will not get tired. **q̇ʷiɫq̇ʷɫt ɫu stipn aẋlsčɫʔeʔ u ničis luḱʷ –** Every Saturday Stephen is capable/does his best to cut wood.

puti i čn q̇ʷiɫ – I am still able/capable.

q̇ʷiłmist, *q̇ʷiłmi* – do one's best; try hard from energy.
q̇ʷiłmist – S/he/it did his/her best. **čn q̇ʷiłmist, kʷ q̇ʷiłmist**
es q̇ʷiłmisti – S/he/it is doing his/her best. **čnes q̇ʷiłmisti, kʷes q̇ʷiłmisti**
qs q̇ʷiłmisti – S/he/it is going to do his/her best. **čiqs q̇ʷiłmisti, kʷqs q̇ʷiłmisti**

čq̇ʷiłmistmis – S/he did one's best toward s.t. **čq̇ʷiłmistmn, čq̇ʷiłmistmntxʷ**
es čq̇ʷiłmistmms – S/he is doing one's best toward s.t. **ies čq̇ʷiłmistmm, as čq̇ʷiłmistmm**

q̇ʷiłmistš – Do your best; try your hardest. *cmd.*

ṅem čn q̇ʷiłmist m čn k̓ʷłči – I will do my best to get there. **čnes q̇ʷiłmisti x̣ʷl̓ čiqs npiyelsi** – I am trying my hardest so I can be happy.

sičstmist – do one's best; try hard from ability. *rt.: **sisyus** – smart; suffix: **...ečst, ...čst** – of the hand; suffix: **...ist** – action for/of the self.*
sičstmist – S/he/it did his/her best. **čn sičstmist, kʷ sičstmist**
es sičstmisti – S/he/it is doing his/her best. **čnes sičstmisti, kʷes sičstmisti**
qs sičstmisti – S/he/it is going to do his/her best. **čiqs sičstmisti, kʷqs sičstmisti**
sičstmíʔist – They did his/her best. **qeʔ sičstmist, p sičstmist**
es sičstmíʔisti – They are doing his/her best. **qeʔes sičstmisti, pes sičstmisti**
qs sičstmíʔisti – They are going to do his/her best. **qeʔqs sičstmisti, pqs sičstmisti**

sičstmistš – Do your best; try your hardest. *cmd.*

čmaqs – perform at the peak of one's ability; best at something; pinnacle. *See: **best.***

> The **i** following uvular consonants (UC) and the glottal stop ʔ sound like English "*ey*" as in the words th*ey*, h*ey*, wh*ey*, etc. Salish UC are: **q**, **q̇**, **qʷ**, **q̇ʷ**, **x̣**, **x̣ʷ**. For example, the suffix **...qin** – head/top, is often spelled using English *ey* as "q*ey*n". So **qi**, **q̇i**, **qʷi**, **q̇ʷi**, **x̣i**, **x̣ʷi**, may be spelled with English *ey* as **q***ey*, **q̇***ey*, **qʷ***ey*, **q̇ʷ***ey*, **x̣***ey*, **x̣ʷ***ey* in other texts.

capture

čnapqn – capture someone.
čnapqis – S/he captured s.o. **čnapqn, čnapqntxʷ**
es čnapqnm – S/he is capturing s.o. **ies čnapqnm, as čnapqnm**
qs čnapqnm – S/he is going to capture s.o. **iqs čnapqnm, aqs čnapqnm**

čnapqntm – S/he was captured.

kʷanx̣n – kidnap; grab the arm. *See: **kidnap.***

t šméṅ qʷo kʷanx̣ntm – The enemy captured me.

car

ṗiṗuyšn – automobile, car. *lit. wrinkled feet. rt.: **ṗuy** – wrinkle; suffix: **...šn** – foot.*
sčṗuyšn – car tire.
łṗiṗuyšn – little car.
esq̇exʷmscu ṗiṗuyšn – sports car.

čn tumíst i t sic ṗiṗuyšn – I bought a new car.

xʷistm – start something; make something go. *(i.e., start a car, etc.) See: **start.***

...sqáx̣eʔ, *...sqá* – suffix indicating horses, domestic animals, or vehicles. *See: **animal.***

pmmm – The sound a car makes.

snqʷq̇ʷapaqstn – something to slide down the road with. *prefix: **sn...** – a place of; suffix: **...tin, ...tn** – means of/device. See: **slide.***

> s.t. - something, the 3rd person
> (s.t.) - something implied
> s.o. - someone, the 3rd person
> *sl.* - singular form
> *pl.* - plural form
> *rt.* - root word
> *cmd.* - command
> *lit.* - literally
> *fig.* - figuratively
> *i.e.,* - for example
> *See:* - Redirection to a related word.

card

ṁéṁscutn – playing cards.

sk̓ʷłq̇eẏi – picture; photograph; postcard.
sk̓ʷłq̇ẏq̇eẏi – pictures; photographs; postcards.

care **čšťncut –** take care of one's self. *rt.: čšťim – guard; suffix: ...cut – action to the self.*
čšťncut – S/he took care of one's self. **čn čšťncut, kʷ čšťncut**
es čšťncuti – S/he is taking care of one's self. **čnes čšťncuti, kʷes čšťncuti**
qs čšťncuti – S/he is going to take care of one's self. **čiqs čšťncuti, kʷqs čšťncuti**
čšťncúˀut – They took care of themselves. **qeˀ čšťncut, p čšťncút**
es čšťncúˀuti – They are taking care of themselves. **qeˀes čšťncuti, pes čšťncuti**
qs čšťncúˀuti – They are going to take care of themselves. **qeˀqs čšťncuti, pqs čšťncuti**

čšťncutš – Take care of yourself. *cmd.*

čštelm – put something in the care of someone else.
čštelmis – S/he put s.t./s.o. in the care of someone else. **čštelmn, čštelmntxʷ**
čštéˀelmis – They put s.t./s.o. in the care of someone else. **qeˀ čštelmntm, čštelmntp**

čštelmntm – S/he/it was put in the care of s.o.

čštltelmntxʷ – You put things in the care of other people; sent things through the mail or with somebody. **čštltelmis –** S/he/it put things in the care of s.o.; sent things through the mail or with s.o.

čtelm – leave something in charge of somebody; give to someone to take care of temporarily.
čtelmis – S/he put s.t. in the care of s.o. **čtelmn, čtelmntxʷ**
es čtelms – S/he is putting s.t. in the care of s.o. **ies čtelm, as čtelm**
qs čtelms – S/he is going to put s.t. in the care of s.o. **iqs čtelm, aqs čtelm**
čtéˀelmis – They put s.t. in the care of s.o. **qeˀ čtelmntm, čtelmntp**
es čtéˀelms – They are putting s.t. in the care of s.o. **qeˀes čtelm, es čtelmp**
qs čtéˀelms – They are going to put s.t. in the care of s.o.; send the mail. **qeˀqs čtelm, qs čtelmp**

čtltelmis – S/he put things in the care of s.o.

čšťim – guard or take care of. *(This term is also used for wakes as it is seen that people are taking care of the dead.) See: **guard**.*
čšťsqáx̣eˀ, *čšťsqá* – guard horses/domestic animals. *See: **guard**.*
čšťeľt – watch over children; babysit. *See: **babysit**.*
es čšťmi – wake. *See: **wake**.*

iscnq̇éˀels – my business.
ascnq̇éˀels – your business.

es nq̇éˀelsi – S/he/it is busy/engaged in business. **čnes nq̇éˀelsi, kʷes nq̇éˀelsi**
es nq̇éˀeˀelsi – They are busy/engaged in business. **qeˀes nq̇éˀelsi, pes nq̇éˀelsi**

nq̇éˀelsmis – S/he/it took care of s.t. **nq̇éˀelsmn, nq̇éˀelsmntxʷ**
es nq̇éˀelsms – S/he/it is taking care of s.t. **ies nq̇éˀelsm, as nq̇éˀelsm**
qs nq̇éˀelsms – S/he/it is going to take care of s.t. **iqs nq̇éˀelsm, aqs nq̇éˀelsm**
nq̇éˀeˀelsmis – They took care of s.t. **qeˀ nq̇éˀelsmntm, nq̇éˀelsmntp**
es nq̇éˀeˀelsms – They are taking care of s.t. **qeˀes nq̇éˀelsm, es nq̇éˀelsmp**
qs nq̇éˀeˀelsms – They are going to take care of s.t. **qeˀqs nq̇éˀelsm, qs nq̇éˀelsmp**

čiqs xʷuy č x̣ʷiˀilqsa čn ep scnq̇éˀels – I am going to Pablo on business. I have business there.

čeṁm – detest; reject something; have no care for something; snub something. *See: **detest**.*

yomšniš – step with tensed leg so as not to slip and/or fall. *(i.e., walking on ice, walking on a wet floor, etc.) See: **step**.*

careless **scṗatša –** something put together carelessly. *rt.: ṗať – s.t. soft/squishy.*

caress **tutéẇ** – use gentleness with something; caress something. *See:* ***gentle.***

caribou **styélsčn,** *stýé* – woodland mountain caribou; *Rangifer tarandus caribou.* *suffix:* ***...elsčn*** *– horn.*

car license plate **čšṅmin** – car license plate. *rt.:* ***šiṅ*** *– flat cover; suffix:* ***...min, ...mn*** *– instrument/tool.*

> The **i** following uvular consonants (UC) and the glottal stop ʔ sound like English "*ey*" as in the words th*ey*, h*ey*, wh*ey*, etc. Salish UC are: **q, q̇, qʷ, q̇ʷ, x̣, x̣ʷ**. For example, the suffix ...**qin** – head/top, is often spelled using English *ey* as "qeyn". So **qi, q̇i, qʷi, q̇ʷi, x̣i, x̣ʷi**, may be spelled with English *ey* as **q***ey*, **q̇***ey*, **qʷ***ey*, **q̇ʷ***ey*, **x̣***ey*, **x̣ʷ***ey* in other texts.

Caroline **kallin** – Caroline.

carpenter **sxʷk̓ʷul̓łxʷm** – someone tasked to build houses; carpenter. *rt:* ***k̓ʷul̓*** *– make/build/do; prefix:* ***sxʷ...*** *– one tasked to do; suffix:* ***...ełxʷ, ...łxʷ*** *– house.*

carpenter shop **sxʷk̓ʷul̓łxʷm snk̓ʷul̓mn** – carpenter's shop/workplace.

carpet **čłxʷépmn** – rug; carpet. *rt.:* ***xʷep*** *– cover; prefix:* ***čł...*** *– surface.*

carrot **sƛ̓uk̓ʷm** – carrot, wild carrot.

carry **q̇ʷełt** – carry on back; pack. *See:* ***pack.***

plim – drift/float away by water or wind; carried away. *See:* ***drift.***
łu t snéẇt plntem – It was carried away by the wind.

kʷenlt – hold a child. *See:* ***hold.***

łqlšax̣n – sit on the arm. *(i.e., as a baby, carried in arm, etc.)* *See:* ***sit.***

cascara **čq̇ʷiq̇ʷisálqʷ,** *čq̇ʷiq̇ʷisá* – cascara; *Rhammus purshiana.*

cash register **syenmn** – cash register; calculator; adding machine.

cassette recorder **snsunuṁtn** – cassette recorder. *prefix:* ***sn...*** *– a place of; suffix:* ***...tin, ...tn*** *– means of/device.*

čx̣ʷax̣ʷnč, *čx̣ʷa* – radio; harp; guitar; stereo; anything that makes music. *rt.:* ***x̣ʷax̣ʷʔey*** *– laugh.*

cast **čcq̇mnłqnełkʷm,** *čcq̇mnłqne* – cast a fishing line. *rt.:* ***cq̇minm*** *– throw.*
čcq̇mnłqnełkʷis – S/he cast the line. **čcq̇mnłqnełkʷn, čcq̇mnłqnełkʷntxʷ**
es čcq̇mnłqnełkʷms – S/he is casting the line. **ies čcq̇mnłqnełkʷm, as čcq̇mnłqnełkʷm**
qs čcq̇mnłqnełkʷms – S/he is going to cast the line. **iqs čcq̇mnłqnełkʷm, aqs čcq̇mnłqnełkʷm**
čcq̇mnłqnéʔełkʷis – They cast the line. **qeʔ čcq̇mnłqnełkʷntm, čcq̇mnłqnełkʷntp**
es čcq̇mnłqnéʔełkʷms – They are casting the line. **qeʔes čcq̇mnłqnełkʷm, es čcq̇mnłqnełkʷmp**
qs čcq̇mnłqnéʔełkʷms – They are going to cast the line. **qeʔqs čcq̇mnłqnełkʷm, qs čcq̇mnłqnełkʷmp**

čqq̇ṁé čox̣me – fishing line.

čt̓kʷqne – bait.

> s.t. - something, the 3rd person
> (s.t.) - something implied
> s.o. - someone, the 3rd person
> *sl.* - singular form
> *pl.* - plural form
> *rt.* - root word
> *cmd.* - command
> *lit.* - literally
> *fig.* - figuratively
> *i.e.,* - for example
> *See:* - Redirection to a related word.

cat **pus** – cat. **pspus** – cats. *pl.*
šeẏ łu kʷtisi pusts – That one is Big Blanket's cat. **ci pspus** – Those cats.

catalogue **snx̣litmn** – catalogue.

catch **kʷnnunm** – catch/grab someone or something.

kʷnnuis – S/he/it caught s.o./s.t. **kʷnnun, kʷnnuntxʷ**
es kʷnnunms – S/he/it is catching s.o./s.t. **ies kʷnnunm, as kʷnnunm**
qs kʷnnunms – S/he/it is going to catch s.o./s.t. **iqs kʷnnunm, aqs kʷnnunm**
kʷnnúˀunts – They caught s.o./s.t. **qeˀ kʷnnuntm, kʷnnuntp**
es kʷnnúˀunms – They are catching s.o./s.t. **qeˀes kʷnnunms, es kʷnnunmp**
qs kʷnnúˀunms – They are going to catch s.o./s.t. **qeˀqs kʷnnunms, qs kʷnnunmp**

kʷnnunt – Catch it. *cmd.*

ta qʷo qs kʷnnuntxʷ – You cannot catch me. **t swe u kʷnnuis** – Who caught it? **qʷo kʷnnunt** – Catch me. **kʷnnuncn** – I caught you.

ncčničṅ – catch up to someone or something. *rt.:* ***čicn** – meet.*
ncčničis – S/he/it caught up to s.o./s.t. **ncčničn, ncčničntxʷ**
es ncčničṅms – S/he/it is catching up to s.o./s.t. **ies ncčničṅm, as ncčničṅm**
qs ncčničṅms – S/he/it is going to catch up to s.o./s.t. **iqs ncčničṅm, aqs ncčničṅm**
ncčníˀičis – They caught up to s.o./s.t. **qeˀ ncčničntm, ncčničntp**

ta qʷo qs ncčničntxʷ – You cannot catch up to me. **qeˀ ncčničiłlt t sčq̓ʷeyq̓ʷe** – The Blackfeet caught up with us.

ncčninčnt – Catch up. *cmd.*

ncčnčnaqs, *ncčnčna* – catch up.
ncčnčnaqs – S/he caught up. **čn ncčnčnaqs, kʷ ncčnčnaqs**
es ncčnčnaqsi – S/he is catching up. **čnes ncčnčnaqsi, kʷes ncčnčnaqsi**
qs ncčnčnaqsi – S/he is going to catch up. **čiqs ncčnaqsi, kʷqs ncčnaqsi**
ncčnčnáˀaqs – They caught up. **qeˀ ncčnčnaqs, p ncčnčnaqs**

ntuṅičṅm – fail to catch up to someone; unable to catch up to someone; behind. *rt.:* ***tuiṅ** – fail/deficient.*
es ntuṅičṅ – S/he cannot catch up. **čnes ntuṅičṅ, kʷes ntuṅičṅ**
es ntuṅčna – S/he cannot catch up.

ntuṅičis – S/he failed to catch up to s.o. **ntuṅičn, ntuṅičntxʷ**
es ntuṅičṅms – S/he/it is failing to catch up to s.o. **ies ntuṅičṅm, as ntuṅičṅm**
qs ntuṅičṅms – S/he/it is going to fail to catch up to s.o. **iqs ntuṅičṅm, aqs ntuṅičṅm**
ntuṅíˀičis – They failed to catch up to s.o. **qeˀ ntuṅičntm, ntuṅičntp**

qeˀ ntuṅča – We cannot catch up.
qʷo ntuṅičíˀis – They cannot catch me.

ac – bind; restrain; tie; trap. *See:* ***tie.***
acsqáx̣eˀ – S/he caught a horse. **čn acsqáx̣eˀ, kʷ acsqáx̣eˀ**
es acsqáx̣eˀi – S/he is catching a horse. **čnes acsqáx̣eˀi, kʷes acsqáx̣eˀi**

acsqáx̣ˀeis – S/he caught his/her horse. **acsqáx̣ˀen, acsqáx̣ˀentxʷ**
es acsqáx̣ˀems – S/he is catching his/her horse. **ies acsqáx̣ˀem, as acsqáx̣ˀem**

acacsqáx̣eˀ, *acacsqá* – break horses; restrain/catch horses. *See:* ***break.***

qq̓ṁéyeˀ, *qq̓ṁé* – angling; fish. *See:* ***angle.***

mul – fish/scoop something out of water. *(i.e., with a net, container, etc.)* *See:* ***fish.***

catch fire

ṗaap – grass/timber caught fire. *See:* ***fire.***

ulip – burn up; catch fire. **ululip** *pl.* *See:* ***fire.***

catch fish

nq̓l̓xʷétkʷ, *nq̓l̓xʷé* – hook/snag fish.

nq̇l̓xʷétkʷm – S/he snagged a fish. **čn nq̇l̓xʷétkʷm, kʷ nq̇l̓xʷétkʷm**
es nq̇l̓xʷétkʷi – S/he is snagging a fish. **čnes nq̇l̓xʷétkʷi, kʷes nq̇l̓xʷétkʷi**
qs nq̇l̓xʷétkʷi – S/he is going to snag a fish. **čiqs nq̇l̓xʷétkʷi, kʷqs nq̇l̓xʷétkʷi**

nq̇l̓q̇l̓xʷétkʷm – S/he snagged fish. **čn nq̇l̓q̇l̓xʷétkʷm, kʷ nq̇l̓q̇l̓xʷétkʷm**

čq̇l̓uxʷ – snag on something.
čq̇l̓xʷmin – hook for pulling or catching.

nq̇l̓xʷétkʷm t kʷtunt sẇéwł – S/he snagged the big fish. **isince łu es nq̇l̓xʷé** – My little brother is snagging it.

qq̇ṁéyeʔ, *qq̇ṁé* – angling; fish. *See:* ***angle.***

mul – fish/scoop something out of water. *(i.e., with a net, container, etc.)* *See:* ***fish.***

The **i** following uvular consonants (UC) and the glottal stop **ʔ** sound like English "*ey*" as in the words th*ey*, h*ey*, wh*ey*, etc. Salish UC are: **q**, **q̇**, **qʷ**, **q̇ʷ**, **x̣**, **x̣ʷ**. For example, the suffix …**qin** – head/top, is often spelled using English *ey* as "q*ey*n". So **qi**, **q̇i**, **qʷi**, **q̇ʷi**, **x̣i**, **x̣ʷi**, may be spelled with English *ey* as **q***ey*, **q̇***ey*, **qʷ***ey*, **q̇ʷ***ey*, **x̣***ey*, **x̣ʷ***ey* in other texts.

caterpillar

čililk̇ʷté – caterpillar; woolly worm.
es yal̓mnscuti – It is coiling itself up *(a caterpillar making a cocoon).*

catfish

upupci – channel catfish; *Ictalurus punctatus*; black bullhead; *Ameiurus melas.*

Catherine

katlin – Catherine.

Catholic

es lpatém – S/he is baptized. *See:* ***baptize.***

cattail

ṗišłp – cattail leaves; *Typha latifolia.*

sq̇ʷástqin, *sq̇ʷástqi* – cattail spike.

caught

kʷnnunm – catch/grab someone or something. *See:* ***catch.***

cause

q̇eʔečst – made to be or do something; cause hardship for someone; cause problems for someone; put someone/something into it *(by holding, by making it one's business to do so, by situational happenstance, etc.).* *See:* ***made.***

cave

es nłx̣ʷenč – cave. *rt.:* ***łox̣ʷ*** *– hole; prefix:* ***n…*** *– inside; suffix:* ***…enč*** *– within.*

ntmwalš – Rocks fell/slid from the side of a cave. *See:* ***crumble.***

k̇ʷłtmip – Rocks caved in/fell from under. *See:* ***crumble.***

caw

es nʔáṅni – The magpie is cawing.

Cayuse Creek

ništé – Cayuse Creek, Montana.

sntťáċetn – place near Cayuse Creek in the Bitterroot.

ep sṗéƛ̓m – place near Cayuse Creek in the Bitterroot.

ceanothus

k̇ʷl̓itčyełp , *k̇ʷl̓itčye* – ceanothus; *Ceanothus sanguineus.*

cease

hoy – quit; stop; finish; okay; that's it; cease. *See:* ***quit.***

Cecille

sisil – Cecille.

cedar

ástqʷ – western red cedar; *Thuja plicata.*

mšéłp – western red cedar boughs.

s.t. - something, the 3rd person
(s.t.) - something implied
s.o. - someone, the 3rd person
sl. - singular form
pl. - plural form
rt. - root word
cmd. - command
lit. - literally
fig. - figuratively
i.e., - for example
See: - Redirection to a related word.

qʷelcn – western red cedar; *Thuja plicata;* grand fir; balsam fir; *Abies grandis. (There is some confusion with this word; it is used by different speakers as western red cedar, Thuja plicata, and grand fir, Abies grandis.)*

cedar waxwing **łkʷkʷusṅ,** *łkʷkʷu* – cedar waxwing; *Bombycilla cedrorum.*

ceiling **nłcenčn** – ceiling.

celebrate **npiyéls** – happy.

celebration **esẏapqini** – powwow; celebration. *suffix:* ***...qin, ...qn*** *– top.*
es ẏapqíʔini – They are celebrating. **qeʔes ẏapqini, pes ẏapqini**

esẏapqini spq̇niʔ – July *(month of celebration). See:* ***July.***
ẏapqin łu t sq̇sip – There were a lot of people celebrating long ago.

celery **sqltmxʷá** – elk thistle; celery; *Cirsium foliosum.*

cell phone **snčsṗálqʷlwistn** – cell phone. *rt.:* ***čsṗálqʷ*** *– hit on wood; prefix:* ***sn...*** *– a place of; suffix:* ***...lwis*** *– indicate going around; suffix:* ***...tin, ...tn*** *– means of/device.*

cent **séns** – cent.
nk̇ʷuʔséns – penny.
cilséns – nickel.

center **nihéẇs,** *nihé* – middle; center.

cereal **x̣am kʷekʷstn** – cereal. *lit. dry breakfast.*

chain **q̇l̓xʷélis,** *q̇l̓xʷé* – link/hook uniformly together; chain. *rt.:* ***q̇l̓uxʷ*** *– hook; suffix:* ***...elis*** *– uniformly.*
q̇l̓xʷélis – S/he linked together (s.t.). **čn q̇l̓xʷélis, kʷ q̇l̓xʷélis**
es q̇l̓xʷélisi – S/he is linking together (s.t.). **čnes q̇l̓xʷélisi, kʷes q̇l̓xʷélisi**
qs q̇l̓xʷélisi – S/he is going to link together (s.t.). **čiqs q̇l̓xʷélisi, kʷqs q̇l̓xʷélisi**

q̇l̓xʷélisis – S/he linked s.t. together. **q̇l̓xʷélisn, q̇l̓xʷélisntxʷ**
es q̇l̓xʷélisms – S/he is linking s.t. together. **ies q̇l̓xʷélism, as q̇l̓xʷélism**
qs q̇l̓xʷélisms – S/he is going to link s.t. together. **iqs q̇l̓xʷélism, aqs q̇l̓xʷélism**

ies q̇lq̇l̓xʷélism inṗiṗuyšn – I am chaining my car.

chair **snčłemutn,** *snčłemu* – chair. *rt.:* ***emut*** *– sit; prefix:* ***sn...*** *– a place of; affix:* ***čł...*** *– surface; suffix:* ***...tin, ...tn*** *– means of/device.*
siyent esyáʔ ci snčłemutn – Count all the chairs.

chalkboard **snčq̇ẏalqʷtn** – writing board; chalkboard; whiteboard.

challenge **nʔawqnm** – call upon/ask for someone; challenge/encourage someone; beseech; exhort. *See:* ***call.***

chameleon **kʷekʷel̓eʔ** – chameleon; little appearance changer.

change **k̇ʷl̓eys** – change into something; change money. *rt.:* ***ey*** *– cross; prefix:* ***k̇ʷl̓...*** *– make.*
k̇ʷl̓eysm – S/he/it changed. **čn k̇ʷl̓eysm, kʷ k̇ʷl̓eysm**
es k̇ʷl̓eysi – S/he/it is changing. **čnes k̇ʷl̓eysi, kʷes k̇ʷl̓eysi**
qs k̇ʷl̓eysi – S/he/it is going to change. **čiqs k̇ʷl̓eysi, kʷqs k̇ʷl̓eysi**

k̇ʷl̓eysis – S/he/it changed s.t. **k̇ʷl̓eysn, k̇ʷl̓eysntxʷ**

es k̓ʷl̓eysms – S/he/it is changing s.t. **ies k̓ʷl̓eysm, as k̓ʷl̓eysm**
qs k̓ʷl̓eysms – S/he/it is going to change s.t. **iqs k̓ʷl̓eysm, aqs k̓ʷl̓eysm**

k̓ʷl̓l̓eysm – S/he changed (into s.t.). **čn k̓ʷl̓l̓eysm, kʷ k̓ʷl̓l̓eysm**

es k̓ʷl̓eys – S/he/it is changed. **čnes k̓ʷl̓eys, kʷes k̓ʷl̓eys**
es k̓ʷl̓eysti – S/he/it is changing one's self. **čnes k̓ʷl̓eysti, kʷes k̓ʷl̓eysti**

sk̓ʷl̓eys – change.
sck̓ʷl̓eys – something that has been changed.
nk̓ʷl̓eystn – something that causes change.

k̓ʷl̓eysiš – Change. *cmd.*
k̓ʷl̓eysnt – Change it. *cmd.*

es k̓ʷl̓eysnwexʷi – They are changing places with each other. **qeʔes k̓ʷl̓eysnwexʷi, pes k̓ʷl̓eysnwexʷi**
es k̓ʷl̓l̓eysnwexʷi – They are changing with each other. **qeʔes k̓ʷl̓l̓eysnwexʷi, pes k̓ʷl̓l̓eysnwexʷi**

The **i** following uvular consonants (UC) and the glottal stop **ʔ** sound like English "*ey*" as in the words th*ey*, h*ey*, wh*ey*, etc. Salish UC are: **q, q̓, qʷ, q̓ʷ, x̣, x̣ʷ**. For example, the suffix …**qin** – head/top, is often spelled using English *ey* as "q*ey*n". So **qi, q̓i, qʷi, q̓ʷi, x̣i, x̣ʷi**, may be spelled with English *ey* as **q***ey*, **q̓***ey*, **qʷ***ey*, **q̓ʷ***ey*, **x̣***ey*, **x̣ʷ***ey* in other texts.

k̓ʷl̓isalqs – change shirt.
k̓ʷl̓isalqs – S/he changed shirts. **čn k̓ʷl̓isalqs, kʷ k̓ʷl̓isalqs**
es k̓ʷl̓isalqsi – S/he is changing shirts. **čnes k̓ʷl̓isalqsi, kʷes k̓ʷl̓isalqsi**
qs k̓ʷl̓isalqsi – S/he is going to change shirts. **čiqs k̓ʷl̓isalqsi, kʷqs k̓ʷl̓isalqsi**

k̓ʷl̓isalqsis – S/he changed s.o.'s shirt. **k̓ʷl̓isalqsn, k̓ʷl̓isalqsntxʷ**
es k̓ʷl̓isalqsms – S/he is changing s.o.'s shirt. **ies k̓ʷl̓isalqsm, as k̓ʷl̓isalqsm**

k̓ʷl̓isalqsiš – Change shirts. *cmd.*
k̓ʷl̓isalqsnt – Change his/her shirt. *cmd.*

k̓ʷl̓isnłxʷpalqs – change clothes.
k̓ʷl̓isnłxʷpalqs – S/he changed clothes. **čn k̓ʷl̓isnłxʷpalqs, kʷ k̓ʷl̓isnłxʷpalqs**
es k̓ʷl̓isnłxʷpalqsi – S/he is changing clothes. **čnes k̓ʷl̓isnłxʷpalqsi, kʷes k̓ʷl̓isnłxʷpalqsi**
qs k̓ʷl̓isnłxʷpalqsi – S/he is going to change clothes. **čiqs k̓ʷl̓isnłxʷpalqsi, kʷqs k̓ʷl̓isnłxʷpalqsi**

k̓ʷl̓isnłxʷpalqsis – S/he changed s.o.'s clothes. **k̓ʷl̓isnłxʷpalqsn, k̓ʷl̓isnłxʷpalqsntxʷ**
es k̓ʷl̓isnłxʷpalqsms – S/he is changing s.o.'s clothes. **ies k̓ʷl̓isnłxʷpalqsm, as k̓ʷl̓isnłxʷpalqsm**

k̓ʷl̓isnłxʷpalqsiš – Change clothes. *cmd.*
k̓ʷl̓isnłxʷpalqsnt – Change his/her clothes. *cmd.*

k̓ʷl̓l̓isqáx̣eʔ, *k̓ʷl̓l̓isqá* **–** change horses.
k̓ʷl̓l̓isqáx̣eʔ – S/he changed horses. **čn k̓ʷl̓l̓isqáx̣eʔ, kʷ k̓ʷl̓l̓isqáx̣eʔ**
es k̓ʷl̓l̓isqáx̣eʔi – S/he is changing horses. **čnes k̓ʷl̓l̓isqáx̣eʔi, kʷes k̓ʷl̓l̓isqáx̣eʔi**
qs k̓ʷl̓l̓isqáx̣eʔi – S/he is going to change horses. **čiqs k̓ʷl̓l̓isqáx̣eʔi, kʷqs k̓ʷl̓l̓isqáx̣eʔi**

s.t. - something, the 3rd person
(s.t.) - something implied
s.o. - someone, the 3rd person
sl. - singular form
pl. - plural form
rt. - root word
cmd. - command
lit. - literally
fig. - figuratively
i.e., - for example
See: - Redirection to a related word.

kʷel – change outward perception; change color; ripening/dying. *(i.e., leaves, grass, berries, etc.)*
i kʷel – Its color is changed; it is ripe; it is completely dead.
kʷeʔel – Its color became changed; ripened/died.
es kʷeelmi – It is changing color; ripening/dying.

es kʷeʔel – Its color has become changed; it is ripe; it is fully dead.

kʷlup – It changed color suddenly.
kʷlešn – the root changed; the root is ripe.
čkʷlełp – The leaves changed color.

es **čkʷlełpi** – The leaves are changing color.
kʷlulexʷ – The ground/grass changed color; becoming yellow.
es **kʷlulexʷi** – The ground/grass is changing color; becoming yellow.

kʷels – face changed color; become enraged; become scared; become embarrassed.

kʷlsmist – S/he got into a state that changed one's face color. **čn kʷlsmist, kʷ kʷlsmist**
es kʷlsmisti – S/he is getting into a state that changed one's face color. **čnes kʷlsmisti, kʷes kʷlsmisti**

nkʷlsncut – S/he caused one's face to change color. **čn nkʷlsncut, kʷ nkʷlsncut**
es nkʷlsncuti – S/he is causing one's face to change color. **čnes nkʷlsncuti, kʷes nkʷlsncuti**

ṅeyxʷéẇs, *ṅeyxʷé* – trade; swap. *See: **trade**.*

nʔeys – pay for something bought. *See: **pay**.*
snʔéys – cost, price.

tumíst, *tumí* – buy. *See: **buy**.*

t̓xʷlmncut – change one's self; to disguise. *See: **disguise**.*

t̓xʷlmist – change one's self spiritually. *See: **disguise**.*

change attitude

nt̓xʷlméls – change attitude. *rt.: **t̓ixʷlm** – different.*
nt̓xʷlmélsm – S/he/it changed one's attitude. **čn nt̓xʷlmélsm, kʷ nt̓xʷlmélsm**
es nt̓xʷlmélsi – S/he/it is changing one's attitude. **čnes nt̓xʷlmélsi, kʷes nt̓xʷlmélsi**
qs nt̓xʷlmélsi – S/he/it is going to change one's attitude. **čiqs nt̓xʷlmélsi, kʷqs nt̓xʷlmélsi**
nt̓xʷlméʔelsm – They changed their attitude. **qeʔ nt̓xʷlmélsm, p nt̓xʷlmélsm**

nk̓ʷl̓isncut, *nk̓ʷl̓isncu* – change one's mind; change one's self.
nk̓ʷl̓isncut – S/he changed one's mind. **čn nk̓ʷl̓isncut, kʷ nk̓ʷl̓isncut**
es nk̓ʷl̓isncuti – S/he is changing one's mind. **čnes nk̓ʷl̓isncuti, kʷes nk̓ʷl̓isncuti**
qs nk̓ʷl̓isncuti – S/he is going to change one's mind. **čiqs nk̓ʷl̓isncuti, kʷqs nk̓ʷl̓isncuti**

nk̓ʷl̓isncutš – Change your mind. *cmd.*

chapped

liẇt – chapped.
es liẇti – It is chapped.

liẇs – chapped face.
liẇs – S/he had a chapped face. **čn liẇs, kʷ liẇs**
es liẇsi – S/he is getting a chapped face. **čnes liẇsi, kʷes liẇsi**
qs liẇsi – S/he is going to get a chapped face. **čiqs liẇsi, kʷqs liẇsi**

es liẇs – S/he has a chapped face. **čnes liẇs, kʷes liẇs**

luliẇčst – chapped hands. *suffix: **...ečst, ...čst** – of the hand.*
luliẇčst – S/he had chapped hands. **čn luliẇčst, kʷ luliẇčst**
es luliẇčsti – S/he is getting chapped hands. **čnes luliẇčsti, kʷes luliẇčsti**
qs luliẇčsti – S/he is going to get chapped hands. **čiqs luliẇčsti, kʷqs luliẇčsti**

es luliẇčst – S/he has chapped hands. **čnes luliẇčst, kʷes luliẇčst**

luliẇšn – chapped feet.
luliẇšn – S/he had chapped feet. **čn luliẇšn, kʷ luliẇšn**
es luliẇšni – S/he is getting chapped feet. **čnes luliẇšni, kʷes luliẇšni**
qs luliẇšni – S/he is going to get chapped feet. **čiqs luliẇšni, kʷqs luliẇšni**

es luliẃšn – S/he has chapped feet. **čnes luliẃšn, kʷes luliẃšn**

χamposqn – chapped/dry lips. *rt.: χam – dry; suffix: ...posqn – lips.*

charcoal
ċáx̣ʷċx̣ʷt, ċáx̣ʷ – powdery ashes.

qʷlmin – ash chunks; charcoal. *(used as a teething medicine)*

charge
čx̣ʷicut – more than one charges toward; attack; rush to; run toward.
rt.: x̣ʷuy – go.

čx̣ʷicúʔut – They charged in. **qeʔ čx̣ʷicut, p čx̣ʷicut**

es čx̣ʷicúʔuti – They are charging in. **qeʔes čx̣ʷicuti, pes čx̣ʷicuti**

qs čx̣ʷicúʔuti – They are going to charge in. **qeʔqs čx̣ʷicuti, pqs čx̣ʷicuti**

čx̣ʷicúʔutmis – They charged s.t./s.o. **qeʔ čx̣ʷicutmn, čx̣ʷicutmntp**

es čx̣ʷicúʔutms – They are charging s.t./s.o. **qeʔes čx̣ʷicutm, es čx̣ʷicutmp**

qs čx̣ʷicúʔutms – They are going to charge s.t./s.o. **qeʔqs čx̣ʷicutm, qs čx̣ʷicutmp**

čx̣ʷicutwi – All of you attack. *cmd.*
čx̣ʷicutmnti – Charge s.t./s.o. *cmd.*

čx̣ʷťpminm – an individual charges toward; run toward; attack; rush to; an individual runs toward. *rt.: x̣ʷťip – run somewhere.*

čx̣ʷťpmis – S/he charged at s.t./s.o. **čx̣ʷťpmin, čx̣ʷťpmintx̣ʷ**

es čx̣ʷťpminms – S/he is charging at s.t./s.o. **ies čx̣ʷťpminm, as čx̣ʷťpminm**

qs čx̣ʷťpminms – S/he is going to charge at s.t./s.o. **iqs čx̣ʷťpminm, aqs čx̣ʷťpminm**

čx̣ʷťpmintm – S/he was charged.

čx̣ʷťpmsqe – S/he attacked. **čn čx̣ʷťpmsqe, kʷ čx̣ʷťpmsqe**

es čx̣ʷťpmnwex̣ʷi – They are charging each other.

k̓ʷl̓x̣ʷlx̣ʷi – make credit.

ťk̓ʷntes – S/he put s.o. in charge; appoint. **ťk̓ʷnten, ťk̓ʷntex̣ʷ**

ťk̓ʷntéʔes – They put s.o. in charge; appoint. **qeʔ ťk̓ʷntem, ťk̓ʷntep**

Charles
čali – Charlie; Charles.

Charlo
sallu – Charlo.

Charlo's Heights
nk̓ʷaliʔps – Charlo's Heights, Montana.

łmq̓ʷcṅé – south of Charlo's Heights in the Bitterroot.

chase
čtqém – chase after. *rt.: tqem – touch.*

čtqem – S/he/it chased (s.t.). **čn čtqem, kʷ čtqem**

es čtqmi – S/he/it is chasing (s.t.). **čnes čtqmi, kʷes čtqmi**

qs čtqmi – S/he/it is going to chase (s.t.). **čiqs čtqmi, kʷqs čtqmi**

čtqéʔem – They chased (s.t.). **qeʔ čtqem, p čtqem**

es čtqmíʔi – They are chasing (s.t.). **qeʔes čtqmi, pes čtqmi**

qs čtqmíʔi – They are going to chase (s.t.). **qeʔqs čtqmi, pqs čtqmi**

čtqntes – S/he/it chased it. **čtqnten, čtqntex̣ʷ**

es čtqems – S/he/it is chasing it. **ies čtqem, as čtqem**

qs čtqems – S/he/it is going to chase it. **iqs čtqem, aqs čtqem**

čtqntéʔes – They chased it. **qeʔ čtqntem, čtqntep**

The **i** following uvular consonants (UC) and the glottal stop **ʔ** sound like English "*ey*" as in the words th*ey*, h*ey*, wh*ey*, etc. Salish UC are: **q, q̓, q̓ʷ, q̓ʷ, x̣, x̣ʷ**. For example, the suffix **...qin** – head/top, is often spelled using English *ey* as "**qeyn**". So **qi, q̓i, q̓ʷi, q̓ʷi, x̣i, x̣ʷi**, may be spelled with English *ey* as **qey, q̓ey, q̓ʷey, q̓ʷey, x̣ey, x̣ʷey** in other texts.

---

s.t. - something, the 3rd person
(s.t.) - something implied
s.o. - someone, the 3rd person
sl. - singular form
pl. - plural form
rt. - root word
cmd. - command
lit. - literally
fig. - figuratively
i.e., - for example
See: - Redirection to a related word.

es čtqéʔems – They are chasing it. **qeʔes čtqem, es čtqemp**
qs čtqéʔems – They are going to chase. **qeʔqs čtqem, qs čtqemp**

es čtqtqmi – S/he/it is chasing this and that. **čnes čtqtqmi, kʷes čtqtqmi**

čtqtqemn – one inclined to chase. *(i.e., a dog that chases cars all the time.) suffix:* ***...emn*** *– one inclined to do.*

čtqent – You chase it. *cmd.*
čtqlwis – S/he/it chased (s.t.) around. **čn čtqlwis, kʷ čtqlwis**
es čtqlwisi – S/he/it is chasing (s.t.) around. **čnes čtqlwisi, kʷes čtqlwisi**
es čtqnnwéxʷi – They're chasing each other. **qeʔes čtqnnwéxʷi, pes čtqnnwéxʷi**

čnes čtqem t ċúʔulixʷ – I chase deer. **ies čtqem ċúʔulixʷ** – I am chasing a deer. **kʷ iqs čtqem** – I am going to chase you.

čtqmsqáx̣eʔ, *čtqmsqá* – chase after domestic animals, mainly horses.
čtqmsqáx̣eʔ – S/he chased after. **čn čtqmsqáx̣eʔ, kʷ čtqmsqáx̣eʔ**
es čtqmsqáx̣eʔi – S/he is chasing after. **čnes čtqmsqáx̣eʔi, kʷes čtqmsqáx̣eʔi**
qs čtqmsqáx̣eʔi – S/he is going to chase after. **čiqs čtqmsqáx̣eʔi, kʷqs čtqmsqáx̣eʔi**
čtqmsqáʔax̣eʔ – They chased after. **qeʔ čtqmsqáx̣eʔ, p čtqmsqáx̣eʔ**
es čtqmsqáʔax̣eʔi – They are chasing after. **qeʔes čtqmsqáx̣eʔi, pes čtqmsqáx̣eʔi**
qs čtqmsqáʔax̣eʔi – They're going to chase after. **qeʔqs čtqmsqáx̣eʔi, pqs čtqmsqáx̣eʔi**

sxʷčtqmsqáx̣eʔ – one tasked to chase away horses. *prefix:* ***sxʷ...*** *– one tasked to do.*

qixʷ – chase/whip/drive away.
qixʷis – S/he/it chased it away. **qixʷn, qixʷntxʷ**
es qixʷms – S/he/is is chasing it away. **ies qixʷm, as qixʷm**
qs qixʷms – S/he is going to chase it away. **iqs qixʷm, aqs qixʷm**
qíʔixʷis – They chased it away. **qeʔ qixʷntm, qixʷntp**
es qíʔixʷm – They are chasing it away. **qeʔes qixʷm, es qixʷmp**
qs qíʔixʷm – They are going to chase it away. **qeʔqs qixʷm, qs qixʷmp**

sxʷqixʷm – one tasked to chase/drive away.
qixʷmn – whip; something used to chase/whip away animals. *suffix:* ***...min, ...mn*** *– instrument/tool.*
łqiqxʷmn – little whip; quirt. *suffix:* ***...min, ...mn*** *– instrument/tool.*

qixʷiš – Chase (s.t.) away. *cmd.*
qixʷnt – Chase it away. *cmd.*
k̓ʷłqixʷcnis – S/he chased s.o./s.t. away from food. **k̓ʷłqixʷcnn, k̓ʷłqixʷcnntxʷ**
k̓ʷłqixʷ – protect; defended. *See:* ***protect.***

t kʷtisi u qʷo qixʷłts isnčłċaʔsqá – Big Blanket chased my horses away.

qixʷsqáx̣eʔ, *qixʷsqá* – chase/whip away horses; drive horses and stock.
qixʷsqáx̣eʔ – S/he chased. **čn qixʷsqáx̣eʔ, kʷ qixʷsqáx̣eʔ**
es qixʷsqáx̣eʔi – S/he is chasing. **čnes qixʷsqáx̣eʔi, kʷes qixʷsqáx̣eʔi**
qs qixʷsqáx̣eʔi – S/he is going to chase. **čiqs qixʷsqáx̣eʔi, kʷqs qixʷsqáx̣eʔi**
qixʷsqáʔax̣eʔ – They chased. **qeʔ qixʷsqáx̣eʔ, p qixʷsqáx̣eʔ**
es qixʷsqáʔax̣eʔi – They are chasing. **qeʔes qixʷsqáx̣eʔi, pes qixʷsqáx̣eʔi**
qs qixʷsqáʔax̣eʔi – They are going to chase. **qeʔqs qixʷsqáx̣eʔi, pqs qixʷsqáx̣eʔi**

qixʷsqáx̣eʔtn – driving horse.

meʔminm – chase/drive away someone; kick someone out.
es meʔminms – S/he is chasing away s.o. **ies meʔminm, as meʔminm**
es meʔmłtumši – S/he is chasing away people. **čnes meʔmłtumši, kʷes meʔmłtumši**

iax̣ – herd/drive animals; make a group of animals go in a certain direction. *See: **herd**.*

cheap **nłkʷk̓ʷim̓áqsm,** *nłkʷk̓ʷim̓á* – cheap; inexpensive; thing of little value. *circumfix: **n...aqsm** – kinds.*

cheat **qʷil** – cheat.
qʷilm – S/he cheated. **čn qʷilm, kʷ qʷilm**
es qʷili – S/he/it is cheating. **čnes qʷili, kʷes qʷili**
qs qʷili – S/he/it is going to cheat. **čiqs qʷili, kʷqs qʷili**
qʷiˀilm – They cheated. **qeˀ qʷilm, p qʷilm**
es qʷiˀili – They are cheating. **qeˀes qʷili, pes qʷili**
qs qʷiˀili – They are going to cheat. **qeˀqs qʷili, pqs qʷili**

qʷilis – S/he cheated him/her. **qʷiln, qʷilntxʷ**
es qʷilms – S/he is cheating him/her/it. **ies qʷilm, as qʷilm**
qs qʷilms – S/he is going to cheat him/her/it. **iqs qʷilm, aqs qʷilm**

es qʷilnwexʷi – They are cheating each other. **qeˀes qʷilnwexʷi, pes qʷilnwexʷi**
es qʷllncuti – S/he is cheating one's self. **čnes qʷllncuti, kʷes qʷllncuti**

qʷl̓qʷl̓muł, *qʷl̓qʷl̓mu* – one that habitually cheats; cheater; con man; someone who trys to get the best of people.

qʷo qʷilis – S/he cheated me. **swe łu es qʷilms t mali** – Who did Mary cheat? **qʷl̓qʷl̓mu łu mali** – Mary is a cheater.

The **i** following uvular consonants (UC) and the glottal stop **ˀ** sound like English "*ey*" as in the words th*ey*, h*ey*, wh*ey*, etc. Salish UC are: **q, q̓, qʷ, q̓ʷ, x̣, x̣ʷ**. For example, the suffix **...qin** – head/top, is often spelled using English *ey* as "q*ey*n". So **qi, q̓i, qʷi, q̓ʷi, x̣i, x̣ʷi**, may be spelled with English *ey* as **q***ey*, **q̓***ey*, **qʷ***ey*, **q̓ʷ***ey*, **x̣***ey*, **x̣ʷ***ey* in other texts.

check **nˀac̓x̣ew̓s** – look at/check out something. *suffix: **...éw̓s** – in between, middle. See: **inspect**.*

cheek **sk̓ʷłčmus** – cheek. *rt.: **čm** – extremity.*
sk̓ʷłcheus – right cheek.
sk̓ʷłc̓q̓ʷeus – left cheek.

cheese **kʷl̓eyn** – cheese.

cherish **q̓ix̣tm** – cherish something or someone; fond of something possessed; treasure something or someone; show respect by cherishing a gift
q̓ix̣tm – S/he cherished. **čn q̓ix̣tm, kʷ q̓ix̣tm**
es q̓ix̣tms – S/he is cherishing. **ies q̓ix̣tm, as q̓ix̣tm**
qs q̓ix̣tms – S/he is going to cherish. **iqs q̓ix̣tm, aqs q̓ix̣tm**

q̓ix̣tmis – S/he cherished s.t./s.o. **q̓ix̣tmn, q̓ix̣tmntxʷ**
es q̓ix̣tms – S/he is cherishing s.t./s.o. **ies q̓ix̣tm, as q̓ix̣tm**
qs q̓ix̣tms – S/he is going to cherish s.t./s.o. **iqs q̓ix̣tm, aqs q̓ix̣tm**

es q̓x̣q̓ix̣tms – S/he is cherishing things. **ies q̓x̣q̓ix̣tm, as q̓x̣q̓ix̣tm**

sq̓ix̣tm – something cherished.
q̓x̣tmncutn – one affectionate to another.

q̓ix̣tiš – Cherish. *cmd.*
q̓ix̣tmnt – Cherish s.t./s.o. *cmd.*
q̓ix̣tmist – cherish one's self.
q̓x̣mscut – act to be admired.
q̓ix̣tmłtumš – fond of people.
q̓ix̣tmsqax̣eˀ – fond of horses/domestic animals/vehicle.
es q̓x̣tmnwexʷi – They are fond of each other. **qeˀes q̓x̣tmnwexʷi, pes q̓x̣tmnwexʷi**

s.t. - something, the 3rd person
(s.t.) - something implied
s.o. - someone, the 3rd person
sl. - singular form
pl. - plural form
rt. - root word
cmd. - command
lit. - literally
fig. - figuratively
i.e., - for example
See: - Redirection to a related word.

chest **sččmaxʷcč** – chest. *rt.:* ***čm*** *– extremity.*
sqpmin – sternum.

chestnut-backed chickadee **ċsqaṅíʔ** – chestnut-backed chickadee; *Poecile rufescens.*

chew **k̓ʷek̓ʷʔém** – chew; bite repeatedly.
k̓ʷek̓ʷʔém – S/he/it chewed. **čn k̓ʷek̓ʷʔém, kʷ k̓ʷek̓ʷʔém**
es k̓ʷek̓ʷʔémi – S/he/it is chewing. **čnes k̓ʷek̓ʷʔémi, kʷes k̓ʷek̓ʷʔémi**
qs k̓ʷek̓ʷʔémi – S/he/it is going to chew. **iqs k̓ʷek̓ʷʔémi, aqs k̓ʷek̓ʷʔémi**
k̓ʷek̓ʷʔéʔem– They chewed. **qeʔ k̓ʷek̓ʷʔém, p k̓ʷek̓ʷʔém**
es k̓ʷek̓ʷʔéʔemi – They are chewing. **qeʔes k̓ʷek̓ʷʔémi, es k̓ʷek̓ʷʔémi**
qs k̓ʷek̓ʷʔéʔemi – They are going to chew. **qeʔqs k̓ʷek̓ʷʔémi, qs k̓ʷek̓ʷʔémi**

k̓ʷek̓ʷʔentes – S/he/it chewed on s.t. **k̓ʷek̓ʷʔenten, k̓ʷek̓ʷʔentexʷ**
es k̓ʷek̓ʷʔéms – S/he/it is chewing on s.t. **ies k̓ʷek̓ʷʔém, as k̓ʷek̓ʷʔém**
qs k̓ʷek̓ʷʔéms – S/he/it is going to chew on s.t. **iqs k̓ʷek̓ʷʔém, aqs k̓ʷek̓ʷʔém**
k̓ʷek̓ʷʔentéʔes – They chewed on s.t. **qeʔ k̓ʷek̓ʷʔentén, k̓ʷek̓ʷʔentép**
es k̓ʷek̓ʷʔéʔems – They are chewing on s.t. **qeʔes k̓ʷek̓ʷʔém, es k̓ʷek̓ʷʔémp**
qs k̓ʷek̓ʷʔéʔems – They are going to chew on s.t. **qeʔqs k̓ʷek̓ʷʔém, qs k̓ʷek̓ʷʔémp**

k̓ʷek̓ʷʔeiš – Chew. *cmd.*
k̓ʷek̓ʷʔent – Chew it. *cmd.*
k̓ʷek̓ʷʔecnilš – chew food. *suffix:* ***...ilš*** *– autonomous.*

x̣ƛ̓im – chew away at something; gnaw.
x̣ƛ̓im – S/he/it chewed away. **čn x̣ƛ̓im, kʷ x̣ƛ̓im**
es x̣ƛ̓mi – S/he/it is chewing away. **čnes x̣ƛ̓mi, kʷes x̣ƛ̓mi**
qs x̣ƛ̓ims – S/he/it is going to chew away. **čiqs x̣ƛ̓mi, kʷqs x̣ƛ̓mi**
x̣ƛ̓im – They chewed away. **qeʔ x̣ƛ̓im, p x̣ƛ̓im**
es x̣ƛ̓míʔi – They are chewing away. **qeʔes x̣ƛ̓mi, pes x̣ƛ̓mi**
qs x̣ƛ̓míʔi – They are going to chew away. **qeʔqs x̣ƛ̓mi, pqs x̣ƛ̓mi**

x̣ƛ̓ntes – S/he/it chewed away at s.t. **x̣ƛ̓nten, x̣ƛ̓ntexʷ**
es x̣ƛ̓ims – S/he/it is chewing away at s.t. **ies x̣ƛ̓im, as x̣ƛ̓im**
qs x̣ƛ̓ims – S/he/it is going to chew away at s.t. **iqs x̣ƛ̓im, aqs x̣ƛ̓im**
x̣ƛ̓ntéʔes – They chewed away at s.t. **x̣ƛ̓ntem, x̣ƛ̓ntep**
es x̣ƛ̓íʔims – They are chewing away at s.t. **qeʔes x̣ƛ̓im, es x̣ƛ̓imp**
qs x̣ƛ̓íʔims – They are going to chew away at s.t. **qeʔqs x̣ƛ̓im, qs x̣ƛ̓imp**

x̣ƛ̓iš – Gnaw. *cmd.*
x̣ƛ̓int – Gnaw it. *cmd.*
x̣ƛ̓epm – chew on a rope.
x̣ex̣iƛ̓eʔ – little chewer, affectionately.

qʷo x̣ƛ̓ntem t k̓ʷekʷt̓neʔ – The mouse chewed something of mine.

čx̣ƛ̓us – chew on something that is round.
čx̣ƛ̓usm – S/he/it chewed (a round object). **čn čx̣ƛ̓usm, kʷ čx̣ƛ̓usm**
es čx̣ƛ̓usi – S/he/it is chewing (a round object). **čnes čx̣ƛ̓usi, kʷes čx̣ƛ̓usi**
qs čx̣ƛ̓usi – S/he/it is going to chew (a round object). **čiqs čx̣ƛ̓usi, kʷqs čx̣ƛ̓usi**
čx̣ƛ̓úʔusm – They chewed (a round object). **qeʔ čx̣ƛ̓usm, p čx̣ƛ̓usm**
es čx̣ƛ̓úʔusi – They are chewing (a round object). **qeʔes čx̣ƛ̓usi, pes čx̣ƛ̓usi**
qs čx̣ƛ̓úʔusi – They are going to chew (a round object). **qeʔqs čx̣ƛ̓usi, pqs čx̣ƛ̓usi**

čx̣ƛ̓usis – S/he/it chewed a round object. **čx̣ƛ̓usn, čx̣ƛ̓usntxʷ**

es čx̣ƛ̓usms – S/he/it is chewing a round object. **ies čx̣ƛ̓usm, as čx̣ƛ̓usm**
qs čx̣ƛ̓usms – S/he/it is going to chew a round object. **iqs čx̣ƛ̓usm, aqs čx̣ƛ̓usm**

čx̣ƛ̓x̣ƛ̓usm – Each one chewed (a round object).

x̣ƛ̓epm – chew on a rope.
x̣ƛ̓epis – S/he/it chewed a rope. **x̣ƛ̓epn, x̣ƛ̓epntxʷ**
es x̣ƛ̓epms – S/he/it is chewing a rope. **ies x̣ƛ̓epm, as x̣ƛ̓epm**
qs x̣ƛ̓epms – S/he/it is going to chew a rope. **iqs x̣ƛ̓epm, aqs x̣ƛ̓epm**
x̣ƛ̓éʔepis – They chewed a rope. **qeʔ x̣ƛ̓epntm, x̣ƛ̓epntp**
es x̣ƛ̓éʔepms – They are chewing a rope. **qeʔes x̣ƛ̓epm, es x̣ƛ̓epmp**
qs x̣ƛ̓éʔepms – They are going to chew a rope. **qeʔqs x̣ƛ̓epm, qs x̣ƛ̓epmp**

čx̣ƛ̓alqʷ – chew on wood.
čx̣ƛ̓alqʷis – S/he/it chewed wood. **čx̣ƛ̓alqʷn, čx̣ƛ̓alqʷntxʷ**

čx̣ƛ̓alqʷn łkʷlkʷaliʔ – I chewed corn.

es x̣ƛ̓ulexʷi – It is grazing, (animals). *See:* ***graze***.

es x̣ƛ̓ełċʔem – It is chewing away at his/her body. *(i.e., cancer)*

k̓ʷłx̣ƛ̓im – chew something off.
k̓ʷłx̣ƛ̓ntes – S/he/it chewed away at s.t. **k̓ʷłx̣ƛ̓nten, k̓ʷłx̣ƛ̓ntexʷ**
es k̓ʷłx̣ƛ̓ims – S/he/it is chewing away at s.t. **ies k̓ʷłx̣ƛ̓im, as k̓ʷłx̣ƛ̓im**
qs k̓ʷłx̣ƛ̓ims – S/he/it is going to chew away at s.t. **iqs k̓ʷłx̣ƛ̓im, aqs k̓ʷłx̣ƛ̓im**

k̓ʷłx̣ƛ̓int – Chew it off. *cmd.*

Cheyenne

čqqayus – Cheyenne. *lit. painted eyes.*

chickadee

ċípana – black-capped chickadee; *Poecile atricapillus.*

ċsqáṅeʔ – mountain chickadee; *Poecile gambeli.*

ċsqaṅíʔ – chestnut-backed chickadee; *Poecile rufescens.*

chicken

skʷiskʷs – spruce grouse; Franklin's grouse; fools hen; *Falcipennis canadensis*; domestic chicken.

čn člqepm t skʷiskʷs – I plucked the feathers off the chicken. **ha es qʷmmims t snčl̓é askʷiskʷs** – Was the coyote killing your chickens? **qʷo pulłtm iskʷiskʷs** – Somebody killed my chickens.

sq̓óxʷlu, *sq̓ó* – sharp-tailed grouse; prairie chicken; *Tympanuchus phasianellus jamesi.*

lipul – domestic chicken. *(approximation to French word)*

likok – domestic rooster. *(approximation to French word)*

chicken hawk

sqqi – chicken hawk; *Accipiter gentilis.*

chicken house

snkʷiskʷstn – chicken house. *prefix:* ***sn...*** *– a place of; suffix:* ***...tin, ...tn*** *– means of/device.*

chicken pox

spoct – chicken pox; smallpox.

chief

ilmixʷm – chief; boss.
łil̓ṁixʷm – little chief.
ilmxʷscutn – one who acts as chief.

The **i** following uvular consonants (UC) and the glottal stop **ʔ** sound like English "*ey*" as in the words th*ey*, h*ey*, wh*ey*, etc. Salish UC are: **q**, **q̓**, **qʷ**, **q̓ʷ**, **x̣**, **x̣ʷ**. For example, the suffix ...**qin** – head/top, is often spelled using English *ey* as "q*ey*n". So **qi**, **q̓i**, **qʷi**, **q̓ʷi**, **x̣i**, **x̣ʷi**, may be spelled with English *ey* as **q***ey*, **q̓***ey*, **qʷ***ey*, **q̓ʷ***ey*, **x̣***ey*, **x̣ʷ***ey* in other texts.

s.t. - something, the 3rd person
(s.t.) - something implied
s.o. - someone, the 3rd person
sl. - singular form
pl. - plural form
rt. - root word
cmd. - command
lit. - literally
fig. - figuratively
i.e., - for example
See: - Redirection to a related word.

ilmxʷemn – one inclined to lead/boss. *suffix:* ***...emn –*** *one inclined to do.*
ilmxʷmuł – one that habitually leads/bosses. *suffix:****...łmuł –*** *one that habitually does.*

ililmxʷscut – bossy; make one's self the boss. *See:* ***boss.***
nilmixʷmels – wants to lead; wants be chief. *circumfix:* ***n...els –*** *want, feel.*

qeʔ qł ililmxʷscúʔutn – They will be our dictators. **uł inʔililmixʷm łu inṗiṗx̣ʷot uł px̣páx̣t –** My elders are my leaders; they are wise.

šʔitmasqe – leader; first people; first to volunteer; first to be there. *rt.:* ***šʔit –*** *first; suffix:* ***...sqe, ...sqelixʷ –*** *people. See:* ***leader.***

Chief Cliff

snpċančštis – Chief Cliff, Flathead Nation.

Chief Mountain

sʔilṁłxʷsċut – Chief Mountain, Montana; *lit. chief of the Rocky Mountains.*

child

skʷḱʷimlt – young; child.
łu puti či skʷḱʷimlt nx̣elmn nq̓ʷiq̓ʷosmi – When I was young I was afraid of dogs.

łox̣ʷtélt – baby.

sšiimišlt – only child.

stʔewtélt – youngest, last born child.

sq̓éẁselt – middle child(ren).

šitmišlt – first born child.

sšitelt – first child.

children

sccṁelt – children.

skʷḱʷimlt – young; child.

sxʷsixʷlt – offspring.

chilled

suẏ – cold; chilled.

chilly

suẏ – cold; chilled.
i suẏ – S/he/it is cold/chilly. **i čn suẏ, i kʷ suẏ**
i łssuẏ – It is a little chilly.

suẏt – S/he/it was cold/chilly. **čn suẏt, kʷ suẏt**
es suẏti – S/he/it is cold/chilly. **čnes suẏti, kʷes suẏti**
qs suẏti – S/he/it is going to be cold/chilly. **čiqs suẏti, kʷqs suẏti**

i suẏ č čo – It is chilly outside. **ha kʷes suẏti –** Are you cold. **x̣iṅe čn suẏt –** I might get chilly.

chimney

ṫpe – pipe; chimney. *See:* ***pipe.***

chin

ḱʷiʔepest, *ḱʷiʔepe* **–** chin.

Chinese

čusẁi – Chinese.

chinook

es cháłqi – A chinook is blowing *(warm dry wind).*
eċx̣i t es cháłqi – It seems like a warm wind is blowing outside.

chipmunk

qʷqʷċẁéyeʔ, *qʷqʷċẁé* **–** yellow-pine chipmunk; *Tamias amoenus;* least chipmunk; *Tamias minimus.*

l esmilk̓ʷ u č̓t̓p̓t̓p̓yew̓t łu qʷqʷċw̓é – Chipmunks were standing all over. **qʷqʷċw̓é łu isuméš –** Chipmunk is my medicine power.

chiropractor **sxʷnplusm –** one tasked to turn heads; chiropractor. *See: **turn**.*

chitchat **xʷaˀscan –** chitchat; speak for nothing. *(i.e., when someone asks to borrow money and they still owe you; idle conversation; gossip; talking to the wall)*
xʷaˀscan – S/he spoke for nothing. **čn xʷaˀscan, kʷ xʷaˀscan**
es xʷaˀscani – S/he is speaking for nothing. **čnes xʷaˀscani, kʷes xʷaˀscani**
qs xʷaˀscani – S/he is going to speak for nothing. **čiqs xʷaˀscani, kʷqs xʷaˀscani**

The **i** following uvular consonants (UC) and the glottal stop **ˀ** sound like English "*ey*" as in the words th*ey*, h*ey*, wh*ey*, etc. Salish UC are: **q, q̓, qʷ, q̓ʷ, x̣, x̣ʷ**. For example, the suffix ...**qin** – head/top, is often spelled using English *ey* as "q*ey*n". So **qi, q̓i, qʷi, q̓ʷi, x̣i, x̣ʷi**, may be spelled with English *ey* as **q***ey*, **q̓***ey*, **qʷ***ey*, **q̓ʷ***ey*, **x̣***ey*, **x̣ʷ***ey* in other texts.

choice **scnk̓ʷéṅ –** choice; something that is taken. *prefix: **sc...** – s.t. that's been done/made/prepared. See: **try**.*
aq scnk̓ʷéṅ – It is going to be your choice.
t aq scnk̓ʷéṅ – It is going to be your choice.

scnte – idea. *prefix: **sc...** – s.t. that's been done/made/prepared.*
aq scnte – It is going to be your idea/choice.

choke **ap̓x̣ʷ –** choke on something.
ap̓x̣ʷ – S/he/it choked. **čn ap̓x̣ʷ, kʷ ap̓x̣ʷ**
es ap̓x̣ʷi – S/he/it is choking. **čnes ap̓x̣ʷi, kʷes ap̓x̣ʷi**
qs ap̓x̣ʷi – S/he/it is going to choke. **čiqs ap̓x̣ʷi, kʷqs ap̓x̣ʷi**

x̣iṅe kʷ ap̓x̣ʷ – You might choke. **x̣i m kʷ ap̓x̣ʷ –** You might choke.

k̓ʷłċip̓cnm – choke somebody. *rt.: **ċip̓** – pinch; prefix: **k̓ʷł...** – under; suffix: **...cin, ...cn** – action of the mouth.*
k̓ʷłċip̓cis – S/he choked s.o. **k̓ʷłċip̓cn, k̓ʷłċip̓cntxʷ**
es k̓ʷłċip̓cnms – S/he is choking s.o. **ies k̓ʷłċip̓cnm, as k̓ʷłċip̓cnm**
qs k̓ʷłċip̓cnms – S/he is going to choke s.o. **iqs k̓ʷłċip̓cnm, aqs k̓ʷłċip̓cnm**

k̓ʷłq̓ʷeˀecin, *k̓ʷłq̓ʷeˀeci* **–** choke from something around the neck.
k̓ʷłq̓ʷeˀecintxʷ – You choke s.o.

chokecherry **łx̣ʷłó –** chokecherry.
łx̣ʷołx̣ʷalqʷ, *łx̣ʷołx̣ʷa* **–** chokecherry tree; *Prunus virginiana.*

nnłx̣ʷło – patch of chokecherry trees.

łx̣ʷłó spq̓niˀ – September *(the month of the chokecherry).*

choose **nk̓ʷéṅm –** choose; pick; select; show the selection. *See: **try**.*

chop **šlim –** chop.
šlim – S/he/it chopped (s.t.). **čn šlim, kʷ šlim**
es šlmi – S/he/it is chopping (s.t.). **čnes šlmi, kʷes šlmi**
qs šlmi – S/he/it is going to chop (s.t.). **čiqs šlmi, kʷqs šlmi**
šlíˀim – They chopped (s.t.). **qeˀ šlim, p šlim**
es šlmíˀi – They are chopping (s.t.). **qeˀes šlmi, pes šlmi**
qs šlmíˀi – They are going to chop (s.t.). **qeˀqs šlmi, pqs šlmi**

šlntes – S/he chopped it. **šlnten, šlntexʷ**
es šlims – S/he is chopping it. **ies šlim, as šlim**
qs šlims – S/he is going to chop it. **iqs šlim, aqs šlim**
šlntéˀes – They chopped it. **qeˀ šlntem, šlntep**

šlmin – axe.

s.t. - something, the 3rd person
(s.t.) - something implied
s.o. - someone, the 3rd person
sl. - singular form
pl. - plural form
rt. - root word
cmd. - command
lit. - literally
fig. - figuratively
i.e., - for example
See: - Redirection to a related word.

šlep – chop down; chop off.
šlepm – S/he chopped (s.t. off/down). **čn šlepm, kʷ šlepm**

šlepis – S/he chopped it down. **šlepn, šlepntxʷ**
es šlepms – S/he is chopping it down. **ies šlepm, as šlepm**
qs šlepms – S/he is going to chop it down. **iqs šlepm, aqs šlepm**
šlé?epis – They chopped it down. **qe? šlepntm, šlepntp**

šlšlepis – S/he chopped things down.
es šlšlepi – S/he is chopping off (branches). **čnes šlšlepi, kʷes šlšlepi**

ṅe l sčace m čn k̓ʷis šlepm t maniłp x̣ʷl̓ incitxʷ – Sunday I will go and chop down balsam for my house.

pič – shave/cut. *(i.e., shaving wood.) See:* ***shave.***

Christ **yesukʷli, yesukli** – Jesus Christ.

Christine **klistin** – Christine

Christmas **nwel** – Noel; Christmas.
nwel sx̣lx̣alts – Christmas day.

syew̓smskʷkʷ?ec – midnight.

sčačacełp – tree decorations. *lit. things hung up on a tree.*

yalełp – wreath.

sčuxʷuxʷełp – garland. *lit. boughs tied together.*

church **snčáwmn** – place to pray; church. *rt.:* ***čaw*** *– pray; prefix:* ***sn...*** *– a place of; suffix:* ***...min, ...mn*** *– instrument/tool*

cider **aplsetkʷ** – cider; apple juice.

cigarette **sčṗl̓ṗl̓k̓ʷiċe?**, *sčṗl̓ṗl̓k̓ʷi* – cigarette. *rt.:* ***ṗulk̓ʷ*** *– fold.*

čṗl̓k̓ʷiċe? – roll a cigarette.
čṗl̓k̓ʷiċ?em – S/he rolled a cigarette. **čn čṗl̓k̓ʷiċ?em, kʷ čṗl̓k̓ʷiċ?em**
es čṗl̓k̓ʷiċe?i – S/he is rolling a cigarette. **čnes čṗl̓k̓ʷiċe?i, kʷes čṗl̓k̓ʷiċe?i**

smenxʷ – something that is smoked.
nłéptmn ismenxʷ u inčpáx̣mn – I forgot my cigarettes and matches.

cinch **k̓ʷłx̣ṗenč**, *k̓ʷłx̣ṗe* – cinch.

circle **syal** – circle.
i yal – It is round.

yalpósqn, *yalpó* – rounded lips. *See:* ***lips.***

yalk̓ʷ – bend/make into a circular shape.
yalk̓ʷmncut – It formed a circle of itself; *i.e., a snake.*
yalk̓ʷmncutš – Make a circle of yourself. *cmd.*

yalk̓ʷmcutist – S/he made a circle. **čn yalk̓ʷmcutist, kʷ yalk̓ʷmcutist**
es yalk̓ʷmcutisti – S/he is making a circle. **čnes yalk̓ʷmcutisti, kʷes yalk̓ʷmcutisti**
qs yalk̓ʷmcutisti – S/he is going to make a circle. **čiqs yalk̓ʷmcutisti, kʷqs yalk̓ʷmcutisti**

yalk̓ʷntés – S/he/it circled it. **yalk̓ʷntén, yalk̓ʷntéxʷ**
es yalk̓ʷúms – S/he/it is circling it. **ies yalk̓ʷúm, as yalk̓ʷúm**
qs yalk̓ʷúms – S/he/it is circling it. **iqs yalk̓ʷúm, aqs yalk̓ʷúm**
yalk̓ʷntéʔes – They circled it. **qeʔ yalk̓ʷntem, yalk̓ʷntep**
es yalk̓ʷúʔums – They are circling it. **qeʔes yalk̓ʷúm, es yalk̓ʷúmp**
qs yalk̓ʷúʔums – They are going to circle it. **qeʔqs yalk̓ʷúm, qs yalk̓ʷúmp**

yalk̓ʷmcutš – Circle (s.t.). *cmd.*
yalk̓ʷúnt – Circle it. *cmd.*
nyalk̓ʷúnt – Put inside the circle. *cmd.*

čiyálk̓ʷ – wrap/circle something with something.
es čiyálk̓ʷms – S/he/it is circling it with s.t. **ies čiyálk̓ʷm, as čiyálk̓ʷm**
čiyalk̓ʷúnt – Circle it with s.t. *(i.e., a rope).*
čiyalk̓ʷic̓éʔ – It is wrapped/circled. *suffix:* ***...ic̓éʔ*** *– covered in.*
čiyalk̓ʷic̓ʔént – Wrap/circle it. *cmd.*

t swe u yalk̓ʷntés – Who circled it? **t swe u čiyalk̓ʷntés** – Who circled it with something?

šlič – go round; turn on an axis; go in a circular course; rotate 360 degrees. *See:* ***around.***

The **i** following uvular consonants (UC) and the glottal stop **ʔ** sound like English "*ey*" as in the words *they, hey, whey,* etc. Salish UC are: **q, q̓, qʷ, q̓ʷ, x̣, x̣ʷ**. For example, the suffix **...qin** – head/top, is often spelled using English *ey* as "q*ey*n". So **qi, q̓i, qʷi, q̓ʷi, x̣i, x̣ʷi**, may be spelled with English *ey* as **q***ey*, **q̓***ey*, **qʷ***ey*, **q̓ʷ***ey*, **x̣***ey*, **x̣ʷ***ey* in other texts.

clam

čk̓ʷlk̓ʷllča – clam; *Sphaeriidae pisidium.*

skʷk̓ʷl̓áneʔ – western pearlshell; oyster; *Margaritifera falcata.*

clap hands

nt̓qʷt̓qʷčn̓ečst – clap hands. *suffix:* ***...ečst, ...čst*** *– of the hand.*
nt̓qʷt̓qʷčn̓ečstm – S/he clapped. **čn nt̓qʷt̓qʷčn̓ečstm, kʷ nt̓qʷt̓qʷčn̓ečstm**
es nt̓qʷt̓qʷčn̓ečsti – S/he is clapping. **čnes nt̓qʷt̓qʷčn̓ečsti, kʷes nt̓qʷt̓qʷčn̓ečsti**
qs nt̓qʷt̓qʷčn̓ečsti – S/he is going to clap. **čiqs nt̓qʷt̓qʷčn̓ečsti, kʷqs nt̓qʷt̓qʷčn̓ečsti**

nt̓qʷt̓qʷčn̓ečstis – S/he clapped s.o.'s hands. **nt̓qʷt̓qʷčn̓ečstn, nt̓qʷt̓qʷčn̓ečstntxʷ**
es nt̓qʷt̓qʷčn̓ečstms – S/he is clapping s.o.'s hands. **ies nt̓qʷt̓qʷčn̓ečstm, as nt̓qʷt̓qʷčn̓ečstm**
qs nt̓qʷt̓qʷčn̓ečstms – S/he is going to clap s.o.'s hands. **iqs nt̓qʷt̓qʷčn̓ečstm, aqs nt̓qʷt̓qʷčn̓ečstm**

nt̓qʷt̓qʷečstniš – Clap. *cmd.*
nt̓qʷt̓qʷečstnt – Clap s.o.'s hands. *cmd.*

qʷo nkʷłnt̓qʷt̓qʷéčsnt – Clap with me. **nt̓qʷt̓qʷečstniš ecx̣i t qʷoyʔe** – Clap like me.

Clara

kloli – Clara; Clarice; Gloria. *(approximation to English)*

Clarice

kloli – Clara, Clarice, Gloria. *(approximation to English)*

Clark Fork River

nmesulétkʷ, *nmesulé* – Clark Fork River, western Montana; *also thought to be the origin of the name Missoula.*

nskʷaʔstétkʷ – Clark Fork River.

Clark's nutcracker

snalqʷ – nutcracker; Clark's nutcracker; *Nucifraga columbiana.*

claw

q̓ʷx̣ʷqinšn, *q̓ʷx̣ʷqi* – toenail; claws. **q̓ʷx̣ʷq̓ʷx̣ʷqinšn** *pl.*

ususšnaqinšn – long claws.

clay

sčiłt – white clay.
l šeý u še txʷtíʔixʷm t sčiłt łu t sq̓sip – That's where they used to get white clay long ago.

s.t. - something, the 3rd person
(s.t.) - something implied
s.o. - someone, the 3rd person
sl. - singular form
pl. - plural form
rt. - root word
cmd. - command
lit. - literally
fig. - figuratively
i.e., - for example
See: - Redirection to a related word.

tixʷm – pick/get a plant object or clay. *See: pick.*

clean

xʷuk̓ʷ – clean; clear out/off; make tidy.

xʷk̓ʷum – S/he got clean. **čn xʷk̓ʷum, kʷ xʷk̓ʷum**
es xʷk̓ʷmi – S/he is getting clean. **čnes xʷk̓ʷmi, kʷes xʷk̓ʷmi**
qs xʷk̓ʷmi – S/he is going to get clean. **čiqs xʷk̓ʷmi, kʷqs xʷk̓ʷmi**

xʷk̓ʷntes – S/he/it cleaned it. **xʷk̓ʷnten, xʷk̓ʷntexʷ**
es xʷk̓ʷums – S/he/it is cleaning it. **ies xʷk̓ʷum, as xʷk̓ʷum**
qs xʷk̓ʷums – S/he/it is going to clean it. **iqs xʷk̓ʷum, aqs xʷk̓ʷum**
xʷk̓ʷntéʔes – They cleaned it. **qeʔ xʷk̓ʷntem, xʷk̓ʷntep**
es xʷk̓ʷúʔums – They are cleaning it. **qeʔes xʷk̓ʷum, es xʷk̓ʷump**
qs xʷk̓ʷúʔums – They are going to clean it. **qeʔqs xʷk̓ʷum, qs xʷk̓ʷump**

xʷk̓ʷpnúis – S/he/it finally got it clean. **xʷk̓ʷpnun, xʷk̓ʷpnuntxʷ**

xʷk̓ʷunt – Clean it. *cmd.*
xʷk̓ʷunti – All of you clean it. *cmd.*
xʷk̓ʷxʷk̓ʷunt – Clean each one/place. *cmd.*
xʷk̓ʷxʷk̓ʷunti – All of you clean each one/place. *cmd.*

i xʷuk̓ʷ – It is clean.

xʷuk̓ʷs – Her/his face is clean. **čn xʷuk̓ʷs, kʷ xʷuk̓ʷs**

čxʷok̓ʷlqʷm – clean wood/pole/log.
nxʷk̓ʷxʷk̓ʷeysm – brush/clean teeth. *See: brush.*

es xʷk̓ʷmi t lukʷ – S/he is cleaning the pole *(peeling bark off)*. **ies xʷk̓ʷum inpus** – I am cleaning my cat. **xʷk̓ʷunt m nc̓éw̓kʷntxʷ asq̓ʷl̓á** – Clean and wash your black tree moss. **čq̓l̓xʷéw̓snt l ascčawálqʷ ṅem i xʷuk̓ʷ** – Throw it over your peeled pole, then it will be clean. **i čxʷók̓ʷlqʷ** – The wood/pole/log is clean.

nxʷk̓ʷaqsm – clean a road.
nxʷk̓ʷaqsm – S/he cleaned a road. **čn nxʷk̓ʷaqsm, kʷ nxʷk̓ʷaqsm**
es nxʷk̓ʷaqsi – S/he is cleaning a road. **čnes nxʷk̓ʷaqsi, kʷes nxʷk̓ʷaqsi**

nxʷk̓ʷaqsis – S/he cleaned the road. **čn nxʷk̓ʷaqsn, kʷ nxʷk̓ʷaqsntxʷ**
es nxʷk̓ʷaqsms – S/he is cleaning the road. **ies nxʷk̓ʷaqsm, as nxʷk̓ʷaqsm**

nxʷk̓ʷaqsnt – Clean the road. *cmd.*

čxʷk̓ʷełpm – clean bark/branches.
čxʷk̓ʷełpm – S/he cleaned bark. **čn čxʷk̓ʷełpm, kʷ čxʷk̓ʷełpm**
es čxʷk̓ʷełpi – S/he is cleaning bark. **čnes čxʷk̓ʷełpi, kʷes čxʷk̓ʷełpi**
qs čxʷk̓ʷełpi – S/he is going to clean bark. **čnqs čxʷk̓ʷełpi, kʷqs čxʷk̓ʷełpi**

čt̓l̓qʷew̓s – gut fish. *See: gut.*

čłc̓sim – sweep/clear the surface. *See: sweep.*

clear

x̣al – clear.
nx̣al – clear water.
i x̣al – It is light.
sx̣lx̣alt – day(light).
łx̣l̓pulexʷ, *łx̣l̓pu* – dawn.

ƛ̓e es x̣lpulexʷi – It is already getting light. **ṅe puti i sx̣al m p eł cxʷixʷuy** – You all come back when it is still light.

i qʷoł – It is hazy/dusty/smokey, not clear.
i qʷłqʷoł t smʔot – It is smokey.
es qʷołmncu – It is a dust storm or blizzard.

wnwinxʷ, *wnwi* – plainly visible; evident; apparent; very clear; obvious. *See:* ***plain.***

ċsim – clear; clear clutter/items/objects.
ċsim – S/he/it cleared. **čn ċsim, kʷ ċsim**
es ċsmi – S/he/it is clearing. **čnes ċsmi, kʷes ċsmi**
qs ċsmi – S/he/it is going to clear. **čiqs ċsmi, kʷqs ċsmi**

ċsntes – S/he/it cleared s.t. **ċsnten, ċsntexʷ**
es ċsims – S/he/it is clearing s.t. **ies ċsim, as ċsim**
qs ċsims – S/he/it is going to clear s.t. **iqs ċsim, aqs ċsim**

ċsiš – Clear. *cmd.*
ċsint – Clear it. *cmd.*
ċsip – disappear; gone; wiped out; cleared out. *See:* ***disappear.***
k̓ʷlċsip – family is wiped out.
čłċsim – sweep/clear the surface. *See:* ***sweep.***

The **i** following uvular consonants (UC) and the glottal stop **ʔ** sound like English "*ey*" as in the words th*ey*, h*ey*, wh*ey*, etc. Salish UC are: **q, q̇, qʷ, q̇ʷ, x̣, x̣ʷ**. For example, the suffix ...**qin** – head/top, is often spelled using English *ey* as "q*ey*n". So **qi, q̇i, qʷi, q̇ʷi, x̣i, x̣ʷi**, may be spelled with English *ey* as **q***ey*, **q̇***ey*, **qʷ***ey*, **q̇ʷ***ey*, **x̣***ey*, **x̣ʷ***ey* in other texts.

Clearwater

čċnpá – Clearwater, Montana.
swipšṅá – Clearwater, Montana.
séwsułkʷ – Clearwater, Montana.

clematis, virgin's bower

čiliyal̓álqʷ, *čiliyal̓á* – orange honeysuckle; *Lonicera ciliosa.*

clever

sisyus – smart; clever; good at something. *See:* ***smart.***
xʷʔit łu sisyus ƛ̓eʔkʷilš – There are lots of smart, powerful medicine men.

px̣páx̣t – smart; clever; have knowledge; have wisdom. *See:* ***smart.***

tam t̓ul̓ – tremendous; outstanding; extreme; excellent. *See:* ***excellent.***

cliff

nšnšnenč – rock cliff; rock bank.

npapaánč, *npapaá* – dirt riverbank; dirt cliff. *See:* ***bank.***

cliff swallow

słṁó, *łṁó* – cliff swallow; *Petrochelidon pyrrhonota.*

climb

čiwlš – climb. *(also used to indicate going upstairs) suffix:* ***...ilš*** *– autonomous.*
čiwlš – S/he/it climbed. **čn čiwlš, kʷ čiwlš**
es čiwlši – S/he/it is climbing. **čnes čiwlši, kʷes čiwlši**
qs čiwlši – S/he/it is going to climb. **čiqs čiwlši, kʷqs čiwlši**
čwíʔiwlš – They climbed. **qeʔ čwiwlš, p čwiwlš**
es čwíʔiwlši – They are climbing. **qeʔes čwiwlši, pes čwiwlši**
qs čwíʔiwlši – They are going to climb. **qeʔqs čwiwlši, pqs čwiwlši**

čiwlšis – S/he/it made s.o. climb. **čiwlšn, čiwlšntxʷ**
es čiwlšms – S/he/it is making s.o. climb. **ies čiwlšm, as čiwlšm**
čwíʔiwlšis – They made s.o. climb. **qeʔ čwíwlšntm, čwíwlšntp**

es łčwiwlši – S/he/it is climbing a little. **čnes łčwiwlši, kʷes łčwiwlši**
es čučiwlši – S/he/it is climbing around. **čnes čučiwlši, kʷes čučiwlši**

s.t. - something, the 3rd person
(s.t.) - something implied
s.o. - someone, the 3rd person
sl. - singular form
pl. - plural form
rt. - root word
cmd. - command
lit. - literally
fig. - figuratively
i.e., - for example
See: - Redirection to a related word.

nčulépm – S/he/it climbed up to a nest. **čn nčulépm, kʷ nčulépm**
es nčulépi – S/he/it climbed up to a nest. **čnes nčulépi, kʷes nčulépi**

snčiwlštn – ladder; stairs. *prefix:* ***sn...*** *– a place of; suffix:* ***...tin, ...tn*** *– means of/device.*
snčučiwlštn – jungle gym. *prefix:* ***sn...*** *– a place of; suffix:* ***...tin, ...tn*** *– means of/device.*
nčučiwlštn – jungle gym; climbing inside. *prefix:* ***n...*** *– inside; suffix:* ***...tin, ...tn*** *– means of/device.*

čiwlš – Climb. *cmd.*
čwiwlšwi – All of you climb. *cmd.*
čiwlšnt – Make him/her climb. *cmd.*

ta kʷ qes čiwlš – Do not climb.

clock

spq̇niʔ – month; moon; sun; clock.

close

łʔem – close in friendship or relationship.
łʔemncutist – S/he got close to (s.o.). **čn łʔemncutist, kʷ łʔemncutist**
es łʔemncutisti – S/he is getting close to (s.o.). **čnes łʔemncutisti, kʷes łʔemncutisti**
qs łʔemncutisti – S/he is going to get close to (s.o.). **čiqs łʔemncutisti, kʷqs łʔemncutisti**

łʔem astéṁils – close to your relatives.

čłeṁncut – get one's self close/next to/against something.
čłeṁncut – S/he got one's self next to it. **čn čłeṁncut, kʷ čłeṁncut**
es čłeṁncuti – S/he is getting one's self next to it. **čnes čłeṁncuti, kʷes čłeṁncuti**
qs čłeṁncuti – S/he is going to get one's self next to it. **čiqs čłeṁncuti, kʷqs čłeṁncuti**

čłeṁncutn – Someone/something that one leans on.

čłeṁncutš – Get yourself next to it.
čłeṁncutwi – All of you get yourselves close to together; bunch up.

isx̣elwi łu inčłeṁncutn – My husband is my support. **ta čn epł čłeṁncutn** – I have no one to lean on; I have no support.

čłałaqmscut – get close/against someone sitting.
čłałaqmscut – S/he got close/against someone sitting. **čn čłałaqmscut, kʷ čłałaqmscut**
es čłałaqmscuti – S/he is getting close/against someone sitting. **čnes čłałaqmscuti, kʷ čłałaqmscuti**

qʷoṁmałq, *qʷoṁma* – get close to doing/finishing something; getting near to some point; close to the end of a journey; winning. *suffix:* ***...ałq*** *– smell, accompaniment.*
qʷoṁmałq – S/he is got close to finishing. **čn qʷoṁmałq, kʷ qʷoṁmałq**
es qʷoṁmałqi – S/he is getting close to finishing. **čnes qʷoṁmałqi, kʷes qʷoṁmałqi**
qs qʷoṁmałqi – S/he is getting close to finishing. **čiqs qʷoṁmałqi, kʷqs qʷoṁmałqi**

qʷoṁmałqis – S/he got close to finishing it. **qʷoṁmałqn, qʷoṁmałqntxʷ**
es qʷoṁmałqms – S/he is getting close to finishing it. **ies qʷoṁmałqm, as qʷoṁmałqm**
qs qʷoṁmałqms – S/he is going to get close to finishing it. **iqs qʷoṁmałqm, aqs qʷoṁmałqm**

qʷoṁmacn – close to ending/finishing a meal.
qʷoṁmasq̇t – close to the end of the day.

ta ies qʷoṁmałqm – I am not even close to finishing it.

k̇ʷłnšṅep – close a hinged door. *rt.:* ***šiṅ*** *– flat cover; circumfix* ***k̇ʷłn...p*** *– opening.*
es k̇ʷłnšṅep – It is closed.

k̇ʷłnšṅépis – S/he closed the door. **k̇ʷłnšṅepn, k̇ʷłnšṅepntxʷ**

es k̓ʷłnšṅepms – S/he is closing the door. **ies k̓ʷłnšṅepm, as k̓ʷłnšṅepm**
qs k̓ʷłnšṅepms – S/he is going to close the door. **iqs k̓ʷłnšṅepm, aqs k̓ʷłnšṅepm**

k̓ʷłnšṅépnt ci k̓ʷłnčmep – Close the door.

k̓ʷál̓čqn – lid, cover. *rt.: k̓ʷel̓č – upturned formed object.*
es k̓ʷál̓čqn – It is closed; it has a lid.

k̓ʷál̓čqis – S/he closed it. **k̓ʷál̓čqn, k̓ʷál̓čqntxʷ**
es k̓ʷál̓čqnms – S/he is closing it. **ies k̓ʷál̓čqnm, as k̓ʷál̓čqnm**
qs k̓ʷál̓čqnms – S/he is going to close it. **iqs k̓ʷál̓čqnm, aqs k̓ʷál̓čqnm**
k̓ʷáʔal̓čqis – They closed it. **qeʔ k̓ʷál̓čqntm, k̓ʷál̓čqntp**
es k̓ʷáʔal̓čqnms – They are closing it. **qeʔes k̓ʷál̓čqnm, es k̓ʷál̓čqnmp**
qs k̓ʷáʔal̓čqnms – They are going to close it. **qeʔqs k̓ʷál̓čqnm, qs k̓ʷál̓čqnmp**

k̓ʷál̓čqniš – Close; put the lid on. *cmd.*
k̓ʷál̓čqnt – Close it; put the lid on it. *cmd.*

k̓ʷál̓čqnt anlepute – Close your bottle. *cmd.*

šṅewṡ – close a book. *rt.: šiṅ – flat cover; suffix: ...éwṡ – in between, middle.*
es šṅewṡ – It is closed.

šṅéwṡis – S/he closed the book. **šṅewṡn, šṅewṡntxʷ**
es šṅewṡms – S/he is closing the book. **ies šṅewṡm, as šṅewṡm**
qs šṅewṡms – S/he is going to close the book. **iqs šṅewṡm, aqs šṅewṡm**

šṅewṡnt – Close it. *cmd.*

šṅewṡnt anččnṗiċéʔ – Close your book.

tukʷ – closed in.
i tukʷ – It is plugged up.
ntukʷpełċeʔ – The inside is plugged up/closed in.

čx̣ssmels, *čx̣ssme* **–** physically affectionate with someone; make out with someone; lucky. *(In the short form this word is also used as an expression for having good luck.) See: **affection**.*

čsax̣m – close to; near. *See: **near**.*

ččʔit – in motion to get close/near someone or something; drawing near. *See: **near**.*

nċipsm – wink; close eye. *See: **wink**.*

> The **i** following uvular consonants (UC) and the glottal stop **ʔ** sound like English "*ey*" as in the words th*ey*, h*ey*, wh*ey*, etc. Salish UC are: **q**, **q̇**, **qʷ**, **q̇ʷ**, **x̣**, **x̣ʷ**. For example, the suffix ...**qin** – head/top, is often spelled using English *ey* as "q*ey*n". So **qi**, **q̇i**, **qʷi**, **q̇ʷi**, **x̣i**, **x̣ʷi**, may be spelled with English *ey* as **q***ey*, **q̇***ey*, **qʷ***ey*, **q̇ʷ***ey*, **x̣***ey*, **x̣ʷ***ey* in other texts.

cloth

łqq̇ẏilxʷ – cloth. *See: **pattern**.*

clothes

x̣cnuṁtn – clothes; thing to get one's self ready.
snx̣cnuṁtn – dresser. *prefix: sn... – a place of; suffix: ...tin, ...tn – means of/device.*

x̣cnuṁtš – Get ready; put your clothes on. *cmd.*
x̣cnuṁt – ready/dressed; put clothes on. *See: **wear**.*

łixʷp – slip/pull/put something fitted over an object. *See: **pull over**.*
nłxʷpncut – dress one's self. *See: **dress**.*
snłxʷpalqstn – clothes.

...alqs – *suffix indicating clothing*, this is in reference to all clothing but can refers to shirt and coat.
x̣salqs – good/beautiful clothing. *prefix: x̣s... – good; suffix: ...lqs, ...alqs – clothes.*
čsalqs – bad/ugly clothing. *prefix: čs... – bad; suffix: ...lqs, ...alqs – clothes.*

> s.t. - something, the 3rd person
> (s.t.) - something implied
> s.o. - someone, the 3rd person
> *sl.* - singular form
> *pl.* - plural form
> *rt.* - root word
> *cmd.* - command
> *lit.* - literally
> *fig.* - figuratively
> *i.e.,* - for example
> *See:* - Redirection to a related word.

suypálqs – white people clothing. *rt.: **suyápi** – white people; suffix: **...lqs, ...alqs** – clothes.*
sot̓lqs – sweater. *rt.: **sut̓** – stretch; suffix: **...lqs, ...alqs** – clothes. lit. stretchy clothes.*
q̓ʷaylqs – black gown; priest. *rt.: **q̓ʷay** – black; suffix: **...lqs, ...alqs** – clothes. lit. black clothes*
mʔamalqs – woman's clothes; dress as a woman; disguised as a woman. *See: **dress**.*

clothes dryer **snčéxʷmn x̣ʷl̓ x̣cnuṁtn** – dryer for clothes.

clothes line **čłqʷeẇstn** – clothes line. *suffix: **...éẇs** – in between, middle.*

čłx̣ʷeẇstn – clothes line. *suffix: **...éẇs** – in between, middle.*

clothes pin **x̣p̓min** – clothes pin.

clothing store **sntumístn l x̣cnuṁtn** – place to buy clothes; clothing store.

cloud **sčtṁip** – clouds.

cloudy **i čtokʷsq̓t,** *i čto* – It is cloudy. *rt.: **tukʷ** – blocked; suffix: **...asq̓t** – sky, day.*
i čtkʷasq̓t – It is clouded over; the whole sky is clouded. *suffix: **...asq̓t** – sky, day.*

čtqpasq̓t, *čtqpa* – clouded over. *rt.: **tqep** – dammed, restricted.*
es čtqpasq̓t – It is clouded over.

i čpaʔsq̓t – It is a clear sky *(no clouds)*. *suffix: **...asq̓t** – sky, day.*

es čsasq̓ti – It is bad weather. *suffix: **...asq̓t** – sky, day.*

club **skʷenlt** – use anything as a club.

čłp̓l̓p̓x̣ʷa – club used by people long ago.

clump **scmalq̓ʷ** – one clump of clay or dirt. *prefix: **sc...** – s.t. that's been done/made/prepared.*
scmlmalq̓ʷ – clumps of clay or dirt. *prefix: **sc...** – s.t. that's been done/made/prepared.*

clumsy **čt̓št̓špšnemn** – clumsy, one inclined to trip. *suffix: **...emn** – one inclined to do.*

coal **ċáx̣ʷċx̣ʷt,** *ċáx̣ʷ* – powdery ashes.

qʷlmin – ash chunks; charcoal. *(used as a teething medicine)*

coast **qʷq̓ʷaancut,** *qʷq̓ʷaancú* – coast, slide. *See: **slide**.*

coat **čłql̓tčalqs,** *čłql̓tča* – coat. *rt.: **qeltč** – meat, body; suffix: **...lqs, ...alqs** – clothes.*
es čql̓tčalqs – S/he is wearing a coat. **čnes čql̓tčalqs, kʷes čql̓tčalqs**

čql̓tčalqsiš – Put your coat on. *cmd.*

lkepu – coat. *(approximation to French word)*
lkepusiš – Put your coat on. *cmd.*

spomlqs – fur coat. *suffix: **...lqs, ...alqs** – clothes.*

sčuptsálqs, *sčuptsá* – hairy coat.

stqyalqs, *stqya* – long coat. *(i.e., a parka)*

nłupax̣nm – put the arm inside. *rt.: **łʔum** – stab; sting. See: **inside**.*

x̣p̓im – layer; line; coat. *See: **layer**.*

coax **tutéẁ –** use gentleness with something; caress something. *See:* ***gentle.***

cocklebur **úˀupupt –** cocklebur; *Xanthium.*

Coeur d'Aléne **sčicwi –** Coeur d'Aléne people. *lit. stay on the point of land where two rivers meet.*

coffee **kapi –** coffee. *(approximation to French word)*
kapists – his/her coffee. **inkapi, ankapi**

ṅcqaus, *ṅcqau* **–** place single object in a fire; cook/make coffee/tea. *rt.:* ***caq*** *– single object placed down; suffix:* ***...us*** *– face, fire. See:* ***place.***
ṅcqau – S/he cooked coffee. **čn ṅcqau, kʷ ṅcqau**
es ṅcqausi – S/he is cooking coffee. **čnes ṅcqausi, kʷes ṅcqausi**
qs ṅcqausi – S/he is going to cook coffee. **čiqs ṅcqausi, kʷqs ṅcqausi**

ṅcqausis – S/he cooked the coffee. **ṅcqausn, ṅcqausntxʷ**
es ṅcqausms – S/he is cooking the coffee. **ies ṅcqausm, as ṅcqausm**
qs ṅcqausms – S/he is going to cook the coffee. **iqs ṅcqausm, aqs ṅcqausm**

čn ṅcqaus t kapi – I cooked coffee.

The **i** following uvular consonants (UC) and the glottal stop **ˀ** sound like English "*ey*" as in the words th*ey*, h*ey*, wh*ey*, etc. Salish UC are: **q, q̇, qʷ, q̇ʷ, x̣, x̣ʷ**. For example, the suffix ...**qin** – head/top, is often spelled using English *ey* as "q*ey*n". So **qi, q̇i, qʷi, q̇ʷi, x̣i, x̣ʷi**, may be spelled with English *ey* as **q***ey*, **q̇***ey*, **qʷ***ey*, **q̇ʷ***ey*, **x̣***ey*, **x̣ʷ***ey* in other texts.

coffee pot **sṅcqaustn,** *sṅcqau* **–** coffee pot. *prefix:* ***sn...*** *– a place of; suffix:* ***...tin, ...tn*** *– means of/device.*

coil **yalim,** *yal* **–** coil up; wrap.
yalim – S/he wrapped. **čn yalim, kʷ yalim**
es yalmi – S/he is wrapping. **čnes yalmi, kʷes yalmi**
qs yalmi – S/he is going to wrap. **čiqs yalmi, kʷqs yalmi**
yalíˀim – They wrapped. **qeˀ yalim, p yalim**
es yalmíˀi – They are wrapping. **qeˀes yalmi, pes yalmi**
qs yalmíˀi – They are going to wrap. **qeˀqs yalmi, pqs yalmi**

yalntes – S/he wrapped s.t. **yalnten, yalntexʷ**
es yalims – S/he is wrapping s.t. **ies yalim, as yalim**
qs yalmi – S/he is going to wrap s.t. **iqs yalim, aqs yalim**
yalntéˀes – They wrapped s.t. **qeˀ yalntem, yalntep**
es yalíˀims – They are wrapping s.t. **qeˀes yalim, es yalimp**
qs yalíˀims – They are going to wrap s.t. **qeˀqs yalim, qs yalimp**

yalil – It got coiled up; wrapped up; tangled.

yalint – Coil it up. *cmd.*
es yal̓mnscuti – It is coiling itself. *(i.e., a caterpillar coiling itself in a cocoon.)*
yalnscut – something you wrap around.

s.t. - something, the 3rd person
(s.t.) - something implied
s.o. - someone, the 3rd person
sl. - singular form
pl. - plural form
rt. - root word
cmd. - command
lit. - literally
fig. - figuratively
i.e., - for example
See: - Redirection to a related word.

coin **sqʷmatye –** coin.
ululim – money.
kʷateˀ – quarter.
nk̓ʷuˀ séns – penny.
cil séns – nickel.
upn séns – dime.

coin purse **snululimtn –** bank *(for money)*, coin purse. *prefix:* ***sn...*** *– a place of; suffix:* ***...tin, ...tn*** *– means of/device.*

coitus **skʷnús –** coitus.

es kʷnúsi – S/he is in the act of coition. **čnes kʷnúsi, kʷes kʷnúsi**

cola **nṫišk̓ʷ** – sweet liquid; pop; Kool-aid.
ċwetiš t nṫišk̓ʷ – Go get a pop.

cold **ċalt** – It is very cold; cold weather.
ċaltm – The weather turned very cold.
es ċalti – The weather is being very cold.

ċalsts – S/he/it made it turn very cold. **ċalstn, ċalstxʷ**
es ċalms – S/he/it is making it turn very cold. **ies ċalm, as ċalm**
qs ċalms – S/he/it is going to make it turn very cold. **iqss ċalm, aqs ċalm**

es ċaltwilši – The weather is becoming very cold. *suffix: **...wilš**– developmental.*

sċalt – the cold.
nċlatkʷ – cold water.

ċalt č čolsqe – It is cold outside.

suẏt – cold, chilled.
es suẏti – S/he/it is cold. **čnes suẏti, kʷes suẏti**
es súˀuẏti – They are cold. **qeˀes suẏti, pes suẏti**

i suẏ – It is chilly.
i łssuẏ – It is a little chilly.

i suẏ č čo – It is chilly outside. **ha kʷes suẏti** – Are you cold? **tam qeˀes sẏuẏti** – We are not cold. **ha es súˀuẏti** – Are they cold? **pes sẏuẏti** – You folks are cold.

ixʷmus – chilled from cold weather; very cold weather. *(time to put **yucmn**(red ochre) on the face)*
ixʷmusm – S/he/it got chilled. **čn ixʷmusm, kʷ ixʷmusm**
es ixʷmusi – S/he/it is chilled/very cold. **čnes ixʷmusi, kʷes ixʷmusi**

čłixʷmusm – S/he/it felt chilly all over. **čn čłixʷmusm, kʷ čłixʷmusm**
es čłixʷmusi – S/he/it is feeling chilly all over. **čnes čłixʷmusi, kʷes čłixʷmusi**

ixʷmusmis – S/he was made very cold by the weather.
es ixʷmusms – S/he is being made very cold by the weather.

sixʷmus – the cold weather; the cold.
čixʷmusm – the North Wind.

suł – froze.
es sulti – S/he/it is freezing. **čnes sulti, kʷes sulti**
es súˀułti – They are freezing. **qeˀes sulti, pes sulti**

es slsulčsti – Her/his hands are freezing/cold. **čnes slsulčsti, kʷes slsulčst**
es slsulšni – Her/his feet are freezing/cold. **čnes slsulšni, kʷes slsulšni**

yo x̣iṅe sult ye čłkʷlkʷlé – This calf might freeze.

qʷós – curly sticking out.
i čqʷosq̓t – it is cold air/sky.
čqʷósqn spq̓niˀ – February *(month of the cold). See: **February**.*

i x̣áˀ – It is cool.

uxʷt – freezing; get frostbite. *See: **frostbite**.*

collapse **mcaq** – collapsed; falls apart. *rt.:* ***caq*** *– single object placed down.*
es mcqmi – It is collapsing.

nmcaq – It fell in on itself.
nmcqus – The fire fell in on itself.

tmim – crumble down/apart. *See:* ***crumble.***

collar **t̓poɫq̓ʷltn** – shirt collar. *rt.:* ***t̓ip*** *– join/add to; suffix:* ***...aɫq̓ʷlt, ...ɫq̓ʷlt*** *– throat*

sq̓l̓psqáx̣eʔtn, *sq̓l̓psqá* – horse collar.

collect **qmin** – put things down; lay things down; place things down. *See:* ***lay.***

y̓amim – gather/collect together. *See:* ***gather.***
scyamin – things that have been collected together.

college **skʷtisnyoʔnuntn** – college; school.

snac̓x̣ɫq̓ey̓mi – college; school.

collide **čtemistmnwéxʷ,** *čtemistmnwé* – bump into each other; collide.

color **sq̓y̓q̓ʔy̓i** – colors; designs.

k̓ʷɫq̓y̓q̓ey̓im – color a picture; color something.
k̓ʷɫq̓y̓q̓ey̓im – S/he colored. **čn k̓ʷɫq̓y̓q̓ey̓im, kʷ k̓ʷɫq̓y̓q̓ey̓im**
es k̓ʷɫq̓y̓q̓ey̓imi – S/he is coloring. **čnes k̓ʷɫq̓y̓q̓ey̓imi, kʷes k̓ʷɫq̓y̓q̓ey̓imi**
qs k̓ʷɫq̓y̓q̓ey̓imi – S/he is going to color. **čiqs k̓ʷɫq̓y̓q̓ey̓imi, kʷqs k̓ʷɫq̓y̓q̓ey̓imi**
k̓ʷɫq̓y̓q̓ey̓íʔim – They colored. **qeʔ k̓ʷɫq̓y̓q̓ey̓im, p k̓ʷɫq̓y̓q̓ey̓im**
es k̓ʷɫq̓y̓q̓ey̓míʔi – They are coloring. **qeʔes k̓ʷɫq̓y̓q̓ey̓imi, pes k̓ʷɫq̓y̓q̓ey̓imi**
qs k̓ʷɫq̓y̓q̓ey̓míʔi – They are going to color. **qeʔqs k̓ʷɫq̓y̓q̓ey̓imi, pqs k̓ʷɫq̓y̓q̓ey̓imi**

k̓ʷɫq̓y̓q̓ey̓ntes – S/he colored it. **k̓ʷɫq̓y̓q̓ey̓nten, k̓ʷɫq̓y̓q̓ey̓ntexʷ**
es k̓ʷɫq̓y̓q̓ey̓ims – S/he is coloring it. **ies k̓ʷɫq̓y̓q̓ey̓im, as k̓ʷɫq̓y̓q̓ey̓im**
qs k̓ʷɫq̓y̓q̓ey̓ims – S/he is going to color it. **iqs k̓ʷɫq̓y̓q̓ey̓im, aqs k̓ʷɫq̓y̓q̓ey̓im**
k̓ʷɫq̓y̓q̓ey̓ntéʔes – They colored it. **qeʔ k̓ʷɫq̓y̓q̓ey̓ntem, k̓ʷɫq̓y̓q̓ey̓ntep**
es k̓ʷɫq̓y̓q̓ey̓íʔims – They are coloring it. **qeʔes k̓ʷɫq̓y̓q̓ey̓im, es k̓ʷɫq̓y̓q̓ey̓imp**
qs k̓ʷɫq̓y̓q̓ey̓íʔims – They are going to color it. **qeʔqs k̓ʷɫq̓y̓q̓ey̓im, qs k̓ʷɫq̓y̓q̓ey̓imp**

k̓ʷɫq̓y̓q̓ey̓iš – Color. *cmd.*
k̓ʷɫq̓y̓q̓ey̓int – Color s.t. *cmd.*

kʷel – change outward perception; change color; ripening/dying. *See:* ***change.***

colt **ɫq̓q̓y̓itš,** *ɫq̓q̓y̓i* – colt.

Columbia Falls **nq̓eyɫkʷm** – Columbia Falls, Montana.

Columbia large-scaled sucker **sl̓aw̓s** – small mouth sucker; Columbia large-scaled sucker; *Catostomus macrocheilus.*

Columbian hawthorn **stm̓óqʷ** – Columbia hawthorn; *Crataegus columbiana.*

Columbian ground squirrel **sisč** – gopher; Columbia ground squirrel; *Spermophilus columbianus.*

The **i** following uvular consonants (UC) and the glottal stop **ʔ** sound like English "*ey*" as in the words th*ey*, h*ey*, wh*ey*, etc. Salish UC are: **q, q̓, qʷ, q̓ʷ, x̣, x̣ʷ**. For example, the suffix **...qin** – head/top, is often spelled using English *ey* as "q*ey*n". So **qi, q̓i, qʷi, q̓ʷi, x̣i, x̣ʷi,** may be spelled with English *ey* as **q***ey*, **q̓***ey*, **qʷ***ey*, **q̓ʷ***ey*, **x̣***ey*, **x̣ʷ***ey* in other texts.

s.t. - something, the 3rd person
(s.t.) - something implied
s.o. - someone, the 3rd person
sl. - singular form
pl. - plural form
rt. - root word
cmd. - command
lit. - literally
fig. - figuratively
i.e., - for example
See: - Redirection to a related word.

Columbia onion **sehč** – onion; Columbia onion; *Allium columbianum;* Geyer's onion; *Allium geyeri.*

Colville people **sxʷyélpetkʷ**, *sxʷye* – Colville.

učnaqin, *učnaqi* – Okanagan. *rt.:* ***wič** – see;*

snq̓a – Southern Okanagan.

snpowilši – San Poil tribe.

smlqmi – Methow tribe.

saáptniša – Nez Perce; southern band.

slapaá – Nez Perce; northern band.

comb **sušmin** – comb.

słušmin – little comb.

łušulexʷtn – hand rake.

ušním – comb something.
ušntés – S/he combed s.t. **ušntén, ušntéxʷ**
es ušníms – S/he is combing s.t. **ies ušním, as ušním**
qs ušníms – S/he is going to comb s.t. **iqs ušním, aqs ušním**
ušntéˀes – They combed s.o.'s hair. **qeˀ ušntém, ušntép**
es ušníˀims – They are combing s.t. **qeˀes ušním, es ušnímmp**
qs ušníˀims – They are going to comb s.t. **qeˀqs ušním, qs ušnímmp**

ušqínm – comb hair on the head. *suffix:* ***...qin, ...qn** – top.*
ušqinm – S/he combed hair. **čn ušqinm, kʷ ušqinm**
es ušqini – S/he is combing hair. **čnes ušqini, kʷes ušqini**
qs ušqini – S/he is going to comb hair. **čiqs ušqini, kʷqs ušqini**
ušqíˀinm – They combed hair. **qeˀ ušqinm, p ušqinm**
es ušqíˀini – They are combing hair. **qeˀes ušqini, pes ušqini**
qs ušqíˀini – They are going to comb hair. **qeˀqs ušqini, pqs ušqini**

ušqis – S/he combed s.o.'s hair. **ušqin, ušqintxʷ**
es ušqinms – S/he is combing s.o.'s hair. **ies ušqinm, as ušqinm**
qs ušqinms – S/he is going to comb s.o.'s hair. **iqs ušqinm, aqs ušqinm**

ušqiniš – Comb your hair. *cmd.*
ušqint – Comb his/her hair. *cmd.*

ušntén inq̓ʷómqn – I combed my hair.

nušepneˀ – comb/brush beard.
nušepneˀ – He combed his beard. **čn nušepneˀ, kʷ nušepneˀ**
es nušepnˀei – He is combing his beard. **čnes nušepnˀei, kʷes nušepnˀei**
qs nušepnˀei – He is going to comb his beard. **čiqs nušepnˀei, kʷqs nušepnˀei**

ušepneˀs – S/he combed s.o.'s beard. **ušepnˀen, ušepnˀentxʷ**
es ušepnˀems – S/he is combing s.o.'s beard. **ies ušepnˀem, as ušepnˀem**
qs ušepnˀems – S/he is going to comb s.o.'s beard. **iqs ušepnˀem, aqs ušepnˀem**

čušepm – comb/brush fur.
čušepis – S/he brushed its fur. **čušepn, čušeptxʷ**
es čušepms – S/he is brushing its fur. **ies čušepm, as čušepm**

qs čušepms – S/he is going to brush its fur. **iqs čušepm, aqs čušepm**

nłṗaw̓sqn – part hair in the middle of the head. *rt.: **łiṗ** – line.*
nłṗaw̓sqnm – S/he parted one's hair. **čn nłṗaw̓sqnm, kʷ nłṗaw̓sqnm**
es nłṗaw̓sqni – S/he is parting one's hair. **čnes nłṗaw̓sqni, kʷes nłṗaw̓sqni**

nłṗaw̓sqis – S/he parted s.o.'s hair. **čn nłṗaw̓sqn, kʷ nłṗaw̓sqntxʷ**
es nłṗaw̓sqni – S/he is parting s.o.'s hair. **čnes nłṗaw̓sqni, kʷes nłṗaw̓sqni**

nłṗaw̓sqniš – Part your hair. *cmd.*
nłṗaw̓sqnt – Part his/her hair. *cmd.*

come

cxʷuy – go in the direction of the speaker; come. *rt.: **xʷuy** – go; prefix: **c...** – indicating toward the speaker.*
cxʷuy – S/he/it came here. **čn cxʷuy, kʷ cxʷuy**
es cxʷuyi – S/he/it is coming here. **čnes cxʷuyi, kʷes cxʷuyi**
qs cxʷuyi – S/he/it is going to come here. **čiqs cxʷuyi, kʷqs cxʷuyi**
cxʷúʔuy – They came. **qeʔ cxʷuy, kʷ cxʷuy**
es cxʷúʔuyi – They are coming. **qeʔes cxʷuyi, pes cxʷuyi**
qs cxʷúʔuyi – They are going to come. **qeʔqs cxʷuyi, pqs cxʷuyi**

es cxʷixʷúʔuyi – Each one is coming. **qeʔes cxʷixʷuyi, pes cxʷixʷuyi**

cxʷuyš – Come here. *cmd.*
cxʷuywi – All of you come here. *cmd.*

xʷuy – go. *See: **go**.*

eł cxʷuy še l sčili – S/he/it came back to Dixon.

cnʔułxʷ – come inside, enter. *sl.*
cnʔułxʷ – S/he/it came inside. **čn cnʔułxʷ, kʷ cnʔułxʷ**
es cnʔułxʷi – S/he/it is coming inside. **čnes cnʔułxʷi, kʷes cnʔułxʷi**
qs cnʔułxʷi – S/he/it is going to come inside. **čiqs cnʔułxʷi, kʷqs cnʔułxʷi**

cnʔułxʷš – Come inside. *cmd.*
nʔułxʷ – go inside; enter. *sl. See: **enter**.*

cnpilš – come inside, enter. *pl. suffix: **...ilš** – autonomous.*
cnpíʔilš – They came inside. **qeʔ cnpilš, p cnpilš**
es cnpíʔilši – They are coming inside. **qeʔes cnpilši, pes cnpilši**
qs cnpíʔilši – They are going to come inside. **qeʔqs cnpilši, pqs cnpilši**

cnpilš – Come in here. *pl. cmd.*
npilš – go inside, enter. *pl. See: **enter**.*

x̣̌e ep sqélixʷ u cnpilš łu uł selíš – There were already people here when the Salish came in.

cʔocqéʔ – come out of something in the direction of the speaker. *sl. prefix: **c...** – indicating toward the speaker.*
cʔocqéʔ – S/he/it came out. **čn cʔocqéʔ, kʷ cʔocqéʔ**
es cʔocqéʔi – S/he/it is coming out. **čnes cʔocqéʔi, kʷes cʔocqéʔi**
qs cʔocqéʔi – S/he/it is going to come out. **čiqs cʔocqéʔi, kʷqs cʔocqéʔi**

cʔocqéʔš – Come out. *cmd.*
cʔocqʔém – bring something out here. *See: **bring**.*
ocqéʔ – go out. *sl. See: **go out**.*

The **i** following uvular consonants (UC) and the glottal stop **ʔ** sound like English "*ey*" as in the words *they, hey, whey*, etc. Salish UC are: **q, q̇, qʷ, q̇ʷ, x̣, x̣ʷ**. For example, the suffix **...qin** – head/top, is often spelled using English *ey* as "q*ey*n". So **qi, q̇i, qʷi, q̇ʷi, x̣i, x̣ʷi**, may be spelled with English *ey* as **q***ey*, **q̇***ey*, **qʷ***ey*, **q̇ʷ***ey*, **x̣***ey*, **x̣ʷ***ey* in other texts.

s.t. - something, the 3rd person
(s.t.) - something implied
s.o. - someone, the 3rd person
sl. - singular form
pl. - plural form
rt. - root word
cmd. - command
lit. - literally
fig. - figuratively
i.e., - for example
See: - Redirection to a related word.

ha ṅem kʷqs cʔocqéʔi – Are you going to come out? **ha ƛ̓e kʷqs cʔocqéʔi –** Are you ready to come outside? **cʔocqéʔ łu mali –** Mary came out. **tas cʔocqéʔ łu mali stṁasts –** Mary's cow did not come out.

cʔoccqeʔ – many come out of something in the direction of the speaker. *pl. prefix:* ***c...*** *– indicating toward the speaker.*
cʔoccqéʔeʔ – They came out. **qeʔ cʔoccqéʔ, p cʔoccqéʔ**
es cʔoccqéʔeʔi – They are coming out. **qeʔes cʔoccqéʔi, pes cʔoccqéʔi**
qs cʔoccqéʔeʔi – They are going to come out. **qeʔqs cʔoccqéʔi, pqs cʔoccqéʔi**

cʔoccqéʔwi – All of you come out. *cmd.*
occqeʔ – more than one go out. *pl. See:* ***go out.***

ci tl̓ʔe cʔoccqéʔi – From right there they came out.

ck̓ʷul̓iš – Come over here to do something. *cmd.*
eł ck̓ʷul̓iš – Come back here to do something. *cmd.*

t̓éʔek̓ʷ – come out of the water.

come down

t̓ipmncut – come down from something high. *(i.e., tree, chair, etc.) rt.:* ***t̓iip*** *– fall.*
t̓ipmncut – S/he/it came down. **čn t̓ipmncut, kʷ t̓ipmncut**
es t̓ipmncuti – S/he/it is coming down. **čnes t̓ipmncuti, kʷes t̓ipmncuti**
qs t̓ipmncuti – S/he/it is going to come down. **čiqs t̓ipmncuti, kʷqs t̓ipmncuti**
t̓ipmncúʔut – They came down. **qeʔ t̓ipmncut, p t̓ipmncut**
es t̓ipmncúʔuti – They are coming down. **qeʔes t̓ipmncuti, pes t̓ipmncuti**
qs t̓ipmncúʔuti – They are going to come down. **qeʔqs t̓ipmncuti, pqs t̓ipmncuti**

t̓ipmncutš – Come down. *cmd.*
ct̓ipmncutš – Come down to me. *cmd. prefix:* ***c...*** *– indicating toward the speaker.*

čn ct̓ipmncu tl̓ es šit̓ – I came down from the tree. **t̓ipmncutš ci tl̓ ṗiṗuyšn –** Get out of that car *(one person).*

t̓oqmncut – Two or more people come down from something high. *(i.e., tree, chair, etc.)*
t̓oqmncúʔut – They came down. **qeʔ t̓oqmncut, p t̓oqmncut**
es t̓oqmncʔuuti – They are coming down. **qeʔes t̓oqmcuti, pes t̓oqmncuti**
qs t̓oqmncúʔuti – They are going to come down. **qeʔqs t̓oqmncuti, pqs t̓oqmncuti**

t̓oqmncutwi – All of you get down. *cmd.*

t̓oqmncutwi ci tl̓ ṗiṗuyšn – All of you get out of that car. *(When there is more than one in car.)*

t̓ipm – take something down from up high. *See:* ***take.***

comfortable

xʷuʔm – get comfortable with someone or something.
xʷuʔmis – S/he got comfortable with s.t./s.o. **xʷuʔmin, xʷuʔmintxʷ**

xʷuʔmnwexʷ – They got comfortable with each other. **qeʔ xʷuʔmnwexʷ, p xʷuʔmnwexʷ**
es xʷuʔmnwexʷi – They are getting comfortable with each other. **qeʔes xʷuʔmnwexʷi, pes xʷuʔmnwexʷi**
es xʷuʔmnwexʷi – They are going to get comfortable with each other. **qeʔqs xʷuʔmnwexʷi, pqs xʷuʔmnwexʷi**

comforter

snq̇ʷomi – comforter; quilt *(stuffed blanket; thick blanket).*

commodities

scpx̣ʷmi – rations; per capita; commodities; pay day. *See:* ***distribute.***

common juniper **ċiqnełp –** common juniper; prickly juniper; *Juniperus communis. rt.:* ***ċiq –*** *prickly; suffix:* ***...ełp, ...łp*** *– tree; floor.*

punłp – Rocky Mountain juniper; *Juniperus scopulorum.*

compact disc **syal člo***ˀ***mintn –** round recording device; compact disc (cd). *suffix:* ***...tin, ...tn*** *– means of/device.*

companion **x̣cut –** partner; share/help in the activities of another; be a comrade; associate as a companion. *See:* ***partner.***

l̓áx̣t – befriend. *See:* ***friend.***

q̇ep – friend/companion to death; someone that will die for one. *See:* ***friend.***

compare **tqʷmew̓s –** compare. *suffix:* ***...éw̓s*** *– in between, middle.*

complete **milk̓ʷ –** complete; whole; all over; all around.
es milk̓ʷ – It is complete, entire.

mlk̓ʷstes – S/he/it made s.t. whole/complete. **mlk̓ʷsten, mlk̓ʷstexʷ**
es mlk̓ʷstes – S/he/it is making s.t. whole/complete. **ies mlk̓ʷsten, as mlk̓ʷstexʷ**
qs mlk̓ʷstes – S/he/it is going to make s.t. whole/complete. **iqs mlk̓ʷsten, aqs mlk̓ʷstexʷ**

mlk̓ʷmulexʷ – all over the place, all over the land.
čmlk̓ʷmasq̇t, *čmlk̓ʷma* **–** all day long. *suffix:* ***...asq̇t*** *– sky, day.*
čmlk̓ʷskʷkʷˀec – all night.
k̓ʷłmilk̓ʷ – whole thing; entire.
mlk̓ʷsqelixʷ – all Indian.
es mlk̓ʷmulexʷ – everywhere.

č ušnełxʷ u čmlk̓ʷma čiqs lciˀi – I am going to be at the Longhouse all day. **l es milk̓ʷ u čt̓pt̓pyew̓t łu qʷqʷċw̓é –** Chipmunks were standing all over. **čmlk̓ʷma čnes ċuˀċa yetłx̣ʷá –** I was swimming all day today. **čmlk̓ʷma u čn sp̓sqé l sqélixʷ –** All day long I was hitting people. **i t milk̓ʷ u čnes ƛ̓emi –** I am looking all around.

es wiˀ – something complete.

...nu... – *transitive suffix indicating something was completed; indicating there was a progression up to the point of completion.*
šƛ̓pnunm – defeat someone. *See:* ***defeat.***
k̓ʷl̓nunm – finally finish making; accomplish something. *See:* ***accomplish.***

qʷoṁmałq, *qʷoṁma* **–** get close to doing/finishing something; getting near to some point; close to the end of a journey; winning. *See:* ***close.***

Complex **x̣ʷiˀilqsa l sqlixʷłˀilmi –** Tribal headquarters in Pablo, Flathead Nation.

computer **snłk̓ʷłk̓ʷłsncutn –** computer; tool with memory. *prefix:* ***sn...*** *– a place of; suffix:* ***...tin, ...tn*** *– means of/device.*
ha kʷ ṅe u čtemmn asnłk̓ʷłk̓ʷłsncutn – Can I use your computer? **člˀont asnłk̓ʷłk̓ʷłsncutn –** Turn on our computer.

k̓ʷékʷt̓neˀ – deer mouse; mouse; computer mouse.
sṅq̇eẏmintn – keyboard.

sck̓ʷl̓łsċṁqin – computer. *lit. made brain. prefix:* ***sck̓ʷl̓...*** *– s.t. that's been made.*

The **i** following uvular consonants (UC) and the glottal stop **ˀ** sound like English "*ey*" as in the words *they, hey, whey*, etc. Salish UC are: **q, q̇, qʷ, q̇ʷ, x̣, x̣ʷ**. For example, the suffix **...qin** – head/top, is often spelled using English *ey* as "q*ey*n". So **qi, q̇i, qʷi, q̇ʷi, x̣i, x̣ʷi**, may be spelled with English *ey* as **q***ey*, **q̇***ey*, **qʷ***ey*, **q̇ʷ***ey*, **x̣***ey*, **x̣ʷ***ey* in other texts.

s.t. - something, the 3rd person
(s.t.) - something implied
s.o. - someone, the 3rd person
sl. - singular form
pl. - plural form
rt. - root word
cmd. - command
lit. - literally
fig. - figuratively
i.e., - for example
See: - Redirection to a related word.

conceal **yelxʷ –** conceal; spread to cover; veil.
yelxʷm – S/he concealed (s.t.). **čn yelxʷm, kʷ yelxʷm**
es yelxʷi – S/he is concealing (s.t.). **čnes yelxʷi, kʷes yelxʷi**
qs yelxʷi – S/he is going to conceal (s.t.). **čiqs yelxʷi, kʷqs yelxʷi**

yelxʷis – S/he concealed s.t. **yelxʷn, yelxʷntxʷ**
es yelxʷms – S/he is concealing s.t. **ies yelxʷm, as yelxʷm**
qs yelxʷms – S/he is going to conceal s.t. **iqs yelxʷm, aqs yelxʷm**

nilxʷustn – veil; curtain.
čiyálxʷqn, *číya* **–** head wrap; scarf. *rt.:* ***yelxʷ*** *– conceal*

conceited **q̇xʷnscut –** conceited; proud of one's self.
q̇xʷnscut – S/he was being conceited. **čn q̇xʷnscut, kʷ q̇xʷnscut**
es q̇xʷnscuti – S/he is being conceited. **čnes q̇xʷnscuti, kʷes q̇xʷnscuti**
qs q̇xʷnscuti – S/he is going to be conceited. **čiqs q̇xʷnscuti, kʷqs q̇xʷnscuti**

q̇exʷ – proud; admire. *See:* ***proud.***
q̇xʷq̇exʷt, *q̇xʷq̇e* **–** proud; vain; think much of; stuck-up. *See:* ***stuck-up.***
q̇exʷmscut – show-off; snobby; arrogant; self admiring. *See:* ***show-off.***

kʷtnlsmist – think highly of one's self; think big of one's self; self-conceited. *See:* ***proud.***

ac̓x̣mscut, *ac̓x̣mscú* **–** conceited; always looking at one's self. *See:* ***show-off.***

condiments **čtxʷcin –** add something to food. *(i.e., mustard, ketchup, etc.) suffix:* ***...cin, ...cn*** *– action of the mouth.*

condom **łxʷpustn –** condom. *rt.:* ***łixʷp*** *– slip/pull over.*
łxʷpusis – S/he put the condom on. **łxʷpusn, łxʷpusntxʷ**

łxʷpusnt – Put the condom on. *cmd.*

cone **sčč̓ic̓éʔ –** pine cone; tree cone.

confess **nmipmist –** tell on one's self; confess. *rt.:* ***nmipa*** *– tattle; suffix:* ***...ist*** *– action to the self*
nmipmist – S/he confessed. **čn nmipmist, kʷ nmipmist**
es nmipmisti – S/he is confessing. **čnes nmipmisti, kʷes nmipmisti**
qs nmipmisti – S/he is going to confess. **čiqs nmipmisti, kʷqs nmipmisti**
nmipmíʔist – They confessed. **qeʔ nmipmist, p nmipmist**
es nmipmíʔisti – They are confessing. **qeʔes nmipmisti, pes nmipmisti**
qs nmipmíʔisti – They are going to confess. **qeʔqs nmipmisti, pqs nmipmisti**

es nmimipmisti – S/he is repeatedly confessing. **čnes nmimipmisti, kʷes nmimipmisti**

es nmimipnwexʷi – They are telling on each other. **qeʔes nmimipnwexʷi, pes nmimipnwexʷi**

confident **muscn –** speak with hope and confidence.
muscnm – S/he spoke with confidence. **čn muscnm, kʷ muscnm**
es muscni – S/he is speaking with confidence. **čnes muscni, kʷes muscni**
qs muscni – S/he is going to speak with confidence. **čiqs muscni, kʷqs muscni**

nmusls – hope; confident feelings.

musčst – do one's best with hope of succeeding; do something with confidence.
musčstm – S/he did one's best. **čn musčstm, kʷ musčstm**
es musčsti – S/he is doing one's best. **čnes musčsti, kʷes musčsti**

qs musčsti – S/he is going to do one's best. **čiqs musčsti, kʷqs musčsti**

confirmation

heʔ – expression seeking confirmation/affirmation; similar to "huh?" in English.

x̣se heʔ – It tastes good, does it not? **es ay̓pmi heʔ** – S/he is going fast, right?
qeʔes susti heʔ – We are drinking, right?

confuse

sil̓ – confused; unable to figure something out; mistaken.
sl̓il̓ – S/he/it got confused. **čn sl̓il̓, kʷ sl̓il̓**
es sll̓ṁi – S/he/it is confused. **čnes sll̓ṁi, kʷes sll̓ṁi**
qs sll̓ṁi – S/he/it is going to be confused. **čiqs sll̓ṁi, kʷqs sll̓ṁi**
sl̓íʔil̓ – They got confused. **qeʔ sl̓il̓, p sl̓il̓**
es sll̓ṁíʔi – They are confused. **qeʔes sll̓ṁi, pes sll̓ṁi**
qs sll̓ṁíʔi – They are going to be confused. **qeʔqs sll̓ṁi, pqs sll̓ṁi**

sll̓mis – S/he is confused about s.t. **sll̓min, sll̓mintxʷ**
es sll̓minms – S/he is confused about s.t. **ies sll̓minm, as sll̓minm**
qs sll̓minms – S/he is going to be confused about s.t. **iqs sll̓minm, aqs sll̓minm**
sll̓míʔis – They are confused about s.t. **qeʔ sll̓mintm, sll̓mintp**
es sll̓míʔinms – They are confused about s.t. **qeʔes sll̓minm, es sll̓minmp**
qs sll̓míʔinms – They are going to be confused about s.t. **qeʔqs sll̓minm, qs sll̓minmp**

sl̓mstes – S/he made s.o. confused. **sl̓msten, sl̓mstexʷ**
es sl̓ims – S/he is making s.o. confused. **ies sl̓im, as sl̓im**
qs sl̓ims – S/he is going to make s.o. confused. **iqs sl̓im, aqs sl̓im**

sl̓ip – S/he/it got puzzled. **čn sl̓ip, kʷ sl̓ip**

sl̓ppnuis – S/he/it finally got confused by s.t./s.o. **sl̓ppnun, sl̓ppnuntxʷ**

sl̓lusis – S/he could not figure out s.o.'s face. **sl̓lusn, sl̓lusntxʷ**

nsl̓sl̓mtumš – confused about people; mixing up people.
sl̓lpcin – confused about what to say. *See: **tongue tied**.*
sl̓lpcan – make a mistake talking; mix up words. *See: **tongue tied**.*
čsl̓lpečst – make a mistake in working. *See: **mistake**.*

con man

qʷl̓qʷl̓mul, *qʷl̓qʷl̓mu* – cheater; con man. *suffix: **...lmul** – one that habitually does.*

connect

nlolosewṡ – connect things together; fit things inside to connect. *(i.e., connector blocks, building block toys, etc.) rt.: **nloʔ** – put inside; suffix: **...éwṡ** – in between, middle.*
nlolosééwṡsis – S/he connected it together. **nlolosééwṡsn, nlolosééwṡsntxʷ**
es nlolosééwṡsms – S/he is connecting it together. **ies nlolosééwṡsm, as nlolosééwṡsm**
qs nlolosééwṡsms – S/he is going to connect it together. **iqs nlolosééwṡsm, aqs nlolosééwṡsm**

es nlolosééwṡ – things are connected together.

nlolosewṡsnt – Connect it together *(to fit it inside the other). cmd.*

ṫip – join to make longer; fasten to make longer. (*i.e., sewing, fastening, etc.)* *See: **join**.*

nṫpséĺis – join things together; fasten things together. *See: **join**.*

nacséĺis – join/tie two things together. *See: **splice**.*

ax̣mewṡ – splice something together; weave ends together. *See: **splice**.*

The **i** following uvular consonants (UC) and the glottal stop **ʔ** sound like English "*ey*" as in the words *they, hey, whey*, etc. Salish UC are: **q, q̓, qʷ, q̓ʷ, x̣, x̣ʷ**. For example, the suffix ...**qin** – head/top, is often spelled using English *ey* as "q*ey*n". So **qi, q̓i, qʷi, q̓ʷi, x̣i, x̣ʷi**, may be spelled with English *ey* as **q***ey*, **q̓***ey*, **qʷ***ey*, **q̓ʷ***ey*, **x̣***ey*, **x̣ʷ***ey* in other texts.

s.t. - something, the 3rd person
(s.t.) - something implied
s.o. - someone, the 3rd person
sl. - singular form
pl. - plural form
rt. - root word
cmd. - command
lit. - literally
fig. - figuratively
i.e., - for example
See: - Redirection to a related word.

connector
nacselistn – connectors; putting things together.

scnlolosewʼs – connectors; things that fit inside each other. *suffix: **...éẃs–** in between, middle.*

scnt̓psewʼs – connectors; things that fit together end to end. *suffix: **...éẃs–** in between, middle.*

Conner
epł msáwiˀ – Conner, Montana.

consent
šeẏ – that in general; there, confirming/concurring; yes, concurring.

ta kʷeṁt łu ƛ̓e qʷo šiẏélsmntm – No, she has already accepted me.

console
łem – console someone.

łemm – S/he consoled (s.o.). **čn łemm, kʷ łemm**
es łemmi – S/he is consoling (s.o.). **čnes łemmi, kʷes łemmi**
qs łemmi – S/he is going to console (s.o.). **čiqs łemmi, kʷqs łemmi**

nłmelsts – S/he consoled s.o. **nłmelstn, nłmelstxʷ**
es nłmelsms – S/he is consoling s.o. **čnes nłmelsm, kʷes nłmelsm**
qs nłmelsms – S/he is going to console s.o. **čiqs nłmelsm, kʷqs nłmelsm**

nłmelskʷ – Console him/her. *cmd.*

constantly
iqʷeṁtm – constantly; forever; without interruption; persevere.

iqʷeṁtmsts – S/he/it persevered s.t. **iqʷeṁtmstn, iqʷeṁtmstxʷ**
es iqʷeṁtms – S/he/it are persevering s.t. **ies iqʷeṁtm, as iqʷeṁtm**

čiqʷṁtečsis – S/he/it finished(killed) s.o. with one blow. **čiqʷṁtečsn, čiqʷṁtečsntxʷ**
qs čiqʷṁtečstms – S/he/it is going to finish s.o. with one blow. **iqs čiqʷṁtečstm, aqs čiqʷṁtečstm**

iqʷeṁtmskʷ – Persevere it. *cmd.*

iqʷeṁtm u ƛ̓lil – S/he/it died for good. **iqʷeṁtmskʷ łu sˀitš** – Sleep without interruption.
iqʷeṁtmstn łu sċaál – I persevered the pain.

constipated
nċopups – constipated.

nċopups – S/he was constipated. **čn nċopups, kʷ nċopups**
es nċopupsi – S/he is being constipated. **čnes nċopupsi, kʷes nċopupsi**
qs nċopupsi – S/he is going to be constipated. **čiqs nċopupsi, kʷqs nċopupsi**

es nċopups – S/he is constipated. **čnes nċopups, kʷes nċopups**

q̇xʷpénč – bloated. *suffix: **...enč–** within.*

constricted
i ċim – It is constricted.

k̓ʷłnċmép – constricted opening. *circumfix: **k̓ʷłn...ep–** opening.*
słċṁċṁépšn – cowboy boots. *See: **boot**.*

ċán – tight; fixed in place; constricted; well fastened. *See: **tight**.*

consume
ċsip – disappear; gone; wiped out; cleared out. *See: **disappear**.*

ċsċspmi – It is disappearing.

iłn – eat, of an individual. *See: **eat**.*

contact lens
sčloˀloˀs – contact lenses.

es čloˀloˀs – S/he is wearing contact lenses. **čnes čloˀloˀs, kʷes čloˀloˀs**

content
nqimls – calm; content; relaxed. *See: **calm**.*

qmqeṁt – S/he is at peace/content. *See: **calm**.*

contract
qin – contract; shrink; cripple.

qnin – It contracted/shrunk.

qnečst – contracted/crippled hand. *(i.e., from arthritis, etc.)*
qnqnečst – contracted/crippled hands.
qnnečst – His/her hand contracted. **čn qnnečst, kʷ qnnečst**
qnqnqinčst – contracted/crippled fingers.
qnax̣n – contracted/crippled arm.
qnesšn – contracted/crippled foot.

control
ṗičmłls – controlling; get the best of.
ṗičmsts – S/he got the best of s.o./s.t. **ṗičmstn, ṗičmstxʷ**
es ṗičmmstms – S/he is getting the best of s.o./s.t. **ies ṗičmmstm, as ṗičmmstm**
qs ṗičmmstms – S/he is going to get the best of s.o./s.t. **iqs ṗičmmstm, aqs ṗičmmstm**

ṗičmłls t scaal – Sickness got the best of him/her.

čiépleʔ – control. *suffix: **...épleʔ** – permanence.*

cook
k̇ʷl̇sncut, *k̇ʷl̇sncu* **–** cook; prepare food.
k̇ʷl̇sncut – S/he cooked. **čn k̇ʷl̇sncut, kʷ k̇ʷl̇sncut**
es k̇ʷl̇sncuti – S/he is cooking. **čnes k̇ʷl̇sncuti, kʷes k̇ʷl̇sncuti**
qs k̇ʷl̇sncuti – S/he is going to cook. **čiqs k̇ʷl̇sncuti, kʷqs k̇ʷl̇sncuti**
k̇ʷl̇sncúʔut – They cooked. **qeʔ k̇ʷl̇sncut, p k̇ʷl̇sncut**
es k̇ʷl̇sncúʔuti – They are cooking. **qeʔes k̇ʷl̇sncuti, pes k̇ʷl̇sncuti**
qs k̇ʷl̇sncúʔuti – They are going to cook. **qeʔqs k̇ʷl̇sncuti, pqs k̇ʷl̇sncuti**

sxʷk̇ʷl̇sncutn, *sxʷk̇ʷl̇sncu* **–** cook; someone tasked to prepare food. *prefix: **sxʷ...** – one tasked to do.*

k̇ʷl̇sncutš – Cook. *cmd.*
k̇ʷl̇sncutwi – All of you cook. *cmd.*

ṅe kʷqs k̇ʷl̇sncut m nṫpusnt – When you are going to cook, boil it.

q̇ʷlexʷs, *q̇ʷle* **–** cooking on a fire or in hot ashes.
q̇ʷlexʷs – S/he cooked by fire. **čn q̇ʷlexʷs, kʷ q̇ʷlexʷs**
es q̇ʷlexʷsi – S/he is cooking by fire. **čnes q̇ʷlexʷsi, kʷes q̇ʷlexʷsi**
qs q̇ʷlexʷsi – S/he is going to cook by fire. **čiqs q̇ʷlexʷsi, kʷqs q̇ʷlexʷsi**

nṫpus, *nṫpu* **–** cook something by boiling. *See: **boil**.*

qʷl̇ep – bake underground; pit bake. *See: **bake**.*

ċáx̣m, *ċá* **–** fry something. *See: **fry**.*

acqʷ – roast something. *See: **roast**.*

cqaẏé – dry/smoke meat over a fire. *See: **dry meat**.*

ṗiqém – make done; ready; ripen. *See: **done**.*

nqʷl̇púlexʷm – make bread. *See: **bread**.*

nłċx̣ċax̣lexʷ – make donuts. *See: **donut**.*

nṗéčlexʷm – make bannock bread. *See: **bannock bread**.*

The **i** following uvular consonants (UC) and the glottal stop ʔ sound like English "*ey*" as in the words *they, hey, whey*, etc. Salish UC are: **q, q̇, qʷ, q̇ʷ, x̣, x̣ʷ**. For example, the suffix **...qin** – head/top, is often spelled using English *ey* as "q*ey*n". So **qi, q̇i, qʷi, q̇ʷi, x̣i, x̣ʷi**, may be spelled with English *ey* as **q***ey*, **q̇***ey*, **qʷ***ey*, **q̇ʷ***ey*, **x̣***ey*, **x̣ʷ***ey* in other texts.

s.t. - something, the 3rd person
(s.t.) - something implied
s.o. - someone, the 3rd person
sl. - singular form
pl. - plural form
rt. - root word
cmd. - command
lit. - literally
fig. - figuratively
i.e., - for example
See: - Redirection to a related word.

čiqs k̓ʷul̓i t scnłl̓ql̓a – I am going to make pancakes. *See: **pancake**.*

cookies **snłcpcuplexʷ** – cookies. *rt.: **łcpcup** – little crumbs; suffix: **...ulexʷ** – land.*

scnłt̓št̓išlexʷ – cookies; little cakes. *prefix: **sc...** – s.t. that's been done/made/prepared.*

cooking pan **snċáx̣mn** – frying pan.

snt̓pustn – cooking pan, boiling pot. *prefix: **sn...** – a place of; suffix: **...tin, ...tn** – means of/device.*

cooking stove **snk̓ʷl̓sncutn** – place to cook; kitchen, range, cooking stove.

cool **x̣aʔ** – cool.
x̣áʔap – It got cool.
es x̣aʔpmi – It is cooling off.
es x̣apulexʷi – a cool breeze is blowing along the ground.

i x̣aʔ č čo – It is cool outside.

nml̓ap – The liquid cooled down. *rt.: **meʔl̓** – be agreeable.*
es nml̓pma – The liquid is cooling down.
qs nml̓pma – The liquid is going to cool down.

nmeʔl̓els, *nmeʔl̓e* – cool off after being angry. *See: **calm**.*

nml̓mel̓čst – act calmly as a child playing with toys. *See: **calm**.*

coot **st̓l̓áqšn** – American coot; mudhen; *Fulica americana.*

łẏé – rail; coot; *Rallus limicola.*

cop car **sxʷnqcqcl̓šaqs,** *sxʷnqcqcl̓ša* – patrol car, cop car. *rt.: **qcqecl̓š** – run around; prefix: **sxʷ...** – one tasked to do.*

copy **q̇ẏus** – copy paper, documents. *rt.: **q̇eẏ** – write, mark; suffix: **...us** – face, fire.*

q̇ẏusis – S/he copied s.t. **q̇ẏusn, q̇ẏusntxʷ**
es q̇ẏusms – S/he is copying s.t. **ies q̇ẏusm, as q̇ẏusm**
qs q̇ẏusms – S/he is going to copy s.t. **iqs q̇ẏusm, aqs q̇ẏusm**

snq̇ẏustn – copy machine.
snq̇ẏq̇ẏus – copies.

q̇ẏusiš – Make copies. *cmd.*
q̇ẏusnt – Copy it. *cmd.*
q̇ẏułnt – Go copy for s.o. *cmd.*

snk̓ʷłq̇ẏq̇eẏmintn – printer. *prefix: **sn...** – a place of; suffix: **...tin, ...tn** – means of/device.*

corn **łkʷlkʷal̓i** – corn. *lit. little yellows.*

corner **sqʷʔeʔ** – corner.
sqʷaqʷʔeʔ – corners.

k̓ʷłqʷʔemstem – corner something.

corral **snk̓ʷłʔox̣ʷsqáx̣eʔtn,** *snk̓ʷłʔox̣ʷsqá* – corral; horse pen. *rt.: **ox̣ʷ** – string out; prefix: **sn...** – a place of; suffix: **...tin, ...tn** – means of/device.*

snk̓ʷłʔox̣ʷelt – playpen; baby corral. *rt.: **ox̣ʷ** – string out; prefix: **sn...** – a place of.*

correct **c̓x̣ʷc̓x̣ʷom** – correct; preach to.
es c̓x̣ʷc̓x̣ʷoms – S/he is correcting s.o. **ies c̓x̣ʷc̓x̣ʷom, as c̓x̣ʷc̓x̣ʷom**
qs c̓x̣ʷc̓x̣ʷoms – S/he is going to correct s.o. **iqs c̓x̣ʷc̓x̣ʷom, aqs c̓x̣ʷc̓x̣ʷom**
es c̓x̣ʷc̓x̣ʷóʔoms – They are correcting s.o. **qeʔes c̓x̣ʷc̓x̣ʷom, es c̓x̣ʷc̓x̣ʷomp**
qs c̓x̣ʷc̓x̣ʷóʔoms – They are going to correct s.o. **qeʔqs c̓x̣ʷc̓x̣ʷom, qs c̓x̣ʷc̓x̣ʷomp**

qes c̓x̣ʷc̓x̣ʷoms – S/he will be correcting s.o. **iqes c̓x̣ʷc̓x̣ʷom, aqes c̓x̣ʷc̓x̣ʷom**
qes c̓x̣ʷc̓x̣ʷóʔoms – They will be correcting s.o. **qeʔqes c̓x̣ʷc̓x̣ʷom**

es c̓x̣ʷc̓x̣ʷɫtu – S/he is correcting/preaching to. **čnes c̓x̣ʷc̓x̣ʷɫtu, kʷes c̓x̣ʷc̓x̣ʷɫtu**
es c̓x̣ʷc̓x̣ʷɫtúʔu – They are correcting/preaching to. **qeʔes c̓x̣ʷc̓x̣ʷɫtu, pes c̓x̣ʷc̓x̣ʷɫtu**

The **i** following uvular consonants (UC) and the glottal stop **ʔ** sound like English "*ey*" as in the words th*ey*, h*ey*, wh*ey*, etc. Salish UC are: **q, q̓, qʷ, q̓ʷ, x̣, x̣ʷ**. For example, the suffix …**qin** – head/top, is often spelled using English *ey* as "q*ey*n". So **qi, q̓i, qʷi, q̓ʷi, x̣i, x̣ʷi**, may be spelled with English *ey* as **q***ey*, **q̓***ey*, **qʷ***ey*, **q̓ʷ***ey*, **x̣***ey*, **x̣ʷ***ey* in other texts.

x̣éʔenim – reprimand; straighten out.
x̣éʔentes – S/he reprimanded s.o. **x̣éʔenten, x̣éʔentexʷ**
es x̣éʔenims – S/he is reprimanding s.o. **ies x̣éʔenim, as x̣éʔenim**
qs x̣éʔenims – S/he is going to reprimand s.o. **iqs x̣éʔenim, aqs x̣éʔenim**
x̣éʔentéʔes – They reprimanded s.o. **qeʔ x̣éʔentem, x̣éʔentep**
es x̣éʔeníʔims – They are reprimanding s.o. **qeʔes x̣éʔenim, es x̣éʔenimp**
qs x̣éʔeníʔims – They are going to reprimand s.o. **qeʔqs x̣éʔenim, qs x̣éʔenimp**

sxʷx̣éʔenɫtu – one tasked to reprimand. *prefix:* ***sxʷ…** – one tasked to do; suffix:* ***…ɫtumš** – of people.*

x̣éʔenel̓t – reprimand children.

kʷ ies x̣éʔenim – I am reprimanding you. **ta es x̣éʔenel̓t** – S/he does not reprimand children. **n̓e ta kʷes x̣éʔenel̓t m kʷ xʷeyt** – If you do not reprimand children you will be in trouble; you will pay later. **qʷo x̣éʔentem** – I was reprimanded.

m̓éy̓eʔ – explain; tell; show; make something known. *See:* ***explain.***

Corvallis **cƛ̓mƛ̓mqi** – Corvallis, Montana.

cost **snʔéys** – cost.

nkʷtnaqs – expensive, costs a large amount.

costive **q̓xʷpénč** – bloat, constipated, costive. *suffix:* ***…enč** – within.*

cottage cheese **scnmlqʷé** – cottage cheese. *prefix:* ***sc…** – s.t. that's been done/made/prepared.*

cottontail **wiw̓slščn, wisšlšn** – cottontail; *Sylvilagus nuttallii.*

cottonwood tree **mulš** – cottonwood; *Populus trichocarpa.* **mlmulš** *pl.*

couch **snčɫay̓ay̓éw̓tn** – couch. *prefix:* ***sn…** – a place of; suffix:* ***…tin, …tn** – means of/device.*

cougar **skʷtismyé** – mountain lion; cougar.

cough **ohóʔ** – cough.
ohóʔ – S/he coughed. **čn ohóʔ, kʷ ohóʔ**
es ohóʔi – S/he is coughing. **čnes ohóʔi, kʷes ohóʔi**
qs ohóʔi – S/he is going to cough. **čiqs ohóʔi, kʷqs ohóʔi**
ohóʔoʔ – They coughed. **qeʔ ohóʔ, p ohóʔ**
es ohóʔoʔi – They are coughing. **qeʔes ohóʔi, pes ohóʔi**
qs ohóʔoʔi – They are going to cough. **qeʔqs ohóʔi, pqs ohóʔi**

s.t. - something, the 3rd person
(s.t.) - something implied
s.o. - someone, the 3rd person
sl. - singular form
pl. - plural form
rt. - root word
cmd. - command
lit. - literally
fig. - figuratively
i.e., - for example
See: - Redirection to a related word.

ta kʷ qes ohóˀ – Do not cough.

nšičsm – cough from choking.
nšičsmntm – S/he/it was made to cough from choking.

Council Grove

člme – Council Grove; west of Missoula, Montana. *(The place where the signing of the Hellgate Treaty in 1855 occurred.)*

count

siyénm – count.
siyénm – S/he counted. **čn siyénm, kʷ siyénm**
es siyéni – S/he is counting. **čnes siyéni, kʷes siyéni**
qs siyéni – S/he is going to count. **čiqs siyéni, kʷqs siyéni**
siyéˀenm – They counted. **qeˀ siyénm, p siyénm**
es siyéˀeni – They are counting. **qeˀes siyéni, pes siyéni**
qs siyéˀeni – They are going to count. **qeˀqs siyéni, pqs siyéni**

siyéis – S/he counted s.t. **siyén, siyéntxʷ**
es siyénms – S/he is counting s.t. **ies siyénm, as siyénm**
qs siyénms – S/he is going to count s.t. **iqs siyénm, aqs siyénm**
siyéˀeis – They counted s.t. **qeˀ siyéntm, siyéntp**
es siyéˀenms – They are counting s.t. **qeˀes siyénm, es siyénmp**
qs siyéˀenms – They are going to count s.t. **qeˀqs siyénm, qs siyénmp**

syeniš – Count. *cmd.*
syént – Count s.t. *cmd.*

siyent č héˀenm – Count to eight. **siyent esyáˀ ci snčłemutn** – Count all the chairs. **ies siyenm inˀululim** – I am counting my money.

čsyenm – count people.
čsyeis – S/he counted people. **čsyen, čsyentxʷ**
es čsyenms – S/he is counting people. **ies čsyenm, as čsyenm**
qs čsyenms – S/he is going to count people. **iqs čsyenm, aqs čsyenm**
čsyéˀeis – They counted people. **qeˀ čsyentm, čsyentp**
es čsyéˀenms – They are counting people. **qeˀes čsyenm, es čsyenmp**
qs čsyéˀenms – They are going to count people. **qeˀqs čsyenm, qs čsyenmp**

ha čsyentxʷ – Did you count the people? **p ies čsyenm** – I am counting all of you. **ha ƛe pes čsyen** – Are all of you counted?

sinásq̓t, *siná* – count days. *See:* ***calendar.***

couple

es čselm – They are two people. *See:* ***people.***
čsel – two people.

nx̣ʷnx̣ʷéw̓s, *nx̣ʷnx̣ʷé* – marry; have a wife. *rt.:* ***nox̣ʷnx̣ʷ*** *– wife; suffix:* ***...éw̓s*** *– in between, middle. lit. coming together with a wife. See:* ***marry.***

nx̣lusew̓s – marry; have a husband. *rt.:* ***sx̣elwi*** *– husband; suffix:* ***...éw̓s*** *– in between, middle. lit. coming together with a husband. See:* ***marry.***

cousin

snkʷsixʷ – cousin; brother; sister. **snkʷsxʷsixʷ** *pl. rt.:* ***sxʷsixʷlt*** *– offspring; prefix:* ***snkʷ...*** *– fellow; member of.*

stmel̓is – relative.

cover

čłxʷépneˀ – cover over something with a pliable object.
čłxʷépnˀeis – S/he covered s.t. **čłxʷépnˀen, čłxʷépnˀentxʷ**

es čłxʷépnʔems – S/he is covering s.t. **ies čłxʷépnʔem, as čłxʷépnʔem**
qs čłxʷépnʔems – S/he is going to cover s.t. **iqs čłxʷépnʔem, aqs čłxʷépnʔem**

es čłxʷépneʔ – It is covered

čłxʷépmn – rug *(a cover).*

čłxʷépnʔent – Cover it. *cmd.*

čłṗnéneʔ – cover something with long objects *(i.e., leaves, sticks, branches). rt.:* ***ṗin*** *– long objects laying; circumfix:* ***čł...eneʔ*** *– cover all over.*
čłṗnenʔeis – S/he covered over s.t. **čłṗnenʔen, čłṗnenʔentxʷ**
es čłṗnenʔems – S/he is covering over s.t. **ies čłṗnenʔem, as čłṗnenʔem**
qs čłṗnenʔems – S/he is going to cover over s.t. **ias čłṗnenʔem, aqs čłṗnenʔem**

čłṗnenʔent – Cover over it. *cmd.*

The **i** following uvular consonants (UC) and the glottal stop **ʔ** sound like English "*ey*" as in the words th*ey*, h*ey*, wh*ey*, etc. Salish UC are: **q**, **q̇**, **qʷ**, **q̇ʷ**, **x̣**, **x̣ʷ**. For example, the suffix …**qin** – head/top, is often spelled using English *ey* as "q*ey*n". So **qi**, **q̇i**, **qʷi**, **q̇ʷi**, **x̣i**, **x̣ʷi**, may be spelled with English *ey* as **q***ey*, **q̇***ey*, **qʷ***ey*, **q̇ʷ***ey*, **x̣***ey*, **x̣ʷ***ey* in other texts.

čłpłqeneʔ – cover something with spread out things. *rt.:* ***płqem*** *– spread/unpack; circumfix:* ***čł...eneʔ*** *– cover all over.*
čłpłqenʔeis – S/he covered s.t. with spread out things. **čłpłqenʔen, čłpłqenʔentxʷ**
es čłpłqenʔems – S/he is covering s.t. with spread out things. **ies čłpłqenʔem, as čłpłqenʔem**
qs čłpłqenʔems – S/he is going cover s.t. with spread out things. **ias čłpłqenʔem, aqs čłpłqenʔem**

čłpłqenʔent – Covering it with spread out things. *cmd.*

čłx̣ceneʔ – fixing the covering of something; cover something; make the bed. *rt.:* ***x̣cim*** *– make ready/orderly; circumfix:* ***čł...eneʔ*** *– cover all over.*
čłx̣cenʔeis – S/he fixed the covering over s.t. **čłx̣cenʔen, čłx̣cenʔentxʷ**
es čłx̣cenʔems – S/he is fixing the covering over s.t. **ies čłx̣cenʔem, as čłx̣cenʔem**
qs čłx̣cenʔems – S/he is going to fix the covering over s.t. **ias čłx̣cenʔem, aqs čłx̣cenʔem**

čłx̣cenʔent – Fix the covering over it. *cmd.*

čłk̇ʷl̓čeneʔ – cover over something with a rigid object. *(i.e., putting a bucket over an object.) circumfix:* ***čł...eneʔ*** *– cover all over.*
čłk̇ʷl̓čenʔeis – S/he covered s.t. **čłk̇ʷl̓čenʔen, čłk̇ʷl̓čenʔentxʷ**
es čłk̇ʷl̓čenʔems – S/he is covering s.t. **ies čłk̇ʷl̓čenʔem, as čłk̇ʷl̓čenʔem**
qs čłk̇ʷl̓čenʔems – S/he is going to cover s.t. **iqs čłk̇ʷl̓čenʔem, aqs čłk̇ʷl̓čenʔem**

es čłk̇ʷl̓čeneʔ – It is covered over.

čłk̇ʷl̓čenʔent – Cover it. *cmd.*

k̇ʷel̓č – turn upside-down a container type object; upturned object. *See:* ***upside-down.***
k̇ʷál̓čqn – lid; cap; cover of a container. *rt.:* ***k̇ʷel̓č*** *– covered over; suffix:* ***...qin, ...qn*** *– top.*
k̇ʷl̓čulexʷ – the area of the sweat. *rt.:* ***k̇ʷel̓č*** *– covered over; suffix:* ***...ulexʷ*** *– land.*
k̇ʷl̓čaw̓qn – covered head.
k̇ʷl̓čapqn – covered head.
čk̇ʷl̓čiċeʔ – soft cover book.

čłlaq̇éneʔ – bury/cover with dirt. *See:* ***bury.***

šiṅ – something upturned is laying down or covering something; something flat against something.
es šiṅ – It is upturned. *(i.e., an upturned plate, etc.)*

čłšneneʔ – cover over something with an upturned object. *circumfix:* ***čł...eneʔ*** *– cover all over.*

s.t. - something, the 3rd person
(s.t.) - something implied
s.o. - someone, the 3rd person
sl. - singular form
pl. - plural form
rt. - root word
cmd. - command
lit. - literally
fig. - figuratively
i.e., - for example
See: - Redirection to a related word.

šneẃsnt – Cover it.

nšnselxʷ, *nšnse* – window. *rt.: **šiṅ** – flat cover; suffix: **...elxʷ**, ...lö – skin/hide.*
čšnšnustn, *čšnšnu* – glasses. *lit. covers the eyes.*

es šnšiṅ asčkʷƛ̓kʷƛ̓us – Your eyes are covered.

ččnṗiċeʔ – hardcover book; book.

čłqtčus – front cover.

čk̓ʷl̓čičṅ – back cover. *suffix: **...ičṅ** – back.*

čcneẃstn – book spine. *suffix: **...éẃs** – in between, middle.*

łixʷp – slip/pull/put something fitted over an object. *See: **pull over**.*

cow

sṫṁa – cow. **sṫṁṁa** – cows. *pl. rt.: **ṫmam** – suck. See: **suck**.*

es ṫmamcni – (The cow) is eating.

sṫṁáltms – buffalo cow.

čususšnelsčn – long horn cow. *rt.: **wisšn** – long; suffix: **...elsčn** – horn.*

snq̇ʷaq̇ʷʔemxʷtn, *snq̇ʷaq̇ʷʔe* – milk cow.

coward

nx̣x̣lemn – one inclined to be scared; coward; scaredy-cat. *suffix: **...emn** – one inclined to do.*

cow elk

snéčłċeʔ, *sné* – cow elk; *Cervus canadensis. See: **elk**.*
snčłċelxʷ – cow elk hide.

cow feet

sṫṁa ucilšn – cow dewclaws/feet.

cow parsnip

xʷtełp, *xʷte* – cow parsnip; *Heracleum lanatum.*

cowry

ṫaṁyócn, *ṫaṁyó* – cowry; snail; leech. *rt.: **ṫam** – lightly suck.*

coyote

snčl̓ép, *snčl̓é* – Coyote; coyote; *Canis latrans.*
spiliye – Coyote. *(Spokane)*
puliaha – Mole; Coyotes' wife. *lit. mole.*
čatnalqs – Coyote's daughter; Horsefly Dress. *suffix: **...lqs, ...alqs** – clothes. lit. horsefly dress or shirt.*
miyołtk̓ʷoṫqn, *miyołtk̓ʷo* – Coyote's first son; knows as he lays his head down.
k̓ʷłṫatłal̓aʔqʷ, *k̓ʷłṫatła* – Coyote's second son; lays down straight under a tree or log.
ṗcalqʷewestšn, *ṗcalqʷe* – Coyote's third son; excrement in the middle crook of his foot.
yelčṅełpaẃastqn, *yelčṅełpaẃa* – Coyote's fourth son.
ċaʔcinšn, *ċaʔci* – Coyote's fifth son; the baby.

nčl̓pscut, *nčl̓pscu* – act as Coyote; foolish. *rt.: **snčl̓ep** – coyote; suffix: **...cut** – action to the self.*
nčl̓pscut – S/he acted like Coyote. **čn nčl̓pscut, kʷ nčl̓pscut**
es nčl̓pscuti – S/he is acting like Coyote. **čnes nčl̓pscuti, kʷes nčl̓pscuti**
qs nčl̓pscuti – S/he is going to act like Coyote. **čiqs nčl̓pscuti, kʷqs nčl̓pscuti**

Coyote wood

snčl̓pálqʷ, *snčl̓pá* – Coyote wood *(thorn bush wood used to make arrows).*

crab

ċoẏx̣é – crab.

crack

sq̇ep – It split naturally; it cracked. *rt.: **saq̇** – split. See: **split**.*

es sq̇pmi – It is cracking.

sq̇pulexʷ – cracked ground.
sq̇skʷetkʷ – cracked ice.
sq̇pqin – cracked head. *suffix:* ***...qin, ...qn** – top.*
nsq̇ew̓s – split in the middle; split in two.
saq̇ – split; parted; cloven. *See:* ***split.***

es til̓ – It is cracked *(of glass).*

crackers

łt̓sa̓s, *łt̓sa̓* – crackers. *rt.:* ***t̓as** – hard; prefix:* ***ł...** – little.*

crack joints

ƛ̓oqʷ – crack a joint. *(i.e. knuckles, wrist, etc.)*
ƛ̓qʷƛ̓oqʷis – S/he cracked the joints. **ƛ̓qʷƛ̓oqʷn, ƛ̓qʷƛ̓oqʷntxʷ**
es ƛ̓qʷƛ̓oqʷms – S/he is cracking the joints. **ies ƛ̓qʷƛ̓oqʷm, as ƛ̓qʷƛ̓oqʷm**
qs ƛ̓qʷƛ̓oqʷms – S/he is going to crack the joints. **iqs ƛ̓qʷƛ̓oqʷm, aqs ƛ̓qʷƛ̓oqʷm**

ƛ̓qʷƛ̓oqʷnt – Crack the joints. *cmd.*
ƛ̓oqʷnt – Crack the joint. *cmd.*

The **i** following uvular consonants (UC) and the glottal stop **ʔ** sound like English "*ey*" as in the words th*ey*, h*ey*, wh*ey*, etc. Salish UC are: **q, q̇, qʷ, q̇ʷ, x̣, x̣ʷ**. For example, the suffix **...qin** – head/top, is often spelled using English *ey* as "q*ey*n". So **qi, q̇i, qʷi, q̇ʷi, x̣i, x̣ʷi**, may be spelled with English *ey* as **q***ey*, **q̇***ey*, **qʷ***ey*, **q̇ʷ***ey*, **x̣***ey*, **x̣ʷ***ey* in other texts.

cracklins

čcix̣mn – cracklins. *(Salish)*

x̣ʷoƛ̓ene – cracklins. *(Pend d'Oreille)*

cradle board

mx̣ʷol̓ – baby board; cradle board.

mx̣ʷsul̓ičn̓ – carry a cradle board on the back. *suffix:* ***...ičn̓** – back.*
es mx̣ʷsul̓ičn̓i – S/he is carrying a cradle board. **čnes mx̣ʷsul̓ičn̓i, kʷes mx̣ʷsul̓ičn̓i**

cramp

es qcim – cramp. *rt.:* ***qcip** – shrink.*

qʷo es qcim – I have a cramp. **es qcmečstm** – S/he has a cramp in the hand. **qʷo es qcšnim** – I have a cramp in my leg.

nc̓kʷełšn – have a cramp in the leg.
nc̓kʷełšn – S/he had a cramped leg. **čn nc̓kʷełšn, kʷ nc̓kʷełšn**
es nc̓kʷełšni – S/he has a cramped leg. **čnes nc̓kʷełšni, kʷes nc̓kʷełšni**
qs nc̓kʷełšni – S/he is going to have a cramped leg. **čiqs nc̓kʷełšni, kʷqs nc̓kʷełšni**

nc̓kʷc̓kʷełšn – S/he has cramps in both legs. **x̣ʷa es nckʷełšni** – Maybe s/he has a leg cramp.

crane

skʷalšin, *skʷalši* – sandhill crane; *Grus canadensis.*

crash

laẏ – sound of a crash; crashing sound.

crave

nełnels, *nełne* – crave food; want to eat. *rt.:* ***iłn** – eat.*
nełnelsm – S/he/it craved food. **čn nełnelsm, kʷ nełnelsm**
es nełnelsi – S/he/it is craving food. **čnes nełnelsi, kʷes nełnelsi**
qs nełnelsi – S/he/it is going to crave food. **čiqs nełnelsi, kʷqs nełnelsi**
nełnéʔelsm – They craved food. **qeʔ nełnelsm, p nełnelsm**
es nełnéʔelsi – They are craving food. **qeʔes nełnelsi, pes nełnelsi**
qs nełnéʔelsi – They are going to crave food. **qeʔqs nełnelsi, pqs nełnelsi**

nełnelsis – S/he/it craved the food. **nełnelsn, nełnelsntxʷ**
es nełnelsms – S/he/it is craving the food. **ies nełnelsm, as nełnelsm**
qs nełnelsms – S/he/it is going to crave the food. **iqs nełnelsm, aqs nełnelsm**
nełnéʔelsis – They craved the food. **qeʔ nełnelsntm, nełnelsntp**

s.t. - something, the 3rd person
(s.t.) - something implied
s.o. - someone, the 3rd person
sl. - singular form
pl. - plural form
rt. - root word
cmd. - command
lit. - literally
fig. - figuratively
i.e., - for example
See: - Redirection to a related word.

es nełnéʔelsms – They are craving the food. **qeʔes nełnelsm, es nełnelsmp**
qs nełnéʔelsms – They are going to crave the food. **qeʔqs nełnelsm, qs nełnelsmp**

t stem̓ u kʷes nełnelsi – What food do you crave? **čnes nełne t swewł –** I am craving fish. **tam čnes nełnelsi –** I am not craving food.

crawl **tiyéš –** crawl.
tiyéš – S/he/it crawled. **čn tiyéš, kʷ tiyéš**
es tiyéši – S/he/it is crawling. **čnes tiyéši, kʷes tiyéši**
qs tiyéši – S/he/it is going to crawl. **čiqs tiyéši, kʷqs tiyéši**
tiyéʔeš – They crawled. **qeʔ tiyéš, p tiyéš**
es tiyéʔeši – They are crawling. **qeʔes tiyéši, pes tiyéši**
qs tiyéʔeši – They are going to crawl. **qeʔqs tiyéši, pqs tiyéši**

čtiyéšmis – S/he/it crawled toward s.t./s.o. **čtiyéšmn, čtiyéšmntxʷ**
es čtiyéšmms – S/he/it is crawling toward s.t./s.o. **ies čtiyéšmm, as čtiyéšmm**
qs čtiyéšmm – S/he/it is going to crawl toward s.t./s.o. **iqs čtiyéšmm, aqs čtiyéšmm**

tišlwis – crawling around.

čtišalqʷ – crawl on a log, railroad track or something long and narrow.

tišulexʷ – bug, a ground crawler.
titišulexʷ – bugs.
ntišulexʷ – crawling under the ground.

tam čnes tiyeši – I was not crawling. **kʷtisi ntiyéš l es nlox̣ʷ –** Big Blanket crawled into a hole. **k̓ʷłtiyéš kʷtisi l p̓ip̓uyšn –** Big Blanket crawled under the car.

crayfish **ċoċiʔx̣é –** crayfish.

crayon **npƛ̓aqstn –** crayon. *rt.:* ***p̓uƛ̓*** *– grease, oil; circumfix:* ***n...aqs*** *– nose, road, pointed.*

crazy **qʷéw –** crazy; drunk.
es qʷéwmi – S/he is being drunk/crazy. **čnes qʷéwmi, kʷes qʷéwmi**

qʷéww – S/he got drunk/crazy. **čn qʷéww, kʷ qʷéww**
es qʷéwwi – S/he is getting drunk/crazy. **čnes qʷéwwi, kʷes qʷéwwi**
qs qʷéwwi – S/he is going to get drunk/crazy. **čiqs qʷéwwi, kʷqs qʷéwwi**

qʷéwis – S/he made s.o. drunk/crazy. **qʷéwn, qʷéwntxʷ**
es qʷéwms – S/he is making s.o. drunk/crazy. **ies qʷéwm, as qʷéwm**
qs qʷéwms – S/he is going to make s.o. drunk/crazy. **iqs qʷéwm, aqs qʷéwm**

es qʷoqʷéwi – S/he is drunk; has altered thinking. **qeʔes qʷoqʷéwi, pes qʷoqʷéwi**
es qʷoqʷéʔewi – They are drunk; have altered thinking. **qeʔes qʷoqʷéwi, pes qʷoqʷéwi**

qʷéwmistmis – S/he got intoxicated with s.t. **qʷéwmistmn, qʷéwmistmntxʷ**
es qʷéwmistms – S/he is getting intoxicated with s.t. **ies qʷéwmistm, as qʷéwmistm**
qs qʷéwmistms – S/he is going to get intoxicated with s.t. **iqs qʷéwmistm, aqs qʷéwmistm**

i qʷéw – S/he/it is crazy. **i čn qʷéw, i kʷ qʷéw**
i qʷqʷéw – S/he/it is a little crazy. **i čn qʷqʷéw, i kʷ qʷqʷéw**

sxʷqʷewm – one tasked to be drunk/crazy; jester. *prefix:* ***sxʷ...*** *– one tasked to do.*
qʷowemn – one inclined to be drunk/crazy; drunkard. *suffix:* ***...emn*** *– one inclined to do.*
qʷéwutn – something that makes drunkenness/crazyness; alcohol. *suffix:* ***...tin, ...tn*** *– means of/device.*
qʷéwncutn – something that one intoxicates one's self with.

qʷaqʷeweʔ – crazy one; little crazy one, affectionately.

qʷéwncut – S/he got one's self intoxicated. **čn qʷéwncut, kʷ qʷéwncut**
es qʷéwncuti – S/he is getting one's self intoxicated. **čnes qʷéwncuti, kʷes qʷéwncuti**

qʷawqʷut – wicked; maddening; unpredictable; intoxicating; vicious.
qʷéwčst – S/he did/made s.t. crazy/funny. **čn qʷéwčst, kʷ qʷéwčst**

čqʷoqʷéwčstmis – S/he did s.t. crazy to s.o./s.t. **čqʷoqʷéwčstmn, čqʷoqʷéwčstmntxʷ**
čqʷoqʷéʔewčstmis – They did s.t. crazy to s.o./s.t. **qeʔ čqʷoqʷéwčstmntm, čqʷoqʷéwčstmntp**

islup m čn qʷéw – At any moment I will go crazy.

qʷoqʷéwlš, *qʷoqʷé* – do something crazy. *suffix:* ***...ilš*** *– autonomous.*
qʷoqʷéwlš – S/he/it did s.t. crazy. **čn qʷoqʷéwlš, kʷ qʷoqʷéwlš**
es qʷoqʷéwlši – S/he/it is doing s.t. crazy. **čnes qʷoqʷéwlši, kʷes qʷoqʷéwlši**
qs qʷoqʷéwlši – S/he/it is going to do s.t. crazy. **čiqs qʷoqʷéwlši, kʷqs qʷoqʷéwlši**
qʷoqʷéʔewlš – They did s.t. crazy. **qeʔ qʷoqʷéwlš, p qʷoqʷéwlš**
es qʷoqʷéʔewlši – They are doing s.t. crazy. **qeʔes qʷoqʷéwlši, pes qʷoqʷéwlši**
qs qʷoqʷéʔewlši – They are going to do s.t. crazy. **qeʔqs qʷoqʷéwlši, pqs qʷoqʷéwlši**

nqʷéwcn – say something crazy; say something insulting to someone. *circumfix:* ***n...cin, cn*** *– action of the mouth.*
nqʷéwcn – S/he said s.t. crazy. **čn nqʷéwcn, kʷ nqʷéwcn**
es nqʷéwcni – S/he is saying s.t. crazy. **čnes nqʷéwcni, kʷes nqʷéwcni**

čqʷéwcnmis – S/he said s.t. crazy to s.o. **čqʷéwcnmn, čqʷéwcnmntxʷ**
es čqʷéwcnms – S/he is saying s.t. crazy to s.o. **ies čqʷéwcnm, as čqʷéwcnm**
qs čqʷéwcnms – S/he is going to say s.t. crazy to s.o. **iqs čqʷéwcnm, aqs čqʷéwcnm**

čqʷoqʷocnmłtumš – speak to the people as fools.

čqʷoqʷéws – crazy/silly eyes. *rt.:* ***qʷeẇ*** *– crazy; circumfix:* ***č...us*** *– spherical object; eyes.*
i čqʷoqʷéws – S/he/it has crazy eyes. **i čn čqʷoqʷéws, i kʷ čqʷoqʷéws**
i čłqʷoqʷéws – S/he/it has little crazy eyes. **i čn čłqʷoqʷéws, i kʷ čłqʷoqʷéws**

qʷqʷiwxʷ – spin one's self until dizzy; *a game played mainly by children. rt.:* ***qʷeẇ*** *– crazy.*
qʷqʷiwxʷ – S/he turned until dizzy. **čn qʷqʷiwxʷ, kʷ qʷqʷiwxʷ**
es qʷqʷiwxʷi – S/he is turning until dizzy. **čnes qʷqʷiwxʷi, kʷes qʷqʷiwxʷi**
qs qʷqʷiwxʷi – S/he is going to turn until dizzy. **čiqs qʷqʷiwxʷi, kʷqs qʷqʷiwxʷi**

čiṁqn – dark in the head; to be crazy.
i čiṁqn – S/he/it is crazy. **i čn čiṁqn, i kʷ čiṁqn**

The **i** following uvular consonants (UC) and the glottal stop **ʔ** sound like English *"ey"* as in the words *they, hey, whey,* etc. Salish UC are: **q, q̇, qʷ, q̇ʷ, x̌, x̌ʷ**. For example, the suffix **...qin** – head/top, is often spelled using English *ey* as "q*ey*n". So **qi, q̇i, qʷi, q̇ʷi, x̌i, x̌ʷi**, may be spelled with English *ey* as **q***ey*, **q̇***ey*, **qʷ***ey*, **q̇ʷ***ey*, **x̌***ey*, **x̌ʷ***ey* in other texts.

cream

sčłťéʔetkʷ – cream.

cream of wheat

spqi – cream of wheat *(hot cereal).*

crease

npʔups – creased pants.
npʔups – S/he has a crease in his/her pants. **čn npʔups, kʷ npʔups**

creator

amotqn – Creator; Sits On Top; president. *rt.:* ***emut*** *– sit; suffix:* ***...qin, ...qn*** *– top.*

k̇ʷl̇ncutn – Creator; Maker of Ways/Mannerisms. *rt.:* ***cuut*** *– one's mannerism; prefix:* ***...k̇ʷl̇*** *– make; suffix:* ***...tin, ...tn*** *– means of/device.*

s.t. - something, the 3rd person
(s.t.) - something implied
s.o. - someone, the 3rd person
sl. - singular form
pl. - plural form
rt. - root word
cmd. - command
lit. - literally
fig. - figuratively
i.e., - for example
See: - Redirection to a related word.

čšyéple? – Creator; Keeper; Protecter. *rt.: **čšťim** – guard; suffix: **...éple?** – permanence.*

čšťncutn – Creator; Protecter. *rt.: **čšťim** – guard; suffix: **...cut** – action to the self.*

Cree

nxʷťu, nxʷťxʷťu – Cree people.

creek

nšiẏétkʷ, *nšiẏé* – creek, stream. *lit. first water. rt.: **š?it** – first; suffix: **...etkʷ, ...tkʷ** – liquid*
nłšiẏétkʷ, *nłšiẏé* – small stream/creek.
nšišiyétkʷ – streams, creeks.

nčłkʷtnetkʷ – big stream/creek.

cricket

silẇéne? – cricket; *Gryllinae.*

sálsl – cricket; *Gryllinae.*

crier

sxʷẇeẇe?m – one tasked to call out. *prefix: **sxʷ...** – one tasked to do.*
łu sxʷẇeẇé?m čłqlšéłxʷ – The crier got on his horse and trotted around the camp.

cripple

tľxʷncut – unable to do anything with one's self; crippled. *rt.: **tľxʷe** – difficult; suffix: **...cut** – action to the self.*
es tľxʷncuti – S/he is crippled. **čnes tľxʷncuti, kʷes tľxʷncuti**

qin – contract; shrink; cripple. *See: **contract.***

crook

sxʷṅaq̇ʷ – thief; crook; one tasked to steal. *rt.: **ṅaq̇ʷ** – steal; prefix: **sxʷ...** – one tasked to do.*
naq̇ʷémn – one inclined to steal; thief. *suffix: **...emn** – one inclined to do.*

crooked

ťiskʷ – crooked; not straight; not aligned.
ťskʷečst – crooked finger. *suffix: **...ečst, ...čst** – of the hand.*
es ťsťiskʷ – zigzag.

čťskʷiċe? – crooked all over.

tkʷmim – bent crooked.
tkʷmstes – S/he bent s.t. crooked. **tkʷmsten, tkʷmstexʷ**
es tkʷmims – S/he is bending s.t. crooked. **ies tkʷmim, as tkʷmim**
qs tkʷmims – S/he is going to bend s.t. crooked. **iqs tkʷmim, aqs tkʷmim**

crop

x̣ʷtim – cut something off. *See: **cut off.***
čx̣ʷtim – cut off; separate from. *See: **cut off.***
čx̣ʷténe? – cropped ear.

k̇ʷóľłq – plant a garden; plant a crop; plant something. *See: **plant.***

cross

eyméẇs – It is crossed. *rt.: **ey** – cross; suffix: **...éẇs** – in between, middle.*
n?eymuseẇs – two lines crossed. *suffix: **...éẇs** – in between, middle.*

n?aymusaqstšnm – cross legs. *rt.: **ey** – cross; suffix: **...aqstšn** – leg.*
n?aymusaqstšnm – S/he crossed his/her legs. **čn n?aymusaqstšnm, kʷ n?aymusaqstšnm**
es n?aymusaqstšni – S/he is crossing his/her legs. **čnes n?aymusaqstšni, kʷes n?aymusaqstšni**

n?aymusaqstšniš – Cross your legs. *cmd.*
n?aymusaqstšnwi – All of you cross your legs. *cmd.*

n?aymusax̣nm – cross arms.
n?aymusax̣nm – S/he crossed his/her arms. **čn n?aymusax̣nm, kʷ n?aymusax̣nm**

nʔaymusax̣niš – Cross your arms. *cmd.*
nʔaymusax̣nwi – All of you cross your arms. *cmd.*
ṅem p nʔaymusax̣nm – You all will have your arms crossed.

es čqqx̣nax̣n – His/her legs are stacked one on the other. **čnes čqqx̣nax̣n, kʷes čqqx̣nax̣n** *See: **stack**.*

es čqqtusaqstšn – His/her legs are stacked one on the other. **čnes čqqtusaqstšn, kʷes čqqtusaqstšn** *See: **stack**.*

> The **i** following uvular consonants (UC) and the glottal stop **ʔ** sound like English "*ey*" as in the words *they*, *hey*, *whey*, etc. Salish UC are: **q**, **q̓**, **qʷ**, **q̓ʷ**, **x̣**, **x̣ʷ**. For example, the suffix **...qin** – head/top, is often spelled using English *ey* as "*qeyn*". So **qi**, **q̓i**, **qʷi**, **q̓ʷi**, **x̣i**, **x̣ʷi**, may be spelled with English *ey* as **q***ey*, **q̓***ey*, **qʷ***ey*, **q̓ʷ***ey*, **x̣***ey*, **x̣ʷ***ey* in other texts.

niʔék̓ʷ – cross water.
niʔék̓ʷ – S/he/it crossed the water. **čn niʔék̓ʷ, kʷ niʔék̓ʷ**
es niʔék̓ʷmi – S/he/it is crossing the water. **čnes niʔék̓ʷmi, kʷes niʔék̓ʷmi**
qs niʔék̓ʷmi – S/he/it is going to cross the water. **čiqs niʔék̓ʷmi, kʷqs niʔék̓ʷmi**
es niʔéʔek̓ʷmi – They are crossing the water. **qeʔes niʔék̓ʷmi, pes niʔék̓ʷmi**

niʔek̓ʷstes – S/he/it ferried s.t./s.o. across the water. **niʔek̓ʷsten, niʔek̓ʷstexʷ**
es niʔék̓ʷms – S/he/it is ferrying s.t./s.o. across the water. **ies niʔék̓ʷm, as niʔék̓ʷm**
qs niʔék̓ʷms – S/he/it is going to ferry s.t./s.o. across the water. **iqs niʔék̓ʷm, aqs niʔék̓ʷm**
niʔek̓ʷstéʔes – They ferried s.t./s.o. across the water. **qeʔ niʔek̓ʷstem, niʔek̓ʷstep**

sniʔek̓ʷtin – water crossing.
niʔek̓ʷtin – ferry; something used to cross water.

niʔek̓ʷskʷ – Take him/her across the water. *cmd.*
niʔek̓ʷɫtumš – ferry people across.
niʔek̓ʷštwexʷ – help one another cross the water.

nx̣ʷcuʔsáqs – cross a road. *circumfix: **n...aqs** – nose, road.*
nx̣ʷcuʔsáqs – S/he/it crossed the road. **čn nx̣ʷcuʔsáqs, kʷ nx̣ʷcuʔsáqs**
es nx̣ʷcuʔsáqsi – S/he/it is crossing the road. **čnes nx̣ʷcuʔsáqsi, kʷes nx̣ʷcuʔsáqsi**
qs nx̣ʷcuʔsáqsi – S/he/it is going to cross the road. **čiqs nx̣ʷcuʔsáqsi, kʷqs nx̣ʷcuʔsáqsi**

nx̣ʷcuʔséẇs – cross to the other side of something. *(i.e., through a stand of trees, through a crowd of people, etc.). suffix: **...éẇs** – in between, middle.*
nx̣ʷcuʔséẇs – S/he/it crossed to the other side. **čn nx̣ʷcuʔséẇs, kʷ nx̣ʷcuʔséẇs**
es nx̣ʷcuʔséẇsi – S/he/it is crossing to the other side. **čnes nx̣ʷcuʔséẇsi, kʷes nx̣ʷcuʔséẇsi**
qs nx̣ʷcuʔséẇsi – S/he/it is going to cross to the other side. **čiqs nx̣ʷcuʔséẇsi, kʷqs nx̣ʷcuʔséẇsi**
nx̣ʷcuʔséʔeẇs – They crossed to the other side. **qeʔ nx̣ʷcuʔséẇs, p nx̣ʷcuʔséẇs**
es nx̣ʷcuʔséʔeẇsi – They are crossing to the other side. **qeʔes nx̣ʷcuʔséẇsi, pes nx̣ʷcuʔséẇsi**
qs nx̣ʷcuʔséʔeẇsi – They are going to cross to the other side. **qeʔqs nx̣ʷcuʔséẇsi, pqs nx̣ʷcuʔséẇsi**

nx̣ʷcuʔséẇsis – S/he/it brought s.t. across. **nx̣ʷcuʔséẇsn, nx̣ʷcuʔséẇsntxʷ**
es nx̣ʷcuʔséẇsms – S/he/it is bringing s.t. across. **ies nx̣ʷcuʔséẇsm, as nx̣ʷcuʔséẇsm**
qs nx̣ʷcuʔséẇsms – S/he/it is going to bring s.t. across. **iqs nx̣ʷcuʔséẇsm, aqs nx̣ʷcuʔséẇsm**
nx̣ʷcuʔséʔeẇs – They brought s.t. across. **qeʔ nx̣ʷcuʔséẇsntm, nx̣ʷcuʔséẇsntp**
es nx̣ʷcuʔséʔeẇsms – They are bringing s.t. across. **qeʔes nx̣ʷcuʔséẇsm, es nx̣ʷcuʔséẇsmp**
qs nx̣ʷcuʔséʔeẇsms – They are going to bring s.t. across. **qeʔqs nx̣ʷcuʔséẇsm, qs nx̣ʷcuʔséẇsmp**

> s.t. - something, the 3rd person
> (s.t.) - something implied
> s.o. - someone, the 3rd person
> *sl.* - singular form
> *pl.* - plural form
> *rt.* - root word
> *cmd.* - command
> *lit.* - literally
> *fig.* - figuratively
> *i.e.,* - for example
> *See:* - Redirection to a related word.

čɫx̣ʷcuʔséẇs – cross to the other side of a plain or any flat land area. *suffix: **...éẇs** – in between, middle.*
čɫx̣ʷcuʔséẇs – S/he/it crossed the plain. **čn čɫx̣ʷcuʔséẇs, kʷ čɫx̣ʷcuʔséẇs**

es **čłx̣ʷcuʔséẇsi** – S/he/it is crossing the plain. **čnes čłx̣ʷcuʔséẇsi, kʷes čłx̣ʷcuʔséẇsi**
qs **čłx̣ʷcuʔséẇsi** – S/he/it is going to cross the plain. **čiqs čłx̣ʷcuʔséẇsi, kʷqs čłx̣ʷcuʔséẇsi**

čłx̣ʷcuʔséẇsis – S/he/it brought s.t. across. **čłx̣ʷcuʔséẇsn, čłx̣ʷcuʔséẇsntxʷ**
es čłx̣ʷcuʔséẇsms – S/he/it is bringing s.t. across. **ies čłx̣ʷcuʔséẇsi, as čłx̣ʷcuʔséẇsi**
qs čłx̣ʷcuʔséẇsms – S/he/it is going to bring s.t. across. **čiqs čłx̣ʷcuʔséẇsi, aqs čłx̣ʷcuʔséẇsi**

čłx̣ʷceẇs – cross over something. *suffix:* ***...éẇs*** *– in between, middle.*
čłx̣ʷceẇs – S/he went over. **čn čłx̣ʷceẇs, kʷ čłx̣ʷceẇs**
es čłx̣ʷceẇsi – S/he is going over. **čnes čłx̣ʷceẇsi, kʷes čłx̣ʷceẇsi**

čłx̣ʷceẇsis – S/he brought s.t. over. **čłx̣ʷceẇsn, čłx̣ʷceẇsntxʷ**
es čłx̣ʷceẇsms – S/he is bringing s.t. over. **ies čłx̣ʷceẇsm, as čłx̣ʷceẇsm**

čłx̣ʷceẇsiš – Go over. *cmd.*

k̇ʷłnx̣ʷcuʔséẇs – cross to the other side of a tunnel. *suffix:* ***...éẇs*** *– in between, middle.*
k̇ʷłnx̣ʷcuʔséẇs – S/he/it crossed the tunnel. **čn k̇ʷłnx̣ʷcuʔséẇs, kʷ k̇ʷłnx̣ʷcuʔséẇs**
es k̇ʷłnx̣ʷcuʔséẇsi – S/he/it is crossing the tunnel. **čnes k̇ʷłnx̣ʷcuʔséẇsi, kʷes k̇ʷłnx̣ʷcuʔséẇsi**
qs k̇ʷłnx̣ʷcuʔséẇsi – S/he/it is going to cross the tunnel. **čiqs k̇ʷłnx̣ʷcuʔséẇsi, kʷqs k̇ʷłnx̣ʷcuʔséẇsi**

k̇ʷłnx̣ʷcuʔséẇsis – S/he/it brought s.t. through. **k̇ʷłnx̣ʷcuʔséẇsn, k̇ʷłnx̣ʷcuʔséẇsntxʷ**
es k̇ʷłnx̣ʷcuʔséẇsms – S/he/it is bringing s.t. through. **ies k̇ʷłnx̣ʷcuʔséẇsi, as k̇ʷłnx̣ʷcuʔséẇsi**
qs k̇ʷłnx̣ʷcuʔséẇsms – S/he/it is going to bring s.t. through. **čiqs k̇ʷłnx̣ʷcuʔséẇsi, aqs k̇ʷłnx̣ʷcuʔséẇsi**

čtlihálqʷ – across anything that is a line; railroad track; or a border.

ntl̓ihaqs – across the road, street or highway.

ntl̓iheẇs, *ntl̓ihe* – across the canyon. *suffix:* ***...éẇs*** *– in between, middle.*

čtl̓iheẇs – across the land/valley. *suffix:* ***...éẇs*** *– in between, middle.*

čtl̓ihičṅ, *čtl̓ihi* – over the hill.

ntl̓ihełċeʔ – across the room.

nisq̇ʷot, *nisq̇ʷo* – across the river. *See:* ***across.***

čxʷstalqʷ – Walk on a log or anything that is narrow and high.

es tqtqncuti – repeatedly touch one's self; *(said when making the sign of the cross). See:* ***touch.***

crossbill

łʔayʔayxʷusáqs, *łʔayʔayxʷusá* – red crossbill; *Loxia curvirostra.*

crouch

łkʷk̇ʷimist – crouch; squat low; make self small. *rt.:* ***k̇ʷim*** *– small.*
łkʷk̇ʷmist – S/he crouched. **čn łkʷk̇ʷimist, kʷ łkʷk̇ʷimist**
es łkʷk̇ʷimisti – S/he is crouching. **čnes łkʷk̇ʷimisti, kʷes łkʷk̇ʷimisti**
qs łkʷk̇ʷimisti – S/he is going to crouch. **čiqs łkʷk̇ʷimisti, kʷqs łkʷk̇ʷimisti**

łkʷk̇ʷimistiš – Crouch. *cmd.*

Crow

stemčiistn, *stemči* – Crow. *lit. down the river people.*
qʷayičint – Mountain Crow people. *something to do with their blue paint.*

crow

scáʔaʔ – American crow; *Corvus brachyrhynchos.*

Crow Creek

ṅmĺá séwłkʷs – Crow Creek, Flathead Nation. *lit. flooding, ravens nesting, the thistle.*

Crow Creek Pass, South **x̣qʷosálqʷ sx̣ʷcuʔsi** – South Crow Creek Pass, Mission Mountain Range, Flathead Nation.

crowd **tuʔ** – crowded together; gathered together.
tuʔmis – S/he put a group together. **tuʔmin, tuʔmintxʷ**
es tuʔmims – S/he is putting a group together. **ies tuʔmim, as tuʔmim**
qs tuʔmims – S/he is going to put a group together. **iqs tuʔmim, aqs tuʔmim**

i tuʔ – It is crowded.

tuʔsqelixʷ – crowd of people.
tuʔsqax̣eʔ – crowd of animals.

ix̣x̣nunm – crowd someone or something so that it has to move over.
ix̣x̣nuis – S/he crowded s.o. over. **ix̣x̣nun, ix̣x̣nuntxʷ**
es ix̣x̣nums – S/he is crowding s.o. over. **ies ix̣x̣nunm, as ix̣x̣nunm**
qs ix̣x̣nums – S/he is going to crowd s.o. over. **iqs ix̣x̣nunm, aqs ix̣x̣nunm**

ix̣x̣nusm – get in someone's face to move them over.

qʷo ix̣x̣nuntm u čn ocqeʔ – I was crowded over and went out.

ċaaw̓t – tightly packed; crowded. *rt.: **ċan** – tight; suffix: **...éw̓t** – group state.*
es ċaaw̓t – They are tightly packed; crowded. **qeʔes ċaaw̓t, pes ċaaw̓t**

čxʷexʷʔit, *čxʷexʷʔi* – many people. *See: **many**.*

čššin – went along involuntarily; get pushed along. *(i.e., in a crowd of people pushing you along.)*

čicn – happen upon; to meet someone; an accidental meeting. *See: **meet**.*
nčcnew̓sts – S/he came into a crowd. **nčcnew̓stn, nčcnew̓stxʷ**
nčcnéʔew̓sts – They came into a crowd. **qeʔ nčcnew̓stm, nčcnew̓stp**

> The **i** following uvular consonants (UC) and the glottal stop **ʔ** sound like English "*ey*" as in the words *they, hey, whey*, etc. Salish UC are: **q, q̇, qʷ, q̇ʷ, x̣, x̣ʷ**. For example, the suffix **...qin** – head/top, is often spelled using English *ey* as "q*ey*n". So **qi, q̇i, qʷi, q̇ʷi, x̣i, x̣ʷi**, may be spelled with English *ey* as **q***ey*, **q̇***ey*, **qʷ***ey*, **q̇ʷ***ey*, **x̣***ey*, **x̣ʷ***ey* in other texts.

crown **łqʷqin** – put on/ wear a crown. *rt.: **łoqʷ** – over lay/around; suffix: **...qin, ...qn** – top.*
łqʷqinm – S/he put on a crown. **čn łqʷqinm, kʷ łqʷqinm**
es łqʷqini – S/he is putting on a crown. **čnes łqʷqini, kʷes łqʷqini**
qs łqʷqini – S/he is going to put on a crown. **čiqs łqʷqini, kʷqs łqʷqini**

łqʷqis – S/he put a crown on s.o. **łqʷqin, łqʷqintxʷ**
es łqʷqinms – S/he is putting a crown on s.o. **ies łqʷqinm, as łqʷqinm**
qs łqʷqinms – S/he is going to put a crown on s.o. **iqs łqʷqinm, aqs łqʷqinm**

es łqʷqin – S/he is crowned. **čnes łqʷqin, kʷes łqʷqin**
łqʷqintm – S/he got crowned. **qʷo łqʷqintm, kʷ łqʷqintm**

łqʷqintn – crown.

łqʷqiniš – Put on a crown. *cmd.*
łqʷqint – Crown him/her. *cmd.*

crucify **čptkʷumnálqʷ**, *čptkʷumná* – crucify; pinned to wood. *See: **pin**.*

crumble **tmim** – crumble down/apart.
tmip – It crumbled down.
es tmpmi – It is crumbling down.

tmis – S/he made it crumble down. **tmin, tmintxʷ**
es tmims – S/he is making it crumble down. **ies tmim, as tmim**

> s.t. - something, the 3rd person
> (s.t.) - something implied
> s.o. - someone, the 3rd person
> *sl.* - singular form
> *pl.* - plural form
> *rt.* - root word
> *cmd.* - command
> *lit.* - literally
> *fig.* - figuratively
> *i.e.,* - for example
> *See:* - Redirection to a related word.

qs tmims – S/he is going to make it crumble down. **iqs tmim, aqs tmim**

tmint – Make it crumble. *cmd.*

ntmip – It crumbled in on itself.

ntmmels – feelings crumbled.
tmpseẁs – crumble in the middle. *suffix: **...éẁs** – in between, middle.*

tmwalš – crumble apart and fall/slide. *(i.e., cliff rocks fall, landslide, etc.) rt.: **tmim** – crumble.*
es tmwalši – It is crumbling and falling.

es tmwalš – It is crumbled and fallen.

tmwalšts – S/he made it crumble and fall. **tmwalštn, tmwalštxʷ**
es tmwalšms – S/he is making it crumble and fall. **ies tmwalšm, as tmwalšm**
qs tmwalšms – S/he is going to make it crumble and fall. **iqs tmwalšm, aqs tmwalšm**

ntmwalš – Rocks fell/slid from the side of a cave.

k̓ʷłtmip – Rocks caved in/fell from under.
es k̓ʷłtmpmi – The rocks are caving in/fell from under.

crumbs

ccup – crumbs.
łcpcup – small crumbs.
ccupcn – crumbs from the mouth. *suffix: **...cin, ...cn** – action of the mouth.*
es ccupcni – crumbs are falling from his/her mouth. **čnes ccupcni, kʷes ccupcni**

cry

ċqʷaqʷ, *ċqʷa* – cry; loud cry. *(i.e., a child in pain, etc.)*
ċqʷaqʷ – S/he cried. **čn ċqʷaqʷ, kʷ ċqʷaqʷ**
es ċqʷaqʷi – S/he is crying. **čnes ċqʷaqʷi, kʷes ċqʷaqʷi**
qs ċqʷaqʷi – S/he is going to cry. **čiqs ċqʷaqʷi, kʷqs ċqʷaqʷi**
es ċqʷáʔaqʷi – They are crying. **qeʔes ċqʷaqʷi, pes ċqʷaqʷi**

es ċqʷċqʷelsi – S/he is crying excessively.

ċqʷaqʷš – Cry. *cmd.*
ċqʷqʷemn – one inclined to cry; crybaby. *suffix: **...emn** – one inclined to do.*

ċqʷqʷllwis – crying around.

cʔot – moan; slow quiet steady cry. *(i.e., mourning, lonesome, hurt feelings, etc.)*
cʔot – S/he moaned. **čn cʔot, kʷ cʔot**
es cʔoti – S/he is moaning. **čnes cʔoti, kʷes cʔoti**
qs cʔoti – S/he is going to moan. **čiqs cʔoti, kʷqs cʔoti**

čcʔot – mourn; cry over. *See: **mourn**.*

cʔotemn – one inclined to moan. *suffix: **...emn** – one inclined to do.*

čawawpus – cry; have tears. *See: **tears**.*

laiʔ – sorrowful cry; cry with tears; weep.
laim – S/he cried. **čn laim, kʷ laim**
es laiʔi – S/he is crying. **čnes laiʔi, kʷes laiʔi**

laiš – Cry. *cmd.*

łoóť – uncontrolled gasping after crying.
łoóť – S/he was gasping. **čn łoóť, kʷ łoóť**
es łoóťi – S/he is gasping. **čnes łoóťi, kʷes łoóťi**

crybaby **c̓qʷqʷemn –** one inclined to cry; crybaby. *suffix:* ***...emn –*** *one inclined to do.*

Crystal Mountain **čłcó –** Crystal Mountain, Montana.

cucumber **słx̣ʷep –** cucumber.

culture **nqlixʷečst –** do something as a human; culture; tradition.
nqlixʷečsis – S/he did s.t. as a human. **nqlixʷečsn, nqlixʷečsntxʷ**
es nqlixʷečstms – S/he is doing s.t. as a human. **ies nqlixʷečstm, as nqlixʷečstm**
qs nqlixʷečstms – S/he is going to do s.t. as a human. **iqs nqlixʷečstm, aqs nqlixʷečstm**

nqlixʷečstn – the human ways; culture; traditions.

nqlixʷcut – be human; be cultural; be Indian.
nqlixʷcut – S/he was cultural. **čn nqlixʷcut, kʷ nqlixʷcut**
es nqlixʷcuti – S/he is being cultural. **čnes nqlixʷcuti, kʷes nqlixʷcuti**
qs nqlixʷcuti – S/he is going to be cultural. **čiqs nqlixʷcuti, kʷqs nqlixʷcuti**

nqlixʷcutn – humanist; one that makes one human; creator.

nk̓ʷul̓mn – ways; customs; habits; culture; traditions; the things one does. *See:* ***customs.***

nˀax̣íłtn – ways; customs; the way one acts. *See:* ***customs.***

cup **snsustn –** something to drink out of; cup. *rt.:* ***sust –*** *drink; prefix:* ***sn... –*** *a place of; suffix:* ***...tin, ...tn –*** *means of/device.* **snssustn** *pl.*

łpó – cup.
inłl̓pó – my cup.

cupboard **snqpéłc̓eˀtn**, *snqpé* **–** place to put dishes; cupboard. *rt.:* ***qpéłc̓eˀ –*** *plate; prefix:* ***sn... –*** *a place of; suffix:* ***...tin, ...tn –*** *means of/device.*

snčsle – cupboard.

cure **p̓aáx̣ –** heal; cure; get well. *See:* ***heal.***

čc̓oqm – cure; pull out from sickness/death.
čc̓oqntes – S/he cured s.o. **čc̓oqnten, čc̓oqntexʷ**
es čc̓oqms – S/he is curing s.o. **ies čc̓oqm, as čc̓oqm**
qs čc̓oqms – S/he is going to cure s.o. **iqs čc̓oqm, aqs čc̓oqm**

čc̓oqint – Cure him/her. *cmd.*

čc̓oqncit – S/he cured you.

malyémm – doctor someone. *See:* ***doctor.***

curlew **wál̓wl̓ –** long-billed curlew; *Numenius americanus.*

curl **qʷos –** curl; crisp.
qʷsip – It got curled.
qʷspmi – It is getting curled.

es qʷsim – It is curled.

qʷsntes – S/he curled s.t. **qʷsnten, qʷsntexʷ**
es qʷsims – S/he is curling s.t. **ies qʷsim, as qʷsim**

The **i** following uvular consonants (UC) and the glottal stop ˀ sound like English "*ey*" as in the words *they, hey, whey,* etc. Salish UC are: **q, q̓, qʷ, q̓ʷ, x̣, x̣ʷ**. For example, the suffix **...qin** – head/top, is often spelled using English *ey* as "*qeyn*". So **qi, q̓i, qʷi, q̓ʷi, x̣i, x̣ʷi**, may be spelled with English *ey* as **q***ey*, **q̓***ey*, **qʷ***ey*, **q̓ʷ***ey*, **x̣***ey*, **x̣ʷ***ey* in other texts.

s.t. - something, the 3rd person
(s.t.) - something implied
s.o. - someone, the 3rd person
sl. - singular form
pl. - plural form
rt. - root word
cmd. - command
lit. - literally
fig. - figuratively
i.e., - for example
See: - Redirection to a related word.

qs qʷsims – S/he is going to curl s.t. **iqs qʷsim, as qʷsim**

qʷspstes – S/he made s.t. curled. **qʷspstes, qʷspstes**
es qʷspims – S/he is making s.t. curl. **ies qʷspim, as qʷspim**
qs qʷspims – S/he is going to make s.t. curl. **iqs qʷspim, as qʷspim**

qʷsint – Curl it. *cmd.*
qʷsmelxʷ – curled fur hide. *(i.e., sheep, dog, etc.)*
čqʷosqn – curled hair; curled on top.

čqʷosmqn – His/her hair got curled. **čn čqʷosmqn, kʷ čqʷosmqn**
es čqʷosmqni – His/her hair is getting curled. **čnes čqʷosmqni, kʷes čqʷosmqni**

čqʷsqnmist – S/he curled one's hair. **čn čqʷsqnmist, kʷ čqʷsqnmist**
es čqʷsqnmisti – S/he is curling one's hair. **čnes čqʷsqnmisti, kʷes čqʷsqnmisti**

čqʷosqis – S/he curled s.o.'s hair. **čqʷosqn, čqʷosqntxʷ**
es čqʷosqnms – S/he is curling s.o.'s hair. **ies čqʷosqnm, as čqʷosqnm**

čqʷosqnepl̓ʔeis – S/he gave s.o. a perm. **čqʷosqnepl̓ʔen, čqʷosqnepl̓ʔentxʷ**
es čqʷosqnepl̓ʔems – S/he is giving s.o. a perm. **ies es čqʷosqnepl̓ʔem, as es čqʷosqnepl̓ʔem**

čqʷosqnepl̓ʔentm – S/he got a perm. **qʷo čqʷosqnepl̓ʔentm, kʷ čqʷosqnepl̓ʔentm**
es čqʷosqneple̓ʔ – S/he has a perm. **čnes čqʷosqneple̓ʔ, kʷes čqʷosqneple̓ʔ**

curling iron
čqʷosqntn – curling iron.

currants
stm̓tu – currants *(berries)*.

curse
q̇ewm – curse; wish bad on somebody; cast/wish bad luck on somebody.
es q̇ewm – S/he is cursed. **čnes q̇ewm, kʷes q̇ewm**

q̇ewis – S/he cursed s.o. **q̇ewn, q̇ewntxʷ**
es q̇ewms – S/he is cursing s.o. **ies q̇ewm, as q̇ewm**
qs q̇ewms – S/he is going to curse s.o. **iqs q̇ewm, aqs q̇ewm**
q̇éʔewis – They wished bad on s.o. **qeʔ q̇éʔewntm, q̇ewntp**

q̇ewntm – S/he/it was witched/wished bad upon.

q̇ewnt – Wish bad on him/her. *cmd.*

hoy n̓em q̇ewnct – Quit, they will wish bad on you. **q̇ewncn –** I cursed you.

čscinm – talk in a bad way; bad mouth. *See:* ***talk.***

Curse words: below are words used to express feelings of anger, disdain, disapproval and aversion toward someone. The words by themselves are not bad or taboo in the sense that English curse words are. It is the feelings behind them that make these words profane.
kʷ p̓at̓qan – You dumby/splat head.
kʷ tin̓mu – You are nothing. *See:* ***worthless.***
kʷ nt̓łups – You dirty butt. *See:* ***dirty.***
kʷ mtmi – You are no good. *See:* ***bad.***
kʷ t̓eyeʔ – You are bad/evil. *See:* ***bad.***

x̣ił – interjection; exclamation; darn; doggone; damn. *See:* ***exclamation.***
ye pn̓ – exclamation to accentuate a word or thought. *See:* ***exclamation.***

ye pṅ kʷ nťłups – You dirty butt! *(derogatory)* **x̣ił kʷ nťłups –** You dirty butt! *(derogatory)* **x̣ił kʷ mtmi –** Damn, you are no good! *(derogatory)* **uł nťłups –** Those dirty butts. **x̣ił kʷ nqʷyutups –** You rich butt. *(derogatory)*

cursive **nk̓ʷłłiṗ q̓eẏim –** cursive write; write with one line.

curtain **nil̓xʷénčtn,** *nil̓xʷé* – drapes; curtain. *lit. to cover. rt.:* ***yelxʷ*** *– conceal.*

nil̓xʷustn – veil; curtain. *rt.:* ***yelxʷ*** *– conceal.*

curve **yalk̓ʷ –** bend/make into a circular shape. *See:* ***circle.***

curved **q̓ʷaťx̣ʷ –** curved object; naturally curved object. *(i.e., banana, macaroni, horn, etc.)*
es q̓ʷaťx̣ʷ – It is curved.

čq̓ʷaťlqpsm – curve the neck.
es čq̓ʷaťlqpsi – S/he is curving the neck. **čnes čq̓ʷaťlqpsi, kʷes čq̓ʷaťlqpsi**

čqʷq̓ʷaťálqʷ – curved wood.

q̓ʷaťx̣ʷ – banana. **q̓ʷťq̓ʷaťx̣ʷ,** *q̓ʷťq̓ʷa* – bananas.

yéṗ – formed/bent into a curve/hook/angle. *(i.e., a wire, etc.)*
iṗiyéṗ – more than one formed bend.
iṗiṗ – It became formed into a bend.
iṗiṗiṗ – It became formed into several bends.
niṗiyaṗqs – road that has more than one curve.

yanq̓ʷ – curved shape within an object.

i ninṗáqs – The road is curvy.
sninṗáqs – curvy road.

custom **nˀax̣íłtn –** ways; customs; the way one acts. *rt.:* ***ax̣il*** *– do, act.*

nk̓ʷul̓mn – ways; customs; habits; culture; traditions; the things one does. *rt.:* ***k̓ʷul̓*** *– make/build/do.*
ye pṅ pspast annk̓ʷul̓mn – Your culture is full of energy. **k̓ʷnšspe u kʷes k̓ʷul̓i l t sq̓sip cúˀuts nk̓ʷul̓mis –** How many years have you been working with the Culture Committee?

cuut – way of doing something; one's mannerism; one's gift from Creator. *See:* ***ways.***

nqlixʷcut – be human; be cultural; be Indian. *See:* ***culture.***

sqʷˀem – habit; practice. *See:* ***accustomed.***

qʷaqʷemncut, *qʷaqʷemncú* – practice, drill, train, study. *See:* ***practice.***

customer **sxʷtumíst –** one tasked to buy; customer. *prefix:* ***sxʷ...*** *– one tasked to do.*

cut **nič –** cut; slice; saw.
ničm – S/he/it cut (s.t.). **čn ničm, kʷ ničm**
es niči – S/he/it is cutting (s.t). **čnes niči, kʷes niči**
qs niči – S/he/it is going to cut (s.t.). **čiqs niči, kʷqs niči**
es níˀiči – They are cutting (s.t.). **qeˀes niči, pes niči**

ničis – S/he/it cut it. **ničn, ničntxʷ**
es ničms – S/he/it is cutting it. **ies ničm, as ničm**

The **i** following uvular consonants (UC) and the glottal stop **ˀ** sound like English "*ey*" as in the words *they, hey, whey,* etc. Salish UC are: **q, q̓, qʷ, q̓ʷ, x̣, x̣ʷ**. For example, the suffix **...qin** – head/top, is often spelled using English *ey* as "q*ey*n". So **qi, q̓i, qʷi, q̓ʷi, x̣i, x̣ʷi,** may be spelled with English *ey* as **q***ey*, **q̓***ey*, **qʷ***ey*, **q̓ʷ***ey*, **x̣***ey*, **x̣ʷ***ey* in other texts.

s.t. - something, the 3rd person
(s.t.) - something implied
s.o. - someone, the 3rd person
sl. - singular form
pl. - plural form
rt. - root word
cmd. - command
lit. - literally
fig. - figuratively
i.e., - for example
See: - Redirection to a related word.

qs nič̓ms – S/he/it is going to cut it. **iqs nič̓m, aqs nič̓m**
níˀičis – They cut it. **qeˀ nič̓ntm, nič̓ntp**

nič̓č̓ – It got cut.
es nič̓ – It is cut.

sxʷnč̓sqelixʷ – surgeon; someone tasked to cut people. *prefix:* ***sxʷ...*** *– one tasked to do.*

nič̓iš – Cut. *cmd.*
nič̓nt – Cut it. *cmd.*
nič̓nti – You all go ahead and cut it up. *cmd.*
nič̓ntwi – You guys cut it. *cmd.*
nič̓elis – cut/sawed in several pieces.
k̓ʷłnič̓ – cut out.

wis nič̓ntm – It is already cut up. **nk̓ʷuˀ nłámqeˀ čnič̓qn –** One bear got cut on the head *(i.e., with a knife).* **ṅem čn wis nič̓m m čn ocqeˀ –** I will finish cutting and I will go out.

štip – get cut accidentally.
štip – S/he got cut. **čn štip, kʷ štip**
es štpmi – S/he is getting cut. **čnes štpmi, kʷes štpmi**
qs štpmi – S/he is going to get cut. **čiqs štpmi, kʷqs štpmi**
štíˀip – They got cut. **qeˀ štip, p štip**

štpnuis – S/he cut s.o. **štpnun, štpnuntxʷ**
es štpnunms – S/he is cutting s.o. **ies štpnunm, as štpnunm**
qs štpnunms – S/he is going to cut s.o. **iqs štpnunm, aqs štpnunm**

sštip – cut; laceration.

štpáyaqn – S/he got cut on the head.

čaˀilqn – cut hair.
čaˀilqnm – S/he cut hair. **čn čaˀilqnm, kʷ čaˀilqnm**
es čaˀilqni – S/he is cutting hair. **čnes čaˀilqni, kʷes čaˀilqni**
qs čaˀilqni – S/he is going to cut hair. **čiqs čaˀilqni, kʷqs čaˀilqni**

čaˀilqis – S/he cut s.o's hair. **čaˀilqn, čaˀilqntxʷ**
es čaˀilqnms – S/he is cutting s.o's hair. **ies čaˀilqnm, as čaˀilqnm**
qs čaˀilqnms – S/he is going to cut s.o's hair. **iqs čaˀilqnm, aqs čaˀilqnm**

snčaˀilqntn – place to cut hair; barber shop. *prefix:* ***sn...*** *– a place of; suffix:* ***...tin, ...tn*** *– means of/device.*
sxʷčaˀilqnm – one tasked to cut hair; barber. *prefix:* ***sxʷ...*** *– one tasked to do.*
čaˀilqnemn – one inclined to cut hair; barber. *prefix:* ***...emn*** *– one inclined to do.*

čaˀilqniš – Cut hair. *cmd.*
čaˀilqnwi – All of you cut hair. *cmd.*
čaˀilqnt – Cut someone's hair. *cmd.*

čaˀilqncut – cut your own hair.
čaˀilqncut – S/he cut his/her own hair. **čn čaˀilqncut, kʷ čaˀilqncut**
es čaˀilqncuti – S/he is cutting his/her own hair. **čnes čaˀilqncuti, kʷes čaˀilqncuti**
qs čaˀilqncuti – S/he is going to cut his/her own hair. **čiqs čaˀilqncuti, kʷqs čaˀilqncuti**

čaˀilqncutš – Cut your own hair. *cmd.*
čaˀilqncutwi – All of you cut your own hair. *cmd.*

ncaxʷk̓ʷqintm – Take the top off (he is scalped).

x̣ʷic – cut bunches of something.
x̣ʷicm – S/he cut the things. **čn x̣ʷicm, kʷ x̣ʷicm**
es x̣ʷici – S/he cut the things. **čnes x̣ʷici, kʷes x̣ʷici**

x̣ʷiclexʷm – cut hay or grass. *See:* ***mow.***

čx̣ʷicp – cut fur off an animal. *rt.:* ***...ep –*** *rope, head hair.*
čx̣ʷicpm – S/he cut off fur. **čn čx̣ʷicpm, kʷ čx̣ʷicpm**
es čx̣ʷicpi – S/he is cutting off fur. **čnes čx̣ʷicpi, kʷes čx̣ʷicpi**
qs čx̣ʷicpi – S/he is going to cut off fur. **čiqs čx̣ʷicpi, kʷqs čx̣ʷicpi**

ṅe wis čxʷntéxʷ m kʷ čx̣ʷicpm t anłṅi – When you finish cutting it (the meat) off, you will cut off the fur with your knife.

pič – shave/cut. *(i.e., shaving wood.) See:* ***shave.***

šlim – chop. *See:* ***chop.***

čalim, ***čali*** **–** cut with scissors. *See:* ***scissors.***

The **i** following uvular consonants (UC) and the glottal stop **ʔ** sound like English "*ey*" as in the words *they, hey, whey*, etc. Salish UC are: **q, q̇, qʷ, q̇ʷ, x̣, x̣ʷ**. For example, the suffix **...qin** – head/top, is often spelled using English *ey* as "q*ey*n". So **qi, q̇i, qʷi, q̇ʷi, x̣i, x̣ʷi**, may be spelled with English *ey* as **q***ey*, **q̇***ey*, **qʷ***ey*, **q̇ʷ***ey*, **x̣***ey*, **x̣ʷ***ey* in other texts.

cut off

x̣ʷtim – cut something off.
x̣ʷtip – S/he cut off (s.t.). **čn x̣ʷtip, kʷ x̣ʷtip**
es x̣ʷtmi – S/he is cutting off (s.t.). **čnes x̣ʷtip, kʷes x̣ʷtmi**
qs x̣ʷtmi – S/he is going to cut off (s.t.). **čiqs x̣ʷtip, kʷqs x̣ʷtmi**
x̣ʷtíʔip – They cut off (s.t.). **qeʔ x̣ʷtip, p x̣ʷtip**
es x̣ʷtmíʔi – They are cutting off (s.t.). **qeʔes x̣ʷtip, pes x̣ʷtmi**

x̣ʷtntes – S/he cut s.t. off. **x̣ʷtnten, x̣ʷtntexʷ**
es x̣ʷtpims – S/he is cutting s.t. off. **čnes x̣ʷtpim, kʷes x̣ʷtpim**
q̇s x̣ʷtpims – S/he is going to cut s.t. off. **čiqs x̣ʷtpim, kʷqs x̣ʷtpim**
x̣ʷtntéʔes – They cut s.t. off. **qeʔ x̣ʷtntem, kʷ x̣ʷtntep**

es x̣ʷtx̣ʷtmi – S/he is repeatedly cutting off. **čnes x̣ʷtx̣ʷtmi, kʷes x̣ʷtx̣ʷtmi**

x̣ʷtepm – cut down.
x̣ʷtelis – cut in several parts.
x̣ʷtseẇsm – cut in half. *suffix:* ***...éẇs –*** *in between, middle.*
es xʷoyt – It is cut off.

čx̣ʷtupsm – cut a tail off; cut off the end of something.
es čx̣ʷtupsi – S/he is cutting off the end. **čnes čx̣ʷtupsi, kʷes čx̣ʷtupsi**

es čx̣ʷtups – Its tail is cut off; it has no ending.

čx̣ʷtx̣ʷtupsntxʷ – You cut off the endings.

k̇ʷłx̣ʷtim – undercut something off; cut off for apportionment.
k̇ʷłx̣ʷtip – S/he cut off (s.t.). **čn k̇ʷłx̣ʷtip, kʷ k̇ʷłx̣ʷtip**
es k̇ʷłx̣ʷtmi – S/he is cutting off (s.t.). **čnes k̇ʷłx̣ʷtip, kʷes k̇ʷłx̣ʷtmi**
qs k̇ʷłx̣ʷtmi – S/he is going to cut off (s.t.). **čiqs k̇ʷłx̣ʷtip, kʷqs k̇ʷłx̣ʷtmi**
k̇ʷłx̣ʷtíʔip – They cut off (s.t.). **qeʔ k̇ʷłx̣ʷtip, p k̇ʷłx̣ʷtip**

k̇ʷłx̣ʷtntes – S/he cut s.t. off. **k̇ʷłx̣ʷtnten, k̇ʷłx̣ʷtntexʷ**
es k̇ʷłx̣ʷtpims – S/he is cutting s.t. off. **čnes k̇ʷłx̣ʷtpim, kʷes k̇ʷłx̣ʷtpim**
qs k̇ʷłx̣ʷtpims – S/he is going to cut s.t. off. **čiqs k̇ʷłx̣ʷtpim, kʷqs k̇ʷłx̣ʷtpim**
k̇ʷłx̣ʷtntéʔes – They cut s.t. off. **qeʔ k̇ʷłx̣ʷtntem, kʷ k̇ʷłx̣ʷtntep**
es k̇ʷłx̣ʷtpíʔims – They are cutting s.t. off. **qeʔes k̇ʷłx̣ʷtpim, es k̇ʷłx̣ʷtpimp**

nx̣ʷtečst – cut off finger. *suffix:* ***...ečst, ...čst –*** *of the hand.*

s.t. - something, the 3rd person
(s.t.) - something implied
s.o. - someone, the 3rd person
sl. - singular form
pl. - plural form
rt. - root word
cmd. - command
lit. - literally
fig. - figuratively
i.e., - for example
See: - Redirection to a related word.

es nx̣ʷtečst – His/her finger is cut off. **čnes nx̣ʷtečst, kʷes nx̣ʷtečst**

nx̣ʷtečstmis – S/he cut off s.o.'s finger. **nx̣ʷtečstmn, nx̣ʷtečstmntxʷ**
es nx̣ʷtečsts – S/he is cutting off s.o.'s finger. **ies nx̣ʷtečstm, as nx̣ʷtečstm**
qs nx̣ʷtečsts – S/he is cutting off s.o.'s finger. **iqs nx̣ʷtečstm, aqs nx̣ʷtečstm**

čx̣ʷt̓éneʔ – cropped/cut off ear.
es čx̣ʷt̓éneʔ – His/her/its ear is cropped/cut off. **čnes čx̣ʷt̓éneʔ, kʷes čx̣ʷt̓éneʔ**

es čx̣ʷt̓énʔems – S/he is cutting off s.o.'s ear. **ies čx̣ʷt̓énʔem, as čx̣ʷt̓énʔem**
qs čx̣ʷt̓énʔems – S/he is going to cut off s.o.'s ear. **iqs čx̣ʷt̓énʔem, aqs čx̣ʷt̓énʔem**

čx̣ʷtim – cut off; separate from.
x̣ʷntés – S/he cut it from s.t. **čx̣ʷntén, čx̣ʷntéxʷ**
es čx̣ʷims – S/he is cutting it from s.t. **ies čx̣ʷim, as čx̣ʷim**
qs čx̣ʷims – S/he is going to cut it from s.t. **iqs čx̣ʷim, aqs čx̣ʷim**

cut out

k̓ʷłnič – cut out; undercut something. *(with a knife)*
k̓ʷłničm – S/he cut out (s.t.). **čn k̓ʷłničm, kʷ k̓ʷłničm**
es k̓ʷłniči – S/he is cutting out (s.t). **čnes k̓ʷłniči, kʷes k̓ʷłniči**
qs k̓ʷłniči – S/he is going to cut out (s.t.). **čiqs niči, kʷqs k̓ʷłniči**

k̓ʷłničis – S/he cut it out. **k̓ʷłničn, k̓ʷłničntxʷ**
es k̓ʷłničms – S/he is cutting it out. **ies k̓ʷłničm, as k̓ʷłničm**
qs k̓ʷłničms – S/he is going to cut it out. **iqs k̓ʷłničm, aqs k̓ʷłničm**

k̓ʷłničiš – Cut out. *cmd.*
k̓ʷłničntwi – All of you cut. *cmd.*
k̓ʷłničnt – Cut it out. *cmd.*
k̓ʷłničnti – All of you cut it up. *cmd.*

k̓ʷłčalim – cut something out with scissors. *See: **scissors**.*
k̓ʷłčalim – S/he cut out. **čn k̓ʷłčalim, kʷ k̓ʷłčalim**
es k̓ʷłčalmi – S/he is cutting out. **čnes k̓ʷłčalmi, kʷes k̓ʷłčalmi**
qs k̓ʷłčalmi – S/he is going to cut out. **čiqs k̓ʷłčalmi, kʷqs k̓ʷłčalmi**

k̓ʷłčalntés – S/he cut s.t. out. **k̓ʷłčalntén, k̓ʷłčalntéxʷ**
es k̓ʷłčalims – S/he is cutting s.t. out. **ies k̓ʷłčalim, as k̓ʷłčalim**
qs k̓ʷłčalims – S/he is going to cut s.t. out. **iqs k̓ʷłčalim, aqs k̓ʷłčalim**

es k̓ʷłčal – It is cut out.

k̓ʷłčališ – Cut. *cmd.*
k̓ʷłčaliwi – All of you cut. *cmd.*
k̓ʷłčalint – Cut it. *cmd.*
k̓ʷłčalinti – All of you cut it. *cmd.*

k̓ʷłčalint ci p̓ip̓uyšn – Cut out the (picture) car.

cutthroat trout

pisł – westslope cutthroat trout; *Oncorhynchus clarkii lewisi.*
pipsł – small trout; little cutthroat trout.
łpspisł – little trout; little cutthroat trout.

cylinder

yult – large in girth. *(a description of cylindrical objects.) See: **girth**.*

łqqalqʷ – narrow in girth. *(a description of cylindrical objects.) See: **narrow**.*

daddy longlegs **stamóľqn –** daddy longlegs, female; *Triaenonychidae.*
stamóľiyaqn – daddy longlegs, male; *Triaenonychidae.*

dagger **x̣tx̣itne –** dagger

łṁinč, *łṁi* – knife.

dam **tqep –** dam; restrict; choke off.
tqep – It got dammed.
es tqpmi – It is getting dammed.
qs tqpmi – It is going to get dammed.

tqépm – S/he/it dammed (s.t.). **čn tqépm, kʷ tqépm**
es tqépi – S/he/it is damming (s.t.). **čnes tqépi, kʷes tqépi**
qs tqépi – S/he/it is going to dam (s.t.). **čiqs tqépi, kʷqs tqépi**

tqépis – S/he/it dammed it. **tqépn, tqépntxʷ**
es tqépms – S/he/it is damming it. **ies tqépm, as tqépm**
qs tqépms – S/he/it is going to dam it. **iqs tqépm, aqs tqépm**

stqép – dam.
tqéptn – material used to dam/restrict; bottle cork.

tqépnt – Dam it. *cmd.*
tqup – suffocate (not dead); restrict air flow; lacking air; winded/out of breath. *See:* ***suffocate.***

damn **x̣ił –** interjection; exclamation; darn; doggone; damn. *See:* ***exclamation.***

damp **ťim –** damp.
i ťim – S/he/it is damp. **i čn ťim, i kʷ ťim**
i łťťim – S/he/it is a little damp. **i čn łťťim, i kʷ łťťim**

ťmip – S/he/it got damp. **čn ťmip, kʷ ťmip**
łťťmip – S/he/it got a little damp. **čn łťťmip, kʷ łťťmip**
ťíʔim – It got damp.
i ťmup – It got damp all of a sudden.

ťmpilš – S/he/it gradually got damp. **čn ťmpilš, kʷ ťmpilš** *suffix:* ***...ilš*** *– autonomous.*
es ťmpilši – S/he/it is getting damp. **čnes ťmpilši, kʷes ťmpilši**
qs ťmpilši – S/he/it is getting damp. **čiqs ťmpilši, kʷqs ťmpilši**
ťmpíʔilš – They gradually got damp. **qeʔ ťmpilš, p ťmpilš**
es ťmpíʔilši – They are getting damp. **qeʔes ťmpilši, pes ťmpilši**
qs ťmpíʔilši – They are going to get damp. **qeʔqs ťmpilši, pqs ťmpilši**

ťmpstes – S/he/it made s.o./s.t. damp. **ťmpsten, ťmpstexʷ**
ťmpstéʔes – They made s.o./s.t. damp. **qeʔ ťmpstem, ťmpstep**

s.t. - something, the 3rd person
(s.t.) - something implied
s.o. - someone, the 3rd person
sl. - singular form
pl. - plural form
rt. - root word
cmd. - command
lit. - literally
fig. - figuratively
i.e., - for example
See: - Redirection to a related word.

łt̓t̓mpstes – S/he/it made s.o./s.t. a little damp. **łt̓t̓mpsten, łt̓t̓mpstexʷ**

t̓imlexʷ – damp ground, swamp.
t̓mpulexʷ – ground/area that got damp.
łt̓t̓mpulexʷ – ground/area that got a little damp.
t̓mic̓eʔ – damp all over; damp blanket.
t̓mt̓imčst – damp hands/fingers.
es t̓mpnwexʷi – They are getting each other damp.

t̓mpalqs – damp clothes. *suffix: **...lqs, ...alqs** – clothes.*
t̓mpalqs – His/her/its clothes got damp. **čn t̓mpalqs, kʷ t̓mpalqs**
t̓mpalqsis – S/he/it got s.o.'s clothes damp. **t̓mpalqsn, t̓mpalqsntxʷ**
es t̓mpalqsms – S/he/it is getting s.o.'s clothes damp. **ies t̓mpalqsm, as t̓mpalqsm**
qs t̓mpalqsms – S/he/it is going to get s.o.'s clothes damp. **iqs t̓mpalqsm, aqs t̓mpalqsm**
t̓mpáʔalqsis – They got s.o.'s clothes damp. **qeʔ t̓mpalqsntm, t̓mpalqsntp**
es t̓mpáʔalqsms – They are getting s.o.'s clothes damp. **qeʔes t̓mpalqsm, es t̓mpalqsmp**
qs t̓mpáʔalqsms – They are going to get s.o.'s clothes damp. **qeʔqs t̓mpalqsm, qs t̓mpalqsmp**

ssalt – damp/wet.
ssaltelxʷ – damp cloth/material.
ssaltulexʷ – damp earth.

dance

wénš – war dance; dance at a powwow. *See: **war dance**.*

es nineʔ – owl dance. *See: **owl dance**.*

snx̣ʷalmncutn – prairie chicken dance. *See: **prairie chicken dance**.*

snsqq̓ostn – prairie chicken dance. *See: **prairie chicken dance**.*

st̓iplscut swenš – lost article dance. *See: **lost article dance**.*

čsplqmncut – old warrior dance. *See: **old warrior dance**.*

nqaqaá – canvas dance. *See: **canvas dance**.*

tlqmi – jump dance; jumping. *(This describes the jumping that occurs at jump dances and medicine dances. This dance is held in the wintertime.) See: **jump dance**.*

nqwistn, *nqwi* **–** jump dance. *(This describes the action of following people in a circle that occurs at jump dances and medicine dances. This dance is held in the wintertime.) See: **jump dance**.*

nx̣asqin – jump dance held anytime of the year. *See: **jump dance**.*

snƛ̓ekʷlšscutn – medicine dance for doctoring. *See: **medicine dance**.*

es qʷásqʷiʔi – become a Blue Jay at a medicine dance. *See: **medicine dance**.*

šlšlčmncutist, *šlšlčmncu* **–** round dancing. *See: **round dance**.*

yul – scalp dance. *See: **scalp dance**.*

ṅiʔṅiṅp̓mncut, *ṅiʔṅiṅp̓mncú* **–** snake dancing. *See: **snake dance**.*

qʷiṁmncut, *qʷiṁmncú* **–** dance; any modern style of dance. *rt.: **q̓ʷiṁ** – hurry; suffix: **...cut** – action to the self.*
qʷiṁmncut – S/he danced. **čn qʷiṁmncut, kʷ qʷiṁmncut**
es qʷiṁmncuti – S/he is dancing. **čnes qʷiṁmncuti, kʷes qʷiṁmncuti**
qs qʷiṁmncuti – S/he is going to dance. **čiqs qʷiṁmncuti, kʷqs qʷiṁmncuti**
qʷiṁmncúʔut – They danced. **qeʔ qʷiṁmncut, p qʷiṁmncut**
es qʷiṁmncúʔuti – They are dancing. **qeʔes qʷiṁmncuti, pes qʷiṁmncuti**

qs qʷiṁmncúʔuti – They are going to dance. **qeʔqs qʷiṁmncuti, pqs qʷiṁmncuti**

snqʷiṁmncutn – place to dance; dance hall. *prefix:* ***sn...*** *– a place of; suffix:* ***...tin, ...tn*** *– means of/device.*

qʷiṁmncutš – Dance. *cmd.*
qʷiṁmncutwi – All of you dance. *cmd.*

es čṅnwexʷ – square dance. *rt.:* ***čṅim*** *– grasp on to; suffix:* ***...wexʷ*** *– action to each other.*
čṅnwéʔexʷ – They square danced. **qeʔ čṅnwéʔexʷ, p čṅnwéʔexʷ**
es čṅnwéʔexʷi – They are square dancing. **qeʔes čṅnwéʔexʷi, pes čṅnwéʔexʷi**
qs čṅnwéʔexʷi – They are going to square dance. **qeʔqs čṅnwéʔexʷi, pqs čṅnwéʔexʷi**

The **i** following uvular consonants (UC) and the glottal stop **ʔ** sound like English "*ey*" as in the words th*ey*, h*ey*, wh*ey*, etc. Salish UC are: **q, q̇, qʷ, q̇ʷ, x̣, x̣ʷ**. For example, the suffix **...qin** – head/top, is often spelled using English *ey* as "q*ey*n". So **qi, q̇i, qʷi, q̇ʷi, x̣i, x̣ʷi**, may be spelled with English *ey* as **q***ey*, **q̇***ey*, **qʷ***ey*, **q̇ʷ***ey*, **x̣***ey*, **x̣ʷ***ey* in other texts.

dance hall
snqʷiṁmncutn – place to dance; dance hall. *prefix:* ***sn...*** *– a place of; suffix:* ***...tin, ...tn*** *– means of/device.*

dance pavilion
snwénštn – place to war dance/war dance song; dance pavilion. *prefix:* ***sn...*** *– a place of; suffix:* ***...tin, ...tn*** *– means of/device.*

dangerous
činčnt – It's dangerous.

čnčnmscut – do something dangerous; put one's self in danger.
čnčnmscut – S/he/it did s.t. dangerous. **čn čnčnmscut, kʷ čnčnmscut**
es čnčnmscuti – S/he/it is doing s.t. dangerous. **čnes čnčnmscuti, kʷes čnčnmscuti**
qs čnčnmscuti – S/he/it is going to do s.t. dangerous. **čiqs čnčnmscuti, kʷqs čnčnmscuti**
čnčnmscúʔut – They did s.t. dangerous. **qeʔ čnčnmscut, p čnčnmscut**

es łčnčnmscuti – S/he/it is doing s.t. a little dangerous. **čnes łčnčnmscuti, kʷes łčnčnmscuti**

čnʔenmutiem – something that's always dangerous.
čnčntmulexʷ – dangerous area.
čnčntičṅ – dangerous ridge. *suffix:* ***...ičṅ*** *– back.*
čnčnetkʷ – dangerous water. *suffix:* ***...etkʷ, ...tkʷ*** *– liquid*
snčintn – particular place of danger. *prefix:* ***sn...*** *– a place of; suffix:* ***...tin, ...tn*** *– means of/device.*
snčnčintn – place of danger. *prefix:* ***sn...*** *– a place of; suffix:* ***...tin, ...tn*** *– means of/device.*
čnčnutm – dangerous.

čx̣enépleʔ – forbidden. *suffix:* ***...épleʔ*** *– permanence.*

činčnt łu asck̓ʷul̓ – Your job is dangerous.

Daniel
tonél̓ – Daniel.

Darby
snk̓ʷłxʷexʷeṁi – Darby, Montana. *lit. the place of lifting. rt.:* ***k̓ʷłxʷʔem*** *– lift; prefix:* ***sn...*** *– a place of:* ***sn...*** *– a place of.*
nłpapʔá – south of Darby.

s.t. - something, the 3rd person
(s.t.) - something implied
s.o. - someone, the 3rd person
sl. - singular form
pl. - plural form
rt. - root word
cmd. - command
lit. - literally
fig. - figuratively
i.e., - for example
See: - Redirection to a related word.

dare
el̓m – dare.
es el̓m – S/he/it is dared.

el̓mcin – dare someone to do something. *suffix:* ***...cin, ...cn*** *– action of the mouth.*
el̓mcis – S/he dared s.o. to do something. **el̓mcin, el̓mcintxʷ**
es el̓mcinms – S/he is daring s.o. to do something. **ies el̓mcinm, as el̓mcinm**
qs el̓mcinms – S/he is going to dare s.o. to do something. **iqs el̓mcinm, aqs el̓mcinm**

el̓mscut – dare one's self.

eľmscut – S/he dared one's self. **čn eľmscut kʷ eľmscut**
es eľmscuti – S/he is daring one's self. **čnes eľmscuti kʷes eľmscuti**
qs eľmscuti – S/he is going to dare one's self. **čiqs eľmscuti kʷqs eľmscuti**

eľmist – dare one's self.

es eľmscutms – S/he is making s.o. dare one's self.

nkʷnmist – dare.
nkʷnmist – S/he dared. **čn nkʷnmist, kʷ nkʷnmist**
es nkʷnmisti – S/he is daring. **čnes nkʷnmisti, kʷes nkʷnmisti**
qs nkʷnmisti – S/he is going to dare. **čiqs nkʷnmisti, kʷqs nkʷnmisti**

nkʷnmistmis – S/he dared s.o. **nkʷnmistmn, nkʷnmistmntxʷ**
es nkʷnmistms – S/he is daring s.o. **ies nkʷnmistm, as nkʷnmistm**
qs nkʷnmistms – S/he is going to dare s.o. **iqs nkʷnmistm, aqs nkʷnmistm**

nłkʷkʷnmist – dare a little.
nkʷkʷnmistemn – one inclined to dare. *suffix: **...emn** – one inclined to do.*
nkʷnmistmnwexʷist – dare each other.

kʷ ies nkʷnmistm – I am daring you. **nkʷnmistmncn** – I dared you.

xʷaˀscan – chitchat; speak for nothing. *See: **chitchat**.*

dark

čiṁ – dark; lacking direct light (not shaded); from dim to total darkness.
i čiṁ – It is dark.
i nčiṁ – It is dark in there.

čmip – It got dark.
es čmpmi – It is getting dark.
qs čmpmi – It is going to get dark.

čmčmpstes – S/he made it go dark. **čmčmpsten, čmčmpstexʷ**
es čmčmpims – S/he is making it go dark. **ies čmčmpim, as čmčmpim**
qs čmčmpims – S/he is going to make it go dark. **iqs čmčmpim, aqs čmčmpim**

čmpstem – S/he was made to go dark; out of it. *See: **faint**.*
es čmip – It remains dark.
čmup – All of a sudden it got dark/disappeared.

čmpim – overly excited; out of control. *See: **excited**.*
čmpqin – faint; get a dark head; black out. *See: **faint**.*
es čmčmpasq̇t – The sky grows dark.

kʷ čiṁqn – something is dark with your brain; you are crazy. **ha kʷ nx̣el łu i l čiṁ** – Are you afraid of the dark?

čłčmpeneˀ – It got dark all over. *circumfix: **čł...eneˀ** – cover all over.*
čłčmpenˀeis – S/he/it made it get dark all over. **čłčmpenˀen, čłčmpenˀentxʷ**
es čłčmpenˀems – S/he/it is making it get dark all over. **ies čłčmpenˀem, as čłčmpenˀem**
qs čłčmpenˀems – S/he/it is going to make it get dark all over. **iqs čłčmpenˀem, aqs čłčmpenˀem**

darn

x̣ił – interjection; exclamation; darn; doggone; damn. *See: **exclamation**.*
x̣ił mtmi uł snčľé – Darn those no-good coyotes!

daughter

sṁmčˀélt, *sṁčˀé* – daughter *(general)*. **sṁtṁčˀélt** – daughters.

isťmčʔélt – my daughter.

šitmišlt – first born daughter or son.
q̇éʔew̓s – middle son or daughter. *suffix:* ***...éw̓s*** *– in between, middle.*
stʔéwtel̓t – youngest daughter.

sépn – daughter-in-law.
sč̓ʔelp – daughter-in-law after son's death.

sck̓ʷl̓sťmčʔé – foster daughter. *prefix:* ***sck̓ʷl̓...*** *– s.t. that's been made.*
skʷenltsťmčʔé – god daughter.

daughter-in-law

sépn – daughter-in-law.

sč̓ʔélp – son or daughter-in-law after death of spouse.

David

tapit – David.

dawn

snṗaq̇cin – dawn, *(before the sun comes up). rt.:* ***ṗaq̇*** *– bright; prefix:* ***sn...*** *– a place of.*

łx̣lpulexʷ, *łx̣lpu* – dawn, *(the first light of the morning). rt.:* ***x̣al*** *– light; prefix:* ***ł...*** *– little; suffix:* ***...ulexʷ*** *– land.*

c̓łe – sunrise, *(just as the sun is peeking over the mountain or land). See:* ***sunrise.***

cƛ̓éʔeč – peeking out, *(when the sun is partially up). See:* ***sunrise.***

sčpƛ̓e – sunrise, *(just when the sun comes off the mountain or land). See:* ***sunrise.***

day

sx̣lx̣alt, *sx̣lx̣a* – day.
x̣est sx̣lx̣alt – good day.

...ásq̇t – suffix indicating day, sky.
čmlk̓ʷmasq̇t, *čmlk̓ʷma* – all day long.
čmlk̓ʷma u čn sṗsqé l sqelixʷ – All day long I was hitting people.

čušnasq̇t – long day.
yetłx̣ʷasq̇t, *yetłx̣ʷa* – today.

ṅe eł nk̓ʷasq̇t – day after tomorrow.
ci t snk̓ʷasq̇t – day before yesterday.
ci t sʔaslasq̇t – two days ago.

snpƛ̓mstasq̇t – last day. *rt.:* ***pƛ̓im*** *– release from.*
x̣sasq̇tm – It was a good day.
čťosq̇t – half day.
łkʷk̓ʷsasq̇t – slow day.

šey̓ łu ṅe eł nk̓ʷasq̇t łu sčłʔeʔ – The day after tomorrow is Saturday.

es sinasq̇ti – counting days. *See:* ***calendar.***
nk̓ʷasq̇t – one day. **aslasq̇t** – two days. **čałlasq̇t** – three days. **mosq̇t** – four days. **clčstasq̇t** – five days. **ťq̇nčstasq̇t** – six days. **sṗl̓čstasq̇t** – seven days. **hʔanmasq̇t** – eight days. **x̣ṅtasq̇t** – nine days. **upnčstasq̇t** – ten days. **upn eł nk̓ʷasq̇t** – eleven days. **xʷʔasq̇t** – lot of days.

daydream

snap – stare off; daydream; become quiet and calm; settled.
snap – S/he daydreamed. **čn snap, kʷ snap**
es snpma – S/he is daydreaming. **čnes snpma, kʷes snpma**

The **i** following uvular consonants (UC) and the glottal stop **ʔ** sound like English "*ey*" as in the words th*ey*, h*ey*, wh*ey*, etc. Salish UC are: **q**, **q̇**, **qʷ**, **q̇ʷ**, **x̣**, **x̣ʷ**. For example, the suffix **...qin** – head/top, is often spelled using English *ey* as "q*ey*n". So **qi**, **q̇i**, **qʷi**, **q̇ʷi**, **x̣i**, **x̣ʷi**, may be spelled with English *ey* as **q***ey*, **q̇***ey*, **qʷ***ey*, **q̇ʷ***ey*, **x̣***ey*, **x̣ʷ***ey* in other texts.

s.t. - something, the 3rd person
(s.t.) - something implied
s.o. - someone, the 3rd person
sl. - singular form
pl. - plural form
rt. - root word
cmd. - command
lit. - literally
fig. - figuratively
i.e., - for example
See: - Redirection to a related word.

qs snpma – S/he is going to daydream. **čiqs snpma, kʷqs snpma**

saṅ – tranquil; quiet and calm; tame; settled. *See: **quiet**.*

Dayton
iʔłixʷ – Dayton, Flathead Nation.

dead
tmtmnéẏ – the dead; deceased; departed.

ƛ̓lil – one dies. *See: **die**.*
es ƛ̓lil – S/he/it is dead.

qʷmip – more than one dies. *See: **die**.*

ƛ̓leẏeʔ – play dead. *See: **die**.*

ƛ̓lƛ̓llmist – making one's self still; play dead. *See: **die**.*

dead tree
čéyeʔ – dead tree; snag; wood dry with age.

q̇ʷéllš – dead tree.

death camas
iẇéstn – death camas; *Zigadenus elegans*.

debt
xʷlxʷilt, *xʷlxʷi* – have debt.
qeʔ xʷlxʷilt – our debts.

k̇ʷl̇xʷlxʷi – get credit; make debt.
k̇ʷl̇xʷlxʷi – S/he made a debt. **čn k̇ʷl̇xʷlxʷi, kʷ k̇ʷl̇xʷlxʷi**
es k̇ʷl̇xʷlxʷi – S/he is making a debt. **čnes k̇ʷl̇xʷlxʷi, kʷes k̇ʷl̇xʷlxʷi**
qs k̇ʷl̇xʷlxʷi – S/he is going to make a debt. **čiqs k̇ʷl̇xʷlxʷi, kʷqs k̇ʷl̇xʷlxʷi**

puti kʷ epł xʷlxʷi – You still have a debt. **iscxʷlxʷi t inṗiṗuyšn –** I got the car on credit. **epł xʷlxʷi l anwi t upn ululim –** S/he owes you ten dollars; s/he has a debt of ten dollars to you. **k̇ʷłʔéṗnt inxʷlxʷi –** Eliminate my debt. *cmd.*

nšƛ̓pus – pay off debts in full. *See: **pay**.*

nk̇ʷlisusm, *nk̇ʷlisu* – pay one's debt. *See: **pay**.*

nsewpm – ask someone to repay their debt *(as a last resort the debtor has not paid and the lender has waited long enough)*.
nsewpm – S/he asked for a debt. **čn nsewpm, kʷ nsewpm**
es nsewpi – S/he is asking for a debt. **čnes nsewpi, kʷes nsewpi**
qs nsewpi – S/he is going to ask for a debt. **čiqs nsewpi, kʷqs nsewpi**

nsewpis – S/he asked s.o. for a debt. **nsewpn, nsewpntxʷ**
es nsewpms – S/he is asking for a debt. **ies nsewpm, as nsewpm**
qs nsewpms – S/he is going to ask for a debt. **iqs nsewpm, aqs nsewpm**

nsewpnt – Ask him/her to pay his/her debt. *cmd.*

decagon
upnčsq̇tq̇it – decagon; has ten flat sides.

December
esʔacṁi spq̇niʔ – December *(trapping month)*.

decide
mippscut, *mippscu* – decide for one's self. *rt.: **mi–** reality, the known; suffix: **...cut–** action to the self.*
mippscut – S/he decided for one's self. **čn mippscut, kʷ mippscut**
es mippscuti – S/he is deciding for one's self. **čnes mippscuti, kʷes mippscuti**

qs mippscuti – S/he is going to decide for one's self. **čiqs mippscuti, kʷqs mippscuti**

mippscutn – one's decision.

mippscutiš – Decide.

deep **nišut** – down inside; deep inside. *rt.: **išut** – down, low; prefix: **n...** – inside. See: **inside**.*
snišut – deep as a measure.
čeɫe sċušin snišut – three feet deep.

qʷést – deep snow.
nqʷést – deep water.
qʷestm – It got deep.
tl̓ ciʔ qʷestm – It got deeper.

l čeṅ u eċx̣lsqʷest ɫu asmek̓ʷt – How deep is your snow? **ha kʷ qʷestm** – Did your (snow) get deep?

The **i** following uvular consonants (UC) and the glottal stop **ʔ** sound like English "*ey*" as in the words *they*, *hey*, *whey*, etc. Salish UC are: **q**, **q̓**, **qʷ**, **q̓ʷ**, **x̣**, **x̣ʷ**. For example, the suffix **...qin** – head/top, is often spelled using English *ey* as "qeyn". So **qi**, **q̓i**, **qʷi**, **q̓ʷi**, **x̣i**, **x̣ʷi**, may be spelled with English *ey* as **q***ey*, **q̓***ey*, **qʷ***ey*, **q̓ʷ***ey*, **x̣***ey*, **x̣ʷ***ey* in other texts.

deer **ċúʔulixʷ**, *ċúʔu* – white-tail doe; *Odocoileus virginianus. See: **white-tail deer**.*
sx̣ʷl̓éščn, *sx̣ʷl̓é* – white-tail buck; *Odocoileus virginianus. See: **white-tail deer**.*
sṫulċeʔ – black-tail doe; female mule deer; mule; *Odocoileus hemionus. See: **black-tail deer**.*
puwélsčn, *puwé* – black-tail buck; male mule deer; *Odocoileus hemionus. See: **black-tail deer**.*
sɫpaʔpi, *paʔpi* – fawn.
sɫqʷq̓ʷɫte – fawn in fall; young deer after six months.

x̣ʷancoʔ – deer's whistle.
es x̣ʷancoʔ – The deer is whistling.

deer head **ċulixʷayaqn** – deer head.
cúʔulixʷ spɫqis – The deer's head.

deer hide **q̓ett** – hide.
ċulixʷélxʷ, *ċulixʷé* – buckskin, white-tail doe hide.
sx̣ʷl̓éščnelxʷ – white-tail buck hide.
sṫulċeʔlxʷ – black-tail doe hide.
puwélsčnelxʷ – black-tail buck hide.

deer lick **ciɫnqs** – deer lick; salt lick.

Deerlodge **sncwe** – Deerlodge, Montana.

deer mouse **k̓ʷék̓ʷṫneʔ** – deer mouse; mouse; *Peromyscus maniculatus.*

sqʷʔópɫxʷ – hole; den *(as of a mouse or rat). rt.: **qʷʔóp** – make soft; suffix: **...eɫxʷ**, **...ɫxʷ** – house.*

defeat **šƛ̓ip**, *šƛ̓i* – lose; defeated. *rt.: **šiƛ̓** – flat, level, aligned.*
šƛ̓ip – S/he/it lost. **čn šƛ̓ip, kʷ šƛ̓ip**
es šƛ̓pmi – S/he/it is losing. **čnes šƛ̓pmi, kʷes šƛ̓pmi**
qs šƛ̓pmi – S/he/it is going to lose. **čiqs šƛ̓pmi, kʷqs šƛ̓pmi**
šƛ̓íʔip – They lost. **qeʔ šƛ̓ip, p šƛ̓ip**
es šƛ̓pmíʔi – They are losing. **qeʔes šƛ̓pmi, pes šƛ̓pmi**
qs šƛ̓pmíʔi – They are going to lose. **qeʔqs šƛ̓pmi, pqs šƛ̓pmi**

šƛ̓pnuis – S/he/it defeated s.o. **šƛ̓pnun, šƛ̓pnuntxʷ**
es šƛ̓pnunms – S/he/it is defeating s.o. **ies šƛ̓pnunm, as šƛ̓pnunm**

s.t. - something, the 3rd person
(s.t.) - something implied
s.o. - someone, the 3rd person
sl. - singular form
pl. - plural form
rt. - root word
cmd. - command
lit. - literally
fig. - figuratively
i.e., - for example
See: - Redirection to a related word.

qs šƛ̓pnunms – S/he/it is going to defeat s.o. **iqs šƛ̓pnunm, aqs šƛ̓pnunm**
šƛ̓pnúˀuis – They defeated s.o. **qeˀ šƛ̓pnun, šƛ̓pnuntp**
es šƛ̓pnúˀunms – They are defeating s.o. **qeˀes šƛ̓pnunm, es šƛ̓pnunmp**
qs šƛ̓pnúˀunms – They are going to defeat s.o. **qeˀqs šƛ̓pnunm, qs šƛ̓pnunmp**

šƛ̓pnuntm – S/he was defeated.

šƛ̓pemn – one inclined to get defeated. *suffix: **...emn** – one inclined to do.*

šƛ̓ipš – Lose. *cmd.*
šƛ̓pnunt – Beat him/her. *cmd.*
šƛ̓pnuɬmn – defeated.
čeɬlšƛ̓ip – S/he lost three times. **čn čeɬlšƛ̓ip, kʷ čeɬlšƛ̓ip**
šƛ̓páqs, *šƛ̓pá* **–** win/defeat/beat at some contest or event. *See: **win.***

šƛ̓pnuncn – I defeated you.

defecate

ṁṅéč, *ṁṅé* **–** excrement; defecate; feces.
ṁṅéčm – S/he defecated. **čn ṁṅéčm, kʷ ṁṅéčm**
es ṁṅeči – S/he is defecating. **čnes ṁṅeči, kʷes ṁṅeči**
qs ṁṅeči – S/he is going to defecate. **čiqs ṁṅeči, kʷqs ṁṅeči**
ṁṅéˀečm – They defecate. **qeˀ ṁṅečm, p ṁṅečm**
es ṁṅéˀeči – They are defecating. **qeˀes ṁṅeči, pes ṁṅeči**
qs ṁṅéˀeči – They are going to defecate. **qeˀqs ṁṅeči, pqs ṁṅeči**

nṁṅčeẇsm – defecate pants. *suffix: **...éẇs** – in between, middle.*
nṁṅčeẇsm – S/he defecated one's pants. **čn nṁṅčeẇsm, kʷ nṁṅčeẇsm**
es nṁṅčeẇsi – S/he is defecating one's pants. **čnes nṁṅčeẇsm, kʷes nṁṅčeẇsi**
qs nṁṅčeẇsi – S/he is going to defecate one's pants. **čiqs nṁṅčeẇsm, kʷqs nṁṅčeẇsi**
nṁṅčéˀeẇsm – They defecated their pants. **qeˀ nṁṅčeẇsm, p nṁṅčeẇsm**
es nṁṅčéˀeẇsi – They are defecating their pants. **qeˀes nṁṅčeẇsm, pes nṁṅčeẇsi**
qs nṁṅčéˀeẇsi – They are going to defecate their pants. **qeˀqs nṁṅčeẇsm, pqs nṁṅčeẇsi**

nṁṅčelsm – want/need to defecate.
nṁṅčelsm – S/he needed to defecate. **čn nṁṅčelsm, kʷ nṁṅčelsm**
es nṁṅčelsi – S/he is needing to defecate. **čnes nṁṅčelsi, kʷes nṁṅčelsi**
qs nṁṅčelsi – S/he is going to need to defecate. **čiqs nṁṅčelsi, kʷqs nṁṅčelsi**

sṅṁṅé – toilet.
sṁṅčsqá – horse feces.

čiqs k̓ʷis ṁṅé – I am going to the outhouse. **mƛ̓miƛ̓šn t ṁṅéč –** Crap got smeared on both feet. **k̓ʷ še smx̣e ɬu epɬ ṁṅéč –** That's right it was the grizzly's crap. **iqs čṗṫaẇɬtm ye ṁṅéčs ye l ɬox̣ʷɬx̣ʷa –** I am going to put his/her crap up in the cherry tree. **ha kʷ ṁṅe –** Did you crap? **ha kʷ nṁṅčeẇsm –** Did you crap your pants?

lˀe u es nṗeṗhem – It pooped right here.

pċam – have diarrhea; evacuate liquid feces; skunk sprays. *See: **diarrhea.***

deficient

k̓ʷɬtwiṅtm – fall short of something; deficient in something; unable to attain something. *(i.e., betting, racing, trying to get something, etc.) rt.: **tuiṅ** – fail/deficient.*
k̓ʷɬtwiṅtm – S/he fell short *(of s.t.).* **čn k̓ʷɬtwiṅtm, kʷ k̓ʷɬtwiṅtm**
es k̓ʷɬtwiṅti – S/he is falling short *(of s.t.).* **čnes k̓ʷɬtwiṅti, kʷes k̓ʷɬtwiṅti**

k̓ʷɬtwiṅsts – S/he fell short of s.t. **čn k̓ʷɬtwiṅstn, kʷ k̓ʷɬtwiṅstxʷ**

es k̓ʷłttwiṅ – S/he is short of the mark. **čnes k̓ʷłttwiṅ, kʷes k̓ʷłttwiṅ**

es k̓ʷłtuṅlsmisti – S/he thinks s/he is lacking. **čnes k̓ʷłtuṅlsmisti, kʷes k̓ʷłtuṅlsmisti**

ntuṅičṅm – fail to catch up to someone; unable to catch up to someone; behind. *See:* ***catch.***

deflate **psas** – swelled object shrinks/flattens; deflate. *See:* ***swell.***

dehydrator **snčéxʷmn x̣ʷl̓ sʔiłn** – dryer for food; dehydrator.
snčéxʷmn x̣ʷl̓ sṗiʔqáłq – dryer for fruit; dehydrator.

demonstrative **lʔé** – this, these.

ci – that one.

den **sqʷʔópłxʷ** – hole; den *(as of a mouse or rat). rt.:* ***qʷʔóp*** *– make soft; suffix:* ***...ełxʷ, ...łxʷ*** *– house.*

nłx̣ʷolexʷ – hole; den. *rt.:* ***łoxʷ*** *– hole; suffix:* ***...ulexʷ*** *– land.*

nłx̣ʷlx̣ʷlalqʷ – hole; den in a log/tree. *rt.:* ***łoxʷ*** *– hole; suffix:* ***...alqʷ*** *– wood.*

dent **ṗé** – dent.
ṗéʔentes – S/he dented s.t. **ṗéʔenten, ṗéʔentexʷ**
es ṗéʔems – S/he is denting s.t. **ies ṗéʔem, as ṗéʔem**
qs ṗéʔems – S/he is going to dent s.t. **iqs ṗéʔem, aqs ṗéʔem**
ṗéʔeʔentes – They dented s.t. **qeʔ ṗéʔentem, ṗéʔentep**
es ṗéʔeʔems – They are denting s.t. **qeʔes ṗéʔem, es ṗéʔemp**
qs ṗéʔeʔems – They are going to dent s.t. **qeʔqs ṗéʔem, qs ṗéʔemp**

es ṗéʔ – It is dented.

ṗeṗʔéʔeʔ – It got dented.
ṗéʔentem – It got dented by s.t./s.o.

čṗéʔepm – indent something. *(i.e., skin, etc.) See:* ***indent.***

dentist **sxʷnċoqeysm** – dentist; someone tasked to pull teeth.

sxʷaċx̣eysm – dentist; someone tasked to look at teeth.

deny **tamm** – not; deny; refuse. *See:* ***refuse.***

łenmt – deny a charge made against one's self. *See:* ***serious.***

Derian **taliyán** – Derian.

descendant **awtmasqelixʷ**, *awtmasqe* – people of today; descendants; the people that follow those that already came. *rt.:* ***awtpa*** *– follow; suffix:* ***...sqe, ...sqelixʷ*** *– people. See:* ***follow.***

sxʷsixʷlt – offspring; children; descendants.

desert parsley **čéyči** – desert parsley; *Lomatium.*

sṗéxʷenč – desert parsley; *Lomatium.*

designs **sq̇iq̇ʔeẏ** – colors, designs.

desire **ṫinúxʷ** – desire something or someone.

The **i** following uvular consonants (UC) and the glottal stop **ʔ** sound like English "*ey*" as in the words *they, hey, whey*, etc. Salish UC are: **q, q̇, qʷ, q̇ʷ, x̣, x̣ʷ**. For example, the suffix **...qin** – head/top, is often spelled using English *ey* as "q*ey*n". So **qi, q̇i, qʷi, q̇ʷi, x̣i, x̣ʷi**, may be spelled with English *ey* as **q***ey*, **q̇***ey*, **qʷ***ey*, **q̇ʷ***ey*, **x̣***ey*, **x̣ʷ***ey* in other texts.

s.t. - something, the 3rd person
(s.t.) - something implied
s.o. - someone, the 3rd person
sl. - singular form
pl. - plural form
rt. - root word
cmd. - command
lit. - literally
fig. - figuratively
i.e., - for example
See: - Redirection to a related word.

ṫinúxʷis – S/he desired s.t./s.o. **ṫinúxʷn, ṫinúxʷntxʷ**
es ṫinúxʷms – S/he is desiring s.t./s.o. **ies ṫinúxʷm, as ṫinúxʷm**
qs ṫinúxʷms – S/he is going to desire s.t./s.o. **iqs ṫinúxʷm, aqs ṫinúxʷm**
ṫinúʔuxʷis – They desired s.t./s.o. **qeʔ ṫinúxʷntm, ṫinúxʷntp**
es ṫinúʔuxʷms – They are desiring s.t./s.o. **qeʔes ṫinúxʷm, es ṫinúxʷmp**
qs ṫinúʔuxʷms – They are going to desire s.t./s.o. **qeʔqs ṫinúxʷm, qs ṫinúxʷm**

ṫinxʷemn – one inclined to desire. *suffix: **...emn** – one inclined to do.*

ṫinúxʷiš – Desire. *cmd.*
ṫinúxʷnt – Desire it. *cmd.*
ṫinúxʷnwexʷ – They desired each other.

ṫinúxʷc – S/he desired you. **ṫinúxʷncn –** I desired you.

q̇xʷmin – desire for something not possessed; fond of something; wish for something that can be had.
q̇xʷmis – S/he desires s.t./s.o. **q̇xʷmin, q̇xʷmintxʷ**
es q̇xʷminms – S/he desires s.t./s.o. **ies q̇xʷminm, es q̇xʷminm**
q̇xʷmíʔis – They desire s.t./s.o. **qeʔ q̇xʷmintm, q̇xʷmintp**

es q̇exʷmscini – S/he is boasting; talk with big words. **čnes q̇exʷmscini, kʷes q̇exʷmscini**
es q̇xʷmnwexʷi – They are fond of/desire each other. **qeʔes q̇xʷmnwexʷi, pes q̇xʷmnwexʷi**

q̇exʷmscut – show-off; snobby; arrogant; self admiring. *See: **show-off**.*

q̇exʷmscutn – someone to desire one's self.

qeʔ qł q̇exʷmscutn – S/he will be the one desiring us.

q̇ix̣t – protective of something; fond of something possessed; attached to something.
q̇ix̣t – S/he was protective. **čn q̇ix̣t, kʷ q̇ix̣t**
es q̇ix̣ti – S/he is being protective. **čnes q̇ix̣ti, kʷes q̇ix̣ti**
qs q̇ix̣ti – S/he is going to be protective. **čiqs q̇ix̣ti, kʷqs q̇ix̣ti**

q̇ix̣tmis – S/he was protective of s.t. **q̇ix̣tmn, q̇ix̣tmntxʷ**
es q̇ix̣tmms – S/he is being protective of s.t. **ies q̇ix̣tmm, as q̇ix̣tmm**
qs q̇ix̣tmms – S/he is going to be protective of s.t. **iqs q̇ix̣tmm, aqs q̇ix̣tmm**

sq̇ix̣t – fondness.
q̇x̣tmncut – fond of one's self; love one's self.
es q̇x̣tmnwexʷi – They are fond of/attached to each other. **qeʔes q̇x̣tmnwexʷi, pes q̇x̣tmnwexʷi**

xʷmminm – yearn; long for; strongly desire. *See: **yearn**.*

q̇mscin – wish; hunger for. *See: **wish**.*

čłyuxʷt, *čłyu* – envious; want to be like; wish for something; feel bad over. *See: **envy**.*

čhomist, *čho* – in awe of something or someone; overwhelmed; see something beautiful/good/wonderful. *See: **awe**.*

desk

snq̇eẏmintn – desk; post office; any place to write. *prefix: **sn...** – a place of; suffix: **...tin, ...tn** – means of/device.*

despair

yéṁmist, *yéṁm* – despaired; frustrated; troubled; worried; have a block; have a dilemma.
i yeṁ – S/he/it is at a block. **i čn yeṁ, i kʷ yeṁ**

yeṁm – S/he was frustrated/despaired. **čn yeṁm, kʷ yeṁmi**
es yeṁmi – S/he is frustrated/despaired. **čnes yeṁmi, kʷes yeṁmi**

qs yeṁmi – S/he is going to be frustrated/despaired. **čiqs yeṁmi, kʷqs yeṁmi**

yeṁmis – S/he was frustrated/despaired at s.t. **yeṁmn, yeṁmntxʷ**
es yeṁmms – S/he is frustrated/despaired at s.t. **ies yeṁmm, as yeṁmm**
qs yeṁmms – S/he is going to be frustrated/despaired at s.t. **iqs yeṁmm, aqs yeṁmm**

yeṁmsts – S/he caused s.o. frustration. **yeṁmstn, yeṁmstxʷ**
es yeṁmsts – S/he is causing s.o. frustration. **es yeṁmstn, es yeṁmstxʷ**
qs yeṁmsts – S/he is going to be causing s.o. frustration. **qs yeṁmstn, qs yeṁmstxʷ**

iṁmscut – S/he was frustrated with one's self. **čn iṁmscut, kʷ iṁmscut**
es iṁmscuti – S/he is frustrated with one's self. **čnes iṁmscuti, kʷes iṁmscuti**
qs iṁmscuti – S/he is going to be frustrated with one's self. **čiqs iṁmscuti, kʷqs iṁmscuti**

niṁmelsm – S/he feels frustrated. **čn niṁmelsm, kʷ niṁmelsm**
es niṁmelsi – S/he is feeling frustrated. **čnes niṁmelsi, kʷes niṁmelsi**
qs niṁmelsi – S/he is going to feel frustrated. **čiqs niṁmelsi, kʷqs niṁmelsi**

The **i** following uvular consonants (UC) and the glottal stop **ʔ** sound like English "*ey*" as in the words th*ey*, h*ey*, wh*ey*, etc. Salish UC are: **q, q̓, qʷ, q̓ʷ, x̣, x̣ʷ**. For example, the suffix **...qin** – head/top, is often spelled using English *ey* as "q*ey*n". So **qi, q̓i, qʷi, q̓ʷi, x̣i, x̣ʷi**, may be spelled with English *ey* as **q***ey*, **q̓***ey*, **qʷ***ey*, **q̓ʷ***ey*, **x̣***ey*, **x̣ʷ***ey* in other texts.

iṁmemn – one inclined to be despaired. *suffix: **...emn** – one inclined to do.*
syeṁm – the despair.
scyeṁm – something that has been despairing.
čyeṁmn – something that is needed.
yeṁyṁt – something despairing; impossible.

yeṁm łu islax̣t – My friend is at a block; my friend is frustrated. **es k̓ʷłyéṁms –** S/he is troubled about s.t. **łu tʔe steṁ u kʷ yéṁm –** You were troubled by anything. **čnes yeṁmi x̣ʷl̓ čn oost –** I am frustrated because I am lost. **yeṁmłcn łu asqʷlqʷelt –** I was troubled with your talk. **ta čn ep syeṁm –** I have no frustration/no despair.

čmšqnmist, *čmšqnmi* **–** give up. *See: **give up**.*

despise

tmals – despise; disregard; spurn; pay no attention to; have no feelings for; have no care for; have no respect for. *rt.: **tam** – not, deny; suffix: **...els, ...ls** – want, feel.*
tmalsi – S/he acted with disregard. **čn tmalsi, kʷ tmalsi**
es tmalsi – S/he is acting with disregard. **čnes tmalsi, kʷes tmalsi**
qs tmalsi – S/he is going to act with disregard. **čiqs tmalsi, kʷqs tmalsi**

tmalsmis – S/he despised s.o. **tmalsmn, tmalsmntxʷ**
es tmalsms – S/he is despising s.o. **ies tmalsm, as tmalsm**
qs tmalsms – S/he is going to despise s.o. **iqs tmalsm, aqs tmalsm**

es tmlsmnwexʷi – They despise each other. **qeʔes tmlsmnwexʷi, pes tmlsmnwexʷi**

s.t. - something, the 3rd person
(s.t.) - something implied
s.o. - someone, the 3rd person
sl. - singular form
pl. - plural form
rt. - root word
cmd. - command
lit. - literally
fig. - figuratively
i.e., - for example
See: - Redirection to a related word.

determined

ta sṗllčusm, *ta sṗllču* **–** determined; does not turn back.

ax̣lwis, *ax̣lwi* **–** hustle around for something; able, determined in doing something. *See: **busy**.*
čn ax̣lwi u k̓ʷul̓n łu k̓ʷłnčmé – I was determined, able in fixing the door. **áx̣lwis u wičts sxʷmalyé –** S/he was determined, able in finding a doctor. **ax̣lwis pasqá u k̓ʷłči –** Through his determination Pascal arrived here or there. **ax̣lwis qʷléwyeʔ uẏé –** Valeria kept at it and got done.

detest

čeṁm – detest; reject something; have no care for something; snub something.
čeṁis – S/he rejected s.t. **čeṁn, čeṁntxʷ**

es čem̓ms – S/he is rejecting s.t. **ies čem̓m, as čem̓m**
qs čem̓ms – S/he is going to reject s.t. **iqs čem̓m, aqs čem̓m**
čéʔem̓is – They rejected s.t. **qeʔ čem̓ntm, čem̓ntp**
es čéʔem̓ms – They reject s.t./s.o. **qeʔes čém̓m, es čém̓mp**
qs čéʔem̓ms – They are going to reject s.t./s.o. **qeʔqs čém̓m, qs čém̓mp**

es čm̓čem̓ms – S/he is rejecting things. **ies čm̓čem̓m, as čm̓čem̓m**

čem̓ntm – S/he/it was rejected.

sččem̓ – something that was rejected.
čem̓istemn – one inclined to reject things. *suffix:* ***...emn*** *– one inclined to do.*
čm̓čm̓mul – one that habitually detests. *suffix:* ***...ɬmuɬ*** *– one that habitually does.*

čem̓iš – Reject. *cmd.*
čem̓nt – Reject it. *cmd.*
čem̓ncut – detest one's self.
čem̓nwexʷ – detest each other.
čm̓čm̓snuxʷ – worthy of rejection.
čem̓małq – rejected when trying to get with someone. *suffix:* ***...ałq*** *– smell, accompaniment.*

ies čém̓m łu incitxʷ – I reject my house; I do not care for my house.

nʔaymls – have bad feelings; have inner anger.
nʔaymlsm – S/he/it had bad feelings. **čn nʔaymlsm, kʷ nʔaymlsm**
es nʔaymlsi – S/he/it has bad feelings. **čnes nʔaymlsi, kʷes nʔaymlsi**
qs nʔaymlsi – S/he/it is going to have bad feelings. **čiqs nʔaymlsi, kʷqs nʔaymlsi**

nʔaymlsis – S/he/it had bad feelings toward s.o. **nʔaymlsn, nʔaymlsntxʷ**
es nʔaymlsms – S/he/it has bad feelings toward s.o. **ies nʔaymlsm, as nʔaymlsm**
qs nʔaymlsms – S/he/it is going to have bad feelings toward s.o. **iqs nʔaymlsm, aqs nʔaymlsm**

nʔaymlsemn – one inclined to have bad feelings. *suffix:* ***...emn*** *– one inclined to do.*

nʔaymlsmnwexʷ – have bad feelings toward each other.

ta kʷ qes nʔayml̓s – Do not have bad feeling. **ta qʷo qs nʔaymlsmstxʷ** – Do not have bad feelings toward me.

aim̓eʔ – hate. *See:* ***hate.***

nčesls – grouchy; angry feelings. *See:* ***grouchy.***

devil

sx̣ʷélmn – devil. *rt.:* ***x̣ʷél*** *– abandon. See:* ***abandon.***

emtep – Sits-at-the-base.

c̓otelixʷ – The-bad-one.

dew

t̓iimutiyeʔ – dew. *suffix:* ***...mutiyeʔ*** *– temporary.*
es t̓iimutiyeʔi – It is dewy.

t̓im – damp.
i t̓im – It is damp.
t̓im̓lexʷ – damp ground, swamp.

diameter

skʷtisyal – diameter; big roundness.
t čen̓ ec̓x̣lskʷtisyal łu pumin – How big is the *(diameter)* drum?

yult – large in girth. *(of cylindrical objects.)* *See:* ***girth.***

t čeṅ ecx̣lsyult – How big is the girth?

łqqalqʷ – narrow in girth. *(of cylindrical objects.)*

diamond **qʷqʷaqʷʔeʔ –** diamond shape.

diaper **nłqʷéẃstn,** *nłqʷé –* diaper.

nłqʷépustšn – diaper; breechcloth; loincloth.

x̣ʷl̓ šeẏ u es nłqʷéẃs – That's why s/he wears a diaper.

The **i** following uvular consonants (UC) and the glottal stop **ʔ** sound like English "*ey*" as in the words th*ey*, h*ey*, wh*ey*, etc. Salish UC are: **q**, **q̓**, **qʷ**, **q̓ʷ**, **x̣**, **x̣ʷ**. For example, the suffix ...**qin** – head/top, is often spelled using English *ey* as "q*ey*n". So **qi**, **q̓i**, **qʷi**, **q̓ʷi**, **x̣i**, **x̣ʷi**, may be spelled with English *ey* as **q***ey*, **q̓***ey*, **qʷ***ey*, **q̓ʷ***ey*, **x̣***ey*, **x̣ʷ***ey* in other texts.

diarrhea **pċam –** have diarrhea; evacuate liquid feces; skunk sprays.

pċam – S/he/it had diarrhea. **čn pċam, kʷ pċam**
es pċma – S/he/it has diarrhea. **čnes pċma, kʷes pċma**
qs pċma – S/he/it is going to have diarrhea. **čiqs pċma, kʷqs pċma**

pċntas – S/he/it evacuated on s.o. **pċntan, pċntaxʷ**
es pċams – S/he/it is evacuating on s.o. **ies pċam, as pċam**
qs pċams – S/he/it is going to evacuate on s.o. **iqs pċam, aqs pċam**

pċmstas – S/he/it made s.o. evacuate diarrhea. **pċmstan, pċmstaxʷ**
es pċmams – S/he/it is making s.o. evacuate diarrhea. **ies pċmam, as pċmam**
qs pċmams – S/he/it is going to make s.o. evacuate diarrhea. **iqs pċmam, aqs pċmam**

pċmanis – S/he/it squirted it out. **pċmanmn, pċmanmntxʷ**
es pċmanms – S/he/it is squirting it out. **ies pċmanm, as pċmanm**
qs pċmanms – S/he/it is going to squirt it out. **iqs pċmanm, aqs pċmanm**

spaċ – diarrhea; fly feces.

pċmantn – laxative.

pċaiš – Squirt it out. *cmd.*
pċmaskʷ – Make s.o. evacuate diarrhea. *cmd.*
es pċncoti – S/he is evacuating diarrhea in one's pants. **čnes pċncoti, kʷes pċncoti**
es pċmalsi – S/he is wanting to evacuate diarrhea. **čnes pċmalsi, kʷes pċmalsi**
pċmlwis – going around with diarrhea.

qʷo pċntas t x̣stéyẏeʔ – The skunk sprayed me. **pċntas sk̓ʷuys t łox̣te –** The baby evacuated diarrhea on his mother. **ta kʷ qes čxʷʔaqsm t sƛ̓ša x̣iṅe m kʷ pċmals –** Don't eat too many huckleberries, you might get diarrhea.

dictionary **nyoʔnuntn q̓eẏmin –** dictionary.

die **ƛ̓lil –** one dies.

ƛ̓lil – S/he/it died. **čn ƛ̓lil, kʷ ƛ̓lil**
es ƛ̓llmi – S/he/it is dying. **čnes ƛ̓llmi, kʷes ƛ̓llmi**
qs ƛ̓llmi – S/he/it is going to be dying. **čiqs ƛ̓llmi, kʷqs ƛ̓llmi**

scƛ̓lil – death. *prefix:* **sc...** *– s.t. that's been done/made/prepared.*
puʔƛ̓lil – spouse of s.o. who died.

ƛ̓lƛ̓elil – have the appearance of dying. *(i.e., to fall from becoming unconscious, as in fainting, etc.)*
ƛ̓lsqá – His/her horse/car is dead. **čn ƛ̓lsqá, kʷ ƛ̓lsqá**

s.t. - something, the 3rd person
(s.t.) - something implied
s.o. - someone, the 3rd person
sl. - singular form
pl. - plural form
rt. - root word
cmd. - command
lit. - literally
fig. - figuratively
i.e., - for example
See: - Redirection to a related word.

ṅe qeʔ čč̓ʔit l qeʔ scƛ̓lil – When we are near death. **t snx̣el u ƛ̓lil –** S/he died of fear. **kʷssusntm u ƛ̓lil –** S/he was startled and died.

ƛ̓lƛ̓lels – feel like dying. *suffix: **...els, ...ls** – want, feel.*
ƛ̓lƛ̓lels – S/he felt like s/he was going to die. **čn ƛ̓lƛ̓lels, kʷ ƛ̓lƛ̓lels**
es ƛ̓lƛ̓lelsi – S/he is feeling like s/he is going to die. **čnes ƛ̓lƛ̓lelsi, kʷes ƛ̓lƛ̓lelsi**

ƛ̓leẏeʔ – play dead.
es ƛ̓leẏeʔi – S/he/it is playing dead. **es ƛ̓leẏeʔi, es ƛ̓leẏeʔi**

ƛ̓lƛ̓llmist – making one's self still; play dead.
ƛ̓lƛ̓llmist – S/he/it played dead. **čn ƛ̓lƛ̓llmist, kʷ ƛ̓lƛ̓llmist**
es ƛ̓lƛ̓llmisti – S/he/it is playing dead. **čnes ƛ̓lƛ̓llmisti, kʷes ƛ̓lƛ̓llmisti**
qs ƛ̓lƛ̓llmisti – S/he/it is going to play dead. **čiqs ƛ̓lƛ̓llmisti, kʷqs ƛ̓lƛ̓llmisti**
es ƛ̓lƛ̓llmíʔisti – They are playing dead. **qeʔes ƛ̓lƛ̓llmisti, pes ƛ̓lƛ̓llmisti**

ƛ̓lƛ̓llmistiš – Play dead. *cmd.*

qʷmip – more than one dies.
qʷmiʔip – They died. **qeʔ qʷmip, p qʷmip**
es qʷmpmi – They are dying. **qeʔes qʷmpmi, pes qʷmpmi**
qs qʷmpmi – They are going to be dying. **qeʔqs qʷmpmi, pqs qʷmpmi**

qʷmpstes – S/he caused them to die. **qʷmpstes, qʷmpstes**
es qʷmpims – S/he is causing them to die. **ies qʷmpim, as qʷmpim**

qʷmpiskʷ – Make them die. *cmd.*

qʷmim – kill more than one at a time; killing them all off. *See: **kill**.*

qeʔes qʷmpmi łu t scsust – We're dying of something that has been drank. **isqʷsqʷseʔ ta ep sʔiłn**
ṅem qʷmiʔip – My sons have no food and are going to die.

es šʔalqin – S/he was unaware s/he was making "final rounds" before dying; preparing for death. *(Said after death, in hindsight; a person went around and visited relatives, friends and old acquaintances; as if the person was saying their final farewells.)*
es šʔalqini – S/he/it is preparing for death. **čnes šʔalqini, kʷes šʔalqini**
es šʔalqíʔini – They are preparing for death. **qeʔes šʔalqini, pes šʔalqini**

k̓ʷ še šʔalqin – Oh that's what s/he was doing; preparing for death.

mix̣ʷt – gravely ill; dying.
es mix̣ʷti – S/he is gravely ill. **čnes mix̣ʷti, kʷes mix̣ʷti**

hoy mix̣ʷt łu šeẏ sqelixʷ – That person is gravely ill.

nc̓spulexʷ – massacre; wiped out from the land. *See: **massacre**.*

kʷel – change outward perception; change color; ripening/dying. *See: **change**.*

different

t̓ixʷlm – different.
łt̓t̓ixʷlm – a little different.

es t̓ixʷlm – It is different.
es t̓xʷt̓ixʷlm – Each one is different.

nt̓xʷlméls – change attitude. *See: **change attitude**.*
t̓xʷlmncut – change one's self; to disguise. *See: **disguise**.*
t̓xʷlmist – change one's self spiritually. *See: **disguise**.*

nt̓xʷt̓xʷlmeẇs – different kinds. *suffix: **...éẇs** – in between, middle.*

t̓xʷlelixʷ – different people.
t̓xʷlmulexʷ – different land.

es ṫxʷṫixʷlm sšeṅš – The rocks are different shapes and colors. **kʷeṁt tl̓ šeẏ cxʷuy łu sqélixʷ u es ṫixʷlm –** Then from there things came to be changed/got different for the people. **cxʷuy łu sqelixʷ u ṫixʷlm łu nuwewlštn –** People came and the language changed.

nšƛ̓aqsm, *nšƛ̓a* – many things not the same grouped together. *rt.:* ***šiƛ̓*** *– flat, level, aligned.*
nšƛ̓aqsm sšeṅš – different kinds of rocks. **nšƛ̓áqsm xʷixʷeẏuł –** all kinds of wildlife. **nšƛ̓aqsm łu ṗiṗuyšn –** all kinds of cars. **nšƛ̓aqsm sqelixʷ –** all kinds of people.

wičm nšƛ̓a xʷixʷeẏuł – I saw all kinds of animals. **nšƛ̓aqsm es ṫxʷṫixʷlm ṗuṗuyšn –** There are all kinds of different cars.

> The **i** following uvular consonants (UC) and the glottal stop **ʔ** sound like English "*ey*" as in the words th*ey*, h*ey*, wh*ey*, etc. Salish UC are: **q**, **q̇**, **qʷ**, **q̇ʷ**, **x̣**, **x̣ʷ**. For example, the suffix **…qin** – head/top, is often spelled using English *ey* as "q*ey*n". So **qi**, **q̇i**, **qʷi**, **q̇ʷi**, **x̣i**, **x̣ʷi**, may be spelled with English *ey* as **q***ey*, **q̇***ey*, **qʷ***ey*, **q̇ʷ***ey*, **x̣***ey*, **x̣ʷ***ey* in other texts.

difficult

tl̓xʷéčst, *tl̓xʷé* – difficult; hard to do; struggle at something; unable to succeed. *suffix:* ***…ečst, …čst*** *– of the hand.*
tl̓xʷe – S/he/it had a difficult time; struggled. **čn tl̓xʷe, kʷ tl̓xʷe**
es tl̓xʷeli – S/he/it is struggling. **čnes tl̓xʷeli, kʷes tl̓xʷeli**
qs tl̓xʷeli – S/he/it is going to struggle. **čiqs tl̓xʷeli, kʷqs tl̓xʷeli**

til̓xʷis – S/he/it failed with s.t. **til̓xʷn, til̓xʷntxʷ**
es til̓xʷms – S/he/it is failing with s.t. **čnes til̓xʷm, kʷes til̓xʷm**
qs til̓xʷms – S/he/it is going to fail with s.t. **čiqs til̓xʷm, kʷqs til̓xʷm**

til̓tl̓xʷt – difficult; hard.
tl̓tl̓xʷsnuxʷ – difficult; impossible. *suffix:* ***…snuxʷ*** *– worthy of.*

tl̓xʷncut – unable to do anything with one's self; crippled. *See:* ***cripple.***

til̓tl̓xʷt łu sʔaq̇m – It is difficult to scrape *(a hide)*. **x̣ił til̓tl̓xʷt łu šeẏ –** That is really difficult.

ƛ̓ic̓t – hard; tough; hard to break. *See:* ***hard.***

dig

ciq – dig.
ciqm – S/he/it dug. **čn ciqm, kʷ ciqm**
es ciqi – S/he/it is digging. **čnes ciqi, kʷes ciqi**
qs ciqi – S/he/it is going to dig. **čiqs ciqi, kʷqs ciqi**
cíʔiqm – They dug. **qeʔ ciqm, p ciqm**
es cíʔiqi – They are digging. **qeʔes ciqi, pes ciqi**
qs cíʔiqi – They are going to dig. **qeʔqs ciqi, pqs ciqi**

ciqis – S/he/it dug s.t. **ciqn, ciqntxʷ**
es ciqms – S/he/it is digging s.t. **ies ciqm, as ciqm**
qs ciqms – S/he/it is going to dig s.t. **iqs ciqm, aqs ciqm**
cíʔiqis – They dug s.t. **qeʔ ciqntm, ciqntp**
es cíʔiqms – They are digging s.t. **qeʔes ciqm, es ciqmp**
qs cíʔiqms – They are going to dig s.t. **qeʔqs ciqm, qs ciqmp**

ciqcq – dig. *pl.*

ṅem nciqm – S/he/it will dig. **ṅem čn nciqm, ṅem kʷ nciqm**
ncíʔiqm – They will dig. **ṅem qeʔ nciqm, ṅem p nciqm**
ṅem qes ciqms – S/he/it will be digging it. **ṅem iqes ciqm, ṅem aqes ciqm**
ṅem qs cíʔiqms – They will be digging it. **ṅem qeʔqes ciqm, ṅem qes ciqmp**
ṅem kʷ nciqm t aq snq̇ʷl̓éptn – You will dig your baking pit.

> s.t. - something, the 3rd person
> (s.t.) - something implied
> s.o. - someone, the 3rd person
> *sl.* - singular form
> *pl.* - plural form
> *rt.* - root word
> *cmd.* - command
> *lit.* - literally
> *fig.* - figuratively
> *i.e.,* - for example
> *See:* - Redirection to a related word.

x̣éct – dig roots.
x̣ect – S/he dug. **čn x̣ect, kʷ x̣ect**
es x̣ecti – S/he is digging. **čnes x̣ecti, kʷes x̣ecti**

qs x̣ecti – S/he is going to dig. **čiqs x̣ecti, kʷqs x̣ecti**
x̣éʔect – They dug. **qeʔ x̣ect, p x̣ect**
es x̣éʔecti – They are digging. **qeʔes x̣ecti, pes x̣ecti**
qs x̣éʔecti – They are going to dig. **qeʔqs x̣ecti, pqs x̣ecti**

x̣ectis – S/he dug the roots. **x̣ectn, x̣ectntxʷ**
es x̣ectms – S/he is digging the roots. **ies x̣ectm, as x̣ectm**
qs x̣ectms – S/he is going to dig the roots. **iqs x̣ectm, aqs x̣ectm**

x̣ecštis – S/he dug the roots for s.o. **x̣ecštn, x̣ecštxʷ**
es x̣ecštms – S/he is digging the roots for s.o. **ies x̣ecštm, as x̣ecštm**
qs x̣ecštms – S/he is going to dig the roots for s.o. **iqs x̣ecštm, aqs x̣ecštm**

sxʷx̣ect – one tasked to dig roots.
scx̣ect – roots that have been dug.

x̣ectiš – Dig. *cmd.*
x̣ectnt – Dig the roots. *cmd.*
x̣cctutm – roots are good to dig; ripe to dig.
x̣cctmutm – roots can be dug, the ground is not too hard.
nx̣ctels – want to dig roots.
nx̣ctmlwis – going around digging roots; digging roots here and there.

ṅem p eł k̓ʷis x̣ect – You guys will go back to dig. **kʷes x̣ecti t sx̣ʷéʔli –** You are digging camas. **tas x̣cctmutmstn –** I could not dig out the roots; the ground was too hard. **ṅe kʷékʷst m qeʔ k̓ʷis x̣ect –** In the morning we are going to go dig. **łoq̓ʷnt esyáʔ ascx̣ect –** Peel everything you dig up. **qeʔes x̣ec̓ti –** We are digging.

nwec̓ – dig something out with a tool. *(i.e., digging out marrow with a stick, etc.)*
nwec̓i – S/he picked (s.t.) out. **čn newc̓, kʷ nwec̓i**
es nwec̓i – S/he is picking (s.t.) out. **čnes nwec̓i, kʷes nwec̓i**
qs nwec̓i – S/he is going to pick (s.t.) out. **čiqs nwec̓i, kʷqs nwec̓i**

nuc̓isncutn, *nuc̓isncu* – toothpick.

digger
péceʔ – digger, digging tool for roots. *(originally made of horn; now metal)*
pcpéceʔ – diggers.

digit
t̓ix̣ – sticks out.
st̓ix̣čst – finger. *suffix: **...ečst, ...čst** – of the hand.*
st̓ix̣šn – toe.
st̓x̣t̓ix̣čst – fingers. *suffix: **...ečst, ...čst** – of the hand.*
st̓x̣t̓ix̣šn – toes.

dilemma
yéṁmist, *yéṁm* – despaired; frustrated; troubled; worried; have a block; have a dilemma. *See: **despair**.*

dining table
snčłeľiłntn, *snčłeľi* – table for many people. *rt.: **iłn** – eat; prefix: **sn...** – a place of; suffix: **...tin, ...tn** – means of/device.*

snčł̓ʔiłntn – table for one person. *rt.: **iłn** – eat; refix: **sn...** – a place of; suffix: **...tin, ...tn** – means of/device.*

dinner
čluxʷm – eat supper/dinner. *See: **supper**.*

dip
es nčuxʷ – dip in the land.
nčxʷulexʷ – It is a dip in the land.

čxʷčxʷulexʷ – dips in the land.

k̇ʷɫmulm – dip/scoop out water. *rt.: **mul**– remove from water/liquid.*
k̇ʷɫmulis – S/he got water. **k̇ʷɫmuln, k̇ʷɫmulntxʷ**
es k̇ʷɫmulms – S/he is getting water. **ies k̇ʷɫmulm, as k̇ʷɫmulm**
qs k̇ʷɫmulms – S/he is going to get water. **iqs k̇ʷɫmulm, aqs k̇ʷɫmulm**
k̇ʷɫmúʔulis – They got water. **qeʔ k̇ʷɫmulntm, k̇ʷɫmulntp**
es k̇ʷɫmúʔulms – They are getting water. **qeʔes k̇ʷɫmulm, es k̇ʷɫmulmp**
qs k̇ʷɫmúʔulms – They are going to get water. **qeʔqs k̇ʷɫmulm, qs k̇ʷɫmulmp**

ṅem k̇ʷɫmulm – S/he will get water. **ṅem čn k̇ʷɫmulm, ṅem kʷ k̇ʷɫmulm**
ṅem k̇ʷɫmúʔulm – They will get water. **ṅem qeʔ k̇ʷɫmulm, ṅem p k̇ʷɫmulm**
ṅem qs k̇ʷɫmulms – S/he will be getting water. **ṅem iqs k̇ʷɫmulm, ṅem aqs k̇ʷɫmulm**
ṅem qs k̇ʷɫmúʔulms – They will be getting water. **ṅem qeʔqs k̇ʷɫmulm, ṅem qs k̇ʷɫmulmp**

The **i** following uvular consonants (UC) and the glottal stop **ʔ** sound like English "*ey*" as in the words th*ey*, h*ey*, wh*ey*, etc. Salish UC are: **q, q̇, qʷ, q̇ʷ, x̣, x̣ʷ**. For example, the suffix ...**qin** – head/top, is often spelled using English *ey* as "q*ey*n". So **qi, q̇i, qʷi, q̇ʷi, x̣i, x̣ʷi**, may be spelled with English *ey* as **q***ey*, **q̇***ey*, **qʷ***ey*, **q̇ʷ***ey*, **x̣***ey*, **x̣ʷ***ey* in other texts.

sxʷk̇ʷɫmulm – one tasked to dip for water. *prefix: **sxʷ...** – one tasked to do.*
ƛ̓mulmn – container to get water.

k̇ʷɫmuliš – Scoop out water. *cmd.*
k̇ʷɫmulškʷ – Scoop out water. *cmd.*

nmulm – fetch water/liquid *(from the sound made dipping a container in water; used to indicate the motion getting water). See: **fetch**.*

k̇ʷɫmuliš stipn – Scoop out some water, Stephen.

nkʷelm – dip/submerge in water/liquid.
nkʷelis – S/he dipped s.t. in water. **nkʷeln, nkʷelntxʷ**
es nkʷelms – S/he is dipping s.t. in water. **ies nkʷelm, as nkʷelm**
qs nkʷelms – S/he is going to dip s.t. in water. **iqs nkʷelm, aqs nkʷelm**

nkʷelnt – Dip it in the water. *cmd.*
es nkʷelčsti – S/he is dipping one's hand in water. **čn es nkʷelčsti, kʷes nkʷelčsti**
es nkʷlkʷelčsti – S/he is dipping one's hands in water. **čn es nkʷlkʷelčsti, kʷes nkʷlkʷelčsti**

nločstetkʷ – put/dip finger in water/liquid.
nločstetkʷm – S/he dipped a finger in water. **čn nločstetkʷm, kʷ nločstetkʷm**

nlawatkʷps – dip into water. *(i.e., birds.)*

nʔoʔopqs – dip into water in search of food. *(i.e., ducks, geese, moose, etc.)*
es nʔoʔopqsi – It is dipping into the water in search of food.

s.t. - something, the 3rd person
(s.t.) - something implied
s.o. - someone, the 3rd person
sl. - singular form
pl. - plural form
rt. - root word
cmd. - command
lit. - literally
fig. - figuratively
i.e., - for example
See: - Redirection to a related word.

dipper

snk̇ʷɫmulmn, *snk̇ʷɫmu* – dipper *(for water)*. *rt.: **nmulm** – get water.*

q̇ʷox̣ʷṁiṅeʔ – American dipper; water osel; *Cinclus mexicanus*.

direction

sc̓altulexʷ – north.
sx̣alptin – east.
sƛ̓aq̇lexʷ – south.
sčlxʷtin – west.
sṫčmíʔis – guide; direction.

tax̣ʷlus – face/head toward a direction; start in a direction. *See: **start**.*

dirt

malt – mud. *See: **mud**.*

sṫulixʷ – ground; earth; land; field. *See:* ***earth.***

dirty

ṫiɫ – dirty.

i ṫiɫ – S/he/it is dirty.

ṫiɫs – dirty face.
ɫṫṫiɫs – little dirty face.
nṫɫups – dirty butt. *rt.:* ***ṫiɫ*** *– dirty; circumfix:* ***n...ups*** *– butt, tail.*

mal – muddy; soiled with mud/dirt. *See:* ***mud.***

čečéʔt – nasty. *See:* ***nasty.***

disability

ntmlsmncot – disability; unable to do something. *rt.:* ***tam*** *– not, deny; circumfix:* ***n...els*** *– want, feel; suffix:* ***...cut*** *– action to the self.*

disagree

q̇eyus – doubt; disbelief; question. *See:* ***doubt.***

disappear

ċsip – disappear; gone; wiped out; cleared out.
ċsip – S/he/it disappeared. **čn ċsip, kʷ ċsip**
es ċspmi – S/he/it is disappearing. **čnes ċspmi, kʷes ċspmi**
qs ċspmi – S/he/it is going to disappear. **čiqs ċspmi, kʷqs ċspmi**
ċsíʔip – They disappeared. **qeʔ ċsip, p ċsip**
es ċspmíʔi – They are disappearing. **qeʔes ċspmi, pes ċspmi**
qs ċspmíʔi – They are going to disappear. **qeʔqs ċspmi, pqs ċspmi**

ċspnuis – S/he/it completed clearing it out. **ċspnun, ċspnuntxʷ**
es ċspnunms – S/he/it is in the process of clearing s.t. out. **ies ċspnunm, as ċspnunm**
qs ċspnunms – S/he/it is going to be in the process of clearing s.t. out. **iqs ċspnunm, aqs ċspnunm**

ċspnuis – S/he/it got wiped out.

es ċsċspmi – Each one is disappearing.

k̇ʷlċsip – family is wiped out.
ċsim – clear; clear clutter/items/objects. *See:* ***clear.***
čɫċsim – sweep/clear the surface. *See:* ***sweep.***

k̇ʷɫčluxʷ – go out of sight around an obstacle. *(i.e., a tree, hill, rock, building, etc.)*
k̇ʷɫčlxʷmncut – S/he/it went out of sight. **čn k̇ʷɫčlxʷmncut, kʷ k̇ʷɫčlxʷmncut**
es k̇ʷɫčlxʷmncuti – S/he/it is going out of sight. **čnes k̇ʷɫčlxʷmncuti, kʷes k̇ʷɫčlxʷmncuti**
qs k̇ʷɫčlxʷmncuti – S/he/it is going to go out of sight. **čiqs k̇ʷɫčlxʷmncuti, kʷqs k̇ʷɫčlxʷmncuti**
k̇ʷɫčlxʷmncúʔut – They went out of sight. **qeʔ k̇ʷɫčlxʷmncut, p k̇ʷɫčlxʷmncut**
es k̇ʷɫčlxʷmncúʔuti – They are going out of sight. **qeʔes k̇ʷɫčlxʷmncuti, pes k̇ʷɫčlxʷmncuti**
qs k̇ʷɫčlxʷmncúʔuti – They are going to go out of sight. **qeʔqs k̇ʷɫčlxʷmncuti, pqs k̇ʷɫčlxʷmncuti**

es k̇ʷɫčluxʷ – S/he/it got out of sight.

aámt – melt; dissolve away. *See:* ***melt.***

disappointed

nmaẇls – disappointed; discouraged; have broken feelings. *rt.:* ***maẇ*** *– break; circumfix:* ***n...els*** *– want, feel.*
nmaẇls – S/he was disappointed. **čn nmaẇls, kʷ nmaẇls**
es nmaẇlsi – S/he is disappointed. **čnes nmaẇlsi, kʷes nmaẇlsi**
qs nmaẇlsi – S/he is going to be disappointed. **čiqs nmaẇlsi, kʷqs nmaẇlsi**
nmáʔaẇls – They were disappointed. **qeʔ nmaẇls, p nmaẇls**

es nmáʔaẇlsi – They are disappointed. **qeʔes nmaẇlsi, pes nmaẇlsi**
qs nmáʔaẇlsi – They are going to be disappointed. **qeʔqs nmaẇlsi, pqs nmaẇlsi**

čnmaẇlsmis – S/he was disappointed in s.t./s.o. **čnmaẇlsmn, čnmaẇlsmntxʷ**
es čnmaẇlsms – S/he is disappointed in s.t./s.o. **ies čnmaẇlsm, as čnmaẇlsm**
qs čnmaẇlsms – S/he is going to be disappointed in s.t./s.o. **iqs čnmaẇlsm, aqs čnmaẇlsm**
čnmáʔaẇlsmis – They were disappointed in s.t./s.o. **qeʔ čnmaẇlsmntm, čnmaẇlsmntp**
es čnmáʔaẇlsms – They are disappointed in s.t./s.o. **qeʔes čnmaẇlsm, es čnmaẇlsmp**
qs čnmáʔaẇlsms – They are going to be disappointed in s.t./s.o. **qeʔqs čnmaẇlsm, qs čnmaẇlsmp**

čnmaẇlsmncn – I was disappointed in you. **čnmaẇlsłmn** – I was disappointed in all of you. **qeʔ čnmaẇlsłlt** – S/he was disappointed in us.

The **i** following uvular consonants (UC) and the glottal stop ʔ sound like English "*ey*" as in the words *they*, *hey*, *whey*, etc. Salish UC are: **q, q̓, qʷ, q̓ʷ, x̣, x̣ʷ**. For example, the suffix **...qin** – head/top, is often spelled using English *ey* as "q*ey*n". So **qi, q̓i, qʷi, q̓ʷi, x̣i, x̣ʷi**, may be spelled with English *ey* as **q***ey*, **q̓***ey*, **qʷ***ey*, **q̓ʷ***ey*, **x̣***ey*, **x̣ʷ***ey* in other texts.

tuṅus – face of disappointment for not receiving any distributed items. *See: **fail**.*

nixʷpels – have hurt feelings; profound sadness. *See: **hurt feelings**.*

disbelieve

q̓eyus – doubt; disbelief; question. *See: **doubt**.*

discipline

x̣eʔe – keep someone in line; correct behavior; forbid bad behavior; prevent misdeeds; make someone behave.
x̣eʔentes – S/he corrected s.o. **x̣eʔenten, x̣eʔentexʷ**
es x̣eʔenims – S/he is correcting s.o. **ies x̣eʔenim, as x̣eʔenim**
qs x̣eʔenims – S/he is is going to correct s.o. **iqs x̣eʔenim, aqs x̣eʔenim**

sxʷx̣eʔem – someone tasked to correct/discipline.
x̣eʔenemn – one inclined to correct/discipline. *suffix: **...emn** – one inclined to do.*
x̣ex̣eʔenmuł – one that habitually corrects/disciplines. *suffix: **...łmuł** – one that habitually does.*

x̣eʔenint – Correct him/her. *cmd.*
es x̣eʔenwexʷi – They are correcting each other. **qeʔes x̣eʔenwexʷi, pes x̣eʔenwexʷi**
es x̣eʔeštwexʷi – They are helping each other in forbiding. **qeʔes x̣eʔeštwexʷi, pes x̣eʔeštwexʷi**
x̣eʔenłtumš – correct people. *suffix: **...łtumš** – of people.*
x̣eʔenelt – correct children. *suffix: **...elt, ...lt** – child, baby*
x̣eʔensqáx̣eʔ, *x̣eʔensqá* – correct domestic animals. *suffix: **...sqax̣eʔ, ...sqa** – domestic animal; generally horse or car*

kʷ qs sxʷx̣eʔem – It is your responsibility to discipline.

discourage

k̓ʷłłpip̓ – unmotivated/discouraged/lazy; unable to do something; depressed. *(This term describes someone who has no motivation, who is discouraged and who is lazy. Many words in Salish are a combination of English words. At times it is hard to give a clear translation.)*
łpip̓ – S/he was hopeless. **čn łpip̓, kʷ łpip̓**
es łpp̓mi – S/he is hopeless. **čnes łpp̓mi, kʷes łpp̓mi**
qs łpp̓mi – S/he is going to be hopeless. **čiqs łpp̓mi, kʷqs łpp̓mi**

k̓ʷłłpip̓ – S/he was unmotivated. **čn k̓ʷłłpip̓, kʷ k̓ʷłłpip̓**
es k̓ʷłłpp̓mi – S/he is unmotivated. **čnes k̓ʷłłpp̓mi, kʷes k̓ʷłłpp̓mi**
qs k̓ʷłłpp̓mi – S/he is going to be unmotivated. **čiqs k̓ʷłłpp̓mi, kʷqs k̓ʷłłpp̓mi**
k̓ʷłłpíʔip̓ – They were unmotivated. **qeʔ k̓ʷłłpip̓, p k̓ʷłłpip̓**
es k̓ʷłłpp̓míʔi – They are unmotivated. **qeʔes k̓ʷłłpp̓mi, pes k̓ʷłłpp̓mi**

s.t. - something, the 3rd person
(s.t.) - something implied
s.o. - someone, the 3rd person
sl. - singular form
pl. - plural form
rt. - root word
cmd. - command
lit. - literally
fig. - figuratively
i.e., - for example
See: - Redirection to a related word.

qs k̓ʷɬpp̓míʔi – They are going to be unmotivated. **qeʔqs k̓ʷɬpp̓mi, pqs k̓ʷɬpp̓mi**

k̓ʷɬpp̓tes – S/he made s.o. be discouraged. **k̓ʷɬpp̓sten, k̓ʷɬpp̓stexʷ**
es k̓ʷɬpp̓ims – S/he is making s.o. be discouraged. **čnes k̓ʷɬpp̓im, kʷes k̓ʷɬpp̓im**
qs k̓ʷɬpp̓im– S/he is going to make s.o. be discouraged. **čiqs k̓ʷɬpp̓im, kʷqs k̓ʷɬpp̓im**

k̓ʷɬpp̓mis – S/he was unmotivated by s.t. **k̓ʷɬpp̓min, k̓ʷɬpp̓mintxʷ**
es k̓ʷɬpp̓minms – S/he is unmotivated by s.t. **ies k̓ʷɬpp̓minm, as k̓ʷɬpp̓minm**
qs k̓ʷɬpp̓minms – S/he is going to be unmotivated by s.t. **iqs k̓ʷɬpp̓minm, aqs k̓ʷɬpp̓minm**
k̓ʷɬpp̓míʔis – They were unmotivated by s.t. **qeʔ k̓ʷɬpp̓mintm, k̓ʷɬpp̓mintp**
es k̓ʷɬpp̓míʔinm – They are unmotivated by s.t. **qeʔes k̓ʷɬpp̓minm, es k̓ʷɬpp̓minmp**
qs k̓ʷɬpp̓míʔinm – They are going to be unmotivated by s.t. **qeʔqs k̓ʷɬpp̓minm, qs k̓ʷɬpp̓minmp**

k̓ʷɬpɬip̓t – difficult to do/learn/catch.
nɬpɬcin – discouraging talker.
k̓ʷɬpɬp̓ulexʷ – difficult to reach place.

k̓ʷɬp̓cinmis – S/he gave up talking with s.o. **k̓ʷɬp̓cinmn, k̓ʷɬp̓cinmntxʷ**
es k̓ʷɬp̓cinms – S/he is giving up talking with s.o. **ies k̓ʷɬpp̓minm, as k̓ʷɬpp̓minm**

čn k̓ʷɬpip̓ x̣ʷl̓ čnes x̣ʷeyti – I am unmotivated because I am lazy.

nmaw̓ls – disappointed; discouraged; have broken feelings. *See: **disappointed**.*

discuss

čq̓mq̓milš, *čq̓mq̓mi* – discuss. *suffix: **...ilš** – autonomous.*

čq̓mq̓míʔilš – They discussed. **qeʔ čq̓mq̓milš, p čq̓mq̓milš**
es čq̓mq̓míʔilši – They are discussing. **qeʔes čq̓mq̓milši, pes čq̓mq̓milši**
qs čq̓mq̓míʔilši – They are going to discuss. **qeʔqs čq̓mq̓milši, pqs čq̓mq̓milši**

čq̓mq̓milšmis – S/he discussed s.t. **čq̓mq̓milšmn, čq̓mq̓milšmntxʷ**
es čq̓mq̓milšmms – S/he is discussing s.t. **ies čq̓mq̓milšmm, as čq̓mq̓milšmm**
qs čq̓mq̓milšmms – S/he is going to discuss s.t. **iqs čq̓mq̓milšmm, aqs čq̓mq̓milšmm**
čq̓mq̓míʔilšmis – They discussed s.t. **qeʔ čq̓mq̓milšmntm, čq̓mq̓milšmntp**
es čq̓mq̓míʔilšmms – They are discussing s.t. **qeʔes čq̓mq̓milšmm, es čq̓mq̓milšmm**
qs čq̓mq̓míʔilšmms – They are going to discuss s.t. **qeʔqs čq̓mq̓milšmm, qs čq̓mq̓milšmm**

sčq̓mq̓milš – something that's been discussed.

čq̓mq̓milšmnt – Discuss it. *cmd.*

stem̓ ɬu qs cčq̓mq̓milš – What are we going to discuss? *(What is on the agenda?)*

q̓mq̓milš, *q̓mq̓mi* – meet and talk; have a meeting; discuss. *See: **meet**.*

disdain

nc̓los – action showing disdain toward someone. *This is done with the arm out and the wrist slightly bent down; then by extending, spreading and curving the index and middle fingers in the direction of the recipient. The literal translation: to poke the eyes. This action is similar to flipping someone off by extending the middle finger.*

nc̓losis – S/he showed disdain toward s.o. **nc̓losn, nc̓losntxʷ**

qʷo nc̓losntm – I was shown disdain by someone.

disengage

nc̓oqew̓sm – disengage from the middle. *rt.: **c̓oʔq** – pull out; suffix: **...éw̓s** – in between, middle.*

nc̓oqew̓sm – S/he disengaged from the middle. **čn nc̓oqew̓sm, kʷ nc̓oqew̓sm**
es nc̓oqew̓si – S/he is disengaging from the middle. **čnes nc̓oqew̓si, kʷes nc̓oqew̓si**

nc̓oqew̓si – S/he disengaged s.t. from the middle. **čn nc̓oqew̓sn, kʷ nc̓oqew̓sntxʷ**

es nċoqeẇsms – S/he is disengaging s.t. from the middle. **ies nċoqeẇsm, as nċoqeẇsm**

disguise **ṫxʷlmncut –** change one's self; to disguise. *rt.: **ṫixʷlm** – different; suffix: **...cut** – action to the self.*

ṫxʷlmscut – S/he disguised one's self. **čn ṫxʷlmscut, kʷ ṫxʷlmscut**
es ṫxʷlmscuti – S/he is disguising one's self. **čnes ṫxʷlmscuti, kʷes ṫxʷlmscuti**
qs ṫxʷlmscuti – S/he is going to disquise one's self. **čiqs ṫxʷlmscuti, kʷqs ṫxʷlmscuti**

ṫxʷlmist – change one's self spiritually. *rt.: **ṫixʷlm** – different; suffix: **...ist** – action to the self.*
ṫxʷlmist – S/he changed one's self. **čn ṫxʷlmist, kʷ ṫxʷlmist**
es ṫxʷlmisti – S/he is changing one's self. **čnes ṫxʷlmisti, kʷes ṫxʷlmisti**
qs ṫxʷlmisti – S/he is going to change one's self. **čiqs ṫxʷlmisti, kʷqs ṫxʷlmisti**

mʔamalqs – woman's clothes; dress as a woman; disguised as a woman. *See: **dress**.*

nṫxʷlméls – change attitude. *See: **change attitude**.*

> The **i** following uvular consonants (UC) and the glottal stop **ʔ** sound like English "*ey*" as in the words th*ey*, h*ey*, wh*ey*, etc. Salish UC are: **q**, **q̇**, **qʷ**, **q̇ʷ**, **x̣**, **x̣ʷ**. For example, the suffix ...**qin** – head/top, is often spelled using English *ey* as "q*ey*n". So **qi**, **q̇i**, **qʷi**, **q̇ʷi**, **x̣i**, **x̣ʷi**, may be spelled with English *ey* as **q***ey*, **q̇***ey*, **qʷ***ey*, **q̇ʷ***ey*, **x̣***ey*, **x̣ʷ***ey* in other texts.

disgusted **néhels –** sick and tired; perturbed; disturbed; fed up. *See: **disturbed**.*

nplus – turn the face/head. *See: **turn**.*
es nplusm – His/her face is turned away. **čnes nplusm, kʷes nplusm**

dish **qpéłċeʔ**, *qpé* – plate.
qpéłċeʔs – his/her plate.

dishpan **snċuʔłqpéłċeʔtn**, *snċuʔłqpé* – dishpan; something used to wash dishes. *prefix: **sn...** – a place of; suffix: **...tin, ...tn** – means of/device.*

dishtowel **nʔeṗłqpełċeʔtn**, *nʔeṗłqpe* – dishtowel; something used to wipe dishes.

dishwasher **snnċuʔłqpéłċeʔtn**, *snnċuʔłqpé* – dishwasher. *prefix: **sn...** – a place of; suffix: **...tin, ...tn** – means of/device.*

nċuʔłqpéłċeʔ, *nċuʔłqpé* – wash dishes.
nċuʔłqpé – S/he washed dishes. **čn nċuʔłqpé, kʷ nċuʔłqpé**
es nċuʔłqpé – S/he is washing dishes. **čnes nċuʔłqpé, kʷes nċuʔłqpé**
qs nċuʔłqpé – S/he is going to wash dishes. **čiqs nċuʔłqpé, kʷqs nċuʔłqpé**
nċuʔłqpéʔe – They washed dishes. **qeʔ nċuʔłqpé, p nċuʔłqpé**
es nċuʔłqpéʔe – They are washing dishes. **qeʔes nċuʔłqpé, pes nċuʔłqpé**
qs nċuʔłqpéʔe – They are going to wash dishes. **qeʔqs nċuʔłqpé, pqs nċuʔłqpé**

sxʷnċuʔłqpéłċeʔ, *sxʷnċuʔłqpé* – one tasked to wash dishes. *prefix: **sxʷ...** – one tasked to do.*

x̣ssxʷnċuʔłqpé – S/he is a good dishwasher. **čn x̣ssxʷnċuʔłqpé, kʷ x̣ssxʷnċuʔłqpé**

ṅe kʷ wis nċułqpéceʔ m sic kʷ ocqeʔ kʷqs pk̓ʷlʔemi – When you finish washing the dishes then you can go outside to play ball.

> s.t. - something, the 3rd person
> (s.t.) - something implied
> s.o. - someone, the 3rd person
> *sl.* - singular form
> *pl.* - plural form
> *rt.* - root word
> *cmd.* - command
> *lit.* - literally
> *fig.* - figuratively
> *i.e.,* - for example
> *See:* - Redirection to a related word.

dislocate **malkʷum –** dislocated joint; disjointed.
malkʷntés – S/he disjointed it. **malkʷntén, malkʷntéxʷ**
es malkʷúms – S/he is disjointing it. **ies malkʷúm, as malkʷúm**
qs malkʷúms – S/he is going to disjoint it. **iqs malkʷúm, aqs malkʷúm**

malukʷ – It got disjointed/dislocated.
es malkʷ – It is disjointed/dislocated.

es malkʷselis – It is disjointed from the other.

malkʷunt – Disjoint/dislocate it. *cmd.*
malkʷsew̓sis – separate or disconnect the joints. *(i.e., cutting joints, etc.) See: **separate**.*
malkʷax̣n – disjointed/dislocated elbow. *See: **elbow**.*
k̓ʷłmalkʷcnéčst – dislocated/disjointed wrist. *See: **wrist**.*
malkʷečst – disjointed/dislocated finger. *See: **finger**.*
malkʷłq̓eyt – dislocate the shoulder. *See: **shoulder**.*
malkʷew̓šn – disjointed/dislocated knee. *See: **knee**.*
malkʷew̓s – disjointed/dislocated spine. *See: **spine**.*

dismount

t̓ipmncut – come down from something high. *(i.e., tree, chair, etc.) See: **come down**.*

disregard

p̓áu – disregard; ignore; lose interest; tire of something; distracted.
p̓áumist – S/he lost interest. **čn p̓áumist, kʷ p̓áumist**
es p̓áumist – S/he is losing interest. **čnes p̓áumisti, kʷes p̓áumisti**
qs p̓áumist – S/he is going to lose interest. **čiqs p̓áumisti, kʷqs p̓áumisti**

p̓áumis – S/he lost interest in s.t./s.o. **p̓áumin, p̓áumintxʷ**
es p̓áuminms – S/he is losing interest in s.t./s.o. **ies p̓áuminm, as p̓áuminm**
qs p̓áuminms – S/he is going to lose interest in s.t./s.o. **iqs p̓áuminm, aqs p̓áuminm**

p̓áusts – S/he did not care for s.t./s.o. **p̓áustn, p̓áustxʷ**
es p̓áums – S/he does not care for s.t./s.o. **ies p̓áum, as p̓áum**
qs p̓áums – S/he is not going to care for s.t./s.o. **iqs p̓áum, aqs p̓áum**

p̓áučstmis – S/he distracted s.t./s.o. **p̓áučstmn, p̓áučstmntxʷ**
es p̓áučstms – S/he is distracting s.t./s.o. **ies p̓áučstm, as p̓áučstm**
qs p̓áučstms – S/he is going to distract s.t./s.o. **iqs p̓áučstm, aqs p̓áučstm**

p̓aup̓ut – indifferent; without interest or concern. *See: **indifferent**.*
p̓aup̓usnuxʷ – something that receives no attention.

p̓up̓utmnelt – no interest for children.
np̓up̓uwenéʔ – ignore; do not pay attention to; do not listen. *See: **ignore**.*
čp̓up̓áus – look distracted.
p̓ausʔiłn – have no care to eat.

np̓áucnmis – S/he spoke disrespectful to s.o. **np̓áucnmn, np̓áucnmntxʷ**
es np̓áucnms – S/he is speaking disrespectful to s.o. **ies np̓áucnm, as np̓áucnm**
qs np̓áucnms – S/he is going to be disrespectful to s.o. **iqs np̓áucnm, aqs np̓áucnm**

qeʔ p̓áumintm łu suyapi nuwewlštn – We lost interest in the English language.

tmals – despise; disregard; spurn; pay no attention to; have no feelings for; have no care for; have no respect for. *See: **despise**.*

dissolve

aámt – melt; dissolve away. *See: **melt**.*

distant

lkʷut – far. *See: **far**.*

č lkʷut – distant.

distracted

p̓áu – disregard; ignore; lose interest; tire of something; distracted. *See: **disregard**.*

distribute

px̣ʷmim – distribute; spread around; pass/hand out.
px̣ʷmim – S/he distributed. **čn px̣ʷmim, kʷ px̣ʷmim**

es pẋʷmi – S/he is distributing. **čnes pẋʷmi, kʷes pẋʷmi**
qs pẋʷmi – S/he is going to distribute. **čiqs pẋʷmi, kʷqs pẋʷmi**
pẋʷmíˀim – They distributed. **qeˀ pẋʷmim, p pẋʷmim**
es pẋʷmíˀi – They are distributing. **qeˀes pẋʷmi, pes pẋʷmi**
qs pẋʷmíˀi – They are going to distribute. **qeˀqs pẋʷmi, pqs pẋʷmi**

pẋʷmstes – S/he distributed s.t. **pẋʷmsten, pẋʷmstexʷ**
es pẋʷmims – S/he is distributing s.t. **ies pẋʷmim, as pẋʷmim**
qs pẋʷmims – S/he is going to distribute s.t. **iqs pẋʷmim, aqs pẋʷmim**
pẋʷmstéˀes – They distributed s.t. **qeˀ pẋʷmstem, pẋʷmstep**
es pẋʷmíˀims – They are distributing s.t. **qeˀes pẋʷmim, es pẋʷmimp**
qs pẋʷmíˀims – They are going to distribute s.t. **qeˀqs pẋʷmim, qs pẋʷmimp**

scpẋʷmi – something that is being distributed *(i.e., rations, per capita, commodities, pay day). prefix:* ***sc...*** *– s.t. that's been done/made/prepared.*

pẋʷmiskʷ – Pass it out. *cmd.*

iqs pẋʷmim inčłq̓iq̓á – I am going to pass out my candy.

tuṅus – face of disappointment for not receiving any distributed items. *See:* ***fail.***

The **i** following uvular consonants (UC) and the glottal stop ˀ sound like English "*ey*" as in the words th*ey*, h*ey*, wh*ey*, etc. Salish UC are: **q, q̓, qʷ, q̓ʷ, ẋ, ẋʷ**. For example, the suffix **...qin** – head/top, is often spelled using English *ey* as "q*ey*n". So **qi, q̓i, qʷi, q̓ʷi, ẋi, ẋʷi**, may be spelled with English *ey* as **q***ey*, **q̓***ey*, **qʷ***ey*, **q̓ʷ***ey*, **ẋ***ey*, **ẋʷ***ey* in other texts.

disturbed

néhels – sick and tired; perturbed; disturbed; fed up.
néhels – S/he got fed up. **čn néhels, kʷ néhels**
es néhelsi – S/he is fed up. **čnes néhelsi, kʷes néhelsi**
qs néhelsi – S/he is going to be fed up. **čiqs néhelsi, kʷqs néhelsi**

nméˀels – disturbed; bothered feelings.
nméˀels – S/he got disturbed. **čn nméˀels, kʷ nméˀels**
es nméˀelsi – S/he is disturbed. **čnes nméˀelsi, kʷes nméˀelsi**
qs nméˀelsi – S/he is going to be disturbed. **čiqs nméˀelsi, kʷqs nméˀelsi**

ditch

sctletkʷ, *sctle* **–** ditch/canal. *rt.:* ***til*** *– tear; prefix:* ***sc...*** *– s.t. that's been done/made/prepared; suffix:* ***...etkʷ, ...tkʷ*** *– liquid.*
ci l sctletkʷ – It is in that ditch.

dive

ust – dive into water.
ust – S/he dove. **čn ust, kʷ ust**
es usti – S/he is diving. **čnes usti, kʷes usti**
qs usti – S/he is going to dive. **čiqs usti, kʷqs usti**
úˀusust – Each one of them dove. **qeˀ usust, p usust**
es úˀususti – Each one is diving. **qeˀes ususti, pes ususti**
qs úˀususti – Each one is going to dive. **qeˀqs ususti, pqs ususti**

ustiš – Dive. *cmd.*
ustwi – All of you dive. *cmd.*

es ustlwisi – S/he is diving around. **čnes ustlwisi, kʷes ustlwisi**

nilmnulexʷ – hit the ground head first.
nilmnulexʷ – S/he hit the ground head first. **čn nilmnulexʷ, kʷ nilmnulexʷ**

s.t. - something, the 3rd person
(s.t.) - something implied
s.o. - someone, the 3rd person
sl. - singular form
pl. - plural form
rt. - root word
cmd. - command
lit. - literally
fig. - figuratively
i.e., - for example
See: - Redirection to a related word.

diver

sxʷˀust – diver; one tasked to dive. *prefix:* ***sxʷ...*** *– one tasked to do.*

łusustuˀ – diver *(bird)*; smaller duck.

divide

ẋʷq̓ʷeẃs – divide/part something; apportion; cut cards. *suffix:* ***...éẃs*** *– in between, middle.*

x̣ʷq̇ʷeẇsis – S/he divided s.t. **x̣ʷq̇ʷeẇsn, x̣ʷq̇ʷeẇsntxʷ**
es x̣ʷq̇ʷeẇsms – S/he is dividing s.t. **ies x̣ʷq̇ʷeẇsm, as x̣ʷq̇ʷeẇsm**
qs x̣ʷq̇ʷeẇsms – S/he is going to divide s.t. **iqs x̣ʷq̇ʷeẇsm, aqs x̣ʷq̇ʷeẇsm**
x̣ʷq̇ʷéʔeẇsis – They divided s.t. **qeʔ x̣ʷq̇ʷeẇsn, x̣ʷq̇ʷeẇsntp**
es x̣ʷq̇ʷéʔeẇsms – They are dividing s.t. **qeʔes x̣ʷq̇ʷeẇsm, es x̣ʷq̇ʷeẇsmp**
qs x̣ʷq̇ʷéʔeẇsms – They are going to divide s.t. **qeʔqs x̣ʷq̇ʷeẇsm, qs x̣ʷq̇ʷeẇsmp**

x̣ʷq̇ʷeẇsnt – Divide it. *cmd.*

x̣ʷq̇ʷeẇsnt t̓aq̇n t esel – Divide six by two. **t̓aq̇n x̣ʷq̇ʷeẇsm t esel še tixʷł čełe** – Six divided by two equals three, *(6 ÷ 2 = 3).*

x̣ʷq̇ʷom – separate something that is together. *(i.e., a pile, a ream of paper, a package of crackers, etc.) See:* ***separate.***

tx̣ʷeẇs – divide something in two; halve something. *See:* ***halve.***

ček̓ʷseẇsm – separate something solid. *(i.e., a rock, bread loaf, pie, etc.) See:* ***separate.***

k̓ʷłx̣ʷtim – undercut something off; cut off for apportionment. *See:* ***cut off.***

saq̇ – split; parted; cloven. *See:* ***split.***

sax̣ʷ – split wood with an instrument. *See:* ***split.***

divorce

x̣ʷq̇ʷpeẇs – get divorced. *suffix:* ***...éẇs*** *– in between, middle.*
es x̣ʷq̇ʷpeẇs – S/he is divorced.

x̣ʷq̇ʷpéʔeẇs – They got divorced.
es x̣ʷq̇ʷpéʔeẇsi – They are getting divorced.
qs x̣ʷq̇ʷpéʔeẇsi – They are going to get divorced.

nx̣ʷq̇ʷomels – want to get divorced.
nx̣ʷq̇ʷomels – S/he wanted to get divorced. **čn nx̣ʷq̇ʷomels, kʷ nx̣ʷq̇ʷomels**
es nx̣ʷq̇ʷomelsi – S/he is wanting to get divorced. **čnes nx̣ʷq̇ʷomelsi, kʷes nx̣ʷq̇ʷomelsi**
qs nx̣ʷq̇ʷomelsi – S/he is going to want to get divorced. **čiqs nx̣ʷq̇ʷomelsi, kʷqs nx̣ʷq̇ʷomelsi**

x̣ʷq̇ʷuscut – divorce one's spouse.
x̣ʷq̇ʷuscut – S/he divorced his/her spouse. **čn x̣ʷq̇ʷuscut, kʷ x̣ʷq̇ʷuscut**
es x̣ʷq̇ʷuscuti – S/he is divorcing his/her spouse. **čnes x̣ʷq̇ʷuscuti, kʷes x̣ʷq̇ʷuscuti**
qs x̣ʷq̇ʷuscuti – S/he is going to divorce his/her spouse. **čiqs x̣ʷq̇ʷuscuti, kʷqs x̣ʷq̇ʷuscuti**

ček̓ʷmscut – separate from one's partner/spouse. *rt.:* ***čehek̓ʷ*** *– separate; suffix:* ***...cut*** *– action to the self.*
ček̓ʷmscuti – S/he separated. **čn ček̓ʷmscuti, kʷ ček̓ʷmscuti**
es ček̓ʷmscuti – S/he is separating. **čnes ček̓ʷmscuti, kʷes ček̓ʷmscuti**
qs ček̓ʷmscuti – S/he is going to separate. **čiqs ček̓ʷmscuti, kʷqs ček̓ʷmscuti**

Dixon

sčilip – Dixon, Flathead Nation. *rt.:* ***ili*** *– pass into/through.*

dizzy

nsĺsĺmtus, *nsĺsĺmtu* – dizzy. *rt.:* ***siĺ*** *– confuse.*
nsĺsĺmtus – S/he/it was dizzy. **čn nsĺsĺmtus, kʷ nsĺsĺmtus**
es nsĺsĺmtusi – S/he/it is dizzy. **čnes nsĺsĺmtusi, kʷes nsĺsĺmtusi**
es nsĺsĺmtúʔusi – They are dizzy. **qeʔes nsĺsĺmtusi, pes nsĺsĺmtusi**

nsĺsĺmtusis – S/he got s.o. dizzy. **nsĺsĺmtusn, nsĺsĺmtusntxʷ**
es nsĺsĺmtusms – S/he is getting s.o. dizzy. **ies nsĺsĺmtusm, as nsĺsĺmtusm**
qs nsĺsĺmtusms – S/he is going to get s.o. dizzy. **iqs nsĺsĺmtusm, aqs nsĺsĺmtusm**
nsĺsĺmtúʔusis – They got s.o. dizzy. **qeʔ nsĺsĺmtusntm, nsĺsĺmtusntp**

es nsl̓sl̓mtúʔusms – They are getting s.o. dizzy. **qeʔes nsl̓sl̓mtusm, es nsl̓sl̓mtusmp**
qs nsl̓sl̓mtúʔusms – They're going to get s.o. dizzy. **qeʔqs nsl̓sl̓mtusm, qs nsl̓sl̓mtusmp**

nsl̓sl̓mtemn – one inclined to get dizzy. *suffix:* ***...emn*** *– one inclined to do.*
nsl̓pstwéʔexʷist – They got each other dizzy. **qeʔ nsl̓pstwéʔexʷist, p nsl̓pstwéʔexʷist**

ta čiqs sust t nx̣ʷoskʷ x̣iṅe čn nsl̓sl̓mtus – I am not going to drink beer so I will not get dizzy. **ṅe kʷ sust t nx̣ʷoskʷ m kʷ nsl̓sl̓mtus** – When you drink beer you get dizzy.

nsl̓pscut – get one's self dizzy. *rt.:* ***sil̓*** *– confuse.*
nsl̓pscut – S/he/it got one's self dizzy. **čn nsl̓pscut, kʷ nsl̓pscut**
es nsl̓pscuti – S/he/it is getting one's self dizzy. **čnes nsl̓pscuti, kʷes nsl̓pscuti**
qs nsl̓pscuti – S/he/it is going to get one's self dizzy. **čiqs nsl̓pscuti, kʷqs nsl̓pscuti**

nsl̓pscutš – Get yourself dizzy. *cmd.*

The **i** following uvular consonants (UC) and the glottal stop **ʔ** sound like English "*ey*" as in the words th*ey*, h*ey*, wh*ey*, etc. Salish UC are: **q, q̇, qʷ, q̇ʷ, x̣, x̣ʷ**. For example, the suffix ...**qin** – head/top, is often spelled using English *ey* as "q*ey*n". So **qi, q̇i, qʷi, q̇ʷi, x̣i, x̣ʷi**, may be spelled with English *ey* as **q***ey*, **q̇***ey*, **qʷ***ey*, **q̇ʷ***ey*, **x̣***ey*, **x̣ʷ***ey* in other texts.

nsl̓pqin – dizzy in the head. *rt.:* ***sil̓*** *– confuse; suffix:* ***...qin, ...qn*** *– top.*
nsl̓pqin – S/he was dizzy. **čn sl̓pqin, kʷ nsl̓pqin**
es nsl̓pqini – S/he is dizzy. **čnes sl̓pqini, kʷes nsl̓pqini**
qs nsl̓pqini – S/he is going to be dizzy. **čiqs sl̓pqini, kʷqs nsl̓pqini**
qs nsl̓sl̓pqíʔini – Each one is going to be dizzy. **qeʔqs nsl̓sl̓pqini, pqs nsl̓sl̓pqini**

nsl̓péʔeẇs, *nsl̓péʔe* – a little dizzy from alcohol; not quite drunk. *rt.:* ***sil̓*** *– confuse; suffix:* ***...éẇs*** *– in between, middle.*
es nsl̓péʔe – S/he is a little dizzy. **čnes nsl̓péʔe, kʷes nsl̓péʔe**

qʷqʷiwxʷ – spin one's self until dizzy; *a game played mainly by children. rt.:* ***qʷeẇ*** *– crazy. See:* ***crazy.***

sil̓ – confused; unable to figure something out; mistaken. *See:**confuse.***

npṁpqan – get knocked out; to be out of the head. *See:* ***knock out.***

do

ax̣íl, *ax̣í* – do as someone/something; imitate; behave a certain way. *See:* ***imitate.***
ax̣ílm – S/he/it did like (s.o./s.t.). **čn ax̣ílm, kʷ ax̣ílm**
es ax̣íli – S/he/it is do it like (s.o./s.t.). **čnes ax̣íli, kʷes ax̣íli**
qs ax̣íli – S/he/it is going to do it like (s.o./s.t.). **čiqs ax̣íli, kʷqs ax̣íli**

ax̣ísts – S/he did it like s.t./s.o. **ax̣ístn, ax̣ístxʷ**
es ax̣ílms – S/he is doing it like s.t./s.o. **ies ax̣ílm, as ax̣ílm**
ax̣íʔists – They did it like s.t./s.o. **qeʔ ax̣ístm, ax̣ístp**

scax̣íl – something that has been done; the way it was done.
ax̣íltn – something used in such a way.

ax̣ískʷ – Do it like him/her/it. *cmd.*
ax̣lmnscut – move one's self in a certain way.
nax̣lels – want to do something a certain way.
ax̣llwís, *ax̣llwí* – hustle around for something; able and determined in doing something. *See:* ***busy.***

l čeṅ m ax̣ístn – How will I do it? **l čeṅ u ax̣ístxʷ** – How did you do it? **lʔe u ax̣ístxʷ** – This is how you did it. **ye lʔe m ax̣ístxʷ** – You will do it like this. **ax̣ístn t seẇłkʷ** – I treat it like water. **ṅem kʷ ax̣ilm** – You do it like this. **l čeṅ u čnes ax̣ili** – How am I being/acting? **čnes ax̣ili t snčłċaʔsqax̣eʔ** – I'm behaving/acting like a horse. **qʷo ax̣istm t čn ilmixʷm** – I was treated like a leader. **ax̣iskʷ t ṗx̣ʷṗx̣ʷot** – Treat him/her like an elder. **tam l šeẏ aqł ax̣iltn** – Don't use it that way.

s.t. - something, the 3rd person
(s.t.) - something implied
s.o. - someone, the 3rd person
sl. - singular form
pl. - plural form
rt. - root word
cmd. - command
lit. - literally
fig. - figuratively
i.e., - for example
See: - Redirection to a related word.

aẋtčim – busy with something. *See: **busy**.*

ećšĉéṅ – question inquiring about the state of someone or something. *See: **happen**.*
 ećšĉéṅ – How is s/he/it? **čn ećšĉéṅ, kʷ ećšĉéṅ**
 ećšećšĉéʔeṅ – How are they? **qeʔ ećšećšĉéṅ, p ećšećšĉéṅ**

 ećšĉéṅts – What did s/he/it do to her/him/it? **ećšĉéṅtxʷ**
 ećšĉéʔeṅts – What did they do to him/her/it? **qeʔ ećšĉéṅtm, ećšĉéṅtp**

 es čésts – What did s/he/it do with s.t./s.o.? **es čéstxʷ, es čéstn**
 es čéʔests – What did they do with s.t./s.o.? **qeʔes čéstm, es čéstp**

 sewnt asłaẋt ećšĉéṅ – Ask your friend how s/he is. **kʷqs ećšĉéṅi ṅe čłʔeʔ** – What are you going to do Saturday? **es čéstxʷ ci q̓ett** – What did you do with that hide.

ećšĉṅmscut – What is someone doing with/of one's self?
 ećšĉṅmscuti – What is s/he/it doing? **čn ećšĉṅmscuti, kʷ ećšĉṅmscuti**

l̓q̓ʷom – can do; prevail; succeed.
 l̓q̓ʷom – S/he prevailed. **čn l̓q̓ʷom, kʷ l̓q̓ʷom**
 es l̓q̓ʷmi – S/he is prevailing. **čnes l̓q̓ʷmi, kʷes l̓q̓ʷmi**
 qs l̓q̓ʷmi – S/he is going to prevail. **čiqs l̓q̓ʷmi, kʷqs l̓q̓ʷmi**

 es l̓q̓ʷncut – S/he can. **čnes l̓q̓ʷncut, kʷes l̓q̓ʷncut**

 l̓q̓ʷntes – S/he prevailed at s.t. **l̓q̓ʷnten, l̓q̓ʷntexʷ**
 es l̓q̓ʷoms – S/he is prevailing at s.t. **ies l̓q̓ʷom, as l̓q̓ʷom**
 qs l̓q̓ʷoms – S/he is going to prevail at s.t. **iqs l̓q̓ʷom, aqs l̓q̓ʷom**

 es l̓q̓ʷq̓ʷnunms – S/he is succeeding to prevail at s.t. **ies l̓q̓ʷq̓ʷnunm, as l̓q̓ʷq̓ʷnunm**

 l̓q̓ʷoš – Prevail. *cmd.*
 l̓q̓ʷont – Prevail at it. *cmd.*

 es l̓q̓ʷstwexʷi – They can do it to one another. **qeʔes l̓q̓ʷstwexʷi, pes l̓q̓ʷstwexʷi**

 es l̓q̓ʷq̓ʷotm – It is possible.
 l̓q̓ʷq̓ʷmutmsts – S/he made it possible. **l̓q̓ʷq̓ʷmutmstn, l̓q̓ʷq̓ʷmutmstxʷ**
 es l̓q̓ʷq̓ʷmutms – S/he can do it. **ies l̓q̓ʷq̓ʷmutm, as l̓q̓ʷq̓ʷmutm**

 ha es l̓q̓ʷq̓ʷotm – Is it possible? **tas l̓q̓ʷq̓ʷotm** – It cannot be done.

k̓ʷul̓ – do; make; fix; work. *See: **work**.*

iše – always; do. *See: **always**.*

uṅuṅexʷist – really/truly do something. *rt.: **unéxʷ** – real, true, yes. See: **true**.*
 qs uṅuṅexʷisti – S/he is really going to do s.t. **čiqs uṅuṅexʷisti, kʷqs uṅuṅexʷisti**

q̓ʷiłmist, *q̓ʷiłmi* – do one's best; try hard from energy. *See: **capable**.*

sičstmist – do one's best; try hard from ability. *See: **capable**.*

čmaqs – perform at the peak of one's ability; best at something; pinnacle. *See: **best**.*

musčst – do one's best with hope of succeeding; do something with confidence. *See: **confident**.*

aytčst – strive; exert one's self in work. *See: **strive**.*

do as

aẋíl, *aẋí* – do as someone/something; imitate; behave a certain way. *See: **imitate**.*

 ẋʷl̓ steṁ u l še u kʷ aẋí – Why did you do it this way?

doctor **sxʷmalyémistn,** *sxʷmalyé* – doctor; one tasked to doctor. *prefix:* ***sxʷ...*** *– one tasked to do.*
t sxʷmalyé kʷ es ṗaax̣nunms – The doctor is curing you.

sxʷnčsqelixʷ – surgeon; someone tasked to cut people. *See:* ***cut.***

malyémm – doctor someone.
malyemis – S/he doctored s.o. **malyemn, malyemntxʷ**
es malyemms – S/he is doctoring s.o. **ies malyemm, as malyemm**
qs malyemms – S/he is going to doctor s.o. **iqs malyemm, aqs malyemm**
malyéʔemis – They doctored s.o. **qeʔ malyemntm, malyemntp**

malyemistn – something to doctor with; medicine.

malyemnt – Doctor s.o. *cmd.*

ṅem qes malyemms – S/he will be doctoring. **ṅem iqes malyemm, ṅem aqes malyemm**
ṅem qes malyéʔemms – They will be doctoring. **ṅem qeʔqes malyemm, ṅem qes malyemmp**

The **i** following uvular consonants (UC) and the glottal stop ʔ sound like English "*ey*" as in the words *they, hey, whey,* etc. Salish UC are: **q, q̓, qʷ, q̓ʷ, x̣, x̣ʷ**. For example, the suffix ...**qin** – head/top, is often spelled using English *ey* as "*qeyn*". So **qi, q̓i, qʷi, q̓ʷi, x̣i, x̣ʷi,** may be spelled with English *ey* as **q***ey*, **q̓***ey*, **qʷ***ey*, **q̓ʷ***ey*, **x̣***ey*, **x̣ʷ***ey* in other texts.

dodge **plutm** – dodge/duck away from something.
plutm – S/he dodged. **čn plutm, kʷ plutm**
plúʔutm – S/he dodged. **qeʔ plutm, p plutm**

plutmis – S/he dodged s.t. **plutmn, plutmntxʷ**
es plutms – S/he is dodging s.t. **ies plutm, as plutm**
qs plutms – S/he is going to dodge s.t. **iqs plutm, aqs plutm**
plúʔutmis – They dodged s.t. **qeʔ plutmn, plutmntp**
es plúʔutms – They are dodging s.t. **qeʔes plutm, es plutmp**

plutmiš – Dodge. *cmd.*
plutmnt – Dodge s.t. *cmd.*

nplus – turn the face/head. *See:* ***turn.***

doe **sṫulċeʔ** – black-tail doe; female mule deer; mule; *Odocoileus hemionus.*

ċúʔulixʷ, *ċúʔu* – white-tail doe; *Odocoileus virginianus.*

dog **nqʷq̓ʷosṁičṅšn,** *nqʷq̓ʷosṁi* – dog. **nqʷiq̓ʷosṁičṅšn** – dogs.
nqʷiq̓ʷosṁičṅšis – his/her dogs.
nqʷiq̓ʷosṁíʔičṅšis – their dogs.

skʷtiłnqʷq̓ʷosṁi – big dog.
nłqʷq̓ʷosṁi – little dog.
sx̣słnqʷq̓ʷosmi – good dog.
sčsłnqʷq̓ʷosmi – bad dog.

kʷtunt nqʷq̓ʷosṁi – big dog. **es k̓ʷéʔems t smx̣é innqʷq̓ʷosṁi** – Grizzly was biting my dog. **es titiẏaqʷti innqʷiq̓ʷosṁi** – My dogs are fighting.

sṫiṫičime, *sṫiṫiči* – pup, little dog.

sṁusłċeʔ, *sṁu* – female animal.

čłkʷicčľš – hair stands up, as on a dog's/bear's back when angry. *See:* ***hair.***

čṫaq̓šnm – raise/lift leg up to the side. *(i.e., as a dog would do to urinate) See:* ***lift.***

s.t. - something, the 3rd person
(s.t.) - something implied
s.o. - someone, the 3rd person
sl. - singular form
pl. - plural form
rt. - root word
cmd. - command
lit. - literally
fig. - figuratively
i.e., - for example
See: - Redirection to a related word.

es nłpqnops – tail is bent down *(between legs)*. *See:* ***bend.***

dogbane **sṗċnalqʷ** – dogbane.

dogcatcher **sxʷkʷnem l nqʷq̓ʷosṁi** – dogcatcher; one tasked to take dogs. *prefix:* ***sxʷ...*** *– one tasked to do.*

dogwood **stečcxʷ** – red osier dogwood; red willow; *Cornus stolonifera.*

doing **ax̣tčim** – busy with something. *See:* ***busy.***

stem łu askʷulm – What are you doing? *See:* ***work.***

do like **ax̣íl,** *ax̣í* – do as someone/something; imitate; behave a certain way. *See:* ***imitate.***

eċx̣i es cháłqi – It seems like it is chinooking outside.

doll **łox̣ʷox̣ʷteĺe** – baby doll.

dollar **nk̓ʷuˀ ululim** – one dollar.
ululim – money, iron.

Dolly Varnden trout **aáycčst,** *aáy* – bull trout; Dolly Varden trout; *Salvelinus confluentus.* *See:* ***bull trout.***

Dominick **tomni** – Dominick.

done **ṗiqém** – make done; ready; ripen. *(of food as in cooking.)*
ṗiyaq – It got done cooking; the berries got ripe.
es ṗiyaqmi – It is getting done cooking; the berries are getting ripe.
qs ṗiyaqmi – It is going to get done cooking; the berries are going to get ripe.

ṗiqstes – S/he made s.t. ready. **ṗiqsten, ṗiqstexʷ**
es ṗiqéms – S/he is making s.t. done/ready. **ies ṗiqém, as ṗiqém**
qs ṗiqéms – S/he is going to make s.t. done/ready. **iqs ṗiqém, aqs ṗiqém**

es ṗiyaq – It is done cooking; the berries are ripe.

sṗiqáłq – berry; fruit; raisin. *rt.:* ***ṗiẏáq*** *– ready, ripe; suffix:* ***...ałq*** *– smell, accompaniment.*

ƛ̓e ṗiyaq – It is already done; the berries are already ripe. **ṗiyaq łu sṫšałq** – The huckleberries got ripe. **ṗiyaq łu scnċáx̣lexʷ** – The frybread got done.

uẏéčst, *uẏé* – finish working; done working; come to an end. *See:* ***finish.***

x̣iˀu – unripe, not done.
es x̣iˀu – It is unripe, not done.

qʷoṁmałq, *qʷoṁma* – get close to doing/finishing something; getting near to some point; close to the end of a journey; winning. *See:* ***close.***

donkey **sṫulċeˀˀ** – black-tail doe; female mule deer; mule; donkey.

do not **ta qes ...** – do not. *The predicate word,* ***ta*** *– no, when used in conjunction with particle,* ***qes,*** *constitute, "do not," when used with a cause transitive pronoun particle as in the examples below.*

ta qes sčq̓ʷamaqsmstxʷ łu ṫeyeˀ – Do not do drugs. **ta qes nłeptmstxʷ** – Do not forget about it.
ta qes čyóqʷstxʷ – Do not lie about s.o. **ta qes mlmelčstmstxʷ** – Do not play with it.

ta qs … – do not. *The predicate word, **ta** – no, when used in conjunction with particle, **qs,** constitute, "do not," when used with a transitive pronoun particle as in the examples below.*
ta qs nłeptmntxʷ – Do not forget it. **čšťntéxʷ ta qs łx̣ʷntéxʷ łu q̓ett** – Be careful, do not make holes in the hide. **ta qs ċulntxʷ** – Do not waste it. **ta qs k̓ʷłax̣lmistmntxʷ łu ťeyeʔ** – Do not give in to evil.

The **i** following uvular consonants (UC) and the glottal stop **ʔ** sound like English "*ey*" as in the words *they, hey, whey,* etc. Salish UC are: **q, q̓, qʷ, q̓ʷ, x̣, x̣ʷ**. For example, the suffix …**qin** – head/top, is often spelled using English *ey* as "*qeyn*". So **qi, q̓i, qʷi, q̓ʷi, x̣i, x̣ʷi,** may be spelled with English *ey* as **q***ey*, **q̓***ey*, **qʷ***ey*, **q̓ʷ***ey*, **x̣***ey*, **x̣ʷ***ey* in other texts.

donut

nłċx̣ċax̣lexʷ – make donuts.
nłċx̣ċax̣lexʷm – S/he made donuts. **čn nłċx̣ċax̣lexʷm, kʷ nłċx̣ċax̣lexʷm**
es nłċx̣ċax̣lexʷi – S/he is making donuts. **čnes nłċx̣ċax̣lexʷi, kʷes nłċx̣ċax̣lexʷi**
qs nłċx̣ċax̣lexʷi – S/he is going to made donuts. **čiqs nłċx̣ċax̣lexʷi, kʷqs nłċx̣ċax̣lexʷi**

scnłċx̣ċax̣léxʷ – donuts. *prefix: **sc...** – s.t. that's been done/made/prepared.*

do one's best

q̓ʷiłmist, *q̓ʷiłmi* – do one's best; try hard from energy. *See: **capable.***

čmaqs – perform at the peak of one's ability; best at something; pinnacle. *See: **best.***

sičstmist – do one's best; try hard from ability. *See: **capable.***

musčst – do one's best with hope of succeeding; do something with confidence. *See: **confident.***

aytčst – strive; exert one's self in work. *See: **strive.***

door

k̓ʷłnčmép, *k̓ʷłnčmé* – door. *rt.: **čm** – extremity; circumfix: **k̓ʷłn...ep** – opening.*
k̓ʷłnčmqnep – top of the door.
k̓ʷłnčmčnep – back of the door.
k̓ʷłnčmcnełp – front of the door.

k̓ʷłnx̣ʷomep – gate. *circumfix: **k̓ʷłn...ep** – opening. See: **gate.***

k̓ʷłnyalep – gate. *circumfix: **k̓ʷłn...ep** – opening. See: **gate.***

door handle

k̓ʷłnmaw̓ptn – door handle.

Dorothy

toloti – Dorothy.

dot

łččeʔ – dot; little spot; little lump.

double

nx̣ppmew̓s – multiply; double up; laminate. *See: **multiply.***

doubt

q̓eyus – doubt; disbelief; question.
es q̓eyus – S/he is not believed. **čnes q̓eyus, kʷes q̓eyus**

q̓eyusncut – S/he was in disbelief. **čn q̓eyusncut, kʷ q̓eyusncut**
es q̓eyusncuti – S/he is in disbelief. **čnes q̓eyusncuti, kʷes q̓eyusncuti**

q̓eyusis – S/he doubted s.o. **q̓eyusn, q̓eyusntxʷ**
es q̓eyusms – S/he is doubting s.o. **ies q̓eyusm, as q̓eyusm**
qs q̓eyusms – S/he is going to doubt s.o. **iqs q̓eyusm, aqs q̓eyusm**

sq̓eyus – the doubt.
q̓eyusemn – one inclined to doubt.
q̓iq̓eyusmuł – one that habitually doubts.
q̓eyusncutn – one's doubter.
čq̓eyustn – the thing that causes doubt.

s.t. - something, the 3rd person
(s.t.) - something implied
s.o. - someone, the 3rd person
sl. - singular form
pl. - plural form
rt. - root word
cmd. - command
lit. - literally
fig. - figuratively
i.e., - for example
See: - Redirection to a related word.

es q̓eyułtumši – S/he doubts the people. **čnes q̓eyułtumši, kʷes q̓eyułtumši**
es q̓eyusnweʔexʷi – They are doubting each other. **qeʔes q̓eyusnwexʷi, pes q̓eyusnwexʷi**

tmalsm – in doubt; no feeling for something. *rt.: **tam** – not, no; suffix: **...els, ...ls** – want, feel.*
tmalsm – S/he felt doubt. **čn tmalsm, kʷ tmalsm**
es tmalsi – S/he is feeling doubt. **čnes tmalsi, kʷes tmalsi**

tmalsis – S/he doubted s.o./s.t. **tmalsn, tmalsntxʷ**
es tmalsms – S/he is doubting s.o./s.t. **ies tmalsm, as tmalsm**

tmalsmis – S/he doubted what s/he was doing. **tmalsmn, tmalsmntxʷ**
es tmalsmms – S/he is doubting what s/he is doing. **ies tmalsmm, as tmalsmm**

tmalsemn – one inclined to doubt. *suffix: **...emn** – one inclined to do.*

x̣ʷa uc – maybe but doubtful.
ƛ̓x̣ʷa – doubt.

dough

scnłucus – dough. *prefix: **sc...** – s.t. that's been done/made/prepared.*

scnméƛ̓ – something that's been mixed. *prefix: **sc...** – s.t. that's been done/made/prepared.*

Douglas fir

cq̓ełp – Douglas fir; *Pseudotsuga menziesii.*

dove

hem̓ishm̓ – dove, mourning dove; *Zenaida macroura.*
x̣ʷc̓x̣ʷo – pigeon; rock dove; *Columba livia.*

down

išut – down, low.
išilšscut – S/he lowered one's self down. **čn išilšscut, kʷ išilšscut**
es išilšscuti – S/he is lowering one's self down. **čnes išilšscuti, kʷes išilšscuti**
qs išilšscuti – S/he is going to lower one's self down. **čiqs išilšscuti, kʷqs išilšscuti**

išilšsts – S/he lowered s.t. down. **išilšstn, išilšstxʷ**
es išilšms – S/he is lowering s.t. down. **ies išilšm, as išilšm**
qs išilšms – S/he is going to lower s.t. down. **iqs išilšm, aqs išilšm**

čišut – down as a measure.
esel sc̓ušin čišut – two feet down.

tl̓ ciʔ išut – lower.

č išut – down; to the low.
k̓ʷłišut – underneath; down below; under; beneath. *See: **under**.*
nišut – down inside; deep inside. *See: **inside**.*

olqʷétkʷ, *olqʷé* – go/travel to water; go to the edge of the water *(often refers to a lake edge).*
olqʷétkʷm – S/he/it went to the water. **čn olqʷétkʷm, kʷ olqʷétkʷm**
es olqʷétkʷi – S/he/it is going to the water. **čnes olqʷétkʷi, kʷes olqʷétkʷi**
qs olqʷétkʷi – S/he/it is going to go to the water. **čiqs olqʷétkʷi, kʷqs olqʷétkʷi**
es olqʷéʔetkʷi – They are going to the water. **qeʔes olqʷétkʷi, pes olqʷétkʷi**

es ololqʷétkʷi – Each one is going to the water. **qeʔes ololqʷétkʷi, pes ololqʷétkʷi**

cʔolqʷétkʷm – S/he/it came to the water. *prefix: **c...** – indicating toward the speaker.*

t̓ipmncut – come down from something high. *(i.e., tree, chair, etc.) See: **come down**.*

t̓ipm – take something down from up high. *See: **take**.*

nčepmn – down; down filling. *rt.: **čep** – soft; prefix: **n...** – inside; suffix: **...min, ...mn** – instrument/tool.*

downhill wełkʷp – go downhill.
wełkʷp – S/he/it went downhill. **čn wełkʷp, kʷ wełkʷp**
es wełkʷpi – S/he/it is going downhill. **čnes wełkʷpi, kʷes wełkʷpi**
qs wełkʷpi – S/he/it is going to go downhill. **čiqs wełkʷpi, kʷqs wełkʷpi**

ułkʷpusis – S/he/it brought s.t. downhill. **ułkʷpusn, ułkʷpusntxʷ**
es ułkʷpusms – S/he/it is bringing s.t. downhill. **ies ułkʷpusm, as ułkʷpusm**
qs ułkʷpusms – S/he/it is going to bring s.t. downhill. **iqs ułkʷpusm, aqs ułkʷpusm**
ułkʷpúʔusis – They brought s.t. downhill. **qeʔ ułkʷpusntm, ułkʷpusntp**
es ułkʷpúʔusms – They are bringing s.t. downhill. **qeʔes ułkʷpusm, es ułkʷpusmp**
qs ułkʷpúʔusms – They are going to bring s.t. downhill. **qeʔqs ułkʷpusm, qs ułkʷpusmp**

čn eł cwełkʷp – I came back down here.

sułqpu – downhill; a description of a slope.

The **i** following uvular consonants (UC) and the glottal stop **ʔ** sound like English "*ey*" as in the words th*ey*, h*ey*, wh*ey*, etc. Salish UC are: **q, q̓, qʷ, q̓ʷ, x̣, x̣ʷ**. For example, the suffix ...**qin** – head/top, is often spelled using English *ey* as "q*ey*n". So **qi, q̓i, qʷi, q̓ʷi, x̣i, x̣ʷi**, may be spelled with English *ey* as **q***ey*, **q̓***ey*, **qʷ***ey*, **q̓ʷ***ey*, **x̣***ey*, **x̣ʷ***ey* in other texts.

downstream nʔax̣ʷt – go downriver by land; go downhill over a long distance.
nʔax̣ʷt – S/he/it went downriver. **čn nʔax̣ʷt, kʷ nʔax̣ʷt**
es nʔax̣ʷti – S/he/it is going downriver. **čnes nʔax̣ʷti, kʷes nʔax̣ʷti**
qs nʔax̣ʷti – S/he/it is going to go downriver. **čiqs nʔax̣ʷti, kʷqs nʔax̣ʷti**
es nʔáʔax̣ʷti – They are going downriver. **qeʔes nʔax̣ʷti, pes nʔax̣ʷti**
qs nʔáʔax̣ʷti – They are going to go downriver. **qeʔqs nʔax̣ʷti, pqs nʔax̣ʷti**

nc̓ʔilš – go upstream by land; go up river by land. *See: **upstream**.*

utemči, *ute* – downriver to another country/land; generally toward the Pacific ocean; west. *See: **west**.*

downy woodpecker st̓lxʷu – downy woodpecker; *Picoides pubescens*.

drag ckʷaqs – drag something. *rt.: **ckʷum** – pull.*
ckʷaqsis – S/he drug something. **čn ckʷaqsn, kʷ ckʷaqsntxʷ**
es ckʷaqsms – S/he is dragging something. **ies ckʷaqsm, as ckʷaqsm**
qs ckʷaqsms – S/he is going to drag something. **iqs ckʷaqsm, aqs ckʷaqsm**

dragonfly x̣ʷatqiṅéʔ – dragonfly.

drain k̓ʷłsixʷ – drain something. *rt.: **sixʷm** – spill; prefix: **k̓ʷł...** – under: **k̓ʷł...** – under.*
k̓ʷłsixʷmis – S/he drained it. **k̓ʷłsixʷmn, k̓ʷłsixʷmntxʷ**
es k̓ʷłsixʷms – S/he is draining it. **ies k̓ʷłsixʷm, as k̓ʷłsixʷm**
qs k̓ʷłsixʷms – S/he is going to drain it. **iqs k̓ʷłsixʷm, aqs k̓ʷłsixʷm**

es k̓ʷłsixʷ – It is drained.

k̓ʷłsixʷmnt – Drain it; flush it. *cmd.*

k̓ʷłsixʷmnt ci snṁṅe – Flush the toilet. **k̓ʷłsixʷmn ci snṁṅe** – I flushed the toilet.

s.t. - something, the 3rd person
(s.t.) - something implied
s.o. - someone, the 3rd person
sl. - singular form
pl. - plural form
rt. - root word
cmd. - command
lit. - literally
fig. - figuratively
i.e., - for example
See: - Redirection to a related word.

drape čłqʷéẁs – drape up high; hang up high over an object; hang up. *rt.: **łoqʷ** – over lay/around; circumfix: **č...eẁs** – up high.*
čłqʷéẁsis – S/he/it draped s.t. over. **čłqʷéẁsn, čłqʷéẁsntxʷ**
es čłqʷéẁsms – S/he/it is draping s.t. over. **ies čłqʷéẁsm, as čłqʷéẁsm**
qs čłqʷéẁsms – S/he/it is going to drape s.t. over. **iqs čłqʷéẁsm, aqs čłqʷéẁsm**
čłqʷéʔéẁsis – They draped s.t. over. **qeʔ čłqʷéẁsntm, čłqʷéẁsntp**

es čłqʷéʔeẁsms – They are draping s.t. over. **qeʔes čłqʷéẁsm, es čłqʷéẁsmp**

es čłqʷéẁs – It is draped over.

čłqʷéẁsntm – S/he/it was draped over. **qʷo čłqʷéẁsntm**

čłqʷéẁsiš – Drape (it) over. *cmd.*
čłqʷéẁsnt – Drape it over. *cmd.*

łqʷax̣n – drape something over the arm. *rt.: **łoqʷ**– over lay/around; suffix: **...ax̣n** – arm.*
łqʷax̣inm – S/he draped (s.t.) over the arm. **čn łqʷax̣nm, kʷ łqʷax̣nm**
es łqʷax̣ni – S/he is draping (s.t.) over the arm. **čnes łqʷax̣ni, kʷes łqʷax̣ni**
qs łqʷax̣ni – S/he is going to drape (s.t.) over the arm. **čiqs łqʷax̣ni, kʷqs łqʷax̣ni**

łqʷax̣is – S/he draped s.t. over s.o.'s arm. **łqʷax̣n, łqʷax̣ntxʷ**
es łqʷax̣nms – S/he is draping s.t. over s.o.'s arm. **ies łqʷax̣nm, as łqʷax̣nm**
qs łqʷax̣nms – S/he is going to drape s.t. over s.o.'s arm. **iqs łqʷax̣nm, aqs łqʷax̣nm**

es łqʷax̣n – S/he is wearing s.t. draped over the arm. **čnes łqʷax̣n, kʷes łqʷax̣n**

łqʷax̣niš – Drape something over the arm. *cmd.*
łqʷax̣nt – Drape something over his/her arm. *cmd.*

sq̇léps, *sq̇lé* – necklace.

drapes

nil̓xʷéẁstn, *nil̓xʷé* – drapes; curtains; *lit. to cover.*

draw

k̓ʷłq̇eẏim – draw a picture.
k̓ʷłq̇eẏim – S/he drew. **čn k̓ʷłq̇eẏim, kʷ k̓ʷłq̇eẏim**
es k̓ʷłq̇eẏimi – S/he is drawing. **čnes k̓ʷłq̇eẏimi, kʷes k̓ʷłq̇eẏimi**
qs k̓ʷłq̇eẏimi – S/he is going to draw. **čiqs k̓ʷłq̇eẏimi, kʷqs k̓ʷłq̇eẏimi**
k̓ʷłq̇eẏíʔim – They drew. **qeʔ k̓ʷłq̇eẏim, p k̓ʷłq̇eẏim**

k̓ʷłq̇eẏntes – S/he drew it. **k̓ʷłq̇eẏnten, k̓ʷłq̇eẏntexʷ**
es k̓ʷłq̇eẏims – S/he is drawing it. **ies k̓ʷłq̇eẏim, as k̓ʷłq̇eẏim**
qs k̓ʷłq̇eẏims – S/he is going to draw it. **iqs k̓ʷłq̇eẏim, aqs k̓ʷłq̇eẏim**
k̓ʷłq̇eẏntéʔes – They drew it. **qeʔ k̓ʷłq̇eẏntem, k̓ʷłq̇eẏntep**
qs k̓ʷłq̇eẏíʔims – They are going to draw it. **qeʔqs k̓ʷłq̇eẏim, qs k̓ʷłq̇eẏimp**

k̓ʷłq̇eẏiš – Draw. *cmd.*
k̓ʷłq̇eẏint – Draw s.t./s.o. *cmd.*

ṅem k̓ʷłq̇eẏim – S/he will draw. **ṅem čn k̓ʷłq̇eẏim, ṅem kʷ k̓ʷłq̇eẏim**
ṅem k̓ʷłq̇eẏíʔim – They will draw. **ṅem qeʔ k̓ʷłq̇eẏim, ṅem p k̓ʷłq̇eẏim**
ṅem k̓ʷłq̇ẏq̇eẏntes – S/he will draw it. **ṅem k̓ʷłq̇ẏq̇eẏnten, ṅem k̓ʷłq̇ẏq̇eẏntexʷ**
ṅem k̓ʷłq̇ẏq̇eẏntéʔes – They will draw it. **ṅem qeʔ k̓ʷłq̇ẏq̇eẏntem, ṅem k̓ʷłq̇ẏq̇eẏntep**

ṅem qeʔ k̓ʷłq̇ẏq̇eẏntem łu qeʔ sumeš – We'll paint pictures of our medicine power. **qeyqeyši sck̓ʷłq̇eẏis łiʔe k̓ʷul̓is** – Qeyqeyshi did his painting here. **k̓ʷłq̇eẏint asq̇ẏq̇eẏi** – Draw you pattern.
čłq̇eẏint asq̇ẏq̇eẏi – Draw your pattern.
łq̇q̇ẏilxʷ – cloth. *See: **pattern**.*

nċoqičṅ – draw an arrow out of a quiver on the back. *rt.: **ċoʔq** – pull out; suffix: **...ičṅ** – back.*
nċoqičṅm – S/he drew out an arrow. **čn nċoqičṅm, kʷ nċoqičṅm**
es nċoqičṅi – S/he is drawing out an arrow. **čnes nċoqičṅi, kʷes nċoqičṅi**
qs nċoqičṅi – S/he is going to draw out an arrow. **čiqs nċoqičṅi, kʷqs nċoqičṅi**

nċoqičṅis – S/he drew out an arrow. **nċoqičṅn, nċoqičṅntxʷ**

es nc̓oqičn̓ms – S/he is drawing out an arrow. **ies nc̓oqičn̓m, as nc̓oqičn̓m**
qs nc̓oqičn̓ms – S/he is going to draw out an arrow. **iqs nc̓oqičn̓m, aqs nc̓oqičn̓m**

nc̓oqičn̓nt – Draw it out. *cmd.*

nc̓oˀqłniut, *nc̓oˀqłni* – draw a knife/sword/gun out of a side mounted sheath; unsheath. *rt.: c̓oˀq – pull out.*
nc̓oˀqłniutm – S/he drew out. **čn nc̓oˀqłniutm, kʷ nc̓oˀqłniutm**
es nc̓oˀqłniuti – S/he is drawing out. **čnes nc̓oˀqłniuti, kʷes nc̓oˀqłniuti**
qs nc̓oˀqłniuti – S/he is going to draw out. **čiqs nc̓oˀqłniuti, kʷqs nc̓oˀqłniuti**

nc̓oˀqłniutmis – S/he drew it out. **nc̓oˀqłniutmn, nc̓oˀqłniutmntxʷ**
es nc̓oˀqłniutms – S/he is drawing it out. **ies nc̓oˀqłniutm, as nc̓oˀqłniutm**
qs nc̓oˀqłniutms – S/he is going to draw it out. **iqs nc̓oˀqłniutm, aqs nc̓oˀqłniutm**

nc̓oˀqłniutmnt – Draw it out. *cmd.*

estóqʷ – ravine; draw.

The **i** following uvular consonants (UC) and the glottal stop **ˀ** sound like English "*ey*" as in the words *they, hey, whey,* etc. Salish UC are: **q, q̓, qʷ, q̓ʷ, x̣, x̣ʷ**. For example, the suffix **...qin** – head/top, is often spelled using English *ey* as "q*ey*n". So **qi, q̓i, qʷi, q̓ʷi, x̣i, x̣ʷi**, may be spelled with English *ey* as **q***ey*, **q̓***ey*, **qʷ***ey*, **q̓ʷ***ey*, **x̣***ey*, **x̣ʷ***ey* in other texts.

dream

nspsupps, *nspsu* – dreaming.
nspsuppsm – S/he/it dreamt. **čn nspsuppsm, kʷ nspsuppsm**
es nspsuppsi – S/he/it is dreaming. **čnes nspsuppsi, kʷes nspsuppsi**
qs nspsuppsi – S/he/it is going to dream. **čiqs nspsuppsi, kʷqs nspsuppsi**
nspsúˀuppsm – They dreamt. **qeˀ nspsuppsm, p nspsuppsm**
es nspsuppsi – They are dreaming. **qeˀes nspsuppsi, pes nspsuppsi**
qs nspsuppsi – They are going to dream. **qeˀqs nspsuppsi, pqs nspsuppsi**

nspsuppsmis – S/he/it dreamt about s.o./s.t. **nspsuppsmn, nspsusppsmntxʷ**
es nspsuppsms – S/he/it is dreaming of s.o./s.t. **ies nspsuppsm, as nspsuppsm**
qs nspsuppsms – S/he/it is going to dream of s.o./s.t. **iqs nspsuppsm, aqs nspsuppsm**

scnspsupps – something that has been dreamt.
snspsupps – dream.

nspsuppsmcn – I dreamt about you. **čn nspsuppsm t islax̣t** – I dreamt of my friend.
nspsuppsmn łu islax̣t – I dreamt of my friend.

qiˀis – nightmare; bad dream; had a nightmare. *See: **nightmare**.*

moyx̣ – extrasensory perception; vision; foretelling dream; clairvoyant. *See: **vision**.*

snap – stare off; daydream; become quiet and calm; settled. *See: daydream.*

dress

ištpálqs, *ištpá* – dress; skirt. *suffix: **...lqs, ...alqs** – clothes.*

sčx̣ʷpxʷálqs, *sčx̣ʷpxʷá* – wing dress; woman's traditional cloth dress. *suffix: **...lqs, ...alqs** – clothes.*

kʷłištálqs, *kʷłištá* – under clothing; slip for a dress. *suffix: **...lqs, ...alqs** – clothes.*

snacłq̓éyt, *snacłq̓é* – dress/shirt. *rt.: **ac** – **tie**; suffix: **...łq̓éyt** – shoulder.*

nłxʷpncut – dress one's self.
nłxʷpncut – S/he dressed one's self. **čn nłxʷpncut, kʷ nłxʷpncut**
es nłxʷpncuti – S/he is dressing one's self. **čnes nłxʷpncuti, kʷes nłxʷpncuti**

es nłxʷpalqs – S/he/it is dressed/in clothes. **čnes nłxʷpalqs, kʷes nłxʷpalqs**

nłxʷpalqs – S/he got dressed. **čn nłxʷpalqs, kʷ nłxʷpalqs**

s.t. - something, the 3rd person
(s.t.) - something implied
s.o. - someone, the 3rd person
sl. - singular form
pl. - plural form
rt. - root word
cmd. - command
lit. - literally
fig. - figuratively
i.e., - for example
See: - Redirection to a related word.

es nłxʷpalqsi – S/he is getting dressed. **čnes nłxʷpalqsi, kʷes nłxʷpalqsi**

nłxʷpalqscut – S/he clothed one's self. **čn nłxʷpalqscut, kʷ nłxʷpalqscut**
es nłxʷpalqscuti – S/he is clothing one's self. **čnes nłxʷpalqscuti, kʷes nłxʷpalqscuti**
qs nłxʷpalqscuti – S/he is going to cloth one's self. **čiqs nłxʷpalqscuti, kʷqs nłxʷpalqscuti**

nłxʷpalqsis – S/he put clothes on s.o. **nłxʷpalqsn, nłxʷpalqsntxʷ**
es nłxʷpalqsms – S/he is putting clothes on s.o. **ies nłxʷpalqsm, as nłxʷpalqsm**
qs nłxʷpalqsms – S/he is going to put clothes on s.o. **iqs nłxʷpalqsm, aqs nłxʷpalqsm**

snłxʷpalqstn – clothes.

nłxʷpncutš – Get dressed; get in your clothes. *cmd.*
nłxʷpalqscutš – Cloth yourself. *cmd.*
nłxʷpalqsnt – Put clothes on him/her. *cmd.*

łixʷp – slip/pull/put something fitted over an object. *See:* ***pull over.***

x̣cnuṁt – ready/dressed; put clothes on. *See:* ***wear.***
x̣cnuṁt – S/he put clothes on. **čn x̣cnuṁt, kʷ x̣cnuṁt**
es x̣cnuṁti – S/he is putting clothes on. **čnes x̣cnuṁti, kʷes x̣cnuṁti**
qs x̣cnuṁti – S/he is going to put clothes on. **čiqs x̣cnuṁti, kʷqs x̣cnuṁti**
es x̣cnúʔumti – They are putting clothes on. **qeʔes x̣cnuṁti, pes x̣cnuṁti**

x̣cnuṁtsts – S/he made s.o. dress. **x̣cnuṁtstn, x̣cnuṁtstxʷ**
es x̣cnuṁtms – S/he is making s.o. dress. **ies x̣cnuṁtm, as x̣cnuṁtm**
qs x̣cnuṁtms – S/he is going to make s.o. dress. **iqs x̣cnuṁtm, aqs x̣cnuṁtm**

es x̣cnuṁt – S/he is dressed. **čnes x̣cnuṁt, kʷes x̣cnuṁt**
qs x̣cnuṁt – S/he is going to be dressed. **čiqs x̣cnuṁt, kʷqs x̣cnuṁt**
es x̣cnúʔumt – They are dressed. **qeʔes x̣cnuṁt, pes x̣cnuṁt**

x̣cnuṁtš – Put your clothes on. *cmd.*
x̣cnuṁtwi – All of you put your clothes on. *cmd.*
x̣cnuṁtskʷ – Make s.o. dress. *cmd.*

tam i t qʷec u qeʔes x̣cnuṁt – We were not dressed warm.

x̣cmncut, *x̣cmncu* – get one's self ready/dressed. *rt.:* ***x̣cim*** *– make ready/orderly. See:* ***ready.***
x̣cmncut – S/he got ready/dressed. **čn x̣cmncut, kʷ x̣cmncut**
es x̣cmncuti – S/he is getting dressed/ready. **čnes x̣cmncuti, kʷes x̣cmncuti**
qs x̣cmncuti – S/he is going to get dressed/ready. **čiqs x̣cmncuti, kʷqs x̣cmncuti**
es x̣cmncúʔuti – They are getting dressed/ready. **qeʔes x̣cmncuti, pes x̣cmncuti**
qs x̣cmncúʔuti – They are going to get dressed/ready. **qeʔqs x̣cmncuti, pqs x̣cmncuti**

x̣cmncutš – Get dressed/ready. *cmd.*
x̣cmncutwi – All of you get dressed/ready. *cmd.*

kʷéṁt qeʔ eł x̣cmncut qeʔqs k̓ʷis ẏapqiṅi – Then, we'll be ready again to go celebrate.

mʔamalqs – woman's clothes; dress as a woman; disguised as a woman. *rt.:* ***mʔem*** *– woman; suffix:* ***...lqs, ...alqs*** *– clothes.*
es mʔamalqsi – S/he is dressed as a woman. **čnes mʔamalqsi, kʷes mʔamalqsi**

čpƛ̓ʔencut – undress one's self. *See:* ***undress.***

dresser

snx̣cnuṁtn – place for clothes; dresser. *prefix:* ***sn...*** *– a place of; suffix:* ***...tin, ...tn*** *– means of/device.*

dribble **čłtetˀem –** dribble; bounce the ball on the ground. *rt: teˀ – hit/bump; prefix: čł... – surface.*
čłtetˀem – S/he dribbled. **čn čłtetˀem, kʷ čłtetˀem**
es čłtetˀemi – S/he is dribbling. **čnes čłtetˀemi, kʷes čłtetˀemi**
qs čłtetˀemi – S/he is going to dribble. **čiqs čłtetˀemi, kʷqs čłtetˀemi**

čłtetˀentes – S/he dribbled it. **čłtetˀenten, čłtetˀententxʷ**
es čłtetˀems – S/he is dribbling it. **ies čłtetˀem, as čłtetˀem**
qs čłtetˀems – S/he is going to dribble it. **iqs čłtetˀem, aqs čłtetˀem**

čłtetˀeiš – Dribble. *cmd.*
čłtetˀent – Dribble. *cmd.*

čłtetˀent sččxʷumeˀ – Dribble the ball. **čłtetˀentes č ntl̓ihełčeˀ –** S/he dribbled it to the otherside.

The **i** following uvular consonants (UC) and the glottal stop **ˀ** sound like English "*ey*" as in the words th*ey*, h*ey*, wh*ey*, etc. Salish UC are: **q, q̓, qʷ, q̓ʷ, x̣, x̣ʷ**. For example, the suffix **...qin** – head/top, is often spelled using English *ey* as "q*ey*n". So **qi, q̓i, qʷi, q̓ʷi, x̣i, x̣ʷi**, may be spelled with English *ey* as **q***ey*, **q̓***ey*, **qʷ***ey*, **q̓ʷ***ey*, **x̣***ey*, **x̣ʷ***ey* in other texts.

drift **plim –** drift/float away by water or wind; carried away.
plim – It drifted it away.
es plmi – It is drifting it away.
qs plmi – It is going to drift it away.

plip – It drifted away.
es plpmi – It is drifting away.
qs plpmi – It is going to drift away.

plntes – S/he/it made s.t. drift away. **plnten, plntexʷ**
es plims – S/he/it is making s.t. drift away. **ies plim, as plim**
qs plims – S/he/it is going to make s.t. drift away. **iqs plim, aqs plim**

pilplt – one that can drift; unstable.

plpnuis – S/he/it succeeded in making s.t. drift away. **plpnun, plpnuntxʷ**
čłpllmetkʷ – drift on the water. *prefix: čł... – surface; suffix: ...etkʷ, ...tkʷ – liquid*

łu t snew̓t plntem – It was carried away by the wind.

laáp – float in a vessel; navigate by water; row; surf internet. *(i.e., boat, canoe, raft, etc.) See: **float**.*

driftwood **stxʷuxʷ –** driftwood.

drill **qʷaqʷemncut,** *qʷaqʷemncú* **–** practice, drill, train, study. *rt.: qʷˀem – get accustomed; suffix: ...cut – action to the self. See: **practice**.*

drink **sust –** drink.
sust – S/he/it drank. **čn sust, kʷ sust**
es susti – S/he/it is drinking. **čnes susti, kʷes susti**
qs susti – S/he/it is going to drink. **čiqs susti, kʷqs susti**
es súˀusti – They are drinking. **qeˀes susti, pes susti**
qs súˀusti – They are going to drink. **qeˀqs susti, pqs susti**

sustis – S/he/it drank s.t. **sustn, sustntxʷ**
es sustms – S/he/it is drinking s.t. **ies sustm, as sustm**
qs sustms – S/he/it is going to drink s.t. **iqs sustm, aqs sustm**
súˀustis – They drank s.t. **qeˀ sustntm, sustntp**
es súˀustims – They are drinking s.t. **qeˀes sustm, es sustmp**

sxʷsust – one tasked to drink. *prefix: sxʷ... – one tasked to do.*
scsust – drink. *prefix: sc... – s.t. that's been done/made/prepared.*

s.t. - something, the 3rd person
(s.t.) - something implied
s.o. - someone, the 3rd person
sl. - singular form
pl. - plural form
rt. - root word
cmd. - command
lit. - literally
fig. - figuratively
i.e., - for example
See: - Redirection to a related word.

snsustn – drinking container; cup. *prefix: **sn...** – a place of; suffix: **...tin, ...tn** – means of/device.*
snssustn, *snssu* – place to drink. *prefix: **sn...** – a place of; suffix: **...tin, ...tn** – means of/device.*
snkʷłsust – drinking partner. *prefix: **nkʷł...** – together with.*

sustiš – Drink. *cmd.*
sustnt – Drink s.t. *cmd.*
es nsstelsi – S/he/it is wanting to drink. **čnes nsstelsi, kʷes nsstelsi**

ułéʔ čiqs susti t nt̓iškʷ – I am going to drink pop again. **qeʔes qʷmpmi łu t scsust** – We're dying from something that has been drank.

łmtq̓ʷolm – take a sip.
łmtq̓ʷolm – S/he took a sip. **čn łmtq̓ʷolm, kʷ łmtq̓ʷolm**
es łmtq̓ʷoli – S/he is taking a sip. **čnes łmtq̓ʷoli, kʷes łmtq̓ʷoli**
qs łmtq̓ʷoli – S/he is going to take a sip. **čiqs łmtq̓ʷoli, kʷqs łmtq̓ʷoli**

łmtq̓ʷolis – S/he sipped it. **łmtq̓ʷoln, łmtq̓ʷolntxʷ**
es łmtq̓ʷolms – S/he is sipping it. **ies łmtq̓ʷolm, as łmtq̓ʷolm**
qs łmtq̓ʷolms – S/he is going sip it. **iqs łmtq̓ʷolm, aqs łmtq̓ʷolm**

łmtq̓ʷoliš – Sip. *cmd.*
łmtq̓ʷolnt – Sip it. *cmd.*

nsʔóp – empty something; drink up; make dry. *See: **empty**.*

nsoʔpetkʷ, *nsoʔpe* – empty the water/liquid. *See: **empty**.*

qʷéwutn – alcohol. *See: **alcohol**.*

drip

aw̓u – drip; drain; leak.
aw̓up – It dripped.
es aw̓pmi – It is dripping.
qs aw̓pmi – It is going to drip.

aw̓is – S/he dripped s.t. **aw̓n, aw̓ntxʷ**
es aw̓ms – S/he is dripping s.t. **ies aw̓m, as aw̓m**

saw̓up – a drop.
saw̓aw̓up – drops.
sčaw̓up – a drop on something.
sčaw̓aw̓up – drops on something.

aw̓nt – Drip it. *cmd.*
čaw̓pmis – S/he felt a drop. **čaw̓pmin, čaw̓pmintxʷ**
es čław̓peneʔ – It is covered in drops.
es čaw̓aw̓pic̓eʔ – S/he/it is dripping (from) all over. **čnes čaw̓aw̓pic̓eʔ, kʷes čaw̓aw̓pic̓eʔ**
awawpew̓s – leak. *See: **leak**.*
čawawpus – cry; to have tears. *See: **tears**.*
nawpcin – drool; to slobber. *See: **drool**.*
nawawpaqs – runny nose. *See: **runny nose**.*

kʷaskʷas, *kʷassss* – sound of grease dripping on the fire.
i kʷaskʷas – Grease is dripping and hitting the fire with that sound.

kʷskʷsalš – grease dripped.
es kʷskʷsalši – grease is dripping.
qs kʷskʷsalši – grease is going to drip.

drive **ntx̣ʷmsqáx̣eʔ,** *ntx̣ʷmsqá* – drive a car, wagon, or team of horses. *rt.: **tox̣ʷ** – straight; prefix: **n...** – inside; suffix: **...sqax̣eʔ, ...sqa** – domestic animal; mainly referring to horse or car.*
ntx̣ʷmsqáx̣eʔ – S/he drove *(a car)*. **čn ntx̣ʷmsqáx̣eʔ, kʷ ntx̣ʷmsqáx̣eʔ**
es ntx̣ʷmsqáx̣eʔi – S/he is driving. **čnes ntx̣ʷmsqáx̣eʔi, kʷes ntx̣ʷmsqáx̣eʔi**
qs ntx̣ʷmsqáx̣eʔi – S/he is going to drive. **čiqs ntx̣ʷmsqáx̣eʔi, kʷqs ntx̣ʷmsqáx̣eʔi**
ntx̣ʷtx̣ʷmsqáʔa – Each one drove. **qeʔ ntx̣ʷtx̣ʷmsqá, p ntx̣ʷtx̣ʷmsqá**
es ntx̣ʷtx̣ʷmsqáʔaxeʔi – Each one is driving. **qeʔes ntx̣ʷtx̣ʷmsqáʔaxeʔi, pes ntx̣ʷtx̣ʷmsqáʔaxeʔi**

sxʷntx̣ʷmsqáx̣eʔ, *sxʷntx̣ʷmsqá* – driver; one tasked to drive.
ntx̣ʷmsqáx̣eʔtn – reins. *suffix: **...tin, ...tn** – means of/device.*

k̓ʷłcaqʷm – bring back runaway animals; drive back horses; head horses off. *See: **herd**.*

iax̣ – herd/drive animals; make a group of animals go in a certain direction. *See: **herd**.*

usšlšisqáx̣eʔ – drive horses/domestic animals further. *See: **herd**.*

qixʷ – chase/whip/drive away. *See: **chase**.*

meʔminm – chase/drive away someone; kick someone out. *See: **chase**.*

The **i** following uvular consonants (UC) and the glottal stop **ʔ** sound like English "*ey*" as in the words th*ey*, h*ey*, wh*ey*, etc. Salish UC are: **q, q̓, qʷ, q̓ʷ, x̣, x̣ʷ**. For example, the suffix **...qin** – head/top, is often spelled using English *ey* as "q*ey*n". So **qi, q̓i, qʷi, q̓ʷi, x̣i, x̣ʷi**, may be spelled with English *ey* as **q***ey*, **q̓***ey*, **qʷ***ey*, **q̓ʷ***ey*, **x̣***ey*, **x̣ʷ***ey* in other texts.

drizzle **nk̓ʷnk̓ʷeys** – drizzle; sprinkle. *rt.: **nk̓ʷuʔ** – one; suffix: **...eys** – rain.*
es nk̓ʷnk̓ʷéysi – It is drizzling.
es nk̓ʷnk̓ʷeysi č čo – It is drizzling outside.

nłk̓ʷnk̓ʷeys – rain a little; drizzle a little. *rt.: **nk̓ʷuʔ** – one; prefix: **ł...** – little; suffix: **ł...** – little**...eys** – rain.*
es nłk̓ʷnk̓ʷeysi – It is drizzling a little.

drool **nawpcin** – drool; slobber. *rt.: **awup** – drip; suffix: **...cin, ...cn** – action of the mouth.*
nawpcin – S/he/it drooled. **čn nawpcin, kʷ nawpcin**
es nawpcini – S/he/it is drooling. **čnes nawpcini, kʷes nawpcini**
qs nawpcini – S/he/it is going to drool. **čiqs nawpcini, kʷqs nawpcini**
es nawawpcíʔin – Each one of them drooled. **qeʔ nawawpcin, p nawawpcin**
es nawawpcíʔini – Each one of them is drooling. **qeʔes nawawpcini, pes nawawpcini**
qs nawawpcíʔini – Each one of them is going to drool. **qeʔqs nawawpcini, pqs nawawpcini**

drop **t̓ipmim** – drop something unintentionally. *rt.: **t̓iip** – fall.*
t̓ipmis – S/he dropped s.t. **t̓ipmin, t̓ipmintxʷ**
es t̓ipmims – S/he is dropping s.t. **ies t̓ipmim, as t̓ipmim**
qs t̓ipmims – S/he going to drop s.t. **iqs t̓ipmim, aqs t̓ipmim**
t̓ipmíʔis – They dropped s.t. **qeʔ t̓ipmintm, t̓ipmintp**
es t̓ipmíʔims – They are dropping s.t. **qeʔes t̓ipmim, es t̓ipmimp**
qs t̓ipmíʔims – They are going to drop s.t. **qeʔqs t̓ipmim, qs t̓ipmimp**

t̓ipmintm – S.t./s.o. was dropped.

čłx̣ʷop – fail to catch something.
čłx̣ʷopečst – fail to catch something with the hand; something glanced off the hand. *suffix: **...ečst, ...čst** – of the hand.*
čłx̣ʷopečstis – S/he dropped s.t. *(catching s.t., hit the hand)*. **čłx̣ʷopečstn, čłx̣ʷopečstntxʷ**
čłx̣ʷopéʔečstis – They dropped s.t. *(catching s.t., hit the hand)*. **qeʔ čłx̣ʷopečstntm, čłx̣ʷopečstntp**

suuʔ – water subsides/drops after a flood.

s.t. - something, the 3rd person
(s.t.) - something implied
s.o. - someone, the 3rd person
sl. - singular form
pl. - plural form
rt. - root word
cmd. - command
lit. - literally
fig. - figuratively
i.e., - for example
See: - Redirection to a related word.

es suumi – the water is subsiding.
qs suumi – the water is going to subside.

es suuʔ – the water is subsided.

iše suuʔ – The water goes up and down.

pƛ̓éčstm – release something from the hand. *See: **release**.*

pƛ̓im – release; free from something; remove something. *See: **release**.*

aw̓u – drip; drain; leak. *See: **drip**.*

drown **nƛ̓llétkʷ**, *nƛ̓llé* – drowning of one; die in the water.
nƛ̓llétkʷ – S/he/it drowned. **čn nƛ̓llétkʷ, kʷ nƛ̓llétkʷ**
es nƛ̓llétkʷi – S/he/it is drowning. **čnes nƛ̓llétkʷi, kʷes nƛ̓llétkʷi**
qs nƛ̓llétkʷi – S/he/it is going to drown. **čiqs nƛ̓llétkʷi, kʷqs nƛ̓llétkʷi**

nqʷmpétkʷ – drowning of more than one; die in the water.
nqʷmpéʔetkʷ – They drowned. **qeʔ nqʷmpétkʷi, p nqʷmpétkʷ**
es nqʷmpéʔetkʷi – They are drowning. **qeʔes nqʷmpétkʷi, pes nqʷmpétkʷi**
qs nqʷmpéʔetkʷi – They are going to drown. **qeʔqs nqʷmpétkʷi, pqs nqʷmpétkʷi**

np̓uwetkʷ – drown; breath water.
np̓uwetkʷm – S/he/it drowned. **čn np̓uwetkʷm, kʷ np̓uwetkʷm**

ntqetkʷm – hold someone or something under/in water.
ntqetkʷis – S/he held s.o. under/in water. **ntqetkʷn, ntqetkʷntxʷ**
es ntqetkʷms – S/he is holding s.o. under/in water. **ies ntqetkʷm, as ntqetkʷm**
qs ntqetkʷms – S/he is going to hold s.o. under/in water. **iqs ntqetkʷm, aqs ntqetkʷm**

ntqetkʷnt – Hold him/her/it under water. *cmd.*

drowsy **čšʔitš –** sleepy. *See: **sleepy**.*

drugs **sčqʷamaqs –** something one is used to; something liked *(i.e., drugs).*
ta qes čqʷamaqsmstxʷ łu t̓eyeʔ – Do not do drugs.

malyémistn – medicine. *See: **medicine**.*

p̓aáx̣ – heal; cure; get well. *See: **heal**.*

čnilm – poison someone. *See: **poison**.*

drum **pumin –** drum. *rt.: **spúʔus** – heart; suffix: **...min, ...mn** – instrument/tool.*
čeṅ łu anpumin – Where is your drum? **maw̓t łu inpumin –** My drum is broken *(broken frame).*
t̓łip łu inpumin – My drum is broken *(the drum head is torn).* **t čeṅ ečx̣lskʷtisyal łu pumin –** How big is the drum?

sp̓łčep, *sp̓łče* – drum; beat a drum. *rt.: **sp̓im** – strike w/ object. See: **hit**.*
sp̓łčep – S/he drummed. **čn sp̓łčep, kʷ sp̓łčep**
es sp̓łčepi – S/he is drumming. **čnes sp̓łčepi, kʷes sp̓łčepi**
qs sp̓łčepi – S/he is going to drum. **čiqs sp̓łčepi, kʷqs sp̓łčepi**
sp̓łčéʔep – They drummed. **qeʔ sp̓łčep, p sp̓łčep**
es sp̓łčéʔepi – They are drumming. **qeʔes sp̓łčepi, pes sp̓łčepi**
qs sp̓łčéʔepi – They are going to drum. **qeʔqs sp̓łčepi, pqs sp̓łčepi**

sp̓łčepis – S/he beat the drum. **sp̓łčepn, sp̓łčepntxʷ**
es sp̓łčepms – S/he is beating the drum. **čnes sp̓łčepm, kʷes sp̓łčepm**

qs sṗłčepms – S/he is going to beat the drum. **čiqs sṗłčepm, kʷqs sṗłčepm**

drummer
sxʷsṗłčepm, *sxʷsṗłče* – drummer; one tasked to drum. *prefix:* ***sxʷ...*** *– one tasked to do.*
sṗłčpemn – drummer; one inclined to drum. *suffix:* ***...emn*** *– one inclined to do.*

drumstick
sṗmintn – something to hit with.

drunk
qʷéw – crazy; drunk. *See:* ***crazy.***

qeʔes qʷmpmi łu t scsust – We're dying of drink. *See:* ***drink.***

nsl̓péʔew̓s, *nsl̓péʔe* – a little dizzy from alcohol; not quite drunk. *See:* ***dizzy.***

nwalqnm – tip the head. *(Also, a saying to be drinking alcohol.) See:* ***tip.***

dry
čéxʷ – dry something with air; remove moisture from something.
čexʷm – S/he dried (s.t.). **čn čexʷm, kʷ čexʷm**
es čexʷi – S/he is drying (s.t.). **čnes čexʷi, kʷes čexʷi**
qs čexʷi – S/he is going to dry (s.t.). **čiqs čexʷi, kʷqs čexʷi**
čéʔexʷm – They dried (s.t.). **qeʔ čexʷm, p čexʷm**

čexʷist – S/he dried one's self. **čn čexʷist, kʷ čexʷist**
es čexʷisti – S/he is drying one's self. **čnes čexʷisti, kʷes čexʷisti**
qs čexʷisti – S/he is going to dry one's self. **čiqs čexʷisti, kʷqs čexʷisti**

čexʷis – S/he dried s.t. **čexʷn, čexʷntxʷ**
es čexʷms – S/he is drying s.t. **ies čexʷm, as čexʷm**
qs čexʷms – S/he is going to dry s.t. **iqs čexʷm, aqs čexʷm**
es čéʔexʷms – They are drying s.t. **qeʔes čexʷm, es čexʷmp**

sčexʷ – the drying.
sččexʷ – something that's dried. *prefix:* ***sc...*** *– s.t. that's been done/made/prepared.*
snčéxʷmn – dryer; place to dry.
nčéxʷmn – something used to dry.

čexʷiš – Dry. *cmd.*
čexʷnt – Dry it. *cmd.*

kʷem̓t čéxʷn sxʷéli – Then I dried the camas.

x̣am̓ – dry; the literal or figurative absence of moisture.
i x̣am̓ – S/he/it is dry. **i čn x̣am̓, i kʷ x̣am̓**
i nx̣am̓ – It is dry inside.

x̣am̓léxʷ –dry land/area.
x̣am̓lqʷ – dry wood.

x̣m̓ip – S/he/it got dry. **čn x̣m̓ip, kʷ x̣m̓ip**
es x̣m̓pmi – S/he/it is getting dry. **čnes x̣m̓pmi, kʷes x̣m̓pmi**
qs x̣m̓pmi – S/he/it is going to get dry. **čiqs x̣m̓pmi, kʷqs x̣m̓pmi**

x̣m̓pstes – S/he/it caused s.t. to dry. **x̣m̓psten, x̣m̓pstexʷ**
es x̣m̓pims – S/he/it is making s.t. become dry. **ies x̣m̓pim, as x̣m̓pim**
qs x̣m̓pims – S/he/it is going to make s.t. become dry. **iqs x̣m̓pim, aqs x̣m̓pim**

nx̣m̓ip – It got dry inside, empty.

x̣m̓puléxʷ – land/area that got dry.
x̣m̓palqʷ – wood got dry.

The **i** following uvular consonants (UC) and the glottal stop ʔ sound like English "*ey*" as in the words th*ey*, h*ey*, wh*ey*, etc. Salish UC are: **q, q̇, qʷ, q̇ʷ, x̣, x̣ʷ**. For example, the suffix **...qin** – head/top, is often spelled using English *ey* as "q*ey*n". So **qi, q̇i, qʷi, q̇ʷi, x̣i, x̣ʷi**, may be spelled with English *ey* as **q***ey*, **q̇***ey*, **qʷ***ey*, **q̇ʷ***ey*, **x̣***ey*, **x̣ʷ***ey* in other texts.

s.t. - something, the 3rd person
(s.t.) - something implied
s.o. - someone, the 3rd person
sl. - singular form
pl. - plural form
rt. - root word
cmd. - command
lit. - literally
fig. - figuratively
i.e., - for example
See: - Redirection to a related word.

es x̣m̓ip sqel̓tč – dry meat.

nx̣mpcin – thirsty; have a dry mouth. *See:* ***thirst.***
nx̣ampłk̓ʷlt – dry throat *(what happens when you eat chokecheries).*

es x̣m̓pmi sic̓m – The blanket is getting dry.

cqay̓é – dry/smoke meat over a fire. *See:* ***dry meat.***

nsʔóp – empty something; to drink up; to make dry. *See:* ***empty.***

čéyeʔ – snag; dead tree; wood dry with age.
sčayalqʷ – dead standing tree; snag.

dryer

snčéxʷmn – place to dry; dryer.
snčéxʷmn x̣ʷl̓ x̣cnum̓tn – dryer for clothes.
snčéxʷmn x̣ʷl̓ sʔiłn – dryer for food; dehydrator.
snčéxʷmn x̣ʷl̓ sp̓iʔqáłq – dryer for fruit; dehydrator.

drying rack

sncqay̓ełc̓eʔ, *sncqay̓e* – rack to smoke and dry meat. *rt.:* ***cqay̓e*** *– dry/smoke meat; prefix:* ***sn...*** *– a place of.*

snłp̓éłc̓eʔtn, *snłp̓é* – drying rack. *rt.:* ***łip̓*** *– line; suffix:* ***...ełc̓eʔ*** *– inside contents, body, meat*

dry meat

cqay̓é – dry/smoke meat over a fire.
cqay̓ém – S/he dried meat. **čn cqay̓ém, kʷ cqay̓ém**
es cqay̓éi – S/he is drying meat. **čnes cqay̓éi, kʷes cqay̓éi**
qs cqay̓éi – S/he is going to dry meat. **čiqs cqay̓éi, kʷqs cqay̓éi**
es cqay̓éʔei – They are drying meat. **qeʔes cqay̓éi, pes cqay̓éi**
qs cqay̓éʔei – They are going to dry meat. **qeʔqs cqay̓éi, pqs cqay̓éi**

cqay̓is – S/he dried the meat. **cqay̓n, cqay̓ntxʷ**
es cqay̓ms – S/he is drying the meat. **ies cqay̓m, as cqay̓m**
qs cqay̓ms – S/he is going to dry the meat. **iqs cqay̓m, aqs cqay̓m**
cqáʔay̓is – They dried the meat. **qeʔ cqay̓ntm, cqay̓ntp**
es cqáʔay̓ms – They are drying the meat. **qeʔes cqay̓m, es cqay̓mp**

cqay̓išts – S/he dried meat for s.o. **cqay̓ištn, cqay̓ištxʷ**
es cqay̓ištms – S/he is drying meat for s.o. **ies cqay̓ištm, as cqay̓ištm**
qs cqay̓ištms – S/he is going to dry meat for s.o. **iqs cqay̓ištm, aqs cqay̓ištm**

sccqay̓ełc̓eʔ, *sccqay̓e* – dried/smoked meat. *rt.:* ***cqay̓e*** *– dry/smoke meat; prefix:* ***sc...*** *– s.t. that's been done/made/prepared.*
sncqay̓ełc̓eʔtn, *sncqay̓e* – rack to smoke and dry meat. *rt.:* ***cqay̓e*** *– dry/smoke meat; prefix:* ***sn...*** *– a place of.*

cqay̓eiš – Dry meat. *cmd.*
cqay̓nt – Dry the meat. *cmd.*

x̣ʷcntén u t̓él̓is łu innox̣ʷnx̣ʷ u cqay̓is. – I skinned it, and my wife sliced it and dried it. **uł sxʷl̓xʷl̓tew̓s es t̓éʔeli u es cqay̓éʔe** – Those people sliced and dried meat. **n̓em iqs cqay̓m** – I will dry it. **iqs cqay̓štm łu inqeneʔ** – I am going to dry meat for my grandma.

es x̣m̓ip sqel̓tč – It is dried meat.

dry meat rope

siy̓én̓p̓ – dry meat rope; strips of greasy dried meat.

duck

sesƛ̓xʷum̓ – duck; female mallard.

qʷinqn – male mallard. *lit. green head.*
stt̓ʔumeʔ – duckling, gosling.
łusustuʔ – diver *(bird)*; smaller duck.
čkʷlqin – redhead, *Aythya Americana. suffix:* ***...qin, ...qn –*** *top.*
sčłčmqni – hooded merganser, *Lophodytes cucullatus.*
kʷl̓kʷlal̓i – merganser, *Mergus merganser.*
q̇lépyeʔ – ring-necked duck, *Aythya collaris.*
tt̓qʷeneʔ – green-winged teal, *Anas carolinensis.*
ċáʔx̣eʔ – duck species.

plutm – dodge/duck away from something. *See:* ***dodge.***

duck hawk

aátat – falcon; Peregrine falcon; duck hawk; *Falco peregrinus.*

duckling

stt̓ʔumeʔ – duckling; gosling.

dull

ilʔilt, *ilʔi –* It is dull.

dumb

ṗat̓qan – An insult indicating someone has a soft sloppy head. *rt.:* ***ṗat̓ –*** *s.t. soft/squishy; suffix:* ***...qin, ...qn –*** *top. See:* ***pile.***
ṗat̓qan – S/he/it is a dumb/splat head. **čn ṗat̓qan, kʷ ṗat̓qan**

ṗat̓oyʔe – jerk; fool. *rt.:* ***ṗat̓ –*** *s.t. soft/squishy. See:* ***pile.***

čq̇awqn – jerk; dumb; stupid; broken head.

tqawqn, *tqaw –* dumb; unable to talk. *lit. plugged up speech.*
es tqaw – S/he is unable to talk.

dump

nṗt̓atkʷm – pour/dump a viscous substance in water *(i.e., brains, wet hide, honey, etc.). rt.:* ***ṗat̓ –*** *s.t. soft/squishy; suffix:* ***...etkʷ, ...tkʷ –*** *liquid*
nṗt̓atkʷm – S/he/it dumped in the water. **čn nṗt̓atkʷn, kʷ nṗt̓atkʷm**
es nṗt̓atkʷi – S/he is dumping in the water. **čnes nṗt̓atkʷi, kʷes nṗt̓atkʷi**
qs nṗt̓atkʷi – S/he is going to dump in the water. **čiqs nṗt̓atkʷi, kʷqs nṗt̓atkʷi**
nṗt̓áʔatkʷm – They dumped in the water. **qeʔ nṗt̓atkʷm, p nṗt̓atkʷm**

nṗt̓atkʷis – S/he/it dumped s.t. in the water. **nṗt̓atkʷn, nṗt̓atkʷntxʷ**
es nṗt̓atkʷms – S/he is dumping s.t. in the water. **ies nṗt̓atkʷm, as nṗt̓atkʷm**
qs nṗt̓atkʷms – S/he is going to dump s.t. in the water. **iqs nṗt̓atkʷm, aqs nṗt̓atkʷm**
es nṗt̓áʔatkʷms – They are dumping s.t. in the water. **qeʔes nṗt̓atkʷm, es nṗt̓atkʷmp**

ṗt̓am – splatter/spill/pour a viscous substance. *(i.e., spit, snow, honey, glue, mud, feces, etc.) See:* ***splatter.***

nṗt̓átkʷnt l séwłkʷ – Dump it into the water. *cmd.*

sixʷm – spill liquid out; pour liquid out. *See:* ***spill.***

pukʷ – spill/pour round objects. *(i.e., rocks, berries, marbles, apples, etc.) See:* ***spill.***
čłpukʷ – spread/pour round things out on a surface of something. *(i.e., berries, marbles, etc.) See:* ***spread.***

poq̇ʷ – spill/pour/dump powdered substances. *(i.e., salt, sugar, flour, gunpowder, ash, etc.) See:* ***spill.***

čqqʷusm – pour something. *See:* ***pour.***

snx̣ʷelmn – place you abandon things; dump; garbage receptacle. *See:* ***abandon.***

dumplings

scnt̓łt̓łe – dumplings. *prefix:* ***sc... –*** *s.t. that's been done/made/prepared.*

The **i** following uvular consonants (UC) and the glottal stop **ʔ** sound like English "*ey*" as in the words *they, hey, whey,* etc. Salish UC are: **q, q̇, qʷ, q̇ʷ, x̣, x̣ʷ**. For example, the suffix **...qin** – head/top, is often spelled using English *ey* as "q*ey*n". So **qi, q̇i, qʷi, q̇ʷi, x̣i, x̣ʷi**, may be spelled with English *ey* as **q***ey*, **q̇***ey*, **qʷ***ey*, **q̇ʷ***ey*, **x̣***ey*, **x̣ʷ***ey* in other texts.

s.t. - something, the 3rd person
(s.t.) - something implied
s.o. - someone, the 3rd person
sl. - singular form
pl. - plural form
rt. - root word
cmd. - command
lit. - literally
fig. - figuratively
i.e., - for example
See: - Redirection to a related word.

nłq̓ľáq̓lexʷ – make pancakes. *See:* ***pancake.***

dusk

łqiqlt, *łqi* – dusk *(when the sun is already down).*

sčsoósqn, *sčsoó* – sunset. *See:* ***sunset.***

sčlux̌ʷ – evening. *See:* ***evening.***

dust

sqʷʔoł – dust.
i qʷʔoł – It is dusty.

qʷołist – S/he/it dusted one's self. **čn qʷołist, kʷ qʷołist**
es qʷołisti – S/he/it is dusting one's self. **čnes qʷołisti, kʷes qʷołisti**
qs qʷołisti – S/he/it is going to dust one's self. **čiqs qʷołisti, kʷqs qʷołisti**

i qʷołs – S/he/it has a dusty face.
qʷołlexʷ – dusty land/area.
nqʷołqs – dusty road/nose.
čqʷołċeʔ – covered in dust.

es qʷułmncuti – There is low visibility from a dust storm or blizzard; *(fig., this can be said of someone really "dancing up a storm," making dust).*

čłsp̓p̓im – hit/wipe dust off things with a duster. *rt.:* ***sp̓im*** *– strike w/ object.*
čłsp̓p̓im – S/he/it dusted. **čn čłsp̓p̓im, kʷ čłsp̓p̓im**
es čłsp̓p̓mi – S/he/it is dusting. **čnes čłsp̓p̓mi, kʷes čłsp̓p̓mi**
qs čłsp̓p̓mi – S/he/it is going to dust. **čiqs čłsp̓p̓mi, kʷqs čłsp̓p̓mi**

čłsp̓p̓ntes – S/he/it dusted s.t. **čłsp̓p̓nten, čłsp̓p̓ntexʷ**
es čłsp̓p̓ims – S/he/it is dusting s.t. **ies čłsp̓p̓im, as čłsp̓p̓im**
qs čłsp̓p̓ims – S/he/it is going to dust s.t. **iqs čłsp̓p̓im, aqs čłsp̓p̓im**

čłsp̓p̓iš – Dust. *cmd.*
čłsp̓p̓int – Dust it. *cmd.*

mal – muddy; soiled with mud/dirt. *See:* ***mud.***

sqʷopt – loose tangled ball of dust, lint, hair, etc. *(usually found under furniture).*

poq̓ʷ – spill/pour/dump powdered substances. *(i.e., salt, sugar, flour, gunpowder, ash, etc.) See:* ***spill.***

dustpan

snnpq̓ʷmin – dustpan; something to put dust inside of.

snčłpq̓ʷmin – dustpan; something to get dust off the surface.

dwell

nłqqełċeʔ – dwell/inhabit the inside; possess. *rt.:* ***łaq*** *– sit; suffix:* ***...ełċeʔ*** *– inside contents, body, meat.*
es nłqqełċeʔ – They dwell within. **qeʔes nłqqełċeʔ, pes nłqqełċeʔ**

nłqqełċʔemis – They inhabited s.o./s.t. **qeʔ nłqqełċʔemntm, nłqqełċʔemntp**
es nłqqełċʔemms – They inhabiting s.o./s.t. **qeʔes nłqqełċʔemm, es nłqqełċʔemmp**
qs nłqqełċʔemms – They are going to inhabit s.o./s.t. **qeʔqs nłqqełċʔemm, qs nłqqełċʔemmp**

qʷo es nłqqełċʔemms – I'm inhabited by them; they dwell in me; I'm possessed.

lciʔ – stays here; remains here; dwells. *See:* ***stay.***

lšeʔ – stays there; roams in that general area; home range. *See:* ***stay.***

k̓ʷléw̓t – gathered/standing together. *(refers to standing; i.e., people, trees, etc.) See:* ***gather***

E

eagle **pqlqin,** *pqlqi* – bald eagle; *Haliaeetus leucocephalus. See:* ***bald eagle.***

mlqnups, *mlqnu* – golden eagle; *Aquila chrysaetos. See:* ***golden eagle.***

sq̇eẏmi – mature spotted eagle.

ilmxʷsq̇iʔmi – chief eagle.

Eagle Pass **ṅnšťeẇs sx̣ʷcuʔsi** – Eagle Pass, Mission Mountain Range, Flathead Nation.

ear **ťéneʔ** – ear. **ťnťéneʔ** – ears.
sčheneʔ – right ear.
sččq̇ʷeneʔ – left ear.
čłq̇łq̇éneʔ – big ears. *rt.:* ***łaq̇t*** *– wide.*
ntqtqéneʔ – plugged ears.
snupupéneʔ – ear hair.

earache **nċaléneʔ** – aching ear. *rt.:* ***ċaál*** *– ache.*
nċaľéneʔ – S/he had an earache. **čn nċaľéneʔ, kʷ nċaľéneʔ**
es nċaľénʔei – S/he has an earache. **čnes nċaľénʔei, kʷes nċaľénʔei**
qs nċaľénʔei – S/he is going to have an earache. **čiqs nċaľénʔei, kʷqs nċaľénʔei**
nċaľéʔeneʔ – They had an earache. **qeʔ nċaľéneʔ, p nċaľéneʔ**
es nċaľéʔenʔei – They have an earache. **qeʔes nċaľénʔei, pes nċaľénʔei**
qs nċaľéʔenʔei – They are going to have an earache. **qeʔqs nċaľénʔei, pqs nċaľénʔei**

snċaléneʔ – an earache.
snċaċaléneʔ – both ears ache.

early **iʔíst,** *iʔí* – early.
iʔísq̇t – early morning.

ṅem iʔíst m qeʔ eťeťitš – We'll go to sleep early. **iʔíst u čn qéiłt t skʷekʷst** – I woke up early this morning. **ṅe eł x̣lip ṅem iʔíst m čn qéiłt** – When it gets to be daylight I will wake up early.

earrings **snacacéneʔ** – earrings. *rt.:* ***ac*** *– tie; suffix:* ***...eneʔ*** *– ear.*
snacéneʔ – earring.
sčptptqʷéneʔ – post earrings. *suffix:* ***...eneʔ*** *– ear.*
sčptqʷéneʔ – one post earring.

nacacéneʔ – wear earrings.
es nacacéneʔ – S/he is wearing earrings. **čnes nacacéneʔ, kʷes nacacéneʔ**

nacacénʔem – S/he put earrings on. **čn nacacénʔem, kʷ nacacénʔem**
es nacacénʔei – S/he is putting earrings on. **čnes nacacénʔei, kʷes nacacénʔei**

s.t. - something, the 3rd person
(s.t.) - something implied
s.o. - someone, the 3rd person
sl. - singular form
pl. - plural form
rt. - root word
cmd. - command
lit. - literally
fig. - figuratively
i.e., - for example
See: - Redirection to a related word.

qs nacacénʔei – S/he is going to put earrings on. **čiqs nacacénʔei, kʷqs nacacénʔei**

nacacénʔeis – S/he put earrings on s.o. **ies nacacénʔen, as nacacénʔentxʷ**
es nacacénʔems – S/he is putting earrings on s.o. **ies nacacénʔem, as nacacénʔem**
qs nacacénʔems – S/he is going to put earrings on s.o. **iqs nacacénʔem, aqs nacacénʔem**

nacacéneʔiš – Put earrings on. *cmd.*
nacacénʔent – Put earrings on s.o. *cmd.*

čɫx̣ʷɫx̣ʷéneʔ – pierce ears. *rt.: **ɫóx̣ʷ** – It has a hole; suffix: **...eneʔ** – ear.*
čɫx̣ʷénʔeis – S/he pierced s.o.'s ear. **čɫx̣ʷénʔen, čɫx̣ʷénʔentxʷ**
es čɫx̣ʷénʔems – S/he is piercing s.o.'s ear. **ies čɫx̣ʷénʔem, as čɫx̣ʷénʔem**
qs čɫx̣ʷénʔems – S/he is going to pierce s.o.'s ear. **iqs čɫx̣ʷénʔem, aqs čɫx̣ʷénʔem**

es nɫx̣ʷɫx̣ʷéneʔ – S/he has pierced ears. **čnes nɫx̣ʷɫx̣ʷéneʔ, kʷes nɫx̣ʷɫx̣ʷéneʔ**

sxʷčɫx̣ʷɫx̣ʷéneʔ – one tasked to pierce ears. *suffix: **sxʷ...** – one tasked to do.*

čɫx̣ʷénʔent – Pierce s.o.'s ear. *cmd.*

earth

smlq̇ʷsťulixʷ – earth.

sťulixʷ – ground; earth; land; field.
mlk̇ʷmulexʷ sťulixʷ – entire earth.
mlq̇ʷmulexʷ sťulixʷ – balled earth.

šiyulexʷ – first land; homeland; place of origin.

čnes k̇ʷl̓sťulixʷ – I am working my land. **i xʷuk̇ʷ ye sťulixʷ** – This land is clean.

earthquake

yatmulexʷ – earthquake. *rt.: **yatt** – shake; suffix: **...ulexʷ** – land.*

ẏiʔiulexʷ – earthquake; moving land. *rt.: **iwu** – move; suffix: **...ulexʷ** – land.*

earthworm

yanáq̇ʷ – angleworm, earthworm.

east

snx̣lptin – east. *rt.: **x̣lip** – light up.*

Easter

paqs sx̣lx̣alt – Easter.

easy

iɫťé – It is easy.

iɫťetmšn – tender footed.

iɫťetmšmiš – Walk lightly. *cmd.*

miɫ iɫťé – It is too easy. **eɫ k̇ʷul̓n inṗiṗuyšn u iɫťé u eɫ wiʔsten** – I worked on my car; it was easy, so I finished it. **exʷ iɫťétmstxʷ** – Oh, you made it easy.

iɫťétmčst – It is easily made. *suffix: **...ečst, ...čst** – of the hand.*
iɫťétmčsts – S/he made s.t. easy. **iɫťétmčstn, iɫťétmčstxʷ**
es ɫťetčnms – S/he is making it easy. **ies ɫťetčnm, as ɫťetčnm**
qs ɫťetčnms – S/he is going to make it easy. **iqs ɫťetčnm, aqs ɫťetčnm**

čťimečst – make easy. *suffix: **...ečst, ...čst** – of the hand.*
čťimečstm – S/he/it made it easy. **čn čťimečstm, kʷ čťimečstm**

čťimečstmis – S/he/it made s.t. easy. **čťimečstmn, čťimečstmntxʷ**
es čťimečstms – S/he/it is making s.t. easy. **ies čťimečstm, as čťimečstm**

čťimečstmn – I made it easy for s.o. **čťiméʔečstmɫtn** – I made it easy for them.

ha t milq̇ʷ čṫiṫimečstmntxʷ – Does it always come easy for you?

x̣sečst – handle something with ease; do something in a good way. *suffix:* ***...ečst, ...čst*** *– of the hand.*
x̣sečstmis – S/he handled something with ease. **x̣sečstmn, x̣sečstmntxʷ**
es x̣sečstms – S/he is handling something with ease. **ies x̣sečstm, as x̣sečstm**
qs x̣sečstms – S/he is going to handle something with ease. **iqs x̣sečstm, aqs x̣sečstm**

łx̣sx̣esečst, *łx̣sx̣ese* – handle something lightly/with ease; not disturbing a situation.

x̣sečstmnt – Handle it with ease. *cmd.*

imše łx̣sx̣esečstmntxʷ x̣iṅe maẁt – You should handle it gently, it might break.

i pel̓ – It is easy/simple. *(Spokane word)*

The **i** following uvular consonants (UC) and the glottal stop ʔ sound like English "*ey*" as in the words th*ey*, h*ey*, wh*ey*, etc. Salish UC are: **q, q̇, qʷ, q̇ʷ, x̣, x̣ʷ**. For example, the suffix ...**qin** – head/top, is often spelled using English *ey* as "q*ey*n". So **qi, q̇i, qʷi, q̇ʷi, x̣i, x̣ʷi**, may be spelled with English *ey* as **q***ey*, **q̇***ey*, **qʷ***ey*, **q̇ʷ***ey*, **x̣***ey*, **x̣ʷ***ey* in other texts.

eat

iłn – eat, of an individual.
iłn – S/he/it ate. **čn iłn, kʷ iłn**
es iłni – S/he/it is eating. **čnes iłni, kʷes iłni**
qs iłni – S/he/it is eating. **čiqs iłni, kʷqs iłni**

iłís – S/he/it ate s.t. **iłn, iłntxʷ**
es iłnms – S/he/it is eating s.t. **ies iłnm, as iłnm**
qs iłnms – S/he/it is eating s.t. **iqs iłnm, aqs iłnm**

iłíšts – S/he/it ate s.t. for s.o. **iłíštn, iłíštxʷ**
iłíłts – S/he/it ate s.t. of s.o.'s. **iłíłtn, iłíłtxʷ**

łʔiiłn – S/he/it ate a little. **čn łʔiiłn, kʷ łʔiiłn**

es iłn – S/he/it eats. **čnes iłn, kʷes iłn**
iłntm – It was eaten.

sʔiłn – food.
scʔiłn – something that's been eaten.
sxʷʔiłn – one tasked to eat. *prefix:* ***sxʷ...*** *– one tasked to do.*
ełnemn – one inclined to eat. *suffix:* ***...emn*** *– one inclined to do*
snʔiłntn – place to eat. *prefix:* ***sn...*** *– a place of; suffix:* ***...tin, ...tn*** *– means of/device.*
snkʷłʔiłn – fellow eater. *prefix:* ***snkʷł...*** *– fellow, member of.*

iłniš – Eat. *cmd.*
iłnš – Eat. *cmd.*
iłnt – Eat it. *cmd.*
iłłnutm – eatable.
es iłłnmutms – S/he/it is able to eat s.t. **ies iłłnmutm, as iłłnmutm**
es nkʷłʔiłnms – S/he/it is eating with s.o. **ies nkʷłʔiłnm, as nkʷłʔiłnm**
es ełnlwisi – S/he/it is eating here and there. **čnes ełnlwisi, kʷes ełnlwisi**
es ełnwexʷisti – They're eating each other.
nełnels, *nełne* – crave food; want to eat. *See:* ***crave.***

iše iłn – S/he/it eats. **iše čn iłn** – I eat; I do eat. **iše čn iłn t q̇itq̇ṁ** – I do eat strawberries. **čnes iłn t q̇itq̇ṁ** – I eat strawberries. **ies iłnm apls** – I am eating apples. **ƛ̓meẏ u čn łʔiiłn t sṫša** – I ate a few huckleberries.

s.t. - something, the 3rd person
(s.t.) - something implied
s.o. - someone, the 3rd person
sl. - singular form
pl. - plural form
rt. - root word
cmd. - command
lit. - literally
fig. - figuratively
i.e., - for example
See: - Redirection to a related word.

eliłn – eat, of more than one person.
elíʔiłnm – They ate. **qeʔ eliłnm, p eliłnm**
es elíʔiłni – They are eating. **qeʔes eliłni, pes eliłni**

qs elíʔiłni – They are going to eat. qeʔqs eliłni, pqs eliłni

elíʔiłis – They ate s.t. qeʔ eliłntm, eliłntp
es elíʔiłnms – They are eating s.t. qeʔes eliłnm, es eliłnmp
qs elíʔiłnm – They are going to eat s.t. qeʔqs eliłnm, qs eliłnmp
eleliłn – Each one ate; each group ate.

eliłnwi – All of you eat. *cmd.*
eliłnti – All of you eat it. *cmd.*

x̌ʷu qeʔqs elíłni – Let's eat.

wiʔcinm – finish eating; eat it all up. *rt.: uẏé – finish; suffix: …cin, …cn – action of the mouth.*
  wiʔcinm – S/he/it finished eating. čn wiʔcinm, kʷ wiʔcinm
  es wiʔcini – S/he/it is finishing eating. čnes wiʔcini, kʷes wiʔcini
  qs wiʔcini – S/he/it is going to finish eating. čiqs wiʔcini, kʷqs wiʔcini
  wiʔcíʔinm – They finished eating. qeʔ wiʔcinm, p wiʔcinm
  es wiʔcíʔini – They are finishing eating. qeʔes wiʔcini, pes wiʔcini
  qs wiʔcíʔini – They are going to finish eating. qeʔqs wiʔcini, pqs wiʔcini

  wiʔcinmis – S/he/it ate it. wiʔcinmn, wiʔcinmntxʷ
  es wiʔcinmms – S/he/it is finishing eating it. ies wiʔcinmm, as wiʔcinmm
  qs wiʔcinmms – S/he/it is going to finish eating it. iqs wiʔcinmm, aqs wiʔcinmm
  wiʔcíʔinmis – They finished eating it. qeʔ wiʔcinmntm, wiʔcinmntp
  es wiʔcíʔinmms – They are finishing eating it. qeʔes wiʔcinmm, es wiʔcinmmp
  qs wiʔcíʔinmms – They are going to finish eating it. qeʔqs wiʔcinmm, qs wiʔcinmmp

  wiʔcinmntm – It got ate up.

  wiʔcinmnt – Eat it all up. *cmd.*
  wiʔcinmnt esyaʔ asʔiłn – Eat up all your food. wiʔcinm isʔiłn – I ate up all my food. ƛ̓e čn
  wiʔcinm – I've already eaten; I am done. ha kʷ wiʔcinm – Did you finish eating?

čx̌ʷʔaqsm, čx̌ʷʔa – eat a lot. *rt: x̌ʷʔit – a lot/many.*
  čx̌ʷʔaqsm – S/he ate a lot. čn čx̌ʷʔaqsm, kʷ čx̌ʷʔaqsm
  es čx̌ʷʔaqsi – S/he is eating a lot. čnes čx̌ʷʔaqsi, kʷes čx̌ʷʔaqsi
  qs čx̌ʷʔaqsi – S/he is going to eat a lot. čiqs čx̌ʷʔaqsi, kʷqs čx̌ʷʔaqsi

  mił čn čx̌ʷʔa – I ate too much. iše čx̌ʷʔaqsm t čłq̇iq̇á – S/he always eats a lot of candy.

nt̓laneʔ – overeat; eat too much; gluttony.
  nt̓lanʔem – S/he/it ate too much. čn nt̓lanʔem, kʷ nt̓lanʔem

  uł nt̓láʔaneʔ – They are overeaters. qeʔ uł nt̓lanʔem, p uł nt̓lanʔem

  šewi kʷ nt̓laneʔ – See, you eat too much.

q̇amaliyeʔ – eat and eat; eat greedily.
  q̇amaliyeʔ – S/he/it ate and ate. čn q̇amaliyeʔ, kʷ q̇amaliyeʔ
  es q̇amaliyeʔi – S/he/it is eating and eating. čnes q̇amaliyeʔi, kʷes q̇amaliyeʔi
  qs q̇amaliyeʔi – S/he/it is going to eat and eat. čiqs q̇amaliyeʔi, kʷqs q̇amaliyeʔi

x̌ʷełcin – eat fast/hurriedly. *rt: x̌ʷełe – hurry; suffix: …cin, …cn – action of the mouth.*
  x̌ʷełcin – S/he ate fast. čn x̌ʷełcin, kʷ x̌ʷełcin
  es x̌ʷełcini – S/he is eating fast. čnes x̌ʷełcini, kʷes x̌ʷełcini
  qs x̌ʷełcini – S/he is going to eat fast. čiqs x̌ʷełcini, kʷqs x̌ʷełcini

  x̌ʷełcinš – Eat fast. *cmd.*

čn xʷełcin u čn wiʔcinm – I ate fast and finished eating.

maʔqcan – eat fast.
maʔqcanm – S/he ate fast. **čn maʔqcanm, kʷ maʔqcanm**
es maʔqcani – S/he is eating fast. **čnes maʔqcani, kʷes maʔqcani**
qs maʔqcani – S/he is going to eat fast. **čiqs maʔqcani, kʷqs maʔqcani**

łmaʔqcan – eat a little, fast; eat a snack.
łmaʔqcanm – S/he snacked. **čn łmaʔqcanm, kʷ łmaʔqcanm**
es łmaʔqcani – S/he is snacking. **čnes łmaʔqcani, kʷes łmaʔqcani**
qs łmaʔqcani – S/he is going to snack. **čiqs łmaʔqcani, kʷqs łmaʔqcani**

čačʔaqs – particular about food; picky.
es čačʔaqs – S/he is particular about food. **čnes čačʔaqs, kʷes čačʔaqs**

čmqnaqs – have a dislike for some food.
es čmqnaqs – S/he has a dislike for some food. **čnes čmqnaqs, kʷes čmqnaqs**

es čmqnaqs ci lipuwá – S/he has a dislike for peas.

t̓us – eat marrow. *See:* ***marrow.***

nt̓išp – eat something sweet. *See:* ***sweet.***

čluxʷm – eat supper/dinner. *See:* ***supper.***

kʷekʷstm – eat breakfast. *See:* ***breakfast.***

ntox̣ʷqinm – eat lunch. *See:* ***lunch.***

x̣ƛ̓ulexʷ – graze on the land. *See:* ***graze.***

x̣ƛ̓cin – graze/eat. *See:* ***graze.***

es t̓macni – (The cow) is eating. *See:* ***cow.***

mq̇enč, *mq̇e* – full from eating. *See:* ***full.***

> The **i** following uvular consonants (UC) and the glottal stop ʔ sound like English "*ey*" as in the words *they, hey, whey,* etc. Salish UC are: **q, q̇, qʷ, q̇ʷ, x̣, x̣ʷ**. For example, the suffix …**qin** – head/top, is often spelled using English *ey* as "q*ey*n". So **qi, q̇i, qʷi, q̇ʷi, x̣i, x̣ʷi,** may be spelled with English *ey* as **q***ey*, **q̇***ey*, **qʷ***ey*, **q̇ʷ***ey*, **x̣***ey*, **x̣ʷ***ey* in other texts.

echo

snṁl̓ṁalk̓ʷáqs, *snṁl̓ṁalk̓ʷá* – echoes.
es nṁl̓ṁalk̓ʷáqsi – It is echoing.

snṁalk̓ʷcán – echo; reflecting voice.
es nṁalk̓ʷáni – It is reflecting.

eclipse

k̓ʷłčlxʷspq̇niʔ – lunar eclipse.

eddie

niṅqʷʔetkʷ, *niṅqʷʔe* – eddie; whirlpool. *suffix:* ***…etkʷ, …tkʷ*** *– liquid*
es niṅqʷʔetkʷi – The water has an eddie.

nxʷlekʷ – whirlpool. *See:* ***whirlpool.***

Edward

itwál – Edward.

eel

kʷutuł – eel; Pacific lamprey; *Lampetra tridentata.*

egg

úʔuseʔ – egg; eggs.
łúʔuseʔ – small eggs.
es nt̓pus úʔuseʔ – boiled eggs.
snʔúʔuseʔtn – nest. *prefix:* ***sn…*** *– a place of; suffix:* ***…tin, …tn*** *– means of/device.*

uʔusʔém – It layed eggs.

> s.t. - something, the 3rd person
> (s.t.) - something implied
> s.o. - someone, the 3rd person
> *sl.* - singular form
> *pl.* - plural form
> *rt.* - root word
> *cmd.* - command
> *lit.* - literally
> *fig.* - figuratively
> *i.e.,* - for example
> *See:* - Redirection to a related word.

es uʔusʔéi – It is laying eggs.

čč̓miċeʔ – eggshell. *rt.: **č̓m** – extremity; suffix: **...iċéʔ** – covered in.*

n...ep – circumfix indicating eggs.
snkʷaliʔep – egg yolk. *rt.: **kʷaliʔ** – yellow.*
čmlk̓ʷcnep – eggshell. *rt.: **milk̓ʷ** – whole.*
nčulépm – climbed up to a nest. *rt.: **čiwlš** – climb. See: **climb**.*

nt̓kʷepm – crack an egg.
nt̓kʷepm – S/he cracked an egg. **čn nt̓kʷepm, kʷ nt̓kʷepm**
es nt̓kʷepi – S/he is cracking an egg. **čnes nt̓kʷepi, kʷes nt̓kʷepi**
qs nt̓kʷepi – S/he is going to crack an egg. **čiqs nt̓kʷepi, kʷqs nt̓kʷepi**

nt̓kʷepis – S/he cracked the egg. **nt̓kʷepn, kʷ nt̓kʷepntxʷ**
es nt̓kʷepms – S/he is cracking the egg. **ies nt̓kʷepm, as nt̓kʷepm**
qs nt̓kʷepms – S/he is going to crack the egg. **iqs nt̓kʷepm, aqs nt̓kʷepms**

es nt̓kʷt̓kʷepi – S/he is cracking eggs. **čnes nt̓kʷt̓kʷepi, kʷes nt̓kʷt̓kʷepi**
es nt̓kʷt̓kʷepms – S/he is cracking the eggs. **ies nt̓kʷt̓kʷepm, as nt̓kʷt̓kʷepm**

nt̓kʷepnt – Crack it. *cmd.*

nsq̓ew̓s – split in the middle; split in two. *See: **split**.*

nƛ̓éʔepm – search for eggs. *rt.: **ƛ̓eʔem** – search.*
nƛ̓éʔepm – S/he searched for eggs. **čn nƛ̓éʔepm, kʷ nƛ̓éʔepm**
es nƛ̓éʔepi – S/he is searching for eggs. **čnes nƛ̓éʔepi, kʷes nƛ̓éʔepi**
qs nƛ̓éʔepi – S/he is going to search for eggs. **čiqs nƛ̓éʔepi, kʷqs nƛ̓éʔepi**

swe łu qs nƛ̓éʔepi t úʔuseʔ – Who is going to search for eggs?

nċax̣pm – fry eggs. *rt.: **ċax̣** – fry.*
nċax̣pm – S/he fried eggs. **čn nċax̣pm, kʷ nċax̣pm**
es nċax̣pi – S/he is frying eggs. **čnes nċax̣pi, kʷes nċax̣pi**
qs nċax̣pi – S/he is going to fry eggs. **čiqs nċax̣pi, kʷqs nċax̣pi**

čiqs nċax̣pi t úʔuseʔ – I am going to fry eggs.

es nsinepi – S/he is counting eggs. *rt.: **syen** – count.*
nkʷep – one egg. **neslep –** two eggs. **čełlep –** three eggs. **nmsep –** four eggs. **nclčstep –** five eggs. **nt̓q̓nčstep –** six eggs. **nsp̓lčstep –** seven eggs. **nhenmep –** eight eggs. **nx̣ntep –** nine eggs. **nʔupnčstep –** ten eggs. **nxʷʔep –** many eggs.

nehk̓ʷep – sit on eggs; incubate eggs.
es nehk̓ʷepi – S/he/it is sitting on eggs.
qs nehk̓ʷepi – S/he is going to sit on eggs.

eight

héʔeṅm – eight. **heʔhéʔenm –** eights. *pl.*
heṅmwilš – become eight.
upn eł héʔeṅm – eighteen.
čhéʔeṅm – eight people.

heṅm... – prefix indicating eight combined with another affix forming a full word.
haṅmásq̓t – eight days. *suffix: **...asq̓t** – sky, day.*
heṅmełxʷ – eight houses. *suffix: **...ełxʷ, ...łxʷ** – house.*
nheṅmep – eight eggs. *circumfix: **n...ep** – egg.*
heṅméssṅ – eight rocks. *suffix: **...essṅ, ...ssṅ** – rock.*

heṅmł... – prefix indicating eight added to a whole word.
heṅmłʔupn – eighty; eight tens.
heṅmłšƛ̓ip – S/he lost eight times. **čn heṅmłšƛ̓ip, kʷ heṅmłšƛ̓ip**
haṅmsqáx̣eʔ, *clčsqá* – eight domestic animals or cars. *The ł is dropped when preceding an s.*
héṅmłʔopnčstqn – eight thousand.

> The **i** following uvular consonants (UC) and the glottal stop **ʔ** sound like English "*ey*" as in the words th*ey*, h*ey*, wh*ey*, etc. Salish UC are: **q**, **q̇**, **qʷ**, **q̇ʷ**, **x̣**, **x̣ʷ**. For example, the suffix ...**qin** – head/top, is often spelled using English *ey* as "q*ey*n". So **qi**, **q̇i**, **qʷi**, **q̇ʷi**, **x̣i**, **x̣ʷi**, may be spelled with English *ey* as **q***ey*, **q̇***ey*, **qʷ***ey*, **q̇ʷ***ey*, **x̣***ey*, **x̣ʷ***ey* in other texts.

eight hundred

héṅmłnk̓ʷoʔqín, *héṅmłnk̓ʷoʔqí* – eight hundred.

eighty

heṅmłʔupn, *heṅmłʔu* – eighty.

elbow

sčmusáx̣n – elbow. *rt.: čm – extremity.*
sčmumusax̣n – elbows.
sčmuʔusáx̣n – elbows.

malkʷax̣n – disjointed/dislocated elbow.
es malkʷax̣n – His/her elbow is disjointed/dislocated. **čnes malkʷax̣n, kʷes malkʷax̣n**

malkʷax̣is – S/he/it disjointed/dislocated s.o.'s elbow. **malkʷax̣n, malkʷax̣ntxʷ**
es malkʷax̣nms – S/he/it is disjointing/dislocating s.o.'s elbow. **ies malkʷax̣nm, as malkʷax̣nm**
qs malkʷax̣nms – S/he/it is going to disjoint/dislocate s.o.'s elbow. **iqs malkʷax̣nm, aqs malkʷax̣nm**

elder

ṗiṗx̣ʷót – old ones; elders.
łpṗx̣ʷot – small elder; lower level elder.
ṗx̣ʷṗx̣ʷot – parents; elders.

ṗx̣ʷtwil̓š – S/he became an elder. *suffix: ...wilš – developmental.*
es ṗx̣ʷtwil̓ši – S/he is becoming an elder. **čnes ṗx̣ʷtwil̓ši, kʷes ṗx̣ʷtwil̓ši**

es ṗx̣ʷtil̓ši – S/he is growing up. **čnes ṗx̣ʷtil̓ši, kʷes ṗx̣ʷtil̓ši** *suffix: ...ilš – autonomous.*
uł inʔililmixʷm łu inṗiṗx̣ʷot uł px̣páx̣t – My elders are my leaders; they are wise.

čewlš – get old. *suffix: ...ilš – autonomous.*
es čewlši – S/he is becoming old. **čnes čewlši, kʷes čewlši**

šiʔelsqelixʷ – first people; elders.
es šiʔelwilši – S/he is becoming an elder. **čnes šiʔelwilši, kʷes šiʔelwilši**

putʔem šiʔelsqelixʷ – Honor the first people/elders.

elderberry

ċkʷikʷ – blue elderberry; *Sambucus cerulea.*

electricity

suwečm – lightning; electricity.
suwečm x̣ʷl̓ anpaqmn – batteries for your flashlight.

elephant

nsṫsoʔ – elephant. *rt.: ṫsoʔ – sneeze.*

elf

sncṁasqélixʷ, *sncṁasqé* – little people. *(similar to elves, gnomes, or leprechauns)*

eliminate

k̓ʷłx̣ʷelm – eliminate something physical; ruin something. *rt.: x̣ʷel – abandon; prefix: k̓ʷł... – under.*
k̓ʷłx̣ʷelm – S/he/it eliminated (s.t.). **čn k̓ʷłx̣ʷelm, kʷ k̓ʷłx̣ʷelm**
es k̓ʷłx̣ʷeli – S/he/it is eliminating (s.t.). **čnes k̓ʷłx̣ʷeli, kʷes k̓ʷłx̣ʷeli**
qs k̓ʷłx̣ʷeli – S/he/it is going to be eliminating (s.t.). **čiqs k̓ʷłx̣ʷeli, kʷqs k̓ʷłx̣ʷeli**
k̓ʷłx̣ʷéʔelm – They eliminated (s.t.). **qeʔ k̓ʷłx̣ʷelm, p k̓ʷłx̣ʷelm**

> s.t. - something, the 3rd person
> (s.t.) - something implied
> s.o. - someone, the 3rd person
> *sl.* - singular form
> *pl.* - plural form
> *rt.* - root word
> *cmd.* - command
> *lit.* - literally
> *fig.* - figuratively
> *i.e.,* - for example
> *See:* - Redirection to a related word.

es k̓ʷɬx̣ʷéʔeli – They're eliminating (s.t.). **qeʔes k̓ʷɬx̣ʷeli, pes k̓ʷɬx̣ʷeli**
qs k̓ʷɬx̣ʷéʔeli – They're going to be eliminating (s.t.) **qeʔqs k̓ʷɬx̣ʷeli, pqs k̓ʷɬx̣ʷeli**

k̓ʷɬx̣ʷelis – S/he/it eliminated it. **k̓ʷɬx̣ʷeln, k̓ʷɬx̣ʷelntxʷ**
es k̓ʷɬx̣ʷelms – S/he/it is eliminating it. **ies k̓ʷɬx̣ʷelm, as k̓ʷɬx̣ʷelm**
qs k̓ʷɬx̣ʷelms – S/he/it is going to eliminate it. **iqs k̓ʷɬx̣ʷelm, aqs k̓ʷɬx̣ʷelm**
k̓ʷɬx̣ʷéʔelis – They eliminated it. **qeʔ k̓ʷɬx̣ʷelntm, k̓ʷɬx̣ʷelntp**
es k̓ʷɬx̣ʷéʔelms – They're eliminating it. **qeʔes k̓ʷɬx̣ʷelm, es k̓ʷɬx̣ʷelmp**
qs k̓ʷɬx̣ʷéʔelms – They're going to eliminate it. **qeʔqs k̓ʷɬx̣ʷelm, qs k̓ʷɬx̣ʷelmp**

es k̓ʷɬx̣ʷlx̣ʷeli – S/he is eliminating (things). **čnes x̣ʷlx̣ʷeli, kʷes k̓ʷɬx̣ʷlx̣ʷeli**
es k̓ʷɬx̣ʷlx̣ʷelms – S/he is eliminating things. **ies k̓ʷɬx̣ʷlx̣ʷelm, as k̓ʷɬx̣ʷlx̣ʷelm**

k̓ʷɬx̣ʷell – S/he got eliminated.
k̓ʷɬx̣ʷelntm – S/he was eliminated.

k̓ʷɬx̣ʷlnuis – S/he finally eliminated it. **k̓ʷɬx̣ʷlnun, k̓ʷɬx̣ʷlnuntxʷ**

sxʷk̓ʷɬx̣ʷelm – one tasked to eliminate. *prefix:* ***sxʷ...** – one tasked to do.*
k̓ʷɬx̣ʷlemn – one inclined to eliminate. **k̓ʷɬx̣ʷlx̣ʷlemn** *pl. suffix:* ***...emn** – one inclined to do.*
sck̓ʷɬx̣ʷel – something that's been eliminated. *prefix:* ***sc...** – s.t. that's been done/made/prepared.*
snx̣ʷelmn – place you eliminate things.

k̓ʷɬx̣ʷeliš – Eliminate (it). *cmd.*
k̓ʷɬx̣ʷelskʷ – Eliminate it. *cmd.*
k̓ʷɬx̣ʷelskʷi – All of you eliminate it. *cmd.*
k̓ʷɬx̣ʷelnt – Eliminate it. *cmd.*
k̓ʷɬx̣ʷelnti – All of you eliminate it. *cmd.*

es k̓ʷɬx̣ʷlmnwexʷi – They're eliminating each other. **qeʔes k̓ʷɬx̣ʷlmnwexʷi, pes k̓ʷɬx̣ʷlmnwexʷi**
k̓ʷɬx̣ʷllwisis – S/he keeps eliminating s.t. **k̓ʷɬx̣ʷllwisn, k̓ʷɬx̣ʷllwisntxʷ**
es nk̓ʷɬx̣ʷlmelsi – S/he is wanting to eliminate (s.t.). **čnes nk̓ʷɬx̣ʷlmelsi, kʷes nk̓ʷɬx̣ʷmelsi**

k̓ʷɬʔep̓ – eliminate; wipe away something. *rt.:* ***ep̓** – wipe; prefix:* ***k̓ʷɬ...** – under.*
k̓ʷɬʔép̓m – S/he/it eliminated (s.t.). **čn k̓ʷɬʔép̓m, kʷ k̓ʷɬʔép̓m**
es k̓ʷɬʔép̓i – S/he/it is eliminating (s.t.). **čnes k̓ʷɬʔép̓i, kʷes k̓ʷɬʔép̓i**
qs k̓ʷɬʔép̓i – S/he/it is going to eliminate (s.t.). **čiqs k̓ʷɬʔép̓i, kʷqs k̓ʷɬʔép̓i**
k̓ʷɬéʔep̓m – They eliminated (s.t.). **qeʔ k̓ʷɬʔép̓m, p k̓ʷɬʔép̓m**
es k̓ʷɬéʔep̓i – They are eliminating (s.t.). **qeʔes k̓ʷɬʔép̓i, pes k̓ʷɬʔép̓i**
qs k̓ʷɬéʔep̓i – They are going to eliminate (s.t.). **qeʔqs k̓ʷɬʔép̓i, pqs k̓ʷɬʔép̓i**

k̓ʷɬép̓is – S/he/it eliminated it. **k̓ʷɬʔép̓n, k̓ʷɬʔép̓ntxʷ**
es k̓ʷɬʔép̓ms – S/he/it is eliminating it. **ies k̓ʷɬʔép̓m, as k̓ʷɬʔép̓m**
qs k̓ʷɬʔép̓ms – S/he/it is going to eliminate it. **iqs k̓ʷɬʔép̓m, aqs k̓ʷɬʔép̓m**
k̓ʷɬʔéʔep̓is – They eliminated it. **qeʔ k̓ʷɬʔép̓ntm, k̓ʷɬʔép̓ntp**
es k̓ʷɬʔéʔep̓ms – They are eliminating it. **qeʔes k̓ʷɬʔép̓m, es k̓ʷɬʔép̓mp**
qs k̓ʷɬʔéʔep̓ms – They are going to eliminate it. **qeʔqs k̓ʷɬʔép̓m, qs k̓ʷɬʔép̓mp**

k̓ʷɬʔép̓iš – Eliminate (s.t.). *cmd.*
k̓ʷɬʔép̓wi – All of you eliminate (s.t.). *cmd.*
k̓ʷɬʔép̓nt – Eliminate it. *cmd.*
k̓ʷɬʔép̓nti – All of you eliminate it. *cmd.*

ṅem k̓ʷɬʔép̓m – S/he/it will eliminate. **ṅem čn k̓ʷɬʔép̓m, ṅem kʷ k̓ʷɬʔép̓m**
ṅem k̓ʷɬʔéʔep̓m – They will eliminate. **ṅem qeʔ k̓ʷɬʔép̓m, ṅem p k̓ʷɬʔép̓m**
ṅem qes k̓ʷɬʔép̓m – S/he/it will be eliminating it. **ṅem iqes k̓ʷɬʔép̓m, ṅem aqes k̓ʷɬʔép̓m**

ṅem qes k̓ʷɫʔéʔep̓m – They will be eliminating it. **ṅem qeʔqes k̓ʷɫʔép̓m, ṅem qes k̓ʷɫʔép̓mp**

ta kʷ qes k̓ʷɫʔép̓m – Do not eliminate (s.t.). *cmd.* **k̓ʷɫʔép̓nt inxʷlxʷi** – Eliminate my debt. *cmd.*

nɫptmist – eliminate something from one's mind; forget on purpose. *rt.: **nɫeptm** – forget; suffix: **...ist** – action for/of the self.*

nɫptmist – S/he eliminated. **čn nɫptmist, kʷ nɫptmist**
es nɫptmisti – S/he is eliminating. **čnes nɫptmisti, kʷes nɫptmisti**
qs nɫptmisti – S/he is going to eliminate. **čiqs nɫptmisti, kʷqs nɫptmisti**
nɫptmíʔist – They eliminated. **qeʔ nɫptmist, p nɫptmist**
es nɫptmíʔisti – They are eliminating. **qeʔes nɫptmisti, pes nɫptmisti**
qs nɫptmíʔisti – They are going to eliminate. **qeʔqs nɫptmisti, pqs nɫptmisti**

The **i** following uvular consonants (UC) and the glottal stop **ʔ** sound like English "*ey*" as in the words *they, hey, whey,* etc. Salish UC are: **q, q̓, qʷ, q̓ʷ, x̣, x̣ʷ**. For example, the suffix **...qin** – head/top, is often spelled using English *ey* as "q*ey*n". So **qi, q̓i, qʷi, q̓ʷi, x̣i, x̣ʷi**, may be spelled with English *ey* as **q***ey*, **q̓***ey*, **qʷ***ey*, **q̓ʷ***ey*, **x̣***ey*, **x̣ʷ***ey* in other texts.

nɫptmistmis – S/he eliminated s.t. **nɫptmistmn, nɫptmistmntxʷ**
es nɫptmistms – S/he is eliminating s.t. **ies nɫptmistm, as nɫptmistm**
qs nɫptmistms – S/he is going to eliminate s.t. **iqs nɫptmistm, aqs nɫptmistm**
nɫptmíʔistmis – They eliminated s.t. **qeʔ nɫptmistmntm, nɫptmistmntp**
es nɫptmíʔistms – They are eliminating s.t. **qeʔes nɫptmistm, es nɫptmistmp**
qs nɫptmíʔistms – They are going to eliminate s.t. **qeʔqs nɫptmistm, qs nɫptmistmp**

nɫptmistmntm – S/he/it was eliminated from s.o.'s mind. **qʷo nɫptmistmntm, kʷ nɫptmistmntm**

nɫptmistš – Erase your mind. *cmd.*
nɫptmistmnt – Eliminate it from your mind. *cmd.*

Elizabeth

elisepé – Elizabeth.
nisepé – Elizabeth.

elk

snéčɫc̓eʔ, *sné* – cow elk; *Cervus canadensis.* **snčnéčɫc̓eʔ** *pl.*
tšec̓ – bull elk; *Cervus canadensis.* **tščšec̓** *pl.*
št̓št̓u – yearling elk; *Cervus canadensis.*
ɫčeʔ – young elk; *Cervus canadensis.*
q̓y̓itš – calf elk; *Cervus canadensis.*

šc̓elxʷ – bull elk hide.
snčɫc̓elxʷ – cow elk hide.

tl̓ čeṅ u es cxʷuyi ye uɫ snéčɫc̓eʔ – Where have all these cow elk come from? **ɫu tšec̓ es čx̣ʷq̓ʷx̣ʷaq̓ʷms ɫu qx̣mis u es npuxʷi** – The bull elk is grinding his antlers and bugling.

snčɫc̓aʔsqá – horse. *rt.: **snéčɫc̓eʔ** – cow elk; suffix: **...sqáx̣eʔ** – domesticated. See: **horse**.*

snq̓axʷmi – elk teeth.

sax̣mqn – rub one's antlers on something such as a tree. *See: **rub**.*

čx̣ʷq̓ʷx̣ʷaq̓ʷm – grind/file on the side of something. *See: **grind**.*

s.t. - something, the 3rd person
(s.t.) - something implied
s.o. - someone, the 3rd person
sl. - singular form
pl. - plural form
rt. - root word
cmd. - command
lit. - literally
fig. - figuratively
i.e., - for example
See: - Redirection to a related word.

Elmer

amlo – Elmer.

Elmo

sqʷʔeʔ – Elmo, Flathead Nation. *lit. inlet in the lake.*

elope

xʷt̓pncut – elope; run away. *rt.: **xʷt̓ip** – run away; suffix: **...cut** – action to the self.*
xʷt̓pncut – S/he eloped. **čn xʷt̓pncut, kʷ xʷt̓pncut**
es xʷt̓pncuti – S/he is eloping. **čnes xʷt̓pncuti, kʷes xʷt̓pncuti**
qs xʷt̓pncuti – S/he is going to elope. **čiqs xʷt̓pncuti, kʷqs xʷt̓pncuti**

emaciated

čt̓ás – thin; skinny; lean; emaciated; hard on the surface. *rt.: **t̓as** – hard.*

i čt̓ás – S/he/it is thin. **i čn čt̓ás, i kʷ čt̓ás**

embarrassed

čc̓eʔšepleʔ – embarrassed. *rt.: c̓ʔeš – ashamed; suffix: ...épleʔ – permanence.*

čc̓eʔšépleʔis – S/he was embarrassed by s.t./s.o. **čc̓eʔšéplen, čc̓eʔšéplentxʷ**
es **čc̓eʔšéplʔems** – S/he is embarrassed by s.t./s.o. **ies čc̓eʔšéplʔem, as čc̓eʔšéplʔem**
qs **čc̓eʔšéplʔems** – S/he is going to be embarrased by s.t./s.o. **iqs čc̓eʔšéplʔem, aqs čc̓eʔšéplʔem**
čc̓eʔšéʔepleʔis – They were embarrassed by s.t./s.o. **qeʔ čc̓eʔšéplentm, čc̓eʔšéplentp**
es **čc̓eʔšéʔeplʔems** – They are embarrassed by s.t./s.o. **qeʔes čc̓eʔšéʔeplʔem, es čc̓eʔšéʔeplʔemp**
qs **čc̓eʔšéʔeplʔems** – They are going to be embarrassed by s.t./s.o. **qeʔqs čc̓eʔšéplem, qs čc̓eʔšéplemp**

čc̓eʔšéplemn – one inclined to get embarrassed. *suffix: ...emn – one inclined to do.*
scčc̓eʔšépleʔist – something that was embarrassing. *prefix: sc... – s.t. that's been done/made/prepared.*

c̓ʔeš – ashamed. *See: ashamed.*

empty

nmiš – There's nothing inside; it is empy.

nsʔóp – empty something; to drink up; to make dry.
nsʔopnuis – S/he emptied s.t. **nsʔopnun, nsʔopnuntxʷ**
es **nsʔopnunms** – S/he is emptying s.t. **ies nsʔopnunm, as nsʔopnunm**
qs **nsʔopnunms** – S/he is going to empty s.t. **iqs nsʔopnunm, aqs nsʔopnunm**

nsosopnúʔuis – They emptied s.t. **qeʔ nsosopnuntm, nsosopnuntp**
es **nsosopnúʔunms** – They are emptying s.t. **qeʔes nsosopnunm, es nsosopnunmp**
qs **nsosopnúʔunms** – They are going to empty s.t. **qeʔqs nsosopnunm, qs nsosopnunmp**

nsopnuntm – It got drank up.

nsopnunt – Empty it. *cmd.*

čmi nsʔóp – It just got dry. **nsopnuntm u nx̣mip** – It got drank up and dried up. **qʷo nsopnułts innt̓išk̓ʷ** – S/he drank all my pop. **tas nsopnuntxʷ** – You did not drink it all up.

nsoʔpetkʷ, *nsoʔpe* – empty the water/liquid. *prefix: n... – inside; suffix: ...etkʷ – liquid.*
nsoʔpetkʷ – S/he emptied (s.t.). **čn nsoʔpetkʷ, kʷ nsoʔpetkʷ**
es **nsoʔpetkʷi** – S/he is emptying (s.t.). **čnes nsoʔpetkʷi, kʷes nsoʔpetkʷi**
qs **nsoʔpetkʷi** – S/he is going to empty (s.t.). **čiqs nsoʔpetkʷi, kʷqs nsoʔpetkʷi**

end

npƛ̓mus – come to the end of a time period, an action, or a place; reach the full extent. *rt.: pƛ̓im – release from.*
npƛ̓mus – S/he/it got to the end. **čn npƛ̓mus, kʷ npƛ̓mus**
es **npƛ̓musi** – S/he/it is getting to the end. **čnes npƛ̓musi, kʷes npƛ̓musi**
qs **npƛ̓musi** – S/he/it is going to get to the end. **čiqs npƛ̓musi, kʷqs npƛ̓musi**

npƛ̓musis – S/he/it got to the end of s.t. **npƛ̓musn, npƛ̓musntxʷ**
es **npƛ̓musms** – S/he/it is getting to the end of s.t. **ies npƛ̓musm, as npƛ̓musm**
qs **npƛ̓musms** – S/he/it is going to get to the end of s.t. **iqs npƛ̓musm, aqs npƛ̓musm**

npƛ̓musts sƛ̓ax̣t – speed limit. **stem̓ łu es q̓ey̓i npƛ̓mus x̣ʷl̓ łu qł čtemtis sqʔem** – What is the expiration date for using the milk? **šey̓ u npƛ̓mus** – That's the end. **es npƛ̓musi łu isk̓ʷul̓** – My job is coming to an end.

nčcnus – arrive at the start of a time period, the beginning of an action, or the edge of a place. *See: arrive.*

łe – end; arrive at the end.
łeʔpus – S/he went to the end. **čn łeʔpus, kʷ łeʔpus**

nłaqnetkʷ – arrive at the top of a dead end canyon going down stream. *See: **canyon**.*

nłapaqs, nçapa – arrive at the end; an expression indicating to go to the extreme. *See: **really**.*
nłapaqs – S/he arrived at the end. **čn nłapaqs, kʷ nłapaqs**
nłapaqsis – S/he arrived at the end of s.t. **nłapaqsn, nłapaqsntxʷ**
es nłapaqms – S/he is arriving at the end of s.t. **ies nłapaqm, as nłapaqm**
qs nłapaqms – S/he is going to arrive at the end of s.t. **iqs nłapaqm, aqs nłapaqm**

łʔesmek̓ʷt – get to an impassable place in the snow.
łʔetkʷ – get to an impassable place in the water.

uẏéčst, *uẏé* – finish working; done working; come to an end. *See: **finish**.*

hoy – quit; stop; finish; okay; that's it; cease. *See: **quit**.*
šehoy – The end, that's all.

qʷoṁmałq, *qʷoṁma* – get close to doing/finishing something; getting near to some point; close to the end of a journey; winning. *See: **close**.*

The **i** following uvular consonants (UC) and the glottal stop **ʔ** sound like English "*ey*" as in the words th*ey*, h*ey*, wh*ey*, etc. Salish UC are: **q, q̇, qʷ, q̇ʷ, x̣, x̣ʷ**. For example, the suffix …**qin** – head/top, is often spelled using English *ey* as "q*ey*n". So **qi, q̇i, qʷi, q̇ʷi, x̣i, x̣ʷi**, may be spelled with English *ey* as **q***ey*, **q̇***ey*, **qʷ***ey*, **q̇ʷ***ey*, **x̣***ey*, **x̣ʷ***ey* in other texts.

enemy

šméṅ – enemy.

čšmšmṅeẇs – double up on an someone; double team someone.
čšmšmṅeʔeẇsm – They doubled up. **qeʔ čšmšmṅeẇsm, p čšmšmṅeẇsm**
es čšmšmṅeʔeẇsi – They are doubling up. **qeʔes čšmšmṅeẇsi, pes čšmšmṅeẇsi**
qs čšmšmṅeʔeẇsi – They are going to double up. **qeʔqs čšmšmṅeẇsi, pqs čšmšmṅeẇsi**

čšmšmṅeʔeẇsis – They doubled up on s.o. **qeʔ čšmšmṅeẇsntm, čšmšmṅeẇsntp**
es čšmšmṅeʔeẇsms – They are doubling up on s.o. **qeʔes čšmšmṅeẇsm, es čšmšmṅeẇsmp**
qs čšmšmṅeʔeẇsms – They are going to double up on s.o. **qeʔqs čšmšmṅeẇsm, qs čšmšmṅeẇsmp**

ewtus – oppose; work against. *See: **oppose**.*

energy

nq̇ʷiłq̇ʷłtn – something that makes one capable; energy. *See: **capable**.*
i q̇ʷił – S/he/it is full of energy. **i čn q̇ʷił, i kʷ q̇ʷił**

xʷaw – have lots of energy.
i xʷaw – S/he/it has lots of energy. **i čn xʷaw, i kʷ xʷaw**

enfold

ččnpiċeʔ – enfold something; put something in a file. *suffix: **…iċéʔ** – covered in.*
ččnpiċʔeis – S/he enfolded s.t. **ččnpiċʔen, ččnpiċʔentxʷ**
es ččnpiċʔems – S/he is enfolding s.t. **ies ččnpiċʔem, as ččnpiċʔem**
qs ččnpiċʔems – S/he is going to enfold s.t. **iqs ččnpiċʔem, aqs ččnpiċʔem**

es ččnpiċeʔ – It is enfolded.

ččnpiċʔent – Enfold it; file it. *cmd.*

ččnṗiċeʔ – hardcover book; book. *suffix: **…iċéʔ** – covered in.*

čṗlk̓ʷiċéʔ – wrap; enfold; roll up. *See: **wrap**.*

Engelmann spruce

ṫsṫsélp, *ṫsṫsé* – spruce; *Picea engelmannii.*

English

snuyapcn – English. *rt.: **suyápi** – white person; circumfix: **n…cin, cn** – action of the mouth.*

s.t. - something, the 3rd person
(s.t.) - something implied
s.o. - someone, the 3rd person
sl. - singular form
pl. - plural form
rt. - root word
cmd. - command
lit. - literally
fig. - figuratively
i.e., - for example
See: - Redirection to a related word.

nuyapcnm – speak English. *suffix: **…cin, …cn** – action of the mouth.*
nuyapcnm – S/he spoke English. **čn nuyapcnm, kʷ nuyapcnm**

es nuyapcni – S/he is speaking English. **čnes nuyapcni, kʷes nuyapcni**
qs nuyapcni – S/he is going to speak English. **čiqs nuyapcni, kʷqs nuyapcni**

es nuyapcan – S/he talks English. **čnes nuyapcan, kʷes nuyapcan**
es nuyáˀapcan – They talk English. **qeˀes nuyapcan, pes nuyapcan**

sxʷnuyapcnm – one tasked to speak English. *prefix:* ***sxʷ...** – one tasked to do.*
nuyapcemn – one inclined to speak English. *suffix:* ***...emn** – one inclined to do.*

nuyapcniš – Speak English. *cmd.*
nuyapcnmnwexʷ – speak English to each other.

ta kʷ qes nuyapcnm – Do not talk English. **ta p qes nuyuyapcnm –** All of you, do not talk English. **ƛ̓e es misten snuyapcn –** I already know English. **yoˀnun čiqs nsuyapcni –** I learned English.

enjoy

x̣stmels, *x̣stme* **–** have fun; have good feelings; enjoy something; entertained. *rt.:* ***x̣es** – good; suffix:* ***...els, ...ls** – want, feel.*
es x̣smelsi – S/he is having fun. **čnes x̣smelsi, kʷes x̣smelsi**
es x̣stméˀelsi – They are having fun. **qeˀes x̣smelsi, pes x̣smelsi**

x̣stmelsm – S/he/it had fun. **čn x̣stmelsm, kʷ x̣stmelsm**
es x̣stmelsi – S/he/it is having fun. **čnes x̣stmelsi, kʷes x̣stmelsi**
qs x̣stmelsi – S/he/it is going to have fun. **čiqs x̣stmelsi, kʷqs x̣stmelsi**
x̣stméˀelsm – They had fun. **qeˀ x̣stmelsm, p x̣stmelsm**
es x̣stméˀelsi – They are having fun. **qeˀes x̣stmelsi, pes x̣stmelsi**

nx̣stmis – S/he/it enjoyed it. **nx̣stmin, nx̣stmintxʷ**
es nx̣stminms – S/he/it is enjoying it. **ies nx̣stminm, as nx̣stminm**
qs x̣stminms – S/he/it is going to enjoy it. **iqs** nx̣stminm, **aqs nx̣stminm**
nx̣stmíˀis – They enjoyed it. **qeˀ nx̣stmintm, nx̣stmintp**
es nx̣stmíˀinms – They are enjoying it. **qeˀes nx̣stminm, es nx̣stminmp**
qs nx̣stmíˀinms – They are going to enjoy it. **qeˀqs nx̣stminm, qs nx̣stminmp**

x̣sx̣stméˀe – Each one of them enjoyed (s.t.).

es nx̣smelstni – S/he is anticipating having good feelings.
ies nx̣smelsnm – S/he is enjoying s.t.

x̣x̣stmé – It is fun.

ṅem nx̣stminm – S/he/it will have fun. **ṅem čn nx̣stminm, ṅem kʷ nx̣stminm**
ṅem nx̣stmíˀinm – They will have fun. **ṅem qeˀ nx̣stminm, ṅem p nx̣stminm**

čx̣saqs, *čx̣sa* **–** enjoy food or drinks.
čx̣saqsm – S/he/it enjoyed food. **čn čx̣saqsm, kʷ čx̣saqsm**
es čx̣saqsi – S/he/it is enjoying food. **čnes čx̣saqsi, kʷes čx̣saqsi**
qs čx̣saqsi – S/he/it is going to enjoy food. **čiqs čx̣saqsi, kʷqs čx̣saqsi**
čx̣sáˀaqsm – They enjoyed food. **qeˀ čx̣saqsm, p čx̣saqsm**
es čx̣sáˀaqsi – They are enjoying food. **qeˀes čx̣saqsi, pes čx̣saqsi**

ṅem čx̣saqsm – S/he/it will enjoy food. **ṅem čn čx̣saqsm, ṅem kʷ čx̣saqsm**
ṅem čx̣sáˀaqsm – They will enjoy food. **ṅem qeˀ čx̣saqsm, ṅem p čx̣saqsm**

čn čx̣saqsm t kapi ye t skʷekʷst – I am enjoying my coffee this morning.

enough

put – just, exactly, even, enough; right then. *See:* ***just.***

enraged **čxʷttels,** *čxʷtte* – enraged; angry; mad; vicious; the extreme of anger.

čxʷttels – S/he/it got enraged. **čn čxʷttels, kʷ čxʷttels**
es čxʷttelsi – S/he/it is enraged. **čnes čxʷttelsi, kʷes čxʷttelsi**
qs čxʷttelsi – S/he/it is going to be enraged. **čiqs čxʷttelsi, kʷqs čxʷttelsi**
čxʷttéˀels – They got enraged. **qeˀ čxʷttels, p čxʷttels**
es čxʷttéˀelsi – They are enraged. **qeˀes čxʷttelsi, pes čxʷttelsi**

čxʷttelsmis – S/he/it got enraged at s.o. **čxʷttelsmn, čxʷttelsmntxʷ**
es čxʷttelsmms – S/he/it is enraged at s.o. **ies čxʷttelsmm, as čxʷttelsmm**
qs čxʷttelsmms – S/he/it is going to be enraged at s.o. **iqs čxʷttelsmm, aqs čxʷttelsmm**
čxʷttéˀelsmis – They got enraged at s.o. **qeˀ čxʷttelsmntm, čxʷttelsmntp**
es čxʷttéˀelsmms – They are enraged at s.o. **qeˀes čxʷttelsmm, es čxʷttelsmmp**

es čłxʷttelsi – S/he/it is slightly enraged. **čnes čłxʷttelsi, kʷes čłxʷttelsi**
es čłxʷttelsmms – S/he/it is slightly enraged at s.o. **ies čłxʷttelsmm, as čłxʷttelsmm**

čxʷttlsemn – one inclined to get enraged. *suffix:* ***...emn*** *– one inclined to do.*
nxʷtxʷttsnuxʷ – S/he/it is deserving of anger.

nxʷtxʷtcin – arrogant talk; talk provoking anger.

The **i** following uvular consonants (UC) and the glottal stop ˀ sound like English "*ey*" as in the words *they, hey, whey,* etc. Salish UC are: **q, q̇, qʷ, q̇ʷ, x̣, x̣ʷ**. For example, the suffix ...**qin** – head/top, is often spelled using English *ey* as "qeyn". So **qi, q̇i, qʷi, q̇ʷi, x̣i, x̣ʷi,** may be spelled with English *ey* as **q***ey*, **q̇***ey*, **qʷ***ey*, **q̇ʷ***ey*, **x̣***ey*, **x̣ʷ***ey* in other texts.

enter **nˀułxʷ** – go inside; enter. *sl.*

nˀułxʷ – S/he/it went inside. **čn nˀułxʷ, kʷ nˀułxʷ**
es nˀułxʷi – S/he/it is going inside. **čnes nˀułxʷi, kʷes nˀułxʷi**
qs nˀułxʷi – S/he/it is going to go inside. **čiqs nˀułxʷi, kʷqs nˀułxʷi**

cnˀułxʷ – S/he/it came inside. **čn cnˀułxʷ, kʷ cnˀułxʷ**
es cnˀułxʷi – S/he/it is coming inside. **čnes cnˀułxʷi, kʷes cnˀułxʷi**
qs cnˀułxʷi – S/he/it is going to come inside. **čiqs cnˀułxʷi, kʷqs cnˀułxʷi**

čnˀułxʷmis – S/he/it went in to see s.o. **čnˀułxʷmn, čnˀułxʷmntxʷ**
es čnˀułxʷms – S/he/it is going in to see s.o. **ies čnˀułxʷm, as čnˀułxʷm**
qs čnˀułxʷms – S/he/it is going to go in to see s.o. **iqs čnˀułxʷm, aqs čnˀułxʷm**

nˀułxʷeẇs – S/he/it entered between. **čn nˀułxʷeẇs, kʷ nˀułxʷeẇs**
es nˀułxʷeẇsi – S/he/it is entering between. **čnes nˀułxʷeẇsi, kʷes nˀułxʷeẇsi**
qs nˀułxʷeẇsi – S/he/it is going to enter between. **čiqs nˀułxʷeẇsi, kʷqs nˀułxʷeẇsi**

nˀułxʷeẇsis – S/he/it entered between s.t. **čn nˀułxʷeẇsn, kʷ nˀułxʷeẇsntxʷ**
es nˀułxʷeẇsms – S/he/it is entering between s.t. **čnes nˀułxʷeẇsm, kʷes nˀułxʷeẇsm**
qs nˀułxʷeẇsms – S/he/it is going to enter between s.t. **čiqs nˀułxʷeẇsm, kʷqs nˀułxʷeẇsm**

nˀułxʷš – Go inside. *cmd.*
cnˀułxʷš – Come inside. *cmd.*

nˀułxʷm – bring an individual person or thing inside. *See:* ***bring.***
nˀułxʷmsqáx̣eˀ, *nˀułxʷmsqá* – bring one domestic animal, horse inside. *See:* ***bring.***
nłxʷpmeẇs – S/he/it happened to enter between. **čn nłxʷpmeẇs, kʷ nłxʷpmeẇs**

čn nˀułxʷ l sntumístn – I went into the store. **kʷłˀułxʷ kʷtisi l p̓ip̓uyšn** – Big Blanket went into the car. **eł cnˀulxʷ łu mali** – Mary came back in. **nˀułxʷ č nk̓ʷełxʷ** – S/he went

s.t. - something, the 3rd person
(s.t.) - something implied
s.o. - someone, the 3rd person
sl. - singular form
pl. - plural form
rt. - root word
cmd. - command
lit. - literally
fig. - figuratively
i.e., - for example
See: - Redirection to a related word.

into another house. **nʔułxʷ ci i nk̓ʷełce̓ʔ –** S/he went into another room. **qeʔ nʔułxʷ l sntumístn –** I went into the store.

npilš – go inside, enter. *pl. suffix:* ***...ilš –*** *autonomous.*
npíʔilš – They went inside. **qeʔ npilš, p npilš**
es npíʔilši – They are going inside. **qeʔes npilši, pes npilši**
qs npíʔilši – They are going to go inside. **qeʔqs npilši, pqs npilši**

npilšwi – All of you go inside. *cmd.*
npilskʷ – Bring things in. *cmd.*
nʔpíʔilšis – They brought s.t. in. **qeʔ nʔpilšntm, nʔpilšntp**

npilšm – bring things inside there. *See:* ***bring.***
nplšsqáx̣eʔ, *nplšsqá –* bring domestic animals, horses inside. *See:* ***bring.***

qeʔ npilš l sntumístn – We went into the store. **nplpíʔilš l sntumístn łu snč̓lé –** The coyotes went into the store one by one. **ƛ̓e ep sqélixʷ u cnpilš łu uł selíš –** There was already people here when the Salish came in. **qeʔ npilš l qecitxʷ –** We went into our house.

nłxʷpmew̓s – slip between something that is tight fitting; go between and through a tight/constricted opening. *rt.:* ***łixʷp –*** *slip/pull over; suffix:* ***...éw̓s –*** *in between, middle.*
nłxʷpmew̓s – S/he/it happened to enter between. **čn nłxʷpmew̓s, kʷ nłxʷpmew̓s**

entire

esyáʔ – everything; everyone; all. *See:* ***all.***

milk̓ʷ – complete; whole; all over; all around. *See:* ***complete.***

envy

čłyuxʷt, *čłyu –* envious; want to be like; wish for something; feel bad over.
čłyuxʷt – S/he/it was envious. **čn čłyuxʷt, kʷ čłyuxʷt**
es čłyuxʷti – S/he/it is being envious. **čnes čłyuxʷti, kʷes čłyuxʷti**

čłyuxʷmis – S/he/it was envious of s.o. **čłyuxʷmin, čłyuxʷmintxʷ**
es čłyuxʷmims – S/he/it is being envious of s.o. **ies čłyuxʷmis, as čłyuxʷmis**

epilepsy

qcqcim – seizures; epilepsy.
qcqcntem – S/he/it had a seizure.

equal

šimew̓s – equal; have the same value with the other. *rt.:* ***šey̓ –*** *there; suffix:* ***...éw̓s –*** *in between, middle.*

i šey̓ – that very one; the same one. *See:* ***that.***

ec̓x̣íl, *ec̓x̣í –* like; same. *See:* ***like.***
ic̓x̣ax̣i – exactly the same.

eraser

xʷk̓ʷmintn – eraser.

ermine

łpápqłce̓ʔ, *łpá –* winter weasel; ermine; *Mustela frenata. rt.:* ***piq –*** *white.*

łčim̓ – summer weasel; ermine; *Mustela frenata.*

escape

k̓ʷłnq̓ʷmist, *k̓ʷłnq̓ʷmi –* run away stealthily; sneak away; leave; escape. *rt.:* ***naq̓ʷ –*** *steal.; prefix:* ***k̓ʷł... –*** *under; suffix:* ***...ist –*** *action to the self.*
k̓ʷłnq̓ʷmist – S/he/it escaped. **čn k̓ʷłnq̓ʷmist, kʷ k̓ʷłnq̓ʷmist**
es k̓ʷłnq̓ʷmisti – S/he/it is escaping. **čnes k̓ʷłnq̓ʷmisti, kʷes k̓ʷłnq̓ʷmisti**
qs k̓ʷłnq̓ʷmisti – S/he/it is going to escape. **čiqs k̓ʷłnq̓ʷmisti, kʷqs k̓ʷłnq̓ʷmisti**
k̓ʷłnq̓ʷmíʔist – They escaped. **qeʔ k̓ʷłnq̓ʷmist, p k̓ʷłnq̓ʷmist**

k̓ʷłn̓q̓ʷmistmis – S/he/it escaped from s.o. **k̓ʷłn̓q̓ʷmistmn, k̓ʷłn̓q̓ʷmistmntxʷ**
es k̓ʷłn̓q̓ʷmistmms – S/he/it is escaping from s.o. **ies k̓ʷłn̓q̓ʷmistmm, as k̓ʷłn̓q̓ʷmistmm**
qs k̓ʷłn̓q̓ʷmistmms – S/he/it is going to escape from s.o. **iqs k̓ʷłn̓q̓ʷmistmm, aqs k̓ʷłn̓q̓ʷmistmm**

k̓ʷłn̓q̓ʷmstmnwexʷ – escaped from each other.

ṅem k̓ʷłn̓q̓ʷmist – S/he/it will escape. **ṅem čn k̓ʷłn̓q̓ʷmist, ṅem kʷ k̓ʷłn̓q̓ʷmist**
ṅem k̓ʷłn̓q̓ʷmíʔist – They will escape. **ṅem qeʔ k̓ʷłn̓q̓ʷmist, ṅem p k̓ʷłn̓q̓ʷmist**

The **i** following uvular consonants (UC) and the glottal stop **ʔ** sound like English "*ey*" as in the words th*ey*, h*ey*, wh*ey*, etc. Salish UC are: **q, q̇, qʷ, q̇ʷ, x̣, x̣ʷ**. For example, the suffix **...qin** – head/top, is often spelled using English *ey* as "q*ey*n". So **qi, q̇i, qʷi, q̇ʷi, x̣i, x̣ʷi**, may be spelled with English *ey* as **q***ey*, **q̇***ey*, **qʷ***ey*, **q̇ʷ***ey*, **x̣***ey*, **x̣ʷ***ey* in other texts.

łx̣ʷoṗ – run off to the outside of something; dash out; suddenly run out of an enclosure.
łx̣ʷṗim – S/he/it ran off to the outside. **čn łx̣ʷṗim, kʷ łx̣ʷṗim**
es łx̣ʷṗmi – S/he/it is running off to the outside. **čnes łx̣ʷṗmi, kʷes łx̣ʷṗmi**
qs łx̣ʷṗmi – S/he/it is going to run off to the outside. **čiqs łx̣ʷṗmi, kʷqs łx̣ʷṗmi**
łx̣ʷṗíʔim – They ran off to the outside. **qeʔ łx̣ʷṗim, p łx̣ʷṗim**

łx̣ʷṗnuis – S/he/it let it run off. **łx̣ʷṗnun, łx̣ʷṗnuntxʷ**
es łx̣ʷṗnunms – S/he/it is letting it run off. **ies łx̣ʷṗnunm, as łx̣ʷṗnunm**
qs łx̣ʷṗnunms – S/he/it is going to let it run off. **iqs łx̣ʷṗnunm, aqs łx̣ʷṗnunm**

łx̣ʷoṗš – Run out. *cmd.*
łx̣ʷoṗwi – All of you run out. *cmd.*
łx̣ʷṗnunt – Let it run off. *cmd.*
nłx̣ʷṗim – run into the inside of something; dash in.

ṅem łx̣ʷṗim – S/he/it will run outside. **ṅem čn łx̣ʷṗim, ṅem kʷ łx̣ʷṗim**
ṅem łx̣ʷṗíʔim – They will run outside. **ṅem qeʔ łx̣ʷṗim, ṅem p łx̣ʷṗim**

łx̣ʷṗim kʷtisi l citxʷ – Big Blanket ran out of the house. **čn łx̣ʷṗim tl̓ incitxʷ** – I ran out of my house. **es łx̣ʷṗmi kʷtisi l citxʷ** – Big Blanket running out of the house. **es nłx̣ʷṗmi kʷtisi l citxʷ** – Big Blanket is running into the house.

t̓loq̓ʷ – run away; flee from danger; flee out of fear. *See: **run away**.*

xʷt̓ip – an individual ran from the spot occupied to somewhere; escape from routine. *See: **run away**.*

Eskimo

ċaltulexʷ sqelixʷ – Eskimo; cold land people.

ethnonyms

sqélixʷ – human; person; Indian. *See: **Indian**.*
sqlqelixʷ – people, Indians.
sqlixʷulexʷ – Indian land.

ƛ̓e ep sqélixʷ u cnpilš łu uł selíš – There were already people here when the Salish came in.

s.t. - something, the 3rd person
(s.t.) - something implied
s.o. - someone, the 3rd person
sl. - singular form
pl. - plural form
rt. - root word
cmd. - command
lit. - literally
fig. - figuratively
i.e., - for example
See: - Redirection to a related word.

selíš – Salish; Bitterroot Salish. *(self identification term)*
t̓at̓ʔayaqn – Bitterroot Salish *(Pend d'Oreille term)*
łq̓ełmlš – Bitterroot Salish *(Pend d'Oreille name for Salish). lit. wide cottonwood.*
łqayaqn, *łqa* – Bitterroot Salish. *lit. wide head; Pend d'Oreille term.*

sčłq̓etkʷmcin – Upper Pend d'Oreille; people of the wide lake. *rt.: **łaq̓t** – wide; suffix: **...etkʷ, ...tkʷ** – liquid (self identification term)*
sčłq̓etkʷmiš – Upper Pend d'Oreille; people of the wide lake. *rt.: **łaq̓t** – wide; suffix: **...etkʷ, ...tkʷ** – liquid (Qlispel term)*

qlispél, *qlispé* – Kalispel; Lower Pend d'Oreille. *rt.: **qal** – fresh, raw. (self identification term)*

snxʷmeneʔ – Spokane.
sntutʔulixʷ – Upper Spokane people. *(Pend d'Oreille term)*

sntuˀtˀuli – Upper Spokane. *(self identification term)*
snxwmeneˀi – Spokane. *(self identification term)*
scqescił ni – Lower Spokane. *(self identification term)*

sčicwi – Coeur d'Aléne.

sxʷyélpetkʷ, *sxʷye* – Colville.

učnaqin, *učnaqi* – Okanagan. *rt.:* ***wič*** *– see;*
snq̓a – Southern Okanagan.

sxʷil̓epiš – San Poil.

smlqmi – Methow.

sqlsé – Kootenai.

sčq̓ʷey̓šn, *sčq̓ʷe* – Blackfeet. *rt.:* ***q̓ʷay*** *– black; suffix:* ***...šin, ...šn*** *– feet.*
snxʷlsčint, *snxʷlsči* – Blood.
sxʷiyesčint – Ant People, a band of the Blackfeet.
łcc̓mic̓eˀ – Small Robes, a band of the Blackfeet.

saáptniša – Nez Perce; southern band.
slapaá – Nez Perce; northern band.

iaqmeˀ – Yakima.

nx̣ʷustaptneˀ, *nx̣ʷusta* – Assiniboine.

nq̓y̓osq̓isčint – Gros Ventres.

čqqayus – Cheyenne.

snuwepcn, *snuwe* – Shoshoni.
snuwepcn, *snuwe* – Lemhi band of the Shoshoni.

slqʷtłłnxʷt̓u, *nxʷt̓u* – Sioux.

nxʷt̓xʷt̓u – Cree.

stemčiistn, *stemči* – Crow.
qʷayičint – Mountain Crow.

ox̣ʷi – Navajo.

čt̓l̓t̓leptn, *čt̓l̓t̓le* – Pueblo.

c̓altulexʷ sqelixʷ – Eskimo.

spayół, *spayó* – Mexican.

čusw̓i – Chinese.

čapni – Japanese.

q̓ʷyós – black person; African-American. *See:* ***African-American.***

suyápi – white people. *(This term is used to describe Caucasian people; generally it refers to people who are not Native American. The term is also used to describe the English language.) See:* ***white people.***
semeˀ – French.
kʷlkʷlta – Canadian.
snołpselixʷ – German.
nłt̓uxʷtn – Italian.

Evaro **snłʔóy̓čn** – Evaro, Flathead Nation. *lit. small clearing on hilltop.*

Evaro Hill **snłp̓upx̣̌m,** *snłp̓u* – Evaro Hill, south of Evaro. *lit. emerge from a narrow opening into the clearing.*

eve **čłʔéʔ** – against; eve. *(The eve of some day/event is seen as being against the day coming.)* *See:* ***against***.

even **put** – just, exactly, even, enough; right then. *See:* ***just***

evening **sčlux̣ʷ** – evening.
x̣est sčlux̣ʷ – good evening.

člux̣ʷm – eat supper/dinner. *See:* ***supper***.

k̓ʷłčlux̣ʷ – go out of sight around an obstacle. *(i.e., a tree, hill, rock, building, etc.)* *See:* ***disappear***.
ṅem qeʔ čsčlux̣ʷ – It will get evening on us.

sčsoósqn, *sčsoó* – sunset. *See:* ***sunset***.

evening grosbeak **nkʷtnáqs** – evening grosbeak, black-headed grosbeak, pine grosbeak.

everyone **esyáʔ** – everything; everyone; all. *See:* ***all***.

everything **esyáʔ** – everything; everyone; all. *See:* ***all***.

every time **ax̣l** – every time.
ax̣lásq̓t, *ax̣lá* – everyday. *suffix:* ***...asq̓t*** *– sky, day.*
ax̣lspentč – every year.
ax̣lṁnux̣ʷist – go through something over and over.
ax̣l čn sust t kapi še čn čsʔitš – Every time I drink coffee, I get sleepy. **put u qeʔ tʔe łu ax̣lṁnux̣ʷist** – Again we're going through this time.

evident **wnwinx̣ʷ,** *wnwi* – plainly visible; evident; apparent; very clear; obvious. *See:* ***plain***.

evil **t̓éyeʔ,** *t̓e* – bad; evil; mean. *See:* ***bad***.
t̓éyeʔ – S/he/it is mean/bad. **čn t̓éyeʔ, kʷ t̓éyeʔ**
łt̓et̓iyeʔ – S/he/it is a little mean/bad. **čn łt̓et̓iyeʔ, kʷ łt̓et̓iyeʔ**

t̓éyeʔm – S/he/it acted mean/bad. **čn t̓éyeʔm, kʷ t̓éyeʔm**
es t̓éyeʔi – S/he/it is acting mean/bad. **čnes t̓éyeʔi, kʷes t̓éyeʔi**

t̓iyewilš – S/he/it became mean/bad. **čn t̓iyewilš, kʷ t̓iyewilš** *suffix:* ***...wilš*** *– developmental.*
es t̓iyewilši – S/he/it is becoming mean/bad. **čnes t̓iyewilši, kʷes t̓iyewilši**

t̓éyešts – S/he/it acted mean/bad toward s.o. **t̓éyeštn, t̓éyeštxʷ**
es t̓éyeštm – S/he/it is acting mean/bad toward s.o. **čnes t̓éyeštm, kʷes t̓éyeštm**

st̓éyeʔ – the bad.
kʷłt̓éyeʔ – sin.

t̓et̓iyeʔ – bad, as a term of endearment; bad as a pet name.
t̓et̓iyeʔ – S/he/it is bad. **čn t̓et̓iyeʔ, kʷ t̓et̓iyeʔ**

st̓et̓iyeʔ – the bad, as a term of endearment.

The **i** following uvular consonants (UC) and the glottal stop **ʔ** sound like English "*ey*" as in the words th*ey*, h*ey*, wh*ey*, etc. Salish UC are: **q**, **q̓**, **qʷ**, **q̓ʷ**, **x̣**, **x̣ʷ**. For example, the suffix ...**qin** – head/top, is often spelled using English *ey* as "q*ey*n". So **qi**, **q̓i**, **qʷi**, **q̓ʷi**, **x̣i**, **x̣ʷi**, may be spelled with English *ey* as **q***ey*, **q̓***ey*, **qʷ***ey*, **q̓ʷ***ey*, **x̣***ey*, **x̣ʷ***ey* in other texts.

s.t. - something, the 3rd person
(s.t.) - something implied
s.o. - someone, the 3rd person
sl. - singular form
pl. - plural form
rt. - root word
cmd. - command
lit. - literally
fig. - figuratively
i.e., - for example
See: - Redirection to a related word.

exactly **put –** just, exactly, even, enough; right then. *See: **just**.*

examine **šƛ̓us –** search/stare around; look from one thing to the next; scan. *See: **search***

excellent **qʷamqʷmt –** excellent; beautiful; pleasing.
qʷam – pleasure; pleasing; pleasant; excellent. *See: **pleasure**.*

nqʷamqʷmetkʷ – excellent water. *rt.: **qʷamqʷmt** – excellent; suffix: **...etkʷ, ...tkʷ** – liquid*

qʷamqʷmt łu asck̓ʷuľ – Your work is excellent. **nłapa qʷamqʷmt –** Really excellent!

tam ťuľ – tremendous; outstanding; extreme; excellent.
tam ťuľ – S/he/it is outstanding. **tam čn ťuľ, tam kʷ ťuľ**

tam nťuľcn – talk in extremes good or bad.

tam es ťuľeysi – It is raining in extreme.

yo tam kʷ ťuľ – You're outstanding. **tam sťuľ sxʷk̓ʷľsncut –** S/he is a excellent cook.

exchange **ṅeyxʷéẇs,** *ṅeyxʷé* **–** trade. *See: **trade**.*

tumíst, *tumí* **–** buy. *See: **buy**.*
tumistmnwe – buy from each other; exchange.

excite **psap –** excited/nervous.
psap – S/he/it got excited. **čn psap, kʷ psap**
es pspma – S/he/it is getting excited. **čnes pspma, kʷes pspma**
qs pspma – S/he/it is going to get excited. **čiqs pspma, kʷqs pspma**

psmntas – S/he/it is nervous about s.t. **psmntan, psmntaxʷ**
es psmams – S/he/it is getting nervous about s.t. **ies psmam, as psmam**
qs psmams – S/he/it is going to get nervous about s.t. **iqs psmam, aqs psmam**

pspstas – S/he/it made s.o. nervous. **pspstan, pspstaxʷ**
es pspams – S/he/it is making s.o. nervous. **ies pspam, as pspam**
qs pspams – S/he/it is going to make s.o. nervous. **iqs pspam, aqs pspam**

psačstmis – S/he/it did s.t. to make s.o. nervous. **psačstmn, psačstmntxʷ**
es psačstms – S/he/it is doing s.t. to make s.o. nervous. **ies psačstm, as psačstm**
qs psačstms – S/he/it is going to do s.t. to make s.o. nervous. **iqs psačstm, aqs psačstm**

pspsamn – someone who always gets excited/nervous.
pspsmuł – one that habitually gets excited nervous. *suffix: **...łmuł** – one that habitually does.*
snpspstantn – someone who always gets excited/nervous.

pspast – excited, full of energy.
psmscut – S/he got one's self excited. **čn psmscut, kʷ psmscut**
pspmals, *pspma* **–** nervously anticipating. *See: **anticipate**.*

ta kʷ qes psap – Do not get excited. **łu ṅe ta qʷo es psap –** If I do not get excited. **t milq̓ʷ u pspsšalš –** S/he is always excited. **uł pspast łu sccmeľt –** Those children are full of energy. **ye pṅ pspast annk̓ʷuľmn –** Your culture is full of energy.

psaẇscn – talk excitedly. *suffix: **...éẇs** – in between, middle.*
psaẇscn – S/he talked excitedly. **čn psaẇscn, kʷ psaẇscn**
es psaẇscni – S/he is talking excitedly. **čnes psaẇscni, kʷes psaẇscni**
qs psaẇscni – S/he is going to talk excitedly. **čiqs psaẇscni, kʷqs psaẇscni**

čmpim – overly excited; out of control. *rt.: čim – dark.*
es čmpim – S/he is overly excited. **čnes čmpim, kʷes čmpim**

exclamation

k̓ʷ uc uṅe – Oh that's right!

hayo – male exclamation.

eni – female exclamation.

enuˀ – female exclamation of pain.

enuč – exclamation of pain.

haˀm – female exclamation indicating pity at a situation or for something.

hoy – "Boy!" "Gee!"
hoy es lemti – Gee, s/he's happy.

exʷ – gee; gee...always/again; oh.
exʷ kʷes susti t kapi – Gee, you are always drinking coffee! **exʷ šeẏ kʷ emut –** Gee, you are sitting again!

x̣ił – interjection; exclamation; darn; doggone; damn. *This word adds emphasis to other words or thoughts.*
x̣ił mtmi uł snčl̓é – Darn those no-good coyotes!

ye pṅ – exclamation to accentuate a word or thought.
ye pṅ pspast annk̓ʷul̓mn – Your culture is full of energy. **ye pṅ čnes čsq̇méltni –** I am really hungry.

> The **i** following uvular consonants (UC) and the glottal stop **ˀ** sound like English "*ey*" as in the words *they*, *hey*, *whey*, etc. Salish UC are: **q**, **q̇**, **qʷ**, **q̇ʷ**, **x̣**, **x̣ʷ**. For example, the suffix ...**qin** – head/top, is often spelled using English *ey* as "*qeyn*". So **qi**, **q̇i**, **qʷi**, **q̇ʷi**, **x̣i**, **x̣ʷi**, may be spelled with English *ey* as **q***ey*, **q̇***ey*, **qʷ***ey*, **q̇ʷ***ey*, **x̣***ey*, **x̣ʷ***ey* in other texts.

excrement

ṁṅéč, *ṁṅé* **–** excrement; defecate; feces. *See:* ***defecate.***
snṁṅéčtn, *snṁṅé* **–** toilet. *prefix:* ***sn...*** *– a place of; suffix:* ***...tin, ...tn*** *– means of/device.*
sṁṅčsqáx̣eˀ – horse/domestic animal feces.

scułm ṁṅéč – steer feces.

excuse

xʷumiˀ – An expression of politeness roughly translated to please or excuse me. *See:* ***please.***

exhausted

picxʷt – exhausted; tired.
picxʷt – S/he got exhausted. **čn picxʷt, kʷ picxʷt**
es picxʷti – S/he is exhausted. **čnes picxʷti, kʷes picxʷti**
qs picxʷti – S/he is going to be exhausted. **čiqs picxʷti, kʷqs picxʷti**

pcxʷmutˀem – sick and tired.

pcxʷus – look exhausted. *suffix:* ***...us*** *– face, fire.*
pcxʷus – S/he/it looked exhausted. **čn pcxʷus, kʷ pcxʷus**
es pcxʷusi – S/he/it is looking exhausted. **čnes pcxʷusi, kʷes pcxʷusi**

npcxʷels – act/want exhausted. *circumfix:* ***n...els*** *– want, feel.*
npcxʷels – S/he/it acted exhausted. **čn npcxʷels, kʷ npcxʷels**
es npcxʷelsi – S/he/it is acting exhausted. **čnes npcxʷelsi, kʷes npcxʷelsi**
qs npcxʷelsi – S/he/it is going to act exhausted. **čiqs npcxʷelsi, kʷqs npcxʷelsi**

illmnaqs – exhausted; played out.

> s.t. - something, the 3rd person
> (s.t.) - something implied
> s.o. - someone, the 3rd person
> *sl.* - singular form
> *pl.* - plural form
> *rt.* - root word
> *cmd.* - command
> *lit.* - literally
> *fig.* - figuratively
> *i.e.,* - for example
> *See:* - Redirection to a related word.

expand

xʷup – straighten something; unfold; extend something. *See* ***stretch.***

expensive

nkʷtnaqsm, *nkʷtna* **–** expensive; costs a large amount; something of great value. *circumfix:* ***n...aqsm*** *– kinds. See* ***important.***

expiration **npλ̓mus –** the full extent; the end. *See **end**.*
steṁ łu es q̇eẏ npλ̓mus x̣ʷl̓ łu qł čtemtis sqʔem – What is the expiration date for using the milk.

explain **ṁéẏeʔ –** explain; tell; show; make something known.
ṁéẏełts – S/he/it explained to s.o. **ṁéẏełtn, ṁéẏełtxʷ**
es ṁéẏełtms – S/he/it is explaining to s.o. **ies ṁéẏełtm, as ṁéẏełtm**
qs ṁéẏełtms – S/he/it is going to explain to s.o. **iqs ṁéẏełtm, aqs ṁéẏełtm**
ṁéʔeyełts – They explained to s.o. **qeʔ ṁéẏeltm, ṁéẏełtp**

ṁéẏešts – S/he/it made s.o. know s.t. **ṁéẏeštn, ṁéẏeštxʷ**
es ṁéẏeštms – S/he/it is make s.o. know s.t. **ies ṁéẏeštm, as ṁéẏeštm**
qs ṁéẏeštms – S/he/it is going to make s.o. know s.t. **iqs ṁéẏeštm, aqs ṁéẏeštm**

sxʷṁeẏštwe – one tasked to tell (stories). *prefix: **sxʷ...** – one tasked to do.*

ṁéẏełt – Show; tell; explain. *cmd.*

ṁiṁéẏeʔ – teach. *See: **teach**.*
ṁiṁiim – tell a story/news; narrate. *See: **tell**.*
es ṁeẏštwexʷisti – They're showing each other. **qeʔes ṁeẏštwexʷisti, pes ṁeẏštwexʷisti**
ṁiyełtumš – show the people; tell the people; explain to the people.

ta qeʔqs cṁéẏeʔ łiʔe sic es ṗox̣ʷtil̓ši – Those who are growing up right now will not have this knowledge. **we ṁéẏełtn –** Well I showed, told, explained. **we ṁéẏeʔ –** Well I told, showed, explained. **qʷo ṁéẏełt łu i tóx̣ʷ –** Tell me straight, tell me the truth. **ta kʷ ies nunxʷenem łu asṁéẏe –** I do not believe what you explained. **ha kʷ iqs ṁéẏełtm –** Should I show you.

nmipáłq, *nmipá* **–** tattle; accuse. *See: **tattle**.*

exponent **nx̣pṗmncut –** multiply by one's self; exponentiation.
nx̣pṗmncutmis – S/he exponentiated it. **nx̣pṗmncutmn, nx̣pṗmncutmntxʷ**
es nx̣pṗmncutmms – S/he is exponentiating it. **ies nx̣pṗmncutmm, as nx̣pṗmncutmm**
qs nx̣pṗmncutmms – S/he is going to exponentiate it. **iqs nx̣pṗmncutmm, aqs nx̣pṗmncutmm**

snx̣pṗmncutn – exponent.

steṁ łu snx̣pṗmncutis – What is its exponent? **nx̣pṗmncutmis čełe t cil –** S/he exponentiated three to the fifth power. **čełe nx̣pṗmncut t cil –** Three to the fifth power, *(3^5).*

expose **čłaq̇ʷiċeʔ –** exposed to view all over; completely exposed. *See: **appear**.*

extend **xʷup –** straighten something; unfold; extend something. *See **stretch**.*

čxʷálšn – extend the foot to something; take a step. *See **step**.*

ṫip – join to make longer; fasten to make longer. (*i.e., sewing, fastening, etc.)* *See: **join**.*

exterior **sčłqel̓tč –** exterior; outside layer. *rt.: **qeltč** – meat, body; prefix: **čł...** – surface.*

extinguish **łeps –** extinguish a fire; turn off a light or electrical appliance. *See: **put out**.*

eye **sčkʷλ̓us –** eye. **sčkʷλ̓kʷλ̓us –** eyes.
sčchus – right eye.
sčċq̓ʷus – left eye.
čxʷexʷʔus – many spherical objects; many eyes.
čxʷexʷemus – many spherical objects; many eyes.

č...us, č...s – circumfix indicating a spherical object such as eyes.

čkʷtkʷtnus – big eyes. *rt.: **kʷtunt** – big.*
čiliyals – round eyes. *rt.: **yal** – round.*
i čpiqs – white of the eye. *rt.: **piq** – white.*
i čpqpiqs – white eyes. *rt.: **piq** – white.*
i čpaqs – bum eye, grey eye, burned eye. *rt.: **paá** – faded.*
i čpqpáqaqs – white eyes, cataracts. *rt.: **paá** – faded.*
i čq̓ʷaẏs – black of the eyes. *rt.: **q̓ʷaẏ** – black.*
i č̓q̓ʷiq̓ʷays – black color of eyes. *rt.: **q̓ʷaẏ** – black.*
i ṅq̓ʷiq̓ʷays – black eyes *(from getting hit)*. *rt.: **q̓ʷaẏ** – black.*
i č̓kʷlkʷils – bloodshot eyes, pink eye. *rt.: **kʷil** – red.*
i čyuyúʔus – sharp eyes, good sight. *rt.: **yoyóot** – strong.*
i čqʷsqʷis – hazy eyes, blurry eyes, poor sight.
i čċk̓ʷċik̓ʷs – seeing spots, lights; seeing double. *rt.: **ċik̓ʷ** – spark.*
es čplplč̓us – cross eyes. *rt.: **plič̓** – red.*
i čqʷnqʷins – green or blue eyes. *rt.: **qʷin** – green.*
čxʷk̓ʷpus – clean/clear eye. *rt.: **xʷuk̓ʷ** – clean.*

čquqaupus – have itchy eyes. *See: **itch**.*
čpipiis – have happy eyes; flirty eyes; gleem in the eye. *See: **happy**.*
sčmċmaċs – have gummy eyes. *See: **awake**.*
čqʷoqʷéws – crazy/silly eyes. *rt.: **qʷeẇ** – crazy. See: **crazy**.*
čmomotus – have smoke in the eyes. *rt.: **mʔot** – smokey. See: **smoke**.*

člč̓ečs – have mean eyes. *rt.: **leč̓** – angry. See: **angry**.*
i člč̓ečs – I have mean eyes. **i čn člč̓ečs, i kʷ člč̓ečs**

p uł člč̓ečs – You all have mean eyes.

nťpos – gummed up eyes.
qʷo nťposntm – My eyes got gummed up

es čnṁqin – blind. *See: **blind**.*

i ċik̓ʷk̓ʷk̓ʷ – seeing spots or stars from getting hit.

čťipus – something fell/got into the eye. **čťiťipus** *pl.*
čťipus – Something fell/got into the his/her eye. **čn čťipus, kʷ čťipus**
es čťipus – S/he/it has s.t that fell/got into one's eye. **čnes čťipus, kʷes čťipus**

i čťipus – as soon as something fell into his/her eye. **i čn čťipus, i kʷ čťipus**

č̓ł̓uús – get poked in the eye.
č̓łuúsis – S/he poked s.o.'s eye. **č̓łuúsn, č̓łuúsntxʷ**
es č̓łuúsms – S/he is poking s.o.'s eye. **ies č̓łuúsm, as č̓łuúsm**
qs č̓łuúsms – S/he is going to poke s.o.'s eye. **iqs č̓łuúsm, aqs č̓łuúsm**

č̓łuúsntm – S/he was poked in the eye. **qʷo č̓łuúsntm, kʷ č̓łuúsntm**

č̓łuúsnt – Poke him/her/it in the eye. *cmd.*

čšťncutš x̣ine kʷ č̓łuúsntm – Take care of yourself, you might get poked in the eye.

nċipsm – wink; close eye. *See: **wink**.*

čkʷƛ̓kʷƛ̓us – open eyes. *See: **open**.*

eyebrow

cpłéẏt, *cpłéẏ* – eyebrow.

The **i** following uvular consonants (UC) and the glottal stop **ʔ** sound like English "*ey*" as in the words th*ey*, h*ey*, wh*ey*, etc. Salish UC are: **q**, **q̓**, **qʷ**, **q̓ʷ**, **x̣**, **x̣ʷ**. For example, the suffix **...qin** – head/top, is often spelled using English *ey* as "q*ey*n". So **qi**, **q̓i**, **qʷi**, **q̓ʷi**, **x̣i**, **x̣ʷi**, may be spelled with English *ey* as **q***ey*, **q̓***ey*, **qʷ***ey*, **q̓ʷ***ey*, **x̣***ey*, **x̣ʷ***ey* in other texts.

s.t. - something, the 3rd person
(s.t.) - something implied
s.o. - someone, the 3rd person
sl. - singular form
pl. - plural form
rt. - root word
cmd. - command
lit. - literally
fig. - figuratively
i.e., - for example
See: - Redirection to a related word.

cpcpłeẏ – eyebrows.

eyedrops **čmaluẏústn –** eye medicine. *circumfix: **č...us** – spherical object; eyes.*

čmaluẏúsis – S/he medicated s.o.'s eye. **čmaluẏúsn, čmaluẏúsntxʷ**
es čmaluẏúsms – S/he is medicating s.o.'s eye. **ies čmaluẏúsm, as čmaluẏúsm**
qs čmaluẏúsms – S/he is going to medicate s.o.'s eye. **iqs čmaluẏúsm, aqs čmaluẏúsm**

čłnmus – put drops in the eye. *rt.: **łin** – splash; circumfix: **č...us** – spherical object; eyes.*
čłnmus – S/he put drops in the eye. **čn čłnmus, kʷ čłnmus**
es čłnmusi – S/he is putting drops in the eye. **čnes čłnmusi, kʷes čłnmusi**
qs čłnmusi – S/he is going to put drops in the eye. **čiqs čłnmusi, kʷqs čłnmusi**

čłnmusis – S/he put drops in the eye. **čłnmusn, čłnmusntxʷ**
es čłnmusi – S/he is putting drops in the eye. **čnes čłnmusi, kʷes čłnmusi**
qs čłnmusi – S/he is going to put drops in the eye. **čiqs čłnmusi, kʷqs čłnmusi**

čłnmusnt – Put drops in his/her eye. *cmd.*

eyeglasses **čšṅšṅustn,** *čšṅšṅu* **–** eyeglasses. *rt.: **šiṅ** – flat cover; circumfix: **č...us** – spherical object; eyes; eyes; suffix: **...tin, ...tn** – means of/device.*

es čšṅšṅus – S/he is wearing eyeglasses. **čnes čšṅšṅus, kʷes čšṅšṅus**

čšṅšṅusiš – Put your eyeglasses on. *cmd.*

eyelash **sčupupus,** *sčupupu* **–** eyelash. *rt.: **čupu** – hairy; circumfix: **č...us** – spherical object; eyes.*

F

fabric softener **nčepplqstn –** fabric softener.

nṗťatkʷnt ci nčepplqstn – Pour the fabric softener in the water.

face **skʷƛ̓us –** face.
skʷƛ̓kʷƛ̓us – faces.

sčłč̓méssn – forehead. *See: **forehead.***
cpłéẏt, *cpłéẏ* **–** eyebrow. *See: **eyebrow.***
sčupupus, *sčupupu* **–** eyelash. *See: **eyelash.***
sčkʷƛ̓kʷƛ̓us – eyes. *See: **eye.***
snṗsáqs, *snṗsá* **–** nose; bird's beak; pencil tip. *See: **nose.***
sk̓ʷłčmus – cheek. *See: **cheek.***
k̓ʷiˀepest, *k̓ʷíˀepe* **–** chin. *See: **chin.***

...s, us – suffix indicating face.
mals – dusty/dirty face.
i mals – You have a dirty face. **i čn mals, i kʷ mals**

kʷils – have a red face.
kʷils – S/he has a red face. **čn kʷils, kʷ kʷils**

nc̓uuys – sour face; the face you get when you eat something sour.

c̓ew̓sm – wash the face. *See: **wash.***
ac̓x̣ʷosm – look at a face. *See: **look.***
mińsm – paint the face. *See: **paint.***
q̇ʷaysm – make the face black. *See: **paint.***

ntax̣ʷlús – face toward some direction. *suffix: **...us** – face.*
ntax̣ʷlúsm – S/he/it faced toward (s.t.). **čn ntax̣ʷlúsm, kʷ ntax̣ʷlúsm**
es ntax̣ʷlúsi – S/he/it is moving to face toward (s.t.). **čnes ntax̣ʷlúsi, kʷes ntax̣ʷlúsi**
qs ntax̣ʷlúsi – S/he/it is going to move to face toward (s.t.). **čiqs ntax̣ʷlúsi, kʷqs ntax̣ʷlúsi**
ntax̣ʷlúˀusm – They faced toward (s.t.). **qeˀ ntax̣ʷlúsm, p ntax̣ʷlúsm**
es ntax̣ʷlúˀusi – They are moving to face toward (s.t.). **qeˀes ntax̣ʷlúsi, pes ntax̣ʷlúsi**
qs ntax̣ʷlúˀusi – They are going to move to face toward (s.t.). **qeˀqs ntax̣ʷlúsi, pqs ntax̣ʷlúsi**

ntax̣ʷlúsmis – S/he/it faced s.o. in some direction. **ntax̣ʷlúsmn, ntax̣ʷlúsmntxʷ**
es ntax̣ʷlúsms – S/he/it is facing s.o. in some direction. **ies ntax̣ʷlúsm, as čntax̣ʷlúsm**
qs ntax̣ʷlúsms – S/he/it is going to face s.o. in some direction. **iqs ntax̣ʷlúsm, aqs ntax̣ʷlúsm**

s.t. - something, the 3rd person
(s.t.) - something implied
s.o. - someone, the 3rd person
sl. - singular form
pl. - plural form
rt. - root word
cmd. - command
lit. - literally
fig. - figuratively
i.e., - for example
See: - Redirection to a related word.

es ntax̣ʷlús – S/he/it is facing toward (s.t.). **čnes ntax̣ʷlús, kʷes ntax̣ʷlús**
es ntax̣ʷlúʔus – They are facing toward (s.t.). **qeʔes ntax̣ʷlús, pes ntax̣ʷlús**

čntax̣ʷlúsmis – S/he/it faced toward s.t./s.o. **čntax̣ʷlúsmn, čntax̣ʷlúsmntxʷ**
es čntax̣ʷlúsms – S/he/it is facing toward s.t./s.o. **ies čntax̣ʷlúsm, as čntax̣ʷlúsm**
qs čntax̣ʷlúsms – S/he/it is going to face toward s.t./s.o. **iqs čntax̣ʷlúsm, aqs čntax̣ʷlúsm**
čntax̣ʷlúʔusmis – They faced toward s.t./s.o. **qeʔ čntax̣ʷlúsmntm, čntax̣ʷlúsmntp**
es čntax̣ʷlúʔusms – They are facing toward s.t./s.o. **qeʔes čntax̣ʷlúsm, es čntax̣ʷlúsmp**
qs čntax̣ʷlúʔusms – They are going to face toward s.t./s.o. **qeʔqs čntax̣ʷlúsm, qs čntax̣ʷlúsmp**

ntax̣ʷlúsis – S/he/it faced s.o. toward s.t./s.o. **ntax̣ʷlúsn, ntax̣ʷlúsntxʷ**
ntax̣ʷlúʔusis – They faced s.o. toward s.t./s.o. **qeʔ ntax̣ʷlúsntm, ntax̣ʷlúsntp**

ntx̣ʷtax̣ʷlúʔusm – Each one faced toward (s.t.). **qeʔ ntx̣ʷtax̣ʷlúsm, p ntx̣ʷtax̣ʷlúsm**

ntax̣ʷlúsiš – Face toward (s.t.). *cmd.*
ntax̣ʷlúswi – All of you face toward (s.t.). *cmd.*
ntax̣ʷlusmnt – Face toward s.o./s.t. *cmd.*
cntax̣ʷlúsiš – Face here toward me. *cmd.*
qʷo ntax̣ʷlusmnt – Face toward me. *cmd.*
ntax̣ʷlúsnt – Face s.o. toward s.t. *cmd.*
es čntax̣ʷlsmnwexʷi – They are facing each other. **qeʔes čntax̣ʷlsmnwexʷi, pes čntax̣ʷlsmnwexʷi**

ṅem ntax̣ʷlúsm – S/he/it will face toward (s.t.). **ṅem čn ntax̣ʷlúsm, ṅem kʷ ntax̣ʷlúsm**
ṅem ntax̣ʷlúʔusm – They will face toward (s.t.). **ṅem qeʔ ntax̣ʷlúsm, ṅem p ntax̣ʷlúsm**
čn ntax̣ʷlúsm č nx̣alptin – I faced toward the east. **es cntax̣ʷlús łu inṗiṗuyšn** – My car is facing me.

face down

łq̇ʷtulexʷ, *łq̇ʷtu* – face down.
łq̇ʷtulexʷis – S/he put s.t./s.o. face down. **łq̇ʷtulexʷn, łq̇ʷtulexʷnxʷ**
es łq̇ʷtulexʷms – S/he is putting s.t./s.o. face down. **ies łq̇ʷtulexʷm, as łq̇ʷtulexʷm**
qs łq̇ʷtulexʷms – S/he is going to put s.t./s.o. face down. **iqs łq̇ʷtulexʷm, aqs łq̇ʷtulexʷm**

es łq̇ʷtulexʷ – S/he/it is face down. **čnes łq̇ʷtulexʷ, kʷes łq̇ʷtulexʷ**

łqq̇lšulexʷ – fall face down.

fade

paá – faded; pale; gray.
i paá – It is faded; it is pale.
i páas – His/her/its face is pale.
es paám – fades.

npaáps – faded pants.
i pa ululim – silver. *lit. faded metal.*

čeʔ i pá – fade.

fail

tuṅéčstm – fail to do/make something. *rt.: **tuiṅ** – fail/deficient; suffix: **...ečst, ...čst** – of the hand.*
es tuṅéčst – S/he failed. **čnes tuṅéčst, kʷes tuṅéčst**

tuṅéčstmis – S/he failed to do it. **tuṅéčstmn, tuṅéčstntxʷ**
es tuṅéčstms – S/he/it is failing at it. **ies tuṅéčstm, as tuṅéčstm**
qs tuṅéčstms – S/he/it is going to fail at it. **iqs tuṅéčstm, aqs tuṅéčstm**
tuṅéʔevstmis – They failed to do it. **qeʔ tuṅéčstmntm, tuṅéčstmntp**
es tuṅéʔečstms – They are failing at it. **qeʔes tuṅéčstm, es tuṅéčstmp**
qs tuṅéʔečstms – They are going to fail at it. **qeʔqs tuṅéčstm, qs tuṅéčstmp**

tuṅulexʷ – shortage of something for land. *(i.e., planting seeds, etc.) rt.: **tuiṅ** – fail/deficient.*
tuṅulexʷ – S/he lacked enough for the land. **čn tuṅulexʷ, kʷ tuṅulexʷ**

tuṅalqs – unfinished clothing for lack of material. *rt.: **tuiṅ** – fail/deficient.*
tuṅalqs – S/he lacked enough material. **čn tuṅalqs, kʷ tuṅalqs**

tuṅus – face of disappointment for not receiving any distributed items. *rt.: **tuiṅ** – fail/deficient.*
tuṅus – S/he got a disappointed face. **čn tuṅus, kʷ tuṅus**

ntuṅičṅm – fail to catch up to someone; unable to catch up to someone; behind. *See: **catch**.*

k̓ʷłtwiṅtm – fall short of something; deficient in something; unable to attain something. *See: **deficient**.*

tas k̓ʷl̓nuis – S/he did not complete it. *See: **accomplish**.*

The **i** following uvular consonants (UC) and the glottal stop ˀ sound like English "*ey*" as in the words *they, hey, whey*, etc. Salish UC are: **q, q̓, qʷ, q̓ʷ, x̣, x̣ʷ**. For example, the suffix ...**qin** – head/top, is often spelled using English *ey* as "q*ey*n". So **qi, q̓i, qʷi, q̓ʷi, x̣i, x̣ʷi**, may be spelled with English *ey* as **q***ey*, **q̓***ey*, **qʷ***ey*, **q̓ʷ***ey*, **x̣***ey*, **x̣ʷ***ey* in other texts.

faint

čmpqin – faint; get a dark head; black out. *rt.: **čim** – dark; suffix: **...qin, ...qn** – top.*
čmpqin – S/he fainted. **čn čmpqin, kʷ čmpqin**
es čmpqini – S/he is fainting. **čnes čmpqini, kʷes čmpqini**
qs čmpqini – S/he is going to faint. **čiqs čmpqini, kʷqs čmpqini**

čmpstem – S/he was made to go dark; out of it. *This term refers to losing control due to being excited or angry, as if the person was about to faint or pass out. rt.: **čim** – dark.*

ha kʷqs čmpsteṁ – Are you going to faint?

npṁpqan – get knocked out; to be out of the head. *See: **knock out**.*

ƛ̓lƛ̓elil – have the appearance of dying. *(i.e., to fall from becoming unconscious, as in fainting, etc.)*
eċx̣i čiqs ƛ̓lƛ̓elil – It is like I am going to faint.

fairy slipper

smˀém q̓ešis – fairy slipper flower; women's shoe.

sčt̓ásšn – shoe; fairy slipper flower.

falcon

aátat – falcon; Peregrine falcon; duck hawk; *Falco peregrinus*.

fall

tk̓ʷuk̓ʷ – fall down.
tk̓ʷuk̓ʷ – S/he/it fell down. **čn tk̓ʷuk̓ʷ, kʷ tk̓ʷuk̓ʷ**
es tk̓ʷk̓ʷmi – S/he/it is falling down. **čnes tk̓ʷk̓ʷmi, kʷes tk̓ʷk̓ʷmi**
qs tk̓ʷk̓ʷmi – S/he/it is going to fall down. **čiqs tk̓ʷk̓ʷmi, kʷqs tk̓ʷk̓ʷmi**

tk̓ʷuk̓ʷš – Fall down. *cmd.*

es tk̓ʷtk̓ʷuli – S/he is really sick; laying down sick for a long time.

qmmin – more than one fell down.
qmmíˀin – They fell down. **qeˀ qmmin, p qmmin**
es qmmíˀini – They are falling down. **qeˀes qmmini, pes qmmini**
qs qmmíˀini – They are going to fall down. **qeˀqs qmmini, pqs qmmini**

t̓iip – fall from something.
t̓iip – S/he/it fell. **čn t̓iip, kʷ t̓iip**
es t̓ipmi – S/he/it is falling. **čnes t̓ipmi, kʷes t̓ipmi**
qs t̓ipmi – S/he/it is going to fall. **čiqs t̓ipmi, kʷqs t̓ipmi**
t̓iíˀip – They fell. **qeˀ t̓iip, p t̓iip**
es t̓ipmíˀi – They are falling. **qeˀes t̓ipmi, pes t̓ipmi**

s.t. - something, the 3rd person
(s.t.) - something implied
s.o. - someone, the 3rd person
sl. - singular form
pl. - plural form
rt. - root word
cmd. - command
lit. - literally
fig. - figuratively
i.e., - for example
See: - Redirection to a related word.

qs t̓ipmí?i – They are going to fall. **qe?qs t̓ipmi, pqs t̓ipmi**

t̓ipmim – drop something. *See:* ***drop****.*
t̓ipm – take something down from up high. *See:* ***take****.*

čt̓ipus – something fell/got into the eye. *See:* ***eye****.*

kʷṅe u čn t̓iip tl̓ nwist – I should have fallen from that high place.

nt̓ipmétkʷ – fall in the water.
nt̓ipmétkʷ – S/he/it fell in the water. **čn nt̓ipmétkʷ, kʷ nt̓ipmétkʷ**
es nt̓ipmétkʷi – S/he/it is falling in the water. **čnes nt̓ipmétkʷi, kʷes nt̓ipmétkʷi**
qs nt̓ipmétkʷi – S/he/it is going to fall in the water. **čiqs nt̓ipmétkʷi, kʷqs nt̓ipmétkʷi**
nt̓ipmé?etkʷ – They fell in the water. **qe? nt̓ipmétkʷ, p nt̓ipmétkʷ**
es nt̓ipmé?etkʷi – They are falling in the water. **qe?es nt̓ipmétkʷi, pes nt̓ipmétkʷi**
qs nt̓ipmé?etkʷi – They are going to fall in the water. **qe?qs nt̓ipmétkʷi, pqs nt̓ipmétkʷi**

est̓ipmétkʷ – waterfall.

nl?óp – fall into some place.
nl?óp l es nłoẋʷ – fall into a hole.
nlolopsew̓s – words falling into place, saying the right things. *suffix:* ***...éw̓s*** *– in between, middle.*
nl?ópetkʷ – fall into water.

cqql̓ičṅ, *cqql̓i* – fall over backward. *suffix:* ***...ičṅ*** *– back.*
cqql̓ičṅ – S/he fell over backward. **čn cqql̓ičṅ, kʷ cqql̓ičṅ**

ẋiṅe kʷ sqql̓i – You might fall over.

łqq̓lšulexʷ – fall face first.
łqq̓lšulexʷ – S/he fell face first. **čn łqq̓lšulexʷ**, **kʷ łqq̓lšulexʷ**

ẋiṅe kʷ łqq̓lšulexʷ – You might fall face first.

cqqšulexʷ – fall backward onto the ground.

nspp̓mnulexʷ – fall hard on the ground; strike the ground with something. *rt.:* ***sp̓im*** *– strike w/ object; suffix:* ***...ulexʷ*** *– land.*

kʷcič – the act of falling pertaining to a single fixed object. *(i.e., tree, post, house, etc.)*
es kʷččmi – It is falling.

kʷččnuis – S/he/it made s.t. fall over. **kʷččnun, kʷččnuntxʷ**
es kʷččnunms – S/he/it is making s.t. fall over. **ies kʷččnunm, as kʷččnunm**
es kʷččnunms – S/he/it going to make s.t. fall over. **iqs kʷččnunm, aqs kʷččnunm**

kʷcičč – It got out of a perpendicular state.

es kʷcič – It is fallen over. *(i.e., a tree/log, post, etc.)*

kʷččnunt – Push it over; make it fall. *cmd.*
kʷckʷcič – Each one fell over.
kʷččalqʷ – The cylindrical object fell over; tree fell over.
čłkʷččene? – It fell over onto something.

ẋʷa es kʷckʷčči smi – Maybe they fell over.

čskʷic – stoop over. *See:* ***stoop****.*

k̓ʷiċšlš – tip an upright thing over/off. *See:* ***tip****.*

tmwalš – crumble apart and fall. *(i.e., cliff rocks fall, landslide, etc.)* *rt.:* ***tmim*** *– crumble. See:* ***crumble****.*

es tmwalš – It is crumbled apart and fallen.

ntmwalš – Rocks fell/slid from the side of a cave.

k̓ʷłtmip – Rocks/earth caved in/fell from under.
es k̓ʷłtmpmi – It is caving in/fell from under.

šnin – a circular discoidal object falls over. *(i.e., coin, tire, lid, etc.)*
x̣ʷollq̓ʷ u šnin – It rolled and fell over.

ntéʔemnulexʷ – land on feet then crumble to the ground. *rt.: **teʔ** – hit/bump. See: **bump***

téʔemist – flop down. *rt.: **teʔ** – hit/bump. See: **bump**.*

qʷo tʔapqntm – It fell on my head. *See: **bump**.*

mcaq – collapsed; falls apart. *See: **collapse**.*

yomšniš – step with tensed leg so as not to slip and/or fall. *(i.e., walking on ice, walking on a wet floor, etc.) See: **step**.*

The **i** following uvular consonants (UC) and the glottal stop ʔ sound like English "*ey*" as in the words *they, hey, whey*, etc. Salish UC are: **q, q̓, qʷ, q̓ʷ, x̣, x̣ʷ**. For example, the suffix ...**qin** – head/top, is often spelled using English *ey* as "*qeyn*". So **qi, q̓i, qʷi, q̓ʷi, x̣i, x̣ʷi**, may be spelled with English *ey* as **q***ey*, **q̓***ey*, **qʷ***ey*, **q̓ʷ***ey*, **x̣***ey*, **x̣ʷ***ey* in other texts.

fall time

sčʔeẏ – fall time; autumn.
ax̣lčʔeẏ – every fall.

es čʔeẏm̓nuxʷisti, *es čʔeẏm̓nuxʷi* – It is again the time of fall. *suffix: **...m̓nuxʷ** – in the time of.*

łu sq̓sip sqelixʷ iše esyaʔ še ep snčʔeytin ax̣lčʔey še iʔimš łu č snčʔeytiʔis – The people long ago all had fall hunting places; every fall they would move to their fall hunting place.

false

tam unéxʷ – not true.

false hellebore

sic̓sečiyeʔ – false hellebore; Indian hellebore; *Veratrum viride.*

sst̓sóʔ – sneeze root; false hellebore root; *Veratrum viride.*

false solomns seal

x̣nx̣néłp, *x̣nx̣né* – field mint, peppermint; false solomns seal; *Mentha arvensis.*

family

nk̓ʷusm – family. *lit. – one fire. rt.: **nk̓ʷuʔ** – one; suffix: **...us** – face, fire.*

nk̓ʷaʔqsus – one band of one family.

sxʷl̓xʷl̓tew̓s – family or a group of people. *rt.: **xʷl̓xʷilt** – live; suffix: **...éw̓s** – in between, middle.*

snk̓ʷelixʷ – one people/family/tribe.

fan

x̣amin – fan; cooling device. *rt.: **x̣a** – cool; suffix: **...min, ...mn** – instrument/tool.*

far

lkʷut – far.
č lkʷut – distant.
sšẏmł člkʷut – farthest.
lkʷulexʷ – place far away.

lkʷukʷ – go far.
lkʷukʷ – S/he went far. **čn lkʷukʷ, kʷ lkʷukʷ**
es lkʷkʷmi – S/he is going far. **čnes lkʷkʷmi, kʷes lkʷkʷmi**
qs lkʷkʷmi – S/he is going to go far. **čiqs lkʷkʷmi, kʷqs lkʷkʷmi**
lkʷúʔukʷ – They went far. **qeʔ lkʷukʷ, p lkʷukʷ**
es lkʷkʷmíʔi – They are going far. **qeʔes lkʷkʷmi, pes lkʷkʷmi**
qs lkʷkʷmíʔi – They are going to go far. **qeʔqs lkʷkʷmi, pqs lkʷkʷmi**

s.t. - something, the 3rd person
(s.t.) - something implied
s.o. - someone, the 3rd person
sl. - singular form
pl. - plural form
rt. - root word
cmd. - command
lit. - literally
fig. - figuratively
i.e., - for example
See: - Redirection to a related word.

lkʷkʷusis – S/he brought s.o./s.t.far. **lkʷkʷusn, lkʷkʷusntxʷ**
es lkʷkʷusms – S/he is bringing s.o./s.t. far. **ies lkʷkʷusm, as lkʷkʷusm**
qs lkʷkʷusms – S/he is going to bring s.o./s.t. far. **iqs lkʷkʷusm, aqs lkʷkʷusm**

lkʷkʷstes – S/he caused s.o. to go far. **lkʷkʷsten, lkʷkʷstexʷ**
es lkʷkʷums – S/he is causing s.o. to go far. **ies lkʷkʷum, as lkʷkʷum**
qs lkʷkʷums – S/he is going to cause s.o. to go far. **iqs lkʷkʷum, aqs lkʷkʷum**
lkʷkʷstéʔes – They caused s.o. to go far. **qeʔ lkʷkʷstem, lkʷkʷstep**
es lkʷkʷúʔums – They are causing s.o. to go far. **qeʔes lkʷkʷum, es lkʷkʷump**
qs lkʷkʷúʔums – They are going to cause s.o. to go far. **qeʔqs lkʷkʷum, qs lkʷkʷump**

lkʷkʷistemn – one inclined to go far. *suffix: …emn – one inclined to do.*
lkʷkʷsteẇs – They are far apart. (emotionally) *suffix: …éẇs – in between, middle.*
lkʷkʷstelis – They are far apart. (physically)
lkʷkʷlwis – travel far.

lkʷkʷusnt – Bring it far. *cmd.*
lkʷkʷuskʷ – Make him/her go far. *cmd.*

č lkʷut łu incitxʷ – My house is far away. č lkʷkʷstexʷ – Move it far away. č lkʷut tỉ citxʷs – S/he/it is far away from her/his/its house. lkʷkʷstumn – I brought you far. lkʷkʷmistmncn – I brought you far. l čeṅ u eċx̣lslkʷut łu ancitxʷ – How far away is your house?

tečnulexʷ – place far away.

fart ṗʔum – fart.

ṗʔum – S/he/it farted. **čn ṗʔum, kʷ ṗʔum**
es ṗumi – S/he/it is farting. **čnes ṗumi, kʷes ṗumi**
qs ṗumi – S/he/it is going to fart. **čiqs ṗumi, kʷqs ṗumi**
ṗʔúʔum – They farted. **qeʔ ṗʔum, p ṗʔum**
es ṗúʔumi – They are farting. **qeʔes ṗumi, pes ṗumi**
qs ṗúʔumi – They are going to fart. **qeʔqs ṗumi, kʷpqs ṗumi**

sṗuʔ – fart. **isṗuʔ, asṗuʔ, sṗuʔs**

ṗqʷṗiqʷlš – farting around.
ṗaṗiqʷeʔ – farting all the time.
ṗuṗumu – stink bug.

ṅe kʷ ṗʔum iše puxʷ łu asṗuʔ – When you fart, it stinks.

ṗuwetkʷm – fart in the water.

ṗuwetkʷm – S/he farted in the water. **čn ṗuwetkʷm, kʷ ṗuwetkʷm**
es ṗuwetkʷi – S/he is farting in the water. **čnes ṗuwetkʷi, kʷes ṗuwetkʷi**
qs ṗuwetkʷi – S/he is going to fart in the water. **čiqs ṗuwetkʷi, kʷqs ṗuwetkʷi**
ṗuwéʔetkʷm – They farted in the water. **qeʔ ṗuwetkʷm, p ṗuwetkʷm**
es ṗuwéʔetkʷi – They are farting in the water. **qeʔes ṗuwetkʷi, pes ṗuwetkʷi**
qs ṗuwéʔetkʷi – They are going to fart in the water. **qeʔqs ṗuwetkʷi, pqs ṗuwetkʷi**

nṗumels – want to fart. *circumfix: n…els – want.*

nṗumels – S/he wanted to fart. **čn nṗumels, kʷ nṗumels**
es nṗumelsi – S/he is wanting to fart. **čnes nṗumelsi, kʷes nṗumelsi**
qs nṗumelsi – S/he is going to want to fart. **čiqs nṗumelsi, kʷqs nṗumelsi**

čsṗuncut – fart while straining; make one's self fart.

čsṗuncut – S/he made one's self fart. **čn čsṗuncut, kʷ čsṗuncut**
es čsṗuncuti – S/he is making one's self fart. **čnes čsṗuncuti, kʷes čsṗuncuti**

qs čsṗuncuti – S/he is going to make one's self fart. **čiqs čsṗuncuti, kʷqs čsṗuncuti**

čn ṫiip u čn čsṗuncut – I fell and farted.

ṗiq̇ʷ – sound of a fart.
es ṗq̇ʷṗiq̇ʷlši – S/he/it is repeatedly farting. **čnes ṗq̇ʷṗiq̇ʷlši, kʷes ṗq̇ʷṗiq̇ʷlši**

fast

aẏip – go fast, hurry. *(i.e., on foot, by car, or on horseback)*
aẏíp – S/he/it went fast. **čn aẏíp, kʷ aẏíp**
es aẏpmi – S/he/it is going fast. **čnes aẏpmi, kʷes aẏpmi**
qs aẏpmi – S/he/it is going to go fast. **čiqs aẏpmi, kʷqs aẏpmi**
aẏíʔip – They went fast. **qeʔ aẏíp, p aẏíp**
es aẏpmíʔi – They are going fast. **qeʔes aẏpmi, pes aẏpmi**
qs aẏpmíʔi – They are going to go fast. **qeʔqs aẏpmi, pqs aẏpmi**

aẏpstés – S/he/it made s.t. go fast. **aẏpstén, aẏpstéxʷ**
es aẏpims – S/he/it is making s.t. go fast. **ies aẏpim, as aẏpim**
qs aẏpims – S/he/it is going to make s.t. go fast. **iqs aẏpim, aqs aẏpim**
aẏpstéʔes – They made s.t. go fast. **qeʔ aẏpstem, aẏpstep**
es aẏpims – They are making s.t. go fast. **qeʔes aẏpim, es aẏpimp**
qs aẏpims – They are going to make s.t. go fast. **qeʔqs aẏpim, qs aẏpimp**

aẏpcnmistm – S/he talked fast. **čn aẏpcnmistm, kʷ aẏpcnmistm**
es aẏpcnmi – S/he is talking fast. **čnes aẏpcnmi, kʷes aẏpcnmi**
qs aẏpcnmi – S/he is going to talk fast. **čiqs aẏpcnmi, kʷqs aẏpcnmi**
aẏpcnmíʔistm – They talked fast. **qeʔ aẏpcnmistm, p aẏpcnmistm**
es aẏpcnmi – They are talking fast. **qeʔes aẏpcnmi, pes aẏpcnmi**
qs aẏpcnmi – They are going to talk fast. **qeʔqs aẏpcnmi, pqs aẏpcnmi**

aẏaẏpuł – one that habitually goes fast.
aẏputm – S/he/it is able to go fast.

ha kʷ aẏip – Did you go fast? **aẏpstés łu ṗiṗuyšis –** S/he made his/her car go fast. **hoy qeʔes aẏpcnmi –** Boy, I am talking fast. *(my mouth is going fast)*

ƛ̓áx̣t – fast, rapid.
ƛ̓x̣etkʷ – water rapid. *suffix:* ***...etkʷ, ...tkʷ*** *– liquid*
sšimł ƛ̓áx̣t – fastest.
ƛ̓x̣tsqáx̣eʔ – fast horse.

wamistš – Go fast. *cmd. See:* ***hurry****.*

xʷau – sound of going fast; to go fast.
i xʷau – S/he/it went like the wind. **i čn xʷau, i kʷ xʷau**

fasten

ċánm – fastened; fixed in position; tight; immovable. *(i.e., lid on a jar; knot; stuck/locked door, etc.)*
ċnap – It got tight/fastened.
es ċnpma – It is tightening; it is becoming fastened.

ċán – tight; fixed in place; constricted; well fastened.

ċanmsts – S/he made s.t. well fastened. **ċanmstn, ċanmstxʷ**
es ċanms – S/he is making s.t. well fastened. **ies ċanm, as ċanm**
qs ċanms – S/he is going to make s.t. well fastened. **iqs ċanm, aqs ċanm**
ċáʔanmsts – They made s.t. well fastened. **ċanmstm, ċanmstp**

The **i** following uvular consonants (UC) and the glottal stop **ʔ** sound like English "*ey*" as in the words *they, hey, whey*, etc. Salish UC are: **q, q̇, qʷ, q̇ʷ, x̣, x̣ʷ**. For example, the suffix **...qin** – head/top, is often spelled using English *ey* as "q*ey*n". So **qi, q̇i, qʷi, q̇ʷi, x̣i, x̣ʷi**, may be spelled with English *ey* as **q***ey*, **q̇***ey*, **qʷ***ey*, **q̇ʷ***ey*, **x̣***ey*, **x̣ʷ***ey* in other texts.

s.t. - something, the 3rd person
(s.t.) - something implied
s.o. - someone, the 3rd person
sl. - singular form
pl. - plural form
rt. - root word
cmd. - command
lit. - literally
fig. - figuratively
i.e., - for example
See: - Redirection to a related word.

ċnpnuis – S/he succeeded in fastening s.t. **ċnpnun, ċnpnuntxʷ**
es ċnpnunms – S/he is succeeding in fastening s.t. **ies ċnpnunm, as ċnpnunm**
qs ċnpnunms – S/he is going to succeed in fastening s.t. **iqs ċnpnunm, aqs ċnpnunm**

ċnċant – firm; immovable; well fastened; tight.

ċánmskʷ – Fasten it; make it tight. *cmd.*
es ċánm – It is tight; it is well fastened.
es nċnmalsms – S/he/it is wanting to fasten s.t. **ies nċnmalsm, as nċnmalsm**
nċnċnmos – put s.t. tightly on the face. *(i.e., hands, etc.)*
k̓ʷłnċnmap – lock a door. *See:* ***lock.***
ċán – tight; fixed in place; constricted; well fastened. *See:* ***tight.***
es čłċnmaneʔ – It has s.t. fastened over it.

čx̣p̓a – neck button; top button. *rt.:* ***x̣p̓*** *– line, coat.*

k̓ʷłx̣p̓énč, *k̓ʷłx̣p̓é* – cinch.

fat

q̓ʷoct – fat.
q̓ʷoc – S/he got fat. **čn q̓ʷoc, kʷ q̓ʷoc**
es q̓ʷcmi – S/he is getting fat. **čnes q̓ʷcmi, kʷes q̓ʷcmi**

q̓ʷcntes – S/he fattened s.o. **q̓ʷcnten, q̓ʷcntexʷ**
es q̓ʷcims – S/he is fattening s.o. **ies q̓ʷcim, as q̓ʷcim**

es łq̓ʷq̓ʷcmi – S/he is getting a little fat. **čnes łq̓ʷq̓ʷcmi, kʷes łq̓ʷq̓ʷcmi**

sq̓ʷoct – grease; lard; oil.

q̓ʷciskʷ – Fattened him/her/it. *cmd.*
q̓ʷaq̓ʷoceʔ – fatty, affectionately.
q̓ʷcncut – fatten one's self.
nq̓ʷcels – feel/want like getting fat.

nṁéƛ̣ t sq̓ʷoct – S/he mixed the grease. **mus q̓ʷcq̓ʷoct nłmłámqeʔ** – four fat bears. **čmu q̓ʷcq̓ʷoct šméṅ** – four fat enemies.

čkʷtṅéẁs – It has a big belly.

fathead minnow

kʷkʷenčn – fathead minnow; *Pimephales promelas. (small warm water fish like a sunfish)*

father

lʔéw – father of a male. **leléw** – fathers. *pl. See:* ***section 3: Kinship terms.***
lʔéw – He is a father of a male. **čn lʔéw, kʷ lʔéw**

es k̓ʷl̓lʔéwi – He is acting as a father. **čn k̓ʷl̓lʔéwi, kʷ k̓ʷl̓lʔéwi**

méstṁ – father of a female.

tam we es itši łu inméstṁ – My father really was not sleeping.

sx̣ax̣éʔ – father-in-law.
łwésten – stepfather.
p̓x̣ʷot – godfather.
sck̓ʷl̓lʔew – foster father of male. *prefix:* ***sck̓ʷl̓...*** *– s.t. that's been made.*
sck̓ʷl̓méstṁ – foster father of female. *prefix:* ***sck̓ʷl̓...*** *– s.t. that's been made.*

father-in-law

sx̣ax̣éʔ – father-in-law. *See:* ***section 3: Kinship terms.***

faucet **snłx̣ʷetkʷtn** – faucet.

favorite **nččṁštin** – favorite place.
čṁmštin – favorite person *(s.o. that is depended on).*

čeṅ łu annččṁštin – Where is your favorite place?

sx̣mnčscut – favorite person. *rt.: **x̣menč** – like/love; suffix: **...cut** – action to the self.*
isx̣mnčscut – my favorite person.

sšẏmłx̣menč – favorite thing liked.
isšẏmłx̣menč p̓ip̓uyšn – my favorite car.

fawn **słpaˀpičqn,** *słpaˀpi* – little fawn.

spaˀpičqn, *spaˀpi* – fawn.

słqʷq̓ʷłte – fawn in fall; young deer after six months.

The **i** following uvular consonants (UC) and the glottal stop **ˀ** sound like English "*ey*" as in the words *they, hey, whey,* etc. Salish UC are: **q, q̓, qʷ, q̓ʷ, x̣, x̣ʷ**. For example, the suffix **...qin** – head/top, is often spelled using English *ey* as "*qeyn*". So **qi, q̓i, qʷi, q̓ʷi, x̣i, x̣ʷi,** may be spelled with English *ey* as **q***ey*, **q̓***ey*, **qʷ***ey*, **q̓ʷ***ey*, **x̣***ey*, **x̣ʷ***ey* in other texts.

fear **ẏaam** – fear; mistrust; in subjugation; not free with feelings. *rt.: **ẏaa** – scarce.*
ẏaam – S/he was in fear. **čn ẏaam, kʷ ẏaam**
es ẏaami – S/he is in fear. **čnes ẏaami, kʷes ẏaami**
qs ẏaami – S/he is going to be in fear. **čiqs ẏaami, kʷqs ẏaami**

čiẏaapleˀ – unapproachable; someone that imposes respect for fear, greatness, or stature. *rt.: **ẏaa** – scarce.*
es čiẏaapleˀ – S/he is a terror; is feared/respected. **čnes čiẏaapleˀ, kʷes čiẏaapleˀ**

čiẏaaplˀeis – S/he feareded to interact with s.o. **čiẏaaplˀen, čiẏaaplˀentxʷ**
es čiẏaaplˀems – S/he is fearing to interact with s.o. **ies čiẏaaplˀem, as čiẏaaplˀem**
qs čiẏaaplˀems – S/he is going to fear to interact with s.o. **iqs čiẏaaplˀem, aqs čiẏaaplˀem**

nẏaẏanus – look with fear/respect. *rt.: **ẏaa** – scarce.*
nẏaẏanusis – S/he looked at s.o./s.t. with fear/respect. **nẏaẏanusn, nẏaẏanusntxʷ**
es nẏaẏanusms – S/he is looking at s.o./s.t. with fear/respect. **es nẏaẏanusm, es nẏaẏanusm**

niẏaaneˀ – no care to listen to someone for fear/respect to hear the person or what is said. *rt.: **ẏaa** – scarce.*
niẏaanˀeis – S/he did not care to hear s.o. **niẏaanˀen, niẏaanˀentxʷ**
es niẏaanˀems – S/he does not care to hear s.o. **čnes niẏaanˀem, kʷes niẏaanˀem**

nx̣él – afraid/scared of something. *See: **scared.***

kʷˀeł – jumpy; nervous; edgy; frantic. *See: **nervous.***

kʷssusm, *kʷssu* – startle. *See: **startle.***

čin – afraid of getting hurt; careful and cautious. *(i.e., falling, etc.) See: **afraid.***

feast **skʷtisyamncut** – big gathering.

skʷtisntox̣qin – big lunch.

skʷtisčluxʷ – big dinner.

feather **sqpuseł,** *sqpu* – feather; wing.
sqpusełs kʷtisi – Big Blanket's feather.

kʷilkʷesčéyp – Red-Feather, a chief of the Salish.

čqʷlpelxʷ, *čqʷlpe* – feather plume.

s.t. - something, the 3rd person
(s.t.) - something implied
s.o. - someone, the 3rd person
sl. - singular form
pl. - plural form
rt. - root word
cmd. - command
lit. - literally
fig. - figuratively
i.e., - for example
See: - Redirection to a related word.

nčepmn – down; down filling. *rt.: **čep** – soft; prefix: **n...** – inside; suffix: **...min, ...mn** – instrument/tool.*

February **čqʷósqn spq̓niʔ** – February *(month of the cold; curled on top).*

feed **eṁtm** – feed.

eṁtm – S/he fed. **čn eṁtm, kʷ eṁtm**
es eṁti – S/he is feeding. **čnes eṁti, kʷes eṁti**
qs eṁti – S/he is going to feed. **čiqs eṁti, kʷqs eṁti**
éʔeṁtm – They fed. **qeʔ eṁtm, p eṁtm**
es éʔeṁti – They are feeding. **qeʔes eṁti, pes eṁti**
qs éʔeṁti – They are going to feed. **qeʔqs eṁti, pqs eṁti**

eṁsts – S/he fed s.o. **eṁstn, eṁstxʷ**
es eṁtms – S/he/it is feeding s.o. **ies eṁtm, as eṁtm**
qs eṁtms – S/he/it is going to feed s.o. **iqs eṁtm, aqs eṁtm**
éʔeṁsts – They fed s.o. **qeʔ eṁstm, eṁstp**
es éʔeṁtms – They are feeding s.o. **qeʔes eṁtm, es eṁtmp**
qs éʔeṁtms – They are going to feed s.o. **qeʔqs eṁtm, qs eṁtmp**

es eṁeṁti – S/he is feeding and feeding. **čnes eṁeṁti, kʷes eṁeṁti**
es eṁeṁtms – S/he/it is feeding and feeding s.o. **ies eṁeṁtm, as eṁeṁtm**
eṁtmnt – Feed him/her/it. *cmd.*

eṁstm – S/he was fed. **eṁtmncn** – I fed you. **emtmncs** – S/he fed you. **qeʔ eṁtmłst** – You fed us.

čk̓ʷink̓ʷnš es éṁstxʷ – How many are you feeding? **čk̓ʷink̓ʷnš łu as eṁtm** – How many are you feeding? **qs eṁtms łu sccmeľt** – S/he is going to feed the children.

eṁinšm – feed animals.

eṁinšm – S/he fed. **čn eṁinšm, kʷ eṁinšm**
es eṁinši – S/he is feeding. **čnes eṁinši, kʷes eṁinši**
qs eṁinši – S/he is going to feed. **čiqs eṁinši, kʷqs eṁinši**
eṁíʔinšm – They fed. **qeʔ eṁinšm, p eṁinšm**
es eṁíʔinši – They are feeding. **qeʔes eṁinši, pes eṁinši**
qs eṁíʔinši – They are going to feed. **qeʔqs eṁinši, pqs eṁinši**

eṁinšis – S/he fed it. **eṁinšn, eṁinšntxʷ**
es eṁinšms – S/he is feeding it. **ies eṁinšm, as eṁinšm**
qs eṁinšms – S/he is going to feed it. **iqs eṁinšm, aqs eṁinšm**
eṁíʔinšis – They fed it. **qeʔ eṁinšntm, p eṁinšntp**
es eṁíʔinšms – They are feeding it. **qeʔes eṁinšm, es eṁinšmp**
qs eṁíʔinšms – They are going to feed it. **qeʔqs eṁinšm, qs eṁinšmp**

sxʷeṁinšm – one tasked to feed animals. *prefix: **sxʷ...** – one tasked to do.*

eṁinšnt – Feed the animals. *cmd.*

ies eṁinšm t supulexʷ – I am feeding the animals hay.

aṁisqáx̣eʔ, *aṁisqá* – feed horses/domestic animals. *suffix: **...sqax̣eʔ, ...sqa** – domestic animal; mainly referring to horse or car.*

aṁisqáx̣eʔ – S/he fed. **čn aṁisqáx̣eʔ, kʷ aṁisqáx̣eʔ**
es aṁisqáx̣eʔi – S/he is feeding. **čnes aṁisqáx̣eʔi, kʷes aṁisqáx̣eʔi**
qs aṁisqáx̣eʔi – S/he is going to feed. **čiqs aṁisqáx̣eʔi, kʷqs aṁisqáx̣eʔi**
aṁisqáʔax̣eʔ – They fed. **qeʔ aṁisqáx̣eʔ, p aṁisqáx̣eʔ**

es aṁisqáʔax̣eʔi – They are feeding. **qeʔes aṁisqáx̣eʔi, pes aṁisqáx̣eʔi**
qs aṁisqáʔax̣eʔi – They are going to feed. **qeʔqs aṁisqáx̣eʔi, pqs aṁisqáx̣eʔi**

sxʷʔaṁisqáx̣eʔ – one tasked to feed horses/domestic animals. *prefix: **sxʷ...** – one tasked to do.*

qʔeméľt – breastfeed; nurse. *See: **breastfeed**.*

The **i** following uvular consonants (UC) and the glottal stop **ʔ** sound like English "*ey*" as in the words th*ey*, h*ey*, wh*ey*, etc. Salish UC are: **q**, **q̇**, **qʷ**, **q̇ʷ**, **x̣**, **x̣ʷ**. For example, the suffix ...**qin** – head/top, is often spelled using English *ey* as "q*ey*n". So **qi**, **q̇i**, **qʷi**, **q̇ʷi**, **x̣i**, **x̣ʷi**, may be spelled with English *ey* as **q***ey*, **q̇***ey*, **qʷ***ey*, **q̇ʷ***ey*, **x̣***ey*, **x̣ʷ***ey* in other texts.

feel

enwenm – feel/sense.
enwéis – S/he sensed s.t. **enwén, enwéntxʷ**

snʔenwncut – feelings.
scʔenwn – something that's been sensed/felt.

es enwncuti – She is feeling/sensing of one's self; starting labor.

enwnm t es xʷťilši – I am aware of something getting up. **t čeṅ eċx̣lsʔenenwn** – How does it feel? **tmłʔenwen** – have no feeling. **steṁ łu enenwis** – What does it feel like? **steṁ łu enuncuts** – What does it feel like?

neč̓nunm – feel a presence.
neč̓nuis – S/he felt a presence. **neč̓nun, neč̓nuntxʷ**
es neč̓nunms – S/he is feeling a presence. **ies neč̓nunm, as neč̓nunm**

neneč̓nemn – one inclined to feel presences. *suffix: **...emn** – one inclined to do.*

čn xʷist l ċlċil i čim kʷemt u neč̓nun tʔe steṁ – I walked in the woods. It was dark. Then I felt a presence.

nneč̓cinm – feel a voice/presence. *suffix: **...cin, ...cn** – action of the mouth.*

čṅuxʷ – touch; perceive by the sense of touch; come in contact physically or spiritually with some part of the body. *See: **touch**.*

tec – touch; the position of touch; to have the finger/hand on something. *See: **touch**.*

feelings

snʔenwncut – feelings.

n...éls – *circumfix indicating want, need, feelings.*
čupélsm, *čupé* – lonesome; miss someone. *See: **lonesome**.*
npiyéls, *npiyé* – feel happy. *See: **happy**.*
nixʷpels – have hurt feelings; profound sadness. *See: **hurt feelings**.*
nʔayml̓s – have bad feelings; have inner anger. *See: **detest**.*
nx̣mnčsels – feel loved/liked. *See: **love**.*
nx̣sels – pleased; have good feelings. *See: **pleased**.*
nx̣smslscut – feel good within one's self. *See: **good**.*
ntmmels – feelings crumbled. *See: **crumble**.*

nčtxʷsels – add feelings. *circumfix: **n...els** – want, feel.*
nčtxʷsels – S/he added feelings. **čn nčtxʷsels, kʷ nčtxʷsels**
es nčtxʷselsi – S/he is adding feelings. **čnes nčtxʷselsi, kʷes nčtxʷselsi**
qs nčtxʷselsi – S/he is going to add feelings. **čiqs nčtxʷselsi, kʷqs nčtxʷselsi**

čn šƛ̓paqs u čn nčtxʷsels tľ ciʔ u čnes npiyélsi – I won and I added to my happy feelings.

s.t. - something, the 3rd person
(s.t.) - something implied
s.o. - someone, the 3rd person
sl. - singular form
pl. - plural form
rt. - root word
cmd. - command
lit. - literally
fig. - figuratively
i.e., - for example
See: - Redirection to a related word.

feet

sċuċušin – feet.

łkʷeykʷnumešn – little feet.

łkʷkʷnumešn – little foot.

ččňčňšnim – Grab/hold someone by the feet. *See: **grasp**.*

Felicite **plisiti** – Felicite.

fellow **snkʷɫ...** – *prefix indicating the one/thing something is done/being together with. The ɫ is lost when preceding an s. See: **with**.*
snkʷsqelixʷ – fellow people; fellow human being.
snk̓ʷélixʷ – fellow people.
snkʷsqltmixʷ – fellow man.
snkʷsmʔem – fellow woman.
snkʷsixʷ – sibling; brother, sister, cousin. *lit. fellow offspring.*

felt **enwenm** – feel/sense. *See: **feel**.*

tec – touch; the position of touch; to have the finger/hand on something. *See: **touch**.*

female **smʔém** – woman, girl; female. *See: **woman**.*

šéšutm – girl up to age of puberty.

pełpłk̓ʷi – women folk.

sṁumšn, *sṁu* – female animal. **sṁmumšn** *pl.*
słṁumšn, *słṁu* – little female animal.

fence **sk̓ʷɫʔox̣ʷ** – fence; field fence. *rt.: **ox̣ʷm** – string out.*
es k̓ʷɫʔox̣ʷ – It is fenced in.
k̓ʷɫʔox̣ʷmíntn – fencing material; fence. *suffix: **...tin, ...tn** – means of/device.*

k̓ʷɫɫʔox̣ʷsqáx̣eʔ – construct a fence for domestic animals.
k̓ʷɫɫʔox̣ʷsqáx̣eʔ – S/he made a fence. **čn k̓ʷɫɫʔox̣ʷsqáx̣eʔ, kʷ k̓ʷɫɫʔox̣ʷsqáx̣eʔ**
es k̓ʷɫɫʔox̣ʷsqáx̣eʔi – S/he is making a fence. **čnes k̓ʷɫɫʔox̣ʷsqáx̣eʔi, kʷes k̓ʷɫɫʔox̣ʷsqáx̣eʔi**
qs k̓ʷɫɫʔox̣ʷsqáx̣eʔi – S/he is going to make a fence. **čiqs k̓ʷɫɫʔox̣ʷsqáx̣eʔi, kʷqs k̓ʷɫɫʔox̣ʷsqáx̣eʔi**

ox̣ʷm – string something out; say someone is skinny, stretched, or boney. *(i.e., fencing, rope, hose, etc.) See: **string**.*

fern **ṫx̣ṫx̣éłp** – fern; lady fern; *Pteridium aquilinum.*

ferruginous hawk **kʷlkʷlši ċlċlšmu** – ferruginous hawk; *Buteo regalis.*

ferry **niʔék̓ʷ** – cross water. *See: **cross**.*

fetch **ċwét** – fetch something out of sight.
ċwetm – S/he fetched. **čn ċwetm, kʷ ċwetm**
es ċweti – S/he is fetching. **čnes ċweti, kʷes ċweti**
qs ċweti – S/he is going to fetch. **čiqs ċweti, kʷqs ċweti**
ċwéʔetm – They fetched. **qeʔ ċwetm, p ċwetm**
es ċwéʔeti – They are fetching. **qeʔes ċweti, pes ċweti**
qs ċwéʔeti – They are going to fetch. **qeʔqs ċweti, pqs ċweti**

ċwetis – S/he fetched s.t. **ċwetn, ċwetntxʷ**
es ċwetms – S/he is fetching s.t. **ies ċwetm, as ċwetm**
qs ċwetms – S/he is going to fetch s.t. **iqs ċwetm, aqs ċwetm**
ċwéʔetis – They fetched s.t. **qeʔ ċwetntm, ċwetntp**
es ċwéʔetms – They are fetching s.t. **qeʔes ċwetm, es ċwetmp**
qs ċwéʔetms – They are going to fetch s.t. **qeʔqs ċwetm, qs ċwetmp**

ċwetš – Go fetch (s.t.). *cmd.*
ċwetnt – Go get s.t. *cmd.*

ha kʷ ṅe u kʷ ċwétm t sʔiłn – Would you go get some food? **ċwétiš t sʔiłn –** Get some food. **čnes ċweti t ululim –** I am going after money. **ies ċwetm łu ululim –** I am going after money. **qʷo ċwetiš nt̓išk̓ʷ –** Get me a pop. **xʷuyš ċwetnt –** Go and get it. **ċwetiš t mlmé –** Go get a toy. **qʷo ċwetłt –** Go get it for me. **ċwetnt anmlmé –** Get your toy. **tl̓ čen u ċwétntxʷ asiċm –** Where did you fetch your blanket from. **ha kʷṅe u qʷo ċwétštxʷ sʔiłn –** Would you go get some food for me? **steṁ as ċwetm –** What are you getting?

The **i** following uvular consonants (UC) and the glottal stop **ʔ** sound like English "*ey*" as in the words *they, hey, whey*, etc. Salish UC are: **q, q̓, qʷ, q̓ʷ, x̣, x̣ʷ**. For example, the suffix ...**qin** – head/top, is often spelled using English *ey* as "*qeyn*". So **qi, q̓i, qʷi, q̓ʷi, x̣i, x̣ʷi**, may be spelled with English *ey* as **q***ey*, **q̓***ey*, **qʷ***ey*, **q̓ʷ***ey*, **x̣***ey*, **x̣ʷ***ey* in other texts.

ċutsqáx̣eʔ, *ċutsqá* **–** fetch domestic animals, horses. *rt.: **ċwet** – fetch; suffix: **...sqax̣eʔ, ...sqa** – domestic animal; generally horse or car.*
ċutsqáx̣eʔ – S/he/it fetched. **čn ċutsqáx̣eʔ, kʷ ċutsqáx̣eʔ**
es ċutsqáx̣eʔi – S/he/it is fetching. **čnes ċutsqáx̣eʔi, kʷes ċutsqáx̣eʔi**
qs ċutsqáx̣eʔi – S/he/it is going to fetch. **čiqs ċutsqáx̣eʔi, kʷqs ċutsqáx̣eʔi**
ċutsqáʔáx̣eʔ – They fetched. **qeʔ ċutsqáx̣eʔ, p ċutsqáx̣eʔ**
es ċutsqáʔáx̣eʔi – They are fetching. **qeʔes ċutsqáx̣eʔi, pes ċutsqáx̣eʔi**
qs ċutsqáʔáx̣eʔi – They are going to fetch. **qeʔqs ċutsqáx̣eʔi, pqs ċutsqáx̣eʔi**

ckʷnem – fetch something that is within the immediate area; *lit. to go take something and bring it back here. rt.: **kʷen** – take; prefix: **c...** – indicating toward the speaker.*
ckʷéis – S/he/it fetched s.t. **ckʷén, ckʷéntxʷ**
es ckʷnems – S/he/it is fetching s.t. **ies ckʷnem, as ckʷnem**
qs ckʷnems – S/he/it is going to fetch s.t. **iqs ckʷnem, aqs ckʷnem**
ckʷéʔeis – They brought s.t. here. **qeʔ ckʷéntm, ckʷéntp**
es ckʷnéʔems – They are fetching s.t. **qeʔes ckʷnem, es ckʷnemp**
qs ckʷnéʔems – They are going to fetch s.t. **qeʔqs ckʷnem, qs ckʷnemp**

ckʷišts – S/he got it for s.o. **ckʷištn, ckʷištxʷ**

ckʷent – Bring it here; hand it to me. *cmd.*
qeʔ ckʷešłt – Get it for us. *cmd.*

eł ckʷént – Bring it back here. **qʷo ckʷełt ink̓ʷłnčexʷk̓ʷé –** Fetch my keys for me. **iqs ckʷnem ci snsustn –** I am going to go get the cup and bring it here. **t atwen u ckʷéis –** Tony got it. **itam łu ckʷen –** I got the wrong one. **nexʷ qʷo ckʷešt –** Get one for me too.

cq̓ʷom – gather and bring things here. *(the plural form of **ckʷnem**) See: **gather**.*

nmulm – fetch water/liquid *(from the sound made dipping a container in water; used to indicate the motion getting water). rt.: **mul** – remove from water/liquid.*
nmulm – S/he got water. **čn nmulm, kʷ nmulm**
es nmuli – S/he is getting water. **čnes nmuli, kʷes nmuli**
qs nmuli – S/he is going to get water. **čiqs nmuli, kʷqs nmuli**
nmúʔulm – They got water. **qeʔ nmulm, p nmulm**
es nmúʔuli – They are getting water. **qeʔes nmuli, pes nmuli**

nmulis – S/he put water in s.t. **nmuln, nmulntxʷ**
es nmulms – S/he is putting water in s.t. **ies nmulm, as nmulm**
qs nmulms – S/he is going to put water in s.t. **iqs nmulm, aqs nmulm**

nmulmis – S/he used s.t. to get water. **nmulmn, nmulmtxʷn**
es nmulmms – S/he is using s.t. to get water. **ies nmulmm, as nmulmm**
qs nmulmms – S/he is going to use s.t. to get water. **iqs nmulmm, aqs nmulmm**

ƛ̓mulmn – container to get water.

s.t. - something, the 3rd person
(s.t.) - something implied
s.o. - someone, the 3rd person
sl. - singular form
pl. - plural form
rt. - root word
cmd. - command
lit. - literally
fig. - figuratively
i.e., - for example
See: - Redirection to a related word.

nmuliš – Get water. *cmd.*
nmulnt – Put the water/liquid in that. *cmd.*

k̓ʷłmulm – dip/scoop out water. *See: **dip**.*

nmuliš, alyé – Go get water, Harriet!

q̓eyẇ – get/fetch fish from a trap/barrier.
q̓eyẇm – S/he got fish from a trap/barrier. **čn q̓eyẇm, kʷ q̓eyẇm**
es q̓eyẇi – S/he is getting fish from a trap/barrier. **čnes q̓eyẇi, kʷes q̓eyẇi**
qs q̓eyẇi – S/he is going to get fish from a trap/barrier. **čiqs q̓eyẇi, kʷqs q̓eyẇi**
sxʷq̓eyẇm – one tasked to get fish from a trap/barrier.

q̓eyẇiš – Get fish from a trap/barrier. *cmd.*

čł..., č... – *prefix to indicate that something is gone after.*
es čłsšeṅši – S/he is going after rocks.
es čsnqʷl̓pú – S/he is going after bread.

čłʔululim – go after money. *See: **money**.*
čsnqʷl̓pú – go after bread. *See: **bread**.*
čłuk̓ʷ – go after wood. *See: **wood**.*

čsteṁ – What did s/he go after? **čn čsteṁ, kʷ čsteṁ**
es čsteṁi – What is s/he going after? **čnes čsteṁi, kʷes čsteṁi**
qs čsteṁi – What is s/he going to go after? **čiqs čsteṁi, kʷqs čsteṁi**

kʷlkʷlscut – repeatedly goes and fetches things.
es kʷlkʷlscuti – S/he keeps going and fetching things. **čnes kʷlkʷlscuti, kʷes kʷlkʷlscuti**

few

ƛ̓méẏ – few, barely, not much.
čmi u ƛ̓meẏ t splqe u kʷ iłn – Only a little bit of sausage you ate.

łłuẇet, *łłu* **–** few, less, little bit.
es łuẇetilši – They are becoming thin/few. **qeʔes łuẇetilši, pes łuẇetilši** *suffix: **...ilš** – autonomous.*

łuẇetilšsts – S/he made them become thin/few. **łuẇetilšstn, łuẇetilšstxʷ**
es łuẇetilšms – S/he is making them become thin/few. **ies łuẇetilšm, as łuẇetilšm**

čłuẇet – few people.
łuẇasq̓t – few days.
łuẇasq̓tilš – the days get fewer. *suffix: **...ilš** – autonomous.*
łutilš – thin; become few; weed. *See: **thin**.*

čmi u łłuẇet – only a little bit.

łk̓ʷik̓ʷnš – few in number. *rt.: **k̓ʷinš** – how many.*
l nk̓ʷuʔ łk̓ʷik̓ʷnš łu es wičstxʷ – In this one place you see a few.

fiddle

čx̣ʷaq̓ʷnčstn – fiddle; cello; bowed string instrument.

field

sṫulixʷ – ground; earth; land; field.

čiqs xʷilwisi x̣ʷl̓ isck̓ʷul̓ – I am going to be in the field (for work); I going to travel around for my work.

fierce

nkʷk̓ʷeʔcin – growl; fierce growl; biting voice.

nłomcn – fierce sounding; fierce voice; scolding voice.

tam cqq̇ʷotm – fierce looking.

nx̣llutm – scary. *rt.: **nx̣el** – afraid.*

fifty

clčɫʔupn, *clčɫʔu* – fifty.

fight

tiyáqʷt, *tiyá* – fight.

tiyáqʷt – S/he fought. **čn tiyáqʷt, kʷ tiyáqʷt**
es tiyáqʷti – S/he/it is fighting. **čnes tiyáqʷti, kʷes tiyáqʷti**
qs tiyáqʷti – S/he/it is going to fight. **čiqs tiyáqʷti, kʷqs tiyáqʷti**
tiyáʔaqʷt – They fought. **qeʔ tiyáqʷt, p tiyáqʷt**
es tiyáʔaqʷti – They are fighting. **qeʔes tiyáqʷti, pes tiyáqʷti**
qs tiyáʔaqʷti – They are going to fight. **qeʔqs tiyáqʷti, pqs tiyáqʷti**

tiyáqʷis – S/he/it fought s.o./s.t. **tiyáqʷn, tiyáqʷntxʷ**
es tiyáqʷms – S/he/it is fighting s.o./s.t. **ies tiyáqʷm, as tiyáqʷm**
qs tiyáqʷms – S/he/it is going to fight s.o./s.t. **iqs tiyáqʷm, aqs tiyáqʷm**
tiyáʔaqʷis – They fought s.o./s.t. **qeʔ tiyáqʷntm, tiyáqʷntp**
es tiyáʔaqʷms – They are fighting s.o./s.t. **qeʔes tiyáqʷm, es tiyáqʷmp**
qs tiyáʔaqʷms – They are going to fight s.o./s.t. **qeʔqs tiyáqʷm, qs tiyáqʷmp**

es titiẏáqʷti – S/he/it is fighting over and over. **čnes titiẏáqʷti, kʷes titiẏáqʷti**
es titiẏáqʷms – S/he/it is fighting s.o. over and over. **ies titiẏáqʷm, as titiẏáqʷm**

sxʷtiyáqʷt – one tasked to fight. *prefix: **sxʷ...** – one tasked to do.*
tiqʷtemn – one inclined to fight. *suffix: **...emn** – one inclined to do.*

tiyáqʷlš – Fight. *cmd.*
tiyáqʷnt – Fight s.o. *cmd.*
nkʷɫtiyaqʷis – S/he/it fought with s.o./s.t. *prefix: **nkʷɫ...** – together with.*
es nkʷɫtiyaqʷti – S/he/it is fighting together with (s.o./s.t.). *prefix: **nkʷɫ...** – together with.*
es tiqʷtncuti – S/he/it is fighting one's self. **čnes tiqʷtncuti, kʷes tiqʷtncuti**

tiqʷšitxʷ – You fought for s.o.

wičtn esél smx̣é es titiẏáqʷti – I saw two grizzly bears fighting. **es titiẏáqʷti ɫu innqʷiq̇ʷsṁi** – My dogs are fighting.

ƛ̓áq̇ʷ – verbally or physically fight one's spouse.
ƛ̓áq̇ʷm – S/he fought one's spouse. **čn ƛ̓áq̇ʷm, kʷ ƛ̓áq̇ʷm**
es ƛ̓áq̇ʷi – S/he is fighting one's spouse. **čnes ƛ̓áq̇ʷi, kʷes ƛ̓áq̇ʷi**
qs ƛ̓áq̇ʷi – S/he is going to fight one's spouse. **čiqs ƛ̓áq̇ʷi, kʷqs ƛ̓áq̇ʷi**

ƛ̓aq̇ʷis – S/he fought his/her spouse. **ƛ̓aq̇ʷn, ƛ̓aq̇ʷntxʷ**
es ƛ̓aq̇ʷms – S/he is fighting his/her spouse. **ies ƛ̓aq̇ʷm, as ƛ̓aq̇ʷm**
qs ƛ̓aq̇ʷms – S/he is going to fight his/her spouse. **iqs ƛ̓aq̇ʷm, aqs ƛ̓aq̇ʷm**

sxʷƛ̓áq̇ʷm – one tasked to fight their spouse. *prefix: **sxʷ...** – one tasked to do.*
ƛ̓aq̇ʷemn – one inclined to fight their spouse. *suffix: **...emn** – one inclined to do.*

čiqs ƛ̓aq̇ʷi l innox̣ʷnx̣ʷ – I going to fight my wife. **kʷqs ƛ̓aq̇ʷi l asx̣elwi** – You are going to fight your husband. **kʷ sxʷƛ̓áq̇ʷm** – You are a wife-beater.

čscnmnwéxʷist, *čscnmnwé* – quarrel; say bad words to each other. *See: **quarrel.***

čxʷṫpminm – an individual charges toward; run toward; attack; rush to; an individual runs toward. *See: **charge.***

The **i** following uvular consonants (UC) and the glottal stop **ʔ** sound like English "*ey*" as in the words th*ey*, h*ey*, wh*ey*, etc. Salish UC are: **q, q̇, qʷ, q̇ʷ, x̣, x̣ʷ**. For example, the suffix ...**qin** – head/top, is often spelled using English *ey* as "q*ey*n". So **qi, q̇i, qʷi, q̇ʷi, x̣i, x̣ʷi**, may be spelled with English *ey* as **q***ey*, **q̇***ey*, **qʷ***ey*, **q̇ʷ***ey*, **x̣***ey*, **x̣ʷ***ey* in other texts.

s.t. - something, the 3rd person
(s.t.) - something implied
s.o. - someone, the 3rd person
sl. - singular form
pl. - plural form
rt. - root word
cmd. - command
lit. - literally
fig. - figuratively
i.e., - for example
See: - Redirection to a related word.

mľk̇ʷstwexʷ, *mľk̇ʷstwe* – all over each other. *rt.: **milk̇ʷ** – complete; suffix: **...wexʷ** – action to each other.*
mľk̇ʷstwéʔexʷ – They were all over each other. **qeʔ mľk̇ʷstwexʷ, p mľk̇ʷstwexʷ**
es mľk̇ʷstwéʔexʷi – They are all over each other. **qeʔes mľk̇ʷstwexʷi, pes mľk̇ʷstwexʷi**
qs mľk̇ʷstwéʔexʷi – They are going to be all over each other. **qeʔqs mľk̇ʷstwexʷi, pqs mľk̇ʷstwexʷi**

pɫstwaxʷ – punching each other out.
es pɫstwaxʷi – punching

fighter
sxʷtiyáqʷt – one tasked to fight. *prefix: **sxʷ...** – one tasked to do.*
tiqʷtemn – one inclined to fight. *suffix: **...emn** – one inclined to do.*

figure out
mipnunm – figure out something; find out about something; complete an understanding; succeed in understanding; learn of something. *See: **learn**.*

siľ – confused; unable to figure something out; mistaken. *See: **confuse**.*

file
x̣ʷaq̇ʷmn – file. *suffix: **...min, ...mn** – instrument/tool.*

x̣ʷáq̇ʷm – grind/file something. *See: **grind**.*

ččnpiċeʔ – enfold something; put something in a file. *See: **enfold**.*

file cabinet
snʔelk̇ʷmn l q̇eẏmin – place to store paper.

filing drawer
snʔelk̇ʷmn l q̇eẏmin – place to store paper.

fill
q̇ʷéċ – filled to the top. *See: **full**.*

filly
sɫṁumšn, *sɫṁu* – little female animal; filly. *See: **female**.*

finally
ax̣í – indicates finality.
ax̣í u xʷk̇ʷpnun – I finally got it clean.
ax̣í u ax̣ʷnun – I finally got it scraped.
ax̣í u čċslxʷnun – I finally got him/her naked.

qʷoṁmaɫq, *qʷoṁma* – get close to doing/finishing something; getting near to some point; close to the end of a journey; winning. *See: **close**.*

fine
x̣est – good.
čn x̣es – I am well.

put – just, exactly, even, enough; right then. *See: **just**.*

find
wič – see; find; perceive; come into view. *See: **see**.*

ƛ̓éʔem – look for; search; find. *See: **search**.*

finger
sťix̣čst – finger. **sťx̣ťix̣čst** – fingers. *pl. rt.: **ťix̣** – protrude; suffix: **...ečst, ...čst** – of the hand.*

sťumčst – thumb. *rt.: **ťum** – lightly suck. See: **suck**.*

syulčst – middle finger; thumb; thick finger. *rt.: **yult** – thick in girth. See: **girth**.*

sq̇aẇqinčst – ring finger. *suffix: **...qinčst** – finger.* **sqq̇aẇqinčst** – ring fingers. *pl.*

sťaẇqinčst – little finger. *suffix: **...qinčst** – finger.* **stťaẇqinčst** – little fingers. *pl.*

ċoq̇ʷmn – pointer finger. **ċq̇ʷċoq̇ʷmn** *pl. rt.: **ċoq̇ʷ** – point; suffix: **...min, ...mn** – instrument/tool.*

čṅxʷqnečstmn, *čṅxʷqne* – finger tip.

sčmqinčst – middle knuckle.

sčmusečst – top knuckle.

ususqnečst – long fingers. *suffix:* ***...qinčst–*** *finger.*

malkʷečst – disjointed/dislocated finger. *suffix:* ***...ečst, ...čst–*** *of the hand.*
es malkʷečst – His/her finger is disjointed/dislocated. **čnes malkʷečst, kʷes malkʷečst**

malkʷečsis – S/he/it disjointed/dislocated s.o.'s finger. **malkʷečsn, malkʷečsntxʷ**
es malkʷečsms – S/he/it is disjointing/dislocating s.o.'s finger. **ies malkʷečsm, as malkʷečsm**
qs malkʷečsms – S/he/it is going to disjoint/dislocate s.o.'s finger. **iqs malkʷečsm, aqs malkʷečsm**

nločstetkʷ – put/dip finger in water/liquid. *See:* ***dip.***

The **i** following uvular consonants (UC) and the glottal stop ʔ sound like English "*ey*" as in the words th*ey*, h*ey*, wh*ey*, etc. Salish UC are: **q, q̇, qʷ, q̇ʷ, x̣, x̣ʷ**. For example, the suffix **...qin** – head/top, is often spelled using English *ey* as "q*ey*n". So **qi, q̇i, qʷi, q̇ʷi, x̣i, x̣ʷi**, may be spelled with English *ey* as **q***ey*, **q̇***ey*, **qʷ***ey*, **q̇ʷ***ey*, **x̣***ey*, **x̣ʷ***ey* in other texts.

fingernail

q̇ʷx̣ʷqinčst, ***q̇ʷx̣ʷqi*** **–** fingernail. **q̇ʷx̣ʷq̇ʷx̣ʷqinčst** *pl. suffix:* ***...qinčst–*** *finger.*

usušnqnečst – long fingernails. *suffix:* ***...qinčst–*** *finger.*
es usušnqnečst – S/he has long fingernails. **čnes usušnqnečst, kʷes usušnqnečst**

čxʷtxʷtqnečst – cut fingernails. *suffix:* ***...qinčst–*** *finger.*
čxʷtxʷtqnečstm – S/he cut fingernails. **čn čxʷtxʷtqnečstm, kʷ čxʷtxʷtqnečstm**
es čxʷtxʷtqnečsti – S/he is cutting fingernails. **čnes čxʷtxʷtqnečsti, kʷes čxʷtxʷtqnečsti**
qs čxʷtxʷtqnečsti – S/he is going to cut fingernails. **čiqs čxʷtxʷtqnečsti, kʷqs čxʷtxʷtqnečsti**

čxʷtxʷtqnečstis – S/he cut s.o.'s fingernails. **čxʷtxʷtqnečstn, čxʷtxʷtqnečstntxʷ**
es čxʷtxʷtqnečstms – S/he is cutting s.o.'s fingernails. **ies čxʷtxʷtqnečstm, as čxʷtxʷtqnečstm**
qs čxʷtxʷtqnečstms – S/he is going to cut s.o.'s fingernails. **čiqs čxʷtxʷtqnečstm, kʷqs čxʷtxʷtqnečstm**

es čxʷtxʷtqnečst – His/her fingernails are cut. **čnes čxʷtxʷtqnečst, kʷes čxʷtxʷtqnečst**

sčxʷtxʷtqnečstn – fingernail cutter.
čxʷtxʷtqnečstiš – Cut fingernails. *cmd.*
čxʷtxʷtqnečsnt – Cut s.o.'s fingernails. *cmd.*

čx̣ƛ̓x̣ƛ̓qnečst – chew fingernails. *suffix:* ***...qinčst–*** *finger.*
čx̣ƛ̓x̣ƛ̓qnečstm – S/he chewed fingernails. **čn čx̣ƛ̓x̣ƛ̓qnečstm, kʷ čx̣ƛ̓x̣ƛ̓qnečstm**
es čx̣ƛ̓x̣ƛ̓qnečsti – S/he is chewing fingernails. **čnes čx̣ƛ̓x̣ƛ̓qnečsti, kʷes čx̣ƛ̓x̣ƛ̓qnečsti**
qs čx̣ƛ̓x̣ƛ̓qnečsti – S/he is going to chew fingernails. **čiqs čx̣ƛ̓x̣ƛ̓qnečsti, kʷqs čx̣ƛ̓x̣ƛ̓qnečsti**

čx̣ƛ̓x̣ƛ̓qnečstis – S/he chewed s.o.'s fingernails. **čx̣ƛ̓x̣ƛ̓qnečstn, čx̣ƛ̓x̣ƛ̓qnečstntxʷ**
es čx̣ƛ̓x̣ƛ̓qnečstms – S/he is chewing s.o.'s fingernails. **ies čx̣ƛ̓x̣ƛ̓qnečstm, as čx̣ƛ̓x̣ƛ̓qnečstm**
qs čx̣ƛ̓x̣ƛ̓qnečstms – S/he is going to chew s.o.'s fingernails. **čiqs čx̣ƛ̓x̣ƛ̓qnečstm, kʷqs čx̣ƛ̓x̣ƛ̓qnečstm**

es čx̣ƛ̓x̣ƛ̓qnečst – His/her fingernails are chewed. **čnes čx̣ƛ̓x̣ƛ̓qnečst, kʷes čx̣ƛ̓x̣ƛ̓qnečst**

čx̣ƛ̓x̣ƛ̓qnečstiš – Chew fingernails. *cmd.*
čx̣ƛ̓x̣ƛ̓qnečsnt – Chew s.o.'s fingernails. *cmd.*

k̇ʷɫxʷk̇ʷxʷk̇ʷqin – clean fingernails. *suffix:* ***...qin, ...qn–*** *top.*

s.t. - something, the 3rd person
(s.t.) - something implied
s.o. - someone, the 3rd person
sl. - singular form
pl. - plural form
rt. - root word
cmd. - command
lit. - literally
fig. - figuratively
i.e., - for example
See: - Redirection to a related word.

k̓ʷɬxʷk̓ʷxʷk̓ʷqinm – S/he cleaned fingernails. **čn k̓ʷɬxʷk̓ʷxʷk̓ʷqinm, kʷ k̓ʷɬxʷk̓ʷxʷk̓ʷqinm**
es k̓ʷɬxʷk̓ʷxʷk̓ʷqini – S/he is cleaning fingernails. **čnes k̓ʷɬxʷk̓ʷxʷk̓ʷqini, kʷes k̓ʷɬxʷk̓ʷxʷk̓ʷqini**
qs k̓ʷɬxʷk̓ʷxʷk̓ʷqini – S/he is going to clean fingernails. **čiqs k̓ʷɬxʷk̓ʷxʷk̓ʷqini, kʷqs k̓ʷɬxʷk̓ʷxʷk̓ʷqini**

k̓ʷɬxʷk̓ʷxʷk̓ʷqis – S/he cleaned s.o.'s fingernails. **k̓ʷɬxʷk̓ʷxʷk̓ʷqin, k̓ʷɬxʷk̓ʷxʷk̓ʷqintxʷ**
es k̓ʷɬxʷk̓ʷxʷk̓ʷqinms – S/he is cleaning s.o.'s fingernails. **ies k̓ʷɬxʷk̓ʷxʷk̓ʷqinm, as k̓ʷɬxʷk̓ʷxʷk̓ʷqinm**
qs k̓ʷɬxʷk̓ʷxʷk̓ʷqinms – S/he is going to clean s.o.'s fingernails. **čiqs k̓ʷɬxʷk̓ʷxʷk̓ʷqinm, kʷqs k̓ʷɬxʷk̓ʷxʷk̓ʷqinm**

es k̓ʷɬxʷk̓ʷxʷk̓ʷqin – His/her fingernails are clean. **čnes k̓ʷɬxʷk̓ʷxʷk̓ʷqin, kʷes k̓ʷɬxʷk̓ʷxʷk̓ʷqin**

k̓ʷɬxʷk̓ʷxʷk̓ʷqiniš – Clean fingernails. *cmd.*
k̓ʷɬxʷk̓ʷxʷk̓ʷqint – Clean s.o.'s fingernails. *cmd.*

x̣ʷq̓ʷx̣ʷq̓ʷqin – file fingernails. *suffix: ...qin, ...qn – top.*
x̣ʷq̓ʷx̣ʷq̓ʷqinm – S/he filed fingernails. **čn x̣ʷq̓ʷx̣ʷq̓ʷqinm, kʷ x̣ʷq̓ʷx̣ʷq̓ʷqinm**
es x̣ʷq̓ʷx̣ʷq̓ʷqini – S/he is filing fingernails. **čnes x̣ʷq̓ʷx̣ʷq̓ʷqini, kʷes x̣ʷq̓ʷx̣ʷq̓ʷqini**
qs x̣ʷq̓ʷx̣ʷq̓ʷqini – S/he is going to file fingernails. **čiqs x̣ʷq̓ʷx̣ʷq̓ʷqini, kʷqs x̣ʷq̓ʷx̣ʷq̓ʷqini**

x̣ʷq̓ʷx̣ʷq̓ʷqis – S/he filed s.o.'s fingernails. **x̣ʷq̓ʷx̣ʷq̓ʷqin, x̣ʷq̓ʷx̣ʷq̓ʷqintxʷ**
es x̣ʷq̓ʷx̣ʷq̓ʷqinms – S/he is filing s.o.'s fingernails. **ies x̣ʷq̓ʷx̣ʷq̓ʷqinm, as x̣ʷq̓ʷx̣ʷq̓ʷqinm**
qs x̣ʷq̓ʷx̣ʷq̓ʷqinms – S/he is going to file s.o.'s fingernails. **čiqs x̣ʷq̓ʷx̣ʷq̓ʷqinm, kʷqs x̣ʷq̓ʷx̣ʷq̓ʷqinm**

es x̣ʷq̓ʷx̣ʷq̓ʷqin – His/her fingernails are filed. **čnes x̣ʷq̓ʷx̣ʷq̓ʷqin, kʷes x̣ʷq̓ʷx̣ʷq̓ʷqin**

x̣ʷq̓ʷx̣ʷq̓ʷqiniš – File fingernails. *cmd.*
x̣ʷq̓ʷx̣ʷq̓ʷqint – File s.o.'s fingernails. *cmd.*

mnminqn – paint fingernails. *suffix: ...qin, ...qn – top.*
mnminqnm – S/he painted fingernails. **čn mnminqnm, kʷ mnminqnm**
es mnminqni – S/he is painting fingernails. **čnes mnminqni, kʷes mnminqni**
qs mnminqni – S/he is going to paint fingernails. **čiqs mnminqni, kʷqs mnminqni**

mnminqis – S/he painted s.o.'s fingernails. **mnminqn, mnminqntxʷ**
es mnminqnms – S/he is painting s.o.'s fingernails. **ies mnminqnm, as mnminqnm**
qs mnminqnms – S/he is going to paint s.o.'s fingernails. **čiqs mnminqnm, kʷqs mnminqnm**

es mnminqn – His/her fingernails are painted. **čnes mnminqn, kʷes mnminqn**

mnminqniš – Paint fingernails. *cmd.*
mnminqnt – Paint s.o.'s fingernails. *cmd.*

ƛ̓m̓qnečst – blood blistered fingernail. *suffix: ...qinčst – finger.*

finish

uẏéčst, *uẏé* – finish working; done working; come to an end. *suffix: ...ečst, ...čst – of the hand.*
uẏéčst – S/he/it finished. **čn uẏéčst, kʷ uẏéčst**
es uẏéčsti – S/he/it is coming to the end. **čnes uẏéčsti, kʷes uẏéčsti**
qs uẏéčsti – S/he/it is going to come to the end. **čiqs uẏéčsti, kʷqs uẏéčsti**

uẏéčstmis – S/he/it used s.t. to finish s.t. **uẏéčstmn, uẏéčstmntxʷ**
es uẏéčstmms – S/he/it is using s.t. to finish s.t. **ies uẏéčstmm, as uẏéčstmm**
as uẏéčstmms – S/he/it is going to use s.t. to finish s.t. **iqs uẏéčstmm, aqs uẏéčstmm**
uẏéčstmis – They used s.t. to finish s.t. **qeʔ uẏéčstmntm, uẏéčstmntp**

olqʷšitn u uẏéčst – I helped till it was finished. **ṅem olqʷšitn m uẏé** – I will help till it is finished. **ha kʷ uẏéčst** – Are you done? **ċyu u čn uẏéčst** – I am not finished yet. **uẏéčstmn łu isck̓ʷul̓ t łteteʔmin** – I finished my work with a hammer.

uẏécn – finish talking. *suffix: **...cin, ...cn** – action of the mouth.*
uẏécn – S/he/it finished talking. **čn uẏécn, kʷ uẏécn**

wis – finish.
wiˀstés – S/he/it finished s.t. **wiˀstén, wiˀstéxʷ**
es uˀims – S/he/it is finishing s.t. **ies uˀim, as uˀim**
qs uˀims – S/he/it is going to finish s.t. **iqs uˀim, aqs uˀim**
wiˀstéˀes – They finished s.t. **qeˀ wiˀstém, wiˀstép**
es uˀíˀims – They are finishing s.t. **qeˀes uˀim, es uˀimp**
qs uˀíˀims – They are going to finish s.t. **qeˀqs uˀim, qs uˀimp**

es wiˀłtems – S/he/it is finishing s.t. **ies wiˀłtem, as wiˀłtem**
qs wiˀłtems – S/he/it is going to finish s.t. **iqs wiˀłtem, aqs wiˀłtem**
es wiˀłtéˀems – They are finishing s.t. **qeˀes wiˀłtem, es wiˀłtemp**
qs wiˀłtéˀems – They are going to finish s.t. **qeˀqs wiˀłtem, qs wiˀłtemp**

qeˀ winumt – We finished doing what we were supposed to do.
wiˀnuis – S/he finally finished it. **wiˀnun, wiˀnuntxʷ**

ṅem čn wis ničm – I will finish cutting. **ṅe wis čluxʷm –** after dinner; when dinner is finished. **ṅem qeˀ wis čáwm m sic qeˀ eḷiłn –** We will finish praying, and then we can eat. **ṅe wis áq̇ntxʷ –** When you are finished scraping it. **ṅe wis q̇ʷéˀentéxʷ m sṫsuṫmstxʷ –** When you finish wringing it, you stretch it. **ƛ̓e čn wis iłn –** I've already eaten; I am done. **ha ƛ̓e wiˀstéxʷ –** Did you finish it? **aċaċx̣n u wiˀsten –** I read it and finished it.

iqs wiˀłltem – I am going to finish s.t. of his.

wiˀsqáx̣eˀ – finished with a horse. *suffix: **...sqax̣eˀ, ...sqa** – domestic animal; generally horse or car.*
wiˀsqáx̣eˀ – S/he is finished with his/her horse. **čn wiˀsqáx̣eˀ, kʷ wiˀsqáx̣eˀ**

wiˀcinm – finish eating; eat it all up. *suffix: **...cin, ...cn** – action of the mouth. See: **eat**.*

uyásq̇t, *uyá* – the storm/weather ended. *See: **storm**.*

qʷoṁmałq, *qʷoṁma* – get close to doing/finishing something; getting near to some point; close to the end of a journey; winning. *See: **close**.*

hoy – quit; stop; finish; okay; that's it; cease. *See: **quit**.*

ƛ̓lip – stop. *See: **stop**.*

čmšqnmist, *čmšqnmi* – give up; come to the end of one's abilities. *See: **give up**.*

> The **i** following uvular consonants (UC) and the glottal stop **ˀ** sound like English "*ey*" as in the words *they, hey, whey*, etc. Salish UC are: **q, q̇, qʷ, q̇ʷ, x̣, x̣ʷ**. For example, the suffix ...**qin** – head/top, is often spelled using English *ey* as "q*ey*n". So **qi, q̇i, qʷi, q̇ʷi, x̣i, x̣ʷi**, may be spelled with English *ey* as q*ey*, q̇*ey*, qʷ*ey*, q̇ʷ*ey*, x̣*ey*, x̣ʷ*ey* in other texts.

Finley Creek
nqpu nłšiˀétkʷs – Finley Creek in the Jocko Valley, Flathead Nation.

Finley Point
sččméple – Finley Point on Flathead Lake, Flathead Nation.

nccṁesšṅ – place near Finley Point. *lit. place with small rocks.*

fir
maniṅłp – alpine/subalpine fir; *Abies lasiocarpa.*

cq̇ełp – Douglas fir; *Pseudotsuga menziesii.*

sṫikʷłp – grand fir; balsam fir; *Abies grandis.*

qʷelcn – grand fir, balsam *fir; Abies* grandis; western red cedar; *Thuja plicata. (There is uncertainty with this word; some speakers identify it as western red cedar, Thuja plicata, while some identify it as grand fir, Abies grandis.)*

> s.t. - something, the 3rd person
> (s.t.) - something implied
> s.o. - someone, the 3rd person
> *sl.* - singular form
> *pl.* - plural form
> *rt.* - root word
> *cmd.* - command
> *lit.* - literally
> *fig.* - figuratively
> *i.e.,* - for example
> *See:* - Redirection to a related word.

fire
solšictn, *solši* – fire, flame.

olšictm – S/he made a fire. **čn olšictm, kʷ olšictm**
es olšicti – S/he is making a fire. **čnes olšicti, kʷes olšicti**
qs olšicti – S/he is going to make a fire. **čiqs olšicti, kʷqs olšicti**

olšictiš – Make a fire. *cmd.*

snolšictn, *snolši* – place of fire; stove; engine.

...us – suffix indicating fire.
čkʷtnus – big fire.
sxʷčk̓ʷulsm – one tasked to take care of fire. *prefix:* ***sxʷ...*** *– one tasked to do.*

ṅcqaus, *ṅcqau* – set in the fire; to make coffee. *See:* ***set.***
ncq̓mnusm – throw in the fire. *See:* ***throw.***
nʔemtus – sit by the fire. *See:* ***sit.***
sxʷlekʷs – fire whirlwind. *See:* ***whirlwind.***

olus – have fire.
olus – S/he has a fire. **čn olus, kʷ olus**
es olusi – S/he has a fire. **čnes olusi, kʷes olusi**
qs olusi – S/he is going to have a fire. **čiqs olusi, kʷqs olusi**

čṗnusm – lay long objects in a fire. *rt.:* ***ṗin*** *– lay.*
čṗnusis – S/he laid it in the fire. **čṗnusn, čṗnusntxʷ**
es čṗnusms – S/he is laying it in the fire. **ies čṗnusm, as čṗnusm**
qs čṗnusms – S/he is going to lay it in the fire. **iqs čṗnusm, aqs čṗnusm**

čṗnusntxʷ t čičitṅé m še čt̓qntéxʷ t ant̓qéłp – Lay alders in the fire, then stack on your ferns.

ulip – burn up; catch fire. **ululip** *pl.*
ulip – S/he/it burned. **čn ulip, kʷ ulip**
es ulpmi – S/he/it is burning. **čnes ulpmi, kʷes ulpmi**
qs ulpmi – S/he/it is going to burn. **čiqs ulpmi, kʷqs ulpmi**
ulíʔip – They burned. **qeʔ ulip, p ulip**
es ulpmíʔi – They are burning. **qeʔes ulpmi, pes ulpmi**

ulntes – S/he/it lit/burned s.t. **ulnten, ulntexʷ**
es ulims – S/he/it is lighting/burning s.t. **ies ulim, as ulim**
qs ulpims – S/he/it is going to light/burn s.t. **iqs ulim, aqs ulim**
ulntéʔes – They lit/burned s.t. **qeʔ ulntem, ulntep**
es ulíʔims – They are lighting/burning s.t. **qeʔes ulim, es ulimp**

ululntéʔes – Each one of them lit a fire. **qeʔ ululntem, ululntep**

čulusnt – Light it up. *cmd.*

x̣sulip – It burned good.
x̣snulpeẘs – It started to burn good. *suffix:* ***...éẘs*** *– in between, middle.*
nulpseẘs – It burned in half. *suffix:* ***...éẘs*** *– in between, middle.*
čulpalqʷ – The wood burned on the outside.

k̓ʷłulip – catch fire from underneath. **k̓ʷłululip** *pl. prefix:* ***k̓ʷł...*** *– under.*
k̓ʷłulip – S/he/it caught fire. **čn k̓ʷłulip, kʷ k̓ʷłulip**
es k̓ʷłulpmi – S/he/it is burning. **čnes k̓ʷłulpmi, kʷes k̓ʷłulpmi**
qs k̓ʷłulpmi – S/he/it is going to burn. **čiqs k̓ʷłulpmi, kʷqs k̓ʷłulpmi**
k̓ʷłulíʔip – They caught fire. **qeʔ k̓ʷłulip, p k̓ʷłulip**
es k̓ʷłulpmíʔi – They are burning. **qeʔes k̓ʷłulpmi, pes k̓ʷłulpmi**

k̇ʷłulntes – S/he/it lit s.t. underneath. **k̇ʷłulnten, k̇ʷłulntexʷ**
es k̇ʷłulims – S/he/it is lighting s.t. underneath. **ies k̇ʷłulim, as k̇ʷłulim**
qs k̇ʷłulims – S/he/it is going to light s.t. underneath. **iqs k̇ʷłulim, aqs k̇ʷłulim**
k̇ʷłulntéʔes – They lit s.t. underneath. **qeʔ k̇ʷłulntem, k̇ʷłulntep**
es k̇ʷłulíʔims – They are lighting s.t. underneath. **qeʔes k̇ʷłulim, es k̇ʷłulimp**

kʷéṁt k̇ʷłul̓usnt asšéṅš – Then make a fire under your rocks.

čolépcn, *čolé* – build a fire for a sweat.
čolépcn – S/he made a sweat fire. **čn čolépcn, kʷ čolépcn**
es čolépcni – S/he is making a sweat fire. **čnes čolépcni, kʷes čolépcni**
qs čolépcni – S/he is going to make a sweat fire. **čiqs čolépcni, kʷqs čolépcni**
čoléʔepcn – They made a sweat fire. **qeʔ čolépcn, p čolépcn**
es čoléʔepcni – They are making a sweat fire. **qeʔes čolépcni, pes čolépcni**
qs čoléʔepcni – They are going to make a sweat fire. **qeʔqs čolépcni, pqs čolépcni**

sxʷčole – one tasked to make fire for a sweat. *prefix:* ***sxʷ...*** *– one tasked to do.*

čolépcniš – Make a sweat fire. *cmd.*

čłolenenis – S/he started the fire on top.
k̇ʷłnolé – Make fire from under.

čn čolépcn x̣ʷl̓ čiqs nolmi – I made a sweat fire to heat up the rocks.

nolím – heat up rocks.
nolím – S/he heated up rocks. **čn nolím, kʷ nolím**
es nolmí – S/he is heating up rocks. **čnes nolmí, kʷes nolmí**
qs nolmí – S/he is going to heat up rocks. **čiqs nolmí, kʷqs nolmí**
nolíʔim – They heated up rocks. **qeʔ nolím, p nolím**
es nolmíʔi – They are heating up rocks. **qeʔes nolmí, pes nolmí**
qs nolmíʔi – They are going to heat up rocks. **qeʔqs nolmí, pqs nolmí**

ṗaap – grass/timber caught fire.
ṗaam – The grass/timber burned.
es ṗaapmi – The grass/forest is burning; it is a forest fire.
qs ṗaapmi – The grass/forest is going to burn; it is going to be a forest fire.

ṗaantes – S/he set fire to the grass/forest. **ṗaanten, ṗaantexʷ**
es ṗaams – S/he is setting fire to the grass/forest. **ies ṗaam, as ṗaam**
qs ṗaams – S/he is going to set fire to the grass/forest. **ias ṗaam, aas ṗaam**

sxʷṗaap – one tasked to make grass/timber fires. *prefix:* ***sxʷ...*** *– one tasked to do.*

ṗaapulexʷ – The land is burned up.
čłṗapeneʔ – It got burned over. *circumfix:* ***čł...eneʔ*** *– cover all over.*

xʷlqpi – make fire by friction; rubbing sticks.
es xʷlq̇pi – S/he is making a fire by friction. **čnes xʷlqpi, kʷes xʷlqpi**

čulus – light up; turn something on; ignite. *See:* ***light.***

n...qneł – *circumfix indicating firing a shot.*
nk̇ʷqneł – S/he fired one shot. **čn nk̇ʷqneł, kʷ nk̇ʷqneł**
naslqneł – S/he fired two shots. **čn naslqneł, kʷ naslqneł**
nčałlqneł – S/he fired three shots. **čn nčałlqneł, kʷ nčałlqneł**

The **i** following uvular consonants (UC) and the glottal stop ʔ sound like English "*ey*" as in the words th*ey*, h*ey*, wh*ey*, etc. Salish UC are: **q, q̇, qʷ, q̇ʷ, x̣, x̣ʷ**. For example, the suffix …**qin** – head/top, is often spelled using English *ey* as "q*ey*n". So **qi, q̇i, qʷi, q̇ʷi, x̣i, x̣ʷi**, may be spelled with English *ey* as **q***ey*, **q̇***ey*, **qʷ***ey*, **q̇ʷ***ey*, **x̣***ey*, **x̣ʷ***ey* in other texts.

s.t. - something, the 3rd person
(s.t.) - something implied
s.o. - someone, the 3rd person
sl. - singular form
pl. - plural form
rt. - root word
cmd. - command
lit. - literally
fig. - figuratively
i.e., - for example
See: - Redirection to a related word.

nmosqneł – four shots. **nclčstqneł** – five shots. **nṫq̇nčstqneł** – six shots. **nsṗl̓čstqneł** – seven shots. **nhenmqneł** – eight shots. **nx̣ntqneł** – nine shots. **nˀupnčstqneł** – ten shots.

firefly
ṗaq̇l̓wisi – firefly *(it flashes around)*.

ṗaq̇l̓uyeˀ – firefly *(it flashes)*.

ṗaq̇l̓i – firefly.

fireman
sxʷłépsm – one tasked to put out fires; fireman; firefighter. *prefix:* ***sxʷ...*** *– one tasked to do.*

fireweed
qʷqʷółnłp, qʷqʷółnéłp – fireweed, blooming Sally.

firewood
luk̓ʷ – wood.

słƛ̓ƛ̓uk̓ʷe – pitch wood.

ṗseš, ***ṗse*** – get firewood; go after firewood; fetch firewood. *See:* ***get****.*

fireworks
lixʷ – fireworks. *(describes how it looks)*

čṫaṫapsqe – firecracker. *(describes the sound)*

ṗaq̇mnscut – something lit up *(i.e., fireworks, lightning, falling star)*.

čṗaq̇asq̇t – lights in the sky. *suffix:* ***...asq̇t*** *– sky, day.*

firm
ċnċant – firm; immovable; well fastened; tight. *rt.:* ***ċan*** *– tight.*

first
šˀitmist, ***šˀit*** – first, ahead.

šˀit – S/he/it was first. **čn šˀit, kʷ šˀit**
es šˀiti – S/he/it is first. **čnes šˀiti, kʷes šˀiti**
qs šˀiti – S/he/it is going to be first. **čiqs šˀiti, kʷqs šˀiti**
šˀíˀit – They were first. **qeˀ šˀit, p šˀit**
es šˀíˀiti – They are first. **qeˀes šˀiti, pes šˀiti**
qs šˀíˀiti – They are going to be first. **qeˀqs šˀiti, pqs šˀiti**

šˀitstes – S/he put s.o./s.t. first. **šˀitsten, šˀitstexʷ**
šˀitstéˀes – They put s.o./s.t. first. **qeˀ šˀitstem, šˀitstep**

es łsšˀiti – S/he/it is a little ahead. **čnes łsšˀiti, kʷes łsšˀiti**

šˀitm – S/he became first. **čn šˀitm, kʷ šˀitm**
šˀitstem – S/he/it was put first.

šˀitemn – one inclined to be first; one inclined to try to be first. *suffix:* ***...emn*** *– one inclined to do.*
šˀitmasqe – leader; first to volunteer; first to be there. *suffix:* ***...sqe, ...sqelixʷ*** *– people. See:* ***leader****.*
sšitṁeľt, šiˀtmišlt – the eldest child. *suffix:* ***...elṫ, ...l̓t*** *– child, baby*

šíˀiscutiš – Be first. *cmd.*
šˀitmiskʷ – Put it first; allow s.o. to be first. *cmd.*
šiṁscut – put one's self first.
šˀitmscut – put one's self first; to want to be first.
es šˀitmscuti – S/he is wanting to be first. **čnes šˀitmscuti, kʷses šˀitmscuti**

kʷes šˀit – You go first.
pes šˀit – You folks go first.
es šˀíˀit – They go first.

qʷoyʔe łu čiqs šʔiti – I will go first. **we čnes šʔit –** I was first. **es nʔeẇtpe es šʔit qeyqeyši –** They followed each other, **Qeyqeyshi** in the lead. **hoy u šʔitm –** It came to be s/he/it was first. **k̇ʷis šíʔiscutiš –** Go be first. *cmd.* **olqʷšíʔisten –** I helped s.o. be first. **mlqʷšʔit –** S/he/it is always first. **swe łu es šʔiti –** Who is first?

fish

sẇewł – fish.
ẇewłm – The fish swam.
es ẇewłi – The fish is swiming.
qs ẇewłi – The fish is going to swim.

ẇewłetkʷ – school of fish.
snsẇewłtn – aquarium.

> The **i** following uvular consonants (UC) and the glottal stop **ʔ** sound like English "*ey*" as in the words *they, hey, whey*, etc. Salish UC are: **q**, **q̇**, **qʷ**, **q̇ʷ**, **x̣**, **x̣ʷ**. For example, the suffix ...**qin** – head/top, is often spelled using English *ey* as "*qeyn*". So **qi**, **q̇i**, **qʷi**, **q̇ʷi**, **x̣i**, **x̣ʷi**, may be spelled with English *ey* as **q***ey*, **q̇***ey*, **qʷ***ey*, **q̇ʷ***ey*, **x̣***ey*, **x̣ʷ***ey* in other texts.

aáycčst, *aáy* **–** bull trout; Dolly Varden trout; *Salvelinus confluentus. See:* ***bull trout.***
pisł – westslope cutthroat trout; *Oncorhynchus clarkii lewisi. See:* ***cutthroat trout.***
sttṁáyľqs, *sttṁá* **–** bullhead trout; brown trout; *Salmo trutta. See:* ***brown trout.***
łxʷxʷiups – lake trout; *Salvelinus namaycush.*
nxʷmeneʔ – steelhead salmon; rainbow trout; *Oncorhynchus mykiss. (native to the area of the Spokane tribe; lit. red/pink around the ears)*
smłič, *smłi* **–** salmon; chinook salmon; *Oncorhynchus tshawytscha.*
nťk̇ʷus – sockeye salmon; kokanee salmon; *Oncorhynchus nerka.*
sčlwes, *sčlwe* **–** pink salmon; humpback salmon; *Oncorhynchus gorbuscha.*
čléneʔ – longnosed sucker; *Catostomus catostomus.*
sľaẇs – small mouth sucker; Columbia large-scaled sucker; *Catostomus macrocheilus.*
tẇeckʷ – small black sucker fish.
qʷq̇ʷéʔčn, *qʷq̇ʷé* **–** northern pikeminnow; *Ptychocheilus oregonensis.*
x̣ʷx̣ʷẏucṅ, *x̣ʷx̣ʷẏu* **–** whitefish; *Prosopium williamsoni.*
nčličṅ – grayling *(fish); Thymallus arcticus.*
upupci – channel catfish; *Ictalurus punctatus*; black bullhead; *Ameiurus melas.*
kʷkʷenčn – fathead minnow; *Pimephales promelas. (small warm water fish like a sunfish)*
ckʷcičṅ – flathead chub; *Platygobio gracilis. (has a shinny back.) suffix:* ***...ičṅ*** *– back.*
kʷutuł – eel; Pacific lamprey; *Lampetra tridentata.*
sċmtus – sturgeon. *rt.:* ***ċim*** *– contricted.*
ċqċiq – trout-perch; *Percopsis omiscomaycus.*
ntťx̣e – little trout.
ččiẇeʔ – fish species.
piqłċeʔ – halibut.
snlšimċeʔ – fish species *(has large scales that are removed before cooking).*

cq̇mstetkʷ – fish jumping out of the water. *rt.:* ***cq̇minm*** *– throw; suffix:* ***...etkʷ, ...tkʷ*** *– liquid*
es cq̇mstetkʷi sẇewł – The fish is jumping out of the water.

> s.t. - something, the 3rd person
> (s.t.) - something implied
> s.o. - someone, the 3rd person
> *sl.* - singular form
> *pl.* - plural form
> *rt.* - root word
> *cmd.* - command
> *lit.* - literally
> *fig.* - figuratively
> *i.e.,* - for example
> *See:* - Redirection to a related word.

łtłatmist – fish out of water; fish flopping around out of water.
es łtłatmisti – It is flopping around.

qq̇ṁéyeʔ, *qq̇ṁé* **–** angling; fish. *See:* ***angle.***

mul – fish/scoop something out of water. *(i.e., with a net, container, etc.)*
muľm – S/he fished with a net. **čn muľm, kʷ muľm**
es muľi – S/he is fishing with a net. **čnes muľi, kʷes muľi**
qs muľi – S/he is going to fish with a net. **čiqs muľi, kʷ qs muľi**

mulis – S/he fished s.t. out of the water. **muln, mulntxʷ**
es mulms – S/he is fishing s.t. out of the water. **ies mulm, as mulm**

qs mulms – S/he is going to fish s.t. out of the water. **iqs mulm, aqs mulm**

mul̓l – the fish got caught with nets.

es mul – S/he/it is fished out of the water; it is caught with a net.

sxʷmulm – one tasked to fish things out of the water.
smul – the thing fished out of the water.
scmul – something that has been fished out of the water.
mul̓lmn – something to fish out of water; scoop net.
nčɫmultn – something to skim the surface of the water.

mul̓liš – Catch fish with nets. *cmd.*
mulnt – Fish it out of the water. *cmd.*

čɫmulis – S/he fished s.t. off the surface of water. **čɫmuln, čɫmulntxʷ**
es čɫmulms – S/he is fishing s.t. off the surface of water. **ies čɫmulm, as čɫmulm**
qs čɫmulms – S/he is going to fish s.t. off the surface of water. **iqs čɫmulm, aqs čɫmulm**

q̓ʷyox̣ʷ – trap fish in a barrier/fence. *See:* ***trap.***
sq̓ʷyokʷétkʷ, *sq̓ʷyokʷé –* fish trap/cage.

snqq̓ećétkʷ – fish trap; fishnet.

Fish Creek **npččél̓ –** place near Alberton, Montana, a creek within Salish and Pend d'Orielle aboriginal territory.

fish eggs, roe **ék̓ʷn –** roe; fish eggs.

fisher **sxʷeyn –** fisher; *Martes pennanti.*

fisherman **sxʷqq̓m̓é –** one tasked to fish; fisherman. *prefix:* ***sxʷ...*** *– one tasked to do.*

fish hawk **ċixʷċxʷ –** fish hawk; osprey; *Pandion haliaetus.*

fishhook **čq̓lxʷqne –** fishhook.

čt̓kʷqne – bait.

fishing line **čqq̓m̓é čox̣me –** fishing line.
čox̣méple? – something hanging off of something. *suffix:* ***...éple?*** *– permanence.*

fishing pole **čqq̓m̓é,** *čqq̓m̓éye?tn –* fishing pole.

čqq̓m̓é čox̣me – fishing line.

čcqmnɫqne – cast line.

fist **mlq̓ʷéčst –** fist. *rt.:* ***malq̓ʷ*** *– balled object; suffix:* ***...ečst*** *– hand.*

fit **lawap –** It just fit.

lmlamist – throw a fit; have a temper tantrum. *See:* ***wiggle.***

five **cil –** five. **clcil –** fives. *pl.*
upn eɫ cil – fifteen.
čcilcl – five people.
cil séns – nickel.

clčst… – prefix indicating five combined with another affix forming a full word.
clčstásq̓t – five days. *suffix:* ***…asq̓t** – sky, day.*
clčsteɫxʷ – five houses. *suffix:* ***…eɫxʷ, …ɫxʷ** – house.*
nclčstep – five eggs. *circumfix:* ***n…ep** – egg.*
clčstéssn̓ – five rocks. *suffix:* ***…essn̓, …ssn̓** – rock.*

clčɫ… – prefix indicating five, with whole word.
clčɫʔupn – fifty, five tens.
clčɫšƛ̓ip – S/he lost five times. **čn clčɫšƛ̓ip, kʷ clčɫšƛ̓ip**
clčsqáx̣eʔ, *clčsqá* – five domestic animals or cars. *The **ɫ** is dropped when preceding an **s**.*
clčɫʔopnčstqn – five thousand.

> The **i** following uvular consonants (UC) and the glottal stop **ʔ** sound like English "*ey*" as in the words th*ey*, h*ey*, wh*ey*, etc. Salish UC are: **q**, **q̓**, **qʷ**, **q̓ʷ**, **x̣**, **x̣ʷ**. For example, the suffix …**qin** – head/top, is often spelled using English *ey* as "q*ey*n". So **qi**, **q̓i**, **qʷi**, **q̓ʷi**, **x̣i**, **x̣ʷi**, may be spelled with English *ey* as **q***ey*, **q̓***ey*, **qʷ***ey*, **q̓ʷ***ey*, **x̣***ey*, **x̣ʷ***ey* in other texts.

five hundred
clčɫnk̓ʷoʔqín, *clčɫnk̓ʷoʔqí* – five hundred.

fix
k̓ʷul̓ – do; make; fix; work. *See:* ***work**.*
k̓ʷul̓n – I fixed it.

čnes k̓ʷul̓i l p̓ip̓uyšn – I am fixing the car. **čn áx̣lwi k̓ʷul̓n k̓ʷɫnčmé** – I was persistent, determined, able in fixing the door.

k̓ʷl̓lexʷeɫp, *k̓ʷl̓lexʷe* – fix a bed. *See:* ***bed**.*

flag
sččacé – flag. *prefix:* ***sc…** – s.t. that's been done/made/prepared.*

sččla – eagle feather staff.

flame
solši – fire, flame. *See:* ***fire**.*

sulip – something that burned up. *See:* ***fire**.*

flap
q̓tq̓atx̣n – move arms/wings up and down; flap.

flash
c̓ik̓ʷ – shiny, flashy, sparkly.
i c̓ik̓ʷ – It is shiny.
čɫc̓ik̓ʷčn – water over ice *(shiny surface)*.

p̓áq̓ – shine, bright. *See:* ***shine**.*

flashlight
p̓áq̓mn – something brightens up; flashlight. *rt.:* ***paq̓** – shine; suffix:* ***…min, …mn** – instrument/tool.*

p̓éxʷmn – something that glows; flashlight. *rt.:* ***p̓éxʷ** – red-hot glow.*

flat
šiƛ̓ – flat/even; aligned; straight; ordered.
i šiƛ̓ – It is flat.

šiƛ̓lexʷ – flat land.
i šiƛ̓lexʷ – The land is all even.
i čɫšiƛ̓kʷ – flat water; calm water.

šƛ̓mulexʷ – level out the land.
šƛ̓elixʷ – visit people/tribes/towns one after another; tour among the various people. *See:* ***visit**.*
šƛ̓eɫxʷ – visit homes one after another; go house to house. *See:* ***visit**.*

> s.t. - something, the 3rd person
> (s.t.) - something implied
> s.o. - someone, the 3rd person
> *sl.* - singular form
> *pl.* - plural form
> *rt.* - root word
> *cmd.* - command
> *lit.* - literally
> *fig.* - figuratively
> *i.e.,* - for example
> *See:* - Redirection to a related word.

šƛ̓mim – put things in a straight line; aligned; ordered; level and even.
šƛ̓mstes – S/he/it put s.t. in a straight line. **šƛ̓msten, šƛ̓mstexʷ**
es šƛ̓mims – S/he/it is putting s.t. in a straight line. **ies šƛ̓mim, as šƛ̓mim**

qs šƛ̓mims – S/he/it is going to put s.t. in a straight line. **iqs šƛ̓mim, aqs šƛ̓mim**

šƛ̓mist – put one's self in a straight line.
šƛ̓mist – S/he/it got in a straight line. **čn šƛ̓mist, kʷ šƛ̓mist**
es šƛ̓misti – S/he/it is getting in a straight line. **čnes šƛ̓misti, kʷes šƛ̓misti**
qs šƛ̓misti – S/he/it is going to get in a straight line. **čiqs šƛ̓misti, kʷqs šƛ̓misti**

šƛ̓mistiš – Get in a straight line. *cmd.*

šƛ̓mncut – make one's self go in a straight line with others.
šƛ̓mncut – S/he/it went in a straight line. **čn šƛ̓mncut, kʷ šƛ̓mncut**
es šƛ̓mncuti – S/he/it is going in a straight line. **čnes šƛ̓mncuti, kʷes šƛ̓mncuti**
qs šƛ̓mncuti – S/he/it is going to to go in a straight line. **čiqs šƛ̓mncuti, kʷqs šƛ̓mncuti**

šƛ̓łtumš – S/he/it put the people in a straight line. **čn šƛ̓łtumš, kʷ šƛ̓łtumš**

łoc – flatten; smash.
łocis – S/he/it flatten s.t. **łocn, łocntxʷ**
łóʔocis – S/he/it flatten s.t. **qeʔ łocntm, łocntp**

łocntm – S/he/it was flattened.

łocntm sp̓l̓q̓ʷa t p̓ip̓uyšn – The turtle was flattened by the car.

p̓aƛ̓ – smooth texture. *See: **smooth**.*

psas – swelled object shrinks/flattens; deflate. *See: **swell**.*

Flathead Indian

selíš – Salish, Bitterroot Salish *(self identification)*.
łq̓ełmlš – Bitterroot Salish *(Pend d'Oreille term)*.
łqayaqn, *łqa* **–** Bitterroot Salish *(Pend d'Oreille term)*.

sčłq̓etkʷmcin – Upper Pend d'Oreille. *rt.: **łaq̓t** – wide; suffix: **...etkʷ, ...tkʷ** – liquid*

sqélixʷ – people, Indian.

Flathead Lake

čłq̓etkʷ – Flathead Lake. *suffix: **...etkʷ, ...tkʷ** – liquid*

skʷtiłčłq̓li – big lake.

Flathead River

ntx̣ʷetkʷ, *ntx̣ʷe* **–** Flathead River; the river. *suffix: **...etkʷ, ...tkʷ** – liquid*

flat land

sičƛ̓lexʷ – flat land; even land. *rt.: **šiƛ̓** – flat. See: **flat**.*

flat tire

čpsšan – flat tire. *rt.: **psas** – deflate.*
čpsšan – S/he has a flat tire. **čn čpsšan, kʷ čpsšan**
čpsšáʔan – They have a flat tire. **qeʔ čpsšan, p čpsšan**

čt̓lpšin – tire blow out.
čt̓lpšin – S/he had a tire blow out. **čn čt̓lpšin, kʷ čt̓lpšin**

flea

k̓ʷt̓k̓ʷit̓ps – flea.

flesh

sqeltč – meat; flesh.

flick

nt̓mčim – flick with the finger; place a bet down as in flicking down a card or money.
nt̓mčim – S/he flicked. **čn nt̓mčim, kʷ nt̓mčim**
es nt̓mčmi – S/he is flicking. **čnes nt̓mčmi, kʷes nt̓mčmi**
qs nt̓mčmi – S/he is going to flick. **čiqs nt̓mčmi, kʷqs nt̓mčmi**

nťmčim – They flicked. **qeˀ nťmčim, p nťmčim**
es nťmčmíˀi – They are flicking. **qeˀes nťmčmi, pes nťmčmi**
qs nťmčmíˀi – They are going to flick. **qeˀqs nťmčmi, pqs nťmčmi**

ťmčim – S/he hit with finger. **čn ťmčim, kʷ ťmčim**
es ťmčmi – S/he is hitting with finger. **čnes ťmčmi, kʷes ťmčmi**
qs ťmčmi – S/he is going to hit with finger. **čiqs ťmčmi, kʷqs ťmčmi**

ťmčntes – S/he hit s.o./s.t. with the finger. **ťmčnten, ťmčntexʷ**
es ťmčims – S/he is hitting s.o./s.t. with the finger. **ies ťmčim, as ťmčim**
qs ťmčims – S/he is going to hit s.o./s.t. with the finger. **iqs ťmčim, aqs ťmčim**
ťmčntéˀes – They hit s.o./s.t. with the finger. **qeˀ ťmčntem, ťmčntep**
es ťmčíˀims – They are hitting s.o./s.t. with the finger. **qeˀes ťmčim, es ťmčimp**
qs ťmčíˀims – They are going to hit s.o./s.t. with the finger. **qeˀqs ťmčim, qs ťmčimp**

ťmťmčmuł – one that habitually hits with the finger/bets. *suffix: **...łmuł** – one that habitually does.*

ťmčiš – Flick your finger. *cmd.*
ťmčint – Flick s.o./s.t. with your finger. *cmd.*
ťmčečsm – snap fingers. *See: **snap**.*

ťmčusis – S/he hit him/her with the finger in the face. **ťmčusnt, ťmčusntxʷ**
čłťmčeššis – S/he hit him/her with the finger on the forehead. **čłťmčeššn, čłťmčeššntxʷ**
čťmčeneˀ – S/he hit with the finger on the ear.
nťmčawqn – S/he hit with the finger on the top of the head.

The **i** following uvular consonants (UC) and the glottal stop **ˀ** sound like English "*ey*" as in the words *they*, *hey*, *whey*, etc. Salish UC are: **q, q̇, qʷ, q̇ʷ, x̣, x̣ʷ**. For example, the suffix **...qin** – head/top, is often spelled using English *ey* as "q*ey*n". So **qi, q̇i, qʷi, q̇ʷi, x̣i, x̣ʷi**, may be spelled with English *ey* as **q***ey*, **q̇***ey*, **qʷ***ey*, **q̇ʷ***ey*, **x̣***ey*, **x̣ʷ***ey* in other texts.

flicker, northern

kʷlkʷlé – northern flicker; red-shafted flicker; *Colaptes auratus*.

flinch

nplus – turn the face/head. *See: **turn**.*

flint

oloľé – chert; flint, *describing its use as a fire starter.*

x̣ʷix̣ʷiyestn – chert, *of a quality for making a sharp edged tool.*
x̣ʷix̣ʷiyeššn – chert, *describing the type of rock.*

flip

nocqayáqn, *nocqayá* – flip over on feet.
nocqayá – S/he flipped over. **čn nocqayá, kʷ nocqayá**

i k̓ʷľčup – It flipped/turned over.

flip off

nčlos – action showing disdain toward someone. *See: **disdain**.*

flirt

sllľstwexʷ, *sllľstwe* – flirt with each other; acting goofy with each other. *suffix: **...wexʷ** – action to each other.*
es sllľstwexʷi – They are flirting with each other. **qeˀes sllľstwexʷi, pes sllľstwexʷi**

q̇xʷuxʷ – flirt. *rt.: **q̇exʷ** – proud, conceited.*
q̇xʷuxʷ – S/he flirted. **čn q̇xʷuxʷ, kʷ q̇xʷuxʷ**
es q̇xʷxʷmi – S/he is flirting. **čnes q̇xʷxʷmi, kʷes q̇xʷxʷmi**
qs q̇xʷxʷmi – S/he is going to flirt. **čiqs q̇xʷxʷmi, kʷqs q̇xʷxʷmi**

s.t. - something, the 3rd person
(s.t.) - something implied
s.o. - someone, the 3rd person
sl. - singular form
pl. - plural form
rt. - root word
cmd. - command
lit. - literally
fig. - figuratively
i.e., - for example
See: - Redirection to a related word.

float

laáp – float in a vessel; navigate by water; row; surf internet. *(i.e., boat, canoe, raft, etc.)*
laáp – S/he floated by boat. **čn laáp, kʷ laáp**
es lapmi – S/he is floating by boat. **čnes lapmi, kʷes lapmi**

qs lapmi – S/he is going to float by boat. **čiqs lapmi, kʷqs lapmi**

lapstes – S/he made the water vessel go. **lapsten, lapstexʷ**
es lapims – S/he is making the water vessel go. **ies lapim, as lapim**
qs lapims – S/he is going to make the water vessel go. **iqs lapim, aqs lapim**

tspisċé u čn laáp – Yesterday I floated *(sailed)*.

plim – drift/float away by water or wind; carried away. *See: **drift**.*

čłt̓k̓ʷetkʷ – place on the water; float. *suffix: **...etkʷ, ...tkʷ** – liquid*
čłt̓k̓ʷetkʷis – S/he placed it on the water. **čłt̓k̓ʷetkʷn, čłt̓k̓ʷetkʷntxʷ**
es čłt̓k̓ʷetkʷms – S/he is placing it on the water. **ies čłt̓k̓ʷetkʷm, as čłt̓k̓ʷetkʷm**
qs čłt̓k̓ʷetkʷms – S/he is going to place it on the water. **iqs čłt̓k̓ʷetkʷm, aqs čłt̓k̓ʷetkʷm**

flood **t̓ečt** – overflow the banks; to flood.
es t̓ečti – It is flooding.

t̓ečt u mlʼpulexʷ – It flooded over the banks and flowed over the land.

es mlʼpulexʷi – It is flooding; it is overflowing onto the land. *See: **overflow**.*

čłmlʼpeneʔ – cover with inundating water. *circumfix: **čł...eneʔ** – cover all over.*
čłmlʼpenʔeis – S/he flooded it. **čłmlʼpenʔen, čłmlʼpenʔentxʷ**
es čłmlʼpenʔems – S/he is flooding it. **ies čłmlʼpenʔem, as čłmlʼpenʔem**
qs čłmlʼpenʔems – S/he is going to flood it. **iqs čłmlʼpenʔem, aqs čłmlʼpenʔem**

floor **x̣lełp** – floor.

t̓qełp – flooring. *(i.e. cedar boughs, blankets, reeds, hide, etc.)*

flop **łtłatmist** – fish out of water; fish flopping around out of water. *See: **fish**.*

lmlamist – throw a fit; have a temper tantrum. *See: **wiggle**.*

lalamist – wiggle/roll around; *toss and turn. (i.e., when in pain; restless in bed; like an animal wallowing in dirt.) See: **wiggle**.*

yananq̓ʷmilš – roll/wiggle, as would happen in bed. *See: **wiggle**.*

Florence **čp̓uƛ̓us** – Florence, Montana.

flour **scx̣ʷaq̓ʷ** – something that's been ground; flour. *rt.: **x̣ʷaq̓ʷ** – grind; prefix: **sc...** – s.t. that's been done/made/prepared. See: **grind**.*

flow **moop** – something flows.
es mopmi – It is flowing.
es čmopmi – It is flowing down something.

sčmoop – something flows down something.

es mopétkʷ – flowing water.
čmopalqʷ – something flowing down a tree. *(i.e., sap, water, etc.)*
čmopełp – something flowing down a branch. *(i.e., sap, water, etc.)*
čłmopeneʔ – flowing over the surface/top of something. *circumfix: **čł...eneʔ** – cover all over.*

flower **sċéʔek̓ʷ** – flower.
es ċek̓ʷmi – It is flowering up.

ċéʔek̓ʷulexʷ – flowered land; flowers all over.

sċekʼʷulexʷ – flower on the ground.
ċekʼʷulexʷm – The land flowered up.
es ċekʼʷulexʷi – The land is flowering up.

sčċekʼʷełp – flower in a tree; blossom, bloom. *See: **bloom**.*
sčċekʼʷełpm – The tree blossoms came out.
es čċekʼʷełpi – The tree blossoms are coming out.

čmkʷkʷełp – bud on a tree.

ťlqʷqin – when buds first open up. *rt.: **ťlip** – it came open; suffix: **...qin, ...qn** – top.*

sčťemp – stem of a flower.

fluctuate

suuʔ – water subsides/drops after a flood. *See: **drop**.*

fluke

x̣ʷncóʔ – fluke.

flush

kʼʷłsixʷm – drain/pour from under; flush. *rt.: **sixʷ** – pour; prefix: **kʼʷł...** – under. See: **pour***
kʼʷłsixʷis – S/he flushed it. **kʼʷłsixʷn, kʼʷłsixʷntxʷ**
es kʼʷłsixʷms – S/he is flushing it. **ies kʼʷłsixʷm, as kʼʷłsixʷm**
qs kʼʷłsixʷms – S/he is going to flush it. **iqs kʼʷłsixʷm, aqs kʼʷłsixʷm**

kʼʷłsixʷnt – Drain it; flush it. *cmd.*

kʼʷłsixʷntxʷ ci snṁṅe – Flush the toilet. **kʼʷłsixʷn ci snṁṅe** – I flushed the toilet.

płpxʷłš – Flush the toilet. *cmd.*

flute

čłłx̣ʷálqʷ, *čłłx̣ʷá* – flute. *rt.: **łox̣ʷ** – hole; suffix: **...alqʷ** – wood; cylindical.*
čłłx̣ʷálqʷm – S/he played the flute. **čn čłłx̣ʷálqʷm, kʷ čłłx̣ʷálqʷm**
es čłłx̣ʷálqʷi – S/he is playing the flute. **čnes čłłx̣ʷálqʷi, kʷes čłłx̣ʷálqʷi**
qs čłłx̣ʷálqʷi – S/he is going to play the flute. **čiqs čłłx̣ʷálqʷi, kʷqs čłłx̣ʷálqʷi**

sxʷčłłx̣ʷálqʷ – one tasked to play the flute.

čłłx̣ʷálqʷiš – Play the flute. *cmd.*

flutter

x̣ʷall – flutter/shake. *See: **shake**.*

fly

x̣máłtn – housefly.
plpulsts łu ułx̣máłtn – S/he killed lots of flies. **čn česle t x̣małtn** – I killed two flies.

čátnłq – horsefly.

ťuxʷt – fly.
ťuxʷt – S/he/it flew. **čn ťuxʷt, kʷ ťuxʷt**
es ťuxʷti – S/he/it is flying. **čnes ťuxʷti, kʷes ťuxʷti**
qs ťuxʷti – S/he/it is going to fly. **čiqs ťuxʷti, kʷqs ťuxʷti**
ťúʔuxʷt – They flew. **qeʔ ťuxʷt, p ťuxʷt**
es ťúʔuxʷti – They are flying. **qeʔes ťuxʷti, pes ťuxʷti**
qs ťúʔuxʷti – They are going to fly. **qeʔqs ťuxʷti, pqs ťuxʷti**

ťuxʷtsts – S/he/it made it fly. **ťuxʷtstn, ťuxʷtstxʷ**
es ťuxʷtsts – S/he/it is making it fly. **ies ťuxʷtstn, as ťuxʷtstn**
qs ťuxʷtsts – S/he/it is going to make it fly. **iqs ťuxʷtstn, aqs ťuxʷtstn**

ťiťuxʷtmuł – one that habitually flies. *suffix: **...tmuł** – one that habitually does.*

The **i** following uvular consonants (UC) and the glottal stop ʔ sound like English "*ey*" as in the words *they, hey, whey*, etc. Salish UC are: **q, q̓, qʷ, q̓ʷ, x̣, x̣ʷ**. For example, the suffix **...qin** – head/top, is often spelled using English *ey* as "q*ey*n". So **qi, q̓i, qʷi, q̓ʷi, x̣i, x̣ʷi**, may be spelled with English *ey* as **q***ey*, **q̓***ey*, **qʷ***ey*, **q̓ʷ***ey*, **x̣***ey*, **x̣ʷ***ey* in other texts.

s.t. - something, the 3rd person
(s.t.) - something implied
s.o. - someone, the 3rd person
sl. - singular form
pl. - plural form
rt. - root word
cmd. - command
lit. - literally
fig. - figuratively
i.e., - for example
See: - Redirection to a related word.

t́uxʷtn – airplane. *suffix: **...tin, ...tn** – means of/device.*
čeṅ łu mlqnu? es t́xʷtlwisi – Where is the eagle? It is flying around.

čt́uxʷtm – fly to something.
čt́uxʷtmis – It flew to s.t./s.o.
es čt́uxʷtmms – It is flying to s.t./s.o.
qs čt́uxʷtmms – It is going to fly to s.t./s.o.

čt́uxʷtmis ci l sc̓éʔek̓ʷ łu x̣małtn – The fly flew toward the flower.

čłt́xʷteneʔ – fly over. *circumfix: **čł...eneʔ** – cover all over.*
čłt́uxʷtenʔeis – S/he/it flew over s.t. **čłt́uxʷtenʔen, čłt́uxʷtenʔentxʷ**
es čłt́uxʷtenʔems – S/he/it is flying over s.t. **ies čłt́uxʷtenʔem, as čłt́uxʷtenʔem**
qs čłt́uxʷtenʔems – S/he/it is going to fly over s.t. **iqs čłt́uxʷtenʔem, aqs čłt́uxʷtenʔem**

čłt́uxʷtenenc ancitxʷ łu t mlqnu – The eagle flew over your house.

xʷexʷéʔe – Each one of the birds lifted off to fly.
xʷéʔe – The birds lifted off to fly.

flying squirrel
sxʷupxʷp – northern flying squirrel; *Glaucomys sabrinus.*

fly swatter
sṗmintn – fly swatter. *rt.: **sṗim** – hit; suffix: **...mintn** – tool that does.*
pulsts x̣máłtn t sṗmintn – S/he killed the fly with a fly swatter.

foam
póʔos – foam; froth; lather.
i póʔos – It is foam; froth; lather.
i npʔoscn – S/he/it is has froth at the mouth.

čłpʔosatkʷ – foam on the water.
snpʔoscn – froth at the mouth.
possm – lather. *See: **lather.***

x̣ʷos – foam; becomes foam.
nx̣ʷóskʷ – beer.
sx̣ʷósm – foamberry, buffalo berry, soap berry.

foamberry
sx̣ʷósm – foamberry; buffaloberry; soapberry; *shepherdia canadensis.*

foe
ewtus – oppose; work against. *See: **oppose.***

čšmšmṅeẇs – double up on an someone; double team someone. *See: **enemy.***

fog
shemip – fog.
hemip – It got foggy.
es hempmi – It is foggy.

fold
ṗulk̓ʷ – fold/roll up, not flat. **ṗlṗulk̓ʷ** *pl.*
ṗulk̓ʷis – S/he folded s.t. **ṗulk̓ʷn, ṗulk̓ʷntxʷ**
es ṗulk̓ʷms – S/he is folding s.t. **ies ṗulk̓ʷm, as ṗulk̓ʷm**
qs ṗulk̓ʷms – S/he is going to fold s.t. **iqs ṗulk̓ʷm, aqs ṗulk̓ʷm**
ṗúʔulk̓ʷis – They folded s.t. **qeʔ ṗulk̓ʷntm, ṗulk̓ʷntp**
es ṗúʔulk̓ʷms – They are folding s.t. **qeʔes ṗulk̓ʷm, es ṗulk̓ʷmp**
qs ṗúʔulk̓ʷms – They are going to fold s.t. **qeʔqs ṗulk̓ʷm, qs ṗulk̓ʷmp**

es ṗlṗulk̓ʷms – S/he is folding and folding things. **ies ṗlṗulk̓ʷm, as ṗlṗulk̓ʷm**

es ṗulk̇ʷ – It is folded.
ṗulk̇ʷntm – It was folded.

ṗulk̇ʷnt – Fold it. *cmd.*
čṗlk̇ʷiċéʔ – wrap; enfold; roll up. *suffix: **...iċéʔ** – covered in. See: **wrap**.*
sčṗl̇ṗl̇k̇ʷiċeʔ, *sčṗl̇ṗl̇k̇ʷí* – cigarette. *See: **cigarette**.*
es nṗl̇k̇ʷenʔei – S/he is folding a pillow.

k̇ʷeṁt ṗulk̇ʷntxʷ – Then you fold it up. **ha ṗulk̇ʷntxʷ** – Did you fold it?

pṅeẇsm – fold/bend something; bend something from the middle. *rt.: **piṅ** – bend; suffix: **...éẇs** – in between, middle. See: **bend**.*
es pṅeẇs – It is folded; it is bent.

pṅeẇsm – S/he folded. **čn pṅeẇsm, kʷ pṅeẇsm**
es pṅeẇsi – S/he is folding. **čnes pṅeẇsi, kʷes pṅeẇsi**
qs pṅeẇsi – S/he is going to fold. **čiqs pṅeẇsi, kʷqs pṅeẇsi**
pṅéʔeẇsm – They folded. **qeʔ pṅeẇsm, p pṅeẇsm**
es pṅéʔeẇsi – They are folding. **qeʔes pṅeẇsi, pes pṅeẇsi**

pṅeẇsis – S/he folded s.t. **pṅeẇsn, pṅeẇsntxʷ**
es pṅeẇsms – S/he is folding s.t. **ies pṅeẇsm, as pṅeẇsm**
qs pṅeẇsms – S/he is going to fold s.t. **iqs pṅeẇsm, aqs pṅeẇsm**
pṅéʔeẇsis – They folded s.t. **qeʔ pṅeẇsntm, pṅeẇsntp**

es pṅpṅeẇsi – S/he is folding things/repeatedly. **čnes pṅpṅeẇsi, kʷes pṅpṅeẇsi**

pṅeẇsnt – Fold it. *cmd.*

piṅ – bend from one position to an curved/angular position. *See: **bend**.*
čpṅeẇsm – fold onto; bend onto. *(i.e., folding the top portion of a paper onto itself.) See: **bend**.*
npṅusncut – bend one's self in the middle. *See: **bend**.*
npṅeẇsis – fold in. *(i.e., folding paper to make a paper airplane.) See: **bend**.*

The **i** following uvular consonants (UC) and the glottal stop **ʔ** sound like English "*ey*" as in the words th*ey*, h*ey*, wh*ey*, etc. Salish UC are: **q**, **q̇**, **qʷ**, **q̇ʷ**, **x̣**, **x̣ʷ**. For example, the suffix **...qin** – head/top, is often spelled using English *ey* as "q*ey*n". So **qi**, **q̇i**, **qʷi**, **q̇ʷi**, **x̣i**, **x̣ʷi**, may be spelled with English *ey* as **q***ey*, **q̇***ey*, **qʷ***ey*, **q̇ʷ***ey*, **x̣***ey*, **x̣ʷ***ey* in other texts.

follow

aẇtpáqs, *aẇtpá* – follow; walk behind someone.
aẇtpáqs – S/he/it followed. **čn aẇtpáqs, kʷ aẇtpáqs**
es aẇtpaqsi – S/he/it is following. **čnes aẇtpáqsi, kʷes aẇtpáqsi**
qs aẇtpáqsi – S/he/it is following. **čiqs aẇtpáqsi, kʷqs aẇtpáqsi**
aẇtpáʔaqs – They followed. **qeʔ aẇtpáqs, p aẇtpáqs**
es aẇtpáʔaqsi – They are following. **qeʔes aẇtpáqsi, pes aẇtpáqsi**

ewtepis – S/he/it followed s.o. **ewtepn, ewtepntxʷ**
es ewtepms – S/he/it is following s.o. **ies ewtepm, as ewtepm**
qs ewtepms – S/he/it is going to follow s.o. **iqs ewtepm, aqs ewtepm**
ewtéʔepis – They followed s.o. **qeʔ ewtepntm, ewtepntp**
es ewtéʔepms – They are following s.o. **qeʔes ewtepm, es ewtepmp**

awtpaqsiš – Follow. *cmd.*
awtpaqswi – You all follow. *cmd.*
ewtépnt – Follow someone. *cmd.*
awtpncutš – Allow yourself to follow. *cmd.*

awtpncut – allow one's self to follow, to give into.
awtpncut – S/he allowed one's self to follow. **čn awtpncut, kʷ awtpncut**
es awtpncuti – S/he is allowing one's self to follow. **čnes awtpncuti, kʷes awtpncuti**
qs awtpncuti – S/he is going to allow one's self to follow. **čiqs awtpncuti, kʷqs awtpncuti**

s.t. - something, the 3rd person
(s.t.) - something implied
s.o. - someone, the 3rd person
sl. - singular form
pl. - plural form
rt. - root word
cmd. - command
lit. - literally
fig. - figuratively
i.e., - for example
See: - Redirection to a related word.

qʷo ewtepnt – Walk behind me. **es aw̓tpa łu kʷtisi l pyel –** Big Blanket followed Pierre. **kʷ ies ewtepm –** I am following you. **ewtepntst –** S/he followed you.

ecċéwt – late, lagging behind. *See: **last**.*

ecċew̓tl̓wil̓š – S/he/it kept getting behind.

nšiẏustšn – follow in the tracks of someone or an animal; follow in someone's footsteps; emulate someone. *rt.: **šiẏust** – pass through.*
nšiẏustšnm – S/he followed in the tracks. **čn nšiẏustšnm, kʷ nšiẏustšnm**
es nšiẏustšni – S/he is following in the tracks. **čnes nšiẏustšni, kʷes nšiẏustšni**
qs nšiẏustšni – S/he is going to follow in the tracks. **čiqs nšiẏustšni, kʷqs nšiẏustšni**

nšiẏustšis – S/he followed in s.o.'s tracks. **čn nšiẏustšn, kʷ nšiẏustšntxʷ**
es nšiẏustšnms – S/he is following in s.o.'s tracks. **ies nšiẏustšnm, as nšiẏustšnm**
qs nšiẏustšnms – S/he is going to follow in s.o.'s tracks. **iqs nšiẏustšnm, aqs nšiẏustšnm**

nšiẏustšncutn – follower.

nšiẏustšnt – Follow in s.o.'s tracks. *cmd.*
nšiẏustšncut – follow one's own tracks.

fond

q̇iẋtm – cherish something or someone; fond of something possessed; treasure something or someone; show respect by cherishing a gift. *See: **cherish**.*

food

sʔiłn – food. **sʔiłis, isʔiłn, asʔiłn**

sqʷaʔmáqs – habitual food.

smʔáw – left over things.
sčmawá – left over food.

...cin – *suffix indicating an action of the mouth; i.e., speaking, eating, & food. See: **mouth**.*
šymłẋscin – favorite food. **šymłẋscis, inšymłẋscin, anšymłẋscin**

skʷumcn – left over food you take with you for later. *suffix: **...cin, ...cn** – action of the mouth.*

sṫipcin – food that has fallen or was dropped. *rt.: **ṫiip** – fall; suffix: **...cin, ...cn** – action of the mouth.*
es ṫipcini – food is falling from his/her mouth. **čnes ṫipcini, kʷes ṫipcini**

łṫṫipcin – little food fell from his/her mouth.

ccupcn – crumbs from the mouth. *suffix: **...cin, ...cn** – action of the mouth.*
es ccupcni – crumbs are falling from his/her mouth. **čnes ccupcni, kʷes ccupcni**

nẋalẋaltcin, *nẋalẋaltci* **–** ask for food. *suffix: **...cin, ...cn** – action of the mouth.*
es nẋalẋaltcini – S/he is asking for food. **čnes nẋalẋaltcini, kʷes nẋalẋaltcini**

snẋalẋaltcin – food that's asked for.

ałnmsqáẋeʔ, *ałnmsqá* **–** oats; horse food. *rt.: **iłn** – eat; suffix: **...sqáẋeʔ** – domestic animal; mainly referring to horse or car.*

nełnels, *nełne* **–** crave food; want to eat. *See: **crave**.*

fool

psayéʔ – fool; foolish.
psayéʔ – S/he/it is a fool. **čn psayéʔ, kʷ psayéʔ**

k̓ʷl̓spsayémis – S/he/it treated s.o. as a fool. **k̓ʷl̓spsayémn, k̓ʷl̓spsayémntxʷ**
es k̓ʷl̓spsayéms – S/he/it is treating s.o. as a fool. **ies k̓ʷl̓spsayém, as k̓ʷl̓spsayém**
qs k̓ʷl̓spsayéms – S/he/it is going to treat s.o. as a fool. **iqs k̓ʷl̓spsayém, aqs k̓ʷl̓spsayém**

psayus – face of a fool.
čpspsayus – eyes of a fool.

x̣ʷa qeʔ uł psayéʔ – Maybe we were foolish. **čn čpspsayusm –** I have the eyes of a fool.

x̣ił exʷ ye ta es k̓ʷłpusncu l sk̓ʷłpáx̣éms – S/he was really acting like a jerk; s/he had no sense in his/her thinking.

The **i** following uvular consonants (UC) and the glottal stop **ʔ** sound like English *"ey"* as in the words *they*, *hey*, *whey*, etc. Salish UC are: **q**, **q̓**, **qʷ**, **q̓ʷ**, **x̣**, **x̣ʷ**. For example, the suffix **...qin** – head/top, is often spelled using English *ey* as "q*ey*n". So **qi**, **q̓i**, **qʷi**, **q̓ʷi**, **x̣i**, **x̣ʷi**, may be spelled with English *ey* as q*ey*, q̓*ey*, qʷ*ey*, q̓ʷ*ey*, x̣*ey*, x̣ʷ*ey* in other texts.

foolish

ċsčsmscut – do something foolish.
ċsčsmscut – S/he/it did s.t. foolish. **čn ċsčsmscut, kʷ ċsčsmscut**
es ċsčsmscuti – S/he/it is doing s.t. foolish. **čnes ċsčsmscuti, kʷes ċsčsmscuti**
qs ċsčsmscuti – S/he/it is going to do s.t. foolish. **čiqs ċsčsmscuti, kʷqs ċsčsmscuti**

nčl̓pscut, *nčl̓pscu* **–** act as Coyote; be foolish; mimic others' actions just because they are doing it. *rt.:* ***snčl̓ep*** *– coyote; suffix:* ***...cut*** *– action to the self.*
nčl̓pscut – S/he acted like Coyote. **čn nčl̓pscut, kʷ nčl̓pscut**
es nčl̓pscuti – S/he is acting like Coyote. **čnes nčl̓pscuti, kʷes nčl̓pscuti**
qs nčl̓pscuti – S/he is going to act like Coyote. **čiqs nčl̓pscuti, kʷqs nčl̓pscuti**

fools hen

skʷiskʷs – spruce grouse; Franklin's grouse; fools hen; *Falcipennis canadensis*; domestic chicken. *See:* ***chicken.***

foot

sċuʔšin – foot. **sċuċušin –** feet.

sčłčmšin – top of foot.
sṫx̣ṫix̣šn – toes.
syulšn – big toe.
q̓ʷx̣ʷqinšn – toenail.
snłčaʔčmqn – tip of foot.
sněmičn̓šn – bottom of foot.

łkʷkʷnumešn – small feet.

sčchesšn – right foot.
sččiq̓ʷesšn – left foot.

nq̓naq̓šn – stink feet.
nq̓naq̓šn – S/he/it had stink feet. **čn nq̓naq̓šn, kʷ nq̓naq̓šn**
es nq̓naq̓šni – S/he/it has stink feet. **čnes nq̓naq̓šni, kʷes nq̓naq̓šni**
qs nq̓naq̓šni – S/he/it is going to have stink feet. **čiqs nq̓naq̓šni, kʷqs nq̓naq̓šni**

slsulšn – cold feet.
slsulšn – S/he/it had cold feet. **čn slsulšn, kʷ slsulšn**
es slsulšni – S/he/it has cold feet. **čnes slsulšni, kʷes slsulšni**
qs slsulšni – S/he/it is going to have cold feet. **čiqs slsulšni, kʷqs slsulšni**

s.t. - something, the 3rd person
(s.t.) - something implied
s.o. - someone, the 3rd person
sl. - singular form
pl. - plural form
rt. - root word
cmd. - command
lit. - literally
fig. - figuratively
i.e., - for example
See: - Redirection to a related word.

for

x̣ʷl̓ – for; because; so; about.
x̣ʷlstém̓, *x̣ʷlsté* **–** why. *See:* ***why.***
x̣ʷl̓ šeẏ – for that.

mił nwist x̣ʷl̓ nplé – It is too high for you guys. **qeʔes čučawi x̣ʷl̓ sṫiplscut –** We are praying for the lost articles. **čnes nx̣saqs łu x̣ʷl̓ isx̣mnčew̓s –** I am on a good path because of my lover. **čn x̣ʷełe x̣ʷl̓ čnes ntelsi čiqs pk̓ʷlʔemi –** I am hurrying because I want to play ball. **čnes xʷeƛ̓misti x̣ʷl̓ čiqs npiyelsi –** I am relaxing so I can be happy. **k̓ʷ x̣ʷl̓ šey̓ u ećx̣i –** Oh, that's why its like that. **qeʔes čsšeńši x̣ʷl̓ qeʔ snlaqi –** We are going after rocks for the sweat. **x̣e ies k̓ʷłpax̣em x̣ʷl̓ anwi –** I am thinking something good about you.

i mi – It is plainly evident; it is absolute; it is fact. *See: **absolute**.*

forbid

čx̣enépleʔm – forbid. *suffix: **...épleʔ** – permanence.*
čx̣enepleʔis – S/he forbade s.t. **čx̣enepleʔn, čx̣enepleʔntxʷ**

x̣eʔe – keep someone in line; correct behavior; forbid bad behavior; prevent misdeeds; make someone behave. *See: **discipline**.*

maq – forbid; prevent; detain someone from doing, going, or starting.
maqm – S/he forbid (s.o.) from going. **čn maqnm, kʷ maqm**
es maqi – S/he is forbiding (s.o.) from going. **ies maqi, as maqi**
qs maqi – S/he is going to forbid (s.o.) from going. **iqs maqi, aqs maqi**

maqis – S/he prevented s.o. from going. **maqn, maqntxʷ**
es maqms – S/he is preventing s.o. from going. **ies maqm, as maqm**
qs maqms – S/he is going to prevent s.o. from going. **iqs maqm, aqs maqm**

maqnt – Prevent him/her. *cmd.*
es nmqmelsi – S/he is wanting to prevent.
es mqcinms – S/he is talking s.o. out of going. **ies mqcinm, as mqcinm**

ta – no; not. *See: **no**.*

čʔemtupsm – keep someone from doing something; hold someone back. *rt.: **emut** – sit; suffix: **...ups, ps** – butt, tail. See: **hold back**.*

forecast

aćx̣nuxʷ – forecast weather. *suffix: **...ṁnuxʷ** – process through/become.*
aćx̣nuxʷi – S/he forcasted weather. **čn aćx̣nuxʷi, kʷ aćx̣nuxʷi**
es aćx̣nuxʷi – S/he is forcasting weather. **čnes aćx̣nuxʷi, kʷes aćx̣nuxʷi**
qs aćx̣nuxʷi – S/he is going to forcast weather. **čiqs aćx̣nuxʷi, kʷqs aćx̣nuxʷi**

sʔaćx̣nuxʷ – weather forecast.

forehead

sčłčméssn – forehead. *rt.: **čm** – extremity.*

forest

nkʷéct, *nkʷé* – forest; backwoods; brush; thicket.

forest fire

ṗaap – grass/timber caught fire. *See: **fire**.*

forever

tšiyeẁs – forever.

forget

nłépt – forget.
nłéptmis – S/he/it forgot s.t./s.o. **nłeptmn, nłeptmntxʷ**
es nłéptms – S/he/it is forgetting s.t./s.o. **ies nłeptm, as nłeptmn**
qs nłéptms – S/he/it is going to forget s.t./s.o. **iqs nłeptm, aqs nłeptmn**
nłéʔeptmis – They forgot s.t./s.o. **qeʔ nłéptmntm, nłéptmntp**
es nłéʔeptms – They are forgetting s.t./s.o. **qeʔes nłéptm, es nłéptmp**

nłéptsts – S/he/it caused s.o. to forgot. **nłeptstn, nłeptstxʷ**
es nłéptsts – S/he/it is making s.o. forget. **es nłeptstn, es nłeptstxʷ**
qs nłéptms – S/he/it is going to make s.o. forget. **iqs nłeptm, aqs nłeptmn**

snłept – something forgotten.

scnłept – something that's been forgotten. *prefix:* ***sc...*** *– s.t. that's been done/made/prepared.*
nłptémn – one inclined to forget. *suffix:* ***...emn*** *– one inclined to do.*
nłpłptmuł – one that habitually forgets. *suffix :****...łmuł*** *– one that habitually does.*
nłptmistemn – one inclined to forget purposely. *suffix:* ***...emn*** *– one inclined to do.*

nłeptmnt – Forget it. *cmd.*
ta qs nłeptmntxʷ – Do not forget it. *cmd.*
ta qes nłeptmstxʷ – Do not forget about it. *cmd.*
ta qes nłeptmštxʷ – Do not forget for s.o. *cmd.*
nłptmist – eliminate something from one's mind; forget on purpose. *See:* ***eliminate.***

nłéptmncn – I forgot you. **ta qs nłeptmn** – I will not forget. **čn nłptémn** – I am forgetful; I forget things all the time. **kʷ nłptémn** – You are forgetful. **nłéptmn ismeṅxʷ u inčpáx̣mn** – I forgot my cigarettes and matches. **nłeptmn łu skʷests** – I forgot his/her name. **es misten čn ep snłept** – I know I have something forgotten; I know I forgot something.

The **i** following uvular consonants (UC) and the glottal stop ʔ sound like English "*ey*" as in the words th*ey*, h*ey*, wh*ey*, etc. Salish UC are: **q**, **q̇**, **qʷ**, **q̇ʷ**, **x̣**, **x̣ʷ**. For example, the suffix **...qin** – head/top, is often spelled using English *ey* as "q*ey*n". So **qi**, **q̇i**, **qʷi**, **q̇ʷi**, **x̣i**, **x̣ʷi**, may be spelled with English *ey* as **q***ey*, **q̇***ey*, **qʷ***ey*, **q̇ʷ***ey*, **x̣***ey*, **x̣ʷ***ey* in other texts.

fork

łek̇ʷpcintn, *łek̇ʷpci* – fork. *rt.:* ***čłk̇ʷum*** *– pick up; suffix:* ***...cin, ...cn*** *– action of the mouth; suffix:* ***...tin, ...tn*** *– means of/device.*
łek̇ʷpcinm – S/he forked (s.t.). **čn łek̇ʷpcinm, kʷ łek̇ʷpcinm**
es łek̇ʷpcini – S/he is forking (s.t.). **čnes łek̇ʷpcini, kʷes łek̇ʷpcini**
qs łek̇ʷpcini – S/he is going to fork (s.t.). **čiqs łek̇ʷpcini, kʷqs łek̇ʷpcini**

łek̇ʷpcinmis – S/he forked s.t. **łek̇ʷpcinmn, łek̇ʷpcinmntxʷ**
es łek̇ʷpcinms – S/he is forking s.t. **ies łek̇ʷpcinm, as łek̇ʷpcinm**
qs łek̇ʷpcinms – S/he is going to fork s.t. **iqs łek̇ʷpcinm, aqs łek̇ʷpcinm**

łek̇ʷpciniš – Fork (s.t.). *cmd.*
łek̇ʷpcinmnt – Fork it. *cmd.*

čsłk̇ʷłk̇ʷmi – pitchfork. *See:* ***pitchfork.***

fort

smituʔ – fort *(for defense).*

Fort Benton

mltałxʷ – Fort Benton, Montana; *lit. mud house.*

Fort Missoula

sxʷpulstwe – Fort Missoula, Montana.
smlk̇ʷšná – mountain near Ft. Missoula.

Fort Owen

npƛ̣u – Fort Owen near Stevensville, Montana.

forty

msłʔupn, *msłʔu* – forty.

forward

issax̣m – move forward.
issax̣m – S/he/it moved forward. **čn issax̣m, kʷ issax̣m**
es issax̣isti – S/he/it is moving forward. **čnes issax̣isti, kʷes issax̣isti**
qs issax̣isti – S/he/it is going to move forward. **čiqs issax̣isti, kʷqs issax̣isti**
isśáʔax̣m – They moved forward. **qeʔ issax̣m, p issax̣m**
es isśáʔax̣isti – They are moving forward. **qeʔes issax̣isti, pes issax̣isti**

issax̣miš – Move forward. *cmd.*

q̇ʷamim – move something. *See:* ***move.***

s.t. - something, the 3rd person
(s.t.) - something implied
s.o. - someone, the 3rd person
sl. - singular form
pl. - plural form
rt. - root word
cmd. - command
lit. - literally
fig. - figuratively
i.e., - for example
See: - Redirection to a related word.

fossil

tsq̇spscoṁ – fossil; ancient bones.

kʷl̓l̓eysšṅ – fossilized; changed to stone.

foster daughter **sck̓ʷl̓sťm̓čʔé** – foster daughter. *prefix:* ***sck̓ʷl̓...*** *– s.t. that's been made.*

foster elder sister **sck̓ʷl̓ƚčíčšeʔ** – foster elder sister. *prefix:* ***sck̓ʷl̓...*** *– s.t. that's been made.*

foster father **sck̓ʷl̓méstm̓** – foster father of a female. *prefix:* ***sck̓ʷl̓...*** *– s.t. that's been made.*

sck̓ʷl̓l̓ʔew – foster father of a male. *prefix:* ***sck̓ʷl̓...*** *– s.t. that's been made.*

foster mother **sck̓ʷl̓tum̓** – foster mother of female. *prefix:* ***sck̓ʷl̓...*** *– s.t. that's been made.*

sck̓ʷl̓sk̓ʷuy – foster mother of male. *prefix:* ***sck̓ʷl̓...*** *– s.t. that's been made.*

foster parents **sck̓ʷl̓p̓x̣ʷp̓x̣ʷót** – foster parents. *prefix:* ***sck̓ʷl̓...*** *– s.t. that's been made.*

foster relative **sck̓ʷl̓ƚčíčšeʔ** – foster elder sister. *prefix:* ***sck̓ʷl̓...*** *– s.t. that's been made.*
sck̓ʷl̓méstm̓ – foster father of a women. *prefix:* ***sck̓ʷl̓...*** *– s.t. that's been made.*
sck̓ʷl̓p̓x̣ʷp̓x̣ʷót – foster parents. *prefix:* ***sck̓ʷl̓...*** *– s.t. that's been made.*
sck̓ʷl̓qecč, sck̓ʷl̓ƚqáqceʔ – foster older brother of a female. *prefix:* ***sck̓ʷl̓...*** *– s.t. that's been made.*
sck̓ʷl̓sqʷséʔ – foster son. *prefix:* ***sck̓ʷl̓...*** *– s.t. that's been made.*

foster younger sister **sck̓ʷl̓ƚccʔups** – foster younger sister. *prefix:* ***sck̓ʷl̓...*** *– s.t. that's been made.*

four **mus** – four. **msmus** – fours. *pl.*
mus sƚqʷá – four rabbits.

mus... prefix indicating four combined with another affix forming a full word.
mosq̓t – four days. *suffix:* ***...asq̓t*** *– sky, day.*
musƚxʷ – four houses. *suffix:* ***...eƚxʷ, ...ƚxʷ*** *– house.*
musšn̓ – four rocks. *suffix:* ***...essn̓, ...ssn̓*** *– rock.*
nmsep – four eggs. *circumfix:* ***n...ep*** *– egg.*
čmusm, *čmu* – four people. *prefix:* ***č...*** *– people. suffix:*

čaƚlásq̓t x̣ʷa mosq̓t – three or four days.

msƚ... – prefix indicating four, add to a full word.
msƚʔupn, *msƚʔu* – forty.
msƚšƛ̓ip – S/he lost four times. **čn msƚšƛ̓ip, kʷ msƚšƛ̓ip**
mssqáx̣eʔ, *mssqá* – four domestic animals. *The* ***ƚ*** *is dropped when preceding an* ***s****.*
msƚʔopnčstqn – four thousand.

four hundred **msƚnk̓ʷoʔqín,** *msƚnk̓ʷoʔqí* – four hundred.

fox **x̣ʷax̣ʷáalixʷ,** *x̣ʷax̣ʷaá* – fox; *Vulpes vulpes.*

fraction **snttx̣ʷew̓s** – something that's divided. *suffix:* ***...éw̓s*** *– in between, middle.*
sntx̣ʷew̓s – something divided; half.
nk̓ʷuʔ čeƚlsntx̣ʷtx̣ʷew̓s – one third, 1/3; one of three divided things.
nk̓ʷuʔ mssntx̣ʷtx̣ʷew̓s – one fourth, 1/4; one of four divided things.
nk̓ʷuʔ clčsntx̣ʷtx̣ʷew̓s – one fifth, 1/5; one of five divided things.
nk̓ʷuʔ t̓q̓nčsntx̣ʷtx̣ʷew̓s – one sixth, 1/6; one of six divided things.
nk̓ʷuʔ sp̓l̓čsntx̣ʷtx̣ʷew̓s – one seventh, 1/7; one of seven divided things.
nk̓ʷuʔ henmsntx̣ʷtx̣ʷew̓s – one eighth, 1/8; one of eight divided things.
nk̓ʷuʔ x̣ntsntx̣ʷtx̣ʷew̓s – one ninth, 1/9; one of nine divided things.
nk̓ʷuʔ upnčsntx̣ʷtx̣ʷew̓s – one tenth, 1/10; one of ten divided things.

nk̓ʷuʔ čełlulexʷ – one of three or 1/3. *(This is in reference to area.) See: **area**.*

Frances
pleswe – Frances.

Francis
plasi – Francis.

Frank
plenk – Frank.
plasi – Francis; Frank.

Franklin's grouse
skʷiskʷs – spruce grouse; Franklin's grouse; fools hen; *Falcipennis canadensis*; domestic chicken. *See: **chicken**.*

free
pƛ̓im – release; free from something; remove something. *See: **release**.*

es ac – S/he/it is tied *(not free). See: **tie**.*

freeze
sult – freeze solid objects.
es sulti – S/he/it is freezing; becoming frozen. **čnes sulti, kʷes sulti**
qs sulti – S/he/it is going to be freezing; become frozen. **čiqs sulti, kʷqs sulti**

es slsulti – Each one is becoming frozen.

sulis – S/he froze s.t. **suln, sulntxʷ**
es sulms – S/he is freezing s.t. **ies sulm, as sulm**
qs sulms – S/he is going to freeze s.t. **iqs sulm, aqs sulm**

nsulusm – freeze berries/round objects.
nsolqs – frozen nose.
slsulšn – His/her foot fell asleep. **čn slsulšn, kʷ slsulšn**

iqs sulm łu isqeltč – I am going to freeze my meat? **iqs nsulusm łu ist̓ša** – I am going to freeze my huckleberries?

nimáp – freeze; water hardened. *rt.: **imáp** – harden by cooling.*
es nimpá – The water is hardening.
qs nimpá – The water is going to harden.

es nimápisti – The water is freezing over.

nimpstás – S/he froze the water. **nimpstán, nimpstáxʷ**
es nimpáms – S/he is freezing the water. **ies nimpám, as nimpám**
qs nimpáms – S/he is going to freeze the water. **iqs nimpám, aqs nimpám**

snimáp – frozen water; ice.
scnimáp – water that's been frozen; ice.

nimpáskʷ – Freeze the water. *cmd.*
i nimc̓natkʷ – frozen river/stream banks.

nyametkʷ – make ice. *rt.: **imáp** – harden by cooling; suffix: **...etkʷ, ...tkʷ** – liquid*
nyametkʷis – S/he made ice. **nyametkʷn, nyametkʷntxʷ**
es nyametkʷms – S/he is making ice. **ies nyametkʷm, as nyametkʷm**
qs nyametkʷms – S/he is going to make ice. **iqs nyametkʷm, aqs nyametkʷm**

ha aqs nyametkʷm – Are you going to freeze the water; are you going to make ice?

p̓ałt – freeze a little. *An indication of this state is when water keeps freezing over the top of ice.*
es p̓ałti – when the water keeps freezing over the ice.

The **i** following uvular consonants (UC) and the glottal stop **ʔ** sound like English "*ey*" as in the words *they, hey, whey*, etc. Salish UC are: **q, q̓, qʷ, q̓ʷ, x̣, x̣ʷ**. For example, the suffix **...qin** – head/top, is often spelled using English *ey* as "q*ey*n". So **qi, q̓i, qʷi, q̓ʷi, x̣i, x̣ʷi**, may be spelled with English *ey* as **q***ey*, **q̓***ey*, **qʷ***ey*, **q̓ʷ***ey*, **x̣***ey*, **x̣ʷ***ey* in other texts.

s.t. - something, the 3rd person
(s.t.) - something implied
s.o. - someone, the 3rd person
sl. - singular form
pl. - plural form
rt. - root word
cmd. - command
lit. - literally
fig. - figuratively
i.e., - for example
See: - Redirection to a related word.

es ṗṗałti – It is freezing a little.

čłčiḱʷčn – water over ice.

nołip – The water/river became one piece; the ice formed all over the water. *rt.:* ***oył*** *– one piece.*
es nołpmi – The water/river is becoming one piece; it is freezing over.
qs nołpmi – The water/river is going to become one piece; it is going to freeze over.

ixʷmus – chilled from cold weather; very cold weather. *See:* ***cold.***

uxʷt – freezing; get frostbite. *See:* ***frostbite.***

freezer

snˀuxʷtn – place to freeze; freezer. *prefix:* ***sn...*** *– a place of; suffix:* ***...tin, ...tn*** *– means of/device.*
snˀuxʷmn – freezer. *prefix:* ***sn...*** *– a place of; suffix:* ***...min, ...mn*** *– instrument/tool.*

snsulmn – refrigerator. *prefix:* ***sn...*** *– a place of; suffix:* ***...min, ...mn*** *– instrument/tool.*

French

semeˀ – French.
semeˀ nuwewlštn – French language. *suffix:* ***...tin, ...tn*** *– means of/device.*

fresh

qeẏl – fresh (meat).

qal – fresh, not dry; green plants/trees; wet meat/hide.
i qal – It is fresh.
qlalqʷ – green wood.
qlałq – fresh roots. *suffix:* ***...ałq*** *– smell, accompaniment.*
qlelxʷ – fresh hide.
qlełċeˀ – fresh meat.
qlesłl – fresh fish.
čqlqlus – fresh berries/fruit.

Friday

clčstasq̇t, *clčsta* – Friday, the fifth day past Sunday. *suffix:* ***...asq̇t*** *– sky, day.*
eł clčstasq̇t – Friday; *lit. again the fifth day past Sunday.*

friend

ľáx̣t – befriend.
ḱʷlsľľáx̣t – S/he/it made friends. **čn ḱʷlsľľáx̣t, kʷ ḱʷlsľľáx̣t**
es ḱʷlsľľáx̣ti – S/he/it is making friends. **čnes ḱʷlsľľáx̣ti, kʷes ḱʷlsľľáx̣ti**
qs ḱʷlsľľáx̣ti – S/he/it is going to make friends. **čiqs ḱʷlsľľáx̣ti, kʷqs ḱʷlsľľáx̣ti**

ľáx̣tmis – S/he/it befriended s.o. **ľáx̣tmn, ľáx̣tmntxʷ**
es ľáx̣tmms – S/he/it is befriending s.o. **ies ľáx̣tmm, as ľáx̣tmm**
qs ľáx̣tmms – S/he/it is going to befriend s.o. **iqs ľáx̣tmm, aqs ľáx̣tmm**

sľáx̣t – friend; partner. **sľľax̣t** *pl.*
lx̣temn – one inclined to be friendly. *suffix:* ***...emn*** *– one inclined to do.*

ľáx̣tmnt – Befriend s.o. *cmd.*
ľx̣teẇs – friends with one other; close friend. *(In the past close friends would join arm in arm when they met.)* *rt.:* ***lax̣t*** *– friend; suffix:* ***...éẇs*** *– in between, middle.*

q̇ep – friend/companion to death; someone that will die for one.
q̇pntes – S/he stayed close to s.o. **q̇pnten, q̇pntexʷ**
es q̇pims – S/he stays close to s.o. **ies q̇pim, as q̇pim**

q̇pncutn – friend to death.

x̣cut – partner; share/help in the activities of another; be a comrade; associate as a companion. *See:* ***partner.***

ihém – regain friendship; make peace; reconcile differences. *See: **peace**.*

fright

čin – afraid of getting hurt. *(i.e., falling, etc.) See: **afraid**.*

nx̣élm – afraid/scared of something. *See: **scare**.*

kʷeɬ – jumpy, nervous, edgy. *See: **nervous**.*

kʷssusm, *kʷssu* **–** startle. *See: **startle**.*

fringe

es cocoo – fringes; things hanging down in a line.
cocoontes – S/he is making fringes of it. **cocoonten, cocoontexʷ**
es cocooms – S/he is making fringes of it. **ies cocoom, as cocoom**
qs cocooms – S/he is going to make fringes of it. **iqs cocoom, aqs cocoom**

cocoont – Make fringes of it. *cmd.*

frog

ɬmɬam̓áyeʔ, *ɬmɬam̓á* **–** frog.
ɬɬm̓ɬam̓á – little frog.

xʷit ɬmɬam̓á – many frogs. **čeʔ ta epɬ ɬmɬam̓á –** There are no frogs.

snakʷkʷá – toad.

ql̓ql̓aqs, *ql̓ql̓a* **–** tadpole.

front

miɬčmels – in the front. *rt.: **čm** – extremity.*
smiɬčmels – front side.

l̓ miɬčmels tšeċ m ṫk̓ʷntexʷ – Put the bull elk in the front.

swe ɬu l asmiɬčmels – Who is in front of you?

sččmaxʷcč – chest. *See: **chest**.*

frost

sq̇ʷéyt – frost.
i q̇ʷéy – It is frosted.
es q̇ʷéyti – It is frosting.
sq̇ʷéylexʷ – frost on the ground.

ixʷmus – chilled from cold weather; very cold weather. *See: **cold**.*

qʷós – curly sticking out.
čqʷósqn spq̇niʔ – February.

frostbite

uxʷt – freezing; get frostbite.
uxʷt – S/he/it froze. **čn uxʷt, kʷ uxʷt**
es uxʷti – S/he/it is freezing. **čnes uxʷti, kʷes uxʷti**
qs uxʷti – S/he/it is going to freeze. **čiqs uxʷti, kʷqs uxʷti**

es uxʷuxʷšn – His/her feet are frostbitten. **čnes uxʷuxʷšn, kʷes uxʷuxʷšn**
es uxʷuxʷčst – His/her hands are frostbitten. **čnes uxʷuxʷčst, kʷes uxʷuxʷčst**
es uxʷuxʷeneʔ – His/her ears are frostbitten. **čnes uxʷuxʷeneʔ, kʷes uxʷuxʷeneʔ**

sʔuxʷt – frostbite.
uxʷuxʷt – frostbitten; very painful frostbite.

froze

sult – freeze solid objects. *See: **freeze**.*

ixʷmus – chilled from cold weather; very cold weather. *See: **cold**.*

The **i** following uvular consonants (UC) and the glottal stop ʔ sound like English "*ey*" as in the words th*ey*, h*ey*, wh*ey*, etc. Salish UC are: **q**, **q̇**, **qʷ**, **q̇ʷ**, **x̣**, **x̣ʷ**. For example, the suffix ...**qin** – head/top, is often spelled using English *ey* as "q*ey*n". So **qi**, **q̇i**, **qʷi**, **q̇ʷi**, **x̣i**, **x̣ʷi**, may be spelled with English *ey* as **q***ey*, **q̇***ey*, **qʷ***ey*, **q̇ʷ***ey*, **x̣***ey*, **x̣ʷ***ey* in other texts.

s.t. - something, the 3rd person
(s.t.) - something implied
s.o. - someone, the 3rd person
sl. - singular form
pl. - plural form
rt. - root word
cmd. - command
lit. - literally
fig. - figuratively
i.e., - for example
See: - Redirection to a related word.

nimáp – freeze; water hardened. *See: **freeze**.*

uxʷt – freezing; get frostbite. *See: **frostbite**.*

fruit **sṗiqáłq** – berry, fruit, raisin. *rt.: **ṗiẏáq** – ready, ripe; suffix: **...ałq** – smell, accompaniment.*

frustrated **yéṁmist,** *yéṁm* – despaired; frustrated; troubled; worried; have a block; have a dilemma. *See: **despair**.*

fry **ċáx̣m,** *ċá* – fry something.

ċax̣m – S/he fried (s.t.). **čn ċax̣m, kʷ ċax̣m**
es ċax̣i – S/he is frying (s.t.). **čnes ċax̣i, kʷes ċax̣i**
qs ċax̣i – S/he is going to fry (s.t.). **čiqs ċax̣i, kʷqs ċax̣i**
es ċáʔax̣i – They are frying (s.t.). **qeʔes ċax̣i, pes ċax̣i**

ċax̣is – S/he fried s.t. **ċax̣n, ċax̣ntxʷ**
es ċax̣ms – S/he is frying s.t. **ies ċax̣m, as ċax̣m**
qs ċax̣ms – S/he is going to fry s.t. **iqs ċax̣m, aqs ċax̣m**
ċáʔax̣is – They fried s.t. **qeʔ ċax̣ntm, ċax̣ntp**

ċax̣mis – S/he used s.t. to fry. **ċax̣mn, ċax̣nmtxʷ**
es ċax̣mms – S/he is using s.t. to fry. **ies ċax̣mm, as ċax̣mm**
qs ċax̣mms – S/he is going to use s.t. to fry. **čiqs ċax̣mm, kʷqs ċax̣mm**

sxʷċax̣m – one tasked to fry. *prefix: **sxʷ...** – one tasked to do.*
ċax̣émn – one inclined to fry. *suffix: **...emn** – one inclined to do.*
scċax̣ – something that's been fried. *prefix: **sc...** – s.t. that's been done/made/prepared.*
snċáx̣mn – frying pan.
čċax̣mn – remains of s.t. that's been fried

ċáx̣iš – Fry (s.t.). *cmd.*
ċáx̣nt – Fry something. *cmd.*
nċax̣pm – fry eggs. *See: **egg**.*
nċax̣lexʷm – make frybread.

t cni u ċax̣is łu lkʷošó – S/he fried the bacon. **čiqs ċáx̣i t úʔuséʔ** – I am going to fry eggs. **ṅem čn nċax̣lexʷm** – I will make frybread. **steṁ łu ċax̣mntxʷ łu sqeltč** – What did you use to fry the meat? **swe łu ċax̣is łu sqeltš** – Who fried the meat?

frybread **nċáx̣lexʷ** – make frybread. *rt.: **ċax̣** – fry; prefix: **sc...** – s.t. that's been done/made/prepared.*

nċáx̣lexʷm – S/he made frybread. **čn nċáx̣lexʷm, kʷ nċáx̣lexʷm**
es nċáx̣lexʷi – S/he is making frybread. **čnes nċáx̣lexʷi, kʷes nċáx̣lexʷi**
nċáʔax̣lexʷm – They made frybread. **qeʔ nċáx̣lexʷm, p nċáx̣lexʷm**

scnċáx̣lexʷ – frybread, bread that's been fried.

nċáx̣lexʷiš – Make frybread. *cmd.*

ṅem čn nċax̣lexʷm – I will make frybread.

frying pan **snċáx̣mn** – place to fry; frying pan.

full **q̓ʷéċ** – filled to the top.

q̓ʷéċt – It got filled full.
es q̓ʷéċti – It is getting full.
qs q̓ʷéċti – It is going to get full.

q̓ʷéċis – S/he/it filled it. **q̓ʷéċn, q̓ʷéċntxʷ**
es q̓ʷéċnms – S/he/it is filling it. **ies q̓ʷéċnm, as q̓ʷéċnm**
qs q̓ʷéċnms – S/he/it is going to fill it. **iqs q̓ʷéċnm, aqs q̓ʷéċnm**

q̓ʷéċsts – S/he/it made it full. **q̓ʷéċstn, q̓ʷéċstxʷ**
es q̓ʷéċms – S/he/it is making it full. **ies q̓ʷéċm, as q̓ʷéċm**
qs q̓ʷéċms – S/he/it is going to make it full. **iqs q̓ʷéċm, aqs q̓ʷéċm**

q̓ʷeċstm – It was filled by someone.

q̓ʷéċnt – Fill it. *cmd.*
q̓ʷéċiskʷ – Fill it; make it full. *cmd.*

nq̓ʷeċłċeʔ – fill the inside.

nsixʷn inłl̓pó t kapi u q̓ʷéct – I filled my cup full of coffee. **q̓ʷeċstm ci łčép t st̓šá** – Somebody filled the bucket with huckleberries. **kʷ nq̓ʷeċłċeʔ łu t x̣ést** – You are full of good.

The **i** following uvular consonants (UC) and the glottal stop **ʔ** sound like English "*ey*" as in the words *they, hey, whey*, etc. Salish UC are: **q, q̓, qʷ, q̓ʷ, x̣, x̣ʷ**. For example, the suffix ...**qin** – head/top, is often spelled using English *ey* as "q*ey*n". So **qi, q̓i, qʷi, q̓ʷi, x̣i, x̣ʷi**, may be spelled with English *ey* as **q***ey*, **q̓***ey*, **qʷ***ey*, **q̓ʷ***ey*, **x̣***ey*, **x̣ʷ***ey* in other texts.

mq̓enč, *mq̓e* – full from eating.
mq̓enč – S/he got full. **čn mq̓enč, kʷ mq̓enč**
es mq̓enči – S/he is full. **čnes mq̓enči, kʷes mq̓enči**
qs mq̓enči – S/he is going to be full. **čiqs mq̓enči, kʷas mq̓enči**

ha kʷ mq̓enč – Are you full?

mq̓nčetkʷ – full from drink.

čxʷʔaqsm, *čxʷʔa* – eat a lot. *See: **eat**.*

ml̓ukʷ – spread all around; propagate; grow, of non-living things. *See: **all around**.*

ml̓ip – overflow; inundate; overwhelm from something. *(i.e., riverbank, a container, etc.)* *See: **overflow**.*

t̓ečt – overflow the banks; to flood. *See: **flood**.*

fun

x̣stmels, *x̣stme* – have fun; have good feelings; enjoy something; entertained. *See: **enjoy**.*
es x̣smelsi – S/he is having fun. **čnes x̣smelsi, kʷes x̣smelsi**

čn x̣stmels łu čnes qq̓m̓eyeʔ – I had fun fishing. **ṅe kʷ sust t nx̣oskʷ šey̓ u kʷ nte x̣stme** – When you drink beer you think you are having fun.

nx̣stminm – enjoy something.
nx̣stminm – S/he/it had fun. **čn nx̣stminm, kʷ nx̣stminm**
es nx̣stmini – S/he/it is having fun. **čnes nx̣stmini, kʷes nx̣stmini**
qs nx̣stmini – S/he/it is going to have fun. **čiqs nx̣stmini, kʷqs nx̣stmini**
nx̣stmíʔinm – They had fun. **qeʔ nx̣stminm, p nx̣stminm**

nx̣stmis – S/he/it enjoyed s.t./s.o. **nx̣stmin, nx̣stmintxʷ**
es nx̣stminms – S/he/it is enjoying s.t./s.o. **ies nx̣stminm, as nx̣stminm**
qs nx̣stminms – S/he/it is going to enjoy s.t./s.o. **iqs nx̣stminm, aqs nx̣stminm**
es nx̣stmíʔinms – They are enjoying s.t./s.o. **qeʔes nx̣stminm, es nx̣stminmp**

ṅem nx̣stminm – S/he/it will have fun. **ṅem čn nx̣stminm, ṅem kʷ nx̣stminm**
ṅem nx̣stmíʔinm – They will have fun. **ṅem qeʔ nx̣stminm, ṅem p nx̣stminm**

s.t. - something, the 3rd person
(s.t.) - something implied
s.o. - someone, the 3rd person
sl. - singular form
pl. - plural form
rt. - root word
cmd. - command
lit. - literally
fig. - figuratively
i.e., - for example
See: - Redirection to a related word.

funeral

lq̓łtmtmnéy – funeral; bury the dead.

tmtmnéy̓ – the dead; deceased; departed. *See: **dead**.*

funny **x̣stmels,** *x̣stme* – have fun; enjoy something; be enertained. *See:* ***enjoy.***

fur **spum** – fur (animal).

spomqn – fur hat.
pomqnm – S/he put on a fur hat. **čn pomqnm, kʷ pomqnm**
es pomqni – S/he putting on a fur hat. **čnes pomqni, kʷes pomqni**

es pomqn – S/he is wearing a fur hat. **čnes pomqn, kʷes pomqn**

pomqniš – Put your fur hat on. *cmd.*

fur coat **spumlqs** – fur coat. *rt.:* ***spum*** *– fur; suffix:* ***...lqs, ...alqs*** *– clothes.*
pumlqsm – S/he put on a fur coat. **čn pumlqsm, kʷ pumlqsm**
es pumlqsi – S/he putting on a fur coat. **čnes pumlqsi, kʷes pumlqsi**

es pumlqs – S/he is wearing a fur coat. **čnes pumlqs, kʷes pumlqs**

pumlqsiš – Put your fur coat on. *cmd.*

sčuptsálqs – fur coat; hairy coat. *rt.:* ***čupu*** *– hairy; suffix:* ***...lqs, ...alqs*** *– clothes.*
es čuptsálqs – S/he is wearing a hairy coat. **čnes čuptsálqs, kʷes čuptsálqs**

čuptsálqsiš – Put your hairy coat on. *cmd.*

furious **léč̓** – furious; really angry; mad; in a rage; violent.
léč̓ – S/he/it got furious. **čn léč̓, kʷ léč̓**
es léč̓i – S/he/it is furious. **čnes léč̓i, kʷes léč̓i**
qs léč̓i – S/he/it is going to be furious. **čiqs léč̓i, kʷqs léč̓i**

léč̓is – S/he/it got furious at s.o. **léč̓n, léč̓ntxʷ**
es léč̓nms – S/he/it is furious at s.o. **ies léč̓nm, as léč̓nm**
es léʔeč̓nms – They are furious at s.o. **qeʔes léč̓nm, es léč̓nmp**

es lč̓léč̓iʔ – S/he/it is repeatedly furious. **čnes lč̓léč̓iʔ, kʷes lč̓léč̓iʔ**
es łl̓él̓č̓iʔ – S/he/it is, slightly, furious. **čnes łl̓él̓č̓iʔ, kʷes łl̓él̓č̓iʔ**
es łl̓él̓č̓nms – S/he/it is, slightly, furious at s.o. **ies łl̓él̓č̓nm, as łl̓él̓č̓nm**

lč̓emn – one inclined to get furious. *suffix:* ***...emn*** *– one inclined to do.*
lč̓lič̓t – furious one.

leč̓iš – Get furious. *cmd.*
ll̓č̓iscut – S/he got furious with one's self. **čn ll̓č̓iscut, kʷ ll̓č̓iscut**
es ll̓č̓iscuti – S/he is getting furious with one's self. **čnes ll̓č̓iscuti, kʷes ll̓č̓iscuti**

es lč̓nwexʷi – They are being furious with each other. **qeʔes lč̓nwexʷi, pes lč̓nwexʷi**
es lč̓lwisi – S/he is going around being furious. **čnes lč̓lwisi, kʷes lč̓lwisi**
člč̓leč̓s – have mean eyes. *circumfix:* ***č...us*** *– spherical object; eyes. See:* ***eye.***
nmlč̓ič̓ṅ – turn one's back in anger to someone. *See:* ***turn.***

čn nte ṅem kʷ leč̓iʔ čn kʷłax̣lmist t anwi – I thought you would be furious. **qʷo es léč̓nms** – S/he is furious with me.

furniture **nqmnl̓scut** – furniture. *rt.:* ***qmin*** *– place things down.*

furry **i čppuṁċeʔ** – It is furry. *suffix:* ***...iċéʔ*** *– covered in.*

future **tʔé pisteṁ** – future, some day.

G

Gabriel **kaplyé –** Gabriel.

gall bladder **nqqlistn –** gall bladder.

gallon **nk̓ʷuʔ čilwi –** one gallon.

gallop **pq̇smi –** gallop.
es pq̇smi – It is galloping. **čnes pq̇smi, kʷes pq̇smi**

es ppq̇msmi – It is slow galloping (horse).

gamble **x̣cx̣cim –** gamble. *rt.:* ***x̣cim*** *– make ready/orderly. See:* ***ready.***
x̣cx̣cim – S/he gambled. **čn x̣cx̣cim, kʷ x̣cx̣cim**
es x̣cx̣cmi – S/he is gambling. **čnes x̣cx̣cmi, kʷes x̣cx̣cmi**
qs x̣cx̣cmi – S/he is going to gamble. **čiqs x̣cx̣cmi, kʷqs x̣cx̣cmi**
x̣cx̣cíʔim – They gambled. **qeʔ x̣cx̣cim, p x̣cx̣cim**
es x̣cx̣cmíʔi – They are gambling. **qeʔes x̣cx̣cmi, pes x̣cx̣cmi**
qs x̣cx̣cmíʔi – They are going to gamble. **qeʔqs x̣cx̣cmi, pqs x̣cx̣cmi**

x̣cx̣cmis – S/he gambled with s.t. **x̣cx̣cmin, x̣cx̣cmintxʷ**
es x̣cx̣cminms – S/he is gambling with s.t. **ies x̣cx̣cminm, as x̣cx̣cminm**
qs x̣cx̣cminms – S/he is going to gamble s.t. **iqs x̣cx̣cminm, aqs x̣cx̣cminm**

sx̣cx̣cim – the gamble.
sx̣cx̣ec – the bet; the thing gambled.
sxʷx̣cx̣cim – one tasked to gamble.
x̣cx̣cmuł – one that habitually gambles.

x̣cx̣ciš – Gamble. *cmd.*

isnacłq̇eyt łu iqsx̣cx̣ec – I'm going to bet my shirt; I'm going to gamble with my shirt.

nx̣cepist – take the place of someone in gambling.
es nx̣cepisti – S/he took the place of s.o. **čnes nx̣cepisti, kʷes nx̣cepisti**

gambling loss **alip –** lose in gambling. *See:* ***lose.***

game **memscutn –** game. *suffix:* ***...tin, ...tn*** *– means of/device. See:* ***play.***

xʷixʷeẏuł tqlse – animal signs. *(a children's game)*

q̇icqleʔ – hoop game. *(a children's game)*

ilmintn – hoop game sticks.

weluqs – card game played frequently during powwows.

s.t. - something, the 3rd person
(s.t.) - something implied
s.o. - someone, the 3rd person
sl. - singular form
pl. - plural form
rt. - root word
cmd. - command
lit. - literally
fig. - figuratively
i.e., - for example
See: - Redirection to a related word.

garage **snṗiṗuẏšntn** – car repair shop; garage. *prefix:* ***sn...** – a place of; suffix:* ***...tin, ...tn** – means of/device.*

garbage **scx̣ʷel** – something that's been thrown away *(i.e., people, child, spouse or item.) prefix:* ***sc...** – s.t. that's been done/made/prepared. See:* ***abondon.***
snx̣ʷelmn – place to abandon things, *(i.e., trash can, dump, etc.).* **snx̣ʷlx̣ʷelmn** *pl.*
čx̣ʷelmn – garbage already thrown away. *suffix:* ***...min, ...mn** – instrument/tool.*

garden **k̓ʷółl̓q** – plant a garden; plant a crop; plant something. *See:* ***plant.***

gargle **nċaẇłq̓ʷl̓t** – gargle. *rt.: ċeẇ – wash; prefix:* ***n...** – inside; suffix:* ***...ałq̓ʷlt, ...łq̓ʷlt** – throat.*
nċaẇłq̓ʷl̓t – S/he gargled. **čn nċaẇłq̓ʷl̓t, kʷ nċaẇłq̓ʷl̓t**
es nċaẇłq̓ʷl̓ti – S/he is gargling. **čnes nċaẇłq̓ʷl̓ti, kʷes nċaẇłq̓ʷl̓ti**
qs nċaẇłq̓ʷl̓ti – S/he is going to gargle. **čiqs nċaẇłq̓ʷl̓ti, kʷqs nċaẇłq̓ʷl̓ti**
nċáʔaẇłq̓ʷl̓t – They gargled. **qeʔ nċaẇłq̓ʷl̓t, p nċaẇłq̓ʷl̓t**
es nċáʔaẇłq̓ʷl̓ti – They are gargling. **qeʔes nċaẇłq̓ʷl̓ti, pes nċaẇłq̓ʷl̓ti**
qs nċáʔaẇłq̓ʷl̓ti – They are going to gargle. **qeʔqs nċaẇłq̓ʷl̓ti, pqs nċaẇłq̓ʷl̓ti**

qx̣ʷx̣ʷx̣ʷ – gargling sound.

Garrison Junction **snx̣ʷq̓ʷpusaqs** – place name for the Garrison Junction, Montana area. *(People would split with one group going toward the Helena area and one going toward the Butte area.)*

garter snake **sčewileʔ** – snake; *Thamnophis sirtalis.*

gas **kaslin** – gasoline, gas.

gas pedal **snčqlwetmn kaslintn** – gas pedal.

gas station **snkaslintn** – place with gas; gas station; gas can. *prefix:* ***sn...** – a place of; suffix:* ***...tin, ...tn** – means of/device.*

gate **k̓ʷłnčmép,** *k̓ʷłnčmé* – door, gate. *rt.:* ***čm** – extremity; circumfix* ***k̓ʷłn...p** – opening.*

k̓ʷłnxʷomep – gate. *circumfix:* ***k̓ʷłn...p** – opening.*

k̓ʷłnox̣ʷep – gate; wire/rope gate. *rt.:* ***ox̣ʷm** – strung across; circumfix* ***k̓ʷłn...p** – opening.*

k̓ʷłnyalep – gate; tied back and forth together. *rt.:* ***yal** – wrap; circumfix* ***k̓ʷłn...p** – opening.*

k̓ʷłnšmep – gate; wood slide gate. *rt.:* ***šim** – slid/rammed through; circumfix* ***k̓ʷłn...p** – opening.*

gather **ẏamim** – gather/collect things together.
ẏamim – S/he/it gathered. **čn ẏamim, kʷ ẏamim**
es ẏaʔmini – S/he/it is gathering. **čnes ẏaʔmini, kʷes ẏaʔmini**
qs ẏaʔmini – S/he/it is going to gather. **čiqs ẏaʔmini, kʷqs ẏaʔmini**
ẏamíʔim – They gathered. **qeʔ ẏamim, p ẏamim**
es ẏamíʔini – They are gathering. **qeʔes ẏaʔmini, pes ẏaʔmini**
qs ẏamíʔini – They are going to gather. **qeʔqs ẏaʔmini, pqs ẏaʔmini**

ẏamstés – S/he/it gathered s.t. **ẏamstén, ẏamstéxʷ**
es ẏamims – S/he/it is gathering s.t. **ies ẏamim, as ẏamim**
qs ẏamims – S/he/it is going to gather s.t. **iqs ẏamim, aqs ẏamim**
ẏamstéʔes – They gathered s.t. **qeʔ ẏamstém, ẏamstép**
es ẏamíʔims – They are gathering s.t. **qeʔes ẏamim, es ẏamimp**
qs ẏamiʔms – They are going to gather s.t. **qeʔqs ẏamim, qs ẏamimp**

es ẏamim – They are gathered/collected together.

scẏamin – things that have been collected together. *prefix:* ***sc...*** *– s.t. that's been done/made/prepared.*

ẏamiskʷ – Gather the things up. *cmd.*
ẏamiskʷi – All of you gather the things up. *cmd.*
ẏamint – Use it to gather the things up. *cmd.*
ẏamsqáx̣eʔ, *ẏamsqá* – gather/round up domestic animals/horses. *See:* ***round up.***

ṅem ẏamstes – S/he/it will gather s.t. **ṅem ẏamsten, ṅem ẏamintxʷ**
ṅem ẏáʔamis – They will gather s.t. **ṅem qeʔ ẏamstem, ṅem ẏamintp**

es ẏapqiṅi – They are powwowing, celebrating.
sẏapqinm – powwow, celebration.
ẏamłtumš – gather people.

ẏamstexʷ sšeṅš – You gathered rocks. **ẏamiskʷ ci anmľmé** – Gather your toys. **i ẏaʔẏaʔi** – They are all together. **ẏaẏamiskʷ l eċx̣ax̣i esyaʔ łu kʷtkʷtunt** – Gather up all the ones that are big. **iʔá łu ilmixʷm łu t šeẏ** – The chief met there. **l še u qeʔ iaʔ** – We met there.

The **i** following uvular consonants (UC) and the glottal stop **ʔ** sound like English "*ey*" as in the words th*ey*, h*ey*, wh*ey*, etc. Salish UC are: **q**, **q̇**, **qʷ**, **q̇ʷ**, **x̣**, **x̣ʷ**. For example, the suffix **...qin** – head/top, is often spelled using English *ey* as "q*ey*n". So **qi**, **q̇i**, **qʷi**, **q̇ʷi**, **x̣i**, **x̣ʷi**, may be spelled with English *ey* as **q***ey*, **q̇***ey*, **qʷ***ey*, **q̇ʷ***ey*, **x̣***ey*, **x̣ʷ***ey* in other texts.

ẏamncut – gather together.
ẏamncúʔut – They gathered together. **qeʔ ẏamncut, p ẏamncut**
es ẏamncúʔuti – They are gathering together. **qeʔes ẏamncuti, pes ẏamncuti**
qs ẏamncúʔuti – They are going to gather together. **qeʔqs ẏamncuti, pqs ẏamncuti**

ẏamncutwi – Everybody gather. *cmd.*

es ẏamncuti łu sqelixʷ – The people are gathering.

k̇ʷléẇt – gathered/standing together. *(refers to standing; i.e., people, trees, etc.) suffix:* ***...éẇt*** *– group state.*
k̇ʷléʔeẇt – They are gathered together. **qeʔ k̇ʷléẇt, p k̇ʷléẇt**

k̇ʷlmncut – gathered together; a close gathering.
es k̇ʷlmncúʔuti – They are gathered together. **qeʔes k̇ʷlmncuti, pes k̇ʷlmncuti**

qʷxʷéẇt – animals standing together. *(refers to standing; i.e., animals, trees, etc.; derogatory, used to describe people standing around.) suffix:* ***...éẇt*** *– group state.*
qʷxʷqʷxʷéẇt – each group of animals standing together.

cq̇ʷom – gather and bring things here. *(the plural form of* ***ckʷnem****)*
cq̇ʷomis – S/he gathered and brought things. **cq̇ʷomn, cq̇ʷomntxʷ**
es cq̇ʷoms – S/he is gathering and bringing things. **ies qom, as cq̇ʷom**
qs cq̇ʷoms – S/he is going to gather and bring things. **iqs qom, aqs cq̇ʷom**
cq̇ʷóʔomis – They gathered and brought things. **qeʔ cq̇ʷomntm, cq̇ʷomntp**
es cq̇ʷóʔoms – They are gathering and bringing things. **qeʔes cq̇ʷom, es cq̇ʷomp**
qs cq̇ʷóʔoms – They are going to gather and bring things. **qeʔqs cq̇ʷom, qs cq̇ʷomp**

čmčeṁ – pick up and gather things cast away and unused.
čmčeṁ – S/he gathered things cast away. **čn čmčeṁ, kʷ čmčeṁ**
es čmčeṁi – S/he is gathering things cast away. **čnes čmčeṁi, kʷes čmčeṁi**
qs čmčeṁi – S/he is going to gather things cast away. **čiqs čmčeṁi, kʷqs čmčeṁi**

čmčmstes – S/he gathered the things cast away. **čmčmsten, čmčmstexʷ**
es čmčmims – S/he is gathering the things cast away. **ies čmčmim, as čmčmim**
qs čmčmims – S/he is going to gather the things cast away. **iqs čmčmim, aqs čmčmim**

s.t. - something, the 3rd person
(s.t.) - something implied
s.o. - someone, the 3rd person
sl. - singular form
pl. - plural form
rt. - root word
cmd. - command
lit. - literally
fig. - figuratively
i.e., - for example
See: - Redirection to a related word.

čmčmuł – one that habitually gathers cast away things.
čmčmnumt – one that is refused by others.

čmčeṁełp, *čmčeṁe* **–** pick up and gather branches and/or small pieces of wood.
čmčeṁełpm – S/he gathered wood. **čn čmčeṁełpm, kʷ čmčeṁełpm**
es čmčeṁełpi – S/he is gathering wood. **čnes čmčeṁełpi, kʷes čmčeṁełpi**
qs čmčeṁełpi – S/he is going to gather wood. **čiqs čmčeṁełpi, kʷqs čmčeṁełpi**
es čmčéʔeṁełpi – They are gathering wood. **qeʔes čmčeṁełpi, pes čmčeṁełpi**

ṗseš, *ṗse* **–** get firewood; go after firewood; fetch firewood. *See:* ***get.***

q̓ʷleẇm – gather/pick berries and fruit. *See:* ***pick.***

tixʷm – pick/get a plant object or clay. *See:* ***pick.***

gauntlets

spčpéčst – gloves; gauntlets. *See:* ***glove.***

gave

xʷiċ – give. *See:* ***give.***

gay

sxʷnṫaław̓s, *sxʷnṫała* **–** lesbian; gay woman.

sxʷnlespsm – gay man.

geese

sṫaq̓ – geese.
ṫaq̓ṫ – geese in formation while flying.

ṫaq̓ṫ k̓ʷsixʷ – The geese gathered.

tptpósqn, *tptppó* **–** Canada goose; *Branta canadensis.*

ẇuʔẇuʔ – snow goose; *Chen caerulescens.*

k̓ʷsixʷ – goose.

gel

čpóƛ̓qntn – styling gel; hair oil. *rt.:* ***puƛ̓*** *– oil; suffix:* ***...tin, ...tn*** *– means of/device.*
čpóƛ̓qnm – S/he put gel/oil in one's hair. **čn čpóƛ̓qnm, kʷ čpóƛ̓qnm**
es čpóƛ̓qni – S/he is putting gel/oil in one's hair. **čnes čpóƛ̓qni, kʷes čpóƛ̓qni**
qs čpóƛ̓qni – S/he is going to put gel/oil in one's hair. **čiqs čpóƛ̓qni, kʷqs čpóƛ̓qni**

čpóƛ̓qis – S/he put gel/oil in s.o.'s hair. **čpóƛ̓qn, čpóƛ̓qntxʷ**
es čpóƛ̓qnms – S/he is putting gel/oil in s.o.'s hair. **ies čpóƛ̓qnm, kʷes čpóƛ̓qnm**
qs čpóƛ̓qnms – S/he is going to put gel/oil in s.o.'s hair. **čiqs čpóƛ̓qnm, kʷqs čpóƛ̓qnm**

čpóƛ̓qniš – Put gel/oil in your hair. *cmd.*
čpóƛ̓qnt – Put gel/oil in his/her hair. *cmd.*

gelding

nq̓ʷaq̓ʷʔépls – gelding. *suffix:* ***...epls*** *– testicle.*

sqltmxʷsqáx̣eʔ, *sqltmxʷsqá* **–** male horse in general. *rt.:* ***sqltmixʷ*** *– man.*

generous

kʷtiłx̣est – great good, generous.
kʷtiłx̣est łu kʷtisi – Big Blanket is generous.

gentle

tutéẇ – use gentleness with something; caress something.
tutéẇ – S/he used gentleness. **čn tutéẇ, kʷ tutéẇ**
es tutéẇi – S/he is using gentleness. **ies tutéẇi, as tutéẇi**
qs tutéẇi – S/he is going to use gentleness. **iqs tutéẇi, aqs tutéẇi**

tutéẇis – S/he was gentle with s.o./s.t. **tutéẇn, tutéẇntxʷ**

es tutéẇms – S/he is being gentle with s.o./s.t. **ies tutéẇm, as tutéẇm**
qs tutéẇms – S/he is going to be gentle with s.o./s.t. **iqs tutéẇm, aqs tutéẇm**

tutéẇnt – Be gentle with it. *cmd.*
tutéẇmist – gentle and caressing of one's self; find excuses with one's self.
tutéẇcin – talk gently; talk coaxingly. *suffix: **...cin, ...cn** – action of the mouth.*

tutéẇis ci nqʷq̓ʷosmičṅ t stipn – Stephen was gentle with the dog.

saṅ – tranquil; quiet and calm; tame; settled. *See: **quiet**.*

The **i** following uvular consonants (UC) and the glottal stop ʔ sound like English "*ey*" as in the words th*ey*, h*ey*, wh*ey*, etc. Salish UC are: **q**, **q̓**, **qʷ**, **q̓ʷ**, **x̣**, **x̣ʷ**. For example, the suffix ...**qin** – head/top, is often spelled using English *ey* as "q*ey*n". So **qi**, **q̓i**, **qʷi**, **q̓ʷi**, **x̣i**, **x̣ʷi**, may be spelled with English *ey* as **q***ey*, **q̓***ey*, **qʷ***ey*, **q̓ʷ***ey*, **x̣***ey*, **x̣ʷ***ey* in other texts.

George

čaʔč – George.

geranium

tt̓qnéłp – sticky wild geranium; *Geranium viscosissimum*.

German

snołpsélixʷ – German.

germinate

k̓ʷl̓l̓ałq – germinate; plant born; crop produce.
es k̓ʷl̓l̓ałqi – It is germinating; crop is producing.

gesture

tql̓sečst – gesture with the hand for somebody's attention; sign. *rt.: **taq** – wave; suffix: **...ečst, ...čst** – of the hand.*
tql̓sečstm – S/he gestured with the hand. **čn tql̓sečstm, kʷ tql̓sečstm**
es tql̓sečsti – S/he is gesturing with the hand. **čnes tql̓sečsti, kʷes tql̓sečsti**
qs tql̓sečsti – S/he is going to gesture with the hand. **čiqs tql̓sečsti, kʷqs tql̓sečsti**

tql̓sečstis – S/he gestured to get s.o.'s attention. **tql̓sečstn, tql̓sečstntxʷ**
es tql̓sečstms – S/he is gesturing to get s.o.'s attention. **ies tql̓sečstm, as tql̓sečstm**
qs tql̓sečstms – S/he is going to gesture to get s.o.'s attention. **iqs tql̓sečstm, aqs tql̓sečstm**

tql̓sečstiš – Gesture with your hand. *cmd.*
tql̓sečstnt – Gesture with your hand to s.o. *cmd.*

swe łu as tql̓sečstm – Whose attention are you trying to get?

qxʷlsečst – gesture with the hand for somebody to leave. *rt.: **qixʷ** – chase away; suffix: **...ečst, ...čst** – of the hand.*
qxʷlsečstm – S/he gestured with the hand. **čn qxʷlsečstm, kʷ qxʷlsečstm**
es qxʷlsečsti – S/he is gesturing with the hand. **čnes qxʷlsečsti, kʷes qxʷlsečsti**
qs qxʷlsečsti – S/he is going to gesture with the hand. **čiqs qxʷlsečsti, kʷqs qxʷlsečsti**

qxʷlsečstis – S/he gestured for s.o. to leave. **qxʷlsečstn, qxʷlsečstntxʷ**
es qxʷlsečstms – S/he is gesturing for s.o. to leave. **ies qxʷlsečstm, as qxʷlsečstm**
qs qxʷlsečstms – S/he is going to gesture for s.o. to leave. **iqs qxʷlsečstm, aqs qxʷlsečstm**

qxʷlsečstiš – Gesture with your hand. *cmd.*
qxʷlsečstnt – Gesture with your hands for s.o. to leave. *cmd.*

swe łu as qxʷlsečstm – Who are you gesturing to, to leave?

s.t. - something, the 3rd person
(s.t.) - something implied
s.o. - someone, the 3rd person
sl. - singular form
pl. - plural form
rt. - root word
cmd. - command
lit. - literally
fig. - figuratively
i.e., - for example
See: - Redirection to a related word.

get

ċwét – fetch something out of sight. *See: **fetch**.*

ckʷnem – fetch something that is within the immediate area; *lit. to go take something and bring it back here. See: **fetch**.*

tixʷł – acquire something; get or receive something; gather. *See: **acquire**.*

tixʷm – pick/get a plant object or clay. *See: **pick**.*

nmulm – fetch water/liquid *(from the sound made dipping a container in water; used to indicate the motion getting water)*. *See: **fetch**.*

čmčem̓ – pick up and gather things cast away and unused. *See: **gather**.*

čmčem̓ełp, *čmčem̓e* – pick up and gather branches and/or small pieces of wood. *See: **gather**.*

p̓seš, *p̓se* – get firewood; go after firewood; fetch firewood.
p̓seš – S/he got firewood. **čn p̓seš, kʷ p̓seš**
es p̓seši – S/he is getting firewood. **čnes p̓seši, kʷes p̓seši**
qs p̓seši – S/he is going to get firewood. **čiqs p̓seši, kʷqs p̓seši**
p̓séʔeš – They got firewood. **qeʔ p̓seš, p p̓seš**
es p̓séʔeši – They are getting firewood. **qeʔes p̓seši, pes p̓seši**
qs p̓séʔeši – They are going to get firewood. **qeʔqs p̓seši, pqs p̓seši**

p̓sešis – S/he got the firewood. **p̓sešn, p̓sešntxʷ**
es p̓sešms – S/he is getting the firewood. **ies p̓sešm, as p̓sešm**
qs p̓sešms – S/he is going to get the firewood. **iqs p̓sešm, aqs p̓sešm**

p̓seššmis – S/he got firewood for s.o. **p̓seššmn, p̓seššmntxʷ**
es p̓seššms – S/he is getting firewood for s.o. **ies p̓seššm, as p̓seššm**
qs p̓seššms – S/he is going to get firewood for s.o. **iqs p̓seššm, aqs p̓seššm**

p̓seššts – S/he helped get firewood for s.o. **p̓sešštn, p̓sešštxʷ**
es p̓sešštms – S/he is helping get firewood for s.o. **ies p̓sešštm, as p̓sešštm**
qs p̓sešštms – S/he is going to help get firewood for s.o. **iqs p̓sešštm, aqs p̓sešštm**

p̓seštn – Something used to fetch firewood. *(i.e., axe, saw, horse, rope, etc.)*

p̓seš – Get firewood. *cmd.*
p̓sešnt – Get the firewood. *cmd.*

n̓em p̓seš – S/he will gather wood. **n̓em čn p̓seš, n̓em kʷ p̓seš**
n̓em p̓séʔeš – They will gather wood. **n̓em qeʔ p̓seš, n̓em p p̓seš**

čn p̓seš t mulš – I got cottonwood. **m še p p̓seš, pes p̓seši –** You will gather, be gathering firewood. **m še kʷ p̓seš –** You will gather firewood.

get on

čłqlšew̓s, *čłqlše* – mount, *of one individual*; straddle. *See: **mount**.*

čłqqew̓s, *čłqqe* – mount, *more than one*; straddle; get on. *See: **mount**.*

get out

x̣̌ékʷ – leave; move off; out of the way. *See: **leave**.*

t̓oqmncut – Two or more people come down from something high. *(i.e., tree, chair, etc.) See: **come down**.*
t̓oqmncutwi ci tl̓ p̓ip̓uyšn – All of you get out of that car (more than one in car).

t̓ipmncut – come down from something high. *(i.e., tree, chair, etc.) See: **come down**.*
t̓ipmncutš ci tl̓ p̓ip̓uyšn – Get out of that car *(one person)*.

get the best of

p̓ic̓młls – controlling; get the best of. *See: **control**.*

qʷl̓qʷl̓mul, *qʷl̓qʷl̓mu* – one that habitually cheats; cheater; con man; someone who trys to get the best of people. *rt.: **qʷil** – cheat. See: **cheat**.*

getting

…wilš – *suffix indcating developmental progression; getting to; in the process of.*
es kʷtntwilši – S/he/it is getting big. **čnes kʷtntwilši, kʷes kʷtntwilši** *See: **grow**.*
es yoyoʔtwilši – S/he/it is getting strong. **čnes yoyoʔtwilši, kʷes yoyoʔtwilši** *See: **strong**.*
es lemtwil̓ši – S/he/it is getting happy. **čnes lemtwil̓ši, kʷes lemtwil̓ši** *See: **glad**.*

es px̣px̣twilši – S/he is getting smart. **čnes px̣px̣twilši, kʷes px̣px̣twilši** *See: **smart.***
es x̣stwilši – S/he/it is getting better. **čnes x̣stwilši, kʷes x̣stwilši** *See: **better.***

...ilš – *suffix indcating autonomous progression; getting to; in the process of.*
es čstilši – S/he/it is getting worse. **čnes čstilši, kʷes čstilši** *See: **bad.***
es px̣ʷtilši – S/he/it is growing up; getting to be an adult. **čnes px̣ʷtilši, kʷes px̣ʷtilši** *See: **grow.***

... ṁnuxʷ – suffix indicating going through the time of; process through something; getting to be/becoming.
es ċʔalṁnuxʷi – S/he is getting sick. **čnes ċʔalṁnuxʷi, kʷes ċʔalṁnuxʷi**
es aymtṁnuxʷi – S/he is getting angry. **čnes aymtṁnuxʷi, kʷes aymtṁnuxʷi**
es qpcṁnuxʷisti, *es qpcṁnuxʷí* – It is again the time of spring.
es anłqṁnuxʷisti, *es anłqṁnuxʷí* – It is again the time of summer.
es čʔeẏṁnuxʷisti, *es čʔeẏṁnuxʷí* – It is again the time of fall.
es istčṁnuxʷisti, *es istčṁnuxʷí* – It is again the time of winter.

put u qeʔ tʔe łu ax̣lṁnuxʷist – Again we're going through this time. *See: **every time.***

The **i** following uvular consonants (UC) and the glottal stop **ʔ** sound like English "*ey*" as in the words *they, hey, whey,* etc. Salish UC are: **q, q̇, qʷ, q̇ʷ, x̣, x̣ʷ**. For example, the suffix **...qin** – head/top, is often spelled using English *ey* as "q*ey*n". So **qi, q̇i, qʷi, q̇ʷi, x̣i, x̣ʷi**, may be spelled with English *ey* as **q***ey*, **q̇***ey*, **qʷ***ey*, **q̇ʷ***ey*, **x̣***ey*, **x̣ʷ***ey* in other texts.

get well
ṗaáx̣ – heal; cure; get well. *See: **heal.***

x̣stwilš – get better. *See: **better.***

get up
xʷṫilš – get up from a resting/laying state; rise. *See: **rise.***

geyser
čłptpatkʷ – geyser.

ghost
k̓ʷsk̓ʷsčasq̇élixʷ, *k̓ʷsk̓ʷsčasq̇é* – ghost.
k̓ʷusčentm – S/he/it was ghosted.
qʷo k̓ʷusčentm – I was ghosted.

giant wild rye
pspsnéwł, papʔá – giant wild rye.

gift
sxʷiċčš – something given; a present. *See: **give.***

sčéppn – present to soothe/soften a bad relationship. *See: **give.***

čṫliċéʔ – tear a covering/wrapping off. *(i.e., a wrapping off a present, etc.)* *See: **tear.***

ččhiċeʔ – unwrap; remove wrapping to reveal. *See: **unwrap.***

gilia
k̓ʷłi – gilia.

giraffe
čusšnelps – giraffe; long neck.

girdle
nqʷlqʷčisqáx̣eʔtn, *nqʷlqʷčisqá* – girdle commonly used for saddle horses.
*suffix: **...tin, ...tn** – means of/device.*
es nqʷlqʷčisqáx̣eʔi – S/he is throwing the girdle on the saddle. **čnes nqʷlqʷčisqáx̣eʔi, kʷ es nqʷlqʷčisqáx̣eʔi**

girl
šéšutm – little girl up to the age of puberty. **šéušutm –** *pl.* little girls.
šéutm – older girl before puberty.

šéšeẇeʔ – affectionate/pet name for a little girl.

es łx̣ʷómʔi – girl/boy during puberty.

s.t. - something, the 3rd person
(s.t.) - something implied
s.o. - someone, the 3rd person
sl. - singular form
pl. - plural form
rt. - root word
cmd. - command
lit. - literally
fig. - figuratively
i.e., - for example
See: - Redirection to a related word.

sṫiċmišlt – girl after the age of puberty.

smˀém – woman.
słmˀém – little woman.
sxʷsmˀém, *sxʷsmˀé* – sister; women.

pełpłk̇ʷi – women folk.

girth **yult –** large in girth. *(of cylindrical objects.)*
čyulps – bulky large tail.
čyullps – big neck.
syulčst – thumb; thick finger. *suffix:* ***...ečst, ...čst*** *– of the hand.*

t čeṅ eċx̣lsyult – How big is the girth/diameter?

łqqalqʷ – narrow in girth. *(of cylindrical objects.) See:* ***narrow.***

give **xʷiċ –** give.
xʷiċłts – S/he/it gave s.t. to s.o. **xʷiċłtn, xʷiċłtxʷ**
es xʷiċłtms – S/he/it is giving s.t. to s.o. **ies xʷiċłtm, as xʷiċłtm**
qs xʷiċłtms – S/he/it is going to give s.t. to s.o. **iqs xʷiċłtm, aqs xʷiċłtm**
xʷíˀiċłts – They gave s.t. to s.o. **qeˀ xʷiċłtm, xʷiċłtp**
es xʷíˀiċłtms – They are giving s.t. to s.o. **qeˀes xʷiċłtm, es xʷiċłtmp**
qs xʷíˀiċłtms – They are going to give s.t. to s.o. **qeˀqs xʷiċłtm, qs xʷiċłtmp**

qʷo xʷiċłts – S/he/it gave s.t. to me. **qʷo xʷiċłtxʷ**
qʷo es xʷiċłtms – S/he/it is giving s.t. to me. **qʷo as xʷiċłtm**
qʷo qs xʷiċłtms – S/he/it is going to give s.t. to me. **qʷo aqs xʷiċłtm**
qʷo xʷíˀiċłts – They gave s.t. to me. **qʷo xʷiċłtp**
qʷo es xʷíˀiċłtms – They are giving s.t. to me. **qʷo es xʷiċłtmp**
qʷo qs xʷíˀiċłtms – They are going to give s.t. to me. **qʷo qs xʷiċłtmp**

xʷiċłtms – S/he/it gave s.t. to you. **xʷiċłtmn**
kʷ es xʷiċłtms – S/he/it is giving s.t. to you. **kʷ ies xʷiċłtm**
kʷ qs xʷiċłtms – S/he/it is going to give s.t. to you. **kʷ iqs xʷiċłtm**
xʷíˀiċłtms – They gave it to you. **qeˀ xʷiċłtmt**
kʷ es xʷíˀiċłtms – They are giving s.t. to s.o. **kʷ qeˀes xʷiċłtm**
kʷ qs xʷíˀiċłtms – They are going to give s.t. to s.o. **kʷ qeˀqs xʷiċłtm**

qeˀ xʷiċłls – S/he/it gave s.t. to us. **qeˀ xʷiċłlt**
qeˀ xʷíˀiċłls – They gave s.t. to us. **qeˀ xʷiċłlp**

xʷiċłms – S/he/it gave it to you all. **xʷiċłmn**
xʷíˀiċłms – They gave it to you all. **xʷiċłmt**

xʷíˀiċłts – S/he/it gave it to them. **xʷíˀiċłtn, xʷíˀiċłtxʷ**
xʷíˀiˀiċłts – They gave it to them. **qeˀ xʷíˀiċłtm, xʷíˀiċłtp**

xʷiċłt – Give it to s.o. *cmd.*
xʷiċšt – Give it for s.o. *cmd.*

ṅem qes xʷiċłtms – S/he/it will be giving s.t. to s.o. **ṅem iqes xʷiċłtm, ṅem aqes xʷiċłtm**

xʷiċšt mlmelčstn – Give him a toy. **qʷo xʷiċłt –** Give it to me. **ha qʷo xʷi** t **sewłkʷ –** Can I have a drink of water? **qʷo xʷiċšt čełe ululim –** Give me $3.00. **xʷiċłt ci pus č stipn –** Give that cat to Stephen. **xʷiċłtn łu pus č stipn –** I gave a cat to Stephen. **xʷiċštn łu stipn t pus –** I gave a cat to Stephen. **qʷo xʷċłnaimlstis –** S/he gave me hate.

xʷċšmist – surrender; give one's self. *rt.:* ***xʷiċ*** *– give; suffix:* ***...ist*** *– action for/of the self. See:* ***surrender.***

xʷċšsqáx̣eʔ, *xʷċšsqá* – give horses and domestic animals.
xʷċšsqáx̣eʔ – S/he gave a horse. **čn xʷċšsqáx̣eʔ, kʷ xʷċšsqáx̣eʔ**
es xʷċšsqáx̣eʔi – S/he is giving a horse. **čnes xʷċšsqáx̣eʔi, kʷes xʷċšsqáx̣eʔi**
qs xʷċšsqáx̣eʔi – S/he is going to give a horse. **čiqs xʷċšsqáx̣eʔi, kʷqs xʷċšsqáx̣eʔi**
xʷċšsqáʔax̣eʔ – They gave a horse. **qeʔ xʷċšsqáx̣eʔ, p xʷċšsqáx̣eʔ**
es xʷċšsqáʔax̣eʔi – They are giving a horse. **qeʔes xʷċšsqáx̣eʔi, pes xʷċšsqáx̣eʔi**
qs xʷċšsqáʔax̣eʔi – They are going to give a horse. **qeʔqs xʷċšsqáx̣eʔi, pqs xʷċšsqáx̣eʔi**

The **i** following uvular consonants (UC) and the glottal stop **ʔ** sound like English "*ey*" as in the words *they*, *hey*, *whey*, etc. Salish UC are: **q**, **q̇**, **qʷ**, **q̇ʷ**, **x̣**, **x̣ʷ**. For example, the suffix ...**qin** – head/top, is often spelled using English *ey* as "q*ey*n". So **qi**, **q̇i**, **qʷi**, **q̇ʷi**, **x̣i**, **x̣ʷi**, may be spelled with English *ey* as **q***ey*, **q̇***ey*, **qʷ***ey*, **q̇ʷ***ey*, **x̣***ey*, **x̣ʷ***ey* in other texts.

čéppm – give a present to soothe/soften a bad relationship. *rt.:* ***čep*** *– soft.*
čéppis – S/he/it gave s.o. a present. **čéppn, čéppntxʷ**
es čéppms – S/he/it is giving s.o. a present. **ies čéppm, as čéppm**
qs čéppms – S/he/it is going to give s.o. a present. **iqs čéppm, aqs čéppm**
čéʔeppis – They gave s.o. a present. **qeʔ čéppntm, čéppntp**
es čéʔeppms – They are giving s.o. a present. **qeʔes čéppm, es čéppmp**
qs čéʔeppms – They are going to give s.o. a present. **qeʔqs čéppm, qs čéppmp**

sčéppn – present to soothe/soften a bad relationship.

give up

čmšqnmist, *čmšqnmi* – give up; come to the end of one's abilities. *rt.:* ***miš*** *– none.*
čmšqnmist – S/he gave up. **čn čmšqnmist, kʷ čmšqnmist**
es čmšqnmisti – S/he is giving up. **čnes čmšqnmisti, kʷes čmšqnmisti**
qs čmšqnmisti – S/he is going to give up. **čiqs čmšqnmisti, kʷqs čmšqnmisti**
čmšqnmíʔist – They gave up. **qeʔ čmšqnmist, p čmšqnmist**
es čmšqnmíʔisti – They are giving up. **qeʔes čmšqnmisti, pes čmšqnmisti**
qs čmšqnmíʔisti – They are going to give up. **qeʔqs čmšqnmisti, pqs čmšqnmisti**

čmšqnmistmsts – S/he gave up on s.t. **čmšqnmistmstn, kʷ čmšqnmistmstxʷ**
es čmšqnmistmsts – S/he is giving up on s.t. **es čmšqnmistmstn, es čmšqnmistmstxʷ**

ta kʷ qes čmšqnmi – Do not give up. **ta qeʔ qes čmšqnmistmstm** – We must never give up.

glacier

sxʷuymaqs – glacier.

glacier lily

máx̣eʔ – glacier lily; *Erythronium grandiflorum.*

glad

lémt – glad; thankful.
lemt – S/he/it was glad. **čn lemt, kʷ lemt**
es lemti – S/he/it is glad. **čnes lemti, kʷes lemti**
qs lemti – S/he/it is going to be glad. **čiqs lemti, kʷqs lemti**
léʔemt – They were glad. **qeʔ lemt, p lemt**
es léʔemti – They are glad. **qeʔes lemti, pes lemti**
qs léʔemti – They are going to be glad. **qeʔqs lemti, pqs lemti**

lemtmis – S/he/it was thankful for s.t. **lemtmn, lemtmntxʷ**
es lemtms – S/he/it is thankful for s.t. **ies lemtm, as lemtm**
qs lemtms – S/he/it is going to be thankful for s.t. **iqs lemtm, aqs lemtm**
léʔemtmis – They were thankful for s.t. **qeʔ lemtmntm, lemtmntp**
es léʔemtms – They are thankful for s.t. **qeʔes lemtm, es lemtmp**
qs léʔemtms – They are going to be thankful for s.t. **qeʔqs lemtm, qs lemtmp**

s.t. - something, the 3rd person
(s.t.) - something implied
s.o. - someone, the 3rd person
sl. - singular form
pl. - plural form
rt. - root word
cmd. - command
lit. - literally
fig. - figuratively
i.e., - for example
See: - Redirection to a related word.

lemtmntm – S/he/it was thanked; was shown gladness. *(i.e., getting applause, getting an award, etc.)*

sxʷlémt – one tasked to thank.
lmtemn – one inclined to be thankful. *suffix:* ***...emn –*** *one inclined to do.*
lémlmt – pleasing; gratifying.
lmlmsnuxʷ – worthy of gratitude. *suffix:* ***...snuxʷ –*** *worthy of.*

lémlmtš – Thank you.
lmmscut – glad with one's self; thankful. *See:* ***thankful.***
lmtstwexʷist – make each other glad.
lmlmsnuxʷmis – S/he found s.o./s.t. worthy of gratitude. **lmlmsnuxʷmn, lmlmsnuxʷmtxʷ**

yo lémlmtš – By golly, thank you. **yo qeʔ lemt –** I am really thankful or really glad.

lemtwiľš – get happy/glad.
lemtwiľš – S/he/it got happy. **čn lemtwiľš, kʷ lemtwiľš**
es lemtwiľši – S/he/it is getting happy. **čnes lemtwiľši, kʷes lemtwiľši**
qs lemtwiľši – S/he/it is going to get happy. **čiqs lemtwiľši, kʷqs lemtwiľši**
lemtwíʔiľš – They got happy. **qeʔ lemtwiľš, p lemtwiľš**
es lemtwíʔiľši – They are getting happy. **qeʔes lemtwiľši, pes lemtwiľši**
qs lemtwíʔiľši – They are going to get happy. **qeʔqs lemtwiľši, pqs lemtwiľši**

lmtmnwexʷist – happy/glad to see one another; thank each other.
es lmtmnwexʷisti – They are happy to see each other. **qeʔes lmtmnwexʷisti, pes lmtmnwexʷisti**

glance

čáliʔ – take a glance at someone or something.
čáliʔ – S/he/it glanced. **čn čáliʔ, kʷ čáliʔ**
es čáliʔi – S/he/it is glancing. **čnes čálíʔi, kʷes čálíʔi**
qs čálíʔi – S/he/it is going to glance. **čiqs čálíʔi, kʷqs čálíʔi**
čáʔaliʔ – They glanced. **qeʔ čáliʔ, p čáliʔ**
es čáʔalíʔi – They are glancing. **qeʔes čálíʔi, pes čálíʔi**
qs čáʔalíʔi – They are going to glance. **qeʔqs čálíʔi, pqs čálíʔi**

čalíʔis – S/he/it glanced at s.o. **čaliʔn, čaliʔntxʷ**
es čaliʔms – S/he/it is glancing at s.o. **ies čaliʔm, as čaliʔm**
qs čaliʔms – S/he/it is going to glance at s.o. **iqs čaliʔm, aqs čaliʔm**
čalíʔiʔis – They glanced at s.o. **qeʔ čaliʔntm, čaliʔntp**
es čalíʔiʔms – They are glancing at s.o. **qeʔes čaliʔm, es čaliʔmp**
qs čalíʔiʔms – They are going to glance at s.o. **qeʔqs čaliʔm, qs čaliʔmp**

es člčálíʔi – S/he/it is glancing around. **čnes člčálíʔi, kʷes člčálíʔi**

sxʷčáliʔ – one tasked to glance. *prefix:* ***sxʷ...*** *– one tasked to do.*

ełččáliʔ łu č sľaẋts – S/he took a little look back at his/her friend. **qʷo čálíʔis –** S/he glanced at me.

čłẋʷop – fail to catch something. *See:* ***drop.***

glass

i ẋal – glass. *lit. it is clear.*

glasses

čšnšnustn, *čšnšnu* **–** glasses. *lit. covers the eyes. rt.:* ***šiṅ*** *– flat cover; circumfix:* ***č...us*** *– spherical object; eyes; suffix:* ***...tin, ...tn –*** *means of/device.*

čšnšnusm – S/he put glasses on. **čn čšnšnusm, kʷ čšnšnusm**
es čšnšnusi – S/he is putting glasses on. **čnes čšnšnusi, kʷes čšnšnusi**
qs čšnšnusi – S/he is going to put glasses on. **čiqs čšnšnusi, kʷqs čšnšnusi**

čšnšnusis – S/he put glasses on s.o. **čšnšnusn, čšnšnusntxʷ**
es čšnšnusms – S/he is putting glasses on s.o. **ies čšnšnusm, as čšnšnusm**

es čšnšnus – S/he is wearing glasses. **čnes čšnšnus, kʷes čšnšnus**

čšnšnusiš – Put your glasses on. *cmd.*

nčičisnutn – sunglasses.

sčloˀloˀs – contact lenses. *See: **contact lens.***

gleem **čpipiis –** have happy eyes; to have flirty eyes; to have a gleem in the eye. *See: **happy.***

ṗáq̇ – shine; bright. *See: **shine.***

glimpse **i mél̓ –** quiver; glimpse of something disappearing.
i mél̓ u k̓ʷɫčlux̣ʷ – Get a glimpse of something *(person, deer, etc.)* and then it disappears. **čnes x̣ʷisti u i mél̓ –** I am walking and saw a glimpse of something.

ƛ̓meẏ u wičtn – I saw a little bit. *rt.: **wič** – come into view. See: **see.***

tqtaqlš – glimpse.

> The **i** following uvular consonants (UC) and the glottal stop **ˀ** sound like English "*ey*" as in the words th*ey*, h*ey*, wh*ey*, etc. Salish UC are: **q**, **q̇**, **qʷ**, **q̇ʷ**, **x̣**, **x̣ʷ**. For example, the suffix ...**qin** – head/top, is often spelled using English *ey* as "q*ey*n". So **qi**, **q̇i**, **qʷi**, **q̇ʷi**, **x̣i**, **x̣ʷi**, may be spelled with English *ey* as **q***ey*, **q̇***ey*, **qʷ***ey*, **q̇ʷ***ey*, **x̣***ey*, **x̣ʷ***ey* in other texts.

glossy **ṗič –** glossy; shine something; *used to describe the shiny surface of rubber, dark sun tans and the skin of black people.*
ṗičis – S/he shined s.t. **ṗičn, ṗičntxʷ**
es ṗičms – S/he is shining s.t. **ies ṗičm, as ṗičm**
qs ṗičms – S/he is going to shine s.t. **iqs ṗičm, aqs ṗičm**

ṗičlxʷ – leather. *rt.: **ṗič** – glossy; suffix: **...lxʷ** – skin, hide.*
čṗiččeˀ – suitcase; leather suitcase.
sṗičlqs – raincoat; glossy coat. *suffix: **...lqs, ...alqs** – clothes.*
sṗčṗičšn, *sṗčṗi* – rubber boots.

ṗičnt – Shine it. *cmd.*

ṗičs – dark, shiny face. *(Also a name of a person.)*
i ṗičs – very black face.
ṗčṗiččst – very black hands. *suffix: **...ečst, ...čst** – of the hand.*
ṗčṗičšn – very black feet.

glove **spéčst –** glove. **spčpečst,** *spčpe* – gloves *pl. suffix: **...ečst, ...čst** – of the hand.*
pčpečstm – S/he put gloves on. **čn pčpečstm, kʷ pčpečstm**
es pčpečsti – S/he is putting gloves on. **čnes pčpečsti, kʷes pčpečsti**

pčpečstis – S/he put gloves on. **pčpečsn, kʷ pčpečsntxʷ**
es pčpečstms – S/he is putting gloves on. **ies pčpečstm, as pčpečstm**

es pčpečst – S/he is wearing gloves. **čnes pčpečst, kʷes pčpečst**

pčpečstiš – Put your gloves on. *cmd.*
pčpečsnt – Put gloves on s.o. *cmd.*

nloˀčnečstiš – Put your hand in. *cmd.* **ha kʷes tx̣ʷtx̣ʷloˀqnečst –** Are your fingers in the right place?

pƛ̓pƛ̓ečst – remove gloves. *rt.: **pƛ̓im** – release from; suffix: **...ečst, ...čst** – of the hand.*
pƛ̓pƛ̓ečst – S/he removed his/her gloves. **čn pƛ̓pƛ̓ečst, kʷ pƛ̓pƛ̓ečst**
es pƛ̓pƛ̓ečsti – S/he is removing his/her gloves. **čnes pƛ̓pƛ̓ečsti, kʷes pƛ̓pƛ̓ečsti**
qs pƛ̓pƛ̓ečsti – S/he is going to remove his/her gloves. **čiqs pƛ̓pƛ̓ečsti, kʷqs pƛ̓pƛ̓ečsti**

pƛ̓pƛ̓ečstis – S/he is removing s.o.'s gloves. **pƛ̓pƛ̓ečstn, pƛ̓pƛ̓ečstntxʷ**

> s.t. - something, the 3rd person
> (s.t.) - something implied
> s.o. - someone, the 3rd person
> *sl.* - singular form
> *pl.* - plural form
> *rt.* - root word
> *cmd.* - command
> *lit.* - literally
> *fig.* - figuratively
> *i.e.,* - for example
> *See:* - Redirection to a related word.

es pƛ̓pƛ̓ečstms – S/he is removing s.o.'s gloves. **ies pƛ̓pƛ̓ečstm, as pƛ̓pƛ̓ečstm**
qs pƛ̓pƛ̓ečstms – S/he is going to remove s.o.'s gloves. **iqs pƛ̓pƛ̓ečstm, aqs pƛ̓pƛ̓ečstm**

es čpƛ̓ečst – S/he has one glove off. **čnes čpƛ̓ečst, kʷes čpƛ̓ečst**
es pƛ̓pƛ̓ečst – S/he has no gloves. **čnes pƛ̓pƛ̓ečst, kʷes pƛ̓pƛ̓ečst**

sxʷpƛ̓pƛ̓ečst – one tasked to remove gloves. *prefix:* ***sxʷ...*** *– one tasked to do.*

pƛ̓pƛ̓ečstiš – Remove your gloves. *cmd.*
pƛ̓pƛ̓ečstnt – Remove his/her gloves. *cmd.*

glue **čt̓łim –** glue, plaster. *rt.:* ***t̓ił*** *– dirty.*
čt̓łim – S/he glued. **čn čt̓łim, kʷ čt̓łim**
es čt̓łmi – S/he is gluing. **čnes čt̓łmi, kʷes čt̓łmi**
qs čt̓łmi – S/he is going to glue. **čiqs čt̓łmi, kʷqs čt̓łmi**
čt̓łíʔim – They glued. **qeʔ čt̓łim, p čt̓łim**
es čt̓łmíʔi – They are gluing. **qeʔes čt̓łmi, pes čt̓łmi**

čt̓łntes – S/he glued s.t. **čt̓łnten, čt̓łntexʷ**
es čt̓łims – S/he is gluing s.t. **čnes čt̓łim, kʷes čt̓łim**
qs čt̓łims – S/he is going to glue s.t. **čiqs čt̓łim, kʷqs čt̓łim**
čt̓łntéʔes – They glued s.t. **qeʔ čt̓łntem, čt̓łntep**
es čt̓łíʔims – They are gluing s.t. **qeʔes čt̓łim, es čt̓łimp**

čt̓łntem – It has been glued.
es čt̓łim – It is glued.

sxʷčt̓łim – one tasked to glue. *prefix:* ***sxʷ...*** *– one tasked to do.*
čt̓łemn – one inclined to glue. *suffix:* ***...emn*** *– one inclined to do.*
čt̓łt̓łmuł – one that habitually glues. *suffix:* ***...łmuł*** *– one that habitually does.*
čt̓łmin – glue, plaster.

čt̓łiš – Glue. *cmd.*
čt̓łint – Glue s.t. *cmd.*

stem̓ łu as čt̓łim – What are you gluing? **ha kʷes čt̓łmi –** Are you gluing? **ha es čt̓łim –** Is it glued? **ha wis čt̓łntexʷ –** Did you finish gluing it?

gnaw **x̣ipt –** gnawed by bugs. *(i.e., dried meat or woolen clothes, bugs got into them)*
es x̣ipi – It is gnawing.

x̣ipis – It gnawed at s.t.
es x̣ipms – It is gnawing at s.t.

x̣ipntm – It was gnawed.

x̣ipncutn – gnawer of one's things.

x̣ƛ̓im – chew away at something; gnaw. *See:* ***chew.***
x̣ƛ̓cin – graze/eat. *See:* ***graze.***
x̣ƛ̓ulexʷ – graze on the land. *See:* ***graze.***

go **xʷuy –** go; movement of no particular direction.
xʷuy – S/he/it went. **čn xʷuy, kʷ xʷuy**
es xʷuyi – S/he/it is going. **čnes xʷuyi, kʷes xʷuyi**
qs xʷuyi – S/he/it is going to go. **čiqs xʷuyi, kʷqs xʷuyi**
xʷúʔuy – They went. **qeʔ xʷuy, kʷ xʷuy**
es xʷúʔuyi – They are going. **qeʔes xʷuyi, pes xʷuyi**

qs xʷúʔuyi – They are going to go. **qeʔqs xʷuyi, pqs xʷuyi**

es xʷixʷúʔuyi – Each one is going. **qeʔes xʷixʷuyi, pes xʷixʷuyi**

xʷuyš – Go. *cmd.*
xʷuywi – All of you go. *cmd.*

cxʷuy – go in the direction of the speaker; come. *See:* ***come.***
nxʷyelsm – want to go. *rt.:* ***xʷuy*** *– go; circumfix:* ***n...els*** *– want, feelings.*
xʷixʷeym – S/he/it goes here and there.
čxʷuym – visit. *rt.:* ***xʷuy*** *– go; prefix:* ***č...*** *– people. See:* ***visit.***
xʷuyš ƛ̓éʔent anłqa – Go and find your big brother. **xʷuyš iłnš –** Go eat! **xʷuyš łaqšlš č snčłeli –** Go and sit down at the table. **qeʔqs xʷuy č sntumístn –** We are going to go to the store. **x̣ʷa ṅem čn xʷuy č esyapqini –** Maybe I will go to the powwow.

The **i** following uvular consonants (UC) and the glottal stop **ʔ** sound like English "*ey*" as in the words th*ey*, h*ey*, wh*ey*, etc. Salish UC are: **q**, **q̇**, **qʷ**, **q̇ʷ**, **x̣**, **x̣ʷ**. For example, the suffix **...qin** – head/top, is often spelled using English *ey* as "q*ey*n". So **qi**, **q̇i**, **qʷi**, **q̇ʷi**, **x̣i**, **x̣ʷi**, may be spelled with English *ey* as **q***ey*, **q̇***ey*, **qʷ***ey*, **q̇ʷ***ey*, **x̣***ey*, **x̣ʷ***ey* in other texts.

nxʷyelsm – want to go. *rt.:* ***xʷuy*** *– go; circumfix:* ***n...els*** *– want, feelings.*
nxʷyelsm – S/he/it wanted to go. **čn nxʷyelsm, kʷ nxʷyelsm**
es xʷyelsi – S/he/it is wanting to go. **čnes nxʷyelsi, kʷes nxʷyelsi**
qs xʷyelsi – S/he/it is going to want to go. **čiqs nxʷyelsi, kʷqs nxʷyelsi**
nxʷyéʔelsm – They wanted to go. **qeʔ nxʷyelsm, p nxʷyelsm**
es xʷyéʔelsi – They are wanting to go. **qeʔes nxʷyelsi, pes nxʷyelsi**
qs xʷyéʔelsi – They are going to want to go. **qeʔqs nxʷyelsi, pqs nxʷyelsi**
qeʔes nxʷyelsi č snłʔo – I am wanting to go to the bathroom.

č čeṅ u kʷes nxʷyelsi – Where are you wanting to go?

eṅés – on the way to somewhere.
eṅés – S/he/it went somewhere. **čn eṅés, kʷ eṅés**
es eṅési – S/he/it is on the way somewhere. **čnes eṅési, kʷes eṅési**
qs eṅési – S/he/it is going to be on the way somewhere. **čiqs eṅési, kʷqs eṅési**
eṅéʔes – They went somewhere. **qeʔ eṅés, p eṅés**
es eṅéʔesi – They are on the way somewhere. **qeʔes eṅési, pes eṅési**
qs eṅéʔesi – They are going to be on the way somewhere. **qeʔqs eṅési, pqs eṅési**

xʷu qeʔqs eṅési – Okay, let's go. **qeʔqł eṅési –** We're going to be going back (home).

k̇ʷis – indicates that the action takes movement; go.
čiqs k̇ʷis iłni – I am going to go eat.
k̇ʷis itš – Go and sleep.
xʷuyš k̇ʷis k̇ʷl̓lexʷe – Go fix your bed.
xʷuyš k̇ʷis ċew̓siš – Go wash your face.

nʔax̣ʷt – go downriver by land; go downhill over a long distance. *See:* ***downstream.***
nċʔilš – go upstream by land; go up river by land. *See:* ***upstream.***

olqʷétkʷ, *olqʷé* – go/travel to water; go to the edge of the water *(often refers to a lake edge). See:* ***down.***
qum – go/travel away from water; go into open country; go to places far from water; go to a place with no water. *See:* ***travel.***

wełkʷp – go downhill. *See:* ***down.***
ššal̓ús, *ššal̓ú* – go uphill. *See:* ***uphill.***

nʔułxʷ – go inside; enter. *sl. See:* ***enter.***
ocqéʔ – go out. *sl. See:* ***go out.***

s.t. - something, the 3rd person
(s.t.) - something implied
s.o. - someone, the 3rd person
sl. - singular form
pl. - plural form
rt. - root word
cmd. - command
lit. - literally
fig. - figuratively
i.e., - for example
See: - Redirection to a related word.

npilš – go inside, enter. *pl. See:* ***enter.***
occqeʔ – more than one go out. *pl. See:* ***go out.***

šiẏust, *šiẏu* – pass through; go through. *See:* ***pass.***
čx̣ʷcim – pass; go by. *See:* ***pass.***

čšin – go with; accompany. *See:* ***accompany.***

ṗl̓čus, *ṗl̓ču* – turn back; go back. *See:* ***turn.***

šlič – go round; turn on an axis; go in a circular course; rotate 360 degrees. *See:* ***around.***

k̓ʷłčluxʷ – go out of sight around an obstacle. *(i.e., a tree, hill, rock, building, etc.) See:* ***disappear.***

lkʷukʷ – go far. *See:* ***far.***

aẏip – go fast, hurry. *(i.e., on foot, by car, or on horseback) See:* ***fast.***

nwéẇpm – move backward in/on something. *(i.e., in a car, on a bike, etc.) See:* ***back up.***

ċwét – fetch something out of sight. *See:* ***fetch.***

xʷau – sound of going fast; to go fast. *See:* ***fast.***

x̣eł – invite to go; invite to travel to someplace. *See:* ***invite.***

ƛ̓ékʷ – leave; move off; out of the way. *See:* ***leave.***

čuw – gone; away; absent. *See:* ***gone.***

go after

ċwét – fetch something out of sight. *See:* ***fetch.***
ċwetm – S/he fetched. **čn ċwetm, kʷ ċwetm**

nmulm – fetch water/liquid *(from the sound made dipping a container in water; used to indicate the motion getting water). See:* ***fetch.***

čł…, *č…* – *prefix to indicate that something is gone after. See:* ***fetch.***

go around

šlič – go round; turn on an axis; go in a circular course; rotate 360 degrees. *See:* ***around.***
nčšličn̓m – go around somebody's back. *See:* ***around.***

nšlič – go around the inside of something. *See:* ***around.***

nšlčełxʷm – go round the inside of a structure or village. *See:* ***around.***

nšlčusm – go around a fire. *See:* ***around.***

čšlčełxʷm – go around the outside of a village/house/tipi. *See:* ***around.***

nčcnšncut – make a complete revolution; make a circle; meet one's own footprints/tracks. *See:* ***around.***

goat

łpxʷpu – goat.

sx̣ʷƛ̓eẏ – mountain goat; *Oreamnos americanus. See:* ***mountain goat.***

go back

ṗl̓čus, *ṗl̓ču* – turn back; go back. *See:* ***turn.***

ṗl̓čmncut, *ṗl̓čmncu* – turn one's self over; turn one's self back; expression indicating defeat. *See:* ***turn.***

go backwards

nwéẇpm – move backward in/on something. *(i.e., in a car, on a bike, etc.) See:* ***back up.***

nupmupsm, *nupmu* – back up; go backward. *See:* ***back up.***

God **amotqn** – Creator; Sits On Top; president. *See:* ***creator.***

k̓ʷl̓ncutn – Creator; Maker of Ways/Mannerisms. *See:* ***creator.***

čšyéple? – Creator; Keeper; Protecter. *See:* ***creator.***

godchild **skʷenlt** – godchild.

goddaughter **skʷenltsɫ̓mč?é** – goddaughter.

godmother **sck̓ʷl̓sk̓ʷuy** – foster mother; godmother. *prefix:* ***sck̓ʷl̓...*** *– s.t. that's been made.*

p̓x̣ʷót – parent.

go down **weɫkʷp** – go downhill. *See:* ***down.***

olqʷétkʷ, *olqʷé* – go/travel to water; go to the *edge of the water (often refers to a lake edge). See:* ***down.***

t̓ipmncut – come down from something high. *(i.e., tree, chair, etc.) See:* ***come down.***

t̓oqmncut – Two or more people come down from something high. *(i.e., tree, chair, etc.) See:* ***come down.***

go downstream **n?ax̣ʷt** – go downriver by land; go downhill over a long distance. *See:* ***downstream.***

godparent **p̓x̣ʷót** – parent.

goes to **qʷay i č qʷay** – blue goes to blue.

go fast **ay̓ip** – go fast, hurry. *(i.e., on foot, by car, or on horseback) See:* ***fast.***

ƛ̓áx̣t – fast, rapid. *See:* ***fast.***

wamist, *wami* – run walk; hurry along; run in a feminine manner. *See:* ***run.***

go in **n?uɫxʷ** – go inside; enter. *sl. See:* ***enter.***

npilš – go inside, enter. *pl. See:* ***enter.***

going **qs** – *particle indicating going to.*
qe?qs eliɫni – We are going to eat. **uɫé? qe?qs susti t nt̓išk̓ʷ** – I am going to drink pop again.
hayo qs tiw̓ɫ nóx̣ʷnx̣ʷi – Hey, he's going to get a wife!

gold **kʷkʷalí?it** – gold.

golden eagle **mlqnups,** *mlqnu* – golden eagle; *Aquila chrysaetos.*
qeɫmlqnups – young golden eagle.
čn wičm t mlqnu – I saw an eagle. **čɫt̓uxʷten?enct ancitxʷ ɫu t mlqnu** – The eagle flew over your house.

golden mantled squirrel **ssa?l̓i** – golden mantled squirrel; *Spermophilus lateralis.*

gone **čuw** – gone; away; absent.
i čuw – S/he/it is gone/absent. **i čn čuw, i kʷ čuw**

The **i** following uvular consonants (UC) and the glottal stop **?** sound like English "*ey*" as in the words th*ey*, h*ey*, wh*ey*, etc. Salish UC are: **q, q̓, qʷ, q̓ʷ, x̣, x̣ʷ**. For example, the suffix ...**qin** – head/top, is often spelled using English *ey* as "q*ey*n". So **qi, q̓i, qʷi, q̓ʷi, x̣i, x̣ʷi,** may be spelled with English *ey* as **q***ey*, **q̓***ey*, **qʷ***ey*, **q̓ʷ***ey*, **x̣***ey*, **x̣ʷ***ey* in other texts.

s.t. - something, the 3rd person
(s.t.) - something implied
s.o. - someone, the 3rd person
sl. - singular form
pl. - plural form
rt. - root word
cmd. - command
lit. - literally
fig. - figuratively
i.e., - for example
See: - Redirection to a related word.

čuwis – S/he/it made s.t. absent. **čuwn, čuwntxʷ**
es čuwms – S/he/it is making s.t. absent. **ies čuwm, as čuwm**
qs čuwms – S/he/it is going to make s.t. absent. **iqs čuwm, aqs čuwm**

k̓ʷłčuwmsts – S/he/it treated s.o. as absent. **k̓ʷłčuwmstn, k̓ʷłčuwmstxʷ**
es k̓ʷłčuwms – S/he/it is treating s.t. as absent. **ies k̓ʷłčuwm, as k̓ʷłčuwm**

čuwncut – S/he/it made one's self be absent. **čn čuwncut, kʷ čuwncut**
es čuwncuti – S/he/it is making one's self be absent. **čnes čuwncuti, kʷes čuwncuti**

čulexʷ – gone all over; deserted.
čupélsi – lonesome.
čawqn – naked; said of gamblers upon losing everything.
es k̓ʷłčuwmnwexʷi – They are treating each other as absent. **qeʔes k̓ʷłčuwmnwexʷi, pes k̓ʷłčuwmnwexʷi**

čuw łu kʷtisi – Big Blanket is gone.

miš – none; out of.
nmiš – empty inside.

miš łu qeʔ sʔiłn – We do not have any food.

ċsip – disappear; gone; wiped out; cleared out. *See: **disappear**.*

k̓ʷłčluxʷ – go out of sight around an obstacle. *(i.e., a tree, hill, rock, building, etc.) See: **disappear**.*

good

x̣est, *x̣e* – good; fine; beautiful.
x̣e łu qeʔ ep sxʷṁiṁeẏʔm – It is good we have teachers.
x̣e łu qesxʷṁiṁeẏʔm – We have good teachers.
x̣est łu inlʔew – My dad is good; nice; kind.
x̣est snyák̓ʷqi – Good afternoon.

x̣est č čo – It is nice, it is beautiful outside. **l čeṅ u eċx̣lsx̣est –** How good is it? **čn eċx̣lsx̣est t anwi –** I am as good as you. **čeṅ łu šymł x̣est –** Which is the best?

nx̣esls – have good actions and feelings, have a kind heart. *circumfix: **n...els** – want, feel.*
es nx̣eslsi – S/he/it is having good feelings. **čnes nx̣eslsi, kʷes nx̣eslsi**
qs nx̣eslsi – S/he/it is going to have good feelings. **qeʔqs nx̣eslsi, kʷqs nx̣eslsi**

ha kʷ nx̣esls yetłx̣ʷa – Are you feeling good today? **ta qs tam qeʔqs nx̣eslsi ṅe qeʔ k̓ʷĺsncut –** We must have good feelings when we cook.

nx̣sels – pleased; have good feelings. *circumfix: **n...els** – want, feel. See: **please**.*

nx̣smslscut – feel good within one's self.
nx̣smslscut – S/he felt good. **čn nx̣smslscut, kʷ nx̣smslscut**
es nx̣smslscuti – S/he is feeling good. **čnes nx̣smslscuti, kʷes nx̣smslscuti**
qs nx̣smslscuti – S/he is going to feel good. **čiqs nx̣smslscuti, kʷqs nx̣smslscuti**
nx̣smslscúʔut – They felt good. **qeʔ nx̣smslscut, p nx̣smslscut**
es nx̣smslscúʔuti – They are feeling good. **qeʔes nx̣smslscuti, pes nx̣smslscuti**

x̣smscut – being good.
x̣smscut – S/he/it was being good. **čn x̣smscut, kʷ x̣smscut**
es x̣smscuti – S/he/it is being good. **čnes x̣smscuti, kʷes x̣smscuti**
qs x̣smscuti – S/he/it is going to be good. **čiqs x̣smscuti, kʷqs x̣smscuti**

x̣es – feel good/well; in good health. *See: **well**.*

x̣s... – prefix indicating good.
*These are examples of the prefix **x̣s** with a full word.*
x̣sʔacċx̣ – good movie. *See: **watch**.*
x̣ssxʷnċuʔłqpé – S/he is a good dishwasher. *See: **dishwasher**.*
x̣sulip – It burned good. *See: **fire**.*
sx̣słnqʷq̓ʷosmi – good little dog. *See: **dog**.*
x̣słqʷacqn – good little hat. *See: **hat**.*

*These are examples of the prefix **x̣s** with a suffix creating a full word.*
x̣sasq̓t – The sky/weather is good. *suffix: **...asq̓t** – sky, day. See: **weather**.*
x̣salqs – good clothing. *suffix: **...lqs, ...alqs** – clothes. See: **clothes**.*
x̣sx̣séčst – capable hands. *suffix: **...ečst, ...čst** – of the hand. See: **hand**.*
x̣sulexʷ – good land/place. **x̣sx̣sulexʷ** *pl. suffix: **...ulexʷ** – land. See: **land**.*
x̣scinm – talk good. *suffix: **...cin, ...cn** – action of the mouth. See: **talk**.*
x̣sałq – S/he/it smells good. *See: **smell**.*

*These are examples of **x̣s** surrounded by a curricumfix or preceded by a prefix creating a full word.*
čx̣sme – infatuated with someone. *prefix: **č...** – people. See: **infatuate**.*
nx̣sels – pleased; to have good feelings. *circumfix: **n...els** – want, feel. See: **pleased**.*
nx̣saqs – good road; good nose. *circumfix: **n...aqs** – nose, road. See: **road**.*
nx̣sx̣seys – good teeth. *circumfix: **n...eys** – teeth. See: **teeth**.*
nx̣setkʷ – good water. *prefix: **n...** – inside; suffix: **...etkʷ** – liquid. See: **water**.*

x̣sełċeʔ, *x̣se* – It tastes good. *See: **taste**.*
ha x̣se – Does it taste good?

nx̣setkʷ – The liquid tastes good. *See: **taste**.*

tam t̓ul̓ – tremendous; outstanding; extreme; excellent. *See: **excellent**.*

x̣ʷawx̣ʷut – very good.

qʷamqʷmt – excellent; beautiful; pleasing. *See: **excellent**.*

put šey̓ – S/he/it is just right; enough; fine; okay. *See: **just***

čhomist, *čho* – in awe of something or someone; overwhelmed; see something beautiful/good/wonderful. *See: **awe**.*

The **i** following uvular consonants (UC) and the glottal stop **ʔ** sound like English "*ey*" as in the words *they*, *hey*, *whey*, etc. Salish UC are: **q**, **q̓**, **qʷ**, **q̓ʷ**, **x̣**, **x̣ʷ**. For example, the suffix ...**qin** – head/top, is often spelled using English *ey* as "q*ey*n". So **qi**, **q̓i**, **qʷi**, **q̓ʷi**, **x̣i**, **x̣ʷi**, may be spelled with English *ey* as **q***ey*, **q̓***ey*, **qʷ***ey*, **q̓ʷ***ey*, **x̣***ey*, **x̣ʷ***ey* in other texts.

goods

sqmnlscut – goods; the things one put down. *pl. rt.: **qmin** – place things down; suffix: **...cut** – action to the self.*
čqmnálqʷ – things sent away.

čqmnálqʷntm – The things were sent away.

st̓k̓ʷlscut – good; the thing one put down. *rt.: **t̓uk̓ʷ** – put/place something down; suffix: **...cut** – action to the self.*

st̓qlscut – goods.

teṁm – use; take care of; have responsibility for. *See: **use**.*
stṁlscut – What kind of goods are they/is it?

teṁtn – What is it used for? goods, thing used.

es kʷests teṁtn łu qs k̓ʷul̓ms – S/he is holding the thing s/he is going to make something with.

s.t. - something, the 3rd person
(s.t.) - something implied
s.o. - someone, the 3rd person
sl. - singular form
pl. - plural form
rt. - root word
cmd. - command
lit. - literally
fig. - figuratively
i.e., - for example
See: - Redirection to a related word.

goose

k̓ʷsixʷ – goose in general. *(This word describes what a goose sounds like.)*
ṅem eł ċk̓ʷłči łu k̓ʷsixʷ – The geese will return.

sťaqt – geese. *(This word describes geese flying in their v formation.)*
ťaqt – Geese in formation while flying.

ťaqt k̓ʷsixʷ – The geese gathered.

tptpósqn, *tptppó* **–** Canada goose. *(This word describes what the goose looks like.)*

ẇuʔẇuʔ – snow goose; *Chen caerulescens.*

gooseberry

nťeťmelps, *nťe* **–** gooseberry.

nťeťmałq, *nťe* **–** green gooseberry. *suffix:* ***...ałq*** *– smell, accompaniment.*

go out

ocqéʔ – go out. *sl.*
ocqéʔ – S/he/it went out. **čn ocqéʔ, kʷ ocqéʔ**
es ocqéʔi – S/he/it is going out. **čnes ocqéʔi, kʷes ocqéʔi**
qs ocqéʔi – S/he/it is going to go out. **čiqs ocqéʔi, kʷqs ocqéʔi**

esocqʔétkʷ – spring (of water).

ocqéʔš – Go outside.
ocqʔém – bring something out there. *See:* ***bring.***
cʔocqéʔ – come out of something in the direction of the speaker. *See:* ***come.***
ocqéʔstxʷ – Bring that out.

ha ṅem kʷqs ocqéʔi – Are you going out? **ha ƛ̓e ocqéʔ –** Are you ready to go outside? **ocqéʔ łu mali –** Mary went out. **x̣iṅé čn ocqéʔ –** I might have to go outside. **tas ocqéʔ łu mali stṁasts –** Mary's cow did not go out.

occqeʔ – more than one go out. *pl.*
occqéʔeʔ – They went out. **qeʔ occqéʔ, p occqéʔ**
es occqéʔeʔi – They are going out. **qeʔes occqéʔi, pes occqéʔi**
qs occqéʔeʔi – They are going to go out. **qeʔqs occqéʔi, pqs occqéʔi**

occqéʔwi – All of you go out.
cʔoccqeʔ – many come out of something in the direction of the speaker. *See:* ***come.***

ci tl̓ʔe occqéʔi – From right there they went out.

ocsqáx̣eʔ – bring/take a horse/domestic animal out of some place. *(i.e., a barn, corral, etc.)* *See:* ***bring.***

pupƛ̓m – go out of the woods/canyon into open land.

go out of sight

k̓ʷłčluxʷ – go out of sight around an obstacle. *(i.e., a tree, hill, rock, building, etc.)* *See:* ***disappear.***

ċsip – disappear; gone; wiped out; cleared out. *See:* ***disappear.***

go outside

ocqéʔ – go out. *sl.* *See:* ***go out.***

č̓ólsqeʔ, *č̓ č̓ó* **–** outside. *See:* ***outside.***

gopher

sisč – gopher; Columbia ground squirrel; *Spermophilus columbianus.*

pul̓yeʔ – mole; northern pocket gopher; *Thomomys talpoides.*

skʷuṁcn – pocket gopher; *Thomomys idahoensis.*

gopher snake

sx̣ʷnu – bull snake; gopher snake; *Pituophis catenifer.*

gorilla

skʷtiłmonqi – gorilla; ape. *prefix:* ***skʷtił...*** *– big.*

gosling **sttʔumeʔ** – duckling; gosling.
k̓ʷsixʷ sttʔumeʔ – gosling.
sesƛ̓xʷuṁ sttʔumeʔ – duckling.

gossip **wekʷcnm** – hide your talk by whispering or by talking a different language; talk secretly; gossip. *suffix:* ***...cin, ...cn*** *– action of the mouth.*
wekʷcnm – S/he talked secretly. **čn wekʷcnm, kʷ wekʷcnm**
es wekʷcni – S/he is talking secretly. **čnes wekʷcni, kʷes wekʷcni**
qs wekʷcni – S/he is going to talk secretly. **čiqs wekʷcnisti, kʷqs wekʷcni**
wéʔekʷcnm – They talked secretly. **qeʔ wekʷcnm, p wekʷcnm**
es wéʔekʷcni – They are talking secretly. **qeʔes wekʷcnisti, pes wekʷcni**

wekʷcis – S/he gossiped about s.o. **wekʷcn , wekʷcntxʷ**
es wekʷcnms – S/he is gossiping about s.o. **ies wekʷcnm, as wekʷcnm**
qs wekʷcnms – S/he is going to gossip about s.o. **iqs wekʷcnm, aqs wekʷcnm**
wéʔekʷcis – They gossiped about s.o. **qeʔ ekʷcntm , wekʷcntp**
es wéʔekʷcnms – They are gossiping about s.o. **qeʔes wekʷcnm, es wekʷcnmp**

xʷaʔscan – chitchat; speak for nothing. *See:* ***chitchat.***

The **i** following uvular consonants (UC) and the glottal stop **ʔ** sound like English "*ey*" as in the words th*ey*, h*ey*, wh*ey*, etc. Salish UC are: **q, q̓, qʷ, q̓ʷ, x̣, x̣ʷ**. For example, the suffix ...**qin** – head/top, is often spelled using English *ey* as "q*ey*n". So **qi, q̓i, qʷi, q̓ʷi, x̣i, x̣ʷi**, may be spelled with English *ey* as **q***ey*, **q̓***ey*, **qʷ***ey*, **q̓ʷ***ey*, **x̣***ey*, **x̣ʷ***ey* in other texts.

go through **čx̣ʷcim** – pass; go by. *See:* ***pass.***

x̣ʷcuʔsičṅ, *x̣ʷcuʔsí* – go over a mountain pass. *See:* ***pass.***

šiẏust, *šiẏu* – pass through; go through. *See:* ***pass.***

čiyek̓ʷ – go through a narrow opening. *See:* ***pass through.***

nc̓lilš – go through trees. *See:* ***tree.***

go up **ššal̓ús,** *ššal̓ú* – go uphill. *See:* ***uphill.***

nwisšlš – go up; raise. *See:* ***up.***

go upstream **nc̓ʔilš** – go upstream by land; go up river by land. *See:* ***upstream.***

go with **čšin** – go with; accompany. *See:* ***accompany.***

gown **q̓ʷaylqs** – black gown, priest. *suffix:* ***...lqs, ...alqs*** *– clothes. lit. black clothes.*

suypálqs – Whiteman's clothing. *suffix:* ***...lqs, ...alqs*** *– clothes. lit. Whiteman's clothes.*

x̣salqs – good clothing. *suffix:* ***...lqs, ...alqs*** *– clothes. lit. good clothes.*

mʔamalqs – woman's clothes. *rt.:* ***mʔem*** *– woman; suffix:* ***...lqs, ...alqs*** *– clothes.*
es mʔamalqsi – S/he is dressed as a woman.

grab **k̓ʷɬčnapqn** – grab the back of the head.
k̓ʷɬčnapqis – S/he grabbed s.o. **k̓ʷɬčnapqn, k̓ʷɬčnapqntxʷ**
es k̓ʷɬčnapqnm – S/he is grabbing s.o. **ies k̓ʷɬčnapqnm, as k̓ʷɬčnapqnm**
qs k̓ʷɬčnapqnm – S/he is going to grab s.o. **iqs k̓ʷɬčnapqnm, aqs k̓ʷɬčnapqnm**

k̓ʷɬčnapqntm – S/he was grabbed by the back of the head.

nčnaw̓sqn – grab the top of the head.
nčnaw̓sqis – S/he grabbed s.o. **nčnaw̓sqn, nčnaw̓sqntxʷ**
es nčnaw̓sqnm – S/he is grabbing s.o. **ies nčnaw̓sqnm, as nčnaw̓sqnm**
qs nčnaw̓sqnm – S/he is going to grab s.o. **iqs nčnaw̓sqnm, aqs nčnaw̓sqnm**

s.t. - something, the 3rd person
(s.t.) - something implied
s.o. - someone, the 3rd person
sl. - singular form
pl. - plural form
rt. - root word
cmd. - command
lit. - literally
fig. - figuratively
i.e., - for example
See: - Redirection to a related word.

nčnaw̓sqntm – S/he was grabbed by the top of the head.

nčnususm – grab the front of the head.
nčnususis – S/he grabbed s.o. **nčnususn, nčnususntxʷ**
es nčnususm – S/he is grabbing s.o. **ies nčnususm, as nčnususm**
qs nčnususm – S/he is going to grab s.o. **iqs nčnususm, aqs nčnususm**

nčnususntm – S/he was grabbed by the front of the head.

čnapqn – capture someone. *See: **capture**.*

čn̓im – grasp on to something. *See: **grasp**.*

kʷestm – hold something in the hand; in possession of something. *See: **hold**.*

kʷanx̣n – kidnap; grab the arm. *See: **kidnap**.*

grain

sp̓qi – wheat.

lewén – oats.

ałnmsqáx̣eʔ, *ałnmsqá* **–** oats; horse food. *rt.: **iłn** – eat; suffix: **...sqáx̣eʔ** – domestic animal; mainly referring to horse or car.*

čsp̓im – thrash oats; gathering huckleberries *(when hitting the bush you make berries fall onto a canvas). rt.: **sp̓im** – strike w/ object. See: **thrash**.*

ql̓wá – thrash wheat; horses stepping on wheat. *See: **thrash**.*

grandchild

yayá – grandchild, *(woman's daughter's children)*; maternal grandmother *(mother's mother). See: **Sec. 3: Kinship terms**.*
ččyeʔ – grandchild, *(woman's daughter's children)*; maternal grandmother, *(mother's mother). (This term is used in some Coyote stories.)*
qéneʔ – grandchild, *(woman's son's children)*; paternal grandmother, *(father's mother).*
síleʔ – grandchild, *(man's daughter's children)*; maternal grandfather, *(mother's father).*
sx̣épeʔ – grandchild, *(man's son's children)*; paternal grandfather, *(father's father).*

grandfather

síleʔ – grandchild, *(man's daughter's children)*; maternal grandfather, *(mother's father). See: **Sec. 3: Kinship terms**.*
sx̣épeʔ – grandchild, *(man's son's children)*; paternal grandfather, *(father's father).*

x̣apqn – grandfather.

grand fir

st̓ikʷłp – grand fir; balsam fir; *Abies grandis.*

qʷelcn – western red cedar; *Thuja plicata;* grand fir; balsam fir; *Abies grandis. (There is some confusion with this word; it is used by different speakers as western red cedar, Thuja plicata, and grand fir, Abies grandis.)*

grandmother

yayá, *ččyeʔ* **–** grandchild, *(woman's daughter's children)*; maternal grandmother *(mother's mother). See: **Sec. 3: Kinship terms**.*
qéneʔ – grandchild, *(woman's son's children)*; paternal grandmother, *(father's mother).*

grandparent

čéweʔ – grandmother/grandfather after death of parents. *(This term is used when the grandparents take over the role of parents after the death of one's parents.) See: **Sec. 3: Kinship terms**.*
nčučeweʔ – grandparents after death of parents.

t̓úpyeʔ – great-grandchild; great-grandparent.
t̓ot̓o – great-grandchild; great-grandparent. *(Salish; some say it is a baby-talk version of **t̓úpyeʔ**.)*
il̓áw̓yeʔ – great-great-grandchild; great-great-grandparent.
y̓ukʷeʔ – great-great-great-grandchild; great-great-great-grandparent.

sčtammqn – great-great-great-great-grandchild; great-great-great-great-grandparent.

grape
čtekʷé – grape.

čtekʷétkʷ – grape juice. *suffix: ...etkʷ, ...tkʷ – liquid*

čłx̣lx̣als, *čłx̣lx̣a* – grape; light colored grape. *rt.: x̣al – clear; prefix: ł... – little; circumfix: č...us – spherical object; eyes.*

sċals – creeping Oregon grape; creeping barberry; *Mahonia repens.*

sqʷoyu – Oregon grape; *Mahonia aquifolium.*

grapefruit
čcicuis, *čcicu* – grapefruit.

graph
sctqʷtqʷqʷmeẃs – graph. *prefix: sc... – s.t. that's been done/made/prepared; suffix: ...éẃs – in between, middle.*

tqʷmeẃs – compare. *See: **compare**.*

grasp
čṅim – grasp on to something.

čṅim – S/he grasped on. **čn čṅim, kʷ čṅim**
es čṅmi – S/he is grasping on. **čnes čṅmi, kʷes čṅmi**
qs čṅmi – S/he is going to grasp on. **čiqs čṅmi, kʷqs čṅmi**
čṅíˀim – They grasped on. **qeˀ čṅim, p čṅim**
es čṅmíˀi – They are grasping on. **qeˀes čṅmi, pes čṅmi**
qs čṅmíˀi – They are going to grasp on. **qeˀqs čṅmi, pqs čṅmi**

čṅntes – S/he grasped on it. **čṅnten, čṅntexʷ**
es čṅim – S/he is grasping on it. **ies čṅim, as čṅim**
qs čṅims – S/he is going to grasp on it. **iqs čṅim, aqs čṅim**
čṅntéˀes – They grasped on it. **qeˀ čṅntem, čṅntep**
es čṅíˀims – They are grasping on it. **qeˀes čṅim, es čṅimp**
qs čṅíˀims – They are going to grasp on it. **qeˀqs čṅim, qs čṅimp**

čṅiš – Grasp. *cmd.*
čṅint – Grasp it. *cmd.*

ččṅim – hold/grasp on to something.

ččṅim – S/he held on. **čn ččṅim, kʷ ččṅim**
es ččṅmi – S/he is holding on. **čnes ččṅmi, kʷes ččṅmi**
qs ččṅmi – S/he is going to hold on. **čiqs ččṅmi, kʷqs ččṅmi**
qs ččṅmíˀi – They are going to hold on. **qeˀqs ččṅmi, pqs ččṅmi**

ččṅntes – S/he held on to it. **ččṅnten, ččṅntexʷ**
es ččṅims – S/he is holding on to it. **ies ččṅim, as ččṅim**
qs ččṅims – S/he is going to hold on to it. **iqs ččṅim, aqs ččṅim**
es ččṅíˀims – They are holding on to it. **qeˀes ččṅim, es ččṅimp**

nččṅmin – handle. *suffix: ...min, ...mn – instrument/tool.*
snččṅmintn – handrail. *prefix: sn... – a place of; suffix: ...mintn – tool that does.*

ččṅiš – Hold on. *cmd.*
ččṅint – Hold on to it. *cmd.*

ččṅépleˀ – lead by the hand. *(i.e., leading a horse.) See: **lead**.*

nslslmtus u ččṅntes l snčłemutn – S/he got dizzy and held on to the chair.

ččṅčṅšnim – Grab/hold someone by the feet.

The **i** following uvular consonants (UC) and the glottal stop ˀ sound like English "*ey*" as in the words th*ey*, h*ey*, wh*ey*, etc. Salish UC are: **q, q̇, qʷ, q̇ʷ, x̣, x̣ʷ**. For example, the suffix ...**qin** – head/top, is often spelled using English *ey* as "q*ey*n". So **qi, q̇i, qʷi, q̇ʷi, x̣i, x̣ʷi**, may be spelled with English *ey* as **q***ey*, **q̇***ey*, **qʷ***ey*, **q̇ʷ***ey*, **x̣***ey*, **x̣ʷ***ey* in other texts.

s.t. - something, the 3rd person
(s.t.) - something implied
s.o. - someone, the 3rd person
sl. - singular form
pl. - plural form
rt. - root word
cmd. - command
lit. - literally
fig. - figuratively
i.e., - for example
See: - Redirection to a related word.

ččňčňšntes – S/he grabbed s.o.'s feet. **ččňčňšnten, ččňčňšntexʷ**
es ččňčňšnims – S/he is grabbing s.o.'s feet. **ies ččňčňšnim, as ččňčňšnim**
qs ččňčňšnims – S/he is going to grab s.o.'s feet. **iqs ččňčňšnim, aqs ččňčňšnim**

čňéčs – hold hands; grasp hands. *See: **shake hands**.*

yomim – hold something steady. *rt.: **yoyoot**– strong. See: **hold**.*

grass

skʷʔalulexʷ – things that grow on the land; grass. *rt.: **kʷʔal**– plants grow; suffix: **...ulexʷ**– land. See: **grow**.*

supulexʷ – grass. *rt.: **up**– hair; suffix: **...ulexʷ**– land.*

kʷel – change outward perception; change color; ripening/dying. *See: **change**.*

grass dance

k̓ʷłpeʔšnulexʷ – flatten grass; grass dance.
es k̓ʷłpeʔšnulexʷ – The grass is flattened.

k̓ʷłpeʔšnulexʷm – S/he grass danced. **čn kʷłpeʔšnulexʷm, kʷ k̓ʷłpeʔšnulexʷm**
es k̓ʷłpeʔšnulexʷi – S/he is grass dancing. **čnes kʷłpeʔšnulexʷi, kʷes k̓ʷłpeʔšnulexʷi**
qs k̓ʷłpeʔšnulexʷi – S/he is going to grass dance. **čiqs kʷłpeʔšnulexʷi, kʷqs k̓ʷłpeʔšnulexʷi**

k̓ʷłpeʔšnulexʷis – S/he flatten the grass. **k̓ʷłpeʔšnulexʷn, k̓ʷłpeʔšnulexʷntxʷ**
es k̓ʷłpeʔšnulexʷms – S/he is flattening the grass. **ies k̓ʷłpeʔšnulexʷm, as k̓ʷłpeʔšnulexʷm**
qs k̓ʷłpeʔšnulexʷms – S/he is going to flatten the grass. **iqs k̓ʷłpeʔšnulexʷm, aqs k̓ʷłpeʔšnulexʷm**

grass fire

ṗaap – grass/timber caught fire. *See: **fire**.*

grasshopper

tt̓áċeʔ – grasshopper.

gravel

pq̓ʷesšn – gravel.

Gravel Bay

nccm̓e – Gravel Bay in Flathead Lake, Flathead Nation.

gravy

scnpq̓ʷetkʷ – gravy.

gray

čx̣i – gray.
i čx̣i – It is gray.

i čx̣i snčłċaʔsqá – gray horse.

páa – faded, pale, gray.
i paá – It is faded; it is pale.
i páas – The face is pale.
es paám – fades.

i pa ululim – silver. *lit. faded metal.*

pqmast – begin to get gray/white hair.
es pqmasti – S/he is getting gray/white hair. **čnes pqmasti, kʷes pqmasti**

čmixʷqn – gray/white and black hair; salt-and-pepper hair.
es čmixʷqn – S/he has gray/white and black hair. **čnes čmixʷqn, kʷes čmixʷqn**

pqmayaqn – gray/white hair.
pqmayaqn – S/he has gray/white hair. **čn pqmayaqn, kʷ pqmayaqn**

gray jay

lk̓ʷłk̓ʷqi – gray jay; Canada jay; camp robber; whiskey jack; *Perisoreus canadensis*.

grayling **nčličn̓** – grayling *(fish); Thymallus arcticus. suffix:* ***...ičn̓*** *– back.*

gray wolf **čx̣i nčiʔcn** – gray wolf. *suffix:* ***...cin, ...cn*** *– action of the mouth.*

graze **x̣ƛ̓ulexʷ** – graze on the land.
x̣ƛ̓ulexʷ – S/he/it grazed on the land.
es x̣ƛ̓ulexʷi – S/he/it is grazing on the land.
qs x̣ƛ̓ulexʷi – S/he/it is going to graze on the land.

x̣ƛ̓cin – graze/eat. *suffix:* ***...cin, ...cn*** *– action of the mouth.*
x̣ƛ̓cin – S/he/it grazed/ate.
es x̣ƛ̓cini – S/he/it is grazing/eating.
qs x̣ƛ̓cini – S/he/it is going to graze/eat.

x̣ƛ̓im – chew away at something; gnaw. *See:* ***chew.***

grease **sq̓ʷoct** – grease; lard. *rt.:* ***q̓ʷoct*** *– fat.*
nm̓éƛ̓ t sq̓ʷoct – S/he mixed the grease.

scocoó – bear rib grease.

kʷaskʷas – sound of grease dripping on the fire.
i kʷaskʷas – It is dripping and hitting the fire *(it is making the sound of grease hitting the fire).*

kʷasss – sound of grease burning.

p̓uƛ̓m – grease/oil something.
p̓uƛ̓m – S/he greased. **čn p̓uƛ̓m, kʷ p̓uƛ̓m**
es p̓uƛ̓i – S/he is greasing. **čnes p̓uƛ̓i, kʷes p̓uƛ̓i**
qs p̓úʔuƛ̓i – S/he is going to grease. **čiqs p̓uƛ̓i, kʷqs p̓uƛ̓i**

p̓uƛ̓is – S/he greased s.t. **p̓uƛ̓n, p̓uƛ̓ntxʷ**
es p̓uƛ̓ms – S/he is greasing s.t. **ies p̓uƛ̓m, as p̓uƛ̓m**
qs p̓úƛ̓ms – S/he is going to grease s.t. **čiqs p̓uƛ̓m, kʷqs p̓uƛ̓m**

p̓uƛ̓iš – Grease. *cmd.*
p̓uƛ̓nt – Grease s.t. *cmd.*

i puƛ̓ – It is greasy.

p̓uƛ̓sm – greasy face.
p̓uƛ̓čstm – greasy hand. *suffix:* ***...ečst, ...čst*** *– of the hand.*

ies p̓uƛ̓m łu isťopqs – I am greasing my thread. **čnes p̓uƛ̓i t isťopqs** – I am greasing my thread.

greasy **i puƛ̓** – It is greasy.

great blue heron **smóq̓ʷeʔ** – heron, great blue heron.

greater yellow legs **nusšnáqs** – greater yellow legs. *lit. long beak/nose.*

great horned owl **snineʔ** – owl; great horned owl; *Bubo virginianus*; great gray owl; *Strix nebulosa.*
wičtn snineʔ t skʷekʷst – I saw an owl this morning.

Great Spirit **amotqn** – Creator; Sits On Top; president. *rt.:* ***emut*** *– sit; suffix:* ***...qin, ...qn*** *– top.*
k̓ʷl̓ncutn – Creator; Maker of Ways/Mannerisms.

The **i** following uvular consonants (UC) and the glottal stop **ʔ** sound like English "*ey*" as in the words *they, hey, whey,* etc. Salish UC are: **q, q̓, qʷ, q̓ʷ, x̣, x̣ʷ**. For example, the suffix **...qin** – head/top, is often spelled using English *ey* as "q*ey*n". So **qi, q̓i, qʷi, q̓ʷi, x̣i, x̣ʷi**, may be spelled with English *ey* as **q***ey*, **q̓***ey*, **qʷ***ey*, **q̓ʷ***ey*, **x̣***ey*, **x̣ʷ***ey* in other texts.

s.t. - something, the 3rd person
(s.t.) - something implied
s.o. - someone, the 3rd person
sl. - singular form
pl. - plural form
rt. - root word
cmd. - command
lit. - literally
fig. - figuratively
i.e., - for example
See: - Redirection to a related word.

čšyéple? – Creator; Keeper; Protecter. *rt.: **čšťim** – guard; suffix: **...éple?** – permanence.*

greed **q̓amaliye?** – eat and eat; eat greedily. *See: **eat**.*

nc̓anps – greedy; literally have a tight butt.

green **qʷin** – green. **qʷnqʷin** – greens. *pl.*

qʷinis – S/he made it green. **qʷinn, qʷinntxʷ**
es qʷinms – S/he is making it green. **ies qʷinm, as qʷinm**
qs qʷinms – S/he is going to make it green. **iqs qʷinm, aqs qʷinm**

i qʷin – It is green.
i łqʷqʷin – It is a little green; greenish.

qʷinnt – Make it green. *cmd.*

qʷeqʷine? – little green one.
čqʷnqʷinc̓e?, *čqʷnqʷi* – watermelon. *suffix: **...ic̓é?** – covered in. lit. it is all green.*

green racer **npƛ̓ác̓e?** – eastern racer, green racer; *Coluber constrictor.*

green wood **ql̓alqʷ** – green/fresh wood. *rt.: **qal̓** – fresh; suffix: **...alqʷ** – wood; cylindical.*

greet **q̓ʷiťs** – nod the head; greet; hail. *See: **nod**.*

čnčsnwéxʷ, *čnčsnwé* – hold hands with each other. *See: **shake hands**.*

čtóls – point with the eyes; show acknowledgement by looking. *See: **acknowledge**.*

tóls – point with the head or face; show acknowledgement. *See: **acknowledge**.*

greetings **?a** – hello; *initial greeting.*

?é – hello; *acknowledgement to initial greeting.*

x̣est skʷekʷst – Good morning; *greeting or parting statement.*
x̣est sx̣lx̣alt – Good day; *greeting or parting statement.*
x̣est snyak̓ʷqi – Good afternoon; *greeting or parting statement.*
x̣est sčluxʷ – Good evening; *greeting or parting statement.*
x̣est skʷkʷec – Good night; *greeting or parting statement.*

grief **pupusénč**, *pupusé* – sad; mourn; grieve. *See: **sad**.*

grin **nťum̓s** – smile, grin. *See: **smile**.*

grind **x̣ʷáq̓ʷm** – grind/file something.

x̣ʷáq̓ʷm – S/he ground. **čn x̣ʷáq̓ʷm, kʷ x̣ʷáq̓ʷm**
es x̣ʷáq̓ʷi – S/he is grinding. **čnes x̣ʷáq̓ʷi, kʷes x̣ʷáq̓ʷi**
qs x̣ʷáq̓ʷi – S/he is going to grind. **čiqs x̣ʷáq̓ʷi, kʷqs x̣ʷáq̓ʷi**

x̣ʷáq̓ʷis – S/he ground s.t. **x̣ʷáq̓ʷn, x̣ʷáq̓ʷntxʷ**
es x̣ʷáq̓ʷms – S/he is grinding s.t. **čnes x̣ʷáq̓ʷm, kʷes x̣ʷáq̓ʷm**
qs x̣ʷáq̓ʷms – S/he is going to grind s.t. **čiqs x̣ʷáq̓ʷm, kʷqs x̣ʷáq̓ʷm**

x̣ʷáq̓ʷmn – file.
scx̣ʷáq̓ʷ – something that's been ground; flour. *prefix: **sc...** – s.t. that's been done/made/prepared.*
x̣ʷáq̓ʷiš – Grind/file. *cmd.*
x̣ʷáq̓ʷnt – Grind/file it. *cmd.*
x̣ʷq̓ʷmutmsts – S/he was able to grind s.t. **x̣ʷq̓ʷmutmstn, x̣ʷq̓ʷmutmstxʷ**

es x̣ʷq̓ʷmutms – S/he can grind s.t. **ies x̣ʷq̓ʷmutm, as x̣ʷq̓ʷmutm**
es x̣ʷq̓ʷq̓ʷutm – It is grindable.

es čx̣ʷq̓ʷx̣ʷaq̓ʷm – It is grinding on the side of something. *(i.e., elk rubbing antlers)*

es x̣ʷáq̓ʷi t sqeľtč – S/he is grinding meat; making hamburger.

grizzly bear **smx̣éy̓čn̓,** *smx̣é* – grizzly bear; *Ursus arctos horribilis. suffix:* ***...ičn̓*** *– back.*
smx̣mx̣éy̓čn̓ – grizzly bears. *pl.*
sɬmx̣x̣éy̓čn̓, *sɬmx̣x̣é* – little grizzly bear.

cil smx̣mx̣é – five grizzly bears. **čn wičm t smx̣é** – I saw a grizzly bear.

groom well **sˀiˀc̓qn** – puccoon groom well; narrow-leaved puccoon; *Lithospermum incisum.*

grosbeak **nkʷtnáqs** – grosbeak, black-headed grosbeak, pine grosbeak. *lit. big beak/nose.*

grouchy **nčesls** – grouchy; angry feelings. *circumfix:* ***n...els*** *– want, feel.*
nčesls – S/he/it was grouchy. **čn nčesls, kʷ nčesls**
es nčeslsi – S/he/it is being grouchy. **čnes nčeslsi, kʷes nčeslsi**

nčeslsmis – S/he/it felt angry at s.o. **nčeslsmn, nčeslsmntxʷ**
es nčeslsms – S/he/it is feeling angry at s.o. **ies nčeslsm, as nčeslsm**

xʷas – grouchy.
i xʷas – S/he/it is grouchy. **i čn xʷas, i kʷ xʷas**

ground **sṫulixʷ** – ground, earth, dirt. *See:* ***land.***

...ulexʷ – suffix indicating ground, land, earth. *See:* ***land.***

ṫk̓ʷṫk̓ʷulexʷ – place things on the ground. *rt.:* ***ṫuk̓ʷ*** *– put/place something down. See:* ***put.***
ṫk̓ʷṫk̓ʷulexʷ – S/he/it placed (s.t.) on the ground. **čn ṫk̓ʷṫk̓ʷulexʷ, kʷ ṫk̓ʷṫk̓ʷulexʷ**
es ṫk̓ʷṫk̓ʷulexʷi – S/he/it is placing (s.t.) on the ground. **čnes ṫk̓ʷṫk̓ʷulexʷi, kʷes ṫk̓ʷṫk̓ʷulexʷi**

malt – mud. *See:* ***mud.***

groundhog **smc̓éc̓** – hoary marmot; *Marmota caligata*; yellow-bellied marmot; *Marmota flaviventris;* groundhog; woodchuck; *(there is no distinction between the two marmot species).*

ground squirrel **sisč** – gopher; Columbia ground squirrel; *Spermophilus columbianus.*

groundwater **k̓ʷɬsixʷlexʷ** – groundwater.

group **sxʷl̓xʷl̓tew̓s** – family or a group of people. *rt.:* ***xʷl̓xʷil̓t*** *– live; suffix:* ***...éw̓s*** *– in between, middle.*

grouse **q̓áɬq̓ɬc̓eˀ,** *q̓á* – ruffed grouse; *Bonasa umbellus.*

skʷiskʷs – spruce grouse; Franklin's grouse; fools hen; *Falcipennis canadensis*; domestic chicken. *See:* ***chicken.***

sq̓ʷóxʷlu, *sq̓ʷó* – sharp-tailed grouse; prairie chicken; *Tympanuchus phasianellus jamesi.*

grouseberry **sipt** – whortleberry; grouseberry; *Vaccinium scoparium.*

The **i** following uvular consonants (UC) and the glottal stop ˀ sound like English "*ey*" as in the words th*ey*, h*ey*, wh*ey*, etc. Salish UC are: **q, q̓, qʷ, q̓ʷ, x̣, x̣ʷ**. For example, the suffix ...**qin** – head/top, is often spelled using English *ey* as "q*ey*n". So **qi, q̓i, qʷi, q̓ʷi, x̣i, x̣ʷi,** may be spelled with English *ey* as **q***ey*, **q̓***ey*, **qʷ***ey*, **q̓ʷ***ey*, **x̣***ey*, **x̣ʷ***ey* in other texts.

s.t. - something, the 3rd person
(s.t.) - something implied
s.o. - someone, the 3rd person
sl. - singular form
pl. - plural form
rt. - root word
cmd. - command
lit. - literally
fig. - figuratively
i.e., - for example
See: - Redirection to a related word.

grow **kʷʔal̓** – grow; grow out from something. *(generally pertaining to plants)*
es kʷʔal̓mi – It is growing.
qs kʷʔal̓mi – It is going to grow.

ckʷakʷʔal̓ – each one grows; each one comes up.
es ckʷakʷʔal̓mi – Each one is growing; each one is coming up.

łkʷkʷʔál̓ – sprout; *lit. grow a little.*
łkʷkʷʔál̓ulexʷ – plants are sprouting on the land.
es kʷʔál̓ulexʷi – plants are coming up *(i.e., in the spring)*.
es nkʷal̓eysi – His/her teeth are growing out. **čnes nkʷʔál̓eysi, kʷes nkʷʔál̓eysi**
es nkʷal̓eplsčni – Its antlers are growing out.

skʷʔal̓ulexʷ – things that grow on the land; grass. *rt.: **kʷʔal̓** – plants grow; suffix: **...ulexʷ** – land.*

čkʷal̓ečst – bud; produce; makes something grow upon. *(the tree/plant is doing the action, it is making something grow)*
es čkʷal̓ečst – It produce new growth on it; it is budding.

es čkʷal̓ečstms – It is producing buds.

čkʷal̓ečstmis łu sc̓éʔek̓ʷ – It made/grew/produced a flower.

sčkʷal̓ečst – produce; what the tree/plant made.

es ox̣ʷx̣ʷépi – roots are growing. *See: **root**.*

px̣ʷtilš – grow up. *(pertaining to people) suffix: **...ilš** – autonomous.*
px̣ʷtilš – S/he/it grew up; got to be an adult. **čn px̣ʷtilš, kʷ px̣ʷtilš**
es px̣ʷtilši – S/he/it is growing up; getting to be an adult. **čnes px̣ʷtilši, kʷes px̣ʷtilši**

qltmwilš – become a man. *suffix: **...wilš** – developmental.*
qltmwilš – He became a man. **čn qltmwilš, kʷ qltmwilš**
es qltmwilši – He is becoming a man. **čnes qltmwilši, kʷes qltmwilši**

kʷtntwilš – get big; grow big. *suffix: **...wilš** – developmental.*
kʷtntwilš – S/he/it got big. **čn kʷtntwilš, kʷ kʷtntwilš**
es kʷtntwilši – S/he/it is getting big. **čnes kʷtntwilši, kʷes kʷtntwilši**
qs kʷtntwilši – S/he/it is going to get big. **čiqs kʷtntwilši, kʷqs kʷtntwilši**

nkʷƛ̓pulexʷ – come out of the ground. *rt.: **kʷƛ̓pim** – detach.*
es nkʷƛ̓pulexʷi – It is coming out of the ground.

ml̓uk̓ʷ – spread all around; propagate; grow, of non-living things. *See: **all around**.*

growl **naʔip** – growl.
es naʔipi – It is growling.

nkʷk̓ʷeʔcin – growl; fierce growl; biting voice. *rt.: **k̓ʷʔem** – bite; suffix: **...cin, ...cn** – action of the mouth.*

nłamqcn – black bear growl. *suffix: **...cin, ...cn** – action of the mouth.*
es nłamqcni – It is growling.

čn sewneʔ es nłamqcni – I hear a black bear growling.

guard **čšt̓im** – guard or take care of. *(This term is also used for wakes as it is seen that people are taking care of the dead.)*
čšt̓im – S/he guarded. **čn čšt̓im, kʷ čšt̓im**
es čšt̓mi – S/he is guarding. **čnes čšt̓mi, kʷes čšt̓mi**

es čšťmíʔi – They are guarding. **qeʔes čšťmi, pes čšťmi**

čšťn̓tes – S/he guarded s.o/s.t. **čšťn̓tén, čšťn̓téxʷ**
es čšťims S/he is guarding s.o./s.t. **ies čšťim, as čšťim**
čšťn̓téʔes – They guarded s.o/s.t. **qeʔ čšťn̓tém, čšťn̓tép**

sxʷčšťim – one tasked to guard. *prefix:* ***sxʷ...*** *– one tasked to do.*
čšťšťmuł – one that habitually guards. *suffix:* ***...łmuł*** *– one that habitually does.*
čšťn̓cutn – warning. *suffix:* ***...tin, ...tn*** *– means of/device.*

čšťiš – Guard/take care. *cmd.*
čšťint – Guard/take care of s.t. *cmd.*

čšťn̓téxʷ ta qs łx̣ʷntéxʷ łu q̇ett – Be careful, do not make holes in the hide.
čšťn̓téxʷ łu anq̇ett – You take care of your hide. **ha kʷ n̓e u čšťn̓téxʷ incitxʷʔ** – Will you take care of my house?

The **i** following uvular consonants (UC) and the glottal stop ʔ sound like English "*ey*" as in the words th*ey*, h*ey*, wh*ey*, etc. Salish UC are: **q, q̇, qʷ, q̇ʷ, x̣, x̣ʷ**. For example, the suffix ...**qin** – head/top, is often spelled using English *ey* as "q*ey*n". So **qi, q̇i, qʷi, q̇ʷi, x̣i, x̣ʷi**, may be spelled with English *ey* as **q***ey*, **q̇***ey*, **qʷ***ey*, **q̇ʷ***ey*, **x̣***ey*, **x̣ʷ***ey* in other texts.

čšťsqáx̣eʔ, *čšťsqá* – guard horses/domestic animals.
čšťsqáx̣eʔ – S/he guarded. **čn čšťsqáx̣eʔ, kʷ čšťsqáx̣eʔ**
es čšťsqáx̣eʔi – S/he is guarding. **čnes čšťsqáx̣eʔi, kʷes čšťsqáx̣eʔi**
es čšťsqáʔax̣eʔi – They are guarding. **qeʔes čšťsqáx̣eʔi, pes čšťsqáx̣eʔi**

sxʷčšťsqáx̣eʔ – one tasked to guard horses/domestic animals/cars. *prefix:* ***sxʷ...*** *– one tasked to do.*

čšťelm – put something in the care of someone else. *See:* ***care.***

čšťn̓cut – take care of one's self. *See:* ***care.***

čšťel̓t – watch over children; babysit. *See:* ***babysit.***

guardian

suméš – guardian spirit; spiritual power; medicine power.
qʷqʷċw̓é łu isuméš – Chipmunk is my medicine power.

guess

k̓ʷłʔawʔáw, *k̓ʷłʔawʔá* – guess. *rt.:* ***aw*** *– speak, pronounce; prefix:* ***k̓ʷł...*** *– under.*
k̓ʷłʔawʔáwm – S/he guessed. **čn k̓ʷłʔawʔáwm, kʷ k̓ʷłʔawʔáwm**
es k̓ʷłʔawʔáwi – S/he is guessing. **čnes k̓ʷłʔawʔáwi, kʷes k̓ʷłʔawʔáwi**
qs k̓ʷłʔawʔáwi – S/he is going to guess. **čiqs k̓ʷłʔawʔáwi, kʷqs k̓ʷłʔawʔáwi**

k̓ʷłʔawʔáwis – S/he guessed it. **k̓ʷłʔawʔáwn, k̓ʷłʔawʔáwntxʷ**
es k̓ʷłʔawʔáwms – S/he is guessing it. **ies k̓ʷłʔawʔáwm, as k̓ʷłʔawʔáwm**

k̓ʷłʔawnuis – S/he succeeded in guessing it. **k̓ʷłʔawnun, k̓ʷłʔawnuntxʷ**

sxʷk̓ʷłʔawʔáwm – one tasked to guess.
k̓ʷłʔawmemn – one that is inclined to guess.
k̓ʷłʔawncutn – guesser of one.

k̓ʷłʔawʔáwiš – Guess. *cmd.*
k̓ʷłʔawʔáwnt – Guess it. *cmd.*
k̓ʷłʔawmnweʔexʷ – They were guessing each other. **qeʔ k̓ʷłʔawmnwexʷ, p k̓ʷłʔawmnwexʷ**

k̓ʷłʔawł – good luck in guessing.

k̓ʷłʔawiš n̓e kʷ k̓ʷłcnnels n̓em anwi n̓e ta kʷ k̓ʷłcnnels n̓em qʷoyʔe – Guess; if you guess right it will be yous, if you guess wrong it will be mine.

k̓ʷłcnnels – guess right.
k̓ʷłcnnels – S/he guessed right. **čn k̓ʷłcnnels, kʷ k̓ʷłcnnels**

s.t. - something, the 3rd person
(s.t.) - something implied
s.o. - someone, the 3rd person
sl. - singular form
pl. - plural form
rt. - root word
cmd. - command
lit. - literally
fig. - figuratively
i.e., - for example
See: - Redirection to a related word.

es k̓ʷłcnnelsi – S/he is guessing right. **čnes k̓ʷłcnnelsi, kʷes k̓ʷłcnnelsi**

guest **xʷicn –** guest. **inxʷicn, anxʷicn, xʷicis**
xʷicnmis – S/he took s.o. as a guest. **xʷicnmn, xʷicnmntxʷ**
es xʷicnms – S/he is taking s.o. as a guest. **ies xʷicnm, as xʷicnm**

sčxʷuy – visitor. **sčxʷixʷuy –** visitors. *pl. rt.: **čxʷuym** – visit. See: **visit**.*
qeʔ ep sčxʷixʷuy – We have visitors.

sčiccn – guest. *rt.: **čicn** – meet someone. See: **meet**.*

guide **sxʷlšitusm –** guide; one tasked to guide. *prefix: **sxʷ...** – one tasked to do.*

sť̓čmíʔis – guide, direction.

mieńcutn – something or someone that guides. *(i.e., spirit, teacher, etc.) suffix: **...tin, ...tn** – means of/device.*
anmieńcutn – Your person/spirit that guides you.
kʷ inmieńcutn qʷo ṁéẏełtxʷ – Show me, my teacher/spirit guide.

guitar **ox̣ʷox̣ʷalqʷmn –** guitar. *rt.: **ox̣ʷom** – strung across; suffix: **...alqʷ** – wood; cylindical; suffix: **...min, ...mn** – instrument/tool.*

čx̣ʷax̣ʷʔanč, *čx̣ʷa* **–** radio, harp, guitar, stereo, anything that makes music. *rt.: **x̣ʷax̣ʷʔey** – laugh.*

gum **tq̓ʷeẏ –** chewing gum.

gums **snálexʷtn –** gums.

gumweed **ťlšisqá –** gumweed; *Grindelia howellii.*

gun **nťq̓nčstéłce,** *nťq̓nčste* **–** pistol; six-shooter. *rt.: **ťaq̓n** – six.*

sululmiňč, *sululmi* **–** rifle. *See: **rifle**.*

gunpowder **npq̓ʷmin –** gunpowder.

ťikʷ – gun blast.
ťkʷťikʷlš – shooting around.

gurgle **mal̓l̓l̓ –** gurgling, bubbling.

gut **čťl̓ewṡ –** gut animals. *suffix: **...éwṡ** – in between, middle.*
čťl̓ewṡis – S/he gutted it. **čťl̓ewṡn, čťl̓ewṡntxʷ**
es čťl̓ewṡms – S/he is gutting it. **ies čťl̓ewṡm, as čťl̓ewṡm**

čťl̓ewṡntxʷ – Gut it. *cmd.*

čťl̓qʷewṡ – gut fish. *suffix: **...éwṡ** – in between, middle.*
čťl̓qʷewṡis – S/he gutted it. **čťl̓qʷewṡn, čťl̓qʷewṡntxʷ**
es čťl̓qʷewṡms – S/he is gutting it. **ies čťl̓qʷewṡm, as čťl̓qʷewṡm**

čťl̓qʷewṡntxʷ – Gut it. *cmd.*

čťl̓qʷéwṡts – S/he gutted s.t. **čťl̓qʷéwṡtn, čťl̓qʷéwṡtxʷ**

ṅe kʷ čnk̓ʷé m še čťl̓qʷéwṡtxʷ – If you get one, you will gut it.

guts **stx̣enč –** guts. *suffix: **...enč** – within.*

sp̓l̓q̓énč, *sp̓l̓q̓é* **–** large intestine.

H

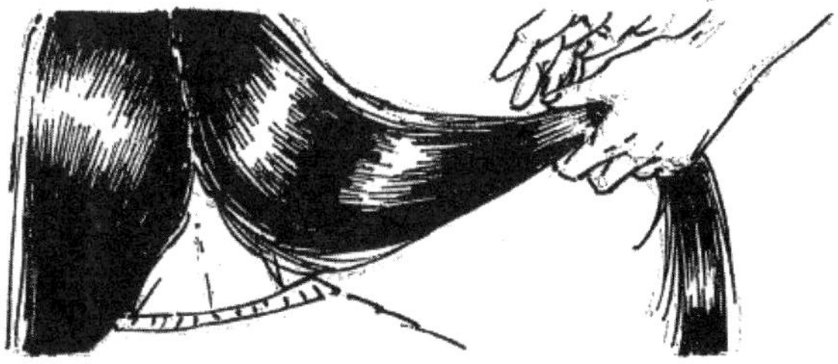

habit **sqʷʔem** – habit; practice. *rt.: **qʷʔem** – get accustomed; See: **accustomed**.*
sqʷéʔms – his/her/its habit; it is his/her/its practice. **isqʷéʔm, asqʷéʔm**

ha kʷ ep sqʷéʔm – Do you have a habit?

nk̓ʷul̓mn – ways; customs; habits; culture; traditions; the things one does. *See: **customs**.*

nʔax̣íłtn – ways; customs; the way one acts. *See: **customs**.*

habitat **snlšeʔtn** – habitat; roaming area.
lšeʔ – stays there; roams in that general area; home range. *See: **stay**.*

l nkʷect łu snlšeʔtis – The forest is its habitat.

habitual **qʷaqʷemncut,** *qʷaqʷemncú* – practice, drill, train, study. *See: **practice**.*

qʷamáqs – get accustomed to food. *See: **accustomed**.*

hail **ssal̓us,** *ssal̓u* – hail, hailstones.
sal̓us – It hailed.
es sal̓usi – It is hailing.
qs sal̓usi – It is going to hail.

sal̓usis – It hailed on s.t.
es sal̓usms – It is hailing on s.t.

qʷo sal̓usntm – I got hailed on.

q̇ʷit̓s – nod the head; greet; hail. *See: **nod**.*

čn q̇ʷit̓s mali – I nodded toward Mary; I hail Mary.

hair **q̇ʷómqn** – head hair. *rt.: **q̇ʷum** – bunched.*

spum – fur; animal hair.

...up... – Infix to indicate hair other than on the head.
supcin – whiskers; beard. *suffix: **...cin, ...cn** – action of the mouth.*
snupupeneʔ – ear hair.
snupupaqs – nose hair.
snupupax̣n – underarm hair.
sčupʔeẇs – belly hair. *suffix: **...éẇs** – in between, middle.*
snupičn̓ – back hair. *suffix: **...ičn̓** – back.*
sčupupus – eye lashes. *circumfix: **č...us** – spherical object; eyes.*

...ep – *suffix indicating rope, head hair.*
xʷʔep – many ropes/hair.
nk̓ʷep – one hair. **eslép** – two hairs. **čełép** – three hairs. **musp** – four hairs.

s.t. - something, the 3rd person
(s.t.) - something implied
s.o. - someone, the 3rd person
sl. - singular form
pl. - plural form
rt. - root word
cmd. - command
lit. - literally
fig. - figuratively
i.e., - for example
See: - Redirection to a related word.

clčstep – five hairs. **t̓q̓nčstep** – six hairs. **sp̓l̓čep** – seven hairs.
henmép – eight hairs. **x̣antep** – nine hairs. **upnčstep** – ten hairs.

pox̣t – pubic hair.

p̓at̓qan – messy hair. *See: **pile**.*
kʷ p̓at̓qan – You have messy hair.

t̓ix̣qn – messy/bushy hair. *rt.: **t̓ix̣** – protrude. See: **messy**.*

i čn x̣opqn – I have bad hair.

pqmast – begin to get gray/white hair.
es pqmasti – S/he is getting gray/white hair. **čnes pqmasti, kʷes pqmasti**

čmixʷqn – gray/white and black hair; salt-and-pepper hair.
es čmixʷqn – S/he has gray/white and black hair. **čnes čmixʷqn, kʷes čmixʷqn**

pqmayaqn – gray/white hair.
pqmayaqn – S/he has gray/white hair. **čn pqmayaqn, kʷ pqmayaqn**

nłppqosusi – put colored powder on the front tuff of hair for protection *(this is done by a medicine man especially during a war dance time).*

čłkʷicċl̓š – hair stands up, as on a dog's/bear's back when angry.
es čłkʷicċl̓ši – Its hair is standing up.

ta kʷ qes čłkʷicċl̓š – Don't raise your hair; don't get angry.

hair oil

čp̓uƛ̓qntn – hair oil; styling gel. *rt.: **p̓uƛ̓** – grease, oil; suffix: **...qin, ...qn** – top; suffix: **...tin, ...tn** – means of/device.*

hairy

čupu – hairy. *infix: **...up...** – hair.*
čłuʔpel̓xʷ es łuʔpus ci čłčče – That brown horse had its winter fur on and little whiskers on its face.

half

tx̣ʷew̓s – divide something in two; halve something. *rt.: **tox̣ʷ** – straight; suffix: **...éw̓s** – in between, middle.*
tx̣ʷew̓sm – S/he is halved. **čn tx̣ʷew̓sm, kʷ tx̣ʷew̓sm**
es tx̣ʷew̓si – S/he is halving. **čnes tx̣ʷew̓si, kʷes tx̣ʷew̓si**
qs tx̣ʷew̓si – S/he is going to halve. **čiqs tx̣ʷew̓si, kʷqs tx̣ʷew̓si**

tx̣ʷew̓sts – S/he/it halved s.t. **tx̣ʷew̓stn, tx̣ʷew̓stxʷ**
es tx̣ʷew̓sms – S/he/it is halving s.t. **ies tx̣ʷew̓sm, as tx̣ʷew̓sm**
qs tx̣ʷew̓sms – S/he/it is going to halve s.t. **iqs tx̣ʷew̓sm, aqs tx̣ʷew̓sm**
tx̣ʷéʔew̓sts – They halved s.t. **qeʔ tx̣ʷew̓stm, tx̣ʷew̓stp**
es tx̣ʷéʔew̓sms – They are halving s.t. **qeʔes tx̣ʷew̓sm, es tx̣ʷew̓smp**
qs tx̣ʷéʔew̓sms – They are going to halve s.t. **qeʔqs tx̣ʷew̓sm, qs tx̣ʷew̓smp**

es tx̣ʷtx̣ʷew̓sms – S/he/it is halving things. **ies tx̣ʷtx̣ʷew̓sm, as tx̣ʷtx̣ʷew̓sm**

es łttx̣ʷew̓sms – S/he/it is halving s.t. a little bit. **ies łttx̣ʷew̓sm, as łttx̣ʷew̓sm**

sctx̣ʷew̓s – something that's been halved. *prefix: **sc...** – s.t. that's been done/made/prepared.*

tx̣ʷew̓snt – Halve s.t. *cmd.*

ha kʷ n̓e u tx̣ʷew̓stxʷ anapl – Would you half your apple? **qʷo xʷic̓štxʷ tx̣ʷew̓s** – Give me half.

syew̓smskʷkʷʔec – midnight.

sčut – Half of an object, number, or time; half of the whole; one side.
čmi sčtasq̓t u čiqs k̓ʷuli – I am going to work only half a day.
mus eł sčut – 4:30 *lit. 4 plus a half.*

sčtm…, sčt… – prefix indicating half of. *rt.: **sčut** – half of.*
sčtasq̓t – half a day. *suffix: **…asq̓t** – sky, day.*
sčtmsqélixʷ, *sčtmsqé* – half-blood Indian.
sčtmsqáx̣eʔ, *sčtmsqá* – half-blood horse.
sčtéłċeʔ – side, half body. *prefix: **sčtm…, sčt…** – half; suffix: **…ełċeʔ** – inside of something, body.*

> The **i** following uvular consonants (UC) and the glottal stop **ʔ** sound like English "*ey*" as in the words *they, hey, whey,* etc. Salish UC are: **q, q̓, qʷ, q̓ʷ, x̣, x̣ʷ**. For example, the suffix …**qin** – head/top, is often spelled using English *ey* as "q*ey*n". So **qi, q̓i, qʷi, q̓ʷi, x̣i, x̣ʷi**, may be spelled with English *ey* as **q***ey*, **q̓***ey*, **qʷ***ey*, **q̓ʷ***ey*, **x̣***ey*, **x̣ʷ***ey* in other texts.

half-blood

sčtmsqélixʷ, *sčtmsqé* – half-blood Indian. *prefix: **sčtm…, sčt…** – half.*
sčtmsqáx̣eʔ, *sčtmsqá* – half-blood horse.

halter

łxʷpusáx̣eʔ, *łxʷpusá* – halter. *lit. slips over the neck. rt.: **łixʷp** – slip/pull over.*
es łxʷpus – S/he/it is haltered.

łax̣ústn, *łax̣ú* – halter. *lit. has lines on the face. rt.: **i ax̣** – it has lines; suffix: **…us** – face; suffix: **…tin, …tn** – means of/device.*

ax̣usm – put on a bridle, hackamore, or halter. *rt.: **i ax̣** – it has lines; suffix: **…us** – face, fire. See: **bridle**.*

pƛ̓usm – take off a bridle, hackamore, or halter. *rt.: **pƛ̓im** – release from; suffix: **…us** – face, fire. See: **bridle***

k̓ʷłaceʔ – bridle. *See: **bridle**.*

čax̣ċasqáx̣eʔtn, *čax̣ċasqá* – harness. *rt.: **i ax̣** – it has lines; suffix: **…tin, …tn** – means of/device. See: **harness**.*

ham

lkʷošó – pig, bacon, pork, ham. *(approximation to French word)*

hamburger

es x̣ʷáq̓ʷ sqeľtč – hamburger; it is ground meat. *See: **grind**.*
es x̣ʷáq̓ʷi t sqeľtč – S/he is grinding meat. **čnes x̣ʷáq̓ʷi t sqeľtč, kʷes x̣ʷáq̓ʷi t sqeľtč**

Hamilton

čłčlčlé – Hamilton, Montana. *rt.: **čil** – upright protrusion; prefix: **čł…** – surface.*

hammer

tʔem – pound; hammer; bump.
tetʔem – S/he hammered. **čn tetʔem, kʷ tetʔem**
es tetʔemi – S/he is hammering. **čnes tetʔemi, kʷes tetʔemi**
qs tetʔemi – S/he is going to hammer. **čiqs tetʔemi, kʷqs tetʔemi**

tetʔentes – S/he hammered s.t. **tetʔenten, tetʔentexʷ**
es tetʔems – S/he is hammering s.t. **ies tetʔem, as tetʔem**
qs tetʔems – S/he is going to hammer s.t. **iqs tetʔem, aqs tetʔem**

tetʔemints – S/he used s.t. to hammer. **tetʔemintn, tetʔemintxʷ**
es tetʔemms – S/he is using s.t. to hammering. **ies tetʔemm, as tetʔemm**
qs tetʔemms – S/he is going to use s.t. to hammer. **iqs tetʔemm, aqs tetʔemm**

łteteʔmin – hammer; tool to pound. *rt.: **teʔ** – hit/bump into; prefix: **ł…** – little; suffix: **…min, …mn** – instrument/tool.*
ntaʔqintn – sledge hammer. *rt.: **ntaʔqin** – hit on top; suffix: **…qin, …qn** – top; suffix: **…tin, …tn** – means of/device.*

tetʔeiš – Hammer. *cmd.*
tetʔent – Hammer it. *cmd.*

tʔenuis – S/he succeeded in hitting s.t. **tʔenun, tʔenuntxʷ**
tetʔenuis – S/he succeeded in hammering s.t. **tetʔenun, tetʔenuntxʷ**

> s.t. - something, the 3rd person
> (s.t.) - something implied
> s.o. - someone, the 3rd person
> *sl.* - singular form
> *pl.* - plural form
> *rt.* - root word
> *cmd.* - command
> *lit.* - literally
> *fig.* - figuratively
> *i.e.,* - for example
> *See:* - Redirection to a related word.

hand **čelš** – one hand. **člčelš** – hands *pl.*
sčłčmečst – back of hand.
snčmčṅečst – palm.
sntpp̓sečst – knuckle.
st̓x̣t̓ix̣čst – fingers.

...ečst – suffix indicating hand.
mlq̓ʷéčst – fist. *rt.: malq̓ʷ – balled object.*
sčchečst – right hand. *See: right side.*
sč̓ciqʷečst – left hand. *See: left side.*
kʷtkʷtnečst – big hands. *rt.: kʷtunt – big.*
t̓mt̓mlačst – hands do not work good.
x̣sx̣séčst – capable hands. *rt.: x̣est – good.*
yuyúwečst – strong hands; capable hands. *rt.: yoyóot – strong.*
nt̓qʷčṅéčst – clap hands. *See: clap.*

ċaléčst – have a sore/achy hand. *rt.: ċaál – ache; suffix: ...ečst, ...čst – of the hand.*
ċaléčst – S/he/it had a sore hand. **čn ċaléčst, kʷ ċaléčst**
es ċaléčsti – S/he/it has a sore hand. **čnes ċaléčsti, kʷes ċaléčsti**
qs ċaléčsti – S/he/it is going to have a sore hand. **čiqs ċaléčsti, kʷqs ċaléčsti**
ċaléˀečst – They had a sore hand. **qeˀ ċaléčst, p ċaléčst**
es ċaléˀečsti – They have a sore hand. **qeˀes ċaléčsti, pes ċaléčsti**
qs ċaléˀečsti – They are going to have a sore hand. **qeˀqs ċaléčsti, pqs ċaléčsti**

ċuċéẇčstm – S/he/it washed his/her/its hands. **čn ċuċéẇčstm, kʷ ċuċéẇčstm**
es ċuċéẇčsti – S/he/it is washing his/her/its hands. **čnes ċuċéẇčsti, kʷes ċuċéẇčsti**
ċuċéẇčstiš – Wash your hands. *cmd.*

kʷnkʷnmičst – lock hands. *suffix: ...ečst, ...čst – of the hand.*
es kʷnkʷnmičsti – S/he has hands locked.

tčšnmisti – hands together.

tcčnčnmisti – hands together.

tčtčšnmisti – hands together.

es nkʷnmičṅisti – S/he has hands behind back. **čnes nkʷnmičṅisti, kʷes nkʷnmičṅisti**

ntqtqłniẇłtni – have hands on hips.

k̓ʷłkʷakʷq aqi – cold, almost frostbitten, hands.

tql̓sečst – gesture with the hand for somebody's attention; sign. *See: gesture.*

qxʷlsečst – gesture with the hand for somebody to leave. *See: gesture.*

handbag **ax̣éṅeˀ** – beaded bag/handbag. *rt.: i ax̣ – it has lines. See: line.*
łax̣éṅeˀ – Small beaded bag/handbag. *See: bag.*

handcuffs **k̓ʷłlolocnečst,** *k̓ʷłlolocn* – handcuffs. *suffix: ...ečst, ...čst – of the hand.*

handkerchief **čiyálxʷqn,** *číya* – head wrap; scarf. *rt.: yalim – coil, wrap; suffix: ...qin, ...qn – top.*

snnostn – Anything used to blow your nose; a device for snot. *See: snot.*

snosmn – Anything used to blow your nose; a utensil for snot. *See: snot.*

nʔap̓aqstn – nose wiper; anything used to wipe the nose. *rt.: **ep̓m –** wipe; suffix: **...tin, ...tn** – means of/**device.** See: **wipe**.*

handle
nčč̓n̓min – handle. *rt.: **č̓n̓im –** grasp on to something. See: **grasp**.*

čč̓n̓épleʔ – lead by the hand. *(i.e., leading a horse.) See: **lead**.*

hand out
px̣ʷmim – distribute; spread around; pass/hand out. *See: **distribute**.*

handrail
snčč̓n̓mintn – handrail. *rt.: **č̓n̓im –** grasp on to something; prefix: **sn... –** a place of; suffix: **...tin, ...tn –** means of/device. See: **grasp**.*

handshake
čn̓č̓łtumš, *čn̓č̓łtu* **–** shake hands with people. *See: **shake hands**.*

sčn̓č̓łtumšs – his/her/its hand shake. **isčn̓č̓łtumš, asčn̓č̓łtumš**

čn̓éčs – hold hands; grasp hands. *See: **shake hands**.*

handsome
swiʔnumt – handsome, pretty.

hang
šal – hang/suspended; something hanging pendulously.

šalntes – S/he made s.t. suspended. **šalnten, šalntenxʷ**
es šalims – S/he is making s.t. suspended. **ies šalim, as šalim**
qs šalims – S/he is going to make s.t. suspended. **iqs šalim, aqs šalim**

šalut – It is suspended; it is in the state of suspension.

es čšaltéw̓s – It is suspended up high.
es čłšalteneʔ – It is suspended over.

čšlšalew̓s, *čšlšale* **–** lamp; lantern.
k̓ʷłnšalpncutn – tipi door.
nšlšaltáqs, *nšlšaltá* **–** turkey.
nšaltsq̓me – uvula.

čacéw̓sm – tie up; to tie and hang up. *rt.: **acim –** tie; circumfix: **č...ew̓s –** up high.*

čacéw̓sm – S/he/it was hung. **čn čacéw̓sm, kʷ čacéw̓sm**
es čacéw̓si – S/he/it is hanging. **čnes čacéw̓si, kʷes čacéw̓si**
qs čacéw̓si – S/he/it is going to hang. **čiqs čacéw̓si, kʷqs čacéw̓si**
čacéʔew̓sm – They were hung. **qeʔ čacéw̓sm, p čacéw̓sm**
es čacéʔew̓si – They are hanging. **qeʔes čacéw̓si, pes čacéw̓si**
qs čacéʔew̓si – They are going to hang. **qeʔqs čacéw̓si, pqs čacéw̓si**

čacéw̓sts – S/he/it hung s.o. **čacéw̓stn, čacéw̓stxʷ**
es čacéw̓sms – S/he/it is hanging s.o. **ies čacéw̓sm, as čacéw̓sm**
qs čacew̓sms – S/he/it is going to hang s.o. **iqs čacéw̓sm, aqs čacéw̓sm**
čacéʔew̓sts – They hung s.o. **qeʔ čacéw̓stm, čacéw̓stp**
es čacéʔew̓sms – They are hanging s.o. **qeʔes čacéw̓sm, es čacéw̓smp**
qs čacéʔew̓sms – They are going to hang s.o. **qeʔqs čacéw̓sm, qs čacéw̓smp**

čacéw̓stm – S/he/it was hung by s.o.

sčacew̓s, *sčace* **–** Sunday.

čox̣mepleʔ – something fastened and hanging/dangling off. *(i.e., a rope tied to something; someone on parole, etc.) suffix: **...epleʔ –** permanence.*

čox̣meplʔeis – S/he fastened s.t. that hangs off. **čox̣meplʔen, čox̣meplʔentxʷ**
es čox̣meplʔems – S/he is fastening s.t. that hangs off. **ies čox̣meplʔem, as čox̣meplʔem**
qs čox̣meplʔems – S/he is going to fasten s.t. that hangs off. **iqs čox̣meplʔem, aqs čox̣meplʔem**

The **i** following uvular consonants (UC) and the glottal stop **ʔ** sound like English "*ey*" as in the words th*ey*, h*ey*, wh*ey*, etc. Salish UC are: **q, q̇, qʷ, q̇ʷ, x̣, x̣ʷ**. For example, the suffix **...qin** – head/top, is often spelled using English *ey* as "q*ey*n". So **qi, q̇i, qʷi, q̇ʷi, x̣i, x̣ʷi**, may be spelled with English *ey* as **q***ey*, **q̇***ey*, **qʷ***ey*, **q̇ʷ***ey*, **x̣***ey*, **x̣ʷ***ey* in other texts.

s.t. - something, the 3rd person
(s.t.) - something implied
s.o. - someone, the 3rd person
sl. - singular form
pl. - plural form
rt. - root word
cmd. - command
lit. - literally
fig. - figuratively
i.e., - for example
See: - Redirection to a related word.

čłqʷéw̓s – drape up high; hang up high over an object; hang up. *See: **drape**.*

es q̓leps – It is hanging off the neck.

hang up

čq̓l̓xʷéw̓s – hang/hook up high; hang on a hook. *circumfix: **č...ew̓s** – up high.*
čq̓l̓xʷéw̓sis – S/he/it hung it up. **čq̓l̓xʷéw̓sn, čq̓l̓xʷéw̓sntxʷ**
es čq̓l̓xʷéw̓sms – S/he/it is hanging it up. **ies čq̓l̓xʷéw̓sm, as čq̓l̓xʷéw̓sm**
qs čq̓l̓xʷéw̓sms – S/he/it is going to hang it up. **iqs čq̓l̓xʷéw̓sm, aqs čq̓l̓xʷéw̓sm**
čq̓l̓xʷéʔéw̓sis – They hung it up. **qeʔ čq̓l̓xʷéw̓sntm, čq̓l̓xʷéw̓sntp**
es čq̓l̓xʷéʔew̓sms – They are hanging it up. **qeʔes čq̓l̓xʷéw̓sm, es čq̓l̓xʷéw̓smp**
qs čq̓l̓xʷéʔew̓sms – They are going to hang it up. **qeʔqs čq̓l̓xʷéw̓sm, qs čq̓l̓xʷéw̓smp**

čq̓l̓xʷéw̓snt – Hang it up. *cmd.*

čq̓l̓xʷéw̓stxʷ – You hung it up.

čq̓l̓xʷéw̓sntm – It was hung up.
qʷo čq̓l̓xʷéw̓sntm – I was hung up.

es čq̓l̓xʷéw̓s – It is hung up.

t kʷtisi čq̓l̓xʷéw̓sis – Big Blanket hung it up. **ye lʔe m čq̓l̓xʷéw̓stnxʷ –** Hang it up right here.
čq̓l̓xʷéw̓snt anlkepu – Hang up your coat. **ta qes čq̓l̓xʷéw̓stxʷ –** Do not hang it up.

čłqʷéw̓s – drape up high; hang up high over an object; hang up. *See: **drape**.*

čłqʷelism – meat hung over something; things hung over something in a line; draped over.
čłqelisis – S/he hung things in a line. **čłqelisn, čłqelisntxʷ**
es čłqelisms – S/he is hanging things in a line. **ies čłqelism, as čłqelism**
qs čłqelisms – S/he is going to hang things in a line. **iqs čłqelism, aqs čłqelism**

es čłqelism – The meat is hung over.

happen

ėčšč́éṅ – question inquiring about the state of someone or something. *See: **do**.*
ėčšč́éṅm – What happened to him/her/it? **čn ėčšč́éṅm, kʷ ėčšč́éṅm**
es ėčšč́éṅi – What is happening/wrong with her/him/it? **čnes ėčšč́éṅi, kʷes ėčšč́éṅi**
qs ėčšč́éṅi – What is going to be happening with her/him/it? **čiqs ėčšč́éṅi, kʷqs ėčšč́éṅi**
ėčšešč́éʔeṅm – What happened to them? **qeʔ ėčšešč́éṅm, p ėčšešč́éṅm**
es ėčšešč́éʔeṅi – What is happening/wrong with them? **qeʔes ėčšešč́éṅi, pes ėčšešč́éṅi**
qs ėčšešč́éʔeṅi – What is going to be happening with them? **qeʔqs ėčšešč́éṅi, pqs ėčšešč́éṅi**

ėčšč́ṅasq̓ti – What is happening with the sky; how's the weather? *suffix: **...asq̓t** – sky, day.*

x̣ʷa ėčšč́eṅm – Maybe something happened to him/her/it? **ėčšč́enm łu qeč́ʔupn –** What happened to our Council? **ėčšč́enstxʷ łu anpspus –** What did you do to your cats? **wis nk̓ʷeʔnis łu smx̣e u ėčšč́eṅm –** What happens after the grizzly makes his/her choice?

nloʔpus – fall into place; happen; come about; answered.
nloʔloʔpštmist – S/he experienced things falling into place. **čn nloʔloʔpštmist, kʷ nloʔloʔpštmist**
es nloʔloʔpštmisti – S/he is experiencing things falling into place. **čnes nloʔloʔpštmisti, kʷes nloʔloʔpštmisti**
qs nloʔloʔpštmisti – S/he is going to experience things falling into place. **čiqs nloʔloʔpštmisti, kʷqs nloʔloʔpštmisti**

es nloʔpusi – It is falling into place.

nloʔpsew̓sis – S/he/it made it happen. **nloʔpsew̓sn, nloʔpsew̓sntxʷ**

es nloˀpseẇsms – S/he/it is making it happen. **ies nloˀpseẇsm, as nloˀpseẇsm**
qs nloˀpseẇsms – S/he/it is going to make it happen. **iqs nloˀpseẇsm, aqs nloˀpseẇsm**

nloˀpštmistmis – S/he/it made it happen for s.o. **nloˀpštmistmn, nloˀpštmistmntxʷ**
es nloˀpštms – S/he/it is making it happen for s.o. **ies nloˀpštm, as nloˀpštm**
qs nloˀpštms – S/he/it is going to make it happen for s.o. **iqs nloˀpštm, aqs nloˀpštm**

snloˀpsiš – happenings.

ṅem nloˀloˀpus łu ascčučawm – Your prayers will fall into place. **nloˀloˀpus łu asčučaw** – Your prayers will come about. **iqs nloˀpuštm łu stipn** – I am going to make it happen for Stephen. **čnes nloˀloˀpštmisti x̣ʷl̓ isčučaw** – I am experiencing my prayers. **šeẏ łu isnloˀpsiš** – That's my happenings.

The **i** following uvular consonants (UC) and the glottal stop **ˀ** sound like English "*ey*" as in the words *they, hey, whey*, etc. Salish UC are: **q, q̇, qʷ, q̇ʷ, x̣, x̣ʷ**. For example, the suffix ...**qin** – head/top, is often spelled using English *ey* as "q*ey*n". So **qi, q̇i, qʷi, q̇ʷi, x̣i, x̣ʷi**, may be spelled with English *ey* as **q***ey*, **q̇***ey*, **qʷ***ey*, **q̇ʷ***ey*, **x̣***ey*, **x̣ʷ***ey* in other texts.

happy

pii – happy; pleasure; bliss; rejoice. *(this describes the actions of happiness)*
pii – S/he rejoiced; expressed happiness. **čn pii, kʷ pii**
es piimi – S/he is rejoicing. **čnes piim, kʷes piim**
qs piimi – S/he is going to rejoice. **čiqs piim, kʷqs piim**

piimis – S/he took pleasure in it. **piimin, piimintxʷ**
es piiminms – S/he is taking pleasure in it. **ies piiminm, as piiminm**
qs piiminms – S/he is going to take pleasure in it. **iqs piiminm, aqs piiminm**

piyečstms – S/he caused s.o. to rejoice. **piyečstmn, piyečstmntxʷ**
es piyečstms – S/he is causing s.o. to rejoice. **ies piyečstm, as piyečstm**
qs piyečstms – S/he is going to cause s.o. to rejoice. **iqs piyečstm, aqs piyečstm**

pipiit – joyful.
piimin – instrument of joy.
spipisnuxʷ – something that is worthy of enjoyment/pleasure. *suffix:* ***...snuxʷ*** *– worthy of.*

piimint – Take pleasure in it. *cmd.*
piyečstmnt – Make s.o. rejoice. *cmd.*
pepiẏeˀ – happy one, affectionately.

npiyéls, *npiyé* – feel happy. *rt.:* ***pii*** *– happy; circumfix:* ***n...els*** *– want, feel.*
npiyéls – S/he/it was happy. **čn npiyéls, kʷ npiyéls**
es npiyélsi – S/he/it is happy. **čnes npiyélsi, kʷes npiyélsi**
qs npiyélsi – S/he/it is going to be happy. **čiqs npiyélsi, kʷqs npiyélsi**
npiyéˀels – They were happy. **qeˀ npiyéls, p npiyéls**
es npiyéˀelsi – They are happy. **qeˀes npiyélsi, pes npiyélsi**
qs npiyéˀelsi – They are going to be happy. **qeˀqs npiyélsi, pqs npiyélsi**

npiyélsmis – S/he/it felt happy with it. **npiyélsmn, npiyélsmntxʷ**
es npiyélsms – S/he/it is feeling happy with it. **ies npiyélsm, as npiyélsm**
qs npiyélsms – S/he/it is going to feel happy with it. **iqs npiyélsm, aqs npiyélsm**

npiyélsts – S/he/it caused s.o. to feel happy. **npiyélstn, npiyélstxʷ**
es npiyélstms – S/he/it is causing s.o. to feel happy. **ies npiyélstm, as npiyélstm**
qs npiyélstms – S/he/it is going to cause s.o. to feel happy. **iqs npiyélstm, aqs npiyélstm**

es npipiyélsi – S/he/it is repeatedly happy. **čnes npipiyélsi, kʷes npipiyélsi**

npiyélstn – something that causes happiness.
snkʷłnpiyéls – someone happiness is shared with. *suffix:* ***snkʷł...*** *– fellow, member of.*

s.t. - something, the 3rd person
(s.t.) - something implied
s.o. - someone, the 3rd person
sl. - singular form
pl. - plural form
rt. - root word
cmd. - command
lit. - literally
fig. - figuratively
i.e., - for example
See: - Redirection to a related word.

npiyélsiš – Feel happy. *cmd.*
npiyélsmist – happy with one's self.
es npiyélsmnwexʷi – They are happy toward each other.
es npiyélstwexʷi – They are making each other happy.
es npiyélsmistms – S/he enjoys one's self with it. **ies npiyélsmistm, as npiyélsmistm**

kʷemt esyáʔ u npiyéls – Then everyone was happy. **we es pupušenči łu mali u eł npiyéls –** Mary was sad and then she got happy again.

čpipiis – have happy eyes; have flirty eyes; have a gleem in the eye. *circumfix:* ***č...us*** *– spherical object; eyes.*
i čpipiis – S/he/it has happy eyes. **i čn čpipiis, i kʷ čpipiis**

čpiismis – S/he/it saw s.o. looking happy. **čpiismn, čpiismntxʷ**
es čpiisms – S/he/it sees s.o. looking happy. **ies čpiism, as čpiism**

npiyusmis – S/he/it happily looked at s.o./s.t. **npiyusmn, npiyusmntxʷ**
es npiyusms – S/he/it is happily looking at s.o./s.t. **ies npiyusm, as npiyusm**

npiyusmnt – Look at it happily. *cmd.*

piis – have a happy face; have a smiling face.
i piis – S/he/it has a happy face. **i čn piis, i kʷ piis**

piyusm – make one's face happy.
piyusm – S/he made a happy face. **čn piyusm, kʷ piyusm**
es piyusi – S/he is making a happy face. **čnes piyusi, kʷs piyusi**
qs piyusi – S/he is going to make a happy face. **kʷqs piyusi, kʷqs piyusi**

piyusis – S/he made a happy face at s.o. **piyusn, piyusntxʷ**
es piyusms – S/he is making a happy face at s.o. **ies piyusm, as piyusm**
qs piyusms – S/he is going to make a happy face at s.o. **iqs piyusm, aqs piyusm**

piyusnt – Make a happy face at him. *cmd.*

npipicin – talk happily. *suffix:* ***...cin, ...cn*** *– action of the mouth.*
picinmis – S/he told s.o. happy words/news. **picinmn, picinmntxʷ**
es picinms – S/he is telling s.o. happy words/news. **ies picinm, as picinm**
qs picinms – S/he is going to tell s.o. happy words/news. **iqs picinm, aqs picinm**

lemtwil̓š – get happy/glad. *See:* ***glad.***

Happy Birthday

čk̓ʷul̓ltn – birthday.
npiyels ančk̓ʷul̓ltn – Happy Birthday.
x̣est ančk̓ʷul̓ltn – Happy/good Birthday.

nčcnšncut – make a complete revolution; make a circle; meet one's own foot prints/tracks. *This word is used to describe cycles such as birthdays, and the telling of time in showing hours. rt.:* ***čicn*** *– meet; infix:* ***...šn...*** *– foot; suffix:* ***...cut*** *– action to the self. See:* ***around.***

Happy New Year

x̣est sčn̓čłtumš – Happy New Year. *rt.:* ***čn̓čłtumš*** *– shake hands w/ people. See:* ***shake hands.***

hard

t̓ás – hard; solid.
i t̓as – It is hard.
t̓sap – It got hard; it solidified.
es t̓spma – It is getting hard; it is solidifying.

t̓ásis – S/he made it hard. **t̓ásn, t̓ásntxʷ**

es t̓ásms – S/he is making it hard. **ies t̓ásm, as t̓ásm**
qs t̓ásms – S/he is going to make it hard. **iqs t̓ásm, aqs t̓ásm**

st̓st̓assšn – shoes.
sčt̓ássšn – shoe.

t̓ásnt – Make it hard/solidify. *cmd.*
t̓sapnuis – S/he succeeded at making it hard. **t̓sapnun, t̓sapnuntxʷ**
es čt̓sapmi – It is hardening on something. *(i.e., glue, etc.)*
es nt̓sapmi – It is hardening inside. *(i.e., glue, etc.)*
t̓ałt̓aseʔ – little hard one, affectionately.
i čłt̓as – The surface is hard.
i čt̓ás – It is poor, lean, skinny.

i t̓as łu luk̓ʷ – The wood is hard. **t̓sap łu smek̓ʷt** – The snow got hard

The **i** following uvular consonants (UC) and the glottal stop ʔ sound like English "ey" as in the words they, hey, whey, etc. Salish UC are: **q, q̓, qʷ, q̓ʷ, x̌, x̌ʷ**. For example, the suffix ...**qin** – head/top, is often spelled using English *ey* as "qeyn". So **qi, q̓i, qʷi, q̓ʷi, x̌i, x̌ʷi**, may be spelled with English *ey* as **qey, q̓ey, qʷey, q̓ʷey, x̌ey, x̌ʷey** in other texts.

ƛ̓ic̓t – hard; tough; hard to break.
ƛ̓c̓im – S/he/it became tough/hard. **čn ƛ̓c̓im, kʷ ƛ̓c̓im**
es ƛ̓c̓mi– S/he is becoming tough/tough. **čnes ƛ̓c̓mi, kʷes ƛ̓c̓mi**
qs ƛ̓c̓mi – S/he is going to become tough/hard. **čiqs ƛ̓c̓mi, kʷqs ƛ̓c̓mi**

ƛ̓c̓stes– S/he made s.t. tough. **ƛ̓c̓sten, ƛ̓c̓stexʷ**
es ƛ̓c̓ims – S/he is making s.t. tough. **ies ƛ̓c̓im, as ƛ̓c̓im**
qs ƛ̓c̓ims – S/he is going to make s.t. tough. **iqs ƛ̓c̓im, aqs ƛ̓c̓im**

ƛ̓ic̓łc̓eʔ – tough meat.
ƛ̓ic̓lqʷ – hard wood.
ƛ̓ic̓lexʷ – hard ground.

ƛ̓ic̓t łu luk̓ʷ – Wood is tough; wood is hard to break.

yoyoscut, *yoyoscú* – do something with a physically strong effort. *See:* ***try.***
čyoyoscutmis – S/he/it worked hard at it. **čyoyoscutmn, čyoyoscutmntxʷ**
čyoyoscúʔutmis – They worked hard at it. **qeʔ čyoyoscutmntm, čyoyoscutmntp**

čyoyoscutmnt – Do it hard, work hard at it. *cmd.*
yoyoscut m cq̓mint – Throw it hard. *cmd.*
yoyoscq̓mint – Throw it hard. *cmd.*
yoyostl̓qent – Kick it hard. *cmd.*
yoyosčłtʔent – Bounce it hard. *cmd.*

imáp – hardened by cooling; solidified; coagulated. *(i.e., grease, plastic, etc.)*
es impmá – It is hardening.

impstás – S/he hardened s.t. **impstán, impstáxʷ**
es impáms – S/he is hardening s.t. **ies impám, as impám**
qs impáms – S/he is going to harden s.t. **iqs impám, aqs impám**

simáp – hardened/ solidified/ coagulated object.
scimáp – something that has been hardened/solidified/coagulated.

impáskʷ – Solidify it. *cmd.*

tl̓xʷé – difficult, hard; struggle. *See:* ***difficult.***

q̓ʷił – energy; motivation; internal drive. *See:* ***capable.***

s.t. - something, the 3rd person
(s.t.) - something implied
s.o. - someone, the 3rd person
sl. - singular form
pl. - plural form
rt. - root word
cmd. - command
lit. - literally
fig. - figuratively
i.e., - for example
See: - Redirection to a related word.

hardship

qʷn̓msc̓ut – pity one's self; have a hard time. *rt.:* ***qʷn̓qʷin̓t*** *– pity; suffix:* ***...cut*** *– action to the self.*

qʷṅmscut – S/he/it had a hard time. **čn qʷṅmscut, kʷ qʷṅmscut**
es qʷṅmscuti – S/he/it is having a hard time. **čnes qʷṅmscuti, kʷes qʷṅmscuti**
qs qʷṅmscuti – S/he/it is going to have a hard time. **čiqs qʷṅmscuti, kʷqs qʷṅmscuti**
qʷṅmscúʔut – They had a hard time. **qeʔ qʷṅmscut, p qʷṅmscut**
es qʷṅmscúʔuti – They are having a hard time. **qeʔes qʷṅmscuti, pes qʷṅmscuti**
qs qʷṅmscúʔuti – They are going to have a hard time. **qeʔqs qʷṅmscuti, pqs qʷṅmscuti**

scqʷṅmscut – hardship. *rt.: **qʷṅqʷiṅt** – pitiful, poor; prefix: **sc...** – s.t. that's been done/made/prepared.*
scqʷṅmscuts – his/her/its hardship. **iscqʷṅmscut, ascqʷṅmscut**

qʷṅečstm – cause someone to have a hard time; play a trick on someone. *rt.: **qʷṅqʷiṅt** – pitiful, poor. See: **trick**.*

q̇eʔečst – made to be or do something; cause hardship for someone; cause problems for someone; put someone/something into it *(by holding, by making it one's business to do so, by situational happenstance, etc.). See: **made**.*

hare

słqʷá – rabbit; *Lepus americanus.*

wiẇslščn, wisšlšn – cottontail; *Sylvilagus nuttallii.*

ususilščn – bunny, small rabbit; *Brachylagus idahoensis.*

hare bell

łl̓el̓puté – hare bell; *Campanula rotundifolia.*

harm

lxʷup – get hurt accidently. *See: **hurt**.*
lxʷpnunm – hurt or harm someone. *See: **hurt**.*

harness

čax̣ċasqáx̣eʔtn, *čax̣ċasqá* – harness. *rt.: **i ax̣** – it has lines; suffix: **...tin, ...tn** – means of/device. See: **line**.*
čax̣ċasqáx̣eʔ – S/he harnessed a horse. **čn čax̣ċasqáx̣eʔ, kʷ čax̣ċasqáx̣eʔ**
es čax̣ċasqáx̣eʔi – S/he is harnessing a horse. **čnes čax̣ċasqáx̣eʔi, kʷes čax̣ċasqáx̣eʔi**
qs čax̣ċasqáx̣eʔi – S/he is going to harness a horse. **čiqs čax̣ċasqáx̣eʔi, kʷqs čax̣ċasqáx̣eʔi**

čax̣ʷċisqáx̣eʔ – harness a horse.
čax̣ʷċisqáx̣eʔ – S/he harnessed a horse. **čn čax̣ʷċisqáx̣eʔ, kʷ čax̣ʷċisqáx̣eʔ**
es čax̣ʷċisqáx̣eʔi – S/he is harnessing a horse. **čnes čax̣ʷċisqáx̣eʔi, kʷes čax̣ʷċisqáx̣eʔi**
qs čax̣ʷċisqáx̣eʔi – S/he is going to harness a horse. **čiqs čax̣ʷċisqáx̣eʔi, kʷqs čax̣ʷċisqáx̣eʔi**

es čax̣iċeʔ – S/he/it is harnessed; covered with lines.

čpƛ̓iċéʔ – take a harness off. *rt.: **pƛ̓im** – release from; suffix: **...iċéʔ** – covered in.*
čpƛ̓iċéʔis – S/he took the harness off. **čpƛ̓iċéʔn, čpƛ̓iċéʔntxʷ**
es čpƛ̓iċʔéms – S/he is taking the harness off. **ies čpƛ̓iċʔém, as čpƛ̓iċʔém**
qs čpƛ̓iċʔéms – S/he is going to take the harness off. **iqs čpƛ̓iċʔém, aqs čpƛ̓iċʔém**

čpƛ̓iċéʔnt – Take the harness off. *cmd.*

čpƛ̓asqáx̣eʔ, *čpƛ̓asqá* – take the harness off.
čpƛ̓asqáx̣eʔ – S/he took the harness off. **čn čpƛ̓asqáx̣eʔ, kʷ čpƛ̓asqáx̣eʔ**
es čpƛ̓asqáx̣eʔi – S/he is taking the harness off. **čnes čpƛ̓asqáx̣eʔi, kʷes čpƛ̓asqáx̣eʔi**
qs čpƛ̓asqáx̣eʔi – S/he is going to take the harness off. **čiqs čpƛ̓asqáx̣eʔi, kʷqs čpƛ̓asqáx̣eʔi**

čpƛ̓asqáx̣eʔiš – Take the harness off. *cmd.*

sq̇alpssqáx̣eʔtn, *sq̇alpssqá* – harness for a packhorse. *suffix: **...tin, ...tn** – means of/device.*

łxʷpusqáx̣eʔ, *łxʷpusqá* – halter. *lit. slips over the face. See: **halter**.*
es łxʷpus – S/he/it is haltered.

ɬax̣ústn, *ɬax̣ú* – halter. *lit. has lines on the face. suffix:* ***...tin, ...tn*** *– means of/device. See:* ***halter.***

harp

čx̣ʷax̣ʷnč, *čx̣ʷa* – radio, harp, guitar, stereo, anything that makes music.

Harriet

alyé – Harriet.

harvest

tixʷɬq – harvest berries/a crop. *rt.:* ***tixʷɬ*** *– acquire.*

tixʷɬq – S/he harvested. **čn tixʷɬq, kʷ tixʷɬq**
es tixʷɬqi – S/he is harvesting. **čnes tixʷɬqi, kʷes tixʷɬqi**
qs tixʷɬqi – S/he is going to harvest. **čiqs tixʷɬqi, kʷqs tixʷɬqi**
tíˀixʷɬq – They harvested. **qeˀ tixʷɬq, p tixʷɬq**
es tíˀixʷɬqi – They are harvesting. **qeˀes tixʷɬqi, pes tixʷɬqi**
qs tíˀixʷɬqi – They are going to harvest. **qeˀqs tixʷɬqi, pqs tixʷɬqi**

tixʷcnm – get food mainly from hunting and fishing. *rt.:* ***tixʷɬ*** *– acquire; suffix:* ***...cin, ...cn*** *– action of the mouth.*

tixʷcnm – S/he got/harvested food. **čn tixʷcnm, kʷ tixʷcnm**
es tixʷcni – S/he is getting/harvesting food. **čnes tixʷcni, kʷes tixʷcni**
qs tixʷcni – S/he is going to get/harvest food. **čiqs tixʷcni, kʷqs tixʷcni**
tíˀixʷcnm – They got/harvested food. **qeˀ tixʷcnm, p tixʷcnm**
es tíˀixʷcni – They are getting/harvesting food. **qeˀes tixʷcni, pes tixʷcni**
qs tíˀixʷcni – They are going to get/harvest food. **qeˀqs tixʷcni, pqs tixʷcni**

tixʷm – pick/get food. *rt.:* ***tixʷɬ*** *– acquire.*

tixʷm – S/he picked. **čn tixʷm, kʷ tixʷm**
es tixʷi – S/he is picking. **čnes tixʷi, kʷes tixʷi**
qs tixʷi – S/he is going to pick. **čiqs tixʷi, kʷqs tixʷi**
tíˀixʷm – They picked. **qeˀ tixʷm, p tixʷm**
es tíˀixʷi – They are picking. **qeˀes tixʷi, pes tixʷi**
qs tíˀixʷi – They are going to pick. **qeˀqs tixʷi, pqs tixʷi**

tixʷis – S/he picked s.t. **tixʷn, tixʷntxʷ**
es tixʷms – S/he is picking s.t. **ies tixʷm, as tixʷm**
qs tixʷms – S/he is going to pick s.t. **iqs tixʷm, aqs tixʷm**
tíˀixʷis – They picked s.t. **qeˀ tixʷntm, tixʷntp**
es tíˀixʷms – They are picking s.t. **qeˀes tixʷm, es tixʷmp**
qs tíˀixʷms – They are going to pick s.t. **qeˀqs tixʷm, qs tixʷmp**

ƛ̓e tixʷntm – It's already been picked.

tixʷɬ – acquire something; get or receive something; gather. *See:* ***acquire.***

hat

qʷácqn – hat. **qʷcqʷacqn** *pl. rt.:* ***qʷec*** *– warm; suffix:* ***...qn*** *– head.*

qʷcqʷáˀacqis – their hats. *pl.*

es qʷácqn – S/he has a hat on. **čnes qʷácqn, kʷes qʷácqn**

qʷacqiš – Put your hat on. *cmd.*

x̣sɬqʷacqn – good little hat.

spomqn – fur hat. *suffix:* ***...qin, ...qn*** *– top. See:* ***fur.***

snsṗqinqn – straw hat. *suffix:* ***...qin, ...qn*** *– top.*

snqápqn – baseball cap. *suffix:* ***...qin, ...qn*** *– top.*

nšṅusu – cap.

The **i** following uvular consonants (UC) and the glottal stop **ˀ** sound like English "*ey*" as in the words *they, hey, whey*, etc. Salish UC are: **q, q̇, qʷ, q̇ʷ, x̣, x̣ʷ**. For example, the suffix **...qin** – head/top, is often spelled using English *ey* as "q*ey*n". So **qi, q̇i, qʷi, q̇ʷi, x̣i, x̣ʷi**, may be spelled with English *ey* as **q***ey*, **q̇***ey*, **qʷ***ey*, **q̇ʷ***ey*, **x̣***ey*, **x̣ʷ***ey* in other texts.

s.t. - something, the 3rd person
(s.t.) - something implied
s.o. - someone, the 3rd person
sl. - singular form
pl. - plural form
rt. - root word
cmd. - command
lit. - literally
fig. - figuratively
i.e., - for example
See: - Redirection to a related word.

snsoťqn – stocking cap. *suffix: **...qin, ...qn** – top.*

nƛ̓imqn – pointed hat. *suffix: **...qin, ...qn** – top.*

pƛ̓qin – remove head cover/hat; bare head. *rt.: **pƛ̓im** – release from; suffix: **...qin, ...qn** – top.*
es pƛ̓qini – S/he is removing his/her head cover. **čnes pƛ̓qini, kʷes pƛ̓qini**
qs pƛ̓qini – S/he is going to remove his/her head cover. **čiqs pƛ̓qini, kʷqs pƛ̓qini**

es pƛ̓qin – S/he is bare headed/no hat. **čnes pƛ̓qin, kʷ es pƛ̓qin**

pƛ̓qiniš – Remove your hat. *cmd.*

hatch

člehxʷk̓ʷi – hatch egg.
es člehxʷk̓ʷi – It is hatching.

člehxʷxʷk̓ʷċéʔ – shell cracked away.

hatchet

łšl̓min – little axe, hatchet.

hate

aiṁeʔ – hate.
aiṁeʔis – S/he/it hates s.t./s.o. **aiṁeʔn, aiṁeʔntxʷ**
es aiṁeʔms – S/he/it is hating s.t./s.o. **ies aiṁeʔm, as aiṁeʔm**
qs aiṁeʔms – S/he/it is going to hate s.t./s.o. **iqs aiṁeʔm, aqs aiṁeʔm**
aiṁéʔeʔis – They hate s.t./s.o. **qeʔ aiṁeʔntm, aiṁeʔntp**
es aiṁéʔeʔms – They are hating s.t./s.o. **qeʔes aiṁeʔm, es aiṁeʔmp**

saiṁeʔ – hate.
saiṁeʔs – S/he/it is his/her/its hate; s/he/it hates s.o./s.t. **isaiṁeʔ, asaiṁeʔs**

naiṁels – hateful feelings.

aiṁeʔn łu incitxʷ – I hate my house. **kʷ isaiṁeʔ** – You are my hate; I hate you. **čn ep saiṁeʔ** – I have someone/something I hate. **qʷo xʷčłnaimlstis** – S/he gave me hate.

čeṁm – detest; reject something; have no care for something; snub something. *See: **detest**.*

nweyls – lazy/tired; hate to do work; do something haphazardly. *See: **lazy**.*

have

epł – have, has, own.
epł ... – S/he/it has... **čn epł ..., kʷ epł ...**
epł ... – They have... **qeʔ epł ..., p epł ...**

epł pus – S/he has a cat. **čn epł pus, kʷ epł pus**
epł púʔus – They have a cat. **qeʔ epł pus, p epł pus**
*The **ł** is dropped when it precedes words beginning with **s**; see example below.*
ep siċm – S/he has a blanket. **čn ep siċm, kʷ ep siċm**
ep síʔiċm – They have a blanket. **qeʔ ep siċm, p ep siċm**

čn epł nťiškʷ – I have pop. **epł citxʷ t i sic łu kʷtisi** – Big Blanket has a new house. **čn ep siċm** – I have a blanket. **ha ƛ̓e kʷ epł cq̓ełp** – Do you already have Douglas fir? **uc kʷ epł ululim** – Perhaps you have money? *(a polite way to ask for money)* **ha kʷ epł ululim** – Do you have any money? **es misten kʷ epł ululim** – I know you have money.

hawk

ċlċlšmu – hawk *(general)*; red-tailed hawk; *Buteo jamaicensis.*

kʷlkʷlši ċl̓ċl̓šmu – ferruginous hawk; *Buteo regalis.*

sʔistč ċl̓ċl̓šmu – rough-legged hawk; *Buteo lagopus* .

sťqnups, *sťqnu* – broad-winged hawk; *Buteo platypterus.*

sqqeẏ – northern goshawk; *Accipiter striatus.*

aátat – falcon; Peregrine falcon; duck hawk; *Falco peregrinus.*

yecic – merlin; *Falco columbarius.*

spiyálqn – American kestrel; *Falco sparverius.*

ċixʷċxʷ – fish hawk; osprey; *Pandion haliaetus.*

The **i** following uvular consonants (UC) and the glottal stop ʔ sound like English "*ey*" as in the words th*ey*, h*ey*, wh*ey*, etc. Salish UC are: **q**, **q̓**, **qʷ**, **q̓ʷ**, **x̣**, **x̣ʷ**. For example, the suffix **...qin** – head/top, is often spelled using English *ey* as "q*ey*n". So **qi**, **q̓i**, **qʷi**, **q̓ʷi**, **x̣i**, **x̣ʷi**, may be spelled with English *ey* as **q***ey*, **q̓***ey*, **qʷ***ey*, **q̓ʷ***ey*, **x̣***ey*, **x̣ʷ***ey* in other texts.

hawk owl

sɫiyeʔ – hawk owl; *Surnia ulula.*

hawthorn

sxʷexʷʔénčeɫp, *sxʷexʷʔenč* – thorn bush, thorn tree, hawthorn; *Crataegus douglasii.*
sxʷeʔneɫq, *sxʷeʔne* – thorn berry.

snčl̓palqʷ, *sncl̓pa* – thorn wood, Coyote wood; *Crataegus chrysocarpa.*

stṁóqʷ – Columbia hawthorn; *Crataegus columbiana.*

hay

supuléxʷ – hay. *rt.:* ***up*** *– hair; suffix:* ***...ulexʷ*** *– land.*
qeʔ t̓qém t supulexʷ – We stacked the hay.

lčéw̓s – tied up around the middle; bale of hay. *See:* ***tie.***

he

cniɫċ, *cni* – It is his/hers/its; it is him/her/it. *See:* ***her.***

head

spɫqin – head. *rt.:* ***pɫiɫt*** *– thick; suffix:* ***...qin, ...qn*** *– top.*
kʷtonqn – big head.
sntx̣ʷaw̓sqn – top of head.
sčɫčmesšn – forehead. *rt.:* ***čm*** *– extremity.*
sčmapqn – back of head. *rt.:* ***čm*** *– extremity.*
sk̓ʷɫčmapqn – base of the back of head. *rt.:* ***čm*** *– extremity.*
sṅčmenéʔ – side of head, by ears. *rt.:* ***čm*** *– extremity.*
nišištus – temples.
ċoṁyaqn – bonehead.

es ncqusm – S/he/it has their head up.

čtoyqn – S/he/it has one's head down/bowed.

čmpqin – get a dark head/to black out. *suffix:* ***...qin, ...qn*** *– top.*

čmpsteṁ – out of it; knocked out.

npṁpqan – out of the head; dizzy, silly, buzzed. *See:* ***dizzy.***

čtaqnulexʷ – hit head on the ground.

s.t. - something, the 3rd person
(s.t.) - something implied
s.o. - someone, the 3rd person
sl. - singular form
pl. - plural form
rt. - root word
cmd. - command
lit. - literally
fig. - figuratively
i.e., - for example
See: - Redirection to a related word.

headache

ċʔalqín – headache. *rt.:* ***ċaál*** *– ache.*
ċʔalqín – S/he/it had a headache. **čn ċʔalqín, kʷ ċʔalqín**
es ċʔalqíni – S/he/it has a headache. **čnes ċʔalqíni, kʷes ċʔalqíni**
qs ċʔalqíni – S/he/it is going to have a headache. **čiqs ċʔalqíni, kʷqs ċʔalqíni**
ċʔalqíʔin – They had a headache. **qeʔ ċʔalqín, p ċʔalqín**
es ċʔalqíʔini – They have a headache. **qeʔes ċʔalqíni, pes ċʔalqíni**
qs ċʔalqíʔini – They are going to have a headache. **qeʔqs ċʔalqíni, pqs ċʔalqíni**

ċʔalqínis – S/he/it gave s.o. a headache. **ċʔalqín, kʷ ċʔalqíntxʷ**
es ċʔalqínms – S/he/it is giving s.o. a headache. **ies ċʔalqínm, as ċʔalqínm**

qs c̓ʔalqínms – S/he/it is going to give s.o. a headache. **iqs c̓ʔalqínm, aqs c̓ʔalqínm**

headband
łxʷpqintn – headband *(i.e., elastic headband). rt.: **łixʷp** – slip/pull over; suffix: **...qin, ...qn** – top; suffix: **...tin, ...tn** – means of/device.*

čiyálxʷqn, *čiya* – head wrap; scarf. *rt.: **yalim** – coil, wrap; suffix: **...qin, ...qn** – top.*

łqʷeẁstn – hat band. *suffix: **...tin, ...tn** – means of/device; suffix: **...éẁs** – in between, middle.*

sqʷlápqn – hat band.

head cheese
lkʷošó scnitkʷé – pig head cheese.

headdress
c̓lqin, *c̓lqi* – feather headdress; war bonnet; headdress. *rt.: **c̓il** – standing upright; suffix: **...qin, ...qn** – top.*

pesyáʔ m p c̓lc̓lqinm – All of you put on headdresses.

snc̓laẁsqn, *snc̓la* – roach. *See: **roach.***

qicqn – buffalo horn/mountain goat horn headdress with white weasel hide. *suffix: **...qin, ...qn** – top.*

sc̓t̓x̣čnqin – round bustle headdress. *rt.: **t̓ix̣** – protrude; suffix: **...qin, ...qn** – top.*

k̓ʷłacepqntn – hair piece; tied to the head. *rt.: **ac** – tie; prefix: **k̓ʷł...** – under; suffix: **...qin, ...qn** – top.*

headlights
c̓ek̓ʷmn – light; vehicle headlight.

headwaters
nłaʔpqnetkʷ – headwaters; where the water begins *(i.e., a spring, fountain, lake). rt.: **łe** – end; suffix: **...qin, ...qn** – top.*

nłaʔpqin – total end of something; very top of something. *rt.: **łe** – end; suffix: **...qin, ...qn** – top.*

snłaʔpqin – place where the water starts from.

heal
p̓aáx̣ – heal; cure; get well.

p̓aáx̣ – S/he/it healed. **čn p̓aáx̣, kʷ p̓aáx̣**
es p̓aáx̣mi – S/he/it is healing. **čnes p̓aáx̣mi, kʷes p̓aáx̣mi**
qs p̓aáx̣mi – S/he/it is going to heal. **čiqs p̓aáx̣mi, kʷqs p̓aáx̣mi**
p̓aáʔax̣ – They healed. **qeʔ p̓aáx̣, p p̓aáx̣**
es p̓aáʔax̣mi – They are healing. **qeʔes p̓aáx̣mi, pes p̓aáx̣mi**
qs p̓aáʔax̣mi – They are going to heal. **qeʔqs p̓aáx̣mi, pqs p̓aáx̣mi**

p̓ax̣ntes – S/he/it healed s.o. **p̓ax̣nten, kʷ p̓ax̣ntexʷ**
es p̓ax̣ems – S/he/it is healing s.o. **ies p̓ax̣em, as p̓ax̣em**
qs p̓ax̣ems – S/he/it is going to heal s.o. **iqs p̓ax̣em, aqs p̓ax̣em**

p̓aax̣stés – S/he/it cured s.o. **p̓aax̣stén, p̓aax̣stéxʷ**
es p̓aax̣minms – S/he/it is curing s.o. **ies p̓aax̣minm, as p̓aax̣minm**
qs p̓aax̣minms – S/he/it is going to cure s.o. **iqs p̓aax̣minm, aqs p̓aax̣minm**

p̓aax̣nuis – S/he/it succeeded at healing s.o. **p̓aax̣nun, p̓aax̣nuntxʷ**
es p̓aax̣nunms – S/he/it is trying to heal s.o. **ies p̓aax̣nunm, as p̓aax̣nunm**
qs p̓aax̣nunms – S/he/it is going to try to heal s.o. **iqs p̓aax̣nunm, aqs p̓aax̣nunm**

sxʷp̓ax̣em – one tasked to heal. *prefix: **sxʷ...** – one tasked to do.*

p̓ax̣ent – Heal him/her/it. *cmd.*
p̓aáx̣ncutš – Heal yourself. *cmd.*
np̓ax̣éls – want to be healed. *circumfix: **n...els** – want, feel.*
p̓aáx̣łtumš – heal the people. *suffix: **...łtumš** – of people.*

es ṗaáx̣ncuti – S/he/it is healing one's self. **čnes ṗaáx̣ncuti, kʷes ṗaáx̣ncuti**
es ṗaáx̣nwexʷi – They are healing each other. **čnes ṗaáx̣nwexʷi, kʷes ṗaáx̣nwexʷi**
nṗax̣ełċeʔ – heal inside. *prefix:* ***n...*** *– inside; suffix:* ***...ełċeʔ*** *– inside contents, body, meat*
ṗaṗax̣enʔem – heal ears. *suffix:* ***...eneʔ*** *– ear..*
čṗaṗax̣úsm – heal eyes. *circumfix:* ***č...us*** *– spherical object; eyes.*

k̇ʷmi ṗaáx̣ – I hope s/he/it heals. **t sxʷmalyé kʷ es ṗaax̣minms –** The doctor is curing you. **t sxʷmalyé kʷ es ṗaax̣nunms –** The doctor is trying to heal you. **čn ṗaṗax̣enʔem –** My ears got well. **t sxʷmalyé qʷ čṗaṗax̣úsntm –** The doctor cured my eyes.

malyémm – doctor someone. *See:* ***doctor.***

x̣stwilš – get better. *See:* ***better.***

The **i** following uvular consonants (UC) and the glottal stop **ʔ** sound like English "*ey*" as in the words th*ey*, h*ey*, wh*ey*, etc. Salish UC are: **q**, **q̇**, **qʷ**, **q̇ʷ**, **x̣**, **x̣ʷ**. For example, the suffix **...qin** – head/top, is often spelled using English *ey* as "q*ey*n". So **qi**, **q̇i**, **qʷi**, **q̇ʷi**, **x̣i**, **x̣ʷi**, may be spelled with English *ey* as **q***ey*, **q̇***ey*, **qʷ***ey*, **q̇ʷ***ey*, **x̣***ey*, **x̣ʷ***ey* in other texts.

hear

séwneʔ – hear; listen.
séwneʔ – S/he/it heard. **čn séwneʔ, kʷ séwneʔ**
es séwneʔi – S/he/it heard. **čnes séwneʔi, kʷes séwneʔi**
qs séwneʔi – S/he/it heard. **čiqs séwneʔi, kʷqs séwneʔi**
séʔewneʔ – They heard. **qeʔ séwneʔ, p séwneʔ**

séwneʔmis – S/he/it heard s.o./s.t. **séwneʔmn, séwneʔmntxʷ**
es séwneʔms – S/he is hearing s.o./s.t. **ies séwneʔm, as séwneʔm**
qs séwneʔms – S/he is going to hear s.o./s.t. **iqs séwneʔm, aqs séwneʔm**
séʔewneʔmis – They heard s.o./s.t. **qeʔ séwneʔmntm, séwneʔmntp**
es séʔewneʔms – They are hearing s.o./s.t. **qeʔes séwneʔm, es séwneʔmp**
qs séʔewneʔms – They are going to hear s.o./s.t. **qeʔqs séwneʔm, qs séwneʔmp**

čn séwneʔ t smx̣e l incitxʷ – I heard a grizzly bear in my house. **ta či séwneʔ –** I did not hear. **ha kʷ séwneʔ –** Did you hear? **séwneʔmncn –** I heard you. **čn séwneʔ steṁ łu es pupéwlši –** I hear something breathing.

nyuyúweneʔ – good hearing. *rt.:* ***yoyóot*** *– strong.*
i nyuyúweneʔ – S/he/it has good hearing. **i čn nyuyúweneʔ, i kʷ nyuyúweneʔ**

lešn – hear something from far off.
lešn – S/he heard from far off. **čn lešn, kʷ lešn**
es lešni – S/he is hearing from far off. **čnes lešni, kʷes lešni**
léʔešn – They hear from far off. **qeʔ lešn, p lešn**

lešnmis – S/he heard s.t. from far off. **lešnmn, lešnmntxʷ**

ntmaneʔ – refuse to hear/listen. *See:* ***listen.***

nṗuṗuwenéʔ – ignore; do not pay attention to; do not listen. *See:* ***ignore.***

exʷkʷunm – make sound of people and animal voices; someone talking in the distance but not being able to discern what is being said. *See:* ***sound.***

tspmncót, *tspmncó* **–** sudden sound of voices shouting. *See:* ***sound.***

tstsalš – sound of a group making noises. *(i.e., children talking, birds chirping, etc.) See:* ***sound.***

s.t. - something, the 3rd person
(s.t.) - something implied
s.o. - someone, the 3rd person
sl. - singular form
pl. - plural form
rt. - root word
cmd. - command
lit. - literally
fig. - figuratively
i.e., - for example
See: - Redirection to a related word.

heart

spúʔus – heart. **spupúʔus –** hearts. *pl.*
kʷtispúʔus – big heart, brave.

ł ispúʔus ƛe es t misten – In my heart I already knew. **tł ispúʔus kʷ isx̣mnčeẇs kʷ innox̣ʷnx̣ʷ –** From my heart you are my love, you are my wife.

npuʔstin – thinking/talking of somebody then they show up or you run into them. *See:* ***think***.

puʔsminm – think about somebody. *rt.:* ***spúʔus*** *– heart. See:* ***think***.

pusulexʷ – thinking of a certain place/area/land. *rt.:* ***spúʔus*** *– heart. See:* ***think***.

k̓ʷłpusncut, *k̓ʷłpusncu* **–** self-conscious; shy, bashful, polite; considerate; not impose. *See:* ***self-conscious***.

pupusénč, *pupusé* **–** sad; to mourn; to grieve. *rt.:* ***spúʔus*** *– heart; suffix:* ***...énč*** *– within. See:* ***sad***.

pumin – drum. *rt.:* ***spúʔus*** *– heart; suffix:* ***...min, ...mn*** *– instrument/tool. See:* ***drum***.

nyoyowáls – strong mind, strong heart. *rt.: yoyoot – strong. See:* ***strong***.

heat

sƛ̓aáq̓ – heat. *See:* ***hot***.

p̓eč – get hot from some heat source; warmed/heated from radiant heat.
p̓ečim – S/he/it got heated up. **čn p̓ečim, kʷ p̓ečim**
es p̓ečmi – S/he/it is getting heated up. **čnes p̓ečmi, kʷes p̓ečmi**
qs p̓ečmi – S/he/it is going to get heated up. **čiqs p̓ečmi, kʷqs p̓ečmi**
p̓ečíʔim – They got heated up. **qeʔ p̓ečim, p p̓ečim**
es p̓ečmíʔi – They are getting heated up. **qeʔes p̓ečmi, pes p̓ečmi**
qs p̓ečmíʔi – They are going to get heated up. **qeʔqs p̓ečmi, pqs p̓ečmi**

p̓ečis – S/he put s.t. into the heat. **p̓ečn, p̓ečntxʷ**
es p̓ečms – S/he is putting s.t. into the heat. **ies p̓ečm, as p̓ečm**
qs p̓ečms – S/he is going to put s.t. into the heat. **iqs p̓ečm, aqs p̓ečm**
p̓éʔečis – They put s.t. into the heat. **qeʔ p̓ečntm, p̓ečntp**
es p̓éʔečms – They are putting s.t. into the heat. **qeʔes p̓ečm, es p̓ečmp**
qs p̓éʔečms – They are going to put s.t. into the heat. **qeʔqs p̓ečm, qs p̓ečmp**

p̓čp̓ečn – I put s.t. into the heat over and over.

p̓éeč – S/he/it got heated. **čn p̓éeč, kʷ p̓éeč**
p̓ečntm – S/he/it was heated. **qʷo p̓ečntm, kʷ p̓ečntm**

sp̓eeč – radiant heat.
scp̓eč – something that's been heated. *prefix:* ***sc...*** *– s.t. that's been done/made/prepared.*

es np̓eččni – S/he is warming his/her body by the fire. **čnes np̓eččni, kʷes np̓eččni**
np̓ečičn̓ – get a hot back. *suffix:* ***...ičn̓*** *– back.*
čp̓ep̓ečeneʔ – get hot ears.
np̓ep̓ečłq̓eẏt – get hot shoulders.
čp̓ap̓ačax̣n – get hot arms.
čłp̓éʔečsšn – get a hot forehead.
čp̓ap̓asaqstšn – get hot legs. *suffix:* ***...aqstšn*** *– leg.*
np̓ečps – get a hot butt.
p̓ečus – get a hot face.
np̓ačaqs – get a hot nose.
np̓ečlexʷm – make bannock bread. *See:* ***bannock bread***.

nolím – heat up rocks. *See:* ***fire***.

es sl̓stwexʷi, *es sl̓stwe* **–** The animals are mating. *See:* ***mate***.

heat waves **sƛ̓aq̇asq̇t –** heat waves. *suffix:* ***...asq̇t –*** *sky, day.*

es ƛ̓aq̇asq̇ti – It has heat waves.

heaven **sččmásq̇t –** sky. *rt.:* ***čm –*** *extremity; suffix:* ***...asq̇t –*** *sky, day.*

heavy **x̣emt –** heavy.

x̣emt – S/he/it is heavy. **čn x̣emt, kʷ x̣emt**

x̣mtwilš – It got heavy. **čn x̣mtwilš, kʷ x̣mtwilš** *suffix:* ***...wilš –*** *developmental.*
es x̣mtwilši – It is getting heavy. **čnes x̣mtwilši, kʷes x̣mtwilši**
qs x̣mtwilši – It is going to get heavy. **čiqs x̣mtwilši, kʷqs x̣mtwilši**

x̣mtełċeʔ – heavy body.

x̣ił kʷ x̣mtełċeʔ – Darn, you have a heavy body.

heel **sčmépšn –** heel. *rt.:* ***čm –*** *extremity.* **sčmčmépšn –** heels. *pl.* **sčmmépšn –** heels. *pl.*

Helena **čłmlše –** Helena, Montana.

hellgramite **čƛ̓áq̇nšn –** stonefly, hellgramite.

hello **ʔa –** hello; *initial greeting.*
ʔé – hello; *acknowledgement to initial greeting.*

All words that start with a vowel naturally produce and have a ʔ (glottal stop). Throughout this book the ʔ (glottal stop) has been left off except on the these two words. These words are so short that the ʔ was left to preserve their stature. In all other cases it is unnecessary and cumbersome.

help **olqʷšcut –** help one's self. *suffix:* ***...cut –*** *action to the self.*
es olqʷšcuti – S/he/it is helping. **čnes olqʷšcuti, kʷes olqʷšcuti**
qs olqʷšcuti – S/he/it is going to help. **čiqs olqʷšcuti, kʷqs olqʷšcuti**
es olqʷšcúʔuti – They are helping. **qeʔes olqʷšcuti, pes olqʷšcuti**
qs olqʷšcúʔuti – They are going to help. **qeʔqs olqʷšcuti, pqs olqʷšcuti**

olqʷšitis – S/he/it helped s.t./s.o. **olqʷšitn, olqʷšitxʷ**
es olqʷšitms – S/he/it is helping s.t./s.o. **ies olqʷšitm, as olqʷšitm**
qs olqʷšitms – S/he/it is going to help s.t./s.o. **iqs olqʷšitm, aqs olqʷšitm**
olqʷšíʔitis – They helped it. **qeʔ olqʷšitm, olqʷšitntp**
es olqʷšíʔitms – They are helping it. **qeʔes olqʷšitm, es olqʷšitmp**
qs olqʷšíʔitms – They are going to help it. **qeʔqs olqʷšitm, qs olqʷšitmp**

olqʷšitmstm – S/he/it was helped.

olqʷšcutn – helper. *(i.e., midwife, subchief.) suffix:* ***...tin, ...tn –*** *means of/device.*
sxʷʔolqʷšcutn – one tasked to help. *prefix:* ***sxʷ... –*** *one tasked to do; suffix:* ***...tin, ...tn –*** *means of/device.*
olqʷštemn – one inclined to help. *suffix:* ***...emn –*** *one inclined to do.*
ololqʷšmuł – one that habitually helps. *suffix:* ***...tmuł –*** *one that habitually does.*
sxʷʔolqʷštumš – one tasked to help people. *prefix:* ***sxʷ... –*** *one tasked to do; suffix:* ***...tumš –*** *of people.*

olqʷšiš – Help. *cmd.*
olqʷšit – Help it. *cmd.*
olqʷštwéxʷ – They helped each other.

The **i** following uvular consonants (UC) and the glottal stop ʔ sound like English "*ey*" as in the words *they, hey, whey,* etc. Salish UC are: **q, q̇, qʷ, q̇ʷ, x̣, x̣ʷ**. For example, the suffix **...qin** – head/top, is often spelled using English *ey* as "q*ey*n". So **qi, q̇i, qʷi, q̇ʷi, x̣i, x̣ʷi**, may be spelled with English *ey* as **q***ey*, **q̇***ey*, **qʷ***ey*, **q̇ʷ***ey*, **x̣***ey*, **x̣ʷ***ey* in other texts.

s.t. - something, the 3rd person
(s.t.) - something implied
s.o. - someone, the 3rd person
sl. - singular form
pl. - plural form
rt. - root word
cmd. - command
lit. - literally
fig. - figuratively
i.e., - for example
See: - Redirection to a related word.

qeʔes olqʷšt̓wéxʷi – We are helping each other.

ṅem qes olqʷšíʔitms – They will be helping it. **ṅem qeʔqes olqʷšitm –** We will be helping s.o./s.t. **ṅem qes olqʷšitmp –** You all will be helping s.o./s.t. **ha kʷ ṅe u qʷo olqʷšitxʷ –** Would you help me. **olqʷšitn u uẏé –** I helped till it was done. **ṅem olqʷšitn m uẏé –** I will help till it is done. **ṅem olqʷšiłmn –** I will help you all. **olqʷšitmn łu kʷes k̓ʷuli t ƛ̓iyéʔ –** I helped you make a canoe. **t tlé u we qeʔes olqʷšiłls u áyx̣ʷt u hoysts –** Teresa really was helping us, but she got tired and quit. **ṅem olqʷšitmstm –** S/he/it will be helped. **qeʔ olqʷšiłls –** S/he/it helped us. **qeʔ olqʷšiłlt –** Help us. **ha kʷes nte kʷ iqs olqʷšitm –** Do you want me to help you?

čutmist – seek/ask for help from the spiritual world. *(i.e., vision quest.) rt.: **čoncut** – prayer/offer.*
čutmisti – S/he sought help. **čn čutmisti, kʷ čutmisti**
es čutmisti – S/he is seeking help. **čnes čutmisti, kʷes čutmisti**
qs čutmisti – S/he is going to seek help. **čiqs čutmisti, kʷqs čutmisti**

es čutmistms – S/he/it is seeking/asking s.t./s.o. for help. **ies čutmistm, as čutmistm**

helper
sxʷʔolqʷšcutn – one tasked to help. *prefix: **sxʷ...** – one tasked to do; suffix: **...tin, ...tn** – means of/device.*

helpless
tmłʔolqʷšcut – helpless.
tmłʔolqʷšcut – S/he/it is helpless. **čn tmłʔolqʷšcut, kʷ tmłʔolqʷšcut**
es tmłʔolqʷšcuti – S/he/it is being helpless. **čnes tmłʔolqʷšcuti, kʷes tmłʔolqʷšcuti**
qs tmłʔolqʷšcuti – S/he/it is going to be helpless. **čiqs tmłʔolqʷšcuti, kʷqs tmłʔolqʷšcuti**
uł tmłʔolqʷšcúʔut – They are helpless. **qeʔ uł tmłʔolqʷšcut, p uł tmłʔolqʷšcut**
es tmłʔolqʷšcúʔuti – They are being helpless. **qeʔes tmłʔolqʷšcuti, pes tmłʔolqʷšcuti**
qs tmłʔolqʷšcúʔuti – They are going to be helpless. **qeʔqs tmłʔolqʷšcuti, pqs tmłʔolqʷšcuti**

hemlock
inixʷ – water hemlock.

płtiṅéłp, *płtiṅé* – western hemlock; *Tsuga heterophylla.*

xʷk̓ʷstnełp, *xʷk̓ʷstne* – mountain hemlock; *Tsuga mertensiana.*

hen
skʷiskʷs – spruce grouse; Franklin's grouse; fools hen; *Falcipennis canadensis*; domestic chicken. *See: **chicken**.*

lipul – domestic chicken. *(approximation to French word) See: **chicken**.*

heptagon
sṗl̓čsq̓tq̓it – heptagon; has seven flat sides.

her
cniłċ, *cni* – It is his/hers/its; it is him/her/it.

*Words that end in a vowel, like **kapi**, add **...sts** to make it third person possessive.*
ƛ̓m kapists – It was her/his/its coffee.
kapists – his/her/its coffee.
qł kapists – It is going to be his/her/its coffee.

*Words that end with an **...n**, like **q̓ʷomqn**, drop the **...n** and add **...is** to make it third person possessive.*
q̓ʷomqis – his/her hair. *Animals have, **spum** – fur, so it doesn't say his/her/**its** hair. "Its" is omitted.*

*Words that end with an **...s**, like **spúʔus**, add **...ts** to make it third person possessive.*
spúʔusts – his/her/its heart.

herd
iax̣ – herd/drive animals; make a group of animals go in a certain direction.
ix̣m – S/he/it herded. **čn ix̣m, kʷ ix̣m**
es ix̣mi – S/he/it is herding. **čnes ix̣mi, kʷes ix̣mi**
qs ix̣mi – S/he/it is going to herd. **čnes ix̣mi, kʷes ix̣mi**

ix̣míʔi – They herded. **qeʔ ix̣mi, p ix̣mi**
es ix̣míʔi – They are herding. **qeʔes ix̣mi, pes ix̣mi**
qs ix̣míʔi – They are going to herd. **qeʔqs ix̣mi, pqs ix̣mi**

ix̣ntes – S/he/it herded them. **ix̣nten, ix̣ntexʷ**
es ix̣ems – S/he/it is herding them. **ies ix̣em, as ix̣em**
qs ix̣ems – S/he/it is going to herd them. **iqs ix̣em, aqs ix̣em**

ix̣eiš – Herd. *cmd.*
ix̣ant – Herd them. *cmd.*

ix̣msqáx̣eʔ, *ix̣msqá* – herd domestic animals; herd up horses.
ix̣msqáx̣eʔ – S/he herded stock. **čn ix̣msqáx̣eʔ, kʷ ix̣msqáx̣eʔ**
es ix̣msqáx̣eʔi – S/he is herding stock. **čnes ix̣msqáx̣eʔi, kʷes ix̣msqáx̣eʔi**
qs ix̣msqáx̣eʔi – S/he is going to herd stock. **čiqs ix̣msqáx̣eʔi, kʷqs ix̣msqáx̣eʔi**
ix̣msqáʔax̣eʔ – They herded stock. **qeʔ ix̣msqáx̣eʔ, p ix̣msqáx̣eʔ**
es ix̣msqáʔax̣eʔi – They are herding stock. **qeʔes ix̣msqáx̣eʔi, pes ix̣msqáx̣eʔi**
qs ix̣msqáʔax̣eʔi – They are going to herd stock. **qeʔqs ix̣msqáx̣eʔi, pqs ix̣msqáx̣eʔi**

k̓ʷłcaqʷm – bring back runaway animals; drive back horses; head horses off.
k̓ʷłcaqʷm – S/he drove back. **čn k̓ʷłcaqʷm, kʷ k̓ʷłcaqʷm**
es k̓ʷłcaqʷi – S/he is driving back. **čnes k̓ʷłcaqʷi, kʷes k̓ʷłcaqʷi**
qs k̓ʷłcaqʷi – S/he is going to drive back. **čiqs k̓ʷłcaqʷi, kʷqs k̓ʷłcaqʷi**
k̓ʷłcáʔaqʷm – They drove back. **qeʔ k̓ʷłcaqʷm, p k̓ʷłcaqʷm**
es k̓ʷłcáʔaqʷi – They are driving back. **qeʔes k̓ʷłcaqʷi, pes k̓ʷłcaqʷi**
qs k̓ʷłcáʔaqʷi – They are going to drive back. **qeʔqs k̓ʷłcaqʷi, pqs k̓ʷłcaqʷi**

k̓ʷłcaqʷis – S/he drove them back. **k̓ʷłcaqʷn, k̓ʷłcaqʷntxʷ**
es k̓ʷłcaqʷms – S/he is driving them back. **ies k̓ʷłcaqʷm, as k̓ʷłcaqʷm**
qs k̓ʷłcaqʷms – S/he is going to drive them back. **iqs k̓ʷłcaqʷm, aqs k̓ʷłcaqʷm**

usšlšisqáx̣eʔ – drive horses/domestic animals further.
usšlšisqáx̣eʔ – S/he herded stock. **čn usšlšisqáx̣eʔ, kʷ usšlšisqáx̣eʔ**
es usšlšisqáx̣eʔi – S/he is herding stock. **čnes usšlšisqáx̣eʔi, kʷes usšlšisqáx̣eʔi**
qs usšlšisqáx̣eʔi – S/he is going to herd stock. **čiqs usšlšisqáx̣eʔi, kʷqs usšlšisqáx̣eʔi**
usšlšisqáʔax̣eʔ – They herded stock. **qeʔ usšlšisqáx̣eʔ, p usšlšisqáx̣eʔ**
es usšlšisqáʔax̣eʔi – They are herding stock. **qeʔes usšlšisqáx̣eʔi, pes usšlšisqáx̣eʔi**
qs usšlšisqáʔax̣eʔi – They are going to herd stock. **qeʔqs usšlšisqáx̣eʔi, pqs usšlšisqáx̣eʔi**

yam̓mełc̓eʔ – herd of animals, mainly elk; gathered together animals. *rt.: **y̓amim** – gather; suffix: **...ełc̓eʔ** – inside contents, body, meat*
es yam̓mełc̓eʔi – The animals (elk) are herding together.
es yam̓mełc̓eʔ – The animals (elk) are herded together.

here

iheʔ – here; this in hand; this at hand. *See: **this**.*
łiheʔ – these here in hand.
iheʔ łu isnʔitštn – This is my bedroom. **ha iheʔ ye lʔe** – Does this one go here?

łiʔe – this; here; specifically this one. *See: **this**.*

lʔe – this here.
lʔe – S/he/it is here. **čn lʔe, kʷ lʔe**

lʔeš – Remain here. *cmd.*

iʔe – this very one here.

The **i** following uvular consonants (UC) and the glottal stop **ʔ** sound like English "*ey*" as in the words th*ey*, h*ey*, wh*ey*, etc. Salish UC are: **q, q̓, qʷ, q̓ʷ, x̣, x̣ʷ**. For example, the suffix ...**qin** – head/top, is often spelled using English *ey* as "q*ey*n". So **qi, q̓i, qʷi, q̓ʷi, x̣i, x̣ʷi**, may be spelled with English *ey* as q*ey*, q̓*ey*, qʷ*ey*, q̓ʷ*ey*, x̣*ey*, x̣ʷ*ey* in other texts.

s.t. - something, the 3rd person
(s.t.) - something implied
s.o. - someone, the 3rd person
sl. - singular form
pl. - plural form
rt. - root word
cmd. - command
lit. - literally
fig. - figuratively
i.e., - for example
See: - Redirection to a related word.

iˀe – S/he/it is here. **čn iˀe, kʷ iˀe**

iˀeš – Remain right here. *cmd.*

šˀeˀ – there.

ye – this right here; this time. *See: **this**.*

hermit thrush **xʷiwxʷu** – northern oriole, Bullock's oriole; hermit thrush.

heron **smóq̓ʷeˀ** – great blue heron; *Ardea herodias*.

smaťqʷul – black crowned night heron; *Nycticorax nycticorax*.

hexagon **ťq̓nčsq̓tq̓it** – hexagon; has six flat sides.

hibernate **nˀestčṁnuxʷ** – hibernate. *rt.: **istč**– winter; prefix: **n...** – inside; suffix: **...ṁnuxʷ** – process through/become.*
es nˀestčṁnuxʷ – It hibernates.
es nˀestčṁnuxʷi – It is hibernating.

hiccup **ẇehi** – hiccup.
es ẇehcni – S/he is hiccuping. **čnes ẇehcni, kʷes ẇehcni**

Hidden Lake **k̓ʷłnčmé čłq̓liˀs** – Hidden Lake, in the Mission Mountain Range, Flathead Nation.

hide **q̓étt** – pelt; hide.
q̓étts – his/her/its hide. **inq̓étt, anq̓étt**

čeṅ łu ci q̓étt – Where's that hide.

...elxʷ, ...lxʷ – suffix indicating hide.
cˀulixʷélxʷ, *ċulixʷé* – buckskin, white-tail doe hide.
sx̣ʷl̓éščnelxʷ – white-tail buck hide.
sťulċeˀlxʷ – black-tail doe hide.
puwélsčnelxʷ – black-tail buck hide.
šċelxʷ – bull elk hide.
snčłċelxʷ – cow elk hide.
sċpselxʷ – beaver hide.

wekʷm – hide out of view.
wekʷm – S/he/it hid. **čn wekʷm, kʷ wekʷm**
es wekʷi – S/he/it is hiding. **čnes wekʷi, kʷes wekʷi**
qs wekʷi – S/he/it is going to hide. **čiqs wekʷi, kʷqs wekʷi**
wéˀekʷm – They hid. **qeˀ wekʷm, p wekʷm**
es wéˀekʷi – They are hiding. **qeˀes wekʷi, pes wekʷi**

wekʷis – S/he/it hid s.t./s.o. **wekʷn, wekʷntxʷ**
es wekʷms – S/he/it is hiding s.t./s.o. **ies wekʷm, as wekʷm**
qs wekʷms – S/he/it is going to hide s.t./s.o. **iqs wekʷm, aqs wekʷm**
wéˀekʷis – They hid s.t./s.o. **qeˀ wekʷntm, wekʷntp**
es wéˀekʷms – They are hiding s.t./s.o. **qeˀes wekʷm, es wekʷmp**

ukʷistmis – S/he/it hid one's self from s.t./s.o. **ukʷistmn, ukʷistmntxʷ**
es ukʷistms – S/he/it is hiding one's self from s.t./s.o. **ies ukʷistm, as ukʷistm**
qs ukʷistms – S/he/it is going to hide one's self from s.t./s.o. **iqs ukʷistm, aqs ukʷistm**

ukʷmistmis – S/he/it hid s.t. of one's self from s.t./s.o. **ukʷmistmn, ukʷmistmntxʷ**
es ukʷmistms – S/he/it is hiding s.t. of one's self from s.t./s.o. **ies ukʷmistm, as ukʷmistm**
qs ukʷmistms – S/he/it is going to hide s.t. of one's self from s.t./s.o. **iqs ukʷmistm, aqs ukʷmistm**

wekʷistemn – one inclined to hide. *suffix: **...emn** – one inclined to do.*
wekʷmn – camouflage.

wekʷiš – Hide. *cmd.*
ukʷwekʷwi – All of you hide. *cmd.*
wekʷnt – Hide it. *cmd.*
wekʷcnm – hide your talk by whispering or by talking a different language; talk secretly; gossip. *See: **gossip**.*
wekʷsm – hide the face. *See: **peek**.*
es nukʷistelsi – S/he/it is wanting to hide. **čnes nukʷistelsi, kʷes nukʷistelsi**
es nukʷukʷistelsi – S/he/it persists in wanting to hide.
es nukʷmelsms – S/he/it is wanting to hide s.t. **ies nukʷmelsm, as nukʷmelsm**
es ukʷstmnwexʷi – They are hiding from each other. **qeʔes ukʷstmnwexʷi, pes ukʷstmnwexʷi**

čn wekʷist – I hid myself. **čnes wekʷisti tḷ inʔilmixʷm –** I am hiding from my boss. **ṅem iqs wekʷm –** I will hide it.

> The **i** following uvular consonants (UC) and the glottal stop **ʔ** sound like English "*ey*" as in the words th*ey*, h*ey*, wh*ey*, etc. Salish UC are: **q**, **q̇**, **qʷ**, **q̇ʷ**, **x̣**, **x̣ʷ**. For example, the suffix **...qin** – head/top, is often spelled using English *ey* as "q*ey*n". So **qi**, **q̇i**, **qʷi**, **q̇ʷi**, **x̣i**, **x̣ʷi**, may be spelled with English *ey* as **q***ey*, **q̇***ey*, **qʷ***ey*, **q̇ʷ***ey*, **x̣***ey*, **x̣ʷ***ey* in other texts.

łoq – hide away from the knowledge of others so as not to be stolen.
łqom – S/he/it hid (s.t.) away. **čn łqom, kʷ łqom**
es łqmi – S/he/it is hiding (s.t.) away. **čnes łqmi, kʷes łqmi**
qs łqmi – S/he/it is going to hide (s.t.) away. **čiqs łqmi, kʷqs łqmi**

łqntes – S/he/it hid s.t. away. **łqnten, łqntexʷ**
es łqoms – S/he/it is hiding s.t. away. **ies łqom, as łqom**
qs łqoms – S/he/it is going to hide s.t. away. **iqs łqom, aqs łqom**

łqont – Hide it away. *cmd.*

high

nwist – up; above; up high.
snwist – high. *(as a measure)*
t čeṅ ecx̣ḷsnwist – How high is it?
mus sċušin snwist – four feet high.

č nwist – up, upstairs, up high.

nwisšlš – raise up. *See: **raise**.*

mił nwist x̣ʷḷ nplé – It is too high for you guys. **kʷ ṅe u čn cṫip tḷ nwist –** I might have fallen from that high place.

łkʷk̇ʷiyomqn – small voice; feminine voice; high pitch voice. *See: **small**.*

hill

es móq̇ʷ – hill, mountain. *rt.: **moq̇ʷ** – a bump.*
łṁq̇ʷmq̇ʷtuḷéxʷ – hills. *lit. little bumps on the land.*
es mq̇ʷmóq̇ʷ – mountains.

xʷṫip č es mq̇ʷmóq̇ʷ – S/he ran to the mountains.

słqá – hilltop.

k̇ʷłx̣sulexʷ – bare hill or mountain.

> s.t. - something, the 3rd person
> (s.t.) - something implied
> s.o. - someone, the 3rd person
> *sl.* - singular form
> *pl.* - plural form
> *rt.* - root word
> *cmd.* - command
> *lit.* - literally
> *fig.* - figuratively
> *i.e.,* - for example
> *See:* - Redirection to a related word.

him

cniłċ, *cni* – It is his/hers/its; it is him/her/it. *See: **her**.*

hindquarters **q̓tq̓almélqstšn,** *q̓tq̓almé* – hindquarters.

t q̓tq̓almé u nuswist – The hindquarters stuck up.

hip **snčmaqstšn** – hip. *rt.: čm – extremity.*

hippopotamus **kʷtnaposqn** – hippopotamus.

his **cniłċ,** *cni* – It is his/hers/its; it is him/her/it. *See: her.*

hiss **kʷaskʷas** – sound of grease dripping on the fire.
i kʷaskʷas – Grease is dripping and hitting the fire with that sound.

snčišmn – teakettle.

hit **sṗim** – hit/strike with an object.
sṗim – S/he struck. **čn sṗim, kʷ sṗim**
es sṗmi – S/he is striking. **čnes sṗmi, kʷes sṗim**
qs sṗmi – S/he is going to strike. **čiqs sṗmi, kʷqs sṗim**
sṗíʔim – They struck. **qeʔ sṗim, p sṗim**
es sṗmíʔi – They are striking. **qeʔes sṗmi, pes sṗmi**
es sṗmíʔi – They are going to strike. **qeʔqs sṗmi, pqs sṗmi**

sṗntes – S/he struck it. **sṗnten, sṗntexʷ**
es sṗims – S/he is striking it. **ies sṗim, as sṗim**
qs sṗims – S/he is going to strike it. **iqs sṗim, aqs sṗim**
sṗntéʔes – They struck it. **qeʔ sṗntes, sṗntep**
es sṗíʔims – They are striking it. **qeʔes sṗim, es sṗimp**
es sṗíʔims – They are going to strike it. **qeʔqs sṗim, qs sṗimp**

sxʷsṗim – one tasked to hit. *prefix: sxʷ... – one tasked to do.*
sṗsṗmuł – one that habitually hits. *suffix: ...łmuł – one that habitually does.*

sṗiš – Strike. *cmd.*
sṗint – Strike it. *cmd.*
sṗinti – All of you strike it. *cmd.*
čsṗiċéʔ – whip; hit someone all over with something. *See: whip.*
sṗłčep, *sṗłče* – drum; beat a drum. *See: drum.*

sṗint sččxʷumeʔ – Hit the ball! **qʷo sṗntés** – S/he hit me.

sṗsqé – strike people; to bat a ball.
sṗsqé – S/he/it struck people. **čn sṗsqé, kʷ sṗsqé**

spapqnm – strike the head with an object.
spapqnm – S/he hit the head. **čn spapqnm, kʷ spapqnm**
es spapqni – S/he is hitting the head. **čnes spapqni, kʷes spapqni**
qs spapqni – S/he is going to hit the head. **čiqs spapqni, kʷqs spapqni**
spáʔapqnm – They hit the head. **qeʔ spapqnm, p spapqnm**
es spáʔapqni – They are hitting the head. **qeʔes spapqni, pes spapqni**
qs spáʔapqni – They are going to hit the head. **qeʔqs spapqni, pqs spapqni**

spapqis – S/he hit s.o. on the head. **spapqn, spapqntxʷ**
es spapqnms – S/he is hitting s.o.'s head. **ies spapqnm, as spapqnm**
qs spapqnms – S/he is going to hit s.o.'s head. **iqs spapqnm, aqs spapqnm**
spáʔapqis – They hit s.o. on the head. **qeʔ spapqntm, spapqntp**

es spáˀapqnms – They are hitting s.o.'s head. **qeˀes spapqnm, es spapqnmp**
qs spáˀapqnms – They are going to hit s.o.'s head. **qeˀqs spapqnm, qs spapqnmp**

spapqntm – S/he/it was hit on the head.

k̓ʷłolocin – hit multiple times.

puˀ – sound of hitting a body.

tˀem – hit someone with a blunt projectile object. *See: **bump**.*
tˀentes – S/he hit s.o. with s.t. **tˀenten, tˀentexʷ**
es tˀems – S/he is hitting s.o. with s.t. **ies tˀem, as tˀem**
qs tˀems – S/he hit s.o. with s.t. **iqs tˀem, aqs tˀem**

tˀapqnm – hit someone on the head.
es tˀapqnms – S/he hit s.o. on the head.
qʷo tˀapqntm – I got hit on the head.

ntˀawsqntm – S/he/it was hit on the head.

ntˀaqsntm – S/he/it was hit on the nose.

soq̓ʷm – almost hit by something; missed by something; almost happened.
soq̓ʷmsts – S/he almost hit s.o. **soq̓ʷmstn, soq̓ʷmstxʷ**

soq̓ʷmstm x̣ił n̓e u čtemistmntm – S/he almost got run into by something.

cúˀum – punch with a fist. *See: **punch**.*

cuncut – punch one's self. *See: **punch**.*

nt̓łoqsm – punch someone in the nose. *See: **punch**.*

čcoqin – beat on. *See: **beat**.*

ƛ̓áq̓ʷ – verbally or physically fight one's spouse. *See: **fight**.*

nt̓mčim – flick with the finger; place a bet down as in flicking down a card or money. *See: **flick**.*

t̓qum – slap; hit with an open hand. *See: **slap**.*

łčim – spank; whip. *(i.e., as to punish)* *See: **spank**.*

ilip – wounded/shot by a bullet, arrow or sharp stick. *See: **wound**.*

hitchhike

sxʷčnq̓ʷnaq̓ʷm, *sxʷčnq̓ʷna* – hitchhiker/hobo;. *rt.: **naq̓ʷ** – steal; prefix: **sxʷ...** – one tasked to do.*

nšt̓t̓aqs – hitchhike. *lit. something on the road.*
es nšt̓t̓aqsi – S/he is hitchhiking. **čnes nšt̓t̓aqsi, kʷes nšt̓t̓aqsi**

nxʷstaqs – walk on the road. *rt.: **xʷist** – walk; circumfix: **n...aqs** – nose, road.*
nxʷstaqsi – S/he/it walked on the road. **čn nxʷstaqsi, kʷ nxʷstaqsi**
es nxʷstaqsi – S/he/it is walking on the road. **čnes nxʷstaqsi, kʷes nxʷstaqsi**
qs nxʷstaqsi – S/he/it is going to walk on the road. **čiqs nxʷstaqsi, kʷqs nxʷstaqsi**

ntkʷutaqs – walk on a road; referring to more than one person. *rt.: **tkʷuut** – they walk; circumfix: **n...aqs** – nose, road.*
ntkʷutáˀaqs – They walked on the road. **qeˀ ntkʷutaqs, p ntkʷutaqs**
es ntkʷutáˀaqsi – They are walking on the road. **qeˀes ntkʷutaqsi, pes ntkʷutaqsi**
qs ntkʷutáˀaqsi – They are going to walk on the road. **qeˀqs ntkʷutaqsi, pqs ntkʷutaqsi**

The **i** following uvular consonants (UC) and the glottal stop **ˀ** sound like English "*ey*" as in the words th*ey*, h*ey*, wh*ey*, etc. Salish UC are: **q, q̓, qʷ, q̓ʷ, x̣, x̣ʷ**. For example, the suffix **...qin** – head/top, is often spelled using English *ey* as "q*ey*n". So **qi, q̓i, qʷi, q̓ʷi, x̣i, x̣ʷi**, may be spelled with English *ey* as **q***ey*, **q̓***ey*, **qʷ***ey*, **q̓ʷ***ey*, **x̣***ey*, **x̣ʷ***ey* in other texts.

s.t. - something, the 3rd person
(s.t.) - something implied
s.o. - someone, the 3rd person
sl. - singular form
pl. - plural form
rt. - root word
cmd. - command
lit. - literally
fig. - figuratively
i.e., - for example
See: - Redirection to a related word.

hive **sqʷuʔɫéɫxʷ** – beehive. *rt.: **sqʷuʔɫ** – bee; suffix: **...eɫxʷ, ...ɫxʷ** – house.*

hoarse **sekʷcin** – hoarse; weak vocalization.

hoary marmot **smėéċ** – hoary marmot; *Marmota caligata*; yellow-bellied marmot; *Marmota flaviventris;* groundhog; woodchuck; *(there is no distinction between the two marmot species).*

hobble **čacšn** – hobble; bind feet.
es čacšn – S/he/it is hobbled. **čns čacšn, kʷes čacšn**

lčlčšisqáx̣eʔ, *lčlčšisqá* – hobble a horse; tie up the horse's legs. *rt.: **lčim** – tie up; suffix: **...sqáx̣eʔ** – domestic animal; mainly referring to horse or car; suffix: **...tin, ...tn** – means of/device.*
lčlčšisqáx̣eʔ – S/he hobbled. **čn lčlčšisqáx̣eʔ, kʷ lčlčšisqáx̣eʔ**
es lčlčšisqáx̣eʔi – S/he is hobbling. **čnes lčlčšisqáx̣eʔi, kʷes lčlčšisqáx̣eʔi**

lčlčšisqáx̣eʔis – S/he hobbled it. **lčlčšisqáx̣eʔn, lčlčšisqáx̣eʔntxʷ**
es lčlčšisqáx̣eʔms – S/he is hobbling it. **ies lčlčšisqáx̣eʔm, as lčlčšisqáx̣eʔm**

lčlčšisqáx̣eʔtn, *lčlčšisqá* – hobbling.

čacšisqáx̣eʔ, *čacšisqá* – hobble/bind a horse's legs. *rt.: **ac** – bind, tie, trap; suffix: **...sqáx̣eʔ** – domestic animal; mainly referring to horse or car; suffix: **...tin, ...tn** – means of/device.*
čacšisqáx̣eʔ – S/he hobbled. **čn čacšisqáx̣eʔ, kʷ čacšisqáx̣eʔ**
es čacšisqáx̣eʔi – S/he is hobbling. **čnes čacšisqáx̣eʔi, kʷes čacšisqáx̣eʔi**

čacšisqáx̣eʔis – S/he hobbled it. **čacšisqáx̣eʔn, čacšisqáx̣eʔntxʷ**
es čacšisqáx̣eʔms – S/he is hobbling it. **ies čacšisqáx̣eʔm, as čacšisqáx̣eʔm**

čacšisqáx̣eʔtn, *čacšisqá* – hobbling.

hobo **sxʷčnq̓ʷnaq̓ʷm**, *sxʷčnq̓ʷna* – hitchhiker/hobo. *rt.: **naq̓ʷ** – steal; prefix: **sxʷ...** – one tasked to do.*

čxʷstalqʷ – walk on wood/railroad track. *rt.: **xʷist** – walk; suffix: **...alqʷ** – wood; cylindical.*
es čxʷstalqʷi – S/he is walking on the tracks. **čnes čxʷstalqʷi, kʷes čxʷstalqʷi**

hog **npɫpɫáqs** – hog; pig. *rt.: **pɫiɫt** – thick; circumfix: **n...aqs** – nose, road.*

lkʷošó – pig; bacon; pork; ham. *(approximation to French word)*

hold **kʷestm** – hold something in the hand; in possession of something. *rt.: **kʷen** – take.*
kʷests – S/he/it held s.t. **kʷestn, kʷestxʷ**
es kʷests – S/he/it is holding s.t. **es kʷestn, es kʷestxʷ**
qs kʷests – S/he/it is going to hold s.t. **qs kʷestn, qs kʷestxʷ**
kʷéʔests – They held s.t. **qeʔ kʷestn, kʷestp**
es kʷéʔests – They are holding s.t. **qeʔes kʷestn, es kʷestp**
qs kʷéʔests – They are going to hold s.t. **qeʔqs kʷestn, qs kʷestp**

es kʷestm – It is being held.
ha es kʷestxʷ – Are you holding it?

kʷenlt – hold a child. *rt.: **kʷen** – take; suffix: **...elt, ...lt** – child, baby.*
kʷenltm – S/he/it held a child. **čn kʷenltm, kʷ kʷenltm**
es kʷenlti – S/he/it is holding a child. **čnes kʷenlti, kʷes kʷenlti**
qs kʷenlti – S/he/it is going to hold a child. **čiqs kʷenlti, kʷqs kʷenlti**

kʷnmtncut – hold yourself. *rt.: **kʷen** – take.*
es kʷnmtncutisti – S/he is holding him/her self. **čnes kʷnmtncutisti, kʷes kʷnmtncutisti**
qs kʷnmtncutisti – S/he is going to hold him/her self. **čiqs kʷnmtncutisti, kʷqs kʷnmtncutisti**

es kʷnmisti – S/he is hugging. **čnes kʷnmisti, kʷes kʷnmisti**

kʷnmist – hug; hold of one's self. *See: **hug**.*

łqlšax̣n – sit on the arm. *(i.e., as a baby, carried in arm, etc.) See: **sit**.*

yomim – hold something steady. *rt.: **yoyoot** – strong.*
yomstes – S/he/it held s.t. steady. **yomsten, yomstexʷ**
es yomims – S/he/it is holding s.t. steady. **ies yomim, as yomim**
qs yomims – S/he/it is going to hold s.t. steady. **iqs yomim, aqs yomim**
yomstéˀes – They held s.t. steady. **qeˀ yomstem, yomstep**
es yomíˀims – They are holding s.t. steady. **qeˀes yomim, es yomimp**
qs yomíˀims – They are going to hold s.t. steady. **qeˀqs yomim, qs yomimp**

yomiš – Hold steady. *cmd.*
yomint – Hold it steady. *cmd.*

yomspewlš – hold breath inside the body. *rt.: **yomim** – hold steady. See: **breathe**.*
yomscin – hold breath by closing the mouth. *rt.: **yomim** – hold steady; suffix: **...cin, ...cn** – action of the mouth. See: **breathe**.*
yomncut, *yomncu* **–** make one's self become rigid/tense. *See: **tense**.*

čṅéčs – hold hands; grasp hands. *See: **shake hands**.*

čṅim – grasp on to something. *See: **grasp**.*

ččṅim – hold/grasp on to something. *See: **grasp**.*

The **i** following uvular consonants (UC) and the glottal stop ˀ sound like English "*ey*" as in the words *they, hey, whey,* etc. Salish UC are: **q, q̓, qʷ, q̓ʷ, x̣, x̣ʷ**. For example, the suffix **...qin** – head/top, is often spelled using English *ey* as "q*ey*n". So **qi, q̓i, qʷi, q̓ʷi, x̣i, x̣ʷi,** may be spelled with English *ey* as **q***ey*, **q̓***ey*, **qʷ***ey*, **q̓ʷ***ey*, **x̣***ey*, **x̣ʷ***ey* in other texts.

hold back

čˀemtupsm – keep someone from doing something; hold someone back. *rt.: **emut** – sit; suffix: **...ups, ps** – butt, tail.*
čˀemtupsis – S/he held s.o. back. **čˀemtupsn, čˀemtupsntxʷ**
es čˀemtupsms – S/he is holding s.o. back. **ies čˀemtupsm, as čˀemtupsm**
qs čˀemtupsms – S/he is going to hold s.o. back. **iqs čˀemtupsm, aqs čˀemtupsm**

es čˀemtupsms kʷtisi t nox̣ʷnx̣ʷs – Big Blanket's wife is keeping him home. *lit. Big Blanket's wife is sitting on his tail.*

maq – forbid; prevent; detain someone from doing, going, or starting. *See: **forbid**.*

x̣eˀe – keep someone in line; correct behavior; forbid bad behavior; prevent misdeeds; make someone behave. *See: **discipline**.*

hole

łóx̣ʷ – make a hole in something; puncture something; bore through.
łx̣ʷom – S/he made a hole through (s.t.). **čn łx̣ʷom, kʷ łx̣ʷom**
es łx̣ʷomi – S/he is making a hole through (s.t.). **čnes łx̣ʷomi, kʷes łx̣ʷomi**
qs łx̣ʷomi – S/he is going to make a hole through (s.t.). **čiqs łx̣ʷomi, kʷqs łx̣ʷomi**

łx̣ʷntes – S/he made a hole through s.t. **łx̣ʷnten, łx̣ʷntexʷ**
es łx̣ʷoms – S/he is making a hole through s.t. **ies łx̣ʷom, as łx̣ʷom**
qs łx̣ʷomi – S/he is going to make a hole through s.t. **iqs łx̣ʷom, aqs łx̣ʷom**

es łóx̣ʷ – It has a hole.
es łx̣ʷeẃs – It has a hole all the way through.
łx̣ʷox̣ʷ – It got punctured; it got a hole.
łx̣ʷntem – S/he/it was punctured.

łx̣ʷmin – hole punch; drill; auger.
słx̣ʷsewłkʷ – water well.

s.t. - something, the 3rd person
(s.t.) - something implied
s.o. - someone, the 3rd person
sl. - singular form
pl. - plural form
rt. - root word
cmd. - command
lit. - literally
fig. - figuratively
i.e., - for example
See: - Redirection to a related word.

łx̣ʷoiš – Make a hole. *cmd.*
łx̣ʷont – Make a hole in it. *cmd.*

čłłx̣ʷálqʷ, *čłłx̣ʷá –* flute. *See: **flute.***
nłx̣ʷéłc̓eʔ – bore out the inside; hollow out the inside. *See: **bore.***
čsłx̣ʷmus, *čsłx̣ʷmu –* pierce all the way through; permeable. *See: **pierce.***
čłx̣ʷłx̣ʷéneʔ – pierce ears. *See: **earrings.***
čłox̣ʷálqʷ – hole in a standing tree.
nłox̣ʷálqʷ – hole in a fallen tree.
nłx̣ʷolexʷ – hole in the ground.
łx̣ʷmutiyeʔ – sewn together quickly. *(there is no hemming and/or the stitching is loose thus leaving gaps or holes)*

nlʔóp – fall into some place. *See: **fall.***

sqʷʔópłxʷ – hole; den (as of a mouse or rat). *rt.: **qʷʔóp** – make soft; suffix: **...etxʷ, ...txʷ** – house.*

x̣ʷlxʷenš – hole in the side of a ridge.

holiday

kʷtunt sx̣lx̣alt – big day; holiday.

holler

wéʔm – yell; holler out; talk while shouting.
wéʔm – S/he hollered. **čn wéʔm, kʷ wéʔm**
es wéʔi – S/he is hollering. **čnes wéʔi, kʷes wéʔi**
qs wéʔi – S/he is going to holler. **čiqs wéʔi, kʷqs wéʔi**
wéʔeʔis – They hollered. **qeʔ wéʔm, p wéʔm**
es wéʔeʔi – They are hollering. **qeʔes wéʔi, pes wéʔi**
qs wéʔeʔi – They are going to holler. **qeʔqs wéʔi, pqs wéʔi**

wéʔis – S/he called to s.o. **wéʔn, wéʔntxʷ**
es wéʔms – S/he is calling to s.o. **ies wéʔm, as wéʔm**
qs wéʔms – S/he is going to call to s.o. **iqs wéʔm, aqs wéʔm**
wéʔeʔis – They called to s.o. **qeʔ wéʔntm, wéʔntp**
es wéʔeʔms – They are calling to s.o. **qeʔes wéʔm, es wéʔmp**
qs wéʔeʔms – They are going to call to s.o. **qeʔqs wéʔm, qs wéʔmp**

sxʷčwewéʔm – one tasked to call out; an auctioneer. *prefix: **sxʷ...** – one tasked to do.*
wewéʔmuł – one that habitually hollers. *suffix: **...tmut** – one that habitually does.*
sxʷk̓ʷłwéʔm – one tasked to holler/repeat at a Medicine Dance. *prefix: **sxʷ...** – one tasked to do.*
čwewéʔm – auction. *See: **auction.***

wéʔiš – Holler. *cmd.*
wéʔnt – Holler at s.o. *cmd.*
wewʔilš – hollering around. *suffix: **...ilš** – autonomous.*
weʔnwexʷ – hollering at each other.

lulucin – make the trilling sound of women. *(i.e., of victory, honor, recognition) suffix: **...cin, ...cn** – action of the mouth.*
lulucin – S/he yelled. **čn lulucin, kʷ lulucin**

coʔim̓cn – scream at the top of one's voice. *See: **scream.***

čošim – yell out; shout out. *(i.e., a war cry) See: **yell.***

x̣lit – call for; holler for; beckon. *See: **call.***

cʔot – moan; slow quiet steady cry. *See: **cry.***

hollow **es nɫx̣ʷéɫc̓eʔ** – It is hollowed out. *rt.: **ɫóx̣ʷ** – It has a hole; suffix: **...eɫc̓eʔ** – the inside of something, body.*
nɫx̣ʷéɫc̓eʔ – bore out the inside; hollow out the inside. *See: **bore**.*

holy **px̣px̣twilš** – S/he became holy. *suffix: **...wilš** – developmental.*
sent spx̣páx̣t – The Holy Ghost.

home **snlciʔtn** – place of living, dwelling; home. *rt.: **lciʔ** – live in; prefix: **sn...** – a place of; suffix: **...tin, ...tn** – means of/device. See: **stay**.*

snlšeʔtn – habitat; roaming area. *See: **stay**.*

emut – at home; sitting.
emut – S/he was at home. **čn emut, kʷ emut**
es emuti – S/he is at home. **čnes emuti, kʷes emuti**
qs emuti – S/he is going to be at home. **čiqs emuti, kʷqs emuti**

homesick **čupélsm,** *čupé* – lonesome; miss someone. *See: **lonesome**.*

honey **sqʷoʔɫups,** *sqʷoʔɫu* – honey.

sqʷoʔɫ lamná – honey; bee syrup.
sqʷoʔɫ sp̓asts – honey, bee's smear.
sqʷoʔɫ mneč – honey, bee excrement.

honeysuckle **čiliyal̓álqʷ**, *čiliyal̓á* – orange honeysuckle; vine; *Lonicera ciliosa.*

nɫámqeʔ sʔiɫis – bearberry honeysuckle; black twin-berry; *Lonicera involucrata.*

hood **snolši čɫk̓ʷl̓čeneʔtn** – engine hood. *circumfix: **čɫ...eneʔ** – cover all over.*

hooded merganser **tt̓qʷéneʔ** – hooded merganser; *Lophodytes cucullatus.*

hoof **sq̓sq̓šin** – cloven hoofs. *rt.: **q̓saq** – split; suffix: **...šin, ...šn** – feet. See: **split**.*

ucilšn – dewclaws.
lkʷošó ucilšn – pig's feet.

hook **q̓l̓uxʷ** – place on a hook-like object.
q̓l̓xʷntes – S/he hooked s.t. **q̓l̓xʷnten, q̓l̓xʷntexʷ**
es q̓l̓xʷums – S/he is hooking s.t. **iess q̓l̓xʷum, as q̓l̓xʷum**

čq̓l̓uxʷ – S/he/it got hooked. **čn čq̓l̓uxʷ, kʷ čq̓l̓uxʷ**
es čq̓l̓xʷmi – S/he/it is getting hooked. **čnes čq̓l̓xʷmi, kʷes čq̓l̓xʷmi**

q̓l̓xʷncut – S/he/it hooked one's self. **čn q̓l̓xʷncut, kʷ q̓l̓xʷncut**

čq̓l̓xʷmin – hook for pulling or catching.
čq̓l̓xʷew̓stn – hook for hanging things on. *suffix: **...éw̓s** – in between, middle.*

čq̓l̓xʷéw̓s – hang/hook up high; hang on a hook. *See: **hang up**.*
čq̓l̓xʷus – snag/hook something by the eye.
nq̓lq̓l̓xʷé – snag fish. *See: **snag**.*
q̓l̓xʷélis, *q̓l̓xʷé* – link/hook uniformly together; chain. *See: **chain**.*

čq̓l̓xʷusntm – S/he/it got snagged/hooked in the eye.

qq̓m̓éyeʔ, *qq̓m̓é* – angling; fish. *See: **angle**.*

The **i** following uvular consonants (UC) and the glottal stop ʔ sound like English "*ey*" as in the words *they, hey, whey*, etc. Salish UC are: **q, q̓, qʷ, q̓ʷ, x̣, x̣ʷ**. For example, the suffix **...qin** – head/top, is often spelled using English *ey* as "qeyn". So **qi, q̓i, qʷi, q̓ʷi, x̣i, x̣ʷi**, may be spelled with English *ey* as **q***ey*, **q̓***ey*, **qʷ***ey*, **q̓ʷ***ey*, **x̣***ey*, **x̣ʷ***ey* in other texts.

s.t. - something, the 3rd person
(s.t.) - something implied
s.o. - someone, the 3rd person
sl. - singular form
pl. - plural form
rt. - root word
cmd. - command
lit. - literally
fig. - figuratively
i.e., - for example
See: - Redirection to a related word.

hoop game **q̓icqleʔ –** hoop game. *(a children's game)*

ilmintn – hoop game sticks. *suffix:* ***...tin,*** *...tn – means of/device.*

hop **nłttlqpncut –** do a little jump; hop.
nłttlqpncut – S/he/it hopped. **čn nłttlqpncut, kʷ nłttlqpncut**
es nłttlqpncuti – S/he/it is hopping. **čnes nłttlqpncuti, kʷes nłttlqpncuti**
qs nłttlqpncuti – S/he/it is going to hop. **čiqs nłttlqpncuti, kʷqs nłttlqpncuti**
nłttlqpncúʔut – They hopped. **qeʔ nłttlqpncut, p nłttlqpncut**
es nłttlqpncúʔuti – They are hopping. **qeʔes nłttlqpncuti, pes nłttlqpncuti**
qs nłttlqpncúʔuti – They are going to hop. **qeʔqs nłttlqpncuti, pqs nłttlqpncuti**

hope **nmusls –** hope; confident feelings.
nmuslsm – S/he/it hoped. **čn nmuslsm, kʷ nmuslsm**
es nmuslsi – S/he/it is hoping. **čnes nmuslsi, kʷes nmuslsi**
qs nmuslsi – S/he/it is going to hope. **čiqs nmuslsi, kʷqs nmuslsi**
nmúʔuslsm – They hoped. **qeʔ nmuslsm, p nmuslsm**
es nmúʔuslsi – They are hoping. **qeʔes nmuslsi, pes nmuslsi**
qs nmúʔuslsi – They are going to hope. **qeʔqs nmuslsi, pqs nmuslsi**

nmuslsis – S/he/it hoped for s.t. **nmuslsn, nmuslsntxʷ**
es nmuslsms – S/he/it is hoping for s.t. **ies nmuslsm, as nmuslsm**
qs nmuslsms – S/he/it is going to hope for s.t. **iqs nmuslsm, aqs nmuslsm**
nmúʔuslsis – They hoped for s.t. **qeʔ nmuslsntm, nmuslsntp**
es nmúʔuslsms – They are hoping for s.t. **qeʔes nmuslsm, es nmuslsmp**
qs nmúʔuslsms – They are going to hope for s.t. **qeʔqs nmuslsm, qs nmuslsmp**

nmuslsts – S/he/it made s.o. hope. **nmuslstn, nmuslstxʷ**
es nmuslstms – S/he/it is making s.o. hope. **ies nmuslstm, as nmuslstm**
qs nmuslstms – S/he/it is going to make s.o. hope. **iqs nmuslstm, aqs nmuslstm**

nmuslstn – Something that causes hope.
musčst – do one's best with hope of succeeding; do something with confidence. *See:* ***confident.***

ṅem qes nmuslsms – S/he/it will be hoping for s.t. **ṅem iqes nmuslsm, ṅem aqes nmuslsm**
ṅem qes nmúʔuslsms – They will be hoping for s.t. **ṅem qeʔqes nmuslsm, ṅem qes nmuslsmp**

k̓ʷmiʔ – hope/wish
k̓ʷmiʔ ċeẃntxʷ ančelš – Wish you would wash you hands. **k̓ʷmiʔ ta qs ťipeys yetłx̣ʷa –** I hope it does not rain today. **k̓ʷmiʔ tam qs ťipeysi ṅe čluxʷ –** I hope it is not raining this evening.

horn **qx̣min –** antlers; horns.

...elsčn – *suffix indicating antler or horn.*
ususšnelsčn – long horn.
ułususšnelsčn – more than one long horn.
čususšnelsčn – long horn cow.
usšnelsčn – unicorn.

čošmin – car horn. *rt.:* ***čošim*** *– yell out; suffix:* ***...min, ...mn*** *– instrument/tool.*

hornet **sqʷuʔł –** wasp; bee; hornet.

horse **snčłċaʔsqáx̣eʔ,** *snčłċaʔsqá* **–** horse. *rt.:* ***snéčłċeʔ*** *– cow elk; suffix:* ***...sqáx̣eʔ*** *– domestic animal, horse, car.*
nmlmlk̓ʷépls, *nmlmlk̓ʷé* **–** stallion. *suffix:* ***...epls*** *– testicle.*

nq̓ʷaq̓ʷʔépls – gelding. *suffix:* ***...epls*** *– testicle.*
sqltmxʷsqáx̣eʔ, *sqltmxʷsqá* – male horse in general. *rt.:* ***sqltmixʷ*** *– man.*
sm̓omšn – mare.
słm̓umšn, *słm̓u* – little female animal; filly. *See:* ***female.***
łqq̓y̓itš, *łqq̓y̓i* – colt. *rt.:* ***q̓y̓itš*** *– calf elk.*
łqʷq̓ʷm̓éw̓s, *łqʷq̓ʷm̓é* – yearling.
łqʷq̓ʷmuʔsqáx̣eʔ, *łqʷq̓ʷmuʔsqá* – yearling.
skʷk̓ʷiml̓tsqáx̣eʔ, *skʷk̓ʷiml̓tsqá* – young horse.
p̓ox̣ʷtsqáx̣eʔ, *p̓ox̣ʷtsqá* – old horse.

x̣ƛ̓cin – horse. *lit. something that grazes. See:* ***graze.***
sncm̓asqáx̣eʔ, *sncm̓asqá* – shetland pony.
sxʷq̓ʷłtsqáx̣eʔ, *sxʷq̓ʷłtsqá* – packhorse; pack mule. *prefix:* ***sxʷ...*** *– one tasked to do.*
snckʷmintn, *snckʷmi* – draft/work horse.
nčłptisqáx̣eʔtn – hunting horse. *suffix:* ***...tin, ...tn*** *– means of/device.*
q̓ay̓élxʷ – pinto.
es q̓ay̓e – pinto.
mn̓mil̓š – pacer/prancer.
snq̓ʷiiq̓ʷoƛ̓štn, snq̓ʷiiq̓ʷo – horse race; race.
suypsqáx̣eʔ – American stock; horses; cattle; etc.
semeʔsqáx̣eʔ – French stock; horses; cattle; etc.
snckʷmi – team of horses.

p̓x̣sqáx̣eʔ – branded horse.
es q̓ašisqáx̣eʔ, *es q̓ašisqá* – It is shod.
es q̓aq̓ešin – It has shoes on.
čsq̓éneʔ – split eared.
čx̣ʷtpéneʔ – cropped eared. *rt.:* ***x̣ʷtim*** *– cut off.*
čxʷmxʷéneʔ – red eared.
čx̣ʷtups – bob tailed. *rt.:* ***x̣ʷtim*** *– cut off.*
čłx̣ʷéneʔ – bore eared. *rt.:* ***łóx̣ʷ*** *– It has a hole.*
čłx̣ʷłox̣ʷéneʔ – bore ears.

kʷaʔalqin – strawberry roan.
čłkʷil – bay or chestnut horse.
čłp̓oq̓ʷlxʷ – brown horse.
čłp̓umelxʷ – light yellow horse
čłičy̓ó – appaloosa.
łiy̓ápł – appaloosa.
sʔaápsqáx̣eʔ – appaloosa. *rt.:* ***saáptniša*** *– Nez Perce.*
xʷamqn – roan horse.
pqaw̓s – bald face horse.
es q̓ʷayqn – blue-gray horse.
esq̓y̓iłxʷ, *esq̓y̓i* – pinto. *lit. it has spots.*
i čłčélxʷ, *i čłčé* – brown; it is brown.
i čłp̓exʷ – buckskin horse.
i čłpálxʷ, *i čłpá* – mouse colored; it is faded.
i kʷil – bay horse; it is red.
i čx̣i – gray; it is gray.
i čpálxʷ, *i čpá* – cream horse with black tail.
i čpiqlps, *i čpi* – palamino. *(cream horse with white tail)*
i p̓exʷ – sorrell horse.

The **i** following uvular consonants (UC) and the glottal stop **ʔ** sound like English "*ey*" as in the words th*ey*, h*ey*, wh*ey*, etc. Salish UC are: **q**, **q̓**, **qʷ**, **q̓ʷ**, **x̣**, **x̣ʷ**. For example, the suffix **...qin** – head/top, is often spelled using English *ey* as "q*ey*n". So **qi**, **q̓i**, **qʷi**, **q̓ʷi**, **x̣i**, **x̣ʷi**, may be spelled with English *ey* as **q***ey*, **q̓***ey*, **qʷ***ey*, **q̓ʷ***ey*, **x̣***ey*, **x̣ʷ***ey* in other texts.

s.t. - something, the 3rd person
(s.t.) - something implied
s.o. - someone, the 3rd person
sl. - singular form
pl. - plural form
rt. - root word
cmd. - command
lit. - literally
fig. - figuratively
i.e., - for example
See: - Redirection to a related word.

i q̓ʷay – black; it is black.

...sqáx̣eʔ, *...sqá* – suffix indicating horses, domestic animals, or vehicles.
k̓ʷl̓čisqáx̣eʔm – pack a horse. *See:* ***pack.***
k̓ʷl̓lisqáx̣eʔ, *k̓ʷl̓lisqá* – change horses. *See:* ***change.***
acacsqáx̣eʔ, *acacsqá* – break horses. *See:* ***break.***
k̓ʷłʔox̣ʷsqáx̣eʔ – construct a fence for domestic animals. *See:* ***fence.***
k̓ʷłtl̓tl̓qnčsqáx̣eʔ, *k̓ʷłtl̓tl̓qnčsqá* – spur a horse. *See:* ***spur.***
k̓ʷłʔacpasqáx̣eʔ – bridle a horse. *See:* ***bridle.***
am̓isqáx̣eʔ, *am̓isqá* – feed horses/domestic animals. *See:* ***feed.***
čtečsqáx̣eʔ – mark a horse/domestic animal with the hand. *See:* ***brand.***
čtqmsqáx̣eʔ, *čtqmsqá* – chase after domestic animals; mainly horses. *See:* ***chase.***
n̓ayxʷmsqáx̣eʔ, *n̓ayxʷmsqá* – trade horses/domestic animals. *See:* ***trade.***
p̓ix̣sqáx̣eʔ – brand a horse/domestic animal with a hot iron. *See:* ***brand.***
kłlisqáx̣eʔ, *kłlisqá* – borrow horses and domestic animals. *See:* ***borrow.***
nplšsqáx̣eʔ, *nplšsqá* – bring domestic animals and/or horses inside. *See:* ***enter.***
nt̓k̓ʷčisqáx̣eʔ – saddle a horse. *See:* ***saddle.***
ntx̣ʷmsqáx̣eʔ, *ntx̣ʷmsqá* – drive a car, wagon, or team of horse. *See:* ***drive.***
nʔułxʷmsqáx̣eʔ, *nʔułxʷmsqá* – bring one domestic animal, horse inside. *See:* ***bring.***
osqáx̣eʔ – lose a domestic animal, horse, car. *See:* ***lost.***
xʷimsqáx̣eʔ, *xʷymsqá* – take/bring along domestic animals/horses. *See:* ***bring.***
qixʷsqáx̣eʔ, *qixʷsqá* – chase/whip away horses; to drive horses and stock. *See:* ***chase.***
talsqáx̣eʔ, *talsqá* – loose/untie a horse/domestic animal. *See:* ***untie.***
tmsqáx̣eʔ, **tmsqá** – bring a horse to water. *See:* ***bring.***
tusqáx̣eʔ, *tusqá* – buy horses and domestic animals. *See:* ***buy.***
ukʷmsqáx̣eʔ, *ukʷmsqá* – bring domestic animals/horses somewhere. *See:* ***bring.***
ƛ̓asqáx̣eʔ, *ƛ̓asqá* – look for domestic animals; horse; car. *See:* ***look.***
ƛ̓xʷpsqáx̣eʔ, *ƛ̓xʷpsqá* – win a domestic animal; horse; car. *See:* ***win.***
usšlšisqáx̣eʔ – drive horses/domestic animals further. *See:* ***drive.***
ałnmsqáx̣eʔ, *ałnmsqá* – oats; horse food. *rt.:* ***iłn*** *– eat.*

horseback

čmtéw̓s, *čmté* – ride/straddle something *(one person). rt.:* ***emut*** *– sit.; suffix:* ***...éw̓s*** *– in between, middle. See:* ***ride.***

čay̓utéw̓sm, *čay̓uté* – ride/straddle something *(several people). rt.:* ***ayew̓t*** *– several people sit; suffix:* ***...éw̓s*** *– in between, middle. See:* ***ride.***

horsefly

čátnłq – horsefly.

horse mint

tiitw̓i – horse mint; nettle-leaf giant-hyssop; *Agastache urticifolia.*

horse race

sq̓ʷiiq̓ʷoƛ̓š, **sq̓ʷiiq̓ʷo** – horse race; race. *rt.:* ***q̓ʷuƛ̓š*** *– run, pl.*

horseshoe

q̇ašisqáx̣eʔtn, *q̇ašisqá* – horseshoe. *suffix:* ***...tin, ...tn*** *– means of/device.*
q̇aq̇ašisqáx̣eʔtn, *q̇aq̇ašisqá* – horseshoes. *suffix:* ***...tin, ...tn*** *– means of/device.*

q̇ašisqáx̣eʔ, *q̇ašisqá* – shod/shoe a horse.
q̇ašisqáx̣eʔ – S/he/it shod. **čn q̇ašisqáx̣eʔ, kʷ q̇ašisqáx̣eʔ**
es q̇ašisqáx̣eʔi – S/he/it is shoeing. **čnes q̇ašisqáx̣eʔi, kʷes q̇ašisqáx̣eʔi**
qs q̇ašisqáx̣eʔi – S/he/it is going to shoe. **čiqs q̇ašisqáx̣eʔi, kʷqs q̇ašisqáx̣eʔi**
q̇ašisqáʔáx̣eʔ – They shod. **qeʔ q̇ašisqáx̣eʔ, p q̇ašisqáx̣eʔ**
es q̇ašisqáʔáx̣eʔi – They are shoeing. **qeʔes q̇ašisqáx̣eʔi, pes q̇ašisqáx̣eʔi**
qs q̇ašisqáʔáx̣eʔi – They are going to shoe. **qeʔqs q̇ašisqáx̣eʔi, pqs q̇ašisqáx̣eʔi**

es q̇aq̇ašisqáx̣eʔi – S/he/it is shoeing horses. **čnes q̇aq̇ašisqáx̣eʔi, kʷes q̇aq̇ašisqáx̣eʔi**

es q̇ašisqáx̣eʔ, *es q̇ašisqá* – It is shod.
es q̇aq̇ešin – It has shoes on.

horsetail, scouring rush **ṫuxʷn** – scouring rush horsetail; *Equisetum laevigatum.*

nšṫsṫsewṡ, *nšṫsṫse* – horse tail; *Equisetum. (something joined together) suffix:* ***...éw̓s*** *– in between, middle.*

hose **nłłx̣ʷełċeʔ** – hose. *rt.:* ***łox̣ʷ*** *– hole; suffix:* ***...ełċeʔ*** *– the inside of something, body.*
ha kʷ epł nłłx̣ʷełċeʔ – Do you have a hose.

nox̣ʷométkʷtn – hose. *rt.:* ***ox̣ʷom*** *– strung out; suffix:* ***...etkʷ, ...tkʷ*** *– liquid; suffix:* ***...tin, ...tn*** *– means of/device.*

łłnulexʷtn – spread water on the ground; water the ground; sprinkle. *See:* ***sprinkle.***

łin – splash/sprinkle and spread liquid. *See:* ***splash.***

The **i** following uvular consonants (UC) and the glottal stop ʔ sound like English "*ey*" as in the words *they, hey, whey*, etc. Salish UC are: **q, q̇, qʷ, q̇ʷ, x̣, x̣ʷ**. For example, the suffix **...qin** – head/top, is often spelled using English *ey* as "q*ey*n". So **qi, q̇i, qʷi, q̇ʷi, x̣i, x̣ʷi**, may be spelled with English *ey* as **q***ey*, **q̇***ey*, **qʷ***ey*, **q̇ʷ***ey*, **x̣***ey*, **x̣ʷ***ey* in other texts.

hospital **snčċalélstn** – hospital; place of the sick. *rt.:* ***čċalels*** *– sick; prefix:* ***sn...*** *– a place of; suffix:* ***...tin, ...tn*** *– means of/device.*

hot **ƛ̓aq̇** – hot.
i ƛ̓aq̇ – It is hot.
es ƛ̓aq̇mi – S/he/it is hot. **čnes ƛ̓aq̇mi, kʷes ƛ̓aq̇mi**
qs ƛ̓aq̇mi – S/he/it is going to be hot. **čiqs ƛ̓aq̇mi, kʷqs ƛ̓aq̇mi**

ƛ̓áʔaq̇ – It got hot.

sƛ̓aáq̇ – heat.
i nƛ̓aq̇łċeʔ – It is hot inside.
ƛ̓áq̇lexʷ – hot land.
nƛ̓aq̇ičn̓ – have a hot back. *suffix:* ***...ičn̓*** *– back.*
ƛ̓aq̇t – when someone sits by you and is hot.

i ƛ̓aq̇ č čo – It is hot outside. **i ƛ̓aq̇ yetłx̣ʷa** – It is hot today. **mił i ƛ̓aq̇** – It is too hot. **ha kʷes ƛ̓aq̇mi** – Are you hot?

ṗéxʷ – bright; the red-hot glow of something heated.
ṗéʔexʷ – It got bright/red-hot.
i čṗxʷṗéxʷs – They're red-hot *(of s.t. round like rocks).*
čṗxʷṗéxʷsšn̓ – red-hot rocks; glowing rocks.
ṗéxʷmn – flashlight *(a thing that glows).*
ṗéxʷełċeʔ – It is light inside.
n̓e i čṗxʷṗéxʷs kʷém̓t m kʷ čtax̣ʷlé kʷqs q̓ʷl̓épi – When they're red-hot, then you start your baking. **qeʔ ṗéxʷełċeʔ** – The room/house we're in lit up.

qʷéc – warm. *See:* ***warm.***

ṗeč – get hot from some heat source; warmed/heated from radiant heat. *See:* ***heat.***

s.t. - something, the 3rd person
(s.t.) - something implied
s.o. - someone, the 3rd person
sl. - singular form
pl. - plural form
rt. - root word
cmd. - command
lit. - literally
fig. - figuratively
i.e., - for example
See: - Redirection to a related word.

hot dog **sṗl̓q̇enč**, *sṗl̓q̇e* – intestine; sausage/hot dog/wiener.

hotel **sncciłštn** – An overnight camping place; hotel, motel. *rt.:* ***cciłš*** *– camp overnight; prefix:* ***sn...*** *– a place of; suffix:* ***...tin, ...tn*** *– means of/device.*

Hot Springs **nayyáykʷ** – hot springs water; Hot Springs, Flathead Nation.

hour **nčcnšncut** – make a complete revolution; to make a circle; to meet one's own foot prints/tracks. *This word is used to describe cycles such as birthdays, and the telling of time in showing hours. rt.: **čicn** – meet; infix: **...šn...** – foot; suffix: **...cut** – action to the self. See: **around**.*

nčcnšncut – S/he/it went clear around, it is his/her birthday. **čn nčcnšncut, kʷ nčcnšncut**

nčcnšncut spq̇niʔ – one time around the clock.

k̇ʷnšłnšncu – How many hours?

ṗlṗlčṁstes łu sqéltč x̣ʷl̓ čełé x̣ʷa mus snčcnšncut – She is turning the meat over and over for three of four hours. **ha kʷ nčcnšncut** – Did you make it clear around; is it your birthday?

nk̇ʷuʔ sšlličč spq̇niʔ – one hour.

nk̇ʷuʔ słšlličč spq̇niʔ – one minute, one second.

house **citxʷ** – house. **ctcitxʷ** – houses.

...ełxʷ, ...łxʷ – suffix indicating house or tipi.
kʷtnéłxʷ – big house.
łkʷk̇ʷnéłxʷ, łkʷk̇ʷiméłxʷ – little house.
nčmqnełxʷ – top or peak of the house.

k̇ʷnšełxʷ – How many houses/tipis are there? *rt.: **k̇ʷinš** – how many; suffix: **...ełxʷ, ...łxʷ** – house.*
nk̇ʷełxʷ – 1 house. **esłełxʷ** – 2 houses. **čełłełxʷ** – 3 houses. **musłxʷ** – 4 houses. **clčstełxʷ** – 5 houses. **ṫq̇nčstełxʷ** – 6 houses. **sṗl̓čełxʷ** – 7 houses. **héʔenmełxʷ** – 8 houses. **upnčstełxʷ** – 10 houses. **upnčstełxʷ eł nk̇ʷuʔ** – 11 houses.
xʷʔełxʷ – many houses.

kʷ k̇ʷnšełxʷ – How many houses do you have. **čmi u čn łl̓k̇ʷełxʷ** – I only have one little house.

housefly **x̣máłtn** – housefly.

čn čsle t x̣małtn – I killed two flies.

how **t čeṅ ecx̣i** – How is; what kind?
t čeṅ ecx̣i łu q̇eẏmintis – How is his/her pencil/pen? *(what color; what kind?)* *(**nk̇ʷuʔ q̇eẏmintn i kʷil u nk̇ʷuʔ q̇eẏmintn i q̇ʷay** – One is red and one is black.)*

l čeṅ u ecx̣i – How is it *(like)*?
l čeṅ u ecx̣i u kʷ ntltlqpncut – How do you jump? *(**ha kʷ iqs ṁéẏełtm** – Should I show you?)* **l čeṅ u ecx̣i u iše k̇ʷuľntxʷ** – How do you fix it? **l čeṅ u ecx̣i u iše es awstxʷ** – How do you say it? **l čeṅ u ecx̣i u iše es k̇ʷuľstxʷ ṅe kʷ k̇ʷl̓sncut t uʔuseʔ** – How do you prepare eggs when you cook them?

l čeṅ m ax̣í – How is it done?
l čeṅ m ax̣ístn – How should I do it.
l čeṅ u ax̣ístxʷ – How did you do it.

l čeṅ m ax̣í m kʷ tixʷł čłq̇iq̇á – How do you get candy?

how is it **ečščéṅ** – question inquiring about the state of someone or something. *See: **happen**.*

howl **qeʔ hewšiłlt** – We are being howled at by a dog scout.

how many **k̇ʷinš** – How many/much? *(of a number, i.e., money, time)*
sk̇ʷnšspentč – How old is s/he/it?
k̇ʷnšełxʷ – How many houses/tipis are there?
k̇ʷnšasq̇t – How many days? *suffix: **...asq̇t** – sky, day.*

k̓ʷnšłnčcnšncut – How many hours?
čk̓ʷink̓ʷnš – How many people are there?

k̓ʷinš kʷ čkʷnšé t sw̓éwł – How many fish did you catch? **t k̓ʷinš u kʷes ntelsi –** How much do you want? **k̓ʷinš łu héʔenm –** How much is eight? **k̓ʷinš łiʔe –** How much is this? **k̓ʷinš u asx̣emt –** How much do you weigh? **p čk̓ʷink̓ʷnš –** How many are there of you?

> The **i** following uvular consonants (UC) and the glottal stop **ʔ** sound like English "*ey*" as in the words *they, hey, whey*, etc. Salish UC are: **q, q̓, qʷ, q̓ʷ, x̣, x̣ʷ**. For example, the suffix ...**qin** – head/top, is often spelled using English *ey* as "q*ey*n". So **qi, q̓i, qʷi, q̓ʷi, x̣i, x̣ʷi**, may be spelled with English *ey* as q*ey*, q̓*ey*, qʷ*ey*, q̓ʷ*ey*, x̣*ey*, x̣ʷ*ey* in other texts.

hubcap

čmičšnenetn – hubcap. *suffix: **...tin, ...tn** – means of/device.*

huckleberry

sṫšałq, *sṫša* – huckleberry; *Vaccinium membranaceum. rt.: **tiš** – sweet; suffix: **...ałq** – smell, accompaniment.*
sṫšalqʷ – huckleberry bush.

čn x̣mnčł sṫša – I like huckleberries.

čsṗim – thrash oats; gathering huckleberries *(when hitting the bush the berries fall onto a canvas). rt.: **sṗim** – strike w/ object. See: **thrash**.*

sipt – whortleberry; grouseberry; *Vaccinium scoparium.*
sptnełp – whortleberry plant.

hug

kʷnmist – hug; hold of one's self. *(a personal hug of care/concern/passion) rt.: **kʷen** – take; suffix: **...ist** – action for/of the self.*
es kʷnmisti – S/he is hugging. **čnes kʷnmisti, kʷes kʷnmisti**
qs kʷnmisti – S/he is going to hug. **čiqs kʷnmisti, kʷqs kʷnmisti**
es kʷnmíʔisti – They are hugging. **qeʔes kʷnmisti, pes kʷnmisti**
qs kʷnmíʔisti – They are going to hug. **qeʔqs kʷnmisti, pqs kʷnmisti**

kʷnmistmis – S/he hugged s.o. **kʷnmistmn, kʷnmistmntxʷ**
es kʷnmismms – S/he is hugging s.o. **ies kʷnmismm, as kʷnmismm**
qs kʷnmismms – S/he is going to hug s.o. **iqs kʷnmismm, aqs kʷnmismm**

es kʷnkʷnmisti – S/he is hugging more than once. **čnes kʷnkʷnmisti, kʷes kʷnkʷnmisti**

kʷnmistš – Hug. *cmd.*
kʷnmistmnt – Hug him/her. *cmd.*
es kʷnmistmnwexʷi – They are hugging each other. **qeʔes kʷnmistmnwexʷi, pes kʷnmistmnwexʷi**

kʷnmutiyeʔ – hug; hold temporarily. *(an impersonal hug) rt.: **kʷen** – take; suffix: **...mutiyeʔ** – temporary.*
kʷnmutiyeʔ – S/he hugged. **čn kʷnmutiyeʔ, kʷ kʷnmutiyeʔ**
es kʷnmutiyeʔi – S/he is hugging. **čnes kʷnmutiyeʔi, kʷes kʷnmutiyeʔi**
qs kʷnmutiyeʔi – S/he is going to hug. **čiqs kʷnmutiyeʔi, kʷqs kʷnmutiyeʔi**

kʷnmutiyeis – S/he hugged s.o. **kʷnmutiyen, kʷnmutiyentxʷ**
es kʷnmutiyems – S/he is hugging s.o. **ies kʷnmutiyem, as kʷnmutiyem**
qs kʷnmutiyems – S/he is going to hug s.o. **iqs kʷnmutiyem, aqs kʷnmutiyem**

kʷnmutiyeš – Hug. *cmd.*
kʷnmutiyent – Hug him/her. *cmd.*

> s.t. - something, the 3rd person
> (s.t.) - something implied
> s.o. - someone, the 3rd person
> *sl.* - singular form
> *pl.* - plural form
> *rt.* - root word
> *cmd.* - command
> *lit.* - literally
> *fig.* - figuratively
> *i.e.,* - for example
> *See:* - Redirection to a related word.

human

sqélixʷ – human; person; Indian. *This word is a combination of the two words, **sqeltč** – meat and **sṫulixʷ** – land, meaning flesh/meat of the earth. Its literal meaning is human but in common speech the term generally refers to Indian. See: **Indian**.*

nqlixʷcut – be human; be cultural; be Indian. *See: **culture**.*

nqlixʷečst – do something as a human; culture; tradition. *See: **culture**.*

humble **łkʷk̓ʷimscut –** humble one's self; be humble; make one's self small. *rt.: **k̓ʷim** – small.*
łkʷk̓ʷimscut – S/he humbled one's self. **čn łkʷk̓ʷimscut, kʷ łkʷk̓ʷimscut**
es łkʷk̓ʷimscuti – S/he is humbling one's self. **čnes łkʷk̓ʷimscut, kʷes łkʷk̓ʷimscuti**
qs łkʷk̓ʷimscuti – S/he is going to humble one's self. **čiqs łkʷk̓ʷimscut, kʷqs łkʷk̓ʷimscuti**

łkʷk̓ʷimscutš – Humble yourself. *cmd.*

hummingbird **łx̣ʷx̣ʷn̓i –** hummingbird; rufous, black-chinned, calliope.

hump **nmq̓ʷičn̓,** *nmq̓ʷi* **–** hump back; hump. *rt.: **moq̓ʷ** – bump; suffix: **...ičn̓** – back.*

humpback salmon **sč̓lwes,** *sč̓lwe* **–** pink salmon; humpback salmon; *Oncorhynchus gorbuscha.*

hundred **nk̓ʷoʔqín,** *nk̓ʷoʔqí* **–** one hundred.

hung **čacéw̓sm –** tie up; to tie and hang up. *See: **hang.***

čql̓xʷéw̓s – hang/hook up high; hang on a hook. *See: **hang up.***

čłqʷéw̓s – drape up high; hang up high over an object; hang up. *See: **drape.***

hungry **čsq̓méltn,** *čsq̓mé* **–** hungry/starving for food; figuratively, spiritually hungry.
čsq̓méltn – S/he/it was hungry. **čn čsq̓méltn, kʷ čsq̓méltn**
es čsq̓méltni – S/he/it is hungry. **čnes čsq̓méltni, kʷes čsq̓méltni**
qs čsq̓méltni – S/he/it is going to be hungry. **čiqs čsq̓méltni, kʷqs čsq̓méltni**
čsq̓méʔeltn – They were hungry. **qeʔ čsq̓méltn, p čsq̓méltn**
es čsq̓méʔeltni – They are hungry. **qeʔes čsq̓méltni, pes čsq̓méltni**
qs čsq̓méʔeltni – They are going to be hungry. **qeʔqs čsq̓méltni, pqs čsq̓méltni**

čsq̓méltsts – S/he/it starved s.o./s.t. **čsq̓méltstn, čsq̓méltstxʷ**
es čsq̓méltnms – S/he/it is starving s.o./s.t. **ies čsq̓méltnm, as čsq̓méltnm**
qs čsq̓méltnms – S/he/it is going to starve s.o./s.t. **iqs čsq̓méltnm, aqs čsq̓méltnm**

es čsłq̓qméltni – S/he/it is a little hungry. **čnes čsq̓méltni, kʷes čsq̓méltni**
čsq̓memélt – Each one was hungry.

sq̓méltn – hunger.
sčq̓méltn – the hungry; the starving.
scčq̓méltn – that have had hunger; that have starved.

čsq̓méltskʷ – Make s.o. starve. *cmd.*
čsq̓méltncut – make one's self hunger; make one's self starve.

nexʷ qeʔes čsq̓méltni – We're hungry too. **cc̓il̓š hoy sčsq̓méltn –** S/he camped and was hungry.
čnes čsq̓méltni t swew̓ł – I am hungry for fish.

nełnels, *nełne* **–** crave food; want to eat. *See: **crave.***

hunt **čłip –** hunt.
čłip – S/he/it hunted. **čn čłip, kʷ čłip**
es čłpmi – S/he/it is hunting. **čnes čłpmi, kʷes čłpmi**
qs čłpmi – S/he/it is going to hunt. **čiqs čłpmi, kʷqs čłpmi**
čłíʔip – They hunted. **qeʔ čłip, p čłip**
es čłpmíʔi – They are hunting. **qeʔes čłpmi, pes čłpmi**
qs čłpmíʔi – They are going to hunt. **qeʔqs čłpmi, pqs čłpmi**

čłpntés – S/he/it hunted s.t. **čłpntén, čłpntéxʷ**

es čłpims – S/he/it is hunting s.t. **ies čłpim, as čłpim**
qs čłpims – S/he/it is going to hunt s.t. **iqs čłpim, aqs čłpim**
čłpntéʔes – They hunted s.t. **qeʔ čłpntém, čłpntép**
es čłpíʔims – They are hunting s.t. **qeʔes čłpim, es čłpimp**
qs čłpíʔims – They are going to hunt s.t. **qeʔqs čłpim, qs čłpimp**

es čłčłpmi – Each one/group is hunting. **čnes čłpmi, kʷes čłpmi**
es čłčłpims – S/he/it is repeatedly hunting s.t. **ies čłčłpim, as čłčłpim**
čłpntém – S/he/it was hunted.

sxʷčłip – hunter; one tasked to hunt. *prefix:* ***sxʷ...*** *– one tasked to do.*
čłpemn – hunter; one inclined to hunt. *suffix:* ***...emn*** *– one inclined to do.*
čłčłpuł – hunter; one that habitually hunts. *suffix:* ***...łmuł*** *– one that habitually does.*
sčłip – hunting; the hunted.
scčłip – something that has been hunted. *prefix:* ***sc...*** *– s.t. that's been done/made/prepared.*
čłpncutn – hunter of someone. *suffix:* ***...cut*** *– action to the self; suffix:* ***...tin, ...tn*** *– means of/device.*
čłpšcutn – hunter for someone. *suffix:* ***...cut*** *– action to the self; suffix:* ***...tin, ...tn*** *– means of/device.*
čłptin – object used for hunting. *(i.e., gun, clothing, truck, horse, etc.) suffix:* ***...tin, ...tn*** *– means of/device.*
snčłptin – hunting place. *prefix:* ***sn...*** *– a place of; suffix:* ***...tin, ...tn*** *– means of/device.*
snčłpmintn – place used for hunting. *prefix:* ***sn...*** *– a place of; suffix:* ***...mintn*** *– tool that does.*

čłipš – Hunt. *cmd.*
čłpint – Hunt it. *cmd.*
čłpšit – Hunt for him/her. *cmd.*
čłpšits – S/he/it hunted for s.o. **čłpšitn, čłpšitxʷ**
es čłpmlwisi – S/he is hunting around. **čnes čłpmlwisi, kʷes čłpmlwisi**
es čłpštweʔexʷi – They are hunting each other. **qeʔes čłpštweʔexʷi, pes čłpštweʔexʷi**
es čłpmnweʔexʷi – They are helping each other hunt. **qeʔes čłpmnweʔexʷi, pes čłpmnweʔexʷi**

čłpntén łu sne – I hunted a cow elk. **čłpšitn łu inyayá –** I hunted for my grandma.

nčłpels – want to hunt; feel like hunting.
nčłpels – S/he is wanting to hunt. **čn nčłpels, kʷ nčłpels**
es nčłpelsi – S/he is wanting to hunt. **čnes nčłpelsi, kʷes nčłpelsi**
qs nčłpelsi – S/he is going to want to hunt. **čiqs nčłpelsi, kʷqs nčłpelsi**

čłpłtumš – hunt for the people.
čłpłtumš – S/he hunted for the people. **čn čłpłtumš, kʷ čłpłtumš**
es čłpłtumši – S/he is hunting for the people. **čnes čłpłtumši, kʷes čłpłtumši**
qs čłpłtumši – S/he is going to hunt for the people. **čiqs čłpłtumši, kʷqs čłpłtumši**
es čłpłtúʔumši – They are hunting for the people. **qeʔes čłpłtumši, pes čłpłtumši**

čłpminm – use something to hunt.
čłpmis – S/he/it used s.t. to hunt. **čłpmin, čłpmintxʷ**
es čłpminms – S/he/it is using s.t. to hunt. **ies čłpminm, as čłpminm**
qs čłpminms– S/he/it is going to use s.t. to hunt. **iqs čłpminm, aqs čłpminm**
čłpmíʔis – They used s.t. to hunt. **qeʔ čłpntém, čłpntép**
es čłpmíʔinms– They are using s.t. to hunt. **qeʔes čłpminm, es čłpminmp**

čłpmint – Use it to hunt. *cmd.*

The **i** following uvular consonants (UC) and the glottal stop **ʔ** sound like English "*ey*" as in the words th*ey*, h*ey*, wh*ey*, etc. Salish UC are: **q, q̇, qʷ, q̇ʷ, x̣, x̣ʷ**. For example, the suffix **...qin** – head/top, is often spelled using English *ey* as "q*ey*n". So **qi, q̇i, qʷi, q̇ʷi, x̣i, x̣ʷi**, may be spelled with English *ey* as **q***ey*, **q̇***ey*, **qʷ***ey*, **q̇ʷ***ey*, **x̣***ey*, **x̣ʷ***ey* in other texts.

s.t. - something, the 3rd person
(s.t.) - something implied
s.o. - someone, the 3rd person
sl. - singular form
pl. - plural form
rt. - root word
cmd. - command
lit. - literally
fig. - figuratively
i.e., - for example
See: - Redirection to a related word.

čłpmin łu ckʷiṅč – I used a bow to hunt. **steṁ łu aqs čłpminm –** What are you going to use to hunt?

čˀeym – fall hunt; hunt during the fall/autumn. *See: **fall time**.*
čˀeym – S/he did a fall time hunt. **čn čˀeym, kʷ čˀeym**
es čˀeymi – S/he is doing a fall time hunting. **čnes čˀeymi, kʷes čˀeymi**
qs čˀeymi – S/he is going to do a fall time hunt. **čiqs čˀeymi, kʷqs čˀeymi**
čˀéˀeym – They did a fall time hunt. **qeˀ čˀeym, p čˀeym**

snčˀeytim – fall time hunting place.

ṅe qʷo čłip l sčˀey še qeˀ awntm qeˀes čˀeymi – When we hunt in the fall time we say we are fall hunting. **łu sq̇sip sqelixʷ iše esyaˀ še ep snčˀeytin ax̣lčˀey še iˀimš łu č snčˀeytiˀis –** The people long ago all had fall hunting places; every fall they would move to their fall hunting place.

es wiqłceˀi – buffalo hunting *(spring/summer)*.

čslqnel̓ – good luck hunting; outsmart game/prey. *(Example: while hunting a hunter is spotted by the game yet s/he is able to out maneuver them and still get one.)*
čslqnel̓ – S/he/it had good luck hunting. **čn čslqnel̓, kʷ čslqnel̓**
es čslqnel̓i – S/he/it is outsmarting game/prey. **čnes čslqnel̓i, kʷes čslqnel̓i**
qs čslqnel̓i – S/he/it is going to outsmart game/prey. **čiqs čslqnel̓i, kʷqs čslqnel̓i**
čslqnéˀel̓ – S/he/it had good luck hunting. **qeˀ čslqnel̓, p čslqnel̓**

čslqnel̓is – S/he/it had good luck hunting s.t. **čslqnel̓n, čslqnel̓ntxʷ**
es čslqnel̓ms – S/he/it is outsmarting the game/prey. **ies čslqnel̓m, as čslqnel̓m**
qs čslqnel̓ms – S/he/it is going to outsmart the game/prey. **iqs čslqnel̓m, aqs čslqnel̓m**

hunting bow

ckʷiṅč – hunting bow. *See: **bow**.*

hurry

x̣ʷełé – hurry; quickly.
x̣ʷełé – S/he/it hurried. **čn x̣ʷełé, kʷ x̣ʷełé**
es x̣ʷełé – S/he/it is hurrying. **čnes x̣ʷełé, kʷes x̣ʷełé**
qs x̣ʷełé – S/he/it is going to hurry. **čiqs x̣ʷełé, kʷqs x̣ʷełé**

i x̣ʷełé – It is hurried.

imše kʷ x̣ʷełé – You should hurry. **k̓ʷul̓n qs x̣ʷełé –** I made her hurry.

x̣ʷełéčst – do work in a hurry; do something quick. *suffix: **...ečst, ...čst** – of the hand.*
x̣ʷełéčst – S/he/it did it quick. **čn x̣ʷełéčst, kʷ x̣ʷełéčst**
es x̣ʷełéčsti – S/he/it is doing it quick. **čnes x̣ʷełéčsti, kʷes x̣ʷełéčsti**
qs x̣ʷełéčsti – S/he/it is going to do it quick. **čiqs x̣ʷełéčsti, kʷqs x̣ʷełéčsti**
x̣ʷełéˀečst – They did it quick. **qeˀ x̣ʷełéčst, p x̣ʷełéčst**
es x̣ʷełéˀečsti – They are doing it quick. **qeˀes x̣ʷełéčsti, pes x̣ʷełéčsti**

x̣ʷełéčstmis – S/he/it did s.t. quick. **x̣ʷełéčstmn, x̣ʷełéčstmntxʷ**
es x̣ʷełéčstmms – S/he/it is doing s.t. quick. **ies x̣ʷełéčstmm, as x̣ʷełéčstmm**
qs x̣ʷełéčstmms – S/he/it is going to do s.t. quick. **iqs x̣ʷełéčstmm, aqs x̣ʷełéčstmm**

x̣ʷełéčsts – S/he/it made s.o. work quick. **x̣ʷełéčstn, x̣ʷełéčstxʷ**
es x̣ʷełéčstms – S/he/it is making s.o. work quick. **ies x̣ʷełéčstm, as x̣ʷełéčstm**
qs x̣ʷełéčstms – S/he/it is going to make s.o. work quick. **iqs x̣ʷełéčstm, aqs x̣ʷełéčstm**

x̣ʷełéčstš – Work quick. *cmd.*
x̣ʷełéčstwi – All of you work quick. *cmd.*
x̣ʷełéčstmnt – Do it quickly. *cmd.*

qʷiṁm – anxious; in a hurry; move quickly.
qʷiṁm – S/he was anxious. **čn qʷiṁm, kʷ qʷiṁm**
es qʷiṁṁi – S/he is anxious. **čnes qʷiṁṁi, kʷes qʷiṁṁi**
qs qʷiṁṁi – S/he is going to be anxious. **čiqs qʷiṁṁi, kʷqs qʷiṁṁi**
es qʷíˀiṁṁi – They are anxious. **qeˀes qʷiṁṁi, pes qʷiṁṁi**

qʷiṁčstmist – S/he hurried to work. **čn qʷiṁčstmist, kʷ qʷiṁčstmist**
es qʷiṁčstmisti – S/he is hurrying to work. **čnes qʷiṁčstmisti, kʷes qʷiṁčstmisti**
qs qʷiṁčstmisti – S/he is going to hurry to work. **čiqs qʷiṁčstmisti, kʷqs qʷiṁčstmisti**

qʷiṁmis – S/he hurried s.o. **qʷiṁmn, qʷiṁmntxʷ**
es qʷiṁṁs – S/he is hurrying s.o. **ies qʷiṁṁ, as qʷiṁṁ**
qs qʷiṁṁs – S/he is going to hurry s.o. **iqs qʷiṁṁ, aqs qʷiṁṁ**

qʷiṁqʷṁt – S/he is a quick/anxious one. **čn qʷiṁqʷṁt, kʷ qʷiṁqʷṁt**

nqʷṁqʷiṁels – busy.
qʷiṁmncut, *qʷiṁmncú* – dance; any modern style of dance. *See:* ***dance.***

aẋlá u es qʷiṁṁi – S/he is always anxious. **ta kʷ qes qʷiṁm** – Do not be in a hurry. **č čeṅ u kʷes qʷiṁṁi** – Where are you in a hurry to?

pmmap – hurry along.
pmmap – S/he/it hurried along. **čn pmmap, kʷ pmmap**
es pmpma – S/he/it is hurrying along. **čnes pmpma, kʷes pmpma**
qs pmpma – S/he/it is going to hurry along. **čiqs pmpma, kʷqs pmpma**

wamist, *wami* – run walk; hurry along; run in a feminine manner. *See:* ***run.***

aẏip – go fast, hurry. *(i.e., on foot, by car, or on horseback) See:* ***fast.***

The **i** following uvular consonants (UC) and the glottal stop **ˀ** sound like English "*ey*" as in the words *they, hey, whey,* etc. Salish UC are: **q, q̓, qʷ, q̓ʷ, x̣, x̣ʷ**. For example, the suffix ...**qin** – head/top, is often spelled using English *ey* as "*qeyn*". So **qi, q̓i, qʷi, q̓ʷi, x̣i, x̣ʷi,** may be spelled with English *ey* as **q***ey*, **q̓***ey*, **qʷ***ey*, **q̓ʷ***ey*, **x̣***ey*, **x̣ʷ***ey* in other texts.

hurt

lxʷup – get hurt accidently.
lxʷup – S/he/it got hurt. **čn lxʷup, kʷ lxʷup**

es lxʷup – S/he/it is hurt. **čnes lxʷup, kʷes lxʷup**

lxʷpnuis – S/he/it hurt s.o. **lxʷpnun, lxʷpnuntxʷ**
es lxʷpnunms – S/he/it is hurting s.o. **ies lxʷpnunm, as lxʷpnunm**
qs lxʷpnunms – S/he/it is going to hurt s.o. **iqs lxʷpnunm, aqs lxʷpnunm**
lxʷpnúˀuis – They hurt s.o. **qeˀ lxʷpnuntm, lxʷpnuntp**
es lxʷpnúˀunm – They are hurting s.o. **qeˀes lxʷpnunm, es lxʷpnunmp**

slxʷup – wound.
slxʷlxʷup – wounds.
lxʷpemn – one inclined to get hurt. *suffix:* ***...emn*** *– one inclined to do.*

lxʷpncut – S/he hurt one's self accidently. **čn lxʷpncut, kʷ lxʷpncut**
lxʷpšin – S/he hurt one's foot. **čn lxʷpšin, kʷ lxʷpšin**
es lxʷpšnmi – His/her foot is getting hurt. **čnes lxʷpšnmi, kʷes lxʷpšnmi**
lxʷpšntes – S/he hurt s.o.'s foot. **lxʷpšnten, lxʷpšntexʷ**
lxʷpečst – S/he hurt one's hand. **čn lxʷpečst, kʷ lxʷpečst**
lxʷpičṅ – S/he hurt one's back. **čn lxʷpičṅ, kʷ lxʷpičṅ**

lemlmtš ta čis lxʷup – Thank you I am not hurt. **ta es čint x̣iṅe lxʷup** – S/he is not afraid to get hurt. **ha kʷ lxʷup** – Did you get hurt? **lxʷup isćušin** – I hurt my foot.

s.t. - something, the 3rd person
(s.t.) - something implied
s.o. - someone, the 3rd person
sl. - singular form
pl. - plural form
rt. - root word
cmd. - command
lit. - literally
fig. - figuratively
i.e., - for example
See: - Redirection to a related word.

nixʷpels – have hurt feelings; profound sadness. *rt.: **ixʷ**– sad, hurt ;suffix: **...els, ...ls**– want, feel.*
nixʷpels – S/he got hurt feelings. **čn nixʷpels, kʷ nixʷpels**
es nixʷpelsi – S/he has hurt feelings. **čnes nixʷpelsi, kʷes nixʷpelsi**
qs nixʷpelsi – S/he is going to have hurt feelings. **čiqs nixʷpelsi, kʷqs nixʷpelsi**
nixʷpéʔels – They got hurt feelings. **qeʔ nixʷpels, p nixʷpels**
nixʷpelsts – S/he hurt s.o.'s feelings. **nixʷpelstn, nixʷpelstxʷ**

es nixʷpelsms – S/he is hurting s.o.'s feelings. **ies nixʷpelsm, as nixʷpelsm**
qs nixʷpelsms – S/he is going to hurt s.o.'s feelings. **iqs nixʷpelsi, aqs nixʷpelsm**
nixʷpéʔelsts – They hurt s.o.'s feelings. **qeʔ nixʷpelstm, nixʷpelstp**
es nixʷpéʔelsms – They are hurting s.o.'s feelings. **qeʔes nixʷpelsm, es nixʷpelsmp**

es nixʷplstwéʔexʷi – They are making each other get hurt feelings. **qeʔes nixʷplstwexʷi, pes nixʷplstwexʷi**

qʷo nixʷpelsts – S/he hurt my feelings.

x̣ṅnumt – get injured; have a long lasting sickness. *See: **injure.***

ċaál, *ċa* **–** achy; sore; hurting; in pain. *See: **ache.***

iłččéṅ – tender; painful to the touch *(as, a sore spot). See: **tender.***

hurtful

nċalċlcn – say hurtful words. *circumfix: **n...cin, cn**– action of the mouth.*
nċalċlcn – S/he said hurtful words. **čn nċalċlcn, kʷ nċalċlcn**
es nċalċlcni – S/he is saying hurtful words. **čnes nċalċlcni, kʷes nċalċlcni**

husband

sx̣élwiʔ – husband.
słx̣ex̣lwiʔ – little husband.

ta tam iqł sx̣elwiʔ – No, he is not going to be my husband.

husky

kʷtisqélixʷ, *kʷtisqé* **–** big person; husky person.

hyena

oẏnctemn nqʷq̓ʷosmi – hyena. *lit. laughing dog.*

I

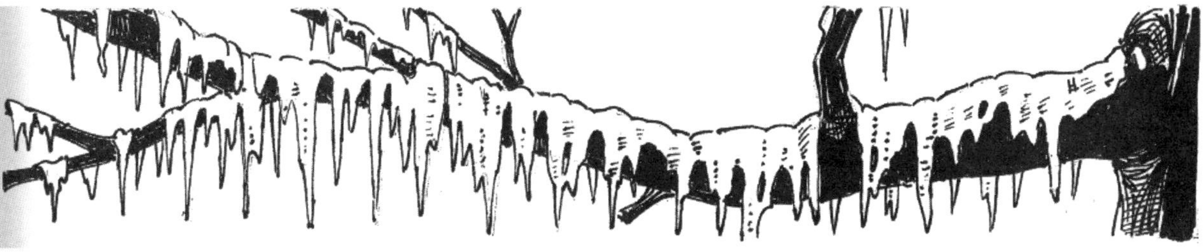

I, me **qʷoyʔé –** me; I; it is me.
qʷoyʔé łu čn ócqeʔ – I am the one that went out. **qʷoyʔé łu čn epł ye kʷtunt ṗiṗuyšn –** This big car is mine, I am the one that has a big car. **ci i nk̓ʷuʔ t qʷoyʔé m kʷén –** The other one I will take. **ta es mistén t qʷoyʔé –** I did not know. **ta, qʷoyʔé łu čn epł pus –** No, that's my cat. **ta, tam l qʷoyʔé u es nsuʔcnmi, šeẏ łu es cčxʷuymms, tam qʷoyʔé. –** No, it is not me he has come proposing to. He has come to visit her, not me.

…n, …ntén, …stén – transitive pronoun suffix 1st person *to* the 3rd person, I *to* him/her/it.
wičtn – I saw it.

čn, čnes, čiqs – intransitive pronoun particle indicating the 1st person, I.
čnes itši – I am sleeping.

ice **sxʷuymtkʷ –** ice.

nimáp – freeze; water hardened. *See: **freeze**.*

es ṗałti – when the water keeps freezing over the ice.

čłċik̓ʷčn – water over ice.

ice skate **čłpekʷp –** ice skate.
čłpekʷpm – S/he is ice skating. **čn čłpekʷpm, kʷ čłpekʷpm**
es čłpekʷpi – S/he is ice skating. **čnes čłpekʷpi, kʷes čłpekʷpi**
qs čłpekʷpi – S/he is going to ice skate. **čiqs čłpekʷpi, kʷqs čłpekʷpi**

ta qs tam qeʔqs čłpekʷpi – We have to go ice skating.

icicle **sxʷixʷuymetkʷ –** icicle. *suffix: **…etkʷ, …tkʷ** – liquid*
sxʷixʷuymełxʷ – icicle off a house.
sxʷixʷuymtalqʷ – icicle off a tree.
nxʷuymaqs – icicle off the nose.
čxʷuymups – icicle off a tail.

idea **scntels –** idea; want. *rt.: **ntels** – want; prefix: **sc…** – s.t. that's been done/made/prepared.*

čn ep scntéls – I have an idea.
kʷ ep scntéls – You have an idea.

sck̓ʷłpáʔx̣em, *sck̓ʷłpáʔx̣* **–** thoughts; idea. *rt.: **k̓ʷłpax̣em** – think; prefix: **sc…** – s.t. that's been done/made/prepared.*

if not **x̣iṅe –** might happen.
x̣iṅe čn xʷeyʔt – I might get in trouble.

s.t. - something, the 3rd person
(s.t.) - something implied
s.o. - someone, the 3rd person
sl. - singular form
pl. - plural form
rt. - root word
cmd. - command
lit. - literally
fig. - figuratively
i.e., - for example
See: - Redirection to a related word.

x̣iṅé čn ócqeʔ – I might have to go outside.

igloo **smek̓ʷtsełxʷ** – igloo; snow house. *suffix: **...ełxʷ, ...łxʷ** – house.*

igneous rock **impasšn** – igneous rock; lava rock. *rt.: **imap** – solidify; suffix: **...esšn̓, ...sšn̓** – rock.*

ignite **čulus** – light up; turn something on; ignite. *See: **light**.*

čulusis – S/he lit it. **čulusn, čulusntxʷ**

ṅem čulusn – I will light it.

ignore **nṗuṗuwenéʔ** – ignore; do not pay attention to; do not listen. *rt.: **ṗau** – disregard.*
nṗuṗuwenéʔ – S/he ignored. **čn nṗuṗuwenéʔ, kʷ nṗuṗuwenéʔ**
es nṗuṗuwenéʔ – S/he is ignoring. **čnes nṗuṗuwenéʔ, kʷes nṗuṗuwenéʔ**
qs nṗuṗuwenéʔ – S/he is going to ignore. **čiqs nṗuṗuwenéʔ, kʷqs nṗuṗuwenéʔ**

x̣ił kʷes nṗuṗuwenéʔ – Gee, you cannot hear.

ṗáu – disregard; ignore; lose interest; tire of something; distracted. *See: **disregard**.*

ntmaneʔ – refuse to hear/listen. *See: **listen**.*

ill **čċaléls,** *čċalé* – ill, sick. **čċax̣ʷéls** – sick to the stomach. *See: **sick**.*

ċaál, *ċa* – achy; sore; hurting; in pain. *See: **ache**.*

čċax̣élsi – hurting inside; sick (in one's mind). *See: **sick**.*

čċax̣ʷéls – sick to the stomach. *See: **sick**.*

čtax̣élsm – have a burning inside your stomach. *(i.e., heartburn) See: **nauseated**.*

ččessls – sick to the stomach; nauseated. *See: **nauseated**.*

imitate **ax̣íl,** *axí* – do as someone/something; imitate; behave a certain way. *See: **do**.*
ax̣ílm – S/he/it did like (s.o./s.t.). **čn ax̣ílm, kʷ ax̣ílm**

ax̣ílmsts – S/he did s.t. like s.t./s.o. **ax̣ílmstn, ax̣ílmstxʷ**
es ax̣lmisms – S/he is doing s.t. like s.t./s.o. **ies ax̣lmism, as ax̣lmism**
qs ax̣lmisms – S/he is going to do s.t. like s.t./s.o. **iqs ax̣lmism, aqs ax̣lmism**
ax̣íʔilmsts – They did s.t. like s.t./s.o. **qeʔ ax̣ílmstm, ax̣ílmstp**
es ax̣lmíʔisms – They are doing s.t. like s.t./s.o. **qeʔes ax̣lmism, es ax̣lmismp**
qs ax̣lmíʔisms – They are going to do s.t. like s.t./s.o. **qeʔqs ax̣lmism, qs ax̣lmismp**

ax̣lmstes – S/he did s.t. with s.t./s.o. **ax̣lmsten, ax̣lmstexʷ**
ax̣lmstéʔes – They did s.t. with s.t./s.o. **qeʔ ax̣lmstem, ax̣lmstep**

ax̣lemn – one inclined to act like s.t./s.o. *suffix: **...emn** – one inclined to do.*
nax̣íltn – ways; customs; the way one acts.

es ax̣lmnwexʷisti – They are acting like each other. **qeʔes ax̣lmnwexʷisti, pes ax̣lmnwexʷisti**

l čeṅ m ax̣ílm – How will it perform/be; what will it do?

x̣ʷl̓ steṁ u l še u kʷ ax̣ílm – Why did you do it this way? **čnes ax̣íli t łox̣ʷte** – I am acting like a baby.

nql̓ql̓wečšnm – imitate a walk or dance. *rt.: **ql̓we** – step.*
nql̓ql̓wečsis – S/he imitated s.o.'s walk/dance. **nql̓ql̓wečsn, nql̓ql̓wečsntxʷ**
es nql̓ql̓wečsnms – S/he/it is imitating s.o.'s walk/dance. **ies nql̓ql̓wečsnm, as nql̓ql̓wečsnm**

qs nql̓ql̓wečsnms – S/he/it is going to imitate s.o.'s walk/dance. **iqs nql̓ql̓wečsnm, aqs nql̓ql̓wečsnm**

nql̓ql̓wečsnt – Imitate s.o.'s walk/dance. *cmd.*

ncucuwečst – act in someone's place; substitute for somebody. *See: **substitute**.*

important **nkʷtnaqsm,** *nkʷtna* – expensive; costs a large amount; something of great value. *See: **expensive**.*
es nkʷtnaqsm – It is important; it is expensive; it has great value.

nkʷtnaqsmsts – S/he made s.t. be important. **nkʷtnaqsmstn, nkʷtnaqsmstxʷ**
es nkʷtnaqsms – S/he is making s.t. be important. **ies nkʷtnaqsm, as nkʷtnaqsm**
qs nkʷtnaqsms – S/he is going to make s.t. be important. **iqs nkʷtnaqsm, aqs nkʷtnaqsm**

nkʷtnaqsmskʷ – Make it important; make it be of great value. *cmd.*

The **i** following uvular consonants (UC) and the glottal stop **ʔ** sound like English "*ey*" as in the words th*ey*, h*ey*, wh*ey*, etc. Salish UC are: **q, q̇, qʷ, q̇ʷ, x̣, x̣ʷ**. For example, the suffix ...**qin** – head/top, is often spelled using English *ey* as "qeyn". So **qi, q̇i, qʷi, q̇ʷi, x̣i, x̣ʷi**, may be spelled with English *ey* as **q***ey*, **q̇***ey*, **qʷ***ey*, **q̇ʷ***ey*, **x̣***ey*, **x̣ʷ***ey* in other texts.

in **l –** *particle indicating in; on; with.*
čmut l es šʔiṫ – S/he sat (perched) in a tree.
čn sewneʔ t smx̣e l incitxʷ – I heard a grizzly bear in my house.

n... – prefix indicating in, inside.
nṫišk̓ʷ – sweet liquid; pop; Kool-aid.
es nṫuk̓ʷ – It lays in.

nʔułxʷ – go inside, enter. *sl. See: **enter**.*

npilš – go inside, enter. *pl. See: **enter**.*

q̇eʔ – put/placed inside something; inserted between. *See: **insert**.*

incite, push **čn ečẏami –** I am inciting to evil.

inclined **čṫuẏ –** bend toward; inclined. *See: **bend**.*

indent **łṗič –** indent in skin. *(i.e., when you take your belt off.)*

čṗéʔepm – indent something. *(i.e., skin, etc.)*
es čṗéʔepi – S/he has an indent. **čnes čṗéʔepi, kʷes čṗéʔepi**

čṗéʔepncut – S/he indented one's self. **čn čṗéʔepncuti, kʷ čṗéʔepncut**
es čṗéʔepncuti – S/he is indenting one's self. **čnes čṗéʔepncuti, kʷes čṗéʔepncuti**
qs čṗéʔepncuti – S/he is going to indent one's self. **čiqs čṗéʔepncuti, kʷqs čṗéʔepncuti**

es ṗéʔ – It is dented. *See: **dent**.*

Indian **sqélixʷ –** human; person; Indian. *This word is a combination of the two words, **sqeltč** – meat and **sṫulixʷ** – land, meaning flesh/meat of the earth. Its literal meaning is human but in common speech the term generally refers to Indian.*
sqlqelixʷ – people, Indians.

sqlixʷulexʷ – Indian land.

x̣̌e ep sqélixʷ u cnpilš łu uł selíš – There were already people here when the Salish came in.

selíš – Salish; Bitterroot Salish *(self identification term).*
ṫaṫʔayaqn – Bitterroot Salish *(self identification term).*
łq̇ełmlš – Bitterroot Salish *(Pend d'Oreille term).*

s.t. - something, the 3rd person
(s.t.) - something implied
s.o. - someone, the 3rd person
sl. - singular form
pl. - plural form
rt. - root word
cmd. - command
lit. - literally
fig. - figuratively
i.e., - for example
See: - Redirection to a related word.

łqayaqn, *łqa* – Bitterroot Salish *(Pend d'Oreille term)*.

qlispél, *qlispé* – Kalispel; Lower Pend d'Oreille. *rt.: **qal** – fresh, raw.*

sčłq̓etkʷmiš – Upper Pend d'Oreille; people of the wide lake. *rt.: **łaq̓t** – wide; suffix: **...etkʷ, ...tkʷ** – liquid (Qlispel term)*

snxʷmeneʔ – Spokane.

sčicwi – Coeur d'Aléne.

sxʷyélpetkʷ, *sxʷye* – Colville.

učnaqin, *učnaqi* – Okanagan. *rt.: **wič** – see;*
snq̓a – Southern Okanagan.

snpowilši – San Poil tribe.

sxʷil̓piš – San Poil tribe.

smlqmi – Methow tribe.

sqlsé – Kootenai. **sqlqlse** *pl.*

sčq̓ʷey̓šn, *sčq̓ʷe* – Blackfeet. *rt.: **q̓ʷay** – black; suffix: **...šin, ...šn** – feet.*
snxʷlsči – Blood.

saáptniša – Nez Perce.
slapaá – Nez Perce.

iaqmeʔ – Yakima.

nx̣ʷustaptneʔ, *nx̣ʷusta* – Assiniboine.

čqqayus – Cheyenne.

snuwepcn, *snuwe* – Shoshoni.
snuwepcn, *snuwe* – Lemhi band of the Shoshoni.

slqʷtłłnxʷt̓u – Sioux.

nxʷt̓xʷt̓u – Cree.

stemčiistn, *stemči* – Crow.

qʷayičint – Mountain Crow.

ox̣ʷi – Navajo.

čt̓lt̓leptn, *čt̓lt̓le* – Pueblo.

c̓altulexʷ sqelixʷ – Eskimo.

Indian broth
sx̣sétkʷ, *sx̣sé* – soup; broth.

Indian carrot
sƛ̓uk̓ʷm – carrot; *Daucus carota.*

Indian Flag
sčc̓la – eagle feather staff.

Indian ice cream
sx̣ʷosm – foam berries; Indian ice cream; *Shepherdia canadensis.*

Indian paintbrush
st̓lt̓lá sc̓iik̓ʷs – Indian paintbrush; Thunder's spark; *Castilleja miniata.*

Indian soup
scnpq̓ʷetkʷ, *scnpq̓ʷe* – soup; something put in the water. *prefix: **sc...** – s.t. that's been done/made/prepared; suffix: **...etkʷ, ...tkʷ** – liquid*

Indian suitcase **čq̓ʔiċéʔ,** *čq̓ʔí* – Indian suitcase; rawhide bag. *lit. it has a pattern around it. See: **pattern**.*

snċʔu – Indian suitcase.

indifferent **p̓aup̓ut** – indifferent; without interest or concern. *See: **disregard**.*
p̓aup̓ut – S/he is an indifferent/uninterested one. **čn p̓aup̓ut, kʷ p̓aup̓ut**

p̓aup̓ut l es k̓ʷłpax̣mi – S/he is distracted in/by his/her thinking.

infatuate **čx̣ssmels,** *čx̣ssme* – physically affectionate with someone; make out with someone; lucky. *(In the short form this word is also used as an expression for having good luck.) See: **affection**.*
čx̣ssmelsis – S/he was infatuated with s.o. **čx̣ssmelsn, kʷ čx̣ssmelsntxw**
es čx̣ssmelsms – S/he is infatuated with s.o. **ies čx̣ssmelsm, as čx̣ssmelsm**
qs čx̣ssmelsms – S/he is going to be infatuated with s.o. **iqs čx̣ssmelsi, aqs čx̣ssmelsi**

ha as čx̣smelsm – Are you infatuated with s.o.?

infect **čnilİ** – got poisoned; got infected.

inflate **npew** – pump up; inflate. *See: **pump**.*

infrequent **łaq̓ʷlwis** – go around showing up/to make appearances here and there. *See: **appear**.*
łaq̓ʷcin – speak up once in a while. *See: **appear**.*

inhabit **nłqqełċeʔ** – dwell/inhabit the inside; possess. *See: **dwell**.*

injure **x̣ṅnumt** – get injured; have a long lasting sickness.
x̣ṅnumt – S/he/it was injured. **čn x̣ṅnumt, kʷ x̣ṅnumt**
es x̣ṅnumti – S/he/it is injured/sick. **čnes x̣ṅnumti, kʷes x̣ṅnumti**
qs x̣ṅnumti – S/he/it is going to be injured/be sick. **čiqs x̣ṅnumti, kʷqs x̣ṅnumti**

sx̣ṅnumt – An unexpected accident; an injury; sickness.
ep sx̣ṅnumt – S/he/it has an injury/sickness. **čn ep sx̣nṅumt, kʷ ep sx̣nṅumt**

in-law **sčéšt** – brother-in-law of a male.
seʔstém – brother-in-law of a female.
łcécč – mother-in-law.
sx̣ax̣éʔ – father-in-law.
isčéẇ – sister-in-law of a female or male.

nq̓ʷiċtn – brother/sister-in-law after death/separation/divorce of spouse.
es nq̓ʷiċtni – marry a brother/sister-in-law after the death of one's spouse.

snéčłxʷ – son-in-law.
sépn – daughter-in-law.
sčʔélp – son- or daughter-in-law after death of spouse.

es nťkʷempi – marry a brother/sister-in-law after separation or divorce.

innards **sništełċéʔ** – innards.

inner tube **nox̣ʷmin** – inner tube.

inquire **sułtumš** – inquire; ask people; ask at large. *rt.: **sew** – ask; suffix: **...łtumš** – of people.*

The **i** following uvular consonants (UC) and the glottal stop **ʔ** sound like English "*ey*" as in the words *they, hey, whey*, etc. Salish UC are: **q, q̓, qʷ, q̓ʷ, x̣, x̣ʷ**. For example, the suffix ...**qin** – head/top, is often spelled using English *ey* as "q*ey*n". So **qi, q̓i, qʷi, q̓ʷi, x̣i, x̣ʷi**, may be spelled with English *ey* as **q***ey*, **q̓***ey*, **qʷ***ey*, **q̓ʷ***ey*, **x̣***ey*, **x̣ʷ***ey* in other texts.

s.t. - something, the 3rd person
(s.t.) - something implied
s.o. - someone, the 3rd person
sl. - singular form
pl. - plural form
rt. - root word
cmd. - command
lit. - literally
fig. - figuratively
i.e., - for example
See: - Redirection to a related word.

sułtumš – S/he inquired. **čn sułtumš, kʷ sułtumš**
es sułtumši – S/he is inquiring. **čnes sułtumši, kʷes sułtumši**
qs sułtumši – S/he is going to inquire. **čiqs sułtumši, kʷqs sułtumši**

sułtumšiš – Inquire. *cmd.*

ha puti kʷ ep scsułtumš – Do you still have any questions?

séw – ask; seek information. *See: **ask**.*

insect

tišulexʷ – insect; bug. *lit. earth crawler. rt.: **tiyeš**– crawl; suffix: **...ulexʷ**– land.*
es tišulexʷi – It is crawling on the ground.

titišulexʷ – insects; bugs.
łttišulexʷ – little insect; bug.

nopoplq̓sétkʷ, *nopoplq̓sé* – water insects, bugs.

yanáq̓ʷ – angleworm; earthworm. *See: **worm**.*

insert

q̓eʔ – put/place/squeeze inside something; inserted between.
q̓eʔeʔ – It got stuck/placed in a snug fitting place. **čn q̓eʔeʔ, kʷ q̓eʔeʔ**

q̓ʔentes – S/he put s.t. in a snug fitting place. **q̓ʔenten, q̓ʔentexʷ**
es q̓ʔems – S/he is putting s.t. in a snug fitting place. **ies q̓ʔem, as q̓ʔem**
qs q̓ʔems – S/he is going to put s.t. in a snug fitting place. **iqs q̓ʔem, aqs q̓ʔem**

q̓ʔent – Put it inside a snug fitting place. *cmd.*

nq̓ʔentes – S/he put s.t. inside a snug fitting place. **nq̓ʔenten, nq̓ʔentexʷ**
čq̓ʔentes – S/he put s.t. on the outer part of a snug fitting place. **čq̓ʔenten, čq̓ʔentexʷ**
q̓em̓elisis – S/he inserted/put things/people between one another. **q̓em̓elisn, q̓em̓elisntxʷ**
nq̓ʔelisis – S/he put s.t. between several. **nq̓ʔelisn, nq̓ʔelisntxʷ**
nq̓emuscut, *nq̓emuscú* – put one's self between things. *See: **between**.*
nq̓eʔulexʷ – put in the ground. *(i.e., planting, etc.) See: **plant**.*
nq̓éʔetkʷ – sink into water. *See: **sink**.*
q̓ešin – footwear; moccasin, shoe, boot, etc. *rt.: **q̓eʔ**– put inside; suffix: **...šin**– foot. lit. anything that is wore on the foot where the foot fits inside. See: **shoe**.*
q̓ašisqáx̣eʔtn, *q̓ašisqá* – horseshoe. *See: **horseshoe**.*
q̓éʔew̓s – middle son or daughter. *lit. placed in the middle. See: **son**.*
nq̓ʔels – busy with something; pay attention to something; involved with something. *See: **business**.*
q̓eʔečst – made to be or do something; cause hardship for someone; cause problems for someone; put someone/something into it *(by holding, by making it one's business to do so, by situational happenstance, etc.). See: **made**.*

nq̓ʔew̓sm – insert something in between things *(i.e., making a sandwich, between objects, etc.). suffix: **...éw̓s**– in between, middle.*
nq̓ʔew̓sis – S/he inserted s.t. in between things. **nq̓ʔew̓sn, nq̓ew̓sntxʷ**
es nq̓ʔew̓sms – S/he is inserting s.t. in between things. **ies nq̓ʔew̓sm, as nq̓ʔew̓sm**
qs nq̓ʔew̓sms – S/he is going to insert s.t. in between things. **iqs nq̓ʔew̓sm, aqs nq̓ʔew̓sm**

scnq̓ʔew̓s – something that's been inserted between; sandwich. *See: **sandwich**.*

nq̓ʔew̓snt – Insert something in between things. *cmd.*

inside

nišut – down inside; deep inside. *rt.: **išut**– down, low; prefix: **n...** – inside.*
č nišut – the inside.

ništełċéˀ – inside a body/hollow object. *rt.: **išut** – down; suffix: **...ełċeˀ** – inside contents, body, meat*

...ełċéˀ – suffix indicating the inside of a hollow object or body.
sništeɫċéˀ – innards. *rt.: **išut** – down.*
nqʷecɫċeˀ – It is warm in here. *rt.: **qʷec** – warm.*
nƛ̓aq̓ɫċeˀ – It is warm in here. *rt.: **ƛ̓aq̓** – hot.*

nlˀóp – fall into some place. *See: **fall**.*

nɫxʷpax̣nm – put the arm inside. *rt.: **ɫixʷp** – slip/pull over.*
nɫxʷpax̣niš – Put your arm inside. *(i.e., inside a sleeve, etc.) cmd.*

nɫxʷpaqstšnm – put the leg inside. *rt.: **ɫixʷp** – slip/pull over; suffix: **...aqstšn** – leg.*
nɫxʷpaqstšniš – Put your leg inside. *(i.e., inside a pant leg, etc.) cmd.*

nˀuɫxʷ – go inside; enter. *sl. See: **enter**.*

npilš – go inside, enter. *pl. See: **enter**.*

q̓eˀ – put/place/squeeze inside something; inserted between. *See: **insert**.*

ɫixʷp – slip/pull/put something fitted over an object. *See: **pull over**.*

insist

áy̓ċ – urge; insist and plead; stubborn.
es ay̓ċisti – S/he is insisting. **čnes ay̓ċisti, kʷes ay̓ċisti**

áy̓ċis – S/he urged s.o. **áy̓ċn, áy̓ċntxʷ**
es áy̓ċms – S/he is urging s.o. **ies áy̓ċm, as áy̓ċm**
qs áy̓ċms – S/he is going to urge s.o. **iqs áy̓ċm, aqs áy̓ċm**
áˀay̓ċíˀis – They urged upon s.o. **qeˀ áy̓ċntm, áy̓ċntp**

áy̓ċmsts – S/he urged s.o. **áy̓ċmstn, áy̓ċmstxʷ**
áˀay̓ċmsts – They urged s.o. **qeˀ áy̓ċmstm, áy̓ċmstp**

čáy̓ċistmis – S/he insisted upon s.t. **čáy̓ċistmn, čáy̓ċistmntxʷ**
es čáy̓ċistms – S/he is insisting upon s.t. **ies čáy̓ċistm, as čáy̓ċistm**
qs čáy̓ċistms – S/he is going to insist upon s.t. **iqs čáy̓ċistm, aqs čáy̓ċistm**

áy̓ċnt – Urge him/her. *cmd.*
áy̓ċistš – Insist. *cmd.*

áy̓ċnemn – one inclined to insist.
áy̓ċaċt – self-willed; insisting one; stubborn.
čáy̓ċistn – what one insists for.
náy̓ċaċls – bent strongly on something. *circumfix: **n...els** – want, feel*
es áy̓ċnmnwexʷi – They are insisting upon each other. **qeˀes áy̓ċnmnwexʷi, pes áy̓ċnmnwexʷi**

steṁ ɫu ančáy̓ċistn – What are you insisting for?

ay̓ċn – have the voice of insisting, begging and pleading.
es ay̓ċn – S/he/it insisted. **čnes ay̓ċn, kʷes ay̓ċn**
es ay̓ċni – S/he/it is insisting. **čnes ay̓ċni, kʷes ay̓ċni**
qs ay̓ċni – S/he/it is going to insist. **čiqs ay̓ċni, kʷqs ay̓ċni**

áy̓ċnš – Insist. *cmd.*

qiˀl – beg; insist; persuade; coaxed into. *See: **beg**.*

The **i** following uvular consonants (UC) and the glottal stop **ˀ** sound like English "*ey*" as in the words *they, hey, whey*, etc. Salish UC are: **q, q̓, qʷ, q̓ʷ, x̣, x̣ʷ**. For example, the suffix **...qin** – head/top, is often spelled using English *ey* as "q*ey*n". So **qi, q̓i, qʷi, q̓ʷi, x̣i, x̣ʷi**, may be spelled with English *ey* as **q***ey*, **q̓***ey*, **qʷ***ey*, **q̓ʷ***ey*, **x̣***ey*, **x̣ʷ***ey* in other texts.

s.t. - something, the 3rd person
(s.t.) - something implied
s.o. - someone, the 3rd person
sl. - singular form
pl. - plural form
rt. - root word
cmd. - command
lit. - literally
fig. - figuratively
i.e., - for example
See: - Redirection to a related word.

inspect **čaċx̣iċeʔ** – look something all over; inspect. *rt.: **áċx̣** – look; prefix: **č...** – upon; suffix: **...iċéʔ** – covered in. See: **look**.*
čaċx̣iċʔem – S/he/it inspected. **čn čaċx̣iċʔem, kʷ čaċx̣iċʔem**
es čaċx̣iċʔei – S/he/it is inspecting. **čnes čaċx̣iċʔei, kʷes čaċx̣iċʔei**
qs čaċx̣iċʔei – S/he/it is going to inspect. **čiqs čaċx̣iċʔei, kʷqs čaċx̣iċʔei**

čaċx̣iċʔeis – S/he/it inspected s.t. **čaċx̣iċʔen, čaċx̣iċʔentxʷ**
es čaċx̣iċʔems – S/he/it is inspecting s.t. **ies čaċx̣iċʔem, as čaċx̣iċʔem**
qs čaċx̣iċʔems – S/he/it is going to inspect s.t. **iqs čaċx̣iċʔem, aqs čaċx̣iċʔem**

sxʷčaċx̣iċʔem – one tasked to inspect; inspector. *prefix: **sxʷ...** – one tasked to do.*

čaċx̣iċʔent – Inspect it. *cmd.*

aċaċx̣m – look at repeatedly; inspect. *rt.: **áċx̣** – look. See: **look**.*
aċáċx̣is – S/he/it inspected s.t. **aċaċx̣n, aċáċx̣ntxʷ**
es aċáċx̣ms – S/he/it is inspecting s.t. **ies aċáċx̣m, as aċáċx̣m**
qs áċx̣ms – S/he/it is going to inspect s.t. **iqs aċáċx̣m, aqs aċáċx̣m**
aċaċáʔaċx̣is – They inspected s.t. **qeʔ aċáċx̣ntm, aċáċx̣ntp**
es aċáʔaċx̣ms – They are inspecting s.t. **qeʔes aċáċx̣m, es aċáċx̣mp**

nʔaċx̣éẇs – look at/check out something. *rt.: **áċx̣** – look; suffix: **...éẇs** – in between, middle. See: **look**.*
nʔaċx̣éẇsis – S/he/it checked out s.t. **nʔaċx̣éẇsn, nʔaċx̣éẇsntxʷ**
es nʔaċx̣éẇsms – S/he/it is checking out s.t. **ies nʔaċx̣éẇsm, as nʔaċx̣éẇsm**
qs nʔaċx̣éẇsms – S/he/it is going to check out s.t. **iqs nʔaċx̣éẇsm, aqs nʔaċx̣éẇsm**
nʔaċx̣éʔeẇsis – They check s.t. **qeʔ nʔáċx̣éẇsntm, nʔáċx̣éẇsntp**
es nʔaċx̣éʔeẇsms – They are checking out s.t. **ies nʔaċx̣éẇsm, as nʔaċx̣éẇsm**
qs nʔaċx̣éʔeẇsms – They are going to check out s.t. **iqs nʔaċx̣éẇsm, aqs nʔaċx̣éẇsm**

nʔaċx̣éẇsnt – Checked out s.t. *cmd.*

niʔaċx̣ – look inside; inspect the inside. *rt.: **áċx̣** – look; prefix: **n...** – inside. See: **look**.*
niʔaċx̣is – S/he/it looked inside s.t. **niʔaċx̣n, niʔaċx̣ntxʷ**
es niʔaċx̣ms – S/he/it is looking inside s.t. **ies niʔaċx̣m, as niʔaċx̣m**
qs niʔaċx̣ms – S/he/it is going to look inside s.t. **iqs niʔaċx̣m, aqs niʔaċx̣m**

niʔaċx̣nt – Inspect the inside of it. *cmd.*

šƛ̓us – search/stare around; look from one thing to the next; scan. *See: **search**.*

instruct **ċox̣ʷ** – impart wisdom, knowledge, and/or experiences of one's self; instruct; lecture; teach; inform.
ċox̣ʷm – S/he instructed. **čn ċox̣ʷm, kʷ ċox̣ʷm**
es ċox̣ʷi – S/he is instructing. **čnes ċox̣ʷi, kʷes ċox̣ʷi**
qs ċox̣ʷi – S/he is going to instruct. **čiqs ċox̣ʷi, kʷqs ċox̣ʷi**

ċx̣ʷntes – S/he instructed s.o. **ċx̣ʷnten, ċx̣ʷntexʷ**
es ċox̣ʷms – S/he is instructing s.o. **ies ċox̣ʷm, as ċox̣ʷm**
qs ċox̣ʷms – S/he is going to instruct s.o. **iqs ċox̣ʷm, aqs ċox̣ʷm**

es ċox̣ʷ – S/he is instructed. **čnes ċox̣ʷ, kʷes ċox̣ʷ**
ċx̣ʷntem – S/he was instructed by s.o. **qʷo ċx̣ʷntem, kʷ ċx̣ʷntem**

ċx̣ʷncutn – the instructor of one; the example setter of one; the model of one.
nċx̣ʷeltn – the model; the example setter.

čċox̣ʷ, *čċo* – premeditated action; do something on purpose; willful intention. *See: **smart**.*

c̓x̣ʷc̓x̣ʷłtumš, *c̓x̣ʷc̓x̣ʷłtu* – preach/lecture the people; make the people mindful of something. *See: **smart**.*

c̓x̣ʷc̓x̣ʷelt – preach/lecture to children; make the children mindful of something. *See: **smart**.*

intelligent

sisyus – smart; clever; good at something. *See: **smart**.*

px̣páx̣t – smart; clever; have knowledge; have wisdom. *See: **smart**.*

tam t̓ul̓ – tremendous; outstanding; extreme; excellent. *See: **excellent**.*

interest

p̓áu – disregard; ignore; lose interest; tire of something; distracted. *See: **disregard**.*

internet

mlk̓ʷmsnyoʔnwexʷistn – internet; all encompassing place to exchange information.

snm̓eẏłtumštn – website; place of showing/teaching.

snƛ̓emintn – search engine; something used to search.

nšiʔstew̓stn – hyper link; link; something used to pass between/among things. *rt.: **šiẏust** – pass through; suffix: **...éw̓s** – in between, middle.*

čp̓ac̓ – press something; click on something. *See: **press**.*
čc̓iq̓ʷłp̓ac̓ – left click.
čchałp̓ac̓ – right click.

q̓ʷamim – move/slide something. *See: **move**.*
q̓ʷamiskʷ č nwist – move it up; scroll up.
q̓ʷamiskʷ č nišut – move it down; scroll down.
q̓ʷamiskʷ č asčchečst – move it to your right; scroll right.
q̓ʷamiskʷ č asčc̓iq̓ʷečst – move it to your left; scroll left.

laáp – float in a vessel; navigate by water; row*; surf internet. (i.e., boat, canoe, raft, etc.) See: **float**.*

interpret

nmicinm – interpret someone's words; know words. *rt.: **mi** – reality, the known; suffix: **...cin, ...cn** – action of the mouth.*
nmicinm – S/he interpreted. **čn nmicinm, kʷ nmicinm**
es nmicini – S/he is interpreting. **čnes nmicini, kʷes nmicini**
qs nmicini – S/he is going to interpret. **čiqs nmicini, kʷes nmicini**
nmicíʔinm – They interpreted. **qeʔ nmicinm, p nmicinm**
es nmicíʔini – They are interpreting. **qeʔes nmicini, pes nmicini**
qs nmiciníʔi – They are going to interpret. **qeʔqs nmicini, pes nmicini**

nmicis – S/he interpreted for s.o. **čn nmicin, kʷ nmicintxʷ**
es nmicinms – S/he is interpreting for s.o. **ies nmicinm, as nmicinm**
qs nmicinms – S/he is going to interpret for s.o. **iqs nmicinm, aqs nmicinm**

sxʷnmicin – one tasked to interpret; interpreter. *prefix: **sxʷ...** – one tasked to do.*

nmiciniš – Interpret. *cmd.*
nmicint – Interpret for him/her. *cmd.*

nmicncut – interpret one's own words.
nmicncut – S/he interpreted his/her words. **čn nmicncut, kʷ nmicncut**
es nmicncuti – S/he is interpreting his/her words. **čnes nmicncuti, kʷes nmicncuti**
qs nmicncuti – S/he is going to interpret his/her words. **čiqs nmicncuti, kʷes nmicncuti**

The **i** following uvular consonants (UC) and the glottal stop **ʔ** sound like English "*ey*" as in the words th*ey*, h*ey*, wh*ey*, etc. Salish UC are: **q, q̓, qʷ, q̓ʷ, x̣, x̣ʷ**. For example, the suffix ...**qin** – head/top, is often spelled using English *ey* as "q*ey*n". So **qi, q̓i, qʷi, q̓ʷi, x̣i, x̣ʷi**, may be spelled with English *ey* as **q***ey*, **q̓***ey*, **qʷ***ey*, **q̓ʷ***ey*, **x̣***ey*, **x̣ʷ***ey* in other texts.

s.t. - something, the 3rd person
(s.t.) - something implied
s.o. - someone, the 3rd person
sl. - singular form
pl. - plural form
rt. - root word
cmd. - command
lit. - literally
fig. - figuratively
i.e., - for example
See: - Redirection to a related word.

nmicncúˀut – They interpreted their words. **qeˀ nmicncut, p nmicncut**
es nmicncúˀuti – They are interpreting their words. **qeˀes nmicncuti, pes nmicncuti**
qs nmicncúˀuti – They are going to interpret their words. **qeˀqs nmicncuti, pqs nmicncuti**

nmicncutn – interpreter of one.

nmicncutš – Interpret your words. *cmd.*

interpreter

sxʷnmicinm, *sxʷnmici* **–** one tasked to interpret. *prefix:* ***sxʷ...*** *– one tasked to do; suffix:* ***...cin, ...cn*** *– action of the mouth.*

interrogate

sumlwism – ask around; interrogate. *rt.:* ***sew*** *– ask; suffix:* ***...lwis*** *– indicates going around.*
sumlwisis – S/he interrogated s.o. **sumlwisn, sumlwisntxʷ**
es sumlwisms – S/he is interrogating s.o. **ies sumlwism, as sumlwism**
qs sumlwisms – S/he is going to interrogate s.o. **iqs sumlwism, aqs sumlwism**

sumlwisnt – Interrogate s.o. *cmd.*

čsewpleˀ – ask permission; ask about someone. *See:* ***permission.***

séw – ask; seek information. *See:* ***ask.***

intestine

sṗlq̓énč, *sṗlq̓é* **–** small intestine; sausage/hot dog/wiener. *suffix:* ***...enč*** *– within.*

sołénč – large intestine. *suffix:* ***...enč*** *– within.*

łq̓łénč, *łq̓łé* **–** large intestine. *suffix:* ***...enč*** *– within.*

invisible

tas uččutm – something that cannot be seen; something invisible. *See:* ***see.***

invite

x̣eł – invite to go; invite to travel to someplace.
x̣ełm – S/he invited (s.o.). **čn x̣ełm, kʷ x̣ełm**
es x̣ełi – S/he is inviting (s.o.). **čnes x̣ełi, kʷes x̣ełi**
qs x̣ełi – S/he is going to invite (s.o.). **čiqs x̣ełi, kʷqs x̣ełi**

x̣ełis – S/he invited s.o. on a trip. **x̣ełn, x̣ełntxʷ**
es x̣ełms – S/he is inviting s.o. on a trip. **čnes x̣ełm, kʷes x̣ełm**
qs x̣ełms – S/he is going to invite s.o. on a trip. **čiqs x̣ełm, kʷqs x̣ełm**

es x̣łłumši – S/he is inviting the people on a trip. **čnes x̣łłumši, kʷes x̣łłumši**
es x̣łmsqax̣eˀi – S/he is calling the dog(domestic animal) to go somewhere. **čnes x̣łmsqax̣eˀi, kʷes x̣łmsqax̣eˀi**

x̣lit – call for; holler for; beckon. *See:* ***call.***

involve

nšeẏ – in there; involved; included; in the party of. *rt.:* ***šeẏ*** *– there.*
nšeẏ – S/he was involved. **čn nšeẏ, kʷ nšeẏ**
es nšeẏ – S/he is involved. **čnes nšeẏ, kʷes nšeẏ**
qs nšeẏ – S/he is going to be involved. **čiqs nšeẏ, kʷqs nšeẏ**

nšeẏsts – S/he made s.o. be involved. **nšeẏstn, nšeẏstxʷ**
es nšeẏms – S/he is making s.o. be involved. **ies nšeẏm, as nšeẏm**
qs nšeẏms – S/he is going to make s.o. be involved. **iqs nšeẏm, aqs nšeẏm**

nšeẏskʷ – Make s.o. be involved. *cmd.*

šišeẏ – in the company of; together with; involved with. *rt.:* ***šeẏ*** *– there.*
šišeẏ – S/he was involved with. **čn šišeẏ, kʷ šišeẏ**

es šišeẏ – S/he is involved with. **čnes šišeẏ, kʷes šišeẏ**
qs šišeẏ – S/he is going to be involved with. **čiqs šišeẏ, kʷqs šišeẏ**

šiyečst – take part in the work; involved with the work. *rt.: šeẏ – there; suffix: ...ečst, ...čst – of the hand.*
šiyečst – S/he was involved with the work. **čn šiyečst, kʷ šiyečst**
es šiyečsti – S/he is involved with the work. **čnes šiyečsti, kʷes šiyečsti**
qs šiyečsti – S/he is going to be involved with the work. **čiqs šiyečsti, kʷqs šiyečsti**

šiyečstmis – S/he was involved in the work with s.o. **šiyečstmn, šiyečstmntxʷ**
es šiyečstms – S/he is involved in the work with s.o. **ies šiyečstm, as šiyečstm**
qs šiyečstms – S/he is going to be involved in the work with s.o. **iqs šiyečstm, aqs šiyečstm**

čšeẏcn – involved in the talk; part of the conversation.
čšeẏcnmis – S/he was involved in that talk. **čšeẏcnmn, čšeẏcnmntxʷ**
es čšeẏcnms – S/he is involved in that talk. **ies čšeẏcnm, as čšeẏcnm**
qs čšeẏcnms – S/he is going to be involved in that talk. **iqs čšeẏcnm, aqs čšeẏcnm**

The **i** following uvular consonants (UC) and the glottal stop ʔ sound like English "*ey*" as in the words th*ey*, h*ey*, wh*ey*, etc. Salish UC are: **q**, **q̇**, **qʷ**, **q̇ʷ**, **x̣**, **x̣ʷ**. For example, the suffix ...**qin** – head/top, is often spelled using English *ey* as "q*ey*n". So **qi**, **q̇i**, **qʷi**, **q̇ʷi**, **x̣i**, **x̣ʷi**, may be spelled with English *ey* as **q***ey*, **q̇***ey*, **qʷ***ey*, **q̇ʷ***ey*, **x̣***ey*, **x̣ʷ***ey* in other texts.

iron

ululim – iron, metal.

ṫeċ – iron/press clothing.
ṫeċis – S/he ironed it. **ṫeċn, ṫeċntxʷ**
es ṫeċms – S/he/it is ironing it. **ies ṫeċm, as ṫeċm**
qs ṫeċms – S/he/it is going to iron it. **iqs ṫeċm, aqs ṫeċm**

ṫeċmn – iron for clothes.

ṫeċnt – Press it. *cmd.*

ha ṫeċntxʷ asnołups – Did you iron your pants? **ṅem pċikʷmntxʷ seẇłk̓ʷ l asnołups m še ṫeċntxʷ** – You will spray water on your pants and then you will iron them.

ironing board

snṫéċmn – ironing board.

irrigate

ṅmẇaẇs, *ṅmẇa* – irrigate/water a field, yard, ground. *(water flows in irrigation channels among/between the plants/field) suffix: ...éẇs – in between, middle.*
ṅmẇaẇsm – S/he irrigated. **čn ṅmẇaẇsm, kʷ ṅmẇaẇsm**
es ṅmẇaẇsi – S/he is irrigating. **čnes ṅmẇaẇsi, kʷes ṅmẇaẇsi**
qs ṅmẇaẇsi – S/he is going to irrigate. **čiqs ṅmẇaẇsi, kʷqs ṅmẇaẇsi**

łin – splash/sprinkle and spread liquid. *See: splash.*

łłnulexʷtn – spread water on the ground; water the ground; sprinkle. *See: sprinkle.*

Isabelle

sepel – Isabelle.

island

čssunkʷ – island.

it

cniłċ, *cni* – It is his/hers/its; it is him/her/it. *See: her.*

Italian

nłṫuxʷtn – Italian.

itch

qaup – itchy.
qaup – S/he got itchy. **čn qaup, kʷ qaup**
es qaupmi – S/he/it is itchy. **čnes qaupmi, kʷes qaupmi**

s.t. - something, the 3rd person
(s.t.) - something implied
s.o. - someone, the 3rd person
sl. - singular form
pl. - plural form
rt. - root word
cmd. - command
lit. - literally
fig. - figuratively
i.e., - for example
See: - Redirection to a related word.

i qau – It is itchy.

čqaupiċeˀ – itchy all over.

qaupqin – have an itchy head. *suffix:* ***...qin, ...qn*** *– top.*
qaupqin – His/her/its head was itchy. **čn qaupqin kʷ qaupqin**
es qaupqini – His/her/its head is itchy. **čnes qaupqini kʷes qaupqini**
qs qaupqini – His/her/its head is going to be itchy. **čiqs qaupqini kʷqs qaupqini**

čquqaupus – have itchy eyes. *circumfix:* ***č...us*** *–spherical object; eyes.*
čquqaupus – His/her/its eyes were itchy. **čn čquqaupus kʷ čquqaupus**
es čquqaupusi – His/her/its eyes are itchy. **čnes čquqaupusi kʷes čquqaupusi**
qs čquqaupusi – His/her/its eyes are going to be itchy. **čiqs čquqaupusi kʷqs čquqaupusi**

nqaupaqs – have an itchy nose.
nqaupaqs – His/her/its nose was itchy. **čn nqaupaqs, kʷ nqaupaqs**
es nqaupaqsi – His/her/its nose is itchy. **čnes nqaupaqsi, kʷes nqaupaqsi**
qs nqaupaqsi – His/her/its nose is going to be itchy. **čiqs nqaupaqsi, kʷqs nqaupaqsi**

nqaupéneˀ – have an itchy ear.
nqaupéneˀ – His/her/its ear was itchy. **čn nqaupéneˀ kʷ nqaupéneˀ**
es nqaupénˀei – His/her/its ear is itchy. **čnes nqaupénˀei kʷes nqaupénˀei**
qs nqaupénˀei – His/her/its ear is going to be itchy. **čiqs nqaupénˀei kʷqs nqaupénˀei**

nqaupáłq̇ʷlt – have an itchy throat.
nqaupáłq̇ʷlt – His/her/its throat was itchy. **čn nqaupáłq̇ʷlt, kʷ nqaupáłq̇ʷlt**
es nqaupáłq̇ʷlti – His/her/its throat is itchy. **čnes nqaupáłq̇ʷlti, kʷes nqaupáłq̇ʷlti**
qsnqaupáłq̇ʷlti – His/her/its throat is going to be itchy. **čiqs nqaupáłq̇ʷlti, kʷqs nqaupáłq̇ʷlti**

nqaupčnéẇs, *nqaupčné* – have an itchy lower back.
nqaupcné – His/her/its back was itchy. **čn nqaupcné kʷ nqaupcné**

nqaupičṅ – have an itchy upper back. *suffix:* ***...ičṅ*** *– back.*
nqaupičṅ – His/her/its back was itchy. **čn nqaupičṅ kʷ nqaupičṅ**
es nqaupičṅi – His/her/its back is itchy. **čnes nqaupičṅi kʷes nqaupičṅi**
qs nqaupičṅi – His/her/its back is going to be itchy. **čiqs nqaupičṅi kʷqs nqaupičṅi**

nqaupečst – have an itchy hand. *suffix:* ***...ečst, ...čst*** *– of the hand.*
nqaupéčst – His/her/its hand was itchy. **čn nqaupéčst kʷ nqaupéčst**
es nqaupéčsti – His/her/its hand is itchy. **čnes nqaupéčsti kʷes nqaupéčsti**
qs nqaupéčsti – His/her/its hand is going to be itchy. **čiqs nqaupéčsti kʷqs nqaupéčsti**

nqaupax̣n – have an itchy arm.
nqaupax̣n – His/her/its arm was itchy. **čn nqaupax̣n kʷ nqaupax̣n**
es nqaupax̣ni – His/her/its arm is itchy. **čnes nqaupax̣ni kʷes nqaupax̣ni**
qs nqaupax̣ni – His/her/its arm is going to be itchy. **čiqs nqaupax̣ni kʷqs nqaupax̣n**

qaupšin – have an itchy foot.
qaupšin – His/her/its foot was itchy. **čn qaupšin kʷ qaupšin**
es qaupšini – His/her/its foot is itchy. **čnes qaupšini kʷes qaupšini**
qs qaupšini – His/her/its foot is going to be itchy. **čiqs qaupšini kʷqs qaupšini**

quqaupšin – have itchy feet.

nqaupups – *literally:* have an itchy butt; *figuratively:* anxious, restless and unable to sit still. *See:* ***anxious.***

J

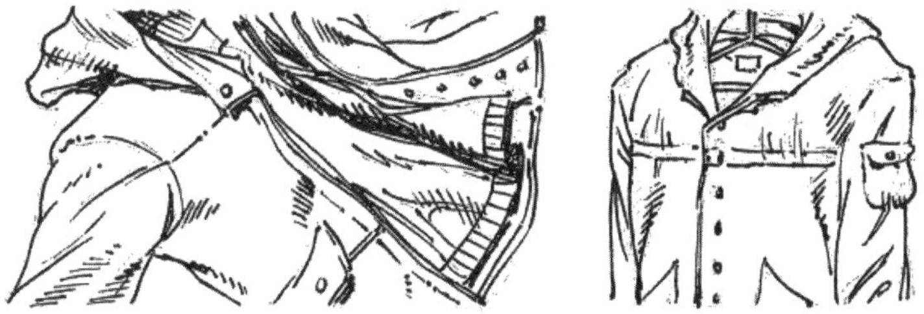

jack **k̓ʷłxʷemin** – jack; car jack.

jacket **čłqal̓tčálqs,** *čłqal̓tčá* – coat; jacket.
lkepu – coat; jacket. *(approximation to French word)*

jail **snlč̓mintn** – place to be tied up; jail. *rt.:* ***lič̓*** *– tied up.*

jam **t̓iš čmiƛ̓mn** – jam; sweet spread.

sṗiqałq čmiƛ̓mn – fruit spread.

January **sčṅčłtu spq̇niʔ** – January *(shaking hands month).*

st̓apsqé spq̇niʔ – January *(shooting month).*

Japanese **čapni** – Japanese.

jar **snṗt̓ṗt̓mán** – jar; a container of soft squishy stuff. *rt.:* ***ṗat̓*** *– s.t. soft/squishy; prefix:* ***sn...*** *– a place of; suffix:* ***...min, ...mn*** *– instrument/tool.*

jaw **k̓ʷiʔépeʔ** – chin; jaw.

jay **qʷásqʷiʔ** – blue jay; Stellar's jay.

lk̓ʷłk̓ʷqi – gray jay; Canada jay; camp robber; whiskey jack; *Perisoreus canadensis*.

snalkʷ – gray jay.

jealous **k̓ʷuxʷs** – jealousy of a partner/spouse; jealous face; look jealous.
k̓ʷuxʷsm – S/he is jealous. **čn k̓ʷuxʷsm, kʷ k̓ʷuxʷsm**
es k̓ʷuxʷsi – S/he is jealous. **čnes k̓ʷuxʷsi, kʷes k̓ʷuxʷsi**
qs k̓ʷuxʷsi – S/he is jealous. **čiqs k̓ʷuxʷsi, kʷqs k̓ʷuxʷsi**

k̓ʷuxʷsemn – one inclined to be jealous. **čn k̓ʷuxʷsemn** *suffix:* ***...emn*** *– one inclined to do.*

k̓ʷuxʷsnmlwi – go around being jealous.

q̇xʷemn – one inclined to be jealous. *suffix:* ***...emn*** *– one inclined to do.*

jerk **ṗat̓oyʔe** – jerk. *rt.:* ***ṗat̓*** *– s.t. soft/squishy. See:* ***pile****.*

čq̇awqn – jerk, dumb, stupid; broken head. *See:* ***dumb****.*

x̣ił exʷ ye ta es k̓ʷłpusncu – S/he was really acting like a jerk.

Jesus Christ **yesukʷli** – Jesus Christ.

s.t. - something, the 3rd person
(s.t.) - something implied
s.o. - someone, the 3rd person
sl. - singular form
pl. - plural form
rt. - root word
cmd. - command
lit. - literally
fig. - figuratively
i.e., - for example
See: - Redirection to a related word.

job **sck̓ʷul̓** – something that's been worked/made/fixed. *prefix:* ***sc...*** *– s.t. that's been done/made/prepared. See:* ***work****.*
snk̓ʷul̓mn – place, to do work/to make/to fix; a work bench; a work place.

Jocko **čxʷtpmnwé** – Jocko Hollow, near Arlee, Flathead Nation.
čcáqʷsšn̓ – lit. rock or tree standing on a rock.
łl̓q̓ʷólexʷ – little clearing.

Jocko Hollow **čxʷtpmnw̓é** – rocky cliffs on both sides.

Jocko Hollow, northwest **čišl̓št̓áqs** – the lower end of a mountain.

Jocko Lake, lower **nisisutétkʷ** – shadows in the water.

Jocko Lake, upper **čłsusuw̓etkʷ** – home of the **usuʔł** (loon). *suffix:* ***...etkʷ, ...tkʷ*** *– liquid*
čłsusuw̓én̓eʔ – something covered with water time to time.

Jocko River **nisisutétkʷ ntx̣ʷe** – Jocko River.

Joe Quequesus Mountain **iʔámsxʷi nmq̓ʷénčs** – Joe Quequesus mountain, in the Mission Mountain Range, Flathead Nation.

John **čon** – John.

Johnny **čoni** – Johnny.

join **t̓ip** – join to make longer; fasten to make longer. *(i.e., sewing, fastening, etc.)*
t̓pntes – S/he joined s.t. to it. **t̓pnten, t̓pntexʷ**
es t̓pims – S/he is joining s.t. to it. **ies t̓pim, as t̓pim**
qs t̓pims – S/he is going to join s.t. to it. **iqs t̓pim, aqs t̓pim**

nt̓psél̓is – join things together; fasten things together. *(i.e., tying ropes together, etc.)*
t̓polqʷltn – shirt collar.

nt̓pséw̓s – fasten something together lengthwise; make an inseparable union. *rt.:* ***t̓ip*** *– join/add to.*
nt̓pséw̓sis – S/he joined the two ends together. **nt̓pséw̓sn, nt̓pséw̓sntxʷ**
es nt̓pséw̓sms – S/he is joining the two ends together. **ies nt̓pséw̓sm, as nt̓pséw̓sm**

es nt̓ppséw̓s – things are joined together. *(i.e., a spine, train cars, etc.)*

snt̓ppséčst – knuckle. *suffix:* ***...ečst, ...čst*** *– of the hand.*

es nt̓ppsew̓s čx̣ʷllq̓ʷa – The train is joined together. **es nt̓pséw̓s łu asččmaqstš l asčmqinšn** – Your leg is joined together at the knee.

nacsél̓is – join/tie two things together. *See:* ***splice****.*

ax̣mew̓s – splice something together; weave ends together. *See:* ***splice****.*

nšt̓st̓sew̓s, *nšt̓st̓se* – horse tail *(something joined together)*. *suffix:* ***...éw̓s*** *– in between, middle.*

čhém – join in with something; get in on something; share in the pursuits of someone; be a part of something.
čhém – S/he joined in. **čn čhém, kʷ čhém**
es čhémi – S/he is joining in. **čnes čhémi, kʷes čhémi**
qs čhémi – S/he is going to join in. **čiqs čhémi, kʷqs čhémi**

čhémis – S/he joined in with s.o. **čhémn, čhémntx^w**
es čhémms – S/he is joining in with s.o. **ies čhémm, as čhémm**

čhémiš – Join in. *cmd.*
čhémnt – Join in with him/her. *cmd.*
cčhémiš – Come join in. *cmd.*
cčhémnt – Come join in with it. *cmd.*

The **i** following uvular consonants (UC) and the glottal stop **ʔ** sound like English "*ey*" as in the words *they, hey, whey*, etc. Salish UC are: **q, q̓, qʷ, q̓ʷ, x̣, x̣ʷ**. For example, the suffix **...qin** – head/top, is often spelled using English *ey* as "q*ey*n". So **qi, q̓i, qʷi, q̓ʷi, x̣i, x̣ʷi**, may be spelled with English *ey* as **q***ey*, **q̓***ey*, **qʷ***ey*, **q̓ʷ***ey*, **x̣***ey*, **x̣ʷ***ey* in other texts.

joke **čposcánm** – tease/joke.
čposcánm – S/he/it joked. **čn čposcánm, kʷ čposcánm**
es čposcáni – S/he/it is joking. **čnes čposcáni, kʷes čposcáni**
čposcáʔanm – They joked. **qeʔ čposcánm, p čposcánm**

es čposcánms – S/he/it is teasing/joking s.o. **ies čposcánm, as čposcánm**
qs čposcánms – S/he/it is going to tease/joke s.o. **iqs čposcánm, aqs čposcánm**

sxʷčposcánm – one tasked to tease/joke. *prefix:* ***sxʷ...*** *– one tasked to do.*
čposcnémn – someone inclined to tease/joke. *suffix:* ***...emn*** *– one inclined to do.*

ha čmi u kʷes poscáni – Are you just joking?

čqʷéwčstmm – play a prank/joke on someone; do something crazy to someone. *suffix:* ***...ečst, ...čst*** *– of the hand.*
čqʷéwčstis – S/he played a joke on s.o. **čqʷéwčstn, čqʷéwčstntxʷ**
es čqʷéwčstmms – S/he is playing a joke on s.o. **ies čqʷéwčstmm, as čqʷéwčstmm**

Joseph **susép, cósep** – Joseph.

Josephine **susét** – Josephine.

jovial **npiyéls,** *npiyé* – feel happy. *circumfix:* ***n...els*** *– want, feel. See:* ***happy****.*

juggle **nttʔečstew̓s** – juggle. *suffix:* ***...ečst, ...čst*** *– of the hand; suffix:* ***...éw̓s*** *– in between, middle.*
nttʔečstew̓s – S/he juggled. **čn nttʔečstew̓s, kʷ nttʔečstew̓s**
es nttʔečstew̓si – S/he is juggling. **čnes nttʔečstew̓si, kʷes nttʔečstew̓si**

nyeuʔusečst – juggle. *rt.:* ***nyeuʔumist*** *– in balance; suffix:* ***...ečst, ...čst*** *– of the hand.*
nyeuʔusečst – S/he juggled. **čn nyeuʔusečst, kʷ nyeuʔusečst**
es nyeuʔusečsti – S/he is juggling. **čnes nyeuʔusečsti, kʷes nyeuʔusečsti**

juice **sk̓ʷłsʔetkʷ** – juice. *suffix:* ***...etkʷ, ...tkʷ*** *– liquid*
sk̓ʷłsóʔo – juice.

čp̓mp̓umsetkʷ – orange juice. *suffix:* ***...etkʷ, ...tkʷ*** *– liquid*
aplsetkʷ – apple juice; cider. *suffix:* ***...etkʷ, ...tkʷ*** *– liquid*
čtekʷétkʷ – grape juice. *suffix:* ***...etkʷ, ...tkʷ*** *– liquid*
nłx̣ʷołx̣ʷetkʷ – cherry juice. *suffix:* ***...etkʷ, ...tkʷ*** *– liquid*
sp̓iqáłqetkʷ – berry juice; fruit juice. *suffix:* ***...etkʷ, ...tkʷ*** *– liquid*
nc̓uykʷ – lemon juice; sour liquid. *suffix:* ***...etkʷ, ...tkʷ*** *– liquid*
sxʷyatkʷ – tomato juice. *suffix:* ***...etkʷ, ...tkʷ*** *– liquid*

s.t. - something, the 3rd person
(s.t.) - something implied
s.o. - someone, the 3rd person
sl. - singular form
pl. - plural form
rt. - root word
cmd. - command
lit. - literally
fig. - figuratively
i.e., - for example
See: - Redirection to a related word.

July **esy̓apqini spq̓niʔ** – July *(month of celebration).*

čuláy – July. *(approximation to English word)*

jump **ntlqpncut** – jump.
ntlqpncut – S/he/it jumped. **čn ntlqpncut, kʷ ntlqpncut**

es ntlqpncuti – S/he/it is jumping. **čnes ntlqpncuti, kʷes ntlqpncuti**
ntlqpncúʔut – They jumped. **qeʔ ntlqpncut, p ntlqpncut**

es ntltlqpncuti – S/he/it is jumping up and down. **čnes ntltlqpncuti, kʷes ntltlqpncuti**

ntlqpncutš – Jump. *cmd.*
nłttlqpncut – do a little jump, hop. *See: **hop**.*

nqƛ̓ip – jump in something. *(i.e., boat, hole, container, etc.)*
nqƛ̓ip – S/he/it jumped in (s.t.). **čn nqƛ̓ip, kʷ nqƛ̓ip**
es nqƛ̓pmi – S/he/it is jumping in (s.t.). **čnes nqƛ̓pmi, kʷes nqƛ̓pmi**

čłqƛ̓ip – jump up onto the surface of something. *(i.e., table, chair, board, etc.)*
čłqƛ̓ip – S/he/it jumped on (s.t.). **čn čłqƛ̓ip, kʷ čłqƛ̓ip**
es čłqƛ̓pmi – S/he/it is jumping on (s.t.). **čnes čłqƛ̓pmi, kʷes čłqƛ̓pmi**

čn čłqƛ̓ip snčłelintn – I jumped on the table.

čqƛ̓pew̓s – jump up onto something. *(i.e., large rock, etc.) suffix: **...éw̓s –** in between, middle.*
čqƛ̓pew̓s – S/he/it jumped on (s.t.). **čn čqƛ̓pew̓s, kʷ čqƛ̓pew̓s**
es čqƛ̓pew̓si – S/he/it is jumping on (s.t.). **čnes čqƛ̓pew̓si, kʷes čqƛ̓pew̓si**

čn čqƛ̓pew̓s l sšeṅš – I jumped up onto the rock.

jump dance

tlqmi – jump dance; jumping. *(This describes the jumping that occurs at jump dances and medicine dances. This dance is held in the wintertime.)*
es tlqmi – S/he is jump dancing. **čnes tlqmi, kʷes tlqmi**

nqwistn, *nqwi* **–** jump dance. *(This describes the action of following people in a circle that occurs at jump dances and medicine dances. This dance is held in the wintertime.) suffix: **...tin, ...tn –** means of/device.*
es nqwistni – S/he is jump dancing.

nx̣asqin – jump dance held anytime of the year.
es nx̣asqini – S/he is jump dancing. **čnes nx̣asqini, kʷes nx̣asqini**

snƛ̓ekʷlšscutn – medicine dance for doctoring. *See: **medicine dance**.*

es qʷásqʷiʔi – become a Blue Jay at a medicine dance. *See: **medicine dance**.*

sxʷk̓ʷłwéʔm – one tasked to repeat what is said in a jump/medicine dance. *prefix: **sxʷ... –** one tasked to do.*

jumpy

kʷʔeł – jumpy, nervous, edgy. *See: **nervous**.*

June

sx̣ʷéʔli spq̇niʔ – June *(month of the camas).*

juneberry

siẏeẏéʔ – juneberry; serviceberry; *Amelanchier alnifolia* var. *alnifolia*.

juniper

punłp – Rocky Mountain juniper; *Juniperus scopulorum*.

ċiqnełp – common juniper; prickly juniper; *Juniperus communis*.

just

put – just, exactly, even, enough; right then.
put – S/he/it is just right. **čn put, kʷ put**

put šeẏ – S/he/it is just right; enough; fine; okay. **put u čis q̇mim t sƛ̓šá –** I just ate a huckleberry. **put u čn itš –** I was just asleep. **ta qeʔqs cxʷuy ṅe ta ps put t sʔiłn –** We will not come if you do not have enough food! **ta es cxʷuy put u čnes nséwcnmi –** She is not coming now that I am proposing. **put u l šeẏ –** Right there. **put u l k̓ʷinš –** What time is it?

K

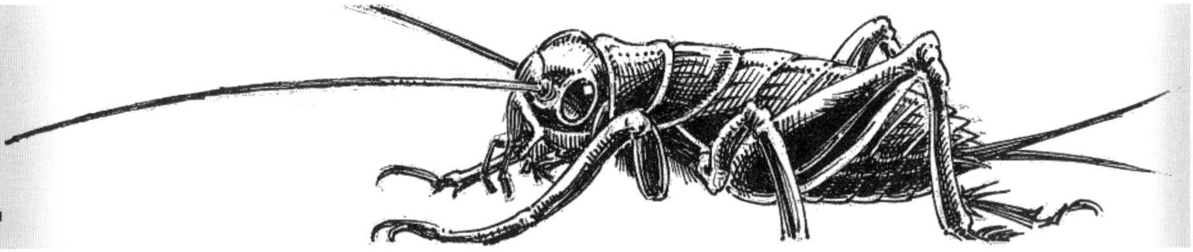

Kalispel **qlispél**, *qlispé* – Kalispel; Lower Pend d'Oreille. *rt.: **qal** – fresh, raw. (Self identification term)*

nqlispélišcn – Kalispel language.

Kalispell **snłaapa** – Kalispell, Montana.

Katy **ketli** – Katy.

katydid **silw̓éneʔ** – cricket.

keep **čšt̓im** – guard; take care of; keep. *See: **guard**.*

ketchup **sxʷya čtxʷcin** – ketchup.

kettle **snčišmn** – teakettle.

key **k̓ʷłnčehk̓ʷéptn**, *k̓ʷłnčehk̓ʷé* – key. *rt.: **čhék̓ʷ** – break free of; circumfix: **k̓ʷłn...ep** – opening; suffix: **...tin, ...tn** – means of/device.*

kick **tl̓qém** – kick.

tl̓qém – S/he/it kicked. **čn tl̓qém, kʷ tl̓qém**
es tl̓qmi – S/he/it is kicking. **čnes tl̓qmi, kʷes tl̓qmi**
qs tl̓qmi – S/he/it is going to kick. **čiqs tl̓qmi, kʷqs tl̓qmi**
tl̓qéʔem – They kicked. **qeʔ tl̓qém, p tl̓qém**
es tl̓qmíʔi – They are kicking. **qeʔes tl̓qmi, pes tl̓qmi**
qs tl̓qmíʔi – They are going to kick. **qeʔqs tl̓qmi, pqs tl̓qmi**

tl̓qntes – S/he/it kicked s.o./s.t. **tl̓qnten, tl̓qntexʷ**
es tl̓qéms – S/he/it is kicking s.o./s.t. **ies tl̓qém, as tl̓qém**
qs tl̓qéms – S/he/it is going to kick s.o./s.t. **iqs tl̓qém, aqs tl̓qém**
tl̓qntéʔes – They kicked s.o./s.t. **qeʔ tl̓qntem, tl̓qntep**
es tl̓qéʔems – They are kicking s.o./s.t. **qeʔes tl̓qém, es tl̓qémp**
qs tl̓qéʔems – They are going to kick s.o./s.t. **qeʔqs tl̓qém, qs tl̓qémp**

tl̓qntém – S/he/it was kicked.

sxʷtl̓qem – one tasked to kick; kicker. *prefix: **sxʷ...** – one tasked to do.*
tl̓qmemn – one inclined to kick. *suffix: **...emn** – one inclined to do.*
tl̓tl̓qmuł – one that habitually kicks. *suffix: **...łmuł** – one that habitually does.*

tl̓qeiš – Kick. *cmd.*
tl̓qent – Kick it. *cmd.*
tl̓qełt – Kick it to somebody. *cmd.*
yoyostl̓qent – Kick it hard. *cmd.*
es tl̓qnwexʷi – They're kicking each other.

s.t. - something, the 3rd person
(s.t.) - something implied
s.o. - someone, the 3rd person
sl. - singular form
pl. - plural form
rt. - root word
cmd. - command
lit. - literally
fig. - figuratively
i.e., - for example
See: - Redirection to a related word.

tl̓qešnm – hit feet against something. *suffix:* ***...šin, ...šn*** *– feet.*
ntl̓qew̓s – kick in the middle. *suffix:* ***...éw̓s*** *– in between, middle.*
čtl̓qqin – kick the head/top. *suffix:* ***...qin, ...qn*** *– top.*
nčtl̓qłniut – kick the head/top. *suffix:* ***...łniut*** *– side.*
ntl̓qepls – kick testicles. *circumfix:* ***n...epls*** *– testicles.*
čtl̓qalqʷ – kick wood/tree. *suffix:* ***...alqʷ*** *– wood; cylindical.*

tl̓qntém łu kʷtisi – Big Blanket got kicked. **tl̓qem sicms –** S/he kicked his/her blanket. **t kʷtisi u tl̓qntés inpus –** Big Blanket kicked my cat. **t swe u tl̓qntes –** Who kicked it? **qʷo tl̓qełt –** Kick it to me.

tl̓qsqélixʷ, *tl̓qsqé* **–** kick a person. *suffix:* ***...sqé, ...sqélixʷ*** *– people.*
tl̓qsqé – S/he/it kicked a person. **čn tl̓qsqé, kʷ tl̓qsqé**
es tl̓qsqé – S/he/it is kicking a person. **čnes tl̓qsqé, kʷes tl̓qsqé**
qs tl̓qsqé – S/he/it is going to kick a person. **čiqs tl̓qsqé, kʷqs tl̓qsqé**

k̓ʷłntl̓qep – kick a door. *circumfix:* ***k̓ʷłn...ep*** *– opening.*
k̓ʷłntl̓qep – S/he kicked the door. **čn k̓ʷłntl̓qep, kʷ k̓ʷłntl̓qep**
es k̓ʷłntl̓qepi – S/he is kicking the door. **čnes k̓ʷłntl̓qepi, kʷes k̓ʷłntl̓qepi**
qs k̓ʷłntl̓qepi – S/he is going to kick the door. **čiqs k̓ʷłntl̓qepi, kʷqs k̓ʷłntl̓qepi**

k̓ʷłntl̓qepis – S/he kicked s.o.'s door. **k̓ʷłntl̓qepn, k̓ʷłntl̓qepntxʷ**
es k̓ʷłntl̓qepms – S/he is kicking s.o.'s door. **ies k̓ʷłntl̓qepm, as k̓ʷłntl̓qepm**
qs k̓ʷłntl̓qepms – S/he is going to kick s.o.'s door. **iqs k̓ʷłntl̓qepm, aqs k̓ʷłntl̓qepm**

es k̓ʷłntl̓tl̓qepi – S/he is repeatedly kicking the door. **čnes k̓ʷłntl̓tl̓qepi, kʷes k̓ʷłntl̓tl̓qepi**

k̓ʷłntl̓qepnt – Kick his/her door. *cmd.*

qeʔ k̓ʷłntl̓tl̓qepłlt – somebody's kicking our door.

ntl̓qups – kick someone in the rear end. *circumfix:* ***n...ups*** *– butt, tail.*
t kʷtisi ntl̓tl̓qupsis – Big Blanket kicked him in the rear end.

meʔminm – chase/drive away someone; kick someone out. *See:* ***chase.***

kidnap

kʷanx̣n – kidnap; grab the arm. *rt.:* ***kʷen*** *– take; suffix:* ***...ax̣n*** *– arm.*
kʷanx̣is – S/he kidnapped s.t. **kʷanx̣n, kʷanx̣ntxʷ**
es kʷanx̣nms – S/he is kidnapping s.t. **ies kʷanx̣nm, as kʷanx̣nm**
qs kʷanx̣nms – S/he is going to kidnap s.t. **iqs kʷanx̣nm, aqs kʷanx̣nm**
kʷáʔanx̣is – They kidnapped s.t. **qeʔ kʷanx̣ntm, kʷanx̣ntp**
es kʷáʔanx̣nms – They are kidnapping s.t. **qeʔes kʷanx̣nm, es kʷanx̣nmp**
qs kʷáʔanx̣nms – They are going to kidnap s.t. **qeʔqs kʷanx̣nm, qs kʷanx̣nmp**

sckʷanx̣n – kidnapped prisoner. *prefix:* ***sc...*** *– s.t. that's been done/made/prepared.*
kʷanx̣nemn – one inclined to kidnap. *suffix:* ***...emn*** *– one inclined to do.*

qʷo kʷanx̣ntxʷ – You kidnapped me. **qʷo kʷanx̣ntm –** I got kidnapped. **t šmén̓ qʷo kʷanx̣ntm –** The enemy captured me.

kidney

mt̓ós – kidney. **mt̓mt̓ós –** kidneys. *pl.*

kids

skʷk̓ʷim̓lt – young; child.
sccm̓élt – children.

sxʷsixʷlt – offspring; children.
sxʷsixʷlts – Your children. **isxʷsixʷlt, asxʷsixʷlt**
sxʷsíʔixʷlts – Their children. **qesxʷsixʷlt, sxʷsixʷltmp**

kill **puls –** kill.

pulsm – S/he/it killed. **čn pulsm, kʷ pulsm**
es pulsi – S/he/it is killing. **čnes pulsi, kʷes pulsi**
qs pulsi – S/he/it is going to kill. **čiqs pulsi, kʷqs pulsi**
púʔulsm – They killed. **qeʔ pulsm, p pulsm**
es púʔulsi – They are killing. **qeʔes pulsi, pes pulsi**
qs púʔulsi – They are going to kill. **qeʔqs pulsi, pqs pulsi**

pulsts – S/he/it killed s.t./s.o. **pulstn, pulstxʷ**
es pulsms – S/he/it is killing s.t./s.o. **ies pulsm, as pulsm**
qs pulsms – S/he/it is going to kill s.t./s.o. **iqs pulsm, aqs pulsm**
púʔulsts – They killed s.t./s.o. **qeʔ pulstm, pulstp**
es púʔulsms – They are killing s.t./s.o. **qeʔes pulsm, es pulsmp**
qs púʔulsms – They are going to kill s.t./s.o. **qeʔqs pulsm, qs pulsmp**

pulstm – S/he/it was killed.

sxʷpuls – one tasked to kill. *prefix:* ***sxʷ...*** *– one tasked to do.*
scpuls – something that's been killed. *prefix: sc... – s.t. that's been done/made/prepared.*
sxʷplstwé – warrior; soldier. *prefix:* ***sxʷ...*** *– one tasked to do.*

pulsiš – Kill. *cmd.*
es plstwéxʷi – They are killing each other.

čn pulsm t tšeċ – I killed the elk. **pulstn tšeċ –** I killed the elk. **qʷo pulłtm iskʷiskʷs –** Somebody killed my chickens. **pulstmt –** You got killed. **x̣iṅe pulstm t sxʷk̓ʷl̓sncutn –** S/he/it might get killed by the cook. **steṁ łu ascpuls –** What did you kill?

plsqélixʷ, *plsqé* **–** killed a person. *rt.:* ***puls*** *– kill; suffix:* ***...sqe, ...sqelixʷ*** *– people.*
plsqélixʷ – S/he/it killed s.o. **čn plsqélixʷ, kʷ plsqélixʷ**
es plsqélixʷi – S/he/it is killing s.o. **čnes plsqélixʷi, kʷes plsqélixʷi**
qs plsqélixʷi – S/he/it is going to kill s.o. **čiqs plsqélixʷi, kʷqs plsqélixʷi**

plsqax̣eʔ, *plsqa* **–** killed domestic animal. *rt.:* ***puls*** *– kill; suffix:* ***...sqe, ...sqelixʷ*** *– people.*
plsqax̣eʔ – S/he/it killed the animal. **čn plsqax̣eʔ, kʷ plsqax̣eʔ**
es plsqax̣eʔi – S/he/it is killing the animal. **čnes plsqax̣eʔi, kʷes plsqax̣eʔi**
qs plsqax̣eʔi – S/he/it is going to kill the animal. **čiqs plsqax̣eʔi, kʷqs plsqax̣eʔi**

pulsta – kill big animals.

qʷmim – kill more than one at a time; killing them all off.
qʷmntes – S/he/it killed them. **qʷmnten, qʷmntexʷ**
es qʷmims – S/he/it is killing them. **ies qʷmim, as qʷmim**
qs qʷmims – S/he/it is going to kill them. **iqs qʷmim, aqs qʷmim**
qʷmntéʔes – They killed them. **qeʔ qʷmntem, qʷmntep**
es qʷmíʔims – They are killing them. **qeʔes qʷmim, es qʷmimp**
qs qʷmíʔims – They are going to kill them. **qeʔqs qʷmim, qs qʷmimp**

es qʷmqʷmims – S/he/it is killing groups at a time. **ies qʷmqʷmim, as qʷmqʷmim**

qʷmqʷmntéʔem – They were all killed off.

qʷmip – more than one dies. *See:* ***die.***

ha es qʷmims t snčl̓é askʷiskʷs – Was the coyote killing your chickens? **ha t snčl̓é u es qʷmims –** Was the coyote killing them?

čxʷełċeʔ, *čxʷe* **–** get/kill many animals for the meat they provide *(for the purpose of eating).*

The **i** following uvular consonants (UC) and the glottal stop **ʔ** sound like English "*ey*" as in the words th*ey*, h*ey*, wh*ey*, etc. Salish UC are: **q, q̇, qʷ, q̇ʷ, x̣, x̣ʷ**. For example, the suffix ...**qin** – head/top, is often spelled using English *ey* as "q*ey*n". So **qi, q̇i, qʷi, q̇ʷi, x̣i, x̣ʷi**, may be spelled with English *ey* as **q***ey*, **q̇***ey*, **qʷ***ey*, **q̇ʷ***ey*, **x̣***ey*, **x̣ʷ***ey* in other texts.

s.t. - something, the 3rd person
(s.t.) - something implied
s.o. - someone, the 3rd person
sl. - singular form
pl. - plural form
rt. - root word
cmd. - command
lit. - literally
fig. - figuratively
i.e., - for example
See: - Redirection to a related word.

čxʷełċeʔ – S/he got/killed many. **čn čxʷełċeʔ, kʷ čxʷełċeʔ**

čnk̓ʷełċeʔ, *čnk̓ʷe* – get/kill fish, birds, big animals for the meat they provide *(for the purpose of eating).*
čnk̓ʷełċeʔ – S/he got/killed one. **čn čnk̓ʷełċeʔ, kʷ čnk̓ʷełċeʔ**

čn čnk̓ʷe t qałqłċeʔ – I killed a grouse.

čsleł ċeʔ, *čsle* – get/kill two animals for the meat they provide *(for the purpose of eating).*
čsleł ċeʔ – S/he got/killed two. **čn čsleł ċeʔ, kʷ čsleł ċeʔ**

čn čsle t x̣małtn – I killed two flies.

ččełleł ċeʔ, *ččełle* – get/kill three animals for the meat they provide *(for the purpose of eating).*
ččełleł ċeʔ – S/he got/killed three. **čn ččełleł ċeʔ, kʷ ččełleł ċeʔ**

t̓at̓apṁi – hunt/kill with small arms.
es t̓at̓apṁi – killing small animals.

čnes t̓apṁi łu t słqʷa – I am killing a rabbit.

nċspulexʷ – massacre; wiped out from the land. *See: **massacre.***

killdeer

stiitšn – killdeer; *Charadrius vociferus.*

ƛ̓leẏeʔ – play dead. *See: **die.***

ƛ̓lƛ̓llmist – making one's self still; play dead. *See: **die.***

kind

nqʷṅqʷṅéls – pity; be a kind person. *rt.: **q̓ʷnq̓ʷint** – pity; circumfix: **n...els** – want, feel.*
nqʷṅqʷṅéls – S/he/it was kind. **čn nqʷṅqʷṅéls, kʷ nqʷṅqʷṅéls**
es nqʷṅqʷṅélsi – S/he/it is being kind. **čnes nqʷṅqʷṅélsi, kʷes nqʷṅqʷṅélsi**
qs nqʷṅqʷṅélsi – S/he/it is going to be kind. **čiqs nqʷṅqʷṅélsi, kʷqs nqʷṅqʷṅélsi**
nqʷṅqʷṅéʔels – They were kind. **qeʔ nqʷṅqʷṅéls, p nqʷṅqʷṅéls**
es nqʷṅqʷṅéʔelsi – They are being kind. **qeʔes nqʷṅqʷṅélsi, pes nqʷṅqʷṅélsi**
qs nqʷṅqʷṅéʔelsi – They are going to be kind. **qeʔqs nqʷṅqʷṅélsi, pqs nqʷṅqʷṅélsi**

nqʷṅqʷṅélsis – S/he/it was kind to s.o. **nqʷṅqʷṅélsn, nqʷṅqʷṅélsntxʷ**
es nqʷṅqʷṅélsms – S/he/it is being kind to s.o. **ies nqʷṅqʷṅélsm, as nqʷṅqʷṅélsm**
qs nqʷṅqʷṅélsi – S/he/it is going to be kind to s.o. **iqs nqʷṅqʷṅélsm, aqs nqʷṅqʷṅélsm**
nqʷṅqʷṅéʔelsis – They were kind to s.o. **qeʔ nqʷṅqʷṅélsntm, nqʷṅqʷṅélsntp**
es nqʷṅqʷṅéʔelsms – They are being kind to s.o. **qeʔes nqʷṅqʷṅélsm, es nqʷṅqʷṅélsmp**
qs nqʷṅqʷṅéʔelsms – They are going to be kind to s.o. **qeʔqs nqʷṅqʷṅélsm, qs nqʷṅqʷṅélsmp**

x̣est – good; kind; nice.

t čeṅ eċx̣i – How is; what kind? *See: **how.***
t čeṅ eċx̣i u sust – What kind did s/he/it drink? **t čeṅ eċx̣i u kʷes nstetkʷi** – What kind do you want to drink?

eċšččéṅ – question inquiring about the state of someone or something. *See: **happen.***
eċščnulexʷi – What kind of land? *rt. **eċščen** – how is it?; suffix: **...asq̓t** – sky, day.*
eċščnełxʷi – What color/kind is the house/lodge? *rt. **eċščen** – how is it?; suffix: **...etxʷ, ...łxʷ** – house.*
eċščnelxʷi – What color/kind is the fur? *rt. **eċščen** – how is it?; suffix: **...elxʷ, ...lxʷ** – skin/hide.*
eċščnalqsi – What color/kind of clothing/shirt? *rt. **eċščen** – how is it?; suffix: **...lqs, ...alqs** – clothes.*
eċščnusi – What kind of face? *rt. **eċščen** – how is it?; suffix: **...us** – face, fire.*

n...aqsm – *circumfix indicating the kind/kinds.*

nḱʷaqsm – one kind. **naslaqsm** – two kinds. **nčałlaqsm** – three kinds. **nmosqsm** – four kinds. **nclčstaqsm** – five kinds. **nt́q̇nčstaqsm** – six kinds. **nsṗlčstaqsm** – seven kinds. **nhanmaqsm** – eight kinds. **nx̣ntaqsm** – nine kinds. **nʔopnčstaqsm** – ten kinds.

nḱʷnšaqsm – How many kinds?
t čeṅ u eċx̣laqsm – How is/are the thing(s)?
nxʷʔaqsm – many kinds.
nkʷtnaqsm, *nkʷtna* – expensive; costs a large amount; something of great value. *See:* ***expensive***.
nłkʷḱʷiṁáqsm, *nłkʷḱʷiṁá* – cheap; inexpensive; thing of little value.
nšƛ̓aqsm, *nšƛ̓a* – many things not the same; many things one after another. *See:* ***all kinds***.

> The **i** following uvular consonants (UC) and the glottal stop **ʔ** sound like English "*ey*" as in the words th*ey*, h*ey*, wh*ey*, etc. Salish UC are: **q**, **q̇**, **qʷ**, **q̇ʷ**, **x̣**, **x̣ʷ**. For example, the suffix …**qin** – head/top, is often spelled using English *ey* as "q*ey*n". So **qi**, **q̇i**, **qʷi**, **q̇ʷi**, **x̣i**, **x̣ʷi**, may be spelled with English *ey* as **q***ey*, **q̇***ey*, **qʷ***ey*, **q̇ʷ***ey*, **x̣***ey*, **x̣ʷ***ey* in other texts.

kingbird

sččáteʔ, *sččá* – western kingbird; *Tyrannus verticalis. (black and white)*
słččáteʔ – small western kingbird.

kingfisher

ċális – belted kingfisher; *Megaceryle alcyon.*

kinnikinnick

skʷlis – kinnikinnick berries; *Arctostaphylos uva-ursi.*
skʷlsełp, *skʷlse* – kinnikinnick plant; *Arctostaphylos uva-ursi.*

kiss

t́mam – kiss something; place lips on something.
t́mam – S/he is kissed. **čn t́mam, kʷ t́mam**
es t́mma – S/he is kissing. **čnes t́mma, kʷes t́mma**
qs t́mma – S/he is going to kiss. **čiqs t́mma, kʷqs t́mma**

t́mstas – S/he kissed s.t. **t́mstan, t́mstaxʷ**
es t́mams – S/he is kissing s.t. **ies t́mams, as t́mams**
qs t́mams – S/he is going to kiss s.t. **iqs t́mams, aqs t́mams**

snt́mcan – kiss.

t́mant – Kiss s.t. *cmd.*
nt́mcnwaxʷ – kiss each other. **qeʔ nt́mcnwaxʷ, p nt́mcnwaxʷ**

nt́aṁcánm – kiss on the lips.
nt́aṁcánm – S/he kissed. **čn nt́aṁcánm, kʷ nt́aṁcánm**
es nt́aṁcáni – S/he is kissing. **čnes nt́aṁcáni, kʷes nt́aṁcáni**
qs nt́aṁcáni – S/he is going to kiss. **čiqs nt́aṁcáni, kʷqs nt́aṁcáni**
nt́aṁcáʔanm – They kissed. **qeʔ nt́aṁcánm, p nt́aṁcánm**
es nt́aṁcáʔani – They are kissing. **qeʔes nt́aṁcáni, pes nt́aṁcáni**
qs nt́aṁcáʔani – They are going to kiss. **qeʔqs nt́aṁcáni, pqs nt́aṁcáni**

nt́aṁcais – S/he kissed s.o. **nt́aṁcan, ntaṁcantxʷ**
es nt́aṁcánms – S/he is kissing s.o. **ies nt́aṁcánm, as nt́aṁcánm**
qs nt́aṁcánms – S/he is going to kiss s.o. **iqs nt́aṁcánm, aqs nt́aṁcánm**
nt́aṁcáʔais – They kissed s.o. **qeʔ nt́aṁcantm, ntaṁcantp**
es nt́aṁcáʔanms – They are kissing s.o. **qeʔes nt́aṁcánm, es nt́aṁcánmp**
qs nt́aṁcáʔanms – They are going to kiss s.o. **qeʔqs nt́aṁcánm, qs nt́aṁcánmp**

nt́aṁcant – Kiss s.o. *cmd.*
es nt́aṁcnwaxʷi – They're kissing each other.

> s.t. - something, the 3rd person
> (s.t.) - something implied
> s.o. - someone, the 3rd person
> *sl.* - singular form
> *pl.* - plural form
> *rt.* - root word
> *cmd.* - command
> *lit.* - literally
> *fig.* - figuratively
> *i.e.,* - for example
> *See:* - Redirection to a related word.

qʷo nt́aṁcánt – Kiss me. **t mali qʷo nt́aṁcanis** – Mary kissed me. **ha iše nt́aṁcantxʷ łu annox̣ʷnx̣ʷ** – Do you kiss your wife?

k̓ʷłt̓mosm – kiss on the cheek.
k̓ʷłt̓mosis – S/he kissed s.o.'s cheek. **k̓ʷłt̓mosn, k̓ʷłt̓mosntxʷ**
es k̓ʷłt̓mosms – S/he is kissing s.o.'s cheek. **ies k̓ʷłt̓mosm, as k̓ʷłt̓mosm**
qs k̓ʷłt̓mosms – S/he is going to kiss s.o.'s cheek. **iqs k̓ʷłt̓mosm, aqs k̓ʷłt̓mosm**
k̓ʷłt̓móˀosis – They kissed s.o.'s cheek. **qeˀ k̓ʷłt̓mosntm, k̓ʷłt̓mosntp**

k̓ʷłt̓mosiš – Kiss the cheek. *cmd.*
k̓ʷłt̓mosnt – Kiss s.o.'s cheek. *cmd.*

qʷo k̓ʷłt̓mosnt – Kiss my cheek.

čt̓messnm – kiss on the forehead.
čt̓messnmis – S/he kissed s.o.'s forehead. **čt̓messnmn, čt̓messnmntxʷ**
es čt̓messnms – S/he is kissing s.o.'s forehead. **ies čt̓messnm, as čt̓messnm**
qs čt̓messnms – S/he is going to kiss s.o.'s forehead. **iqs čt̓messnm, aqs čt̓messnm**
čt̓messnmis – They kissed s.o.'s forehead. **qeˀ čt̓messnmntm, čt̓messnmntp**

čt̓messniš – Kiss the forehead. *cmd.*
čt̓messnmnt – Kiss s.o.'s forehead. *cmd.*

qʷo čt̓messnmnt – Kiss my forehead.

čt̓malpsm – kiss on the neck.
čt̓malpsis – S/he kissed s.o.'s neck. **čt̓malpsn, čt̓malpsntxʷ**
es čt̓malpsms – S/he is kissing s.o.'s neck. **ies čt̓malpsm, as čt̓malpsm**
qs čt̓malpsms – S/he is going to kiss s.o.'s neck. **iqs čt̓malpsm, aqs čt̓malpsm**
čt̓máˀalpsis – They kissed s.o.'s neck. **qeˀ čt̓malpsntm, čt̓malpsntp**

čt̓malpsiš – Kiss the neck. *cmd.*
čt̓malpsnt – Kiss s.o.'s neck. *cmd.*

qʷo čt̓malpsnt – Kiss my neck.

t̓mačst – kiss on the hand. *suffix:* ***...ečst, ...čst*** *– of the hand.*
t̓mačsis – S/he kissed s.o.'s hand. **t̓mačsn, t̓mačstntxʷ**
es t̓mačsms – S/he is kissing s.o.'s hand. **ies t̓mačstm, as t̓mačsm**
qs t̓mačsms – S/he is going to kiss s.o.'s hand. **iqs t̓mačsm, aqs t̓mačsm**
t̓máˀačsis – They kissed s.o.'s hand. **qeˀ t̓mačsntm, t̓mačsntp**

t̓mačsiš – Kiss the hand. *cmd.*
t̓mačsnt – Kiss s.o.'s hand. *cmd.*

qʷo t̓mačsnt – Kiss my hand.

t̓mawsm – kiss on the belly.
t̓mawsis – S/he kissed s.o.'s belly. **t̓mawsn, t̓mawsntxʷ**
es t̓mawsms – S/he is kissing s.o.'s belly. **ies t̓mawsm, as t̓mawsm**
qs t̓mawsms – S/he is going to kiss s.o.'s belly. **iqs t̓mawsm, aqs t̓mawsm**
t̓máˀawsis – They kissed s.o.'s belly. **qeˀ t̓mawsntm, t̓mawsntp**

t̓mawsiš – Kiss the belly. *cmd.*
t̓mawsnt – Kiss s.o.'s belly. *cmd.*

qʷo t̓mawsnt – Kiss my belly.

nt̓mačn̓m – kiss on the back.
nt̓mačn̓mis – S/he kissed s.o.'s back. **nt̓mačn̓mn, nt̓mačn̓mntxʷ**
es nt̓mačn̓ms – S/he is kissing s.o.'s back. **ies nt̓mačn̓m, as nt̓mačn̓m**

qs nt̓mačn̓ms – S/he is going to kiss s.o.'s back. **iqs nt̓mačn̓m, aqs nt̓mačn̓m**
nt̓máʔačn̓mis – They kissed s.o.'s back. **qeʔ nt̓mačn̓mntm, nt̓mačn̓mntp**

nt̓mačn̓iš – Kiss the back. *cmd.*
nt̓mačn̓mnt – Kiss s.o.'s back. *cmd.*

qʷo nt̓mačn̓mnt – Kiss my back.

čt̓maqstšnm – kiss on the leg. *suffix: **...aqstšn** – leg.*
čt̓maqstšnmis – S/he kissed s.o.'s leg. **čt̓maqstšnmn, čt̓maqstšnmntxʷ**
es čt̓maqstšnms – S/he is kissing s.o.'s leg. **ies čt̓maqstšnm, as čt̓maqstšnm**
qs čt̓maqstšnms – S/he is going to kiss s.o.'s leg. **iqs čt̓maqstšnm, aqs čt̓maqstšnm**
čt̓máʔaqstšnmis – They kissed s.o.'s leg. **qeʔ čt̓maqstšnmntm, čt̓maqstšnmntp**

čt̓maqstšniš – Kiss the leg. *cmd.*
čt̓maqstšnmnt – Kiss s.o.'s leg. *cmd.*

qʷo čt̓maqstšnmnt – Kiss my leg.

The **i** following uvular consonants (UC) and the glottal stop ʔ sound like English "*ey*" as in the words *they, hey, whey*, etc. Salish UC are: **q, q̓, qʷ, q̓ʷ, x̣, x̣ʷ**. For example, the suffix **...qin** – head/top, is often spelled using English *ey* as "q*ey*n". So **qi, q̓i, qʷi, q̓ʷi, x̣i, x̣ʷi**, may be spelled with English *ey* as **q***ey*, **q̓***ey*, **qʷ***ey*, **q̓ʷ***ey*, **x̣***ey*, **x̣ʷ***ey* in other texts.

čt̓mšinm – kiss on the foot.
čt̓mšinmis – S/he kissed s.o.'s foot. **čt̓mšinmn, čt̓mšinmntxʷ**
es čt̓mšinms – S/he is kissing s.o.'s foot. **ies čt̓mšinm, as čt̓mšinm**
qs čt̓mšinms – S/he is going to kiss s.o.'s foot. **iqs čt̓mšinm, aqs čt̓mšinm**
čt̓maʔšinmis – They kissed s.o.'s foot. **qeʔ čt̓mšinmntm, čt̓mšinmntp**

čt̓mšiniš – Kiss the foot. *cmd.*
čt̓mšinmnt – Kiss s.o.'s foot. *cmd.*

qʷo čt̓mšinmnt – Kiss my foot.

t̓molexʷm – kiss the ground.
t̓molexʷm – S/he/it kissed the ground. **čn t̓molexʷm, kʷ t̓molexʷm**
es t̓molexʷi – S/he/it is kissing the ground. **čnes t̓molexʷi, kʷes t̓molexʷi**
qs t̓molexʷi – S/he/it is going to kiss the ground. **čiqs t̓molexʷi, kʷqs t̓molexʷi**
t̓moléʔexʷm – They kissed the ground. **qeʔ t̓molexʷm, p t̓molexʷm**

kitchen

snk̓ʷl̓sncutn, *snk̓ʷl̓sncu* – place to cook; kitchen, range, cooking stove. *prefix: **sn...** – a place of; suffix: **...tin, ...tn** – means of/device.*

kite

čaceplé t t̓uxʷtn – kite. *lit. tied flyer.*

kitten tails

čečłu – red bessya, kitten tails, red kitten tails; *Synthyris canbyi*.

kleenex

snnostn – anything used to blow your nose; a snot device. *prefix: **sn...** – a place of; suffix: **...tin, ...tn** – means of/device.*

snosmn – Anything used to blow your nose; a snot instrument. *prefix: **sn...** – a place of.*

nosiš – Blow your nose. *See: **snot**.*

nʔap̓aqstn – nose wiper; anything used to wipe the nose. *rt.: **ep̓m** – wipe; suffix: **...tin, ...tn** – means of/device.*

s.t. - something, the 3rd person
(s.t.) - something implied
s.o. - someone, the 3rd person
sl. - singular form
pl. - plural form
rt. - root word
cmd. - command
lit. - literally
fig. - figuratively
i.e., - for example
See: - Redirection to a related word.

knee

sčmqinšn, *sčmqin* – knee. *rt.: **čm** – extremity.*
sčmew̓sšn – back of knee.

malkʷew̓šn – disjointed/dislocated knee.
es malkʷew̓šn – His/her knee is disjointed/dislocated. **čnes malkʷew̓šn, kʷes malkʷew̓šn**

malkʷeẁšis – S/he/it disjointed/dislocated s.o.'s knee. **malkʷeẁšn, malkʷeẁšntxʷ**
es malkʷeẁšnms – S/he/it is disjointing/dislocating s.o.'s knee. **ies malkʷeẁšnm, as malkʷeẁšnm**
qs malkʷeẁšnms – S/he/it is going to disjoint/dislocate s.o.'s knee. **iqs malkʷeẁšnm, aqs malkʷeẁšnm**

kneel

nčlxʷépšn, *nčlxʷé* – kneel.
nčlxʷepšn – S/he/it knelt. **čn nčlxʷepšn, kʷ nčlxʷepšn**
es nčlxʷepšni – S/he/it is kneeling. **čnes nčlxʷepšni, kʷes nčlxʷepšni**
qs nčlxʷepšni – S/he/it is going to kneel. **čiqs nčlxʷepšni, kʷqs nčlxʷepšni**

snčlxʷé – kneeler *(as in a church).*

nčlxʷepšniš – Kneel. *cmd.*
nčlxʷepšnwi – All of you kneel. *cmd.*
nčlčlxʷepšnwi – Each one of you kneel. *cmd.*

knife

łṅinč, *łṅi* – knife. **łṅłṅinč,** *łṅłṅi* – knives. *pl.*
skʷtiłłṅinč, *skʷtiłłṅi* – big knife.
x̣ʷċmin łṅi – hunting knife.
sx̣ʷċim – hunting knife.

čxʷmin – tool with handle and with serrated edge on the bottom *(for cutting meat off a hide).*

čl̓olopálqʷ, *čl̓olopá* – pocketknife.

x̣tx̣itne – dagger, knife.

sṅṅi – sheath. *(for a knife)*

knock

k̓ʷłncucuẁép, *k̓ʷłncucuẁé* – knock on a door. *circumfix:* ***k̓ʷłn...ep*** *– opening.*
k̓ʷłncucuẁép – S/he knocked. **čn k̓ʷłncucuẁép, kʷ k̓ʷłncucuẁép**
es k̓ʷłncucuẁépi – S/he is knocking. **čnes k̓ʷłncucuẁépi, kʷes k̓ʷłncucuẁépi**
qs k̓ʷłncucuẁépi – S/he is going to knock. **čiqs k̓ʷłncucuẁépi, kʷqs k̓ʷłncucuẁépi**
k̓ʷłncucuẁéʔep – They knocked. **qeʔ k̓ʷłncucuẁép, p k̓ʷłncucuẁép**
es k̓ʷłncucuẁéʔepi – They are knocking. **qeʔes k̓ʷłncucuẁépi, pes k̓ʷłncucuẁépi**
qs k̓ʷłncucuẁéʔepi – They are going to knock. **qeʔqs k̓ʷłncucuẁépi, pqs k̓ʷłncucuẁépi**

epł es k̓ʷłncucuẁé – somebody is knocking at the door.

cułteł – knocked once. *See:* ***hit.***

knock out

npṁpqan – get knocked out; to be out of the head.
es npṁpqan – S/he is knocked out. **čnes npṁpqan, kʷes npṁpqan**

npṁpqais – S/he knocked out s.o. **npṁpqan, npṁpqantxʷ**
es npṁpqanms – S/he is knocking out s.o. **ies npṁpqanm, as npṁpqanm**
qs npṁpqanms – S/he is going to knock out s.o. **iqs npṁpqanm, aqs npṁpqanm**

qʷo npṁpqantm – I got knocked out.

knot

acséẁs – make a knot. *rt.:* ***ac*** *– bind, tie, trap.*
acséẁsm – S/he made a knot. **čn acséẁsm, kʷ acséẁsm**
es acséẁsi – S/he is making a knot. **čnes acséẁsi, kʷes acséẁsi**
qs acséẁsi – S/he is going to make a knot. **čiqs acséẁsi, kʷqs acséẁsi**

acselism – S/he made knots. **čn acselism, kʷ acselism**
es acselisi – S/he is making knots. **čnes acselisi, kʷes acselisi**

qs acselisi – S/he is going to make knots. **čiqs acselisi, kʷqs acselisi**

acséẇsis – S/he tied them together in a knot. **acséẇsn, acséẇsntxʷ**
es acséẇsms – S/he is tying them together in a knot. **ies acséẇsm, as acséẇsm**
qs acséẇsms – S/he is going to tie them together in a knot. **iqs acséẇsm, aqs acséẇsm**

The **i** following uvular consonants (UC) and the glottal stop **ʔ** sound like English "*ey*" as in the words th*ey*, h*ey*, wh*ey*, etc. Salish UC are: **q**, **q̇**, **qʷ**, **q̇ʷ**, **x̣**, **x̣ʷ**. For example, the suffix ...**qin** – head/top, is often spelled using English *ey* as "q*ey*n". So **qi**, **q̇i**, **qʷi**, **q̇ʷi**, **x̣i**, **x̣ʷi**, may be spelled with English *ey* as **q***ey*, **q̇***ey*, **qʷ***ey*, **q̇ʷ***ey*, **x̣***ey*, **x̣ʷ***ey* in other texts.

snacséẇs – knot.
snacselis – knots.

acséẇsiš – Make a knot. *cmd.*
acséẇsnt – Tie them together in a knot. *cmd.*

know

mi – fact; knowing; reality; certainty.
i mi – It is plainly evident; it is absolute; it is fact. *See: **absolute**.*
es mi – It is certain; it is fact.
miíp – It became known. *See: **learn**.*

es mistes – S/he/it knows s.t. **es misten, es mistéxʷ**
es mistéʔes – They know s.t. **qeʔes mistém, es mistép**

es t mistén – I already knew it.

ha es mistéxʷ u es ṫipeysi – Do you know it's raining? **ta es misten łu skʷests** – I do not know his/her name. **ta es mistén** – I do not know. **ha es mistéxʷ** – Do you know?

nmiels – want to know. *suffix: **n...els** – want, feel.*
nmielsm – S/he wanted to know. **čn nmielsm, kʷ nmielsm**
es nmielsi – S/he is wanting to know. **čnes nmielsi, kʷes nmielsi**
qs nmielsi – S/he is going to want to know. **čiqs nmielsi, kʷqs nmielsi**

nmielsmis – S/he wanted to know s.t. **nmielsmn, nmielsmntxʷ**
es nmielsms – S/he is wanting to know s.t. **ies nmielsm, as nmielsm**
qs nmielsms – S/he is going to want to know s.t. **iqs nmielsm, aqs nmielsm**

mielsm – S/he thought s/he knew. **čn mielsm, kʷ mielsm**
es mielsi – S/he is thinking s/he knows. **čnes mielsi, kʷes mielsi**
qs mielsi – S/he is going to think s/he knows. **čiqs mielsi, kʷqs mielsi**

mielsmis – S/he thought s/he knew s.t. **mielsmn, mielsmntxʷ**
es mielsms – S/he is thinking s/he knows s.t. **ies mielsm, asnmielsm**
qs mielsms – S/he is going to think s/he knows s.t. **iqs mielsm, aqs mielsm**

es nmilsmisti – S/he knows his/her self. **čnes nmilsmisti, kʷes nmilsmisti**

miulexʷ – know a place or area. *suffix: **...ulexʷ** – land.*
es miulexʷsts – S/he/it knows the place. **es miulexʷstn, es miulexʷstxʷ**
es miuléʔexʷsts – They know the place. **qeʔes miulexʷstm, es miulexʷstmp**

ta es miulexʷstn – I do not know that place. **es mimiulexʷstn** – I know those places. **ha es miulexʷstxʷ** – Do you know that place?

s.t. - something, the 3rd person
(s.t.) - something implied
s.o. - someone, the 3rd person
sl. - singular form
pl. - plural form
rt. - root word
cmd. - command
lit. - literally
fig. - figuratively
i.e., - for example
See: - Redirection to a related word.

miełxʷ – know location of someone's home/house. *suffix: **...etxʷ, ...łxʷ** – house.*
es miełxʷsts – S/he/it knows the location of s.o.'s home. **es miełxʷstn, es miełxʷstxʷ**
es miuléʔexʷsts – They know the location of s.o.'s home. **qeʔes miełxʷstm, es miełxʷstmp**

ha es miełxʷstxʷ – Do you know where his/her house is? **ta es miełxʷstn** – I do not know that place. **es mimiełxʷstn** – I know the location of their homes.

nmiaqs – know a road/way. *circumfix:* ***n...aqs*** *– nose, road, pointed.*
nmiaqsis – S/he/it knew that road. **nmiaqsn, nmiaqsntxʷ**
es nmiaqsms – S/he/it knows that road. **ies miulexʷm, as nmiaqsm**

sxʷnmiaqsm – one charged with knowing a road; guide. *prefix:* ***sxʷ...*** *– one tasked to do.*

čsnnmiep – know about something; aware of something. *(of something far-off)*
es čsnnmiepsts – S/he knows about it. **es čsnnmiepstn, es čsnnmiepstxʷ**
es čsnnmiéˀepstms – They know about it. **qeˀes čsnnmiepstm, es čsnnmiepstm**

es t čsnnmiepstn – I already knew it *(definitely knew it)*.

ha kʷ ep sčsnnmiep ṅe čupcin – Do you have knowledge/an idea of when s/he will be quiet?

miscut, *miscu* – know of one's self; aware; conscious. *(something in the immediate area)*
es miscut – S/he knows one's self. **čnes miscut, kʷes miscut**
es miscúˀut – They know about one's self. **qeˀes miscut, pes miscut**

ta es miscut – S/he is unaware.

es t miscut – S/he had prior awareness. **čnes t miscut, kʷes t miscut**
es t miscúˀut – They knew it.

mipnunm – figure out something; find out about something; complete an understanding; succeed in understanding; learn of something. *See:* ***learn.***

suxʷ – know; recognize; acquainted with. *See:* ***recognize.***
es suxʷsts – S/he knows him/her. **es suxʷstn, es suxʷstxʷ**
es súˀuxʷsts – They know him/her. **qeˀes suxʷstm, es suxʷstp**

ta es suxʷstn – I do not know him/her. **ta es sxʷsuxʷstn** – I do not know them. **ha es sxʷsuxʷstxʷ** – Do you know them?

yoˀ... – learn; gain/have knowledge. *See:* ***learn.***
yoˀstes – S/he/it is learning how to do s.t. **yoˀsten, yoˀstexʷ**
es yoˀstes – S/he/it knows how to do s.t. **es yoˀsten, es yoˀstexʷ**
yoˀstéˀes – They are learning how to do s.t. **qeˀ yoˀstem, yoˀstep**
es yoˀstéˀes – They know how to do s.t. **qeˀes yoˀstem, es yoˀstep**

ha yoˀstexʷ kʷqs syeni – Do you know how to count? **nexʷ ta es yoˀstép łu sčłip** – Also, you all do not know how to hunt. **ha yoˀstéxʷ łu stql̓séˀ** – Do you know sign language? **ha es yoˀstéxʷ sk̓ʷl̓ƛ̓iyéˀ** – Do you know how to make a canoe? **ċẏu es yoˀnusten** – I do not know how yet.

ta wi – I don't know.

ta we – I don't know.

knuckle

sntpṗsečst – knuckle. **sntptpṗsečst** – knuckles. *rt.:* ***ṫip*** *– join/add to; suffix:* ***...ečst, ...čst*** *– of the hand.*

sčmqinčst – middle knuckle of finger.

sčmusečst – top knuckle of finger.

Kool-aid

nṫišk̓ʷ – sweet liquid; pop; Kool-aid.
ċwetiš t nṫišk̓ʷ – Go get a pop.

Kootenai

sqlsé – Kootenai. **sqlqlse** *pl.*

L

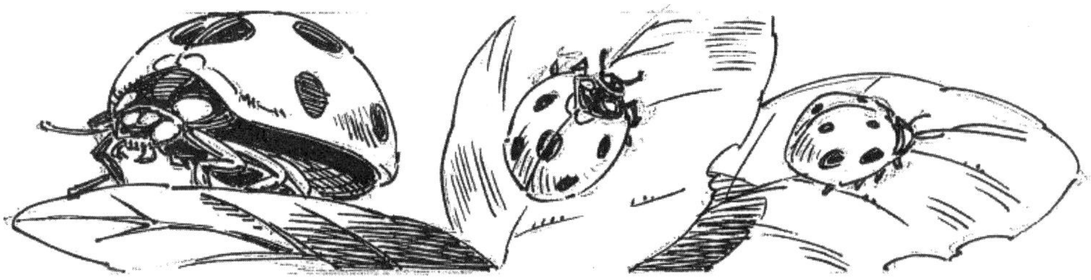

labium **splimn –** labium.

labor **k̓ʷul̓ –** do; make; fix; work. *See: **work**.*

Labrador tea **sčt̓x̌ʷičn̓ liti, sčt̓x̌ʷčłliti –** mountain tea; labrador tea; *Ledum glandulosum.*

lacing **scq̓eċ –** something that's been laced together. *prefix: **sc...** – s.t. that's been done/made/prepared.*
es q̓eċi – S/he is lacing. **čnes q̓eċi, kʷes q̓eċi**

sip̓iˀ – buckskin; buckskin rope; buckskin lacing.
łsisp̓iˀ – little lacing; little piece of buckskin.

lack **y̓apcin –** lack something. *rt.: **y̓aa** – scarce.*
es y̓apcini – S/he is lacking (s.t.). **čnes y̓apcini, kʷes y̓apcini**

y̓apcinmis – S/he lacked s.t. **y̓apcinmn, y̓apcinmntxʷ**
es y̓apcinmms – S/he is lacking s.t. **ies y̓apcinmm, as y̓apcinmm**
qs y̓apcinmms – S/he is going to lack s.t. **iqs y̓apcinmm, aqs y̓apcinmm**

y̓apcnemn – one inclined to lack something. *suffix: **...emn** – one inclined to do.*

k̓ʷły̓apcin – in need of something; miss something. *See: **need**.*

čnes y̓apcini t sˀiłn – I am lacking food. **hayo čn y̓apcin t kapi –** I am in need of coffee. **ta qeˀ qes y̓apcin –** We will not be in need.

k̓ʷłtwin̓tm – fall short of something; deficient in something; unable to attain something. *See: **deficient**.*

ladder **snčiwlštn –** ladder. *prefix: **sn...** – a place of; suffix: **...tin, ...tn** – means of/device.*

sqluwetn – stepladder.

ladybug **st̓lt̓la –** ladybug.

lady fern **t̓x̌t̓x̌éłp –** lady fern; *Pteridium aquilinum.*

lag **čén –** tarry; slowpoke. *See: **slowpoke**.*

ecċéwt – late, lagging behind. *See: **last**.*

lake **čłq̓lip,** *čłq̓li* **–** lake.
čłqq̓lip, *čłqq̓li* **–** pond; little lake.

kʷ y̓amim t sšén̓š tam t šiˀmi tam tl̓ ntx̌ʷé u tl̓ čłq̓li – You gather rocks, not just any old rocks, not from the river or from the lake.

s.t. - something, the 3rd person
(s.t.) - something implied
s.o. - someone, the 3rd person
sl. - singular form
pl. - plural form
rt. - root word
cmd. - command
lit. - literally
fig. - figuratively
i.e., - for example
See: - Redirection to a related word.

nła?pqin – headwaters; where the water begins *(i.e., a spring, fountain, lake). rt.:* ***łe*** *– end; suffix:* ***...qin, ...qn*** *– top.*

olqʷétkʷm, *olqʷé* – go down to the water's edge *(often refers to a lake edge). See:* ***down.***

lake trout

łxʷxʷiups – lake trout; *Salvelinus namaycush.*

lamb

łłmotó – lamb; little sheep.
xʷłxʷa – lamb.

lame

tl̓xʷncut – lame.
es tl̓xʷncut – S/he/it walks lame.

laminate

nqq̓?eple? – laminate; put something permanently in between. *rt.:* ***q̓e?*** *– insert; prefix:* ***n...*** *– inside; suffix:* ***...eple?*** *– permanence.*
nqq̓?epl?em – S/he laminated. **nqq̓?epl?en, nqq̓?epl?entxʷ**
es nqq̓?epl?ei – S/he is laminating. **ies nqq̓?epl?ei, as nqq̓?epl?ei**
qs nqq̓?epl?ei – S/he is going to laminate. **iqs nqq̓?epl?ei, aqs nqq̓?epl?ei**

nqq̓?epl?eis – S/he laminated s.t. **nqq̓?epl?en, nqq̓?epl?en**
es nqq̓?epl?ems – S/he is laminating s.t. **ies nqq̓?epl?em, as nqq̓?epl?em**
qs nqq̓?epl?ems – S/he is going to laminate s.t. **iqs nqq̓?epl?em, aqs nqq̓?epl?em**

es nqq̓?eple? – It is laminated.

snqq̓?eple?tn – laminator.

nqq̓?epl?en – Laminate it. *cmd.*

ha es nqq̓?eple? – Is it laminated? **ha aqs nqq̓?epl?em** – Are you going to laminate it?

nx̣pp̓mew̓s – multiply; double up; laminate. *See:* ***multiply.***

nttl̓ew̓s – laminate wood. *suffix:* ***...éw̓s*** *– in between, middle.*
nttl̓ew̓sis – S/he laminated the wood. **nttl̓ew̓sn, nttl̓ew̓sntxʷ**
es nttl̓ew̓sms – S/he is laminating the wood. **ies nttl̓ew̓sm, as nttl̓ew̓sm**
qs nttl̓ew̓sms – S/he is going to laminate the wood. **iqs nttl̓ew̓sm, aqs nttl̓ew̓sm**

nttl̓ew̓snt – Laminate it. *cmd.*

ha es nttl̓ew̓s – Is it laminated? **ha aqs nttl̓ew̓sm** – Are you going to laminate it?

lamp

čšlšalew̓s, *čšlšale* – lamp; lantern.

c̓ék̓ʷmn – light.

c̓ék̓ʷsšn̓ – light.

lance

smul̓mn – lance; spear.

land

sṫulixʷ – earth, land.
ši?elixʷ – first people.

čnes k̓ʷul̓sṫulixʷ – I am working my land. **x̣ʷa tl̓ ši?elixʷ** – Where's s/he from; where's his/her first land?

...ulexʷ – suffix indicating land, place, or area.
x̣sulexʷ – good land/place. **x̣sx̣sulexʷ** *pl. prefix:* ***x̣s...*** *– good; suffix:* ***...ulexʷ*** *– land.*
naslé xʷ – wet land/place. *rt.:* ***nas*** *– wet; suffix:* ***...ulexʷ*** *– land.*
ƛ̓áq̓lexʷ – hot land; south. *rt.:* ***ƛ̓aq̓*** *– hot; suffix:* ***...ulexʷ*** *– land.*

sqlixʷulexʷ – Indian land. *rt.:* ***sqelixʷ*** *– people; suffix:* ***...ulexʷ*** *– land.*
ṫxʷlmulexʷ – different land/place. *rt.:* ***ṫixʷlm*** *– different; suffix:* ***...ulexʷ*** *– land.*
šiyulexʷ – first land; homeland; place of origin.**stṁulexʷ** – what land/place? *rt.:* ***steṁ*** *– what; suffix:* ***...ulexʷ*** *– land. See:* ***what.***

nk̓ʷulexʷ – one place/land. **eslulexʷ** – two places/lands. **čeɬlulexʷ** – three places/lands. **msulexʷ** – four places/lands. **clčstulexʷ** – five places/lands. **ṫq̇nčstulexʷ** – six places/lands. **spl̓čstulexʷ** – seven places/lands. **hˀenmulexʷ** – eight places/lands. **x̣ntulexʷ** – nine places/lands. **upnčstulexʷ** – ten places/lands.

xʷeˀulexʷ – many places.

> The **i** following uvular consonants (UC) and the glottal stop ˀ sound like English "*ey*" as in the words th*ey*, h*ey*, wh*ey*, etc. Salish UC are: **q, q̇, qʷ, q̇ʷ, x̣, x̣ʷ**. For example, the suffix ...**qin** – head/top, is often spelled using English *ey* as "q*ey*n". So **qi, q̇i, qʷi, q̇ʷi, x̣i, x̣ʷi**, may be spelled with English *ey* as **q***ey*, **q̇***ey*, **qʷ***ey*, **q̇ʷ***ey*, **x̣***ey*, **x̣ʷ***ey* in other texts.

čɬqqlšeẇs – land on something. *suffix:* ***...éẇs*** *– in between, middle.*
čɬqqlšeẇs – S/he landed. **čn čɬqqlšeẇs, kʷ čɬqqlšeẇs**

cqqepšnm – land softly. *(i.e., birds and bugs)*
qʷo cqqepšnmis t x̣maɬtn – The fly landed on me.

cqqulexʷ – land on the land. *(i.e., airplane)*
cqqulexʷ ɬu ṫuxʷtn – The airplane landed.

čṫuxʷtm – fly toward something. *See:* ***fly.***

lane

nx̣qeẇs – lane. *suffix:* ***...éẇs*** *– in between, middle.*

language

nqʷlqʷel̓tn – language; the way an individual or family group speaks/talks. *suffix:* ***...tin, ...tn*** *– means of/device. rt.:* ***qʷlqʷelt*** *– speak.*
qeˀes yoˀnunm qenqʷlqʷel̓tn – We are learning our language. **ƛ̓ičt ɬu seliš nqʷlqʷel̓tn qs yoˀnunm** – Salish is hard to learn.

nuwewlštn – language; what a people/person speaks. *rt.:* ***uwewlš*** *– speak formally; suffix:* ***...tin, ...tn*** *– means of/device.*
čiqs ax̣llwisi iqs yoˀnunm ɬu qenuwewlštn – I am going to be able to learn our language. **semeˀ nuwewlštn** – French language.

nsélišcn – Salish language. *See:* ***Salish.***

nqlispélišcn – Kalispel language. *See:* ***Kalispel.***

snuyapcn – English. *See:* ***English.***

...cin – *suffix indicating an action of the mouth; i.e., speaking, eating, & food. See:* ***mouth.***
es nċkʷscan – S/he does not say words right. **čnes nċkʷscan, kʷes nċkʷscan**
es nṫixʷlcn – S/he speaks a different language.

nmemeˀcin – talk in a bothersome way. *rt.:* ***memeˀt*** *– bothersome. See:* ***talk.***
x̣scinm – talk in a good way; talk good about someone or something. *See:* ***talk.***
čscinm – talk in a bad way; bad mouth. *See:* ***talk.***
ɬaqʷcin – spoke up (once in a while). *See:* ***talk.***
nk̓ʷnk̓ʷucin – saying one word at a time. *See:* ***talk.***

> s.t. - something, the 3rd person
> (s.t.) - something implied
> s.o. - someone, the 3rd person
> *sl.* - singular form
> *pl.* - plural form
> *rt.* - root word
> *cmd.* - command
> *lit.* - literally
> *fig.* - figuratively
> *i.e.,* - for example
> *See:* - Redirection to a related word.

lantern

čšlšaleẇs, *čšlšale* – lamp; lantern.

ċék̓ʷmn – light.

ċék̓ʷsšṅ – light.

lap

sččmélpstšn – thighs. *rt.:* ***čm*** *– extremity.*

larch

cáqʷlš – western larch; tamarack; *Larix occidentalis.*

lard **sq̇ʷoct** – grease, lard. *rt.: q̇ʷoct – fat.*

scocoó – bear rib grease.

large **k̇ʷtunt** – It is big. *See: big.*

kʷtił... – prefix indicating something is great or big. *See: big.*

lark **wewickʷl̓eʔ,** *wewi* – female western meadowlark; *Sturnella neglecta.*
wewickʷl̓om, *wewi* – male western meadowlark; *Sturnella neglecta.*

lark bunting **ƛ̓čƛ̓á esq̇ẏe** – lark bunting; *Calamospiza melanocorys.*

larkspur **nłqʷiqʷayá** – mountain bluebird; *Sialia currucoides*; western bluebird; *Sialia mexicana.*

laryngitis **nsekʷ** – laryngitis; hoarse.

last **ecc̓éwt** – late, lagging behind.
ecc̓éwt – S/he/it was late. **čn ecc̓éwt, kʷ ecc̓éwt**
es eʔc̓ewti – S/he/it is last. **čnes eʔc̓ewti, kʷes eʔc̓ewti**
qs eʔc̓ewti – S/he/it is going to be last. **čiqs eʔc̓ewti, kʷqs eʔc̓ewti**

ecc̓ewtl̓wil̓š – S/he kept getting behind.

ecc̓mtums – deliberately fall behind.
ecc̓mtums – S/he deliberately fell behind. **čn ecc̓mtums, kʷ ecc̓mtums**
es ecc̓mtumsi – S/he is deliberately falling behind. **čnes ecc̓mtumsi, kʷes ecc̓mtumsi**
qs ecc̓mtumsi – S/he is going to deliberately fall behind. **čiqs ecc̓mtumsi, kʷqs ecc̓mtumsi**

ecc̓mtumsiš – Deliberately fall behind. *cmd.*

swe łu es eʔc̓ewti – Who is last? **yetłx̣ʷa łu es ec̓éw̓ti kʷqs ac̓x̣łq̇eẏmi** – Today is the last day of school.

late **ecc̓éwt** – late, lagging behind. *See: last.*

later **k̇ʷe ṅe** – in a while/wait; after while.

k̇ʷe ṅe – wait.

ṅe x̣ił ṅe – in a little while.

ṅe qeʔ wis čluxʷm – after we finish supper.

lather **possm** – lather.
possm – S/he lathered. **čn possm, kʷ possm**
es possi – S/he is lathering. **čnes possi, kʷes possi**
qs possi – S/he is going to lather. **čiqs possi, kʷqs possi**

possis – S/he lathered s.o./s.t. **possn, possntxʷ**
es possms – S/he is lathering s.o./s.t. **ies possm, as possm**
qs possms – S/he is going to lather s.o./s.t. **iqs possm, aqs possm**

laugh **oẏncut** – for a single person to laugh.
oẏncut – S/he/it laughed. **čn oẏncut, kʷ oẏncut**
es oẏncuti – S/he/it is laughing. **čnes oẏncuti, kʷes oẏncuti**
qs oẏncuti – S/he/it is going to laugh. **čiqs oẏncuti, kʷqs oẏncuti**
oẏncúʔut – They laughed. **qeʔ oẏncut, p oẏncut**

es oẏncúʔuti – They are laughing. **qeʔes oẏncuti, pes oẏncuti**
qs oẏncúʔuti – They are going to laugh. **qeʔqs oẏncuti, pqs oẏncuti**

oẏncutmsts – S/he/it made s.o. laugh. **oẏncutmstn, oẏncutmstxʷ**
es oẏncutms – S/he/it is making s.o. laugh. **ies oẏncutm, as oẏncutm**
qs oẏncutms – S/he/it is going to is make s.o. laugh. **iqs oẏncutm, aqs oẏncutm**

oẏnstemn – one inclined to laugh. *suffix:* ***...emn*** *– one inclined to do.*
nčoẏoẏci – person who always makes fun of others.
oẏnctmlwis – laughing around.

łoẏncutš – Smile (little laugh). *cmd.*

čoẏncutmis – S/he/it laughed at s.o./s.t. **čoẏncutmn, čoẏncutmntxʷ**
es čoẏncutmms – S/he/it is laughing at s.o./s.t. **ies čoẏncutmm, as čoẏncutmm**
qs čoẏncutmms – S/he/it is going to laugh at s.o./s.t. **iqs čoẏncutmm, aqs čoẏncutmm**
čoẏncúʔutmis – They laughed at s.o./s.t. **qeʔ čoẏncutmntm, čoẏncutmntp**
es čoẏncúʔutmms – They are laughing at s.o./s.t. **qeʔes čoẏncutmm, es čoẏncutmmp**
qs čoẏncúʔutmms – They are going to laugh at s.o./s.t. **qeʔqs čoẏncutmm, qs čoẏncutmmp**

The **i** following uvular consonants (UC) and the glottal stop **ʔ** sound like English "*ey*" as in the words th*ey*, h*ey*, wh*ey*, etc. Salish UC are: **q, q̇, qʷ, q̇ʷ, x̣, x̣ʷ**. For example, the suffix **...qin** – head/top, is often spelled using English *ey* as "q*ey*n". So **qi, q̇i, qʷi, q̇ʷi, x̣i, x̣ʷi**, may be spelled with English *ey* as q*ey*, q̇*ey*, qʷ*ey*, q̇ʷ*ey*, x̣*ey*, x̣ʷ*ey* in other texts.

čoẏoẏłtém – laugh at someone or something; to make fun of.
es čoẏoẏłtéms – S/he/it is laughing at s.o./s.t. **ies čoẏoẏłtém, as čoẏoẏłtém**
qs čoẏoẏłtéms – S/he/it is going to laugh at s.o./s.t. **iqs čoẏoẏłtém, aqs čoẏoẏłtém**
es čoẏoẏłtéʔems – They are laughing at s.o./s.t. **qeʔes čoẏoẏłtém, es čoẏoẏłtémp**
qs čoẏoẏłtéʔems – They are going to laugh at s.o./s.t. **qeʔqs čoẏoẏłtém, qs čoẏoẏłtémp**

čoẏoẏłtúmš, *čoẏoẏłtú* – laugh at someone; make fun of someone. *See:* ***make fun of.***

qʷo es čoẏoẏłtéms inṗiṗuyšn – He's laughing at my car. **qeʔes čoẏoẏłul̓t** – They are laughing at us. **qʷo čoẏoẏłtem isqʷseʔ** – S/he laughed at my son. **qʷo čẏoẏołtem** – I was laughed at. **čoẏncutmncn** – I laughed at you.

x̣ʷax̣ʷʔéy – for more than one person to laugh.
čx̣ʷax̣ʷʔéyminm – more than one person laughs at/toward someone.

x̣ʷax̣ʷʔéy esyáʔ sqélixʷ – All the people laughed.

laundry

nq̇ʷʔétkʷ, *nq̇ʷʔé* – wash clothes; do laundry. *See:* ***wash.***

laundry soap

ċéẇmn – soap. *rt.:* ***ċeẇ*** *– wash; suffix:* ***...min, ...mn*** *– instrument/tool.*

lava

mopesšn – lava.

impasšn – igneous rock; lava rock. *See:* ***igneous rock.***

law

snčċx̣ʷx̣ʷepletn – rules; laws. *rt.:* ***čċox̣ʷ*** *– willful action of one's self; prefix:* ***sn...*** *– a place of; suffix:* ***...epleʔ*** *– permanence ; suffix:* ***...tin, ...tn*** *– means of/device.*

snčċx̣ʷx̣ʷepletn sqelixʷ – the people's laws.

ċox̣ʷ – impart wisdom, knowledge, and/or experiences of one's self; instruct; lecture; teach; inform. *See:* ***instruct.***

iheʔ łu qeʔ snčċx̣ʷx̣ʷepletn ṅe qeʔ yamncut – These are our rules when we gather.

s.t. - something, the 3rd person
(s.t.) - something implied
s.o. - someone, the 3rd person
sl. - singular form
pl. - plural form
rt. - root word
cmd. - command
lit. - literally
fig. - figuratively
i.e., - for example
See: - Redirection to a related word.

Lawrence

loló – Lawrence.

laxative **pċmantn –** laxative. *See: **diarrhea**.*

lay **es čiċ –** one long object put in a lying position.
čċntes – S/he laid one stick *(long object)* down. **čċnten, čċntexʷ**
es čċims – S/he is laying one stick *(long object)* down. **ies čċim, as čċim**
qs čċims – S/he is going to lay one stick *(long object)* down. **iqs čċim, aqs čċim**

es čiċ – It is lying down.
es čċeẃs – one log/long object spans over. *(i.e., over a creek, over a ditch, etc.)*

čłk̓ʷitšl̓š l es čiċ – S/he stepped over a log.

ṗin – long objects put in a lying position.
ṗnntes – S/he laid sticks *(long object)* down. **ṗnnten, ṗnntexʷ**
es ṗnims – S/he is laying sticks *(long object)* down. **ies ṗnim, as ṗnim**
qs ṗnims – S/he is going to lay sticks *(long object)* down. **iqs ṗnim, aqs ṗnim**

ṗnṗin – groups of long objects in a lying position.
es ṗin – They are in a lying postion.
es ṗnṗin – Each group is in a lying postion.

es ṗnalqʷ – Logs/wood are lying down.
es ṗnṗnalqʷ – Groups of logs are lying down.

ṗnełxʷ – log house.
es ṗnulexʷ – They are lying on the ground.

čṗnusm – lay long objects in a fire. *See: **fire**.*
čṗnusntxʷ t čičitńé m še čt̓qntéxʷ t ant̓qéłp – Lay alders in the fire, then stack on your ferns.

ṗnṗnši – have legs and feet in a prone position; legs in a state of laziness. *rt.: **ṗin** – long object lying.*
es ṗnṗnši – S/he is lying; his/her legs are in a prone position. **čnes ṗnṗnši, kʷes ṗnṗnši**

kʷ qes ṗnṗši – Lay down with your legs out. *cmd.*
ta kʷ qes ṗnṗši – Do not lay down with your legs out. *cmd.*

łq̇ilš – lie down; in the motion of lying down. *suffix: **...ilš** – autonomous.*
łq̇ilš – S/he/it layed down. **čn łq̇ilš, kʷ łq̇ilš**
es łq̇ilši – S/he/it is lying down. **čnes łq̇ilši, kʷes łq̇ilši**
qs łq̇ilši – S/he/it is going to lay down. **čiqs łq̇ilši, kʷqs łq̇ilši**

łq̇ilšsts – S/he made s.o. lie down. **łq̇ilšstn, łq̇ilšstxʷ**
es łq̇ilšms – S/he is making s.o. lie down. **ies łq̇ilšm, as łq̇ilšm**
qs łq̇ilšms – S/he/it is going to make s.o. lie down. **iqs łq̇ilšm, aqs łq̇ilšm**

čłq̇ilšmis – S/he layed down by s.o. **čłq̇ilšmn, čłq̇ilšmntxʷ**
es čłq̇ilšmms – S/he is laying down by s.o. **ies čłq̇ilšmm, as čłq̇ilšmm**
qs čłq̇ilšmms – S/he/it is going to lay down by s.o. **iqs čłq̇ilšmm, aqs čłq̇ilšmm**

nkʷłłq̇ilšmis – S/he layed down with s.o. **nkłłq̇ilšmn, nkłłq̇ilšmntxʷ**
es nkłłq̇ilšms – S/he is laying down with s.o. **ies nkłłq̇ilšm, as nkłłq̇ilšm**
qs nkłłq̇ilšms – S/he/it is going to lay down with s.o. **iqs nkłłq̇ilšm, aqs nkłłq̇ilšm**

łq̇ilš – Lay down. *cmd.*
łq̇lilšwi – All of you lay down. *cmd.*
łq̇ilšmskʷ – Make him/her lay down. *cmd.*
łq̇lilšmskʷi – Make all of them lay down. *cmd.*

łq̇lšulexʷ – laying on the ground.

łq̇ot – laying down. *(sl.)*
łq̇ot – S/he was laying. **čn łq̇ot, kʷ łq̇ot**
es łq̇oti – S/he is laying. **čnes łq̇oti, kʷes łq̇oti**
qs łq̇oti – S/he is going to be laying. **čiqs łq̇oti, kʷqs łq̇oti**

łq̇tstes – S/he made s.o. lay. **łq̇tsten, łq̇tstexʷ**
es łq̇tims – S/he is making s.o. lay. **čnes łq̇tim, kʷes łq̇tim**
qs łq̇tims – S/he is going to make s.o. lay. **čiqs łq̇tim, kʷqs łq̇tim**

nłq̇otn – place to lay.

es łq̇otš – Stay laying down. *cmd.*
łq̇tmiskʷ – Make him/her lay. *cmd.*
nłq̇otetkʷ – lie in the water. *suffix: **...etkʷ, ...tkʷ** – liquid*

łq̇lut – laying down of more than one person. *pl.*
łq̇lúˀut – They were laying. **qeˀ łq̇lut, p łq̇lut**
es łq̇lúˀuti – They are laying. **qeˀes łq̇luti, pes łq̇luti**
qs łq̇lúˀuti – They are going to lay. **qeˀqs łq̇luti, pqs łq̇luti**

łq̇łq̇lut – Each one was laying. **qeˀ łq̇łq̇lut, p łq̇łq̇lut**
es łq̇łq̇luti – Each one is laying. **qeˀes łq̇łq̇luti, pes łq̇łq̇luti**
qs łq̇łq̇luti – Each one is going to lay. **qeˀqs łq̇łq̇luti, pqs łq̇łq̇luti**

łq̇ʷtulexʷ, *łq̇ʷtu* – face down. *See: **face down.***

qqtuˀsaqstšn, *qqtuˀsa* – lay with one leg over the other.
qqtuˀsaqstšn – S/he is laying w/ one leg over. **čn qqtuˀsaqstšn, kʷ qqtuˀsaqstšn**

cql̓ut – lie on the back.
cql̓tsˀitš – lie on the back.
k̓ʷłcql̓ut – lie on the back under something.
ncql̓tetkʷ – lie on the back in the water. *suffix: **...etkʷ, ...tkʷ** – liquid*
cql̓úˀut qeyqeyši u nk̓ʷuˀskʷkʷˀe – Qeyqeyshi and One-Night were lying around.

t̓uk̓ʷ – put something down; lay something down; place something down. *See: **put.***
t̓k̓ʷncut – place one's self down.

qmin – put things down; lay things down; place things down. *See: **put.***

sil – place more than one object upright. *See: **place.***

caq – place a single object upright; set down. *See: **place.***

pkʷéw̓t – round objects lying/sitting around. *See: **scatter.***

łoqʷ – overlay; place something on/over something else *(not to cover)*; lay something on; drape something over a narrow/smaller object. *See: **lay over.***

uˀusˀém – It layed eggs. *See: **egg.***

lay ears back

čmčmłéneˀ – an angry horse laying his/her ears back.

layer

x̣p̓im – layer; line; coat. *rt.: **x̣p̓** – line, coat.*
x̣p̓ip̓ – S/he/it got coated. **čn x̣p̓ip̓, kʷ x̣p̓ip̓**
es x̣p̓p̓mi – S/he/it is getting coated. **ies x̣p̓p̓mi, as x̣p̓p̓mi**
qs x̣p̓p̓mi – S/he/it is going to get coated. **iqs x̣p̓p̓mi, aqs x̣p̓p̓mi**

The **i** following uvular consonants (UC) and the glottal stop **ˀ** sound like English "*ey*" as in the words *they, hey, whey*, etc. Salish UC are: **q, q̇, qʷ, q̇ʷ, x̣, x̣ʷ**. For example, the suffix **...qin** – head/top, is often spelled using English *ey* as "q*ey*n". So **qi, q̇i, qʷi, q̇ʷi, x̣i, x̣ʷi**, may be spelled with English *ey* as **q***ey*, **q̇***ey*, **qʷ***ey*, **q̇ʷ***ey*, **x̣***ey*, **x̣ʷ***ey* in other texts.

s.t. - something, the 3rd person
(s.t.) - something implied
s.o. - someone, the 3rd person
sl. - singular form
pl. - plural form
rt. - root word
cmd. - command
lit. - literally
fig. - figuratively
i.e., - for example
See: - Redirection to a related word.

x̣p̓ntes – S/he layered it. **x̣p̓nten, x̣p̓ntexʷ**
es x̣p̓ims – S/he is layering it. **ies x̣p̓im, as x̣p̓im**
qs x̣p̓ims – S/he is going to layer it. **iqs x̣p̓im, aqs x̣p̓im**

nx̣p̓ewsis – S/he lined it. **nx̣p̓ewsn, nx̣p̓ewsntxʷ**
es nx̣p̓ewsms – S/he is lining it. **ies nx̣p̓ewsm, as nx̣p̓ewsm**
qs nx̣p̓ewsms – S/he is going to line it. **iqs nx̣p̓ewsm, aqs nx̣p̓ewsm**

x̣p̓eẇsis – S/he doubled it. **x̣p̓eẇsn, x̣p̓eẇsntxʷ**
es x̣p̓eẇsms – S/he is doubling it. **ies x̣p̓eẇsm, as x̣p̓eẇsm**
qs x̣p̓eẇsms – S/he is going to double it. **iqs x̣p̓eẇsm, aqs x̣p̓eẇsm**

x̣p̓int – Layer it; button it. *cmd.*

es x̣p̓eẇs – It doubled.
es nx̣p̓eẇs – It lined.
es x̣p̓elis – It has several coatings/layers.
es nx̣p̓elis – It is lined with several coatings; it has many layers within.
nx̣p̓p̓meẇs – multiply; double up; laminate. *See:* ***multiply.***
x̣p̓eẇstn – buckle together. *See:* ***buckle.***
snx̣p̓éẇs – lining the inside; soul. *See:* ***soul.***
nx̣p̓melis – stack solid objects. *See:* ***stack.***

es nx̣p̓eẇs łu inlkepu – My coat has a lining. **k̓ʷinš łu sx̣p̓elis –** How many layers does it have? **ha es nx̣p̓eẇs łu anlkepu –** Is your coat lined? **t čeṅ u ecx̣lsx̣p̓elis –** What kind of layers does it have?

lay over

łoqʷ – overlay; place something on/over something else *(not to cover)*; lay something on; drape something over a narrow/smaller object.
łoqʷm – S/he overlayed. **čn łoqʷm, kʷ łoqʷm**
es łqʷmi – S/he is overlaying. **čnes łqʷmi, kʷes łqʷmi**
qs łqʷmi – S/he is going to overlay. **čiqs łqʷmi, kʷqs łqʷmi**

łqʷntes – S/he overlayed s.t. **łqʷnten, łqʷntexʷ**
es łoqʷms – S/he is overlaying s.t. **ies łoqʷm, as łoqʷm**
qs łoqʷms – S/he is going to overlay s.t. **iqs łoqʷm, aqs łoqʷm**

es łoqʷ – It is placed over.

łoqʷiš – Lay it over. *cmd.*
łqʷont – Lay it over it. *cmd.*
čłqʷéẇs – drape up high; hang up high over an object; hang up. *See:* ***drape.***
łqʷax̣n – drape something over the arm. *See:* ***drape.***
łqʷłqʷemxʷ – put on/wear a bra. *See:* ***bra.***
łqʷłqʷłq̓eyt, *łqʷłqʷłq̓e* **–** put on/wear suspenders. *See:* ***suspenders.***
łqʷqin – put on/ wear a crown. *See:* ***crown.***
čłqʷesšṅtn – sling to hurl projectiles. *See:* ***sling.***

lazy

nweyls – lazy/tired; hate to do work; do something haphazardly. *(This term refers to the way a person does work or tasks. Someone haphazardly performing work, being lazy, is an example of this term.)*
es nweylsi – S/he is being lazy. **čnes nweylsi, kʷes nweylsi**
es nwéʔeylsi – They are being lazy. **qeʔes nweylsi, pes nweylsi**

nwilsemn – one inclined to be lazy. *suffix:* ***...emn*** *– one inclined to do.*

ha kʷes nwéylsi – Do not you feel up to it?

x̣ʷopt – lazy; unable to do work. *(This term is used to describe a person who is unable or unwilling to do work. An example is an elderly person who is no longer able to perform tasks. This term could also apply to a person that will not do work.)*

x̣ʷopt – S/he/it is lazy. **čn x̣ʷopt, kʷ x̣ʷopt**

če čn x̣ʷopt – I cannot do anything anymore. **t qʷoyʔe k̓ʷuĺn u če x̣ʷopt –** I made him/her lazy. **ƛ̓m u we sisyu u xʷuy u če x̣ʷopt –** S/he used to be smart now s/he is lazy.

x̣ʷeyti – lazy; take it easy. *(This term is used to describe a person who is taking it easy. It almost means to be relaxing. This term would be used for someone taking a vacation or a person not working.)*

es x̣ʷeyti – S/he is being lazy. **čnes x̣ʷeyti, kʷes x̣ʷeyti**
qs x̣ʷeyti – S/he is going to be lazy. **čiqs x̣ʷeyti, kʷqs x̣ʷeyti**
es x̣ʷeyʔiti – They are being lazy. **qeʔes x̣ʷeyti, pes x̣ʷeyti**

es x̣ʷix̣ʷeyti – Each one them is being lazy. **qeʔes x̣ʷix̣ʷeyti, pes x̣ʷix̣ʷeyti**

x̣ʷax̣ʷeẏm – someone who is always lazy.

mił čnes x̣ʷeyti – I am too lazy.

k̓ʷłłpip̓ – unmotivated/discouraged/lazy; *unable to do something; depressed. (This term describes someone who has no motivation, who is discouraged and who is lazy. Many words in Salish are a combination of English words. At times it is hard to give a clear translation.) See:* ***discourage***.

The **i** following uvular consonants (UC) and the glottal stop **ʔ** sound like English "*ey*" as in the words *they, hey, whey*, etc. Salish UC are: **q, q̓, qʷ, q̓ʷ, x̣, x̣ʷ**. For example, the suffix ...**qin** – head/top, is often spelled using English *ey* as "q*ey*n". So **qi, q̓i, qʷi, q̓ʷi, x̣i, x̣ʷi**, may be spelled with English *ey* as **q***ey*, **q̓***ey*, **qʷ***ey*, **q̓ʷ***ey*, **x̣***ey*, **x̣ʷ***ey* in other texts.

lead

x̣ʷl̓šiitus – lead someone.

x̣ʷl̓šitusis – S/he/it led him/her/it. **x̣ʷl̓šitusn, x̣ʷl̓šitusntxʷ**
es x̣ʷl̓šitusms – S/he/it is leading him/her/it. **ies x̣ʷl̓šitusm, as x̣ʷl̓šitusm**
qs x̣ʷl̓šitusms – S/he/it is going to lead him/her/it. **iqs x̣ʷl̓šitusm, aqs x̣ʷl̓šitusm**
x̣ʷl̓šitúʔusis – They led him/her/it. **qeʔ x̣ʷl̓šitusntm, x̣ʷl̓šitusntp**

x̣ʷl̓šitúʔusn – I led them. **x̣ʷl̓šitusmncn –** I am leading you.

x̣ʷl̓šiʔcut – lead.

nčṅelsm – lead the blind by taking their hand. *rt.:* ***čṅim** – grasp on to s.t. See:* ***grasp***.

nčṅelsis – S/he led s.o. **nčṅelsn, nčṅelsntxʷ**
es nčṅelsms – S/he is leading s.o. **ies nčṅelsm, as nčṅelsm**
qs nčṅelsms – S/he is going to lead s.o. **iqs nčṅelsm, aqs nčṅelsm**
nčṅéʔelsis – They led s.o. **qeʔ nčṅelsntm, nčṅelsntp**

nčṅelsnt – Lead s.o. *cmd.*

ččṅépleʔ – lead by the hand. *(i.e., leading a horse.) rt.:* ***čṅim** – grasp on to s.t.; suffix:* ***...épleʔ** – permanence. See:* ***grasp***.

ččṅeplʔéis – S/he lead s.o. **ččṅeplʔén, ččṅeplʔéntxʷ**
es ččṅeplʔéms – S/he is leading s.o. **ies ččṅepléʔm, as ččṅeplʔém**
qs ččṅeplʔéms – S/he is going to lead s.o. **iqs ččṅepʔlém, aqs ččṅeplʔém**
ččṅeplʔéʔeis – They lead s.o. **qeʔ ččṅeplʔéntm, ččṅeplʔéntp**
es ččṅeplʔéʔems – They are leading s.o. **qeʔes ččṅeplʔém, es ččṅeplʔémp**
qs ččṅeplʔéʔems – They are going to lead s.o. **qeʔqs ččṅeplʔém, qs ččṅeplʔémp**

ččṅeplʔént – Lead him/her/it. *cmd.*

s.t. - something, the 3rd person
(s.t.) - something implied
s.o. - someone, the 3rd person
sl. - singular form
pl. - plural form
rt. - root word
cmd. - command
lit. - literally
fig. - figuratively
i.e., - for example
See: - Redirection to a related word.

ččṅmutiyeʔ – lead to move a little. *(i.e., readjusting s.o.'s position, etc.) rt.:* ***čṅim** – grasp on to s.t.; suffix:* ***...mutiyeʔ** – temporary. See:* ***grasp***.

ččṅmutiyeis – S/he moved s.o. **ččṅmutiyen, ččṅmutiyentxʷ**

es ččṅmutiyems – S/he is moving s.o. **ččṅmutiyem, ččṅmutiyem**

leader **š'itmasqe –** leader; first to volunteer; first to be there. *rt.: š'it – first; suffix: ...sqe, ...sqelixʷ – people.*
sxʷšiitusm – leader; one tasked to lead. *prefix: sxʷ... – one tasked to do.*

šitmscut – appoint one's self to lead.
šitmscut – S/he became a leader. **čn šitmscut, kʷ šitmscut**
es šitmscutisti – S/he is becoming a leader. **čnes šitmscutisti, kʷes šitmscutisti**
qs šitmscutisti – S/he is going to become a leader. **čiqs šitmscutisti, kʷqs šitmscutisti**

nši'telixʷ – head person in the lodge/house.

ilmixʷm – chief; boss. *See: **chief**.*

leaf **picčł –** leaf; cabbage, lettuce. **pcpicčł** *pl.*

čtt̓ekʷełp – leaf bud opened.
es čtt̓ekʷełpi – The leaf bud is opening.

kʷel – change outward perception; change color; ripening/dying. *See: **change**.*

leak **awawpeẇs –** leak.
es awawpeẇsi – It is leaking/dripping.

es nawawpełċe'i – It is leaking inside. *(i.e., boat, container, etc.)*

awpemn – one inclined to drip/leak; leaky container; leaky faucet.

aẇu – drip; drain; leak. *See: **drip**.*

lean **čła'qin –** lean the top of something against something.
es čła'qin – S/he/it is leaned against something.

čnes čła'qini l es šit̓ – I am leaning my head against the tree.

čt̓ásels, *čt̓a* **–** skinny; thin; lean. *(i.e., person, horse, tree)*
i čt̓á – thin.
i čt̓ás – poor; lean; hard on the surface.

i čx̣aṁłċe' – The animal is skinny/lean.

łiip– became skinny/lean. *See: **skinny**.*

learn **yo'... –** learn; gain/have knowledge. *See: **know**.*
yo'nuis – S/he/it learned it. **yo'nun, yo'nuntxʷ**
es yo'nunms – S/he/it is learning it. **ies yo'nunm, as yo'nunm**
qs yo'nunms – S/he/it is going to learn it. **iqs yo'nunm, aqs yo'nunm**
yó'o'nuis – They learned it. **qe' yo'nuntm, yo'nuntp**
es yó'o'nunms – They are learning it. **qe'es yo'nunm, es yo'nunmp**
qs yó'o'nunms – They are going to learn it. **qe'qs yo'nunm, qs yo'nunmp**

ṅem yo'nuis – S/he/it will learn it. **ṅem yo'nun, ṅem yo'nuntxʷ**
ṅem yó'o'nuis – They will learn it. **ṅem qe' yo'nuntm, ṅem yo'nuntp**

yo'nunt – Learn it. *cmd.*

kʷemt steṁ łu qe'qs yo'nunm yetłx̣ʷa – Then what are we going to learn today? **qe'es yo'nunm qe' nqʷlqʷeľtn –** We are learning our language. **eni ƛ̓ičt łu seliš nqʷlqʷeľtn qs yo'nunm –** Gee,

Salish is hard to learn *(woman speaking)*. **nexʷ ta es yoʔstép łu sčłip** – Also you guys do not know how to hunt. **ha es yoʔstéxʷ łu stqlséʔ** – Do you know sign language?

miíp – It became known.
  es mipmi – It is becoming known.
  qs mipmi – It is going to become known.

  mi – fact; knowing; reality; certainty. *See: know.*

  mipnwe – S/he learned part of something. **čn mipnwe, kʷ mipnwe**
  łmipnwe – S/he learned a little part of something. **čn łmipnwe, kʷ łmipnwe**

  mipstwexʷ – They are found out about each other. **qeʔ mipstwexʷ, p mipstwexʷ**
  es mipstwexʷi – They are finding out about each other. **qeʔes mipstwexʷi, pes mipstwexʷi**
  qs mipstwexʷi – They are going to find out about each other. **qeʔqs mipstwexʷi, pqs mipstwexʷi**

  es mipštwexʷi – They are finding out s.t. for each other. **qeʔes mipštwexʷi, pes mipštwexʷi**

  mimipmuł – one that habitually learns about things. *suffix: ...łmuł – one that habitually does.*

mipnunm – figure out something; find out about something; complete an understanding; succeed in understanding; learn of something.
  mipnuis – S/he/it found s.t. out. **mipnun, mipnuntxʷ**
  es mipnunms – S/he/it is finding s.t. out. **ies mipnunm, as mipnunm**
  qs mipnunms – S/he/it is going to find s.t. out. **iqs mipnunm, aqs mipnunm**
  mipnúʔuis – They found s.t. out. **qeʔ mipnuntm, mipnuntp**
  es mipnúʔunms – They are finding s.t. out. **qeʔes mipnunm, es mipnunmp**
  qs mipnúʔunms – They are going to find s.t. out. **qeʔqs mipnunm, qs mipnunmp**

  mipnwemn – one inclined to learn about things. *suffix: ...emn – one inclined to do.*
  mimipnwemn – one inclined to constantly learn about things. *suffix: ...emn – one inclined to do.*

  mipnunt – Find out. *cmd.*

  ṅem mipnuis – S/he/it will find s.t. out. **ṅem mipnun, ṅem mipnuntxʷ**
  ṅem mipnúʔuis – They will find s.t. out. **ṅem qeʔ mipnuntm, ṅem mipnuntp**
  ṅem qes mipnunms – S/he/it will be finding s.t. out. **ṅem iqes mipnunm, ṅem aqes mipnunm**

mipulexʷ – learn to recognize a place/area; figure out where one is at. *suffix: ...ulexʷ – land.*
  mipulexʷis – S/he/it learned the place. **mipulexʷn, mipulexʷntxʷ**
  es mipulexʷms – S/he/it is learning the place. **ies mipulexʷm, as mipulexʷm**
  qs mipulexʷms – S/he/it is going to learn the place. **iqs mipulexʷm, aqs mipulexʷm**

mipełxʷ – learn to recognize a home/house/lodge; figure out the house/lodge; come to know the house/lodge. *suffix: ...ełxʷ, ...łxʷ – house.*
  mipełxʷis – S/he/it learned to recognize the house. **mipełxʷn, mipełxʷntxʷ**
  es mipełxʷms – S/he/it is learning to recognize the house. **ies mipełxʷm, as mipełxʷm**
  qs mipełxʷms – S/he/it is going to learn to recognize the house. **iqs mipełxʷm, aqs mipełxʷm**

nmipaqs – learn to recognize a road. *circumfix: n...aqs – nose, road, pointed.*
  nmipaqsis – S/he/it learned the road. **nmipaqsn, nmipaqsntxʷ**

> The **i** following uvular consonants (UC) and the glottal stop **ʔ** sound like English "*ey*" as in the words th*ey*, h*ey*, wh*ey*, etc. Salish UC are: **q, q̇, qʷ, q̇ʷ, x̣, x̣ʷ**. For example, the suffix **...qin** – head/top, is often spelled using English *ey* as "q*eyn*". So **qi, q̇i, qʷi, q̇ʷi, x̣i, x̣ʷi**, may be spelled with English *ey* as q*ey*, q̇*ey*, qʷ*ey*, q̇ʷ*ey*, x̣*ey*, x̣ʷ*ey* in other texts.

> s.t. - something, the 3ʳᵈ person
> (s.t.) - something implied
> s.o. - someone, the 3ʳᵈ person
> *sl.* - singular form
> *pl.* - plural form
> *rt.* - root word
> *cmd.* - command
> *lit.* - literally
> *fig.* - figuratively
> *i.e.,* - for example
> *See:* - Redirection to a related word.

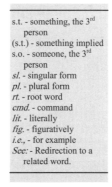

es nmipaqsms – S/he/it is learning the road. **ies mipaqsm, as nmipaqsm**
qs nmipaqsms – S/he/it is going to learn the road. **iqs nmipaqsm, aqs nmipaqsm**

čmipeneʔ – learn by hearing.
čmipenʔemis – S/he learned by hearing it. **čmipenʔemn, čmipenʔemntxʷ**
es čmipenʔems – S/he is learning by hearing it. **ies čmipenʔem, as čmipenʔem**
qs čmipenʔems – S/he is going to learn by hearing it. **iqs čmipenʔem, aqs čmipenʔem**

sxʷčmipeneʔ – one tasked to learn by hearing.
čmipenʔemn – one inclined to learn by hearing.

čmipus – learn by seeing.
čmipusmis – S/he learned by seeing it. **čmipusmn, čmipusmntxʷ**
es čmipusms – S/he is learning by seeing it. **ies čmipusm, as čmipusm**
qs čmipusms – S/he is going to learn by seeing it. **iqs čmipusm, aqs čmipusm**
čmipúʔusmis – They learned by seeing it. **qeʔ čmipusmntm, čmipusmntp**
es čmipúʔusms – They are learning by seeing it. **qeʔes čmipusm, es čmipusmp**
qs čmipúʔusms – They are going to learn by seeing it. **qeʔqs čmipusm, qs čmipusmp**

čmipusis – S/he knows what it is/recognizes it. **čmipusn, čmipusntxʷ**

sxʷčmipusm – one tasked to learn by seeing.
čmimipsemn – one inclined to learn by seeing.
čmipustn – visual signal/sign.

čmipusmnt – Figure it out by seeing. *cmd.*

čmipečst – learn by doing/working; hands-on learning.
čmipečsmis – S/he learned by doing it. **čmipečsmn, čmipečsmntxʷ**
es čmipečstms – S/he is learning by doing it. **ies čmipečstm, as čmipečstm**
qs čmipečstms – S/he is going to learn by doing it. **iqs čmipečstm, aqs čmipečstm**

sxʷčmipečstm – one tasked to learn by doing.
čmimipčsemn – one inclined to learn by doing.

čmipečstmnt – Figure it out by doing. *cmd.*

nmipels – want to figure something out; want to learn.
nmipelsmis – S/he/it wanted to learn it. **nmipelsmn, nmipelsmntxʷ**
es nmipelsmms – S/he/it is wanting to learn it. **ies nmipelsmm, as nmipelsmm**
qs mipnunms – S/he/it is going to want to learn it. **iqs nmipelsmm, aqs nmipelsmm**
nmipéʔelsmis – They want to learn it. **qeʔ mipnuntm, mipnuntp**
es nmipéʔelsmms – They are wanting to learn it. **qeʔes nmipelsmm, es nmipelsmm**
qs nmipéʔelsmms – They are going to want to learn it. **qeʔqs nmipelsmm, qs nmipelsmm**

nmiplsemn – one inclined to want to learn about things. *suffix: **...emn –** one inclined to do.*
nmimiplsemn – one inclined to constantly want to learn about things. *suffix: **...emn –** one inclined to do.*
nmimiplsmuł – one that habitually wants to learn about things. *suffix: **...łmuł –** one that habitually does.*

least **sšẏmłłuweʔ –** least.

leather **ṗičlxʷ –** leather. *rt.: **ṗič –** glossy; suffix: **...lxʷ –** skin, hide.*
čṗičċeʔ – suitcase; leather suitcase. *rt.: **ṗič –** glossy; suffix: **...iċéʔ –** covered in.*

ċulixʷélxʷ, *ċulixʷé* **–** buckskin, white-tail doe hide.

leave **q̇ʷmepm –** more than one person leaving.

q̓ʷméʔepm – They left. **qeʔ q̓ʷmepm, p q̓ʷmepm**

ƛ̓ékʷ – leave; move off; out of the way.
ƛ̓ékʷ – S/he/it got out of the way. **čn ƛ̓ékʷ, kʷ ƛ̓ékʷ**
es ƛ̓ékʷi – S/he/it is getting out of the way. **čnes ƛ̓ékʷi, kʷes ƛ̓ékʷi**
qs ƛ̓ékʷi – S/he/it is going to get out of the way. **čiqs ƛ̓ékʷi, kʷqs ƛ̓ékʷi**

ƛ̓ékʷsts – S/he/it removed s.t. out of the way. **ƛ̓ékʷstn, ƛ̓ékʷstxʷ**
es ƛ̓ékʷms – S/he/it is removing s.t. out of the way. **ies ƛ̓ékʷm, as ƛ̓ékʷm**
qs ƛ̓ékʷms – S/he/it is going to remove s.t. out of the way. **iqs ƛ̓ékʷm, aqs ƛ̓ékʷm**

es ƛ̓ékʷ – S/he/it is out of the way. **čnes ƛ̓ékʷ, kʷes ƛ̓ékʷ**

ƛ̓ékʷš – Leave, get out of here, get out of the way. *cmd.*
ƛ̓ékʷwi – All of you get out of the way. *cmd.*
ƛ̓ékʷskʷ – Move it out of the way. *cmd.*
ƛ̓ékʷskʷi – All of you move it out of the way. *cmd.*
ƛ̓ékʷšts – S/he/it removed s.t. out of the way for s.o. **ƛ̓ékʷstn, ƛ̓ékʷstxʷ**
k̓ʷłƛ̓kʷmist – move one's self under something to get out of a storm. *(i.e., tree, shelter, etc.)*
nƛ̓kʷmist – move one's self into something to get out of a storm. *(i.e., house, tipi, tent, etc.)*

łqʷom – leave/hide something temporarily in a safe place.
łqʷntes – S/he/it left s.t. temporarily. **łqʷnten, łqʷntexʷ**
es łqʷoms – S/he/it is leaving s.t. temporarily. **ies łqʷom, as łqʷom**
qs łqʷoms – S/he/it is going to leave s.t. temporarily. **iqs łqʷom, aqs łqʷom**

słqʷom – Something left temporarily.

łqʷmint – Leave/hide s.t. temporarily. *cmd.*
słqʷelt – leave/hide a child temporarily.

ƛ̓il – still; no movement. *See:* ***still.***
ƛ̓ilskʷ – Let it be still; leave it alone. *cmd.*
ƛ̓ilskʷwi – All of you let it be still; leave it alone. *cmd.*

x̣ʷel – abandon; throw away; leave. *See:* ***abandon.***

eṅés – on the way to somewhere. *See:* ***go.***

hoy – quit; stop; finish; okay; that's it; cease. *See:* ***quit.***

k̓ʷłn̓q̓ʷmist, *k̓ʷłn̓q̓ʷmi* – run away stealthily; sneak away; leave; escape. *See:* ***escape.***

The **i** following uvular consonants (UC) and the glottal stop **ʔ** sound like English "*ey*" as in the words th*ey*, h*ey*, wh*ey*, etc. Salish UC are: **q**, **q̓**, **qʷ**, **q̓ʷ**, **x̣**, **x̣ʷ**. For example, the suffix ...**qin** – head/top, is often spelled using English *ey* as "q*ey*n". So **qi**, **q̓i**, **qʷi**, **q̓ʷi**, **x̣i**, **x̣ʷi**, may be spelled with English *ey* as **q***ey*, **q̓***ey*, **qʷ***ey*, **q̓ʷ***ey*, **x̣***ey*, **x̣ʷ***ey* in other texts.

leaves
picčł – leaf; cabbage; lettuce. **pcpicčł** *pl.*

ledge
łʔamqṅe – ledge.

leech
ťaṁyó – cowry; leech; slug; snail.

left over
smʔáw – left over things.
qeʔ ep smʔáw – We have left overs.

sčmawáqs, *sčmawá* – left over food.

skʷumcn – left over food you take with you for later. *suffix: **...cin, ...cn** – action of the mouth.*

s.t. - something, the 3rd person
(s.t.) - something implied
s.o. - someone, the 3rd person
sl. - singular form
pl. - plural form
rt. - root word
cmd. - command
lit. - literally
fig. - figuratively
i.e., - for example
See: - Redirection to a related word.

left side
sččiq̓ʷečst, *sčči* – left hand.
es ččiq̓ʷečst – S/he is left-handed. **čnes ččiq̓ʷečst, kʷes ččiq̓ʷečst**

sččiq̓ʷessn – left foot.
sčq̓ʷax̣n – left arm.
sččq̓ʷus – left eye.
sčq̓ʷaqstšn – left leg.
sččq̓ʷeneʔ – left ear.
sk̓ʷłčq̓ʷeus – left cheek.
sččq̓ʷepneʔ – left braid.

leg

sččmáqstšn – leg. *rt.: **čm** – extremity.* **sčmčmáqstšn** *pl.*
sččmelpstšn – thigh; lap.
sčmelqstšn – hamstring.
snčmusšn – inner thigh.
sčmqinšn – knee.
sčmeẁsšn – back of knee.
sčx̣maqstšn – shin.
snq̓ʷmšin – calf.
sk̓ʷłčmcinšn – ankle.

...áqstšn – *suffix indicating leg.*
schaqstšn – right leg.
sčq̓ʷaqstšn – left leg.
čłxʷixʷcáqstšn – short legged person.
čłqiqʔáqstšn – skinny legs.
čususnáqstšn – long legged person.

talaqstšn – move/shake/bounce leg; releasing/relaxing from the leg and foot. *rt.: **tal** – loosen/untie; suffix: **...aqstšn** – leg. See: **untie**.*
es talaqstšni – S/he is bouncing his/her leg. **čnes talaqstšni, kʷes talaqstšni**

p̓np̓nšin – have legs and feet in a laying position; almost in a lazy state. *See: **lay**.*
kʷ qes p̓np̓nšin – Lay down with your legs out. *cmd.*
ta kʷ qes p̓np̓šin – Do not lay down with your legs out. *cmd.*

nx̣ʷlx̣ʷallpussni – shaky tired legs. *See: **shake**.*
nx̣ʷlx̣ʷallpussn – S/he/it had shaky legs. **čn nx̣ʷlx̣ʷallpussn, kʷ nx̣ʷlx̣ʷallpussn**

es čqqtusaqstšn – His/her legs are stacked one on the other. **čnes čqqtusaqstšn, kʷes čqqtusaqstšn** *See: **stack**.*

leggings

sx̣éƛ̓išn – legging. **sx̣ƛ̓x̣eƛ̓išn** *pl.*

lemon

čkʷlkʷaliʔ – lemon.

lend

kʷułn – borrow; lend. *See: **borrow**.*

lent, Catholic

putʔéy – showing respect; holding sacred; fasting.

leopard frog

łm̓łam̓áyeʔ, *łm̓łam̓á* – frog; spotted frog.

lesbian

sxʷntaʔłaẁs, *sxʷntaʔła* – lesbian.

less

łłuẁet, *łłu* – few; less.

ssy̓młłu – least.

let

lciʔm – let it be; yield to; permit it; allow to continue. *rt.: **ci** – that.*

lciʔsts – S/he let it be. **lciʔstn, lciʔstxʷ**
es lciʔms – S/he is letting it be. **ies lciʔm, as lciʔm**
qs lciʔms – S/he is going to let it be. **iqs lciʔm, aqs lciʔm**

lciʔnt – Let it be. *cmd.*
lciʔskʷ – Yield to it. *cmd.*

lci ʔ – stays here; remains here; dwells. *See: **stay**.*

let go **pλ̓éčstm –** release something from the hand. *See: **release**.*

letter **q̇eẏmin –** paper; book.

scq̇eẏi – written word; alphabetic letter; something that's written. *prefix: **sc...** – s.t. that's been done/made/prepared.*
scq̇ẏq̇eẏi – written words; written alphabetic letters. *prefix: **sc...** – s.t. that's been done/made/prepared.*
steṁ ẏe scq̇eẏi – What letter is this?
l čeṅ u nʔečx̣ilcn ẏe scq̇eẏi – How does this letter sound?

scʔawʔaw – spoken words; something that's said. *prefix: **sc...** – s.t. that's been done/made/prepared.*

lettuce **picčł –** leaf; cabbage; lettuce.

Lewis and Clark Pass **smitu sx̣ʷcuʔsičṅ –** Lewis and Clark Pass, near Lincoln, Montana.

Lewis' woodpecker **ciwcu –** Lewis' woodpecker; *Melanerpes lewis*.

liar **sxʷyoqʷistm,** *sxʷyoqʷi* **–** one tasked to lie. *rt.: **yoqʷist** – lie; tell falsehood; prefix: **sxʷ...** – one tasked to do.*
iqʷistémn – one inclined to lie. *suffix: **...emn** – one inclined to do.*
sxʷʔiqʷistmlwis – one tasked to go around lying. *prefix: **sxʷ...** – one tasked to do.*

qʷl̓qʷl̓muł, *qʷl̓qʷl̓mu* **–** one that habitually cheats; cheater; con man; someone who trys to get the best of people. *See: **cheat**.*

library **sňčłq̇eẏmintn –** post office; library. *rt.: **q̇eẏmin** – paper, book; prefix: **sn...** – a place of; suffix: **...tin, ...tn** – means of/device.*

lice **qʷtáx̣ʷeʔ –** louse.

ččsťineʔ – nit.

λ̓osqnm – look for/search the head. *See: **search**.*
kʷ iqs λ̓oʔosqnm łu qʷtáx̣ʷeʔ – I am going to search your head for lice. **es λ̓oʔosqnms łu qʷtáx̣ʷeʔ –** S/he is searching for lice on his/her head.

nučyanmqn – find lice/nits on the head.
nučyanmqis – S/he found lice/nits on s.o.'s head. **nučyanmqn, nučyanmqntxʷ**
es nučyanmqnms – S/he is finding lice/nits on s.o.'s head. **ies nučyanmqnm, as nučyanmqnm**
qs nučyanmqnms – S/he is going to find lice/nits on s.o.'s head. **iqs nučyanmqnm, aqs nučyanmqnm**

nučnayqn – find something on the head.
nučnayqis – S/he found s.t. on s.o.'s head. **nučnayqn, nučnayqntxʷ**
es nučnayqnms – S/he is finding s.t. on s.o.'s head. **ies nučnayqnm, as nučnayqnm**
qs nučnayqnms – S/he is going to find s.t. on s.o.'s head. **iqs nučnayqnm, aqs nučnayqnm**

The **i** following uvular consonants (UC) and the glottal stop **ʔ** sound like English "*ey*" as in the words *they, hey, whey,* etc. Salish UC are: **q, q̇, qʷ, q̇ʷ, x̣, x̣ʷ**. For example, the suffix **...qin** – head/top, is often spelled using English *ey* as "q*ey*n". So **qi, q̇i, qʷi, q̇ʷi, x̣i, x̣ʷi**, may be spelled with English *ey* as **q***ey*, **q̇***ey*, **qʷ***ey*, **q̇ʷ***ey*, **x̣***ey*, **x̣ʷ***ey* in other texts.

s.t. - something, the 3rd person
(s.t.) - something implied
s.o. - someone, the 3rd person
sl. - singular form
pl. - plural form
rt. - root word
cmd. - command
lit. - literally
fig. - figuratively
i.e., - for example
See: - Redirection to a related word.

ƛ̓up – pull a louse/nit out of the hair.
ƛ̓upm – S/he pulled a louse/nit out of the hair. **čn ƛ̓upm, kʷ ƛ̓upm**
es ƛ̓upi – S/he is pulling a louse/nit out of the hair. **čnes ƛ̓upi, kʷes ƛ̓upi**
qs ƛ̓upi – S/he is going to pull a louse/nit out of the hair. **čiqs ƛ̓upi, kʷqs ƛ̓upi**

ƛ̓upis – S/he pulled a louse/nit out of s.o.'s hair. **ƛ̓upn, ƛ̓upntxʷ**
es ƛ̓upms – S/he is pulling a louse/nit out of s.o.'s hair. **ies ƛ̓upm, as ƛ̓upm**
qs ƛ̓upms – S/he is going to pull a louse/nit out of s.o.'s hair. **iqs ƛ̓upm, aqs ƛ̓upm**

es ƛ̓pƛ̓upi – S/he is pulling lice/nits out of the hair. **čnes ƛ̓pƛ̓upi, kʷes ƛ̓pƛ̓upi**

ƛ̓upiš – Pull a louse/nit out of the hair. *cmd.*
ƛ̓upnt – Pull a louse/nit out of his/her hair. *cmd.*

license **čšnmintn** – car license.

lichen **skʷályo** – yellow lichen.

sqʷl̓ápqn, *sqʷl̓á* – black tree moss.
kʷ čsqʷl̓á kʷ ẏamim – You gather black tree moss.

šáwtmqn – black tree moss.

lick **ťaqʷ** – lick.
ťaqʷm – S/he/it licked. **čn ťaqʷm, kʷ ťaqʷm**
es ťaqʷi – S/he/it is licking. **čnes ťaqʷi, kʷes ťaqʷi**
qs ťaqʷi – S/he/it is going to lick. **čiqs ťaqʷi, kʷqs ťaqʷi**
ťáʔaqʷm – They licked. **qeʔ ťaqʷm, p ťaqʷm**

ťáqʷis – S/he/it licked s.t. **ťáqʷn, ťáqʷntxʷ**
es ťaqʷms – S/he/it is licking s.t. **ies ťaqʷm, as ťaqʷm**
qs ťaqʷms – S/he/it is going to lick s.t. **iqs ťaqʷm, aqs ťaqʷm**
ťáʔaqʷis – They licked s.t. **qeʔ ťáqʷntm, ťáqʷntp**

ťaqʷnt – Lick it. *cmd.*

ťaťaqʷeʔ – little licker, affectionately.
ťqʷečst – lick the hand. *suffix:* ***...ečst, ...čst*** *– of the hand.*
čťqʷax̣n – lick the arm.

ṅem ťaqʷm – S/he/it will lick. **ṅem čn ťaqʷm, ṅem kʷ ťaqʷm**
ṅem ťáʔaqʷm – They will lick. **ṅem qeʔ ťaqʷm, ṅem p ťaqʷm**
ṅem ťáqʷis – S/he/it will lick it. **ṅem ťáqʷn, ṅem ťáqʷntxʷ**
ṅem ťáʔaqʷis – They will lick it. **ṅem qeʔ ťáqʷntm, ṅem ťáqʷntp**

ťmam – suck/lick/kiss something. *(i.e., ice-cream, lollipop)* *See:* ***kiss.***

licorice root **ṗx̣ʷcuxʷeʔ**, *ṗx̣ʷcu* – meadow rue; licorice root; *Glycyrrhiza lepidota.*

lid **k̓ʷál̓čqn** – lid, cap, cover of a container. *rt.:* ***k̓ʷel̓č*** *– upturned formed object; suffix:* ***...qin, ...qn*** *– top.*

lie **yóqʷistm**, *yóqʷi* – lie; tell a falsehood; not telling the truth.
yóqʷistm – S/he/it lied. **čn yóqʷistm, kʷ yóqʷistm**
es yóqʷisti – S/he/it is lying. **čnes yóqʷisti, kʷes yóqʷisti**
qs yóqʷisti – S/he/it is going to lie. **čiqs yóqʷisti, kʷqs yóqʷisti**
yóʔoqʷistm – They lied. **qeʔ yóqʷistm, p yóqʷistm**
es yóʔoqʷisti – They are lying. **qeʔes yóqʷisti, pes yóqʷisti**

qs yóʔoqʷisti – They are going to lie. **qeʔqs yóqʷisti, pqs yóqʷisti**

yóqʷis – S/he/it lied to it. **yóqʷn, yóqʷntxʷ**
es yóqʷms – S/he/it is lying to s.o. **ies yóqʷm, as yóqʷm**
qs yóqʷms – S/he/it is going to lie to s.o. **iqs čyóqʷm, aqs yóqʷm**
yóʔoqʷis – They lied to s.o. **qeʔ yóqʷntm, yóqʷntp**

iqʷyóqʷis – S/he/it told lies to it. **iqʷyóqʷn, iqʷyóqʷntxʷ**
iqʷyóʔoqʷis – They told lies to it. **qeʔ iqʷyóqʷntm, iqʷyóqʷntp**

yoqʷntm – S/he/it was lied to.

syóqʷm – lies.
sxʷyoqʷistm, *sxʷyoqʷí* – one tasked to lie. *prefix:* ***sxʷ...*** *– one tasked to do.*
iqʷistémn – one inclined to lie. *suffix:* ***...emn*** *– one inclined to do.*
sxʷʔiqʷistmlwis – one tasked to go around lying. *prefix:* ***sxʷ...*** *– one tasked to do.*

iqʷistmlwis – lying around.
iqʷistmnwexʷ – They lied to each other. **qeʔ iqʷistmnwe, p iqʷistmnwe**

ṅem yóqʷm – S/he/it will lie. **ṅem čn yóqʷi, ṅem kʷ yóqʷm**
ṅem yóʔoqʷm – They will lie. **ṅem qeʔ yóqʷm, ṅem p yóqʷm**
ṅem čyóqʷis – S/he/it will lie about s.t. **ṅem čyóqʷn, ṅem čyóqʷntxʷ**
ṅem yóʔoqʷis – They will lie about s.t. **ṅem qeʔ čyóqʷntm, ṅem čyóqʷntp**
qes yóqʷms – S/he/it is going to be lying to s.o. **iqes yóqʷm, aqes yóqʷm**
qes yóʔoqʷms – You all are going to be lying to s.o. **qeʔqes yóqʷm, qes yóqʷmp**

qʷo yoqʷntm – I was lied to.

čyóqʷm – tell a lie about someone.
čyóqʷis – S/he/it lied about s.o. **čyóqʷn, čyóqʷntxʷ**
es čyóqʷms – S/he/it is lying about s.o. **ies čyóqʷm, as čyóqʷm**
qs čyóqʷms – S/he/it is going to lie about s.o. **iqs čyóqʷm, aqs čyóqʷm**
čyóʔoqʷis – They lied about s.o. **qeʔ čyóqʷntm, čyóqʷntp**
es čyóʔoqʷms – They are lying about s.o. **qeʔes čyóqʷm, es čyóqʷmp**
qs čyóʔoqʷms – They are going to lie about s.o. **qeʔqs čyóqʷm, qs čyóqʷmp**

čiqʷyóqʷis – S/he/it told lies about it. **čiqʷyóqʷn, čiqʷyóqʷntxʷ**
čiqʷyóʔoqʷis – They told lies about it. **qeʔ čiqʷyóqʷntm, čiqʷyóqʷntp**

čiqʷyóqʷłmn – I told lies about you. **ta qes čyóqʷstxʷ –** You must not lie about s.o.

nyoqʷcnm – lie about something that was said to benefit the speaker. *suffix:* ***...cin, ...cn*** *– action of the mouth.*
es nyóqʷcnms – S/he is lying about what was said. **ies nyóqʷcnm, as nyóqʷcnm**

ha as nyóqʷcnm – Are you lying about what was said?

lifetime

scxʷlxʷilt – lifetime. *prefix:* ***sc...*** *– s.t. that's been done/made/prepared.*

es šʔiti – beginning of time or first time.

lift

ḱʷłxʷʔém – lift something up.
ḱʷłxʷʔeʔis – S/he lifted up s.t. **ḱʷłxʷʔen, ḱʷłxʷʔentxʷ**
es ḱʷłxʷʔéms – S/he is lifting up s.t. **ies ḱʷłxʷʔém, as ḱʷłxʷʔém**
qs ḱʷłxʷʔéms – S/he is going to lift up s.t. **iqs ḱʷłxʷʔém, aqs ḱʷłxʷʔém**
ḱʷłxʷʔéʔeʔis – They lifted up s.t. **qeʔ ḱʷłxʷʔentm, ḱʷłxʷʔentp**
es ḱʷłxʷʔéʔems – They are lifting up s.t. **qeʔes ḱʷłxʷʔém, es ḱʷłxʷʔémp**

The **i** following uvular consonants (UC) and the glottal stop ʔ sound like English "*ey*" as in the words *they, hey, whey,* etc. Salish UC are: **q, q̓, qʷ, q̓ʷ, x̣, x̣ʷ**. For example, the suffix **...qin** – head/top, is often spelled using English *ey* as "q*ey*n". So **qi, q̓i, qʷi, q̓ʷi, x̣i, x̣ʷi,** may be spelled with English *ey* as q*ey*, q̓*ey*, qʷ*ey*, q̓ʷ*ey*, x̣*ey*, x̣ʷ*ey* in other texts.

s.t. - something, the 3rd person
(s.t.) - something implied
s.o. - someone, the 3rd person
sl. - singular form
pl. - plural form
rt. - root word
cmd. - command
lit. - literally
fig. - figuratively
i.e., - for example
See: - Redirection to a related word.

qs k̓ʷɫxʷʔéʔems – They are going to lift up s.t. **qeʔqs k̓ʷɫxʷʔém, qs k̓ʷɫxʷʔémp**

k̓ʷɫxʷeʔxʷémi – repeatedly lift something; picking something up.
es k̓ʷɫxʷeʔxʷemi – S/he is picking up. **čnes k̓ʷɫxʷeʔxʷemi, kʷes k̓ʷɫxʷeʔxʷemi**

k̓ʷɫxʷʔent – Pick it up. *cmd.*

qʷo k̓ʷɫxʷʔent – Pick me up. **kʷ iqs k̓ʷɫxʷʔem** – I am going to pick you up.

nwisšlšm – raise/lift something up. *See: **raise**.*

čťaq̇šnm – raise/lift leg up to the side.
čťaq̇šnm – S/he raised one's leg up to the side. **čn čťaq̇šnm, kʷ čťaq̇šnm**
es čťaq̇šni – S/he is raising one's leg to the side. **čnes čťaq̇šni, kʷes čťaq̇šni**
qs čťaq̇šni – S/he is going to raise one's leg to the side. **čiqs čťaq̇šni, kʷqs čťaq̇šni**

čťaq̇šnmis – S/he lifted s.o.'s leg up to the side. **čťaq̇šnmn, čťaq̇šnmntxʷ**
es čťaq̇šnms – S/he is lifting s.o.'s leg to the side. **ies čťaq̇šnm, as čťaq̇šnm**

čťaq̇šniš – Raise your leg to the side. *cmd.*
čťaq̇šnint – Lift his/her/its leg to the side. *cmd.*

light

ċék̓ʷsšṅ – light.
ċk̓ʷċek̓ʷsšṅ – lights.
ċék̓ʷsšk̓ʷmn – lamp.
ċek̓ʷmn – light.

čulusnt ci ċék̓ʷsšṅ – Turn the light on. **ɫepsnt ci ċék̓ʷsšṅ** – Turn off the light.

ṗáq̇ – shine; bright. *See: **shine**.*
snčṗaq̇ustn – light bulb. *rt.: **ṗaq̇** – bright; circumfix; **č...us** – spherical shape; prefix: **...tin, ...tn** – means of/device.*

ṗéxʷ – bright; the red-hot glow of something heated. *See: **hot**.*
snṗéṗexʷups – tail light.
ṗaṗaxʷaqn – cab/roof light.
nisaqm sṗéʔexʷ – turn signal lights.

čulus – light up; turn something on; ignite.
čulusis – S/he/it turned it on. **čulusn, čulusntxʷ**
es čulusms – S/he/it is turning it on. **ies čulusm, as čulusm**
qs čulusms – S/he/it is going to turn it on. **iqs čulusm, aqs čulusm**
čulúʔusis – They turned it on. **qeʔ čulusntm, čulusntp**

es čulus – It is lit; it is turned on.

čulustn – lighter; light switch.
čulusnt – Light it up; turn it on. *cmd.*
čulsncut – light one's self up; turn one's self on.

čulusnt ci ċék̓ʷsšṅ – Turn the light on.

i x̣al – It is clear; it is daylight.
snx̣alptin – East; where the light comes.
x̣alpulexʷ – first light of the day.
čɫx̣alpeneʔ – first light of the day. *circumfix: **čɫ...eneʔ** – cover all over.*

x̣lip – It lit up; day light.

x̣lup – All of a sudden it lit up.

łppeš, *łppe* – light in weight; featherlike; gentle.
i łppeš – It is light.
i łppełċeʔ – It is a light body.

łppe łu aspúus – Your heart is light.

lighter

čulustn – make flame, lighter, light switch. *prefix:* ***sn...*** *– a place of; suffix:* ***...tin, ...tn*** *– means of/device.*

lightning

suwéčm – lightning.
es uwéči – It is lightning.

es uwéči č čo – It is lightning outside.

ċq̓em – struck by lightning. *See:* ***struck.***

light switch

čulustn – make flame, lighter, light switch. *prefix:* ***sn...*** *– a place of; suffix:* ***...tin, ...tn*** *– means of/device.*

> The **i** following uvular consonants (UC) and the glottal stop **ʔ** sound like English "*ey*" as in the words th*ey*, h*ey*, wh*ey*, etc. Salish UC are: **q, q̓, qʷ, q̓ʷ, x̣, x̣ʷ**. For example, the suffix ...**qin** – head/top, is often spelled using English *ey* as "q*ey*n". So **qi, q̓i, qʷi, q̓ʷi, x̣i, x̣ʷi**, may be spelled with English *ey* as **q***ey*, **q̓***ey*, **qʷ***ey*, **q̓ʷ***ey*, **x̣***ey*, **x̣ʷ***ey* in other texts.

like

eċx̣íl, *eċx̣í* – like; same.
iċx̣ax̣i – exactly the same.

eċx̣íli – S/he/it is acting like. **čn eċx̣íli, kʷ eċx̣íli**
eċx̣íʔili – They are acting like. **qeʔ eċx̣íli, p eċx̣íli**

eċx̣íʔili t ilmixʷm – They are acting like the boss. **x̣ił eċx̣íli t ilmixʷm** – S/he's really acting like a chief.

q̓eċx̣i – like that.
eċx̣ax̣íl, *eċx̣ax̣í* – alike; same. *See:* ***alike.***
eċx̣lmutm – S/he/it has become like s.o.
eċx̣lmutisti – S/he is making/becoming/acting like s.o.
eċx̣lnuxʷisti – S/he is working toward becoming like s.o.
eċx̣llmisti – S/he appears like/is similar to s.o.

eċx̣l̓lus – two people look alike. *suffix:* ***...us*** *– face.*
i eċx̣l̓lus – They look alike. *suffix:* ***...us*** *– face.*
eċx̣lx̣lus – Each one looks alike. *suffix:* ***...us*** *– face.*
i eċx̣ax̣lúʔus – They all look alike.

i eċx̣ax̣lsqe – They look alike *(bodies; tall, fat, big belly, etc.).*
eċx̣ax̣lsqá – The horses look alike.
eċx̣lsmisti – S/he is trying to be like/match s.o.

l čeṅ u kʷ eċx̣íli – How are you acting? **x̣ił eċx̣ili t ilmixʷm** – He's acting like a chief. **eċx̣i ye tʔe m k̓ʷul̓ntxʷ** – Make it just like this. **ha kʷ epł eċx̣ax̣lsqá** – Do you have horses that look alike? **t šeẏ eċx̣i** – It is the same kind. **eċx̣i es chááłqi** – It seems like it is chinooking outside. **kʷ eċx̣lx̣sałq t sċéʔek̓ʷ** – You smell good like a flower.

ṗáu – disregard; ignore; lose interest; tire of something; distracted. *See:* ***disregard.***
ƛ̓e ṗáumin – I already lost interest in it.

x̣menč – love; like. *suffix:* ***...enč*** *– within. See:* ***love.***

čłyuxʷt, *čłyu* – envious; want to be like; wish for something; feel bad over. *See:* ***envy.***

xʷmminm – yearn; long for; strongly desire. *See:* ***yearn.***

> s.t. - something, the 3rd person
> (s.t.) - something implied
> s.o. - someone, the 3rd person
> *sl.* - singular form
> *pl.* - plural form
> *rt.* - root word
> *cmd.* - command
> *lit.* - literally
> *fig.* - figuratively
> *i.e.,* - for example
> *See:* - Redirection to a related word.

lily **máx̣eʔ –** glacier lily; *Erythronium grandiflorum.*

qʷónmłp – yellow pond-lily; *Nuphar lutea.*

line **es łiṗ –** line; stripe.
łṗim – S/he made a line. **čn łṗim, kʷ łṗim**
es łṗmi – S/he making a line. **čnes łṗmi, kʷes łṗmi**
qs łṗmi – S/he going to make a line. **čiqs łṗmi, kʷqs łṗmi**

łṗntes – S/he made a line on s.t. **łṗnten, łṗntexʷ**
es łṗims – S/he making a line on s.t. **ies łṗim, as łṗim**
qs łṗims – S/he going to make a line on s.t. **iqs łṗim, aqs łṗim**

łṗiš – Make a line. *cmd.*
łṗint – Make a line on it. *cmd.*

łṗmncut – line one's self up. *See:* ***line up.***
łṗmintn – pencil; carpenter's pencil. *See:* ***pencil.***

łaqšlš l es łiṗ – Sit on the line. **ye l es łiṗ m p łṗmncut –** All of you will line up on this line.
łṗmncutwi ye l es łiṗ – All of you line up on this line.

šiƛ̓ – flat/even; aligned; straight; ordered. *See:* ***flat.***
šƛ̓milš – row, line. *See:* ***row.***
šƛ̓mim – put things in a straight line; aligned; ordered; level and even. *See:* ***flat.***

i ax̣ – It has lines; it is interlaced/crosses over.
es aax̣ – It is interlaced, crosses over.

čáʔax̣iċeʔ – striped. *suffix:* ***...iċéʔ*** *– covered in.*
es čax̣iċeʔ – It is all wrapped up.
čax̣iċeʔnt – Wrap it up. *cmd.*

ax̣ccné – lacing that wraps around; laces back and forth.
čax̣ċasqá – harness. *See:* ***harness.***
ax̣usnt – put the hackamore/bridle on it. *See:* ***bridle.***
ax̣éṅeʔ – beaded bag/handbag. *rt.:* ***i ax̣*** *– it has lines.*
łax̣éṅeʔ – small beaded bag/handbag

x̣ṗim – layer; line; coat. *See:* ***layer.***

line up **łṗmncut –** line one's self up.
łṗmncut – S/he lined up. **čn łṗmncut, kʷ łṗmncut**
es łṗmncuti – S/he is lining up. **čnes łṗmncuti, kʷes łṗmncuti**
qs łṗmncuti – S/he is going to line up. **čiqs łṗmncuti, kʷqs łṗmncuti**
łṗmncúʔut – They lined up. **qeʔ łṗmncut, p łṗmncut**
es łṗmncúʔuti – They are lining up. **qeʔes łṗmncuti, pes łṗmncuti**
qs łṗmncúʔuti – They are going to line up. **qeʔqs łṗmncuti, pqs łṗmncuti**

łṗmncutš – Line up. *cmd.*
łṗmncutwi – All of you line up. *cmd.*

hoy kʷeṁt ƛ̓e es łṗmncuti – They were already lining up.

lion **upayaqn –** lion. *lit. furry head.*

skʷtismyé – mountain lion, cougar; *Puma concolor.*

lip **splimcn** – lip; mouth.

...pósqn, ***...pó*** – *suffix indicating lip.*
t̓išpósqn, *t̓išpó* – sweet lips.
kʷilpósqn, *kʷilpó* – red lips *(lipstick on).*
ƛ̓um̓pósqn, *ƛ̓um̓pó* – purple lips.
poƛ̓pósqn, *poƛ̓pó* – purple lips.
q̓ʷaposqncut – squeeze one's lips together. *See:* ***mouth.***
łispó – smelly lips/face; fishy smell. *See:* ***smell.***

yalpósqn, *yalpó* – rounded lips.
yalpósqn – S/he had rounded lips. **čn yalpósqn, kʷ yalpósqn**

i yalpósqn – S/he has rounded lips. **i čn yalpósqn, i kʷ yalpósqn**

yalposqniš – Round your lips. *cmd.*

> The **i** following uvular consonants (UC) and the glottal stop **ˀ** sound like English "*ey*" as in the words *they, hey, whey,* etc. Salish UC are: **q, q̓, qʷ, q̓ʷ, x̣, x̣ʷ**. For example, the suffix **...qin** – head/top, is often spelled using English *ey* as "*qeyn*". So **qi, q̓i, qʷi, q̓ʷi, x̣i, x̣ʷi,** may be spelled with English *ey* as **q***ey*, **q̓***ey*, **qʷ***ey*, **q̓ʷ***ey*, **x̣***ey*, **x̣ʷ***ey* in other texts.

liquid **...etkʷ, ...tkʷ, ...kʷ** – *suffix indicating liquid.*
sew̓łkʷ – water.
nt̓iškʷ – sweet liquid; pop; Kool-aid.
nyoywátkʷ – strong liquid (esp. coffee).
nc̓áw̓kʷ – weak, tasteless liquid. *(i.e., coffee)*
sq̓ʷłséˀetkʷ – juice.

liquor **qʷéwutn** – liquor. *lit. something that makes you crazy. suffix:* ***...tin, ...tn*** *– means of/device.*

nx̣ʷoskʷ – beer. *lit. foamy liquid.*

listen **sunum̓t** – listen.
sunum̓t – S/he/it listened. **čn sunum̓t, kʷ sunum̓t**
es sunum̓ti – S/he/it is listening. **čnes sunum̓ti, kʷes sunum̓ti**
qs sunum̓ti – S/he/it is going to listen. **čiqs sunum̓ti, kʷqs sunum̓ti**
sunúˀum̓t – They listened. **qeˀ sunum̓t, p sunum̓t**
es sunúˀum̓ti – They are listening. **qeˀes sunum̓ti, pes sunum̓ti**
qs sunúˀum̓ti – They are going to listen. **qeˀqs sunum̓ti, pqs sunum̓ti**

sunum̓tmis – S/he/it listened to s.o. **sunum̓tmn, sunum̓tmntxʷ**
es sunum̓tms – S/he/it is listening to s.o. **ies sunum̓tm, as sunum̓tm**
qs sunum̓tms – S/he/it is going to listen to s.o. **iqs sunum̓tm, aqs sunum̓tm**
sunúˀum̓tmis – They listened to s.o. **qeˀ sunum̓tmntm, sunum̓tmntp**
es sunúˀum̓tms – They are listening to s.o. **qeˀes sunum̓tm, es sunum̓tmp**
qs sunúˀum̓tms – They are going to listen to s.o. **qeˀqs sunum̓tm, qs sunum̓tmp**

es susunum̓ti – S/he/it keeps listening. **čnes susunum̓ti, kʷes susunum̓ti**
es susunum̓tms – S/he/it keeps listening to s.o. **ies susunum̓tm, as susunum̓tm**

susułmuł – one that habitually listens. *suffix:* ***...łmuł*** *– one that habitually does.*

sunum̓tš, *sunu* – Listen. *cmd.*
sunum̓twi – All of you listen. *cmd.*
sunum̓tmnt – Listen to s.o. *cmd.*

sunum̓tmncn – I listened to you. **qʷo sunum̓tmnt** – Listen to me. *cmd.* **čnes**

> s.t. - something, the 3rd person
> (s.t.) - something implied
> s.o. - someone, the 3rd person
> *sl.* - singular form
> *pl.* - plural form
> *rt.* - root word
> *cmd.* - command
> *lit.* - literally
> *fig.* - figuratively
> *i.e.,* - for example
> *See:* - Redirection to a related word.

sunuṁti ye sqltmixʷ – I am listening to this man. **iše čn susumuṁt t čx̣ʷa –** I listen to the radio. **čiqs susunuṁti t isxʷṁiṁéẏˀm –** I am going to listen to my teacher. **sunuṁtwi es nkʷneyi tˀe swe –** All of you listen, somebody is singing.

ntmaneˀ – refuse to hear/listen.
ntmanˀem – S/he refused to hear. **čn ntmanˀem, kʷ ntmanˀem**
es ntmanˀei – S/he is refusing to hear. **čnes ntmanˀei, kʷes ntmanˀei**
qs ntmanˀei – S/he is going to refuse to hear. **čiqs ntmanˀei, kʷqs ntmanˀei**

ntmanˀeis – S/he refused to listen to s.o. **ntmanˀen, ntmanˀentxʷ**
es ntmanˀems – S/he is refusing to listen to s.o. **ies ntmanˀem, as ntmanˀem**
qs ntmanˀems – S/he is going to refuse to listen to s.o. **iqs ntmanˀem, aqs ntmanˀem**

sewnéˀ – hear. *See: **hear**.*

little

łkʷk̓ʷṅumet, *k̓ʷk̓ʷṅume* **–** little thing; small thing. *See: **small**.*
łkʷk̓ʷiyomqn – small voice; feminine voice; high pitch voice. *See: **small**.*
k̓ʷimł... – *prefix indicating something is little. See: **small**.*

ł... – *prefix that indicates a word meaning is diminished or that the word is little in comparison to the full word.*
łx̣x̣e – little cute one.
łtt̓iłs – little dirty face.

łčečwlš – little old.

sk̓ʷṅšspé – few years.

ƛ̓méẏ – few, barely, not much. *See: **few**.*

č łxʷect nk̓ʷuˀ – little after one.

little brown bat

t̓lt̓el̓ẇé, *t̓lt̓el̓ẇéliyeˀ* **–** bat, little brown bat.

live

xʷlxʷilt – alive; living.
es xʷlxʷilt – S/he/it is alive. **čnes xʷlxʷilt, kʷes xʷlxʷilt**

nxʷlxʷiltn – life.
sxʷlxʷilt – life; the living.
scxʷlxʷilt – lifetime. *prefix: **sc...** – s.t. that's been done/made/prepared.*

es xʷl̓l̓misti – S/he/it is coming alive *(born, hatched)*.
es xʷllmscutisti – S/he/it is making one's self come alive.

eł xʷl̓il̓ – S/he/it came back to life. **qeˀ xʷlxʷilt łu tl̓ t̓eyeˀ –** Deliver us from evil.

lciˀ – stays here; remains here; dwells. *See: **stay**.*

lšeˀ – stays there; roams in that general area; home range. *See: **stay**.*

kʷléẇt – dwell together.

lively

qʷiṁqʷṁmt – lively in working.

liver

pṅinč – liver.

living room

snłexʷlstn – living room; a place to relax. *prefix: **sn...** – a place of; suffix: **...tin, ...tn** – means of/device.*

lizard

šl̓šl̓čé – lizard, salamander.

load **q̓ʷelt** – load.
q̓ʷélt – S/he/it loaded (s.o./s.t.). **čn q̓ʷélt, kʷ q̓ʷélt**
es q̓ʷélti – S/he/it is loading (s.o./s.t.). **čnes q̓ʷélti, kʷes q̓ʷélti**
qs q̓ʷélti – S/he/it is going to load (s.o./s.t.). **čiqs q̓ʷélti, kʷqs q̓ʷélti**

q̓ʷéltis – S/he/it loaded s.o./s.t. **q̓ʷéltn, q̓ʷéltntxʷ**
es q̓ʷéltms – S/he/it is loading s.o./s.t. **ies q̓ʷéltm, as q̓ʷéltm**
qs q̓ʷéltms – S/he/it is going to load s.o./s.t. **iqs q̓ʷéltm, aqs q̓ʷéltm**

es q̓ʷélt – S/he/it is loaded. **čnes q̓ʷélt, kʷes q̓ʷélt**

kʷtnečl̓ – big load of provisions.

čłqminm – load; put things on the surface. *See: **put**.*

snč̓ʔinč, *snč̓ʔi* – bullet; the loading of a gun. *See: **bullet**.*

lobster **coyx̣eʔ** – lobster; crayfish.

lock **k̓ʷłnč̓ʔeptn**, *k̓ʷłnč̓ʔe* – padlock. *circumfix **k̓ʷłn...p** – **opening**.*

es k̓ʷłnč̓ʔep – It is padlocked.

k̓ʷłnc̓nmap – lock a door. *rt.: **c̓an** – tight; circumfix: **k̓ʷłn...p** – opening.*
k̓ʷłnc̓nmapis – S/he locked the door. **k̓ʷłnc̓nmapn, k̓ʷłnc̓nmapntxʷ**
es k̓ʷłnc̓nmapms – S/he is locking the door. **ies k̓ʷłnc̓nmapm, as k̓ʷłnc̓nmapm**
qs k̓ʷłnc̓nmapms – S/he is going to lock the door. **iqs k̓ʷłnc̓nmapm, aqs k̓ʷłnc̓nmapm**

k̓ʷłnc̓nmapnt – Lock it. *cmd.*

ha es k̓ʷłnc̓nmap – Is it locked?

locomotive **čx̣ʷllq̓ʷálqʷ**, *čx̣ʷllq̓ʷá* – train, locomotive, railroad cars.

lodge **sq̓eymułxʷ**, *sq̓eymu* – tipi.
q̓eyq̓eymułxʷ – more than one tipi.

spc̓néłxʷ, *spc̓né* – tipi; canvas lodge.
sp̓iʔełxʷ – tipi; buckskin tipi.
soxʷełxʷ – willow/reed tipi; medicine lodge.
scwéłxʷ – medicine lodge; thatched lodge. *prefix: **sc...** – s.t. that's been done/made/prepared.*
snlaq̓ist, *snlaq̓i* – sweat lodge. *See: **sweat lodge**.*
citxʷ – house.
nšiʔtelixʷ – head person in the lodge/house.

lodgepole pine **qʷqʷliʔt** – lodgepole pine; *Pinus contorta*.

log **smlk̓ʷtalqʷ** – log.
smlmlk̓ʷtalqʷ – logs.

kʷcič – the act of falling pertaining to a *single fixed object. (i.e., tree, post, house, etc.) See: **fall**.*
es kʷcič – It is fallen over. *(i.e., a tree/log, post, etc.)*

p̓in – long objects put in a lying position. *See: **lay**.*
p̓nełxʷ – log house.

nič – cut; slice; saw. *See: **cut**.*

The **i** following uvular consonants (UC) and the glottal stop **ʔ** sound like English "*ey*" as in the words th*ey*, h*ey*, wh*ey*, etc. Salish UC are: **q, q̓, qʷ, q̓ʷ, x̣, x̣ʷ**. For example, the suffix ...**qin** – head/top, is often spelled using English *ey* as "q*ey*n". So **qi, q̓i, qʷi, q̓ʷi, x̣i, x̣ʷi**, may be spelled with English *ey* as **q***ey*, **q̓***ey*, **qʷ***ey*, **q̓ʷ***ey*, **x̣***ey*, **x̣ʷ***ey* in other texts.

s.t. - something, the 3rd person
(s.t.) - something implied
s.o. - someone, the 3rd person
sl. - singular form
pl. - plural form
rt. - root word
cmd. - command
lit. - literally
fig. - figuratively
i.e., - for example
See: - Redirection to a related word.

loincloth **nłqʷépustšn** – diaper; breechcloth; loincloth.

Lolo **tmsmłi** – Lolo, Montana.

nccq̓łpé – mountain near Lolo.

Lolo Hot Springs **smtt̓m̓čqi** – Lolo Hot Springs area, Montana.

q̓ʷlótqne, čmulši – areas around Lolo Hot Springs.

Lolo Trail **naptnišaqs** – Lolo Trail, Montana and Idaho. *lit. Nez Perce trail/road/path.*

Lomah **lomé** – Lomah.

lone **łn̓k̓ʷuʔ** – just one.
čłn̓áqsm, *čłn̓á* – lone person.
i čnaqsm – one peson.

Lone Pine **qaliye** – Lone Pine, Flathead Nation.

lonesome **čupélsm,** *čupé* – lonesome; miss someone.
čupélsm – S/he/it was lonesome. **čn čupelsm, kʷ čupelsm**
es čupelsi – S/he/it is lonesome. **čnes čupelsi, kʷes čupelsi**
qs čupelsi – S/he/it is going to be lonesome. **čiqs čupelsi, kʷqs čupelsi**
es čupéʔelsi – They are lonesome. **qeʔes čupelsi, pes čupelsi**

čupélsmis – S/he/it was lonesome for s.o. **čupelsmn, kʷ čupelsmntxʷ**
es čupelsms – S/he/it is lonesome for s.o. **ies čupelsm, as čupelsm**
qs čupelsms – S/he/it is going to be lonesome for s.o. **iqs čupelsm, aqs čupelsm**
es čupéʔelsms – They are lonesome for s.o. **qeʔes čupelsm, es čupelsmp**

long **wisšn** – long in length.
swisšn – long; as a measure.
cil sc̓ušin swisšn – five feet long.

nʔusšnáqs – long road/nose.
čwisqn – longhair.
čususnaqstšn – long legged person. *suffix:* ***...aqstšn*** *– leg.*
usšnalqʷ – long wood/log.
čusšnelps – long neck.

ci sk̓ʷl̓snʔiłntm u tečeṅ suswisšn – The time in eating was really long.

q̓sip – long time. *See:* ***long time.***

xʷmminm – yearn; long for; strongly desire. *See:* ***yearn.***

long-billed curlew **wál̓wi, wal̓wí, sq̓l̓wí** – long-billed curlew; *Numenius americanus.*

longhair **čwisqn,** *čwi* – longhair.

Longhouse **usšnełxʷ** – Longhouse in St. Ignatius, Flathead Nation.

long johns **snsut̓ps** – long johns. *lit. stretchy pants. rt.:* ***sut̓*** *– stretch; circumfix:* n...ups – butt, tail.

longnosed sucker **čléneʔ** – longnosed sucker; *Catostomus catostomus.*

long tailed weasel **łpápqłc̓eˀ**, *łpá* – winter weasel; ermine; *Mustela frenata. rt.: **piq** – white.*

łčim̓ – summer weasel; ermine; *Mustela frenata.*

long time **q̓sip**, *q̓si* – long time.

q̓sip – S/he/it did for a long time. **čn q̓sip, kʷ q̓sip**
es q̓spmi – S/he/it is doing for a long time. **čnes q̓spmi, kʷes q̓spmi**

q̓spstes – S/he made it last a long time. **q̓spsten, q̓spstexʷ**
es q̓spims – S/he is making it last a long time. **ies q̓spim, as q̓spim**

nq̓sptin – place where one stays a long time.
q̓spemn – one inclined to be late in coming.

es q̓sipš – Stay a long time. *cmd.*
kʷtiłq̓sip – really long time.
łq̓q̓sip – little long time.
t sq̓sps – ancient; a very long time ago.
t słq̓q̓sip – a little while ago.
t sq̓sip – long time ago.
q̓spcinm – talk for a long time; endless talker. *See: **talk**.*

t sq̓sip u es wičtmncn – I have not seen you for a long time. **ha wičtxʷ łu toki łu tam t sq̓sip** – Did you see Toki not too long ago? **mił q̓sip u čn k̓ʷulm̓** – I worked too long. **ta qs q̓sip** – It will not be a long time. **łu t sq̓sip sqélixʷ** – The people of long ago. **tma łu t sq̓sip xʷˀit łu xʷixʷey̓uł** – Because, long ago there were lots of animals. **t sq̓sip ta ep suyápi** – Long ago there were not any white people.

q̓spqin – live for a long time. *suffix: **...qin, ...qn** – top.*
q̓spqin – S/he/it lived a long time. **čn q̓spqin, kʷ q̓spqin**

t slˀe – recently; not too long ago. *See: **recent**.*

The **i** following uvular consonants (UC) and the glottal stop ˀ sound like English "*ey*" as in the words th*ey*, h*ey*, wh*ey*, etc. Salish UC are: **q**, **q̓**, **qʷ**, **q̓ʷ**, **x̣**, **x̣ʷ**. For example, the suffix **...qin** – head/top, is often spelled using English *ey* as "q*ey*n". So **qi**, **q̓i**, **qʷi**, **q̓ʷi**, **x̣i**, **x̣ʷi**, may be spelled with English *ey* as **q***ey*, **q̓***ey*, **qʷ***ey*, **q̓ʷ***ey*, **x̣***ey*, **x̣ʷ***ey* in other texts.

look **ác̓x̣** – look at something.

ác̓x̣m – S/he/it looked. **čn ác̓x̣m, kʷ ác̓x̣m**
es ác̓x̣i – S/he/it is looking. **čnes ác̓x̣i, kʷes ác̓x̣i**
es ác̓x̣i – S/he/it is going to look. **čnes ác̓x̣i, kʷes ác̓x̣i**
áˀac̓x̣m – They looked. **qeˀ ác̓x̣m, p ác̓x̣m**
es áˀac̓x̣i – They are looking. **qeˀes ác̓x̣i, pes ác̓x̣i**

ác̓x̣is – S/he/it looked at it. **ác̓x̣n, ác̓x̣ntxʷ**
es ác̓x̣ms – S/he/it is looking at it. **ies ác̓x̣m, as ác̓x̣m**
qs ác̓x̣ms – S/he/it is going to look at it. **iqs ác̓x̣m, aqs ác̓x̣m**
áˀac̓x̣is – They looked at it. **qeˀ ác̓x̣ntm, ác̓x̣ntp**
es áˀac̓x̣ms – They are looking at it. **qeˀes ác̓x̣m, es ác̓x̣mp**

es ác̓ac̓x̣i – S/he/it is looking. **čnes ác̓ac̓x̣i, kʷes ác̓ac̓x̣i**
es ác̓x̣c̓x̣ms – S/he/it is watching/staring . **ies ác̓x̣c̓x̣m, as ác̓x̣c̓x̣m**

sxʷˀác̓x̣m – one tasked to look. *prefix: **sxʷ...** – one tasked to do.*

ác̓x̣iš – Look. *cmd.*
ác̓x̣wi – All of you look. *cmd.*
ác̓x̣nt – Look at it. *cmd.*
ác̓x̣nti – All of you look at it. *cmd.*
čac̓x̣ˀencu – looking into your past; reflecting on your past.

s.t. - something, the 3rd person
(s.t.) - something implied
s.o. - someone, the 3rd person
sl. - singular form
pl. - plural form
rt. - root word
cmd. - command
lit. - literally
fig. - figuratively
i.e., - for example
See: - Redirection to a related word.

es aċx̣ulexʷi – S/he is looking at the land/area/country. **čnes aċx̣ulexʷi, kʷes aċx̣ulexʷi**
áċx̣nwexʷ – look at each other.
áċx̣nwéʔexʷ – They looked at each other. **qeʔ áċx̣nwexʷ, p áċx̣nwexʷ**
es áċx̣nwéʔexʷi – They are looking at each other. **qeʔes áċx̣nwexʷi, pes áċx̣nwexʷi**
aċaċx̣m – look at repeatedly; inspect. *See: **inspect**.*
čaċx̣iċeʔ – look something all over; inspect. *See: **inspect**.*
niʔaċx̣ – look inside; inspect the inside. *See: **inspect**.*
nʔaċx̣éẇs – look at/check out something. *See: **inspect**.*
áċċx̣ – watch something. *rt.: **áċx̣** – look. See: **watch**.*

ṅem áċx̣ – S/he/it will look. **ṅem čn áċx̣, ṅem kʷ áċx̣**
ṅem áʔaċx̣ – They will look. **ṅem qeʔ áċx̣, ṅem p áċx̣**
ṅem áċx̣is – S/he/it will look at it. **ṅem áċx̣n, ṅem áċx̣ntxʷ**
ṅem áʔaċx̣is – They will look at it. **ṅem qeʔ áċx̣ntm, ṅem áċx̣ntp**

qʷo áċx̣is – S/he looked at me. **qesyáʔ u qeʔes aċx̣i łu sxʷwenš** – We are all staring at the dancer. **es áʔaċx̣ms nqʷq̓ʷosṁi** – They are looking at a dog. **es cʔáċx̣i** – She is looking toward me. **t šeẏ u iše eċx̣i qeʔes aċx̣łlt łu steṁ qeʔ sck̓ʷul̓** – That's the way it is, they look at what we do.

aċx̣sncut – look at one's self; look at your reflection.
aċx̣sncut – S/he/it looked at one's self. **čn aċx̣sncut, kʷ aċx̣sncut**
es aċx̣sncuti – S/he is looking at one's self. **čnes aċx̣sncuti, kʷes aċx̣sncuti**
qs aċx̣sncuti – S/he is going to look at one's self. **čiqs aċx̣sncuti, kʷqs aċx̣sncuti**

aċx̣sncutš – Look at yourself (in a mirror). *cmd.*

ax̣la u kʷ aċx̣sncu – You always look at yourself.

aċx̣osm – look at a face.
aċx̣osm – S/he/it looked at (s.o.'s) face. **čn aċx̣osm, kʷ aċx̣osm**
es aċx̣osi – S/he/it is looking at (s.o.'s) face. **čnes aċx̣osi, kʷes aċx̣osi**
qs aċx̣osi – S/he/it is going to look at (s.o.'s) face. **čiqs aċx̣osi, kʷqs aċx̣osi**
aċx̣óʔosm – They looked at (s.o.'s) face. **qeʔ aċx̣osm, p aċx̣osm**

aċx̣osis – S/he/it looked at s.o.'s face. **aċx̣osn, kʷ aċx̣osntxʷ**
es aċx̣osms – S/he/it is looking at s.o.'s face. **ies aċx̣osm, as aċx̣osm**
qs aċx̣osms – S/he/it is going to look at s.o.'s face. **iqs aċx̣osm, aqs aċx̣osm**
aċx̣óʔosis – They looked at s.o.'s face. **qeʔ aċx̣osntm, aċx̣osntp**

aċx̣osiš – Look at the face. *cmd.*
aċx̣osnt – Look at his/her face. *cmd.*

kʷ iqs aċx̣osm – I am going to look at your face.

čaċaċx̣osm – look at/into eyes. *circumfix: **č...us** – spherical object; eyes.*
čaċaċx̣osm – S/he/it looked (at s.o.'s) eyes. **čn čaċaċx̣osm, kʷ čaċaċx̣osm**
es čaċaċx̣osi – S/he/it is looking (at s.o.'s) eyes. **čnes čaċaċx̣osi, kʷes čaċaċx̣osi**
qs čaċaċx̣osi – S/he/it is going to look (at s.o.'s) eyes. **čiqs čaċaċx̣osi, kʷqs čaċaċx̣osi**
čaċaċx̣óʔosm – They looked (at s.o.'s) eyes. **qeʔ čaċaċx̣osm, p čaċaċx̣osm**

čaċaċx̣osis – S/he/it looked at s.o.'s eyes. **čaċaċx̣osn, kʷ čaċaċx̣osntxʷ**
es čaċaċx̣osms – S/he/it is looking at s.o.'s eyes. **ies čaċaċx̣osm, as čaċaċx̣osm**
qs čaċaċx̣osms – S/he/it is going to look at s.o.'s eyes. **iqs čaċaċx̣osm, aqs čaċaċx̣osm**
čaċaċx̣óʔosis – They looked at s.o.'s eyes. **qeʔ čaċaċx̣osntm, čaċaċx̣osntp**

čaċaċx̣osiš – Look at the eyes. *cmd.*
čaċaċx̣osnt – Look at his/her eyes. *cmd.*

kʷ iqs čaċaċx̣osm – I am going to look into your eyes.

qʷo čaċaċx̣osnt – Look me in the eye.

čx̣aˀx̣apsuɬ – S/he/it is staring .
uɬ čx̣aˀx̣apsuɬ – Those ones are staring .

čyuyúˀusm – look at something with a sharp eye; look closely at something . *rt.: **yoyóot** – strong.*
čyuyúˀusmis – S/he looked at s.t. with a sharp eye. **čyuyúˀusmn, čyuyúˀusmntxʷ**
es čyuyúˀusms – S/he is looking at s.t. with a sharp eye. **ies čyuyúˀusm, as čyuyúˀusm**
qs čyuyúˀusms – S/he is going to look at s.t. with a sharp eye. **iqs čyuyúˀusm, aqs čyuyúˀusm**

i čyuyúˀus – S/he/it has sharp eyes, good sight. *rt.: **yoyóot** – strong.*

čtkʷk̓ʷusm – look closely at something; zero-in on something .
čtkʷk̓ʷusmis – S/he looked closely at s.t . **čtkʷk̓ʷusmn, čtkʷk̓ʷusmntxʷ**
es čtkʷk̓ʷusms – S/he is looking closely at s.t . **ies čtkʷk̓ʷusm, as čtkʷk̓ʷusm**
qs čtkʷk̓ʷusms – S/he is going to look closely at s.t . **iqs čtkʷk̓ʷusm, aqs čtkʷk̓ʷusm**

ƛ̓éˀem – look for; search; find. *See: **search**.*

šƛ̓us – search/stare around; look from one thing to the next; scan. *See: **search**.*

ƛ̓úˀusm – look in on somebody. *See: **search**.*

ƛ̓uƛ̓uscutist – seek a vision. *See: **vision**.*

ƛ̓asqáx̣eˀ, *ƛ̓asqá* – look for domestic animals, horse, car. *See: **search**.*

čáliˀ – take a glance at someone or something. *See: **glance**.*

čtóls – point with the eyes; show acknowledgement by looking. *See: **acknowledge**.*

loon

usuˀɬ – loon; *Gavia immer*.

loose

háw̓m – loosen something; slacken. *(i.e., knot, jar lid, tense person, etc.)*
háw̓w̓ – S/he/it got loosened/relaxed. **čn háw̓w̓, kʷ háw̓w̓**
es háw̓w̓i – S/he is loosening/relaxing. **čnes háw̓w̓i, kʷes háw̓w̓i**
qs háw̓w̓i – S/he is going to loosen/relaxing. **čiqs háw̓w̓i, kʷqs háw̓w̓i**

háw̓msts – S/he loosened s.t. **háw̓mstn, háw̓mstxʷ**
es háw̓ms – S/he is loosening s.t. **ies háw̓m, as háw̓m**
qs háw̓ms – S/he is going to loosen s.t. **iqs háw̓m, aqs háw̓m**
háˀaw̓msts – They loosened s.t. **qeˀ háw̓mstm, háw̓mstp**
es háˀaw̓ms – They are loosening s.t. **qeˀes háw̓m, es háw̓mp**

háw̓ntm – It was loosened.
i háw̓ – It is loose.

háw̓ – S/he is loose/relaxed. **čn háw̓, kʷ háw̓**

háw̓mskʷ – Loosen it. *cmd.*
es nháw̓elsi – S/he wants to be relieved/loosened. **čnes nháw̓elsi, kʷes nháw̓elsi**

kʷƛ̓im – take something out; detach; loose/free embedded object. *See: **take**.*
čkʷƛ̓pep – shed fur. *See: **shed**.*

The **i** following uvular consonants (UC) and the glottal stop **ˀ** sound like English "*ey*" as in the words *they*, *hey*, *whey*, etc. Salish UC are: **q, q̓, qʷ, q̓ʷ, x̣, x̣ʷ**. For example, the suffix **...qin** – head/top, is often spelled using English *ey* as "q*ey*n". So **qi, q̓i, qʷi, q̓ʷi, x̣i, x̣ʷi**, may be spelled with English *ey* as **q***ey*, **q̓***ey*, **qʷ***ey*, **q̓ʷ***ey*, **x̣***ey*, **x̣ʷ***ey* in other texts.

s.t. - something, the 3rd person
(s.t.) - something implied
s.o. - someone, the 3rd person
sl. - singular form
pl. - plural form
rt. - root word
cmd. - command
lit. - literally
fig. - figuratively
i.e., - for example
See: - Redirection to a related word.

łiyat – loose; not fastened well.
čehéķʷ – separate; detatch; break free of; loosen. *See: **separate**.*
talip, *tal* **–** untie; loose. *See: **untie**.*
čťoʔq̇ép – molt feathers. *See: **molt**.*
čttoqqin – loose hair; balding. *See: **bald**.*
nawpncut – shed skin as a snake. *See: **shed**.*

lord

čelltč – owner; master; lord.

amotqn – Creator; Sits On Top; president. *See: **creator**.*

ķʷl̓ncutn – Creator; Maker of Ways/Mannerisms.

čšyépleʔ – Creator; Keeper; Protecter.

lose

šƛ̓ip, *šƛ̓i* **–** lose; defeated. *See: **defeat**.*

alip – lose in gambling.
alip – S/he lost. **čn alip, kʷ alip**
es alpmi – S/he is losing. **čnes alpmi, kʷes alpmi**
qs alpmi – S/he is going to lose. **čiqs alpmi, kʷqs alpmi**
es áʔalpmi – They are losing. **qeʔes alpmi, pes alpmi**

sʔalip – gambling loss.

alpiċeʔ – lose blankets in gambling.

ṗáu – disregard; ignore; lose interest; tire of something; distracted. *See: **disregard**.*

loss

salip – lose in gambling.

lost

oóst – lost.
oóst – S/he/it was lost. **čn oóst, kʷ oóst**
es oósti – S/he/it is lost. **čnes oósti, kʷes oósti**
qs oósti – S/he/it is going to be lost. **čiqs oósti, kʷqs oósti**
es oóʔosti – They are lost. **qeʔes oósti, pes oósti**

oósis – S/he/it lost s.t/s.o. **oósn, oósntxʷ**
oóʔosis – They lost s.t/s.o. **qeʔ oósntm, oósntp**

oostlwist – go around being lost.
es oostlwisti – S/he is going around lost. **čnes oostlwisti, kʷes oostlwisti**

čosoóssn – lost shoes. *suffix: **...šin, ...šn** – feet.*

osqáx̣eʔ – lose a domestic animal; horse; car. *suffix: **...sqax̣eʔ, ...sqa** –domestic animal; mainly referring to horse or car.*
osqáx̣eʔ – S/he lost a horse. **čn osqáx̣eʔ, kʷ osqáx̣eʔ**
es osqáx̣eʔi – S/he is losing a horse. **čnes osqáx̣eʔi, kʷes osqáx̣eʔi**
qs osqáx̣eʔi – S/he is going to lose a horse. **čiqs osqáx̣eʔi, kʷqs osqáx̣eʔi**

niap – lost for good.

lost article dance

sťiplscut swenš – lost article dance. *rt.: **ťiip** – fall; suffix: **...cut** – action to the self.*
es ťiplscuti – S/he is dancing. **čnes ťiplscuti, kʷes ťiplscuti**
es ťiplscúʔuti – They are dancing. **qeʔes ťiplscuti, pes ťiplscuti**

qeʔes čučawi x̣ʷl̓ sťiplscut – We are praying for the lost articles.

sṫiplscut qʷelm – lost article song.

lots

miɫ – too much, too many. *See: too much.*

xʷʔit – many; a lot; much; have plenty. *See: many.*

yapqin – a lot; big gathering; gathering of many things/people.
ƛ̓e qeʔ čiyyapqin – There are lots of us now. **néɫi ṅem ẏapqin qeʔqs cq̓ʷeɫt –** Because there will be lots for us to pack out.

The **i** following uvular consonants (UC) and the glottal stop **ʔ** sound like English "*ey*" as in the words th*ey*, h*ey*, wh*ey*, etc. Salish UC are: **q**, **q̓**, **qʷ**, **q̓ʷ**, **x̣**, **x̣ʷ**. For example, the suffix …**qin** – head/top, is often spelled using English *ey* as "q*ey*n". So **qi**, **q̓i**, **qʷi**, **q̓ʷi**, **x̣i**, **x̣ʷi**, may be spelled with English *ey* as **q***ey*, **q̓***ey*, **qʷ***ey*, **q̓ʷ***ey*, **x̣***ey*, **x̣ʷ***ey* in other texts.

loud

nƛ̓x̣cin – loud in singing or talking; make loud noises. *suffix: ...cin, ...cn – action of the mouth.*
nƛ̓x̣cinm – S/he was loud. **čn nƛ̓x̣cinm, kʷ nƛ̓x̣cinm**
es nƛ̓x̣cini – S/he is being loud. **čnes nƛ̓x̣cini, kʷes nƛ̓x̣cini**
qs nƛ̓x̣cini – S/he is going to be loud. **čiqs nƛ̓x̣cini, kʷqs nƛ̓x̣cini**

nƛ̓x̣ciniš – Be loud; talk loud; sing loud. *cmd.*
nƛ̓x̣cinwi – All of you be loud; talk loud; sing loud. *cmd.*

sšymɫ nƛ̓x̣cin – loudest.

l čeṅ u ecx̣lsnƛ̓x̣cin – How loud is it? **kʷtnelsiš nƛ̓x̣ciniš –** Be proud, speak loud. **miɫ nƛ̓x̣cin –** It is too loud.

Louie

lwi – Louie.

louse

qʷtáx̣ʷeʔ – louse, lice.

lovage

x̣ásx̣s – lovage; *Ligusticum.*

love

x̣menč – love; like. *suffix: ...enč – within.*
x̣menčm – S/he/it liked/loved. **čn x̣menčm, kʷ x̣menčm**
es x̣menči – S/he/it is liking/loving. **čnes x̣menči, kʷes x̣menči**
qs x̣menči – S/he/it is going to like/love. **čiqs x̣menči, kʷqs x̣menči**
es x̣méʔenči – They are liking/loving. **qeʔes x̣menči, pes x̣menči**

x̣menčs – S/he/it likes/love. **inx̣menč, anx̣menč**
x̣méʔenčs – They like/love. **qeʔ x̣menč, x̣menčmp**

x̣mnčscut – S/he loved one's self. **čn x̣mnčscut, kʷ x̣mnčscut**
es x̣mnčscuti – S/he is loving one's self. **čnes x̣mnčscuti, kʷes x̣mnčscuti**

nx̣menčis – S/he/it likes/loves s.o/s.t. **nx̣menčn, nx̣menčntxʷ**
es x̣ménčms – S/he/it is loving s.o/s.t. **ies x̣ménčm, as x̣menčm**
qs x̣ménčms – S/he/it is loving s.o/s.t. **iqs x̣ménčm, aqs x̣menčm**
x̣méʔenčis – They like/love s.o/s.t. **qeʔ x̣menčntm, x̣menčntp**

es ɫx̣x̣ménčms – S/he/it is loving s.o/s.t. a little. **ies ɫx̣x̣ménčm, as ɫx̣x̣menčm**

sxʷx̣ménč – lover; one tasked to love/like. *prefix: sxʷ... – one tasked to do.*
x̣mnčemn – lover; one inclined to love/like. *suffix: ...emn – one inclined to do.*
x̣mnčutm – loveable.
sx̣mx̣mnčsnuxʷ – lovely; something worthy of love.
čx̣menčtn – why one is loved.
sx̣mnčsqáx̣eʔs – the horse s/he loves. **isx̣mnčsqáx̣eʔ, asx̣mnčsqáx̣eʔ**
sx̣mnčscut – favorite person.

x̣mnčscutš – Love your self. *cmd.*

s.t. - something, the 3rd person
(s.t.) - something implied
s.o. - someone, the 3rd person
sl. - singular form
pl. - plural form
rt. - root word
cmd. - command
lit. - literally
fig. - figuratively
i.e., - for example
See: - Redirection to a related word.

x̣mnčłtumš – love the people.
x̣mnčelt – love children.

x̣menčstmn – I love/like you. **x̣menčstmncn –** I like/love you. **x̣menčłmn –** I liked/loved you all. **kʷ inx̣menč –** You are my love/like; I love/like you. **kʷ ies x̣menčm –** I am loving you. **kʷ nx̣menčs –** S/he/it likes/loves you. **x̣méʔenčis t suyápi –** The white people liked this. **inx̣me łu smx̣e –** I like grizzy bear. **inqecč tam x̣ménčis qs pulsi t xʷixʷéẏuł –** My older brother does not like killing animals. **ta l stém̓ u es x̣méʔenčstm łu t snk̓ʷélixʷs –** None of their tribesmen liked them at all. **sxʷx̣ménč t kapi –** coffee lover. **x̣mnčłkapi –** coffee lover. **inx̣meč čiqs mntwi –** I like running. **es nx̣selsi łu inčx̣menčtn –** Her good way is the reason I love her. **swinumt kʷ swinumt t̓išpo tl̓ ispuus kʷ inx̣menč –** Beautiful, you are beautiful sweet lips; from my heart I love you.

x̣mnčelis – love of two or more; love equally; community love.
es x̣mnčéʔelisi – The group is loving each other. **qeʔes x̣mnčelisi, pes x̣mnčelisi**

x̣mnčelists – S/he made the group love each other. **x̣mnčelistn, x̣mnčelistxʷ**
es x̣mnčelisms – S/he is making the group love each other. **ies x̣mnčelism, as x̣mnčelism**

nx̣mnčelistn – love; what makes people love one another.

x̣mnčew̓s – love one another.
x̣mnčéʔew̓s – They loved each other. **qeʔ x̣mnčew̓s, p x̣mnčew̓s**
es x̣mnčéʔew̓si – They are loving each other. **qeʔes x̣mnčew̓si, pes x̣mnčew̓si**
qs x̣mnčéʔew̓si – They are going to love each other. **qeʔqs x̣mnčew̓si, pqs x̣mnčew̓si**

x̣mnčew̓sts – S/he caused them to love each other. **x̣mnčew̓stn, x̣mnčew̓stxʷ**
es x̣mnčew̓sms – S/he is causing them to love each other. **ies x̣mnčew̓sm, as x̣mnčew̓sm**
qs x̣mnčew̓sms – S/he is going to cause them to love each other. **iqs x̣mnčew̓sm, aqs nx̣mnčew̓sm**

es nx̣mnčéʔew̓s – They love one another. **qeʔes nx̣mnčew̓s, pes nx̣mnčew̓s**

snx̣mnčew̓sts – his/her beloved. **isnx̣mnčew̓s, asnx̣mnčew̓s**
sx̣mnčew̓s – mutual love. *suffix:* ***...éw̓s*** *– in between, middle.*

čnes nx̣saqs łu x̣ʷl̓ isx̣mnčew̓s – I am on a good path because of my lover.

nx̣mnčsels – feel loved/liked.
nx̣mnčsels – S/he felt loved. **čn nx̣mnčsels, kʷ nx̣mnčsels**
es nx̣mnčselsi – S/he is feeling loved. **čnes nx̣mnčselsi, kʷes nx̣mnčselsi**
qs nx̣mnčselsi – S/he is going to feel loved. **čiqs nx̣mnčselsi, kʷqs nx̣mnčselsi**
nx̣mnčséʔels – They felt loved. **qeʔ nx̣mnčsels, p nx̣mnčsels**

x̣mmnčils – begin to love/like.
x̣mmnčils – S/he began to love. **čn x̣mmnčils, kʷ x̣mmnčils**
es x̣mmnčilsi – S/he is beginning to love. **čnes x̣mmnčilsi, kʷes x̣mmnčilsi**
qs x̣mmnčilsi – S/he is going to begin to love. **čiqs x̣mmnčilsi, kʷqs x̣mmnčilsi**

x̣mmnčilsis – S/he began to love s.o. **x̣mmnčilsn, x̣mmnčilsntxʷ**
es x̣mmnčilsms – S/he is beginning to love s.o. **ies x̣mmnčilsm, as x̣mmnčilsm**
qs x̣mmnčilsms – S/he is going to begin to love s.o. **iqs x̣mmnčilsm, aqs x̣mmnčilsm**

pux̣mnčscut – love one's spouse.
pux̣mnčscut – S/he loved his/her spouse. **čn pux̣mnčscut, kʷ pux̣mnčscut**
es pux̣mnčscuti – S/he loves his/her spouse. **čnes pux̣mnčscuti, kʷes pux̣mnčscuti**

pux̣mnčscutš – Love your spouse. *cmd.*

pux̣menč – love someone's spouse; adulterous love.
es pux̣emnč – S/he loves a married person. **čnes pux̣emnč, kʷes pux̣emnč**

pux̣menčsts – S/he loved s.o.'s spouse. **pux̣menčstn, pux̣menčstxʷ**
es pux̣menčm – S/he is loving s.o.'s spouse. **ies pux̣menčm, as pux̣menčm**
qs pux̣menčm – S/he is going to love s.o.'s spouse. **iqs pux̣menčm, aqs pux̣menčm**

The **i** following uvular consonants (UC) and the glottal stop **ʔ** sound like English "*ey*" as in the words th*ey*, h*ey*, wh*ey*, etc. Salish UC are: **q, q̇, qʷ, q̇ʷ, x̣, x̣ʷ**. For example, the suffix ...**qin** – head/top, is often spelled using English *ey* as "q*ey*n". So **qi, q̇i, qʷi, q̇ʷi, x̣i, x̣ʷi**, may be spelled with English *ey* as **q***ey*, **q̇***ey*, **qʷ***ey*, **q̇ʷ***ey*, **x̣***ey*, **x̣ʷ***ey* in other texts.

ṗałkʷ – preferential affection. *See: **affection**.*

čx̣ssmels, *čx̣ssme* – physically affectionate with someone; make out with someone; lucky. *(In the short form this word is also used as an expression for having good luck.) See: **affection**.*

q̇ix̣tm – cherish something or someone; fond of something possessed; treasure something or someone; show respect by cherishing a gift. *See: **cherish**.*

čołip – become attached to something to form one whole. *See: **attach**.*
es ołeẇs – The two are one piece; the two hearts are united. **qeʔes ołeẇs, pes ołeẇs**

nk̇ʷuwilš – They became one. *See: **one**.*

xʷmminm – yearn; long for; strongly desire. *See: **yearn**.*

low

išut – down, low. *See: **down**.*

k̇ʷłišut – underneath; down below; under; beneath. *See: **under**.*

nišut – down inside; deep inside. *See: **inside**.*

lower

tl̓ ciʔ išut – lower. *See: **down**.*

k̇ʷłt̓ipstes – S/he lowered the price. **k̇ʷłt̓ipsten, k̇ʷłt̓ipstexʷ**

sʔuʔ – water fluctuates; water goes up and down.
iše sʔuʔ – The water goes up and down.
sʔu łu sewłkʷ – It just got low, the water.

luck

x̣stšitm – good luck.
es x̣stšitm – S/he/it has good luck. **qʷo es x̣stšitm, kʷ es x̣stšitm**

čstšitm – good luck.
es čstšitm – S/he/it has bad luck. **qʷo es čstšitm, kʷ es čstšitm**

...el̓ – *Suffix: intransitive success; indicating luck, ablility to outsmart, ablility to out maneuver. Whether the luck is perceived as good or bad depends on the context of the root word meaning.*
čslqnel̓ – good luck hunting; outsmart game/prey. *See: **hunt**.*
k̇ʷłʔawl̓ – good luck guessing.
łx̣ʷṗel̓ – luck in escaping.
t̓l̓xʷel̓ – bad luck; could not succeed.
xʷcpel̓ – unlucky, too late.
čcnel̓ – luck in winning.
ƛ̓xʷpel̓ – luck in winning.
čtewl̓ – luck in hitting the mark.
ilpel̓ – luck in stricking with a projectile.
x̣lwiʔel̓ – luck in getting a husband.

s.t. - something, the 3rd person
(s.t.) - something implied
s.o. - someone, the 3rd person
sl. - singular form
pl. - plural form
rt. - root word
cmd. - command
lit. - literally
fig. - figuratively
i.e., - for example
See: - Redirection to a related word.

nx̣ʷnx̣ʷel̓ – good luck in getting a wife.

accel̓ – luck in catching.
accel̓ – S/he was luck to catch him. **čn accel̓, kʷ accel̓**
es accel̓i – S/he is catching by luck. **čnes accel̓i, kʷes accel̓i**

čswilqn – chance in overcoming/winning/beating.
čswilqis – S/he overcame s.o./s.t. by chance. **čswilqn, čswilqntxʷ**
es čswilqnms – S/he is overcoming s.o./s.t. by chance. **ies čswilqnm, as čswilqnm**

lucky
čx̣ssmels, *čx̣ssme* – physically affectionate with someone; make out with someone; lucky. *(In the short form this word is also used as an expression for having good luck.) See:* ***affection.***

łu čnes nxʷstaqsi u čn čx̣ssme – I was hitchhiking and got lucky. **čx̣ssme u pulsm t sx̣ʷleščn** – He was lucky and killed a white-tail buck.

Lucy
luci – Lucy.

lug nut
sčx̣ʷlx̣ʷlq̓ʷšin – lug nut. *See:* ***nut.***

luke warm
i nmal̓kʷ – The liquid is luke warm.

lumber
łq̓lq̓alqʷ – lumber. *suffix:* ***...alqʷ*** *– wood; cylindical.*
łq̓álqʷ – board. *suffix:* ***...alqʷ*** *– wood; cylindical.*

scpič – lumber. *rt.:* ***pič*** *– shave/cut; prefix:* ***sc...*** *– s.t. that's been done/made/prepared.*

lumber mill
snpičmn – lumber mill. *rt.:* ***pič*** *– shave/cut; prefix:* ***sn...*** *– a place of; suffix:* ***...min, ...mn*** *– instrument/tool.*

snničmn – lumber mill. *rt.:* ***nič*** *– cut; prefix:* ***sn...*** *– a place of; suffix:* ***...min, ...mn*** *– instrument/tool.*

lump
čéʔ – lump; something just sitting there.
es čéʔ – S/he/it is a lump. **čnes čéʔ, kʷes čéʔ**
nčʔéneʔ – pillow; lump for the ear.

scmlmálq̓ʷ – clumps. *prefix:* ***sc...*** *– s.t. that's been done/made/prepared.*

lunch
sťečl – lunch/snack.
iqs k̓ʷul̓m sťečl – I am going to make a lunch/snack.

ntox̣ʷqinm – eat lunch. *suffix:* ***...qin, ...qn*** *– top.*
ntox̣ʷqinm – S/he/it ate lunch. **čn ntox̣ʷqinm, kʷ ntox̣ʷqinm**
es ntox̣ʷqini – S/he/it is eating lunch. **čnes ntox̣ʷqini, kʷes ntox̣ʷqini**
qs ntox̣ʷqini – S/he/it is going to eat lunch. **čiqs ntox̣ʷqini, kʷqs ntox̣ʷqini**
es ntóʔox̣ʷqini – They are eating lunch. **qeʔes ntox̣ʷqini, pes ntox̣ʷqini**

sntox̣ʷqinm – lunchtime.

t stem̓ u kʷ ntox̣ʷqinm – What did you eat for lunch?

lungs
spew̓pu – lungs.

lupine
nq̓naq̓tétp, *nq̓naq̓té* – lupine; *Lupinus.*

ťaťaqnétp – lupine; *Lupinus.*

lynx
p̓ičn̓ – lynx; *Lynx canadensis.*

M

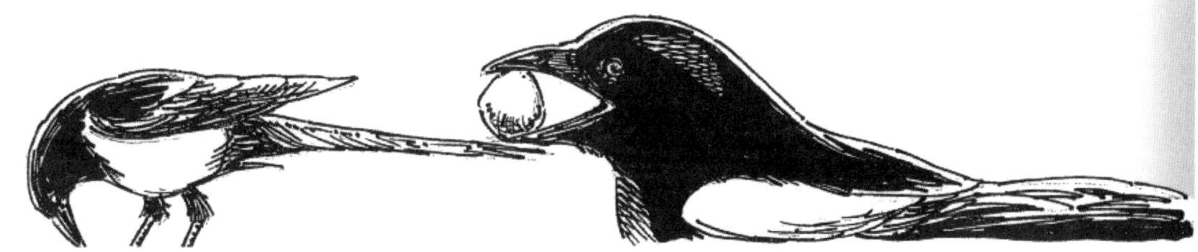

macaroni **scnłx̣ʷłłx̣ʷé –** macaroni. *rt.: **łox̣ʷ**– hole; prefix: **sc...** – s.t. that's been done/made/prepared.*

mad **áym –** angry, mad. *See: **angry**.*

léč – furious; really angry; mad; in a rage; violent. *See: **furious**.*

čxʷttels, *čxʷtte* – enraged; angry; mad; vicious; the extreme of anger. *See: **enraged**.*

nq̇aupáqs – have a broken nose. An expression indicating someone is angry. *See: **angry**.*

nšiwm – have angry/nasty/bad actions or words. *See: **angry**.*

hawawlš – tell off; yell at someone. *See: **tell off**.*

made **k̓ʷul̓ –** do; make; fix; work. *See: **work**.*

q̇eʔečst – made to be or do something; cause hardship for someone; cause problems for someone; put someone/something into it *(by holding, by making it one's business to do so, by situational happenstance, etc.). rt.: **q̇eʔ** – put inside; suffix: **...ečst, ...čst** – of the hand.*
q̇eʔečstmis – S/he made s.o. do s.t. **q̇eʔečstmn, q̇eʔečstmntxʷ**
es q̇eʔečstms – S/he is making s.o. do s.t. **ies q̇eʔečstm, as q̇eʔečstm**
qs q̇eʔečstms – S/he is going to make s.o. do s.t. **iqs q̇eʔečstm, aqs q̇eʔečstm**

q̇eʔečstmnt – Get in his/her business/way. *cmd.*

qʷo q̇eʔečstmntm u nʔemtewsn – I had to wait for it; I was made to wait for it.

maggot **čéčłuʔ –** maggot.
čéčłuʔxʷntm – It got maggots on it.

x̣máłtn – housefly.

magnet **čołpmin –** something that attaches to something to form a solid whole; magnet. *rt.: **oył** – one piece, whole.*
čołpmew̓stn – something that attaches two things together to form a whole; magnet. *rt.: **oył** – one piece, whole.*

magpie **áṅn –** magpie; *Pica hudsonia.*
es nʔáṅncni – The magpie is cawing.

anʔáṅnmuł – magpie that habitually caws; one that habitually is like the magpie. *suffix: **...łmuł** – one that habitually does.*

Magpie **qʷacqisʔá,** *qʷacqisʔáṅn* – Magpie, an area in the Flathead Nation. *lit. Magpie's hat.*

mail **sck̓ʷłxʷic̓š q̇ey̓min –** mail. *prefix:f **sc...** – s.t. that's been done/made/prepared.*

s.t. - something, the 3rd person
(s.t.) - something implied
s.o. - someone, the 3rd person
sl. - singular form
pl. - plural form
rt. - root word
cmd. - command
lit. - literally
fig. - figuratively
i.e., - for example
See: - Redirection to a related word.

čtqʷalqʷm – ship something off.

Main Gambling Grounds

słeʔi – Main Gambling Grounds, a place name.

make

k̓ʷul̓ – do; make; fix; work. *See:* ***work***.

qʷo k̓ʷul̓is čiqs oyencuti – S/he/it made me laugh. **qʷo k̓ʷul̓ntxʷ čiqs tkʷk̓ʷmi –** You made me fall.
ta qʷo qs k̓ʷul̓ntxʷ čiqs oyencuti – Do not make me laugh. **k̓ʷul̓nt qs mntwi –** Make him/her run.

nqʷl̓pulexʷm – make bread. *See:* ***bread***.

nċax̣lexʷm – make frybread. *See:* ***frybread***.

np̓ečlexʷm – make bannock bread. *See:* ***bannock bread***.

nłċx̣ċax̣lexʷm – make donuts. *See:* ***donut***.

make fun of

čoẏoẏłtúmš, *čoẏoẏłtú* **–** laugh at someone; make fun of someone.
čoẏoẏłtúmš – S/he laughed at someone. **čn oẏoẏłtúmš, kʷ čoẏoẏłtúmš**
es čoẏoẏłtúmši – S/he is laughing at someone. **čnes oẏoẏłtúmši, kʷes čoẏoẏłtúmši**
qs čoẏoẏłtúmši – S/he is going to laugh at someone. **čiqs oẏoẏłtúmši, kʷqs čoẏoẏłtúmši**

ta kʷ qes čoẏołtúmš – Do not make fun of s.o.

čoẏoẏłtém – laugh at someone or something; to make fun of. *See:* ***laugh***.
nčoẏoẏci – person who always makes fun of others.

makeup

snt̓eċstn – makeup face. *prefix:* ***sn...*** *– a place of; suffix:* ***...tin, ...tn*** *– means of/device.*
ihém – regain friendship; make peace; reconcile differences. *See:* ***peace***.

male

sqltmixʷ, *sqltmi* **–** man; male sex.

nmlmlk̓ʷépls, *nmlmlk̓ʷé* **–** male animal; bull, stallion. *suffix:* ***...epls*** *– testicle.*

mallard

sesƛ̓xʷuṁ – duck; female mallard.

qʷinqn – male mallard.

mammoth

neṁmlaqs, *neṁmla* **–** mammoth.

man

sqltmixʷ, *sqltmi* **–** man; male sex.
sqlqltmixʷ, *sqlqltmi* **–** men; menfolk.
sqql̓tṁixʷ – small man.

sqltmxʷalqs – men's clothes/dress.
qlqltmxʷus – look like a man.
nqltmixʷcn – talk/sound like a man.

nyowalqn – deep voice; low voice.

nkʷtonqn – big voice.

mane

sčiċelps – horse mane. *suffix:* ***...elps, ...lps*** *– neck.*

čx̣ilps – grey horse mane. *suffix:* ***...elps, ...lps*** *– neck.*

many

xʷʔit – many; a lot; much; have plenty.
xʷʔitm – S/he/it got many. **čn xʷʔitm, kʷ xʷʔitm**
es xʷʔitmi – S/he/it is getting many. **čnes xʷʔitmi, kʷes xʷʔitmi**
qs xʷʔitmi – S/he/it is going to get many. **čiqs xʷʔitmi, kʷqs xʷʔitmi**

xʷetilš – They became many. **qeʔ xʷetilš, p xʷetilš**
es xʷetilši – S/he/it is becoming many. **qeʔes xʷetilši, pes xʷetilši**
qs xʷetilši – S/he/it is going to become many. **qeʔqs xʷetilši, pqs xʷetilši**

xʷetilš – They became many. **qeʔ xʷetilš, p xʷetilš**
es xʷetilši – S/he/it is becoming many. **qeʔes xʷetilši, pes xʷetilši**
qs xʷetilši – S/he/it is going to become many. **qeʔqs xʷetilši, pqs xʷetilši**

xʷeʔtstes – S/he/it made s.t. be many. **xʷeʔtsten, xʷeʔtstexʷ**
es xʷeʔtims – S/he/it is making s.t. be many. **ies xʷeʔtim, as xʷeʔtim**
qs xʷeʔtims – S/he/it is going to make s.t. be many. **iqs xʷeʔtim, aqs xʷeʔtim**

xʷʔitmis – S/he/it used a lot of s.t. **xʷʔitmn, xʷʔitmntxʷ**
es xʷʔitmms – S/he/it is using a lot of s.t. **ies xʷʔitmm, as xʷʔitmm**
qs xʷʔitmms – S/he/it is going to use a lot of s.t. **iqs xʷʔitmm, aqs xʷʔitmm**

xʷʔáłq – S/he got a lot of berries. **čn xʷʔáłq, kʷ xʷʔáłq**
es xʷʔáłqi – S/he is getting a lot of berries. **čnes xʷʔáłq, kʷes xʷʔáłqi**

The **i** following uvular consonants (UC) and the glottal stop **ʔ** sound like English "*ey*" as in the words *they, hey, whey,* etc. Salish UC are: **q, q̓, qʷ, q̓ʷ, x̣, x̣ʷ**. For example, the suffix **...qin** – head/top, is often spelled using English *ey* as "q*ey*n". So **qi, q̓i, qʷi, q̓ʷi, x̣i, x̣ʷi,** may be spelled with English *ey* as **q***ey*, **q̓***ey*, **qʷ***ey*, **q̓ʷ***ey*, **x̣***ey*, **x̣ʷ***ey* in other texts.

čxʷełċeʔ, *čxʷe* – get/kill many animals for the meat they provide *(for the purpose of eating)*. *See:* ***kill.***
xʷexʷʔit – many groups.
čxʷexʷʔit, *čxʷexʷʔi* – many people.
xʷexʷʔel̓t – many children.
xʷʔasqá – many domestic animals.
xʷeʔšin – many feet, many tracks.
xʷʔeššn̓ – many rocks.
xʷʔełxʷ – many houses.

xʷʔit łu l ispúʔus – There is a lot in my heart. **xʷʔit łu isck̓ʷłpa** – There is a lot on my mind. **l čen̓ u eċx̣lsxʷʔit** – How many is it? **eċx̣lsxʷʔit t sq̓pq̓epe** – It is as many as sand. **čen̓ łu šymł xʷʔit** – Which is the most? **ƛ̓e čxʷʔéʔ t sw̓ewł** – There is already a lot of fish. **čxʷoyqntp néłi ƛ̓e čxʷʔéʔ t ċúʔulixʷ** – You guys pile it up, because there are already a lot of deer. **iše čxʷexʷʔi łu sqélixʷ** – There are a lot of people. **une xʷʔit łu sqel̓tč** – Yes, it is a lot of meat.

map
scq̓y̓ulexʷ – map. *rt.:* ***q̓ey̓i*** *– write/mark; prefix:* ***sc...*** *– s.t. that's been done/made/prepared; suffix:* ***...ulexʷ*** *– land.*

maple
sx̣ʷƛ̓ulalqʷ, *sx̣ʷƛ̓ula* – Rocky Mountain maple; *Acer glabrum.*

marble
čmilqʷs – marble.

March
k̓ʷsixʷ spq̓niʔ – March *(month of the geese).*

mare
smómšn – mare.
sm̓usłċeʔ, *sm̓u* – female animal.

mark
es łip̓ – line; stripe. *See:* ***line.***

čt̓čim – mark/brand with the hand. *See:* ***brand.***

p̓ix̣ – brand with a hot iron. *See:* ***brand.***

ċałxʷ – piled rock shelter/marker. *See:* ***rock.***

s.t. - something, the 3rd person
(s.t.) - something implied
s.o. - someone, the 3rd person
sl. - singular form
pl. - plural form
rt. - root word
cmd. - command
lit. - literally
fig. - figuratively
i.e., - for example
See: - Redirection to a related word.

marker
nt̓maqstn q̓ey̓mintn – marker; damp tipped writing tool. *rt.:* ***t̓im̓*** *– damp; circumfix:* ***n...aqs*** *– nose, road, pointed.*

market **nˀeys –** pay for something bought. *See:* ***pay****.*
nˀeysts – S/he was in the market for s.t. **nˀeystn, nˀeystxʷ**
es nˀeysts – S/he is in the market for s.t. **es nˀeystn, es nˀeystxʷ**
qs nˀeysts – S/he is going to be in the market for s.t. **qs nˀeystn, qs nˀeystxʷ**

es nˀeysts łu snčłċaˀsqaχeˀ – S/he is in the market for horses. **es nˀeystm łu sewłkʷ –** There is a market for water.

marmot **smċėċ –** hoary marmot; *Marmota caligata*; yellow-bellied marmot; *Marmota flaviventris;* groundhog; woodchuck; *(there is no distinction between the two marmot species).*

marrow **sťus –** marrow.

ťus – eat marrow.
ťusm – S/he/it ate marrow. **čn ťusm, kʷ ťusm**
es ťusi – S/he/it is eating marrow. **čnes ťusi, kʷes ťusi**
qs ťusi – S/he/it is going to eat marrow. **čiqs ťusi, kʷqs ťusi**
ťúˀusm – They ate marrow. **qeˀ ťusm, p ťusm**
es ťúˀusi – They are eating marrow. **qeˀes ťusi, pes ťusi**
qs ťúˀusi – They are going to eat marrow. **qeˀqs ťusi, pqs ťusi**

ha iše kʷ ťusm – Do you eat marrow?

skʷlqin – backbone marrow.

marrow gut **sołénč –** marrow gut. *suffix:* ***...enč*** *– within.*

marry **nχ̣ʷnχ̣ʷéẃs,** *nχ̣ʷnχ̣ʷé* **–** marry; together with a wife. *rt.:* ***noχ̣ʷnχ̣ʷ*** *– wife; suffix:* ***...éẃs*** *– in between, middle. lit. coming together with a wife.*
es nχ̣ʷnχ̣ʷeẃsi – He is getting married. **čnes nχ̣ʷnχ̣ʷeẃsi, kʷes nχ̣ʷnχ̣ʷeẃsi**
qs nχ̣ʷnχ̣ʷeẃsi – He is going to get married. **čiqs nχ̣ʷnχ̣ʷeẃsi, kʷqs nχ̣ʷnχ̣ʷeẃsi**

es nχ̣ʷnχ̣ʷeẃs – He is married. **čnes nχ̣ʷnχ̣ʷeẃs, kʷes nχ̣ʷnχ̣ʷeẃs**

hayo qs tiẃł nóχ̣ʷnχ̣ʷi – Hey, he's going to get a wife!
qł nóχ̣ʷnχ̣ʷs – his bride-to-be. **iqł nóχ̣ʷnχ̣ʷ, aqł nóχ̣ʷnχ̣ʷ**

nχ̣useẃs – marry; together with a husband. *rt.:* ***sχ̣elwi*** *– husband; suffix:* ***...éẃs*** *– in between, middle. lit. coming together with a husband.*
es nχ̣useẃsi – She is getting married. **čnes nχ̣useẃsi, kʷes nχ̣useẃsi**
qs nχ̣useẃsi – She is going to get married. **čiqs nχ̣useẃsi, kʷqs nχ̣useẃsi**

es nχ̣useẃs – She is married. **čnes nχ̣useẃs, kʷes nχ̣useẃs**

q sχ̣elwists – her husband-to-be. **iq sχ̣elwi, aq sχ̣elwi** *Rule:* ***ł*** *of* ***qł*** *is drop before* ***s****.*

es nq̓ʷiċtni – marry a brother/sister-in-law after the death of one's spouse. *See:* ***in-law****.*

es nťkʷempi – marry a brother/sister-in-law after separation or divorce.

nkʷłk̓ʷul̓l – made with; married.
es nkʷłk̓ʷúˀul̓l – They are married. **qeˀes nkʷłk̓ʷúˀul̓l, pes nkʷłk̓ʷúˀul̓l**
snkʷłk̓ʷul̓l – the one married.

šeẏ łu isnkʷłk̓ʷul̓l – S/he is the one married to me.

marten **ol̓ó –** marten; *Martes americana.*
łoˀl̓ó – pine marten, marten.

marterial **łqq̓íʔilxʷ** – material, patterned material.

Martin **maltá** – Martin.
łmaltá – little Martin.

Mary **mali** – Mary.
łmali – little Mary.

mash **łóc** – smash, mash. *See: **smash**.*

mask **k̓ʷl̓čustn** – mask. **k̓ʷl̓k̓ʷl̓čustn** *pl. rt.: **k̓ʷelč̓** – upturned formed object; suffix: **...us** – face, fire; suffix: **...tin, ...tn** – means of/device.*
k̓ʷl̓čusm – S/he put on a mask. **čn k̓ʷl̓čusm, kʷ k̓ʷl̓čusm**
es k̓ʷl̓čusi – S/he is putting on a mask. **čnes k̓ʷl̓čusi, kʷes k̓ʷl̓čusi**

es k̓ʷl̓čus – S/he is wearing a mask. **čnes k̓ʷl̓čus, kʷes k̓ʷl̓čus**

The **i** following uvular consonants (UC) and the glottal stop **ʔ** sound like English "*ey*" as in the words th*ey*, h*ey*, wh*ey*, etc. Salish UC are: **q, q̓, qʷ, q̓ʷ, x̌, x̌ʷ**. For example, the suffix **...qin** – head/top, is often spelled using English *ey* as "q*ey*n". So **qi, q̓i, qʷi, q̓ʷi, x̌i, x̌ʷi**, may be spelled with English *ey* as **q***ey*, **q̓***ey*, **qʷ***ey*, **q̓ʷ***ey*, **x̌***ey*, **x̌ʷ***ey* in other texts.

massacre **nc̓spulexʷ** – massacre; wiped out from the land. *rt.: **c̓sip** – disappear; suffix: **...ulexʷ** – land.*
nc̓spulexʷis – S/he massacred them. **nc̓spulexʷn, nc̓spulexʷntxʷ**
es nc̓spulexʷms – S/he is massacring them. **ies nc̓spulexʷm, as nc̓spulexʷm**
qs nc̓spulexʷms – S/he is going to massacre them. **iqs nc̓spulexʷm, aqs nc̓spulexʷm**

nc̓spúʔulexʷntm – They got massacred.

massage **p̓c̓pac̓m** – massage. *rt.: **p̓ac̓** – press.*
p̓c̓pac̓is – S/he/it massaged s.o. **p̓c̓pac̓n, p̓c̓pac̓ntxʷ**
es p̓c̓pac̓ms – S/he/it is massaging s.o. **ies p̓c̓pac̓m, as p̓c̓pac̓m**
qs p̓c̓pac̓ms – S/he/it is going to massage s.o. **iqs p̓c̓pac̓m, aqs p̓c̓pac̓m**

p̓c̓pac̓nt – Massage him/her. *cmd.*

master **čelltč** – owner; master; lord.

mat **syey** – woven mat.

match **t̓qʷmew̓s** – match something together. *suffix: **...éw̓s** – in between, middle.*
t̓qʷmew̓sm – S/he matched (s.t.). **čn t̓qʷmew̓sm, kʷ t̓qʷmew̓sm**
es t̓qʷmew̓si – S/he is matching (s.t.). **čnes t̓qʷmew̓si, kʷes t̓qʷmew̓si**
qs t̓qʷmew̓si – S/he is going to match (s.t.). **čiqs t̓qʷmew̓si, kʷqs t̓qʷmew̓si**
t̓qʷméʔew̓sm – They matched (s.t.). **qeʔ t̓qʷmew̓sm, p t̓qʷmew̓sm**
es taméʔew̓si – They are matching (s.t.). **qeʔes t̓qʷmew̓si, pes t̓qʷmew̓si**
qs taméʔew̓si – They are going to match (s.t.). **qeʔqs t̓qʷmew̓si, pqs t̓qʷmew̓si**

t̓qʷmew̓sis – S/he matched s.t. **t̓qʷmew̓sn, t̓qʷmew̓sntxʷ**
es t̓qʷmew̓si – S/he is matching s.t. **ies t̓qʷmew̓si, as t̓qʷmew̓si**
qs t̓qʷmew̓si – S/he is going to match s.t. **iqs t̓qʷmew̓si, aqs t̓qʷmew̓si**
t̓qʷméʔew̓sis – They matched s.t. **qeʔ t̓qʷmew̓sntm, t̓qʷmew̓sntp**
es t̓qʷméʔew̓sms – They are matching s.t. **qeʔes t̓qʷmew̓sm, es t̓qʷmew̓smp**
qs t̓qʷméʔew̓sms – They are going to match s.t. **qeʔqs t̓qʷmew̓sm, qs t̓qʷmew̓smp**

es t̓qʷt̓qʷmew̓si – S/he is matching repeatedly. **čnes t̓qʷt̓qʷmew̓si, kʷes t̓qʷt̓qʷmew̓si**

t̓qʷmew̓siš – Match. *cmd.*

s.t. - something, the 3rd person
(s.t.) - something implied
s.o. - someone, the 3rd person
sl. - singular form
pl. - plural form
rt. - root word
cmd. - command
lit. - literally
fig. - figuratively
i.e., - for example
See: - Redirection to a related word.

ṫqʷmeẁsnt – Match it together. *cmd.*
ṫqʷṫqʷmeẁskʷ – Match it together. *cmd.*

kʷ ƛ̓éʔ**em ec̓x̣ax̣i m ṫqʷṫqʷmeskʷ –** You look for the same ones and match them up. **ƛ̓é**ʔ**ent ci sṫqʷmeẁsts łiʔe –** Look for its match/mate to this.

ṫqʷseẁs – match/connect something together. *suffix: ...éẁs – in between, middle.*
ṫqʷseẁsm – S/he matched (s.t.). **čn ṫqʷseẁsm, kʷ ṫqʷseẁsm**
es ṫqʷseẁsi – S/he is matching (s.t.). **čnes ṫqʷseẁsi, kʷes ṫqʷseẁsi**
qs ṫqʷseẁsi – S/he is going to match (s.t.). **čiqs ṫqʷseẁsi, kʷqs ṫqʷseẁsi**
ṫqʷséʔeẁsm – They matched (s.t.). **qeʔ ṫqʷseẁsm, p ṫqʷseẁsm**
es ṫqʷséʔeẁsi – They are matching (s.t.). **qeʔes ṫqʷseẁsi, pes ṫqʷseẁsi**

ṫqʷseẁsis – S/he matched s.t. **čn ṫqʷseẁsn, kʷ ṫqʷseẁsntxʷ**
es ṫqʷseẁsi – S/he is matching s.t. **čnes ṫqʷseẁsi, kʷes ṫqʷseẁsi**
qs ṫqʷseẁsi – S/he is going to match s.t. **čiqs ṫqʷseẁsi, kʷqs ṫqʷseẁsi**
ṫqʷséʔeẁsis – They matched s.t. **qeʔ ṫqʷseẁsntm, ṫqʷseẁsntp**
es ṫqʷséʔeẁsms – They are matching s.t. **qeʔes ṫqʷseẁsm, es ṫqʷseẁsmp**

es ṫqʷṫqʷseẁsi – S/he is matching repeatedly. **čnes ṫqʷṫqʷseẁsi, kʷes ṫqʷṫqʷseẁsi**

ṫqʷṫqʷseẁskʷ – Match it up. *cmd.*

kʷ ƛ̓éʔem ec̓x̣ax̣i m ṫqʷṫqʷseskʷ – You look for the same ones and match them up.

matchstick **čpáx̣mn –** matches; matchstick.
nłéptmn ismenxʷ u inčpáx̣mn – I forgot my cigarettes and matches.

mate **es sl̓stwexʷi,** *es sl̓stwe* **–** The animals are mating. *rt.: **sil̓** – confuse.*

Matthew **matiya –** Matthew.

mattress **ṫk̓ʷéłp –** bedding; mattress. *rt.: **ṫuk̓ʷ** – place down; suffix: **...ełp, ...łp** – tree; floor.*

May **sṗéƛ̓m spq̇niʔ –** May *(month of the bitterroot).*

may **ha kʷ ṅe u –** question of politeness, as in, *“may I.”*

ha kʷ ṅe u qeʔqs occqeʔi qeʔqs k̓ʷis memscuti – May we go outside and play? **ha kʷ ṅe u čiqs k̓ʷis susti t sewłkʷ –** May I go drink water? **ha kʷ ṅe u čiqs xʷuyi č snłʔo –** May I go to the bathroom? **ha kʷ ṅe u qʷo olqʷšitxʷ –** Would you help me?

maybe **x̣ʷa –** perhaps; maybe.
x̣ʷa we – maybe so.

x̣ʷa ṅem ṫipéys – Maybe it will rain. **x̣ʷa u x̣ʷa ta –** Maybe, maybe not. **x̣ʷa ṅem x̣ʷa ta –** Maybe it will, maybe not. **x̣ʷa ṅem kʷ tixʷ scpupušénč –** Maybe you will get saddness. **x̣ʷa es ncqelši –** Maybe s/he has a leg cramp. **x̣ʷa es kʷckʷc̓c̓smi –** Maybe they fell over. **x̣ʷa qeʔ uł psayéʔ –** Maybe we were foolish. **całlásq̇t x̣ʷa mosq̇t –** three or four days. **x̣ʷa ṅem čn xʷuy č esyapqini –** Maybe I will go to the powwow.

x̣i m – maybe.

McGruder **łq̇ʷó –** Little Prairie; McGruder, *(near the middle fork of the Jocko River, Flathead Nation).*

me **qʷoyʔé –** mine; me.

meadow **l̓q̓ʷólexʷ**, *l̓q̓ʷó* – meadow.
łl̓q̓ʷólexʷ, *łl̓q̓ʷó* – little meadow.

meadowlark **wewickʷl̓eʔ**, *wewi* – female western meadowlark; *Sturnella neglecta.*
wewickʷl̓om, *wewi* – male western meadowlark; *Sturnella neglecta.*

meadow rue **p̓x̣ʷcuxʷeʔ**, *p̓x̣ʷcu* – meadow rue; licorice root; *Glycyrrhiza lepidota.*

meadow vole **sc̓msx̣ʷné** – meadow vole; *Microtus pennsylvanicus.*

The **i** following uvular consonants (UC) and the glottal stop **ʔ** sound like English "*ey*" as in the words th*ey*, h*ey*, wh*ey*, etc. Salish UC are: **q**, **q̓**, **qʷ**, **q̓ʷ**, **x̣**, **x̣ʷ**. For example, the suffix ...**qin** – head/top, is often spelled using English *ey* as "q*ey*n". So **qi**, **q̓i**, **qʷi**, **q̓ʷi**, **x̣i**, **x̣ʷi**, may be spelled with English *ey* as **q***ey*, **q̓***ey*, **qʷ***ey*, **q̓ʷ***ey*, **x̣***ey*, **x̣ʷ***ey* in other texts.

mean **łen** – stoic; serious; unexpressive. *See: **serious**.*

člč̓lečs – have angry/mean eyes. *rt.: **leč̓** – angry; circumfix: **č...us** – spherical object; eyes.*

lč̓us – have angry/mean face. *rt.: **leč̓** – angry; suffix: **...us** – face, fire.*
es lč̓lč̓usi es moq̓ʷ – The mountains look mean.

t̓éyeʔ, *t̓e* – bad; evil; mean. *See: **bad**.*
čn t̓éyeʔ – I am mean, evil, bad. **ma še we cuncn epł t̓it̓éye sm̓tm̓a** – See, I told you there are a lot of mean cows.

mtmitt, *mtmi* – no-good. *See: **no-good**.*

measles **sčłʔo** – measles.

measure **suxʷmeʔ** – measure.
suxʷmeʔm – S/he/it measured. **čn suxʷmeʔm, kʷ suxʷmeʔm**
es suxʷmeʔi – S/he/it is measuring. **čnes suxʷmeʔi, kʷes suxʷmeʔi**
qs suxʷmeʔi – S/he/it is going to measure. **čiqs suxʷmeʔi, kʷqs suxʷmeʔi**

suxʷmeʔis – S/he/it measured s.t. **suxʷmeʔn, suxʷmeʔntxʷ**
es suxʷmeʔms – S/he/it is measuring s.t. **ies suxʷmeʔm, as suxʷmeʔm**
qs suxʷmeʔms – S/he/it is going to measure s.t. **iqs suxʷmeʔm, aqs suxʷmeʔm**

suxʷmeʔnt – Measured it. *cmd.*

suxʷmeʔtn – ruler; yard stick; measuring tape. *suffix: **...tin, ...tn** – means of/device.*

suxʷmełxʷ – measure a house.
suxʷmełxʷ – S/he measured a house. **čn suxʷmełxʷ, kʷ suxʷmełxʷ**
es suxʷmełxʷi – S/he is measuring a house. **čnes suxʷmełxʷi, kʷes suxʷmełxʷi**
qs suxʷmełxʷi – S/he is going to measure a house. **čiqs suxʷmełxʷi, kʷqs suxʷmełxʷi**

suxʷmulexʷ – measure land/area.
suxʷmulexʷ – S/he measured the land. **čn suxʷmulexʷ, kʷ suxʷmulexʷ**
es suxʷmulexʷi – S/he is measuring the land. **čnes suxʷmulexʷi, kʷes suxʷmulexʷi**
qs suxʷmulexʷi – S/he is going to measure the land. **čiqs suxʷmulexʷi, kʷqs suxʷmulexʷi**

ƛ̓e łu es wis suxʷmeʔntm ye sqlixʷulexʷs – They had already finished measuring out Indian land.

s.t. - something, the 3rd person
(s.t.) - something implied
s.o. - someone, the 3rd person
sl. - singular form
pl. - plural form
rt. - root word
cmd. - command
lit. - literally
fig. - figuratively
i.e., - for example
See: - Redirection to a related word.

measuring tape **suxʷmeʔtn** – ruler; yard stick; measuring tape. *suffix: **...tin, ...tn** – means of/device.*

meat **sqeľtč** – meat, body. **sqľqeľtč** *pl.*
słqaqľtč – little meat, body.

sccqaẏełċeʔ, *sccqaẏe* – dried/smoked meat. *See:* ***dry meat.***

sppq̓ʷé – pounded dried meat.

scq̓ʷlé – meat roasted over a fire. *prefix:* ***sc...*** *– s.t. that's been done/made/prepared.*

snčxʷmin – meat on a hide.

es x̣ṁip sqeľtč – dry meat.

siẏéṅṗ – dry meat rope.

medicine **malyémistn**, *malyé* – medicine. *rt:* ***malyém*** *– doctor;* ***heal;*** *suffix:* ***...tin, ...tn*** *– means of/device. See:* ***doctor.***
čmi cníʔilc łu epł malyéʔe – Only they had medicines.

medicine dance **snƛ̓ekʷlšscutn** – medicine dance for doctoring. *prefix:* ***sn...*** *– a place of; suffix:* ***...tin, ...tn*** *– means of/device.*

es x̣ċmscuti – medicine dance.

es qʷásqʷiʔi – become a Blue Jay at a medicine dance.

tlqmi – jump dance; jumping. *(This describes the jumping that occurs at jump dances and medicine dances. This dance is held in the wintertime.) See:* ***jump dance.***

nqwistn, *nqwi* – jump dance. *(This describes the action of following people in a circle that occurs at jump dances and medicine dances. This dance is held in the wintertime.) See:* ***jump dance.***

nx̣asqin – jump dance held anytime of the year. *See:* ***jump dance.***

sxʷk̓ʷłwéʔm – one tasked to repeat what is said in the medicine dance. *prefix:* ***sxʷ...*** *– one tasked to do.*

medicine lodge **scwéłxʷ** – medicine lodge. *prefix:* ***sc...*** *– s.t. that's been done/made/prepared; suffix:* ***...etxʷ, ...łxʷ*** *– house.*
es cwéłxʷi – S/he is putting up a medicine lodge. **čnes cwéłxʷi, kʷes cwéłxʷi**

łu istč še k̓ʷuľ scwéłxʷ – In winter a medicine lodge was made.

snculexʷ – place of the medicine lodge.

k̓ʷľčulexʷ – place of the sweat lodge.

ṅšiʔtelixʷ – head person in the medicine lodge.

nšiʔtelixʷ – head person in the lodge/house.

medicine person **ƛ̓eʔkʷilš** – medicine person. **ƛ̓eƛ̓eʔkʷilš** *pl. suffix:* ***...ilš*** *– autonomous.*

ṅšiʔtelixʷ – head person in the medicine lodge.

suméš – guardian spirit; spiritual power; medicine power.
qʷqʷċwé łu isuméš – Chipmunk is my medicine power.

Medicine Tree **čq̓ʔe** – the Medicine Tree, near Darby, Montana.

meet **čic** – happen upon; meet someone; an accidental meeting.
čicis – S/he/it met s.o./s.t. **čicn, čicntxʷ**
es čicnms – S/he/it is meeting s.o./s.t. **ies čicnm, as čicnm**

qs čicnms – S/he/it is going to meet s.o./s.t. **iqs čicnm, aqs čicnm**
číʔicis – They met s.o./s.t. **qeʔ čicntm, čicntp**

čicntm – S/he was met by someone.

nčicntn – the place one ends up.
čicncutn – someone that arrives/happens upon one.

čicnt – Meet somebody. *cmd.*
es ččnwexʷi – They are meeting each other.
qeʔqs ččnwexʷi – We are going to meet each other.

nčcneẇsts – S/he came into a crowd. **nčcneẇstn, nčcneẇstxʷ**
nčcnéʔeẇsts – They came into a crowd. **qeʔ nčcneẇstm, nčcneẇstp**

kʷłčicš, *kʷłčí* – arrived there. *See: arrive.*
nčcnus – arrive at the start of a time period, the beginning of an action, or the edge
   of a place. *See: arrive.*
nčcnšncut – make a complete revolution; make a circle; meet one's own
   footprints/tracks. *See: around.*

kʷmiʔ čicn isínceʔ – I hope I run into my younger brother.

q̇mq̇milš, *q̇mq̇mi* – meet and talk; have a meeting; discuss. *suffix: …ilš– autonomous.*
   q̇mq̇míʔilš – They spoke. **qeʔ q̇mq̇milš, p q̇mq̇milš**
   es q̇mq̇míʔilši – They are speaking. **qeʔes q̇mq̇milši, pes q̇mq̇milši**
   qs q̇mq̇míʔilši – They are going to speak. **qeʔqs q̇mq̇milši, pqs q̇mq̇milši**

čq̇mq̇milš, *čq̇mq̇mi* – discuss about something.

čq̇mq̇míʔilšmis – They discussed s.t. **qeʔ čq̇mq̇milšmntm, čq̇mq̇milšmntp**
es čq̇mq̇míʔilšms – They are discussing s.t. **qeʔes čq̇mq̇milšm, es čq̇mq̇milšmp**
qs čq̇mq̇míʔilšms – They are going to discuss s.t. **qeʔqs čq̇mq̇milšm, qs čq̇mq̇milšmp**

q̇mq̇míʔi we eł iáʔa – They talked together when they met again. **čiqs xʷuyi č čʔupn es q̇mq̇mi –**
I am going to go to the council meeting. **čiqs xʷuyi č es q̇mq̇mi** – I am going to go to a meeting.
ṅem l kʷinš m qeʔ čtax̣ʷle m qeʔ q̇mq̇milš – What time will we start our meeting? **steṁ łu**
čq̇mq̇milšmntp – What did you all discuss?

ẏamim – gather/collect things together. *See: gather.*

melt

aámt – melt; dissolve away.
   es aamti – It is melting.

ecx̣i es aamti łu qeʔ nuwewlštn – It is like our language is melting away.

oʔiṁ – melt; thaw.
   es oʔiṁi – It is melting/thawing.
   es oʔimṁi – It is melting slowly.

oʔimetkʷ – melt snow/ice in water. *suffix: …etkʷ, …tkʷ– liquid*
   oʔimetkʷ – S/he melted ice in water. **čn oʔimetkʷ, kʷ oʔimetkʷ**
   es oʔimetkʷi – S/he is melting ice in water. **čnes oʔimetkʷi, kʷes oʔimetkʷi**
   qs oʔimetkʷi – S/he is going to melt ice in water. **čiqs oʔimetkʷi, kʷqs oʔimetkʷi**

nʔoʔiml – melt something metal.
   nʔoʔimls – S/he melted the metal. **nʔoʔimln, nʔoʔimlntxʷ**
   es nʔoʔimlms – S/he is melting the metal. **ies nʔoʔimlm, as nʔoʔimlm**

The i following uvular consonants (UC) and the glottal stop ʔ sound like English "*ey*" as in the words th*ey*, h*ey*, wh*ey*, etc. Salish UC are: q, q̇, qʷ, q̇ʷ, x̣, x̣ʷ. For example, the suffix …**qin** – head/ top, is often spelled using English *ey* as "qeyn". So qi, q̇i, qʷi, q̇ʷi, x̣i, x̣ʷi, may be spelled with English *ey* as q*ey*, q̇*ey*, qʷ*ey*, q̇ʷ*ey*, x̣*ey*, x̣ʷ*ey* in other texts.

s.t. - something, the 3rd
      person
(s.t.) - something implied
s.o. - someone, the 3rd
      person
sl. - singular form
pl. - plural form
rt. - root word
cmd. - command
lit. - literally
fig. - figuratively
i.e., - for example
See: - Redirection to a
      related word.

ncmetkʷ – melt snow. *suffix: **...etkʷ, ...tkʷ** – liquid*
ncmetkʷ – S/he melted snow. **čn ncmetkʷ, kʷ ncmetkʷ**
es ncmetkʷi – S/he is melting snow. **čnes ncmetkʷi, kʷes ncmetkʷi**
qs ncmetkʷi – S/he is going to melt snow. **čiqs ncmetkʷi, kʷqs ncmetkʷi**
ncmé?etkʷ – They melted snow. **qe? ncmetkʷ, p ncmetkʷ**

men **sqlqltmixʷ**, *sqlqltmi* – men, menfolk.

merganser **kʷl̓kʷlal̓i** – merganser; *Mergus merganser.*

tt̓qʷéne? – hooded merganser; *Lophodytes cucullatus.*

merry **pii** – happy; pleasure; bliss; rejoice. *(this describes the actions of happiness) See: **happy**.*

npiyéls, *npiyé* – feel happy. *See: **happy**.*

mess **łit̓m** – scatter something; mess something up. *See: **scatter**.*

message **nłk̓ʷelsm** – message.

messy **łp̓łap̓lš** – messy.

scp̓at̓ša – something put together carelessly.

p̓at̓qan – messy hair. *rt.: **p̓at̓** – s.t. soft/squishy; suffix: **...qin, ...qn** – top. See: **pile**.*
p̓at̓qan – S/he/it has messy hair. **čn p̓at̓qan, kʷ p̓at̓qan**

t̓ix̣qn – messy hair. *rt.: **t̓ix̣** – protrude; suffix: **...qin, ...qn** – top.*
t̓ix̣qn – S/he/it had messy hair. **čn t̓ix̣qn, kʷ t̓ix̣qn**
es t̓ix̣qn – S/he/it has messy hair. **čnes t̓ix̣qn, kʷes t̓ix̣qn**

c̓lixʷqn – messy hair; bushy hair. *rt.: **c̓il** – protrude; suffix: **...qin, ...qn** – top.*

x̣opqn – have bad hair.
i x̣opqn – S/he/it has bad hair. **i čn x̣opqn, i kʷ x̣opqn**

metamorphic rock **k̓ʷl̓isp̓c̓pesšn** – metamorphic rock. *rt.: **p̓ic̓** – pressure; prefix: **k̓ʷl̓is** – change; suffix: **...esšn̓, ...sšn̓** – rock.*

Methow **smlqmi** – Methow tribe.

Mexican **spayół,** *spayó* – Mexican. **spipayół** – Mexicans. *pl.*

Michael **misél** – Michael; Mike.

middle **nihéw̓s** – middle, center.
t̓k̓ʷunt skʷiskʷs nihéw̓sms l snčłemutn u snčłelilntn – Put the antelope and cow in the middle. 1
nihéw̓s staán u st̓m̓a m tkʷntexʷ – Put the antelope and cow in the middle. **swe łu l snihéw̓sm** – Who is in the middle? **stem̓ łu nihéw̓sm ci staán u ci st̓m̓a** – What is in between the antelope and the cow?

...éw̓s – *suffix indicating middle, center.*
čłkʷk̓ʷimew̓s – S/he/it has a little belly.
čkʷtnew̓s – big belly.
ččełlew̓s – three bellies.
nłp̓p̓ew̓s – skinny belly (from starvation).
łqq?ew̓s – skinny belly.

q̓eʔ – put/place/squeeze inside something; inserted between. *See: **insert**.*

midnight **tx̣ʷéw̓sm łu skʷkʷʔéc** – midnight came.
syew̓smskʷkʷʔéc – midnight, Christmas.

midwife **olqʷšcutn** – helper; midwife. *suffix: **...tin, ...tn** – means of/device.*

might **x̣in̓e** – might. *(Indicates the next statement may happen if the previous is not followed.)*
ta čiqs sust t nx̣oskʷ x̣in̓e čn nslslmtu – I am not going to drink beer, I might get dizzy. **ta kʷ qes čečečmscut x̣in̓e kʷ tixʷł łox̣te** – Do not be nasty, you might get a baby. **iłnt asʔiłn x̣in̓e čsp̓ic̓éʔncn** – Eat your food or I might whip you!

migrate **es t̓áqti** – The geese are flying *(in formation)*.

mile **suxʷmeʔtn** – measure; often referred to as a mile. *prefix: **sn...** – a place of; suffix: **...tin, ...tn** – means of/device.*
nk̓ʷuʔ suxʷmeʔtn – one mile.

milfoil **nkʷk̓ʷá** – yarrow, milfoil.

milk **sqʔém** – milk.

qʔeméł̓t – breastfeed; nurse. *See: **breastfeed**.*

q̓ʷaq̓ʷʔemxʷ – milking; squeeze breasts. *rt.: **q̓ʷʔe** – wring, squeeze; suffix:**...emxʷ** – breasts.*
q̓ʷaq̓ʷʔemxʷm – S/he milked. **čn q̓ʷaq̓ʷʔemxʷm, kʷ q̓ʷaq̓ʷʔemxʷm**
es q̓ʷaq̓ʷʔemxʷi – S/he is milking. **čnes q̓ʷaq̓ʷʔemxʷi, kʷes q̓ʷaq̓ʷʔemxʷi**
qs q̓ʷaq̓ʷʔemxʷi – S/he is going to milk. **čiqs q̓ʷaq̓ʷʔemxʷi, kʷqs q̓ʷaq̓ʷʔemxʷi**

q̓ʷaq̓ʷʔemxʷis – S/he milked it. **q̓ʷaq̓ʷʔemxʷn, q̓ʷaq̓ʷʔemxʷntxʷ**
es q̓ʷaq̓ʷʔemxʷms – S/he is milking it. **ies q̓ʷaq̓ʷʔemxʷm, as q̓ʷaq̓ʷʔemxʷm**
qs q̓ʷaq̓ʷʔemxʷms – S/he is going to milk it. **iqs q̓ʷaq̓ʷʔemxʷm, aqs q̓ʷaq̓ʷʔemxʷm**

q̓ʷaq̓ʷʔemxʷnt – Milk it. *cmd.*
q̓ʷaq̓ʷʔemxʷmncut – extract milk from one's self.

milk cow **snq̓ʷaq̓ʷʔemxʷtn,** *snq̓ʷaq̓ʷʔe* – milk cow.

Milk River **npiqkʷ** – Milk River, river in northern Montana. *lit. white waters.*

milkweed **snlqʷó** – milkweed; *Asclepias syriaca.*

mill **snpičmn** – lumber mill. *rt.: **pič** – shave/cut; prefix: **sn...** – a place of; suffix: **...min, ...mn** – instrument/tool.*

snnič̓mn – lumber mill. *rt.: **nič̓** – cut; prefix: **sn...** – a place of; suffix: **...min, ...mn** – instrument/tool.*

Millie **mili** – Millie.

million **opʔopnčstqn** – million. *lit. a thousand thousands.*

mind **npax̣mintn** – human mind; wisdom's tool.

snk̓ʷłpax̣min – human mind; place of thoughts.

séwneʔš – command to listen.

The **i** following uvular consonants (UC) and the glottal stop **ʔ** sound like English "*ey*" as in the words th*ey*, h*ey*, wh*ey*, etc. Salish UC are: **q**, **q̓**, **qʷ**, **q̓ʷ**, **x̣**, **x̣ʷ**. For example, the suffix **...qin** – head/top, is often spelled using English *ey* as "q*ey*n". So **qi**, **q̓i**, **qʷi**, **q̓ʷi**, **x̣i**, **x̣ʷi**, may be spelled with English *ey* as **q***ey*, **q̓***ey*, **qʷ***ey*, **q̓ʷ***ey*, **x̣***ey*, **x̣ʷ***ey* in other texts.

s.t. - something, the 3rd person
(s.t.) - something implied
s.o. - someone, the 3rd person
sl. - singular form
pl. - plural form
rt. - root word
cmd. - command
lit. - literally
fig. - figuratively
i.e., - for example
See: - Redirection to a related word.

nyoywáls – strong heart; strong mind.

mine
qʷoyʔé – mine; me.

inkapi – my coffee.
iqł kapi – It is going to be my coffee.
ƛ̓m inkapi – It was my coffee.

*Words that begin with **s**, like **sʔiłn**, drop the **...ł** of **iqł**.*
iq sʔiłn – It is going to be my food.

*Words that begin with **s**, like **sʔiłn**, drop the **...n** on **in**.*
isʔiłn – my food.

mink
ċx̣lé – mink; *Mustela vison.*

minnow
sxʷiymineʔ – minnow.

łq̓eneʔč – minnow.

mint
x̣nx̣nélp, *x̣nx̣né* – field mint, peppermint; false solomns seal; *Mentha arvensis.*

tiitẁi – horse mint; nettle-leaf giant-hyssop; *Agastache urticifolia.*

minute
nk̓ʷu łššllič – minute.

mirror
snaċx̣sncutn, *snaċx̣sncu* – mirror. *rt.: **aċx̣** – look; prefix: **sn...** – a place of; suffix: **...tin, ...tn** – means of/device.*

aċx̣sncut – S/he/it looked at one's self. **čn aċx̣sncut, kʷ aċx̣sncut**
es aċx̣sncuti – S/he/it is looking at one's self. **čnes aċx̣sncuti, kʷes aċx̣sncuti**
qs aċx̣sncuti – S/he/it is going to look at one's self. **čiqs aċx̣sncuti, kʷqs aċx̣sncuti**

aċx̣sncutš – Look at yourself in the mirror. *cmd.*
aċx̣sncutwi – All of you look at yourselves in the mirror. *cmd.*

ax̣le u kʷ aċx̣sncu – You always look at yourself.

k̓ʷnmesncu – mirror.

miscarry
x̣ent – miscarry; abort.

x̣ent – She miscarried. **čn x̣ent, kʷ x̣ent**
es x̣enti – She is miscarrying. **čnes x̣enti, kʷes x̣enti**

x̣entsts – S/he caused her to miscarry. **x̣entstn, x̣entstxʷ**
es x̣entms – S/he is making her miscarry. **ies x̣entm, as x̣entm**
qs x̣entms – S/he is going to make her miscarry. **iqs x̣entm, aqs x̣entm**

miser
ẏekʷmist – being miserly.

ẏekʷmist – S/he was miserly. **čn ẏekʷmist, kʷ ẏekʷmist**
es ẏekʷmisti – S/he is being miserly. **čnes ẏekʷmisti, kʷes ẏekʷmisti**
qs ẏekʷmisti – S/he is going to be miserly. **čiqs ẏekʷmisti, kʷqs ẏekʷmisti**

miss
šič̓t – miss something targeted.

šič̓t – S/he/it missed. **čn šič̓t, kʷ šič̓t**
es šič̓ti – S/he/it is missing. **čnes šič̓ti, kʷes šič̓ti**
qs šič̓ti – S/he/it is going to miss. **čiqs šič̓ti, kʷqs šič̓ti**
es šíʔič̓ti – They are missing. **qeʔes šič̓ti, pes šič̓ti**

šičis – S/he/it missed it. **šičn, šičntxʷ**
es šičms – S/he/it is missing it. **ies šičm, as šičm**
qs šičms – S/he/it is going to miss it. **iqs šičm, aqs šičm**
šíʔičis – They missed it. **qeʔ šičntm, šičntp**

qeʔ ščnwe – We missed each other.

šičšnm – miss with the foot.

čłx̌ʷop – fail to catch something.
čłx̌ʷopnuis – S/he failed to catch s.t. **čłx̌ʷopnun, čłx̌ʷopnuntxʷ**
es čłx̌ʷopnunms – S/he is failing to catch s.t. **ies čłx̌ʷopnunm, as čłx̌ʷopnunm**
qs čłx̌ʷopnunms – S/he is going to fail to catch s.t. **iqs čłx̌ʷopnunm, aqs čłx̌ʷopnunm**

čłx̌ʷopečst – fail to catch something with the hand; something glanced off the hand. *suffix: **...ečst, ...čst** – of the hand.*
čłx̌ʷopečstis – S/he failed to catch s.t. **čłx̌ʷopečstn, čłx̌ʷopečstntxʷ**
es čłx̌ʷopečstms – S/he is failing to catch s.t. **ies čłx̌ʷopečstm, as čłx̌ʷopečstm**
qs čłx̌ʷopečstms – S/he is going to fail to catch s.t. **iqs čłx̌ʷopečstm, aqs čłx̌ʷopečstm**
čłx̌ʷopéʔečstis – They failed to catch s.t. **qeʔ čłx̌ʷopečstntm, čłx̌ʷopečstntp**

čupélsm, *čupé* – lonesome; miss someone. *See: **lonesome**.*

soq̓ʷm – almost hit by something; missed by something; almost happened. *See: **hit**.*

> The **i** following uvular consonants (UC) and the glottal stop **ʔ** sound like English "*ey*" as in the words th*ey*, h*ey*, wh*ey*, etc. Salish UC are: **q, q̓, qʷ, q̓ʷ, x̌, x̌ʷ**. For example, the suffix **...qin** – head/top, is often spelled using English *ey* as "q*ey*n". So **qi, q̓i, qʷi, q̓ʷi, x̌i, x̌ʷi**, may be spelled with English *ey* as **q***ey*, **q̓***ey*, **qʷ***ey*, **q̓ʷ***ey*, **x̌***ey*, **x̌ʷ***ey* in other texts.

Mission

snyéľmn – St. Ignatius; Mission, Flathead Nation. *lit. a place where something was surrounded.*

Mission Dam Lake

snyéľmn čłq̓liʔs – Mission Lake, near St. Ignatius, Flathead Nation.

Missoula

nłʔaycčstm, *nłʔay* – Missoula, Montana; place of little bull trout.

nmesuletkʷ – Clark Fork River; *also thought to be the origin of the name Missoula. rt.: **suuʔ** – subsided water; suffix: **...etkʷ, ...tkʷ** – liquid*

Missouri River

epł yu ntx̌ʷetkʷs – Missouri River. *lit. river of the red paint.*

mistake

qʷomscut, *qʷomscu* – make a mistake.

čsľlpečst – make a mistake in working. *rt.: **siľ** – confuse; suffix: **...ečst, ...čst** – of the hand.*
čsľlpečst – S/he made a mistake in the work. **čn čsľlpečst, kʷ čsľlpečst**
es čsľlpečsti – S/he is making a mistake in the work. **čnes čsľlpečsti, kʷes čsľlpečsti**
qs čsľlpečsti – S/he is going to make a mistake in the work. **čiqs čsľlpečsti, kʷqs čsľlpečsti**

čsľlpečststmis – S/he made a mistake in doing s.t. **čsľlpečststmn, čsľlpečststmntxʷ**
es čsľlpečststms – S/he is making a mistake in doing s.t. **ies čsľlpečststm, as čsľlpečststm**
qs čsľlpečststms – S/he is going to make a mistake in doing s.t. **iqs čsľlpečststm, aqs čsľlpečststm**

siľ – confused; unable to figure something out; mistaken. *See: **confuse**.*
sľlpcan – make a mistake talking; mix up words. *See: **tongue tied**.*
sľlpcin – confused about what to say. *See: **tongue tied**.*

> s.t. - something, the 3rd person
> (s.t.) - something implied
> s.o. - someone, the 3rd person
> *sl.* - singular form
> *pl.* - plural form
> *rt.* - root word
> *cmd.* - command
> *lit.* - literally
> *fig.* - figuratively
> *i.e.,* - for example
> *See:* - Redirection to a related word.

mitten

smlmlq̓ʷtečst – mittens. *suffix: **...ečst, ...čst** – of the hand.*

mix **nméx̣̌** – mix.

nméx̣̌m – S/he/it mixed. **čn nméx̣̌m, kʷ nméx̣̌m**
es nméx̣̌i – S/he/it is mixing. **ies nméx̣̌i, as nméx̣̌i**
qs nméx̣̌i – S/he/it is going to mix. **iqs nméx̣̌i, aqs nméx̣̌i**
es nméˀex̣̌i – They are mixing. **qeˀes nméx̣̌i, pes nméx̣̌i**

nméx̣̌is – S/he/it mixed s.t. **nméx̣̌n, nméx̣̌ntxʷ**
es nméx̣̌ms – S/he/it is mixing s.t. **ies nméx̣̌m, as nméx̣̌m**
qs nméx̣̌ms – S/he/it is going to mix s.t. **iqs nméx̣̌m, aqs nméx̣̌m**

es nméx̣̌ – It is mixed.
nméx̣̌ntm – It was mixed.

scnméx̣̌ – something that's been mixed*; i.e., dough. prefix:* ***sc...*** *– s.t. that's been done/made/prepared.*
nméx̣̌mn – baking powder. *suffix:* ***...min, ...mn*** *– instrument/tool.*

nméx̣̌iš – Mix. *cmd.*
nméx̣̌nt – Mix it. *cmd.*

nméx̣̌nt łu mulš t ml̓ml̓té u nexʷ ppo u nexʷ t apłsálqʷ łu ṅe kʷ wičm – Mix cottonwood with aspen and willow and also applewood, if you can find it.

sil̓ – confused; unable to figure something out; mistaken. *See:* ***confuse.***

moccasin **siṗišn** – one moccasin. **sṗsiṗišn** – moccasins.

es sṗsiṗišn – S/he is wearing moccasins. **čnes sṗsiṗišn, kʷes sṗsiṗišn**

siṗišnm – S/he put on moccasins. **čn siṗišnm, kʷ siṗišnm**
es siṗišni – S/he is putting on moccasins. **čnes siṗišni, kʷes siṗišni**
qs siṗišni – S/he is going to put on moccasins. **čiqs siṗišni, kʷqs siṗišni**

siṗišnis – S/he put on s.o.'s moccasins. **siṗišn, siṗišntxʷ**
es siṗišnms – S/he is putting on s.o.'s moccasins. **ies siṗišnm, as siṗišnm**
qs siṗišnms – S/he is going to put on s.o.'s moccasins. **iqs siṗišnm, aqs siṗišnm**

q̇ešin – footwear; moccasin, shoe, boot, etc. *rt.:* ***q̇eˀ*** *– put inside; suffix:* ***...šin*** *– foot. lit. anything that is wore on the foot where the foot fits inside. See:* ***shoe.***

mock orange **wax̣íłp** – mock orange; syringe; *Philadelphus lewisii.*

moisten **łuc** – soak; moisten. *See:* ***soak.***

mold **spaq̇m** – mold.

es paq̇m – It is moldy.
qs paq̇mi – It is going to get moldy.

paq̇qt – It has molded; expression of frustration.

x̣̌e paq̇m asnqʷlpu – Your bread is already moldy.

mole **pul̓ye** – mole.

Mollman Pass **słipu sx̣ʷcuˀsi** – Mollman Pass, in the Mission Mountain Range, Flathead Nation.

mul̓mn sx̣ʷcuˀsi. – Mollman Pass, in the Mission Mountain Range, Flathead Nation.

molt **čt̓oʔq̇ép** – molt feathers.
es čt̓oʔq̇épi – It is molting.

es čt̓oʔq̇ép – It is molted.

sčt̓oʔq̇ép – molted feathers.

moment **islup** – at any moment; any second; any time now.

islup čn hoyyho – Any moment I will finish. **islup m čn qʷéw** – At any moment I will go crazy.

Monday **sčx̣ʷéct,** *sčx̣ʷé* – Monday. *lit. past; meaning the day past Sunday.*

čp̓ƛ̓w̓m – Monday.

money **ululim** – money, metal.
séns – cents.
nk̓ʷuʔséns – penny.
cilséns – nickel.
upnséns – dime.
kʷateʔ – quarter.
sčut – half dollar.
nk̓ʷuʔ ululim – one dollar.

i pa ululim – silver. *lit. faded metal.*

ies siyenm inʔululim – I am counting my money. **uc kʷ epɫ ululim** – Perhaps you have money? *(nice way to ask for money)* **ha kʷ epɫ ululim** – Do you have any money? **esmisten kʷ epɫ ululim** – I know you have money.

čɫʔululim – go after money.
čɫʔululimi – S/he went after money. **čn čɫʔululimi, kʷ čɫʔululimi**
es čɫʔululimi – S/he is going after money. **čnes čɫʔululimi, kʷes čɫʔululimi**
qs čɫʔululimi – S/he is going to go after money. **čiqs čɫʔululimi, kʷqs čɫʔululimi**

monkey **monqi** – monkey.

monster **naɫisqélixʷtn,** *naɫisqé* – monster.

month **spq̇niʔ** – month, moon, sun, clock.
nk̓ʷuʔ spq̇niʔ – one month.
esel spq̇niʔ – two months.
cil spq̇niʔ – five months.
upn eɫ nk̓ʷuʔ spq̇niʔ – eleven months.
eslʔupn spq̇niʔ – twenty months.

sčx̣ʷcspq̇niʔ – the past month.

months **sčn̓čɫtu spq̇niʔ** – January *(month of shaking hands). See: **January**.*
čqʷósqn spq̇niʔ – February *(month of the cold). See: **February**.*
k̓ʷsixʷ spq̇niʔ – March *(month of the geese). See: **March**.*
sčiyál̓mn spq̇niʔ – April *(month of the buttercup). See: **April**.*
sp̓éƛ̓m spq̇niʔ – May *(month of the bitterroot). See: **May**.*
sx̣ʷéʔli spq̇niʔ – June *(month of the camas). See: **June**.*
esy̓apqini spq̇niʔ – July *(month of celebration). See: **July**.*

The **i** following uvular consonants (UC) and the glottal stop **ʔ** sound like English "*ey*" as in the words *they, hey, whey*, etc. Salish UC are: **q, q̇, qʷ, q̇ʷ, x̣, x̣ʷ**. For example, the suffix ...**qin** – head/top, is often spelled using English *ey* as "q*ey*n". So **qi, q̇i, qʷi, q̇ʷi, x̣i, x̣ʷi**, may be spelled with English *ey* as **q***ey*, **q̇***ey*, **qʷ***ey*, **q̇ʷ***ey*, **x̣***ey*, **x̣ʷ***ey* in other texts.

s.t. - something, the 3rd person
(s.t.) - something implied
s.o. - someone, the 3rd person
sl. - singular form
pl. - plural form
rt. - root word
cmd. - command
lit. - literally
fig. - figuratively
i.e., - for example
See: - Redirection to a related word.

sť̓šá spq̇ni? – August *(month of the huckleberry). See:* ***August.***
łx̣ʷłó spq̇ni? – September *(month of the chokecherry). See:* ***September.***
sčłip spq̇ni? – October *(month of hunting). See:* ***October.***
sqʷllu spq̇ni? – November *(month of storytelling). See:* ***November.***
es?ácm̓i spq̇ni? – December *(month of trapping). See:* ***December.***

sťapsqé spq̇ni? – January *(month of the shooting; referring to shooting during New Years). See:* ***January.***
siqʷiqʷnw̓é spq̇ni? – April *(month of the fooling each other). See:* ***April.***
čuláy – July. *See:* ***July.***

moon **spq̇ni?** – month; moon; sun; clock.
eł ctešlš – new moon.
sčut, sččutt – half moon.
eł sčut – 3/4 moon.
nk̓ʷu? sṗqni? – full moon.

moose **sx̣áslqs** – moose; *Alces alces.*
smčsx̣áslqs, *smčsx̣á* – cow moose.

moose nose **sx̣áslqs snṗsáqs** – moose nose.

mop **čł?éṗm** – mop; wipe the surface. *rt.:* ***eṗ*** *– wipe; prefix:* ***čł...*** *– surface.*
čł?éṗm – S/he/it mopped. **čn čł?éṗm, kʷ čł?éṗm**
es čł?éṗi – S/he/it is mopping. **čnes čł?éṗi, kʷes čł?éṗi**
qs čł?éṗi – S/he/it is going to mop. **čiqs čł?éṗi, kʷqs čł?éṗi**
es čł?é?eṗi – They are mopping. **qe?es čł?éṗi, pes čł?éṗi**

čł?éṗis – S/he/it mopped it. **čł?éṗn, čł?éṗntxʷ**
es čł?éṗms – S/he/it is mopping it. **ies čł?éṗm, as čł?éṗm**
qs čł?éṗms – S/he/it is going to mop it. **iqs čł?éṗm, aqs čł?éṗm**

čł?éṗmn – mop; something to wipe a surface.

čł?éṗiš – Mop. *cmd.*
čł?éṗnt – Mop it. *cmd.*

čł?éṗłptn – mop. *rt.:* ***eṗ*** *– wipe; prefix:* ***čł...*** *– surface; affix:* ***...ełp, ...łp*** *– tree; floor; suffix:* ***...tin, ...tn*** *– means of/device.*

morchella mushroom **ṗax̌qine?** – mushroom; morel or morchella mushroom. *rt.:* ***ṗax̌*** *– smooth; suffix:* ***...qin, ...qn*** *– top.*

more **tl̓ ci?** – more than.
tl̓ ci? kʷ čenčnt – You are more of a slowpoke. **tl̓ ci? išut** – lower. **ṅem tl̓ ci? qʷaqʷemncú** – I will study harder. **tl̓ ci? qʷestm** – It got deeper. **q̇ʷomnt esel tl̓ ci? kʷ čtxʷum t esel** – Take two from there and add two. **tl̓ ci? q̇ʷomiš esel kʷemt k̓ʷinš łu l šeẏ** – From five take two; then how many do you have?

ułé? – again, more.
m čłťkʷntexʷ ułé? – You will put it on top again. **ułé? čiqs susti t nťiškʷ** – I am going to drink pop again.

morning **skʷékʷst** – morning.
x̣est skʷékʷst – good morning.

kʷémt ṅe kʷékʷst m qe? k̓ʷis x̣éct – Then in the morning we're going to go dig.

kʷekʷstm – eat breakfast. *See:* ***breakfast.***

Mose **muwi** – Mose.

mosquito **sláqs** – mosquito.

mosquito hawk **sṗáas** – nighthawk, night bat, mosquito hawk; *Chordeiles minor.*

moss **šawtmqn** – black tree moss; black lichen.

sqʷl̓ápqn, *sqʷl̓á* – black tree moss when used with camas baking; black lichen.
kʷ čsqʷl̓á – You gather black tree moss.

sčkʷalip – yellow/green tree moss.

snupleʔxʷe – moss *(plant in water).*

most **sšy̓mł** – ..."est" of words like in widest.
sšy̓mł łaq̓t – widest. **sšy̓mł ƛ̓ax̣t** – fastest. **sšy̓mł šept** – slowest. **sšy̓mł xʷʔit** – most.

moth **čkʷk̓ʷʔéneʔ** – moth *(general term).*

čqcqá, čqsqá – large moth.

čéčłuʔ – maggot.

mother **sk̓ʷuy** – mother of a male. *See:* ***Sec. 3: Kinship Terms.***
tum̓ – mother of female.
tétmtn – mother and father of daughter-in-law.
tum̓mp – your mother *(talking to two sisters).*

sxʷl̓xʷl̓tew̓s – mother and daughter. *suffix:* ***...éw̓s*** *– in between, middle.*

mother-in-law **łcécč** – mother-in-law. *See:* ***Sec. 3: Kinship Terms.***

motorcycle **snṗṗiq̓ʷps** – motorcycle. *lit. riding something that farts. rt.:* ***ṗiq̓ʷ*** *– fart sound.*
čn epł i kʷil snṗṗiq̓ʷps – I have a red motorcycle.

nttl̓qʷo – motorcycle.

mount **čłqqew̓s,** *čłqqe* – mount, *more than one*; straddle; get on. *rt.:* ***łaqq*** *– sit down many; suffix:* ***...éw̓s*** *– in between, middle.*
čłqqew̓s – S/he got on. **čn čłqqew̓s, kʷ čłqqew̓s**

čłqqew̓swi – All of you mount. *cmd.*

čłqqew̓s snčłcaʔsqáx̣eʔs – They got on his/her horse.

čłqlšew̓s, *čłqlše* – mount, *of one individual*; straddle. *rt.:* ***łaqšlš*** *– sit down; suffix:* ***...éw̓s*** *– in between, middle.*
čłqlšew̓s – S/he mounted. **čn čłqlšew̓s, kʷ čłqlšew̓s**
es čłqlšew̓si – S/he is mounting. **čnes čłqlšew̓si, kʷes čłqlšew̓si**
qs čłqlšew̓si – S/he is going to mount. **čiqs čłqlšew̓si, kʷqs čłqlšew̓si**

čłqlšew̓siš – Mount. *cmd.*

t̓ipmncut – come down from something high *(i.e., tree, chair, etc.). rt.:* ***t̓iip*** *– fall. See:* ***come down.***

The **i** following uvular consonants (UC) and the glottal stop **ʔ** sound like English "*ey*" as in the words th*ey*, h*ey*, wh*ey*, etc. Salish UC are: **q, q̓, qʷ, q̓ʷ, x̣, x̣ʷ**. For example, the suffix **...qin** – head/top, is often spelled using English *ey* as "q*ey*n". So **qi, q̓i, qʷi, q̓ʷi, x̣i, x̣ʷi**, may be spelled with English *ey* as **q***ey*, **q̓***ey*, **qʷ***ey*, **q̓ʷ***ey*, **x̣***ey*, **x̣ʷ***ey* in other texts.

s.t. - something, the 3rd person
(s.t.) - something implied
s.o. - someone, the 3rd person
sl. - singular form
pl. - plural form
rt. - root word
cmd. - command
lit. - literally
fig. - figuratively
i.e., - for example
See: - Redirection to a related word.

mountain **es móq̇ʷ** – hill, mountain.
es mqʷmóq̇ʷ – mountains.

xʷṫip č es mq̇ʷmóq̇ʷ – S/he ran away to the mountains. **es mx̣ʷpmi ci č es mq̇ʷmoq̇ʷ** – It is snowing in the mountains.

sɬqá – hilltop.

k̇ʷɬx̣sulexʷ – bare hill or mountain.

čkʷtonqn – big mountain. *circumfix:* ***č...qn*** *– mountain.*

mountain alder **čičitṅéɬp,** *čičitṅé* – alder tree; *Alnus incana.*

mountain ash **smx̣é sʔiɫis** – mountain ash; *Sorbus scopulina.*

mountain bistort **iẇéstn** – mountain bistort; *Polygonum bistortoides.*

mountain bluebird **nɬqʷiqʷayáċeʔ,** *nɬqʷiqʷayá* – mountain bluebird; *Sialia currucoides.*

mountain caribou **styélsčn,** *styé* – woodland mountain caribou; *Rangifer tarandus caribou.*
suffix: ***...elsčn*** *– horn.*

mountain chickadee **ċsqáṅeʔ** – mountain chickadee; *Poecile gambeli.*

mountain goat **sx̣ʷƛ̓eẏ** – mountain goat; *Oreamnos americanus.*
sx̣ʷƛ̓inelxʷ – mountain goat hide/skin.

nlimqe – male mountain goat.

mountain hemlock **xʷk̇ʷstneɬp,** *xʷk̇ʷstne* – mountain hemlock; *Tsuga mertensiana.*

pɬtiṅéʔ – western hemlock; *Tsuga heterophylla.*

mountain lion **skʷtismyé** – mountain lion, cougar; *Puma concolor.*

mountain pass **sx̣ʷcuʔsi** – mountain pass. *See:* ***pass.***

mountain sheep **ɫʔumnélsčn,** *ɫʔumné* – bighorn sheep, mountain sheep; *Ovis canadensis.*
nɫmqélsčn, *nɫmqé* – bighorn sheep ewe, mountain sheep ewe; *Ovis canadensis.*

mountain tea **sčtx̣ʷičṅ liti, sčtx̣ʷčɫliti** – mountain tea; labrador tea; *Ledum glandulosum.*

mountain whitefish **x̣ʷx̣ʷẏucṅ,** *x̣ʷx̣ʷẏu* – whitefish; *Prosopium williamsoni.*

mourn **ɫwelmt** – in mourning.
ɫwelmt – S/he was in mourning. **čn ɫwelmt, kʷ ɫwelmt**
es ɫwelmti – S/he is in mourning. **čn ɫwelmti, kʷ ɫwelmti**

nɫulmtepmis – S/he mourned s.o. **nɫulmtepmn, nɫulmtepmntxʷ**
es nɫulmtepms – S/he is mourning s.o. **ies nɫulmtepm, as nɫulmtepm**

es k̇ʷɫɫulmtenči – She is mourning with child. **čnes k̇ʷɫɫulmtenči, kʷes k̇ʷɫɫulmtenči**

sɫwél̓mt – widow/widower during mourning.

čcʔot – mourn; cry over. *rt.:* ***cʔot*** *– cry.*
čcʔot – S/he mourned. **čn čcʔot, kʷ čcʔot**
es čcʔoti – S/he is mourning. **čnes čcʔoti, kʷes čcʔoti**

qs čcʔoti – S/he is going to mourn. **čiqs čcʔoti, kʷqs čcʔoti**

čcʔotmis – S/he mourned for s.o. **čcʔotmn, čcʔotmntxʷ**
es čcʔotms – S/he is mourning for s.o. **ies čcʔotm, as čcʔotm**
qs čcʔotms – S/he is going to mourn for s.o. **iqs čcʔotm, aqs čcʔotm**

pupusénč, *pupusé* – sad; sorry; mourn; grieve. *See:* ***sad.***

mourning dove

heṁishṁ – dove, mourning dove; *Zenaida macroura.*

mouse

k̓ʷék̓ʷt̓neʔ – deer mouse; mouse.

sqʷʔópłxʷ – hole; den *(as of a mouse or rat). rt.:* ***qʷʔóp*** *– make soft; suffix:* ***...ełxʷ, ...łxʷ*** *– house.*

mouth

splimcn – lips; mouth.

...cin – *suffix indicating an action of the mouth; i.e., speaking, eating, & food.*

saq̇cn – have the mouth open; part lips. *rt.:* ***saq̇*** *– split; suffix:* ***...cin, ...cn*** *– action of the mouth.*
saq̇cn – S/he had an open mouth. **čn saq̇cn, kʷ saq̇cn**
es saq̇cni – His/her mouth is open. **čnes saq̇cni, kʷes saq̇cni**

saq̇cniš – Open your mouth. *cmd.*
saq̇cnwi – All of you open your mouth. *cmd.*

xʷpmaẇsqn – open mouth wide; stretch mouth. *rt.:* ***xʷup*** *– stretch, unfold.*
xʷpmaẇsqn – S/he opened his/her mouth wide. **čn xʷpmaẇsqn, kʷ xʷpmaẇsqn**
es xʷpmaẇsqn – His/her mouth is opened wide. **čnes xʷpmaẇsqn, kʷes xʷpmaẇsqn**

xʷpmaẇsqniš – Open your mouth wide. *cmd.*

kʷtcin – have a mouthful. *suffix:* ***...cin, ...cn*** *– action of the mouth.*
kʷtcin – S/he had a mouthful. **čn kʷtcin, kʷ kʷtcin**
es kʷtcini – S/he has a mouthful. **čnes kʷtcini, kʷes kʷtcini**
qs kʷtcini – S/he is going to have a mouthful. **čiqs kʷtcini, kʷqs kʷtcini**

ta kʷ qes qʷlqʷel̓t ṅe kʷes kʷtcini – Do not talk when you have a mouthful.

nšt̓cin – have something sticking out of the mouth. *(i.e., cigarette, straw, pencil, etc.) rt.:* ***šit̓*** *– stand upright; suffix:* ***...cin, ...cn*** *– action of the mouth.*
nšt̓cin – S/he had s.t. sticking out of the mouth. **čn nšt̓cin, kʷ nšt̓cin**
es nšt̓cini – S/he has s.t. sticking out of the mouth. **čnes nšt̓cini, kʷes nšt̓cini**
qs nšt̓cini – S/he is going to have s.t. sticking out of the mouth. **čiqs nšt̓cini, kʷqs nšt̓cini**

nšt̓cinmis – S/he put s.t. in s.o.'s mouth. **nšt̓cinmn, nšt̓cinmntxʷ**
es nšt̓cinms – S/he is putting s.t. in s.o.'s mouth. **ies nšt̓cinm, as nšt̓cinm**
qs nšt̓cinms – S/he is going to put s.t. in s.o.'s mouth. **iqs nšt̓cinm, aqs nšt̓cinm**

nšt̓ciniš – Put it in your mouth. *cmd.*
nšt̓cinmnt – Put it in s.o.'s mouth. *cmd.*

es laxʷk̓ʷa – His/her/its mouth is wide open.

q̇ʷaċłq̇ʷlt – have a mouthful. *rt.:* ***q̇ʷeċt*** *– full; suffix:* ***...ałq̇ʷlt, ...łq̇ʷlt*** *– throat.*
i q̇ʷaċłq̇ʷlt – S/he/it has a mouthful. **i čn q̇ʷaċłq̇ʷlt, i kʷ q̇ʷaċłq̇ʷlt**

n...epneʔ – *circumfix indicating taking a mouthful.*
neslepneʔ – S/he took two mouthfuls. **čn neslepneʔ, kʷ neslepneʔ**

The **i** following uvular consonants (UC) and the glottal stop **ʔ** sound like English "*ey*" as in the words th*ey*, h*ey*, wh*ey*, etc. Salish UC are: **q, q̇, qʷ, q̇ʷ, x̣, x̣ʷ**. For example, the suffix ...**qin** – head/top, is often spelled using English *ey* as "q*ey*n". So **qi, q̇i, qʷi, q̇ʷi, x̣i, x̣ʷi**, may be spelled with English *ey* as **q***ey*, **q̇***ey*, **qʷ***ey*, **q̇ʷ***ey*, **x̣***ey*, **x̣ʷ***ey* in other texts.

s.t. - something, the 3rd person
(s.t.) - something implied
s.o. - someone, the 3rd person
sl. - singular form
pl. - plural form
rt. - root word
cmd. - command
lit. - literally
fig. - figuratively
i.e., - for example
See: - Redirection to a related word.

nčeɫlepneʔ – S/he took three mouthfuls. **nmuspneʔ** – S/he took four mouthfuls. **nclčstepneʔ** – S/he took five mouthfuls. **nt̓q̓nšstepneʔ** – S/he took six mouthfuls. **nsp̓l̓čstepneʔ, nhenmepneʔ, nx̣ntepneʔ, nʔupnčstepneʔ**

...pósqn, *...pó* – *suffix indicating lip. See:* ***lip.***

q̇ʷaposqncut – squeeze one's lips together. *rt.:* ***q̇ʷʔe*** *– wring, squeeze; suffix:* ***...posqn*** *– lips; suffix:* ***...cut*** *– action to the self.*
q̇ʷaposqncut – S/he squeezed one's lips together. **čn q̇ʷaposqncut, kʷ q̇ʷaposqncut**
es q̇ʷaposqncuti – S/he is squeezing one's lips together. **čnes q̇ʷaposqncuti, kʷes q̇ʷaposqncuti**
qs q̇ʷaposqncuti – S/he is going to squeeze one's lips together. **čiqs q̇ʷaposqncuti, kʷqs q̇ʷaposqncuti**

q̇ʷaposqncutš – Squeeze your lips together. *cmd.*

ɫq̇aposqn – wide mouth.

move

iṁš – move camp; move to another home/place; journey.
iṁš – S/he moved. **čn iṁš, kʷ iṁš**
es iṁši – S/he is moving. **čnes iṁši, kʷes iṁši**
qs iṁši – S/he is going to move. **čiqs iṁši, kʷqs iṁši**
es íʔiṁši – They are moving. **qeʔes iṁši, pes iṁši**

iṁšstes – S/he made s.o. move. **iṁšsten, iṁšstexʷ**
es iṁšms – S/he is making s.o. move. **ies iṁšm, as iṁšm**
qs iṁšms – S/he is going to make s.o. move. **iqs iṁšm, aqs iṁšm**

es ṁʔiṁši – Each one is moving. **qeʔes ṁʔiṁši, pes ṁʔiṁši**

es cʔiṁši – S/he is moving here. **čnes cʔiṁši, kʷes cʔiṁši**
qs cʔiṁši – S/he is going to move here. **čiqs cʔiṁši, kʷqs cʔiṁši**

snṁšlwistn – place where one is moving.

es iṁšlwisi – S/he/it is moving place to place. **čnes iṁšlwisi, kʷes iṁšlwisi**

tsnkʷspé u cʔiṁš kʷtisi – Big Blanket moved here a year ago. **qeʔes iṁši čč̓ʔit čɫčéwm** – We were moving close to the plains. **ṅe eɫ cwis íʔiṁš m qeʔ wénš** – When they finish moving back here again, we'll war dance.

qʷmep – move off as a group; start the move; group journey.
qʷmeʔep – They started off. **qeʔ qʷmep, p qʷmep**
es qʷmpiʔi – They are starting off. **qeʔes qʷmpi, pes qʷmpi**
qs qʷmpiʔi – They are going to start off. **qeʔqs qʷmpi, pqs qʷmpi**

qʷmepsts – S/he made them start off. **qʷmepstn, qʷmepstxʷ**
es qʷmepms– S/he is making them start off. **ies qʷmepm, as qʷmepm**
qs qʷmepms– S/he is going to make them start off. **iqs qʷmepm, aqs qʷmepm**

čqʷmeʔepmis – They started off to. **qeʔ čqʷmepstm, čqʷmepstp**
es qʷmepms– S/he is making them start off. **ies qʷmepm, as qʷmepm**
qs qʷmepms– S/he is going to make them start off. **iqs qʷmepm, aqs qʷmepm**

sipšlš – moving something from one place to another; make someone move off; transport; transplant; shift. *suffix:* ***...ilš*** *– autonomous.*
sipšlšm – S/he moved (s.t.). **čn sipšlšm, kʷ sipšlšm**
es sipšlši – S/he is moving (s.t.). **čnes sipšlši, kʷes sipšlši**
qs sipšlši – S/he is going to move (s.t.). **čiqs sipšlši, kʷqs sipšlši**

sipšlšsts – S/he moved s.t. **sipšlšstn, sipšlšstxʷ**
es sipšlšms – S/he is moving it. **ies sipšlšm, as sipšlšm**
qs sipšlšms – S/he is going to move it. **iqs sipšlšm, aqs sipšlšm**

sipšlšskʷ – Move it. *cmd.*

sipšlšstxʷ snčłemutn č sčċiq̓ʷečsts nqʷq̓ʷosmi – You moved the chair to the left side of the dog.

q̓ʷamim – move/slide something.
q̓ʷamstes – S/he/it moved s.t. **q̓ʷamsten, q̓ʷamstexʷ**
es q̓ʷamims – S/he/it is moving s.t. **ies q̓ʷamim, as q̓ʷamim**
qs q̓ʷamims – S/he/it is going to move s.t. **iqs q̓ʷamim, aqs q̓ʷamim**
es q̓ʷamíʔims – They are moving s.t. **qeʔes q̓ʷamim, es q̓ʷamimp**

q̓ʷṁq̓ʷamuł – one that habitually moves around. *suffix:* ***...łmuł –*** *one that habitually does.*

q̓ʷamiskʷ – Move s.t. over. *cmd.*
q̓ʷamint – Move it forward. *cmd.*

q̓ʷamepl – move/scoot on a chair.
q̓ʷamups – move/scoot on the butt.

q̓ʷamncut – move one's self over; slide over. *See:* ***slide.***

q̓ʷamiskʷ ci č nk̓ʷuʔ – Move s.t. over to the next one. **q̓ʷamiskʷ t esel –** Move s.t. over two.

iwu – movement of something voluntary as moving a body part or involuntary as a quiver, shake, or tremble.
iwm – S/he shook. **čn iwm, kʷ iwm**
es iwi – S/he is shaking. **čnes iwi, kʷes iwi**
qs iwi – S/he is going to shake. **čiqs iwi, kʷqs iwi**

iwmsts – S/he made s.t. move (shake). **iwmstn, iwmstxʷ**
es iwms – S/he is making s.t. move (shake). **ies iwm, as iwm**
qs iwms – S/he is going to make s.t. move (shake). **iqs iwm, aqs iwm**

iwmist – S/he shook one's self. **čn iwmist, kʷ iwmist**
es iwmisti – S/he is shaking one's self. **čnes iwmisti, kʷes iwmisti**
qs iwmisti – S/he is going to shake one's self. **čiqs iwmisti, kʷqs iwmisti**

iwimskʷ – Shake it. *cmd.*
iwést – trembled/twitched. *See:* ***quiver.***
yumi – pregnant. *(have movement inside.)* *See:* ***pregnant.***
niwłċe – movement inside.
iwiwmqnečst – move fingers.
iwiwmečst – move hands.
iwiwls – blood moves; pulse. *rt.:* ***iwu –*** *move.* *See:* ***pulse.***
čiwċeʔ – shiver; move/shake all over. *rt.:* ***iwu –*** *move.* *See:* ***shiver.***

iwimskʷ ančlčelš – Shake your hands.

čtčit – move lightly; move gently.
čtčit – S/he moved lightly. **čn čtčit, kʷ čtčit**
es čtčiti – S/he is moving lightly. **čnes čtčiti, kʷes čtčiti**
qs čtčiti – S/he is going to move lightly. **čiqs čtčiti, kʷqs čtčiti**

čtčitiš – Move lightly. *cmd.*

The **i** following uvular consonants (UC) and the glottal stop ʔ sound like English "*ey*" as in the words *they*, *hey*, *whey*, etc. Salish UC are: **q**, **q̓**, **qʷ**, **q̓ʷ**, **x̣**, **x̣ʷ**. For example, the suffix **...qin** – head/top, is often spelled using English *ey* as "q*ey*n". So **qi**, **q̓i**, **qʷi**, **q̓ʷi**, **x̣i**, **x̣ʷi**, may be spelled with English *ey* as **q***ey*, **q̓***ey*, **qʷ***ey*, **q̓ʷ***ey*, **x̣***ey*, **x̣ʷ***ey* in other texts.

s.t. - something, the 3rd person
(s.t.) - something implied
s.o. - someone, the 3rd person
sl. - singular form
pl. - plural form
rt. - root word
cmd. - command
lit. - literally
fig. - figuratively
i.e., - for example
See: - Redirection to a related word.

čtčits – scout on foot; sneak and look around. *See:* ***scout.***
čtčitšn – walk lightly; walk gently. *See:* ***walk.***

movie **sʔaccx̣** – movie, show. *rt.:* ***accx̣*** *– watch.* *See:* ***watch.***
scʔaccx̣ – something that's been watched. *prefix:* ***sc...*** *– s.t. that's been done/made/prepared.*
x̣sʔaccx̣ – good movie.
čsʔaccx̣ – bad movie.
snʔaccx̣tn – television, movie house. *prefix:* ***sn...*** *– a place of; suffix:* ***...tin, ...tn*** *– means of/device.*

mow **x̣ʷiclexʷ** – mow grass or hay.
x̣ʷiclexʷm – S/he mowed. **čn x̣ʷiclexʷm, kʷ x̣ʷiclexʷm**
es x̣ʷiclexʷi – S/he is mowing. **čnes x̣ʷiclexʷi, kʷes x̣ʷiclexʷi**
qs x̣ʷiclexʷi – S/he is going to mow. **čiqs x̣ʷiclexʷi, kʷqs x̣ʷiclexʷi**
x̣ʷíʔiclexʷm – They mowed. **qeʔ x̣ʷiclexʷm, p x̣ʷiclexʷm**
es x̣ʷíʔiclexʷi – They are mowing. **qeʔes x̣ʷiclexʷi, pes x̣ʷiclexʷi**

x̣ʷiclexʷiš – Mow. *cmd.*
x̣ʷiclexʷnt – Mow the grass. *cmd.*

much **xʷʔit** – many; a lot; much; have plenty. *See:* ***many.***

miɫ – too much, too many. *See:* ***too much.***

k̓ʷinš – How many/much? *(of a number, i.e., money, time)* *See:* ***how many.***

ƛ̓méẏ – few, barely, not much. *See:* ***few.***

mud **mal** – muddy; soiled with mud/dirt.
malis – S/he soiled s.t./s.o. with mud. **maln, malntxʷ**
es malms – S/he is soiling s.t./s.o. with mud. **ies malm, as malm**
qs malms – S/he is going to soil s.t./s.o. with mud. **iqs malm, aqs malm**

malt – mud.

malnt – Soil it with mud. *cmd.*
i mállexʷ – It is muddy *(ground is muddy).*

čmalċeʔ – covered in mud.
es čmalċeʔ – S/he is covered in mud. **čnes čmalċeʔ, kʷes čmalċeʔ**

mals – soiled face.
malsncut – S/he muddied one's face. **čn malsncut, kʷ malsncut**
es malsncuti – S/he is muddying one's face. **čnes malsncuti, kʷes malsncuti**
qs malsncuti – S/he is going to muddy one's face. **čiqs malsncuti, kʷqs malsncuti**

malsis – S/he muddied s.o.'s face. **malsn, malsntxʷ**
es malsms – S/he is muddying s.o.'s face. **ies malsm, as malsm**
qs malsms – S/he is going to muddy s.o.'s face. **iqs malsm, aqs malsm**

i mals – S/he/it has a soiled face. **i čn mals, i kʷ mals**
es mals – His/her/its face is soiled. **čnes mals, kʷes mals**

malsncutiš – Muddy your face. *cmd.*
malsnt – Muddy s.o.'s face. *cmd.*

mlmalčst – soiled hands. *suffix:* ***...ečst, ...čst*** *– of the hand.*
mlmalčsncut – S/he muddied one's hands. **čn mlmalčsncut, kʷ mlmalčsncut**
es mlmalčsncuti – S/he is muddying one's hands. **čnes mlmalčsncuti, kʷes mlmalčsncuti**

qs mlmalčsncuti – S/he is going to muddy one's hands. **čiqs mlmalčsncuti, kʷqs mlmalčsncuti**

mlmalčsis – S/he muddied s.o.'s hands. **mlmalčsn, mlmalčsntxʷ**
es mlmalčsms – S/he is muddying s.o.'s hands. **ies mlmalčsm, as mlmalčsm**
qs mlmalčsms – S/he is going to muddy s.o.'s hands. **iqs mlmalčsm, aqs mlmalčsm**

i mlmalčst – S/he/it has soiled hands. **i čn mlmalčst, i kʷ mlmalčst**
es mlmalčst – His/her/its hands are soiled. **čnes mlmalčst, kʷes mlmalčst**

mlmalčsncutiš – Muddy your hands. *cmd.*
mlmalčsnt – Muddy s.o.'s hands. *cmd.*

mlmalšn – soiled feet.
mlmalšnncut – S/he muddied one's feet. **čn mlmalšncut, kʷ mlmalšnncut**
es mlmalšnncuti – S/he is muddying one's feet. **čnes mlmalšnncuti, kʷes mlmalšnncuti**
qs mlmalšnncuti – S/he is going to muddy one's feet. **čiqs mlmalšnncuti, kʷqs mlmalšnncuti**

mlmalšnis – S/he muddied s.o.'s feet. **mlmalšn, mlmalšntxʷ**
es mlmalšnms – S/he is muddying s.o.'s feet. **ies mlmalšnm, as mlmalšnm**
qs mlmalšnms – S/he is going to muddy s.o.'s feet. **iqs mlmalšnm, aqs mlmalšnm**

i mlmalšn – S/he/it has soiled feet. **i čn mlmalšn, i kʷ mlmalšn**
es mlmalšn – His/her/its feet are soiled. **čnes mlmalšn, kʷes mlmalšn**

mlmalšncutiš – Muddy your feet. *cmd.*
mlmalšnt – Muddy s.o.'s feet. *cmd.*

mallqs – muddy clothes.
mallqsis – S/he muddied s.o.'s clothes. **mallqsn, mallqsntxʷ**
es mallqsms – S/he is muddying s.o.'s clothes. **ies mallqsm, as mallqsm**
qs mallqsms – S/he is going to muddy s.o.'s clothes. **iqs mallqsm, aqs mallqsm**

mallqsnt – Muddy s.o.'s clothes. *cmd.*

ƛ̓awač̓ – muddy; squishy mud.
i ƛ̓awač̓ – S/he/it is muddy. **i čn ƛ̓awač̓, i kʷ ƛ̓awač̓**

ƛ̓awač̓is – S/he/it got s.t./s.o. muddy. **ƛ̓awač̓n, ƛ̓awač̓ntxʷ**
es ƛ̓awač̓ms – S/he/it is getting s.t./s.o. muddy. **ies ƛ̓awač̓m, asƛ̓awač̓m**

ƛ̓awač̓lexʷ – muddy land/place.
čƛ̓awač̓lqʷ – muddy wood/tree.
nƛ̓awač̓ – stuck in mud. *See: **stuck**.*

muddler **sttṁá** – slimy muddler, slimy sculpin; *Cottus cognatus*.

mudhen **st̓láqšn** – American coot; mudhen; *Fulica americana*.

łẏé – rail; coot; *Rallus limicola*.

mugwort **qpqptéłp,** *qpqpté* – sage; mug worm; tarragon.

mule **st̓ulċeʔ** – black-tail doe; female mule deer; mule; *Odocoileus hemionus*.

sxʷq̓ʷéłt – packhorse; pack mule. *prefix: **sxʷ...** – one tasked to do.*

mule deer **st̓ulċeʔ** – black-tail doe; female mule deer; mule; *Odocoileus hemionus*. **stl̓t̓ulċeʔ** *pl.*

The **i** following uvular consonants (UC) and the glottal stop **ʔ** sound like English "*ey*" as in the words th*ey*, h*ey*, wh*ey*, etc. Salish UC are: **q**, **q̓**, **qʷ**, **q̓ʷ**, **x̣**, **x̣ʷ**. For example, the suffix ...**qin** – head/top, is often spelled using English *ey* as "q*ey*n". So **qi**, **q̓i**, **qʷi**, **q̓ʷi**, **x̣i**, **x̣ʷi**, may be spelled with English *ey* as **q***ey*, **q̓***ey*, **qʷ***ey*, **q̓ʷ***ey*, **x̣***ey*, **x̣ʷ***ey* in other texts.

s.t. - something, the 3rd person
(s.t.) - something implied
s.o. - someone, the 3rd person
sl. - singular form
pl. - plural form
rt. - root word
cmd. - command
lit. - literally
fig. - figuratively
i.e., - for example
See: - Redirection to a related word.

sṫulċeˀlxʷ – black-tail doe hide.

puwélsčn, *puwé* – black-tail buck; male mule deer; Odocoileus *hemionus.* **pupuwélsčn** *pl.*

puwélsčnelxʷ – black-tail buck hide/buckskin.

multiply

nx̣pṗmeẇs – multiply; double up; laminate. *rt.: x̣ṗ – line, coat; suffix: ...éẇs – in between, middle.*

nx̣pṗmeẇsm – S/he multiplied (s.t.). **čn nx̣pṗmeẇsm, kʷ nx̣pṗmeẇsm**
es nx̣pṗmeẇsi – S/he is multiplying (s.t.). **čnes nx̣pṗmeẇsi, kʷes nx̣pṗmeẇsi**
qs nx̣pṗmeẇsi – S/he is going to multiply (s.t.). **čiqs nx̣pṗmeẇsi, kʷqs nx̣pṗmeẇsi**

nx̣pṗmeẇsis – S/he multiplied s.t. **nx̣pṗmeẇsn, nx̣pṗmeẇsntxʷ**
es nx̣pṗmeẇsms – S/he is multiplying s.t. **ies nx̣pṗmeẇsm, as nx̣pṗmeẇsm**
qs nx̣pṗmeẇsms – S/he is going to multiply s.t. **iqs nx̣pṗmeẇsm, aqs nx̣pṗmeẇsm**

nx̣pṗmeẇsnt – Multiply it. *cmd.*

ha es nx̣pṗmeẇs – Is it multiplied/doubled? **ha aqs nx̣pṗmeẇsm** – Are you going to multipy it?
esel nx̣pṗmeẇsnt čeɫe kʷemt eɫ ṫaq̇n – Two times three equals six, *(2 x 3 = 6).*

mummy

čiyaliicmis – mummy. *lit. wraped-up.*

murder

plsqélixʷ, *plsqé* – kill people.

muscle

nyoyoscutn – muscle. *suffix: ...tin, ...tn – means of/device.*

sqelṫč – meat.

mushroom

ṗaƛ̓qineˀ – mushroom; morel or morchella mushroom. *rt.: ṗaƛ̓ – smooth; suffix: ...qin, ...qn – top.*

muskrat

ččl̓éxʷ – muskat; *Ondatra zibethicus.*

mustard

kʷaliˀ čtxʷcin – mustard.

tax̣t – mustard.

my

iqɫ – It is going to be mine.
iqɫ mlmelčstn – It is going to be my toy.

in, i – It is mine; my.
inmlmelčstn – my toy.

incitxʷ – my house.
innṫišk – my pop.
isqʷséˀ – my son.
iskʷiskʷs – my chicken.

ƛ̓m in, ƛ̓m i – It was mine.
ƛ̓m inmlmelčstn – It was my toy.

qʷoyˀé – mine; me.

N

nail **lṗx̣ʷmin,** *lṗx̣ʷmi* – nail. *suffix:* ***...min, ...mn*** *– instrument/tool.*
łlṗlṗx̣ʷmin, *łlṗlṗx̣ʷmi* – little nail.

lṗx̣ʷom – pin/nail something to something.
lṗx̣ʷomis – S/he pinned s.t. to s.t. **lṗx̣ʷomn, lṗx̣ʷomntxʷ**
es lṗx̣ʷoms – S/he is pinning s.t. to s.t. **ies lṗx̣ʷom, as lṗx̣ʷom**
qs lṗx̣ʷoms – S/he is going to pin s.t. to s.t. **iqs lṗx̣ʷom, aqs lṗx̣ʷom**
lṗx̣ʷóʔomis – They pinned s.t. to s.t. **qeʔ lṗx̣ʷomn, lṗx̣ʷomntp**

lṗx̣ʷomnt – Pin it to something. *cmd.*

člṗx̣ʷalqʷm – nail wood. *suffix:* ***...alqʷ*** *– wood; cylindical.*
člṗx̣ʷalqʷis – S/he nailed s.t. **člṗx̣ʷalqʷn, člṗx̣ʷalqʷntxʷ**
es člṗx̣ʷalqʷms – S/he is nailing s.t. **ies člṗx̣ʷalqʷm, as člṗx̣ʷalqʷm**
qs člṗx̣ʷalqʷms – S/he is going to nail s.t. **iqs člṗx̣ʷalqʷm, aqs člṗx̣ʷalqʷm**
člṗx̣ʷáʔalqʷis – They nailed s.t. **qeʔ člṗx̣ʷalqʷntm, člṗx̣ʷalqʷntp**

člṗlṗx̣ʷalqʷtn – railroad spike. *suffix:* ***...tin, ...tn*** *– means of/device.*

člṗx̣ʷalqʷnt – Nail it. *cmd.*

q̓ʷx̣ʷqinčst, *q̓ʷx̣ʷqi* – fingernail. *See:* ***fingernail.***

q̓ʷx̣ʷqinšn, *q̓ʷx̣ʷqi* – toenail; claws. *See:* ***toenail.***

naked **čtmélxʷ,** *čtmé* – naked; without clothes. *rt.:* ***tam*** *– none; prefix:* ***č...*** *– up on; suffix:* ***...elxʷ*** *– skin/hide.*
čtmelxʷ – S/he was naked. **čn čtmelxʷ, kʷ čtmelxʷ**
čtméʔelxʷ – They were naked. **qeʔ čtmelxʷ, p čtmelxʷ**

i čtmelxʷ – S/he is naked. **i čn čtmelxʷ, i kʷ čtmelxʷ**

čtmtmelxʷwis – S/he goes around naked. **čn čtmtmelxʷwis, kʷ čtmtmelxʷwis**

čċslexʷ – get naked; get cleared of clothing.
čċslexʷis – S/he got s.o. naked. **čċslexʷn, čċslexʷntxʷ**
es čċslexʷms – S/he is getting s.o. naked. **ies čċslexʷm, as čċslexʷm**
qs čċslexʷms – S/he is going to get s.o. naked. **iqs čċslexʷm, aqs čċslexʷm**
čċsléʔexʷis – They got s.o. naked. **qeʔ čċxʷelxʷntm, čċxʷelxʷntp**
es čċsléʔexʷms – They are getting s.o. naked. **qeʔes čċslexʷm, es čċslexʷmp**
qs aisléʔexʷms – They are going to get s.o. naked. **qeʔqs čċxʷelxʷm, qs čċslexʷmp**

čċslxʷnuis – S/he succeeded in getting s.o. naked. **čċslxʷnun, čċslxʷnuntxʷ**

čċslexʷnt – Get s.o. naked. *cmd.*
es čċslxʷmnwexʷi – They are getting each other naked.

s.t. - something, the 3rd person
(s.t.) - something implied
s.o. - someone, the 3rd person
sl. - singular form
pl. - plural form
rt. - root word
cmd. - command
lit. - literally
fig. - figuratively
i.e., - for example
See: - Redirection to a related word.

axí u ččslxʷnun – I finally got s.o. naked.

ččslxʷncut – get one's self naked. *rt.: ċslexʷ– make bare/clean; suffix: ...cut– action to the self.*
ččslxʷncut – S/he got naked. **čn ččslxʷncut, kʷ ččslxʷncut**
es ččslxʷncuti – S/he is getting naked. **čnes ččslxʷncut, kʷes ččslxʷncuti**
qs ččslxʷncuti – S/he is going to get naked. **čiqs ččslxʷncut, kʷqs ččslxʷncuti**
ččslxʷncúʔut – They got naked. **qeʔ ččslxʷncut, p ččslxʷncut**
es ččslxʷncúʔuti – They are getting naked. **qeʔes ččslxʷncut, pes ččslxʷncuti**
qs ččslxʷncúʔuti – They are going to get naked. **qeʔqs ččslxʷncut, pqs ččslxʷncuti**

ččslxʷncutš – Get yourself naked. *cmd.*

ččxʷelxʷ – get naked.
ččxʷelxʷis – S/he got s.o. naked. **ččxʷelxʷn, ččxʷelxʷntxʷ**
es ččxʷelxʷms – S/he is getting s.o. naked. **ies ččxʷelxʷm, as ččxʷelxʷm**
qs ččxʷelxʷms – S/he is going to get s.o. naked. **iqs ččxʷelxʷm, aqs ččxʷelxʷm**
ččxʷéʔelxʷis – They got s.o. naked. **qeʔ ččxʷelxʷntm, ččxʷelxʷntp**
es ččxʷéʔelxʷms – They are getting s.o. naked. **qeʔes ččxʷelxʷm, es ččxʷelxʷmp**
qs ččxʷéʔelxʷms – They are going to get s.o. naked. **qeʔqs ččxʷelxʷm, qs ččxʷelxʷmp**

ččxʷelxʷnt – Get s.o. naked. *cmd.*
es čččxʷlmnwexʷi – They are getting each other naked.

kʷ iqs ččxʷelxʷm – I am going to get you naked.

čpƛ̓ʔencut – undress one's self. *See: **undress**.*

npƛ̓alqs, *npƛ̓a* **–** remove/take off clothes. *See: **undress**.*
npƛ̓alqsiš – Remove your clothes. *cmd.*

name

skʷést – name; title.
skʷests – his/her name. **iskʷest, askʷest**
sšʔitmskʷest – first name.
snq̓eskʷest – middle name.
snk̓ʷlixʷskʷest – last name; family name.
ušiskʷest – long name.
skʷstulexʷ – place name; name of the land.
skʷskʷstulexʷ – place names; names of the land.

swe łu askʷest – What is your name? **steṁ łu askʷest –** What is your name; what is it about? *i.e., jump dance name, animal name, etc.* **steṁ łu skʷests –** What is its name? **nłeptmn łu skʷests –** I forgot his/her name. **ta esmisten łu skʷests –** I do not know her/his/its name.

kʷestšmis – name someone.
kʷestšmis – S/he named s.o. **kʷestšmn, kʷestšmntxʷ**
es kʷestšms – S/he is naming s.o. **ies kʷestšm, as kʷestšm**
qs kʷestšms – S/he is going to name s.o. **iqs kʷestšm, aqs kʷestšm**
kʷéʔestšmis – They named s.o. **qeʔ kʷestšmntm, kʷestšmntp**
es kʷéʔestšms – They are naming s.o. **qeʔes kʷestšm, es kʷestšmp**
qs kʷéʔestšms – They are going to name s.o. **qeʔqs kʷestšm, qs kʷestšmp**

kʷestšmnt – Named him/her/it. *cmd.*

steṁ łu aqs kʷestšm – What are you going to name him/her? **steṁ u kʷestšmntxʷ –** What did you name him/her?

nkʷestšnm – named after someone.

nkʷestšnmis – S/he named him/her after s.o. **nkʷestšnmn, nkʷestšnmntxʷ**
es nkʷestšnms – S/he is naming him/her after s.o. **ies nkʷestšnmn, as nkʷestšnm**
qs nkʷestšnms – S/he is going to name him/her after s.o. **iqs nkʷestšnmn, aqs nkʷestšnm**
nkʷéʔestšnmis – They named him/her after s.o. **qeʔ nkʷestšnmntm, nkʷestšnmntp**
es nkʷéʔestšnms – They are naming him/her after s.o. **qeʔes nkʷestšnmn, es nkʷestšnmp**
qs nkʷéʔestšnms – They are going to name him/her after s.o. **iqs nkʷestšnmn, qs nkʷestšnmp**

nkʷestšnmntm skʷtismyeʔ – S/he was named after a mountain lion. **qʷo**
nkʷestšnmntm łu isíleʔ – I was named after my mother's father.

The **i** following uvular consonants (UC) and the glottal stop **ʔ** sound like English "*ey*" as in the words th*ey*, h*ey*, wh*ey*, etc. Salish UC are: **q, q̇, qʷ, q̇ʷ, x̣, x̣ʷ**. For example, the suffix ...**qin** – head/top, is often spelled using English *ey* as "q*ey*n". So **qi, q̇i, qʷi, q̇ʷi, x̣i, x̣ʷi**, may be spelled with English *ey* as **q***ey*, **q̇***ey*, **qʷ***ey*, **q̇ʷ***ey*, **x̣***ey*, **x̣ʷ***ey* in other texts.

naẇkʷestm – give the name of someone.
naẇkʷestmis – S/he gave him/her the name of s.o. **naẇkʷestmn, naẇkʷestmntxʷ**
es naẇkʷestms – S/he is giving him/her the name of s.o. **ies naẇkʷestm, as naẇkʷestm**
qs naẇkʷestms – S/he is going to give him/her the name of s.o. **iqs naẇkʷestm, aqs naẇkʷestm**

snqlixʷskʷest – name in Salish.
snqlixʷskʷests – his/her name in Salish. **isnqlixʷskʷest, asnqlixʷskʷest**

swe łu asnqlixʷskʷest – What is your name in Salish?

suyapskʷest – English name.
suyapskʷests – his/her English name. **isuyapskʷest, asuyapskʷest**

swe łu asuyapskʷest – What is your English name?

nčnqinm – sign one's name. *See: **signature**.*

nq̇eẏustšnm – copy a name; write a name. *See: **signature**.*

sʔaẇẇ – called; something said. *See: **say**.*
steṁ łu sʔaẇẇs – What is it called?

es custm – It is called; it is said about. *See: **say**.*
ṅe eł ctešlš še es custm k̇ʷsixʷ spq̇niʔ – When it emerges, March is called the month of the geese.

nap

łʔiitš – sleep a little while; take a nap. *rt.: **itš** – sleep; prefix: **ł...** – little.*
łʔiitši – S/he/it slept a little while. **čn łʔiitš, kʷ łʔiitš**
es łʔiitši – S/he/it is sleeping a little while. **čnes łʔiitši, kʷes łʔiitši**
qs łʔiitši – S/he/it is going to sleep a little while. **čiqs łʔiitši, kʷqs łʔiitši**

ťk̇ʷncut – put one's self down; take a nap.
ťk̇ʷncut – S/he/it put one's self down. **čn ťk̇ʷncut, kʷ ťk̇ʷncut**
es ťk̇ʷncuti – S/he/it is putting one's self down. **čnes ťk̇ʷncuti, kʷes ťk̇ʷncuti**
qs ťk̇ʷncuti – S/he/it is going to put one's self down. **čiqs ťk̇ʷncuti, kʷqs ťk̇ʷncuti**
ťk̇ʷncúʔut – They put themselves down. **qeʔ ťk̇ʷncut, p ťk̇ʷncut**
es ťk̇ʷncúʔuti – They are putting themselves down. **qeʔes ťk̇ʷncuti, pes ťk̇ʷncuti**
qs ťk̇ʷncúʔuti – They are going to put themselves down. **qeʔqs ťk̇ʷncuti, pqs ťk̇ʷncuti**

łtťk̇ʷncut – S/he/it took a short nap.

ťk̇ʷncutš – Put yourself down. *cmd.*
ťk̇ʷncutwi – All of you put yourselves down. *cmd.*

s.t. - something, the 3rd person
(s.t.) - something implied
s.o. - someone, the 3rd person
sl. - singular form
pl. - plural form
rt. - root word
cmd. - command
lit. - literally
fig. - figuratively
i.e., - for example
See: - Redirection to a related word.

q̓etyus, *q̓etyu* – nod off; have heavy eyes; cannot hold up head; *literally: weighted face. rt.: **q̓et**– weigh down; suffix: **...us**– face, fire.*
q̓etyus – S/he/it is nodding off. **čn q̓etyus, kʷ q̓etyus**
es q̓etyusi – S/he/it is nodding off. **čnes q̓etyusi, kʷes q̓etyusi**

narrow **łqq̓éw̓t,** *łqq̓é* – narrow/skinny.
i łqq̓ew̓t – It is narrow.
łqq̓ew̓tsts – S/he made s.t. narrow. **łqq̓ew̓tstn, łqq̓ew̓tstxʷ**
es łqq̓ew̓tms – S/he is making s.t. narrow. **ies łqq̓ew̓tm, as łqq̓ew̓tm**
qs łqq̓ew̓tms – S/he is going to make s.t. narrow. **iqs łqq̓ew̓tm, aqs łqq̓ew̓tm**

sck̓ʷłłqq̓e – It was made narrow.
łqq̓asqelixʷ – S/he is a slim person.

łqqˀełc̓eˀ – S/he is skinny.
nłqqˀełc̓eˀ – narrow opening/room.

łqq̓alqʷ – narrow cylinder; tree.
i łqq̓alqʷ anq̓ey̓mintn – Your pencil is skinny.
łqq̓alqʷ ci es šiť – That tree is narrow.
nłqq̓alqʷ – inside narrow trees.

nłqq̓aqs – narrow road.

nłqq̓etkʷ – narrow stream or lake. *suffix: **...etkʷ, ...tkʷ**– liquid*

łqq̓esšn̓ – narrow rock.

nasty **čečeˀt** – nasty.
čečeˀt – S/he is nasty. **čn čečeˀt, kʷ čečeˀt**
es čečeˀilši – S/he is being nasty. **čnes čečeˀilši, kʷes čečeˀilši** *suffix: **...ilš**– autonomous.*

čečnmscut – S/he was nasty. **čn čečnmscut, kʷ čečnmscut**
es čečnmscuti – S/he is being nasty. **čnes čečnmscuti, kʷes čečnmscuti**
qs čečnmscuti – S/he is going to be nasty. **čiqs čečnmscuti, kʷqs čečnmscuti**
čečnmscúˀut – They were nasty. **qeˀ čečnmscut, p čečnmscut**
es čečnmscúˀuti – They are being nasty. **qeˀes čečnmscuti, pes čečnmscuti**
qs čečnmscúˀuti – They are going to be nasty. **qeˀqs čečnmscuti, pqs čečnmscuti**

čečeplmis – S/he was nasty to s.o. **čečeplmn, čečeplmntxʷ**
es čečeplms – S/he is being nasty to s.o. **ies čečeplm, as čečeplm**
qs čečeplms – S/he is going to be nasty to s.o. **iqs čečeplm, aqs čečeplm**
čečéˀeplmis – They were nasty to s.o. **qeˀ čečeplmntm, čečeplmntp**
es čečéˀeplms – They are being nasty to s.o. **qeˀes čečeplm, es čečeplmp**

ččesmcutmis – S/he was nasty to s.o. **ččesmcutmn, ččesmcutmntxʷ**
es ččesmcutmms – S/he is being nasty to s.o. **ies ččesmcutmm, as ččesmcutmm**
qs ččesmcutmms – S/he is going to be nasty to s.o. **iqs ččesmcutmm, aqs ččesmcutmm**
ččesmcúˀutmis – They were nasty to s.o. **qeˀ ččesmcutmntm, ččesmcutmntp**
es ččesmcúˀutmms – They are being nasty to s.o. **qeˀes ččesmcutmm, es ččesmcutmmp**

čečnmscutš – Be nasty. *cmd.*
ččesmcutmnt – Be nasty to s.o. *cmd.*
qeˀes čečestmnwexʷisti – We are being nasty with each other.

es nčečeˀtmisti – S/he is wanting to be nasty. **čnes nčečeˀtmisti, kʷes nčečeˀtmisti**
es nčečeˀtmscuti – S/he is wanting to be nasty. **čnes nčečeˀtmscuti, kʷes nčečeˀtmscuti**

ta kʷ qes čečečmscut x̣iṅe kʷ tixʷł łox̣te – Do not be nasty, you might acquire a baby.

nčečecin – say nasty words. *suffix:* ***...cin, ...cn*** *– action of the mouth.*
nčečecinm – S/he said nasty words. **čn nčečecinm, kʷ nčečecinm**
es nčečecinisti – S/he is saying nasty words. **čnes nčečecinisti, kʷes nčečecinisti**
qs nčečecinisti – S/he is going to say nasty words. **čiqs nčečecinisti, kʷqs nčečecinisti**

nčečecíʔinm – They said nasty words. **qeʔ nčečecinm, p nčečecinm**
es nčečecíʔinisti – They are saying nasty words. **qeʔes nčečecinisti, pes nčečecinisti**

sxʷnčečecinm – one tasked to talk nasty. *prefix:* ***sxʷ...*** *– one tasked to do.*
nčečecnemn – one inclined to talk nasty. *suffix:* ***...emn*** *– one inclined to do.*

nčečeciniš – Talk nasty. *cmd.*
nčečecint – Talk nasty to s.o. *cmd.*

nčečecnwexʷist – They said nasty words to each other. **qeʔ nčečecnwexʷist, p nčečecnwexʷist**
es nčečecnwexʷisti – They are saying nasty words to each other. **qeʔes nčečecnwexʷisti, pes nčečecnwexʷisti**
es nčečecnwéʔexʷisti – They *(more than 2 people)* are saying nasty words to each other.

The **i** following uvular consonants (UC) and the glottal stop **ʔ** sound like English "*ey*" as in the words th*ey*, h*ey*, wh*ey*, etc. Salish UC are: **q, q̇, qʷ, q̇ʷ, x̣, x̣ʷ**. For example, the suffix ...**qin** – head/top, is often spelled using English *ey* as "q*ey*n". So **qi, q̇i, qʷi, q̇ʷi, x̣i, x̣ʷi**, may be spelled with English *ey* as **q***ey*, **q̇***ey*, **qʷ***ey*, **q̇ʷ***ey*, **x̣***ey*, **x̣ʷ***ey* in other texts.

nauseated

čc̓essls – sick to the stomach; nauseated.
čc̓esslsm – S/he was nauseated. **čn čc̓esslsm, kʷ čc̓esslsm**
es čc̓esslsi – S/he is nauseated. **čnes čc̓esslsi, kʷes čc̓esslsi**
qs čc̓esslsi – S/he is going to be nauseated. **čiqs čc̓esslsi, kʷqs čc̓esslsi**
es čc̓éʔesslsi – They are nauseated. **qeʔes čc̓esslsi, pes čc̓esslsi**

čtax̣élsm – have a burning inside your stomach. *(i.e., heartburn) rt.:* ***tax̣*** *– bitter; spicy.*
čtax̣élsm – S/he had heartburn. **čn čtax̣élsm , kʷ čtax̣élsm**
es čtax̣élsi – S/he has heartburn. **čnes čtax̣élsi, kʷes čtax̣élsi**
qs čtax̣élsi – S/he is going to have heartburn. **čiqs čtax̣élsi, kʷqs čtax̣élsi**
es čtax̣éʔelsi – They have heartburn. **qeʔes čtax̣élsi, pes čtax̣élsi**

čċax̣ʷélsi – Sick to your stomach. *(i.e., heartburn, ate too much) See:* ***sick.***

Navajo

ox̣ʷiċeʔ, *ox̣ʷi* – Navajo.

navel

témuʔ – belly button, navel.

near

čc̓ʔit – in motion to get close/near someone or something; drawing near.
čc̓ʔit – S/he got close. **čn čc̓ʔit, kʷ čc̓ʔit**
es čc̓itmi – S/he is getting close. **čnes čc̓itmi, kʷes čc̓itmi**
qs čc̓itmi – S/he is going to get close. **čiqs čc̓itmi, kʷqs čc̓itmi**
čc̓ʔíʔit – They got close. **qeʔ čc̓ʔit, p čc̓ʔit**

čc̓ʔitmis – S/he/it got near s.t. **čc̓ʔitmn, čc̓ʔitmntxʷ**
es čc̓ʔitmnms – S/he/it is getting near s.t. **ies čc̓ʔitmnm, as čc̓ʔitmnm**
qs čc̓ʔitmnms – S/he/it is going to get near s.t. **iqs čc̓ʔitmnm, aqs čc̓ʔitmnm**
čc̓ʔíʔitmis – S/he/it got near s.t. **qeʔ čc̓ʔitmntm, čc̓ʔitmntp**

čc̓ʔitmstes – S/he/it made s.o. advance near it. **čc̓ʔitmsten, čc̓ʔitmstexʷ**
es čc̓ʔitms – S/he/it is making s.o. advance near it. **ies čc̓ʔitm, as čc̓ʔitm**
qs čc̓ʔitms – S/he/it is going to make s.o. advance near it. **iqs čc̓ʔitm, aqs čc̓ʔitm**

s.t. - something, the 3rd person
(s.t.) - something implied
s.o. - someone, the 3rd person
sl. - singular form
pl. - plural form
rt. - root word
cmd. - command
lit. - literally
fig. - figuratively
i.e., - for example
See: - Redirection to a related word.

čitmint – Get near him/her/it. *cmd.*
čč̓ʔitmntm – something/someone got near him/her/it.

es čč̓ʔitmnwexʷi – They are drawing near to each other.

qeʔes im̓ši čč̓ʔit čłčéwm – We were moving close to the plains. **tnk̓ʷuʔ qʷoyʔe u isqwseʔ qeʔ čč̓ʔitmntm nk̓ʷuʔ tšeċ –** One time my son and I got close to a bull elk.

čsax̣m – close to; near.
čsáx̣x̣m – getting close/near.
čsax̣x̣m – S/he/it got close. **čn čsax̣x̣m, kʷ čsax̣x̣m**
es čsax̣x̣mi – S/he/it is getting close. **čnes čsax̣x̣mi, kʷes čsax̣x̣mi**
qs čsax̣x̣mi – S/he/it is going to get close. **čiqs čsax̣x̣mi, kʷqs čsax̣x̣mi**
es čsáʔax̣x̣mi – They are getting close. **qeʔes čsax̣x̣mi, pes čsax̣x̣mi**

čsax̣x̣mis – S/he/it got close to s.o./s.t. **čsax̣x̣mn, čsax̣x̣mntxʷ**
es čsax̣x̣ms – S/he/it is getting close to s.o./s.t. **ies čsax̣x̣m, as čsax̣x̣m**
qs čsax̣x̣ms – S/he/it is going to get close to s.o./s.t. **iqs čsax̣x̣m, aqs čsax̣x̣m**
es čsáʔax̣x̣ms – They are getting close to s.o./s.t. **qeʔes čsax̣x̣m, es čsax̣x̣mp**

čsx̣mis – S/he/it worked at getting close to s.o./s.t. **čsx̣min, čsx̣mintxʷ**
čsx̣míʔis – They worked at getting close to s.o./s.t. **qeʔ čsx̣mintm, čsx̣mintp**
es čx̣smnwexʷisti – They are getting close to each other.
es čsx̣mncutisti – S/he is getting close to one's self. **čnes čsx̣mncutisti, kʷes čsx̣mncutisti**

čsax̣x̣mstmn – I got close to you.

čn čsax̣x̣m l inp̓ip̓uyšn – I got close to my car. **čsax̣x̣mn łu inp̓ip̓uyšn –** I got close to my car. **es mistén u esél nłámqeʔ es čsáx̣x̣mi l ancitxʷ –** I know two bears have been around your house. **čn wičm t nłámqeʔ l isčsáx̣x̣m x̣ił n̓e u qeʔ tʔamnqnwe –** I saw a bear so close we almost bumped heads.

čłʔéʔ – against; pressed against something; leaned against something; eve of any day. *See: **against**.*
čłʔems – his/her close thing/person. **inčłʔem, ančłʔem**
čłʔéʔems – their close thing/person. **qečłʔem, čłʔemmp**

čłʔem – S/he is close/against. **čn čłʔem, kʷ čłʔem**

čłʔemnwexʷ – They are close to each other *(i.e., relatives/friends)*. **qeʔ čłʔemnwexʷ, p čłʔemnwexʷ**

kʷ čłʔem kʷ istmelis – You are a close relative of mine. **čłʔem islax̣t –** My friend is close.

čx̣ssmels, *čx̣ssme* **–** physically affectionate with someone; make out with someone; lucky. *(In the short form this word is also used as an expression for having good luck.) See: **affection**.*

qʷom̓małq, *qʷom̓ma* **–** get close to doing/finishing something; getting near to some point; close to the end of a journey; winning. *See: **close**.*

neat

tuc – neat; in order; clean; preen; groomed.
i tuc – It is neat. **i čn tuc, i kʷ tuc**
i tctuc – Each of them are neat. **i qeʔ tctuc, i p tctuc**

es tucmi – S/he/it is fixing one's self up. **čnes tucmi, kʷes tucmi**
es ttucmisti – S/he/it is preening a little. **čnes ttucmisti, kʷes ttucmisti**

x̣est, *x̣e* **–** good; fine; beautiful. *See: **good**.*

neck

čspin – neck.

sččmčn̓elps – back of the neck.

sx̣ʷopłq̓ʷlt – throat; wind pipe. *See:* ***throat.***

...lpus, lps – *suffix indicating neck.*
čyullps – big neck. *rt.:* ***yult –*** *thick in girth. See:* ***girth.***

ntlpus – broken neck.
ntlpus – S/he broke his/her neck. **čn ntlpus, kʷ ntlpus**
es ntlpusi – S/he has a broken neck. **čnes ntlpusi, kʷes ntlpusi**

nc̓alpus – hurt neck.
nc̓alpus – S/he hurt his/her neck. **čn nc̓alpus, kʷ nc̓alpus**
es nc̓alpusi – S/he has a sore/hurting neck. **čnes nc̓alpusi, kʷes nc̓alpusi**

...elps – *suffix indicating the neck.*
čusšnelps – long neck; giraffe.

cq̓awelps – The neck of a bottle/item broke.
es cq̓awelpsi – His/her/its neck is broken.

cq̓awpelps – The neck of an animal broke.
es cq̓awpelpsi – The animal's neck is broken.

The **i** following uvular consonants (UC) and the glottal stop ʔ sound like English "*ey*" as in the words th*ey*, h*ey*, wh*ey*, etc. Salish UC are: **q**, **q̓**, **qʷ**, **q̓ʷ**, **x̣**, **x̣ʷ**. For example, the suffix **...qin** – head/top, is often spelled using English *ey* as "q*ey*n". So **qi**, **q̓i**, **qʷi**, **q̓ʷi**, **x̣i**, **x̣ʷi**, may be spelled with English *ey* as **q***ey*, **q̓***ey*, **qʷ***ey*, **q̓ʷ***ey*, **x̣***ey*, **x̣ʷ***ey* in other texts.

neck ache

č̓caʔlelps – have a neck ache. *rt.:* ***c̓aál –*** *ache.*

nc̓alpus – have a neck ache. *rt.:* ***c̓aál –*** *ache.*

neckerchief

sk̓ʷłyalcim – neckerchief.

necklace

sq̓lélps, *sq̓lé* **–** necklace.

need

k̓ʷłẏapcin – in need of something; miss something. *rt.:* ***ẏaa –*** *scarce.*
k̓ʷłẏapcinmis – S/he was in need of s.t. **k̓ʷłẏapcinmn, k̓ʷłẏapcinmntxʷ**
es k̓ʷłẏapcinmms – S/he is in need of s.t. **ies k̓ʷłẏapcinmm, as k̓ʷłẏapcinmm**
qs k̓ʷłẏapcinmms – S/he is going to be in need of s.t. **iqs k̓ʷłẏapcinmm, aqs k̓ʷłẏapcinmm**
es k̓ʷłẏapcíʔinmms – They are in need of s.t. **qeʔes k̓ʷłẏapcinmm, es k̓ʷłẏapcinmmp**

k̓ʷłẏapcnemn – one inclined to be in need of something. *suffix:* ***...emn –*** *one inclined to do.*

ẏapcin – lack something. *See:* ***lack.***

ies k̓ʷłẏapcinmm łu ululim – I need money.

yéṁmist, *yéṁm* **–** despaired; frustrated; troubled; worried; have a block; have a dilemma. *See:* ***despair***

needle

č̓łx̣ʷé – needle.

čnšn̓i – buckskin needle.

čemeʔ – pine needle.

sčq̓ʷomq̓ʷmełp – needle bunches. *rt.:* ***q̓ʷum –*** *bunched.*

needle holder

snč̓łx̣ʷé – needle holder, sewing kit, pin cushion.

neighbor

sčsx̣x̣méłxʷ – neighbor, the house nearby. *rt.:* ***čsax̣x̣m –*** *near; suffix:* ***...ełxʷ, ...łxʷ –*** *house.*

nephew

smamáʔ, *sméʔł* **–** paternal uncle *(father's brother)*; man's nephew/niece *(brother's children). See:* ***Sec. 3: Kinship Terms.***
nunumeʔ, *nunu* **–** maternal uncle *(mother's brother)*; man's nephew/niece *(sister's children).*

s.t. - something, the 3rd person
(s.t.) - something implied
s.o. - someone, the 3rd person
sl. - singular form
pl. - plural form
rt. - root word
cmd. - command
lit. - literally
fig. - figuratively
i.e., - for example
See: - Redirection to a related word.

sk̓ʷúk̓ʷiʔ – paternal aunt of a male *(father's sister)*; woman's nephew *(brother's son)*.
tetíkʷeʔ, *tikʷł* – paternal aunt of a female *(father's sister)*; woman's niece *(brother's daughter)*.
qáx̣eʔ – maternal aunt *(mother's sister)*; woman's nephew/niece *(sister's children)*.

słwélt – orphaned nephew/niece, child of brother/sister after death of connecting relative.

nervous

kʷʔeł – jumpy; nervous; edgy; frantic.
i kʷʔeł – S/he/it is edgy. **i čn kʷʔeł, i kʷ kʷʔeł**
i kʷʔéʔeł – They are edgy. **i qeʔ kʷʔeł, i p kʷʔeł**

kʷʔeł – S/he/it was edgy. **čn kʷʔeł, kʷ kʷʔeł**
es kʷʔełmi – S/he/it is edgy. **čnes kʷʔełmi, kʷes kʷʔełmi**
qs kʷʔełmi – S/he/it is going to be edgy. **čiqs kʷʔełmi, kʷqs kʷʔełmi**
es kʷʔéʔełmi – They are edgy. **qeʔes kʷʔełmi, pes kʷʔełmi**

kʷʔełmis – S/he/it was scared of s.t. **kʷʔełmin, kʷʔełmintxʷ**
es kʷʔełminms – S/he/it is scared of s.t. **ies kʷʔełminm, as kʷʔełminm**
qs kʷʔełminms – S/he/it is going to be scared of s.t. **iqs kʷʔełminm, aqs kʷʔełminm**

kʷʔełšits – S/he/it was edgy about s.t. for s.o. **kʷʔełšitn, kʷʔełšitntxʷ**
kʷʔełšíʔits – They were edgy about s.t. for s.o. **qeʔ kʷʔełšitntm, kʷʔełšitntp**

kʷłkʷeł – Each one is edgy.

es łkʷkʷełmi – S/he/it is a little edgy.

kʷʔełemn – one inclined to be nervous/edgy. *suffix: **...emn** – one inclined to do.*
kʷekʷʔełmuł – one that is habitually nervous/edgy. *suffix: **...łmuł** – one that habitually does.*

kʷełšict – frantic for someone.
es kʷʔełcuti – S/he/it is scaring itself. **čnes kʷʔełcuti, kʷes kʷʔełcuti**
es kʷʔełmnwexʷisti – They are scaring each other. **qeʔes kʷʔełmnwexʷisti, pes kʷʔełmnwexʷisti**

i kʷłkʷʔeł łu ċúʔulixʷ – The deer are edgy. **čn sewneʔ tʔe stem̓ u čn kʷʔeł** – I heard something and got nervous/scared. **čn łkʷkʷʔeł t skʷkʷec** – I got a little nervous/edgy of the night.

psap – excited/nervous. *See: **excited**.*

nx̣ʷeʔłels – anxious; want to hurry. *See: **anxious**.*

nest

snʔúʔuseʔtn – nest. *prefix: **sn...** – a place of; suffix: **...tin, ...tn** – means of/device.*

es ntqqełpi – It is making a nest.

es q̓ċełxʷi – Magpie is making a nest. *rt.: **q̓eċ** – weave; suffix: **...etxʷ, ...łxʷ** – house.*

net

scq̓eċ – something that's been woven; net. *prefix: **sc...** – s.t. that's been done/made/prepared.*
es q̓éċ – It is woven; net.

snqq̓eċétkʷ – fish trap; fishnet.

mul̓lmn – scoop net. *rt.: **mul** – remove from water/liquid.*

nettles

ċċax̣éłp – stinging nettles; *Urtica dioica*.

never

tapistém̓, *tapisté* – never.

new

sic – new; right then; right now; recent.
i sic – It is new; it is just finished.

i t sic – recently.

i sicłxʷ łu kʷtisi – Big Blanket's house is new. **i sic łu kʷtisi citxʷs –** Big Blanket's house is new. **epł citxʷ t i sic łu kʷtisi –** Big Blanket has a new house. **kʷtnéłxʷ u i sicłxʷ łu kʷtisi –** Big Blanket has a big new house. **ha i sic łu anlkepu –** Is your coat new? **čn tumíst t i sic p̓ip̓uyšn –** I bought a new car. **ṅem qeʔ wis čáwm m sic qeʔ eł̓iłn –** We will finish praying, and then we can eat. **iʔe t sic u wisten –** I recently finshed it. **t spistem u wistexʷ? i sic –** When did you finsh it? It is new (just finished).

The **i** following uvular consonants (UC) and the glottal stop **ʔ** sound like English "*ey*" as in the words *they, hey, whey*, etc. Salish UC are: **q, q̓, qʷ, q̓ʷ, x̣, x̣ʷ**. For example, the suffix **…qin** – head/top, is often spelled using English *ey* as "q*ey*n". So **qi, q̓i, qʷi, q̓ʷi, x̣i, x̣ʷi**, may be spelled with English *ey* as **q***ey*, **q̓***ey*, **qʷ***ey*, **q̓ʷ***ey*, **x̣***ey*, **x̣ʷ***ey* in other texts.

news **sṁiṁiʔ –** story; news; something that's been told. *See:* ***tell.***

newspaper **sṁiṁiʔštwe q̓eẏmin –** newspaper.

New Year **sčnčłtumš,** *sčnčłtu* **–** the time of shaking hands; the new year. *See:* ***shake hands.***

sťapsqélixʷ, *sťapsqé* **–** the time of shooting; the new year. *See:* ***shoot.***

next **sčtl̓cis –** next to him/her/it (other side of).

asčtl̓cis – other side of you.

isčtl̓cis – other side of me.

nkʷł… – *prefix indicating together with, do with. The* ***ł*** *is lost when preceding an* ***s.***

snkʷłʔemuts – S/he/it sits with him/her/it. **isnkʷłʔemut, asnkʷłʔemut**

snkʷłʔečswíšs – S/he/it stands with him/her/it. **isnkʷłʔečswíš, asnkʷłʔečswíš**

swe łu asnkʷłʔemut – Who is sitting next to you?

čsax̣m – close to.

swe łiciʔ l asčsax̣m u emut – Who is that sitting next to you?

eł t – indicates next.

eł t čeṅ – Which one goes next?

eł t čeṅ sq̓íʔi – What color goes next?

eł t swe – Who is next?

eł t steṁ – What is next?

ha eł t anwi – Are you next?

eł t anwi – You are next.

łu eł t steṁ sq̓iq̓ʔeẏ łu aqs čtxʷum – What is next in the pattern that you are going to add?

ṅe ye tʔe – next time.

Nez Perce **saáptniša –** Nez Perce; southern band.

slapaá – Nez Perce; northern band.

nice **x̣est,** *x̣e* **–** good; fine; beautiful. *See:* ***good.***

nickel **cilséns –** nickel.

niece **smamáʔ,** *sméʔł* **–** paternal uncle *(father's brother)*; man's nephew/niece *(brother's children).*

nunumeʔ, *nunu* **–** maternal uncle *(mother's brother)*; man's nephew/niece *(sister's children). See:* ***Sec. 3: Kinship Terms.***

sk̓ʷúk̓ʷiʔ – paternal aunt of a male *(father's sister)*; woman's nephew *(brother's son).*

tetíkʷeʔ, *tikʷł* **–** paternal aunt of a female *(father's sister)*; woman's niece *(brother's daughter).*

s.t. - something, the 3rd person
(s.t.) - something implied
s.o. - someone, the 3rd person
sl. - singular form
pl. - plural form
rt. - root word
cmd. - command
lit. - literally
fig. - figuratively
i.e., - for example
See: - Redirection to a related word.

qáx̣eʔ – maternal aunt *(mother's sister)*; woman's nephew/niece *(sister's children)*.

słwélt – orphaned nephew/niece, child of brother/sister after death of connecting relative.

night

skʷkʷʔéc, *skʷkʷʔé* – night.

kʷkʷʔéc – It became night.
es kʷkʷécm̓i – It is becoming night.
qs kʷkʷécm̓i – It is going to become night.

čłkʷkʷéceneʔ – S/he/it was overcome by the night. **čn čłkʷkʷéceneʔ, kʷ čłkʷkʷéceneʔ**
es čłkʷkʷéceneʔi – S/he/it is being overcome by the night. **čnes čłkʷkʷéceneʔi, kʷes čłkʷkʷéceneʔi**
qs čłkʷkʷéceneʔi – S/he/it is going to get overcome by the night. **čiqs čłkʷkʷéceneʔi, kʷqs čłkʷkʷéceneʔi**

t skʷkʷʔéc – last night.
ṅe kʷkʷʔéc – tonight.
čmlk̓ʷskʷkʷʔec – all night.
nk̓ʷskʷkʷʔéc – one night.

ta čis itš t skʷkʷʔec – I did not sleep last night.

nighthawk

sp̓áas – nighthawk, night bat, mosquito hawk; *Chordeiles minor*.

nightmare

qey̓s – have nightmare; bad dream.

qey̓s – S/he/it had a nightmare. **čn qey̓s, kʷ qey̓s**
es qey̓si – S/he/it is having a nightmare. **čnes qey̓si, kʷes qey̓si**
qs qey̓si – S/he/it is going to have a nightmare. **čiqs qey̓si, kʷqs qey̓si**

qey̓smis – S/he/it had a nightmare about s.o./s.t. **qey̓smn, qey̓smntxʷ**
es qey̓sms – S/he/it is having a nightmare about s.o./s.t. **ies qey̓sm, as qey̓sm**
qs qey̓sms – S/he/it is going to have a nightmare about s.o./s.t. **iqs qey̓sm, aqs qey̓sm**

es qiqey̓si – Each one is having a nightmare. **qeʔes qiqey̓si, pes qiqey̓si**
es qiqey̓sms – Each one is having a nightmare about s.o./s.t. **qeʔes qiqey̓sm, es qiqey̓smp**

łqiqey̓s – S/he had a little nightmare.

scqey̓s – nightmare. *prefix:* ***sc...*** *– s.t. that's been done/made/prepared.*
qey̓semn – one inclined to have nightmares. *suffix:* ***...emn*** *– one inclined to do.*

qey̓siš – Have a nightmare. *cmd.*
qey̓smnt – Have a nightmare about s.o./s.t. *cmd.*
qey̓smncut – S/he had a nightmare about one's self. **čn qey̓smncut, kʷ qey̓smncut**
es qey̓smncuti – S/he is having a nightmare about one's self. **čnes qey̓smncuti, kʷes qey̓smncuti**
qey̓slwis – S/he has nightmares everywhere. **čn qey̓slwis, kʷ qey̓slwis**

qey̓smncn – I had a nightmare about you. **qʷo aqs qey̓sm** – You are going to have a nightmare about me.

nine

x̣ṅut – nine. **x̣ṅx̣ṅut** – nines. *pl.*

upn eł x̣ṅut – nineteen.
čx̣ṅut – nine people.

x̣ṅt... – *prefix indicating nine combined with another affix forming a full word.*
x̣ṅtásq̓t – nine days. *suffix:* ***...asq̓t*** *– sky, day.*
x̣ṅtełxʷ – nine houses. *suffix:* ***...ełxʷ, ...łxʷ*** *– house.*
x̣ṅtep – nine eggs. *circumfix:* ***n...ep*** *– egg.*

x̣n̓téssn̓ – nine rocks. *suffix:* ***...essn̓, ...ssn̓** – rock.*

x̣n̓tł... – *prefix indicating nine added to a whole word.*
x̣n̓tłˀupn – ninety; nine tens.
x̣n̓tłšƛ̓ip – S/he lost nine times. **čn x̣n̓tłšƛ̓ip, kʷ x̣n̓tłšƛ̓ip**
x̣n̓tsqáx̣eˀ, *x̣n̓tsqá* – nine domestic animals or cars.
x̣n̓tłˀopnčstqn – nine thousand.

nine hundred **x̣n̓tłnk̓ʷoˀqín,** *x̣n̓tłnk̓ʷoˀqí* – nine hundred.

x̣n̓tłnk̓ʷoˀqín opnčstqn – nine hundred thousand.

nineteen **upn eł x̣n̓ut** – nineteen.

ninety **x̣n̓tłˀupn,** *x̣n̓tłˀu* – ninety.

x̣n̓tłˀupn opnčstqn – ninety thousand.

nipple **sčqˀemtn** – nipple.
qeˀmtin – nipple.

tatameˀ – suck on the nipple. *See:* ***suck.***

Nirada **nčˀaqs** – Nirada, Flathead Nation.

nit **ččstineˀ** – nit.

qʷtáx̣ʷeˀ – louse; lice.

no **ta** – no; not.

ax̣ax̣l̓usm – shake your head side to side to say no. *See:* ***shake.***

oyš – *said in disgruntlement to doing some task, as if to say "to hell with you I am not going to do it."*

nobody **taswé** – nobody.
ta t swe čmi t čnaqs – It wasn't nobody; it was just the one person.

nod **q̓ʷit̓s** – nod the head; greet; hail.
nq̓ʷit̓sm – S/he nodded. **čn nq̓ʷit̓sm, kʷ nq̓ʷit̓sm**
es nq̓ʷit̓si – S/he is nodding. **čnes nq̓ʷit̓si, kʷes nq̓ʷit̓si**
qs nq̓ʷit̓si – S/he is going to nod. **čiqs nq̓ʷit̓si, kʷqs nq̓ʷit̓si**
es nq̓ʷit̓ˀit̓si – They are nodding. **qeˀes nq̓ʷit̓si, pes nq̓ʷit̓si**

q̓ʷit̓sts – S/he nodded to s.o. **q̓ʷit̓stn, q̓ʷit̓stxʷ**
q̓ʷit̓ˀit̓sts – They nodded to s.o. **qeˀ q̓ʷit̓stm, q̓ʷit̓stp**

nq̓ʷit̓smis – S/he nodded to s.o. in acknowledgement. **nq̓ʷit̓smn, nq̓ʷit̓smntxʷ**
nq̓ʷit̓ˀit̓smis – They nodded to s.o. in acknowledgement. **qeˀ nq̓ʷit̓smntm, nq̓ʷit̓smntp**

es nq̓ʷt̓q̓ʷit̓si – S/he keeps nodding. **čnes nq̓ʷt̓q̓ʷit̓si, kʷes nq̓ʷt̓q̓ʷit̓si**

q̓ʷit̓siš – Nod. *cmd.*
q̓ʷit̓smnt – Nod at s.o. *cmd.*
čnq̓ʷt̓smnwexʷ – They nodded at each other. **qeˀ čnq̓ʷt̓smnwexʷ, p čnq̓ʷt̓smnwexʷ**
es čnq̓ʷt̓smnwexʷi – They are nodding at each other. **qeˀes čnq̓ʷt̓smnwexʷi, p es čnq̓ʷt̓smnwexʷi**

> The **i** following uvular consonants (UC) and the glottal stop **ˀ** sound like English "*ey*" as in the words th*ey*, h*ey*, wh*ey*, etc. Salish UC are: **q, q̓, qʷ, q̓ʷ, x̣, x̣ʷ**. For example, the suffix ...**qin** – head/top, is often spelled using English *ey* as "q*ey*n". So **qi, q̓i, qʷi, q̓ʷi, x̣i, x̣ʷi**, may be spelled with English *ey* as **q***ey*, **q̓***ey*, **qʷ***ey*, **q̓ʷ***ey*, **x̣***ey*, **x̣ʷ***ey* in other texts.

> s.t. - something, the 3rd person
> (s.t.) - something implied
> s.o. - someone, the 3rd person
> *sl.* - singular form
> *pl.* - plural form
> *rt.* - root word
> *cmd.* - command
> *lit.* - literally
> *fig.* - figuratively
> *i.e.,* - for example
> *See:* - Redirection to a related word.

q̓ʷt̓q̓ʷt̓smnwexʷ – They keep nodding at each other.

čn q̓ʷit̓s mali – I salute Mary, hail Mary. **łu snq̓ʷit̓s łu anš –** The angel's greeting.

ncqosm – nod/throw the head back.
ncqosm – S/he/it threw the head back. **čn ncqosm, kʷ ncqosm**
es ncqosi – S/he/it is throwing the head back. **čnes ncqosi, kʷes ncqosi**
qs ncqosi – S/he/it is going to the throw head back. **čiqs ncqosi, kʷqs ncqosi**

čtóls – point with the eyes; show acknowledgement by looking. *See:* ***acknowledge.***

tóls – point with the head or face; show acknowledgement. *See:* ***acknowledge.***

nodding onion

qʷléwyeʔ – onion; *Allium cernuum.*

no-good

mtmitt, *mtmi* **–** no-good.
mtmitt – S/he is no-good. **čn mtmitt, kʷ mtmitt**
es mttmscutisti – S/he is being no-good. **čnes mttmscutisti, kʷes mttmscutisti**

nmtmtcin – talk no-good words. *See:* ***talk.***

ṅem čiqł mtmi ṅex̣li – I will be the no-good one tomorrow, I am going to become no-good tomorrow. **x̣ił kʷ mtmitt –** You are really no-good.

tam l tʔestéṁ u čtemtn – S/he/it has no use. *See:* ***use.***

noise

nmemecin – noisy; bothersome noise. *rt.:* ***memeʔt*** *– bothersome; suffix:* ***...cin, ...cn*** *– action of the mouth.*

exʷkʷunm – make sound of people and animal voices; someone talking in the distance but not being able to discern what is being said. *See:* ***sound.***

tstsalš – sound of a group making noises. *(i.e., children talking, birds chirping, etc.)* *See:* ***sound.***

tspmncót, *tspmncó* **–** sudden sound of voices shouting. *See:* ***sound.***

kʷemt m puwau – Then s/he/it will make a lot of noise.

nonagon

x̣ṅtsq̓tq̓it – nonagon; has nine flat sides.

none

miš – none; out of.
mišlexʷ – the land/place is empty; there is none all over.
nmiš – empty.
čmšqnmist, *čmšqnmi* **–** give up; come to the end of one's abilities. *See:* ***give up.***

miš łu qeʔ sʔiłn – We do not have any food.

i čmi – only.

tastéṁ – nothing; none.

noon

sntx̣ʷqin, *sntx̣ʷqi* **–** noon. *rt.:* ***tox̣ʷ*** *– straight; suffix:* ***...qin, ...qn*** *– top.*
x̣est snyak̓ʷqi – Good afternoon.

čč̓ʔit sntox̣ʷqi – It is almost noon. **ƛ̓e qeʔqs ntox̣ʷqini –** We are ready to eat lunch. **ƛ̓e qeʔ wis ntox̣ʷqinm –** We already ate lunch.

north

sċaltulexʷ – north.

northern flicker

kʷlkʷlé – northern flicker; red-shafted flicker; *Colaptes auratus.*

northern flying squirrel **sxʷupxʷp –** northern flying squirrel; *Glaucomys sabrinus.*

northern oriole **xʷiwxʷu –** Bullock's oriole; northern oriole; *Icterus bullockii.*

northern pikeminnow **qʷq̓ʷéʔčn,** *qʷq̓ʷé* – northern pikeminnow; *Ptychocheilus oregonensis.*

northern pocket gopher **pul̓yeʔ –** mole; *Thomomys talpoides.*

sisč̓ – gopher; Columbia ground squirrel; *Spermophilus columbianus.*

northern saw-whet owl **sqq̓éxʷʔe –** northern saw-whet owl; *Aegolius acadicus.*

nose **snp̓sáqs,** *snp̓sá* – nose; bird's beak; pencil tip.
sn̓p̓sáqstn, *sn̓p̓sá* – nostril.
nxʷaʔamaqs – many noses.
nq̓aw̓paqs – broken nose; angry.

snupupaqs – nose hair.

nawawpaqs – runny nose.
es nawawpaqsi – One's nose is running.

nʔap̓qsncutš – Wipe your nose. *cmd.*
nʔap̓qsiš – Wipe a nose. *cmd.*

nosiš – Blow your nose. *See: **snot**.*

nsumsqnm – good sniffer (like a dog).

nkʷtnáqs – big nose; high-priced.
nkʷtnáqs łu citxʷs kʷtisi – Big Blanket's house is high-priced.

nosebleed **mll̓áqs,** *ml̓l̓á* – have a nosebleed. *rt.: **mlip** – overflow; suffix: **...aqs** – nose, road.*
ml̓l̓áqs – S/he/it had a nosebleed. **čn ml̓l̓áqs, kʷ ml̓l̓áqs**
es ml̓l̓áqsi – S/he/it has a nosebleed. **čnes ml̓l̓áqsi, kʷes ml̓l̓áqsi**
es ml̓l̓áʔaqsi – They have a nosebleed. **qeʔes ml̓l̓áqsi, pes ml̓l̓áqsi**

ml̓l̓áqsis – S/he/it gave s.o. a nosebleed. **ml̓l̓áqsn, ml̓l̓áqsntxʷ**
ml̓l̓áʔaqsis – They gave s.o. a nosebleed. **qeʔ ml̓l̓áqsntm, ml̓l̓áqsntp**

sml̓l̓áqs, *sml̓l̓á* – nosebleed.

not **tá –** no; not.

tamm – not; deny; refuse. *See: **refuse**.*

nothing **tastém̓ –** none; nothing. *See: **refuse**.*

tmmamn – one inclined to get nothing. *rt.: **tam** – not, deny; suffix: **...emn** – one inclined to do.*

tmstem̓ – have nothing.
tmstem̓ – S/he/it has/got nothing. **čn tmstem̓, kʷ tmstem̓**

tmotm – nothing; good for nothing; *(term of belittlement). rt.: **tam** – not, deny.*
tmotm – S/he is good for nothing. **čn tmotm, kʷ tmotm**

k̓ʷłtmotmis – S/he treated s.o. as nothing. **k̓ʷłtmotmn, k̓ʷłtmotmntxʷ**
es k̓ʷłtmotms – S/he is treating s.o. as nothing. **ies k̓ʷłtmotm, as k̓ʷłtmotm**

The **i** following uvular consonants (UC) and the glottal stop **ʔ** sound like English "*ey*" as in the words th*ey*, h*ey*, wh*ey*, etc. Salish UC are: **q, q̓, qʷ, q̓ʷ, ẋ, ẋʷ**. For example, the suffix **...qin** – head/top, is often spelled using English *ey* as "q*ey*n". So **qi, q̓i, qʷi, q̓ʷi, ẋi, ẋʷi**, may be spelled with English *ey* as **q***ey*, **q̓***ey*, **qʷ***ey*, **q̓ʷ***ey*, **ẋ***ey*, **ẋʷ***ey* in other texts.

s.t. - something, the 3rd person
(s.t.) - something implied
s.o. - someone, the 3rd person
sl. - singular form
pl. - plural form
rt. - root word
cmd. - command
lit. - literally
fig. - figuratively
i.e., - for example
See: - Redirection to a related word.

qs k̓ʷłtmotms – S/he is going to treat s.o. as nothing. **iqs k̓ʷłtmotm, aqs k̓ʷłtmotm**

tnm̓us – nothing, worthless.
tnm̓us – S/he/it is worthless. **čn tnm̓us, kʷ tnm̓us**

i tn̓m̓u – S/he/it is nothing/worthless.

not often
tam tméy̓ – rare; not often.
tam qʷi – not often.

not yet
c̓y̓u – not yet.
c̓y̓u u es yoʔnusten – I do not know it yet. **c̓y̓u u čn uy̓écst** – I am not done yet. **c̓y̓u u es yoʔnusten łu sqʷllumt** – I do not know the story yet. **puti c̓y̓u** – It is still not done.

November
sqʷllumt spq̓niʔ – November *(month of storytelling).*

now
yetłx̣ʷásq̓t, *yetłx̣ʷá* – now; today. *suffix: **...asq̓t** – sky, day.*

sic – new; right then; right now; recent.
sic čn lʔe – Now I am here. **sic kʷes čšʔitši** – Now you are sleepy. **ta qeʔqs cm̓éyyé łiʔe sic es p̓ox̣ʷtil̓ši** – Those who are growing up right now will not have this knowledge.

nude
čtmélxʷ, *čtmé* – naked; without clothes. *See: **naked**.*

npƛ̓alqs, *npƛ̓a* – remove/take off clothes. *See: **undress**.*
npƛ̓alqsiš – Remove your clothes. *cmd.*

numb
čsulšn – foot "fell asleep," or went numb.
čsulčst – hand "fell asleep," or went numb. *suffix: **...ečst, ...čst** – of the hand.*
čsolx̣n – arm "fell asleep," or went numb.

number
sisiyen – numbers.

scsiyen – number; something that's counted. *prefix: **sc...** – s.t. that's been done/made/prepared.*

nun
smem q̓ʷaylqs – nun. *suffix: **...lqs, ...alqs** – clothes.*

nurse
qʔeméłt – breastfeed; nurse. *See: **breastfeed**.*

sxʷmalyé olqʷšcutis – nurse; doctor's helper.

nut
q̓ép̓xʷeʔ – nut; nuts; peanut.

sčx̣ʷlx̣ʷolq̓ʷ – nut, *used with a bolt.*
sčx̣ʷlx̣ʷlq̓ʷšin – lug nut.

čx̣ʷlx̣ʷolq̓ʷm – screw a nut onto a bolt. *See: **screw**.*

snƛ̓čtew̓s, *snƛ̓čte* – seed from the inside of something. *(i.e., fruit, nuts, etc.) See: **seed**.*

nutcracker
snálkʷ – Clark's nutcracker; *Nucifraga columbiana.*

nuthatch
k̓ʷłx̣ʷlx̣ʷlq̓ʷmálqʷ – nuthatch; *Sitta.*

Nuttall's cottontail
wiw̓slščn, wisšlšn – cottontail; *Sylvilagus nuttallii.*

O

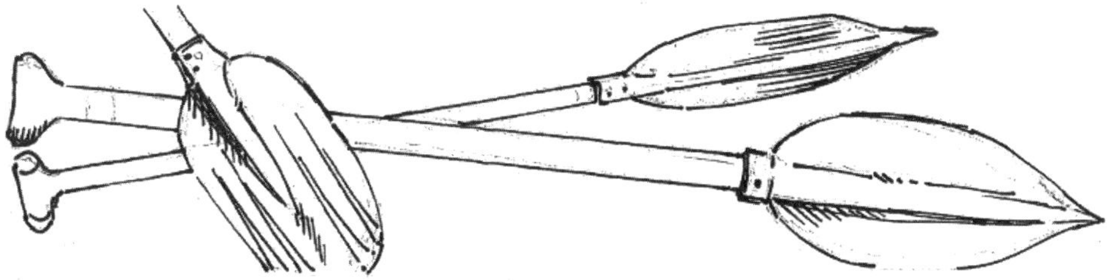

oar **laaptin –** oar. *rt.:* ***laap*** *– float; suffix:* ***...tin, ...tn*** *– means of/device.*

laapmin – oar. *rt.:* ***laap*** *– float; suffix:* ***...min, ...mn*** *– instrument/tool.*

ƛ̓mo – paddle.

oatmeal **moš –** mush oatmeal.

oats **lewén –** oats; oatmeal.

ałnmsqáx̣eʔ, *ałnmsqá* – oats; horse food. *rt.:* ***iłn*** *– eat; suffix:* ***...sqáx̣eʔ*** *– domestic animal; mainly referring to horse or car.*

čsp̓im – thrash oats; gathering huckleberries *(when hitting the bush the berries fall onto a canvas).* *See:* ***thrash****.*

ql̓wá – thrash wheat; stepping on wheat. *See:* ***thrash****.*

obvious **i mi –** It is plainly evident; it is absolute; it is fact. *See:* ***absolute****.*

wnwinxʷ, *wnwi* – plainly visible; evident; apparent; very clear; obvious. *See:* ***plain****.*

occasionally **łaq̓ʷlwis –** go around showing up/to make appearances here and there. *See:* ***appear****.*

łaq̓ʷcin – speak up once in a while. *See:* ***appear****.*

ocean **sčłpƛ̓métkʷ**, *sčłpƛ̓mé* – ocean. *rt.:* ***pƛ̓im*** *– release from.*

octagon **henmsq̓tq̓it –** octagon; has eight flat sides.

October **sčłip spq̓niʔ –** October *(month of hunting).*

čłip – hunt. *See:* ***hunt****.*

odor **spxʷup –** odor; taste.

puxʷ – has an odor; smells. *See:* ***smell****.*

t čeṅ u ecx̣lspxʷup – how does it smell/taste?

sin – pleasant odor; smell of perfume. *See:* ***smell****.*
náq̓ – smell rotten; the smell of rotten meat; smell of excrement. *See:* ***smell****.*
qax̣ – smell bad; stink. *See:* ***smell****.*
łis – smelly; the smell of fish. *See:* ***smell****.*
ix̣ʷwey – smell of animal in rut. *See:* ***smell****.*
q̓ʷiʔ – smell like smoke. *See:* ***smell****.*
suṁm – smell something; sniff. *See:* ***smell****.*

offer **nweym –** make prayful offerings in sacrifice to the creator.
nweym – S/he offered. **čn nweym, kʷ nweym**

s.t. - something, the 3rd person
(s.t.) - something implied
s.o. - someone, the 3rd person
sl. - singular form
pl. - plural form
rt. - root word
cmd. - command
lit. - literally
fig. - figuratively
i.e., - for example
See: - Redirection to a related word.

es nweymi – S/he is offering. **čnes nweymi, kʷes nweymi**
qs nweymi – S/he is going to offer. **čiqs nweymi, kʷqs nweymi**

nweymis – S/he offered s.t. in sacrifice. **nweymn, nweymntxʷ**
es nweyms – S/he is offering s.t. in sacrifice. **ies nweym, as nweym**

nweymn – something used as an offering.
nweytn – offerings that have prayers.

č̓oncutist – give offerings/pray. *See: **pray**.*

office
snk̓ʷul̓mn – office, any work place.

often
tméẏ – often.

i qʷit – often.
tam qʷit – not often.

i qʷit łu wičntxʷ łu ċúʔulixʷ – You often see white-tail deer. **tam qʷi ṅem wičtxʷ łu es tptpk̓ʷuli** – You will not often see a lot of sickly people. **tam qʷi ṅem wičtxʷ łu es tkʷtkʷk̓ʷuli** – You will not often see a lot of sickly people. **tam i qʷit u čn ċalax̣n** – I hardly ever get sore arms.

oh!
eni – Oh, my *(woman's exclamation)*.

hayo – Oh, gee *(man's exclamation)*.

k̓ʷ uc unexʷ, *k̓ʷ uc une* – Oh! That is right; Oh! Yes.

oil
sq̓ʷoculexʷ – motor oil. *lit. fat of the land.*

sq̓ʷocełp – vegetable oil. *lit. fat of the branches.*

sq̓ʷocalqʷ – tree oil. *lit. fat of the tree.*

Okanagan
učnaqin, *učnaqi* – Okanagan. *rt.: **wič** – see; suffix: **...qin, ...qn** – top.*

snq̓a – Southern Okanagan.

okay
xʷu – Okay, all right.
xʷu qeʔqs tkʷtkʷúʔuti – Okay, let's go walk.

put šeẏ – S/he/it is just right; enough; fine; okay. *See: **just**.*

hoy – quit; stop; finish; okay; that's it; cease. *See: **quit**.*

old
čéwlš – age; get old.
čéwlš – S/he got old. **čn čéwlš, kʷ čéwlš**
es čéwlši – S/he is getting old. **čnes čéwlši, kʷes čéwlši**
qs čéwlši – S/he is going to get old. **čiqs čéwlši, kʷqs čéwlši**

es łčéčwlši – S/he getting a little old.

kʷes tax̣ʷlu č sčéwlš – You are starting to age. **qʷo ask̓ʷul̓m čiqs čéwlši** – You are making me old.
ƛ̓e čéwlš – S/he is already getting old.

ṗx̣ʷót – old.
ṗox̣ʷtwil̓š – become an elder.
ṗiṗx̣ʷót – old ones; elders.
ṗx̣ʷót – parent, godparent. **ṗx̣ʷṗx̣ʷót** *pl.*

x̣ipt – gnawed by bugs. *(i.e., dried meat or woolen clothes, bugs got into them) See: **gnaw**.*

es paq̓m – It is moldy. *See: **mold**.*

old warrior dance

čsplqmncut – dance the old warrior dance.
es čsplqmncuti – He is dancing the old warior dance. **čnes čsplqmncuti, kʷes čsplqmncuti**

snčsplqmncutn – old warrior dance song. *prefix: **sn...** – a place of; suffix: **...tin, ...tn** – means of/device.*

on

l – in; on; with.
čn ła l snčłemu – I sat on a chair. **łq̓iłš ci l asnitštn** – Lay down on your bed. **lʔe** – this here; this place; here.

once

tnk̓ʷuʔ – one time before.
tʔe u tnk̓ʷuʔ – once in awhile. **x̣̌m tnk̓ʷuʔ** – there was once.

one

nk̓ʷuʔ – one; single. **nk̓ʷnk̓ʷuʔ** – ones. *pl.*
nk̓ʷuʔmnsts – S/he made it be one. **nk̓ʷuʔmnstn, nk̓ʷuʔmnstxʷ**
es nk̓ʷuʔm – S/he is making it be one. **ies nk̓ʷuʔm, as nk̓ʷuʔm**
qs nk̓ʷuʔm – S/he is going to make it be one. **iqs nk̓ʷuʔm, aqs nk̓ʷuʔm**

nk̓ʷuʔmskʷ – Make them be one/united. *cmd.*

nk̓ʷuwilš – They became one. **qeʔ nk̓ʷuwilš, p nk̓ʷuwilš** *suffix: **...wilš** – developmental.*
es nk̓ʷuwilši – They are becoming one. **qeʔes nk̓ʷuwilši, pes nk̓ʷuwilši**
es nk̓ʷuwilši – They are going to be becoming one. **qeʔes nk̓ʷuwilši, pes nk̓ʷuwilši**

nk̓ʷusm – family. *lit. one fire.*
nk̓ʷuʔséns – penny.
i łnk̓ʷuʔ – single.
nk̓ʷélixʷ – tribe.
nk̓ʷoʔqín, *nk̓ʷoʔqí* – one hundred.
čnáqs, *čna* – one person, a single person.
čłnáqs, *čłná* – one person, alone.

nk̓ʷ... – *prefix indicating one combined with another affix forming full word.*
nk̓ʷásq̓t – one day. *suffix: **...asq̓t** – sky, day.*
nk̓ʷełxʷ – one house. *suffix: **...ełxʷ, ...łxʷ** – house.*
nnk̓ʷep – one egg. *circumfix: **n...ep** – egg.*
nk̓ʷéssn̓ – one rock. *suffix: **...essn̓, ...ssn̓** – rock.*
nk̓ʷsqáx̣eʔ, *nk̓ʷsqá* – one domestic animal or car.

es nk̓ʷúʔumnwexʷi – They are becoming one with each other; they agree with each other.
nkʷłnk̓ʷúʔumncn – I became one with you; I agreed with you. *prefix: **nkʷł...** – together with.*

łnk̓ʷúʔumnwexʷ – They are a little ways toward becoming one with each other.

oył – one piece; whole; no holes/breaks/tears.
ołip – It became one piece; it became whole.
es ołpmi – It is becoming one piece; it is becoming whole.

i oył – It is one piece; it is whole.
es ołew̓s – The two are one piece; the two hearts are united.
čoyłc̓eʔ – one piece all around something.
es nołelis – the objects are one piece.
nołip – The water/river became one piece; the ice formed all over the water. *See: **freeze**.*

The **i** following uvular consonants (UC) and the glottal stop **ʔ** sound like English "*ey*" as in the words *they, hey, whey*, etc. Salish UC are: **q, q̓, qʷ, q̓ʷ, x̣, x̣ʷ**. For example, the suffix **...qin** – head/top, is often spelled using English *ey* as "q*ey*n". So **qi, q̓i, qʷi, q̓ʷi, x̣i, x̣ʷi**, may be spelled with English *ey* as **q***ey*, **q̓***ey*, **qʷ***ey*, **q̓ʷ***ey*, **x̣***ey*, **x̣ʷ***ey* in other texts.

s.t. - something, the 3rd person
(s.t.) - something implied
s.o. - someone, the 3rd person
sl. - singular form
pl. - plural form
rt. - root word
cmd. - command
lit. - literally
fig. - figuratively
i.e., - for example
See: - Redirection to a related word.

čołip – become attached to something to form one whole. *See: **attach**.*

onion

qʷléwyeˀ – nodding onion; *Allium cernuum.*

sehč – onion; Columbia onion; *Allium columbianum;* Geyer's onion; *Allium geyeri.*

only

čmi – only.
i čmi – It is only.

čmi ṅe qʷo x̣aq̓ntxʷ – Only if you pay me. **x̣ʷa čmi u tˀe u tnk̓ʷuˀ še kʷ łexʷls** – It seems you only rest once in a while. **čmi u es nc̓pc̓ipsi** – S/he only blinks. **i čmi u stipn u k̓ʷis swenš** – Alone, Stephen went to dance. **čmi u ƛ̓mey̓ t splqe u kʷ iłn** – Only a little bit of sausage you ate. **čmi u łłuw̓et** – It is only a little bit. **čmi sčtasq̓t u čiqs k̓ʷul̓i** – I am going to work only half a day. **čmi u čn łl̓k̓ʷełxʷ** – I only have one little house. **ha čmi u kʷes poscáni** – Are you just joking? **čmi cníˀilc łu epł malyé** – Only they had medicines. **ta swe čmi t čnaqs** – nobody, just one person.

open

k̓ʷłnmaw̓pm – open a hinged door. *rt.: **maw** – break; circumfix: **k̓ʷłn...p** – opening.*
es k̓ʷłnmaw̓p – It is opened.

k̓ʷłnmaw̓pis – S/he/it opened it. **k̓ʷłnmaw̓pn, k̓ʷłnmaw̓pntxʷ**
es k̓ʷłnmaw̓pms – S/he/it is opening it. **ies k̓ʷłnmaw̓pm, as k̓ʷłnmaw̓pm**
qs k̓ʷłnmaw̓pms – S/he/it is going to open it. **iqs k̓ʷłnmaw̓pm, aqs k̓ʷłnmaw̓pm**

k̓ʷłnmaw̓pnt – Open the door. *cmd.*

k̓ʷłnmaw̓pnt ci k̓ʷłnčmep – Open the door. *cmd.* **es k̓ʷłnmaw̓pms nšnse** – S/he is opening the window.

k̓ʷłnčhepm – open a flap. *rt.: **čhém** – reveal; circumfix: **k̓ʷłn...p** – opening.*
es k̓ʷłnčhép – It is opened.

k̓ʷłnčhépis – S/he opened it. **k̓ʷłnčhépn k̓ʷłnčhépntxʷ**
es k̓ʷłnčhépms – S/he/it is opening it. **ies k̓ʷłnčhépm, as k̓ʷłnčhépm**
qs k̓ʷłnčhépms – S/he/it is going to open it. **iqs k̓ʷłnčhépm, aqs k̓ʷłnčhépm**

k̓ʷłnčhépnt – Open a flap. *cmd.*

k̓ʷłncoqép – open a bottle or anything that has a lid. *circumfix: **k̓ʷłn...p** – opening.*
es k̓ʷłncoqép – It is opened.

k̓ʷłncoqépis – S/he/it opened it. **k̓ʷłncoqépn, k̓ʷłncoqépntxʷ**
es k̓ʷłncoqépms – S/he/it is opening it. **ies k̓ʷłncoqépm, as k̓ʷłncoqépm**
qs k̓ʷłncoqépms – S/he/it is going to open it. **iqs k̓ʷłncoqépm, aqs k̓ʷłncoqépm**

k̓ʷłncoqépnt – Open the lid/bottle. *cmd.*

čkʷƛ̓kʷƛ̓us – open eyes.
čkʷƛ̓kʷƛ̓usm – S/he opened one's eyes. **čn čkʷƛ̓kʷƛ̓usm, kʷ čkʷƛ̓kʷƛ̓usm**

es čkʷƛ̓kʷƛ̓us – His/her eyes are open. **čnes čkʷƛ̓kʷƛ̓us, kʷes čkʷƛ̓kʷƛ̓us**

čkʷƛ̓kʷƛ̓usiš – Open your eyes. *cmd.*
čkʷƛ̓kʷƛ̓uswi – All of you open your eyes. *cmd.*

čxʷpxʷpnus – open eyes wide; stretch eyes. *rt.: **xʷup** – stretch, unfold.*
čxʷpxʷpnus – S/he opened his/her eyes wide. **čn čxʷpxʷpnus, kʷ čxʷpxʷpnus**
es čxʷpxʷpnus – His/her eyes are opened wide. **čnes čxʷpxʷpnus, kʷes čxʷpxʷpnus**

čxʷpxʷpmusmis – S/he opened one's eyes wide to s.t./s.o. **čxʷpxʷpmusmn, čxʷpxʷpmusmntxʷ**

es čxʷpxʷpmusms – S/he is opening one's eyes wide to s.t./s.o. **čnes čxʷpxʷpmusm, kʷes čxʷpxʷpmusm**

čxʷpxʷpnusiš – Open your eyes wide. *cmd.*
čxʷpxʷpmusmnt – Open your eyes wide to it. *cmd.*

xʷpmaw̓sqn – open mouth wide; stretch mouth. *See:* ***mouth.***

saq̓cn – have the mouth open; part lips. *See:* ***mouth.***

open up

čt̓lpew̓s – tear open from the middle. *rt.:* ***t̓lip*** *– rip; suffix:* ***...éw̓s*** *– in between, middle.*
sčt̓lt̓lpew̓s łkʷlkʷali – popcorn.

t̓lqʷqin – When the bud first opens up. *rt.:* ***t̓lip*** *– rip; suffix:* ***...qin, ...qn*** *– top.*

n̓e kʷ čnk̓ʷé m še čt̓l̓qʷéw̓stxʷ – If you get one, you gut it.

čt̓lič̓éʔ – tear a covering/wrapping off. *(i.e., a wrapping off a present, etc.)* *See:* ***tear.***

čč̓hič̓eʔ – unwrap; remove wrapping to reveal. *See:* ***unwrap.***

k̓ʷłnmaw̓pm – open a hinged door. *See:* ***open.***

oppose

ewtus – oppose; work against. *(i.e., competition, sickness, gambling, war, etc.)*
ewtusis – S/he opposed s.o. **ewtusn, ewtusntxʷ**
es ewtusms – S/he is opposing s.o. **ies ewtusm, as ewtusm**
qs ewtusms – S/he is going to oppose s.o. **iqs ewtusm, aqs ewtusm**

čʔewtusmis – S/he was s.o.'s opponent. **čʔewtusmn, čʔewtusmntxʷ**
es čʔewtusmms – S/he is s.o.'s opponent. **ies čʔewtusmm, as čʔewtusmm**
qs čʔewtusmms – S/he is going to be s.o.'s opponent. **iqs čʔewtusmm, aqs čʔewtusmm**

ewtsew̓s – They become foes. **qeʔ ewtsew̓s, p ewtsew̓s**
es ewtsew̓si – They are becoming foes. **qeʔes ewtsew̓si, pes ewtsew̓si**

nʔewtus – opponent; adversary; foe.

ewtusnt – Oppose him/her. *cmd.*
čewtusmnt – Be his/her opponent. *cmd.*
ewtselis – several oppose each other; several nations at war.
es ewtusmnwexʷi – They are each other's foe. **qeʔes ewtusmnwexʷi, pes ewtusmnwexʷi**

kʷ iqs ewtusm, ta kʷ ies nunxʷenem łu ascʔuwewlš – I am going to oppose you, I do not believe what you said. **čn ewtusmncut** – I am my own foe.

čšmšmn̓ew̓s – double up on an someone; double team someone. *See:* ***enemy.***

nx̣ctus – take sides; side with someone in some activity. *See:* ***side.***

opposite

es čmenm – the opposite.

st̓ixʷlms – It is opposite. *See:* ***different.***
unexʷ st̓ixʷlms ta – Yes is no's opposite.

orange

p̓um – brownish orange; tan orange; smoke. **p̓mp̓um** *pl.*
p̓umis – S/he made it orange. **p̓umn, p̓umntxʷ**
es p̓umms – S/he is making it orange. **ies p̓umm, as p̓umm**
qs p̓umms – S/he is going to make it orange. **iqs p̓umm, aqs p̓umm**

i p̓um – It is orange.

The **i** following uvular consonants (UC) and the glottal stop **ʔ** sound like English "*ey*" as in the words *they, hey, whey,* etc. Salish UC are: **q, q̓, qʷ, q̓ʷ, x̣, x̣ʷ**. For example, the suffix **...qin** – head/top, is often spelled using English *ey* as "q*ey*n". So **qi, q̓i, qʷi, q̓ʷi, x̣i, x̣ʷi,** may be spelled with English *ey* as **q***ey*, **q̓***ey*, **qʷ***ey*, **q̓ʷ***ey*, **x̣***ey*, **x̣ʷ***ey* in other texts.

---

s.t. - something, the 3rd person
(s.t.) - something implied
s.o. - someone, the 3rd person
sl. - singular form
pl. - plural form
rt. - root word
cmd. - command
lit. - literally
fig. - figuratively
i.e., - for example
See: - Redirection to a related word.

i łṗṗum – It is a little orange; orangish.

ṗumnt – Make it orange. *cmd.*
ṗeṗuṁe? – orangy, affectionately.

čṗmṗums, *čṗmṗu* – orange *(the fruit). rt.: **ṗum** – orange; circumfix: **č...us** – spherical object; eyes.*
es x̣ʷic čṗmṗu – sliced orange.
čṗmṗumsetkʷ – orange juice. *suffix: **...etkʷ, ...tkʷ** – liquid*

order **x̣cim** – prepare something; make ready; put in order. *(i.e., put disarrayed things in order, getting things ready for travel, etc.) See: **ready**.*

Oregon grape **sqʷoyu** – Oregon grape; *Mahonia aquifolium*.

sċals – creeping Oregon grape; creeping barberry; *Mahonia repens*.

oriole **xʷiwxʷu** – Northern oriole, Bullock's oriole; hermit thrush.

orphan **čtmaple?** – orphan; has no parents. *rt.: **tam** – negative; prefix: **č...** – people; suffix: **...éple?** – permanence.*
čtmaple?m – S/he/it became an orphan. **čn čtmaple?m, kʷ čtmaple?m**

słwélt – orphaned nephew/niece; brother's or sister's child after their death; aunt or uncle after death of parent(s).

osel **q̇ʷox̣ʷṁiṅe?** – American dipper; water osel; *Cinclus mexicanus*.

osprey **ċixʷċxʷ** – fish hawk; osprey; *Pandion haliaetus*.

other **čtl̓cis** – next to him/her/it (other side of).
asčtl̓cis – other side of you.
isčtl̓cis – other side of me.

ci i nk̓ʷu? – the other one.
ci i nk̓ʷełċe? – the other room.

k̓ʷiƛ̓t – some; other; several. *See: **some**.*

otter **ltkʷups,** *ltkʷu* – river otter; *Lontra canadensis*.
łltkʷu – otter pelt.
łltkʷhe – otter braid wraps.

ouch **áẇ** – man says.
enuč – woman says.

our **qe? énple** – ours; us.

outhouse **sṅṁṅéčtn,** *sṅṁṅé* – toilet.
čiqs k̓ʷis ṁṅé – I am going to go to the outhouse.

nanax̣, *naná* – potty.
čiqs k̓ʷis nanax̣i – I am going to the potty.

out of **miš** – none; out of. *See: **none**.*
nmiš – empty inside.

miš łu qe? s?iłn – We do not have any food.

ċsip – disappear; gone; wiped out; cleared out. *See:* ***disappear.***

outside

čólsqeʔ, *č čó* – outside.
č čó u čiqs k̓ʷis meṅxʷi – I am going to go outside and smoke.

sčłqel̓tč – exterior; outside layer. *See:* ***exterior.***
i qʷin łu čłqel̓tčs čqʷnqʷinċeʔ – The watermelon's exterior is green.

ocqéʔ – go out. *sl.* *See:* ***go out.***

pupƛ̓m – go out of the woods/canyon into open land.

npƛ̓mus – go out of a confined area into an open area. *(i.e., forest, crowd of people, etc.)*

outstanding

yopiyewt – outstanding, stand out from others; survive. *See:* ***strength.***

tam t̓ul̓ – tremendous; outstanding; extreme; excellent. *See:* ***excellent.***

The **i** following uvular consonants (UC) and the glottal stop **ʔ** sound like English "*ey*" as in the words th*ey*, h*ey*, wh*ey*, etc. Salish UC are: **q**, **q̇**, **qʷ**, **q̇ʷ**, **x̣**, **x̣ʷ**. For example, the suffix **...qin** – head/top, is often spelled using English *ey* as "q*ey*n". So **qi**, **q̇i**, **qʷi**, **q̇ʷi**, **x̣i**, **x̣ʷi**, may be spelled with English *ey* as **q***ey*, **q̇***ey*, **qʷ***ey*, **q̇ʷ***ey*, **x̣***ey*, **x̣ʷ***ey* in other texts.

oval

i wisšn syal – oval; a long circle.

oven

nk̓ʷłoʔmin – oven.

k̓ʷłʔo – put something in an enclosure; put in the oven.
k̓ʷłʔois – S/he put s.t. in the oven. **k̓ʷłʔon, k̓ʷłʔontxʷ**
es k̓ʷłʔoms – S/he is putting s.t. in the oven. **ies k̓ʷłʔom, as k̓ʷłʔom**

k̓ʷłʔont – Put s.t. in the oven. *cmd.*

k̓ʷłkʷƛ̓im – take something out of an enclosure; take out of the oven. *See:* ***take.***

over

čłx̣ʷceẁs – cross over something. *See:* ***cross.***

čłqʷéẁs – drape up high; hang up high over an object; hang up. *See:* ***drape.***

čłṫxʷteneʔ – fly over. *See:* ***fly.***

čłk̓ʷel̓č – turn a rigid container type object upside-down on a flat surface ; roll/tip over. *(i.e., car, hat, lid, etc.)* *See:* ***upside down.***

łixʷp – slip/pull/put something fitted over an object. *See:* ***pull over.***

overcast

čtkʷpásq̇t, *čtkʷpá* – overcast. *suffix:* ***...asq̇t*** *– sky, day.*

overcoat

sk̓ʷtnálqs – overcoat; big coat. *rt.:* ***k̓ʷtunt*** *– big; suffix:* ***...lqs, ...alqs*** *– clothes.*

x̣ṗim – layer; line; coat. *See:* ***layer.***

overflow

ml̓ip – overflow; inundate; overwhelm from something. *(i.e., riverbank, a container, etc.)*
ml̓ip – It overflowed.
es ml̓pmi – It is overflowing.
qs ml̓pmi – It is going to overflow.

es ml̓pulexʷi – It is flooding; it is overflowing onto the land.
ml̓l̓áqs, *ml̓l̓á* – have a nosebleed. *See:* ***nosebleed.***

ml̓ip inkapi – My coffee over filled.

ṫečt – overflow the banks; to flood. *See:* ***flood.***

s.t. - something, the 3rd person
(s.t.) - something implied
s.o. - someone, the 3rd person
sl. - singular form
pl. - plural form
rt. - root word
cmd. - command
lit. - literally
fig. - figuratively
i.e., - for example
See: - Redirection to a related word.

overlay **łoqʷ** – overlay; place something on/over something else *(not to cover)*; lay something on; drape something over a narrow/smaller object. *See:* ***lay over.***

overnight camp **ccil̓š** – overnight camp; overnight stay. *See:* ***camp.***

overturn **čłk̓ʷél̓č** – overturn.
k̓ʷel̓č – turn upside-down a container type object; upturned object. *See:* ***upside-down.***

overwhelm **čhomist,** *čho* – in awe of something or someone; overwhelmed; see something beautiful/good/wonderful. *See:* ***awe.***

owe **xʷlxʷilt,** *xʷlxʷí* – have debt. *See:* ***debt.***

owl **snineʔ** – owl; great horned owl; *Bubo virginianus*; great gray owl; *Strix nebulosa.*
es nineʔ – owl dance. **wičtn snineʔ t skʷekʷst** – I saw an owl this morning.

nsp̓šnmé – snowy owl; *Bubo scandiacus.*
nčcw̓éʔ – burrowing owl; *Athene cunicularia.*
čočošmuł – screech owl; *Megascops kennicottii.* *suffix:* ***...łmuł*** *– one that habitually does.*
nččxʷéls, *nččxʷé* – short-eared owl; *Asio flammeus.*
sqq̓éxʷʔe – northern saw-whet owl; *Aegolius acadicus.*
sčušnma – northern pygmy owl; *Glaucidium gnoma.*

owl dance **es nineʔ** – owl dance.
nineʔm – S/he owl danced. **čn nineʔm, kʷ nineʔm**
es nineʔi – S/he is owl dancing. **čnes nineʔi, kʷes nineʔi**
qs nineʔi – S/he is going to owl dance. **čiqs nineʔi, kʷqs nineʔi**
es nin̓neʔi – They are owl dancing. **qeʔes nin̓neʔi, pes nin̓neʔi**

nkʷłninemis – S/he owl danced with s.o. **nkʷłninemn, nkʷłninemntxʷ**
es nkʷłnin̓ems – S/he is owl dancing with s.o. **ies nkʷłnin̓em, as nkʷłnin̓em**
qs nkʷłnin̓ems – S/he is going to owl dance with s.o. **iqs nkʷłnin̓em, aqs nkʷłnin̓em**

łnin̓ʔem – S/he owl danced a little. **čn łnin̓ʔem, kʷ łnin̓ʔem**

ninʔemn – one inclined to owl dance. *suffix:* ***...emn*** *– one inclined to do.*
snnineʔtn – owl dance song. *prefix:* ***sn...*** *– a place of; suffix:* ***...tin, ...tn*** *– means of/device.*

nineʔiš – Owl dance. *cmd.*
nkʷłninemnt – Owl dance with someone. *cmd.*

ninšels – S/he wanted to owl dance. **čn ninšels, kʷ ninšels**
es ninšelsi – S/he is wanting to owl dance. **čnes ninšelsi, kʷes ninšelsi**

own **epł** – have, has, own. *See:* ***have.***

tixʷł – acquire something; get or receive something; gather. *See:* ***acquire.***

owner **čelltč** – owner; master; lord.
kʷ qł čelltč t esyáʔ spúʔus – May you be every heart's master.

oyster **skʷk̓ʷl̓áneʔ** – western pearlshell; oyster; *Margaritifera falcata.*

čk̓ʷlk̓ʷllča – clam; *Sphaeriidae pisidium.*

Oyster Creek **epskʷk̓ʷl̓án̓eʔ** – Oyster Creek, a creek in the Flathead Nation. *lit. has oysters.*

P

Pablo **x̣ʷiʔilqsa –** Pablo. *lit. long narrow strip of trees.*

pack **q̓ʷeɫt –** carry on back; pack.
q̓ʷéɫtm – S/he/it carried (s.t.). **čn q̓ʷéɫtm, kʷ q̓ʷéɫtm**
es q̓ʷéɫti – S/he/it is carrying (s.t.). **čnes q̓ʷéɫti, kʷes q̓ʷéɫti**
qs q̓ʷéɫti – S/he/it is going to carry (s.t.). **čiqs q̓ʷéɫti, kʷqs q̓ʷéɫti**

q̓ʷéɫtmis – S/he/it carried s.t. **q̓ʷéɫtmn, q̓ʷéɫtmntxʷ**
es q̓ʷéɫtms – S/he/it is carrying s.t. **ies q̓ʷéɫtm, as q̓ʷéɫtm**
qs q̓ʷéɫtms – S/he/it is going to carry s.t. **iqs q̓ʷéɫtm, aqs q̓ʷéɫtm**
q̓ʷéʔeɫtmis – They carried s.t. **qeʔ q̓ʷéɫtmntm, q̓ʷéɫtmntp**
es q̓ʷéʔeɫtms – They are carrying s.t. **qeʔes q̓ʷéɫtm, es q̓ʷéɫtmp**

sxʷq̓ʷéɫt – somebody who packs. *prefix: **sxʷ...** – one tasked to do.*
sq̓ʷeɫt – pack.
snq̓ʷeɫtn – backpack. *prefix: **sn...** – a place of; suffix: **...tin, ...tn** – means of/device.*
snq̓ʷɫté – arrow quiver.
čq̓ʷeɫtn – packsaddle. *suffix: **...tin, ...tn** – means of/device.*
sxʷq̓ʷɫtsqáx̣eʔ, *sxʷq̓ʷɫtsqá* – packhorse; pack mule. *prefix: **sxʷ...** – one tasked to do.*

eɫ q̓ʷeɫtmn č qeʔ sq̓eymuɫxʷ – I carried it back to our tipi. **sxʷq̓ʷéɫt ci sṫulċeʔ –** That is a pack mule.

q̓ʷáɫq̓ʷɫt – pack the meat of an animal after hunting.
q̓ʷáɫq̓ʷɫt – S/he packed game. **čn q̓ʷáɫq̓ʷɫt, kʷ q̓ʷáɫq̓ʷɫt**

k̓ʷl̓čisqáx̣eʔm – pack a horse.
k̓ʷl̓čisqáx̣eʔm – S/he packed a horse. **čn k̓ʷl̓čisqáx̣eʔm, kʷ k̓ʷl̓čisqáx̣eʔm**
es k̓ʷl̓čisqáx̣eʔi – S/he is packing a horse. **čnes k̓ʷl̓čisqáx̣eʔi, kʷes k̓ʷl̓čisqáx̣eʔi**
qs k̓ʷl̓čisqáx̣eʔi – S/he is going to pack a horse. **čiqs k̓ʷl̓čisqáx̣eʔi, kʷqs k̓ʷl̓čisqáx̣eʔi**

packhorse **sxʷq̓ʷɫtsqáx̣eʔ,** *sxʷq̓ʷɫtsqá* – packhorse; pack mule. *prefix: **sxʷ...** – one tasked to do.*

q̓ʷɫox̣mups – tail strap on packhorse.

pack rat **héw̓t –** pack rat, bushy-tailed wood rat; *Neotoma cinerea.*

sqʷʔópɫxʷ – hole; den *(as of a mouse or rat). rt.: **qʷʔóp** – make soft; suffix: **...eɫxʷ, ...ɫxʷ** – house.*

pack up **p̓lk̓ʷmncut –** pack one's self up. *rt.: **p̓ulk̓ʷ** – fold; suffix: **...cut** – action to the self.*
p̓lk̓ʷmncut – S/he/it packed up. **čn p̓lk̓ʷmncut, kʷ p̓lk̓ʷmncut**
es p̓lk̓ʷmncuti – S/he/it is packing up. **čnes p̓lk̓ʷmncuti, kʷes p̓lk̓ʷmncuti**
qs p̓lk̓ʷmncuti – S/he/it is going to pack up. **čiqs p̓lk̓ʷmncuti, kʷqs p̓lk̓ʷmncuti**
p̓lk̓ʷmncúʔut – They packed up. **qeʔ p̓lk̓ʷmncut, p p̓lk̓ʷmncut**

s.t. - something, the 3rd person
(s.t.) - something implied
s.o. - someone, the 3rd person
sl. - singular form
pl. - plural form
rt. - root word
cmd. - command
lit. - literally
fig. - figuratively
i.e., - for example
See: - Redirection to a related word.

es ṗlk̓ʷmncúʔuti – They are packing up. **qeʔes ṗlk̓ʷmncuti, pes ṗlk̓ʷmncuti**

ṗlk̓ʷmncutš – Pack up. *cmd.*
ṗlk̓ʷmncutwi – All of you pack up. *cmd.*

p ṗlk̓ʷmncut m p imš – All of you pack up and move.

pełqmncut – unpack one's self. *See: **unpack**.*

paddle **ƛ̓mo** – paddle. *See: **oar**.*

pail **łčepeʔ,** *łčep* – bucket, pail.

pain **ċaál,** *ċa* – achy; sore; hurting; in pain. *See: **ache**.*

paint **miṅm** – paint.
miṅm – S/he painted. **čn miṅm, kʷ miṅm**
es miṅi – S/he is painting. **čnes miṅi, kʷes miṅi**
qs miṅi – S/he is going to paint. **čiqs miṅi, kʷqs miṅi**
míʔiṅm – They painted. **qeʔ miṅm, p miṅm**
es míʔiṅi – They are painting. **qeʔes miṅi, pes miṅi**

čmiṅis – S/he painted s.t. **čmiṅn, čmiṅntxʷ**
es čmiṅms – S/he is painting s.t. **ies čmiṅm, as čmiṅm**
qs čmiṅms – S/he is going to paint s.t. **iqs čmiṅm, aqs čmiṅm**
čmíʔiṅis – They painted s.t. **qeʔ čmiṅntm, čmiṅntp**
es čmíʔiṅms – They are painting s.t. **qeʔes čmiṅm, es čmiṅmp**

es miṅ – It is painted.

sxʷmiṅm – one tasked to paint; painter. *prefix: **sxʷ...** – one tasked to do.*
miṅtn – paintbrush. *suffix: **...tin, ...tn** – means of/device.*
miṅmn – paint.
miṅłxʷtn – house paint.

miṅiš – Paint. *cmd.*
čmiṅnt – Paint it. *cmd.*
es miṅisti – S/he is painting one's self. **čnes miṅisti, kʷes miṅisti**

ṅem miṅm – S/he will paint. **ṅem čn miṅm, ṅem kʷ miṅm**
ṅem míʔiṅm – They will paint. **ṅem qeʔ miṅm, ṅem p miṅm**

kʷtkʷtnulexʷ łu scmṅíʔis – S/he painted on big, wide areas. **steṁ łu as miṅm** – What are you painting? **swe łu es nte qs miṅi** – Who wants to paint? **sic čn epł miṅmn** – Now I have paint.

miṅsm – paint the face. *suffix: **...us** – face, fire.*
miṅsm – S/he painted his/her face. **čn miṅsm, kʷ miṅsm**
es miṅsi – S/he is painting his/her face. **čnes miṅsi, kʷes miṅsi**
qs miṅsi – S/he is going to paint his/her face. **čiqs miṅsi, kʷqs miṅsi**
míʔiṅsm – They painted his/her face. **qeʔ miṅsm, p miṅsm**
es míʔiṅsi – They are painting their faces. **qeʔes miṅsi, pes miṅsi**

xʷem – red paint/dye.
xʷem – S/he painted with red. **čn xʷem, kʷ xʷem**
es xʷemi – S/he is painting with red. **čnes xʷemi, kʷes xʷemi**

es xʷem – It is painted/dyed red.

xʷemiš – Paint it red. *cmd.*
čxʷmalqʷ – red painted wood.
xʷamlqs – red painted clothing.

xʷemsm – put red paint on the face. *suffix:* ***...us*** *– face, fire.*
xʷemsm – S/he painted his/her face red. **čn xʷemsm, kʷ xʷemsm**
es xʷemsi – S/he is painting his/her face red. **čnes xʷemsi, kʷes xʷemsi**
qs xʷemsi – S/he is going to paint his/her face red. **čiqs xʷemsi, kʷqs xʷemsi**
xʷéʔemsm – They painted his/her face red. **qeʔ xʷemsm, p xʷemsm**
es xʷéʔemsi – They are painting their faces red. **qeʔes xʷemsi, pes xʷemsi**

xʷemsiš – Put red paint on the face. *cmd.*

q̓ʷaysm – make/paint the face black. *suffix:* ***...us*** *– face, fire.*
q̓ʷaysm – S/he painted his/her face black. **čn q̓ʷaysm, kʷ q̓ʷaysm**
es q̓ʷaysi – S/he is painting his/her face black. **čnes q̓ʷaysi, kʷes q̓ʷaysi**
qs q̓ʷaysi – S/he is going to paint his/her face black. **čiqs q̓ʷaysi, kʷqs q̓ʷaysi**

The **i** following uvular consonants (UC) and the glottal stop **ʔ** sound like English "*ey*" as in the words th*ey*, h*ey*, wh*ey*, etc. Salish UC are: **q**, **q̓**, **qʷ**, **q̓ʷ**, **x̣**, **x̣ʷ**. For example, the suffix ...**qin** – head/top, is often spelled using English *ey* as "q*ey*n". So **qi**, **q̓i**, **qʷi**, **q̓ʷi**, **x̣i**, **x̣ʷi**, may be spelled with English *ey* as **q***ey*, **q̓***ey*, **qʷ***ey*, **q̓ʷ***ey*, **x̣***ey*, **x̣ʷ***ey* in other texts.

paintbrush

miṅtn – paintbrush. *suffix:* ***...tin, ...tn*** *– means of/device.*

st̓lt̓lá sc̓iik̓ʷs – Indian paintbrush; Thunder's spark; *Castilleja miniata.*

painted turtle

sṗl̓q̓ʷáqs, *sṗl̓q̓ʷá* – turtle; *Chrysemys picta.*

pale

i paá – It is faded/pale.
paas – pale face *(when you see a ghost or when you are really sick). suffix:* ***...us*** *– face, fire.*

es paám – fades.

i pa ululim – silver. *lit. faded metal.*

palm

snčmčnečst – palm. **snčmčmčnečst** – palms.

Palm Sunday

qʷélcn – Palm Sunday.

palomino

čpi – palomino horse.

pan

snc̓áx̣mn – skillet, frying pan.
snt̓pustn – boiling pot.

qpéłc̓eʔ, *qpé* – plate; dishpan.

pancake

nłlq̓l̓áq̓lexʷ – make pancakes. *rt:* ***łaq̓*** *– wide; suffix:* ***...ulexʷ*** *– land.*
nłlq̓l̓áq̓lexʷm – S/he made pancakes. **čn nłlq̓l̓áq̓lexʷm, kʷ nłlq̓l̓áq̓lexʷm**
es nłlq̓l̓áq̓lexʷi – S/he is making pancakes. **čnes nłlq̓l̓áq̓lexʷi, kʷes nłlq̓l̓áq̓lexʷi**
qs nłlq̓l̓áq̓lexʷi – S/he is going to make pancakes. **čiqs nłlq̓l̓áq̓lexʷi, kʷqs nłlq̓l̓áq̓lexʷi**

scnłlq̓l̓áq̓lexʷ, *scnłlq̓l̓á* – pancakes.

s.t. - something, the 3rd person
(s.t.) - something implied
s.o. - someone, the 3rd person
sl. - singular form
pl. - plural form
rt. - root word
cmd. - command
lit. - literally
fig. - figuratively
i.e., - for example
See: - Redirection to a related word.

panda

čuswi nłamqeʔs – panda bear.

pants

snołups, *snołu* – pants; trousers. *rt.:* ***oył*** *– one piece, whole.*
nołupsm – S/he put pants on. **čn nołupsm, kʷ nołupsm**
es nołupsi – S/he is putting pants on. **čnes nołupsi, kʷes nołupsi**
qs nołupsi – S/he is going to put pants on. **čiqs nołupsi, kʷqs nołupsi**

nołupsis – S/he put pants on s.o. **nołupsn, nołupsntxʷ**
es nołupsms – S/he is putting pants on s.o. **ies nołupsm, as nołupsm**
qs nołupsms – S/he is going to put pants on s.o. **iqs nołupsm, aqs nołupsm**

es nołups – S/he is wearing pants. **čnes nołups, kʷes nołups**

nołupsiš – Put your pants on. *cmd.*
nołupsntxʷ – Put your pants on him/her/it. *cmd.*

ta snołupsm – There were no trousers. **hoy maw̓is snołupsts –** S/he took off his/her pants. **sxʷuxʷyeʔ l snołupsts –** ants in his/her pants. **miš snołups –** There were no trousers. **tas snołups –** S/he doesn't wearing pants. **tam es snołupsi –** S/he isn't wearing pants.

n...ups – *circumfix indicating the butt, tail, or pants.*
nłiqps – torn/raggy pants.
nkʷalups – yellow pants; yellow tail; yellow butt.

nłxʷpaqstšnm – put the leg inside. *rt.: **łixʷp** – slip/pull over See: **inside**.*

paper
q̓ey̓min – paper; book.

paper birch
čqʷłn̓ałp, *čqʷłn̓a* – white birch; *Betula papyifera.*

sicqn̓ełp – red birch; *Betula occidentalis.*

paper puncher
łx̣ʷłx̣ʷmintn l q̓ey̓min – paper puncher. *rt.: **łox̣ʷ** – hole; suffix: **...mintn** – tool that does.*

parade
sntkʷutew̓s, *sntkʷute* – parade. *rt.: **tkʷúut** – walk pl.; suffix: **...éw̓s** – in between, middle.*
es ntkʷutew̓si – They are parading. **qeʔes ntkʷutew̓si, pes ntkʷutew̓si**
qs ntkʷutew̓si – They are going to parade. **qeʔqs ntkʷutew̓si, pqs ntkʷutew̓si**

Paradise
čłl̓q̓ʷe – Paradise, Montana.

parent
p̓x̣ót – parent; godparent.
p̓x̣p̓x̣ot – parents.
sck̓ʷl̓p̓x̣ót – foster parent. *prefix: **sck̓ʷl̓...** – s.t. that's been made. See: **Sec. 3: Kinship Terms**.*
sck̓ʷl̓p̓x̣p̓x̣ót – foster parents. *prefix: **sck̓ʷl̓...** – s.t. that's been made.*

seʔxʷnémt – parents of son or daughter-in-law.
tétmtn – parents of son or daughter-in-law.

park
es cqsqá – S/he is parked.
cqsqáx̣ʔeis – S/he parked the vehicle. **cqsqáx̣ʔen, cqsqáx̣ʔentxʷ**
es cqsqáx̣ʔems – S/he is parking the vehicle. **ies cqsqáx̣ʔem, as cqsqáx̣ʔem**
qs cqsqáx̣ʔems – S/he is going to park the vehicle. **iqs cqsqáx̣ʔem, aqs cqsqáx̣ʔem**

cqsqáx̣ʔent – Park it. *cmd.*

ha cqsqáx̣ʔentxʷ – Did you part the vehicle? **l čen̓ u cqsqáx̣ʔentxʷ –** Where did you park the vehicle? **ac̓x̣nt ci č̓ ci es cqsqáx̣eʔ łu sxʷkʷnem –** Look, the police officer(patrol car) is parked over there. **nłeptmn łu l čen̓ u cqsqáx̣ʔen łu inp̓ip̓uyšn –** I forgot where I parked my car.

es cqeuł – They are parked.

parole
čox̣mepleʔ – something fastened and hanging/dangling off. *(i.e., a rope tied to something; someone on parole, etc.) See: **hang**.*

es čoẋmepleʔ – S/he/it is fastened and hanging off; s/he is on parole. **čnes čoẋmepleʔ, kʷes čoẋmepleʔ**

parsnip
xʷtełp, *xʷte* – cow parsnip; *Heracleum lanatum.*

part
ẋʷq̓ʷeẇs – divide/part something; apportion; cut cards. *See:* ***divide.***

čehék̓ʷ – separate; detatch; break free of; loosen. *See:* ***separate.***

iheʔ łu qł qʷoyʔé – This part will be mine.

partner
ẋcut – partner; share/help in the activities of another; be a comrade; associate as a companion. *(the opposite is to oppose)*
ẋcut – S/he/it partnered. **čn ẋcut, kʷ ẋcut**
es ẋcuti – S/he/it is partnering. **čnes ẋcuti, kʷes ẋcuti**
qs ẋcuti – S/he/it is going to partner. **čiqs ẋcuti, kʷqs ẋcuti**

ẋcutsts – S/he/it made s.o. take a companion. **ẋcutstn, ẋcutstxʷ**
es ẋcutms – S/he/it is making s.o. take a companion. **ies ẋcutm, as ẋcutm**
qs ẋcutms – S/he/it is going to make s.o. take a companion. **iqs ẋcutm, aqs ẋcutm**

ẋcutmis – S/he/it had s.o. for a companion. **ẋcutmn, ẋcutmntxʷ**
es ẋcutmms – S/he/it is having s.o. for a companion. **ies ẋcutmm, as ẋcutmm**
qs ẋcutmms – S/he/it is going to have s.o. for a companion. **iqs ẋcutmm, aqs ẋcutmm**

es ẋcut – S/he/it shares in activity of (s.o.); s/he/it is a partner. **čnes ẋcut, kʷes ẋcut**

sẋcut – partner; comrade; companion. **insẋcut, ansẋcut, sẋcuts**
sẋcẋcut – partners; comrades; companions; teammates. **insẋcut, ansẋcut, sẋcuts**

ẋcutš – Partner. *cmd.*
ẋcteẇswi – You all partner up. *cmd.*
ẋcutmnt – Take him/her as your partner. *cmd.*
ẋcutskʷ – Make him/her have a partner. *cmd.*
es ẋcteẇs – They are comrades.
es ẋctelis – They are several comrades.
ẋccmutiyeʔ – become traveling partners for a short period.
nẋctus – take sides; side with someone in some activity. *See:* ***side.***

swe łu asẋcut – Who is your partner?

l̓áẋt – befriend. *See:* ***friend.***

q̓ep – friend/companion to death; someone that will die for one. *See:* ***friend.***

nkʷł... – *prefix indicating together with, do with.* *See:* ***with.***
snkʷłsust – drinking partner. *prefix:* ***nkʷł...*** *– together with.*

Pascal
pasqá – Pascal.

pass
čẋʷcim – pass; go by.
čẋʷcim – S/he/it passed by. **čn čẋʷcim, kʷ čẋʷcim**
es čẋʷcmi – S/he/it is passing by. **čnes čẋʷcmi, kʷes čẋʷcmi**
qs čẋʷcmi – S/he/it is going to pass by. **čiqs čẋʷcmi, kʷqs čẋʷcmi**

čẋʷcntes – S/he/it passed s.t./s.o. **čẋʷcnten, čẋʷcntexʷ**
es čẋʷcims – S/he/it is passing s.t./s.o. **ies čẋʷcim, as čẋʷcim**
qs čẋʷcims – S/he/it is going to pass s.t./s.o. **iqs čẋʷcim, aqs čẋʷcim**

The **i** following uvular consonants (UC) and the glottal stop **ʔ** sound like English "*ey*" as in the words th*ey*, h*ey*, wh*ey*, etc. Salish UC are: **q, q̓, qʷ, q̓ʷ, ẋ, ẋʷ**. For example, the suffix **...qin** – head/top, is often spelled using English *ey* as "q*ey*n". So **qi, q̓i, qʷi, q̓ʷi, ẋi, ẋʷi**, may be spelled with English *ey* as **q***ey*, **q̓***ey*, **qʷ***ey*, **q̓ʷ***ey*, **ẋ***ey*, **ẋʷ***ey* in other texts.

s.t. - something, the 3rd person
(s.t.) - something implied
s.o. - someone, the 3rd person
sl. - singular form
pl. - plural form
rt. - root word
cmd. - command
lit. - literally
fig. - figuratively
i.e., - for example
See: - Redirection to a related word.

čx̣ʷcntéʔes – They passed s.t./s.o. **qeʔ čx̣ʷcntem, čx̣ʷcntep**
es čx̣ʷcíʔims – They are passing s.t./s.o. **qeʔes čx̣ʷcim, es čx̣ʷcimp**

čx̣ʷccnuis – S/he/it succeeded in passing s.t./s.o. **čx̣ʷccnun, čx̣ʷccnuntxʷ**
es čx̣ʷccnunms – S/he/it is working at passing s.t./s.o. **ies čx̣ʷccnunm, as čx̣ʷccnunm**
es čx̣ʷcx̣ʷcmi – S/he/it is repeatedly passing by. **čnes čx̣ʷcx̣ʷcmi, kʷes čx̣ʷcx̣ʷcmi**

es čłx̣ʷex̣ʷcti – S/he/it is passing by a little. **čnes čłx̣ʷex̣ʷcti, kʷes čłx̣ʷex̣ʷcti**

čx̣ʷctemn – one inclined to pass by. *suffix:* ***...emn*** *– one inclined to do.*
čx̣ʷcx̣ʷcmuł – one that habitually passes by. *suffix:* ***...łmuł*** *– one that habitually does.*
čx̣ʷcncutn – passer of one.

čx̣ʷciš – Pass by. *cmd.*
čx̣ʷcint – Pass by s.t./s.o. *cmd.*
čx̣ʷéct – It went past/through.
nčx̣ʷctels – want to pass by.
es čx̣ʷccutm – It is passable.
es čx̣ʷcnwexʷisti – They are passing each other.

čx̣ʷcntes ci kʷtunt ssenš – S/he went passed that big rock. **čn nq̓eq̓emuscut u čn čx̣ʷect –** I went into a crowd and passed through. **ṅe l upn eł cil čx̣ʷéct l nk̓ʷuʔ –** 15 past 1, 1:15. **upn čx̣ʷéct ntx̣ʷqi –** ten past noon.

x̣ʷcuʔsičṅ, *x̣ʷcuʔsi* – go over a mountain pass. *suffix:* ***...ičṅ*** *– back.*
x̣ʷcuʔsičṅ – S/he/it went over. **čn x̣ʷcuʔsičṅ, kʷ x̣ʷcuʔsičṅ**
es x̣ʷcuʔsičṅi – S/he/it is going over. **čnes x̣ʷcuʔsičṅi, kʷes x̣ʷcuʔsičṅi**
qs x̣ʷcuʔsičṅi – S/he/it is going to go over. **čiqs x̣ʷcuʔsičṅi, kʷqs x̣ʷcuʔsičṅi**
x̣ʷcuʔsíʔičṅ – They went over. **qeʔ x̣ʷcuʔsičṅ, p x̣ʷcuʔsičṅ**
es x̣ʷcuʔsíʔičṅi – They are going over. **qeʔes x̣ʷcuʔsičṅi, pes x̣ʷcuʔsičṅi**

sx̣ʷcuʔsi – mountain pass.

ƛ̓e šʔél̓ qeʔqs x̣ʷcuʔsi č snyél̓mn – Pretty soon we are going to go over the big mountains to Mission.

šiẏust, *šiẏu* – pass through; go through. *See:* ***pass through.***

px̣ʷmim – distribute; spread around; pass/hand out. *See:* ***distribute.***

pass through

šiẏust, *šiẏu* – pass through; go through.
šiẏustm – S/he passed through. **čn šiẏustm, kʷ šiẏustm**
es šiẏusti – S/he is passing through. **čnes šiẏusti, kʷes šiẏusti**
qs šiẏusti – S/he is going to pass through. **čiqs šiẏusti, kʷqs šiẏusti**

šiẏustmis – S/he passed by s.o./s.t. **šiẏustmn, šiẏustmntxʷ**
es šiẏustms – S/he is passing by s.o./s.t. **ies šiẏustm, as šiẏustm**
qs šiẏustms – S/he is going to pass by s.o./s.t. **iqs šiẏustm, aqs šiẏustm**

šiẏustiš – Pass through. *cmd.*
šiẏustwi – All of you pass through. *cmd.*
šiẏustmnt – Pass by/through it. *cmd.*
šiẏustmnti – All of you pass by/through it. *cmd.*
nšiẏust – pass by in the woods.
nšiʔstetkʷ – pass by in the water.
nšiʔstičṅ – pass behind someone's back. *suffix:* ***...ičṅ*** *– back.*

nšiẏustšn – follow in the tracks of someone or an animal; follow in someone's footsteps; emulate someone. *See: **follow**.*

xʷumiˀ tˀe u čiqs šiẏusti – Excuse me, I am going to go through here.

čiyek̓ʷ – go through a narrow opening. *(i.e., narrow gate; baby being born; thread a needle, etc.)*
čiyek̓ʷm – S/he went through. **čn čiyek̓ʷm, kʷ čiyek̓ʷm**
es čiyek̓ʷi – S/he is going through. **čnes čiyek̓ʷi, kʷes čiyek̓ʷi**
qs čiyek̓ʷi – S/he is going to go through. **čiqs čiyek̓ʷi, kʷqs čiyek̓ʷi**

čiyek̓ʷntes – S/he made s.t. go through. **čiyek̓ʷnten, čiyek̓ʷntexʷ**
es čiyek̓ʷms – S/he is making s.t. go through. **čnes čiyek̓ʷm, kʷes čiyek̓ʷm**
qs čiyek̓ʷms – S/he is going to make s.t. go through. **čiqs čiyek̓ʷm, kʷqs čiyek̓ʷm**

čiyek̓ʷiš – Pass through. *cmd*
čiyek̓ʷont – Pass s.t. through. *cmd*

The **i** following uvular consonants (UC) and the glottal stop **ˀ** sound like English "*ey*" as in the words th*ey*, h*ey*, wh*ey*, etc. Salish UC are: **q**, **q̇**, **qʷ**, **q̇ʷ**, **x̣**, **x̣ʷ**. For example, the suffix …**qin** – head/top, is often spelled using English *ey* as "q*ey*n". So **qi**, **q̇i**, **qʷi**, **q̇ʷi**, **x̣i**, **x̣ʷi**, may be spelled with English *ey* as **q***ey*, **q̇***ey*, **qʷ***ey*, **q̇ʷ***ey*, **x̣***ey*, **x̣ʷ***ey* in other texts.

past

ƛ̓m – past, used to be.
ƛ̓m inṗiṗuyšn – It used to be my car.
ƛ̓m kʷ swe – What was your name?

pat

łecm – smooth hair; pet. *See: **pet**.*
łacqnm – smooth hair of the head; pet the head. *See: **pet**.*

tutéẇ – use gentleness with something; caress something. *See: **gentle**.*
tutéẇis ci nqʷq̇ʷosmičṅ t stipn – Stephen was gentle with the dog.

patch

nšnus – patch a tire/tube. *rt.: **šiṅ** – flat cover.*
nšnusis – S/he patched it. **nšnusn, nšnusntxʷ**
es nšnusms – S/he is patching it. **ies nšnusm, as nšnusm**
qs nšnusms – S/he is going to patch it. **iqs nšnusm, aqs nšnusm**

nšnusmn – tire/tube patch.

path

q̇áx̣ – path/trail.

q̇x̣šits – S/he made a path for s.o. **q̇x̣šitn, q̇x̣šitx**
es q̇x̣šitms – S/he is making a path for s.o. **ies q̇x̣šitm, as q̇x̣šitm**
qs q̇x̣šitms – S/he is going to make a path for s.o. **iqs q̇x̣šitm, aqs q̇x̣šitm**

es łqq̇áx̣ – small path/trail. *See: **trail**.*

patience

niwals – have patience with something; bear something; tolerate something. *rt.: **yóo** – strong; circumfix: **n…els** – want, feel.*
niwalsm – S/he had patience. **čn niwalsm, kʷ niwalsm**
es niwals – S/he is patient. **čnes niwals, kʷes niwals**

niyolsmist – S/he was patient. **čn niyolsmist, kʷ niyolsmist**
es niyolsmisti – S/he is being patient. **čnes niyolsmisti, kʷes niyolsmisti**
qs niyolsmisti – S/he is going to be patient. **čiqs niyolsmisti, kʷqs niyolsmisti**

niyolsmistmis – S/he was patient with s.o./s.t. **niyolsmistmn, niyolsmistmntxʷ**
es niyolsmistms – S/he is being patient with s.o./s.t. **ies niyolsmistm, as niyolsmistm**
qs niyolsmistms – S/he is going to be patient with s.o./s.t. **iqs niyolsmistm, aqs niyolsmistm**

niwalsmis – S/he had patience with s.o./s.t. **niwalsmn, niwalsmntxʷ**

s.t. - something, the 3rd person
(s.t.) - something implied
s.o. - someone, the 3rd person
sl. - singular form
pl. - plural form
rt. - root word
cmd. - command
lit. - literally
fig. - figuratively
i.e., - for example
See: - Redirection to a related word.

es niwalsms – S/he is having patience with s.o./s.t. **ies niwalsm, as niwalsm**
qs niwalsms – S/he is going to have patience with s.o./s.t. **iqs niwalsm, aqs niwalsm**

niwalstes – S/he made s.o. have patience. **niwalsten, niwalstexʷ**
es niwalstems – S/he is making s.o. have patience. **ies niwalstem, as niwalstem**
qs niwalstems – S/he is going to make s.o. have patience. **iqs niwalstem, aqs niwalstem**

siyosčint – patient one.
sniwalstn – patience; the thing that makes one patient.
čniwalstn – patience; the reason one is patient.
sniawiyols – having patience; enduring feelings.

niwalsiš – Be patient. *cmd.*
niwalsmnt – Be patient with s.o./s.t. *cmd.*
qeˀqs niyolsmnwéxʷi – We have patience with each other.
iwaqsm – bear/tolerate the taste of something. *See: **taste**.*
iwenˀem – stand to hear something or someone.

nqimls – feel calm; feel content; relaxed; patient. *See: **calm**.*

patrol car

sxʷnqcqcl̓šaqs, *sxʷnqcqcl̓ša* **–** patrol car, cop car. *rt.: **qcqecl̓š** – run around; prefix: **sxʷ...** – one tasked to do.*

patrol man

sxʷnkʷanqsm – patrol man. *prefix: **sxʷ...** – one tasked to do.*

Pattee Canyon

sloˀté – Pattee Canyon; southeast of Missoula, Montana.

pattern

k̓ʷul̓iš t sq̓iq̓ˀey̓ – Make a pattern. *cmd.*
ułeˀ k̓ʷul̓nt sq̓iq̓ˀey̓ – Make the same pattern. **łu eł t stem̓ sq̓iq̓ˀey̓ łu aqs čtxʷum –** What is next in the pattern that you are going to add?

es čq̓ˀic̓éˀ – It has a pattern around it.
čq̓ˀic̓éˀ, *čq̓ˀi* **–** Indian suitcase, rawhide bag. *lit. it has a pattern around it.*

pave

es nt̓łaqs – The road is paved. *rt.: **t̓ił** – dirty; circumfix: **n...aqs** – nose, road, pointed.*

pay

nˀeys – pay for something bought.
nˀeysm – S/he paid. **čn nˀeysm, kʷ nˀeysm**
es nˀeysi – S/he is paying. **čnes nˀeysi, kʷes nˀeysi**
qs nˀeysi – S/he is going to pay. **čiqs nˀeysi, kʷqs nˀeysi**

nˀeysis – S/he paid for s.t. **nˀeysn, nˀeysntxʷ**
es nˀeysms – S/he is paying for s.t. **ies nˀeysm, as nˀeysm**
qs nˀeysms – S/he is going to pay for s.t. **iqs nˀeysm, aqs nˀeysm**

nˀeyšmis – S/he paid for s.t. for s.o. **nˀeyšmn, nˀeyšmntxʷ**
es nˀeyšms – S/he is paying for s.t. for s.o. **ies nˀeyšm, as nˀeyšm**
qs nˀeyšms – S/he is going to pay for s.t. for s.o. **iqs nˀeyšm, aqs nˀeyšm**

nˀeyšts – S/he helped s.o. pay for it. **nˀeyštn, nˀeyštxʷ**
es nˀeyštms – S/he is helping s.o. paying for it. **ies nˀeyštm, as nˀeyštm**
qs nˀeyštms – S/he is going to help pay for it. **iqs nˀeyštm, aqs nˀeyštm**

nˀeysmis – S/he paid it with s.t. **nˀeysmn, nˀeysmntxʷ**
es nˀeysmms – S/he is paying it with s.t. **ies nˀeysmm, as nˀeysmm**
qs nˀeysmms – S/he is going to pay it with s.t. **iqs nˀeysmm, aqs nˀeysmm**

sxʷnʔeysm – customer; one tasked to pay.
snʔeys – price; cost.
scnʔeys – something that has been paid for.
nʔeystn – purchase; what is paid for.
nʔeysmn – what is used to pay.

nʔeysiš – Pay. *cmd.*
nʔeysnt – Pay for it. *cmd.*
nʔeysts – S/he was in the market for s.t. *See:* ***market.***

nʔeysn łu inṗiṗuyšn – I paid for my car. **nʔeysmn łu inululim –** I paid for it with my money. **ha es nʔeys –** Is it paid? **steṁ łu as nʔeysmm –** What are you using to pay for it? **ṅe tas nʔeyłts ṅem t qoyʔe m nʔeyštn –** If s/he does not pay it to you, I will pay for him/her. **steṁ łu snʔeysts –** What is its price?

The **i** following uvular consonants (UC) and the glottal stop **ʔ** sound like English "*ey*" as in the words th*ey*, h*ey*, wh*ey*, etc. Salish UC are: **q**, **q̇**, **qʷ**, **q̇ʷ**, **x̣**, **x̣ʷ**. For example, the suffix …**qin** – head/top, is often spelled using English *ey* as "q*ey*n". So **qi**, **q̇i**, **qʷi**, **q̇ʷi**, **x̣i**, **x̣ʷi**, may be spelled with English *ey* as **q***ey*, **q̇***ey*, **qʷ***ey*, **q̇ʷ***ey*, **x̣***ey*, **x̣ʷ***ey* in other texts.

x̣aq̇ – pay someone; salary.
x̣aq̇is – S/he paid s.o. **x̣aq̇n, x̣aq̇ntxʷ**
es x̣aq̇ms – S/he is paying s.o. **ies x̣aq̇m, as x̣aq̇m**
qs x̣aq̇ms – S/he is going to pay s.o. **iqs x̣aq̇m, aqs x̣aq̇m**
x̣áʔaq̇is – They paid s.o. **qeʔ x̣aq̇ntm, x̣aq̇ntp**
es x̣áʔaq̇ms – They are paying s.o. **qeʔes x̣aq̇m, es x̣aq̇mp**

x̣aq̇ntm – S/he was paid.

x̣aq̇nt – Pay s.o. *cmd.*

ṅe qʷo x̣aq̇ntxʷ – If you pay me. **čmi ṅe qʷo x̣aq̇ntxʷ –** Only if you pay me. **čmi ṅe qʷo x̣aq̇ntm –** Only if I get paid. **čmi ṅe qʷo x̣aq̇is –** Only if they pay me.

nšƛ̓pus – pay off debts in full. *rt.:* ***šiƛ̓*** *– flat, level, aligned.*
nšƛ̓pusm – S/he paid debts/squared up. **čn nšƛ̓pusm, kʷ nšƛ̓pusm**
es nšƛ̓pusi – S/he is paying debts/square up. **čnes nšƛ̓pusi, kʷes nšƛ̓pusi**
qs nšƛ̓pusi – S/he is going to pay debts/square up. **čiqs nšƛ̓pusi, kʷqʷ nšƛ̓pusi**

es nšƛ̓pus – S/he is debt free/all squared up.

nk̓ʷlisusm, *nk̓ʷlisu* **–** pay one's debt.
nk̓ʷlisusm – S/he paid their debt. **čn nk̓ʷlisusm, kʷ nk̓ʷlisusm**

pay day

scpx̣ʷmi – something that has been handed out *(i.e., rations, per capita, commodities, pay day). prefix:* ***sc…*** *– s.t. that's been done/made/prepared.*
px̣ʷmim – distribute; spread around; pass/hand out. *See:* ***distribute.***

peace

ihém – regain friendship; make peace; reconcile differences.
ihémis – S/he/it regained s.o.'s friendship. **ihémn, ihémntxʷ**
es ihéms – S/he/it is regaining s.o.'s friendship. **ies ihém, as ihém**
qs ihéms – S/he/it is going to regain s.o.'s friendship. **iqs ihém, aqs ihém**

ihemtwexʷ – make up after a fight; make peace with one another.
es ihemtwéʔexʷi – They are making peace with each other. **qeʔes ihemtwexʷi, pes ihemtwexʷi**

ihemtwéxʷsts – S/he made them reconcile with each other. **ihemtwéxʷstn, ihemtwéxʷstxʷ**
ihemtwéxʷms – S/he is making them reconcile with each other. **ies ihemtwéxʷm, pes ihemtwéxʷm**

s.t. - something, the 3rd person
(s.t.) - something implied
s.o. - someone, the 3rd person
sl. - singular form
pl. - plural form
rt. - root word
cmd. - command
lit. - literally
fig. - figuratively
i.e., - for example
See: - Redirection to a related word.

nihemtwéxʷtn – peace; something that makes peace; something that makes differences reconciled.

qmqemt – S/he is at peace/content. *See: **calm**.*

peanuts **q̓ép̓xʷeʔ –** nut; nuts; peanut.

pear **čċmċmus,** *čċmċmu* **–** pear. *rt.: **ċim** – constricted; circumfix: **č...us** – spherical object; eyes.*

peas **lipuwá –** peas. *(approximation to French word)*

iłnt anlipuwá – Eat your peas.

peek **ƛ̓éʔeč,** *ƛ̓éʔe* **–** peek out; come out.

ƛ̓éʔeč – S/he/it peeked out. **čn ƛ̓éʔeč, kʷ ƛ̓éʔeč**
es ƛ̓éʔečmi – S/he/it is peeking out. **čnes ƛ̓éʔečmi, kʷes ƛ̓éʔečmi**
qs ƛ̓éʔečmi – S/he/it is going to peek out. **čiqs ƛ̓éʔečmi, kʷqs ƛ̓éʔečmi**

ƛ̓ečis – S/he/it made s.t. peek out. **ƛ̓ečn, ƛ̓ečntxʷ**
es ƛ̓ečms – S/he/it is making s.t. peek out. **ies ƛ̓ečm, as ƛ̓ečm**
qs ƛ̓ečms – S/he/it is going to make s.t. peek out. **iqs ƛ̓ečm, aqs ƛ̓ečm**

ƛ̓ečč – It peeked out.

ƛ̓ečš – Peeked out. *cmd.*
ƛ̓ečwi – All of you peeked out. *cmd.*
ƛ̓ečnt – Peeked it out. *cmd.*
ƛ̓ečnti – All of you peeked it out. *cmd.*
nƛ̓čmew̓s – peek out among the middle things. *suffix: **...éw̓s** – in between, middle.*
ƛ̓ečulexʷ – peek out of the ground. *(i.e., when first noticed that plants/grass is growing, etc.)*
sƛ̓éʔeč – sunrise; the sun just peeked out.
ƛ̓eččin – sound off; make voice appear. *suffix: **...cin, ...cn** – action of the mouth.*
ƛ̓eččn – stick out the tongue. *See: **tongue**.*
ƛ̓čim̓ – protrude out; bulge out. *See: **protrude**.*

ƛ̓ačqn – peek over; show the head.
ƛ̓ačqnm – S/he peeked over. **čn ƛ̓ačqnm, kʷ ƛ̓ačqnm**
es ƛ̓ačqni – S/he is peeking over. **čnes ƛ̓ačqni, kʷes ƛ̓ačqni**
qs ƛ̓ačqni – S/he is going to peek over. **čiqs ƛ̓ačqni, kʷqs ƛ̓ačqni**

ƛ̓ačqniš – Peek over. *cmd.*

nƛ̓ečs – peek the face in something.
nƛ̓ečsm – S/he peeked one's face in. **čn nƛ̓ečsm, kʷ nƛ̓ečsm**
es nƛ̓ečsi – S/he is peeking one's face in. **čnes nƛ̓ečsi, kʷes nƛ̓ečsi**
qs nƛ̓ečsi – S/he is going to peek one's face in. **čiqs nƛ̓ečsi, kʷqs nƛ̓ečsi**

ƛ̓ečs – peek the face out.

wekʷsm – hide the face; play peek-a-boo. *rt.: **wekʷ** – hide; suffix: **...us** – face, fire.*
wekʷsm – S/he hid his/her face. **čn wekʷsm, kʷs wekʷsm**
es wekʷsi – S/he is hiding his/her face. **čnes wekʷsi, kʷes wekʷsi**
qs wekʷsi – S/he is going to hide his/her face. **čiqs wekʷsi, kʷsqs wekʷsi**
wéʔekʷsm – They hid his/her face. **qeʔ wekʷsm, p wekʷsm**
es wéʔekʷsi – They are hiding his/her face. **qeʔes wekʷsi, pes wekʷsi**
qs wéʔekʷsi – They are going to hide his/her face. **qeʔqs wekʷsi, pqs wekʷsi**

wekʷsis – S/he hid s.o.'s face. **wekʷsn, wekʷsntxʷ**
es wekʷsms – S/he is hiding s.o.'s face. **ies wekʷsm, as wekʷsm**

qs wekʷsms – S/he is going to hide s.o.'s face. **iqs wekʷsm, aqs wekʷsm**
wéʔekʷsis – They hid s.o.'s face. **qeʔ wekʷsntm, wekʷsntp**
es wéʔekʷsms – They are hiding s.o.'s face. **qeʔes wekʷsm, es wekʷsmp**
qs wéʔekʷsms – They are going to hide s.o.'s face. **qeʔqs wekʷsm, qs wekʷsmp**

es ukʷwekʷsi – S/he/it is playing peek-a-boo. **čnes ukʷwekʷsi, kʷes ukʷwekʷsi**

wekʷsiš – Hide your face. *cmd.*
wekʷsnt – Hide his/her face. *cmd.*

k̓ʷłʔiq̓iyaq̓ist, *k̓ʷłʔiq̓iya* **–** peeking around something. *(i.e., looking out a window, peeking around a corner, etc.)*
k̓ʷłʔiq̓iyaq̓ist – S/he peeked around. **čn k̓ʷłʔiq̓iyaq̓ist, kʷ k̓ʷłʔiq̓iyaq̓ist**
es k̓ʷłʔiq̓iyaq̓isti – S/he is peeking around. **čnes k̓ʷłʔiq̓iyaq̓isti, kʷes k̓ʷłʔiq̓iyaq̓isti**
qs k̓ʷłʔiq̓iyaq̓isti – S/he is going to peek around. **čiqs k̓ʷłʔiq̓iyaq̓isti, kʷqs k̓ʷłʔiq̓iyaq̓isti**

peel

ewm – peel with a knife/peeler. *(i.e., apple, potato, carrot, etc.)*
ewm – S/he peeled. **čn ewm, kʷ ewm**
es ewmi – S/he is peeling. **čnes ewmi, kʷes ewmi**
qs ewmi – S/he is going to peel. **čiqs ewmi, kʷqs ewmi**

ewis – S/he peeled s.t. **ewn, ewntxʷ**
es ewms – S/he is peeling s.t. **ies ewm, as ewm**
qs ewms – S/he is going to peel s.t. **iqs ewm, aqs ewm**

ewnuis – S/he succeeded in peeling s.t. **ewnun, ewnuntxʷ**
es ewnunms – S/he is succeeding in peeling s.t. **ies ewnunm, as ewnunm**
qs ewnunms – S/he is going to succeed in peeling s.t. **iqs ewnunm, aqs ewnunm**

ewup – It peeled; it peeled by itself.
es ewpmi – It is peeling.
qs ewpmi – It is going to peel.

ewmemn – one inclined to peel. *suffix:* ***...emn –*** *one inclined to do.*
sxʷewm – one tasked to peel. *prefix:* ***sxʷ... –*** *one tasked to do.*
ewncutn – one that peels for one. *suffix:*
scewm – something that's been peeled. *prefix:* ***sc... –*** *s.t. that's been done/made/prepared.*
ewmintn – peelings.
ewmin – something used to peel. *suffix:* ***...min, ...mn –*** *instrument/tool*

ewiš – Peel. *cmd.*
ewnt – Peel it. *cmd.*

čewic̓éʔ – peel the entire skin off; peel all around. *(i.e., apple, potato, carrot, etc.) rt.:* ***ew –*** *peel; suffix:* ***...ic̓éʔ –*** *covered in.*
čewic̓ʔéis – S/he peeled the entire skin off it. **čewic̓ʔén, čewic̓ʔéntxʷ**
es čewic̓ʔéms – S/he is peeling the entire skin off it. **ies čewic̓ʔém, as čewic̓ʔém**
qs čewic̓ʔéms – S/he is going to peel the entire skin off it. **iqs čewic̓ʔém, aqs čewic̓ʔém**

es čewic̓éʔ – The entire object is peeled.

sččewic̓éʔ – peelings.

čewic̓ʔéš – Peel the whole thing. *cmd.*

The **i** following uvular consonants (UC) and the glottal stop **ʔ** sound like English "*ey*" as in the words *they, hey, whey,* etc. Salish UC are: **q, q̓, qʷ, q̓ʷ, x̣, x̣ʷ**. For example, the suffix ...**qin** – head/top, is often spelled using English *ey* as "q*ey*n". So **qi, q̓i, qʷi, q̓ʷi, x̣i, x̣ʷi**, may be spelled with English *ey* as **q***ey*, **q̓***ey*, **qʷ***ey*, **q̓ʷ***ey*, **x̣***ey*, **x̣ʷ***ey* in other texts.

s.t. - something, the 3rd person
(s.t.) - something implied
s.o. - someone, the 3rd person
sl. - singular form
pl. - plural form
rt. - root word
cmd. - command
lit. - literally
fig. - figuratively
i.e., - for example
See: - Redirection to a related word.

čewiċʔént – Peel all of it. *cmd.*

čawálqʷm – peel bark; peel flower stems; peel cylindrical objects. *rt.: **ew** – peel.*
čawálqʷm – S/he peeled bark. **čn čawálqʷm, kʷ čawálqʷm**
es čawálqʷi – S/he is peeling bark. **čnes čawálqʷi, kʷes čawálqʷi**
qs čawálqʷi – S/he is going to peel bark. **čiqs čawálqʷi, kʷqs čawálqʷi**

čawálqʷis – S/he peeled the bark. **čawálqʷn, čawálqʷntxʷ**
es čawálqʷm – S/he is peeling the bark. **ies čawálqʷm, as čawálqʷm**
qs čawálqʷm – S/he is going to peel the bark. **iqs čawálqʷm, aqs čawálqʷm**

sččawálqʷ – something that's been peeled. *prefix: **sc...** – s.t. that's been done/made/prepared.*

čawálqʷiš – Peel. *cmd.*
čawálqʷnt – Peel it. *cmd.*

čłqʷéw̓snt l asččawálqʷ ṅem i xʷuk̓ʷ – Throw it over your peeled pole so it'll be clean.

čawełpm – peel fibers off of bark. *rt.: **ew** – peel.*
čawełpm – S/he peeled bark. **čn čawełpm, kʷ čawełpm**
es čawełpi – S/he is peeling bark. **čnes čawełpi, kʷes čawełpi**
qs čawełpi – S/he is going to peel bark. **čiqs čawełpi, kʷqs čawełpi**

čawełpis – S/he peeled the bark. **čawełpn, čawełpntxʷ**
es čawełpms – S/he is peeling the bark. **ies čawełpms, as čawełpm**
qs čawełpms – S/he is going to peel the bark. **iqs čawełpms, aqs čawełpms**

čawełpiš – Peel bark fibers. *cmd.*
čawełpnt – Peel the bark fibers. *cmd.*

čq̓iċéʔ – peel the entire skin off; peel all around; take the topping off. *(i.e., orange, lemon, etc.) suffix: **...iċéʔ** – covered in.*
čq̓iċʔéis – S/he peeled the entire skin off it. **čq̓iċʔén, čq̓iċʔéntxʷ**
es čq̓iċʔéms – S/he is peeling the entire skin off it. **ies čq̓iċʔém, as čq̓iċʔém**
qs čq̓iċʔéms – S/he is going to peel the entire skin off it. **iqs čq̓iċʔém, aqs čq̓iċʔém**

čq̓iċʔéš – Peel. *cmd.*
čq̓iċʔént – Peel it. *cmd.*

ṅawep – skin; peel the skin off an animal. *See: **skin**.*

es ṅawepi t ččl̓exʷ – S/he is peeling the muskrat.

łoq̓ʷ – make bare; peel *(i.e., peeling bitterroot, peeling camas, plucking the fuzz off a bird).*
łoq̓ʷm – S/he/it peeled. **čn łoq̓ʷm, kʷ łoq̓ʷm**
es łoq̓ʷi – S/he is peeling. **čnes łoq̓ʷi, kʷes łoq̓ʷi**
qs łoq̓ʷi – S/he is going to peel. **čiqs łoq̓ʷi, kʷqs łoq̓ʷi**
łóʔoq̓ʷm – They peeled. **qeʔ łoq̓ʷm, p łoq̓ʷm**
es łóʔoq̓ʷi – They are peeling. **qeʔes łoq̓ʷi, pes łoq̓ʷi**
qs łóʔoq̓ʷi – They are going to peel. **qeʔqs łoq̓ʷi, pqs łoq̓ʷi**

łoq̓ʷis – S/he/it peeled s.t. **łoq̓ʷn, łoq̓ʷntxʷ**
es łoq̓ʷms – S/he is peeling s.t. **ies łoq̓ʷm, as łoq̓ʷm**
qs łoq̓ʷms – S/he is going to peel s.t. **iqs łoq̓ʷm, aqs łoq̓ʷm**
łóʔoq̓ʷis – They peeled s.t. **qeʔ łoq̓ʷntm, łoq̓ʷntp**
es łóʔoq̓ʷms – They are peeling s.t. **qeʔes łoq̓ʷm, es łoq̓ʷmp**
qs łóʔoq̓ʷms – They are going to peel s.t. **qeʔqs łoq̓ʷm, qs łoq̓ʷmp**

i łoq̓ʷ – It is bare; it is peeled.

scłoq̓ʷm – something that's been peeled. *prefix:* ***sc...*** *– s.t. that's been done/made/prepared.*
sccłoq̓ʷ – peelings. *prefix:* ***sc...*** *– s.t. that's been done/made/prepared.*

łoq̓ʷiš – Peel. *cmd.*
łoq̓ʷwi – All of you peel. *cmd.*
łoq̓ʷnt – Peel s.t. *cmd.*

nłóq̓ʷoʔ – bald. *rt.:* ***łoq̓ʷm*** *– make bare.*
nłóq̓ʷoʔ – S/he is bald. **čn nłóq̓ʷoʔ, kʷ nłóq̓ʷoʔ**

łóq̓ʷlexʷ – bare land.

łóq̓ʷnt esyáʔ ascx̣éct – Peel everything you dig up.

es xʷk̓ʷpmi – S/he is cleaning. *(i.e., scraping, peeling down something) See:* ***clean.***
i čxʷók̓ʷlqʷ – The pole is clean.

> The **i** following uvular consonants (UC) and the glottal stop **ʔ** sound like English "*ey*" as in the words th*ey*, h*ey*, wh*ey*, etc. Salish UC are: **q**, **q̓**, **qʷ**, **q̓ʷ**, **x̣**, **x̣ʷ**. For example, the suffix ...**qin** – head/top, is often spelled using English *ey* as "q*ey*n". So **qi**, **q̓i**, **qʷi**, **q̓ʷi**, **x̣i**, **x̣ʷi**, may be spelled with English *ey* as **q***ey*, **q̓***ey*, **qʷ***ey*, **q̓ʷ***ey*, **x̣***ey*, **x̣ʷ***ey* in other texts.

pelt

q̓étt – hide; pelt.
anq̓étt – your hide.
čen łu ci q̓étt? – Where's that hide?

pen

q̓eỷmintn – writing utensil; pen; pencil.

nmlq̓ʷasq q̓eỷmintn – ball point pen. *rt.:* ***malq̓ʷ*** *– balled object; circumfix:* ***n...aqs*** *– nose, road, pointed.*

nmopaqs q̓eỷmintn – fountain pen. *rt.:* ***moo*** *– flowing; circumfix:* ***n...aqs*** *– nose, road, pointed.*

pencil

q̓eỷmintn – pen; pencil. *rt.:* ***q̓eỷ*** *– write, mark; suffix:* ***...mintn*** *– tool that does.*

łp̓mintn – pencil; carpenter's pencil. *rt.:* ***łip̓*** *– line; suffix:* ***...mintn*** *– tool that does.*

nšmaqs q̓eỷmintn – lead pencil. *rt.:* ***šim*** *– rammed through; circumfix:* ***n...aqs*** *– nose, road, pointed.*

snp̓sáqs – nose; bird's beak; pencil tip.

nłƛ̓ƛ̓imaqstn – sharpener; pencil sharpener. *suffix:* ***...tin, ...tn*** *– means of/device. See:* ***sharp.***

Pend d'Oreille

sčłq̓etkʷmcin – Upper Pend d'Oreille; people of the wide lake. *rt.:* ***łaq̓t*** *– wide; suffix:* ***...etkʷ, ...tkʷ*** *– liquid (self identification term)*
sčłq̓etkʷmiš – Upper Pend d'Oreille; people of the wide lake. *rt.:* ***łaq̓t*** *– wide; suffix:* ***...etkʷ, ...tkʷ*** *– liquid (Qlispel term)*
sčłq̓tkʷmsči – Upper Pend d'Oreille; people of the wide lake. *rt.:* ***łaq̓t*** *– wide; suffix:* ***...etkʷ, ...tkʷ*** *– liquid (Salish term)*

qlispél, *qlispé* – Kalispel; Lower Pend d'Oreille. *rt.:* ***qal*** *– fresh, raw. (self identification term)*

penguin

wl̓wel̓ – It waddles; penguin.

kʷl̓kʷališn wl̓wel̓ – yellow foot penguin. *lit. a yellow footed waddler.*

q̓lepswl̓wel̓ – chin strapped penguin.

penny

nk̓ʷuʔséns – penny.

pentagon

clčsq̓tq̓it – pentagon; has five flat sides.

people

sqélixʷ – human; person; Indian. *See:* ***Indian.*** *rt.:* ***qeltč*** *– meat, body; rt.:* ***sṫulixʷ*** *– land, earth.*
sṫlsqelixʷ – people at large; *tore from the land. rt.:* ***sqeltč*** *– meat, flesh; rt.:* ***sṫulixʷ*** *– land, earth; prefix:* ***ṫil*** *– ripped.*
snkʷsqelixʷ – fellow people; fellow human being.

> s.t. - something, the 3rd person
> (s.t.) - something implied
> s.o. - someone, the 3rd person
> *sl.* - singular form
> *pl.* - plural form
> *rt.* - root word
> *cmd.* - command
> *lit.* - literally
> *fig.* - figuratively
> *i.e.,* - for example
> *See:* - Redirection to a related word.

qlixʷnxʷistn – walk like a human; walk like an Indian.
nqlixʷcut – be human; be cultural; be Indian. *See: **culture**.*
nqlixʷečst – do something as a human; culture; tradition. *See: **culture**.*

…elixʷ, **…lixʷ**, **…lxʷ –** *suffix indicating people.*
sncm̓asqélixʷ, *sncm̓asqé* **–** little people. *(similar to elves, gnomes, or leprechauns)*
snk̓ʷélixʷ – tribespeople, those who live in the same place, one people. *rt.: **nk̓ʷuʔ** – one.*

stmélixʷ – what people/tribe. *rt.: **stem̓** – what.*
t̓xʷlélixʷ – different people/tribe; stranger. *rt.: **t̓ixʷlm** – different.*

kʷ stmélixʷ – What people/tribe are you? **ep stmélixʷ łu č łu –** There's some family/people over there.

čnaqs – one person.
čnaqsm – S/he is alone/is one person. **čn čnaqsm, kʷ čnaqsm**
es čnaqsm – S/he is one person. **čnes čnaqsm, kʷes čnaqsm**
čnčnaqs – each one of them.
čnáʔaqs – those ones individually.

čsel – two people.
čselm – those two people. **qeʔ čselm, p čselm**
es čselm – There are two people. **qeʔes čselm, pes čselm**

ččečeɫe – three people.
ččečeɫe – those three people. **qeʔ ččečeɫe, p ččečeɫe**
es ččečeɫe – there are three people. **qeʔ ččečeɫe, p ččečeɫe**

ččeɫl sisp̓l̓ – three groups of seven.

čmusms – four people.
čmusms – those four people. **qeʔ čmusms, p čmusms**
es čmusms – There are four people. **qeʔes musms, pes čmusms**

čmčmus – groups of four people.
es čmčmnúʔus – those groups of four.

čcilcl – five people.
čcilcl – those five people. **qeʔ čcilcl, p čcilcl**
es čcilcl – There are five people. **qeʔes čcilcl, pes čcilcl**

čclcil – groups of five.

čt̓aq̓n – six people.
čt̓aq̓n – those six people. **qeʔ čt̓aq̓n, p čt̓aq̓n**
es čt̓aq̓n – There are six people. **qeʔes čt̓aq̓n, pes čt̓aq̓n**

čt̓q̓t̓aq̓n – groups of six.

čsisp̓l̓ – seven people.
čsisp̓l̓ – those seven people. **qeʔ čsisp̓l̓, p čsisp̓l̓**
es čsisp̓l̓ – There are seven people. **qeʔes čsisp̓l̓, pes čsisp̓l̓**

čsisiʔsp̓l̓ – groups of seven.

čhéʔenm – eight people.
čhéʔenm – those eight people. **qeʔ čhéʔenm, p čhéʔenm**
es čhéʔenm – There are eight people. **qeʔes čhéʔenm, pes čhéʔenm**

čheʔhéʔenm – groups of eight.

čx̣ṅut – nine people.
čx̣ṅut – those nine people. **qeʔ čx̣ṅut, p čx̣ṅut**
es čx̣ṅut – There are nine people. **qeʔes čx̣ṅut, pes čx̣ṅut**

čx̣nx̣nut – groups of nine.

čʔupn – ten people.
čʔupn – those ten people. **qeʔ čʔupn, p čʔupn**
es čʔupn – There are ten people. **qeʔes čʔupn, pes čʔupn**

čupʔupn – groups of ten.

čʔupn eł čnaqs – eleven people.

čxʷexʷʔi – lots of people.

p čk̇ʷink̇ʷnš – How many are there of you? *See:* ***how many****.*

sxʷl̇xʷl̇teẇs – family or a group of people. *suffix:* ***...éẇs*** *– in between, middle.*

The **i** following uvular consonants (UC) and the glottal stop **ʔ** sound like English "*ey*" as in the words *they, hey, whey*, etc. Salish UC are: **q, q̇, qʷ, q̇ʷ, x̣, x̣ʷ**. For example, the suffix **...qin** – head/top, is often spelled using English *ey* as "q*ey*n". So **qi, q̇i, qʷi, q̇ʷi, x̣i, x̣ʷi**, may be spelled with English *ey* as **q***ey*, **q̇***ey*, **qʷ***ey*, **q̇ʷ***ey*, **x̣***ey*, **x̣ʷ***ey* in other texts.

pepper

łtx̣tax̣, *łtx̣ta* – pepper.
łtx̣tax̣m – S/he peppered (s.t.) **čn łtx̣tax̣m, kʷ łtx̣tax̣m**
es łtx̣tax̣i – S/he is peppering (s.t.) **čnes łtx̣tax̣i, kʷes łtx̣tax̣i**
qs łtx̣tax̣i – S/he is going to pepper (s.t.) **čiqs łtx̣tax̣i, kʷqs łtx̣tax̣i**

łtx̣tax̣is – S/he peppered it. **łtx̣tax̣n, łtx̣tax̣ntxʷ**
es łtx̣tax̣ms – S/he is peppering it. **ies łtx̣tax̣m, as łtx̣tax̣m**
qs łtx̣tax̣ms – S/he is going to pepper it. **iqs łtx̣tax̣m, aqs łtx̣tax̣m**

es łtx̣tax̣ – It is peppered.
i łtx̣tax̣ – It is peppery.

snłtx̣tax̣ – pepper shaker.

łtx̣tax̣nt – Pepper it. *cmd.*

peppermint

x̣nx̣néłp, *x̣nx̣né* – field mint, peppermint; false solomns seal; *Mentha arvensis.*

tiitẇi – horse mint; nettle-leaf giant-hyssop; *Agastache urticifolia.*

per capita

scpx̣ʷmi – something that has been handed out *(i.e., rations, per capita, commodities, pay day). rt.:* ***px̣ʷum*** *– distribute; prefix:* ***sc...*** *– s.t. that's been done/made/prepared.*

perceive

séw – ask; seek information. *See:* ***ask****.*
séwneʔ – hear; listen. *See:* ***hear****.*

sunuṁt – listen. *See:* ***listen****.*

s.t. - something, the 3rd person
(s.t.) - something implied
s.o. - someone, the 3rd person
sl. - singular form
pl. - plural form
rt. - root word
cmd. - command
lit. - literally
fig. - figuratively
i.e., - for example
See: - Redirection to a related word.

perch

čmut – sit up high; perch.
čmut l es šiṫ – S/he/it sat in a tree.

peregrine falcon

aátat – falcon; Peregrine falcon; duck hawk; *Falco peregrinus.*

perform

ax̣í – busy with; mess around with; perform. *See:* ***busy****.*

ax̣tčim – busy with something. *See:* ***busy****.*

perfume

senistn – Indian perfume. *suffix:* ***...tin, ...tn*** *– means of/device.*

sinmn – something used to make a pleasant smell.

nsinkʷ – pleasant smelling liquid; perfume.

qmepeˀ – beaver testicles *(used for scent/fragrance)*.

perhaps **x̣ʷa –** perhaps or maybe.
x̣ʷa ṅem t̓ipéys – Maybe it will rain.
x̣ʷa u x̣ʷa ta – Maybe, maybe not.

uc – *particle expressing perhaps in a question form.*
uc kʷep sp̓eƛ̓m – Perhaps you have bitterroot?
uc kʷ epł ululim – Perhaps you have money? *(nice way to ask for money)*
x̣ʷa uc kʷep sp̓eƛ̓m – Is it possible you have bitterroot.

perm **qʷos –** curl; crisp. *See: **curl**.*

Perma **sˀolqʷelšwetkʷ,** *sˀolqʷelšwe* **–** Perma, Flathead Nation. *lit. to come out of a canyon to the water.*
*suffix: **...etkʷ, ...tkʷ** – liquid*

permission **čsewpleˀ –** ask permission; ask about someone.
čsewpleˀ – S/he asked permission. **čn čsewpleˀ, kʷ čsewpleˀ**
es čsewplˀei – S/he is asking permission. **čnes čsewplˀei, kʷes čsewplˀei**
qs čsewplˀei – S/he is going to ask permission. **čiqs čsewplˀei, kʷqs čsewplˀei**

čsewplˀeis – S/he interrogated s.o; s/he asked s.o.'s permission. **čsewplˀen, čsewplˀentxʷ**
es čsewplˀems – S/he is interrogating s.o.; s/he is asking s.o.'s permission. **ies čsewplˀem, as čsewplˀem**
qs čsewplˀems – S/he is going to interrogate s.o.; s/he is going to ask s.o.'s permission. **iqs čsewplˀem, aqs čsewplˀem**

čsewplˀeiš – Ask permission. *cmd.*
čsewplˀent – Interrogate s.o.; ask s.o. permission. *cmd.*

séw – ask; seek information. *See: **ask**.*

persistent **ax̣lnumt –** persistent.
ax̣lnumt – S/he/it was persistent. **čn ax̣lnumt, kʷ ax̣lnumt**
ṅem ax̣lnumt – S/he/it will be persistent. **ṅem čn ax̣lnumt, ṅem kʷ ax̣lnumt**

ax̣llwís, *ax̣llwí* **–** hustle around for something; able and determined in doing something. *See: **busy**.*

nq̓aq̓ˀels – always busy; snoopy; nosy; prying. *See: **business**.*

person **sqélixʷ –** human; person; Indian. *See: **Indian**.*

perspire **čskʷilt –** sweat; perspire. *See: **sweat**.*

persuade **áẏċ –** urge; insist and plead; stubborn. *See: **insist**.*

aẏċn – have the voice of insisting, begging and pleading. *See: **insist**.*

qiˀl – beg; insist; persuade; coaxed into. *See: **beg**.*

pest **meméˀt –** bothersome; pesty. *See: **bother**.*

pester **mˀečstm –** bother with behavior or actions. *See: **bother**.*

hetiṁ – tease *(more a playful tease than a bothersome tease)*. *See: **tease**.*

pet **čem̓u** – pet.

čelltč – owner; master; lord.

łecm – smooth hair; pet.
łec – S/he petted. **čn łecn, kʷ łecm**
es łeci – S/he is petting it. **čnes łeci, kʷes łeci**

łecis – S/he petted it. **łecn, łecntxʷ**
es łecms – S/he is petting it. **ies łecm, as łecm**
qs łecms – S/he is going to pet it. **iqs łecm, aqs łecm**
łéˀecis – They pet it. **qeˀ łecn, łecntp**
es łéˀecms – They are petting it. **qeˀes łecm, es łecmp**

łecš – Pet. *cmd.*
łecnt – Pet it. *cmd.*

łacqnm – smooth hair of the head; pet the head.
łacqnis – S/he petted it. **łacqn, łacqntxʷ**
es łacqnms – S/he is petting it. **ies łacqnm, as łacqnm**
qs łacqnms – S/he is going to pet it. **iqs łacqnm, aqs łacqnm**
łáˀacqis – They pet it. **qeˀ łacqn, łacqntp**
es łáˀacqnms – They are petting it. **qeˀes łacqnm, es łacqnmp**
qs łáˀacqnms – They are going to pet it. **qeˀqs łacqnm, qs łacqnmp**

łacqnt – Pet its head. *cmd.*

tutéw̓ – use gentleness with something; caress something. *See:* ***gentle.***

Peter **piyél** – Peter; Pete; Pierre.

Petty Creek **snċemċm** – Petty Creek near Alberton, Montana.

phallus **spalq** – phallus.

pheasant **čusw̓i skʷiskʷs** – ring-necked pheasant; *Phasianus colchicus.*
čusuwisšn – pheasant.

Phillip **pli** – Phillip.

photocopying machine **snk̓ʷłq̓y̓q̓ey̓mintn** – printer, copier. *prefix:* ***sn...*** *– a place of; suffix:* ***...tin, ...tn*** *– means of/device.*

photograph **sk̓ʷłq̓ˀey̓** – picture; photograph; postcard.
sk̓ʷłq̓iq̓ˀey̓ – pictures; photographs; postcards.

k̓ʷłq̓ey̓im – draw a picture. *See:* ***draw.***
ṅem qeˀ k̓ʷłq̓y̓q̓ey̓ntem łu qeˀ sumeš – We'll paint pictures of our medicine power.

piano **čłtqeneˀtn** – piano. *rt.:* ***tq*** *– touch action; circumfix:* ***čł...eneˀ*** *– cover all over.*
čłtqenˀem – S/he played the piano. **čn čłtqenˀem, kʷ čłtqenˀem**
es čłtqenˀei – S/he is playing the piano. **čnes čłtqenˀei, kʷes čłtqenˀei**
qs čłtqenˀei – S/he is going to play the piano. **čiqs čłtqenˀei, kʷqs čłtqenˀei**

čłtqtqenˀeiš – Play the piano. *cmd.*

The **i** following uvular consonants (UC) and the glottal stop **ˀ** sound like English "*ey*" as in the words *they, hey, whey*, etc. Salish UC are: **q, q̓, qʷ, q̓ʷ, x̣, x̣ʷ**. For example, the suffix **...qin** – head/top, is often spelled using English *ey* as "q*ey*n". So **qi, q̓i, qʷi, q̓ʷi, x̣i, x̣ʷi**, may be spelled with English *ey* as **q***ey*, **q̓***ey*, **qʷ***ey*, **q̓ʷ***ey*, **x̣***ey*, **x̣ʷ***ey* in other texts.

s.t. - something, the 3rd person
(s.t.) - something implied
s.o. - someone, the 3rd person
sl. - singular form
pl. - plural form
rt. - root word
cmd. - command
lit. - literally
fig. - figuratively
i.e., - for example
See: - Redirection to a related word.

pick **tixʷm** – pick/get a plant object or clay.
tixʷm – S/he picked. **čn tixʷm, kʷ tixʷm**
es tixʷi – S/he is picking. **čnes tixʷi, kʷes tixʷi**
qs tixʷi – S/he is going to pick. **čiqs tixʷi, kʷqs tixʷi**
tíʔixʷm – They picked. **qeʔ tixʷm, p tixʷm**
es tíʔixʷi – They are picking. **qeʔes tixʷi, pes tixʷi**
qs tíʔixʷi – They are going to pick. **qeʔqs tixʷi, pqs tixʷi**

tixʷis – S/he picked s.t. **tixʷn, tixʷntxʷ**
es tixʷms – S/he is picking s.t. **ies tixʷm, as tixʷm**
qs tixʷms – S/he is going to pick s.t. **iqs tixʷm, aqs tixʷm**
tíʔixʷis – They picked s.t. **qeʔ tixʷntm, tixʷntp**
es tíʔixʷms – They are picking s.t. **qeʔes tixʷm, es tixʷmp**
qs tíʔixʷms – They are going to pick s.t. **qeʔqs tixʷm, qs tixʷmp**

es txʷtixʷi – S/he is picking (things). **čnes tixʷi, kʷes tixʷi**
es txʷtixʷms – S/he is picking things. **ies txʷtixʷm, as txʷtixʷm**

es łtitxʷi – S/he is picking a little. **čnes łtitxʷi, kʷes łtitxʷi**
es łtitxʷms – S/he is picking a little of s.t. **ies łtitxʷm, as łtitxʷm**

tixʷxʷ – It was picked.
tixʷxʷn – I was able to pick it.
tixʷntm – It was picked by somebody.

tixʷnuis – S/he/it finally picked s.t. **tixʷnuin, tixʷnuintxʷ**
tixʷšts – S/he/it picked s.t. for s.o. **tixʷštn, tixʷštxʷ**

sxʷtixʷm – one tasked to gather things. *prefix:* ***sxʷ...*** *– one tasked to do.*
txʷemn – one inclined to gather. *suffix:* ***...emn*** *– one inclined to do.*
txʷtxʷmuł – one that habitually gathers. *suffix:* ***...łmuł*** *– one that habitually does.*
sctixʷ – something that's been gathered. *prefix:* ***sc...*** *– s.t. that's been done/made/prepared.*
sntixʷtn – place to gather.
tixʷmn – something used to gather. *(i.e.,* ***peċeʔ****)*

tixʷiš – Gather. *cmd.*
tixʷwi – You all gather. *cmd.*
tixʷnt – Gather s.t. *cmd.*
tixʷnti – You all gather s.t. *cmd.*

tixʷlwis – go around and gather.
es tixʷlwisi – S/he is gathering here and there. **čnes tixʷlwisi, kʷes tixʷlwisi**
tixʷlwisiš – Gather here and there. *cmd.*
tixʷcnm – get/harvest food. *See:* ***harvest.***
tixʷłq – harvest. *See:* ***harvest.***

xʷu qeʔqs k̓ʷis tixʷi t sčiłt – Let's go get some white clay. **l šeẏ u iše txʷtíʔixʷm t sčiłt łu t sqsi** – That is where they got white clay long ago. **ha kʷ sxʷtixʷm** – Are you someone who gathers? **aẋí u tixʷxʷn** – I finally acquired it. **ƛ̓e tixʷntm** – It has already been picked. **tixʷntxʷ łu sċʔekʷ** – You picked a flower.

čłk̓ʷum – pick something up using an instrument or tool. *(i.e., a needle for beads, a pitchfork for hay/rocks, etc.)*
čłk̓ʷum – S/he picked up. **čn čłk̓ʷum, kʷ čłk̓ʷum**
es čłk̓ʷmi – S/he is picking up. **čnes čłk̓ʷmi, kʷes čłk̓ʷmi**
qs čłk̓ʷmi – S/he is going to pick up. **čiqs čłk̓ʷmi, kʷqs čłk̓ʷmi**

č̓łk̓ʷúʔum – They picked up. **qeʔ č̓łk̓ʷum, p č̓łk̓ʷum**
es č̓łk̓ʷmíʔi – They are picking up. **qeʔes č̓łk̓ʷmi, pes č̓łk̓ʷmi**
qs č̓łk̓ʷmíʔi – They are going to pick up. **qeʔqs č̓łk̓ʷmi, pqs č̓łk̓ʷmi**

č̓łk̓ʷntes – S/he picked s.t. up. **č̓łk̓ʷnten, č̓łk̓ʷntexʷ**
es č̓łk̓ʷums – S/he is picking s.t. up. **ies č̓łk̓ʷum, kʷes č̓łk̓ʷum**
qs č̓łk̓ʷums – S/he is going to pick s.t. up. **čiqs č̓łk̓ʷum, kʷqs č̓łk̓ʷum**
č̓łk̓ʷntéʔes – They picked s.t. up. **qeʔ č̓łk̓ʷntem, č̓łk̓ʷntep**
es č̓łk̓ʷums – They are picking s.t. up. **qeʔes č̓łk̓ʷum, es č̓łk̓ʷump**
qs č̓łk̓ʷums – They are going to pick s.t. up. **qeʔqs č̓łk̓ʷum, qs č̓łk̓ʷump**

č̓łk̓ʷunt – Pick it up. *cmd.*

ṅem č̓łk̓ʷntes – S/he will pick s.t. up. **ṅem č̓łk̓ʷnten, ṅem č̓łk̓ʷntexʷ**
ṅem č̓łk̓ʷntéʔes – They will pick s.t. up. **ṅem qeʔ č̓łk̓ʷntem, ṅem č̓łk̓ʷntep**
ṅem qs č̓łk̓ʷums – S/he will be picking s.t. up. **ṅem iqs č̓łk̓ʷum, ṅem aqs č̓łk̓ʷum**
ṅem qs č̓łk̓ʷúʔums – They will be picking s.t. up. **ṅem qeʔqs č̓łk̓ʷum, ṅem qs č̓łk̓ʷump**

č̓łk̓ʷunt l tins – Put (the bead) on the sinew. **č̓łk̓ʷunt l č̓łl̓x̣ʷé –** Put (the bead) on the needle.

q̇ʷleẇm – gather/pick berries and fruit.
q̇ʷléẇm – S/he picked. **čn q̇ʷléẇm, kʷ q̇ʷléẇm**
es q̇ʷléẇi – S/he is picking. **čnes q̇ʷléẇi, kʷes q̇ʷléẇi**
qs q̇ʷléẇi – S/he is going to pick. **čiqs q̇ʷléẇi, kʷqs q̇ʷléẇi**
es q̇ʷléʔeẇi – They are picking. **qeʔes q̇ʷléẇi, pes q̇ʷléẇi**

q̇ʷléẇis – S/he/it picked berries. **q̇ʷléẇn, q̇ʷléẇntxʷ**
es q̇ʷléẇms – S/he is picking berries. **ies q̇ʷléẇm, as q̇ʷléẇm**
qs q̇ʷléẇms – S/he is going to pick berries. **iqs q̇ʷléẇm, aqs q̇ʷléẇm**
es q̇ʷléʔeẇms – They are picking berries. **qeʔes q̇ʷléẇm, es q̇ʷléẇmp**

nq̇ʷléẇtn – container for berries.
scq̇ʷléẇm – something that's been picked. *prefix:* ***sc...*** *– s.t. that's been done/made/prepared.*

q̇ʷléẇiš – Pick berries. *cmd.*
q̇ʷléẇnt – Pick the berries. *cmd.*

ṅem p k̓ʷis q̇ʷléẇm t q̇itq̇m – You will all go picking strawberries.

q̇ʷl̓q̇ʷluscin, *q̇ʷl̓q̇ʷlusci* – pick and eat berries. *suffix:* ***...cin, ...cn*** *– action of the mouth.*
q̇ʷl̓q̇ʷluscinm – S/he picked and ate berries. **čn q̇ʷl̓q̇ʷluscinm, kʷ q̇ʷl̓q̇ʷluscinm**
es q̇ʷl̓q̇ʷluscini – S/he is picking and eating berries. **čnes q̇ʷl̓q̇ʷluscini, kʷes q̇ʷl̓q̇ʷluscini**
qs q̇ʷl̓q̇ʷluscini – S/he is going to pick and eat berries. **čiqs q̇ʷl̓q̇ʷluscini, kʷqs q̇ʷl̓q̇ʷluscini**

q̇ʷl̓q̇ʷlusciniš – Pick and eat berries. *cmd.*

ṅe p q̇ʷl̓q̇ʷlusci ṅem p wičm t nłámqeʔ – If you pick berries, you will see bears.

čsp̓im – thrash oats; gathering huckleberries *(when hitting the bush the berries fall onto a canvas). See:* ***thrash****.*

k̓ʷłxʷʔém – lift something up. *See:* ***lift****.*
k̓ʷłxʷeʔxʷʔémi – repeatedly lift something; picking something up.
es k̓ʷłxʷeʔxʷeʔmi – S/he is picking up. **čnes k̓ʷłxʷeʔxʷeʔmi, kʷes k̓ʷłxʷeʔxʷeʔmi**

The **i** following uvular consonants (UC) and the glottal stop **ʔ** sound like English "*ey*" as in the words th*ey*, h*ey*, wh*ey*, etc. Salish UC are: **q**, **q̇**, **qʷ**, **q̇ʷ**, **x̣**, **x̣ʷ**. For example, the suffix **...qin** – head/top, is often spelled using English *ey* as "q*ey*n". So **qi**, **q̇i**, **qʷi**, **q̇ʷi**, **x̣i**, **x̣ʷi**, may be spelled with English *ey* as **q***ey*, **q̇***ey*, **qʷ***ey*, **q̇ʷ***ey*, **x̣***ey*, **x̣ʷ***ey* in other texts.

s.t. - something, the 3rd person
(s.t.) - something implied
s.o. - someone, the 3rd person
sl. - singular form
pl. - plural form
rt. - root word
cmd. - command
lit. - literally
fig. - figuratively
i.e., - for example
See: - Redirection to a related word.

tixʷɫ – acquire something; get or receive something; gather. *See: **acquire**.*
ƛ̓e tixʷntm – It has already been picked. **tixʷntxʷ ɫu sċʔek̓ʷ** – You picked a flower. **l šeẏ u iše txʷtíʔixʷm t sčiɫt ɫu t sqsi** – That is where they got white clay long ago.

nk̓ʷéṅm – choose; pick; select; show the selection. *See: **try**.*

ẏamim – gather/collect things together. *See: **gather**.*

čmčeṁ – pick up and gather things cast away and unused. *See: **gather**.*

čmčeṁeɫp, *čmčeṁe* – pick up and gather branches and/or small pieces of wood. *See: **gather**.*

nweċ – dig something out with a tool. *See: **dig**.*

hetiṁ – tease *(more a playful tease than a bothersome tease)*. *See: **tease**.*

pickup truck

snʔukʷʔu – truck; pickup truck.

picture

sk̓ʷɫq̇ʔẏi – picture; photograph; postcard.
sk̓ʷɫq̇iq̇ʔeẏ – pictures; photographs; postcards.

k̓ʷɫq̇eẏim – draw a picture. *See: **draw**.*
ṅem qeʔ k̓ʷɫq̇ẏq̇eẏntem ɫu qeʔ sumeš – We'll paint pictures of our medicine power.

pie

pay – pie.

piece

ɫttil – piece; small shard. *rt: **til**– break.*
oiɫ – single piece.

pierce

čsɫx̣ʷmus, *čsɫx̣ʷmu* – pierce all the way through; permeable. *rt.: **ɫóx̣ʷ**– It has a hole.*
čsɫx̣ʷmusm – It let water/substances through. (i.e., cloth, filter, etc.)
es čsɫx̣ʷmus – It is pierced all the way through; it is permeable.

es čsɫx̣ʷmusi – S/he/it is piercing all the way through.

ɫóx̣ʷ – make a hole in something; puncture something; bore through. *See: **hole**.*
čɫx̣ʷɫx̣ʷéneʔ – pierce ears. *See: **earrings**.*

ƛ̓qʷómn – awl.

čptkʷumnálqʷ, *čptkʷumná* – crucify; pinned to wood. *See: **pin**.*

ilip – wounded/shot by a bullet, arrow or sharp stick. *See: **wound**.*

ilim – throw and strike something with a pointed object. *(throw an arrow, spear, sharp stick, etc.)* *See: **throw**.*

Pierre

pyél, piyél – Peter, Pete, Pierre.

pig

lkʷošó – pig; bacon; pork; ham. *(approximation to French word)*
lkʷlkʷošó – pigs.
ɫlkʷošó – piglets; little pig.
snlkʷošótn – pigpen. *prefix: **sn...** – a place of; suffix: **...tin, ...tn** – means of/device.*

npl̓pl̓qáqs – hog; pig *(has a flared nose)*. *rt.: **pelq** – thick.*

pigeon

x̣ʷċx̣ʷo – pigeon; rock dove; *Columba livia*.

pig feet

lkʷošó ucilšn – pig feet.

pika

sčiṅ – pika; rock rabbit; *Ochotona princeps*.

pikeminnow, northern **qʷq̓ʷéčn,** *qʷq̓ʷé* – northern pikeminnow; *Ptychocheilus oregonensis.*

pile **čx̣ʷoyqn** – pile things.
čx̣ʷoyqis – S/he piled s.t. **čx̣ʷoyqn, čx̣ʷoyqntxʷ**
es čx̣ʷoyqnms – S/he is piling s.t. **ies čx̣ʷoyqnm, as čx̣ʷoyqnm**
qs čx̣ʷoyqnms – S/he is going to pile s.t. **iqs čx̣ʷoyqnm, aqs čx̣ʷoyqnm**
čx̣ʷóʔoyqis – They piled s.t. **qeʔ čx̣ʷoyqntm, čx̣ʷoyqntp**
es čx̣ʷóʔoyqnms – They are piling s.t. **qeʔes čx̣ʷoyqnm, es čx̣ʷoyqnmp**

es čx̣ʷoyqn – It is piled.

čx̣ʷoyqnt – Pile it. *cmd.*

čx̣ʷoyqn tspisce – I piled it yesterday. **čx̣ʷoyqntxʷ tspisce** – You piled it yesterday. **čx̣ʷoyqntp néłi ƛ̓e čxʷʔéʔ t sw̓ewł** – You guys pile it up, because there are already a lot of fish.

> The **i** following uvular consonants (UC) and the glottal stop **ʔ** sound like English "*ey*" as in the words th*ey*, h*ey*, wh*ey*, etc. Salish UC are: **q, q̓, qʷ, q̓ʷ, x̣, x̣ʷ**. For example, the suffix **...qin** – head/top, is often spelled using English *ey* as "q*ey*n". So **qi, q̓i, qʷi, q̓ʷi, x̣i, x̣ʷi**, may be spelled with English *ey* as **q***ey*, **q̓***ey*, **qʷ***ey*, **q̓ʷ***ey*, **x̣***ey*, **x̣ʷ***ey* in other texts.

es p̓aṫ – It is something soft and squishy *(i.e., excrement, brains, a wet hide, etc.) (If someone has a big belly* ***es p̓aṫ*** *can be said about it.)*; figuratively when a person feels tired and loose.
es p̓aṫ – S/he feels tired and loose. **čnes p̓aṫ, kʷes p̓aṫ**

x̣ił čnes p̓aṫ – I do not feel good or I feel tired and loose.

snp̓ṫp̓ṫmán – jar; a container of soft squishy stuff. *rt.:* ***p̓aṫ*** *– s.t. soft/squishy; prefix:* ***sn...*** *– a place of; suffix:* ***...min, ...mn*** *– instrument/tool.*

p̓aṫqan – have messy hair; *derogatory*, dumb/splat head. *See:* ***dumb.***
p̓aṫoyʔe – jerk. *See:* ***dumb.***
p̓ṫaṫ – played out; have no energy; tired. *See:* ***tired.***

c̓ałxʷ – piled rock shelter/marker. *See:* ***rock.***

ṫqem – stack things; piled things; lying in a heap. *See:* ***stack.***

pileated woodpecker **spuwál̓qn** – pileated woodpecker; red-headed woodpecker; *Dryocopus pileatus.*

pill **scčq̓mus,** *scčq̓mu* – pill. *prefix:* ***sc...*** *– s.t. that's been done/made/prepared.*
exʷ x̣ʷa kʷ ep scčq̓mu čq̓musiš – Suppose you have pills, swallow it.

pillow **nčʔéneʔ** – pillow. *rt.:* ***čeʔ*** *– lump; suffix:* ***...eneʔ*** *– ear.*

pimple **sčečeʔus** – pimples; acne. *rt.:* ***čeʔ*** *– lump; suffix:* ***...us*** *– face, fire.*
sčeʔus – pimple; zit.

pin **čłččʔe** – headpin.

utčl̓e – safety pin.

čutčlenč – lacing pins of a tipi. *suffix:* ***...enč*** *– within. See:* ***tipi.***

lp̓x̣ʷoms – pin something to something.
es lp̓x̣ʷoms – S/he is pinning s.t. to s.t. **ies lp̓x̣ʷom, as lp̓x̣ʷom**

čptqʷalqʷ – tack something to something.
čptqʷalqʷm – S/he tacked. **čn čptqʷalqʷm, kʷ čptqʷalqʷm**
es čptqʷalqʷi – S/he is tacking. **čnes čptqʷalqʷi, kʷes čptqʷalqʷi**
qs čptqʷalqʷi – S/he is going to tack. **čiqs čptqʷalqʷi, kʷqs čptqʷalqʷi**

> s.t. - something, the 3rd person
> (s.t.) - something implied
> s.o. - someone, the 3rd person
> *sl.* - singular form
> *pl.* - plural form
> *rt.* - root word
> *cmd.* - command
> *lit.* - literally
> *fig.* - figuratively
> *i.e.,* - for example
> *See:* - Redirection to a related word.

čptqʷalqʷism – S/he tacked s.t. to the wall. **čptqʷalqʷn, čptqʷalqʷntxʷ**
es čptqʷalqʷms – S/he is tacking s.t. to the wall. **ies čptqʷalqʷm, as čptqʷalqʷm**
qs čptqʷalqʷms – S/he is going to tack s.t. to the wall. **iqs čptqʷalqʷm, aqs čptqʷalqʷm**

čtptqʷntes – S/he tacked s.t. to the wall. **čtptqʷnten, čtptqʷntexʷ**

čptkʷumnálqʷ, *čptkʷumná* – crucify; pinned to wood.

pinch **ċiṗ** – pinch.
ċiṗłċeʔ – S/he pinched (s.o.). **čn ċiṗłċeʔ, kʷ ċiṗłċeʔ**
es ċiṗłċʔei – S/he is pinching (s.o.). **čnes ċiṗłċʔei, as ċiṗłċʔei**
qs ċiṗłċʔei – S/he is going to pinch (s.o.). **čiqs ċiṗłċʔei, kʷqs ċiṗłċʔei**

ċiṗis – S/he pinched s.t. **ċiṗn, ċiṗntxʷ**
es ċiṗms – S/he is pinching s.t. **ies ċiṗm, as ċiṗm**
qs ċiṗms – S/he is going to pinch s.t. **iqs ċiṗm, aqs ċiṗm**

ċiṗntm – S/he got pinched by him/her. **qʷo ċiṗntm, kʷ ċiṗntm**

ċiṗnt – Pinch it. *cmd.*
ċiṗłċeʔ – pinch the body/flesh.
nċipsm – wink; close eye. *See: **wink**.*
k̇ʷłċiṗcnm – choke somebody. *See: **choke**.*

ta kʷ qes ċiṗłċeʔ – Don't pinch.

čiṗ – pinch with a device.
čiṗis – S/he pinch s.t. with a device. **čiṗn, čiṗntxʷ**
es čiṗms – S/he is pinching s.t. with a device. **ies čiṗm, as čiṗm**
q čiṗms – S/he is going to pinch s.t. with a device. **iqs čiṗm, aqs čiṗm**

čiṗṗ – S/he/it got pinched. **čn čiṗṗ, kʷ čiṗṗ**
čiṗntm – S/he/it got pinched by something. **qʷo čiṗntm, kʷ čiṗntm**

čiṗmn – pliers.

čiṗnt – Pinch it with a device. *cmd.*

čn čiṗṗ t čalmin – I got pinched by the scissors.

pine **sʔátqʷłp** – Ponderosa pine; bull pine; *Pinus ponderosa.*

qʷqʷliʔt – lodgepole pine; *Pinus contorta.*

ƛ̓iyalqʷ – white pine; *Pinus monticola.*

pineapple weed **nclclx̌ʷqin** – pineapple weed; *Matricaria discoidea. suffix: **...qin, ...qn** – top.*

pine beetle **sxʷyalqʷ** – wood worm; pine beetle worm.

pine cone **sččiċéʔ** – pine cone; tree cone.

pine drops **snčl̓ép ṫapmis** – pine drops. *lit. Coyote's arrow.*

pine grosbeak **nkʷtnáqs** – evening grosbeak, black-headed grosbeak, pine grosbeak.

pine marten **łoʔl̓ó** – pine marten, marten.

pine needles **čemeʔ** – pine needles.

pine squirrel **iscč** – pine squirrel; *Tamiasciurus hudsonicus.*

pink **i hen** – It is pink. **hnhen** – pinks. *pl.*
hnntes – S/he made it pink. **hnnten, hnntexʷ**
es henms – S/he is making it pink. **ies henm, as henm**
qs henms – S/he is going to make it pink. **iqs henm, aqs henm**

i łhhen – It is a little pink; pinkish.

hnint – Make it pink. *cmd.*

łkʷkʷil – pink. *lit. little red.*

pink eye **i čkʷlkʷils** – bloodshot eyes; pink eye. *circumfix:* ***č...us*** *– spherical object; eyes.*

pint **ppil̓** – pint.

pinto **q̇ay̓élxʷ** – pinto.
es q̇ay̓e – pinto.
q̇ay̓élxʷs – His/her pinto.

epł q̇ay̓é łu qeyqeyši – Qeyqeyshi had a pinto horse.

pipe **snmeṅxʷtn**, *snmé* – smoking pipe. *rt.:* ***meṅxʷ*** *– smoke; prefix:* ***sn...*** *– a place of; suffix:* ***...tin, ...tn*** *– means of/device.*

t̓peptn, *t̓pe* – pipe stem; chimney. *rt.:* ***t̓ip*** *– join/add to.*
łu es nt̓psnwéxʷi – Those who were smoking the pipe. **qeʔqs mnmé qeʔqs snt̓psnwéxʷi** – We'll pass the peace pipe.

pipsissewa **sčx̣lx̣lpu** – prince's pine; pipsissewa; *Chimaphila umbellata.*

pistol **nt̓q̇nčstéłċe**, *nt̓q̇nčste* – pistol, six-shooter. *lit. six hollows inside. prefix:* ***n...*** *– inside; prefix:* ***t̓q̇nčst...*** *– six; suffix:* ***...ełċeʔ*** *– inside contents, body, meat.*

Pistol Creek **čxʷqne** – Pistol Creek area, Flathead Nation. *rt.:* ***čuxʷ*** *– bowl formation.*

nq̇ʷsq̇ʷey – east end of Pistol Creek Mountain, Flathead Nation.

pitch **t̓ełtn** – pitch gum; Ponderosa pine pitch; sap. *rt.:* ***t̓eł*** *– make sticky.*

sƛ̓ƛ̓ukʷe – pitch wood.

łkʷkʷiyomqn – small voice; feminine voice; high pitch voice. *See:* ***small.***

cq̇minm – throw an object. *See:* ***throw.***

pitchfork **čłk̓ʷłk̓ʷmintn**, *čłk̓ʷłk̓ʷmi* – pitchfork. *rt.:* ***čłk̓ʷum*** *– pick up; suffix:* ***...min, ...mn*** *– instrument/tool. See:* ***pick.***

čłk̓ʷłk̓ʷum – pick things up repeatedly with an instrument/tool. *(i.e., using a pitchfork, picking up beads with a needle.)*
čłk̓ʷłk̓ʷum – S/he picked up repeatedly. **čn čłk̓ʷłk̓ʷum, kʷ čłk̓ʷłk̓ʷum**
es čłk̓ʷłk̓ʷmi – S/he is picking up repeatedly. **čnes čłk̓ʷłk̓ʷmi, kʷes čłk̓ʷłk̓ʷmi**
qs čłk̓ʷłk̓ʷmi – S/he is going to pick up repeatedly. **čiqs čłk̓ʷłk̓ʷmi, kʷqs čłk̓ʷłk̓ʷmi**
čłk̓ʷłk̓ʷúʔum – They picked up repeatedly. **qeʔ čłk̓ʷłk̓ʷum, p čłk̓ʷłk̓ʷum**
es čłk̓ʷłk̓ʷmíʔi – They are picking up repeatedly. **qeʔes čłk̓ʷłk̓ʷmi, pes čłk̓ʷłk̓ʷmi**

The **i** following uvular consonants (UC) and the glottal stop **ʔ** sound like English "*ey*" as in the words th*ey*, h*ey*, wh*ey*, etc. Salish UC are: **q, q̇, qʷ, q̇ʷ, x̣, x̣ʷ**. For example, the suffix **...qin** – head/top, is often spelled using English *ey* as "q*ey*n". So **qi, q̇i, qʷi, q̇ʷi, x̣i, x̣ʷi**, may be spelled with English *ey* as **q***ey*, **q̇***ey*, **qʷ***ey*, **q̇ʷ***ey*, **x̣***ey*, **x̣ʷ***ey* in other texts.

s.t. - something, the 3rd person
(s.t.) - something implied
s.o. - someone, the 3rd person
sl. - singular form
pl. - plural form
rt. - root word
cmd. - command
lit. - literally
fig. - figuratively
i.e., - for example
See: - Redirection to a related word.

qs čłk̓ʷłk̓ʷmíˀi – They are going to pick up repeatedly. **qeˀqs čłk̓ʷłk̓ʷmi, pqs čłk̓ʷłk̓ʷmi**

čłk̓ʷłk̓ʷntes – S/he picked up the things repeatedly. **čłk̓ʷłk̓ʷnten, čłk̓ʷłk̓ʷntexʷ**
es čłk̓ʷłk̓ʷmi – S/he is picking up the things repeatedly. **ies čłk̓ʷłk̓ʷum, as čłk̓ʷłk̓ʷum**
qs čłk̓ʷłk̓ʷmi – S/he is going to pick up the things repeatedly. **iqs čłk̓ʷłk̓ʷum, aqs čłk̓ʷłk̓ʷum**
čłk̓ʷłk̓ʷúˀum – They picked up the things repeatedly. **qeˀ čłk̓ʷłk̓ʷntem, čłk̓ʷłk̓ʷntep**
es čłk̓ʷłk̓ʷmíˀi – They are picking up the things repeatedly. **qeˀes čłk̓ʷłk̓ʷum, es čłk̓ʷłk̓ʷump**
qs čłk̓ʷłk̓ʷúˀums – They are going to pick up the things repeatedly. **qeˀqs čłk̓ʷłk̓ʷum, qs čłk̓ʷłk̓ʷump**

pitch wood

sƛ̓ƛ̓uk̓ʷe – pitch wood.

pity

qʷn̓qʷin̓t – pitiful; poor.
qʷn̓qʷin̓t – S/he/it is pitiful. **čn qʷn̓qʷin̓t, kʷ qʷn̓qʷin̓t**
qʷn̓qʷiˀin̓t – They are pitiful. **qeˀ qʷn̓qʷin̓t, p qʷn̓qʷin̓t**

nqʷn̓mis – S/he/it pitied s.o. **nqʷn̓min, nqʷn̓mintxʷ**
es nqʷn̓minms – S/he/it is pitying s.o. **ies nqʷn̓minm, as nqʷn̓minm**
nqʷn̓míˀis – They pitied s.o. **qeˀ nqʷn̓mintm, nqʷn̓mintp**

nqʷn̓qʷn̓éls – pity; be a kind person. *circumfix: **n…els** – want, feel. See: **kind**.*

qʷn̓qʷn̓us – S/he has a pitiful face. **čn qʷn̓qʷn̓us, kʷ qʷn̓qʷn̓us**
qʷn̓qʷn̓scin – S/he had pitiful words. **čn qʷn̓qʷn̓scin, kʷ qʷn̓qʷn̓scin**
qʷn̓mscut – pity one's self; have a hard time. *See: **hardship**.*
qʷn̓ečstm – cause someone to have a hard time; play a trick on someone. *See: **trick**.*

qʷo nqʷn̓mintm – I was pitied. **n̓e we qʷn̓qʷin̓t n̓em kʷen** – Even if he is poor, I will take him. **qeˀ uł qʷn̓qʷin̓t** – We are pitiful.

qiˀl – beg; insist; persuade; coaxed into. *See: **beg**.*

place

caq – place a single object upright; set down. *(the placement of a single object not the action of placing something down.)*
cqntés – S/he placed s.t./s.o. **cqntén, cqntéxʷ**
es cqéms – S/he is placing s.t./s.o. **ies cqém, as cqém**
qs cqéms – S/he is going to place s.t./s.o. **iqs cqém, aqs cqém**
cqntéˀes – They placed s.t./s.o. **qeˀ cqntém, cqntép**

es caq – It is placed.

cqent – Place it. *cmd.*
es cqsqá – S/he is parked; the car is set down. *See: **park**.*
es cqeuł – They are parked. *See: **park**.*

ncaq – place something upright inside. *rt.: **caq** – single object placed down.*
ncaq – S/he set it in. **čn ncaq, kʷ ncaq**
es ncaqi – S/he is setting it in. **čnes ncaqi, kʷes ncaqi**
qs ncaqi – S/he is going to set it in. **čiqs ncaqi, kʷqs ncaqi**
ncáˀaq – They set it in. **qeˀ ncaq, p ncaq**
es ncáˀaqi – They are setting it in. **qeˀes ncaqi, pes ncaqi**
qs ncáˀaqi – They are going to set it in. **qeˀqs ncaqi, pqs ncaqi**

sncaq – something used for setting something in.

ncqent – Set it in. *cmd.*
n̓cqaus, *n̓cqau* – place single object in a fire; cook/make coffee/tea. *See: **coffee**.*

ha ƛ̓e kʷ wis ṅcqaus t liti – Did you set the tea in/on the fire, stove, pot?

sil – place more than one object upright. *(the placement of objects not the action of placing something down.)*
slntes – S/he placed them. **slnten, slntexʷ**
es slims – S/he is placing them. **ies slim, as slim**
qs slims – S/he is going to place them. **iqs slim, aqs slim**

es sil – They are placed.

slint – Place them. *cmd.*

čłsil – set down more than one object upright on a surface. *(the placement of a more than one object not the action of placing things down.)*
es čłsil – It is set; the objects are placed.

čłslint – Set the table. *cmd.*
čłsliwi – Set the table, all of you. *cmd.*

ṫukʷ – put something down; lay something down; place something down. *See:* ***put.***

qmin – put things down; lay things down; place things down. *See:* ***put.***

čłqmin – put things on a surface. *See:* ***put.***

nqmnetkʷ – put things in the water. *See:* ***put.***

ye lʔe – in this place.
ye tl̓ʔe – from this place.

l šeẏ – in that place.
šeẏ tl̓ – from that place; from that time.

nk̓ʷulexʷ – another/one place/land.
č nk̓ʷulexʷ – at another place.

pusulexʷ – thinking of a certain place/area/land. *rt.:* ***spúʔus*** *– heart; suffix:* ***...ulexʷ*** *– land.*
es pusulexʷi – S/he is thinking of a place. **čnes pusulexʷi, kʷes pusulexʷi**

es miulexʷsts – S/he knows the place/area/land. **es miulexʷstn, es miulexʷstxʷ**
es miúʔulexʷsts – They know the place/area/land. **qeʔes miulexʷstm, es miulexʷstp**

ta es miulexʷstn – I do not know that place. **ha es miulexʷstxʷ –** Do you know that place?

łoqʷ – overlay; place something on/over something else *(not to cover)*; lay something on; drape something over a narrow/smaller object. *See:* ***lay over.***

q̇eʔ – put/place/squeeze inside something; inserted between. *See:* ***insert.***

The **i** following uvular consonants (UC) and the glottal stop ʔ sound like English "*ey*" as in the words *they, hey, whey,* etc. Salish UC are: **q, q̇, qʷ, q̇ʷ, x̣, x̣ʷ**. For example, the suffix **...qin** – head/top, is often spelled using English *ey* as "q*ey*n". So **qi, q̇i, qʷi, q̇ʷi, x̣i, x̣ʷi,** may be spelled with English *ey* as **q***ey*, **q̇***ey*, **qʷ***ey*, **q̇ʷ***ey*, **x̣***ey*, **x̣ʷ***ey* in other texts.

Placid Lake

čłq̇lʔe – Placid Lake, Montana.

plain

wnwinxʷ, *wnwi* – plainly visible; evident; apparent; very clear; obvious.
i wnwinxʷ – It is plainly visible; evident; apparent; very clear; it is obvious.

i wnwi łu skʷkʷlil – It is very clear and sunshiny. **wnwnwi łu sxʷtxʷtips –** Its ribs were showing, sticking out. **ṅem i wnwi łu anšušẇéł –** Your path will be very clear.

nunwinxʷps – The buttocks are plainly visible.
i nunwinxʷps – His/her buttocks are plainly visible.

s.t. - something, the 3rd person
(s.t.) - something implied
s.o. - someone, the 3rd person
sl. - singular form
pl. - plural form
rt. - root word
cmd. - command
lit. - literally
fig. - figuratively
i.e., - for example
See: - Redirection to a related word.

plains

čłčéwm – plain; mountainless land.

Plains **nčk̓ʷi** – Plains, Montana.

plant **k̓ʷólłq** – plant a garden; plant a crop; plant something. *rt.: k̓ʷul̓ – make/build/do.*
k̓ʷól̓łqm – S/he planted. **čn k̓ʷól̓łqm, kʷ k̓ʷól̓łqm**
es k̓ʷól̓łqi – S/he is planting. **čnes k̓ʷól̓łqi, kʷes k̓ʷól̓łqi**
qs k̓ʷól̓łqi – S/he is going to plant. **čiqs k̓ʷól̓łqi, kʷqs k̓ʷól̓łqi**

sk̓ʷól̓łq – garden; crop; plant.

k̓ʷól̓łqiš – Plant; make a garden. *cmd.*

k̓ʷl̓k̓ʷóʔol̓łq t spqi lewén k̓ʷl̓k̓ʷl̓áʔała xʷʔit – They planted wheat, oats, plants, lots.

es kʷʔál̓ulexʷi – Plants are coming up *(i.e., in the spring). See: **grow**.*
skʷʔal̓ulexʷ – things that grow on the land; grass. *rt.: **kʷʔal̓** – plants grow; suffix: **...ulexʷ** – land.*

nq̓eʔulexʷ – put in the ground. *(i.e., planting, etc.) rt.: **q̓eʔ** – put inside; suffix: **...ulexʷ** – land.*
es nq̓eʔulexʷms – S/he is putting s.t. in the ground. **ies nq̓eʔulexʷm, as nq̓eʔulexʷm**

snq̓eʔulexʷtn – place where s.t. is put in the ground. *(i.e., garden, field, etc.)*

plantain **nčʔéw̓s** – rattlesnake plantain; *Goodyera oblongifolia.*
nłmłmqʔéneʔ, sčłmłmqʔéneʔ – plantain; *Plantago.*

plaster **čpt̓áċeʔ** – plastered/cover in something. *suffix: **...iċéʔ** – covered in.*

čpt̓áċeʔ t malt – S/he/it is covered in mud.

čt̓łim – glue, plaster. *See: **glue**.*

plastic **nx̣lx̣listn** – plastic.

plate **qpéłċeʔ**, *qpé* – plate; dish. **qpqpéłċeʔ** – plates; dishes *pl.*
łqpéłċeʔ – little plate. **łqpqpéłċeʔ** *pl.*
kʷtiłqpéłċeʔ – big plate.

qpéłċeʔs – his/her plate. **inqpéłċeʔ, qnqpéłċeʔ**
qpéʔełċeʔs – their plate. **qeʔqpéłċeʔ, qnqpéłċʔemp**

tl̓ip łu qpé – plate broke.

play **memscut** – play; amuse one's self.
memscut – S/he/it played. **čn memscut, kʷ memscut**
es memscuti – S/he/it is playing. **čnes memscuti, kʷes memscuti**
qs memscuti – S/he/it is going to play. **čiqs memscuti, kʷqs memscuti**
memscúʔut – They played. **qeʔ memscut, p memscut**
es memscúʔuti – They are playing. **qeʔes memscuti, pes memscuti**
qs memscúʔuti – They are going to play. **qeʔqs memscuti, pqs memscuti**

memscutn – game. *suffix: **...tin, ...tn** – means of/device.*
m̓ém̓scu – playing cards.

memscutš – Play. *cmd.*

ha kʷ ṅé u čn k̓ʷis mémscut – May I go play? **es nte qs memscuti l anwi** – S/he wants to play with you. **čmlk̓ʷmasq̓t u memscut** – S/he played all day long. **xʷuyš memscutš** – Go play.

ml̓mel̓čstm – play with something. *rt.: **meʔl̓** – be agreeable; suffix: **...ečst, ...čst** – of the hand.*
ml̓mel̓čstm – S/he played with (s.t.). **čn lmel̓čstm, kʷ ml̓mel̓čstm**

es mlmelčsti – S/he is playing with (s.t.). **čnes mlmelčsti, kʷes mlmelčsti**
qs mlmelčsti – S/he is going to play with (s.t.). **čiqs mlmelčsti, kʷqs mlmelčsti**
mlméʔelčstm – They played with (s.t.). **qeʔ mlmelčstm, p mlmelčstm**
es mlméʔelčsti – They are playing with (s.t.). **qeʔes mlmelčsti, pes mlmelčsti**
qs mlméʔelčsti – They are going to play with (s.t.). **qeʔqs mlmelčsti, pqs mlmelčsti**

mlmelčstmsts – S/he played with s.t. **mlmelčstmstn, mlmelčstmstxʷ**
es mlmelčstmms – S/he is playing with s.t. **ies mlmelčstmm, as mlmelčstmm**
qs mlmelčstmms – S/he is going to play with s.t. **iqs mlmelčstmm, aqs mlmelčstmm**
mlméʔelčstmsts – They played with s.t. **qeʔ mlmelčstmstm, mlmelčstmstp**
es mlméʔelčstmms – They are playing with s.t. **qeʔes mlmelčstmm, es mlmelčstmmp**
qs mlméʔelčstmms – They are going to play with s.t. **qeʔqs mlmelčstmm, qs mlmelčstmmp**

The **i** following uvular consonants (UC) and the glottal stop **ʔ** sound like English "*ey*" as in the words th*ey*, h*ey*, wh*ey*, etc. Salish UC are: **q, q̓, qʷ, q̓ʷ, x̣, x̣ʷ**. For example, the suffix **...qin** – head/top, is often spelled using English *ey* as "q*ey*n". So **qi, q̓i, qʷi, q̓ʷi, x̣i, x̣ʷi**, may be spelled with English *ey* as **q***ey*, **q̓***ey*, **qʷ***ey*, **q̓ʷ***ey*, **x̣***ey*, **x̣ʷ***ey* in other texts.

mlmelčstiš – Play with (it). *cmd.*
mlmelčstmskʷ – Play with it. *cmd.*

ta qes mlmelčstmstxʷ – Do not play with it. **es mlmelčstmms ululims** – S/he is playing with his/her money. **es mlmelčsti l nqʷq̓ʷosmičn̓ sʔiłn** – S/he is playing with the dog food. **ta qes mlmelčstmstxʷ łu annuwewlštn** – Do not play with your language.

ƛ̓leẏeʔ – play dead. *See: **die**.*

ƛ̓lƛ̓llmist – making one's self still; play dead. *See: **die**.*

play ball

pk̓ʷlʔem – playing ball. *(i.e., basketball, baseball, football, etc.)*
es pk̓ʷlʔemi – S/he is playing ball. **čnes pk̓ʷlʔemi, kʷes pk̓ʷlʔemi**

sxʷpk̓ʷlʔem – one tasked to play ball. *prefix: **sxʷ...** – one tasked to do.*

či sxʷpk̓ʷlʔem – I am a ballplayer. **n̓e kʷ wis nčułqpéceʔ m sic kʷ ocqeʔ kʷqs pk̓ʷlʔemi** – When you finish washing the dishes then you can go outside to play ball. **čn x̣ʷełe x̣ʷl̓ čnes ntelsi čiqs pk̓ʷlʔemi** – I am hurrying because I want to play ball.

playing cards

m̓ém̓scutn, *m̓ém̓scu* – playing cards. *suffix: **...tin, ...tn** – means of/device.*

nx̣ʷq̓ʷew̓siš – Split (cut the cards). *cmd. See: **split**.*
nx̣ʷq̓ʷew̓sntxʷ – Split it (you cut the deck). *See: **split**.*

please

xʷumiʔ – An expression of politeness roughly translated to please or excuse me.

xʷumiʔ ci t̓iš – Please pass the sugar. **xʷumiʔ tʔe u čiqs šiẏu** – Excuse me, I am going to go through here.

pleased

nx̣sels – pleased; have good feelings. *rt.: **x̣est** – good; circumfix: **n...els** – want, feel.*
nx̣sels – S/he felt pleased. **čn nx̣sels, kʷ nx̣sels**
es nx̣selsi – S/he is feeling pleased. **čnes nx̣selsi, kʷes nx̣selsi**
qs nx̣selsi – S/he is going to feel pleased. **čiqs nx̣selsi, kʷqs nx̣selsi**
nx̣séʔels – They felt pleased. **qeʔ nx̣sels, p nx̣sels**
es nx̣séʔelsi – They are feeling pleased. **qeʔes nx̣selsi, pes nx̣selsi**
qs nx̣séʔelsi – They are going to feel pleased. **qeʔqs nx̣selsi, pqs nx̣selsi**

s.t. - something, the 3rd person
(s.t.) - something implied
s.o. - someone, the 3rd person
sl. - singular form
pl. - plural form
rt. - root word
cmd. - command
lit. - literally
fig. - figuratively
i.e., - for example
See: - Redirection to a related word.

nx̣selsmis – S/he was pleased with s.t./s.o. **nx̣selsmn, nx̣selsmntxʷ**
es nx̣selsms – S/he is feeling pleased with s.t./s.o. **čnes nx̣selsm, kʷes nx̣selsm**
qs nx̣selsi – S/he is going to feel pleased with s.t./s.o. **čiqs nx̣selsm, kʷqs nx̣selsm**
nx̣séʔelsmis – They felt pleased with s.t./s.o. **qeʔ nx̣selsmntm, nx̣selsmntp**
es nx̣séʔelsms – They are feeling pleased wih s.t./s.o. **qeʔes nx̣selsm, es nx̣selsmp**
qs nx̣séʔelsms – They are going to feel pleased with s.t./s.o. **qeʔqs nx̣selsm, qs nx̣selsmp**

nx̣selsiš – Be pleased. *cmd.*

nx̣selsmncn – I was pleased with you. **qeʔ nx̣selsłlt –** S/he was pleased with us.

pleasure

qʷam – pleasure; pleasing; pleasant; excellent.
nqʷmlsmist – S/he felt pleasure. **čn nqʷmlsmist, kʷ nqʷmlsmist**
es nqʷmlsmisti – S/he is feeling pleasure. **čnes nqʷmlsmisti, kʷes nqʷmlsmisti**
qs nqʷmlsmisti – S/he is going to feel pleasure. **čiqs nqʷmlsmisti, kʷqs nqʷmlsmisti**

nqʷmels – S/he took pleasure. **čn nqʷmels, kʷ nqʷmels**
es nqʷmelsi – S/he is taking pleasure. **čnes nqʷmelsi, kʷes nqʷmelsi**
qs nqʷmelsi – S/he is going to take pleasure. **čiqs nqʷmelsi, kʷqs nqʷmelsi**

nqʷmelsts – S/he made s.o. take pleasure. **nqʷmelstn, nqʷmelstxʷ**
es nqʷmelsms – S/he is making s.o. take pleasure. **ies nqʷmelsm, as nqʷmelsm**
qs nqʷmelsms – S/he is going to make s.o. take pleasure. **iqs nqʷmelsm, aqs nqʷmelsm**

nqʷmelsmis – S/he took pleasure in s.t./s.o. **nqʷmelsmn, nqʷmelsmntxʷ**
es nqʷmelsmms – S/he is taking pleasure in s.t./s.o. **ies nqʷmelsmm, as nqʷmelsmm**
qs nqʷmelsmms – S/he is going to take pleasure in s.t./s.o. **iqs nqʷmelsmm, aqs nqʷmelsmm**

nqʷmelsmnt – Take pleasure in it. *cmd.*

es qʷamqʷmcnmist – S/he speaks pleasantly. **čn qʷamqʷmcnmist, kʷ qʷamqʷmcnmist**

nqʷamqʷmcin – S/he spoke pleasantly. **čn nqʷamqʷmcin, kʷ nqʷamqʷmcin**
es nqʷamqʷmcini – S/he is speaking pleasantly. **čnes nqʷamqʷmcini, kʷes nqʷamqʷmcini**

nqʷamqʷmcis – S/he spoke pleasantly to s.o. **nqʷamqʷmcin, nqʷamqʷmcintxʷ**
es nqʷamqʷmcinms – S/he is speaking pleasantly to s.o. **ies nqʷamqʷmcinm, as nqʷamqʷmcinm**

nqʷamqʷmetkʷ – excellent water. *rt.: **qʷamqʷmt** – excellent; suffix: **...etkʷ, ...tkʷ** – liquid*

qʷamqʷmt – excellent; beautiful; pleasing. *See: **excellent**.*

qʷamqʷmt łu asck̓ʷul̓ – Your work is excellent. **nłapa qʷamqʷmt –** Really excellent!

plenty

qʷyulexʷ – rich, wealthy. *See: **rich**.*

pliers

čip̓mn – pliers. *lit. something that pinches.*

k̓ʷʔemin – pliers. *lit. something that bites.*

plow

t̓ulexʷ – plow. *rt.: **t̓il** – tear; suffix: **...ulexʷ** – land.*
t̓ulexʷm – S/he plowed. **čn t̓ulexʷm, kʷ t̓ulexʷm**
es t̓ulexʷi – S/he is plowing. **čnes t̓ulexʷi, kʷes t̓ulexʷi**
qs t̓ulexʷi – S/he is going to plow. **čiqs t̓ulexʷi, kʷqs t̓ulexʷi**

t̓ulexʷtn – plow. *suffix: **...tin, ...tn** – means of/device.*

pluck

čłqepm – pluck feathers.
čn čłqepm t skʷiskʷs – I plucked the feathers off the chicken.

čċoʔqep – pluck/pull feathers.
čċoʔqepm – S/he/it plucked feathers. **čn čċoʔqepm, kʷ čċoʔqepm**
es čċoʔqepi – S/he/it is plucking feathers. **čnes čċoʔqepi, kʷes čċoʔqepi**

łoq̇ʷ – make bare; peel *(i.e., peeling bitterroot, peeling camas, plucking the fuzz off a bird). See: **peel**.*

> The **i** following uvular consonants (UC) and the glottal stop **ʔ** sound like English "*ey*" as in the words th*ey*, h*ey*, wh*ey*, etc. Salish UC are: **q**, **q̇**, **qʷ**, **q̇ʷ**, **x̣**, **x̣ʷ**. For example, the suffix ...**qin** – head/top, is often spelled using English *ey* as "q*ey*n". So **qi**, **q̇i**, **qʷi**, **q̇ʷi**, **x̣i**, **x̣ʷi**, may be spelled with English *ey* as **q***ey*, **q̇***ey*, **qʷ***ey*, **q̇ʷ***ey*, **x̣***ey*, **x̣ʷ***ey* in other texts.

plug **k̓ʷłntqep** – It is plugged inside. *circumfix: **k̓ʷłn...p** – opening.*

plum **čťeťeʔus**, *čťeťeʔu* – wild plum; plum.

čťaťasalqʷ – plum tree.

plume **čqʷlpelxʷ**, *čqʷlpe* – feather plume.

pocket **snlulwá** – pocket.

ƛ̓áqneʔ – pocket.

pocket gopher **puľyeʔ** – mole; northern pocket gopher; *Thomomys talpoides*.

skʷuṁcn – pocket gopher; *Thomomys idahoensis*.

pocketknife **čľoľopa** – pocketknife.

point **ċóq̇ʷ** – point.
ċóq̇ʷm – S/he pointed. **čn ċóq̇ʷm, kʷ ċóq̇ʷm**
es ċóq̇ʷi – S/he is pointing. **čnes ċóq̇ʷi, kʷes ċóq̇ʷi**
qs ċóq̇ʷi – S/he is going to point. **čiqs ċóq̇ʷi, kʷqs ċóq̇ʷi**
ċóʔoq̇ʷm – They pointed. **qeʔ ċóq̇ʷm, p ċóq̇ʷm**
es ċóʔoq̇ʷi – They are pointing. **qeʔes ċóq̇ʷi, pes ċóq̇ʷi**

ċóq̇ʷis – S/he pointed at it. **ċóq̇ʷn, ċóq̇ʷntxʷ**
es ċóq̇ʷms – S/he is pointing at it. **ies ċóq̇ʷm, as ċóq̇ʷm**
qs ċóq̇ʷms – S/he is going to point at it. **iqs ċóq̇ʷm, aqs ċóq̇ʷm**
ċóʔoq̇ʷis – They pointed at it. **qeʔ ċóq̇ʷntm, ċóq̇ʷntp**
es ċóʔoq̇ʷms – They are pointing at it. **qeʔes ċóq̇ʷm, es ċóq̇ʷmp**

ċóq̇ʷntm – S/he was pointed at. **qʷo ċóq̇ntm, kʷ ċóq̇ʷntm**

sxʷċóq̇ʷm – one tasked to point *(as in stickgame). prefix: **sxʷ...** – one tasked to do.*
ċóq̇ʷmn – pointer finger. *suffix: **...min, ...mn** – instrument/tool.*

ċóq̇ʷiš – Point. *cmd.*
ċóq̇ʷnt – Point at it. *cmd.*

ċóq̇ʷnt ci snčłeʔľiłntn – Point at the table.
ċóq̇ʷnt łu ṗaq̇mn č anwi – Point the flashlight at yourself.

tolposqn – point with the lips. *rt.: **tol** – straight vertical; suffix: **...posqn** – lips*
tolposqn – S/he pointed with the lips. **čn tolposqn, kʷ tolposqn**
es tolposqni – S/he is pointing with the lips. **čnes tolposqni, kʷes tolposqni**
qs tolposqni – S/he is going to point with the lips. **čiqs tolposqni, kʷqs tolposqni**

tolposqnmis – S/he pointed at s.t./s.o. with the lips. **tolposqnmn, tolposqnmntxʷ**
es tolposqnms – S/he is pointing at s.t./s.o. with the lips. **ies tolposqnm, as tolposqnm**
qs tolposqnms – S/he is going to point at s.t./s.o. with the lips. **iqs tolposqnm, aqs tolposqnm**

> s.t. - something, the 3rd person
> (s.t.) - something implied
> s.o. - someone, the 3rd person
> *sl.* - singular form
> *pl.* - plural form
> *rt.* - root word
> *cmd.* - command
> *lit.* - literally
> *fig.* - figuratively
> *i.e.,* - for example
> *See:* - Redirection to a related word.

tolposqniš – Point with your lips. *cmd.*
tolposqnmnt – Point at it with your lips. *cmd.*

čtóls – point with the eyes; show acknowledgement by looking. *See:* ***acknowledge.***

tóls – point with the head or face; show acknowledgement. *See:* ***acknowledge.***

ƛ̓im – comes to a point.
es nƛ̓mƛ̓maqs – It has points.

i nłƛ̓ƛ̓imaqs – It has a sharp point. *See:* ***sharp.***

xʷƛ̓im – whittle. *See:* ***whittle.***

nƛ̓mawsqn – pointed head *(used as a derogatory statement).*

n...aqs, n...qs – *circumfix indicating that something goes to a point, typically used in words involving the nose or a road.*
es nƛ̓mƛ̓maqs – It has points.
nxʷaʔamaqs – many noses; many roads.
nawawpaqs – runny nose.
nx̣saqs – good road; good nose. *prefix:* ***x̣s...*** *– good.*
nčsaqs – bad road; bad nose. *prefix:* ***čs...*** *– bad.*
ntx̣ʷaqs – straight road. *rt.:* ***tox̣ʷ*** *– straight.*
nusšnáqs – long road. *rt.:* ***wisšn*** *– long.*

poison

čnilm – poison someone.
čnilis – S/he poisoned s.o. **čniln, čnilntxʷ**
es čnilms – S/he is poisoning s.o. **ies čnilm, as čnilm**
qs čnilms – S/he is going to poison s.o. **iqs čnilm, aqs čnilm**
čníʔilis – They poisoned s.o. **qeʔ čnilntm, čnilntp**
es čníʔilms – They are poisoning s.o. **qeʔes čnilm, es čnilmp**

es čnil – S/he is poisoned. **čnes čnil, kʷes čnil**
čnil̓l – infected; s/he got poisoned.
čnilntm – S/he was poisoned. **qʷo čnilntm, kʷ čnilntm**

čnilmn, *čnil* – poison. *suffix:* ***...min, ...mn*** *– instrument/tool.*

čnilnt – Poison him/her/it. *cmd.*
čnilncut – S/he/it poisoned one's self. **čn čnilncut, kʷ čnilncut**
čnilscut – S/he poisoned one's self purposely. **čn čnilscut, kʷ čnilscut**

nixʷ – poisonous.

poison ivy

sul̓aqeʔ – poison ivy; *Toxicodendron radicans.*

poke

łwepł – poke an orifice.
łwepł – S/he poked an orifice. **čn łwepł, kʷ łwepł**

łwepłis – S/he poked the orifice. **łwepłn, łwepłntxʷ**
es łwepłms – S/he is poking the orifice. **ies łwepłm, as łwepłm**
qs łwepłms – S/he is going to poke the orifice. **iqs łwepłm, aqs łwepłm**

łwepłntm – S/he/it was poked.

łwepł t sululmi – S/he poked/cleaned the rifle.

x̣ʷoiqʷm – poke at something. *(i.e., pile, fire, etc.)*

x̣ʷoiqʷm – S/he poked at s.t. **čn x̣ʷoiqʷm, kʷ x̣ʷoiqʷm**
es x̣ʷoiqʷi – S/he is poking at s.t. **čnes x̣ʷoiqʷi, kʷes x̣ʷoiqʷi**

caqʷm – poke/stick into/through something with a cylindrical object.
caqʷis – S/he poked it into/through something. **caqʷn, caqʷntxʷ**
es caqʷms – S/he is poking it into/through something. **ies caqʷm, as caqʷm**
qs caqʷms – S/he is poking it into/through something. **iqs caqʷm, aqs caqʷm**

ncaqʷmn – something used to poke/stick into/through something, *(i.e., stick used in the camas bake; stick used to poke at the fire; etc.). (The stick is placed in the middle prior to putting the contents used in the camas baking pit. After the pit is prepared the stick is pulled out and water is poured in the hole left by the stick.)*

caqʷnt – Put it in/through it. *cmd.*

čłłuús – get poked in the eye. *See: **eye**.*

łˀum – pierce something with a sharp object. *See: **stab**.*

łóx̣ʷ – make a hole in something; puncture something; bore through. *See: **hole**.*

ċiq – prickly. *See: **prickly**.*

> The **i** following uvular consonants (UC) and the glottal stop **ˀ** sound like English "*ey*" as in the words *they, hey, whey,* etc. Salish UC are: **q, q̇, qʷ, q̇ʷ, x̣, x̣ʷ**. For example, the suffix **...qin** – head/top, is often spelled using English *ey* as "q*ey*n". So **qi, q̇i, qʷi, q̇ʷi, x̣i, x̣ʷi**, may be spelled with English *ey* as **q***ey*, **q̇***ey*, **qʷ***ey*, **q̇ʷ***ey*, **x̣***ey*, **x̣ʷ***ey* in other texts.

poker **x̣ʷoiqʷmn** – something used to poke around at something. *(i.e., fire poker)*

polar bear **čpqłpuṁċeˀ** – polar bear; *Ursus maritimus*.

pole **sq̇eẏmn** – pole; tipi pole.

čqq̇ṁé – fishing pole.

yollqʷ – big pole.

police **sxʷkʷnem** – one tasked to take/grab; police. *prefix: **sxʷ...** – one tasked to do.*

sxʷlčim – one tasked to tie up; police. *prefix: **sxʷ...** – one tasked to do.*

polite **k̓ʷłpusncut**, *k̓ʷłpusncu* – self-conscious; backward; shy; bashful; polite; considerate; does not impose. *See: **self-conscious**.*

xʷumiˀ – An expression of politeness roughly translated to please or excuse me. *See: **please**.*

pollution **i ṫił sx̣aap** – The air is dirty, polluted.

Polson **nčmqnetkʷ**, *nčmqne* – Polson, Flathead Nation. *lit. head/top of the water. suffix: **...etkʷ, ...tkʷ** – liquid*

polygon **es q̇tq̇it** – square; has flat sides.
clčsq̇tq̇it – pentagon; has five flat sides.
ṫqnčsq̇tq̇it – hexagon; has six flat sides.
sṗl̓čsq̇tq̇it – heptagon; has seven flat sides.
henmsq̇tq̇it – octagon; has eight flat sides.
x̣ntsq̇tq̇it – nonagon; has nine flat sides.
upnčsq̇tq̇it – decagon; has ten flat sides.

pond **čłqq̇lip**, *čłqq̇li* – pond; little lake.

nsixʷlexʷ – puddle; pond. *rt.: **sixʷ** – pour/spill; suffix: **...ulexʷ** – land.*
słsesixʷ – puddle. *rt.: **sixʷ** – pour/spill.*

> s.t. - something, the 3rd person
> (s.t.) - something implied
> s.o. - someone, the 3rd person
> *sl.* - singular form
> *pl.* - plural form
> *rt.* - root word
> *cmd.* - command
> *lit.* - literally
> *fig.* - figuratively
> *i.e.,* - for example
> *See:* - Redirection to a related word.

Ponderosa pine **sʔátqʷɫp** – Ponderosa pine; bull pine; *Pinus ponderosa.* **sʔatátqʷɫp** *pl.*

t̓el̓tn – Ponderosa pine sap.

pony **sncṁasqáx̣eʔ,** *sncṁasqá* – shetland pony.

pool **čɫx̣ʷlx̣ʷlq̓ʷi** – playing pool/billiards.
čɫx̣ʷlx̣ʷlq̓ʷi – S/he played pool. **čn čɫx̣ʷlx̣ʷlq̓ʷi, kʷ čɫx̣ʷlx̣ʷlq̓ʷi**
es čɫx̣ʷlx̣ʷlq̓ʷi – S/he is playing pool. **čnes čɫx̣ʷlx̣ʷlq̓ʷi, kʷes čɫx̣ʷlx̣ʷlq̓ʷi**
qs čɫx̣ʷlx̣ʷlq̓ʷi – S/he is going to play pool. **čiqs čɫx̣ʷlx̣ʷlq̓ʷi, kʷqs čɫx̣ʷlx̣ʷlq̓ʷi**

ha kʷqs k̓ʷis čɫx̣ʷlx̣ʷlq̓ʷi – Are you going to go play pool?

pool table **snčɫx̣ʷlx̣ʷlq̓ʷi** – pool table.

poor **qʷṅqʷiṅt** – pitiful; poor. *See:* ***pity.***

scqʷṅmscut – hardship. *prefix:* ***sc...*** *– s.t. that's been done/made/prepared. See:* ***hardship.***

yéṁmist, *yéṁm* – despaired; frustrated; troubled; worried; have a block; have a dilemma. *See:* ***despair.***

pop **nt̓išk̓ʷ** – sweet liquid; pop; Kool-aid.

čnes susti t nt̓išk̓ʷ – I am drinking pop. **uɫéʔ čiqs susti t nt̓išk̓ʷ** – I am going to drink pop again.

t̓ikʷ – pop sound.
t̓ikʷ – gun blast.

t̓kʷt̓ikʷlš – shooting around.

popcorn **čtltl̓péw̓s ɫkʷlkʷáli** – popcorn.

staq̓ʷt ɫkʷlkʷali – popcorn.

porcupine **sk̓ʷil̓** – porcupine; *Erethizon dorsatum.*

pork **lkʷošó** – pig; bacon; pork; ham. *(approximation to French word)*

possess **nɫqqeɫċeʔ** – dwell/inhabit the inside; possess. *See:* ***dwell.***

possible **k̓ʷl̓lutm** – It can be made; possible. *See:* ***work.***

post **nšt̓ulexʷtn** – post. *rt.:* ***šit̓*** *– stand upright; suffix:* ***...ulexʷ*** *– land; suffix:* ***...tin, ...tn*** *– means of/device.*

nčlulexʷtn – posts. *rt.:* ***čil*** *– standing upright; suffix:* ***...ulexʷ*** *– land; suffix:* ***...tin, ...tn*** *– means of/device.*

postage stamp **čcpq̓min** – postage stamp. *rt.:* ***čcpaq̓*** *– sticky; suffix:* ***...min*** *– instrument.*

postcard **sk̓ʷɫq̓ʔiʔ** – picture; photograph; postcard.
sk̓ʷɫq̓iq̓ʔey̓ – pictures; photographs; postcards.

Post Creek **k̓ʷɫnčmé** – Post Creek, Flathead Nation. *lit. trees growing in circle with small gateway. rt.:* ***čim*** *– constriction; circumfix:* ***k̓ʷɫn...p*** *– opening.*

post office **snčɫq̓ey̓mintn** – post office; library. *rt.:* ***čɫq̓ey̓min*** *– go after paper; prefix:* ***sn...*** *– a place of; suffix:* ***...tin, ...tn*** *– means of/device.*
čiqs k̓ʷis čɫq̓ey̓mini – I am going to go to the post office.

snčtelmn – post office. *prefix:* ***sn...*** *– a place of.*

pot **snṫpustn,** *snṫpu* – cooking pot; boiling pot. *rt.:* ***nṫpus*** *– boil; prefix:* ***sn...*** *– a place of; suffix:* ***...tin, ...tn*** *– means of/device.*

sṅcqaustn, *sṅcqau* – coffee pot. *rt.:* ***caq*** *– single object placed down; prefix:* ***sn...*** *– a place of; affix:* ***...us*** *– face, fire; suffix:* ***...tin, ...tn*** *– means of/device.*

potato **patáq** – potato.

skʷṅkʷinm, *skʷṅkʷi* – spring beauty; Indian potato.

sqáqʷocn – arrowleaf; wapato; water potato; *Sagittaria latifolia.*

scʔacqʷ – something that's been roasted. *(i.e., a potato, meat, etc.) prefix:* ***sc...*** *– s.t. that's been done/made/prepared.*

potent **yoyoót** – strong. *See:* ***strong.***

Potomac **qľsa** – Potomac, Montana.

pound **tʔem** – pound; hammer; bump. *See:* ***hammer.***

łteteʔmin – hammer; tool to pound.

ṅem qeʔ ntéʔeʔeľistm – We're going to beat them up. **t q̓ʷi u es ṫeṫemi ci kʷtisi t sppq̓ʷé** – Big Blanket is pounding the dried meat with a round rock.

sppq̓ʷé – pound dried meat.

sx̣emt – pound in weight. *See:* ***heavy.***

pour **npkʷétkʷ** – pour round objects in water. *(i.e., berries, rocks, etc.) rt.:* ***pukʷ*** *– pour round objects; suffix:* ***...etkʷ, ...tkʷ*** *– liquid*
es npkʷetkʷ – It is spawning. *suffix:* ***...etkʷ, ...tkʷ*** *– liquid*

npkʷétkʷis – S/he poured s.t. in the water. **npkʷétkʷn, npkʷétkʷntxʷ**
es npkʷétkʷms – S/he is pouring s.t. in the water. **ies npkʷétkʷm, as npkʷétkʷm**
qs npkʷétkʷms – S/he is going to pour s.t. in the water. **iqs npkʷétkʷm, aqs npkʷétkʷm**
npkʷéʔetkʷis – They poured s.t. in the water. **qeʔ npkʷétkʷntm, npkʷétkʷntp**
es npkʷéʔetkʷms – They are pouring s.t. in the water. **qeʔes npkʷétkʷm, es npkʷétkʷmp**
qs npkʷéʔetkʷms – They are going to pour s.t. in the water. **qeʔqs npkʷétkʷm, qs npkʷétkʷmp**

npkʷétkʷnt – Pour s.t. in the water. *cmd.*
pukʷ – spill/pour round objects. *(i.e., rocks, berries, marbles, apples, etc.) See:* ***spill.***
čłpukʷ – spread/pour round things out on a surface of something. *(i.e., berries, marbles, etc.) See:* ***spread.***

čn npkʷetkʷm t sṫša – I put huckleberries in the water.

sixʷm – spill liquid out; pour liquid out. *See:* ***spill.***
nsixʷm – S/he/it poured in (s.t.). **čn nsixʷm, kʷ nsixʷm**
es nsixʷi – S/he/it is pouring in (s.t.). **čnes nsixʷi, kʷes nsixʷi**
qs nsixʷi – S/he/it is going to pour in (s.t.). **čiqs nsixʷi, kʷqs nsixʷi**
nsixʷis – S/he/it poured s.t. in. **nsixʷn, nsixʷntxʷ**
es nsixʷms – S/he/it is pouring s.t. in. **ies nsixʷm, as nsixʷm**
qs nsixʷms – S/he/it is going to pour s.t. in. **iqs nsixʷm, aqs nsixʷm**

čqqʷusm – pour/dump large objects.
čqqʷusis – S/he/it poured it. **čqqʷusn, čqqʷusntxʷ**
čqqʷúʔusis – They poured it. **qeʔ čqqʷusntm, čqqʷusntp**

The **i** following uvular consonants (UC) and the glottal stop ʔ sound like English "*ey*" as in the words th*ey*, h*ey*, wh*ey*, etc. Salish UC are: **q, q̓, qʷ, q̓ʷ, x̣, x̣ʷ**. For example, the suffix ...**qin** – head/top, is often spelled using English *ey* as "q*ey*n". So **qi, q̓i, qʷi, q̓ʷi, x̣i, x̣ʷi**, may be spelled with English *ey* as **q***ey*, **q̓***ey*, **qʷ***ey*, **q̓ʷ***ey*, **x̣***ey*, **x̣ʷ***ey* in other texts.

s.t. - something, the 3rd person
(s.t.) - something implied
s.o. - someone, the 3rd person
sl. - singular form
pl. - plural form
rt. - root word
cmd. - command
lit. - literally
fig. - figuratively
i.e., - for example
See: - Redirection to a related word.

ṅem čqqʷusntxʷ anyóq̓ʷi – You will dump your rotten wood.

np̓ťatkʷm – pour/dump a viscous substance in water *(i.e., brains, wet hide, honey, etc.). See: **dump**.*

poq̓ʷ – spill/pour/dump powdered substances. *(i.e., salt, sugar, flour, gunpowder, ash, etc.) See: **spill**.*

laqʷm – splash/pour water. *(i.e., in a sweat, etc.) See: **splash**.*

pout **x̣ił kʷ speƛ̓m –** You are bitterroot; you are pouting.

powder **es p̓oqʷm –** It is powder. *(i.e., dust, dirt, etc.)*
pq̓ʷmin – powder.
npq̓ʷmin – gunpowder.
sppq̓ʷé – pound dried meat.

nméƛ̓mn – baking powder.

powder room **snxʷémstn –** powder room. *prefix: **sn...** – a place of; suffix: **...tin, ...tn** – means of/device.*

power **syoyoot –** physical strength/power.

sumeš – spiritual/medicine power; guardian/medicine spirit. *It is not common for someone to talk about their **sumeš**. It is so personal that even a closest friend or family member might not know.*
ṅem qeʔ k̓ʷłq̓y̓q̓eyntem łu qeʔ sumeš – We'll paint pictures of our medicine power.

powerful **sisyus –** smart; clever; good at something. *See: **smart**.*
xʷʔit łu sisyus ƛ̓eʔkʷilš – There are lots of smart, powerful medicine men.

yoyoót – strong. *See: **strong**.*

powwow **yapqin –** gather for celebration; powwow. *rt.: **iap** – more than one arrived there; suffix: **...qin, ...qn** – top.*
es yapqiʔini – They are gathering for a powwow.

es yapqin – It is a gathering; a celebration; a powwow.

syapqin – celebration; powwow.

y̓ay̓at łu syapqinm – rare powwow; celebration.

practice **qʷaqʷemncut,** *qʷaqʷemncú* **–** practice, drill, train, study. *rt.: **qʷʔem** – get accustomed; suffix: **...cut** – action to the self. See: **accustomed**.*
qʷaqʷemncut – S/he/it practiced. **čn qʷaqʷemncut, kʷ qʷaqʷemncut**
es qʷaqʷemncuti – S/he/it is practicing. **čnes qʷaqʷemncuti, kʷes qʷaqʷemncuti**
qs qʷaqʷemncuti – S/he/it is going to practice. **čiqs qʷaqʷemncuti, kʷqs qʷaqʷemncuti**
qʷaqʷemncúʔut – They practiced. **qeʔ qʷaqʷemncut, p qʷaqʷemncut**
es qʷaqʷemncúʔuti – They are practicing. **qeʔes qʷaqʷemncuti, pes qʷaqʷemncuti**
qs qʷaqʷemncúʔuti – They are going to practice. **qeʔqs qʷaqʷemncuti, pqs qʷaqʷemncuti**

isqʷéʔm – my habit; it is my practice.

qʷaqʷemncutš – Practice. *cmd.*

ṅem tl̓ ciʔ qʷaqʷemncú – I will study harder. **es qʷaqʷemncuti qs sxʷṁiṁey̓ʔm –** S/he is practicing to be a teacher.

prairie **es łq̓ʷólexʷ –** meadow.
łq̓ʷólexʷ, *łq̓ʷó* **–** Little Prairie *(along the middle fork of the Jocko River, Flathead Nation).*

es nq̓li – little opening/meadow.

prairie chicken **sq̓óxʷlu,** *sq̓ó* – sharp-tailed grouse; prairie chicken; *Tympanuchus phasianellus jamesi.*

prairie chicken dance **snsqq̓ostn** – prairie chicken dance. *rt.:* ***sq̓o*** *– prairie chicken; prefix:* ***sn...*** *– a place of; suffix:* ***...tin, ...tn*** *– means of/device.*

es nsqq̓ostni – S/he is prairie chicken dancing. **čnes nsqq̓ostni, kʷes nsqq̓ostni**
es nsqq̓óʔostni – They are prairie chicken dancing. **qeʔes nsqq̓ostni, pes nsqq̓ostni**

es qqowisti – S/he is prairie chicken dancing.
es nqqowistelsi – S/he is wanting to prairie chicken dance.

ha es yostexʷ snsqq̓ostn – Do you know how to prairie chicken dance?

snx̣ʷalmncutn – prairie chicken dance. *rt.:* ***x̣ʷal*** *– flutter/shake; prefix:* ***sn...*** *– a place of; suffix:* ***...tin, ...tn*** *– means of/device.*

es x̣ʷalmncuti – S/he is prairie chicken dancing. **čnes x̣ʷalmncuti, kʷes x̣ʷalmncuti**
es x̣ʷalmncúʔuti – They are prairie chicken dancing. **qeʔes x̣ʷalmncuti, pes x̣ʷalmncuti**

es nx̣ʷalmnstelsi – S/he is wanting to prairie chicken dance.

> The **i** following uvular consonants (UC) and the glottal stop **ʔ** sound like English "*ey*" as in the words *they, hey, whey,* etc. Salish UC are: **q, q̓, qʷ, q̓ʷ, x̣, x̣ʷ**. For example, the suffix ...**qin** – head/top, is often spelled using English *ey* as "*qeyn*". So **qi, q̓i, qʷi, q̓ʷi, x̣i, x̣ʷi,** may be spelled with English *ey* as **q***ey*, **q̓***ey*, **qʷ***ey*, **q̓ʷ***ey*, **x̣***ey*, **x̣ʷ***ey* in other texts.

prairie dog **heẇheẇmuł** – black-tailed prairie dog; *Cynomys ludovicianus. lit. one that habitually barks.*

słkʷu – white-tailed prairie dog; *Cynomys leucurus.*

praise **kʷtncinm** – praise; talk highly of someone; speak big of someone. *suffix:* ***...cin, ...cn*** *– action of the mouth.*

kʷtncinmis – S/he praised s.o. **kʷtncinmn, kʷtncinmntxʷ**
es kʷtncinms – S/he is praising s.o. **ies kʷtncinm, as kʷtncinm**
qs kʷtncinms – S/he is going to praise s.o. **iqs kʷtncinm, aqs kʷtncinm**

kʷtncinmnt – Praise s.o. *cmd.*

kʷtncnmist – praise one's self.

prance **mṅmilš** – prance. *suffix:* ***...ilš*** *– autonomous.*

es mṅmilši – S/he/it is prancing.

pray **čáw** – pray.

čáwm – S/he/it prayed. **čn čáwm, kʷ čáwm**
es čáwi – S/he/it is praying. **čnes čáwi, kʷes čáwi**
qs čáwi – S/he/it is going to pray. **čiqs čáwi, kʷqs čáwi**
čáʔawm – They prayed. **qeʔ čáwm, p čáwm**
es čáʔawi – They are praying. **qeʔes čáwi, pes čáwi**

čáwis – S/he/it prayed for s.o./s.t. **čáwn, čáwntxʷ**
es čáwms – S/he/it is praying for s.o./s.t. **ies čáwm, as čáwm**
qs čáwms – S/he/it is going to pray for s.o./s.t. **iqs čáwm, aqs čáwm**
čáʔawis – They prayed for s.o./s.t. **qeʔ čáwntm, čáwntp**
es čáʔawms – They are praying for s.o./s.t. **qeʔes čáwm, es čáwmp**

čáwntm – S/he/it was prayed for.

snčáwmn – place to pray.

> s.t. - something, the 3rd person
> (s.t.) - something implied
> s.o. - someone, the 3rd person
> *sl.* - singular form
> *pl.* - plural form
> *rt.* - root word
> *cmd.* - command
> *lit.* - literally
> *fig.* - figuratively
> *i.e.,* - for example
> *See:* - Redirection to a related word.

čočomuł – one that habitually prays. *suffix:* ***...łmuł*** *– one that habitually does.*

čáwiš – Pray. *cmd.*
čáwnt – Pray for s.o./s.t. *cmd.*
čáwštm – pray for someone's sake.
nčomels – want to pray.
čáwšłtumš – pray for the people.
čáwštwexʷ – pray for each other.
čáwšcut – pray for one's self.
ččáwpleˀ – pray for/over something; bless. *See:* ***bless.***

ṅem čáwm – S/he will pray. **ṅem čn čáwm, ṅem kʷ čáwm**
ṅem čáˀawm – They will pray. **ṅem qeˀ čáwm, ṅem p čáwm**
ṅem qs čáwms – S/he/it will be praying for s.o./s.t. **ṅem iqes čáwm, ṅem aqes čáwm**
ṅem qs čáˀawms – They will be praying for s.o./s.t. **ṅem qeˀqs čáwm, ṅem qs čáwmp**
xʷu qeˀqs čáwi – Let's pray. **ṅem qeˀ wis čáwm m sic qeˀ eł̓iłn** – We will finish praying, and then we will eat.

nčáwcnm – say prayers for someone that is incapable of saying prayers; pray in a way that someone else would pray. *suffix:* ***...cin, ...cn*** *– action of the mouth.*
es nčáwcnms – S/he is saying prayers for s.o. **ies nčáwcnm, as nčáwcnm**

nčáwcnmn – I said prayers for you.

čoncutist – give offerings/pray.
es čoncuti – S/he is praying. **čnes čoncuti, kʷes čoncuti**
es čoncúˀuti – They are praying. **qeˀes čoncuti, pes čoncuti**

čonumt – S/he offered.
nčoncutmis – S/he offered it. **nčoncutmn, nčoncutmntxʷ**
nčoncúˀutmis – They offered it. **qeˀ nčoncutmntm, nčoncutmntp**

nčoncutmntm – It was offered.

nčoncutn – thing or place to pray to. *suffix:* ***...tin, ...tn*** *– means of/device.*
nčoncutis – Her/his thing or place to pray to.

snčoncutn – place of offering/prayer *(i.e., the Medicine Tree; a special place in mountains; a place you get your nyopiyewtn/strength). prefix:* ***sn...*** *– a place of; suffix:* ***...tin, ...tn*** *– means of/device.*

sčmaqʷncut – words to get rid of evil/bad feelings/sickness. *(i.e., prayer.) See:* ***rid.***

prayer
nčáwmn – prayer.

preach
ċx̣ʷċx̣ʷłtumš, *ċx̣ʷċx̣ʷłtu* – preach/lecture the people; make the people mindful of something. *rt.:* ***ċox̣ʷ*** *– imparting of one's self; suffix:* ***...łtumš*** *– of people.*
ċx̣ʷċx̣ʷłtumš – S/he preached. **čn ċx̣ʷċx̣ʷłtumš, kʷ ċx̣ʷċx̣ʷłtumš**
es ċx̣ʷċx̣ʷłtumši – S/he is preaching. **čnes ċx̣ʷċx̣ʷłtumši, kʷes ċx̣ʷċx̣ʷłtumši**
qs ċx̣ʷċx̣ʷłtumši – S/he is going to preach. **čiqs ċx̣ʷċx̣ʷłtumši, kʷqs ċx̣ʷċx̣ʷłtumši**

ċox̣ʷ – impart wisdom, knowledge, and/or experiences of one's self; instruct; lecture; teach; inform. *See:* ***instruct.***

ċx̣ʷċx̣ʷelt – preach/lecture to children; make the children mindful of something. *rt.:* ***ċox̣ʷ*** *– imparting of one's self; suffix:* ***...eł̓t, ...ł̓t*** *– child, baby.*
ċx̣ʷċx̣ʷelt – S/he preached. **čn ċx̣ʷċx̣ʷelt, kʷ ċx̣ʷċx̣ʷelt**
es ċx̣ʷċx̣ʷelti – S/he is preaching. **čnes ċx̣ʷċx̣ʷelti, kʷes ċx̣ʷċx̣ʷelti**
qs ċx̣ʷċx̣ʷelti – S/he is going to preach. **čiqs ċx̣ʷċx̣ʷelti, kʷqs ċx̣ʷċx̣ʷelti**

predator **ťeyeʔxʷixʷeyuł –** bad animal; predator.

preen **tucmi –** preen/clean self.
es tucmisti – S/he/it is preening one's self. **čnes tucmisti, kʷes tucmisti**

pregnant **yumi –** pregnant. *(have movement inside.) rt.: **iwu** – move.*
es yumi – She is pregnant. **čnes yumi, kʷes yumi**

ntkʷk̓ʷeľt – She is pregnant; she has a baby inside. *rt.: **nťuk̓ʷ** – place inside; suffix: **...eľt, ...ľt** – child, baby.*

nťk̓ʷełc̓eʔ – She has a baby inside. *rt.: **nťuk̓ʷ** – place inside; suffix: **...ełc̓eʔ** – inside the body.*

The **i** following uvular consonants (UC) and the glottal stop **ʔ** sound like English "*ey*" as in the words *they, hey, whey,* etc. Salish UC are: **q, q̓, qʷ, q̓ʷ, x̣, x̣ʷ**. For example, the suffix **...qin** – head/top, is often spelled using English *ey* as "q*ey*n". So **qi, q̓i, qʷi, q̓ʷi, x̣i, x̣ʷi,** may be spelled with English *ey* as **q***ey,* **q̓***ey,* **qʷ***ey,* **q̓ʷ***ey,* **x̣***ey,* **x̣ʷ***ey* in other texts.

prepare **x̣cim –** prepare something; make ready; put in order. *(i.e., put disarrayed things in order, getting things ready for travel, etc.) See: **ready**.*

nx̣cels – feel/want/be prepared for whatever may happen. *See: **ready**.*

x̣cečst – fix something; make something prepared for whatever; make someone behave so as to be ready and prepared next time; punish someone to teach a lesson of preparation. *(i.e. telling a dog to go after someone to teach them a lesson so that should the same event happen again the person will be prepared; as fixed is used in the phrase "that'll fix 'em.") See: **ready**.*

present **sxʷic̓c̓š –** something given; a present. *See: **give**.*

sčéppn – present to soothe/soften a bad relationship. *See: **give**.*

čtľic̓éʔ – tear a covering/wrapping off *(i.e., a wrapping off a present, etc.). See: **open up**.*

president **amotqn –** Creator; Sits On Top; president.

press **čeťm –** press on something.
čeťis – S/he pressed on s.t. **čeťn, čeťntxʷ**
es čeťms – S/he is pressing on s.t. **ies čeťm, as čeťm**
qs čeťms – S/he is going to press on s.t. **iqs čeťm, aqs čeťm**

es čťčeťms – S/he is repeatedly pressing on s.t. **ies čťčeťm, as čťčeťm**

es čłčeťms – S/he is pressing down on s.t. **ies čłčeťm, as čłčeťm**

čeťnt – Press it. *cmd.*

čťčeťťeneʔ – something got weighted down.

p̓ac̓ – press as would be done in massage.
p̓ac̓is – S/he/it pressed s.t. **p̓ac̓n, p̓ac̓ntxʷ**
es p̓ac̓ms – S/he/it is pressing s.t. **ies p̓ac̓m, as p̓ac̓m**
qs p̓ac̓ms – S/he/it is going to press s.t. **iqs p̓ac̓m, aqs p̓ac̓m**

čp̓ac̓is – S/he/it pressed on s.t. **čp̓ac̓n, čp̓ac̓ntxʷ**

p̓cp̓ac̓m – massage.
es čp̓ac̓ – It is pressed.

čp̓ac̓iš – Press. *cmd.*

čp̓ac̓ntxʷ snčłemutn – You pressed the chair.

ťec̓ – iron/press clothing. *See: **iron**.*

p̓é – dent. *See: **dent**.*

s.t. - something, the 3rd person
(s.t.) - something implied
s.o. - someone, the 3rd person
sl. - singular form
pl. - plural form
rt. - root word
cmd. - command
lit. - literally
fig. - figuratively
i.e., - for example
See: - Redirection to a related word.

pressure **čłéˀeẁs** – internal pressure. *suffix:* ***...éẁs*** *– in between, middle.*
tmsčłéˀeẁs – no pressure.
čłéˀeẁsétkʷ – liquid pressure.

ha ep sčłéˀeẁs – Does it have pressure?

p̓iċm – put violent pressure on something.
qeˀes p̓iċmłels – controlling; getting the best of us.

el – tease; bother. *See:* ***bother.***

pretty **swiˀnumt**, *swiˀnu* – beautiful; pretty/handsome.

prevail **l̓q̓ʷom** – can do; prevail; succeed. *See:* ***do.***

prevent **čˀemtupsm** – keep someone from doing something; hold someone back. *See:* ***hold back.***

maq – forbid; prevent; detain someone from doing, going, or starting. *See:* ***forbid.***

x̣eˀe – keep someone in line; correct behavior; forbid bad behavior; prevent misdeeds; make someone behave. *See:* ***discipline.***

price **snˀeys** – price; cost.
nˀeys – pay for something bought. *See:* ***pay.***

stem̓ łu snˀeysts – What is its price?

prickly **ċiq** – prickly.
ċiqp – horse hair rope; bristly/rough rope.
ċiqnełp – common juniper; prickly juniper; *Juniperus communis. rt.:* ***ċiq*** *– prickly; suffix:* ***...ełp, ...łp*** *– tree; floor.*

prickly pear cactus **sxʷyéneˀ** – prickly pear cactus; *Opuntia polyacantha.*

priest **q̓ʷáylqs** – priest. *rt.:* ***q̓ʷáy*** *– black; suffix:* ***...lqs, ...alqs*** *– clothes.*

prince's pine **sčx̣lx̣lpu** – prince's pine; pipsissewa; *Chimaphila umbellata.*

print **łp̓łip̓łq̓ey̓im** – print words.

printer **snk̓ʷłq̓y̓q̓ey̓mintn** – printer. *prefix:* ***sn...*** *– a place of; suffix:* ***...tin, ...tn*** *– means of/device.*

prison **snloˀ** – prison.

snlčmintn – place to be tied up; jail. *rt.:* ***lič*** *– tied up.*

prisoner **sčkʷánx̣n** – kidnapped prisoner.

scnloˀ – something that is put inside. *(i.e., a prisoner) prefix:* ***sc...*** *– s.t. that's been done/made/prepared.*

probably **i mi** – It is plainly evident; it is absolute; it is fact.
x̣ʷa i mi – probably; I suppose.

x̣ʷa i mi u ta es mistexʷ – I suppose you do not know it. **i mi lkʷut** – Of course it is far. **i mi u ta es mistexʷ** – Of course you do not know it.

problem **q̓eʔečst** – made to be or do something; cause hardship for someone; cause problems for someone; put someone/something into it *(by holding, by making it one's business to do so, by situational happenstance, etc.)*. *See:* ***made.***

produce **k̓ʷl̓l̓ałq** – germinate; plant born; crop produce. *rt.:*
k̓ʷl̓l̓ałq – S/he produced a crop; seeds germinated. **čn k̓ʷl̓l̓ałq, kʷ k̓ʷl̓l̓ałq**
es k̓ʷl̓l̓ałqi – His/her crop is in production; seeds are germinating. **čnes k̓ʷl̓l̓ałqi, kʷes k̓ʷl̓l̓ałqi**

sk̓ʷl̓l̓ałq – produce; fruit, vegatable, and crop produce.

ta či sk̓ʷl̓l̓ałq – My crop did not produce; my seeds didn't grow.

čk̓ʷal̓ečst – bud; produce; makes something grow upon. *See:* ***grow.***

The **i** following uvular consonants (UC) and the glottal stop **ʔ** sound like English *"ey"* as in the words *they, hey, whey*, etc. Salish UC are: **q, q̓, qʷ, q̓ʷ, x̌, x̌ʷ**. For example, the suffix ...**qin** – head/top, is often spelled using English *ey* as "q*ey*n". So **qi, q̓i, qʷi, q̓ʷi, x̌i, x̌ʷi**, may be spelled with English *ey* as **q***ey*, **q̓***ey*, **qʷ***ey*, **q̓ʷ***ey*, **x̌***ey*, **x̌ʷ***ey* in other texts.

projectile **...eł** – *suffix indicating a projectile.*
k̓ʷul̓ł – make arrowheads/projectiles.
łcċmeł – small projectile; bb. *See:* ***bullet.***

promise **ċox̌ʷš** – promise; pledge. *rt.:* ***ċox̌ʷ*** *– imparting of one's self.*
es ċox̌ʷšitms – S/he is promising. **ies ċox̌ʷšitm, as ċox̌ʷšitm**
qs ċox̌ʷšitms – S/he is going to promise. **iqs ċox̌ʷšitm, aqs ċox̌ʷšitm**
es ċóʔox̌ʷšitms – They are promising. **qeʔes ċox̌ʷšitm, es ċox̌ʷšitmp**

ṅem qs ċox̌ʷšitms – S/he will be promising. **ṅem iqes ċox̌ʷšitm, ṅem aqes ċox̌ʷšitm**
es ċox̌ʷštwéʔexʷi – They are promising each other. **qeʔes ċox̌ʷštwexʷi, pes ċox̌ʷštwexʷi**

ċox̌ʷ – impart wisdom, knowledge, and/or experiences of one's self; instruct; lecture; teach; inform. *See:* ***instruct.***

kʷ ies ċox̌ʷšitm – I am promising you.

pronghorn **staán** – antelope; pronghorn; *Antilocapra americana.*

propagate **ml̓uk̓ʷ** – spread all around; propagate; grow, of non-living things. *See:* ***all around.***

propose **nsucnmist** – propose marriage to someone; ask permission to marry.
nsucnmistm – S/he proposed (to s.o). **čn nsucnmistm, kʷ nsucnmistm**
es nsucnmisti – S/he is proposing (to s.o.). **čnes nsucnmisti, kʷes nsucnmisti**
qs nsucnmisti – S/he is going to propose (to s.o.). **čiqs nsucnmisti, kʷqs nsucnmisti**

nsucnmistmis – S/he proposed to s.o. **nsucnmistmn, nsucnmistmtnxʷ**
es nsucnmistms – S/he is proposing to s.o. **ies nsucnmistm, as nsucnmistm**
qs nsucnmistms – S/he is going to propose to s.o. **iqs nsucnmistm, aqs nsucnmistm**

es nsucnmélsi – S/he is wanting to propose (to s.o.). **čnes nsucnmélsi, kʷes nsucnmélsi**

hoy čiqs k̓ʷis nsucnmi – Okay, I am going to go propose. **ta, tam l qʷoyʔé u es nsucnmi šey̓ łu es ccx̌ʷuyms, tam qʷoyʔé** – No, it is not me he's come proposing to; he's come for her, not me. **ta es cxʷuy put u čnes nsucnmi** – She is not coming now that I am proposing. **m cnʔułxʷ łu es nsucnmisti łu sqltmi** – man comes in and proposes. **es nsucnmistms** – S/he is asking (parents) to marry their daughter/son. **čnes nsucnmisti t px̌px̌ots** – I am asking the parents to marry their daughter/son.

s.t. - something, the 3rd person
(s.t.) - something implied
s.o. - someone, the 3rd person
sl. - singular form
pl. - plural form
rt. - root word
cmd. - command
lit. - literally
fig. - figuratively
i.e., - for example
See: - Redirection to a related word.

protect **k̓ʷłqixʷ** – protect; defended. *rt.: **qixʷ**– chase away.*
k̓ʷłqixʷis – S/he/it protected s.o./s.t. **k̓ʷłqixʷn, k̓ʷłqixʷntxʷ**
es k̓ʷłqixʷms – S/he/it is protecting s.o./s.t. **ies k̓ʷłqixʷm, as k̓ʷłqixʷm**
k̓ʷłqíʔixʷis – They protected s.o./s.t. **qeʔ k̓ʷłqixʷntm, k̓ʷłqixʷntp**

es k̓ʷłqxʷncuti – S/he is protecting one's self. **čnes k̓ʷłqxʷncuti, kʷes k̓ʷłqxʷncuti**

k̓ʷłqixʷntm – S/he/it was protected.

k̓ʷłqxʷncutn – protector. *suffix: **...tin, ...tn**– means of/device.*

k̓ʷłqixʷłt – Protect s.o. *cmd.*

ṅem t cni m qeʔ k̓ʷłqixʷłs – S/he will protect us. **qeʔ k̓ʷłqixʷłt** – Protect us.

k̓ʷłhemm – defend someone; stick up for someone; protect someone.
es k̓ʷłhemmi – S/he is sticking up for (s.o.). **čnes k̓ʷłhemmi, kʷes k̓ʷłhemmi**

čšt̓im – guard or take care of. *(This term is also used for wakes as it is seen that people are taking care of the dead.) See: **guard**.*

protrude **t̓ix̣** – scattered outward protrusions; jut out in a scattered fashion; stick out here and there.
i t̓ix̣ – It is sticking out.

ƛ̓čiṁ – protrude out; bulge out.
sƛ̓čƛ̓čim – bulges; protrusions.
ƛ̓éʔeč, *ƛ̓éʔe* – peek out; come out. *See: **peek**.*
ƛ̓ečcn – stick out the tongue. *See: **tongue**.*

proud **q̇exʷ** – proud; admire.
q̇xʷnscut – conceited; proud of one's self. *See: **conceited**.*
q̇exʷmscut – show-off; snobby; arrogant; self admiring. *See: **show-off**.*
q̇xʷq̇exʷt, *q̇xʷq̇e* – proud; vain; think much of; stuck-up. *See: **stuck-up**.*

čq̇xʷq̇exʷtn – thing of admiration; thing of pride.

čq̇xʷq̇exʷtmis – S/he was proud of s.t. **čq̇xʷq̇exʷtmn, čq̇xʷq̇exʷtmntxʷ**
es čq̇xʷq̇exʷtms – S/he is proud of s.t. **ies čq̇xʷq̇exʷtm, as čq̇xʷq̇exʷtm**

kʷtnels – proud; think highly; have confidence. *rt.: **kʷtunt**– big; circumfix: **n...els**– want, feel.*
kʷtnelsmis – S/he was proud of s.o. **kʷtnelsmn, kʷtnelsmntxʷ**
es kʷtnelsms – S/he is being proud of s.o. **ies kʷtnelsm, as kʷtnelsm**
qs kʷtnelsms – S/he is going to be proud of s.o. **iqs kʷtnelsm, aqs kʷtnelsm**

skʷtnels – that which is thought highly of.
kʷtnlsmncutn – admirer; fan.

kʷtnelsiš – Be proud. *cmd.*
kʷtnelsmnt – Be proud of s.o. *cmd.*
kʷtnlsmnwexʷ – think highly of each other.
kʷtnlsmist – think highly of one's self; think big of one's self; self-conceited.

kʷtnelsiš nƛ̓x̣ciniš – Be proud, speak loud. **łu kʷ amotqn tma tl̓ askʷtnels še yetłx̣ʷasq̇t qeʔ lʔe łu sqelixʷ** – Creator, because of your esteem, humans are still here today.

kʷtnlscutist – proud of one's accomplishments.
kʷtnlscutist – S/he was proud of one's self. **čn kʷtnlscutist, kʷ kʷtnlscutist**
es kʷtnlscutisti – S/he is taking pride in one's self. **čnes kʷtnlscutisti, kʷes kʷtnlscutisti**

qs kʷtnlscutisti – S/he is going to take pride in one's self. **čiqs kʷtnlscutisti, kʷqs kʷtnlscutisti**

imše kʷ kʷtnlscutist – Be proud of your accomplishments.

kʷtiscut – make one's self important, great; brag. *See: **brag**.*

provide **eṁtm –** feed. *See: **feed**.*

prune **čq̓ʷiq̓ʷá –** prunes.

pry **nq̓aq̓ʔels –** always busy; snoopy; nosy; prying. *See: **business**.*

k̓ʷłutčent – pry something up.

k̓ʷłwečnt – pry something off.

puberty **es łx̣ʷómʔey̓ –** boy/girl going through puberty; at the age of puberty.

pubic hair **pox̣t –** pubic hair.

puccoon **sʔiʔc̓qn –** puccoon groom well; narrow-leaved puccoon; *Lithospermum incisum*.

puddle **słsesixʷ –** puddle. *rt.: **sixʷ** – pour/spill.*

snsixʷlexʷ – pond, puddle. *rt.: **sixʷ** – pour/spill; suffix: **...ulexʷ** – land. See: **pond**.*

ṅṅłƛ̓awačl̓exʷ – puddle. *rt.: **ƛ̓awač** – mud; suffix: **...ulexʷ** – land. See: **mud**.*

Pueblo **čt̓lt̓le –** Pueblo people.

puff **łpčim –** take a puff of smoke such as from a cigarette.
łpčim – S/he took a puff. **čn łpčim, kʷ łpčim**
es łpčmi – S/he is taking a puff. **čnes łpčmi, kʷes łpčmi**
qs łpčmi – S/he is going to take a puff. **čiqs łpčmi, kʷqs łpčmi**

łpłpčim – S/he took several puffs.

puffball **sʔitš –** puffball.

pull **ckʷum –** pull. *(Caution: this word is nearly the same as rape.)*
ckʷum – S/he pulled. **čn ckʷum, kʷ ckʷum**

ckʷntes – S/he pulled s.t./s.o. **ckʷnten, ckʷntexʷ**
es ckʷums – S/he is pulling s.t./s.o. **ies ckʷum, as ckʷum**
qs ckʷums – S/he is going to pull s.t./s.o. **iqs ckʷum, aqs ckʷum**

ckʷntem – S/he/it got pulled.

ckʷunt – Pull it. *cmd.*
ckʷkʷnuis – S/he finally pulled s.t. **ckʷkʷnun, ckʷkʷnuntxʷ**

qʷo ckʷšit – Pull it for me. **qʷo ckʷułt –** Pull that for me. **ckʷaqłten –** I pulled it on the road for him.

čłcckʷičṅ – pull on ice; drag across ice.
čłcckʷičis – S/he pulled s.t./s.o. on ice. **čłcckʷičṅ, čłcckʷičṅtxʷ**
es čłcckʷičṅms – S/he is pulling s.t./s.o. on ice. **ies čłcckʷičṅm, as čłcckʷičṅm**
qs čłcckʷičṅms – S/he is going to pull s.t./s.o. on ice. **iqs čłcckʷičṅm, aqs čłcckʷičṅm**

sntm̓qʷolexʷtn – pulled out of the ground. *prefix: **sn...** – a place of; suffix: **...tin, ...tn** – means of/device.*

The **i** following uvular consonants (UC) and the glottal stop **ʔ** sound like English "*ey*" as in the words th*ey*, h*ey*, wh*ey*, etc. Salish UC are: **q, q̓, qʷ, q̓ʷ, x̣, x̣ʷ**. For example, the suffix **...qin** – head/top, is often spelled using English *ey* as "q*ey*n". So **qi, q̓i, qʷi, q̓ʷi, x̣i, x̣ʷi**, may be spelled with English *ey* as **q***ey*, **q̓***ey*, **qʷ***ey*, **q̓ʷ***ey*, **x̣***ey*, **x̣ʷ***ey* in other texts.

s.t. - something, the 3rd person
(s.t.) - something implied
s.o. - someone, the 3rd person
sl. - singular form
pl. - plural form
rt. - root word
cmd. - command
lit. - literally
fig. - figuratively
i.e., - for example
See: - Redirection to a related word.

čq̓lx̓ʷmin – hook for pulling or catching.

pull out **ċoˀq** – pulled something out.
ċoˀqm – S/he pulled (s.t) out. **čn ċoˀqm, kʷ ċoˀqm**
es ċoˀqmi – S/he is pulling (s.t) out. **čnes ċoˀqmi, kʷes ċoˀqmi**
qs ċoˀqmi – S/he is going to pull (s.t) out. **čiqs ċoˀqmi, kʷqs ċoˀqmi**

nċoqntes – S/he pulled s.t. out. **nċoqnten, kʷ nċoqntexʷ**
es nċoqms – S/he is pulling s.t. out. **ies nċoqm, as nċoqm**
qs nċoqms – S/he is going to pull s.t. out. **iqs nċoqm, aqs nċoqm**

nċoqeys – pull a tooth out. *See: **pull teeth**.*
nċoqičn̓ – draw an arrow out of a quiver on the back. *See: **draw**.*
nċoˀqłniut, *nċoˀqłni* – draw a knife/sword/gun out of a side mounted sheath; unsheath. *See: **draw**.*
nċoqeẁsm – disengage from the middle. *See: **disengage**.*
čċoqalqʷ – pull something out of a tree/wood.
čċoqm – cure; pull out from sickness/death. *See: **cure**.*

nċuwaq – suddenly pull something out.
nċuwaqis – S/he suddenly pulled s.t. out. **nċuwaqn, nċuwaqntxʷ**

nċuwaqntm anx̣lexʷ – Your tooth was pulled out.

lq̓em – pull a rooted thing out; root out. *(i.e., plants, hair, etc.)*
lq̓ntes – S/he pulled s.t. out. **lq̓nten, lq̓ntexʷ**
es lq̓ems – S/he is pulling s.t. out. **ies lq̓em, as lq̓em**
qs lq̓ems – S/he is going to pull s.t. out. **iqs lq̓em, aqs lq̓em**

lq̓pesn̓cut, *lq̓pesn̓cu* – tweezers.

čsx̣qin – pull hair out one by one.
čsx̣qncut – S/he pulled one's hair out. **čn čsx̣qncut, kʷ čsx̣qncut**
es čsx̣qncuti – S/he is pulling one's hair out. **čnes čsx̣qncuti, kʷes čsx̣qncuti**

čsx̣qis – S/he pulled s.o.'s hair out. **čsx̣qin, čsx̣qintxʷ**
es čsx̣qinms – S/he is pulling s.o.'s hair out. **ies čsx̣qinm, as čsx̣qinm**

nkʷƛ̓etkʷ – pull/take out of the water.
nkʷƛ̓etkʷis – S/he pulled s.t. out of the water. **nkʷƛ̓etkʷn, nkʷƛ̓etkʷntxʷ**
es nkʷƛ̓etkʷms – S/he is pulling s.t. out of the water. **ies nkʷƛ̓etkʷm, as nkʷƛ̓etkʷm**
qs nkʷƛ̓etkʷms – S/he is going to pull s.t. out of the water. **iqs nkʷƛ̓etkʷm, aqs nkʷƛ̓etkʷm**

cnkʷƛ̓etkʷn łu ƛ̓iyéˀ – I pulled the boat out of the water toward me.

kʷƛ̓im – take something out; detach; loose/free embedded object. *See: **take**.*

pull over **łixʷp** – slip/pull/put something fitted over an object. *(i.e., clothing, etc.)*
es łixʷp – It is pulled over something.
es nłixʷp – S/he/it has s.t. pulled over.

łxʷpntes – S/he pulled something tightly fitted over s.t. **łxʷpnten, łxʷpntexʷ**
es łxʷpims – S/he is pulling something tightly fitted over s.t. **ies łxʷpim, as łxʷpim**
qs łxʷpims – S/he is going to pull something tightly fitted over s.t. **iqs łxʷpim, aqs łxʷpim**

łxʷpint – Pulled something tightly fitted over it. *cmd.*

nłxʷpncut – dress one's self. *See: **dress**.*
nłxʷpncutš – Get dressed; get in your clothes. *cmd.*

łxʷpax̌nm – put something over the arm. *rt.: **łixʷp** – slip/pull over; suffix: **...ax̌n** – arm.*
nłxʷpax̌niš – Put your arm inside. *(i.e., inside a sleeve, etc.) cmd.*

łxʷpaqstšnm – put something over the leg. *rt.: **łixʷp** – slip/pull over; suffix: **...aqstšn** – leg.*
nłxʷpaqstšniš – Put your leg inside. *(i.e., inside a pant leg, etc.) cmd.*

pull teeth

nċoqeys – pull a tooth out.
nċoqeysm – S/he pulled a tooth. **čn nċoqeysm, kʷ nċoqeysm**
es nċoqeysi – S/he is pulling a tooth. **čnes nċoqeysi, kʷes nċoqeysi**
qs nċoqeysi – S/he is going to pull a tooth. **čiqs nċoqeysi, kʷqs nċoqeysi**

nċoqeysis – S/he pulled s.o.'s tooth. **nċoqeysn, nċoqeysntxʷ**
es nċoqeysms – S/he is pulling s.o.'s tooth. **ies nċoqeysm, as nċoqeysm**
qs nċoqeysms – S/he is going to pull s.o.'s tooth. **iqs nċoqeysm, aqs nċoqeysm**

nċoqeysntm – His/her tooth was pulled. **qʷo nċoqeysntm, kʷ nċoqeysntm**

sxʷnċoqeysm – dentist; someone tasked to pull teeth.

nċoqeysiš – Pull a tooth. *cmd.*
nċoqeysnt – Pull s.o.'s tooth. *cmd.*

ha kʷ ṅe u qʷo aqs nċoqeysm – Would you pull my tooth?

The **i** following uvular consonants (UC) and the glottal stop **ʔ** sound like English "*ey*" as in the words th*ey*, h*ey*, wh*ey*, etc. Salish UC are: **q**, **q̇**, **qʷ**, **q̇ʷ**, **x̌**, **x̌ʷ**. For example, the suffix **...qin** – head/top, is often spelled using English *ey* as "q*ey*n". So **qi**, **q̇i**, **qʷi**, **q̇ʷi**, **x̌i**, **x̌ʷi**, may be spelled with English *ey* as **q***ey*, **q̇***ey*, **qʷ***ey*, **q̇ʷ***ey*, **x̌***ey*, **x̌ʷ***ey* in other texts.

pulse

ttmtmwils – pulse; heart beat.
es ttmtmwilsi – It is pulsing; it is beating.

iwiwls – blood moves; pulse. *rt.: **iwu** – move.*
es iwiwlsi – It is moving; it is pulsing.

l čeṅ u ecx̌lsʔiwiwls – How is my pulse?

pump

npew – pump up; inflate.
npewis – S/he pumped s.t. up. **npewn, npewntxʷ**
es npewms – S/he is pumping s.t. up. **ies npewm, as npewm**
qs npewms – S/he is going to pump s.t. up. **iqs npewm, aqs npewm**

npewmn – pump; something used to inflate.

npewnt – Inflate it. *cmd.*

npewn łu innox̌ʷmin – I inflated my inner tube.

pumpkin

sqalixʷqn – pumpkin.

pumpkin bread

sqalixʷqn scnqʷl̓pulexʷ – pumpkin bread.

punch

cúʔum – punch with a fist.
cuʔntes – S/he punched s.t./s.o. **cuʔnten, cuʔntexʷ**
es cúʔums – S/he is punching s.o./s.t. **ies cúʔum, as cúʔum**
qs cúʔums – S/he is punching s.o./s.t. **iqs cúʔum, aqs cúʔum**
cuʔntéʔes – They punched s.t./s.o. **qeʔ cuʔntem, cuʔntep**

cʔuncin – I hit you.

k̇ʷłcuncinm – punch someone in the chin.
k̇ʷłcuncis – S/he punched s.o.'s chin. **k̇ʷłcuncin, k̇ʷłcuncintxʷ**
es k̇ʷłcuncinms – S/he is punching s.o's chin. **ies k̇ʷłcuncinm, as k̇ʷłcuncinm**
qs k̇ʷłcuncinms – S/he is going to punch s.o.'s chin. **iqs k̇ʷłcuncinm, aqs k̇ʷłcuncinm**

s.t. - something, the 3rd person
(s.t.) - something implied
s.o. - someone, the 3rd person
sl. - singular form
pl. - plural form
rt. - root word
cmd. - command
lit. - literally
fig. - figuratively
i.e., - for example
See: - Redirection to a related word.

es k̓ʷłcúʔuncinms – They are punching s.o.'s chin. **qeʔes k̓ʷłcuncinm, es k̓ʷłcuncinmp**

ncuʔáqsm – punch someone in the nose.
ncuʔáqsis – S/he punched s.o.'s nose. **ncuʔáqsn, ncuʔáqsntxʷ**
es ncuʔáqsms – S/he is punching s.o.'s nose. **ies ncuʔáqsm, as ncuʔáqsm**
qs ncuʔáqsms – S/he is going to punch s.o.'s nose. **iqs ncuʔáqsm, aqs ncuʔáqsm**

sxʷncuʔáqsm – one tasked to punch in the nose.

ncuʔáqsnt – Punch s.o. in the nose. *cmd.*

ncʔusm – punch someone in the eye.
ncʔusis – S/he punched s.o. in the eye. **ncʔusn, ncʔusntxʷ**
es ncʔusms – S/he is punching s.o. in the eye. **ies ncʔusm, as ncʔusm**
qs ncʔusms – S/he is going to punch s.o. in the eye. **iqs ncʔusm, aqs ncʔusm**

ncʔusnt – Punch s.o. in the nose. *cmd.*

cẇapqnm – punch someone in the head.
cẇapqis – S/he punched s.o.'s head. **cẇapqn, cẇapqntxʷ**
es cẇapqnms – S/he is punching s.o.'s head. **ies cẇapqnm, as cẇapqnm**
qs cẇapqnms – S/he is going to punch s.o.'s head. **iqs cẇapqnm, aqs cẇapqnm**
cẇáʔapqis – They punched s.o.'s head. **qeʔ cẇapqntm, cẇapqntp**

k̓ʷłcẇapqnm – punch someone in the back of the head.
k̓ʷłcẇapqis – S/he punched the back of s.o.'s head. **k̓ʷłcẇapqn, k̓ʷłcẇapqntxʷ**
es k̓ʷłcẇapqnms – S/he is punching the back of s.o.'s head. **ies k̓ʷłcẇapqnm, as k̓ʷłcẇapqnm**
qs k̓ʷłcẇapqnms – S/he is going to punch the back of s.o.'s head. **iqs k̓ʷłcẇapqnm, aqs k̓ʷłcẇapqnm**

nċwenеʔ – punch someone in the ear.
nċwenʔeis – S/he punched s.o.'s ear. **nċwenʔen, nċwenʔentxʷ**
es nċwenʔems – S/he is punching s.o.'s ear. **ies nċwenʔem, as nċwenʔem**
qs nċwenʔems – S/he is going to punch s.o.'s ear. **iqs nċwenʔem, aqs nċwenʔem**

cwax̣nm – punch someone in the arm.
cwax̣is – S/he punched s.o. in the arm. **cwax̣n, cwax̣ntxʷ**
es cwax̣nms – S/he is punching s.o. in the arm. **ies cwax̣nm, as cwax̣nm**
qs cwax̣nms – S/he is going to punch s.o. in the arm. **iqs cwax̣nm, aqs cwax̣nm**

cuncut – punch one's self.
cuncut – S/he hit one's self. **čn cuncut, kʷ cuncut**
es cuncuti – S/he is hitting one's self. **čnes cuncuti, kʷes cuncuti**
qs cuncuti – S/he is going to hit one's self. **čiqs cuncuti, kʷqs cuncuti**

nƛ̓oqsm – punch someone in the nose.
nƛ̓oqsis – S/he punched s.o. in the nose. **nƛ̓oqsn, nƛ̓oqsntxʷ**
es nƛ̓oqsms – S/he is punching s.o. in the nose. **ies nƛ̓oqsm, as nƛ̓oqsm**
qs nƛ̓oqsms – S/he is going to punch s.o. in the nose. **iqs nƛ̓oqsm, aqs nƛ̓oqsm**
nƛ̓óʔoqsis – They punched s.o. in the nose. **qeʔ nƛ̓oqsntm, nƛ̓oqsntp**

nƛ̓osm – punch someone in the eye.
nƛ̓osis – S/he punched s.o. in the eye. **nƛ̓osn, nƛ̓osntxʷ**
es nƛ̓osms – S/he is punching s.o. in the eye. **ies nƛ̓osm, as nƛ̓osm**
qs nƛ̓osms – S/he is going to punch s.o. in the eye. **iqs nƛ̓osm, aqs nƛ̓osm**

nƛ̓oposqnm – punch someone in the mouth.

nt̓łoposqis – S/he punched s.o. in the mouth. **nt̓łoposqn, nt̓łoposqntxʷ**
es nt̓łoposqnms – S/he is punching s.o. in the mouth. **ies nt̓łoposqnm, as nt̓łoposqnm**
qs nt̓łoposqnms – S/he is going to punch s.o. in the mouth. **iqs nt̓łoposqnm, aqs nt̓łoposqnm**

nt̓łososm – punch someone in the face.
t̓łososis – S/he punched s.o. in the face. **nt̓łososn, nt̓łososntxʷ**
es nt̓łososms – S/he is punching s.o. in the face. **ies nt̓łososm, as nt̓łososm**
qs nt̓łososms – S/he is going to punch s.o. in the face. **iqs nt̓łososm, aqs nt̓łososm**

puncture

łóx̣ʷ – make a hole in something; puncture something; bore through. *See:* ***hole.***

čłx̣ʷsew̓s – punch a hole in some container; puncture a container. *(i.e., a can, a balloon, etc.) rt.:* ***łox̣ʷ*** *– hole; prefix:* ***č...*** *– upon; suffix:* ***...éw̓s*** *– in between, middle.*
čłx̣ʷsew̓s – S/he punctured (s.t.). **čn čłx̣ʷsew̓s, kʷ čłx̣ʷsew̓s**
es čłx̣ʷsew̓si – S/he is puncturing (s.t.). **čnes čłx̣ʷsew̓si, kʷes čłx̣ʷsew̓si**
qs čłx̣ʷsew̓si – S/he is going to puncture (s.t.). **čiqs čłx̣ʷsew̓si, kʷqs čłx̣ʷsew̓si**

čłx̣ʷsew̓sis – S/he punctured s.t. **čłx̣ʷsew̓sn, čłx̣ʷsew̓sntxʷ**
es čłx̣ʷsew̓sms – S/he is puncturing s.t. **ies čłx̣ʷsew̓sm, as čłx̣ʷsew̓sm**
qs čłx̣ʷsew̓sms – S/he is going to puncture s.t. **iqs čłx̣ʷsew̓sm, aqs čłx̣ʷsew̓sm**

čłx̣ʷsew̓siš – Make a hole. *cmd.*
čłx̣ʷsew̓snt – Make a hole in it. *cmd.*

punish

ttx̣ʷeplʔem – punish. *rt.:* ***tox̣ʷ*** *– straight; suffix:* ***...epleʔ*** *– permanence.*

łc̓im – spank; whip. *(i.e., as to punish) See:* ***spank.***

čsp̓ic̓éʔ – whip; hit someone all over with something. *See:* ***whip.***

éyčst – revenge; got even; avenge wrongs done. *See:* ***revenge.***

pup, puppy

st̓it̓iʔčime, *st̓it̓iʔči* – pup; little dog.

nnłqqʷcm̓i – puppy.

pure

siš – pure; purify; sterile.
sšip – It became pure.
es sšpmi – It is becoming pure.

sišis – S/he purified/sterilized s.t. **sišn, sišntxʷ**
es sišms – S/he is purifying/sterilizing s.t. **ies sišm, as sišm**
qs sišms – S/he is going to purify/sterilize s.t. **iqs sišm, aqs sišm**

i siš – It is pure.

sišnt – Purify/sterilize it. *cmd.*
nsiškʷ – pure water.

purple

ƛ̓um̓ – deep purple; dark blood. **ƛ̓m̓ƛ̓um̓** *pl.*
ƛ̓umis – S/he made it purple. **ƛ̓um̓n, ƛ̓um̓ntxʷ**
es ƛ̓um̓ms – S/he is making it purple. **ies ƛ̓um̓m, as ƛ̓um̓m**
qs ƛ̓um̓ms – S/he is going to make it purple. **iqs ƛ̓um̓m, aqs ƛ̓um̓m**

i ƛ̓um̓ – It is purple; it is dark blood.
i łƛ̓ƛ̓um̓ – It is a little purple; purplish.

The **i** following uvular consonants (UC) and the glottal stop **ʔ** sound like English "*ey*" as in the words th*ey*, h*ey*, wh*ey*, etc. Salish UC are: **q, q̓, qʷ, q̓ʷ, x̣, x̣ʷ**. For example, the suffix ...**qin** – head/top, is often spelled using English *ey* as "q*ey*n". So **qi, q̓i, qʷi, q̓ʷi, x̣i, x̣ʷi**, may be spelled with English *ey* as **q***ey*, **q̓***ey*, **qʷ***ey*, **q̓ʷ***ey*, **x̣***ey*, **x̣ʷ***ey* in other texts.

s.t. - something, the 3rd person
(s.t.) - something implied
s.o. - someone, the 3rd person
sl. - singular form
pl. - plural form
rt. - root word
cmd. - command
lit. - literally
fig. - figuratively
i.e., - for example
See: - Redirection to a related word.

ƛuṁnt – Make it purple. *cmd.*
ƛeƛuṁeʔ – little purple one, affectionately.

purpose **čċox̣ʷ**, *čċo* – premeditated action; do something on purpose; willful intention. *rt.: ċox̣ʷ– imparting of one's self.*
čċx̣ʷntes – S/he did it willfully. **čċx̣ʷnten, čċx̣ʷntexʷ**
es čċx̣ʷoms – S/he is doing it willfully. **ies čċx̣ʷom, as čċx̣ʷom**

es čċx̣ʷečsti – S/he is purposely doing something out of spite. **čnes čċx̣ʷečsti, kʷes čċx̣ʷečsti**

čċox̣ʷemn – one inclined to have premeditated actions. *suffix: ...emn – one inclined to do; prefix: sc... – s.t. that's been done/made/prepared.*

ċox̣ʷ – impart wisdom, knowledge, and/or experiences of one's self; instruct; lecture; teach; inform. *See: instruct.*

tam iscčċox̣ʷ – I did not mean to; I am sorry.

purr **nx̣ʷllpcin** – cat's purr. *rt.: x̣ʷall – flutter/shake; suffix: ...cin, ...cn – action of the mouth. See: shake.*
es nx̣ʷllpcini – It is purring.

purse **ax̣éṅeʔ** – beaded bag/handbag. *rt.: i ax̣ – it has lines. See: line.*
łax̣éṅeʔ – small beadedbag/handbag.

snululimtn – coin purse; bank. *prefix: sn... – a place of; suffix: ...tin, ...tn – means of/device.*

pus **mċołt** – pus.

push **kʷup** – push; shove.
kʷupm – S/he pushed. **čn kʷupm, kʷ kʷupm**
es kʷupi – S/he is pushing. **čnes kʷupi, kʷes kʷupi**
qs kʷupi – S/he is going to push. **čiqs kʷupi, kʷqs kʷupi**

kʷupis – S/he pushed s.o./s.t. **kʷupn, kʷupntxʷ**
es kʷupms – S/he is pushing s.o./s.t. **ies kʷupm, as kʷupm**
qs kʷupms – S/he is going to push s.o./s.t. **iqs kʷupm, aqs kʷupm**
kʷúʔupis – They pushed s.o./s.t. **qeʔ kʷupntm, kʷupntp**

kʷułtm – S/he/it was pushed.

kʷupiš – Push. *cmd.*
kʷupnt – Push it. *cmd.*
es nkʷupmelsi – S/he is wanting to push. **čnes nkʷupmelsi, kʷes nkʷupmelsi**
kʷppnuis – S/he succeeded in pushing s.o./s.t. **kʷppnun, kʷppnuntxʷ**
es kʷupnwexʷi – They are pushing each other. **qeʔes kʷupnwexʷi, pes kʷupnwexʷi**

ta qʷo qes kʷupstxʷ – Do not push me! **kʷupis łu snkʷsixʷs u tk̓ʷuk̓ʷ** – My cousin pushed him down. **qʷo kʷupis** – S/he pushed me. **t swe u qʷo kʷupis** – Who pushed me?

nkʷpiṅč – push someone's back; push someone forward.
nkʷpiṅčis – S/he pushed s.o.'s back. **nkʷpiṅčn, nkʷpiṅčntxʷ**
es nkʷpiṅčms – S/he is pushing s.o.'s back. **ies nkʷpiṅčm, as nkʷpiṅčm**
qs nkʷpiṅčms – S/he is going to push s.o.'s back. **iqs nkʷpiṅčm, aqs nkʷpiṅčm**

nkʷpiṅčnt – Push his/her back. *cmd.*

ċq̓ʷšnim – push off with one foot/leg.
ċq̓ʷšnim – S/he pushed off. **čn ċq̓ʷšnim, kʷ ċq̓ʷšnim**

ċq̓ʷċq̓ʷšnim – push off repeatedly with one foot/leg.

tečim – push with the tip of a slender object. *(i.e., tip of finger, tip of a stick, etc.)*
tečntes – S/he pushed s.t. with a tip. **tečnten, tečntexʷ**
es tečims – S/he is pushing s.t. with a tip. **ies tečim, as tečim**
qs tečims – S/he is going to push s.t. with a tip. **iqs tečim, aqs tečim**

ntčaqs – push out something from inside an pipe with a stick/wire.

ta qʷo qes elstxʷ – Do not bug me; do not push me.

čnes čyami – I am inciting to evil.

pussy willow

sɫt̓it̓ič̓i – pussy willow; *Salix discolor.*

put

t̓uk̓ʷ – put something down; lay something down; place something down. *(i.e., an object, bet, wager, etc.)*
t̓k̓ʷum – put something down/to place someone in charge/to appoint.
t̓k̓ʷntes – S/he put s.t. down. **t̓k̓ʷntén, t̓k̓ʷntéxʷ**
es t̓k̓ʷums – S/he is putting s.t. down. **ies t̓k̓ʷum, as t̓k̓ʷum**
qs t̓k̓ʷums – S/he is going to put s.t. down. **iqs t̓k̓ʷum, aqs t̓k̓ʷum**
t̓k̓ʷntéʔes – They put s.t. down. **qeʔ t̓k̓ʷntém, t̓k̓ʷntép**
es t̓k̓ʷúʔums – They are putting s.t. down. **qeʔes t̓k̓ʷum, es t̓k̓ʷump**

es t̓uk̓ʷ – It is put down.

t̓k̓ʷunt – Put it down. *cmd.*
eɫ t̓k̓ʷunt – Put it back down. *cmd.*

t̓k̓ʷncut – place one's self down.
t̓k̓ʷncutš – Put yourself down. *cmd.*

t̓k̓ʷmstes – S/he laid s.t./s.o. down. **t̓k̓ʷmsten, t̓k̓ʷmstexʷ**
es t̓k̓ʷmstes – S/he is laying s.t./s.o. down. **es t̓k̓ʷmsten, es t̓k̓ʷmstexʷ**
es t̓k̓ʷmstems – S/he is laying s.t./s.o. down. **ies t̓k̓ʷmstem, as t̓k̓ʷmstem**
qs t̓k̓ʷmstems – S/he is going to lay s.t./s.o. down. **iqs t̓k̓ʷmstem, aqs t̓k̓ʷmstem**

t̓k̓ʷmstem – S/he/it was laid down.

t̓k̓ʷmstem t sċʔal – The sickness put me down.

čɫt̓k̓ʷum – put something down on the surface.
čɫt̓k̓ʷntes – S/he put s.t. down on the surface. **čɫt̓k̓ʷntén, čɫt̓k̓ʷntéxʷ**
es čɫt̓k̓ʷums – S/he is putting s.t. down on the surface. **ies čɫt̓k̓ʷum, as čɫt̓k̓ʷum**
qs čɫt̓k̓ʷums – S/he is going to put s.t. down on the surface. **iqs čɫt̓k̓ʷum, aqs čɫt̓k̓ʷum**
čɫt̓k̓ʷntéʔes – They put s.t. down on the surface. **qeʔ čɫt̓k̓ʷntém, čɫt̓k̓ʷntép**

čɫt̓uk̓ʷ – placed upon; laid.

čɫt̓k̓ʷunt – Put it on the surface. *cmd.*

ṅem čɫt̓k̓ʷntexʷ uɫéʔ – You will put it on top again.

čɫt̓k̓ʷetkʷm – place something on the surface of the water.
čɫt̓k̓ʷetkʷis – S/he put s.t. on the water. **čɫt̓k̓ʷetkʷn, čɫt̓k̓ʷetkʷntxʷ**
es čɫt̓k̓ʷetkʷms – S/he is placing s.t. on the water. **ies čɫt̓k̓ʷetkʷm, as čɫt̓k̓ʷetkʷm**
qs čɫt̓k̓ʷetkʷms – S/he is going to place s.t. on the water. **iqs čɫt̓k̓ʷetkʷm, aqs čɫt̓k̓ʷetkʷm**

čɫt̓k̓ʷetkʷnt – Put it on the water. *cmd.*

The **i** following uvular consonants (UC) and the glottal stop **ʔ** sound like English "*ey*" as in the words th*ey*, h*ey*, wh*ey*, etc. Salish UC are: **q, q̓, qʷ, q̓ʷ, x̣, x̣ʷ**. For example, the suffix ...**qin** – head/top, is often spelled using English *ey* as "q*ey*n". So **qi, q̓i, qʷi, q̓ʷi, x̣i, x̣ʷi**, may be spelled with English *ey* as **q***ey*, **q̓***ey*, **qʷ***ey*, **q̓ʷ***ey*, **x̣***ey*, **x̣ʷ***ey* in other texts.

s.t. - something, the 3rd person
(s.t.) - something implied
s.o. - someone, the 3rd person
sl. - singular form
pl. - plural form
rt. - root word
cmd. - command
lit. - literally
fig. - figuratively
i.e., - for example
See: - Redirection to a related word.

čłťk̓ʷetkʷn ƛ̓iyeʔ u čn laap – I put the canoe on the water and floated.

nťk̓ʷetkʷm – place something in the water.
nťk̓ʷetkʷis – S/he put s.t. in the water. **nťk̓ʷetkʷn, nťk̓ʷetkʷntxʷ**
es nťk̓ʷetkʷms – S/he is placing s.t. in the water. **ies nťk̓ʷetkʷm, as nťk̓ʷetkʷm**
qs nťk̓ʷetkʷms – S/he is going to place s.t. in the water. **iqs nťk̓ʷetkʷm, aqs nťk̓ʷetkʷm**

nťk̓ʷetkʷnt – Put it in the water. *cmd.*

nťk̓ʷetkʷn sšenš l łčepeʔ – I put the rock in the bucket of water.

nťk̓ʷum – put something inside.
nťk̓ʷntes – S/he put s.t. inside. **nťk̓ʷntén, nťk̓ʷntéxʷ**
es nťk̓ʷums – S/he is putting s.t. inside. **ies nťk̓ʷum, as nťk̓ʷum**
qs nťk̓ʷums – S/he is going to put s.t. inside. **iqs nťk̓ʷum, aqs nťk̓ʷum**

nťk̓ʷunt – Put it down. *cmd.*

nťk̓ʷnten sččxʷumeʔ l čluk̓ʷċeʔ kʷemt k̓ʷis elk̓ʷn – I put the ball in the box and then I went and put it away.

k̓ʷłťk̓ʷum – put something underneath.
k̓ʷłťk̓ʷntes – S/he put s.t. underneath. **k̓ʷłťk̓ʷntén, k̓ʷłťk̓ʷntéxʷ**
es k̓ʷłťk̓ʷums – S/he is putting s.t. underneath. **ies k̓ʷłťk̓ʷum, as k̓ʷłťk̓ʷum**
qs k̓ʷłťk̓ʷums – S/he is going to put s.t. underneath. **iqs k̓ʷłťk̓ʷum, aqs k̓ʷłťk̓ʷum**

es k̓ʷłťuk̓ʷ – It is placed underneath.

k̓ʷłťk̓ʷunt – Place it underneath. *cmd.*

k̓ʷłťk̓ʷntén l snčłʔitštn – I put it under my bed. ci **k̓ʷłnčehk̓ʷéptn es k̓ʷłťuk̓ʷ l sšenš čsax̣x̣m l k̓ʷłnčmep** – The key is under the rock near the door.

čťk̓ʷum – put something on the side.
čťk̓ʷntes – S/he put s.t. on the side. **čťk̓ʷntén, čťk̓ʷntéxʷ**
esč ťk̓ʷums – S/he is putting s.t. on the side. **ies čťk̓ʷum, as čťk̓ʷum**
qs čťk̓ʷums – S/he is going to put s.t. on the side. **iqs čťk̓ʷum, aqs čťk̓ʷum**

čťk̓ʷunt – Put it on the side. *cmd.*

qmin – put things down; lay things down; place things down.
qmin – S/he put things down. **čn qmin, kʷ qmin**
es qmini – S/he is putting things down. **čnes qmini, kʷes qmini**
qs qmini – S/he is going to put things down. **čiqs qmini, kʷqs qmini**

qmis – S/he put the things down. **qmin, qmintxʷ**
es qminms – S/he is putting the things down. **ies qminm, as qminm**
qs qminms – S/he is going to put the things down. **iqs qminm, aqs qminm**

es qmin – They are placed down.

qmniẏeẇt – things placed down here and there. *suffix:* ***...éẇt*** *– group state.*
čqmnálqʷ – things sent away.
sqmnlscut – goods. *pl.*

nqmint – Put the things inside. *cmd.*

ye sťsťasšis še snołupsts es qmin – His/her shoes and pants are there.

čłqmin – put things on a surface.
čłqmin – S/he placed things on a surface. **čn čłqmin, kʷ čłqmin**

es č̓łqmini – S/he is placing things on a surface. **čnes č̓łqmini, kʷes č̓łqmini**
qs č̓łqmini – S/he is going to place things on a surface. **čiqs č̓łqmini, kʷqs č̓łqmini**

nqmnetkʷ – put things in the water. *suffix:* ***...etkʷ, ...tkʷ*** *– liquid*
nqmnetkʷm – S/he put (things) in the water. **čn nqmnetkʷm, kʷ nqmnetkʷm**
es nqmnetkʷi – S/he is placing (things) in the water. **čnes nqmnetkʷi, kʷes nqmnetkʷi**
qs nqmnetkʷi – S/he is going to put (things) in the water. **čiqs nqmnetkʷi, kʷqs nqmnetkʷi**
nqmnéʔetkʷm – They put (things) in the water. **qeʔ nqmnetkʷm, p nqmnetkʷm**

nqmnetkʷis – S/he put things in the water. **nqmnetkʷn, nqmnetkʷntxʷ**
es nqmnetkʷms – S/he is placing things in the water. **ies nqmnetkʷm, as nqmnetkʷm**
qs nqmnetkʷms – S/he is going to place things in the water. **iqs nqmnetkʷm, aqs nqmnetkʷm**
nqmnéʔetkʷis – They put things in the water. **qeʔ qmnetkʷntm, nqmnetkʷntp**

nqmnetkʷnt – Put them in the water. *cmd.*

nqmnéʔetkʷis łu sʔíʔiłis – They put their food in the water. **čn nqmnetkʷm t sicm̓ –** I put the blankets in the water.

> The **i** following uvular consonants (UC) and the glottal stop **ʔ** sound like English "*ey*" as in the words th*ey*, h*ey*, wh*ey*, etc. Salish UC are: **q, q̇, qʷ, q̇ʷ, x̣, x̣ʷ**. For example, the suffix **...qin** – head/top, is often spelled using English *ey* as "q*ey*n". So **qi, q̇i, qʷi, q̇ʷi, x̣i, x̣ʷi**, may be spelled with English *ey* as **q***ey*, **q̇***ey*, **qʷ***ey*, **q̇ʷ***ey*, **x̣***ey*, **x̣ʷ***ey* in other texts.

sil – place more than one object upright. *See:* ***place.***

caq – place a single object upright; set down. *See:* ***place.***

k̇ʷłlʔo – put something in an enclosure; put in the oven. *See:* ***oven.***

npkʷétkʷ – pour round objects in water. *(i.e., berries, rocks, etc.)* *See:* ***pour.***

nt̓qetkʷm – stack/put it in the water. *rt.:* ***t̓qem*** *– stack.*
nt̓qetkʷis – S/he put it in the water. **nt̓qetkʷn, nt̓qetkʷntxʷ**
es nt̓qetkʷms – S/he is putting it in the water. **ies nt̓qetkʷm, as nt̓qetkʷm**
qs nt̓qetkʷms – S/he is going to put it in the water. **iqs nt̓qetkʷm, aqs nt̓qetkʷm**

nt̓qétkʷnt l séwłkʷ – You put it in the water.

ṗeč̓ – get hot from some heat source; warmed/heated from radiant heat. *See:* ***heat.***

łoqʷ – overlay; place something on/over something else *(not to cover)*; lay something on; drape something over a narrow/smaller object. *See:* ***lay over.***

q̇eʔ – put/place/squeeze inside something; inserted between. *See:* ***insert.***

łixʷp – slip/pull/put something fitted over an object. *See:* ***pull over.***

put away

elk̇ʷm – store away; put away; save.
elk̇ʷis – S/he put s.t. away. **elk̇ʷn, elk̇ʷntxʷ**
es elk̇ʷms – S/he is putting s.t. away. **ies elk̇ʷm, as elk̇ʷm**
qs elk̇ʷms – S/he is going to put s.t. away. **iqs elk̇ʷm, aqs elk̇ʷm**

elk̇ʷent – Put it away. *cmd.*

sʔelk̇ʷlscut – souvenir.
sʔelk̇ʷmn – keepsake, memorial gift.

kʷum – save; stash. *See:* ***save.***

> s.t. - something, the 3rd person
> (s.t.) - something implied
> s.o. - someone, the 3rd person
> *sl.* - singular form
> *pl.* - plural form
> *rt.* - root word
> *cmd.* - command
> *lit.* - literally
> *fig.* - figuratively
> *i.e.,* - for example
> *See:* - Redirection to a related word.

put down

caq – place a single object upright; set down. *See:* ***set.***

ṗin – long objects put in a lying position. *See: **lay**.*

es čiċ – one long object put in a lying position. *See: **lay**.*

put in

q̇eʔ – put/place/squeeze inside something; inserted between. *See: **insert**.*

put on

qmin – put things down; lay things down; place things down. *See: **lay**.*

x̣cnum̓t – ready/dressed; put clothes on. *See: **wear**.*

łixʷp – slip/pull/put something fitted over an object. *See: **pull over**.*

put out

łeps – extinguish a fire; turn off a light or electrical appliance. *See: **light up**.*

łepsis – S/he/it turned it off. **łepsn, łepsntxʷ**
es łepsms – S/he/it is turning it off. **ies łepsm, as łepsm**
qs łepsms – S/he/it is going to turn it off. **iqs łepsm, aqs łepsm**

łepsnt – Turn it off. *cmd.*
łepsncut – extinguish one's self; turn one's self off.

łepsnt ci ċék̓ʷsšn – Turn off the light.

puzzled

sil̓ – confused; unable to figure something out; mistaken. *See: **confuse**.*

Q

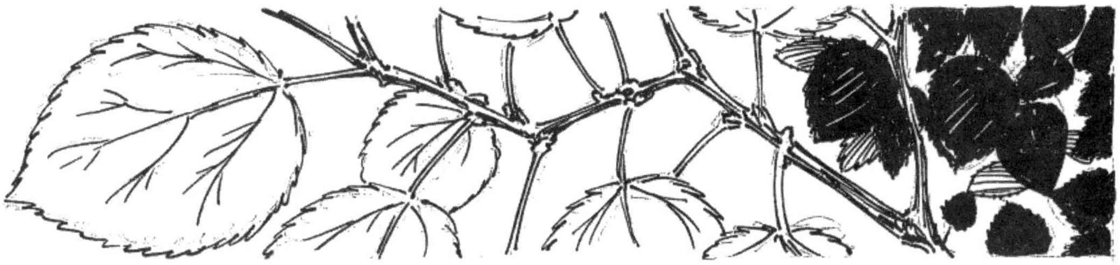

Qeyqeyshi **qeyqeyši** – man's name.

Q-tip **nxʷl̓k̓ʷpe** – ear tickler, ear scratcher. *(in the past, the tip of a feather was used)*

quaking aspen **ml̓ml̓téłp**, *ml̓ml̓té* – quaking aspen; *Populus tremuloides*.

quarrel **čscnmnwéxʷist**, *čscnmnwé* – quarrel; say bad words to each other.
*prefix: **čs...** – bad; suffix: **...cin, ...cn** – action of the mouth; suffix: **...wexʷ** – action to each other.*
čscnmnwéxʷist – They quarreled. **qeʔ čscnmnwéxʷist, p čscnmnwéxʷist**
es čscnmnwéxʷisti – They are quarreling. **qeʔes čscnmnwéxʷisti, pes čscnmnwéxʷisti**
qs čscnmnwéxʷisti – They're going to quarrel. **qeʔqs čscnmnwéxʷisti, pqs čscnmnwéxʷisti**

quarter **kʷateʔ** – quarter.

question **nsumels** – want to question; want to ask.
nsumels – S/he wanted to question. **čn nsumels, kʷ nsumels**
es nsumelsi – S/he is wanting to question. **čnes nsumelsi, kʷes nsumelsi**
qs nsumelsi – S/he is going to want to question. **čiqs nsumelsi, kʷqs nsumelsi**

nsumelsmis – S/he wanted to question s.o. **nsumelsmn, nsumelsmntxʷ**
es nsumelsms – S/he is wanting to question s.o. **ies nsumelsm, as nsumelsm**
qs nsumelsms – S/he is going to want to question s.o. **iqs nsumelsm, aqs nsumelsm**

séw – ask; seek information. *See: **ask**.*

sułtumš – inquire; ask people; ask at large. *See: **inquire**.*
ha puti kʷ ep scsułtumš – Do you still have any questions?

q̇eyus – doubt; disbelief; question. *See: **doubt**.*

quick **qʷim̓m** – anxious; in a hurry; move quickly. *See: **hurry**.*

x̣ʷełé – hurry; quickly. *See: **hurry**.*

x̣ʷełéčst – do work in a hurry; do something quick. *See: **hurry**.*

quiet **čúʔup** – quiet.
čúʔup – S/he stopped talking. **čn čúʔup, kʷ čúʔup**
es čupmi – S/he is keeping silent. **čnes čupmi, kʷes čupmi**
qs čupmi – S/he is going to keep silent. **čiqs čupmi, kʷqs čupmi**

čupstes – S/he/it made s.o. quit talking. **čupsten, čupstexʷ**
es čupims – S/he/it is making s.o. quit talking. **ies čupim, as čupim**
qs čupims – S/he/it is going to make s.o. quit talking. **iqs čupim, aqs čupim**
čupstéʔes – They made s.o. quit talking. **qeʔ čupstem, čupstep**
es čupíʔims – They are making s.o. quit talking. **qeʔes čupim, qs čupimmp**
qs čupíʔims – They are going to make s.o. quit talking. **qeʔqs čupim, qs čupimmp**

s.t. - something, the 3rd person
(s.t.) - something implied
s.o. - someone, the 3rd person
sl. - singular form
pl. - plural form
rt. - root word
cmd. - command
lit. - literally
fig. - figuratively
i.e., - for example
See: - Redirection to a related word.

čupmistmis – S/he/it quit talking to s.o. **čupmistmn, čupmistntxʷ**
qs čupmistmms – S/he/it is going to quit talking to s.o. **iqs čupmistmm, aqs čupmistmm**
čupmíˀistmis – They quit talking to s.o. **qeˀ čupmistmntm, čupmistmntp**

čupemn – one inclined to stop others from talking. *suffix: **...emn** – one inclined to do.*

čúˀupš – Be quiet. *cmd.*
čúˀupwi – All of you be quiet. *cmd.*
čupskʷ – Make s.o. quit talking. *cmd.*
čupmistmnt – Stop talking to s.o. *cmd.*
čucn čúˀupš – Be quiet.
čupłtumš – stop the people from talking.

čupcin – quiet the talk. *suffix: **...cin, ...cn** – action of the mouth.*
čewep – shut up all of a sudden.

čúˀupš es itši – Be quiet s/he/it is sleeping. **ta qes čupmistmntxʷ łu asxʷsixʷlt –** Do not stop talking to your children. **hoy čupcincn –** I quit talking to you.

čucn – say nothing. *suffix: **...cin, ...cn** – action of the mouth.*
čucn – S/he did not say anything. **čn čucn, kʷ čucn**

ṅem čucn – S/he will not say anything. **ṅem čn čucn, ṅem kʷ čucn**

čucnš – Do not say anything. *cmd.*

hoycn – quit talking; quit making noise; quit crying. *suffix: **...cin, ...cn** – action of the mouth.*
hoycn – S/he quit talking. **čn hoycn, kʷ hoycn**
es hoycni – S/he is remaining silent. **čnes hoycni, kʷes hoycni**
qs hoycni – S/he is going to quit talking. **čiqs hoycni, kʷqs hoycni**

hoycnis – S/he made s.o. quit talking. **hoycn, hoycntxʷ**
es hoycnms – S/he is keeping s.o. silent. **ies hoycnm, as hoycnm**
qs hoycnms – S/he is going to make s.o. quit talking. **iqs hoycnm, aqs hoycnm**

hoycnmis – S/he quit talking about s.t. **hoycnmn, hoycnmntxʷ**
es hoycnmms – S/he is keeping silent about s.t. **ies hoycnmm, as hoycnmm**
qs hoycnmms – S/he is going to quit talking about s.t. **iqs hoycnmm, aqs hoycnmm**

hoycnemn – one inclined to stop talking. *suffix: **...emn** – one inclined to do.*

hoycnš – Quit talking. *cmd.*
hoycnt – Make s.o. quit talking. *cmd.*

nłkʷḱʷiyecn, *nłkʷḱʷi* **–** whisper; talk little; talk quiet. *suffix: **...cin, ...cn** – action of the mouth. See: **whisper**.*

qmqémlš – person who is very quiet, reserved.
qmqemt – S/he is at peace/content. *See: **calm**.*

saṅ – tranquil; quiet and calm; tame; settled.
snap – stare off; daydream; become quiet and calm; settled. *See: **daydream**.*
sṅap – S/he became settled. **čn sṅap, kʷ sṅap**
es sṅpma – S/he is becoming settled. **čnes sṅpma, kʷes sṅpma**
qs sṅpma – S/he is going to become settled. **čiqs sṅpma, kʷqs sṅpma**

sṅpstas – S/he made s.o. settle down. **sṅpstan, sṅpstaxʷ**
es sṅpams – S/he is making s.o. settle down. **ies sṅpam, as sṅpam**
qs sṅpams – S/he is going to make s.o. settle down. **iqs sṅpam, aqs sṅpam**

sṅpnois – S/he succeeded in making s.o. settled. **sṅpnon, sṅpnontxʷ**

es sṅpnonms – S/he is succeeding in making s.o. settled. **ies sṅpnonm, as sṅpnonm**
qs sṅpnonms – S/he is going to succeed in making s.o. settled. **iqs sṅpnonm, aqs sṅpnonm**

sṅapš – Settle down. *cmd.*
sṅpstakʷ – Settle him/her/it down. *cmd.*
sṅpstwaxʷ – settle each other down.

sṅsáṅt, *sṅsá* – gentle; tame; settled; calm and quiet. *See: **tame**.*

> The **i** following uvular consonants (UC) and the glottal stop ʔ sound like English "*ey*" as in the words th*ey*, h*ey*, wh*ey*, etc. Salish UC are: **q**, **q̇**, **qʷ**, **q̇ʷ**, **x̣**, **x̣ʷ**. For example, the suffix ...**qin** – head/top, is often spelled using English *ey* as "q*ey*n". So **qi**, **q̇i**, **qʷi**, **q̇ʷi**, **x̣i**, **x̣ʷi**, may be spelled with English *ey* as **q***ey*, **q̇***ey*, **qʷ***ey*, **q̇ʷ***ey*, **x̣***ey*, **x̣ʷ***ey* in other texts.

quilt

snq̇ʷomi – comforter; quilt *(stuffed blanket; thick blanket).*

sṫqʷṫaqʷi – quilt *(pieces sewn together).*

quirt

łqiqxʷmn – little whip; quirt. *suffix: **...min, ...mn** – instrument/tool.*

quit

hoy – quit; stop; finish; okay; that's it; cease.
hoym – S/he/it quit/finished. **čn hoym, kʷ hoym**
es hoymi – S/he/it is quiting/finishing. **čnes hoymi, kʷes hoymi**

hoyho – S/he/it finished. **čn hoyho, kʷ hoyho**
hoyhóʔo – They finished. **qeʔ hoyho, p hoyho**

i hoy – S/he/it is finished/ is at the end. **i čn hoy, i kʷ hoy**

hoysts – S/he/it quit s.t./s.o. **hoystn, hoystxʷ**
es hoyms – S/he/it is quitting s.t./s.o. **ies hoym, as hoym**
qs hoyms – S/he/it is going to quit s.t./s.o. **iqs hoym, aqs hoym**
hóʔoysts – They quit s.t./s.o. **qeʔ hoystm, hoystp**
es hóʔoyms – They are quitting s.t./s.o. **qeʔes hoym, es hoymp**
qs hóʔoyms – They are going to quit s.t./s.o. **qeʔqs hoym, qs hoymp**

shoy – the end; the ending.
čhoytn – the thing/reason something/someone ended/quit.

hoyskʷ – Quit, leave s.o./s.t. alone. *cmd.*
hoywi – All of you quit. *cmd.*
t hoyskʷ – Quit that first. *cmd.*
hoycnš – Stop talking; stop crying. *(said to a baby when it's crying) cmd.*

hoystm – It was ended.

čhoysts – S/he/it quit because of s.t./s.o. **čhoystn, čhoystxʷ**
es čhoyms – S/he/it is quitting because of s.t./s.o. **ies čhoym, as čhoym**
qs čhoyms – S/he/it is going to quit because of s.t./s.o. **iqs čhoym, aqs čhoym**
čhóʔoysts – They quit because of s.t./s.o. **qeʔ čhoystm, čhoystp**
es čhóʔoyms – They are quitting because of s.t./s.o. **qeʔes čhoym, es čhoymp**
qs čhóʔoyms – They are going to quit because of s.t./s.o. **qeʔqs čhoym, qs čhoymp**

es hoyčsti – S/he quit working. **čnes hoyčsti, kʷes hoyčsti**

islup čn hoyho – At any moment I will finish. **ta qes hoystn** – I will never quit. **ta qeʔ qes hoystm** – We must never quit. **t tlé u we qeʔes olqʷšiłls u áyx̣ʷt u hoysts** – Teresa really was helping us, but she got tired and quit. **šehoy** – That is all.

> s.t. - something, the 3rd person
> (s.t.) - something implied
> s.o. - someone, the 3rd person
> *sl.* - singular form
> *pl.* - plural form
> *rt.* - root word
> *cmd.* - command
> *lit.* - literally
> *fig.* - figuratively
> *i.e.,* - for example
> *See:* - Redirection to a related word.

hoyčst – quit working. *suffix: **...ečst, ...čst** – of the hand.*
hoyčstm – S/he quit the work. **čn hoyčstm, kʷ hoyčstm**

es hoyčsti – S/he is quiting the work. **čnes hoyčsti, kʷes hoyčsti**
qs hoyčsti – S/he is going to quit the work. **čiqs hoyčsti, kʷqs hoyčsti**

hoyčstis – S/he quit working on s.t. **hoyčstn, hoyčstntxʷ**
es hoyčsms – S/he is quiting the work on s.t. **ies hoyčsm, as hoyčsm**
qs hoyčsms – S/he is going to quit working on s.t. **iqs hoyčsm, aqs hoyčsm**

nhoyls – want to quit something; feel like quiting. *circumfix:* ***n...els*** *– want, feel.*
nhoylsm – S/he wanted to quit. **čn nhoylsm, kʷ nhoylsm**
es nhoylsi – S/he wants to quit. **čnes nhoylsi, kʷes nhoylsi**
qs nhoylsi – S/he is going to want to quit. **čiqs nhoylsi, kʷqs nhoylsi**

nhoylsmis – S/he wanted to quit s.t. **nhoylsmn, nhoylsmntxʷ**
es nhoylsms – S/he wants to quit s.t. **ies nhoylsm, as nhoylsm**
qs nhoylsms – S/he is going to want to quit s.t. **iqs nhoylsm, aqs nhoylsm**

es nhoylsmnwéʔexʷi – We want to quit each other. **qeʔes nhoylsmnwexʷi, pes nhoylsmnwexʷi**

čṗʔum – *Figuratively*, quit or give up; *literally*, fart on it.

quitter **sxʷhóym –** one tasked to quit. *prefix:* ***sxʷ...*** *– one tasked to do.*

quiver **mél̓ –** quiver; glimpse of something disappearing.
ml̓ml̓téłp, *ml̓ml̓té* – quaking aspen; *Populus tremuloides.*

iwu – movement of something voluntary as moving a body part or involuntary as a quiver, shake, or tremble. *See:* ***move.***
iwést – S/he trembled/twitched. **čn iwést, kʷ iwést**
es iwésti – S/he is trembling/twitching. **čnes iwésti, kʷes iwésti**

x̣ʷall – flutter/shake. *See:* ***shake.***

quiver for arrows **snq̓ʷłté –** arrow quiver.

nċoqičṅ – draw an arrow out of a quiver on the back. *See:* ***draw.***

R

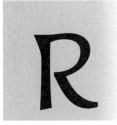

rabbit **sɫqʷá –** rabbit; *Lepus americanus.*

sɫqʷaqʷċeʔ – little or young rabbit.
sɫqʷa scq̓ʷlé – roasted rabbit. **sɫqʷásts kʷtisi –** Big Blanket's rabbit.

wiẇslščn, wisšlšn – cottontail; *Sylvilagus nuttallii.*

ususilščn – bunny, small rabbit; *Brachylagus idahoensis.*

raccoon **mhuyeʔ –** raccoon; *Procyon lotor.*

race **q̓ʷiiq̓ʷóƛ̓š,** *q̓ʷiiq̓ʷó* – race. *rt.:* ***q̓ʷuƛ̓š*** *– run, pl.*

q̓ʷiiq̓ʷó – S/he raced. **čn q̓ʷiiq̓ʷó, kʷ q̓ʷiiq̓ʷó**
es q̓ʷiiq̓ʷó – S/he is racing. **čnes q̓ʷiiq̓ʷó, kʷes q̓ʷiiq̓ʷó**
qs q̓ʷiiq̓ʷó – S/he is going to race. **čiqs q̓ʷiiq̓ʷó, kʷqs q̓ʷiiq̓ʷó**
q̓ʷiiq̓ʷóʔo – They raced. **qeʔ q̓ʷiiq̓ʷó, p q̓ʷiiq̓ʷó**
es q̓ʷiiq̓ʷóʔo – They are racing. **qeʔes q̓ʷiiq̓ʷó, pes q̓ʷiiq̓ʷó**
qs q̓ʷiiq̓ʷóʔo – They are going to race. **qeʔqs q̓ʷiiq̓ʷó, pqs q̓ʷiiq̓ʷó**

es q̓ʷiq̓ʷiq̓ʷó – Each one of them is racing. **qeʔes q̓ʷq̓ʷiq̓ʷó, pes q̓ʷq̓ʷiq̓ʷó**

sq̓ʷiiq̓ʷoƛ̓š – horse race.
snq̓ʷiiq̓ʷoƛ̓š, *snq̓ʷiiq̓ʷo* – place of racing; racetrack; race course.

qeʔes q̓ʷiq̓ʷiq̓ʷo qeʔes eɫiɫni – We were each racing while we were eating.

race horse **snq̓ʷiiq̓ʷoƛ̓štn, snq̓ʷiiq̓ʷo –** horse race.

racer **npƛ̓áċeʔ –** eastern racer, green racer; *Coluber constrictor.*

rack **snɫṗé –** drying rack.

sncqaẏe – rack to smoke and dry meat. *rt.:* ***cqaẏe*** *– dry/smoke meat; prefix:* ***sn...*** *– a place of.*

čɫcqmin – truck rack. *rt.:* ***caq*** *– single object placed down; prefix:* ***čɫ...*** *– surface.*

radio **čx̣ʷax̣ʷnč,** *čx̣ʷa* – radio; harp; guitar; stereo; anything that makes music.

čx̣ʷax̣ʷnčs – his/her radio, etc.

raft **lčéwl –** make a wooden raft. *rt.:* ***lič*** *– tied together.*

lčéwlm – S/he made a wooden raft. **lčéwlm, lčéwlm**
es lčéwli – S/he is making a wooden raft. **čnes lčéwli, kʷes lčéwli**
qs lčéwli – S/he is going to make a wooden raft. **čiqs lčéwli, kʷqs lčéwli**

lčéwlis – S/he made that wooden raft. **lčéwln, lčéwlntxʷ**
es lčéwlms – S/he is making that wooden raft. **ies lčéwlm, as lčéwlm**
qs lčéwlms – S/he is going to make that wooden raft. **iqs lčéwlm, aqs lčéwlm**

s.t. - something, the 3rd person
(s.t.) - something implied
s.o. - someone, the 3rd person
sl. - singular form
pl. - plural form
rt. - root word
cmd. - command
lit. - literally
fig. - figuratively
i.e., - for example
See: - Redirection to a related word.

slčéwl – wooden raft.
slčéwlxʷ – raft.

lčéwlš – Make a wooden raft. *cmd.*
lčéwlnt – Make the wooden raft. *cmd.*

raggy **čkʷskʷsċiċéʔ** – raggy cloth. *suffix: **...iċéʔ** – covered in.*

x̣ipt – gnawed by bugs. *(i.e., dried meat or woolen clothes, bugs got into them) See: **gnaw**.*

łiqt – shredded, torn cloth; raggy. *See: **shred**.*

t̓łip – pull apart something; rip something. *See: **rip**.*

raid **x̣eyílš** – go on a raid of the enemy. *suffix: **...ilš** – autonomous.*
x̣eyílš – S/he raided. **čn x̣eyílš, kʷ x̣eyílš**
es x̣eyílši – S/he is raiding. **čnes x̣eyílši, kʷes x̣eyílši**
qs x̣eyílši – S/he is going to raid. **čiqs x̣eyílši, kʷqs x̣eyílši**
x̣eyíʔilš – They raided. **qeʔ x̣eyílš, p x̣eyílš**
es x̣eyíʔilši – They are raiding. **qeʔes x̣eyílši, pes x̣eyílši**
qs x̣eyíʔilši – They are going to raid. **qeʔqs x̣eyílši, pqs x̣eyílši**

čx̣eyílšmis – S/he raided the enemy. **čx̣eyílšmn, čx̣eyílšmntxʷ**
es čx̣eyílšmms – S/he is raiding the enemy. **ies čx̣eyílšmm, as čx̣eyílšmm**
qs čx̣eyílšmms – S/he is going to raid the enemy. **iqs čx̣eyílšmm, aqs čx̣eyílšmm**
čx̣eyíʔilšmis – They raided the enemy. **qeʔ čx̣eyílšmntm, čx̣eyílšmntp**
es čx̣eyíʔilšmms – They are raiding the enemy. **qeʔes čx̣eyílšmm, es čx̣eyílšmmp**
qs čx̣eyíʔilšmms – They are going to raid the enemy. **qeʔqs čx̣eyílšmm, qs čx̣eyílšmmp**

sxʷx̣eyílš – one tasked to raid; warrior.

railroad cars **čx̣ʷllq̓ʷálqʷtn,** *čx̣ʷllq̓ʷá* – train, locomotive, railroad cars. *suffix: **...tin, ...tn** – means of/device.*

railroad tracks **čx̣ʷllq̓ʷa sxʷuytis** – railroad tracks.
čx̣ʷišalqʷ sxʷuytis – railroad tracks.

rain **st̓ipéys** – rain.
t̓ipéys – It rained.
es t̓ipéysi – It is raining.
qs t̓ipeysi – It is going to rain.

t̓ipéysis – It rained on s.o./s.t.
es t̓ipéysms – It is raining on s.o./s.t.
qs t̓ipeysms – It is going to rain on s.o./s.t.

t̓ipeysmntm – S/he/it got rained on. **qʷo t̓ipeysmntm, kʷ t̓ipeysmntm**

es t̓ipéysi č čo – It is raining outside. **x̣ʷa ṅem t̓ipéys** – Maybe it'll rain; if it rains. **es t̓ipeysi ci č es moq̓ʷ** – It is raining in/on that mountain. **eċx̣i qs t̓ipeysi** – It looks like it is going to rain.

łtt̓ipéys – It rained a little; it drizzled.
es łtt̓ipéysi – It is raining a little.
qs łtt̓ipéysi – It is going to rain a little.

xʷʔéys – It rained hard/a lot.
es xʷʔéysi – It is raining/snowing hard/a lot.
qs xʷʔéysi – It is going to rain hard/a lot.

es łk̓ʷṅk̓ʷéysi – It is sprinkling; one drop is falling here and there.

es łuweysi – The rain is letting up. *rt.:* ***łuwet*** *– few.*
qs łuweysi – The rain is going to let up.

es pt́ncoti, *es pt́nco* – It is raining slush*; it is making itself stick to something. (wet slushy snow) See:* ***slush****.*

es ołépiʔi – It is raining sleet.

uyásq̇t, *uyá* – the storm/weather ended. *See:* ***storm****.*

rainbow

skʷumiwtšn – rainbow.

nq̇l̓ye – rainbow around the sun or moon.

sʔuluáx̣n – sun dogs; sun flares.
es uluáx̣n – It is the sun dogs. *(sun flares)*

rainbow trout

nxʷmeneʔ – steelhead salmon; rainbow trout; *Oncorhynchus mykiss. (native to the area of the Spokane tribe; lit. red/pink around the ears)*

The **i** following uvular consonants (UC) and the glottal stop **ʔ** sound like English "*ey*" as in the words th*ey*, h*ey*, wh*ey*, etc. Salish UC are: **q**, **q̇**, **qʷ**, **q̇ʷ**, **x̣**, **x̣ʷ**. For example, the suffix …**qin** – head/top, is often spelled using English *ey* as "q*ey*n". So **qi**, **q̇i**, **qʷi**, **q̇ʷi**, **x̣i**, **x̣ʷi**, may be spelled with English *ey* as **q***ey*, **q̇***ey*, **qʷ***ey*, **q̇ʷ***ey*, **x̣***ey*, **x̣ʷ***ey* in other texts.

raincoat

sṗičlqs – raincoat; glossy coat. *rt.:* ***ṗič*** *– glossy; suffix:* ***…lqs, …alqs*** *– clothes.*

es ṗičlqs – S/he is wearing a raincoat. **čnes ṗičlqs, kʷes ṗičlqs**

ṗičlqsiš – Put your raincoat on. *cmd.*

raise

nwisšlš – go up; to raise. *rt.:* ***nwist*** *– up, up high.*
nwisšlšis – S/he raised s.t. up. **nwisšlšn, nwisšlšntxʷ**
es nwisšlšms – S/he is raising s.t. up. **ies nwisšlšm, as nwisšlšm**
qs nwisšlšms – S/he is going to raise s.t. up. **iqs nwisšlšm, aqs nwisšlšm**
nwíʔisšlšis – They raised s.t. up. **qeʔ nwisšlšntm, nwisšlšntp**
es nwíʔisšlšms – They are raising s.t. up. **qeʔes nwisšlšm, es nwisšlšmp**
qs nwíʔisšlšms – They are going to raise s.t. up. **qeʔqs nwisšlšm, qs nwisšlšmp**

nwisšlšnt – Raise it up. *cmd.*
nwisšlšiš – Go up. *cmd. See:* ***up****.*

es nwisšlši – S/he is going up. *See:* ***up****.*

nwisšlšnt asčuwax̣n – Raise your arm.

x̣ccmi – family raised (grew up) at a certain place.

raisin

sṗiqáłq – berry; fruit; raisin. *rt.:* ***ṗiẏáq*** *– ready, ripe; suffix:* ***…ałq*** *– smell, accompaniment.*
słpṗiqáłq – raisin.

rake

ušulexʷ – rake the ground. *rt.:* ***uš*** *– comb; suffix:* ***…ulexʷ*** *– land.*
ušulexʷ – S/he raked. **čn ušulexʷ, kʷ ušulexʷ**
es ušulexʷi – S/he is raking. **čnes ušulexʷi, kʷes ušulexʷi**
qs ušulexʷi – S/he is going to rake. **čiqs ušulexʷi, kʷqs ušulexʷi**

ušulexʷis – S/he raked it. **ušulexʷn, ušulexʷntxʷ**
es ušulexʷms – S/he is raking it. **ies ušulexʷm, as ušulexʷm**
qs ušulexʷms – S/he is going to rake it. **iqs ušulexʷm, aqs ušulexʷm**

ušulexʷtn – rake. *rt.:* ***uš*** *– comb; affix:* ***…ulexʷ*** *– land; suffix:* ***…tin, …tn*** *– means of/device.*
łušulexʷtn – hand rake. *rt.:* ***uš*** *– comb; affix:* ***…ulexʷ*** *– land; suffix:* ***…tin, …tn*** *– means of/device.*

s.t. - something, the 3rd person
(s.t.) - something implied
s.o. - someone, the 3rd person
sl. - singular form
pl. - plural form
rt. - root word
cmd. - command
lit. - literally
fig. - figuratively
i.e., - for example
See: - Redirection to a related word.

y̓ay̓am̓min – farm rake. *rt.: **y̓amim** – gather; suffix: **...min** – instrument.*

ram **tʔamnqnmwexʷ**, *tʔamnqnwe* – bump/ram each other's heads together. *rt.: **teʔ** – hit/bump into.*
es tʔamnqnmwexʷi – They are bumping heads together. *(The action of bighorn sheep rams.)*

nllsew̓s – ram/smash something together permanently. *suffix: **...éw̓s** – in between, middle.*
nllsew̓sis – S/he/it rammed s.t. together. **nllsew̓sn, nllsew̓sntxʷ**
es nllsew̓sms – S/he/it is ramming s.t. together. **ies nllsew̓sm, as nllsew̓sm**
qs nllsew̓sms – S/he/it is going to ram s.t. together. **iqs nllsew̓sm, aqs nllsew̓sm**

range **snk̓ʷl̓sncutn,** *snk̓ʷl̓sncu* – place to cook; kitchen; kitchen range; cooking stove. *prefix: **sn...** – a place of; suffix: **...tin, ...tn** – means of/device.*

rape **ċk̓ʷum** – thrust; rape. *(literally describs the action; suggests rape.)*
ċk̓ʷum – He raped. **čn ċk̓ʷum, kʷ ċk̓ʷum**

ċk̓ʷntes – He raped s.o. **ċk̓ʷnten, ċk̓ʷntexʷ**
es ckʷums – He is raping s.o. **ies ċk̓ʷums, as ċk̓ʷums**
qs ċk̓ʷums – He is going to rape s.o. **iqs ċk̓ʷum, aqs ċk̓ʷum**

ċk̓ʷntem – S/he got raped.

qʷo ċk̓ʷntem – I was raped.

rapid **ay̓ip** – go fast, hurry. *(i.e., on foot, by car, or on horseback) See: **fast**.*

ƛ̓áx̣t – fast, rapid. *See: **fast**.*

rare **tam tméy̓** – rare; not often.

y̓ay̓áat – rare; scarce; hard to acquire. *rt.: **y̓aa** – scarce.*
y̓ay̓áat łu ululim – Money is scarce. **y̓ay̓áat łu stem̓** – something is hard to get. **y̓ay̓áat łu esy̓apqinm** – rare powwow, celebration.

heheʔt – rarely, when it used to be common.
heheʔt tʔe u qeʔ uwewlš – We rarely talk anymore.

tʔe u tnk̓ʷuʔ – once in awhile.

łaqʷlwi – shows up once in awhile. *See: **infrequent**.*
łaqʷcin – spoke up (once in a while). *suffix: **...cin, ...cn** – action of the mouth.*

x̣iʔu – rare; raw. *See: **raw**.*

raspberry **ll̓ác** – red raspberry.

mcukʷ – black raspberry; blackberry; blackcap; *Rubus occidentalis*.

rat **héw̓t** – pack rat, bushy-tailed wood rat; *Neotoma cinerea*.

sqʷʔópłxʷ – hole, den *(as of a mouse or rat). rt.: **qʷʔóp** – make soft; suffix: **...ełxʷ, ...łxʷ** – house.*

rather **k̓ʷ še** – rather; supposed to be; preferably; evidently then. *In conjunction these two particles express preferability, expected or required, in an action/object as opposed to an understood or stated action/object.*

k̓ʷ še qʷoyʔe – It is supposed to be me. **k̓ʷ še qeʔes elisłni tam qeʔes memscuti** – We are supposed to be eating not playing. **k̓ʷ še qeʔqs xʷuyi č sntumístn** – We're supposed to be going to the store. **k̓ʷ še kʷ sewneʔ** – You are supposed to hear.

ration **scpx̣ʷmi** – something that is passed out. *(i.e., rations, per capita, commodities, pay day) prefix:* ***sc...*** *– s.t. that's been done/made/prepared.*

rattle **ċós**, *ċó* – rattle.

ċaľé – rattle.

čťxʷalqʷ, *čťxʷa* – hoof rattle.

rattlesnake **x̣eʔulexʷ** – rattlesnake; *Crotalus viridis.*

rattlesnake plantain **nčʔéw̓s** – rattlesnake plantain; *Goodyera oblongifolia.*

Ravalli **sk̓ʷłʔólqʷe,** *sk̓ʷłʔó* – Ravalli, Flathead Nation. *lit. getting back to the water.*

eł k̓ʷłʔólqʷe – S/he went back to the water again.

raven **m̓lá** – raven; *Corvus corax.*

ravine **es tóqʷ** – ravine, draw; slope walled canyon.

raw **x̣iʔu** – rare; raw.
es x̣iʔu – It is raw; rare *(not fully cooked).*

rawhide **qlélxʷ** – rawhide.

q̓étt – pelt, hide.

sčłq̓ʷastn, *sčłq̓ʷa* – basket made of bark; rawhide bucket. *See:* ***basket.***

čq̓ʔiċéʔ, *čq̓ʔi* – Indian suitcase, rawhide bag. *lit. it has a pattern around it. See:* ***pattern.***

rawhide bag **čq̓ʔi** – Indian suitcase; rawhide bag.

razor **áx̣ʷstn** – razor. *suffix:* ***...tin, ...tn*** *– means of/device.*

amx̣ʷsncu – razor; shaver.

reach **xʷálčst** – reach for something; extend the arm/hand. *suffix:* ***...ečst, ...čst*** *– of the hand.*
xʷálčstm – S/he reached. **čn xʷálčstm, kʷ xʷálčstm**
es xʷálčsti – S/he is reaching. **čnes xʷálčsti, kʷes xʷálčsti**
qs xʷálčsti – S/he is going to reach. **čiqs xʷálčsti, kʷqs xʷálčsti**

čxʷálčstis – S/he reached for s.t. **čxʷálčstn, čxʷálčstntxʷ**
es čxʷálčstms – S/he is reaching for s.t. **ies čxʷálčstm, as čxʷálčstm**
qs čxʷálčstms – S/he is going to reach for s.t. **iqs čxʷálčstm, aqs čxʷálčstm**

es xʷlxʷálčsti – S/he is reaching. **čnes xʷlxʷálčsti, kʷes xʷlxʷálčsti**

xʷálčstiš – Reach. *cmd.*
čxʷálčsnt – Reached for it. *cmd.*

read **aċx̣łq̓ey̓mi** – read; look at a paper with words. *rt.:* ***aċx̣*** *– look;* ***q̓ey̓im*** *– write.*
aċx̣łq̓ey̓im – S/he read. **čn aċx̣łq̓ey̓im, kʷ aċx̣łq̓ey̓im**
es aċx̣łq̓ey̓mi – S/he is reading. **čnes aċx̣łq̓ey̓mi, kʷes aċx̣łq̓ey̓mi**
qs aċx̣łq̓ey̓mi – S/he is going to read. **čiqs aċx̣łq̓ey̓mi, kʷqs aċx̣łq̓ey̓mi**

aċx̣łq̓ey̓mistš – Read. *cmd.*

The **i** following uvular consonants (UC) and the glottal stop **ʔ** sound like English "*ey*" as in the words th*ey*, h*ey*, wh*ey*, etc. Salish UC are: **q, q̓, qʷ, q̓ʷ, x̣, x̣ʷ**. For example, the suffix **...qin** – head/top, is often spelled using English *ey* as "qeyn". So **qi, q̓i, qʷi, q̓ʷi, x̣i, x̣ʷi**, may be spelled with English *ey* as **q***ey*, **q̓***ey*, **qʷ***ey*, **q̓ʷ***ey*, **x̣***ey*, **x̣ʷ***ey* in other texts.

s.t. - something, the 3rd person
(s.t.) - something implied
s.o. - someone, the 3rd person
sl. - singular form
pl. - plural form
rt. - root word
cmd. - command
lit. - literally
fig. - figuratively
i.e., - for example
See: - Redirection to a related word.

awʔawm – say words out loud; read aloud. *See: **say**.*
awʔawm – S/he read out loud. **čn awʔawm, kʷ awʔawm**
es awʔawi – S/he is reading out loud. **čnes awʔawi, kʷes awʔawi**
qs awʔawi – S/he is going to read out loud. **čiqs awʔawi, kʷqs awʔawi**

ready

es wiʔ – ready; complete.
ta čnes wiʔ – I am not ready.

ṗiẏáq – ready; ripe.
še ṗiẏáq łu asqeľtč – Then your meat is ready.
ṅe ṗiẏáq m k̓ʷłq̓ʷʔentéxʷ – When it is ready, you strain it.

ƛ̓e – ready.
ha ƛ̓e – Are you ready?
ha ƛ̓e ocqe – Did s/he go outside?
ha ƛ̓e kʷ qʷoṁma – Are you almost ready?

x̣cim – prepare something; make ready; put in order. *(i.e., put disarrayed things in order, getting things ready for travel, etc.)*
x̣cim – S/he prepared (s.t.). **čn x̣cim, kʷ x̣cim**
es x̣cmi – S/he is preparing (s.t.). **čnes x̣cmi, kʷes x̣cmi**
qs x̣cmi – S/he is going to prepare (s.t.). **čiqs x̣cmi, kʷqs x̣cmi**

x̣cmstes – S/he prepared it. **x̣cmsten, x̣cmstexʷ**
es x̣cmims – S/he is preparing it. **ies x̣cmim, as x̣cmim**
qs x̣cmims – S/he is going to prepare it. **iqs x̣cmim, aqs x̣cmim**

x̣ccnuis – S/he succeeded in preparing it. **x̣ccnun, x̣ccnuntxʷ**
es x̣ccnunms – S/he is succeeding in preparing it. **ies x̣ccnunm, as x̣ccnunm**

es x̣cmilši – S/he is getting back in order. **čnes x̣cmilši, kʷes x̣cmilši** *suffix: **...ilš** – autonomous.*
es čx̣cmilši – S/he is in line with something. **čnes čx̣cmilši, kʷes čx̣cmilši**

x̣cint – Put it in order. *cmd.*
es nx̣cels – S/he has one's self prepared. **čnes nx̣cels, kʷes nx̣cels**
x̣cmncut, *x̣cmncu* – get one's self ready/dressed. *See: **dress**.*

es čx̣ccusi łu sṗiqáłq – The berries are getting ready. **es x̣ccmi łu es ċéʔek̓ʷ –** The buds are getting ready to flower.

x̣cus – ready eyes; eyes peeled.
x̣cx̣cusm – His/her eyes were ready. **čn x̣cx̣cusm, kʷ x̣cx̣cusm**
es x̣cx̣cusi – His/her eyes are ready. **čnes x̣cx̣cusi, kʷes x̣cx̣cusi**
qs x̣cx̣cusi – His/her eyes are going to be ready. **čiqs x̣cx̣cusi, kʷqs x̣cx̣cusi**

x̣cx̣cusiš – Make your eyes ready; keep your eyes peeled. *cmd.*

čn x̣cx̣cusm u wičtn sx̣ʷľéščn – My eyes were ready and I saw a white-tail buck.

nx̣cels – feel/want/be prepared for whatever may happen. *circumfix: **n...els** – want, feel.*
nx̣cels – S/he prepared one's self. **čn nx̣cels, kʷ nx̣cels**
es nx̣celsi – S/he is preparing one's self. **čnes nx̣celsi, kʷes nx̣celsi**
qs nx̣celsi – S/he is going to prepare one's self. **čiqs nx̣celsi, kʷqs nx̣celsi**

es nx̣cels – S/he has one's self prepared. **čnes nx̣cels, kʷes nx̣cels**

nx̣celsmis – S/he prepared one's self for s.t. **nx̣celsmn, nx̣celsmntxʷ**
es nx̣celsms – S/he is preparing one's self for s.t. **ies nx̣celsm, as nx̣celsm**

qs nx̣celsms – S/he is going to prepare one's self for s.t. **iqs nx̣celsm, aqs nx̣celsm**

nx̣celsiš – Prepare yourself. *cmd.*
nx̣celsmnt – Prepare yourself for it. *cmd.*
nx̣celstn – something used for preparation.

ha nx̣celsmntxʷ łu aqs x̣ʷċim – Did you prepare yourself to argue with him/her?
qeʔ čxʷicutmłlt u ta qeʔ epł nx̣celstn – We were attacked and had nothing prepared.

x̣cečst – fix something; make something prepared for whatever; make someone behave so as to be ready and prepared next time; punish someone to teach a lesson of preparation. *(i.e. telling a dog to go after someone to teach them a lesson so that should the same event happen again the person will be prepared; as fixed is used in the phrase "that'll fix 'em.")*
x̣cečstmis – S/he fixed s.o. **x̣cečstmn, x̣cečstmntxʷ**
es x̣cečstms – S/he is fixing s.o. **ies x̣cečstm, as x̣cečstm**
qs x̣cečstms – S/he is going to fix s.o. **iqs x̣cečstm, aqs x̣cečstm**

x̣cečstmnt – Fix s.o. *cmd.*

uẏéčst, *uẏé* **–** finish working; done working; come to an end. *See:* ***finish.***

ċẏu – Not yet *(answer to question are you ready).*
ċẏu čnes uẏé – I am still not done/finished/ ready.

> The **i** following uvular consonants (UC) and the glottal stop ʔ sound like English "*ey*" as in the words th*ey*, h*ey*, wh*ey*, etc. Salish UC are: **q**, **q̇**, **qʷ**, **q̇ʷ**, **x̣**, **x̣ʷ**. For example, the suffix ...**qin** – head/top, is often spelled using English *ey* as "q*ey*n". So **qi**, **q̇i**, **qʷi**, **q̇ʷi**, **x̣i**, **x̣ʷi**, may be spelled with English *ey* as **q***ey*, **q̇***ey*, **qʷ***ey*, **q̇ʷ***ey*, **x̣***ey*, **x̣ʷ***ey* in other texts.

real

unéxʷ, *uné* **–** real; true; yes.
u l šeẏ u eċx̣i unéxʷ – That is how it really was.
tam unéxʷ – false.

ha kʷes unéxʷisti – Are you telling the truth?

nunxʷéneʔ, *nunxʷé* **–** believe. *See:* ***believe.***

really

nłapaqs, *nłapa* **–** arrive at the end; an expression indicating to go to the extreme. *rt.:* ***łe–*** *end.*
nłapa qʷamqʷmt – Really excellent! **es čselm nłapa es npiyéʔelsi –** Those two are really happy.
nłapa k̓ʷłċa tʔe u ƛ̓lil sqelixʷ – Death can be very painful.

receive

tixʷł – acquire something; get or receive something; gather. *See:* ***acquire.***

recent

t slʔe – recently; not too long ago.
t spistem̓ u k̓ʷul̓ntxʷ t slʔe – When did you do it? Recently.

sic – new; right then; right now; recent. *See:* ***new.***

recognize

suxʷ – know; recognize; acquainted with. *See:* ***know.***
suxʷis – S/he/it recognized it. **suxʷn, suxʷntxʷ**
es suxʷms – S/he/it is recognizing it. **ies suxʷm, as suxʷm**
qs suxʷms – S/he/it is going to recognize it. **iqs suxʷm, aqs suxʷm**
súʔuxʷis – They recognized it. **qeʔ suxʷntm, suxʷntp**
es súʔuxʷms – They are recognizing it. **qeʔes suxʷm, es suxʷmp**
qs suʔuxʷms – They are going to recognize it. **qeʔqs suxʷm, qs suxʷmp**

nsuxʷcn – recognize a voice/sound.
nsuxʷcn – S/he/it recognized a voice/sound. **čn nsuxʷcn, kʷ nsuxʷcn**
es nsuxʷcni – S/he/it is recognizing a voice/sound. **ies nsuxʷcni, kʷes nsuxʷcni**
qs nsuxʷcni – S/he/it is going to recognize a voice/sound. **čiqs nsuxʷcni, kʷqs nsuxʷcni**

> s.t. - something, the 3rd person
> (s.t.) - something implied
> s.o. - someone, the 3rd person
> *sl.* - singular form
> *pl.* - plural form
> *rt.* - root word
> *cmd.* - command
> *lit.* - literally
> *fig.* - figuratively
> *i.e.,* - for example
> *See:* - Redirection to a related word.

nsuxʷcis – S/he/it recognized s.o.'s voice. **nsuxʷcn, nsuxʷcntxʷ**
es nsuxʷcnms – S/he/it is recognizing s.o.'s voice. **ies nsuxʷcnm, as nsuxʷcnm**
qs nsuxʷcnms – S/he/it is going to recognize s.o.'s voice. **iqs nsuxʷcnm, aqs nsuxʷcnm**

x̣iṅe qʷo nsuxʷcis – S/he/it might recognize my voice. **es nsuxʷcn t inṗiṗuyšn –** S/he/it recognizes the sound of my car.

reconcile **ihém –** regain friendship; make peace; reconcile differences. *See: **peace**.*

record **člo**ʔ**m –** record.
es čloʔ**ms –** S/he is recording s.t. **ies člo**ʔ**m, as člo**ʔ**m**
qs čloʔ**ms –** S/he is going to record s.t. **iqs člo**ʔ**m, aqs člo**ʔ**m**

sččloʔ **–** something that's been put onto; a recording.
čloʔ**mintn –** something to put onto; recording tape. *suffix: **...tin, ...tn** – means of/device.*
syal čloʔ**mintn –** round recording device; compact disc (cd). *suffix: **...tin, ...tn** – means of/device.*

recreation **xʷeƛ̓mist –** relax; do what one wants; pass time; recreate. *See: **relax**.*
snxʷeƛ̓mistn – place to relax, recreate; a recreation area. *prefix: **sn...** – a place of; suffix: **...tin, ...tn** – means of/device.*

nxʷxʷeƛ̓mistn – certain place to relax, recreate, do what you want *(i.e., fishing hole, some place in the mountains, your shop, etc.). suffix: **...tin, ...tn** – means of/device.*

recreational entertainment **čx̣ʷƛ̓xʷe –** recreational entertainment.

recreational vehicle **esxʷilwis citxʷ –** recreational vehicle; RV. *lit. moving house.*

rectangle **i wisšn q̓tq̓it –** rectangle; a long square.

red **kʷil –** red. **kʷlkʷil –** reds. *pl.*
kʷilis – S/he made it red. **kʷiln, kʷilntxʷ**
es kʷilms – S/he is making it red. **ies kʷilm, as kʷilm**
qs kʷilms – S/he is going to make it red. **iqs kʷilm, aqs kʷilm**

i kʷil – It is red.
i łkʷikʷl – It is a little red; redish; pink.
kʷiil̓ – It turned red.

kʷilnt – Make it red. *cmd.*

kʷekʷil̓eʔ – little red one, affectionately.
čkʷilċeʔ – red all over it; covered in red.
kʷils – red face.
nkʷilqs – red nose.
nkʷilkʷ – wine. *lit. red liquid.*
kʷlkʷlé – red-headed woodpecker.

ikʷlkʷil łu isnq̓ʷóƛ̓šn – My socks are red.

xʷem – red paint/dye. *See: **paint**.*

yuċmn – red ochre, red paint.

red besseya **čečłu –** red besseya; kitten tails; *Besseya rubra.*

red birch **sicqṅełp –** red birch; *Betula occidentalis.*

red crossbill **łˀayˀayxʷusáqs**, *łˀayˀayxʷusá* – red crossbill; *Loxia curvirostra.*

red fox **x̣ʷax̣ʷaálixʷ**, *x̣ʷax̣ʷaá* – fox; *Vulpes vulpes.*

redhead **skʷaˀqin**. **čkʷilqn** – redhead. *suffix:* ***...qin, ...qn*** *– top.*

red-headed woodpecker **kʷlkʷlé** – red-headed woodpecker; *Melanerpes erythrocephalus.*

spuwáľqn – pileated woodpecker; red-headed woodpecker; *Dryocopus pileatus.*

red-hot **ṗéxʷ** – bright; the red-hot glow of s.t. heated. *See:* ***hot.***

red oshier dogwood **stečcxʷ** – red osier dogwood; red willow; *Cornus stolonifera.*

red paint **xʷem** – red paint/dye. *See:* ***paint.***

yuċmn – red ochre; red paint.

red raspberry **lľac** – raspberry.

red salmon **smłič**, *smłi* – salmon *general term*; chinook salmon; *Oncorhynchus tshawytscha. See:* ***salmon.***

red-shafted flicker **kʷlkʷlé** – red-shafted flicker; common flicker; northern flicker.

red-tailed chipmunk **qʷqʷċẇé** – yellow pine chipmunk; red-tailed chipmunk.

red-winged blackbird **čłq̓ẏe ƛ̓čƛ̓á** – red-winged blackbird; *Agelaius phoeniceus.*

refrigerator **snsulmn** – refrigerator. *rt.:* ***sult*** *– freeze.*

refuse **tamm** – not; deny; refuse.

tamm – S/he/it refuses/denies to. **čn tamm, kʷ tamm**
es tami – S/he/it is refusing. **čnes tami, kʷes tami**
qs tami – S/he/it is going to refuse. **čiqs tami, kʷqs tami**

tamsts – S/he refused it. **tamstn, tamstxʷ**
es tamms – S/he is refusing it. **ies tamm, as tamm**
qs tamms – S/he is going to refuse it. **iqs tamm, aqs tamm**
táˀamsts – They refused it. **qeˀ tamstm, tamstp**
es táˀamsts – They are refusing it. **qeˀes tamstm, es tamstp**
qs táˀamsts – They are going to refuse it. **qeˀqs tamstm, qs tamstp**

es tmtami – S/he/it is refusing repeatedly. **čnes tmtami, kʷes tmtami**
es tmtamms – S/he is repeatedly refusing it. **ies tmtamm, as tmtamm**

tmtmmuł – one that habitually refuses.
ntamtn – refusal.
čtamtn – reason for refusal.

tamiš – Refuse. *cmd.*
tamskʷ – Refuse it. *cmd.*
tmals – despise; disregard; spurn; pay no attention to; have no feelings for; have no care for; have no respect for. *See:* ***despise.***

The **i** following uvular consonants (UC) and the glottal stop **ˀ** sound like English "*ey*" as in the words th*ey*, h*ey*, wh*ey*, etc. Salish UC are: **q**, **q̓**, **qʷ**, **q̓ʷ**, **x̣**, **x̣ʷ**. For example, the suffix ...**qin** – head/top, is often spelled using English *ey* as "q*ey*n". So **qi**, **q̓i**, **qʷi**, **q̓ʷi**, **x̣i**, **x̣ʷi**, may be spelled with English *ey* as **q***ey*, **q̓***ey*, **qʷ***ey*, **q̓ʷ***ey*, **x̣***ey*, **x̣ʷ***ey* in other texts.

s.t. - something, the 3rd person
(s.t.) - something implied
s.o. - someone, the 3rd person
sl. - singular form
pl. - plural form
rt. - root word
cmd. - command
lit. - literally
fig. - figuratively
i.e., - for example
See: - Redirection to a related word.

tmłtomš – deny people.
tmsteṁ – have nothing.
tmsteṁ – S/he/it has/got nothing. **čn tmsteṁ, kʷ tmsteṁ**

tmotm – nothing; good for nothing; *(term of belittlement). See: **nothing**.*
tmsteṁ – have nothing. *See: **nothing**.*
tamcnm – refuse what is said. *suffix: **...cin, ...cn** – action of the mouth.*
ntmcan – say no.
tmstawexʷ – refuse each other.
tmštawexʷ – refuse something to each other.

ta qes tamstxʷ – Do not refuse it. **ta tamstn** – No, I refused it. **ha tamstxʷ** – Did you refuse it?
x̣ʷa uc tamstn – Perhaps I will not accept it.

ntmaneʔ – refuse to hear; not listening.
ntmanʔem – S/he refused to hear. **čn ntmanʔem, kʷ ntmanʔem**
es ntmanʔei – S/he is refusing to hear. **čnes ntmanʔei, kʷes ntmanʔei**
qs ntmanʔei – S/he is going to refuse to hear. **čiqs ntmanʔei, kʷqs ntmanʔei**

ntmanʔemis – S/he refused to hear s.o. **ntmanʔemn, ntmanʔemntxʷ**
es ntmanʔems – S/he is refusing to hear s.o. **ies ntmanʔem, as ntmanʔem**
qs ntmanʔems – S/he is going to refuse to hear s.o. **iqs ntmanʔem, aqs ntmanʔem**

ntmanmnwexʷ – refuse to hear each other.

ẏekʷ – refuse to give; stingy.
ẏekʷminm – S/he refused to give. **čn ẏekʷminm, kʷ ẏekʷminm**
es ẏekʷmini – S/he is refusing to give. **čnes ẏekʷmini, kʷes ẏekʷmini**
qs ẏekʷmini – S/he is going to refuse to give. **čiqs ẏekʷmini, kʷqs ẏekʷmini**

ẏekʷmis – S/he refused to give s.t. **ẏekʷminm, kʷ ẏekʷmintxʷ**
es ẏekʷminms – S/he is refusing to give s.t. **ies ẏekʷminm, as ẏekʷmini**
qs ẏekʷminms – S/he is going to refuse to give s.t. **iqs ẏekʷmini, aqs ẏekʷmini**

sẏekʷmin – the thing refused to give.
scẏekʷmin – the thing not given.
ẏeẏukʷeʔ – stingy one.
ikʷmemn – one inclined to refuse to give. *suffix: **...emn** – one inclined to do.*

ẏekʷminiš – Don't give. *cmd.*
ẏekʷmint – Don't give it. *cmd.*
ẏekʷmełxʷ – refused to give a lodge.
ẏakʷmnalqs – refused to give clothes.
ẏakʷmsqax̣eʔ – refused to give a horse/car.

čeṁm – detest; reject something; have no care for something; snub something. *See: **detest**.*

es nx̣lx̣lmi – S/he is refusing. *rt.: **nx̣el** – afraid.*

regret

čłqʷṅcut – blame one's self; regret.
es čłqʷṅcutisti – S/he is regreting. **čnes čłqʷṅcutisti, kʷes čłqʷṅcutisti**

reins

ntx̣ʷmsqáx̣eʔtn – reins. *suffix: **...tin, ...tn** – means of/device.*

ččṅplasqáx̣eʔ – rein a horse.
es ččṅplasqáx̣eʔi – S/he is reining the horse. **čnes ččṅplasqáx̣eʔi, kʷes ččṅplasqáx̣eʔi**

ntnmusqáx̣eʔ – hold the reins tight.

es ntnmusqáx̣eʔi – S/he is holding the reins tight. **čnes ntnmusqáx̣eʔi, kʷes ntnmusqáx̣eʔi**

reject **čeṁm** – detest; reject something; have no care for something; snub something. *See: **detest**.*

tamm – not; deny; refuse. *See: **refuse**.*

aiṁeʔ – hate. *See: **hate**.*

relative **stṁélis** – relative.
stmṁélis – relatives.
čɫʔe stṁélis – close relative.

ṅem qeʔ čxʷimsqe č astṁélis – We will visit your relative.

snċʔew̓s – distant relative. *suffix: **...éw̓s** – in between, middle.*

relax **xʷeƛ̓mist** – relax; do what one wants; pass time; recreate.
xʷeƛ̓mist – S/he relaxed. **čn xʷeƛ̓mist, kʷ xʷeƛ̓mist**
es xʷeƛ̓misti – S/he is relaxing. **čnes xʷeƛ̓misti, kʷes xʷeƛ̓misti**
qs xʷeƛ̓misti – S/he is going to relax. **čiqs xʷeƛ̓misti, kʷqs xʷeƛ̓misti**
xʷeƛ̓míʔist – They relaxed. **qeʔ xʷeƛ̓mist, p xʷeƛ̓mist**
es xʷeƛ̓míʔisti – They are relaxing. **qeʔes xʷeƛ̓misti, pes xʷeƛ̓misti**
qs xʷeƛ̓míʔisti – They are going to relax. **qeʔqs xʷeƛ̓misti, pqs xʷeƛ̓misti**

snxʷeƛ̓mistn – place to relax/pass time; recreation area. *prefix: **sn...** – a place of; suffix: **...tin, ...tn** – means of/device.*
nxʷxʷeƛ̓mistn – specific place to relax; recreate; do what you want *(i.e., fishing hole, some place in the mountains, your shop, etc.). suffix: **...tin, ...tn** – means of/device.*

čnes xʷeƛ̓misti x̣ʷl̓ čiqs npiyelsi – I am relaxing so I can be happy.

xʷxʷṁqncut, *xʷxʷṁqncú* – relax one's self; to make one's self have no cares; to have no worries.
xʷxʷṁqncut – S/he relaxed. **čn xʷxʷṁqncut, kʷ xʷxʷṁqncut**
es xʷxʷṁqncuti – S/he is relaxing. **čnes xʷxʷṁqncuti, kʷes xʷxʷṁqncuti**
qs xʷxʷṁqncuti – S/he is going to relax. **čiqs xʷxʷṁqncuti, kʷqs xʷxʷṁqncuti**
xʷxʷṁqncúʔut – They relaxed. **qeʔ xʷxʷṁqncut, p xʷxʷṁqncut**
es xʷxʷṁqncúʔuti – They are relaxing. **qeʔes xʷxʷṁqncuti, pes xʷxʷṁqncuti**
qs xʷxʷṁqncúʔuti – They are going to relax. **qeʔqs xʷxʷṁqncuti, pqs xʷxʷṁqncuti**

xʷxʷuṁ – relaxed/safe/secure; have no worries; have no cares; out of danger. *See: **secure**.*

ɫexʷésčt, *ɫexʷé* – rest; relax; take a break. *See: **rest**.*

qim – calm; undisturbed. *See: **calm**.*

háw̓m – loosen something; *slacken. (i.e., knot, jar lid, tense person, etc.) See: **loose**.*

release **pƛ̓éčstm** – release something from the hand. *rt.: **pƛ̓im** – release from; suffix: **...ečst, ...čst** – of the hand.*
pƛ̓éčstm – S/he let go. **čn pƛ̓éčstm, kʷ pƛ̓éčstm**
es pƛ̓éčsti – S/he is letting go. **čnes pƛ̓éčsti, kʷes pƛ̓éčsti**
qs pƛ̓éčsti – S/he is going to let go. **čiqs pƛ̓éčsti, kʷqs pƛ̓éčsti**
pƛ̓éʔečstm – They let go. **qeʔ pƛ̓éčstm, p pƛ̓éčstm**
es pƛ̓éʔečsti – They are letting go. **qeʔes pƛ̓éčsti, pes pƛ̓éčsti**
qs pƛ̓éʔečsti – They are going to let go. **čiqs pƛ̓éčsti, pqs pƛ̓éčsti**

pƛ̓éčstmis – S/he let go of s.t./s.o. **pƛ̓éčstmn, pƛ̓éčstmntxʷ**
es pƛ̓éčstms – S/he is letting go of s.t./s.o. **ies pƛ̓éčstm, as pƛ̓éčstm**

The **i** following uvular consonants (UC) and the glottal stop **ʔ** sound like English "*ey*" as in the words *they, hey, whey*, etc. Salish UC are: **q, q̓, qʷ, q̓ʷ, x̣, x̣ʷ**. For example, the suffix **...qin** – head/top, is often spelled using English *ey* as "q*ey*n". So **qi, q̓i, qʷi, q̓ʷi, x̣i, x̣ʷi**, may be spelled with English *ey* as *qey, q̓ey, qʷey, q̓ʷey, x̣ey, x̣ʷey* in other texts.

s.t. - something, the 3rd person
(s.t.) - something implied
s.o. - someone, the 3rd person
sl. - singular form
pl. - plural form
rt. - root word
cmd. - command
lit. - literally
fig. - figuratively
i.e., - for example
See: - Redirection to a related word.

qs pƛ̓éčstms – S/he is going to let go of s.t./s.o. **iqs pƛ̓éčstm, aqs pƛ̓éčstm**
pƛ̓éʔečstmis – They let go of it. **qeʔ pƛ̓éčstmntm, pƛ̓éčstmntp**
es pƛ̓éʔečstms – They are letting go of s.t./s.o. **qeʔes pƛ̓éčstm, es pƛ̓éčstmp**
qs pƛ̓éʔečstms – They are going to let go of s.t./s.o. **qeʔqs pƛ̓éčstm, qs pƛ̓éčstmp**

pƛ̓éčstmnt – Let go of it! *cmd.*

ṅem pƛ̓éčstmis – S/he/it will let go of it. **ṅem pƛ̓éčstmn, ṅem pƛ̓éčstmntxʷ**
ṅem pƛ̓éʔečstmis – They will let go of it. **ṅem qeʔ pƛ̓éčstmntm, ṅem pƛ̓éčstmntp**

čpƛ̓éčšnmist – release something held by the foot. *rt.: **pƛ̓im** – release from; suffix: **...šin, ...šn** – feet.*
čpƛ̓éčšnmist – S/he let go. **čn čpƛ̓éčšnmist, kʷ čpƛ̓éčšnmist**
es čpƛ̓éčšnmisti – S/he is letting go. **čnes čpƛ̓éčšnmisti, kʷes čpƛ̓éčšnmisti**
qs čpƛ̓éčšnmisti – S/he is going to let go. **čiqs čpƛ̓éčšnmisti, kʷqs čpƛ̓éčšnmisti**

čpƛ̓éčšnmistmis – S/he let go of s.t. **čpƛ̓éčšnmistmn, čpƛ̓éčšnmistmntxʷ**
es čpƛ̓éčšnmistms – S/he is letting go of s.t. **ies čpƛ̓éčšnmistm, as čpƛ̓éčšnmistm**
qs čpƛ̓éčšnmistms – S/he is going to let go of s.t. **iqs čpƛ̓éčšnmistm, aqs čpƛ̓éčšnmistm**

čpƛ̓éčšnmistmnt – Let go of it! *cmd.*

čpƛ̓mist – release one's self from something. *(i.e., emotions, hanging onto s.t. over head, etc.)*
čpƛ̓mist – S/he released one's self. **čn čpƛ̓mist, kʷ čpƛ̓mist**
es čpƛ̓misti – S/he is releasing one's self. **čnes čpƛ̓misti, kʷes čpƛ̓misti**
qs čpƛ̓misti – S/he is going to release one's self. **čiqs čpƛ̓misti, kʷqs čpƛ̓misti**

čpƛ̓mistmis – S/he released s.t. from one's self. **čpƛ̓mistmn, čpƛ̓mistmntxʷ**
es čpƛ̓mistmms – S/he is releasing s.t. from one's self. **ies čpƛ̓mistmm, as čpƛ̓mistmm**
qs čpƛ̓mistmm – S/he is going to release s.t. from one's self. **iqs čpƛ̓mistmm, aqs čpƛ̓mistmm**

čpƛ̓mistmnt – Release it from yourself. *cmd.*

pƛ̓im – release; free from something; remove something.
pƛ̓ntes – S/he/it released it from s.t. **pƛ̓nten, pƛ̓ntexʷ**
es pƛ̓ims – S/he/it is releasing it from s.t. **ies pƛ̓im, as pƛ̓im**
qs pƛ̓ims – S/he/it is going to release it from s.t. **iqs pƛ̓im, aqs pƛ̓im**
pƛ̓ntéʔes – They release it from s.t. **qeʔ pƛ̓ntem, pƛ̓ntep**
es pƛ̓íʔims – They are releasing it from s.t. **qeʔes pƛ̓im, es pƛ̓imp**
qs pƛ̓íʔims – They are going to release it from s.t. **qeʔqs pƛ̓im, qs pƛ̓imp**

pƛ̓ntem – S/he/it was released from s.t.
es pƛ̓im – It is released/removed.

pƛ̓int – Remove it, take it off. *cmd.*
pƛ̓int anlkepu – Take off you coat. *cmd.*

pƛ̓ip – It slipped away/ended. *See: **slip**.*
čpƛ̓ip – It came undone. *See: **undone**.*
npƛ̓alqs, *npƛ̓a* **–** remove/take off clothes. *See: **undress**.*
pƛ̓qin – remove head cover/hat; bare head. *See: **hat**.*
npƛ̓ičṅm – remove a saddle. *See: **saddle**.*
pƛ̓usm – take a bridle/hackamore/halter off. *See: **bridle**.*
pƛ̓pƛ̓šnim – remove footwear. *See: **shoe**.*
npƛ̓mus – come to the end of a time period, an action, or a place; reach the full extent. *See: **end**.*

remain

lciʔ – stays here; remains here; dwells. *See: **stay**.*

člciʔm – stay by it; remain with it. *See: **stay**.*

nkʷɫciʔm – stay together with someone; remain together with someone. *See:* ***stay.***

remember **nɫk̓ʷk̓ʷmin** – remember.

nɫk̓ʷk̓ʷmis – S/he/it remembered s.t. **nɫk̓ʷk̓ʷmin, nɫk̓ʷk̓ʷmintxʷ**
es nɫk̓ʷk̓ʷminms – S/he/it is remembering s.t. **ies nɫk̓ʷk̓ʷminm, as nɫk̓ʷk̓ʷminm**
qs nɫk̓ʷk̓ʷminms – S/he/it is going to remember s.t. **iqs nɫk̓ʷk̓ʷminm, aqs nɫk̓ʷk̓ʷminm**
nɫk̓ʷk̓ʷmíʔis – They remembered s.t. **qeʔ nɫk̓ʷk̓ʷmintm, nɫk̓ʷk̓ʷmintp**
es nɫk̓ʷk̓ʷmíʔinms – They are remembering s.t. **qeʔes nɫk̓ʷk̓ʷminm, es nɫk̓ʷk̓ʷminmp**
qs nɫk̓ʷk̓ʷmíʔinms – They are going to remember s.t. **qeʔqs nɫk̓ʷk̓ʷminm, qs nɫk̓ʷk̓ʷminmp**

es nɫk̓ʷk̓ʷmists – S/he/it is remembering s.t. **es nɫk̓ʷk̓ʷmistn, es nɫk̓ʷk̓ʷmistxʷ**
qs nɫk̓ʷk̓ʷmists – S/he/it is going to remember s.t. **qs nɫk̓ʷk̓ʷmistn, qs nɫk̓ʷk̓ʷmistxʷ**
es nɫk̓ʷk̓ʷmists – S/he/it is remembering s.t. **es nɫk̓ʷk̓ʷmistn, es nɫk̓ʷk̓ʷmistxʷ**
qs nɫk̓ʷk̓ʷmists – S/he/it is going to remember s.t. **qs nɫk̓ʷk̓ʷmistn, qs nɫk̓ʷk̓ʷmistxʷ**

nɫk̓ʷɫk̓ʷmin – I remembered things.

nk̓ʷɫk̓ʷɫsemn – one inclined to remember. *suffix:* ***...emn*** *– one inclined to do.*
nɫk̓ʷk̓ʷnemn – one inclined to remember. *suffix:* ***...emn*** *– one inclined to do.*
nk̓ʷɫk̓ʷeɫs – The individual that remembers.

nɫk̓ʷk̓ʷmint – Remember it. *cmd.*

ha eɫ nɫk̓ʷk̓ʷmintxʷ – Do you remember it? **nɫk̓ʷk̓ʷmistmn** – I remembered you. **steṁ ɫu es nɫk̓ʷk̓ʷmistxʷ** – What do you remember? **ha es nɫk̓ʷk̓ʷmintxʷ** – Do you remember it? **ta qs tam nɫk̓ʷk̓ʷmistxʷ** – You have to remember it.

k̓ʷɫk̓ʷɫsncut – reflect back within one's self; search one's mind.
es k̓ʷɫk̓ʷɫsncuti – S/he is searching his/her mind. **čnes k̓ʷɫk̓ʷɫsncuti, kʷes k̓ʷɫk̓ʷɫsncuti**

> The **i** following uvular consonants (UC) and the glottal stop **ʔ** sound like English *"ey"* as in the words *they, hey, whey,* etc. Salish UC are: **q, q̓, qʷ, q̓ʷ, x̣, x̣ʷ**. For example, the suffix **...qin** – head/top, is often spelled using English *ey* as "q*ey*n". So **qi, q̓i, qʷi, q̓ʷi, x̣i, x̣ʷi,** may be spelled with English *ey* as **q***ey,* **q̓***ey,* **qʷ***ey,* **q̓ʷ***ey,* **x̣***ey,* **x̣ʷ***ey* in other texts.

remind **nɫk̓ʷɫk̓ʷelsm** – remind someone.

nɫk̓ʷɫk̓ʷelsis – S/he reminded s.o. **nɫk̓ʷɫk̓ʷelsn, nɫk̓ʷɫk̓ʷelsntxʷ**
es nɫk̓ʷɫk̓ʷelsms – S/he is reminding s.o. **ies nɫk̓ʷɫk̓ʷelsm, as nɫk̓ʷɫk̓ʷelsm**
qs nɫk̓ʷɫk̓ʷelsms – S/he is going to remind s.o. **iqs nɫk̓ʷɫk̓ʷelsm, aqs nɫk̓ʷɫk̓ʷelsm**

nɫk̓ʷɫk̓ʷelsnt – Remind s.o. *cmd.*

kʷ ies nɫk̓ʷɫk̓ʷelsm x̣iṅe nɫeptmntxʷ – I am reminding you because you might forget it.

remove **pƛ̓im** – release; free from something; remove something. *See:* ***release.***

pƛ̓int – Remove it, take it off. *cmd.*
pƛ̓qin – remove head cover/hat; bare head. *See:* ***hat.***
pƛ̓pƛ̓šnim – remove footwear. *See:* ***shoe.***
čpƛ̓ʔencut – undress one's self. *See:* ***undress.***
npƛ̓alqs, *npƛ̓a* – remove/take off clothes. *See:* ***undress.***
npƛ̓ičn̓m – remove a saddle. *See:* ***saddle.***
pƛ̓usm – take a bridle/hackamore/halter off. *See:* ***bridle.***

kʷƛ̓im – take something out; detach; loose/free embedded object. *See:* ***take.***

> s.t. - something, the 3rd person
> (s.t.) - something implied
> s.o. - someone, the 3rd person
> *sl.* - singular form
> *pl.* - plural form
> *rt.* - root word
> *cmd.* - command
> *lit.* - literally
> *fig.* - figuratively
> *i.e.,* - for example
> *See:* - Redirection to a related word.

repair **eɫ k̓ʷul̓** – repair something. *rt.:* ***k̓ʷul̓*** *– do.*

eɫ k̓ʷul̓m – S/he repaired (s.t.). **čn eɫ k̓ʷul̓m, kʷ eɫ k̓ʷul̓m**

es eɬ k̓ʷul̓i – S/he is repairing (s.t.). **čnes eɬ k̓ʷul̓i, kʷes eɬ k̓ʷul̓i**
qs eɬ k̓ʷul̓i – S/he is going to repair (s.t.). **čiqs eɬ k̓ʷul̓i, kʷqs eɬ k̓ʷul̓i**

eɬ k̓ʷul̓is – S/he repaired s.t. **eɬ k̓ʷul̓n, eɬ k̓ʷul̓ntxʷ**
es eɬ k̓ʷul̓ms – S/he/it is repairing s.t. **ies eɬ k̓ʷul̓m, as eɬ k̓ʷul̓m**
qs eɬ k̓ʷul̓ms – S/he/it is going to repair s.t. **iqs eɬ k̓ʷul̓m, aqs eɬ k̓ʷul̓m**

eɬ k̓ʷul̓ɬxʷ – repair a house.

repeat

ineẏcn, *ine* – repeat words; repeat something already said; say something again. *suffix:* ***...cin, ...cn*** *– action of the mouth.*
ineẏcnm – S/he repeated words. **čn ineẏcnm, kʷ ineẏcnm**
es ineẏcni – S/he is repeating words. **čnes ineẏcni, kʷes ineẏcni**
qs ineẏcni – S/he is going to repeat words. **čiqs ineẏcni, kʷqs ineẏcni**

sxʷineẏcnm – one tasked to repeat words. *prefix:* ***sxʷ...*** *– one tasked to do.*
ineẏcnemn – one inclined to repeat words. *suffix:* ***...emn*** *– one inclined to do.*

ineẏcniš – Say it again. *cmd.*

milk̓ʷ – always; repeatedly.
tmilk̓ʷ es emuti l es šit̓ ɬu mali – Mary always sits in that tree.

eċínt, *eċí* – question inquiring about what was said. *See:* ***say.***

reservation

sqlixʷulexʷ – Indian land.
sqelixʷ sṫulixʷ – reservation; people's land.

reserved

héʔemist – restrain one's self; reserved; in awe of. *rt.:* ***héʔe*** *– conserve, respect.*
héʔemist – S/he was reserved. **čn héʔemist, kʷ héʔemist**
es héʔemisti – S/he is being reserved. **čnes héʔemisti, kʷes héʔemisti**
qs héʔemisti – S/he is going to be reserved. **čiqs héʔemisti, kʷqs héʔemisti**

héʔemistmis – S/he was reserved with s.o./s.t. **héʔemistmn, héʔemistmntxʷ**
es héʔemistms – S/he is being reserved with s.o./s.t. **ies héʔemistm, as héʔemistm**
qs héʔemistms – S/he is going to be reserved with s.o./s.t. **iqs héʔemistm, aqs héʔemistm**

héʔemistmn ɬu smʔem – I keep myself in reserve with women.

ɬén – stoic; serious; look mean. *See:* ***serious.***

ẏaamin – shy; reserved; *lacking some quality, i.e., confidence, etc. See:* ***shy.***

respect

putʔem – respect something or somebody; hold something or someone sacred.
putʔeʔis – S/he respected s.o./s.t. **putʔen, putʔentxʷ**
es putʔems – S/he is respecting s.o./s.t. **ies putʔem, as putʔem**
qs putʔems – S/he is going to respect s.o./s.t. **iqs putʔem, aqs putʔem**
putʔéʔeʔis – They respected s.o./s.t. **qeʔ putʔentm, putʔentp**
es putʔéʔems – They are respecting s.o./s.t. **qeʔes putʔem, es putʔemp**
qs putʔéʔems – They are going to respect s.o./s.t. **qeʔqs putʔem, qs putʔemp**

putʔentm – It was respected.

scputʔe – sacred; something that's been respected. *prefix:* ***sc...*** *– s.t. that's been done/made/prepared.*
nputʔélstn – something used to respect; sacred. *suffix:* ***...tin, ...tn*** *– means of/device.*
putʔéncut – respect one's self.

putʔent – Respect it. *cmd.*

nkʷtnelsm – think highly of somebody; show respect for somebody; have trust for somebody. *rt.: **kʷtunt–** big; circumfix: **n...els–** want, feel.*

nkʷtnelsis – S/he thought highly of s.o. **nkʷtnelsn, nkʷtnelsntxʷ**
es nkʷtnelsms – S/he is thinking highly of s.o. **ies nkʷtnelsm, as nkʷtnelsm**
qs nkʷtnelsms – S/he is going to think highly of s.o. **iqs nkʷtnelsm, aqs nkʷtnelsm**
nkʷtnéʔelsis – They thought highly of s.o. **qeʔ nkʷtnelsn, nkʷtnelsntp**
es nkʷtnéʔelsms – They are thinking highly of s.o. **qeʔes nkʷtnelsm, es nkʷtnelsmp**
qs nkʷtnéʔelsms – They are going to think highly of s.o. **qeʔqs nkʷtnelsm, qs nkʷtnelsmp**

čnes sunumti ye sqltmixʷ es qʷlqʷeľti u ies nkʷtnelsm – I am listening to this man speak; I think highly of him.

héʔem – put away to keep something in its original state; show respect by using sparingly; conserve and protect something.

héʔem – S/he conserved. **čn héʔem, kʷ héʔem**
es héʔemi – S/he is conserving. **čnes héʔemi, kʷes héʔemi**
qs héʔemi – S/he is going to conserve. **čiqs héʔemi, kʷqs héʔemi**

héʔentes – S/he saved away s.t. **héʔenten, héʔentexʷ**
es héʔems – S/he is saving away s.t. **ies héʔem, as héʔem**
qs héʔems – S/he is going to save away s.t. **iqs héʔem, aqs héʔem**

héʔeiš – Conserve. *cmd.*
héʔemłtumš – show respect for people.
nhéʔemelsm – want to conserve something; act in a way that respects someone's feelings.
hehesnuxʷ – S/he/it is deserving/worthy of respect.
héʔemist – restrain one's self; reserved; in awe of. *See: **reserved**.*

imše kʷ héʔemłtumš – You should be respectful.

nhéʔelsm – oblige someone out of respect; oblige someone out of pity; appease someone's feelings.

nhéʔelsis – S/he obliged s.o. **nhéʔelsn, nhéʔelsntxʷ**
es héʔems – S/he is obliging s.o. **ies héʔem, as héʔem**
qs héʔems – S/he is going to oblige s.o. **iqs héʔem, aqs héʔem**

nhéʔelsmist – oblige one's self.

hoy nhéʔelsn u cun "xʷu ṅem čšncin" – I felt sorry for him and told him, "Okay I will go with you."

q̇ix̣tm – cherish something or someone; fond of something possessed; treasure something or someone; show respect by cherishing a gift. *See: **cherish**.*

The **i** following uvular consonants (UC) and the glottal stop **ʔ** sound like English "*ey*" as in the words *they, hey, whey*, etc. Salish UC are: **q, q̇, qʷ, q̇ʷ, x̣, x̣ʷ**. For example, the suffix **...qin** – head/top, is often spelled using English *ey* as "q*ey*n". So **qi, q̇i, qʷi, q̇ʷi, x̣i, x̣ʷi**, may be spelled with English *ey* as **q***ey*, **q̇***ey*, **qʷ***ey*, **q̇ʷ***ey*, **x̣***ey*, **x̣ʷ***ey* in other texts.

response

pṅ – but *(contradictory)*, well *(as a rebuke)*, yet *(in spite of)*. *This particle is interjectory in emphasizing contrariness or exception to a preceding statement. As a response it rebukes a statement, request, question, or an understood or implied statement.*

ye pṅ – exclamation to accentuate a word or thought. *See: **exclamation**.*

pṅ swe łu askʷest – Well! What is your name? **pṅ x̣ʷa steṁ łu šeẏ –** Well! What is that? **pṅ tam čnes ntelsi –** But! I don't want to? **pṅ x̣ʷľ steṁ –** But! Why? **pṅ t swe u cunct –** Well! Who told you? **pṅ x̣ʷa ẇe l še u eċx̣i –** Well! Maybe that's the way it is. **pṅ i mi u tam l šeẏ u eċx̣i –** Well! What is your name? **pṅ čn nte i tox̣ʷ łu šeẏ –** But! I thought that was right.

s.t. - something, the 3rd person
(s.t.) - something implied
s.o. - someone, the 3rd person
sl. - singular form
pl. - plural form
rt. - root word
cmd. - command
lit. - literally
fig. - figuratively
i.e., - for example
See: - Redirection to a related word.

k̓ʷ – evidently; yet; apparently; but; oh. *This particle marks a casual opposition or contrast to the preceding statement. Used as an intensifier inference to express casual surprise of an occurence, statement, or presented knowledge.*

cuntm t px̣px̣ots k̓ʷ np̓up̓uwenéʔ – S/he was told by his/her elders, yet s/he paid no attention. **qʷo cuntm xʷuyiš k̓ʷ čn č̓łemut** – I was told to go, yet I sat there. **mipnun k̓ʷ kʷ yoyoot** – I found out that you are strong. **mipnuis k̓ʷ es yoqʷisti łu sqltmixʷ** – S/he found out that the man had lied. **k̓ʷ stem̓ łu as k̓ʷul̓m** – But what are you doing. **k̓ʷ x̣ʷa stem̓ łu šey̓** – Well, I wonder what that is. **k̓ʷ uc unexʷ** – Oh, that's right. **k̓ʷ t šey̓ u ec̓x̣i** – Oh, that's the way it is. **k̓ʷ x̣ʷl̓ šey̓ u ec̓x̣i** – Oh, that's why it is like that.

m – respectful affirmative response; attentive response. *(usually said in a drawn out fashion.)*

rest

łexʷésčt, *łexʷé* – rest; relax; take a break.

łexʷesčt – S/he relieved one's tiredness. **čn łexʷesčt, kʷ łexʷesčt**
es łexʷesčti – S/he is relieving one's tiredness. **čnes łexʷesčti, kʷes łexʷesčti**
qs łexʷesčti – S/he is going to relieve one's tiredness. **čiqs łexʷesčti, kʷqs łexʷesčti**

łexʷls – S/he felt rested. **čn łexʷls, kʷ łexʷls**
es łexʷlsi – S/he is feeling rested. **čnes łexʷlsi, kʷes łexʷlsi**
qs łexʷlsi – S/he is going to feel rested. **čiqs łexʷlsi, kʷqs łexʷlsi**
es łéʔexʷlsi – They are feeling rested. **qeʔes łexʷlsi, pes łexʷlsi**
qs łéʔexʷlsi – They are going to feel rested. **qeʔqs łexʷlsi, pqs łexʷlsi**

es łexʷls – S/he is rested. **čnes łexʷls, kʷes łexʷls**

łexʷlsiš – Be rested. *cmd.*
łexʷesčtš – Relieve your weariness; take a break. *cmd.*
łexʷesčtwi – All of you relieve your weariness; take a break. *cmd.*

ṅem x̣ʷa m x̣ʷa esel sčacé qeʔqs łéxʷlsi – Then we'll rest for maybe two weeks. **x̣ʷa čmi u tʔe u tnk̓ʷuʔ še kʷ łexʷls** – It seems you only rest once in a while. **xʷu qeʔqs łexʷlsi** – Okay, let's take a break; take five; break time.

młuxʷls – fresh; vigorous; rested.
es młuxʷls – S/he is fresh. **čnes młuxʷls, kʷes młuxʷls**

młxʷels – S/he took a rest. **čn młxʷels, kʷ młxʷels**
es młxʷelsi – S/he is taking a rest. **čnes młxʷelsi, kʷes młxʷelsi**
qs młxʷelsi – S/he is going to take a rest. **čiqs młxʷelsi, kʷqs młxʷelsi**

młxʷelsts – S/he let s.o./s.t. take a rest. **młxʷelstn, młxʷelstxʷ**
es młxʷelsms – S/he is letting s.o./s.t. take a rest. **ies młxʷelsm, as młxʷelsm**
qs młxʷelsms – S/he is going to let s.o./s.t. take a rest. **iqs młxʷelsm, aqs młxʷelsm**

młxʷlsqax̣eʔ – S/he rested one's horse. **čn młxʷlsqax̣eʔ, kʷ młxʷlsqax̣eʔ**

młxʷłxʷels – one fresh to work; rested.
epł młxʷłxʷels – S/he has a fresh (horse). **čn epł młxʷłxʷels, kʷ epł młxʷłxʷels**

restaurant

snʔel̓iłntn, *snʔel̓i* – café; cafeteria; restaurant. *lit. a place where many people eat. prefix:* ***sn...*** *– a place of; suffix:* ***...tin, ...tn*** *– means of/device. See:* ***eat.***

restless

k̓ʷłulupšin – restless; antsy; raring to go; have cabin fever. *lit. to have your feet on fire. prefix:* ***k̓ʷł...*** *– under; rt.:* ***ulip*** *– burn; suffix:* ***...šin*** *– foot.*
k̓ʷłulupšin – S/he was restless. **čn k̓ʷłulupšin, kʷ k̓ʷłulupšin**
es k̓ʷłulupšini – S/he is restless. **čnes k̓ʷłulupšini, kʷes k̓ʷłulupšini**
qs k̓ʷłulupšini – S/he is going to be restless. **čiqs k̓ʷłuluspšini, kʷqs k̓ʷłulupšini**

lalamist – wiggle/roll around; *toss and turn. (i.e., when in pain; restless in bed; like an animal wallowing in dirt.) See:* ***wiggle.***

lmlamist – throw a fit; have a temper tantrum. *See:* ***wiggle.***

restrain

ac – bind; restrain; tie; trap. *See:* ***tie.***

resurrect

nkʷƛ̓lexʷncut – resurrect. *rt.:* ***kʷƛ̓pim*** *– detach.*
es nkʷƛ̓lex̣ʷncuti – S/he/it is resurrecting. **čnes nkʷƛ̓lex̣ʷncuti, kʷes nkʷƛ̓lex̣ʷncuti**

retrieve

emlš – retrieve something hidden/cached and take it away.
emlš – S/he retrieved (s.t.). **čn emlš, kʷ emlš**
es emlši – S/he is retrieving (s.t.). **čnes emlši, kʷes emlši**
qs emlši – S/he is going to retrieve (s.t.). **čiqs emlši, kʷqs emlši**

emlšis – S/he retrieved s.t. **emlšn, emlšntxʷ**
es emlšms – S/he is retrieving s.t. **ies emlšm, as emlšm**
qs emlšms – S/he is going to retrieve s.t. **iqs emlšm, aqs emlšm**

emlšiš – Retrieve. *cmd.*
emlšnt – Retrieve it. *cmd.*

> The **i** following uvular consonants (UC) and the glottal stop **ʔ** sound like English "*ey*" as in the words th*ey*, h*ey*, wh*ey*, etc. Salish UC are: **q, q̇, qʷ, q̇ʷ, x̣, x̣ʷ**. For example, the suffix **...qin** – head/top, is often spelled using English *ey* as "q*ey*n". So **qi, q̇i, qʷi, q̇ʷi, x̣i, x̣ʷi**, may be spelled with English *ey* as **q***ey*, **q̇***ey*, **qʷ***ey*, **q̇ʷ***ey*, **x̣***ey*, **x̣ʷ***ey* in other texts.

Revais Creek

ncwetkʷ – Revais Creek, a creek that flows in the Flathead Nation. *lit. tree roots visible near stream. suffix:* ***...etkʷ, ...tkʷ*** *– liquid*

reveal

čłaq̇ʷiċeʔ – exposed to view all over; completely exposed. *See:* ***appear.***

čhem – uncover; reveal. *See:* ***reveal.***

revenge

éyčst – revenge; got even; avenge wrongs done.
éyčst – S/he got revenge. **čn éyčst, kʷ éyčst**
es éyčsti – S/he is getting revenge. **čnes éyčsti, kʷes éyčsti**
qs éyčsti – S/he is going to get revenge. **čiqs éyčsti, kʷqs éyčsti**

éymt – S/he was vengeful. **čn éymt, kʷ éymt**
es éymti – S/he is being revengeful. **čnes éymti, kʷes éymti**
qs éymti – S/he is going to be revengeful. **čiqs éymti, kʷqs éymti**

éycn – S/he spoke revengefully. **čn éycn, kʷ éycn**
es éycni – S/he is speaking revengefully. **čnes éycni, kʷes éycni**
qs éycni – S/he is going to speak revengefully. **čiqs éycni, kʷqs éycni**

éyčstis – S/he got revenge on s.o. **éyčstn, kʷ éyčstntxʷ**
es éyčstms – S/he is getting revenge on s.o. **ies éyčstm, as éyčstm**
qs éyčstms – S/he is going to get revenge on s.o. **iqs éyčstm, aqs éyčstm**

sʔéyčst – vengence.
čʔéyčstn – thing/act that causes one to take revenge.

éyčstemn – one inclined to get revenge.

nʔéyls – S/he felt revengeful. **čn nʔéyls, kʷ nʔéyls**
es nʔéylsi – S/he is feeling revengeful. **čnes nʔéylsi, kʷes nʔéylsi**
qs nʔéylsi – S/he is going to feel revengeful. **čiqs nʔéylsi, kʷqs nʔéylsi**

> s.t. - something, the 3rd person
> (s.t.) - something implied
> s.o. - someone, the 3rd person
> *sl.* - singular form
> *pl.* - plural form
> *rt.* - root word
> *cmd.* - command
> *lit.* - literally
> *fig.* - figuratively
> *i.e.,* - for example
> *See:* - Redirection to a related word.

review

šƛ̓us – search/stare around; look from one thing to the next; scan. *See:* ***search.***

revive **kʷeƛ̓ep** – revived; came out of it.
i kʷeƛ̓ep – S/he/it revived; s/he/it came out of it.

pispiskʷeƛ̓ep – Fox revived Coyote.

rib **sxʷtip** – rib. **sxʷtxʷtip** – ribs. *pl.*
wnwnwi łu sxʷtxʷtips – Its ribs were showing and sticking out.

ribbon **k̓ʷłłp̓min** – ribbon. *rt.:* ***łip̓*** *– line.*

rice **sxʷuxʷyeʔ** – ants; rice.

rich **qʷyulexʷ** – rich, wealthy.
qʷyulexʷ – S/he is rich. **čn qʷyulexʷ, kʷ qʷyulexʷ**

qʷilexʷwilš – S/he became rich. **čn qʷilexʷwilš, kʷ qʷilexʷwilš** *suffix:* ***...wilš*** *– developmental.*
es qʷilexʷwilši – S/he is becoming rich. **čnes qʷilexʷwilši, kʷes qʷilexʷwilši**
qs qʷilexʷwilši – S/he is going to become rich. **čiqs qʷilexʷwilši, kʷqs qʷilexʷwilši**

ha p qʷyulexʷ – Are you all rich? **ha kʷ qʷyulexʷ** – Are you rich?

rid **čmaqʷncut** – get rid of evil/bad feeling/sickness of one's self.
čmaqʷncut – S/he got rid of the bad. **čn čmaqʷncut, kʷ čmaqʷncut**
es čmaqʷncuti – S/he is getting rid of the bad. **čnes čmaqʷncuti, kʷes čmaqʷncuti**
qs čmaqʷncuti – S/he is going to get rid of the bad. **čiqs čmaqʷncuti, kʷqs čmaqʷncuti**
čmaqʷncúʔut – They got rid of the bad. **qeʔ čmaqʷncut, p čmaqʷncut**
es čmaqʷncúʔuti – They are getting rid of the bad. **qeʔes čmaqʷncuti, pes čmaqʷncuti**
qs čmaqʷncúʔuti – They are going to get rid of the bad. **qeʔqs čmaqʷncuti, pqs čmaqʷncuti**

es čmaqʷncutmms – S/he is getting rid of the bad. **ies čmaqʷncutmm, as čmaqʷncutmm**

sčmaqʷncut – Words to get rid of evil/bad feelings/sickness. *(i.e., prayer.)*

ride **čmtéw̓sm,** *čmté* – ride/straddle something *(one person). rt.:* ***emut*** *– sit.; suffix:* ***...éw̓s*** *– in between, middle.*
čmtéw̓sm – S/he rode. **čnes čmtéw̓sm, kʷes čmtéw̓sm**
es čmtéw̓si – S/he is riding. **čnes čmtéw̓si, kʷes čmtéw̓si**
qs čmtéw̓si – S/he is going to ride. **čiqs čmtéw̓si, kʷqs čmtéw̓si**

čmtéw̓s l snčłc̓aʔsqáx̣eʔs – S/he rode his/her horse.

čay̓utéw̓sm, *čay̓uté* – ride/straddle something *(several people). rt.:* ***ayew̓t*** *– several people sit; suffix:* ***...éw̓s*** *– in between, middle.*
čay̓utéʔew̓sm – They rode. **qeʔ čay̓utéw̓sm, p čay̓utéw̓sm**
es čay̓utéʔew̓si – They are riding. **qeʔes čay̓utéw̓si, pes čay̓utéw̓si**
qs čay̓utéʔew̓si – They are going to ride. **qeʔqs čay̓utéw̓si, pqs čay̓utéw̓si**

nt̓qʷmew̓s – riding side by side.

čłqqew̓s, *čłqqe* – mount, *more than one*; straddle; get on. *See:* ***mount.***

čłqlšew̓s, *čłqlše* – mount, of one *individual*; straddle. *See:* ***mount.***

čnaq̓ʷlqʷi – stealing a ride on a train, bus or car. *rt.:* ***naq̓ʷ*** *– steal; suffix:* ***...lqʷ*** *– s.t. that rolls.*

ridge **sčtx̣ʷičn̓** – ridge. *suffix:* ***...ičn̓*** *– back.*
čnčntičn̓ – dangerous ridge.
x̣ʷlxʷenš – hole in the side of a ridge.

mx̣ʷičṅ – snow spot on mountain; snowed on the ridge.
čxʷstičṅ – walk on a ridge.

rifle

sululmiṅč, *sululmi* – rifle. *suffix:* ***...iṅč*** *– weapon.*

right

tx̣ʷmscut, *tx̣ʷmscú* – make one's self do right. *rt.:* ***tox̣ʷ*** *– straight; suffix:* ***...cut*** *– action to the self.*

tx̣ʷmscut – S/he did right. **čn tx̣ʷmscut, kʷ tx̣ʷmscut**
es tx̣ʷmscuti – S/he is doing right. **čnes tx̣ʷmscut, kʷes tx̣ʷmscuti**
qs tx̣ʷmscuti – S/he is going to do right. **čiqs tx̣ʷmscut, kʷqs tx̣ʷmscuti**
tx̣ʷmscúʔut – They did right. **qeʔ tx̣ʷmscut, p tx̣ʷmscut**
es tx̣ʷmscúʔuti – They are doing right. **qeʔes tx̣ʷmscut, pes tx̣ʷmscuti**
qs tx̣ʷmscúʔuti – They are going to do right. **qeʔqs tx̣ʷmscut, pqs tx̣ʷmscuti**

tx̣ʷnuis – S/he did it right. **tx̣ʷnun, tx̣ʷnuntxʷ**
es tx̣ʷnunms – S/he is doing it right. **ies tx̣ʷnunm, as tx̣ʷnunm**
qs tx̣ʷnunm– S/he is going to do it right. **iqs tx̣ʷnunm, aqs tx̣ʷnunm**

tx̣ʷmscutš – Straighten yourself up; do right. *cmd.*

eni ta kʷes tx̣ʷmscuti – You are not doing right. *(What you say when you catch somebody doing something wrong. i.e., stealing, drinking) (man says* ***hayo*** *instead of* ***eni****)* **ṅe ta kʷes tx̣ʷmscuti ṅem kʷ xʷéẏt** – If you do not do right you will be in trouble. **k̓ʷinš łu tx̣ʷnuntxʷ** – How many did you get right?

k̓ʷucuṅe – Oh that's right.

put – just, exactly, even, enough; right then. *See:* ***just***

> The **i** following uvular consonants (UC) and the glottal stop **ʔ** sound like English "*ey*" as in the words *they*, *hey*, *whey*, etc. Salish UC are: **q, q̇, qʷ, q̇ʷ, x̣, x̣ʷ**. For example, the suffix **...qin** – head/top, is often spelled using English *ey* as "q*ey*n". So **qi, q̇i, qʷi, q̇ʷi, x̣i, x̣ʷi**, may be spelled with English *ey* as **q***ey*, **q̇***ey*, **qʷ***ey*, **q̇ʷ***ey*, **x̣***ey*, **x̣ʷ***ey* in other texts.

right side

sččhéčst, *sččhé* – right hand.
es čchéčst – S/he is right handed. **čnes čchéčst, kʷes čchéčst**

sčchesšn – right foot.
schax̣n – right arm.
sčchus – right eye.
schaqstšn – right leg.
sčcheneʔ – right ear.
sk̓ʷłcheus – right cheek.
sčchepeney – right braid.

łáqšlš łu l sččhéčsts – Sit at his/her right hand side.

rigid

yomncut, *yomncu* – become rigid; tense.
yomncut – S/he got rigid. **čn yomncut, kʷ yomncut**
es yomncuti – S/he is rigid. **čnes yomncuti, kʷes yomncuti**
qs yomncuti – S/he is going to be rigid. **čiqs yomncuti, kʷqs yomncuti**

yomncutš – Toughen up; become rigid/tense. *cmd.*

ċuk̓ʷ – stiff; rigid; taut; erect.
i ċuk̓ʷ – It is rigid/stiff.
ċk̓ʷuk̓ʷ – It got rigid/stiff.

ċk̓ʷmin – ear pole of a tipi.

> s.t. - something, the 3rd person
> (s.t.) - something implied
> s.o. - someone, the 3rd person
> *sl.* - singular form
> *pl.* - plural form
> *rt.* - root word
> *cmd.* - command
> *lit.* - literally
> *fig.* - figuratively
> *i.e.,* - for example
> *See:* - Redirection to a related word.

ring

čmṗqinčst, *čmṗqi* – band; finger ring. *suffix:* ***...ečst, ...čst*** *– of the hand.*

liwm – ring a bell.
liwmsts – S/he/it rang the bell. **liwmstn, liwmstxʷ**

liwmstm – The bell was rung.

qeʔ liwmłt – Our doorbell is ringing.

sq̓aw̓qinčst – ring finger. *suffix:* ***...qinčst –*** *finger.*

ring-necked pheasant

čusw̓i skʷiskʷs – ring-necked pheasant; *Phasianus colchicus.*

rip

t̓l̓ip – pull apart something; rip something.
t̓l̓ntés – S/he/it ripped it. **t̓l̓ntén, t̓l̓ntéxʷ**
es t̓l̓pims – S/he/it is ripping s.t. **ies t̓l̓pim, as t̓l̓pim**
qs t̓l̓pims – S/he/it is going to rip s.t. **iqs t̓l̓pim, aqs t̓l̓pim**
t̓l̓ntéʔes – They ripped it. **qeʔ t̓l̓ntém, t̓l̓ntép**
es t̓l̓pims – They are ripping s.t. **qeʔes t̓l̓pim, es t̓l̓pimp**
qs t̓l̓pims – They are going to rip s.t. **qeʔqs t̓l̓pim, qs t̓l̓pimp**

t̓l̓t̓l̓ntés – S/he/it ripped it to shreds.

es t̓il – It is ripped/tore.

sct̓l̓etkʷ – canal. *rt.:* ***t̓il –*** *tear; suffix:* ***...etkʷ, ...tkʷ –*** *liquid.*

t̓l̓t̓l̓ntés isċm t smx̣é – The grizzly ripped my blanket to shreds. **t̓l̓ip łu inpumin –** My drum is broke *(the hide is torn).*

ripe

p̓iqém – make done; ready; ripen. *See:* ***done.***
sp̓iqáłq – berry; fruit; raisin. *rt.:* ***p̓iy̓áq –*** *ready, ripe; suffix:* ***...ałq –*** *smell, accompaniment.*

kʷel – change outward perception; change color; ripening/dying. *See:* ***change.***

x̣iʔu – unripe, not done. *See:* ***unripe.***
es x̣iʔu – It is unripe, not done.

rise

xʷt̓ilš – get up from a resting/laying state; rise. *suffix:* ***...ilš –*** *autonomous.*
xʷt̓ilš – S/he/it got up. **čn xʷt̓ilš, kʷ xʷt̓ilš**
es xʷt̓ilši – S/he/it is getting up. **čnes xʷt̓ilši, kʷes xʷt̓ilši**
qs xʷt̓ilši – S/he/it is going to get up. **čiqs xʷt̓ilši, kʷqs xʷt̓ilši**
xʷt̓íʔilši – They got up. **qeʔ xʷt̓ilš, p xʷt̓ilš**
es xʷt̓íʔilši – They are getting up. **qeʔes xʷt̓ilši, pes xʷt̓ilši**
qs xʷt̓íʔilši – They are going to get up. **qeʔqs xʷt̓ilši, pqs xʷt̓ilši**

xʷt̓ilšsts – S/he/it made s.o. get up. **xʷt̓ilšstn, xʷt̓ilšstxʷ**
es xʷt̓ilšms – S/he/it is making s.o. get up. **ies xʷt̓ilšm, as xʷt̓ilšm**
qs xʷt̓ilšms – S/he/it is going to make s.o. get up. **iqs xʷt̓ilšm, aqs xʷt̓ilšm**

xʷt̓ilš – Rise; get up. *cmd.*
xʷt̓ilšskʷ – Make him/her/it rise/get up. *cmd.*
nxʷt̓l̓šetkʷ – rise from water.
nxʷt̓l̓šew̓s – S/he/it got up from in between. **čn nxʷt̓l̓šew̓s, kʷ nxʷt̓l̓šew̓s**

ṅem i kʷékʷst m qeʔ xʷt̓l̓ilš – In the morning we will get up. **enwnm t es xʷt̓ilši –** I am aware of something getting up. **čn qéiłt u čn xʷt̓ilš –** I woke and got up.

tlxʷmist, *tlxʷmi* **–** unable to rise/get up. *See:* ***stuck.***

qiłt – wake up. *See:* ***wake.***

nkʷƛ̓im – take something out from inside something. *rt.:* ***kʷƛ̓im –*** *take out. See:* ***take.***
nkʷƛ̓ip – it rose out of the restriction.

kʷƛ̓im – take something out; detach; loose/free embedded object. *See:* ***take.***

river **ntx̣ʷétkʷ,** *ntx̣ʷé* – river. *rt.:* ***tox̣ʷ*** *– straight; suffix:* ***...etkʷ, ...tkʷ*** *– liquid*

łntx̣ʷetkʷ – little river. *suffix:* ***...etkʷ, ...tkʷ*** *– liquid*

nqqʔetkʷ – little river. *suffix:* ***...etkʷ, ...tkʷ*** *– liquid*

stem̓ łiše l ntx̣ʷetkʷ – What is that in the river.

snx̣ʷq̓ʷpsetkʷ – place where the river forms from a lake.

nisq̓ʷot, *nisq̓ʷo* – across the river. *See:* ***across.***

nilew̓s – main waterway, which tributaries flow into.

sčilip – mouth of a river or stream; town name of Dixon, Flathead Nation. *rt.:* ***ili*** *– pass into/through.*

es čilpmi – The waterway flows into another waterway; it is a tributary.

snčilptin – tributary waterway.

The **i** following uvular consonants (UC) and the glottal stop **ʔ** sound like English "*ey*" as in the words th*ey*, h*ey*, wh*ey*, etc. Salish UC are: **q**, **q̓**, **qʷ**, **q̓ʷ**, **x̣**, **x̣ʷ**. For example, the suffix **...qin** – head/top, is often spelled using English *ey* as "q*ey*n". So **qi**, **q̓i**, **qʷi**, **q̓ʷi**, **x̣i**, **x̣ʷi**, may be spelled with English *ey* as **q***ey*, **q̓***ey*, **qʷ***ey*, **q̓ʷ***ey*, **x̣***ey*, **x̣ʷ***ey* in other texts.

riverbank **npapaánč,** *npapaá* – dirt riverbank; dirt cliff.

es npapaánč – It is a dirt bank.

river otter **ltkʷups,** *ltkʷu* – river otter; *Lontra canadensis.*

roach **sncl̓aw̓sqn,** *sncl̓a* – roach. *rt.:* ***c̓il*** *– standing upright; suffix:* ***...éw̓s*** *– in between, middle; suffix:* ***...qin, ...qn*** *– top.*

es ncl̓aw̓sqn – S/he is wearing a roach. **čnes ncl̓aw̓sqn, kʷes ncl̓aw̓sqn**

road **šušw̓éł** – road. **šušušw̓eł** – roads. *pl.*

stém̓ łišé l šušw̓éł – What is that on the road?

n...aqs, n...qs *– circumfix indicating that something goes to a point, typically used in words involving the nose or a road. See:* ***point.***

nx̣saqs – good road. *prefix:* ***x̣s...*** *– good.*

nčsaqs – bad road. *prefix:* ***čs...*** *– bad.*

ntx̣ʷaqs – straight road. *rt.:* ***tox̣ʷ*** *– straight.*

nušnáqs – long road. *rt.:* ***wisšn*** *– long.*

nkʷtnaqs – big road. *rt.:* ***kʷtunt*** *– big.*

nłq̓áqs, *nłq̓á* – wide road. *rt.:* ***łaq̓t*** *– wide.*

i noolqs – slippery road. *rt.:* ***ool*** *– slippery.*

nx̣maqs – dry road. *rt.:* ***x̣am*** *– dry.*

nƛ̓awačqs – muddy road. *rt.:* ***ƛ̓awač*** *– muddy.*

ntłaqs – paved road; dirty road; something is on the road. *rt.:* ***t̓ił*** *– dirty.*

nt̓saqs – hard road; paved road. *rt.:* ***t̓as*** *– hard.*

npkʷaqs – gravel/dirt road. *rt.:* ***pukʷ*** *– round objects poured.*

nx̣ʷq̓ʷpaqs – split road. *rt.:* ***t̓as*** *– hard.*

nx̣iqaqs – washboard road. *rt.:* ***x̣iq*** *– rub.*

npq̓ʷaqs – powdered road from blasting. *rt.:* ***poq̓ʷ*** *– granular substance poured.*

nšičqs – run off the road. *rt.:* ***šičt*** *– miss a target.*

nšičqs – S/he ran off the road. **čn nšičqs, kʷ nšičqs**

nisaqm – go off the road; to go to the side of the road.

nxʷstaqs – walk on the road. *rt.:* ***xʷist*** *– walk; circumfix:* ***n...aqs*** *– nose, road. See:* ***hitchhike.***

s.t. - something, the 3rd person
(s.t.) - something implied
s.o. - someone, the 3rd person
sl. - singular form
pl. - plural form
rt. - root word
cmd. - command
lit. - literally
fig. - figuratively
i.e., - for example
See: - Redirection to a related word.

ntkʷutaqs – walk on a road; referring to more than one person. *rt.: **tkʷuut–** they walk; circumfix: **n...aqs** – nose, road. See: **hitchhike**.*

nk̓ʷol̓qs – work on a road. *rt.: **k̓ʷul̓–** work.*
nk̓ʷol̓qs – S/he worked on the road. **čn nk̓ʷol̓qs, kʷes nk̓ʷol̓qs**
es nk̓ʷol̓qsi – S/he is working on the road. **čnes nk̓ʷol̓qsi, kʷes nk̓ʷol̓qsi**
qs nk̓ʷol̓qsi – S/he is going to work on the road. **čiqs nk̓ʷol̓qsi, kʷqs nk̓ʷol̓qsi**

nk̓ʷol̓qsis – S/he made the road. **nk̓ʷol̓qsn, nk̓ʷol̓qsntxʷ**
es nk̓ʷol̓qsms – S/he is making the road. **ies nk̓ʷol̓qsm, as nk̓ʷol̓qsm**
qs nk̓ʷol̓qsms – S/he is going to make the road. **iqs nk̓ʷol̓qsm, aqs nk̓ʷol̓qsm**

nk̓ʷol̓qšts – S/he made a road for s.o. **nk̓ʷol̓qštn, nk̓ʷol̓qštxʷ**

sxʷnk̓ʷol̓qsm – one tasked to work on the roads. *prefix: **sxʷ...** – one tasked to do.*

k̓ʷul̓ – do; make; fix; work. *See: **work**.*

roan

kʷlaqin – strawberry roan. *suffix: **...qin, ...qn** – top.*

xʷámqn – roan.

roast

acqʷ – roast something.
acqʷm – S/he roasted. **čn acqʷm, kʷ acqʷm**
es acqʷi – S/he is roasting. **čnes acqʷi, kʷes acqʷi**
qs acqʷi – S/he is going to roast. **čiqs acqʷi, kʷqs acqʷi**
áʔacqʷm – They roasted. **qeʔ acqʷm, p acqʷm**
es áʔacqʷi – They are roasting. **qeʔes acqʷi, pes acqʷi**
qs áʔacqʷi – They are going to roast. **qeʔqs acqʷi, pqs acqʷi**

acqʷis – S/he roasted s.t. **acqʷn, acqʷntxʷ**
es acqʷms – S/he is roasting s.t. **ies acqʷm, as acqʷm**
qs acqʷms – S/he is going to roast s.t. **iqs acqʷm, aqs acqʷm**
áʔacqʷis – They roasted s.t. **qeʔ acqʷntm, acqʷntp**
es áʔacqʷms – They are roasting s.t. **qeʔes acqʷm, es acqʷmp**
qs áʔacqʷms – They are going to roast s.t. **qeʔqs acqʷm, qs acqʷmp**

scʔacqʷ – something that's been roasted. *(i.e., a potato, meat, etc.) prefix: **sc...** – s.t. that's been done/made/prepared.*

čiqs acqʷi t pataq – I am going to roast potatoes.

qʷl̓ełċeʔ – roast meat on a fire.
es qʷl̓ełċeʔi – S/he is roasting meat. **čnes qʷl̓ełċeʔi, kʷes qʷl̓ełċeʔi**

qʷl̓ełċʔeis – S/he is roasting meat. **qʷl̓ełċʔen, qʷl̓ełċʔentxʷ**
es qʷl̓ełċʔems – S/he is roasting the meat. **ies qʷl̓ełċʔem, as qʷl̓ełċʔem**

scnlóʔ – something put in the oven. *(i.e., a roast, bread, etc.) prefix: **sc...** – s.t. that's been done/made/prepared.*

kʷl̓sncut, *k̓ʷl̓sncu* **–** cook; prepare food. *See: **cook**.*

qʷl̓ep – bake underground; pit bake. *See: **bake**.*

rob

náq̓ʷ – steal; rob. *See: **steal**.*
naq̓ʷéṁn – someone who always steals; a thief.

nčṁełxʷ – steal; rob.

k̓ʷłnq̓ʷmist, *k̓ʷłnq̓ʷmi* **–** run away stealthily; sneak away; leave; escape. *See: **escape**.*

robin **sx̣ax̣l̓č** – robin; *Turdus migratorius.*

rock **sšeṅš** – rock.

sšṅšeṅš – rocks.
sŧšešṅš – little rock.
kʷtnesšṅ – big rock.
ŧqlqesšṅ – wide rock.
t̓ik̓ʷsšṅ – sweat rocks.
impasšn – igneous rock; lava rock. *See: **igneous rock**.*
k̓ʷl̓isṗċpesšn – metamorphic rock. *See: **metamorphic rock**.*
ṅċnċansšn – sedimentary rock. *See: **sedimentary rock**.*
čmomotesšṅ – smokey rocks.
kʷaliˀnše – yellowstone.
x̣ʷl̓x̣ʷl̓q̓ʷqʷse – rolling rocks down hill.

nk̓ʷesšṅ – one rock. **eslesšṅ** – two rocks. **čeŧlesšṅ** – three rocks. **musšṅ** – four rocks. **clčstesšṅ** – five rocks. **tq̓nčstesšṅ** – six rocks. **sṗlčesšṅ** – seven rocks. **héˀenmesšṅ** – eight rocks. **x̣ṅtesšṅ** – nine rocks. **upnčstesšṅ** – ten rocks.
upn eŧ nk̓ʷesšṅ – eleven rocks.
nk̓ʷoˀqstesšṅ – one hundred rocks.
xʷˀesšṅ – bunch of rocks.

nšƛ̓aqsm ŧu sšeṅš – different kinds of rocks. **es ŧṗŧiṗ sšeṅš** – striped rock. **kʷ y̓amim t sšéṅš tam tl̓ ntx̣ʷé u tl̓ čŧq̓ali** – You gather rocks, but not from the river or from the lake.

čsšeṅš – go after rocks.
čsšeṅš – S/he went after rocks. **čn čsšeṅš, kʷ čsšeṅš**
es čsšeṅši – S/he is going after rocks. **čnes čsšeṅši, kʷes čsšeṅši**
qs čsšeṅši – S/he is going to go after rocks. **čiqs čsšeṅši, kʷqs čsšeṅši**

qeˀes čsšeṅši x̣ʷl̓ qeˀ snlaqi – We are going after rocks for the sweat.

ċaŧxʷ – piled rock shelter/marker.
ċŧxʷntes – S/he made a rock shelter/marker. **ċŧxʷnten, ċŧxʷntexʷ**
es ċaŧxʷms – S/he is making a rock shelter/marker. **ies ċaŧxʷm, as ċaŧxʷm**
qs ċaŧxʷms – S/he is going to make a rock shelter/marker. **iqs ċaŧxʷm, aqs ċaŧxʷm**

es ċaŧxʷ – It is a rock shelter/marker.

ċaŧxʷsšṅ – piled rock marker.

rock dove **x̣ʷċx̣ʷo** – pigeon; rock dove; *Columba livia.*

rock rabbit **sčiṅ** – pika; rock rabbit; *Ochotona princeps.*

rock slide **snccosls** – rock slide.

rock worm **ččnčṗi** – rock worm.

rocky **nsšeṅšm** – rocky.

Rocky Mountain juniper **punŧp** – Rocky Mountain juniper; *Juniperus scopulorum.*

Rocky Mountain maple **sx̣ʷƛ̓ula** – maple; Rocky Mountain maple; *Acer glabrum.*

The **i** following uvular consonants (UC) and the glottal stop **ˀ** sound like English "*ey*" as in the words th*ey*, h*ey*, wh*ey*, etc. Salish UC are: **q**, **q̓**, **qʷ**, **q̓ʷ**, **x̣**, **x̣ʷ**. For example, the suffix **...qin** – head/top, is often spelled using English *ey* as "q*ey*n". So **qi**, **q̓i**, **qʷi**, **q̓ʷi**, **x̣i**, **x̣ʷi**, may be spelled with English *ey* as **q***ey*, **q̓***ey*, **qʷ***ey*, **q̓ʷ***ey*, **x̣***ey*, **x̣ʷ***ey* in other texts.

s.t. - something, the 3rd person
(s.t.) - something implied
s.o. - someone, the 3rd person
sl. - singular form
pl. - plural form
rt. - root word
cmd. - command
lit. - literally
fig. - figuratively
i.e., - for example
See: - Redirection to a related word.

Rocky Mountain oyster **mčméčp –** testicles; Rocky Mountain oyster.

Rocky Mountain Range **xʷc̓xʷc̓ut –** Rocky Mountains.
xʷc̓ut – Rocky Mountain.

rodent **q̓ʷłq̓ʷłšulexʷ –** little animals; rodents. *(q̓ʷłq̓ʷł – sound/action little animals make/do.)*
łxʷxʷcuseʔ – rodent species.

roe **úʔuséʔek̓ʷn –** fish eggs; roe.

roll **x̣ʷollq̓ʷ –** roll.
x̣ʷóllq̓ʷm – S/he/it rolled. **čn x̣ʷóllq̓ʷm, kʷ x̣ʷóllq̓ʷm**
es x̣ʷóllq̓ʷi – S/he/it is rolling. **čnes x̣ʷóllq̓ʷi, kʷes x̣ʷóllq̓ʷi**
qs x̣ʷóllq̓ʷi – S/he/it is going to roll. **čiqs x̣ʷóllq̓ʷi, kʷqs x̣ʷóllq̓ʷi**
x̣ʷóʔollq̓ʷm – They rolled. **qeʔ x̣ʷóllq̓ʷm, p x̣ʷóllq̓ʷm**
es x̣ʷóʔollq̓ʷi – They are rolling. **qeʔes x̣ʷóllq̓ʷi, pes x̣ʷóllq̓ʷi**
qs x̣ʷóʔollq̓ʷi – They are going to roll. **qeʔqs x̣ʷóllq̓ʷi, pqs x̣ʷóllq̓ʷi**

x̣ʷóllq̓ʷis – S/he/it rolled it. **x̣ʷóllq̓ʷn, x̣ʷóllq̓ʷntxʷ**
es x̣ʷóllq̓ʷms – S/he/it is rolling it. **ies x̣ʷóllq̓ʷm, as x̣ʷóllq̓ʷm**
qs x̣ʷóllq̓ʷms – S/he/it is going to roll it. **iqs x̣ʷóllq̓ʷm, aqs x̣ʷóllq̓ʷm**
x̣ʷóʔollq̓ʷis – They rolled it. **qeʔ x̣ʷóllq̓ʷntm, x̣ʷóllq̓ʷntp**
es x̣ʷóʔollq̓ʷms – They are rolling it. **qeʔes x̣ʷóllq̓ʷm, es x̣ʷóllq̓ʷmp**
qs x̣ʷóʔollq̓ʷms – They are rolling it. **qeʔqs x̣ʷólq̓ʷm, qs x̣ʷóllq̓ʷmp**

x̣ʷóllq̓ʷnuis – S/he/it succeeded in rolling it. **x̣ʷóllq̓ʷnun, x̣ʷóllq̓ʷnuntxʷ**
es x̣ʷóllq̓ʷnunms – S/he/it is succeeding in rolling it. **ies x̣ʷóllq̓ʷnunm, as x̣ʷóllq̓ʷnunm**
qs x̣ʷóllq̓ʷnunms – S/he/it is going to succeed in rolling it. **iqs x̣ʷóllq̓ʷnunm, aqs x̣ʷóllq̓ʷnunm**

es x̣ʷlx̣ʷóllq̓ʷi – S/he/it is rolling and rolling. **čnes x̣ʷlx̣ʷóllq̓ʷi, kʷes x̣ʷlx̣ʷóllq̓ʷi**
es x̣ʷlx̣ʷóllq̓ʷms – S/he/it is rolling and rolling it. **ies x̣ʷlx̣ʷóllq̓ʷm, as x̣ʷlx̣ʷóllq̓ʷm**

x̣ʷóllq̓ʷntm – S/he/it was rolled. **qʷo x̣ʷóllq̓ʷntm, kʷ x̣ʷóllq̓ʷntm**
čłx̣ʷl̓q̓ʷentm – S/he/it was rolled over by s.t. **qʷo čłx̣ʷl̓q̓ʷentm, kʷ čłx̣ʷl̓q̓ʷentm**

čx̣ʷllq̓ʷálqʷtn, *čx̣ʷllq̓ʷá* – railroad cars, train. *suffix:* ***...tin, ...tn*** *– means of/device.*
x̣ʷóllq̓ʷ – wagon.

x̣ʷóllq̓ʷmistš – Roll over. *cmd.*
x̣ʷóllq̓ʷnt – Roll it. *cmd.*
cx̣ʷóllq̓ʷnt – Roll it toward me. *cmd.*
x̣ʷollq̓ʷłt – Roll it to somebody. *cmd.*
yoyosx̣ʷollq̓ʷnt – Roll it hard. *cmd.*
x̣ʷl̓x̣ʷl̓q̓ʷqʷse – S/he rolled rocks down hill. **čn x̣ʷl̓x̣ʷl̓q̓ʷqʷse, kʷ x̣ʷl̓x̣ʷl̓q̓ʷqʷse**
čłx̣ʷl̓q̓ʷeis – S/he rolled over s.t. **čłx̣ʷl̓q̓ʷen, čłx̣ʷl̓q̓ʷentxʷ**

t swe u x̣ʷollq̓ʷis – Who rolled it? **qʷo cx̣ʷollq̓ʷłt –** Roll it to me.

x̣ʷllq̓ʷncut – roll one's self.
x̣ʷllq̓ʷncut – S/he/it rolled one's self. **čn x̣ʷllq̓ʷncut, kʷ x̣ʷllq̓ʷncut**
es x̣ʷllq̓ʷncuti – S/he/it is rolling one's self. **čnes x̣ʷllq̓ʷncuti, kʷes x̣ʷllq̓ʷncuti**
qs x̣ʷllq̓ʷncuti – S/he/it is going to roll one's self. **čiqs x̣ʷllq̓ʷncuti, kʷqs x̣ʷllq̓ʷncuti**

čx̣ʷllq̓ʷncutmis – S/he/it rolled one's self to s.t. **čx̣ʷllq̓ʷncutmn, čx̣ʷllq̓ʷncutmntxʷ**
es čx̣ʷllq̓ʷncutms – S/he/it is rolling one's self to s.t. **ies čx̣ʷllq̓ʷncutm, as čx̣ʷllq̓ʷncutm**

qs čx̣ʷllq̓ʷncutms – S/he/it is going to roll one's self to s.t. **iqs čx̣ʷllq̓ʷncutm, aqs čx̣ʷllq̓ʷncutm**

x̣ʷllq̓ʷncutš – Roll yourself. *cmd.*
čx̣ʷllq̓ʷncutmnt – Roll yourself to it. *cmd.*

čłx̣ʷllq̓ʷeneʔ – roll over something.
čłx̣ʷllq̓ʷeneʔm – S/he/it rolled over. **čn čłx̣ʷllq̓ʷeneʔm, kʷ čłx̣ʷllq̓ʷeneʔm**
es čłx̣ʷllq̓ʷeneʔi – S/he/it is rolling over. **čnes čłx̣ʷllq̓ʷeneʔi, kʷes čłx̣ʷllq̓ʷeneʔi**
qs čłx̣ʷllq̓ʷeneʔi – S/he/it is going to roll over. **čiqs čłx̣ʷllq̓ʷeneʔi, kʷqs čłx̣ʷllq̓ʷeneʔi**

čłx̣ʷllq̓ʷenʔeis – S/he/it rolled over s.t. **čłx̣ʷllq̓ʷenʔen, čłx̣ʷllq̓ʷenʔentxʷ**
es čłx̣ʷllq̓ʷenʔems – S/he/it is rolling over s.t. **ies čłx̣ʷllq̓ʷenʔem, as čłx̣ʷllq̓ʷenʔem**
qs čłx̣ʷllq̓ʷenʔems – S/he/it is going to roll over s.t. **iqs čłx̣ʷllq̓ʷenʔem, aqs čłx̣ʷllq̓ʷenʔem**

čłx̣ʷllq̓ʷeneʔiš – Roll over. *cmd.*
čłx̣ʷllq̓ʷenʔent – Roll over it. *cmd.*

k̓ʷel̓č – turn upside-down a container type object; upturned object. *See:* ***upside-down.***

čp̓lk̓ʷic̓éʔ – wrap; enfold; roll up. *See:* ***wrap.***

The **i** following uvular consonants (UC) and the glottal stop **ʔ** sound like English "*ey*" as in the words *they, hey, whey,* etc. Salish UC are: **q, q̓, qʷ, q̓ʷ, x̣, x̣ʷ**. For example, the suffix **...qin** – head/top, is often spelled using English *ey* as "q*ey*n". So **qi, q̓i, qʷi, q̓ʷi, x̣i, x̣ʷi,** may be spelled with English *ey* as **q***ey*, **q̓***ey*, **qʷ***ey*, **q̓ʷ***ey*, **x̣***ey*, **x̣ʷ***ey* in other texts.

roller skates

nx̣ʷlx̣ʷlq̓ʷšintn – roller skates. *suffix:* ***...tin, ...tn*** *– means of/device.*
x̣ʷlx̣ʷlq̓ʷepšn – roller shoes.

čłx̣ʷlx̣ʷlq̓ʷšintn – skate board. *suffix:* ***...tin, ...tn*** *– means of/device.*

rolling

es x̣ʷóllq̓ʷi – S/he/it is rolling.
x̣ʷlx̣ʷl̓q̓ʷqʷse – rolling rocks down hill.

čx̣ʷllq̓ʷalqʷ – rolling down a line or log. *(i.e., ball rolling on a log, train on tracks, etc.)*

Rollins

qʷłqʷłi – Rollins, Montana.

Ronan

ocqʔetkʷ, *ocqʔe* – Ronan, Flathead Nation. *lit. the spring water. suffix:* ***...etkʷ, ...tkʷ*** *– liquid*

roof

nčmqnéłxʷ, *nčmqné* – roof. *rt.:* ***čm*** *– extremity.*

room

nk̓ʷimełc̓eʔ – room. *suffix:* ***...ełc̓eʔ*** *– the inside of something.*
nłkʷk̓ʷimełc̓eʔ – small room.
ntl̓ihełc̓eʔ – across the room.
ci i nk̓ʷełc̓eʔ – the other room.

ci i nk̓ʷełc̓eʔ u es itši – S/he/it is sleeping in the other room.

snlcitn – place of living; home. *prefix:* ***sn...*** *– a place of; suffix:* ***...tin, ...tn*** *– means of/device.*

rooster

sqltmxʷskʷiskʷs – rooster.

likók – rooster. *(approximation to French word)*

root

sox̣ʷép – root.
es ox̣ʷx̣ʷépi – roots are growing.

rope

sp̓éc̓n – canvas/hemp/flax rope.

sip̓iʔ – hide/leather rope; lacing.

s.t. - something, the 3rd person
(s.t.) - something implied
s.o. - someone, the 3rd person
sl. - singular form
pl. - plural form
rt. - root word
cmd. - command
lit. - literally
fig. - figuratively
i.e., - for example
See: - Redirection to a related word.

ċiqp – horse hair rope; bristly/rough rope. *rt.: **ċiq** – prickly.*

qalmuˀteˀ – square plaited rope.

es sitčeˀ – three braided rope.

es q̓eċ – flat plaited rope.

acqáx̣eˀtn – buffalo hair rope; 3, 4, 6, 8 braided rope. *suffix: **...tin, ...tn** – means of/device.*

aclaw̓sqáx̣eˀtn – picket rope. *rt.: **ac** – bind, tie, trap; suffix: **...tin, ...tn** – means of/device.*

k̓ʷłacacšintn – hobbling rope. *rt.: **ac** – bind, tie, trap; suffix: **...tin, ...tn** – means of/device.*

čacíntn – tie on rope. *rt.: **ac** – bind, tie, trap; prefix: **č...** – upon; suffix: **...tin, ...tn** – means of/device.*

acmíntn – rope for catching. *rt.: **ac** – bind, tie, trap; suffix: **...tin, ...tn** – means of/device.*

čacélpstn – rope to put around neck. *rt.: **ac** – bind, tie, trap; prefix: **č...** – upon; suffix: **...tin, ...tn** – means of/device.*

k̓ʷłˀacépstn – rope to bridle horse in the mouth. *rt.: **ac** – bind, tie, trap; prefix: **k̓ʷł...** – under; suffix: **...tin, ...tn** – means of/device.*

ax̣ʷaw̓stn – rope to wind around the nozzle. *suffix: **...tin, ...tn** – means of/device.*

...ep *– suffix indicating rope, head hair.*
l̓ttimép – feeble rope.
łuwép – few ropes.
xʷˀep – many ropes.
łq̓ep – wide rope; belt. *rt.: **łaq̓** – wide.*

nk̓ʷep – one rope. **eslép** – two ropes. **čełép** – three ropes. **musp** – four ropes.
clčstep – five ropes. **t̓q̓nčstep** – six ropes. **sp̓l̓čep** – seven ropes.
henmép – eight ropes. **x̣antep** – nine ropes. **upnčstep** – ten ropes.

łxʷpusm – rope around the neck. *suffix: **...us** – face, fire. lit. slips over the face.*
łxʷpusis – S/he roped it. **łxʷpusn, łxʷpusntxʷ**
es łxʷpusms – S/he is roping it. **ies łxʷpusm, as łxʷpusm**
qs łxʷpusms – S/he is going to rope it. **iqs łxʷpusm, aqs łxʷpusm**

łxʷpusnt – Rope it around the neck. *cmd.*

čtqnten łxʷpusn snčłċaˀsqá – I chased and roped the horse around the neck.

siy̓én̓p̓ – dry meat rope.

iyutm – rub.

łiqt – shredded, torn cloth; raggy. *See: **shred**.*

t̓uwáq – break rope/cord. *See: **break**.*

x̣ƛ̓epm – chew a rope. *See: **chew**.*

roper

sxʷacacim – cattle roper; one tasked to tie up. *prefix: **sxʷ...** – one tasked to do.*

sxʷłxʷpusm – roper; one tasked to rope. *prefix: **sxʷ...** – one tasked to do.*

rosary

łik̓ʷ – string things together; putting things on thread, yarn or string. *(i.e., a rosary.)*

Rose

useli – Rosalie; Rose.

rose **xʷxʷẏépełp,** *xʷxʷẏé* – wild rose bush; *Rosa virginiana.*
sxʷẏapałq – wild rose hips. *suffix:* ***...ałq*** *– smell, accompaniment.*

snqáupups, *snqáupu* – rose hips, wild rose fruit; this term is used in Coyote stories.

Ross' Hole **kʷtiłṗupƛ̓m̓** – Ross' Hole, in the Bitterroot Valley, Montana. *lit. coming out into a big hole.*

rot **ituk͏ʷ** – rotted.
es ituk͏ʷ – It is rotten.
es itkʷmi – It is getting rotten; an expression referring to one's spouse.
es nitkʷełċeʔ – The inside is rotten. *(i.e., a log, etc.)*

itituk͏ʷ – Things are rotten here and there.

nitkʷeẇs – several things are rotten. *suffix:* ***...éẇs*** *– in between, middle.*

náq̓ – smell rotten; the smell of rotten meat; smell of excrement. *See:* ***smell.***

x̣ipt – gnawed by bugs. *(i.e., dried meat or woolen clothes, bugs got into them) See:* ***gnaw.***

rough **ƛ̓ox̣** – rough abrasive texture.
i ƛ̓ox̣ – It is rough.

čƛ̓ox̣ċeʔ – It is rough all over.

moƛ̓ – rough/bumpy texture.
i moƛ̓ – It is bumpy.

čmoƛ̓ċeʔ – It is rough/bumpy all over.

round dance **šlšlčmncutist,** *šlšlčmncu* – round dancing.
šlšlčmncut – S/he round danced. **čn šlšlčmncut, kʷ šlšlčmncut**
es šlšlčmncuti – S/he is round dancing. **čnes šlšlčmncuti, kʷes šlšlčmncuti**
qs šlšlčmncuti – S/he is going to round dance. **čiqs šlšlčmncuti, kʷqs šlšlčmncuti**
šlšlčmncúʔut – They round danced. **qeʔ šlšlčmncut, p šlšlčmncut**
es šlšlčmncúʔuti – They are round dancing. **qeʔes šlšlčmncuti, pes šlšlčmncuti**
qs šlšlčmncúʔuti – They are going to round dance. **qeʔqs šlšlčmncuti, pqs šlšlčmncuti**

nłšlčmncut – S/he round danced a little.

snšlšlčmncutn – round dance. *prefix:* ***sn...*** *– a place of; suffix:* ***...tin, ...tn*** *– means of/device.*
šlšlčmnsemn – one inclined to round dance. *suffix:* ***...emn*** *– one inclined to do.*

šlšlčmncutš – Round dance. *cmd.*
šlšlčmncutwi – All of you round dance. *cmd.*

es nšlšlčmstemisti – S/he wants to round dance. **čnes nšlšlčmstemisti, kʷes nšlšlčmstemisti**

round object **syal** – circle. *See:* ***circle.***

málq̓ʷ – rounded/spherical; balled object; accumulate. *See:* ***ball.***

čéʔ – lump; something just sitting there. *See:* ***lump.***

yult – large in girth. *(of cylindrical objects.) See:* ***girth.***

npkʷétkʷ – pour round objects in water. *(i.e., berries, rocks, etc.) See:* ***pour.***

The **i** following uvular consonants (UC) and the glottal stop **ʔ** sound like English "*ey*" as in the words th*ey*, h*ey*, wh*ey*, etc. Salish UC are: **q**, **q̓**, **qʷ**, **q̓ʷ**, **x̣**, **x̣ʷ**. For example, the suffix ...**qin** – head/top, is often spelled using English *ey* as "q*ey*n". So **qi**, **q̓i**, **qʷi**, **q̓ʷi**, **x̣i**, **x̣ʷi**, may be spelled with English *ey* as **q***ey*, **q̓***ey*, **qʷ***ey*, **q̓ʷ***ey*, **x̣***ey*, **x̣ʷ***ey* in other texts.

s.t. - something, the 3rd person
(s.t.) - something implied
s.o. - someone, the 3rd person
sl. - singular form
pl. - plural form
rt. - root word
cmd. - command
lit. - literally
fig. - figuratively
i.e., - for example
See: - Redirection to a related word.

round up **ẏamsqáx̣eʔ**, *ẏamsqá* – gather/round up domestic animals/horses.
ẏamsqáx̣eʔ – S/he gathered horses. **čn ẏamsqáx̣eʔ, kʷ ẏamsqáx̣eʔ**
es ẏamsqáx̣eʔi – S/he is gathering horses. **čnes ẏamsqáx̣eʔi, kʷes ẏamsqáx̣eʔi**
qs ẏamsqáx̣eʔi – S/he is going to gather horses. **čiqs ẏamsqáx̣eʔi, kʷqs ẏamsqáx̣eʔi**
ẏamsqáʔax̣eʔ – They gathered horses. **qeʔ ẏamsqáx̣eʔ, p ẏamsqáx̣eʔ**
es ẏamsqáʔax̣eʔi – They are gathering horses. **qeʔes ẏamsqáx̣eʔi, pes ẏamsqáx̣eʔi**
qs ẏamsqáʔax̣eʔi – They are going to gather horses. **qeʔqs ẏamsqáx̣eʔi, pqs ẏamsqáx̣eʔi**

row **šƛ̓milš** – row, line. *rt: šiƛ̓ – flat, level, aligned.*
es šƛ̓milš – They are in line/row.

šiƛ̓ – flat/even; aligned; straight; ordered. *See: **flat**.*
šƛ̓mim – put things in a straight line; aligned; ordered; level and even. *See: **flat**.*

eslep es šƛ̓šƛ̓milš – second row.
šƛ̓milš p̓ip̓uyšn – row of cars.
šƛ̓šƛ̓milš p̓ip̓uyšn – rows of cars.

laáp – float in a vessel; navigate by water; *row; surf internet. (i.e., boat, canoe, raft, etc.) See: **float**.*

rub **yilk̓ʷ** – rub something with hands or fingers.
yilk̓ʷis – S/he rubbed s.t. **yilk̓ʷn, yilk̓ʷntxʷ**
es yilk̓ʷms – S/he is rubbing s.t. **ies yilk̓ʷm, as yilk̓ʷm**
qs yilk̓ʷms – S/he is going to rub s.t. **iqs yilk̓ʷm, aqs yilk̓ʷm**

nilk̓ʷčnečsis – S/he rubbed s.t. in the hand. **nilk̓ʷčnečsn, nilk̓ʷčnečsntxʷ**
es nilk̓ʷčnečsms – S/he is rubbing s.t. in the hand. **ies nilk̓ʷčnečsm, as nilk̓ʷčnečsm**
qs nilk̓ʷčnečsms – S/he is going to rub s.t. in the hand. **iqs nilk̓ʷčnečsm, aqs nilk̓ʷčnečsm**

yilk̓ʷnt – Rub it. *cmd.*
ilk̓ʷax̣nm – rub the arm.
čyilk̓ʷšnm – rub the foot.
ilk̓ʷax̣nm – rub the arm.
ililk̓ʷčsncut – rub one's hands.
čililk̓ʷsncut – rub one's eyes.
nilk̓ʷčnečstmis – S/he rubbed the palm of s.o.'s hand. **nilk̓ʷčnečstmn, nilk̓ʷčnečstmntxʷ**
nilk̓ʷčnečstm – S/he rubbed the palm of the hand. **čn nilk̓ʷčnečstm, kʷ nilk̓ʷčnečstm**

yilk̓ʷnt sx̣ʷéʔli – rub the camas *(to remove dirt)*. **ha kʷ ṅe u qʷo čyililk̓ʷšntxʷ** – Would you rub my feet?

yut – make soft, supple or limber by rubbing with the hands.
yut – S/he rubbed (s.t.). **čn yut, kʷ yut**
es yuti – S/he is rubbing (s.t.). **čnes yuti, kʷes yuti**
qs yuti – S/he is going to rub (s.t.). **čiqs yuti, kʷqs yuti**

yutis – S/he rubbed s.t. **yutn, yutntxʷ**
es yutms – S/he is rubbing s.t. **ies yutm, as yutm**
qs yutms – S/he is going rub s.t. **iqs yutm, aqs yutm**

yutmskʷ – Rub it. *cmd.*

k̓ʷis yutmskʷ – Go rub it.

sax̣mqn – rub one's antlers on something such as a tree.
es sax̣mqni – It is rubbing its antlers.

es sax̣si – It is rubbing its antlers.

snsax̣mqntn – place where animals rub their antlers.
snsax̣stn – place where animals rub their antlers.

x̣iq – rub against; the sound of rubbing.
x̣iq – S/he/it rubbed against (s.t.). **čn x̣iq, kʷ x̣iq**
es x̣iqi – S/he/it is rubbing against (s.t.). **čnes x̣iqi, kʷes x̣iqi**
qs x̣iqi – S/he/it is going to rub against (s.t.). **čiqs x̣iqi, kʷqs x̣iqi**

x̣iqis – S/he/it rubbed against s.t. **x̣iqn, x̣iqntxʷ**
es x̣iqms – S/he/it is rubbing against s.t. **ies x̣iqm, as x̣iqm**
qs x̣iqms – S/he/it is going to rub against s.t. **iqs x̣iqm, aqs x̣iqm**

čx̣iqis – S/he/it rubbed s.t. against s.t. **čx̣iqn, čx̣iqntxʷ**
es čx̣iqms – S/he/it is rubbing s.t. against s.t. **ies čx̣iqm, as čx̣iqm**
qs čx̣iqms – S/he/it is going to rub s.t. against s.t. **iqs čx̣iqm, aqs čx̣iqm**

snčx̣iqmn – washboard; rubbing device. *(i.e., something used for tanning hides, etc.)*

x̣qx̣iqlš – something is rubbing.

ha čx̣iqntxʷ łu anċulixʷélxʷ – Did you rub your buckskin? **x̣ʷa steṁ łu x̣qx̣iqlš –** What is that rubbing?

miƛ̓ – smear; rub something; spread something on something. *See: **smear**.*

čx̣ʷq̓ʷx̣ʷaq̓ʷm – grind/file on the side of something. *See: **grind**.*

ṅe qʷʔóp m łuxʷntxʷ – When it is soften up, you rub it back and forth.

rubber

łsṫsuṫ, *łsṫsu* **–** rubber. *rt.: **suṫ** – stretch.*

ṗič – glossy; *shine something; used to describe the shiny surface of rubber, dark sun tans and the skin of black people. See: **glossy**.*

rubber boots

sṗčṗičšn, *sṗčṗi* **–** rubber boots. *lit. glossy feet.*

rude

q̓xʷq̓exʷt, *q̓xʷq̓e* **–** proud; vain; think much of; stuck-up. *See: **stuck-up**.*

q̓xʷnscut – conceited; proud of one's self. *See: **conceited**.*

rue

ṗx̣ʷcuxʷeʔ, *ṗx̣ʷcu* **–** meadow rue; licorice root; *Glycyrrhiza lepidota*.

ruffed grouse

qáłqłċeʔ, *qá* **–** ruffed grouse; *Bonasa umbellus*.

rufous hummingbird

łx̣ʷx̣ʷṅi – hummingbird; rufous, black-chinned, calliope.

rug

čłxʷépmn – rug; carpet. *rt.: **xʷep** – cover; prefix: **čł...** – surface.*

ruin

k̓ʷłx̣ʷellm – ruin something; let something waste away. *rt.: **x̣ʷel** – abandon; prefix: **k̓ʷł...** – under.*
k̓ʷłx̣ʷellm – S/he/it wasted away. **čn k̓ʷłx̣ʷellm, kʷ k̓ʷłx̣ʷellm**
es k̓ʷłx̣ʷelli – S/he/it is wasting away. **čnes k̓ʷłx̣ʷelli, kʷes k̓ʷłx̣ʷelli**
qs k̓ʷłx̣ʷelli – S/he/it is going to waste away. **čiqs k̓ʷłx̣ʷelli, kʷqs k̓ʷłx̣ʷelli**
k̓ʷłx̣ʷéʔellm – They wasted away. **qeʔ k̓ʷłx̣ʷellm, p k̓ʷłx̣ʷellm**
es k̓ʷłx̣ʷéʔelli – They are wasting away. **qeʔes k̓ʷłx̣ʷelli, pes k̓ʷłx̣ʷelli**
qs k̓ʷłx̣ʷéʔelli – They are going to waste away. **qeʔqs k̓ʷłx̣ʷelli, pqs k̓ʷłx̣ʷelli**

The **i** following uvular consonants (UC) and the glottal stop **ʔ** sound like English "*ey*" as in the words th*ey*, h*ey*, wh*ey*, etc. Salish UC are: **q, q̓, qʷ, q̓ʷ, x̣, x̣ʷ**. For example, the suffix **...qin** – head/top, is often spelled using English *ey* as "q*ey*n". So **qi, q̓i, qʷi, q̓ʷi, x̣i, x̣ʷi**, may be spelled with English *ey* as **q***ey*, **q̓***ey*, **qʷ***ey*, **q̓ʷ***ey*, **x̣***ey*, **x̣ʷ***ey* in other texts.

s.t. - something, the 3rd person
(s.t.) - something implied
s.o. - someone, the 3rd person
sl. - singular form
pl. - plural form
rt. - root word
cmd. - command
lit. - literally
fig. - figuratively
i.e., - for example
See: - Redirection to a related word.

k̓ʷɬx̣ʷellis – S/he/it wasted it. **k̓ʷɬx̣ʷelln, k̓ʷɬx̣ʷellntxʷ**
es k̓ʷɬx̣ʷellms – S/he/it is wasting it. **ies k̓ʷɬx̣ʷellm, as k̓ʷɬx̣ʷellm**
qs k̓ʷɬx̣ʷellms – S/he/it is going to waste it. **iqs k̓ʷɬx̣ʷellm, aqs k̓ʷɬx̣ʷellm**
k̓ʷɬx̣ʷéʔelis – They wasted it. **qeʔ k̓ʷɬx̣ʷelntm, k̓ʷɬx̣ʷelntp**
es k̓ʷɬx̣ʷéʔellms – They are wasting it. **qeʔes k̓ʷɬx̣ʷellm, es k̓ʷɬx̣ʷellmp**
qs k̓ʷɬx̣ʷéʔellms – They are going to waste it. **qeʔqs k̓ʷɬx̣ʷellm, qs k̓ʷɬx̣ʷellmp**

es k̓ʷɬx̣ʷlx̣ʷelli – S/he is continuously wasting away. **čnes x̣ʷlx̣ʷelli, kʷes k̓ʷɬx̣ʷlx̣ʷelli**
es k̓ʷɬx̣ʷlx̣ʷellms – S/he is wasting things. **ies k̓ʷɬx̣ʷlx̣ʷellm, as k̓ʷɬx̣ʷlx̣ʷellm**

k̓ʷɬx̣ʷelll – S/he/it got ruined.
k̓ʷɬx̣ʷellntm – S/he/it was left to ruin; s/he/it was allowed to waste away.

k̓ʷɬx̣ʷllnuis – S/he finally wasted it. **k̓ʷɬx̣ʷllnun, k̓ʷɬx̣ʷllnuntxʷ**

sxʷk̓ʷɬx̣ʷellm – one tasked to waste. *prefix:* ***sxʷ...*** *– one tasked to do.*
k̓ʷɬx̣ʷllemn – one inclined to waste. **k̓ʷɬx̣ʷllemn** *pl. suffix:* ***...emn*** *– one inclined to do.*
sck̓ʷɬx̣ʷell – something that has been wasted. *prefix:* ***sc...*** *– s.t. that's been done/made/prepared.*
snx̣ʷellmn – place things are ruined or wasted.

k̓ʷɬx̣ʷelliš – Waste. *cmd.*
k̓ʷɬx̣ʷellskʷ – Ruin it. *cmd.*
k̓ʷɬx̣ʷellnt – Ruin it. *cmd.*
es k̓ʷɬx̣ʷllmnwexʷi – They are wasting each other away. **qeʔes k̓ʷɬx̣ʷllmnwexʷi, pes k̓ʷɬx̣ʷllmnwexʷi**
k̓ʷɬx̣ʷllwisis – S/he keeps going around wasting things. **k̓ʷɬx̣ʷllwisn, k̓ʷɬx̣ʷllwisntxʷ**
es nk̓ʷɬx̣ʷllmelsi – S/he is wanting to waste (s.t.). **čnes nk̓ʷɬx̣ʷllmelsi, kʷes nk̓ʷɬx̣ʷllmelsi**

ṅem k̓ʷɬx̣ʷéllm – S/he/it will waste away. **ṅem čn k̓ʷɬx̣ʷéllm, ṅem kʷ k̓ʷɬx̣ʷéllm**
ṅem k̓ʷɬx̣ʷéʔellm – They will waste away. **ṅem qeʔ k̓ʷɬx̣ʷélm, ṅem p k̓ʷɬx̣ʷélm**

ċulm – let something go to waste; do away with something by destruction or nonuse; not using something properly. *See:* ***waste.***

ruler

suxʷmeʔtn – ruler; yard stick; measuring tape. *rt.:* ***suxʷmeʔ*** *– measure; suffix:* ***...tin, ...tn*** *– means of/device.*

rules

snčċx̣ʷx̣ʷepleʔtn – rules; laws. *prefix:* ***sn...*** *– a place of; suffix:* ***...epleʔ*** *– permanence ; suffix:* ***...tin, ...tn*** *– means of/device.*
iheʔ ɬu qesnčċx̣ʷx̣ʷepleʔtn x̣ʷl ṅe qeʔ memscut – Here are our rules for when we play.

run

mntwilš, *mntwi* – run. *(This word describes running as a type of motion) suffix:* ***...ilš*** *– autonomous.*
mntwilš – S/he/it ran. **čn mntwilš, kʷ mntwilš**
es mntwilši – S/he/it is running. **čnes mntwilši, kʷes mntwilši**
qs mntwilši – S/he/it is going to run. **čiqs mntwilši, kʷqs mntwilši**
mnmntwíʔilš – Each on of them ran. **qeʔ mnmntwilš, p mnmntwilš**
es mnmntwíʔilši – Each on of them are running. **qeʔes mnmntwilši, pes mnmntwilši**
qs mnmntwíʔilši – Each one of them are going to run. **qeʔqs mnmntwilši, pqs mnmntwilši**

ṅem mntwilš – He/it will run. **ṅem čn mntwilš, ṅem kʷ mntwilš**
ṅem mnmntwíʔilš – They will run. **ṅem qeʔ mnmntwilš, ṅem p mnmntwilš**

mntwilšiš, *mntwi* – Run. *cmd.*

qéclš – run of an individual; run leisurely. *(This word describes the action of running as an activity; i.e., running for exercise, jogging, etc.) suffix:* ***...ilš*** *– autonomous.*
qéclš – S/he ran. **čn qéclš, kʷ qéclš**

es qéclši – S/he is running. **čnes qéclši, kʷes qéclši**
qs qéclši – S/he is going to run. **čiqs qéclši, kʷqs qéclši**

čqéclšmis – S/he ran to s.t./s.o. **čqéclšmn, čqéclšmntxʷ**
es čqéclšmms – S/he is running to s.t./s.o. **ies čqéclšmm, as čqéclšmm**
qs čqéclšmms – S/he is going to run to s.t./s.o. **iqs čqéclšmm, aqs čqéclšmm**

qicqleʔ – hoop game.

qéclš – Run. *cmd.*
čqeclšmnt – Run/caper to it. *cmd.*

qcqéclš – individually bound/caper; run around leisurely; repeatedly run as an activity. *suffix:* ***...ilš*** *– autonomous.*
qcqeclš – S/he ran around. **čn qcqeclš, kʷ qcqeclš**
es qcqeclši – S/he is running around. **čnes qcqeclši, kʷes qcqeclši**
qs qcqeclši – S/he is going to run around. **čiqs qcqeclši, kʷqs qcqeclši**

ta kʷ qes qcqeclš – Do not run around. **čnes ntelsi čiqs qcqeclši –** I want to run around.

q̇ʷoƛ̓š – run of two or more; run of animals. *(This word describes the action of running as an activity)*
q̇ʷóʔoƛ̓š – They ran. **qeʔ q̇ʷóƛ̓š, p q̇ʷóƛ̓š**
es q̇ʷóʔoƛ̓ši – They are running. **qeʔes q̇ʷóƛ̓ši, pes q̇ʷóƛ̓ši**
qs q̇ʷóʔoƛ̓ši – They are going to run. **qeʔqs q̇ʷóƛ̓ši, pqs q̇ʷóƛ̓ši**

čq̇ʷóʔoƛ̓šmis – They ran to s.o./s.t. **qeʔ čq̇ʷoƛ̓šmntm, čq̇ʷoƛ̓šmntp**
es čq̇ʷóʔoƛ̓šmms – They are running to s.o./s.t. **qeʔes čq̇ʷoƛ̓šmm, es čq̇ʷoƛ̓šmmp**
qs čq̇ʷóʔoƛ̓šmms – They are going to rn to s.o./s.t. **qeʔqs čq̇ʷoƛ̓šmm, qs čq̇ʷoƛ̓šmmp**

q̇ʷoƛ̓šwi – All of you run. *cmd.*
čq̇ʷoƛ̓šmnti – All of you run to it. *cmd.*

q̇ʷƛ̓q̇ʷƛ̓šin – two or more bound/caper; run around leisurely; run repeatedly as an activity.
k̇ʷƛ̓k̇ʷƛ̓šíʔin – They ran around. **qeʔ q̇ʷƛ̓q̇ʷƛ̓šin, p q̇ʷƛ̓q̇ʷƛ̓šin**
es q̇ʷƛ̓q̇ʷƛ̓šnmíʔi – They are running around. **qeʔes q̇ʷƛ̓q̇ʷƛ̓šnmi, pes q̇ʷƛ̓q̇ʷƛ̓šnmi**
qs q̇ʷƛ̓q̇ʷƛ̓šnmíʔi – They are going to run around. **qeʔqs q̇ʷƛ̓q̇ʷƛ̓šnmi, pqs q̇ʷƛ̓q̇ʷƛ̓šnmi**

wamist, *wami* – run walk; hurry along; run in a feminine manner.
wamistm – S/he/it ran. **čn wamistm, kʷ wamistm**
es wamisti – S/he/it is running. **čnes wamisti, kʷes wamisti**
qs wamisti – S/he/it is going to run. **čiqs wamisti, kʷqs wamisti**
wamíʔistm – They ran. **qeʔ wamistm, p wamistm**
es wamíʔisti – They are running. **qeʔes wamisti, pes wamisti**
qs wamíʔisti – They are going to run. **qeʔqs wamisti, pqs wamisti**

wamstes – S/he/it made s.o. hurry along. **wamsten, wamistexʷ**
es wamstms – S/he/it is making s.o. hurry along. **ies wamstm, as wamstm**
qs wamstms – S/he/it is going make s.o. hurry along. **iqs wamstm, aqs wamstm**

čwamistmis – S/he/it hurried to s.t./s.o. **čwamistmn, čwamistmntxʷ**
es čwamistms – S/he/it is hurrying to s.t./s.o. **ies čwamistm, as čwamistm**
qs čwamistms – S/he/it is going hurry to s.t./s.o. **iqs čwamistm, aqs čwamistm**

wamistš – Walk fast. *cmd.*
wamistwi – All of you walk fast. *cmd.*
cwamistš – Walk fast to me. *cmd.*

The **i** following uvular consonants (UC) and the glottal stop **ʔ** sound like English "*ey*" as in the words th*ey*, h*ey*, wh*ey*, etc. Salish UC are: **q, q̇, qʷ, q̇ʷ, x̣, x̣ʷ**. For example, the suffix **...qin** – head/top, is often spelled using English *ey* as "q*ey*n". So **qi, q̇i, qʷi, q̇ʷi, x̣i, x̣ʷi**, may be spelled with English *ey* as **q***ey*, **q̇***ey*, **qʷ***ey*, **q̇ʷ***ey*, **x̣***ey*, **x̣ʷ***ey* in other texts.

s.t. - something, the 3rd person
(s.t.) - something implied
s.o. - someone, the 3rd person
sl. - singular form
pl. - plural form
rt. - root word
cmd. - command
lit. - literally
fig. - figuratively
i.e., - for example
See: - Redirection to a related word.

wamstmskʷ – Make him/her hurry. *cmd.*
čwamistmnt – Hurry to it. *cmd.*

ṅem čn wamistm – I will run.

xʷṫip – an individual ran from the spot occupied to somewhere; escape from routine. *See:* ***run away.***

čxʷṫpminm – an individual charges toward; run toward; attack; rush to; an individual runs toward. *See:* ***charge.***

xʷicut – more than one ran from the spot occupied to somewhere; escaped from routine. *See:* ***run away.***

čxʷicut – more than one charges toward; attack; rush to; run toward. *See:* ***charge.***

ṫloq̇ʷ – run away; flee from danger; flee out of fear. *See:* ***run away.***

łx̣ʷoṗ – run off to the outside of something; dash out; suddenly run out of an enclosure. *See:* ***escape.***

pq̇smi – gallop. *See:* ***gallop.***

cilšlš – trot (man, horse, animal). *See:* ***trot.***

k̓ʷłnq̇ʷmist, *k̓ʷłnq̇ʷmi* **–** run away stealthily; sneak away; leave; escape. *See:* ***escape.***

čic – happen upon; meet someone; an accidental meeting. *See:* ***meet.***

čtéˀemistm, *čtéˀe* **–** bump against something *(i.e., wall, person, etc.).* *See:* ***bump.***

run away

ṫloq̇ʷ – run away; flee from danger; flee out of fear.
ṫloq̇ʷ – S/he/it ran away. **čn ṫloq̇ʷ, kʷ ṫloq̇ʷ**
es ṫlq̇ʷmi – S/he/it is running away. **čnes ṫlq̇ʷmi, kʷes ṫlq̇ʷmi**
qs ṫlq̇ʷmi – S/he/it is going to run away. **čiqs ṫlq̇ʷmi, kʷqs ṫlq̇ʷmi**
ṫlóˀoq̇ʷ – They ran away. **qeˀ ṫloq̇ʷ, p ṫloq̇ʷ**
es ṫlq̇ʷmíˀi – They are running away. **qeˀes ṫlq̇ʷmi, pes ṫlq̇ʷmi**
qs ṫlq̇ʷmíˀi – They are going to run away. **qeˀqs ṫlq̇ʷmi, pqs ṫlq̇ʷmi**

ṫlq̇ʷstes – S/he/it caused s.o. to flee. **ṫlq̇ʷsten, ṫlq̇ʷsntexʷ**
es ṫlq̇ʷoms – S/he/it is causing s.o. to flee. **ies ṫlq̇ʷom, as ṫlq̇ʷom**
qs ṫlq̇ʷoms – S/he/it is going to cause s.o. to flee. **iqs ṫlq̇ʷom, aqs ṫlq̇ʷom**

ṫlq̇ʷmis – S/he/it fled from s.o./s.t. **ṫlq̇ʷmin, ṫlq̇ʷmintxʷ**
es ṫlq̇ʷminms – S/he/it is fleeing from s.o./s.t. **ies ṫlq̇ʷminm, as ṫlq̇ʷminm**
qs ṫlq̇ʷminms – S/he/it is going to flee from s.o./s.t. **iqs ṫlq̇ʷminm, aqs ṫlq̇ʷminm**

ṫlq̇ʷusis – S/he/it took s.o. away in flight. **ṫlq̇ʷusn, ṫlq̇ʷusntxʷ**
es ṫlq̇ʷusms – S/he/it is taking s.o. away in flight. **ies ṫlq̇ʷusm, as ṫlq̇ʷusm**
qs ṫlq̇ʷusms – S/he/it is going to take s.o. away in flight. **iqs ṫlq̇ʷusm, aqs ṫlq̇ʷusm**

čṫlq̇ʷmis – S/he/it fled to s.o./s.t. **čṫlq̇ʷmin, čṫlq̇ʷmintxʷ**
es čṫlq̇ʷminms – S/he/it is fleeing to s.o./s.t. **ies čṫlq̇ʷminm, as čṫlq̇ʷminm**
qs čṫlq̇ʷminms – S/he/it is going to flee to s.o./s.t. **iqs čṫlq̇ʷminm, aqs čṫlq̇ʷminm**

ṫlṫloq̇ʷ – Each one ran away.

sṫloq̇ʷ – the flight.
ṫlq̇ʷomn – one inclined to flee. *suffix:* ***...emn*** *– one inclined to do*
sxʷṫlq̇ʷom – one charged to flee. *prefix:* ***sxʷ...*** *– one tasked to do.*
sxʷṫloq̇ʷ – the ones that fled. *prefix:* ***sxʷ...*** *– one tasked to do.*
čṫlq̇ʷtin – the reason for flight; the thing that causes one to flee.
nṫlq̇ʷtin – the way to flee; the means to escape.

ṫloq̇ʷš – Flee. *cmd.*
ṫlq̇ʷoskʷ – Make s.o./s.t. flee. *cmd.*

ṫlq̇ʷmnwéʔexʷ – They ran away from each other. **qeʔ ṫlq̇ʷmnwexʷ, p ṫlq̇ʷmnwéʔexʷ**

xʷṫip – an individual ran from the spot occupied to somewhere; escape from routine.
xʷṫip – S/he/it ran away. **čn xʷṫip, kʷ xʷṫip**
es xʷṫpmi – S/he/it is running away. **čnes xʷṫpmi, kʷes xʷṫpmi**
qs xʷṫpmi – S/he/it is going to run away. **čiqs xʷṫpmi, kʷqs xʷṫpmi**

xʷṫpusis – S/he/it took s.o. away; make it run away. **xʷṫpusn, xʷṫpusntxʷ**
es xʷṫpusms – S/he/it is taking s.o. away. **ies xʷṫpusm, as xʷṫpusm**
qs xʷṫpusms – S/he/it is going to take s.o. away. **iqs xʷṫpusm, aqs xʷṫpusm**

es xʷṫxʷṫpmi – S/he/it is repeatedly running away. **čnes xʷṫpmi, kʷes xʷṫpmi**

xʷṫipš – Run to. *cmd.*
t xʷṫip – run away before/ahead of s.t./s.o.
xʷṫpsalqʷ – come out of the forest when traveling.
xʷṫpnumt – succeed in running away.
xʷṫpelt – child run away.
xʷṫplwis – run away here and there.
xʷṫpncut – elope; run away. *See: **elope**.*
čxʷṫpminm – an individual charges toward; run toward; attack; rush to; an individual runs toward. *See: **charge**.*

ṅem xʷṫip – S/he/it will run away. **ṅem čn xʷṫip, ṅem kʷ xʷṫip**
ṅem xʷṫíʔip – They will run away. **ṅem qeʔ xʷṫip, ṅem p xʷṫip**

xʷṫip č esmq̇ʷmóq̇ʷ – S/he ran to the mountains. **xʷṫpusn isnčłċasqax̣eʔ –** I made my horse run away. **qs xʷṫpusms innox̣ʷnx̣ʷ –** He's going to run somewhere with my wife. **xʷṫpelt łu isqʷseʔ–** My son ran somewhere. **čn puxʷṫip –** My spouse ran away; I am the one with the spouse who ran away.

The **i** following uvular consonants (UC) and the glottal stop **ʔ** sound like English "*ey*" as in the words *they, hey, whey,* etc. Salish UC are: **q, q̇, qʷ, q̇ʷ, x̣, x̣ʷ**. For example, the suffix ...**qin** – head/top, is often spelled using English *ey* as "q*ey*n". So **qi, q̇i, qʷi, q̇ʷi, x̣i, x̣ʷi,** may be spelled with English *ey* as **q***ey*, **q̇***ey*, **qʷ***ey*, **q̇ʷ***ey*, **x̣***ey*, **x̣ʷ***ey* in other texts.

nxʷṫpmels – want to run away; want to escape from routine. *circumfix: **n...els** – want, feel.*
nxʷṫpmels – S/he wanted to run away. **čn nxʷṫpmels, kʷ nxʷṫpmels**
es nxʷṫpmelsi – S/he is wanting to run away. **čnes nxʷṫpmelsi, kʷes nxʷṫpmelsi**
qs nxʷṫpmelsi – S/he is going to want to run away. **čiqs nxʷṫpmelsi, kʷqs nxʷṫpmelsi**
nxʷṫpméʔels – They wanted to run away. **qeʔ nxʷṫpmels, p nxʷṫpmels**
es nxʷṫpméʔelsi – They are wanting to run away. **qeʔes nxʷṫpmelsi, pes nxʷṫpmelsi**
qs nxʷṫpméʔelsi – They are going to want to run away. **qeʔqs nxʷṫpmelsi, pqs nxʷṫpmelsi**

ṅem nxʷṫpmels – S/he will want to run away. **ṅem čn nxʷṫpmels, ṅem kʷ nxʷṫpmels**
ṅem nxʷṫpméʔels – They will want to run away. **ṅem qeʔ nxʷṫpmels, ṅem p nxʷṫpmels**

xʷicut – more than one ran from the spot occupied to somewhere; escaped from routine. *rt.: **xʷuy** – go.*
xʷicúʔut – They ran away. **qeʔ xʷicut, p xʷicut**
es xʷicúʔuti – They are running away. **qeʔes xʷicuti, pes xʷicuti**
qs xʷicúʔuti – They are going to run away. **qeʔqs xʷicuti, pqs xʷicuti**

xʷicutwi – All of you attack. *cmd.*
čxʷicut – more than one charges toward; attack; rush to; run toward. *See: **charge**.*

s.t. - something, the 3rd person
(s.t.) - something implied
s.o. - someone, the 3rd person
sl. - singular form
pl. - plural form
rt. - root word
cmd. - command
lit. - literally
fig. - figuratively
i.e., - for example
See: - Redirection to a related word.

runny nose

nawawpaqs – runny nose. *rt.: **awup** – drip.*

nawapaqs – One's nose was running. **čn nawapaqs, kʷ nawapaqs**
es nawapaqsi – One's nose is running. **čnes nawapaqsi, kʷes nawapaqsi**
qs nawapaqsi – One's nose is going to run. **čiqs nawapaqsi, kʷqs nawapaqsi**

rupture

xʷaʔlip – rupture; tear; slit.
xʷaʔlip – S/he tore (s.t.). **čn xʷaʔlip, kʷ xʷaʔlip**
es xʷaʔlpmi – S/he is tearing (s.t.). **čnes xʷaʔlpmi, kʷes xʷaʔlpmi**
qs xʷaʔlpmi – S/he is going to tear (s.t.). **čiqs xʷaʔlpmi, kʷqs xʷaʔlpmi**

xʷaʔlntes – S/he tore s.t. **xʷaʔlnten, xʷaʔlntexʷ**
es xʷaʔlims – S/he is tearing s.t. **ies xʷaʔlim, as xʷaʔlim**
qs xʷaʔlims – S/he is going to tear s.t. **iqs xʷaʔlim, aqs xʷaʔlim**

xʷaʔlip ispúʔus – My heart ruptured/split.

rush

čxʷṫpminm – an individual charges toward; run toward; attack; rush to; an individual runs toward. *See:* ***charge***.

x̣ʷełé – hurry; quickly. *See:* ***hurry***.

qʷiṁm – anxious; in a hurry; move quickly. *See:* ***hurry***.

wamist, *wami* – run walk; hurry along; run in a feminine manner. *See:* ***run***.

aẏip – go fast, hurry. *(i.e., on foot, by car, or on horseback)* *See:* ***fast***.

rut

es sl̓stwexʷi, *es sl̓stwe* – The animals are mating. *See:* ***mate***.

S

sack **čk̓ʷxʷépleʔ,** *čk̓ʷxʷé* – bag with a handle. *suffix:* ***...épleʔ*** *– permanence.*

q̓éc̓ – woven sack/bag. *See:* ***weave.***

čq̓ʔic̓éʔ, *čq̓ʔi* – Indian suitcase; rawhide bag. *lit. it has a pattern around it. See:* ***pattern.***

ax̣éṅeʔ – beaded bag/handbag. *rt.:* ***i ax̣*** *– it has lines. See:* ***line.***
łax̣éṅeʔ – small beaded bag/handbag

čtk̓ʷłc̓ełniut, *čtk̓ʷłc̓e* – something on the side to stuff in; pouch on a belt. *See:* ***side.***

qq̓epeʔ – cornhusk bag.

sqtté – baby sack. *(a wrap for babies)*

sacred **scputʔe –** sacred. *prefix:* ***sc...*** *– s.t. that's been done/made/prepared. See:* ***respect.***
nputʔélstn – something used for respect; sacred. *suffix:* ***...tin, ...tn*** *– means of/device.*

sacrifice **čptkʷumnálqʷ,** *čptkʷumná* – crucify; pinned to wood. *See:* ***pin.***

nweym – make prayful offerings in sacrifice to the creator. *See:* ***offer.***

sad **pupusénč,** *pupusé* – sad; sorry; mourn; grieve. *rt.:* ***spúʔus*** *– heart; suffix:* ***...énč*** *– within.*
pupusénč – S/he got sad. **čn pupusénč, kʷ pupusénč**
es pupusénči – S/he is sad. **čnes pupusénči, kʷes pupusénči**
qs pupusénči – S/he is going to be sad. **čiqs pupusénči, kʷqs pupusénči**
pupuséʔenč – They got sad. **qeʔ pupusénč, p pupusénč**
es pupuséʔenči – They are sad. **qeʔes pupusénči, pes pupusénči**
qs pupuséʔenči – They are going to be sad. **qeʔqs pupusénči, pqs pupusénči**

pupusénčmist – S/he was sad for one's self. **čn pupusénčmist, kʷ pupusénčmist**
es pupusénčmisti – S/he is sad for one's self. **čnes pupusénčmisti, kʷes pupusénčmisti**
qs pupusénčmisti – S/he is going to be sad for one's self. **čiqs pupusénčmisti, kʷqs pupusénčmisti**

pupusénčmis – S/he got sad for s.o./s.t. **pupusénčmn, pupusénčmntxʷ**
es pupusénčmms – S/he is sad for s.o./s.t. **ies pupusénčmm, as pupusénčmm**
qs pupusénčmms – S/he is going to be sad for s.o./s.t. **iqs pupusénčmm, aqs pupusénčmm**

pupusénčsts – S/he made s.o. sad. **pupusénčstn, pupusénčstxʷ**
es pupusénčms – S/he is making s.o. sad. **ies pupusénčm, as pupusénčm**
qs pupusénčms – S/he is going to make s.o. sad. **iqs pupusénčm, aqs pupusénčm**

čpupusénčmis – S/he got sad because of s.o./s.t. **čpupusénčmn, čpupusénčmntxʷ**
es čpupusénčmms – S/he is sad because of s.o./s.t. **ies čpupusénčmm, as čpupusénčmm**

s.t. - something, the 3rd person
(s.t.) - something implied
s.o. - someone, the 3rd person
sl. - singular form
pl. - plural form
rt. - root word
cmd. - command
lit. - literally
fig. - figuratively
i.e., - for example
See: - Redirection to a related word.

qs čpupusénčmms – S/he is going to be sad because of s.o./s.t. **iqs čpupusénčmm, aqs čpupusénčmm**

spupusénč – sadness.
scpupusénč – past sadness.
npupusénčtn – sorrow.
čnpupusénčtn – something that causes sadness/sorrow.

pupusnčstwexʷ – make each other sad.
pupusnčmnwexʷ – sad for each other.

x̣ʷa ṅem kʷ tixʷ scpupusénč – Maybe you will get sad.

ixʷ – sad; hurt; mental pain.
ixʷup – S/he got sad. **čn ixʷup, kʷ ixʷup**
es ixʷpmi – S/he is becoming sad. **čnes ixʷpmi, kʷes ixʷpmi**

ixʷpmis – S/he was saddened by s.t. **ixʷpmin, ixʷpmintxʷ**
es ixʷpminms – S/he is saddened by s.t. **ies ixʷpminm, as ixʷpminm**

nixʷels – S/he felt sad/hurt. **čn nixʷels, kʷ nixʷels**
es nixʷelsi – S/he is feeling sad/hurt. **čnes nixʷelsi, kʷes nixʷelsi**

nixʷelsis – S/he made s.o. feel sad/hurt. **nixʷelsn, nixʷelsntxʷ**
es nixʷelsms – S/he is making s.o. feel sad/hurt. **ies nixʷelsm, as nixʷelsm**

ixʷiẇuxʷt – saddening.
nixʷeneʔ – S/he/it heard sad/hurtful news. **čn nixʷeneʔ, kʷ nixʷeneʔ**
ixʷixʷsuxʷ – S/he/it is deserving of compassion.
čixʷixʷus – sad/hurt eyes.

nixʷpels – have hurt feelings; profound sadness. *See:* ***hurt.***

yaṁqʷs – look sad; sad face.
i yaṁqʷs – S/he looks sad. **i čn yaṁqʷs, i kʷ yaṁqʷs**

nłenmnt – Look sad. *cmd. rt.:* ***łén*** *– unexpressive. See:* ***serious.***

saddle

nt̓k̓ʷčisqáx̣eʔtn, *nt̓k̓ʷčisqá* **–** saddle. *rt.:* ***t̓uk̓ʷ*** *– place down; affix:* ***...sqax̣eʔ, ...sqa*** *–domestic animal; mainly referring to horse or car; suffix:* ***...tin, ...tn*** *– means of/device.*

nt̓k̓ʷčisqáx̣eʔ – saddle a horse.
nt̓k̓ʷčisqáx̣eʔ – S/he saddled a horse. **čn nt̓k̓ʷčisqáx̣eʔ, kʷ nt̓k̓ʷčisqáx̣eʔ**
es nt̓k̓ʷčisqáx̣eʔi – S/he is saddling a horse. **čnes nt̓k̓ʷčisqáx̣eʔi, kʷes nt̓k̓ʷčisqáx̣eʔi**
qs nt̓k̓ʷčisqáx̣eʔi – S/he's going to saddle a horse. **čiqs nt̓k̓ʷčisqáx̣eʔi, kʷqs nt̓k̓ʷčisqáx̣eʔi**

nt̓k̓ʷčisqáx̣eʔiš – Saddle the horse.

nčłxʷčisqáx̣eʔtn, *nčłxʷčisqá* **–** woman's saddle. *suffix:* ***...tin, ...tn*** *– means of/device.*

nt̓k̓ʷičṅ – saddle. *rt.:* ***t̓uk̓ʷ*** *– place down; suffix:* ***...ičṅ*** *– back. lit. put on the back.*
es nt̓k̓ʷičṅ – S/he/it is saddled.

aṁaṁta – saddle *(made of wood and bones). rt.:* ***emut*** *– sit.*

nc̓lx̣ʷčisqax̣eʔtn – packsaddle. *rt.:* ***c̓alx̣ʷ*** *– poles lashed together; suffix:* ***...tin, ...tn*** *– means of/device.*

čq̓ʷełtn – packsaddle. *suffix:* ***...tin, ...tn*** *– means of/device. See:* ***pack.***

nc̓lx̣ʷčisqáx̣eʔtn, *nc̓lx̣ʷčisqá* **–** packsaddle. *rt.:* ***c̓alx̣ʷ*** *– poles lashed together.*

snčql̓ql̓wew̓tn, *snčql̓ql̓we* – stirrups. *suffix: **...tin, ...tn** – means of/device.*

nqʷlqʷčisqáx̣eʔtn, *nqʷlqʷčisqá* – girdle commonly used for saddle horses. *suffix: **...tin, ...tn** – means of/device.*

npƛ̓ičn̓m – remove a saddle. *rt.: **pƛ̓im** – release from; suffix: **...ičn̓** – back.*
npƛ̓ičn̓m – S/he removed a saddle. **čn npƛ̓ičn̓m, kʷ npƛ̓ičn̓m**
es npƛ̓ičn̓i – S/he is removing a saddle. **čnes npƛ̓ičn̓i, kʷes npƛ̓ičn̓i**
qs npƛ̓ičn̓i – S/he is going to remove a saddle. **čiqs npƛ̓ičn̓i, kʷqs npƛ̓ičn̓i**
es npƛ̓íʔičn̓i – They are removing a saddle. **qeʔes npƛ̓ičn̓i, pes npƛ̓ičn̓i**

npƛ̓ičis – S/he removed the saddle. **npƛ̓ičn̓, npƛ̓ičn̓txʷ**
es npƛ̓ičn̓i – S/he is removing the saddle. **ies npƛ̓ičn̓m, kʷes npƛ̓ičn̓m**
qs npƛ̓ičn̓i – S/he is going to remove the saddle. **čiqs npƛ̓ičn̓m, kʷqs npƛ̓ičn̓m**
es npƛ̓íʔičn̓ms – They are removing the saddle. **qeʔes npƛ̓ičn̓m, es npƛ̓ičn̓mp**

npƛ̓ičn̓iš – Remove a saddle. *cmd.*
npƛ̓ičn̓wi – All of you remove a saddle. *cmd.*
npƛ̓ičn̓t – Remove the saddle. *cmd.*

ha npƛ̓ičn̓txʷ – Did you take the saddle off?

> The **i** following uvular consonants (UC) and the glottal stop **ʔ** sound like English "*ey*" as in the words th*ey*, h*ey*, wh*ey*, etc. Salish UC are: **q, q̇, qʷ, q̇ʷ, x̣, x̣ʷ**. For example, the suffix **...qin** – head/top, is often spelled using English *ey* as "q*ey*n". So **qi, q̇i, qʷi, q̇ʷi, x̣i, x̣ʷi**, may be spelled with English *ey* as **q***ey*, **q̇***ey*, **qʷ***ey*, **q̇ʷ***ey*, **x̣***ey*, **x̣ʷ***ey* in other texts.

saddle blanket

nqpčisqáx̣eʔtn, *nqpčisqá* – saddle blanket. *suffix: **...tin, ...tn** – means of/device.*

nqpops – put a saddle blanket on under the saddle.
nqpopsm – S/he put a saddle blanket on. **čn nqpopsm, kʷ nqpopsm**
es nqpopsi – S/he is putting a saddle blanket on. **čnes nqpopsi, kʷes nqpopsi**
qs nqpopsi – S/he is going to put a saddle blanket on. **čiqs nqpopsi, kʷqs nqpopsi**

nqpopčisqáx̣eʔtn, *nqpopčisqá* – saddle blanket under a saddle. *suffix: **...tin, ...tn** – means of/device.*

nqpičn̓ – put a saddle blanket on. *suffix: **...ičn̓** – back.*
nqpičn̓m – S/he put a saddle blanket on. **čn nqpičn̓m, kʷ nqpičn̓m**
es nqpičn̓i – S/he is putting a saddle blanket on. **čnes nqpičn̓i, kʷes nqpičn̓i**
qs nqpičn̓i – S/he is going to put a saddle blanket on. **čiqs nqpičn̓i, kʷqs nqpičn̓i**

čqpew̓s – put on a blanket for on top of the saddle. *suffix: **...éw̓s** – in between, middle.*
čqpew̓sm – S/he put a blanket on the saddle. **čn čqpew̓sm, kʷ čqpew̓sm**
es čqpew̓si – S/he is putting a blanket on the saddle. **čnes čqpew̓si, kʷes čqpew̓si**
qs čqpew̓si – S/he is going to put a blanket on the saddle. **čiqs čqpew̓si, kʷqs čqpew̓si**

čpqew̓sqáx̣eʔtn, *čpqew̓sqá* – blanket for on top of a saddle. *suffix: **...tin, ...tn** – means of/device.*

safe

xʷxʷum̓ – relaxed/safe/secure; have no worries; have no cares; out of danger. *See: **secure**.*

nxʷlxʷiltn – life. *See: **live**.*

> s.t. - something, the 3rd person
> (s.t.) - something implied
> s.o. - someone, the 3rd person
> *sl.* - singular form
> *pl.* - plural form
> *rt.* - root word
> *cmd.* - command
> *lit.* - literally
> *fig.* - figuratively
> *i.e.,* - for example
> *See:* - Redirection to a related word.

safety pin

utčl̓é – safety pin.

sag

uxʷ – droop; hang down; sag. *(i.e., breasts, etc.)*
es uxʷ – It is drooped.

sage

qpqptéłp, *qpqpté* – sage; mug worm; tarragon.

sagebrush

ṗuṗunéłp – sagebrush; big sagebrush; *Artemisia tridentata.*

sagebrush buttercup

sčyal̓mn – sage buttercup; *Ranunculus glaberrimus.*

Sahaptin **saáptniša –** Nez Perce; southern band.
slapaá – Nez Perce; northern band.

sail **laáp –** float in a vessel; navigate by water; *row; surf internet. (i.e., boat, canoe, raft, etc.) See:* ***float.***
tspisċé u čn laáp – Yesterday I floated (sailed).

nłq̓ultn – sail. *rt.:* ***łaq̓*** *– wide.*

pl̓ip – float.

čł̓k̓ʷetkʷ – float. *suffix:* ***...etkʷ, ...tkʷ*** *– liquid*

St. Ignatius **snyél̓mn –** St. Ignatius, Flathead Nation. *lit. a place where something was surrounded.*

St. Mary's Lake **sent mali cłq̓liˀs –** St. Mary's Lake, near St. Ignatius, Flathead Nation.

St. Regis **čxʷtpe –** St. Regis, Montana; *lit. rocky point coming to an end.*

salamander **šl̓šl̓čé –** salamander, lizard.

Salish **selíš –** Salish; Bitterroot Salish.
nsélišcn – Salish language.
ṫaṫˀayaqn – Bitterroot Salish. *lit. hair stands up on the head.*
łqayaqn, *łqa* **–** Bitterroot Salish. *lit. wide head.*
łq̓ełmlš – Bitterroot Salish *(Pend d'Oreille name for Salish).*
sčq̓ltčisci – Bitterroot Salish *(Spokane name for Salish).*

sqélixʷ – human; person; Indian. *See:* ***Indian.***

salmon **smłič,** *smłi* **–** salmon *general term*; chinook salmon; *Oncorhynchus tshawytscha.*
smłič sṗłqin – salmon head.
smłič sups – salmon tail.
smłič úˀuseˀek̓ʷn – salmon eggs.

nxʷmeneˀ – steelhead salmon; rainbow trout; *Oncorhynchus mykiss. (native to the area of the Spokane tribe; lit. red/pink around the ears)*
nṫkʷus – sockeye salmon; kokanee salmon; *Oncorhynchus nerka.*
sčlwes, *sčlwe* **–** pink salmon; humpback salmon; *Oncorhynchus gorbuscha.*

Salmon Lake **soli –** Salmon Lake, Idaho.

salt **ċol –** salt.
ċolis – S/he salted it. **ċoln, ċolntxʷ**
es ċolms – S/he is salting it. **ies ċolm, as ċolm**
qs ċolms – S/he is going to salt it. **iqs ċolm, aqs ċolm**

es ċol – It is salted.
i ċol – It is salty.
i nċolkʷ – It is salty *(liquid).*

snċol – salt shaker.

ċolnt – Salt it. *cmd.*

inx̣menč iqs ċolm łu iscṫel – I like salting the meat I cut for drying.

salt lick **ciłnqs –** deer lick, salt lick.

salute **q̓ʷitˈs** – nod the head; greet; hail. *See: **nod**.*

same **eċx̣íl,** *eċx̣í* – like; same. *See: **like**.*
iċx̣ax̣i – exactly the same.

i šeẏ – that very one; the same one. *See: **that**.*
nexʷ epɫ tšeẏ – S/he has the same.

Samuel **samwél** – Samuel.

sand **sq̓pq̓epé** – sand.

sandhill crane **skʷalšin,** *skʷalši* – sandhill crane; *Grus canadensis*.

sandles **sɫxʷɫxʷpšin** – slippers; sandles; anything you slip on the feet.

sandpiper **nuˀsšṅáqs,** *nuˀsšṅá* – sandpiper.

sandwich **scnq̓ˀeẇs,** *scnq̓ˀe* – sandwich. *prefix: **sc...** – s.t. that's been done/made/prepared; suffix: **...éẇs** – in between, middle.*

San Poil **sxʷil̓epiš** – San Poil.

sap **ṫeɫtn** – pitch gum, Ponderosa pine pitch, sap.

nˀawpálqʷ ṫeɫtn – sap is running *(inside the bark)*.

smċemċm – honey sap. *(rendered from tamarack sap)*

sčmx̣ʷcin, *sčmx̣ʷci* – inside of the bark, or sap, of the cottonwood or bull-pine.

sčmoop – something flows down something. *(i.e., sap, water, etc.) See: **flow**.*
čmopalqʷ – something flowing down a tree. *(i.e., sap, water, etc.)*
čmopeɫp – something flowing down a branch. *(i.e., sap, water, etc.)*

sassy **eycn** – sassy; talk back. *suffix: **...cin, ...cn** – action of the mouth.*
eycnm – S/he talked back. **čn eycnm, kʷ eycnm**
es eycni – S/he is talking back. **čnes eycni, kʷes eycni**
es eycni – S/he is going to talk back. **čnes eycni, kʷes eycni**

eycnemn – one inclined to talk back. *suffix: **...emn** – one inclined to do.*

Saturday **sčɫˀeˀ** – Saturday; end of the week. *rt.: **čɫˀeˀ** – against.*

sausage **ɫlkʷošó es naċeẇs** – sausage. *lit. tied/hooked together pig.*

ɫlkʷlkʷošó – sausage; little pigs.

sp̓l̓q̓enč, *sp̓l̓q̓e* – intestine; sausage/hot dog/wiener.

savage **uˀẇáq̓uˀq̓t** – wild; savage; untamed physically and morally; one that keeps away.

save **kʷum** – save; stash.
kʷumis – S/he saved s.t. **kʷumn, kʷumntxʷ**
es kʷumms – S/he is saving s.t. **ies kʷumm, as kʷumm**

sckʷum – something that has been saved; stashed.

The **i** following uvular consonants (UC) and the glottal stop **ˀ** sound like English "*ey*" as in the words th*ey*, h*ey*, wh*ey*, etc. Salish UC are: **q**, **q̓**, **qʷ**, **q̓ʷ**, **x̣**, **x̣ʷ**. For example, the suffix ...**qin** – head/top, is often spelled using English *ey* as "q*ey*n". So **qi**, **q̓i**, **qʷi**, **q̓ʷi**, **x̣i**, **x̣ʷi**, may be spelled with English *ey* as **q***ey*, **q̓***ey*, **qʷ***ey*, **q̓ʷ***ey*, **x̣***ey*, **x̣ʷ***ey* in other texts.

s.t. - something, the 3rd person
(s.t.) - something implied
s.o. - someone, the 3rd person
sl. - singular form
pl. - plural form
rt. - root word
cmd. - command
lit. - literally
fig. - figuratively
i.e., - for example
See: - Redirection to a related word.

skʷumcn – left over food you take with you for later. *suffix:* ***...cin, ...cn*** *– action of the mouth.*

elk̓ʷm – store away; put away; save. *See:* ***put away****.*

saw

nič̓mn – saw.

nič̓ – cut; slice; saw. *See:* ***cut****.*

wič – see; find; perceive; come into view. *See:* ***see****.*

čswič – see an object on something or someone. *(i.e., a stain on a shirt, spot on the wall, etc.)* *See:* ***see****.*

uč̓twéxʷ, *uč̓twé* – see each other. *See:* ***see****.*

sawdust

čnič̓mn – sawdust.

saw-whet owl, northern

sqq̓éxʷʔe – northern saw-whet owl; *Aegolius acadicus*.

say

áwm – say/speak; pronounce; annunciate.

áwm – S/he said. **čn áwm, kʷ áwm**
es áwi – S/he is saying. **čnes áwi, kʷes áwi**
qs áwi – S/he is going to say. **čiqs áwi, kʷqs áwi**
áʔawm – They said. **qeʔ áwm, p áwm**
es áʔawi – They are saying. **qeʔes áwi, pes áwi**
qs áʔawi – They are going to say. **qeʔqs áwi, pqs áwi**

áwis – S/he said s.t. **áwn, áwntxʷ**
es áwms – S/he is saying s.t. **ies áwm, as áwm**
qs áwms – S/he is going to say s.t. **iqs áwm, aqs áwm**
áʔawis – They said s.t. **qeʔ áwntm, áwntp**
es áʔawms – They are saying s.t. **qeʔes áwm, es áwmp**
qs áʔawms – They are going to say s.t. **qeʔqs áwm, qs áwmp**

es awʔáwi – S/he is repeatedly saying. **čnes awʔáwi, kʷes awʔáwi**
es awʔáwms – S/he is repeatedly saying s.t. **ies awʔáwm, as awʔáwm**

áwnuis – S/he finally said it. **áwnun, áwnuntxʷ**
es áwnunms – S/he is finally saying it. **ies áwnunm, as áwnunm**

sʔaw̓w̓ – called; something said.
scʔáw – something that's been said; spoken word. *prefix:* ***sc...*** *– s.t. that's been done/made/prepared.*
scʔawʔáw, *scʔawʔá* – something that's been said; spoken words. *prefix:* ***sc...*** *– s.t. that's been done/made/prepared.*

áwiš – Say/speak; pronounce. *cmd.*
áwnt – Say it. *cmd.*
áwlqʷ – say the name of a tree.
áwłq – say the name of a berry.
áwulexʷ – say the name of an area.
áwawsnuxʷ – It is worth saying.
nʔawqnm – call upon/ask for someone; challenge/encourage someone; beseech; exhort. *See:* ***call****.*
k̓ʷłʔawʔáw, *k̓ʷłʔawʔá* – guess. *See:* ***guess****.*
awʔawm – say words out loud; read aloud. *See:* ***read****.*
čáw – pray. *See:* ***pray****.*

es awʔawi – S/he is reading out loud. **čnes awʔawi, kʷes awʔawi**

stem̓ łu sʔaw̓w̓s – What is it called?

cu – say/speak to somebody; inform; provide information about something.
cúnm – S/he/it said. **čn cúnm, kʷ cúnm**
es cuti – S/he/it is saying. **čnes cuti, kʷes cuti**
qs cuti – S/he/it is going to say. **čiqs cuti, kʷqs cuti**
cúʔunm – They said. **qeʔ cúnm, p cúnm**
es cúʔuti – They are saying. **qeʔes cuti, pes cuti**
qs cúʔuti – They are going to say. **qeʔqs cuti, pqs cuti**

cúis – S/he/it said it to s.o. **cún, cúntxʷ**
es cunms – S/he/it is saying it to s.o. **ies cunm, as cunm**
qs cunms – S/he/it is going to say it to s.o. **iqs cunm, aqs cunm**
cúʔuis – They said it to s.o. **qeʔ cúntm, cúntp**
es cúʔunms – They are saying it to s.o. **qeʔes cunm, es cunmp**
qs cúʔunms – They are going to say it to s.o. **qeʔqs cunm, qs cunmp**

cúntm – something was said to him/her/it. **qʷo cúntm, kʷ cúntm**

cunt – Say it to s.o. *cmd.*
es custm – It is called; it is said about.

čscúis – S/he/it said it about s.o. **čscún, čscúntxʷ**
es čscunms – S/he/it is saying it about s.o. **ies čscunm, as čscunm**
qs čscunms – S/he/it is going to say it about s.o. **iqs čscunm, aqs čscunm**

cúłts – S/he said it to s.o. **cúłtn, cúłtxʷ**
es cułtms – S/he is saying it to s.o. **ies cułtm, as cułtm**
qs cułtms – S/he is going to say it to s.o. **iqs cułtm, aqs cułtm**

ṅem cunm – S/he will say. **ṅem čn cunm, ṅem kʷ cunm**
ṅem cúʔunm – They will say. **ṅem qeʔ cunm, ṅem p cunm**

ṅem cuis – S/he will say it to s.o. **ṅem cun, ṅem cuntxʷ**
ṅem qs cunms – S/he will be saying it to s.o. **ṅem iqs cunm, ṅem aqs cunm**
ṅem cúʔuis – They will say it to s.o. **ṅem qeʔ cuntm, ṅem cuntp**
ṅem qs cúʔunms – They will be saying it to s.o. **ṅem qeʔqs cunm, ṅem qs cunmp**

cuntm kʷ eċi x̣ʷĺ qʷoyʔe – S/he was told, "What did you say for me?" **qeʔ cułls** – S/he said to us. **qeʔ cułlt** – We were told. **łiʔe ies cunm** – This I am telling. **we cun** – I did tell. **ma še we cuncn epł ṫiṫéẏe sṁtṁa** – See, I told you there's a lot of mean cows. **ṅe eł ctešlš še es custm k̇ʷsixʷ spq̇niʔ** – When it emerges, March is called the month of the geese.

exʷkʷunm – make indiscernible speech; make chatter; hear people/animals making sounds; people talking in the distance.
exʷkʷunm – S/he made sounds. **čn exʷkʷunm, kʷ exʷkʷunm**
es exʷkʷuni – S/he is making sounds. **čnes exʷkʷuni, kʷes exʷkʷuni**

exʷkʷúʔunm – They made sounds. **qeʔ exʷkʷunm, p exʷkʷunm**
es exʷkʷúʔuni – They are making sounds. **qeʔes exʷkʷuni, pes exʷkʷuni**

exʷkʷunis – S/he/it said it. **exʷkʷunn, exʷkʷunntxʷ**
exʷkʷúʔunis – They said it. **qeʔ exʷkʷunntm, exʷkʷunntp**

exʷexʷkʷunm – Each is making sounds.

eċínt, *eċí* – question inquiring about what was said.
eċínt – What did s/he say? **čn eċínt, kʷ eċínt**
es eċínti – What is s/he saying? **čnes eċínti, kʷes eċínti**

The **i** following uvular consonants (UC) and the glottal stop ʔ sound like English "*ey*" as in the words *they, hey, whey*, etc. Salish UC are: **q, q̇, qʷ, q̇ʷ, x̣, x̣ʷ**. For example, the suffix ...**qin** – head/top, is often spelled using English *ey* as "*qeyn*". So **qi, q̇i, qʷi, q̇ʷi, x̣i, x̣ʷi**, may be spelled with English *ey* as **q***ey*, **q̇***ey*, **qʷ***ey*, **q̇ʷ***ey*, **x̣***ey*, **x̣ʷ***ey* in other texts.

s.t. - something, the 3rd person
(s.t.) - something implied
s.o. - someone, the 3rd person
sl. - singular form
pl. - plural form
rt. - root word
cmd. - command
lit. - literally
fig. - figuratively
i.e., - for example
See: - Redirection to a related word.

qs ečínti – What is s/he going to be saying? **čiqs ečínti, kʷqs ečínti**
ečíˀint – What did they say? **qeˀ ečínt, p ečínt**
es ečíˀinti – What are they saying? **qeˀes ečínti, pes ečínti**
qs ečíˀinti – What are they going to be saying? **qeˀqs ečínti, pqs ečínti**

ečinnsts – What did s/he say to s.o.? **ečinnstn, ečinnstxʷ**
es ečíntms – What is s/he saying to s.o.? **ies ečíntm, as ečíntm**
qs ečíntms – What is s/he going to say to s.o.? **iqs ečíntm, aqs ečíntm**
ečíˀinnsts – What did they say to s.o.? **qeˀ ečinnstm, ečinnstp**
es ečíˀintms – What are they saying to s.o.? **ies ečíntm, as ečíntm**
qs ečíˀintms – What are they going to say to s.o.? **iqs ečíntm, aqs ečíntm**

ečintm – What was said to him/her?

cuntm kʷ eči x̣ʷl̓ qʷoyˀe – S/he was told, "What did you say for me?" **ta tˀeys eči** – I did not say anything. **unexʷ tˀe kʷ eči** – You did say something.

...cin – *suffix indicating an action of the mouth; i.e., speaking, eating, & food.* *See:* ***mouth.***

ineẏcn, *ine* – repeat words; repeat something already said; say something again. *See:* ***repeat.***

k̓ʷéṅcn – try to say something. *See:* ***try.***

ṁéẏeˀ – explain; tell; show; make something known. *See:* ***explain.***

scale

iliš – fish scales.

scalp

sóqʷqn – scalp someone.
sóqʷqis – S/he scalped s.o. **sóqʷqn, sóqʷqntxʷ**
es sóqʷqnms – S/he is scalping s.o. **ies sóqʷqnm, as sóqʷqnm**
qs sóqʷqnms – S/he is scalping s.o. **iqs sóqʷqnm, aqs sóqʷqnm**
sóˀoqʷqis – They scalped s.o. **qeˀ sóqʷqntm, sóqʷqntp**
es sˀóqʷqnms – They are scalping s.o. **qeˀes sóqʷqnm, es sóqʷqnmp**
qs sóˀoqʷqnms – They are scalping s.o. **qeˀqs sóqʷqnm, qs sóqʷqnmp**

soqʷqntm – S/he was scalped.
es soqʷqn – S/he is scalped.

nčak̓ʷqintm – Take the top off (scalped).

scalp dance

yul – scalp dance.
yulm – S/he scalp danced. **čn yulm, kʷ yulm**
es yuli – S/he is scalp dancing. **čnes yuli, kʷes yuli**
qs yuli – S/he is scalp dancing. **čiqs yuli, kʷqs yuli**

es yúˀuli – They are scalp dancing. **qeˀes yuli, pes yuli**

yulis – S/he made s.o. scalp dance. **yuln, yulntxʷ**
es yulms – S/he is making s.o. scalp dance. **ies yulm, as yulm**
qs yulms – S/he is going to make s.o. scalp dance. **iqs yulm, aqs yulm**

sxʷyulm – one tasked to scalp dance.

kʷeṁt łiˀe l es custm es yuli – Then there is what is called the scalp dance.

scar

qt̓iṁ – scar formation.
qtt̓iṁ – a scar formed.
es qtt̓iṁi – a scar is forming.

sqt̓im̓ – scar.

čłqt̓m̓essn – scar on the forehead.
čłqt̓m̓essn – scar on the forehead.
qt̓m̓ax̣n – scar on the arn.

scarce

y̓aa – scarce; commanding respect; uninviting.
i y̓aa – It is scarce.

y̓aam – fear; mistrust; in subjugation; not free with feelings. *See: **fear**.*

iy̓aastes – S/he was scarce of s.t. **iy̓aasten, iy̓aastexʷ**
es iy̓aams – S/he is scarce of s.t. **ies iy̓aam, as iy̓aam**

y̓aamemn – coward; reserved.
y̓ay̓aascut – S/he was being hard to approach. **čn y̓ay̓aascut, kʷ y̓ay̓aascut**
y̓aasqelixʷ – shy/reserved of people. *See: **shy**.*
y̓ay̓áat – rare; scarce; hard to acquire. *See: **rare**.*
k̓ʷły̓apcin – in need of something; miss something. *See: **need**.*
y̓apcin – lack something. *See: **lack**.*
čiy̓aapleʔ – unapproachable; someone that imposes respect for fear, greatness, or stature. *See: **fear**.*
ny̓ay̓anus – look with fear/respect. *See: **fear**.*
niy̓aaneʔ – no care to listen to someone for fear/respect to hear the person or what is said. *See: **fear**.*
niy̓ay̓aals – scarce/rare feelings; selfish. *See: **selfish**.*
y̓ay̓aawulexʷ – poor; place hard to reach; place hard to comprehend.

The **i** following uvular consonants (UC) and the glottal stop **ʔ** sound like English "*ey*" as in the words th*ey*, h*ey*, wh*ey*, etc. Salish UC are: **q, q̓, qʷ, q̓ʷ, x̣, x̣ʷ**. For example, the suffix ...**qin** – head/top, is often spelled using English *ey* as "q*ey*n". So **qi, q̓i, qʷi, q̓ʷi, x̣i, x̣ʷi**, may be spelled with English *ey* as **q***ey*, **q̓***ey*, **qʷ***ey*, **q̓ʷ***ey*, **x̣***ey*, **x̣ʷ***ey* in other texts.

scared

nx̣él – afraid/scared of something.
nx̣elm – S/he/it was afraid. **čn nx̣elm, kʷ nx̣elm**
es nx̣éli – S/he/it is scared. **čnes nx̣éli, kʷes nx̣éli**
qs nx̣éli – S/he/it is going to be scared. **čiqs nx̣éli, kʷqs nx̣éli**
es nx̣éʔeli – They are scared. **qeʔes nx̣éli, pes nx̣éli**
qs nx̣éʔeli – They are going to be scared. **qeʔqs nx̣éli, pqs nx̣éli**

nx̣elmis – S/he/it got afraid of s.o./s.t. **nx̣elmn, nx̣elmntxʷ**
es nx̣elmms – S/he/it is afraid of s.o./s.t. **ies nx̣elmm, as nx̣elmm**
qs nx̣elmms – S/he/it is going to be afraid of s.o./s.t. **iqs nx̣elmm, aqs nx̣elmm**
nx̣éʔelmis – They got afraid of s.o./s.t. **qeʔ nx̣elmntm, nx̣elmntp**
es nx̣éʔelmms – They are afraid of s.o./s.t. **qeʔes nx̣elmm, es nx̣elmmp**
qs nx̣éʔelmms – They are going to be afraid of s.o./s.t. **qeʔqs nx̣elmm, qs nx̣elmmp**

es nx̣lx̣éli – S/he/it is afraid (of things). **čnes nx̣lx̣éli, kʷes nx̣lx̣éli**
es nx̣lx̣élms – S/he/it is afraid of things. **ies nx̣lx̣élm, as nx̣lx̣élm**

es nłx̣ax̣li – S/he/it is a little afraid. **čnes nłx̣ax̣li, kʷes nłx̣ax̣li**

nx̣x̣lemn – one inclined to be scared; coward; scaredy-cat. *suffix: **...emn** – one inclined to do.*
nx̣lx̣elmn – something used to scare.
nx̣llutm – something to be feared.
snx̣lx̣lsnuxʷ – something worth to be feared.
snx̣lx̣lsnu – something that is spooky.

nx̣lx̣eliš – Scare. *cmd.*
nx̣lx̣elwi – All of you scare. *cmd.*
nx̣lx̣elnt – Scare it. *cmd.*
nx̣lx̣elnti – All of you scare it. *cmd.*

s.t. - something, the 3rd person
(s.t.) - something implied
s.o. - someone, the 3rd person
sl. - singular form
pl. - plural form
rt. - root word
cmd. - command
lit. - literally
fig. - figuratively
i.e., - for example
See: - Redirection to a related word.

nx̣lx̣lłtumšiš – Scare them. *cmd.*
nx̣lx̣lłtumš, *nx̣lx̣lłtu* – scare people.
es nx̣l̓x̣l̓łtumši – S/he is scaring people. **čnes nx̣l̓x̣l̓łtumši, kʷes nx̣l̓x̣l̓łtumši**
es nx̣elmnscuti – S/he/it is scaring one's self. **čnes nx̣elmnscuti, kʷes nx̣elmnscuti**
es nx̣llncuti – S/he/it is scaring one's self. **čnes nx̣llncuti, kʷes nx̣llncuti**
es nx̣lx̣l̓lmisti – S/he is scaring one's self. **čnes nx̣lx̣l̓lmisti, kʷes nx̣lx̣l̓lmisti**
es nx̣lx̣lnwexʷisti – They are scaring each other. **qeʔes nx̣lx̣lnwexʷisti, pes nx̣lx̣lnwexʷisti**

nx̣lx̣el̓lwis – go around scaring.
nx̣l̓x̣l̓m̓lwis, *nx̣l̓x̣l̓m̓lwi* – go around being scared; scared, on the run.

kʷ es nx̣elmms – S/he/it is afraid of you. **es nx̣elmms esyaʔ –** S/he/it is afraid of them. **qʷo as nx̣elmm –** You are afraid of me. **as nx̣éʔelmm –** You are afraid of them. **kʷ ies nx̣elmm –** I am afraid of you. **čn nx̣elemn l skʷkʷʔec tʔe u čn susewneʔ –** I am afraid of sounds in the dark. **kʷ nx̣elm t sč̓ey̓t –** You are afraid of spiders. **ha kʷ nx̣elm łu i l čim̓ –** Are you afraid of the dark? **ha kʷ nx̣el t nqʷq̓ʷosmi –** Are you afraid of the dog? **čn nx̣elemn t sč̓ewileʔ –** I am afraid of snakes. **čn nx̣elemn t nwist –** I am afraid of heights. **uł nx̣éʔelemn t st̓lt̓la –** They are afraid of thunder. **čn nx̣el t anwi –** I am afraid of you. **łu puti čis skʷk̓ʷiml̓t čn nx̣elemn t nqʷiq̓ʷosmi –** When I was younger I was afraid of dogs. **p ies nx̣elmm pesyaʔ –** I am afraid of you all. **tam kʷ ies nx̣elmm –** I am not afraid of you. **es nx̣éʔeli t nałisqe –** They are scared of monsters. **t scnx̣el t u ƛ̓lil t sckʷssu –** S/he died of fear. **ha iše kʷ nx̣el –** Do you get scared? **kʷ nx̣lx̣lsnu –** You are spooky. **ax̣í u nx̣lx̣lnun –** I finally scared him/her. **qʷo nx̣lx̣el̓št –** Scare him/her for me. **nx̣lx̣éʔelnt –** Scare them. *cmd.*

k̓ʷłax̣lmist – afraid; give into; scared to offend; timid. *See:* ***afraid.***

č̓in – afraid of getting hurt; careful and cautious. *(i.e., falling, etc.)* *See:* ***afraid.***

kʷʔeł – jumpy; nervous; edgy; frantic. *See:* ***nervous.***

kʷssusm, *kʷssu* – startle. *See:* ***startle.***

scaredy-cat

nx̣x̣lemn – one inclined to be scared; coward; scaredy-cat.
nx̣l̓x̣l̓m̓lwis, *nx̣l̓x̣l̓m̓lwi* – go around being scared; scared and on the run.

scarf

čiyálxʷqn, *čiya* – head wrap; scarf. *rt.:* ***yelxʷ*** *– conceal; suffix:* ***...qin, ...qn*** *– top.*

scatter

isk̓ʷl – scatter things out; throw things away. *(i.e., peelings, scraps, etc.)*
isk̓ʷlis – S/he scattered things out. **isk̓ʷln, isk̓ʷlntxʷ**
es isk̓ʷlms – S/he is scattering things out. **ies isk̓ʷlm, as isk̓ʷlm**
qs isk̓ʷlms – S/he is going to scatter things out. **iqs isk̓ʷlm, aqs isk̓ʷlm**
iʔisk̓ʷlis – They scatter things out. **qeʔ isk̓ʷlntm, isk̓ʷlntp**
es iʔisk̓ʷlms – They are scattering things out. **qeʔes isk̓ʷlm, es isk̓ʷlmp**
qs iʔisk̓ʷlms – They are going to scatter things out. **qeʔqs isk̓ʷlm, qs isk̓ʷlmp**

isk̓ʷlnt – Scatter the things out. *cmd.*

n̓e kʷ wis łoq̓ʷm m še isk̓ʷlnt łu sccłoq̓ʷ – When you finish peeling you will scatter out the peelings.

łit̓m – scatter something; mess something up.
łit̓msts – S/he scattered s.t. **łit̓mstn, łit̓mstxʷ**
es łit̓mms – S/he is scattering s.t. **ies łit̓mm, as łit̓mm**
qs łit̓mms – S/he is going to scatter s.t. **iqs łit̓mm, aqs łit̓mm**

łitt̓ – scattered.

łiťmskʷ – Scatter it. *cmd.*

pkʷéw̓t – round objects lying/sitting around. *suffix: **...éw̓t** – group state.*
łiˀe scmlmálq̓ʷ eł es x̣ʷlx̣ʷélm pkʷéw̓t – There were clumps left lying all over.

čłpukʷ – spread/pour round things out on a surface of something. *(i.e., berries, marbles, etc.) See: **spread**.*

npkʷétkʷ – pour round objects in water. *(i.e., berries, rocks, etc.) See: **pour**.*

y̓ay̓áat – rare; scarce; hard to acquire. *See: **rare**.*

px̣ʷum – distribute, spread around, pass/hand out. *See: **distribute**.*

The **i** following uvular consonants (UC) and the glottal stop **ˀ** sound like English "*ey*" as in the words *they*, *hey*, *whey*, etc. Salish UC are: **q**, **q̓**, **qʷ**, **q̓ʷ**, **x̣**, **x̣ʷ**. For example, the suffix ...**qin** – head/top, is often spelled using English *ey* as "q*ey*n". So **qi**, **q̓i**, **qʷi**, **q̓ʷi**, **x̣i**, **x̣ʷi**, may be spelled with English *ey* as **q***ey*, **q̓***ey*, **qʷ***ey*, **q̓ʷ***ey*, **x̣***ey*, **x̣ʷ***ey* in other texts.

Schley

snłáˀcna – Schley, Flathead Nation.

school

snaċx̣łq̓eẏmíntn, *snaċx̣łq̓eẏmí* – school; schoolhouse. *rt.: **aċx̣łq̓eẏm** – read; prefix: **sn...** – a place of; suffix: **...mintn** – instrument/tool.*

scissors

čalmin – scissors.
člčalmin – more than one scissors.
łččalmin – little scissors.
kʷtiłčalmin – big scissors.

čalim, *čali* – cut with scissors.
čalim – S/he cut. **čn čalim, kʷ čalim**
es čalmi – S/he is cutting. **čnes čalmi, kʷes čalmi**
qs čalmi – S/he is going to cut. **čiqs čalmi, kʷqs čalmi**
čalíˀim – They cut. **qeˀ čalim, p čalim**
es čalmíˀi – They are cutting. **qeˀes čalmi, pes čalmi**
qs čalmíˀi – They are going to cut. **qeˀqs čalmi, pqs čalmi**

čalntés – S/he cut s.t. **čalntén, čalntéxʷ**
es čalims – S/he is cutting s.t. **ies čalim, as čalim**
qs čalims – S/he is going to cut s.t. **iqs čalim, aqs čalim**
čalntéˀes – They cut s.t. **qeˀ čalntém, čalntép**
es čalíˀims – They are cutting s.t. **qeˀes čalim, es čalimp**
qs čalíˀims – They are going to cut s.t. **qeˀqs čalim, qs čalimp**

es čal – It is cut.

sččal – something that is cut with scissors. *prefix: **sc...** – s.t. that's been done/made/prepared.*

čališ – Cut. *cmd.*
čalint – Cut it. *cmd.*
k̓ʷłčalim – cut something out with scissors. *See: **cut out**.*

čn čipṗ t čalmin – The scissors pinched me. **kʷent ye sččal** – Take these that have been cut. **čališ t q̓ešin** – Cut out moccasins.

s.t. - something, the 3rd person
(s.t.) - something implied
s.o. - someone, the 3rd person
sl. - singular form
pl. - plural form
rt. - root word
cmd. - command
lit. - literally
fig. - figuratively
i.e., - for example
See: - Redirection to a related word.

scold

łm̓łoˀmlš – scold someone.
łm̓łoˀmlš – S/he scolded. **čn łm̓łoˀmlš, kʷ łm̓łoˀmlš**
es łm̓łoˀmlši – S/he is scolding. **čnes łm̓łoˀmlši, kʷes łm̓łoˀmlši**
qs łm̓łoˀmlši – S/he is going to scold. **čiqs łm̓łoˀmlši, kʷqs łm̓łoˀmlši**

łm̓łoˀmlšsts – S/he scolded s.o. **łm̓łoˀmlšstn, łm̓łoˀmlšstxʷ**
es łm̓łoˀmlšms – S/he is scolding s.o. **ies łm̓łoˀmlšm, as łm̓łoˀmlšm**
qs łm̓łoˀmlšms – S/he is going to scold s.o. **iqs łm̓łoˀmlšm, aqs łm̓łoˀmlšm**

ɫṁɫóʔoʔmlšts – They scolded s.o. **qeʔ ɫṁɫoʔmlštm, ɫṁɫoʔmlštp**

čɫṁɫoʔmlšsts – S/he scolded him/her because of s.t. **čɫṁɫoʔmlšstn, čɫṁɫoʔmlšstxʷ**
es čɫṁɫoʔmlšms – S/he is scolding him/her because of s.t. **ies čɫṁɫoʔmlšm, as čɫṁɫoʔmlšm**

ɫṁɫoʔmlšskʷ – Scold him/her. *cmd.*
ɫṁɫoʔmstwexʷ – Scold each other.

nɫṁɫmlšaẃs, *nɫṁɫmlša* – scold somebody; tell off; chew out; ball out. *suffix:* ***...éẃs*** *– in between, middle.*
nɫṁɫmlša – S/he scolded. **čn nɫṁɫmlša, kʷ nɫṁɫmlša**
nɫṁɫmlšáʔa – They scolded. **qeʔ nɫṁɫmlša, p nɫṁɫmlša**

nɫṁɫmlšaẃskʷ – Scold him/her. *cmd.*

scoop **k̓ʷɫmulm –** dip/scoop out water. *See:* ***dip.***
k̓ʷɫmuliš, alyé – Scoop out some water, Harriet!

mul – fish/scoop something out of water. *(i.e., with a net, container, etc.)* *See:* ***fish.***

score **sk̓ʷɫɫq̓q̓eʔeẏ –** score.

scout **čtčits –** scout on foot; sneak and look around.
čtčitsm – S/he scouted. **čn čtčitsm, kʷ čtčitsm**
es čtčitsi – S/he is scouting. **čnes čtčitsi, kʷes čtčitsi**
qs čtčitsi – S/he is going to scout. **čiqs čtčitsi, kʷqs čtčitsi**

sxʷčtčitsm, *sxʷčtči* – one tasked to scout. *prefix:* ***sxʷ...*** *– one tasked to do.*

scrape **ax̣ʷ –** scrape.
ax̣ʷm – S/he scraped. **čn ax̣ʷm, kʷ ax̣ʷm**
es ax̣ʷi – S/he is scraping. **čnes ax̣ʷi, kʷes ax̣ʷi**
qs ax̣ʷi – S/he is going to scrape. **čiqs ax̣ʷi, kʷqs ax̣ʷi**
áʔax̣ʷm – They scraped. **qeʔ ax̣ʷm, p ax̣ʷm**

ax̣ʷis – S/he scraped s.t. **ax̣ʷn, ax̣ʷntxʷ**
es ax̣ʷms – S/he is scraping s.t. **ies ax̣ʷm, as ax̣ʷm**
qs ax̣ʷms – S/he is going to scrape s.t. **iqs ax̣ʷm, aqs ax̣ʷm**
áʔax̣ʷis – They scraped s.t. **ax̣ʷntm, ax̣ʷntp**

es ax̣ʷʔax̣ʷi – S/he is scraping. **čnes ax̣ʷʔax̣ʷi, kʷes ax̣ʷʔax̣ʷi**
es ax̣ʷʔax̣ʷms – S/he is scraping s.t. **ies ax̣ʷʔax̣ʷm, as ax̣ʷʔax̣ʷm**

ax̣ʷnuis – S/he finally scraped s.t. **ax̣ʷnun, ax̣ʷnuntxʷ**
ax̣ʷnúʔuis – They finally scraped s.t. **qeʔ ax̣ʷnuntm, ax̣ʷnuntp**

ax̣ʷmn – scraper.
ax̣ʷečstn – hand scraper.

ax̣ʷiš – Scrape. *cmd.*
ax̣ʷnt – Scrape it. *cmd.*
čɫʔax̣ʷ – scrape the surface.
čɫʔax̣ʷneʔ – scrape all over the surface.
čɫʔax̣ʷɫp – scrape the floor.
ax̣ʷlexʷ – scrape the ground. *(i.e., shoveling snow, etc.)*

ax̣í u ax̣ʷnun – I finally got it scraped.

ax̣ʷlxʷm – scrape fur off a hide.

ax̣ʷlxʷm – S/he scraped. **čn ax̣ʷlxʷm, kʷ ax̣ʷlxʷm**
es ax̣ʷlxʷi – S/he is scraping. **čnes ax̣ʷlxʷi, kʷes ax̣ʷlxʷi**
qs ax̣ʷlxʷi – S/he is going to scrape. **čiqs ax̣ʷlxʷi, kʷqs ax̣ʷlxʷi**
áʔax̣ʷlxʷm – They scraped. **qeʔ ax̣ʷlxʷm, p ax̣ʷlxʷm**
es áʔax̣ʷlxʷi – They are scraping. **qeʔes ax̣ʷlxʷi, pes ax̣ʷlxʷi**
qs áʔax̣ʷlxʷi – They are going to scrape. **qeʔqs ax̣ʷlxʷi, pqs ax̣ʷlxʷi**

ax̣ʷlxʷis – S/he scraped s.t. **ax̣ʷlxʷn, ax̣ʷlxʷntxʷ**
es ax̣ʷlxʷms – S/he is scraping s.t. **ies ax̣ʷlxʷm, as ax̣ʷlxʷm**
qs ax̣ʷlxʷms – S/he is going to scrape s.t. **iqs ax̣ʷlxʷm, aqs ax̣ʷlxʷm**
áʔax̣ʷlxʷis – They scraped s.t. **qeʔ ax̣ʷlxʷntm, ax̣ʷlxʷntp**
es ax̣ʷlxʷms – They are scraping s.t. **qeʔes ax̣ʷlxʷm, es ax̣ʷlxʷmp**
qs ax̣ʷlxʷms – They are going to scrape s.t. **qeʔqs ax̣ʷlxʷm, qs ax̣ʷlxʷmp**

es ax̣ʷʔax̣ʷlxʷi – S/he is scraping. **čnes ax̣ʷʔax̣ʷlxʷi, kʷes ax̣ʷʔax̣ʷlxʷi**
es ax̣ʷʔax̣ʷlxʷms – S/he is scraping s.t. **ies ax̣ʷʔax̣ʷlxʷm, as ax̣ʷʔax̣ʷlxʷm**

ax̣ʷlxʷnuis – S/he finally scraped s.t. **ax̣ʷlxʷnun, ax̣ʷlxʷnuntxʷ**
ax̣ʷlxʷnúʔuis – They finally scraped s.t. **qeʔ ax̣ʷlxʷnuntm, ax̣ʷlxʷnuntp**

ax̣ʷlxʷmn – scraper.

ax̣í u ax̣ʷlxʷnun – I finally got it scraped.

čxʷum – scrape the inside of a hide.
čxʷum – S/he scraped. **čn čxʷum, kʷ čxʷum**
es čxʷmi – S/he is scraping. **čnes čxʷmi, kʷes čxʷmi**
qs čxʷmi – S/he is going to scrape. **čiqs čxʷmi, kʷqs čxʷmi**
čxʷúʔum – They scraped. **qeʔ čxʷum, p čxʷum**
es čxʷmíʔi – They are scraping. **qeʔes čxʷmi, pes čxʷmi**
qs čxʷmíʔi – They are going to scrape. **qeʔqs čxʷmi, pqs čxʷmi**

čxʷmin – tool for cutting meat off a hide; scraper.

áq̇i – scrape a wet rawhide to soften it.
áq̇m – S/he scraped (hide). **čn áq̇m, kʷ áq̇m**
es áq̇i – S/he is scraping (hide). **čnes áq̇i, kʷes áq̇i**
qs áq̇i – S/he is going to scrape (hide). **čiqs áq̇i, kʷqs áq̇i**
áʔaq̇m – They scraped (hide). **qeʔ áq̇m, p áq̇m**
es áʔaq̇i – They are scraping (hide). **qeʔes áq̇i, pes áq̇i**
qs áʔaq̇i – They are going to scrape (hide). **qeʔqs áq̇i, pqs áq̇i**

áq̇is – S/he scraped the rawhide. **áq̇n, áq̇ntxʷ**
es áq̇ms – S/he is scraping the rawhide. **ies áq̇m, as áq̇m**
qs áq̇ms – S/he is going to scrape the rawhide. **iqs áq̇m, aqs áq̇m**
áʔaq̇is – They scraped the rawhide. **qeʔ áq̇ntm, áq̇ntp**
es áʔaq̇ms – They are scraping the rawhide. **qeʔes áq̇m, es áq̇mp**
qs áʔaq̇ms – They are going to scrape the rawhide. **qeʔqs áq̇m, qs áq̇mp**

áq̇mn – rawhide scraper.

ṅem kʷ áq̇m t anʔáq̇mn – You will scrape it with your scraper. **ṅe wis áq̇ntxʷ m q̇ʷʔentexʷ –** When you are finished scraping it, wring it out.

xʷikʷ – scraping a hide to soften/fluff it, a part of the tanning process. *See: **tan**.*

xʷuk̇ʷ – clean; clear out/off; make tidy. *See: **clean**.*

The **i** following uvular consonants (UC) and the glottal stop **ʔ** sound like English "*ey*" as in the words th*ey*, h*ey*, wh*ey*, etc. Salish UC are: **q**, **q̇**, **qʷ**, **q̇ʷ**, **x̣**, **x̣ʷ**. For example, the suffix …**qin** – head/top, is often spelled using English *ey* as "q*ey*n". So **qi**, **q̇i**, **qʷi**, **q̇ʷi**, **x̣i**, **x̣ʷi**, may be spelled with English *ey* as **q***ey*, **q̇***ey*, **qʷ***ey*, **q̇ʷ***ey*, **x̣***ey*, **x̣ʷ***ey* in other texts.

s.t. - something, the 3rd person
(s.t.) - something implied
s.o. - someone, the 3rd person
sl. - singular form
pl. - plural form
rt. - root word
cmd. - command
lit. - literally
fig. - figuratively
i.e., - for example
See: - Redirection to a related word.

es xʷk̓ʷpmi – S/he is scraping, peeling down.

i čxʷók̓ʷlqʷ – The wood/pole/log is clean.

čpáx̣mn – matchstick.

scratch

emuk̓ʷ – scratch; slight injury.
nʔamk̓ʷaqs – scraped/scratched nose.
nʔamk̓ʷax̣n – scraped/scratched arm.

qsim – scratch, as to relieve an itch.
qsim – S/he scratched. **čn qsim, kʷ qsim**
es qsmi – S/he is scratching. **čnes qsmi, kʷes qsmi**
qs qsmi – S/he is going to scratch. **čiqs qsmi, kʷqs qsmi**
qsíʔim – They scratched. **qeʔ qsim, p qsim**
es qsmíʔi – They are scratching. **qeʔes qsmi, pes qsmi**
qs qsmíʔi – They are going to scratch. **qeʔqs qsmi, pqs qsmi**

qsntes – S/he scratched s.o. **qsnten, qsntexʷ**
es qsims – S/he is scratching s.o. **ies qsim, as qsim**
qs qsims – S/he is going to scratch s.o. **iqs qsim, aqs qsim**
qsntéʔes – They scratched s.o. **qeʔ qsntem, qsntep**
es qsíʔims – They are scratching s.o. **qeʔes qsim, es qsimp**
qs qsíʔims – They are going to scratch s.o. **qeʔqs qsim, qs qsimp**

sxʷqsim – one tasked to scratch. *prefix:* ***sxʷ...*** *– one tasked to do.*
qsemn – one inclined to scratch. *suffix:* ***...emn*** *– one inclined to do.*
qsqsmuł – one that habitually scratches. *suffix:* ***...łmuł*** *– one that habitually does.*

qsiš – Scratch. *cmd.*
qsmiskʷ – Scratch s.t. *cmd.*
qsint – Scratch s.t. *cmd.*
k̓ʷłqsuscut – scratch one's cheek.
qsqncut – scratch one's head.

qsncut, *qsncu* – scratch one's self to relieve an itch.
qsncut – S/he scratched one's self. **čn qsncut, kʷqsncut**
es qsncuti – S/he is scratching one's self. **čnes qsncuti, kʷes qsncuti**
qs qsncuti – S/he is going to scratch one's self. **čiqs qsncuti, kʷqs qsncuti**
qsncúʔut – They scratch themselves. **qeʔ qsncut, p qsncut**
es qsncúʔuti – They are scratching themselves. **qeʔes qsncuti, pes qsncuti**
qs qsncúʔuti – They are going to scratch themselves. **qeʔqs qsncuti, pqs qsncuti**

qsn̓cutš – Scratch yourself. *cmd.*

nqsičn̓m – scratch the back of someone to relieve an itch. *suffix:* ***...ičn̓*** *– back.*
nqsičn̓m – S/he/it scratched a back. **čn nqsičn̓m, kʷ nqsičn̓m**
es nqsičn̓i – S/he/it is scratching a back. **čnes nqsičn̓i, kʷes nqsičn̓i**
qs nqsičn̓i – S/he/it is going to scratch a back. **čiqs nqsičn̓i, kʷqs nqsičn̓i**

nqsičn̓mis – S/he/it scratched s.o.'s back. **nqsičn̓mn, nqsičn̓mntxʷ**
es nqsičn̓ms – S/he/it is scratching s.o.'s back. **ies nqsičn̓m, as nqsičn̓m**
qs nqsičn̓ms – S/he/it is going to scratch s.o.'s back. **iqs nqsičn̓m, aqs nqsičn̓m**

nqsičn̓mntm – His/her back was scratched.

nqsičn̓tn – back scratcher.

nqsičṅiš – Scratch the back. *cmd.*
nqsičṅmnt – Scratch his/her back. *cmd.*

ṅem qs nqsičṅms – S/he/it will be scratching s.o.'s back. **ṅem iqs nqsičṅm, ṅem aqs nqsičṅm**
ṅem qs nqsíˀičṅms – They will be scratching s.o.'s back. **ṅem qeˀqs nqsičṅm, ṅem qs nqsičṅmp**

kʷ iqs nqsičṅm – I am going to scratch your back. **ha kʷ ṅe u q̓ʷo aqs nqsičṅm –** Would you scratch my back?

The **i** following uvular consonants (UC) and the glottal stop **ˀ** sound like English "*ey*" as in the words th*ey*, h*ey*, wh*ey*, etc. Salish UC are: **q**, **q̇**, **qʷ**, **q̇ʷ**, **x̣**, **x̣ʷ**. For example, the suffix **…qin** – head/top, is often spelled using English *ey* as "q*ey*n". So **qi**, **q̇i**, **qʷi**, **q̇ʷi**, **x̣i**, **x̣ʷi**, may be spelled with English *ey* as **q***ey*, **q̇***ey*, **qʷ***ey*, **q̇ʷ***ey*, **x̣***ey*, **x̣ʷ***ey* in other texts.

t̓l̓q̇em – scratch to cause injury.
t̓l̓q̇em – S/he scratched. **čn t̓l̓q̇em , kʷ t̓l̓q̇em**
es t̓l̓q̇mi – S/he is scratching. **čnes t̓l̓q̇mi, kʷes t̓l̓q̇mi**
qs t̓l̓q̇mi – S/he is going to scratch. **čiqs t̓l̓q̇mi, kʷqs t̓l̓q̇mi**
t̓l̓q̇éˀem – They scratched. **qeˀ t̓l̓q̇em , p t̓l̓q̇em**
es t̓l̓q̇míˀi – They are scratching. **qeˀes t̓l̓q̇mi, pes t̓l̓q̇mi**
qs t̓l̓q̇míˀi – They are going to scratch. **qeˀqs t̓l̓q̇mi, pqs t̓l̓q̇mi**

t̓l̓q̇ntes – S/he scratched s.o. **t̓l̓q̇nten, t̓l̓q̇ntexʷ**
es t̓l̓q̇ems – S/he is scratching s.o. **ies t̓l̓q̇em , as t̓l̓q̇em**
qs t̓l̓q̇ems – S/he is going to scratch s.o. **iqs t̓l̓q̇em , aqs t̓l̓q̇em**
t̓l̓q̇ntéˀes – They scratched s.o. **qeˀ t̓l̓q̇ntem, t̓l̓q̇ntep**
es t̓l̓q̇éˀems – They are scratching s.o. **qeˀes t̓l̓q̇em , es t̓l̓q̇emp**
qs t̓l̓q̇éˀems – They are going to scratch s.o. **qeˀqs t̓l̓q̇em , qs t̓l̓q̇emp**

t̓l̓q̇ent – Scratch s.o. *cmd.*
t̓l̓q̇ncut – scratch one's self causing injury.

l̓q̇l̓q̇em – scratch using an object.
l̓q̇l̓q̇em – S/he scratched. **čn l̓q̇l̓q̇em , kʷ l̓q̇l̓q̇em**
es l̓q̇l̓q̇mi – S/he is scratching. **čnes l̓q̇l̓q̇mi, kʷes l̓q̇l̓q̇mi**
qs l̓q̇l̓q̇mi – S/he is going to scratch. **čiqs l̓q̇l̓q̇mi, kʷqs l̓q̇l̓q̇mi**
t̓l̓q̇éˀem – They scratched. **qeˀ l̓q̇l̓q̇em , p l̓q̇l̓q̇em**
es l̓q̇l̓q̇míˀi – They are scratching. **qeˀes l̓q̇l̓q̇mi, pes l̓q̇l̓q̇mi**
qs l̓q̇l̓q̇míˀi – They are going to scratch. **qeˀqs l̓q̇l̓q̇mi, pqs l̓q̇l̓q̇mi**

l̓q̇l̓q̇ntes – S/he scratched s.t. **l̓q̇l̓q̇nten, l̓q̇l̓q̇ntexʷ**
es l̓q̇l̓q̇ems – S/he is scratching s.t. **ies l̓q̇l̓q̇em , as l̓q̇l̓q̇em**
qs l̓q̇l̓q̇ems – S/he is going to scratch s.t. **iqs l̓q̇l̓q̇em , aqs l̓q̇l̓q̇em**
l̓q̇l̓q̇ntéˀes – They scratched s.t. **qeˀ l̓q̇l̓q̇ntem, l̓q̇l̓q̇ntep**
es t̓l̓q̇éˀems – They are scratching s.t. **qeˀes l̓q̇l̓q̇em , es l̓q̇l̓q̇emp**
qs t̓l̓q̇éˀems – They are going to scratch s.t. **qeˀqs l̓q̇l̓q̇em , qs l̓q̇l̓q̇emp**

l̓q̇l̓q̇ent – Scratch s.t. *cmd.*

x̣ʷocm – scratch with claws, animals.
x̣ʷocm – S/he/it scratched. **čn x̣ʷocm, kʷ x̣ʷocm**
es x̣ʷoci – S/he/it is scratching. **čnes x̣ʷoci, kʷes x̣ʷoci**
qs x̣ʷoci – S/he/it is going to scratch. **čiqs x̣ʷoci, kʷqs x̣ʷoci**
x̣ʷóˀocm – They scratched. **qeˀ x̣ʷocm, p x̣ʷocm**
es x̣ʷóˀoci – They are scratching. **qeˀes x̣ʷoci, pes x̣ʷoci**
qs x̣ʷóˀoci – They are going to scratch. **qeˀqs x̣ʷoci, pqs x̣ʷoci**

x̣ʷocis – S/he/it scratched s.o./s.t. **x̣ʷocn, x̣ʷocntxʷ**
es x̣ʷocms – S/he/it is scratching s.o./s.t. **ies x̣ʷocm, as x̣ʷocm**
qs x̣ʷocms – S/he/it is going to scratch s.o./s.t. **iqs x̣ʷocm, aqs x̣ʷocm**

s.t. - something, the 3rd person
(s.t.) - something implied
s.o. - someone, the 3rd person
sl. - singular form
pl. - plural form
rt. - root word
cmd. - command
lit. - literally
fig. - figuratively
i.e., - for example
See: - Redirection to a related word.

x̣ʷóʔocis – They scratched s.o./s.t. **qeʔ x̣ʷocntm, x̣ʷocntp**
es x̣ʷóʔocms – They are scratching s.o./s.t. **qeʔes x̣ʷocm, es x̣ʷocmp**
qs x̣ʷóʔocms – They are going to scratch s.o./s.t. **qeʔqs x̣ʷocm, qs x̣ʷocmp**

es x̣ʷcx̣ʷoci – S/he/it is scratching repeatedly. **čnes x̣ʷcx̣ʷoci, kʷes x̣ʷcx̣ʷoci**
es x̣ʷcx̣ʷocms – S/he/it is scratching s.o./s.t. repeatedly. **ies x̣ʷcx̣ʷocm, as x̣ʷcx̣ʷocm**

ṅem x̣ʷocm – S/he/it will scratch. **ṅem čn x̣ʷocm, ṅem kʷ x̣ʷocm**
ṅem x̣ʷóʔocm – They will scratch. **ṅem qeʔ x̣ʷocm, ṅem p x̣ʷocm**
ṅem qes x̣ʷocms – S/he/it will be scratching it. **ṅem iqes x̣ʷocm, ṅem aqes x̣ʷocm**
ṅem qes x̣ʷóʔocms – They will be scratching it. **ṅem qeʔqes x̣ʷocm, ṅem qes x̣ʷocmp**

scream

coʔiṁcn – scream at the top of one's voice.
coʔiṁcn – S/he/it screamed. **čn coʔiṁcn, kʷ coʔiṁcn**
es coʔiṁcni – S/he/it is screaming. **čnes coʔiṁcni, kʷes coʔiṁcni**
qs coʔiṁcni – S/he/it is going to scream. **čiqs coʔiṁcni, kʷqs coʔiṁcni**

es coʔilši – S/he/it is screaming around. **čnes coʔilši, kʷes coʔilši** *suffix: **...ilš–** autonomous.*

coʔiṁcniš – Scream. *cmd.*

ċiwm – shrill sound; scream.
ċiwm – S/he/it screamed. **čn ċiwm, kʷ ċiwm**
es ċiwi – S/he/it is screaming. **čnes ċiwi, kʷes ċiwi**
qs ċiwi – S/he/it is going to scream. **čiqs ċiwi, kʷqs ċiwi**

es ċiwċiwlši – S/he/it is screaming around. **čnes ċiwċiwlši, kʷes ċiwċiwlši**

caa – scream from pain or fright.
es caa – S/he is screaming from pain. **čnes caa, kʷes caa**

cʔot – moan; slow quiet steady cry. *See: **cry**.*

čošim – yell out; shout out. *(i.e., a war cry) See: **yell**.*

screech owl

čočošmuɬ – screech owl; *Megascops kennicottii. suffix: **...ɬmuɬ–** one that habitually does.*

screw

čx̣ʷlx̣ʷolq̓ʷm – screw a nut onto a bolt.
čx̣ʷlx̣ʷolq̓ʷis – S/he screwed it on. **čx̣ʷlx̣ʷolq̓ʷn, čx̣ʷlx̣ʷolq̓ʷntxʷ**
es čx̣ʷlx̣ʷolq̓ʷms – S/he is screwing it on. **ies čx̣ʷlx̣ʷolq̓ʷm, as čx̣ʷlx̣ʷolq̓ʷm**
qs čx̣ʷlx̣ʷolq̓ʷms – S/he is going to screw it on. **iqs čx̣ʷlx̣ʷolq̓ʷm, aqs čx̣ʷlx̣ʷolq̓ʷm**

sčx̣ʷlx̣ʷolq̓ʷ – nut, *used with a bolt.*
sčx̣ʷlx̣ʷlq̓ʷšin – lug nut.

scrunch

ṗeẏṗism – scrunch the face.
ṗeẏṗism – S/he scrunched his/her face. **čn ṗeẏṗism, kʷ ṗeẏṗism**

sculpin

sttṁá – slimy muddler, slimy sculpin; *Cottus cognatus.*

seagull

smq̓áma – seagull. *rt.: **q̓amaliyeʔ–** eat and eat. See: **eat**.*

lqʷlq̓oxqi – seagull.

search

ƛ̓éʔem – look for; search; find.
ƛ̓éʔem – S/he/it searched. **čn ƛ̓éʔem, kʷ ƛ̓éʔem**
es ƛ̓éʔemi – S/he/it is searching. **čnes ƛ̓éʔemi, kʷes ƛ̓éʔemi**
qs ƛ̓éʔemi – S/he/it is going to search. **čiqs ƛ̓éʔemi, kʷqs ƛ̓éʔemi**

ƛ̓éʔeʔm – They searched. **qeʔ ƛ̓éʔem, p ƛ̓éʔem**
es ƛ̓éʔeʔmi – They are searching. **qeʔes ƛ̓éʔemi, pes ƛ̓éʔemi**
qs ƛ̓éʔeʔmi – They are going to search. **qeʔqs ƛ̓éʔemi, pqs ƛ̓éʔemi**

ƛ̓éʔentes – S/he/it searched for s.o./s.t. **ƛ̓éʔenten, ƛ̓éʔentexʷ**
es ƛ̓éʔems – S/he/it is searching for s.o./s.t. **ies ƛ̓éʔem, as ƛ̓éʔem**
qs ƛ̓éʔems – S/he/it is going to search for s.o./s.t. **iqs ƛ̓éʔem, aqs ƛ̓éʔem**
ƛ̓éʔeʔm – They searched for s.o./s.t. **qeʔ ƛ̓éʔem, p ƛ̓éʔem**
es ƛ̓éʔeʔms – They are searching for s.o./s.t. **qeʔes ƛ̓éʔem, es ƛ̓éʔemp**
qs ƛ̓éʔeʔms – They are going to search for s.o./s.t. **qeʔqs ƛ̓éʔemi, qs ƛ̓éʔemp**

sxʷƛ̓éʔem – one tasked to search. *prefix: sxʷ... – one tasked to do.*

ƛ̓éʔent – Search for s.o./s.t. *cmd.*
ƛ̓éʔenti – You all search for s.o./s.t. *cmd.*
ƛ̓asqáx̣eʔ, *ƛ̓asqá* – look for domestic animals; horse; car.
nƛ̓eƛ̓estnels – search within one's self; to soul search. *(done when something is bothering one's self.)*
es nƛ̓eƛ̓estnelsi – S/he is soul searching. **čnes nƛ̓eƛ̓estnelsi, kʷes nƛ̓eƛ̓estnelsi**
čƛ̓eċʔencu – search for something on one's self. *(i.e., an object, memory)*

čnes ƛ̓éʔemi t ululim – I am looking for money. **ƛ̓éʔenti péceʔmp u sčłq̓ʷastnmp** – All of you look for your diggers and your bark bags. **xʷuyš ƛ̓éʔent anłqaqċeʔ** – Go and find your older brother. **qʷo ƛ̓eʔłt ink̓ʷłnčexʷk̓ʷé** – Go find me my keys. **ies ƛ̓éʔem inʔilmixʷm** – I am looking for my boss. **stem̓ łu es ƛ̓éʔeʔms** – What are they looking for? **ha qʷo aqs ƛ̓éʔem** – Are you going to look for me?

> The **i** following uvular consonants (UC) and the glottal stop ʔ sound like English "*ey*" as in the words *they*, *hey*, *whey*, etc. Salish UC are: **q**, **q̓**, **qʷ**, **q̓ʷ**, **x̣**, **x̣ʷ**. For example, the suffix ...**qin** – head/top, is often spelled using English *ey* as "q*ey*n". So **qi**, **q̓i**, **qʷi**, **q̓ʷi**, **x̣i**, **x̣ʷi**, may be spelled with English *ey* as **q***ey*, **q̓***ey*, **qʷ***ey*, **q̓ʷ***ey*, **x̣***ey*, **x̣ʷ***ey* in other texts.

ƛ̓úʔusm – look in on somebody.
ƛ̓úʔusm – S/he/it looked in on (s.o.). **čn ƛ̓úʔusm, kʷ ƛ̓úʔusm**
es ƛ̓úʔusi – S/he/it is looking in on (s.o.). **čnes ƛ̓úʔusi, kʷes ƛ̓úʔusi**
qs ƛ̓úʔusi – S/he/it is going to look in on (s.o.). **čiqs ƛ̓úʔusi, kʷqs ƛ̓úʔusi**
ƛ̓úʔuʔusm – They looked in on (s.o.). **qeʔ ƛ̓úʔusm, p ƛ̓úʔusm**
es ƛ̓úʔuʔusi – They are looking in on (s.o.). **qeʔes ƛ̓úʔusi, pes ƛ̓úʔusi**
qs ƛ̓úʔuʔusi – They are going to look in on (s.o.). **qeʔqs ƛ̓úʔusi, pqs ƛ̓úʔusi**

ƛ̓uƛ̓úʔusis – S/he/it looked in on s.o. **ƛ̓uƛ̓úʔusn, ƛ̓uƛ̓úʔusntxʷ**
es ƛ̓úʔumsms – S/he/it is looking in on s.o. **ies ƛ̓úʔumsm, as ƛ̓úʔumsm**
qs ƛ̓úʔumsms – S/he/it is going to look in on s.o. **iqs ƛ̓úʔumsm, aqs ƛ̓úʔumsm**
ƛ̓uƛ̓úʔuʔusis – They looked in on s.o. **qeʔ ƛ̓uƛ̓úʔusntm, ƛ̓uƛ̓úʔusntp**
es ƛ̓úʔuʔumsms – They are looking in on s.o. **qeʔes ƛ̓úʔumsm, es ƛ̓úʔumsmp**
qs ƛ̓úʔuʔumsms – They are going to look in on s.o. **qeʔqs ƛ̓úʔumsm, qs ƛ̓úʔumsmp**

ƛ̓úʔusiš – Look in on. *cmd.*

ƛ̓asqáx̣eʔ, *ƛ̓asqá* – look for domestic animals, horse, car.
ƛ̓asqáx̣eʔ – S/he/it looked for a horse. **čn ƛ̓asqáx̣eʔ, kʷ ƛ̓asqáx̣eʔ**
es ƛ̓asqáx̣eʔi – S/he/it is looking for a horse. **čnes ƛ̓asqáx̣eʔi, kʷes ƛ̓asqáx̣eʔi**
qs ƛ̓asqáx̣eʔi – S/he/it is going to look for a horse. **čiqs ƛ̓asqáx̣eʔi, kʷqs ƛ̓asqáx̣eʔi**
ƛ̓asqáʔáx̣eʔ – They looked for a horse. **qeʔ ƛ̓asqáx̣eʔ, p ƛ̓asqáx̣eʔ**
es ƛ̓asqáʔáx̣eʔi – They are looking for a horse. **qeʔes ƛ̓asqáx̣eʔi, pes ƛ̓asqáx̣eʔi**
qs ƛ̓asqáʔáx̣eʔi – They are going to look for a horse. **qeʔqs ƛ̓asqáx̣eʔi, pqs ƛ̓asqáx̣eʔi**

es ƛ̓aƛ̓asqáx̣eʔi – S/he/it is looking for many horses. **čnes ƛ̓aƛ̓asqáx̣eʔi, kʷes ƛ̓aƛ̓asqáx̣eʔi**

> s.t. - something, the 3rd person
> (s.t.) - something implied
> s.o. - someone, the 3rd person
> *sl.* - singular form
> *pl.* - plural form
> *rt.* - root word
> *cmd.* - command
> *lit.* - literally
> *fig.* - figuratively
> *i.e.,* - for example
> *See:* - Redirection to a related word.

ƛ̓osqnm – look for/search the head.
ƛ̓osqis – S/he searched s.o.'s head. **ƛ̓osqn, ƛ̓osqntxʷ**
es ƛ̓osqnms – S/he is searching s.o.'s head. **ies ƛ̓osqnm, as ƛ̓osqnm**
qs ƛ̓osqnms – S/he is going to search s.o.'s head. **iqs ƛ̓osqnm, aqs ƛ̓osqnm**

ƛ̓osqntm – His/her head was searched.

ƛ̓osqnt – Search s.o.'s head. *cmd.*

kʷ iqs ƛ̓osqnm łu qʷtáx̣ʷeʔ – I am going to search your head for lice. **es ƛ̓osqnms łu qʷtáx̣ʷeʔ –** S/he is searching for lice on his/her head.

ƛ̓uƛ̓uscutist – seek a vision. *See:* ***vision.***

nƛ̓éʔepm – search for eggs. *See:* ***egg.***

šƛ̓us – search/stare around; look from one thing to the next; scan. *rt.:* ***šiƛ̓*** *– flat, level, aligned.*
šƛ̓usm – S/he/it scanned around. **čn šƛ̓usm, kʷ šƛ̓usm**
es šƛ̓usi – S/he/it is scanning around. **čnes šƛ̓usi, kʷes šƛ̓usi**
qs šƛ̓usi – S/he/it is going to scan around. **čiqs šƛ̓usi, kʷqs šƛ̓usi**

šƛ̓usis – S/he/it searched/stared around for s.t./s.o. **šƛ̓usn, šƛ̓usntxʷ**
es šƛ̓usms – S/he/it is searching/staring around for s.t./s.o. **ies šƛ̓usm, as šƛ̓usm**
qs šƛ̓usms – S/he/it is going to search/stare around for s.t./s.o. **iqs šƛ̓usm, aqs šƛ̓usm**

šƛ̓usmis – S/he/it looked at them in examination. **šƛ̓usmn, šƛ̓usmntxʷ**
es šƛ̓usmms – S/he/it is looking at them in examination. **ies šƛ̓usmm, as šƛ̓usmm**
qs šƛ̓usmms – S/he/it is going to look at them in examination. **iqs šƛ̓usmm, aqs šƛ̓usmm**

šƛ̓pusis – S/he/it passed and looked at them. **šƛ̓pusn, šƛ̓pusntxʷ**
es šƛ̓pusms – S/he/it is passing and looking at them. **ies šƛ̓pusm, as šƛ̓pusm**
qs šƛ̓pusms – S/he/it is going to pass and look at them. **iqs šƛ̓pusm, aqs šƛ̓pusm**

šƛ̓usiš – Search/stare around. *cmd.*

seat **snčłemutn –** chair; a place to sit. *prefix:* ***sn...*** *– a place of; suffix:* ***...tin, ...tn*** *– means of/device.*

seaweed **sčsnkʷʔaletkʷ –** seaweed. *suffix:* ***...etkʷ, ...tkʷ*** *– liquid*

second **aw̓tpáqs,** *aw̓tpá* **–** follow; walk behind someone. *See:* ***follow.***

secondhand store **snq̓splscutn,** *snq̓splscu* **–** secondhand store. *prefix:* ***sn...*** *– a place of; suffix:* ***...tin, ...tn*** *– means of/device.*

secret **wekʷcnm –** hide your talk by whispering or by talking a different language; talk secretly; gossip. *See:* ***gossip***

secretary **sxʷq̓íʔim –** one tasked to write; secretary. *prefix:* ***sxʷ...*** *– one tasked to do.*

secure **xʷxʷum̓ –** relaxed/safe/secure; have no worries; have no cares; out of danger.
es xʷxʷm̓qini – S/he is safe. **čnes xʷxʷm̓qini, kʷes xʷxʷm̓qini**
qs xʷxʷm̓qini – S/he is going to be safe. **čiqs xʷxʷm̓qini, kʷqs xʷxʷm̓qini**

xʷxʷm̓qnulexʷ – place of no cares.
snxʷxʷm̓qncutn – personal place of no worries. *prefix:* ***sn...*** *– a place of; suffix:* ***...tin, ...tn*** *– means of/device.*
scxʷxʷm̓qncut – something that relaxes a person. *prefix:* ***sc...*** *– s.t. that's been done/made/prepared.*

xʷxʷṁqncut, *xʷxʷṁqncú* – relax one's self; to make one's self have no cares; to have no worries. *See:* ***relax****.*

yo łu xʷxʷṁqnulexʷ – This is really a safe area.

sedimentary rock

ṅcṅċansšn – sedimentary rock. *rt.:* ***ċan*** *– tight; suffix:* ***...essṅ, ...sšṅ*** *– rock.*

see

wič – see; find; perceive; come into view.

wičm – S/he/it saw (s.t.). **čn wičm, kʷ wičm**
wíˀičm – They saw/found (s.t.). **qeˀ wičm, p wičm**

wičis – S/he/it saw/found it. **wičtn, wičtxʷ**
es wičms – S/he/it is seeing it. **ies wičm, as wičm**
qs wičms – S/he/it is going to see it. **iqs wičm, aqs wičm**
wíˀičis – They saw/found it. **qeˀ wičtm, wičtp**
es wíˀičms – They are seeing it. **qeˀes wičm, es wičmp**

wičtmntm – S/he/it was found/seen. **qʷo wičtmntm, kʷ wičtmntm**
wíˀičłlt – They were seen. **qeˀ wičłlt, wičłls**

scwič – something has been found/seen.
sˀučučsnuxʷ – something worthy of being seen. *suffix:* ***...snuxʷ*** *– worthy of.*
uččutm – something that can be seen.
tas uččutm – something that cannot be seen; something invisible.

wičnt – Perceive it. *cmd.*
wičłxʷ – S/he saw/found a house. **čn wičłxʷ, kʷ wičłxʷ**
wičłċéˀ – see animals.
wičsq̇t – see the sky.
učsqax̣eˀ – find horses; find domestic animals.
uččnuis – S/he/it succeeded in seeing it. **uččnun, uččnun**
učscut – S/he/it perceives one's self. **čn učscut, kʷ učscut**
učncut – S/he/it made one's self be seen. **čn učncut, kʷ učncut**
nučmélsis – S/he/it wanted to see s.o./s.t. **nučmélsn, nučmélsntxʷ**

wičtms – S/he saw you. **wičtmncn**
wičnts – S/he saw you.

ṅem wičm – S/he/it will see (s.t). **ṅem čn wičm, ṅem kʷ wičm**
ṅem wíˀičm – They will see (s.t.). **ṅem qeˀ wičm, ṅem p wičm**
ṅem wičis – S/he/it will see it. **ṅem wičtn, ṅem wičtxʷ**
ṅem wíˀičis – They will see it. **ṅem qeˀ wičtm, ṅem wičtp**
ṅem qs wičms – S/he/it will be seeing it. **ṅem iqs wičm, ṅem aqs wičm**
ṅem qs wíˀičms – They will be seeing it. **ṅem qeˀqs wičm, ṅem qs wičmp**

čn wičm tˀésteṁ – I saw something. **čn wičm t k̓ʷsixʷ** – I saw geese. **čn wičm t ululim** – I found money. **wičtn łu ancitxʷ** – I found your house *(was looking for it)*. **wičn łu ancitxʷ** – I saw your house *(saw it)*. **ṅem še eł es wičtmncn** – I will see you again. **ṅe itšeṅe m eł wičtmncn** – I will see you soon. **ṅe č̓luxʷ l heˀenm m eł wičtmncn** – I will see you at eight this evening. **ṅex̣li m eł wičłmn** – Tomorrow I will see you again. **qeˀ eł cwičłlt** – We were seen again. **qeˀ wičtm atwen es wenši** – We saw Tony dance. **t kʷtisi u eł wičts** – Big Blanket found it. **wičłxʷ łu kʷtisi** – Big Blanket saw a house. **ta swe swičts ci smx̣é es iłnms sť̓šá** – Nobody saw that grizzly eating the huckleberries. **łu es cxʷuy łu susep č qecitxʷ tspisċé u wičłċéˀ t sné** – While Joe was coming to our house yesterday, he saw a cow elk. **t čmu sqélixʷ u qʷo ck̓ʷis**

The **i** following uvular consonants (UC) and the glottal stop **ˀ** sound like English "*ey*" as in the words th*ey*, h*ey*, wh*ey*, etc. Salish UC are: **q, q̇, qʷ, q̇ʷ, x̣, x̣ʷ**. For example, the suffix **...qin** – head/top, is often spelled using English *ey* as "q*ey*n". So **qi, q̇i, qʷi, q̇ʷi, x̣i, x̣ʷi**, may be spelled with English *ey* as **q***ey*, **q̇***ey*, **qʷ***ey*, **q̇ʷ***ey*, **x̣***ey*, **x̣ʷ***ey* in other texts.

s.t. - something, the 3rd person
(s.t.) - something implied
s.o. - someone, the 3rd person
sl. - singular form
pl. - plural form
rt. - root word
cmd. - command
lit. - literally
fig. - figuratively
i.e., - for example
See: - Redirection to a related word.

wí?ičis – Four people came to see me. **qesyá? u qe? wičtm –** We all saw. **čn wičm t nłámqe? l isčsáx̣x̣m x̣iłṅe u qe? t?amnqnwe –** I saw a bear so close we almost bumped heads.

čswič – see an object on something or someone. *(i.e., a stain on a shirt, spot on the wall, etc.)*
čswičis – S/he/it saw s.t. on it. **čswičtn, čswičtxʷ**
es čswičms – S/he/it is seeing s.t. on it. **ies čswičm, as čswičm**
qs čswičms – S/he/it is going to see s.t. on it. **iqs čswičm, aqs čswičm**

učsqélixʷ, *učsqé* – see people.
učsqélixʷ – S/he saw people. **čn učsqélixʷ, kʷ učsqelixʷ**
učsqé?elixʷ – They saw people. **qe? učsqélixʷ, p učsqelixʷ**

čn učsqélixʷ t sqélixʷ – I saw some people. **čn učsqé t čsel –** I saw two people. **čn učsqé t smx̣é –** I saw Grizzly Bear. **čn učsqé t mlqnu –** I saw Eagle.

učtwéxʷ, *učtwé* – see each other.
učtwé?exʷ – They saw each other. **qe? učtwéxʷ, p učtwéxʷ**
es učtwé?exʷi – They are seeing each other. **qe?es učtwéxʷi, pes učtwéxʷi**
qs učtwé?exʷi – They are going to see each other. **qe?qs učtwéxʷi, pqs učtwéxʷi**

es nučmlsmnwé?exʷi – They are wanting to see each other. **qe?es nučmlsmnwéxʷi, pes nučmlsmnwéxʷi**

ṅem qe? eł učtwéxʷ – We will see each other again.

šewi – See; there; that's what you get.
šewi kʷ t̓eye? – See, you are mean.
šewi kʷ nt̓lane? – See, you eat too much.

ma – see.
ma še we cuncn epł t̓it̓éẏe łu st̓ṁa – See, I told you there are a lot of mean cows.
tma łu t sq̇sip xʷ?it łu xʷixʷeẏuł – Because, long ago there were lots of animals.

iseẇt – know/see something or someone is there but they cannot be seen; see just an outline or vision of something.

seed

snƛ̓čteẇs, *snƛ̓čte* – seed from the inside of something. *(i.e., fruit, nuts, etc.) suffix:* ***...éẇs*** *– in between, middle.*

snƛ̓ƛ̓i – seed from the top of something.

saqin – plant that has seeds on top that can blow away. *(i.e., dandelion) suffix:* ***...qin, ...qn*** *– top.*

ƛ̓é?ečłełp – seeds opened up; seeds grew.
es ƛ̓é?ečłełpi – seeds are opening up; seeds are growing to a plant.

seizure

qcmim – seizure. *rt.:* ***qcip*** *– shrink.*
es qcmim – S/he is having a seizure. **čnes qcmim, kʷes qcmim**

qcqcmim – seizures; epilepsy.
qcqcntem – S/he had a seizure.

select

nk̓ʷéṅm – choose; pick; select; show the selection. *See:* ***try.***

k̓ʷéṅ – try; sample; attempt; show out; make attention to. *See:* ***try.***

self-conscious

k̓ʷłpusncut, *k̓ʷłpusncu* – self-conscious; backward; shy; bashful; polite; considerate; does not impose.
k̓ʷłpusncut – S/he/it was self-conscious. **čn k̓ʷłpusncut, kʷ k̓ʷłpusncut**

es k̓ʷłpusncuti – S/he/it is being self-conscious. **čnes k̓ʷłpusncuti, kʷes k̓ʷłpusncuti**
qs k̓ʷłpusncuti – S/he/it is going to be self-conscious. **čiqs k̓ʷłpusncuti, kʷqs k̓ʷłpusncuti**
es k̓ʷłpusncúˀuti – They are being self-conscious. **qeˀes k̓ʷłpusncuti, pes k̓ʷłpusncuti**

k̓ʷłpusncutš – Be self-conscious. *cmd.*

ta kʷ qes k̓ʷłpusncut – Do not be self-conscious. **x̣ił exʷ ye ta es k̓ʷłpusncu –** S/he was really acting like a jerk. **tas k̓ʷłpusncut –** S/he was not self-conscious.

> The **i** following uvular consonants (UC) and the glottal stop **ˀ** sound like English "*ey*" as in the words th*ey*, h*ey*, wh*ey*, etc. Salish UC are: **q, q̇, qʷ, q̇ʷ, x̣, x̣ʷ**. For example, the suffix ...**qin** – head/top, is often spelled using English *ey* as "q*ey*n". So **qi, q̇i, qʷi, q̇ʷi, x̣i, x̣ʷi**, may be spelled with English *ey* as q*ey*, q̇*ey*, qʷ*ey*, q̇ʷ*ey*, x̣*ey*, x̣ʷ*ey* in other texts.

selfish

niẏaẏaals – scarce/rare feelings; selfish.
niẏaẏaals – S/he was selfish. **čn niẏaẏaals, kʷ niẏaẏaals**
es niẏaẏaalsi – S/he is being selfish. **čnes niẏaẏaalsi, kʷes niẏaẏaalsi**
qs niẏaẏaalsi – S/he is going to be selfish. **čiqs niẏaẏaalsi, kʷqs niẏaẏaalsi**

niẏaẏaalsis – S/he had no care for s.o. **niẏaẏaalsn, niẏaẏaalsntxʷ**
es niẏaẏaalsms – S/he is having no care for s.o. **ies niẏaẏaalsm, as niẏaẏaalsm**
qs niẏaẏaalsms – S/he is going to have no care for s.o. **iqs niẏaẏaalsm, aqs niẏaẏaalsm**

es čsniẏaẏaalsms – S/he is having no care for s.t. **ies čsniẏaẏaalsm, as čsniẏaẏaalsm**

send

kʷul – send someone somewhere.
kʷulsts – S/he sent him/her. **kʷulstn, kʷulstxʷ**
kʷúˀulsts – They sent him/her. **qeˀ kʷulstm, kʷulstp**

kʷulstms – S/he sent you. **kʷulstmn –** I sent you.
kʷúˀulstms – They sent you. **kʷulstmt –** We sent you.

kʷultms – S/he sent you all. **kʷultmłt –** I sent you all.
kʷúˀultms – They sent you all. **qeˀ kʷultmt –** We sent you all.

qeˀ kʷulłls – S/he sent us. **qeˀ kʷulłlt –** You sent us.
qeˀ kʷuˀlłls – They sent us. **qeˀ kʷulłlp –** You all sent us.

kʷuˀlstxʷ – You sent them. **kʷuˀlstn –** I sent them.
kʷuˀlsts – S/he sent them. **qeˀ kʷuˀlstm –** We sent them.

kʷlkʷúˀulstm – Each one was sent.
kʷulstm – S/he was sent. **qʷo kʷulstm, kʷ kʷulstm**
qʷo kʷulsts – S/he sent me. **t mali qeˀ kʷulłls č sntumístn –** Mary sent us to the store.

k̓ʷłxʷiċšm – send something.
k̓ʷłxʷiċšmis – S/he sent s.t. **k̓ʷłxʷiċšmn, k̓ʷłxʷiċšmntxʷ**
es k̓ʷłxʷiċšms – S/he is sending s.t. **ies k̓ʷłxʷiċšm, as k̓ʷłxʷiċšm**
qs k̓ʷłxʷiċšms – S/he is going to send s.t. **iqs k̓ʷłxʷiċšm, aqs k̓ʷłxʷiċšm**

sck̓ʷłxʷiċšm – something that's been sent. *prefix:* ***sc...** – s.t. that's been done/made/prepared.*
sck̓ʷłxʷiċšm q̇eẏmin – mail; sent paper.

k̓ʷłxʷiċšmnt – Send it. *cmd.*

> s.t. - something, the 3rd person
> (s.t.) - something implied
> s.o. - someone, the 3rd person
> *sl.* - singular form
> *pl.* - plural form
> *rt.* - root word
> *cmd.* - command
> *lit.* - literally
> *fig.* - figuratively
> *i.e.,* - for example
> *See:* - Redirection to a related word.

sense

enwenm – feel/sense. *See:* ***feel.***

separate

čehék̓ʷ – separate; detatch; break free of; loosen. *rt.:* ***čhék̓ʷ** – detach.*
čehk̓ʷmscut – separate from one's partner or spouse.
čehk̓ʷmscuti – S/he separated (s.t.). **čn čehk̓ʷmscuti, kʷ čehk̓ʷmscuti**
es čehk̓ʷmscuti – S/he is separating (s.t.). **čnes čehk̓ʷmscuti, kʷes čehk̓ʷmscuti**

qs čehk̓ʷmscuti – S/he is going to separate (s.t.). **čiqs čehk̓ʷmscuti, kʷqs čehk̓ʷmscuti**

es čečhk̓ʷsew̓si – It is separating. *suffix:* ***...éw̓s –*** *in between, middle.*

čłčhék̓ʷnt – Uncover it. *cmd.*

k̓ʷłnčehk̓ʷéptn, *k̓ʷłnčehk̓ʷé* **–** key. *rt.:* ***čhék̓ʷ –*** *detach; circumfix:* ***k̓ʷłn...ep –*** *opening; suffix:* ***...tin, ...tn –*** *means of/device.*

isc̓ápq čhék̓ʷ – My glued thing came loose, came off.

čłčhék̓ʷm – uncover something; separate the surface. *See:* ***uncover.***

čeluk̓ʷ – It came apart.
člehxʷk̓ʷi – hatch egg. *See:* ***hatch.***

ček̓ʷsew̓sm – separate something solid. *(i.e., a rock, bread loaf, pie, etc.) suffix:* ***...éw̓s –*** *in between, middle.*
ček̓ʷsew̓sis – S/he separated s.t. **ček̓ʷsew̓sn, ček̓ʷsew̓sntxʷ**
es ček̓ʷsew̓sms – S/he is separating s.t. **ies ček̓ʷsew̓sm, as ček̓ʷsew̓sm**
qs ček̓ʷsew̓sms – S/he is separating s.t. **iqs ček̓ʷsew̓sm, aqs ček̓ʷsew̓sm**

ček̓ʷsew̓snt – Separate s.t. *cmd.*

ček̓ʷsew̓sn łiheʔ u sic x̣ʷq̓ew̓sn – I separated this and then I divided it up.

x̣ʷq̓ʷom – separate something that is together. *(i.e., a pile, a ream of paper, a package of crackers, etc.)*
x̣ʷq̓ʷom – S/he/it divided. **čn x̣ʷq̓ʷom, kʷ x̣ʷq̓ʷom**
es x̣ʷq̓ʷmi – S/he/it is dividing. **čnes x̣ʷq̓ʷmi, kʷes x̣ʷq̓ʷmi**
qs x̣ʷq̓ʷmi – S/he/it is going to divide. **čiqs x̣ʷq̓ʷmi, kʷqs x̣ʷq̓ʷmi**
es x̣ʷq̓ʷmíʔi – They are dividing. **qeʔes x̣ʷq̓ʷmi, pes x̣ʷq̓ʷmi**

x̣ʷq̓ʷmstes – S/he/it divided s.t. **x̣ʷq̓ʷmsten, x̣ʷq̓ʷmstexʷ**
es x̣ʷq̓ʷmims – S/he/it is dividing s.t. **ies x̣ʷq̓ʷmim, as x̣ʷq̓ʷmim**
qs x̣ʷq̓ʷmims – S/he/it is going to divide s.t. **iqs x̣ʷq̓ʷmim, aqs x̣ʷq̓ʷmim**
x̣ʷq̓ʷmstéʔes – They divided s.t. **qeʔ x̣ʷq̓ʷmstem, x̣ʷq̓ʷmstep**

x̣ʷq̓ew̓stn – separator; screen.
x̣ʷq̓ʷmiš – Separate. *cmd.*
x̣ʷq̓ʷmiskʷ – Separate it. *cmd.*

x̣ʷq̓ʷq̓ʷmnutmsts – S/he was able to separable. **x̣ʷq̓ʷq̓ʷmnutmstn, x̣ʷq̓ʷq̓ʷmnutmstxʷ**
es x̣ʷq̓ʷq̓ʷotm – It is separable.
tas x̣ʷq̓ʷq̓ʷotm – It is inseparable.
x̣ʷq̓ew̓s – divide/part something; apportion; cut cards. *See:* ***divide.***
x̣ʷq̓ʷpew̓s – get divorced. *See:* ***divorce.***

k̓ʷlčlim – separate from the main source/bulk/group and put aside.
k̓ʷlčlim – S/he/it put (s.t.) aside. **čn k̓ʷlčlim, kʷ k̓ʷlčlim**
es k̓ʷlčlmi – S/he/it is putting (s.t.) aside. **čnes k̓ʷlčlmi, kʷes k̓ʷlčlmi**
qs k̓ʷlčlmi – S/he/it is going to put (s.t.) aside. **čiqs k̓ʷlčlmi, kʷqs k̓ʷlčlmi**

k̓ʷlčlmncut – S/he/it separated one's self from the group. **čn k̓ʷlčlmncut, kʷ k̓ʷlčlmncut**
es k̓ʷlčlmncuti – S/he/it is separated one's self from the group. **čnes k̓ʷlčlmncuti, kʷes k̓ʷlčlmncuti**

k̓ʷlčlmstes – S/he/it separated and put s.t. aside. **k̓ʷlčlmsten, k̓ʷlčlmstexʷ**
es k̓ʷlčlmims – S/he/it is separating and putting s.t. aside. **ies k̓ʷlčlmim, as k̓ʷlčlmim**
qs k̓ʷlčlmims – S/he/it is going to separate and put s.t. aside. **iqs k̓ʷlčlmim, aqs k̓ʷlčlmim**

k̓ʷlčlmłtes – S/he/it put s.t. aside for s.o. **k̓ʷlčlmłten, k̓ʷlčlmłtexʷ**

k̓ʷlčlmiskʷ – Put it aside. *cmd.*
k̓ʷlčlmiɫt – Put it aside for him/her. *cmd.*

malkʷsew̓sis – separate or disconnect the joints. *(i.e., cutting joints, etc.) suffix:* ***...éw̓s*** *– in between, middle.*
malkʷsew̓sis – S/he separated the joint. **malkʷsew̓sn, malkʷsew̓sntxʷ**
es malkʷsew̓sms – S/he is separating the joint. **ies malkʷúm, as malkʷúm**
qs malkʷsew̓sms – S/he is going to separate the joint. **iqs malkʷúm, aqs malkʷúm**

tx̣ʷew̓s – divide something in two; halve something. *See:* ***half.***

sax̣ʷ – split wood with an instrument. *See:* ***split.***

saq̓ – split; parted; cloven. *See:* ***split.***

The **i** following uvular consonants (UC) and the glottal stop ʔ sound like English "*ey*" as in the words *they*, *hey*, *whey*, etc. Salish UC are: **q**, **q̓**, **qʷ**, **q̓ʷ**, **x̣**, **x̣ʷ**. For example, the suffix **...qin** – head/top, is often spelled using English *ey* as "q*ey*n". So **qi**, **q̓i**, **qʷi**, **q̓ʷi**, **x̣i**, **x̣ʷi**, may be spelled with English *ey* as **q***ey*, **q̓***ey*, **qʷ***ey*, **q̓ʷ***ey*, **x̣***ey*, **x̣ʷ***ey* in other texts.

September

ɫx̣ʷɫó spq̓niʔs – September *(month of the chokecherry).*

serious

ɫen – stoic; serious; unexpressive.
i ɫen – S/he is unexpressive. **i čn ɫen, i kʷ ɫen**
ɫenɫnt – unexpressive; person who refrains from talking.

ɫens – have an unexpressive/serious face, almost mean looking.
i ɫens – S/he has a serious face. **i čn ɫens, i kʷ ɫens**

ɫnusm – S/he was unexpressive. **čn ɫnusm, kʷ ɫnusm**
es ɫnusi – S/he is being unexpressive. **čnes ɫnusi, kʷes ɫnusi**

ɫnusmis – S/he looked serious at s.o. **ɫnusmn, ɫnusmntxʷ**
es ɫnusms – S/he is looking serious at s.o. **ies ɫnusm, as ɫnusm**

ta kʷqs nt̓um̓sm i kʷ ɫén – Do not smile, look serious. *cmd.*

ɫenmt – S/he denied an accusation. **čn ɫenmt, kʷ ɫenmt**
es ɫenmti – S/he is denying an accusation. **čnes ɫenmti, kʷes ɫenmti**
qs ɫénmti – S/he is going to deny an accusation. **čiqs ɫenmti, kʷqs ɫenmti**

ɫenmtmis – S/he denied the accusation. **ɫenmtmn, ɫenmtmntxʷ**
es ɫenmti – S/he is denying the accusation. **čnes ɫenmti, kʷes ɫenmti**
qs ɫénmti – S/he is going to deny the accusation. **čiqs ɫenmti, kʷqs ɫenmti**

serviceberry

sɫáq – serviceberry; sarviceberry.
sqaɫpálqʷ – serviceberry tree; *Amelanchier alnifolia var. pumila.*

siy̓ey̓éʔ – juneberry; serviceberry; *Amelanchier alnifolia* var. *alnifolia.*

set

t̓ukʷ – put something down; lay something down; place something down. *See:* ***put.***

qmin – put things down; lay things down; place things down. *See:* ***put.***

sil – place more than one object upright. *See:* ***place.***

caq – place a single object upright; set down. *See:* ***place.***

s.t. - something, the 3rd person
(s.t.) - something implied
s.o. - someone, the 3rd person
sl. - singular form
pl. - plural form
rt. - root word
cmd. - command
lit. - literally
fig. - figuratively
i.e., - for example
See: - Redirection to a related word.

seven

sispl̓ – seven. **spsispl̓** – sevens. *pl.*
es spl̓čstwilši – S/he/it is becoming seven. **čnes spl̓čstwilši, kʷes spl̓čstwilši**
upn eɫ sispl̓ – seventeen.
čsispl̓ – seven people.

spl̓čst... – *prefix indicating seven combined with another affix forming a full word.*

sṗl̓čstásq̇t – seven days. *suffix: ...asq̇t – sky, day.*
sṗl̓čsteɫxʷ – seven houses. *suffix: ...eɫxʷ, ...ɫxʷ – house.*
nsṗl̓čstep – seven eggs. *circumfix: n...ep – egg.*
sṗl̓čstéssn̓ – seven rocks. *suffix: ...essn̓, ...ssn̓ – rock.*

sṗl̓čɫ... – *prefix indicating seven added to a whole word.*
sṗl̓čɫʔupn – seventy, seven tens.
sṗl̓čɫšƛ̓ip – S/he lost seven times. **čn sṗl̓čɫšƛ̓ip, kʷ sṗl̓čɫšƛ̓ip**
sṗl̓čsqáx̣eʔ, *sṗl̓čsqá* – seven domestic animals or cars. *The ɫ is dropped when preceding an s.*
sṗl̓čɫʔopnčstqn – seven thousand.

seven hundred **sṗl̓čɫnk̓ʷoʔqín**, *sṗl̓čɫnk̓ʷoʔqí* – seven hundred.

seventy **sṗl̓čɫʔupn**, *sṗl̓čɫʔu* – seventy.

several **k̓ʷiƛ̓t** – some; other; several. *See: some.*

k̓ʷnk̓ʷinš – several. *See: how many.*
ɫk̓ʷik̓ʷnš – several; a few.
x̣ʷa k̓ʷinš – several; some.

sew **t̓qʷom** – sew.
t̓qʷom – S/he sewed. **čn t̓qʷom, kʷ t̓qʷom**
es t̓qʷmi – S/he is sewing. **čnes t̓oqʷmi, kʷes t̓oqʷmi**
qs t̓qʷmi – S/he is going to sew. **čiqs t̓oqʷmi, kʷqs t̓oqʷmi**

t̓qʷntes – S/he sewed it. **t̓qʷnten, t̓qʷntexʷ**
es t̓qʷoms – S/he is sewing it. **ies t̓qʷom, as t̓qʷom**
qs t̓qʷoms – S/he is going to sew it. **iqs t̓qʷom, aqs t̓qʷom**

es t̓qʷt̓oqʷmi – S/he is sewing and sewing. **čnes t̓qʷt̓oqʷmi, kʷes t̓qʷt̓oqʷmi**
es t̓qʷt̓qʷoms – S/he is sewing and sewing it. **ies t̓qʷt̓qʷom, as t̓qʷt̓qʷom**

čt̓qʷntexʷ anʔištpa – Sew on your skirt.

nɫqʷpusi – thread a needle.
čɫqʷntéʔes – They threaded the needle. **čɫqʷntem, čɫqʷntep**
čɫqʷntes – S/he threaded the needle. **čɫqʷnten, čɫqʷntexʷ**

čɫqʷntéxʷ – You put the thread in the needle; also picking up rocks for the sweat.

sewing kit **snčɫl̓x̣ʷé** – sewing kit. *See: needle.*

sewing machine **snt̓qʷmintn**, *snt̓qʷmin* – sewing machine. *prefix: sn... – a place of; suffix: ...tin, ...tn – means of/device.*

shade **čéy** – have shade.
čɫčéyist – S/he/it shaded one's self. **čn čɫčéyist, kʷ čɫčéyist**
es čɫčéyisti – S/he/it is shading one's self. **čnes čɫčéyisti, kʷes čɫčéyisti**
qs čɫčéyisti – S/he/it is is going to shade one's self. **čiqs čɫčéyisti, kʷqs čɫčéyisti**

čɫčéyis – S/he/it shaded s.t./s.o. **čɫčéyn, čɫčéyntxʷ**
es čɫčéyms – S/he/it is shading s.t./s.o. **ies čɫčéym, as čɫčéym**
qs čɫčéyms – S/he/it is going to shade s.t./s.o. **iqs čɫčéym, aqs čɫčéym**

es k̓ʷɫčeymi – S/he/it is sitting in the shade. **čnes k̓ʷɫčeymi, kʷes k̓ʷɫčeymi**
qs k̓ʷɫčeymi – S/he/it is going to sit in the shade. **čiqs k̓ʷɫčeymi, kʷqs k̓ʷɫčeymi**

sčéy – shade.
sčéylexʷ – shaded place.
sččéy – something shaded.
čłččeẏmn – umbrella.

ci sk̓ʷl̓sn̓ʔiłntm u tʔečéṅ suswissn cłt̓qt̓aqntém t es čłčičéy – The places made for eating were very long; they covered them with brush for shade.

The **i** following uvular consonants (UC) and the glottal stop **ʔ** sound like English "*ey*" as in the words *they, hey, whey*, etc. Salish UC are: **q, q̓, qʷ, q̓ʷ, x̣, x̣ʷ**. For example, the suffix ...**qin** – head/ top, is often spelled using English *ey* as "qeyn". So **qi, q̓i, qʷi, q̓ʷi, x̣i, x̣ʷi**, may be spelled with English *ey* as **q***ey*, **q̓***ey*, **qʷ***ey*, **q̓ʷ***ey*, **x̣***ey*, **x̣ʷ***ey* in other texts.

shadow
smłmeĺk̓ʷé – shadow.

shake
yatt – shake.
itiẏatmsts – S/he/it shook s.t. **itiẏatmstn, itiẏatmstxʷ**
es itiẏatmsts – S/he/it is shaking s.t. **es itiẏatmstn, es itiẏatmstxʷ**
qs itiẏatmsts – S/he/it is going to shake s.t. **qs itiẏatmstn, qs itiẏatmstxʷ**

itiẏatmstm – S/he/it was shook.

yátmskʷ – Shake it.
yatmistwi – All of you shake yourselves.
itiẏatt – shakable; unstable.
yatmulexʷ – earthquake.

x̣ʷall – flutter/shake.
x̣ʷallip – S/he/it fluttered/shook. **čn x̣ʷallip, kʷ x̣ʷallip**
i x̣all – It is fluttering.

x̣ʷallmstes – S/he/it shook s.t. **x̣ʷallmsten, x̣ʷallmstexʷ**

nx̣ʷllpcin – cat's purr. *suffix:* ***...cin, ...cn*** *– action of the mouth. See:* ***purr.***
nx̣ʷlx̣ʷallpusšni – shaky tired legs. *See:* ***leg.***

x̣ʷallip ispúʔus – My heart fluttered. **i x̣ʷall łu ispúʔus** – My heart is fluttering. **es x̣ʷallippi łu ispúʔus** – My heart is shaking.

ax̣ax̣l̓ečstm – shook him side to side.
ax̣ax̣l̓usm – shake your head side to side to say no.

iwu – movement of something voluntary as moving a body part or involuntary as a quiver, shake, or tremble. *See:* ***move.***

čṅéčs – hold hands; grasp hands. *See:* ***shake hands.***

talaqstšn – move/shake/bounce leg; releasing/relaxing from the leg and foot. *See:* ***leg.***

shake hands
čṅéčs – hold hands; grasp hands. *rt.:* ***čṅim*** *– grasp on to s.t. See:* ***grasp.***
čṅéčsis – S/he held s.o.'s hand. **čṅéčsn, čṅéčsntxʷ**
es čṅečsms – S/he is holding s.o.'s hand. **ies čṅečsm, as čṅečsm**
qs čṅečsms – S/he is going to hold s.o.'s hand. **iqs čṅečsm, aqs čṅečsm**
čṅéʔečsis – They held s.o.'s hand. **qeʔ čṅéčsntm, čṅéčsntp**
es čṅéʔečsms – They are holding s.o.'s hand. **qeʔes čṅečsm, es čṅečsmp**

čṅéčsnt – Hold s.o.'s hand. *cmd.*

čnčsnwéxʷ, *čnčsnwé* – hold hands with each other.
es čnčsnwéxʷi – They are holding each other's hands. **qeʔes čnčsnwéxʷi, pes čnčsnwéxʷi**
čnčṅčsnwéxʷ – Each one held hands with each other.

s.t. - something, the 3rd person
(s.t.) - something implied
s.o. - someone, the 3rd person
sl. - singular form
pl. - plural form
rt. - root word
cmd. - command
lit. - literally
fig. - figuratively
i.e., - for example
See: - Redirection to a related word.

čṅéčsnt asl̓ax̣t – Shake hands with your friend. *cmd.*

čṅčłtumš, *čṅčłtu –* shake hands with people. *rt.:* ***čṅim*** *– grasp on to s.t. See:* ***grasp.***
čṅčłtumš – S/he shook hands. **čn čṅčłtumš, kʷ čṅčłtumš**
es čṅčłtumši – S/he is shaking hands. **čnes čṅčłtumši, kʷes čṅčłtumši**
qs čṅčłtumši – S/he is going to shake hands. **čiqs čṅčłtumši, kʷqs čṅčłtumši**

sččṅčłtu – handshake. *prefix:* ***sc...*** *– s.t. that's been done/made/prepared.*

shallow

nłx̣x̣letkʷ – shallow water. *rt.:* ***x̣al*** *– clear; prefix:* ***ł...*** *– little; suffix:* ***...etkʷ, ...tkʷ*** *– liquid*
i nłx̣x̣letkʷ – It is shallow water.

łx̣x̣álkʷ, *łx̣x̣á –* shallow water; little Clearwater. *rt.:* ***x̣al*** *– clear; prefix:* ***ł...*** *– little; suffix:* ***...etkʷ, ...tkʷ*** *– liquid*
i łx̣x̣álkʷ – It is shallow water.

shame

ċʔeš – ashamed. *See:* ***ashamed.***
ċešċšt – shameful.

shampoo

čċáẁqntn – shampoo. *suffix:* ***...tin, ...tn*** *– means of/device.*

shape

sk̓ʷull – shape of something; how something is made.

šeẏ łu sk̓ʷulls łiʔe – That is the shape of this.

sʔaccx̣ – shape of something; how something looks.

share

maẁšít – share. *rt.:* ***maẁ*** *– break.*
maẁšít – S/he shared. **čn maẁšít, kʷ maẁšít**
es maẁšíti – S/he is sharing. **čnes maẁšíti, kʷes maẁšíti**
qs maẁšíti – S/he is going to share. **čiqs maẁšíti, kʷqs maẁšíti**
maẁšíʔit – They shared. **qeʔ maẁšít, p maẁšít**
es maẁšíʔiti – They are sharing. **qeʔes maẁšíti, pes maẁšíti**
qs maẁšíʔiti – They are going to share. **qeʔqs maẁšíti, pqs maẁšíti**

es maẁštwéxʷisti – They are sharing with each other. **qeʔes maẁštwéxʷisti, pes maẁštwéxʷisti**

maẁšítmis – S/he shared with s.o. **maẁšítmn, maẁšítmntxʷ**
es maẁšítms – S/he is sharing with s.o. **čnes maẁšítm, kʷes maẁšítm**
qs maẁšíti – S/he is going to share with s.o. **čiqs maẁšítm, kʷqs maẁšítm**
maẁšíʔitmis – They shared with s.o. **qeʔ maẁšítmntm, maẁšítmntp**
es maẁšíʔitm – They are sharing with s.o. **qeʔes maẁšítm, es maẁšítmp**
qs maẁšíʔitm – They are going to share with s.o. **qeʔqs maẁšítm, qs maẁšítmp**

maẁšítiš – Share. *cmd.*
maẁšítmnt – Share with him/her. *cmd.*

maẁsaqsm – share food.
maẁsaqsm – S/he shared food. **čn maẁsaqsm, kʷ maẁsaqsm**
es maẁsaqsi – S/he is sharing food. **čnes maẁsaqsi, kʷes maẁsaqsi**
qs maẁsaqsi – S/he is going to share food. **čiqs maẁsaqsi, kʷqs maẁsaqsi**
maẁsáʔaqsm – They shared food. **qeʔ maẁsaqsm, p maẁsaqsm**
es maẁsáʔaqsi – They are sharing food. **qeʔes maẁsaqsi, pes maẁsaqsi**
qs maẁsáʔaqsi – They are going to share food. **qeʔqs maẁsaqsi, pqs maẁsaqsi**

maẁsaqsis – S/he shared food with s.o. **maẁsaqsn, maẁsaqsntxʷ**
es maẁsaqsms – S/he is sharing food with s.o. **ies maẁsaqsm, as maẁsaqsm**
qs maẁsaqsms – S/he is going to share food with s.o. **iqs maẁsaqsm, aqs maẁsaqsm**

maẁsáʔaqsis – They shared food with s.o. **qeʔ maẁsaqsntm, maẁsaqsntp**
es maẁsáʔaqsms – They are sharing food with s.o. **qeʔes maẁsaqsm, es maẁsaqsmp**
qs maẁsáʔaqsms – They are going to share food with s.o. **qeʔqs maẁsaqsm, qs maẁsaqsmp**

maẁsaqsiš – Share your food. *cmd.*
maẁsaqsnt – Share your food with s.o. *cmd.*

čhém – join in with something; get in on something; share in the pursuits of someone; be a part of something. *See: **join**.*

nk̓ʷłk̓ʷul̓mnt – Use it together with something. *cmd.*

ṅeyxʷnwexʷist – trade with each other; share. *See: **trade**.*
ṅeyxʷnwéʔexʷist – They traded with each other. **qeʔ ṅeyxʷnwéʔexʷist, p ṅeyxʷnwéʔexʷist**
es ṅeyxʷnwéʔexʷisti – They are trading with each other. **qeʔes ṅeyxʷnwéʔexʷist, pes ṅeyxʷnwéʔexʷisti**
qs ṅeyxʷnwéʔexʷisti – They are going to trade with each other. **qeʔqs ṅeyxʷnwéʔexʷist, pqs ṅeyxʷnwéʔexʷisti**

The **i** following uvular consonants (UC) and the glottal stop **ʔ** sound like English "*ey*" as in the words th*ey*, h*ey*, wh*ey*, etc. Salish UC are: **q**, **q̓**, **qʷ**, **q̓ʷ**, **x̣**, **x̣ʷ**. For example, the suffix ...**qin** – head/top, is often spelled using English *ey* as "q*ey*n". So **qi**, **q̓i**, **qʷi**, **q̓ʷi**, **x̣i**, **x̣ʷi**, may be spelled with English *ey* as **q***ey*, **q̓***ey*, **qʷ***ey*, **q̓ʷ***ey*, **x̣***ey*, **x̣ʷ***ey* in other texts.

sharp

nłƛ̓ƛ̓imaqs, *nłƛ̓ƛ̓i* – sharp point. *circumfix: **n...aqs** – nose, road.*
i nłƛ̓ƛ̓imaqs, *i nłƛ̓ƛ̓i* – It has a sharp point.

anq̓ʷx̣ʷqi mił i nłƛ̓ƛ̓i – Your fingernail is sharp.

nłƛ̓ƛ̓imaqs – sharpen something to a point. *(i.e., pencil, stick, etc.)*
nłƛ̓ƛ̓imaqsis – S/he sharpened s.t. **nłƛ̓ƛ̓imaqsn, nłƛ̓ƛ̓imaqsntxʷ**
es nłƛ̓ƛ̓imaqsms – S/he is sharpening s.t. **ies nłƛ̓ƛ̓imaqsm, as nłƛ̓ƛ̓imaqsm**
qs nłƛ̓ƛ̓imaqsms – S/he is going to sharpen s.t. **iqs nłƛ̓ƛ̓imaqsm, aqs nłƛ̓ƛ̓imaqsm**

nłƛ̓ƛ̓imaqstn – sharpener, pencil sharpener. *suffix: **...tin, ...tn** – means of/device.*

nłƛ̓ƛ̓imaqsnt – Sharpen it. *cmd.*

ha kʷ ṅe u nłƛ̓ƛ̓imaqsn inq̓eẏmintn – May I sharpen my pencil?

nx̣ʷƛ̓aqs – sharpen something using a knife, axe or anything with an edge. *(i.e., stick, pole, pencil, etc.)*
nx̣ʷƛ̓aqsis – S/he sharpened s.t. **nx̣ʷƛ̓aqsn, nx̣ʷƛ̓aqsntxʷ**
es nx̣ʷƛ̓aqsms – S/he is sharpening s.t. **ies nx̣ʷƛ̓aqsm, as nx̣ʷƛ̓aqsm**
qs nx̣ʷƛ̓aqsms – S/he is going to sharpen s.t. **iqs nx̣ʷƛ̓aqsm, aqs nx̣ʷƛ̓aqsm**

x̣ʷix̣ʷit – sharp edge.

c̓iq – prickly. *See: **prickly**.*

xʷƛ̓im – whittle. *See: **whittle**.*

sharpener

nłƛ̓ƛ̓imaqstn – sharpener, pencil sharpener. *suffix: **...tin, ...tn** – means of/device.*

pƛ̓se – knife sharpener; stone sharpener.

sharp-tailed grouse

sq̓óxʷlu, *sq̓ó* – sharp-tailed grouse; prairie chicken; *Tympanuchus phasianellus jamesi.*

shatter

til̓ – shatter/break into pieces of stone, glass, iron or teeth.
tlip – It broke.
es tlpmi – It is breaking.
qs tlpmi – It is going to break.

s.t. - something, the 3rd person
(s.t.) - something implied
s.o. - someone, the 3rd person
sl. - singular form
pl. - plural form
rt. - root word
cmd. - command
lit. - literally
fig. - figuratively
i.e., - for example
See: - Redirection to a related word.

tlíˀip – They broke.

tlntés – S/he/it broke s.t. **tl̓ntén, tl̓ntexʷ**
es tlims – S/he/it is breaking s.t. **ies tl̓im, as tl̓im**
qs tlims – S/he/it is going to break s.t. **iqs tl̓im, aqs tl̓im**
tlntéˀes – They broke s.t. **qeˀ tl̓ntém, tl̓ntép**

tltlip – It shattered.
es til – It is broke.
tlil – It got broke/shattered.
łttil – It broke a little.

ntlpus – S/he/it has a broken neck. **čn ntlpus, kʷ ntlpus**
ntlpeys – S/he/it has a broken tooth. **čn ntlpeys, kʷ ntlpeys**
ntltlpeys – S/he/it has broken teeth. **čn ntltlpeys, kʷ ntltlpeys**
ntl̓eysis – S/he/it broke s.o.'s tooth. **ntleysn, ntleysntxʷ**

qʷo ntleysntxʷ – You broke my tooth. **ha tlntexʷ qeˀaċx̣snċu –** Did you break our mirror. **tlip łu qpé –** plate broke. **t swe u tl̓ntés łu qpéłċeˀ –** Who broke the plate? **tlntén łu qpéłċeˀ –** I broke the plate. **es til nšṅse –** The window is broken. **tlip łu innšṅse –** My window broke. **tl̓tl̓ip łu innšṅse –** My window broke into pieces. **tl̓ip łu inpumin –** My drum is broken (hide is torn).

shave

ax̣ʷsncut, *ax̣ʷsncu* **–** shave one's face; scrape one's face. *rt.:* ***ax̣ʷ*** *– scrape.*
ax̣ʷsncut – S/he shaved one's face. **čn ax̣ʷsncut, kʷ ax̣ʷsncut**
es ax̣ʷsncuti – S/he is shaving one's face. **čnes ax̣ʷsncuti, kʷes ax̣ʷsncuti**
qs ax̣ʷsncuti – S/he is going to shave one's face. **čiqs ax̣ʷsncuti, kʷqs ax̣ʷsncuti**

ax̣ʷs – S/he shaved a face. **čn ax̣ʷs, kʷ ax̣ʷs**
es ax̣ʷsi – S/he is shaving a face. **čnes ax̣ʷsi, kʷes ax̣ʷsi**
qs ax̣ʷsi – S/he is going to shave a face. **čiqs ax̣ʷsi, kʷqs ax̣ʷsi**

łx̣mcut, *łx̣mcu* **–** shave one's self.
łx̣mcut – S/he shaved one's self. **čn łx̣mcut, kʷ łx̣mcut**
es łx̣mcuti – S/he is shaving one's self. **čnes łx̣mcuti, kʷes łx̣mcuti**
qs łx̣mcuti – S/he is going to shave one's self. **čiqs łx̣mcuti, kʷqs łx̣mcuti**

pič – shave/cut. *(i.e., shaving wood.)*
pičm – S/he shaved/cut. **čn pičm, kʷ pičm**
es piči – S/he is shaving/cutting. **čnes piči, kʷes piči**
qs piči – S/he is going to shave/cut. **čiqs piči, kʷqs piči**

scpič – lumber. *rt.:* ***pič*** *– shave/cut; prefix:* ***sc...*** *– s.t. that's been done/made/prepared.*

pčalqʷm – shave/cut wood.

čaˀilqn – cut hair. *See:* ***cut.***

shaver

áx̣ʷstn – razor, shaver. *suffix:* ***...tin, ...tn*** *– means of/device.*

shaving cream

x̣ʷˀustn – shaving cream. *suffix:* ***...tin, ...tn*** *– means of/device.*

posmn – shaving cream. *suffix:* ***...min, ...mn*** *– instrument/tool.*

shawl

sk̓ʷłcowi – shawl.

she

cniłċ, *cni* **–** It is his/hers/its; it is him/her/it. *See:* ***her.***

sheath

sṅṅi – sheath.

skʷiłłniut, *skʷiłłni* – knife sheath.

nc̓oˀqłniut, *nc̓oˀqłni* – draw a knife/sword/gun out of a side mounted sheath; unsheath. *See:* ***draw.***

snq̓ʷłté – gun holster.

čt̓k̓ʷłc̓ełniut, *čt̓k̓ʷłc̓e* – something on the side to put stuff in; pouch on a belt. *See:* ***side.***

The **i** following uvular consonants (UC) and the glottal stop ˀ sound like English "*ey*" as in the words th*ey*, h*ey*, wh*ey*, etc. Salish UC are: **q**, **q̓**, **qʷ**, **q̓ʷ**, **x̣**, **x̣ʷ**. For example, the suffix **...qin** – head/top, is often spelled using English *ey* as "q*ey*n". So **qi**, **q̓i**, **qʷi**, **q̓ʷi**, **x̣i**, **x̣ʷi**, may be spelled with English *ey* as **q***ey*, **q̓***ey*, **qʷ***ey*, **q̓ʷ***ey*, **x̣***ey*, **x̣ʷ***ey* in other texts.

shed

snluk̓ʷłtn, snluk̓ʷtn – woodshed. *suffix:* ***...tin, ...tn*** *– means of/device.*

čkʷƛ̓pep – shed fur. *rt.:* ***kʷƛ̓im*** *– take out.*
es čkʷƛ̓pepi – It is shedding fur.

es čkʷƛ̓pep – Its fur is shedded.

nawpncut – shed skin as a snake.
es nawpncuti – It is shedding its skin.

sheep

lmotó – sheep. *(approximation to French word)*

łˀumnélsčn, *łˀumné* – bighorn sheep, mountain sheep; *Ovis canadensis.*

nłmqélsčn, *nłmqé* – bighorn sheep ewe, mountain sheep ewe; *Ovis canadensis.*

x̣ʷłx̣ʷá, łox̣ʷłx̣ʷá – sheep.

sheepskin

x̣ʷłx̣ʷłsélxʷ – sheepskin.

shelf

snčcqew̓stn – shelf. *rt.:* ***caq*** *– single object placed down; prefix:* ***sn...*** *– a place of; suffix:* ***...éw̓s*** *– in between, middle; suffix:* ***...tin, ...tn*** *– means of/device.*

shell

čk̓ʷllčic̓eˀtn – turtle shell.

Shetland pony

sncm̓asqá – Shetland pony; small horse.

shield

šƛ̓e – war shield.

shifter

sččloˀloˀ – gear shifter.

shin

sčx̣máqstšn – shin. *suffix:* ***...aqstšn*** *– leg.*

shine

c̓ik̓ʷ – shiny, flashy, sparkly; reflects light.
i c̓ik̓ʷ – It is shiny.

čc̓k̓ʷic̓eˀ – shiny all over; covered in reflective material.
c̓ec̓ik̓ʷeˀ – shiny one, affectionately.
čłc̓ik̓ʷetkʷ – shiny water.
čłc̓ik̓ʷčn̓ – water over ice *(shiny surface, glazed surface).*

nc̓k̓ʷlus – snow-blind. *See:* ***snow-blind.***

p̓áq̓ – shine; bright.
i p̓áq̓ – It is bright.
p̓aaq̓ – It got bright.

p̓áq̓mn – flashlight.

np̓aq̓éłc̓eˀ – light up the inside.
p̓aq̓mnscu – something lit up *(i.e., fireworks, lightning, falling star; something that lights up the sky).*

s.t. - something, the 3rd person
(s.t.) - something implied
s.o. - someone, the 3rd person
sl. - singular form
pl. - plural form
rt. - root word
cmd. - command
lit. - literally
fig. - figuratively
i.e., - for example
See: - Redirection to a related word.

čṗaq̇asq̇t – lights in the sky. *suffix: **...asq̇t –** sky, day.*
snčṗaq̇ustn – light bulb. *rt.: **ṗaq̇ –** bright; circumfix; **č...us –** spherical shape; prefix: **...tin, ...tn –** means of/device.*
ṗaq̇l̓wi, ṗaq̇l̓uye? – firefly *(it flashes).*

cí?itxʷs nṗaq̇éłċe? – Their house was all lit up.

ṗič – glossy; *shine something; used to describe the shiny surface of rubber, dark sun tans and the skin of black people. See: **glossy**.*

shinny
pk̓ʷlemi – shinny game.
sččxʷume? – shinny ball; ball.
sṗint sččxʷume? – Hit the ball!

shirt
snacłq̇éyt, *snacłq̇é* **–** shirt. *rt.: **ac –** tie; suffix: **łq̇éyt –** shoulder.*
es nacłq̇éyt – S/he is wearing a shirt. **čnes nacłq̇éyt, kʷes nacłq̇éyt**

nacłq̇éytš – Put on your shirt. *cmd.*

x̣salqs – good shirt. *suffix: **...lqs, ...alqs –** clothes.*
čsalqs – bad shirt. *suffix: **...lqs, ...alqs –** clothes.*

kʷ x̣salqs – You have a good shirt.

sṗčsta – sleeve.
łuxʷca – short sleeve.
t̓połq̓ʷltn – shirt collar. *rt.: **t̓ip –** join/add to; suffix: **...ałq̓ʷlt, ...łq̓ʷlt –** throat*

sṗiyalqs – buckskin shirt. *suffix: **...lqs, ...alqs –** clothes.*
sšinmči – woman's holy shirt; woman's war shirt.
słikʷlqs – man's holy shirt for war; shirt with holes. *suffix: **...lqs, ...alqs –** clothes.*
sčpqłċa?álqs, *sčpqłċa?á* **–** buckskin shirt.
sčppq̇łt̓a – white buckskin shirt.
sčppqłċ?e? – white buckskin shirt.

es nṗl̓čsalqs – His/her shirt is on backwards.

nłupax̣nm – put the arm inside. *rt.: **ł?um –** pierce, sting. See: **inside**.*

shiver
x̣ʷalmim – shiver. *rt.: **x̣ʷall –** flutter/shake. See: **shake**.*
es x̣ʷalpmi – S/he is shivering. **čnes x̣ʷalpmi, kʷes x̣ʷalpmi**
es x̣ʷalpmí?i – They are shivering. **qe?es x̣ʷalpmi, pes x̣ʷalpmi**

x̣ʷalmstém – S/he/it was made to shiver. **qʷo x̣ʷalmstém, kʷ x̣ʷalmstém**

x̣ʷlx̣ʷalmuł – one that habitually shivers. *suffix: **...łmuł –** one that habitually does.*

čiwċe? – shiver; move/shake all over. *rt.: **iwu –** move.*
čiwċ?em – S/he/it shivered. **čn čiwċ?em, kʷ čiwċ?em**
es čiwċ?ei – S/he/it is shivering. **čnes čiwċ?ei, kʷes čiwċ?ei**

shoe
q̇ešin – footwear; moccasin, shoe, boot, etc. *rt.: **q̇e? –** put inside; suffix: **...šin –** foot. lit. anything that is wore on the foot where the foot fits inside.*
es q̇ešin – S/he is wearing footwear. **čn q̇ešin, kʷ q̇ešin**

q̇ešnim – S/he put on footwear. **čn q̇ešnim, kʷ q̇ešnim**
es q̇ešnmi – S/he is putting on footwear. **čnes q̇ešnmi, kʷes q̇ešnmi**
qs q̇ešnmi – S/he is going to put on footwear. **čiqs q̇ešnmi, kʷqs q̇ešnmi**

q̓ešntes – S/he put on s.o.'s footwear. **q̓ešnten, q̓ešntexʷ**
es q̓ešnims – S/he is putting on s.o.'s footwear. **ies q̓ešnim, as q̓ešnim**
qs q̓ešnims – S/he is going to put on s.o.'s footwear. **iqs q̓ešnim, aqs q̓ešnim**

q̓ašisqáx̣eʔtn, *q̓ašisqá* **–** horseshoe. *See:* ***horseshoe.***

q̓ešniš – Put shoes on. *cmd.*
q̓ešnint – Put on his/her shoes. *cmd.*

t sk̓ʷuys u acntés łu q̓ešis – his/her mother tied his/her shoes.

sčt̓ássn – shoe; hard sole footwear. *rt.:* ***t̓as*** *– hard; suffix:* ***...šin, ...šn*** *– foot.*
st̓st̓ássn – shoes.

słxʷłxʷpšin – slippers, sandles, anything you slip on. *rt.:* ***łxʷp*** *– slip over; suffix:* ***...šin, ...šn*** *– foot.*

pƛ̓pƛ̓šnim – remove footwear. *rt.:* ***pƛ̓im*** *– remove, free.*
pƛ̓pƛ̓šnim – S/he removed his/her footwear. **čn pƛ̓pƛ̓šnim, kʷ pƛ̓pƛ̓šnim**
es pƛ̓pƛ̓šnmi – S/he is removing his/her footwear. **čnes pƛ̓pƛ̓šnmi, kʷes pƛ̓pƛ̓šnmi**
qs pƛ̓pƛ̓šnmi – S/he is going to remove his/her footwear. **čiqs pƛ̓pƛ̓šnmi, kʷqs pƛ̓pƛ̓šnmi**

pƛ̓pƛ̓šntes – S/he is removing s.o.'s footwear. **pƛ̓pƛ̓šnten, pƛ̓pƛ̓šntexʷ**
es pƛ̓pƛ̓šnims – S/he is removing s.o.'s footwear. **ies pƛ̓pƛ̓šnim, as pƛ̓pƛ̓šnim**
qs pƛ̓pƛ̓šnims – S/he is going to remove s.o.'s footwear. **čiqs pƛ̓pƛ̓šnim, kʷqs pƛ̓pƛ̓šnim**

es čpƛ̓šin – S/he has one shoe off; one foot is bare. **čnes čpƛ̓šin, kʷes čpƛ̓šin**
es pƛ̓pƛ̓šin – S/he is barefoot. **čnes pƛ̓pƛ̓šin, kʷes pƛ̓pƛ̓šin**

sxʷpƛ̓pƛ̓šnim – one tasked to remove footwear. *prefix:* ***sxʷ...*** *– one tasked to do.*

pƛ̓pƛ̓šniš – Remove your footwear. *cmd.*
pƛ̓pƛ̓šnint – Remove his/her footwear. *cmd.*

maw̓nt ast̓st̓assn – Take your shoes off.

shoehorn

čloštin – shoehorn.

shoelace

acnenešn, *accné* **–** shoelace.

ax̣ccné – lacing that wraps around; laces back and forth. *See:* ***line.*** *See:* ***wrap***
es aax̣ – It is interlaced, crosses over.

shoot

t̓apim – shoot something with an arrow or a bullet.
t̓apntes – S/he shot at it. **t̓apnten, t̓apntexʷ**
es t̓apims – S/he is shooting at it. **ies t̓apim, as t̓apim**
qs t̓apims – S/he is going to shoot at it. **iqs t̓apim, aqs t̓apim**
t̓apntéʔes – They shot at it. **qeʔ t̓apntem, t̓apntep**

t̓apminmis – S/he shot the arrow/bullet. **t̓apminmn, t̓apminmntxʷ**
es t̓apminms – S/he is shooting the arrow/bullet. **ies t̓apminm, as t̓apminm**
qs t̓apminms – S/he is going to shoot the arrow/bullet. **iqs t̓apminm, aqs t̓apminm**

t̓apntém – S/he was shot. **qʷo t̓apntem**

t̓apmin – arrow.

t̓apiš – Shoot. *cmd.*
t̓apint – Shoot it. *cmd.*

The **i** following uvular consonants (UC) and the glottal stop **ʔ** sound like English "*ey*" as in the words th*ey*, h*ey*, wh*ey*, etc. Salish UC are: **q, q̓, qʷ, q̓ʷ, x̣, x̣ʷ**. For example, the suffix **...qin** – head/top, is often spelled using English *ey* as "q*ey*n". So **qi, q̓i, qʷi, q̓ʷi, x̣i, x̣ʷi**, may be spelled with English *ey* as **q***ey*, **q̓***ey*, **qʷ***ey*, **q̓ʷ***ey*, **x̣***ey*, **x̣ʷ***ey* in other texts.

s.t. - something, the 3rd person
(s.t.) - something implied
s.o. - someone, the 3rd person
sl. - singular form
pl. - plural form
rt. - root word
cmd. - command
lit. - literally
fig. - figuratively
i.e., - for example
See: - Redirection to a related word.

t̓apsqé – shoot people.
nt̓at̓apetkʷ – shoot in the water.
es t̓aplwisi – S/he is shooting around/shooting several times. **čnes t̓aplwisi, kʷes t̓aplwisi**
es t̓aplwisms – S/he is shooting several times at s.t./s.o. **ies t̓aplwism, as t̓aplwism**

ṅem t̓apntes – S/he will shoot you. **ṅem t̓apnten, ṅem t̓apntexʷ**
ṅem t̓apntéʔes – They will shoot it. **ṅem qeʔ t̓apntem, ṅem t̓apntep**

ṅem t̓apncis – S/he will shoot you. **ṅem t̓apncíʔis –** They will shoot you. **t̓apncis –** S/he shot you. **t̓apncin –** I shot you. **t̓apncíʔis –** They shot you. **t̓apiš tox̣ –** Shoot straight. **ṅem t̓apncin –** I will shoot you. **t̓apntés łu puwé łu t intuṁ –** My mother shot the deer.

t̓ikʷ – gun blast.
t̓kʷt̓ikʷlš – shooting around.

t̓lt̓lqʷilš – hear shooting; someone is shooting. *suffix: **...ilš** – autonomous.*

ilip – wounded/shot by a bullet, arrow or sharp stick. *See: **wound**.*

shooting star
nccl̓ó – shooting star.

x̣awitx̣aw – shooting star.

likók spłqis – shooting star flower. *lit. rooster's head.*

shore
łʔémcne – shore.

sx̣cin – shore.

npapaánč, *npapaá* **–** dirt riverbank; dirt cliff. *See: **bank**.*

short
łxʷiceʔ – short in length.
čłxʷixʷcaqstšn – short legged person. *suffix: **...aqstšn** – leg.*

łkʷk̓ʷiṁálqʷ, *łkʷk̓ʷiṁá* **–** short person.

k̓ʷłtwiṅtm – fall short of something; deficient in something; unable to attain something. *See: **deficient**.*
es k̓ʷłttwin – S/he does not have enough. **čnes k̓ʷłttwi, kʷes k̓ʷłttwi**

short-eared owl
nččxʷé – short-eared owl; *Asio flammeus*.

Shoshone
snuwepcn, *snuwe* **–** Shoshone.
snuwepcn, *snuwe* **–** Lemhi band of the Shoshone.

shot
t̓apim – shoot something with an arrow or a bullet. *See: **shoot**.*

łuʔax̣nm – stab or give a shot in the arm.
łuʔax̣is – S/he gave s.o. a shot in the arm. **łuʔax̣n, łuʔax̣ntxʷ**
es łuʔax̣nms – S/he is giving s.o. a shot in the arm. **ies łuʔax̣nm, as łuʔax̣nm**
qs łuʔax̣nms – S/he is going to give s.o. a shot in the arm. **iqs łuʔax̣nm, aqs łuʔax̣nm**

łuʔax̣ntm – S/he/it got a shot/stabbed in the arm.

łuʔax̣nt – Give him/her a shot in the arm. *cmd.*

łuʔax̣ncut – give one's self a shot in the arm.
łuʔax̣ncut – S/he gave one's self a shot in the arm. **čn łuʔax̣ncut, kʷ łuʔax̣ncut**
es łuʔax̣ncuti – S/he is giving one's self a shot in the arm. **čnes łuʔax̣ncuti, kʷes łuʔax̣ncuti**
qs łuʔax̣ncuti – S/he is going to give one's self a shot in the arm. **čiqs łuʔax̣ncuti, kʷqs łuʔax̣ncuti**

łuwep – get a shot; get stabbed.
łuweplentm – S/he/it got a shot/stabbed in the buttocks.
łuwepusšnm – get a shot/stabbed in the hip.

ilip – wounded/shot by a bullet, arrow or sharp stick. *See: **wound**.*

should

imše – it should be.
imše kʷ x̣scinm – You should talk good. **imše čłyuxʷstmstxʷ** – You should admire it. **imše kʷ čint** – You should be afraid. **imše nunxʷénʔemnt anpx̣px̣ot** – You should believe your elders. **imše kʷ x̣ʷełé** – You should hurry. **imše kʷ kʷtlcutist** – Be proud of your accomplishments. **imše kʷ x̣scinm** – You should talk good.

kʷ še – you should.
kʷ še cuntxʷ łu mal iłniš – You should tell Mary to eat.

The **i** following uvular consonants (UC) and the glottal stop ʔ sound like English "*ey*" as in the words *they*, *hey*, *whey*, etc. Salish UC are: **q**, **q̓**, **qʷ**, **q̓ʷ**, **x̣**, **x̣ʷ**. For example, the suffix ...**qin** – head/top, is often spelled using English *ey* as "q*ey*n". So **qi**, **q̓i**, **qʷi**, **q̓ʷi**, **x̣i**, **x̣ʷi**, may be spelled with English *ey* as **q***ey*, **q̓***ey*, **qʷ***ey*, **q̓ʷ***ey*, **x̣***ey*, **x̣ʷ***ey* in other texts.

shoulder

snčmłq̓éyt, *snčmłq̓é* – shoulder. *rt.: **čm** – extremity.*
snčmčmłq̓éyt, *snčmčmłq̓é* – shoulders.

nmq̓ʷłq̓eyt – shrug the shoulder. *rt.: **moq̓ʷ** – bump; suffix: **łq̓éyt** – shoulder. See: **shrug**.*
nmq̓ʷmq̓ʷłq̓eyt – S/he shrugged the shoulders. **čn nmq̓ʷmq̓ʷłq̓eyt, kʷ nmq̓ʷmq̓ʷłq̓eyt**

nmq̓ʷmq̓ʷłq̓eytš – Shrug your shoulders. *cmd.*

malkʷłq̓eyt – dislocate the shoulder.
es malkʷłq̓eyt – His/her shoulder is dislocated. **čnes malkʷłq̓eyt, kʷes malkʷłq̓eyt**

malkʷłq̓eytis – S/he/it dislocated s.o.'s shoulder. **malkʷłq̓eytn, malkʷłq̓eytntxʷ**
es malkʷłq̓eytms – S/he/it is dislocating s.o.'s shoulder. **ies malkʷłq̓eytm, as malkʷłq̓eytm**
qs malkʷłq̓eytms – S/he/it is going to dislocate s.o.'s shoulder. **iqs malkʷłq̓eytm, aqs malkʷłq̓eytm**

malkʷłq̓eytnt – Dislocate s.o.'s shoulder. *cmd.*
malkʷłq̓eytncut – dislocate one's shoulder.

shoulder blade

sxʷƛ̓elnčst, *sxʷƛ̓e* – blade.

łq̓éyt – shoulder blade.

shout

čošim – yell out; shout out. *(i.e., a war cry) See: **yell**.*

tspmncót, *tspmncó* – sudden sound of voices shouting. *See: **sound**.*

wéʔm – yell; holler out; talk while shouting. *See: **holler**.*

shove

kʷup – push; shove. *See: **push**.*

shovel

nqľotłq̓éytn, *nqľotłq̓é* – shovel. *rt.: **qľwet** – step; suffix: **łq̓éyt** – shoulder.*

ax̣ʷmn – shovel for scraping. *(i.e., shoveling snow) rt.: **ax̣ʷ** – scrape. See: **scrape**.*
čnes ax̣ʷi t smek̓ʷt – I am scraping (shoveling) snow.

show

k̓ʷéṅ – try; sample; attempt; show out; make attention to. *See: **try**.*
es k̓ʷéṅ – S/he/it is showed out/tried. **čnes k̓ʷéṅ, kʷes k̓ʷéṅ**

k̓ʷéṅš – show for inspection; show out; exhibit for sampling.
k̓ʷéṅšm – S/he/it showed. **čnes k̓ʷéṅšm, kʷes k̓ʷéṅšm**
es k̓ʷéṅši – S/he/it is showing. **čnes k̓ʷéṅši, kʷes k̓ʷéṅši**

s.t. - something, the 3rd person
(s.t.) - something implied
s.o. - someone, the 3rd person
sl. - singular form
pl. - plural form
rt. - root word
cmd. - command
lit. - literally
fig. - figuratively
i.e., - for example
See: - Redirection to a related word.

qs k̓ʷéṅši – S/he/it is going to show. **čiqs k̓ʷéṅši, kʷqs k̓ʷéṅši**

k̓ʷéṅšmis – S/he showed s.t. **k̓ʷéṅšmn, k̓ʷéṅšmntxʷ**
es k̓ʷéṅšmms – S/he is showing s.t. **ies k̓ʷéṅšmm, as k̓ʷéṅšmm**
qs k̓ʷéṅšmms – S/he is going to show s.t. **iqs k̓ʷéṅšmm, aqs k̓ʷéṅšmm**

k̓ʷéṅłts – S/he showed s.t. to s.o. **k̓ʷéṅłtn, k̓ʷéṅłtxʷ**
es k̓ʷéṅłtms – S/he is showing s.t. to s.o. **ies k̓ʷéṅłtm, as k̓ʷéṅłtm**
qs k̓ʷéṅłtms – S/he is going to show s.t. to s.o. **iqs k̓ʷéṅłtm, aqs k̓ʷéṅšmm**

k̓ʷéṅšmnt – Show it. *cmd.*
k̓ʷeṅłt – Show s.t to someone. *cmd.*
k̓ʷṅšmist – attempt; make a personal attempt. *See: **attempt**.*
k̓ʷṅk̓ʷeṅ – try out something. *See: **try out**.*
k̓ʷaṅmaqs – taste food. *See: **taste**.*
nk̓ʷéṅkʷ – taste liquid. *See: **taste**.*

xʷuyš słqʷa k̓ʷeṅłt – Go Rabbit show it to him/her.

scacc̓x̣ – movie, show. *rt.: **acc̓x̣** – watch; prefix: **sc...** – s.t. that's been done/made/prepared. See: **watch**.*
x̣sacc̓x̣ – good movie.
čsacc̓x̣ – bad movie.
snʔacc̓x̣tn – television, movie house. *prefix: **sn...** – a place of; suffix: **...tin, ...tn** – means of/device.*

ṁéẏeʔ – explain; tell; show; make something known. *See: **explain**.*

łaq̓ʷš – show something to someone by making it appear or exposing it to view; reveal something to someone. *See: **appear**.*

shower

nc̓aẇlšłečsušeẇs – shower. *rt.: **ečswíš** – stand.*
nc̓uʔłečsušeẇs – shower. *rt.: **ečswíš** – stand.*

k̓ʷłečsušeẇs l snc̓aẇlštn – shower.

es čłsxʷeneʔi – It's pouring over.

show house

snʔacc̓x̣tn – show house, drive-in, TV. *prefix: **sn...** – a place of; suffix: **...tin, ...tn** – means of/device.*

show-off

q̓exʷmscut – show-off; snobby; arrogant; self admiring.
q̓exʷmscut – S/he/it was showing off. **čn q̓exʷmscut, čn q̓exʷmscut**
es q̓exʷmscuti – S/he/it is showing off. **čnes q̓exʷmscuti, čnes q̓exʷmscuti**
es q̓exʷmscuti – S/he/it is going to show off. **čnes q̓exʷmscuti, čnes q̓exʷmscuti**
es q̓exʷmscúʔuti – They are being snobby. **qeʔes q̓exʷmscuti, pes q̓exʷmscuti**

qeʔ qł q̓exʷmscutn – We'll show off.

ac̓x̣mscut, *ac̓x̣mscú* – conceited; always looking at one's self.
ac̓x̣mscut – S/he was conceited. **čn ac̓x̣mscut, kʷ ac̓x̣mscut**
es ac̓x̣mscuti – S/he is being conceited. **čnes ac̓x̣mscut, kʷes ac̓x̣mscuti**
qs ac̓x̣mscuti – S/he is going to be conceited. **čiqs ac̓x̣mscut, kʷqs ac̓x̣mscuti**
ac̓x̣mscúʔut – They were conceited. **qeʔ ac̓x̣mscut, p ac̓x̣mscut**
es ac̓x̣mscuti – They are being conceited. **qeʔes ac̓x̣mscut, pes ac̓x̣mscuti**
qs ac̓x̣mscuti – They are going to be conceited. **qeʔqs ac̓x̣mscut, pqs ac̓x̣mscuti**

sisiscut – a smart aleck; smarty; know-it-all; show-off. *See: **smart**.*
es sisiscuti – S/he is being a smart aleck. **čnes sisiscuti, kʷes sisiscuti**

shred **ɫiqt –** shredded, torn cloth; raggy.
es ɫiqt – It is shredded; torn in many places.
es ɫiqti – It is tearing in pieces.

ɫiqis – S/he made it raggy. **ɫiqn, as ɫiqntxʷ**
es ɫiqms – S/he is making it raggy. **ies ɫiqm, as ɫiqm**
qs ɫiqms – S/he is going to make it raggy. **iqs ɫiqm, aqs ɫiqm**

ɫiqq – It got raggy.

nɫiqps – torn/raggy pants.

t̓ɫip – pull apart something; rip something. *See:* ***rip.***

shrink **qcip –** shrink; contract.
qcip – S/he/it shrank. **čn qcip, kʷ qcip**
es qcpmi – S/he/it is shrinking. **čnes qcpmi, kʷes qcpmi**
qs qcpmi – S/he/it is going to shrink. **čiqs qcpmi, kʷqs qcpmi**

qcmis – S/he shrunk s.t. **qcmin, qcmintxʷ**
es qcims – S/he is shrinking s.t. **ies qcim, as qcim**
qs qcims – S/he is going to shrink s.t. **iqs qcim, aqs qcim**
qcmíʔis – They shrunk s.t. **qeʔ qcmintm, qcmintp**

qcip ɫu q̇ett – The hide shrunk.

qin – contract; shrink; cripple. *See:* ***contract.***

psas – swelled object shrinks/flattens; deflate. *See:* ***swell.***

shrug **nmq̇ʷɫq̇eyt –** shrug the shoulders. *rt.:* ***moq̇ʷ*** *– bump; suffix:* ***ɫq̇éyt*** *– shoulder.*
nmq̇ʷɫq̇eyt – S/he shrugged his/her shoulders. **čn nmq̇ʷɫq̇eyt, kʷ nmq̇ʷɫq̇eyt**
es nmq̇ʷɫq̇eyt – His/her shoulders are shrugged. **čnes nmq̇ʷɫq̇eyt, kʷes nmq̇ʷɫq̇eyt**

nmq̇ʷɫq̇eytš – Shrug your shoulders. *cmd.*

shut **k̓ʷɫnšn̓ep –** close a hinged door. *See:* ***close.***

shut-up **čúʔup –** quiet. *See:* ***quiet.***
čúʔupš – Be quiet. *cmd.*

čucn – say nothing. *See:* ***quiet.***
čucnš – Do not say anything. *cmd.*

hoycn – quit talking; quit making noise; quit crying. *See:* ***quiet.***
hoycnš – Quit talking. *cmd.*

shy **ẏaamin –** shy; reserved; *lacking some quality, i.e., confidence, etc. rt.:* ***ẏaa*** *– scarce.*
ẏaamis – S/he was reserved with s.o. **ẏaamin, ẏaamintxʷ**
es ẏaaminms – S/he is reserved with s.o. **ies ẏaaminm, as ẏaaminm**
qs ẏaaminms – S/he is going to be reserved with s.o. **iqs ẏaaminm, aqs ẏaaminm**

yaamemn – one inclined to be shy, reserved.
yayaasnuxʷ – S/he/it brings about shyness; causes reserved attitudes.

ẏaam – fear; mistrust; in subjugation; not free with feelings. *See:* ***fear.***

The **i** following uvular consonants (UC) and the glottal stop **ʔ** sound like English "*ey*" as in the words th*ey*, h*ey*, wh*ey*, etc. Salish UC are: **q, q̇, qʷ, q̇ʷ, x̣, x̣ʷ**. For example, the suffix ...**qin** – head/top, is often spelled using English *ey* as "q*ey*n". So **qi, q̇i, qʷi, q̇ʷi, x̣i, x̣ʷi**, may be spelled with English *ey* as **q***ey*, **q̇***ey*, **qʷ***ey*, **q̇ʷ***ey*, **x̣***ey*, **x̣ʷ***ey* in other texts.

s.t. - something, the 3rd person
(s.t.) - something implied
s.o. - someone, the 3rd person
sl. - singular form
pl. - plural form
rt. - root word
cmd. - command
lit. - literally
fig. - figuratively
i.e., - for example
See: - Redirection to a related word.

y̓aasqelixʷ – shy/reserved of people. *rt.: **y̓aa** – scarce.*
es y̓aasqelixʷ – S/he is shy of people. **čnes y̓aasqelixʷ, kʷes y̓aasqelixʷ**

y̓aasqlixʷemn – one inclined to be shy/reserved of people. *suffix: **...emn** – one inclined to do.*

c̓ʔeš – ashamed. *See: **ashamed.***

sibling

snkʷsixʷ – sibling; brother, sister, cousin. *prefix: **snkʷ...** – fellow; member of; rt.: **sxʷsixʷlt** – offspring.*
snkʷsxʷsixʷ – siblings; brothers, sisters, cousins.

sick

čc̓aléls, *čc̓alé* – ill, sick. *rt.: **c̓aál** – ache.*
čc̓aléls – S/he/it was sick. **čn čc̓aléls, kʷ čc̓aléls**
es čc̓alélsi – S/he/it is sick. **čnes čc̓alélsi, kʷes čc̓alélsi**
qs čc̓alélsi – S/he/it is going to be sick. **čiqs čc̓alélsi, kʷqs čc̓alélsi**
čc̓aléʔels – They were sick. **qeʔ čc̓aléls, p čc̓aléls**
es čc̓aléʔelsi – They are sick. **qeʔes čc̓alélsi, pes čc̓alélsi**
qs čc̓aléʔelsi – They are going to be sick. **qeʔqs čc̓alélsi, pqs čc̓alélsi**

čc̓ax̣ʷéls – sick to the stomach. *(i.e., heartburn, ate to much)*
čc̓ax̣ʷéls – S/he/it was sick. **čn čc̓ax̣ʷéls, kʷ čc̓ax̣ʷéls**
es čc̓ax̣ʷélsi – S/he/it is sick. **čnes čc̓ax̣ʷélsi, kʷes čc̓ax̣ʷélsi**
qs čc̓ax̣ʷélsi – S/he/it is going to be sick. **čiqs čc̓ax̣ʷélsi, kʷqs čc̓ax̣ʷélsi**
čc̓ax̣ʷéʔels – They were sick. **qeʔ čc̓ax̣ʷéls, p čc̓ax̣ʷéls**
es čc̓ax̣ʷéʔelsi – They are sick. **qeʔes čc̓ax̣ʷélsi, pes čc̓ax̣ʷélsi**
qs čc̓ax̣ʷéʔelsi – They are going to be sick. **qeʔqs čc̓ax̣ʷélsi, pqs čc̓ax̣ʷélsi**

mix̣ʷt – sick; dying; gravely ill.
es mix̣ʷti – S/he is dying/sick. **čnes mix̣ʷti, kʷes mix̣ʷti**

es tkʷtk̓ʷuli – S/he is really sick; laying down sick for a long time.

čtax̣élsm – have a burning inside your stomach. *(i.e., heartburn) See: **nauseated.***

ččessls – sick to the stomach; nauseated. *See: **nauseated.***

weyt – sick of animals.
weyt – It got sick.
es weyt – It is sick.
es weyti – It is getting sick.

weytstes – S/he caused it to get sick. **weytsten, weytstexʷ**
es weytms – S/he causing it to get sick. **ies weytm, as weytm**
qs weytms – S/he is going to cause it to get sick. **iqs weytm, aqs weytm**

sweyt – sickness of animals.
witemn – one inclined to be sick; sickly animal.

sick and tired

néhels – sick and tired; perturbed; disturbed; fed up. *See: **disturbed.***

sickness

sc̓aál – ache. *See: **ache.***

sweyt – sickness of animals.

čpxʷpqneltn – morning sickness.
es čpxʷpqneltni – She has morning sickness. **čnes čpxʷpqneltni, kʷes čpxʷpqneltni**

side

snčmłniut – side of the body. *rt.: **čm** – extremity.*

čťk̓ʷłċełniut, *čťk̓ʷłċe* – something on the side to put stuff in; pouch on a belt.

naċaċłniut – hanging on the side *(i.e., side panels on a dance outfit.)*

sčtéłċeʔ – side, half body. *rt.: **sčut** – half; suffix: **...ełċeʔ** – the inside of something, body.*

sčtłtéłceʔ – sides.

sčmeẃs – one side of an object; waist. *rt.: **čm** – extremity; suffix: **...éẃs** – in between, middle.*

nisq̓ʷot, *nisq̓ʷo* – across the river. *See: **across**.*

sčchéčst, *sčché* – right hand. *See: **right side**.*

sčċiq̓ʷečst, *sčċi* – left hand. *See: **left side**.*

smiłčmels – front side. *See: **front**.*

nx̣ctus – take sides; side with someone in some activity. *rt.: **x̣cut** – partner.*
nx̣ctusm – S/he/it took sides. **čn nx̣ctusm, kʷ nx̣ctusm**
es nx̣ctusi – S/he/it is taking sides. **čnes nx̣ctusi, kʷes nx̣ctusi**
qs nx̣ctusi – S/he/it is going to take sides. **čiqs nx̣ctusi, kʷqs nx̣ctusi**

nx̣ctusis – S/he/it sided with s.o. **nx̣ctusn, nx̣ctusntxʷ**
es nx̣ctusms – S/he/it is siding with s.o. **ies nx̣ctusm, as nx̣ctusm**
qs nx̣ctusms – S/he/it is going to side with s.o. **iqs nx̣ctusm, aqs nx̣ctusm**

čnx̣ctusmis – S/he/it sided with s.o. to that purpose. **čnx̣ctusmn, čnx̣ctusmntxʷ**
es čnx̣ctusmms – S/he/it is siding with s.o. to that purpose. **ies čnx̣ctusmm, as čnx̣ctusmm**
qs čnx̣ctusmms – S/he/it is going to side with s.o. to that purpose. **iqs čnx̣ctusmm, aqs čnx̣ctusmm**

es nłx̣x̣ctusms – S/he/it is siding with s.o. a little. **ies nłx̣x̣ctusm, as nłx̣x̣ctusm**

nx̣ctusiš – Take sides. *cmd.*
nx̣ctusnt – Side with him/her/it. *cmd.*
es nx̣ctsmnwexʷi – They are siding with each other. **qeʔes nx̣ctsmnwexʷi, pes nx̣ctsmnwexʷi**
x̣cut – partner; share/help in the activities of another; be a comrade; associate as a companion. *See: **partner**.*

ewtus – oppose; work against. *See: **oppose**.*

sight

čswič – see an object on something or someone. *(i.e., a stain on a shirt, spot on the wall, etc.) See: **see**.*

učtwéxʷ, *učtwé* – see each other. *See: **see**.*

sightsee

aċx̣ulexʷ – sightsee; look at the land/area/country.
aċx̣ulexʷm – S/he was sightseeing. **čn aċx̣ulexʷm, kʷ aċx̣ulexʷm**
es aċx̣ulexʷi – S/he is sightseeing. **čnes aċx̣ulexʷi, kʷes aċx̣ulexʷi**
qs aċx̣ulexʷi – S/he is going to sightsee. **čiqs aċx̣ulexʷi, kʷqs aċx̣ulexʷi**
aċx̣úʔulexʷm – They were sightseeing. **qeʔ aċx̣ulexʷm, p aċx̣ulexʷm**
es aċx̣úʔulexʷi – They are sightseeing. **qeʔes aċx̣ulexʷi, pes aċx̣ulexʷi**
qs aċx̣úʔulexʷi – They are going to sightsee. **qeʔqs aċx̣ulexʷi, pqs aċx̣ulexʷi**

sign

sčšṅalqʷ – sign. *(i.e., stop sign, street signs, etc.)*

nčnqinm – sign one's name.

stqlsé – sign language.

The **i** following uvular consonants (UC) and the glottal stop **ʔ** sound like English "*ey*" as in the words *they, hey, whey,* etc. Salish UC are: **q, q̓, qʷ, q̓ʷ, x̣, x̣ʷ**. For example, the suffix **...qin** – head/top, is often spelled using English *ey* as "q*ey*n". So **qi, q̓i, qʷi, q̓ʷi, x̣i, x̣ʷi,** may be spelled with English *ey* as **q***ey*, **q̓***ey*, **qʷ***ey*, **q̓ʷ***ey*, **x̣***ey*, **x̣ʷ***ey* in other texts.

s.t. - something, the 3rd person
(s.t.) - something implied
s.o. - someone, the 3rd person
sl. - singular form
pl. - plural form
rt. - root word
cmd. - command
lit. - literally
fig. - figuratively
i.e., - for example
See: - Redirection to a related word.

signal **taq** – wave; gesture with the hand. *See: **wave**.*

xʷixʷeẏuł tql̓sé – animal signs. *(a children's game)*

tql̓sečst – gesture with the hand for somebody's attention; sign. *See: **gesture**.*
stql̓sé – sign language.

signature **nčnqinm** – sign one's name. *suffix: **...qin, ...qn** – top.*
nčnqinm – S/he signed one's name. **čn nčnqinm, kʷ nčnqinm**

nq̇eẏustšnm – copy a name; write a name.
nq̇eẏusm – S/he co-signed. **čn nq̇eẏusm, kʷ nq̇eẏusm**
es nq̇eẏusi – S/he is co-signing. **čnes nq̇eẏusi, kʷes nq̇eẏusi**
qs nq̇eẏusi – S/he is going to co-sign. **čiqs nq̇eẏusi, kʷqs nq̇eẏusi**
nq̇eẏúˀusm – They co-signed. **qeˀ nq̇eẏusm, p nq̇eẏusm**
es nq̇eẏúˀusi – They are co-signing. **qeˀes nq̇eẏusi, pes nq̇eẏusi**
qs nq̇eẏúˀusi – They are going to co-sign. **qeˀqs nq̇eẏusi, pqs nq̇eẏusi**

nq̇eẏusis – S/he co-signed it. **nq̇eẏusn, nq̇eẏusntxʷ**
es nq̇eẏusms – S/he is co-signing it. **ies nq̇eẏusm, as nq̇eẏusm**
qs nq̇eẏusms – S/he is going to co-sign it. **iqs nq̇eẏusm, aqs nq̇eẏusm**
nq̇eẏúˀusis – They co-signed it. **qeˀ nq̇eẏusntm, nq̇eẏusntp**
es nq̇eẏúˀusms – They are co-signing it. **qeˀes nq̇eẏusm, es nq̇eẏusmp**
qs nq̇eẏúˀusms – They are going to co-sign it. **qeˀqs nq̇eẏusm, qs nq̇eẏusmp**

nq̇eẏuštis – S/he co-signed it for s.o. **nq̇eẏuštn, nq̇eẏuštntxʷ**
es nq̇eẏuštms – S/he is co-signing it for s.o. **ies nq̇eẏuštm, as nq̇eẏuštm**
qs nq̇eẏuštms – S/he is going to co-sign it for s.o. **iqs nq̇eẏuštm, aqs nq̇eẏuštm**
nq̇eẏúˀuštis – They co-signed it for s.o. **qeˀ nq̇eẏuštntm, nq̇eẏuštntp**
es nq̇eẏúˀuštms – They are co-signing it for s.o. **qeˀes nq̇eẏuštm, es nq̇eẏuštmp**
qs nq̇eẏúˀuštms – They are going to co-sign it for s.o. **qeˀqs nq̇eẏuštm, qs nq̇eẏuštmp**

sign language **stql̓sé** – sign language.
ha es yostéxʷ łu stql̓sé – Do you know sign language?

tql̓sečst – gesture with the hand for somebody's attention; sign. *See: **gesture**.*

silent **i čucn** – silent. *See: **quiet**.*

łen – stoic; serious; unexpressive. *See: **serious**.*

silver **i pa ululim** – silver. *lit. faded metal.*

similar **eċx̣íl**, *eċx̣í* – like; same. *See: **like**.*

sin **kʷtiłt̓éyeˀ** – really bad; sin.

sinew **tinš** – sinew; tendons. *rt.: **tin** – tight, taut, tense.*

sq̇eyi – strip of sinew from the back; back strap.

sing **nkʷnem** – sing.
nkʷnem – S/he sang. **čn nkʷnem, kʷ nkʷnem**
es nkʷneyi – S/he is singing. **čnes nkʷneyi, kʷes nkʷneyi**
qs nkʷneyi – S/he is going to sing. **čiqs nkʷneyi, kʷqs nkʷneyi**
nkʷnéˀem – They sang. **qeˀ nkʷnem, p nkʷnem**

es nkʷnéʔeyi – They are singing. **qeʔes nkʷneyi, pes nkʷneyi**
qs nkʷnéʔeyi – They are going to sing. **qeʔqs nkʷneyi, pqs nkʷneyi**

nkʷeis – S/he sang it. **nkʷen, nkʷentxʷ**
es nkʷnems – S/he is singing it. **ies nkʷnem, as nkʷnem**
qs nkʷnems – S/he is going to sing it. **iqs nkʷnem, aqs nkʷnem**
nkʷéʔeis – They sang it. **qeʔ nkʷentm, nkʷentp**
es nkʷnéʔems – They are singing it. **qeʔes nkʷnem, es nkʷnemp**
qs nkʷnéʔems – They are going to sing it. **qeʔqs nkʷnem, qs nkʷnemp**

sxʷnkʷnem – one tasked to sing; a singer. *prefix:* ***sxʷ...*** *– one tasked to do.*
sxʷnkʷnkʷnem – singers. *prefix:* ***sxʷ...*** *– one tasked to do.*
kʷélm – song.

nkʷneyiš – Sing. *cmd.*
nkʷnkʷneywi – Each one of you sing. *cmd.*

ƛ̓e es nkʷnéʔei – They're already singing. **nkʷnéʔem łu sqélixʷ** – The people sang.

nqnestšm – sing a song from an animal.
nqnestšis – S/he sang a song from an animal. **nqnestšn, nqnestšntxʷ**
es nqnestšms – S/he is singing a song from an animal. **ies nqnestšm, as nqnestšm**
qs nqnestšms – S/he is going to sing a song from an animal. **iqs nqnestšm, aqs nqnestšm**

ies nqnestšm ci skʷalšin – I am singing the crane's song.

nqnecnm, *nqncinm* – sing a song from a person. *suffix:* ***...cin, ...cn*** *– action of the mouth.*
nqnecis – S/he sang a song from s.o. **nqnecn, nqnecntxʷ**
es nqnecnms – S/he is singing a song from s.o. **ies nqnecnm, as nqnecnm**
qs nqnecnms – S/he is going to sing a song from s.o. **iqs nqnecnm, aqs nqnecnm**

singer
sxʷnkʷnem – singer. **sxʷnkʷnkʷnem** *pl. prefix:* ***sxʷ...*** *– one tasked to do.*

single
nk̓ʷuʔ – one; single. *See:* ***one.***

čnáqs x̣ʷix̣ʷit – single knife.

sink
snčuʔłqpéłčeʔ, *snčuʔłqpé* – sink to wash dishes.

nq̓éʔetkʷ – sink into water. *rt.:* ***q̓eʔ*** *– put inside.*

q̓etm – make weighty as a means to counter balance; make weighty to make something sink down. *See:* ***balance.***
nq̓ʔét – S/he/it sank *(in water)* from weight. **čn nq̓ʔét, kʷ nq̓ʔét**
es nq̓ʔéti – S/he/it is sinking *(in water)* from weight. **čnes nq̓ʔéti, kʷes nq̓ʔéti**

Sioux
slqʷtłłnxʷťu, *nxʷťu* – Sioux.

sip
łmtq̓ʷol – sip.
łmtq̓ʷolm – S/he/it sipped. **čn łmtq̓ʷolm, kʷ łmtq̓ʷolm**
es łmtq̓ʷoli – S/he/it is sipping. **čnes łmtq̓ʷoli, kʷes łmtq̓ʷoli**
qs łmtq̓ʷoli – S/he/it is going to sip. **čiqs łmtq̓ʷoli, kʷqs łmtq̓ʷoli**

łmtq̓ʷolis – S/he/it sipped s.t. **łmtq̓ʷoln, łmtq̓ʷolntxʷ**
es łmtq̓ʷolms – S/he/it is sipping s.t. **ies łmtq̓ʷolm, as łmtq̓ʷolm**
qs łmtq̓ʷolms – S/he/it is going to sip s.t. **iqs łmtq̓ʷolm, aqs łmtq̓ʷolm**

łmtq̓ʷoliš – Sip. *cmd.*

The **i** following uvular consonants (UC) and the glottal stop **ʔ** sound like English "*ey*" as in the words th*ey*, h*ey*, wh*ey*, etc. Salish UC are: **q, q̓, qʷ, q̓ʷ, x̣, x̣ʷ**. For example, the suffix **...qin** – head/top, is often spelled using English *ey* as "q*ey*n". So **qi, q̓i, qʷi, q̓ʷi, x̣i, x̣ʷi**, may be spelled with English *ey* as **q***ey*, **q̓***ey*, **qʷ***ey*, **q̓ʷ***ey*, **x̣***ey*, **x̣ʷ***ey* in other texts.

s.t. - something, the 3rd person
(s.t.) - something implied
s.o. - someone, the 3rd person
sl. - singular form
pl. - plural form
rt. - root word
cmd. - command
lit. - literally
fig. - figuratively
i.e., - for example
See: - Redirection to a related word.

łmtq̓ʷolnt – Sip it. *cmd.*

sister
łčíčšeʔ – older sister of male or female.
łčíčšeʔs – his/her older sister. **inłčíčšeʔ, anłčíčšeʔ**

łccʔups, *łccʔu* **–** younger sister of male or female. **łcicʔups,** *łcicʔu* **–** younger sisters. *pl.*
łccʔupsts – his/her younger sister. **inłccʔups, anłccʔups**

snkʷsixʷ – brother/sister/cousin. **snkʷsxʷsixʷ** *pl. rt.: **sxʷsixʷlt** – offspring; prefix: **snkʷ...** – fellow; member of.*
snkʷsixʷs – his/her brother/sister/cousin. **isnkʷsixʷ, asnkʷsixʷ**
snkʷsíʔixʷs – their brother/sister/cousin. **qesnkʷsixʷ, snkʷsixʷmp**

sxʷsmʔé – sister *(general)*; women in the household.

isčéẇ – sister-in-law of a female or male.

sck̓ʷl̓łčíčšeʔ – foster older sister of male or female. *prefix: **sck̓ʷl̓...** – s.t. that's been made.*
sck̓ʷl̓łccʔups – foster younger sister of male or female. *prefix: **sck̓ʷl̓...** – s.t. that's been made.*

sister-in-law
isčéẇ – sister-in-law of a female or male.
nq̓ʷiċtn – brother/sister-in-law after death/separation/divorce of spouse.

sit
čłemút – one person sitting down.
čłemút – S/he/it sat. **čn čłemút, kʷ čłemút**
es čłemúti – S/he/it is sitting. **čnes čłemúti, kʷes čłemúti**
qs čłemúti – S/he/it is going to be sitting. **čiqs čłemúti, kʷqs čłemúti**

k̓ʷłemút – sit under something.
k̓ʷłemút – S/he/it sat under (s.t.). **čn k̓ʷłemút, kʷ k̓ʷłemút**
es k̓ʷłemúti – S/he/it is sitting under (s.t.). **čnes k̓ʷłemúti, kʷes k̓ʷłemúti**
qs k̓ʷłemúti – S/he/it is going to be sitting under (s.t.). **čiqs k̓ʷłemúti, kʷqs k̓ʷłemúti**

snčłemutn – chair. *prefix: **sn...** – a place of; suffix: **...tin, ...tn** – means of/device.*
snkʷłʔemut – The one someone sits with. *prefix: **nkʷł...** – together with.*

nʔemtéẇs – wait for something. *rt.: **emut** – sit; suffix: **...éẇs** – in between, middle. See: **wait**.*
k̓ʷłamtalqʷm – sit under a tree. *rt.: **emut** – sit; suffix: **...alqʷ** – wood; cylindical.*
čmtéẇsm, *čmté* **–** ride/straddle something *(one person). See: **ride**.*
čʔemtupsm – keep someone from doing something; hold someone back. *See: **hold back**.*

swe łiciʔ l asčsax̣m u emut – Who is that sitting next to you? **t swe u kʷ es čemutmms –** Who is sitting by you? **swe u emut č asčhečst –** Who is that sitting to your right?

emcnetkʷm – sit by the water.
emcnetkʷm – S/he/it sat by the water. **čn emcnetkʷm, kʷ emcnetkʷm**
es emcnetkʷi – S/he/it is sitting by the water. **čnes emcnetkʷi, kʷes emcnetkʷi**
qs emcnetkʷi – S/he/it is going to be sitting by the water. **čiqs emcnetkʷi, kʷqs emcnetkʷi**

nʔemtetkʷm – sit in the water.
nʔemtetkʷm – S/he/it sat in the water. **čn nʔemtetkʷm, kʷ nʔemtetkʷm**
es nʔemtetkʷi – S/he/it is sitting in the water. **čnes nʔemtetkʷi, kʷes nʔemtetkʷi**
qs nʔemtetkʷi – S/he/it is going to be sitting in the water. **čiqs nʔemtetkʷi, kʷqs nʔemtetkʷi**

nʔemtus – sit by the fire.
nʔemtus – S/he/it sat by the fire. **čn nʔemtus, kʷ nʔemtus**
es nʔemtusi – S/he/it is sitting by the fire. **čnes nʔemtusi, kʷes nʔemtusi**
qs nʔemtusi – S/he/it is going to be sitting by the fire. **čiqs nʔemtusi, kʷqs nʔemtusi**

čłčmcne – sit in the back.
čłčmcne – S/he/it sat in the back. **čn čłčmcne, kʷ čłčmcne**
es čłčmcne – S/he/it is sitting in the back. **čnes čłčmcne, kʷes čłčmcne**
qs čłčmcne – S/he/it is going to be sitting in the back. **čiqs čłčmcne, kʷqs čłčmcne**

čemtšnm – sit at the feet of someone.
čemtšnmis – S/he/it sat at s.o's feet. **čemtšnmn, čemtšnmntxʷ**
es čemtšnms – S/he/it is sitting at s.o.'s feet. **ies čemtšnm, as čemtšnm**
qs čemtšnms – S/he/it is going to be sitting at s.o.'s feet. **iqs čemtšnm, aqs čemtšnm**

čmut – perched; sitting up high.
čmut – S/he/it sat up high. **čn čmut, kʷ čmut**
es čmuti – S/he/it is sitting up high. **čnes čmuti, kʷes čmuti**
qs čmuti – S/he/it is going to be sitting up high. **čiqs čmuti, kʷqs čmuti**

ay̓ew̓t – many people sitting. *suffix: **...éw̓t** – group state.*
ay̓é⁹ew̓t – They were sitting around. **qe⁹ ay̓ew̓t, p ay̓ew̓t**
es ay̓é⁹ew̓ti – They are sitting around. **qe⁹es ay̓ew̓ti, pes ay̓ew̓ti**
qs ay̓é⁹ew̓ti – They are going to be sitting around. **qe⁹qs ay̓ew̓ti, pqs ay̓ew̓ti**

es ay̓ay̓ew̓ti – each group is sitting around.

snčłay̓éw̓tn – couch. *prefix: **sn...** – a place of; suffix: **...tin, ...tn** – means of/device.*

čay̓utéw̓sm, *čay̓uté* – ride/straddle something *(several people). See: **ride**.*

ċaw̓t – many people sitting around; *said in a derogatory manner. suffix: **...éw̓t** – group state.*
l⁹e u ċaw̓t – These people are just sitting around right here; *said in a derogatory manner.*

łaqšlš, *ła* – sit down; in the motion of sitting down.
kʷ łaqšlš – You sat down. **čn łaqšlš, kʷ łaqšlš**
es łaqšlši – S/he is sitting down. **čnes łaqšlši, kʷes łaqšlši**
qs łaqšlši – S/he is going to sit down. **čiqs łaqšlši, kʷqs łaqšlši**

čłaqšlšmis – S/he sat s.o. down. **čłaqšlšmn, čłaqšlšmntxʷ**
es łaqšlšms – S/he is sitting s.o. down. **ies łaqšlšm, as łaqšlšm**
qs łaqšlšms – S/he is going to sit s.o. down. **iqs łaqšlšm, aqs łaqšlšm**

čłaqšlšmis – S/he sat down by s.o.; s/he sat upon s.t. **čłaqšlšmn, čłaqšlšmntxʷ**
es čłaqšlšms – S/he is sitting down by s.o. **ies čłaqšlšm, as čłaqšlšm**
qs čłaqšlšms – S/he is going to sit down by s.o. **iqs čłaqšlšm, aqs čłaqšlšm**
čłá⁹aqšlšmis – They sat down by s.o. **qe⁹ čłaqšlšmntm, čłaqšlšmntp**

łáqšlš – Sit down. *cmd.*
łáqšlšskʷ – Sit s.o. down. *cmd.*
čłqlšew̓s, *čłqlše* – mount, *of one individual*; straddle. *See: **mount**.*
łqlšulexʷ – sit down on the ground.
čłqlšalqʷ – sit on a log.
čłłqlšene⁹ – sit and cover over something.
čłałaqmscut – get close/against someone sitting. *See: **close**.*

kʷitisi łaqšlš – Big Blanket sat down. **ṅem čn łaqšlš –** I will sit down. **ṅem łaqšlš –** S/he/it will sit down. **qʷo čłaqšlšmnt –** Sit down by me. *cmd.*

łaqq – for more than one person to sit down; people in the motion of sitting down.
łá⁹aqq – They sat down. **qe⁹ łaqq, p łaqq**

The **i** following uvular consonants (UC) and the glottal stop ⁹ sound like English "*ey*" as in the words *they, hey, whey*, etc. Salish UC are: **q, q̇, qʷ, q̇ʷ, x̣, x̣ʷ**. For example, the suffix **...qin** – head/top, is often spelled using English *ey* as "q*ey*n". So **qi, q̇i, qʷi, q̇ʷi, x̣i, x̣ʷi**, may be spelled with English *ey* as **q***ey*, **q̇***ey*, **qʷ***ey*, **q̇ʷ***ey*, **x̣***ey*, **x̣ʷ***ey* in other texts.

s.t. - something, the 3rd person
(s.t.) - something implied
s.o. - someone, the 3rd person
sl. - singular form
pl. - plural form
rt. - root word
cmd. - command
lit. - literally
fig. - figuratively
i.e., - for example
See: - Redirection to a related word.

es łáˀaqqi – They are sitting down. **qeˀes łaqqi, pes łaqqi**
qs łáˀaqqi – They are going to sit down. **qeˀqs łaqqi, pqs łaqqi**

łaqqsts – S/he sat them down. **łaqqstn, łaqqstxʷ**
es łaqqms – S/he is sitting them down. **ies łaqqm, as łaqqm**
qs łaqqms – S/he is going to sit them down. **iqs łaqqm, aqs łaqqm**

łaqqwi – All of you sit down. *cmd.*
čłqqeẇs, *čłqqe* – mount, *more than one*; straddle; get on. *See:* ***mount.***
łqqulexʷ – two or more sit down on the ground.
nłqqetkʷ – two or more people sit down in the water.

łqlšax̣n – sit on the arm. *(i.e., as a baby, carried in arm, etc.)*
łqlšax̣n – S/he sat on the arm. **čn łqlšax̣n, kʷ łqlšax̣n**
es łqlšax̣n – S/he is sitting in the arm. **čnes łqlšax̣n, kʷes łqlšax̣n**

łqlšax̣is – S/he sat in s.o.'s arm. **łqlšax̣n, łqlšax̣ntxʷ**
es łqlšax̣nms – S/he is sitting in s.o.'s arm. **ies łqlšax̣nm, as łqlšax̣nm**
qs łqlšax̣nms – S/he is going to sit in s.o.'s arm. **iqs łqlšax̣nm, aqs łqlšax̣nm**

łqlšax̣nmis – S/he sat s.o. on one's arm. **łqlšax̣nmn, łqlšax̣nmntxʷ**
es łqlšax̣nmms – S/he is sitting s.o. on one's arm. **ies łqlšax̣nmm, as łqlšax̣nmm**

łqlšax̣nt – Sit in his/her arm. *cmd.*
łqlšax̣nmnt – Sit him/her in his/her arm. *cmd.*

qʷo łqlšax̣nt – Sit in my arm. **ha qʷo asnłqlšax̣nlsm** – Do you want to sit on my arm? **es ntelsi**
kʷqs łqlšax̣nms – S/he wants to sit in your arm.

nṫq̓meẇs – sitting by each other. *suffix:* ***...éẇs*** *– in between, middle.*
es nṫq̓meẇs – They are sitting by each other. **qeˀes nṫq̓meẇs, pes nṫq̓meẇs**

es nṫq̓ṫq̓meẇs – Each group is sitting by each other. *(i.e., on bleachers at a game)*

pkʷéẇt – round objects lying/sitting around.
łiˀe scmlmálq̓ʷ eł esx̣ʷlx̣ʷélm pkʷéẇt – There were clumps left lying all over.

lawlosšn – sit with legs stretched out.
es lawlosšni – S/he is sitting with legs stretched out. **čnes lawlosšni, kʷes lawlosšni**

six

ṫáq̓n – six. **ṫq̓ṫaq̓n** – sixes. *pl.*
upn eł ṫáq̓n – sixteen.
čṫáq̓n – six people.

ṫq̓nčst... – *prefix indicating six when combined with a suffix or circumfix to form a full word.*
ṫq̓nčstásq̓t – six days. *suffix:* ***...asq̓t*** *– sky, day.*
ṫq̓nčsteɫxʷ – six houses. *suffix:* ***...eɫxʷ, ...ɫxʷ*** *– house.*
nṫq̓nčstep – six eggs. *circumfix:* ***n...ep*** *– egg.*
ṫq̓nčstéssn̓ – six rocks. *suffix:* ***...essn̓, ..ssn̓*** *– rock.*
nṫq̓nčstéłċeˀ – six-shooter, pistol. *suffix:* ***...ełċeˀ*** *– inside contents, body, meat*

ṫq̓nčł... – *prefix indicating six added to a whole word.*
ṫq̓nčłˀupn – sixty, six tens.
ṫq̓nčłšƛ̓ip – S/he lost six times. **čn ṫq̓nčłšƛ̓ip, kʷ ṫq̓nčłšƛ̓ip**
ṫq̓nčsqáx̣eˀ, *ṫq̓nčsqá* – six domestic animals or cars. *The* ***ł*** *is dropped when preceding an* ***s.***
ṫq̓nčłˀopnčstqn – sx thousand.

six hundred

tq̓nčłnkʷoˀqín, *tq̓nčłnkʷoˀqí* – six hundred.

sixty **ṫq̓nčłˀupn** – sixty, six tens.

size **skʷtunt** – bigness.
k̓ʷinš skʷtunts łu asnq̓ʷóƛ̓šn – What size are your socks.

Skalkaho Pass **sq̓x̣q̓x̣o** – Skalkaho Pass, in the Bitterroot Mountains, Montana. *rt.: q̓ax̣ – trail, path.*

skate **nx̣ʷlx̣ʷlq̓ʷšintn** – roller skates. *suffix: ...tin, ...tn – means of/device.*
čłx̣ʷlx̣ʷlq̓ʷšintn – skate board. *suffix: ...tin, ...tn – means of/device.*

čłpekʷpi – ice skate. *See: ice skate.*

skeleton **spasċóṁ**, *spasċó* – animal skeleton.
sqlixʷsċoṁ – human skeleton.

ski **čkʷkʷixʷšn** – ski.
čkʷkʷixʷšn – S/he skied. **čn čkʷkʷixʷšn, kʷ čkʷkʷixʷšn**
es čkʷkʷixʷšni – S/he is skiing. **čnes čkʷkʷixʷšni, kʷes čkʷkʷixʷšni**

Skidoo Bay **čołeneˀ** – Skidoo Bay, Flathead Lake, Flathead Nation.

skillet **snċáx̣mn** – skillet, frying pan. *rt.: ċax̣ – fry; prefix: sn... – a place of; suffix: ...min, ...mn – instrument/tool.*

snṫpustn, *snṫpu* – cooking pan, boiling pot. *rt.: nṫpus – boil.*

skin **q̓ett** – hide, skin, pelt.

xʷcim – skin hoofed animals.
xʷcim – S/he skinned. **čn xʷcim, kʷ xʷcim**
es xʷcmi – S/he is skinning. **čnes xʷcmi, kʷes xʷcmi**
qs xʷcmi – S/he is going to skin. **čiqs xʷcmi, kʷqs xʷcmi**
xʷcíˀim – They skinned. **qeˀ xʷcim, p xʷcim**
es xʷcmíˀi – They are skinning. **qeˀes xʷcmi, pes xʷcmi**

xʷcntés – S/he skinned it. **xʷcntén, xʷcntéxʷ**
es xʷcims – S/he is skinning it. **čnes xʷcim, kʷes xʷcim**
qs xʷcims – S/he is going to skin it. **čiqs xʷcim, kʷqs xʷcim**
xʷcntéˀes – They skinned it. **qeˀ xʷcntém, xʷcntép**
es xʷcíˀims – They are skinning it. **qeˀes xʷcim, es xʷcimp**

xʷcntén u ṫéľm łu innóx̣ʷnx̣ʷ u cqaẏis – I skinned it and my wife sliced it and dried it.

čłsuwalxʷm – skin non-hoofed animals.
čłsuwal̥xʷm – S/he skinned. **čn čłsuwalxʷm, kʷ čłsuwalxʷm**
es čłsuwalxʷi – S/he is skinning. **čnes čłsuwalxʷi, kʷes čłsuwalxʷi**
qs čłsuwalxʷi – S/he is going to skin. **čiqs čłsuwalxʷi, kʷqs čłsuwalxʷi**

ṅawep – skin; peel the skin off an animal. *(i.e., mink, ferret, rabbit, etc.) rt.: ew – peel.*
ṅawep – S/he peeled the skin off. **čn ṅawep, kʷ ṅawep**
es ṅawepi – S/he is peeling the skin off. **čnes ṅawepi, kʷes ṅawepi**
qs ṅawepi – S/he is going to peel the skin off. **čiqs ṅawepi, kʷqs ṅawepi**

es ṅawepi t ččľexʷ – S/he is peeling the ferret.

The **i** following uvular consonants (UC) and the glottal stop **ˀ** sound like English "*ey*" as in the words th*ey*, h*ey*, wh*ey*, etc. Salish UC are: **q**, **q̓**, **qʷ**, **q̓ʷ**, **x̣**, **x̣ʷ**. For example, the suffix **...qin** – head/top, is often spelled using English *ey* as "q*ey*n". So **qi**, **q̓i**, **qʷi**, **q̓ʷi**, **x̣i**, **x̣ʷi**, may be spelled with English *ey* as **q***ey*, **q̓***ey*, **qʷ***ey*, **q̓ʷ***ey*, **x̣***ey*, **x̣ʷ***ey* in other texts.

s.t. - something, the 3rd person
(s.t.) - something implied
s.o. - someone, the 3rd person
sl. - singular form
pl. - plural form
rt. - root word
cmd. - command
lit. - literally
fig. - figuratively
i.e., - for example
See: - Redirection to a related word.

c̓ˀulixʷélxʷ, *c̓ulixʷé* – deer hide.

skinny **čt̓ás,** *čt̓á* – poor, lean, skinny. *rt.: **t̓as** – hard.*
i čt̓ás – S/he/it is thin. *lit. the surface is hard.*

łqqe – narrow.
łqqełc̓eˀ – S/he has a skinny body. *suffix: **...ełc̓eˀ** – the inside of something, body.*

łqqaˀsqélixʷ, *łqqaˀsqé* – skinny person.

ox̣ʷm – string something out; say someone is skinny, stretched, or boney. *(i.e., fencing, rope, hose, etc.) See: **string**.*

łiip– became skinny/lean.
łiip– S/he/it became skinny. **čn łiip, kʷ łiip**
es łipmi– S/he/it is becoming skinny. **čnes łipmi, kʷes łipmi**
qs łipmi– S/he/it is going to become skinny. **čiqs łipmi, kʷqs łipmi**

łipstes– S/he/it made s.o./s.t. become skinny. **łipsten, łipstexʷ**
es łipims– S/he/it is making s.o./s.t. become skinny. **čnes łipim, kʷes łipim**
qs łipims – S/he/it is going to make s.o./s.t. become skinny. **čiqs łipim, kʷqs łipim**

skip **qqetsšnim** – skip.
qqetsšnim – S/he skipped. **čn qqetsšnim, kʷ qqetsšnim**
es qqetsšnmi – S/he is skipping. **čnes qqetsšnmi, kʷes qqetsšnmi**
qs qqetsšnmi – S/he is going to skip. **čiqs qqetsšnmi, kʷqs qqetsšnmi**
qqetsšníˀim – They skipped. **qeˀ qqetsšnim, p qqetsšnim**
es qqetsšnmíˀi – They are skipping. **qeˀes qqetsšnmi, pes qqetsšnmi**

qqetsšniš – Skip. *cmd.*

čłteˀtˀetkʷm – skip on the water.
es čłteˀtˀetkʷms – S/he is skipping it on the water.

čłtatasqetkʷ – skip a rock on water. *suffix: **...etkʷ, ...tkʷ** – liquid*
čłtatasqetkʷm – S/he skipped a rock. **čn čłtatasqetkʷm, kʷ čłtatasqetkʷm**
es čłtatasqetkʷi – S/he is skipping a rock. **čnes čłtatasqetkʷi, kʷes čłtatasqetkʷi**
qs čłtatasqetkʷi – S/he is going to skip a rock. **čiqs čłtatasqetkʷi, kʷqs čłtatasqetkʷi**

čx̣ʷcew̓s – skip past something, skip over something, skip something. *(i.e., skipping numbers in counting, etc.) rt.: **čx̣ʷect** – pass; suffix: **...éw̓s** – in between, middle.*

skipper **ntt̓laceˀ** – water skipper *(insect)*.

skirt **ištpalqs,** *ištpa* – dress; skirt.

skull **sqlixʷsc̓om̓yaˀqn** – skull.

skunk **x̣stéyy̓eˀ** – skunk; *Mephitis mephitis.*

pc̓am – have diarrhea; evacuate liquid feces; skunk sprays. *See: **diarrhea**.*

skunk cabbage **timuˀ** – yellow skunk cabbage; *Lysichiton americanus.*

sky **sččmásq̓t** – sky; heaven. *rt.: **čm** – extremity; suffix: **...asq̓t** – sky, day.*

i čpáˀsq̓t – It is a clear sky (no clouds). *suffix: **...asq̓t** – sky, day.*

čqʷinsq̓t – blue sky. *suffix: **...asq̓t** – sky, day.*

i kʷkʷliľ – It is sunny.

slap **t̓qum** – slap; hit with an open hand.
t̓qntes – S/he slapped s.o. **t̓qnten, t̓qntexʷ**
es t̓qums – S/he is slapping s.o. **ies t̓qum, as t̓qum**
qs t̓qums – S/he is going to slap s.o. **iqs t̓qum, aqs t̓qum**

nt̓qt̓qanaqn – slap the ears.
nt̓qaw̓sqn – slap the top of the head.
čłt̓qesšn – slap the forehead.
t̓qečst – slap the hand.

t̓qosusm – slap in the face.
t̓qosusis – S/he slapped s.o.'s face. **t̓qosusn , t̓qosusntxʷ**
es t̓qosusms – S/he is slapping s.o.'s face. **ies t̓qosusm, as t̓qosusm**
qs t̓qosusms – S/he is going to slap s.o.'s face. **iqs t̓qosusm, aqs t̓qosusm**
t̓qosúʔusis – They slapped s.o.'s face. **qeʔ t̓qosusntm , t̓qosusntp**
t̓qosusntm – S/he was slapped. **qʷo t̓qosusntm, kʷ t̓qosusntm**

kʷ qs t̓qosusms – S/he is going to slap you.

t̓ał – the sound of a slap.

slaughter **plsqax̣eʔm** – kill domestic animals.

sled **snq̓ʷoq̓ʷaw̓istn** – sled.

q̓ʷoq̓ʷaw̓ist, *q̓ʷoq̓ʷaw̓i* – slide; sled.
q̓ʷoq̓ʷaw̓ist – S/he sled. **čn q̓ʷoq̓ʷaw̓ist, kʷ q̓ʷoq̓ʷaw̓ist**
es q̓ʷoq̓ʷaw̓isti – S/he is sledding. **čnes q̓ʷoq̓ʷaw̓isti, kʷes q̓ʷoq̓ʷaw̓isti**
qs q̓ʷoq̓ʷaw̓isti – S/he is going to sled. **čiqs q̓ʷoq̓ʷaw̓isti, kʷqs q̓ʷoq̓ʷaw̓isti**

qʷq̓ʷaancut, *qʷq̓ʷaancú* – coast one's self; slide one's self. *See:* ***slide.***

cckʷiʔu – sleigh. *See:* ***sleigh.***

sledge hammer **ntaʔqintn** – sledge hammer. *rt.:* ***ntaʔqin*** *– hit on top; suffix:* ***...qin, ...qn*** *– top; suffix:* ***...tin, ...tn*** *– means of/device.*

sleep **itš** – sleep.
itš – S/he/it slept. **čn itš, kʷ itš**
es itši – S/he/it is sleeping. **čnes itši, kʷes itši**
qs itši – S/he/it is going to sleep. **čiqs itši, kʷqs itši**
eťitš – They slept. **qeʔ eťitš, p eťitš**
es eťitši – They are sleeping. **qeʔes eťitši, pes itši**
qs eťitši – They are going to sleep. **qeʔqs eťitši, pqs itši**

itšis – S/he made s.o. sleep. **itštn, itštntxʷ**
es itšmms – S/he is making s.o. sleep. **ies itšmm, as itšmm**
qs itšmms – S/he is going to make s.o. sleep. **iqs itšmm, aqs itšmm**

es łʔiitši – S/he/it is sleeping a little while. **čnes łʔiitši, kʷes łʔiitši** *See:* ***nap.***

etšémn – one inclined to sleep; one who sleeps too much. *suffix:* ***...emn*** *– one inclined to do.*
snʔitštn – bedroom. *prefix:* ***sn...*** *– a place of; suffix:* ***...tin, ...tn*** *– means of/device.*
snčłʔitštn – bed. *prefix:* ***sn...*** *– a place of; suffix:* ***...tin, ...tn*** *– means of/device.*

The **i** following uvular consonants (UC) and the glottal stop **ʔ** sound like English "*ey*" as in the words th*ey*, h*ey*, wh*ey*, etc. Salish UC are: **q, q̓, qʷ, q̓ʷ, x̣, x̣ʷ**. For example, the suffix **...qin** – head/top, is often spelled using English *ey* as "q*ey*n". So **qi, q̓i, qʷi, q̓ʷi, x̣i, x̣ʷi**, may be spelled with English *ey* as **q***ey*, **q̓***ey*, **qʷ***ey*, **q̓ʷ***ey*, **x̣***ey*, **x̣ʷ***ey* in other texts.

s.t. - something, the 3rd person
(s.t.) - something implied
s.o. - someone, the 3rd person
sl. - singular form
pl. - plural form
rt. - root word
cmd. - command
lit. - literally
fig. - figuratively
i.e., - for example
See: - Redirection to a related word.

itš – Sleep. *cmd.*
eṫitšwi – All of you sleep. *cmd.*
es netšelsi – S/he wants to sleep. **čnes netšelsi, kʷes netšelsi**

čúˀupš es itši – Be quiet, s/he is sleeping.

čšˀitš – sleepy. *See: **sleepy**.*

nˀestčṁnuxʷ – hibernate. *See: **hibernate**.*

čxʷusminm – lose sleep over something; worried.
es čxʷusminm – S/he is losing sleep over s.t./s.o. **ies čxʷusminm, as čxʷusminm**
qs čxʷusminm – S/he is going to lose sleep over s.t./s.o. **iqs čxʷusminm, aqs čxʷusminm**
es čxʷusmíˀinm – S/he is losing sleep over s.t./s.o. **ies čxʷusminm, as čxʷusminm**
qs čxʷusmíˀinm – S/he is going to lose sleep over s.t./s.o. **iqs čxʷusminm, aqs čxʷusminm**

npċosntm – got gummed up eyes; slept late.
qʷo npċosntm – I got gummed eyes; I slept late.

q̇etyus, *q̇etyu* – nod off; have heavy eyes; cannot hold up head; *literally: weighted face. See: **nap**.*

Sleeping Child

snetetšé – Sleeping Child Hot Springs, near Lolo, Montana. *rt.: **itš** – sleep; prefix: **sn...** – a place of.*

sleepwalker

qeẏs – have nightmare; bad dream. *See: **nightmare**.*

sleepy

čšˀitš – sleepy.
čšˀitš – S/he/it was sleepy. **čn čšˀitš, kʷ čšˀitš**
es čšˀitši – S/he/it is sleepy. **čnes čšˀitši, kʷes čšˀitši**
qs čšˀitši – S/he/it is going to be sleepy. **čiqs čšˀitši, kʷqs čšˀitši**
čšˀeṫitš – There were sleepy. **qeˀ čšˀeṫitš, p čšˀeṫitš**
es čšˀeṫitši – There are sleepy. **qeˀes čšˀeṫitši, pes čšˀeṫitši**
qs čšˀeṫitši – There are going to be sleepy. **qeˀqs čšˀeṫitši, pqs čšˀeṫitši**

es čšeṫeṫíˀitši – Each one is sleepy. **qeˀes čšeṫeṫíˀitši, p es čšeṫeṫíˀitši**

sleet

sṗtnco – sleet.
es pṫncoti, ***es*** *pṫnco* – It is raining slush; it is making itself stick to something. *(wet slushy snow) See: **slush**.*

sołépíˀi – sleet.
es ołépíˀi – It is sleeting.

sleeve

sṗčstax̣n, *sṗčsta* – sleeve.
łxʷcax̣n, *łxʷca* – short sleeve.

ptptax̣n – roll up sleeves.
ptptax̣nm – S/he rolled up sleeves. **čn ptptax̣nm, kʷ ptptax̣nm**
es ptptax̣ni – S/he is rolling up sleeves. **čnes ptptax̣ni, kʷes ptptax̣ni**
qs ptptax̣ni – S/he is going to roll up sleeves. **čiqs ptptax̣ni, kʷqs ptptax̣ni**

ptptax̣is – S/he rolled up s.o.'s sleeves. **ptptax̣n, ptptax̣ntxʷ**
es ptptax̣nms – S/he is rolling up s.o.'s sleeves. **ies ptptax̣nm, as ptptax̣nm**
qs ptptax̣nms – S/he is going to roll up s.o.'s sleeves. **iqs ptptax̣nm, aqs ptptax̣nm**

es ptptax̣n – His/her sleeves are rolled up**.** **čnes ptptax̣n, kʷes ptptax̣n**

ptptax̣niš – Roll up your sleeves. *cmd.*

ptptax̣nt – Roll up his/her sleeves. *cmd.*

łxʷpax̣nm – put something over the arm. *rt.: łixʷp – slip/pull over.* See: ***pull over.***

es nłxʷpax̣n – His/her arm is in the sleeve. **čnes nłxʷpax̣n, kʷes nłxʷpax̣n**

nłxʷpax̣is – S/he put his/her arm in the sleeve. **nłxʷpax̣n, nłxʷpax̣ntxʷ**

es nłxʷpax̣nms – S/he is putting his/her arm in the sleeve. **ies nłxʷpax̣nm, as nłxʷpax̣nm**

qs nłxʷpax̣nms – S/he is going to put his/her arm in the sleeve. **iqs nłxʷpax̣nm, aqs nłxʷpax̣nm**

nłxʷpax̣niš – Put your arm inside. *(i.e., inside a sleeve, etc.) cmd.*

nłxʷpax̣nnt – Put his/her arm inside. *(i.e., inside a sleeve, etc.) cmd.*

sleigh   cckʷiʔu – sleigh.

slice   t̓élm – slice meat for drying.

t̓élm – S/he sliced meat. **čn t̓élm, kʷ t̓élm**

es t̓éli – S/he is slicing meat. **čnes t̓éli, kʷes t̓éli**

qs t̓éli – S/he is going to slice meat. **čiqs t̓éli, kʷqs t̓éli**

t̓éʔelm – They sliced meat. **qeʔ t̓élm, p t̓élm**

es t̓éʔeli – They are slicing meat. **qeʔes t̓éli, pes t̓éli**

qs t̓éʔeli – They are going to slice meat. **qeʔqs t̓éli, pqs t̓éli**

t̓élis – S/he sliced the meat. **t̓éln, t̓élntxʷ**

es t̓élms – S/he is slicing the meat. **ies t̓élm, as t̓élm**

qs t̓élms – S/he is going to slice the meat. **iqs t̓élm, aqs t̓élm**

t̓éʔelis – They sliced the meat. **qeʔ t̓élntm, t̓élntp**

es t̓éʔelms – They are slicing the meat. **qeʔes t̓élm, es t̓élmp**

qs t̓éʔelms – They are going to slice the meat. **qeʔqs t̓élm, qs t̓élmp**

n̓em iqs t̓elm – I will prepare it for drying; I will slice it.

uł sxʷÏxʷÏtew̓s es t̓éʔeli u es cqéʔey̓i – Those people sliced and dried meat. **xʷcntén u t̓éÍm łu innóx̣ʷnx̣ u cqay̓is** – I skinned it and my wife sliced it and dried it.

slide   q̓ʷaap – move/slide by natural occurence.

q̓ʷaap – It slid. **čn q̓ʷaap, kʷ q̓ʷaap**

es q̓ʷapmi – It is sliding. **čnes q̓ʷapmi, kʷes q̓ʷapmi**

qs q̓ʷapmi – It is going to slide. **čiqs q̓ʷapmi, kʷqs q̓ʷapmi**

nq̓ʷapaqs – slide down the road.

q̓ʷamim – move/slide something. *See: **move**.*

qʷq̓ʷaancut, *qʷq̓ʷaancú* – coast one's self; slide one's self.

qʷq̓ʷaancut – S/he/it slid. **čn qʷq̓ʷaancut, kʷ qʷq̓ʷaancut**

es qʷq̓ʷaancuti – S/he/it is sliding. **čnes qʷq̓ʷaancuti, kʷes qʷq̓ʷaancuti**

qs qʷq̓ʷaancuti – S/he/it is going to slide. **čiqs qʷq̓ʷaancuti, kʷqs qʷq̓ʷaancuti**

qʷq̓ʷaancúʔut – They slid. **qeʔ qʷq̓ʷaancut, p qʷq̓ʷaancut**

es qʷq̓ʷaancúʔuti – They are sliding. **qeʔes qʷq̓ʷaancuti, pes qʷq̓ʷaancuti**

qs qʷq̓ʷaancúʔuti – They are going to slide. **čiqs qʷq̓ʷaancuti, kʷqs qʷq̓ʷaancuti**

snqʷq̓ʷaancutn – slide. *prefix: **sn…** – a place of; suffix: **…tin, …tn** – means of/device.*

qʷq̓ʷaancutš – Slide. *cmd.*

qʷq̓ʷaancutwi – All of you slide. *cmd.*

q̓ʷoq̓ʷaw̓ist, *q̓ʷoq̓ʷaw̓i* – slide; sled. *See: **sled**.*

The **i** following uvular consonants (UC) and the glottal stop **ʔ** sound like English "*ey*" as in the words th*ey*, h*ey*, wh*ey*, etc. Salish UC are: **q, q̓, qʷ, q̓ʷ, x̣, x̣ʷ**. For example, the suffix **…qin** – head/top, is often spelled using English *ey* as "q*ey*n". So **qi, q̓i, qʷi, q̓ʷi, x̣i, x̣ʷi**, may be spelled with English *ey* as q*ey*, q̓*ey*, qʷ*ey*, q̓ʷ*ey*, x̣*ey*, x̣ʷ*ey* in other texts.

---

s.t. - something, the 3ʳᵈ person
(s.t.) - something implied
s.o. - someone, the 3ʳᵈ person
sl. - singular form
pl. - plural form
rt. - root word
cmd. - command
lit. - literally
fig. - figuratively
i.e., - for example
See: - Redirection to a related word.

q̓ʷamncut – move one's self over; slide over.
q̓ʷamncut – S/he/it slid over. **čn q̓ʷamncut, kʷ q̓ʷamncut**
es q̓ʷamncuti – S/he/it is sliding over. **čnes q̓ʷamncuti, kʷes q̓ʷamncuti**
qs q̓ʷamncuti – S/he/it is going to slide over. **čiqs q̓ʷamncuti, kʷqs q̓ʷamncuti**
q̓ʷamncúʔut – They slid over. **qeʔ q̓ʷamncut, p q̓ʷamncut**
es q̓ʷamncúʔuti – They are sliding over. **qeʔes q̓ʷamncuti, pes q̓ʷamncuti**
qs q̓ʷamncúʔuti – They are going to slide over. **qeʔqs q̓ʷamncuti, pqs q̓ʷamncuti**

q̓ʷamncutš – Slide over. *cmd.*
q̓ʷamncutwi – All of you slide over. *cmd.*
cq̓ʷamncutš – Slide over to me. *cmd.*
q̓ʷamiskʷ – Move it over.

q̓ʷamiskʷ ci č nk̓ʷuʔ – Move it over to the next one. **q̓ʷamiskʷ t esel –** Move it over two.

čłpekʷp – ice skate. *See: **ice skate**.*

slight

x̣ʷem – slight; disparage.
x̣ʷemčst – S/he acted with slight. **čn x̣ʷemčst, kʷ x̣ʷemčst**
es x̣ʷemčsti – S/he is acting with slight. **čnes x̣ʷemčsti, kʷes x̣ʷemčsti**
qs x̣ʷemčsti – S/he is going to act with slight. **čiqs x̣ʷemčsti, kʷqs x̣ʷemčsti**

x̣ʷmelsmis – S/he slighted s.o. **x̣ʷmelsmn, x̣ʷmelsmntxʷ**
es x̣ʷmelsmms – S/he is slighting s.o. **ies x̣ʷmelsmm, as x̣ʷmelsmm**
qs x̣ʷmelsmms – S/he is going to slight s.o. **iqs x̣ʷmelsmm, aqs x̣ʷmelsmm**

slimy muddler

sttm̓á – slimy muddler, slimy sculpin; *Cottus cognatus*.

sling

snčtatasqe – sling to hurl projectiles.

čłqʷesšn̓tn – sling to hurl projectiles. *rt.: **łoqʷ** – over lay/around; suffix: **...esšn̓, ...sšn̓** – rock; suffix: **...tin, ...tn** – means of/device.*

slingshot

tatasqe – slingshot.

slip

pƛ̓ip – It slipped away/ended. *rt.: **pƛ̓im** – remove, free.*
es pƛ̓pmi – It is slipping away.

es ax̣osi snčłc̓aʔsqá x̣ʷa čen̓ u ax̣í u pƛ̓pus – The hackamore slipped off the horse.

čłax̣ʷq̓ʷpšin, *čłax̣ʷq̓ʷpši* **–** slip. **čłax̣ʷax̣ʷq̓ʷpšin –** slip on both feet.
čłax̣ʷax̣ʷq̓ʷpšin – S/he slipped. **čn čłax̣ʷax̣ʷq̓ʷpšin, kʷ čłax̣ʷax̣ʷq̓ʷpšin**

čn čłax̣ʷax̣ʷq̓ʷpšin u čn tk̓ʷuk̓ʷ – I slipped and fell down.

i oól̓ – It is slippery.
i nʔoólqs – slippery road.

k̓ʷłištalqs, *k̓ʷłišta* **–** under clothing; slip for a dress. *suffix: **...lqs, ...alqs** – clothes.*

łixʷp – slip/pull/put something fitted over an object. *See: **pull over**.*

yomšniš – step with tensed leg so as not to slip and/or fall. *(i.e., walking on ice, walking on a wet floor, etc.) See: **step**.*

slipper

słxʷłxʷpšin – slippers, sandles, anything you slip on. *rt.: **łxʷp** – slip over; suffix: **...šin, ...šn** – foot.*

slippery

i oól̓ – It is slippery.

i čł'oóľ – The surface is slippery.
oóľlexʷ – slippery ground.
i oóľlexʷ – The ground is slippery.
i n'oóľqs – The road is slippery.

čł'oóľ x̣lełp – The floor is slick. **iše i oóľ łu sxʷuymtkʷ** – Ice is slippery.

The **i** following uvular consonants (UC) and the glottal stop ʔ sound like English "*ey*" as in the words *they, hey, whey*, etc. Salish UC are: **q, q̇, qʷ, q̇ʷ, x̣, x̣ʷ**. For example, the suffix ...**qin** – head/top, is often spelled using English *ey* as "q*ey*n". So **qi, q̇i, qʷi, q̇ʷi, x̣i, x̣ʷi**, may be spelled with English *ey* as **q***ey*, **q̇***ey*, **qʷ***ey*, **q̇ʷ***ey*, **x̣***ey*, **x̣ʷ***ey* in other texts.

slit

nič – cut; slice; saw. *See:* ***cut.***

slither

čewileʔ – movement of a snake; slither.
i čewileʔ – It slithers.

es čewileʔi – It is slithering.

sčewileʔ – snake; garter snake; general term for snake.

yananq̇ʷ – wiggle. *See:* ***wiggle.***
i yanaq̇ʷ – It slithers.
yanaq̇ʷ – worm.

sliver

łuwečst – get a sliver in the hand/finger. *rt.:* ***ł'um*** *– pierce with sharp object; suffix:* ***...ečst, ...*** *âst – of the hand.*

łuwečstmntm – S/he got a sliver. **qʷo łuwečstmntm, kʷ łuwečstmntm**

łuwečstmis – S/he poked s.o.'s hand/finger. **łuwečstmn, kʷ łuwečstmntxʷ**

slobber

nawpcin – drool; slobber. *See:* ***drool.***

slope

ułkʷpulexʷ, *ułkʷpu* – downward slope.
es ułkʷpulexʷ – It is downward sloping.
es łułkʷpulexʷ – It is slightly downward sloping.

łšlšált – upward slope.

slow

šept – slow.
šept – S/he/it is slow. **čn šept, kʷ šept**
sšymł šept – S/he/it is the slowest.

łkʷk̓ʷiyet, *łkʷk̓ʷi* – go slow; slowly.
łkʷk̓ʷiyet – S/he went slow. **čn łkʷk̓ʷiyet, kʷ łkʷk̓ʷiyet**
es łkʷk̓ʷiyeti – S/he is going slow. **čnes łkʷk̓ʷiyeti, kʷes łkʷk̓ʷiyeti**

łkʷk̓ʷiyetsts – S/he made s.o. go slow. **łkʷk̓ʷiyetstn, łkʷk̓ʷiyetstxʷ**
es łkʷk̓ʷiyetms – S/he is going to make s.o. go slow. **ies łkʷk̓ʷiyetm, as łkʷk̓ʷiyetm**

łkʷk̓ʷiyetš – Go slow. *cmd.*
łkʷk̓ʷiyetmskʷ – Make him/her/it go slow. *cmd.*

x̣ił i łkʷk̓ʷi – Slow a little.

łkʷk̓ʷiyasq̇t – slow day.

nkʷk̓ʷiyecin – speak slowly; speak gently.
nkʷk̓ʷiyecini – S/he is speaking slowly. **čn nkʷk̓ʷiyecin, kʷ nkʷk̓ʷiyecin**
es nkʷk̓ʷiyecini – S/he is speaking slowly. **čnes nkʷk̓ʷiyecini, kʷes nkʷk̓ʷiyecini**

nkʷk̓ʷiyecinmis – S/he spoke slowly to s.o. **nkʷk̓ʷiyecinmn, kʷ nkʷk̓ʷiyecinmntxʷ**

s.t. - something, the 3rd person
(s.t.) - something implied
s.o. - someone, the 3rd person
sl. - singular form
pl. - plural form
rt. - root word
cmd. - command
lit. - literally
fig. - figuratively
i.e., - for example
See: - Redirection to a related word.

es nkʷk̓ʷiyecinmms – S/he is speaking slowly to s.o. **ies nkʷk̓ʷiyecinmm, as nkʷk̓ʷiyecinmm**

nkʷk̓ʷiyeciniš – Speak slowly. *cmd.*
nkʷk̓ʷiyecinmnt – Speak slowly to him/her. *cmd.*

slowpoke **čén –** tarry; slowpoke.
čnčénmist – S/he was being a slowpoke. **čn čnčénmist, kʷ čnčénmist**
es čnčénmisti – S/he is being a slowpoke. **čnes čnčénmist, kʷes čnčénmisti**
qs čnčénmisti – S/he is going to be a slowpoke. **čiqs čnčénmist, kʷqs čnčénmisti**

čénčnt – be a slowpoke.
čéčeṅeˀ – slow one, affectionately.
čnčénlš – S/he was poking around; S/he was being a slowpoke.
es čénmscuti – S/he is being slow. **čnes čénmscuti, kʷes čénmscuti**

slush **es ṗṅcoti,** *es ṗṅco* – It is raining slush; it is making itself stick to something. *(wet slushy snow) rt.:* ***ṗṫam*** *– splatter. See:* ***splatter.***

es ołépíˀi – It is sleeting.

small **łkʷk̓ʷṅumet,** *kʷk̓ʷṅume* – little thing; small thing.
łkʷk̓ʷnéłxʷ – little house.

ye exʷ łkʷk̓ʷṅu – gee this little one. *(said in surprise)* **čeṅ łu šymł łkʷkʷnumeˀ –** Which is the smallest?

k̓ʷiyumeˀ – tiny one.
łkʷk̓ʷiyumsts – S/he made s.t. be small. **łkʷk̓ʷiyumsts, łkʷk̓ʷiyumsts**
es łkʷk̓ʷiyumm – S/he is making s.t. be small. **ies łkʷk̓ʷiyum, as łkʷk̓ʷiyum**
qs łkʷk̓ʷiyumm – S/he is going to make s.t. be small. **iqs łkʷk̓ʷiyum, aqs łkʷk̓ʷiyum**

es łkʷk̓ʷistlsmisti – S/he has a small opinion of one's self. **čnes łkʷk̓ʷistlsmisti, kʷes łkʷk̓ʷistlsmisti**

k̓ʷiyusqax̣e – tiny horse.
skʷk̓ʷimlt – young; child.

łkʷk̓ʷiyumeˀ – little tiny one.
łkʷk̓ʷimalqʷ, *łkʷk̓ʷima* – short person; short wood.
łkʷk̓ʷimélxʷ – little house.
łkʷk̓ʷimspuus – small hearted.
łkʷk̓ʷimesšn – small stone.
łkʷk̓ʷimaposqn – small mouth.
łkʷk̓ʷimist – crouch; squat low; make self small. *See:* ***crouch.***
łkʷk̓ʷimscut – humble one's self; be humble; make one's self small. *See:* ***humble.***

łkʷk̓ʷiyomqn – small voice; feminine voice; high pitch voice.
es łkʷk̓ʷiyomqn – S/he/it has a small voice. **kʷes łkʷk̓ʷiyomqn, kʷes łkʷk̓ʷiyomqn**
es łkʷk̓ʷiyomqni – S/he/it is speaking with a small voice. **kʷes łkʷk̓ʷiyomqni, kʷes łkʷk̓ʷiyomqni**

łkʷk̓ʷiyet, *łkʷk̓ʷi* – go slow; slowly. *See:* ***slow.***
nkʷk̓ʷiyecin – speak slowly; speak gently. *See:* ***slow.***

k̓ʷimł... – *prefix indicating something is little.*
k̓ʷimłqpełc̓eˀ – big plate.
k̓ʷimłx̣est – kinda good.
k̓ʷimłpx̣pax̣t – little wise.

k̇ʷimsmłič – small salmon.
k̇ʷimsiċm – small blanket.

k̇ʷimłq̇sip – short time.

łccimet, *łccime* – little things; small things.
sccṁelt – children.
nłccṁeys – little teeth.
č̇łccṁus, *č̇łccṁu* – beads.

smallpox

spoct – chicken pox; smallpox.

smart

px̣páx̣t – smart; clever; have knowledge; have wisdom.
px̣px̣twilš – become smart. *suffix:* ***...wilš*** *– developmental.*
es px̣px̣twilši – S/he is getting smart. **čnes px̣px̣twilši, kʷes px̣px̣twilši**

spx̣páx̣t – that which is guidance, wisdom and smarts; spirit.
pepáx̣eʔ – wise one, affectionately.

sisyus – smart; clever; good at something.
sisyus – S/he is smart. **čn sisyus, kʷ sisyus**

uł sisyus – those smart ones.
sesiẏeʔ – clever one, affectionately.

xʷʔit łu sisyus ƛ̓eʔkʷilš – There are lots of smart, powerful medicine men. **swe łu sisyus** – Who is smart?

siscut – act better; smarty.
siscut – S/he was acting smart. **čn siscut, kʷ siscut**
es siscuti – S/he is acting smart. **čnes siscuti, kʷes siscuti**
qs siscuti – S/he is going to act smart. **čiqs siscuti, kʷqs siscuti**
siscúʔut – They were acting smart. **qeʔ siscut, p siscut**
es siscúʔuti – They are acting smart. **qeʔes siscuti, pes siscuti**
qs siscúʔuti – They are going to act smart. **qeʔqs siscuti, pqs siscuti**

sisiscut – know-it-all; show-off.
sisiscut – S/he was showing off. **čn sisiscut, kʷ sisiscut**
es sisiscuti – S/he is showing off. **čnes sisiscuti, kʷes sisiscuti**
qs sisiscuti – S/he is going to show off. **čiqs sisiscuti, kʷqs sisiscuti**

tam ṫul̇ – tremendous; outstanding; extreme; excellent. *See:* ***excellent.***

wil – faulty; wrong; wicked. *See:* ***wicked.***

smash

łóc – smash, mash.
łócm – S/he smashed. **čnł ócm, kʷ łócm**
es łóci – S/he is smashing. **ies łóci, as łóci**
qs łóci – S/he is going to smash. **iqs łóci, aqs łóci**

łócis – S/he smashed s.t. **łócn, łócntxʷ**
es łócms – S/he is smashing s.t. **ies łócm, as łócm**
qs łócms – S/he is going to smash s.t. **iqs łócm, aqs łócm**
łóʔocis – They smashed s.t. **qeʔ łócntm, łócntp**
es łócms – They are smashing s.t. **qeʔes łócm, es łócmp**
qs łócms – They are going to smash s.t. **qeʔqs łócm, qs łócmp**

łóct – It is mashed.

The **i** following uvular consonants (UC) and the glottal stop ʔ sound like English *"ey"* as in the words *they, hey, whey,* etc. Salish UC are: **q, q̇, qʷ, q̇ʷ, x̣, x̣ʷ**. For example, the suffix ...**qin** – head/top, is often spelled using English *ey* as "q*ey*n". So **qi, q̇i, qʷi, q̇ʷi, x̣i, x̣ʷi**, may be spelled with English *ey* as **q***ey*, **q̇***ey*, **qʷ***ey*, **q̇ʷ***ey*, **x̣***ey*, **x̣ʷ***ey* in other texts.

s.t. - something, the 3rd person
(s.t.) - something implied
s.o. - someone, the 3rd person
sl. - singular form
pl. - plural form
rt. - root word
cmd. - command
lit. - literally
fig. - figuratively
i.e., - for example
See: - Redirection to a related word.

es łóct – It got smashed.

łóccnuis – S/he smashed s.t. **łóccnun, łóccnuntxʷ**
es łócms – S/he is smashing s.t. **ies łócm, as łócm**

sxʷłócm – one tasked to smash.
łócmn – something used to smash.
scłóc – something that has been smashed.

łóciš – Smash. *cmd.*
łócnt – Smash it. *cmd.*
łocčst – S/he smashed his/her hand. **čn łocčst, kʷ łocčst**
łocqn – smashed head.

łócntxʷ łu sċmqin – Mash the brains. **łócn isťumčst** – I smashed my thumb.

tmwalš – crumble apart and fall. *(i.e., cliff rocks fall, landslide, etc.) See: **fall**.*

smear **miƛ̓** – smear; rub something; spread something on something.
i miƛ̓ – It is smeared.

miƛ̓is – S/he smeared s.t. **miƛ̓n, miƛ̓ntxʷ**
es miƛ̓ms – S/he is smearing s.t. **ies miƛ̓m, as miƛ̓m**
qs miƛ̓ms – S/he is going to smear s.t. **iqs miƛ̓m, aqs miƛ̓m**
míʔiƛ̓is – They smeared s.t. **qeʔ miƛ̓ntm, miƛ̓ntp**

čmiƛ̓mn – butter.

mƛ̓miƛ̓šn – smear something on the feet.
mƛ̓miƛ̓šnm – S/he/it smeared one's feet. **čn mƛ̓miƛ̓šnm, kʷ mƛ̓miƛ̓šnm**
es mƛ̓miƛ̓šni – S/he/it is smearing one's feet. **čnes mƛ̓miƛ̓šni, kʷes mƛ̓miƛ̓šni**
qs mƛ̓miƛ̓šni – S/he/it is going to smear one's feet. **čiqs mƛ̓miƛ̓šni, kʷqs mƛ̓miƛ̓šni**

mƛ̓miƛ̓čst – smear something on the hands. *suffix: **...ečst, ...čst** – of the hand.*
mƛ̓miƛ̓čstm – S/he/it smeared one's hands. **čn mƛ̓miƛ̓čstm, kʷ mƛ̓miƛ̓čstm**
es mƛ̓miƛ̓čsti – S/he/it is smearing one's hands. **čnes mƛ̓miƛ̓čsti, kʷes mƛ̓miƛ̓čsti**
qs mƛ̓miƛ̓čsti – S/he/it is going to smear one's hands. **čiqs mƛ̓miƛ̓čsti, kʷqs mƛ̓miƛ̓čsti**

miƛ̓stmn – I smeared you. **mƛ̓miƛ̓šn t ṁṅéč** – Crap smeared on both feet. **ṅe cxʷuy qs mƛ̓miƛ̓čsti** – When s/he comes s/he will smear his/her hands.

smell **suṁm** – smell something; sniff.
smsuṁm – S/he/it smelled. **čn smsuṁm, kʷ smsuṁm**
es smsuṁi – S/he/it is smelling. **čnes smsuṁi, kʷes smsuṁi**
qs smsuṁi – S/he/it is going to smell. **čiqs smsuṁi, kʷqs smsuṁi**
smsúʔuṁm – They smelled. **qeʔ smsuṁm, p smsuṁm**
es smsúʔuṁi – They are smelling. **qeʔes smsuṁi, pes smsuṁi**
qs smsúʔuṁi – They are going to smell. **qeʔqs smsuṁi, pqs smsuṁi**

suṁis – S/he/it smelled s.t. **suṁn, suṁntxʷ**
es suṁms – S/he/it is smelling s.t. **ies suṁm, as suṁm**
qs suṁms – S/he/it is going to smell s.t. **iqs suṁm, aqs suṁm**
súʔuṁis – They smelled s.t. **qeʔ suṁntm, suṁntp**
es súʔuṁms – They are smelling s.t. **qeʔes suṁm, es suṁmp**
qs súʔuṁms – They are going to smell s.t. **qeʔqs suṁm, qs suṁmp**

suṁiš – Smell. *cmd.*

suṁnt – You smell it. *cmd.*
nsuṁkʷnt – Smell the water/liquid. *cmd.*

es suṁlexʷi – It is smelling the ground. *suffix: **...ulexʷ**– land.*

qʷo suṁnt – Smell me. **ha aqs suṁm –** Are you going to smell it?

nsuṁkʷ – smell liquids.
nsuṁkʷm – S/he/it smelled the liquid. **čn nsuṁkʷm, kʷ nsuṁkʷm**
es nsuṁkʷi – S/he/it is smelling the liquid. **čnes nsuṁkʷi, kʷes nsuṁkʷi**
qs nsuṁkʷi – S/he/it is going to smell the liquid. **čiqs nsuṁkʷi, kʷqs nsuṁkʷi**

nsuṁkʷis – S/he/it smelled the liquid. **nsuṁkʷn, kʷ nsuṁkʷntxʷ**
es nsuṁkʷms – S/he/it is smelling the liquid. **ies nsuṁkʷm, as nsuṁkʷm**
qs nsuṁkʷms – S/he/it is going to smell the liquid. **iqs nsuṁkʷm, aqs nsuṁkʷm**

The **i** following uvular consonants (UC) and the glottal stop **ʔ** sound like English "*ey*" as in the words th*ey*, h*ey*, wh*ey*, etc. Salish UC are: **q**, **q̇**, **qʷ**, **q̇ʷ**, **x̣**, **x̣ʷ**. For example, the suffix ...**qin** – head/top, is often spelled using English *ey* as "q*ey*n". So **qi**, **q̇i**, **qʷi**, **q̇ʷi**, **x̣i**, **x̣ʷi**, may be spelled with English *ey* as **q***ey*, **q̇***ey*, **qʷ***ey*, **q̇ʷ***ey*, **x̣***ey*, **x̣ʷ***ey* in other texts.

es susawqsi – sniffing the air. *(Animals often do this when they put their nose up and look for a smell, when they are being alert.)*

nsoṁqs – sniff something. *circumfix: **n...aqs**– nose, road, pointed. See: **sniff**.*

...ałq – *suffix indicating a smell, accompaniment.*
x̣sałq – S/he/it smells good. **čn x̣sałq, kʷ x̣sałq**
č̇sałq – S/he/it smells bad. **čn č̇sałq, kʷ č̇sałq**
yoyowałq – strong smell.

sṗiqáłq – berry, fruit, raisin. *rt.: **ṗiẏáq**– ready, ripe; suffix: **...ałq**– smell, accompaniment.*
sṫšałq, *sṫša* **–** huckleberry. *rt.: **ṫiš**– sweet; suffix: **...ałq**– smell, accompaniment.*
eċx̣lx̣sałq – smell good like something.
eċx̣lč̇sałq – smell bad like something.
eċx̣lałq – smell like something.
t čeṅ eċx̣lałq – What does it smell like?

x̣sáłq łu sṫšá – The huckleberries smell good. **kʷ eċx̣lx̣sałq t sċéʔeḱʷ –** You smell good like a flower.

puxʷ – has an odor; smells.
i puxʷ – S/he/it smells. **i čn puxʷ, i kʷ puxʷ**

pxʷup – S/he/it had an odor. **čn pxʷup, kʷ pxʷup**
es pxʷpmi – S/he/it is giving off an odor. **čnes pxʷpmi, kʷes pxʷpmi**
qs pxʷpmi – S/he/it is giving off an odor. **čiqs pxʷpmi, kʷqs pxʷpmi**
pxʷúʔup – They had an odor. **qeʔ pxʷup, p pxʷup**

pxʷpnuis – S/he/it succeeded in smelling s.t. **pxʷpnun, pxʷpnuntxʷ**
es pxʷpnunms – S/he/it is smelling s.t. **ies pxʷpnunm, as pxʷpnunm**
qs pxʷpnunms – S/he/it is going to smell s.t. **iqs pxʷpnunm, aqs pxʷpnunm**

s.t. - something, the 3rd person
(s.t.) - something implied
s.o. - someone, the 3rd person
sl. - singular form
pl. - plural form
rt. - root word
cmd. - command
lit. - literally
fig. - figuratively
i.e., - for example
See: - Redirection to a related word.

spxʷup – odor; taste.

pxʷpnunt – Smell it. *cmd.*
pxʷpnwexʷ – They smelled each other. **qeʔ pxʷpnwexʷ, p pxʷpnwexʷ**

pxʷpnuncn – I smell you. **ha p pxʷpnwe t isṗuʔ –** Did you folks smell my fart?
ta ep spxʷup – It has no odor.

sin – pleasant odor; smell of perfume.
i sin – S/he/it has a pleasant odor. **i čn sin, i kʷ sin**

snmscut – S/he/it made one's self smell pleasant. **čn snmscut, kʷ snmscut**

es snmscuti – S/he/it is making one's self smell pleasant. **čnes snmscuti, kʷes snmscuti**
qs snmscuti – S/he/it is going to make one's self smell pleasant. **čiqs snmscuti, kʷqs snmscuti**

senistmis – S/he made s.t./s.o. smell pleasant. **senistmn, senistmntxʷ**
es senistms – S/he is making s.t./s.o smell pleasant. **ies senistm, as senistm**
qs senistms – S/he is going to make s.t./s.o. smell pleasant. **iqs senistm, aqs senistm**

sinmn – something used to make a pleasant smell.
nsinkʷ – pleasant smelling liquid; perfume.

sinałq – smells pleasant. *suffix:* ***...ałq** – smell, accompaniment.*
čsinċeˀ – smells pleasant all over something.

qax̣ – smell bad; stink. *(i.e., body odor, etc.)*
i qax̣ – S/he/it stinks. **i čn qax̣, i kʷ qax̣**

es qax̣mi – S/he/it is giving off a stink smell. **čnes qax̣mi, kʷes qax̣mi**

náq̇ – smell rotten; the smell of rotten meat; smell of excrement.
i náq̇ – It is rotten smelling.

i náq̇ sqeľtč – The meat smeals rotten. **t kʷtisi u qʷo x̣ʷiċšts t ináq̇ sqeľtč –** Big Blanket gave me rotten meat. **ha i kʷ náq̇ –** Did you mess; are you smelly?

łis – smelly; the smell of fish.
i łis – S/he/it is smelly. **i čn łis, i kʷ łis**

łispó – smelly lips/face, fishy smell. *See:* ***lip.***

ix̣ʷwey – smell of animal in rut.

q̇ʷiˀ – smell like smoke.
i q̇ʷiˀ – S/he/it smells like smoke. **i čn q̇ʷiˀ, i kʷ q̇ʷiˀ**

smile

nťuṁs – smile, grin.
es nťuṁsi – S/he/it is smiling. **čnes nťuṁsi, kʷes nťuṁsi**
qs nťuṁsi – S/he/it is going to smile. **čiqs nťuṁsi, kʷqs nťuṁsi**

es nłtťuṁsi – S/he/it is smiling a little. **čnes nłtťuṁsi, kʷes nłtťuṁsi**

nťuṁsiš – Smile; grin. *cmd.*

ta kʷ qes nťuṁsm i kʷ łén – Do not smile, look real mean.

łoyncut – smile; laugh a little.
łoyncut – S/he laughed a little. **čn łoyncut, kʷ łoyncut**
es łoyncuti – S/he is laughing a little. **čnes łoyncuti, kʷes łoyncuti**
qs łoyncuti – S/he is going to laugh a little. **čiqs łoyncuti, kʷqs łoyncuti**

łoyncutš – Smile. *(little laugh) cmd.*

smoke

smˀot – smoke.
i mˀot – It is smoky.

mˀotulexʷ – smoky land.
es mˀotulexʷi – It is smoky all over.
nmotqnełxʷ, *nmotqne* **–** smoke coming our of a house/tipi/chimney.

čmomotus – have smoke in the eyes. *circumfix:* ***č...us** – spherical object; eyes.*
čmotus – have smoke in one eye.

čmomotus – S/he/it had smoke in the eyes. **čn čmomotus, kʷ čmomotus**
es čmomotusi – S/he/it is getting smoke in the eyes. **čnes čmomotusi, kʷes čmomotusi**
qs čmomotusi – S/he/it is going to get smoke in the eyes. **čiqs čmomotusi, kʷqs čmomotusi**

méṅxʷ – smoke something. *(i.e., tobacco, etc.)*
meṅxʷ – S/he smoked. **čn meṅxʷ, kʷ meṅxʷ**
es meṅxʷi – S/he is smoking. **čnes meṅxʷi, kʷes meṅxʷi**
qs meṅxʷi – S/he is going to smoke. **čiqs meṅxʷi, kʷqs meṅxʷi**
méʔeṅxʷ – They smoked. **qeʔ meṅxʷ, p meṅxʷ**
es méʔeṅxʷi – They are smoking. **qeʔes meṅxʷi, pes meṅxʷi**
qs méʔeṅxʷi – They are going to smoke. **qeʔqs meṅxʷi, pqs meṅxʷi**

es mnmeṅxʷi – S/he is smoking and smoking. **čnes mnmeṅxʷi, kʷes mnmeṅxʷi**

mnxʷemn – one inclined to smoke. *suffix: **...emn** – one inclined to do.*
snméṅxʷ, *snmé* – smoking pipe.

čiqs k̓ʷis meṅxʷi – I am going to go smoke. **kʷ mnxʷemn –** You smoke a lot.

q̇ʷiʔ – smell like smoke.
i q̇ʷiʔ – S/he/it smells like smoke. **i čn q̇ʷiʔ, i kʷ q̇ʷiʔ**

ṗumlxʷm – smoke buckskin. *rt.: **ṗum** – orange; suffix: **...elxʷ** – skin/hide.*
ṗumlxʷm – S/he smoked buckskin. **čn ṗumlxʷm, kʷ ṗumlxʷm**
es ṗumlxʷi – S/he is smoking buckskin. **čnes ṗumlxʷi, kʷes ṗumlxʷi**
qs ṗumlxʷi – S/he is going to smoke buckskin. **čiqs ṗumlxʷi, kʷqs ṗumlxʷi**

scṗumlxʷ – smoked hide. *prefix: **sc...** – s.t. that's been done/made/prepared.*

smoke alarm

liwmn smʔót – smoke alarm.

smooth

ṗaƛ̓ – smooth texture.
ṗaƛ̓is – S/he made it smooth. **ṗaƛ̓n, ṗaƛ̓ntxʷ**
es ṗaƛ̓ms – S/he is making it smooth. **ies ṗaƛ̓m, as ṗaƛ̓m**
qs ṗaƛ̓ms – S/he is going to make it smooth. **iqs ṗaƛ̓m, aqs ṗaƛ̓m**

i ṗaƛ̓ – It is smooth.
ṗaƛ̓ntm – It was made smooth.

ṗaƛ̓nt – Make it smooth. *cmd.*
ṗaƛ̓mskʷ – Smooth it. *cmd.*
ṗaƛ̓mulexʷ – smooth area; smooth land.
ṗaƛ̓mulexʷnt – Smooth the area. *cmd.*

ṗaƛ̓qineʔ – mushroom, morel.

šiƛ̓ – flat/even; aligned; straight; ordered. *See: **flat**.*

smother

tqup – suffocate (not dead); restrict air flow; lacking air; winded/out of breath. *See: **suffocate**.*

smudge

npomqstn – smudge; a plant used to purify one's self referred to as smudge. *(i.e., juniper, cedar, sweetgrass, etc.) suffix: **...tin, ...tn** – means of/device.*
npomqsm – S/he/it smudged. **čn npomqsm, kʷ npomqsm**
es npomqsi – S/he/it is smudging. **čnes npomqsi, kʷes npomqsi**
qs npomqsi – S/he/it is going to smudge. **čiqs npomqsi, aqs npomqsi**

npomqsis – S/he/it smudged s.o./s.t. **npomqsn, npomqsntxʷ**

The **i** following uvular consonants (UC) and the glottal stop **ʔ** sound like English "*ey*" as in the words th*ey*, h*ey*, wh*ey*, etc. Salish UC are: **q, q̇, qʷ, q̇ʷ, x̣, x̣ʷ**. For example, the suffix **...qin** – head/top, is often spelled using English *ey* as "q*ey*n". So **qi, q̇i, qʷi, q̇ʷi, x̣i, x̣ʷi**, may be spelled with English *ey* as **q***ey*, **q̇***ey*, **qʷ***ey*, **q̇ʷ***ey*, **x̣***ey*, **x̣ʷ***ey* in other texts.

s.t. - something, the 3rd person
(s.t.) - something implied
s.o. - someone, the 3rd person
sl. - singular form
pl. - plural form
rt. - root word
cmd. - command
lit. - literally
fig. - figuratively
i.e., - for example
See: - Redirection to a related word.

es npomqsms – S/he/it is smudging s.o./s.t. **ies npomqsm, as npomqsm**
qs npomqsms – S/he/it is going to smudge s.o./s.t. **iqs npomqsm, aqs npomqsm**

npomqsiš – Smudge. *cmd.*
npomqsnt – Smudge him/her. *cmd.*

smutt **nt̓mčim –** flick with the finger; place a bet down as in flicking down a card or money. *See: **flick**. Reservation colloquial English.*

snack **łmaʔqcan –** eat a little, fast; eat a snack. *See: **eat**.*

snag **nq̇lq̇l̓xʷé –** snag fish. *See: **hook**.*
nq̇lq̇l̓xʷé – S/he snagged fish. **čn nq̇lq̇l̓xʷé, kʷ nq̇lq̇l̓xʷé**
es nq̇lq̇l̓xʷé – S/he is snagging fish. **čnes nq̇lq̇l̓xʷé, kʷes nq̇lq̇l̓xʷé**
qs nq̇lq̇l̓xʷé – S/he is going to snag fish. **čiqs nq̇lq̇l̓xʷé, kʷqs nq̇lq̇l̓xʷé**

wičtn ci sqltmi łu nq̇l̓xʷé t kʷtunt sw̓éwł – I saw the man who caught that big fish. **isc̓éšt či es nq̇l̓xʷé. –** My brother-in-law is the one who caught it.

čéyeʔ – snag; dead tree; wood dry with age.

es nq̇aqʷin – tree snag.

q̇ʷéllš – dead tree.

kʷcič – the act of falling pertaining to a *single fixed object. (i.e., tree, post, house, etc.) See: **fall**.*

snail **t̓am̓yócn,** *t̓am̓yó* **–** cowry; snail; leech. *rt.: **t̓am –** lightly suck. See: **suck**.*

čyalk̓ʷičn̓ – snail. *suffix: **...ičn̓ –** back.*

snake **sčewileʔ –** snake; garter snake; general term for snake.
x̣eʔulexʷ – rattlesnake; *Crotalus viridis.*
sx̣ʷnu – bull snake; gopher snake; *Pituophis catenifer.*
npƛ̓áċeʔ – eastern racer, green racer; *Coluber constrictor.*

čewileʔ – movement of a snake; slither. *See: **slither**.*

snake dance **ṅiʔṅiṅṗmncut,** *ṅiʔṅiṅṗmncú* **–** snake dancing.
ṅiʔṅiṅṗmncut – S/he snake danced. **čn ṅiʔṅiṅṗmncut, kʷ ṅiʔṅiṅṗmncut**
es ṅiʔṅiṅṗmncuti – S/he is snake dancing. **čnes ṅiʔṅiṅṗmncuti, kʷes ṅiʔṅiṅṗmncuti**
qs ṅiʔṅiṅṗmncuti – S/he is going to snake dance. **čiqs ṅiʔṅiṅṗmncuti, kʷqs ṅiʔṅiṅṗmncuti**
ṅiʔṅiṅṗmncúʔut – They snake danced. **qeʔ ṅiʔṅiṅṗmncut, p ṅiʔṅiṅṗmncut**
es ṅiʔṅiṅṗmncúʔuti – They are snake dancing. **qeʔes ṅiʔṅiṅṗmncuti, pes ṅiʔṅiṅṗmncuti**
qs ṅiʔṅiṅṗmncúʔuti – They are going to snake dance. **qeʔqs ṅiʔṅiṅṗmncuti, pqs ṅiʔṅiṅṗmncuti**

sṅiʔṅiṅṗmncutn – snake dance.
ṅiʔṅiṅṗmstemn – one inclined to snake dance. *suffix: **...emn –** one inclined to do.*
sṅiʔṅiṅṗmnsqin – snake dance song.

ṅiʔṅiṅṗmncutš – Snake dance. *cmd.*
ṅiʔṅiṅṗmncutwi – All of you snake dance. *cmd.*
es ṅiʔṅiṅṗmnwelsi – S/he wants to snake dance.

es ṅiʔṅiṅṗmstemisti – S/he is wanting to snake dance. **čnes ṅiʔṅiṅṗmstemisti, kʷes ṅiʔṅiṅṗmstemisti**

es ṅiʔṅiṅṗmnsqiʔini – S/he is singing a snake dance song. **čnes ṅiʔṅiṅṗmnsqiʔini, kʷes ṅiʔṅiṅṗmnsqiʔini**

snap

nmals – snap eyes in disgust.
nmalsmis – S/he snapped eyes in disgust at s.o. **nmalsmn, nmalsmntxʷ**
nmáʔalsmis – They snapped eyes in disgust at s.o. **qeʔ nmalsmntm, nmalsmntp**

nmlmalsmis – S/he snapped eyes in disgust at s.o. several times. **nmlmalsmn, nmlmalsmntxʷ**

sxʷnmalsm – one tasked to snap eyes at people. *prefix:* ***sxʷ...*** *– one tasked to do.*
nmlmalsmemn – one inclined to snap eyes at people. *suffix:* ***...emn*** *– one inclined to do.*

nmalsmnt – Snap eyes at s.o. *cmd.*

ťmčečsm – snap fingers.
ťmčečsm – S/he snapped one's fingers. **čn ťmčečsm, kʷ ťmčečsm**
es ťmčečsi – S/he is snapping one's fingers. **čnes ťmčečsi, kʷes ťmčečsi**
qs ťmčečsi – S/he is going to snap one's fingers. **čiqs ťmčečsi, kʷqs ťmčečsi**

nťmčim – flick with the finger; place a bet down as in flicking down a card or money. *See:* ***flick.***

> The **i** following uvular consonants (UC) and the glottal stop ʔ sound like English "*ey*" as in the words *they, hey, whey,* etc. Salish UC are: **q, q̇, qʷ, q̇ʷ, x̣, x̣ʷ**. For example, the suffix **...qin** – head/top, is often spelled using English *ey* as "q*ey*n". So **qi, q̇i, qʷi, q̇ʷi, x̣i, x̣ʷi,** may be spelled with English *ey* as **q***ey,* **q̇***ey,* **qʷ***ey,* **q̇ʷ***ey,* **x̣***ey,* **x̣ʷ***ey* in other texts.

snare

čṅeyn – snare something; trap something with a snare.
čṅeynm – S/he snared. **čn čṅeynm, kʷ čṅeynm**
es čṅeyni – S/he is snaring. **čnes čṅeyni, kʷes čṅeyni**
qs čṅeyni – S/he is going to snare. **čiqs čṅeyni, kʷqs čṅeyni**

čṅeyis – S/he snared s.t. **čṅeyn, čṅeyntxʷ**
es čṅeyms – S/he is snaring s.t. **ies čṅeym, as čṅeym**
qs čṅeyms – S/he is going to snare s.t. **iqs čṅeym, aqs čṅeym**

čṅeymn – snare.

čnes čṅeyni t słqʷa – I am trapping rabbits.

sneak

k̓ʷłnq̓ʷmist, *k̓ʷłnq̓ʷmi* **–** run away stealthily; sneak away; leave; escape. *See:* ***escape.***

sneak up

eẇet – sneak up on someone or something.
eẇetm – S/he/it sneaked up. **čn eẇetm, kʷ eẇetm**
es eẇeti – S/he/it is sneaking up. **čnes eẇeti, kʷes eẇeti**
qs eẇeti – S/he/it is going to sneak up. **čiqs eẇeti, kʷqs eẇeti**
eẇéʔetm – They sneaked up. **qeʔ eẇetm, p eẇetm**
es eẇéʔeti – They are sneaking up. **qeʔes eẇeti, pes eẇeti**
qs eẇéʔeti – They are going to sneak up. **qeʔqs eẇeti, pqs eẇeti**

sneeze

ťsóʔ – sneeze.
ťsóʔm – S/he sneezed. **čn ťsóʔm, kʷ ťsóʔm**
es ťsóʔi – S/he is sneezing. **čnes ťsóʔi, kʷes ťsóʔi**
qs ťsóʔi – S/he is going to sneeze. **čiqs ťsóʔi, kʷqs ťsóʔi**

ťsóʔiš – Sneeze. *cmd.*

qʷo puʔsmis – S/he thought of me. *(said after you sneeze.)* *See:* ***think.***
puʔsminc – S/he thought of you. *(said to someone after s/he sneezes.)*

> s.t. - something, the 3rd person
> (s.t.) - something implied
> s.o. - someone, the 3rd person
> *sl.* - singular form
> *pl.* - plural form
> *rt.* - root word
> *cmd.* - command
> *lit.* - literally
> *fig.* - figuratively
> *i.e.,* - for example
> *See:* - Redirection to a related word.

sneeze root
sićsečiyeʔ – false hellebore; Indian hellebore; *Veratrum viride.*

sst́sóʔ – sneeze root; false hellebore root; *Veratrum viride.*

sniff
nsoṁqs – sniff something. *circumfix:* ***n...aqs*** *– nose, road, pointed.*
nsoṁqs – S/he/it sniffed (s.t.). **čn nsoṁqs, kʷ nsoṁqs**
es nsoṁqsi – S/he/it is sniffing (s.t.). **čnes nsoṁqsi, kʷes nsoṁqsi**
qs nsoṁqsi – S/he/it is going to sniff (s.t.). **čiqs nsoṁqsi, kʷqs nsoṁqsi**
nsoṁqsis – S/he/it sniffed s.t. **nsoṁqsn, nsoṁqsntxʷ**
es nsoṁqsms – S/he/it is sniffing s.t. **ies nsoṁqsm, as nsoṁqsm**
qs nsoṁqsms – S/he/it is going to sniff s.t. **iqs nsoṁqsm, aqs nsoṁqsm**

ntmaqsm – suck/snort/sniffle through the nose. *(i.e., snot, drugs, etc.) rt.:* ***ṫum*** *– suck; circumfix:* ***n...aqs*** *– nose, road.*
ntmaqsm – S/he sniffled. **čn ntmaqsm, kʷ ntmaqsm**
es ntmaqsi – S/he is sniffling. **čnes ntmaqsi, kʷes ntmaqsi**
qs ntmaqsi – S/he is going to sniffle. **čiqs ntmaqsi, kʷqs ntmaqsi**
ntmáʔaqsm – They sniffled. **qeʔ ntmaqsm, p ntmaqsm**
es ntmáʔaqsi – They are sniffling. **qeʔes ntmaqsi, pes ntmaqsi**
ntmaqsis – S/he snorted s.t. **ntmaqsn, ntmaqsntxʷ**

es ntmaqsms – S/he is sniffling. **ies ntmaqsm, as ntmaqsm**
qs ntmaqsi – S/he is going to sniffle. **čiqs ntmaqsm, kʷqs ntmaqsm**
ntmáʔaqsis – They snorted s.t. **qeʔ ntmaqsntm, ntmaqsntp**
es ntmáʔaqsms – They are snorting s.t. **qeʔes ntmaqsm, es ntmaqsmp**

ntmaqsnt – Snort it. *cmd.*

suṁm – smell something; sniff. *See:* ***smell.***

snore
x̣ʷoq̇ʷlqʷs – snore.
x̣ʷoq̇ʷlqʷs – S/he/it snored. **čn x̣ʷoq̇ʷlqʷs, kʷ x̣ʷoq̇ʷlqʷs**
es x̣ʷoq̇ʷlqʷsi – S/he/it is snoring. **čnes x̣ʷoq̇ʷlqʷsi, kʷes x̣ʷoq̇ʷlqʷsi**
qs x̣ʷoq̇ʷlqʷsi – S/he/it is going to snore. **čiqs x̣ʷoq̇ʷlqʷsi, kʷqs x̣ʷoq̇ʷlqʷsi**

snort
ntmaqsm – suck/snort/sniffle through the nose. *(i.e., snot, drugs, etc.) See:* ***sniff.***

snot
snos – snot.
nosiš – Blow your nose. *cmd.*

snnostn – Anything used to blow your nose; a device for snot. *prefix:* ***sn...*** *– a place of; suffix:* ***...tin, ...tn*** *– means of/device.*

snosmn – Anything used to blow your nose; a utensil for snot. *prefix:* ***sn...*** *– a place of; suffix:* ***...min, ...mn*** *– instrument/tool.*

nʔaṗaqstn – nose wiper; anything used to wipe the nose. *rt.:* ***eṗm*** *– wipe; suffix:* ***...tin, ...tn*** *– means of/device.*

nawawpaqs – have a runny nose.
es nawapaqsi – S/he/it has a runny nose. **čnes nawapaqsi, kʷes nawapaqsi**

snow
sméḱʷt – snow on the ground.
słṁemḱʷt – little snow. *(When the ground isn't all covered).*

es amti łu smeḱʷt – The snow is melting.
smḱʷtseys – snowflake.

łq̓łq̓eys – big snowflakes. *rt.: **łaq̓** – wide.*
smlq̓ʷtsmek̓ʷt – snowball.
smk̓ʷtselixʷ – snowman.

l čeṅ u ečx̣lsqʷest łu asmek̓ʷt – How deep is your snow?

čmuk̓ʷt – snow building up on something.
čmk̓ʷeẃt – The snow built up on it.

es čmuk̓ʷt – It has snow on it.
es čmuk̓ʷti t smek̓ʷt – Snow is building up on it.

mx̣ʷop – It snowed.
es mx̣ʷpmi – It is snowing.
qs mx̣ʷpmi – It is going to snow.

mx̣ʷntes – It snowed on s.t.
es mx̣ʷoms – It is snowing on s.t.

es łmx̣ʷpmi – It is snowing a little.

mx̣ʷntem – S/he/it got snowed on.
qʷo mx̣ʷntem – I got snowed on.

smx̣ʷóp – snows; age; year.

mx̣ʷqinm – It snowed on top. *suffix: **...qin, ...qn** – top.*
es mx̣ʷqini – It is snowing on the mountaintops.

mx̣ʷpmi ci č esmq̓ʷmoq̓ʷ – It is snowing in the mountains.

mx̣ʷičṅ – snow spot on mountain; snowed on the ridge. *suffix: **...ičṅ** – back.*
čmx̣ʷmx̣ʷičṅ – snow spots on mountain.

qʷést – deep snow. *See: **deep**.*

es pt̓ncoti, ***es pt̓nco*** **–** It is raining slush; it is making itself stick to something. *(wet slushy snow) See: **slush**.*

es ołépiˀi – It is sleeting

es xʷˀéysi – It is raining/snowing hard.

pxʷtṅi – snowdrift. *See: **snowdrift**.*

čsačtásq̓t, ***čsačtá*** **–** winter's last attempt at a big snow storm. *(In early spring, often indicated by having snow on one side of s.t. such as trees or poles.)*

nq̓oƛ̓šis – spring snows, off and on snowing.

titimulexʷ – place of no snow during the winter.
k̓ʷłtitimulexʷ – no snow under something but snow is everywhere else. *(i.e., trees, logs, etc.)*

uyásq̓t, ***uyá*** **–** the storm/weather ended. *See: **storm**.*

snowball
smlq̓ʷtsmek̓ʷt – snowball.

snowberry
stmtmniˀáłq, ***stmtmniˀá*** **–** snowberry; *Symphoricarpos albus.*

snow-blind
nčk̓ʷlus – snow-blind. *rt.: **čik̓ʷ** – shiny; prefix: **n...** – inside; suffix: **č...us** – spherical object; eyes.*

The **i** following uvular consonants (UC) and the glottal stop **ˀ** sound like English "*ey*" as in the words *they, hey, whey*, etc. Salish UC are: **q, q̓, qʷ, q̓ʷ, x̣, x̣ʷ**. For example, the suffix **...qin** – head/top, is often spelled using English *ey* as "q*ey*n". So **qi, q̓i, qʷi, q̓ʷi, x̣i, x̣ʷi**, may be spelled with English *ey* as **q***ey*, **q̓***ey*, **qʷ***ey*, **q̓ʷ***ey*, **x̣***ey*, **x̣ʷ***ey* in other texts.

s.t. - something, the 3rd person
(s.t.) - something implied
s.o. - someone, the 3rd person
sl. - singular form
pl. - plural form
rt. - root word
cmd. - command
lit. - literally
fig. - figuratively
i.e., - for example
See: - Redirection to a related word.

nċk̓ʷlus – S/he got snow-blinded. **čn nċk̓ʷlus, kʷ nċk̓ʷlus**
es nċk̓ʷlusi – S/he is snow-blinded. **čnes nċk̓ʷlusi, kʷes nċk̓ʷlusi**
qs nċk̓ʷlusi – S/he is going to become snow-blinded. **čiqs nċk̓ʷlusi, kʷqs nċk̓ʷlusi**

x̣iṅe m kʷ nċk̓ʷlus – You might get snow-blinded.

snow bunting **łṁṁék̓ʷt** – snow bunting.

snowdrift **pxʷtṅi** – snowdrift.

snowflake **smk̓ʷtseys** – snowflake.

snow goose **ẇuʔẇuʔ** – snow goose; *Chen caerulescens.*

snowman **smk̓ʷtselixʷ** – snowman.

snowshoe **ċewéčšn** – snowshoe; walk in snowshoes.
ċewéčšnm – S/he went snowshoeing. **čn ċewéčšnm, kʷ ċewéčšnm**
es ċewéčšni – S/he is snowshoeing. **čnes ċewéčšni, kʷes ċewéčšni**
qs ċewéčšni – S/he is going to go snowshoeing. **čiqs ċewéčšni, kʷqs ċewéčšni**

sċewéčšn – snowshoes; Bigfoot tracks.

sċwené – Bigfoot; Sasquatch.

snowshoe hare **słqʷá** – rabbit; *Lepus americanus.*

snowy owl **nsp̓šnmé** – snowy owl; *Bubo scandiacus.*

snub **čeṁm** – detest; reject something; have no care for something; snub something. *See:* ***detest.***

soak **łuc** – soak; moisten.
łucis – S/he moisten s.t. **łucn, łucntxʷ**
es łucms – S/he is moistening s.t. **ies łucm, as łucm**
qs łucms – S/he is going to moisten s.t. **iqs łucm, aqs łucm**

nłuckʷ – soak in water.
łcposqncut – moisten one's lips.
čłocqnm – S/he soaked hair. **čn čłocqnm, kʷ čłocqnm**

soap **ċéẇstn** – hand soap. *rt.:* ***ċeẇ*** *– wash; suffix:* ***...tin, ...tn*** *– means of/device.*
ċéẇmn – cloths soap. *suffix:* ***...min, ...mn*** *– instrument/tool.*

soapberry **sx̣ʷósm** – foamberry; buffaloberry; soapberry; *shepherdia canadensis.*

sock **snq̓ʷoƛ̓šn,** *snq̓ʷó* – sock. *rt.:* ***q̓ʷuƛ̓*** *– pad.*
es nq̓ʷoƛ̓šn – S/he is wearing socks. **čnes nq̓ʷoƛ̓šn, kʷes nq̓ʷoƛ̓šn**

nq̓ʷoƛ̓šniš – Put your socks on. *cmd.*

tas nq̓ʷoƛ̓šnm – S/he had no socks on.

sockeye salmon **nt̓kʷus** – sockeye salmon; kokanee salmon; *Oncorhynchus nerka.*

soda **nt̓íškʷ** – sweet liquid; pop; Kool-aid.

čnes susti t nt̓íškʷ – I am drinking pop.

soft **čep** – soft.
i čep – It is soft.
łččép – little soft.
i łččép – It is a little soft.

nčepmn – down; down filling. *rt.: **čep** – soft; prefix: **n...** – inside; suffix: **...min, ...mn** – instrument/tool.*

čéppm – give a present to soothe/soften a bad relationship. *rt.: **čep** – soft.*

łmṁoc – soft; squishy.
łmṁocčst – soft hands. *suffix: **...ečst, ...čst** – of the hand.*
łṁocčst – soft hand. *suffix: **...ečst, ...čst** – of the hand.*

cim – fatty; smooth; soft.
i cmup – It is mellow out, soft.

qʷʔóp – make soft. *(i.e., hide tanning.)*
qʷopstés – S/he made it soft. **qʷopstén, qʷopstéxʷ**
es qʷopims – S/he is making it soft. **ies qʷopim, as qʷopim**

es łqʷqʷop – It's a little soft.

sqʷʔópłxʷ – hole, den *(as of a mouse or rat). rt.: **qʷʔóp** – make soft; suffix: **...etxʷ, ...łxʷ** – house.*

qʷopiskʷ – Make it soft. *cmd.*

ṅe qʷʔóp m ṫqʷntexʷ – When it is softened, you sew it up. **ṅe qʷʔóp m łuxʷntxʷ** – When it is softened up, you rub it back and forth.

uẇał – soften a hide with brains. *(i.e., the process of the hide getting soft from brains.)*
es uẇałi – It is softening.

uẇałis – S/he softened the hide. **uẇałn, uẇałntxʷ**
es uẇałms – S/he is softening the hide. **ies uẇałm, as uẇałm**

yut – make soft, supple or limber by rubbing with the hands. *See: **rub**.*

es ṗaṫ – It is something soft and squishy *(i.e., excrement, person, brains, a wet hide, etc.)*; figuratively to feel tired and loose. *See: **pile**.*

softly **x̣sečstm** – do s.t. softly/gently; do something in a good way. *suffix: **...ečst, ...čst** – of the hand.*
i x̣sečstmnt – Do it softly/gently, pertaining to yourself. *cmd.*
čx̣sečstmnt – Do it softly/gently. *cmd.*

soldier **sólte** – soldier.

sxʷplstwéxʷ – warrior/soldier. *rt.: **puls** – kill; prefix: **sxʷ...** – one tasked to do; suffix: **...wexʷ** – action to each other.*

sxʷx̣eyílš – one tasked to raid; warrior. *See: **raid**.*

šinmsči – woman warrior/soldier.

sole **snčmičn̓šn** – bottom of foot or shoe. *rt.: **čm** – extremity.*

solidfy **imáp** – hardened by cooling; solidified; coagulated. *(i.e., grease, plastic, etc.) See: **hard**.*

solitary **nk̓ʷukʷk̓ʷwilš** – solitary. *suffix: **...wilš** – developmental.*

The **i** following uvular consonants (UC) and the glottal stop **ʔ** sound like English "*ey*" as in the words th*ey*, h*ey*, wh*ey*, etc. Salish UC are: **q, q̇, qʷ, q̇ʷ, x̣, x̣ʷ**. For example, the suffix ...**qin** – head/top, is often spelled using English *ey* as "q*ey*n". So **qi, q̇i, qʷi, q̇ʷi, x̣i, x̣ʷi**, may be spelled with English *ey* as **q***ey*, **q̇***ey*, **qʷ***ey*, **q̇ʷ***ey*, **x̣***ey*, **x̣ʷ***ey* in other texts.

s.t. - something, the 3rd person
(s.t.) - something implied
s.o. - someone, the 3rd person
sl. - singular form
pl. - plural form
rt. - root word
cmd. - command
lit. - literally
fig. - figuratively
i.e., - for example
See: - Redirection to a related word.

es nḱʷukʷḱʷwilši – S/he/it is being solitary. **čnes nḱʷukʷḱʷwilši, kʷes nḱʷukʷḱʷwilši**

es nḱʷukʷḱʷwilš xʷixʷeyuł – It is a solitary animal.

Solomon **salwén** – Solomon.

some **ḱʷiƛ̓t** – some; other; several.
ḱʷiƛ̓t qs cxʷúʔuy – Some are coming. **kʷeṁt čtax̣ʷlé łu ḱʷiƛ̓t še ax̣llá** – Then the others started to do the same.

čn epł tšeẏ ecx̣i pṅ tam xʷʔit – I have some like that but not many.

ałqalqs – have some cloth to make clothing.
ałqalqs – S/he has cloth to make clothing. **čn ałqalqs, kʷ ałqalqs**

ałqełxʷ – have some material to make a house.
ałqełxʷ – S/he has material to make a house. **čn ałqełxʷ, kʷ ałqełxʷ**

somebody **tʔé swe** – somebody.

someday **tʔé piste** – someday.
ṅe tʔe piste – someday. *(more specific)*
ṅe t nḱʷa – one day in the future.

Somers **čšl̓šá** – Somers, Montana.

something **tʔésteṁ** – something.
słetṁ – a little thing.
wičtn tʔésteṁ – I saw something.

sometime **łaqʷlwi** – shows up once in awhile. *See: **infrequent**.*

somewhere **tʔé l čeṅ** – somewhere.

tʔé č čeṅ – somewhere.

son **sqʷséʔ** – son; of mother or father. **sqʷsqʷsé** *pl.*
sqʷqʷsélt, *sqʷqʷsé* – young son; child son.
q̇éʔeẇs – middle son or daughter. *lit. placed in the middle. rt.: **q̇eʔ** – put inside; suffix: **...éẇs** – in between, middle.*
šitmišlt – first born son or daughter.

sckʷ̓l̓sqʷséʔ – foster son. *prefix: **sckʷ̓l̓...** – s.t. that's been made.*
skʷnltsqʷséʔ – godson.
słqʷqʷséʔ – small boy.

isqʷséʔ – my son. **kʷtisi sqʷséʔs** – Big Blanket's son.

song **kʷélm** – song. **kʷlkʷélm** *pl.*
ƛ̓e es nkʷnéʔems łu snwénštn kʷélm – They're already singing the war dance song.

čmštin – personal song.
inčmštin – my song.

snčsplqmncutn – old warrior dance song. *suffix: **...tin, ...tn** – means of/device.*

son-in-law **snéčłxʷ** – son-in-law.
sčʔélp – son/daughter-in-law after death of spouse.

soon **i t šeṅé –** soon.

Sophie **supi –** Sophie.

sore **tẇič –** get sore/stiff from being in one position.
tẇič – S/he got stiff. **čn tẇič, kʷ tẇič**
es tučmisti – S/he is getting stiff. **čnes tučmisti, kʷes tučmisti**
qs tučmisti – S/he is going to get stiff. **čiqs tučmisti, kʷqs tučmisti**

ha ƛ̓e kʷ tẇič – Are you stiff yet? Have you been there a long time? Is it time to go?

ċaál, *ċa* **–** achy; sore; hurting; in pain. *See:* ***ache.***
čn ċaal̓éčst – My hand is aching. *suffix:* ***...ečst, ...čst*** *– of the hand.*
čcax̣élsi – Hurting inside, sick *(in one's mind).*
čċax̣ʷélsi – Sick to your stomach. *(i.e., heartburn, ate to much)*

The **i** following uvular consonants (UC) and the glottal stop **ʔ** sound like English "*ey*" as in the words th*ey*, h*ey*, wh*ey*, etc. Salish UC are: **q**, **q̇**, **qʷ**, **q̇ʷ**, **x̣**, **x̣ʷ**. For example, the suffix ...**qin** – head/top, is often spelled using English *ey* as "q*ey*n". So **qi**, **q̇i**, **qʷi**, **q̇ʷi**, **x̣i**, **x̣ʷi**, may be spelled with English *ey* as **q***ey*, **q̇***ey*, **qʷ***ey*, **q̇ʷ***ey*, **x̣***ey*, **x̣ʷ***ey* in other texts.

i łččéṅ – tender. *(as, a sore spot)*
łččéṅšn – tender footed horse.

mṅmi – single footed horse; horse with a sore foot.

spóct – runny sore.

sorry **ččox̣ʷ,** *čċo* **–** premeditated action; do something on purpose; willful intention. *See:* ***purpose.***
tam isččox̣ʷ – It is not my will; I am sorry.

soul **snx̣ṗéẇs –** lining the inside; soul. *rt.:* ***x̣ṗ*** *– line, coat.*
isnx̣ṗéẇs – my soul.

es cotelixʷ – It takes your soul; startled.

sound **tspmncót,** *tspmncó* **–** sudden sound of voices shouting.

es tspmncóti łu sqelixʷ – The people are starting to shout.

tstsalš – sound of a group making noises. *(i.e., children talking, birds chirping, etc.)*
tstsalš – They made noise. **qeʔ tstsalš, p tstsalš**
es tstsalši – They are making noise. **qeʔes tstsalši, pes tstsalši**
qs tstsalši – They are going to make noise. **qeʔqs tstsalši, pqs tstsalši**

exʷkʷunm – make sound of people and animal voices; someone talking in the distance but not being able to discern what is being said.
exʷkʷunm – S/he made sounds. **čn exʷkʷunm, kʷ exʷkʷunm**
exʷkʷúʔunm – They made sounds. **qeʔ exʷkʷunm, p exʷkʷunm**

exʷkʷunis – S/he/it said it. **exʷkʷunn, exʷkʷunntxʷ**
exʷkʷúʔunis – They said it. **qeʔ exʷkʷunntm, exʷkʷunntp**

exʷexʷkʷunm – Each is making sounds.
cʔexʷexʷkʷunm – hear people coming, talking.

snʔexʷkʷuncn – sound of s.t./s.o. *suffix:* ***...cin, ...cn*** *– action of the mouth.*
snʔexʷkʷuntn – sounds; song. *suffix:* ***...tin, ...tn*** *– means of/device.*

steṁ łu snʔexʷkʷuncis – What is its sound? **steṁ łu snʔexʷkʷuncn x̣ʷl̓ p –** What is the sound for the letter "p"? **iše nʔexʷkʷuncnm łu nqʷq̇ʷosmi –** Dogs make sounds.

s.t. - something, the 3rd person
(s.t.) - something implied
s.o. - someone, the 3rd person
sl. - singular form
pl. - plural form
rt. - root word
cmd. - command
lit. - literally
fig. - figuratively
i.e., - for example
See: - Redirection to a related word.

nt̓ixʷxʷlcn – It is a different sound. *rt.:* ***t̓ixʷlm*** *– different; suffix:* ***...cin, ...cn*** *– action of the mouth. See:* ***different.***

čn nx̣lemn l skʷkʷʔec tʔe u čn susewneʔ – I am afraid of sounds in the dark. *See:* ***hear.***

ca ca ca – sound of tantrum, pitful or wailing cry.

ċiʔ ċiʔ – sound of a mouse squeak.

ċio ċio – sound of a bird squeak.

čaxʷ čaxʷ čaxʷ – sound of hitting wood; knocking sound.

cos – sound of a rattle.

hammm – sound of buzzing flies.

hu hu – sound of an owl.

iox̣ʷ – sound of rushing water.

kʷasss – sound of grease burning.

kʷaskʷas – sound of grease dripping on the fire.

k̇ʷss – sound of water put on a fire.

k̇ʷičč – sound of a falling tree.

laẏ – sound of a single crashing tin/plate.
  laẏiʔiʔ – sound of a single crashing tin/plate.

liq – sound of a string break.

liw – sound of a bell ring.

lox̣ʷ – sound of a heavy object hitting a floor; foot step.

luʔ – sound of a thump; muted foot step.

łakʷ – sound of a slap.

łaṗ – sound of bare feet on a floor.

łiċċċ – sound of a seam tearing.

ło – sound of a continuous rain.

łox̣ łox̣ łox̣ – sound of a mouse scratching.

mal̇l̇l̇ – sound of bubbling liquid.

miyu – sound of a cat meow.

pat pat – sound a bubbling boiling liquid.
  pattt – sound of air/gas expelling.

pmmm – sound a car makes.

pppuwa pppuwa – sound of thunder.

puʔ – sound of hitting a body.

putuie – sound of a rooster cawing *(cock-a-doodle-do).*

ṗaċċ – sound of diarrhea.

ṗaq̇q̇ – sound of dry grass burning.

ṗat̓t̓ – sound of a splattering substance.

ṗiq̓ʷ – sound of a fart.

qx̣ʷx̣ʷx̣ʷ – gargling sound.

t̓aċċċ – sound of a grasshopper.

t̓ał – sound of a slap.

t̓ałłt̓ałł – sound of a galloping horse.

t̓apaxʷ – sound of a large splash.

we – sound a dog makes when barking.

xʷkʷ xʷkʷ – sound of walking in snow.

xʷau – sound of going fast; to go fast. *See:* ***fast.***

yiq̓ – sound of creaking trees.

> The **i** following uvular consonants (UC) and the glottal stop ʔ sound like English "*ey*" as in the words th*ey*, h*ey*, wh*ey*, etc. Salish UC are: **q**, **q̓**, **qʷ**, **q̓ʷ**, **x̣**, **x̣ʷ**. For example, the suffix …**qin** – head/top, is often spelled using English *ey* as "q*ey*n". So **qi**, **q̓i**, **qʷi**, **q̓ʷi**, **x̣i**, **x̣ʷi**, may be spelled with English *ey* as **q***ey*, **q̓***ey*, **qʷ***ey*, **q̓ʷ***ey*, **x̣***ey*, **x̣ʷ***ey* in other texts.

soup

sx̣sétkʷ, *sx̣sé* – soup.

snsx̣sestn – bowl. *prefix:* ***sn…*** *– a place of; suffix:* ***…tin, …tn*** *– means of/device.*

scnpq̓ʷetkʷ, *scnpq̓ʷe* – soup, something put in the water. *prefix:* ***sc…*** *– s.t. that's been done/made/prepared; suffix:* ***…etkʷ, …tkʷ*** *– liquid*

łx̣ʷło scnpq̓ʷe – chokecherry soup.
st̓ša scnpq̓ʷe – huckleberry soup.
x̣mip sqelt̓č scnpq̓ʷe – dry meat soup.

sour

ċuy – sour.

i ċuy – It is sour.
i nċuycn – It tastes sour.
i nċuykʷ – It is sour liquid.
nċuuys – sour face; the face you get when you eat something sour.

south

ƛ̓aq̓lexʷ – south. *rt.:* ***ƛ̓aq̓*** *– hot; suffix:* ***…ulexʷ*** *– land.*

souvenir

sʔélk̓ʷmn – souvenir. *rt.:* ***elk̓ʷ*** *– store away.*

sʔélk̓ʷlscut, *sʔélk̓ʷlscu* – something kept for one's self. *rt.:* ***elk̓ʷ*** *– store away; suffix:* ***…cut*** *– action to the self.*

spaghetti

scnxʷeyƛ̓kʷ – something broke into water; spaghetti. *prefix:* ***sc…*** *– s.t. that's been done/made/prepared.*

ox̣ʷox̣ʷm – spaghetti; things strung out. *See:* ***string.***

scnšmetkʷ – something standing in water; spaghetti. *prefix:* ***sc…*** *– s.t. that's been done/made/prepared*

> s.t. - something, the 3rd person
> (s.t.) - something implied
> s.o. - someone, the 3rd person
> *sl.* - singular form
> *pl.* - plural form
> *rt.* - root word
> *cmd.* - command
> *lit.* - literally
> *fig.* - figuratively
> *i.e.,* - for example
> *See:* - Redirection to a related word.

spank

łċim – spank; whip. *(i.e., as to punish)*

łċim – S/he spanked. **čn łċim, kʷ łċim**
es łċmi – S/he is spanking. **čnes łċmi, kʷes łċmi**
qs łċmi – S/he is going to spank. **čiqs łċmi, kʷqs łċmi**
łċíʔim – They spanked. **qeʔ łċim, p łċim**
es łċmíʔi – They are spanking. **qeʔes łċmi, pes łċmi**

łċntes – S/he spanked s.o. **łċnten, łċntexʷ**
es łċims – S/he is spanking s.o. **ies łċim, as łċim**
qs łċims – S/he is going to spank s.o. **iqs łċim, aqs łċim**

łċntéʔes – They spanked s.o. **qeʔ łċntem, łċntep**
es łċíʔims – They are spanking s.o. **qeʔes łċim, es łċimp**

es łċim – S/he/it is being spanked.

sxʷłċim – one tasked to spank. *prefix: **sxʷ...** – one tasked to do.*
łċłċmuł – one that habitually spanks. *suffix: **...łmuł** – one that habitually does.*
słċiċ – the whip.
słiċċ – the whipping.
słċiċeʔ – lash marks.

łċiš – Spank. *cmd.*
łċint – Spank him/her. *cmd.*
łċelt – whip a child.
łċncut – whip one's self.
čłċiċeʔ – whip all over.
łċelisis – S/he whipped each one. **łċelisn, łċelisntxʷ**

kʷqs łċim – You are going to be spanked.

čsṗiċéʔ – whip; hit someone all over with something. *See: **whip**.*

spark
ċiḱʷ – shiny, flashy, sparkly.
i ċiḱʷ – It is shiny.
čłċiḱʷčn – water over ice (shiny surface).

ṗáq̓ – shine; bright. *See: **shin**.*

sparrow
łososi – sparrow.

sparrow hawk
spiyálqn – American kestrel; *Falco sparverius*.

yecic – merlin; *Falco columbarius*.

spawn
es npkʷétkʷi – spawning. *rt.: **npkʷétkʷ** – put/pour round objects in water. See: **pour**.*

speak
qʷlqʷélt, *qʷlqʷé* **–** speak/talk; the act of talking; saying words.
qʷlqʷélt – S/he spoke. **čn qʷlqʷélt, kʷ qʷlqʷélt**
es qʷlqʷélti – S/he is speaking. **čnes qʷlqʷélti, kʷes qʷlqʷélti**
qs qʷlqʷélti – S/he is going to speak. **čiqs qʷlqʷélti, kʷqs qʷlqʷélti**
qʷlqʷéʔelt – They spoke. **qeʔ qʷlqʷélt, p qʷlqʷélt**
es qʷlqʷéʔelti – They are speaking. **qeʔes qʷlqʷélti, pes qʷlqʷélti**
qs qʷlqʷéʔelti – They are going to speak. **qeʔqs qʷlqʷélti, pqs qʷlqʷélti**

qʷlqʷelsts – S/he spoke to s.o. **qʷlqʷelstn, qʷlqʷelstxʷ**
es qʷlqʷelstms – S/he is speaking to s.o. **ies qʷlqʷelstm, as qʷlqʷelstm**
qs qʷlqʷelstms – S/he is going to speak to s.o. **iqs qʷlqʷelstm, aqs qʷlqʷelstm**
qʷlqʷéʔelsts – They spoke to s.o. **qeʔ qʷlqʷelstm, as qʷlqʷelstp**
es qʷlqʷéʔelstms – They are speaking to s.o. **qeʔes qʷlqʷelstm, es qʷlqʷelstmp**
qs qʷlqʷéʔelstms – They are going to speak to s.o. **qeʔqs qʷlqʷelstm, qs qʷlqʷelstmp**

qʷlqʷéltmis – S/he used s.t. to speak. **qʷlqʷéltmn, qʷlqʷéltmntxʷ**
es qʷlqʷéltms – S/he is using s.t. to speak. **ies qʷlqʷéltm, as qʷlqʷéltm**
qs qʷlqʷélti – S/he is going to use s.t. to speak. **iqs qʷlqʷéltm, aqs qʷlqʷéltm**

čqʷlqʷéltmis – S/he spoke about s.t. **čqʷlqʷéltmn, čqʷlqʷéltmntxʷ**
es čqʷlqʷéltms – S/he is speaking about s.t. **ies čqʷlqʷéltm, as čqʷlqʷéltm**

qs čqʷlqʷélti – S/he is going to speak about s.t. **iqs čqʷlqʷéltm, aqs čqʷlqʷéltm**

qʷlqʷelstm – S/he/it was spoken to.

qʷlqʷeltš – Speak. *cmd.*
qʷlqʷelskʷ – Speak to s.o. *cmd.*
qʷlqʷltmuł – one that habitually speaks. *suffix:* ***...łmuł*** *– one that habitually does*
nqʷlqʷel̓tn – language; how an individual or family group speaks. *suffix:* ***...tin, ...tn*** *– means of/device.*
sxʷqʷlqʷelt, *sxʷqʷlqʷe* **–** attorney; someone tasked to talk; speaker. *prefix:* ***sxʷ...*** *– one tasked to do.*
es qʷlqʷeltwexʷ – They are saying words to each other. **qeʔes qʷlqʷeltwexʷ, pes qʷlqʷeltwexʷ**

tas yoʔstén łu selíš nqʷlqʷéltis – I do not know how to speak Salish. **yoʔnun čiqs qʷlqʷé t sql̓sé –** I learned how to speak Kootenai. **ṅe tas k̓ʷis sust t kapi m ta qs qʷlqʷé –** If s/he does not drink coffee, s/he cannot talk. **p ies qʷlqʷelstm –** I am speaking to you all. **qeʔes qʷlqʷel̓tłls –** S/he is speaking to us. **kʷ es qʷlqʷelstms –** S/he is speaking to you. **qʷlqʷelstem –** It talked to him.

The **i** following uvular consonants (UC) and the glottal stop **ʔ** sound like English "*ey*" as in the words th*ey*, h*ey*, wh*ey*, etc. Salish UC are: **q, q̇, qʷ, q̇ʷ, x̣, x̣ʷ**. For example, the suffix ...**qin** – head/top, is often spelled using English *ey* as "qeyn". So **qi, q̇i, qʷi, q̇ʷi, x̣i, x̣ʷi**, may be spelled with English *ey* as **q***ey*, **q̇***ey*, **qʷ***ey*, **q̇ʷ***ey*, **x̣***ey*, **x̣ʷ***ey* in other texts.

uwéwlš – communicate; speak formally; convey meaning through speech.
uwéwlš – S/he spoke. **čn uwéwlš, kʷ uwéwlš**
es uwéwlši – S/he is speaking. **čnes uwéwlši, kʷes uwéwlši**
qs uwéwlši – S/he is going speak. **čiqs uwéwlši, kʷqs uwéwlši**
uwéʔewlš – They spoke. **qeʔ uwéwlš, p uwéwlš**
es uwéʔewlši – They are speaking. **qeʔes uwéwlši, pes uwéwlši**
qs uwéʔewlši – They are going speak. **qeʔqs uwéwlši, pqs uwéwlši**

uwéwlšiš – Speak something. *cmd.*
čuwéwlšm – talk about.
nuwewlštn – language; the way a people speaks. *suffix:* ***...tin, ...tn*** *– means of/device.*
sxʷẇeẇéʔ – one tasked to call out; crier. *prefix:* ***sxʷ...*** *– one tasked to do.*
sxʷk̓ʷłwéʔm – one tasked to repeat what is said in the medicine dance. *prefix:* ***sxʷ...*** *– one tasked to do.*

x̣ʷl̓ steṁ u tam t seliš u kʷes uwewlši – Why are you not speaking Salish. **ha iše kʷ uwewlš t seliš –** Do you speak Salish? **ƛ̓mey u iše čn łuwewlš –** I speak a little bit. **tam x̣e čnes nsuxʷne i kʷ łkʷk̓ʷi m kʷ uwewlš –** I do not understand good, speak slowly. **ta qeʔqs čuwewlšm łu inṗiṗuyšn –** We're not going to talk about my car.

áwm – say/speak; pronounce; annunciate. *See:* ***say***.

cu – say/speak to somebody; inform; provide information about something. *See:* ***say***.

...cin – *suffix indicating an action of the mouth; i.e., speaking, eating, & food. See:* ***mouth***.
nmemeʔcin – talk in a bothersome way. *rt.:* ***memeʔt*** *– bothersome. See:* ***talk***.
x̣scinm – talk in a good way; talk good about someone or something. *See:* ***talk***.
č̓scinm – talk in a bad way; bad mouth. *See:* ***talk***.
łaqʷcin – spoke up (once in a while). *See:* ***talk***.
nk̓ʷnk̓ʷucin – saying one word at a time. *See:* ***talk***.
aytcin – speak with passion; speak with effort; speak over. *See:* ***strive***.
xʷaʔscan – chitchat; speak for nothing. *See:* ***chitchat***.

s.t. - something, the 3rd person
(s.t.) - something implied
s.o. - someone, the 3rd person
sl. - singular form
pl. - plural form
rt. - root word
cmd. - command
lit. - literally
fig. - figuratively
i.e., - for example
See: - Redirection to a related word.

spear

smul̓mn – lance, spear.
łumin – spear.

snululmu – spear.

nłwetkʷtn – fishing spear. *suffix: **...tin, ...tn** – means of/device.*

spices **nmex̌mn** – something that's mixed; spices. *rt.: **mex̌** – mix; prefix: **n...** – inside; suffix: **...min, ...mn** – instrument/tool*

spider **sčéy̓t** – spider.
kʷ nx̣el t sčey̓t – You are afraid of spiders.

stamólqn – daddy longlegs. *See: **daddy longlegs**.*
tupn – black widow.
nttmičn̓, *nttmi* – barn spider. *rt.: **iłttim** – tender; suffix: **...ičn̓** – back.*

spill **sixʷm** – spill liquid out; pour liquid out.
sixʷm – S/he/it spilled/poured. **čn sixʷm, kʷ sixʷm**
es sixʷi – S/he/it is spilling/pouring. **čnes sixʷi, kʷes sixʷi**
qs sixʷi – S/he/it is going to spill/pour. **čiqs sixʷi, kʷqs sixʷi**
síˀixʷm – They spilled/poured. **qeˀ sixʷm, p sixʷm**
es síˀixʷi – They are spilling/pouring. **qeˀes sixʷi, pes sixʷi**
qs síˀixʷi – They are going to spill/pour. **qeˀqs sixʷi, pqs sixʷi**

sixʷis – S/he/it spilled/poured on s.t./s.o. **sixʷn, sixʷntxʷ**
es sixʷms – S/he/it is spilling/pouring on s.t./s.o. **ies sixʷm, as sixʷm**
qs sixʷms – S/he/it is going to spill/pour on s.t./s.o. **iqs sixʷm, aqs sixʷm**
síˀixʷis – They spilled/poured on s.t./s.o. **qeˀ sixʷntm, sixʷntp**
es síˀixʷms – They are spilling/pouring on s.t./s.o. **qeˀes sixʷm, es sixʷmp**
qs síˀixʷms – They are going to spill/pour on s.t./s.o. **qsqs sixʷm, qs sixʷmp**

sixʷmis – S/he/it spilled/poured s.t. **sixʷmn, sixʷmntxʷ**
es sixʷmms – S/he/it is spilling/pouring s.t. **ies sixʷmm, as sixʷmm**
qs sixʷmms – S/he/it is going to spill/pour s.t. **iqs sixʷmm, aqs sixʷmm**

čsixʷmis – S/he/it spilled s.t. upon s.t./s.o. **čsixʷmn, čsixʷmntxʷ**
es čsixʷms – S/he/it is spilling s.t. upon s.t./s.o. **ies čsixʷm, as čsixʷm**
qs čsixʷms – S/he/it is going to spill s.t. upon s.t./s.o. **iqs čsixʷm, aqs čsixʷm**

es sixʷ – It is spilled/poured.
sixʷxʷ – It got spilled by accident.
čsixʷxʷ – It got spilled upon by accident.
nsixʷxʷ – It got poured inside by accident.

sixʷiš – Pour. *cmd.*
sixʷnt – Pour/spill it. *cmd.*
nsixʷmis – S/he/it poured s.t. inside it. **nsixʷmn, nsixʷmntxʷ**
čłsixʷnˀeis – S/he/it poured s.t. over it. **čłsixʷnˀen, čłsixʷnˀentxʷ**
čłsxʷnncut – S/he/it spilled/poured s.t. on one's self. **čn čłsxʷnncut, kʷ čłsxʷnncut**
čsixʷnc̓eˀ – Spill all over something.

n̓em sixʷm – S/he/it will spill/pour. **n̓em čn sixʷm, n̓em kʷ sixʷm**
n̓em síˀixʷm – They will spill/pour. **n̓em qeˀ sixʷm, n̓em p sixʷm**

nsixʷn u q̓ʷéc̓t – I filled it full. **čłsxʷnncut t kapi** – S/he spilled coffee on one's self.

poq̓ʷ – spill/pour/dump powdered substances. *(i.e., salt, sugar, flour, gunpowder, ash, etc.)*
es pq̓ʷmi – S/he/it spilling a powder substance. **es pq̓ʷmi, es pq̓ʷmi**

pq̓ʷntes – S/he/it spilled it. **pq̓ʷnten, pq̓ʷntexʷ**
es pq̓ʷoms – S/he/it is spilling it. **ies pq̓ʷom, as pq̓ʷom**

qs pq̓ʷoms – S/he/it is going to spill it. **iqs pq̓ʷom, aqs pq̓ʷom**

pq̓ʷmis – S/he/it used s.t. to spill it. **pq̓ʷmin, pq̓ʷmintxʷ**
es pq̓ʷminms – S/he/it is using s.t. to spill it. **ies pq̓ʷminm, as pq̓ʷminm**
qs pq̓ʷminms – S/he/it is going to use s.t. to spill it. **iqs pq̓ʷminm, aqs pq̓ʷminm**
pq̓ʷmíʔis – They used s.t. to spill it. **qeʔ pq̓ʷmintm, pq̓ʷmintp**
es pq̓ʷmíʔinms – They are using s.t. to spill it. **qeʔes pq̓ʷminm, es pq̓ʷminmp**
qs pq̓ʷmíʔinms – They are going to use s.t. to spill it. **qeʔqs pq̓ʷminm, qs pq̓ʷminmp**

pq̓ʷoq̓ʷ – The powder substance got spilled.

pq̓ʷont – Spill the powdery substance. *cmd.*
npq̓ʷont – Spill the powdery substance inside the container. *cmd.*
čłpq̓ʷont – Spill the powdery substance on the flat surface. *cmd.*
čpq̓ʷus – spill/pour powder onto the eye or fire.
pq̓ʷew̓t – The powdery substance is scattered. *suffix: **...éw̓t** – group state.*
npq̓ʷčnečstmis – S/he poured s.t. into his/her hand. **npq̓ʷčnečstmn, npq̓ʷčnečstmntxʷ**

ṅem qs pq̓ʷminms – S/he/it will be spilling it. **ṅem iqs pq̓ʷminm, ṅem aqs pq̓ʷminm**

pq̓ʷoq̓ʷ łu ċol – The salt got spilled.

The **i** following uvular consonants (UC) and the glottal stop **ʔ** sound like English "*ey*" as in the words *they*, *hey*, *whey*, etc. Salish UC are: **q**, **q̓**, **qʷ**, **q̓ʷ**, **x̣**, **x̣ʷ**. For example, the suffix **...qin** – head/top, is often spelled using English *ey* as "q*ey*n". So **qi**, **q̓i**, **qʷi**, **q̓ʷi**, **x̣i**, **x̣ʷi**, may be spelled with English *ey* as **q***ey*, **q̓***ey*, **qʷ***ey*, **q̓ʷ***ey*, **x̣***ey*, **x̣ʷ***ey* in other texts.

pukʷ – spill/pour round objects. *(i.e., rocks, berries, marbles, apples, etc.)*
pkʷntes – S/he/it spilled s.t. **pkʷnten, pkʷntexʷ**
es pkʷums – S/he/it is spilling s.t. **ies pkʷum, as pkʷum**
qs pkʷums – S/he/it is going to spill s.t. **iqs pkʷum, aqs pkʷum**
pkʷntéʔes – They spilled s.t. **qeʔ pkʷntém, pkʷntép**
es pkʷúʔums – They are spilling s.t. **qeʔes pkʷum, es pkʷump**
qs čłpkʷúʔums – They are going to spill s.t. **qeʔqs pkʷum, qs pkʷump**

es pkʷpkʷums – S/he/it is pouring things. **ies pkʷpkʷum, as pkʷpkʷum**

pkʷunt – Spill the round objects. *cmd.*
npkʷétkʷ – pour round objects in water. *(i.e., berries, rocks, etc.) See: **pour**.*
čłpukʷ – spread/pour round things out on a surface of something. *(i.e., berries, marbles, etc.) See: **spread**.*

p̓t̓am – splatter/spill/pour a viscous substance. *(i.e., spit, snow, honey, glue, mud, feces, etc.) See: **splatter**.*
np̓t̓atkʷm – pour/dump a viscous substance in water *(i.e., brains, wet hide, honey, etc.). See: **dump**.*

čqqʷusm – pour/dump large objects. *See: **pour**.*

laq̓ʷm – splash water; scoop and splash water; pour and splash water; throw water. *See: **splash**.*

spin

šllčmncutist – spin or twirl one's self.
es šllčmncutist – S/he/it is spinning. **čnes šllčmncutist, kʷes šllčmncutist**

šllčmis – S/he/it spun/twirled s.t./s.o. **šllčmin, šllčmintxʷ**
es šllčminms – S/he/it is spinning/twirling s.t./s.o. **ies šllčminm, as šllčminm**
qs šllčminms – S/he/it is going to spin/twirl s.t./s.o. **iqs šllčminm, aqs šllčminm**

šlličmskʷ – Spin/twirl s.t./s.o. *cmd.*

qʷqʷiwxʷ – spin one's self until dizzy; a game played mainly by children. *rt.: **qʷew̓** – crazy. See: **crazy**.*

s.t. - something, the 3rd person
(s.t.) - something implied
s.o. - someone, the 3rd person
sl. - singular form
pl. - plural form
rt. - root word
cmd. - command
lit. - literally
fig. - figuratively
i.e., - for example
See: - Redirection to a related word.

spine

ásx̣m̓ – backbone.

snṫx̣ʷičṅ – spine. *suffix:* ***...ičṅ*** *– back.*

malkʷeẇs – disjointed/dislocated spine. *suffix:* ***...éẇs*** *– in between, middle.*
es malkʷeẇs – S/he has a disjointed/dislocated spine. **čnes malkʷeẇs, kʷes malkʷeẇs**

malkʷeẇsis – S/he disjointed/dislocated s.o.'s spine. **malkʷeẇsn, malkʷeẇsntxʷ**
es malkʷeẇsms – S/he is disjointing/dislocating s.o.'s spine. **ies malkʷeẇsm, as malkʷeẇsm**
qs malkʷeẇsms – S/he is going to disjoint/dislocate s.o.'s spine. **iqs malkʷeẇsm, aqs malkʷeẇsm**

spirit

spx̣páx̣t – that which is guidance, wisdom and smarts; spirit.

spiritual power

sumeš – spiritual/medicine power; guardian/medicine spirit.

ṅem qeʔ k̓ʷłq̓ẏq̓eẏntm łu qeʔ sumeš – We'll paint our medicine power.

spit

ptáx̣ʷ – spit.
ptáx̣ʷm – S/he spit. **čn ptáx̣ʷm, kʷptáx̣ʷm**
es ptáx̣ʷi – S/he is spitting. **čnes ptáx̣ʷi, kʷes ptáx̣ʷi**
qs ptáx̣ʷi – S/he is going to spit. **čiqs ptáx̣ʷi, kʷqs ptáx̣ʷi**
ptáʔax̣ʷm – They spit. **qeʔ ptáx̣ʷm, p ptáx̣ʷm**
es ptáʔax̣ʷi – They are spitting. **qeʔes ptáx̣ʷi, pes ptáx̣ʷi**
qs ptáʔax̣ʷi – They are going to spit. **qeʔqs ptáx̣ʷi, pqs ptáx̣ʷi**

ptáx̣ʷmis – S/he spit s.t. out. **ptáx̣ʷmn, ptáx̣ʷmntxʷ**
es ptáx̣ʷmms – S/he is spitting s.t. out. **ies ptáx̣ʷmm, as ptáx̣ʷmm**
qs ptáx̣ʷms – S/he is going to spit s.t. out. **iqs ptáx̣ʷm, aqs ptáx̣ʷmm**
ptáʔax̣ʷmis – They spit s.t. out. **qeʔ ptáx̣ʷmntm, ptáx̣ʷmntp**
es ptáʔax̣ʷmms – They are spitting s.t. out. **qeʔes ptáx̣ʷmm, es ptáx̣ʷmmp**
qs ptáʔax̣ʷmms – They are going to spit s.t. out. **qeʔqs ptáx̣ʷmm, qs ptáx̣ʷmmp**

ptáx̣ʷis – S/he spit on s.o. **ptáx̣ʷn, ptáx̣ʷntxʷ**
es ptáx̣ʷms – S/he is spitting on s.o. **ies ptáx̣ʷm, as ptáx̣ʷm**
qs ptáx̣ʷms – S/he is going to spit on s.o. **iqs ptáx̣ʷm, aqs ptáx̣ʷm**
ptáʔax̣ʷis – They spit on s.o. **qeʔ ptáx̣ʷntm, ptáx̣ʷntp**
es ptáʔax̣ʷms – They are spitting on s.o. **qeʔes ptáx̣ʷm, es ptáx̣ʷmp**
qs ptáʔax̣ʷms – They are going to spit on s.o. **qeʔqs ptáx̣ʷm, qs ptáx̣ʷmp**

ptáx̣ʷntm – S/he/it was spit on.

sptax̣ʷ – spit.
snptáx̣ʷmn – spittoon.

ptáx̣ʷiš – Spit. *cmd.*
ptáx̣ʷmnt – Spit it out. *cmd.*
ptáx̣ʷnt – Spit on him/her/it. *cmd.*

eł ptáx̣ʷmn łu i táx̣ – Again, I spit out the bitter part.

spittoon

snptáx̣ʷmn – thing to spit in; spittoon.

snptáx̣ʷtn – place to spit in; spittoon. *prefix:* ***sn...*** *– a place of; suffix:* ***...tin, ...tn*** *– means of/device.*

splash

laq̓ʷm – splash water; scoop and splash water; pour and splash water; throw water.
laq̓ʷm – S/he splashed. **čn laq̓ʷm, kʷ laq̓ʷm**
es laq̓ʷi – S/he is splashing. **čnes laq̓ʷi, kʷes laq̓ʷi**
qs laq̓ʷi – S/he is going to splash. **čiqs laq̓ʷi, kʷqs laq̓ʷi**
láʔaq̓ʷm – They splashed. **qeʔ laq̓ʷm, p laq̓ʷm**

es láʔaq̇ʷi – They are splashing. **qeʔes laq̇ʷi, pes laq̇ʷi**
qs láʔaq̇ʷi – They are going to splash. **qeʔqs laq̇ʷi, pqs laq̇ʷi**

laq̇ʷis – S/he splashed it. **laq̇ʷn, laq̇ʷntxʷ**
es laq̇ʷms – S/he is splashing it. **ies laq̇ʷm, as laq̇ʷm**
qs laq̇ʷms – S/he is going to splash it. **iqs laq̇ʷm, aqs laq̇ʷm**
láʔaq̇ʷis – They splashed it. **qeʔ laq̇ʷntm, laq̇ʷntp**
es láʔaq̇ʷms – They are splashing it. **qeʔes laq̇ʷm, es laq̇ʷmp**
qs láʔaq̇ʷms – They are going to splash it. **qeʔqs laq̇ʷm, qs laq̇ʷmp**

es lq̇ʷlaq̇ʷi – S/he is splashing repeatedly. **čnes lq̇ʷlaq̇ʷi, kʷes lq̇ʷlaq̇ʷi**
es lq̇ʷlaq̇ʷms – S/he is splashing it over and over. **ies lq̇ʷlaq̇ʷm, as lq̇ʷlaq̇ʷm**

laq̇ʷiš – Pour/splash. *cmd.*
lq̇ʷlaq̇ʷiš – Splash around. *cmd.*
laq̇ʷnt – Pour/splash it. *cmd.*
člq̇ʷlaq̇ʷšnm – splash water on legs.
es člq̇ʷncuti – S/he/it is splashing one's self with water. **čnes člq̇ʷncuti, kʷes člq̇ʷncuti**
es člq̇ʷnwexʷi – They are splashing each other with water. **qeʔes člq̇ʷnwexʷi, pes člq̇ʷnwexʷi**

ṅem laq̇ʷm – S/he will pour/splash. **ṅem čn laq̇ʷm, ṅem kʷ laq̇ʷm**
ṅem láʔaq̇ʷm – They will pour/splash. **ṅem qeʔ laq̇ʷm, ṅem p laq̇ʷm**

laq̇ʷsšṅ – splash water on rocks. *(i.e., in a sweat, etc.) suffix:* ***...essṅ, ...sšṅ*** *– rock.*
laq̇ʷsšṅ – S/he splashed on rocks. **čn laq̇ʷsšṅ, kʷ laq̇ʷsšṅ**
es laq̇ʷsšṅi – S/he is splashing on rocks. **čnes laq̇ʷsšṅi, kʷes laq̇ʷsšṅi**
qs laq̇ʷsšṅi – S/he is going to splash on rocks. **čiqs laq̇ʷsšṅi, kʷqs laq̇ʷsšṅi**

laq̇ʷsšṅiš – Splash water on rocks. *cmd.*

łin – splash/sprinkle and spread liquid.
łnap – It splashed/sprinkled out as a natural process.

łnntes – S/he splashed water on it. **łnnten, łnntexʷ**
es łinms – S/he is splashing water on it. **ies łinm, as łinm**
qs łinms – S/he is going to splash water on it. **iqs łinm, aqs łinm**

łnint – Splash it. *cmd.*

łnesšṅ – splash/sprinkle water on rocks. *(i.e., in a sweat, etc.) suffix:* ***...essṅ, ...sšṅ*** *– rock.*
łnesšṅ – S/he splashed water on rocks. **čn łnesšṅ, kʷ łnesšṅ**
es łnesšṅi – S/he is splashing water on rocks. **čnes łnesšṅi, kʷes łnesšṅi**
qs łnesšṅi – S/he is going splash water on rocks. **čiqs łnesšṅi, kʷqs łnesšṅi**

sxʷłnesšṅ – one tasked to splash rocks. *prefix:* ***sxʷ...*** *– one tasked to do.*

łnesšṅiš – Splash the rocks. *cmd.*

łins – splash something liquid on the face.
łins – S/he splashed water on the face. **čn łins, kʷ łins**
es łinsi – S/he is splashing water on the face. **čnes łinsi, kʷes łinsi**
qs łinsi – S/he is going splash water on the face. **čiqs łinsi, kʷqs łinsi**

łinsis – S/he splashed water on s.o.'s face. **łinsn, łinsntxʷ**
es łinsms – S/he is splashing water on s.o.'s face. **ies łinsm, as łinsm**
qs łinsms – S/he is going splash water on s.o.'s face. **iqs łinsm, aqs łinsm**

The **i** following uvular consonants (UC) and the glottal stop ʔ sound like English "*ey*" as in the words *they, hey, whey*, etc. Salish UC are: **q, q̇, qʷ, q̇ʷ, x̣, x̣ʷ**. For example, the suffix **...qin** – head/top, is often spelled using English *ey* as "q*ey*n". So **qi, q̇i, qʷi, q̇ʷi, x̣i, x̣ʷi**, may be spelled with English *ey* as **q***ey*, **q̇***ey*, **qʷ***ey*, **q̇ʷ***ey*, **x̣***ey*, **x̣ʷ***ey* in other texts.

s.t. - something, the 3rd person
(s.t.) - something implied
s.o. - someone, the 3rd person
sl. - singular form
pl. - plural form
rt. - root word
cmd. - command
lit. - literally
fig. - figuratively
i.e., - for example
See: - Redirection to a related word.

łinsnt – Splash water on his/her face. *cmd.*

qʷo łinsntm – I got water splashed on my face.

čłnáyaqn – splash something liquid on the head.
čłnáyaqn – S/he splashed on the head. **čn čłnáyaqn, kʷ čłnáyaqn**
es čłnáyaqni – S/he is splashing on the head. **čnes čłnáyaqni, kʷes čłnáyaqni**
qs čłnáyaqni – S/he is going splash on the head. **čiqs čłnáyaqni, kʷqs čłnáyaqni**

čłnáyaqis – S/he splashed on s.o.'s head. **čłnáyaqn, čłnáyaqntxʷ**
es čłnáyaqnms – S/he is splashing on s.o.'s head. **ies čłnáyaqnm, as čłnáyaqnm**
qs čłnáyaqnms – S/he is going splash on s.o.'s head. **iqs čłnáyaqnm, aqs čłnáyaqnm**

qʷo čłnáyaqntm – I got water splashed on my head.

splatter

p̓t̓am – splatter/spill/pour a viscous substance. *(i.e., spit, snow, honey, glue, mud, feces, etc.)*
p̓t̓ntas – S/he/it splattered s.t./s.o. with s.t. **p̓t̓ntan, p̓t̓ntaxʷ**
es p̓t̓ams – S/he/it is splattering s.t./s.o. with s.t. **ies p̓t̓am, as p̓t̓am**
qs p̓t̓ams – S/he/it is going to splatter s.t./s.o. with s.t. **iqs p̓t̓am, aqs p̓t̓am**

p̓t̓at̓ – It got splattered.

p̓t̓mantn – something used to splatter something with. *(i.e., paper for a spitwad, etc.)*

p̓t̓ant – pour/spill/splatter it. *cmd.*
p̓t̓ntakʷ – Splatter him/her/it with s.t. *cmd.*
čp̓t̓qanm – splatter the head.
čp̓t̓alqʷm – splatter wood.
čp̓t̓asm – splatter/spit in the eye.
čp̓t̓ačst – splatter the hand. *suffix:* ***...ečst, ...čst*** *– of the hand.*
np̓t̓atkʷm – pour/dump a viscous substance in water *(i.e., brains, wet hide, honey, etc.). See:* ***dump****.*
es pt̓ncoti, *es pt̓nco* **–** It is raining slush; it is making itself stick to something. *(wet slushy snow) See:* *slush.*

p̓t̓ntas łu snčłemutn t malt – S/he/it splattered the chair with mud.

spleen

stx̣enč – spleen. *suffix:* ***...enč*** *– within.*

hlipe – spleen.

splice

ax̣meẃs – splice something together; weave ends together. *suffix:* ***...éẃs*** *– in between, middle.*

nacsél̓is – join/tie two things together.
nacselistn – connectors; putting things together. *suffix:* ***...tin, ...tn*** *– means of/device.*

t̓ip – join to make longer; fasten to make longer. (*i.e., sewing, fastening, etc.) See:* ***join****.*

split

sax̣ʷ – split wood with an instrument.
sax̣ʷm – S/he split wood. **čn sax̣ʷm, kʷ sax̣ʷm**
es sax̣ʷi – S/he is splitting wood. **čnes sax̣ʷi, kʷes sax̣ʷi**
qs sax̣ʷi – S/he is going to split wood. **čiqs sax̣ʷi, kʷqs sax̣ʷi**
sáʔax̣ʷm – They split wood. **qeʔ sax̣ʷm, p sax̣ʷm**
es sáʔax̣ʷi – They are splitting wood. **qeʔes sax̣ʷi, pes sax̣ʷi**
qs sáʔax̣ʷi – They are going to split wood. **qeʔqs sax̣ʷi, pqs sax̣ʷi**

es sax̣ʷms – S/he is splitting wood. **ies sax̣ʷm, as sax̣ʷm**
es sáʔax̣ʷms – They are splitting wood. **qeʔes sax̣ʷm, es sax̣ʷmp**

sxʷsax̣ʷm – one tasked to split wood.

ṅem sax̣ʷm – S/he will split wood. **ṅem čn sax̣ʷm, ṅem kʷ sax̣ʷm**
ṅem sáʔax̣ʷm – They will split wood. **ṅem qeʔ sax̣ʷm, ṅem p sax̣ʷm**

sax̣ʷm t luk̇ʷ – S/he split wood. **čn sax̣ʷm t mulš –** I split cottonwood.

nx̣ʷq̇ʷeẇs – split something apart from within. *suffix: **...éẇs**– in between, middle.*
nx̣ʷq̇ʷeẇsis – S/he split s.t. **nx̣ʷq̇ʷeẇsn, nx̣ʷq̇ʷeẇsntxʷ**
es nx̣ʷq̇ʷeẇsms – S/he is splitting s.t. **ies nx̣ʷq̇ʷeẇsm, as nx̣ʷq̇ʷeẇsm**
qs nx̣ʷq̇ʷeẇsms – S/he is going to split s.t. **iqs nx̣ʷq̇ʷeẇsm, aqs nx̣ʷq̇ʷeẇsm**
nx̣ʷq̇ʷéʔeẇsis – They split s.t. **qeʔ nx̣ʷq̇ʷeẇsn, nx̣ʷq̇ʷeẇsntp**
es nx̣ʷq̇ʷéʔeẇsms – They are splitting s.t. **qeʔes nx̣ʷq̇ʷeẇsm, es nx̣ʷq̇ʷeẇsmp**
qs nx̣ʷq̇ʷéʔeẇsms – They are going to split s.t. **qeʔqs nx̣ʷq̇ʷeẇsm, qs nx̣ʷq̇ʷeẇsmp**

nx̣ʷq̇ʷeẇsiš – Split; *also cut the cards. cmd.*

saq̇ – split; parted; cloven.
sq̇em – S/he/it split (s.t.). **čn sq̇em, kʷ sq̇em**
es sq̇mi – S/he/it is splitting (s.t.). **čnes sq̇mi, kʷes sq̇mi**
qs sq̇mi – S/he/it is going to split (s.t.). **čiqs sq̇mi, kʷqs sq̇mi**

sq̇ntes – S/he/it split s.t. **sq̇nten, sq̇ntexʷ**
es sq̇ems – S/he/it is splitting s.t. **ies sq̇em, as sq̇em**
qs sq̇ems – S/he/it is going to split s.t. **iqs sq̇em, aqs sq̇em**

sq̇q̇nuis – S/he/it succeed in splitting s.t. **sq̇q̇nun, sq̇q̇nuntxʷ**
sq̇šišts – S/he/it split s.t. for s.o. **sq̇šištn, sq̇šištxʷ**

sq̇aq̇ – It split/cracked/parted.
es saq̇ – It is split/cracked/parted.
es sq̇saq̇ – It is split.
es sq̇aq̇ – It splits; it can be split.

sxʷsq̇em – one tasked to split something.

sq̇eiš – Split (s.t.). *cmd.*
sq̇ent – Split it. *cmd.*
nsq̇elis – split in several pieces.
saq̇cn – have the mouth open; part lips. *See: **mouth.***
sq̇sq̇šin – cloven hooves.

sq̇ep – It split naturally; it cracked. *See: **crack.***
es sq̇pmi – It is splitting naturally.
es nsq̇peẇsi – It is splitting/cracking in two naturally.
es nsq̇pelisi – It is split into several pieces naturally.

nsq̇eẇs – split in the middle; split in two. *suffix: **...éẇs**– in between, middle.*
nsq̇eẇsis – S/he split s.t. in two. **nsq̇eẇsn, nsq̇eẇsntxʷ**
es nsq̇eẇsms – S/he is splitting s.t. in two. **ies nsq̇eẇsm, as nsq̇eẇsm**
qs nsq̇eẇsms – S/he is going to split s.t. in two. **iqs nsq̇eẇsm, aqs nsq̇eẇsm**

es nsq̇eẇs – It is split in the middle; it is split in two.

nsq̇eẇstn – wedge.

nsq̇eẇsnt – Split it in half. *cmd.*

The **i** following uvular consonants (UC) and the glottal stop **ʔ** sound like English "*ey*" as in the words *they, hey, whey*, etc. Salish UC are: **q, q̇, qʷ, q̇ʷ, x̣, x̣ʷ**. For example, the suffix **...qin** – head/top, is often spelled using English *ey* as "q*ey*n". So **qi, q̇i, qʷi, q̇ʷi, x̣i, x̣ʷi**, may be spelled with English *ey* as **q***ey*, **q̇***ey*, **qʷ***ey*, **q̇ʷ***ey*, **x̣***ey*, **x̣ʷ***ey* in other texts.

s.t. - something, the 3rd person
(s.t.) - something implied
s.o. - someone, the 3rd person
sl. - singular form
pl. - plural form
rt. - root word
cmd. - command
lit. - literally
fig. - figuratively
i.e., - for example
See: - Redirection to a related word.

x̣ʷq̓ʷeẁs – divide/part something; apportion; cut cards. *See: **divide**.*

x̣ʷq̓ʷom – separate something that is together. *(i.e., a pile, a ream of paper, a package of crackers, etc.) See: **separate**.*

ček̓ʷseẁsm – separate something solid. *(i.e., a rock, bread loaf, pie, etc.) See: **separate**.*

x̣ʷq̓ʷpeẁs – get divorced. *See: **divorce**.*

tx̣ʷeẁs – divide something in two; halve something. *See: **half**.*

xʷaˀlip – rupture; tear; slit. *See: **rupture**.*

spoil

k̓ʷłx̣ʷellm – ruin something; let something waste away. *See: **ruin**.*

Spokane people

snxʷmeneˀ – Spokane people. *(named after the steelhead salmon)*
snxwmeneˀi – Spokane. *(self identification term)*
sntutˀulixʷ – Upper Spokane people. *(Pend d'Oreille term)*
sntuˀtˀuli – Upper Spokane. *(self identification term)*
scqesciłni – Lower Spokane. *(self identification term)*

snxʷmeneˀcn – Spokane language.

spooky

xʷtelis – look spooky; scary looking.
i xʷtelis – S/he is spooky looking, scary looking. **i čn xʷtelis, i kʷ xʷtelis**

spoon

łuˀmn – spoon. **łmuṁn** *pl.*

šnšˀinu – spoon.

sports car

esq̓exʷmscu p̓ip̓uyšn – sports car.

spouse

snkʷłk̓ʷull – spouse. *prefix: **nkʷł...** – together with.*

nóx̣ʷnx̣ʷ – wife.

sx̣élwi – husband.

x̣ʷllałq – abandoned spouse. *suffix: **...ałq** – smell, accompaniment.*

puˀ – spouse of somebody who is...
puˀt̓eyeˀ – spouse of somebody who is mean.
puˀx̣ʷopt – spouse of somebody who is lazy.
puˀsuyápi – spouse of somebody who is a white person.

puˀčsel – spouse with two wives/husbands. *Count wives/husbands, add **puˀ** to the counting of people. See **people**.*

es itkʷmi – It is getting rotten; also an expression referring to one's spouse. *See: **rot**.*

ƛ̓áq̓ʷ – verbally or physically fight one's spouse. *See: **fight**.*

spray

pc̓am – have diarrhea; evacuate liquid feces; skunk sprays. *See: **diarrhea**.*

spread

čłpiłm – spread things out *(i.e., bitterroot)*.
čłpłntes – S/he spread things out. **čłpłnten, čłpłntexʷ**
es čłpiłms – S/he is spreading things out. **ies čłpiłm, as čłpiłm**
qs čłpiłms – S/he is going to spread things out. **iqs čłpiłm, aqs čłpiłm**
čłpłnteˀes – They spread things out. **qeˀ čłpłntem, čłpłntep**
es čłpiˀiłms – They are spreading things out. **qeˀes čłpiłm, es čłpiłmp**

qs čłpiʔiłms – They are going to spread things out. **qeʔqs čłpiłm, qs čłpiłmp**

es čłpiłm – It is spread out.

čłpłint – Spread it out. *cmd.*
čłpiłmskʷ – Spread it out. *cmd.*

čłpiłmskʷ l aspéčn – Spread it out on your canvas. **ṅe wis nčeẃtkʷntxʷ m še čłpiłntxʷ łu aspeƛ̓m –** When you finish washing your bitterroot, you will spread it out.

płqem – lay things out; unpack.
płqem – S/he laid (things) out. **čn płqem, kʷ płqem**
es pełqmisti – S/he is laying (things) out. **čnes pełqmisti, kʷes pełqmisti**
qs pełqmisti – S/he is going to lay (things) out. **čiqs pełqmisti, kʷqs pełqmisti**
płqéʔem – They laid (things) out. **qeʔ płqem, p płqem**
es pełqmíʔisti – They are laying (things) out. **qeʔes pełqmisti, pes pełqmisti**
qs pełqmíʔisti – They are going to lay (things) out. **qeʔqs pełqmisti, pqs pełqmisti**

płqntes – S/he laid things out. **płqnten, płqntexʷ**
es płqems – S/he is laying things out. **ies płqem, as płqem**
qs płqems – S/he is going to lay things out. **iqs płqem, aqs płqem**
płqntéʔes – They laid things out. **qeʔ płqntem, płqntep**
es płqéʔems – They are laying things out. **qeʔes płqem, es płqemp**

płqint – Lay it out. *cmd.*
pełqmncut – unpack one's self. *See: **unpack**.*

The **i** following uvular consonants (UC) and the glottal stop **ʔ** sound like English "*ey*" as in the words *they*, *hey*, *whey*, etc. Salish UC are: **q**, **q̇**, **qʷ**, **q̇ʷ**, **x̣**, **x̣ʷ**. For example, the suffix ...**qin** – head/top, is often spelled using English *ey* as "q*ey*n". So **qi**, **q̇i**, **qʷi**, **q̇ʷi**, **x̣i**, **x̣ʷi**, may be spelled with English *ey* as **q***ey*, **q̇***ey*, **qʷ***ey*, **q̇ʷ***ey*, **x̣***ey*, **x̣ʷ***ey* in other texts.

čłpukʷ – spread/pour round things out on a surface of something. *(i.e., berries, marbles, etc.) rt.: **pukʷ** – pour round objects; prefix: **čł...** – surface.*
čłpkʷntés – S/he spread the round things out. **čłpkʷntén, čłpkʷntéxʷ**
es čłpkʷums – S/he is spreading the round things out. **ies čłpkʷum, as čłpkʷum**
qs čłpkʷums – S/he is going to spread the round things out. **iqs čłpkʷum, aqs čłpkʷum**
čłpkʷntéʔes – They spread the round things out. **qeʔ čłpkʷntém, čłpkʷntép**
es čłpkʷuʔums – They are spreading the round things out. **qeʔes čłpkʷum, es čłpkʷump**

es čłpukʷ – It is poured/spread out.

čłpkʷunt – Spread the round things out. *cmd.*
pukʷ – spill/pour round objects. *(i.e., rocks, berries, marbles, apples, etc.) See: **spill**.*
npkʷétkʷ – pour round objects in water. *(i.e., berries, rocks, etc.) See: **pour**.*

čłpkʷntéxʷ l spéčn – You pour it onto the canvas. **es čłpukʷ l x̣lełp ci nqʷq̇ʷosmičn sʔiłn –** The dog food is poured on the floor. **steṁ łu es čłpukʷ –** What is poured? **m še čłpkʷntep l spečn –** Then you pour it onto the canvas.

xʷep – cover; spread something out.
čłxʷépmn – cover.
čłxʷepneʔ – cover.
xʷeplentxʷ – Spread it on the ground.

čłxʷépnéntxʷ łu asx̣ʷéʔli – Cover your camas with wet dirt, lots of dirt; make a mound. **ha ṅem xʷepntxʷ isičm –** Will you spread my blanket? **ha ṅem xʷeplentxʷ t isičm –** Will you spread my blanket on the ground? **ha ṅem čłxʷepnentxʷ t isičm –** Will you cover it with my blanket?

miƛ̓ – smear; rub something; spread something on something. *See: **smear**.*

s.t. - something, the 3rd person
(s.t.) - something implied
s.o. - someone, the 3rd person
sl. - singular form
pl. - plural form
rt. - root word
cmd. - command
lit. - literally
fig. - figuratively
i.e., - for example
See: - Redirection to a related word.

mḷukʷ – spread all around; propagate; grow, of non-living things. *See: **all around**.*

px̣ʷmim – distribute; spread around; pass/hand out. *See: **distribute**.*

łin – splash/sprinkle and spread liquid. *See: **splash**.*

isk̓ʷl – scatter things out; throw things away. *See: **scatter**.*

spring

sqépc – spring season.

es qpcṁnuxʷisti, *es qpcṁnuxʷi* – It is again the time of spring. *suffix: **...ṁnuxʷ** – in the time of.*

l sqépc u l sʔanłq – In spring and summer. **ččʔit łu sqépc** – It is almost spring.

es kʷálulexʷi – plants are coming up. *See: **grow**.*
es x̣ecti – digging. *See: **dig**.*
es wiq̓łceʔi – hunt to get bull buffalo (for their hides). *See: **hunt**.*

es ocqʔétkʷ – The water is coming out; spring. *suffix: **...etkʷ, ...tkʷ** – liquid*
ocqʔetkʷ, *ocqʔe* – Ronan, Flathead Nation.

nłaʔpqnetkʷ – headwaters; where the water begins *(i.e., a spring, fountain, lake)*. *See: **headwater**.*

iłpṗóc – wire spring.

spring beauty

skʷṅkʷinm, *skʷṅkʷi* – spring beauty; Indian potato.

sprinkle

łłnulexʷtn – spread water on the ground; water the ground; sprinkle. *rt.: **łin** – spread liquid; suffix: **...ulexʷ** – land; suffix: **...tin, ...tn** – means of/device.*
łłnulexʷm – S/he watered the ground. **čn łłnulexʷm, kʷ łłnulexʷm**
es łłnulexʷi – S/he is watering the ground. **čnes łłnulexʷi, kʷes łłulexʷi**
qs łłnulexʷi – S/he is going to water the ground. **čiqs łłnulexʷi, kʷqs łłnulexʷi**

čiqs k̓ʷis łłnulexʷi t supulexʷ – I am going to go water the lawn.

łin – splash/sprinkle and spread liquid. *See: **splash**.*

sprinkler

pċikʷmn – sprinkler. *See: **squirt**.*
pčkʷċikʷ – It squirts repeatedly.

sprout

łkʷkʷʔáḷ – sprout. *lit. grow a little. See: **grow**.*

spruce

ṫsṫséłp, *ṫsṫsé* – spruce; *Picea engelmannii*.

spruce grouse

skʷiskʷs – spruce grouse; Franklin's grouse; fools hen; *Falcipennis canadensis*; domestic chicken. *See: **chicken**.*

spur

k̓ʷłṫḷṫḷqnčsqáx̣eʔ, *k̓ʷłṫḷṫḷqnčsqá* – spur a horse.
k̓ʷłṫḷṫḷqnčsqáx̣eʔ – S/he spurred a horse. **čn k̓ʷłṫḷṫḷqnčsqáx̣eʔ, kʷ k̓ʷłṫḷṫḷqnčsqáx̣eʔ**
es k̓ʷłṫḷṫḷqnčsqáx̣eʔi – S/he is spurring a horse. **čnes k̓ʷłṫḷṫḷqnčsqáx̣eʔi, kʷes k̓ʷłṫḷṫḷqnčsqáx̣eʔi**
qs k̓ʷłṫḷṫḷqnčsqáx̣eʔi – S/he is going to spur a horse. **čiqs k̓ʷłṫḷṫḷqnčsqáx̣eʔi, kʷqs k̓ʷłṫḷṫḷqnčsqáx̣eʔi**

k̓ʷłṫḷṫḷqnčsqáx̣eʔtn – spur. *suffix: **...tin, ...tn** – means of/device.*

k̓ʷłṫḷṫḷqnčsqáx̣eʔiš – Spur. *cmd.*

sċḷċlepšn – spur.

square

q̓tq̓it – square; has flat sides.
es q̓tq̓it – It is square.

squash **skʷašiš** – squash.

sq̇álixʷqn – pumpkin; squash.

squat **laq̇ʷq̇ʷmist** – squat; sit low.
laq̇ʷq̇ʷmist – S/he squatted. **čn laq̇ʷq̇ʷmist, kʷ laq̇ʷq̇ʷmist**
es laq̇ʷq̇ʷmisti – S/he is squatting. **čnes laq̇ʷq̇ʷmisti, kʷes laq̇ʷq̇ʷmisti**
qs laq̇ʷq̇ʷmisti – S/he is going to squat. **čiqs laq̇ʷq̇ʷmisti, kʷqs laq̇ʷq̇ʷmisti**

łkʷk̓ʷimist – crouch; squat low; make self small. *See:* ***crouch.***

squeak **iq̇iq̇lš** – squeak noise.

ċmċumłš łu k̓ʷékʷt̓neʔ – The mouse is squeaking.

squeeze **ċán** – tight; fixed in place; constricted; well fastened. *See:* ***tight.***

ċip̓ – pinch.
nċip̓s – wink.
k̓ʷłċip̓cnm – choke somebody.
ies k̓ʷłċip̓cnm – I am choking him/her.

p̓iċ – squeeze; put pressure on something.
p̓iċm – put violent pressure on.
qeʔes p̓iċmłls – controlling, getting the best of us.
qʷo es p̓iċmłls – controlling, getting the best of me.
kʷ es p̓iċmłls – controlling, getting the best of you.

p̓ulk̓ʷ – fold/roll up, not flat. *See:* ***fold.***

q̇ʷʔe – wring; twist; squeeze. *See:* ***wring.***

squirrel **iscč** – pine squirrel; *Tamiasciurus hudsonicus.*
es iscči – S/he is being like a squirrel *(eating or acting like).* **čnes iscči, kʷes iscči**

sxʷupxʷp – northern flying squirrel; *Glaucomys sabrinus.*

sisč – gopher; Columbia ground squirrel; *Spermophilus columbianus.*

squirt **pċikʷm** – squirt; spray.
čpċikʷmis – S/he sprayed s.t. **čpċikʷmn, čpċikʷmntxʷ**
es čpċikʷmnms – S/he is spraying s.t. **ies čpċikʷmnm, as čpċikʷmnm**

pċikʷmn – sprinkler.

čpċikʷmnt – Spray it. *cmd.*

pċkʷċikʷ – It squirts repeatedly.

pċam – have diarrhea; evacuate liquid feces; skunk sprays. *See:* ***diarrhea.***

squish **łóc** – smash, mash. *See:* ***smash.***

es p̓at̓ – It is something soft and squishy *(i.e., excrement, brains, a wet hide, etc.) (If someone has a big belly* ***es p̓at̓*** *can be said about it.)*; figuratively when a person feels tired and loose. *See:* ***pile.***

stab **łʔum** – pierce something with a sharp object. *(i.e., stab w/ knife, sting by a bee, a shot in the arm, pricked with a needle, etc.)*

The **i** following uvular consonants (UC) and the glottal stop ʔ sound like English "*ey*" as in the words th*ey*, h*ey*, wh*ey*, etc. Salish UC are: **q**, **q̇**, **qʷ**, **q̇ʷ**, **x̣**, **x̣ʷ**. For example, the suffix ...**qin** – head/top, is often spelled using English *ey* as "q*ey*n". So **qi**, **q̇i**, **qʷi**, **q̇ʷi**, **x̣i**, **x̣ʷi**, may be spelled with English *ey* as **q***ey*, **q̇***ey*, **qʷ***ey*, **q̇ʷ***ey*, **x̣***ey*, **x̣ʷ***ey* in other texts.

s.t. - something, the 3rd person
(s.t.) - something implied
s.o. - someone, the 3rd person
sl. - singular form
pl. - plural form
rt. - root word
cmd. - command
lit. - literally
fig. - figuratively
i.e., - for example
See: - Redirection to a related word.

ɬˀuntés – S/he stabbed it. **ɬˀuntén, ɬˀuntéxʷ**
es ɬˀums – S/he is stabbing it. **ies ɬˀum, as ɬˀum**
qs ɬˀums – S/he is going to stab it. **iqs ɬˀum, aqs ɬˀum**
ɬˀuntéˀes – They stabbed it, they poked it. **qeˀ ɬˀuntém, ɬˀuntép**

ɬˀuntém – S/he/it was stung/stabbed.

ɬumin – spear.
ɬuɬẇé – thorn.

ɬˀunt – Stab it. *cmd.*
ɬuˀax̣nm – stab or give a shot in the arm. *See: **shot**.*
ɬuwep – get a shot; get stabbed. *See: **shot**.*
ɬwepɬ – poke an orifice. *See: **poke**.*

kʷ ɬwenšntm – You were stabbed/poked. **qʷo ɬˀuntés –** S/he/it stung/stabbed me. **qʷo ɬˀuntém –** I was stung/stabbed.

stable **snt̓pyutsqá –** barn, stable. *rt.: **t̓pyeẇt** – stand around pl.; suffix: **...sqáx̣eˀ** – domestic animal; mainly referring to a horse or car.*

stack **čqteẇs –** stack one thing on top of another.
čqteẇsis – S/he stacked s.t. on. **čqteẇsn, čqteẇsntxʷ**
es čqteẇsms – S/he is stacking s.t. on. **ies čqteẇsm, as čqteẇsm**
qs čqteẇsms – S/he is going to stack s.t. on. **iqs čqteẇsm, aqs čqteẇsm**

čqtelisis – S/he stacked several things. **čqtelisn, čqtelisntxʷ**
es čqtelisms – S/he is stacking s.t. on. **ies čqtelism, as čqtelism**
qs čqteẇsms – S/he is going to stack s.t. on. **iqs čqtelism, aqs čqtelism**

es čqteẇs – They are stacked one on the other.
es čqtelis – They are stacked evenly.

es čqqx̣nax̣n – His/her legs are stacked one on the other. **čnes čqqx̣nax̣n, kʷes čqqx̣nax̣n**
es čqqtusaqstšn – His/her legs are stacked one on the other. **čnes čqqtusaqstšn, kʷes čqqtusaqstšn**

t̓qem – stack things; piled things; lying in a heap.
t̓qem – S/he stacked. **čn t̓qem, kʷ t̓qem**
es t̓qmi – S/he is stacking. **čnes t̓qmi, kʷes t̓qmi**
qs t̓qmi – S/he is going to stack. **čiqs t̓qmi, kʷqs t̓qmi**

čt̓qntés – S/he stacked s.t. on. **čt̓qntén, čt̓qntéxʷ**
es čt̓qems – S/he is stacking s.t. on. **ies čt̓qem, as čt̓qem**
qs čt̓qems – S/he is going to stack s.t. on. **iqs čt̓qem, aqs čt̓qem**

es t̓aq – It is piled; lying in a heap.

čt̓qent – Stack it. *cmd.*
nt̓qetkʷm – stack/put it in the water.

qeˀ t̓qém t supulexʷ – We stacked the hay.

čp̓nusntxʷ t čičitn̓é m še čt̓qntéxʷ t ant̓qéɬp – Lay alders in the fire, then stack on your ferns.

nx̣p̓melis – stack solid objects. *(i.e., boxes, books, etc.) rt.: **x̣p̓** – line, coat.*
nx̣p̓melisis – S/he stacked objects. **nx̣p̓melisn, nx̣p̓melisntxʷ**
es nx̣p̓melisms – S/he is stacking objects. **ies nx̣p̓melism, as nx̣p̓melism**
qs nx̣p̓melisms – S/he is going to stack objects. **iqs nx̣p̓melism, aqs nx̣p̓melism**

nx̣pmelisnt – Stack it. *cmd.*

staff **sčċla** – eagle feather staff.

stagger **plpillš** – stagger.
es plpillši – S/he is staggering. **čnes plpillši, kʷes plpillši**

pillš – stagger once. *(as in getting up from a chair)*
łpl̓pil̓l̓ – staggering a little.

stairs **snčiwlštn** – stairs; ladder. *prefix:* ***sn...*** *– a place of; suffix:* ***...tin, ...tn*** *– means of/device.*
č nwist – up; upstairs; up high.

stake **ċq̇ʷpełxʷ**, *ċq̇ʷpe* – tipi stakes. *rt.:* ***ċóq̇ʷ*** *– point; suffix:* ***...ełxʷ, ...łxʷ*** *– house.*

stall **snačsušsqá** – stall. *rt.:* ***ečswíš*** *– stand; prefix:* ***sn...*** *– a place of; suffix:* ***...sqax̣eʔ, ...sqa*** *–domestic animal; mainly referring to horse or car.*

čč̓sme – the car stalls.

stallion **nmlmlk̓ʷépls**, *nmlmlk̓ʷé* – male animal; bull, stallion. *suffix:* ***...epls*** *– testicle.*

stamp **čcpq̇min** – postage stamp.

stand **ečswíš** – in a standing position; on one's feet.
ečswíš – S/he/it was standing. **čn ečswíš, kʷ ečswíš**
es ečswiši – S/he/it is standing. **čnes ečswíši, kʷes ečswíši**
qs ečswíši – S/he/it is going to be standing. **čiqs ečswíši, kʷqs ečswíši**

ečswíšis – S/he/it made s.o. stand on one's feet. **ečswíšn, ečswíšntxʷ**
es ečswíšms – S/he/it is making s.o. stand on one's feet. **ies ečswíšm, as ečswíšm**
qs ečswíšms – S/he/it is going to make s.o. stand on one's feet. **iqs ečswíšm, aqs ečswíšm**

snkʷłʔečswíš – the one stands with one. *prefix:* ***nkʷł...*** *– together with.*

ečswíšiš – Be on your feet. *cmd.*
ečswíšnt – Put s.o. on their feet. *cmd.*
čłečsušetkʷ – stand on the water. *suffix:* ***...etkʷ, ...tkʷ*** *– liquid*
k̓ʷłečsušetkʷ – stand under the water. *suffix:* ***...etkʷ, ...tkʷ*** *– liquid*
ečsušcnetkʷ – stand by the water. *suffix:* ***...etkʷ, ...tkʷ*** *– liquid*
čłečswiš – stand on the surface of something.
čłečsušeneʔ – stand over something. *circumfix:* ***čł...eneʔ*** *– cover all over.*
k̓ʷłnečsušep – stand at a door.
čečsušep – stand by a door.
čačsušqin – stand on top/mountain. *suffix:* ***...qin, ...qn*** *– top.*
čačsušalqʷ – stand on a log/wood.

nʔečsušétkʷ – S/he/it was standing in the water. **čn nʔečsušétkʷ, kʷ nʔečsušétkʷ**
es nʔečsušétkʷi – S/he/it was standing in the water. **čnes nʔečsušétkʷi, kʷes nʔečsušétkʷi**

l čeṅ u ečswíš łu sṁma – Where is the cow standing? **q̇si l šeẏ čn ečswíš i čn ƛ̓il** – I stood there a long time, I did not move.

ṫpyeẁt – more than one standing. *suffix:* ***...éẁt*** *– group state.*
ṫpip – They stood up. **qeʔ ṫpip, p ṫpip**

The **i** following uvular consonants (UC) and the glottal stop **ʔ** sound like English "*ey*" as in the words th*ey*, h*ey*, wh*ey*, etc. Salish UC are: **q, q̇, qʷ, q̇ʷ, x̣, x̣ʷ**. For example, the suffix ...**qin** – head/top, is often spelled using English *ey* as "q*ey*n". So **qi, q̇i, qʷi, q̇ʷi, x̣i, x̣ʷi**, may be spelled with English *ey* as **q***ey*, **q̇***ey*, **qʷ***ey*, **q̇ʷ***ey*, **x̣***ey*, **x̣ʷ***ey* in other texts.

s.t. - something, the 3rd person
(s.t.) - something implied
s.o. - someone, the 3rd person
sl. - singular form
pl. - plural form
rt. - root word
cmd. - command
lit. - literally
fig. - figuratively
i.e., - for example
See: - Redirection to a related word.

ṫpyéˀeẇt – They are standing around. **qeˀ ṫpyeẇt, p ṫpyeẇt**

ṫppstes – S/he made them stand. **ṫppsten, ṫppstexʷ**
es ṫppims – S/he is making them stand. **ies ṫppim, as ṫppim**
qs ṫppims – S/he is going to make them stand. **iqs ṫppim, aqs ṫppim**

ṫpṫpyeẇt – Two or more groups are standing around.

ṫpipwi – All of you stand up. *cmd.*

snṫpyutsqá – barn, stable.

ṫpmncut – They stood up.

wičtn xʷˀit snčłċásqá nṫpyeẇt – I saw a lot of horses standing around. **l es milkʷ u ṫpṫpyeẇt łu qʷqʷċẇé –** Chipmunks were standing all over.

tešlš – the motion of standing up; also in reference to something coming up/coming about *(i.e., moon, month, sun).*
tešlš – S/he/it stood up. **čn tešlš, kʷ tešlš**
es tešlši – S/he/it is standing up. **čnes tešlši, kʷes tešlši**
qs tešlši – S/he is going to stand up. **čiqs tešlši, kʷqs tešlši**

sxʷtéšlš – temporary getter-upper. *prefix:* ***sxʷ...*** *– one tasked to do.*

téšlš – Stand up. *cmd.*
k̓ʷłtšlšalqʷ – stand under a tree/log. *prefix:* ***k̓ʷł...*** *– under; suffix:* ***...alqʷ*** *– wood; cylindical.*
ntšlšétkʷ – S/he/it stood up in the water. **čn ntšlšétkʷ, kʷ ntšlšétkʷ**
es ntšlšétkʷi – S/he/it is standing up in the water. **čnes ntšlšétkʷi, kʷes ntšlšétkʷi**

téšlš l x̣lep – Stand on the floor. **k̓ʷłtéšlš l es šiṫ –** S/he stood under a tree. **kʷitisi tešlš – kʷitisi** stood up. **ntšlšétkʷ łu sṫṁá –** The cow stood up in the water. **tleˀešlš –** They stood up *(i.e., animals).*

šiṫ – an object stands upright, not a person.
šṫntés – S/he/it stood s.t. up. **šṫntén, šṫntéxʷ**
es šṫims – S/he/it is standing s.t. up. **ies šṫim, as šṫim**
qs šṫims – S/he/it is going to stand s.t. up. **iqs šṫim, aqs šṫim**
šṫntéˀes – They stood s.t. up. **qeˀ šṫntém, šṫntép**
es šṫíˀims – They are standing s.t. up. **qeˀes šṫim, es šṫimp**

es nšṫšṫulexʷ – each one is standing up in the ground. *(i.e., power poles, fence posts)*
es šiṫ – It is standing upright; tree.
nšṫeẇs – It stood up in the middle. *suffix:* ***...éẇs*** *– in between, middle.*
nšṫnten – I stood it up inside of something.

l̓ es nšṫulexʷ m čṫk̓ʷntéxʷ anq̓étt – Put your hide on a pole in the ground. **ṅnšṫéẇs –** Standing-In-Middle *(Eagle pass in the Mission Mountain Range, Flathead Nation; a pillar of rock stands in the middle of the pass).*

ċil – more than one object stands upright, not people.
ċlntés – S/he/it put them upright. **ċlntén, ċlntéxʷ**
es ċlims – S/he/it is putting them upright. **ies ċlim, as ċlim**
qs ċlims – S/he/it is going to put them upright. **iqs ċlim, aqs ċlim**

es nċlulexʷ – They are standing up in the ground. *(i.e., power poles, fence posts)*
es ċlċil – They are standing upright.
ċlċil – trees. *rt.:* ***ċil*** *– standing upright.*

ċáaẇt – standing around. *(i.e., small grove of trees, group of people; derogatory, used to describe people) suffix:* ***...éẇt*** *– group state.*

ċlċil ċáawt – small stand of trees.

k̓ʷléw̓t – gathered/standing together. *(refers to standing; i.e., people, trees, etc.) See:* ***gather***.

qʷaxʷ – animals standing.
qʷaxʷm – The animal was standing.
es qʷaxʷi – The animal is standing.
es qʷáˀaxʷm – They were standing.
es qʷáˀaxʷi – They are standing.

qʷaxʷis – S/he made the animal stand. **qʷaxʷn, qʷaxʷntxʷ**
es qʷaxʷms – S/he is making the animal stand. **ies qʷaxʷm, as qʷaxʷm**

qʷxʷéw̓t – animals standing together. *(refers to standing; i.e., animals, trees, etc.; derogatory, used to describe people standing around.) See:* ***gather***.

xʷt̓ilš – get up from a resting/laying state; rise. *See:* ***rise***.

The **i** following uvular consonants (UC) and the glottal stop **ˀ** sound like English "*ey*" as in the words *they*, *hey*, *whey*, etc. Salish UC are: **q**, **q̓**, **qʷ**, **q̓ʷ**, **x̣**, **x̣ʷ**. For example, the suffix **...qin** – head/top, is often spelled using English *ey* as "q*ey*n". So **qi**, **q̓i**, **qʷi**, **q̓ʷi**, **x̣i**, **x̣ʷi**, may be spelled with English *ey* as **q***ey*, **q̓***ey*, **qʷ***ey*, **q̓ʷ***ey*, **x̣***ey*, **x̣ʷ***ey* in other texts.

staple

x̣p̓éw̓stn – staple. *rt.:* ***x̣p̓*** *– line, coat; suffix:* ***...tin, ...tn*** *– means of/device.*

stapler

q̓ey̓min x̣p̓ew̓stn – stapler.

čip̓mn l q̓ey̓min – stapler; pinches paper.

star

kʷkʷusm̓ – star.

smx̣éy̓čn̓asq̓t – North Star.

st̓ips kʷkʷusm̓ – shooting star; falling star.

stare

čx̣aˀx̣apsus, *čx̣aˀx̣apsu* **–** stare.
čx̣apłtumš – S/he/it stared at people. **čn čx̣apłtumš, kʷ čx̣apłtumš**
es čx̣apłtumši – S/he/it is staring at people. **čnes čx̣apłtumši, kʷes čx̣apłtumši**
qs čx̣apłtumši – S/he/it is going to stare at people. **čiqs čx̣apłtumši, kʷqs čx̣apłtumši**

čx̣aˀx̣apłtemn – one inclined to stare. *suffix:* ***...emn*** *– one inclined to do.*
čx̣aˀx̣apsuł – one who stares all the time.
uł čx̣aˀx̣apsuł – They are the ones who stare all the time.

šƛ̓us – search/stare around; look from one thing to the next; scan. *See:* ***search***.

es áċċx̣m – I am watching, staring . *See:* ***watch***.
qesyaˀ u qeˀes acċx̣m łu sxʷwenš – We are all staring at the dancer.

čƛ̓lƛ̓lpus – not blinking; eyes are still. *rt.:* ***ƛ̓il*** *– no movement; circumfix:* ***č...us*** *– spherical object; eyes.*

snap – stare off; daydream; become quiet and calm; settled. *See:* ***daydream***.

start

čtax̣ʷléčst, *čtax̣ʷlé* **–** start; begin; make something go a certain way/direction.
čtax̣ʷléčst – S/he is started. **čn čtax̣ʷléčst, kʷes čtax̣ʷléčst**
es čtax̣ʷléčsti – S/he is starting. **čnes čtax̣ʷléčsti, kʷes čtax̣ʷléčsti**
qs čtax̣ʷléčsti – S/he is going to start. **čiqs čtax̣ʷléčsti, kʷqs čtax̣ʷléčsti**

čtax̣ʷléčsis – S/he made s.t. start. **čtax̣ʷléčsn, čtax̣ʷléčsntxʷ**
es čtax̣ʷléčstms – S/he is making s.t. start. **ies čtax̣ʷléčstm, as čtax̣ʷléčstm**
qs čtax̣ʷléčstms – S/he is going to make s.t. start. **iqs čtax̣ʷléčstm, aqs čtax̣ʷléčstm**

s.t. - something, the 3rd person
(s.t.) - something implied
s.o. - someone, the 3rd person
sl. - singular form
pl. - plural form
rt. - root word
cmd. - command
lit. - literally
fig. - figuratively
i.e., - for example
See: - Redirection to a related word.

ṅem lk̓ʷinš m qeʔ čtax̣ʷle m qeʔ q̓mq̓mi – What time will we start our meeting? **ṅe i čp̓xʷp̓éxʷs kʷéṁt m kʷ čtax̣ʷlé kʷqs qʷl̓épi –** When they are red-hot, then you start your baking.

tax̣ʷlus – face/head toward a direction; start in a direction.
tax̣ʷlus – S/he/it headed in that direction. **čn tax̣ʷlus, kʷ tax̣ʷlus**
es tax̣ʷlusi – S/he/it is heading in that direction. **čnes tax̣ʷlusi, kʷes tax̣ʷlusi**
qs tax̣ʷlusi – S/he/it is going to head in that direction. **čiqs tax̣ʷlusi, kʷqs tax̣ʷlusi**

es tax̣ʷlus – S/he/it continues in that direction. **čnes tax̣ʷlus, kʷes tax̣ʷlus**

tl̓ʔe es tax̣ʷlus – It starts from here. **č ƛ̓aq̓lexʷ u es tax̣ʷlus –** S/he/it is heading in toward the south. **tl̓ člxʷtin u es ctax̣ʷlus –** S/he/it is heading this way from the west.

xʷistm – start something; make something go. *(i.e., start a car, etc.)*
xʷistis – S/he started it. **xʷistn, xʷistntxʷ**
es xʷistms – S/he is starting it. **ies xʷistm, as xʷistm**
qs xʷistms – S/he is going to start it. **iqs xʷistm, aqs xʷistm**

qʷmep – move off as a group; start the move; group journey. *See: **move**.*

nčcnus – arrive at the start of a time period, the beginning of an action, or the edge of a place. *See: **arrive**.*

startle

kʷssusm, *kʷssu* **–** startle.
kʷssus – S/he got startled. **čn kʷssus, kʷ kʷssus**
kʷssúʔus – They got startled. **qeʔ kʷssus, p kʷssus**

kʷsusis – S/he/it startled s.o./s.t. **kʷsusn, kʷsusntxʷ**
es kʷssusms – S/he/it is startling s.o./s.t. **ies kʷssusm, as kʷssusm**
qs kʷssusms – S/he/it is going to startle s.o./s.t. **iqs kʷssusm, aqs kʷssusm**
kʷsúʔusis – They startled s.o./s.t. **qeʔ kʷsusntm, kʷsusntp**

kʷsusts – S/he/it caused s.o./s.t. to get startled. **kʷsustn, kʷsustxʷ**
kʷsúʔusts – They caused s.o./s.t. to get startled. **qeʔ kʷsustm, kʷsustp**

łkʷkʷsus – S/he/it got a little startled. **čn łkʷkʷsus, kʷ łkʷkʷsus**
łkʷkʷsusts – S/he/it caused s.o./s.t. to get a little startled. **łkʷkʷsustn, łkʷkʷsustxʷ**

kʷsustm – S/he/it got startled.
kʷsstnuis – S/he finally startled s.o./s.t. **kʷsstnun, kʷsstnuntxʷ**
kʷsustšts – S/he startled s.o./s.t. for s.o. **kʷsustštn, kʷsustštxʷ**

sxʷkʷskʷsusm – one tasked to startle. *prefix: **sxʷ...** – one tasked to do.*
kʷskʷsemn – one inclined to startle. *suffix: **...emn** – one inclined to do.*
kʷssemn – one inclined to get startled. *suffix: **...emn** – one inclined to do.*
kʷsustn – something used to startle.

kʷsusiš – Startle. *cmd.*
kʷsuswi – You all startle. *cmd.*
kʷsuskʷ – Startle someone. *cmd.*
kʷsusnt – Startle s.o. *cmd.*
kʷuskʷst – ugly; scary looking. *See: **ugly**.*
kʷsscut – S/he/it startled one's self. **čn kʷsscut, kʷ kʷsscut**
es kʷsscuti – S/he/it is startling one's self. **čnes kʷsscuti, kʷes kʷsscuti**
es kʷssnwexʷisti – They are startling each other. **qeʔes kʷssnwexʷisti, pes kʷssnwexʷisti**
nkʷskʷscin – startling noise.
es kʷskʷtlwisi – S/he is going around startling. **čnes kʷskʷtlwisi, kʷes kʷskʷtlwisi**

qʷo kʷsustštxʷ – Startle s.o. for me. **qʷo kʷsustm** – I was startled. **em u kʷsustn** – Finally I startled s.o. **ax̣í u kʷsustn** – I finally startled s.o. **ha kʷsustmn** – Did I startle you?

nx̣él – afraid/scared of something. *See:* ***scared.***

kʷˀeɫ – jumpy; nervous; edgy; frantic. *See:* ***nervous.***

čin – afraid of getting hurt; careful and cautious. *(i.e., falling, etc.) See:* ***afraid.***

> The **i** following uvular consonants (UC) and the glottal stop **ˀ** sound like English "*ey*" as in the words th*ey*, h*ey*, wh*ey*, etc. Salish UC are: **q**, **q̇**, **qʷ**, **q̇ʷ**, **x̣**, **x̣ʷ**. For example, the suffix …**qin** – head/top, is often spelled using English *ey* as "q*ey*n". So **qi**, **q̇i**, **qʷi**, **q̇ʷi**, **x̣i**, **x̣ʷi**, may be spelled with English *ey* as **q***ey*, **q̇***ey*, **qʷ***ey*, **q̇ʷ***ey*, **x̣***ey*, **x̣ʷ***ey* in other texts.

starve

čsq̇méltn, *čsq̇mé* – hungry/starving for food; figuratively, spiritually hungry. *See:* ***hungry.***

stay

lciˀ – stays here; remains here; dwells. *rt.:* ***ci*** *– that.*
lciˀ – S/he/it stayed/remained here. **čn lciˀ, kʷ lciˀ**
es lciˀ – S/he/it stays/remains here. **čnes lciˀ, kʷes lciˀ**

snlciˀtn – place of living, dwelling; home. *prefix:* ***sn…*** *– a place of; suffix:* ***…tin, …tn*** *– means of/device.*

lciˀš – stay here.
lciˀm – let it be; yield to; permit it; allow to continue. *See:* ***let.***

ṅe qeˀ wis k̓ʷul̓łxʷ ṁ l šey̓ ṁ qeˀ lciˀ – When we finish building the house, we'll live in it.

člciˀm – stay by it; remain with it. *rt.:* ***ci*** *– that; prefix:* ***č…*** *– upon.*
člciˀmis – S/he stayed by it. **člciˀmn, člciˀmnxʷ**
es člciˀms – S/he is staying by it. **ies člciˀm, as člciˀm**
qs člciˀms – S/he is going to stay by it. **iqs člciˀm, aqs člciˀm**

člciˀmncutn – one that remains/stays by someone.

člciˀmnt – Stay by it; stay with it. *cmd.*

nkʷɫciˀm – stay together with someone; remain together with someone. *rt.:* ***ci*** *– that; prefix:* ***snkʷɫ…*** *– fellow, member of.*
nkʷɫciˀmis – S/he stayed by it. **nkʷɫciˀmn, nkʷɫciˀmntxʷ**
es nkʷɫciˀms – S/he is staying by it. **ies nkʷɫciˀm, as nkʷɫciˀm**
qs nkʷɫciˀms – S/he is going to stay by it. **iqs nkʷɫciˀm, aqs nkʷɫciˀm**

nkʷɫciˀmnt – Stay together with him/her; stay together with him/her. *cmd.*

lšeˀ – stays there; roams in that general area; home range. *rt.:* ***še*** *– that.*
lšeˀ– S/he/it stayed there. **čn lšeˀ, kʷ lšeˀ**
es lšeˀ– S/he/it stays there. **čnes lšeˀ, kʷes lšeˀ**

snlšeˀtn – habitat; roaming area.

lšeˀš – stay there.

lˀe – this here. *See:* ***here.***

iˀe – this very one here. *See:* ***here.***

steal

náq̇ʷ – steal; rob.
náq̇ʷm – S/he stole. **čn náq̇ʷm, kʷ náq̇ʷm**
es náq̇ʷi – S/he is stealing. **čnes náq̇ʷm, kʷes náq̇ʷi**
qs náq̇ʷi – S/he is going to steal. **čiqs náq̇ʷm, kʷqs náq̇ʷi**
náˀaq̇ʷm – They stole. **qeˀ náq̇ʷm, p náq̇ʷm**

náq̇ʷmis – S/he stole. **náq̇ʷmn, náq̇ʷmntxʷ**
es náq̇ʷms – S/he is stealing. **ies náq̇ʷm, as náq̇ʷm**

> s.t. - something, the 3rd person
> (s.t.) - something implied
> s.o. - someone, the 3rd person
> *sl.* - singular form
> *pl.* - plural form
> *rt.* - root word
> *cmd.* - command
> *lit.* - literally
> *fig.* - figuratively
> *i.e.,* - for example
> *See:* - Redirection to a related word.

qs náq̓ʷms – S/he is going to steal. **iqs náq̓ʷm, aqs náq̓ʷm**
náʔaq̓ʷmis – They stole. **qeʔ náq̓ʷmntm, náq̓ʷmntp**

sxʷnaq̓ʷ – one tasked to steal; a thief. *prefix:* ***sxʷ...*** *– one tasked to do.*
naq̓ʷémn – one inclined to steal; a thief. *suffix:* ***...emn*** *– one inclined to do.*
scnaq̓ʷ – something that's been stolen. *prefix:* ***sc...*** *– s.t. that's been done/made/prepared.*
čnaq̓ʷlqʷi – stealing a ride on a train, bus or car. *rt.:* ***naq̓ʷ*** *– steal.; suffix:* ***...lqʷ*** *– s.t. that rolls.*
čnq̓ʷnáq̓ʷm, *čnq̓ʷná* – hitcherhiker; hobo.
nq̓ʷsqáx̣eʔ, *nq̓ʷsqá* – steal a horse/car.
puʔnaq̓ʷmn – I stole his/her spouse.

k̓ʷ še eł p̓lč̓ʔu eł k̓ʷis náʔaq̓ʷ – They turned back, and stole. **qʷo náq̓ʷmłts isicm** – S/he stole my blanket. **náq̓ʷłtm** – S/he stole from s.o. **qʷo náq̓ʷłtm iscpuls** – My kill was stolen.

k̓ʷłnq̓ʷmist, *k̓ʷłnq̓ʷmi* – run away; to sneak away; to leave; escape. *rt.:* ***naq̓ʷ*** *– steal; prefix:* ***k̓ʷł...*** *– under. See:* ***escape****.*

nčm̓éłxʷ – rob.

steam
sxʷul – steam.
es xʷulmi – It is evaporating; steaming.

ssalut – white from steam or fog.

steep
šlšalt – upward slope.
łšlšalt – little upward slope.

steering wheel
sntx̣ʷsqax̣eʔtn – steering wheel.

Stellar's jay
qʷásqʷiʔ – blue jay, Stellar's jay.

stem
sčt̓emp – stem of a flower; tree trunk.
es čt̓emp – It comes to the core.

nilemp – stem of a feather/branch/leaf.
es nilemp – It comes to the stem/center.

step
ql̓wet, *ql̓we* – step on something.
ql̓wet – S/he/it stepped. **čn ql̓wet, kʷ ql̓wet**
es ql̓weti – S/he/it is stepping. **čnes ql̓weti, kʷes ql̓weti**
qs ql̓weti – S/he/it is going to step. **čiqs ql̓weti, kʷqs ql̓weti**

ql̓wetis – S/he/it stepped on s.t./s.o. **ql̓wetn, ql̓wetntxʷ**
es ql̓wetms – S/he/it is stepping on s.t./s.o. **ies ql̓wetm, as ql̓wetm**
qs ql̓wetms – S/he/it is going to step on s.t./s.o. **iqs ql̓wetm, aqs ql̓wetm**
ql̓weʔetis – They stepped on s.t./s.o. **qeʔ ql̓wetntm, ql̓wetntp**

ql̓wetiš – Step. *cmd.*
ql̓wetnt – Step on it. *cmd.*
nql̓utetkʷ – step into the water.
nql̓utelis – step/trample things uniformly/uniform things.
nk̓ʷuʔscql̓we – yard (one step).
čłql̓uteneʔ – cover something with a step.

nql̓otłq̓eytm – step on shoulders.
nql̓otłq̓eytis – S/he stepped on s.o.'s shoulders. **nql̓otłq̓eytn, nql̓otłq̓eytntxʷ**
es nql̓otłq̓eytms – S/he is stepping on s.o.'s shoulders. **ies nql̓otłq̓eytm, as nql̓otłq̓eytm**

qs nqľotłq̓eytms – S/he is going to step on s.o.'s shoulders. **iqs nqľotłq̓eytm, aqs nqľotłq̓eytm**

nqľotłq̓éytn, *nqľotłq̓é* – shovel.

čxʷálšn – extend the foot to something; take a step.
čxʷálšn – S/he/it stepped. **čn čxʷálšn, kʷ čxʷálšn**
es čxʷálšni – S/he/it is stepping. **čnes čxʷálšni, kʷes čxʷálšni**
qs čxʷálšni – S/he/it is going to step to s.t. **čiqs čxʷálšni, kʷqs čxʷálšni**

čxʷálšnmis – S/he/it stepped to s.t. **čn čxʷálšn, kʷ čxʷálšn**
es čxʷálšnmms – S/he/it is stepping to s.t. **ies čxʷálšnmm, as čxʷálšnmm**
qs čxʷálšnmms – S/he/it is going to step to s.t. **iqs čxʷálšnmm, aqs čxʷálšnmm**

čxʷálšnmnt – Step to it. *cmd.*

yomšniš – step with tensed leg so as not to slip and/or fall. *(i.e., walking on ice, walking on a wet floor, etc.) rt.: **yóo** – strong; suffix: **...šin, ...šn** – feet.*
yoyomšniš – S/he stepped with tensed legs. **čn yoyomšniš, kʷ yoyomšniš**
es yoyomšniš – S/he is stepping with tensed legs. **čnes yoyomšniš, kʷew yoyomšniš**

The **i** following uvular consonants (UC) and the glottal stop ʔ sound like English "*ey*" as in the words *they, hey, whey*, etc. Salish UC are: **q, q̓, qʷ, q̓ʷ, x̣, x̣ʷ**. For example, the suffix **...qin** – head/top, is often spelled using English *ey* as "q*ey*n". So **qi, q̓i, qʷi, q̓ʷi, x̣i, x̣ʷi**, may be spelled with English *ey* as **q***ey*, **q̓***ey*, **qʷ***ey*, **q̓ʷ***ey*, **x̣***ey*, **x̣ʷ***ey* in other texts.

stepchild

słweľt – stepchild.

step over

čłk̓ʷitšľš – step over something.
čłk̓ʷitšľš l es čiċ – S/he stepped over a log.

stepparent

łwéstn – aunt/uncle after death of connecting relative; stepparent.

sternum

sqpmin – sternum.

stereo

čx̣ʷax̣ʷnč, *čx̣ʷa* – radio; harp; guitar; stereo; anything that makes music.

sterile

siš – pure; purify; sterile. *See: **pure**.*

Stevensville

łq̓éłmlš – Stevensville, Montana. *lit. wide cottonwood.*

stick

łľulk̓ʷ – small wood; stick.

ilmintn – hoop game sticks. *suffix: **...tin, ...tn** – means of/device.*

stmtmniʔálqʷ, *stmtmniʔá* – snowberry (sticks).
q̓aw̓nt ci stmtmniʔá – Break those snowberry (sticks).

čc̓lalqʷtn – stickgame sticks. *suffix: **...tin, ...tn** – means of/device.*

nšťulexʷtn – stick used in the camas bake. *(The stick is placed in the middle prior to putting the contents used in the camas baking pit. After the pit is prepared the stick is pulled out and water is poured in the hole left by the stick.) See: **stand**.*

ncaqʷmn – something used to poke/stick into/through something, *(i.e., stick used in the camas bake, stick used to poke at the fire, etc.). (The stick is placed in the middle prior to putting the contents used in the camas baking pit. After the pit is prepared the stick is pulled out and water is poured in the hole left by the stick.) See: **poke**.*

nšťew̓stn – something that stands up in the middle of something, *(i.e., stick used in the camas bake; etc.). See: **stand**.*

ċax̣ʷmn – stick used to poke at ashes/fire. *rt.: **ċax̣ʷċx̣ʷt** – ashes.*

čc̓p̓aq̓ – stick/adhere something onto something; tape. *See: **sticky**.*

s.t. - something, the 3rd person
(s.t.) - something implied
s.o. - someone, the 3rd person
sl. - singular form
pl. - plural form
rt. - root word
cmd. - command
lit. - literally
fig. - figuratively
i.e., - for example
See: - Redirection to a related word.

čcpq̓em – tape something. *See: **tape**.*

stickgame **c̓alqʷ**, *c̓la* – play stickgame. *rt.: **c̓il** – standing upright; suffix: **...alqʷ** – wood; cylindical.*
c̓alqʷm – S/he played stickgame. **čn c̓alqʷm, kʷ c̓alqʷm**
es c̓alqʷi – S/he is playing stickgame. **čnes c̓alqʷi, kʷes c̓alqʷi**
qs c̓alqʷi – S/he is going to play stickgame. **čiqs c̓alqʷi, kʷqs c̓alqʷi**
es c̓láʔalqʷi – They are playing stickgame. **qeʔes c̓alqʷi, pes c̓alqʷi**

sc̓alqʷ łu l ispúʔus – Stickgame is in my heart. **ha iše kʷ c̓alqʷm** – Do you play stickgame?

sc̓alqʷ, *sc̓la* – stickgame.
sxʷc̓oq̓ʷm – one tasked to point; a pointer. *rt.: **c̓oq̓ʷ** – point; prefix: **sxʷ...** – one tasked to do.*
sxʷwekʷm – one tasked to hide; a hider. *rt.: **wekʷ** – hide; prefix: **sxʷ...** – one tasked to do.*
sxʷminm – hider. *prefix: **sxʷ...** – one tasked to do.*
palq̓i – outside (point).
sčc̓hečst – right (point).
sčciqʷečst – left (point).
nihe – middle (point).

piqlq̓ – point the white bone in stickgame. *rt.: **piq** – white.*
piqlq̓ – S/he pointed the white bone. **čn piqlq̓, kʷ piqlq̓**
es piqlq̓i – S/he is pointing the white bone. **čnes piqlq̓i, kʷes piqlq̓i**
qs piqlq̓i – S/he is going to point the white bone. **čiqs piqlq̓i, kʷqs piqlq̓i**

pqpiqlq̓ – S/he pointed both white bones. **čn pqpiqlq̓, kʷ pqpiqlq̓**
es pqpiqlq̓i – S/he is pointing both white bones. **čnes pqpiqlq̓i, kʷes pqpiqlq̓i**
qs pqpiqlq̓i – S/he is going to point both white bones. **čiqs pqpiqlq̓i, kʷqs pqpiqlq̓i**

šičt – miss something targeted. *See: **miss**.*

nc̓oqʷulexʷ – pull the stick out of the ground.

cqcqminm – switching bones; cheating at stickgame. *rt.: **cqmin** – throw.*

stickgame bones **k̓ʷnk̓ʷi** – stickgame bones.

stickgame poles **snčsp̓alqʷtn** – stickgame poles. *rt.: **sp̓im** – hit; prefix: **sn...** – a place of; suffix: **...tin, ...tn** – means of/device.*

stickgame sticks **čc̓alqʷtn** – stickgame sticks. *rt.: **c̓alqʷ** – stickgame; suffix: **...tin, ...tn** – means of/device.*

stick out **tix̣** – scattered outward protrusions; jut out in a scattered fashion; stick out here and there. *See: **protrude**.*

sticky **i cpaq̓** – It is sticky. *(This word describes the stickiness of substances.)*

cpqq̓milš – It became sticky. *suffix: **...ilš** – autonomous.*
es cpqq̓milš – It is becoming sticky.

cpq̓stes – S/he/it got s.t. sticky. **cpq̓sten, cpq̓stexʷ**
es cpq̓ems – S/he/it is getting s.t. sticky. **ies cpq̓em, as cpq̓em**
qs cpq̓ems – S/he/it is going to get s.t. sticky. **iqs cpq̓em, aqs cpq̓em**

cpq̓ncut – get one's self sticky.
čcpq̓em – tape something. *See: **tape**.*

čc̓p̓aq̓ – stick/adhere something onto something; tape.

čċṗq̇ntes – S/he stuck s.t. on it. **čċṗq̇nten, čċṗq̇ntexʷ**

čċṗq̇ant – Stick it onto it. *cmd.*

ťeɫ – make something sticky; apply paste/sticky substance. *(This word describes making something have a sticky feel by the application of a sticky substance; cause something to become sticky.)*

ťeɫis – S/he made s.t. sticky. **ťeɫn, ťeɫntxʷ**
es ťeɫms – S/he is making s.t. sticky. **ies ťeɫm, as ťeɫm**
qs ťeɫms – S/he is going to make s.t. sticky. **iqs ťeɫm, aqs ťeɫm**

ťeɫtn – pitch gum; Ponderosa pine pitch; sap.

The **i** following uvular consonants (UC) and the glottal stop ʔ sound like English "*ey*" as in the words th*ey*, h*ey*, wh*ey*, etc. Salish UC are: **q**, **q̇**, **qʷ**, **q̇ʷ**, **x̣**, **x̣ʷ**. For example, the suffix ...**qin** – head/top, is often spelled using English *ey* as "q*ey*n". So **qi**, **q̇i**, **qʷi**, **q̇ʷi**, **x̣i**, **x̣ʷi**, may be spelled with English *ey* as **q***ey*, **q̇***ey*, **qʷ***ey*, **q̇ʷ***ey*, **x̣***ey*, **x̣ʷ***ey* in other texts.

sticky purple geranium

tťqnéɫp – sticky purple geranium.

stiff

ƛ̓áx̣ – stiff; hard to move.

ƛ̓x̣ap – S/he/it got stiff. **čn ƛ̓x̣ap, kʷ ƛ̓x̣ap**
es ƛ̓x̣pmi – S/he/it is getting stiff. **čnes ƛ̓x̣pmi, kʷes ƛ̓x̣pmi**

ƛ̓x̣ƛ̓áx̣ – stiff. *pl.*

ƛ̓x̣ƛ̓x̣pšin – legs get stiff.
ƛ̓x̣ƛ̓x̣pax̣n – arms get stiff.

i ƛ̓áx̣ – S/he/it is stiff. **i čn ƛ̓áx̣, i kʷ ƛ̓áx̣**

tẇič – get sore/stiff from being in one position. *See: **sore**.*

still

puti – still.

x̣ʷl̓ šeẏ u puti yetɫx̣ʷasq̇t es cu ɫmɫamá – That is why frog still says that today. **ha puti es xʷlxʷilt –** Is s/he/it still alive? **puti čn q̇ʷiɫ –** I am still able/capable. **ɫu puti či skʷk̓ʷiml̓t nx̣elmn nq̇ʷiq̇ʷosmi –** When I was younger I was afraid of dogs. **ṅe puti isx̣al m p eɫ cxʷixʷuy –** You all come back when it is still light. **puti ċẏu –** It is still not done. **ha puti kʷ epɫ es suɫtumš –** Do you still have any questions?

ƛ̓il – still; no movement.
i ƛ̓il – It is still. **i čn ƛ̓il, i kʷ ƛ̓il**

ƛ̓ilš – Be still. *cmd.*
ƛ̓ilskʷ – Let it be still; leave it alone. *cmd.*
ƛ̓ilskʷwi – All of you leave it still; leave it alone. *cmd.*

ṅem i kʷ ƛ̓il – You will be still.

sting

ɫʔum – pierce something with a sharp object. *See: **stab**.*

ɫuntém – S/he/it was stung by it. **qʷo ɫuntém, kʷ ɫuntém**
ɫuntés – It stung him/her/it. **qʷo ɫuntés**

ɫuẇečst – stung in the hand.
ɫuẇečst – S/he/it got stung on hand. **čn ɫuẇečst, kʷ ɫuẇečst**
es ɫuẇečst – S/he/it is stung on hand. **čnes ɫuẇečst, kʷes ɫuẇečst**

ɫuẇečsis – It stung s.o.'s hand. **qʷo ɫuẇečsis, ɫuẇečsnc**
es ɫuẇečsms – It is stinging s.o.'s hand. **qʷo es ɫuẇečsms, kʷ es ɫuẇečsms**

ɫuẇaẇsqn – stung on the top of the head.
čɫoqin – stung on the head.
nɫuẇeneʔ – stung in the ear.
ɫuẇus – stung in the face.

s.t. - something, the 3rd person
(s.t.) - something implied
s.o. - someone, the 3rd person
sl. - singular form
pl. - plural form
rt. - root word
cmd. - command
lit. - literally
fig. - figuratively
i.e., - for example
See: - Redirection to a related word.

čłuẇus – stung on the eye.
čłłuẇesšn – stung on the forehead.
łuẇaqs – stung in the nose.
k̓ʷłłuẇus – stung in the cheek.
łuẇaposqn – stung in the lip.
łuẇepest – stung on the chin.
čłuẇelps – stung in the neck.
nłuẇičṅ – stung on the back.
čłuẇeẇs – stung in the belly.
łuẇaqstšn – stung in the leg.
čłuẇšin – stung in the foot.

stinger **łumin** – stinger.

stinging nettles **ċċax̣éłp** – stinging nettles; *Urtica dioica.*

stingy **y̓ekʷ** – refuse to give something; be stingy.
y̓ekʷminm – S/he was stingy. **čn y̓ekʷminm, kʷ y̓ekʷminm**
es y̓ekʷmini – S/he is being stingy. **čnes y̓ekʷmini, kʷes y̓ekʷmini**
qs y̓ekʷmini – S/he is going to be stingy. **čiqs y̓ekʷmini, kʷqs y̓ekʷmini**

y̓ekʷmis – S/he refused to give s.t. **y̓ekʷmin, y̓ekʷmintxʷ**
es y̓ekʷminms – S/he is refusing to give s.t. **ies y̓ekʷminm, as y̓ekʷminm**
qs y̓ekʷminms – S/he is going to refuse to give s.t. **iqs y̓ekʷminm, aqs y̓ekʷminm**

y̓ey̓ukʷeʔ – stingy one.

y̓ekʷmemn – one inclined to be stingy. *suffix:* ***...emn*** *– one inclined to do.*
scy̓ekʷmin – something that has been refused to give.

y̓ekʷminš – Be stingy. *cmd.*
y̓ekʷmint – Do not give s.t. *cmd.*
es y̓ekʷmštwexʷi – refuse to give to each other. **qeʔes y̓ekʷmštwexʷi, pes y̓ekʷmštwexʷi**
y̓akʷmnalqs – refuse to give clothing.
y̓ekʷmnełxʷ – refuse to give lodging.
y̓akʷmsqax̣eʔ – refuse to give a horse.
y̓ekʷmist – being miserly. *See:* ***miser.***

stink **čsáłq** – stink; bad smell.

puxʷ – smell bad; stink.
i puxʷ – S/he/it smells. **i čn puxʷ, i kʷ puxʷ**

pxʷup – S/he/it smells/stinks.
qeʔ pxʷup – We smell; we stink.

pxʷpnuis – S/he/it finally smelled s.t. **pxʷpnun, pxʷpnuntxʷ**

spxʷup – an odor.
łpxʷpu – goat.

pxʷpnunt – Smell it. *cmd.*
pxʷpnwexʷ – They smelled each other. **qeʔ pxʷpnwexʷ, p pxʷpnwexʷ**
pepuxʷeʔ – stinky, affectionately.

pxʷpnuncn – I smell you. **ha p pxʷpnwe t isṗuʔ** – Did you folks smell my fart? **ipxʷpuxʷ łu isnq̓ʷóƛ̓šn** – My socks stink.

náq̇ – smell rotten; the smell of rotten meat, crap.
i náq̇ – It is rotten.

i náq̇ps – His/her/its butt is smelly.

nq̇nq̇šin – have stink feet.

i náq̇ sqelt̓č – rotten meat. **t kʷtisi u qʷo x̣ʷičšts t ináq̇ sqelt̓č** – Big Blanket gave me rotten meat. **ha i kʷ náq̇** – Did you mess; are you smelly?

łis – smelly; the smell of fish.
i łis – S/he/it is smelly. **i čn łis, i kʷ łis**

łispósqn, *łispó* – smelly lips/face, fishy smell. *suffix:* ***...posqn*** *– lips. See:* ***lip.***

ix̣ʷwey – smell of an animal in rut.

q̇ʷiˀ – smell like smoke.
i q̇ʷiˀ – S/he/it smells like smoke. **i čn q̇ʷiˀ, i kʷ q̇ʷiˀ**

peˀxʷénč – bloat. *suffix:* ***...enč*** *– within.*

The **i** following uvular consonants (UC) and the glottal stop ˀ sound like English "*ey*" as in the words *they, hey, whey*, etc. Salish UC are: **q, q̇, qʷ, q̇ʷ, x̣, x̣ʷ**. For example, the suffix ...**qin** – head/top, is often spelled using English *ey* as "q*ey*n". So **qi, q̇i, qʷi, q̇ʷi, x̣i, x̣ʷi**, may be spelled with English *ey* as **q***ey*, **q̇***ey*, **qʷ***ey*, **q̇ʷ***ey*, **x̣***ey*, **x̣ʷ***ey* in other texts.

stink bug

p̓up̓umuł, *p̓up̓umu* – stink bug; *Halyomorpha halys. suffix:* ***...łmuł*** *– one that habitually does.*

stir

nax̣letkʷ – stir liquid. *suffix:* ***...etkʷ, ...tkʷ*** *– liquid*
nax̣letkʷ – S/he stirred. **čn nax̣letkʷ, kʷ nax̣letkʷ**
es nax̣letkʷi – S/he is stirring. **čnes nax̣letkʷi, kʷes nax̣letkʷi**
qs nax̣letkʷi – S/he is going to stir. **čiqs nax̣letkʷi, kʷqs nax̣letkʷi**

nax̣letkʷis – S/he stirred it. **nax̣letkʷn, nax̣letkʷntxʷ**
es nax̣letkʷms – S/he is stirring it. **ies nax̣letkʷm, as nax̣letkʷm**
qs nax̣letkʷms – S/he is going to stir it. **iqs nax̣letkʷi, aqs nax̣letkʷi**

sxʷnax̣letkʷ – one tasked to stir. *prefix:* ***sxʷ...*** *– one tasked to do.*
nax̣letkʷtn – stirring tool. *suffix:* ***...tin, ...tn*** *– means of/device.*

nax̣letkʷnt – Stirr it. *cmd.*

nax̣letkʷnt t anłuˀmn – Stirr it with your spoon.

stirrups

snčql̓ql̓wetn, *snčql̓ql̓we* – stirrups. *prefix:* ***sn...*** *– a place of; suffix:* ***...tin, ...tn*** *– means of/device.*
snčql̓wetn, *snčql̓we* – stirrup.

stocking cap

snsot̓qn – stocking cap. *rt.:* ***sut̓*** *– stretch; prefix:* ***sn...*** *– a place of; suffix:* ***...qin, ...qn*** *– top.*

stomach

olin – belly, stomach.
ƛ̓e es kʷłncucw̓e inolin – My stomach's knocking.

nc̓alénč – have a bellyache. *rt.:* ***c̓aál*** *– ache; prefix:* ***n...*** *– inside; suffix:* ***...enč*** *– within.*
nc̓alénč – S/he had a bellyache. **čn nc̓alénč, kʷ nc̓alénč**
es nc̓alénči – S/he has a bellyache. **čnes nc̓alénči, kʷes nc̓alénči**
qs nc̓alénči – S/he going to have a bellyache. **čiqs nc̓alénči, kʷqs nc̓alénči**

čč̓essls – sick to the stomach; nauseated. *See:* ***nauseated.***

s.t. - something, the 3rd person
(s.t.) - something implied
s.o. - someone, the 3rd person
sl. - singular form
pl. - plural form
rt. - root word
cmd. - command
lit. - literally
fig. - figuratively
i.e., - for example
See: - Redirection to a related word.

stone

sšeńš – rock.
es łp̓łip̓ sšeńš – striped rock.
nšƛ̓aqsm sšeńš – different kinds of rocks.

kʷaliˀnše – yellow stone.

pesł – stone for pounding dried meat on.

q̓ʷi – war hammer; stone hammer.
t q̓ʷi u es t̓et̓emi ci kʷtisi t sppq̓ʷé – Big Blanket is pounding the dried meat with a round stone.

stonefly **čt̓áq̓nšn** – stonefly; hellgramite.

stoop **čskʷic** – stoop over.
čskʷicm – S/he stooped over. **čn čskʷicm, kʷ čskʷicm**
es čskʷicmi – S/he is stooping over. **čnes čskʷicmi, kʷes čskʷicmi**
qs čskʷicmi – S/he is going to stoop over. **čiqs čskʷicmi, kʷqs čskʷicmi**
es čskʷíˀicm – They are stooping over. **qeˀes čskʷicmi, pes čskʷicmi**

es čskʷckʷicm – Each one is stooping over.

nqʷayutups – stooped over naked. *circumfix: **n...ups** – butt, tail.*

stop **ƛ̓lip** – stop.
ƛ̓lip – S/he/it stopped. **čn ƛ̓lip, kʷ ƛ̓lip**
es ƛ̓lpmi – S/he/it is stopping. **čnes ƛ̓lpmi, kʷes ƛ̓lpmi**
qs ƛ̓lpmi – S/he/it is going to stop. **čiqs ƛ̓lpmi, kʷqs ƛ̓lpmi**
ƛ̓líˀip – They stopped. **qeˀ ƛ̓lip, p ƛ̓lip**
es ƛ̓lpmíˀi – They are stopping. **qeˀes ƛ̓lpmi, pes ƛ̓lpmi**
qs ƛ̓lpmíˀi – They are going to stop. **qeˀqs ƛ̓lpmi, pqs ƛ̓lpmi**

ƛ̓lpntes – S/he/it stopped it. **ƛ̓lpnten, ƛ̓lpntexʷ**
es ƛ̓lpims – S/he/it is stopping s.t. **ies ƛ̓lpim, as ƛ̓lpim**
qs ƛ̓lpims – S/he/it is going to stop s.t. **iqs ƛ̓lpim, aqs ƛ̓lpim**
ƛ̓lpntéˀes – They stopped it. **qeˀ ƛ̓lpntem, ƛ̓lpntep**
es ƛ̓lpíˀims – They are stopping s.t. **qeˀes ƛ̓lpim, es ƛ̓lpimp**

es ƛ̓lƛ̓lpmi – S/he/it is stopping. **čnes ƛ̓lpmi, kʷes ƛ̓lpmi**
es ƛ̓lƛ̓lpims – S/he/it is stopping s.t. **ies ƛ̓lpim, as ƛ̓lpim**

ƛ̓lpstem – S/he/it got stopped.

ƛ̓lipš – Stop. *cmd.*
ƛ̓lipwi – You all stop. *cmd.*
ƛ̓lpiskʷ – Stop s.o./s.t. *cmd.*

ṅem ƛ̓lip – S/he/it will stop. **ṅem čn ƛ̓lip, ṅem kʷ ƛ̓lip**
ṅem ƛ̓líˀip – They will stop. **ṅem qeˀ ƛ̓lip, ṅem p ƛ̓lip**
ƛ̓lpsten – I stopped it. **ƛ̓lpmin** – I used s.t. to stop it. **iqs ƛ̓lpnunm łu t̓eyeˀ** – I am going to succeed in stopping the bad. **ƛ̓lpšitn** – I stopped it for s.o.'s benefit.

hoy – quit; stop; finish; okay; that's it; cease. *See: **quit**.*

uẏéčst, *uẏé* – finish working; done working; come to an end. *See: **finish**.*

store **sntumistn,** *sntumi* – store; a place to buy something. *prefix: **sn...** – a place of; suffix: **...tin, ...tn** – means of/device.*
snłttumíst – little store.

elk̓ʷm – store away; put away; save. *See: **put away**.*
sˀélk̓ʷlscut – souvenir.

kʷum – save; stash. *See: **save**.*

storm **es qʷułmncuti –** There is low visibility from a dust storm or blizzard; *(fig., this can be said of someone really "dancing up a storm," making dust). See: **dust**.*

čsač̓tásq̇t, *čsač̓tá* **–** winter's last attempt at a big snow storm. *(In early spring, often indicated by having snow on one side of s.t. such as trees or poles.) See: **snow**.*

uyásq̇t, *uyá* **–** the storm/weather ended.
es uy,ssq̇ti – the storm is ending.
qs uyásq̇ti – the storm is going to end.

story **sṁiṁiʔ –** story; news; something that's been told. *See: **tell**.*

ṁéẏeʔ – explain; tell; show; make something known. *See: **explain**.*
sxʷṁeẏštwe – one tasked to tell (stories). *prefix: **sxʷ...** – one tasked to do.*
qeʔqs ṁeẏštwexʷisti – The two of us are telling each other stories.

sqʷllumt, *sqʷllu* **–** animal stories; creation stories; Coyote stories. *(These stories can only be told when the ground is covered with snow and all hibernating animals have gone into hibernation. A good indication that these stories can be told is when the weather is very cold causing trees to pop.)*
qʷllumt – S/he told a story. **čn qʷllumt, kʷ qʷllumt**
es qʷllumti – S/he is telling a story. **čnes qʷllumti, kʷes qʷllumti**
qs qʷllumti – S/he is going to tell a story. **čiqs qʷllumti, kʷqs qʷllumti**

qʷllumtmis – S/he told a story about it. **qʷllumtmn, qʷllumtmntxʷ**

qʷllumtšts – S/he applied a story to s.o. **qʷllumtštn, qʷllumtštxʷ**

šeẏ łu pṅ sqʷllumt – Now that's a Coyote story. **qeʔ qʷllumšłlt –** Tell us a story. **ha kʷ ṅe u qʷllumtmnt smx̣éẏčṅ –** Would you tell a story about grizzly?

snitqʷa – old story.

sniqʷista – made up story. *rt.: **yoqʷist** – lie.*

sq̇spscin – long talk. *rt.: **sq̇sip** – a long time; suffix: **...cin, ...cn** – action of the mouth.*

stove **snolši –** wood stove. *rt.: **solši** – fire; prefix: **sn...** – a place of.*

straddle **čłqlšews,** *čłqlše* **–** mount, *of one individual*; straddle. *suffix: **...éẇs** – in between, middle.*
čłql̓šeẇs – S/he straddled. **čn čłql̓šeẇs, kʷ čłql̓šeẇs**
es čłql̓šeẇsi – S/he is straddling. **čnes čłql̓šeẇsi, kʷes čłql̓šeẇsi**
es čłql̓šeẇsi – S/he is going to straddle. **čnes čłqlšeẇsi, kʷes čłqlšeẇsi**

čłql̓šeẇsis – S/he straddled s.t. **čłql̓šeẇsn, čłql̓šeẇsntxʷ**
es čłql̓šeẇsms – S/he is straddling s.t. **ies čłql̓šeẇsm, as čłql̓šeẇsm**
qs čłql̓šeẇsms – S/he is going to straddle s.t. **iqs čłql̓šeẇsm, aqs čłql̓šeẇsm**

čłql̓šéłxʷ – straddle s.t. (and ride around a camp).
nčłql̓šéłxʷ – straddle s.t. (and ride around the inside of a camp).

łu sxʷẇeẇéʔ čłql̓šéłxʷ – The crier trotted around the camp.

straight **tox̣ʷ –** straight/right; straight/true; undistorted; not curved; not wrong.
i tox̣ʷ – It is straight/true.

tx̣ʷmim – S/he/it made (s.t.) straight/right. **čn tx̣ʷmim, kʷ tx̣ʷmim**
es tx̣ʷmi – S/he/it is making (s.t.) straight/right. **čnes tx̣ʷmi, kʷes tx̣ʷmi**
qs tx̣ʷmi – S/he/it is going to make (s.t.) straight/right. **čiqs tx̣ʷmi, kʷqs tx̣ʷmi**

The **i** following uvular consonants (UC) and the glottal stop **ʔ** sound like English "*ey*" as in the words *they, hey, whey*, etc. Salish UC are: **q, q̇, qʷ, q̇ʷ, x̣, x̣ʷ**. For example, the suffix **...qin** – head/top, is often spelled using English *ey* as "q*ey*n". So **qi, q̇i, qʷi, q̇ʷi, x̣i, x̣ʷi**, may be spelled with English *ey* as **q***ey*, **q̇***ey*, **qʷ***ey*, **q̇ʷ***ey*, **x̣***ey*, **x̣ʷ***ey* in other texts.

s.t. - something, the 3rd person
(s.t.) - something implied
s.o. - someone, the 3rd person
sl. - singular form
pl. - plural form
rt. - root word
cmd. - command
lit. - literally
fig. - figuratively
i.e., - for example
See: - Redirection to a related word.

tx̣ʷmncut – S/he/it made one's self straight/right. **čn tx̣ʷmncut, kʷ tx̣ʷmncut**
es tx̣ʷmncuti – S/he/it is making one's self straight/right. **čnes tx̣ʷmncuti, kʷes tx̣ʷmncuti**
qs tx̣ʷmncuti – S/he/it is going to make one's self straight/right. **čiqs tx̣ʷmncuti, kʷqs tx̣ʷmncuti**

tx̣ʷmstes – S/he straightened s.o. up. **tx̣ʷmsten, tx̣ʷmstexʷ**
es tx̣ʷmims – S/he is straightening s.o. up. **ies tx̣ʷmim, as tx̣ʷmim**
qs tx̣ʷmims – S/he is going to straighten s.o. up. **iqs tx̣ʷmim, aqs tx̣ʷmim**

tx̣ʷnuis – S/he succeeded in straightening s.t./s.o. up. **tx̣ʷnun, tx̣ʷnuntxʷ**
es tx̣ʷnunms – S/he is succeeding in straightening s.t./s.o. up. **ies tx̣ʷnunm, as tx̣ʷnunm**

tx̣ʷox̣ʷ – It became straight/right/tame. **čn tx̣ʷox̣ʷ, kʷ tx̣ʷox̣ʷ**
es tx̣ʷx̣ʷmi – It is becoming straight/right/tame. **čnes tx̣ʷx̣ʷmi, kʷes tx̣ʷx̣ʷmi**

i łtox̣ʷ – It is a little straight/right.

stox̣ʷ – straight; right; just.
tx̣ʷtox̣ʷt – straight; right; just.
ntx̣ʷtin – straight edge; ruler; level; tool to make something straight.

tox̣ʷš – Straighten up; behave. *cmd.*
tx̣ʷmncutš – Straighten yourself up; behave. *cmd.*
tox̣ʷwi – All of you straighten up; behave. *cmd.*
tx̣ʷmiskʷ – Make s.t./s.o. straight. *cmd.*
tx̣ʷtx̣ʷsew̓s – opposite each other.
ntx̣ʷmels – want to be straight.
čłtx̣ʷeneʔ – straight over.
ntx̣ʷawsqn – straight over head.
tx̣ʷmin̓č – aim a weapon *(i.e., bow, gun, etc.). See: **aim**.*
ntx̣ʷaqs – straight road.
tx̣ʷcin – talk straight; talk right; talk correct. *See: **talk**.*
es čtx̣ʷmncutms – S/he/it is going straight to s.o./s.t. **ies čtx̣ʷmncutm, as čtx̣ʷmncutm**

qʷo m̓éy̓ełt łu i tóx̣ʷ – Tell me straight, tell me the truth.

tól – straight vertical.
tltólist – S/he stretched (with arms up). **čn tltólist, kʷ tltólist**
es tltólisti – S/he is stretching (with arms up). **čnes tltólisti, kʷes tltólisti**
qs tltólisti – S/he is going to stretch (with arms up). **čiqs tltólisti, kʷqs tltólisti**

tólmiš – Stretch (with arms up). *cmd.*

čtóls – point with the eyes; show acknowledgement by looking. *See: **acknowledge**.*
tóls – point with the head or face; show acknowledgement. *See: **acknowledge**.*

ta es šƛ̓usn – They did not look anywhere *(stare straight ahead, not looking either way).*

xʷup – straighten something; unfold; extend something. *See: **stretch**.*

strain
k̓ʷłq̓ʷeʔ – strain something.
k̓ʷłq̓ʷʔentés – S/he strained it. **k̓ʷłq̓ʷʔentén, k̓ʷłq̓ʷʔentéxʷ**

stranger
t̓xʷlélixʷ – different people/tribe; stranger. *See: **people**.*

straw
tumn – straw (for drinking). *rt.: **tum** – suck. See: **suck**.*

čqul̓wa – straw.

strawberry **q̇itq̇m** – strawberry.
čq̇tq̇tmeɫp – strawberry plant.

ṅem p kʷis q̇ʷléẁm t q̇itq̇m – You will all go picking strawberries.

strawberry roan **kʷlaqin** – strawberry roan.

straw hat **snsṗqinqn, snsṗqna** – straw hat. *suffix: **...qin, ...qn** – top.*

straw worm **ččl̓čl̓ṗi** – caddisworm, straw worm.

stream **nšiẏétkʷ**, *nšiẏé* – creek, stream. *lit. first water. rt.: **š**ˀ**it** – first. See: **creek**.*

snčilptin – tributary waterway.

nileẁs – main waterway, which tributaries flow into.

strength **yopiyewt** – strength; fortitude; financially sound.
yopiyewt – S/he has strength. **čn yopiyewt, kʷ yopiyewt**

yopiyewtsts – S/he made s.o. strong and able. **yopiyewtstn, yopiyewtstxʷ**
es yopiyewtms – S/he is making s.o. strong and able. **ies yopiyewtm, as yopiyewtm**
qs yopiyewtms – S/he is going to make s.o. strong and able. **iqs yopiyewtm, aqs yopiyewtm**

nyopiyewtn – thing or place where one gets strength. *(i.e., a sweat house, mountains, etc.)*

stretch **sut̓m** – stretch by pulling.
sut̓m – S/he stretched. **čn sut̓m, kʷ sut̓m**
es sut̓i – S/he is stretching. **čnes sut̓i, kʷes sut̓i**
qs sut̓i – S/he is going to stretch. **čiqs sut̓i, kʷqs sut̓i**

sut̓msts – S/he stretched it. **sut̓mstn, sut̓mstxʷ**
súˀut̓msts – They stretched it. **qeˀ sut̓mstm, sut̓mstp**

sut̓mstm – S/he was stretched.

ssot̓lqs – sweater.

sut̓miš – Stretch. *cmd.*

ṅe wis q̇ʷˀentéxʷ m st̓sut̓mstxʷ – When you finish wringing it, stretch it.

xʷup – straighten something; unfold; extend something. *(i.e., unfold a dry hide, unfold s.t., etc.)*
xʷpmim – S/he stretched. **čn xʷpmim, kʷ xʷpmim**
es xʷpmi – S/he is stretching. **čnes xʷpmi, kʷes xʷpmi**
qs xʷpmi – S/he is going to stretch. **čiqs xʷpmi, kʷqs xʷpmi**

xʷpmstes – S/he unfolded s.t. **xʷpmsten, xʷpmstexʷ**
es xʷpmims – S/he is unfolding s.t. **ies xʷpmim, as xʷpmim**
qs xʷpmims – S/he is going to unfold s.t. **iqs xʷpmim, aqs xʷpmim**

xʷpip – S/he/it got stretched. **čn xʷpip, kʷ xʷpip**
es xʷpip – S/he/it is straightened. **čnes xʷpip, kʷes xʷpip**

xʷpmmintn – something used to straighten.

xʷpmiš – Straighten. *cmd.*
xʷpmiskʷ – Straighten it. *cmd.*
xʷpmncut – straighten/stretch one's self.

The **i** following uvular consonants (UC) and the glottal stop ˀ sound like English "*ey*" as in the words *they, hey, whey,* etc. Salish UC are: **q, q̇, qʷ, q̇ʷ, x̣, x̣ʷ**. For example, the suffix ...**qin** – head/top, is often spelled using English *ey* as "q*ey*n". So **qi, q̇i, qʷi, q̇ʷi, x̣i, x̣ʷi**, may be spelled with English *ey* as **q***ey*, **q̇***ey*, **qʷ***ey*, **q̇ʷ***ey*, **x̣***ey*, **x̣ʷ***ey* in other texts.

s.t. - something, the 3rd person
(s.t.) - something implied
s.o. - someone, the 3rd person
sl. - singular form
pl. - plural form
rt. - root word
cmd. - command
lit. - literally
fig. - figuratively
i.e., - for example
See: - Redirection to a related word.

x^{w}pmilš – become straightened/unfolded. *suffix: **...ilš**– autonomous.*
x^{w}palqs – straighten/unfold clothing/shirt.
x^{w}pmiċeʔ – straighten/unfold a blanket.
čx^{w}px^{w}pnus – open eyes wide; stretch eyes. *See: **open**.*
x^{w}pmaẇsqn – open mouth wide; stretch mouth. *See: **mouth**.*
nx^{w}pmičṅm – straighten/stretch the back. *suffix: **...ičṅ**– back.*
x^{w}pmečst – straighten/stretch the hand. *suffix: **...ečst, ...čst**– of the hand.*
x^{w}px^{w}pmax̣nm – straighten/stretch the arms.
x^{w}px^{w}pmaqstšnm – straighten/stretch the legs.
x^{w}px^{w}pmšnim – S/he stretched his/her feet. **čn x^{w}px^{w}pšnim, k^w x^{w}px^{w}pšnim**

ƛ̓e čn x^{w}px^{w}paqstšn – I already stretched my legs. **x^{w}pmsten u tas x^{w}pip –** I stretched it and it did not get straightened. **eł x^{w}pmsten u x^{w}ppnun –** I stretched it again and succeeded in straightening it.

tólmiš – Stretch (with arms up). *cmd. See: **straight**.*

ox̣^{w}m – string something out; say someone is skinny, stretched, or boney. *(i.e., fencing, rope, hose, etc.) See: **string**.*

strike

ilim – throw and strike something with a pointed object. *(throw an arrow, spear, sharp stick, etc.) See: **throw**.*

sṗim – hit/strike with an object. *See: **hit**.*

string

siṗiʔ – lacing.
łsisṗiʔ – little lacing.

accné – shoestring.

łiḱ^w – string things together; putting things on thread, yarn or string. *(i.e., a rosary.)*
łiḱ^w – S/he strung (s.t.) together. **čn łiḱ^w, k^w łiḱ^w**
es łiḱ^{w}i – S/he is stringing (s.t.) together. **čnes łiḱ^{w}i, k^{w}es łiḱ^{w}i**
qs łiḱ^{w}i – S/he is going to string (s.t.) together. **čiqs łiḱ^{w}i, k^{w}qs łiḱ^{w}i**
es łíʔiḱ^{w}i – They are stringing (s.t.) together. **qeʔes łiḱ^{w}i, pes łiḱ^{w}i**

łiḱ^{w}is – S/he strung the things together. **łiḱ^{w}n, łiḱ^{w}ntx^w**
es łiḱ^{w}ms – S/he is stringing the things together. **ies łiḱ^{w}m, as łiḱ^{w}m**
qs łiḱ^{w}ms – S/he is going to string the things together. **iqs łiḱ^{w}m, aqs łiḱ^{w}m**
es łíʔiḱ^{w}ms – They are stringing the things together. **qeʔes łiḱ^{w}m, es łiḱ^{w}mp**

es łḱ^{w}łiḱ^{w}i – S/he is repeatedly stringing (s.t.) together. **čnes łḱ^{w}łiḱ^{w}i, k^{w}es łḱ^{w}łiḱ^{w}i**

scłiḱ^w – something that's been strung together. *prefix: **sc...** – s.t. that's been done/made/prepared.*

łiḱ^{w}iš – String it together. *cmd.*
łiḱ^{w}wi – All of you string it together. *cmd.*

swe łu es nte qs łiḱ^{w}i – Who wants to string things together?

nłułuq^{w}peẇs – string things together using a needle; poking a needle through. *suffix: **...éẇs**– in between, middle.*
nłułuq^{w}peẇsm – S/he strung (s.t.) together. **čn nłułuq^{w}peẇsm, k^w nłułuq^{w}peẇsm**
es nłułuq^{w}peẇsi – S/he is stringing (s.t.) together. **čnes nłułuq^{w}peẇsi, k^{w}es nłułuq^{w}peẇsi**
qs nłułuq^{w}peẇsi – S/he is going to string (s.t.) together. **čiqs nłułuq^{w}peẇsi, k^{w}qs nłułuq^{w}peẇsi**
nłułuq^{w}péʔeẇsm – They strung (s.t.) together. **qeʔ nłułuq^{w}peẇsm, p nłułuq^{w}peẇsm**

scnłułuq^{w}peẇs – something that has been strung together with a needle. *(i.e., popcorn garland.) prefix: **sc...** – s.t. that's been done/made/prepared.*

nłułuqʷpeẃsiš – String it together with the needle. *cmd.*
nłuqʷpeẃsiš – Put the needle through it. *cmd.*

ox̣ʷm – string something out; say someone is skinny, stretched, or boney. *(i.e., fencing, rope, hose, etc.)*
ox̣ʷox̣ʷm – S/he/it is skinny. **čn ox̣ʷox̣ʷm, kʷ ox̣ʷox̣ʷm**

ox̣ʷm – S/he strung (s.t.). **čn ox̣ʷm, kʷ ox̣ʷm**
es ox̣ʷmi – S/he is stringing (s.t.). **čnes ox̣ʷmi, kʷes ox̣ʷmi**
qs ox̣ʷmi – S/he is going to string (s.t.). **čiqs ox̣ʷmi, kʷqs ox̣ʷmi**

ox̣ʷntes – S/he strung s.t. **ox̣ʷnten, ox̣ʷntexʷ**
es ox̣ʷms – S/he is stringing s.t. **ies ox̣ʷm, as ox̣ʷm**
qs ox̣ʷms – S/he is going to string s.t. **iqs ox̣ʷm, aqs ox̣ʷm**

es ox̣ʷox̣ʷmi – S/he is stringing repeatedly (s.t.). **čnes ox̣ʷox̣ʷmi, kʷes ox̣ʷox̣ʷmi**

ox̣ʷont – String it out. *cmd.*

čłk̓ʷum – pick something up using an instrument or tool. *(i.e., a needle for beads, a pitchfork for hay/rocks, etc.) See:* ***pick.***

The **i** following uvular consonants (UC) and the glottal stop ʔ sound like English "*ey*" as in the words *they, hey, whey*, etc. Salish UC are: **q, q̓, qʷ, q̓ʷ, x̣, x̣ʷ**. For example, the suffix ...**qin** – head/top, is often spelled using English *ey* as "q*ey*n". So **qi, q̓i, qʷi, q̓ʷi, x̣i, x̣ʷi**, may be spelled with English *ey* as **q***ey*, **q̓***ey*, **qʷ***ey*, **q̓ʷ***ey*, **x̣***ey*, **x̣ʷ***ey* in other texts.

strip

čc̓slexʷ – get naked; get cleared of clothing. *See:* ***naked.***

npƛ̓alqs, *npƛ̓a* **–** remove/take off clothes. *See:* ***undress.***
npƛ̓alqsiš – Remove your clothes. *cmd.*

sq̓eyi – strip of sinew from the back.

sẏeṅṗ – long strips of elk/deer meat.

stripe

es łiṗ – line; stripe. *See:* ***line.***
es łṗłiṗ sšeṅš – striped rock.

čáʔax̣ic̓eʔ – It is striped; it is covered in lines. *See:* ***line.***

striped skunk

x̣stéyẏeʔ – skunk; *Mephitis mephitis.*

strive

aytčst – strive; exert one's self in work.
aytčst – S/he strived. **čn aytčst, kʷ aytčst**
es aytčsti – S/he is striving. **čnes aytčsti, kʷes aytčsti**
qs aytčsti – S/he is going to strive. **čiqs aytčsti, kʷqs aytčsti**

aytčstmis – S/he exerted effort in s.t. **aytčstmn, aytčstmntxʷ**
es aytčstmms – S/he is is exerting effort in s.t. **ies aytčstmm, as aytčstmm**
qs aytčstmms – S/he is going to exert effort in s.t. **iqs aytčstmm, aqs aytčstmm**

aytcin – speak with passion; speak with effort; speak over.
aytcin – S/he spoke passionately. **čn aytcin, kʷ aytcin**
es aytcini – S/he is speaking passionately. **čnes aytcini, kʷes aytcini**
qs aytcini – S/he is going to speak passionately. **čiqs aytcini, kʷqs aytcini**

aytcinmis – S/he spoke passionately to s.o. **aytcinmn, aytcinmntxʷ**
es aytcinmms – S/he is speaking passionately to s.o. **ies aytcinmm, as aytcinmm**
qs aytcinmms – S/he is going to speak passionately to s.o. **iqs aytcinmm, aqs aytcinmm**

s.t. - something, the 3rd person
(s.t.) - something implied
s.o. - someone, the 3rd person
sl. - singular form
pl. - plural form
rt. - root word
cmd. - command
lit. - literally
fig. - figuratively
i.e., - for example
See: - Redirection to a related word.

strong

yoyoót – strong.
yoyoót – S/he is strong. **čn yoyoót, kʷ yoyoót**

syoyoot – physical strength/power.
nyoyoscutn – muscle. *suffix: **...tin, ...tn** – means of/device.*

yomncut, *yomncu.* **–** make one's self become rigid/tense. *See: **tense**.*
yomncutš – Toughen up; become rigid/tense. *cmd.*

nyoowáls – Strong mind; strong heart.
nyawálš – Be strong; do not cry out in pain. *cmd. See: **tough**.*
nyoyowáls – strong minded; strong hearted; able to endure pain.
nyawlsm – brace feelings; make feelings strong; tough something out. *(i.e., in preparation for bad news, etc.) See: **brace**.*
yomim – hold something steady. *See: **hold**.*
yomspewlš – hold breath inside the body. *rt.: **yomim** – hold steady. See: **breathe**.*
yomscin – hold breath by closing the mouth. *rt.: **yomim** – hold steady. See: **breathe**.*
i čyuyúʔus – sharp eyes; good sight. *rt.: **yoyóot** – strong.*
nyuyúweneʔ – good hearing. *rt.: **yoyóot** – strong. See: **hear**.*
yuyúwečst – strong hands; capable hands. *rt.: **yoyóot** – strong; suffix: **...ečst, ...čst** – of the hand.*
yopiyewt – strength; fortitude; financially sound. *See: **strength**.*
yoyoscut, *yoyoscú* **–** make one's self try hard with a physically strong effort; to give all one's effort. *See: **try hard**.*

yoyoscq̇mint – Throw it hard. **sčx̣ʷéct u yoyoót čn k̓ʷul̓m –** All day Monday I worked hard.
yoyosčƚtʔent – Bounce it hard. *cmd.*

yoyoʔtwilš – get strong. *suffix: **...wilš** – developmental.*
yoyoʔtwilš – S/he got strong. **čn yoyoʔtwilš, kʷ yoyoʔtwilš**
es yoyoʔtwilši – S/he is getting strong. **čnes yoyoʔtwilši, kʷes yoyoʔtwilši**
qs yoyoʔtwilši – S/he is going to get strong. **čiqs yoyoʔtwilši, kʷqs yoyoʔtwilši**

nyoyoʔcin – say strong/powerful words. *suffix: **...cin, ...cn** – action of the mouth.*
nyoyoʔcin – S/he said strong words. **čn nyoyoʔcin, kʷ nyoyoʔcin**
es nyoyoʔcini – S/he is saying strong words. **čnes nyoyoʔcini, kʷes nyoyoʔcini**
qs nyoyoʔcini – S/he is going to say strong words. **čiqs nyoyoʔcini, kʷqs nyoyoʔcini**

čmaqs – perform at the peak of one's ability; best at something; pinnacle. *See: **best**.*

lx̣lix̣t – strong; able to lead into hard situations victoriously.
lx̣lix̣t ci sqltmixʷ – That man is a strong leader.

x̣ʷax̣ʷat – strong.

struck

ċq̇em – struck by lightning.
es ċq̇em – It is struck by lightning.
ċq̇ntem – S/he/it was struck by lightning.

sċq̇lsšit̓ – The tree was struck by lightning.

es uweči u ċq̇ntšʔi – It was lightning and a tree was struck on top of the mountain.

struggle

tl̓xʷéčst, *tl̓xʷé* **–** difficult; hard to do; struggle at something; unable to succeed. *See: **difficult**.*

yéṁmist, *yéṁm* **–** despaired; frustrated; troubled; worried; have a block; have a dilemma. *See: **despair***

strung

ox̣ʷm – string something out; say someone is skinny, stretched, or boney. *(i.e., fencing, rope, hose, etc.) See: **string**.*

ƚik̓ʷ – string things together; putting things on thread, yarn or string. *(i.e., a rosary.) See: **string**.*

stub **čťppšin,** *čťppši* – trip; stub a toe. *See:* ***trip.***
čťppšin – S/he stubbed one's toe; s/he tripped. **čn čťppšin, kʷ čťppšin**

čn čťčťppšin – I stubbed my toes.

stubborn **áẏċaċt** – self-willed; insisting one; stubborn. *See:* ***insist.***

stuck **nƛ̓awač** – stuck in mud.
nƛ̓awač – S/he got stuck in the mud. **čn nƛ̓awač, kʷ nƛ̓awač**

ta kʷ qes nƛ̓awač – Do not get stuck in the mud.

čċṗaq – stuck to something.
čċṗaq – S/he/it is stuck. **čn čċṗaq, kʷ čċṗaq**

čċṗqmin – tape.

tlxʷmist, *tlxʷmi* – unable to rise/get up.
tlxʷmist – S/he was unable to get up. **čn tlxʷmist, kʷ tlxʷmist**
es tlxʷmisti – S/he is unable to get up. **čnes tlxʷmisti, kʷes tlxʷmisti**

čn łaqšlš u čn eł tlxʷmist – I sat down and could not get up.

stuck-up **q̇xʷq̇exʷt,** *q̇xʷq̇e* – proud; vain; think much of; stuck-up.
q̇xʷq̇exʷt – S/he/it is vain. **čn q̇xʷq̇exʷt, kʷ q̇xʷq̇exʷt**

q̇exʷ – proud; admire. *See:* ***proud.***
q̇xʷnscut – conceited; proud of one's self. *See:* ***conceited.***

student **sṁiṁéẏei** – student; scholar; the one taught.

sxʷaċx̣łq̇eẏmi – one tasked to be in school; student. *prefix:* ***sxʷ...*** *– one tasked to do.*

sxʷyoʔnwe – one tasked to learn. *prefix:* ***sxʷ...*** *– one tasked to do.*

study **k̓ʷłpax̣em** – think. *See:* ***think.***

qʷaqʷemncut, *qʷaqʷemncú* – practice, drill, train, study. *See:* ***practice.***
ṅem tl̓ ciʔ čn qʷaqʷemncut – I will study harder.

stuff **nťq̇ʷom** – stuff something.
nťq̇ʷom – S/he stuffed. **čn nťq̇ʷom, kʷ nťq̇ʷom**
es nťq̇ʷmi – S/he is stuffing. **čnes nťq̇ʷmi, kʷes nťq̇ʷmi**
qs nťq̇ʷmi – S/he is going to stuff. **čiqs nťq̇ʷmi, kʷqs nťq̇ʷmi**
es nťq̇ʷmíʔi – They are stuffing. **qeʔes nťq̇ʷmi, pes nťq̇ʷmi**

nťq̇ʷntes – S/he stuffed it. **nťq̇ʷnten, nťq̇ʷntexʷ**
es nťq̇ʷoms – S/he is stuffing it. **ies nťq̇ʷom, as nťq̇ʷom**
qs nťq̇ʷoms – S/he is going to stuff it. **iqs nťq̇ʷom, aqs nťq̇ʷom**
es nťq̇ʷóʔoms – They are stuffing it. **qeʔes nťq̇ʷom, es nťq̇ʷomp**

nq̇ʷomeẇsm – stuff as in making a quilt; stuff in between. *suffix:* ***...éẇs*** *– in between, middle.*
nq̇ʷomeẇsm – S/he stuffed. **čn nq̇ʷomeẇsm , kʷ nq̇ʷomeẇsm**
es nq̇ʷomeẇsi – S/he is stuffing. **čnes nq̇ʷomeẇsi, kʷes nq̇ʷomeẇsi**
qs nq̇ʷomeẇsi – S/he is going to stuff. **čiqs nq̇ʷomeẇsi, kʷqs nq̇ʷomeẇsi**
es nq̇ʷoméʔeẇsi – They are stuffing. **qeʔes nq̇ʷomeẇsi, pes nq̇ʷomeẇsi**

nq̇ʷomeẇsmis – S/he stuffed it. **nq̇ʷomeẇsmn, nq̇ʷomeẇsmntxʷ**

The **i** following uvular consonants (UC) and the glottal stop **ʔ** sound like English "*ey*" as in the words *they, hey, whey,* etc. Salish UC are: **q, q̇, qʷ, q̇ʷ, x̣, x̣ʷ**. For example, the suffix **...qin** – head/top, is often spelled using English *ey* as "q*ey*n". So **qi, q̇i, qʷi, q̇ʷi, x̣i, x̣ʷi,** may be spelled with English *ey* as **q***ey*, **q̇***ey*, **qʷ***ey*, **q̇ʷ***ey*, **x̣***ey*, **x̣ʷ***ey* in other texts.

s.t. - something, the 3rd person
(s.t.) - something implied
s.o. - someone, the 3rd person
sl. - singular form
pl. - plural form
rt. - root word
cmd. - command
lit. - literally
fig. - figuratively
i.e., - for example
See: - Redirection to a related word.

es nq̓ʷomeẁsms – S/he is stuffing it. **ies nq̓ʷomeẁsm, as nq̓ʷomeẁsm**
qs nq̓ʷomeẁsms – S/he is going to stuff it. **iqs nq̓ʷomeẁsm, aqs nq̓ʷomeẁsm**
es nq̓ʷomé?eẁsms – They are stuffing it. **qe?es nq̓ʷomeẁsm, es nq̓ʷomeẁsmp**

stumble
pillš – stagger once. *(as in getting up from a chair) See: **stagger**.*

stump
nx̣ʷċulexʷ, *nx̣ʷċu* – tree stump.

sturgeon
sċmtus – sturgeon. *rt.: **ċim** – contricted.*

styling gel
čpóƛ̓qntn – hair oil; styling gel. *rt.: **puƛ̓** – grease; suffix: **...tin, ...tn** – means of/device.*

submit
k̓ʷłax̣ltmistm – submit; give into; surrender; yield to; succumb to; capitulate.
ta qes k̓ʷłax̣ltmistmstm łu t̓eye? – Do not submit to evil.

subside
suu? – water subsides/drops after a flood. *See: **drop**.*

substitute
ncucuwečst – act in someone's place; substitute for somebody. *suffix: **...ečst, ...čst** – of the hand.*
ncucuwečst – S/he/it acted in s.o.'s place. **čn ncucuwečst, kʷ ncucuwečst**
es ncucuwečsti – S/he/it is acting in s.o.'s place. **čnes ncucuwečsti, kʷes ncucuwečsti**
qs ncucuwečsti – S/he/it is going to act in s.o.'s place. **čiqs ncucuwečsti, kʷqs ncucuwečsti**

ncucuwečsis – S/he/it made s.o. act as one's self. **ncucuwečsn, ncucuwečsntxʷ**
es ncucuwečsms – S/he/it is making s.o. act as one's self. **ies ncucuwečsm, as ncucuwečsm**

ncucuwečsnt – Make s.o./s.t. act as you. *cmd.*

ncucuwečsnt monqi – Make the monkey act as you. **ncucuwečsis t ilmixʷm łu stipn** – The boss made Stephen act in his place.

subtract
k̓ʷłt̓ipmim – subtract from something. *rt.: **t̓iip** – fall; prefix: **k̓ʷł...** – under.*
k̓ʷłt̓ipstes – S/he is subtracting s.t. **k̓ʷłt̓ipsten, k̓ʷłt̓ipstexʷ**
es k̓ʷłt̓ipmims – S/he is subtracting s.t. **ies k̓ʷłt̓ipmim, as k̓ʷłt̓ipmim**
qs k̓ʷłt̓ipmims – S/he is going to subtract s.t. **iqs k̓ʷłt̓ipmim, aqs k̓ʷłt̓ipmim**
k̓ʷłt̓ipsté?es – They subtracted s.t. **qe? k̓ʷłt̓ipstem, k̓ʷłt̓ipstep**
es k̓ʷłt̓ipmí?ims – They are subtracting s.t. **ies k̓ʷłt̓ipmim, es k̓ʷłt̓ipmimp**

es k̓ʷłt̓ipstes – S/he is subtracting s.t. **es k̓ʷłt̓ipsten, es k̓ʷłt̓ipstexʷ**

k̓ʷłt̓ipmiskʷ – Subtract it/ take it away. *cmd.*

qe?qs k̓ʷłt̓it̓ipmisti yetłxʷa – We're going to be subtracting today. **esel k̓ʷłt̓ipmim t nk̓ʷu? še tixʷł nk̓ʷu?** – Two minus one equals one, *(2 – 1 = 1).*

q̓ʷom – take more than one thing. *See: **take**.*

succeed
l̓q̓ʷom – can do; prevail; succeed. *See: **do**.*

***...nu...** – pronoun suffix creating expressions indicating that an agent's action(s) to a object was successfully completed. **...nuis** – s/he/it; **...nun** – I; **...nuntxʷ** – you; **...nú?uis** – they; **qe...nuntm** – we; **...nuntp** – you all.*
k̓ʷłpax̣nuis – S/he just thought of it. **accpnun** – I succeeded in catching s.t. in a trap. **ep̓p̓nuntxʷ** – You succeeded in wiping s.t. **ilpnun** – I wounded it. **x̣ʷl̓nuis** – S/he finally abandoned it. **k̓ʷl̓nuis** – S/he accomplished s.t. **kʷnnuis** – S/he/it caught s.o./s.t. **šƛ̓pnuis** – S/he/it defeated s.o. **ies šƛ̓pnunms** – I am defeating s.o. **ċspnuis** – S/he/it completed clearing it out.

suck **tum** – suck with puckered lips; kiss and drawing in with a suck.
tumm – S/he sucked. **čn tumm, kʷ tumm**
es tumi – S/he is sucking. **čnes tumi, kʷes tumi**
qs tumi – S/he is going to suck. **čiqs t̓umi, kʷqs tumi**

tumis – S/he sucked s.t. **tumn, tumntxʷ**
es tumms – S/he is sucking s.t. **ies tumm, as tumm**
qs tumms – S/he is going to suck s.t. **iqs tumm, aqs tumm**

stum̓čst – thumb; sucking finger. *suffix:* ***...ečst, ...čst*** *– of the hand.*
tumn – straw (for drinking).

tumiš – Suck. *cmd.*
tumnt – Suck it. *cmd.*
tetum̓eʔ – little sucker, affectionately.
tumčstm – suck fingers.

t̓am̓ – slightly suck.
es t̓am̓i – S/he is sucking. **čnes t̓am̓i, kʷes t̓am̓i**

t̓am̓yó – cowry; snail; leech.

es t̓mamcni – It is sucking. *(i.e., a cow eating)*
st̓m̓a – cow. **st̓m̓m̓a** – cows. *pl.* *rt.:* ***t̓mam*** *– kiss.*

t̓mt̓malš – making sucking noise.
t̓mt̓mcin – making sucking noise while eating.

še kʷ t̓mt̓malš – then you made a sucking noise.

tatameʔ – suck on the nipple.
tatameʔ – S/he/it sucked the nipple. **čn tatameʔ, kʷ tatameʔ**
es tatameʔi – S/he/it is sucking the nipple. **čnes tatameʔi, kʷes tatameʔi**
qs tatameʔi – S/he/it is going to suck the nipple. **čiqs tatameʔi, kʷqs tatameʔi**

łop – deep suck; strong suck; to draw blood. *(i.e., extracting poison, etc.)*
łop – S/he sucked. **čn łop, kʷ łop**
es łopi – S/he is sucking. **čnes łopi, kʷes łopi**

łopis – S/he sucked s.o. **łopn, łopntxʷ**
es łopms – S/he is sucking s.o. **ies łopm, as łopm**
qs łopms – S/he is going to suck s.o. **iqs łopm, aqs łopm**

łopcnis – S/he sucked s.o.

t̓mam – kiss something; place lips on something. *See:* ***kiss.***

sucker **čléneʔ** – longnosed sucker; *Catostomus catostomus.*

sl̓aw̓s – small mouth sucker; Columbia large-scaled sucker; *Catostomus macrocheilus.*

tw̓eckʷ – small black sucker fish.

suffer **nxʷcxʷcmél̓s** – suffer; tormented feelings.
nxʷcxʷcmél̓s – S/he had tormented feelings. **čn nxʷcxʷcmél̓s, kʷ nxʷcxʷcmél̓s**
es nxʷcxʷcmél̓si – S/he has tormented feelings. **čnes nxʷcxʷcmél̓si, kʷes nxʷcxʷcmél̓si**

suffocate **tqup** – suffocate (not dead); restrict air flow; lacking air; winded/out of breath.

The **i** following uvular consonants (UC) and the glottal stop **ʔ** sound like English "*ey*" as in the words th*ey*, h*ey*, wh*ey*, etc. Salish UC are: **q, q̇, qʷ, q̇ʷ, x̣, x̣ʷ**. For example, the suffix ...**qin** – head/top, is often spelled using English *ey* as "q*ey*n". So **qi, q̇i, qʷi, q̇ʷi, x̣i, x̣ʷi**, may be spelled with English *ey* as **q***ey*, **q̇***ey*, **qʷ***ey*, **q̇ʷ***ey*, **x̣***ey*, **x̣ʷ***ey* in other texts.

s.t. - something, the 3rd person
(s.t.) - something implied
s.o. - someone, the 3rd person
sl. - singular form
pl. - plural form
rt. - root word
cmd. - command
lit. - literally
fig. - figuratively
i.e., - for example
See: - Redirection to a related word.

tqup – S/he was suffocating. **čn tqup, kʷ tqup**
es tqupmi – S/he is suffocating. **čnes tqupmi, kʷes tqupmi**
qs tqupmi – S/he is going to be suffocating. **čiqs tqupmi, kʷqs tqupmi**

tqpstes – S/he suffocated s.o./s.t. **tqpsten, tqpstexʷ**
es tqpims – S/he is suffocating s.o./s.t. **ies tqpim, as tqpim**
qs tqpims – S/he is going to suffocate s.o./s.t. **iqs tqpim, aqs tqpim**

sugar

t̓iš – sugar; sweet.
iqʷił t̓iš – imitation sugar.
sck̓ʷl̓t̓iš – made sugar.

nt̓išk̓ʷm – put sugar in a liquid.
nt̓iškʷm – S/he put sugar in the liquid. **čn nt̓iškʷm, kʷ nt̓iškʷm**
es nt̓iškʷi – S/he is putting sugar in the liquid. **čnes nt̓iškʷi, kʷes nt̓iškʷi**
qs nt̓iškʷi – S/he is going to put sugar in the liquid. **čiqs nt̓iškʷi, kʷqs nt̓iškʷi**

nt̓išpkʷis – S/he sweetened the liquid. **nt̓išpkʷn, nt̓išpkʷntxʷ**
es nt̓iškʷms – S/he is sweetening the liquid. **ies nt̓iškʷm, as nt̓iškʷm**
qs nt̓iškʷms – S/he is going to sweeten the liquid. **iqs nt̓iškʷm, aqs nt̓iškʷm**

nt̓iškʷ – sweet liquid; pop; Kool-aid.

ha kʷ nt̓iškʷm – Did you put sugar in the liquid?

suicide

plscut, *plscu* – kill one's self.
plscut – S/he killed one's self.
es plscuti – S/he is killing one's self. **čnes plscuti, kʷes plscuti**
qs plscuti – S/he is going to kill one's self. **čiqs plscuti, kʷqs plscuti**

suitcase

čp̓ičceʔ – suitcase; leather suitcase. *rt.: **p̓ič** – glossy; suffix: **...ic̓é**ʔ – covered in.*

čq̓ʔic̓éʔ, *čq̓ʔi* – Indian suitcase, rawhide bag. *lit. it has a pattern around it. See: **pattern**.*

sntqálscu – trunk, suitcase.

summer

sʔánłq – summer.
es anłqm̓nuxʷisti, *es anłqm̓nuxʷi* – It is again the time of summer. *suffix: **...m̓nuxʷ** – in the time of.*

l sqépc u l sʔanłq – in spring and summer. **ha n̓em kʷ k̓ʷul̓m n̓e anłq** – Will you work this summer?

esẏapqini – celebrating; powwowing.

es upčstasq̓t – It is the ten days. *suffix: **...asq̓t** – sky, day.*

es qʷleʔwi – gathering berries.

sun

spq̓niʔ – month; moon; sun; clock.

sun dance

čt̓uscut, *čt̓uscu* – sun dance.

Sunday

sčacew̓s, *sčace* – Sunday. *See: **hang**.*
nk̓ʷuʔ sčacéw̓s – one week.

sunflower

mtčw̓éłp, *mtčw̓é* – sunflower plant.

táqʷu – sunflower root; balsamroot.

sunlight **skʷkʷl̓iʔl**, *skʷkʷl̓iʔ* – sunshine; sunlight.
i kʷkʷl̓iʔl – It is sun shiny.

sunrise **ċłe** – sunrise, *(just as the sun is peeking over the mountain or land).*

cƛ̓éʔeč – peeking out, *(when the sun is partially up). rt.:* ***ƛ̓éʔeč** – peek.*
cƛ̓éččnm łu spq̓niʔ – The sun is peeking over, *(when the sun is partially up).*

scƛ̓éʔeč – sunrise; the sun just peeked out.

es cƛ̓éʔeč – The sun is up.

sčpƛ̓e – sunrise, *(just when the sun comes off the mountain or land). rt.:* ***pƛ̓im** – release from.*

skʷƛ̓ip – sunrise; the sun came out.
es kʷƛ̓pmi – The sun is coming out.

skʷƛ̓ptin – place where the sun comes out.

kʷƛ̓im – take something out; detach; loose/free embedded object. *See:* ***take**.*

łx̣lpulexʷ, *łx̣lpu* – dawn, *(the first light of the morning). See:* ***dawn**.*

snṗaq̓cin – dawn, *(before the sun comes up). See:* ***sunrise**.*

sunset **sčsoósqn, sčsoó** – sunset.

łqiqlt, *łqi* – *dusk (when the sun is already down). See:* ***dusk**.*

sčluxʷ – evening. *See:* ***evening**.*

sunshine **skʷkʷl̓iʔl**, *skʷkʷl̓iʔ* – sunshine; sunlight.
i kʷkʷl̓iʔl – It is sun shiny.

es uluʔáx̣n – It is the sun dogs *(sun flares, rainbow around sun or moon).*

es x̣sásq̓ti – It is good weather. *suffix:* ***...asq̓t** – sky, day.*

i čpáʔsq̓t – It is a clear sky *(no clouds). suffix:* ***...asq̓t** – sky, day.*

supper **čluxʷm** – eat supper/dinner.
čluxʷm – S/he/it ate dinner. **čn čluxʷm, kʷ čluxʷm**
es čluxʷi – S/he/it is eating dinner. **čnes čluxʷi, kʷes čluxʷi**
qs čluxʷi – S/he/it is going to eat dinner. **čiqs čluxʷi, kʷqs čluxʷi**
es člúʔuxʷi – They are eating dinner. **qeʔes čluxʷi, pes čluxʷi**

t stem̓ u kʷ čluxʷm – What did you eat for dinner? **č čen̓ u kʷqs k̓ʷis čluxʷi** – Where are you going to eat supper?

supple **yut** – make soft, supple or limber by rubbing with the hands. *See:* ***rub**.*

support **čłem̓ncut** – get one's self close/next to/against something. *See:* ***close**.*

suppose **k̓ʷ še** – rather; supposed to be; preferably; evidently then. *See:* ***rather**.*

sure **i mi** – It is plainly evident; it is absolute; it is fact. *See:* ***absolute**.*

surprise **kʷssusm**, *kʷssu* – startle. *See:* ***startle**.*

surrender **xʷčšmist** – surrender; give one's self. *rt.:* ***xʷic̓** – give; suffix:* ***...ist** – action for/of the self.*

The **i** following uvular consonants (UC) and the glottal stop **ʔ** sound like English "*ey*" as in the words th*ey*, h*ey*, wh*ey*, etc. Salish UC are: **q, q̓, qʷ, q̓ʷ, x̣, x̣ʷ**. For example, the suffix **...qin** – head/top, is often spelled using English *ey* as "q*ey*n". So **qi, q̓i, qʷi, q̓ʷi, x̣i, x̣ʷi**, may be spelled with English *ey* as **q***ey*, **q̓***ey*, **qʷ***ey*, **q̓ʷ***ey*, **x̣***ey*, **x̣ʷ***ey* in other texts.

s.t. - something, the 3rd person
(s.t.) - something implied
s.o. - someone, the 3rd person
sl. - singular form
pl. - plural form
rt. - root word
cmd. - command
lit. - literally
fig. - figuratively
i.e., - for example
See: - Redirection to a related word.

xʷċšmist – S/he surrendered. **čn xʷċšmist, kʷ xʷċšmist**
es xʷċšmisti – S/he is surrendering. **čnes xʷċšmisti, kʷes xʷċšmisti**
qs xʷċšmisti – S/he is going to surrender. **čiqs xʷċšmisti, kʷqs xʷċšmisti**

čnes xʷċšmisti č sxʷkʷnem – I am surrendering to the police.

surveyor **sxʷłṗulexʷm –** one tasked to put lines on the ground; surveyor.

Susan **susán –** Susan.

suspenders **łqʷłqʷłq̇eyt,** *łqʷłqʷłq̇e* – put on/wear suspenders. *rt.: **łoqʷ**– over lay/around; suffix: **...łq̇éyt**– shoulder.*
łqʷłqʷłq̇eytm – S/he put on suspenders. **čn łqʷłqʷłq̇eytm, kʷ łqʷłqʷłq̇eytm**
es łqʷłqʷłq̇eyti – S/he is putting on suspenders. **čnes łqʷłqʷłq̇eyti, kʷes łqʷłqʷłq̇eyti**
qs łqʷłqʷłq̇eyti – S/he is going to put on suspenders. **čiqs łqʷłqʷłq̇eyti, kʷqs łqʷłqʷłq̇eyti**

łqʷłqʷłq̇eytis – S/he put suspenders on s.o. **čn łqʷłqʷłq̇eytn, kʷ łqʷłqʷłq̇eytntxʷ**
es łqʷłqʷłq̇eytms – S/he is putting suspenders on s.o. **ies łqʷłqʷłq̇eytm, as łqʷłqʷłq̇eytm**
qs łqʷłqʷłq̇eytms – S/he is going to put suspenders on s.o. **iqs łqʷłqʷłq̇eytm, aqs łqʷłqʷłq̇eytm**

es łqʷłqʷłq̇eyt – S/he is wearing suspenders. **čnes łqʷłqʷłq̇eyt, kʷes łqʷłqʷłq̇eyt**
łqʷłqʷłq̇eytn – suspenders.

łqʷłqʷłq̇eytiš – Put suspenders on. *cmd.*
łqʷłqʷłq̇eytnt – Put suspenders on him/her. *cmd.*

suspicious **čtmtmłtumš,** *čtmtmłtu* – suspicious of people.
čtmtmłtu – S/he got suspicious of people. **čn čtmtmłtu, kʷ čtmtmłtu**

swallow **q̇mim –** swallow something.
q̇mim – S/he swallowed. **čn q̇mim, kʷ q̇mim**

q̇mntes – S/he/it swallowed s.t. **q̇mnten, q̇mntexʷ**
es q̇mims – S/he is swallowing s.t. **ies q̇mim, as q̇mim**
qs q̇mims – S/he is going to swallow s.t. **iqs q̇mim, aqs q̇mim**
q̇mntéˀes – They swallowed s.t. **qeˀ q̇mntem, q̇mntep**
es q̇míˀims – They are swallowing s.t. **qeˀes q̇mim, es q̇mimp**

čsq̇méltn, *čsq̇mé* – hungry/starving for food; figuratively, spiritually hungry. *See: **hungry**.*
qq̇m̓éyeˀ, *qq̇m̓é* – angling; fish. *See: **angle**.*

čn q̇mim t kapi – I swallow coffee. **q̇mntén łu sṫšá –** I swallowed a huckeberry. **xʷˀit u čn q̇mim –** I swallowed a lot of them. **ṅem q̇mntexʷ –** You will swallow it. **q̇mq̇mntén –** I swallowed them/repeatedly.

nq̇mep – devour/swallow something.
nq̇mep – S/he devoured (s.t.). **čn nq̇mep, kʷ nq̇mep**
es nq̇mepi – S/he is devouring (s.t.). **čnes nq̇mepi, kʷes nq̇mepi**
qs nq̇mepi – S/he is going to devour (s.t.). **čiqs nq̇mepi, kʷqs nq̇mepi**
nq̇méˀep – They devoured (s.t.). **qeˀ nq̇mepi, p nq̇mep**

nq̇mepis – S/he/it devoured s.t. **nq̇mepn, nq̇mepntxʷ**
es nq̇mepms – S/he is devouring s.t. **ies nq̇mepm, as nq̇mepm**
qs nq̇mepms – S/he is going to devour s.t. **iqs nq̇mepm, aqs nq̇mepm**
nq̇méˀepis – They devoured s.t. **qeˀ nq̇mepntm, nq̇mepntp**

nq̇mepnt – Devour it. *cmd.*

nq̇mepn sťšá – I devoured the huckleberries. **čn nq̇mep t sťšá** – I devoured huckleberries.

q̇mcinm – The action of swallowing. *suffix: **...cin, ...cn** – action of the mouth.*
q̇mcinm – S/he/it swallowed. **čn q̇mcinm, kʷ q̇mcinm**
es q̇mcini – S/he/it is swallowing. **čnes q̇mcini, kʷes q̇mcini**
qs q̇mcini – S/he/it is going to swallow. **čiqs q̇mcini, kʷqs q̇mcini**
q̇mcíˀinm – They swallowed. **qeˀ q̇mcinm, p q̇mcinm**

słṁómqcin, *słṁó* – cliff swallow.

swamp

ťiṁlexʷ – damp ground; swamp. *rt.: **ťiṁ** – damp.*

swan

spqmi – swan; tundra swan; whistling swan.

sweat

čskʷilt – sweat; perspire.
čskʷilt – S/he sweated. **čn čskʷilt, kʷ čskʷilt**
es čskʷilti – S/he is sweating. **čnes čskʷilti, kʷes čskʷilti**
qs čskʷilti – S/he is going to sweat. **čiqs čskʷilti, kʷqs čskʷilti**
es čskʷíˀilti – They are sweating. **qeˀes čskʷilti, pes čskʷilti**

sčskʷilt – sweat.

sčskʷltmalqs – sweaty clothes. *suffix: **...lqs, ...alqs** – clothes.*
es čskʷltmalqsi – S/he has sweaty clothes. **čnes čskʷltmalqsi, kʷes čskʷltmalqsi**

laq̇ist, *laq̇i* – sweat in a sweat lodge.
laq̇ist – S/he/it sweated. **čn laq̇ist, kʷ laq̇ist**
es laq̇isti – S/he/it is sweating. **čnes laq̇isti, kʷes laq̇isti**
qs laq̇isti – S/he/it is going to sweat. **čiqs laq̇isti, kʷqs laq̇isti**
lq̇láˀaq̇ – They sweated. **qeˀ lq̇laq̇, p lq̇laq̇**

lq̇aq̇išts – S/he/it sweated for s.o. **lq̇aq̇ištn, lq̇aq̇ištxʷ**
es lq̇aq̇ištms – S/he/it is sweating for s.o. **ies lq̇aq̇ištm, as lq̇aq̇ištm**
qs lq̇aq̇ištms – S/he/it is going to sweat for s.o. **iqs lq̇aq̇ištm, aqs lq̇aq̇ištm**

sxʷlaq̇m – one tasked to sweat in the sweat lodge. *prefix: **sxʷ...** – one tasked to do.*
lq̇laq̇istenm – someone who always sweats in the sweat lodge.

ṅem laq̇i – S/he/it will sweat. **ṅem čn laq̇i, ṅem kʷ laq̇i**
ṅem lq̇láˀaq̇ – They will sweat. **ṅem qeˀ lq̇laq̇, ṅem p lq̇laq̇**

sweater

ssoťlqs – sweater. *rt.: **suť** – stretch; suffix: **...lqs, ...alqs** – clothes.*

sweat lodge

snlaq̇ist, *snlaq̇i* – sweat lodge.
ha t anwi u k̓ʷuḷntxʷ łu snlaq̇ist – Did you fix the sweat lodge?

k̓ʷl̓čulexʷ – the area of the sweat. *rt.: **k̓ʷelč̓** – cover with; suffix: **...ulexʷ** – land.*

nšiˀtelixʷ – head person in the lodge/house.

čolépcn, *čolé* – build a fire for a sweat. *See: **fire**.*
sxʷčole – one tasked to make fire for a sweat. *prefix: **sxʷ...** – one tasked to do.*

nolím – heat sweat rocks. *See: **fire**.*

nplšesšṅm – bring rocks in there. *rt.: **npilš** – go in pl.; suffix: **...sšṅ** – rock. See: **bring**.*
sxʷnplšesšṅm – one tasked to bring rocks in. *prefix: **sxʷ...** – one tasked to do. See: **bring**.*

The **i** following uvular consonants (UC) and the glottal stop **ˀ** sound like English "*ey*" as in the words *they, hey, whey*, etc. Salish UC are: **q, q̇, qʷ, q̇ʷ, x̣, x̣ʷ**. For example, the suffix **...qin** – head/top, is often spelled using English *ey* as "qeyn". So **qi, q̇i, qʷi, q̇ʷi, x̣i, x̣ʷi**, may be spelled with English *ey* as *qey, q̇ey, qʷey, q̇ʷey, x̣ey, x̣ʷey* in other texts.

s.t. - something, the 3rd person
(s.t.) - something implied
s.o. - someone, the 3rd person
sl. - singular form
pl. - plural form
rt. - root word
cmd. - command
lit. - literally
fig. - figuratively
i.e., - for example
See: - Redirection to a related word.

čłk̓ʷum – pick something up using an instrument or tool. *(i.e., a needle for beads, a pitchfork for hay/rocks, etc.) See:* ***pick.***

čqʷlqʷel̓tn – Sticks used in the sweat. *rt.:* ***qʷlqʷel̓t*** *– talk; suffix:* ***...tin, ...tn*** *– means of/device.*

snpkʷessn̓ – sweat lodge rock pit. *rt.:* ***pukʷ*** *– round objects poured; suffix:* ***...essn̓, ...ssn̓*** *– rock.*

sweat lodge rocks

t̓ik̓ʷssn̓ – sweat lodge rocks.
ƛ̓e i čkʷlkʷil łu t̓ik̓ʷssn̓ – The rocks are ready *(the rocks are red)*. **ƛ̓e i pxʷpexʷ łu t̓ik̓ʷssn̓** – The rocks are glowing hot. **ƛ̓e i čpxʷpexʷssn̓** – The rocks are glowing hot.

sweep

ċslexʷéłpm, *ċslexʷé* – sweep/clear the floor. *rt.:* ***ċslexʷ*** *– make bare/clean; suffix:* ***...ełp, ...łp*** *– tree; coming from floor covering which were boughs in the past.*
ċslexʷéłpm – S/he swept. **čn ċslexʷéłpm, kʷ ċslexʷéłpm**
es ċslexʷéłpi – S/he is sweeping. **čnes ċslexʷéłpi, kʷes ċslexʷéłpi**
qs ċslexʷéłpi – S/he is going to sweep. **čiqs ċslexʷéłpi, kʷqs ċslexʷéłpi**

ċslexʷéłpis – S/he swept it. **ċslexʷéłpn, kʷ ċslexʷéłpntxʷ**
es ċslexʷéłpms – S/he is sweeping it. **čnes ċslexʷéłpm, kʷes ċslexʷéłpm**
qs ċslexʷéłpms – S/he is going to sweep it. **čiqs ċslexʷéłpm, kʷqs ċslexʷéłpm**

ċslexʷéłpntm – It was swept.

ċslexʷéłpmn – broom.

ċslexʷéłpiš – Sweep. *cmd.*
ċslexʷéłpntxʷ – Sweep it. *cmd.*
ċsim – clear; clear clutter/items/objects. *See:* ***clear.***

čłʔáx̣ʷłp – sweep/scrape. *rt.:* ***ax̣ʷ*** *– scrape; prefix:* ***čł...*** *– surface; suffix:* ***...ełp, ...łp*** *– tree; coming from floor covering which were boughs in the past.*
čłʔáx̣ʷłpm – S/he swept. **čn čłʔáx̣ʷłpm, kʷ čłʔáx̣ʷłpm**
es čłʔáx̣ʷłpi – S/he is sweeping. **čnes čłʔáx̣ʷłpi, kʷes čłʔáx̣ʷłpi**
qs čłʔáx̣ʷłpi – S/he is going to sweep. **čiqs čłʔáx̣ʷłpi, kʷqs čłʔáx̣ʷłpi**

čłʔáx̣ʷłpis – S/he swept it. **čłʔáx̣ʷłpn, kʷ čłʔáx̣ʷłpntxʷ**
es čłʔáx̣ʷłpms – S/he is sweeping it. **čnes čłʔáx̣ʷłpm, kʷes čłʔáx̣ʷłpm**
qs čłʔáx̣ʷłpms – S/he is going to sweep it. **čiqs čłʔáx̣ʷłpm, kʷqs čłʔáx̣ʷłpm**

čłʔáx̣ʷłpntm – It was swept.

čłʔáx̣ʷłpmn – broom.

čłʔáx̣ʷłpiš – Sweep. *cmd.*
čłʔáx̣ʷłpntxʷ – Sweep it. *cmd.*

čłċsim – sweep/clear the surface. *rt.:* ***ċsip*** *– disappear; prefix:* ***čł...*** *– surface.*
čłċsim – S/he cleared the surface. **čn čłċsim, kʷ čłċsim**
es čłċsmi – S/he is clearing the surface. **čnes čłċsmi, kʷes čłċsmi**
qs čłċsmi – S/he is going to clear the surface. **čiqs čłċsmi, kʷqs čłċsmi**

sweet

t̓iš – sugar; sweet.
i t̓iš – It is sweet.
i łt̓t̓iš – It is a little sweet.
i nt̓iškʷ – It is sweet (liquid).

iqʷił t̓iš – It is imitation sugar.
sck̓ʷl̓t̓iš – made sugar; artificial sugar.

t̓et̓išeʔ – sweetie.
t̓išłc̓eʔ – sweet inside.
nt̓iškʷm – put sugar in a liquid. *See: **sugar**.*
st̓šałq, *st̓ša* – huckleberry. *rt.: **t̓iš** – sweet; suffix: **...ałq** – smell, accompaniment.*
nt̓iškʷ – sweet liquid; pop; Kool-aid. *rt.: **t̓iš** – sweet; prefix: **n...** – inside; suffix: **...etkʷ** – liquid.*

nt̓išp – eat something sweet.
nt̓išpm – S/he ate s.t. sweet. **čn nt̓išpm, kʷ nt̓išpm**
es nt̓išpi – S/he is eating s.t. sweet. **čnes nt̓išpi, kʷes nt̓išpi**
qs nt̓išpi – S/he is going to eat s.t. sweet. **čiqs nt̓išpi, kʷqs nt̓išpi**

čiqs nt̓išpi t pay – I am going to eat pie. **t čeṅ ec̓x̣lst̓iš** – How sweet is it?

> The **i** following uvular consonants (UC) and the glottal stop ʔ sound like English "*ey*" as in the words *they, hey, whey,* etc. Salish UC are: **q, q̓, qʷ, q̓ʷ, x̣, x̣ʷ**. For example, the suffix ...**qin** – head/top, is often spelled using English *ey* as "q*ey*n". So **qi, q̓i, qʷi, q̓ʷi, x̣i, x̣ʷi**, may be spelled with English *ey* as **q***ey*, **q̓***ey*, **qʷ***ey*, **q̓ʷ***ey*, **x̣***ey*, **x̣ʷ***ey* in other texts.

sweetbread
ckʷckʷu – sweetbread.

sweet cicely
x̣ʷit msṁsá – sweet cicely; sweet root.

sweet grass
sx̣séstiyeʔ – sweet grass. *suffix: **...st̓iyeʔ** – grass.*

Sweet Grass Hills
ččałalqn – Sweet Grass Hills, Montana. *lit. three peaks.*

sweet rolls
scnt̓išlexʷ – sweet rolls. *rt.: **t̓iš** – sweet; prefix: **sc...** – s.t. that's been done/made/prepared.*

sweet-root
x̣ʷit msṁsá – American sweet cicely; sweet root.

swell
sukʷ – swell slowly.
i sukʷ – It is swollen.
sukʷt – It swelled.

sukʷtečst – swollen hand. *suffix: **...ečst, ...čst** – of the hand.*
sukʷšin – swollen foot.

pew – swell rapidly.
i pewt – It is swollen.
pewt – It swelled rapidly.

pewčst – His/her hand swelled rapidly. **čn pewčst, kʷ pewčst**

psas – swelled object shrinks/flattens; deflate.
čpsšan – flat tire. *See: **flat tire**.*

psas łu inolin – My swollen belly went down/shrank.

swim
nčalip, *nčalí* – swim.
nčalip – S/he/it swam. **čn nčalip, kʷ nčalip**
es nčalpmi – S/he/it is swimming. **čnes nčalpmi, kʷes nčalpmi**
qs nčalpmi – S/he/it is going to swim. **čiqs nčalpmi, kʷqs nčalpmi**
nčalíʔip – They swam. **qeʔ nčalip, p nčalip**

nčalpstes – S/he/it made s.o. swim. **nčalpsten, nčalpstexʷ**
es nčalpims – S/he/it is making s.o. swim. **ies nčalpim, as nčalpim**
qs nčalpims – S/he/it is going to make s.o. swim. **iqs nčalpim, aqs nčalpim**

es nłččalpmi – S/he/it is swimming a little. **čnes nłččalpmi, kʷes nłččalpmi**

nčalipš – Swim. *cmd.*
nčalipwi – All of you swim. *cmd.*

> s.t. - something, the 3rd person
> (s.t.) - something implied
> s.o. - someone, the 3rd person
> *sl.* - singular form
> *pl.* - plural form
> *rt.* - root word
> *cmd.* - command
> *lit.* - literally
> *fig.* - figuratively
> *i.e.,* - for example
> *See:* - Redirection to a related word.

es nčalpelsi – S/he is wanting to swim. **čnes nčalpelsi, kʷes nčalpelsi**

ha kʷes nčalpmi – Are you swimming? **čiqs nčalpmi –** I am going to swim.

ċuˀċaw̓lš, *ċuˀċa* – bathe; swim/play in the tub; moving around in the water. *See: **bathe**.*

ẇewłm – The fish swam.
es ẇewłi – The fish is swimming.
qs ẇewłi – The fish is going to swim.

sẇewł – fish.

swing **q̓eṫẇéẇs,** *q̓eṫẇé* – swing.
q̓eṫẇe – S/he/it swung. **čn q̓eṫẇe, kʷ q̓eṫẇe**
es q̓eṫẇe – S/he/it is swinging. **čnes q̓eṫẇe, kʷes q̓eṫẇe**
qs q̓eṫẇe – S/he/it is going to swing. **čiqs q̓eṫẇe, kʷqs q̓eṫẇe**

snq̓eṫẇé – swing.

q̓ṫq̓ṫax̣n – swing arms.
es q̓ṫq̓ṫax̣ni – S/he is swinging his/her arms. **čnes q̓ṫq̓ṫax̣ni, kʷes q̓ṫq̓ṫax̣ni**

sword **ilmin –** sword.

syringe **wax̣íłp –** mock orange; syringe; *Philadelphus lewisii.*

syrup **lamná –** syrup.

nsuṫkʷ – syrup; stretchy liquid. *rt.: **suṫ–** stretch; suffix: **...etkʷ–** liquid.*

T

table **snčłel̓il̓ntn** – table for more than one person. *rt.:* ***iłn*** *– eat; prefix:* ***sn...*** *– a place of; suffix:* ***...tin, ...tn*** *– means of/device.*
snčłʔiłntn – table for one person; place to eat. *rt.:* ***iłn*** *– eat; prefix:* ***sn...*** *– a place of; suffix:* ***...tin, ...tn*** *– means of/device.*
snčłʔíʔiłntn – little table/TV tray for one person. *rt.:* ***iłn*** *– eat; prefix:* ***sn...*** *– a place of; suffix:* ***...tin, ...tn*** *– means of/device.*

tablecloth **k̓ʷłxʷépmn** – tablecloth.

tadpole **ql̓ql̓aqs**, *ql̓ql̓a* – tadpole.

pt̓y̓oseʔ – newly born fish; tadpole.

tag **ttqnnwexʷ** – put hands on each other; play tag. *rt.:* ***tqem*** *– touch.*
ttqnnweʔexʷ – They putting hands on each other. **qeʔ ttqnnwexʷ, pes ttqnnwexʷ**
es ttqnnweʔexʷi – They are putting hands on each other. **qeʔes ttqnnwexʷi, pes ttqnnwexʷi**
qs ttqnnweʔexʷi – They are going to put hands on each other. **qeʔqs ttqnnwexʷi, pqs ttqnnwexʷi**

čtqnnwexʷ – chasing each other; play tag. *rt.:* ***čtqem*** *– chase.*
čtqnnweʔexʷ – They chased each other. **qeʔ čtqnnweʔexʷ, p čtqnnweʔexʷ**
es čtqnnweʔexʷi – They are chasing each other. **qeʔes čtqnnweʔexʷi, pes čtqnnweʔexʷi**
qs čtqnnweʔexʷi – They are going to chase each other. **qeʔqs čtqnnweʔexʷi, pqs čtqnnweʔexʷi**

tail **sups** – tail.
łssusps – little tail.
łspsups – many little tails.
čłłaq̓ps – wide tail. *rt.:* ***łaq̓t*** *– wide.*
čkʷtnups – big tail. *rt.:* ***kʷtunt*** *– big.*
čyulps – bulky large tail. *rt.:* ***yult*** *– thick in girth. See:* ***girth.***
čłk̓ʷk̓ʷiups – small tail.
čłqqups – narrow tail.

čilyelps – wag a tail. *See:* ***wag.***

tailbone **sxʷtups** – tailbone.

tailgate **čsx̣mups** – tailgate.
čsx̣mupsm – S/he tailgated. **čn čsx̣mupsm, kʷ čsx̣mupsm**
es čsx̣mupsi – S/he is tailgating. **čnes čsx̣mupsi, kʷes čsx̣mupsi**
qs čsx̣mupsi – S/he is going to tailgate. **čiqs čsx̣mupsi, kʷqs čsx̣mupsi**

čsx̣mupsis – S/he tailgated s.o. **čsx̣mupsn, čsx̣mupsntxʷ**
es čsx̣mupsms – S/he is tailgating s.o. **ies čsx̣mupsm, as čsx̣mupsm**
qs čsx̣mupsms – S/he is going to tailgate s.o. **iqs čsx̣mupsm, aqs čsx̣mupsm**

s.t. - something, the 3rd person
(s.t.) - something implied
s.o. - someone, the 3rd person
sl. - singular form
pl. - plural form
rt. - root word
cmd. - command
lit. - literally
fig. - figuratively
i.e., - for example
See: - Redirection to a related word.

take **kʷnem –** take one thing; grab.
kʷnem – S/he/it took. **čn kʷnem, kʷ kʷnem**
es kʷnei – S/he/it is taking. **čnes kʷnei, kʷes kʷnei**
qs kʷnei – S/he/it is going to take. **čiqs kʷnei, kʷqs kʷnei**

kʷéis – S/he/it took s.t./s.o. **kʷen, kʷentxʷ**
es kʷnems – S/he/it is taking s.t./s.o. **ies kʷnem, as kʷnem**
qs kʷnems – S/he/it is going to take s.t./s.o. **iqs kʷnem, aqs kʷnem**
kʷéʔeis – They took s.t./s.o. **qeʔ kʷéntm, kʷéntp**
es kʷnéʔems – They are taking s.t./s.o. **qeʔes kʷnem, es kʷnemp**
qs kʷnéʔems – They are going to take s.t./s.o. **qeʔqs kʷnem, qs kʷnemp**

sxʷkʷnem – one tasked to take/grab; police.

kʷeiš – Take. *cmd.*
kʷent – Take it. *cmd.*
ckʷent – Give it to me. *cmd.*
nkʷenxʷcn – the words were taken.
kʷenp – take fire.
kʷestm – hold something in the hand; in possession of something. *See: **hold**.*
kʷenlt – hold a child. *See: **hold**.*
kʷnmtncut – hold yourself. *See: **hold**.*
kʷnmist – hug; hold of one's self. *See: **hug**.*

t atwen u kʷeis – Tony took it. **itam łu kʷen –** I took the wrong one. **ckʷeštms –** S/he took it for you. **qeʔ ckʷešłls –** S/he took it for us. **qʷo kʷent –** Take me.

q̇ʷom – take more than one thing.
q̇ʷom – S/he/it took things. **čn q̇ʷom, kʷ q̇ʷom**
es q̇ʷomi – S/he/it is taking things. **čnes q̇ʷomi, kʷes q̇ʷomi**
qs q̇ʷomi – S/he/it is going to take things. **čiqs q̇ʷomi, kʷqs q̇ʷomi**

q̇ʷomis – S/he/it took the things. **q̇ʷomn, q̇ʷomntxʷ**
es q̇ʷoms – S/he/it is taking the things. **ies q̇ʷom, as q̇ʷom**
qs q̇ʷoms – S/he/it is going to take the things. **iqs q̇ʷom, aqs q̇ʷom**

scq̇ʷom – things that have been taken.

q̇ʷomiš – Take (things). *cmd.*
q̇ʷomnt – Take them. *cmd.*
q̇ʷomštweʔexʷ – They took things for each other. **qeʔ q̇ʷomštwexʷ, p q̇ʷomštwexʷ**
q̇ʷomnweʔexʷ – They took things from each other. **qeʔ q̇ʷomnwexʷ, p q̇ʷomnwexʷ**

q̇ʷomnt esel tl̓ ciʔ kʷ čtxʷum t esel – Take two from there and add two. **tl̓ cil q̇ʷomiš esel kʷemt k̇inš łu l šeẏ –** From five take two; then how many do you have?

k̇ʷłxʷuym – take/bring away. *rt.: **xʷuy** – go; prefix: **k̇ʷł...** – under.*
k̇ʷłxʷuymis – S/he/it took it away. **k̇ʷłxʷuymn, k̇ʷłxʷuymntxʷ**
es k̇ʷłxʷuyms – S/he/it is taking it away. **ies k̇ʷłxʷuym, as k̇ʷłxʷuym**
qs k̇ʷłxʷuyms – S/he/it is going to take it away. **iqs k̇ʷłxʷuym, aqs k̇ʷłxʷuym**

cnkʷƛ̓étkʷm – pull out of water.
cnkʷƛ̓étkʷis – S/he pulled it out of the water. **cnkʷƛ̓étkʷn, cnkʷƛ̓étkʷntxʷ**

młim – take down/dismantle something.
młntés – S/he took something down. **młntén, młntéxʷ**
es młims – S/he is taking something down. **ies młim, as młim**

qs młims – S/he is going to take something down. **iqs młim, aqs młim**

młnté'es łu sq̇eẏmis – They took down the tipi poles.

ṫipm – take something down from up high.
ṫipmstes – take something down from up high. **ṫipmsten, ṫipmstexʷ**

kʷƛ̓im – take something out; detach; loose/free embedded object.
kʷƛ̓ip – It came out naturally.
es kʷƛ̓pmi – It is coming out naturally.
qs kʷƛ̓pmi – It is going to come out naturally.

čkʷƛ̓ip – The handle came off/out.
es čkʷƛ̓pmi – The handle is coming off/out.
qs čkʷƛ̓pmi – The handle is going to come off/out.

kʷƛ̓ntes – S/he took s.t. out. **kʷƛ̓nten, kʷƛ̓ntexʷ**
es kʷƛ̓ims – S/he is taking s.t. out. **ies kʷƛ̓im, as kʷƛ̓im**
qs kʷƛ̓ims – S/he is going to take s.t. out. **iqs kʷƛ̓im, aqs kʷƛ̓im**

čkʷƛ̓pep – shed fur. *See: **shed**.*

k̇ʷłkʷƛ̓im – take something out of an enclosure; take out of the oven. *rt.: **kʷƛ̓im** – take out.*
k̇ʷłkʷƛ̓ntes – S/he took something out of the oven. **k̇ʷłkʷƛ̓nten, k̇ʷłkʷƛ̓ntexʷ**
es k̇ʷłkʷƛ̓ims – S/he is taking something out of the oven. **ies k̇ʷłkʷƛ̓im, as k̇ʷłkʷƛ̓im**

k̇ʷłkʷƛ̓int – Take it out. *cmd.*

nkʷƛ̓im – take something out from inside something.
nkʷƛ̓ntes – S/he took s.t. out of it. **nkʷƛ̓nten, nkʷƛ̓ntexʷ**
es nkʷƛ̓ims – S/he is taking s.t. out of it. **ies nkʷƛ̓im, as nkʷƛ̓im**
qs nkʷƛ̓ims – S/he is going to take s.t. out of it. **iqs nkʷƛ̓im, aqs nkʷƛ̓im**

nkʷƛ̓int – Take it out. *cmd.*

nkʷƛ̓etkʷ – take something out of water.
nkʷƛ̓etkʷis – S/he took s.t. out of water. **nkʷƛ̓etkʷn, nkʷƛ̓etkʷntxʷ**
es nkʷƛ̓etkʷms – S/he is taking s.t. out of water. **ies nkʷƛ̓etkʷm, as nkʷƛ̓etkʷm**
qs nkʷƛ̓etkʷms – S/he is going to take s.t. out of water. **iqs nkʷƛ̓etkʷm, aqs nkʷƛ̓etkʷm**

nkʷƛ̓etkʷnt – Take it out of the water. *cmd.*

nkʷƛ̓us – take something out of a fire.
nkʷƛ̓usis – S/he took s.t. out of the fire. **nkʷƛ̓usn, nkʷƛ̓usntxʷ**
es nkʷƛ̓usms – S/he is taking s.t. out of the fire. **ies nkʷƛ̓usm, as nkʷƛ̓usm**
qs nkʷƛ̓usms – S/he is going to take s.t. out of the fire. **iqs nkʷƛ̓usm, aqs nkʷƛ̓usm**

take care of

nq̇é'elsm – engaged in some activity; have business; take care of something.
nq̇é'elsm – S/he/it was engaged in business. **čn nq̇é'elsm, kʷ nq̇é'elsm**
es nq̇é'elsi – S/he/it is engaged in business. **čnes nq̇é'elsi, kʷes nq̇é'elsi**
qs nq̇é'elsi – S/he/it is going to be engaged in business. **čiqs nq̇é'elsi, kʷqs nq̇é'elsi**
nq̇é'e'élsm – They are engaged in business. **qe' nq̇é'elsm, p nq̇é'elsm**
es nq̇é'e'élsi – They are engaged in business. **qe'es nq̇é'elsi, pes nq̇é'elsi**
qs nq̇é'e'élsi – They are going to be engaged in business. **qe'qs nq̇é'elsi, pqs nq̇é'elsi**

The **i** following uvular consonants (UC) and the glottal stop ' sound like English "*ey*" as in the words *they*, *hey*, *whey*, etc. Salish UC are: **q**, **q̇**, **qʷ**, **q̇ʷ**, **x̣**, **x̣ʷ**. For example, the suffix ...**qin** – head/top, is often spelled using English *ey* as "*qeyn*". So **qi**, **q̇i**, **qʷi**, **q̇ʷi**, **x̣i**, **x̣ʷi**, may be spelled with English *ey* as **q***ey*, **q̇***ey*, **qʷ***ey*, **q̇ʷ***ey*, **x̣***ey*, **x̣ʷ***ey* in other texts.

s.t. - something, the 3rd person
(s.t.) - something implied
s.o. - someone, the 3rd person
sl. - singular form
pl. - plural form
rt. - root word
cmd. - command
lit. - literally
fig. - figuratively
i.e., - for example
See: - Redirection to a related word.

nq̇é?elsmis – S/he/it took care of s.t. **nq̇é?elsmn, nq̇é?elsmntxʷ**
es nq̇é?elsms – S/he/it is taking care of s.t. **ies nq̇é?elsm, as nq̇é?elsm**
qs nq̇é?elsms – S/he/it is going to take care of s.t. **iqs nq̇é?elsm, aqs nq̇é?elsm**
nq̇é?e?élsmis – They took care of s.t. **qe? nq̇é?elsmntm, nq̇é?elsmntp**
es nq̇é?e?élsms – They are taking care of s.t. **qe?es nq̇é?elsm, es nq̇é?elsmp**
qs nq̇é?e?élsms – They are going to take care of s.t. **qe?qs nq̇é?elsm, qs nq̇é?elsmp**

scnq̇é?elsts – his/her/its business. **iscnq̇é?els, ascnq̇é?els**

čiqs xʷuy č x̣ʷi?ilqsa čn ep scnq̇é?els – I am going to Pablo. I have business there.

čšťim – guard or take care of. *(This term is also used for wakes as it is seen that people are taking care of the dead.) See:* ***guard.***

čštelm – put something in the care of someone else. *See:* ***care.***

čšťncut – take care of one's self. *See:* ***care.***

čšťeľt – watch over children; babysit. *See:* ***babysit.***

es čšťmi – S/he is guarding. *(during a wake people are taking care of the dead.) rt.:* ***čšťim –*** *guard. See:* ***guard.***

take off

pƛ̕im – release; free from something; remove something. *See:* ***release.***
pƛ̕int – Remove it; take it off. *cmd.*
pƛ̕qin – remove head cover/hat; bare head. *See:* ***hat.***
pƛ̕pƛ̕šin – remove footwear. *See:* ***shoe.***
čpƛ̕?encut – undress one's self. *See:* ***undress.***
npƛ̕alqs, *npƛ̕a* **–** remove/take off clothes. *See:* ***undress.***
pƛ̕aqslšiš – Remove your clothes. *cmd. See:* ***undress.***
npƛ̕ičn̓t – Remove the saddle. *cmd. See:* ***saddle.***
pƛ̕usnt – Remove the bridle. *cmd. See:* ***bridle.***

čċslexʷ – get naked; get cleared of clothing. *See:* ***naked.***

tale

sqʷllumt, *sqʷl̓lu* **–** animal stories; creation stories; Coyote stories. *(These stories are customarily told when the ground is covered with snow and all hibernating animals have gone into hibernation. A good indication that these stories can be told is when the weather is very cold causing trees to pop.) See:* ***story.***

sm̓im̓i? – story; news; something that's been told. *See:* ***tell.***

talk

qʷlqʷélt, *qʷl̓qʷé* **–** speak/talk; the act of talking; saying words. *See:* ***speak.***

uwéwlš – communicate; speak formally; convey meaning through speech. *See:* ***speak.***

sqʷllumt, *sqʷl̓lu* **–** animal stories; creation stories; Coyote stories. *(These stories can only be told when the ground is covered with snow and all hibernating animals have gone into hibernation. A good indication that these stories can be told is when the weather is very cold causing trees to pop.) See:* ***story.***
sqʷllumt spq̇ni? – November *(month of storytelling).*

q̇mq̇milš, *q̇mq̇mi* **–** meet and talk; have a meeting; discuss. *See:* ***meet.***

nk̓ʷ?elsm – talk about someone in a bad way.
nk̓ʷ?elsis – S/he talked about s.o. **nk̓ʷ?elsn, nk̓ʷ?elsntxʷ**
es nk̓ʷ?elsms – S/he is talking about s.o. **ies nk̓ʷ?elsm, as nk̓ʷ?elsm**
qs nk̓ʷ?elsms – S/he is going to talk about s.o. **iqs nk̓ʷ?elsm, aqs nk̓ʷ?elsm**
nk̓ʷ?é?elsis – They talked about s.o. **qe? nk̓ʷ?elsntm, nk̓ʷ?elsntp**
es nk̓ʷ?é?elsms – They are talking about s.o. **qe?es nk̓ʷ?elsm, es nk̓ʷ?elsmp**
qs nk̓ʷ?é?elsms – They are going to talk about s.o. **qe?qs nk̓ʷ?elsm, qs nk̓ʷ?elsmp**

exʷkʷunm – people/animals making sounds; make sounds/voices/talk in a certain way, *(i.e., people talking/singing in the distance; to hear voices you can't understand; animals making sounds; speaking in a certain way: nice, mean, like animal, etc.).*
exʷkʷunm – S/he/it made sounds. **čn exʷkʷunm, kʷ exʷkʷunm**
es exʷkʷuni – S/he/it is making sounds. **čnes exʷkʷuni, kʷes exʷkʷuni**
exʷkʷúʔunm – They were making sounds. **qeʔ exʷkʷúʔunm, p exʷkʷúʔunm**

exʷexʷkʷunm – Each is making sounds.

exʷkʷunis – S/he/it made the sounds of s.t. **exʷkʷunn, exʷkʷunntxʷ**
es exʷkʷunms – S/he/it is making the sounds of s.t. **ies exʷkʷunm, as exʷkʷunm**
qs exʷkʷunms – S/he/it is going to make the sounds of s.t. **iqs exʷkʷunm, aqs exʷkʷunm**
exʷkʷúʔunis – They made the sounds of s.t. **qeʔ exʷkʷunntm, exʷkʷunntp**

k̇ʷłexʷkʷunis – S/he/it spoke flatteringly to s.o. **k̇ʷłexʷkʷunn, k̇ʷłexʷkʷunntxʷ**
es k̇ʷłexʷkʷunms – S/he/it is speaking flatteringly to s.o. **ies k̇ʷłexʷkʷunm, as k̇ʷłexʷkʷunm**
qs k̇ʷłexʷkʷunms – S/he/it is going to speak flatteringly to s.o. **iqs k̇ʷłexʷkʷunm, aqs k̇ʷłexʷkʷunm**

l čeṅ u qʷo es exʷkʷustxʷ – How do you talk to me? **čnes exʷkʷunm t čn npiyels –** I spoke like I was happy. **x̣ʷl̓ steṁ u qeʔes exʷkʷułls –** Why did s/he speak to us that way?

nexʷkʷuncn – speak as something/someone; sound like something/someone.
es nexʷkʷuncni – S/he/it is sounding like (s.o./s.t.). **čnes nexʷkʷuncni, kʷes nexʷkʷuncni**

snʔexʷkʷuncn – the voice/song that sounds like s.o./s.t. *suffix:* ***...cin, ...cn*** *– action of the mouth.*

wéʔm – yell; holler out; talk while shouting. *See:* ***holler.***

...cin – *suffix indicating an action of the mouth; i.e., speaking, eating, & food.* *See:* **mouth.**

nmemeʔcin – talk in a bothersome way; interrupting speach. *rt.:* ***memeʔt*** *– bothersome; suffix:* ***...cin, ...cn*** *– action of the mouth.*
nmecinm – S/he/it talked in a bothersome way. **čn nmecinm, kʷ nmecinm**
es nmecini – S/he/it is talking in a bothersome way. **čnes nmecini, kʷes nmecini**
qs nmecini – S/he/it is going to talk in a bothersome way. **čiqs nmecini, kʷqs nmecini**
es nmecíʔini – They are talking in a bothersome way. **qeʔes nmecini, pes nmecini**

nmecinmis – S/he/it interrupted s.o. **nmecinmn, nmecinmntxʷ**
es nmecinms – S/he/it is interrupting s.o. **ies nmecinm, as nmecinm**
qs nmecinms – S/he/it is going to interrupt s.o. **iqs nmecinm, aqs nmecinm**
es nmecíʔinms – They are interrupting s.o. **qeʔes nmecinm, es nmecinmp**
qs nmecíʔinms – They are going to interrupt s.o. **qeʔqs nmecinm, qs nmecinmp**

nmemeʔcin – have bothersome talk; talk too much.

x̣scinm – talk in a good way; talk good about someone or something. *rt.: w/prefix:* ***x̣s...*** *– good; suffix:* ***...cin, ...cn*** *– action of the mouth.*
x̣scinm – S/he talked good. **čn x̣scinm, kʷ x̣scinm**
es x̣scini – S/he is talking good. **čnes x̣scini, kʷes x̣scini**
qs x̣scini – S/he is going to talk good. **čiqs x̣scini, kʷqs x̣scini**
x̣scíʔinm – They talked good. **qeʔ x̣scinm, p x̣scinm**
es x̣scíʔini – They are talking good. **qeʔes x̣scini, pes x̣scini**
qs x̣scíʔini – They are going to talk good. **qeʔqs x̣scini, pqs x̣scini**

x̣scinmis – S/he talked good about s.o. **x̣scinmn, x̣scinmntxʷ**

The **i** following uvular consonants (UC) and the glottal stop **ʔ** sound like English "*ey*" as in the words th*ey*, h*ey*, wh*ey*, etc. Salish UC are: **q, q̇, qʷ, q̇ʷ, x̣, x̣ʷ**. For example, the suffix **...qin** – head/top, is often spelled using English *ey* as "q*ey*n". So **qi, q̇i, qʷi, q̇ʷi, x̣i, x̣ʷi**, may be spelled with English *ey* as **q***ey*, **q̇***ey*, **qʷ***ey*, **q̇ʷ***ey*, **x̣***ey*, **x̣ʷ***ey* in other texts.

s.t. - something, the 3rd person
(s.t.) - something implied
s.o. - someone, the 3rd person
sl. - singular form
pl. - plural form
rt. - root word
cmd. - command
lit. - literally
fig. - figuratively
i.e., - for example
See: - Redirection to a related word.

es x̣scinms – S/he is talking good about s.o. **ies x̣scinm, as x̣scinm**
qs x̣scinms – S/he is going to talk good about s.o. **iqs x̣scinm, aqs x̣scinm**
x̣scíˀinmis – They talked good about s.o. **qeˀ x̣scinmntm, x̣scinmntp**
es x̣scíˀinms – They are talking good about s.o. **qeˀes x̣scinm, es x̣scinmp**
qs x̣scíˀinms – They are going to talk good about s.o. **qeˀqs x̣scinm, qs x̣scinmp**

imše kʷ x̣scinm – You should talk good.

čscinm – talk in a bad way; bad mouth. *rt.: w/prefix: **čs...** – bad; suffix: **...cin, ...cn** – action of the mouth.*
čscinm – S/he talked bad. **čn čscinm, kʷ čscinm**
es čscini – S/he is talking bad. **čnes čscini, kʷes čscini**
qs čscini – S/he is going to talk bad. **čiqs čscini, kʷqs čscini**
čscíˀinm – They talked bad. **qeˀ čscinm, p čscinm**
es čscíˀini – They are talking bad. **qeˀes čscini, pes čscini**
qs čscíˀini – They are going to talk bad. **qeˀqs čscini, pqs čscini**

čscinmis – S/he talked bad about s.o. **ies čscinmn, čscinmntxʷ**
es čscinms – S/he is talking bad about s.o. **ies čscinm, as čscinm**
qs čscinms – S/he is going to talk bad about s.o. **iqs čscinm, aqs čscinm**
čscíˀinmis – They talked bad about s.o. **qeˀ čscinmntm, čscinmntp**
es čscíˀinms – They are talking bad about s.o. **qeˀes čscinm, es čscinmp**
qs čscíˀinms – They are going to talk bad about s.o. **qeˀqs čscinm, qs čscinmp**

čscnmnwéxʷist, *čscnmnwé* – quarrel; say bad words to each other. *prefix: **čs...** – bad; suffix: **...cin, ...cn** – action of the mouth.; suffix: **...wexʷ** – action to each other. See: **quarrel**.*

ta kʷ qes čscinm – Do not talk bad. **tam kʷ ies čscinm –** I am not saying anything bad about you.

nťeyecnm – evil/bad talk; saying evil things. *suffix: **...cin, ...cn** – action of the mouth.*
nťeyecnm – S/he talked evil. **čn nťeyecnm, kʷ nťeyecnm**
es nťeyecni – S/he is talking evil. **čnes nťeyecni, kʷes nťeyecni**
qs nťeyecni – S/he is going to talk evil. **čiqs nťeyecni, kʷqs nťeyecni**

ta kʷ qes nťeyecnm – Do not talk evil.

tx̣ʷcin – talk straight; talk right; talk correct. *rt.: **tox̣ʷ** – straight.*
tx̣ʷcinm – S/he talked straight. **čn tx̣ʷcinm, kʷ tx̣ʷcinm**
es tx̣ʷcini – S/he is talking straight. **čnes tx̣ʷcini, kʷes tx̣ʷcini**
qs tx̣ʷcini – S/he is going to talk straight. **čiqs tx̣ʷcini, kʷqs tx̣ʷcini**

čtx̣ʷcinmis – S/he talked straight at s.o./s.t. **čtx̣ʷcinmn, čtx̣ʷcinmntxʷ**
es čtx̣ʷcinms – S/he is talking straight at s.o./s.t. **ies čtx̣ʷcinm, as čtx̣ʷcinm**
qs čtx̣ʷcinms – S/he is going to talk straight at s.o./s.t. **iqs čtx̣ʷcinm, aqs čtx̣ʷcinm**

tx̣ʷciniš – Talked straight. *cmd.*

nmtmtcin – talk with no-good words. *suffix: **...cin, ...cn** – action of the mouth. See: **no-good**.*
nmtmtcin – S/he talked no-good words. **čn nmtmtcin, kʷ nmtmtcin**
es nmtmtcini – S/he is talking no-good words. **čnes nmtmtcini, kʷes nmtmtcini**
qs nmtmtcini – S/he is going to talk no-good words. **čiqs nmtmtcini, kʷqs nmtmtcini**
nmtmtcíˀin – They talked no-good words. **qeˀ nmtmtcin, p nmtmtcin**
es nmtmtcíˀini – They are talking no-good words. **qeˀes nmtmtcini, pes nmtmtcini**
qs nmtmtcíˀini – They are going to talk no-good words. **qeˀqs nmtmtcini, pqs nmtmtcini**

ta kʷ qes nmtmtcinm – Do not talk with no-good words.

q̇spcinm – talk for a long time; endless talker. *suffix: **...cin, ...cn** – action of the mouth.*
q̇spcinm – S/he talked for a long time. **čn q̇spcinm, kʷ q̇spcinm**

es q̇spcini – S/he is talking for a long time. **čnes q̇spcini, kʷes q̇spcini**
qs q̇spcini – S/he is going to talk for a long time. **čiqs q̇spcini, kʷqs q̇spcini**

q̇spcinmis – S/he talked to s.o. a long time. **q̇spcinmn, q̇spcinmntxʷ**
es q̇spcinms – S/he is talking to s.o. a long time. **čnes q̇spcinm, kʷes q̇spcinm**
qs q̇spcinms – S/he is going to talk to s.o. a long time. **čiqs q̇spcinm, kʷqs q̇spcinm**

čq̇spcinmis – S/he talked a long time about s.t. **čq̇spcinmn, čq̇spcinmntxʷ**
es čq̇spcinms – S/he is talking a long time about s.t. **čnes čq̇spcinm, kʷes čq̇spcinm**
qs čq̇spcinms – S/he is going to talk a long time about s.t. **čiqs čq̇spcinm, kʷqs čq̇spcinm**

q̇spcnemn – one inclined to talk long; endless talker.

tam čiqs q̇spcini – I am not going to talk long.

wekʷcnm – hide your talk by whispering or by talking a different language; talk secretly; gossip. *See:* ***gossip.***

uẏécn – finish talking. *suffix:* ***...cin, ...cn*** *– action of the mouth.*
uẏécn – S/he/it finished talking. **čn uẏécn, kʷ uẏécn**

kʷtnmscin – talk big; to brag. *See:* ***brag.***

łaqʷcin – speak up once in a while.

nk̓ʷnk̓ʷucin – Saying one word at a time. *suffix:* ***...cin, ...cn*** *– action of the mouth.*

łkʷkʷnuṁeẏecn – talk small. *suffix:* ***...cin, ...cn*** *– action of the mouth.*

sllpcin – cannot figure out what to say. *rt.:* ***sllim*** *– confused. See:* ***confuse.***
sllpcan – make a mistake; mixed up words.

k̓ʷinšcn – talk some. *rt.:* ***k̓ʷinš*** *– how much; some; suffix:* ***...cin, ...cn*** *– action of the mouth.*
k̓ʷinšcn – S/he talked some. **čn k̓ʷinšcn, kʷ k̓ʷinšcn**
es k̓ʷinšcni – S/he is talking some. **čnes k̓ʷinšcni, kʷes k̓ʷinšcni**
qs k̓ʷinšcni – S/he is going to talk some. **čiqs k̓ʷinšcni, kʷqs k̓ʷinšcni**

tall

kʷtnálqʷ – tall. *rt.:* ***kʷtunt*** *– big; suffix:* ***...alqʷ*** *– wood; cylindical.*
kʷtnlqʷilš – become tall. *suffix:* ***...ilš*** *– autonomous.*
kʷtnlqʷilš – S/he/it became tall. **čn kʷtnlqʷilš, kʷ kʷtnlqʷilš**
es kʷtnlqʷilši – S/he/it is becoming tall. **čnes kʷtnlqʷilši, kʷes kʷtnlqʷilši**
qs kʷtnlqʷilši – S/he/it is going to become tall. **čiqs kʷtnlqʷilši, kʷqs kʷtnlqʷilši**

tallow

sčťk̓ʷe – tallow.

tamarack

cáqʷlš – western larch; tamarack; *Larix occidentalis.*

tame

saṅ – tranquil; quiet and calm; tame; settled. *See:* ***quiet.***
sṅsṅtwalš – S/he/it became tame/settled. **čn sṅsṅtwalš, kʷ sṅsṅtwalš**
es sṅsṅtwalši – It is becoming tame/settled. **čnes sṅsṅtwalši, kʷes sṅsṅtwalši**
qs sṅsṅtwalši – It is going to become tame/settled. **čiqs sṅsṅtwalši, kʷqs sṅsṅtwalši**

sṅsáṅt, *sṅsá* – gentle; tame; settled; calm and quiet.

esyáʔ uł sṅsáṅt – They are all tame.

The **i** following uvular consonants (UC) and the glottal stop **ʔ** sound like English "*ey*" as in the words *they, hey, whey*, etc. Salish UC are: **q, q̇, qʷ, q̇ʷ, x̌, x̌ʷ**. For example, the suffix **...qin** – head/top, is often spelled using English *ey* as "q*ey*n". So **qi, q̇i, qʷi, q̇ʷi, x̌i, x̌ʷi**, may be spelled with English *ey* as **q***ey*, **q̇***ey*, **qʷ***ey*, **q̇ʷ***ey*, **x̌***ey*, **x̌ʷ***ey* in other texts.

s.t. - something, the 3rd person
(s.t.) - something implied
s.o. - someone, the 3rd person
sl. - singular form
pl. - plural form
rt. - root word
cmd. - command
lit. - literally
fig. - figuratively
i.e., - for example
See: - Redirection to a related word.

es tx̣ʷox̣ʷ – S/he/it is tame/straight.
tx̣ʷx̣ʷnuntm – S/he/it was straightened out/trained.

tampon **ntq̓pewstn** – tampon.

tan **čxʷum** – scrape the inside of a hide. *See: **scrape**.*

ax̣ʷlxʷm – scrape fur off a hide. *See: **scrape**.*

áq̓i – scrape a wet rawhide to soften it. *See: **scrape**.*

q̓ʷʔe – wring; twist; squeeze. *See: **wring**.*

uw̓ał – soften a hide with brains. *(i.e., the process of the hide getting soft from brains.) See: **soft**.*

xʷikʷ – scraping a hide to soften/fluff it, a part of the tanning process.
xʷikʷ – S/he scraped. **čn xʷikʷ, kʷ xʷikʷ**
es xʷikʷi – S/he is scraping. **čnes xʷikʷi, kʷes xʷikʷi**
qs xʷikʷi – S/he is going to scrape. **čiqs xʷikʷi, kʷqs xʷikʷi**
xʷíʔikʷ – They scraped. **qeʔ xʷikʷ, p xʷikʷ**
es xʷíʔikʷi – They are scraping. **qeʔes xʷikʷi, pes xʷikʷi**
qs xʷíʔikʷi – They are going to scrape. **qeʔqs xʷikʷi, pqs xʷikʷi**

es xʷkʷxʷikʷi – S/he is tanning hides repeatedly. **čnes xʷkʷxʷikʷi, kʷes xʷkʷxʷikʷi**

qʷʔóp – make soft. *(i.e., hide tanning.) See: **soft**.*
ṅe qʷʔóp m łuxʷntxʷ – When it is softened up, you rub it back and forth. **ṅe qʷʔóp m t̓q̓ʷntexʷ** – When it is softened, you sew it up.

x̣iq – rub against; the sound of rubbing. *See: **rub**.*
snčx̣iqmn – washboard; rubbing device. *(i.e., something used for tanning hides, etc.)*

p̓umlxʷm – smoke buckskin. *See: **smoke**.*
scp̓umlxʷ – smoked hide. *prefix: **sc...** – s.t. that's been done/made/prepared.*

i pá – faded/tan in color.
čłpá – buckskin horse (color).

tangle **yalim,** *yal* – coil up; wrap. *See: **coil**.*

tape **čcpq̓em** – tape something. *rt.: **cpaq̓** – sticky.*
čcpq̓em – S/he taped. **čn čcpq̓em, kʷ čcpq̓em**
es čcpq̓mi – S/he is taping. **čnes čcpq̓mi, kʷes čcpq̓mi**
qs čcpq̓mi – S/he is going to tape. **čiqs čcpq̓mi, kʷqs čcpq̓mi**
čcpq̓éʔem – They taped. **qeʔ čcpq̓em, p čcpq̓em**
es čcpq̓míʔi – They are taping. **qeʔes čcpq̓mi, pes čcpq̓mi**
qs čcpq̓míʔi – They are going to tape. **qeʔqs čcpq̓mi, pqs čcpq̓mi**

čcpq̓ntes – S/he taped s.t. **čcpq̓nten, čcpq̓ntexʷ**
es čcpq̓ems – S/he is taping s.t. **ies čcpq̓em, as čcpq̓em**
qs čcpq̓ems – S/he is going to tape s.t. **iqs čcpq̓em, aqs čcpq̓em**
čcpq̓ntéʔes – They taped s.t. **qeʔ čcpq̓ntem, čcpq̓ntep**
es čcpq̓éʔems – They are taping s.t. **qeʔes čcpq̓em, es čcpq̓emp**
qs čcpq̓éʔems – They are going to tape s.t. **qeʔqs čcpq̓em, qs čcpq̓emp**

sččcpq̓min – something that's been taped. *prefix: **sc...** – s.t. that's been done/made/prepared.*
čcpq̓min – tape.

čcpq̇miš – Tape. *cmd.*
čcpq̇mint – Tape it. *cmd.*

steṁ łu as čcpq̇em – What are you taping? **ha aqs čcpq̇em –** Are you going to tape it?

čloʔmintn – something to put onto; recording tape. *See: **record**.*

tarragon
qpqptéłp, *qpqpté* **–** sage; mug worm; tarragon.

taste
k̓ʷaṅmaqs – taste food. *rt.: **k̓ʷeṅ** – try; suffix: **...aqs** – food, kind. See: **try**.*
k̓ʷaṅmaqsm – S/he/it tasted. **čn k̓ʷaṅmaqsm, kʷ k̓ʷaṅmaqsm**
es k̓ʷaṅmaqsi – S/he/it is tasting. **čnes k̓ʷaṅmaqsi, kʷes k̓ʷaṅmaqsi**
qs k̓ʷaṅmaqsi – S/he/it is going to taste. **čiqs k̓ʷaṅmaqsi, kʷqs k̓ʷaṅmaqsi**

k̓ʷaṅmaqsis – S/he/it tasted s.t. **k̓ʷaṅmaqsn, k̓ʷaṅmaqsntxʷ**
es k̓ʷaṅmaqsms – S/he/it is tasting s.t. **ies k̓ʷaṅmaqsm, as k̓ʷaṅmaqsm**
qs k̓ʷaṅmaqsms – S/he/it is going to taste s.t. **iqs k̓ʷaṅmaqsm, aqs k̓ʷaṅmaqsm**

k̓ʷaṅmaqsnt – Taste it. *cmd.*

nk̓ʷéṅkʷ – taste liquid. *rt.: **k̓ʷeṅ** – try. See: **try**.*
nk̓ʷéṅkʷm – S/he/it tasted. **čn nk̓ʷéṅkʷm, kʷ nk̓ʷéṅkʷm**
es nk̓ʷéṅkʷi – S/he/it is tasting. **čnes nk̓ʷéṅkʷi, kʷes nk̓ʷéṅkʷi**
qs nk̓ʷéṅkʷi – S/he/it is going to taste. **čiqs nk̓ʷéṅkʷi, kʷqs nk̓ʷéṅkʷi**

nk̓ʷéṅkʷis – S/he/it tasted s.t. **nk̓ʷéṅkʷn, nk̓ʷéṅkʷntxʷ**
es nk̓ʷéṅkʷms – S/he/it is tasting s.t. **ies nk̓ʷéṅkʷm, as nk̓ʷéṅkʷm**
qs nk̓ʷéṅkʷms – S/he/it is going to taste s.t. **iqs nk̓ʷéṅkʷm, aqs nk̓ʷéṅkʷm**

nk̓ʷéṅkʷnt – Tasted it. *cmd.*

x̣sełċeʔ, *x̣se* **–** It tastes good.
ha x̣se – Does it taste good? **x̣se heʔ –** It tastes good, does it not?

nx̣setkʷ – The liquid tastes good. *suffix: **...etkʷ, ...tkʷ** – liquid*

čsełċeʔ, *čse* **–** It tastes bad.
ha čse – Does it taste bad? **čse heʔ –** It tastes bad, does it not?

nčsetkʷ – The liquid tastes bad. *suffix: **...etkʷ, ...tkʷ** – liquid*

iwaqsm – bear/tolerate the taste of something.
iwaqsmis – S/he bore the taste of it. **iwaqsmn, iwaqsmntxʷ**

es iwaqsms – S/he is bearing the taste of it. **ies iwaqsm, as iwaqsm**
qs iwaqsms – S/he is going to bear the taste of it. **iqs iwaqsm, aqs iwaqsm**

tasteless
ċáw – tasteless; weak tasting *(not strong)*.
nċáw̓kʷ – weak; tasteless liquid *(i.e., coffee, water, etc.)*.

tattle
nmipáłq, *nmipá* **–** tattle; accuse.
nmipa – S/he tattled. **čn nmipa, kʷ nmipa**
es nmipałqi – S/he is tattling. **čnes nmipałqi, kʷes nmipałqi**
qs nmipałqi – S/he is going to tattle. **čiqs nmipałqi, kʷqs nmipałqi**
nmipáʔa – They tattled. **qeʔ nmipa, p nmipa**
es nmipáʔałqi – They are tattling. **qeʔes nmipałqi, pes nmipałqi**
qs nmipáʔałqi – They are going to tattle. **qeʔqs nmipałqi, pqs nmipałqi**

es nmipałq – S/he is accused. **čnes nmipałq, kʷes nmipałq**

The **i** following uvular consonants (UC) and the glottal stop **ʔ** sound like English "*ey*" as in the words th*ey*, h*ey*, wh*ey*, etc. Salish UC are: **q, q̇, qʷ, q̇ʷ, x̣, x̣ʷ**. For example, the suffix **...qin** – head/top, is often spelled using English *ey* as "q*ey*n". So **qi, q̇i, qʷi, q̇ʷi, x̣i, x̣ʷi**, may be spelled with English *ey* as **q***ey*, **q̇***ey*, **qʷ***ey*, **q̇ʷ***ey*, **x̣***ey*, **x̣ʷ***ey* in other texts.

s.t. - something, the 3rd person
(s.t.) - something implied
s.o. - someone, the 3rd person
sl. - singular form
pl. - plural form
rt. - root word
cmd. - command
lit. - literally
fig. - figuratively
i.e., - for example
See: - Redirection to a related word.

sxʷnmimipa – one tasked to tattle; a tattletale. *prefix:* ***sxʷ...*** *– one tasked to do.*

es nmimipnwexʷi – They are telling on each other. **qeʔes nmimipnwexʷi, pes nmimipnwexʷi**
nmipmist – tell on one's self; confess. *See:* ***confess.***

ṅem nmipa – S/he will tattle. **ṅem čn nmipa, ṅem kʷ nmipa**
ṅem nmipáʔa – They will tattle. **ṅem qeʔ nmipa, ṅem p nmipa**

nmipa ci šešutm – The little girl tattled.

nmyép – tattle on someone.
nmyépis – S/he tattled on s.o. **nmyépn, nmyépntxʷ**
es nmyépms – S/he is tattling on s.o. **ies nmyépm, as nmyépm**
qs nmyépms – S/he is going to tattle on s.o. **iqs nmyépm, aqs nmyépm**

sxʷnmyépm – one tasked to tattle. *prefix:* ***sxʷ...*** *– one tasked to do.*

nmipncut – tattle on one's self.
nmipncut – S/he tattled on one's self. **čn nmipncut, kʷ nmipncut**
es nmipncuti – S/he is tattling on one's self. **čnes nmipncuti, kʷes nmipncuti**
qs nmipncuti – S/he is going to tattle on one's self. **čiqs nmipncuti, kʷqs nmipncuti**

tattoo

čq̓íʔiċeʔ – tattoo; draw on the outside.
čq̓íʔiċeʔm – S/he tattooed. **čn čq̓íʔiċeʔm, kʷ čq̓íʔiċeʔm**
es čq̓íʔiċeʔi – S/he is tattooing. **čnes čq̓íʔiċeʔi, kʷes čq̓íʔiċeʔi**
qs čq̓íʔiċeʔi – S/he is going to tattoo. **čiqs čq̓íʔiċeʔi, kʷqs čq̓íʔiċeʔi**

čq̓íʔiċʔeis – S/he tattooed s.o. **čq̓íʔiċʔen, čq̓íʔiċʔentxʷ**
es čq̓íʔiċʔems – S/he is tattooing s.o. **ies čq̓íʔiċʔem, as čq̓íʔiċʔem**
qs čq̓íʔiċʔems – S/he is going to tattoo s.o. **iqs čq̓íʔiċʔem, aqs čq̓íʔiċʔem**

es čq̓íʔiċeʔ – S/he is tattooed. **čnes čq̓íʔiċeʔ, kʷes čq̓íʔiċeʔ**

čq̓íʔiċʔentm – S/he got tattooed by s.o.

sčq̓íʔiċeʔ – tattoo.

ha kʷ ep sčq̓íʔiċeʔ – Do you have a tattoo? **steṁ łu asčq̓íʔiċeʔ** – What is your tattoo? **l čeṅ łu asčq̓íʔiċeʔ** – Where is your tattoo? **t swe u kʷ čq̓íʔiċʔentm** – Who tattooed you? **eł t steṁ łu aq sčq̓íʔiċeʔ** – What are you going to get tattooed next?

tavern

snssustn, *snssu* – tavern; barroom. *prefix:* ***sn...*** *– a place of; suffix:* ***...tin, ...tn*** *– means of/device.*

tea

liti – tea.

sčtx̣ʷčłliti – mountain tea; labrador tea; *Ledum glandulosum.*
sčtx̣ʷičṅ liti – mountain tea; labrador tea; *Ledum glandulosum.*

ṅcqaus, *ṅcqau* – place single object in a fire; cook/make coffee/tea. *See:* ***place.***

teach

ṁiṁéẏeʔ – teach.
ṁiṁéẏeis – S/he taught s.o. **ies ṁiṁéẏen, as ṁiṁéẏentxʷ**
es ṁiṁéẏems – S/he is teaching s.o. **ies ṁiṁéẏem, as ṁiṁéẏem**
qs ṁiṁéẏems – S/he is going to teach s.o. **iqs ṁiṁéẏem, aqs ṁiṁéẏem**

sṁiṁéẏei – student; scholar; the one taught.
scṁiṁéẏeʔ – something that has been taught; teachings.

ṁiṁéẏeʔiš – Teach him/her. *cmd.*

ṁiṁéẏent – Teach him/her. *cmd.*

ṁéẏeʔ – explain; tell; show; make something known. *See: **explain**.*

teacher

sxʷṁiṁéẏem – teacher; one tasked to teach/tell/explain. *prefix: **sxʷ...** – one tasked to do.*
uł sxʷṁiṁéẏem – those teachers.

ṁiencutn – the teacher of one; teacher. *suffix: **...tin, ...tn** – means of/device.*
sxʷṁiełq̓eẏmi – teacher. *prefix: **sxʷ...** – one tasked to do.*
sxʷṁiṁielt – one tasked to teach children; teacher.

teakettle

snčišmn – teakettle.

snƛ̓áq̓mn – teakettle.

tear

t̓lip – rip; tear; pull apart.
t̓lip – S/he/it ripped (s.t.). **čn t̓lip, kʷ t̓lip**
es t̓lpmi – S/he/it is tearing (s.t.). **čnes t̓lpmi, kʷes t̓lpmi**
qs t̓lpmi – S/he/it is going to tear (s.t.). **čiqs t̓lpmi, kʷqs t̓lpmi**
t̓líʔip – They ripped (s.t.). **qeʔ t̓lip, p t̓lip**
es t̓lpmíʔi – They are tearing (s.t.). **qeʔes t̓lpmi, pes t̓lpmi**
qs t̓lpmíʔi – They are going to tear (s.t.). **qeʔqs t̓lpmi, pqs t̓lpmi**

t̓l̓ntés – S/he/it ripped it. **t̓l̓ntén, t̓l̓ntéxʷ**
es t̓lims – S/he/it is tearing s.t. **ies t̓lim, as t̓lim**
qs t̓lims – S/he/it is going to tear s.t. **iqs t̓lim, aqs t̓lim**
t̓l̓ntéʔes – They ripped it. **qeʔ t̓l̓ntém, t̓l̓ntép**
es t̓líʔims – They are tearing s.t. **qeʔes t̓lim, es t̓limp**
qs t̓líʔims – They are going to tear s.t. **qeʔqs t̓lim, qs t̓limp**

es t̓lt̓lpmi – S/he/it is repeatedly tearing (s.t.). **čnes t̓lt̓lpmi, kʷes t̓lt̓lpmi**
t̓lt̓l̓ntés – S/he/it ripped s.t. to shreds. **t̓lt̓l̓ntén, t̓lt̓l̓ntéxʷ**

es t̓il – It is torn.
t̓l̓ntém – It was ripped by s.o./s.t.

t̓lulexʷ – plow. *rt.: **t̓il** – tear; suffix: **...ulexʷ** – land. See: **plow**.*

t̓lt̓l̓ntés isiċm t smx̌é – The grizzly ripped my blanket to shreds. **t̓lip łu inpumin –** My drum is broke (hide is torn). **aċx̌nt es t̓lt̓lpmi ci q̓eẏmin –** Look, s/he is shredding that paper.

čt̓liċéʔ – tear a covering/wrapping off. *(i.e., a wrapping off a present, etc.) rt.: **t̓lip** – rip; suffix: **...iċéʔ** – covered in.*
čt̓liċéʔ – S/he tore the covering off. **čn čt̓liċéʔ, kʷ čt̓liċéʔ**
es čt̓liċéʔi – S/he is tearing the covering off. **čnes čt̓liċéʔi, kʷes čt̓liċéʔi**
qs čt̓liċéʔi – S/he is going to tear the covering off. **čiqs čt̓liċéʔi, kʷqs čt̓liċéʔi**

čt̓liċéʔis – S/he tore the covering off s.t. **čt̓liċéʔn, čt̓liċéʔntxʷ**
es čt̓liċʔéms – S/he is tearing the covering off s.t. **ies čt̓liċʔém, as čt̓liċʔém**
qs čt̓liċʔéms – S/he is going to tear the covering off s.t. **iqs čt̓liċʔém, aqs čt̓liċʔém**
čt̓liċéʔeʔis – They tore the covering off s.t. **qeʔ čt̓liċéʔntm, čt̓liċéʔntp**

xʷaʔlip – rupture; tear; slit. *See: **rupture**.*

tears

čawawpus – cry; have tears.
čawawpus – S/he had tears. **čn čawawpus, kʷ čawawpus**

The **i** following uvular consonants (UC) and the glottal stop **ʔ** sound like English "*ey*" as in the words *they, hey, whey,* etc. Salish UC are: **q, q̓, qʷ, q̓ʷ, x̌, x̌ʷ**. For example, the suffix **...qin** – head/top, is often spelled using English *ey* as "q*ey*n". So **qi, q̓i, qʷi, q̓ʷi, x̌i, x̌ʷi**, may be spelled with English *ey* as **q***ey*, **q̓***ey*, **qʷ***ey*, **q̓ʷ***ey*, **x̌***ey*, **x̌ʷ***ey* in other texts.

s.t. - something, the 3rd person
(s.t.) - something implied
s.o. - someone, the 3rd person
sl. - singular form
pl. - plural form
rt. - root word
cmd. - command
lit. - literally
fig. - figuratively
i.e., - for example
See: - Redirection to a related word.

es čawawpusi – S/he has tears. **čnes čawawpusi, kʷes čawawpusi**
qs čawawpusi – S/he is going to have tears. **čiqs čawawpusi, kʷqs čawawpusi**

čawawpusmis – S/he had tears for s.o. **čawawpusmn, čawawpusmntxʷ**
es čawawpusms – S/he has tears for s.o. **ies čawawpusm, as čawawpusm**
qs čawawpusms – S/he is going to have tears for s.o. **iqs čawawpusm, aqs čawawpusm**

sčawawpus – tears. *rt.: **awup**– drip; circumfix: **č...us, s**– eyes.*

čawawpusmntm łu tmtmnéẏ – The dead was cried over.

tease **hetim̓** – tease *(more a playful tease than a bothersome tease).*
hetntes – S/he/it teased him/her/it. **hetnten, hetntexʷ**
es hetim̓s – S/he/it is teasing him/her/it. **ies hetim̓, as hetim̓**
es hetíˀim̓s – They are teasing him/her/it. **qeˀes hetim̓, es hetim̓p**

hetnumn – one inclined to tease. *suffix: **...emn**– one inclined to do.*
hetetmuł – one that habitually teases. *suffix: **...łmuł**– one that habitually does.*

hetint – Tease him/her/it. *cmd.*

čłheˀenˀem – bother someone who is sleeping. *See: **wake**.*

kʷ ies hetim̓ – I am teasing you.

łm̓łoˀmlš – scold someone. *See: **scold**.*

el – tease; bother. *See: **bother**.*

čposcánm – tease/joke. *See: **joke**.*

teeter totter **snq̓tq̓atáx̣**, *snq̓tq̓atá* – teeter totter. *rt.: **q̓et**– weigh down.*
q̓tq̓atáx̣ – S/he teeter tottered. **čn q̓tq̓atáx̣, kʷ q̓tq̓atáx̣**
es q̓tq̓atáx̣i – S/he is teeter tottering. **čnes q̓tq̓atáx̣i, kʷes q̓tq̓atáx̣i**
qs q̓tq̓atáx̣i – S/he is going to teeter totter. **čiqs q̓tq̓atáx̣i, kʷqs q̓tq̓atáx̣i**
q̓tq̓atáˀax̣ – They teeter tottered. **qeˀ q̓tq̓atáx̣, p q̓tq̓atáx̣**
es q̓tq̓atáˀax̣i – They are teeter tottering. **qeˀes q̓tq̓atáx̣i, pes q̓tq̓atáx̣i**
qs q̓tq̓atáˀax̣i – They are going to teeter totter. **qeˀqs q̓tq̓atáx̣i, pqs q̓tq̓atáx̣i**

q̓tq̓etew̓s – teeter totter; counter balance back and forth. *rt.: **q̓et**– weigh down.*
q̓tq̓etéˀew̓s – They teeter tottered. **qeˀ q̓tq̓etew̓s, p q̓tq̓etew̓s**
es q̓tq̓etéˀew̓si – They are teeter tottering. **qeˀes q̓tq̓etew̓si, pes q̓tq̓etew̓si**
qs q̓tq̓etéˀew̓si – They are going to teeter totter. **qeˀqs q̓tq̓etew̓si, pqs q̓tq̓etew̓si**

teeth **x̣l̓éxʷ** – tooth. **x̣l̓x̣l̓éxʷ** – teeth.

n...eys – *circumfix indicating teeth.*
nx̣seys – good tooth.
nx̣sx̣seys – good teeth.
nx̣seystn – orthodontics; braces. *suffix: **...tin, ...tn**– means of/device.*

ntmtmeys – no teeth.
nčseys – bad tooth.
nčsčseys – bad teeth.

ntlpeys – break a tooth.
ntlpeys – S/he broke a tooth. **čn ntlpeys, kʷ ntlpeys**
ntlpeysis – S/he broke s.o.'s tooth. **ntlpeysn, ntlpeysntxʷ**
es ntlpeysms – S/he is breaking s.o.'s tooth. **ies ntlpeysm, as ntlpeysm**

qs ntlpeysms – S/he going to break s.o.'s tooth. **iqs ntlpeysm, aqs ntlpeysm**

ntltlpeys – S/he broke teeth. **čn ntltlpeys, kʷ ntltlpeys**
ntltlpeysis – S/he broke s.o.'s teeth. **ntltlpeysn, ntltlpeysntxʷ**

qʷo ntlpeysntxʷ – You broke my tooth. **xʷk̓ʷunt anx̣l̓x̣l̓exʷ ṅe kʷ wis iłn –** Brush (clean) your teeth after eating.

es nkʷʔál̓eysi – His/her teeth are growing out. **čnes nkʷʔál̓eysi, kʷes nkʷʔál̓eysi**
ntoʔx̣qeys – lose teeth.
ṅem kʷ ntoʔx̣qeys – You will lose your teeth.

nhaweys – loose teeth.

nk̓ʷl̓k̓ʷl̓eys – work on teeth.
nk̓ʷl̓k̓ʷl̓eysis – S/he worked on s.o.'s teeth. **nk̓ʷl̓k̓ʷl̓eysn, nk̓ʷl̓k̓ʷl̓eysntxʷ**

nululmeys – metal teeth; metal capped teeth.

nċoqeys – pull a tooth out. *See:* ***pull teeth.***
nxʷk̓ʷxʷk̓ʷeysm – brush/clean teeth. *See:* ***brush.***

snq̇axʷmi – elk teeth.

The **i** following uvular consonants (UC) and the glottal stop ʔ sound like English "*ey*" as in the words th*ey*, h*ey*, wh*ey*, etc. Salish UC are: **q**, **q̇**, **qʷ**, **q̇ʷ**, **x̣**, **x̣ʷ**. For example, the suffix ...**qin** – head/top, is often spelled using English *ey* as "q*ey*n". So **qi**, **q̇i**, **qʷi**, **q̇ʷi**, **x̣i**, **x̣ʷi**, may be spelled with English *ey* as **q***ey*, **q̇***ey*, **qʷ***ey*, **q̇ʷ***ey*, **x̣***ey*, **x̣ʷ***ey* in other texts.

telephone

snčqʷlqʷltálqʷtn – telephone; talk with wood. *rt.:* ***čqʷlqʷltalqʷ*** *– talk on wood; prefix:* ***sn...*** *– a place of; suffix:* ***...tin, ...tn*** *– means of/device.*

snčsṗálqʷtn – telephone; telegraph; hit wood. *rt.:* ***čsṗálqʷ*** *– hit wood; prefix:* ***sn...*** *– a place of; suffix:* ***...tin, ...tn*** *– means of/device.*

kʷ es čsṗalqʷštm – You have a phone call.

snčsṗálqʷlwistn – cell phone. *rt.:* ***čsṗálqʷ*** *– hit on wood; prefix:* ***sn...*** *– a place of; suffix:* ***...lwis*** *– indicate going around; suffix:* ***...tin, ...tn*** *– means of/device.*

television

snʔacċx̣tn – television; movie. *prefix:* ***sn...*** *– a place of; suffix:* ***...tin, ...tn*** *– means of/device.*

tell

ṁiṁiim – tell a story/news; narrate.
qs ṁiṁiim – S/he is going to tell a story. **čiqs ṁiṁiim, kʷqs ṁiṁiim**

ṁiṁiʔšits – S/he told s.o. **ṁiṁiʔšitn, ṁiṁiʔšitxʷ**

ṁiṁiʔšit – Tell him/her your news. *cmd.*
ṁiṁiʔšíʔit – Tell them your news. *cmd.*

sxʷṁiṁiim – one tasked to tell stories. *prefix:* ***sxʷ...*** *– one tasked to do.*
sṁiṁiʔ – story; news; something that's been told.
es ṁiṁiʔštwexʷi – They're telling each other stories. **qeʔes ṁiṁiʔštwexʷi, pes ṁiṁiʔštwexʷi**
es ṁiṁišcutisti – S/he is telling stories to him/her self. **čnes ṁiṁišcutisti, kʷes ṁiṁišcutisti**

ha kʷep sṁiṁiʔ – Do you have news? **steṁ asṁiṁiʔ –** What is your news?
steṁ łu sṁiṁiʔ – What is the news? **t steṁ m qeʔ ṁiṁišitm łu qeʔ sxʷṁiṁeẏʔm –** What will we tell our teacher? **qeʔ ṁiṁišiłls tʔesteṁ –** Tell us something. **sṁiṁíʔis –** their stories.

cu – say/speak to somebody; inform; provide information about something. *See:* ***say.***

ṁéẏeʔ – explain; tell; show; make something known. *See:* ***explain.***

s.t. - something, the 3rd person
(s.t.) - something implied
s.o. - someone, the 3rd person
sl. - singular form
pl. - plural form
rt. - root word
cmd. - command
lit. - literally
fig. - figuratively
i.e., - for example
See: - Redirection to a related word.

tell off **hawawlš** – tell off; yell at someone.
hawawlš – S/he told off (s.o.). **čn hawawlš, kʷ hawawlš**
es hawawlši – S/he is telling off (s.o.). **čnes hawawlši, kʷes hawawlši**
qs hawawlši – S/he is going to tell off (s.o.). **čiqs hawawlši, kʷqs hawawlši**

hawawsts – S/he told s.o. off. **hawawstn, hawawstxʷ**
es hawawms – S/he is telling s.o. off. **čnes hawawm, kʷes hawawm**
qs hawawms – S/he is going to tell s.o. off. **čiqs hawawm, kʷqs hawawm**

hawawlšemn – one inclined to tell off someone. *suffix: **...emn** – one inclined to do.*
hawawlšmuł – one that habitually tells off. *suffix: **...łmuł** – one that habitually does.*

hawawskʷ – Tell him/her off. *cmd.*
es hawstwaxʷi – They are telling each other off. **qeˀes hawstwaxʷi, pes hawstwaxʷi**

łm̓łoˀmlš – scold someone. *See: **scold**.*

temples **nišištus** – temples.

ten **upn** – ten. **upˀupn** – tens. *pl.*
čˀupn – ten people.
upn séns – dime.

upnčst... – *prefix indicating ten with a suffix forming a full word.*
upnčstásq̓t – ten days. *suffix: **...asq̓t** – sky, day.*
upnčstełxʷ – ten houses. *suffix: **...ełxʷ, ...łxʷ** – house.*
nˀupnčstep – ten eggs. *circumfix: **n...ep** – egg.*
upnčstéssn̓ – ten rocks. *suffix: **...essn̓, ...ssn̓** – rock.*

upnčł... – *prefix indicating ten with a whole word.*
upnčłšƛ̓ip – S/he lost ten times. **čn upnčłšƛ̓ip, kʷ upnčłšƛ̓ip**
upnčsqáx̣eˀ, *upnčsqá* – ten domestic animals or cars.
upnčłˀopnčstqn – ten thousand.

tender **iłččén̓** – tender; painful to the touch *(as, a sore spot).*

iłččén̓ isčuwáx̣n – my arm is tender.

ċsċótšn, *ċsċó* – tender foot *(as a horse).*

mn̓mišn, *mn̓mi* – smooth gaited horse; single foot.
es mn̓mišni – Its gait is smooth..

iłtt̓é – It is easy. *See: **easy**.*
iłtt̓etmšn – tender footed.

iłtt̓im – tender spot; fragile; easily broken.

es nitkʷe – It falls apart easily; it is tender. *(i.e., meat.)*
mił es nitkʷe – The (meat) is too tender; it falls apart easily.

tender foot **ċsċótšn**, *ċsċó* – tender foot *(as a horse).*

tense **yomncut**, *yomncu* – make one's self become rigid/tense.
yomncut – S/he became tense. **čn yomncut, kʷ yomncut**
es yomncuti – S/he is becoming tense. **čnes yomncuti, kʷes yomncuti**
qs yomncuti – S/he is going to become tense. **čiqs yomncuti, kʷqs yomncuti**

yomncutš – Toughen up; become rigid/tense. *cmd.*
yomim – hold something steady. *See:* ***hold.***

kʷʔeł – jumpy; nervous; edgy; frantic. *See:* ***nervous.***

tent

sk̓ʷlč̓éłxʷ, *sk̓ʷlč̓é* – tent.

testes

méč̓p – testicle. **mč̓méč̓p –** testes.

...epls – *suffix indicating testicle.*
nmlmlk̓ʷépls, *nmlmlk̓ʷé* – male animal; bull, stallion. *suffix:* ***...epls*** *– testicle.*
nq̓ʷaq̓ʷʔépls – gelding. *suffix:* ***...epls*** *– testicle.*

es nc̓ułmépls – castrated.

text

čp̓ac̓łq̓ey̓im – text. *rt.:* ***p̓ac̓*** *– press; rt.:* ***q̓ey̓*** *– write, mark.*

The **i** following uvular consonants (UC) and the glottal stop **ʔ** sound like English "*ey*" as in the words th*ey*, h*ey*, wh*ey*, etc. Salish UC are: **q**, **q̓**, **qʷ**, **q̓ʷ**, **x̣**, **x̣ʷ**. For example, the suffix **...qin** – head/top, is often spelled using English *ey* as "q*ey*n". So **qi**, **q̓i**, **qʷi**, **q̓ʷi**, **x̣i**, **x̣ʷi**, may be spelled with English *ey* as **q***ey*, **q̓***ey*, **qʷ***ey*, **q̓ʷ***ey*, **x̣***ey*, **x̣ʷ***ey* in other texts.

thankful

lémt – glad; thankful. *See:* ***glad.***

lmmscut – glad with one's self; thankful.
lmmscut – S/he was thankful. **čn lmmscut, kʷ lmmscut**
es lmmscuti – S/he is being thankful. **čnes lmmscuti, kʷes lmmscuti**
qs lmmscuti – S/he is going to be thankful. **čiqs lmmscuti, kʷqs lmmscuti**

lmtemn – one inclined to be thankful. *suffix:* ***...emn*** *– one inclined to do.*

thanks

lémlmtš – thanks. *rt.:* ***lémt*** *– glad; thankful. See:* ***glad.***

that

šey̓ – that in general; there, confirming/concurring; yes, concurring.
łu šey̓ – that.
łišeʔ – that specifically.
č šey̓ – to there; to that.
l šey̓ – in/on there; with that.
i šey̓ – that very one; the same one.
nšiy̓elsm – in favor of s.t./s.o.; in acceptance of s.t.; show preference for s.t./s.o. *See:* ***agree.***
nšey̓ – in there; involved; included; in the party of. *See:* ***involve.***
šišey̓ – in the company of; together with; involved with. *See:* ***involve.***
šiyečst – take part in the work; involved with the work. *See:* ***involve.***

stem̓ łu šey̓ – What is that? **šey̓ łu kʷtisi pusts –** That one's Big Blanket's cat. **es nšey̓ –** S/he was in it, s/he was involved. **ta tam l qʷoyʔé u es nsuʔcnmi šey̓ łu es cčxʷuyms tam qʷoyʔé –** No, it is not me he's come proposing to, he's come for her, not me. **šʔeʔ l sčsax̣ms šušw̓eł –** It is that thing close to the road. **x̣ʷl̓ stem̓ u l šé u kʷ ax̣í –** Why did you do that? **še ye x̣ił lʔe še nk̓ʷuʔ še ye x̣ił lʔe –** This darn one here, that darn one there.

ci – those; that.
ci yéʔ – that.

lciʔ – stays here; remains here; dwells. *See:* ***stay.***
lciʔm – let it be; yield to; permit it; allow to continue. *See:* ***let.***

es čéstxʷ ci q̓ett – What did you do with that hide? **ci pspus –** those cats.

s.t. - something, the 3rd person
(s.t.) - something implied
s.o. - someone, the 3rd person
sl. - singular form
pl. - plural form
rt. - root word
cmd. - command
lit. - literally
fig. - figuratively
i.e., - for example
See: - Redirection to a related word.

thaw

oʔim̓ – melt; thaw.
es oʔim̓ – It is thawed.
es oʔim̓i – It is thawing.

qs oʔiṁi – It is going to thaw.

oʔiṁis – S/he thawed s.t. **oʔiṁn, oʔiṁntxʷ**
es oʔiṁms – S/he is thawing s.t. **ies oʔiṁm, as oʔiṁm**
qs oʔiṁms – S/he is going to thaw s.t. **iqs oʔiṁm, aqs oʔiṁm**

es oẏmulexʷi – The ground is starting to thaw *(at the end of winter)*.

their **cníʔiłċ**, *cníʔi* – It is theirs; them.

ƛ̓m słqʷáʔasts – It was their rabbit.
słqʷáʔasts – their rabbit.
qł słqʷáʔasts – It is going to be their rabbit.

qʷóʔomqis – their hair.
spúʔuʔusts – their heart.

them **cníʔiłċ**, *cníʔi* – It is theirs; them.

then **sic** – new; right then; right now; recent. *See: **new**.*
ṅem qeʔ wis čáwm m sic qeʔ eľiłn – We will finish praying, and then we can eat. **ṅe kʷ wis nċułqpéceʔ m sic kʷ ocqeʔ kʷqs pk̓ʷlʔemi** – When you finish washing the dishes then you can go outside to play ball.

kʷemt – then; in continuation.
i kʷemt – then; in continuation.

kʷemt esyáʔ u npiyels – Then everyone was happy. **kʷemt steṁ łu qeʔqs yoʔnunm yetłx̣ʷa** – Then what are we going to learn today? **i kʷemt u mipnuis u qeʔes acċx̣stm u tloq̓ʷ** – Just then he found out we were watching him and he ran away.

še – then.
še ye x̣ił lʔe še nk̓ʷuʔ še ye x̣ił lʔe – (Then) this darn one here, (then) that darn one there. **m šé kʷ k̓ʷis tumíst t sʔiłn** – Then go buy some food.

there **šeẏ** – that in general; there, confirming/concurring; yes, concurring. *See: **that**.*
č šeẏ – to there.
l šeẏ – in/on there.

put u l šeẏ – It is right there. **ƛ̓m šé l šeẏ** – It used to be there. **l šeẏ u iše txʷtíʔixʷm t sčiłt łu t sq̓sip** – There's where they got white clay long ago. **ha l šeẏ** – Is it there? **šeẏ łu incitxʷ** – There is my house.

łiciʔ – that very one over there *(specific)*.
łiciʔ łu incitxʷ – My house is that very one over there.

ci č ciʔ – over there *(specific)*.
ci č ciʔ łu incitxʷ – My house is that one over there.

lciʔ – stays here; remains here; dwells. *See: **stay**.*

łuweʔ – that over there.
łuweʔ łu incitxʷ – My house is over there.

łu č łu – over there *(general)*.
łu č łu łu incitxʷ – My house is over in that direction.

ci yeʔ – those over there.

ye č̓ eʔ – over there *(redirecting)*.
  ye cčč̓ éʔe – little this way *(toward speaker)(redirecting)*.
  ye čč̓ éʔe – little over there *(redirecting)*.
  ye l eʔ – here; this place.

  ye č̓ eʔ łu incitxʷ – My house is over this way.

Theresa **tlé** – Theresa.

thick **płiłt** – thick.
  eċx̣lspłiłt – How thick is it?
  steṁ łu spłiłts – What is its thickness?

  spłqin – head. *(thick top)*

yult – large in girth. *(of cylindrical objects.)* *See:* ***girth***.

łáq̇t – wide. *See:* ***wide***.

thicket **nkʷéct,** *nkʷé* – forest; backwoods; brush; thicket.

thief **sxʷṅaq̇ʷ** – thief; crook. *prefix:* ***sxʷ...*** *– one tasked to do.*

  naq̇ʷéṁn – thief; one inclined to steal. *suffix:* ***...emn*** *– one inclined to do.*

  t snk̓ʷspéntč łu čn čuw t uł wilwłt u qʷo náʔaq̇ʷmis – Last year when I went away those sly ones stole from me.

thieving **náq̇ʷ** – steal; rob. *See:* ***steal***.

wil – faulty; wrong; wicked. *See:* ***wicked***.

thigh **sčč̓mélpstšn** – thigh; lap. *rt.:* ***č̓m*** *– extremity.*
sč̓melqstšn – hamstring.
snč̓mussšn – inner thigh.

thimble **łxʷpéčstn**; *łxʷpé* – thimble. *rt.:* ***łxʷp*** *– slip over; suffix:* ***...ečst, ...čst*** *– of the hand.*
  łxʷpečstm – S/he used a thimble. **čn łxʷpečstm, kʷ łxʷpečstm**
  es łxʷpečsti – S/he is using a thimble. **čnes łxʷpečsti, kʷes łxʷpečsti**
  qs łxʷpečsti – S/he is going to use a thimble. **čiqs łxʷpečsti, kʷqs łxʷpečsti**

thimble berry **pólplqn** – thimble berry.

thin **łl̓láq** – thin.
  i łl̓láq – It is thin.

i čt̓ás – poor; lean; skinny.

sal̓ – thin liquid substance. *(i.e., soup, oatmeal, mud, etc.)*
  es sal̓mi – It is getting thin.

  saal̓ – It got thinned.
  i sal̓ – It is thin

  sal̓is – S/he thinned s.t. **sal̓n, sal̓ntxʷ**
  es sal̓ms – S/he is thinning s.t. **ies sal̓m, as sal̓m**
  qs sal̓ms – S/he is going to thin s.t. **iqs sal̓m, aqs sal̓m**

  sal̓nt – Thin it. *cmd.*

The **i** following uvular consonants (UC) and the glottal stop **ʔ** sound like English "*ey*" as in the words th*ey*, h*ey*, wh*ey*, etc. Salish UC are: **q, q̇, qʷ, q̇ʷ, x̣, x̣ʷ**. For example, the suffix **...qin** – head/ top, is often spelled using English *ey* as "q*ey*n". So **qi, q̇i, qʷi, q̇ʷi, x̣i, x̣ʷi**, may be spelled with English *ey* as **q***ey*, **q̇***ey*, **qʷ***ey*, **q̇ʷ***ey*, **x̣***ey*, **x̣ʷ***ey* in other texts.

s.t. - something, the 3rd person
(s.t.) - something implied
s.o. - someone, the 3rd person
sl. - singular form
pl. - plural form
rt. - root word
cmd. - command
lit. - literally
fig. - figuratively
i.e., - for example
See: - Redirection to a related word.

łutilš – thin; become few; weed. *rt.:* ***łuwet*** *– few; suffix:* ***...ilš*** *– autonomous.*
łutilšsts – S/he thinned them out. **łutilšstn, łutilšstxʷ**
es łutilšms – S/he is thinning them out. **ies łutilšm, as łutilšm**
qs łutilšms – S/he is going to thin them out. **iqs łutilšm, aqs łutilšm**

łqqéw̓t, *łqqé* – narrow/skinny. *See:* ***narrow.***

łqqʔełc̓eʔ – S/he is skinny. *See:* ***narrow.***

things

stm̓tem̓ – things; stuff.

nšƛ̓aqsm – many things not the same.

think

k̓ʷłpax̣em – think.
k̓ʷłpax̣em – S/he thought. **čn k̓ʷłpax̣em, kʷ k̓ʷłpax̣em**
es k̓ʷłpax̣mi – S/he is thinking. **čnes k̓ʷłpax̣mi, kʷes k̓ʷłpax̣mi**
qs k̓ʷłpax̣mi – S/he is going to think. **čiqs k̓ʷłpax̣mi, kʷqs k̓ʷłpax̣mi**
k̓ʷłpáʔax̣em – They thought. **qeʔ k̓ʷłpax̣em, p k̓ʷłpax̣em**
es k̓ʷłpáʔax̣mi – They are thinking. **qeʔes k̓ʷłpax̣mi, pes k̓ʷłpax̣mi**
qs k̓ʷłpáʔax̣mi – They are going to think. **qeʔqs k̓ʷłpax̣mi, pqs k̓ʷłpax̣mi**

k̓ʷłpax̣ntés – S/he thought about s.o./s.t. **k̓ʷłpax̣ntén, k̓ʷłpax̣ntéxʷ**
es k̓ʷłpax̣ems – S/he is thinking about s.o./s.t. **ies k̓ʷłpax̣em, as k̓ʷłpax̣em**
qs k̓ʷłpax̣ems – S/he is going to think about s.o./s.t. **iqs k̓ʷłpax̣em, aqs k̓ʷłpax̣em**
k̓ʷłpax̣ntéʔes – They thought about s.o./s.t. **qeʔ k̓ʷłpax̣ntém, k̓ʷłpax̣ntép**
es k̓ʷłpax̣éʔems – They are thinking about s.o./s.t. **qeʔes k̓ʷłpax̣em, es k̓ʷłpax̣emp**
qs k̓ʷłpax̣éʔems – They are going to think about s.o./s.t. **qeʔqs k̓ʷłpax̣em, qs k̓ʷłpax̣emp**

k̓ʷłpax̣stés – S/he thought about s.o./s.t. **k̓ʷłpax̣stén, k̓ʷłpax̣stéxʷ**
es k̓ʷłpax̣stes – S/he is thinking about s.o./s.t. **es k̓ʷłpax̣sten, es k̓ʷłpax̣stexʷ**
qs k̓ʷłpax̣stes – S/he is going to think about s.o./s.t. **qs k̓ʷłpax̣sten, qs k̓ʷłpax̣stexʷ**
k̓ʷłpax̣stéʔes – They thought about s.o./s.t. **qeʔ k̓ʷłpax̣stém, k̓ʷłpax̣stép**
es k̓ʷłpax̣stéʔes – They are thinking about s.o./s.t. **qeʔes k̓ʷłpax̣stem, es k̓ʷłpax̣step**
qs k̓ʷłpax̣stéʔes – They are going to think about s.o./s.t. **qeʔqs k̓ʷłpax̣stem, qs k̓ʷłpax̣step**

es k̓ʷłpx̣pax̣mi – S/he is thinking things over. **čnes k̓ʷłpapax̣mi, kʷes k̓ʷłpapax̣mi**
es k̓ʷłpapax̣mi – S/he is repeatedly thinking. **čnes k̓ʷłpapax̣mi, kʷes k̓ʷłpapax̣mi**
es k̓ʷłpapax̣ems – S/he is repeatedly thinking about s.o./s.t. **ies k̓ʷłpapax̣em, as k̓ʷłpapax̣em**

k̓ʷłpax̣nuis – S/he just thought of it. **k̓ʷłpax̣nun, k̓ʷłpax̣nuntxʷ**
es k̓ʷłpax̣nunms – S/he is just thinking of it. **ies k̓ʷłpax̣nunm, as k̓ʷłpax̣nunm**

k̓ʷłpx̣pax̣mul – one that habitually thinks about things. *suffix:* ***...łmuł*** *– one that habitually does.*
px̣pax̣mul – one that habitually thinks. *suffix:* ***...łmuł*** *– one that habitually does.*
sck̓ʷłpáx̣ – thought; an idea; something that is thought of. *prefix:* ***sc...*** *– s.t. that's been done/made/prepared.*

k̓ʷłpax̣ent – Think about it. *cmd.*
es px̣px̣twilši – S/he is getting smart. **čnes px̣px̣twilši, kʷes px̣px̣twilši** *suffix:* ***...wilš*** *– developmental.*
scntt̓kʷsew̓s m nk̓ʷłpax̣min – estimate.

ṅem k̓ʷłpax̣em – S/he will think. **ṅem čn k̓ʷłpax̣em, ṅem kʷ k̓ʷłpax̣em**
ṅem k̓ʷłpáʔax̣em – They will think. **ṅem qeʔ k̓ʷłpax̣em, ṅem p k̓ʷłpax̣em**
x̣e ies k̓ʷłpax̣em x̣ʷl̓ anwi – I am thinking something good about you. **ta es k̓ʷłpax̣sten łu šey̓** – I did not think that. **t smx̣e tas k̓ʷłpax̣nuis x̣ʷl̓ stem̓ u šƛ̓puntm** – Grizzly could not think of why s/he got beat.

ntels, *nte* **–** want; think about. *See:* ***want.***
n̓e nte – What does s/he think/want?
kʷ n̓e nte – What do you think/want?

čnes nté t ululim – I am thinking about money. **tam čnes nté –** I do not want to. **ntéˀe u hoyyho łu splstwé –** They decided to quit killing each other. **kʷ nte sk̓ʷnšpentč łu cniłċ –** How old do you think s/he is?

puˀsminm – think about somebody. *rt.:* ***spúˀus*** *– heart.*
puˀsmis – S/he thought about s.o. **puˀsmin, puˀsmintxʷ**
es puˀsminms – S/he is thinking of s.o. **ies puˀsminm, as puˀsminm**
qs puˀsminms – S/he is going to think of s.o. **iqs puˀsminm, aqs puˀsminm**

qʷo puˀsmis – S/he thought of me. *(said after you sneeze.)* **puˀsminc –** S/he thought of you. *(said to someone after s/he sneezes.)*

npuˀstin – thinking/talking of somebody then they show up or you run into them. *rt.:* ***spúˀus*** *– heart.*
šey łu npuˀstin – That's who I was thinking of. **kʷ ies npuˀstinmm –** I was just thinking about you.

pusulexʷ – thinking of a certain place/area/land. *rt.:* ***spúˀus*** *– heart.*
es pusulexʷi – S/he is thinking of a place. **čnes pusulexʷi, kʷes pusulexʷi**

nmyels – reminiscence; think about memories.
nmyelsmis – S/he reminisced about s.t. **nmyelsmn, nmyelsmntxʷ**
es nmyelsmms – S/he is reminiscencing about s.t. **ies nmyelsmm, as nmyelsmm**
qs nmyelsmms – S/he is going to reminiscence about s.t. **iqs nmyelsmm, aqs nmyelsmm**

nkʷtnelsm – think highly of somebody; show respect for somebody; have trust for somebody. *See:* ***respect.***

thirst

nx̣mpcin, *nx̣mpci* **–** thirsty; have a dry mouth. *rt:* ***x̣am̓*** *– dry; suffix:* ***...cin, ...cn*** *– action of the mouth.*
nx̣mpcin – S/he/it was thirsty. **čn nx̣mpcin, kʷ nx̣mpcin**
es nx̣mpcini – S/he/it is thirsty. **čnes nx̣mpcini, kʷes nx̣mpcini**
qs nx̣mpcini – S/he/it is going to be thirsty. **čiqs nx̣mpcini, kʷqs nx̣mpcini**

es nx̣mpcíˀini – S/he/it is thirsty. **qeˀes nx̣mpcini, pes nx̣mpcini**
es nx̣mx̣mpcini – Each one of them is thirsty. **qeˀes nx̣mx̣mpcini, pes nx̣mx̣mpcini**

thirteen-lined squirrel

ssaˀl̓i – golden mantled squirrel; thirteen-lined squirrel.

thirty

čełlˀupn, *čełlˀu* **–** thirty.

this

iheˀ – here; this in hand; this at hand.
łiheˀ – these here in hand.

iheˀ łu isnˀitštn – This is my bed.

łiˀe – this; here; specifically this one.
stem̓ łiˀe – What is this?

ƛ̓iˀe – this. *(more specific than* ***łiˀe****. An answer to a question as if saying "Well, this is the one.")*

ye – this right here; this time.
ye lˀe – here; in this place; in this time.

> The **i** following uvular consonants (UC) and the glottal stop ˀ sound like English "*ey*" as in the words *they, hey, whey*, etc. Salish UC are: **q, q̓, qʷ, q̓ʷ, x̣, x̣ʷ**. For example, the suffix **...qin** – head/top, is often spelled using English *ey* as "q*ey*n". So **qi, q̓i, qʷi, q̓ʷi, x̣i, x̣ʷi**, may be spelled with English *ey* as **q***ey*, **q̓***ey*, **qʷ***ey*, **q̓ʷ***ey*, **x̣***ey*, **x̣ʷ***ey* in other texts.

> s.t. - something, the 3rd person
> (s.t.) - something implied
> s.o. - someone, the 3rd person
> *sl.* - singular form
> *pl.* - plural form
> *rt.* - root word
> *cmd.* - command
> *lit.* - literally
> *fig.* - figuratively
> *i.e.,* - for example
> *See:* - Redirection to a related word.

ye l citxʷ – in this house. **ye l town** – in this town. **ye l qepc** – in this spring. **cˀim̓š yé l citxʷ** – S/he moved into this house. **še ye x̣ił lˀe še nk̓ʷuˀ še ye x̣ił lˀe** – This darn one here, that darn one there. **cun ye smˀem** – I told this woman.

lˀe – this here. *See: **here**.*

iˀe – this very one here. *See: **here**.*

thistle
sql̓tmxʷá – elk thistle, celery.

ċqċiq – cocklebur.

Thompson Falls
sq̇eyłkʷum – Thompson Falls, Montana.

thorn
łułw̓é – thorn.

thorn tree
sxʷexʷˀénčełp, *sxʷexʷˀenč* – thorn bush; thorn tree; hawthorn.
sxʷeˀne – thornberry.

snčl̓palqʷ, *snčl̓pa* – thorn wood; coyote wood.

thought
sck̓ʷłpáx̣ – thought; an idea; something that is thought of. *prefix: **sc...** – s.t. that's been done/made/prepared.*
isck̓ʷłpax̣ – my thought/idea.

k̓ʷłpax̣em – think. *See: **think**.*

thousand
opnčstqn – one thousand.
eslˀopnčstqn – two thousand.
hénmłˀopnčstqn – eight thousand.

thrash
čsṗim – thrash oats; gathering huckleberries *(when hitting the bush the berries fall onto a canvas). rt.: **sṗim** – strike w/ object. See: **hit**.*
čsṗim – S/he thrashed. **čn čsṗim, kʷ čsṗim**
es čsṗmi – S/he is thrashing. **čnes čsṗmi, kʷes čsṗim**
qs čsṗmi – S/he is going to thrash. **čiqs čsṗmi, kʷqs čsṗim**
čsṗíˀim – They thrashed. **qeˀ čsṗim, p čsṗim**
es čsṗmíˀi – They are thrashing. **qeˀes čsṗmi, pes čsṗmi**
es čsṗmíˀi – They are going to thrash. **qeˀqs čsṗmi, pqs čsṗmi**

čsṗntes – S/he thrashed it. **čsṗnten, čsṗntexʷ**
es čsṗims – S/he is thrashing it. **ies čsṗim, as čsṗim**
qs čsṗims – S/he is going to thrash it. **iqs čsṗim, aqs čsṗim**
čsṗntéˀes – They thrashed it. **qeˀ čsṗntes, čsṗntep**
es čsṗíˀims – They are thrashing it. **qeˀes čsṗim, es čsṗimp**
es čsṗíˀims – They are going to thrash it. **qeˀqs čsṗim, qs čsṗimp**

čsṗiš – Thrash. *cmd.*
čsṗint – Thrash it. *cmd.*

ql̓wá – thrash wheat; stepping on wheat.
es ql̓wa – S/he is walking on the wheat to thrash it.

nql̓ql̓utew̓s – thrash wheat. *suffix: **...éw̓s** – in between, middle.*

thread
sṫópqs – thread.

three
čeɬé – three. **čeˀčeɬé** – threes. *pl.*

upn eł čełé – thirteen.
ččečełé – three people.

čełl... – *prefix indicating three combined with another affix forming a full word.*
čałłásq̓t – three days. *suffix:* ***...asq̓t –*** *sky, day.*
čełłełxʷ – three houses. *suffix:* ***...ełxʷ, ...łxʷ –*** *house.*
nčełłep – three eggs. *circumfix:* ***n...ep –*** *egg.*
čełłéssn̓ – three rocks. *suffix:* ***...essn̓, ...ssn̓ –*** *rock.*

čełl... – *prefix indicating three with whole word.*
čełlˀupn – thirty; three tens.
čełlšƛ̓ip – S/he lost three times. **čn čełlšƛ̓ip, kʷ čełlšƛ̓ip**
čałlsqáx̣eˀ, *čałlsqá* **–** three domestic animals or cars. *The ł is dropped when preceding an s.*
čełlˀopnčstqn – two thousand.

The **i** following uvular consonants (UC) and the glottal stop **ˀ** sound like English "*ey*" as in the words *they, hey, whey,* etc. Salish UC are: **q, q̓, qʷ, q̓ʷ, x̣, x̣ʷ**. For example, the suffix **...qin** – head/top, is often spelled using English *ey* as "q*ey*n". So **qi, q̓i, qʷi, q̓ʷi, x̣i, x̣ʷi,** may be spelled with English *ey* as **q***ey*, **q̓***ey*, **qʷ***ey*, **q̓ʷ***ey*, **x̣***ey*, **x̣ʷ***ey* in other texts.

Three Forks

čxʷxʷttpe – Three Forks of the Missouri River, near Bozeman, Montana. *lit. confluence of rivers.*

three hundred

čełlnk̓ʷoˀqín, *čełlnk̓ʷoˀqí* **–** three hundred.

threw

cq̓minm – throw an object. *See:* ***throw.***

throat

sx̣ʷopłq̓ʷlt – throat; wind pipe.

...ałq̓ʷlt, ...łq̓ʷlt – *suffix indicating throat.*
sčq̓ʷopłq̓ʷlt – left side of throat.
nqopáłq̓ʷlt – My throat itches.
nx̣ampłq̓ʷlt – dry throat. *(i.e., eating chokecherries, etc.)*
nłmpołq̓ʷlt – burned mouth.

nłmpsq̓ameltn – burned throat.

čspin – neck.

through

čx̣ʷcim – pass; go by. *See:* ***pass.***

šiy̓ust, *šiy̓u* **–** pass through; go through. *See:* ***pass.***

nc̓lilš – go through trees. *See:* ***tree.***

x̣ʷcuˀsičn̓, *x̣ʷcuˀsí* **–** go over a mountain pass. *See:* ***pass.***

uy̓éčst, *uy̓é* **–** finish working; done working; come to an end. *See:* ***finish.***

čsłx̣ʷm̓u – through something.

es šmšim – They are pushed/slid/rammed through.
es šim – It is pushed/slid/rammed through.

ilip – wounded/shot by a bullet, arrow or sharp stick. *See:* ***wound.***

ilim – throw and strike something with a pointed object. *(throw an arrow, spear, sharp stick, etc.) See:* ***throw.***

throw

cq̓minm – throw an object.
cq̓mis – S/he/it threw s.t. **cq̓min, cq̓mintxʷ**
es cq̓minms – S/he/it is throwing s.t. **ies cq̓minm, as cq̓minm**
qs cq̓minms – S/he/it is going to throw s.t. **iqs cq̓minm, aqs cq̓minm**

s.t. - something, the 3rd person
(s.t.) - something implied
s.o. - someone, the 3rd person
sl. - singular form
pl. - plural form
rt. - root word
cmd. - command
lit. - literally
fig. - figuratively
i.e., - for example
See: - Redirection to a related word.

cq̇míˀis – They threw s.t. **qeˀ cq̇mintm, cq̇mintp**
es cq̇míˀinms – They are throwing s.t. **qeˀes cq̇minm, es cq̇minmp**
qs cq̇míˀinms – They are going to throw s.t. **qeˀqs cq̇minm, qs cq̇minmp**

cq̇mint – Throw it. *cmd.*
ccq̇mint – Throw it to me. *cmd.*
cq̇miłt – Throw it to somebody. *cmd.*
ncq̇mint – Throw it inside. *cmd.*

ncq̇mncinmis – S/he threw s.t. in the mouth. **ncq̇mncinmn, ncq̇mncinmntxʷ**

qʷo ccq̇miłt – Throw it to me. **t swe u cq̇mis –** Who threw it? **yoyoscq̇mint –** Throw it hard.

ncq̇mnetkʷ – throw objects into the water. *suffix:* ***...etkʷ, ...tkʷ*** *– liquid*
ncq̇mnetkʷis – S/he threw it in the water. **ncq̇mnetkʷn, ncq̇mnetkʷntxʷ**
es ncq̇mnnetkʷms – S/he is throwing it in the water. **ies ncq̇mnnetkʷm, as ncq̇mnnetkʷm**
qs ncq̇mnnetkʷms – S/he is going to throw it in the water. **iqs ncq̇mnnetkʷm, aqs ncq̇mnnetkʷm**

čcq̇mnasq̇tm – throw up into the sky. *suffix:* ***...asq̇t*** *– sky, day.*
čcq̇mnasq̇tis – S/he threw it up to the sky. **čcq̇mnasq̇tn, čcq̇mnasq̇tntxʷ**
es čcq̇mnasq̇tms – S/he is throwing it up to the sky. **ies čcq̇mnasq̇tm, as čcq̇mnasq̇tm**
qs čcq̇mnasq̇tms – S/he is going to throw it up to the sky. **iqs čcq̇mnasq̇tm, aqs čcq̇mnasq̇tm**

ncq̇mnusm – throw in the fire.
ncq̇mnusis – S/he threw it in the fire. **ncq̇mnusn, ncq̇mnusntxʷ**
es ncq̇mnusms – S/he is throwing it in the fire. **ies ncq̇mnusm, as ncq̇mnusm**
qs ncq̇mnusms – S/he is going to throw it in the fire. **iqs ncq̇mnusm, aqs ncq̇mnusm**

ilim – throw and strike something with a pointed object. *(throw an arrow, spear, sharp stick, etc.) rt.:* ***ili*** *– pass into/through.*
ilim – S/he threw and hit (s.t.). **čn ilim, kʷ ilim**
es ilmi – S/he is throwing and hit (s.t.). **čnes ilmi, kʷes ilmi**
qs ilmi – S/he is going to throw and hit (s.t.). **čiqs ilmi, kʷqs ilmi**

ilntes – S/he threw and hit s.t. **ilnten, ilntexʷ**
es ilims – S/he is throwing and hit s.t. **ies ilim, as ilim**
qs ilims – S/he is going to throw and hit s.t. **iqs ilim, aqs ilim**

silpeł – the luck of wounding/hitting with an arrow/spear flung.
silil – the arrow/spear flung.
silim – the striking with an arrow/spear flung.
ilmintn – hoop game sticks. *suffix:* ***...tin, ...tn*** *– means of/device.*

ilip – wounded/shot by a bullet, arrow or sharp stick. *See:* ***wound.***

isk̓ʷl – scatter things out; throw things away. *See:* ***scatter.***

x̣ʷel – abandon; throw away; leave. *See:* ***abandon.***

thrush

xʷiwxʷu – northern oriole, Bullock's oriole; hermit thrush.

thumb

stuṁčst – thumb; sucking finger. *rt.:* ***ṫum*** *– suck; suffix:* ***...ečst, ...čst*** *– of the hand. See:* ***suck.***

syulčst – thumb; thick finger. *rt.:* ***yult*** *– thick in girth; suffix:* ***...ečst, ...čst*** *– of the hand. See:* ***girth.***

thumb wrestle

tumčstwexʷist – thumb wrestle each other. *suffix:* ***...ečst, ...čst*** *– of the hand.*
es tumčstwexʷisti – They are thumb wrestling each other. **qeˀes tumčstwexʷisti, pes tumčstwexʷisti**

kʷ iqs tumčstm – I am going to thumb wrestle you.

thunder **sṫlṫlásq̇t,** *sṫlṫlá* – thunder. *rt.:* ***ṫil*** *– tear; suffix:* ***...asq̇t*** *– sky, day.*
es ṫlṫlasq̇ti, *es ṫlṫla* – It is thundering.

pppuwa pppuwa – sound of thunder.

Thursday **mosq̇t,** *mo* – Thursday. *suffix:* ***...asq̇t*** *– sky, day.*
eł tixʷł mósq̇t – It is Thursday again.
ci t smosq̇t – last Thursday. **ci tixʷł mosq̇t u čn eł cǩʷłči** – On the fourth day I got back.

tick **čččéľsčn** – woodtick.

tickle **qsqsénč** – tickle. *rt.:* ***qsim*** *– scratch, suffix:* ***...enč*** *– within.*
nqsqsenčis – S/he tickled s.o. **nqsqsenčn, nqsqsenčntxʷ**
es qsqsenčms – S/he is tickling s.o. **ies qsqsenčm, as qsqsenčm**
qs qsqsenčms – S/he is going to tickle s.o. **iqs qsqsenčm, aqs qsqsenčm**
nqsqséˀ**enčis** – They tickled s.o. **nqsqsenčntm, nqsqsenčntp**
es qsqséˀ**enčms** – They are tickling s.o. **qe**ˀ**es qsqsenčm, es qsqsenčmp**

ṅem qes qsqsenčms – S/he will be tickling s.o. **ṅem iqes qsqsenčm, ṅem aqes qsqsenčm**
nqsqsenčnt – Tickle him/her. *cmd.*

kʷ iqs nqsqsenčm – I am going to tickle you. **qʷo nqsqsenčnt** – Tickle me.

tie **ľčim** – tie up something or things.
ľčim – S/he tied (s.t.) up. **čn ľčim, kʷ ľčim**
es ľčmi – S/he is tying (s.t.) up. **čnes ľčmi, kʷes ľčmi**
qs ľčmi – S/he is going to tie (s.t.) up. **čiqs ľčmi, kʷqs ľčmi**
ľčíˀ**im** – They tied (s.t.) up. **qe**ˀ **ľčim, ľčim**
es ľčmíˀ**i** – They are tying (s.t.) up. **qe**ˀ**es ľčmi, pes ľčmi**
qs ľčmíˀ**i** – They are going to tie (s.t.) up. **qe**ˀ**qs ľčmi, pqs ľčmi**

ľčntes – S/he tied s.o./s.t. up. **ľčnten, ľčntexʷ**
es ľčims – S/he is tying s.o./s.t. up. **ies ľčim, as ľčim**
qs ľčims – S/he is going to tie s.o./s.t. up. **iqs ľčim, aqs ľčim**
ľčntéˀ**es** – They tied s.o./s.t. up. **qe**ˀ **ľčntem, ľčntep**
es ľčíˀ**ims** – They are tying s.o./s.t. up. **qe**ˀ**es ľčim, es ľčimp**
qs ľčíˀ**ims** – They are going to tie s.o./s.t. up. **qe**ˀ**qs ľčim, qs ľčimp**

es ľčľčmi – S/he is repeatedly tying (s.t.) up. **čnes ľčľčmi, kʷes ľčľčmi**
es ľčľčims – S/he is repeatedly tying s.o./s.t. up. **ies ľčľčim, as ľčľčim**

ľčntem – S/he/it was tied up by s.o. **qʷo ľčntem, kʷ ľčntem**
es ľič – S/he/it is tied up. **čnes ľič, kʷes ľič**

sxʷľčim – one tasked to tie up. *prefix:* ***sxʷ...*** *– one tasked to do.*
ľčemn – one inclined to tie up. *suffix:* ***...emn*** *– one inclined to do.*
ľčľčmuł – one that habitually ties up. *suffix:* ***...łmuł*** *– one that habitually does.*
snlčeẃstn, *snlče* – belt. *rt.:* ***ľič*** *– tie up; prefix:* ***sn...*** *– a place of; suffix:* ***...éẃs*** *– in between, middle; suffix:* ***...tin, ...tn*** *– means of/device.*

ľčiš – Tie up. *cmd.*
ľčmiskʷ – Tie it up. *cmd.*
ľčint – Tie it up. *cmd.*

The **i** following uvular consonants (UC) and the glottal stop ˀ sound like English "*ey*" as in the words *they, hey, whey*, etc. Salish UC are: **q, q̇, qʷ, q̇ʷ, x̣, x̣ʷ**. For example, the suffix **...qin** – head/top, is often spelled using English *ey* as "*qeyn*". So **qi, q̇i, qʷi, q̇ʷi, x̣i, x̣ʷi**, may be spelled with English *ey* as **q***ey*, **q̇***ey*, **qʷ***ey*, **q̇ʷ***ey*, **x̣***ey*, **x̣ʷ***ey* in other texts.

s.t. - something, the 3rd person
(s.t.) - something implied
s.o. - someone, the 3rd person
sl. - singular form
pl. - plural form
rt. - root word
cmd. - command
lit. - literally
fig. - figuratively
i.e., - for example
See: - Redirection to a related word.

lč̓éẇs – tied up around the middle; bale of hay.
lč̓lč̓šisqáxeʔ, *lč̓lč̓šisqá* **–** hobble a horse.
l̓č̓peẇsšnmis – S/he tied s.t. to s.o.'s leg. **l̓č̓peẇsšnmn, l̓č̓peẇsšnmntxʷ**
l̓č̓uscutmis – S/he tied s.t. around one's waist. **l̓č̓uscutmn, l̓č̓uscutmntxʷ**

ac – bind; restrain; tie; trap. *See:* ***trap.***
acim – S/he tied/trapped. **čn acim, kʷ acim**
es acmi – S/he is tying/trapping. **čnes acmi, kʷes acmi**
qs acmi – S/he is going to tie/trap. **čiqs acmi, kʷqs acmi**
acíʔim – They tied/trapped. **qeʔ acim, acim**
es acmíʔi – They are tying/trapping. **qeʔes acmi, es acmi**

acntés – S/he tied/trapped s.t. **acntén, acntéxʷ**
es aciṁs – S/he is tying/trapping s.t. **ies aciṁ, as aciṁ**
qs aciṁs – S/he is going to tie/trap s.t. **iqs aciṁ, aqs aciṁ**
acntéʔes – They tied/trapped s.t. **qeʔ acntém, acntép**
es acíʔiṁs – They are tying/trapping s.t. **qeʔes aciṁ, es aciṁp**

es acacmi – S/he is repeated tying/restraining. **čnes acacmi, kʷes acacmi**
es acaciṁs – S/he is repeatedly tying/restraining s.t. **ies acaciṁ, as acaciṁ**

es ac – S/he/it is tied *(not free)*. **čnes ac, kʷes ac**

sxʷacim – one tasked to tie/trap/catch. *prefix:* ***sxʷ...*** *– one tasked to do.*
acemn – one inclined to tie/trap/catch. *suffix:* ***...emn*** *– one inclined to do.*
acacmuł – one that habitually ties/traps/catches. *suffix:* ***...łmuł*** *– one that habitually does.*
accne – shoestring.

aciš – Tie. *cmd.*
acint – Tie/trap it. *cmd.*
acmiskʷ – Tie it. *cmd.*
acelis – tie together in equal amounts.
accutm – S/he/it is easy to catch.
accmutm – S/he/it easily catches.
aceẇs – tied together. *suffix:* ***...éẇs*** *– in between, middle.*
čacéẇsm – tie up; to tie and hang up. *See:* ***hang.***
acacíṁ – repeatedly catching/restraining; break horses. *See:* ***break.***
acacsqáx̣eʔ, *acacsqá* **–** break horses; restrain/catch horses. *See:* ***break.***
acacnúnm – succeed in breaking a horse; succeed in catching/restraining a horse.

iqs acłtem – I am going to tie something of his. **ies acłteṁ –** I am tying something of his. **accncin –** I tied you. **acint asťsťassšn –** Tie your shoes.

aculexʷ – tied to the ground; staked to the ground; restrained to the ground.
aculexʷ – S/he/it was tied. **čn aculexʷ, kʷ aculexʷ**
es aculexʷi – S/he/it is tied. **čnes aculexʷi, kʷes aculexʷ**
qs aculexʷi – S/he/it is going to be tied. **čiqs aculexʷi, kʷqs aculexʷ**

tiger

skʷtismye – mountain lion; cougar.

tight

c̓án – tight; fixed in place; constricted; well fastened.
i c̓án – It is tight; well fastened.
c̓nap – It got tight.
es c̓npma – It is tightening.

es c̓ánm – It is tight; it is well fastened.

ċnċant – firm; immovable; well fastened; tight.
ċánm – fastened; fixed in position; tight; immovable. *See: **fasten**.*

tin – tight; taut; tense.
i tin – It is tight.
es tnpmi – It is getting tight.

tnstes – S/he made it tight. **tnsten, tnstexʷ**
es tnmims – S/he is making it tight. **ies tnmim, as tnmim**
qs tnmims – S/he is going to make it tight. **iqs tnmim, aqs tnmim**

tnup – It suddenly got tight.

tinš – sinew; tendons.

tnmiskʷ – Make it tight. *cmd.*
čtinċeˀ – tight covering. *(i.e., tight fitting clothes, etc.)*
tins – tight face.
čtntins – tight eyes.

The **i** following uvular consonants (UC) and the glottal stop ˀ sound like English "*ey*" as in the words *they*, *hey*, *whey*, etc. Salish UC are: **q**, **q̇**, **qʷ**, **q̇ʷ**, **x̣**, **x̣ʷ**. For example, the suffix ...**qin** – head/top, is often spelled using English *ey* as "q*ey*n". So **qi**, **q̇i**, **qʷi**, **q̇ʷi**, **x̣i**, **x̣ʷi**, may be spelled with English *ey* as **q***ey*, **q̇***ey*, **qʷ***ey*, **q̇ʷ***ey*, **x̣***ey*, **x̣ʷ***ey* in other texts.

tilt

wéľ – tilt; tip from a standing postion. *(i.e., tree, pole, etc.)*
es wéľm – It is tilted; it is tipped.

wľweľ – tipping from side to side.

wľwéľľš – I am waddling *(as a duck)*. *See: **waddle**.*

timber wolf

nċiˀcn – timber wolf. *suffix: **...cin, ...cn** – action of the mouth.*
čx̣i nċiˀcn – gray wolf.

time

spéntč – year.
tapisté – never.
tspisċé – yesterday.
słesľspé – two-year-old.
es šˀiti – beginning of time; first time.

upn čx̣ʷéct ntx̣ʷqi – ten past noon. **upn čx̣ʷéct upn –** ten past ten. **če t upn m l ntx̣ʷqin –** ten 'til noon. **če t upn m l upn –** ten 'til ten. **sċut čx̣ʷéct syeẇsmskʷkʷe –** half past midnight. **čłx̣ʷa esel –** a little after 2:00.

ľ k̇ʷinš – At what time?
ľ k̇ʷinš m kʷ qéiłt – What time will you wake? **ƛ̓e l k̇ʷinš –** What time is it already? **put u l k̇ʷinš –** Exactly, what time is it? **l k̇ʷinš m kʷ eł ckʷłči –** What time will you get back?

... ṁnuxʷ – *suffix indicating going through the time of; process through something; getting to be/becoming. See: **getting**.*

nčcnus – arrive at the start of a time period, the beginning of an action, or the edge of a place. *See: **arrive**.*

Timothy grass

ččstiṅé, ččntsqáyn – Timothy grass.

s.t. - something, the 3rd person
(s.t.) - something implied
s.o. - someone, the 3rd person
sl. - singular form
pl. - plural form
rt. - root word
cmd. - command
lit. - literally
fig. - figuratively
i.e., - for example
See: - Redirection to a related word.

tin

stpčé – can; tin.

tip

sṅłča – tip.

k̇ʷiċšľš – tip an upright thing over/off.
nk̇ʷiċšľš – S/he/it tipped over into (s.t.) **čn nk̇ʷiċšľš, kʷ nk̇ʷiċšľš**

k̓ʷiċšlsts – S/he tipped s.t. over. **k̓ʷiċšlstn, k̓ʷiċšlstxʷ**
k̓ʷíˀiċšlsts – They tipped s.t. over. **qeˀ k̓ʷiċšlstm, k̓ʷiċšlstp**

nk̓ʷiċšlš l snlkʷošótn łu supi – Sophie tipped over into the pigpen.

nwalqn – tip the head back. *(Also, a saying to be drinking alcohol.)*
es nwalqni – S/he/it is tipping his/her head. **čnes nwalqni, kʷes nwalqni**
es nwlwalqni – S/he/it is tipping his/her head side to side.
nwalqiš – Tip your head. *cmd.*

čłk̓ʷel̓č – turn a rigid container type object upside-down on a flat surface ; roll/tip over. *(i.e., car, hat, lid, etc.) See:* ***upside down.***

wél̓l̓ – tilt; tip from a standing position. *(i.e., tree, pole, etc.) See:* ***tilt.***

tipi

sq̇imułxʷ, *sq̇imu,* – tipi. **sq̇iq̇imu –** more than one tipi.
es q̇imu – The tipi is up.

sq̇iłxʷ – tipi.

es číˀiċ l sq̇imu – They were lying down in the tipi. **nšlíˀič l es q̇i –** They went around the camp.

spċnéłxʷ, *spċné* **–** tipi; canvas lodge.

sṗiˀełxʷ – tipi; buckskin tipi.

soxʷełxʷ – reed tipi; medicine lodge.

scwéłxʷ – medicine lodge. *prefix:* ***sc...*** *– s.t. that's been done/made/prepared.*
łu istč še k̓ʷul̓ scwéłxʷ – In winter a medicine lodge was made.

sq̇eẏmn – pole, tipi pole. **sq̇ẏq̇eẏmn –** tipi poles.
ċq̇ʷpełxʷ, *ċq̇ʷpe* **–** stake.
k̓ʷłnšalpncutn – tipi door. *rt.:* ***šal*** *– suspended; circumfix:* ***k̓ʷłn...ep*** *– opening.*
čutčlenč – lacing pins. *suffix:* ***...enč*** *– within.*
nčmpełxʷ, *nčmpe* **–** back of the tipi *(inside). rt.:* ***čm*** *– extremity.*
čmpełxʷ, *čmpe* **–** back of the tipi *(outside). rt.:* ***čm*** *– extremity.*
nčmep – front of the tipi. *rt.:* ***čm*** *– extremity.*
čmqnełxʷ, *čmqne* **–** top of a tipi *(outside). rt.:* ***čm*** *– extremity.*
nčmqnełxʷ, *nčmqne* **–** top of a tipi *(inside). rt.:* ***čm*** *– extremity.*

ċl̓x̣ʷom – put up the tied poles. *(i.e., tipi poles, etc.) See:* ***tipi poles.***

...ełxʷ, **...łxʷ –** *suffix indicating tipi, house, lodge.*

q̇eẏłxʷm – put up a tipi.
q̇eẏłxʷm – S/he put up a tipi. **čn q̇eẏłxʷm, kʷ q̇eẏłxʷm**
es q̇eẏłxʷi – S/he is putting up a tipi. **čnes q̇eẏłxʷi, kʷes q̇vłxʷi**
qs q̇eẏłxʷi – S/he is going to put up a tipi. **čiqs q̇eẏłxʷi, kʷqs q̇eẏłxʷi**

q̇eẏłxʷis – S/he put up the tipi. **q̇eẏłxʷn, q̇eẏłxʷntxʷ**
q̇éˀeẏłxʷis – They put up the tipi. **qeˀ q̇eẏłxʷntm, q̇eẏłxʷntp**

ċq̇ʷpełxʷm – put a stake in the ground for the tipi.
ċq̇ʷpełxʷm – S/he put the stake in. **čn ċq̇ʷpełxʷm, kʷ ċq̇ʷpełxʷm**
es ċq̇ʷpełxʷi – S/he is putting the stake in. **čnes ċq̇ʷpełxʷi, kʷes ċq̇ʷpełxʷi**
qs ċq̇ʷpełxʷi – S/he is going to put the stake in. **čiqs ċq̇ʷpełxʷi, kʷqs ċq̇ʷpełxʷi**
ċq̇ʷpéˀełxʷm – They put the stake in. **qeˀ ċq̇ʷpełxʷm, p ċq̇ʷpełxʷm**
es ċq̇ʷpéˀełxʷi – They are putting the stake in. **qeˀes ċq̇ʷpełxʷi, pes ċq̇ʷpełxʷi**

qs ċq̓ʷpéʔełxʷi – They are going to put the stake in. **qeʔqs ċq̓ʷpełxʷi, pqs ċq̓ʷpełxʷi**

ċq̓ʷpełxʷiš – Put the stake in. *cmd.*

nacqnełxʷ – The poles are tied at the top.
nacqnełxʷm – S/he tied the top of the poles. **čn nacqnełxʷm, kʷ nacqnełxʷm**
es nacqnełxʷi – S/he is tying the top of the poles. **čnes nacqnełxʷi, kʷes nacqnełxʷi**
qs nacqnełxʷi – S/he is going to tie the top of the poles. **čiqs nacqnełxʷi, kʷqs nacqnełxʷi**
nacqnéʔełxʷm – They tied the top of the poles. **qeʔ nacqnełxʷm, p nacqnełxʷm**
es nacqnéʔełxʷi – They are tying the top of the poles. **qeʔes nacqnełxʷi, pes nacqnełxʷi**
qs nacqnéʔełxʷi – They are going to tie the top of the poles. **qeʔqs nacqnełxʷi, pqs nacqnełxʷi**

The **i** following uvular consonants (UC) and the glottal stop **ʔ** sound like English "*ey*" as in the words *they, hey, whey,* etc. Salish UC are: **q, q̓, qʷ, q̓ʷ, x̣, x̣ʷ**. For example, the suffix ...**qin** – head/top, is often spelled using English *ey* as "q*ey*n". So **qi, q̓i, qʷi, q̓ʷi, x̣i, x̣ʷi,** may be spelled with English *ey* as **q***ey*, **q̓***ey*, **qʷ***ey*, **q̓ʷ***ey*, **x̣***ey*, **x̣ʷ***ey* in other texts.

nk̓ʷełxʷ – one house. **esłełxʷ** – two houses. **čełłełxʷ** – three houses. **musłxʷ** – four houses. **clčstełxʷ** – five houses. **t̓q̓nčstełxʷ** – six houses. **spl̓čełxʷ** – seven houses. **héʔenmełxʷ** – eight houses. **x̣n̓tełxʷ** – nine houses. **upnčstełxʷ** – ten houses.
upn eł nk̓ʷełxʷ – eleven houses.
xʷʔełxʷ – bunch of houses.

tipi poles

sq̓eẏmn – pole, tipi pole. **sq̓ẏq̓eẏmn** – tipi poles.

ċk̓ʷmin – ear pole of a tipi. *rt.: **ċuk̓ʷ** – erect; suffix: **...min, ...mn** – instrument/tool.*
ċk̓ʷċk̓ʷmin – ear poles of a tipi.

ċl̓x̣ʷom – put up the tied poles. *(i.e., tipi poles, etc.) rt.: **ċalx̣ʷ** – poles lashed together.*
ċl̓x̣ʷntes – S/he put up the tied poles. **ċl̓x̣ʷnten, ċl̓x̣ʷntexʷ**
es ċl̓x̣ʷoms – S/he is putting up the tied poles. **ies ċl̓x̣ʷom, as ċl̓x̣ʷom**
qs ċl̓x̣ʷoms – S/he is going to put up the tied poles. **iqs ċl̓x̣ʷom, aqs ċl̓x̣ʷom**
ċl̓x̣ʷntéʔes – They put up the tied poles. **qeʔ ċl̓x̣ʷntem, ċl̓x̣ʷntep**
es ċl̓x̣ʷóʔom – They are putting up the tied poles. **qeʔes ċl̓x̣ʷom, es ċl̓x̣ʷomp**
qs ċl̓x̣ʷóʔom – They are going to put up the tied poles. **qeʔqs ċl̓x̣ʷom, qs ċl̓x̣ʷomp**

ċl̓x̣ʷent – Put up the poles that are tied together; make the base. *cmd.*

tire

sčṗuẏšn – car tire. **sčṗiṗuẏšn** – car tire.

čmičšnenetn – hubcap. *suffix: **...tin, ...tn** – means of/device.*

tired

áyx̣ʷt – physically tired.
ayx̣ʷt – S/he got tired. **čn ayx̣ʷt, kʷ ayx̣ʷt**
es ayx̣ʷti – S/he is tired. **čnes ayx̣ʷti, kʷes ayx̣ʷti**
qs ayx̣ʷti – S/he is going to be tired. **čiqs ayx̣ʷti, kʷqs ayx̣ʷti**
es ayʔayx̣ʷti – Each one is tired. **qeʔes ayʔayx̣ʷti, pes ayʔayx̣ʷti**

ayx̣ʷtmis – S/he got tired of s.t./s.o. **ayx̣ʷtmn, ayx̣ʷtmntxʷ**
es ayx̣ʷtms – S/he is tired of s.t./s.o. **ies ayx̣ʷtm, as ayx̣ʷtm**

sʔáyx̣ʷt – the being tired.
scʔáyx̣ʷt – the having been tired.
čʔáyx̣ʷtn – something that make one tired.

ayáyx̣ʷt – tiresome.
ayáyx̣ʷsnuxʷ – tiresome; makes one tired.

s.t. - something, the 3rd person
(s.t.) - something implied
s.o. - someone, the 3rd person
sl. - singular form
pl. - plural form
rt. - root word
cmd. - command
lit. - literally
fig. - figuratively
i.e., - for example
See: - Redirection to a related word.

ayx̣ʷmscut, *ayx̣ʷmscu* – tire out one's self.
es ayx̣ʷmscuti – S/he is tiring out one's self. **čnes ayx̣ʷmscuti, kʷes ayx̣ʷmscuti**
es ayx̣ʷtmnwexʷi – They are tiring each other. **qeʔes ayx̣ʷtmnwexʷi, pes ayx̣ʷtmnwexʷi**
es ayx̣ʷtstwexʷi – They are making each other tired. **qeʔes ayx̣ʷtstwexʷi, pes ayx̣ʷtstwexʷi**
áyx̣ʷtutm – S/he/it easily tires.

es ayx̣ʷti łu mali x̣ʷl̓ tas itš tskʷkʷʔe – Mary is tired because she did not sleep last night. **ayx̣ʷtmncn** – I am tired of you. **ta qʷo qes ayx̣ʷtmntxʷ** – Do not get tired of me. **we čnes ayx̣ʷti** – I was tired. **we qeʔes ayʔayx̣ʷti** – We were tired.

ayx̣ʷstumn – I got you tired.
ayx̣ʷstumncn – I got you tired.

ayx̣ʷstums – S/he/it got you tired. **qʷo ayx̣ʷstes** – It made me tired. **qʷo ayx̣ʷstem łu qeʔ scxʷist** – Our walk made me tired.

es ṗaṫ – It is something soft and squishy *(i.e., excrement, brains, a wet hide, etc.) (If someone has a big belly* ***es ṗaṫ*** *can be said about it.)*; figuratively when a person feels tired and loose. *See:* ***pile.***
es ṗaṫ – S/he feels tired and loose. **čnes ṗaṫ, kʷes ṗaṫ**

x̣ił čnes ṗaṫ – I do not feel good or I feel loose.

ṗṫaṫ – played out; have no energy; tired.
hoy ṗṫaṫ – S/he is played out, no more energy. **hoy čn ṗṫaṫ** – I am tired, just laying there like mud.

nweyls – lazy/tired; hate to do work; do something haphazardly. *See:* ***lazy.***

picxʷt – exhausted; tired. *See:* ***exhausted.***

illmnaqs – exhausted; played out. *See:* ***exhausted.***

čšʔitš – sleepy. *See:* ***sleepy.***

háw̓m – loosen something; slacken. *(i.e., knot, jar lid, tense person, etc.) See:* ***loosen.***

šáll – bored; tiresome; weary from dullness. *See:* ***bored.***

ṗáu – disregard; ignore; lose interest; tire of something; distracted. *See:* ***disregard.***

q̇etyus, *q̇etyu* – nod off; have heavy eyes; cannot hold up head; *literally: weighted face. See:* ***nap.***

tiresome
ayáyx̣ʷt – tiresome.

toad
snakʷkʷáneʔ, *snakʷkʷá* – toad.

toast
es ṗeʔč – toast.

toaster
snx̣ʷʔustn – toaster. *prefix:* ***sn...*** *– a place of; suffix:* ***...tin, ...tn*** *– means of/device.*

tobacco
sméṅxʷ – something smoked. *(i.e., tobacco, etc.)*
méṅxʷ – smoke. *See:* ***smoke.***
snméṅxʷtn, *snmé* – smoking pipe.

q̇ʷiʔ – smell like smoke. *See:* ***smoke.***

snṫq̇o – chewing tobacco.

tobacco root
msawiyeʔ – tobacco root; Valerian; *Valeriana edulis.*

today
yetłx̣ʷásq̇t, *yetłx̣ʷá* – now, today. *suffix:* ***...asq̇t*** *– sky, day.*
čmlk̓ʷmasq̇t čnes ċuʔċa yetłx̣ʷásq̇t – I was swimming all day today.

toe **st̓ix̣šn** – toe. **st̓x̣t̓ix̣šn** – toes. *rt.:* ***t̓ix̣** – protrude; suffix:* ***...šin, ...šn** – feet.*

toenail **q̓ʷx̣ʷqinšn,** *q̓ʷx̣ʷqi* – toenail; claws. **q̓ʷx̣ʷq̓ʷx̣ʷqinšn** *pl.*

čxʷtxʷtqinšn – cut toenails.
čxʷtxʷtqinšnm – S/he cut toenails. **čn čxʷtxʷtqinšnm, kʷ čxʷtxʷtqinšnm**
es **čxʷtxʷtqinšni** – S/he is cutting toenails. **čnes čxʷtxʷtqinšni, kʷes čxʷtxʷtqinšni**
qs **čxʷtxʷtqinšni** – S/he is going to cut toenails. **čiqs čxʷtxʷtqinšni, kʷqs čxʷtxʷtqinšni**

čxʷtxʷtqinšis – S/he cut s.o.'s toenails. **čxʷtxʷtqinšn, čxʷtxʷtqinšntxʷ**
es **čxʷtxʷtqinšnms** – S/he is cutting s.o.'s toenails. **ies čxʷtxʷtqinšnm, as čxʷtxʷtqinšnm**
qs **čxʷtxʷtqinšnms** – S/he is going to cut s.o.'s toenails. **čiqs čxʷtxʷtqinšnm, kʷqs čxʷtxʷtqinšnm**

es **čxʷtxʷtqinšn** – His/her toenails are cut. **čnes čxʷtxʷtqinšn, kʷes čxʷtxʷtqinšn**

čxʷtxʷtqinšniš – Cut toenails. *cmd.*
čxʷtxʷtqinšnt – Cut s.o.'s toenails. *cmd.*

The **i** following uvular consonants (UC) and the glottal stop **ʔ** sound like English "*ey*" as in the words *they, hey, whey*, etc. Salish UC are: **q, q̓, qʷ, q̓ʷ, x̣, x̣ʷ**. For example, the suffix **...qin** – head/top, is often spelled using English *ey* as "*qeyn*". So **qi, q̓i, qʷi, q̓ʷi, x̣i, x̣ʷi**, may be spelled with English *ey* as **q***ey*, **q̓***ey*, **qʷ***ey*, **q̓ʷ***ey*, **x̣***ey*, **x̣ʷ***ey* in other texts.

čx̣ƛ̓x̣ƛ̓qinšn – chew toenails.
čx̣ƛ̓x̣ƛ̓qinšnm – S/he chewed toenails. **čn čx̣ƛ̓x̣ƛ̓qinšnm, kʷ čx̣ƛ̓x̣ƛ̓qinšnm**
es **čx̣ƛ̓x̣ƛ̓qinšni** – S/he is chewing toenails. **čnes čx̣ƛ̓x̣ƛ̓qinšni, kʷes čx̣ƛ̓x̣ƛ̓qinšni**
qs **čx̣ƛ̓x̣ƛ̓qinšni** – S/he is going to chew toenails. **čiqs čx̣ƛ̓x̣ƛ̓qinšni, kʷqs čx̣ƛ̓x̣ƛ̓qinšni**

čx̣ƛ̓x̣ƛ̓qinšis – S/he chewed s.o.'s toenails. **čx̣ƛ̓x̣ƛ̓qinšn, čx̣ƛ̓x̣ƛ̓qinšntxʷ**
es **čx̣ƛ̓x̣ƛ̓qinšnms** – S/he is chewing s.o.'s toenails. **ies čx̣ƛ̓x̣ƛ̓qinšnm, as čx̣ƛ̓x̣ƛ̓qinšnm**
qs **čx̣ƛ̓x̣ƛ̓qinšnms** – S/he is going to chew s.o.'s toenails. **čiqs čx̣ƛ̓x̣ƛ̓qinšnm, kʷqs čx̣ƛ̓x̣ƛ̓qinšnm**

es **čx̣ƛ̓x̣ƛ̓qinšn** – His/her toenails are chewed. **čnes čx̣ƛ̓x̣ƛ̓qinšn, kʷes čx̣ƛ̓x̣ƛ̓qinšn**

čx̣ƛ̓x̣ƛ̓qinšniš – Chew toenails. *cmd.*
čx̣ƛ̓x̣ƛ̓qinšnt – Chew s.o.'s toenails. *cmd.*

k̓ʷłxʷk̓ʷxʷk̓ʷqinšn – clean toenails.
k̓ʷłxʷk̓ʷxʷk̓ʷqinm – S/he cleaned toenails. **čn k̓ʷłxʷk̓ʷxʷk̓ʷqinm, kʷ k̓ʷłxʷk̓ʷxʷk̓ʷqinm**
es **k̓ʷłxʷk̓ʷxʷk̓ʷqini** – S/he is cleaning toenails. **čnes k̓ʷłxʷk̓ʷxʷk̓ʷqini, kʷes k̓ʷłxʷk̓ʷxʷk̓ʷqini**

k̓ʷłxʷk̓ʷxʷk̓ʷqis – S/he cleaned s.o.'s toenails. **k̓ʷłxʷk̓ʷxʷk̓ʷqin, k̓ʷłxʷk̓ʷxʷk̓ʷqintxʷ**
es **k̓ʷłxʷk̓ʷxʷk̓ʷqinms** – S/he is cleaning s.o.'s toenails. **ies k̓ʷłxʷk̓ʷxʷk̓ʷqinm, as k̓ʷłxʷk̓ʷxʷk̓ʷqinm**

es **k̓ʷłxʷk̓ʷxʷk̓ʷqin** – His/her toenails are clean. **čnes k̓ʷłxʷk̓ʷxʷk̓ʷqin, kʷes k̓ʷłxʷk̓ʷxʷk̓ʷqin**

k̓ʷłxʷk̓ʷxʷk̓ʷqiniš – Clean toenails. *cmd.*
k̓ʷłxʷk̓ʷxʷk̓ʷqint – Clean s.o.'s toenails. *cmd.*

s.t. - something, the 3rd person
(s.t.) - something implied
s.o. - someone, the 3rd person
sl. - singular form
pl. - plural form
rt. - root word
cmd. - command
lit. - literally
fig. - figuratively
i.e., - for example
See: - Redirection to a related word.

x̣ʷq̓ʷx̣ʷq̓ʷqinšn – file toenails.
x̣ʷq̓ʷx̣ʷq̓ʷqinm – S/he filed toenails. **čn x̣ʷq̓ʷx̣ʷq̓ʷqinm, kʷ x̣ʷq̓ʷx̣ʷq̓ʷqinm**

x̣ʷq̓ʷx̣ʷq̓ʷqis – S/he filed s.o.'s toenails. **x̣ʷq̓ʷx̣ʷq̓ʷqin, x̣ʷq̓ʷx̣ʷq̓ʷqintxʷ**

es **x̣ʷq̓ʷx̣ʷq̓ʷqin** – His/her toenails are filed. **čnes x̣ʷq̓ʷx̣ʷq̓ʷqin, kʷes x̣ʷq̓ʷx̣ʷq̓ʷqin**

x̣ʷq̓ʷx̣ʷq̓ʷqiniš – File toenails. *cmd.*
x̣ʷq̓ʷx̣ʷq̓ʷqint – File s.o.'s toenails. *cmd.*

mnminqnši – paint toenails.
mnminqnm – S/he painted toenails. **čn mnminqnm, kʷ mnminqnm**

es mnminqni – S/he is painting toenails. **čnes mnminqni, kʷes mnminqni**
qs mnminqni – S/he is going to paint toenails. **čiqs mnminqni, kʷqs mnminqni**

mnminqis – S/he painted s.o.'s toenails. **mnminqn, mnminqntxʷ**
es mnminqnms – S/he is painting s.o.'s toenails. **ies mnminqnm, as mnminqnm**
qs mnminqnms – S/he is going to paint s.o.'s toenails. **čiqs mnminqnm, kʷqs mnminqnm**

es mnminqn – His/her toenails are painted. **čnes mnminqn, kʷes mnminqn**

mnminqniš – Paint toenails. *cmd.*
mnminqnt – Paint s.o.'s toenails. *cmd.*

ususqinšn – long toenails.
es ususqinšn – S/he has long toenails. **čnes ususqinšn, kʷes ususqinšn**

ƛ̓m̓qinšn – blood blistered toenail.

together

qmim – connect together.
qmis – S/he/it connected s.t. together. **qmin, qmintxʷ**
esyaʔ ci eċx̣ax̣i sq̇iq̇ʔeẏ m qmintxʷ – Connect all the same colors together.

t̓qʷméẇs – standing together. *suffix: **...éẇs** – in between, middle.*
es nt̓q̇meẇs – They are sitting by each other.
qeʔes nt̓q̇meẇs – We are sitting by each other.
pes nt̓q̇meẇs – You all are sitting by each other.
es nt̓q̇t̓q̇meẇs – Each group is sitting by each other *(i.e., on bleachers at a game)*.

es sesélm – both; together.
es čsélm – both people; two people are together.

i ẏaʔẏaʔi – all together.

nkʷł... – *prefix indicating together with, do with. See: **with**.*
nkʷłwenš – dance together with someone. *See: **war dance**.*

nloloseẇs – connect things together; fit things inside to connect. *(i.e., connector blocks, building block toys, etc.) See: **connect**.*

t̓ip – join to make longer; fasten to make longer. *(i.e., sewing, fastening, etc.) See: **join**.*

nacsél̓is – join/tie two things together. *See: **splice**.*

ax̣meẇs – splice something together; weave ends together. *See: **splice**.*

toilet

snm̓ṅéčtn – toilet. *prefix: **sn...** – a place of; suffix: **...tin, ...tn** – means of/device.*
čiqs k̓ʷis m̓ṅé – I am going to go crap.

snłʔó – toilet; outhouse. *prefix: **sn...** – a place of.*

nanax̣i, *naná* – potty.
čiqs k̓ʷis nanax̣i – I am going to the potty.

k̓ʷłsixʷm – drain/pour from under; flush. *See: **flush**.*

toilet paper

nep̓psncutn, *nep̓psncu* – toilet paper. *rt.: **ep̓** – wipe; suffix: **...tin, ...tn** – means of/device. See: **wipe**.*

told

cu – say/speak to somebody; inform; provide information about something. *See: **say**.*

m̓éẏeʔ – explain; tell; show; make something known. *See: **explain**.*

sṁiṁiʔ – story; news; something that's been told. *See: **tell**.*

tolerable

ṫul – tolerable.

ṫulist – S/he made one's self tolerable. **čn ṫulist, kʷ ṫulist**
es ṫulisti – S/he is making one's self tolerable. **čnes ṫulisti, kʷes ṫulisti**
qs ṫulisti – S/he is going to make one's self tolerable. **čiqs ṫulisti, kʷqs ṫulisti**

ṫulntes – S/he made it tolerable. **ṫulnten, ṫulntexʷ**
es ṫulims – S/he is making it tolerable. **ies ṫulim, as ṫulim**
qs ṫulims – S/he is going to make it tolerable. **iqs ṫulim, aqs ṫulim**

ṫuul – It diminished.
es ṫuulmi – It is diminishing.

es ṫuleysi – The rain is becoming tolerable.

tam ṫul̓ – tremendous; outstanding; extreme; excellent. *See: **excellent**.*

The **i** following uvular consonants (UC) and the glottal stop **ʔ** sound like English "*ey*" as in the words *they, hey, whey*, etc. Salish UC are: **q, q̇, qʷ, q̇ʷ, x̣, x̣ʷ**. For example, the suffix **...qin** – head/top, is often spelled using English *ey* as "q*ey*n". So **qi, q̇i, qʷi, q̇ʷi, x̣i, x̣ʷi**, may be spelled with English *ey* as **q***ey*, **q̇***ey*, **qʷ***ey*, **q̇ʷ***ey*, **x̣***ey*, **x̣ʷ***ey* in other texts.

tomahawk

ƛ̓šl̓min – hatchet.

tomato

sxʷya – tomato.

tomorrow

ṅex̣lip, *ṅex̣li* – tomorrow; when it is light.

ṅe eł x̣lip – When it is light again; tomorrow.

tongue

tixʷcč – tongue.

ƛ̓ečcn – stick out the tongue. *rt.: **ƛ̓éʔeč** – peek; suffix: **...cin, ...cn** – action of the mouth.*

ƛ̓ečcnm – S/he stuck out the tongue. **čn ƛ̓ečcnm, kʷ ƛ̓ečcnm**
es ƛ̓ečcni – S/he is sticking out the tongue. **čnes ƛ̓ečcni, kʷes ƛ̓ečcni**
qs ƛ̓ečcni – S/he is going to stick out the tongue. **čiqs ƛ̓ečcni, kʷqs ƛ̓ečcni**

ƛ̓ečcis – S/he made s.o. stick out their tongue. **ƛ̓ečcn, ƛ̓ečcntxʷ**
es ƛ̓ečcnms – S/he is making s.o. sick out their tongue. **ies ƛ̓ečcnm, as ƛ̓ečcnm**
qs ƛ̓ečcnms – S/he is going to make s.o. stick out their tongue. **iqs ƛ̓ečcnm, aqs ƛ̓ečcnm**

ƛ̓ečcnmistmis – S/he stuck out the tongue at s.o. **ƛ̓ečcnmistmn, ƛ̓ečcnmistmntxʷ**
es ƛ̓ečcnmistms – S/he is sticking out the tongue at s.o. **ies ƛ̓ečcnmistm, as ƛ̓ečcnmistm**

tongue tied

sl̓lpcan – make a mistake talking; mix up words. *rt.: **sil̓** – confuse; suffix: **...cin, ...cn** – action of the mouth.*

sl̓lpcan – S/he made a mistake; mixed up words. **čn sl̓lpcan, kʷ sl̓lpcan**
es sl̓lpcani – S/he is mixing up words. **čnes sl̓lpcani, kʷes sl̓lpcani**

sl̓lpcin – confused about what to say. *rt.: **sil̓** – confuse; suffix: **...cin, ...cn** – action of the mouth.*

sl̓lpcin – S/he could not figure out what to say. **čn sl̓lpcin, kʷ sl̓lpcin**
es sl̓lpcini – S/he cannot figure out what to say. **čnes sl̓lpcini, kʷes sl̓lpcini**

tmmcan – tongue tied; have no words. *rt.: **tam** – not/none; suffix: **...cin, ...cn** – action of the mouth.*

sil̓ – confused; unable to figure something out; mistaken. *See: **confuse**.*

s.t. - something, the 3rd person
(s.t.) - something implied
s.o. - someone, the 3rd person
sl. - singular form
pl. - plural form
rt. - root word
cmd. - command
lit. - literally
fig. - figuratively
i.e., - for example
See: - Redirection to a related word.

tonight

ṅe kʷkʷʔéc, *ṅe kʷkʷʔé* – tonight; when it is night.

tonsil

k̓ʷck̓ʷucł – tonsils.

too **nexʷ** – too; also.

tool **k̓ʷuľmn** – something to work with; tool.

too much **mił** – too much, too many.
mił i čťá łu mali – Mary's too skinny. **mił x̣emt ci pus** – That cat is too heavy. **ci skʷk̓ʷimľt iłn mił t xʷˀit sťšá** – That child ate too many huckleberries. **ta mił pqs čxʷˀé** – Do not get too many. **mił čnes x̣ʷeyti** – I am too lazy.

tooth **x̣ľéxʷ** – tooth. **x̣ľx̣ľéxʷ** – teeth. *See:* ***teeth.***

toothache **nċaléys** – have a toothache. *rt.:* ***ċaál*** *– ache.*
nċaléys – S/he got a toothache. **čn nċaléys, kʷ nċaléys**
es nċaléysi – S/he has a toothache. **čnes nċaléysi, kʷes nċaléysi**
qs nċaléysi – S/he is going to have a toothache. **čiqs nċaléysi, kʷqs nċaléysi**

toothbrush **nxʷk̓ʷxʷk̓ʷeystn** – toohbrush. *suffix:* ***...tin, ...tn*** *– means of/device.*

nxʷk̓ʷxʷk̓ʷeysm – brush/clean teeth. *rt.:* ***xʷuk̓ʷ*** *– clean; circumfix:* ***n...eys*** *– teeth.*
nxʷk̓ʷxʷk̓ʷeysm – S/he brushed his/her teeth. **čn nxʷk̓ʷxʷk̓ʷeysm, kʷes nxʷk̓ʷxʷk̓ʷeysm**
es nxʷk̓ʷxʷk̓ʷeysi – S/he is brushing his/her teeth. **čnes nxʷk̓ʷxʷk̓ʷeysi, kʷes nxʷk̓ʷxʷk̓ʷeysi**
qs nxʷk̓ʷxʷk̓ʷeysi – S/he is going to brush his/her teeth. **čiqs nxʷk̓ʷxʷk̓ʷeysi, kʷqs nxʷk̓ʷxʷk̓ʷeysi**

nxʷk̓ʷxʷk̓ʷeysiš – Brush your teeth. *cmd.*

nxʷk̓ʷxʷk̓ʷeysiš ṅe kʷ wis iłn – Brush your teeth after meals.

toothpaste **nċuċéẇistn** – toothpaste. *rt.:* ***ċeẇ*** *– wash; suffix:* ***...tin, ...tn*** *– means of/device.*

toothpick **nuċisncutn,** *nuċisncu* – toothpick. *rt.:* ***wiċ*** *– pick/dig; suffix:* ***...cut*** *– action to the self; suffix:* ***...tin, ...tn*** *– means of/device.*

nuċiċisncut – pick your teeth with a toothpick.
nuċiċisncut – S/he picked one's teeth. **čn nuċiċisncut, kʷ nuċiċisncut**
es nuċiċisncuti – S/he is picking one's teeth. **čnes nuċiċisncuti, kʷes nuċiċisncuti**
qs nuċiċisncuti – S/he's going to pick one's teeth. **čiqs nuċiċisncuti, kʷqs nuċiċisncuti**

top **čłqeẇs,** *čłqe* – on top of. *suffix:* ***...éẇs*** *– in between, middle.*
čłťk̓ʷunt l čłqeẇs – Place it on the top. *cmd.*

qaqlt – arrive at the top.
qaqlt – S/he arrived at the top. **čn qaqlt, kʷ qaqlt**
es qaqlti – S/he is arriving at the top. **čnes qaqlti, kʷes qaqlti**
qs qaqlti – S/he is going to arrive at the top. **čiqs qaqlti, kʷqs qaqlti**

łqqltilš – S/he was getting to the hilltop. **čn łqqltilš, kʷ łqqltilš**
es łqqltilši – S/he is getting to the hilltop. **čnes łqqltilši, kʷes łqqltilši**
qs łqqltilši – S/he is going to be getting to the hilltop. **čiqs łqqltilši, kʷqs łqqltilši**

čqaltqn – S/he arrived at the mountain top. **čn čqaltqn, kʷ čqaltqn**
es čqaltqni – S/he is arriving at the mountain top. **čnes čqaltqni, kʷes čqaltqni**
qs čqaltqni – S/he is going to arrive at the mountain top. **čiqs čqaltqni, kʷqs čqaltqni**

qaqltsts – S/he made s.o. go to the top. **qaqltstn, qaqltstxʷ**
es qaqltms – S/he is making s.o. go to the top. **čnes qaqltm, kʷes qaqltm**
qs qaqltms – S/he is going to make s.o. go to the top. **čiqs qaqltm, kʷqs qaqltm**

qltusis – S/he brought s.o./s.t. to the top. **qltusn, qltusntxʷ**
es qltusms – S/he is bringing s.o./s.t. to the top. **ies qltusm, as qltusm**
qs qltusms – S/he is going to bring s.o./s.t. to the top. **iqs qltusm, aqs qltusm**

łqaqlt, *łqa* **–** arrive at the top of a hill.
łqaqlt – S/he/it arrived at the top of the hill. **čn łqaqlt, kʷ łqaqlt**

sqaqlt – top.
słqaqlt – hilltop.
sč̓qaltqn – mountain top. *circumfix:* ***č̓...qn*** *– mountain.*

qaqltiš – Arrive at the top. *cmd.*
qaqltskʷ – Make s.o. go to the top. *cmd.*
qltusnt – Bring it to the top. *cmd.*
nqltels – want to arrive at the top.

čqé – up above.

č̓mqnéłxʷ – the top of a house/tipi. *rt.:* ***č̓m*** *– extremity.*
nč̓mqnéłxʷ – the top of a house/tipi inside; ceiling.

sntx̣ʷaw̓sqn – top of the head.

č̓łtetʔey – top *(a toy)*.

> The **i** following uvular consonants (UC) and the glottal stop **ʔ** sound like English "*ey*" as in the words th*ey*, h*ey*, wh*ey*, etc. Salish UC are: **q**, **q̓**, **qʷ**, **q̓ʷ**, **x̣**, **x̣ʷ**. For example, the suffix ...**qin** – head/top, is often spelled using English *ey* as "q*ey*n". So **qi**, **q̓i**, **qʷi**, **q̓ʷi**, **x̣i**, **x̣ʷi**, may be spelled with English *ey* as **q***ey*, **q̓***ey*, **qʷ***ey*, **q̓ʷ***ey*, **x̣***ey*, **x̣ʷ***ey* in other texts.

tornado

kʷtisxʷlekʷ – tornado, big whirlwind.
sxʷlekʷ – whirlwind.

es p̓ic̓łqi – strong/big wind; tornado or hurricane like weather; blizzard, but does not refer to snow.

touch

tec – touch; the position of touch; to have the finger/hand on something.
técis – S/he touched it. **técn, técntxʷ**
es tecms – S/he/it is touching it. **ies tecm, as tecm**
qs tecms – S/he/it is going to touch it. **iqs tecm, aqs tecm**
téʔecis – They touched it. **qeʔ tecntm, tecntp**
es téʔecms – They are touching it. **qeʔes tecm, es tecmp**
qs téʔecms – They are going to touch it. **qeʔqs tecm, qs tecmp**

tecnt – Touch it. *cmd.*
es tecnt – Keep you finger on it. *cmd.*

ctécl̓š – S/he felt toward it.
tecnt asnč̓łemutn – Touch the chair.

tqem – touch; the action of touch; to put the finger/hand on something.
tqem – S/he/it touched. **čn tqem, kʷ tqem**
es tqmi – S/he/it is touching. **čnes tqmi, kʷes tqmi**
qs tqmi – S/he/it is going to touch. **čiqs tqmi, kʷqs tqmi**

tqncut – S/he touched one's self. **čn tqncut, kʷ tqncut**
es tqncuti – S/he is touching one's self. **čnes tqncuti, kʷes tqncuti**

tqntes – S/he/it touched s.t. **tqnten, tqntexʷ**
es tqems – S/he/it is touching s.t. **ies tqem, as tqem**
qs tqems – S/he/it is going to touch s.t. **iqs tqem, aqs tqem**

es tqtqmi – S/he/it is repeatedly touching. **čnes tqtqmi, kʷes tqtqmi**
es tqtqncuti – repeatedly touch one's self; *(said when making the sign of the cross)*.

> s.t. - something, the 3rd person
> (s.t.) - something implied
> s.o. - someone, the 3rd person
> *sl.* - singular form
> *pl.* - plural form
> *rt.* - root word
> *cmd.* - command
> *lit.* - literally
> *fig.* - figuratively
> *i.e.,* - for example
> *See:* - Redirection to a related word.

tqtqemn – one inclined to touch something. *suffix: **...emn** – one inclined to do.*

tqeiš – Touch. *cmd.*
tqent – Touch it. *cmd.*
tqncutš – Touch your self. *cmd.*
es tqnnwéxʷi – They are touching each other. **qeʔes tqnnwéxʷi, pes tqnnwéxʷi**
ttqnnwexʷ – put hands on each other; play tag. *See: **tag**.*

tqayaqn – touch the head.
ntqaẇsqn – touch the top of the head.
ntqaẇsqncut – touch one's own head.
čłtqesšn – touch the forehead.
k̓ʷłtqtqus – touch both cheeks.
k̓ʷłtqus – touch one cheek.
čtqtqus – touch both eyes.
čtqus – touch one eye.
ntqtqšncut – touch both of one's own eyes.
ntaqqs – touch the nose.
tqposqn – touch the mouth/lips.
ntqičṅ – touch the back. *suffix: **...ičṅ** – back.*
ntqups – touch the buttock.
tqulexʷ – touch the ground.

čnes tqe t tt̓áċeʔ – I touch grasshoppers. **ies tqem łmłaṁáyeʔ –** I am touching a frog. **kʷ iqs tqem –** I am going to touch you.

čṅuxʷ – touch; perceive by the sense of touch; come in contact physically or spiritually with some part of the body.
čṅuxʷ – S/he got touched. **čn čṅuxʷ, kʷ čṅuxʷ**
es čṅuxʷi – S/he is getting touched. **čnes čṅuxʷi, kʷes čṅuxʷi**
qs čṅuxʷi – S/he is going to get touched. **čiqs čṅuxʷi, kʷqs čṅuxʷi**

čṅxʷum – S/he touched. **čn čṅxʷum, kʷ čṅxʷum**
es čṅxʷmi – S/he is touching. **čnes čṅxʷmi, kʷes čṅxʷmi**
qs čṅxʷmi – S/he is going to touch. **čiqs čṅxʷmi, kʷqs čṅxʷmi**

čṅxʷncut – S/he touched one's self. **čn čṅxʷncut, kʷ čṅxʷncut**
es čṅxʷncuti – S/he is touching one's self. **čnes čṅxʷncuti, kʷes čṅxʷncuti**
qs čṅxʷncuti – S/he is going to touch one's self. **čiqs čṅxʷncuti, kʷqs čṅxʷncuti**

čṅxʷntes – S/he touched/felt s.o./s.t. **čṅxʷnten, čṅxʷntexʷ**
es čṅxʷums – S/he is touching/feeling s.o./s.t. **ies čṅxʷum, as čṅxʷum**
qs čṅxʷums – S/he is going to touch/feel s.o./s.t. **iqs čṅxʷum, aqs čṅxʷum**

ččṅxʷmis – S/he felt the touch of s.t./s.o. **ččṅxʷmin, ččṅxʷmintxʷ**
es ččṅxʷminms – S/he is feeling the touch of s.o./s.t. **ies ččṅxʷminm, as ččṅxʷminm**

sčṅxʷum – the touch; the feel.
scčṅxʷum – something that's been touched; something that's been felt.
čṅxʷmemn – one inclined to touch/feel.
čṅxʷtin – the thing touched; the thing felt.

čṅxʷuwiš – Touch/feel. *cmd.*
čṅxʷunt – Touch/feel it. *cmd.*
es čṅxʷmnweʔexʷi – They feel each other touching/pressing each other. **qeʔes čṅxʷmnwexʷi, pes čṅxʷmnwexʷi**

es **nčṅxʷewsi** – They are touching/pressing each other. **qeʔes nčṅxʷewsi, pes nčṅxʷewsi**
es **nčṅxʷmelsi** – S/he is wanting to touch. **čnes nčṅxʷmelsi, kʷes nčṅxʷmelsi**
es **nčṅxʷmelsms** – S/he is wanting to touch/feel s.t./s.o. **ies nčṅxʷmelsm, as nčṅxʷmelsm**

l čeṅ u ečx̣lsčṅxʷum – How does it feel? **šeẏ łu iscčṅxʷum** – That is what I touched/felt.

enwenm – feel/sense. *See: **feel**.*

čṅéčs – hold hands; grasp hands. *See: **shake hands**.*

The **i** following uvular consonants (UC) and the glottal stop **ʔ** sound like English "*ey*" as in the words *they, hey, whey*, etc. Salish UC are: **q, q̓, qʷ, q̓ʷ, x̣, x̣ʷ**. For example, the suffix **...qin** – head/top, is often spelled using English *ey* as "q*ey*n". So **qi, q̓i, qʷi, q̓ʷi, x̣i, x̣ʷi**, may be spelled with English *ey* as **q***ey*, **q̓***ey*, **qʷ***ey*, **q̓ʷ***ey*, **x̣***ey*, **x̣ʷ***ey* in other texts.

tough

yoyoót – strong. *See: **strong**.*

yomncut, *yomncu* – make one's self become rigid/tense. *See: **tense**.*

nyawlsm – brace feelings; make feelings strong; tough something out. *(i.e., in preparation for bad news, etc.) See: **brace**.*

ƛ̓ic̓t – hard; tough; hard to break. *See: **hard**.*

tl̓xʷéčst, *tl̓xʷé* – difficult; hard to do; struggle at something; unable to succeed. *See: **difficult**.*

towel

eṗstn – towel. *rt: **eṗ** – wipe; suffix: **...tin, ...tn** – means of/device.*

Townsend's big-eared bat

ṫlṫel̓ẇé, *ṫlṫel̓ẇéliyeʔ* – bat; Townsend's big-eared bat.

toy

ml̓méĺčstn, *ml̓mé* – toy; toys. *rt.: **meʔl̓** – be agreeable; suffix: **...tin, ...tn** – means of/device. See: **calm**.*

toy store

sntumístn l ml̓mé – toy store.

track

sxʷuytn – mark left in passing; track. **sxʷixʷuytn** – tracks. *rt.: **xʷuy** – go; suffix: **...tin, ...tn** – means of/device.*

nxʷixʷuym – track.
nxʷixʷuym – S/he tracked. **čn nxʷixʷuym, kʷ nxʷixʷuym**
es **nxʷixʷuyi** – S/he is tracking. **čnes nxʷixʷuyi, kʷes nxʷixʷuyi**
qs **nxʷixʷuyi** – S/he is going to track. **čiqs nxʷixʷuyi, kʷqs nxʷixʷuyi**

sxʷnxʷixʷuym – tracker.

nxʷuyełc̓eʔ – tracking an animal.

nšiẏustšn – follow in the tracks of someone or an animal; follow in someone's footsteps; emulate someone. *See: **follow**.*

es nčicnełc̓eʔi – S/he is approaching an animal.

nšiʔłcnełc̓eʔ – S/he tracked an animal.

nqlqlwečšn – walk in/cover tracks. *Done after the death of someone.*

eṗeṗšnm – wipe away tracks.

xʷeʔšin – lots of feet, lots of tracks.

s.t. - something, the 3rd person
(s.t.) - something implied
s.o. - someone, the 3rd person
sl. - singular form
pl. - plural form
rt. - root word
cmd. - command
lit. - literally
fig. - figuratively
i.e., - for example
See: - Redirection to a related word.

trade

ṅeyxʷéẇs, *ṅeyxʷé* – trade; swap. *rt.: **ey** – cross; suffix: **...éẇs** – in between, middle.*
ṅeyxʷéẇsm – S/he traded. **čn ṅeyxʷéẇsm, kʷ ṅeyxʷéẇsm**
es **ṅeyxʷéẇsi** – S/he is trading. **čnes ṅeyxʷéẇsi, kʷes ṅeyxʷéẇsi**
qs **ṅeyxʷéẇsi** – S/he is going to trade. **čiqs ṅeyxʷéẇsi, kʷqs ṅeyxʷéẇsi**

ṅeyxʷéẇsis – S/he traded for s.t. **ṅeyxʷéẇsn, ṅeyxʷéẇsntxʷ**

es ṅeyxʷéẇsms – S/he is trading for s.t. **ies ṅeyxʷéẇsm, as ṅeyxʷéẇsm**
qs ṅeyxʷéẇsms – S/he is going to trade for s.t. **iqs ṅeyxʷéẇsm, aqs ṅeyxʷéẇsm**
ṅeyxʷéʔeẇsis – They traded for s.t. **qeʔ ṅeyxʷéẇsntm, ṅeyxʷéẇsntp**
es ṅeyxʷéʔeẇsms – They are trading for s.t. **qeʔes ṅeyxʷéẇsm, es ṅeyxʷéẇsmp**
qs ṅeyxʷéʔeẇsms – They are going to trade for s.t. **qeʔqs ṅeyxʷéẇsm, qs ṅeyxʷéẇsmp**

ṅeyeyxʷéẇsms – S/he traded s.t. off. **ṅeyeyxʷéẇsmn, ṅeyxʷéẇsmntxʷ**
es ṅeyeyxʷéẇsms – S/he is trading for s.t. **ies ṅeyeyxʷéẇsm, as ṅeyeyxʷéẇsm**
es ṅeyxʷéẇsmms – S/he is trading s.t. off. **ies ṅeyxʷéẇsmm, as ṅeyxʷéẇsmm**
qs ṅeyxʷéẇsmms – S/he is going to trade s.t. off. **iqs ṅeyxʷéẇsmm, aqs ṅeyxʷéẇsmm**

es ṅeyxʷéẇsi – S/he is trading. **čnes ṅeyxʷéẇsi, kʷes ṅeyxʷéẇsi**
ṅeyeyxʷsemn – one inclined to trade. *suffix: **...emn** – one inclined to do.*
snʔéys – cost; price.

ṅeyxʷéẇsiš – Trade. *cmd.*
ṅeyxʷéẇsnt – Trade it. *cmd.*
qeʔes neyeyxʷłtumš – We are trading with each other.
ṅeyxʷnwexʷist – trade with each other; sharing. *See: **share**.*
ṅeyxʷéẇsšts – S/he traded s.t. off. **ṅeyxʷéẇsštn, ṅeyxʷéẇsštxʷ**
nʔeys – pay for something bought. *See: **pay**.*

ṅayxʷmsqáx̣eʔ, *ṅayxʷmsqá* – trade horses/domestic animals.
ṅayxʷmsqáx̣eʔ – S/he traded. **čṅ ṅayxʷmsqáx̣eʔ, kʷ ṅayxʷmsqáx̣eʔ**
es ṅayxʷmsqáx̣eʔi – S/he is trading. **čṅes ṅayxʷmsqáx̣eʔi, kʷes ṅayxʷmsqáx̣eʔi**
qs ṅayxʷmsqáx̣eʔi – S/he is going to trade. **čiqs ṅayxʷmsqáx̣eʔi, kʷqs ṅayxʷmsqáx̣eʔi**
ṅayxʷmsqáʔax̣eʔ – They traded. **qeʔ ṅayxʷmsqáx̣eʔ, p ṅayxʷmsqáx̣eʔ**
es ṅayxʷmsqáʔax̣eʔi – They are trading. **qeʔes ṅayxʷmsqáx̣eʔi, pes ṅayxʷmsqáx̣eʔi**
qs ṅayxʷmsqáʔax̣eʔi – They are going to trade. **qeʔqs ṅayxʷmsqáx̣eʔi, pqs ṅayxʷmsqáx̣eʔi**

sxʷṅayxʷmsqáx̣eʔ – one tasked to trade horses/domestic animals. *prefix: **sxʷ...** – one tasked to do.*

tumíst, *tumí* – buy. *See: **buy**.*

tradition

nk̓ʷul̓mn – ways, customs, habits, culture, traditions; the things one does.

trail

q̇áx̣ – path/trail. *See: **path**.*
es q̇áx̣ – trail/path. *(a beaten path)*
es łqq̇áx̣ – small path/trail.

es q̇x̣ulexʷ – land trail/path.

trailer

sṅacups – tied to the tail; trailer. *rt.: **ac** – tie; circumfix: **n...ups** – butt, tail.*

trailer court

sṅacupstn – place of the trailers; trailer court. *prefix: **sn...** – a place of; suffix: **...tin, ...tn** – means of/device.*

train

čx̣ʷllq̓ʷálqʷtn, *čx̣ʷllq̓ʷá* – train, locomotive, railroad cars. *rt.: **x̣ʷollq̓ʷ** – roll; suffix: **...tin, ...tn** – means of/device.*

čqql̓ixʷṁa – speeder.

training

qʷaqʷemncut, *qʷaqʷemncú* – practice, drill, train, study. *See: **practice**.*

es tx̣ʷox̣ʷ – S/he/it is tame/straight.
tx̣ʷx̣ʷnúis – S/he straightened s.o./s.t. out. **tx̣ʷx̣ʷnún, tx̣ʷx̣ʷnúntxʷ**
es tx̣ʷx̣ʷnúnms – S/he is straightening s.o./s.t. out. **ies tx̣ʷx̣ʷnúnm, as tx̣ʷx̣ʷnúnm**

qs tx̣ʷx̣ʷnúnms – S/he is going to straighten s.o./s.t. out. **iqs tx̣ʷx̣ʷnúnm, aqs tx̣ʷx̣ʷnúnm**
tx̣ʷx̣ʷnúʔuis – They straightened s.o./s.t. out. **qeʔ tx̣ʷx̣ʷnúntm, tx̣ʷx̣ʷnúntp**
es tx̣ʷx̣ʷnúʔunms – They are straightening s.o./s.t. out. **qeʔes tx̣ʷx̣ʷnúnm, es tx̣ʷx̣ʷnúnmp**
qs tx̣ʷx̣ʷnúʔunms – They are going to straighten s.o./s.t. out. **qeʔqs tx̣ʷx̣ʷnúnm, qs tx̣ʷx̣ʷnúnmp**

tx̣ʷx̣ʷnuntm – S/he/it was straightened out/trained.

tranquil **saṅ –** tranquil; quiet and calm; tame; settled. *See: **quiet**.*

transmission **snloʔloʔpin –** transmission gear unit.

trap **ac –** bind; restrain; tie; trap. *See: **tie**.*
acip – S/he got trapped. **čn acip, kʷ acip**
es acpmi – S/he is unknowingly getting trapped. **čnes acpmi, kʷes acpmi**
qs acpmi – S/he is going to unknowingly get trapped. **čiqs acpmi, kʷqs acpmi**

accpnuis – S/he succeeded in catching s.t. in a trap. **accpnun, accpnuntxʷ**
es accpnunms – S/he is succeeding in catching s.t. in a trap. **ies accpnunm, as accpnunm**

accnuis – S/he succeeded in restraining s.t. **accnun, accpnuntxʷ**

acmin – trap; that someone uses.
acmintn – trap; that traps something.

acipš – Get trapped. *cmd.*
accpnunt – Trap it. *cmd.*
snʔacptin – place to get caught/trapped.
esʔácmi spq̓niʔ – December *(month of trapping).*

tas accutm – S/he/it is difficult to catch/restrain/trap.

q̓ʷyox̣ʷ – trap fish in a barrier/fence.
q̓ʷyox̣ʷm – S/he made a fish trap/barrier. **čn q̓ʷyox̣ʷm, kʷ q̓ʷyox̣ʷm**
es q̓ʷyox̣ʷi – S/he is making a fish trap/barrier. **čnes q̓ʷyox̣ʷm, kʷes q̓ʷyox̣ʷi**

sxʷq̓ʷyox̣ʷ – one tasked to make a fish trap/barrier.
sq̓ʷyox̣ʷ – fish trap/barrier.
sq̓ʷyokʷétkʷ, *sq̓ʷyokʷé* **–** fish trap/cage.

q̓ʷyox̣ʷiš – Make a fish barrier/fence.

snqq̓eċétkʷ – fish trap; fishnet.

čṅeyn – snare; trap. *See: **snare**.*

q̓eyẇ – get/fetch fish from a trap/barrier. *See: **fetch**.*

travel **xʷilwis –** go around; travel around. *rt.: **xʷuy** – go; suffix: **...lwis** – indicate going around.*
nxʷilwistn – something used to travel around in/on. *suffix: **...tin, ...tn** – means of/device.*

ict – go/travel by night.
ictm – S/he traveled by night. **čn ictm, kʷ ictm**
es icti – S/he is traveling by night. **čnes icti, kʷes icti**
qs icti – S/he is going to travel by night. **čiqs icti, kʷqs icti**

ictsts – S/he made s.o. travel by night. **ictstn, ictstxʷ**

The **i** following uvular consonants (UC) and the glottal stop **ʔ** sound like English "*ey*" as in the words *they*, *hey*, *whey*, etc. Salish UC are: **q**, **q̓**, **qʷ**, **q̓ʷ**, **x̣**, **x̣ʷ**. For example, the suffix **...qin** – head/top, is often spelled using English *ey* as "q*ey*n". So **qi**, **q̓i**, **qʷi**, **q̓ʷi**, **x̣i**, **x̣ʷi**, may be spelled with English *ey* as **q***ey*, **q̓***ey*, **qʷ***ey*, **q̓ʷ***ey*, **x̣***ey*, **x̣ʷ***ey* in other texts.

s.t. - something, the 3rd person
(s.t.) - something implied
s.o. - someone, the 3rd person
sl. - singular form
pl. - plural form
rt. - root word
cmd. - command
lit. - literally
fig. - figuratively
i.e., - for example
See: - Redirection to a related word.

es ictms – S/he is making s.o. travel by night. **čnes ictm, kʷes ictm**
qs ictms – S/he is going to make s.o. travel by night. **čiqs ictm, kʷqs ictm**

ictskʷ – Make him/her travel by night. *cmd.*
es nectelsi – S/he wants to travel by night. **čnes nectelsi, kʷes nectelsi**

qum – go/travel away from water; go into open country; go to places far from water; go to a place with no water.
qumšlš – S/he went away from water. **čn qumšlš, kʷ qumšlš**
es qumšlši – S/he is going away from water. **čnes qumšlši, kʷes qumšlši**
qs qumšlši – S/he is going to go away from water. **čiqs qumšlši, kʷqs qumšlši**

qumšlšsts – S/he made s.o. go away from water. **qumšlšstn, qumšlšstxʷ**
es qumšlšms – S/he is is making s.o. go away from water. **ies qumšlšm, as qumšlšm**
qs qumšlšms – S/he is going to make s.o. go away from water. **iqs qumšlšm, aqs qumšlšm**

qumšlšskʷ – Make him/her go away from water.

qʷmep – move off as a group; start the move; group journey. *See:* ***move.***

qéclš – run of an individual; run leisurely. *See:* ***run.***

nʔax̣ʷt – go downriver by land; go downhill over a long distance. *See:* ***downstream.***

x̣eɬ – invite to go; invite to travel to someplace. *See:* ***invite.***

tray

snčɬʔíʔiɬntn – little table; dinner tray. *prefix:* ***sn...*** *– a place of; suffix:* ***...tin, ...tn*** *– means of/device.*

treasure

q̓ix̣tm – cherish something or someone; fond of something possessed; treasure something or someone; show respect by cherishing a gift. *See:* ***cherish.***

tree

es šiť – tree. *rt.:* ***šiť*** *– standing upright. See:* ***stand.***
štičṅ – tree on a cliff. *suffix:* ***...ičṅ*** *– back.*

ċlċil – trees. *rt.:* ***ċil*** *– standing upright.*

nċlilš – go through trees. *suffix:* ***...ilš*** *– autonomous.*
nċlilš – S/he/it went through trees. **čn nċlilš, kʷ nċlilš**
es nċlilši – S/he/it is going through trees. **čnes nċlilši, kʷes nċlilši**
qs nċlilši – S/he/it is going to go through trees. **čiqs nċlilši, kʷqs nċlilši**

snčmaqn – top of the tree; top of the head. *rt.:* ***čm*** *– extremity.*

snɬčalqʷ – tip of the tree.

yul – thick tree; dense trees.

q̓ʷéllš – dead tree.

apɬsálqʷ – apple tree; applewood.

qľalqʷ – green wood (not dry).

es ṗin – log; bunch of logs; piled wood.

tree snag

čéyeʔ – dead tree; wood dry with age; snag.

nq̓aw̓pqin – The tree top broke. *suffix:* ***...qin, ...qn*** *– top.*
es nq̓aw̓qin – The tree top is broken.

tree stump

nx̣ʷx̣ʷċu – tree stump.

triangle **čnšni –** triangle.
es čnšni – It is triangular.

tribe **nk̓ʷélixʷ –** one people.
snk̓ʷélixʷ – tribesman; family; people; those who live in the same place.

stmelixʷ łu aslax̣t – What tribe is your friend from?

tribesman **snk̓ʷélixʷ –** fellow people.
snkʷsqelixʷ – fellow people; fellow human beings. *prefix:* ***nkʷł... –*** *together with.*
snkʷsqltmixʷ – fellow man. *prefix:* ***nkʷł... –*** *together with.*
snkʷsmʔem – fellow woman. *prefix:* ***nkʷł... –*** *together with.*
snkʷsixʷ – sibling; brother, sister, cousin. *prefix:* ***nkʷł... –*** *together with.*

trick **sl̓pstem –** play a trick on someone; cause someone to get confused. *rt.:* ***sil̓ –*** *confuse.*
sl̓pstes – S/he/it played a trick on s.o. **sl̓psten, sl̓pstexʷ**
es sl̓pstes – S/he/it is playing a trick on s.o. **es sl̓psten, es sl̓pstexʷ**
qs sl̓pstes – S/he/it is going to play a trick on s.o. **qs sl̓psten, qs sl̓pstexʷ**

qʷṅečstm – cause someone to have a hard time; play a trick on someone. *rt.:* ***qʷṅqʷiṅt –*** *pitiful, poor; suffix:* ***...ečst, ...čst –*** *of the hand.*
qʷṅečstmis – S/he/it made s.o. have a hard time. **qʷṅečstmn, qʷṅečstmntxʷ**
es qʷṅečstms – S/he/it is making s.o. have a hard time. **ies qʷṅečstm, as qʷṅečstm**
qs qʷṅečstms – S/he/it is going to make s.o. have a hard time. **iqs qʷṅečstm, aqs qʷṅečstm**
qʷṅéʔečstmis – They made s.o. have a hard time. **qeʔ qʷṅečstmntm, qʷṅečstmntp**
es qʷṅéʔečstms – They are making s.o. have a hard time. **qeʔes qʷṅečstm, es qʷṅečstmp**
qs qʷṅéʔečstms – They are going to make s.o. have a hard time. **qeʔqs qʷṅečstm, qs qʷṅečstmp**

qʷṅečstumn – someone who causes others to have a hard time.

qʷo qʷṅečstmntm – I was made to have a hard time.

trim **k̓ʷłx̣ʷic –** trim off. *rt.:* ***x̣ʷic –*** *cut bunches.*

trip **čt̓ppšin,** *čt̓ppši* **–** trip; stub a toe.
čt̓ppšin – S/he tripped. **čn čt̓ppšin, kʷ čt̓ppšin**
es čt̓ppšnmi – S/he is tripping. **čnes čt̓ppšnmi, kʷes čt̓ppšnmi**
qs čt̓ppšnmi – S/he is going to trip. **čiqs čt̓ppšnmi, kʷqs čt̓ppšnmi**

čt̓št̓špšnemn – clumsy; one inclined to trip. *suffix:* ***...emn –*** *one inclined to do.*

tripod **es ċalx̣ʷ –** poles lashed together.
čełċalx̣ʷ – tripod; three poles lashed together. *rt.:* ***ċalx̣ʷ –*** *poles lashed together.*

trot **cilšlš –** trot (man, horse, animal). *suffix:* ***...ilš –*** *autonomous.*
es cilšlši – S/he/it is trotting. **čnes cilšlši, kʷes cilšlši**
es cíʔilšlši – They are trotting. **qeʔes cilšlši, pes cilšlši**

pq̇smi – gallop. *See:* ***gallop.***

trouble **ƛ̓éṁscut –** get one's self in trouble.
ƛ̓éṁscut – S/he/it got in trouble. **čn ƛ̓éṁscut, kʷ ƛ̓éṁscut**
es ƛ̓éṁscuti – S/he/it is getting in trouble. **čnes ƛ̓éṁscuti, kʷes ƛ̓éṁscuti**
qs ƛ̓éṁscuti – S/he/it is going to get in trouble. **čiqs ƛ̓éṁscuti, kʷqs ƛ̓éṁscuti**
ƛ̓éṁscúʔut – They got in trouble. **qeʔ ƛ̓éṁscut, p ƛ̓éṁscut**

The **i** following uvular consonants (UC) and the glottal stop ʔ sound like English "*ey*" as in the words *they, hey, whey,* etc. Salish UC are: **q, q̇, qʷ, q̇ʷ, x̣, x̣ʷ**. For example, the suffix **...qin** – head/top, is often spelled using English *ey* as "q*ey*n". So **qi, q̇i, qʷi, q̇ʷi, x̣i, x̣ʷi**, may be spelled with English *ey* as **q***ey*, **q̇***ey*, **qʷ***ey*, **q̇ʷ***ey*, **x̣***ey*, **x̣ʷ***ey* in other texts.

s.t. - something, the 3rd person
(s.t.) - something implied
s.o. - someone, the 3rd person
sl. - singular form
pl. - plural form
rt. - root word
cmd. - command
lit. - literally
fig. - figuratively
i.e., - for example
See: - Redirection to a related word.

es ƛ̓émscúʔuti – They are getting in trouble. **qeʔes ƛ̓émscuti, pes ƛ̓émscuti**
qs ƛ̓émscúʔuti – They are going to get in trouble. **qeʔqs ƛ̓émscuti, pqs ƛ̓émscuti**

qeʔ ƛ̓emłult – S/he got us in trouble. **ƛ̓émstumt** – They got you in trouble.

xʷéẏt – in trouble.
xʷéẏt – S/he is in trouble. **čn xʷéẏt, kʷ xʷéẏt**

ṅem qeʔ xʷéẏt – We will be in trouble. **hayo hoy qeʔ xʷéẏt čłx̣ʷlq̓ʷenʔen x̣stéẏẏeʔ** – Oh no! Now we are in trouble, I ran over a skunk.

tx̣ʷmscut, *tx̣ʷmscú* – make one's self do right. *See:* ***right.***

yéṁmist, *yéṁm* – despaired; frustrated; troubled; worried; have a block; have a dilemma. *See:* ***despair.***

trousers

snołups, *snołu* – pants, trousers. *See:* ***pants.***

trout

pisł – westslope cutthroat trout; *Oncorhynchus clarkii lewisi. See:* ***cutthroat trout.***

aáycčst, *aáy* – bull trout; Dolly Varden trout; *Salvelinus confluentus. See:* ***bull trout.***

sttṁáẏl̓qs, *sttṁá* – bullhead trout; brown trout; *Salmo trutta. See:* ***brown trout.***

nxʷmeneʔ – steelhead salmon; rainbow trout; *Oncorhynchus mykiss. (native to the area of the Spokane tribe; lit. red/pink around the ears)*

łxʷxʷiups – lake trout; *Salvelinus namaycush.*

łkʷikʷẏu – small trout species.
ččiw̓eʔ – small trout species.

trout-perch

c̓qc̓iq – trout-perch; *Percopsis omiscomaycus.*

truck

snukʷʔukʷmn, *snukʷʔu* – truck; pickup truck.

true

unéxʷ, *uné* – real; true; yes.
tam unéxʷ – false.

unéxʷ l šeẏ u ec̓x̣i – That's how it really was.

uṅexʷist – truthful; being real.
uṅexʷist – S/he was truthful. **čn uṅexʷist, kʷ uṅexʷist**
es uṅexʷisti – S/he is being truthful. **čnes uṅexʷisti, kʷes uṅexʷisti**
qs uṅexʷisti – S/he is going to be truthful. **čiqs uṅexʷisti, kʷqs uṅexʷisti**

uṅuṅexʷist – really/truly do something. *See:* ***do.***

ha kʷes unéxʷisti – Are you telling the truth?

i tóx̣ʷ – It is straight, true. *See:* ***straight.***
qʷo ṁéẏełt łu i tóx̣ʷ – Tell me straight, tell me the truth.

we – really; was; even though. *evidential particle expressing that the statement is unsupported by the apparent condition or situation.*
we čnes ayx̣ʷti – I really am tired. **we čn xʷuy č ancitxʷ u kʷ čuw** – I really went to your house and you were gone. **tam we es itši** – S/he really is not sleeping. **t tlé u we qeʔes olqʷšiłls u áyx̣ʷt u hoysts** – Teresa really was helping us, but she got tired and quit. **ma še we cuncn epł t̓it̓éẏe sṫmṫṁa** – See, I told you there are a lot of mean cows. **q̇mq̇míʔi we eł iáʔa** – They talked together when they met again. **we cun** – Really, I did tell him/her/it.

trunk

snt̓qálscutn, *snt̓qálscu* – trunk; suitcase.

sčṫemp – tree trunk.
es čṫmepleʔ – bottom/stem of a tree/plant/post. *suffix: **...épleʔ** – permanence.*
es čṫmmepleʔ – stems *(of a plant or flower)*. *suffix: **...épleʔ** – permanence.*
es čṫmṫmepleʔ – trunks *(of a tree)*. *suffix: **...épleʔ** – permanence.*

sčṫemps ci es šiṫ – that tree's trunk. **es čṫmmepleʔ ci sċéʔekʷ** – stems of flowers.
es čṫmṫmepleʔ ci ċlċil – trunks of trees.

sqltčalqʷ – tree trunk; body of the tree. *rt.: **qeltč** – meat, body; suffix: **...alqʷ** – wood; cylindical.*

The **i** following uvular consonants (UC) and the glottal stop **ʔ** sound like English "*ey*" as in the words th*ey*, h*ey*, wh*ey*, etc. Salish UC are: **q**, **q̓**, **qʷ**, **q̓ʷ**, **x̣**, **x̣ʷ**. For example, the suffix **...qin** – head/top, is often spelled using English *ey* as "q*ey*n". So **qi**, **q̓i**, **qʷi**, **q̓ʷi**, **x̣i**, **x̣ʷi**, may be spelled with English *ey* as **q***ey*, **q̓***ey*, **qʷ***ey*, **q̓ʷ***ey*, **x̣***ey*, **x̣ʷ***ey* in other texts.

trust

ṫkʷels – trust. *rt.: **ṫukʷ** – place; suffix: **...els, ...ls** – want, feel.*
ṫkʷelsis – S/he/it trusted s.o. **ṫkʷelsn, ṫkʷelsntxʷ**
es ṫkʷelsms – S/he/it is trusting s.o. **ies ṫkʷelsm, as ṫkʷelsm**
qs ṫkʷelsms – S/he/it is going to trust s.o. **iqs ṫkʷelsm, aqs ṫkʷelsm**

ṫkʷlscut – S/he/it trusted in one's self. **čn ṫkʷlscut, kʷ ṫkʷlscut**
es ṫkʷlscuti – S/he/it is trusting in one's self. **ies ṫkʷlscuti, as ṫkʷlscuti**
qs ṫkʷlscuti – S/he/it is going to trust in one's self. **iqs ṫkʷlscuti, aqs ṫkʷlscuti**

ṫkʷlscutš – Trust in yourself. *cmd.*
ṫkʷelsntxʷ – Trust him/her/it. *cmd.*
ṫkʷelsmsts – S/he/it made s.o. trust. **ṫkʷelsmstn, ṫkʷelsmstxʷ**

ta qes ṫkʷelsmstxʷ łu anšmen – Do not trust your enemy. **ta ies ṫkʷelsm łu isxʷqʷlqʷelt še čmi u čnes ṫkʷlscuti** – I do not trust my lawyer; I only trust myself.

nkʷtnelsm – think highly of somebody; show respect for somebody; have trust for somebody. *See: **respect**.*

čheṁm – allowed to use something of someones; trusted with something.
čheṁm – S/he was trusted. **čn čheṁm, kʷ čheṁm**

try

k̓ʷéṅ – try; sample; attempt; show out; make attention to.
k̓ʷéṅm – S/he/it tried. **čn k̓ʷéṅm, kʷ k̓ʷéṅm**
es k̓ʷéṅi – S/he/it is trying. **čnes k̓ʷéṅi, kʷes k̓ʷéṅi**
qs k̓ʷéṅi – S/he/it is going to try. **čiqs k̓ʷéṅi, kʷqs k̓ʷéṅi**
k̓ʷéʔeṅm – They tried. **qeʔ k̓ʷéṅm, p k̓ʷéṅm**
es k̓ʷéʔeṅi – They are trying. **qeʔes k̓ʷéṅi, pes k̓ʷéṅi**
qs k̓ʷéʔeṅi – They are going to try. **qeʔqs k̓ʷéṅi, pqs k̓ʷéṅi**

k̓ʷéṅis – S/he/it tried s.t. **k̓ʷéṅn, k̓ʷéṅntxʷ**
es k̓ʷéṅms – S/he/it is trying s.t. **ies k̓ʷéṅm, as k̓ʷéṅm**
qs k̓ʷéṅms – S/he/it is going to try s.t. **iqs k̓ʷéṅm, aqs k̓ʷéṅm**
k̓ʷéʔeṅis – They tried s.t. **qeʔ k̓ʷéṅntm, k̓ʷéṅntp**
es k̓ʷéʔeṅms – They are trying s.t. **qeʔes k̓ʷéṅm, es k̓ʷéṅmp**
qs k̓ʷéʔeṅms – They are going to try s.t. **qeʔqs k̓ʷéṅm, qs k̓ʷéṅmp**

es łk̓ʷek̓ʷṅi – S/he/it is trying. **čnes łk̓ʷek̓ʷṅi, kʷes łk̓ʷek̓ʷṅi**
es łk̓ʷek̓ʷṅms – S/he/it is trying s.t. **ies łk̓ʷek̓ʷṅm, as łk̓ʷek̓ʷṅm**

k̓ʷeṅnt – Try it. *(i.e., food, drink, dance, etc.) cmd.*
łk̓ʷek̓ʷṅt – Try a little of it. *(i.e., food, drink, dance, etc.) cmd.*
k̓ʷéṅš – show for inspection; show out; exhibit for sampling. *See: **show**.*
k̓ʷṅšmist – attempt; make a personal attempt. *See: **attempt**.*
k̓ʷṅk̓ʷeṅ – try out something. *See: **try out**.*
k̓ʷaṅmaqs – taste food. *See: **taste**.*

s.t. - something, the 3rd person
(s.t.) - something implied
s.o. - someone, the 3rd person
sl. - singular form
pl. - plural form
rt. - root word
cmd. - command
lit. - literally
fig. - figuratively
i.e., - for example
See: - Redirection to a related word.

nk̓ʷéṅkʷ – taste liquid. *See: **taste**.*

ułeʔ eł k̓ʷeṅnt – Try it again. **es k̓ʷéṅms qs xʷisti –** S/he is trying to walk. **ha aqs k̓ʷeṅm –** Are you going to try it? **k̓ʷéṅis qs kʷnems –** S/he tried to take it. **k̓ʷéṅn čiqs x̣esti –** I tried to be good.

k̓ʷéṅcn – try to say something.
k̓ʷéṅcnm – S/he/it tried to say. **čn k̓ʷéṅcnm, kʷ k̓ʷéṅcnm**
es k̓ʷéṅcni – S/he/it is trying to say. **čnes k̓ʷéṅcni, kʷes k̓ʷéṅcni**
qs k̓ʷéṅcni – S/he/it is going to try to say. **čiqs k̓ʷéṅcni, kʷqs k̓ʷéṅcni**

k̓ʷéṅcis – S/he/it tried to say s.t. **k̓ʷéṅcn, k̓ʷéṅcntxʷ**
es k̓ʷéṅcnms – S/he/it is trying to say s.t. **ies k̓ʷéṅcnm, as k̓ʷéṅcnm**
qs k̓ʷéṅcnms – S/he/it is going to try to say s.t. **iqs k̓ʷéṅcnm, aqs k̓ʷéṅcnm**

k̓ʷéṅcnt – Try to say it. *cmd.*

nk̓ʷéṅm – choose; pick; select; show the selection.
nk̓ʷéṅm – S/he/it selected. **čn nk̓ʷéṅm, kʷ nk̓ʷéṅm**
nk̓ʷéʔeṅm – They selected. **qeʔ nk̓ʷéṅm, p nk̓ʷéṅm**

nk̓ʷéṅis – S/he/it choose s.t./s.o. **nk̓ʷéṅn, nk̓ʷéṅntxʷ**
es nk̓ʷéṅms – S/he/it is choosing s.t./s.o. **ies nk̓ʷéṅm as nk̓ʷéṅm**
qs nk̓ʷéṅms – S/he/it is going to choose s.t./s.o. **iqs nk̓ʷéṅm aqs nk̓ʷéṅm**
nk̓ʷéʔeṅis – They choose s.t./s.o. **qeʔ nk̓ʷéṅntm, nk̓ʷéṅntp**
es nk̓ʷéʔeṅms – They are choosing s.t./s.o. **qeʔes nk̓ʷéṅm es nk̓ʷéṅmp**
qs nk̓ʷéʔeṅms – They are going to choose s.t./s.o. **qeʔqs nk̓ʷéṅm qs nk̓ʷéṅmp**

scnk̓ʷéṅ – something that's been chosen/selected. *prefix: **sc...** – s.t. that's been done/made/prepared.*

nk̓ʷéṅnt – Select it. *cmd.*
nk̓ʷnšmist – appoint; make a personal choice. *See: **appoint**.*

ṅem nk̓ʷéṅm – S/he/it will select. **ṅem čn nk̓ʷéṅm, ṅem kʷ nk̓ʷéṅm**
ṅem nk̓ʷéʔeṅm – They will select. **ṅem qeʔ nk̓ʷéṅm, ṅem p nk̓ʷéṅm**

ṅem nk̓ʷéṅis – S/he/it will select it. **ṅem nk̓ʷéṅn, ṅem nk̓ʷéṅntxʷ**
ṅem qs nk̓ʷéṅms – S/he will be selecting s.t./s.o. **ṅem iqs nk̓ʷéṅm, ṅem aqs nk̓ʷéṅm**
ṅem qes nk̓ʷéṅms – S/he should be selecting s.t./s.o. **ṅem qeʔqes nk̓ʷéṅm, ṅem qes nk̓ʷéṅmp**
ṅem nk̓ʷéʔeṅis – They will select it. **ṅem qeʔ nk̓ʷéṅntm, ṅem nk̓ʷéṅntp**

ṅem steṁ nk̓ʷeṅis t smx̣e – What will Grizzly pick? **wis nk̓ʷeṅis łu smx̣e u ecščeṅm –** What happens after Grizzly finishes picking?

ax̣lmist – try at something; put effort into something.
sʔax̣lmist – the effort of something.

t sʔax̣lmist u ta čis xʷuy – Because of the weather I did not go.

try hard

yoyoscut, *yoyoscú* **–** do something with a physically strong effort.
yoyoscut – S/he tried hard. **čn yoyoscut, kʷ yoyoscut**
es yoyoscuti – S/he is trying hard. **čnes yoyoscuti, kʷes yoyoscuti**
qs yoyoscuti – S/he is going to try hard. **čiqs yoyoscuti, kʷqs yoyoscuti**
es yoyoscúʔuti – They are trying hard. **qeʔes yoyoscuti, pes yoyoscuti**

čyoyoscutmis – S/he/it worked hard at it. **čyoyoscutmn, čyoyoscutmntxʷ**
es čyoyoscutms – S/he/it is working hard at it. **ies čyoyoscutm, as čyoyoscutm**
qs čyoyoscutms – S/he/it is going to work hard at it. **iqs čyoyoscutm, aqs čyoyoscutm**
čyoyoscúʔutmis – They worked hard at it. **qeʔ čyoyoscutmntm, čyoyoscutmntp**

es čyoyoscúˀutms – They are working hard at it. **qeˀes čyoyoscutm, es čyoyoscutmp**

čyoyoscutmnt – Do it hard, work hard at it. *cmd.*
yoyoscut m cq̓mint – Throw it hard. *cmd.*
yoyoscq̓mint – Throw it hard. *cmd.*

q̓ʷiɫ – energy; motivation; internal drive. *See:* ***capable.***

q̓ʷiɫmist, *q̓ʷiɫmi* – do one's best; try hard from energy. *See:* ***capable.***

sičstmist – do one's best; try hard from ability. *See:* ***capable.***

čmaqs – perform at the peak of one's ability; best at something; pinnacle. *See:* ***best.***

musčst – do one's best with hope of succeeding; do something with confidence. *See:* ***confident.***

aytčst – strive; exert one's self in work. *See:* ***strive.***

> The **i** following uvular consonants (UC) and the glottal stop **ˀ** sound like English "*ey*" as in the words th*ey*, h*ey*, wh*ey*, etc. Salish UC are: **q, q̓, qʷ, q̓ʷ, x̣, x̣ʷ**. For example, the suffix ...**qin** – head/top, is often spelled using English *ey* as "q*ey*n". So **qi, q̓i, qʷi, q̓ʷi, x̣i, x̣ʷi,** may be spelled with English *ey* as **q***ey*, **q̓***ey*, **qʷ***ey*, **q̓ʷ***ey*, **x̣***ey*, **x̣ʷ***ey* in other texts.

try out

k̓ʷṅk̓ʷeṅ – try out something.
k̓ʷṅk̓ʷéṅis – S/he/it tried s.t. out. **k̓ʷṅk̓ʷéṅn, k̓ʷṅk̓ʷéṅntxʷ**
es k̓ʷéṅms – S/he/it is trying s.t. out. **ies k̓ʷṅk̓ʷéṅm, as k̓ʷṅk̓ʷéṅm**
qs k̓ʷéṅms – S/he/it is going to try s.t. out. **iqs k̓ʷṅk̓ʷéṅm, aqs k̓ʷṅk̓ʷéṅm**

k̓ʷṅk̓ʷeṅnt – Try it out. *(i.e., food, dance, etc.) cmd.*

tub

snċuˀċaw̓lštn, *snċuˀċa* – bathtub; tub. *prefix:* ***sn...*** *– a place of; suffix:* ***...tin, ...tn*** *– means of/device.*

snnqʷˀetkʷ, *snnqʷˀe* – washer tub; tub. *prefix:* ***sn...*** *– a place of; suffix:* ***...etkʷ, ...tkʷ*** *– liquid*

tube

nox̣ʷmin – inner tube.

Tuesday

aslásq̓t, *aslá* – Tuesday; two days; i.e., two days past Sunday. *suffix:* ***...asq̓t*** *– sky, day.*
eɫ tiw̓ɫ aslásq̓t – Again, another Tuesday is here.
eɫ aslásq̓t – It is Tuesday again.

tule

syeyiqn – tule reed mat. *rt.:* ***yey*** *– cross weave.*

tundra swan

spqmi – swan; tundra swan; whistling swan.

turkey

nšlšaltáqs, *nšlšaltá* – turkey. *lit. it has a hanging nose. rt.:* ***šal*** *– suspended.*

turkey vulture

cáqʷuyeˀ – buzzard, vulture.

turn

p̓il̓č – turn something over.
p̓l̓čm̓im – S/he/it turned over (s.t.). **čn p̓l̓čm̓im, kʷ p̓l̓čm̓im**
es p̓l̓čm̓i – S/he/it is turning over (s.t.). **čnes p̓l̓čm̓i, kʷes p̓l̓čm̓i**
qs p̓l̓čm̓i – S/he/it is going to turn over (s.t.). **čiqs p̓l̓čm̓i, kʷqs p̓l̓čm̓i**
es p̓l̓čm̓íˀi – They are turning over (s.t.). **qeˀes p̓l̓čm̓i, pes p̓l̓čm̓i**

p̓l̓čm̓stes – S/he/it turned s.t./s.o. over. **p̓l̓čm̓sten, p̓l̓čm̓stexʷ**
es p̓l̓čims – S/he/it is turning s.t./s.o. over. **ies p̓l̓čim, as p̓l̓čim**
qs p̓l̓čims – S/he/it is going to turn s.t./s.o. over. **iqs p̓l̓čim, aqs p̓l̓čim**
p̓l̓čm̓stéˀes – They turned s.t./s.o. over. **qeˀ p̓l̓čm̓stem, p̓l̓čm̓step**

es p̓l̓p̓l̓čm̓i – S/he/it is turning (s.t.) over and over. **čnes p̓l̓p̓l̓čm̓i, kʷes p̓l̓p̓l̓čm̓i**
es p̓l̓p̓l̓čims – S/he/it is turning s.t./s.o. over and over. **ies p̓l̓p̓l̓čim, as p̓l̓p̓l̓čim**

p̓lličč – It is turned over.

> s.t. - something, the 3rd person
> (s.t.) - something implied
> s.o. - someone, the 3rd person
> *sl.* - singular form
> *pl.* - plural form
> *rt.* - root word
> *cmd.* - command
> *lit.* - literally
> *fig.* - figuratively
> *i.e.,* - for example
> *See:* - Redirection to a related word.

ṗl̓čint – Turn it over. *cmd.*

ṗl̓ṗl̓čmstes łu sqéltč x̣ʷl̓ čełé x̣ʷa mus snčcnšncut – She is turning the meat over and over for three or four hours.

ṗl̓čus, *ṗl̓ču –* turn back; go back.
ṗl̓čus – S/he/it turned back. **čn ṗl̓čus, kʷ ṗl̓čus**
es ṗl̓čusi – S/he/it is turning back. **čnes ṗl̓čusi, kʷes ṗl̓čusi**
ṗl̓čúʔus – They turned back. **qeʔ ṗl̓čus, p ṗl̓čus**

ṗl̓čusts – S/he/it turned s.o. back. **ṗl̓čustn, ṗl̓čustxʷ**
es ṗl̓čusms – S/he/it is turning s.o. back. **ies ṗl̓čusm, as ṗl̓čusm**

ṗl̓čsemn – one inclined to turn back.

ṗl̓čqnwexʷ – turn away from each other.

eł ṗl̓čúʔus – They went back. **eł cṗl̓čus –** S/he/it came back. **še eł ṗl̓čúʔus –** They turned back.
eł ṗl̓čus – It turned back.

ṗl̓čmncut, *ṗl̓čmncu –* turn one's self over; turn one's self back; expression indicating defeat.
ṗl̓čmncut – S/he/it turned over/back around. **čn ṗl̓čmncut, kʷ ṗl̓čmncut**
es ṗl̓čmncuti – S/he/it is turning over/back around. **čnes ṗl̓čmncuti, kʷes ṗl̓čmncuti**
qs ṗl̓čmncuti – S/he/it is going to turn over/back around. **čiqs ṗl̓čmncuti, kʷqs ṗl̓čmncuti**

ṗl̓čmncutš – Turn over/back around. *cmd.*

ṗl̓ṗl̓čłq̇eẏmin – turn pages in a book.
ṗl̓ṗl̓čłq̇eẏim – S/he turned pages. **čn ṗl̓ṗl̓čłq̇eẏim, kʷ ṗl̓ṗl̓čłq̇eẏim**
es ṗl̓ṗl̓čłq̇eẏmi – S/he is turning pages. **čnes ṗl̓ṗl̓čłq̇eẏmi, kʷes ṗl̓ṗl̓čłq̇eẏmi**
qs ṗl̓ṗl̓čłq̇eẏmi – S/he is going to turn pages. **čiqs ṗl̓ṗl̓čłq̇eẏmi, kʷqs ṗl̓ṗl̓čłq̇eẏmi**

ṗl̓čłq̇eẏiš – Turn the page. *cmd.*

nisaqm – turn off the path/road.
nisaqm – S/he/it turned off the path. **čn nisaqm, kʷ nisaqm**

łu čn nisaqm u čn oost – I turned off the path and got lost. **ta kʷ qes nisaqm –** Do not turn off the path.

nmnčim – turn one's back to someone or something.
nmnčmstes – S/he turned one's back to s.o. **nmnčmsten, nmnčmstexʷ**
es nmnčims – S/he is turning one's back to s.o. **ies nmnčim, as nmnčim**
qs nmnčims – S/he is going to turn one's back to s.o. **iqs nmnčim, aqs nmnčim**

nmnčmnwexʷ – turn back to back with each other.

nmlčičṅ – turn one's back in anger to someone. *suffix:* ***...ičṅ*** *– back.*
nmlčičis – S/he turned one's back in anger to s.o. **nmlčičn, nmlčičntxʷ**
es nmlčičṅms – S/he is turning one's back in anger to s.o. **ies nmlčičṅm, as nmlčičṅm**

nplus – turn the face/head. *rt.:* ***plutm*** *– dodge.*
nplusis – S/he turned s.o.'s head. **nplusn, nplusntxʷ**
es nplusms – S/he is turning s.o.'s head. **ies nplusm, as nplusm**
qs nplusms – S/he is going to turn s.o.'s head. **iqs nplusm, aqs nplusm**

sxʷnplusm – one tasked to turn heads; chiropractor.

člʔont – Turn something on. *cmd.*
člʔontes – S/he/it turned it on. **člʔonten, člʔontexʷ**

čl̓ʔonté̓ʔes – They turned it on. **qeʔ čl̓ʔontem, čl̓ʔontep**
čl̓ʔont asnɬk̓ʷɬk̓ʷɬsncutn – Turn on your computer.

čulus – light up; turn something on; ignite. *See: **light**.*
čulusnt ci ċék̓ʷsšṅ – Turn the light on.

ɬeps – extinguish a fire; turn off a light or electrical appliance. *See: **put out**.*
ɬepsnt ci ċék̓ʷsšṅ – turn off the light.

plutm – dodge/duck away from something. *See: **dodge**.*

ntax̣ʷlús – face toward some direction. *suffix: **...us** – face. See: **face**.*

šlčmncut – make one's self turn around/on an axis. *See: **around**.*

nčcnšncut – make a complete revolution; make a circle; meet one's own footprints/tracks. *See: **around**.*

nʔemɬtumš – wait for people; wait for a turn. *See: **wait**.*

čx̣ʷlx̣ʷolq̓ʷm – turn a bolt or similar object.

čɬk̓ʷel̓č – turn a rigid container type object upside-down on a flat surface *; roll/tip over. (i.e., car, hat, lid, etc.) See: **upside down**.*

The **i** following uvular consonants (UC) and the glottal stop ʔ sound like English "*ey*" as in the words *they*, *hey*, *whey*, etc. Salish UC are: **q**, **q̓**, **qʷ**, **q̓ʷ**, **x̣**, **x̣ʷ**. For example, the suffix ...**qin** – head/top, is often spelled using English *ey* as "q*ey*n". So **qi**, **q̓i**, **qʷi**, **q̓ʷi**, **x̣i**, **x̣ʷi**, may be spelled with English *ey* as **q***ey*, **q̓***ey*, **qʷ***ey*, **q̓ʷ***ey*, **x̣***ey*, **x̣ʷ***ey* in other texts.

turtle
sp̓l̓q̓ʷáqs, *sp̓l̓q̓ʷá* – turtle; *Chrysemys picta*.

Turtle Lake
čɬqq̓liʔ – Turtle Lake; a lake in northeastern Flathead Nation near Flathead Lake. *lit. a small lake.*

TV
snʔacċx̣tn – show house; drive-in; TV; movie screen. *prefix: **sn...** – a place of; suffix: **...tin, ...tn** – means of/device.*

nƛ̓x̣cin – loud in singing or talking; make loud noises. *See: **loud**.*

tweezers
lqpesncutn, *lqpesncu* – tweezers.

twenty
eslʔupn, *eslʔu* – twenty.

Twin Buttes
ɬmq̓ʷmóq̓ʷ, *ɬmq̓ʷmó* – Twin Buttes, near Ronan, Flathead Nation.

Twin Lakes
čɬesél̓ čɬq̓iʔq̓l̓i – Twin Lakes in the Jocko drainage, Flathead Nation. *lit. two small lakes.*

twins
ṅésselm – twins.

sncʔeẇs – twin; brother or sister. *suffix: **...éẇs** – in between, middle.*

twirl
šllčmncutist – spin or twirl one's self. *See: **spin**.*

twist
ṫuṗ – twist something together.
ṫuṗ – S/he twisted (s.t.). **čn ṫuṗ, kʷ ṫuṗ**
es ṫuṗi – S/he is twisting (s.t.). **čnes ṫuṗi, kʷes ṫuṗi**
qs ṫuṗi – S/he is going to twist (s.t.). **čiqs ṫuṗi, kʷqs ṫuṗi**

ṫuṗis – S/he twisted s.t. **ṫuṗn, ṫuṗntxʷ**
es ṫuṗms – S/he is twisting s.t. **ies ṫuṗm, as ṫuṗm**
qs ṫuṗms – S/he is going to twist s.t. **iqs ṫuṗm, aqs ṫuṗm**

ṫuṗnt – Twist s.t. together. *cmd.*

s.t. - something, the 3rd person
(s.t.) - something implied
s.o. - someone, the 3rd person
sl. - singular form
pl. - plural form
rt. - root word
cmd. - command
lit. - literally
fig. - figuratively
i.e., - for example
See: - Redirection to a related word.

t̓óp – twist into thread.
t̓ópis – S/he twisted s.t. into thread. **t̓ópn, t̓ópntxʷ**
es t̓ópms – S/he is twisting s.t. into thread. **ies t̓ópm, as t̓ópm**
qs t̓ópms – S/he is going to twist s.t. into thread. **iqs t̓ópm, aqs t̓ópm**

st̓ópqs – thread.

t̓ópnt – Twist s.t. into thread. *cmd.*

y̓eluʔ – twist.
y̓elwis – S/he twisted s.t. **y̓elwn, y̓elwntxʷ**
es y̓elwms – S/he is twisting s.t. **ies y̓elwm, as y̓elwm**
qs y̓elwms – S/he is going to twist s.t. **iqs y̓elwm, aqs y̓elwm**

y̓alqʷ – twisted wood; tree that grows twisted.

q̓ʷʔe – wring; twist; squeeze. *See:* ***wring.***

two

esél – two. **esʔesél** – twos. *pl.*
upn eł esél – twelve.
čsel – two people.

esl... – *prefix indicating two combined with another affix forming a full word.*
aslásq̓t – two days. *suffix:* ***...asq̓t** – sky, day.*
eslełxʷ – two houses. *suffix:* ***...ełxʷ, ...łxʷ** – house.*
nʔeslep – two eggs. *circumfix:* ***n...ep** – egg.*
esléssn̓ – two rocks. *suffix:* ***...essn̓, ...ssn̓** – rock.*

esl... – *prefix indicating two added to a whole word.*
eslʔupn – twenty, two tens.
aslšƛ̓ip – S/he lost two times. **čn aslšƛ̓ip, kʷ aslšƛ̓ip**
aslsqáx̣eʔ, *aslsqá* – two domestic animals or cars.
eslʔopnčstqn – two thousand.

two hundred

esélnk̓ʷoʔqín, *esélnk̓ʷoʔqí* – two hundred.

two-year-old

słesl̓spéntč, *słesl̓spé* – little two-year-old (horse).

type

nq̓ey̓im – type.

ƛ̓áx̣t snq̓ey̓mintn – typewriter. *suffix:* ***...tin, ...tn** – means of/device.*

U

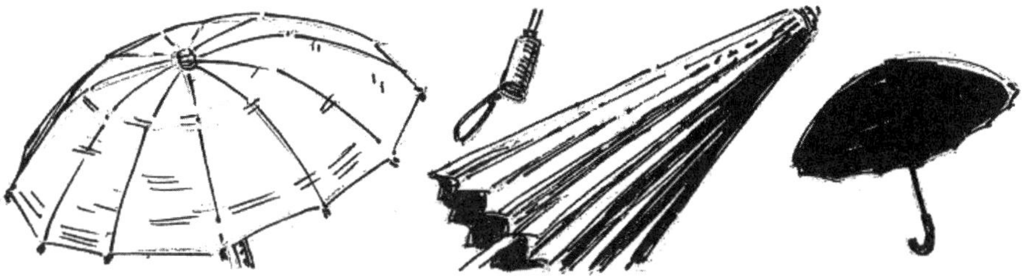

ugly **kʷuskʷst –** ugly; scary looking.

kʷuskʷst – S/he is an ugly person *(did s.t. bad).* **čn kʷuskʷst, kʷ kʷuskʷst**

nkʷskʷstelsm – S/he was being ugly. **čn nkʷskʷstelsm, kʷ nkʷskʷstelsm**
es nkʷskʷstelsi – S/he is being ugly. **čnes nkʷskʷstelsi, kʷes nkʷskʷstelsi**
qs nkʷskʷstelsi – S/he is going to be ugly. **čiqs nkʷskʷstelsi, kʷqs nkʷskʷstelsi**
nkʷskʷstéʔelsm – They were being ugly. **qeʔ nkʷskʷstelsm, p nkʷskʷstelsm**

nkʷskʷstelsmis – S/he was being ugly to s.o. **nkʷskʷstelsmn, nkʷskʷstelsmntxw**
es nkʷskʷstelsms – S/he is being ugly to s.o. **ies nkʷskʷstelsm, as nkʷskʷstelsm**
qs nkʷskʷstelsms – S/he is going to be ugly to s.o. **iqs nkʷskʷstelsm, aqs nkʷskʷstelsm**
es nkʷskʷstéʔelsms – They are being ugly to s.o. **qeʔes nkʷskʷstelsm, es nkʷskʷstelsmmp**

es nkʷskʷsew̓si – S/he is being ugly among the people. **čnes nkʷskʷsew̓si, kʷes nkʷskʷsew̓si**

kʷskʷsus – S/he has an ugly face. **čn kʷskʷsus, kʷ kʷskʷsus**

ta kʷ qes nkʷskʷselš – Do not be ugly. **kʷuskʷst łišeʔ –** That's ugly.

č̓s… – *prefix indicating ugly; unsightly; bad.*
č̓sus – ugly face; unsightly face.
č̓sáłq – stink; bad smell.

t̓éyeʔ, *t̓e* – bad; evil; mean. *See:* ***bad.***

ulcer **es nłikʷłceʔ –** ulcer.

umbrella **čłč̓č̓ey̓mn –** umbrella. *rt.:* ***č̓ey*** *– shade.*

unaware **ta es miscutisti –** not know about something.

ta es miscutisti – S/he does not know anything (about it). **ta čnes miscutisti, ta kʷes miscutisti**

es šʔalqin – S/he was unaware s/he was making "final rounds" before dying. *(Said after death, in hindsight the person visited relatives, friends and old acquaintances; as if the person was saying their final farewells.)*

uncle **smamáʔ**, *sméʔł* – paternal uncle *(father's brother)*; man's nephew/niece *(brother's children).*

nunumeʔ, *nunu* – maternal uncle *(mother's brother)*; man's nephew/niece *(sister's children).*

łwéstn – aunt/uncle after death of connecting relative; stepparent.
słwélt – aunt/uncle after death of connecting relative.

uncover **čhem –** uncover; reveal.

čhmist – S/he revealed (s.t.). **čn čhmist, kʷ čhmist**
es čhmisti – S/he is revealing (s.t.). **čnes čhmisti, kʷes čhmisti**

s.t. - something, the 3rd person
(s.t.) - something implied
s.o. - someone, the 3rd person
sl. - singular form
pl. - plural form
rt. - root word
cmd. - command
lit. - literally
fig. - figuratively
i.e., - for example
See: - Redirection to a related word.

qs čhmisti – S/he is going to reveal (s.t.). **čiqs čhmisti, kʷqs čhmisti**

čhmscut – S/he revealed one's self. **čn čhmscut, kʷ čhmscut**
es čhmscuti – S/he is revealing one's self. **čnes čhmscuti, kʷes čhmscuti**
qs čhmscuti – S/he is going to reveal one's self. **čiqs čhmscuti, kʷqs čhmscuti**

čhntes – S/he revealed s.t. **čhnten, čhntexʷ**
es čhems – S/he is revealing s.t. **ies čhem, as čhem**
qs čhems – S/he is going to reveal s.t. **iqs čhem, aqs čhem**

čhent – Reveal it. *cmd.*
čłčhenʔent – Remove the coverings. *cmd.*

esččhusms – S/he is revealing s.o.'s eyes. **ies ččhusm, as ččhusm**
es čhposqni – S/he is revealing one's mouth. **čnes čhposqni, kʷes čhposqni**
es ččhqini – S/he is revealing one's head. **čnes ččhqini, kʷes ččhqini**
es čheɫxʷi – S/he is removing the lodge covering. **čnes čheɫxʷi, kʷes čheɫxʷi**
ččhiċeʔ – unwrap; remove wrapping to reveal. *See:* ***unwrap****.*
k̓ʷɫnčhepm – open a flap. *circumfix* ***k̓ʷɫn...p*** *–* ***opening****. See:* ***open****.*

čɫčhék̓ʷm – uncover something; separate the surface. *rt.:* ***čhék̓ʷ*** *– detach; prefix:* ***čɫ...*** *– surface.*
čɫčhék̓ʷis – S/he uncovered s.t. **čɫčhék̓ʷn, čɫčhék̓ʷntxʷ**
es čɫčhék̓ʷms – S/he is uncovering s.t. **ies čɫčhék̓ʷm, as čɫčhék̓ʷm**
qs čɫčhék̓ʷms – S/he is going to uncover s.t. **iqs čɫčhék̓ʷm, aqs čɫčhék̓ʷm**

čɫčhék̓ʷnt – Uncover it. *cmd.*

under **k̓ʷɫišut** – underneath; down below; under; beneath. *rt.:* ***išut*** *– down, low; prefix:* ***k̓ʷɫ...*** *– under.*
k̓ʷɫištétkʷ – under water.
ništétkʷ – deep water.
k̓ʷɫišta – slip for a dress.

k̓ʷɫišut l isoq̇me – It is under my buttocks.

k̓ʷɫʔuɫxʷ – go under something.
k̓ʷɫʔuɫxʷm – S/he/it went under (s.t.). **čn k̓ʷɫʔuɫxʷm, kʷ k̓ʷɫʔuɫxʷm**
es k̓ʷɫʔuɫxʷi – S/he/it is going under (s.t.). **čnes k̓ʷɫʔuɫxʷi, kʷes k̓ʷɫʔuɫxʷi**
qs k̓ʷɫʔuɫxʷi – S/he/it is going to go under (s.t.). **čiqs k̓ʷɫʔuɫxʷi, kʷqs k̓ʷɫʔuɫxʷi**
es k̓ʷɫpíʔilši – They are going under (s.t.). **qeʔes k̓ʷɫʔpilši, pes k̓ʷɫpilši**

k̓ʷɫʔuɫxʷš – Go under (s.t.). *cmd.*
k̓ʷɫpilšwi – All of you go under (s.t.). *cmd.*

qs k̓ʷɫʔuɫxʷi t snčɫeliɫntn – S/he is going to go under the table.

underarm **snčmáx̣n** – armpit. *See:* ***armpit****.*

underground **k̓ʷɫištulexʷ** – underground. *rt.:* ***išut*** *– down, low; prefix:* ***n...*** *– inside; suffix:* ***...ulexʷ*** *– land.*
ništulexʷ – in the ground. *rt.:* ***išut*** *– down, low; prefix:* ***n...*** *– inside; suffix:* ***...ulexʷ*** *– land.*

underline **k̓ʷɫɫip̓** – underline something.
k̓ʷɫɫp̓ntes – S/he underlined s.t. **k̓ʷɫɫp̓nten, k̓ʷɫɫp̓ntexʷ**
es k̓ʷɫɫp̓ims – S/he is underlining s.t. **ies k̓ʷɫɫp̓im, as k̓ʷɫɫp̓im**
qs k̓ʷɫɫp̓ims – S/he is underlining s.t. **iqs k̓ʷɫɫp̓im, aqs k̓ʷɫɫp̓im**

es k̓ʷɫɫip̓ – It is underlined.

sk̓ʷɬip̓ – underline.

k̓ʷɬp̓int – Underline it. *cmd.*

understand

nsuxʷneʔ – understand something.
nsuxʷneʔ – S/he/it understood. **čn nsuxʷneʔ, kʷ nsuxʷneʔ**
es nsuxʷneʔi – S/he/it is understanding. **čnes nsuxʷneʔi, kʷes nsuxʷneʔi**
qs nsuxʷneʔi – S/he/it is going to understand. **čiqs nsuxʷneʔi, kʷqs nsuxʷneʔi**
es nsúʔuxʷneʔi – They are understanding. **qeʔes nsuxʷneʔi, pes nsuxʷneʔi**

nsuxʷnemis – S/he/it understood it. **nsuxʷnemn, nsuxʷnemntxʷ**
es nsuxʷnemms – S/he/it is understanding it. **ies nsuxʷnemm, as nsuxʷnemm**
qs nsuxʷnemms – S/he/it is going to understand it. **iqs nsuxʷnemm, aqs nsuxʷnemm**
es nsúʔuxʷnemms – They are understanding it. **qeʔes nsuxʷnemm, es nsuxʷnemmp**

es nsuxʷneʔ – S/he/it understands. **čnes nsuxʷneʔ, kʷes nsuxʷneʔ**

nsxʷsuxʷneʔ – Each one understood. **qeʔ nsxʷsuxʷneʔ, p nsxʷsuxʷneʔ**
es nsxʷsuxʷneʔ – Each one is understanding. **qeʔes nsxʷsuxʷneʔ, pes nsxʷsuxʷneʔ**

es nsxʷnemnwe – They are understanding each other.

nsuxʷnemncn – I understand you.
qeʔ nsuxʷnemɬlt – You understand us.

ha kʷ nsuxʷneʔ – Did you understand? **ta čis nsuxʷneʔ –** I did not understand. **ha p nsuxʷneʔ –** Did you folks understand? **ta čnes nsuxʷneʔ –** I do not understand. **ta qes nsxʷnemnwe –** We do not understand each other. **ta p snsxʷnemnwe –** You folks did not understand each other. **x̣ʷl̓ tá čnes nsuxʷneʔ –** Because I do not understand. **ta es suxʷstn –** I do not recognize her/him.

ta es čsnmyepstn – I do not understand what it is about/for.

> The **i** following uvular consonants (UC) and the glottal stop ʔ sound like English "*ey*" as in the words th*ey*, h*ey*, wh*ey*, etc. Salish UC are: **q, q̓, qʷ, q̓ʷ, x̣, x̣ʷ**. For example, the suffix **...qin** – head/top, is often spelled using English *ey* as "q*ey*n". So **qi, q̓i, qʷi, q̓ʷi, x̣i, x̣ʷi,** may be spelled with English *ey* as **q***ey*, **q̓***ey*, **qʷ***ey*, **q̓ʷ***ey*, **x̣***ey*, **x̣ʷ***ey* in other texts.

underwater

k̓ʷɬištétkʷ – underwater. *rt.: **išut** – down, low.*
ništétkʷ – deep water. *rt.: **išut** – down, low.*

underwear

kʷɬištalqs, ***k̓ʷɬišta*** **–** under clothing. *suffix: **...lqs, ...alqs** – clothes.*
ha kʷes k̓ʷɬišta – Do you have underwear/underskirt on?

snsut̓ps – Long Johns; stretchy underwear.

undone

čpƛ̓ip – It came undone. *rt.: **pƛ̓im** – release from.*

undress

čpƛ̓ʔencut – undress one's self. *rt.: **pƛ̓im** – release from.*
čpƛ̓ʔencut – S/he undressed. **čn čpƛ̓ʔencut, kʷ čpƛ̓ʔencut**
es čpƛ̓ʔencuti – S/he is undressing. **čnes čpƛ̓ʔencuti, kʷes čpƛ̓ʔencuti**
qs čpƛ̓ʔencuti – S/he is going to undress. **čiqs čpƛ̓ʔencuti, kʷqs čpƛ̓ʔencuti**
es čpƛ̓ʔencúʔuti – They are undressing. **qeʔes čpƛ̓ʔencuti, pes čpƛ̓ʔencuti**

čpƛ̓ʔencutš – Undress yourself. *cmd.*

čpƛ̓ic̓éʔ – remove coverings/clothes. *rt.: **pƛ̓im** – release from; suffix: **...ic̓éʔ** – covered in.*
čpƛ̓ic̓éʔ – S/he removed coverings. **čn čpƛ̓ic̓éʔ, kʷ čpƛ̓ic̓éʔ**
es čpƛ̓ic̓éʔi – S/he is removing coverings. **čnes čpƛ̓ic̓éʔi, kʷes čpƛ̓ic̓éʔi**
qs čpƛ̓ic̓éʔi – S/he is going to remove coverings. **čiqs čpƛ̓ic̓éʔi, kʷqs čpƛ̓ic̓éʔi**

čpƛ̓ic̓éʔis – S/he removed s.o.'s coverings. **čpƛ̓ic̓éʔn, čpƛ̓ic̓éʔntxʷ**

> s.t. - something, the 3rd person
> (s.t.) - something implied
> s.o. - someone, the 3rd person
> *sl.* - singular form
> *pl.* - plural form
> *rt.* - root word
> *cmd.* - command
> *lit.* - literally
> *fig.* - figuratively
> *i.e.,* - for example
> *See:* - Redirection to a related word.

es čpƛ̓iċʔéms – S/he is removing s.o.'s coverings. **ies čpƛ̓iċʔém, as čpƛ̓iċʔém**
qs čpƛ̓iċʔéms – S/he is going to remove s.o.'s coverings. **iqs čpƛ̓iċʔém, kʷqs čpƛ̓iċʔém**

sxʷčpƛ̓iċéʔ – one tasked to remove/take off coverings/clothes.

čpƛ̓iċʔéiš – Remove your coverings. *cmd.*

npƛ̓alqs, *npƛ̓a* – remove/take off clothes. *rt.: **pƛ̓im** – release from; suffix: **...lqs, ...alqs** – clothes.*
npƛ̓alqs – S/he removed clothes. **čn npƛ̓alqs, kʷ npƛ̓alqs**
es npƛ̓alqsi – S/he is removing clothes. **čnes npƛ̓alqsi, kʷes npƛ̓alqsi**
qs npƛ̓alqsi – S/he is going to remove clothes. **čiqs npƛ̓alqsi, kʷqs npƛ̓alqsi**
es npƛ̓áʔalqsi – They are removing clothes. **qeʔes npƛ̓alqsi, pes npƛ̓alqsi**

npƛ̓alqsis – S/he removed s.o.'s clothes. **npƛ̓alqsn, npƛ̓alqsntxʷ**
es npƛ̓alqsms – S/he is removing s.o.'s clothes. **ies pƛ̓alqsm, as pƛ̓alqsm**
qs npƛ̓alqsms – S/he is going to remove s.o.'s clothes. **iqs pƛ̓alqsm, kʷqs pƛ̓alqsm**
es npƛ̓áʔalqsms – They are removing s.o.'s clothes. **qeʔes pƛ̓alqsm, es pƛ̓alqsmp**

sxʷnpƛ̓alqs – one tasked to remove/take off clothes.

npƛ̓alqsiš – Remove clothes. *cmd.*
npƛ̓alqsnt – Remove s.o.'s clothes. *cmd.*

npƛ̓áʔƛ̓aʔ – They stripped down, they were finished.
pƛ̓aqslšiš – Remove your clothes. *cmd.*

pƛ̓int – Remove it, take it off. *cmd. See: **remove**.*

pƛ̓qin – remove head cover/hat; bare head. *rt.: **pƛ̓im** – release from. See: **hat**.*

pƛ̓pƛ̓šnim – remove footwear. *rt.: **pƛ̓im** – remove, free. See: **shoe**.*

unfold
xʷup – straighten something; unfold; extend something. *See: **stretch**.*

unhappy
pupusénč, *pupusé* – sad; sorry; mourn; grieve. *See: **sad**.*

unicorn
usšnelsčn – unicorn. *rt.: **wisšn** – long; suffix: **...elsčn** – horn.*

unmotivated
k̓ʷłpiṗ – unmotivated/discouraged/lazy; *unable to do something; depressed. (This term describes someone who has no motivation, who is discouraged and who is lazy. Many words in Salish are a combination of English words. At times it is hard to give a clear translation.) See: **discourage**.*

unpack
pełqmncut – unpack one's self. *rt.: **płqem** – spread out; suffix: **...cut** – action to the self.*
pełqmncut – S/he/it unpacked. **čn pełqmncut, kʷ pełqmncut**
es pełqmncuti – S/he/it is unpacking. **čnes pełqmncuti, kʷes pełqmncuti**
qs pełqmncuti – S/he/it is going to unpack. **čiqs pełqmncuti, kʷqs pełqmncuti**

pełqmncutš – Pack up. *cmd.*
pełqmncutwi – All of you pack up. *cmd.*

p pełqmncut m p imš – All of you pack up and move.

ṗlk̓ʷmncut – pack one's self up. *See: **pack up**.*

unripe
x̣iʔu – unripe, not done.
es x̣iʔu – It is unripe, not done.

unsheath
nċoʔqłniut, *nċoʔqłni* – draw a knife/sword/gun out of a side mounted sheath; unsheath. *See: **draw**.*

untamed **uẇáq̓uq̓t,** *uẇá* – wild, savage, untamed. *See:* ***wild.***

untie **talip,** *tal* – untie; loose.
talip – S/he/it got untied. **čn talip, kʷ talip**
es talpmi – S/he/it is getting untied. **čnes talpmi, kʷes talpmi**
qs talpmi – S/he/it is going to get untied. **čiqs talpmi, kʷqs talpmi**
es talpmíˀi – They are getting untied. **qeˀes talpmi, pes talpmi**

talntes – S/he/it untied s.t. **talnten, talntexʷ**
es talíms – S/he/it is untying s.t. **čnes talim, kʷes talim**
qs talpmi – S/he/it is going to untie s.t. **čiqs talim, kʷqs talim**

es tal – S/he/it is untied; loose. **čnes tal, kʷes tal**

talint – Untie it. *cmd.*

taleẇsm – untie something around the middle. *suffix:* ***...éẇs*** *– in between, middle.*
taleẇsm – S/he untied (s.t.) from around the middle. **čn taleẇsm, kʷ taleẇsm**
es taleẇsi – S/he is untying (s.t.) from around the middle. **čnes taleẇsi, kʷes taleẇsi**
qs taleẇsi – S/he is going to untie (s.t.) from around the middle. **čiqs taleẇsi, kʷas taleẇsi**

k̓ʷłtalncut – untie one's self.
k̓ʷłtalncut – S/he/it untied one's self. **čn k̓ʷłtalncut, kʷ k̓ʷłtalncut**
es k̓ʷłtalncuti – S/he/it is untying one's self. **čnes k̓ʷłtalncuti, kʷes k̓ʷłtalncuti**
qs k̓ʷłtalncuti – S/he/it's going to untie one's self. **čiqs k̓ʷłtalncuti, kʷqs k̓ʷłtalncuti**

čtaliċˀem – untie something/someone; untie a covering. *suffix:* ***...iċéˀ*** *– covered in.*
čtaliċˀem – S/he untied. **čn čtaliċˀem, kʷ čtaliċˀem**
es čtaliċeˀi – S/he is untying. **čnes čtaliċeˀi, kʷes čtaliċeˀi**
qs čtaliċeˀi – S/he is going to untie. **čiqs čtaliċeˀi, kʷas čtaliċeˀi**

talsqáx̣eˀ, *talsqá* – let loose a horse/domestic animal; untie a horse/domestic animal.
talsqáx̣eˀ – S/he untied a horse. **čn talsqáx̣eˀ, kʷ talsqáx̣eˀ**
es talsqáx̣eˀi – S/he is untying a horse. **čnes talsqáx̣eˀi, kʷes talsqáx̣eˀi**
qs talsqáx̣eˀi – S/he is going to untie a horse. **čiqs talsqáx̣eˀi, kʷqs talsqáx̣eˀi**

unwrap **ččhiċeˀ** – unwrap; remove wrapping to reveal. *rt.:* ***čhém*** *– reveal.*
ččhiċˀem – S/he unwrapped. **čn ččhiċˀem, kʷ ččhiċˀem**
es ččhiċeˀi – S/he is unwrapping. **čnes ččhiċeˀi, kʷes ččhiċeˀi**
qs ččhiċeˀi – S/he is going to unwrap. **čiqs ččhiċeˀi, kʷqs ččhiċeˀi**

ččhiċˀeis – S/he unwrapped s.t. **ččhiċˀen, ččhiċˀentxʷ**
es ččhiċˀems – S/he is unwrapping s.t. **ies ččhiċˀem, as ččhiċˀem**
qs ččhiċˀems – S/he is going to unwrap s.t. **iqs ččhiċˀem, aqs ččhiċˀem**

es ččhiċeˀ – S/he/it is unwrapped. **čnes ččhiċeˀ, kʷes ččhiċeˀ**

ččhiċeˀiš – Unwrap. *cmd.*
ččhiċeˀwi – All of you unwrap. *cmd.*
ččhiċˀent – Unwrap it. *cmd.*
ččhiċˀenti – All of you unwrap it. *cmd.*

čt̓liċéˀ – tear a covering/wrapping off. *(i.e., a wrapping off a present, etc.)* *See:* ***tear.***

up **nwisšlš** – go up; raise. *rt.:* ***nwist*** *– up, up high.* *See:* ***raise.***
nwisšlš – S/he went up. **čn nwisšlš, kʷ nwisšlš**
es nwisšlši – S/he is going up. **čnes nwisšlši, kʷes nwisšlši**

The **i** following uvular consonants (UC) and the glottal stop ˀ sound like English "*ey*" as in the words th*ey*, h*ey*, wh*ey*, etc. Salish UC are: **q, q̓, qʷ, q̓ʷ, x̣, x̣ʷ**. For example, the suffix **...qin** – head/top, is often spelled using English *ey* as "q*ey*n". So **qi, q̓i, qʷi, q̓ʷi, x̣i, x̣ʷi**, may be spelled with English *ey* as **q***ey*, **q̓***ey*, **qʷ***ey*, **q̓ʷ***ey*, **x̣***ey*, **x̣ʷ***ey* in other texts.

s.t. - something, the 3rd person
(s.t.) - something implied
s.o. - someone, the 3rd person
sl. - singular form
pl. - plural form
rt. - root word
cmd. - command
lit. - literally
fig. - figuratively
i.e., - for example
See: - Redirection to a related word.

qs nwisšlšms – S/he is going to go up. **čiqs nwisšlši, kʷqs nwisšlši**

nwisšlšiš – Go up. *cmd.*
nwisšlšwi – All of you go up. *cmd.*

nwisšlšnt asčuwax̣n – Raise your arm.

čłqeẃs, *čłqe* **–** on top of. *See:* ***top.***

qaqlt – arrive at the top. *See:* ***top.***

ššal̓ús, *ššal̓ú* **–** go uphill. *See:* ***uphill.***

čqe – upstream. *See:* ***upstream.***

čiwlš – climb. *(also used to indicate going upstairs)* *See:* ***climb.***

nwist – up; above; up high. *See:* ***high.***

x̣ʷcuʔsičṅ, *x̣ʷcuʔsi* **–** go over a mountain pass. *See:* ***pass.***

čłqʷéẃs – drape up high; hang up high over an object; hang up. *See:* ***drape.***

uphill

ššal̓ús, *ššal̓ú* **–** go uphill.
ššal̓ús – S/he/it went uphill. **čn ššal̓ús, kʷ ššal̓ús**
es ššal̓úsi – S/he/it is going uphill. **čnes ššal̓úsi, kʷes ššal̓úsi**
qs ššal̓úsi – S/he/it is going to go uphill. **čiqs ššal̓úsi, kʷqs ššal̓úsi**

šal̓túsis – S/he/it brought it uphill. **šal̓túsn, šal̓túsntxʷ**
es šal̓tmúsms – S/he/it is bringing s.t./s.o. uphill. **ies šal̓tmúsm, as šal̓tmúsm**
qs šal̓tmúsms – S/he/it is going to bring s.t./s.o. uphill. **iqs šal̓tmúsm, aqs šal̓tmúsm**

ššal̓tmusmkʷ – Take it uphill. *cmd.*

čn ššal̓us u čn łqaqlt – I climbed and I made it to the top.

upside-down

nʔawyoqn – upside-down.
nʔawyoqis – S/he turned s.o./s.t. upside-down. **nʔawyoqn, nʔawyoqntxʷ**
es nʔawyoqnms – S/he is turning s.o./s.t. upside-down. **ies nʔawyoqnm, as nʔawyoqnm**
qs nʔawyoqnms – S/he is going to turn s.o./s.t. upside-down. **iqs nʔawyoqnm, aqs nʔawyoqnm**

kʷ iqs nʔawyoqnms – I am going to turn you upside-down.

k̓ʷel̓č – turn upside-down a container type object; upturned object. *(i.e., car, box, cup, bucket, etc.)*
k̓ʷel̓čm – S/he upturned (s.t.). **čn k̓ʷel̓čm, kʷ k̓ʷel̓čm**
es k̓ʷel̓či – S/he is upturning (s.t.). **ies k̓ʷel̓či, as k̓ʷel̓či**
qs k̓ʷel̓či – S/he is going to upturn (s.t.). **iqs k̓ʷel̓či, aqs k̓ʷel̓či**

k̓ʷel̓čis – S/he upturned s.t. **k̓ʷel̓čn, k̓ʷel̓čntxʷ**
es k̓ʷel̓čms – S/he is upturning s.t. **ies k̓ʷel̓čm, as k̓ʷel̓čm**
qs k̓ʷel̓čms – S/he is going to upturn s.t. **iqs k̓ʷel̓čm, aqs k̓ʷel̓čm**

es łk̓ʷek̓ʷl̓či – S/he is upturning (s.t.) a little. **ies łk̓ʷek̓ʷl̓či, as łk̓ʷek̓ʷl̓či**
es łk̓ʷek̓ʷl̓čms – They are upturning s.t. a little. **qeʔes łk̓ʷek̓ʷl̓čm, es łk̓ʷek̓ʷl̓čmp**

es k̓ʷel̓č – It is upturned.

k̓ʷel̓čnt – Upturn it. *cmd.*

čłk̓ʷel̓č – turn a rigid container type object upside-down on a flat surface ; roll/tip over. *(i.e., car, hat, lid, etc.)*
čłk̓ʷel̓čis – S/he tipped it over. **čłk̓ʷel̓čn, čłk̓ʷel̓čntxʷ**

čłk̓ʷéʔel̓čis – They tipped it over. **qeʔ čłk̓ʷel̓čntm, čłk̓ʷel̓čntp**

čłk̓ʷel̓l̓č – It got turned over. *(i.e., car accident when it lands on its top.)*

upstairs

čiwlš – climb. *(also used to indicate going upstairs) See: **climb**.*
es čiwlši – S/he/it is climbing. **čnes čiwlši, kʷes čiwlši**

snčiwlštn – ladder, stairs. *prefix: **sn...** – a place of; suffix: **...tin, ...tn** – means of/device.*

upstream

nc̓ʔilš – go upstream by land; go up river by land. *suffix: **...ilš** – autonomous.*
nc̓ʔilš – S/he/it went upstream. **čn nc̓ʔilš, kʷ nc̓ʔilš**
es nc̓ʔilši – S/he/it is going upstream. **čnes nc̓ʔilši, kʷes nc̓ʔilši**
qs nc̓ʔilši – S/he/it is going to go upstream. **čiqs nc̓ʔilši, kʷqs nc̓ʔilši**

nc̓ic̓ʔilš – Each one went upstream.
qeʔqs nc̓ic̓ʔilši – Each one of us is going to go upstream.

nʔax̣ʷt – go downriver by land; go downhill over a long distance. *See: **downstream**.*

eł nc̓ʔilš – S/he/it went back up the river.

čqe – upstream.
ci tl̓ čqe iscqq̓m̓e – From upstream I caught fish.

urge

áy̓c̓ – urge; insist and plead; stubborn. *See: **insist**.*
ay̓cn – have the voice of insisting, begging and pleading. *See: **insist**.*

urinate

tčey̓ – urinate.
tčey̓m – S/he/it urinated. **čn tčey̓m, kʷ tčey̓m**
es tčey̓i – S/he/it is urinating. **čnes tčey̓i, kʷes tčey̓i**
qs tčey̓i – S/he/it is going to urinate. **čiqs tčey̓i, kʷqs tčey̓i**
es tčéʔey̓i – They are urinating. **qeʔes tčey̓i, pes tčey̓i**

tčey̓is – S/he/it urinated on s.t./s.o. **tčey̓n, tčey̓ntxʷ**
es tčey̓ms – S/he/it is urinating on s.t./s.o. **ies tčey̓m, as tčey̓m**
qs tčey̓ms – S/he/it is going to urinate on s.t./s.o. **iqs tčey̓m, aqs tčey̓m**

ntčimélsm – S/he/it wanted to urinate. **čn ntčimelsm, kʷ ntčimelsm**
es ntčimelsi – S/he/it is wanting to urinate. **čnes ntčimelsi, kʷes ntčimelsi**
qs ntčimelsi – S/he/it is going to want to urinate. **čiqs ntčimelsi, kʷqs ntčimelsi**

ntčtčimuł – one that habitually urinates. *suffix: **...łmuł** – one that habitually does.*

čiqs k̓ʷis tčéy̓i – I am going to go pee. **x̣in̓e kʷ ntčimels** – You might need to pee.

ntčiyéw̓s – urinated pants. *(refers to urinating the middle; more commonly used) prefix: **n...** – inside; suffix: **...éw̓s** – in between, middle.*
ntčiyew̓sm – S/he urinated his/her pants. **čn ntčiyew̓sm, kʷ ntčiyew̓sm**
es ntčiyew̓si – S/he/it is urinating his/her pants. **čnes ntčiyew̓si, kʷes ntčiyew̓si**
qs ntčiyew̓si – S/he/it is going to urinate his/her pants. **čiqs ntčiyew̓si, kʷqs ntčiyew̓si**

ha kʷ ntčiyew̓sm – Did you pee your pants?

ntčiyups – urinate pants. *circumfix: **n...ups** – butt, tail.*
ntčiyupsm – S/he urinated his/her pants. **čn ntčiyupsm, kʷ ntčiyupsm**
es ntčiyupsi – S/he/it is urinating his/her pants. **čnes ntčiyupsi, kʷes ntčiyupsi**
qs ntčiyupsi – S/he/it is going to urinate his/her pants. **čiqs ntčiyupsi, kʷqs ntčiyupsi**

The **i** following uvular consonants (UC) and the glottal stop **ʔ** sound like English "*ey*" as in the words th*ey*, h*ey*, wh*ey*, etc. Salish UC are: **q, q̓, qʷ, q̓ʷ, x̣, x̣ʷ**. For example, the suffix **...qin** – head/top, is often spelled using English *ey* as "q*ey*n". So **qi, q̓i, qʷi, q̓ʷi, x̣i, x̣ʷi**, may be spelled with English *ey* as **q***ey*, **q̓***ey*, **qʷ***ey*, **q̓ʷ***ey*, **x̣***ey*, **x̣ʷ***ey* in other texts.

s.t. - something, the 3rd person
(s.t.) - something implied
s.o. - someone, the 3rd person
sl. - singular form
pl. - plural form
rt. - root word
cmd. - command
lit. - literally
fig. - figuratively
i.e., - for example
See: - Redirection to a related word.

tčiyełp – urinated the bed. *suffix: ...ełp, ...łp – tree; floor, bed.*
tčiyełpm – S/he urinated the bed. **čn tčiyełpm, kʷ tčiyełpm**
es tčiyełpi – S/he/it is urinating the bed. **čnes tčiyełpi, kʷes tčiyełpi**
qs tčiyełpi – S/he/it is going to urinate the bed. **čiqs tčiyełpi, kʷqs tčiyełpi**

ntčyetkʷ – urinate in the water.
ntčyetkʷm – S/he/it urinated in water. **čn ntčyetkʷm, kʷ ntčyetkʷm**
es ntčyetkʷi – S/he/it is urinating in water. **čnes ntčyetkʷi, kʷes ntčyetkʷi**
qs ntčyetkʷi – S/he/it is going to urinate in water. **čiqs ntčyetkʷi, kʷqs ntčyetkʷi**

tčyalqʷqn – urinate up a pole/log/tree.

čťaq̓šnm – raise/lift leg up to the side. *(i.e., as a dog would do to urinate) See: **lift**.*

urine
stčéẏ – urine.
sntčeẏtn – urinary bladder. *prefix: sn... – a place of; suffix: ...tin, ...tn – means of/device.*

us
qeʔnple – us; we; ours.

qeʔ – us; we; ours.
ƛ̓m qeʔmlmelčst – It was our toy.
qeʔmlmelčstn – our toy.
qeʔqł mlmelčstn – It is going to be our toy.

qʷo – me; us as a unit; us together.
qʷo qs susti – We are going to drink. *lit. as a unit we are going to drink.*
i qʷo nk̓ʷuʔ – We are one.

use
teṁm – use; take care of; have responsibility for.
čteṁmis – S/he/it used s.t. **čteṁmn, čteṁmntxʷ**
es čteṁms – S/he/it is using it. **ies čteṁm, as čteṁm**
qs čteṁms – S/he/it is going to use it. **iqs čteṁm, aqs čteṁm**
čtéʔeṁmis – They used s.t. **qeʔ čteṁmntm, čteṁmntp**

teṁtn – What is it used for?
teṁmis – What did s/he/it do with s.t.? **teṁmn, teṁmntxʷ**
es teṁmnwexʷi – They use/need each other. **qeʔes teṁmnwexʷi,pes teṁmnwexʷi**

ṅem qs čtéʔeṁms – They will be using it. **ṅem qeʔqs čtemm, ṅem qs čteṁmp**
ha kʷṅe u čteṁmn asnłk̓ʷłk̓ʷłsncutn – Can I use your computer? **čeʔ tam es čtéʔeṁms** – They are not using it anymore. **t čeṅ sq̓íʔiʔ łu as čteṁm** – What color are you using? **tam l tʔestéṁ u čteṁtn** – S/he/it has no use. **aqł teṁtn** – What are you going to use it for?

k̓ʷl̓k̓ʷul̓mn – the things used in making/building something.
k̓ʷl̓k̓ʷul̓mis – his/her building things. **ink̓ʷl̓k̓ʷul̓mn, ank̓ʷl̓k̓ʷul̓mn**

t stmteṁ łu aqł k̓ʷl̓k̓ʷul̓mn x̣ʷl̓ pumin – What do you use to make a drum?

used to
qʷʔem – get accustomed/used to somebody or something. *See: **accustomed**.*

use together
cčhémnt – Use it together with something.

uterus
snsixʷltn – uterus.

uvula
nšaltsq̓me – uvula. *rt.: šal – suspended.*

V

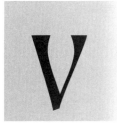

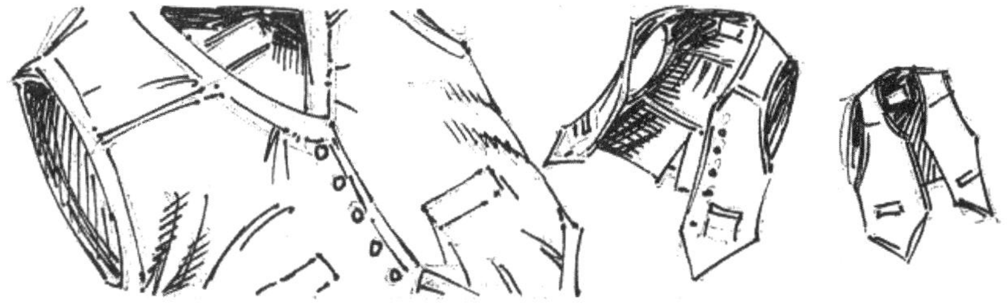

vacuum **čłtumełp –** vacuum a floor. *rt.: **tum** – suck; prefix: **čł...** – surface; suffix: ...ełp, ...łp – tree; floor, bed.*

čłtumełpm – S/he vacuumed a floor. **čn čłtumełpm, kʷ čłtumełpm**
es čłtumełpi – S/he is vacuuming a floor. **čnes čłtumełpi, kʷes čłtumełpi**
qs čłtumełpi – S/he is going to vacuum a floor. **čiqs čłtumełpi, kʷqs čłtumełpi**

čłtumełptn – vacuum cleaner.

čłtumełpš – Vacuum the floor. *cmd.*

čłxʷk̓ʷmintn – vacuum cleaner. *rt.: **xʷuk̓ʷ** – clean; ; prefix: **čł...** – surface; suffix: **...tin, ...tn** – means of/device.*

valerian **msawiyeʔ –** tobacco root; Valerian; *Valeriana edulis*.

valley **x̣sulexʷ ikʷtnulexʷ –** valley. *lit. good big land.*
kʷtnulexʷ eslqʷo – big valley.

łp̓u – coming into a valley.

Valley Creek **łqʷkʷeʔu –** Valley Creek area, in the Jocko Valley, Flathead Nation.

van **snukʷnwe p̓ip̓uyšn –** van.
skʷtnewłkʷ – something big.

vanish **čuw –** gone; away; absent. *See: **gone**.*

ċsip – disappear; gone; wiped out; cleared out. *See: **disappear**.*

k̓ʷłčluxʷ – go out of sight around an obstacle. *(i.e., a tree, hill, rock, building, etc.) See: **disappear**.*

vehicle **...sqáx̣eʔ, *...sqá*** – *suffix indicating horses, domestic animals, or vehicles.* *See: **animal**.*

vein **q̓áq̓łuʔ –** vein.

vest **sk̓ʷłčnčnp̓álqs,** *sk̓ʷłčnčnp̓á* – vest.

k̓ʷłčnčnp̓álqsm – S/he put a vest on. **čn k̓ʷłčnčnp̓álqsm, kʷ k̓ʷłčnčnp̓álqsm**
es k̓ʷłčnčnp̓álqsi – S/he is putting a vest on. **čnes k̓ʷłčnčnp̓álqsi, kʷes k̓ʷłčnčnp̓álqsi**
qs k̓ʷłčnčnp̓álqsi – S/he is going to put a vest on. **čiqs k̓ʷłčnčnp̓álqsi, kʷqs k̓ʷłčnčnp̓álqsi**

k̓ʷłčnčnp̓álqsis – S/he put a vest on s.o. **k̓ʷłčnčnp̓álqsn, k̓ʷłčnčnp̓álqsntxʷ**
es k̓ʷłčnčnp̓álqsms – S/he is putting a vest on s.o. **ies k̓ʷłčnčnp̓álqsm, as k̓ʷłčnčnp̓álqsm**
qs k̓ʷłčnčnp̓álqsms – S/he is going to put a vest on s.o. **iqs k̓ʷłčnčnp̓álqsm, aqs k̓ʷłčnčnp̓álqsm**

s.t. - something, the 3rd person
(s.t.) - something implied
s.o. - someone, the 3rd person
sl. - singular form
pl. - plural form
rt. - root word
cmd. - command
lit. - literally
fig. - figuratively
i.e., - for example
See: - Redirection to a related word.

es k̓ʷłčnčnp̓álqs – S/he is wearing a vest. **čnes k̓ʷłčnčnp̓álqs, kʷes k̓ʷłčnčnp̓álqs**

k̓ʷłčnčnp̓álqsiš – Put a vest on. *cmd.*

Victoria **pitolia** – Victoria.

vine **čiliyal̓álqʷ**, *čiliyal̓á* – orange honeysuckle; vine; *Lonicera ciliosa.*

violet **msm̓sá** – wild violet.
x̣ʷit msm̓sá – American sweet cicely; sweet-root.

virgin **sti̓čmišlt**, *sti̓čmi* – girl after age of puberty; girl in teens; unmarried woman.

virgin's bower, clematis **čiliyal̓álqʷ**, *čiliyal̓á* – orange honeysuckle; *Lonicera ciliosa.*

vision **moyx̣** – extrasensory perception; vision; foretelling dream; clairvoyant.
moyx̣ – S/he perceived with extrasensory clairvoyance. **čn moyx̣, kʷes moyx̣**
es moyx̣i – S/he is perceiving with extrasensory clairvoyance. **čnes moyx̣i, kʷes moyx̣i**
qs moyx̣i – S/he is going to perceive with extrasensory clairvoyance. **čiqs moyx̣i, kʷqs moyx̣i**

moyx̣is – S/he perceived s.t. with extrasensory clairvoyance. **moyx̣n, moyx̣ntxʷ**
es moyx̣ms – S/he is perceiving s.t. with extrasensory clairvoyance. **ies moyx̣m, as moyx̣m**
qs moyx̣ms – S/he is going to perceive s.t. with extrasensory clairvoyance. **iqs moyx̣m, aqs moyx̣m**

tmoyx̣is – S/he foresaw s.t. **tmoyx̣n, tmoyx̣ntxʷ**
es tmoyx̣ms – S/he is foreseeing s.t. **ies tmoyx̣m, as tmoyx̣m**
qs tmoyx̣ms – S/he is going to foresee s.t. **iqs tmoyx̣m, aqs tmoyx̣m**

sxʷmoyx̣ – one tasked to perceive with extrasensory clairvoyance; clairvoyant.

ƛ̓uƛ̓uscutist – seek a vision.
es ƛ̓uƛ̓uscutisti – S/he is seeking a vision. **čnes ƛ̓uƛ̓uscutisti, kʷes ƛ̓uƛ̓uscutisti**

čutmist – seek/ask for help from the spiritual world. *(i.e., vision quest.) rt.: **čoncut** – prayer/offer. See: **help**.*

visit **čxʷuym** – visit. *rt.: **xʷuy** – go; prefix: **č...** – people.*
čxʷuymis – S/he visited s.o. **čxʷuymn, čxʷuymntxʷ**
es čxʷuymms – S/he is visiting s.o. **ies čxʷuymm, as čxʷuymm**
qs čxʷuymms – S/he is going to visit s.o. **iqs čxʷuymm, aqs čxʷuymm**
čxʷúˀuymis – They visited s.o. **qeˀ čxʷuymntm, čxʷuymntp**
qs čxʷúˀuymms – They are going to visit s.o. **qeˀqs čxʷuymm, qs čxʷuymmp**

čxʷuymnt – Visit s.o. *cmd.*

čxʷimsqelixʷ, *čxʷimsqe* – visit people.

qs wis čxʷuymms – S/he is going to visit s.o. first. **iqs wis čxʷuymm, aqs wis čxʷuymm**
qs wis čxʷúˀuymms – They are going to visit s.o. first. **qeˀqs wis čxʷuymm, qs wis čxʷuymmp**
es wis čxʷuymms – S/he just visited s.o. **ies wis čxʷuymm, as wis čxʷuymm**
es wis čxʷúˀuymms – They just visited s.o. **qeˀes wis čxʷuymm, es wis čxʷuymmp**
qʷo čxʷuymis – S/he visited me. **qʷo čxʷúˀuymis** – They visited me. **ha as wis čxʷuymm łu aqł nox̣ʷnx̣ʷ** – Have you been visiting your wife-to-be? **xʷuyš k̓ʷis čxʷuymnt asíleˀ** – Go visit your grandpa. **ha ṅem qeˀ čxʷimsqe č astmm̓élis** – Will we visit your relative? **ta tam l qʷoyˀé u es nsuˀcnmi šey̓ łu es ccxʷuyms, tam qʷoyˀé** – No, it is not me he's come proposing to, he's come for her, not me.

nxʷiyelsm, *nxʷiye* – want to visit somebody; want to go.
nxʷiyelsm – S/he wanted to visit s.o. **čn nxʷiyelsm, kʷ nxʷiyelsm**
es nxʷiyelsi – S/he is wanting to visit s.o. **čnes nxʷiyelsi, kʷes nxʷiyelsi**
nxʷiyéʔelsm – They wanted to visit s.o. **qeʔ nxʷiyelsm, p nxʷiyelsm**
es nxʷiyéʔelsi – They are wanting to visit s.o. **qeʔes nxʷiyelsi, pes nxʷiyelsi**

nxʷiyelsmis – S/he wanted to visit s.o. **nxʷiyelsmn, nxʷiyelsmntxʷ**
es nxʷiyelsms – S/he is wanting to visit s.o. **ies nxʷiyelsm, as nxʷiyelsm**
nxʷiyéʔelsmis – They wanted to visit s.o. **qeʔ nxʷiyelsmntm, nxʷiyelsmntp**
es nxʷiyéʔelsms – They are wanting to visit s.o. **qeʔes nxʷiyelsm, es nxʷiyelsmp**

šƛ̓elixʷ – visit people/tribes/towns one after another; tour among the various people. *rt.: **šiƛ̓** – flat, level, aligned; suffix: **...sqe, ...sqelixʷ** – people.*
es šƛ̓elixʷi – S/he is visiting people one after another. **čnes šƛ̓elixʷi, kʷes šƛ̓elixʷi**
qs šƛ̓elixʷi – S/he is going to visit people one after another. **čiqs šƛ̓elixʷi, kʷqs šƛ̓elixʷi**

šƛ̓ełxʷ – visit homes one after another; go house to house. *rt.: **šiƛ̓** – flat, level, aligned; suffix: **...ełxʷ, ...łxʷ** – house.*
es šƛ̓ełxʷi – S/he is visiting house after house. **čnes šƛ̓ełxʷi, kʷes šƛ̓ełxʷi**
qs šƛ̓ełxʷi – S/he is going to visit house after house. **čiqs šƛ̓ełxʷi, kʷqs šƛ̓ełxʷi**

The **i** following uvular consonants (UC) and the glottal stop **ʔ** sound like English "*ey*" as in the words th*ey*, h*ey*, wh*ey*, etc. Salish UC are: **q, q̓, qʷ, q̓ʷ, x̣, x̣ʷ**. For example, the suffix **...qin** – head/top, is often spelled using English *ey* as "q*ey*n". So **qi, q̓i, qʷi, q̓ʷi, x̣i, x̣ʷi**, may be spelled with English *ey* as **q***ey*, **q̓***ey*, **qʷ***ey*, **q̓ʷ***ey*, **x̣***ey*, **x̣ʷ***ey* in other texts.

visitor

sčxʷuy – visitor.
sčxʷixʷuy – visitors.
qeʔ ep sčxʷixʷuy – We have visitors.

voice

tspmncót, *tspmncó* – sudden sound of voices shouting. *See: **sound.***

łkʷk̓ʷiyomqn – small voice; feminine voice; high pitch voice. *See: **small.***

nkʷtonqn – big voice; deep voice.

volcano

es tlpqin es moq̓ʷ – volcano; torn topped mountain.

vole

sṁmsx̣ʷené – meadow vole.

volume

nƛ̓x̣cin – loud in singing or talking; make loud noises. *suffix: **...cin, ...cn** – action of the mouth. See: **loud.***
nƛ̓x̣cinmis – S/he made s.t./s.o. loud. **nƛ̓x̣cinmn, nƛ̓x̣cinmntxʷ**
es nƛ̓x̣cinms – S/he is making s.t./s.o. loud. **ies nƛ̓x̣cinm, as nƛ̓x̣cinm**
qs nƛ̓x̣cinms – S/he is going to make s.t./s.o. loud. **iqs nƛ̓x̣cinm, aqs nƛ̓x̣cinm**

nƛ̓x̣cinmnt – Make it loud; turn it up. *cmd.*

mił nƛ̓x̣cin – It is too loud; turn it down.

nłkʷk̓ʷiyecn, *nłkʷk̓ʷi* – whisper; talk little; talk quiet. *suffix: **...cin, ...cn** – action of the mouth. See: **whisper.***
nłkʷk̓ʷiecinmis – S/he made s.t./s.o. talk quiet. **nłkʷk̓ʷiecinmn, nłkʷk̓ʷiecinmntxʷ**
es nłkʷk̓ʷiecinms – S/he is making s.t./s.o. talk quiet. **ies nłkʷk̓ʷiecinm, as nłkʷk̓ʷiecinm**
qs nłkʷk̓ʷiecinms – S/he is going to make s.t./s.o. talk quiet. **iqs nłkʷk̓ʷiecinm, aqs nłkʷk̓ʷiecinm**

nłkʷk̓ʷiecinmnt – Make it talk quiet; turn the volume down. *cmd.*

s.t. - something, the 3rd person
(s.t.) - something implied
s.o. - someone, the 3rd person
sl. - singular form
pl. - plural form
rt. - root word
cmd. - command
lit. - literally
fig. - figuratively
i.e., - for example
See: - Redirection to a related word.

volunteer

šʔitmasqe – leader; first people; first to volunteer; first to be there. *rt.: **šʔit** – first; suffix: **...sqe, ...sqelixʷ** – people. See: **leader.***

nʔawqnm – call upon/ask for someone; challenge/encourage someone; beseech; exhort. *See: **call**.*

vomit **noccqecin –** vomit. *suffix: **...cin, ...cn** – action of the mouth.*

noccqecin – S/he vomited. **čn noccqecin, kʷ noccqecin**
es noccqecini – S/he is vomiting. **čnes noccqecini, kʷes noccqecini**
qs noccqecini – S/he is going to vomit. **čiqs noccqecini, kʷqs noccqecini**

noccqecists – S/he made s.o. vomit. **noccqecistn, noccqecistxʷ**
es noccqecists – S/he is making s.o. vomit. **es noccqecistn, es noccqecistxʷ**
qs noccqecists – S/he is going to make s.o. vomit. **qs noccqecistn, qs noccqecistxʷ**

noccqecinmis – S/he vomited s.t. **noccqecinmn, noccqecinmntxʷ**
es noccqecinms – S/he is vomiting s.t. **ies noccqecinm, as noccqecinm**
qs noccqecinms – S/he is going to vomit s.t. **iqs noccqecinm, aqs noccqecinm**

snoccqecin – vomit.

noccqeciniš – Vomit. *cmd.*
noccqecinmnt – Vomit it. *cmd.*
noccqeciskʷ – Make s.o. vomit. *cmd.*

ččessls – sick to the stomach; nauseated. *See: **nauseated**.*

vulture **caqʷuyéʔ –** buzzard, turkey vulture.

W

waddle **wl̓wél̓l̓š –** waddle *(i.e., ducks; elderly people; etc.). rt.:* ***wel̓–*** *tilt. See:* ***tilt.***
wl̓wél̓l̓š – S/he/it waddled. **čn wl̓wél̓l̓š, kw wl̓wél̓l̓š**
es wl̓wél̓l̓ši – S/he/it is waddling. **čnes wl̓wél̓l̓ši, kʷes wl̓wél̓l̓ši**
qs wl̓wél̓l̓ši – S/he/it is going to waddle. **čiqs wl̓wél̓l̓ši, kʷqs wl̓wél̓l̓ši**

wl̓wél̓l̓š – Waddle. *cmd.*
wl̓wél̓l̓šwi – All of you waddle. *cmd.*

wade **nxʷstetkʷ,** *nxʷste* **–** walk in the water; wade. *suffix:* ***...etkʷ, ...tkʷ–*** *liquid*
nxʷstetkʷm – S/he/it walked in the water. **čn nxʷstetkʷm, kʷ nxʷstetkʷm**
es nxʷstetkʷi – S/he/it is walking in the water. **čnes nxʷstetkʷi, kʷes nxʷstetkʷi**
qs nxʷstetkʷi – S/he/it is going to walk in the water. **čiqs nxʷstetkʷi, kʷqs nxʷstetkʷi**

xʷstnetkʷ – walk by the water. *suffix:* ***...etkʷ, ...tkʷ–*** *liquid*
xʷstnetkʷm – S/he/it walked by the water. **čn xʷstnetkʷm, kʷ xʷstnetkʷm**
es xʷstnetkʷi – S/he/it walked by the water. **čnes xʷstnetkʷi, kʷes xʷstnetkʷi**
qs xʷstnetkʷi – S/he/it is going to walk by the water. **čiqs xʷstnetkʷi, kʷqs xʷstnetkʷi**

waffle **łq̓tq̓itlexʷ –** waffle.
łq̓tq̓itlexʷm – S/he made waffles. **čn łq̓tq̓itlexʷm, kʷ łq̓tq̓itlexʷm**
es łq̓tq̓itlexʷi – S/he is making waffles. **čnes łq̓tq̓itlexʷi, kʷes łq̓tq̓itlexʷi**
qs łq̓tq̓itlexʷi – S/he is going to make waffles. **čiqs łq̓tq̓itlexʷi, kʷqs łq̓tq̓itlexʷi**

scłq̓tq̓itlexʷ – waffles.

ṅem čn łq̓tq̓itlexʷm – I will make waffles.

wag **čilyelps –** wag a tail.
čilyelpsm – It wagged its tail.
es čilyelpsi – It is wagging its tail.
qs čilyelpsi – It is going to wag its tail.

čilyelpsiš – Wag your tail. *cmd.*

wagon **x̣ʷóllq̓ʷ –** wagon.

x̣ʷllq̓ʷaqs – wagon trail.

waist **sčmeẇs –** one side of an object; waist. *rt.:* ***čm –*** *extremity; suffix:* ***...éẇs –*** *in between, middle.*
snčmusičṅ – lower back; waist.

wait **nʔemtéẇs –** wait for something. *rt.:* ***emut –*** *sit; suffix:* ***...éẇs –*** *in between, middle.*
nʔemtéẇsm – S/he/it waited. **čn nʔemtéẇsm, kʷ nʔemtéẇsm**
es nʔemtéẇsi – S/he/it is waiting. **čnes nʔemtéẇsi, kʷes nʔemtéẇsi**
qs nʔemtéẇsi – S/he/it is going to wait. **čiqs nʔemtéẇsi, kʷqs nʔemtéẇsi**

s.t. - something, the 3rd person
(s.t.) - something implied
s.o. - someone, the 3rd person
sl. - singular form
pl. - plural form
rt. - root word
cmd. - command
lit. - literally
fig. - figuratively
i.e., - for example
See: - Redirection to a related word.

nʔemtéʔeẇsm – They waited. **qeʔ nʔemtéẇsm, p nʔemtéẇsm**
es nʔemtéʔeẇsi – They are waiting. **qeʔes nʔemtéẇsi, pes nʔemtéẇsi**
qs nʔemtéʔeẇsi – They are going to wait. **qeʔqs nʔemtéẇsi, pqs nʔemtéẇsi**

nʔemtéẇsis – S/he/it waited for s.o./s.t. **nʔemtéẇsn, nʔemtéẇsntxʷ**
es nʔemtéẇsms – S/he/it is waiting for s.o./s.t. **ies nʔemtéẇsm, as nʔemtéẇsm**
qs nʔemtéẇsms – S/he/it going to wait s.o./s.t. **iqs nʔemtéẇsm, aqs nʔemtéẇsm**
nʔemtéʔeẇsis – They waited for s.o./s.t. **qeʔ nʔemtéẇsntm, nʔemtéẇsntp**
es nʔemtéʔeẇsms – They are waiting for s.o./s.t. **qeʔes nʔemtéẇsm, es nʔemtéẇsmp**
qs nʔemtéʔeẇsms – They are going to wait for s.o./s.t. **qeʔqs nʔemtéẇsm, qs nʔemtéẇsmp**

nʔemtéẇsiš – Wait. *cmd.*
nʔemtéẇskʷ – Make s.o. wait for s.o. *cmd.*
nʔemtéẇsnt – Wait for s.o. *cmd.*

ṅem nʔemtéẇstxʷ ṅe wis uwewlš m sic kʷ eɫ t uwewlš – You wait till they get through talking, then you can talk. **steṁ ɫu as nʔemtéẇsm** – What are you waiting for? **nʔemteẇscn** – I waited for you. **qʷo nʔemteẇskʷ** – Wait for me.

nʔemɫtumš – wait for people; wait for a turn. *rt.: **emut–** sit; suffix: **...ɫtumš–** of people.*
es nʔemɫtumši – S/he/it is waiting for people/a turn. **čnes nʔemɫtumši, kʷes nʔemɫtumši**

nʔemɫtumsiš – Wait your turn.

k̓ʷe ṅe – in a while/wait.
ṅe k̓ʷe ṅe – later.

wake

qiɫt – wake up.
qiɫt – S/he/it woke up. **čn qiɫt, kʷ qiɫt**

qiɫis – S/he/it woke s.o./s.t. up. **qéiɫn, kʷ qiɫntxʷ**
es qiɫms – S/he/it is waking s.o./s.t. up. **ies qiɫm, as qiɫm**
qs qiɫms – S/he/it is going to wake s.o./s.t. up. **iqs qiɫm, aqs qiɫm**

es qiɫt – S/he/it is awake. **čnes qiɫt, kʷes qiɫt**
es qlíʔiɫt – They are awake. **qeʔes qliɫt, pes qliɫt**

qɫtumn – something that wakes you *(i.e., alarm clock, wake up song, etc.)*.
qɫtemn – one inclined to wake easy. *suffix: **...emn–** one inclined to do.*

qiɫtš – Wake up. *cmd.*
es qiɫtš – Stay awake. *cmd.*
qliɫtwi – All of you wake up. *cmd.*
qiɫnt – Wake s.o./s.t. up. *cmd.*
qɫtumš – wake people.
čɫqiɫneʔ – wake someone unintentionally.

ỉ k̓ʷinš m kʷ qiɫt – What time will you wake? **qiɫnts** – S/he/it woke you up. **qeʔqs k̓ʷis qɫtumši** – We're going to go wake up the people. **čn qiɫt u čn xʷt̓ilš** – I woke and got up.

čɫheʔenʔem – bother someone who is sleeping.
čɫheʔenʔeis – S/he bothered s.o. sleeping. **čɫheʔenʔen, čɫheʔenʔentxʷ**
es čɫheʔenʔems – S/he is bothering s.o. sleeping. **ies čɫheʔenʔem, as čɫheʔenʔem**
qs čɫheʔenʔems – S/he is going to bother s.o. sleeping. **iqs čɫheʔenʔem, aqs čɫheʔenʔem**

xʷus – wide awake, open-eyed. *See: **awake**.*

čšťim – guard or take care of. *(This term is also used for wakes as it is seen that people are taking care of the dead.) See:* ***guard.***

walk **xʷist** – walk, *referring to a single person. rt.:* ***xʷuy*** *– go; suffix:* ***...ist*** *– action for/of the self.*
xʷist – S/he/it walked. **čn xʷist, kʷ xʷist**
es xʷisti – S/he/it is walking. **čnes xʷisti, kʷes xʷisti**
qs xʷisti – S/he/it is going to walk. **čiqs xʷisti, kʷqs xʷisti**

xʷistmsts – S/he/it made s.o./s.t. go/walk. **xʷistmstn, xʷistmstxʷ**
es xʷistmsts – S/he/it is making s.o./s.t. go/walk. **es xʷistmstn, es xʷistmstxʷ**
qs xʷistmsts – S/he/it is going to make s.o./s.t. go/walk. **qs xʷistmstn, qs xʷistmstxʷ**

es łxʷixʷsti – S/he/it is walking a little *(small steps).* **čnes łxʷixʷsti, kʷes łxʷixʷsti**

xʷistš – Walk. *cmd.*
xʷsxʷistwi – Each one of you walk. *cmd.*

es xʷstlwisi – S/he/it is walking around. **čnes xʷstlwisi, kʷes xʷstlwisi**
es čxʷstlwisms – S/he/it is walking around after s.t. **ies čxʷstlwism, as čxʷstlwism**

mił lkʷut u čn xʷist – I walked too far.

tkʷuút – walk, *referring to more than one person.*
tkʷuúʔut – They walked. **qeʔ tkʷuút, p tkʷuút**
es tkʷuúʔuti – They are walking. **qeʔes tkʷuúti, pes tkʷuúti**
qs tkʷuúʔuti – They are going to walk. **qeʔqs tkʷuúti, pqs tkʷuúti**

tkʷtkʷuút – Each one walked.

čtkʷuútalqʷ – More than one person walks on a narrow object, *i.e., log, railroad tracks, etc.*
čtkʷuúʔutalqʷm – They walked on a narrow object. **qeʔ čtkʷuútalqʷm, p čtkʷuútalqʷm**
es čtkʷuúʔutalqʷi – They're walking on a narrow object. **qeʔes čtkʷuútalqʷi, pes čtkʷuútalqʷi**

es ntkʷutáʔaqsi – S/he/it is walking on the road. **čnes ntkʷutaqsi, kʷes ntkʷutaqsi**

u tkʷuút łu pyel u kʷtisi – Pierre and Big Blanket walked away. **čtkʷtkʷuúʔułṅi** – They were walking side by side. **xʷu qeʔqs tkʷtkʷuúti** – Okay, let's go walk.

čxʷstalqʷ – walk on a narrow object. *(i.e., log, railroad tracks, board, etc.)*
čxʷstalqʷm – S/he/it walked on a narrow object. **čn čxʷstalqʷm, kʷ čxʷstalqʷm**
es čxʷstalqʷi – S/he/it is walking on a narrow object. **čnes čxʷstalqʷi, kʷes čxʷstalqʷi**

sxʷčxʷstalqʷ – hobo; one tasked to walk on railroad tracks. *prefix:* ***sxʷ...*** *– one tasked to do.*

xʷstnetkʷ – walk near water. *suffix:* ***...etkʷ, ...tkʷ*** *– liquid*
xʷstnetkʷm – S/he/it walked near water. **čn xʷstnetkʷm, kʷ xʷstnetkʷm**
es xʷstnetkʷi – S/he/it is walking near water. **čnes xʷstnetkʷi, kʷes xʷstnetkʷi**

čxʷstnetkʷ – walk next to the water. *suffix:* ***...etkʷ, ...tkʷ*** *– liquid*
čxʷstetkʷm – S/he/it walked next to the water. **čn čxʷstetkʷm, kʷ čxʷstetkʷm**
es čxʷstetkʷi – S/he/it is walking next to the water. **čnes čxʷstetkʷi, kʷes čxʷstetkʷ**

čłxʷstetkʷ – walk on the water.

nxʷstetkʷ, *nxʷste* – walk in the water; wade. *See:* ***wade.***

čxʷstičṅ – walk on a ridge. *suffix:* ***...ičṅ*** *– back.*
čxʷstičṅm – S/he/it walked on the ridge. **čn čxʷstičṅm, kʷ čxʷstičṅm**
es čxʷstičṅi – S/he/it is walking on the ridge. **čnes čxʷstičṅi, kʷes čxʷstičṅi**

The **i** following uvular consonants (UC) and the glottal stop ʔ sound like English "*ey*" as in the words *they, hey, whey,* etc. Salish UC are: **q, q̇, qʷ, q̇ʷ, x̣, x̣ʷ**. For example, the suffix ...**qin** – head/top, is often spelled using English *ey* as "q*ey*n". So **qi, q̇i, qʷi, q̇ʷi, x̣i, x̣ʷi**, may be spelled with English *ey* as **q***ey*, **q̇***ey*, **qʷ***ey*, **q̇ʷ***ey*, **x̣***ey*, **x̣ʷ***ey* in other texts.

s.t. - something, the 3rd person
(s.t.) - something implied
s.o. - someone, the 3rd person
sl. - singular form
pl. - plural form
rt. - root word
cmd. - command
lit. - literally
fig. - figuratively
i.e., - for example
See: - Redirection to a related word.

čxʷsxʷstičṅ – walks all the time on the ridge.
sxʷčxʷstičṅ – one tasked to walk on the ridge. *prefix: **sxʷ...** – one tasked to do.*
sxʷčxʷsxʷstič – one tasked to walk on ridges. *prefix: **sxʷ...** – one tasked to do.*

čxʷstqin – walk up on the mountains or on top. *suffix: **...qin, ...qn** – top.*
čxʷstqinm – S/he/it walked on the mountaintop. **čn čxʷstqinm, kʷ čxʷstqinm**
es čxʷstqini – S/he/it is walking on the mountaintop. **čnes čxʷstqini, kʷes čxʷstqini**

xʷlxʷstenč – walk on the side of a mountain or hill. *suffix: **...enč** – within.*
xʷlxʷstenčm – S/he/it walked on the side of the mountain. **čn xʷlxʷstenčm, kʷ xʷlxʷstenčm**
es xʷlxʷstenči – S/he/it is walking on the side of the mountain. **čnes xʷlxʷstenči, kʷes xʷlxʷstenči**
sxʷxʷlxʷstenč – one tasked to walk on the side hill. *prefix: **sxʷ...** – one tasked to do.*

nxʷstliwis – walk around inside. *(i.e., forest; shopping center) suffix: **...lwis** – indicates going around.*
nxʷstliwis – S/he/it walked around inside. **čn nxʷstliwis, kʷ nxʷstliwis**
es nxʷstliwisi – S/he/it is walking around inside. **čnes nxʷstliwisi, kʷes nxʷstliwisi**
qs nxʷstliwisi – S/he/it is going to walk around inside. **čiqs nxʷstliwisi, kʷqs nxʷstliwisi**

nxʷstaqs – walk on the road. *rt.: **xʷist** – walk; circumfix: **n...aqs** – nose, road. See: **hitchhike**.*

ntkʷutaqs – walk on a road; referring to more than one person. *rt.: **tkʷuut** – they walk; circumfix: **n...aqs** – nose, road. See: **hitchhike**.*

iłtt̓etmšm – walk lightly, easily. *rt.: **iłtt̓e** – easy.*
iłtt̓etmšm – S/he walked lightly. **čn iłtt̓etmšm, kʷ iłtt̓etmšm**
es iłtt̓etmšmi – S/he is walking lightly. **čnes iłtt̓etmšmi, kʷes iłtt̓etmšmi**

iłtt̓etmšmiš – Walk lightly. *cmd.*

wamist, *wami* – run walk; hurry along; run in a feminine manner. *See: **run**.*

čtčitšn – walk lightly; walk gently.
čtčitšn – S/he walked lightly. **čn čtčitšn, kʷ čtčitšn**
es čtčitšni – S/he is walking lightly. **čnes čtčitšni, kʷes čtčitšni**
qs čtčitšni – S/he is going to walk lightly. **čiqs čtčitšni, kʷqs čtčitšni**

čtčitšniš – Walk lightly. *cmd.*

wall **nčṁénč** – wall. *rt.: **čm** – extremity; suffix: **...enč** – within.*

wallow **ƛ̓očncot,** *ƛ̓očnco* – wallow in mud.
ƛ̓očncot – S/he/it wallowed in mud. **čn ƛ̓očncot, kʷ ƛ̓očncot**
es ƛ̓očncoti – S/he/it is wallowing in mud. **čnes ƛ̓očncoti, kʷes ƛ̓očncoti**
qs ƛ̓očncoti – S/he/it is going to wallow in mud. **čiqs ƛ̓očncoti, kʷqs ƛ̓očncoti**

qʷołist – dust one's self. *See: **dust**.*

want **ntels,** *nte* – want; think about.
ntelsm – S/he/it wanted (s.t.). **čn ntelsm, kʷ ntelsm**
es ntelsi – S/he/it is wanting (s.t.). **čnes ntelsi, kʷes ntelsi**
qs ntelsi – S/he/it is going to want (s.t.). **čiqs ntelsi, kʷqs ntelsi**
ntéˀelsm – They wanted (s.t.). **qeˀ ntelsm, p ntelsm**
es ntéˀelsi – They are wanting (s.t.). **qeˀes ntelsi, pes ntelsi**

ntelsis – S/he/it wanted s.t./s.o. **ntelsn, ntelsntxʷ**
es ntelsms – S/he/it is wanting s.t./s.o. **ies ntelsm, as ntelsm**
qs ntelsms – S/he/it is going to want s.t./s.o. **iqs ntelsm, aqs ntelsm**
ntéˀelsis – They wanted s.t./s.o. **qeˀ ntelsntm, ntelsntp**

ṅem qes ntelsms – S/he/it will be wanting s.t./s.o. **ṅem iqes ntelsm, ṅem aqes ntelsm**
ṅem qes nté?elsms – They will be wanting s.t./s.o. **ṅem qe?qes ntelsm, ṅem qes ntelsmp**
ṅe nte – What does s/he think/want?
kʷ ṅe nte – What do you think/want?

t steṁ u kʷes ntélsi – What do you want? **čnes nté t ululim –** I am thinking about money. **t k̓ʷinš u kʷes nte –** How much do you want? **u nté?e u hoyyhó?o łu splstwé –** And they decided to quit killing each other. **tam čnes nté –** I do not want to.

The **i** following uvular consonants (UC) and the glottal stop **?** sound like English "*ey*" as in the words *they, hey, whey*, etc. Salish UC are: **q, q̓, qʷ, q̓ʷ, x̣, x̣ʷ**. For example, the suffix **...qin** – head/top, is often spelled using English *ey* as "q*ey*n". So **qi, q̓i, qʷi, q̓ʷi, x̣i, x̣ʷi**, may be spelled with English *ey* as **q***ey*, **q̓***ey*, **qʷ***ey*, **q̓ʷ***ey*, **x̣***ey*, **x̣ʷ***ey* in other texts.

n...els – *circumfix indicating a want/desire/need to do some action.*
nwnšels – want to war dance. *See: **war dance**.*
nčšnmels – want to accompany. *circumfix: **n...els** – want. See: **accompany**.*
nq̓aq̓?els – always busy, snoopy, nosy, prying. *See: **business**.*
nx̣ʷq̓ʷomels – want to get divorced. *See: **divorce**.*
npcxʷels – act exhausted. *circumfix: **n...els** – want, feel. See: **exhausted**.*
np̓umels – want to fart. *circumfix: **n...els** – want. See: **fart**.*
ntčimelsm – S/he/it wanted to urinate. *See: **urinate**.*
ninšels – want to owl dance. *See: **owl dance**.*
nxʷyelsm – want to go. *rt.: **xʷuy** – go; circumfix: **n...els** – want, feelings. See: **go**.*
nxʷt̓pmels – want to run away. *circumfix: **n...els** – want, feel. See: **run away**.*

ha kʷes nxʷiyelsi č sntumíst – Do you want to go to the store?

nstetkʷ– want water/liquid. *(Refering to some beverage or drink.)*
nstetkʷm – S/he/it wanted a drink. **čn nstetkʷm, kʷ nstetkʷm**
es nstetkʷi – S/he/it is wanting a drink. **čnes nstetkʷi, kʷes nstetkʷi**
qs nstetkʷi – S/he/it is going to want a drink. **čiqs nstetkʷi, kʷqs nstetkʷi**

nstetkʷis – S/he/it wanted to drink s.t. **nstetkʷn, nstetkʷntxʷ**
es nstetkʷms – S/he/it is wanting to drink s.t. **ies nstetkʷm, as nstetkʷm**
qs nstetkʷms – S/he/it is going to want to drink s.t. **iqs nstetkʷm, aqs nstetkʷm**

t steṁ u kʷes nstetkʷi – What do you want to drink? **t čeṅ ečx̣i u kʷes nstetkʷi –** What kind do you want to drink?

nełnels, *nełne* **–** crave food; want to eat. *See: **crave**.*

čhomist, *čho* **–** in awe of something or someone; overwhelmed; see something beautiful/good/wonderful. *See: **awe**.*

q̓mscin – wish; hunger for. *See: **wish**.*

war

plstwéxʷ, *plstwé* **–** kill each other. *rt.: **puls** – kill; suffix: **...wexʷ** – action to each other.*
es plstwé?exʷi – They are killing each other. **qe?es plstwéxʷi, pes plstwéxʷi**

s.t. - something, the 3rd person
(s.t.) - something implied
s.o. - someone, the 3rd person
sl. - singular form
pl. - plural form
rt. - root word
cmd. - command
lit. - literally
fig. - figuratively
i.e., - for example
See: - Redirection to a related word.

war bonnet

člqin, *člqi* **–** war bonnet. *rt.: **čil** – standing upright; suffix: **...qin, ...qn** – top.*

war dance

wénš – war dance, dance at a powwow.
wénš – S/he danced. **čn wénš, kʷ wénš**
es wénši – S/he is dancing. **čnes wénši, kʷes wénši**
qs wénši – S/he is going to dance. **čiqs wénši, kʷqs wénši**
wé?enš – They danced. **qe? wénš, p wénš**
es wé?enši – They are dancing. **qe?es wénši, pes wénši**

es wéʔenši – They are going to dance. **qeʔqs wénši, pqs wénši**

es wnwenši – Each one is dancing. **qeʔes wnwenši, pes wnwenši**

łw̓ew̓nš – S/he danced a little. **čn łw̓ew̓nš, kʷ łw̓ew̓nš**

sxʷwénš – one tasked to war dance. *prefix:* ***sxʷ...*** *– one tasked to do.*
wnšemn – one inclined to dance. *suffix:* ***...emn*** *– one inclined to do.*
wnwnšmuł – one that habitually dances. *suffix:* ***...łmuł*** *– one that habitually does.*
snwénštn – place to war dance/war dance song. *prefix:* ***sn...*** *– a place of; suffix:* ***...tin, ...tn*** *– means of/device.*

wenš – Dance. *cmd.*

nunšels – S/he wanted to dance. **čn nunšels, kʷ nunšels**
es nunšelsi – S/he is wanting to dance. **čnes nunšelsi, kʷ nunšelsi**

es nkʷłwéʔenši – They are dancing together. **qeʔes nkʷłwenši, pes nkʷłwenši**
es nkʷłwnwéʔenši – They are dancing together in groups.

n̓e npilš l snwénštn m wéʔenš – When they go into the dance arbor they will dance. **iheʔ łu inwenštn –** Here is my dance regalia. **kʷqs k̓ʷis wenši –** You go and dance. **snwénštn qʷélm ƛ̓e es nkʷnéʔems –** They're already singing the war dance song. **n̓e eł cwis íʔim̓š m qeʔ wénš –** When they finish moving back here again, we'll war dance. **čeʔt mosq̓t m qeʔ wenš –** Four days till we dance.

čsplqmncut – old warrior dance.
es čsplqmncuti – He is dancing the old warior dance. **čnes čsplqmncuti, kʷes čsplqmncuti**
snčsplqmncutn – old warrior dance song. *prefix:* ***sn...*** *– a place of; suffix:* ***...tin, ...tn*** *– means of/device.*

es qʷułmncuti – There is low visibility from a dust storm or blizzard*; (fig., this can be said of someone really "dancing up a storm," making dust). See:* ***dust.***

war dancer

sxʷwénš – one tasked to war dance.
sxʷwnwenš – war dancers. *prefix:* ***sxʷ...*** *– one tasked to do.*
wnšemn – one inclined to dance. *suffix:* ***...emn*** *– one inclined to do.*
wnwnšmuł – one that habitually dances. *suffix:* ***...łmuł*** *– one that habitually does.*

warm

qʷéc – warm.
es qʷecmi – S/he/it is getting warm. **čnes qʷecmi, kʷes qʷecmi**
es qʷcncuti – S/he/it is warming ones's self. **čnes qʷcncuti, kʷes qʷcncuti**

qʷecis – S/he/it warmed s.t. **qʷecn, qʷecntxʷ**
es qʷecms – S/he/it is warming s.t. **ies qʷecm, as qʷecm**

qʷqʷʔec – It got warm.
i qʷqʷʔec – It is warm.
es qʷqʷeʔcmi – It is warming up.

qʷecnt – Warm it. *cmd.*
qʷecmnwexʷ – warm each other.

i nqʷecłc̓eʔ – It is warm inside.

qʷácqn – hat.

x̣e i qʷec – good and warm. **sčey̓t es qʷqʷeʔcnuxʷi –** The spider is bringing warm weather.

p̓eč – get hot from some heat source; warmed/heated from radiant heat. *See:* ***heat.***
es np̓eččni – Warming your body by the fire. *See:* ***heat.***

čskʷilt – sweat; perspire. *See: **sweat**.*

warn

čšťncutš – Take care of yourself. *cmd.*

čšťncut – take care of one's self. *rt.: **čšťim** – guard; suffix: **...cut** – action to the self. See: **care**.*

warrior

sxʷplstwéxʷ – warrior; one tasked to kill others. *prefix: **sxʷ...** – one tasked to do; suffix: **...wexʷ** – action to each other.*

sxʷx̣eyílš – one tasked to raid; warrior. *See: **raid**.*

sólte – soldier. *(approximation to English word)*

šinmsči – woman warrior.

nttx̣ʷte – woman warrior.

sněsplqmncutn – old warrior dance song. *prefix: **sn...** – a place of; suffix: **...tin, ...tn** – means of/device.*

The **i** following uvular consonants (UC) and the glottal stop **ʔ** sound like English "*ey*" as in the words th*ey*, h*ey*, wh*ey*, etc. Salish UC are: **q**, **q̇**, **qʷ**, **q̇ʷ**, **x̣**, **x̣ʷ**. For example, the suffix **...qin** – head/top, is often spelled using English *ey* as "q*ey*n". So **qi**, **q̇i**, **qʷi**, **q̇ʷi**, **x̣i**, **x̣ʷi**, may be spelled with English *ey* as **q***ey*, **q̇***ey*, **qʷ***ey*, **q̇ʷ***ey*, **x̣***ey*, **x̣ʷ***ey* in other texts.

was

ƛ̓ṁ – used to be; was.

ƛ̓ṁ steṁ łiʔe – What was this? **ƛ̓ṁ kʷ swe** – What was your name? **ƛ̓ṁ swe łišeʔ** – Who was that?

wash

ċeẇ – wash.

ċéẇm – S/he/it washed. **čn ċéẇm, kʷ ċéẇm**
es ċéẇi – S/he/it is washing. **čnes ċéẇi, kʷes ċéẇi**
qs ċéẇi – S/he/it is going to wash. **čiqs ċéẇi, kʷqs ċéẇi**

ċéẇist – S/he/it washed one's self. **čn ċéẇist, kʷ ċéẇist**
es ċéẇisti – S/he/it is washing one's self. **čnes ċéẇisi, kʷes ċéẇisti**
qs ċéẇisti – S/he/it is going to wash one's self. **čiqs ċéẇisti, kʷqs ċéẇisti**

ċéẇis – S/he/it washed it. **ċéẇn, ċéẇntxʷ**
es ċéẇms – S/he/it is washing it. **ies ċéẇm, as ċéẇm**
qs ċéẇms – S/he/it is going to wash it. **iqs ċéẇm, aqs ċéẇm**

nċéẇis – S/he/it washed it out. **nċéẇn, nċéẇntxʷ**
es nċéẇms – S/he/it is washing it out. **ies nċéẇm, as nċéẇm**
qs nċéẇms – S/he/it is going to wash it out. **iqs nċéẇm, aqs nċéẇm**
nċéʔeẇis – They washed it out. **qeʔ nċéẇntm, nċéẇntp**

es ċéẇ – S/he/it is washed.
es ċuċéẇi – S/he/it is repeatedly washing. **čnes ċuċéẇi, kʷes ċuċéẇi**

scċéẇ – something that has been washed. *prefix: **sc...** – s.t. that's been done/made/prepared.*
ċéẇmn – soap. *suffix: **...min, ...mn** – instrument/tool.*
ċuċéẇčstn – hand soap. *suffix: **...min, ...mn** – instrument/tool.*
ċuʔłqpéłċeʔtn – dish soap. *suffix: **...min, ...mn** – instrument/tool.*
ċéẇstn – face soap. *suffix: **...tin, ...tn** – means of/device.*

ċéẇnt – Wash it. *cmd.*
nċéẇnt – Wash it out. *cmd.*
ċunwexʷ – wash each other. *suffix: **...wexʷ** – action to each other*
ċumlwis – wash around here and there. *suffix: **...lwis** – indicates going around*
čċaẇqn – wash the head.
ċuċeẇšn – wash feet.
ċuelt – wash children.

s.t. - something, the 3rd person
(s.t.) - something implied
s.o. - someone, the 3rd person
sl. - singular form
pl. - plural form
rt. - root word
cmd. - command
lit. - literally
fig. - figuratively
i.e., - for example
See: - Redirection to a related word.

nċeẇłċeʔ – wash the inside out.
nċuʔłqpéłċeʔ, *nċuʔłqpé* – wash dishes. *See: **dishwasher.***
ċaẇlš – bathe; sit in the tub. *See: **bathe.***

nċéẇkʷ – wash in the water.
nċéẇkʷis – S/he/it washed it in the water. **nċéẇkʷn, nċéẇkʷntxʷ**
es nċéẇkʷms – S/he/it is washing it in the water. **ies nċéẇkʷm, as nċéẇkʷm**
qs nċéẇkʷms – S/he/it is going to wash it in the water. **iqs nċéẇkʷm, aqs nċéẇkʷm**
nċéʔeẇkʷis – They washed it in the water. **qeʔ nċéẇkʷntm, nċéẇkʷntp**

nċéẇkʷnt – Wash it in the water. *cmd.*

nċéẇkʷnt asṗéƛ̓m – Wash your bitterroot. **xʷk̓ʷunt m nċéẇkʷntxʷ asq̇ʷl̓á –** Clean and wash your black tree moss.

ċuċéẇčst – wash hands.
ċuċéẇčstm – S/he/it washed hands. **čn ċuċéẇčstm, kʷ ċuċéẇčstm**
es ċuċéẇčsti – S/he/it is washing hands. **čnes ċuċéẇčsti, kʷes ċuċéẇčsti**
qs ċuċéẇčsti – S/he/it is going to wash hands. **čiqs ċuċéẇčsti, kʷqs ċuċéẇčsti**

ċuċéẇčstis – S/he/it washed s.o.'s hands. **čn ċuċéẇčstn, kʷ ċuċéẇčstntxʷ**
es ċuċéẇčstms – S/he/it is washing s.o.'s hands. **ies ċuċéẇčstm, as ċuċéẇčstm**
qs ċuċéẇčstms – S/he/it is going to wash s.o.'s hands. **iqs ċuċéẇčstm, aqs ċuċéẇčstm**

ċuċéẇčstiš – Wash your hands. *cmd.*
ċuċéẇčsnt – Wash his/her hands. *cmd.*

ha kʷ ċuċéẇčstm – Did you wash your hands?

ċeẇsm – wash the face.
ċeẇsm – S/he/it washed one's face. **čn ċeẇsm, kʷ ċeẇsm**
es ċeẇsi – S/he/it is washing one's face. **čnes ċeẇsi, kʷes ċeẇsi**
qs ċeẇsi – S/he/it is going to wash one's face. **čiqs ċeẇsi, kʷqs ċeẇsi**

ċeẇsis – S/he/it washed s.o.'s face. **ċeẇsn, ċeẇsntxʷ**
es ċeẇsms – S/he/it is washing s.o.'s face. **ies ċeẇsm, as ċeẇsm**
qs ċeẇsms – S/he/it is going to wash s.o.'s face. **iqs ċeẇsm, aqs ċeẇsm**

ċeẇsiš – Wash your face. *cmd.*
ċeẇsnt – Wash his/her face. *cmd.*

nq̇ʷʔétkʷ, *nq̇ʷʔé* – wash clothes; do laundry. *rt.: **q̇ʷʔe** – wring out; suffix: **...etkʷ, ...tkʷ** – liquid**...etkʷ, ...tkʷ** – liquid*
nq̇ʷʔétkʷm – S/he washed clothes. **čn nq̇ʷʔétkʷm, kʷ nq̇ʷʔétkʷm**
es nq̇ʷʔétkʷi – S/he is washing clothes. **čnes nq̇ʷʔétkʷi, kʷes nq̇ʷʔétkʷi**
qs nq̇ʷʔétkʷi – S/he is going to wash clothes. **čiqs nq̇ʷʔétkʷi, kʷqs nq̇ʷʔétkʷi**

nq̇ʷʔétkʷis – S/he washed the clothes. **nq̇ʷʔétkʷn, nq̇ʷʔétkʷntxʷ**
es nq̇ʷʔétkʷms – S/he is washing the clothes. **ies nq̇ʷʔétkʷm, as nq̇ʷʔétkʷm**
qs nq̇ʷʔétkʷms – S/he is going to wash the clothes. **iqs nq̇ʷʔétkʷm, aqs nq̇ʷʔétkʷm**

nq̇ʷʔétkʷiš – Wash clothes. *cmd.*
nq̇ʷʔétkʷnt – Wash the clothes. *cmd.*

qs nq̇ʷʔétkʷ – It is going to be washed; laundry.

swe łu nq̇ʷʔétkʷis insnołups – Who washed my pants?

q̇ʷʔe – wring; twist; squeeze. *See: **wring.***

wash basin **snċéẇstn –** place to wash; wash basin. *prefix:* ***sn...** – a place of; suffix:* ***...tin, ...tn** – means of/device.*

washboard **snčx̣iqmn –** washboard.

washbowl **snċéẇstn –** place to wash; washbowl. *prefix:* ***sn...** – a place of; suffix:* ***...tin, ...tn** – means of/device.*

washer **snq̓ʷʔétkʷn,** *snq̓ʷʔé* **–** washing machine, wash tub. *prefix:* ***sn...** – a place of.*

washing machine **snq̓ʷʔétkʷtn,** *snq̓ʷʔé* **–** washing machine, wash tub. *prefix:* ***sn...** – a place of.*

wasp **sqʷuʔł –** wasp, bee, hornet.

waste **ċulm –** let something go to waste; do away with something by destruction or nonuse; not using something properly.
ċulis – S/he wasted it. **ċuln, ċulntxʷ**
es ċulms – S/he/it is wasting it. **ies ċulm, as ċulm**
qs ċulms – S/he/it is going to waste it. **iqs ċulm, aqs ċulm**
ċúʔulis – They wasted it. **qeʔ ċulntm, ċulntp**
es ċúʔulms – They are wasting it. **qeʔes ċulm, es ċulmp**
qs ċúʔulms – They are going to waste it. **qeʔqs ċulm, qs ċulmp**

ṅem qs ċulms – S/he/it will be wasting. **ṅem iqs ċulm, ṅem aqs ċulm**
ṅem qs ċúʔulms – They will be wasting. **ṅem qeʔqs ċulm, ṅem qs ċulmp**
ṅem ċulis – S/he/it will waste it. **ṅem ċuln, ṅem ċulntxʷ**
ṅem ċúʔulis – They will waste it. **ṅem qeʔ ċulntm, ṅem ċulntp**

ċulemn – one inclined to let something waste. *suffix:* ***...emn** – one inclined to do.*

ċuln łu sṗeƛ̓m – I wasted and ruined the bitterroot; I let the bitterroot spoil. **ta qs ċulntxʷ –** Do not waste it.

qʷiqʷeyéčst, *qʷiqʷeyé* **–** waste by using foolishly; not using something to its full potential. *suffix:* ***...ečst, ...čst** – of the hand.*
qʷiqʷeyéčstis – S/he wasted s.t. **qʷiqʷeyéčstn, qʷiqʷeyéčstntxʷ**
es qʷiqʷeyéčstmms – S/he is wasting s.t. **ies qʷiqʷeyéčstmm, as qʷiqʷeyéčstmm**
qs qʷiqʷeyéčstmms – S/he is going to waste s.t. **iqs qʷiqʷeyéčstmm, aqs qʷiqʷeyéčstmm**

qʷiqʷeyéčstn łu sṗeƛ̓m – I wasted the bitterroot; I used it foolishly.

k̓ʷłx̣ʷellm – ruin something; let something waste away. *See:* ***ruin***

watch **áċċx̣ –** watch; stare at something. *rt.:* ***áċx̣** – look. See:* ***look.***
áċċx̣m – S/he/it watched. **čn áċċx̣m, kʷ áċċx̣m**
es áċċx̣i – S/he/it is watching. **čnes áċċx̣i, kʷes áċċx̣i**
es áċċx̣i – S/he/it is going to watch. **čnes áċċx̣i, kʷes áċċx̣i**
áʔaċċx̣m – They watched. **qeʔ áċċx̣m, p áċċx̣m**
es áʔaċċx̣i – They are watching. **qeʔes áċċx̣i, pes áċċx̣i**
qs áʔaċċx̣i – They are going to watch. **qeʔqs áċċx̣i, pqs áċċx̣i**

áċċx̣is – S/he/it watched it. **áċċx̣n, áċċx̣ntxʷ**
es áċċx̣ms – S/he/it is watching it. **ies áċċx̣m, as áċċx̣m**
qs áċċx̣ms – S/he/it is going to watch it. **iqs áċċx̣m, aqs áċċx̣m**

The **i** following uvular consonants (UC) and the glottal stop **ʔ** sound like English "*ey*" as in the words *they, hey, whey,* etc. Salish UC are: **q, q̓, qʷ, q̓ʷ, x̣, x̣ʷ**. For example, the suffix ...**qin** – head/top, is often spelled using English *ey* as "q*ey*n". So **qi, q̓i, qʷi, q̓ʷi, x̣i, x̣ʷi,** may be spelled with English *ey* as **q***ey*, **q̓***ey*, **qʷ***ey*, **q̓ʷ***ey*, **x̣***ey*, **x̣ʷ***ey* in other texts.

s.t. - something, the 3rd person
(s.t.) - something implied
s.o. - someone, the 3rd person
sl. - singular form
pl. - plural form
rt. - root word
cmd. - command
lit. - literally
fig. - figuratively
i.e., - for example
See: - Redirection to a related word.

áʔaccx̣is – They watched it. **qeʔ áccx̣ntm, áccx̣ntp**
es áʔaccx̣ms – They are watching it. **qeʔes áccx̣m, es áccx̣mp**
qs áʔaccx̣ms – They are going to watch it. **qeʔqs áccx̣m, qs áccx̣mp**

es áċx̣ċx̣ms – S/he/it is watching/staring . **ies áċx̣ċx̣m, as áċx̣ċx̣m**
es áʔaċx̣ċx̣m – They are watching/staring . **qeʔes áċx̣ċx̣m, es áċx̣ċx̣mp**

sxʷʔáccx̣m – one tasked to watch. *prefix:* ***sxʷ...*** *– one tasked to do.*
sʔaccx̣ – movie, show. *See:* ***movie.***
x̣sʔaccx̣ – good movie.

áccx̣iš – Watch. *cmd.*
áccx̣wi – All of you watch. *cmd.*
áccx̣nt – Watch it. *cmd.*
áccx̣nti – All of you watch it. *cmd.*
nʔáccx̣cin – watch someone eat. *suffix:* ***...cin, ...cn*** *– action of the mouth.*

qeʔes áccx̣łls – S/he's watching us. **t šeẏ u iše eċx̣i qeʔes aċx̣łlt łu steṁ qeʔ scḱʷul̓** – That's the way it is, they look at what we do.

sppq̇niʔ – watch, time piece.

water

séwłkʷ – water.

...etkʷ, ...tkʷ, ...kʷ – *suffix indicating water; liquid.* **n...** – *prefix indicating inside. These two affixes frequently co-occur. Descriptions of water usually describe the inside of water or liquid.*

nƛ̓aq̇kʷ – hot water. *rt.:* ***ƛ̓aq̇*** *– hot.*
nmal̓kʷ – luke warm water.
nċlatkʷ – cold water. *rt.:* ***ċalt*** *– cold.*
nsulkʷ – cold water. *rt.:* ***sult*** *– cold.*
nqʷamqʷmetkʷ – excellent water. *rt.:* ***qʷamqʷmt*** *– excellent; suffix:* ***...etkʷ, ...tkʷ*** *– liquid*
nx̣setkʷ – good water. *rt.:* ***x̣est*** *– good.*
nt̓iškʷ – sweet liquid; pop; Kool-aid.
nt̓q̇étkʷnt l séwłkʷ – You put it in the water. *See:* ***put.***

es ocqʔétkʷ – the water is coming out; spring. *See:* ***spring.***
ništétkʷ – underwater, deep stream. *rt.:* ***išut*** *– down, low. See:* ***underwater.***
ntx̣ʷétkʷ, *ntx̣ʷé* – river. *rt.:* ***tox̣ʷ*** *– straight. See:* ***river.***
nšiẏétkʷ, *nšiẏé* – creek, stream. *lit. first water. rt.:* ***šʔit*** *– first. See:* ***creek.***
es mopétkʷ – flowing water.
ḱʷłnċmétkʷ – constricted waterway.
čłeʔusétkʷ – obstructed waterway. *(i.e., rock, log, etc.)*

sʔolqʷelšwetkʷ – where water flows into another waterway. *suffix:* ***...etkʷ, ...tkʷ*** *– liquid*

nileẃs – main waterway, which tributaries flow into.

nqʷést – deep water.

čłq̇li – lake. *See:* ***lake.***

nsixʷlexʷ – pond, puddle. *rt.:* ***sixʷ*** *– pour/spill; suffix:* ***...ulexʷ*** *– land. See:* ***pond.***

ṅmẇaẃs, *ṅmẇa* – irrigate/water a field, yard, ground. *See:* ***irrigate.***

t̓iṁlexʷ – damp ground; swamp. *See:* ***swamp.***

łin – splash/sprinkle and spread liquid. *See:* ***splash.***

iox̣ʷ – sound of rushing water.

nmulm – fetch water/liquid *(from the sound made dipping a container in water; used to indicate the motion getting water). See:* ***fetch.***

łłnulexʷtn – spread water on the ground; water the ground; sprinkle. *See:* ***sprinkle.***

watercress **snkʷalétkʷ** – watercress.

water crossing **snyek̓ʷtin** – place to cross the water; a water crossing.

waterfall **es t̓ipmétkʷ** – waterfall; the water is falling.

water insect **nopoplq̓sétkʷ**, *npoplq̓sé* – water insects, bugs.

ntt̓laceʔ – water skipper *(insect).*

watermelon **čqʷnqʷinc̓eʔ**, *čqʷnqʷi* – watermelon. *suffix:* ***...ic̓éʔ*** *– covered in. lit. it is all green.*

ččqʷáyic̓éʔ – watermelon. *suffix:* ***...ic̓éʔ*** *– covered in. lit. it is all blue.*

water osel **q̓ʷox̣ʷm̓in̓eʔ** – American dipper; water osel; *Cinclus mexicanus.*

water skipper **ntt̓laceʔ** – water skipper *(insect).*

wave **taq** – wave; gesture with the hand.

taqm – S/he waved. **čn taqm, kʷ taqm**
es taqi – S/he is waving. **čnes taqi, kʷes taqi**
qs taqi – S/he is going to wave. **čiqs taqi, kʷqs taqi**

taqis – S/he waved at s.o. **taqn, taqntxʷ**
es taqms – S/he is waving at s.o. **ies taqm, as taqm**
qs taqms – S/he is going to wave at s.o. **iqs taqm, aqs taqm**

es tqtaqi – S/he is waving with both hands. **čnes tqtaqi, kʷes tqtaqi**

taqiš – Wave; gesture with the hand. *cmd.*
taqnt – Wave at s.o. *cmd.*

tql̓sečst – gesture with the hand for somebody's attention; sign. *See:* ***gesture.***

qxʷlsečst – gesture with the hand for somebody to leave. *See:* ***gesture.***

acnew̓kʷ – waves on water.

wax **snloqʷneʔ** – ear wax.

waxwing **łkʷkʷusn̓**, *łkʷkʷu* – cedar waxwing.

way **cuut** – way of doing something; one's mannerism; one's gift from Creator.

cuuts – his/her way of acting/doing. **incuut, ancuut**

x̣słcuut – little good ways.
čsłcuut – little bad ways.

n̓e t iqł cuut – It is going to happen; I will take it no matter what happens to me. **t aqł cuut** – However you do it (so be it). **čn lemt x̣ʷl̓ innunumeʔ łu x̣ʷl̓ cuuts x̣est łu nk̓ʷul̓mis** – I am grateful for my uncle's ways, he has a good way of life.

The **i** following uvular consonants (UC) and the glottal stop **ʔ** sound like English "*ey*" as in the words th*ey*, h*ey*, wh*ey*, etc. Salish UC are: **q**, **q̓**, **qʷ**, **q̓ʷ**, **x̣**, **x̣ʷ**. For example, the suffix ...**qin** – head/top, is often spelled using English *ey* as "q*ey*n". So **qi**, **q̓i**, **qʷi**, **q̓ʷi**, **x̣i**, **x̣ʷi**, may be spelled with English *ey* as **q***ey*, **q̓***ey*, **qʷ***ey*, **q̓ʷ***ey*, **x̣***ey*, **x̣ʷ***ey* in other texts.

s.t. - something, the 3rd person
(s.t.) - something implied
s.o. - someone, the 3rd person
sl. - singular form
pl. - plural form
rt. - root word
cmd. - command
lit. - literally
fig. - figuratively
i.e., - for example
See: - Redirection to a related word.

...cut – *suffix indicating an action to or of the self; it is derived from* ***cuut*** *– one's mannerism.*

k̓ʷl̓ncutn – Creator; Maker of Ways/Mannerisms.

nčl̓pscut, *nčl̓pscu* – act as Coyote; be foolish; mimic others' actions just because they are doing it. *rt.:* ***snčl̓ep*** *– coyote; suffix:* ***...cut*** *– action to the self. See:* ***foolish.***

k̓ʷłpusncut, *k̓ʷłpusncu* – self-conscious; backward; shy; bashful; polite; considerate; does not impose. *See:* ***self-conscious.***

nk̓ʷul̓mn – ways; customs; habits; culture; traditions; the things one does. *See:* ***customs.***

nʔax̣íłtn – ways; customs; the way one acts. *See:* ***customs.***

we

qeʔnple – us, we.

ƛ̓m qemlmelčstn – It was our toy.
qemlmelčstn – our toy.
qeʔqł mlmelčstn – It is going to be our toy.

qeq̓ʷomqn – our hair.
qespúʔus – our heart.

qeʔ uł sccmel̓t – We are children.

člipust – ours, us, we.

weak

c̓áw̓ –tasteless; weak tasting, *(not strong).*
nc̓áw̓kʷ – weak, tasteless liquid *(i.e., coffee).*

wealthy

qʷyulexʷ – rich, wealthy. *See:* ***rich.***

wear

x̣cnum̓t – ready/dressed; put clothes on. *rt.:* ***x̣cim*** *– make ready/orderly. See:* ***ready.***
x̣cnum̓t – S/he put clothes on. **čn x̣cnum̓t, kʷ x̣cnum̓t**
es x̣cnum̓t – S/he is wearing clothes. **čnes x̣cnum̓t, kʷes x̣cnum̓t**
qs x̣cnum̓t – S/he is going to wear clothes. **čiqs x̣cnum̓t, kʷqs x̣cnum̓t**

es qʷacqn – S/he is wearing a hat. *See:* ***hat.***
čnes nołups – I am wearing pants. *See:* ***pants.***
kʷes sic̓m – You are wearing a blanket. *See:* ***blanket.***
es nacłq̓éyt – S/he is wearing a shirt. *See:* ***shirt.***
čnes nq̓ʷoƛ̓šn – I am wearing socks. *See:* ***sock.***
kʷes čqal̓tčalqs – You are wearing a coat. *See:* ***coat.***

łixʷp – slip/pull/put something fitted over an object. *See:* ***pull over.***
nłxʷpncut – dress one's self. *See:* ***dress.***

weasel

łpápqłc̓eʔ, *łpá* – winter weasel; ermine; *Mustela frenata. rt.:* ***piq*** *– white.*

łčim̓ – summer weasel; ermine; *Mustela frenata.*

weather

ec̓ščnasq̓ti – what is happening with the sky; how's the weather? *suffix:* ***...asq̓t*** *– sky, day.*

es nt̓xʷt̓xʷlasq̓ti – The weather is changing.

ac̓x̣asq̓t – look at the sky/weather.

x̣sasq̓t – The sky/weather is good. *prefix:* ***x̣s...*** *– good; suffix:* ***...asq̓t*** *– sky, day.*
es x̣sáq̓ti – It is good weather; the sky is good.
ha x̣sáq̓t – Is it good weather?

čsasq̇t – The sky/weather is bad. *prefix:* ***čs...*** *– bad; suffix:* ***...asq̇t*** *– sky, day.*
es čsásq̇ti – It is bad weather; the sky is bad.

ac̓x̣nuxʷ – forecast weather.

weave **q̇č̓im –** weave; draw material together. *rt.:* ***q̇eč̓*** *– shrink.*
q̇éč̓ – S/he weaved. **čn q̇éč̓, kʷ q̇éč̓**
es q̇éč̓i – S/he is weaving. **čnes q̇éč̓i, kʷes q̇éč̓i**
qs q̇éč̓i – S/he is going to weave. **čiqs q̇éč̓i, kʷqs q̇éč̓i**
q̇éʔeč̓ – They weaved. **qeʔ q̇éč̓, p q̇éč̓**
es q̇éʔeč̓i – They are weaving. **qeʔes q̇éč̓i, pes q̇éč̓i**

q̇č̓ntes – S/he weaved s.t. **q̇č̓nten, q̇č̓ntexʷ**
es q̇č̓ims – S/he is weaving s.t. **ies q̇č̓im, as q̇č̓im**
qs q̇éč̓ms – S/he is going to weave s.t. **iqs q̇č̓im, aqs q̇č̓im**
q̇č̓ntéʔes – They weaved s.t. **qeʔ q̇č̓ntem, q̇č̓ntep**
es q̇č̓íʔims – They are weaving s.t. **qeʔes q̇č̓im, es q̇č̓imp**

es q̇éč̓ – It is woven. *(i.e., sack, net)*

snq̇č̓á – basket.

es q̇č̓int – Weave it. *cmd.*
es čq̇č̓ič̓éʔ – It has a woven cover.

ha as čq̇č̓ič̓ʔém – Are you weaving around it?

yey – weave; cross interweave.
yeyis – S/he weaved it. **yeyn, yeyntxʷ**
es yeyms – S/he is weaving it. **ies yeym, as yeym**
qs yeyms – S/he is going to weave it. **iqs yeym, aqs yeym**
yéʔeyis – They weaved it. **qeʔ yeyntm, yeyntp**
es yéʔeyms – They are weaving it. **qeʔes yeym, es yeymp**
qs yéʔeyms – They are going to weave it. **qeʔqs yeym, qs yeymp**

syey – woven mat.
scyeym – something that's been woven.

yeynt – Weave it. *cmd.*

web **sṫupłxʷ –** spider web. *rt.:* ***ṫup*** *– twist; suffix:* ***...ełxʷ, ...łxʷ*** *– house.*

sʔacims sčeẏt – spider web; spider's trap.

wedge **nsq̇eẇstn –** wedge. *rt.:* ***saq̇*** *– split; prefix:* ***n...*** *– inside; suffix:* ***...éẇs*** *– in between, middle; suffix:* ***...mintn*** *– tool that does...****tin, ...tn*** *– means of/device.*

Wednesday **čałłásq̇t**, *čałłá* **–** Wednesday, three days; *i.e., three days past Sunday. suffix:* ***...asq̇t*** *– sky, day.*
eł tiẇł čałłásq̇t – Again, another Wednesday is here.
eł čałłásq̇t – It is Wednesday again.

weed **nlq̇eẇs –** pull rooted weeds out in a garden; root out weeds; pull a rooted thing out from in between something. *rt.:* ***lq̇e*** *– pull out rooted thing; suffix:* ***...éẇs*** *– in between, middle.*
nlq̇eẇsm – S/he weeded. **čn nlq̇eẇsm, kʷ nlq̇eẇsm**
es nlq̇eẇsi – S/he is weeding. **čnes nlq̇eẇsi, kʷes nlq̇eẇsi**

The **i** following uvular consonants (UC) and the glottal stop **ʔ** sound like English "*ey*" as in the words th*ey*, h*ey*, wh*ey*, etc. Salish UC are: **q**, **q̇**, **qʷ**, **q̇ʷ**, **x̣**, **x̣ʷ**. For example, the suffix ...**qin** – head/top, is often spelled using English *ey* as "q*ey*n". So **qi**, **q̇i**, **qʷi**, **q̇ʷi**, **x̣i**, **x̣ʷi**, may be spelled with English *ey* as **q***ey*, **q̇***ey*, **qʷ***ey*, **q̇ʷ***ey*, **x̣***ey*, **x̣ʷ***ey* in other texts.

s.t. - something, the 3rd person
(s.t.) - something implied
s.o. - someone, the 3rd person
sl. - singular form
pl. - plural form
rt. - root word
cmd. - command
lit. - literally
fig. - figuratively
i.e., - for example
See: - Redirection to a related word.

qs nlq̇ewẉsi – S/he is going to weed. **čiqs nlq̇ewẉsi, kʷqs nlq̇ewẉsi**

nlq̇ewẉsis – S/he weeded it. **nlq̇ewẉsn, nlq̇ewẉsntxʷ**
es nlq̇ewẉsms – S/he is weeding it. **ies nlq̇ewẉsm, as nlq̇ewẉsm**
qs nlq̇ewẉsms – S/he is going to weed it. **iqs nlq̇ewẉsm, aqs nlq̇ewẉsm**

nlq̇ewẉsiš – Weed. *cmd.*
nlq̇ewẉswi – All of you weed. *cmd.*
nlq̇ewẉsnt – Weed it. *cmd.*
lq̇em – pull a rooted thing out; root out. *See: **pull out**.*

sc̆supulexʷ – bad grass; weeds.

łutilš – thin; become few; weed. *See: **thin**.*

week

sčacéẉs – Sunday, week.
nk̓ʷuʔ sčacéẉs – one week.
esel sčacéẉs – two weeks.
čełe sčacéẉs – three weeks.
mus sčacéẉs – four weeks.
upn sčacéẉs – ten weeks.

sčx̣ʷcsčacéẉs – the past week.

weep

ċqʷaqʷ, *ċqʷa* **–** cry; loud cry. *(i.e., a child in pain, etc.) See: **cry**.*

cʔot – moan; slow quiet steady cry. *See: **cry**.*

čawawpus – cry; have tears. *See: **tears**.*

weight

sx̣emt – weight; heaviness. *See: **heavy**.*

q̇etm – make weighty as a means to counter balance; make weighty to make something sink down. *See: **balance**.*

well

x̣es – feel good/well; in good health. *rt.: **x̣est** – good.*
x̣es – S/he/it is well. **čn x̣es, kʷ x̣es**
i x̣es – S/he/it is feeling well. **i čn x̣es, i kʷ x̣es**

x̣sx̣es – They are well. **qeʔ x̣sx̣es, p x̣sx̣es**
i x̣sx̣éʔes – They are feeling well. **i qeʔ x̣sx̣es, i p x̣sx̣es**

nexʷ i čn x̣es – I am also well. **ha i kʷ x̣es –** Are you well? **nexʷ i x̣éʔes –** They are also fine. **kʷeṁt esyaʔ u i x̣sx̣es –** Then each one is well, good, fine. **ʔe qeʔesyaʔ u i qeʔ x̣sx̣es –** Yes we are all fine, well, good.

ṗaáx̣ – heal; cure; get well. *See: **heal**.*

pṅ – but *(contradictory)*, well *(as a rebuke)*, yet *(in spite of)*. *See: **response**.*

słx̣ʷsewłkʷ – water well. *See: **bore**.*

west

sc̆lxʷtin – west.

utemči, *ute* **–** downriver to another country/land; generally toward the Pacific ocean; west.

čiqs nʔax̣ʷti č ute – I am going to go downriver to the west.

western birch

sicqṅełp – red birch; *Betula occidentalis*.

western bluebird **nłqʷiqʷayačn̓** – western bluebird; *Sialia mexicana.*

western hemlock **płtin̓éłp,** *płtin̓é* – western hemlock; *Tsuga heterophylla.*

western kingbird **sččáteʔ,** *sččá* – western kingbird. *(black and white)*
słččáteʔ – small western kingbird.

western larch **cáqʷlš** – western larch; tamarack; *Larix occidentalis.*

western meadowlark **wewickʷl̓eʔ,** *wewi* – female western meadowlark; *Sturnella neglecta.*
wewickʷl̓om, *wewi* – male western meadowlark; *Sturnella neglecta.*

western red cedar **ástqʷ** – western cedar; *Thuja plicata.*

qʷelcn – grand fir, balsam fir; *Abies grandis*; western red cedar; *Thuja plicata. (There is uncertainty with this word; some speakers identify it as western red cedar, Thuja plicata, while some identify it as grand fir, Abies grandis.)*

mšéłp – western cedar boughs.

western yew **ckʷn̓čálqʷ,** *ckʷn̓čá* – yew *(used to make bows –* ***ckʷin̓č****).*

wet **nás** – wet.
es naʔsma – S/he is getting wet. **čnes naʔsma, kʷes naʔsma**
qs naʔsma – S/he is going to get wet. **čiqs naʔsma, kʷqs naʔsma**

i nás – S/he/it is wet. **i čn nás, i kʷ nás**
naʔás – S/he/it got wet. **čn naʔás, kʷ naʔás**

naʔnʔas – Each one got wet.

nasléxʷ – wet land.
čnasus – His/her face was wet.

nłuckʷ – soak. *rt.:* ***łuc*** *– moisten; suffix:* ***...etkʷ, ...tkʷ*** *– liquid*
es nłuckʷi – S/he is soaking (s.t.). **čnes nłuckʷi, kʷes nłuckʷi**

ssalt – damp/wet.

whale **smtus** – whale.

what **stem̓** – What; what is s/he/it? *It can also be a generic term such as "thing" in English. In the plural form it is a filler word similar to thing-a-ma-jig.*
stm̓tem̓ – things, stuff.
tʔe stem̓ – something.

stem̓ – What is s/he/it? **čn stem̓, kʷ stem̓**
stem̓s – Its his/her/its thing. **istem̓, astem̓**
tʔe stem̓s – Its something of his/hers/its. **tʔe istem̓, tʔe astem̓**

u stem̓ – And what?
u eł t stem̓ – Now what?

čstem̓ – What did s/he go after? **čn čstem̓, kʷ čstem̓**
es čstem̓i – What is s/he going after? **čnes čstem̓i, kʷes čstem̓i**
qs čstem̓i – What is s/he going to go after? **čiqs čstem̓i, kʷqs čstem̓i**

ep stem̓ – What does s/he/it have? **čn ep stem̓, kʷ ep stem̓**

The **i** following uvular consonants (UC) and the glottal stop **ʔ** sound like English "*ey*" as in the words th*ey*, h*ey*, wh*ey*, etc. Salish UC are: **q, q̇, qʷ, q̇ʷ, x̣, x̣ʷ**. For example, the suffix **...qin** – head/top, is often spelled using English *ey* as "q*ey*n". So **qi, q̇i, qʷi, q̇ʷi, x̣i, x̣ʷi**, may be spelled with English *ey* as **q***ey*, **q̇***ey*, **qʷ***ey*, **q̇ʷ***ey*, **x̣***ey*, **x̣ʷ***ey* in other texts.

s.t. - something, the 3rd person
(s.t.) - something implied
s.o. - someone, the 3rd person
sl. - singular form
pl. - plural form
rt. - root word
cmd. - command
lit. - literally
fig. - figuratively
i.e., - for example
See: - Redirection to a related word.

q ep stem̓ – What is s/he/it going to have? **čiq ep stem̓, kʷq ep stem̓**

stm̓elixʷ – What people/nationality is s/he? **čn stm̓elixʷ, kʷ stm̓elixʷ**
stm̓ulexʷ – What land?

kʷem̓t stém̓ qeʔ qłtém̓tn – Then, what will we do with it?

wheat **sp̓qin,** *sp̓qi* – wheat.

čsp̓im – thrash oats; gathering huckleberries *(when hitting the bush the berries fall onto a canvas). See:* ***thrash.***

qľwá – thrash wheat; stepping on wheat. *See:* ***thrash.***

wheel **čx̣ʷolqʷšn** – wheel.

sčyalšn – wheel.

sčp̓uyšn – tire.

when **pistem̓,** *piste* – when; inquiring about a day/month/year. *(i.e., asking for a time measured in days)*
t pistem̓ – When in the past?
n̓e pistem̓ – When? *(more specific, i.e., what day?)*
n̓e pistem̓ m kʷ xʷuy – When are you going to go?
t pistem̓ u kʷ eł ck̓ʷłčicš – When did you get back?
tʔe pistem – someday; whenever.

put t čen̓ – when; inquiring about a time in general.
put t čen̓ m eł ck̓ʷłčic – When is s/he going to get back here?

put l k̓ʷinš – what time; inquiring about a time referring to the clock.

n̓e t čen̓ – when ever.

where **čen̓** – Where?
č čen̓ – Where to?
l čen̓ – Where at?
n̓e l čen̓ – Where ever.
kʷ čen̓ – Where are you?

l čen̓ łu ancitxʷ – Where is your house? **l čen̓ łu anp̓umin** – Where is your drum? **l čen̓ u kʷes wis xʷuy** – Where have you been? **l čen̓ u kʷes lcíʔi** – Where have you been living?

es mlk̓ʷmulexʷ – everywhere.

which **čen̓** – Where?
čen̓ łu šymł kʷtunt – Which is the biggest?
čen̓ łu šymł łkʷkʷnumeʔ – Which is the smallest?

whine **nttucin** – whine. *suffix:* ***...cin, ...cn*** *– action of the mouth.*
es nttucini – S/he is whining. **čnes nttucini, kʷes nttucini**

nttucnemn – one inclined to whine. *suffix:* ***...emn*** *– one inclined to do.*

ta kʷ qes nttucinm – Do not whine.

ttucnmist – act with a whine.
es ttucnmisti – S/he is acting with a whine. **čnes ttucnmisti, kʷes ttucnmisti**

nc̓iups – say someone is a whiner; sour butt. *rt.:* ***c̓uy*** *– sour; circumfix:* ***n...ups*** *– butt, tail.*
x̣ił kʷ nc̓iups – Gee, you are a whiner.

whip **čspiċéʔ** – whip; hit someone all over with something. *rt.: **spim** – strike w/ object; suffix: **...iċéʔ** – covered in.*

čspiċʔém – S/he whipped. **čn čspiċʔém, kʷ čspiċʔém**
es čspiċéʔi – S/he is whipping. **čnes čspiċéʔi, kʷs čspiċéʔi**
qs čspiċéʔi – S/he is going to whip. **čiqs čspiċéʔi, kʷqs čspiċéʔi**
čspiċéʔeʔm – They whipped. **qeʔ čspiċʔém, p čspiċʔém**
es čspiċéʔeʔi – They are whipping. **qeʔes čspiċéʔi, pes čspiċéʔi**
qs čspiċéʔeʔi – They are going to whip. **qeʔqs čspiċéʔi, pqs čspiċéʔi**

čspiċéʔis – S/he whipped s.o. **čspiċéʔn, čspiċéʔntxʷ**
es čspiċʔéms – S/he is whipping s.o. **ies spiċʔém, as čspiċʔém**
qs čspiċʔéms – S/he is going to whip s.o. **iqs spiċʔém, aqs čspiċʔém**
čspiċéʔeʔis – They whipped s.o. **qeʔ čspiċéʔntm, čspiċéʔntp**
es čspiċéʔeʔms – They are whipping s.o. **qeʔes spiċʔém, es čspiċʔémp**
qs čspiċéʔeʔms – They are going to whip s.o. **qeʔqs spiċʔém, qs čspiċʔémp**

iɫniš t asʔiɫn x̣iṅe čspiċeʔncn – Eat your food, or I will whip you!

ɫċim – spank; whip. *(i.e., as to punish) See: **spank**.*

qixʷ – chase/whip/drive away. *See: **chase**.*
qixʷmn – whip; something used to chase/whip away animals.

ṫaʔla – whip; flogger.

whirlpool **niṅqʷʔétkʷ**, *niṅqʷʔé* – eddie; whirlpool.

nxʷlekʷ – whirlpool.
es nxʷlekʷi – The water is whirling.

nxʷlekʷis – S/he made the water whirl. **nxʷlekʷn, nxʷlekʷntxʷ**
es nxʷlekʷms – S/he is making the water whirl. **ies nxʷlekʷm, as nxʷlekʷm**
qs nxʷlekʷms – S/he is going to make the water whirl. **iqs nxʷlekʷm, aqs nxʷlekʷm**
nxʷléʔekʷis – They made the water whirl. **qeʔ nxʷlekʷntm, nxʷlekʷntp**
es nxʷléʔekʷms – They are making the water whirl. **qeʔes nxʷlekʷm, es nxʷlekʷmp**
qs nxʷléʔekʷms – They are going to make the water whirl. **qeʔqs nxʷlekʷm, qs nxʷlekʷmp**

es nxʷlxʷlekʷms – S/he is repeatedly making the water whirl. **ies nxʷlxʷlekʷm, as nxʷlxʷlekʷm**

nxʷlekʷnt – Whirl the water. *cmd.*

whirlwind **sxʷlékʷ** – whirlwind.
es xʷlékʷi – It is whirl winding.

sxʷlekʷs – whirlwind originating from fire.
es xʷlekʷsi – It is whirl winding from a fire.

whiskers **supcin**, *supci* – whiskers. *suffix: **...cin, ...cn** – action of the mouth.*

whiskey jack **lk̓ʷɫk̓ʷqi** – gray jay; Canada jay; camp robber; whiskey jack; *Perisoreus canadensis.*

whisper **nɫkʷk̓ʷiyecn**, *nɫkʷk̓ʷi* – whisper; talk little; talk quiet. *suffix: **...cin, ...cn** – action of the mouth.*
nɫkʷk̓ʷiyecn – S/he whispered. **čn nɫkʷk̓ʷiyecn, kʷ nɫkʷk̓ʷiyecn**
es nɫkʷk̓ʷiyecni – S/he is whispering. **čnes nɫkʷk̓ʷiyecni, kʷes nɫkʷk̓ʷiyecni**
qs nɫkʷk̓ʷiyecni – S/he is going to whisper. **čiqs nɫkʷk̓ʷiyecni, kʷqs nɫkʷk̓ʷiyecni**

The **i** following uvular consonants (UC) and the glottal stop ʔ sound like English "*ey*" as in the words th*ey*, h*ey*, wh*ey*, etc. Salish UC are: **q, q̓, qʷ, q̓ʷ, x̣, x̣ʷ**. For example, the suffix **...qin** – head/top, is often spelled using English *ey* as "qeyn". So **qi, q̓i, qʷi, q̓ʷi, x̣i, x̣ʷi**, may be spelled with English *ey* as **q***ey*, **q̓***ey*, **qʷ***ey*, **q̓ʷ***ey*, **x̣***ey*, **x̣ʷ***ey* in other texts.

s.t. - something, the 3rd person
(s.t.) - something implied
s.o. - someone, the 3rd person
sl. - singular form
pl. - plural form
rt. - root word
cmd. - command
lit. - literally
fig. - figuratively
i.e., - for example
See: - Redirection to a related word.

wekʷcnm – hide your talk by whispering or by talking a different language; talk secretly; gossip. *See: **gossip**.*

whistle

sikʷ – whistle.
sikʷm – S/he/it whistled. **čn sikʷm, kʷ sikʷm**
es sikʷi – S/he/it is whistling. **čnes sikʷi, kʷes sikʷi**
qs sikʷi – S/he/it is going to whistle. **čiqs sikʷi, kʷqs sikʷi**

sikʷis – S/he/it whistled at/for s.o./s.t. **sikʷn, sikʷntxʷ**
es sikʷms – S/he/it is whistling at/for s.o./s.t. **ies sikʷm, as sikʷm**
qs sikʷms – S/he/it is going to whistle at/for s.o./s.t. **iqs sikʷm, aqs sikʷm**

sikʷcn – S/he/it whistled a tune. **čn sikʷcn, kʷ sikʷcn**
es sikʷcni – S/he/it is whistling a tune. **čnes sikʷcni, kʷes sikʷcni**
qs sikʷcni – S/he/it is going to whistle a tune. **čiqs sikʷcni, kʷqs sikʷcni**

sikʷiš – Whistle. *cmd.*
sikʷcniš – Whistle a tune. *cmd.*
sikʷwi – All of you whistle. *cmd.*
sikʷcnwi – All of you whistle a tune. *cmd.*
sesikʷeʔ – whistling one, affectionately.

yalpósqn, *yalpó* – rounded lips. *See: **lips**.*

x̣ʷancoʔ – deer's whistle.
es x̣ʷancoʔ – The deer is whistling.

whistle swan

spqmi – swan, tundra swan, whistling swan.

white

piq – white. **pqpiq** – whites. *pl.*
piqis – S/he made it white. **piqn, piqntxʷ**
es piqms – S/he is making it white. **ies piqm, as piqm**
qs piqms – S/he is going to make it white. **iqs piqm, aqs piqm**

i piq – It is white.
i łppiq – It is a little white; whitish.

piqnt – Make it white. *cmd.*
pepiqeʔ – whitey, affectionately.
spqmi – swan, tundra swan, whistling swan.
čpi – palamino.
pqlqin, *pqlqi* – bald eagle; *Haliaeetus leucocephalus. See: **bald eagle**.*
pqayaqn – white headed. *(white headed person or animal.)*

u x̣mx̣mip u pqpiq – And it dried nice and white. **l šeẏ u še txʷtíʔixʷm t sčiłt łu t sq̇sip i piq x̣e** – That's where they used to get white clay long ago, it was white and good.

pqmayaqn – gray/white hair.
pqmayaqn – S/he has gray/white hair. **čn pqmayaqn, kʷ pqmayaqn**

pqmast – get gray/white hair.
es pqmasti – S/he is getting gray/white hair. **čnes pqmasti, kʷes pqmasti**

whitebark pine

ččeẏłp – whitebark pine; *Pinus albicaulis.*

white birch

čqʷłṅalqʷ, *čqʷłṅa* – white birch; *Betula papyifera.*

whiteboard **snčq̓ẏalqʷtn** – writing board; chalkboard; whiteboard.

white camas **pčľu** – biscuit root, white camas; *Lomatium piperi.*

whitefish **x̣ʷx̣ʷẏucṅ**, *x̣ʷx̣ʷẏu* – whitefish; *Prosopium williamsoni.*

Whitefish **epłx̣ʷx̣ʷẏu** – Whitefish, Montana. *lit. has whitefish.*

white people **suyápi** – white people. *(This term is used to describe Caucasian people; generally it refers to people who are not Native American. The term is also used to describe the English language.)*
słuyápi – little bit white (people).
snuyapcn – English. *See:* ***English.***
puʔsuyápi – spouse of somebody who is a white person. *See:* ***spouse.***
suypálqs – American dress. *See:* ***clothes.***
suypsqáx̣e – American stock, horses, cattle, etc.

t sq̓sip ta ep suyápi – Long ago there were not any white people. **x̣méʔenčis t suyápi** – The white people liked this.

semeʔ – French.
kʷlkʷlta – Canadian.
snołpselixʷ – German.
nłťuxʷtn – Italian.

white pine **ƛ̓iyalqʷ** – white pine; *Pinus monticola.*

white-tail deer **sx̣ʷľéščn**, *sx̣ʷľé* – white-tail buck; *Odocoileus virginianus.*
sx̣ʷľéščnelxʷ – white-tail buck hide.

c̓úʔulixʷ, *c̓úʔu* – white-tail doe; *Odocoileus virginianus.*
c̓ulixʷélxʷ, *c̓ulixʷé* – buckskin, white-tail doe hide.

whittle **xʷƛ̓im** – whittle.
xʷƛ̓im – S/he whittled. **čn xʷƛ̓im, kʷ xʷƛ̓im**
es xʷƛ̓mi – S/he is whittling. **čnes xʷƛ̓mi, kʷes xʷƛ̓mi**
qs xʷƛ̓mi – S/he is going to whittle. **čiqs xʷƛ̓mi, kʷqs xʷƛ̓mi**

xʷƛ̓ntes – S/he whittled s.t. **xʷƛ̓nten, xʷƛ̓ntexʷ**
es xʷƛ̓ims – S/he is whittling s.t. **ies xʷƛ̓im, as xʷƛ̓im**
qs xʷƛ̓ims – S/he is going to whittle s.t. **iqs xʷƛ̓im, aqs xʷƛ̓im**

es xʷƛ̓xʷƛ̓míʔi – S/he is whittling. **qeʔes xʷƛ̓xʷƛ̓mi, pes xʷƛ̓xʷƛ̓mi**

xʷƛ̓int – Whittle it. *cmd.*

es čxʷƛ̓alqʷi – S/he is removing bark. **čnes čxʷƛ̓alqʷi, kʷes čxʷƛ̓alqʷi**

who **swe** – Who?
uł swe – Who are they?
ta swe – Nobody.
tʔe swe – Anybody; anyone; somebody. *See:* ***anyone.***
p suswe – Who are each one of you?

t swe u tľntés łu qpe – Who broke the plate? **u łu anwi ha tʔe swe ck̓ʷis wičnts** – What about you; did anyone come to see you? **ta swe qs xʷuyi č nłay** – No one is going to go to Missoula. **ṅe suswéʔe ntéls m še ck̓ʷis laq̓i** – Whoever wants to, will come sweat. **swe t ep stéṁ**

The **i** following uvular consonants (UC) and the glottal stop **ʔ** sound like English "*ey*" as in the words *they, hey, whey,* etc. Salish UC are: **q, q̓, qʷ, q̓ʷ, x̣, x̣ʷ**. For example, the suffix **...qin** – head/top, is often spelled using English *ey* as "q*ey*n". So **qi, q̓i, qʷi, q̓ʷi, x̣i, x̣ʷi**, may be spelled with English *ey* as **q***ey*, **q̓***ey*, **qʷ***ey*, **q̓ʷ***ey*, **x̣***ey*, **x̣ʷ***ey* in other texts.

s.t. - something, the 3rd person
(s.t.) - something implied
s.o. - someone, the 3rd person
sl. - singular form
pl. - plural form
rt. - root word
cmd. - command
lit. - literally
fig. - figuratively
i.e., - for example
See: - Redirection to a related word.

łiciʔ – Who owns that? **swe łu l asnčmičn̓** – Who is behind you? **swe łu l asmiłčmels** – Who is in front of you? **swe łu l snihéw̓sm** – Who is in the middle? **uł swe łu es q̓ʷiiq̓ʷo** – Who are they, those racing?

whole **milk̓ʷ** – complete; whole; all over; all around. *See: **complete**.*

oył – one piece; whole; no holes/breaks/tears.

whortleberry **sipt** – whortleberry; grouseberry; *Vaccinium scoparium*.

why **x̣ʷlstém̓**, *x̣ʷlsté* – why.
x̣ʷl̓ – for, because.

x̣ʷl̓ stem̓ u tám t selíš u kʷes uwéwlši – Why are you not speaking Salish? **x̣ʷl̓ stem̓ u l še u kʷ ax̣íʔ** – Why did you do that? **x̣ʷl̓ šey̓ u puti yetłx̣ʷasq̓t es cu łmłamá** – That's why frog still says that today.

wick **nox̣ʷmełc̓e** – candle wick.

wicked **wil** – faulty; wrong; wicked.
i wil – S/he/it is faulty. **i čn wil, i kʷ wil**

wilwlt – being smart in a sly way.

uł wilwlt u qʷo náʔaq̓ʷmis – Those sly ones stole from me.

qʷawqʷut – wicked; maddening; unpredictable; intoxicating; vicious. *rt.: **qʷéw** – crazy.*
qʷqʷtstes – S/he made s.o. wicked. **qʷqʷtsten, qʷqʷtstexʷ**
es qʷqʷtims – S/he is making s.o. wicked. **ies qʷqʷtim, as qʷqʷtim**

qʷqʷtilš – S/he became wicked. **čn qʷqʷtilš, kʷ qʷqʷtilš** *suffix: **...ilš** – autonomous.*
es qʷqʷtilši – S/he is becoming wicked. **čnes qʷqʷtilši, kʷes qʷqʷtilši**

wide **łáq̓t** – wide.
słaq̓t – wide as a measure.
sšy̓mł łáq̓t – widest.
kʷtisłaq̓t – really wide.
nłq̓etkʷ – wide water. *suffix: **...etkʷ, ...tkʷ** – liquid*
łq̓ep – wide rope; belt.
nłq̓aqs – wide road/path; broad way.
łq̓ew̓t – It appears wide.

t̓aq̓n sc̓ušin słaq̓t – It is 6 feet wide. **t čen̓ u ec̓x̣lsłaq̓t** – How wide is it?

płiłt – thick. *See: **thick**.*

łqqéw̓t, *łqqé* – narrow/skinny. *See: **narrow**.*

widow **słwél̓mt** – widow/widower during mourning.
nc̓lišk̓ʷeʔ – widow/widower after mourning.

wiener **sp̓l̓q̓enč**, *sp̓l̓q̓e* – intestine; sausage/hot dog/wiener.

wife **nóx̣ʷnx̣ʷ** – wife.
hayo qs tiw̓ł nóx̣ʷnx̣ʷi – Hey, he's going to get a wife! **qł nóx̣ʷnx̣ʷ** – Going to be his bride/wife.

nx̣ʷnx̣ʷéw̓s, *nx̣ʷnx̣ʷé* – marry; together with a wife. *See: **marry**.*

puʔ – spouse of somebody who is… *See: **spouse**.*

wiggle

yananq̇ʷ – wiggle.
yananq̇ʷmncut – wiggle one's self.
yananq̇ʷmncut – S/he/it wiggled. **čn yananq̇ʷmncut, kʷ yananq̇ʷmncut**
es yananq̇ʷmncuti – S/he/it is wiggling. **čnes yananq̇ʷmncuti, kʷes yananq̇ʷmncuti**
qs yananq̇ʷmncuti – S/he/it is going to wiggle. **čiqs yananq̇ʷmncuti, kʷqs yananq̇ʷmncuti**
yananq̇ʷmncúʔut – They wiggled. **qeʔ yananq̇ʷmncut, p yananq̇ʷmncut**

yananq̇ʷmilš – roll/wiggle, as would happen in bed. *suffix: **...ilš** – autonomous.*
yananq̇ʷmilš – S/he/it rolled. **čn yananq̇ʷmilš, kʷ yananq̇ʷmilš**
es yananq̇ʷmilši – S/he/it is rolling. **čnes yananq̇ʷmilši, kʷes yananq̇ʷmilši**
qs yananq̇ʷmilši – S/he/it is going to roll. **čiqs yananq̇ʷmilši, kʷqs yananq̇ʷmilši**
yananq̇ʷmíʔilš – They rolled. **qeʔ yananq̇ʷmilš, p yananq̇ʷmilš**

The **i** following uvular consonants (UC) and the glottal stop **ʔ** sound like English "*ey*" as in the words th*ey*, h*ey*, wh*ey*, etc. Salish UC are: **q**, **q̇**, **qʷ**, **q̇ʷ**, **x̣**, **x̣ʷ**. For example, the suffix ...**qin** – head/top, is often spelled using English *ey* as "q*ey*n". So **qi**, **q̇i**, **qʷi**, **q̇ʷi**, **x̣i**, **x̣ʷi**, may be spelled with English *ey* as **q***ey*, **q̇***ey*, **qʷ***ey*, **q̇ʷ***ey*, **x̣***ey*, **x̣ʷ***ey* in other texts.

yl̓yel̓ – wiggle, as a worm or snake would do.
es yl̓yelk̓ʷilši – It is wiggling, the snake or worm. *suffix: **...ilš** – autonomous.*
es yl̓yel̓ms – S/he/it is wiggling s.t., in the form of a snake or worm. **ies yl̓yel̓m, as yl̓yel̓m**

es yl̓yel̓ms ci sp̓ecn – S/he/it is wiggling the rope like a snake or worm.

lalamist – wiggle/roll around; toss and turn. *(i.e., when in pain; restless in bed; like an animal wallowing in dirt.)*
lalamist – S/he/it rolled around. **čn lalamist, kʷ lalamist**
es lalamisti – S/he/it is rolling around. **čnes lalamisti, kʷes lalamisti**
qs lalamisti – S/he/it is going to roll around. **čiqs lalamisti, kʷqs lalamisti**

es nlalamistetkʷi – S/he/it is wiggling around in the water. **čnes nlalamistetkʷi, kʷes nlalamistetkʷi**

lmlamist – throw a fit; have a temper tantrum.
lmlamist – S/he threw a fit. **čn lmlamist, kʷ lmlamist**
es lmlamisti – S/he is throwing a fit. **čnes lmlamisti, kʷes lmlamisti**
qs lmlamisti – S/he is going to throw a fit. **čiqs lmlamisti, kʷqs lmlamisti**

iiw̓ – move, shake, wiggle something.
iiw̓iw̓sts – S/he/it wiggled s.t./s.o. **iiw̓iw̓stn, iiw̓iw̓stxʷ**
es iiw̓iw̓ms – S/he/it wiggled s.t./s.o. **ies iiw̓iw̓m, as iiw̓iw̓m**

iw̓iw̓mskʷ – Move, wiggle it. *cmd.*

es iiw̓iw̓ms łu sčuwax̣is – S/he/it is moving/wiggling its arm. **iw̓iw̓mskʷ ančelš** – Move/wiggle your hand.

wild

uw̓áq̇uq̇t, *uw̓á* – wild, savage, untamed.
w̓iw̓a xʷixʷey̓uł – wild animals.
w̓iw̓a – wild.

aič̓eč̓lt – wild, untame.

tas tx̣ʷox̣ʷ – S/he/it is not tame/straight. *See: **straight**.*

s.t. - something, the 3rd person
(s.t.) - something implied
s.o. - someone, the 3rd person
sl. - singular form
pl. - plural form
rt. - root word
cmd. - command
lit. - literally
fig. - figuratively
i.e., - for example
See: - Redirection to a related word.

wilderness

č̓w̓éw̓t – wilderness. *rt.: **č̓u** – gone; suffix: **...éw̓t** – group state.*

will

k̓ʷułq̇ey̓min – last will and testament.

ṅem – will.

ha ṅem kʷ k̓ʷul̓m ṅe anłq – Will you work this summer? **ṅem x̣ʷelntxʷ –** You will throw it away. **ha ṅem kʷ čšt̓el̓t –** Will you babysit?

willow **ppóxʷpnełp,** *ppó* – shinning willow; *Salix lucida.*

q̓ʷl̓salqʷ, *q̓ʷl̓sa* – willow tree; *Salix scouleriana.*

haw̓ełp – peachleaf willow; *Salix amygdaloides. rt.: **haw̓w̓** – loosen.*

čiliyalqʷ – diamond willow; *Salix bebbiana.*

xʷlqełp – Pacific willow; *Salix lasiandra.*

q̓ʷyokʷełp, *q̓ʷyokʷe* – fishtrap willow; *Salix drummondiana.*

sł̓t̓it̓iči – pussy willow; *Salix discolor.*

smx̣ʷnełp – silverberry; wolf-willow; *Elaeagnus commutate.*

stečcxʷ – red osier dogwood; red willow; *Cornus stolonifera.*

q̓oq̓opuł – willow. *lit. breaks easily.*

wilt **sax̣ʷx̣ʷqn –** flowers wilted. *rt.: **sax̣ʷ** – split.*

win **ƛ̓xʷupist,** *ƛ̓xʷup* – win something; ahead *(i.e., a bet, card game, etc.).*
ƛ̓xʷup – S/he/it was winning. **čn ƛ̓xʷup, kʷ ƛ̓xʷup**
es ƛ̓xʷupisti – S/he/it is winning. **čnes ƛ̓xʷupisti, kʷes ƛ̓xʷupisti**
qs ƛ̓xʷupisti – S/he/it is going to be winning. **čiqs ƛ̓xʷupisti, kʷqs ƛ̓xʷupisti**
ƛ̓xʷúʔup – They were winning. **qeʔ ƛ̓xʷup, p ƛ̓xʷup**
es ƛ̓xʷúʔupisti – They are winning. **qeʔes ƛ̓xʷupisti, pes ƛ̓xʷupisti**

es ƛ̓xʷƛ̓xʷupisti – S/he/it is repeatedly winning. **čnes ƛ̓xʷƛ̓xʷupisti, kʷes ƛ̓xʷƛ̓xʷupisti**

sƛ̓xʷup – win.

ƛ̓xʷpsqáx̣eʔ, *ƛ̓xʷpsqá* – win a domestic animal, horse, car.
ƛ̓xʷpsqáx̣eʔ – S/he/it won. **čn ƛ̓xʷpsqáx̣eʔ, kʷ ƛ̓xʷpsqáx̣eʔ**
es ƛ̓xʷpsqáx̣eʔi – S/he/it is winning. **čnes ƛ̓xʷpsqáx̣eʔi, kʷes ƛ̓xʷpsqáx̣eʔi**
qs ƛ̓xʷpsqáx̣eʔi – S/he/it is going to win. **čiqs ƛ̓xʷpsqáx̣eʔi, kʷqs ƛ̓xʷpsqáx̣eʔi**
ƛ̓xʷpsqáʔáx̣eʔ – They won. **qeʔ ƛ̓xʷpsqáx̣eʔ, p ƛ̓xʷpsqáx̣eʔ**
es ƛ̓xʷpsqáʔáx̣eʔi – They are winning. **qeʔes ƛ̓xʷpsqáx̣eʔi, pes ƛ̓xʷpsqáx̣eʔi**

šƛ̓páqs, *šƛ̓pá* – win/defeat/beat at some contest or event. *rt.: **šiƛ̓** – flat, level, aligned.*
šƛ̓páqs – S/he/it won. **čn šƛ̓páqs, kʷ šƛ̓páqs**
es šƛ̓páqsi – S/he/it is winning. **čnes šƛ̓páqsi, kʷes šƛ̓páqsi**

šƛ̓ip, *šƛ̓i* – lose; defeated. *See: **defeat.***

šƛ̓pnuntm – S/he was defeated.

es šƛ̓pstwexʷi – They are defeating each other. **qeʔes šƛ̓pstwexʷi, pes šƛ̓pstwexʷi**

x̣ʷa ṅe łu ssẏmł ƛ̓áx̣t m šƛ̓pá – May the fastest win. **šƛ̓pnum –** I defeated him. **ṅem swe łu šƛ̓pa –** Who will win? **ṅe es šʔit x̣ʷtew̓s šeẏ łu ṅem šƛ̓pa –** Whoever cuts it in half will win. **iqs šƛ̓pnunm łu t̓eyeʔ –** I am going to beat evil.

qʷoṁmałq, *qʷoṁma* – get close to doing/finishing something; getting near to some point; close to the end of a journey; winning. *See: **close.***

wind **snéw̓t –** wind.

néẇt – The wind blew.
es néẇti – It is windy.
es łṅéṅuʔti – It is a little windy; breezy.

néẇis – The wind blew on s.t.
es néẇms – The wind is blowing on s.t.
qʷo néẇntm – The wind blew on me.

es naẇlqʷi – wind is blowing through the trees.

es ṗičłqi – strong/big wind; tornado or hurricane like weather; blizzard, but does not refer to snow.
ṗičłqi – The wind blew really hard.

es x̣apulexʷi – cool breeze is blowing along the ground.

sxʷlékʷ – whirlwind.
es xʷlékʷi – It is whirl winding.

es qʷułmncuti – It is a dust storm or blizzard.

es cháłqi – chinook is blowing (warm dry wind).

es uwawlqʷi – The trees are talking from the wind blowing through. *rt.:* ***uwewlš*** *– talk; suffix:* ***...alqʷ*** *– wood; cylindical.*
suwawlqʷ – sound of wind.

qim – calm; undisturbed. *See:* ***calm.***

q̇ʷoẏ – calm; serene. *(i.e., place with no wind, etc.) See:* ***calm.***

plim – drift/float away by water or wind; carried away. *See:* ***drift.***
łu t snéẇt plntem – It was carried away by the wind.

The **i** following uvular consonants (UC) and the glottal stop ʔ sound like English "*ey*" as in the words th*ey*, h*ey*, wh*ey*, etc. Salish UC are: **q**, **q̇**, **qʷ**, **q̇ʷ**, **x̣**, **x̣ʷ**. For example, the suffix **...qin** – head/top, is often spelled using English *ey* as "q*ey*n". So **qi**, **q̇i**, **qʷi**, **q̇ʷi**, **x̣i**, **x̣ʷi**, may be spelled with English *ey* as **q***ey*, **q̇***ey*, **qʷ***ey*, **q̇ʷ***ey*, **x̣***ey*, **x̣ʷ***ey* in other texts.

wind chimes
snéẇt luli – wind bells.

winded
tqup – suffocate (not dead); restrict air flow; lacking air; winded/out of breath. *See:* ***suffocate.***

window
nšnselxʷ, *nšnse* – window. *rt.:* ***šiṅ*** *– flat cover; suffix:* ***...elxʷ, ...lxʷ*** *– skin/hide*
t spisćé u wičis t mali ci smx̣é qʷo es mumáẇłtm innšnse – Yesterday Mary saw that grizzly bear breaking my window.

aʔćx̣sncut – mirror.

windshield wiper
eṗʔéṗmn – windshield wipers.

wine
nkʷilkʷ – wine. *lit. red liquid.*

ppil – wine.

wing
sčuwáx̣n – arm; wing.

sqpusłáx̣n – wing.
sqpuséł, *sqpu* – feather, wing.

wink
nċipsm – wink; close eye.
nċipsis – S/he winked at s.o. **nċipsn, nċipsntxʷ**

nċipsiš – Wink; close one eye. *cmd.*

s.t. - something, the 3rd person
(s.t.) - something implied
s.o. - someone, the 3rd person
sl. - singular form
pl. - plural form
rt. - root word
cmd. - command
lit. - literally
fig. - figuratively
i.e., - for example
See: - Redirection to a related word.

nčpčipsiš – Close both eyes. *cmd.*
nčpčipswi – All of you close your eyes. *cmd.*
nčppsimiš – Wink. *cmd.*

qʷo nčipsis – S/he/it winked at me. **qʷo nčip̓smis –** S/he winked at me. **čmi u es nčpčipsi –** S/he is only blinking.

čcaps – blink. *See:* ***blink.***

winter

sʔistč – wintertime.
es istčm̓nuxʷisti, *es istčm̓nuxʷi –* It is again the time of winter. *suffix:* ***...m̓nuxʷ–*** *in the time of.*

ṅe l sʔistč m kʷ ux̣ʷłxʷm – If it is winter, you will freeze it.

wipe

éṗ – wipe.
eṗm – S/he/it wiped (s.t.). **čn eṗm, kʷ eṗm**
es eṗi – S/he/it is wiping (s.t.). **čnes eṗi, kʷes eṗi**
qs eṗi – S/he/it is going to wipe (s.t.). **čiqs eṗi, kʷqs eṗi**
éʔeṗm – They wiped (s.t.). **qeʔ eṗm, p eṗm**
es éʔeṗi – They are wiping (s.t.). **qeʔes eṗi, pes eṗi**
qs éʔeṗi – They are going to wipe (s.t.). **qeʔqs eṗi, pqs eṗi**

eṗist – S/he/it wiped one's self. **čn eṗist, kʷ eṗist**
es eṗisti – S/he/it is wiping one's self. **čnes eṗisti, kʷes eṗisti**
qs eṗisti – S/he/it is going to wipe one's self. **čiqs eṗisti, kʷqs eṗisti**

eṗncut – S/he/it wiped by his/her self. **čn eṗncut, kʷ eṗncut**
es eṗncuti – S/he/it is wiping by his/her self. **čnes eṗncuti, kʷes eṗncuti**
qs eṗncuti – S/he/it is going to wipe by his/her self. **čiqs eṗncuti, kʷqs eṗncuti**

eṗmncut – S/he/it wiped by one's self with s.t. **čn eṗmncut, kʷ eṗmncut**
es eṗmncuti – S/he/it is wiping by one's self with s.t. **čnes eṗmncuti, kʷes eṗmncuti**
qs eṗmncuti – S/he/it is going to wipe by one's self with s.t. **čiqs eṗmncuti, kʷqs eṗmncuti**

eṗis – S/he/it wiped it. **eṗn, eṗntxʷ**
es eṗms – S/he/it is wiping it. **ies eṗm, as eṗm**
qs eṗms – S/he/it is going to wipe it. **iqs eṗm, aqs eṗm**
éʔeṗis – They wiped it. **qeʔ eṗntm, eṗntp**
es éʔeṗms – They are wiping it. **qeʔes eṗm, es eṗmp**
qs éʔeṗms – They are going to wipe it. **qeʔqs eṗm, qs eṗmp**

eṗmis – S/he/it used s.t. to wipe. **eṗmn, eṗmntxʷ**
es eṗmms – S/he/it is using s.t. to wipe. **ies eṗmm, as eṗmm**
qs éṗmms – S/he/it is going to use s.t. to wipe. **iqs eṗmm, aqs eṗmm**

eṗṗnuis – S/he/it succeeded in wiping s.t. **eṗṗnun, eṗṗnuntxʷ**
es eṗṗnunms – S/he/it is succeeding in wiping s.t. **ies eṗṗnunm, as eṗṗnunm**
qs eṗṗnunms – S/he/it is going to succeed in wiping s.t. **iqs eṗṗnunm, aqs eṗṗnunm**

es eṗ – S/he/it is wiped/clean/dry. **čnes eṗ, kʷes eṗ**
eṗṗ – S/he/it got wiped. **čn eṗṗ, kʷ eṗṗ**
es eṗeṗi – S/he/it is wiping repeatedly. **čnes eṗeṗi, kʷes eṗeṗi**

eṗmn – wiper; towel.
éṗstn – towel, something to wipe with. *suffix:* ***...tin, ...tn –*** *means of/device.*
sxʷéṗm – one tasked to wipe. *prefix:* ***sxʷ... –*** *one tasked to do.*
čłʔéṗłptn – mop. *prefix:* ***čł... –*** *surface; affix:* ***...ełp, ...łp*** *– tree; floor; suffix:* ***...tin, ...tn –*** *means of/device.*

čłʔéṗmn – mop. *prefix:* ***čł...*** *– surface*
eṗeṗčstn – hand towel. *suffix:* ***...ečst, ...čst*** *– of the hand; suffix:* ***...tin, ...tn*** *– means of/device.*
aṗposqntn – napkin. *suffix:* ***...tin, ...tn*** *– means of/device.*

éṗiš – Wipe (s.t.). *cmd.*
éṗnt – Wipe it. *cmd.*
eṗłtumš – wipe someone at large.
eṗmlwis – wipe around, here and there.
eṗnwexʷ – wipe each other.
eṗštwexʷ – help each other wipe.
čłʔéṗ – wipe the surface/floor.
neṗmels – want to wipe.
čʔeṗċeʔ – wipe all around/over something.
nʔeṗłċeʔ – wiped the inside of something.
eṗs – wipe the face.
k̇ʷłʔéṗs – wipe the cheek.
nʔeṗeṗs – wipe the eyes.
aṗaṗax̣n – wipe the arms.
aṗaṗaqstšn – wipe the legs.
aṗqn – wipe the head.

ṅem éṗm – S/he/it will wipe. **ṅem čn éṗm, ṅem kʷ éṗm**
ṅem éʔeṗm – They will wipe. **ṅem qeʔ éṗm, ṅem p éṗm**
ṅem qes éṗms – S/he/it will be wiping it. **ṅem iqes éṗm, ṅem aqes éṗm**
ṅem qes éʔeṗms – They will be wiping it. **ṅem qeʔqes éṗm, ṅem qes éṗmp**

ta kʷ qes éṗm – Do not wipe (s.t.). **ta qes éṗstxʷ –** Do not wipe s.t.

The **i** following uvular consonants (UC) and the glottal stop **ʔ** sound like English "*ey*" as in the words th*ey*, h*ey*, wh*ey*, etc. Salish UC are: **q, q̇, qʷ, q̇ʷ, x̣, x̣ʷ**. For example, the suffix ...**qin** – head/top, is often spelled using English *ey* as "q*ey*n". So **qi, q̇i, qʷi, q̇ʷi, x̣i, x̣ʷi**, may be spelled with English *ey* as **q***ey*, **q̇***ey*, **qʷ***ey*, **q̇ʷ***ey*, **x̣***ey*, **x̣ʷ***ey* in other texts.

eṗeṗčstm – wipe hands. *suffix:* ***...ečst, ...čst*** *– of the hand.*
eṗeṗčstm – S/he/it wiped hands. **čn eṗeṗčstm, kʷ eṗeṗčstm**
es eṗeṗčsti – S/he/it is wiping hands. **čnes eṗeṗčsti, kʷes eṗeṗčsti**
qs eṗeṗčsti – S/he/it is going to wipe hands. **čiqs eṗeṗčsti, kʷqs eṗeṗčsti**
éʔeṗeṗčstm – They wiped hands. **qeʔ eṗeṗčstm, p eṗeṗčstm**
es éʔeṗeṗčsti – They are wiping hands. **qeʔes eṗeṗčsti, pes eṗeṗčsti**
qs éʔeṗeṗčsti – They are going to wipe hands. **qeʔqs eṗeṗčsti, pqs eṗeṗčsti**

eṗeṗčstis – S/he/it wiped s.o.'s hands. **eṗeṗčstn, eṗeṗčstntxʷ**
es eṗeṗčstms – S/he/it is wiping s.o.'s hands. **ies eṗeṗčstm, as eṗeṗčstm**
qs eṗeṗčstms – S/he/it is going to wipe s.o.'s hands. **iqs eṗeṗčstm, aqs eṗeṗčstm**
éʔeṗeṗčstis – They wiped s.o.'s hands. **qeʔ eṗeṗčstntm, eṗeṗčstntp**
es éʔeṗeṗčstms – They are wiping s.o.'s hands. **qeʔes eṗeṗčstm, es eṗeṗčstmp**
qs éʔeṗeṗčstms – They are going to wipe s.o.'s hands. **qeʔqs eṗeṗčstm, qs eṗeṗčstmp**

eṗeṗčstn – hand towel. *suffix:* ***...tin, ...tn*** *– means of/device.*

eṗeṗčstniš – Wipe hands. *cmd.*
eṗeṗčstncutš – Wipe your hands. *cmd.*
eṗeṗčstnt – Wipe his/her hands. *cmd.*
es eṗeṗčstncuti – S/he is wiping his/her hands. **čnes eṗeṗčstncuti, kʷes eṗeṗčstncuti**

s.t. - something, the 3rd person
(s.t.) - something implied
s.o. - someone, the 3rd person
sl. - singular form
pl. - plural form
rt. - root word
cmd. - command
lit. - literally
fig. - figuratively
i.e., - for example
See: - Redirection to a related word.

aṗposqnm – wipe the mouth/lips. *suffix:* ***...posqn*** *– lips.*
aṗposqnm – S/he/it wiped the mouth. **čn aṗposqnm, kʷ aṗposqnm**
es aṗposqni – S/he/it is wiping the mouth. **čnes aṗposqni, kʷes aṗposqni**

qs aṗposqni – S/he/it is going to wipe the mouth. **čiqs aṗposqni, kʷqs aṗposqni**
aṗpóˀosqnm – They wiped the mouth. **qeˀ aṗposqnm, p aṗposqnm**
es aṗpóˀosqni – They are wiping the mouth. **qeˀes aṗposqni, pes aṗposqni**
qs aṗpóˀosqni – They are going to wipe the mouth. **qeˀqs aṗposqni, pqs aṗposqni**

aṗposqnis – S/he/it wiped s.o.'s mouth. **aṗposqn, aṗposqntxʷ**
es aṗposqnms – S/he/it is wiping s.o.'s mouth. **ies aṗposqnm, as aṗposqnm**
qs aṗposqnms – S/he/it is going to wipe s.o.'s mouth. **iqs aṗposqnm, aqs aṗposqnm**
aṗpóˀosqnis – They wiped s.o.'s mouth. **qeˀ aṗposqntm, aṗposqntp**
es aṗpóˀosqnms – They are wiping s.o.'s mouth. **qeˀes aṗposqnm, es aṗposqnmp**
qs aṗpóˀosqnms – They are going to wipe s.o.'s mouth. **qeˀqs aṗposqnm, qs aṗposqnmp**

aṗposqntn – napkin. *suffix: **...tin, ...tn** – means of/device.*

aṗposqniš – Wipe the mouth. *cmd.*
aṗposqncutš – Wipe your mouth. *cmd.*
aṗposqnnt – Wipe his/her mouth. *cmd.*
es aṗposqncuti – S/he is wiping his/her mouth. **čnes aṗposqncuti, kʷes aṗposqncuti**

nˀaṗqsm – wipe the nose. *circumfix: **n...aqs** – nose, road, pointed.*
nˀaṗqsm – S/he/it wiped the nose. **čn nˀaṗqsm, kʷ nˀaṗqsm**
es nˀaṗqsi – S/he/it is wiping the nose. **čnes nˀaṗqsi, kʷes nˀaṗqsi**
qs nˀaṗqsi – S/he/it is going to wipe the nose. **čiqs nˀaṗqsi, kʷqs nˀaṗqsi**

nˀaṗqsis – S/he/it wiped s.o.'s nose. **nˀaṗqs, nˀaṗqstxʷ**
es nˀaṗqsms – S/he/it is wiping s.o.'s nose. **ies nˀaṗqsm, as nˀaṗqsm**
qs nˀaṗqsms – S/he/it is going to wipe s.o.'s nose. **iqs nˀaṗqsm, aqs nˀaṗqsm**

nˀaṗqstn – napkin. *suffix: **...tin, ...tn** – means of/device.*

nˀaṗqsiš – Wipe the nose. *cmd.*
nˀaṗqsncutš – Wipe your nose. *cmd.*
nˀaṗqsnt – Wipe his/her nose. *cmd.*
es nˀaṗqsncuti – S/he is wiping his/her nose. **čnes nˀaṗqsncuti, kʷes nˀaṗqsncuti**

neṗpsncut, *neṗpsncu* – wipe one's self with toilet paper. *rt.: **eṗ** – wipe; circumfix: **n...ups** – butt, tail; suffix: **...cut** – action to the self.*
neṗpsncut – S/he wiped one's self. **čn neṗpsncut, kʷ neṗpsncut**
es neṗpsncuti – S/he wiping one's self. **čnes neṗpsncuti, kʷes neṗpsncuti**
qs neṗpsncuti – S/he is going to wipe one's self. **čiqs neṗpsncuti, kʷqs neṗpsncuti**

neṗpsncutn, *neṗpsncu* – toilet paper.

neṗpsncutš – Wipe yourself. *cmd.*

eṗeṗšnm – wipe away tracks; wipe feet.
eṗeṗšnm – S/he wiped away tracks. **čn eṗeṗšnm, kʷ eṗeṗšnm**
es eṗeṗšni – S/he is wiping away tracks. **čnes eṗeṗšni, kʷes eṗeṗšni**
qs eṗeṗšni – S/he is going to wipe away tracks. **čiqs eṗeṗšni, kʷqs eṗeṗšni**

eṗeṗšis – S/he wiped away s.o./s.t.'s tracks. **eṗeṗšn, eṗeṗšntxʷ**
es eṗeṗšnms – S/he is wiping away s.o./s.t.'s tracks. **ies eṗeṗšnm, as eṗeṗšnm**
qs eṗeṗšnms – S/he is going to wipe away s.o./s.t.'s tracks. **iqs eṗeṗšnm, aqs eṗeṗšnm**

ċsip – disappear; gone; wiped out; cleared out. *See: **disappear**.*

wire **łuḷuḷiṁ –** metal wire.

ox̣ʷm – string something out; say someone is skinny, stretched, or boney. *(i.e., fencing, rope, hose, etc.)* *See:* ***string***.

wise **px̣páx̣t –** smart; clever; have knowledge; have wisdom. *See:* ***smart***.

wish **q̇mscin –** wish; hunger for.
q̇mscinm – S/he/it wished. **čn q̇mscinm, kʷ q̇mscinm**
es q̇mscini – S/he/it is wishing. **čnes q̇mscini, kʷes q̇mscini**
qs q̇mscini – S/he/it is going to wish. **čiqs q̇mscini, kʷqs q̇mscini**
q̇mscíʔinm – They wished. **qeʔ q̇mscinm, p q̇mscinm**
es q̇mscíʔini – They are wishing. **qeʔes q̇mscini, pes q̇mscini**
qs q̇mscíʔini – They are going to wish. **qeʔqs q̇mscini, pqs q̇mscini**

q̇mscis – S/he/it wished for s.t./s.o. **q̇mscin, q̇mscintxʷ**
es q̇mscinms – S/he/it is wishing for s.t./s.o. **ies q̇mscinm, as q̇mscinm**
qs q̇mscinms – S/he/it is wishing for s.t./s.o. **iqs q̇mscinm, aqs q̇mscinm**
q̇mscíʔis – They wished for s.t./s.o. **qeʔ q̇mscintm, q̇mscintp**
es q̇mscíʔinms – They are wishing for s.t./s.o. **qeʔes q̇mscinm, es q̇mscinmp**
qs q̇mscíʔinms – They are going to wish for s.t./s.o. **qeʔqs q̇mscinm, qs q̇mscinmp**

q̇mscinmsts – S/he/it wished for s.t. **q̇mscinmstn, q̇mscinmstxʷ**

ta qes q̇mscinmstxʷ – Do not wish for it. **es q̇mscini t smʔem –** He is wishing for a woman.

k̓ʷmiʔ – hope; wish.
k̓ʷmiʔ ċew̓ntxʷ ančlčelš – Wish you would wash you hands. **k̓ʷmiʔ ta qs t̓ipeys yetłx̣ʷa –** I hope it does not rain today. **k̓ʷmiʔ tam qs t̓ipeysi n̓e čluxʷ –** I hope it is not raining this evening.

im̓im̓snuxʷ – wish for something but having a hard time getting it.

p̓isp̓sm – wish, putting bundle out to wish for something or to change into something.
es p̓isp̓si – S/he is taking the medicine bundle up to the mountains.

t̓inúxʷ – desire something or someone. *See:* ***desire***.

q̇xʷmin – desire for something not possessed; fond of something; wish for something that can be had. *See:* ***desire***.

q̇ix̣t – protective of something; fond of something possessed; attached to something. *See:* ***desire***.

xʷmminm – yearn; long for; strongly desire. *See:* ***yearn***.

q̇ewm – curse; wish bad on somebody; cast/wish bad luck on somebody. *See:* ***curse***.

čłyuxʷt, *čłyu* **–** envious; want to be like; wish for something; feel bad over. *See:* ***envy***.

witch **q̇ewm –** curse; wish bad on somebody; cast/wish bad luck on somebody. *See:* ***curse***.

with **nkʷł… –** *prefix indicating together with/do with. The ł is lost when preceding an s.*
nkʷłwenš – dance together with someone. *See:* ***war dance***.
nkʷłmistmm – in agreement with something or someone. *See:* ***agree***.
nkʷłnk̓ʷúʔumncn – I became one with you; I agreed with you. *See:* ***agree***.
nkʷłnt̓qʷt̓qʷéčs – clap with someone. *See:* ***clap***.
nkʷłtiyaqʷt – fight with someone. *See:* ***fight***.
nkʷłninem – owl dance with someone. *See:* ***owl dance***.

The **i** following uvular consonants (UC) and the glottal stop **ʔ** sound like English "*ey*" as in the words th*ey*, h*ey*, wh*ey*, etc. Salish UC are: **q, q̇, qʷ, q̇ʷ, x̣, x̣ʷ**. For example, the suffix …**qin** – head/top, is often spelled using English *ey* as "q*ey*n". So **qi, q̇i, qʷi, q̇ʷi, x̣i, x̣ʷi**, may be spelled with English *ey* as **q***ey*, **q̇***ey*, **qʷ***ey*, **q̇ʷ***ey*, **x̣***ey*, **x̣ʷ***ey* in other texts.

s.t. - something, the 3rd person
(s.t.) - something implied
s.o. - someone, the 3rd person
sl. - singular form
pl. - plural form
rt. - root word
cmd. - command
lit. - literally
fig. - figuratively
i.e., - for example
See: - Redirection to a related word.

snk̉ʷɫ... – *prefix indicating the one/thing something is done/being together with.* *The ɫ is lost when preceding an s.*

snk̉ʷsqelixʷ – fellow people; fellow human being. *See:* ***people***.

snk̉ʷsixʷ – sibling; brother, sister, cousin. *See:* ***sibling***.

snk̉ʷɫʔemut – the one someone sits with. *See:* ***sit***.

snk̉ʷɫʔečswíš – the one someone stands with. *See:* ***stand***.

snk̉ʷɫsust – drinking partner. *See:* ***drink***.

snk̉ʷɫk̉ʷull – spouse. *See:* ***spouse***.

wolf

nčỉʔcn – wolf; timber wolf. *suffix:* ***...cin, ...cn*** – *action of the mouth.*

čx̣i nčỉʔcn – gray wolf.

nčỉʔcnewɫ – wolf pack.

es neči – It howls.
es nčỉʔcni – It is howling/singing.

wolverine

cišps – wolverine; *Gulo gulo.*

q̉ʷo maẉɫx̣ʷis t cišps – Wolverine wrecked my tipi.

woman

smʔém – woman, girl; female. **smmʔem** – women, girls; females.

sx̌ʷsmʔém, *sx̌ʷsmʔé* – sister *(of a male).*

sɫmʔém – little women; girl. **sɫmʔémm** *pl.*
smmʔemus – woman's look; woman's eyes.

mʔamalqs – woman's clothes; dress as a woman; disguised as a woman. *See:* ***dress***.

peɫpɫk̉ʷi – women folk.

ɫk̉ʷk̉ʷiyomqn – small voice; feminine voice; high pitch voice. *See:* ***small***.

wonder

čhomist, *čho* – in awe of something or someone; overwhelmed; see something beautiful/good/wonderful. *See:* ***awe***.

wood

luk̉ʷ – wood.

ɫk̉ʷluk̉ʷ – little wood; stick.

čɫluk̉ʷ – go after wood. *See:* ***go after***.
čɫluk̉ʷ – S/he went after wood. **čn čɫluk̉ʷ, k̉ʷ čɫluk̉ʷ**
es čɫluk̉ʷi – S/he is going after wood. **čnes čɫluk̉ʷi, k̉ʷes čɫluk̉ʷi**
qs čɫluk̉ʷi – S/he is going to go after wood. **čiqs čɫluk̉ʷi, k̉ʷqs čɫluk̉ʷi**
čɫlúʔuk̉ʷ – They went after wood. **qeʔ čɫluk̉ʷ, p čɫluk̉ʷ**
es čɫlúʔuk̉ʷi – They are going after wood. **qeʔes čɫluk̉ʷi, pes čɫluk̉ʷi**
qs čɫlúʔuk̉ʷi – They are going to go after wood. **qeʔqs čɫluk̉ʷi, pqs čɫluk̉ʷi**

luk̉ʷis – S/he picked wood pieces from s.t./s.o. **luk̉ʷn, luk̉ʷntxʷ**
es luk̉ʷms – S/he is picking wood pieces from s.t./s.o. **ies luk̉ʷm, as luk̉ʷm**
qs luk̉ʷms – S/he is going to pick wood pieces from s.t./s.o. **iqs luk̉ʷm, aqs luk̉ʷm**

čɫluk̉ʷš – Go get wood. *cmd.*
luk̉ʷnt – Pick the wood pieces from him/her/it. *cmd.*

...alqʷ – *suffix indicating wood/tree/log.*

es sinalqʷi – S/he is counting wood/logs/trees.

nk̓ʷalqʷ – one log. **aslalqʷ** – two logs. **čałlalqʷ** – three logs. **moslqʷ** – four logs. **clčstalqʷ** – five logs. **t̓q̓nčalqʷ** – six logs. **hanmalqʷ** – eight logs. **x̣ntalqʷ** – nine logs. **upnčstalqʷ** – ten logs. **nk̓ʷoqnalqʷ** – 100 logs. **opnčstalqʷ** – 1000 logs.

aplsálqʷ – applewood.
łq̓álqʷ – board. *See:* ***lumber.***
łq̓lq̓álqʷ – lumber. *See:* ***lumber.***
ql̓alqʷ – green wood (not dry).
es pn̓alqʷ – The wood is bent. *rt.:* ***pin̓** – bent. See:* ***bend.***

es p̓in – log; bunch of logs; piled wood.

słƛ̓ƛ̓uk̓ʷe – pitch wood.

čéyeˀ – dead tree; snag; wood dry with age.

q̓ʷéllš – dead tree.

p̓seš, *p̓se* – get firewood; go after firewood; fetch firewood. *See:* ***get.***

sax̣ʷ – split wood with an instrument. *See:* ***split.***

čmčemen̓łp, *čmčemé* – pick up and gather branches and/or small pieces of wood. *See:* ***gather.***

pič – shave/cut. *(i.e., shaving wood.) See:* ***shave.***

The **i** following uvular consonants (UC) and the glottal stop **ˀ** sound like English "*ey*" as in the words th*ey*, h*ey*, wh*ey*, etc. Salish UC are: **q**, **q̓**, **qʷ**, **q̓ʷ**, **x̣**, **x̣ʷ**. For example, the suffix …**qin** – head/top, is often spelled using English *ey* as "q*ey*n". So **qi**, **q̓i**, **qʷi**, **q̓ʷi**, **x̣i**, **x̣ʷi**, may be spelled with English *ey* as **q***ey*, **q̓***ey*, **qʷ***ey*, **q̓ʷ***ey*, **x̣***ey*, **x̣ʷ***ey* in other texts.

wood chopper

sxʷšlim – one tasked to chop wood. *prefix:* ***sxʷ…** – one tasked to do.*

woodchuck

smčéč – hoary marmot; *Marmota caligata*; yellow-bellied marmot; *Marmota flaviventris;* groundhog; woodchuck; *(there is no distinction between the two marmot species).*

woodcock

spuwál̓qn – pileated woodpecker; red-headed woodpecker; *Dryocopus pileatus.*
čełlspuwá – three woodcocks.

woodland mountain caribou

styélsčn, *stye* – woodland mountain caribou; *Rangifer tarandus caribou. suffix:* ***…elsčn** – horn.*

woodpecker

spuwál̓qn – pileated woodpecker; red-headed woodpecker; *Dryocopus pileatus.*

kʷlkʷlé – red-headed woodpecker.

st̓lx̣ʷu – downy woodpecker.

ciwcu – Lewis's woodpecker.

woods

nkʷéct, *nkʷé* – forest, backwoods, brush, thicket.

woodshed

snluk̓ʷłté – woodshed.

snluk̓ʷtn – place of wood; woodshed. *prefix:* ***sn…** – a place of; suffix:* ***…tin, …tn** – means of/device.*

s.t. - something, the 3rd person
(s.t.) - something implied
s.o. - someone, the 3rd person
sl. - singular form
pl. - plural form
rt. - root word
cmd. - command
lit. - literally
fig. - figuratively
i.e., - for example
See: - Redirection to a related word.

woodtick

čččél̓sčn – woodtick.

woodworm

sxʷyálqʷ – woodworm.

qepqqepté – woodworm.

wool

spum – fur; wool.

woolly worm

čililk̓ʷté – caterpillar, woolly worm.

words **scq̇ẏi –** written letter; something that's written. *prefix: **sc...** – s.t. that's been done/made/prepared.*
scq̇ẏq̇ẏi – written words/letters. *prefix: **sc...** – s.t. that's been done/made/prepared.*
steṁ ẏe scq̇ẏi – What letter is this?
l čeṅ u nʔeċx̣ilcn ẏe scq̇ẏi – How does this letter sound?

scʔaw – spoken word. *prefix: **sc...** – s.t. that's been done/made/prepared.*
scʔawʔaw – spoken words; a sentence; something that's said. *prefix: **sc...** – s.t. that's been done/made/prepared.*

ta kʷ ies nunxʷenem łu asʔawʔaw – I do not believe your words.

...cin – *suffix indicating an action of the mouth; i.e., speaking, eating, & food. See: **mouth**.*
nmemeʔcin – talk in a bothersome way. *rt.: **memeʔt** – bothersome. See: **talk**.*
x̣scinm – talk in a good way; talk good about someone or something. *See: **talk**.*
čscinm – talk in a bad way; bad mouth. *See: **talk**.*
łaqʷcin – spoke up (once in a while). *See: **talk**.*
nk̇ʷnk̇ʷucin – saying one word at a time. *See: **talk**.*

work **k̇ʷul̓ –** do; make; fix; work.
k̇ʷul̓m – S/he/it made/did (s.t.). **čn k̇ʷul̓m, kʷ k̇ʷul̓m**
es k̇ʷul̓i – S/he/it is making/doing (s.t.). **čnes k̇ʷul̓i, kʷes k̇ʷul̓i**
qs k̇ʷul̓i – S/he/it is going to make/do (s.t.). **čiqs k̇ʷul̓i, kʷqs k̇ʷul̓i**
k̇ʷúʔul̓m – They made/did (s.t.). **qeʔ k̇ʷul̓m, p k̇ʷul̓m**
es k̇ʷúʔul̓i – They are making/doing (s.t.). **qeʔes k̇ʷul̓i, pes k̇ʷul̓i**

k̇ʷul̓is – S/he/it made/built/did s.t. **k̇ʷul̓n, k̇ʷul̓ntxʷ**
es k̇ʷul̓ms – S/he/it is making/building/doing it. **ies k̇ʷul̓m, as k̇ʷul̓m**
qs k̇ʷul̓ms – S/he/it is going to make/build/do it. **iqs k̇ʷul̓m, aqs k̇ʷul̓m**
k̇ʷúʔul̓is – They made/built/did s.t. **qeʔ k̇ʷul̓ntm, k̇ʷul̓ntp**
es k̇ʷúʔul̓ms – They are making/building/doing it. **qeʔes k̇ʷul̓m, es k̇ʷul̓mp**

k̇ʷul̓šts – S/he/it did s.t. for s.o. **k̇ʷul̓štn, k̇ʷul̓štxʷ**
es k̇ʷul̓štms – S/he/it is doing s.t. for s.o. **ies k̇ʷul̓štm, as k̇ʷul̓štm**
qs k̇ʷul̓štms – S/he/it is going to do s.t. for s.o. **iqs k̇ʷul̓štm, aqs k̇ʷul̓štm**

k̇ʷul̓mis – S/he/it used s.t. to make s.t. **k̇ʷul̓mn, k̇ʷul̓mntxʷ**
es k̇ʷul̓mms – S/he/it is using s.t. to make s.t. **ies k̇ʷul̓mm, as k̇ʷul̓mm**
qs k̇ʷul̓mms – S/he/it is going to use s.t. to make s.t. **iqs k̇ʷul̓mm, aqs k̇ʷul̓mm**

k̇ʷl̓mutmsts – It was possible for him/her to make s.t. **k̇ʷl̓mutmstn, k̇ʷl̓mutmstxʷ**
es k̇ʷl̓mutms – It is possible for him/her to make s.t. **ies k̇ʷl̓mutm, as k̇ʷl̓mutm**

es k̇ʷl̓k̇ʷul̓i – S/he/it is repeatedly doing (s.t.). **čnes k̇ʷl̓k̇ʷul̓i, kʷes k̇ʷl̓k̇ʷul̓i**
es k̇ʷl̓k̇ʷul̓ms – S/he/it is repeatedly making s.t. **ies k̇ʷl̓k̇ʷul̓m, as k̇ʷl̓k̇ʷul̓m**

es łk̇ʷuk̇ʷl̓i – S/he/it is working a little. **čnes k̇ʷl̓k̇ʷul̓i, kʷes k̇ʷl̓k̇ʷul̓i**
es łk̇ʷuk̇ʷl̓ms – S/he/it is making s.t. with little enthusiasm. **ies łk̇ʷuk̇ʷl̓m, as łk̇ʷuk̇ʷl̓m**

es łk̇ʷuk̇ʷl̓i – S/he/it is doing a little; doing for a short time. **čnes łk̇ʷuk̇ʷl̓i, kʷes łk̇ʷuk̇ʷl̓i**
es łk̇ʷuk̇ʷl̓ms – S/he/it is making a little s.t.; doing it for a short time. **ies łk̇ʷuk̇ʷl̓m, as łk̇ʷuk̇ʷl̓m**

es k̇ʷul̓ – It is built/made/done.
k̇ʷul̓ntm – It got built/made/done.

sk̇ʷul̓ – the work.
sck̇ʷul̓ – something that's been worked/made/done/fixed. *prefix: **sc...** – s.t. that's been done/made/prepared.* **sck̇ʷul̓s, isck̇ʷul̓, asck̇ʷul̓**

snk̓ʷul̓mn – place of work; place to make; place to fix; work bench.
k̓ʷul̓mn – tool; materials to make something.
sxʷk̓ʷul̓m – one tasked to work/make/fix; worker. *prefix:* ***sxʷ...*** *– one tasked to do.*
k̓ʷl̓k̓ʷl̓muł – one that habitually works; worker. *suffix:* ***...łmuł*** *– one that habitually does.*
k̓ʷl̓memn – one inclined to work; worker. *suffix:* ***...emn*** *– one inclined to do.*

k̓ʷul̓iš – Make/do/fix. *cmd.*
k̓ʷul̓wi – All of you make/do/fix. *cmd.*
k̓ʷul̓mistš – Prepare yourself. *cmd.*
k̓ʷul̓mistwi – All of you arrange yourself. *cmd.*
k̓ʷul̓nt – Make/do it. *cmd.*
es k̓ʷul̓iš – Keep working. *cmd.*
es k̓ʷul̓nt – Keep doing it. *cmd.*
k̓ʷul̓nti – All of you make/do it. *cmd.*
k̓ʷul̓št – Make s.t. for s.o.; do it for s.o. *cmd.*
k̓ʷul̓łt – Fix s.t. of his/hers/its. *cmd.*
eł k̓ʷul̓ – repair something. *See:* ***repair.***
k̓ʷl̓nunm – succeed making something; accomplish something. *See:* ***accomplish.***
nk̓ʷol̓qs – work on a road. *See:* ***road.***
k̓ʷul̓łxʷ – work on a house; build a house; carpentry work. *See:* ***build.***

ṅem k̓ʷul̓m – S/he/it will work. **ṅem čn k̓ʷul̓m, ṅem kʷ k̓ʷul̓m**
ṅem k̓ʷúˀul̓m – They will work. **ṅem qeˀ k̓ʷul̓m, ṅem p k̓ʷul̓m**

čn k̓ʷul̓m t citxʷ – I built a house. **kʷtisi es nté qs k̓ʷul̓i t ƛ̓iyéˀ –** Big Blanket wants to make a canoe. **čnes k̓ʷul̓i t ƛ̓iyéˀ –** I am making a boat. **či qeł k̓ʷul̓i t nk̓ʷuˀ –** I am going to make another one. **čiqs k̓ʷul̓i t scnłl̓qľa –** I am going to make pancakes. **k̓ʷnšspe u kʷes k̓ʷul̓i l t sq̇sip cúˀuts nk̓ʷul̓mn –** How many years have you been working with the Culture Committee? **ha ṅem kʷ k̓ʷul̓m ṅe anłq –** Will you work this summer. **čiqs xʷilwisi x̌ʷl̓ isck̓ʷul̓ –** I going to travel around for my work; I will be in the field. **čmlk̓ʷma sčx̌ʷéct u yoyoót čn k̓ʷul̓m –** All day Monday I worked hard. **mił q̇sip čn k̓ʷul̓m –** I worked too long. **šey̓ łu es k̓ʷul̓ms –** That's what s/he is doing. **steṁ łu aqs k̓ʷul̓m ṅex̌li –** What are you going to do tomorrow? **qʷo k̓ʷul̓is čiqs oyencuti –** S/he/it made me laugh. **qʷo k̓ʷul̓ntxʷ čiqs tk̓ʷk̓ʷmi –** You made me fall. **ta qʷo qs k̓ʷul̓ntxʷ čiqs oyencuti –** Do not make me laugh. **k̓ʷul̓nt qs mntwi –** Make him/her run. **k̓ʷul̓štn łu stipn łu t pumin –** I made Stephen a drum. **k̓ʷul̓łtn łu pumin łu x̌ʷl̓ stipn –** I made a drum for Stephen.

nk̓ʷl̓mels – want to do something; want to work; want to be busy.
nk̓ʷl̓mels – S/he wanted to be doing s.t. **čn nk̓ʷl̓mels, kʷ nk̓ʷl̓mels**
es nk̓ʷl̓melsi – S/he is wanting to be doing s.t. **čnes nk̓ʷl̓melsi, kʷes nk̓ʷl̓melsi**
qs nk̓ʷl̓melsi – S/he is going to want to be doing s.t. **čiqs nk̓ʷl̓melsi, kʷqs nk̓ʷl̓melsi**

nk̓ʷl̓melsmis – S/he wanted to do s.t. **nk̓ʷl̓melsmn, nk̓ʷl̓melsmntxʷ**
es nk̓ʷl̓melsms – S/he is wanting to do s.t. **ies nk̓ʷl̓melsm, as nk̓ʷl̓melsm**
qs nk̓ʷl̓melsms – S/he is going to want to do s.t. **iqs nk̓ʷl̓melsm, aqs nk̓ʷl̓melsm**

k̓ʷul̓mist – Prepare one's self to do s.t.; arrange one's self.
k̓ʷul̓mist – S/he/it prepared one's self to do s.t. **čn k̓ʷul̓mist, kʷ k̓ʷul̓mist**
es k̓ʷul̓misti – S/he/it is preparing one's self to do s.t. **čnes k̓ʷul̓misti, kʷes k̓ʷul̓misti**
qs k̓ʷul̓misti – S/he/it is going to prepare one's self to do s.t. **čiqs k̓ʷul̓misti, kʷqs k̓ʷul̓misti**

k̓ʷl̓mlwis – work here and there; work now and then; be frequently busy.

The **i** following uvular consonants (UC) and the glottal stop ˀ sound like English "*ey*" as in the words th*ey*, h*ey*, wh*ey*, etc. Salish UC are: **q, q̇, qʷ, q̇ʷ, x̌, x̌ʷ**. For example, the suffix **...qin** – head/top, is often spelled using English *ey* as "q*ey*n". So **qi, q̇i, qʷi, q̇ʷi, x̌i, x̌ʷi**, may be spelled with English *ey* as **q***ey*, **q̇***ey*, **qʷ***ey*, **q̇ʷ***ey*, **x̌***ey*, **x̌ʷ***ey* in other texts.

s.t. - something, the 3rd person
(s.t.) - something implied
s.o. - someone, the 3rd person
sl. - singular form
pl. - plural form
rt. - root word
cmd. - command
lit. - literally
fig. - figuratively
i.e., - for example
See: - Redirection to a related word.

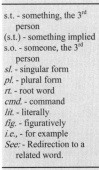

k̓ʷl̓mlwis – S/he worked here and there. **čn k̓ʷl̓mlwis, kʷ k̓ʷl̓mlwis**
es k̓ʷl̓mlwisi – S/he is working here and there. **čnes k̓ʷl̓mlwisi, kʷes k̓ʷl̓mlwisi**
qs k̓ʷl̓mlwisi – S/he is going to work here and there. **čiqs k̓ʷl̓mlwisi, kʷqs k̓ʷl̓mlwisi**

k̓ʷl̓ɫtumš – work for the people.
k̓ʷl̓ɫtumš – S/he worked for the people. **čn k̓ʷl̓ɫtumš, kʷ k̓ʷl̓ɫtumš**
es k̓ʷl̓ɫtumši – S/he is working for the people. **čnes k̓ʷl̓ɫtumši, kʷes k̓ʷl̓ɫtumši**

k̓ʷl̓lutm – It can be made; possible.
qs k̓ʷl̓lutm – It is possible.
ta qs k̓ʷl̓lutm – It is impossible.

k̓ʷl̓mutm – It can be done.
k̓ʷl̓mutmsts – S/he was able to do s.t. **k̓ʷl̓mutmstn, k̓ʷl̓mutmstxʷ**
es k̓ʷl̓mutms – S/he can make s.t. **ies k̓ʷl̓mutm, as k̓ʷl̓mutm**

k̓ʷl̓mutiyeʔ – make/do something haphazardly. *suffix: **...mutiyeʔ** – temporary.*
k̓ʷl̓mutiyeʔ – S/he did (s.t.) haphazardly. **čn k̓ʷl̓mutiyeʔ, kʷ k̓ʷl̓mutiyeʔ**
es k̓ʷl̓mutiyeʔi – S/he is doing (s.t.) haphazardly. **čnes k̓ʷl̓mutiyeʔi, kʷes k̓ʷl̓mutiyeʔi**

k̓ʷl̓mutiyeis – S/he did s.t. haphazardly. **k̓ʷl̓mutiyen, k̓ʷl̓mutiyentxʷ**
es k̓ʷl̓mutiyems – S/he is doing s.t. haphazardly. **ies k̓ʷl̓mutiyem, as k̓ʷl̓mutiyem**

q̓ʷiɫmist, *q̓ʷiɫmi* – do one's best; try hard from energy. *See: **capable**.*

sičstmist – do one's best; try hard from ability. *See: **capable**.*

čmaqs – perform at the peak of one's ability; best at something; pinnacle. *See: **best**.*

musčst – do one's best with hope of succeeding; do something with confidence. *See: **confident**.*

aytčst – strive; exert one's self in work. *See: **strive**.*

work bench **snk̓ʷul̓mn –** place of work; place to make; place to fix; work bench.

worker **sxʷk̓ʷul̓m –** one tasked to work; worker. *prefix: **sxʷ...** – one tasked to do.*

work place **snk̓ʷul̓mn –** place of work; place to make; place to fix; work bench.

worm **ntišulexʷ –** worm, insect, bug. *lit. underground crawlers. prefix: **n...** – inside; rt.: **tiyeš** – crawl; suffix: **...ulexʷ** – land.*
es ntišulexʷi – It is crawling underground/in the ground.

ntitišulexʷ – worms, insects, bugs.
nɫttišulexʷ – little worm, insect, bug.

yanáq̓ʷ – angleworm; earthworm.
yananq̓ʷ – wiggle. *See: **wiggle**.*

ččn̓čn̓pi – caddisworm, straw worm.

čililk̓ʷté – caterpillar, woolly worm.

sxʷyálqʷ – woodworm.

qepqqepté – woodworm.

worry **k̓ʷɫtqpelsm –** feel worried.
k̓ʷɫtqpelsm – S/he felt worried. **čn k̓ʷɫtqpelsm, kʷ k̓ʷɫtqpelsm**
es k̓ʷɫtqpelsi – S/he is feeling worried. **čnes k̓ʷɫtqpelsi, kʷes k̓ʷɫtqpelsi**

qs k̓ʷłtqpelsi – S/he is going to feel worried. **čiqs k̓ʷłtqpelsi, kʷqs k̓ʷłtqpelsi**
k̓ʷłtqpéʔelsm – They felt worried. **qeʔ k̓ʷłtqpelsm, ps k̓ʷłtqpelsm**

yéṁmist, *yéṁm* – despaired; frustrated; troubled; worried; have a block; have a dilemma. *See:* ***despair***.

čxʷusminm – lose sleep over something; worried. *rt.:* ***xʷus*** *– wide awake.*
es čxʷusminms – S/he is losing sleep over s.t./s.o. **ies čxʷusminm, as čxʷusminm**
qs čxʷusminms – S/he is going to lose sleep over s.t./s.o. **iqs čxʷusminm, aqs čxʷusminm**
es čxʷusmíʔinms – S/he is losing sleep over s.t./s.o. **ies čxʷusminm, as čxʷusminm**
qs čxʷusmíʔinms – S/he is going to lose sleep over s.t./s.o. **iqs čxʷusminm, aqs čxʷusminm**

ṅem qes čxʷusminms – S/he will be losing sleep over s.t. **ṅem iqes čxʷusminm, ṅem aqes čxʷusminm**
ṅem qes čxʷusmíʔinms – They will be losing sleep over s.t. **ṅem qeʔqes čxʷusminm, ṅem qes čxʷusminmp**

The **i** following uvular consonants (UC) and the glottal stop **ʔ** sound like English "*ey*" as in the words th*ey*, h*ey*, wh*ey*, etc. Salish UC are: **q**, **q̇**, **qʷ**, **q̇ʷ**, **x̣**, **x̣ʷ**. For example, the suffix …**qin** – head/top, is often spelled using English *ey* as "q*ey*n". So **qi**, **q̇i**, **qʷi**, **q̇ʷi**, **x̣i**, **x̣ʷi**, may be spelled with English *ey* as **q***ey*, **q̇***ey*, **qʷ***ey*, **q̇ʷ***ey*, **x̣***ey*, **x̣ʷ***ey* in other texts.

pupusénč, *pupusé* – sad; sorry; mourn; grieve. *See:* ***sad***.

worthless

sqmł – indicates worthlessness.
sqmłsqelixʷ – worthless man.
sqmsmʔem – worthless woman.
sqmłƛ̓x̣cin – worthless horse.

tṅmusist, *tṅmu* – worthless.
es tṅmusisti – You are not worth anything. **čnes tṅmusisti, kʷes tṅmusisti**

worthy

mi – fact; knowing; reality; certainty. *See:* ***know***.

wound

ilip – wounded/shot by a bullet, arrow or sharp stick. *rt.:* ***ili*** *– pass into/through.*
ilip – S/he/it got wounded. **čn ilip, kʷ ilip**
es ilpmi – S/he/it is getting wounded. **čnes ilpmi, kʷes ilpmi**
qs ilpmi – S/he/it is going to get wounded. **čiqs ilpmi, kʷqs ilpmi**

ilpnuis – S/he wounded it. **ilpnun, ilpnuntxʷ**
es ilpnunms – S/he is wounding it. **ies ilpnunm, as ilpnunm**
qs ilpnunms – S/he is going to wound it. **iqs ilpnunm, aqs ilpnunm**

es ilip – It is wounded. **čnes ilip, kʷes ilip**

ilpncut – wound one's self.
ilpstwéxʷ – wounding each other; battle, war.

ilim – throw and strike something with a pointed object. *(throw an arrow, spear, sharp stick, etc.) See:* ***throw***.

illnun u es ilip – I hit it, and it is wounded.

s.t. - something, the 3rd person
(s.t.) - something implied
s.o. - someone, the 3rd person
sl. - singular form
pl. - plural form
rt. - root word
cmd. - command
lit. - literally
fig. - figuratively
i.e., - for example
See: - Redirection to a related word.

wrap

čṗlk̓ʷiċéʔ – wrap; enfold; roll up. *rt.:* ***ṗulk̓ʷ*** *– fold; suffix:* ***…iċéʔ*** *– covered in. See:* ***fold***.
čṗlk̓ʷiċʔéis – S/he wrapped s.t. **čṗlk̓ʷiċʔén, čṗlk̓ʷiċʔéntxʷ**
es čṗlk̓ʷiċʔéms – S/he is wrapping s.t. **ies čṗlk̓ʷiċʔém, as čṗlk̓ʷiċʔém**
qs čṗlk̓ʷiċʔéms – S/he is going to wrap s.t. **iqs čṗlk̓ʷiċʔém, aqs čṗlk̓ʷiċʔém**

es čṗlk̓ʷiċéʔ – It is wrapped.

čp̓lk̓ʷic̓ʔént – Wrap it. *cmd.*

sčp̓l̓p̓l̓k̓ʷic̓eʔ, *sčp̓l̓p̓l̓k̓ʷí* – cigarette. *See:* ***cigarette.***

čp̓lk̓ʷic̓ʔén uʔuseʔ l snqʷlpulexʷ – I wrapped the eggs in the bread.

sqq̓tté – baby sack (wrap for babies).

čax̣ic̓eʔ – wrap with rope/lace/string. *rt.:* ***i ax̣*** *– it has lines; suffix:* ***...ic̓éʔ*** *– covered in.*
es čax̣ic̓eʔ – S/he/it is all wrapped up. **čnes čax̣ic̓eʔ, kʷes čax̣ic̓eʔ**

čax̣ic̓ʔeis – S/he wrapped s.t. up. **čax̣ic̓ʔen, čax̣ic̓ʔentxʷ**
es čax̣ic̓ʔems – S/he is wrapping s.t. up. **ies čax̣ic̓ʔem, as čax̣ic̓ʔem**
qs čax̣ic̓ʔems – S/he is going to wrap s.t. up. **iqs čax̣ic̓ʔem, aqs čax̣ic̓ʔem**

čax̣ic̓eʔnt – Wrap it up. *cmd.*

čyayalaqtšn – wrap around the legs.

čyayalax̣n – wrap around the arms.

yalim, *yal* – coil up; wrap. *See:* ***coil.***

wreck

čłk̓ʷelč – turn a rigid container type object upside-down on a flat surface *; roll/tip over. (i.e., car, hat, lid, etc.) See:* ***upside down.***

máw̓t – break. *See:* ***break.***
maw̓łxʷn – I wrecked/broke the house, tipi, lodge. **qʷo maw̓łxʷis t cišps** – wolverine wrecked (broke) my tipi.

wrestle

q̓ʷmq̓ʷmnwexʷ, *q̓ʷmnwé* – wrestle each other.

wring

q̓ʷʔe – wring; twist; squeeze.
q̓ʷʔem – S/he twisted/wrung. **čn q̓ʷʔem, kʷ q̓ʷʔem**
es q̓ʷʔemi – S/he is wringing. **ies q̓ʷʔemi, as q̓ʷʔemi**
qs q̓ʷʔemi – S/he is going to wring. **iqs q̓ʷʔemi, aqs q̓ʷʔemi**

q̓ʷʔentes – S/he twisted/wrung s.t. **q̓ʷʔenten, q̓ʷʔentexʷ**
es q̓ʷʔems – S/he is wringing s.t. **ies q̓ʷʔem, as q̓ʷʔem**
qs q̓ʷʔems – S/he is going to wring s.t. **iqs q̓ʷʔem, aqs q̓ʷʔem**
q̓ʷʔentéʔes – They twisted/wrung it. **qeʔ q̓ʷʔentem, q̓ʷʔentep**

q̓ʷʔemin – twisting stick.

q̓ʷʔeiš – Twist; wring. *cmd.*
q̓ʷʔent – Twist it; wring it. *cmd.*
q̓ʷaq̓ʷʔemxʷ – milking; squeeze breasts. *See:* ***milk.***
q̓ʷaposqncut – squeeze one's lips together. *See:* ***mouth.***
nq̓ʷʔétkʷ, *nq̓ʷʔé* – wash clothes; do laundry. *See:* ***wash.***
k̓ʷłq̓ʷʔe – strain something.

n̓e wis q̓ʷʔentéxʷ m sťsuťmstxʷ – When you finish wringing it, stretch it.

ťup̓ – twist something together. *See:* ***twist.***

wrinkle

p̓uy – wrinkled.
es p̓uymi – It is getting wrinkled.

i p̓uy – It is wrinkle.
i p̓uys – The face is wrinkled.

i ṗuyšn – His/her/its foot is wrinkled.

sṗuy – wrinkle.

ṗiṗuyšn – automobile, car. *lit. wrinkled feet. rt.: **ṗuy**– wrinkle; suffix: **...šn**– foot.*
sčṗuyšn – car tire.

The **i** following uvular consonants (UC) and the glottal stop ʔ sound like English "*ey*" as in the words *they, hey, whey*, etc. Salish UC are: **q, q̇, qʷ, q̇ʷ, x̣, x̣ʷ**. For example, the suffix **...qin** – head/top, is often spelled using English *ey* as "q*ey*n". So **qi, q̇i, qʷi, q̇ʷi, x̣i, x̣ʷi**, may be spelled with English *ey* as **q***ey*, **q̇***ey*, **qʷ***ey*, **q̇ʷ***ey*, **x̣***ey*, **x̣ʷ***ey* in other texts.

wrist

sk̇ʷłčmcnéčst, *sk̇ʷłčmcné* – wrist. *rt.: **čm**– extremity.*

k̇ʷłċalcnéčst – sore/hurting wrist. *rt.: **ċaál**– ache; suffix: **...cnečst**– wrist.*
k̇ʷłċalcnéčst – S/he/it had a sore wrist. **čn k̇ʷłċalcnéčst, kʷ k̇ʷłċalcnéčst**
es k̇ʷłċalcnéčsti – S/he/it has a sore wrist. **čnes k̇ʷłċalcnéčsti, kʷes k̇ʷłċalcnéčsti**

k̇ʷłmalkʷcnéčst – dislocated/disjointed wrist. *suffix: **...cnečst**– wrist.*
es k̇ʷłmalkʷcnéčst – His/her wrist is dislocated/disjointed. **čnes k̇ʷłmalkʷcnéčst, kʷes k̇ʷłmalkʷcnéčst**

es malkʷax̣n – His/her elbow is disjointed/dislocated. **čnes malkʷax̣n, kʷes malkʷax̣n**
k̇ʷłmalkʷcnéčsis – S/he/it dislocated/disjointed s.o.'s wrist. **k̇ʷłmalkʷcnéčsn, k̇ʷłmalkʷcnéčsntxʷ**
es k̇ʷłmalkʷcnéčsms – S/he/it is dislocating/disjointing s.o.'s wrist. **ies k̇ʷłmalkʷcnéčsm, as k̇ʷłmalkʷcnéčsm**
qs k̇ʷłmalkʷcnéčsms – S/he/it is going to dislocate/disjoint s.o.'s wrist. **qes k̇ʷłmalkʷcnéčsm, aqs k̇ʷłmalkʷcnéčsm**

write

q̇eẏim – write.
q̇eẏim – S/he wrote. **čn q̇eẏim, kʷ q̇eẏim**
es q̇eẏmi – S/he is writing. **čnes q̇eẏmi, kʷes q̇eẏmi**
qs q̇eẏmi – S/he is going to write. **čiqs q̇eẏmi, kʷqs q̇eẏmi**
q̇eẏíʔim – They wrote. **qeʔ q̇eẏim, p q̇eẏim**
es q̇eẏmíʔi – They are writing. **qeʔes q̇eẏmi, pes q̇eẏmi**
qs q̇eẏmíʔi – They are going to write. **qeʔqs q̇eẏmi, pqs q̇eẏmi**

q̇eẏntes – S/he wrote s.t. **q̇eẏnten, q̇eẏntexʷ**
es q̇eẏims – S/he is writing s.t. **ies q̇eẏim, as q̇eẏim**
qs q̇eẏims – S/he is going to write s.t. **iqs q̇eẏim, aqs q̇eẏim**
q̇eẏntéʔes – They wrote s.t. **qeʔ q̇eẏntem, q̇eẏntep**
es q̇eẏíʔims – They are writing s.t. **qeʔes q̇eẏim, es q̇eẏimp**

q̇eẏminmis – S/he wrote with s.t. **q̇eẏminmn, q̇eẏminmntxʷ**
es q̇eẏminms – S/he is writing with s.t. **ies q̇eẏminm, as q̇eẏminm**
qs q̇eẏminms – S/he is going to write with s.t. **iqs q̇eẏminm, aqs q̇eẏminm**

es q̇ẏq̇eẏmi – S/he is writing and writing. **čnes q̇ẏq̇eẏmi, kʷes q̇ẏq̇eẏmi**
q̇ẏq̇eẏntes – S/he wrote several things. **q̇ẏq̇eẏnten, q̇ẏiq̇eẏntexʷ**
es q̇ẏq̇eẏims – S/he is writing several things. **ies q̇ẏq̇eẏim, as q̇ẏq̇eẏim**

es łq̇q̇eẏmi – S/he is writing a little. **čnes łq̇q̇eẏmi, kʷes łq̇q̇eẏmi**

q̇eẏntem – It was written.
es q̇eẏi – It is written.

sxʷq̇eẏim – one tasked to write. *prefix: **sxʷ...** – one tasked to do.*
q̇ẏq̇ẏmuł – one that habitually writes. *suffix: **...tmuł**– one that habitually does.*
scq̇ẏi – something that's been written.
q̇eẏmin – paper, book.
q̇eẏmintn – pen, pencil.

s.t. - something, the 3rd person
(s.t.) - something implied
s.o. - someone, the 3rd person
sl. - singular form
pl. - plural form
rt. - root word
cmd. - command
lit. - literally
fig. - figuratively
i.e., - for example
See: - Redirection to a related word.

snčłq̓eẏmintn – writing desk.
ƛ̓áx̣t nq̓eẏmintn – typewriter.

q̓eẏmiš – Write. *cmd.*
q̓eẏint – Write it. *cmd.*
es q̓eẏštwexʷi – They are writing for each other.
es nq̓ẏmelsi – S/he is wanting to write. **čnes nq̓ẏmelsi, kʷes nq̓ẏmelsi**
čnes q̓eẏmi č̓ islax̣t – I am writing to my friend. **ha kʷ n̓e u q̓ʷo q̓eẏšitxʷ –** Would you write a letter for me?

k̓ʷłq̓ẏq̓eẏim – color a picture; color something. *See:* ***color.***

k̓ʷłq̓eẏim – draw a picture. *See:* ***draw.***

nčnqinm – sign one's name. *See:* ***signature.***

wrong

česčst – do something bad/wrong; make something bad/wrong.
česčstm – use something or someone for bad; to wrong to someone.
česčstmis – S/he wronged s.o. **česčstmn, česčstmntxʷ**
es česčstmms – S/he is wronging s.o. **ies česčstmm, as česčstmm**
qs česčstmms – S/he is going to wrong s.o. **iqs česčstmm, aqs česčstmm**

č̓smscut – behave badly/wrong. *suffix:* ***...cut–*** *action to the self.*
č̓smscut – S/he/it acted badly. **čn č̓smscut, kʷ č̓smscut**
es č̓smscuti – S/he/it is acting badly. **čnes č̓smscuti, kʷes č̓smscuti**
qs č̓smscuti – S/he/it is going to act badly. **čiqs č̓smscuti, kʷqs č̓smscuti**
č̓smscúʔut – They acted badly. **qeʔ čč̓smscut, p č̓smscut**
es č̓smscúʔuti – They are acting badly. **qeʔes č̓smscuti, pes č̓smscuti**
qs č̓smscúʔuti – They are going to act badly. **qeʔqs č̓smscuti, pqs č̓smscuti**

éyčsšłtumš – avenge wrongs done to the people.
es éyčsšłtumši – S/he is avenging wrongs done to the people. **čnes éyčsšłtumši, kʷes éyčsšłtumši**

éyčst – revenge; got even; avenge wrongs done. *See:* ***revenge.***

i tám – It is not; wrong.
tam – not.

ulmscut – act wrong; act wicked. *rt.:* ***wil–*** *wicked.*
ulmscut – S/he acted wrong. **čn ulmscu, kʷ ulmscut**
es ulmscuti – S/he is acting wrong. **čnes ulmscuti, kʷes ulmscuti**

nwilcn – talk wrong; talk faulty.

wil – faulty; wrong; wicked. *See:* ***wicked.***

sil̓ – confused; unable to figure something out; mistaken. *See:* ***confuse.***

X

x-ray **sčsłx̣musʔacċx̣** – x-ray.

s.t. - something, the 3rd person
(s.t.) - something implied
s.o. - someone, the 3rd person
sl. - singular form
pl. - plural form
rt. - root word
cmd. - command
lit. - literally
fig. - figuratively
i.e., - for example
See: - Redirection to a related word.

Y

yak **čłusšneľxʷ q̓ʷiq̓ʷáy** – yak.

Yakima **iaqmeʔ** – Yakima people.

yard **scqľwét** – yard as a measure. *rt.: **qľwe** – step; prefix: **sc...** – s.t. that's been done/made/prepared.*
nk̓ʷuʔ scqlwét – one yard.

skʷalulexʷ – area where plants/grass grows. *(i.e., a yard, lawn, field, etc.)*

x̣ʷiclexʷ – mow grass or hay. *See: **mow**.*

čmčnełxʷ – front yard. *rt.: **čm** – extremity.*

nčmčnełxʷ – backyard. *rt.: **čm** – extremity.*

yarn belt **npuľčaw̓stn,** *npuľča* – yarn belt. *suffix: **...éw̓s** – in between, middle; suffix: **...tin, ...tn** – means of/device.*

yarrow **nkʷk̓ʷá** – yarrow; milfoil.

yawn **héwlš** – yawn.
héwlš – S/he yawned. **čn héwlš, kʷ héwlš**
es héwlši – S/he is yawning. **čnes héwlši, kʷes héwlši**
qs héwlši – S/he is going to yawn. **čiqs héwlši, kʷqs héwlši**

héwlšts – S/he/it made s.o. yawn. **čn héwlštn, kʷ héwlštnxʷ**
es héwlšms – S/he is making s.o. yawn. **čnes héwlšm, kʷes héwlšm**
qs héwlšms – S/he is going to make s.o. yawn. **čiqs héwlšm, kʷqs héwlšm**

es hewhéwlši – S/he is yawning repeatedly. **čnes hewhéwlši, kʷes hewhéwlši**

huhéwlšemn – one inclined to yawn. *suffix: **...emn** – one inclined to do.*

héwlšiš – Yawn. *cmd.*
héwlšsk̓ʷ – Make s.o. yawn. *cmd.*

year **smx̣ʷóp** – age, year, snow.
sk̓ʷn̓šsmx̣ʷóp – ask how many snows; how old someone is.

spéntč – year.
słesľspé – two-year-old.

čn clčspentč – I am five years old. **čis eslʔu eł cil** – I am 25. **kʷ esel** – You are 2. **uł esel u upn eł cil u eslʔupn eł cil** – They are 2, 15, and 25. **pesyaʔ u p uł taq̓n smx̣ʷop** – All of you are 6 years old.

s.t. - something, the 3rd person
(s.t.) - something implied
s.o. - someone, the 3rd person
sl. - singular form
pl. - plural form
rt. - root word
cmd. - command
lit. - literally
fig. - figuratively
i.e., - for example
See: - Redirection to a related word.

nk̓ʷspéntč – one year. **eslspentč** – two years. **čeɫlspentč** – three years. **mspentč** – four years. **clčspentč** – five years. **t̓qnčspentč** – six years. **sp̓l̓čspentč** – seven years. **henmspentč** – eight years. **x̣l̓tspentč** – nine years. **upnčspentč** – ten years. **eslˀupnčspentč** – twenty years.

sk̓ʷn̓šspéntč, *sk̓ʷn̓šspé* – ask, how many years; how old is someone. *See:* ***age***.

tapistém̓, *tapisté* – never.

tspisc̓é – yesterday.

es šˀiti – S/he/it is first. *(i.e., beginning of time.)*

yearling

ɫqʷq̓ʷm̓é – yearling.

yearn

xʷmminm – yearn; long for; strongly desire.

xʷmmis – S/he longed for s.t./s.o. **xʷmmin, xʷmmintxʷ**
es xʷmminms – S/he is longing for s.t./s.o. **ies xʷmminm, as xʷmminm**
qs xʷmminms – S/he is going to long for s.t./s.o. **iqs xʷmminm, aqs xʷmminm**

es xʷmmnwexʷi – They are longing for each other. **qees xʷmmnwexʷi, pes xʷmmnwexʷi**

xʷmmin – something longed for.
xʷmmaqs – food desired/longed for.
xʷmmulexʷ – place longed for.

yeast

npeulexʷtn – yeast.

nméƛ̓mn – baking powder. *rt.* ***meƛ̓*** *– mix; prefix:* ***n...*** *– inside; suffix:* ***...min, ...mn*** *– instrument/tool.*

yell

čošim – yell out; shout out. *(i.e., a war cry)*

čošim – S/he/it yelled. **čn čošim, kʷ čošim**
es čošmi – S/he/it is yelling. **čnes čošmi, kʷes čošmi**
qs čošmi – S/he/it is going to yell. **čiqs čošmi, kʷqs čošmi**
čošíˀim – They yelled. **qeˀ čošim, p čošim**
es čošmíˀi – They are yelling. **qeˀes čošmi, pes čošmi**
qs čošmíˀi – They are going to yell. **qeˀqs čošmi, pqs čošmi**

čošiš – Shout, yell. *cmd.*

ha es čošmi – Is s/he/it yelling? **čnes čošmi ɫu x̣ʷl̓ isnkʷsqelixʷ** – I am shouting out for my fellow people.

coˀim̓cn – scream at the top of one's voice. *See:* ***scream***.

tspmncót, *tspmncó* – sudden sound of voices shouting. *See:* ***sound***.

wéˀm – yell; holler out; talk while shouting. *See:* ***holler***.

hawawlš – tell off; yell at someone. *See:* ***tell off***.

yellow

kʷaliˀ – yellow. **kʷlkʷaliˀ** – yellows. *pl.*

es kʷal̓li – It is becoming yellow.

kʷaliˀis – S/he made it yellow. **kʷaliˀn, kʷaliˀntxʷ**
es kʷaliˀms – S/he is making it yellow. **ies kʷaliˀm, as kʷaliˀm**
qs kʷaliˀms – S/he is going to make it yellow. **iqs kʷaliˀm, aqs kʷaliˀm**

i kʷaliˀ – It is yellow.
i ɫkʷakʷliˀ – It is a little yellow; yellowish.

kʷaliʔnt – Make it yellow. *cmd.*
kekʷal̓iyeʔ – little yellow one, affectionately.

Yellow Bay **čkʷłkʷl̓a** – Yellow Bay, Flathead Lake, Montana.

yellow bell **q̇áwx̣e** – yellow bell *(flower).*

yellow-bellied marmot **smċėċ** – hoary marmot; *Marmota caligata*; yellow-bellied marmot; *Marmota flaviventris;* groundhog; woodchuck; *(there is no distinction between the two marmot species).*

yellow-headed blackbird **čkʷaliyoqn ƛ̓čƛ̓á** – yellow-headed blackbird; *Xanthocephalus xanthocephalus.*

yellow-jacket **sqʷuʔł** – wasp, bee, hornet.

yellow lichen **skʷályo** – yellow lichen.

yellow pine chipmunk **qʷqʷċw̓é** – yellow pine chipmunk, red-tailed chipmunk.

yellow pond lily **qʷónmłp** – yellow pond-lily; *Nuphar lutea.*

yes **eu,** *e* – yes.

ʔa – yes, consenting.
ʔa eu – Oh, yes.

unexʷ, *une* – true; yes, acknowledged.

šey̓ – yes, concurring.

ṅem – yes, I will.

néłi – yes, naturally; in surprise that one should ask.

ah – yes, in surprise.

xʷu – okay, in agreement.

yesterday **tspisċé** – yesterday.
tspisċé u čn laáp – Yesterday I sailed. **tspisċé u wičis t mali ci ttwit qʷo es máw̓łtms innšnse** – Yesterday Mary saw that boy breaking my window.

yet **ċy̓u** – not yet.

pṅ – but *(contradictory)*, well *(as a rebuke)*, yet *(in spite of)*. *See:* ***response***.

yew **ckʷṅčálqʷ,** *ckʷṅčá* – western yew; *taxus brevifolia (used to make* ***ckʷiṅč*** *– bows.).*

yolk **snkʷaliʔep** – egg yolk. *rt.:* ***kʷaliʔ*** *– yellow.*

yonder **ci č ciʔ** – over there, over yonder.

you **anwi** – you, yours.

ƛ̓m asłqʷamp – It was your rabbit.
asłqʷa – your rabbit.
qł asłqʷa – It is going to be your rabbit.

The **i** following uvular consonants (UC) and the glottal stop **ʔ** sound like English "*ey*" as in the words th*ey*, h*ey*, wh*ey*, etc. Salish UC are: **q**, **q̇**, **qʷ**, **q̇ʷ**, **x̣**, **x̣ʷ**. For example, the suffix …**qin** – head/top, is often spelled using English *ey* as "q*ey*n". So **qi**, **q̇i**, **qʷi**, **q̇ʷi**, **x̣i**, **x̣ʷi**, may be spelled with English *ey* as **q***ey*, **q̇***ey*, **qʷ***ey*, **q̇ʷ***ey*, **x̣***ey*, **x̣ʷ***ey* in other texts.

s.t. - something, the 3rd person
(s.t.) - something implied
s.o. - someone, the 3rd person
sl. - singular form
pl. - plural form
rt. - root word
cmd. - command
lit. - literally
fig. - figuratively
i.e., - for example
See: - Redirection to a related word.

anq̓ʷomqn – your hair.
aspúʔus – your heart.

mił nwist x̣ʷl̓ anwi – It is too high for you.

you all

nplemp – all of you; all of yours.

ƛ̓m słqʷamp – It was you folks' rabbit.
słqʷamp – you folks' rabbit.
qł słqʷamp – It is going to be you folks' rabbit.

q̓ʷomqnmp – you folks' hair.
spúʔusmp – you folks' heart.

pesyáʔ – all of you, you all.
lémlmtš pesyáʔ – thanks, all of you.

p uł – you all; you guys; all of you individuals. *rt.: **uł**– those individuals.*
p uł čenčnt – All you individuals are slowpokes.

young

skʷk̓ʷim̓lt – young; child.

k̓ʷilmscut – act/play young.
k̓ʷilmscut – S/he/it acted young. **čn k̓ʷilmscut, kʷ k̓ʷilmscut**
es k̓ʷilmscuti – S/he/it is acting young. **čnes k̓ʷilmscuti, kʷes k̓ʷilmscuti**
qs k̓ʷilmscuti – S/he/it is going to act young. **čiqs k̓ʷilmscuti, kʷqs k̓ʷilmscuti**
k̓ʷilmscúʔut – They acted young. **qeʔ k̓ʷilmscut, p k̓ʷilmscut**
es k̓ʷilmscúʔuti – They are acting young. **qeʔes k̓ʷilmscuti, pes k̓ʷilmscuti**
qs k̓ʷilmscúʔuti – They are going to act young. **qeʔqs k̓ʷilmscuti, pqs k̓ʷilmscuti**

qeł – young; offspring of animals.
qełmlqnups – young golden eagle.
qełpqlqin – young bald eagle.
qełskʷiskʷs – young chickens.

youngest

tʔéw – young boy.
stʔewtélt – youngest daughter; last born child.
stʔéwti – younger of two children.

your

anwi – you, yours.

ƛ̓m asłqʷa – It was your rabbit.
asłqʷa – your rabbit.
qł asłqʷa – It is going to be your rabbit.

anq̓ʷomqn – your hair.
aspúʔus – your heart.

youth

skʷk̓ʷim̓lt – young, child.

Z

zebra **esłp̓łip̓ snč̓łcaʔsqá** – zebra. *lit. a horse that has lines.*

zig zag **es t̓st̓isk̓ʷ** – It is crooked.

n̓in̓in̓pmncut – a line of objects *(people, animals, etc.)* moving in a zig zag fashion.
n̓in̓petkʷ – turning water. *suffix:* ***...etkʷ, ...tkʷ*** *– liquid*

zipper **nlopeys** – zip a zipper. *lit. fitting teeth together.*
nlopeysis – S/he zipped it. **nlopeysn, nlopeysntxʷ**
es nlopeysms – S/he is zipping it. **ies nlopeysm, as nlopeysm**
qs nlopeysms – S/he is going to zip it. **iqs nlopeysm, aqs nlopeysm**

nlopeysnt – Zip it. *cmd.*

nlopeysnt anlkepu – Zip your coat.

npƛ̓pƛ̓eys – unzip a zipper. *lit. release teeth.*
npƛ̓pƛ̓eysis – S/he unzipped it. **npƛ̓pƛ̓eysn, npƛ̓pƛ̓eysntxʷ**
es npƛ̓pƛ̓eysms – S/he is unzipping it. **ies npƛ̓pƛ̓eysm, as npƛ̓pƛ̓eysm**
qs npƛ̓pƛ̓eysms – S/he is going to unzip it. **iqs npƛ̓pƛ̓eysm, aqs npƛ̓pƛ̓eysm**

npƛ̓pƛ̓eysnt – Unzip it. *cmd.*

npƛ̓pƛ̓eysnt anlkepu – Unzip your coat.

zit **sčečeʔus** – pimples; acne.
sčeʔus – pimple; zit.

zoo **snloʔloʔ xʷixʷeyuł** – zoo. *lit. fenced in wild animals.*

s.t. - something, the 3rd person
(s.t.) - something implied
s.o. - someone, the 3rd person
sl. - singular form
pl. - plural form
rt. - root word
cmd. - command
lit. - literally
fig. - figuratively
i.e., - for example
See: - Redirection to a related word.

malt sqeltč *body*

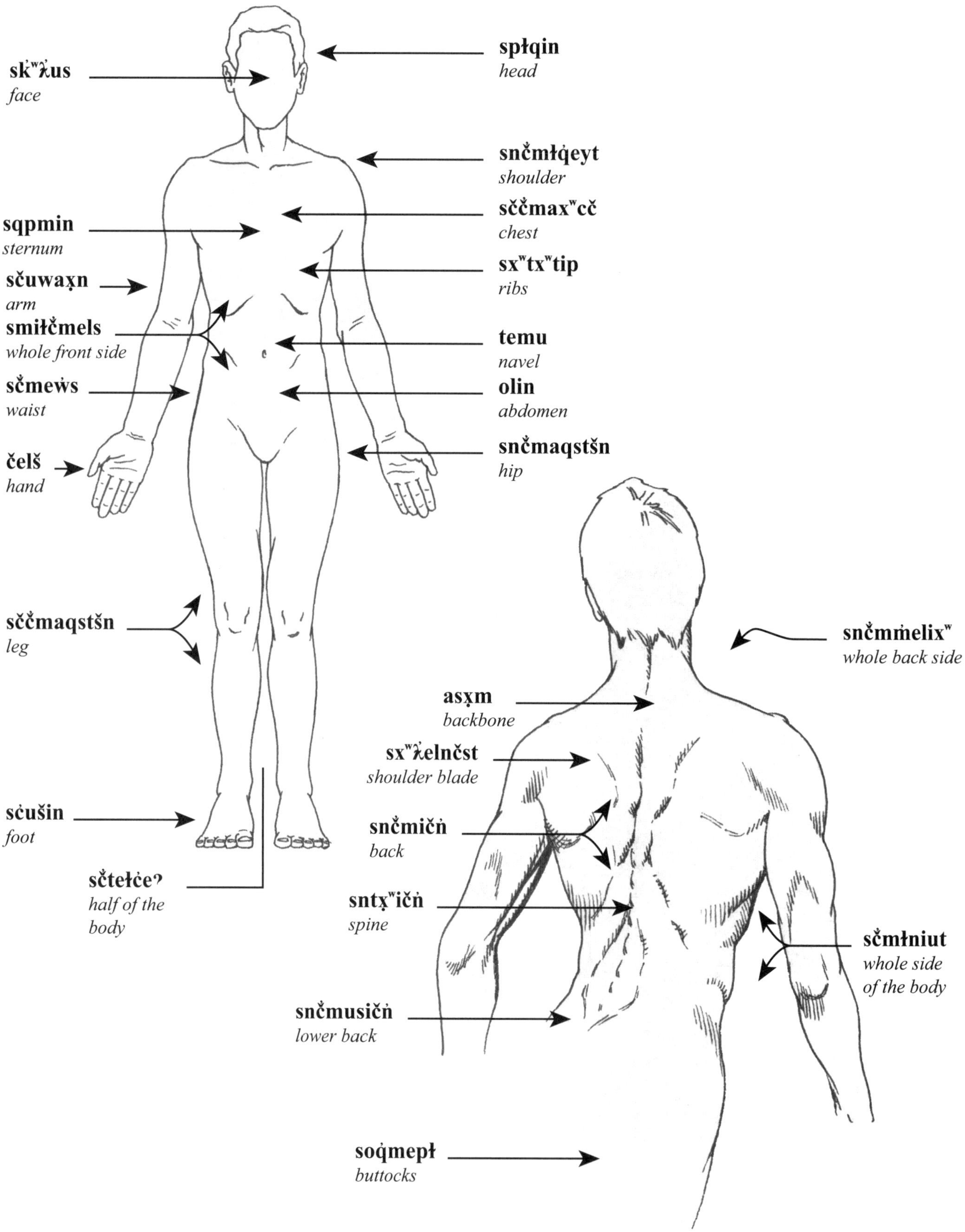

sk̓ʷƛ̓us
face
spłqin
head
snč̓młq̇eyt
shoulder
sqpmin
sternum
sčč̓maxʷcč
chest
sxʷtxʷtip
ribs
sčuwax̣n
arm
smiłč̓mels
whole front side
temu
navel
sč̓meẇs
waist
olin
abdomen
čelš
hand
snč̓maqstšn
hip
sčč̓maqstšn
leg
snč̓mṁelixʷ
whole back side
asx̣m
backbone
sxʷƛ̓elnčst
shoulder blade
sc̓ušin
foot
snč̓mičṅ
back
sč̓tełc̓eʔ
half of the body
sntx̣ʷičṅ
spine
sč̓młniut
whole side of the body
snč̓musičṅ
lower back
soq̇mepł
buttocks

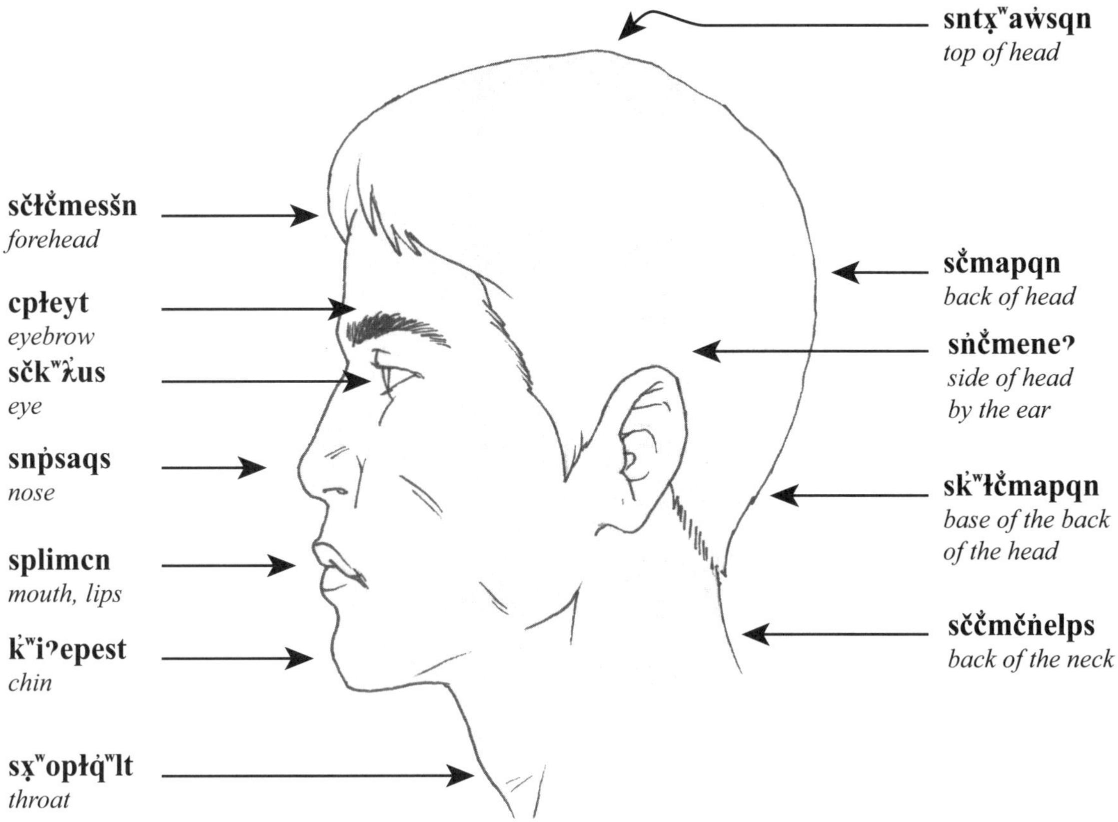
sntx̣ʷaw̓sqn
top of head
sčłčmesšn
forehead
cpłeyt
eyebrow
sčk̓ʷƛ̓us
eye
snp̓saqs
nose
splimcn
mouth, lips
k̓ʷiʔepest
chin
sx̣ʷopłq̓ʷlt
throat
sčmapqn
back of head
sn̓čmeneʔ
side of head by the ear
sk̓ʷłčmapqn
base of the back of the head
sččmčn̓elps
back of the neck

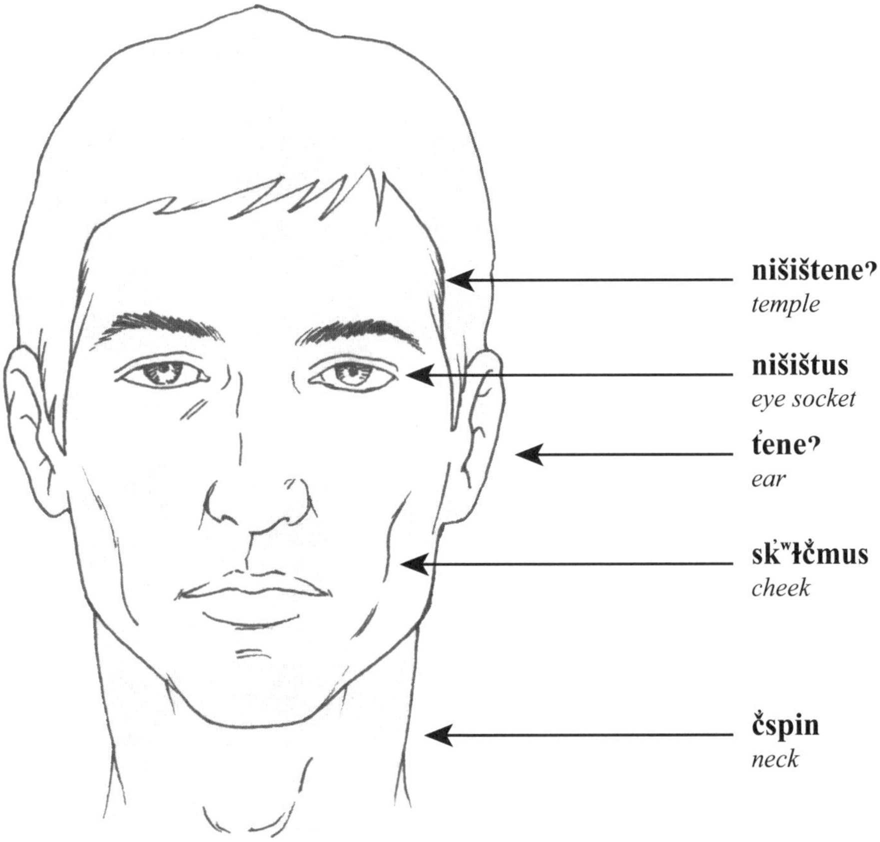
nišišteneʔ
temple
nišištus
eye socket
t̓eneʔ
ear
sk̓ʷłčmus
cheek
čspin
neck

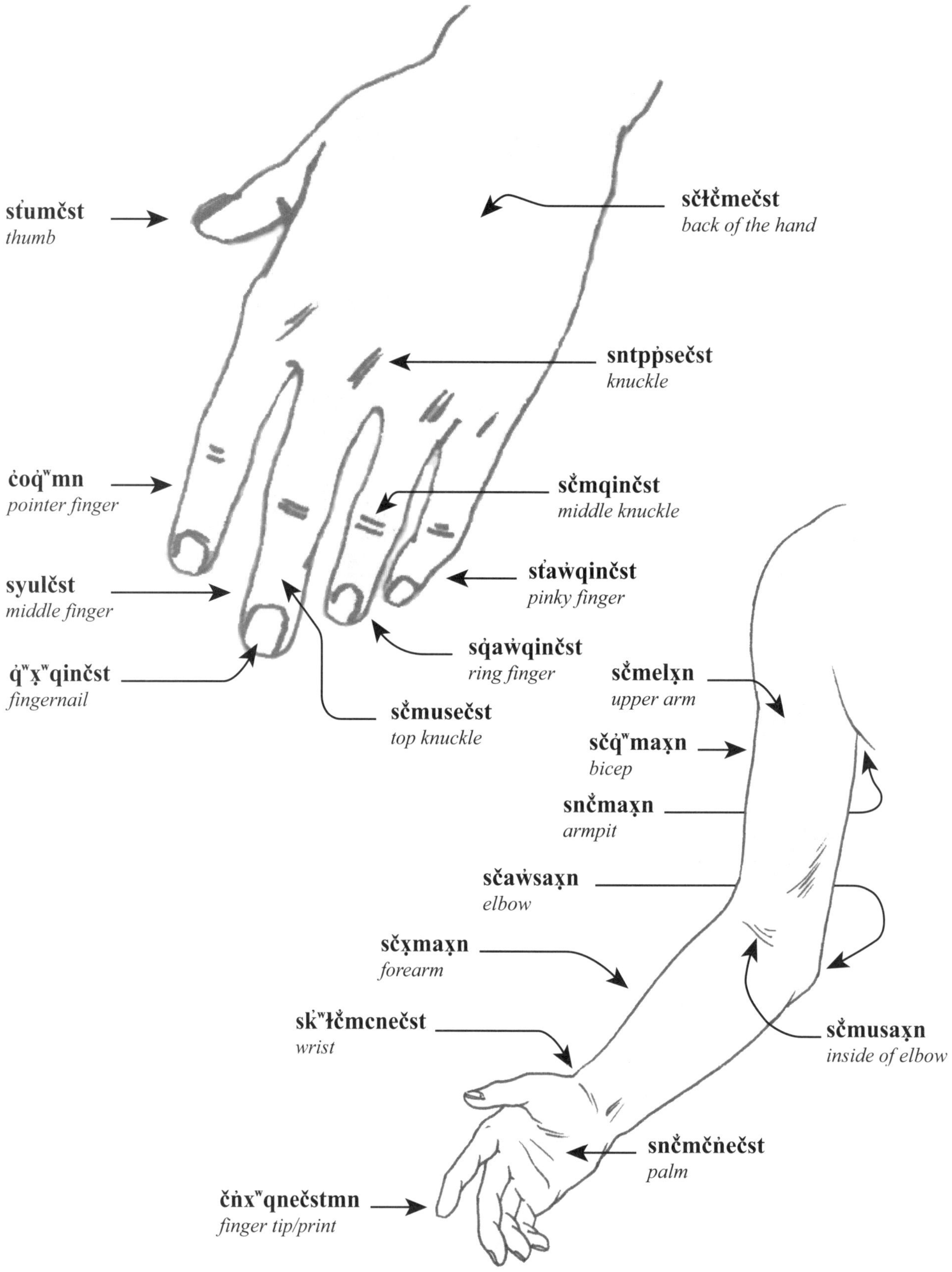
sťumčst
thumb
sčłč̓mečst
back of the hand
sntpp̓sečst
knuckle
c̓oq̓ʷmn
pointer finger
sč̓mqinčst
middle knuckle
sťaw̓qinčst
pinky finger
syulčst
middle finger
sq̓aw̓qinčst
ring finger
q̓ʷx̣ʷqinčst
fingernail
sč̓musečst
top knuckle
sč̓melx̣n
upper arm
sčq̓ʷmax̣n
bicep
snč̓max̣n
armpit
sčaw̓sax̣n
elbow
sčx̣max̣n
forearm
sk̓ʷłč̓mcnečst
wrist
sč̓musax̣n
inside of elbow
snč̓mčn̓ečst
palm
čn̓xʷqnečstmn
finger tip/print

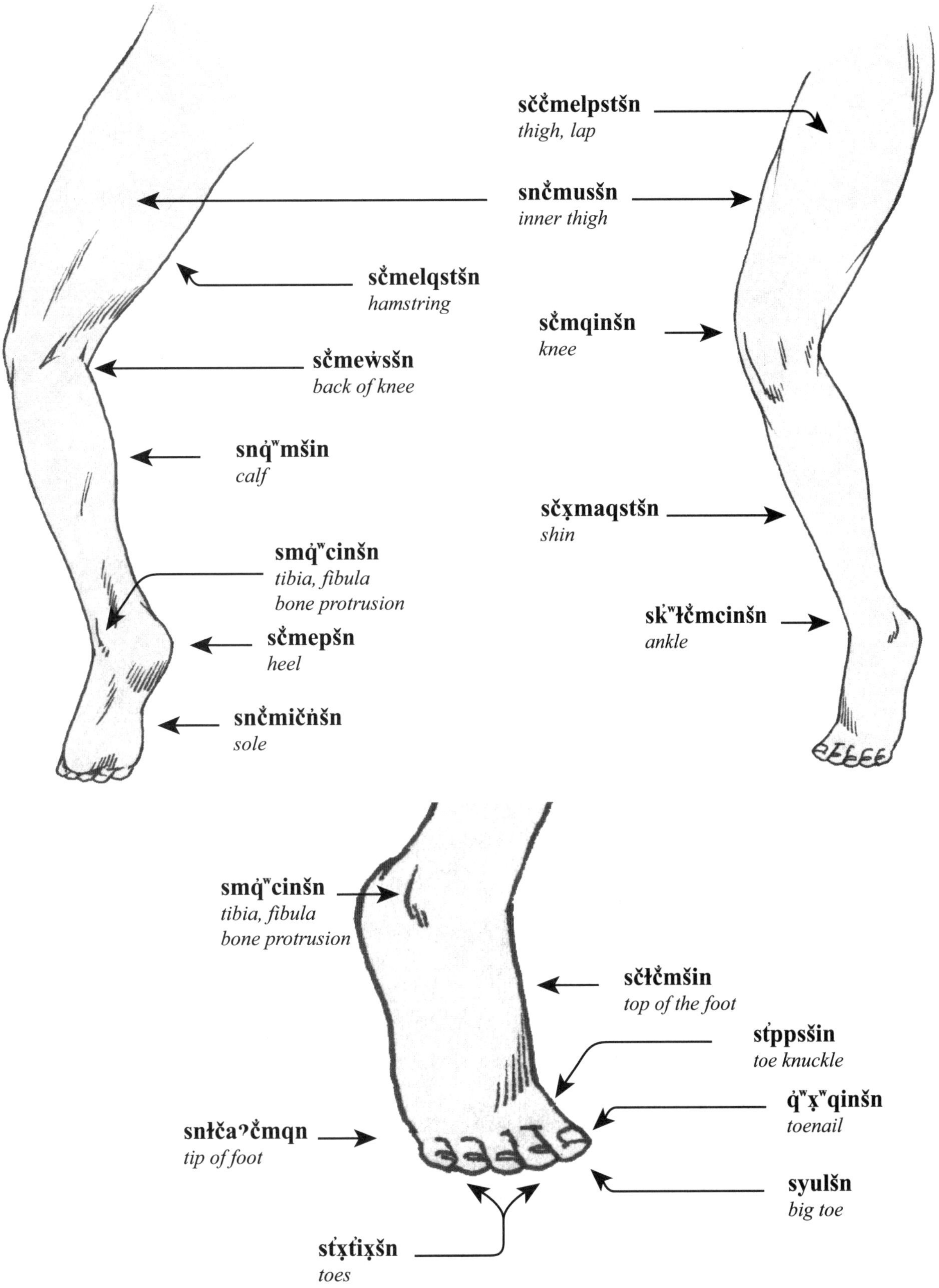
sčč̓melpstšn
thigh, lap
snč̓musšn
inner thigh
sč̓melqstšn
hamstring
sč̓mqinšn
knee
sč̓meẇssšn
back of knee
snq̓ʷmšin
calf
sčx̣maqstšn
shin
smq̓ʷcinšn
tibia, fibula
bone protrusion
sč̓mepšn
heel
sk̓ʷɬč̓mcinšn
ankle
snč̓mičn̓šn
sole
smq̓ʷcinšn
tibia, fibula
bone protrusion
sčɬč̓mšin
top of the foot
sṫppsšin
toe knuckle
q̓ʷx̣ʷqinšn
toenail
snɬča͗č̓mqn
tip of foot
syulšn
big toe
sṫx̣ṫix̣šn
toes

Section 2:

Mature Terminology

The following covers terms that are considered taboo in Western-thought and Christian views; these terms include sexual and genitalial subjects. The dictionary staff chose to place these terms in a separate section so that they may be easily censored from young learners. These terms are generally used in private personal settings between couples. It is not the intent of the dictionary staff to foster a vulgar use of the language. Please respect the teachings of our ancestors and our elders. Please use these words only in appropriate situations. The focus of this book is on language learning and communication. It would be wrong to exclude this information as all language is important and must be preserved and revitalized. Fear and censor of any part of our language and culture will lead to a loss of identity. We must ensure all parts of the language are maintained otherwise we endanger the communicative ability of future speakers.

> *I'm honored to have an input on this section of the Dictionary along with other Elders' comments pertaining to the "Terms of A Mature Nature"*
>
> *A person studying the language must remember that our Native People here and throughout all tribes, never went about using their language in a vulgar way. The Native People were always very sacred and respectful, honoring their language. It was after the coming of the Non-Indians that brought vulgar language and sexual behaviors in everyday life. You can see this example in the movies and other parts of our normal life.*
>
> *Today, it is easier for one to learn these terms and use them in a vulgar way, than it is to learn the Native Language.*
>
> *As a Native Person, you must remember that our Ancestors were a proud, honorable, spiritual, truthful, mindful, helpful, clean and respectful people and so in turn, you must pattern your life in this manner and not misuse our language.*
>
> *Using the Native language in a vulgar way, lowers your own lifestyle and values as a Native Person. Others see this in you, and you become a marked person as "nčečeʔcín," "the one who speaks in a dirty way."*

F. Johnny Arlee, spiritual leader, Salish elder

buttock **nč̓eʔups –** object lodged between the buttocks. *rt.:* ***č̓eʔ*** *– lump.*

nšič̓ps – unsuccessful in some way concerning the pelvic area.

nt̓mopsm – kiss buttocks. *circumfix:* ***n...ups*** *– butt, tail.*

coitus **skʷnús –** coitus.

es kʷnúsi – S/he is in the act of coition. **čnes kʷnúsi, kʷes kʷnúsi**

nyekʷmnups – refuse coition. *rt.:* ***ẏeẏukʷeʔ*** *– stingy; circumfix:* ***n...ups*** *– butt, tail.*

nxʷċšnmups – accept coition. *rt.:* ***xʷiċ*** *– give; circumfix:* ***n...ups*** *– butt, tail.*

xʷċšmist – surrender; give one's self. *rt.:* ***xʷiċ*** *– give; suffix:* ***...ist*** *– action for/of the self. See:* ***surrender****.*

nlesps – male homosexual act.
sxʷnlesps – homosexual male.

cunnilingus **nt̓aław̓s,** *nt̓ała* – cunnilingus.
sxʷnt̓aław̓s, *sxʷnt̓ała* – lesbian.

disengage **nċoqew̓sm** – disengage from the middle. *suffix:* ***...éw̓s*** *– in between, middle.*

nċoqupsm – disengage from the anus.

insert **nx̣ʷiqʷpsm** – insert in an anus.

nq̓eupsm – rectal insertion. *rt.:* ***q̓eʔ*** *– put inside; circumfix:* ***n...ups*** *– butt, tail.*

nq̓ʔew̓sm – insert something in between *(i.e., place between objects, etc.). rt.:* ***q̓eʔ*** *– put inside; suffix:* ***...éw̓s*** *– in between, middle.*

nq̓emuscut, *nq̓emuscú* – put one's self between objects *(i.e., between legs, etc.). See:* ***between.***

masturbate **čsplplqncut,** *čsplplqncu* – self stimulation of the phallus. *rt.:* ***pelq*** *– flared/rolled out.*
plplqem – masturbate him. *rt.:* ***pelq*** *– flared/rolled out.*

nililk̓ʷusncut – repeatedly rub the middle of one's self. *rt.:* ***yilk̓ʷ*** *– rub.*
nililk̓ʷew̓sm – masturbate her. *rt.:* ***yilk̓ʷ*** *– rub.*

orgasm **eṅest** – orgasm.

phallus **spalq** – phallus.
spapál̓q – small phallus.

čs...alq – *circumfix indicating a phallus.*
čsċuk̓ʷ – erect.
čswisšn – long. *rt.:* ***wisšn*** *– long.*
čsyult, *čsyu* – thick. *rt.:* ***yult*** *– thick girth. See:* ***girth.***
čsq̓ʷat̓álq – curved. *rt.:* ***q̓ʷat̓*** *– bent/curved.*
čst̓malqm – kiss. *rt.:* ***t̓am*** *– suck.*
čstomalq – fellate. *rt.:* ***tum*** *– suck.*
čsčṅalq – grab. *rt.:* ***čṅim*** *– grasp.*
čstqalq – touch. *rt.:* ***tqem*** *– touch.*

poke **nx̣ʷiqʷpsm** – poke someone's anus.

semen **nq̓ʷeċłċeʔ** – semen in the oral cavity.

testicle **méčp** – testicle. **mčméčp** – testes.

n...epls – *circumfix indicating testicles.*

nt̓maplsm – kiss testicles.

vagina **sxʷuʔt** – vagina.

niac̓x̣ – look between.

vulva **sṅšaltew̓s** – labia.

Section 3:

Kinship Tables

Kinship terminology in the Salish language is very complex. It is indicative of the value placed on family relationships. The terminology requires 12 tables to show the various levels and changes that occur from marriage and upon death of a connecting relative. The following passage is copied from a Wikipedia.org article on kinship.

> Kinship is a relationship between any entities that share a genealogical origin, through either biological, cultural, or historical descent. In anthropology the kinship system includes people related both by descent and marriage, while usage in biology includes descent and mating. Human kinship relations through marriage are commonly called "affinity" in contrast to "descent" (also called "consanguinity"), although the two may overlap in marriages among those of common descent. Family relations as sociocultural genealogy lead back to gods, animals that were in the area or natural phenomena (as in origin stories).
>
> Kinship is one of the most basic principles for organizing individuals into social groups, roles, categories, and genealogy. Family relations can be represented concretely (mother, brother, grandfather) or abstractly after degrees of relationship. A relationship may have relative purchase (e.g., father is one regarding a child), or reflect an absolute (e.g., status difference between a mother and a childless woman). Degrees of relationship are not identical to heirship or legal succession. Many codes of ethics consider the bond of kinship as creating obligations between the related persons stronger than those between strangers, as in Confucian filial piety.

The colors used to represent the male and female gender are derived from traditional beliefs. Red is the color of war. In the time of our ancestors a major role and duty of males in tribe was protection of the people. Blue represents life giving water. A major role of females to this day is to bring new life to this world. Women are blessed with the gift of being the life givers.

3.01 - Forebears

Male kinship terms.

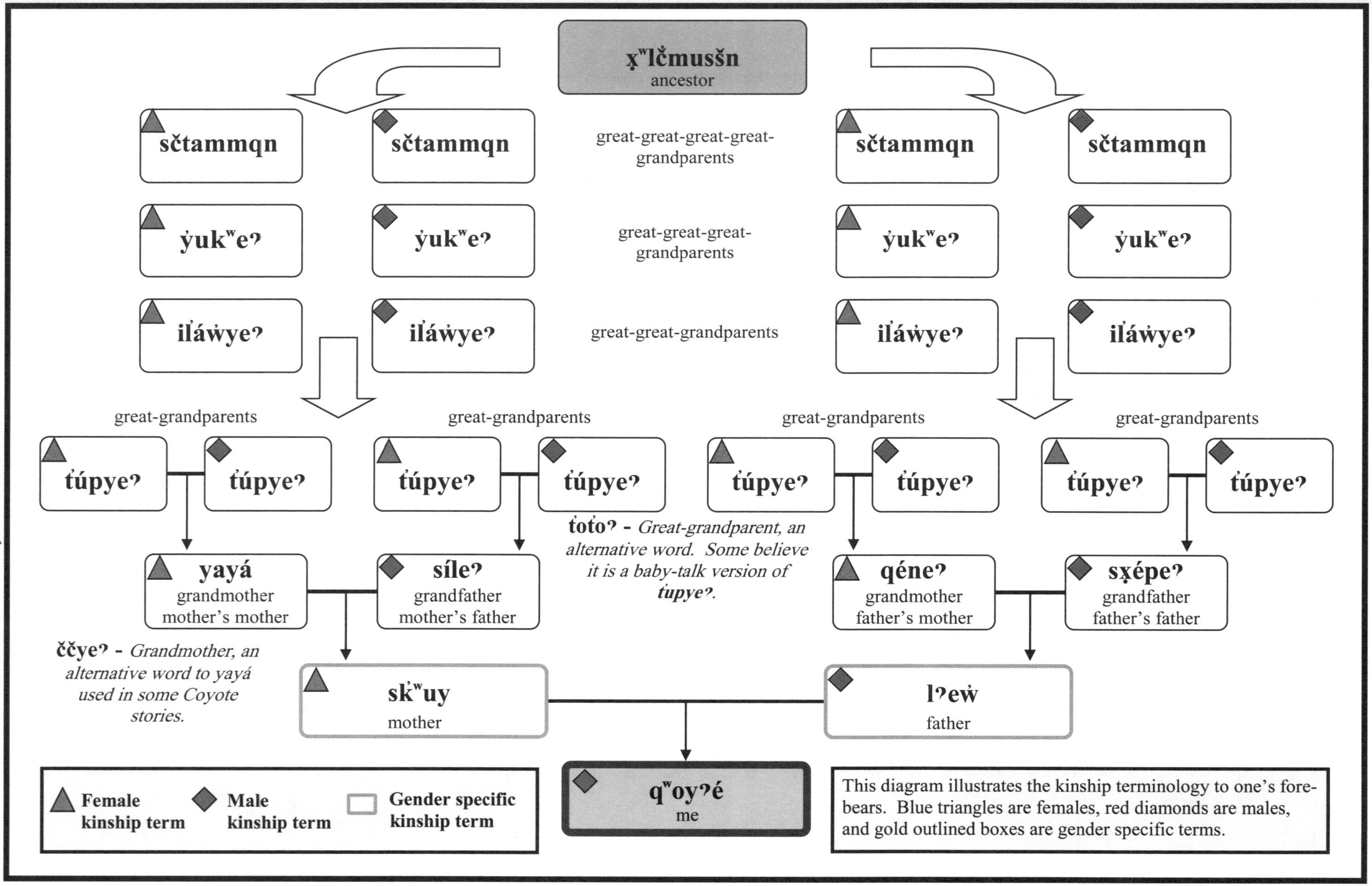

3.02 - Forebears
Female kinship terms.

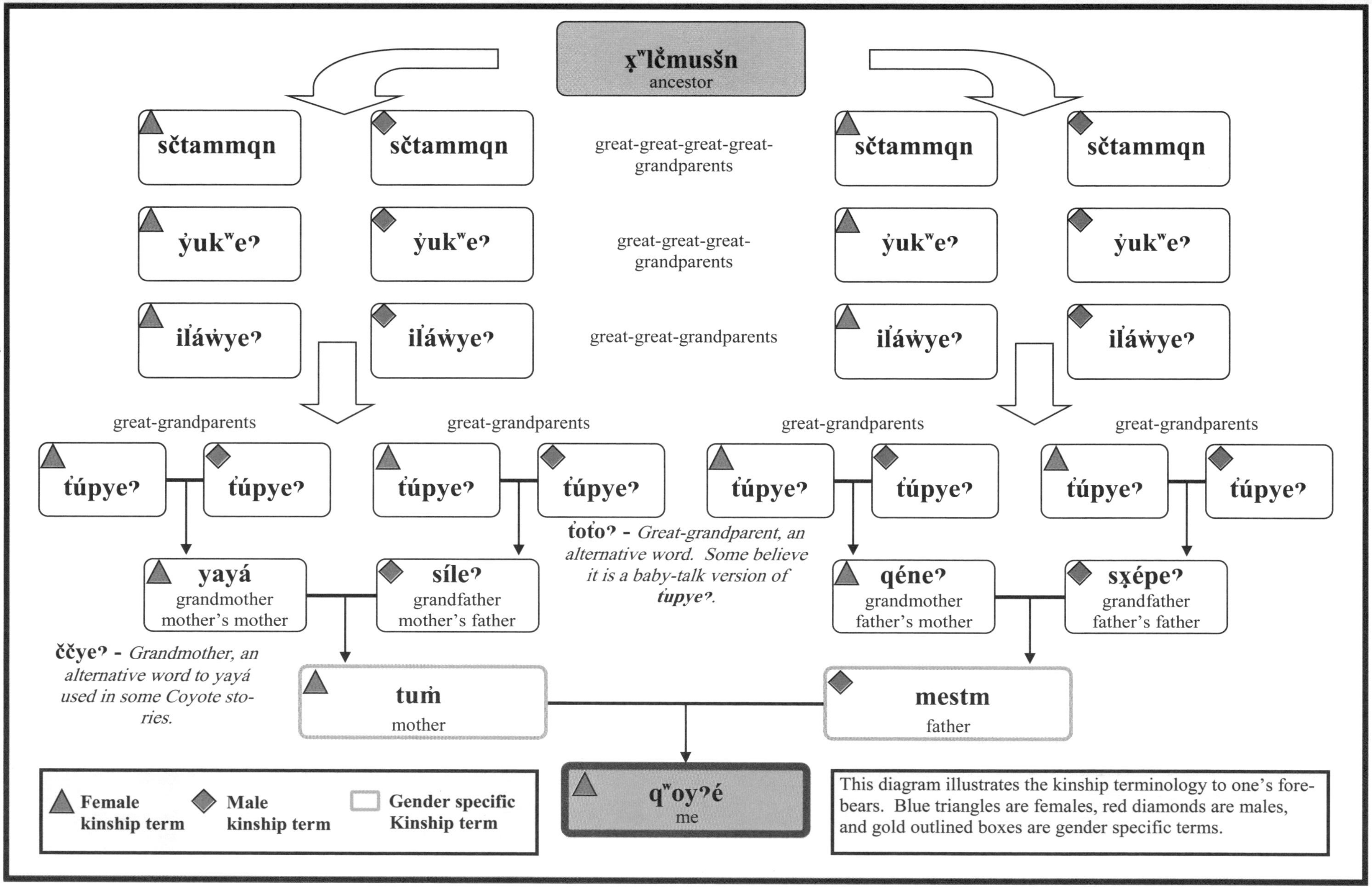

3.03 - Family Unit

Male kinship terms.

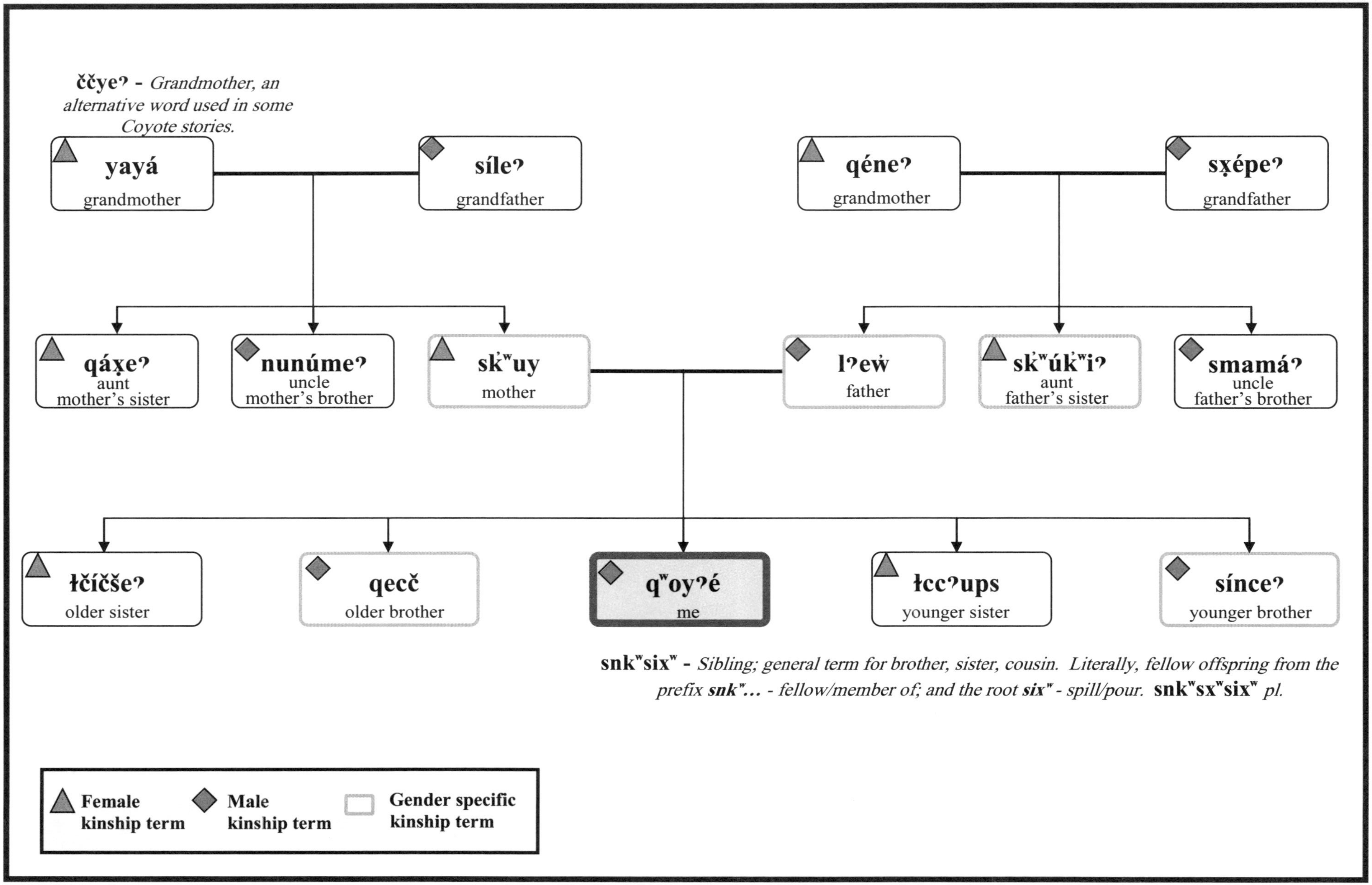

ččyeʔ - Grandmother, an alternative word used in some Coyote stories.
yayá
grandmother
síleʔ
grandfather
qéneʔ
grandmother
sx̣épeʔ
grandfather
qáx̣eʔ
aunt
mother's sister
nunúmeʔ
uncle
mother's brother
sk̓ʷuy
mother
lʔeẁ
father
sk̓ʷúk̓ʷiʔ
aunt
father's sister
smamáʔ
uncle
father's brother
łčíčšeʔ
older sister
qecč
older brother
qʷoyʔé
me
łccʔups
younger sister
sínceʔ
younger brother
snkʷsixʷ - Sibling; general term for brother, sister, cousin. Literally, fellow offspring from the prefix snkʷ... - fellow/member of; and the root sixʷ - spill/pour. snkʷsxʷsixʷ pl.
Female kinship term
Male kinship term
Gender specific kinship term

3.04 - Family Unit
Female kinship terms.

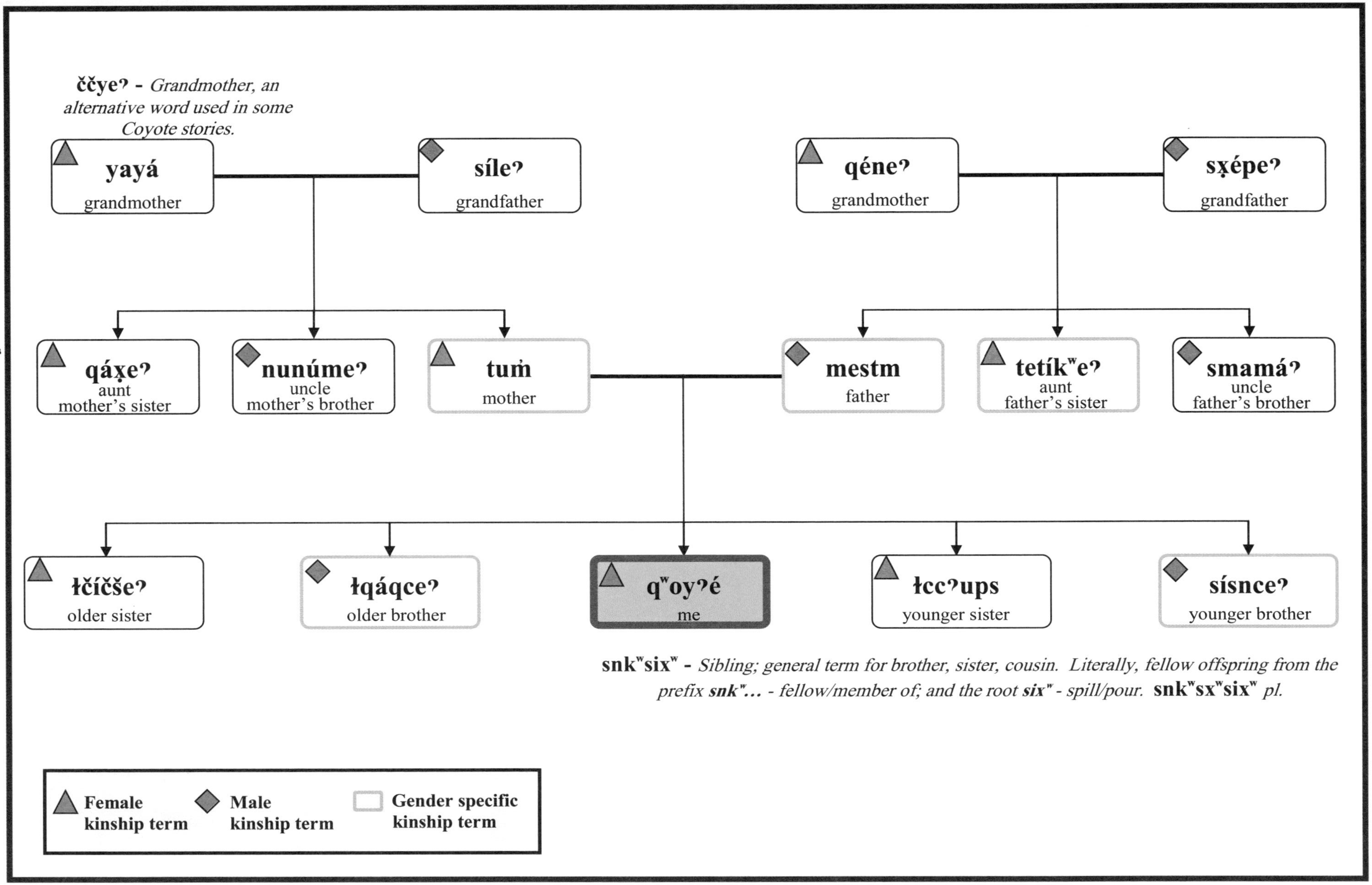

3.05 - Marriage

Male kinship terms

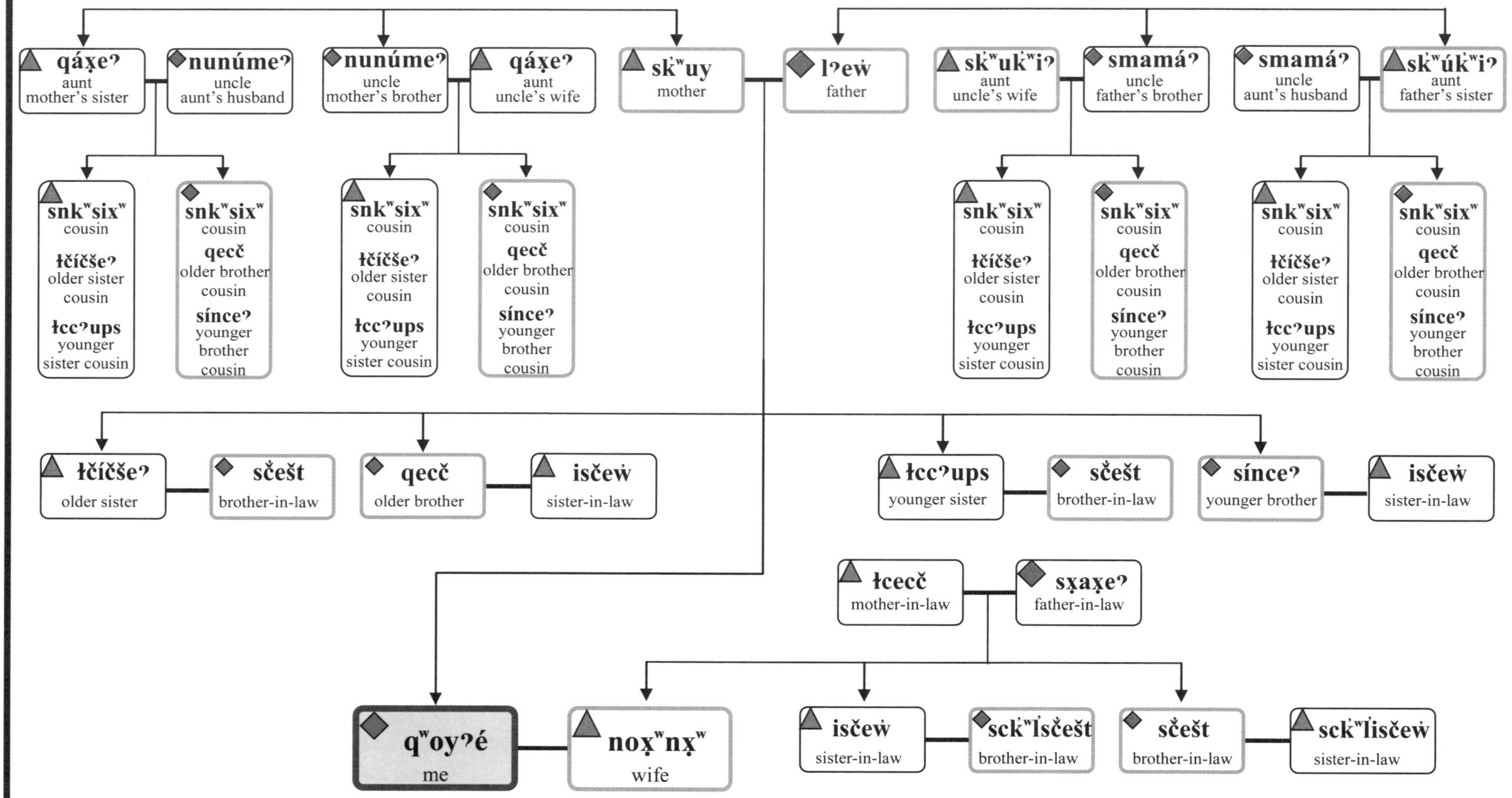

Female kinship term · Male kinship term · Gender specific kinship term

snkʷsixʷ - *Sibling; general term for brother, sister, cousin. Literally, fellow offspring from the prefix* ***snkʷ...*** *- fellow/member of; and the root* ***sixʷ*** *- spill/pour.* **snkʷsxʷsixʷ** *pl.*

3.06 - Marriage
Female kinship terms

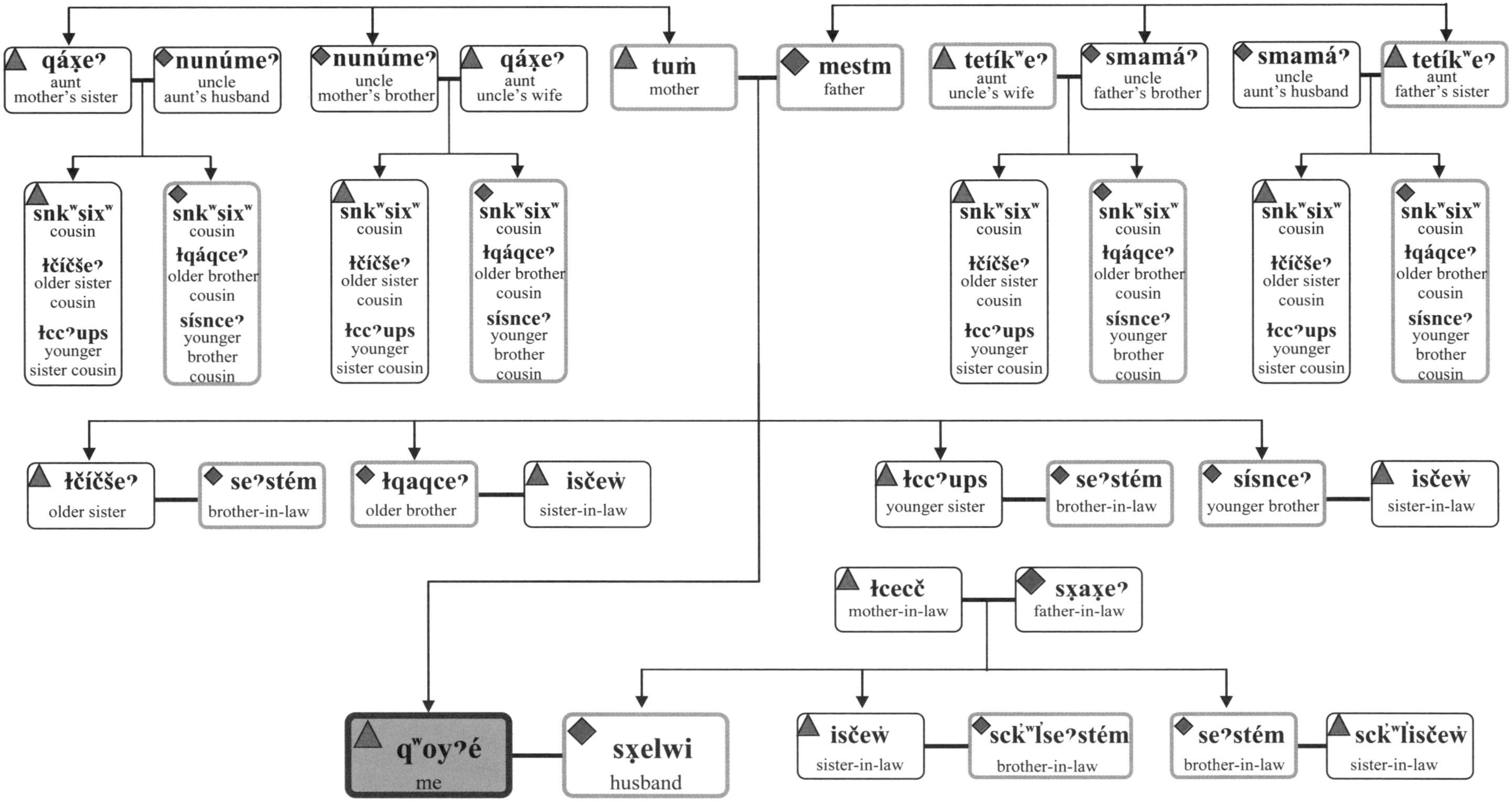

Female kinship term | **Male kinship term** | **Gender specific kinship term**

snkʷsixʷ - *Sibling; general term for brother, sister, cousin. Literally, fellow offspring from the prefix* ***snkʷ...*** *- fellow/member of; and the root* ***sixʷ*** *- spill/pour.* **snkʷsxʷsixʷ** *pl.*

3.07 - Offspring
Male kinship terms

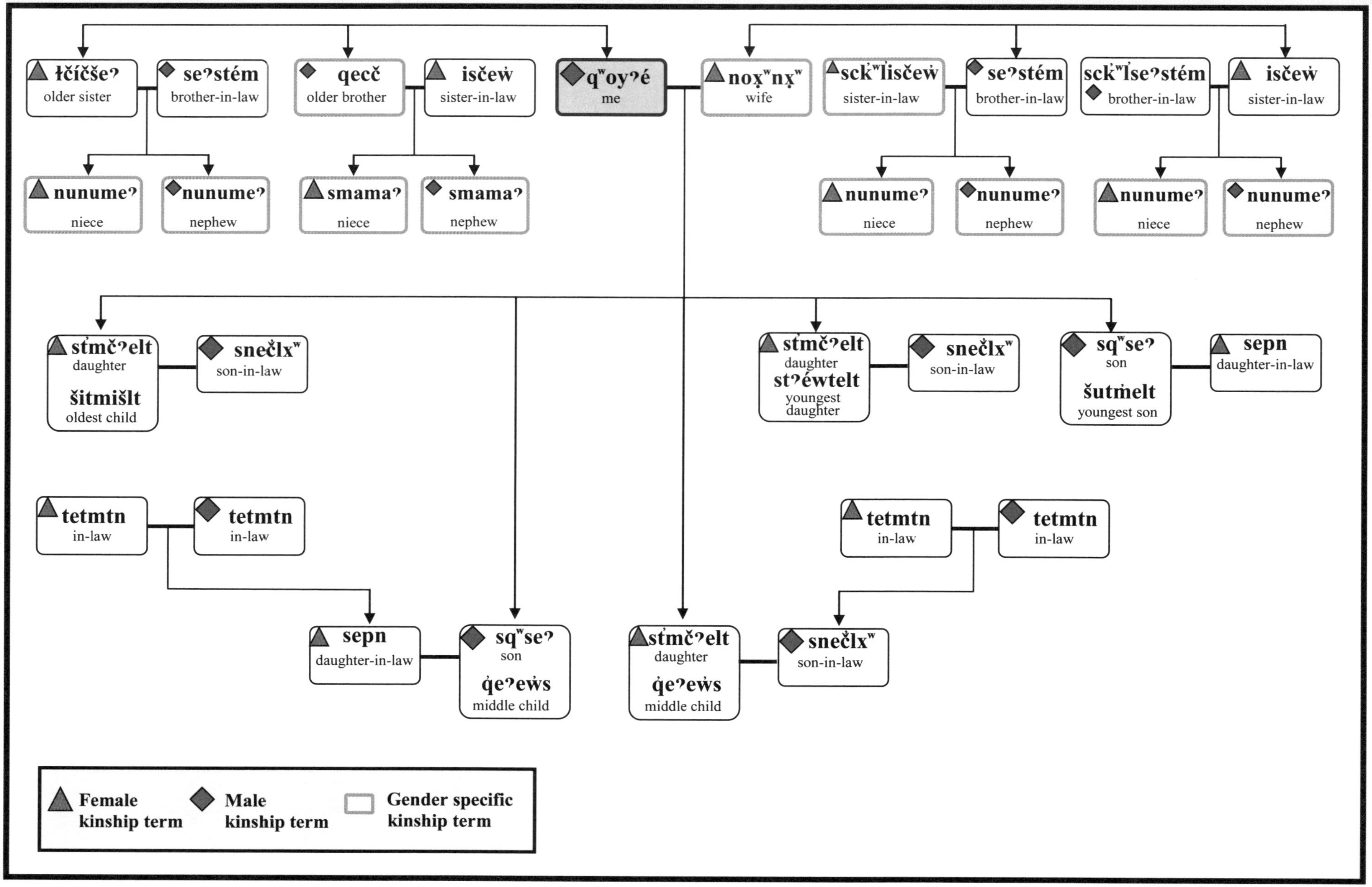

3.08 - Offspring
Female kinship terms

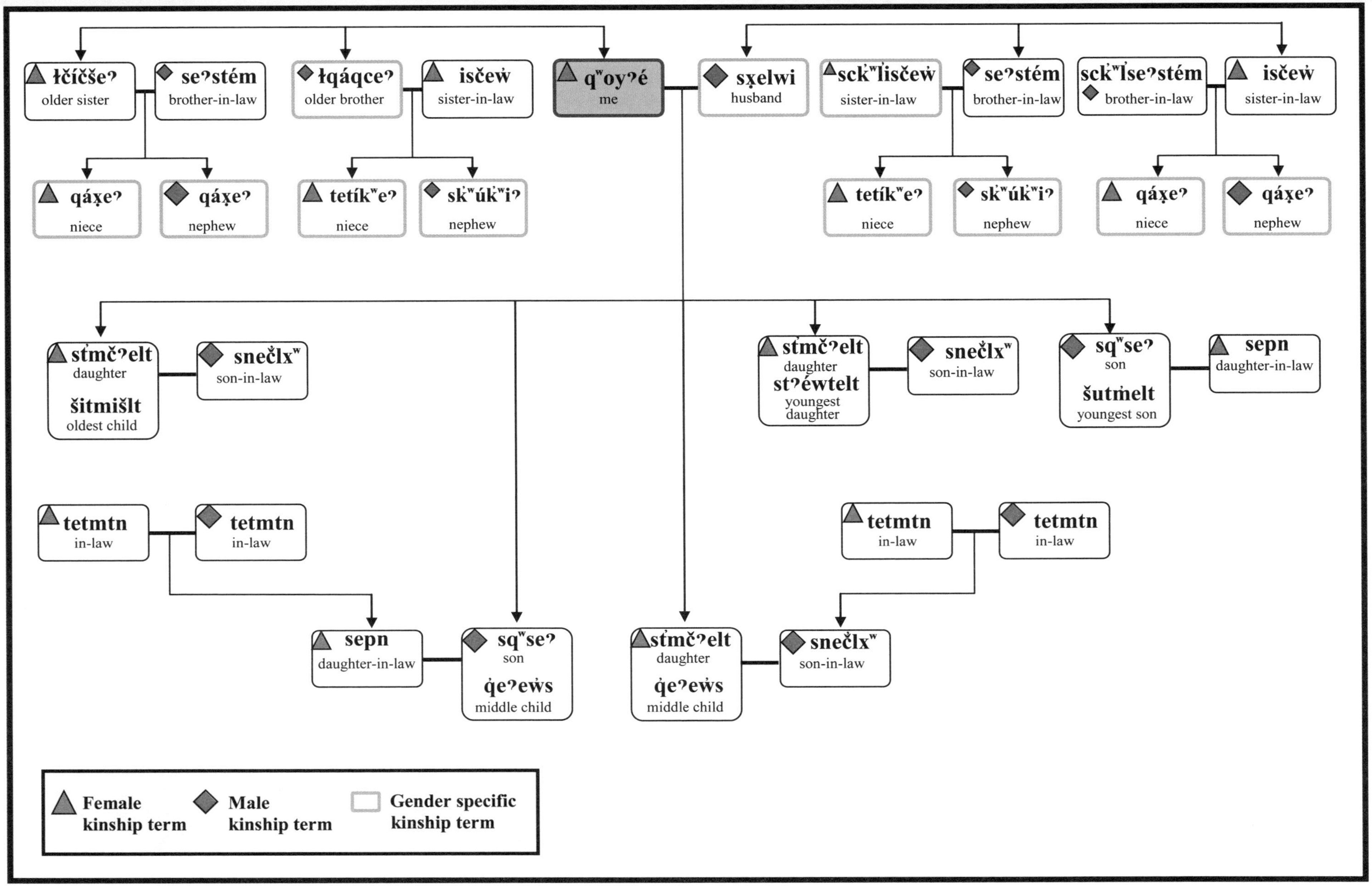

3.09 - After Death of connecting kin

Male kinship terms

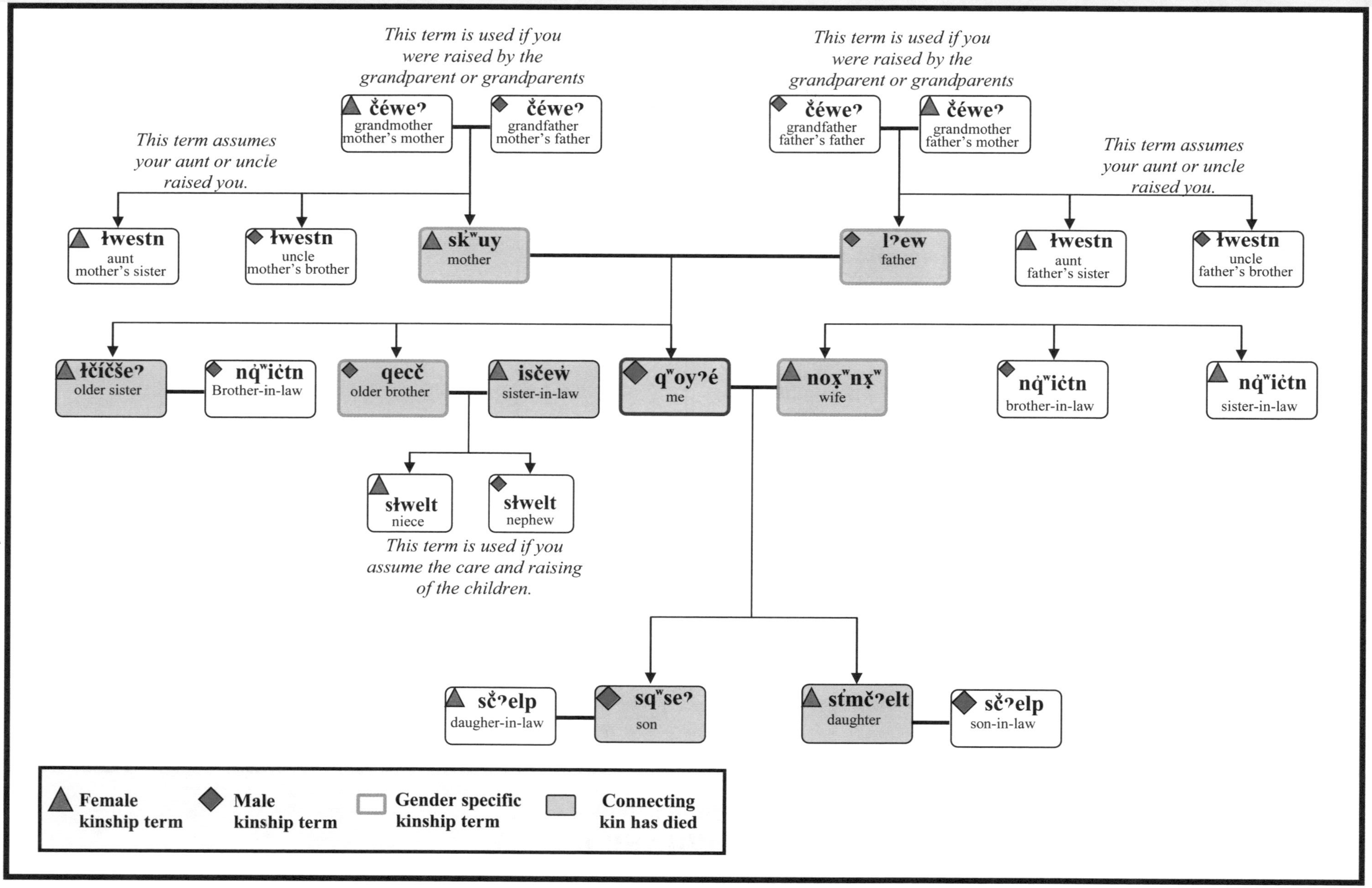

This term is used if you were raised by the grandparent or grandparents
čéweʔ
grandmother
mother's mother
čéweʔ
grandfather
mother's father
This term is used if you were raised by the grandparent or grandparents
čéweʔ
grandfather
father's father
čéweʔ
grandmother
father's mother
This term assumes your aunt or uncle raised you.
łwestn
aunt
mother's sister
łwestn
uncle
mother's brother
skʼʷuy
mother
lʔew
father
This term assumes your aunt or uncle raised you.
łwestn
aunt
father's sister
łwestn
uncle
father's brother
łčíčšeʔ
older sister
nq̓ʷiċtn
Brother-in-law
qecč
older brother
isčeẇ
sister-in-law
qʷoyʔé
me
nox̣ʷnx̣ʷ
wife
nq̓ʷiċtn
brother-in-law
nq̓ʷiċtn
sister-in-law
słwelt
niece
słwelt
nephew
This term is used if you assume the care and raising of the children.
sč̓ʔelp
daugher-in-law
sqʷseʔ
son
sṁčʔelt
daughter
sč̓ʔelp
son-in-law
Female kinship term
Male kinship term
Gender specific kinship term
Connecting kin has died

3.10 - After Death of connecting kin

Female kinship terms

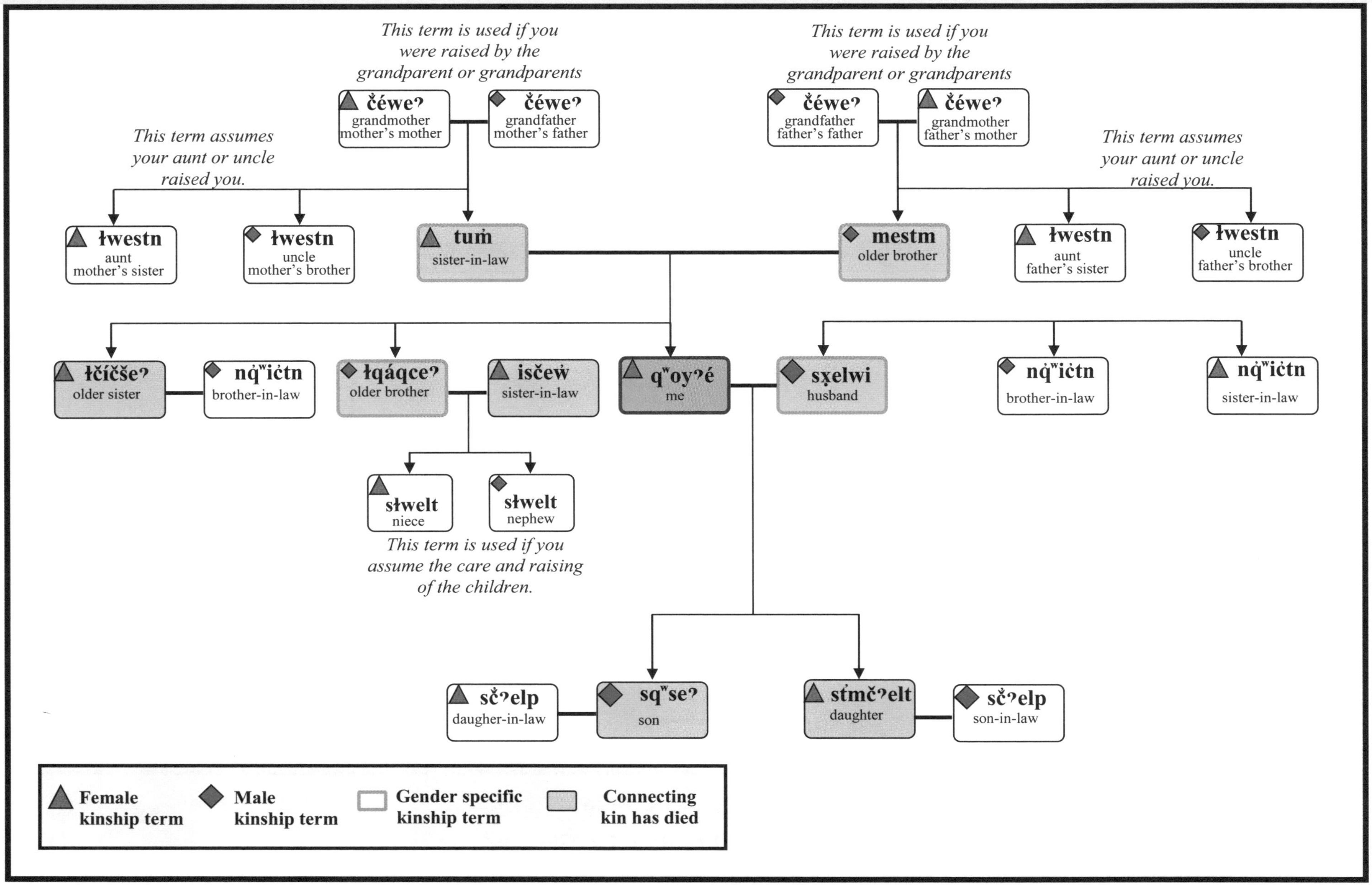

3.11 - Descendants

Male kinship terms.

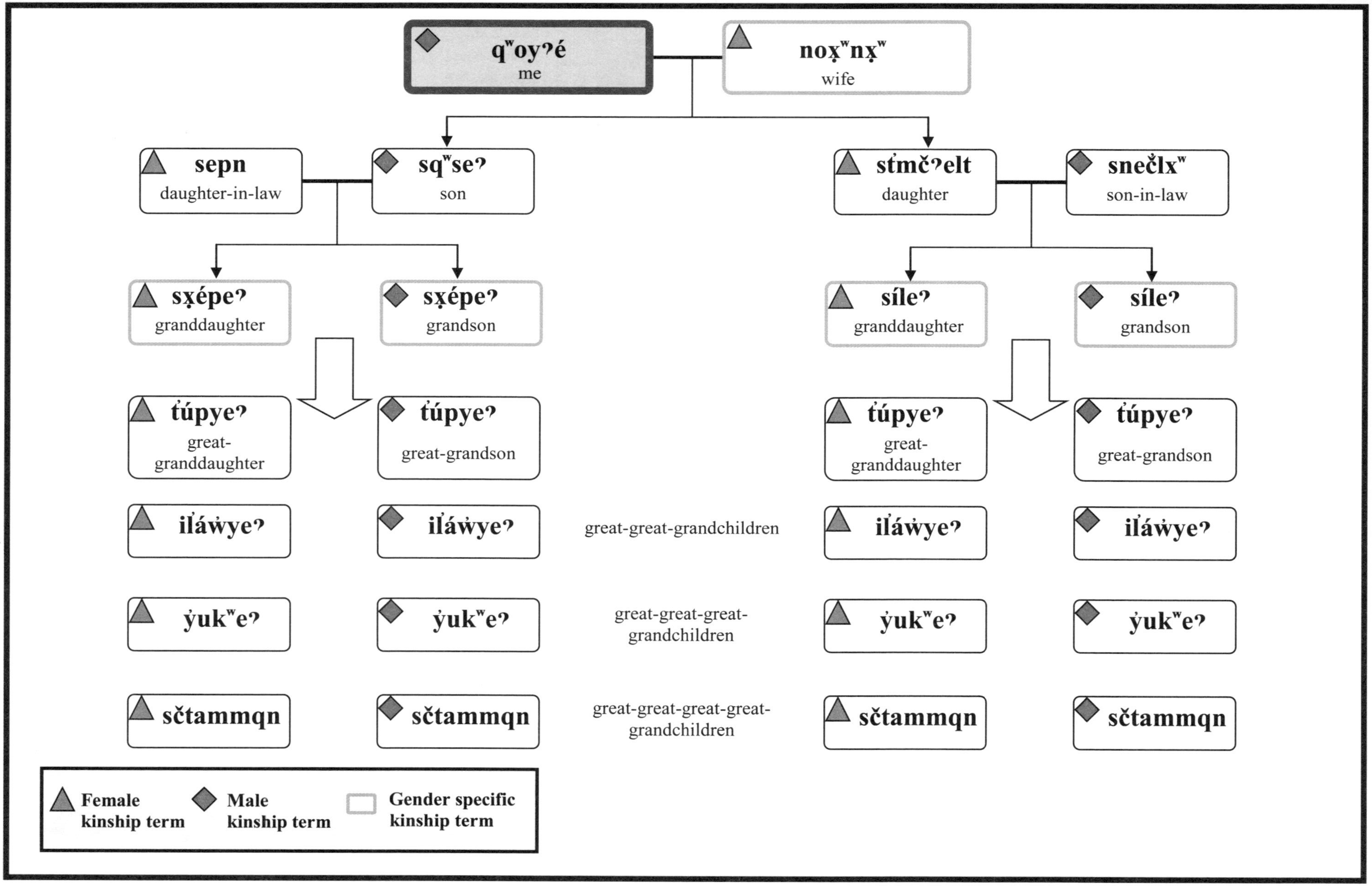

3.12 - Descendants

Female kinship terms.

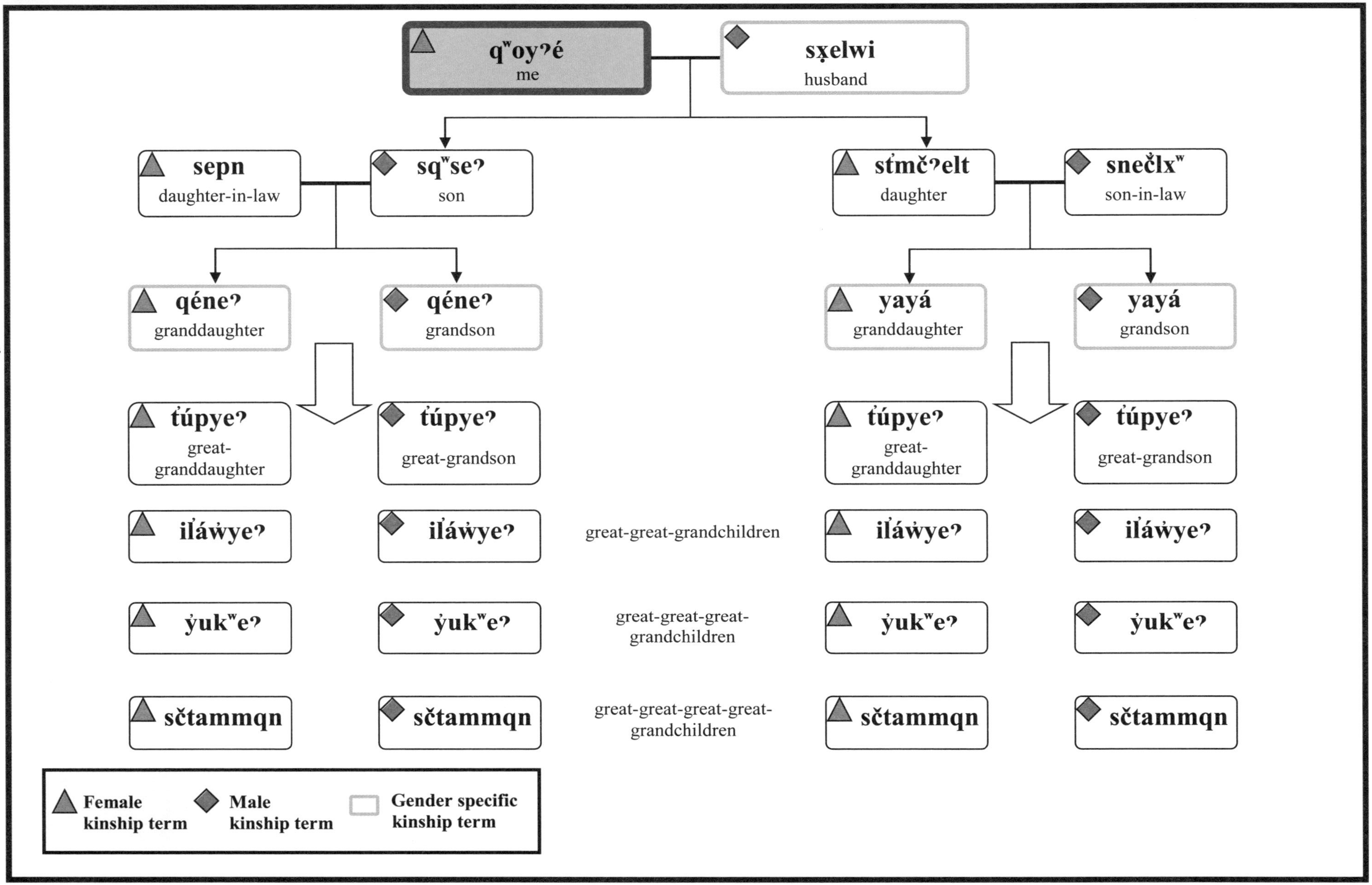

Section 4:

Grammar

This section is provided to help people learning the Salish language. It is presented in a format that shows patterns of the language: grammar. Salish grammar is very precise and consistent. There are clear-cut rules that apply throughout the language. There are few exceptions to these rules. The following is a brief overview of these grammar rules. Look to the future *Salish Grammar* book for more thorough and extensive rules of the Salish language. This section explains the rules using commonly understood terms along with the sometimes confusing linguistic terms. This work is inspired by the dissertation, *A Grammar of Spokane, A Salish Language of Eastern Washington* submitted by *Barry F. Carlson,* University of Hawaii, 1972. In addition, the help Steven M. Egesdal provided was invaluable. His suggestions aided in making this section more refined.

Contents:

One of the most frustrating obstacles in learning Salish has been the creation and use of sentences. Salish is very foreign to English speakers. Speaking Salish can be best explained by using painting as a metaphor. When painting, a person chooses to be simple or detailed in displaying some representation. The artist can choose one color or use the shades of many colors. The same is true of Salish. Think of speaking as painting a picture. A speaker chooses word complexity from simple to ultra specific to convey meaning; she paints a picture of understanding. One's knowledge of grammar and vocabulary are the palette of the speaker.

Simply, languages have their own unique grammar, which include semantics, morphology, syntax, and pragmatics. Grammar is the overall structure, the rules that govern the usage of the language. Semantics covers the meanings expressed in a language. Morphology is the study of the internal structure of words through formation and alteration. Syntax is the rules that determine the way words combine to form phrases and sentences within a language. Pragmatics is concerned with the meaning or information a speaker is trying to convey in the literal sentence being said. Pragmatics is interested in utterances said in general conversation that subtly change meaning. These linguistic subjects provide tools to help the learner better understand how Salish works.

The study of the Salish language is still relatively new. The work presented in this section is still in a state of development. **This is not the final word on the Salish grammar.** It is often difficult to describe the way Salish works in an English context. The descriptions in this section are presented in a draft form to help people begin to grasp meaning of the language. Use this section to help understand the patterns you will surely encounter as you learn the language.

With learning in mind, this book shows grammatical patterns of Salish throughout the many entries. Salish words fall into two categories; full words (predicative words) and particles. Full words are made of a root word or a root with affixes. Full words can occur by themselves and constitute a complete sentence (a predication). In Salish, all full words are complete sentences; this includes words that would normally be nouns in English. It is hard to comprehend that in Salish there are no nouns in the sense of English nouns. This concept can be fully appreciated once the philosophical aspect of the language is understood. Particles are connector words. Particles are used to add information and to connect full words.

Salish thought processes are very different from English. Actions (verbs) hold high importance and thus usually come first in sentences. All sentences in Salish are of three types: simple sentences consisting of a single clause; compound sentences composed of two independent clauses; and complex sentences with a dependent clause. With this begins a brief look at Salish grammar, specifically syntax and morphology as it relates to the process of reduplication.

a. Simple Sentences

A simple sentence is made up of a word or words to form a clause. A clause is a grammatical structure that contains a subject and a predicate. The predicate is a full word with or without an adjunct and attendant particles. In Salish a clause constitutes a complete sentence. Every sentence is made up of at least one clause. A predicate is a single full word or verb phrase. All single verbs and noun like words are predicates. Adjuncts, discussed below, add information. In Salish a single word is a whole sentence as it contains a subject and predicate. You can think of the construction of the sentence as an order of importance. Words closest to the beginning of the sentence hold more importance. Often in a sentence or a thought, the action is more important than the actors.

Throughout this section word order or sentence structure diagrams will be presented in the following format:

Diagram a.1 – Simple Sentence Structure
Predicate/predicate phrase + optional adjunct/adjunct phrase + optional adjunct phrase
qʷo čxʷuymntm + t islax̣t + łu qs lkʷkʷmi
I was visited by my friend that/who is going to go far away.

1. **Predicates**: A predicate is any full word or interrogative (question word) with its attendant particles. Predicates can be single words or verb phrases.

Example: iłn – S/he/it ate.
This complete sentence is an example of a predicate. The full word is **iłn**. The subject is the third person, she/he/it, while the predicate is the act of eating, the verb. Contained in the example, **čn iłn –** *I ate,* is the pronoun particle *čn*, I, and the full word **iłn**. Combined, they form a simple sentence in the form of a predicate verb phrase. The subject is I, and the verb is ate.

čiqs xʷuy č̓ x̣ʷiˀilqsa čn ep scnq̇éˀels – I am going to Pablo. I have business there.

This complete sentence has two independent clauses. The translation requires two English sentences. In Salish it is one complete sentence. The second clause, **čn ep scnq̇éˀels –** I have business there, is an example of an adjunct phrase. The adjunct phrase adds more information to the predicate phrase.

Words that are nouns in English are complete sentences or verb like words in Salish, including names. In Salish, **sˀiłn**, is translated as, *it is food*, whereas in English it would be the noun, *food.* Saying **sˀiłn** is a complete simple sentence.

Particles are dependant words (proclitic and enclitic). ***Particles*** add information to their independent word. An example of a particle are the following intransitive pronoun particles.

2. **Intransitive pronoun particles**: Intransitive pronoun particles are the simplest grammar structure to recognize in Salish. This may be due to the easily discernable comparisons to English grammar. For this reason an introduction to intransitive pronoun particles is included with simple sentences. Pronoun particles identify the person performing the action in the predicate phrase. **All full words or predicates are defaulted to the third person, he, she, it.** Third person plural is handled with a reduplication of the stressed vowel of the predicate. Reduplication is explained later in more detail.

S/he/it, all words are naturally in the third person.
čn – I
kʷ – you

qeˀ – we
p – you all
They, handled with an infix pronoun particle in the form of a reduplication of the stressed vowel as in: **ƛ̓lip –** s/he/it stopped; with infix reduplication **(initial stressed vowel)** (ˀ) **(reduplicated vowel)** as in: **ƛ̓líˀip –** they stopped.

Note: reduplication explanations will be written in an abbreviated fashion as in the above pronoun particle example with **vˀv** to represent **vowel ˀ reduplicated vowel**.

Examples: iłn – S/he/it ate. **čn iłn –** I ate. **kʷ iłn –** You ate. **elíˀiłn –** They ate. **qeˀ eliłn –** We ate. **p eliłn –** You all ate.

These conjugated predicate phrases or simple sentence examples use intransitive pronoun particles. <u>**Notice the order they are presented: third person singular, first person singular, second person singular; third person plural, first person plural, second person plural.**</u> This order is used throughout the book.

A predicate can be an interrogative word such as ***čeṅ* –** where? Interrogatives are explained later.
Examples: čeṅ łu islax̣t – Where is my friend?

3. **Adjuncts**: In addition to the predicate, a clause may have one or more adjuncts or adjunct phrases. These are optional and follow the predicate. Adjuncts add information relating to the predicate. There may be more than one adjunct or adjunct phrase. An adjunct is a full word or phrase. Adjunct phrases are almost always preceded by a demonstrative particle and other optional particles.
   a. Demonstrative particles include:
   Particle **łu** indicates the preceding is of secondary importance. *The particle* **łu** *is very versatile. It can be used as a pause as in English "um."*
      iłn łu stipn – Stephen ate. **łu stipn** is the adjunct phrase. The adjunct is **stipn**. The particle is **łu**. The predicate is **iłn**.

   particle ***x̣ʷl̓*** indicates "for; because."
      ƛ̓lip x̣ʷl̓ x̣stéyy̓eʔ łu stipn – Stephen stopped for the skunk. This sentence has two adjunct phrases with the predicate **ƛ̓lip**. **x̣ʷl̓ x̣steyeʔ** is the first adjunct phrase. **łu stipn** is the second adjunct phrase.

   particle ***t*** indicating the article acted on by an intransitive verb; the actor doing the action of a transitive verb; or the tool or item used in the action of an intransitive verb. *(In time reference sentences with* ***t*** *is a reference to the past.)*
      iłn t pataq łu stipn – Stephen ate potatoes.
      iłis łu pataq t stipn – Stephen ate potatoes.
      t łek̓ʷpci u iłis łu pataq t stipn – Stephen ate potatoes with a fork.

   še is a relative pronoun particle indicating that the following is a condition of the preceding. It is most closely similar to *then* in English.
      iłn t pataq še nmq̓enč – S/he ate potatoes and then got full.
      iłn t nšlšaltáqs še itš – S/he ate turkey and then fell asleep.

   kʷemt is a particle that indicates that a different thought is going to start in continuation of the overall story/speech. It is also similar to *then* in English.

   In review the simple sentence or clause is constructed as follows:

Predicate or predicate phrase **+** optional adjunct phrase **+** optional adjunct phrase

b. Compound Sentences

Compound sentences are composed of two or more independent clauses; in simple terms the sentence contains two or more action phrases. The particle *u* joins two clauses to form a compound sentence.

Diagram b.1 – Compound Sentence Structure
independent clause **+** particle u **+** independent clause
čn čxʷuym t islax̣t + u + čn lkʷukʷ
I visited my friend and I went far away.

Example: iłn u sust – S/he/it ate and drank. This is an example of a compound sentence. Both words are independent clauses joined by ***u***. Each clause can be as complex as a simple sentence. Adjuncts can be added to form predicate clauses. Each must be independent to form a compound sentence.

i łaqšlš u ṫapntem – Right when s/he/it sat down s/he/it was shot.

x̣ʷa i mi u ta es mistexʷ – It is most likely you do not know it.

i mi u ta es mistexʷ – Of course you do not know it.

nłapaqs k̇ʷłċa tʔe u ƛ̓lil sqelixʷ – Death can be very painful.

kʷ sk̇ʷṅšspetč u kʷ xʷist – How old were you when you first walked?

wis iłn u xʷl̇il̇ – S/he finished eating and came alive.

kʷ xʷist u kʷ x̣ʷcuʔsičṅ t esmq̇ʷmoq̇ʷ – You walked and crossed over the mountain.

Compound sentences that reference something that hasn't happened yet use the particle *m* to join the independent clauses. The independent clause can be an interrogative or an imperative. Adjuncts may be used to form predicate clauses. Below are some examples that use the particle *m* to join two clauses to form a compound sentence.

xʷk̇ʷunt m nċeẁk̇ʷntxʷ asq̇ʷl̇á – Clean and wash your black tree moss. In this compound sentence example the first clause is an imperative. The second clause includes additional instruction to the imperative clause.

pesyáʔ m p ċl̇ċl̇qinm – All of you put on headdresses. *The literal translation is: all of you and you all will have put on headdresses.*

tmilq̇ʷ m qeʔes nṫums – We will always have a smile. *The literal translation is: it is always and we will be smiling.*

ta kʷ qes ċʔeš m kʷ qʷlqʷe – Do not be ashamed when you talk. *The literal translation is: do not be ashamed and you will be talking.*

łu as k̇ʷul̇m snlaqi m še pṅpṅalqʷntxʷ – While making a sweat house you have to bend poles. *The literal translation is: while you are making a sweat lodge and then you will bend wooden poles.*

l čeṅ m ax̣í m kʷ tixʷł čłq̇iq̇á – How do you get candy? *The literal translation is: at where and it will be done such a way and you will have gotten candy.*

c. Complex Sentences

Complex sentences contain an independent clause and a semantically dependent clause. The particle **ṅe** creates a semantically dependent clause. A semantically dependent clause, if isolated, is grammatically independent but in the presence of the particle **ṅe** needs another clause to qualify its meaning. The semantically dependent clause can be said alone without the other clause. Salish particle ***ṅe*** sets up a conditional clause/phrase followed by a qualifying independent clause. In a dialogue the response is conditional to a remark or understood subject. The particle *m* precedes the semantically dependent clause. The English conjunctions when and if are equivalent to ***ṅe***. This is a particle expressing conditionality.

Diagram c.1 – Complex Sentence Structure
ṅe + conditional dependent clause **+** particle **m +** independent clause
ṅe + čxʷuymntxʷ łu islax̣t + m + cuntxʷ łu čiqs lkʷkʷmi
When you visit my friend tell him/her that I'm going to go far away.

ṅe člux̣ʷ m eł wičtmncn – I will see you this evening. *The literal translation is: when it-is-evening I'll see you again.*

ṅe pisteṁ m kʷ xʷuy – When are you going to go? *The literal translation is: when, when will you go.*

ṅe l sčace m čn k̓ʷis šlepm t maniłp x̣ʷl̓ incitxʷ – Sunday I will go and chop down balsam for my house. *The literal translation is: when at Sunday I will go to chop down balsam tree for my house.*
ṅe tʔe swe qs ácṁi m še čšin – If anyone is going to trap they should come along. *The literal translation is: when whoever is going trapping then I'll accompany.*
ṅe kʷ upn eł cil m lcíʔistmn kʷqs ntx̣ʷmsqá – When you are fifteen I will let you drive. *The literal translation is: when you are fifteen then I'll-let-you you are going to drive.*
ṅe eł cłʔaq̓ʷ m qeʔ xʷuy – When s/he/it appears again we'll go.
ṅe qeʔ wis k̓ʷul̓łxʷ m šeẏ l qeʔ lciʔ – When we finish building the house, we'll live in it.
ṅe puti i sx̣al m p eł cxʷixʷuy – You all come back when it is still light.
ṅe kʷqs k̓ʷl̓sncut m nt̓pusnt – When you are going to cook boil it.
ṅe ta kʷes x̣éʔenel̓t m kʷ xʷeyt – If you do not reprimand children you will be in trouble/pay later.
ṅe wis čxʷntéxʷ m kʷ čx̣ʷicpm t anłṅi – When you finish cutting it (the meat) off, you will cut off the fur with your knife.
ṅe eł cwis íʔiṁš tl̓ čłčéwm m qeʔ wenš – When they finish moving back here from the plains, we'll war dance.
ṅe kʷékʷst m qeʔ k̓ʷis x̣ect – In the morning we are going to go dig.
ṅe kʷ sust t nx̣ʷoskʷ m kʷ nslslmtus – When you drink beer you get dizzy.

ta qs tam qeʔqs nx̣eslsi ṅe qeʔ k̓ʷl̓sncut – We must have good feelings when we cook.
nméƛ̓nt łu mulš t ml̓ml̓té u nexʷ ppo u nexʷ t apłsálqʷ łu ṅe kʷ wičm – Mix cottonwood with aspen and willow and also applewood, if you can find it.
hoy ṅem čn šáll ṅe eł cxʷuy – I will be (get) tired when s/he comes back.
nxʷk̓ʷxʷk̓ʷeysiš ṅe kʷ wis iłnm – Brush your teeth after meals.
šeẏ łu ṅe eł nk̓ʷasq̓t łu sčłʔeʔ – The day after tomorrow is Saturday.
k̓ʷmiʔ tam qs t̓ipeysi ṅe člux̣ʷ – I hope it's not raining this evening.

ha kʷqs čšt̓el̓ti ṅe člux̣ʷ – Are you going to babysit this evening?
ečx̣i u iše es k̓ʷul̓stxʷ ṅe kʷ k̓ʷl̓sncut t uʔuseʔ – How do you prepare eggs when you cook them?

łu ṅe ta qʷo es psap – If I do not get excited.
ṅe eł nk̓ʷasq̓t – day after tomorrow.

d. Particles and Affixes

Particles are dependant words. Particles add flavor to their independent word. Affixes are elements added to word stems to form a new word or altered meaning to a word. Particles and affixes fall into twenty one categories: intransitive pronouns, six types of transitive pronouns, exclamations, evidential, interrogative, possibility, modality, aspect, negative, future, imperfect, demonstrative, prepositional, imperative, and auxiliary.

1. **Intransitive pronoun** *particles are used to indicate person. These particles always precede the predicate word (verb). In addition intransitive pronoun particles are used in conjunction with indicative mood present tense particle* ***es****, and include:*

   čn – I ***kʷ*** – you ***qeʔ*** – we ***p*** – you all
   plural infix pronoun particle they, *vowel* ***ʔ vowel*** as in ***ƛ̓líʔip*** **–** they stopped.

1.1. Intransitive pronoun particles conjugated in all tenses. Each of the following are examples of simple sentences. Each is complete with a predicate and a pronoun particle. In the tables below, notice that the example predicate word by itself is defaulted to third person singular. This is very important to understand, all words in isolation without a pronoun particle are always in the third person state.

Table d.1 – Intransitive Pronoun Conjugation: Stop		
ƛ̓lip – S/he/it stopped.	čn ƛ̓lip – I stopped.	kʷ ƛ̓lip – You stopped.
es ƛ̓lpmi – S/he/it is stopping.	čnes ƛ̓lpmi – I am stopping.	kʷes ƛ̓lpmi – You are stopping.
qs ƛ̓lpmi – S/he/it is going to stop.	čiqs ƛ̓lpmi – I am going to stop.	kʷqs ƛ̓lpmi – You are going to stop.
ƛ̓líʔip – They stopped.	qe ƛ̓lip – We stopped.	p ƛ̓lip – You all stopped.
es ƛ̓lpmíʔi – They are stopping.	qe es ƛ̓lpmi – We are stopping.	pes ƛ̓lpmi – You all are stopping.
qs ƛ̓lpmíʔi – They're going to stop.	qeʔqs ƛ̓lpmi – They're going to stop.	pqs ƛ̓lpmi – You all are going to stop.

Table d.2 – Intransitive Pronoun Conjugation: Work		
k̓ʷul̓m – S/he/it worked.	čn k̓ʷul̓m – I worked.	kʷ k̓ʷul̓m – You worked.
es k̓ʷul̓i – S/he/it is working.	čnes k̓ʷul̓i – I am working.	kʷes k̓ʷul̓i – You are working.
qs k̓ʷul̓i – S/he/it is going to work.	čiqs k̓ʷul̓i – I am going to work.	kʷqs k̓ʷul̓i – You are going to work.
k̓ʷúʔul̓m – They worked.	qe k̓ʷul̓m – We worked.	p k̓ʷul̓m – You all worked.
es k̓ʷúʔul̓i – They are working.	qe es k̓ʷul̓i – We are working.	pes k̓ʷul̓i – You all are working.
qs k̓ʷúʔul̓i – They are going to work.	qeʔqs k̓ʷul̓i – We are going to work.	pqs k̓ʷul̓i – You all are going to work.

Table d.3 – Intransitive Pronoun Conjugation: Eat		
iɬn – S/he/it ate.	čn iɬn – I ate.	kʷ iɬn – You ate.
es iɬni – S/he/it is eating.	čnes iɬni – I am eating.	kʷes iɬn – You are eating.
qs iɬni – S/he/it is going to eat.	čiqs iɬni – I am going to eat.	kʷqs iɬni – You are going to eat.
elíʔiɬn – They ate.	qe eliɬn – We ate.	p eliɬn – You all ate.
es elíʔiɬni – They are eating.	qe es eliɬni – We are eating.	pes eliɬni – You all are eating.
qs elíʔiɬni – They are going to eat.	qeʔqs eliɬni – We are going to eat.	pqs eliɬni – You all are going to eat.

2. **Transitive pronoun** *prefixes and suffixes. A transitive verb is one which has both a subject and an object. Two types exist depending on the root word being stressed or unstressed. These affixes include:*

2.1. Unstressed with root word, **k̓ʷul̓ –** work/do/make. *See: tables d.4 and d.5.*

...is **–** s/he/it ***...n*** **–** I ***...ntxʷ*** **–** you

... *ʔ vowel repetition* ***...is*** **–** they ***qe...ntm*** **–** we ***...ntp*** **–** you all

k̓ʷul̓is – S/he/it made s.t. **k̓ʷul̓n, k̓ʷul̓ntxʷ**

es k̓ʷul̓ms – S/he/it is making s.t. **ies k̓ʷul̓m, as k̓ʷul̓m**

qs k̓ʷul̓ms – S/he/it is going to make s.t. **iqs k̓ʷul̓m, aqs k̓ʷul̓m**

k̓ʷúʔul̓is – They made s.t. **qeʔ k̓ʷul̓ntm, k̓ʷul̓ntp**

es k̓ʷúʔul̓ms – They are making s.t. **qeʔes k̓ʷul̓m, es k̓ʷul̓mp**

qs k̓ʷúʔul̓ms – They are going to make s.t. **qeʔqs k̓ʷul̓m, qs k̓ʷul̓mp**

2.2. Stressed with root word **ƛ̓lip –** stop:

...ntes **–** s/he/it ***...nten*** **–** I ***...ntexʷ*** **–** you

...ntéʔes **–** they ***qe...ntem*** **–** we ***...ntep*** **–** you all

ƛ̓lpntes – S/he/it stopped s.t./s.o. **ƛ̓lpnten, ƛ̓lpntexʷ**

es ƛ̓lpims – S/he/it is stopping s.t./s.o. **ies ƛ̓lpm, as ƛ̓lpim**

qs ƛ̓lpims – S/he/it is going to stop s.t./s.o. **iqs ƛ̓lpim, aqs ƛ̓lpim**

ƛ̓lpntéʔes – They stopped s.t./s.o. **qeʔ ƛ̓lpntem, ƛ̓lpntep**

es ƛ̓lpíʔims – They are stopping s.t./s.o. **qeʔes ƛ̓lpim, es ƛ̓lpimp**

qs ƛ̓lpíʔims – They are going to stop s.t./s.o. **qeʔqs ƛ̓lpim, qs ƛ̓lpimp**

Table d.4 - Transitive Conjugation: Look

	Future Tense			Future Continuate		
1st Singular	1-2	**kʷ iqs aċx̣m**	I am going to look at you.	1-2	**kʷ iqes aċx̣m**	I must remain looking at you.
	1-3	**iqs aċx̣m**	I am going to look at him/her.	1-3	**iqes aċx̣m**	I must remain looking at him/her.
	1-5	**p iqs aċx̣m**	I am going to look at you all.	1-5	**p iqes aċx̣m**	I must remain looking at you all.
	1-6	**iqs aʔaċx̣m**	I am going to look at them.	1-6	**iqes aʔaċx̣m**	I must remain looking at them.
1st Plural	4-2	**kʷ qs aċx̣m**	We are going to look at you.	4-2	**kʷ qes aċx̣m**	We must remain looking at you.
	4-3	**qeʔqs aċx̣m**	We are going to look at him/her.	4-3	**qeʔ qes aċx̣m**	We must remain looking at him/her.
	4-5	**p qs aċx̣m**	We are going to look at you all.	4-5	**p qes aċx̣m**	We must remain looking at you all.
	4-6	**qeʔqs aʔaċx̣m**	We are going to look at them.	4-6	**qeʔ qes aʔaċx̣m**	We must remain looking at them.
2nd Singular	2-1	**qʷo aqs aċx̣m**	You are going to look at me.	2-1	**qʷo aqes aċx̣m**	You must remain looking at me.
	2-3	**aqs aċx̣m**	You are going to look at him/her.	2-3	**aqes aċx̣m**	You must remain looking at him/her.
	2-4	**qeʔ aqs aċx̣ɬt**	You are going to look at us.	2-4	**qeʔ aqes aċx̣ɬt**	You must remain looking at us.
	2-6	**aqs aʔaċx̣m**	You are going to look at them.	2-6	**aqes aʔaċx̣m**	You must remain looking at them.
2nd Plural	5-1	**qʷo qs aċx̣mp**	You all are going to look at me.	5-1	**qʷo qes aċx̣mp**	You all must remain looking at me.
	5-3	**qs aċx̣mp**	You all are going to look at him/her.	5-3	**qes aċx̣mp**	You all must remain looking at him/her.
	5-4	**qeʔqs aċx̣ɬt**	You all are going to look at us.	5-4	**qeʔ qes aċx̣ɬt**	You all must remain looking at us.
	5-6	**qs aʔaċx̣mp**	You all are going to look at them.	5-6	**qes aʔaċx̣mp**	You all must remain looking at them.
3rd Singular	3-1	**qʷo qs aċx̣ms**	S/he/it is going to look at me.	3-1	**qʷo qes aċx̣ms**	S/he/it must remain looking at me.
	3-2	**kʷ qs aċx̣ms**	S/he/it is going to look at you.	3-2	**kʷ qes aċx̣ms**	S/he/it must remain looking at you.
	3-3	**qs aċx̣ms**	S/he/it is going to look at him/her.	3-3	**qes aċx̣ms**	S/he/it must remain looking at him/her.
	3-4	**qeʔqs aċx̣ɬs**	S/he/it is going to look at us.	3-4	**qeʔ qes aċx̣ɬs**	S/he/it must remain looking at us.
	3-5	**p qs aċx̣ms**	S/he/it is going to look at you all.	3-5	**p qes aċx̣ms**	S/he/it must remain looking at you all.
	3-6	**qs aʔaċx̣ms**	S/he/it is going to look at them.	3-6	**qes aʔaċx̣ms**	S/he/it must remain looking at them.
3rd Plural	6-1	**qʷo qs aʔaċx̣ms**	They are going to look at me.	6-1	**qʷo qes aʔaċx̣ms**	They must remain looking at me.
	6-2	**kʷ qs aʔaċx̣ms**	They are going to look at you.	6-2	**kʷ qes aʔaċx̣ms**	They must remain looking at you.
	6-3	**qs aʔaċx̣ms**	They are going to look at him/her.	6-3	**qes aʔaċx̣ms**	They must remain looking at him/her.
	6-4	**qeʔqs aʔaċx̣ɬs**	They are going to look at us.	6-4	**qeʔ qes aʔaċx̣ɬs**	They must remain looking at us.
	6-5	**p qs aʔaċx̣ms**	They are going to look at you all.	6-5	**p qes aʔaċx̣ms**	They must remain looking at you all.
	6-6	**qs aʔaʔaċx̣ms**	They are going to look at them.	6-6	**qes aʔaʔaċx̣ms**	They must remain looking at them.

The numbers in the initial column represent the actor - patient in the three persons.
1 is first person singular, 2 is second person singular, 3 is third person singular,
4 is first person plural, 5 is second person plural, 6 is third person plural.

Table d.5 - Transitive Conjugation: Look

	Past Perfect Tense			Present Continuous Tense			Prefect Continuate		
1st Singular	1-2	**acx̣ncn**	I looked at you.	1-2	**kʷ ies acx̣m**	I look at you.	1-2	**es acx̣stmn**	I am looking at you.
	1-3	**acx̣n**	I looked at him/her.	1-3	**ies acx̣m**	I look at him/her.	1-3	**es acx̣stn**	I am looking at him/her.
	1-5	**acx̣łmn**	I looked at you all.	1-5	**p ies acx̣m**	I look at you all.	1-5	**es acx̣łmn**	I am looking at you all.
	1-6	**aˀacx̣n**	I looked at them.	1-6	**ies aˀacx̣m**	I look at them.	1-6	**es aˀacx̣stn**	I am looking at them.
1st Plural	4-2	**acx̣nct**	We looked at you.	4-2	**kʷ es acx̣m**	We look at you.	4-2	**es acx̣stmt**	We are looking at you.
	4-3	**qeˀ acx̣ntm**	We looked at him/her.	4-3	**qeˀes acx̣m**	We look at him/her.	4-3	**qeˀes acx̣stm**	We are looking at him/her.
	4-5	**acx̣łmt**	We looked at you all.	4-5	**p es acx̣m**	We look at you all.	4-5	**es acx̣łmn**	We are looking at you all.
	4-6	**qeˀaˀacx̣ntm**	We looked at them.	4-6	**qeˀes aˀacx̣m**	We look at them.	4-6	**qeˀes aˀacx̣stm**	We are looking at them.
2nd Singular	2-1	**qʷo acx̣ntxʷ**	You looked at me.	2-1	**qʷo as acx̣m**	You look at me.	2-1	**qʷo es acx̣stxʷ**	You are looking at me.
	2-3	**acx̣ntxʷ**	You looked at him/her.	2-3	**as acx̣m**	You look at him/her.	2-3	**es acx̣stxʷ**	You are looking at him/her.
	2-4	**qeˀ acx̣łlt**	You looked at us.	2-4	**qeˀ es acx̣łlt**	You look at us.	2-4	**qeˀ es acx̣łlt**	You are looking at us.
	2-6	**aˀacx̣ntxʷ**	You looked at them.	2-6	**as aˀacx̣m**	You look at them.	2-6	**es aˀacx̣stxʷ**	You are looking at them.
2nd Plural	5-1	**qʷo acx̣ntp**	You all looked at me.	5-1	**qʷo es acx̣mp**	You all look at me.	5-1	**qʷo es acx̣stp**	You all are looking at me.
	5-3	**acx̣ntp**	You all looked at him/her.	5-3	**es acx̣mp**	You all look at him/her.	5-3	**es acx̣stp**	You all are looking at him/her.
	5-4	**qeˀ acx̣łlt**	You all looked at us.	5-4	**qeˀ es acx̣łlt**	You all look at us.	5-4	**qeˀ es acx̣łlt**	You all are looking at us.
	5-6	**aˀacx̣ntp**	You all looked at them.	5-6	**es aˀacx̣mp**	You all look at them.	5-6	**es aˀacx̣stp**	You all are looking at them.
3rd Singular	3-1	**qʷo acx̣is**	S/he/it looked at me.	3-1	**qʷo es acx̣ms**	S/he/it looks at me.	3-1	**qʷo es acx̣sts**	S/he/it is looking at me.
	3-2	**acx̣nc**	S/he/it looked at you.	3-2	**kʷ es acx̣ms**	S/he/it looks at you.	3-2	**es acx̣stms**	S/he/it is looking at you.
	3-3	**acx̣is**	S/he/it looked at him/her.	3-3	**es acx̣ms**	S/he/it looks at him/her.	3-3	**es acx̣sts**	S/he/it is looking at him/her.
	3-4	**qeˀ acx̣łls**	S/he/it looked at us.	3-4	**qeˀ es acx̣łls**	S/he/it looks at us.	3-4	**qeˀ es acx̣łls**	S/he/it is looking at us.
	3-5	**acx̣łms**	S/he/it looked at you all.	3-5	**p es acx̣ms**	S/he/it looks at you all.	3-5	**es acx̣łms**	S/he/it is looking at you all.
	3-6	**aˀacx̣is**	S/he/it looked at them.	3-6	**es aˀacx̣ms**	S/he/it looks at them.	3-6	**es aˀacx̣sts**	S/he/it is looking at them.
3rd Plural	6-1	**qʷo aˀacx̣is**	They looked at me.	6-1	**qʷo es aˀacx̣ms**	They look at me.	6-1	**qʷo es aˀacx̣sts**	They are looking at me.
	6-2	**aˀacx̣nc**	They looked at you.	6-2	**kʷ es aˀacx̣ms**	They look at you.	6-2	**es aˀacx̣stms**	They are looking at you.
	6-3	**aˀacx̣is**	They looked at him/her.	6-3	**es aˀacx̣ms**	They look at him/her.	6-3	**es aˀacx̣sts**	They are looking at him/her.
	6-4	**qeˀ aˀacx̣łls**	They looked at us.	6-4	**qeˀ es aˀacx̣łls**	They look at us.	6-4	**qeˀ es aˀacx̣łls**	They are looking at us.
	6-5	**aˀacx̣łms**	They looked at you all.	6-5	**p es aˀacx̣ms**	They look at you all.	6-5	**es aˀacx̣łms**	They are looking at you all.
	6-6	**aˀaˀacx̣is**	They looked at them.	6-6	**es aˀaˀacx̣ms**	They look at them.	6-6	**es aˀaˀacx̣sts**	They are looking at them.

Causative transitive pronoun affixes. *A causative form is an expression of an agent causing or forcing a patient to perform an action or to be in a certain condition. Causative transitive pronouns create verbs noting causation of a subject to an object.*

2.3. Unstressed with root word, **k̓ʷul̓** – work/do/make:

...sts – s/he/it ***...stn*** – I ***...stxʷ*** – you
... *ʔ vowel repetition* ***...sts*** – they ***qe...stm*** – we ***...stp*** – you all

k̓ʷul̓sts – S/he/it prepared s.t. **k̓ʷul̓stn, k̓ʷul̓stxʷ**
es k̓ʷul̓sts – S/he/it is preparing s.t. **es k̓ʷul̓stn, es k̓ʷul̓stxʷ**
qs k̓ʷul̓sts – S/he/it is going to prepare s.t. **qs k̓ʷul̓stn, qs k̓ʷul̓stxʷ**
k̓ʷúʔul̓sts – They prepared s.t. **qeʔ k̓ʷul̓stm, k̓ʷul̓stp**
es k̓ʷúʔul̓sts – They are preparing s.t. **qeʔes k̓ʷul̓stm, es k̓ʷul̓stp**
qs k̓ʷúʔul̓sts – They are going to prepare s.t. **qeʔqs k̓ʷul̓stm, qs k̓ʷul̓stp**

2.4. Stressed with root word **ƛ̓lip** – stop:

...stes – s/he/it ***...sten*** – I ***...stexʷ*** – you
...stéʔes – they ***qe...stem*** – we ***...step*** – you all

ƛ̓lpstes – S/he/it caused s.t./s.o. to stop. **ƛ̓lpsten, ƛ̓lpstexʷ**
es ƛ̓lpstes – S/he/it is causing s.t./s.o. to stop. **es ƛ̓lpsten, es ƛ̓lpstexʷ**
qs ƛ̓lpstes – S/he/it is going to cause s.t./s.o. to stop. **qs ƛ̓lpsten, qs ƛ̓lpstexʷ**
ƛ̓lpstéʔes – They caused s.t./s.o. to stop. **qeʔ ƛ̓lpstem, ƛ̓lpstep**
es ƛ̓lpstéʔes – They are causing s.t./s.o. to stop. **qeʔes ƛ̓lpstem, es ƛ̓lpstep**
qs ƛ̓lpstéʔes – They are going to cause s.t./s.o. to stop. **qeʔqs ƛ̓lpstem, qs ƛ̓lpstep**

3. **Benefactive transitive pronoun** affixes. *These affixives create an expression indicating an agent is performing an action for the positive benefit of a patient (someone or something). Benefactive expressions can only be positive in nature. They cannot take on a negative aspect unlike substitutive expressions.*

3.1. Unstressed with root word, **k̓ʷul̓** – work/do/make:

...šts – s/he/it ***...štn*** – I ***...štxʷ*** – you
... *ʔ vowel repetition* ***...šts*** – they ***qe...štm*** – we ***...štp*** – you all

k̓ʷul̓šts – S/he/it made s.t. for s.o. **k̓ʷul̓štn, k̓ʷul̓štxʷ**
es k̓ʷul̓štms – S/he/it is making s.t. for s.o. **ies k̓ʷul̓štm, as k̓ʷul̓štm**
qs k̓ʷul̓štms – S/he/it is going to make s.t. for s.o. **iqs k̓ʷul̓štm, aqs k̓ʷul̓štm**
k̓ʷúʔul̓šts – They made s.t. for s.o. **qeʔ k̓ʷul̓štm, k̓ʷul̓štp**
es k̓ʷúʔul̓štms – They are making s.t. for s.o. **qeʔes k̓ʷul̓štm, es k̓ʷul̓štmp**
qs k̓ʷúʔul̓štms – They are going to make s.t. for s.o. **qeʔqs k̓ʷul̓štm, qs k̓ʷul̓štmp**

3.2. Stressed with root word **ƛ̓lip** – stop:

...šits – s/he/it ***...šitn*** – I ***...šitxʷ*** – you
...šíʔits – they ***qe...šitm*** – we ***...šitp*** – you all

ƛ̓lpšits – S/he/it stopped s.o./s.t. for s.o. **ƛ̓lpšitn, ƛ̓lpšitxʷ**
es ƛ̓lpšitms – S/he/it is stopping s.t./s.o. for s.o. **es ƛ̓lpšitm, es ƛ̓lpšitm**
qs ƛ̓lpšitms – S/he/it is going to stop s.t./s.o. for s.o. **qs ƛ̓lpšitm, qs ƛ̓lpšitm**
ƛ̓lpšíʔits – They stopped s.t./s.o. for s.o. **qeʔ ƛ̓lpšitm, ƛ̓lpšitp**
es ƛ̓lpšíʔitm– They are stopping s.t./s.o. for s.o. **qeʔes ƛ̓lpšitm, es ƛ̓lpšitmp**
qs ƛ̓lpšíʔitm– They are going to stop s.t./s.o. for s.o. **qeʔqs ƛ̓lpšitm, qs ƛ̓lpšitmp**

4. **Substitutive transitive pronoun** affixes. *These affixives create an expression indicating an agent is performing an action for the benefit or in substitution of a patient (someone or something). Substitutive expressions can be positive or negative in aspect.*

4.1. Unstressed with root word, **k̓ʷul̓** – work/do/make:

...łts – s/he/it ***...łtn*** – I ***...łtxʷ*** – you
... *ʔ vowel repetition* ***...łts*** – they ***qe...łtm*** – we ***...łtp*** – you all

k̓ʷul̓łts – S/he/it made s.t. in place of s.o. **k̓ʷul̓łtn, k̓ʷul̓łtxʷ**
es k̓ʷul̓łtms – S/he/it is making s.t. in place of s.o. **ies k̓ʷul̓łtm, as k̓ʷul̓łtm**
qs k̓ʷul̓łtms – S/he/it is going to make s.t. in place of s.o. **iqs k̓ʷul̓łtm, aqs k̓ʷul̓łtm**
k̓ʷúʔul̓łts – They made s.t. in place of s.o. **qeʔ k̓ʷul̓łtm, k̓ʷul̓łtp**
es k̓ʷúʔul̓łtms – They are making s.t. in place of s.o. **qeʔes k̓ʷul̓łtm, es k̓ʷul̓łtmp**
qs k̓ʷúʔul̓łtms – They are going to make s.t. in place of s.o. **qeʔqs k̓ʷul̓łtm, qs k̓ʷul̓łtmp**

4.2. Stressed with root word **ƛ̓lip –** stop:

...łtes – s/he/it	***...łten –*** I	***...łtexʷ –*** you
...łtéʔes – they	***qe...łtem –*** we	***...łtep –*** you all

ƛ̓lpłtes – S/he/it stopped s.o./s.t. in place of s.o. **ƛ̓lpłten, ƛ̓lpłtexʷ**
es ƛ̓lpłtems – S/he/it is stopping s.t./s.o. in place of s.o. **ies ƛ̓lpłtem, as ƛ̓lpłtem**
qs ƛ̓lpłtems – S/he/it is going to stop s.t./s.o. in place of s.o. **iqs ƛ̓lpłtem, aqs ƛ̓lpłtem**
ƛ̓lpłtéʔes – They stopped s.t./s.o. in place of s.o. **qeʔ ƛ̓lpłtem, ƛ̓lpłtep**
es ƛ̓lpłtéʔem – They are stopping s.t./s.o. in place of s.o. **qeʔes ƛ̓lpłtem, es ƛ̓lpłtemp**
qs ƛ̓lpłtéʔem – They are going to stop s.t./s.o. in place of s.o. **qeʔqs ƛ̓lpłtem, qs ƛ̓lpłtemp**

5. **Instrumentive transitive pronoun** affixes. *These affixes create an expression indicating an agent is using something in performing an action to a patient. In other words, a person or animate object is using an instrument, device, or tool in performing an action to something or someone.*

5.1. Unstressed with root word, **k̓ʷul̓ –** work/do/make:

...mis – s/he/it	***...mn –*** I	***...mntxʷ –*** you
...ʔ** vowel repetition **...mis – they	***qe...mntm –*** we	***...mntp –*** you all

k̓ʷul̓mis – S/he/it used s.t. to make s.t. **k̓ʷul̓mn, k̓ʷul̓mntxʷ**
es k̓ʷul̓mms – S/he/it is using s.t. to make s.t. **ies k̓ʷul̓mm, as k̓ʷul̓mm**
qs k̓ʷul̓mms – S/he/it is going to use s.t. to make s.t. **iqs k̓ʷul̓mm, aqs k̓ʷul̓mm**
k̓ʷúʔul̓mis – They used s.t. to make s.t. **qeʔ k̓ʷul̓ntm, k̓ʷul̓mntp**
es k̓ʷúʔul̓mms – They are using s.t. to make s.t. **qeʔes k̓ʷul̓mm, es k̓ʷul̓mmp**
qs k̓ʷúʔul̓mms – They are going to use s.t. to make s.t. **qeʔqs k̓ʷul̓mm, qs k̓ʷul̓mmp**

5.2. Stressed with root word **ƛ̓lip –** stop:

...mntes – s/he/it	***...mnten –*** I	***...mntexʷ –*** you
...mntéʔes – they	***qe...mntem –*** we	***...mntep –*** you all

ƛ̓lpmntes – S/he/it used s.t. to stop s.t./s.o. **ƛ̓lpmnten, ƛ̓lpmntexʷ**
es ƛ̓lpminms – S/he/it is using s.t. to stop s.t./s.o. **ies ƛ̓lpminm, as ƛ̓lpminm**
qs ƛ̓lpminms – S/he/it is going to use s.t. to stop s.t./s.o. **iqs ƛ̓lpminm, aqs ƛ̓lpminm**
ƛ̓lpmntéʔes – They used s.t. to stop s.t./s.o. **qeʔ ƛ̓lpmntem, ƛ̓lpmntep**
es ƛ̓lpmíʔinms – They are using s.t. to stop s.t./s.o. **qeʔes ƛ̓lpminm, es ƛ̓lpminmp**
qs ƛ̓lpmíʔinms – They are going to use s.t. to stop s.t./s.o. **qeʔqs ƛ̓lpminm, qs ƛ̓lpminmp**

6. **Purposive transitive pronoun** affixes. *This group is a combination of the the prefix č.. – purposive and the relational transitive form. These affixes create an expression indicating an agent is doing an action with or toward a certain purpose. In other words, a person or animate object is acting toward or acting with a direct goal/purpose.*

6.1. With root word, **t̓uxʷt –** fly:

č...mis – s/he/it	***č...mn –*** I	***č...mntxʷ –*** you
č...ʔ** vowel repetition **...mis – they	***qeʔ č...mntm –*** we	***č...mntp –*** you all

čt̓uxʷtmis – S/he/it used s.t. to make s.t. **čt̓uxʷtmn, čt̓uxʷtmntxʷ**
es čt̓uxʷtmms – S/he/it is using s.t. to make s.t. **ies čt̓uxʷtmm, as čt̓uxʷtmm**
qs čt̓uxʷtmms – S/he/it is going to use s.t. to make s.t. **iqs čt̓uxʷtmm, aqs čt̓uxʷtmm**
čt̓úʔuxʷtmis – They used s.t. to make s.t. **qeʔ čt̓uxʷtntm, čt̓uxʷtmntp**
es čt̓úʔuxʷtmms – They are using s.t. to make s.t. **qeʔes čt̓uxʷtmm, es čt̓uxʷtmmp**
qs čt̓úʔuxʷtmms – They are going to use s.t. to make s.t. **qeʔqs čt̓uxʷtmm, qs čt̓uxʷtmmp**

6.2. With root word **x̣ʷus.**– wide awake; alert:

č...mntes – s/he/it ***č...mnten*** – I ***č...mntexʷ*** – you
č...mntéʔes – they ***qeʔ č...mntem*** – we ***č...mntep*** – you all

čxʷusmntes – S/he/it lost sleep over s.t. **čxʷusmnten, čxʷusmntexʷ**
es čxʷusminms – S/he/it is losing sleep over s.t. **ies čxʷusminm, as čxʷusminm**
qs čxʷusminms – S/he/it is going to lose sleep over s.t. **iqs čxʷusminm, aqs čxʷusminm**
čxʷusmntéʔes – They lost sleep over s.t. **qeʔ čxʷusmntem, čxʷusmntep**
es čxʷusmíʔinms – They are losing sleep over s.t. **qeʔes čxʷusminm, es čxʷusminm**
qs čxʷusmíʔinms – They are going to lose sleep over s.t. **qeʔqs čxʷusminm, qs čxʷusminmp**

7. **Successful transitive pronoun** affixes. *These pronoun affixes create expressions indicating that an agent's action to a patient was successfully completed.*

...nuis – s/he/it ***...nun*** – I ***...nuntxʷ*** – you
...núʔuis – they ***qe...nuntm*** – we ***...nuntp*** – you all

ƛ̓lpnuis – S/he/it succeeded in stopping s.t./s.o. **ƛ̓lpnun, ƛ̓lpnuntxʷ**
es ƛ̓lpnunms – S/he/it is succeeding in stopping s.t./s.o. **ies ƛ̓lpnunm, as ƛ̓lpnunm**
qs ƛ̓lpnunms – S/he/it is going to succeed in stopping s.t./s.o. **iqs ƛ̓lpnunm, aqs ƛ̓lpnunm**
ƛ̓lpnúʔuis – They succeeded in stopping s.t./s.o. **qeʔ ƛ̓lpnuntm, ƛ̓lpnuntp**
es ƛ̓lpnúʔunms – They are succeeding in stopping s.t./s.o. **qeʔes ƛ̓lpnunm, es ƛ̓lpnunmp**
qs ƛ̓lpúʔunms – They are going to succeed in stopping s.t./s.o. **qeʔqs ƛ̓lpnunm, qs ƛ̓lpnunmp**

8. **Exclamations** – *Exclamations are full particles or complete sentences. When used in a sentence, exclamations generally go before the predicate.*

8.1. **hayo** – *An exclamation of astonishment said by a male.*
hayo čn ẏapcin t kapi – Gee, I am in need of coffee.

8.2. **eni** – *An exclamation of astonishment said by a female.*
eni ta kʷes tx̣ʷmscuti – Gee, you are not doing right.

8.3. **k̓ʷ** – evidently; yet; apparently; but. *This particle marks a casual opposition or contrast to the preceding statement. Used as an intensifier inference to express casual surprise of an occurence, statement, or presented knowledge. An exclamation used to express pleasant wonderment. See:* ***Evidential****. The word order for this type of sentence is:*
k̓ʷ x̣ʷa stem̓ łu šeẏ – Well, I wonder what that is.
k̓ʷ x̣l̓ šeẏ u ečx̣i – Oh, that's why it is like that.
k̓ʷ stem̓ łu ask̓ʷul̓m – But, what are you doing.
k̓ʷ x̣ʷa stem̓ łu šeẏ – Well, I wonder what that is.

8.3.1. **k̓ʷ uc unexʷ**, *k̓ʷ uc une* – Oh! That is right; Oh! Yes. *An affirmative reply to a recollection as in the English phrases: " oh, that is right"; "oh, yes."*
α: **yetłx̣ʷasq̇t m qeʔ xʷuy č esmq̇ʷmoq̇ʷ** ***β:*** **k̓ʷucune č šeẏ m qeʔ xʷuy** – ***α:*** We are going to the mountains today. ***β:*** That's right, we are going there.

8.3.2. **k̓ʷ šeẏ** – Evidently that. *An exclamation of affirmation.*
k̓ʷ šeẏ łu iskʷest – Oh, that is my name.
k̓ʷ šeẏ u čn iłn – Oh, that is right, I did eat.
k̓ʷ t šeẏ u čn iłn – Oh, that is right, I did eat.

8.4. **yo** – *a mild exclamation used to express pleasure in something as in the English phrase, "by golly."*

8.5. **ma** – *an exclamation to give abrupt attention to a particular positive or negative act as in the English phrases: "see, I told you"; "there, I told you"; "see what you did."*
ma še we cuncn epł t̓it̓éẏe sm̓tm̓a – See, I told you there are a lot of mean cows.

8.6. **šewi –** *an exclamation to express regret of a particular negative act as in the English phrases: "see, there"; "see what happens"; "that is what happens."*
šewi kʷ nt̓lane? – See, you eat too much.
šewi kʷ t̓eye? – See, you are mean.

8.7. **hoh –** surprise in hearing something. *An exclamation used when an unexpected sound is heard.*

8.8. **hoy –** *An exclamation used to indicate a sudden action or an abrupt change. It is usually used in narrative statements.*

8.9. **eh –** surprise; wow. *An interruptive exclamation used to add excitement and drama. It is often heard used as a pause when telling stories.*

8.10. **x̣iɬ –** interjection; exclamation; darn; doggone; damn. *An exclamatory predicate that emphasizes or intensifies a clause.*

x̣iɬ til̓tl̓xʷt ɬu šeẏ – That is really difficult.
x̣iɬ ci č ci? – beyond; way over there.
x̣iɬ mtmi uɬ snč̓l̓é – Darn those no-good coyotes!
x̣iɬ x̣e sunumtmnt – Listen really good to him/her. *cmd.*
x̣iɬ kʷ x̣mteɬċe? – Darn, you have a heavy body.
x̣iɬ kʷes nṗuṗuwené? – Gee, you cannot hear.
x̣iɬ čnes ṗat̓ – I do not feel good or I feel tired and loose.

8.11. **ye pṅ –** exclamation to accentuate a word or thought.
ye pṅ čnes čsq̇méltni – I am really hungry.

9. **Evidential –** *a form, such as a verbal affix, that is a grammatical expression of evidentiality. Evidentiality is an epistemic modality that connotes the speaker's assessment of the evidence for his or her statement. "There's no answer; he must have already left."*

9.1. **k̇ʷ –** evidently; yet; apparently; but. *This particle marks a casual opposition or contrast to the preceding statement. Used as an intensifier inference to express casual surprise of an occurence, statement, or presented knowledge. An exclamation used to express pleasant wonderment. The word order for this type of sentence is:*

Diagram d.6 – Evidential Sentence Structure
predicate phrase + k̇ʷ + opposition/contrast predicate phrase
cuntm lkʷukʷ ɬu slax̣ts + k̇ʷ + nte qs k̇ʷis čxʷuyms
S/he was told that his/her friend went far away yet s/he wants to go visit him/her.

cuntm t px̣px̣ots k̇ʷ nṗuṗuwené? – S/he was told by his/her elders, yet s/he ignored them.
qʷo cuntm xʷuyiš k̇ʷ čn čɬemut – I was told to go, yet I sat there.
mipnun k̇ʷ kʷ yoyoot – I found out that you are strong.
mipnuis k̇ʷ es yoqʷisti ɬu sqltmixʷ – S/he found out that the man had lied.

k̇ʷ steṁ ɬu as k̇ʷul̓m – But what are you doing.
k̇ʷ x̣ʷa steṁ ɬu šeẏ – Well, I wonder what that is.
k̇ʷ uc unexʷ – Oh, that's right.
k̇ʷ t šeẏ u eċx̣i – Oh, that's the way it is.
k̇ʷ x̣ʷl̓ šeẏ u eċx̣i – Oh, that's why it's like that.

9.1.1. **k̇ʷ še –** rather; preferably; evidently then. *This particle expresses preferability, expected or required, in an action/object as opposed to an understood or stated action/object. The word order for this type of sentence is:*

Diagram d.7 – Preferability Sentence Structure
k̓ʷ še + predicate phrase (expected action/object) **+** opposition/contrast predicate phrase
k̓ʷ še + ies čxʷuym łu islax̣t + tam čnes lkʷkʷmi
I am supposed to be visiting my friend, not going far away.

k̓ʷ še qʷoy̓ʔe – Rather than him/her/it, it is supposed to be me.
k̓ʷ še qeʔes elilni tam qeʔes memscuti – Preferably, we are supposed to be eating not playing.
k̓ʷ še qeʔqs xʷuyi č̓ sntumíst – Rather than this, we are supposed to be going to the store.
k̓ʷ še kʷ sewneʔ – Rather than not, you are supposed to hear.

9.1.2. **k̓ʷ šey̓** – Evidently that. *An exclamation of affirmation. See:* ***Exclamations****.*

9.2. **pn̓** – but *(contradictory)*, well *(as a rebuke)*, yet *(in spite of). This particle is interjectory in emphasizing contrariness or exception to a preceding statement. As a response it rebukes an understood or implied statement. The word order for this type of sentence is:*

Diagram d.8 – Contrary Sentence Structure
predicate phrase (implied or stated) **+ pn̓ +** contrary predicate phrase
ƛ̓e lkʷukʷ łu islax̣t + pn̓ + puti ies nxʷuyelsmn
My friend already went far away, yet I still want to visit him/her.

čn epł t šey̓ ec̓x̣i pn̓ tam xʷʔit – I have some like that but not many.
pn̓ swe łu askʷest – Well! What is your name?
pn̓ x̣ʷa stem̓ łu šey̓ – Well! What is that?
pn̓ tam čnes ntelsi – But! I don't want to?
pn̓ x̣ʷl̓ stem̓ – But! Why?
pn̓ t swe u cunct – Well! Who told you?
pn̓ x̣ʷa w̓e l še u ec̓x̣i – Well! Maybe that's the way it is.
pn̓ i mi u tam l šey̓ u ec̓x̣i – Well! For sure it won't be like that.
pn̓ čn nte i tox̣ʷ łu šey̓ – But! I thought that was right.

9.3. **exʷ** – gee whiz, not again. *An exclamation that connotates the English expressions "gee whiz" and "not again" combined.*
exʷ šey̓ kʷ emut – Gee whiz, you are sitting again!
x̣ił exʷ ye ta es k̓ʷłpusncu – S/he was really acting like a jerk.
exʷ iłt̓t̓étmstxʷ – Gee whiz, you made it easy.

exʷ pn̓ anwi – Oh you!? *derogatory*

9.4. **xʷu** – Okay. This predicate is said in response to a statement or command.
α: **čiqs xʷuy č̓ esmq̓ʷmoq̓ʷ** ***β:*** **xʷu n̓e čluxʷ m eł wičtmncn** – ***α:*** I am going to go to the mountains. ***β:*** Okay, I will see you this evening.

9.4.1. **xʷumiʔ** – polite attention.
9.4.2. **xʷuxʷa** – Okay, then.

9.5. **we** – really; even though; was. *The negative evidential particle* ***we*** *indicates a statement is unsupported by the apparent condition or situation.*
we čnes šʔit – Really, I was first *(even though it appears I wasn't)*.
we cun – Really, I did tell him/her *(even though it seems I didn't)*.

we čnes ayx̣ʷti – Really, I am tired *(even though it looks like I'm not).*
we čn xʷuy č ancitxʷ u kʷ čuw – I really went to your house and you were gone.
em we čn iłn puti čnes čsq̓meltni – Even though I did eat, I am still hungry.
ƛ̓m u we sisyus u xʷuy u če x̣ʷopt – S/he really used to be capable; as time went by s/he became unable to work.
tam we es itši – S/he really isn't sleeping.

9.6. **néłi** – naturally because; matter of fact.
néłi łu t sq̓sip ta ep suyapi – Naturally there were no white people long ago.
néłi łu t sq̓sip łiʔe sqelixʷ łu es xʷlxʷilt l milkʷ – Naturally because there were people living all over long ago.
néłi ṅem ẏapqiṅ qeʔqs cq̓ʷełt – Naturally because there will be lots for us to pack out.

10. Interrogative – *Interrogative words are function words used to obtain information; to ask questions.*

10.1. **ha** – Question? ***ha*** *is an interrogative particle. A clause can be changed to a question by adding* ***ha*** *at the beginning. Any clause that is preceded by* ***ha*** *is a question or interrogative clause. It can be said that* ***ha*** *denotes a question just the same as a question mark (?) does at the end of a sentence in English.*
ha tamstxʷ – Did you reject it?
ha qʷʔemintxʷ kʷqs xʷuy č nłʔay – Are you getting used to going to Missoula.
ha kʷes ċʔalqini – Do you have a headache.
ha puti es xʷlxʷilt – Is s/he/it still alive?
ha iše nṫaṁcantxʷ łu annox̣ʷnx̣ʷ – Do you kiss your wife?
ha iše kʷ k̓ʷis čawm – Do you go and pray?
ha kʷes ċʔešmi kʷqs wenš – Are you ashamed to dance?
ha kʷṅe u kʷ čšṫeḷt – Would you babysit?
ha kʷ łmaq̓ – Did you get burned?

10.2. **čeṅ** – location/state. Where? ***čeṅ*** *is an inerrogative particle inquiring about the state/location of something.* ***čeṅ*** *is often preceded by prepositional particles* ***č, l,*** *and* ***tl.***

Diagram d.9 – Location/State Sentence Structure
modifying particle **+ čeṅ +** predicate phrase
č + čeṅ + u qs lkʷkʷmi łu islax̣t
Where far away is my friend going to go?

10.2.1. **čeṅ** – Where? *Used to ask about the general locative state of something.*
čeṅ ancitxʷ – Where is your house?

10.2.2. **č čeṅ** – Where to? *Used to ask in what direction something is.*
č čeṅ u es xʷuyi – To where is s/he going?

10.2.3. **l čeṅ** – Where at? *This interrogative phrase is used to ask about the specific locative state of something.*
l čeṅ łu inq̓ešin – At where are my shoes?

10.2.3.1. **l čeṅ u eċx̣i** – How is it? *This compound sentence inquires about information on the manner of something. It is translated as, how is it like (something)? Literally it asks: at (**l**) where (**čeṅ**) and (**u**) it is like something (**eċx̣i**)*
l čeṅ u eċx̣i u kʷ ntltlqpncut – How do you jump?

10.2.3.2. **l čeṅ m ax̣i** – How is it done? *This compound sentence inquires about information on the manner of something. It is translated as, how is it done? Literally it asks: at (**l**) where (**čeṅ**) and (**m**) do/act like (**ax̣i**).*
l čeṅ m ax̣í m kʷ tixʷł čłq̓iq̓á – How do you get candy?

10.2.4. **tl̓ čeṅ –** Where from? *This phrase is used to inquire about the source or origin point in spatial movement.*

tl̓ čeṅ u kʷ sqelixʷ – from where are you a person; where are you from?

10.2.5. **eċščeṅ –** How is s/he? *This phrase is used to inquire about one's physiological state.*

eċščenstxʷ łu anpspus – What did you do to your cats?

10.3. **steṁ –** What? Interrogative pronoun; non-human object. *This interrogative particle inquires about a characteristic of something. It always precedes the clause statement.*

Diagram d.10 – Interrogative, what, Sentence Structure
modifying particle **+ steṁ +** predicate phrase
x̣ʷl̓ + steṁ + u kʷqs lkʷkʷmi
Why are you going to go far away?

steṁ łu askʷest – What is your name? *This simple interrogative sentence is inquiring about the characteristic of your name, meaning what object or animal does your name come from.*

steṁ łu ask̓ʷul̓m – What are you doing?

10.3.1. **t steṁ –** Interrogative determiner. What? *Used to ask what an intransitive verb is acting on. Also used to inquire about the object used in a transitive verb action.*

t steṁ u kʷ kʷekʷstm – What did you eat for breakfast?
t steṁ łu nič̓mntxʷ – What did you use to cut it with?

10.3.2. **x̣ʷl̓ steṁ –** Reason. Why? *Used to clarify.*

x̣ʷl̓ steṁ u tam t seliš u kʷes uwewlši – Why are you not speaking Salish?
x̣ʷl̓ steṁ u l še u kʷ ax̣ílm – Why did you do it this way?
x̣ʷl̓ steṁ u kʷes ayx̣ʷti – Why are you tired.

10.3.3. **pisteṁ –** Time. When? *Used to inquire about a time in the future.*

t spisteṁ u kʷ eł ck̓ʷłčicš – When did you get back?
ṅe pisteṁ m kʷ xʷuy – When are you going to go?

10.3.4. **ep steṁ –** What does s/he/it have? *Used to inquire about possession.*

kʷ ep steṁ – What do you have?

10.3.5. **tl̓ steṁ –** *Used to inquire about the source, cause or origin of something.*

tl̓ steṁ u es k̓ʷul̓ – What is it made from?

10.3.6. **l steṁ –** *Used to inquire about the characteristics of the locative state such as in what, at what, on what, with what.*

10.3.7. **steṁ** can be used with an affix to create an interrogative phrase.

stṁulexʷ – Some place; What area?
stṁulexʷ łu šeẏ – What place is that?

10.4. **swe –** Interrogative pronoun, human. who? ***swe*** *is used to inquire about a human or human-like subject.*

Diagram d.11 – Interrogative, who, Sentence Structure
modifying particle **+ swe +** predicate phrase
ƛ̓m + swe + łu qs lkʷkʷmi
Who was it that was going to go far away?

swe łu askʷest – What/who is your name? *This simple interrogative sentence is inquiring about your name, meaning who you are.*

kʷ swe – Who are you?
ƛ̓m kʷ swe – What was your name?
p suswe – Who are each one of you?
pṅ swe łu askʷest – Well! What is your name?
tʔe swe – anybody; anyone; somebody.
ta swe – nobody.

10.5. **k̓ʷinš –** Interrogative inquiring about the quantity of a set of objects.

Diagram d.12 – Interrogative, quantity, Sentence Structure

modifying particle **+ k̓ʷinš +** predicate phrase

k̓ʷinš + suxʷmeʔtn łu kʷqs lkʷkʷmi

How far away are you going to go? How many miles is it that you are going?

k̓ʷinš kʷ čk̓ʷnšé t sw̓éwł – How many fish did you catch?
t k̓ʷinš u kʷes nte – How much do you want?

10.5.1. **l k̓ʷinš –** Time. What time? *This interrogative phrase refers to the measure of time. It is believed to originate from the arrangement of numbers on an analog clock. It literally asks "at how many" referring to hand placement on the numbers of a clock.*
l k̓ʷinš m kʷ qéiłt – What time will you wake?

10.5.2. **k̓ʷnš… –** prefix inquiring about the quantity of a set of objects specific to the root word.
k̓ʷnšełxʷ – How many houses/tipis are there?
k̓ʷnšasq̇t – How many days?
čk̓ʷink̓ʷnš – How many people are there?

10.6. **eċint –** An interrogative requesting for a repeat of spoken words.
kʷes eċinti – What are you saying?

10.7. **tma –** as you know; so? A rhetorical interrogative similar to so, because or as you know.
tma iše kʷ sust t sewłkʷ x̣ʷl̓ kʷes nx̣mpci – As you know you drink water, because you are thirsty.

10.8. **Interrogative content clauses** inquire about content implied by or commented on by the main clause.
l šeẏ čeṅ łu es k̓ʷul̓l – It is there where s/he was born.
es misten č čeṅ u es xʷuyi – I know where s/he is going.
xʷixʷuy č nłʔay x̣ʷa čk̓ʷink̓ʷnš – Some people went to Missoula.
čn xʷuy č stṁulexʷ u čn eł cxʷuy – I went some place and came back.
ta es misten steṁ łu es k̓ʷul̓ms – I do not know what s/he is doing.
t smx̣e tas k̓ʷłpax̣nuis x̣ʷl̓ steṁ u šƛ̓puntm – Grizzly could not think of why s/he got beat.

11. **Possibility** – *Possibility is a form of modality. Possibilities consider the conception of counterfactual situations of the actual world or whether a situation could be true.*

11.1. **x̣ʷa –** a particle expressing uncertainty.

Diagram d.13 – Uncertainty Sentence Structure

x̣ʷa + predicate phrase

x̣ʷa + čiqs lkʷkʷmi

Maybe I am going to go far away.

x̣ʷa es čsq̇meltni – Maybe s/he is hungry.

x̣ʷa es kʷckʷcčsmi – Maybe they fell over.
čaɫlásq̇t x̣ʷa mosq̇t – three or four days.

11.1.1. In combination with an interrogative predicate the uncertainty particle x̣ʷa creates an expression that resembles an indefinite pronoun. An indefinite pronoun refers to one or more unspecified beings, objects, or places. The following examples can be used as placeholders. A placeholder is a general term which is used in place of an unknown term or value.

x̣ʷa eċšče̓nm – Maybe something happened to him/her/it?

x̣ʷa k̇ʷinš – some. *Literally it says maybe how many.*
k̇ʷul̓is x̣ʷa k̇ʷinš – S/he made some *(an undetermined amount).*

x̣ʷa swe – someone. *Literally it says maybe who.*
sewnt x̣ʷa swe – Ask someone *(an undetermined person).*

x̣ʷa stem̓ – something.
k̇ʷʔentén x̣ʷa stem̓ – I bit something *(an undetermined object).*

11.2. **uc** – a particle expressing doubt.

uc kʷep sṗeƛ̓m – Perhaps you have bitterroot?
uc kʷ epɫ ululim – Perhaps you have money? *(nice way to ask for money)*
x̣ʷa uc kʷep sṗeƛ̓m – Is it possible you have bitterroot.
x̣ʷa uc tamstn – Perhaps I will not accept it.

11.3. **n̓e** – a particle expressing conditionality; when.

12. **Modality** – *The classification of prepositions on the basis of whether they assert or deny the possibility, impossibility, contingency, or necessity of their content. Also called **mode**. In language, modality is the subject concerning so-called modal auxiliary verbs like can, must, and should, that are customarily used to modify the meaning of other verbs (which in turn tend to take an infinitive form). Modal verbs express possibility (and impossibility, necessity, contingency, etc.), permissibility (and obligation, proscription, etc.), probability (and improbability, etc.). A distinction can be made between both grammatical modality and grammatical mood. Linguistic modality can also refer to the type of communication, whether vocal, signed, or written.*

12.1. **xʷumiʔ** – please. *A predicate of permissibility.*
xʷumiʔ ci t̓iš – Please (pass) the sugar.
xʷumiʔ tʔe u čiqs šiẏu – Excuse me, I am going to go through here.

12.2. **em** – in vain; although; even though. *This particle creates a phrase that indicates the action performed was in vain. The consequence or result of this futile action is either implied or stated directly after as in the examples below.*
em u čn k̇ʷl̓k̇ʷul̓m u čn čmšqnmist – Although I worked and worked, I gave up.
em we čn iɫn puti čnes čsq̇meltni – Even though I did eat, I am still hungry.
em we čn sičstmist ta qs k̇ʷl̓nun – Although I did try my best, I couldn't get it done.

12.3. **i mi** – It is plainly evident; it is absolute; it is fact. *The particle **mi** is translated as: fact; knowing; or the reality. This means that **mi** is the reality of something as it is known. The demonstrative particle **i** is used to mark speciality. Literally it would translate as: specially noted this is the reality/fact.*
i mi lkʷut – Of course it is far.
i mi u šeẏ – It is plain to see that's what it is.
i mi u sṁma – It is plain to see it is a cow.
i mi u ta – For sure no.
i mi u unexʷ – It is certainly true.
i mi u čiqs xʷuyi – I am going for sure.
i mi u ta es mistexʷ – Of course you do not know it.

x̣ʷa i mi u ta es mistexʷ – It is most likely you do not know it.
ha i mi – Is it for sure?

12.4. **ta qs tam** – absolutely must. *This clause demands absolute necessity. It is literally translated as: no going to be not; it cannot be refused.*
ta qs tam čiqs xʷuyi – I absolutely am going to go.
ta qs tam nkʷłmistmnt – You have to agree with him/her.
ta qs tam qeʔqs nx̣eslsi ṅe qeʔ k̓ʷl̓sncut – We must have good feelings when we cook.
ta qs tam nłk̓ʷk̓ʷmistxʷ – You have to remember it.

12.5. **imše** – it should be; it must be. *This particle is used to encourage action.*
imše kʷ x̣scinm – You must talk good.
imše čłyuxʷstmstxʷ – You should admire it.
imše kʷ čint – You should be afraid.
imše nunxʷénʔemnt anpx̣px̣ot – You should believe your elders.
imše kʷ x̣ʷełé – You should hurry.
imše kʷ kʷtlcutist – Be proud of your accomplishments.
imše kʷ x̣scinm – You should talk good.

12.6. **kʷ ṅe u** – perhaps/should. *This clause is used to offer suggestion with an open ended statement. It leaves the suggested action that proceeds it up to the individual to perform. With the interrogative **ha** it creates a polite open ended question. This clause is directed to the second person, you.*
kʷ ṅe u čšťntéxʷ incitxʷʔ – Perhaps you would take care of my house. *In this sentence, the act of taking-care-of-my-house, is open ended and left with the individual to decide.*
čn nte kʷ ṅe u qʷo olqʷšitxʷ – I think you could help me.
ha kʷ ṅe u čšťntéxʷ incitxʷʔ – Would you take care of my house? *In this interrogative sentence the question is indirect and open ended, seeking a response as to whether the individual will take-care-of-my-house.*
ha kʷ ṅe u qʷo xʷiyusnt č nisq̓ʷot – Would you take me across the water?
ha kʷ ṅe u qʷo q̓eẏšitxʷ – Would you write a letter for me?
ha kʷ ṅe u qʷllumtmnt smx̣éẏčṅ – Would you tell a story about grizzly?

12.7. **mše** – you better/should. *This particle indicates a firm insistence to perform. It is directed to the second person, you.*
mše k̓ʷul̓ntxʷ – You better fix it.
mše maẇntxʷ – You better break it.

12.8. **kʷ še** – you should. *This clause is a polite suggestion to perform a preceding action. It is directed to the second person, you.*
kʷ še u ax̣istxʷ – You could do it that way.
kʷ še cuntxʷ łu mal iłniš – You should tell Mary to eat.

12.9. **x̣iṅe** – might. *This particle is used to indicate the possibility. It directly precedes the phrase the speaker wants to indicate may happen.*
x̣iṅe čn xʷeyʔt – I might get in trouble.
x̣iṅe čn suẏt – I might get chilly.
x̣iṅe kʷ ap̣x̣ʷ – You might choke.
ta es čint x̣iṅe lxʷup – S/he/it is not afraid to get hurt.
ta kʷ qes čxʷʔaqsm t sťša x̣iṅe m kʷ p̣čmals – Don't eat too many huckleberries, you might get diarrhea.
imše łx̣sx̣esečstmntxʷ x̣iṅe maẇt – You should handle it gently, it might break.

13. **Aspect** – *A category of the verb designating primarily the relation of the action to the passage of time, especially in reference to completion, duration, or repetition.*

13.1. **ƛ̓e** – already. *This particle indicates that there is an occurence prior in time, specified or implied, than to what is now spoken about. Something has occurred prior to when it is mentioned.*

ƛ̓e ṗiyaq – It is already done; the berries are already ripe. *In this sentence the ripening or readiness of the berries has occurred.* ***ƛ̓e*** *brings attention to this readiness that has occurred.*
ƛ̓e ptaq – It is already sore. *The fact that a blister occurred is established with the particle* ***ƛ̓e****.*
ƛ̓e ṗáumin – I already lost interest in it.
ƛ̓e paq̓m asnqʷlpu – Your bread is already moldy.
ƛ̓e es nkʷnéʔei – They're already singing.
ƛ̓e es x̣lpulexʷi – It is already getting light.
ƛ̓e qeʔqs ntox̣ʷqini – We are ready to eat lunch. *In this sentence* ***ƛ̓e*** *indicates that the readiness of we-are-going-to-eat-lunch has occurred.*
ƛ̓e es misten snuyapcn – I already know English.
ha ƛ̓e kʷqs cʔocqéʔi – Are you ready to come outside?
ha ƛ̓e wiʔstéxʷ – Did you finish it?
ƛ̓e l ḱʷinš – What time is it already?

13.2. **če** – now, indicating progression or continuation. *This particle marks the point of a progression in reaching a different state. This means that through the passage of time either natural or caused, something has become something else. This something else is marked with* ***če****.*
če čn x̣ʷopt – Now I became lazy/unable.
če nłptemn – Now s/he is forgetful.
če t upn m l ntx̣ʷqin – ten till noon.
če t cil m l upn – five till ten.
če l šey̓ u ec̓x̣i – Now it is become like this.
ax̣i u če ƛ̓mey̓ – It was done that way and now there are just a few.
ƛ̓m u we sisyus u xʷuy u če x̣ʷopt – S/he used to be smart; as time went by s/he became lazy/unable.

13.3. **sic** – now; new; right then. *This particle marks the point of a new state. This is a place of sudden change as opposed to a progressive change with particle* ***če****.*
sic kʷes čšʔitši – Now you are sleepy.
sic čn epł miṅmn – Now I have paint.
čeḱʷsew̓sn łiheʔ u sic x̣ʷq̓ew̓sn – I separated this and then I divided it up.
ta qeʔqs cm̓éy̓eʔ łiʔe sic es ṗox̣ʷtil̓ši – Those who are growing up right now will not have this knowledge.
ṅem qeʔ wis čáwm m sic qeʔ elił̓n – We will finish praying, and then we can eat.
ṅe kʷ wis nc̓ułqpéceʔ m sic kʷ ocqeʔ kʷqs pḱʷlʔemi – When you finish washing the dishes, then you can go outside to play ball.
ṅem nʔemtéw̓stxʷ ṅe wis uwewlš m sic kʷ eł t uwewlš – You wait till s/he gets through talking, then you can talk.

13.4. **nexʷ** – also; too.
nexʷ epł t šey̓ – S/he also has the same.
nexʷ qʷo ckʷešt – Get one for me too.
nexʷ qeʔes čsq̓méltni – We're hungry too.
nexʷ ta es yoʔstép łu sčłip – Also, you all do not know how to hunt.
nexʷ i čn x̣es – I am also well.
nméƛ̓nt łu mulš t ml̓ml̓té u nexʷ ppo u nexʷ t apłsálqʷ łu ṅe kʷ wičm – Mix cottonwood with aspen and willow and also applewood, if you can find it.

13.5. **ƛ̓m** – it was; used to be. *This particle indicates that something was a certain way before and now it is different.*
ƛ̓m kapists – It was her/his/its coffee.
ƛ̓m inkapi – It was my coffee.
ƛ̓m inṗiṗuy̓šn – It used to be my car.

ƛ̓m šé l šeẏ – It used to be there.
ƛ̓m kʷ swe – What was your name?
ƛ̓m u we sisyus u xʷuy u če x̣ʷopt – S/he used to be smart now s/he is lazy.

13.6. **wis** – completion. *This particle marks the completion of some action. Particle* ***wis*** *will always directly preceed the predicate it is modifying. As in the examples below* ***wis*** *in between the pronoun particles and the whole word. The particle behaves like a prefix.*
wis iłn u xʷl̓il̓ – S/he finished eating and came alive.
wis nič̓ntm – It is already cut up.
wis nk̓ʷeʔnis łu smx̣e u ečš̓čeṅm – What happens after the grizzly makes his/her choice?
ƛ̓e čn wis iłn – I've already finished eating; I am done.
ƛ̓e qeʔ wis ntox̣ʷqinm – We already finished lunch.
ƛ̓e łu es wis suxʷumentm ye sqlixʷulexʷ – They had already finished measuring out Indian land.
ṅe wis q̓ʷéʔentéxʷ m sṫsuṁstxʷ – When you finish wringing it, you stretch it.
ṅe eł cwis íʔiṁš tl̓ čłčéwm m qeʔ wenš – When they finish moving back here from the plains, we'll war dance.
ṅe kʷ wis nx̣cménʔem m kʷ itš – When you finish fixing your bed, you will sleep.
ṅe qeʔ wis k̓ʷul̓łxʷ m šeẏ l qeʔ lciʔ – When we finish building the house, we'll live in it.
ṅe kʷ wis łoq̓ʷm m še isk̓ʷlnt łu sccłoq̓ʷ – When you finish peeling, you will scatter out the peelings.
ṅem čn wis nič̓m m čn ocqeʔ – I will finish cutting and I will go out.
ṅem qeʔ wis čáwm m sic qeʔ el̓iłn – We will finish praying, and then we can eat.
ha wis čt̓łntexʷ – Did you finish gluing it?
ha ƛ̓e kʷ wis ncqaus t liti – Did you set the tea in/on the (fire, stove, pot)?
qs wis čxʷuymms – S/he is going to visit s.o. first.
l čeṅ u kʷes wis xʷuy – Where have you been?

13.7. **puti** – still. *This particle indicates an action is on going or a state remains in effect.*
puti i čn q̓ʷił – I am still able/capable.
łu puti či skʷk̓ʷiml̓t nx̣elmn nq̓ʷiq̓ʷosmi – When I was young I was afraid of dogs.
x̣ʷl̓ šeẏ u puti yetłx̣ʷasq̓t es cu łmłamá – That is why frog still says that today.
ṅe puti i sx̣al m p eł cxʷixʷuy – You all come back when it is still light.
ha puti es xʷlxʷilt – Is s/he/it still alive?
ha puti kʷ ep scsułtumš – Do you still have any questions?
puti ċẏu – It is still not done.

13.8. **ċẏu** – not yet. *This particle indicates an action has yet to be performed or completed. The particle is often said just as a response. In that instance the action is understood from the interrogative content.*
ċẏu čnes uẏéčsti – I am still not finished yet.
ċẏu u čn uẏéčst – I did not finish yet.
ċẏu ta čnes iłni – I didn't eat yet.
ċẏu es yoʔnusten – I do not know how yet.
ċẏu u es yoʔnusten łu sqʷllumt – I do not know the story yet.

13.9. **ułeʔ** – again. *This particle indicates the repetitive aspect, again.*
ha ułeʔ – Again? Are you going to (do it) again?
ułéʔ čiqs susti t nt̓íškʷ – I am going to drink pop again.
kʷeṁt ułéʔ ye l sčx̣ʷéct – Well, it is Monday again.
k̓ʷmiʔ ułéʔ čiqs susti – I hope to drink again.
ułeʔ eł k̓ʷeṅnt – Try it again.

13.10. **eɫ –** in addition; back as a preposition. *This particle indicates something is returning to a previous state, condition or location. For instance in counting, when the numbers get above ten* ***eɫ*** *is used to indicate that the base set of numbers from one to ten has been established. In essence,* ***upn eɫ nk̓ʷuˀ,*** *eleven, says there are 10 and there is the addition/return of 1 which has been established previously.*
čn eɫ itš – I went back to sleep.
čn eɫ es itši – I am going back to sleep.
i eɫ es kʷupm – I am pushing s.o. again.
čn eɫ xʷuy č nɫq̓a – I went back to Arlee.
eɫ cˀukʷn – I brought it back here.
ṅe eɫ cwis íˀiṁš tl̓ čɫčéwm m qeˀ wenš – When they finish moving back here from the plains, we'll war dance.
eɫ t qʷoyˀe – It's my turn; back to me.
eɫ t anwi – It's your turn; back to you.

13.11. These transitive pronoun affixes indicate an ongoing action is/has complete/finished:

...nuis – s/he/it	***...nun*** – I	***...nuntxʷ*** – you
...núˀuis – they	***qe...nuntm*** – we	***...nuntp*** – you all

13.12. **...i –** continutive aspectual suffix. **...a –** continutive aspectual suffix for root words with a strong ...a... *This suffix indicates that an action is continuing or is in process.*
čnes susti t seẁɫkʷ – I am drinking water.
čnes xʷisti – I am walking.
es nkʷneyi – S/he is singing.

13.13. **...t –** stative aspectual suffix. *Belonging to or designating a class of verbs that express a state or condition*
px̣pax̣t – smart/wise
maẁt – it is broken
til̓tl̓xʷt – it is difficult; hard
pspast – excited, full of energy.
pipiit – happiness.
x̣est – it is good
yoyoót –it is strong

13.14. **ax̣l –** episodic aspectual particle and prefix. *This particle indicates an action occurs episodically. In English this aspect is marked with the use of the word "every." The underlined portion shows the area of the sentence that is influenced by the particle* ***ax̣l.***
ax̣l čn k̓ʷul̓m še čn ayx̣ʷt – Every time I work I get tired.
ax̣l čn sust t kapi še čn čsˀitš – Every time I drink coffee, I get sleepy.
ax̣lásq̇t – everyday.
ax̣lspentč – every year.
ax̣lsˀistč – every winter.

14. Negative

14.1. **ta –** a negative particle that negates parts of speech, and responses to interrogative content clauses. It translates to English *no*. Negative, **ta** and the imperfect particle, **es** form **tas** in a morphological process; so **ta** is really **ta es**.
ta čnes xʷist – I do not walk.
ta čnes nacɫq̓eẏt – I do not wear a shirt.
ta čnes sust t kapi – I do not drink coffee.
tas čteṁstn – I do not use it.
ta i skʷil– It is not red.

14.2. **tam –** It will not be; it is not. A negative predicate.

tam čnes xʷisti – I am not walking.
tam čnes nacłq̓ey̓ti – I am not wearing a shirt.
tam čnes susti t kapi – I am not drinking coffee.
tam ies čtem̓m – I am not using it.
tam i k̓ʷil – It is not red.
tam es moq̓ʷ – It is not a mound/bump/hill.

15. **Future**

15.1. **ṅem** – A particle indicating that something will absolutely happen in the future.
ṅem čn iłn – I will eat. *The particle **ṅem** makes it certain that "I will eat."*
ṅem čn q̓ʷiłmist m čn k̓ʷłči – I will do my best to get there.
ṅem yoʔnun – I will learn it.
ṅem x̣ʷelntxʷ – You will throw it away.
ṅem olqʷšitn m uy̓é – I will help till it is finished.
ṅem čiqs čk̓ʷul̓i yetłx̣ʷa – I am going to bead today. *With certainty, I'm going to bead today.*

x̣ʷa ṅem čn xʷuy č esyapqini – Maybe I will go to the powwow. *The particle **x̣ʷa** modifies **ṅem** to lesser certainty.*

ha ṅem kʷ čšt̓el̓t – Will you babysit?
ha ṅem kʷqs ocqéʔi – Are you going out?

15.2. **qs** – an affix indicating the irrealis; to convey that an action has yet to occur; an action is not real yet.
čiqs čk̓ʷul̓i yetłx̣ʷa – I am going to bead today. *The **qs** affix makes it mean: the act of me beading has yet to occur; as opposed to, **čnes čk̓ʷul̓i** – I am beading, or, **ṅem čn čk̓ʷul̓m** – I will bead.*

steṁ łu anx̣meč aqs iłnm – What do you like to eat?
k̓ʷeṅnt aqs awm – Try and say it.
l čeṅ m kʷ ax̣i aqs k̓ʷul̓m łu pumin – How do you make a drum?

16. **Imperfect** – The imperfect is a grammatical aspect that refers to an action that is seen from some viewpoint as ongoing or habitual in nature.

16.1. **es** – *This particle creates the imperfect aspect. This means that an action is in process or that something remains in a certain state.*
es susti t seẃłkʷ – S/he/it is drinking water. *In this example **es** with the continutive aspect suffix **...i**, conveys the meaning that someone is in the process of drinking the water. The fact that the action of drinking the water is incomplete requires the use of **es**.*
es sust t nt̓iškʷ – S/he/it drinks pop. *In this example **es** conveys the meaning that someone drinks pop (sweet liquid). In this instance without the continutive aspect suffix **...i**, the action is not in process but rather the action becomes a state. This indicates that this person remains in the state of a pop (sweet liquid) drinker.*
es nołups – S/he is wearing pants. *As in the example above, this sentence indicates that someone remains in the state of wearing pants.*
es łiṗ – It is a line. *This sentence indicates that a line remains in the state of being a line.*

16.2. **iše** – The particle indicates the imperfect aspect. It means that an action is something that is always or customarily done.
ha iše nt̓am̓cantxʷ łu annox̣ʷnx̣ʷ – Do you kiss your wife?
ha iše kʷ k̓ʷis čawm – Do you go and pray?
iše čn sust t kapi – I drink coffee.
iše iłn – S/he/it eats.
ṅe kʷ ṗʔum iše puxʷ łu asṗuʔ – When you fart it stinks.
iše t̓uxʷt łu t̓łt̓el̓ẃé – Bats fly.
iše čxʷʔaqsm t čłq̓iq̓á – S/he always eats a lot of candy.

l čeṅ u ec̓x̣i u **<u>iše k̓ʷul̓ntxʷ</u>** – How do you fix it?
tma **<u>iše kʷ sust</u>** **t sewłkʷ x̣ʷl̓ kʷes nx̣mpcin** – As you know, you drink water because you are thirsty.

17. **Demonstrative** – Demonstratives are words or particles that indicate which entity a speaker refers to and/or to distinguish one entity from another.

17.1. **i** – specially noted.

<u>i kʷil</u> – It is red.
<u>i čn x̣es</u> – I am well.
<u>i łaqšlš</u> **u t̓apntem** – Right when s/he/it sat down s/he/it was shot.

17.2. **ʔe** – here. *This particle refers to the presence of something.*

17.2.1. **lʔe** – this here. *These two particles combined indicate the present state of something.*

lʔe u ax̣ístxʷ – This is how you did it.
sic čn lʔe – Now I am here.
lʔe u c̓aw̓t – These people are just sitting around right here; *said in a derogative manner.*

17.2.2. **iʔe** – this very one here.

iʔe t sic u wisten – I recently finshed it.

17.2.3. **tʔe** – here in general. *These two particles combined create a generalization.*

<u>tʔe pistem</u> – someday; whenever.
<u>tʔe stem</u> – something.
<u>tʔe swe</u> – someone.
ṅe **<u>tʔe swe</u>** **qs ácṁi m še ččin** – If anyone is going to trap, they should come along.
čn sewneʔ **<u>tʔe t steṁ</u>** **y̓e tl̓ est̓eṁp** – I heard something in the bush.
łu **<u>tʔe steṁ</u>** **u kʷ yéṁm** – You were troubled by anything.
čn sewneʔ **<u>tʔe steṁ</u>** **u čn kʷʔeł** – I heard something and got nervous/scared.
put u qeʔ **<u>tʔe łu ax̣lṁnuxʷist</u>** – Again we're going through this time.
<u>tʔe u tnk̓ʷuʔ</u> – once in awhile.
xʷumiʔ **<u>tʔe u čiqs šiy̓u</u>** – Excuse me, I am going to go through here.
čn nx̣lemn l skʷkʷʔec **<u>tʔe u čn susewneʔ</u>** – I am afraid of sounds in the dark.

17.2.4. **šʔeʔ** – here. *Said as someone would make it known they were giving something.*

17.3. **ci** – that *(of something nearby). This particle is used to specify something that is within the vision of the speaker. It can also be in reference to something in the mind's eye of someone.*

es k̓ʷʔaqsi t sqel̓tč **<u>ci mla</u>** – That raven has meat in its mouth.
čtl̓ihičis **<u>ci es moq̓ʷ</u>** – on the other side of that mountain/hill.
siyent esyáʔ **<u>ci snčłemutn</u>** – Count all the chairs.
k̓ʷłnšṅépnt **<u>ci k̓ʷłnčmep</u>** – Close the door.
t̓ipmncutš **<u>ci tl̓</u>** **p̓ip̓uyšn** – Get out of that car *(one person)*.
esčéstxʷ **<u>ci q̓ett</u>** – What did you do with that hide.
nʔułxʷ **<u>ci i nk̓ʷełc̓eʔ</u>** – S/he went into another room.
iqs ckʷnem **<u>ci snsustn</u>** – I am going to go get the cup and bring it here.
čt̓uxʷtmis **<u>ci l</u>** **sc̓éʔekʷ łu x̣małtn** – The fly flew toward the flower.
y̓amint **<u>ci anml̓mé</u>** – Gather your toys.
čulusnt **<u>ci c̓ék̓ʷssṅ</u>** – Turn the light on.

17.4. **ye** – this *(close to the speaker physically or in the passage of time). This particle is used to specify something that is in close proximity to the speaker.*

<u>ye l</u> **citxʷ** – In this house.
<u>ye l</u> **qepc** – In this spring.

ye l es łiṗ m p łṗmncut – All of you will line up on this line.
ye lʔe m aẋístxʷ – You will do it like this.
ċa ye isčwaẋn – My arm hurts.
i q̓ʷáy ye ṗiṗuyšn – This car is black.
i xʷuk̓ʷ ye sṫulixʷ – This land is clean.
ha iheʔ ye lʔe – Does this one go here?
tl̓ čeṅ u es cxʷuyi ye uł snéčłceʔ – Where have all these cow elk come from?
čn čẋsaqsm t kapi ye t sk̓ʷekʷst – I am enjoying my coffee this morning.
eċẋi ye tʔe m k̓ʷul̓ntxʷ – Make it just like this.

17.5. **łu** – *This particle is used to differentiate primary information and background information. In the following examples **łu** is usually followed by a noun-like word. In the few cases where it doesn't, **łu** indicates additive information.*
qʷʔemin łu snlaq̓i – I got used to; accustomed to the sweat. *In this example **qʷʔemin**, the act of getting accustomed to something is primary. The **łu** indicates that **snlaq̓i**, the physical sweat lodge, is the secondary or background information of the main action.*
ẋʷllwisn łu stipn – I keep leaving Stephen behind.
qeʔ qʷl̓epntm łu sẋʷéʔli – We baked the camas.
ta qs k̓ʷłaẋlmistmntxʷ łu ṫeyeʔ – Do not give in to evil.
q̓eẏint łu ask̓ʷṅšspe – Write how old you are.
čteʔmistmntm łu ẋʷaẋʷaa t čẋʷllq̓ʷa – The fox was hit by a train.
iqs čšníʔim łu isxʷsixʷlt qs k̓ʷis q̓q̓méʔe – I am going along with my children, they're going to go fishing.
nméẋ̓nt łu mulš t ml̓ml̓té u nexʷ ppo u nexʷ t apłsálqʷ łu ṅe kʷ wičm – Mix cottonwood with aspen and willow and also applewood, if you can find it.
l es milk̓ʷ u čṫpṫpyeẇt łu qʷqʷċẇé – Chipmunks were standing all over.
kʷeṁt tl̓ šeẏ cxʷuy łu sqélixʷ u es ṫixʷlm – Then from there things came to be changed/got different for the people.
isčqʷamaqs łu kapi – I am used to coffee.
miš łu inʔululim – I do not have any money.
i tam łu tkʷen – I accepted the wrong one.
čn čẋssmels łu čnes memscuti – I got lucky when I was playing. *In this example the main point is that "I got lucky." The **łu** separates and indicates that "I was playing" is the secondary information of the thought.*
steṁ łu asẋʷċiċ – What is your argument?
t swe u tl̓ntés łu qpełċeʔ – Who broke the plate?
ha kʷ nẋel łu i l čiṁ – Are you afraid of the dark?
ha iše nṫaṁcantxʷ łu annoẋʷnẋʷ – Do you kiss your wife?

17.6. **ẋʷl̓** – for; because; so.
kʷes aẋllwísi ẋʷl̓ ululim – You are hustling around for money.
l še u ccil̓š ẋʷl̓ k̓ʷnšasq̓t – S/he went camping for so many days.
čnes q̓ʷiłmisti ẋʷl̓ čiqs npiyelsi – I am trying my hardest so I can be happy.
čnes yeṁmi ẋʷl̓ čn oost – I am frustrated because I am lost.
k̓ʷłpiṗ ẋʷl̓ čnes ẋʷeyti – I am unmotivated because I am lazy.

17.7. **t** – this particle has two uses, one is demonstrative and the other is prepositional. The demonstrative form is explained in this section. This section covers six uses of the demonstrative form. As a demonstrative **t** denotes secondary and specially marked information.

17.7.1. Agentive source. *The **t** denotes the source, who or what, that performs the action.*

a. **cuntm t sk̓ʷuys** – He was told by his mother.

*In this clause the **t** denotes who the "someone" is in the action of the transitive verb, **cuntm** – s/he/it was told by someone. In this clause it's some man/boy's mother. We need more information to determine who the man/boy is. **cuntm łu ttwit t sk̓ʷuys** – the boy was told by his mother.*

b. **qʷo es k̓ʷʔems <u>t slaqs</u>** – Mosquitoes are biting me.
*In this clause the **t** denotes what the "it" is in the action of the transitive verb, **qʷo es k̓ʷʔems** – It is biting me. In this clause the mosquitoes, denoted by the **t**, are doing the biting.*

c. **qʷo maw̓łxʷis <u>t cišps</u>** – The wolverine broke my tipi.
*In this clause the **t** denotes what the "it" is in the action of the transitive verb, **qʷo maw̓łxʷis** – It broke my lodge/tipi. In this clause the wolverine, denoted by the **t**, broke the lodge.*

d. **qʷo x̣ƛ̓ntem <u>t k̓ʷekʷt̓neʔ</u>** – The mouse chewed something of mine.
*In this clause the **t** denotes what the "it" is in the action of the transitive verb, **qʷo x̣ƛ̓ntem** – Something of mine was chewed by it.*

e. **qʷo pċntas <u>t x̣stéẏẏeʔ</u>** – The skunk sprayed me.
*In this clause the **t** denotes who the "it" is in the action of the transitive verb, **qʷo pċntas** – It sprayed me.*

f. **<u>t swe</u> u tl̓ntés łu qpełċeʔ** – Who broke the plate?
*In this interrogative clause the **t** indicates that the question is inquiring about who of the "s/he/it" performed the action transitive verb, **tl̓ntes łu qpełċeʔ** – S/he/it broke the plate.*

g. **es čʔemtupsms kʷtisi <u>t nox̣ʷnx̣ʷs</u>** – Big Blanket's wife is keeping him home.
*In this clause the t denotes who the "someone" is that is performing the action to **kʷtisi** (Big Blanket) in the transitive verb, **es čʔemtupsms** – S/he/it is keeping someone home.*

h. **pċntas sk̓ʷuys <u>t łox̣te</u>** – The baby evacuated diarrhea on his mother.

i. **<u>t sqltmixʷ</u> u sṗntes łu pus <u>t luk̓ʷ</u>** – The man hit the cat with a stick. *In this clause the **t** denotes the double agents in the action of: **sṗim** - stricking something with an object; by indicating who hit and with what was used to hit. The two agents are interchangeable; alternately the sentence could say: **<u>t luk̓ʷ</u> u sṗntes łu pus <u>t sqltmixʷ</u>**.*

17.7.2. Instrumentive agentive source. *The **t** denotes the object used in instrumentive transitive pronoun particles. The **t** points to what object was used in the action. The word order for this type of clause is: <u>Instrumentive Trans. Verb</u> + <u>**łu**(optional)</u> + <u>Object</u> + <u>**t**</u> + <u>Indirect Object (object used)</u>; see example sentence b. The word order for an interrogative clause is: <u>**t**</u> + <u>interrogative</u> + <u>**u**</u> + <u>Instrumentive Trans. Verb</u> + <u>**łu**(optional)</u> + <u>Object</u>; see example sentence e. See: **pronoun particles**.*

a. **čteʔmistmntm <u>t ṗiṗuyšn</u>** – It was hit by a car.
*In this clause the **t** denotes what was used, the "something," in performing the action in the transitive verb, **čteʔmistmntm** – It was hit by "something."*

b. **čteʔmistmntm łu x̣ʷax̣ʷaa <u>t čx̣ʷllq̓ʷa</u>** – The fox was hit by a train.
*In this clause the **t** denotes what was used, the "something," in performing the action in the transitive verb, **čteʔmistmntm** – S/he/it was hit by something.*

c. **čsixʷmis <u>t kapi</u>** – S/he spilled coffee on something.
*In this clause the **t** denotes what was used, the "something," in performing the action in the transitive verb, **čsixʷmis** – S/he spilled "something" on something/someone.*

d. **čsixʷmn smʔem <u>t sewłkʷ</u>** – I spilled water on the woman.
*In this clause the t denotes what was used, the "something," in performing the action in the transitive verb, **čsixʷmn smʔem** – I spilled "something" on the woman.*

e. **<u>t steṁ</u> u uẏéčstmntxʷ** – What did you use to finish it?
*In this interrogative clause the **t** indicates that the question is inquiring about what was used, the "it," in performing the transitive verb, **uẏéčstmntxʷ** – You used "it" to finish something.*

17.7.3. Benefactive agentive source. *The **t** marks the indirect goal while **łu** marks the direct goal in benefactive transitives. The **t** points to what object was used in the action. The word order for this type of clause is: <u>Benefactive Trans. Verb</u> + <u>**łu**(optional)</u> + <u>Primary Goal</u> + <u>**t**</u> + <u>Indirect Goal</u>.*

k̓ʷuľštn łu pumin t stipn – I made a drum for Stephen.

17.7.4. **t** – used to mark the possessor of intransitive possessives.
kʷ sk̓ʷuys t stipn – you are the mother of Stephen.
qʷo sxʷmimeyems t sťša – I am the teacher of Huckleberry.

17.7.5. **t** – used to mark the result of an intransitive predicative phrase.
čnes iłni t sqeltš – I am eating meat.
k̓ʷuľiš t esel – make two.
es k̓ʷʔaqsi t sqeľtč ci mla – That raven has meat in its mouth.

17.7.6. **t** – used to mark the result of an unexpressed predicative phrase.
t sšeňš – a rock.

17.8. **ihéʔ** – here; this in hand; this at hand.
iheʔ łu isnʔitštn – This is my bedroom.

17.9. **łiheʔ** – these here in hand.
ček̓ʷsew̓sn łiheʔ u sic x̣ʷq̓ew̓sn – I separated this and then I divided it up.

17.10. **łiʔe** – this; here; specifically this one.
steṁ łiʔe – What is this?

17.11. **ƛ̓iʔe** – this. *(more specific than **łiʔe**. An answer to a question as if saying "Well this is the one.")*

17.12. **šeẏ** – that in general; there, confirming/concurring; yes, concurring. *As a demonstrative this particle is used to indicate something in general away from the speaker but within sight.*

17.13. **łišeʔ** – that specifically. *This particle is used when indicating something specific away from the speaker but within sight.*
steṁ łišeʔ – What is that (very one)?
kʷuskʷst łišeʔ – That is ugly.
ƛ̓ṁ swe łišeʔ – Who was that?

17.14. **łiciʔ** – that very one. *This particle is used when indicating a specific object at a distance.*
łiciʔ łu incitxʷ – My house is that very one over there.
steṁ łiciʔ č nisq̓ʷot – What is that on the other side of the river?
swe łiciʔ l asčsax̣m u emut – Who is that sitting next to you?
swe tʔepstéṁ łiciʔ – Who owns that?

17.15. **łiłuʔ** – that one in general.

18. Prepositional

18.1. **l** – locative particle indicating in, on, with, or at.
l citxʷ u es k̓ʷľsncut – S/he cooks in the house.
l snčłelił ntn u es ťuk̓ʷ – It is placed on the table.
čnes memscuti l innqʷq̓ʷosminčnšn – I am playing with my dog.
k̓ʷłčlxʷmncut l es šiť – S/he/it went behind the tree.
nťqétkʷnt ťiš l ankapi – Put your bitterroot in water.
tmilq̓ʷ čʔemtew̓s l es šiť łu łlqʷó – Little Prairie always sits in that tree.
k̓ʷłtiyéš l p̓ip̓uy̓šn łu kʷtisi – Big Blanket crawled under the car.
čłpiłmskʷ l asp̓ečn – Spread it out on your canvas.
ṅe l sčace m čn k̓ʷis šlepm t maniłp x̣ʷľ incitxʷ – Sunday I will go and chop down balsam for my house.
l es milk̓ʷ u čťpťpyew̓t łu qʷqʷc̓w̓é – Chipmunks were standing all over.

ha kʷ nx̣el łu i l čiṁ – Are you afraid of the dark?
čn nʔułxʷ l sntumístn – I went into the store.

18.2. **č** – directional movement particle indicating spatial reference.
čn eł xʷuy č nłq̓a – I went back to Arlee.
čiqs xʷuyi č snłʔo – I am going to the bathroom.
siyent č héʔenm – Count to eight.
čn ntax̣ʷlúsm č nx̣alptin – I faced toward the east.
x̣ʷa ṅem čn xʷuy č esyapqini – Maybe I will go to the powwow.
xʷťip č es mq̓ʷmóq̓ʷ – S/he ran to the mountains.
čiqs xʷuyi č es q̓mq̓mi – I am going to go to a meeting.
eł q̓ʷełtmn č qeʔ sq̓imu – I carried it back to our tipi.
č čeṅ u kʷes qʷiṁṁi – Where are you in a hurry to?

18.3. **tł̓** – particle indicating a source, cause or point of origin.
čn cťipmncut tł̓ es šiť – I came down from the tree.
čn ťiip tł̓ nwist – I fell from up high.
čn łx̣ʷṗim tł̓ incitxʷ – I ran out of/*(from)* my house.
čnes wekʷisti tł̓ inʔilmixʷm – I am hiding from my boss.
tł̓ ispúʔus kʷ isx̣mnčeẇs kʷ innox̣ʷnx̣ʷ – From my heart you are my love, you are my wife.
tł̓ člxʷtin u es ctax̣ʷlus – S/he/it is heading this way from the west.
ci tł̓ čqe iscq̓q̓ṁe – From upstream I caught fish.
kʷeṁt tł̓ šeẏ cxʷuy łu sqélixʷ u es ťixʷlm – Then from there things came to be changed/got different for the people.
č lkʷut tł̓ citxʷs – S/he/it is far away from her/his/its house.
tł̓ ciʔ qʷestm – It got deeper. *In this clause **tł̓** with **ci** makes the phase comparative which denotes a degree by which something has a quality greater with regular predicates or lesser in diminutive predicates. In this clause **qʷestm** means "it got deep" and **tł̓ ciʔ** means from that. Together it literally says "from that it got deep," translated it means "it got deeper."*
tł̓ ciʔ išut – It got lower.
čn šƛ̓paqs u čn nčtxʷsels tł̓ ciʔ u čnes npiyélsi – I won and I added to my happy feelings.
tł̓ čeṅ u es cxʷuyi ye uł snéčłceʔ – Where have all these cow elk come from?
tł̓ čen u ċwétntxʷ asicm – Where did you get your blanket from?

18.4. **k̓ʷis** – particle indicating spatial movement. *This particle directly precedes the verb it is modifying before all other modifying particles such as **eł**, **c**, and pronoun particles.*
čiqs k̓ʷis ċuʔċawlš – I am going to go bathing.
čiqs k̓ʷis čsṗalqʷi č inʔilmixʷm – I am going to go call my boss.
qeʔqs k̓ʷis ccil̓ši – We are going to go and camp.
čiqs k̓ʷis iłni – I am going to go eat.
xʷu qeʔqs k̓ʷis tixʷi t sčiłt – Let's go get some white clay.
i čmi u stipn u k̓ʷis swenš – Alone, Stephen went to dance.
ṅem p eł k̓ʷis x̣ect – You guys will go back to dig.
k̓ʷis šíʔiscutiš – Go be first. *cmd.*
k̓ʷis itš – Go and sleep. *cmd.*
ha iše kʷ k̓ʷis čawm – Do you go and pray?
ha kʷ ṅé u čn k̓ʷis mémscut – May I go play?

18.5. **t** – this particle has five different meanings *(see demonstrative)*. As a prepositional particle it references a past point in time.
tspisċé – yesterday.
t sčluxʷ – the past evening.

t sq̓sip – long time ago.
t sq̓sip u es wičtmncn – I have not seen you for a long time.
t sl̓ʔe – recently; not too long ago.
t spistem̓ u k̓ʷul̓ntxʷ t slʔe – When did you do it? Recently.
ci t snk̓ʷasq̓t – day before yesterday.
ci t sʔaslasq̓t – two days ago.

18.6. **eɫ** – in addition; back as a preposition
čn eɫ itš – I went back to sleep.
čn eɫ es itši – I am going back to sleep.
i eɫ es kʷupm – I am pushing s.o. again.
čn eɫ xʷuy č̓ nɫq̓a – I went back to Arlee.
eɫ cʔukʷn – I brought it back here.
n̓e eɫ cwis íʔim̓š tl̓ čɫčéwm m qeʔ wenš – When they finish moving back here from the plains, we'll war dance.

18.7. **č...** – affixed to; upon.
čxʷstičn̓ – walk on a ridge.
čq̓isšis – S/he built camp on a large rock.
i čq̓áyalqʷ – The cylindrical object is marked.
čx̣ƛ̓alqʷ – chew on wood.
čx̣ʷq̓ʷx̣ʷaq̓ʷm – grind/file on the side of something.
čt̓ás – thin; skinny; lean; emaciated; hard on the surface.
čp̓nusm – lay long objects in a fire.
čulpalqʷ – The wood burned on the outside.
čn̓im – grasp on to something.

18.8. **...wilš** – suffix indicating developmental progression.
es kʷtntwilši – S/he/it is getting big.
es yoyoʔtwilši – S/he/it is getting strong.
es lemtwil̓ši – S/he/it is getting happy.
es px̣px̣twilši – S/he is getting smart.
es x̣stwilši – S/he/it is getting better.

18.9. **...ilš** – suffix indicating autonoumous movement/progression.
winmtstilš – S/he/it became beautiful.
es čstilši – S/he/it is getting worse.
es px̣ʷtilši – S/he/it is growing up; getting to be an adult.

18.10. **...m̓nuxʷ** – suffix indicating progression.
es ċʔalm̓nuxʷi – S/he is getting sick.
es aymtm̓nuxʷi – S/he is getting angry.
es qpcm̓nuxʷisti, *es qpcm̓nuxʷi* – It is again the time of spring.
es anɫqm̓nuxʷisti, *es anɫqm̓nuxʷi* – It is again the time of summer.
es č̓ʔey̓m̓nuxʷisti, *es č̓ʔey̓m̓nuxʷi* – It is again the time of fall.
es istčm̓nuxʷisti, *es istčm̓nuxʷi* – It is again the time of winter.
put u qeʔ tʔe ɫu ax̣lm̓nuxʷist – Again we're going through this time.

18.11. **n...** – locative prefix indicating inside.
nišut – down inside; deep inside.
ništeɫċéʔ – inside a body/hollow object.
nɫupax̣nm – put the arm inside.
npilš – go inside, enter. *pl.*

nʔułxʷ – go inside; enter. *sl.*
nṫk̓ʷum – put something inside.
nsixʷxʷ – It got poured inside by accident.
nsixʷmis – S/he/it poured s.t. inside it.

18.12. **c…** – directional prefix indicating in the direction of the speaker.
cxʷuy – go in the direction of the speaker; come.
cʔocqéʔ łu mali – Mary came out.
eł ck̓ʷuliš – Come back here to do something.
ci tl̓ʔe cʔoccqéʔi – From right there they came out.
eł cxʷuy še l sčili – S/he/it came back to Dixon.
ƛ̓e ep sqélixʷ u cnpilš łu uł selíš – There were already people here when the Salish came in.
t čmu sqélixʷ u qʷo ck̓ʷis wíʔičis – Four people came to see me.
ṅe suswéʔe ntéls m še ck̓ʷis laq̇i – Whoever wants to, will come sweat.
i ččnaqsm u ck̓ʷłči – All alone s/he arrived here.
ṅe eł cłʔaq̇ʷ m qeʔ xʷuy – When s/he/it appears again we'll go.

18.13. **čł…** – prefix indicating the fetching of, when used with noun-like words.
es čłsšeṅši – S/he is going after rocks.
es čłsnqʷl̓pú – S/he is going after bread.
čłʔululim – go after money.
čłsnqʷl̓pú – go after bread.
čłłuk̓ʷ – go after wood.

18.14. **čł…** – prefix indicating the surface when used with action words.
čłx̣ʷlx̣ʷlq̇ʷi – play pool/billiards.
čłneẁtkʷ – waves on water.
čłtʔem – bounce something. *prefix: **čł…** – on the surface; rt.: **teʔ** – hit/bump into.*

18.15. **k̓ʷł…** – prefix indicating under.
k̓ʷłʔac̓x̣mist – look behind/under.
k̓ʷłʔac̓x̣is – S/he looked under s.t.
k̓ʷłpuxʷm – blow from underneath, blew from underneath.
k̓ʷłq̇ʷoim – S/he got out of the wind.
k̓ʷłtmip – rocks caved in/fell from under.
k̓ʷłtwiṅtm – fall short of something; deficient in something; unable to attain something.
k̓ʷłsixʷ – drain something.
k̓ʷłʔeṗ – eliminate; wipe away something.
k̓ʷłulip – catch fire from underneath.
k̓ʷłṫk̓ʷum – put something underneath.

18.16. **k̓ʷłn…ep** – circumfix indicating an opening.
k̓ʷłnčmep – door.

19. Imperative suffixes

19.1. intransitive

19.1.1. **…š** – suffix changing an action into a singular imperative. This creates a command for an individual to perform

Table d.14 – Intransitive Imperatives

	Imperative Mood	
Singular	**ac̓x̣iš**	Look.
Singular	**ocqeʔš**	Go out.
Singular	**sunumtš**	Listen.
Singular	**iłniš**	Eat.
Plural	**ac̓x̣wi**	You all look.
Plural	**occqeʔwi**	You all go out.
Plural	**sunumtwi**	You all listen.
Plural	**elilnwi**	You all eat.
	Imperative Mood Continuate	
Singular	**es ac̓x̣iš**	Keep looking.
Singular	**es ocqeʔš**	Keep going out.
Singular	**es sunumtš**	Keep listening.
Singular	**es iłniš**	Keep eating.
Plural	**es ac̓x̣wi**	You all keep looking.
Plural	**es occqeʔwi**	You all keep going out.
Plural	**es sunumtwi**	You all keep listening.
Plural	**es elilnwi**	You all keep eating.

some action.

k̓ʷul̓iš – Work.

ƛ̓lipš – Stop.

19.1.2. **... wi** – suffix changing an action into a plural imperative. This creates a command for a group of two or more to perform some action.

k̓ʷul̓wi – All of you work.

ƛ̓lipwi – All of you stop.

19.2. **intransitive continuate**

19.2.1. **es ...š** – imperfect aspect particle **es** and the singular imperative suffix create a continuative imperative. This creates a command to an individual to continue performing some action.

es k̓ʷul̓iš – Continue working; keep working.

es q̓ey̓iš – Continue writing; keep writing.

19.2.2. **es ... wi** – imperfect aspect particle **es** and the plural imperative suffix create a continuative imperative. This creates a command to a group of two or more to continue performing some action.

es k̓ʷul̓wi – All of you continue working.

es q̓ey̓wi – All of you continue writing.

19.3. **transitive**

19.3.1. **...nt** – suffix changing an action to a singular transitive imperative. This creates a command for an individual to perform some action to something or someone.

sustnt – Drink it.

awnt – Pronounce/say it.

19.3.2. **... nti** – suffix changing an action to a plural transitive imperative. This creates a command to a group of two or more to perform some action to something or someone.

ac̓x̣nti – All of you look at it.

sp̓inti – All of you hit it.

19.4. **transitive inflection for causative stems**

19.4.1. **... skʷ** – suffix changing an action to a singular transitive imperative. This creates a command to an individual to cause some action to happen to something or someone.

hoyskʷ – Leave it alone.

liwmskʷ – Ring the bell.

19.4.2. **... skʷi** – suffix changing an action to a plural transitive imperative. This creates a command to a group of two or more to cause some action to happen to something or someone.

k̓ʷul̓skʷi – All of you do it.

ẏamiskʷi – All of you gather the things up.

19.5. **substitutive transitive**. To do something in place of someone else.

19.5.1. **... łt –** suffix changing an action to a singular substitutive imperative. This creates a command to an individual to perform an action in substitution for someone else.

ċwetłt – Go get it for him/her.
qʷo ckʷełt ink̓ʷłnč̓exʷk̓ʷé – Fetch my keys for me.
tl̓qełt – Kick it to somebody. *(in substitute for someone)*

19.5.2. **... łti –** suffix changing an action into a plural substitutive imperative. This creates a command for a group of two or more to perform an action in substitution for someone else.

ċwetłti – All of you go get it for him/her.
kʷełti – All of you grab it for him/her.
tl̓qełti – All of you kick it for him/her.

Table d.15 – Transitive Imperatives

Imperative Mood			
Singular	2-1	**qʷo aċx̣nt**	You look at me.
	2-3	**aċx̣nt**	You look at him/her.
	2-4	**qe aċx̣łlt**	You look at us.
	2-6	**aˀaċx̣nt**	You look at them.
Plural	2-1	**qʷo aċx̣nti**	You all look at me.
	2-3	**aċx̣nti**	You all look at him/her.
	2-4	**qe aċx̣łlt**	You all look at us.
	2-6	**aˀaċx̣nti**	You all look at them.
Imperative Mood Continuate			
Singular	2-1	**qʷo es aċx̣skʷ**	You remain looking at me.
	2-3	**es aċx̣skʷ**	You remain looking at him/her.
	2-4	**qe es aċx̣łlt**	You remain looking at us.
	2-6	**es aˀaċx̣skʷ**	You remain looking at them.
Plural	2-1	**qʷo es aċx̣skʷi**	You all remain looking at me.
	2-3	**es aċx̣skʷi**	You all remain looking at him/her.
	2-4	**qe es aċx̣łlt**	You all remain looking at us.
	2-6	**es aˀaċx̣skʷi**	You all remain looking at them.

19.6. **benefactive transitive**. To do something for the benefit of someone else.

19.6.1. **... šit –** suffix changing an action to a singular benefactive imperative. This creates a command to an individual to perform an action for the benefit of someone who otherwise isn't able to perform the action.

qʷo x̣ʷčšit – Argue for me.
čłpšit – Hunt for him/her.
q̇x̣šits – Make a path for him/her.
qʷo ckʷšit – Pull it for me.
qʷo q̇eẏšit – Write a letter for me.

19.6.2. **... šiti –** suffix changing an action into a plural benefactive imperative. This creates a command for a group of two or more to perform an action for the benefit of someone who otherwise isn't able to perform the action.

qʷo x̣ʷčšiti – You all argue for me.
čłpšiti – You all hunt for him/her.
q̇x̣šiti – You all make a path for s.o.
qʷo ckʷšiti – You all pull it for me.
q̇eẏšiti – You all write for him/her.

20. Auxiliary particles

20.1. **ax̣i –** like
20.2. **čmi –** only
20.3. **x̣ił ṅe u –** almost
20.4. **puti –** still

e. Pronominals

1. Pronominal full words

1.1. **qʷoyʔe** – me
t qʷoyʔe u nṫpusn łu pataq – I boiled the potatoes.
nṫqʷṫqʷečstniš eċx̣i t qʷoyʔe – Clap like me.
qʷoyʔe łu čiqs šʔiti – I will go first.

1.2. **anwi** – you
ha eł t anwi – Are you next?
es nte qs memscuti l anwi – S/he wants to play with you.
ha t anwi u k̓ʷuĺntxʷ łu snlaq̇ist – Did you fix the sweat lodge?

1.3. **cniłċ**, *cni* – him/her/it
t cniłċ u ċax̣is łu lkʷošó – S/he fried the bacon.
ṅem t cniłċ m qeʔ k̓ʷłqixʷłs – S/he will protect us.
kʷ nte sk̓ʷnšpentč łu cniłċ – How old do you think s/he is?

1.4. **qeʔ nple** – us
1.5. **nple** – you all
1.6. **cníʔiłc** – them

2. Pronominal particles

2.1. **uł** – collected, refers to two or more referents as a group or as members of a certain category. *This particle uses pronoun particles to modify the referent group, such as* ***qeʔ*** *– us and* ***p*** *– you all. It could be interpreted also as the "gang of." In the first example,* ***uł snč̓lé****, could be in reference to the ones that are in the company of coyote or coyote and his gang.*
mtmi uł snč̓lé – Those coyotes are no-good!
qeʔ uł qʷṅqʷiṅt – We are pitiful. *We are the ones in the category of being pitiful.*
uł pspast łu sccmeĺt – Those children are full of energy.
pesyaʔ u p uł taq̇n smx̣ʷop – All of you are 6 years old.
uł inʔililmixʷm łu inṗiṗx̣ʷot uł pxpáx̣t – My elders are my leaders; they are wise.
ƛ̓e ep sqélixʷ u cnpilš łu uł selíš – There were already people here when the Salish came in.
x̣ił uł swe łu es q̇ʷiiq̇ʷo – Who are they, those racing?

2.2. **qʷo** – me; us as a unit; us together. *Generally* ***qʷo*** *is used to reference the individual self but when used to reference a group it signifies that the group is closely bonded as if it were one.*
qʷo tkʷent – Accept me.
qʷo čšnint – Come with me.
ha kʷ ṅe u qʷo xʷiyusnt č nisq̇ʷot – Would you take me across the water?
qʷo x̣éʔentem – I was reprimanded.
qʷo qs susti – We are going to drink. *lit. as a unit we are going to drink.*
i qʷo nk̓ʷuʔ – We are one; I am one.

3. Reflexive suffixes

– *reflexive suffixes create words that receive action pertaining to the self. A comprehensive understanding of these suffixes wasn't known at the time this book was published. This list includes suggested interpretations of meaning. It is presented to stimulate further study and exploration for the language learner.*

3.1. **...cut** – action to the self.
čn emcut – I fed myself.
es nʔawqncuti – S/he is calling upon one's self.

3.2. **...ncut** – action by one's self.
čłʔemncut – get one's self close/next to/against something.
k̓ʷĺsncut – S/he cooked. **čn k̓ʷĺsncut, kʷ k̓ʷĺsncut**

qʷéwncut – S/he got one's self intoxicated. **čn qʷéwncut, kʷ qʷéwncut**
čem̓ncut – detest one's self.
čšt̓ncutš x̣ine kʷ čłusntm – Take care of yourself, you might get poked in the eye. **awtpncut** – allow yourself to follow, to give into.
ep̓ncut – wipe by one's self

3.3. **...scut** – action to something for one's benefit.
čn emscut – I give myself as food.
es xʷl̓l̓mscutisti – S/he/it is making one's self come alive.
áymscut – S/he/it got angry at one's self.
łaq̓ʷmscut – S/he made one's self appear.
es winmtscuti – S/he/it is making one's self beautiful.
es ax̣tčmscuti – S/he is busy with his/her self.
es yal̓mnscuti – It is coiling itself up *(a caterpillar making a cocoon).*
čnčnmscut – do something dangerous; put one's self in danger.
mippscut – S/he decided for one's self.
ček̓ʷmscut – separate from one's partner/spouse.

3.4. **...mncut** – something to one's self.
čnes x̣cmncuti – I am getting ready.
čn ewtusmncut – I am my own foe.
šlčmncut – S/he/it turned around. **čn šlčmncut, kʷ šlčmncut**
p̓l̓čmncut – turn one's self over/back.
k̓ʷłčlxʷmncut, *k̓ʷłčlxʷmncu* – make one's self go out of sight.

3.5. **...ist** – action of the self.
xʷist – walk.
ep̓ist – wipe one's self.
y̓ekʷmist – being miserly.
iwmist – S/he shook one's self.
čmšqnmist – S/he gave up.

3.6. **...mist** – action to the self.
ep̓mist – wipe something belonging to one's self.
es xʷl̓l̓misti – S/he/it is coming alive *(born, hatched).*
nk̓ʷnšmist – appoint; make a personal choice.
nsucnmist – propose marriage to someone; ask permission to marry.
kʷtnlsmist – think highly of one's self; think big of one's self; self conceited.
čnes xʷeƛ̓misti – I am passing time; relaxing; doing what I want.

4. **Reciprocal suffix**

4.1. **...nwexʷ** – do to each other.
es čšnwexʷi – They're accompanying each other.
sxʷnwexʷ, *sxʷnwe* – get more acquainted with each other.
łałaq̓ʷcnwexʷ – They showed up with each other.
es čmumusax̣nwexʷi – They are twisting each other's arms.
es čcoqnwexʷi – They are beating each other up.
čteʔmistmnwexʷ – They bumped/ran into each other.

4.2. **...stwexʷ** – cause each other.
ml̓k̓ʷstwexʷ, *ml̓k̓ʷstwe* – all over each other.
sl̓l̓stwexʷ, *sl̓l̓stwe* – They are flirting with each other, acting goofy with each other.

lmtstwexʷ – make each other glad.
es npiyélstwexʷi – They are making each other happy.
es mipstwexʷi – They are learning from each other.
es šƛ̓pstwexʷi – They are defeating each other.

4.3. **...mnwexʷ –** the thing we are to each other.
qeʔes ewtusmnwexʷi – We are each other's foe.
tlsmnwexʷ – They acknowledged each other.
es šiẏelsmnwexʷi – They are favoring each other.
xʷuʔmnwexʷ – They got comfortable with each other.
es tmlsmnwexʷi – They despise each other.

4.4. **...štwexʷ –** help one another.
niʔek̇ʷštwexʷ – help one another cross the water.
es ṁeẏštwexʷi – They're showing each other.
čáwštwexʷ – pray for each other.
qeʔqs ṁeẏštwexʷi – The two of us are telling each other stories.
es ṁiṁiʔštwexʷi – They're telling each other stories.

f. Nominals

Nominals are words that function as nouns. In Salish full words can be changed to noun-like words, nominals, by adding an affix. This section wasn't fully developed at the time of publication.

1. **s –** nominal prefix
2. **sn –** locative nominal prefix
3. **sc –** nominal prefix product
4. **sxʷ –** agentive nominal prefix; one tasked to do.
5. **...cutn –** agentive nominal suffix; the one that does something for someone/something.
6. **...emn –** agentive nominal suffix; one inclined to do something.
7. **...łmuł –** agentive nominal suffix; one that habitually does something.
   q̓ʷṁq̓ʷamuł – one that habitually moves around.
   x̣ʷlx̣ʷalmuł – one that habitually shivers.
   wnwnšmuł – one that habitually dances.
   čnčnłmuł – one that is habitually fearful.
   susułmuł – one that habitually asks questions.

g. Ownership

Ownership is the state of control of an object.

1. **epł –** have.
   epł pus – S/he has a cat. **čn epł pus, kʷ epł pus**
   epł púʔus – They have a cat. **qeʔ epł pus, p epł pus**
   The ł is dropped when it precedes words beginning with s; see example below:
   ep sičm – S/he has a blanket. **čn ep sičm, kʷ ep sičm**
   ep síʔičm – They have a blanket. **qeʔ ep sičm, p ep sičm**

h. Possession

The table on the next page shows possession of the first, second and third person plural and singular. This table is provided to illustrate all the possible ways possession can be used in all tenses.

Table h.1 - Possession: parent

	past		present		future	
Singular	**ƛ̓m px̣ots**	S/he was his/her parent.	**px̣ots**	S/he is his/her parent.	**qł px̣ots**	S/he is going to be his/her parent.
	ƛ̓m inpx̣ot	S/he was my parent.	**inpx̣ot**	S/he is my parent.	**inqł px̣ot**	S/he is going to be my parent.
	ƛ̓m anpx̣ot	S/he was your parent.	**anpx̣ot**	S/he is your parent.	**anqł px̣ot**	S/he is going to be your parent.
	ƛ̓m px̣óʔots	S/he was their parent.	**px̣óʔots**	S/he is their parent.	**qł px̣óʔots**	S/he is going to be their parent.
	ƛ̓m qeʔ px̣ot	S/he was our parent.	**qeʔ px̣ot**	S/he is our parent.	**qeʔqł px̣ot**	S/he is going to be our parent.
	ƛ̓m px̣otmp	S/he was you alls parent.	**px̣otmp**	S/he is you alls parent.	**qł px̣otmp**	S/he is going to be you alls parent.
	ƛ̓m qʷo px̣ots	I was his/her parent.	**qʷo px̣ots**	I am his/her parent.	**qʷo qł px̣ots**	I am going to be his/her parent.
	ƛ̓m qʷo anpx̣ot	I was your parent.	**qʷo anpx̣ot**	I am your parent.	**qʷo anqł px̣ot**	I am going to be your parent.
	ƛ̓m qʷo px̣óʔots	I was their parent.	**qʷo px̣óʔots**	I am their parent.	**qʷo qł px̣óʔots**	I am going to be their parent.
	ƛ̓m qʷo px̣ot	I was you alls parent.	**qʷo px̣ot**	I am you alls parent.	**qʷo qł px̣ot**	I am going to be you alls parent.
	ƛ̓m kʷ px̣ots	You were his/her parent.	**kʷ px̣ots**	You are his/her parent.	**kʷ qł px̣ots**	You are going to be his/her parent.
	ƛ̓m kʷ inpx̣ot	You were my parent.	**kʷ inpx̣ot**	You are my parent.	**kʷ inqł px̣ot**	You are going to be my parent.
	ƛ̓m kʷ px̣óʔots	You were their parent.	**kʷ px̣óʔots**	You are their parent.	**kʷ qł px̣óʔots**	You are going to be their parent.
	ƛ̓m kʷ px̣ot	You were our parent.	**kʷ px̣ot**	You are our parent.	**kʷ qł px̣ot**	You are going to be our parent.
Plural	**ƛ̓m px̣óʔots**	They were his/her parents.	**px̣óʔots**	They are his/her parents.	**qł px̣óʔots**	They are going to be his/her parents.
	ƛ̓m inpx̣óʔot	They were my parents.	**inpx̣óʔot**	They are my parents.	**inqł px̣óʔot**	They are going to be my parents.
	ƛ̓m anpx̣óʔot	They were your parents.	**anpx̣óʔot**	They are your parents.	**anqł px̣óʔot**	They are going to be your parents.
	ƛ̓m px̣óʔoʔots	They were their parents.	**px̣óʔoʔots**	They are their parents.	**qł px̣óʔoʔots**	They are going to be their parents.
	ƛ̓m qeʔ px̣óʔot	They were our parents.	**qeʔ px̣óʔot**	They are our parents.	**qeʔqł px̣óʔot**	They are going to be our parents.
	ƛ̓m px̣óʔotmp	They were you alls parents.	**px̣óʔotmp**	They are you alls parents.	**qł px̣óʔotmp**	They are going to be you alls parents.
	ƛ̓m qeʔ px̣otłls	We were his/her parents.	**qeʔ px̣otłls**	We are his/her parents.	**qeʔqł px̣otłls**	We are going to be his/her parents.
	ƛ̓m qeʔ px̣otłlt	We were your parents.	**qeʔ px̣otłlt**	We are your parents.	**qeʔqł px̣otłlt**	We are going to be your parents.
	ƛ̓m qeʔ px̣óʔotłls	We were their parents.	**qeʔ px̣óʔotłls**	We are their parents.	**qeʔqł px̣óʔotłls**	We are going to be their parents.
	ƛ̓m qeʔ px̣óʔotłlt	We were you alls parents.	**qeʔ px̣óʔotłlt**	We are you alls parents.	**qeʔqł px̣óʔotłlt**	We are going to be you alls parents.
	ƛ̓m p px̣ots	You all were his/her parents.	**p px̣ots**	You all are his/her parents.	**p qł px̣ots**	You all are going to be his/her parents.
	ƛ̓m p inpx̣ot	You all were my parents.	**p inpx̣ot**	You all are my parents.	**p inqł px̣ot**	You all going to be my parents.
	ƛ̓m p px̣óʔots	You all were their parent.	**p px̣óʔots**	You all are their parents.	**p qł px̣óʔots**	You all going to be their parents.
	ƛ̓m p px̣ot	You all were our parents.	**p px̣ot**	You all are our parents.	**p qł px̣ot**	You all going to be our parents.
Plural Individuality	**ƛ̓m px̣px̣ots**	Each one was his/her parent.	**px̣px̣ots**	Each one is his/her parent.	**qł px̣px̣ots**	Each one is going to be his/her parent.
	ƛ̓m inpx̣px̣ot	Each one was my parent.	**inpx̣px̣ot**	Each one is my parent.	**inqł px̣px̣ot**	Each one is going to be my parent.
	ƛ̓m anpx̣px̣ot	Each one was your parent.	**anpx̣px̣ot**	Each one is your parent.	**anqł px̣px̣ot**	Each one is going to be your parent.
	ƛ̓m px̣px̣óʔots	Each one was their parent.	**px̣px̣óʔots**	Each one is their parent.	**qł px̣px̣óʔots**	Each one is going to be their parent.
	ƛ̓m qeʔ px̣px̣ot	Each one was our parent.	**qeʔ px̣px̣ot**	Each one is our parent.	**qeʔqł px̣px̣ot**	Each one is going to be our parent.
	ƛ̓m px̣px̣otmp	Each one was you alls parent.	**px̣px̣otmp**	Each one is you alls parent.	**qł px̣px̣otmp**	Each one is going to be you alls parent.

i. Reduplication

Reduplication is a morphological process. It is the process of reproducing certain letters in a word to change its meaning, among others to pluralize, to show a diminutive state, or to show developmental progress. The rules governing this process are provided below. The abbreviations used are: **c_1** for consonant one, **v** for vowel, **c_2** for consonant two, **$\dot{c}_1$** for stressed consonant one, **$\dot{c}_2$** for stressed consonant two. The first set of consonant, vowel, consonant abbreviations show the original word state. The second set of abbreviations shows the reduplicated word state based on the original.

1. **Plural reduplication** is the process of changing a word to show a plural state.
   1.1. The following pattern is the most common form of reduplication. This pattern occurs on roots that are stressed. It reduplicates the consonates around the stressed vowel in the pattern illustrated in the following: root – **c_1•v•c_2** changes to **c_1•c_2•c_1•v•c_2** in the plural form.
   The word, **qʷin** – *green*, changes to, **qʷnqʷin** – *greens*.
   The word, **pus** – *cat*, changes to, **pspus** – *cats*.

   1.2. This pattern occurs on suffixed stressed words. These are words that are formed with a root and a suffix where the suffix retains the stress. The root in the form of **c_1•c_2** becomes **c_1•c_2•c_1•c_2**
   The word, **tx̣ʷeẇs** – *divide something in two; halve something*, is created from the root word **tox̣ʷ** – *straight*, and the suffix **eẇs** – *in between, middle*. When reduplicated it changes to, **tx̣ʷtx̣ʷeẇs** – *divide repeatedly*.

   1.3. In words that contain an initial ***i*** or ***u*** in the root the reduplication pattern is as follows: **v•c_1** becomes **v•c_1•v•c_1**.
   The word, **ilmixʷm** – *chief*, becomes, **ililmixʷm** – *chiefs*.
   The word, **upn** – *ten*, becomes, **upupn** – *tens*.

   1.4. In words that contain a glottal stop in the root the reduplication pattern is as follows: with **c_1•v•ʔ** as the root becomes **c_1•v•ʔ•c_1•v•ʔ** in the reduplication form.
   čhéʔenm – *eight people*, becomes, **čheʔhéʔenm** – *groups of eight people*.

   1.5. In words that contain a glottalized *l* or *m* before a vowel in the root word the reduplication pattern is as follows: **$\dot{c}_1$•v•** as the root becomes **$\dot{c}_1$• $\dot{c}_1$•v•** in the reduplication form.
   st̓ṁa – *cow*, becomes, **st̓ṁṁa** – *cows*.
   sl̓ax̣t – *friend*, becomes, **sl̓l̓ax̣t** – *friends*.

   1.6. Pronominal, *they*, reduplication happens on the stressed vowel of a word as the following shows: **c_1•v•c_2** becomes **c_1•v•ʔ•v•c_2** with the first vowel being stressed.
   šlntes – *S/he chopped it*, becomes, **šlntéʔes** – *They chopped it.*
   es kʷnems – *S/he/it is taking s.t./s.o.*, becomes, **es kʷnéʔems** – *They are taking s.t./s.o.*
   es áymti – *S/he/it is angry*, becomes, **es áʔaymti** – *They are angry.*

2. **Distributive plural reduplication**
   2.1. **čn qʷaqʷemncut** – I practiced *(implying repetition)*.

   2.2. **es šlšlepi** – S/he is chopping off (branches).

3. **Infix i plural reduplication**.
   3.1. **ttwit** – boy; **titwit** – boys

   3.2. **ččyeʔ** – mother's mother; **čičyeʔ** – daughter's children.

4. **Diminutive reduplication** is the process of changing a word to show a diminished or smaller state.

4.1. In root stressed words a **ł** – little, is added to the front of the word with the pattern: **c₁•v•c₂** changes to **ł•c₁•v•c₁•c₂**.
ṅičmn – cross cut tool, *i.e., saw, large knife.* **łṅiṅčmn** – little knife; knife.
es łxʷixʷsti – S/he/it is walking a little *(small steps)*.

4.2. Resonants are commonly glottalized in diminutive forms in the pattern: **c₁•v•c₂** changes to **ł•ċ₁•v•ċ₁•c₂**.
luk̓ʷ– wood, becomes **łl̓ul̓k̓ʷ** – little wood/stick.

čaw – pray, becomes **łčačw** – little prayer. a4h_5DevelopmentalRedup

4.3. In suffixed stressed words the following pattern is used: **c₁•c₂** changes to **ł•c₁•c₁•c₂**.
x̣ƛ̓cin become **łx̣x̣ƛ̓cin** – graze/eat a little. *In this case, **x̣ƛ̓** – chew, is the root and, ...**cin** – action of the mouth, is the stressed suffix.*
t̓ipeys – rained becomes **łt̓t̓ipeys** – rained a little. *In this case, **t̓iip** – fall, is the root and, ...**eys** – rain, is the stressed suffix.*

5. **Developmental reduplication** is the process of changing a word to show a state of developmental progression.

5.1. Showing development: **c₁•v•c₂** becomes **c₁•v•c₂•c₂**
nič – cut becomes **ničč** – it got cut.

k̓ʷl̓ličč – It got covered over.
čnill̓ – It got poisoned; got infected.
háw̓w̓ – S/he/it got loosened/relaxed.
łiqq – It got raggy.
x̣ʷell – S/he/it got abandoned.
sixʷxʷ – It got spilled by accident.

5.2. In a stress shifting root the form is: **c₁•v•c₂** becomes **c₁•c₂•v•c₂**
xʷuk̓ʷ – clean becomes **xʷk̓ʷuk̓ʷ** – it got clean.

łx̣ʷox̣ʷ – It got punctured. From: **łox̣ʷ** – puncture something.
tlil – It got broke/shattered. From: **til̓** – shatter/break.
p̓t̓at̓ – It got splattered. From: **p̓at̓** – soft and squishy.

5.3. To show development to a particular state the following is used: **c₁ • v • c₂** becomes **c₁ • v • v • c₂**.
ƛ̓aq̓ – hot becomes **ƛ̓aáq̓** – it got hot.

p̓aaq̓ – It got bright.
p̓éeč – S/he/it got heated.
t̓iim – It got damp.
p̓ʔeeʔ – It got dented.
p̓eexʷ – It got bright/red-hot.
naas – S/he/it got wet.

6. **Nominal Adjective reduplication** is the process of changing a root word to make a nominal adjective state. The following are used depending on the root form: for **cvc** roots use: **c₁ • v • c₂** becomes **c₁ • v • c₂ • c₁ • c₂ • t** ; for **cvv** roots use: **c₁ • v₁ • v₂** becomes **c₁ • v • c₁ • v₁ • v₂ • t**.

6.1. **qʷamqʷmt** – excellent; beautiful; pleasing. *From **qʷam**, pleasure, reduplicated to form the meaning: the thing, action or person is one which causes pleasure.*

6.2. **pilplt** – one that can drift; unstable. *From **pil**, drift/float, reduplicated to form the meaning: the thing, action or person is one which drift/float.*

6.3. **pipiit** – joyful. *From **pii**, rejoice, reduplicated to form the meaning: the thing, action or person is one which causes joy.*
6.4. **šálšlt** – dull; uninteresting; causing boredom.

7. **Affective reduplication** is the process of creating terms of endearment or pet names such as "cutie" in English. The following process is the basic pattern for roots: **c_1 • v • c** or **c_1 • c** or **c_1 • v** becomes **c_1 • e • c_1 • v • c • eʔ**. Other morphological rules apply such as if the root word contains a resonant.
   7.1. **t̓et̓íšeʔ** – sweetie, from **t̓iš** – sweet.
   7.2. **sesíkʷeʔ** – little whistler, from **sikʷ** – whistle.
   7.3. **seséw̓eʔ** – little questioner, from **sew** – ask.
   7.4. **kʷekʷíl̓eʔ** – little red one, from **kʷil** – red.
   7.5. **pepíy̓eʔ** – happy one, from **pii** – happy.
   7.6. **x̣ʷex̣ʷc̓eʔ** – little arguer, from **x̣ʷc̓** – argue.
   7.7. **q̓ʷaq̓ʷáy̓eʔ** – blackie, from **q̓ʷay̓** – black.

A *verb* (derived from Latin **verbum,** *word*) is *the* word of a sentence: it asserts something about the subject of the sentence. *Tense* (Latin **tempus,** *time*) indicates the time of the verb as present, past, future, etc. *Voice* (**vocis, vox,** *voice*) is the way of speaking which shows whether the subject performs the action of the verb (active voice) or receives the action of the verb (passive voice). *Mood,* or *mode* (**modus,** *manner*), is the manner of expressing the action of the verb as a fact (indicative mood), a command (imperative mood), etc. To conjugate (**coniugare,** *to join together*) a verb is to give together the inflected forms of the verb according to the requirements of person, number, tense, mood, and voice.

Section 5:

Root Words & Affixes

Root Words*

aax̣ – *has lines,* a descriptive root word indicating parallel or uniform lines as they would appear naturally in the environment or in the process of making artifacts by people. It does not describe the deliberate creation of lines by marking or drawing.

aċx̣łq̇eẏim – *read,* a compound stem word formed from, **aċx̣**, to look, and, **q̇eẏ**, to make markings. Its literal meaning is to look at markings.

ac – *bind, tie, trap,* an action root word indicating the action of tying or restraining. The restraining is a description of catching something such as in a trap or to get a rope around something to prevent further escape.

aċx̣ – *look,* an action root word indicating the action of looking or seeing.

ax̣ʷ – *scrape,* an action root word indicating the action of scraping something with the flat edge of some tool or instrument.

ax̣il – *do, act,* an action root word indicating the action of acting or doing in a similar way; copying the actions of something.

aw – *speak, pronounce,* an action root word indicating the action of deliberate production of speech; deliberate pronunciation of speech/words/sounds of words; speech that flows out slowly and deliberately.

awup – *drip,* an action root word indicating the action of a naturally occurring slow flow of liquid dripping and/or leaking. It is related to, **aw**, to pronounce, in that they both describe a slow flow of something.

ayeẇt – *several people sit,* an action root word indicating the action of two or more people being in a sitting position.

caq – *single object placed down,* a descriptive root word, describing the state of a hollow object set down.

caqʷ – *insert a cylindrical object,* a descriptive root word, describing the state of a cylindrical object inserted into or through an opening.

ccil̓š – *camp overnight,* an action root word, indicating the action of staying in a temporary location, not a permanent or extended stay/camp.

ckʷum – *pull,* an action root word, indicating the action of pulling something.

cpaq̇ – *sticky,* a descriptive stem word, describing something with an adhesive substance on it.

cqaẏe – *dry/smoke meat,* an action root word indicating the action of drying meat with smoke and heat.

cq̇minm – *throw,* an action stem word, indicating the action of propelling one thing away from another, usually the hand.

cup – *particle ridden, rough,* a descriptive root word describing paticles or objects that create an uneven surface or a particle ridden surface.

cuut – *one's mannerism,* a descriptive root word describing a way in which one acts; one's mannerism.

ċʔeš – *ashamed,* a condition root word indicating that someone/something is in a state of being ashamed.

ċaál – *ache,* a stative root word indicating that someone/something is in a state of pain.

ċalx̣ʷ – *poles lashed together,* a descriptive root word, describing poles lashed together.

ċan – *tight,* a descriptive root word, describing something firmly or closely fixed in place.

ċax̣ – *fry,* an action root word indicating the action of frying something. It is believed to originate from the sound grease makes while cooking.

ċax̣ʷċx̣ʷt – *ashes,* a nominal root word describing hot or cold powdery ashes .

ċeẇ – *wash,* an action root word indicating the action of washing something with water to make it clean.

ċik̓ʷ – *shiny,* a descriptive root word describing an object's surface with a bright or glossy finish, something that reflects light.

ċil – *upright protrusion,* a descriptive root word, describing a group of objects that are affixed in some manner and protruding upward or outward; generally in an upright position.

ċim – *constricted,* a descriptive root word describing a constricted opening or passage.

ċiṗ – *pinch,* an action root word describing the action of pinching something.

ċiq – *prickly,* a descriptive root word indicating the feel of something prickly or bristly; that is something with many sharp points.

ċlalqʷ – *stickgame,* a compound stem word indicating the playing of stickgame; from, **ċil**, upright protrusion, and the suffix, **alqʷ**, cylindrical object.

ċoʔq – *pull out,* an action root word describing the action of pulling something out of something or the removal of an infixed object.

ċoq̇ʷ – *point,* an action root word indicating the action of pointing with a long object usually the index finger.

ċox̣ʷ – *imparting of one's self,* an action word describing the action of imparting things from one's self, instruct from one's wisdom, knowledge, and/or experiences, from one's heart.

ċsip – *disappear,* an action root word indicating the action of something spontaneously disappearing.

ċslexʷ – *make bare/clean,* an action root word indicating the action of making something bare/clean of debris.

ċuk̓ʷ – *erect,* a descriptive root word indicating some thing that is stiff, rigid, and erect.

čċalels – *sick,* a condition root word indicating that someone/something is in a state of being sick/ill.

čċox̣ʷ – *willful action of one's self,* an action word describing the action of imparting things from one's self, instruct from one's wisdom, knowledge, and/or experiences, from one's heart.

čeʔl̓ – *alert,* a stative root word, describing the state of being alert. For example, as dogs are alert to the approach of something unknown.

čep – *soft,* a descriptive root word, describing something soft and spongy.

čic – *happen upon,* an action root word indicating the action of arriving/meeting some person, point or place by chance.

čić – *long object laid down,* a stative root word, describing a cylindrical object in the state of laying down.

čilil – *branch off,* a compound stem word describing the branching of some object; from **ilim** to penetrate as to break some kind of barrier into something with a object generally pointed.

čłq̇eẏmin – *go after paper,* a compound stem word indicating the action of going after paper or to go in search of paper.

čłʔe – *against,* a prepositional root word describing the state of being right up against something physically, mentally or perceived. It does not mean that there is an obstruction but merely that something is located next to or against something.

čṅčłtumš – *shake hands w/ people,* a compound stem word formed; from **čṅim** to grasp and the suffix **łtumš** among the people.

čṅim – *grasp on to,* an action root word describing the hand grasping an object either to hold or to hold onto.

čošim – *yell out,* an action root word indicating the action of whooping, crying out in excitement, to make call sounds as to show encouragement and/or agreement.

čsaẋẋ – *near,* a prepositional root word describing the state of being near or close to something.

čsṗálqʷ – *hit on wood,* a compound stem word describing the action of hitting wood and also now applied to telephone calling. This comes from the way communication took place with telegraphs.

čšťim – *guard,* an action root word indicating the action of guarding against something or to be on the watch for some danger

čtqem – *chase,* an action root word indicating the action of chasing or pursuing something or somebody.

čupu – *hairy,* a stative root word, describing the state of an object having a hair/fur like surface.

čxʷuy – *visit,* a stem word from **xʷuy**, to go, indicating going to someplace or somebody. More commonly it is used to describe the action of visiting someone as in going to someone.

čẋʷect – *pass,* a stative root word, describing the state of passing some point either physically or in the marking of time.

čyall – *wrap; encircle,* a compound stem word describing the encircling of some object such as wrapping something with a cord or ropelike object.

čaw – *pray,* an action root word indicating the action of prayer.

čhékʷ – *detach,* an action root word indicating the action of something detatching or breaking free from an object; something getting separated from an object.

čhém – *reveal,* an action root word indicating the action of something revealing a covered/veiled object.

čey – *shade,* a descriptive root word, describing shade as the casting of a shadow.

čim – *dark,* a stative root word, describing the state of a whole area lacking direct light from the sun or from electrical light. The spectrum is from dim or shaded to total darkness but not describing shade.

čiwlš – *climb,* an action root word indicating the action of climbing.

***člux*ʷ** – *go out of sight,* an action root word indicating the action of the setting sun going out of sight.

čm – *extremity,* a descriptive root word, describing the extremity of some object. It is used often in body part descriptors.

čoncut – *prayer/offer.* This root word describes praying and offering.

ču – *gone,* a descriptive root word, describing the absence of something.

ečswíš – *stand,* a stative root word, describing the state of being in a standing position

elḱʷ – *store away,* an action root word indicating the action of storing away some object for future use.

emut – *sit, be home,* a stative root word, describing the state of a singular person sitting, such as one would do while at home.

eṗ – *wipe,* an action root word indicating the action of wiping or scrubbing some object.

ey – *cross,* a descriptive root word, describing objects that are crossed or have a crossed like appearance; make equal, just, square.

héʔe – *conserve, respect,* an action root word indicating the action of being conservative with something or with some action, to hold something in esteem and thus use sparingly.

ia – *assemble, gather,* an action root word indicating the action of assembling or gathering things together.

iap – *more than one arrived there,* a stem word indicating the action of the natural gathering of people as would happen when people arrive as some point; from the root word, **ia** to gather.

ilim – *penetrate w/ pointed object,* an action root word indicating the action of penetrating, as to break some kind of barrier into something with a object, generally a pointed object.

iłn – *eat,* an action root word indicating the action of eating or ingesting food to provide sustenance.

iłtťe – *easy,* a stative root word, describing the state of easiness, being easy to do/make.

iłtťim – *tender,* a stative root word, describing the state of something being tender.

išut – *down, low,* a prepositional root word describing the state of being down/below from some established or understood point.

itš – *sleep,* an action root word indicating the action of sleeping.

iwu – *move,* an action root word indicating the action of making something move, to move things randomly from place to place.

ixʷ – *sad, hurt,* a stative root word, describing the state of sadness and hurt.

kʷʔal – *plants grow,* an action root word indicating the action of the coming forth of a growing thing such as plants, antlers, etc.

kʷaliʔ – *yellow,* a descriptive root word, describing the color.
kʷen – *take.* This root word describes the action of taking an object or an idea. It does not have any connotation of stealing.
kʷil – *red.* a descriptive root word, describing the color red.
kʷtunt – *big,* a descriptive root word, describing large in size, appearance, and/or quality.
kʷƛ̓im – *detach,* an action root word indicating the action of detaching something from another object or when used with other affixes to extract from an object from some place.
k̓ʷel̓č̓ – *upturned formed object.* This root word describes an upturned formed object such as a bucket. It also pertains to something that is overturned, that is something that would normally be on one side. For instance a car is normally on its wheels and therefore if turned over would be described using this root word.
k̓ʷim – *small,* a descriptive root word, describing small in size, appearance, and/or quality.
k̓ʷinš – *how many,* an interrogative root word inquiring about the quantity of some thing.
k̓ʷłq̓ey̓im – *draw,* a compound stem word describing the action of drawing; from **q̓ey̓**, to write/mark and the prefix **k̓ʷł**, under.
k̓ʷłpax̣em – *think,* a compound stem word describing the action of thinking; from **pax̣**, wisdom and the prefix **k̓ʷł**, under.
k̓ʷul̓ – *make/build/do.* an action root word encompassing the actions of making, building, doing, and working. This root can also be found as a compound prefix as in **sck̓ʷl̓**.
k̓ʷul̓l̓ – *born/produced,* a compound stem word describing the action of something produced or made as a process of nature such as being born. This root can also be found as a compound prefix as in **sck̓ʷl̓**.
laap – *float, navigate,* an action root word indicating the navigation and travel of a floating vessel in water. To cause a water vessel to go in a certain direction.
lax̣ – *friend,* a descriptive root word describing friendship or the act of befriending.
laq̓ʷ – *splash; throw water,* an action root word indicating the action of splashing water onto something as with a scooped hand or a flat object to splash at or to scoop and throw water.
lciʔ – *remain there,* a stative root word, describing the state of unobtrusive and unintrusive existence.
leč̓ – *angry,* a stative root word, describing the state of being furious, angry. To bring violence to actions.
lémt – *glad; thankful,* a stative root word, describing the state of being thankful, content, glad.
lo – *out of,* a stative root word, describing the state of something poked out of a literal or figurative formed space.
lq̓e – *pull out rooted thing,* an action root word indicating the action of pulling rooted things out such as plants or hair.
l̓ič̓ – *tied up,* an action root word indicating the action of tying things up to bind things together or prevent movement and/or separation.
łaq – *sit,* an action root word describing the action of sitting down, to occupy a space by sitting down.
łaq̓ – *wide,* a descriptive root word describing the appearance of something wide or broad in width.
łe – *end,* a stative root word, describing the state of arriving or coming to an end or impassable place.
łʔu – *prick, sting,* an action root word indicating the action of penetrating skin with a sharp object such as a spear, thorn, needle or stinger.
łén – *unexpressive,* a descriptive root word describing no expression as a way to deny access to one's feelings.
łin – *sprinkle,* an action root word indicating the action of sprinkling water or a liquid substance in small droplets.
łip̓ – *line,* a descriptive root word describing a line, a marking as a long stroke or something arranged in a series.
łoqʷ – *over lay/around,* an action root word indicating the action of over laying something on another object such as putting a blanket over a horizontal pole.
łoq̓ʷ – *bare, denude,* a descriptive root word describing something that has become bare where it normally would have some covering or growth.
łox̣ʷ – *hole,* a descriptive root word, describing a hole in some object.
łixʷp – *slip/pull over,* an action root word describing the action of slipping/pulling something tightly fitted over an object to partially cover it.
ƛ̓aq̓ – *hot,* a descriptive root word, describing something that is hot to the touch.
ƛ̓awač̓ – *mud,* a descriptive root word describing mud covering or smeared on an object.
ƛ̓čim̓ – *protrude,* a descriptive root word, describing the protrusion or bulging from a plane.
ƛ̓éʔeč̓ – *peek,* an action root word indicating the action describing something peeking/poking out from within or behind something.
ƛ̓eʔem – *search,* an action root word indicating the action of searching for something not in sight.
ƛ̓il – *no movement,* a descriptive root word, describing the absence of movement of some object that would otherwise be able to have movement.
ƛ̓im – *pointed,* a descriptive root word describing an object that comes to a point.
ƛ̓mu – *sound of scooping out water,* a descriptive root word describing sound of scooping out water.
malq̓ʷ – *balled object,* a descriptive root word describing the appearance of some object in a balled state.
maw̓ – *break,* an action root word indicating the action of breaking or breaking down of something.
mʔem – *woman,* a stative root word, describing the state of being a woman.
memeʔt – *bothersome,* a compound stem word describing the state of something or someone having bothersome qualities.
meńxʷ – *smoke,* an action root word indicating the action of inhaling the smoke of dried plants such as tobacco.

meλ̓ – *mix,* an action root word indicating the action of mixing two substances together.

mi – *reality, the known,* a stative root word, describing the state of reality as viewed from each individual.

milk̓ʷ – *whole,* a descriptive root word describing the entirety of something.

mlip – *overflow,* a compound stem word describing an overflow of some liquid from its usual place.

mˀot – *smokey,* a descriptive root word, describing the presence of smoke.

moo – *flowing,* a descriptive root word, describing a flowing fluid mass.

moq̓ʷ – *bump/hill/mtn,* a descriptive root word describing a raised mass from its surrounding area in a mounded form.

m̓tos – *kidney,* a nominal root word describing a kidney or kidney shaped object.

mul – *remove from water/liquid,* an action root word indicating the action of scooping from water or liquid.

nas – *wet,* a descriptive root word, describing the presence of liquid in or on an object.

nk̓ʷéṅ – *choose, pick, select, or try,* a compound stem word describing the selection of something as a way to give something a try.

nk̓ʷuˀ – *one,* a descriptive root word, describing a singular object.

nlo – *put inside,* a stative root word, describing the state of something put inside of a literal or figurative formed space.

nłeptm – *forget,* a stem word describe the act of forgetting; from **łep**, to extinguish.

nmipa – *tattle,* a stem word describe the act of telling on or tattling; from **mi**, reality.

nmulm – *get water,* an action root word indicating the action of getting water from some location.

nox̣ʷnx̣ʷ – *wife,* a stative root word, describing the state of of having a wife.

npilš – *go in pl.,* an action root word indicating the action of more than one entering into an enclosed space.

npkʷétkʷ – *put/pour round objects in water,* a compound stem word describing the action of pouring granular to large objects from a container into water; from **pkʷum**, pour globoid-shaped objects.

ntaˀqin – *hit on top,* a stem word describing the action of hitting something on the top from **teˀ**, bump/hit.

ntels – *want,* a stative root word, describing the state of desire or need. It also describes a thought, as in "what do you think" or "how do you feel" and "what is your opinion on any given subject."

nt̓pus – *boil,* a stem word describing the action of boiling as a way to cook food.

nt̓uk̓ʷ – *placed inside,* a stem word describing the state of something put inside something.

nwist – *up, up high,* a stative root word, describing the state of something being up high.

nx̣el – *afraid,* a condition root word describing a state of fear or of being afraid.

ṅaq̓ʷ – *steal,* an action root word indicating the action of stealing something from someone or something.

ocqeˀ – *go out,* an action root word indicating the action of exiting an enclosed space.

ool – *slippery,* a descriptive root word, describing a slippery surfuce.

ox̣ʷ – *string out.* a descriptive root word, describing things that are strung out such as wire for a fence.

paá – *faded,* a descriptive root word, describing the appearance of a color that has become faded due to sun exposure or use.

pelq – *flared/rolled out,* a descriptive root word describing something that is rolled and flared.

pƚiƚt – *thick,* a descriptive root word, describing a flat object having relatively great extent between both surfaces.

pƚqem – *spread/unpack,* an action root word indicating the action of spreading out objects packed together.

pii – *happy,* a stative root word, describing the state of happiness.

piṅ – *bend,* a descriptive root word, describing an object bent in a sharp angular fashion such as folding, not a rounded bend.

piq – *white,* a descriptive root word, describing the color of white.

plič̓ – *turn over/around,* an action root word indicating the action of turning something in an opposite/reverse way as in turning a flat object over, having clothing inside out or turning in the opposite direction.

plutm – *dodge,* an action root word indicating the action of turning in a direction from the normal course as to avoid something.

pƚiƚt – *thick,* a descriptive root word, describing something with relative great extent from one surface to the other surface.

pλ̓im – *release from,* an action root word indicating the action of removing or releasing something from something else.

poq̓ʷ – *granular substance poured,* an action root word indicating the action of pouring granular or powdered substances.

psap – *excited/nervous,* a stem word describing a state of being excited.

psas – *deflate,* an action root word indicating the action of an inflated object deflating

pukʷ – *round objects poured,* an action root word indicating the action of pouring globoid shaped objects.

puls – *kill,* an action root word indicating the action of killing.

púˀus – *heart,* a descriptive root word describing the heart as well as thought and actions from the heart.

puxʷ – *blow,* an action root word indicating the action of exhaling air or blowing air.

px̣ʷu – *distribute,* an action root word indicating the action of distributing something to individuals.

ṗać – *press,* an action root word indicating the action of pressing with the fingers.

ṗeč̓ – *radiant heat,* a descriptive root word describing the feel of radiant heat or of the action of putting something near a radiant heat source.

ṗulk̓ʷ – *fold/roll,* an action root word indicating the action of folding/rolling a pliable flat object.

ṗuƛ́ – *grease, oil,* a descriptive root word, describing fatty or oily matter.

ṗum – *orange,* a descriptive root word, describing the color of orange from the color of a smoked tanned buckskin.

ṗuy – *wrinkle,* a descriptive root word, describing the presences of wrinkles

qal – *fresh, raw,* a descriptive root word, describing that something is freshly cut, picked or still green with moisture.

qci – *shrink,* a descriptive root word describing the shinking or contracting of some object.

qeltč – *meat, body,* a nominal root word describing meat or muscle

ql̓we – *step,* an action root word indicating the action of stepping or stepping on something.

qmin – *place things down,* an action root word indicating the action of placing more than one object down.

qpéłċeʔ – *plate,* a stem word describing a plate or dishes in general.

qq̇méyeʔ – *fish, angle,* an action root word indicating the action of angling for fish.

q̇ax̣ – *trail, path,* a descriptive root word describing a path beaten and trodden by people and/or animals.

q̇eʔ – *put inside,* a descriptive root word describing something put into an snug enclosed space literally or figuratively.

q̇eċ – *weave,* an action root word indicating the action of interlacing material to weave into a object.

q̇l̓ – *hooked on to,* an action root word indicating the action of putting something onto a protruding or hook-like object.

q̇eẏ – *write, mark.* This root word pertains to making marks such as writing.

q̇sip – *a long time,* a descriptive root word describing a period of time as being relatively long.

qʷʔem – *get accustomed,* a condition root word indicating being or getting accustomed or habituated.

qʷʔóp – *make soft,* an action root word indicating the action of making something soft.

qʷamqʷmt – *excellent,* a stem word making an exclamation showing something is excellent.

qʷáy – *blue,* a descriptive root word, describing the color blue.

qʷec – *warm,* a descriptive root word, describing the feeling of warmth.

qʷéw – *crazy,* a stative root word, describing the state of being crazy.

qʷin – *green,* a descriptive root word, describing the color green to light blue.

qʷlqʷelt – *talk/speak,* a stem word describing the action of talking.

qʷṅqʷiṅt – *pity,* a stem word describing a state of poor quality.

q̇ʷáy – *black,* a descriptive root word, describing the color black.

q̇ʷiṁ – *hurry,* a stative root word, describing the state of being hurried.

q̇ʷoct – *fat,* a descriptive root word describing something with excessive body.

q̇ʷom – *take things,* an action root word indicating the action of taking more than one object or idea. It does not have any connotation of stealing.

saáptniša – *Nez Perce,* a nominal root word describing the Nez Perce people.

saq̇ – *split,* a descriptive root word describing the parting or appearance of parting of objects.

sčut – *half of,* a descriptive root word describing half of an object.

sew – *ask,* an action root word indicating the action of inquiring for information or permission.

sic – *new,* a descriptive root word, describing something being new as an object or as a moment in time.

sil̓ – *confuse,* a descriptive root word, describing the state of being confused or mixed up.

siṗiʔ – *buckskin,* a descriptive root word describing buckskin.

sitč – *braid,* an action root word indicating the action of braiding.

sixʷ – *pour/spill,* an action root word indicating the action of pouring or spilling liquid.

siyen – *count,* an action root word indicating the action of counting things.

snčlep – *coyote,* a nominal root word describing coyote as the central figure in creation stories.

snéčłċeʔ – *cow elk,* a nominal root word describing a cow elk.

solši – *fire,* a nominal root word describing a fire.

spentč – *year,* a nominal root word describing a year.

sṗim – *strike w/ object,* an action root word indicating the action striking something with an object.

sq̇o – *prairie chicken,* a nominal root word describing a prairie chicken

sqʷuʔł – *bee,* a nominal root word describing a bee.

sṫulixʷ – *land, earth,* a nominal root word describing the earth or land.

sult – *freeze,* a descriptive root word describing the state of freezing.

sut̓ – *stretch,* a descriptive root word describing something that has an elasitic quality.

sust – *drink,* an action root word indicating the action of drinking liquid.

suxʷ – *recognition.* This root word pertains to the recognition as in getting to know something.

suxʷmeʔ – *measure,* an action root word indicating the action of measuring something.

suyápi – *white people,* a nominal root word describing people of caucasian decsent.

sx̣elwi – *husband,* a nominal root word describing a husband.

sxʷsixʷlt – *offspring,* a stem word indicating offspring.

šʔit – *first,* a stative root word, describing the state of something being first.

šal – *suspended,* a descriptive root word, describing something pendulous, something suspended.

še – *then,* an aspectual root word indicating the shift of action as referenced to time order.

šeẏ – *there,* a prepositional root word indicating a position of something in spacial, time and/or mental references.

šič̓t – *miss a target,* a stative root word, describing an action attempting to achieve some target and that it has missed.

šil – *chop,* an action root word indicating the action of chopping something in one motion.

šiƛ̓ – *flat, level, aligned.* a descriptive root word, describing something level, aligned, inline; that is things arranged in line or things that follow a successive order.

šiṅ – *flat cover,* a descriptive root word, describing a flat object placed over or next to something.

šim – *rammed through,* a descriptive root word, describing something pushed or rammed through an opening.

šit̓ – *stand upright,* a descriptive root word, describing the state of a long object standing upright.

šlič – *around,* an action root word indicating the action of of going around something.

tam – *not, deny,* this root word can stand alone to mean, not, or in composition it means the negation of its affix.

tax̣ – *bitter,* a descriptive root word, describing something with a bitter, strong or spicy taste or smell.

teʔ – *hit/bump into,* an action root word indicating the action of an object abuptly making contact with another object.

teṁ – *what,* an interrogative root word that inquires about the use of something.

tin – *tight, taut, tense,* a descriptive root word, describing something taut.

tixʷł – *acquire,* an action root word indicating the action of acquiring things.

tiyeš – *crawl,* an action root word indicating the action of crawling near the ground.

tkʷúut – *walk pl.,* an action root word indicating the action of two of more people walking together.

tmim – *crumble,* a stem word indicating something that crumbled; from the root word **tam**, not.

tol – *straight vertical.* a descriptive root word, describing something that is put into a straight vertical position.

tox̣ʷ – *straight,* a descriptive root word, describing something that has a straight or true quality as opposed to a crooked, faulty, or inaccurate quality.

tqem – *touch,* an action root word indicating the action of touching something.

tuiṅ – *fail/deficient,* a stative root word, describing something that has a deficiency or is insufficient.

tukʷ – *blocked,* a stative root word, describing something that has a blockage

tuwaq – *fall apart,* an action root word indicating the action of falling/breaking apart into pieces or widely separated. This word is generally used to describe the coming apart of a rope.

t̓am – *suck,* an action root word indicating the action of sucking.

t̓ap – *shoot* an action root word indicating the action of shooting a projectile weapon.

t̓as – *hard,* a descriptive root word, describing an object that has a hard/solid composition.

t̓eł – *make sticky,* an action root word indicating the action of making something become sticky.

t̓iip – *fall,* an action root word indicating the action of something falling.

t̓il – *tear,* an action root word describing the action of tearing pliable material or the parting of a plane such as the flat surface of the ground.

t̓ił – *dirty,* a descriptive root word, describing the appearance of something that has another substance on it such as soiled hands.

t̓iṁ – *damp,* an descriptive root word, describing something with the feel of moisture within or on the object.

t̓ip – *join/add to,* an action root word indicating the action of adding to something.

t̓iš – *sweet,* a descriptive root word, describing something with a sweet taste or smell.

t̓ix̣ – *protrude,* a descriptive root word, describing a jutted protrusion from main body of a uniform surface/object.

t̓ixʷlm – *different,* a stative root word, describing something that is comparatively different than something else

t̓mam – *suck, kiss,* an action root word indicating the action of kissing.

t̓pip – *stand pl.,* an action root word indicating the action of more than one person rising up in a standing position.

t̓qem – *stack,* an action root word indicating the action of stacking non-rigid objects such as clothing, grass, etc.

t̓soʔ – *sneeze,* an action root word indicating the action of sneezing.

t̓uk̓ʷ – *put/place something down,* an action root word indicating the action of placing an object onto something.

t̓um – *lightly suck,* an action root word indicating the action of lighly sucking.

t̓up – *twist,* an action root word indicating the action of twisting fiber together.

t̓uxʷt – *fly,* an action root word indicating the action of flying.

uẇaq̓uq̓t – *wild,* a stative root word, describing a wild demeanor such as how animals behave.

ukʷm – *bring,* an action root word indicating the action of bringing or hauling something to some place.

ulip – *burn,* a stem root word describing an object in the act of combustion; to be on fire.

ululim – *money,* a stem root word describing metal, coins and common currency.

unéxʷ – *real, true, yes,* a condition root word indicating that something is in accordance with the actual state or condition and/or that something conforms with reality or fact.

up – *hair,* a descriptive root word, describing an aggregate of long slender strands growing from a surface such as hair, grass or trees as seen from a distance.

uš – *comb,* an action root word describing the action of combing through hair or grass.

uwewlš – *speak formally,* an action root word describing the action of conveying information in the form of speech.

uxʷ – *hang, sag,* a descriptive root word, describing an object that hangs or sags.

uẏé – *finish,* a stative root word that describes bringing something to an end or completion.

weʔm – *yell, holler,* an action root word describing the action of speaking words in a very loud voice.
wekʷ – *hide,* an action root word describing the action of concealing something from awareness of others.
weľ – *tilt,* a descriptive root word, describing something that is out of a perpendicular orientation.
wič – *see,* an action root word indicating the action of something coming into view.
wil – *faulty,* a descriptive root word, describing something faulty as in actions.
wisšn – *long,* a stative root word, describing a narrow object having a relative linear extent.
x̣a – *cool,* a descriptive root word, describing the feel of something with a cool temperature.
x̣al – *clear,* a descriptive root word, describing something that has the property to allowing light to transmit through.
x̣alip – *light up,* a stem root word describing the action of something lighting up; from the root word **x̣al**, clear.
x̣am – *dry,* a descriptive root word, describing something free from moisture.
x̣ṗ – *line, coat,* an action root word indicating the action of line/double/coat something.
x̣cim – *make ready/orderly,* an action root word indicating the action of getting something in an orderly fashion in order to make ready for some future or preceding action.
x̣es – *good,* a descriptive root word, describing with a good quality.
x̣iq – *rub,* a descriptive root word, describing the sound of rubbing hard objects together.
x̣menč – *like/love,* a condition root word indicating a feeling of love or desire of something.
xʷist – *walk,* a stem root word describing the action of walking; from the root word **xʷuy**, go.
xʷuy – *go,* an action root word indicating the action of directional movement.
xʷuk̓ʷ – *clean,* a descriptive root word, describing an orderly appearance.
xʷṫip – *run away,* an action root word indicating the action of someone or something running away from something.
xʷeƚe – *hurry,* an action root word indicating the action of hurrying about.
xʷič̓ – *give,* an action root word indicating the action of giving something.
xʷl̓xʷil̓t – *live,* a stem word describing the state of living.
xʷep – *cover,* an action root word indicating the action of covering something with an object such as a blanket or similar object.
x̣ʷal – *flutter/shake,* a descriptive root word, describing rapid irregular movements.
x̣ʷax̣ʷʔey – *laugh,* an action root word indicating the action of more than one person laughing.
x̣ʷel – *abandon,* an action root word indicating the action of abandoning something as getting rid of garbage.
x̣ʷic – *cut bunches,* a descriptive root word, describing the cutting of bunched together strand-like objects such as hair or grass.
x̣ʷollq̓ʷ – *roll,* an action root word indicating the action of rolling an object.
x̣ʷos – *foam,* a descriptive root word, describing the formation of small bubbles in a liquid substance.
yal – *round,* a descriptive root word, describing an appearance of something with a round circular quality.
yalim – *coil, wrap,* a stative root word, of encircling an object with cordage or strips of material; from **yal**, round.
yatt – *shake,* a stative root word, describing irregular movements of an object as a whole.
yelxʷ – *conceal,* an action root word indicating the action of concealing something as to cover or veil.
yey – *cross weave,* a descriptive root word, describing the crossing of rigid material.
yomim – *hold steady,* a stem word describing the action of holding something with one's strength; from the root word **yóo**, strong.
yóo – *strong,* a descriptive root word, describing physical strength literally and figuratively.
yult – *thick in girth,* a stative root word, describing a cylindrical object that has a big/thick girth.
ẏaa – *scarce,* a descriptive root word, describing that something is scarce in quality and/or quantity.
ẏamim – *gather,* a stem word describing the action of gathering objects together; from the root word **ia** assemble, gather.

* The root words in this section are classified to help distinguish and understand meaning. The classifications are open to criticism. Do not use this section as a definitive source. Future editions will include expansion and clarification. The following is the classification: **action** root words describe an action; **aspectual** root words describe a time reference; **compound** stem words are the combination of multiple stem roots; **condition** root words describe a condition; **descriptive** root words describe an attribute; **interrogative** root words create a question; **nominal** root words create speech forms from a noun like word; **prepositional** root words indicate position in space and time; **stem** root words are the combination of a root and some other modifier; **stative** root words describe a state.

Circumfix *A circumfix is an affix added to both ends of a word that changes its meaning. It may be that circumfixes are co-occurrences of a prefix and a suffix.*

circumfix: ***č...eẇs*** *– up high.*
circumfix: ***č...qn*** *– mountain.*
circumfix: ***č...us*** *– spherical object; eyes.*
circumfix: ***čł...eneʔ*** *– cover all over.*
circumfix: ***čł...esšn*** *– forehead.*
circumfix: ***čł...us*** *– cheek.*
circumfix: ***čs...alq*** *– penis.*
circumfix: ***k̓ʷłn...ep*** *– opening.*
circumfix: ***n...aqs*** *– nose, road, pointed.*
circumfix: ***n...aqsm*** *– kinds.*
circumfix: ***n...cin*** *– action of the mouth.*
circumfix: ***n...elis*** *– uniformly.*
circumfix: ***n...els*** *– want, feel.*
circumfix: ***n...eneʔ*** *– inside the ear.*
circumfix: ***n...ep*** *– egg.*
circumfix: ***n...epls*** *– testicles.*
circumfix: ***n...epneʔ*** *– mouthful.*
circumfix: ***n...eys*** *– teeth.*
circumfix: ***n...qneł*** *– fire shot.*
circumfix: ***n...ups*** *– butt, tail.*

Suffix *A suffix is an affix added to the end of a word that changes its meaning.*

suffix: **...alqʷ** – *wood; cylindical.*
suffix: **...lqs, ...alqs** – *clothes.*
suffix: **...ałq** – *smell, accompaniment.*
suffix: **...ałq̇ʷlt, ...łq̇ʷlt** – *throat.*
suffix: **...apqn** – *back of head.*
suffix: **...aqs** – *food, kind.*
suffix: **...aqstšn** – *leg.*
suffix: **...asq̇t** – *sky, day.*
suffix: **...aẇsqn** – *top of head.*
suffix: **...ax̣n** – *arm.*
suffix: **...axʷcč** – *chest.*
suffix: **...ayaqn** – *head.*
suffix: **...cin, ...cn** – *action of the mouth.*
suffix: **...cnečst** – *wrist.*
suffix: **...cut** – *action to the self.*
suffix: **...cutn** – *s.o. who does for one.*
suffix: **...ečst, ...čst** – *of the hand.*
suffix: **...elis** – *uniformly.*
suffix: **...elxʷ, ...lxʷ** – *skin/hide.*
suffix: **...ełp, ...łp** – *tree; floor, bed.*
suffix: **...elps, ...lps** – *neck.*
suffix: **...els, ...ls** – *want, feel.*
suffix: **...elsčn** – *horn.*
suffix: **...el̓t, ...l̓t** – *child, baby.*
suffix: **...ełċeʔ** – *inside contents, body, meat.*
suffix: **...ełxʷ, ...łxʷ** – *house.*
suffix: **...emxʷ** – *breasts.*
suffix: **...emn** – *one inclined to do.*
suffix: **...eneʔ** – *ear.*
suffix: **...énč** – *within.*
suffix: **...ep** – *rope, head hair.*
suffix: **...epleʔ** – *permanence.*
suffix: **...epls** – *testicle.*
suffix: **...eššṅ, ...ššṅ** – *rock.*
suffix: **...etkʷ, ...tkʷ** – *liquid.*
suffix: **...éẇs** – *in between, middle.*
suffix: **...éẇt** – *group state.*
suffix: **...eys** – *rain.*
suffix: **...iċéʔ** – *covered in.*
suffix: **...ičṅ** – *back.*
suffix: **...ilš** – *autonomous.*
suffix: **...iṅč** – *weapon.*
suffix: **...ist** – *action for/of the self.*
suffix: **...ip** – *action of natural cause.*
suffix: **...łmuł** – *one that habitually does.*
suffix: **...łniut** – *side.*
suffix: **...łtumš** – *of people.*
suffix: **...łq̇éyt** – *shoulder.*
suffix: **...lwis** – *indicates going around.*
suffix: **...messn** – *forehead.*
suffix: **...min, ...mn** – *instrument/tool.*
suffix: **...mintn** – *tool that does.*
suffix: **...ṁnuxʷ** – *process through/become.*
suffix: **...mutiyeʔ** – *temporary.*
suffix: **...mutm** – *active possibility.*
suffix: **...numt** – *reach a state.*
suffix: **...nu...** – *transitive suffix indicating success.*
suffix: **...posqn** – *lips.*
suffix: **...qin, ...qn** – *top.*
suffix: **...qinčst** – *finger.*
suffix: **...q̇eẏmin** – *paper; book.*
suffix: **...snuxʷ** – *worthy of.*
suffix: **...sqax̣eʔ, ...sqa** – *domestic animal; generally horse or car.*
suffix: **...sqe, ...sqelixʷ** – *people.*
suffix: **...st̓iyeʔ** – *grass.*
suffix: **...šin, ...šn** – *feet.*
suffix: **...tin, ...tn** – *means of/device.*
suffix: **...ulexʷ** – *land.*
suffix: **...up** – *sudden action of natural cause.*
suffix: **...us** – *face, fire.*
suffix: **...utm** – *passive possibility.*
suffix: **...wexʷ** – *action to each other.*
suffix: **...wilš** – *developmental.*

Prefix *A prefix is an affix added to the front of a word that changes its meaning.*

prefix: **c...** – *indicating toward the speaker.*
prefix: **č...** – *people.*
prefix: **č...** – *upon.*
prefix: **čł...** – *surface.*
prefix: **čs...** – *bad.*
prefix: **k̓ʷimł...** – *small.*
prefix: **k̓ʷl̓...** – *make.*
prefix: **k̓ʷł...** – *under.*
prefix: **ł...** – *little.*
prefix: **mił...** – *front.*
prefix: **n...** – *inside.*
prefix: **nkʷł...** – *together with.*
prefix: **qeł...** – *offspring of.*
prefix: **s...** – *nominal.*
prefix: **sc...** – *s.t. that's been done/made/prepared.*
prefix: **sck̓ʷl̓...** – *something that's been made.*
prefix: **skʷtił...** – *big.*
prefix: **sk̓ʷnš...** – *how many*
prefix: **sn...** – *a place of.*
prefix: **snkʷł...** – *fellow, member of.*
prefix: **ssymł...** – *comparative extreme.*
prefix: **sxʷ...** – *one tasked to do.*
prefix: **tms...** – *not.*
prefix: **t̓q̇nčst...** – *six.*
prefix: **xʷċł...** – *give.*
prefix: **x̣s...** – *good.*

Selected Bibliography

Arlee, Johnny. *Malí Npnaqs*. Pablo, MT: Salish Kootenai College Press, 2003.

Boas, Franz, et al. *Folk-Tales of Salishan and Sahaptin Tribes*. Memoirs of the American Folk-Lore Society, No. 11. Lancaster, PA: American Folk-Lore Society, 1917.

Carlson, Barry F. *A Grammar of Spokane: A Salish Language of Eastern Washington.* Ph.D. diss. University of Hawaii, 1972.

Carlson, Barry F. *Unstressed Root Vowels in Spokane.* University of Hawaii Working Papers in Linguistics, No. 3, Honolulu, HI: 1972.

Carlson, Barry F. *Spokane Dictionary.* Occasional Papers in Linguistics, No. 6, Missoula, MT: University of Montana, 1989.

Flathead Culture Committee. *Common Names of the Flathead Language*. St. Ignatius, MT: The Committee, 1981.

Giorda, Rev. J. *A Dictionary of the Kalispel or Flat-head Indian Language.* Part 1. Kalispel-English. St. Ignatius, MT: Missionaries of the Society of Jesus, 1879.

Giorda, Rev. J. *A Dictionary of the Kalispel or Flat-head Indian Language.* Part 2. English-Kalispel. St. Ignatius, MT: Missionaries of the Society of Jesus, 1879.

Kroeber, Paul D. *The Salish Language Family: Reconstructing Syntax*. Lincoln: University of Nebraska Press in cooperation with the American Indian Studies Research Institute, Indiana University, Bloomington, 1999.

Nesfield, J. C. *Aids To The Study and Composition of English.* London: Macmillan, 1967.

Newman, Stanley. *A History of the Salish Possessive and Subject Forms*. International Journal of Linguistics, Vol. 45, No. 3. (July, 1979): 207–223.

Newman, Stanley. *Functional Change in the Salish Pronominal System*. International Journal of Linguistics, Vol. 46, No. 3. (July, 1980): 155–167.

Speck, Brenda J. *An Edition of Father Post's Kalispell Grammar.* Ph.D. diss. University of Montana, 1977.

Swan, Michael. *Practical English Usage.* 3rd ed. New York: Oxford, 2005.

Pete, Tachini. *nyoʔnuntn q̓éymin Flathead Nation Salish Dictionary*. Pablo, MT: Bilingual Education Department, Salish Kootenai College, 1998.

Salish-Pend d'Oreille Culture Committee. *The Salish People and the Lewis and Clark Expedition*. Lincoln: University of Nebraska Press, 2005.

Thomason, Sarah. *Flathead Dictionary.* First Draft, Ms., 1987.

Turney-High, Harry H. *The Flathead Indians of Montana*. Memoirs of the American Anthropological Association, No. 48. Menasha, WI: American Anthropological Association, 1937.

Vogt, Hans. *The Kalispel Language.* Oslo: Det Norske Videnskaps-Akademi, 1940.

Wheelock, Frederic M. *Latin: An Introduction Course Based on Ancient Authors.* 3rd ed. New York: Barnes & Noble Books, 1963.